HANDBOOK FOR
PROFESSIONAL MANAGERS

Editors

Lester Robert Bittel, M.B.A.

School of Business, James Madison University

and

Jackson Eugene Ramsey, M.B.A., Ph.D., P.E.

School of Business, James Madison University

Managing Editor

Muriel Albers Bittel

McGraw-Hill Book Company

New York   St. Louis   San Francisco   Auckland
Bogotá   Hamburg   Johannesburg   London   Madrid
Mexico   Montreal   New Delhi   Panama   Paris
São Paulo   Singapore   Sydney   Tokyo   Toronto

Portions of this book were previously published under the title *Encyclopedia of Professional Management*.

Library of Congress Cataloging in Publication Data

Main entry under title:

Handbook for professional managers.

  Originally published under title: Encyclopedia of
professional management.
    1. Management—Handbooks, manuals, etc.   2. Business—
Handbooks, manuals, etc.   I. Bittel, Lester R.
II. Ramsey, Jackson Eugene, 1938–   .   III. Bittel,
Muriel Albers.   IV. Title: Encyclopedia of professional
management.
HD31.H31245   1985   658'.003'21   84-20106
ISBN 0-07-005469-X

1234567890   HAL/HAL   898765

ISBN 0-07-005469-X

The editors for this book were William A. Sabin and Jim Bessent, the art director was Naomi Auerbach, the designer was Mark E. Safran, and the production supervisor was Teresa F. Leaden. It was set in Auriga by University Graphics, Inc.

Printed and bound by Halliday Lithograph.

DEDICATION

This new edition of the *Handbook for Professional Managers* is dedicated to the memory of two towering figures in the management field:

Harold F. Smiddy, M.B.A., Ph.D., J.D., P.E., vice president and founder of the General Electric Management Research & Development Institute at Crotonville, New York, and author of the watershed paper "Management as a Profession," presented at the annual conference of the American Society of Mechanical Engineers at New York City in 1960,

and

Lt. Col. Lyndall F. Urwick, the international management consultant and author of the landmark books *The Theory of Organization* (1952) and, with Ernest Dale, *Staff in Organization* (1960).

Both of these distinguished individuals made contributions of great breadth and immeasurable consequence to the profession of management. And both were kind enough to offer considerable advice and guidance in the development of an earlier version of this work.

ABOUT THE EDITORS

Both Lester R. Bittel and Jackson E. Ramsey are professors of management and marketing as well as directors of the Center for Supervisory Research at the James Madison University School of Business. In addition, Dr. Ramsey directs the MBA Program and Management Development Center at James Madison.

Professor Bittel has served as a national officer of the Society for Advancement of Management, the Institute of Certified Professional Managers, the American Production and Inventory Control Society, the Management Division of the American Society of Mechanical Engineers, and the International Management Council. He is an internationally recognized authority on the subject of management.

Professor Bittel's earlier books include *Nine Master Keys of Management, What Every Supervisor Should Know,* and the *Encyclopedia of Professional Management* (all published by McGraw-Hill).

CONTENTS

HOW TO FIND WHAT YOU ARE LOOKING FOR

Terms, definitions, subjects, and subject "fields" can be located by following one, or all, of four different search approaches.

1. *Search the main pages of the text alphabetically.* Some 239 major entries and reference entries are arranged in alphabetical sequence.

2. *Check the "See also" listing at the end of each entry.* These items direct you to other closely related entries in which similar terms or subjects are discussed from another point of view.

3. *Consult the Table of Contents and Subject Locator Guide.* This appears on pages vii–xviii. There are 50 locators covering the most important subject fields in management and business. Under each heading are given the major entries that are particularly relevant to the subject field. For example, under *Computers and Computer Systems,* 19 entries are suggested as being especially useful. Other entries also contain pertinent information for this field, and they can be found by looking in the index.

4. *Search the comprehensive index in the back of the book.* Approximately 17,500 items are listed there. They are cross-referenced in about every reasonable variation of term or subject matter, including proper names of people, organizations, and laws.

TABLE OF CONTENTS AND SUBJECT LOCATOR GUIDE

This table lists in alphabetical order 50 vital areas of concern to the professional manager. Under each of the 50 headings is a list of major entries in the handbook that contain information most relevant to the heading. Entries in the list are found in alphabetical sequence within the main pages of this volume. Several thousand additional terms and subjects can be found in the index in the back of this book.

Budgets and Budgeting

Communications, Internal and External

Compensation and Incentive Plans

Computers and Computer Systems

ix

Productivity Improvement

Profits and Profit Making

Project Management

CONTRIBUTING AUTHORS

This distinguished group of some 229 authors includes businesspeople of outstanding managerial achievement, management consultants who are leaders in their profession, and academic figures who are recognized authorities in their fields. The entries are original and, with few exceptions, were prepared expressly for this handbook. These articles have been reviewed by their colleagues and by a panel of editorial advisers. The contributing authors are listed here alphabetically, followed in each instance by the titles of their entries.

Roy Abel, P.E.
Vice President
Albert Ramond and Associates, Inc.
Management Consultants
Chicago, Illinois
WORK MEASUREMENT

Earl W. Adams, Ph.D.
Andrew Wells Robertson Professor
Department of Economics
Allegheny College
Meadville, Pennsylvania
MARKETS, GOVERNMENT

Robert Albanese
Professor of Management
Department of Management
Texas A&M University
College Station, Texas
OBJECTIVES AND GOALS

Arthur Alkins
Director
Management Science Institute
United States Government
Office of Personnel Management
Philadelphia, Pennsylvania
OFFICE AUTOMATION; WORD PROCESSING

Willard Allan, A.M., F.S.C.A., C.F.A.
President
Lanfri Company
Mt. Pleasant, Michigan
FINANCIAL MANAGEMENT, FINANCING

James M. Apple (deceased)
Georgia Institute of Technology
Atlanta, Georgia
MATERIAL HANDLING

James M. Apple, Jr.
Systecon, Inc.
Atlanta, Georgia
MATERIAL HANDLING

Roger M. Atherton, Jr., Ph.D.
Baldwin Associate Professor of Management
College of Business Administration
University of Oklahoma
Norman, Oklahoma
YOUNGER EMPLOYEES, MANAGEMENT OF

Guy J. Bacci, II, P.E.
Manager, Corporate Industrial Engineering
International Harvester Company
Chicago, Illinois
COMPENSATION, WAGE AND SALARY POLICY
    ADMINISTRATION

David L. Bain
President
David Bain Associates
Joliet, Illinois
PRODUCTIVITY IMPROVEMENT

Robert Douglas Bain
Telemarketing Manager
North American Marketing Corporation
Richmond, Virginia
POLITICAL ACTION COMMITTEES (PACs)

Gregory Balestrero
Manager
Technical Services
American Institute of Industrial Engineers,
    Inc.
Atlanta, Georgia
ENGINEERING, INDUSTRIAL

Philip S. Bannevich
Production Shop Superintendent
Norfolk Naval Shipyard
Portsmouth, Virginia
QUALITY CIRCLES

Dean J. Barron, LL.B., J.D., C.P.A.
Attorney at Law
Fairfax, Virginia
TAX MANAGEMENT

Douglas C. Basil, Ph.D.
Professor of Management
Graduate School of Business
University of Southern California
Los Angeles, California
MARKETING OF SERVICES

Arthur G. Bedeian, D.B.A.
Edward L. Lowder Professor of Management
School of Business
Auburn University
Auburn, Alabama
MANAGEMENT, HISTORICAL DEVELOPMENT OF

Howard Berrian
President
Berrian Associates, Inc.
Morristown, New Jersey
SALES MANAGEMENT

Thomas M. Bertsch, Ph.D.
Marketing Research Consultant
Associate Professor of Marketing
School of Business
James Madison University
Harrisonburg, Virginia
MARKETING RESEARCH

Charles P. Bilbrey, Ph.D.
Associate Professor
School of Business
James Madison University
Harrisonburg, Virginia
COMPUTER HARDWARE, MINICOMPUTERS

John J. Bilon
Professor and Director
Hotel & Restaurant Management Program
James Madison University
Harrisonburg, Virginia
HOSPITALITY MANAGEMENT

Lester R. Bittel, M.B.A.
School of Business
James Madison University
Harrisonburg, Virginia
(contributor of selected entries)

Erwin A. Blackstone, Ph.D.
Department of Economics
School of Business Administration
Temple University
Philadelphia, Pennsylvania
COST-BENEFIT ANALYSIS

Paul W. Bockley
Vice President
Compensation and Industrial Relations
Honeywell, Inc.
Minneapolis, Minnesota
LABOR-MANAGEMENT RELATIONS

Paul M. Bons, Ph.D.
Colonel (retired)
U.S. Army
Centerville, Utah
LEADERSHIP

Donald D. Bowen, Ph.D.
Professor of Management
University of Tulsa
Tulsa, Oklahoma
DEVELOPMENT AND TRAINING: CAREER PLANNING PATHS FOR
   MANAGERS

James W. Bradley
Managing Director
Ulin, Morton, Bradley & Welling, Inc.
One Boston Place
Boston, Massachusetts 02108
ACQUISITIONS AND MERGERS

William H. Bryan
Corporate Credit Manager (retired)
Alton Packaging
Orleans, Massachusetts
CREDIT MANAGEMENT

Victor P. Buell
Professor of Marketing, Emeritus
University of Massachusetts
Editor, Handbook of Modern Marketing
Amherst, Massachusetts
MARKETING, CONCEPTS AND SYSTEMS

Elmer H. Burack
Professor of Management
College of Business Administration
University of Illinois at Chicago
Chicago, Illinois
ORGANIZATION STRUCTURES AND CHARTING

Lee B. Burgunder, J.D., M.B.A.
Associate Professor of Business Law
California Polytechnic State University
San Luis Obispo, California
LEGAL AFFAIRS, MANAGEMENT OF CORPORATE

Madelyn Burley-Allen, M.A.
Founder and President
Dynamics of Human Behavior
San Mateo, California
ASSERTIVENESS TRAINING

William C. Byham, Ph.D.
President
Development Dimensions, Inc.
Pittsburgh, Pennsylvania
ASSESSMENT CENTER METHOD

Bruce A. Campbell
Principal
Campbell & Associates
Lake Forest, Illinois
ATTITUDE SURVEYS

Peter J. Cannon, B.S., M.S., M.B.A.
President
Cannon Associates
Marketing Consultants
Edgewater, Maryland
GOVERNMENT RELATIONS

A. William Capone
Senior Vice President and Chief Financial Officer
Koppers Company, Inc.
Pittsburgh, Pennsylvania
FINANCIAL MANAGEMENT, CAPITAL STRUCTURE AND DIVIDEND
   POLICY

D. R. Carmichael, Ph.D., C.P.A.
Professor of Accounting
Baruch College of the City University of New York
New York, New York
AUDITING, FINANCIAL

Ronald E. Carrier, Ph.D.
President
James Madison University
Harrisonburg, Virginia
COLLEGE AND UNIVERSITY ADMINISTRATION

Archie B. Carroll
Professor of Management
University of Georgia
Athens, Georgia
ETHICS, MANAGERIAL

John M. Carroll, Dr. Eng. Sc., P.E.
Professor
Department of Computer Science
University of Western Ontario
London, Ontario, Canada
COMPUTER SECURITY

Richard E. Cheney
Chairman
Hill and Knowlton, U.S.A.
New York, New York
SHAREHOLDER RELATIONS

John W. Cogger, Ed.D., APD
Senior Vice President
Drake Beam Morin, Inc.
Morristown, New Jersey
INTERVIEWING, EMPLOYEE

Stephen D. Cohen, Ph.D.
Professor
School of International Service
American University
Washington, District of Columbia
INTERNATIONAL TRADE

Bernard Conrad Cole
Consultant
BCC, Inc.
Berkeley, California
COMPUTER SOFTWARE, LANGUAGES

Tracy D. Connors, M.A.
Washington Manager
Gould, Incorporated
Defense Electronics Division
Washington, District of Columbia
NONPROFIT ORGANIZATIONS, MANAGEMENT OF

James W. Cortada, Ph.D.
National Accounts Division
IBM Corporation
Nashville, Tennessee
COMPUTER HARDWARE, MAINFRAMES

Philip B. Crosby
Chairman and CEO
PCA, Inc.
Winter Park, Florida
QUALITY MANAGEMENT

Philip T. Crotty, Ed.D.
Senior Vice President; acting Provost
Northeastern University
Boston, Massachusetts
OLDER EMPLOYEES, MANAGEMENT OF

David A. Cunningham, Ph.D.
Associate Professor
Faculty of Physical Education and Department of
    Physiology
University of Western Ontario
London, Ontario, Canada
STRESS MANAGEMENT

Robert J. Davenport, Jr.
Hay Associates
Management Consultants
Philadelphia, Pennsylvania
COMPENSATION, SALES

Burton V. Dean, Ph.D.
Professor
Department of Operations Research
Case Western Reserve University
Cleveland, Ohio
NETWORK PLANNING METHODS; ZERO-BASE BUDGETING

Kenyon B. De Greene, Ph.D.
Professor
Human Factors Department
Institute of Safety and Systems Management
University of Southern California
Los Angeles, California
HUMAN FACTORS ENGINEERING

M. Wayne DeLozier, Ph.D.
Associate Professor of Marketing
College of Business Administration
University of South Carolina
Columbia, South Carolina
ADVERTISING CONCEPTS

William A. Dempsey, D.B.A.
Chairman
Department of Marketing
School of Business Administration
Temple University
Philadelphia, Pennsylvania
COST-BENEFIT ANALYSIS

Robert H. Doktor
Professor
University of Hawaii at Manoa
Honolulu, Hawaii
INTERPERSONAL RELATIONSHIPS

Stahrl W. Edmunds
Director
Dry Lands Research Institute
Professor
Graduate School of Management
University of California
Riverside, California
ENVIRONMENT, PHYSICAL

Joseph Eisenberg
President
Profit-Improvement, Inc.
Management Consultants
New York, New York
PROFIT IMPROVEMENT

Bruce R. Ellig
Vice President, Employee Relations
Pfizer Inc.
New York, New York
COMPENSATION, EMPLOYEE BENEFIT PLANS

James C. Emery
Professor and Chairman
Decision Sciences Department
The Wharton School
University of Pennsylvania
Philadelphia, Pennsylvania
CONTROL SYSTEMS, MANAGEMENT

Anthony X. Farmer, Ph.D.
Professional Development Consultant
The Personnel Laboratory, Inc.
New York, New York
EMPLOYMENT PROCESS

Gerald R. Ferrera, J.D.
Professor of Law and Chairman
Department of Law
Bentley College
Waltham, Massachusetts
BOARDS OF DIRECTORS, LEGAL LIABILITY GUIDELINES

Fred E. Fiedler, Ph.D.
Professor of Psychology and of Management and
    Organization
University of Washington
Seattle, Washington
LEADERSHIP

Alan C. Filley, Ph.D.
Professor
Department of Management
Graduate School of Business
University of Wisconsin
Madison, Wisconsin
ORGANIZATIONAL ANALYSIS AND PLANNING

Robert D. Foley
Assistant Professor
Department of Industrial Engineering and
    Operations Research
Virginia Polytechnic Institute and State University
Blacksburg, Virginia
SIMULATIONS, BUSINESS AND MANAGEMENT

Jack P. Friedman, Ph.D., C.P.A.
Associate Professor
The University of Texas at Arlington
Arlington, Texas
REAL ESTATE MANAGEMENT, CORPORATE

Ralph M. Gaedeke
Professor of Marketing
School of Business and Public Administration
California State University
Sacramento, California
CONSUMERISM AND CONSUMER PROTECTION LEGISLATION

Philip D. Gardner
Assistant Professor
Department of Soils and Environmental Sciences
University of California
Riverside, California
ENVIRONMENTAL PROTECTION LEGISLATION

Dennis E. Garrett
Department of Business Administration
University of Illinois at Urbana-Champaign
Champaign, Illinois
CONSUMER BEHAVIOR, MANAGERIAL RELEVANCE OF

William F. Glueck (deceased)
Distinguished Professor of Management
College of Business Administration
University of Georgia, Athens
PLANNING, STRATEGIC MATERIAL

William Gomberg, Ph.D., P.E.
Professor Emeritus of Management
The Wharton School
University of Pennsylvania
Philadelphia, Pennsylvania
LABOR (TRADE) UNIONS

Ben S. Graham, Jr., Ph.D.
President
The Ben Graham Corporation
Paperwork Simplification Division
Tipp City, Ohio
PAPERWORK SIMPLIFICATION

James H. Graves
Vice President, Banking
First National Bank in Dallas
Dallas, Texas
FINANCIAL MANAGEMENT, BANK RELATIONS

Jack Gray, Ph.D., C.P.A.
Professor of Accounting and Management
    Information Systems
School of Management
University of Minnesota
Minneapolis, Minnesota
ACCOUNTING, COST ANALYSIS AND CONTROL

E. T. Grether, Ph.D., LL.D., ekon.dr (hon.c.)
Flood Professor of Economics, Emeritus
Dean Emeritus, School of Business Administration
Dean Emeritus, Graduate School of Business
    Administration, Teaching, Research
University of California
Berkeley, California
COMPETITION

Frank K. Griesinger
Frank K. Griesinger and Associates, Inc.
Superior Building, Suite 1412
815 Superior Avenue
Cleveland, Ohio 44114
TELECOMMUNICATIONS

Paul J. Grogan
Professor of Engineering
University of Wisconsin—Extension
Madison, Wisconsin
CONTINUING EDUCATION UNIT (CEU)

Douglas T. Hall, Ph.D.
Professor of Organizational Behavior
School of Management
Boston University
Boston, Massachusetts
DEVELOPMENT AND TRAINING: CAREER PLANNING PATHS FOR
    MANAGERS

William O. Hall, Jr., Ed.D.
Professor of Psychology
Dean of the Graduate School, Sponsored Programs,
    and Continuing Education
James Madison University
Harrisonburg, Virginia
GRANTS MANAGEMENT

Arthur J. Hamilton, J.D., M.B.A.
Associate Professor of Business Law
School of Business
James Madison University
Harrisonburg, Virginia
GOVERNMENT REGULATIONS, BUSINESS LAW; GOVERNMENT
    REGULATIONS, FEDERAL REGULATION OF COMPETITION

Fred G. Harold, D.B.A.
Associate Professor
Department of Computer and Information Systems
College of Business and Public Administration
Florida Atlantic University
Boca Raton, Florida
MANAGEMENT INFORMATION SYSTEMS (MIS)

Joseph Harrington, Jr., Sc.D., P.E.
Consulting Engineer
Senior Consultant to Arthur D. Little, Inc.
Cambridge, Massachusetts
AUTOMATION

Lindley R. Higgins
President
Piedmont Publishing Company
Old Bridge, New Jersey
FIELD SERVICE MANAGEMENT

Thomas J. Hindelang, D.B.A., C.P.A.
Professor of Finance and Chairperson
Department of Finance
Drexel University
Philadelphia, Pennsylvania
LEASING, EQUIPMENT

William J. Hirsch, Attorney at Law
Principal Consultant
Hirsch Associates
Stratford, Pennsylvania
CONTRACTS MANAGEMENT

Dorothy Hogan
Vice President, Communications
American National Standards Institute, Inc.
New York, New York
STANDARDS AND STANDARDIZATION PROGRAMS

John H. Howard, D.B.A.
Associate Professor of Business Administration
University of Western Ontario
London, Ontario, Canada
STRESS MANAGEMENT

Elbert W. Hubbard, Ph.D.
Associate Professor
Department of Real Estate and Urban Affairs
School of Business Administration
Georgia State University
Atlanta, Georgia
REAL ESTATE MANAGEMENT, CORPORATE

John M. Ivancevich
Hugh Roy and Lillie Cranz Cullen Chair
Professor of Organizational Behavior and
    Management
College of Business Administration
University of Houston
Houston, Texas
MANAGEMENT, FUTURE OF

John S. Jenness, M.B.A.
Assistant to the Vice President, Employee Relations
Consolidated Edison Company of New York, Inc.
New York, New York
HUMAN RESOURCES PLANNING

Alton C. Johnson, Ph.D.
Professor of Business (Management)
Graduate School of Business
University of Wisconsin
Madison, Wisconsin
HEALTH INSTITUTIONS, MANAGEMENT OF

Frank J. Johnson, P.E., C.V.S.
Johnson Management Corporation
Smyrna (Atlanta), Georgia
VALUE ANALYSIS

Howard W. Johnson
Chairman of the Corporation
Massachusetts Institute of Technology
Cambridge, Massachusetts
TECHNOLOGY, MANAGEMENT IMPLICATIONS

Rodney Johnson, Ph.D.
City of Philadelphia
Philadelphia, Pennsylvania
STATISTICAL ANALYSIS FOR MANAGEMENT

Anthony F. Jurkus, Ph.D.
Professor of Management
College of Administration and Business
Louisiana Tech University
Ruston, Louisiana
PROFESSIONALISM IN MANAGEMENT

Robert N. Katz
Attorney at Law
Berkeley, California
GOVERNMENT SERVICES

Barry P. Keating, Ph.D.
Associate Professor of Finance and Business
    Economics
University of Notre Dame
South Bend, Indiana
ECONOMIC CONCEPTS

John W. Kendrick, Ph.D.
Professor of Economics
George Washington University
Formerly Chief Economist
United States Department of Commerce
Washington, District of Columbia
PRODUCTIVITY MEASUREMENT

James H. Kennedy
Editor and Publisher
Consultants News
Fitzwilliam, New Hampshire
CONSULTANTS, MANAGEMENT

Donald W. King
President
King Research, Inc.
President (1983–1984)
American Society for Information Science
Rockville, Maryland
INFORMATION SCIENCE

Donald L. Kirkpatrick, Ph.D.
Professor of Management
Management Institute
University of Wisconsin
Milwaukee, Wisconsin
DEVELOPMENT AND TRAINING, MANAGEMENT

Louis H. Knapp
Vice President
Cresap, McCormick, and Paget Division
Towers, Perrin, Forster, & Crosby
Washington, District of Columbia
AUDIT, MANAGEMENT

Blair J. Kolasa, Ph.D.
Professor
School of Business and Administration
Duquesne University
Pittsburgh, Pennsylvania
CONFORMITY IN MANAGEMENT

Harold Koontz, Ph.D. (deceased)
Mead Johnson Professor of Management
Graduate School of Management
University of California
Los Angeles, California
MANAGEMENT THEORY, SCIENCE AND APPROACHES

Donald H. Korn
Senior Management Consultant
Arthur D. Little, Inc.
Cambridge, Massachusetts
ACQUISITIONS AND MERGERS

Lester B. Korn
Chairman and Chief Executive Officer
Korn/Ferry International
New York, New York
SEARCH AND RECRUITMENT, EXECUTIVE

Philip Kotler, Ph.D.
Harold T. Martin Professor of Marketing
Graduate School of Management
Northwestern University
Evanston, Illinois
MARKETING OF SERVICES, PROFESSIONAL

Seymour D. Kramer
President
Revere Business Graphics, Inc.
New York, New York
FORMS DESIGN AND CONTROL

William A. W. Krebs
Vice President
Arthur D. Little, Inc.
Cambridge, Massachusetts
DEVELOPING COUNTRIES, MANAGEMENT IN

Donald W. Kroeber, Ph.D.
Head
Department of Information and Decision Sciences
School of Business
James Madison University
Harrisonburg, Virginia
DECISION SUPPORT SYSTEMS; MANAGEMENT INFORMATION
    SYSTEMS, TRANSACTION PROCESSING SYSTEMS

Robert Lawrence Kuhn, Ph.D.
Senior Research Fellow
Ic² Institute
University of Texas, Austin, Texas
Adjunct Professor of Management
Graduate School of Business Administration
New York University
New York, New York
NEGOTIATING

John C. Lere, Ph.D.
Assistant Professor of Accounting
University of Minnesota
Minneapolis, Minnesota
PRODUCT AND SERVICE PRICING

Stanley H. Lieberstein, Attorney at Law
Partner
Ostrolenk, Faber, Gerb, and Soffen
New York, New York
PATENTS AND VALUABLE INTANGIBLE RIGHTS

William E. Linane, S.I.R.
President
Linane and Company, Inc.
Industrial Real Estate
Rosemont, Illinois
SITE SELECTION

George C. Lodge
Professor of Business Administration
Graduate School of Business Administration
Harvard University
Cambridge, Massachusetts
SOCIAL RESPONSIBILITY OF BUSINESS

Wallace G. Lonergan, Ph.D.
Vice President
HRC & Associates, Inc.
Chicago, Illinois
APPRAISAL, PERFORMANCE

Marvin Loper
Hawaiian Telephone Company
Honolulu, Hawaii
INTERPERSONAL RELATIONS

James P. Low
President
Dynamics, Inc.
Washington, District of Columbia
ASSOCIATIONS, TRADE AND PROFESSIONAL

William M. Luther
President
Luther Company
Stamford, Connecticut
MARKETING MANAGEMENT

Edward O. Malott, Jr.
American Management Associations
New York, New York
CONFERENCES AND MEETINGS, PLANNING FOR

Burton H. Marcus, Ph.D.
Associate Professor of Marketing
Graduate School of Business
University of Southern California
Los Angeles, California
MARKETING OF SERVICES

Charles J. Mathey
Senior Consultant
The Futures Group
76 Eastern Boulevard
Glastonbury, Connecticut 06033
PRODUCT PLANNING AND DEVELOPMENT

Philip H. Maxwell, Ph.D.
Associate Professor of Finance
School of Business
James Madison University
Harrisonburg, Virginia
VALUATION OF A FIRM

Linda L. May
Research Assistant
Department of Soils and Environmental Science
University of California
Riverside, California
ENVIRONMENTAL PROTECTION LEGISLATION

William K. McAleer
President (retired)
Peter F. Loftus Corporation
Pittsburgh, Pennsylvania
ENGINEERING MANAGEMENT

Dalton E. McFarland
Professor Emeritus
School of Business
University of Alabama, Birmingham
BOARDS OF DIRECTORS; COMMITTEES; MANAGEMENT,
    DEFINITIONS OF; MANAGER, DEFINITION OF; OFFICERS,
    CORPORATE

David J. McLaughlin
McLaughlin and Company, Inc.
New York, New York
COMPENSATION, EXECUTIVE

Randolph B. McMullen
Principal
Cooper, Behrens & McMullen, Inc.
Beach Haven, New Jersey
MARGINAL INCOME ANALYSIS

Keith L. McRoberts, Ph.D.
Professor and Chairman
Department of Industrial Engineering
Iowa State University
Ames, Iowa
INVENTORY CONTROL

Peter J. McTague, J.D., P.E., C.F.A.
President and Chief Executive Officer (retired)
Green Mountain Power Corporation
Burlington, Vermont
REGULATED INDUSTRIES, MANAGEMENT OF

Dileep R. Mehta, Ph.D.
Professor of Finance
College of Business Administration
Georgia State University
Atlanta, Georgia
RISK ANALYSIS AND MANAGEMENT

Bert L. Metzger
President
Profit Sharing Research Foundation
Evanston, Illinois
PROFIT SHARING

Bryan E. Milling, B.S., M.B.A.
University of Colorado
Boulder, Colorado
CASH MANAGEMENT

John B. Miner, Ph.D.
Research Professor
Department of Management
Georgia State University
Atlanta, Georgia
COMMUNICATIONS, ORGANIZATIONAL

Mary Green Miner
Director of Surveys
Bureau of National Affairs, Inc.
Washington, District of Columbia
COMMUNICATIONS, ORGANIZATIONAL

Allan H. Mogensen
Work Simplification Conferences
Lake Placid, New York
WORK SIMPLIFICATION AND IMPROVEMENT

William James Morin
Chairman and Chief Executive Officer
Drake Beam Morin, Inc.
New York, New York
OUTPLACEMENT

David G. Muller, A.E.P.
Vice President and Personnel Director
Ohio National Life Insurance Company
Cincinnati, Ohio
PERSONNEL ADMINISTRATION

Edward L. Nash
President and Chief Executive Officer
BBDO Direct
New York, New York
MARKETING, DIRECT

Edward A. Nelson, Ph.D.
Associate Professor of Business
Northern Arizona University
Flagstaff, Arizona
EXCHANGE, FOREIGN, MANAGEMENT OF

Chester A. Newland, Ph.D.
Professor of Public Administration
University of Southern California
Sacramento, California
PUBLIC ADMINISTRATION

Herbert L. Newmark
Planning Consultant
Corporate Headquarters Development
Pompano Beach, Florida
OFFICE SPACE PLANNING

John W. Newstrom, Ph.D.
Professor of Management and Industrial Relations
School of Business and Economics
University of Minnesota
Duluth, Minnesota
DEVELOPMENT AND TRAINING, EMPLOYEE

David W. Nylen, Ph.D.
Eugene M. Lynn Professor of Marketing
School of Business Administration
Stetson University
DeLand, Florida
INNOVATION AND CREATIVITY

George S. Odiorne
Harold G. Holder Professor of Management
Eckerd College
St. Petersburg, Florida
OBJECTIVES, MANAGEMENT BY (MBO)

Tai K. Oh, Ph.D.
Professor of Management
School of Business Administration and Economics
California State University
Fullerton, California
JAPANESE INDUSTRIES, MANAGEMENT IN

Lonnie L. Ostrom, Ph.D.
Director of Development
Professor of Marketing
Arizona State University
Tempe, Arizona
PRODUCT LIABILITY

James A. Parsons, Ph.D.
Director of Manufacturing Systems
Lederle Laboratories
A Division of American Cyanamid Company
Pearl River, New York
PRODUCTION/OPERATIONS MANAGEMENT

Walter W. Perlick, Ph.D.
Professor of Finance
Business Administration Department
California Polytechnic State University
San Luis Obispo, California
OWNERSHIP, LEGAL FORMS OF

Victor H. Pooler, C.P.M.
Director of Purchasing
Carrier Corporation
Syracuse, New York
PURCHASING MANAGEMENT

Avner M. Porat, Ph.D.
Partner
Hay Associates
Management Consultants
Philadelphia, Pennsylvania
COMPENSATION, SALES

Walter J. Primeaux, Jr., Ph.D.
Professor of Business Administration
College of Commerce and Business Administration
University of Illinois at Urbana-Champaign
Champaign, Illinois
PROFITS AND PROFIT MAKING

Robert E. Pritchard, M.B.A., Ed.D.
Professor of Finance and Chairperson
Accounting and Finance
Glassboro State College
Glassboro, New Jersey
LEASING, EQUIPMENT

Harold F. Puff, D.B.A., C.P.M.
Professor of Management, Emeritus
School of Business Administration
Miami University
Oxford, Ohio
COST IMPROVEMENT

**Reverend Theodore V. Purcell, S.J., Ph.D.
(deceased)**
Research Professor
Jesuit Center for Social Studies
Georgetown University
Washington, District of Columbia
EQUAL EMPLOYMENT OPPORTUNITY, MINORITIES AND WOMEN

Inez L. Ramsey, Ed.D.
Assistant Professor
Department of Educational Resources
James Madison University
Harrisonburg, Virginia
COMPUTER-ASSISTED INSTRUCTIONS; DATA BASES,
    COMMERCIAL; INFORMATION SOURCES

Jackson E. Ramsey, M.B.A., Ph.D., P.E.
School of Business
James Madison University
Harrisonburg, Virginia
(contributor of selected entries)

Peter A. Rechnitzer, M.D.
Clinical Professor of Medicine
University of Western Ontario
London, Ontario, Canada
STRESS MANAGEMENT

Larry D. Redinbaugh, Ph.D.
Professor of Administration
College of Business
Creighton University
Omaha, Nebraska
RETAILING MANAGEMENT

Frank K. Reilly, Ph.D.
Dean
College of Business Administration
University of Notre Dame
South Bend, Indiana
MARKETS, SECURITIES; MARKETS, STOCK INDICATOR SERIES

James W. Rice, Ph.D., P.E., CPIM
Professor
College of Business Administration
University of Wisconsin-Oshkosh
Oshkosh, Wisconsin
PRODUCTION PLANNING AND CONTROL

Wallace James Richardson
Professor of Industrial Engineering
Lehigh University
Bethlehem, Pennsylvania
WORK SAMPLING

Al Ries
Trout & Ries Advertising, Inc.
New York, New York
POSITIONING

J. Robin Roark, Ph.D.
Partner
Hay Associates
Management Consultants
Philadelphia, Pennsylvania
WAGES AND HOURS LEGISLATION

Robotics Industries Association
Dearborn, Michigan
ROBOTICS

Simcha Ronen, Ph.D., P.E.
Associate Professor of Organizational Behavior
Graduate School of Business
New York University
New York, New York
WORK SCHEDULES, ALTERNATE

Bernard L. Rosenbaum, Ed.D.
President
MOHR Development, Inc.
Stamford, Connecticut
BEHAVIOR MODELING

Stuart Rosenthal, M.S., M.D.
Clinical Instructor
Department of Psychiatry
Harvard Medical School
Cambridge, Massachusetts
HEALTH, MENTAL

John E. Russell, P.E., C.S.P.
Vice President
Executive in Charge of the Loss Control Division
Maryland Casualty Company
Baltimore, Maryland
SAFETY AND HEALTH MANAGEMENT, EMPLOYEE

Burt K. Scanlan, Ph.D.
Professor of Management
College of Business Administration
University of Oklahoma
Norman, Oklahoma
YOUNGER EMPLOYEES, MANAGEMENT OF

David Schirm, Ph.D.
Assistant Professor
Department of Economics
John Carroll University
Cleveland, Ohio
VALUE-ADDED TAX

Donald P. Schwab, Ph.D.
Slichter Research Professor
Graduate School of Business and Industrial
    Relations Research Institute
University of Wisconsin, Madison
Madison, Wisconsin
MOTIVATION IN ORGANIZATIONS

Eleanor Brantley Schwartz, D.B.A.
Dean
College of Business and Public Administration
University of Missouri-Kansas City
Kansas City, Missouri
WOMEN IN BUSINESS AND MANAGEMENT

Rex A. Sebastian
Senior Vice President, Operations
Dresser Industries, Inc.
Dallas, Texas
INTERNATIONAL OPERATIONS AND MANAGEMENT IN
    MULTINATIONAL COMPANIES

Robert E. Seiler, C.P.A., Ph.D.
Professor of Accounting
University of Houston
Houston, Texas
ACCOUNTING, MANAGERIAL CONTROL

David D. Seltz
President
Seltz Franchising Developments, Inc.
New Rochelle, New York
FRANCHISING

Robert E. Shannon, Ph.D., P.E.
Professor
Department of Industrial Engineering
Texas A&M University
College Station, Texas
OPERATIONS RESEARCH AND MATHEMATICAL MODELING

Richard G. Sheehan
Federal Reserve Bank of St. Louis
St. Louis, Missouri
ECONOMIC MEASUREMENTS

Jagdish N. Sheth, Ph.D.
Brooker Professor of Research
School of Business
University of California
Los Angeles, California
CONSUMER BEHAVIOR, MANAGERIAL RELEVANCE OF

Robert A. Shiff, C.M.C., C.R.M.
President
Naremco Services, Inc.
New York, New York
RECORDS MANAGEMENT

Julian L. Simon
Professor of Economics and Marketing
College of Commerce and Business Administration
University of Illinois at Urbana
Urbana, Illinois
PROFITS AND PROFIT MAKING

E. Ralph Sims, Jr., P.E., C.M.C.
President
The Sims Consulting Group, Inc.
Lancaster, Ohio
MATERIALS MANAGEMENT

Bernard R. Siskin, Ph.D.
Professor
Temple University
Philadelphia, Pennsylvania
STATISTICAL ANALYSIS FOR MANAGEMENT

C. Ray Smith
Tipton R. Snavely Professor of Business
    Administration
The Colgate Darden Graduate School of Business
    Administration
University of Virginia
Charlottesville, Virginia
BUDGETING, CAPITAL

Larry A. Smith, Ph.D.
College of Business Administration
Florida International University
North Miami, Florida
PROJECT MANAGEMENT

William A. Smith, Jr.
Director, Applied Research and Technology Transfer
Professor, Industrial Engineering
North Carolina State University
Raleigh, North Carolina
SYSTEM CONCEPT, TOTAL

Neil H. Snyder
Associate Professor
McIntire School of Commerce
University of Virginia
Charlottesville, Virginia
PLANNING, STRATEGIC MANAGERIAL

Roger A. Soenksen, Ph.D.
Assistant Professor
Department of Communication Arts
James Madison University
Harrisonburg, Virginia
PRIVACY IN THE WORKPLACE

Harriet Premack Soll
Business and Industry Specialist
Central Office
United States Small Business Administration
Washington, District of Columbia
CONTRACTING OUT; SMALL BUSINESS ADMINISTRATION

Martin K. Solomon, Ph.D.
Associate Professor
Department of Computer and Information Systems
College of Business and Public Administration
Florida Atlantic University
Boca Raton, Florida
COMPUTER SOFTWARE, DATA-BASE MANAGEMENT

Edwin H. Sonnecken
Former Vice President, Goodyear Tire and Rubber
    Company, Akron, Ohio
Chairman, Marketing Science Institute
Cambridge, Massachusetts
BRANDS AND BRAND NAMES

Rajendra K. Srivastava, Ph.D.
Associate Professor
Department of Marketing Administration
Graduate School of Business
University of Texas
Austin, Texas
MARKET ANALYSIS

Steven J. Stanard, Ph.D.
Stanard & Associates
Psychologists
Chicago, Illinois
TESTING, PSYCHOLOGICAL

Thomas C. Stanton
President
Francis Marion College
Florence, South Carolina
ACCOUNTING, FINANCIAL

Lawrence L. Steinmetz, Ph.D.
President
High Yield Management, Inc.
Boulder, Colorado
DELEGATION

David C. Stewart
Chairman
Carlisle Engineering Management, Inc.
Carlisle, Massachusetts
FACILITIES AND SITE PLANNING AND LAYOUT

Morris Stone
Vice President (retired)
American Arbitration Association
New York, New York
ARBITRATION, COMMERCIAL; ARBITRATION, LABOR

Paul J. Stonich
Senior Vice President
Management Analysis Center, Inc.
Northbrook, Illinois
BUDGETS AND BUDGET PREPARATION

C. Ian Sym-Smith
General Partner
Hay Associates
Management Consultants
Philadelphia, Pennsylvania
COMPENSATION, SALES

Robert W. Taft
Senior Vice President
Hill and Knowlton, Inc.
New York, New York
SHAREHOLDER RELATIONS

Daniel A. Tagliere
President
ODS—Organization Development Services, Inc.
Chicago, Illinois
ORGANIZATION DEVELOPMENT (OD)

Alden R. Taylor, Jr.
Principal
Cresap, McCormick, and Paget Division
Towers, Perrin, Forster & Crosby
New York, New York
AUDIT, MANAGEMENT

Robert L. Taylor, D.B.A., Lt. Col., USAF
Associate Professor
Department of Economics, Geography, and
    Management
United States Air Force Academy
Colorado Springs, Colorado
PROGRAM PLANNING AND IMPLEMENTATION

Weldon J. Taylor, Ph.D.
Professor of Marketing
Dean Emeritus
College of Business
Brigham Young University
Provo, Utah
MARKETING, CHANNELS OF DISTRIBUTION

Frederick A. Teague
President
Frederick A. Teague & Company, Inc.
Chicago, Illinois
JOB ANALYSIS; JOB EVALUATION

Daphyne Saunders Thomas
Assistant Professor of Business Law
School of Business
James Madison University
Harrisonburg, Virginia
GOVERNMENT REGULATIONS, UNIFORM COMMERCIAL CODE

Albert Thumann, P.E., C.E.M.
Executive Director
Association of Energy Engineers
Atlanta, Georgia
ENERGY MANAGEMENT

Curtis J. Tompkins, Ph.D.
Dean
College of Engineering
West Virginia University
Morgantown, West Virginia
FORECASTING BUSINESS CONDITIONS

Paul E. Torgersen
Dean
College of Engineering
Virginia Polytechnic Institute and State University
Blacksburg, Virginia
SIMULATIONS, BUSINESS AND MANAGEMENT

Benjamin B. Tregoe, Ph.D.
Chairman, Kepner-Tregoe, Inc.
Strategic and Operational Decision Making
Princeton, New Jersey
DECISION-MAKING PROCESS

Joseph M. Trickett, Ph.D.
Professor of Management
Graduate School of Business and Administration
University of Santa Clara
Santa Clara, California
AUTHORITY, RESPONSIBILITY, AND ACCOUNTABILITY

Jack Trout
President
Trout & Ries Advertising, Inc.
New York, New York
POSITIONING

Peter A. Veglahn
Associate Professor
School of Business
James Madison University
Harrisonburg, Virginia
LABOR LEGISLATION

Walter Bernhard Waetjen, Ed.D.
President
Cleveland State University
Cleveland, Ohio
WOMEN IN BUSINESS AND MANAGEMENT

Samuel Wagner
Professor of Business Administration
Franklin and Marshall College
Lancaster, Pennsylvania
TECHNOLOGY TRANSFER

Timothy J. Walsh, J.D., CPP
President
Harris & Walsh Management Consultants, Inc.
New Rochelle, New York
SECURITY MANAGEMENT

Loren E. Waltz
Professor of Business Administration
Indiana University at South Bend
South Bend, Indiana
SOCIETIES, PROFESSIONAL

A. John Ward
President, Strategus Associates
Former Vice President, Management Consulting
    Division,
The Austin Company
Englewood, Florida
MARKETING, INDUSTRIAL

David Warren, C.P.C.U.
Risk Management Consultant
Orinda, California
INSURANCE AND RISK MANAGEMENT

Howard Way and Associates, Inc.
Alexandria, Virginia
INVENTORY STOCK-KEEPING SYSTEMS

Norman Weissman
President
Ruder Finn & Rotman Inc.
New York, New York
PUBLIC AND COMMUNITY RELATIONS

Merle T. Welshans
Adjunct Professor of Finance
School of Business and Public Administration
Washington University
St. Louis, Missouri
FINANCIAL MANAGEMENT

Raymond P. Wenig
President
International Management Services, Inc.
Framingham, Massachusetts
COMPUTER HARDWARE, MICROS/PERSONAL; COMPUTER
    SOFTWARE PACKAGES

J. Fred Weston, Ph.D.
Professor of Managerial Economics and Finance
Graduate School of Management
University of California at Los Angeles
Los Angeles, California
FINANCIAL STATEMENT ANALYSIS

Basil J. Whiting
Senior Partner
Work Life Development Systems, Inc.
Detroit, Michigan
QUALITY OF WORK LIFE

David A. Whitsett
Professor of Psychology
University of Northern Iowa
Cedar Falls, Iowa
WORK DESIGN, JOB ENLARGEMENT, AND JOB ENRICHMENT

Kenneth C. Williamson, Ph.D.
Associate Professor
Department of Management and Marketing
James Madison University
Harrisonburg, Virginia
LOGISTICS, BUSINESS

George W. Wilson, Ph.D.
Distinguished Professor of Business Administration
Professor of Economics
Indiana University
Bloomington, Indiana
ECONOMIC SYSTEMS

Gerald Zaltman, Ph.D.
Albert Wesley Frey Professor of Marketing
Graduate School of Business
University of Pittsburgh
Pittsburgh, Pennsylvania
MARKET ANALYSIS

Carle C. Zimmerman, Ph.D.
Manager
Instrumentation and Engineering Department
Denver Research Center
Marathon Oil Company
Littleton, Colorado
RESEARCH AND DEVELOPMENT MANAGEMENT

D. Kent Zimmerman, Ph.D.
Associate Professor
Department of Management and Marketing
James Madison University
Harrisonburg, Virginia
NOMINAL GROUP TECHNIQUE; POWER AND INFLUENCE

PREFACE

The purpose of this handbook is to provide managers in all kinds of organizations with (1) clear explanations of fundamental concepts and widely practiced techniques and (2) specific advice about how to apply them successfully. The material was selected and shaped to serve managers and potential managers in both the private and public sectors, and they will find here not only *why* a particular principle is accepted but also *how* to use it effectively. The emphasis is primarily on business usage, but considerable attention is given to management practices in public administration and not-for-profit organizations.

The entries in this volume reflect the considered judgment of more than 200 qualified people. These authors have employed a professional approach on the basis of several pivotal factors elaborated upon below.

Scope.   Three intimately related areas were considered in selecting subject matter:

1. *Primary management functions,* such as planning, organizing, activating, controlling, and decision making
2. *Major business activities,* such as finance and accounting, operations and production, marketing and sales, and information management
3. *Environmental resources and constraints,* such as human resources, materials, funds, equipment and facilities, consumer demand, economic con-

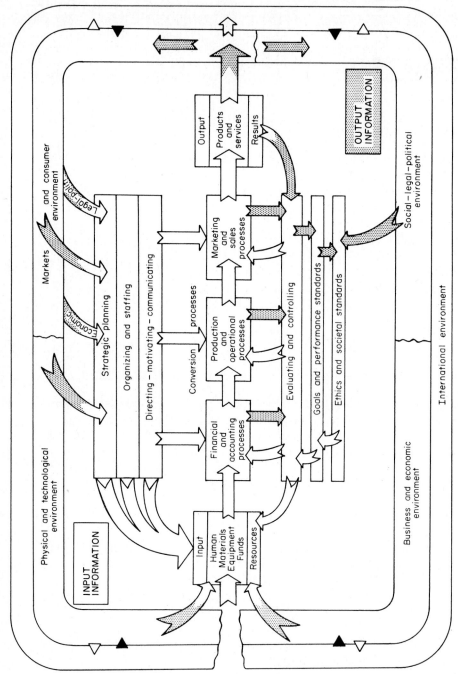

Conceptual rationale for determining scope of subject matter.

ditions, natural resources, community influences, and government regulations

The management process and the business system are examined in each
of their parts, from assembling resources to converting them into value-
added outputs as products and services. These, in turn, are placed in context
with the various environments in which they operate. Thus, the reader will
find definitions, explanations, and application instructions on most significant aspects of management as it applies to business and resources conversion. The accompanying figure graphically illustrates the process involved,
and the handbook includes almost everything that our advisors decided was
of value for the practice of professional management.

Historical information about a concept or technique is included only
where it contributes to understanding some application. Specific figures and
statistics that may be outdated quickly are included only when absolutely
necessary to provide a frame of reference for immediate usage.

A difficult decision, arrived at with the help of the editorial advisers, was
to eliminate biographical sketches of significant managers or contributors to
managerial theories and practices. Some coverage is given to individuals,
however, under Management, historical development of. Throughout the
text, reference is also made to notable contributors, but no biographical
sketches as such are included.

Entry Coverage.   In this work there are 239 comprehensive entries, which
contain over 3000 specific definitions. In general, each major entry provides
(1) a definition of the underlying principle or concept; (2) application opportunities, techniques, procedures, and examples; (3) an evaluation of the usefulness of the concept or technique; and (4) a list of other sources of information available either in the handbook or elsewhere. The key definitions in
the major entries are highlighted in italics.

Perspective.   Regardless of how abstract the subject, contributors were
encouraged to use simple language and to furnish practical examples. Most
important, the authors emphasized the place of every subject within the managerial purview. Because of this, in the eyes of some specialists, depth may
seem to be lacking in some areas. If this is the case, it has not been accidental. With such breadth of subject matter, the controlling guideline throughout
has been to demonstrate the techniques of managerial usage and the suitability for management application.

Disciplines.   Many terms and subjects appear under more than one subject
heading. This reflects the multidisciplinary nature of many managerial and
business activities. Inevitably, and intentionally, there are areas of overlap.
Occasionally there are differing points of view. This reflects the nature of
management, which precludes flat statements of conclusions and unqualified
prescriptions for behavior without first taking the nature of the situation and
the various forces at play fully into account. In many management areas, the
study is fragmented because of the specialized attitudes, training, and expe-

rience of those who practice it. From an academic view, broad disciplines, such as sociology, psychology, information sciences, communications theory, economics, statistics, mathematics, physics, and engineering enter into its discussion. From an experiential view, various business disciplines, such as accounting, finance, marketing, and operations prevail—based also on the individual's experience in a particular industry, such as construction, manufacturing, banking, insurance, public administration, or not-for-profit institutions.

Topic Selection. Topics were selected by a panel of distinguished authorities in their fields. Priorities were assigned to techniques, methods, and concepts most commonly used by professional managers. Practical applications for day-to-day use and for long-term planning and analysis were emphasized. As a consequence, this handbook constitutes a desk reference for dealing professionally with contemporary problems and issues such as those associated with information management, computer optimization, financial strategy, marketing analysis, government restrictions, international awareness, and operational productivity.

Terminology. No claim is made that the definitions here represent standard terminology. At best, they reflect popular business usage and academic consensus. It is especially difficult to reach a standard (or consensus) for management terms because of their unique origin. Management is widely practiced and has its source in many countries, cultures, and languages. Furthermore, it is derived from and grows from many disciplines or fields such as the social and physical sciences, mathematics and statistics, economics and philosophy, and language and communications. It is truly multidisciplinary in character and thus resists the efforts to place its elements under universal restraints, even those imposed by terminology.

Where possible, however, the contributors have respected the efforts to standardize management terms. They have drawn on the works of those professional societies that have developed glossaries of terms acceptable to their members (notably the American Institute of Industrial Engineers, which has a published standard) and on the efforts of the accounting and financial professions to develop standard practices based upon agreement on definitions of terms. They have also consulted the hundreds of textbooks and occasional management dictionaries which have tried separately to solve the problem. In the main, however, the standard for a great many terms remains the basic dictionaries of the English language. Our instruction to authors was to define only those terms for which the established dictionary definition was inadequate or misleading. Accordingly, most terms with a meaning unique to management or its practice are italicized in the text with their definition following immediately.

Indexing. The arrangement of entries is alphabetical and is self-indexing. This is based upon the original decision to arrange this work alphabetically
rather than according to disciplines or functional fields. Because of the many

disciplines involved, it makes sense, but it cannot be denied that management and business subjects do not lend themselves easily to alphabetizing. For this reason, every effort has been made to assist the reader in finding the specific subject matter desired—either in the Table of Contents and Subject Locator Guide or in the comprehensive Index at the back of the book.

Lester R. Bittel
Jackson E. Ramsey

ACKNOWLEDGMENTS

This new work was greatly assisted by a number of individuals who generously shared their expertise with us. Of particular value was the advice of Dr. Donald W. Kroeber for areas related to computers, information management systems, and decision sciences; Dr. Philip H. Maxwell for financial management and investments; and Dr. Inez L. Ramsey for data bases and information sciences. Additionally, we received valued assistance from Robert L. Craig, Stahrl W. Edmunds, Mack Hanan, John W. Hannon, Joseph Harrington, Jr., Joel E. Ross, William G. Sharwell, and William Stocker.

We are also indebted to our colleagues at James Madison University who offered so much support and consultation. They include, in particular, Ronald B. Carrier, president; Robert E. Holmes, dean of the School of Business; Paul H. Kipps, associate dean; and Ross H. Johnson, head of the department of management and marketing.

Finally, we acknowledge the contributions of Pavey L. Hoke and Alice Smith, who did so much of the research for an earlier version of this work, and Helen Turner Royall, who continued her perfection in copy editing and word processing.

Lester R. Bittel
Jackson E. Ramsey
Muriel Albers Bittel

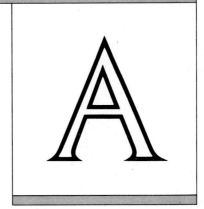

Accounting, Cost Analysis and Control

What is often called cost accounting serves two fairly distinct purposes. Using information prepared for one purpose for the other purpose can lead to incorrect decisions. Two illustrations will suffice. Your accountants report that the average cost per unit of a product produced this July is $4, while for July last year the cost was $4.50. Does this mean that production has been more efficient this year than last? Not necessarily. In another company, accountants report that the average cost of producing a subassembly is $15 per unit, while the purchasing department reports that the identical subassembly can be purchased from a subcontractor for $11 per unit. Does this mean that the subassembly should be purchased from the subcontractor rather than produced internally? Not necessarily. Both cases illustrate situations in which information produced for one purpose might be used inappropriately for another purpose.

Domain of Cost Accounting. The two distinct purposes of cost accounting are sometimes called cost finding and management accounting. *Cost finding* was originally the sole interest of cost account-

ing. Its purpose is to calculate the average cost per unit of products produced by a manufacturer. The accounting rules for determining the average cost per unit are established to facilitate preparation of income statements and balance sheets. Generally accepted accounting principles require that inventories be reported on the basis of their cost. When the units are sold, they are reported in the income statement as cost of goods sold at this same cost. In a manufacturing organization, cost must be determined by an averaging process which satisfies generally accepted accounting principles.

Management accounting is the newer interest of cost accounting. Its purpose is to provide managers with information which aids decision making. There are no generally accepted principles which specify how management accounting information is to be reported. While systems such as direct costing and standard costing exist in management accounting, each accounting report should be tailored to the needs of the decision and the decision maker. The most effective systems result when the manager-decision maker and the accountant work together until the accountant understands the decision to be made and the manager understands the source of the information that the accountant will report.

Cost-Volume Relations

The relation of total cost to volume of operations has its most important application in management accounting, but is also used in cost finding. It is important in management accounting because managers frequently face decisions involving changes in volume of operations (along with other changes). To determine the profit impact of a decision, it is necessary to predict the resulting changes in cost. This requires knowledge of existing cost-volume relations. In cost finding, a predetermined overhead rate (burden rate) can be calculated only after the total amount of overhead cost for the year has been predicted. Since the volume of output is important to the amount of variable costs which should be expected, it is necessary to know the cost-volume relation in order to predict the total amount of overhead cost.

The relation of cost to volume generally falls into two categories, fixed and variable, explained below. Other possibilities exist, and the most important one—semivariable costs—will also be discussed.

Fixed Costs. A fixed cost is one for which the total amount of the cost per period is independent of the volume of operations, within a relevant range of volume. Graphically, it can be shown as indicated in Fig. A-1. The graph shows that as the volume of operations fluctuates within the relevant range, as shown

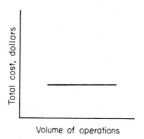

FIG. A-1 Graph of a fixed cost.

by the length of the line, the total amount of this expense, as measured on the vertical scale, remains constant. Examples include the salary of the factory manager, property taxes, and insurance on the factory building and equipment. Note that the definition does not say that a fixed cost will never change. Managers know that salaries, taxes, and insurance do change. The significant point is that the amount of the fixed cost is not directly changed by changes in volume. It would be most unusual, for example, if a factory manager's salary were to fluctuate from month to month based on the production volume of the factory. (If this were to happen, the salary would no longer be an example of a fixed expense.) If there is a significant expansion of the factory capacity, the factory manager's salary might be increased at the next salary review. In addition, the expansion of fac-

tory capacity would probably increase the amount of insurance and taxes. However, these changes would not make these costs variable costs. Rather, the amount of cost would have changed from one fixed level to another fixed level. The new line on the graph would be higher than the old line, but it would still be horizontal. If this were to happen, management would have to replan a variety of activities and also alter the overhead rate used in the factory.

Variable Costs. A variable cost is one in which the total amount varies in direct proportion to the volume of operations but the per-unit cost remains constant within a relevant range. This can be illustrated as shown on the graph in Fig. A-2. To meet this

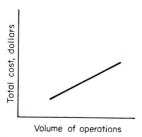

FIG. A-2 Graph of a variable cost.

rather strict definition, the line of the variable cost must be pointed so that it would pass through the origin of the graph (0,0), if the relevant range extended that far back. A prime example of a variable cost is direct materials used in the production of a product. Increasing production by 10 percent will increase the amount of direct materials used by 10 percent. Further, one should expect that a reduction in volume of operations by, say, 15 percent, would reduce the amount of direct materials required by 15 percent. This is because the amount of direct materials used per unit of product is constant.

The idea of a relevant range is important because experience shows that if a manager were to consider doubling volume or cutting volume by two-thirds, cost levels would change in an erratic manner. But such large changes are the exceptions; dealing with them requires a special study. In the normal situation, managers have found that cost can be expected to fluctuate in a predictable manner within the relevant range in which most decisions are made.

Semivariable Costs. If a cost increases as a result of volume changes, it cannot, by definition, be a fixed cost. But there are costs which increase as a result of volume changes but do not fit the rather strict definition of variable cost. Maintenance and electricity costs are examples. These costs often fall into the category of semivariable costs. Within the relevant range, a semivariable cost will increase as a result of changes in the volume of operations but not in direct proportion to volume. A graph of a semivariable cost is shown in Fig. A-3. Note that the line

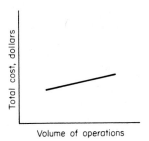

FIG. A-3 Graph of a semivariable cost.

slopes upward as volume increases but that it would not pass through the origin if the relevant range extended back that far.

Semivariable costs present no new problems in analysis, however, because they can be broken into a fixed component and a variable component. This can probably be seen most easily by referring to the graph in Fig. A-4. The graph is the same as that in Fig. A-3

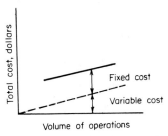

FIG. A-4 Graph of a semivariable cost showing fixed and variable components.

except that the dashed line is added to illustrate that the semivariable cost can be thought of as a variable cost with a fixed amount added on top. The dashed line shows the variable-cost component. The amount added on top is a fixed amount, the same at all volumes, thus fitting the definition of a fixed cost. For analysis, a semivariable expense is broken into its fixed and variable components.

Considering the examples of maintenance and electricity, one can understand why a fixed and variable component would exist. The routine preventive maintenance is the fixed component. The balance of the maintenance could be expected to increase or decrease as the volume of operations resulted in greater or less use of the machines. Electricity used in lighting is likely to be a fixed cost. The plant must be lighted whether it operates at 70 percent capacity or 80 percent capacity; the lighting cost does not vary with volume. The electricity used to power the machines, however, could be expected to increase or decrease as the volume of operations resulted in greater or less use of the machines. Thus, the total electricity cost would have a fixed and a variable

component; therefore it would be a semivariable cost.

Cost Finding

One of the important generally accepted accounting principles (*See* Accounting, financial) is that assets, including inventories, shall be reported at their cost. As the inventory items are sold, the inventory asset account is reduced by the cost of the item sold, and that cost is reported in the income statement as an expense—cost of goods sold. For a retailing or wholesaling firm, the inventory cost can generally be taken from a purchase invoice, adjusted for transportation costs to the warehouse and perhaps some minor preparation costs. In other words, determining the cost of inventory items (and the subsequent cost-of-goods-sold expense) is relatively easy. But in a manufacturing concern, material is purchased and converted through the use of production labor, supplies, equipment, plant facilities, supervision, etc., into the finished inventory ready for sale. The cost of the finished-goods inventory cannot be determined by referring to a purchase invoice. Many other items are a part of the cost. The major task of cost finding is to take the total pool of manufacturing costs and find an average cost of each unit of product produced.

The determination of the average cost per unit is made as follows: The total costs of operating the production facility for a month or a year are determined. If a single product is produced, the total number of units produced is also counted. The average cost per unit is calculated by dividing the total cost by the total number of units. In other words,

Average cost per unit
$$= \frac{\text{total product costs for the period}}{\text{total units produced during the period}}$$

Cost Definitions. For a single product company the only serious problem in determining the average cost per unit is distinguishing between product costs and period costs. In the formula above, to obtain the average cost per unit, only product costs are divided by units produced. Of course, most manufacturing organizations produce more than one product, so they have other problems in cost finding. But all firms must distinguish between product costs and period costs.

Product Costs. Certain costs are physically traceable to a product and are generally agreed to be a part of the cost of the product. The major examples of these product costs are direct materials and direct labor. *Direct materials* are the materials incorporated into the product. They may be basic materials like steel, sand, and ore, or they may be sophisticated subassemblies such as engines and computer modules. In like manner, some production labor is performed directly on the product (perhaps using

3

machinery and equipment). Direct labor is also physically traceable to the product since one can observe and time the work done on a particular product. Thus *direct labor* is that production labor which is performed directly on the product and which can be observed being performed on the product.

Supplies, electricity, heating of the plant, and property taxes and insurance on the plant and equipment are examples of the production costs and are included as part of the average cost of a product. Any cost incurred solely because the firm is in manufacturing is a product cost.

Period Costs. Costs which are not product costs are period costs. Period costs are *not* included in the average cost of the product produced; rather, they are considered an expense in the income statement of the period. Generally speaking, period costs include the selling expenses and general administrative expenses. A wholesaler or retailer incurs selling expenses and general administrative expenses. Of course, the nature and amount of selling and general administrative expenses depend on the nature of the company, its products, and how they are sold. But these types of costs are incurred by all businesses; therefore it cannot be argued that these costs are incurred solely as a result of being in manufacturing.

Overhead Costs. One further definition is needed before the ideas of product and period costs can be summarized. Overhead costs are all product costs other than direct materials and direct labor. Notice that a rather special definition is applied. In general conversation, general administration such as sales management, credit management, customer billing, and similar items might be considered overhead. Not so in this definition. All these items are examples of period costs. They are not product costs and therefore are not overhead. Any organization—retail, wholesale, or manufacturing—would have them.

Schematically, the distinctions and definitions just discussed can be illustrated as shown in Fig. A-5. The significance of the distinctions is that period costs are accounted for as income statement expense items for all retailers, wholesalers, and manufacturers. Product costs would not exist in a retailing or wholesaling organization. For the manufacturer, they are added together and divided by the number of units produced during the period to determine the

average cost per unit of manufactured product. This average cost per unit is first accounted for as an addition to the inventory asset account. When the product is sold, the inventory (asset) is reduced and the expense (cost of goods sold) is increased.

Overhead Rates. In the single product firm, the process of cost finding—determining the average cost per unit—consists of the following three steps:

1. Determine which of the costs incurred by the firm during a year are product costs.

2. Determine the number of units of product produced during the year.

3. Divide the total product costs for the year by the number of units produced.

But what if the company produces several products in a single plant? A new problem exists. The same three-step process cannot be followed because it does not make sense to add units of different products as if they were the same. For example, a company produces color and black-and-white television sets in the same factory. Further, there are several models of each type of television. If product costs were totaled and divided by the total number of television sets produced, all units would be found to have the same cost, a conclusion which is obviously erroneous. Each type and model uses some different parts, requires different direct labor time to produce, and makes use of some different facilities.

Direct Measurement. How does cost accounting find a more reasonable answer? Since the direct material is physically incorporated into the product, it is possible to ask production workers to record the amount of material used in producing each model and type of set. Also, the direct labor workers can be asked to record on their time cards the amount of time spent producing each model and type of set. If questions arise about the accuracy of either direct material or direct labor cost, it is possible to send someone into the factory to observe the production process and to record the material and direct labor going into each model and type of set. The resulting figures should agree with records kept by the production workers, since direct materials are physically incorporated into the set and the direct labor is performed on a particular set. Although it requires some careful record keeping, this is the easy part of the accounting process.

Overhead Measurement. The accounting for the overhead, however, presents three different problems for consideration.

1. Most of the overhead costs will be incurred for the benefit of several or all the products rather than for a single product. There is no physical link to the product as there is in the case of direct materials and direct labor. It is plain that if the product is to be produced, the plant must be heated during the cold months of the year. The

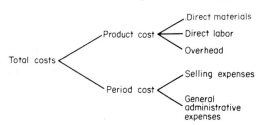

FIG. A-5 Relationships of various cost definitions.

heating of the factory is a product cost and must be included in the average cost of the products produced. But the heat cost benefits not a particular set but all sets produced. There is no way of tracing the amount of heat going into each set as can be done with direct labor.

2. Many costs are cyclical. For example, the heating cost is seasonal. It will be incurred in cold months and not in warm months. But should physically identical sets which were produced in the month of January be said to cost more than the same set produced in June? The accounting answer is no. If the sets were produced in the same facilities, by the same methods, and with the same general level of production efficiency, accountants argue that the sets should have the same average cost. So the heat costs should be averaged over all sets produced during the year.

3. Much production is cyclical. This is similar to the seasonality problem but relates to the fact that the number of units produced varies from month to month because of seasonal sales patterns. This presents no serious problems with direct materials and direct labor because these are usually variable costs, and the cost per unit is constant at any volume in the relevant range. Many overhead costs are fixed, however. What happens if the fixed total monthly costs are divided by varying monthly production totals? The average cost per unit varies from month to month for physically identical products. This is illustrated below.

	June	September
Monthly total fixed costs	$35,000	$35,000
Monthly total production of sets	10,000 sets	14,000 sets
Average fixed cost per unit	$3.50	$2.50

Again accountants argue that these cost variations should be averaged out in cost finding.

Overhead Rates. All three problems are solved by use of predetermined overhead rates which average the fixed costs and serve as a basis for dividing common costs among different products. (These rates are also called burden rates.) A predetermined overhead rate is calculated and used as follows:

1. A decision is made to allocate the overhead in proportion to some base, often direct labor hours, direct labor cost, or machine hours. This decision solves the common cost problem.

2. The total expected production volume for the next year is estimated. The volume is converted to units of the base selected in step 1.

3. The total overhead cost to be incurred for the next year is estimated.

4. The predetermined overhead rate is determined by dividing the total estimated overhead cost for next year by the total estimated production volume, estimated in step 2. The annual estimates used in this step solve the seasonality problems mentioned earlier.

5. Overhead cost is applied (or allocated) to each product by multiplying the predetermined overhead rate by the amount of base (direct labor hours, etc.) contained in the product.

Here is an example of the process. Vinz Corporation produces three products. The expected material and labor content of each product is given below.

	Product R	Product C	Product D
Materials	$11	$8	$17
Direct labor @ $6 per hour	$ 3 (½ hour)	$4 (⅔ hour)	$ 6 (1 hour)

For next year, Vinz estimates sales of R will be 18,000 units, C will be 15,000 units, and D will be 6000 units. It is further estimated that the fixed overhead costs will total $50,000 for the year. Variable overhead is estimated to be $5 per direct labor.

How is the predetermined overhead rate found? Management examines the nature of the overhead items and discovers that the largest part of the overhead consists of supervision, fringe benefits, and other personnel-related costs. Further, the accounting system is already recording and totaling direct labor hours incurred. Thus management decides to base the predetermined overhead rate on direct labor hours. Had the production process been more automated and the overhead costs primarily machine-related costs such as property taxes, insurance, maintenance, and depreciation, management might have decided to base the overhead rate on machine hours. If there had been heavy components of both personnel-related costs and machine-related costs, management might have considered using two predetermined rates, one based on direct labor hours and the other based on machine hours. Most often a single rate is used.

The total production volume had already been estimated in units. All that was needed was to convert the volume estimate to direct labor hours, the base of the predetermined overhead rate. It was done as follows:

Product R	18,000 units @ ½ hour per unit	9,000 hours
Product C	15,000 units @ ⅔ hour per unit	10,000
Product D	6,000 units @ 1 hour per unit	6,000
Total estimated volume for next year		25,000 hours

Next the total overhead cost for next year was estimated as follows:

Fixed overhead	$ 50,000
Variable overhead 25,000 hours @ $5 per hour . .	125,000
Total estimated overhead for next year	$175,000

The predetermined overhead rate is then

$$\frac{\text{Total estimated overhead for next year}}{\text{Total estimated volume for next year}} = \frac{\$175,000}{25,000}$$
$$= \$7 \text{ per direct labor hour}$$

Determining the Average Unit Cost. The Vinz Corporation example is used to complete the illustration of how the average cost per unit is calculated. During the first month of the new year, the company produced 1200 units of R, 1000 units of C, and 500 units of D. The direct materials used for each product were determined by totaling the requisitions from the materials storeroom. The direct labor cost incurred on each product was identified on time tickets prepared by the direct labor workers.

	Product R	Product C	Product D
Direct materials used	$13,464	$7,840	$9,010
Direct labor cost incurred	$ 3,852 (647 hours)	$4,200 (706 hours)	$3,013 (506 hours)

(The reader who recalls the expected direct labor content given earlier in the entry may note that Vinz Corporation used more hours than should have been used for the number of units of products R, C, and D produced. Further, the average cost per direct labor hour was slightly below the expected rate. In a standard cost system—to be discussed later—these facts would give rise to an unfavorable direct labor price variance.)

The average direct labor cost and direct materials cost per unit are determined by dividing the total cost for each product by the number of units produced in the period. The overhead cost per unit is determined by calculating the overhead cost applied to each product during the first month and then dividing it by the number of units produced. The overhead cost applied is the predetermined overhead rate of $7 per direct labor hour times the number of direct labor hours spent on each product during the month.

Product R $7 per hour × 647 hours = $4529
Product C $7 per hour × 706 hours = $4942
Product D $7 per hour × 506 hours = $3542

The average cost per unit of product R is:

Direct materials $13,464/1200 units	=	$11.22 per unit
Direct labor $3852/1200 units	=	3.21 per unit
Overhead $4529/1200 units	=	3.77 per unit
Average cost		$18.20 per unit

In like manner, the average cost of the other two products produced in the first month is reckoned:

	Product C	Product D
Direct materials	$ 7.84	$18.02
Direct labor	4.20	6.03
Overhead	4.94	7.08
Average cost	$16.98 per unit	$31.13 per unit

Standard Costs. Standard costs are estimates of what the material, direct labor, and overhead cost per unit *should* be. They are often determined by adjusting past cost levels, as shown in the accounting records, for any inefficiencies discovered in discussions with production workers and production supervisors. Industrial engineering estimates, though expensive, are also helpful. Sometimes engineering estimates can be obtained as a by-product of designing or redesigning the product or designing the production process.

In the initial Vinz Corporation example, the expected material and labor content of the products was given. They were not labeled as standard costs, although in fact they were. A standard overhead cost per unit was not given, but it is usually included in the standard cost for completeness. The standard overhead cost per unit is determined by applying the predetermined overhead rate to the standard direct labor content in hours. Vinz' predetermined overhead rate is $7 per direct labor hour. The standard direct labor hour content of product R is ½ hour. Thus the standard overhead cost per unit of product R is $3.50 (½ hour × $7 per hour). In like manner, the standard overhead cost per unit of product C is $4.67; of product D, $7.

Advantages. The system for determining average cost, discussed prior to this section, could be referred to as an *actual cost* or *historical cost* system. The primary advantage of a standard cost system over an actual cost system is that the standard cost system with up-to-date standards produces variances which signal possible cost control opportunities. Of course if the standards do not reflect attainable performance, the variances become mixed in meaning and difficult to interpret.

Another important advantage of the standard cost system is that it simplifies certain bookkeeping problems by recording all inventories at their standard cost rather than their actual cost. Actual costs will fluctuate from month to month because of variations in production efficiency. Because units are entering inventory at differing costs per unit, one must follow an inventory method such as first-in first-out (FIFO) average, last-in first-out (LIFO) average, or some other method. In a standard cost system, the ending inventories are determined by multiplying the number of units on hand by the standard cost per unit. The cost-of-goods-sold expense is determined by multiplying the number of units sold by the standard cost per unit.

These advantages of standard costs must be weighed against the cost of establishing the standards and updating them when significant changes in production methods or prices occur.

Job Order Cost Versus Process Cost Systems. The discussions thus far have implicitly assumed that cost finding (either actual or standard costing) follows the process costing system. It has been assumed that the average cost per unit is determined by taking the product costs for a *period of time* and dividing them by the number of units produced during that *period of time*. While no great attention has been given to the appropriate period of time, most of the discussion has implied that the appropriate period of time for determining direct material and direct labor costs is a month. For overhead, the appropriate period of time has been implied to be a year (through the predetermined overhead rate). But the time period selected is arbitrary. A month was used in the discussion because it corresponds to the reporting cycle of many manufacturers. But occasionally a time period of a day, a week, a quarter, or a year is used for direct materials and direct labor. In a situation in which a certain product is produced in a more or less continuous process, such as a production line, continuous molding, or mixing, there is no natural dividing line, and a process cost system is applied.

In other production situations, products are produced in batches or jobs. A machine shop is a good example where an order may come in for 100 units of a certain machined piece. The production of the order or batch is scheduled, and the units are produced. The batches provide a natural basis for determining the average material and direct labor cost per unit. Materials requisitions show the quantity of direct material requisitioned for the batch of production. Time cards show the amount of direct labor spent on the batch. When the batch is completed, it is easy to count the number of good pieces which result (which might be slightly different from the 100 ordered, depending on spoilage). Then the average direct material cost is determined in the usual manner:

Average direct material cost per unit
$$= \frac{\text{total cost of direct material used for this batch}}{\text{total number of good units in this batch}}$$

The same approach can be followed for direct labor cost. The overhead cost is applied to the batch by using the predetermined overhead rate, and the average overhead cost per unit is then also determined by dividing the total overhead cost applied to this batch by the number of good units in the batch.

Differences. In a *job order cost system*, the average cost per unit is determined by taking the total product costs incurred in producing the *batch* or *job* and dividing them by the total number of good units in the batch or job. In a *process cost system*, the average cost per unit is determined by dividing the total product cost incurred for a *period of time* by the number of good units produced during that period of time. In other words, the differences between the systems are not very profound. If the product is produced in batches or jobs, then the batch or job is a convenient basis for calculating the average cost per unit. In a more or less continuous process, time is the most convenient basis for calculating the average cost per unit. Both job order and process costing can be done on an actual cost basis or a standard cost basis. Most complex manufacturing companies use both job order and process costing in different departments of the company, depending on the production process in that department.

Management Accounting

The purpose of management accounting is to provide managers with information which aids decision making. It is convenient to classify management decisions into two categories: planning decisions and control decisions.

Planning Decisions. These are made at all levels but have the objectives of finding a course of action which is feasible and which also reaches organizational objectives. Feasibility implies that the plan is workable and that the organization has the resources to implement the plan. Since a major set of resources is financial resources, accounting information is useful in determining the feasibility of plans. Cash budgets, capital budgets, and projected balance sheets are examples of contributions which accounting can make to resource planning.

A major organizational objective is usually that some minimum level of profit be achieved. In a profit-directed organization, the achievement of a minimum profit is necessary to provide investors with the incentive to invest in the company. A not-for-profit organization may seek to break even or to limit losses in various activities in order that funding sources will provide the resources necessary for the continuance of the organization. A symphony orchestra might anticipate operating at a loss during a year, but a loss which was twice the anticipated loss might make it impossible for the orchestra to continue. Outside funding is anticipated, but it is limited in

7

amount, and careful planning may be necessary to limit the operating losses to levels which can be covered by donations. Thus profit planning is important to most organizations because one objective normally relates to achieving a specified level of profit (or loss). Accounting statements, including projected income statements, are important in this planning activity.

One profit-planning decision which frequently arises is whether to make or buy a component of a company product. The decisions to sell a by-product in its raw state or to process it further before selling are similar. Another decision is whether to sell existing products to private label merchandisers. A decision with major profit and resource implications is the addition of a new product line. Finally, the annual profit plan, incorporating the results of both continuing operations and new operations, is a significant part of the planning process in which management accounting plays a major role.

Control Decisions. These naturally follow the planning decisions. After a feasible plan is developed which meets organizational objectives, management action is required to implement it. Accounting reports provide feedback for control to signal situations in which management action may be required. Control reports inform managers when activities which are part of their responsibility are deviating from the plan.

Accounting in Planning Decisions. The focus of accounting here comes from the particular decision. The data to be reported should be relevant to the decision being considered. The only data relevant to a decision are those which will change as a result of the decision. Any data which will not change as a result of a decision are not relevant to the decision and can safely be ignored in making the decision.

Suppose a company is in the business of making poster-size enlargements from ordinary-size photographs. It has an eastern and western sales location, but the processing equipment is in the east and serves both locations. The company's annual volume is 1000 posters. The cost of making the 1000 posters is as follows:

Photographic paper and chemicals	$900
Fixed annual rental of equipment	400
Insurance	120
Maintenance contract ($200 per year plus 10 cents per poster)	300
Total	$1720

Sales and Promotion. Management is considering a promotional plan that might increase sales by 400 posters per year. The management accountant was asked to predict the increase in cost of making the posters. It was concluded that the relevant costs were the variable paper and chemical costs and the variable portion of the semivariable maintenance

cost. Photographic paper and chemicals were estimated to be 90 cents per poster ($900/1000), and the variable component of the maintenance contract was noted to be 10 cents per poster. Thus the cost of making the posters would increase by $1 per poster, and the total cost of making the 1400 posters was predicted to increase by $400, to $2120. Management weighed these costs and the cost of the added promotion against the added sales revenue which could be achieved and decided that the promotion would add to company profits.

Facilities and Location. At another time, the manager of the western location suggested that it would be convenient to have poster-making equipment at both locations. It was assumed that the number of posters to be made and sold would be unchanged. Since qualified operators were already available at both locations, the management accountant concluded that the relevant expenses were the fixed expenses of renting and insuring the added machine and the fixed component of a second maintenance contract. It was reasoned that the total paper and chemical usage would remain unchanged since the total number of posters to be produced would be unchanged. These variable costs would be incurred at two locations, but the total for the two locations would be the same as the total at the present single location. Thus the relevant cost increases were $400 per year additional machine rental, $120 per year additional insurance, and $200 per year fixed maintenance. Management decided that $720 per year was too much to pay for the convenience of having a machine at each location. It was suggested that if added sales could be generated by having two machines and providing quicker service, the decision could be reconsidered.

Notice that if the accountant had taken the cost-finding approach of determining the average cost per poster, the result would have been $1.72 per poster ($1720 total annual cost divided by 1000 posters per year). But the $1.72 per poster would not have been useful information for either decision. It is important not to confuse cost-finding information with management-accounting information.

Accounting in Control Decisions. There are two key elements in accounting for control. First is responsibility accounting, and second is management by exception.

Responsibility Accounting. This requires that a manager's financial responsibilities be defined in advance. Any revenues, expenses, and assets which the manager is responsible for controlling must be identified. The management accountant would then establish a system of regular reports which show the planned results in one column, the actual results in an adjoining column, and the variances in a third column. The important point is that the report is tailored to the responsibilities of the particular manager. Items which are not the responsibility of the manager are generally not included on the report of that manager. The reason is that the report should focus the manager's attention on those items for which he or she is responsible.

Management by Exception. The variance column of the accounting control report aids management by exception by indicating the items which have deviated from the plan. Managers usually add most to profitability by spending their control efforts on the exceptional items where variances have occurred.

Application. Probably the most widely applied accounting control reports are based on standard costs, and the following example will illustrate how a standard cost system is used to compute variances which are reported to the responsible manager. While a standard cost system produces variances for both direct materials and direct labor costs, the example will consider only direct labor cost since direct material variances are calculated in exactly the same manner.

There are only two reasons for an actual direct labor cost to exceed planned or standard direct labor costs. One is that the hourly rate paid for the direct labor was higher than the standard rate. The second is that the number of direct labor hours used were more than the standard allowed for the work done during the period. Since the type of management action called for might differ depending on which reason caused the variance, a standard cost system reports both a rate and a quantity variance.

The *rate variance* simply shows what the total dollar cost was of paying a higher than standard rate. Suppose that a standard allowed paying $5 per hour for labor in a certain department but that the rate actually paid was $5.30 per hour. Assume further that during the month in question 800 hours of labor were used. The direct labor rate variance would then be ($5.30 − $5.00) × 800 hours, or $240 unfavorable. In this month, the cost of paying 30 cents an hour above standard totaled $240 because 800 hours of direct labor were used. The variance was unfavorable because the actual rate exceeded the standard rate.

More information is needed to compute the *quantity variance.* Suppose that the standard allowed ¼ hour per unit of product produced, and accounting records show that 2800 units were produced during the month. According to the standard, 700 hours should have been used in producing 2800 units (2800 units × ¼ hour per unit). Eight hundred hours were actually used, or an excess of a hundred hours. The dollar cost is found by multiplying this excess by the standard labor rate; in this example $5 per hour times 100 excess hours equals $500. The standard suggests that this unfavorable labor quantity variance might have been avoided. The job of management is to find the causes of the variance and to seek means of avoiding a similar variance in the future.

See also Accounting, managerial control; Budgets and budget preparation; Control systems, management; Marginal income analysis; Product and service pricing.

REFERENCES

Gray, Jack, and Kenneth S. Johnson: *Accounting and Management Action,* 2d ed., McGraw-Hill, New York, 1977.

Gray, Jack, and Donald Ricketts: *Cost and Managerial Accounting,* McGraw-Hill, New York, 1982.

Horngren, Charles T.: *Cost Accounting: A Managerial Emphasis,* 5th ed., Prentice-Hall, Englewood Cliffs, N.J., 1982.

JACK GRAY, *University of Minnesota*

Accounting, Financial

Financial accounting identifies, classifies, records, and summarizes the monetary aspects of business transactions in a systematic enough way to permit managers, investors, and creditors to measure and evaluate an entity's activities. Although double-entry bookkeeping was described as early as 1494 by the Franciscan friar Luca Pacioli, the greatest determining forces in the development of modern accounting were the industrial revolution and the use of the corporate form of organization that was occasioned by it. In the United States, some twentieth century influences have been (1) the growth in the government's tendency to tax economic activity and (2) the government's determination to regulate business.

Whether performed for a fifteenth century Italian merchant or for a twentieth century conglomerate, accounting deals with questions concerning the firm's stocks and flows of wealth. To answer the stock question, "What is the entity's financial position at a particular point in time?", a statement of financial condition, or a balance sheet, is prepared. To answer the flow question, "What profit (or loss) has the entity realized over some period of time?" a statement of income is prepared.

Generally Accepted Accounting Principles. For these statements to have predictive value and to be otherwise useful to the decision makers for whom they are prepared, a body of knowledge has evolved concerning the standards, assumptions, measuring methods, and reporting procedures that the accounting profession will follow. Taken together, these are referred to as *generally accepted accounting principles* (GAAP), which by definition are principles that enjoy substantial authoritative support.

Under the securities laws of 1933 and 1934, the U.S. Congress empowered the Securities and Exchange Commission (SEC) to establish the accounting principles to be followed by companies issuing their securities to the public or having them traded on organized stock exchanges. For over a generation, the SEC chose not to use its powers and instead allowed the accounting profession to take the lead in establishing GAAP. The most influential voice of the profession during this period was the American Institute of Certified Public Accountants (AICPA), which prior to 1957 was the American Institute of Accountants (AIA). In the 1960s and especially in the 1970s, however, the SEC showed a growing willingness to direct a particular practice when the profession faltered or permitted wide areas of difference in GAAP.

Nevertheless, the work done by the AICPA through its Committee on Accounting Procedures, established in the mid-1930s, and subsequently by its Accounting Principles Board (APB), established in 1959 to advance the written expression of GAAP, has been substantial. Until it was superseded in 1973 by the Financial Accounting Standards Board (FASB), the APB issued 31 opionions, 4 statements, and other letters and bulletins that served to shape the financial accounting profession. In spite of its success, the APB increasingly came under criticism from investors and the public at large because of the large number of alternatives allowed in the acceptable methods of accounting for business transactions. A significant criticism was that the APB was dominated by certified public accountants who, according to some, gave inadequate weight to the full range of accounting problems confronting investors and managers.

In an attempt to correct the deficiencies expressed by these critics, the FASB was formed to include membership from business, government, and industry. Some of its work has dealt with clarifying previously issued APB opinions and extending the work that was done by this precedent body. In spite of its broader membership, the FASB was unable to avoid controversies similar to those that troubled the APB, thus giving evidence to the observation that accounting principles, being pragmatic as opposed to self-evident, will always be open to criticism.

The Measurement Problem. Financial accounting is concerned with the application of GAAP to the analysis of economic transactions in a consistent enough manner for an entity's stock of wealth, its flows of wealth, and the changes in the resulting obligations to be accurately measured and reliably reported. The problems associated with the efforts to make these measurements and to report the results of economic transactions can be appreciated through a description of two of the more important financial statements—the balance sheet and the income statement.

Balance Sheet

The balance sheet reflects the fundamental accounting model which describes the financial position of a firm in terms of an equality between its assets on one side and its liabilities plus owners' equities on the other ($A = L + OE$). Hence, the balance sheet is a widely used term but is somewhat less descriptive than the more appropriate designation—statement of financial position.

Assets are economic resources and benefits owned by an entity, valued generally at acquisition cost less accumulated write-offs.

Liabilities are the debts of the entity and other claims against its assets which may oblige the firm to provide goods or services. Usually, liabilities are measured at their current cash equivalent or the maturity value of a debt.

Owners' equities are the residual amounts, $A - L = OE$, but bear little resemblance to the current market value of an entity.

The components of the fundamental accounting model are defined by GAAP, which in turn are defined by the accountants. Managers and investors, irked by this implied circularity, press for more realism in the measurement and reporting process. Nowhere is the pressure more intense than in the problem of accounting for the effects of inflation. For example, productive assets, such as buildings, machinery, and other equipment have traditionally been carried on a firm's books at the acquisition cost less the accumulated depreciation to date.

Inflation Accounting. Alternatives to this historical cost method have been proposed to account for inflation.

Price level adjustments can be made to balance sheet values by applying to them a price index designed to measure the impact of inflation on a firm's financial statements. Both the FASB and the SEC have examined this issue. The problem is dramatized by the separate directions taken by these two bodies; i.e., the FASB sought a solution in general price level adjustments (GPLA), while the SEC was concerned with the specific price changes. The FASB approach is easier for the accountant to take since it retains historical costs and makes adjustments based on changes in the purchasing power of the dollar, using readily available indexes such as the *GNP implicit price deflator* or the *wholesale price index*. But the GPLA may produce results as misleading as the historical cost method it seeks to improve since a particular company's experience may be totally unrelated to general trends in the economy. On the other hand, the SEC's approach deals with the firm's specific experience, but in so doing, it may risk a loss in objectivity and comparability.

Replacement cost accounting, as an alternative to historical cost accounting, addresses the problem from two slightly different views: (1) the cost of replacing the asset as such or (2) the cost of maintaining a comparable productive capacity. Dangers persist. Suppose a firm is using a converted castle for a garment factory. What is the cost of replacing the asset as such? How are the highly subjective assumptions for maintaining a productive capacity handled in industries experiencing rapid changes in technology? While there are no answers to these questions, merely raising them serves to explain the pressure accountants endure in attempting to cope with inflation accounting using this method.

Current (fair) value accounting has a conceptual potential for dealing with the problem of inflation accounting, even though its origin is found in legal proceedings where it is defined as an exchange price that a willing and well-informed buyer and an equally willing and well-informed seller would reach through negotiation. Theoretically, the best way to estimate the fair value of an asset is to calculate the *present value* of the net cash inflows attributable to the asset, using a discount factor that takes into account the effects of inflation as well as the time value of money and the asset's risks and rewards characteristics. That this method is not more widely used is due to the great difficulty involved in estimating future net cash inflows and the highly subjective nature of the choice of a rate at which these inflows should be discounted.

Income Statement

Accountants avoid using the word *profit* on the grounds that it applies so generally to a wide variety of concepts that precision is lost; e.g., profit for tax purposes is not defined the same as profit for internal decision making. This problem of definition can be illustrated with the economist and the accountant, both of whom agree with the fundamental idea that revenues minus cost equal profit ($R - C = P$). The economist holds that a cost is that payment which keeps resources out of alternative employment; therefore, profit is the amount remaining after all costs (including opportunity costs) have been subtracted from revenues. The accountant maintains that profit is determined on the basis of completed transactions; therefore, profit is the amount remaining after all verifiable costs have been subtracted from revenues.

The actual profitability of a firm can be determined by subtracting its net worth at inception from its net worth at termination. Owners and investors are not usually willing to wait such a long period of time to participate in the returns from their investments; therefore, financial accounting must attempt to measure *net income,* the designation preferred by accountants to the more general term *profit,* over a specific segment of time. This attempt necessarily introduces a degree of arbitrariness, but the measurement problem is handled by preparing an income statement that summarizes all transactions of revenue and expenses according to GAAP for a particular period of time, usually a business year ($R - E = NI$).

The first obstacle to income measurement is in determining when revenues and expenses are to be recognized. Basically, there are two methods.

1. The *cash basis* of accounting recognizes revenue and expenses when cash or some other assets are exchanged in completed transactions.

2. Under the *accrual method,* the *realization principle* is followed; i.e., revenues and expenses are recognized when goods are exchanged or when services are provided and the right to revenues is realized.

The next obstacle to income measurement lies in the difficulty in determining what expenses should be matched with what revenues during a period. For example, the calculation of cost of goods sold for a merchandising firm enjoying stable prices would be made by subtracting the ending inventory from the sum of the beginning inventory and the purchase of new merchandise during the period. Because prices are not stable, and because business conditions affect firms differently, GAAP allow certain assumptions to be made concerning the flow of inventories. In choosing from these alternative assumptions, the accountant considers their effects not only on a periodic net income but also on the inventory valuations of the goods remaining at the end of the period.

Last-In First-Out (LIFO). This method assumes that goods most recently purchased will be sold first. During periods of rising prices, this method tends to match current revenues with the costs of replacing merchandise and, consequently, produces a more accurate income statement.

First-In First-Out (FIFO). This method assumes that the oldest goods in stock are sold first, an assumption that usually corresponds to reality. During periods of rising prices, however, this method produces inventory profits because current revenue is matched against costs that are below prices being paid for inventory replacements.

Weighted-Average Method. This method assumes that goods in inventory are so intermixed that stocks are withdrawn at random. Thus, the cost of goods sold is calculated first by stating inventories at average prices paid, weighted according to the quantity purchased at each price, and then subtracting the ending inventory from the cost of goods available for sale. Results produced by this method lie between those obtained by the LIFO and FIFO methods.

Specific-Identification Method. This method allows management to identify sales with specific purchases. While this method is essential and practical for high-cost items, such as boats, cars, jewelry, and serially numbered items, it opens avenues for profit manipulation when applied to commodities and other goods that are commingled in inventories.

The third obstacle to income measurement involves distinguishing between income or losses obtained from normal operations and those caused by windfalls or disasters. Two fundamentally different approaches for dealing with this obstacle are possible.

1. The *all-inclusive concept of income,* holding to the view that income is the aggregate of all transactions affecting an entity's equity over a period of time, reports both recurrent and nonrecurrent operations as income.

2. The *current operating performance approach,* seeking to separate the normal earning power of the firm from its extraordinary gains and losses, reports only the results of recurrent operations on the income statement and makes direct adjustments to retained earnings for extraordinary items.

The APB's Opinion No. 9 of 1966 mandated the all-inclusive concept for reporting income but allowed for the segregation of extraordinary items from the results of normal operations on the income statement. In 1973, the APB issued Opinion No. 30 which made more stringent the conditions an event must satisfy to be regarded as extraordinary; i.e., it must be unusual in nature and not expected to recur in the foreseeable future. Under these rules, losses from an earthquake, since it is both unusual and unforeseeable, would be an extraordinary item; devaluation of foreign currencies, unforeseeable but not unusual, would not qualify as extraordinary.

Conceptual Framework

The development of accounting has been characterized by pragmatism. The practice of dealing with single issues and the problems at hand has created a system of GAAP that lacks conceptual underpinnings. Contemporary problems created by conceptual deficiencies include the following areas troublesome to management.

Accounting for Human Resources. Clearly, one of the most critical factors for the success of an enterprise is the personnel who work for it. These people represent a cost to the firm, a value to it, and an investment that it must maintain. Yet, financial accounting has not accepted the concepts needed to account for a firm's human resources.

Income Tax Accounting. Governed by law rather than GAAP, income tax accounting presents some features that dramatize the need for a conceptual framework to support financial accounting.

Accounting for Installment Sales. Tax laws allow dealers in personal property to spread income from their installment sales over the years in which collections are made. GAAP require revenues to be accounted for at the time the transaction is made.

Investment Tax Credits. Accepting the idea of economics that investments in plants and equipment have an accelerator effect on the economy as a whole, Congress often includes incentives in tax laws to get businesses to make these investments. Although the rate varies from time to time, the laws allow a percentage of the investment to be deducted from the firm's income taxes. How to account for this "gain" is an accounting problem. Two alternatives are available, either of which is permissible under current tax laws.

1. The *flow-through method* takes the view that the investment tax credit is intended to reduce taxes in the year of the investment only.

2. The *cost reduction method* holds to the position that it is the use, not acquisition, of assets that produces benefits to a firm; therefore, the investment tax credit is prorated over the productive life of the asset, and a proportionate amount is deducted from the taxes due each year.

While the FASB has taken the lead in developing a conceptual framework for accounting, the success of that undertaking depends on cooperation from all segments of society—business, industry, government, academia, and the professions.

See also Accounting, cost analysis and control; Accounting, managerial control; Acquisitions and mergers; Auditing, financial; Budgets and budget preparation; Control systems, management; Financial management; Financial management, capital structure and dividend policy; Forecasting business conditions; Inventory control; Leasing, equipment; Marginal income analysis; Program planning and implementation; Risk analysis and management; Tax management.

REFERENCES

Carey, John L.: *The Rise of the Accounting Profession,* 2 vols., American Institute of Certified Public Accountants, New York, 1969–1970.

Davidson, Sidney, and Roman L. Weil: *Handbook of Modern Accounting,* 3d ed., McGraw-Hill, New York, 1983.

Kohler, Eric L.: *Dictionary for Accountants,* 6th ed., Prentice-Hall, Englewood Cliffs, N.J., 1983.

THOMAS C. STANTON, *Francis Marion College*

Accounting, Managerial Control

The accounting process is the primary vehicle within a company for capturing and reporting data on a systematic basis. These data are summarized for the organization as a whole, thus providing a measure of enterprise profitability and financial position; for better-managed companies, data are also accumulated by subsegments of the business to provide a basis for more detailed operational control.

Enterprise Measurement. The profitability of the organization as a whole is reported in the income statement (also called the profit and loss statement), while the financial position of the firm is reported in the balance sheet (also called the statement of financial position). When these two statements are released to stockholders, creditors, governmental agencies, or other groups outside the immediate management of the company, they must conform with generally accepted accounting principles. Although the data which these two reports contain are used by management at the upper levels of the organization and are thus an integral part of the top management control process, their complexity and the need for uniformity warrant separate discussions in this handbook. (*See* Accounting, financial; Financial statement analysis.)

Segment Measurement. Data for sound operational control, detailed planning, and day-to-day decisions are accumulated for each major segment of the business. Segments in this context include any of the fractional parts into which the business may be divided. Examples of the type of segmentation most frequently used are cost centers, departments, products or product lines, territories, manufacturing processes or activities, and customer outlets. The organization may be divided into segments in an almost infinite number of ways, and while many businesses have utilized too few, it is possible to utilize too many. Ascertaining the appropriate subdivisions for data accumulation purposes is the foundation of the accounting control process, since too much detail is costly and at times obscures the more significant points, while too little detail does not provide enough facts for proper operational planning and control.

Relationship to Other Accounting Processes. *Management accounting,* also referred to as *internal accounting,* is directed primarily toward the needs of managers and provides the data needed for controlling their specific activities. The same accounting processes which are utilized to prepare financial reports for external groups (*see* Accounting, financial) are employed to gather the data which appear in management control reports, and separate information systems for these two related, but different, reporting processes are not normally required. Thus the detailed internal data concerning segments of the business are accumulated upward to provide the overall summaries contained in reports submitted to outsiders.

The federal and state tax returns which must be filed are also prepared from the same data base used for financial and managerial reports. A large number of adjustments to these data are necessary to satisfy the statutory tax regulations, but a separate accounting system for tax purposes is rarely maintained.

Budgetary plans for the coming months also follow the same format as the basic financial data-gathering system. Plans for future periods are expressed in dollar amounts through the budget plan; following the same format used for financial and managerial reports permits actual costs to be compared with the budget plan on a regular basis.

Relevance. Management needs an almost infinite amount of information, yet there is no universally accepted body of principles surrounding internal business reporting. Management is free to construct its reports in any way deemed appropriate, to use or not to use a budgetary system, or to change its method of calculating return on investment any time it wishes. For internal management purposes, *relevancy* is the most important attribute of the information and control system. Relevant data are those facts that apply to the problem being analyzed. Thus, they are data that *do not* remain constant across decision alternatives. They are facts that change as the decision alternative is changed. For example, if an increase in production is being considered, associated fixed costs such as building depreciation would be *irrelevant* (assuming excess capacity existed) while variable costs (such as raw materials) would be *relevant.* The inclusion of irrelevant costs in a cost report, for example, could lead to incorrect operating decisions and an ultimate reduction in the profits of the company.

Fitting the Accounting System to the Organization

The management accounting system must be designed to fit the organizational structure of the company, including the responsibility centers of individual managers. Each revenue and cost must be recorded and traced to the manager who has primary responsibility for it. The terms *responsibility accounting, activity accounting,* and *profitability accounting* are used interchangeably to describe this type of accounting framework.

Responsibility Accounting Systems. An accounting system built around managerial responsibilities must be based upon a sound organizational structure with well-defined responsibilities. Each cost must be studied separately to ascertain which executive has primary responsibility for its incurrence or has the strongest influence over its incurrence. This is not an easy task, for few costs are clearly the responsibility of a single individual. Where several persons influence the amount of a cost, the temptation to prorate the cost is strong but should be resisted. Prorations frequently lead to conflicts concerning their fairness and equity and thus weaken the control framework.

Since supervisors are responsible for the costs that both they and their subordinates incur, a responsibility accounting system accumulates costs upward. Lower-level reports at the first-line supervisory level show only the costs for that individual's activities, but a plant superintendent's reports will contain aggregate costs of all the supervisors under his or her control. A vice president of manufacturing, in turn, will receive reports reflecting the activities of all superintendents or other managers under his or her supervision. In this way a pyramid of cost reports is constructed to follow the organizational framework of the company.

Controllable and Uncontrollable Costs. A controllable cost cannot be defined neatly, since costs are controllable only over time and usually by the combined efforts of several persons. The raw material costs entering into a product are affected by (1) their price, which may be the purchasing officer's responsibility, and (2) the efficiency of use, which may be the responsibility of the production officers. A general guide is to assign a cost which cannot be separated causally to that one person who has primary control responsibility for it or who most closely supervises the day-to-day actions which influence it. The control reports which are submitted to that individual should ideally contain only those costs considered controllable at that level. Should any costs considered uncontrollable at that level be included in the report, such as an allocated amount for building depreciation appearing on a production supervisor's report, those costs should be clearly separated and designated as uncontrollable.

Cost Centers. A cost center is an activity within the organization to which costs are assigned. While responsibility centers are established for individuals, cost centers may be established for a machine, a group of machines, a process, or any physical activity for which separate cost information is needed. A single responsibility center sometimes contains a number of cost centers. Information about a physical activity, accumulated through cost centers, is used primarily to accumulate the cost of producing individual products or performing specific services for customers.

Profit Centers. A profit center exists where both cost and revenue data can be traced directly to an activity. Each retail outlet of a chain store is a profit center, since both sales revenues and cost may be recorded for each outlet separately. Internal billing, sometimes of an arbitrary nature, makes artificial profit centers out of such areas as the data processing center, the equipment repairs center, or similar service arms of the organization. The justification for these arbitrary profit centers is that they utilize the profit motive as a motivation device. Any resulting artificial profit is eliminated when a true profit or loss for the company is calculated.

Investment Centers. An investment center exists where the investment required to create and operate a profit center is separable and a return on investment can be calculated. The rate of return earned by the divisions or profit centers within a company is carefully monitored in most instances to provide a measure of divisional performance. The differences in the investment base which result from varying depreciation methods on fixed properties, from different inventory valuation methods, or from leased instead of owned assets must be taken into account when comparing the rates of return.

Intracompany Pricing. Where investment centers or profit centers exist and one center provides products or services for another center, an intracompany pricing system must be established. Methods used to determine the *transfer price* of products or services between autonomous divisions of the same company may be based upon (1) the full cost, (2) the variable cost, (3) the market price if sold to outside customers, or (4) a negotiated price. Variations of these methods are often used, and in all cases care must be exercised when interpreting the resulting profit, especially if a return-on-investment calculation is used as a performance measure.

Direct and Indirect Costs. Many cost analyses require a distinction between those costs which are direct and those which are indirect to the segment being studied. The concept of controllable or uncontrollable, discussed earlier, is related to the managerial control process; the concept of direct or indirect relates to the question of whether the cost is necessary to support a given segment of the company.

Direct costs. A direct cost is one which is directly traceable to the particular segment of the business under study and is incurred specifically for that segment. In a retail establishment the salaries of salesclerks are direct expenses of the departments in which they work, but these same salaries would be indirect to the several product lines sold in the department. A direct cost is usually one which could be eliminated if that segment of the business were to be eliminated.

Indirect Costs. An indirect cost is one that is not directly traceable to specific segments and probably could not be eliminated if that segment of the business were terminated. Since indirect costs are not directly traceable and in many cases could not be eliminated, they are sometimes allocated or prorated, utilizing an appropriate allocation base. Many allocation bases exist, and the only criterion which must be satisfied when selecting an allocation base is that a reasonable relationship exist between the expense and the selected base. Building occupancy costs, such as rent, depreciation, property taxes, and insurance, may be allocated to departments or processes on a cubic space basis, on a square footage basis, or on a percentage basis, calculated to take into account the value of strategic locations near doors or passageways. When indirect costs are allocated to segments, the resulting costs are open to serious question and care must be exercised in interpreting the results. The *contribution margin approach*, discussed later in this section, is a more reliable method and is basically a subtraction of only direct costs from revenues to arrive at the contribution margin produced by that segment. Any indirect or allocated costs are then considered, but only to the extent that they increase or decrease as a result of the specific action being considered.

Internal Control. A company's system of internal control consists of all the measures taken to protect the company's assets against irregularities, to ensure the accuracy of recorded transactions, and to assure management that the information on which it must base decisions is authentic and reliable. The system includes the arrangement of duties and the flow of paperwork which ensure a minimum of clerical errors and maximum security against theft and embezzlement.

Internal Check. The system of internal checks follows two basic principles:

1. Responsibilities of all personnel must be fixed and clearly communicated.

2. Each clerical activity in the organization should be checked as much as possible by another clerical activity, automatically and with a minimal duplication of effort.

The construction of sound systems of internal checks is based upon the separation of three functions. These are (1) the authority to move or transfer assets, (2) physical control of the asset itself, and (3) the record-keeping process. Only when these three activities are separated will the internal check system be strong.

Analysis of Cost Behavior. Knowledge of the reaction of individual costs and expenses to changes in the volume of activity is the foundation for (1) planning the amount of costs to be incurred in future periods, (2) estimating profits from future activities, and (3) determining whether costs have been adequately controlled by those responsible for their incurrence. The relations between changes in a cost and changes in the volume of activity are charted as variable, fixed, and semivariable (also called semifixed or mixed) costs.

Variable costs are those which will fluctuate in close relation to a selected activity or volume measure. Units sold, dollars of sales, units produced, labor hours, and labor costs are the more frequently used volume measures. When volume increases, the amount of a variable cost will increase proportionately. The raw material used in the manufacture of a finished product is almost always a variable cost. The expense for wrapping paper, twine, shopping bags, or other supplies will usually vary with the amount of sales activity in a retail store. Sales commissions, when based upon a percentage of sales, are another example of an expense which is completely variable.

Fixed costs are those which are related to the passage of time and have only a minimal relationship to

the volume of activity which has been or is expected to be undertaken. An annual lease expense which is incurred for building space will be fixed in amount regardless of the manufacturing or sales volume. Depreciation expense is usually fixed, as are many types of insurance; office salaries and property taxes are also examples of costs which in most cases are fixed and have little relationship to the volume of activity. Most fixed costs are committed or programmed costs. Given a long enough time period, all fixed costs would appear variable, and their fixed nature, usually within a 1-year planning period, is the result of management decisions which have committed the company to incur the cost. Depreciation on equipment, certain types of insurance coverage, and salaries of key personnel are examples of *committed costs. Programmed costs* are the result of appropriation decisions and include such costs as advertising and research and development. A programmed cost can be any sum which management wishes, but once it has been budgeted, it must be considered a fixed cost of the period.

Semivariable (or mixed) costs are those which change when volume changes, but not in exact proportion. Salaries of salesclerks in retail stores are an example of this type of expense. When the store's sales are expected to increase, as they are prior to Easter or Christmas, additional salesclerks will be employed, so the total salaries paid to salesclerks will move up or down with the amount of sales. The change will not be in exact proportion, however, for a minimum number of salesclerks will be necessary at all times, and at peak times all clerks will be busier and will produce a larger dollar volume of sales.

The three types of cost behavior are shown graphically in Fig. A-6.

Methods of Measuring Cost Behavior. Ways of measuring the behavior of a cost range from simple estimation methods to sophisticated mathematical formulas. Where historical records are available, they may be the basis for utilizing (1) the scattergraph (or graphic) method, (2) the high-low points method, or (3) the least-squares method. Where no past history is available, the high-low points method may be utilized, the points being carefully selected estimates of two cost amounts.

Scattergraph. Historical cost data, usually by monthly periods, are plotted on a graph, with the volume index on the horizontal axis and the cost amounts on the vertical axis (Fig. A-7). Unusual cost amounts which arise from nonrecurring events, such as a fire, labor strike, or major equipment failure, should be eliminated. After the data are plotted, a trend line is drawn through the points to reflect the general movement. The fixed portion of the cost would be that point at which the trend line intersects the vertical axis. The variable portion is stated in terms of cost per unit volume and is calculated by relating the change in cost between any two points

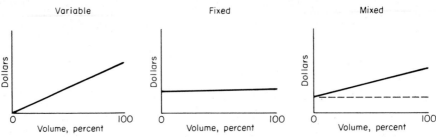

FIG. A-6 Graphic representation of variations in cost behavior.

on the trend line with the change in volume between the same two points.

High-Low Points Method. Since two points determine a straight line, the trend line can be determined by selecting any two volume levels and estimating the cost which would be incurred at those two levels. The points selected should be representative

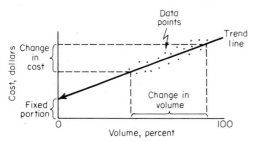

FIG. A-7 Scattergraph.

high and low levels. The two points may be based upon historical data but must be estimated where no prior history exists. The fixed and variable portions of the cost would then be determined in the same way as in the scattergraph method.

Least-Squares Method. This method is based upon a mathematical computation to fit the line to a set of data points. Historical amounts must be available. The method is based upon the solution to a set of simultaneous equations. The amounts which go into the two equations are ΣX (total of all individual volume amounts), ΣY (total of all individual cost amounts), ΣX^2 (total of each volume amount multiplied by itself), N (number of data points), and ΣXY (total of each volume point multiplied by its related cost amount). The formulas, which are solved for a and b, are

$$\Sigma Y = Na + \Sigma Xb$$
$$\Sigma XY = \Sigma Xa + \Sigma X^2 b$$

The calculation can easily be done on a computer or on a hand calculator which is able to store a simple program. The a value, once determined, is the fixed portion of the expense, and the b value, which will

be stated as a cost per unit of volume, will be the variable portion.

The Contribution Margin. A company's overall cost structure is made up of the total of all its fixed costs and the total of all its variable costs. The mixed costs, once analyzed into their fixed and variable components, can be included in the summation of these totals. Knowledge of this overall cost-behavior structure provides a powerful information base for major planning decisions. This is the result of having isolated and measured the variable costs, which move with the volume, and separating them from the fixed costs, which will not change. The projected profit from a contemplated course of action is thus readily determined by subtracting the expected variable costs from the anticipated revenues, leaving the contribution margin. The *contribution margin* is, simply stated, the contribution a particular segment makes toward covering the general pool of fixed costs. If a unit sells for $1 per unit and the variable costs of manufacturing and selling the unit are 80 cents, each unit contributes 20 cents toward the company's fixed costs. The concept of contribution margin is both logical and easily applied and is one of the most universal applications of variable- and fixed-cost data. The level of sales at which losses stop and profits start, for example, can be determined by calculating the sales volume which will produce the amount of contribution margin necessary to cover the firm's total fixed costs exactly.

Another example of the use of this concept is found in calculating the point at which a company should temporarily cease operations. When a company is incurring losses, it may minimize these losses in the short run by continuing in operation, rather than temporarily closing down, so long as it has a contribution margin on present sales to cover a part of its fixed costs, which continue.

Break-Even Analysis. *Break-even analysis* is the analysis of a company's cost, volume, and profit relationships to determine the amount of revenue it must earn to break even with neither a profit nor a loss. The analysis is dependent upon knowledge of the firm's fixed and variable costs and is based upon the concept of the contribution margin. For example, if a company has $1 million of fixed costs, and variable costs equal 60 percent of sales, the break-even point would be calculated as follows:

$$\text{Total revenues} = \text{fixed expenses}$$
$$+ \text{variable expenses}$$
$$+ \text{zero profit}$$
$$R = \$1,000,000 + 0.6R + 0$$
$$R - 0.6R = \$1,000,000$$
$$0.4R = \$1,000,000$$
$$R = \$2,500,000$$

Stated verbally, each dollar of revenue received must be used to pay 60 cents of variable costs, leaving 40 cents to cover fixed costs. At this 40-cent rate of contribution the company must have $2.5 million in sales to cover $1 million in fixed costs.

Estimating the Effect of Future Actions. Break-even analysis is a useful tool to measure the effect of future actions. The following questions illustrate how answers are determined for complex questions utilizing the break-even analysis technique:

Question	Answer
Assuming the cost structure given above, what level of sales must be realized to produce a profit of $200,000?	$0.4S = \$1,000,000 + \$200,000$ $S = \$3,000,000$
How high (measured in dollars) must sales be to cover a $50,000 increase in fixed costs and still produce a profit of $200,000?	$0.4S = \$1,000,000 + \$50,000 +$ $\$200,000$ $S = \$3,125,000$
What amount of sales will be needed to break even if variable costs can be reduced to 55% but with an increase in fixed costs to $1,100,000?	$0.45S = \$1,100,000$ $S = \$2,444,444$

The Break-Even Graph. The cost-volume-profit relationships which are inherent in break-even analysis may be shown graphically, as in Fig. A-8. When this is done, the total fixed costs are shown separately from the total variable costs, usually with the fixed costs in the lower position. The point at which the revenue line crosses the total cost line will represent the break-even point. (*See also* Marginal income analysis.)

An additional concept, that of the *relevant range,* has been superimposed upon the illustrative break-

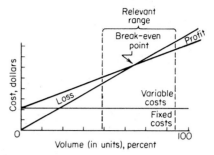

FIG. A-8 Break-even graph.

even chart. The analysis of fixed and variable costs which underlies the break-even concept will be valid only within a certain volume range; that is, the assumption is made that costs will be linear and will not hold at very high or very low ranges of activity. The relevant range must be considered when the fixed- and variable-cost analysis is originally undertaken and is therefore implicit in break-even analysis.

Margin of Safety. One measure which is utilized in the analysis of the financial affairs of a company is the margin of safety. This may be defined as the amount by which present sales exceed the break-even point. When two companies or two divisions of the same company are being compared, their relative margins of safety will indicate which is in the most vulnerable profit position.

Limiting Assumptions. The break-even analysis is based upon a number of assumptions, and its use must be undertaken with awareness of them. The most important assumption is that cost behavior is linear. The behavior of each cost will approach linearity, but careful study will reveal that few costs are actually linear. Another assumption is that the relationship of cost change is sufficiently causal; there may be forces other than volume which produce changes in cost. Finally, if several products are manufactured or sold, the analysis assumes that the product mix will remain constant and that sales prices will not shift. Should this occur, the revenue line will not be portrayed correctly and the relationship of revenue to cost will no longer hold. However, these assumptions are usually not so overpowering that they preclude the use of the technique for overall broad analysis of the effect of contemplated managerial actions. (*See* Marginal income analysis.)

See also Accounting, cost analysis and control; Accounting, financial; Budgeting, capital; Budgets and budget preparation; Control systems, management; Credit management; Financial management; Financial statement analysis; Marginal income analysis; Product and service pricing; Tax management; Zero-base budgeting.

REFERENCES

Anthony, Robert N., and James Reece: *Management Accounting Text and Cases*, 5th ed., Richard D. Irwin, Homewood, Ill., 1983.

Horngren, Charles T.: *Cost Accounting: A Managerial Emphasis*, 5th ed., Prentice-Hall, Englewood Cliffs, N.J., 1982.

Seiler, Robert, and Frank Collins: *Accounting Principles for Management*, 3d ed., Charles E. Merrill, Englewood Cliffs, N.J., 1980.

ROBERT E. SEILER, *University of Houston*

Acquisitions and Mergers

The acquisition of another firm can be both the most exciting and creative and the most expensive and risky venture an executive will undertake. While some acquisitions are highly successful, a great number can best be characterized as mediocre and many are outright failures. The material below is intended to give the reader a basic grounding in both the concepts and the current methods used to grow, to create value, and to reach other objectives through mergers and acquisitions. Included are considerations of economic, strategic, financial, accounting, legal, and organizational issues involved. While directed at acquisitions, the material is equally applicable to divestitures.

Historical Perspective

Although mergers have always been part of the corporate scene, major surges of activities occurred during three earlier periods of economic history: (1) horizontal mergers and market product growth (1895–1905); (2) vertical integration (the 1920s); and (3) the evolution of broader-based firms beginning in the 1950s and 1960s. Members of this last group are not necessarily highly diversified companies, but for the most part they no longer represent single business or single market companies. This is in keeping with current strategic planning philosophy, including product/market portfolio concepts and the balancing of activity between units with both different maturities and different financial characteristics. In addition, the inherent difficulties, long-time requirements, and risks of failure from internal development projects have become better appreciated.

More recently heavy activity has occurred in the financial service industries as banks, insurance companies, brokerage firms, and others attempt to gain a broader participation in the overall financial services market made feasible by deregulation and advances in technology. At the same time a considerable part of the present merger activity represents the purchase of parts of companies by other firms as a result of a movement toward rationalization and away from unrelated diversification.

In 1982, the total value of acquisitions in the United States exceeded the amount of new corporate stock issued by industrial corporations. Moreover, the estimated value of these transactions was approximately 25 percent of new plant and equipment expenditures. A substantial number of acquisitions are much smaller, as shown in Table A-1. Further-

TABLE A-1 Value of Acquisitions by Size of Transaction

	Percentage of transactions where price disclosed		
	1981	1982	1983
$5 million or less	35	32	30
$5.1–$25.0 million	38	36	35
$25.1–$99.9 million	17	20	22
$100 million or more	10	12	13

Source: W. T. Grimm & Co., Chicago.

more, approximately half of all reported transactions represented private or closely held sellers.

While the number of acquisition transactions varies each year and the merger movement is clearly cyclical in nature, a substantial number of acquisitions occur regardless of the point in the cycle. Opportunities exist for acquisition (and divestiture) at all times, and prudent managers must be prepared to cope with the opportunities and risks presented.

Internal Versus External Development

The options for corporate growth can be characterized as *internal development* involving expansion through investment in research, product development, plant and equipment, and so on, on the one hand, and as *acquisition* on the other. Companies should weigh the costs and risks of internal development programs against renewed opportunities for acquisition, which can often provide more rapid, "stepwise," and predictable results for corporate growth. Recent research indicates, for example, that it requires an average of 8 years for new ventures of major U.S. corporations to become profitable.

Financial Factors in the Environment. There are always a number of external, financial, and economic conditions that influence corporate management attitudes toward the choice and the mix between acquisition and internal development. These cyclical conditions largely account for the type and level of corporate development. In the early 1970s, low liquidity, conservative accounting rules, major political and economic uncertainties, and wage and price controls were conducive to stepping up internal development activities. In 1981 and 1982 it appeared that acquisition deals were encouraged by relatively low price/earnings (P/E) ratios, selective liquidity, and expectations about inflationary trends. Conversely, a rising stock market, together with high costs of borrowing and the inability to forecast trends for unfamiliar businesses, might reduce the number of acquisition transactions and favor internal development projects.

Forces that Make Buyers and Sellers. At the same time that buyers are active, forces within the business environment encourage some companies to become prospective sellers. This is illustrated in Fig. A-9. There "selling" forces often motivate corporations to carry out acquisitions and mergers outside of "normal" diversification considerations. These forces can be classified as internal or external, positive or negative, and controllable or uncontrollable; for example, forces opposing acquisition and merger are represented by arrows pointing away from the company.

Acquisition Strategies

In theory, acquisitions are the result of decisions intended to maximize the value of the firm's stock. In practice, however, other, more managerial, objectives often take precedence. These include the simple desires to demonstrate growth, to keep up with competitors, to demonstrate entry into new fields, to ward off potential acquirers, and so forth.

Strategic Objectives. Rational acquisition objectives "in creating values for the stockholders" often include the following:

Greater Income. Combining businesses can mean economic synergies in finance, operations, and marketing.

Less Cyclicity of Income. Income might be stabilized, for example, by means of a highly cyclical company combining with another of lower or opposite cyclicity.

Greater Market Recognition. This can be attained by entering a "favored field."

Spreading of Risk. Acquisitions and mergers can help companies with narrow product or market bases balance their business "portfolios." This can also apply to political and geographic risk-taking.

A More Financially Balanced Enterprise. This places emphasis on balanced cash flow and individual business-unit maturities.

These reasons are not mutually exclusive; usually, a combination of corporate objectives is sought.

Strategic Implementation. Options available to implement strategy are:

- Vertical or horizontal integration
- Divestiture
- International or foreign business
- Business merger (pooling of interests with another corporation of comparable size)
- True diversification versus related diversification
- Special situation investing

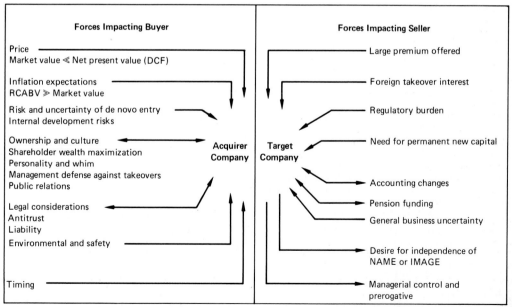

FIG. A-9 Current forces impacting business combinations.

Vertical integration involves acquiring or merging with supply sources (backward integration) or with consumers of present output (forward integration). *Horizontal integration* entails acquiring or merging with competing firms. Antitrust laws, however, preclude certain business combinations. *Divestitures* may be desirable because businesses do not fit into a strategic plan or simply because the firm must raise cash and may not have other alternatives. In recent years, a large number of acquisitions have resulted from divestitures by companies of previously acquired businesses which did not work out or were no longer suitable for the owner's corporate strategy. *International diversification* opens avenues for growth. *Business pooling* strengthens financial and operating bases. True diversification and special situation investing warrant more detailed definition.

True Diversification. The objectives of diversification are twofold: to spread corporate risk and to enlarge corporate opportunities. A corporation undergoes *true diversification* when it acquires a business in a completely different industry from its own—one in which the demand for the products or services is driven by different factors. In some other cases, true diversification denotes an entirely different technology serving the same general marketplace. An example of true diversification would be the acquisition of an oil and gas producer by a cigarette manufacturer. Examples of *related diversifica-*

tion would be the acquisition of a laser-hologram entertainment manufacturer by a video tape recorder-player manufacturer and that of a foreign-based business by a related, entirely U.S.-based business.

Special Situation Investing. Some corporations purchase or sell shares in other corporations much as a portfolio manager or individual investor manages a portfolio of stocks and bonds. This activity is subordinate to the conduct of the main corporate operations but suggests a somewhat controversial strategy for a publicly owned company. Several corporations, including City Investing and Teledyne, have employed this modus operandi.

Identification of Acquisition Candidates

Systematic approaches such as those outlined below can be useful, particularly in the early stages of planning for an acquisition program. They should nearly always be coupled, however, with more opportunistic, intense, pragmatic, and active techniques, at least at the point at which interest in specific industry subsegments has been identified and acquisition objectives have been quantified.

Industry Identification. In most cases, criteria designed to select both industries and potential candidates within an industry include elements of at least some of those shown in Table A-2. Publicly

TABLE A-2   Sample Criteria Headings

1. Preference, if any, for service versus manufacturing industries.
   Additional preferences for type of industry and level of technology.
   Geographic preferences or restrictions.
2. Degree of fit (or lack of it) with the acquirer.
   Includes issues of management comprehension.
   Likely image and market effects if a company in the industry is acquired.
3. Size range of transaction contemplated.
4. Statement as to whether acquisition of a leading company is required or not, and other desired characteristics.
5. Industry makeup of sector(s) considered.
   Number and size distribution of participants.
6. Overall historical profitability.
   Return on assets, total invested capital, sales, and other measures.
   Average price-to-earnings ratio and the rough range of price-to-earnings ratios for the industry.
   Cyclicity of sales and earnings.
   Variability among companies and reasons for same.
7. Overall past and expected growth trends in terms of sales (dollars and physical output).
   Short term.
   Long term.
   Expected future financial performance (freestanding and if acquired).
8. Capital intensity (useful to screen heavy-capital-requirement industries as opposed to "cash generators").
   Dollars of invested capital per dollar of sales.
   Cash-utilization ratio (cash flow in relation to invested capital).
9. Technological, market, regulatory, and political risks.
10. Perceived risk relative to the capital market in general, as measured by the "betas" of major companies in the industry.
11. Projections of selected-company financial performance.
    Cash flow.
    Internal rate of return (IRR).
    Return on total invested capital for selected years.
    Earnings-per-share (EPS) effects, including dilution, if applicable.

Note: Additional factors must be considered when selecting individual companies within an industry, including issues of management, "culture," and value creation.

available information can be helpful in conducting initial screening based on historical performance. This includes data from government sources, such as the *Census of Manufactures* of the U.S. Department of Commerce and the annual *U.S. Industrial Outlook;* Standard and Poor's industry data; *The Value Line Investment Survey;* and a host of others. If one is starting from scratch and wants to look at a very wide range of industries, computer screening techniques can be useful, particularly where quantitative data are concerned. A screening based on more detailed qualitative insights that can be "machine searched," however, is usually desirable. Although the past must be considered, the true test, and obviously the most relevant, is expected future performance.

Company Identification. Once the appropriate industry has been selected, analysis must address the practical tasks both of identifying appropriate acquisition candidates and of developing sufficient information about them so that they can be screened, analyzed, and placed in perspective in relation to the corporation's interests and criteria. This methodical approach is often engaged in concurrently with an opportunistic approach in which potentially available candidates are brought to the attention of the company by outsiders.

Need for Criteria. The two most important factors in identifying and later analyzing potential acquisition candidates are: (1) knowing what you are looking for in terms of specifics—financial parameters and industry position, growth potential, and so on; and (2) knowing how and where to locate them. The development of criteria in order to initiate a systematic search is often arduous and time-consuming. Financial objectives in terms of size, profitability, debt-to-equity ratios, and the effect of the potential acquiree on the income statement and balance sheet of the acquirer need to be specified as part of the criteria. Establishing realistic, acceptable criteria is a difficult task; staff groups engaged in identifying and analyzing potential candidates, along with top management, must constantly test and revise both criteria and possible candidates as the process proceeds.

Candidate Search. Assuming that tentative criteria covering appropriate financial and industry attributes have been developed, where does one go to identify prospects or candidates? Basic directories and data banks usually are a first step. These include Dun & Bradstreet's *Million Dollar Directories* and Standard & Poor's *Register of Corporations Directories.* Internal sources such as marketing and sales departments should also be included as a first step because of their possible knowledge and field contacts. One's own key officers, directors, and other employees are often good sources of candidates.

Publicly Held Companies as Candidates. The identification of publicly held companies is facilitated by the number of different sources from which to choose. When one is beginning from scratch, often the most efficient way to extract a list of companies is to use the Compustat or a similar computerized data base. This procedure will enable the user to define its parameters and select a listing of publicly held companies. There are other initial avenues of pursuit, but most are generally more time-consuming. If no other alternative is available, the investigation can proceed manually by using the Dun & Bradstreet *Million Dollar Directories* (product-code listing) and checking its lists against the Securities and Exchange Commission's list of firms that must file reports with the SEC.

The most important sources for public companies are the SEC Form 10-K and the annual report to shareholders. Also significant are the other SEC documents, such as the 10-Q, Proxy, Registration Statement Prospectus, 13-D, and 14-D1. Sources such as Standard & Poor's *Stock Reports*, Moody's *Investors Service*, and *The Value Line Survey* should not be overlooked.

The basic industry group to which companies belong is important. Industry information is usually easily accessible. Standard & Poor's prepares *Industry Surveys*, which are updated periodically throughout the year. The Department of Commerce publishes the *U.S. Industrial Outlook* annually; it gives a composite view of selected industries. Various statistics are available from *Predicasts* (an annual) and from *Predicasts Basebook*, which is historical in nature; and every industry has trade journals that address subjects such as new-product development, changes in management, regulations, and price trends.

Privately Held Candidates. Industry information is accessed in the same way for private firms as for public firms. The problem lies in securing information on individual privately held firms. One might begin the search with a brief examination of such directories as Dun & Bradstreet's *Million Dollar Directories* and *Middle Market Directory*, Standard & Poor's *Register of Corporations*, and *Thomas' Register.* Computerized references include the *EIS Industrial Plants*, which lists both public and private manufacturing establishments with annual sales exceeding $900,000, and *EIS Non-Manufacturing Establishments*, which covers more than 200,000 companies.

Additional Information. To find out about a privately held company, the next step is to consult one or more of the following sources: (a) state filings: In some states records are kept and are made available about the company's business operation, its board members, and some financials; (b) Dun & Bradstreet credit reports: These reports give various data on companies, including lines of business, history, management, ownership, and credit information; (c) The Robert Morris Associates *Annual Statement Studies:* In its reports, Robert Morris Associates summarizes average financial data for companies in a wide range of industries; (d) field interviews; (e)

21

product literature; (f) trade exhibition shows; (g) editors of selected periodicals; (h) special trade directories; (i) industry associations; (j) probate court estate and divorce records: These can sometimes provide information about control or ownership of small firms; (k) special industry studies; (l) the *Congressional Information Service Index*, which gives information on hearings and transcripts; (m) Senate and House committees; and (n) government reports.

Valuation

There are a variety of techniques used in valuing a business; they are listed below. The emphasis here is on the technical approaches used to determine what a business or a company is worth; that is, to put a price tag on the stock or assets. The negotiating strategy is another factor to be considered. It reflects the time horizons, risk/return preferences, and experiences of the parties to the transaction and is colored by emotional factors such as optimism, pessimism, and ego. Thus there is normally no one value; rather, there is a floor, a ceiling price, and a range of reasonableness for negotiation of a deal between the buyer(s) and seller(s).

A number of methods of valuation should be considered:

1. Liquidation value (the floor)
2. Book value (a reference)
3. Public-market value
4. Public-market values of related firms
5. Acquisition values of related firms
6. Normalized price-to-earnings ratio times current normalized earnings
7. Present value of expected cash flow

All except the last rely on historical information. But since, in most acquisitions, one is "buying the future," one needs to estimate how it will differ from the past. Thus, depending on the views of the parties, more or less attention is paid to historically based values. The negotiated price tends to fall between a future-based (uncertain) valuation and historically based (certain) results.

Accounting, Financial, and Tax Considerations

The details and options open in the structuring of transactions and the consideration of the financial reporting and tax effects are best left to specialized professionals. Early and continuing consultation with accounting, financial, and legal counsel is essential. Nevertheless, executives responsible for planning, implementing, and overseeing acquisitions, as well as all those concerned with the acquisition process, must have at least a preliminary appreciation of these factors. Without this it is impossible to begin to think in terms of a transaction that meets the objectives of all parties.

The main focus here is on transactions involving the acquisition of 80 percent or more of the stock or assets of a company. *In general, acquisition of 20 percent or less of another company's stock is carried on the investor's (acquirer's) balance sheet as an investment at cost. For less than 50 percent but at least 20 percent interest, some control or influence is implied. Here, typically, the equity method is required, with the stock carried on the balance sheet of the acquiring company at cost and adjusted for the proportional share of subsequent net earnings or losses. Where 50 percent (or more) ownership is involved, consolidation of the balance sheets and income statements occurs (with breakout of any minority interest).*

The following material is intended to summarize broadly some of the important financial and accounting issues of acquisitions from the standpoint of both the corporate buyer and the seller, as well as from the point of view of the selling stockholder.

Types of Transactions. The five basic types of transactions employed to effect a business combination—three nontaxable and two taxable—are described below. The discussion assumes that 80 percent or more of the assets or stock of a company are acquired.

Nontaxable Transactions. These transactions are nontaxable in the sense that neither the acquired corporation nor its stockholders incur a tax liability as a result of the acquisition for stock of the acquirer. (When such stockholders do sell their stock, however, a tax liability is incurred if the stock is sold at a gain.) Consideration other than stock or sometimes other securities is termed *boot* and is taxable.

To be tax-free, a reorganization must satisfy a number of requirements, including business purpose, continuity of interest by the stockholders, and continuity of business purpose.

STATUTORY MERGER OR CONSOLIDATION: This type of transaction involves the merger or consolidation of two or more corporations under the laws of the states involved. For purposes of this discussion, a *consolidation* is the combination of two or more corporations into a third, new corporation; a *merger* occurs where one corporation continues as a survivor. A *statutory merger or consolidation* is commonly known as an *A reorganization*, so named for Section 368 (A)(1)(a) of the Internal Revenue Code.

A statutory merger can apply only when the directors of the companies involved and usually the stockholders of at least the acquired company specifically approve the transaction. Obviously, then, this is not a vehicle for an unfriendly tender offer. A major advantage of the statutory-merger route is that acquisition can be for a combination of stock, cash, or other consideration, as long as stock represents 50 percent or more of the total price. Selling stockholders who are not concerned about their tax liabilities can accept cash, and others can have a tax-free exchange. Thus the buyer has considerable flexibility in terms of payment.

Exchange of Stock of Stockholders in the Selling Company for Voting Stock of the Acquiring Corporation: This is the so-called *B reorganization.* Although, as in the statutory merger, it can be a tax-free exchange, here 100 percent of the consideration must consist of the voting stock of the acquiring company. In addition, the acquirer must achieve ownership of stock possessing 80 percent of total combined voting power of all classes of stock entitled to vote and 80 percent of the total number of shares of all other classes of stock. Minority stockholders who choose not to exchange their stock may remain.

Purchase of Assets of the Selling Company for the Acquiring Corporation's Stock: This, the so-called *C reorganization,* involves exchange of voting stock in the acquiring company for substantially all the assets of the acquired company. Under such circumstances it can be a tax-free transaction. The shell of the acquired company may be liquidated after the assets have been exchanged for the acquirer's stock. The transaction may remain tax-free with a small percentage of the purchase price—up to 20 percent—in the form of cash. The rule requiring acquisition of substantially all the assets must be carefully observed. For example, if appreciable assets have been sold off by the seller prior to the transaction, it may not be construed as a tax-free reorganization.

A principal advantage of the acquisition of assets is that the acquirer can select those liabilities that it chooses to assume. Also, this transaction differs from the *B* reorganization previously described (stock-for-stock transaction) in that a small percentage of the purchase price may be permitted to be nonstock. On the other hand, asset transactions involve transfers of titles, which by nature are more complex than transfers of stock.

Taxable Transactions. These are taxable transactions in the sense that the stockholders of the selling company may incur a long-term capital-gains liability at the time of the transaction. (If the stock has been held for less than the minimum required for long-term capital-gains treatment, the stockholders will be subject to taxes at short-term capital-gains rates.) In taxable transactions, a new tax basis would develop for the selling corporation's assets where the assets are purchased directly or the acquired corporation is liquidated in accordance with provisions of the Internal Revenue Code. The effect on taxes of the allocation of purchase price among assets can be a major issue.

Purchase of the Selling Company's Stock from Its Stockholders for Cash or Nonvoting Securities of the Acquirer: Unlike the *A, B,* and *C* tax-free transactions previously discussed, this is always a taxable transaction. Beyond the question of taxes, there are other important advantages from the purchaser's standpoint, since board approval by the selling company is not required and the purchase transaction is with existing stockholders. Therefore, this is a route frequently taken with tender offers. Minority stockholders remain and may be a factor.

Purchase of Assets of the Acquired Company for Cash or Nonvoting Securities of the Buyer: Except for its taxable nature, this is quite similar to a *C* tax-free reorganization. The advantage of purchase of assets rather than of stock is primarily that the liabilities to be assumed can be selected. The shell of the acquired corporation typically is liquidated within 12 months of the plan of liquidation adopted prior to the asset sale in order to avoid double taxation.

Pooling Versus Purchase Accounting. From an accounting standpoint, a merger is treated either as (1) a pooling of interests or (2) a purchase. Important differences in balance-sheet and income-statement effects for the combined company can result from these two approaches. In some instances these differences can be very great: some acquisitions that would be attractive to a buyer on a pooling basis would be difficult or impossible to justify if purchase accounting were required. These are cases where, under purchase accounting only, the purchase price exceeds the fair value of the seller and the difference becomes goodwill that must be amortized against after-tax earnings.

Acquisitions must be accounted for by one of these two methods according to specific rules. APB's Opinion No. 16, issued in 1970, sets up criteria for the conditions under which pooling is mandatory; if these conditions are not met, acquisition must be treated as a purchase. The net effect is to restrict the number of deals in which pooling is possible. It is often difficult or impossible to meet the conditions required to effect a pooling. Generally speaking, where companies desire purchase accounting, this can often be effected by seeing that one or more of the conditions required for pooling is not met. Effecting a pooling, if that is desired, is usually far more difficult.

Pooling of Interests. In the pooling-of-interests method, the balance sheets of the two firms are simply added together and treated as if they had always been one entity. No write-up or change in asset values occurs. Regardless of purchase price, no goodwill is created by the transaction. Earnings of the combined entity can be restated from the beginning of the accounting period as if the two firms had been merged for the entire period. For pooling to be allowed, some of the requirements are that 90 percent or more of the stock of the selling company must be acquired for voting stock of the acquirer; the acquisition must be made in one step; contingent **23** payments (earnouts) are not allowed; each of the two companies must have been an independent entity for at least 2 years; and the new entity cannot dispose of a significant portion of the assets of the combined companies for a 2-year period. If any of these conditions is not satisfied, the combination must be accounted for as a purchase.

Purchase. As previously indicated, purchase accounting must take place where one or more of the conditions for pooling does not exist. As a practical matter, where purchase accounting is desired, conditions can usually be set up to make it happen.

In a purchase transaction, the assets and liabilities of the acquired companies are not recorded at book value, but are shown at "fair market value," as described in APB's Opinion No. 16. Where purchase price exceeds the fair market value of tangible assets—a fairly common occurrence today—the difference must be attributed to identifiable intangible assets, such as patents, or to goodwill. Goodwill typically is not a desirable balance-sheet item, and only after revaluation of other assets does goodwill come into play.

Sometimes patents, technology, and other intangible assets can be determined to have substantial values and an expected life for amortization purposes; thus the creation of goodwill can be minimized or eliminated. However, any goodwill created must be written off for financial-reporting purposes against after-tax income on a straight-line basis over 40 years or less. This is outlined under APB's Opinion No. 17 issued in 1970. It should be noted that this goodwill amortization, unlike identifiable intangible assets, is not a deductible expense for tax purposes. On the other hand, if the purchase price is less than the fair market value of the assets, the property assets are written up. A purchase differs from a pooling of interests in that earnings of the combined entity are reported only as of the date of the transaction.

Impact. Where both the reported book value of the net assets of the selling company and their fair market value approximate the purchase price, the question of pooling versus purchase treatment should largely be a matter of indifference, since no recurring balance-sheet or income-statement effects occur with regard to tax liability or goodwill amortization.

In a more probable situation, however, where the purchase price exceeds reported net book value, the effects can be quite important. A revaluation of assets and liabilities to fair market values may or may not result in creation of goodwill or an attendant non-tax-deductible charge to net income. Even where goodwill can be avoided, revaluation can create a new depreciable base for assets and higher depreciation charges, which may or may not be desirable. Certainly, under such circumstances, reported earnings will be reduced and cash flow increased. This

has proven to be a factor in many recent leveraged buyouts.

Under pooling-of-interests accounting, unlike purchasing accounting, the reported financial statements can reflect the combined companies for the full fiscal year even though the merger took place at some point during the year.

Installment Purchases. Installment purchases can be desirable and come into play for taxable transactions where selling stockholders want to reduce or defer taxes by spreading the gain on the sale of stock over several taxable years and where the buyer agrees to pay for the purchase over the same period. Only purchase accounting applies. Debt is issued for future payments; interest (stated or imputed) on such debt will be taxed at ordinary rather than capital-gains rates.

Earnouts (Contingent Purchase Price). At times the seller's price is such that the transaction can only be justified by the buyer at levels of future earnings considerably above what the buyer can expect with any degree of certainty. Here an earnout may allow the deal to be consummated. Basically, earnouts call for part of the purchase price to be paid in later periods based on future earnings according to a formula worked out between buyer and seller.

Earnouts may qualify as nontaxable transactions if the usual conditions for a tax-free reorganization are met and if all stock used in the purchase is issued within 5 years of closing. Usually an upper limit to the potential number of shares is stated, and 50 percent or more must be issued at the time of closing.

A contingent purchase may allow some deals to go through that would otherwise be impossible. However, a series of difficult management and control problems between buyer and seller during the earnout period may easily develop when the seller's management is attempting to meet its earnings goals. Purchase accounting applies to earnouts.

Antitrust and Other Legal Issues

In observance of the public interest, antitrust legislation proscribes any acquisition or merger that substantially lessens competition or encourages monopolizing behavior. Indeed, the principal concern of antitrust policy is to maintain competitive industry and market structures. The major authority under which the U.S. government or competing companies may challenge a merger is Section 7 of the Clayton Act, enforced by the Department of Justice (DOJ) and the Federal Trade Commission (FTC). Section 5 of the FTC Act gives the FTC additional jurisdiction over alleged unfair business practices. The FTC and DOJ rules relating to premerger notifications and business review clearances and the SEC disclosure requirements governing tender offers and proxy statements also influence merger trends. State laws are becoming more influential as well.

The law distinguishes mergers by their effect on the nature of the acquiring firm and by their competitive impact on the industry or relevant market. Vertical mergers involve acquisition of existing or potential suppliers or customers. Horizontal mergers involve acquisition of existing or potential competitors. Conglomerate mergers typically involve diversification into one or more substantially unrelated businesses.

In 1982 the DOJ issued new simplified merger guidelines which the FTC is also substantially following . The key factor here is the Herfindahl-Hirschman index. This index compares the product market shares of the acquiring and selling firms to the relevant overall market. Use of this quantitative measure involves calculating a numerical score in terms of the squares of percentage market shares. The score can then be compared with the DOJ guidelines to estimate the likelihood of an antitrust challenge.

Various states are active in ways which can delay or effect mergers. Onerous regulations, such as information filing requirements to precede closings of deals and hearings before state commissions, have been adopted by some states to slow the progress of merger negotiations. At the same time, companies that are takeover candidates may amend their bylaws to extend the terms of friendly directors or raise the percentage of shares that must approve an offer. Although these and other more drastic defensive actions may delay some transactions, they are unlikely significantly to deter the present trend toward more mergers.

On the federal level, the Williams Act is the statute governing cash takeovers. Congress has also enacted antitrust legislation (the Hart-Scott-Rodino Act) requiring the submission of a premerger notification to the FTC and DOJ for all mergers and acquisitions in which one of the companies has sales or assets in excess of $100 million and the other company has sales or assets in excess of $10 million.

The SEC and IRS are currently reviewing leveraged buyouts and "going" private practices for potential new valuation, disclosure, tax, and other procedural regulations.

Managing the Acquisition Process

There are few general rules pertaining to functions and roles in this acquisition process. Each corporation has its own personality, style, culture, and biases. In the last analysis, these factors will determine the types of situations that will be of interest and ultimately approved, as well as the approach and organization of the acquisition effort itself.

Analytical Process. In the past, acquisitions were too often made largely on the basis of a situation brought to the parties by outsiders (reactive mode) and after only brief analysis of short-term earnings potential, plus some consideration of fit and longer-term issues. Although the services of finders and intermediaries remain important, and although short-term earnings effects cannot be overlooked, today's efforts are more likely to involve heavier staff inputs, with much more consideration given to an organized search than to a reactive or opportunistic mode. Also, more attention is paid to the analysis of alternative strategic possibilities, longer-range implications, and postmerger management questions. Portfolio theory, asset management, and related concepts from contemporary corporate finance and managerial economics are increasingly a part of the work of investment bankers, consultants, and staff groups within large corporations.

Organizational Approaches. For most companies, a formal corporate-development-acquisition function is of relatively recent origin. Merger and acquisition activities are commonly, although not always, part of or allied with strategic planning and general corporate development.

Unless tied in with operational planning, business analysis, or economics—as opposed to mainly strategic planning activities—most acquisition departments tend to be very small, with one to four professional staff members working with the department head.

Ad hoc groups or task forces are commonly formed by corporate-development departments to address questions of industry outlook, to search for and analyze candidates, and to conduct detailed reviews of promising situations. Finance, legal, economic, and tax staff are often involved, along with managers from operating divisions. Clearly, unusually good working interpersonal relationships and the ability to "sell" or "unsell" ideas to top management are key.

The permanent corporate-development staff will also be interacting with outsiders—investment bankers, finders, consultants, and others. In fact, a significant portion of the director's time may be spent developing and analyzing ideas with outsiders. Some departments regularly meet with selected groups of outsiders to explore acquisition ideas. This contact may include not only investment and commercial bankers and financial consultants, but also former company presidents, headhunters, and other knowledgeable individuals. However done, informing the financial community and others of the corporation's goals and "needs" is important to generating the leads for a successful acquisition program. Formal steps may include speeches and putting such information in the annual report. Communicating the company's financial and management culture can also be crucial.

The effectiveness of the corporate-development-acquisition function depends to a major degree on its relationship to the chief executive officer or chairman; to the heads of operating units who often must support the proposed acquisition or other course of action; and to staff heads, such as those of finance, legal, and marketing departments, with whom corporate-development staff must work.

Acquisition Protocol. Although a series of steps or a protocol can be useful in conceptualizing the overall role of corporate development and the steps in carrying out an active acquisition effort, such a scheme or methodology represents at best only a guide or checklist. It should not serve to create obstacles to opportunities that present themselves and meet the company's criteria. One useful protocol, summarized and adapted from that developed by Robert K. Mueller, chairman of Arthur D. Little, is shown in Table A-3.

Conditions for Success. From our experience with more than 100 corporate assignments relating to mergers and acquisitions, we find that most successes are characterized by the following:

1. Top management involvement and commitment
2. Sound rationale for acquisition, with explicit objectives
3. Flexible, realistic screening criteria
4. Persistence in the acquisition process and sound negotiating skills
5. Willingness to take significant risk
6. Favorable business climate and timing
7. Availability of adequate financial and management resources
8. Appropriate corporate linkage and integration

See also Accounting, financial; Financial management, financing; Financial statement analysis; Government regulations, federal regulation of competition; International operations and management in multinational companies; Legal affairs, management of corporate; Negotiating; Planning, strategic managerial; Risk analysis and management; Tax management; Valuation of a firm.

REFERENCES

Bradley, James W., and Donald H. Korn: *Acquisition and Corporate Development*, Lexington Books/D. C. Heath, Lexington, Mass., 1981.

Davis, F. T., Jr.: *Business Acquisition Desk Book*, Institute for Business Planning, Englewood Cliffs, N.J., 1981.

Salter, Malcolm S., and Wolf A. Weinhold: *Diversification Through Acquisition*, Free Press, New York, 1979.

JAMES W. BRADLEY, *Ulin, Morton, Bradley & Welling Incorporated*

DONALD H. KORN, *Arthur D. Little, Inc.*

Advertising Concepts

This entry examines the economic value and cost of advertising, the functions of advertising, how advertising goals and strategies are developed, basic advertising appeals, and the functions and characteristics of media.

Economic Values and Costs

There are three ways to view the economic value and costs of advertising. One way is to view advertising's aggregate effect on the economy of a nation. The second is to view the value and cost to the individual firm. The third is to look at the value and cost to the consumer.

Aggregate Effect. There is much debate on the value and cost of advertising to an economy. Critics

TABLE A-3 A Protocol for the Acquisition Process

Determinative stage
  Clarify and state acquisition objectives.
  Determine top management and board commitment to the extent possible.
Scouting stage
  Search for and/or otherwise identify acquisition candidates.
  Make initial candidate assessment.
Consultation stage
  Consult with outside legal, accounting, banking, and other professionals, possibly including consultants.
Strategic stage
  Determine impact of the transaction on both parties.
  Develop negotiating strategy and more detailed company analysis, including consideration of accounting/financial and legal issues as well as personalities of the key players.
"Sensor" stage
  Determine likelihood of potential interest via direct or indirect contact.
"Vamp" stage
  Carry out the "act of seduction" coupled with regulatory notice and approvals.
Proposal stage
Deal stage (execution)
Management (postacquisition) stage

believe that advertising is wasteful by adding to product costs, misallocating billions of dollars to unproductive use rather than to production of goods and services, setting up barriers by large firms to the entry of new firms into an industry, and making consumers buy products they do not really need.

Advocates of advertising feel that advertising plays an important role in lessening the negative effects of a recession, extending product life cycles, supporting the media from which we obtain news and entertainment, reducing the prices of products by increasing demand and realizing economies of scale in production, informing consumers of product improvements and new products and thereby contributing to economic growth, and helping to satisfy psychological needs of consumers (e.g., status). Although the debate over the costs and benefits of advertising to an economy has not been, nor is it likely to be, resolved, it probably is fair to say that both sides of the issue have merit.

Individual Firm. Firms benefit from advertising in different ways and to a different extent, depending upon several factors. A company that is unknown or whose brands are unknown is likely to benefit most from advertising. Where products are physically similar, advertising can create a psychological differentiation for a brand in the minds of consumers and increase company sales and profits. Advertising also is more beneficial to a company which is in an industry with expanding sales as opposed to one in which sales are declining. For example, companies which sell citizen band radios will benefit from advertising more than ones selling slide rules. Companies which manufacture products having "hidden" or unobservable qualities will tend to benefit more from advertising than companies in which product features are more apparent.

Advertising also provides a relatively inexpensive means of informing consumers about a company's brands, especially when compared with the cost of a sales force performing the same function. Advertising also benefits a company by making its sales representatives more efficient. That is, advertising provides an entrée for the sales representative. The prospective customer is made aware of the company and its product offerings through advertising. Good advertising may have created an interest in the brand and have stimulated questions about the brand. Thus, advertising can help open the door for sales representatives, inform prospective buyers of product features, and stimulate interest and desire for a product, all of which make sales representatives more efficient.

The Consumer. Advertising is certainly a cost which consumers incur; however, when we consider the alternatives, the benefits of advertising outweigh the cost. To make a product and brand choice, a consumer must have some knowledge of what is available. Advertising is an economical way for consumers to reduce their search time for products and brands which can satisfy a need or solve a problem. Advertising also helps create images and psychological values which can help satisfy the psychological and social needs of consumers. In the United States economy, psychological needs are very important, since basic physiological needs of food, clothing, and shelter have generally been met.

It is generally agreed that many companies do waste some of their money in advertising. Some companies either spend too little on advertising to gain significant economic benefits or spend too much, incurring negative marginal returns. The net effect of advertising in the United States, however, is beneficial to the economy by stimulating demand for new products and by helping firms achieve mass production, economies of scale, and higher employment. The consumer benefits from reduced search costs and psychological and social satisfaction. The firms benefit from higher sales and profits through an efficient means of informing consumers of product offerings.

Functions of Advertising

Advertising performs at least seven basic functions for a company.[1]

Information. Advertising informs consumers of the existence of a brand, its characteristics and benefits, its price, where it can be purchased, and the terms of purchase.

Entertainment. Advertising is very often entertaining. The humor of Miller Lite and Federal Express commercials and the adventuresomeness of the U.S. Army recruiting commercials are examples of how advertising can entertain consumers.

Persuasion. Advertising attempts to create or change consumer attitudes toward the company brand. To influence consumer attitudes, companies use celebrities (credible sources), consumer testimonials, two-sided messages, comparison advertising, logical-factual argumentation, and psychological or social benefits which will accrue to the purchasers of the brand.

Reminder. Because of its repetitive nature, advertising continually reminds consumers of the product and its benefits. Furthermore, heavy reminder advertising tends to create consumer confidence for a brand because of increased familiarity.

Reassurance. Advertising serves to reduce postpurchase doubt for products which require a large investment, such as an automobile. Consumers seek out information which supports a major purchase decision they have made. Advertising is one source which helps to alleviate the doubt they have after a purchase decision.

Assistance to Other Company Efforts. Advertising facilitates other company efforts. Advertis-

27

ing can generate leads for sales representatives, provide an entrée to clients for sales representatives, help consumers to identify product packages in the store more easily, desensitize consumers to the higher-than-average price of a brand, enhance the image and reputation of the firm and stores carrying the brand, improve employee morale, and create a favorable image among present stockholders and potential investors and lending institutions

Addition of Value.[2] Advertising adds value to a product by associating intangible attributes with the brand. A cigarette is ''masculine'' (Marlboro) or ''feminine'' (Virginia Slims) because of the meanings which advertisers associate with the brand names. Thus, advertisers influence consumers' perceptions of products by attributing socially significant values to brands, such as status, sex appeal, and elegance.

Advertising Strategy[3]

There are five basic steps in developing a strategy.

1. Assess opportunities.
2. Analyze corporate resources.
3. Set objectives.
4. Develop and evaluate alternative strategies.
5. Assign specific tasks.

Environmental Factors. The initial step in developing an advertising strategy is to identify and evaluate market opportunities. Market opportunities are created and destroyed by changes in environmental factors. The major environmental factors an advertiser must consider are (1) technological factors, (2) economic factors, (3) sociocultural factors, and (4) legal-political factors.

1. *Technological changes* affect the kinds of media that can be used and how these media can be used. A relatively recent innovation in media is the shopper-talker. It is a device that shows films or slides to consumers at the point of purchase while playing a recorded message about the product. It can be located on counters in department stores or in thoroughfares within shopping malls. Similarly, microfragrance and vinyl sound sheets have been used in magazines to bring the dimension of smell and sound to the print medium. A development on the horizon is the ''television newspaper.'' Because of newsprint shortages and other factors, consumers may only have to push a button on their television to read the comics, the sports page, or Dear Abby. This prospect could have serious implications for the future of newspaper advertising.

2. *Economic changes* can both create and destroy opportunities for advertisers. When economic times are prosperous and discretionary income increases, the demand for amusements, travel, high-quality products, and status goods increases. Advertisers of these goods and services must be ready to increase their effort in times of prosperity. The energy crisis of 1973 to 1974 is an example of how advertisers adapted to a change in the economic environment. Automobile manufacturers began to advertise economy and gas efficiency; gasoline cap locks and antisiphoning devices were advertised; AT&T advertised the energy-saving usage of telephone conferences as opposed to travel by plane or other transportation methods. Electric and gas companies provided consumers with fuel-saving suggestions through their advertising.

3. Changes in the *social* and *cultural* behavior of consumers create and destroy advertising opportunities. The women's liberation movement provides an opportunity for advertisers to develop a new theme associating women's liberation with their products—e.g., cigarettes. Changing societal attitudes toward feminine hygiene deodorants and contraceptives opened up opportunities for advertising these and other products.

4. Changes in the *legal-political* environment affect what can be advertised and how it can be advertised. Cigarettes and liquor are two prime examples of products for which the federal government regulates advertising. Claims advertisers can make about mouthwashes are another example. Changes in the political relations with foreign countries, such as Russia and China, affect where advertisements can be shown. Another influence of government on advertising has been the Federal Trade Commission's (FTC) encouragement of comparison advertising (discussed later). During the 1970s the FTC caused many firms (e.g., in the mouthwash industry) to spend money on corrective advertising.

Advertisers must continually monitor environmental changes, such as those cited above, to adapt and create their advertising messages.

Product-Oriented Strategy. There are two broad categories of advertising strategies—those which use a product-oriented approach and those which use a consumer-oriented approach.[4] At least three advertising strategies use a product-oriented approach. They are (1) *feature-oriented* strategy, in which the advertising campaign stresses specific attributes or characteristics of a brand, such as ''our cigarette has only 2 milligrams of tar and 0.2 milligrams of nicotine''; (2) *use-oriented* strategy, in which the advertising campaign stresses the in-operation and/or postoperation benefits of a brand, such as ''Auto-wax is easier to apply in half the time''; and (3) *product comparison-oriented* strategy, where the advertising campaign stresses differences between a client's brand and a competing brand. Comparative advertising, a form of the product-comparison approach, is increasingly popular. This strategy has its critics and its advocates. Critics believe that comparative advertising reduces the credibility of claims, creates greater consumer awareness of competitors, and confuses consumers. Advocates claim that comparative advertising increases sales of better brands, informs consumers, and forces competitors to upgrade their brands.[5]

Consumer-Oriented Strategy. The second broad set of advertising strategies uses a consumer-oriented approach. At least four strategies use this approach. The first is an *attitude-oriented* strategy, which presents a message consistent with the consumer's attitude-value-belief structure. The second is a *significant group–oriented* approach, which stresses the group that uses or approves of the client's brand. The group must be important to the target market and is usually a reference or social group. The third is a *lifestyle-oriented* approach, which develops its theme around the lifestyle of a distinct target market. Finally, some advertisers use a *subconsciously oriented* approach by appealing to subconscious (or unconscious) consumer needs through symbolism. This approach uses veiled appeals to repressed human desires.

Image-Oriented Strategy. This strategy cannot be classified exclusively under the product- or consumer-oriented approaches. Although all advertising strategies create some kind of brand image in the minds of consumers, an image-oriented strategy is a conscious attempt on the part of advertisers to create a brand "personality" or to develop a brand image consistent with a consumer's self-image.

Positioning. One last strategy which may be categorized as either product- or consumer-oriented creates a "position" or brand niche in the consumer's mind by relating the client's brand to those of its competitors or by attaching the brand to something already in the consumer's mind. This strategy, which became popular in the 1970s, is *product positioning*.[6] Avis positioned itself as second to Hertz, Volkswagen (initially) created the "ugly" position, and 7-Up positioned itself as an "uncola" against the colas. Supporters of product positioning say the strategy has become successful because of the high noise level and clutter resulting from the enormous volume of advertising and the volume of products and brands. The positioning approach allows consumers to hang the brand on a product ladder or attach it to something with which they are familiar and therefore enables them to remember the brand more easily.

The advertising strategy which a company selects depends upon the product type as well as the market segment to whom it chooses to sell.

Appeals, Messages, and Communications

Communication is an inherent part of advertising. To advertise effectively, advertisers should adhere to basic communications principles, such as stating the message in terms familiar to the target audience. A message which is successful in the white Anglo-Saxon market is not very likely to appeal to the black subculture.

From communications research several basic advertising principles have evolved. The following are a few of these principles:

1. A *two-sided advertising message* (i.e., one in which strengths and weaknesses of a brand are brought out or strengths of a competitive brand are mentioned) is more effective than a one-sided message if (a) the audience is well-educated, and (b) the audience uses a competing brand.[7]

2. *Fear appeals* are an effective means of persuading an audience. Mouthwashes, breath mints, and toothpaste are among the product categories which use this appeal by communicating fear of social ostracism.

3. *Pleasant forms of distraction* presented with the advertised message can increase the effectiveness of persuasive appeals.

4. A *message which actively involves the audience* can increase effectiveness. Camera angles can place the audience in a position of vicariously trying the product. Permitting the audience to complete a jingle will actively involve audience members. An example is the earlier television commercial, "You can take Salem out of the country, but. . . ."

5. Advertising practitioners believe that *emotional appeals* are more successful than rational appeals.

6. *Humor* has not proven to be an effective persuasive appeal, but it can be effective in gaining audience attention and in aiding consumer recall of the brand and its message.

7. *Nonverbal communications* are often more important than the verbal message. Facial expressions, voice qualities, dress, gestures, music, and eye movement are examples.

The Media: An Overview

Communications research provides us with several characteristics of the broadcast and print media. Some of the more important are the following:

1. An audience will retain complex factual material better when it is presented in print as opposed to oral presentation. On the other hand, the broadcast media are more effective for simple material.

2. The print media permit easy reexposure, whereas the broadcast media are fleeting.

3. The broadcast media offer consumers a greater sense of realism than the print media.

4. Print allows the reader to develop the topic in depth, because the reader can control the time, pace, and direction of the exposure.

5. Multiple-channel messages are more effective than single-channel presentations. That is, advertising is more effective when the message stimulates more than one sense. This idea helps to explain the powerful effects of television.

Each medium has its strengths and weaknesses. The media mix which an advertiser selects should be based upon the objectives, the advertising strategy used, the characteristics of the product, and the characteristics of the target market.

Print Media. Some of the distinguishing *strengths of a newspaper* are the following:

1. It has high geographic flexibility; i.e., ads can be placed in some markets to the exclusion of others and therefore have copy tailored to each.

2. It has short closing time; ads usually can be placed in newspapers within a 24- to 48-hour period.

3. It is read most widely by well-educated and high socioeconomic groups.

4. It has highly involved readers.

5. It is used as a shopping guide.

6. It is a habitual (daily) activity.[8]

Some of the *newspaper's major weaknesses* are poor reproduction quality and a short life span, i.e., they are usually kept in the home for one day and do not permit frequent reexposure.

Over the past several years, *magazines,* the other major print medium, have become very specialized in order to survive. *Life* and *Look* magazines, once very popular general magazines, have died, although *Life* has been resurrected as a pale image of its former self. One of the major strengths of magazines is their *long life span.* They are retained in the home for long periods of time (often several months) and permit frequent reexposure.

Magazines which have survived into the eighties have done so because of their high degree of *audience selectivity.* Advertisers can zero in on consumers with specific product interests (e.g., *Tennis World*) and specific sex, income, and age groups. Magazines also have increased their geographic flexibility by offering regional editions. Thus, some ads can run in the Northeast which have little relevance to people in the Southeast. Magazines also have advantages of high quality in reproduction and a high level of credibility and prestige.

Business publications, such as *Purchasing* and *Advertising Age,* are high-interest publications to which industry and professionals look for information relevant to their businesses. Other print media available to advertisers are the *yellow pages* of telephone books, which 92 million Americans use an average of 40 times a year.[9] *Outdoor advertising,* a very inexpensive means of delivering a message, and *transit advertising,* found on buses, trains, taxicabs, etc., are also important print media for advertisers.

Broadcast Media. *Television* has the highest overall impact of any medium. Television can reach an enormous audience with a single advertisement, yet cost per exposure is relatively low. Because television uses sight, sound, motion, and color, it delivers a message with great realism. Even though television reaches extremely large audiences, it still maintains a good degree of audience selectivity due mostly to programming. A major advantage of television is *psychology of attention*; that is, an audience will continue to watch a commercial message rather than get up to switch channels.[10]

Among the disadvantages of television are the large absolute (versus relative) cost of a national advertisement, the poor availability of desired times or programs to air the commercial, and the lack of easy reexposure (as opposed to print).

Even with these disadvantages television has high psychological impact because it is realistic and has a multichannel nature, it provides manufacturers with an opportunity to demonstrate their products, and it has the ability to build strong brand images.

Radio was the most pervasive medium until the advent of television. Since the arrival of television, radio has undergone great change. Technologically, radio developed into a highly portable medium as the transistor was ushered in. Now radio can be found in the home, car, factory, beach, stores, and office. Although radio has a massive audience, it is still a very highly selective medium. Its selectivity (well-defined target audience) is due to the plethora of program formats. Advertisers can select nearly any age, race, or socioeconomic class they wish with radio. Radio attracts a larger audience than television until 6:00 P.M. It offers geographic and time flexibility and is less expensive than television or newspapers.

It has, however, the major disadvantage of all broadcast media. It is fleeting, thereby lacking in easy reexposure, and, moreover, it cannot deliver the visual impact of television. Finally, radio lacks the prestige of television and is subject to a higher degree of message distortion.

Media Planning. As we can see, each medium possesses its strengths and weaknesses. To aid the advertiser in making a media-mix decision, a media-planning matrix should be evaluated. A partial representation of a media-planning matrix is given in Fig. A-10.[11]

Media characteristics and functions / Media	Reputation	Life span	Target market/ Total audience	Cost	Flexibility	Reseller support	Message reproduction	Editorial climate	Availability	Psychological impact
Newspapers										
Magazines										
Radio										
Television										
Yellow pages										
Outdoor										
Transit										

FIG. A-10 Media-planning matrix.

To use the matrix, one should place some value or weight on each dimension for each medium. The following are brief descriptions of each medium characteristic or function:

1. *Reputation:* the credibility, trustworthiness, or prestige of the medium.
2. *Life span:* the length of time a medium remains in the home to permit reexposure.
3. *Target market/total audience:* the proportion of total audience which are prime prospects for the firm's product. Thus, *total* circulation and listener or viewer figures are not good criteria.
4. *Cost:* at least two costs must be considered—*absolute* and *relative* costs. The relative cost (cost per prime contact) might be low, but the absolute cost of the medium prohibitive.
5. *Flexibility:* should be judged in terms of *timing* (when the message will be exposed to the audience), *geography* (the physical location of the audience), and *lead time* (advance notice time to the medium).
6. *Reseller support:* the degree of importance that resellers perceive that a medium gives them in selling a product. The producer often needs to obtain shelf space, and this dimension becomes very important.
7. *Message reproduction:* the level of quality in producing a client's message in a medium; for example, color reproduction in magazines versus newspapers.
8. *Editorial climate:* the philosophy or tone of programs or articles which appear within the medium.
9. *Availability:* the degree of ease or difficulty in obtaining media space or time.
10. *Psychological impact:* the level of impression and emotion with which a medium imparts the advertiser's message.

Not only each medium but also the specific vehicles within each medium (i.e., *Popular Computing* magazine versus *Personal Computer,* or *Stereo Review* versus *High Fidelity*) should be evaluated with a media-planning matrix.

After evaluating the media using the media-planning matrix, management should develop the media mix which will achieve stated advertising objectives.

See also Brands and brand names; Consumer behavior, managerial relevance of; Forecasting business conditions; Market analysis; Marketing management; Marketing research; Patients and valuable intangible rights; Positioning; Public and community relations.

NOTES

[1] M. Wayne DeLozier, *The Marketing Communications Process,* McGraw-Hill, New York, 1976, pp. 216–219.

[2] Ivan L. Preston, "Theories of Behavior and the Concept of Rationality in Advertising," *Journal of Communication,* vol. 17, no. 3, pp. 211–222, September 1967.

[3] DeLozier, op. cit.., pp. 272–281.

[4] Ibid., pp. 232–234, for more in-depth discussion.

[5] "Tannenbaum: Comparative Ads Can Work; Kershaw Says No," *Advertising Age,* May 17, 1976.

[6] Jack Trout and Al Ries, "The Positioning Era Cometh," *Advertising Age,* April 24, May 1, and May 8, 1972.

[7] E. W. J. Faison, "Effectiveness of One-sided and Two-sided Mass Communications in Advertising," *The Public Opinion Quarterly,* vol 25, pp. 468–469, 1961.

[8] *Advertising Age,* November 21, 1973, p. 66.

[9] "The *Yellow Pages* in Marketing and Advertising," American Telephone and Telegraph Company, 1970, pp. 6–7.

[10] J. F. Engel, H. G. Wales, and M. R. Warshaw, *Promotional Strategy,* rev. ed., Richard D. Irwin, Homewood, Ill., 1971, p. 261.

[11] DeLozier, op. cit., pp. 245–247.

REFERENCES

Aaker, David A., and John G. Myers: *Advertising Management,* 2d ed., Prentice-Hall, Englewood Cliffs, N.J., 1982.

Bovée, Courtland L., and William F. Arens: *Contemporary Advertising,* Richard D. Irwin, Homewood, Ill., 1982.

Ogilvy, David: *Ogilvy on Advertising,* Crown, New York, 1983.

M. Wayne DeLozier, *University of South Carolina*

Affirmative Action

Affirmative action is positive action taken to ensure nondiscriminatory treatment of all groups protected by legislation forbidding discrimination in employment because of race, religion, sex, age, handicap, or national origin.

The criterion for determining whether affirmative action is needed is not the intent of the employment practices but the results. If company statistics (e.g., on pay or promotion) indicate that the current status of a protected group is inferior to that of the general run of employees, affirmative action may be ordered, including preferential hiring and promotion.

The concept of affirmative action grew out of the Civil Rights Act of 1964, with all its titles and sections. The concept was broadened to include discrimination against age and the handicapped by Section 504 of the Rehabilitation Act of 1973. Of special importance was the implication that discrimination is allowable in cases of "bona fide occupational qualification" (BFOQ). The burden of proof in all BFOQ defenses, however, is upon the employer.

All companies with federal contracts or subcontracts over $50,000 and more than 50 employees are required to have written affirmative action plans. Monitoring is by the Office of Federal Contract Compliance, and violations may result in loss of the contracts. Other companies are monitored by the Equal Employment Opportunity Commission, which may resort to the courts to enforce the demand for affirmative action.

Program Essentials. Equal Employment Opportunity Commission guidelines establish eight essential elements for a complying affirmative action program:

1. A written, and published, statement of an equal employment policy and an affirmative action commitment.

2. Appointment of a highly placed official with the responsibility and authority to implement the program.

3. Publication of the steps the organization will take to make the affirmative action program effective.

4. A survey and analysis of minority and female employment by department and by job classification.

5. Established goals and timetables for attaining them.

6. Development and implementation of specific programs to reach the stated goals.

7. An internal auditing and reporting system to monitor and evaluate progress in each aspect of the program.

8. Development of supportive in-house communications and community awareness programs.

See also Employment process; Labor legislation; Personnel administration; Women in business and management.

REFERENCES

Affirmative Action and Equal Employment: A Guidebook for Employers, U.S. Equal Employment Opportunity Commission, vol. 1, January 1974. (Volume 2 provides specific reference materials.)

Fernandez, John P.: *Racism and Sexism in Corporate Life*, Lexington Books, Lexington, Mass., 1981.

Meyer, John L., and M. W. Donahoe: *Get the Right Person for the Job*, Prentice-Hall, Englewood Cliffs, N.J., 1979.

Peres, Richard: *Preventing Discrimination Complaints: A Guide for Supervisors*, McGraw-Hill, New York, 1979.

LESTER R. BITTEL, *James Madison University*

Appraisal, Performance

Top management in the United States generally agrees that one of the key factors in developing a smoothly functioning and efficient organization is the full utilization of its human resources. Management of the work force is no different from other areas of operation. Effective policies cannot be formulated nor effective action taken without first obtaining reliable and relevant information. Accurate information is needed about each employee's present performance on the job, potential for other jobs, and promotability, and about the requirements of the organization in relation to the talents an individual can offer.

Appraisal of an employee's performance is but one step in a developmental sequence for strengthening the total organization. It is a crucial step which, unfortunately, has often been carried out with only indifferent success. This indifferent success is largely a result of the sensitivity of the process to human errors of judgment, aggravated by a lack of clarity as to just what is being appraised and why.

Objective Appraisal. Too many appraisal programs have been launched without a clear definition of the objective to be achieved. Worse, they may be planned with the vague expectation of achieving a number of overlapping objectives at once. For example, appraisal of performance on the present job is often undertaken in order to:

Identify people who need training.

Determine wage and salary increases.

Compare the effectiveness of two departments performing the same operation.

Determine transfers and policies for internal reorganization.

Identify people who deserve promotion.

Objectives Should Be Realistic. It is doubtful whether appraisal programs could validly provide the primary criterion for most of the objectives mentioned above. For example, if performance on the present job were the only criterion for promotion, all employees performing satisfactorily could rightfully expect to be promoted regardless of age, experience, length of service, availability of positions, talent for other and different occupations, and the general financial position of the company. Again, if excellent performance on the present job were a prerequisite for promotion, many a misplaced individual with talent and potential for other, possibly more responsible and specialized, jobs would be lost to the company.

Objectives Should Be Positive and Constructive. Appraisal programs are doomed to failure if employees associate them with determination of firing and layoffs. Such negative associations not only engender resentment and distrust on the part of employees but also put the assessing supervisor on the spot. Similarly, if appraisal programs become associated with favorable management action, a supervisor, wishing to show the department in a good light, might understandably upgrade an employee's ratings, thus adding deliberate distortion to already biased human judgment.

Objectives Should Be Unitary. If appraisal programs cannot, on their own, validly accomplish a single objective, it is unlikely that they will be effective in serving different or overlapping objectives.

For example, suppose that one objective of an appraisal program is to determine salary increases. In this case, assessing supervisors frequently emphasize the strengths of an employee if they feel that the employee deserves an increase. Suppose that at the same time the appraisal program is being used to improve performance. With this objective in mind, the assessing supervisor may feel obligated to point out an employee's relative weaknesses in order to identify areas for improvement. Inevitably, the assessing supervisors will find themselves in a frustrating, if not untenable, position in attempting to use the assessments for these differing purposes.

Individual Development as an Objective. Using appraisal as a basis for purely administrative decision making is generally unsatisfactory. A far better utilization of it is for the development of the individual employee. Setting individual development as the objective of an appraisal program has a number of advantages.

1. The program is likely to be more acceptable to employees and to gain their support rather than arouse their resentment.

2. There is less obvious reason for the assessing supervisors to introduce deliberate distortion into the assessments to achieve their own ends.

3. Feelings of stress and strain on the part of both the assessing supervisors and the employees are lessened.

4. Assessments will probably reflect the facts better.

Approaches to Appraisal. There are three clearly definable approaches in making an appraisal.

The Work-Centered Approach. In this approach, the *content* of the appraisal is limited to the way in which the person actually performs the significant functions of the job. The items to be evaluated consist of concrete job elements, such as the ability to meet scheduled deadlines. Some of the advantages of the work-centered approach are as follows:

1. It focuses on concrete and observable behavior.

2. The supervisor can cite observable behavior.

3. It supplies an objective basis for discussion between supervisor and employee.

4. It is likely to arouse less resentment and be less damaging to the employee's ego than a discussion of the employee's personality deficiencies and shortcomings.

5. It is amenable to concrete plans for corrective action. Coaching an employee on how to schedule his or her work more realistically is an easier task than advising the employee to cooperate better.

The Person-Centered Approach. In this approach, the *content* of the appraisal concerns the personal characteristics of the person involved. The items to be evaluated consist of personality traits, such as an ability to cooperate.

These approaches sometimes overlap, and some appraisal forms in current use contain items of both types scattered throughout in apparently random order. Certainly, the assessment of behavior traits *and* personality characteristics is an important aspect of determining an employee's potential and formulating plans for personal development. The latter should not be a responsibility of the line supervisor, however. It is a job for a specialist, assisted by the discriminating use of psychological measuring instruments.

The Results-Centered Approach. With the rapid growth of large service organizations in fields like finance, health care, and the professions, an approach which is adaptable and acceptable to large groups of professional and technical people is required.

In its ideal form, this approach allows for an unlimited number of top performers. The premise is that everyone is capable of excellence. The process usually consists of several negotiation sessions between superior and subordinates in which goals to be achieved and expected results are agreed on—goals and results that flow from the organization's mission and long-range objectives.

The goals are of two types:

1. Operating Goals
   a. Doing more of the same thing
   b. Doing things better
   c. Doing things differently
2. Development Goals
   a. Acquiring new knowledge
   b. Upgrading skill
   c. Modifying behavior

At the end of the time period—quarterly or annually—the results expected are weighed against the results achieved, the differences are discussed, and, as far as possible, the supervisor and the subordinate agree on the subordinate's performance.

Once the judgment is made, a new appraisal period begins, with the negotiation of another set of mutually acceptable goals and results. The coaching skills of the employee's immediate supervisor are critical to the success of this approach.

After an organization has decided on the approach to performance appraisal, it has to select the method it will use. Techniques of appraisal may be divided into two major types according to the criteria used in making the judgments about performance on the job.

Appraisal Techniques Employing Objective Criteria

Appraisal techniques of the first type employ objective criteria. The person's performance on the job is judged solely in terms of some measurable index associated with the work, computed for a given period of time. For example, indexes include amount produced, amount of avoidable scrap, or the number of assembled parts found defective. Objective criteria can also be more complex—for example, labor turnover in a supervisor's department or volume of sales adjusted for market potential in different geographical areas. Where such indexes are available, they fulfill a useful purpose. They do, however, suffer from a number of deficiencies, such as the emphasis on quantity rather than quality of work performed. Also, it is difficult to combine quantitative ratings, unless you take into consideration the operating conditions for different plants or market conditions in different sales territories.

In spite of these limitations, the concept of applying objective criteria to present performance is a popular one and has become an integral part of many management-by-objectives programs. When objective criteria are used in this way, the manager or rater serves as the human link between quantitative data and qualitative judgments or evaluations based upon an analysis of quantitative results. Raters are able to take account of rapidly changing circumstances and conditions which affect quantitative measures of work performance. For example, a sales manager for a chemical company was able to take into account the adverse impact of a specific ruling made by the Environmental Protection Agency on the sales of a specific pesticide in different regions of the country with different markets and crop cycles. In another study of sales behavior, it was clearly shown that food sales territories differed markedly in their potential, and that viewing dollar volume sold as a direct measure of sales success greatly oversimplified the sales evaluation process.

Appraisal Techniques Based on Human Judgment

Appraisal techniques of the second type are based on human judgment. These range all the way from completely unquantified subjective judgments to ones based on data from refined instruments employing psychometric methods. No real substitute has been found for the practice of accepting the judgment of peers or supervisors in attempting to determine how well a person is performing the job. The history of appraisal techniques consists, basically, of various attempts to make these judgments quantitative, objective, and reliable.

The Graphic Rating Scale. Typical items from a graphic rating scale are shown in Fig. A-11. The scale has two features earlier rating methods lacked.

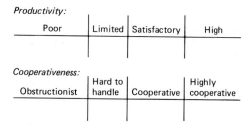

FIG. A-11   Example of a graphic rating scale.

First, the scale is descriptive, and there is no need for the rater to make quantitative judgments. Second, the fact that raters can indicate their assessment at any point along the scale line means that they can discriminate as finely as they choose. It has become evident, however, that even though supervisors place the same person in the same general rank order, they use different standards of assessment. Such different standards result in what the psychologists have called constant errors of judgment. This is a major weakness of this technique.

Forced-Distribution Technique. This method improves on the graphic rating technique. An illustration of it is given in Fig. A-12. Supervisors are forced to allocate a definite percentage of their

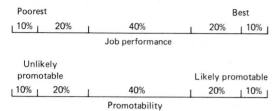

FIG. A-12 Example of a forced distribution report.

TABLE A-4 Example of a Forced-Choice Performance Report

a. Always criticizes, never praises.	M	L
b. Carries out orders by "passing the buck."	M	L
c. Knows the job and performs it well.	M	L
d. Plays no favorites.	M	L
a. Commands respect by his or her actions.	M	L
b. Cool-headed.	M	L
c. Indifferent.	M	L
d. Overbearing.	M	L

Which is *most* and *least* characteristic of the employee?

assessments to each point on the scale. Generally, a five-point scale is used with 10:20:40:20:10 distribution of assessments. This procedure obviates the necessity of applying statistical adjustments to ensure uniform standards. It forces raters to place only 10 percent of their subordinates as top performers and 10 percent as poor performers, with the other 80 percent distributed normally. The same concept can be applied to promotability as well. Since most employees want to know why they are given a high or low job performance rating, supervisors are given a previously prepared checklist of traits and simply check off those that apply to the employee's performance. The disadvantages of this technique are that it assumes either a normal or at least a comparable distribution of proficiency or performance in each rating group. Also it is a relative rather than an absolute measure of performance, and no reasons or explanations are given for the ratings which are made. Because of these limitations, it becomes unwieldy with large groups of employees.

Forced-Choice Technique. In this performance report, instead of indicating how much or how little of each characteristic a person possesses, the rater is required to select from several sets of four adjectives or phrases, one of which is *most* characteristic and one of which is *least* characteristic of the person being rated. The sets of four adjectives, known as tetrads, are so constructed that each contains two favorable and two unfavorable characteristics.

Only one of the favorable statements in each tetrad will yield a point on the report if it is chosen as "most characteristic" of the person being rated. Similarly, only one of the unfavorable statements will yield a point if it is selected as "least characteristic." The reason for this lies in the construction of the tetrads. In each tetrad, the two favorable items are matched with respect to their preference index but differ with respect to their discrimination index. The same holds true for the two unfavorable items. In other words, although the favorable items in each pair appear equally favorable to the rater, and the unfavorable items in each pair appear equally unfavorable, only one item in each pair has been demonstrated to discriminate between good and poor performers. An example of this technique is given in Table A-4.

Although forced-choice ratings have not lived up to their first bright promise, they are still successfully used for specific purposes and populations. A large law enforcement agency has used the forced-choice rating technique for a number of years. The implementation of the technique was based upon essays describing the most effective and successful agent known to respondents. Scale items were developed which were matched for social desirability or preference value but which had high differentiation in separating above-average and below-average employee groups. The continuing success of this implementation of the forced-choice technique is due to strong support from top management, limiting access to the scale scoring key to personnel division staff, periodically updating the content of the scale, and using selected items to form diagnostic subscales for coaching and counseling employees to help them improve their performance.

When the use of forced-choice techniques declined, the search for objective ratings of performance branched off in two rather disparate directions, as characterized by ratings of observable behavior and in the refinement of the classical psychometric methods of ranking or pairing.

Critical Incident Ratings. Ratings of observed behavior which depend upon the identification of incidents of behavior which indicate either exceptionally good or exceptionally poor performance have been grouped under the broad category known as *critical* incident ratings. These ratings assume that the supervisor, who is in daily contact with employees, will be able to observe and identify critical incidents or occurrences that represent either effective or ineffective performance and will record them in an objective manner. It also presumes that supervisors can be trained to identify critical job requirements and specify the kind of behavior incidents which contribute to each requirement. For certain types of work, this can be a very effective method. In the opinion of many who have used it, the greatest contribution, however, has been in establishing a good basis for supervisors' appraisal interviews with their people. It points the way to constructive dialogue about performance. It is equally clear, however, that its

35

claims to objectivity are overdrawn. While it is true that the procedure deals with concrete behavior incidents, what is actually reported will be only that which appears in the eye of the observer.

In contrast to methods employing critical incident ratings, which are of fairly recent origin, the application of classical psychometric methods goes back to about the middle of the nineteenth century. Those most often employed today are the method of rank order and the method of paired comparisons.

Method of Rank Order. When this is applied to appraisal of job performance, the supervisor is required to rank the people in order from the best to the poorest performer according to their overall worth to the organization. A popular variation, called the alternation ranking method, requires that the supervisor first select the best performer and then, from the people remaining, the poorest performer. After this, the supervisor selects the next best and the second poorest, and so on, in sequence, until all employees have been ranked. A typical ranking could look like the example in Fig. A-13.

Employees to be ranked	Rank
Art	1—Highest _____
Bill	2—Next highest _____
Bob	3—Next highest _____
Carla	4—Next highest _____
Charlie	5—Next highest _____
Dan	6—Next highest _____
Edward	7—Next highest _____
Frances	8—Next highest _____
Fred	9—Next highest _____
George	10—Next highest _____
Mary	10—Next lowest _____
Ora	9—Next lowest _____
Paul	8—Next lowest _____
Ralph	7—Next lowest _____
Rose	6—Next lowest _____
Sam	5—Next lowest _____
Ted	4—Next lowest _____
Verna	3—Next lowest _____
Walter	2—Next lowest _____
Yvonne	1—Lowest _____

FIG. A-13 Example of an alternation ranking report.

The comparisons which are made by the supervisor or supervisors in determining the rankings in the method of rank order are made explicitly and more systematically in what is known as the method of paired comparisons.

Method of Paired Comparisons. The principles underlying this method require that every individual to be assessed be compared with every other individual and an explicit judgment made as to who is the better performer. If five employees were to be assessed on job performance, the comparisons required would be those shown in Table A-5.

Comparisons are not made sequentially as presented here, but in random order, and precautions are taken to ensure that no employee is involved in two successive judgments.

TABLE A-5 Example of Comparative Judgments Required by the Method of Paired Comparisons in Assessing Performance of Five Employees

1 vs. 2	2 vs. 3	3 vs. 4	4 vs. 5
1 vs. 3	2 vs. 4	3 vs. 5	
1 vs. 4	2 vs. 5		
1 vs. 5			

$$\text{Total} = \frac{5 \times 4}{2} = 10 \text{ judgments}$$

In spite of the reliability and validity of assessments made with the paired-comparisons technique, the method has not been widely used. The reasons for this are twofold: (1) the time and effort required of the judges and (2) the computational labor called for in obtaining the scale values. The problem of the raters' time and effort is particularly acute when large groups of employees are involved, since the number of comparisons which must be made rises as an exponential function of the number of individuals being assessed.

The consistency of the results obtained in validation studies corroborates the long-held belief that the paired-comparisons technique minimizes the influence of personal bias in subjective judgments, thereby increasing objectivity, reliability, and validity. Mechanization of this technique, using computer programs, has resulted in considerable savings of time and effort in the administration and scoring of the results.

Performance Appraisal Interview

Any discussion of appraisal would be incomplete if it did not conclude with a discussion of the performance interview, since the appraisal is primarily developmental in nature. It is based on the belief that individual improvement will ultimately lead to organization improvement. Managers should be cautioned, however, that there are a few rules that, if followed, lead to a successful relationship. This is particularly true of the appraisal interview, which involves highly sensitive relationships; nevertheless here is how an effective interview might develop:

1. The superior makes it clear that he or she is not taking over the subordinate's problem. It is still the subordinate who has the responsibility for and who must think about the problem. The individual may resent not getting an immediate solu-

tion, but the superior helps the subordinate see that only the individual can solve the problem.

2. The superior indicates in many ways that the subordinate is neither stupid nor unusual for having a problem. The individual is not made to feel a failure.

3. The superior helps the subordinate see the value and importance of working on the problem, pointing out that it would be very worthwhile to seek the best answer to the problem. An atmosphere of encouragement must prevail.

4. The superior may be aware of reasons for the subordinate's difficulty, but guards against telling what is wrong. The superior helps the employee find a positive approach to the problem so as to recognize faulty or short-sighted thinking.

5. The superior then asks insightful questions about the nature of the problem, why it occurred, and what symptoms of it are evident. This helps the subordinate see the need for diagnosing the problem before developing solutions for it.

6. As the two talk further, the superior helps set up criteria for selecting a solution from among the alternatives.

Principles Involved. A review of this ideal appraisal interview highlights some important elements:

1. The purpose of the interview was made clear from the beginning.

2. Nothing was done to emphasize differences in power or authority.

3. The two did not argue.

4. The superior did not tell the subordinate what to do or how to do it.

5. The subordinate helped to solve the problem. Both superior and subordinate gained in self-confidence and in problem-solving skills.

6. Both came out with their own self-respect intact. Their motivation to work on the problem was increased.

The temptation is always present for the superior to take the ball and run with it. If the superior does, however, he or she is playing the game and not coaching. The ability to observe accurately and objectively is left on the bench when the boss joins the contest.

Appraising people is a complex job. It involves understanding other people and the processes of individual change. It also involves understanding ourselves and how we affect others. It requires that manager and managed control and modify their own behavior as required. Above all, it involves establishing relationships between people in which help can be both given and received most effectively.

See also Compensation, wage and salary policy and administration; Development and training, employee; Motivation in organizations.

REFERENCES

Blasingame, Margaret C., Katie R. Schneider, and Donald L. Hawk: *Performance Appraisal Bibliography of Recent Publications,* Center for Creative Leadership, Greensboro, N.C., 1981.

Cummings, Larry L., and Donald P. Schwab: *Performance in Organizations: Determinants and Appraisal,* Scott, Foresman, Glenview, Ill., 1973.

Kellogg, Marion S.: *What To Do About Performance Appraisal,* rev. ed. American Management Association, New York, 1975.

King, Patricia: *Performance Planning and Appraisal: A How-To Book for Managers,* McGraw-Hill, New York, 1983.

WALLACE G. LONERGAN, *HRC and Associates*

Arbitration, Commercial

With few exceptions, any controversy which might be the subject of civil litigation may be submitted by the disputing parties to an impartial person for final and binding determination. Essentially, *commercial arbitration* is a business executive's court—an alternative to the more complex and time-consuming procedures of the official court system.

This process is used mostly where issues turn on questions of fact, such as the quality of merchandise, rather than law. In such cases, parties may want a decision made by one who is familiar with trade customs rather than by a judge who may or may not be knowledgeable in such areas.

Other reasons for resorting to arbitration are that informal procedures can be put in motion quickly and result in decisions which are not subject to appeal on the merits. Even if an arbitrator should err on matters of fact or law, the decision would be final. Under federal law and the arbitration statutes of 42 states, awards are subject to reversal only if the arbitrator was biased or committed gross procedural errors which prejudiced the rights of a party.

No one can be compelled to arbitrate unless that person has agreed in some manner to forgo the right to litigate the issue in court. The agreement to arbitrate is commonly expressed in a future-dispute arbitration clause of a contract. It may also be expressed in a submission agreement signed by both parties, who affirm their willingness to abide by the decision.

Most commercial arbitration in the United States is conducted through the American Arbitration Association (AAA), a nonprofit organization that is available to parties in all industries and fields of activity. AAA charges an administrative fee, based upon the

amount claimed, but its arbitrators generally serve without fee, except where a case involves many days of hearings. Arbitration is also administered by some organized trades, but these procedures are usually available only to members of the trade association.

Although arbitration is less formal than litigation, hearings follow the conventional pattern of opening statements, examination and cross-examination of witnesses, summations, and occasional posthearing briefs. Unlike labor arbitrators, who usually write opinions setting forth the arguments and explaining how they reached their decision, commercial arbitrators write only a brief award, telling the disputants what they must do to resolve the controversy.

Arbitration decisions seldom have meaning for persons other than the parties themselves, and awards are therefore not published.

Many years ago, it was common for judges to disapprove of commercial arbitration on the ground that it "ousted the courts" of jurisdiction. Many lawyers were hostile because they feared that basic concepts of due process would be lost for the sake of speed and economy. Moreover, some advocates of arbitration, hostile to lawyers, urged procedures which would bar legal counsel from participating.

But those attitudes have changed in the wake of laws which, while enforcing agreements to arbitrate and awards, provide remedies if arbitrators should exceed their authority. Lawyers, too, have accepted arbitration as a form of law practice. Today, it is only in cases involving very small sums of money that parties enter into arbitration without the guidance of lawyers.

See also Consumerism and consumer protection legislation; Credit management; Government regulations, uniform commercial code; Legal affairs, management of corporate; Patents and valuable intangible rights; Product liability.

REFERENCES

Bernstein, Merton C.: *Private Dispute Settlement: Cases and Materials on Arbitration*, vol. 14, The Free Press, New York, 1968.

Coulson, Robert: *Business Arbitration—What You Need to Know*, 2d. ed., American Arbitration Association, New York, 1982.

Lazarus, Steven, et al.: *Resolving Business Disputes: The Potential of Commercial Arbitration*, American Management Association, New York, 1965.

MORRIS STONE, *Vice President (Retired), American Arbitration Association*

Arbitration, Labor

Virtually every union contract in the United States contains a provision called an *arbitration clause,* providing for final and binding resolution of employee grievances. Although strikes over alleged violations of existing contracts still occur, work stoppages have for the most part been supplanted by arbitration as the conventional way to deal with disputes over the interpretation or application of collective agreements.

The situation is different with respect to new contract terms. Most private employers and unions prefer not to let an "outsider" determine basic wages and working conditions. They negotiate to a conclusion, even if this means enduring a strike on occasion. In public employment, however, there is a growing trend toward third-party intervention in contract impasses, under the impact of laws which forbid strikes and provide machinery for alternative methods of settlement—binding arbitration, advisory arbitration, fact-finding, etc.

Most employers and unions use ad hoc, or case-by-case, procedures for arbitration. They anticipate too few cases to warrant making full-time arrangements. Instead, they select an arbitrator when he or she is needed, although this does not exclude the possibility that they will make the same selection in the future. Each call to service is for the specific grievance or group of grievances with which the parties are momentarily concerned.

In some industries, however—steel, auto, airlines, and construction, for example—companies and unions set up permanent machinery and name arbitrators or a rotating panel of arbitrators who will be called upon for the life of the contract. In this way, they are assured of decisions that follow established precedents, a circumstance that does not necessarily prevail when a different arbitrator is chosen for each case.

For companies and unions favoring ad hoc procedures, there are two major sources of arbitrators. One is the American Arbitration Association (AAA), a private organization which functions through regional offices throughout the country. AAA charges each party $75 for each case it administers. The other major source is the Federal Mediation and Conciliation Service (FMCS), which operates from Washington, and which does not charge for submitting lists of proposed arbitrators.

Although there are some differences in the way the two organizations operate, they are basically alike in the arbitrators on their panels and in procedures by which a mutual choice of arbitrator is determined from proposed lists. Arbitrators tend to charge about $300 per day of hearing and day of study (study time also includes the writing of an opinion explaining the reason for the decision), and this figure is likely to be the same whether the arbitrator is appointed by the AAA, the FMCS, or directly by the parties, who may have called upon the arbitrator without the assistance of any agency.

The most common subject of labor grievance arbitration is discipline and discharge. Most union con-

tracts forbid disciplinary action by management except for *just cause*. But just cause is seldom defined so completely as to preclude controversy in particular cases. It is then left to the arbitrator to determine whether, in the light of past practice, contract language, and the factual situation, the penalty was appropriate.

Another source of conflict centers around the phrase *seniority versus ability*. A chief objective of unions is to favor senior employees over juniors in matters of promotion, layoff, selection of shifts, and other terms of employment. But the exercise of seniority rights is usually dependent upon the employee having sufficient ability, and contracts seldom are explicit in their definition of terms. Whether a grievant had the contractually required ability to "bump" a junior during a reduction of the work force is a common subject in arbitration.

For decades, labor arbitration awards and opinions have been published by several commercial award-reporting services including: The Bureau of National Affairs, Washington, D.C.; Commerce Clearing House, Chicago, Illinois; and the American Arbitration Association, New York, New York. There is also a considerable amount of interchange of awards within the labor movement and among management groups. Thus, despite the absence of any requirement that ad hoc arbitrators follow precedents, the total body of published decisions has created what the U.S. Supreme Court called "the common law of the shop." These awards, offering insight into practical problems of the workplace, have had a profound influence on American industrial relations.

See also Labor legislation; Labor-management relations; Labor (trade) unions.

REFERENCES

Elkouri, Frank, and Edna Asper Elkouri: *How Arbitration Works*, vol. 12, Bureau of National Affairs, Washington, D.C., 1952; vol. 17, rev. ed., 1960; vol. 25, 3d ed., 1973.

Stone, Morris: *Managerial Freedom and Job Security*, vol. 8, Harper & Row, New York, 1964.

MORRIS STONE, *Vice President (retired), American Arbitration Association*

Assertiveness Training

Assertiveness training is based on humanistic values and is defined as (1) an active and initiating, rather than reacting, mode of behavior; (2) a caring position, emphasizing the positive nature of self and others; (3) self-expression through which one stands up for her or his basic rights without denying the rights of others and without experiencing undue anxiety or guilt; (4) a nonjudgmental attitude that diminishes

the use of labels, stereotypes, and prejudices; and (5) communication of wants, dislikes, and feelings in a clear, direct manner without threatening and attacking.

The overall goal of assertiveness training is to increase confidence, professionalism, the ability to deal effectively with job-related people problems, and the ability to express oneself without violating the rights of self and others.

Building Blocks

A comprehensive approach to assertiveness training encompasses eight building blocks: (1) building self-esteem, (2) knowing how to listen, (3) taking risks, (4) knowing how to say no, (5) knowing how to give constructive feedback, (6) handling criticism, (7) knowing how to express and receive positive feedback, and (8) knowing what you want. Three of these are especially critical to the success of any program.

Knowing How to Say No. The success of a person who manages others depends heavily on that person's own ability to meet goals, implement plans, distribute resources, and mediate and negotiate. Assertiveness training helps such a person to learn to establish boundaries and to say no to requests that are unreasonable. Nonassertive managers often feel that saying no will lead to disapproval. Consequently, they often say yes when they want to say no. Their reluctance to say no leads to procrastination, unmet deadlines, and stress. Guidelines that strengthen a person's ability to say no, when appropriate, include the following:

1. *Question yourself.* Do I want to do this, or am I trying to please someone else? What will I receive for my participation? If I agree to do this, will it continue to be rewarding or will it become oppressive?
2. *Think it over.* Give yourself time to evaluate the request. Assess whether the request is reasonable or unreasonable. It's not necessary to commit yourself to something as soon as you are asked to do it.
3. *Look for clues to unreasonable requests.* Do you find yourself hesitating or hedging? Do you feel cornered or trapped? Do you feel a tightness somewhere in your body?
4. *Ask for further clarification.*
5. *Maintain a negotiable attitude.* Seek resolution from a win-win framework.
6. *Allow for differences of opinions.* Bring them out into the open and discuss them.
7. *Focus on the problem, not on personalities.* Move toward negotiating on points of difference.
8. *Don't overcommit yourself.*

Giving Constructive Feedback. One of the major barriers to expressing negative feedback is lack of familiarity with appropriate techniques. Also, people giving criticism often have a problem doing it because they have difficulty receiving it themselves. Most people want to improve at what they are doing, but when criticisms are stated with a fault-finding attitude or are expressed with judgments and threats, the person receiving the criticism may respond with anger, hurt feelings, or defensiveness. Assertive managers, on the other hand, call attention to problems in ways that motivate employees to improve. Emphasis is upon letting employees know what needs to be changed. Such constructive feedback follows this pattern:

- State the criticism in specific terms instead of vague or general ones.
- Direct comments toward behavior rather than personalities.
- Make statements that are observations of events rather than labels or emotional judgments.
- Focus on a supportive coaching style instead of deflating put-downs.
- Allow the receiver to solve his or her problem.

Handling Criticism. People who manage from the assertive approach generally have confidence in their ability to handle criticism from others effectively. They can discriminate between unjust and just criticism. They are aware of situations in which they react to criticism poorly and have a plan of action to help them respond more effectively the next time around. As a result, their ability to handle criticism improves along with their sense of dignity and self-respect.

Constructively assertive individuals believe that human beings make mistakes and can learn from them. They are aware that it is natural and unavoidable to experience occasional rejection. Having the belief that they are not always or fully responsible for the way others react and feel helps assertive individuals to deal with criticisms objectively and calmly. They are able to meet the critic halfway by asking themselves pertinent questions, such as:

Why is this person making this criticism?

What is she or he attempting to say?

What would be the best way to solve the problem?

Training Results

Assertive managers learn to value those who bring mistakes and oversights to their attention. As a consequence, others in their work groups know they have the right to approach these managers about an error or to provide critical suggestions without being subjected to defensive rebuttals. A number of impor-

tant companies have implemented assertiveness training programs. These include State Compensation Insurance Fund of California, IBM, and Bank of America. These companies have testified that people completing the program are more systematic in their approach to handling on-the-job people problems constructively, are able to handle conflict in a rational manner, can work productively with others to build cooperation and teamwork, and can confront problems effectively instead of putting them off.

See also Affirmative action; Appraisal, performance; Authority, responsibility, and accountability; Behavior modeling; Communications, organizational; Conformity in management; Delegation; Development and training, management; Equal employment opportunity, minorities and women; Laboratory (sensitivity) training; Power and influence; Women in business and management.

REFERENCES

Burley-Allen, Madelyn: *Managing Assertively—How to Improve Your People Skills,* John Wiley, New York, 1983.

Fersterheim, Herbert, and Jean Baer: *Don't Say Yes When You Want To Say No,* Dell, New York, 1975.

Shaw, Malcolm E.: *Assertive-Responsive Management; A Personal Handbook,* Addison-Wesley, Reading, Mass., 1979.

MADELYN BURLEY-ALLEN, *Dynamics of Human Behavior*

Assessment Center Method

The assessment center method is used by many business, government, and nonprofit organizations to improve the accuracy of personnel selection and of development decisions. It has a threefold purpose: (1) to evaluate the potential of candidates for supervisory, sales, or management positions; (2) to help determine training and development needs of individual employees; and (3) to facilitate more accurate work force planning.

An *assessment center* is a method, not a place. Assessment center participants engage in a variety of job-related simulations designed to bring out behavior relevant to skills or dimensions determined by the organization to be critical to success in a target job or jobs. Managers familiar with the requirements of the target-level jobs, and who have been trained in the assessment process, observe and evaluate this behavior.

By placing participants in situations similar to the ones in which they will be required to perform after promotion or assignment, the process is made relevant and fair to all participants. The odds for the accurate prediction of future job success are improved by (1) training the manager-assessors, (2) providing a structured method for observing and ana-

lyzing behavior, and (3) subjecting each participant to the same treatment.

The end result of an assessment center is a written report summarizing the strengths and weaknesses of the individual and, depending upon the center, providing an estimate of the candidate's potential for a higher-level position. This report usually becomes part of the individual's personnel file and serves as a basis for discussion between the individual and the center administrator. Assessment center feedback discussions are unique in their emphasis on behavioral observations. Specific observations, which lead assessors to make certain decisions about dimensions, are shared with the participant.

In addition to rational arguments, the increased accuracy of this technique in comparison with supervisory ratings and tests has been demonstrated in more than 25 well-controlled research studies conducted in both large and small organizations.[1]

Dimensions often measured in assessment centers include:

Impact	Planning and organization
Creativity	Judgment
Stress tolerance	Decisiveness
Leadership	Use of delegation
Sales ability	Flexibility
Sensitivity	Tenacity
Initiative	Management control
Independence	Risk-taking
Problem analysis	

Affirmative Action. Recent research findings indicate that the assessment center method is valid for minority and nonminority group members. Many companies use the method as a component of their program for achieving affirmative action goals. The landmark 1973 Equal Employment Opportunity Commission/AT&T compliance agreement established AT&T's assessment centers as the means for identifying management potential among previously overlooked employees.[2]

Other organizations use the method to identify the management potential of minority groups and women early in their business careers so that development can be accelerated. The method also has proven useful in diagnosing training and developmental needs, thus maximizing the impact of training expenditures.

Flexibility. Assessment centers should be designed as solutions to specific problems. Details of these problems and the environments in which they occur differ greatly from organization to organization; therefore, so do the assessment centers designed to aid in solving the problems. Experience has shown the assessment center method to be flexible and effective in generating valid data under a variety of different situations and circumstances. In addition, the assessment center format can easily be changed in order to evaluate candidates individually rather than in groups.

Objectives. The most frequent reason for initiating an assessment center program is to provide additional sources of data for making promotional decisions. Many other reasons also exist, but the most common program goals are (1) aid in making immediate promotional decisions; (2) early determination of potential so that an individual can be placed in special training and development programs; and (3) diagnosis of individual strengths and weaknesses in order to devise targeted training and developmental activities.

Application. Small and large organizations of all types use the assessment center method to make a wide variety of personnel decisions. Selection, identification of supervisory-managerial potential, and the diagnosis of an individual's strengths and weaknesses relative to present and future positions are the most popular applications. Initial selection of salespeople, management trainees, stationary engineers, police and fire fighters, and highly skilled blue-collar workers are increasingly popular applications.

Length. The number of exercises and the total time required vary greatly with the assessment center purpose and the organizational level of the target job for which it is used. First-line supervisory centers and centers designed to select salespeople, management trainees, or blue-collar employees typically last for a day or less. High-level executive centers can involve 2½ days of exercises. Generally, centers designed to generate developmental recommendations last longer than those designed primarily to yield selection or promotion recommendations.

Size. Typically, six or twelve people are assessed simultaneously, although centers designed for initial selection often assess only one person at a time. Most centers involve one assessor to every two participants; some operate on a one-to-one ratio.

Steps in Starting an Assessment Center. Methods vary, of course, but the following steps ought to be included in most programs.

Establish Goals. The purposes of an assessment center must be clearly defined prior to planning. Several goals may be accomplished by the same center, but the more goals an organization sets for it, the longer and more expensive the program will be. The most fundamental decision is the relative weight to be assigned to the goals of selection versus identification of training and developmental needs.

Plan Program. Planning must concern all aspects of the center, from identification of dimensions to feedback of assessment information to the participants and to management. Fitting the center program into current programs and practices and the need to be sensitive to the attitudes of center participants and nonparticipants in the organization often require many difficult decisions.

Identify Dimensions of Job Performance. Some or all of the following steps should be taken to determine the dimensions to be observed in the assessment center: (1) Examine professional literature and company records. (2) Conduct a systematic job analysis. (3) Observe a sampling of individuals performing the job, and interview higher management about the needed dimensions. (4) Conduct a questionnaire survey of management's views of job requirements. (5) Arrange a "brainstorming" meeting of key managers familiar with the position or positions for which the candidates are being assessed. (6) Obtain critical incidents of behavior leading to particularly successful or unsuccessful performance. (7) Focus not only on present job requirements but also on future ones. (8) Eliminate those dimensions that can be assessed adequately on a person's present job. (9) Obtain a rough ranking of remaining dimensions.

Select Exercises. More than 100 specially developed and tested assessment center exercises are commercially available.[3] They include such techniques as business games, in-baskets, leaderless group discussions (nonassigned roles and assigned roles), analysis (presentation and/or group discussion), individual fact-finding and decision-making exercises, interview simulations, and written presentation and oral presentation exercises.

Exercises should be selected according to the following criteria: (1) level of sophistication and education of the assessees; (2) relative importance of the various dimensions; (3) actual job content of the target position(s); (4) need to observe the participants in a variety of situations; (5) need to observe critical dimensions in several different exercises; and (6) time available for assessment.

Train Assessors. Minimum training should include (1) discussion of the definitions of the dimensions; (2) practice in observing and recording behavior and in writing reports on at least one of each type of exercise used in the center; (3) practice in conducting interviews; and (4) familiarization with the procedure for reaching final decisions.

As an aid in assessor training, videotapes of exercises, sample exercises, and sample final reports are frequently used.

Conduct Center. Centers may be conducted at an organization's own facilities, a conveniently located motel, or other similar locations. The role of the administrator is critical, and the individual performing this function should be thoroughly trained in the process beforehand.

Operational Considerations. Assessment centers are usually initially designed by a trained psychologist familiar with the method but are generally administered by representatives of the organization's training or personnel department who are not psychologists. This representative must administer the exercises, write a final report summarizing the consensus of the assessors on each participant, and, usually, be responsible for feeding back assessment center information to the participants. Administrators must go through assessor training and must have had additional training for their special responsibilities prior to serving in this function.

Most organizations end the administrator's role with the feedback discussion. In some highly developmentally oriented programs, the administrator has continued to be involved in counseling the participant and the participant's supervisor regarding appropriate developmental action and acts as a catalyst to ensure that developmental actions take place.

The percentage of candidates who do well in assessment centers varies markedly between and within organizations. In general, at the presupervisory level approximately one-third of those individuals assessed are thought to have supervisory potential. The percentage goes up in higher-level centers, where there is more opportunity for preselection of the assessees.

Management is, of course, always concerned with the effect of assessment center findings on participants who do poorly. They fear possible morale or turnover implications. Although there are few published research studies in this area, a number of organizations have collected sufficient data to disprove any specific negative reaction. The apparent key to minimizing the negative effects of assessment center reports is in providing effective feedback of the data. Proper feedback stresses that the assessment center is designed to predict potential for a specific job, not a generalized area of potential. It also stresses the training and developmental aspects of center results.

Many small organizations have considered forming a consortium where they can pool resources to operate a cooperative assessment center. To this author's knowledge, this has never worked out. The organizations disagree on the dimensions to be sought and on the scheduling of centers. The advent of new techniques which apply the assessment center method to individual selection has somewhat diminished the motivation of smaller companies to consider cooperative centers.

Consulting Specialists. Most assessment centers have been installed with the advice of consulting specialists. Organizations deem the use of specialists to be advisable in order to establish an effective program which is job-related and thus acceptable to the Equal Employment Opportunity Commission. The EEOC guidelines stress the need for professionally conducted job analyses. A properly qualified outside consultant provides this service and helps the organization choose the most appropriate job-related exercises and design the most efficient assessment.

Assessment centers require a great deal of management time, and an investment in qualified assistance can more than pay off by freeing up executive time.

See also Development and training, career path planning for managers; Development and training management; Equal employment opportunity, minorities and women; Labor legislation; Leadership; Search and recruitment, executive; Testing, psychological.

NOTES

[1] B. Cohen, J. L. Moses, and W. C. Byham, "The Validity of Assessment Centers: A Literature Review," *Monograph II,* Development Dimensions, Pittsburgh, 1974.

[2] D. F. Hoyle, "AT&T Completes Assessment of Nearly 1700 Women Under Consent Agreement," *Assessment and Development,* vol. 12, pp. 4–5.

[3] *Catalog of Assessment and Development Exercises,* Development Dimensions, Pittsburgh, 1977.

REFERENCES

Cohen, S. L.: "Validity and Assessment Center Technology," *Human Resources Management,* vol. 19, 1980, pp. 2–11.

Keil, C. C.: *Assessment Centers: A Guide for Human Resources Management,* Addison-Wesley, Reading, Mass., 1982.

WILLIAM C. BYHAM, *Development Dimensions, Inc.*

Associations, Trade and Professional

America's trade associations and professional societies are a powerful force in the private sector—representing more than 40 million organized individuals and business firms that use their organizational machinery, work force, and resources to help solve business, economic, and social problems. There are some 15,000 national, state, and local trade and professional associations. Most have full-time paid executives.

Although the central purpose of the voluntary association has always been to serve the needs and to protect the interests of the industry or profession it represents, the present trend is for the trade association to broaden its purpose and to serve the overall needs of the nation.

Associations traditionally have performed services in marketing, education, and other areas that business people understand and support. But in carrying out these activities, business executives have traditionally expected the association to take a low profile. Much of this has changed as a result of government initiatives in health and safety, consumerism, the environment, and the economy. Business executives today demand help from associations in explaining new laws and administrative rulings that affect their companies. They look to associations to take public stands they do not want to take individually. More and more the operation of the association is the responsibility of a paid executive rather than of volunteers. The business executive members are too busy running their own businesses. The government, too, relies on associations to present a single voice for an industry or profession. In other words, if there is to be a finger pointed by someone, the association philosophy is: Let it be pointed at the industry as a whole and not at the individual firm.

Scope of Services

Voluntary associations are widening their scope of services and raising their sights. A nationwide survey conducted by the American Society of Association Executives (ASAE) shows that 73 percent of all associations in the United States are involved in helping resolve economic, social, and human problems. Nearly half the associations conduct programs designed to improve consumer satisfaction. More than a third of the associations have programs aimed at safeguarding and improving the environment, and more than a third have programs aimed at aiding the disadvantaged.

Improving Consumer Satisfaction. In this area, associations engage in such activities as:

Publishing and putting into operation a code of ethics that includes requirements for consumer protection.

Encouraging the buying public to report to the association about unsatisfactory products and services.

Educating and urging members to adhere strictly to truth in advertising.

Working closely with federal, state, and local offices of consumer affairs.

Maintaining a task force of members and consumers to study and analyze consumer problems and to find ways to correct them.

Conducting tests and inspections and grading services to help ensure consumer satisfaction.

Developing standards of grade and quality labeling to help others choose the right products to meet their needs.

Operating consumer relations committees on the local level to deal with consumer complaints and to correct the causes.

Improving the Environment. In this area, associations, in increasing numbers, engage in such activities as:

Working for legislation—state and national—to establish standards for environmental control.

Maintaining a task force of members to study sound ways to reduce air, water, and land pollution.

Conducting research to devise better methods of waste disposal on the part of industry.

Conducting educational programs to reduce waste and pollution on the part of users.

Sponsoring programs to encourage clean-up campaigns.

Aiding the Disadvantaged. In this area, associations engage in such activities as:

Encouraging members to hire the disadvantaged.

Helping members provide on-the-job training.

Working with government—federal and state—to aid in job training and creating new job opportunities.

Encouraging entrepreneur programs for minority groups.

Operating placement services for the disadvantaged.

Providing accounting, merchandising, and other business assistance to minority and underprivileged business firms and individuals.

Government Relations. Although government relations has always been a key association function, it is now dominant, according to the ASAE survey. Ninety-two percent of the associations surveyed say they keep their members informed about federal legislative developments. (*See* Table A-6.) Some 96 percent of ASAE's members see a likelihood that association expenditures for government relations will increase significantly in the coming years.

Legislative Activities of Associations. Many associations engage in legislative activities on both the state and federal levels. In fact, many legislators prefer to deal with an association representative rather than deal individually with member companies. In turn, member companies often prefer to deal through an association.

There is nothing sinister about the lobbying activities of associations. The United States has a representative government, and the open struggle among special interests is precisely what marks democracy as a system resting on the consent of the governed.

One problem which arises in connection with lobbying is whether an association must register under the Federal Regulation of Lobbying Act. The act requires that any person engaged in attempting to influence the passage or defeat of any federal legislation (1) must register with the clerk of the House of Representatives and the secretary of the Senate and (2) must periodically disclose certain information about his or her activities. In view of the fact that

TABLE A-6 Government Relations Programs Offered by Associations and Percentage of Associations Conducting Them

Program	%
Informs members of congressional developments	92
Equips members to express views to representatives and senators	87
Informs members of federal administrative actions	87
Informs members of state and local legislative developments	81
Testifies before Congress or state legislatures	76
Maintains a committee to study and make recommendations on state and national legislation	71
Provides data to state governments	66
In convention programs, includes speakers on national legislation	57
Drafts legislation	55
Lobbies	54
Provides data to federal government	49
Reports federal court decisions	46
Trains members to become active in politics	29
Collects and distributes political funds to candidates	27
Arranges plant tours to help government demonstrate U.S. industry to foreign visitors	23
Sponsors courses on political participation	15
Assists members with customs, tariffs, and trade agreements	12
Represents industry in tariff negotiations	9
Assists government in foreign trade fair participation	8

there are very few associations whose principal purpose is influencing the passage or defeat of federal legislation, it is arguable that the lobbying act does not require multipurpose organizations such as associations to register. Since the act is ambiguous on this point, most cautious associations do register.

Another troublesome area to associations in regard to the present concept of lobbying lies in the difficulty of distinguishing between *influencing* and *informing* members of Congress. Since associations are engaged in activities which are informational in character, they are conduits of business information. They collect information from their members, from government agencies, from related agencies, and from other sources. The material collected is ordinarily distributed to anyone who has an interest in it—to members primarily, but also to government officials, including members of Congress. Certainly legislators desire to have access to all sources of information so that they can continue to perform their legislative functions intelligently.

If informing a legislator were to become tantamount to influencing that individual, everyone seeking to assist in making information available to elected representatives would have to register as lobbyists under the act. Such a reading of the present act would certainly prove counterproductive because it would result in blocking the flow of information to federal legislators. Accordingly, if new lobbying legislation were forthcoming, it would appear beneficial if it provided an exemption for those activities which serve to inform as opposed to those which attempt to influence.

Membership Costs and Returns

Each association in a particular field of business offers a variety of valuable services which are obtained at a reasonable cost through payment of company or individual membership dues and through company and individual participation in the work of the association.

Business people expect a return for their dues investment. Many not only lean on their association's representation and guidance but also look upon the association as one of their business departments.

Association dues vary according to the group and the amount of services it offers. Generally, dues are a fraction of 1 percent on the member's annual volume of business. Some associations charge a uniform fee. A few use a combination figure derived from the rate based on volume plus a specific flat charge. Many groups also have a ceiling on the dues they charge.

See also Competition; Government relations; Political action committees (PACs); Public and community relations; Social responsibility of business; Societies, professional.

REFERENCES

Encyclopedia of Associations, vol. 1: *National Organizations of the U.S.*, 18th ed., Gale Research Company, Detroit, 1984.

Low, James P.: *Association Services for Small Business*, U.S. Small Business Administration, Washington, D.C., 1976.

Webster, George D., and Arthur L. Herold: *Antitrust Guide for Association Executives*, American Society of Association Executives, Washington, D.C., 1976.

JAMES P. LOW, *Dynamics Inc.*

Attitude Surveys

Employee morale is considered an important and quantifiable indicator of the success of employer-employee relationships. Early industrial surveys of morale were called inventories and were based on the idea that management should inventory human resources as it does raw materials and finished goods. Such inventories, now called morale scales, opinion surveys, or *attitude surveys* are a valuable management tool providing a systematic measure of how employees view and react to various policies of management. At the same time they provide employees with an opportunity to share opinions and activate change.

Attitude surveys are not tests; there are no right or wrong answers, only reactions or opinions, indicating how a particular individual regards an action or condition.

Management commonly uses three methods to survey employee attitudes: (1) questioning the employee's immediate supervisor; (2) interviewing employees; and (3) administering professionally constructed and normed attitude surveys. The latter is the most economical, efficient, and objective source of information. Questions can be administered quickly to large groups and scored and interpreted readily. The responses provide an objective measure of attitudes concerning both general and particular work situations and a basis for comparison useful to management.

Criteria for Effective Use. The ultimate goal of an attitude survey program is positive—to increase awareness and understanding of employee feelings and to initiate the changes necessary to improve company working conditions and relationships.

An attitude survey should be professionally developed for effective use. It must be reliable, with standardized items and normed results to permit meaningful comparisons between various groups of employees. The survey should be designed to allow individual companies to insert supplementary items on subjects of special concern to that company's management. The program should allow for feedback discussion of the results between employees and management so that each may more fully understand the other's point of view and so that the appropriate action may be initiated. This is crucial because *the decision to initiate an attitude survey carries with it the commitment from management that it is ready and willing to do something.* The attitude survey properly used is a visible sign to employees that management values their opinions: Steps must be taken to ensure employee participation in feedback discussions; plans must be made to change (or attempt to change) objectionable conditions; employees should be informed of actions taken and progress made.

Program Benefits. The attitude survey program is a self-critical process—measuring a company's strengths and weaknesses—to a constructive end—improvement of that company. The information derived is useful on many levels: It can measure the impact of a benefit or policy adjustment, build goodwill, provide information about company operations, ease scheduled mergers through transition phases, and elicit information relating to existing or potential unions; it can be used to assess sources and reasons for such costly problems as low morale, high turnover, absenteeism, and substandard production; it can confirm problem areas but also measure the magnitude and therefore the priority of problems; it can be used to evaluate and promote communication

45

in a company; and it can help management discover how its company compares with others like it across the country.

Well-designed and administered surveys can uncover areas of discontent *before* they become major issues. Thus, often, employees can warn management when equipment is malfunctioning before it actually breaks down, when customers are reacting unfavorably to a product before sales results reflect this, when safety hazards are becoming serious before major accidents occur, or even when employees are becoming disenchanted with a company action, program, or condition *before* organized resistance or a strike results. Surveys provide an early warning to management while there is still time to act. Conversely, such a program can reassure management that programs are working properly and serving the purpose for which they were designed.

Survey Components and Procedures. A typical attitude survey might have three components: a core survey, a section for write-in comments, and a tailor-built survey. The core survey is composed of a number of items or questions that have been tested and retested for validity, reliability, and clarity. For example, "The people I work with get along well together." Typical survey categories are working conditions, pay, benefits, relations with fellow employees and supervisors, effectiveness of management, and adequacy of intracompany communication. Standardization of items permits comparison of a company's results with national, industrial, occupational, or other norms compiled from responses of thousands of employees and employee groups.

Experts find that the most useful survey provides both (1) standardized items, to permit comparisons between companies based on statistical norms, and (2) custom-made items, designed to meet the needs of the specific company. Areas of concern that might be included in a custom-built survey are company benefits, personnel policies, plant changes, parking, unions, and quality controls.

Procedure. The survey program normally proceeds as follows: (1) Appoint survey administrator. (2) Determine date, time, and place for survey. (3) Assign code numbers for various groups in the company taking the survey to facilitate eventual analysis and to reassure employees that their responses are anonymous. (4) Determine norm groups for comparison with the particular company. (5) Conduct survey in a positive psychological climate, making employees feel that the survey is important to them. (6) When finished, have employees put materials in locked box for mailing to administrative company for scoring.

Interpretation. When survey results are returned to the company, management reviews and interprets the summarized results. The idea is to look first at organization problems and then at significant variations in the various coded groups, observing general morale level, noting specific strong and weak points, and interpreting profile patterns for each coded group. Management also takes note of favorable and unfavorable comments. Where profiles are uniformly low, employees probably have unfavorable attitudes toward the organization, apathy toward their jobs, or depressed attitudes about working conditions. Job satisfaction is often found to be related to productivity; conversely, there is strong evidence that a relationship exists between low morale and turnover and absenteeism.

Feedback. After top management has reviewed the findings, it discusses them with middle management. The information can then be sent back to employees via written report or, more effectively, through departmental employee meetings, which provide an opportunity to discuss personally the problems revealed by the survey. Session leaders are sometimes managers of the department, sometimes outside supervisors. Ideally, session leaders are trained to draw out group comments with sensitivity and maturity. These *feedback sessions are considered the crucial part of an attitude survey*, for it is here that a sharing of management decisions takes place. It is here also that suggestions and creative solutions to acknowledged problems are born. Feedback is beneficial in several ways: It builds employee morale and confidence in management, making every member feel important to the organization; the person-to-person discussion is valuable, for it is one of the few times the average employee has the opportunity to discuss working conditions, benefits, and other concerns with a responsible company executive; it stimulates upward and downward communication between management and employees; and it often provides the first step in solving problems revealed by the attitude survey.

A one-time survey is of some immediate value, but a continuous program, with follow-up surveys 1 to 2 years later, serves better to monitor the effectiveness of a company's action plan, as well as employee reactions to management's activities. The initial survey provides a benchmark; succeeding surveys indicate improvement or deterioration.

Applications in Business and Industry. Attitude surveys are in extensive use: Medium- and small-sized companies tend to use standardized surveys developed and constructed by outside testing companies; large corporations often develop their own individualized surveys. Many companies using attitude surveys cultivate their own nuances of use. (The following four examples are excerpted from Science Research Associates' (SRA) Employee Attitude Surveys cassette program.)

Reynolds Metals suggests that a representative of the group being surveyed be involved in initial planning of the program to gain cooperation of all employees. It uses an outside expert to administer the survey and train feedback leaders, thus emphasizing the import of the survey and giving credibility to the anonymous nature of the survey. No decisions are made at the feedback sessions; changes, if any, are made by top management after thorough study of all feedback sessions.

At *Parke-Davis*, those working up the survey prepare tables of critical and favorable written comments by subject. All agreed-upon changes (resulting from feedback sessions and management review) are put into effect immediately. A highly effective aspect of its feedback program is that employees are told that their comments are read, not only by their own line supervisor and plant management, but also by the president of the company and several vice presidents as well, emphasizing the importance top management places on the attitude survey results. Examples of matters learned about and corrected as a result of surveys and feedback meetings are: customer service at distribution centers not up to par; sales promotion material late getting to sales representatives; training programs not achieving objectives; some departments overstaffed, while others overworked.

Sears, Roebuck, and Co. uses several versions of an extensive questionnaire in each of its different locations. Each version is question-specific for particular work groups. As internal conditions change or such things as new government regulations are introduced, new questions are introduced. A core group of general items remains as a permanent measure of employee feelings and expressed motivation. This portion, identical in all versions, provides a comparative base measure of all groups within the organization. The local manager gets results ahead of the next lower level to allow the manager time to digest the report and to indicate that the situation, positive or negative, is her or his responsibility. Numerous individual meetings with employee groups are then held to discuss the findings. This is considered the heart of the program—time-consuming but effective and important. The whole program is designed to encourage continuous attention to the human organization. Because the program is long-established, numerous senior executives have participated in it and therefore are confident of it. In addition, supervisory training programs are specifically related to the issues and needs indicated in the survey.

At *IBM*, management has found that administering the questionnaires on company time rather than mailing them home increases participation 15 to 20 percent. Acceptance and use of the survey by first-level managers improved when they were given report results for their respective departments; it makes survey data relevant to their unique management situation. Employees' perceptions of management's use of survey findings were influenced by whether or not they received feedback. In IBM's attitude survey, 50 percent of the questions in any questionnaire are specific to a particular program, policy, or practice of concern to the unit being surveyed. They resurvey approximately every 1½ to 2 years to give managers feedback on the effectiveness of the actions taken.

Evaluation. In evaluating an attitude survey program it appears that it is correct management attitude and usage that makes such a program successful and incorrect attitude and usage that dooms it to fail.

1. For a survey to "work," support and involvement of all line and staff managers must be real and explicit. Management must see the program as a constructive tool. The tacit commitment by management to accept and respect the results and to respond or act upon them where possible is the backbone of the program. Using the survey simply as a means for employees to "get it off their chests" is of temporary value and can actually lower morale.

2. The survey should seek out information specifically relevant to the needs of the users.

3. Feedback of information must be done in a timely and skillful manner, informing employees of survey results and what progress is being made toward realization of changes.

4. The commitment to anonymity must not be violated. Subordinates should not be questioned about their answers to survey questions or comments. Supervisors must be convinced that the intention of the survey is positive, not punitive, that there will be no recriminations; they must be made to feel that the survey is their tool also, to provide them with the knowledge to deal more effectively with their superiors, peers, and subordinates.

The increased use of attitude surveys reflects growing concern with the assessment and management of human resources. They keep responsible management in touch with large numbers of people, and in a time of fast-paced technological and social change, they provide a way for policymakers to take the pulse among different occupational groups and different generations so that they can respond in a responsible manner. These needs, together with the increasingly available technology of computers—permitting processing and analysis of thousands of questionnaires quickly and skillfully, create an atmosphere receptive to an attitude survey program.

See also Appraisal, performance; Communications, organizational; Interpersonal relationships; Motivation in organizations; Nominal group technique; Suggestion systems.

REFERENCES

Bowditch, James L., and Anthony F. Buono: *Quality of Work Life Assessment: A Survey Based Approach*, Auburn House, Boston, 1982.

Davidson, William L.: *How to Develop and Conduct Successful Employee Attitude Surveys*, Dartnell, Chicago, 1979. **47**

Dunham, Randall B., and Frank J. Smith: *Organizational Surveys: An Internal Assessment of Organizational Health*, Scott, Foresman, Glenview, Ill., 1979.

Bruce A. Campbell, *Campbell & Associates*

Audit, Management

Few business terms have had as many meanings in so short a period of time as *management audit*. For this reason, the modern management audit is often confused with its better-known (and understood) historical antecedent—the financial audit. Both, of course, involve the gathering of information that can aid in decision making—a process as old as human history. But as the requirements of an increasingly complex society transformed the king's court of simpler times into today's "executive court" of economic forecasters, lawyers, accountants, and management consultants, so, too, have the demands of the contemporary business environment created a need for analysis broader in scope and purpose than the financial audit.

Unique Characteristics. The modern management audit meets this need and can be distinguished from its financial "relative" in the following ways:

Purpose. The management audit is an evaluation *of* management. As such, it challenges both the effectiveness of established policies, practices, and procedures and their underlying concepts and principles. The financial audit, in contrast, is a tool *for* management. Although a financial audit can challenge accepted fiscal practices, it more often focuses on an organization's degree of compliance with such practices.

Information Base. The management audit is as dependent on factual evidence as the financial audit. But it also provides informed conclusions and recommendations about leadership and administration that include—but extend beyond—the financial realm.

Range of Inquiry. The management audit generally involves a different level of qualitative evaluation than the financial audit. Specifically, it must consider the insightfulness of leadership; the soundness of objectives, goals, and strategies; and the relative efficiency of operations and administration.

Frame of Reference. The management audit looks at the future implications of management decisions and actions and, in contrast to the financial audit, places significantly greater emphasis on both the business planning process and the identification and fulfillment of related resource needs.

Three-Party Relationship. In addition to the above characteristics, a management audit has come to imply a specific three-party relationship:

- The first party is a focal point of authority—an external government agency, a board of directors, a management team, or the head of a business group or function within a large institution (e.g., a divisional manager or newly appointed head of a particular unit). This party may or may not initiate an audit, but it is always the target audience for the audit's findings.

- The second party—the auditee—is an entity accountable in some way to the first party, thus encompassing virtually any level of a business or public enterprise, from a corporation to a particular division, group, or other organizational unit.

- The third party is an individual or group directed or retained to study the second (e.g., a special committee of the board of directors, an internal task force or study group, or an outside consultant).

An inquiry initiated by the first party is termed a *mandated management audit*. An inquiry introduced by the auditee is called a *voluntary audit*. Variations have also evolved, including the *preaudit*, which is sponsored by the second party in order to prepare for a mandated analysis.

Applications. The three-party audit is generally reserved for situations that involve sensitive or complex issues; for example, when the auditee's performance appears to have fallen short of expectations; when the auditee is accountable to outside constituencies; when adversarial relationships cloud objectivity; or when major or abrupt changes in business circumstances occur. In addition, the situation must be urgent enough to warrant the commitment of necessary resources. All three parties also must be willing or, if necessary, induced to participate in the process.

In recent years, for example, management audits have been commissioned for the following reasons:

- One business is acquired by another, and the acquiring enterprise seeks an objective assessment of the factors involved in integrating the two concerns.

- A public utility commission—troubled by rate increase requests—wishes to reassure itself and the public that a particular utility is well-managed or, if not, that appropriate action will be taken.

- One unit of a successful multidivision company is experiencing a decline in market share and earnings, despite favorable market conditions and several attempts to correct its problems.

- A top-level elected official (e.g., a governor or mayor), facing media criticism about the activities of a major agency under his or her control, wishes to resolve the matter objectively to avoid accusations of political bias.

Structural Variables

Although all management audits have a common purpose and employ a similar analytical approach, their structure can vary markedly, depending on how the following key elements are defined:

Role of the Parties. Very different roles may be assumed by the sponsor, auditee, and auditor, depending on the nature or circumstances of the audit. In a mandated audit, for example, the sponsor's representatives (key executives or staff) may participate actively or may remain uninvolved to avoid any perception of bias. In a voluntary or preaudit, the auditee is likely to take an active stance, while the sponsor (the target audience) may have only limited—or no—awareness of the study until it is completed.

Scope. Depending on the interests and concerns of the parties, an audit can be comprehensive (scrutinizing everything "from the boardroom to the boiler room") or limited to a particular function or project (e.g., the results of a specific marketing program or the effectiveness of a major construction project). The scope of an audit should be agreed upon by all parties involved to ensure uniform interpretation. All parties should, therefore, understand the background and events leading up to the audit, as well as one another's particular concerns.

Objectives. Audit objectives also differ in degree and can influence the conduct of the analysis. Most audits pinpoint the particular strengths and opportunities for improvement evident in the areas under study. Some audits include a broader review of business circumstances and other environmental factors.

Depth of Analysis. The level of scrutiny involved in an audit often reflects a compromise between needs and costs. The three most common levels are: (1) the *reconnaissance audit,* which offers a quick (and economical) overview of the designated area of inquiry; (2) the *comprehensive audit,* which is an in-depth probe; and (3) the *phased audit,* which usually involves initial reconnaissance followed by more exhaustive examination of the specific areas most in need of such attention.

Audit Procedures

Although the actual handling of audits may differ, depending upon the variable elements, most mandated management audits involve the following steps:

1. *Orientation and initial interviews.* The study team meets with sponsor and auditee management to discuss prospective interviewees, sites to be visited, and the kind of information to be gathered. Through these initial meetings, the study team can get to know key executives, meet the individuals assigned to act as their liaison, and arrange other administrative matters.

   During this phase, the study team verifies the audit's structure with senior executives and begins to collect data on organization, activities, and systems. This may include plans, budgets, financial statements, operating reports, organization manuals, policy and procedure statements, systems manuals, minutes of key committee meetings, prior studies, and biographical and employment data on key personnel.

   The preparatory phase enables the study team to pinpoint the most productive areas of inquiry, which will, therefore, receive concentrated attention.

2. *Preparation of a plan of study.* Using the information gathered and analyzed in the preceding step, the study team prepares a detailed plan and time schedule that identifies interviewees inside and outside the enterprise, specific facilities to be visited, and other necessary fact-finding. Management generally approves this plan before subsequent steps are pursued.

3. *Internal fact-finding.* At this point, the study team begins investigating the auditee through interviews, documentation review, and observation of facilities and work processes. Interviews—generally the key source of information—may be conducted with all officers, all key managers, and selected lower-level personnel in all areas of the business. The depth of these interviews will vary, depending on the interviewee's level or function and the audit's scope and objectives.

   The purpose of these interviews is threefold. First, the study team can ascertain each individual's responsibilities and specific functions, scope of authority, relationships with others, and level of involvement in key management and administrative processes. Second, the team can solicit ideas about improving organization and operations and suggestions for solving any problems that have been identified. Finally, the team can seek (in confidence) opinions about qualified candidates who could assume specific management positions following an emergency or retirement.

   Through this internal analysis, the study team develops a thorough understanding of the auditee's strategic challenges and plans; its organizational structure; its human, physical, and financial resources; and its operations.

4. *External fact-finding.* During this step (which usually overlaps those preceding and following it), the study team interviews knowledgeable "outside" observers. Typical candidates might

include representatives from customer or vendor firms; competitors; financial institutions; financial auditors; and federal, state, and local government agencies.

Through these interviews, the team can evaluate the auditee's relationship to its external environment. Issues explored may include sourcing, product policy, manufacturing policy, distribution, market share, cost control, profitability, and overall strategy. This broader perspective facilitates a more objective assessment of the auditee's performance and the challenges it confronts.

5. *Analysis.* After analyzing all information gathered previously, the study team develops a profile of the auditee's performance that generally provides interindustry or intraindustry comparisons on the basis of efficiency and effectiveness. Although many of the criteria used to evaluate performance can be measured quantitatively (in terms of dollars or units of production), truly comparable benchmarks are not always readily available. For this reason, the study team should consider the auditee's performance within the context of its unique environment and apply seasoned judgment, both in tempering quantitative evaluations and in measuring less tangible performance factors (e.g., the enterprise's "public image" and/or reputation within its industry).

6. *Development of conclusions and recommendations.* From the analysis described above, the study team develops conclusions about the efficiency and effectiveness of the auditee's management and operations. The team will confirm all operations and/or functional areas deemed sound, document the apparent sources of any problems—and the potential consequences if they are not resolved—and recommend a course of action.

7. *Communication of the audit's results.* In general, results are communicated in three stages. During the audit, the study team will meet periodically with sponsor and auditee management to review findings, conclusions, and recommendations informally as they evolve. If all parties agree that specific improvement steps are in order, action may begin immediately.

Once the audit is completed, a final report is prepared and usually presented to management in draft form first to ensure accuracy and thoroughness. If necessary, it is revised and then submitted officially (often accompanied by oral-visual presentations). If the report is to be released to broad audiences (e.g., the media or major employee groups), a summary of key findings is usually prepared.

Common Pitfalls

Because auditee and sponsor do not necessarily have the same perspectives or concerns, the three-party audit can raise sensitive issues that may heighten any existing tension. Through intelligent planning and anticipatory management, however, most stumbling blocks can be successfully circumvented. Four common problems are highlighted below:

Lack of Agreement About Audit Structure. If all three parties do not share an understanding of their working relationship and the audit's scope, objectives, and level of scrutiny, they may become frustrated and disenchanted—which can delay the audit itself or hamper acceptance and/or adoption of findings and recommendations. To avoid this problem, structure should be defined (in writing) before the audit begins.

Failure to Establish Confidentiality Provisions. When an audit involves extensive interviewing, confidentiality must be affirmed (also preferably in writing) to encourage auditee personnel to share knowledge and viewpoints that could be helpful to the audit process. Without such a provision, personnel will be reluctant—at best—to communicate openly, and fact-finding efforts may prove largely fruitless. Information will then have to be gathered in other ways, which can dramatically increase the cost of the audit. For similar reasons, the study team should confirm that sponsor and auditee management will be available for informal dialogue during the audit itself.

Insufficient Corroboration of Data. The conclusions of virtually every management audit are based on information from a variety of internal and external sources. Such data must be corroborated, preferably with senior management, before they are included in any final analysis. Factual errors can undermine the credibility of the analysis, and arguments about accuracy can distract attention from substantive findings.

Imbalances in the Portrayal of Analytical Results. A final report that overemphasizes the auditee's strengths or weaknesses can affect the ultimate usefulness of the process itself. Disagreeing factions inside and outside the organization are likely to label the audit a "whitewash" or a "witch-hunt," thus diverting attention from important results. To avoid this problem, the final report should offer a balanced picture of the organization and should devote appropriate attention to recommendations for improvement.

Trends in Usage

As the management audit has evolved in recent years, four important trends have been observed.

1. *Increased use.* A key advantage of the management audit is the opportunity to examine otherwise divisive issues in an atmosphere of analytical objectivity rather than adversarial rancor. This makes it a particularly useful vehicle in a business environment characterized by increasing accountability to shareholders and public entities and growing demands for more productive use of resources.

2. *Decreasing reliance on the comprehensive management audit.* Because a comprehensive audit can be quite costly, a growing number of companies are opting for the phased audit, which provides a more targeted analysis of key problem areas.

3. *Increased use of preaudits.* As use of the mandated audit increases, aggressive managements are initiating more preaudits to identify and mitigate problems before the externally directed review begins.

4. *Greater attention to study team expertise.* Whether audits are conducted by internal study teams or outside consultants, the auditors' experience, judgment, and skill must be considered carefully. Auditors must not only be able to recognize operational realities but also, if necessary, challenge arbitrary, inconsistent, or impractical behavioral and decision-making patterns that have become "accepted standards." For this reason, auditors' technical expertise must be balanced by a broad perspective and a base of experience that extends well beyond the immediate area of inquiry.

The management audit has become a distinctive analytical tool that can provide material benefits when used judiciously. Appropriate use, however, is critical if benefits are to outweigh the often considerable costs of a management audit.

See also Acquisitions and mergers; Auditing, financial; Boards of directors, legal liability guidelines; Consultants, management; Control systems, management; Management information systems (MIS); Organizational analysis and planning; Planning, strategic managerial; Social responsibility of business.

REFERENCES

Flesher, D. L., and S. Siewert: *Independent Auditor's Guide to Operational Auditing,* John Wiley, New York, 1982.

Internal Auditing, Report No. 748, The Conference Board, New York, 1978.

Leonard, William P.: *The Management Audit: An Appraisal of Management Methods and Performance,* Prentice-Hall, Englewood Cliffs, N.J., 1962.

Louis H. Knapp, *Cresap, McCormick and Paget Division: Towers, Perrin, Forster & Crosby*

Alden R. Taylor, Jr., *Cresap, McCormick and Paget Division: Towers, Perrin, Forster & Crosby*

Auditing, Financial

A *financial audit* is an objective investigation to validate the representations in financial statements by obtaining reasonable assurance of the accuracy and reliability of the underlying accounting data.

Since management has a personal interest in the way that its performance is measured in financial statements, the custom has developed of having those statements audited by an independent firm of auditors to provide an outside expert opinion on management's representations.

The Auditor's Standard Report

The *auditor's report* is a formal communication by a firm of independent auditors, describing its examination of financial statements and expressing its professional opinion on those statements.

The typical report has two paragraphs. The first identifies the financial statements examined—typically, comparative balance sheets, income statements, statements of retained earnings, and changes in financial position—and describes the nature and scope of the examination made by the auditor. The second (the opinion) paragraph states whether the financial statements identified in the scope paragraph fairly present the company's financial position, results of operations, and changes in financial position in conformity with generally accepted accounting principles and whether those principles have been applied consistently.

Much of the significance that users of financial statements attach to the report comes from the underlying meaning of two key phrases: generally accepted auditing standards and generally accepted accounting principles.

Generally Accepted Auditing Standards. Independent auditors typically distinguish auditing procedures from auditing standards. *Auditing procedures* are acts performed by auditors to gather evidential matter concerning the underlying accounting data and corroborating data supporting financial statements. *Generally accepted auditing standards* is a technical term that defines accepted auditing practice at a particular time. It includes broad objectives to be achieved in the audit and more detailed technical guidance.

The membership of the American Institute of Certified Public Accountants (AICPA) has officially adopted 10 formal standards—divided into general standards, standards of fieldwork, and standards of reporting.

The general standards broadly describe the qualifications of an independent auditor and the quality his or her work should achieve. The fieldwork standards describe in general terms the minimum requirements of a financial audit, and the reporting standards describe the essential requirements for the form and content of the auditor's report.

The 10 formal standards provide only broad guidance. The AICPA's Auditing Standards Division issues Statements on Auditing Standards (SAS) that provide interpretation of the 10 formal standards. SASs have been referred to in many court cases as the minimum requirements for financial audits.

Generally Accepted Accounting Principles. The first standard of reporting requires the independent auditor's report to state whether the financial statements conform with generally accepted accounting principles. Like generally accepted auditing standards, *generally accepted accounting principles* is a technical term that describes the guidance necessary to define accepted accounting practice at a particular time. The task of developing generally accepted accounting principles now rests principally with the Financial Accounting Standards Board (FASB), an independent organization in the private sector. The Council of the AICPA has designated the FASB as the authoritative source of accounting principles for AICPA members.

Modifications of the Standard Report. The standard report described is referred to as an unqualified opinion. It communicates the fact that the auditor has gathered evidence to support the validity of the events and transactions underlying the statements and that in the auditor's judgment those events and transactions are adequately presented and disclosed in accordance with their economic substance. Anything less than an unqualified opinion is usually considered undesirable by management and may be unacceptable to users of the financial statements. An independent auditor, however, may be forced to express something other than an unqualified opinion if the financial statements depart in a material manner from generally accepted accounting principles, the auditor's examination is not adequate to support an opinion, or the financial statements are affected by a material uncertainty that may at a future date require adjustment of financial statements.

Auditing Practice and Methods

The audit report is signed by a CPA firm rather than by the individual auditor or auditors who conduct the examination.

CPA Firms. A management's choice of a CPA firm can be expected to receive scrutiny by users of financial statements who rely chiefly on the reputation of the CPA firms. Underwriters of large public offerings of securities may demand an international or national firm of wide-known reputation. Bankers and other credit grantors are known to keep lists of acceptable CPA firms based on their own and other creditors' experience.

The Audit Examination. The first examination of a new client is normally extensive. In subsequent audits the end of one engagement blends into the beginning of the next, and each engagement builds on the experience of prior ones. An audit depends heavily on the independent auditor's understanding of the accounting system in use and the controls over it as well as the accounting principles used.

The auditor must be familiar with the characteristics of the company's operations that could have an accounting effect and with management's policies and procedures that have an effect on the reliability of the accounting records and the financial statements prepared from them. The auditor must also consider the effect of changes in the business environment, in the company, and in its operations, and the legal requirements under which the company must operate.

An audit normally begins with a *preliminary review* and evaluation of the client's operations and controls. The auditor may conduct initial interviews with the client's management and supervisory personnel, tour the offices and principal plants, read company manuals on practices and procedures, and in other ways become familiar with the client, its industry, and its particular problems.

The *study and evaluation of internal control* is a significant part of modern audits. The first step is normally a review of the system to obtain an understanding of the controls that are supposed to be in effect. A preliminary evaluation is then made of those controls to see if the auditor can rely on them to ensure the accuracy and reliability of the accounting records. If the auditor plans to rely on particular controls, she or he will then test compliance with them by (1) observing controls, such as separation of key functions in operation, and (2) sampling transactions by inspection of supporting documents.

The study and evaluation of internal control is correlated with analytical procedures and tests of transactions and balances on a sample basis. *Analytical review procedures* include (1) reading important documents, looking for matters of financial and accounting significance; (2) scanning the activity in accounts and summary entries, looking for unusual items; and (3) comparing account balances in one or more other accounting periods or in the budget, looking for unusual or unexpected deviations. Tests of transactions and balances include such procedures as (1) confirming receivables and bank balances with outside parties, (2) physically inspecting assets and comparing asset counts with accounting records, and (3) scrutinizing the documents supporting transactions.

Client-Auditor Relations and Communications

Because independent auditors must have contact with many levels in the organization, it is advisable to fix responsibility on some one individual for coordinating these matters.

Establishing Responsibility within the Organization. Generally, it is the chief financial officer or chief internal auditor who is charged with coordination. The chief executive officer, however, should know the independent auditor well enough to consult with him or her in advance as frequently as necessary on significant matters involving the presentation of the company's financial statements or on significant transactions that are being planned.

Letters of Representation. A generally accepted auditing procedure is to obtain a letter of representation from a company's legal counsel concerning litigation, contingent liabilities, and, in some cases, interpretation of specific contracts and agreements. If a company has a general counsel, it would be common practice for the auditor to work with that person in obtaining the necessary information and representation.

Another common audit procedure is to obtain a representation letter from top officers of the corporation concerning significant representations in the financial statements. Representations obtained from management are not a substitute for audit procedures. They are used by the independent auditor to make a record of significant inquiries and responses during the engagement and to record management's belief that the auditor has been informed of all matters within its knowledge that could have a material bearing on the work.

Audit Committees. Many companies have established audit committees composed primarily of the outside directors of the board of directors. The existence of an audit committee helps to demonstrate that the board of directors is fulfilling its responsibility to shareholders concerning financial reporting and disclosure. Through the audit committee, the board of directors is able to evaluate the work of the independent auditor and understand the nature and limitations of a financial audit.

CPA Firm Selection and Termination. For many companies, the selection of the independent auditor is approved by the board of directors and often ratified by its shareholders. Top management should take the initiative in seeing that the board of directors is adequately informed to make an appropriate selection. CPA firms should be expected to make a proposal explaining their qualifications and abilities to conduct the audit and provide other services.

Just as the company should conduct an investigation in the selection of auditors, independent auditors commonly investigate the reputation and business standing of potential clients. An auditor considering the acceptance of an engagement must also communicate with the independent auditor who preceded her or him on the engagement. In addition, a regulation of the Securities and Exchange Commission may require a company to disclose any dispute with the predecessor auditor about accounting principles or disclosures in a filing.

Working Relations During the Audit. A client's staff may often assist the independent auditor by preparing schedules and analyses of accounts and by searching files for needed information and documents. The cost of an audit can be reduced if this assistance is provided.

If a company has an internal audit department, the independent auditor can be expected to obtain an understanding of the work of the internal audit staff and may be able to make use of the work normally done by the internal audit staff in his or her study and evaluation of internal control. The independent auditor may also be able to get direct assistance from members of the internal audit staff in portions of the examination.

Conferences during the Audit. From time to time during the audit, the partner in charge of the engagement must meet with the chief financial officer or the chief executive officer or the audit committee to discuss accounting policies and controls and the company's financial reporting practices. The level of the communication usually depends on the nature and significance of the matter in question. Important decisions about accounting matters should not be put off until the end of the year, and communications should take place continuously during the audit. The independent auditor and top management should adopt the policy of mutual nonsurprise.

Top management will want to consult with the independent auditor, for example, prior to engaging in major transactions, such as the acquisition of another corporation, to find out how the transaction will be reflected in the financial statements and what prospective changes in accounting principles and in accounting systems or controls may occur.

If the auditor and top management cannot reach agreement on accounting principles or disclosures, it may be necessary for the matter to be resolved by the audit committee or the board of directors itself. Some matters of significance such as major weaknesses in controls may need to be brought to the attention of the board of directors in any event.

Written Communications from the Auditor. Independent auditors may prepare a number of reports for use within the client organization—the most frequent form is the so-called management letter. *Management letters* draw attention to weaknesses in accounting systems and related controls, make constructive suggestions about correcting weaknesses, and explore other possibilities for improvements.

Annual Meetings. It is desirable for the independent auditor to be available at annual meetings to answer the questions of shareholders. Independent auditors are frequently able to explain the safeguards that the company has adopted to prevent material fraud or similar problems. Also, independent auditors are able to answer questions concerning the accounting policies followed by the company and how those policies compare with those of other companies in the industry.

See also Accounting, cost analysis and control; Accounting, financial; Accounting, managerial control; Acquisitions and mergers; Audit, management; Control systems, management; Exchange, foreign, management of; Financial management; Financial statement analysis; Management information systems (MIS); Shareholder relations; Tax management.

REFERENCES

Auditing Standards Division, *Statements on Auditing Standards,* American Institute of Certified Public Accountants, New York: Codification of Statements on Auditing Standards, nos. 1 to 44, January 1983.

Carmichael, D. R., and John J. Willingham: *Perspectives in Auditing,* 3d ed., McGraw-Hill, New York, 1979.

Defliese, Philip L., Kenneth P. Johnson, and Roderick K. Macleod: *Montgomery's Auditing,* 9th ed., Ronald Press, New York, 1975.

D. R. CARMICHAEL, *Baruch College, City University of New York*

Authority, Responsibility, and Accountability

Authority encompasses the concepts of power, responsibility, accountability, delegation, and decentralization; it is "the key to the management job."[1] The changing applications and implications of authority have concerned and confused many managers. However, today's managers can use several approaches to achieve an integrated view of authority. These are based upon (1) status and rank, (2) function or job, and (3) subordinate acceptance. In this entry, responsibility and accountability are considered in their relationship to authority. Delegation, its role in decentralized authority, and its importance to effective management are also considered.

Meaning and Relationships

Authority and responsibility have long been linked in management theory—usually with the admonition that they must be coincidental, corresponding, coequal, coterminous, coexistent, and, often, delegated simultaneously.

Accountability is a concomitant, a derivative, or an adjunct of responsibility.

Power is considered by some to be an element of authority; by others, as related to but different from authority. Still others view authority as an aspect, type, or derivative of power and use the terms interchangeably. Power has not always been discussed freely in management literature, but it needs to be recognized, and its role as an activator in organizations needs to be explored. In this discussion, *power* is defined as an ingredient of all organizational activities and as an underlying basis for the sharing of responsibility and the granting of authority. (*See also* Power and influence.)

Authority is derived from the Latin word *auctoritas,* indicating one who increases or produces. How it should be interpreted and applied in a modern organization depends upon the orientation of the person who is wielding it.

Authority

Authority will be considered from three points of view, followed by a synthesis of these (*see* Table A-7) and a consideration of its relationship to responsibility and its role in the essential managerial act of delegation.

Authority Based upon Power, Status, or Rank. This is the traditional or classical concept. It stresses two elements: (1) a *right* to do something (issue orders, make decisions, command, demand obedience) and (2) the *power* to enforce compliance. It is often stated quite boldly as "the right to tell other people what you want them to do and the power to see that they do it." This interpretation presumes that total, final, or complete authority within each organization resides at some top level where it was placed by a sovereign authority (witness the divine right of kings). In a democracy, the analogy would be the citizenry through their elected representatives. This top level (group, position, person) has been granted the authority to use property or things in an approved way. It then passes parts of this authority downward in the organization, through prescribed channels or paths, to the persons who must take the intended action. The right and power of these action-level people to perform, hence, can be traced upward to their ultimate source within the organization—the charter or grant. Traditional authority has had many exponents and still retains quite a few, as indicated in Table A-7.

Within an organizational hierarchy, *authority based upon position* is actually a part of traditional authority and sometimes is considered to be a subset thereof. It is closely related to status or rank and is spoken of as a level of authority within the organization. In all organizations, people become quite conscious of these levels and refer to top management, middle management, and first-line management as indicative of these respective levels of authority. Thus, a certain position, at a certain level, is presumed to be endowed with a certain amount or degree of authority.

Authority Based upon Function or Job. In this approach, the authority to act is essentially another part of whatever job is committed to take the final or intended action. In other words, the capacity to act resides in and is part of the job. There is no continuing pathway of delegation other than the assignment of the job. Once the job assignment has been accepted, full or complete authority resides in the job and with the person on the job. M. P. Follett is recognized as the first management theorist to propose this concept and to point out that the person on a job and the job itself are interdependent ("authority belongs to the job and stays with the job"[2]). She was objecting to a supreme or final authority which then delegated bits and pieces downward throughout the organization. Thus, the *immediate* source of authority becomes the assignment-acceptance of a job, and the only *ultimate* source is the one who determined and assigned the work.

Closely akin to the concept of job authority, *staff authority* is related directly to and is based solely upon the specialized knowledge and capabilities of a particular staff member (e.g., an attorney). This professional-staff specialization puts such a person in the position to say, "When you do thus and so, do it *this* way." In some cases, there are various levels or locations of staff within a specialized field (e.g., personnel). Here, the top-level staff member is sometimes granted staff authority or *functional authority* over corresponding functions at lower levels in the organization. Such top-level staff may be given authority for surveillance of lower-level performance and for directing work-level personnel. This is frequently the cause of conflict with the local or immediate line authority involved (e.g., accounting versus production). A number of students of management have analyzed these causes of conflict and sought ways to alleviate them.[3] There is no foolproof solution to this specialist-generalist authority problem, although openness, frankness, and joint responsibility for results can alleviate much of it.

Authority Based upon Acceptance, Consent, or Assent. Increasingly popular since Chester Barnard's[4] monumental contribution to the field in 1938, this approach avers that authority resides with the subordinate who is to take the prescribed action and that the subordinate grants an authority to the superordinate by consenting to perform. In short, subordinates *accept* the boss's right to direct them. Thus, as Barnard pointed out, this acceptance is based upon an interpersonal relationship, a communication between persons, and, therefore, is actually passed upward in the organization—just the reverse of the traditional idea of a downward passage. Most exponents of this concept have been classed as *behaviorists* who see the authority relationship as a set of behaviors or interactions; hence the appellation *behavioral authority* in Table A-7.

An Integrated Approach to Authority. Authority based upon an integration of applicable elements from each of the previous approaches would seem most practicable for modern managers. Each has its merits, and some of the elements of each are needed in today's organizations. Observers have pointed out that those who espouse traditional authority view the employee (who does the work and takes the action) as passive and inert, as an instrument of the organization; that M. P. Follett and the adherents of authority based upon function or job see the employee and his or her work as interdependent; and that the behavioral approach considers the employee as separate and apart from the organization. The first approach has been labeled as considering organizations without people; the second, as only observing people within organizations; and the third, as studying people without organizations.

Practicing managers can integrate or combine today's beliefs concerning individual freedom, worth, and opportunities with current developments in human work behavior (including the growing awareness of a person's capacity for self-direction) and with historical evidence and experience in effective organizational functioning. Now, authority can be seen as freedom or opportunity to act, to decide, to perform; the essential elements being *permission* (the consent to do or use something) and *ability* (the capability to take the action). This, of course, requires the manager not only to give permission for the proposed action but also to see that the one who will perform is ready and prepared to act. This will require further that there be agreement as to just *what* is to be done and *how* it is to be done, and *the acceptance* by the subordinate of these objectives. This acceptance equals the responsibility to perform, and it is from this acceptance that the authority to act arises. Thus, this authority is unitary or monolithic and resides with the one who is to perform, whereas the responsibility for action is shared and pluralistic. That is, the responsibility for effective action is shared among the actor, the superordinate, the superordinate's superordinate, and so forth, to the very top of the organization.

TABLE A-7 Concepts of Authority—A Comparison and an Integration

Type and basis	Elements of meaning	Characteristics and assumptions	Immediate source	Ultimate source and path of delegation	Exponents*
Traditional authority—based on power, status, rank	A right and power: to enforce, to require obedience, to demand compliance, to make decisions, to issue orders, to command, to control the action of others	Stems from ownership and use of property Paths or lines of delegation downward through organization to work level Person viewed as passive and inert, an instrument of production or of the organization Manager issues orders or commands and makes decisions	Organizational superordinate	Citizens → Government → Organizational charter → Owners → Officers → Managers → Supervisors → Workers	Alford Davis Fayol Hopf Koontz Mooney Schell Taylor Terry
Functional authority—based on function or job	Inherent in function or work In effect, created by the offer and acceptance of a work assignment	Resides in and is a part of a function, responsibility, job Moves with job assignment—stays with the job—no path Person and work interdependent	A work assignment or job	One who determines and assigns work—no path	Follett

Behavioral authority—based on acceptance, consent, assent	Acceptance of another's right to direct An interpersonal relationship A communication A set of behaviors—interaction between persons	Resides with subordinate, granted to superordinate; subordinate consents to perform Path of authority upward, conferred on boss when subordinate assents to orders Person viewed as independent of organization Manager gets acceptance of proposed action and decisions	The individual subordinate		Argyris Barnard Froman Mayo Roethlisberger Simon
Integrational authority—based on pertinent elements from all the above	Freedom to act, to decide—requiring permission and ability Permission to take action Opportunity to perform Opportunity to innovate Comes into being with the specification of responsibility and its acceptance	Resides with but one person at work, at any one time No path or channel; monolithic, unitary, indivisible, integrated Optimum self-direction Person and work interdependent Manager as a transfer agent transfers authority to those who are to take action (work) Combines freedom and opportunity for self-direction with organizational objectives and job goals	When responsibility is offered to and accepted by a subordinate, he or she is delegated the authority to perform	An organization's permission to exist and operate—its charter, license, etc.—no path	Golembiewski Mandeville Trickett

Owners → Officers → Managers → Supervisors → Workers

* Named exponents are merely a sampling of some of the management theorists who have espoused all or parts of the respective interpretations of authority.

57

Responsibility and Accountability

Responsibility and accountability are terms that are often confused and are frequently used synonymously. *Responsibility,* from the French *responsable,* means liable to respond, answerable. In common parlance, it implies an accountability or answerability to a person or body imposing a task or duty. *If* responsibility has to be accepted (not imposed) and if this acceptance creates an obligation to perform, to do something, then there is an implicit answerability or *accountability.* It is this acceptance and sharing of responsibility which causes the accountability for results that is the very essence of the superordinate-subordinate reporting relationship. With the relationship agreed to and established, the permission to take the intended action naturally follows. And this permission, involving preparation to perform and the inducement to do what has to be done, is the substance of authority as a derivative of responsibility. What, then, *is* delegated by a manager?

Delegation

Delegation has been called the essence of the manager's job, and some observers have claimed that the greatest cause of manager failure is the inability or unwillingness of a manager to delegate. *Delegate,* from the Latin *delegatus,* means to send one with a commission—hence, to empower or trust another person to take action or to perform. Managerial inadequacy in delegation appears to come from the fact that managers are selected to be managers because they are effective doers; whereas when they become managers, they must get things done through other people. Henry Taylor's 1832 admonition, published in *The Statesman,* could well be directed to today's managers:

> The most important qualification of an executive is his ability to act through others, since the value of his operations vicariously effected ought to predominate greatly over the importance of his direct activity. But it is a snare into which men in business and statesmen are apt to fall, that in attaching weight to the immediately visible effects of their efforts they lose sight of what they might accomplish if they applied their powers through the widest possible instrumentalities.

It should be clear by now that managers delegate authority—as permission and inducement to take some action—but that they do *not* delegate responsibility, which they *share* with subordinates. Thus, responsibility, as accepted by the one to take the action, exists and is shared from this point of acceptance upward, level by level, to the top of the organization. Is it this acceptance of accountability for results that the behaviorists find passing upward with the organization (see Table A-7)?

Decentralized authority results from delegation. Decentralization is the keynote of Jethro's ancient advice to Moses (*Exodus* 18:17) that implemented two of the oldest of management precepts—that decisions affecting the work of the organization should be made as close as possible to the level (and location) at which the action is to be taken and that only unusual or exceptional problems should be passed upward for decision—i.e., the principle of decentralized authority and the principle of management by exception.

See also Delegation; Exception, management by; Leadership; Management, definitions of; Management theory, science, and approaches; Organizational analysis and planning.

NOTES

[1] H. Koontz and C. O'Donnell, ''The Functions and Authority of the Manager,'' *Principles of Management; An Analysis of Managerial Functions,* 5th ed., McGraw-Hill, New York, 1972, chap. 3.

[2] M. P. Follett, ''The Basis of Authority,'' *Freedom and Coordination,* Management Publications Trust, London, 1949, p. 1.

[3] D. E. McFarland, *Management: Principles and Practices,* 4th ed., Macmillan, New York, 1974.

[4] C. I. Barnard, *The Functions of the Executive,* Harvard University Press, Cambridge, Mass., 1938, p. 183.

REFERENCES

Ford, Jeffrey D.: ''The Administrative Component in Growing and Declining Organizations,'' *Academy of Management Journal,* vol. 23, December 1980, pp. 615–630.

Jackson, John H., and Cyril P. Morgan: *Organization Theory,* Prentice-Hall, Englewood Cliffs, N.J., 1982.

Satow, R. L.: ''Value-Rational Authority and Professional Organizations,'' *Administrative Science Quarterly,* vol. 20, December 1975, p. 526.

JOSEPH M. TRICKETT, *University of Santa Clara*

Automation

Automation or automatization is the act of increasing the degree to which a process is automatic. The word *automatic* is an adjective describing a mechanism or process which is self-acting and does not rely upon human direction. A mechanism or process is commonly described as automatic if it requires less human direction and control than the predecessor mechanism or process. Automation is therefore a time-related word, and must be understood in the time frame in which it is used. Yesterday's automated mechanism is today's conventional mechanism.

Because automation is a coined word, it is hard to trace its origin with accuracy, but records do show that the economist John Diebold, writing in 1959 on the subject, used automation rather than automatization—which he considered to be the equivalent—because it was easier to use in writing and speaking. Del Harder, a senior manufacturing engineer with the Ford Motor Company, simultaneously and apparently quite independently adopted automation as a verbal shortcut for automatization in his staff meetings on the subject.

At about the same time, Prof. Norbert Weiner of M.I.T. remarked, in ''The Human Use of Human Beings,'' that society had all the necessary technology at its command to make labor completely obsolete in ten years. The reaction of Labor was negative: automation, which in the popular mind of the day meant the elimination of labor, was immediately perceived as a threat. But ten years later employment was higher, and where automation had been introduced, human beings were relieved of some of their most onerous and dangerous tasks. Automation ceased to be a public issue, and the word fell into relative disuse for a decade. Labor unions do not now oppose the introduction of automation.

The Automation Decision

Automation of a mechanism or a process should be undertaken when, and only when, the advantages will outweigh the disadvantages. Said another way, the cost of automating should always be less than the value of the benefits attained by it.

Advantages of Automation. These vary according to the industrial environment, but may include some or all of the following:

- The repeatability of the function and the uniformity of the production are improved.
- The reliability of the function is improved, because it does not depend on human actions; indeed, a fully automated machine may run unattended or with only a monitor.
- The skill required of the operator or the monitor is reduced.
- The function performed may transcend that which any human-operated mechanism can perform.
- The speed of the automated mechanism may exceed that of any human-controlled mechanism.
- The cost of the operation may be reduced.
- The time consumed in the operation may be reduced.
- Automated mechanisms can work in environments that are undesirable for human beings—high temperatures, toxicity of materials or the atmosphere, proximity of hazardous mechanisms

(drop forges, die casting machines), need to perform in darkness (as in photographic work), need to perform in low temperatures (cold storage warehouses), etc.

Disadvantages of Automation. These, too, vary according to the environment, but they may include any or all of the following:

- The automated equipment may very well cost more than the unautomated version. The components which offer the added features of control will also add to the cost and may require a revision of the controlled mechanism as well.
- The automated equipment may be less flexible in its application. While, for example, a human operator can make a wide variety of objects on an engine lathe, if that lathe is converted to an automatic turret lathe, it is limited to the production of a certain class of objects.
- If the automated lathe is made adaptable to a more varied class of product by the addition, for example, of numerical control, that flexibility adds further cost.
- The design, development, and maintenance of automated equipment require special, scarce, and sometimes costly skills.
- The operation of automated equipment requires different labor skills from the operation of nonautomated equipment.
- The optimum automation of a mechanism may require the redesign of the product being manufactured by the mechanism.
- When automation takes the form of a concatenation of simpler machines, as for example in a transfer line for machining auto engine parts, it may be necessary to intersperse automatic inspection stations to ensure quality, thus adding to cost and complexity.
- The magnitude of the effort involved and the cost require a relatively large volume of production of a given product before the incremental savings can justify the effort. Low-volume or infrequent processes are not good candidates for automation.

Some or all of these advantages and disadvantages may be present in any given automation effort. Their balance will determine the course of action.

Application of Automation

The introduction of automation follows a well-known and proven sequence of steps.

Step 1. *Perceive an opportunity.* This may take place on a local level, where a spot improvement can be made, or on a broader level, where a system improvement can be made. In either case, the first step is to determine the needs to be fulfilled by the automation effort. These must be stated carefully in terms that will not predetermine a solution, but will leave room for consideration of several alternatives.

A *high-level* perception might, for example, call for the introduction of a computerized control system. Such a change will affect a large portion of an enterprise. It is most likely to be perceived by top management and will certainly have to be supported by it. A *spot* revision may be perceived by a local supervisor and can be supported by his or her efforts.

Step 2. *Identify and list all the possible alternatives for meeting the needs.* This step should also include an initial assessment of the potential cost and return of each alternative. It does *not* call for a complete design of each alternative, but merely enough so that the most attractive approach may be selected.

Step 3. *Define very carefully the selected alternative.* Special attention should be given to the system or machine specifications. This will provide the engineers or developers with a specific target for their work.

Step 4. *Justify the effort and expense of the project.* This should be done before the actual development begins. Current costs for the process are compared with computed costs for the improved process. A return-on-investment calculation will generally serve the justification purpose for a new automatic mechanism, for example, although some projects, such as corporate market objectives, are undertaken on the basis of noneconomic justifications. Justification of a major system change will, however, involve a lengthy investigation. For example, in the introduction of a *computer integrated manufacturing* system, it might well be impossible to run a complete economic analysis of before and after costs. In this case the decision might be made on the basis of corporate strategy dependent upon the ability of the enterprise to survive in a competitive world with and without the system.

Step 5. *Develop the automated system.* This may be done by in-house engineers, if any are available and able, or by an outside contractor. If a contract is to be let, it should be on the basis of carefully drawn and complete specifications.

Step 6. *Install and debug the mechanism, system, or process.* Do this before it is put into routine use. This task is one of the greatest sources of trouble and contention, and it must be carefully planned for and supervised.

Step 7. *Evaluate the system's performance and results.* A retrospective analysis of the project should always be made to determine the validity of the planning methods and the lessons to be learned for future guidance in automation.

The Stages of Automation

"Automation" is chiefly used to describe the process of evolution of manufacturing mechanisms and processes. This evolution has progressed historically through two stages and is now entering a third.

Labor-Intensive Manufacture. From the dawn of civilization human beings have conceived of and utilized tools and materials that extended human muscular skills and powers. Tools were refined over the centuries, but the control and the motive power of the tools were principally human muscle and brains.

Capital-Intensive Manufacture. When steam power arrived in the late eighteenth century, simple mechanisms were devised to hold and guide the working tool, while the steam engine provided the thrust. The next 2 centuries saw an almost explosive rate of development of these mechanisms and processes into today's industrial equipment. Electric motive power was added to steam power at the close of the nineteenth century, and this power source accelerated the evolution well into the middle of the twentieth century.

Data-Intensive Manufacture. The last 2 decades have seen the beginning of another massive change in the character of manufacturing. *It is changing from capital-intensive to data-intensive.* Furthermore, data processing competence has extended to the benefit of service-oriented industries and processes. Just as in the prior phase human muscle and physical skills were replaced by steam and electric power, human mental skills are being replaced or supplemented by data processing equipment. This change depends upon two facts: (1) all activities in manufacturing may be expressed as data, and (2) very powerful data processing equipment has appeared.

Human control capabilities can now be augmented or replaced by automated devices for handling data, commonly termed *computers*—hence the commonly used term *computer aided manufacturing.* The complex processes of manufacturing and their control require managers to make frequent decisions to adapt to changing circumstances—both long-term trends and unforeseen catastrophes. Some of these decisions may be made according to rules, or through simulation and optimization techniques. Insofar as the decision rules can be codified and lodged in the manager's computers, decision making, too, may be automated. When decisions must be left to human judgment, the manager's computers may be used to collect and display status data and to simulate future results if any one of several decisions is made. This is called an *automated decision-support system.* The term *automation* is once again used frequently but now refers to the automatization of data handling systems.

Advantages and Disadvantages. The change from capital-intensive to data-intensive manufacture has the same characteristics discussed above, but some of the advantages and disadvantages have a new dimension. The speed of data processing in an electronic computer far, far transcends the computational skill of the human mind. Not only can a computer make millions of calculations per second but it can deal with equations or data matrixes whose size transcends the comprehension of the human mind.

For example, finite element analysis is a method of calculating stress or temperature distribution in a machine part. While the theory has been known for a hundred years, its use was limited to relatively simple structures. But with computers, it has been possible to calculate the stress concentration in the wing spar of a large aircraft; the computer has to deal with more than 200 simultaneous differential equations and 2.5 billion bits of data. Such a calculation could not be made by human minds.

On the other side of the coin, the cost of the electronic computers may be as large as, or larger than, the cost of the automated machinery they control. Data processing facilities call for a whole new gamut of technical skills and displace a whole array of clerical workers. Finally, the installation of automated systems will affect the organization of an enterprise from top to bottom.

Future Trends. Automation today is only at the very beginning of the transition from capital- to data-intensive manufacturing systems. Its ultimate possibilities are but dimly perceived. These may include flexible manufacturing systems in which the economic lot size approaches 1 and the unmanned operation of the material conversion part of the production. *Manufacturing is changing from an art to a science.*

Impact of Automation

The introduction of automation—of data handling as well as of mechanisms—affects the productivity of an organization, the cost of the products, and the speed of production, all as might be expected. It also has an impact on the organization of the enterprise,

on the labor force of the company and of the nation in general, and on society.

Impact on the Organization. The most likely impact of automation on the organization of an enterprise is to simplify, stabilize, and rationalize the structure. When the structure is so rationalized, its analogy to other similar structures will be more obvious. This will mean that managerial tools and skills may be learned, acquired, and implemented more readily, to the benefit of the enterprise.

Impact on the Labor Force. Whenever a process is automated, whether it be by the purchase of a standard tool to replace a manual operation or by the installation of some brand-new invention or computer system, the prior operator may be replaced. The replacement may be by another operator of lower, higher, or different skill level or by no operator at all. This undeniably produces a dislocation of that individual worker. Over the long term, automation has increased the productivity of the worker, so that for the same total output, fewer workers are required. However, the provision of the facilities of automation has more often than not created new employment. Over the long term, the level of society's consumption has increased, with the result that today the total level of employment is higher than ever before. The average level of skill of the workers engaged in manufacturing and service industries has also increased as automation has been introduced. Particularly there is a greater need for engineering and mathematical talent in the design and operation of the automated systems.

Impact on Society. When machinery was first introduced, handworkers feared that their jobs would be lost forever. When a weaver in Danzig, Poland, in 1519 invented a powered loom, his fellow weavers summarily destroyed the invention and drowned the inventor. The Luddites of early nineteenth-century England smashed knitting machines and looms which they felt threatened their livelihood. French workers threw their wooden shoes (sabots) into machines to destroy them—hence the term *saboteur.* In consideration of the impact on labor, labor laws have been enacted to protect the workers and labor unions have been organized to represent the workers' point of view in discussions with management.

It is important, however, to keep automation in perspective. Automation is *only one* of the many factors that have contributed to the development of the social structure of modern life. It has, however, contributed *substantially* to the complete revolution of the methods and the mechanisms of manufacturing. Increased productivity achieved by this revolution supports a larger population along with an increased consumption of goods. And when the economy is healthy and in balance, automation tends to provide an increase in leisure time, with greater opportunities for arts, education, and human fulfillment.

See also Computer software, data base management; Control systems, management; Human factors engineering; Office automation; Production/operations management; Robotics.

REFERENCES

Bright, James R.: *Automation and Management,* Graduate School of Business Administration, Harvard University, Cambridge, Mass., 1958.

Diebold, John: *Automation: The Advent of the Automatic Factory,* D. Van Nostrand, New York, 1952.

Harrington, Joseph, Jr.: *Understanding the Manufacturing Process,* Marcel-Dekker, New York, 1984.

————, *Computer Integrated Manufacturing,* Robert E. Krieger, Melbourne, Fla., 1979.

JOSEPH HARRINGTON, JR., *Consulting Engineer*

B

Behavior Modeling

In the 1980 *Annual Review of Psychology*, Goldstein summarizes more than 300 of the most important research articles on training that appeared during the 1970s. He concludes that "during this decade, the method that has generated the most excitement is clearly behavioral role modeling."

Many major corporations are teaching managers to translate motivational theory into action successfully through the process known as "behavior modeling." Modeling was originally confined to laboratory studies of social development in children (see Bandura). Applications of the process in industry in the early 1970s achieved behavior change that traditional management development training designs seldom approached. Hundreds of companies are now using the approach to teach skills in such areas as supervision, selling, sales management, negotiation, interviewing, and performance appraisal.

Behavior modeling is based on a fundamental learning principle: After people are shown an example of an effective behavior and are given the opportunity to practice that behavior in a reinforcing environment, they are better equipped to adopt the behavior for their own use.

Six Basic Steps. Outwardly, the methodology is simple. Rosenbaum (1982) outlined the six basic steps used to provide the participant with new interpersonal skills and the confidence to apply these skills in specific on-the-job situations (see Fig. B-1).

1. *Cognitive presentation.* The initial phase of the developmental process involves the presentation of a series of basic concepts about the key skills to be learned and the steps necessary to implement them in a problem situation. This process occurs in a typical lecture fashion and is designed to provide the conceptual base necessary to facilitate permanent behavior change. It is during this phase that general principles are introduced through lecture, videotape, and workbook exercises. These are central mediating principles or rationales around which a host of more specific skills cluster.

2. *Modeling.* In groups of six to nine, supervisors view films or videotapes in which a model supervisor is shown effectively dealing with an employee in an effort to improve or maintain the subordinate's performance (or salespeople see a salesperson interacting with a customer, someone in personnel interviewing an applicant, or some other similar scene). Each film presents an

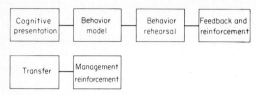

FIG. B-1 Workshop model.

8- to 10-minute demonstration of specific action steps. Instead of making a broad generalization, the model shows at least one effective way of dealing with the situation. Step-by-step guidelines are provided, and the film or videotape shows situations containing real-life problems, not hypothetical situations, with which the participants can identify immediately.

Goldstein and Sorcher (1974) point out that trainees will identify more readily with the person to be imitated (the model) if this individual (a) exhibits competence or expertise, (b) is in a high-status position, (c) controls resources desired by the observer, and (d) is rewarded. Field testing has shown that trainees identify best with models who are shown in familiar surroundings as opposed to unrelated work environments. For the model to have maximum impact, observers should be able to identify with the situation or problem, the surroundings, the language, and the people displayed in the model.

3. *Behavior rehearsal.* Trainees participate in intensive practice and rehearsal of the behavior demonstrated by the models. In fact, the greatest percentage of the training time is spent in skill practice sessions. Most theory-based interpersonal-skills training does not provide the participants with specific information about what to do and also falls short in permitting them to learn how to do it. Behavior rehearsal, or structured role-playing, allows the trainees to practice a new behavior pattern in increasingly difficult situations. Participants thus develop confidence in its use before they are back on the job and are expected to use it.

4. *Feedback and reinforcement.* Praise, approval, encouragement, and attention are all examples of social reinforcers that a trainee receives from the trainer and other trainees as her or his behavior increasingly resembles that of the model. But at no time is the trainee instructed to use only the behavior being learned when handling the situation being depicted. Each pattern is represented as an alternative that should be considered. It is added to the participant's behavioral repertoire, since research indicates that a key ingredient of effective interpersonal behavior is flexibility—the ability to choose a way to cope successfully with a given situation.

The trainee receives immediate feedback on how successfully the behavior is being used and at what point it should be transferred to the job. The confidence of the supervisor, salesperson, negotiator, or other trainee in his or her ability to use the new behavior is built through practice and positive reinforcement in the classroom setting. Videotaping the behavior rehearsals effectively aids the feedback and reinforcement processes.

5. *Transferring training to the job.* The principles of transfer enhancement are emphasized throughout the training period. For example:

- The training groups are kept relatively small (no more than nine in a group).

- In addition to specific behaviors, the general principles of the subject being addressed (sales, supervision, etc.) are practiced; the interpersonal skills taught are determined by the needs of the company. Eventually, participants are able to apply the general principles to new situations that were never modeled.

- Between classes, participants are assigned homework designed to help them transfer the behavior practiced during the training sessions to their jobs. At the start of each training period, the participants describe, discuss, and demonstrate their experiences in applying behavior routines learned previously. This permits further shaping and reinforcement of the training for application on the job.

6. *Management reinforcement.* Managers of the trainees are trained in reinforcement techniques and maintain responsibility for coaching and counseling the trainees and reinforcing their use of their newly learned skills.

Practice and Application. It is important to recognize that while there is overwhelmingly positive behavior change from the observation of a model, this is only one part of a system of learning. Goldstein and Sorcher point out that "modeling alone is insufficient because, though it yields many positive effects, they are often not enduring effects." The value of rehearsal, feedback, and the rapid transfer of newly learned skills to the job should not be underestimated.

Expanding the Application. Behavior modeling, a training technique originally introduced to industry to teach supervisors to handle people better, is being applied successfully in increasingly diverse situations:

- Bankers are developing skills that are vital for effective customer service, marketing leadership, and increasing sales.

- Buyers are learning how to negotiate effectively with vendors.

- Sales managers are acquiring coaching skills that are essential for managing today's salesperson effectively.

- Salespeople are learning critical selling skills directly related to their specific product or service.

- Specialized applications of modeling have included meeting management, supervision of safety, career counseling, employment interviewing, attitude survey feedback, union avoidance, business and social skills training for disadvantaged youths, and telemarketing skills for telephone sales agents.

Verified Results. Although behavior modeling has been applied in industry only for the past decade, significant quantitative data attest to its validity in effecting improved performance levels. For example:

1. Studies of plant efficiency and effectiveness showed that workers reporting to trained supervisors increased their average daily production 25 percent more than control groups.

2. Salespeople trained in behavior modeling programs have increased order flow, retail positioning of products, and the quality of distribution more than untrained and "traditionally" trained sales groups.

3. In general, users of behavior modeling report significant changes in on-the-job behavior as well as in organizational improvement. Participants at all levels of the organization tend to react enthusiastically to the learning design and welcome the practical, skills-building emphases of the training.

The record so far suggests that we have developed a meaningful learning model based on sound learning theory and research. With continued intensive work-related research, behavior modeling may avoid the faddism that has typified other interpersonal-skills training programs.

See also Assertiveness training; Conference leadership; Development and training, Employee; Development and training, management; Discipline; Motivation in organizations.

REFERENCES

Bandura, A.: *Social Learning Theory*, Prentice-Hall, Englewood Cliffs, N.J., 1977.

Goldstein, A. P., and M. Sorcher: *Changing Supervisor Behavior*, Pergamon Press, Elmsford, N.Y., 1974.

Rosenbaum, B. L.: *How to Motivate Today's Workers*, McGraw-Hill, New York, 1982.

BERNARD L. ROSENBAUM, *MOHR Development, Inc.*

Boards of Directors

The *board of directors* is the highest level of management in the modern corporation. Over three-fourths of the state laws of the United States under which corporations are chartered require corporations to be managed by a board of directors. Although corporations are legal entities with attributes of their own, actual persons, such as directors, are responsible for their management.

Board members are elected by stockholders to represent them as a group. Legally they are not agents required to carry out the direct orders of stockholders. They are more akin to elected government officials, such as members of Congress, who represent their constituents but make decisions according to their own best judgment.

Authority and Responsibilities of the Board. It is the board's duty to manage the business in the best interests of the owners, whom they represent, but it also has the responsibility of recognizing the associated interests of other groups, such as employees, customers, and the public.

Directors have the necessary authority to run the corporation, subject to the restrictions of state and federal laws and limitations of the corporate charge and bylaws. These limitations, however, are very general, giving the board a wide scope of authority. Charters typically specify broad and general corporate purposes, and except for cases in which stockholder approval is required, boards have the power to change the bylaws.

Directors are guided by procedures for governance and operations by corporate bylaws, which typically include statements concerning the rights of stockholders; the powers, qualifications, and responsibilities of the directors; and the procedures for conducting corporation affairs. Directors are free to exercise their best judgment in running the company, but they must do so lawfully and prudently in the best interests of the owners.

The Balance of Interests. While the primary responsibility for owner (stockholder) interests is widely recognized, boards must also face demand and pressures from other interested parties, such as employees, customers, and the public. Difficult decisions must be made where the various interests appear to be in conflict.

Two opposing views of these contending influences prevail: (1) that the sole responsibility is to owners and (2) that the board should take a balanced approach to the issues posed by the various interest groups involved. The first view is prevalent where the principal owners are also the top management group and are few in number and where the directors are "insiders" whose jobs depend on pleasing the owners. The second view, the most widely held, does not regard responsibilities to the other groups as necessarily incompatible with stockholder interests. This approach recognizes that acting in socially responsible ways and in awareness of the interests of the various claimant groups is feasible and desirable. In the main, this balanced view is generally consistent with actions in the best interests of the owners.

Specific Tasks, Duties, and Responsibilities. The board is responsible for six major activities: trusteeship, determination of objectives, selection of officers and executives, approval of plans and policies, decision making, and monitoring of results.

Trusteeship. A central responsibility, known as trusteeship, is to safeguard and husband the corporation's assets and resources and to use them in the best interests of the stockholders. The idea of trusteeship includes the balanced view noted above, in which obligations to society and to other constituent groups are regarded as consistent with the primary obligations to stockholders.

Objectives. Boards also determine the corporation's general objectives and a number of corporationwide specific objectives. Boards identify and authenticate major goals, providing priorities and clarification of these goals. They are concerned with the corporation's long-term stability and growth and with a consequent need to keep objectives matched to changing conditions inside the organization and arising from the environment.

Selection of Officers and Executives. The board elects the corporate officers and assigns their general responsibilities. This is the beginning of the delegation process. Some officers are primarily concerned with board matters; most are delegated operating responsibilities through the chief executive officer. Most boards allow the chief executive officer a wide scope for choosing those who serve under him or her, but may reserve a ratifying power over the selection of all key executives who may or may not be elected as officers.

Plans and Policies. Major plans and policies having corporationwide significance are approved by the board. This has the effect of attesting to their importance and reinforcing the commitments of operating managers. Budgets are developed to assist in planning and controlling the company's activities.

Decisions. Major decisions result in the adoption of objectives, plans, and policies. In addition, major operating decisions are often made. Such major decisions as mergers, expansions, or commitments of investment capital often represent critical turning points for the company. Resource allocation decisions are extremely vital. These include declaring dividends, investing profits, and acquiring or disposing of assets. Major organizational design problems are often decided by boards.

Monitoring of Results. To fulfill their responsibilities for the stability, success, and welfare of the corporation, boards continuously exercise control through reviewing operating results, executive performance, market and economic conditions, and the extent to which objectives, plans, and policies are succeeding. The monitoring of production, financial, and other performance data is important, as is the surveillance of conditions in the external environment. Reviews of financial statements, cash position, revenues and expenses, and budgetary control are needed. Financial and management audits are conducted.

Board Operations. The chairperson of the board is the key executive in board operations and is responsible for planning board meetings, agendas, and proposals. He or she has a leadership role and a strong voice in determining the matters that come before the board for action. The chairperson may also be the chief executive officer, but if not, the president and/or the chief executive officer share a joint work load with the chairperson. Sometimes the position is an honorary one or one for which contacts with outside agencies or groups are important.

Running board meetings requires parliamentary and conference-discussion leading skills, as well as substantive knowledge of the problems discussed and the information being provided. As leader, the chairperson must deal with a diversity of persons and interests, guide deliberations, handle arguments and dissent, and cope with conflict and divisiveness.

Such matters as the frequency and duration of meetings, the obtaining and handling of information and staff support work, and the use of committees are important for board operations. Boards generally meet quarterly, but in large firms they may meet monthly, and in small firms, annually.

Directors. There is no standard ideal size for the board of directors. The needs of companies vary, and the board size may depend on the range of experience and talent required. Five to six members appears to be a minimum, while fifteen members approaches the upper limit of most boards. The board needs to be large enough to provide the managerial capabilities required but compact enough to function as a reasonably efficient committee.

Time Requirements. Most board members are part time, but some large companies utilize full-time directors. In addition to attending regular board meetings, directors may perform committee work and must have additional time for studying documents and reports in preparation for board meetings. Directors must be able to devote enough time to their responsibilities to make an effective contribution.

Qualifications. Boards need a variety of capabilities, depending on the nature of the company and its operations. Experience, intelligence, proven capability for making judgments, and analytical skills are highly important for all directors. In addition, particular directors may be chosen for their expertise in certain areas of management. It is important for a board to be composed of a good balance of the capabilities needed. A record of success, maturity, community standing, and interests in the company or industry also are often taken into account in choosing directors. Other qualities of extreme importance include those of independence—the willingness and ability to speak out on issues of importance, of character, of integrity, and of ethical behavior.

Insiders versus Outsiders. A much-debated issue regarding directors is what the balance should be between inside and outside directors. An inside director is generally defined as one having a full-time employment commitment with the firm. An outside director does not have a full-time appointment with the firm. Too much reliance on inside directors runs the risks of inbreeding and lack of independence. However, inside directors do rate high on commitment and on knowledge of the company and its operations. Outside directors, on the other hand, can be relatively independent and bring into consideration fresh points of view and the influence of outside factors, although they may lack intimate knowledge of the firm's operations and may also be overcommitted by serving on other boards.

In recent years there has been substantial pressure in corporations to elect some board members as representatives of interest groups, such as consumers, employees, or the general public. While many are ready to acknowledge the wisdom and benefit of having at least some outside directors, the practice of requiring boards to have directors representing nonstockholder groups is not widely accepted. In a sense, an outside director, if truly independent, can be viewed as representative of the public interest.

Compensation. Board memberships generally have a high status in society. Directors may be paid by per diem fees or by annual retainers. Some companies also provide directors with fringe benefits, such as company-paid insurance programs and reimbursement for travel and other expenses.

Legal Liabilities. Those accepting directorship appointments thereby are subject to complex legal obligations and legal risks. Before accepting an appointment on a board of directors, the individual should consult a personal attorney for a review of obligations and possible risks.

See also Audit, management; Boards of directors, legal liability guidelines; Ethics, managerial; Management, definitions of; Management theory, science and approaches; Organization structures and charting; Ownership, legal forms of; Shareholder relations.

REFERENCES

Brown, Courtney: *Putting the Corporate Board to Work,* Macmillan, New York, 1976.
Mueller, Robert K.: *Board Score: How to Judge Board Worthiness,* D. C. Heath, Lexington, Mass., 1982.
Vance, Stanley C.: *Corporate Leadership: Boards, Directors, and Strategy,* McGraw-Hill, New York, 1983.

DALTON E. McFARLAND, *University of Alabama in Birmingham*

Boards of Directors, Legal Liability Guidelines

General Corporate Board Liability

Upon accepting a position as a corporate board member, a director assumes various legal duties and responsibilities, the noncompliance of which could result in civil and/or criminal liability. A professionally managed company should maintain standards for measuring and evaluating board efficiency. This is especially important because personal knowledge of a wrongdoing or an intent to violate the law is not always necessary to establish board liability. Directors are not the *agents* of the stockholders who elected them, but rather their fiduciaries, because they manage the corporation on their behalf by exercising independent business judgments. Hence, the directors must act within the common-law *fiduciary duties* of due care and loyalty.

Federal statutory laws also provide liability exposure to a director. For example, a corporation that violates antitrust laws or a corporation with registered securities with the Securities and Exchange Commission (SEC) that violates its laws and regulations might cause its directors to be subject to a lawsuit. Federal laws, such as the Employee Retirement Income Security Act and the Foreign Corrupt Practices Act, that require board compliance will also be discussed in this article.

Directors can be sued by the corporation or, if it refuses to bring suit, by the stockholders in a derivative shareholders' action. The SEC, other federal agencies, and the state attorney general's office may also sue the directors for wrongdoing and in some instances prosecute them for criminal conduct with resulting fines and/or imprisonment if they are convicted. Board members may not act contrary to the articles of organization and the bylaws of the corporation. In some instances stockholder approval of board action, such as increasing authorized stock or approving a corporate merger, is necessary. Judgments on the declaration of dividends and appointment of corporate officers are primary board duties. In view of this vast liability exposure, based on the common-law duties of the board as a fiduciary, state law, administrative regulatory laws, and federal statutory laws, directors are obtaining liability insurance to indemnify their conduct.

Common-Law Duties of Directors as Fiduciaries

The legal relationship between the directors and the stockholders is that of a fiduciary. This relationship is based on the function of a director who manages the corporation on behalf of the stockholders rather than under their control. Although the directors exercise independent business judgments, they owe the shareholders the common-law fiduciary duties of due care and loyalty.

State statutory corporate laws generally define the *director's duty of care* as one similar to that cited in the 1983 *Revised Model Business Corporation Act,* sec. 8.30 [2 and 3], which states: "with the care an ordinary prudent person in a like position would exercise under similar circumstances; and when exercising his business judgment, with the belief, premised on a rational basis, that his decision is in the best interest of the corporation." The courts refer to this duty of care as the *business judgment rule.* Under this rule a director will not be held personally liable for an honest and rationally informed business judgment that turns out to be wrong. The American Law Institute in *Tentative Draft No. 1, Principles of Corporate Governance and Structure: Restatement and Recommendations, 1983,* sec. 4.01 (d), suggests a "safe harbor" for directors, providing they made an *informed rational decision* based on a *reasonable inquiry* with respect to the business judgment and acted in *good faith* without a *disabling conflict of interest.* Hence, directors are not liable for honest mistakes in exercising a business judgment.

A *conflict of interest* can arise when a director is a member of interlocking boards or makes a contract with the corporation on which he or she serves. State statutory laws generally allow such a contract if it is fair and reasonable to the corporation and the "conflicting" relationship is *disclosed* to the corporate board and/or stockholders if they must approve the contract. Courts place the burden on the director to prove that the contract was fair and reasonable and that adequate disclosure was made to the appropriate parties.

The *corporate opportunity doctrine* prohibits directors from using their position of trust with the stockholders to make a profit for themselves. The fiduciary *duty of loyalty* requires directors to make a full disclosure to the board and/or stockholders and obtain their approval before seizing a self-serving corporate opportunity. Failure to do so will result in a director being held liable to the corporation and/or the stockholders for any profits made from taking advantage of the corporate opportunity.

Federal Statutory Duties of Directors

Various federal laws subject directors to both civil and criminal liability for their violation. Some of the more common federal laws that expand the liability of directors beyond the common law follow.

Employee Retirement Income Security Act of 1974. ERISA extends the common-law fiduciary duties that a director owes to shareholders to employees and the beneficiaries of their pension plans. Although the board can assign to a committee the administration of the plan, it cannot delegate the responsibility of reviewing their findings to ensure that the administration of the plan is performed in a reasonable manner. Directors must become adequately informed about the administrative policies of employee plans and carefully review their periodic reports. The U.S. Department of Labor, the plan employee, and employees' beneficiaries may sue the directors for violating their fiduciary duties as defined by the statute.

Securities Exchange Act of 1934. The SEA includes a director within its definition of an "insider" as one who may have access to confidential corporate information, allowing her or him to make a profit by the purchase or sale of the corporate securities. If the company has registered securities, the directors must file a report with the SEC at the end of any month in which they purchase or sell the corporate securities. The corporation or its shareholders may sue the directors as "insiders" to recover *short-swing* profits made within a 6-month period caused by the sale or purchase of company securities.

Foreign Corrupt Practices Act of 1977. FCPA requires corporations that report to the SEC to comply with specific *accounting provisions* and prohibits any interstate business association, including those not subject to the act, from engaging in *corrupt practices* with foreign officials. Rule 13B2-2 provides, in part, that "no director . . . shall make a materially false or misleading statement, or omit to state, or cause another person to omit to state, any material fact . . . to an accountant in connection with any required audit or any preparation of a required document or report."

The antibribery section of the act applies to directors of any corporation engaged in interstate commerce that corruptly pay any official of a foreign government for the purpose of influencing any decision in order to obtain or retain business. Violation of the act may subject a director to civil as well as criminal liability. Conviction of a director for a willful violation of the act could mean a fine of up to $10,000 and/or imprisonment for up to 5 years.

Audit Committee

Any company with a listing on the New York Stock Exchange (NYSE) must maintain "an Audit Committee comprised solely of directors independent of management. . . . Directors who are affiliates of the company or officers or employees of the company or its subsidiaries would not be qualified for Audit Committee membership." The audit committee should recommend to management the accounting firm to be employed as the independent auditor. Its primary responsibility is to review the corporate annual and quarterly financial statements filed with the SEC or other regulatory bodies as well as those issued to shareholders and creditors. Failure of a corporate board whose company is listed on the NYSE to install an audit committee would subject it to liability. The board may, in discharging its duties, rely on committee information and reports, providing that the directors reasonably believe the committee is "reliable, competent, and disinterested."

Indemnification of Corporate Board

In view of the potential liability of a board member, companies are providing indemnification for any costs incurred by a director exercising his or her duties. State statutory laws commonly provide authorization for corporate indemnification. The Delaware statute, sec. 145(a), states in part that a director may be indemnified if he "acted in good faith and in a manner he reasonably believed to be in or not opposed to the best interests of the corporation, and with respect to any criminal action or proceeding, had no reasonable cause to believe his conduct was unlawful." A company will often purchase directors' insurance coverage from a third-party insurance carrier to fund this potential indemnification.

Suggested Liability Guidelines

A professionally managed company should establish guidelines to assist the board in avoiding a lawsuit. Keep in mind that directors are not liable for honest mistakes under the business judgment rule. However, a reasonable inquiry into transactions before the board, although not requiring a detailed inspection of day-to-day activity, does obligate the directors to monitor corporate affairs and policies.

A typical law compliance program for a large, publicly held corporation should include (1) an antitrust compliance program with a company statement on antitrust compliance, (2) an SEC compliance program, and (3) a monitoring program to alert directors of any managerial problems that could affect the company. The corporate bylaws should clearly define the function and duties of the board members and each of its committees. Detailed board minutes of frequent meetings should be recorded and distributed to board members reflecting prudent inquiry into committee reports evidencing directors' due diligence. Advance agendas should be distributed to members that will allow them to make astute recommendations. The minutes should make reference to a dissenting director's objection to a resolution as a permanent record in the event of a subsequent lawsuit. Corporate opportunity and conflicts of interest should be disclosed in writing to the board. The minutes should reflect the resolution of the conflict and, where appropriate, stockholders' approval. Compliance with federal regulatory agencies should be ensured by following an outside legal counsel's advice. Directors may rely upon legal counsel, providing they read and review documents before their approval.

Boards are clearly accountable for directorial management. Any conduct short of intense professional monitoring of managerial oversight will be viewed as a violation of a director's duty. Contemporary corporate governance demands of a professionally managed company a corporate board fully accountable to management, to the stockholders, and to federal and state regulatory agencies.

REFERENCES

Commentaries on Corporate Structure and Governance, The American Law Institute, Philadelphia, 1979.

1983 Revised Model Business Corporation Act, American Bar Foundation, Chicago, 1983.

Principles of Corporate Governance and Structure: Restatement and Recommendations, The American Law Institute, Philadelphia, 1982.

GERALD R. FERRERA, *Bentley College*

Brands and Brand Names

Brand names are to products or services what personal names are to human beings. They distinguish or set apart each individual product offering. They are the means by which users or purchasers can identify a product or service of a specific origin, with a reputation or characteristic which is unique or distinct.

Brand names differ from generic names. A *generic name* denotes a category of product or service. A *brand name* identifies a particular version of a generic product or service offered by a particular seller. The analogy to human beings is useful here also. The term *woman* applies to a certain category of human being. *Sue Smith* identifies a specific individual within the generic category of *woman*. The word *automobile* denotes a generic product, a vehicle with four wheels usually propelled by an internal combustion engine. The words *Ford Thunderbird* denote a specific version of an automobile offered by the Ford Motor Company.

Value of Brand Names. The reputation, or image, of brands potentially has great value to users and purchasers as well as to those who offer the product or service. Here, again, a fundamental distinction emerges between a brand name and a generic name. A *generic name* denotes a category of product or service which may be defined in tangible terms (dimensions, chemical makeup, performance). A *brand name* stands for something else: It represents the total image or reputation of the company or individual offering the product or service. Two different brands may, in fact, apply to products or services which, by tangible measurements, are identical. Yet users may view them differently for a host of reasons. They may bear different prices. They may be sold through different outlets. The advertising and promotion may differ in quantity or quality. Users' experience in obtaining service or adjustments may vary.

Thus, the brand or brand name synthesizes the entire complex of physical and psychological factors that affect attitudes toward the product or service which bears that name. Just as Sue Smith stands for a specific image or reputation among those who know her, so, too, Ford Thunderbird evokes an attitudinal response among individuals who have an awareness of that product. The value companies place on a name was shown during the breakup of A.T.&T. A major decision by the court was whether the name "Bell" (and its trademark) would go to the parent companies or the operating companies.

Families of Names. Brand names, like human names, may embrace an entire family, or they may apply to an entity within the family. In the case of Sue Smith, Sue is an individual in the Smith family. Thunderbird is an individual entity in the Ford family of automobiles.

Collective Policy. One aspect of brand policy is a decision to use the family name on all products offered by a seller, such as Del Monte for canned fruits and vegetables. Another decision is whether differing products of the same seller should bear brand names in addition to the family name or be given a combination of a family name and a generic name. For example, under the family name of General Electric, the General Electric Company offers General Electric washers, General Electric refrigerators, General Electric irons, and so on. On the other hand, a company like Sunbeam Electric offers its electric mixer under the name Sunbeam Mixmaster rather than Sunbeam mixer. Eastman offers Kodak Instamatic cameras.

Modified Policy. Sometimes the family name is dropped altogether. Certain products or services may be so different in nature or character that it would be unwise or inappropriate to apply the family name. (This policy can be compared with that of individuals who enter the public forum as actors and decide their family name is inappropriate for the personality they are selling the public and therefore adopt a different name for their public life.) Classic examples of this are found in the products of the Johnson & Johnson Company. The Johnson & Johnson family of products

includes a wide line of health and beauty aids, such as Johnson & Johnson bandages and Johnson & Johnson baby powder. Under this family name are products which also bear their own brand names, such as Johnson & Johnson Bandaids.

Concealment Policy. The options may extend further. For example, Johnson & Johnson has also elected to offer a series of products which carry no Johnson & Johnson identity. These include feminine hygiene products sold under the brand name Modess by a subsidiary known as the Personal Products Company. They include pressure-sensitive tapes sold under the name Texcel by a subsidiary known as the Industrial Tape Company; and they include specialty products for women sold under the Ortho name by the Ortho Products Company. This brand strategy is based on the belief that it is more beneficial to conceal the family relationship of these products than to disclose it.

A reason for this decision may be the belief that these products are so different from the basic family line that they would not benefit from the family name and would have greater acceptance with a name more suited to the character of the product or service. The reasoning may be the other way, of course. It may be felt that some products might adversely affect the reputation or image of the basic family product members. If so, it would be better that users or purchasers did not know of the association between the two.

Selecting Brand Names. Several options are open to a marketer in selecting a brand name.

Personal Identification. When marketing was less sophisticated (and perhaps less competitive) than today, many individuals bestowed their personal family names on their companies and on their products. Henry Ford and Walter Chrysler did so. B. F. Goodrich and Harvey Firestone gave their names to tire companies. But personal names are not always easy to pronounce. They seldom carry an image that relates to the product being sold. Sometimes they are less than appealing. The advertising agency which was asked to promote a line of jams and jellies called Smucker's felt its client's name was more of a handicap than an advantage. To turn this handicap into a benefit, it coined the slogan, "With a name like Smucker's, it has to be good," implying that the product was so superior it overcame the name.

Generic Implications. Some entrepreneurs saw that there was far more to be gained by preempting a name with broad generic implications than by trying to glorify their personal names. These marketing-oriented businesspeople opted for corporate cognomens, like The General Electric Company, Radio Corporation of America, International Harvester Corporation, and International Business Machines.

Value by Association. Sometimes companies were named after famous inventors to lend an aura of scientific authority to the products or services. Bell

Telephone System is a widely known example. Consolidated Edison in New York and Commonwealth Edison in Chicago are regional utilities capitalizing on the name of the famous inventor. When the Seiberling brothers decided to enter the rubber manufacturing business, they concluded that the name Seiberling stood for nothing in rubber, but Charles Goodyear was renowned for discovering vulcanization of rubber. So in his honor they named their new company The Goodyear Tire and Rubber Company. They judged correctly that while a name like Seiberling might eventually acquire a reputation for outstanding rubber products, their marketing task would be eased with a name like Goodyear that would readily be perceived as standing for quality and innovation in the types of products they were selling.

Investigative Selection. As products proliferate and brand names multiply, the hunt for names that will be appropriate, favorable, and distinctive becomes more difficult but more necessary. This hunt has spawned a corps of specialists, both as consultants and within the marketing concerns themselves. These specialists utilize psychologists, consumer researchers, computers, graphic designers, and allied professionals and techniques to solve the brand name equation.

Abstract versus Relevant Names. A constant dilemma confronts those charged with finding the right name: If the name is descriptive enough to convey the product characteristics quickly, it may not be protectable under U.S. trademark law. Corporate executives frequently seek an abstract name, like Kodak, which is distinctive yet has wide recognition as denoting a brand of photographic products. Such a choice tends to overlook or minimize the fact that a major marketing investment was required to give Kodak the status it achieved.

Given the enormous levels of advertising required today to give meaning to abstract words, a marketer who can find a product name with meaning can get off the starting blocks faster in the race against competition. Two refrigerator makers made such an effort. One named his product after Lord Kelvin, who discovered the principles on which refrigeration is based. While Kelvinator may have had meaning to some learned prospective buyers, Frigidaire probably said it more quickly to those who wanted to get rid of their drippy iceboxes. Finding names like Frigidaire which are protectable is an arduous task, however.

So, despite examples of success in finding distinctive names which project correct images of products or services, many marketers have adopted a policy of creating names which, like Kodak, are meaningless in themselves. Du Pont has stated that it follows such a policy, although its adoption of the names Zerone and Zerex for antifreeze are apparent exceptions. Names for synthetic fibers such as Dacron, Qiana, and Kevlar—which indicate neither the corporate origin nor the generic nature of the product—are an outgrowth of this policy. In contrast, Eastman Kodak's name for its polyester fiber Kodel indicates an effort to associate the product with the parent Kodak company.

Trademarks. Trademarks are synonymous with brand names. They are not to be confused with trade names. *Trade names* are sometimes called "commercial names," for they represent the name of the company that makes the product. The name of the product is its brand or trademark. For example, General Motors Corporation makes Cadillacs.

There are exceptions—Johnson & Johnson and Polaroid are examples—where the trade name is the same or is the major part of the trademark. In general, however, the trade name identifies the company, and the trademark or brand is the name of the product. A trade name, unlike a brand name, cannot be registered. Handled separately, as in the Johnson & Johnson case where it is used on products as a trademark, it can qualify for registration for the company's products.

The visual treatment of a brand or trademark plays a vital role in making that name distinctive and meaningful. The use of design, including logotypes, lettering styles, typefaces, package layout, and the like plays a key role in communicating the essence of the offering. (*See* Fig. B-2.) This is a marketing aspect which goes far beyond trademarks and trade names.

Legal Requirements. Distinction in the name is one means of legal protection for the name—but only one! Legal pitfalls abound for the unwary marketer who seeks to reserve for exclusive use a brand name for a company's product. Some marketers have lost the use of names which they believed to be well-established properties of their company. A classic case was Du Pont's loss of the rights to cellophane as a brand name for a variety of transparent packaging film. The courts ruled that by calling the product simply cellophane, with no generic designation, Du Pont had made the word *cellophane* a generic term. For this reason, it lost the rights to the word *cellophane,* and other producers could describe their product as cellophane. Since this ruling, users of brand names must accompany the name with a generic description of the product or service. *Frigidaire* is not enough. It must be a Frigidaire refrigerator. It is instructive that General Foods carefully guards against the name "Sanka" becoming generic for decaffeinated coffee by calling it "Sanka brand." It takes no such precautions with Brim, another of its decaffeinated brands.

Under U.S. trademark law, registration of a name is no guarantee of a right to its use. Prior use is a vital consideration, even though registration has not been accomplished. It is possible that some obscure local user will turn up, claiming infringement of rights. Ownership must also be preserved by regular use of the mark. In short, registration alone should not be

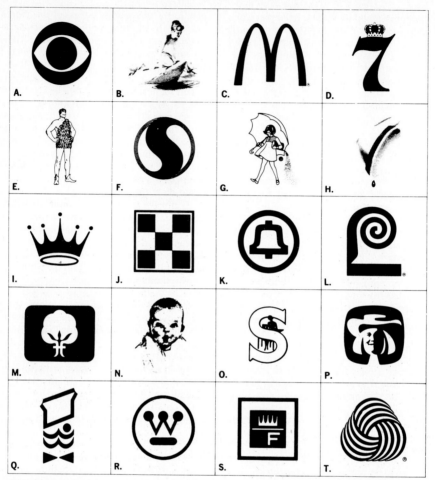

FIG. B-2 Examples of well-known trademarks: (A) CBS; (B) White Rock Psyche; (C) McDonald's arch symbol; (D) Seagram's 7 Crown; (E) Green Giant; (F) Safeway; (G) Morton International umbrella girl; (H) Maxwell House Division of General Foods cup and drop symbol; (I) Hallmark crown symbol; (J) Checkerboard square of Ralston Purina Co.; (K) bell symbol of American Telephone and Telegraph; (L) Lawrey's; (M) cotton bud symbol of Cotton Incorporated; (N) Gerber baby; (O) Singer Company; (P) Quaker Oats; (Q) Mister Donut; (R) Circle "W" of Westinghouse Electric Corp.; (S) Frigidaire crown symbol; (T) Woolmark of the Wool Bureau Inc. (Source: U.S. Trademark Association.)

relied on to protect a trademark. Not only is constant use important, but so is constant vigilance in challenging unauthorized use. Companies like Coca-Cola and Xerox police this territory intensively.

Private Brands. Throughout this entry, the term offered has been used to describe the ownership of the brand or brand name. This is because the ownership of the name may be vested in a variety of parties in the chain, from the original producers of the product or service to the final purchaser. It may be a manufacturer's brand, wholesaler's brand, or distributor's brand. The brand may be owned by one party

and rented, leased, or franchised to another party. A widespread example of this is found in the franchising of retail or service establishments, such as fast food restaurants or gasoline service stations.

The essential fact to keep in mind is that the owner of the brand is the party to whom the purchaser looks for satisfaction. Today, many so-called private brands exist. Generally this means that the brands are not owned by the manufacturer of the product but instead are owned by some reseller—either at the wholesale or at the retail level. This says nothing about the quality, the value, or the price of the product. Many examples may be found of private brands, retailers' brands, distributors' brands, or custom brands (or whatever they may be called) which sell for higher prices than manufacturers' brands. Exclusive retail shops, for example, frequently put their own labels on merchandise manufactured by others and obtain premium prices for such goods. The reason is clear. The consumer has great confidence in the establishment whose name is on the merchandise and feels the fashion or the quality will be superior. Therefore, the consumer does not insist on knowing the name of the manufacturer.

On the other hand, some consumers patronize establishments in which they have little confidence and are reluctant to purchase goods which do carry only the retailer's label and not the manufacturer's brand. They would like to resolve their dilemma by knowing the name of the manufacturer while still paying the low prices of the retailer. Having one's cake and eating it too is a common desire, and it exists in the world of brands.

To the extent that manufacturers of brands with high consumer acceptance also supply comparable products to private brands, and such merchandise is represented to consumers as being identical to the brand product, sales of the higher-priced brand product will suffer. A Gresham's law of brand policy might be stated as follows:

> To the extent that consumers perceive a lower-priced private brand to be from the same source and/or of the same quality as a higher-priced manufacturer's brand, the private brand will drive out the manufacturer's brand.

Outlook for Name Marketing. In the age of consumerism, there appears to be constant pressure to wipe out purchasing by brand and to foster purchasing of generically described merchandise. Yet closer examination suggests that brand buying is far from extinct. What is really occurring is that as product categories mature, more and more generic purchasing occurs. Products become commodities rather than specialties, and the progression from manufacturers' brands to private brands to no brands may occur.

But the market is constantly entered by new and distinctive products, by innovations in technology, fashion, or function. So new manufacturers' brands win popularity and achieve user preference. It is not atypical for the same people who purchase some items on a near-generic basis to pay significant premium prices for manufacturers' brands in other categories of products. The lesson for marketers is that purchasers continue to seek and pay for distinction and quality in products that are important in their ever-changing scale of values. Identifying those wants, fulfilling them, and labeling products with brand names that enable consumers to differentiate

their product selections thus continue to be important factors in marketing success.

See also Advertising concepts; Consumer behavior, managerial relevance of; Patents and valuable intangible rights; Product planning and development; Product and service pricing.

REFERENCES

Crowley, Ellen T.: *Trade Names Dictionary*, Gale Research, Detroit, 1976.

Oathout, John D.: *Trademarks: A Guide to Selection, Administration and Protection*, Scribner, New York, 1981.

Uhr, Ernest, and William Wallace: *Brands: A Selected Bibliography*, American Marketing Association, Chicago, 1972.

EDWIN H. SONNECKEN, *(Retired) Goodyear Tire & Rubber Company*

Budgeting, Capital

Expenditures for property, plant, and equipment, known as capital expenditures, are major decisions for most companies. The money involved is significant, the management time involved is significant, the investment is permanent and not easily reversible, and the company's future profitability is at stake. Therefore, the process of evaluating capital expenditures, called capital budgeting, is extremely important.

Capital Budgeting. *Capital budgeting* is a loosely used term to describe the process of allocating cash expenditures to investments which have a life longer than the operating period—normally 1 year. Traditionally, capital investments have been thought of as those involving *capitalized assets,* or property, plant, and equipment. Actually, property, plant, and equipment comprise only 30 to 40 percent of the total balance sheet assets of the typical manufacturing company. The percentage is greater for process industries and less for service-oriented industries. A certain amount of permanent investment in cash, receivables, and inventory is just as necessary to support an increase in sales, for example, as is the investment in property, plant, and equipment. If one commits $100,000 to buy a new machine to product "tingler," a new product just approved by the marketing department, the additional working capital requirements to support the new sales are just as much a part of the company's investment portfolio as is the new equipment.

Methods Used to Make Investment Decisions. A number of methods are used in business today to allocate a company's limited resources to the most profitable investments. The three most widely used methods are payback, accounting return, and present value.

73

Payback

Payback is a widely used measure in business for making investment decisions. Payback is computed as follows:

$$\frac{\text{Cash outlay}}{\text{Net annual cash inflow}} = x \text{ years}$$

For example, a company has an opportunity to invest $10,000 in a new machine which will result in annual cash savings of $2000. Payback is

$$\frac{\$10,000}{2000} = 5 \text{ years}$$

The same company has an opportunity to invest $10,000 in a piece of equipment which will return $2500 per year. If the company has only $10,000 to invest, presumably, using the payback criterion, it will take the opportunity to invest $10,000/2500 = 4-year payback in preference to the 5-year payback.

Advantages. Payback, given a cash outlay and a cash inflow, is easy to compute and easily understood. The worker on the shop floor understands that if one invests $5 and gets back $1 per year, the investment will be returned in 5 years. It is a measure which is especially suited to the early stages of an investment decision when the figures will necessarily be rough. For a project with a long life, the reciprocal of the payback gives a reasonable estimate of return on investment.

Disadvantages. Payback does not take into consideration the following:

1. Life of the project. For how many years will the cash flow be received? If $10,000 is invested and $2500 received each year for 4 years and if the machine lasts only 4 years, the investment is returned but nothing more. Payback gives return *of* investment, not return *on* investment.

2. Uneven cash flow. Many cash outlays are made in anticipation of future net cash inflows which vary from year to year. For example, there may be heavy start-up costs, and positive cash flow may not occur until several years in the future. Another project may generate high positive cash flow for 2 or 3 years and then decrease rapidly.

To illustrate these problems, consider the question of which of the projects detailed below is the best investment.

Each of these projects involves the outlay of $10,000 today in return for $14,000 over 5 years. Each project has a payback of 4 years. Common sense indicates that project B is the better investment because more dollars are received earlier. If project A continued to return cash flows of $4000 for years 6 to 10 and project B ends at year 5, one would not have to make too many calculations to know that project A would be preferable to project B. (*See* table on page 75.)

Accounting or Unadjusted Return

Many companies measure the performance of operating units by accounting return (unadjusted), better known as examining the *return on investment* (ROI). This is calculated as follows:

$$\text{ROI} = \frac{\text{income}}{\text{investment}}$$

There are a number of variations on this formula. Some companies use operating income (income before interest, taxes, and corporate overhead). Others use net income. Some use gross investment; others use net investment (after accumulated depreciation). Some use average investment.

ROI, however calculated, is also used in making investment decisions. For example, suppose a company has two investment alternatives:

1. $10,000 investment with $2000 income
2. $10,000 investment with $2500 income

The return on project 1 is $2000/$10,000 = 20 percent. The return on project 2 is $2500/$10,000 = 25 percent.

Using the accounting return as a measure, if the company had only $10,000 to invest, it would take project 2.

Advantages. The major advantage of the accounting return is that it is consistent with the way in which many managers have their performance measured. If managers are held responsible for and their bonus is based on getting a 15 percent ROI defined as income/investment, they will be inclined to take only investments which will deliver at least this return.

Disadvantages. The accounting return is similar to payback in that it does not consider the life of a project or the time flow of money. For example:

Cash flow \ Year	0	1	2	3	4	5
A	−$10,000 investment	+1000	+1000	+1000	+7000	+4000
B	−$10,000 investment	+3000	+3000	+3000	+1000	+4000

Cash flow \ Year	0	1	2	3	4	5	6 to 10
A	−$10,000	+$2500	+$2500	+$2500	+$2500	+$2500	0
B	−$10,000	+$2000	+$2000	+$3000	+$3000	+$2500	+$2500

The average return for both projects A and B is $2500/$10,000 = 25 percent. Project A has a life of 5 years, and project B has a life of 10 years. Again, common sense indicates that one would rather invest in project B. Yet the accounting return, literally applied, would indicate no difference between the two projects because each has an average return on investment of 25 percent.

Present Value

Analysis of capital expenditures, using the concept of present value, is widely used. It is a rather new approach, significant application in the United States being developed only in the late 1950s. Present value is the reciprocal of compound interest. The *present value* of a dollar to be received at a future date is the amount which, if invested today at a specified rate, would grow to a dollar at the future date. Present value is used when there is an opportunity to invest *x* dollars today in return for *y* dollars in the future.

In applying the present-value concept to capital investment decisions, four items are involved. They are:

1. Investment—cash outlay
2. Savings—cash inflow
3. Life—economic life of the project
4. Rate of return—rate desired or computed rate on a specific project

A discussion of each item follows.

Investment. Investment represents the incremental cash outlay required to install a machine, build a plant, or whatever the capital investment involves. For example, the cash outlay for a new machine to reduce labor costs would involve the purchase price of the equipment, the freight in, and the cost of installation and start-up.

Savings. Savings represents the incremental cash inflow to be realized by making the investment. This would be the additional cash flow associated with a new product. For a new machine, the savings would be the net labor and other savings to be realized if the machine is installed. The savings are computed for each year of the estimated useful life of the investment.

Life. The life to be used in computing the return on investment is the useful or economic life of the project. This would be the shortest of either the physical life, technological life, or market life. For example, if a special-purpose machine is purchased, its physical life may be estimated at 20 years and its technological life at 12 years, but if the product produced on the machine is estimated to have a life of only 10 years, the useful life is market life—10 years.

Rate of Return. A company must determine what an acceptable rate of return is on a specific project, a class of projects, or an overall rate. In computing rates of return, present-value tables are used. (*See* Tables B-1, B-2, B-3, and B-4.) Today, with computers easily available, the computer is often used to perform the calculations.

For example, assume the following situation.

Invest $10,000 in a laborsaving machine.

Labor savings = $2500 per year.

Useful life = 10 years.

Company desires 10 percent return on investment.

Machine will be depreciated for tax purposes over 10 years on a straight-line basis.

Company has 50 percent tax rate.

Machine will have no salvage value.

Annual Cash-Flow Computations. Compute the annual cash flow as follows (in this example, the savings are the same each year):

Cash in from labor savings	$2500
Cash out for taxes	750*
Annual net cash inflow	$1750

*Income subject to tax = $2500 − $1000 depreciation = $1500 at 50 percent = $750.

Rate-of-Return Calculations. The investment outlay is $10,000. The annual cash savings is $1750. A 10 percent return is desired. Look at Table B-4. Under the 10 percent column, read down to 10 years. The factor is 6.44. Multiply 6.44 by the annual savings of $1750. The result is $11,270. This means that the present value of the future cash inflows of $1750 per year is worth $11,270 today if a 10 percent return on investment is desired. Since the investment is only $10,000 and the present value of future inflows is $11,270, the investment would be made.

If the actual return is desired, divide the investment by the annual savings, $10,000/$1750 = 5.71. Again, look at Table B-4 and read across from year 10. The factor 5.71 is between 12 and 14 percent or about a 13 percent return on investment.

The future cash inflow discounted at 13 percent will be equal to the $10,000 investment today. Finding the rate of return, rather than discounting at a predetermined rate, is called the discounted cash-flow (DCF) method or the internal rate-of-return method.

Based on the example above, one can see that the mechanics of computing the rate of return on a project are relatively easy, given the information for the four items of investment, savings, life, and desired return.

Judgment. The difficult part in the decision-making process is the judgment involved in estimating the savings and the useful life and determining the rate of return desired. It is usually easier to get a fairly accurate figure for the investment—especially for equipment purchased when there is a firm price. Estimating savings for a cost-reduction project is easier than estimating savings for producing a new product.

Complexities. Variable Annual Savings. The cash savings generated from a capital project are seldom the same for each year of the life of the project. The savings may be different because of the use of accelerated depreciation, varying production levels, changes in tax rates, and other related items. The discounted cash-flow concept can be used with varying annual savings in two ways, as illustrated in the following example: A company has the opportunity to invest $1000 in one of four alternative projects. Each project has an estimated life of 6 years and a total return of $1800. The flow of the savings is as shown in this array.

Project C: 16 percent

Project D: 25 percent

Thus, project B gives the highest rate of return because more dollars are received in the early years.

Net Present Value. The *net present value* of an investment is the difference between future cash inflows discounted at a specified rate and the amount of the original investment. If a desired rate of return is known, the present value of the future flow can be determined. Assume the company wants a 20 percent return on investment. The present-value factors for 20 percent for each year are given in Table B-2. Applying these factors to the flows for the four projects, a present value for each project is as follows:

Project	Investment	Present value @ 20%	Net present value
A	$1000	$1092	$ 92
B	1000	1188	188
C	1000	996	−4
D	1000	1142	142

Using the net-present-value (NPV) approach, we see that project B has the highest net present value. Projects A, B, and D all have positive net present values, which means that these projects all return more than 20 percent. Project B has the highest NPV, which makes it the most attractive alternative. Project C, with a negative NPV, returns slightly less than 20 percent.

How would you rank projects if the original outlay is different? The one with the highest investment is likely to have the highest absolute dollar NPV but may have a smaller return. Projects of this nature can be ranked by the use of a profitability index.

Project \ Year	1	2	3	4	5	6	Total
A—$1000	+300	+300	+300	+300	+300	+300	$1800
B—$1000	+400	+400	+400	+200	+200	+200	$1800
C—$1000	+200	+200	+200	+400	+400	+400	$1800
D—$1000	+400	+400	+400	+0	+0	+600	$1800

Internal Rate of Return. One approach is to calculate the rate of return on each project. The *internal rate of return* is the rate which is being earned on the unamortized balance of the investment, such as the rate on a home mortgage. Using Table B-4, the calculation is made using a trial-and-error approach. What rate will bring the future cash flow back to $1000 today? The rates are

Project A: 25 + percent

Project B: 30 + percent

Profitability Index. The profitability index is applied as shown in the table on page 77, left column.

Project A has the lowest dollar NPV. It also has the lowest investment outlay. The index shows, however, that it has the highest return; i.e., the dollars received discounted at 20 percent are higher relative to the investment than the dollars received in either project B or project C.

Uneven Lives. In making a decision to replace an existing piece of equipment with a new one, the

Pro-ject	Invest-ment	Present value @ 20%	NPV @ 20%	Profitability index
A	$10,000	$11,200	$1200	$\dfrac{11,200}{10,000} = 1.12$
B	$20,000	$22,000	$2000	$\dfrac{22,000}{20,000} = 1.10$
C	$80,000	$84,000	$4000	$\dfrac{84,000}{80,000} = 1.05$

differential cash flows must be computed to arrive at the cash savings. If the existing equipment will last as long as the economic life of the proposed new piece of equipment, the cash flows are computed each year over the economic life. If, however, the existing equipment would have to be replaced before the end of the economic life of the new equipment, there would be no savings for the period after the existing equipment is replaced.

One way to handle this problem is to estimate a terminal value for the new equipment at the end of the comparable period of the two pieces of equipment. The least amount of the terminal value would be the tax savings on the write-off of the unallocated cost of the new equipment.

An example follows:

Postaudit

In practice, more emphasis has been put on the techniques of financial analysis than on an audit of a project after completion to see if it is in fact giving the estimated return. A good postaudit procedure should aid in refining the methodology used in appraising capital expenditures and help in isolating further investment opportunities.

There are a number of more specific reasons for an organized postaudit effort. Several reasons mentioned in Research Report 43, *Financial Analysis to Guide Capital Expenditures Decisions,* published by the National Association of Accountants, are:

1. To develop information about the pattern of error that is associated with different project organizations or organizational units which submit investment proposals.

2. To learn lessons from project exposure which can be used in increasing estimating proficiency and to improve estimating procedures.

3. To measure the ability of project engineers, planning analysts, or others who are directly concerned with project organization and evaluation.

4. To provide an overall framework of control so that project origination, approval, and implementation will be a disciplined management process; and to advise both manager and specialists in advance that their project work will be subject to review.

Year	1	2	3	4	5	6	7	8
Existing cash cost	$3000	3000	4000	4000	5000	Replace		
New cash cost	$1500	1500	1500	2000	2000	2000	2000	2000
Savings	$1500	1500	2500	2000	3000 + terminal value			

If the cost of the new piece of equipment is $8000 and it is depreciated over 8 years on a straight-line basis, there would be $3000 unallocated cost at the end of 5 years. The tax write-off terminal value, at a 50 percent tax rate, would be $1500 at the end of 5 years. Thus, savings to be compared with the $8000 investment would be the operating savings for 5 years plus the terminal value of the new equipment at the end of the fifth year.

MAPI. The Machinery and Allied Products Institute (MAPI) published a MAPI study and manual, *Business Investment Management,* in 1967. This book and accompanying charts have been widely used in business, especially for equipment-replacement problems. The approach used by MAPI approximates DCF return, yet it is based on short-cut procedures. The MAPI methodology handles the problem of uneven lives, which is more common in equipment-replacement situations than in most other capital budgeting problems.

Without a disciplined postaudit procedure, there is a tendency for project proposals to show a satisfactory return in order to justify the project when, in fact, the assumptions used may be faulty.

Lease/Purchase Analysis

Leasing on a long-term noncancelable basis is a means of financing an asset, e.g., building or equipment. A commitment to make lease payments on a long-term noncancelable lease is similar to a commitment to make payments on a term loan.

Most sophisticated lenders today look at a company's lease commitments as well as its other debt obligations in appraising the company's ability to carry additional debt.

After a company has made an investment decision

to obtain an asset, how does it decide whether it is cheaper to borrow and buy or to lease the asset? There are two basic approaches:

1. Determine the effective rate of interest paid for lease financing and compare this rate with the borrowing rate.

2. Determine the present-value cash outlay for leasing compared with the present-value outlay for purchasing.

In approaching a lease/purchase analysis, certain assumptions are made:

1. The lease commitment is substantially equivalent to a debt obligation.

2. Depreciation tax savings associated with the purchase alternative and tax savings associated with the lease payments are similar in their certainty. The certainty of tax savings depends upon the certainty that the company will pay taxes in the future. If it is highly probable that the company will pay income taxes in the future, the appropriate rate to use to discount both depreciation tax savings (under purchase) and after-tax lease payments (under leasing) is the company's after-tax interest cost of a term loan.

Effective Rate of Interest. In order to find the effective rate of interest paid for leasing, it is first necessary to compute the after-tax present-value cost of the purchase alternative. The following example will be used (see table at top of right column):

Cost of equipment	$100,000
Estimated life	15 years
Before-tax cost of borrowing	8%
Tax rate	50%
Depreciable life	20 years
Method of depreciation	Straight line
Lease payments for 15 years	$12,550 annually
Salvage value of equipment at end of 15 years (conservative)	-0-

The present-value cost of purchasing is

Cash outlay today	$100,000
Depreciation tax savings ($5000 × 0.50) = $2500 per year for 15 years, present value at 4%, factor 11.34 = 2500 × 11.34 =	(28,350)
Write-off of unallocated cost at end of 15 years = $25,000 × 0.50 × 0.55 (present-value factor for 4% at end of 15 years)	(6875)
Present-value cost of purchasing	$ 64,775

In order to find the effective cost of leasing, the rate which will bring the lease payments to a present value of $64,775 must be calculated.

Gross lease payment	$12,550
After-tax lease payment	$ 6275

What rate will bring 15 annual after-tax lease payments of $6275 back to $64,775?

TABLE B-1 Present Value of $1 Received at End of Year Indicated
Present value $= 1 \div (1 + i)^n$

End of year	2%	4%	6%	8%	10%	12%	14%	16%	18%	20%	25%	30%
1	.98	.96	.94	.93	.91	.89	.88	.86	.85	.83	.80	.77
2	.96	.92	.89	.86	.83	.80	.77	.75	.71	.70	.64	.59
3	.94	.89	.84	.79	.75	.71	.67	.64	.61	.58	.51	.46
4	.93	.86	.79	.73	.68	.63	.59	.55	.52	.48	.41	.35
5	.90	.82	.75	.68	.62	.57	.52	.47	.44	.40	.33	.27
6	.89	.79	.71	.63	.56	.51	.46	.41	.37	.34	.26	.20
7	.87	.76	.66	.59	.51	.45	.40	.36	.31	.28	.21	.16
8	.85	.73	.63	.54	.47	.41	.35	.30	.27	.23	.17	.12
9	.84	.70	.59	.50	.42	.36	.31	.26	.22	.19	.13	.10
10	.82	.68	.56	.46	.39	.32	.27	.23	.19	.16	.11	.07
11	.81	.65	.52	.43	.35	.29	.23	.20	.16	.14	.09	.06
12	.79	.63	.50	.40	.32	.26	.21	.17	.14	.11	.07	.04
13	.77	.60	.47	.37	.29	.23	.18	.14	.12	.09	.05	.03
14	.76	.58	.44	.34	.26	.20	.16	.13	.10	.08	.04	.03
15	.74	.55	.42	.31	.24	.18	.14	.11	.08	.07	.04	.02
20	.67	.45	.31	.22	.15	.10	.07	.05	.04	.03	.01	.01
25	.61	.37	.23	.15	.09	.06	.04	.03	.02	.01	*	*
30	.55	.31	.17	.10	.06	.03	.02	.01	.01	*	*	*
35	.50	.25	.13	.07	.04	.02	.01	.01	*	*	*	*
40	.45	.21	.10	.05	.02	.01	*	*	*	*	*	*

TABLE B-2   Present Value of $1 Received at Middle of Year Indicated
Present value $= 1 \div (1 + i)^{n-1/2}$

Middle of year	2%	4%	6%	8%	10%	12%	14%	16%	18%	20%	25%	30%
1	.99	.98	.97	.96	.95	.95	.94	.93	.92	.91	.89	.88
2	.97	.94	.92	.89	.87	.84	.82	.80	.78	.76	.72	.67
3	.95	.91	.86	.83	.79	.75	.72	.69	.66	.63	.57	.52
4	.93	.87	.82	.76	.72	.67	.63	.60	.56	.53	.46	.40
5	.92	.84	.77	.71	.65	.60	.55	.51	.48	.44	.37	.31
6	.90	.81	.72	.65	.59	.54	.49	.44	.40	.37	.29	.23
7	.88	.77	.69	.61	.54	.48	.43	.38	.34	.31	.23	.18
8	.86	.75	.64	.56	.49	.43	.37	.33	.29	.25	.19	.14
9	.84	.71	.61	.52	.44	.38	.33	.28	.24	.21	.15	.11
10	.83	.69	.58	.48	.40	.34	.29	.25	.21	.18	.12	.08
11	.81	.66	.54	.45	.37	.31	.25	.21	.18	.15	.10	.07
12	.80	.64	.51	.41	.33	.27	.22	.18	.15	.12	.07	.05
13	.78	.61	.48	.38	.30	.24	.20	.15	.12	.10	.06	.04
14	.76	.59	.46	.36	.28	.22	.17	.14	.11	.09	.05	.03
15	.75	.57	.43	.33	.25	.19	.15	.11	.09	.07	.04	.02
20	.68	.47	.32	.22	.16	.11	.08	.05	.04	.03	.01	*
25	.61	.38	.24	.15	.10	.06	.04	.03	.02	.02	*	*
30	.56	.31	.18	.10	.06	.04	.02	.01	.01	.01	*	*
35	.50	.26	.13	.07	.04	.02	.01	.01	*	*	*	*
40	.46	.21	.10	.05	.02	.01	*	*	*	*	*	*

$$\frac{64,775}{6275} = 10.33 \text{ factor for 15 years, or slightly more than 6\%}$$

Therefore, the after-tax cost of leasing is about 6 percent compared with an after-tax cost of borrowing of 4 percent. In this case it is more attractive to purchase.

Present-Value Outlays. Using the example given above, the net-present-value outlay if the asset is purchased is $64,775.

What is the present value of the lease payments?

TABLE B-3   Present Value of $1 Received at End of Each Year for N Years

Period in years	2%	4%	6%	8%	10%	12%	14%	16%	18%	20%	25%	30%
1	.98	.96	.94	.93	.91	.89	.88	.86	.85	.83	.80	.77
2	1.94	1.88	1.83	1.79	1.74	1.69	1.65	1.61	1.56	1.53	1.44	1.36
3	2.88	2.77	2.67	2.58	2.49	2.40	2.32	2.25	2.17	2.11	1.95	1.82
4	3.81	3.63	3.46	3.31	3.17	3.03	2.91	2.80	2.69	2.59	2.36	2.17
5	4.71	4.45	4.21	3.99	3.79	3.60	3.43	3.27	3.13	2.99	2.69	2.44
6	5.60	5.24	4.92	4.62	4.35	4.11	3.89	3.68	3.50	3.33	2.95	2.64
7	6.47	6.00	5.58	5.21	4.86	4.56	4.29	4.04	3.81	3.61	3.16	2.80
8	7.32	6.73	6.21	5.75	5.33	4.97	4.64	4.34	4.08	3.84	3.33	2.92
9	8.16	7.43	6.80	6.25	5.75	5.33	4.95	4.60	4.30	4.03	3.46	3.02
10	8.98	8.11	7.36	6.71	6.14	5.65	5.22	4.83	4.49	4.19	3.57	3.09
11	9.79	8.76	7.88	7.14	6.49	5.94	5.45	5.03	4.65	4.33	3.66	3.15
12	10.58	9.39	8.38	7.54	6.81	6.20	5.66	5.20	4.79	4.44	3.73	3.19
13	11.35	9.99	8.85	7.91	7.10	6.43	5.84	5.34	4.91	4.53	3.78	3.22
14	12.11	10.57	9.29	8.25	7.36	6.63	6.00	5.47	5.01	4.61	3.82	3.25
15	12.85	11.12	9.71	8.56	7.60	6.81	6.14	5.58	5.09	4.68	3.86	3.27
20	16.35	13.59	11.47	9.82	8.51	7.47	6.62	5.93	5.35	4.87	3.95	3.32
25	19.52	15.62	12.78	10.68	9.08	7.85	6.88	6.09	5.47	4.95	3.99	3.33
30	22.40	17.30	13.76	11.26	9.43	8.06	7.01	6.18	5.52	4.98	4.00	3.33
35	25.00	18.67	14.49	11.65	9.64	8.18	7.07	6.21	5.54	4.99	4.00	3.33
40	27.36	19.80	15.04	11.92	9.78	8.25	7.11	6.23	5.55	5.00	4.00	3.33

TABLE B-4 Present Value of $1 Received at Middle of Each Year for *N* Years

Period in years	2%	4%	6%	8%	10%	12%	14%	16%	18%	20%	25%	30%
1	.99	.98	.97	.96	.95	.95	.94	.93	.92	.91	.89	.88
2	1.96	1.92	1.89	1.85	1.89	1.79	1.76	1.73	1.70	1.67	1.61	1.55
3	2.91	2.83	2.75	2.68	2.61	2.54	2.48	2.42	2.36	2.30	2.18	2.07
4	3.84	3.70	3.57	3.44	3.33	3.21	3.11	3.02	2.92	2.83	2.64	2.47
5	4.76	4.54	4.34	4.15	3.98	3.81	3.66	3.53	3.40	3.27	3.01	2.78
6	5.66	5.35	5.06	4.80	4.57	4.35	4.15	3.97	3.80	3.64	3.30	3.01
7	6.54	6.12	5.75	5.41	5.11	4.83	4.58	4.35	4.14	3.95	3.53	3.19
8	7.40	6.87	5.39	5.97	5.60	5.26	4.95	4.68	4.43	4.20	3.72	3.33
9	8.24	7.58	7.00	6.49	6.04	5.64	5.28	4.96	4.67	4.41	3.87	3.44
10	9.07	8.27	7.58	6.97	6.44	5.98	5.57	5.21	4.88	4.59	3.99	3.52
11	9.88	8.93	8.12	7.42	6.81	6.29	5.82	5.42	5.06	4.74	4.09	3.59
12	10.68	9.57	8.63	7.83	7.14	6.56	6.04	5.60	5.21	4.86	4.16	3.64
13	11.46	10.18	9.11	8.21	7.44	6.80	6.24	5.75	5.33	4.96	4.22	3.68
14	12.22	10.77	9.57	8.57	7.72	7.02	6.41	5.89	5.44	5.05	4.27	3.71
15	12.97	11.34	10.00	8.90	7.97	7.21	6.56	6.00	5.53	5.12	4.31	3.73
20	16.51	13.86	11.81	10.20	8.93	7.91	7.07	6.38	5.81	5.33	4.42	3.78
25	19.72	15.93	13.16	11.09	9.52	8.30	7.34	6.56	5.94	5.42	4.45	3.80
30	22.62	17.64	14.18	11.70	9.88	8.53	7.48	6.65	5.99	5.46	4.46	3.80
35	25.25	19.04	14.93	12.11	10.11	8.66	7.55	6.69	6.02	5.47	4.46	3.80
40	27.63	20.19	15.50	12.39	10.26	8.73	7.58	6.71	6.03	5.48	4.47	3.80

First, it is necessary to state the discount rate which is to be used to discount the lease payments. This rate is the after-tax cost of debt rate, applied to the after-tax lease payments, if the same rate is deemed to be applicable to the tax savings associated with the lease payments.

Using the example above, the after-tax lease payments are $6275 annually. The 15-year 4 percent discount factor is 11.34. Thus, the present value of the lease alternative is

$$\$6275 \times 11.34 = \$71{,}160$$

The same conclusion is reached: It is less expensive to purchase than it is to lease—$64,775 compared with $71,160.

Exceptional Cases. An abbreviated explanation of two methods of approaching a straightforward lease versus purchase analysis has been presented. But not all lease/purchase situations are as simple as that illustrated. Some of the more common exceptional cases are:

1. Under the purchase alternative, the company owns an asset which at the end of the estimated life, used for comparative purposes, is "worth" something; i.e., land or a building useful for other purposes. In the illustration used above, it was assumed that the asset had no terminal value, and consequently it was written off for tax purposes. If it is probable that the asset has some

value at the end of the estimated life, the situation can be handled in two ways:

a. Estimate the value at the end of the useful life, consider taxable gains or write-offs, apply a present-value factor, and bring the present-value amount back to reduce the purchase cost. Continuing with the example used above, if it is assumed that the equipment would be salable for $50,000 at the end of 15 years, this would result in a $25,000 gain on sale ($50,000 sales price less $25,000 unallocated cost). If the gain is taxed at 25 percent, the net cash inflow at the end of the 15 years would be $50,000 − $6250 taxes, or $43,750. Applying a present-value factor of 0.55 (4 percent, 15 years) would result in $24,063. The present-value cost of purchasing would then be:

Same	$100,000
Same	(28,350)
Present value of salvage value	(24,063)
Present value cost of purchasing	$ 47,587

b. If it is difficult to estimate a precise figure for the salvage (or terminal) value, it is possible to determine what this value would have to be in order to make the purchase alternative as attractive as the lease alternative, assuming the lease alternative has a lower cost without considering salvage value. (This was not the case in the previous example.)

Examine another case with the following situation:

Present-value cost of purchasing, before
considering salvage value $50,000
Present-value cost of leasing $40,000

What would the after-tax salvage value of the asset owned under the purchase alternative have to be to make purchasing as attractive as leasing? There is a present-value difference of $10,000 ($50,000 − 40,000). Using the 4 percent present-value factor for the fifteenth year, the after-tax salvage value would have to be

$$\frac{\$10,000}{0.55} = \$18,182$$

Using this method, it is possible to highlight the unknown; i.e., by determining what the value has to be, rather than by attempting to assign a definite figure.

2. A second type of exceptional case is one in which a company is a marginal credit risk or for some reason appears to have access to more lease than debt capacity. A company in this category may not be able to get term loans, yet it may be able to lease assets, particularly if it can lease equipment from the company manufacturing the equipment. If leasing is the only alternative and the asset is a good investment, a lease/purchase analysis is not applicable.

New Techniques

Companies today are combining other quantitative techniques with capital project analysis. Some of them are:

Sensitivity Analysis. This method, in effect, uses different sets of assumptions relative to the projected savings to look at a proposed project. What would the savings be if the selling price of the product produced on the machine increased by 10 percent? Decreased by 10 percent? What would the savings be if volume decreased by 20 percent? Increased by 20 percent? It is useful to apply sensitivity analysis when any of the factors involved in the savings calculation are likely to be unstable.

Probability. Sensitivity analysis can be combined with the use of probability theory. What is the probability that prices may increase or decrease by 10 percent? The probability factors can be applied to the various price alternatives to get an expected return. A simple example:

Price	Probability	Expected price
$12	25%	$3.00
$10	50%	5.00
$ 8	15%	1.20
$ 6	10%	0.60
		$9.60

The use of probability analysis provides a disciplined way of injecting subjective hunches into the analysis process.

Summary

Various methods are used in practice to appraise the desirability of long-term investments. The three most commonly used are payback, accounting return, and discounted cash flow. Each of these methods has its advantages and disadvantages.

See also Accounting, cost analysis and control; Accounting, financial; Accounting, managerial control; Budgets and budget preparation; Financial management; Financial management, capital structure and dividend policy; Marginal income analysis; Risk analysis and management; Tax management; Valuation of a firm.

REFERENCES

Bierman, Harold, Jr., and Seymour Smidt: *The Capital Budgeting Decision*, 5th ed., Macmillan, New York, 1980.

Financial Analysis to Guide Capital Expenditure Decisions, Research Report 43, National Association of Accountants, New York, 1967.

Terbough, George W.: *Business Investment Management*, Machinery and Allied Products Institute, Washington, D.C., 1967.

C. RAY SMITH, *University of Virginia*

Budgets and Budget Preparation

Budgeting is the process by which costs are assigned to specific functions or activities that are planned within a designated upcoming period (usually 12 months). It is a widely used management tool that facilitates utilization of the vast amounts of information available today. Effective budgeting can improve decision making, provide a benchmark to measure and control performance, increase general communication and analysis within the organization, and establish an understanding between managers about goals and objectives. The three components of budgeting dealt with in this entry are (1) sales and volume budgets, (2) variable-cost budgets, and (3) overhead budgets. (These three components are the core of a basic budgeting system. There are, of course, other special components, such as project budgets, which do not have the same degree of general applicability; those will not be presented here.)

Effect of the Budgeting Process. All organizations have a limited amount of resources. Decisions must be made about how to allocate the available resources to meet the organization's objectives most effectively. The quality of those decisions can be greatly enhanced by a good planning and budgeting process—one that emphasizes input from all levels of management and rationalizes each allocation along the way.

Budgeting measures and controls performance. Goals must be set before any budgeting begins. As the budgeting process unfolds, feedback tells us if the partial results are leading in the appropriate direction. Corrective action can be undertaken at this point if the thrust seems off target.

A good budgeting process improves communication within the organization. Budgeting encourages managers to think analytically. Improved analysis and communication ultimately lead to better decision making at the grass roots of the organization, as well as at the general manager level.

Strategy Formulation and the Budget. Budgeting is merely one tool that management has at its disposal to improve decision making and effect favorable results. Figure B-3 shows the interrelationship between strategy formulation and implementation as decisions are made in the organization. Developing a sound strategy without effective implementation is just as unsuccessful as not developing a strategy at all.

Sound strategy formulation is a prerequisite to truly effective implementation and budgeting. It requires thorough analysis of the environment, competitors, customers, the company, and the company's businesses. A strategy differentiates the company by way of its comparative advantages and is a necessary condition for success.

Implementation requires careful understanding, design, and use of human resources, organization structure, culture, and management processes. Clearly, implementation and strategy need to be coordinated and thought of together; they are both critical to the organization.

Budgeting, of course, is one of the management processes. The others are measurement and rewards, planning, and programming. Budgeting is a key management tool because it assigns dollar costs to the activities planned in the upcoming year (or other period of time). It is a tangible method by which resources can be allocated and strategies implemented.

Budgets provide data that can be used to control performance and determine rewards.

Budgeting encourages communications and uses the communications systems established in the organization.

Organization structure helps determine how the budgeting process will work.

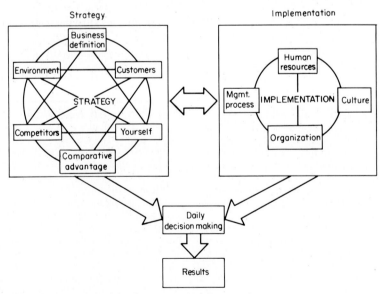

FIG. B-3 Interrelationship of strategy and implementation.

Components of the Budgeting Process. The budget is completed in three major steps which result in:

Sales and volume budgets

Variable-cost budgets

Overhead-cost budgets

The components of budgeting are completed sequentially. Sales and volume budgets are prepared prior to the other two components because the volume forecast serves as input to the other budgets. A description of each of these budgets follows.

Sales and Volume Budgeting

Sales and volume budgeting is a process by which revenues and the quantity of goods to be produced are forecast for the upcoming year. Usually, the budget is broken down by product lines, by month, and by producing location.

Different types of sales and volume budgets are produced for a variety of uses. Sales quotas are generally developed as a means to measure and motivate sales personnel. The sales quotas may differ from the budget since quotas are meant to motivate the employees. General sales forecasts usually are based on estimated economic conditions and generally are produced by economists or others not directly involved in line management. Sales budgets, on the other hand, are produced by line management. They become a part of the overall company budget and are used by others as input to their budgets.

The sales and volume budget is necessary for three reasons:

1. Line executives responsible for sales need to be involved in planning their activities and the expected results. The act of budgeting increases their analytical involvement in planning sales activities.

2. A benchmark for measuring results and monitoring performance should be established.

3. Sales and volume budgets are a necessary and vital input to the variable-cost budgets and overhead-cost budgets.

Table B-5 shows examples of sales and volume budgets. Note that the budget is broken down by product line and by region within each product line. The needs of various organizations may dictate other breakdowns, but these are the most common.

Four Major Steps. The sales and volume budgeting process is composed of the following four major steps:

1. Overall sales goals are prepared and provided to the manager responsible for sales. These goals are established through (a) an economist's sales

TABLE B-5 Example of Sales Budget

Sales budget summary		
	Sales	
Product line	$000	Volume (units)
Widgets	1000	12,000
Buggy whips	525	15,500
Hoola hoops	610	13,250
	2135	

Widget sales budget by region		
	Sales by region	
Region	$000	Volume (units)
Midwest	500	6000
West	250	3000
East	200	2500
South	50	500
	1000	12,000

outlook, (b) sales forecasts prepared via forecasting models, (c) historical sales trends, and (d) the chief executive's judgment. The goals are somewhat arbitrary at this point and are prepared on a top-down basis with little input from the sales force manager. (*See also* Forecasting business conditions.)

2. The product line managers or their counterparts prepare their sales budgets. This process involves a series of substeps: (a) examination of industry, economic, and market-share data; (b) examination of historical trends; (c) determination of the market approach in terms of use of sales force, advertising, promotion, pricing, channels of distribution, packaging, product modifications, etc.; and (d) estimation of sales by month by major product line.

3. Sales management and manufacturing management estimate production requirements and inventory levels. An estimate of production volume for each plant and for each product is prepared.

4. The finance group works with sales and manufacturing to develop estimates and ensure that the production volume estimates, inventory level estimates, and sales forecasts tie in.

The final sales and volume plan is approved only after significant interaction among many levels of management.

Since many factors influence sales volume, a range of sales volume should be provided, indicating pessimistic, most likely, and optimistic assessments.

This contingency budget provides management with data to deal effectively with uncertainty.

Pitfalls of the Sales and Volume Budgeting Process. Perhaps the greatest hazard of this process is the tendency of some organizations to budget sales without first carefully planning the marketing approach. Well-thought-out marketing plans behind the numbers are a prerequisite to meaningful budgets.

Another pitfall is the diverse use of budgets. If the salesperson's quota is based on the same budget prepared for company planning purposes, trouble can arise. The salesperson may want a low quota; the sales manager may want a high or a low quota, depending upon the motivation involved. Such pressures can cause the budget to be unrealistic.

A third pitfall is overreliance on economic and forecasting models for sales budgeting. The common denominator in most successful modeling applications is the use of practical models that are responsive to the manager's own perspective.

Design and Use of Decision Models. There are at least seven critical ingredients in the successful design and use of decision models:

1. Closing the designer-user gap. There is usually a gulf between the model designer and the model user that must be explicitly resolved to avoid failure. The model designer has a technical knowledge that is likely to be far greater than that of the user. The user, on the other hand, has a finer appreciation of the problems that she or he must face and the operating or policy decisions that must be made.

2. Defining the problem before selecting a solution. Much time and effort is wasted finding a problem to fit a solution. Implicit in not allowing the management scientist to predetermine the solution is the recognition that there are many problems for which models are not useful.

3. Being willing to sacrifice technical efficiency for communication. It is more important for the user to understand the model than it is to save computing time.

4. Building models for people and not for organization charts. Models are used by people and not by titles, positions, or job descriptions.

5. Making the model small enough to be manageable and to address specific well-defined problems.

6. Ensuring that the problem addressed by the model is large (in potential impact on profits) and/or repetitive so that the model can prove its value.

7. Utilizing management judgment as well as hard data in the model. The model should complement management judgment but not replace it.

The successful model uses a small number of critical pieces of data which more often than not must be estimated by judgment and/or special studies rather than accounting or other regularly collected data.

In summary, people, rather than models, make decisions, and the people who generally make the best decisions are those who are closely involved in the marketing function. Thus it is vital to avoid abrogating the sales budgeting responsibility to a model.

Variable-Cost Budgets

Variable costs are those that vary directly with increases and decreases in the volume of goods manufactured. Variable costs traditionally are associated with three categories of expense:

Direct material expense

Direct labor expense

Portions of manufacturing or plant overhead expense which vary with volume

Other departmental expenses (such as corporate administrative, marketing, and research and development) are generally considered fixed overhead expenses. These, together with the nonvariable portions of plant overhead, are addressed more fully in this entry in the section on overhead budgets.

Variable-cost budgeting begins with the development of the sales forecast, since inventory and production cost estimates are related to the anticipated sales volume. Completion of the forecast enables management to proceed to the production budget (by product and expressed in units). The production budget is based on the expected level of sales for the year, plus expected inventory additions for the year. The completion of these steps allows management to establish budgets for

1. Material usage and purchases

2. Direct labor costs

3. A portion of manufacturing or plant overhead costs

Budgeting for Direct Costs of Production. The budgeting process for material usage and purchases and that for direct labor costs are similar. Standard costs are generally considered unit costs, while budgeted costs typically refer to the standard or unit costs multiplied by the expected production for the year. When variable budgets are used, the use of multiple production levels results in multiple budgets for each standard or unit cost, as shown in Table B-6.

The budget for the direct costs of production is developed through establishing standards for both labor and material factors.

TABLE B-6 Example of Flexible Budget*

Cost category	Standard cost	Budgeted cost for indicated volume levels		
		20,000 hours 10,000 units	22,000 hours 11,000 units	24,000 hours 12,000 units
Direct labor cost	$ 5.00/hour	$100,000	$110,000	$120,000
Material cost	$15.00/unit	$150,000	$165,000	$180,000
Total direct cost		$250,000	$275,000	$300,000

*Flexible Budgeting for Direct Costs for Widgets

Labor Standards. Direct labor costs are composed of two factors: the quantity of labor utilized and the rate paid to the productive work force.

Labor rates are generally not controllable by a company since they are most often the result of union contract negotiations and/or local conditions of labor supply-and-demand factors. The rates to be used for standard-setting purposes are those that are anticipated for the forthcoming year.

The quantity of labor utilized, on the other hand, is of much greater importance, for actual labor efficiency measured by the labor-efficiency standard is largely controllable by management.

Time-and-motion studies and associated work-measurement techniques are the most widely used method of setting labor standards. Meaningful method studies evaluate both the operation and the environment in arriving at realistic objectives. Critical questions to answer are these: "Is the standard to be an average of expected production that will most accurately price inventory and allow for overachievement as well as underachievement? Is the standard to be established as a goal for the work force to strive toward, and hence be set more stringently than management's expectation of actual performance?" For planning and budgeting purposes, the standard should reflect what manufacturing management expects to happen. Other standards can be used for motivational purposes.

Other methods utilized as a basis for establishing labor-efficiency standards involve evaluation of past standards and actual times, times used in similar operations, and industry guidelines.

Material Standards. The various costs for raw material entering into the product have both a price and a usage factor.

The price factor is generally determined by a purchasing group within the corporation and is based either upon the current prices or upon average expected prices during the forthcoming year. Price budgeting is mainly a predictive task, since the major variation in price is usually an external phenomenon. Nonetheless, wise purchase timing, lot ordering, discount planning, and alternative transportation evaluation all can produce better prices. In budgeting for prices, the possible economies available through effective purchasing management, particularly within the current economic climate, should be recognized.

Budgets for material quantities are prepared through the development of the standard bill of materials. The preparation of the standard bill of materials (see Table B-7) is based upon formal engi-

TABLE B-7 Example of Bill of Materials*

Part number	Quantity required per unit	Description
X1416	140 cubic inches	Cement block
X2372	3 ounces	Epoxy
Q0002	10 pieces	Catch lever
K1000	2 boxes	Expansion bolt kit

*Standard Bill of Materials for Superwidgets

neering test standards, trial runs, historical experience when the job is already in production, and industry experience. The responsibility for setting the material standards is generally that of the engineering department, with the assistance of the production and accounting staffs.

In order to arrive at a unit material budget for each raw material or part entering into the production of an item, the quantity of material or number of parts required per unit produced (taken from the standard bill of materials) is multiplied by the estimated price for that type of material or part. Once this has been done for all materials, parts, and components that make up the item being manufactured, the unit material budgets are added to a total material budget for the production of one item. (In Table B-6, this is the $15.00 per unit shown as the material cost.)

Budgeting for Variable Indirect Costs of Production. In addition to direct material and labor costs, a number of other plant, or manufacturing, costs vary with volume. Examples of these include *portions of* maintenance, utilities, expendable supplies, and certain indirect labor costs. An analysis of numerous corporate budgets would show that these particular indirect product costs are often mixed in with managed or overhead costs for budgeting and expense-reporting purposes. Separate reporting is preferable due to the varied nature of the controllability of these costs.

Three characteristics of indirect product costs are important:

1. Like direct material and labor, a quantity required per unit of production can be established on the basis of engineering studies (utility expense for heavy machinery, for example).

2. Some items may have a fixed element of cost as well as a variable element.

3. Like managed costs, levels of organizational efficiency can be identified with various levels of expenditures for indirect product costs.

The most common approach to the evaluation of these costs is through the flexible budgeting technique, which establishes volume-cost relationships (see Fig. B-4). While individual items may not bear

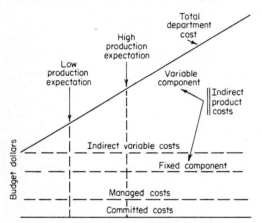

FIG. B-4 A simple flexible budget for departmental costs.

direct relationships to production, the aggregate departmental relationships often do.

Hazards in Flexible Budgeting. A word of caution is in order, however, since flexible budgeting does not address the following questions:

1. What is the excess cost built into the standard or budgeted indirect costs that have been used in the past?

2. How much lower could the variable budgeting line be set (by reducing the fixed component of indirect costs, managed costs, and committed costs) and still meet production schedules in the short run or in the long run?

These questions can be answered better by evaluating the relative necessity of various service levels per unit of production for different departments or categories of indirect variable expense. A fuller explanation of this service-level approach (zero-base

planning and budgeting) is presented in the following section on overhead budgets.

Overhead Budgets

Overhead budgets are prepared for all costs that do not vary directly with volume. There are two major types of overhead costs, as shown in Fig. B-4.

Committed Costs. Committed costs are expenses that the organization will incur in the short term no matter what decisions are made; e.g., depreciation, insurance, rental charges, and certain taxes. Obviously, these costs can be changed by drastic action or in the long term.

Managed Costs. Managed costs do not vary directly with volume, but they can be changed. Examples include all overhead activities such as finance, research, development, office services, quality control, production planning, and engineering. The difference between these costs and committed costs is that decisions can be made about the level of service and cost that can be provided in the current year. Note that some manufacturing and plant overhead costs (e.g., the fixed component of indirect product costs) vary directly with volume and can be changed.

The managed costs are important for two reasons: (1) management can make decisions about what level of service and cost is provided, and (2) the increases or decreases in these costs have a dramatic impact on profit. Table B-8 shows how a 5 percent

TABLE B-8 Impact of Managed Costs on Profits

	$000	Change
Sales	750,000	
Variable costs	496,000	
Managed costs	204,200	(10,210) − 5%
Profit before taxes	49,800	60,010 + 20%

reduction in managed costs has a 20 percent positive impact on profits before taxes.

Problems Posed by Overhead Costs. Traditionally, organizations have had a difficult time dealing with overhead costs. No neat standard cost formulas can be developed readily, and managers have felt uneasy about determining the relative merits of various overhead activities. Thus the usual approach is to concentrate in one of the following ways:

1. Examine new overhead activities very carefully.

2. Examine particular line items, such as travel, with a fine-tooth comb.

3. Reduce or expand all overhead activities across the board.

The problem with this approach, of course, is that overhead costs are not scrutinized in terms of their value to the organization. Furthermore, the *base* activities that have gone on for years are not examined systematically. These flaws result in management's inability to reallocate resources intelligently to the uses most appropriate to the organization.

Zero-Base Planning and Budgeting. A new approach for overhead budgeting, called zero-base planning and budgeting, attacks overhead in a different way. The effects of the zero-base planning and budgeting process include (1) selective cost and activity reductions or expansions, (2) reallocations of resources among overhead activities, and (3) a variety of analytical and communication benefits.

Zero-base planning and budgeting is a tool that helps cost center managers analyze their operations better and allows general managers to allocate resources more effectively through:

Examination of expected work loads.

Proper compartmentalization of overhead costs.

Rigorous analysis of each overhead-cost compartment.

Allocation of critical resources to appropriate activities.

Preparation of detailed budgets.

The process can be summarized briefly in four steps.

Proper Identification of Decision Units. The decision unit is the grouping of activities around which analysis is centered. In many cases, the decision unit corresponds to the traditional cost center or budget unit. In other cases, the decision unit encompasses a group of activities that can be analyzed effectively by management. Decision units may include special projects or programs, activities that apply across the organization (e.g., marketing), objects of expense, or services rendered.

It is important to note that decision units are established so that units of activities can be analyzed and discretionary trade-off decisions can be made. While managed costs are broken into decision units, committed costs are separated and not analyzed through zero-base planning and budgeting.

Rigorous Analysis of Each Decision Unit. The zero-base process is designed to involve all levels of management in the analysis. After the managers analyze their decision units, higher-level managers use the information to make resource allocation decisions.

Each decision unit is analyzed in three different ways: (1) the managers examine the purpose of their functions and their current methods of operation; (2) alternative ways of operating are examined; (3) incremental cost-benefit analysis is performed once the method of operation is determined.

A decision-unit manager usually begins the analysis by specifying exactly how he or she currently operates and by describing the number of people and dollars involved in the activity. Performance measures are developed to examine the strengths and weaknesses of the manager's current approach.

The manager then considers alternative ways of operating. After reviewing the alternatives (including the current method), the manager chooses the best method of operation. To begin the incremental analysis, the decision-unit manager determines, from a base of zero, which of the service needs provided by the unit is most important. These highest-priority needs constitute the first or minimum increment of service. In all cases, the first increment requires lower expenditure than is currently provided and offers either a narrower range of services than is presently provided or a reduced quality or quantity of service. Additional increments of service and cost are developed, with each successive increment containing those services which are next in order of priority. Several increments may be required before the cumulative total approximates or exceeds current service levels.

Performance measures are included in each analysis since they identify meaningful quantitative measures that assist in evaluating the effectiveness and efficiency of each increment. Measures may include work load (e.g., divisions served, number of work units, or tasks performed), performance (e.g., cost effectiveness, unit cost), or other pertinent data.

Allocation of Critical Resources. The increments developed by decision-unit managers provide the basic information from which higher-level managers allocate critical resources to high-priority activities.

Figure B-5 shows how the reallocation process works. Suppose a corporate division is divided into three decision units: purchasing, A; stores, B; and maintenance, C. Further assume that each decision unit is broken down into four increments. After analysis is provided by the decision-unit manager, the division head ranks the 12 increments in priority order. Figure B-5 shows that A-1, B-1, and C-1, the minimum increments, are ranked first. Then the manager ranks C-2 and C-3 before approving A-2 and B-2. If the current level of expenditure for each decision unit is between 2 and 3, it is obvious that the manager prefers funding a new increment for C before funding the current increments for A and B.

Furthermore, if the total budget available is represented by the cutoff line, the manager would have approved expenditures through increment C-4. Note that different amounts of cost and service were approved for each decision unit. This tool, therefore, can be used to allocate resources to the activities with the highest payoff.

How are the trade-offs made? The ranking man-

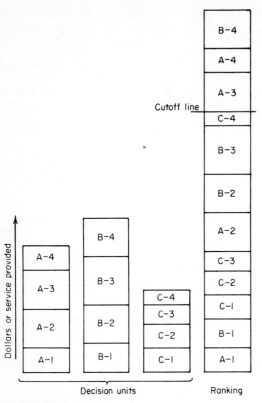

FIG. B-5 Reallocation process.

A: Purchasing   B: Stores   C: Maintenance

ager examines increments and analyses for each decision unit and makes the decision on the basis of the cost-benefit analysis by increment. Of course, the decision is made in consultation with the decision-unit managers.

The initial ranking of increments occurs at the organizational level, where the analysis is developed to allow each manager to evaluate the relative importance of her or his own operations. Thus, the managers are able to make trade-offs between discrete levels of services, optimizing the return on expenditures. This ranking is reviewed at higher organizational levels and used as a guide for merging those rankings.

Preparation of Detailed Budgets.   Once the allocation decisions have been made, detailed budgets are prepared. The ranking table prepared by management provides the basis for this clerical function.

Preparing the Final Budget

The sales and volume budgets, variable-cost budgets, and overhead budgets are the three major compo-

nents of the total final budget. Top management must review each of the budgets, determine the effect on the organization, and make decisions leading to the preparation of the final budget.

Figure B-6 shows that top management first examines the three components separately. Reviews

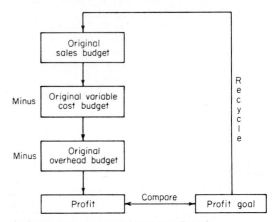

FIG. B-6   Integrating budgets with profit goals.

of the plans and budgets should be conducted for each individual component. Then the three should be combined to determine the likely profit. A comparison is made with the profit goal for the organization.

Management then simulates various effects of sales levels. It is relatively simple to simulate variable-cost margins at different sales levels. (Computer simulation models are useful for this exercise.) Given a certain level of overhead, the break-even points and profit levels are developed. (*See* Marginal income analysis.)

Once a good estimate of revenue minus variable costs is determined, overhead costs can be estab-

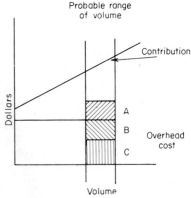

FIG. B-7   Adjustable funding line.

lished. Figure B-7 indicates that overhead is not fixed. The zero-base analysis, for example, ends with a ranking of overhead activities. Management can adjust the funding line to level A, B, or C, as shown in Fig. B-7, to increase or decrease the profit levels.

See also Accounting, managerial control; Budgeting, capital; Control systems, management; Financial management; Forecasting business conditions; Marginal income analysis; Planning, strategic managerial; Program planning and implementation; Tax management; Zero-base budgeting.

REFERENCES

Bump, Jack A.: "Profit Planning and Budgeting," in Richard F. Vancil (ed.), *Financial Executive's Handbook*, Dow Jones-Irwin, Homewood, Ill., 1970.

Stonich, Paul J. (ed.): *Implementing Strategy: Making It Happen*, Ballinger-Harfax, Cambridge, Mass., September 1982.

Stonich, Paul J. "Zero-Base Planning: A Management Tool," *Managerial Planning*, July–August 1976.

PAUL J. STONICH, *Management Analysis Center, Inc. (MAC)*

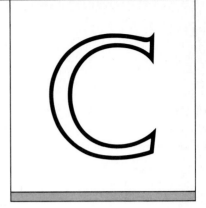

Cash Management

Effective cash management is essential for the success of a business. In fact, cash management can be more important than the ability to deliver every customer order promptly. A business can lose a customer without sustaining irreparable damage. However, a gap in its cash flow that results in a missed payroll can force a business to close its doors.

A cash-flow budget provides the essential foundation for effective cash management. That budget helps anticipate potential gaps in a firm's cash flow and provides management with the time necessary to avoid or fill those gaps before they develop. The need for a cash-flow budget, in addition to a financial budget, arises from the critical distinction between financial and cash transactions in a business.

Remember that, except for retailers, few businesses generate sales directly in exchange for cash. Instead, manufacturers and wholesalers sell their products in exchange for customers' promises to pay for their purchases in accordance with their designated selling terms. However, the traditional accounting process does not always distinguish between financial and cash transactions.

Thus, on the seller's side, the accounting process requires a record of a sale on the day it occurs, even though no cash actually changes hands. Instead, the proceeds from the sale enter into the firm's accounts receivable. The buyer's side similarly records a purchase (although not necessarily an expense), and at the same time records an increase in accounts payable. However, the sale initially represents a financial transaction that has no immediate impact on either firm's cash reserves.

Accrual accounting enables a business to evaluate its financial performance by properly matching its revenues and expenses when they occur. At the same time, accrual accounting does not provide the correct picture of the cash flow through a business. Some business managers find this confusing, since the accounting process also records the exchange of cash that completes a financial transaction. Yet the buyer does not record an expense nor does the seller record any revenue at the time the cash exchange occurs.

The exchange of cash completes a business transaction: It represents either a customer's payment for a purchase or a business's final fulfillment of its own liabilities. The record of cash receipts and disbursements, then, reflects the actual cash flow into and out of a business. Indeed, that record provides the proper picture of a firm's cash flow, whether or not the *financial* transactions coincide with the *cash* transactions.

Proceeding from that distinction, a cash-flow budget projects the future cash receipts and disbursements anticipated in the normal course of business. However, that budget goes beyond the simple summation of the year's upcoming activity. Indeed, it projects the actual time that cash will flow into and out of a business. The illustration employed here projects that flow on a monthly basis, but note that a business can also project a weekly or even a daily cash flow.

Budgeting Process

The cash-flow budgeting process can be separated into five distinct steps:

1. The sales forecast
2. The projection of the firm's cash receipts
3. The projection of the firm's cash disbursements
4. The projection of the interrelationships between the receipts and disbursements
5. The elimination of any potential gaps in the firm's cash flow

The discussion below provides a detailed review of each step in the cash-flow budgeting process. Notice that the process isn't an esoteric exercise reserved for large corporations with professional staff accountants. Indeed, any business manager with a grasp of the fundamental concepts can develop an effective cash-flow budget for the firm.

The Sales Forecast. Every cash budget must begin with a sales forecast. Of course, every forecast includes some uncertainty. An erratic economy makes absolute predictability impossible. Nevertheless, the lack of precision does not eliminate the value of that forecast. Even an intuitive projection— e.g., perhaps the previous year's sales volume, adjusted for inflation—provides a reasonable start for the cash-flow budgeting process.

As the basis for illustration, we will use a portion of the annual sales forecast for the Prudent Company. For the first four months of its upcoming business year, Prudent's monthly sales projections (in $1000s) stand as follows:

Month	Jan.	Feb.	Mar.	Apr.
Projected sales in $1000s	$70	$50	$100	$150

That sales forecast then provided the basis for the second step in the cash-flow budgeting process—projecting the firm's cash receipts.

Projecting Cash Receipts. As noted above, the need for a projection of a firm's cash receipts—apart from a sales forecast—arises from the fact that the primary source of cash flow into a business comes from the collection of accounts receivable, rather than sales. Indeed, the cash from a sale flows into a business only when a business collects the accounts receivable that represent the original proceeds from the sale.

Of course, a business may supplement the cash flow from sales with borrowed funds. But the cash-flow budget is a necessary precedent that helps anticipate the need for that supplement. Consequently, this step of the budgeting process does not look beyond the cash flow anticipated from the collection of a firm's accounts receivable. Note that a business also should add any expected cash sales to the anticipated cash flow from collections.

A business usually must rely on historical experience to project the cash flow from its collections. In the Prudent Company's circumstance, this history indicates that the company collects its receivables according to the following pattern: 70 percent in the month immediately following the sale, 20 percent in the second month following the sale, and 10 percent in the third month following the sale. Presumably that historical experience will extend into the future. Noting that the firm's actual sales in October, November, and December of the current year are expected to be $80,000 each month, the expected cash inflows from collections (in $1000s) for the budget months appear as follows:

Projected collections	Jan.	Feb.	Mar.	Apr.
70% of previous month's sales	$56	$49	$35	$70
20% of 2nd previous month's sales	$16	$16	$14	$10
10% of 3rd previous month's sales	$ 8	$ 8	$ 8	$ 7
Total monthly cash collections	$80	$73	$57	$87

The Prudent Company expects to receive $80,000 in cash collections in January. That total includes customer payments for 70 percent of December's sales, 20 percent of November's sales, and the remaining 10 percent uncollected portion of October's sales. Monthly collections in February and March then decline, lagging the projected drop in sales for January and February.

Note that the projections for March indicate sales of $100,000 but collections from previous sales of only $57,000. This emphasizes that the cash inflow to a business represents collections from prior sales, not the current month's.

Projecting Cash Expenditures. The sales forecast also provides the starting point for the next step in the cash budgeting process—i.e., anticipating a firm's cash expenditure requirements. Typically, most business expenditures fall into one of three predictable categories: (1) payment for purchases, (2) payment for operating expenses, and (3) debt payments.

The projected cash expenditures for the Prudent Company develop from the following characteristics of its operations:

1. The cost of goods sold averages 55 percent of sales.

2. Prudent purchases the inventory for each month's forecasted sales volume 1 month in advance; that is, the firm purchases the stock necessary for March's anticipated sales in February.

3. Suppliers allow Prudent 30 days to pay for its purchases; consequently, the firm pays for all inventory in the month following the actual purchase.

4. Monthly cash operating expenses average $30,000; that includes salaries, wages, rent, utilities, and other repetitive monthly expenses.

5. Prudent has $5000 in monthly debt-service requirements.

Proceeding from the above sales forecast, the projected cash expenditures (in $1000s) for the Prudent Company become:

	Sales			
	Jan.	Feb.	Mar.	Apr.
	$70	$50	$100	$150
	Projected expenditures			
Purchases (55% of sales)	$38.5	$27.5	$ 55	$ 82.5
Operating expenses	$30	$30	$ 30	$ 30
Debt service	$ 5	$ 5	$ 5	$ 5
Total cash expenditures	$73.5	$62.5	$ 90	$117.5

In January, Prudent will need $38,500 to pay for inventory purchases made in December. The company will make those purchases based on the January sales forecast. The company's cash operating expenses and debt-service requirements increase Prudent's total cash needs for the month to $73,500.

Repeating the projection process for the next three months, we find a drop in Prudent's cash expenditure requirements for February. This reflects a seasonal reduction in demand for Prudent's products. The firm's cash requirements increase in March and April as demand picks up.

Interrelating Receipts and Disbursements. The fourth step in the cash-flow budgeting process interrelates the previous two projections and measures the net effect those flows will have on the company's cash reserves each month. This identifies the net increase or decrease in cash (in $1000s) the company can expect each month:

	Jan.	Feb.	Mar.	Apr.
Projected cash collections	$80	$73	$57	$ 87
Projected cash expenditures	$73.5	$62.5	$90	$117.5
Net effect on cash reserves	+$ 6.5	+$10.5	($33)	($ 30.5)

Thus, the projection indicates that the Prudent Company can expect a $6500 net increase in cash in January. The business also can expect another $10,500 increase in cash in February, even though a drop in sales is forecast for that month. The next two months are projected to have deficit cash flows, despite (actually, because of) an anticipated increase in sales.

Filling in the Gaps. The final step in the cash-flow budgeting process interrelates a firm's cash reserves with the projected monthly inflows and outflows of cash. That identifies any potential cash-flow problems a business might have.

Of course, no problem exists so long as the net cash outflow in any month doesn't drain a firm's cash reserves below some practical operating minimum. However, if any monthly drain drops those reserves below that minimum, the company must seek external financing to fill in the cash shortage. Alternatively, management can exert the necessary effort to avoid the cash shortage without the help of borrowed funds, perhaps by accelerating collections or operating with a smaller investment in inventory.

Again using the Prudent Company for illustration, note three additional facts about its circumstances:

1. Prudent will open the year with a $20,000 cash operating balance.

2. The company has a $50,000 bank line of credit.

3. Company policy requires $20,000 in cash as the minimum operating balance necessary to begin any month.

Interrelating those facts with the previous projections helps identify the potential gaps in Prudent's cash flow over the forecast period. This final step also identifies the extent to which the company must use its line of credit to meet its cash operating requirements and avoid any cash-flow problems.

	Jan.	Feb.	Mar.	Apr.
Beginning cash	$20	$26.5	$37	$20
Net change	+$ 6.5	+$10.5	($33)	($30.5)
Ending cash (before borrowing)	$26.5	$37	$ 4	($10.5)
Borrowing	—	—	$16	$30.5
Ending cash (after borrowing)	$26.5	$37	$20	$20
Cumulative borrowing	—	—	$16	$46.5

The Prudent Company has no cash-flow problem in January. In fact, the net $6500 gain during the month enables the company to enter February with a $26,500 cash balance. That balance increases again during February and the company enters March with $37,000 on hand.

However, in March, the Prudent Company feels the first impact from the seasonal sales increase on its cash reserves. While the $33,000 drain during that month leaves the firm with a positive cash balance, it makes the Prudent use its line of credit to meet its minimum cash operating balance.

Finally, the $30,500 net cash drain projected in April emphasizes the critical need for the cash-flow budgeting process. The failure to foresee that deficit would leave Prudent with a severe cash-flow problem. Indeed, the ability to anticipate that deficit with the help of the budget provides the primary justification for obtaining the bank line of credit necessary to fill the gap.

Variations. Remember that any business, regardless of its size, can use the five steps illustrated here to anticipate its potential cash-flow problems. Begin with a sales forecast, then complete the remaining four steps in order. Of course, a firm's unique circumstances might require some alteration of the budgeting format.

For example, the illustration does not reflect any cash sales or income from investment of surplus cash. Also, cash anticipated from the sale of any business assets should be included. Certainly, such refinements can be added quite easily.

More important, the budget here presumes that cash inflows and outflows occur evenly throughout each month. If a firm's cash flows are not uniform, a monthly projection may understate or overstate a firm's financing requirements. For example, if all payments must be made on the tenth of each month but collections come in uniformly throughout the month, a business may need to borrow a larger amount than that apparent in a monthly budget. Indeed, many businesses may find it necessary to prepare budgets that project cash flows on a weekly or daily basis.

Note also that a cash budget represents a forecast, so all values are *expected* values. If actual sales, collections, expenses, or purchases are different from the forecasted levels, the forecasted cash requirements also will be incorrect. However, even inaccurate forecasts provide a reasonable foundation for effective cash management. The foundation dissolves in the absence of a budget.

Finally, recognize that a cash budget actually represents only the starting point for effective cash management. While it can help a business avoid embarrassing cash-flow problems, it also provides the basis for improving the firm's cash flow.

Thus, a business might reduce or eliminate the need to borrow by arranging a better balance between the timing of its cash receipts and disbursements. That balance might develop from an effort to accelerate collections from customers or from processing payments more efficiently. Or a business might find it beneficial to delay disbursements or utilize float to reduce the size of its minimum cash operating balance.

In any circumstance, a cash-flow budget represents the necessary prerequisite for effecting any of those management actions. A cash-flow budget does not shield a business from cash problems, but it helps provide management with the foresight necessary to hold those problems in check.[1]

See also Accounting, cost analysis and control; Accounting, managerial control; Budgets and budget preparation; Credit management; Financial management, capital structure and dividend policy; Financial management, financing.

NOTES

[1] Article excerpted from *Cash Flow Problem Solver* by Bryan E. Milling. Copyright 1982 by the author. Reprinted with the permission of the publisher, Chilton Book Company, Radnor, Pa., 19089.

REFERENCES

Brigham, Eugene F.: *Fundamentals of Financial Management*, Dryden Press, Chicago, 1983.

Harrington, Diana R., and Brent D. Wilson: *Corporate Financial Analysis*, Business Publications, Plano, Tex., 1983.

Van Horne, James C.: *Fundamentals of Financial Management*, Prentice-Hall, Englewood Cliffs, N.J., 1983.

BRYAN E. MILLING, *University of Colorado*

College and University Administration

While a college or university surely cannot be considered in the same manner as a large corporation, there can be no doubt that higher education in this country today is indeed a business—a very big business.

Statistics concerning higher education in this country are staggering. In the fall of 1982, there were some 12.3 million full-time and part-time students enrolled in the nation's 3000 colleges and universities. The number of students represented some 5.5 percent of the entire population of the United States. In other words, about 1 person in each 18 was enrolled as a college student.

Budgetary figures also clearly point out the magnitude—and big business characteristics—of higher education. In 1980, higher education in America had expenditures totaling some $61 billion. In the entire world, only one corporation, Exxon Corporation, had revenues exceeding the expenditures of higher education. The total spent by higher education is roughly equal to the annual sales of General Motors Corporation or Mobil Oil.

About one-third of the total expenditures in higher education went directly to instructional programs. Other major expenditures went, however, into areas such as plant operation ($4.7 billion); operation of dormitories, dining facilities, etc. ($6.4 billion); and extension and public service programs ($1.8 billion). Massive expenditures also went into research on college campuses, which continued to be the chief spawning ground for scientific breakthroughs and innovative approaches to problems. More than $5.1 billion was spent on research during 1980, in addition to several billion dollars within regular academic programs.

On a balance sheet, higher education certainly resembles a gargantuan corporation, and to varying degrees, each of the nation's institutions of higher learning is similar to a business or corporation.

But higher education poses special problems of management—problems that are unlike those faced on the corporate level. Foremost among these is the fact that each college and university has a broad-based constituency, one composed of many distinct groups with each viewing the institution in a different light. The job of managing the institution then is to maintain a proper balance among each of these groups and to attempt to satisfy each group.

Constituent Relations. The major constituent groups that each college or university must serve are alumni, students, faculty, and the general public, including legislators for the state-supported institutions.

Each of these groups views the institution through glasses of varying tints. Each has its own distinct idea on how the institution should be run, on what it should be doing and what it should not be doing. Alumni, for example, tend to view the institution the way it was "back then." As a rule, they are reluctant to accept change or to support fully any move that would alter the institution from the way it

was in their undergraduate days. Most frequently, students represent the opposite end of the spectrum. They carry a philosophy advocating change that would fulfill their aims of the moment. In terms of change, faculty generally are split, with younger faculty members resembling students in seeking change and older faculty members paralleling alumni concerns about change. Faculty members are united, however, in their desire to carry out their jobs with as little interference as possible from the management level. Their concern is for total academic freedom in their classrooms without influences from the outside. As would be expected, concerns of the general public run the widest possible range and all must be considered. These range from the strictly parochial concerns of the college's neighbors over parking regulations to the broader concerns of state legislators over accountability for expenditure of public funds.

From this complexity of desires, the college administrator has a job which is simple in description but highly difficult in practice: He or she must balance the objectives of all these diverse groups into a common direction for the institution. In simplest terms, the best solution is a utilitarian one, as expressed by John Stuart Mill: the greatest happiness for the greatest number of people. In practice, however, equal weight cannot possibly be given strictly on the basis of numbers. Additional importance must be assigned to the feelings of students and faculty in particular, for it is they who constitute the living fiber of the institution.

For determining the mission and role of the institution and for carrying out the functions of the institution, a precise plan must be adopted.

Plan Development. The first, and by far the most important, portion of the plan should deal with the institution's purpose. Purposes of different institutions of higher learning vary widely. Is the institution a major university with a multitude of undergraduate and graduate programs? Is it a small, single-purpose college? Is it primarily for lower-level undergraduate work, upper-level undergraduate work, or graduate work? Is its appeal mainly to urban students? Is it a residential campus? All these questions, and many more, must be answered before the institution's true purpose can be ascertained. And not only does the purpose of today need to be determined, but the purposes of 10, 20, and 30 years in the future must also be projected.

One method of answering the questions of purpose and objectives is through the action of a blue-ribbon committee composed of representatives of all constituent groups: alumni, students, faculty, public, and legislators.

Once the plan is developed, it is essential that it be fully understood by all members of the college or university community. It must be asserted and reasserted. Of particular importance is that the institution's board of trustees be in full support of the plan and completely understand the plan and its purposes.

Carrying out the plan, however, depends not on the institution's constituent groups but on its administrators. The next important job of the college chief executive is similar to that of her or his corporate colleagues: to select able lieutenants. It is crucial for the president of the institution to have efficient and conscientious assistants in carrying out the institution's plan.

Organization Development. First attention in the organization of the college or university should go to the budget and personnel areas. Staff members in these areas must have the expertise to handle problems and establish budgets, as they would if they were employed by industry. However, they must also have the ability to realize that while institutions of higher learning must be operated in a businesslike manner, they have special characteristics that business firms do not have. Budget and personnel staff members must recognize these differences and keep in mind that the primary mission of an institution of higher learning is the teaching of young men and women.

Another vital prerequisite for good college management is for the president to have a solid cadre of experienced and knowledgeable vice presidents. Each distinct area of the college or university's operation should be headed by a divisional head or vice president. The number of divisions and vice presidents will of, course, vary greatly, depending upon the size of the institution. A larger institution, for example, might have vice presidents in academic, business, administrative, public service, student service, and development areas as well as in any major specialized area such as medicine. The vice presidents must be given sufficient authority and latitude to handle the day-to-day decisions in their respective areas, and they should meet frequently with the president to determine answers to broader questions.

Above all, there must be active and easily accessible means of communication between the president and vice presidents and among the vice presidents themselves. The entire organization system could easily collapse if vice president A did not know which areas were being handled by vice president B. The president cannot expect—and should not want—complete agreement among all the vice presidents on all matters. He or she should, however, demand full and frank input from all key aides on every pressing matter.

In many institutions of higher education, the computer, personnel, budgeting, auditing, and institutional research are generally placed under a vice president who has line responsibility in the organization. These functions can be carried out more effectively if they are under a division head or a vice pres-

ident who reports directly to the president and has staff responsibility in the organization.

By and large, these functions are being performed to assist the other vice presidents in planning for resource utilization within the institution. The president should be directly involved in this type of planning. The allocation of resources to accomplish the mission of the institution is paramount in the responsibilities of the president. After the plans are made and the budget is established, the vice presidents responsible for operating divisions can carry out the mission of the institution within the resources allocated by the president's budget advisers. A division of administrative services and systems development enables the president to stay involved in the important responsibility of planning and resource allocation, but gives the vice presidents the responsibility for the day-in and day-out conduct of the affairs of the institution. This administrative structure allows the president to have input from the various constituents of the campus in developing the mission and objectives of the institution and in allocating the resources to achieve these objectives.

Unique Aspects. Even if all the institution's objectives are set forth clearly and the organization is established in flawless fashion, there are unique difficulties of management which must be faced in higher education.

As mentioned before, there is a general resistance to change, particularly among alumni and older faculty members. But when change is indicated, change must take place. And it is the singular role of the institution's chief executive officer to effect this change.

An important ingredient in a college or university environment is trust among the different constituencies. The faculty, the students, the alumni, and the public who trust each other will be able to carry through on projects more effectively than would be the case if there were a feeling of anxiety, uncertainty, and fear.

In order to establish an environment in which there is mutual trust, the president must believe she or he is dealing with intelligent and competent individuals who can make a contribution to the institution, not only in handling classroom instruction and research but also in helping to delineate and to achieve the purpose and the mission of the institution. There must be a formal structure for the ideas of faculty and students to emerge in the institution. It is essential that faculty and student organizations exist and that these organizations have a degree of autonomy in their operations. It is by having these organizations that the faculty and students can feel that they are making an input into the direction and operation of the institution. Their input not only contributes to a feeling of involvement but also can be very beneficial to the president and vice presidents of the institution because of the insight which faculty and students have with regard to program development.

In addition to the formal organization for the faculty and students, an institution can also combine representatives from these two groups with administrators and will benefit from the combined efforts of the three groups involved in the operation of the institution. The president, then, has the full benefit of views on the college from various sections of the campus, and the various sections of the campus will feel that they have been heard in regard to their interest in the institution. There should be a faculty senate and a student senate, and these organizations should act on matters of concern to them. In addition, there should be a body that brings representatives from these two groups into contact with administrators for discussion of broader issues of the campus. This provides full involvement of all the groups and helps to create an environment that is responsive to change.

Curriculum Development. At the core of the success of the college is the curriculum. The curriculum of a college or university must reflect the needs of society in given areas; however, there is a time lag problem. The students of today must meet the needs of a society that is 1 to 4 years in the future. Therefore, it is the role of the institution not only to recognize society's needs of today but also to forecast correctly the needs of the future. The curriculum must be geared to fill future voids in professional and vocational markets. One way of tackling this problem is to establish a department which deals with the future society and the curriculum needed to accommodate that society, as well as the scholarly and professional talents needed by faculty members for the new curriculum. The institution can deal with the instructional changes that will come about in the future if it involves the faculty and students in describing the curriculum of the future. It can also provide the resources and assistance whereby faculty members can make changes in their own scholarly efforts in order to accommodate the new instructional requirements.

Commitment and Change. Colleges and universities are currently coping with the problems of declining enrollments and a shortage of resources. These problems can be managed more easily if there is a feeling on the campus that all the constituents are committed to the institution and its mission. In the absence of an orderly process for change, the pressures of declining enrollment and resources will engender fear and hostility. The campus which does not overcome these problems becomes less effective in terms of its pursuit of scholarship, freedom, and the expansion of learning. It is this matter that is the most important to effective management of an institution—recognizing the need to deal with change

and to involve faculty and students in the process of change. After all, the institution of higher education is essentially one which deals with the human factor.

See also Nonprofit organizations, management of; Organizational analysis and planning; Program planning and implementation; Public administration.

REFERENCES

Carnegie Council on Policy Studies in Higher Education: *Three Thousand Futures*, Jossey-Bass, San Francisco, 1981.

Jedamus, Paul, Marvin W. Peterson, and Associates: *Improving Academic Management, A Handbook of Planning and Institutional Research*, Jossey-Bass, San Francisco, 1980.

National Center for Education Statistics: *Digest of Education Statistics*, U.S. Government Printing Office, Washington, D.C., 1982.

RONALD E. CARRIER, *James Madison University*

Committees

The use of committees is widespread in all organizations. In some, permanent committees are established, but temporary committees of various types are the most numerous.

Deploring or disparaging committees is fashionable, both because they entail an extra burden for their members and because they are often poorly directed and hence ineffectual. Properly managed, however, committees are an effective way of coping with special tasks and problems, particularly of the kind that cut across more than one organizational unit.

Advantages

Committees are useful for working directly on problems that require integration and coordination for better linkages between otherwise separate units. If left to their own devices, the individual units would have to rely on a weaker strategy—that of cooperation—or on the coercive coordinating decision of a higher manager.

The most outstanding advantage is that committees bring together the special human capabilities that each problem or activity area requires.

Another advantage is that a committee can focus intensely in a problem area. It can concentrate its efforts in a shorter time span. Decisions needing quick action can be sped up. By contrast, problems that continue over long periods of time can be kept under constant review. Thus committees provide flexibility for meeting a wide range of needs.

A further benefit occurs for the individual members themselves. It provides a means of involvement and participation. Members learn skills needed for working with other people in a less structured way, removed, usually, from direct boss-subordinate roles. Both written and oral communications skills can be developed through practice and observation. Members often learn interpersonal and group skills and acquire technical insight and practice not possible to them in their regular jobs.

Disadvantages

Most of the possible disadvantages stem from inept handling of the committee's deliberations or problems in the way a committee is set up. Such drawbacks may include an excessive amount of time spent to complete the work, a failure of communications among members, and the possibility that a committee will prevent or delay action rather than accelerate it. Committees may be unable to attain worthwhile results. Such difficulties add unnecessarily to an organization's costs.

Roles and Types of Committees

Permanent Committees. These include standing committees and committees integrated into the organization's basic structure. Standing committees may be at any level, and they deal with problems that continue to exist over time. The safety committee in an organization is a good example.

Organization-Based Committees. These are more or less permanent committees usually consisting of high-level officers of the corporation and continuing over substantial periods of time. The executive committee of the board of directors is an example. Since the board may meet only quarterly, the day-to-day policy actions may be entrusted to an executive committee. Another common type is the finance committee, given the responsibility for long-range financial planning and the financial security of the enterprise. The board of directors of a corporation also functions much like a permanent organization committee.

Voluntary associations make wise use of permanent committees, which include advisory or administrative groups. The conceptual difference between committees, boards, councils, and advisory groups is often unclear.

Temporary Committees. These committees provide maxiumum flexibility and adaptation to changing needs. Most organizations employ an enormous variety of them. They are also called ad hoc committees.

The roles and tasks of such committees should be stated specifically in an initial written charge to the committees. The charge details the purposes, aims, or intended uses of the work. Among the common tasks are (1) investigating problem areas; (2) making recommendations to managers or action units; (3) planning new activities or programs; (4) doing research to support new plans, policies, or programs; and (5) evaluating or auditing practices, programs, or procedures. A terminal date is usually indicated, so that a temporary committee knows when it should be disbanded. A moderator may be appointed or elected from the group by committee members.

Setting up Committees

It is important to provide permanent, standing, or ad hoc committees with a specific, clearly written charge which gives the scope and purpose of their work. The creating authority should establish the committee's authority and designate the individual or group to which it reports or refers its results. A target date of completion is important for ad hoc committees.

The selection of members is a key element. The criteria include the capabilities of individuals, the specific interests or constituencies of each member, the balance of power resulting from the association of group members, and the amount of the members' time to be required.

The committee should make sure its tasks, goals, and authority are understood by members. A minimum structure is achieved by electing or appointing a moderator. Subcommittees may be needed to divide the work into related parts. Meeting schedules should be worked out.

Chairing a committee requires skill in conference leading, group discussion, and human relations. Special training in small-group leadership may be given to those who frequently are chosen to chair committees.

See also Boards of directors; Interpersonal relationships; Management, definitions of; Manager, definition of; Officers, corporate; Organization structures and charting; Project management.

REFERENCES

Trecker, Harleigh B.: *Working with Groups, Committees, and Communities,* Association Press, Chicago, 1979.

Tropman, John E.: *The Essentials of Committee Management,* Nelson Hall, Chicago, 1979.

DALTON E. MCFARLAND, *University of Alabama in Birmingham*

Communications, Organizational

The communications processes within organizations are vital for the achievement of organizational goals.

They are the processes that link the various components of the organization together; they are found at all levels of the organization, and they affect every individual working for the organization in one way or another. The effectiveness of the communications system—the way in which it is managed—has a significant impact on the ultimate effectiveness of the total organization.

Communications have a major influence on both types of organizational goals—task and maintenance. With respect to *task (or productivity) goals,* without some means for downward communications, employees would not know what work they were expected to perform and when and how to do their work. Without adequate provision for upward communications, managers would not have the information needed to decide what to tell employees to do in the future. As organizations grow and become more complex, communications related to the organizational *maintenance goal* become increasingly important. Employees, including those at managerial levels, want to know how their work and their departments fit into the total operation, and they want to be informed about changes that might have some effect on their jobs or job environment. Thus in very large organizations, the management effort involved in communications processes can, and should, be considerable.

Communications Policy. While the extent of the management effort in the area of communications is important, the most crucial ingredient for the success of the communications program is the attitude of top management. Perhaps more than in any other aspect of management, the communications system requires the involvement and support of the highest levels of the organization. Unless there is a climate of trust and sincerity from the top, little real communication is likely to occur, no matter how much time and money are spent on formal communications techniques.

The basic requirements for effective organizational communications may be summarized as follows:

1. Top management must recognize the need for and benefits of good communications throughout the organization, and take the steps necessary to provide a climate conducive to effective communication.

2. Managers at all levels need to be aware of their role in the communications system and, if necessary, be given training to help them in this role.

3. Professionals in the field of organizational communications should be called upon to assist management in planning the communications system, in implementing it, and in measuring its effectiveness.

Communications Systems

Essentially, communication is the transmission of a *message* from one person (referred to as the *source*) to one or more other persons *(receivers).* In the organizational context, the message may involve a directive or order to do something; it may be a suggestion for changing a procedure; it may be an expression of approval or disapproval for the way a job has been performed; and so forth. The vehicle for transmitting the message is called the *channel.* Communication channels may be oral or written, formal or informal, and one-to-one or one-to-many. A supervisor's casual conversation with one of his or her subordinates uses an oral, informal, one-to-one channel; a letter from the company president mailed to all employees' homes is a written, formal, one-to-many channel.

For the successful transmission of messages, there has to be some assurance that the source and the receiver have some common basis for understanding the message—that it means the same thing to the person sending the message as to the person or persons receiving it. To achieve this, communications systems frequently include *feedback mechanisms,* which in essence send another message from the receiver to the source saying the original message has been received and understood. One common mechanism is a question-and-answer period at the end of a meeting in which an executive reports on the company's financial situation or on plans for new products.

Communications Networks. Within organizations, communication, or the transmission of messages, occurs through formal structures or through informal processes, both of which involve communications *networks.* A network, essentially, is a pattern of channels for the communication of messages to and from, or among, a specific group of people.

Figure C-1 illustrates five possible networks involving five persons; these networks are commonly found in the literature on communication because they have been studied widely by researchers on communication effectiveness. In the wheel network, person A is in the central position through which messages from B, C, D, and E must be transmitted. In the chain network, person A also is in a central position for transmitting messages, but messages to person C must go through person B, and messages to person E must go through person D. In the Y network, person C is in a central position with respect to persons A, B, and D, but messages to person E must go through person D. In the circle, each person can communicate with the persons on either side, and in the all-channel network, messages can be transmitted by each person from and to all other persons.

In ongoing organizations, it is unlikely that exact replicas of such networks will be found to any degree. The networks, both formal and informal, in the typ-

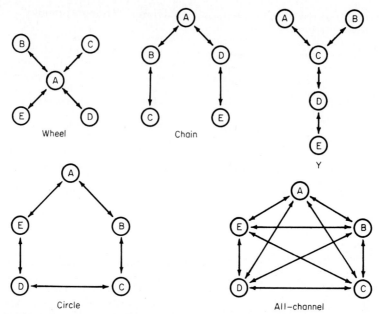

FIG. C-1 Communications network.

ical company usually involve many more than five people, and often they are a combination of two or more of the ones illustrated. One important concept that is illustrated by three of the networks—the wheel, chain, and Y—is that of the *gatekeeper,* or a person who is in a position to decide what messages should, or need to be, transmitted to others. In the wheel, person A is the gatekeeper with respect to all other persons, and in the chain, person A is the gate-

keeper for persons B and D, while B is the gatekeeper for C, and D is the gatekeeper for E.

The Formal Communications System. In most large organizations, the formal communications system is based on a chain of command from the top of the organization down, and the communications network can be depicted in the form of an organization chart, as shown in Fig. C-2. Within the formal system, messages are transmitted through the channels

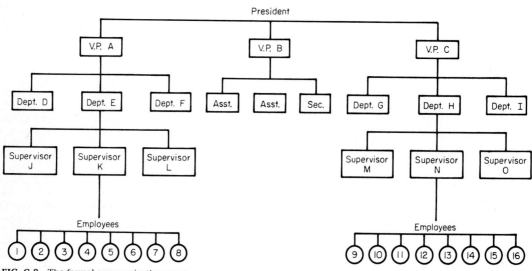

FIG. C-2 The formal communications system.

specified, and there are gatekeepers at each level of the organization for the persons at the next lower level. In the formal organizational context, these people also have been referred to as *linking pins.* Thus, in Fig. C-2, supervisor K is the linking pin between the supervisory level and employees 1 through 8.

The formal communications system is used for all official messages, including directives, procedures, policies, explanatory memorandums, job instructions, and so forth. It is predominantly a downward system, although there usually are provisions for some upward communications through the formal system in the form of production and sales reports, performance appraisals, and the like. In the case of upward commmunications, the person at the lower level is the gatekeeper for messages being transmitted upward. In Fig. C-2, for example, the head of department E is the gatekeeper for information concerning work units directed by supervisors J, K, and L, that is transmitted to vice president A.

For purposes of efficiency, there are frequent instances where horizontal communication is desirable. For example, if the job assignment of employee 5 requires communication with employee 12, the formal network in its strictest sense would require communication from employee 5 through supervisor K, department head E, vice president A, to the president and then back down through vice president C, department head H, and supervisor N. It is generally recognized that in such a situation, horizontal communication should be encouraged as long as it is authorized by the immediate superiors. In the situation described, supervisors K and N would be what are called the *authorizing agents* for the creation of a *bridge* of horizontal communication between employees 5 and 12. This process frequently is referred to as *Fayol's bridge* after management theorist Henri Fayol, who first discussed this principle of management.

The Informal Communications System. As any manager knows, many messages are transmitted in organizations every day that do not go through the formal channels. In contrast to the formal system, which relies predominantly on written channels, the informal communications system is primarily oral. Furthermore, much of the information transmitted through the informal system is not crucial to the functioning of the organization; often it is "scuttlebutt." The opportunity to engage in such communication may serve a purpose insofar as organizational maintenance is concerned and have a positive effect on the company's reputation as a place to work, but it does not contribute directly to the achievement of task goals.

There are some informal communications, however, that do affect organizational productivity, either positively or negatively; thus, the informal system cannot be ignored. The networks of the informal system can be very complex, and usually they involve relationships outside the formal hierarchy. A car pool can be the basis of a communications network; perhaps employees 3, 4, and 8 are in a car pool with supervisor N and one of the assistants to president B. Another opportunity for informal communication is the golf or tennis game that might involve supervisor J, department heads F and H, and vice president B. These situations provide an opportunity for the transmission of information in channels not accounted for in the formal system. Furthermore, the persons involved who receive messages through the informal system are in a position to transmit the messages to the persons directly above or below them in the formal system. Thus, the informal networks can become very extensive.

The Grapevine. An informal communications network found in nearly all organizations is the *grapevine,* so called because of its tendency to wander in and out of the formal, hierarchical lines of communication. The grapevine is the channel, usually an oral, one-to-one channel, through which rumors can be spread throughout the organization extremely rapidly. When the rumors involve possible changes in company policies, production plans, or top-level personnel, their effect on both productivity and organization climate can be devastating. Because of this, the grapevine generally is viewed negatively by employees although it often is perceived as influential since the rumors frequently have an element of truth to them. However, most messages transmitted through the grapevine are either groundless or distorted in some way.

It has been suggested that the best way to deal with the grapevine is to try to identify the persons in the organization who are the active transmitters on the grapevine, and who may constitute about 10 percent of the total personnel of the company. These people can then be "used" by top management to transmit messages quickly. This is a risky approach, however, because there is such frequent distortion on the grapevine and because there usually are many persons who are completely isolated from the grapevine and would never receive the messages. It is generally conceded that there is no way to eliminate the grapevine, and there may actually be some positive aspects to its existence. Probably the most effective approach for offsetting the harmful effects of the grapevine is to make sure that formal channels are established and used for all information managers and employees need or want to know.

Communications Techniques

A variety of techniques or methods are used in most companies to transmit information through the formal communications system. They may be oral or written or a combination of the two, and they usually are described in terms of downward techniques or **101** upward techniques. Communications methods commonly used in organizations are listed in Table C-1.

Many of the oral methods listed may involve both downward and upward communications; one-to-one telephone conversations or interviews typically provide an opportunity for information to be transmitted upward. Of the more formal oral communications methods, meetings frequently are used for two-way communications, particularly such meetings as those of an executive with her or his immediate staff or those of a supervisor with his or her work group. Most written communications, however, are strictly one way—either downward or upward.

Downward Communications. As noted, communications from the top of the organization down are essential to any operation; they translate management policy planning and decision making into orders directing employees on their jobs. It is not surprising, therefore, that most organizations spend much more time and effort on downward than on upward communications. As the methods listed in Table C-1 indicate, however, much of the communications effort involves information designed to enhance the organizational climate and build a loyal group of employees and managers. Many of the written methods used for all employees, particularly

employee publications, have no direct bearing on productivity.

Where it is essential for information to be communicated downward, the same message may be transmitted by several methods. This approach provides for a certain amount of *redundancy*, but it has been found that some redundancy may be necessary for effective communication. Research studies involving employee communications have reinforced the notion that a combination of communication methods, including both oral and written, are the best assurance that information will be received.

To determine which downward technique to use for a particular type of information, a number of factors are relevant. Some techniques are much faster than others; some are appropriate only for certain levels of employees; some are viewed as more authoritative than others. Another factor that should be considered is whether the information is likely to be viewed as positive or negative.

The figures in Table C-2 indicate the methods used most frequently by more than 200 companies for communicating three different types of information to employees. For information on changes in pay, which usually is viewed positively, the most frequently used method is an individual verbal com-

TABLE C-1 Communications Methods

Direction	Oral	Written

Downward:
  Among
    managerial
    levels
	Directives over the telephone
	One-to-one conferences or interviews
	Staff meetings
	Committee meetings
	Lunch or dinner meetings
		Policy and procedure manuals
		Job descriptions
		Organization charts
		Memoranda
		Reports of committee meetings and decisions
		    reached
		Progress and planning reports
		Management newsletters

Downward:
  To all
    employees
	Job instructions from supervisor or trainer
	Appraisal interviews
	Orientation and training meetings
	Departmental or work-unit meetings
	Mass meetings or annual meetings of all
	    employees
	Closed-circuit TV addresses
	Public address systems
	Videotapes or cassettes
	Open house and plant tours
	Recorded telephone messages
		Assignment sheets or lists of job duties
		Bulletin board notices
		Posters
		Memos or announcements
		Employee publications
		Pay inserts
		Letters to employees' homes
		Handbooks, pamphlets or brochures on
		    company policies, benefits, etc.
		Annual reports
		News stories and/or advertisements in the local
		    press or TV

Upward:	Informal discussions with employees, first-
	    level supervisors, union representatives
	Employee or staff meetings
	Counseling sessions
	Exit interviews
	Telephone "hot lines" for employee
	    questions
		Formal attitude surveys
		Written grievances or complaints filed
		Company performance reports on production,
		    sales, finances, personnel, etc.
		Suggestion systems
		Question-and-answer column in employee
		    publications
		Gripe boxes

TABLE C-2 Methods Used for Communicating Different Types of Information

Type of information/method of communication	Percentage of 219 companies using method indicated
Changes in wage or salary levels	
Individual oral communication	45
Memos or letters to employees	31
Group meetings	29
Articles in employee publications	14
Through union/union contract	13
Posted on bulletin boards	12
Other (cassette recordings, public address system, local press)	5
Changes in operations that might result in layoffs, transfers, etc.	
Group meetings	44
Individual oral communication	31
Memos or letters to employees	21
Articles in employee publications	13
Posted on bulletin boards	12
Through union/union contract	8
Changes in top-level personnel	
Memo or letters to employees	44
Articles in employee publications	43
Posted on bulletin boards	36
Group meetings	13
Local news media	8
Individual oral communication	5

Source: Adapted from *Employee Communications*, Bureau of National Affairs, Inc., Personnel Policies Forum Survey, no. 110, Washington, D.C., 1975, p. 16.

munication between the employee and the immediate supervisor. To communicate changes in operations, where the information may be negative, the most frequent method is a group meeting, which usually provides an opportunity for answering employees' questions and presenting more information on future prospects. For information of a relatively neutral variety, such as changes in top-level personnel, the more impersonal, written techniques are used most frequently.

Employee Publications. In many companies, particularly large ones with a number of work locations, considerable time and money are spent on employee publications. These may take the form of a newsletter, a newspaper, or a magazine complete with color photographs. They are published as frequently as weekly or as infrequently as quarterly, with a monthly publication schedule being most common. Distribution most often is by mail to employees' homes, although sometimes the publications are distributed at work—sent through the company mail system, handed out by supervisors, or picked up at the plant gate or other distribution points. Frequently the publications are prepared by professional journalists on the company staff; another approach is for the company's advertising agency to do the final layout and artwork with the company personnel writing the material to be included.

In view of the expense of the employee publication effort in most companies, often little is done to find out if management is getting its money's worth from its efforts. In some companies, management is reluctant to use employee publications for other than chitchat or announcements about retirements and service anniversaries. In cases where companies have conducted readership surveys of their employee publications, however, they have found that employees generally are interested in material that is more company-oriented and gives them information on company progress and future plans.

Upward Communications. While most communication in organizations is downward from the top of the hierarchy, upward communication is essential as well. The two most important aspects of upward communication are that it (1) provides management with some feedback indicating whether messages communicated downward have been received and (2) transmits upward the information needed for higher-level decisions. It is also important because it gives lower-level managers and employees an opportunity to ask questions, make complaints, express satisfaction or dissatisfaction with the way things are being managed, and make suggestions for improvements in methods or changes in policies.

As indicated in Table C-1, there are fewer methods for upward than for downward communications; furthermore, the methods that generally are considered most effective for upward communications are informal discussions with employees or first-level supervisors. In one survey of personnel executives, the formal upward method considered most effective was the attitude survey; however, less than one-third of the companies participating in the survey had ever conducted a formal employee attitude survey. Because of the time and expense involved in conducting such surveys, it is usually the larger companies that use them as a means for upward communications.

A major problem in upward communications is associated with the hierarchical system of most business organizations. Supervisors and department heads, in essence, are the gatekeepers with respect to messages upward, and in many cases they can effectively stifle employee complaints or reports of dissatisfaction. Many of the formal upward channels are designed to get around this problem in that they set up a channel around the immediate superior. This is true, for example, of attitude surveys, formal grievance procedures, gripe boxes, and suggestion systems. In recent years, a number of companies have established private "hot line" systems to provide a method for employees to communicate anonymously on any matter of concern with the company official best qualified to discuss the issue. Inquiries may be made through a special telephone line or company mail forms. One such program has a coordinating staff to transmit the inquiries to the appropriate person for reply. The employee making the inquiry receives a direct response, and questions that are of general interest are discussed in the company newspaper. In this way, both upward and downward communications are served.

Employee Meetings. Employee meetings also provide a method for both upward and downward communications. Some meetings are almost all downward in nature; this is true, for example, of meetings held to present information on the company's environmental position, to explain a new safety procedure, or to train a group of employees in a new method of handling orders. For these types of meetings, there often are elaborate visual aids, such as slides, videotapes, or films, and a good deal of preparation. While there may be some opportunity for feedback in the way of questions related to the subject at hand, these meetings are not aimed at providing a general channel of upward communication.

In some companies, a general upward channel is provided through special employee meetings on a regular basis. One example of how such meetings may be arranged is shown in Table C-3, taken from the policy and procedure bulletin of a large manufacturing company with a number of plants in different locations.

Management Information Systems. With the advent of computer technology in the 1950s, business organizations began to develop management information systems (MIS). These systems are in essence a complex communications network linking all parts of an organization no matter how geographically dispersed they may be. Such a system permits input of data from any point within the organization, data transmission, data processing, and information storage and retrieval; in effect, it is capable of gathering and processing all the data needed to provide information for planning, operating, and controlling the organization.

While the potential value of MIS as a communications channel is great, the technology appears to be far ahead of actual or effective application to date. Most organizations have not yet developed their systems to the extent possible. In part, this is because many top-level managers are reluctant to put certain data into the computer data bank for fear it will become available to unauthorized persons. There are many applications, however, where management information systems have proved worthwhile, particularly in such areas as production planning and sales forecasting. A major benefit of the use of computer networks for communications is that the information can be transmitted directly from the operating levels of the organization to the highest levels without having to be processed through the several hierarchical levels in between. This both saves time and reduces

TABLE C-3 An Example of Upward Communications

Employee Discussion Groups—Hourly

1. The Plant will conduct bi-monthly (more often if necessary) employee discussion groups.

2. The group representation will consist of 8–10 hourly employees, the Plant Manager and Personnel Manager.

3. The selection will include both sexes, all races and a mixture of old and new employees to assure representation from each operating segment of the plant.

4. The notice of each group discussion will be posted on all bulletin boards two days prior to the meeting. The notice will include the employee's name, department, time and location of the meeting. Copies of the notice will be mailed to Department Heads and to each individual employee's supervisor.

5. Discussion groups will cover all shifts. It is recommended the discussions begin 1½ hours before shift end and conclude at shift end. The meeting will be held in the Plant Manager's office.

6. The meeting will be opened by the Plant Manager introducing himself and informing the group that all statements made by himself or the Personnel Manager may be repeated throughout the plant. The group will be assured that their statements, suggestions, and complaints will not be repeated except where follow-up is required. The group will then introduce themselves and the discussion will begin.

7. The purpose of these group discussions is to allow the employee an opportunity to register complaints regarding working conditions, equipment, wages, classifications, overtime, etc., either for himself or fellow workers. The Plant Manager and Personnel Manager will answer questions and explain management's position.

8. Immediately following the meeting the Personnel Manager will follow up on all items and instigate corrective action if warranted. The action taken will be reported back to the employee registering the complaint or suggestion. A written record of reported items and corrective action will be maintained by the Personnel Department.

Source: Employee Communications, Bureau of National Affairs, Inc., Personnel Forum Survey, no. 110, Washington, D.C., 1975, pp. 25–26.

the chances of distortion of the information transmitted.

Barriers to Effective Communications

In any type of communication, there are inherent difficulties associated with the different perceptions, values, experiences, standards, and biases of the sender and the receiver of the message involved. In the organizational context, these problems are amplified by such factors as physical distance between the sender and the receiver, emotional distance resulting from status differences between higher management and the lower levels, fears and anxieties related to boss-subordinate roles, and so forth.

Communications Breakdown. Probably the most common problem in organizational communications is the failure to transmit the message intended to those who should receive it: a communications breakdown. Studies in ongoing organizations indicate that often only about 50 percent of the communicational interactions between people result in real communication. In other words, as many as half the people for whom a message is intended either do not receive it at all or else receive a distorted version of the message.

There are two major approaches to reducing the incidence of communications breakdown. The first is repetition or redundancy: The same message is sent to the same people through more than one channel and using various methods. The more often a message is transmitted and the more ways it is sent, the more likely it will in fact reach the intended receivers without error or distortion. The drawback to this approach is that it reduces the amount of information that can be communicated at any point in time. There also is the possibility that some persons may, in effect, "tune out" the communications channel when they perceive the message is redundant.

Another approach to preventing communications breakdown is to provide a means for the receiver of a message to verify it through some feedback process or two-way interaction. Studies consistently have shown that two-way communication is viewed as more accurate and more satisfying to the parties involved; however, it is more time-consuming (about 50 percent longer on the average) and thus not feasible for all kinds of information.

Distortion in Upward Communications. The breakdown in communications is of particular concern in the downward system because it is essential for those at lower levels to know what management expects them to do. In the upward system, the major difficulty involves distortion. This may involve the transmission upward of only "good" news and suppression of bad performance reports, employee complaints, and the like. In some instances, superiors may completely block the upward transmission of information—either because it might be interpreted to reflect negatively on the superior or because it does not appear important enough to bother higher-level management with it.

As noted earlier, some formal upward communications channels, such as attitude surveys and employee complaint procedures, may permit the bypassing of lower-level managers. Computerized information systems also tend to transmit information directly to top management. Unless these programs are administered effectively and considered legitimate communications channels, there may be considerable resentment on the part of the lower-level managers who are bypassed in the process.

Information Overload. A problem, particularly for those at the highest levels of management, is that of information overload. Full information on every detail of the company's operation and the activities of every employee is more than most executives can cope with. The information-producing capabilities of the computer have added greatly to the overload problem.

There is one area where each manager has to decide for himself or herself what information is really needed and how frequently it should be updated. Often, information processing can be delegated; where delegation and decentralization are used as a means of avoiding overload, however, there has to be some means to ensure that crucial messages get through. It is important that decision makers have all the relevant information before deciding the future course of the organization.

As noted, top management has to set the stage for effective organizational communications. In many organizations, unfortunately, management thinks of communications only in terms of orders downward and progress reports upward; frequently managers fail to communicate because they assume everyone knows as much as they do. A relatively new approach to assessing the communications climate in organizations is the *communications audit.* Through a variety of procedures, including questionnaires and interviews, the audit provides a comprehensive picture of the organization's communications system, including the sources and causes of communications failure. Such an audit, in addition to suggesting areas in which more formal communications techniques may be needed, also can indicate points in the organization where management needs to concentrate on providing a more effective communications climate.

See also Attitude surveys; Information sources; Interpersonal relationships; Management information systems (MIS); Public and community relations; Suggestion systems.

REFERENCES

Employee Communications, Personnel Policies Forum Survey, no. 110, Bureau of National Affairs, Inc., Washington, D.C., July 1975.

Haney, William V.: *Communications and Organizational Behavior*, 4th ed., Richard D. Irwin, Homewood, Ill., 1981.

Lesikar, Raymond V.: *Business Communications: Theory and Applications*, Richard D. Irwin, Homewood, Ill., 1980.

MARY GREEN MINER, *Bureau of National Affairs, Inc.*

JOHN B. MINER, *Georgia State University*

Compensation, Employee Benefit Plans

Originally identified as fringe benefits because of their minimal role, forms of indirect compensation for work have become known popularly as employee benefits as their importance has increased relative to direct compensation (i.e., wages, salaries, and bonuses in the form of cash and/or stock payments). Defined most simply, an *employee benefit* is compensation in cash or its equivalent which is not paid directly or specifically for time spent discharging work assignments.

Most forms of employee benefits may be classified into one of six categories: time off with pay, employee services, special payments, health care, survivor protection, and retirement.

Employee Benefit Categories

Time Off with Pay. As the phrase implies, this is payment for hours not worked (thereby differentiating it from wage or salary, which is pay for time worked). Basically, time off with pay covers pay while not at the work site, but it may also cover pay for not working while on the company premises.

Included in this grouping of payments for time not spent at the work site are pay for leisure time (e.g., holidays and vacations), for meeting social and civic responsibilities (e.g., funeral leave, court duty, and military reserve training allowance), for accident or illness which incapacitates a person (e.g., workers' compensation and disability), and for termination of employment (e.g., unemployment compensation and severance pay).

Rest-Period Pay. Probably the most widely known recuperation period is the coffee break—a scheduled stoppage in work for 10 or 15 minutes while the individual is paid to enjoy a drink and the companionship of fellow workers. Other short paid periods of time not worked include wash and cleanup at the end of the day and a meal period taken at the work station (often required by state law when insufficient time is given for one meal during a shift).

Leisure-Time Pay. Many companies now provide 10 or more paid holidays each year. In addition to what is referred to as the "basic six" (i.e., New Year's Day, Memorial Day, Fourth of July, Labor Day, Thanksgiving, and Christmas), the other popular holidays are Good Friday, Washington's Birthday, Columbus Day, Veteran's Day, the day after Thanksgiving, and personal floaters to be used when the employee chooses. Normally an employee is eligible for holiday pay after a minimum period of employment (e.g., 1 month).

Vacation pay, on the other hand, normally increases with additional years of company service (e.g., 2 weeks after 1 year, 3 weeks after 5 years, 4 weeks after 12 years, and 5 weeks after 20 years, and 6 weeks after 30 years employment). The scheduling of vacations ranges from approval of employee request for specified dates to company-dictated locationwide shutdown for prescribed periods.

The sabbatical is a more restricted form of time off with pay, whereby the recipient receives 6 months or more to accomplish a specific objective. Sabbaticals are used to meet specific educational needs of the individual (e.g., completing doctorate work in a technical discipline), to respond to social needs (e.g., working with a worthy nonprofit organization such as a drug rehabilitation center), or simply to allow a person a longer period to "get away from it all" in order to return with renewed enthusiasm.

Because of the cost, sabbaticals are usually very limited in number. Recipients are chosen typically on the basis of organizational level and/or some form of competitive examination.

Social Responsibility Pay. A death in the immediate family normally allows the employee a maximum number of days of paid absence (e.g., 3) for funeral leave—time off for bereavement.

Court duty pay is usually the difference between normal pay and what the individual receives from the court for serving as a juror.

A military reserve training allowance is payment for all or a portion of the time off which an employer is required to give an employee to fulfill military training commitments.

Disability Pay. Another paid absence, which may be for a long time, is a period of inability to work due to accident or illness. If the disability is work-related, payment is covered under workers' compensation. Today all states have laws requiring employers to be responsible for all costs of work-related disabilities, regardless of who is at fault. All disabilities are categorized as either permanent or temporary and either total or partial. Benefits are either in the form of lump sum awards and/or weekly payments for a specified period of time in recognition of treatment, rehabilitation, and extent of injury and permanence.

Only five states (California, Hawaii, New Jersey, New York, and Rhode Island) and Puerto Rico have statutes covering nonoccupational accident or illness absences. These provide limited payments usually for a maximum of 6 months and are called disability pay plans. In spite of the lack of legislated benefits, most companies have instituted voluntary programs to provide benefits similar to workers' compensation. In most companies this is split into two different programs: short-term and long-term. As the words denote, the difference is in the duration of benefits.

Short-term disability benefits normally cover the first 6 (maybe 12) months of the disability: Such programs are usually self-insured in larger companies. Long-term plans pick up where short-term plans end and are normally more formally insured or self-funded through a 501 (c) (9) Trust, a section of the Internal Revenue Code (IRC) covering "voluntary employees' beneficiary associations." In most instances long-term disability plans are integrated with disability benefits provided by Social Security.

Unemployment and Termination Pay. Unemployment compensation is pay to a person no longer employed. Provision for such programs was established in the Social Security Act of 1935. This law made the individual states responsible for setting up and administering their own programs.

The level and extent of benefits vary significantly by state, although most states provide up to 26 weeks, depending upon eligibility. Some provide higher benefits, depending on the number of dependents, and a few include workers who are on strike. A number also provide automatic extension of benefits during periods of high unemployment.

The amount of tax each employer will pay on covered compensation is based on an experience rating formula which penalizes those companies with an unstable work force. The formulas, while similar, do vary from state to state.

Termination or severance pay is the final form of pay for time not worked. In many instances, it is pay for time not worked in lieu of notice. Under such conditions the employee may receive notice on Friday of being terminated, effective immediately, and of being given two additional weeks of pay. The assumption is that during the next 2 weeks he or she can find employment elsewhere and therefore not suffer any loss of income.

Some companies differentiate between individual terminations and plant closings. When they do, greater termination or severance pay benefits are given in the latter situation—often scaled upward in relation to years of service (e.g., 2 weeks plus 1 additional week for every year of service).

Severance pay for higher-paid employees is often more generous than that for lower-paid individuals—probably a reflection that higher-paid employees may have fewer suitable employment opportunities available elsewhere.

Employee Services. This covers a wide range of items which are either provided at no cost to the employee or made available at a discounted price. Included in this category are a company cafeteria, parking facilities, recreation programs, company medical facilities, and company products.

Many companies are offering additional services in response to social pressures. These services include providing child-care facilities, thus enabling mothers to work, scheduling car pools and sometimes providing minibuses to reduce commuting costs and fuel consumption, and providing a full array of protective clothing for those who might be exposed to health-threatening gases and substances.

Another service is making employee-authorized deductions through the company's payroll system. These run the range from mass-merchandised insurance programs for automobile and homeowner policies to credit unions.

Relatively new on the benefit scene are the following: legal insurance (where legal services are paid for in whole or in part by the employer); auto insurance (with the company passing on discounted rates to its employees, who usually pay through a payroll deduction); homeowners' insurance (similar in operation to auto insurance); and liability insurance (normally provided only to officers and directors to protect them from legal actions arising out of performance of their duties).

Counseling is another service which is provided by a number of companies and which can take many forms. Financial counseling for executives normally includes advice on estate building as well as estate conservation (including tax aspects). A more broadly based benefit is preretirement planning. Under such a program, employees are invited to a number of company-sponsored seminars focusing on legal, financial, and personal considerations of retirement.

Special Payments. These are cash benefits paid in recognition of certain events. An example is the attendance bonus (paid either in cash or in paid time off) for specified periods of perfect attendance (e.g., week, month, or year). An extension of this is the length-of-service bonus which increases with every additional year of company service (e.g., $25 for 1 year of service, $50 for 2 years of service, etc.). A more common modification is the service award program where 5-year milestones are commemorated with a special pin or other item displaying the company emblem. Normally a special recognition is taken of 25 years of service. Many companies sponsor a quarter-century club with annual dinners for past and new members at company expense.

Special-event gifts are common, especially among smaller companies. The Thanksgiving turkey, the Christmas ham, the wedding cake knife, and the baby sweater are among the more common examples. Suggestion awards ranging from token recognition to significant amounts are often given to employees for improving product quality and/or reducing business expenses.

Educational Assistance. Company recognition of the importance of continued education is often reinforced with an educational assistance program for its employees. This usually takes the form of reimbursement of a percentage of college tuition (e.g., 75 percent) but typically does not include other expenses such as books.

In providing scholarships for dependents of employees, a company will invariably specify the number it is prepared to give each year. Often the employee's dependent is required to submit a formal application and take a competitive examination.

Another educational benefit is the matching gift program, whereby the company will match (possibly to a stated individual maximum amount) a contribution by the employee to a qualified institute of higher learning.

Relocation Reimbursement. Relocation expenses are often reimbursed to a significant extent when the company wishes an individual to move to a different company location. Usually such coverage is only provided to management-level employees, but there are instances of coverage to lower-paid employees who possess unique technical skills. In addition to paying the actual moving costs, many companies will pay all or part of the selling costs of a house (including loss against appraised value), travel and lodging costs while the employee seeks new accommodations (or waits for a new home to become available), carrying costs on a former residence until sold, and low-cost or no-cost loans until the former residence is sold.

Reimbursement for travel, meals, and lodging in conjunction with business responsibilities is covered under expense accounts, not employee benefits, and usually is limited to sales representatives and management personnel. Many companies, however, pay blue-collar and lower-paid office employees a supper allowance if their work extends into a meal period which is after normal working hours.

Overtime and Premiums. Some authorities consider penalty pay as a form of benefit. The most significant form of penalty pay is overtime pay. In 1938, the federal Fair Labor Standards Act became law. Among its provisions was the requirement that all employees who could not be exempted from the act (i.e., outside salespeople, executives, professionals, and administrators) had to be paid time and one-half for all hours worked in excess of 40 hours per week if the company was engaged in interstate commerce. Previously, in 1936, the Walsh-Healey Act stated that similar people must be compensated at the rate of time and one-half for all hours worked in excess of 8 hours per day if the employer had a federal government contract of $10,000 or more.

In addition to overtime pay, most companies will pay a premium if the employee works on a company-paid holiday or on Sunday. A number of companies also pay a special premium for Saturday, regardless of the number of hours the employee otherwise works.

Especially disagreeable work often commands an additional hourly premium. Similarly, a guarantee of 2 to 4 hours is used by many when the employee is called back to the site after having left for the day or is called in on a nonscheduled workday. This assures the individual of a minimum amount of pay, even though the task may only take a few minutes. A similar approach is used to cover the employee who reports in on a regularly scheduled workday and finds there is no work (possibly owing to an unforeseen calamity, such as a power failure). In each case the difference between the pay for the hours actually worked and those paid for can be considered a benefit.

Health Care. Reimbursement for various types of medical expenses is a prevalent employee benefit. Employers have a great deal of flexibility in designing programs to ease the financial burden that can be imposed on the employee through various types of health-care expenses. However, male and female workers must be treated equally, as must their spouses. Additionally, the employer must comply with the requirements of the Employee Retirement Income Security Act (commonly called ERISA). Although this act deals primarily with pension plans, it supersedes the earlier Welfare and Pension Plans Disclosure Act as it relates to reporting financial and other information on health care plans.

The major portion of employer-provided health care coverage is provided under group health insurance plans. As implied, the word *group* indicates that the contract covers a designated group of employees rather than a specific person. Financing ranges from a fully insured program (the typical group contract placed with an insurance company) to a self-insured plan (whereby the company directly assumes the risk). The premium paid to insurance companies covers benefit payments, expenses, taxes, commissions, and the insurance company profits. If the insurance company is asked to evaluate and process claims under a self-insured plan, it is called an ASO (administrative services only). When the carrier agrees to make all payments above a prescribed level, it has a stop-loss feature.

Since the premium of an insured plan is generally experience-rated for each group, there can be differences in cost from one group to another. The inherent efficiencies of a large group generally provide lower premiums than comparable coverage under an individual policy. When a high-risk group is able to take additional coverage, the plan suffers from the risk of adverse selection.

Well known in the area of health care protection are Blue Cross and Blue Shield—independent, nonprofit membership corporations. The first provides protection against the cost of hospital charges; the second focuses on surgical and other medical care items.

Another form of community-rated health care plan is the health care maintenance organization (HMO). For a fixed monthly charge every covered employee and her or his family receive no-cost health care instead of pay-for-repair health care. The incentive to those responsible for administering health care is to diagnose problems early and treat them before they become major problems, which require more time and expense to treat. This concept of prepaid health care was essentially the model for the Health Maintenance Organization Act of 1973. An HMO meeting the act's standards must be offered employees as an alternative to other coverage, if the HMO makes the request.

The normal group insurance contract providing health care is either a comprehensive or a schedule plan (usually with a major medical override). A comprehensive plan has a corridor or deductible (e.g., $100), which the employee pays in full. The plan then pays a percentage (e.g., 80 percent) of all remaining expenses in a calendar year up to a maximum (e.g., $250,000). The advantage of this plan is its simplicity.

The schedule plan identifies each covered expense and the maximum amount that will be paid. Normally, such a plan also has a major medical coinsurance feature, which, after a deductible (e.g., $100), will pay a percentage of all remaining expenses (e.g.., 80 percent). While more complicated than a comprehensive type, a schedule plan makes it possible for the individual to get full reimbursement of all expenses if the charges are equal to or less than the allowable schedule. Under either the comprehensive or the scheduled plan, it is possible to add a stop-loss clause (i.e., maximum amount the employee would have to pay).

Since July 1966, a major role in health care for disabled and retired employees has been played by Medicare, under title XVIII of the Social Security law. This program specifies two types of coverage: (1) basic coverage (providing benefits to cover the cost of hospital and related care) and (2) a voluntary supplement to cover certain doctor charges and other medical services not covered by the basic plan. Eligible employees receive basic benefits at no cost and are automatically enrolled in the supplemental plan at a monthly premium set by the government (although they can, of course, withdraw from the voluntary portion). In addition to Medicare, many retired employees are eligible for some form of coverage under the company health care plan.

Title XIX of the Social Security Act is also significant in the discussion of health care, for it introduced Medicaid—a program which provides matching federal funds to those states granting a specified minimum degree of health care protection to defined low-income people. Since these medical benefits are provided to those normally on welfare, they should not be considered part of a company employee benefit program.

Most medical insurance programs cover prescription drugs only if administered as part of hospital care, so a number of companies have also set up prescription care plans. Under such plans the employee normally pays the first $1 or $2 and the plan covers the remaining expenses.

In addition, vision care insurance (a plan which covers all or part of eye examinations, prescription lenses, and frames), has become more prevalent. Some provide audio care covering corrective hearing devices. Many extend dental insurance to cover both preventive oral care (e.g., checkups, cleaning, and x-rays) and repair and replacement.

The cost of health care has caused many companies to develop cost containment programs, including tighter claims monitoring and self-insuring a large portion of the expenses. Additionally, many health care or wellness programs attempt to mini-mize illness-related risks. These wellness programs also provide counseling services for those with chemical dependency, emotional, and other problems.

Survivor Protection. This includes all forms of compensation paid to the beneficiary (i.e., designated survivor). The most common is provided under group life insurance plans. A majority of these plans (especially for salaried employees) provide an amount equal to a specified portion of salary (e.g., two times). In many companies this cost is paid, at least in part, by the employee, though the trend is to company-pay all coverage. The right to purchase individual insurance of the same amount without a medical exam after the group coverage is canceled is called "the conversion privilege."

Many companies also have an accidental death and dismemberment (AD&D) policy. The former pays an additional amount of insurance if the death is accidental; the latter, specified amounts for loss of eyesight or limbs.

An additional form of survivor protection is business travel accident insurance. Normally, such programs provide for death benefits equal to some multiple of salary if death occurs while traveling on company business. For cost considerations, some plans will exclude high-exposure risks (e.g., salespersons traveling within their territory).

Retirement. Benefits included in this category are all deferred payments which commence on the date the employee leaves the active employment of the company (and usually the work force). The payment may be either in a lump sum or in an annuity (regular payments over a specified period). Typically, companies will periodically make retiree adjustments (i.e., increase the annuity amount of retired employees to offset the reduced purchasing power of fixed pensions during inflationary periods).

Defined Benefit Plans. Retirement plans are either defined benefit or defined contribution plans. The former indicates the annuity amount that the individual will receive upon meeting certain age and/or service requirements. Such plans are subdivided into career service (e.g., $15 per month per year of service), career earnings (e.g., 1.4 percent per $1000 earned with the company), and final pay (e.g., 1.1 percent per $1000 of the average compensation during the highest paid 5 years of the 10 years immediately preceding retirement, multiplied by the years of service). Some have modified their career earnings plans to take on the appearance of final pay plans by periodically weighting later years of employment more heavily.

With most defined benefit plans, benefits are scheduled to begin at age 65 (although a number of plans now specify 62, and some, age 60). If benefits begin before this normal retirement date, there is a discount for each year, the rationale being that the individual probably will receive benefits for a longer period of time because of this early retirement. Some plans provide for nondiscounted pensions when certain age and years-of-service combinations are attained (e.g., 85 or 90). In addition to the formal early retirement program, special-opportunity programs may be designed to provide liberalized early retirement pensions for those who retire within certain prescribed periods or "windows." Usually such plans are in response to a company need to reduce manning levels and attendant payroll costs.

Additionally, many plans will integrate benefits with those provided under Social Security. This allows the company to minimize the possibility of the employee retiring with combined net income greater than that while employed since, depending on income level, up to one-half of the Social Security benefits could be taxable. It also allows the company to provide greater plan benefits to the higher-paid individuals (since it gives lesser benefits to the lower-paid) at the same cost.

Integrated plan formulas are essentially of two types and are used with both career earnings and final-pay-type plans. The more common is the carve-out or step-up approach. This uses one value for all earnings up to the Social Security tax base (e.g., 1 percent) and a higher value for all earnings in excess of that amount (e.g., 1.5 percent). The other approach employs an offset formula which uses one value (e.g., 1.5 percent) for all earnings but then subtracts a percentage (e.g., 50 percent) of the primary Social Security benefit at age 65. Although there is a considerable amount of flexibility in designing integrated pension plans, there are a number of specific Internal Revenue Service rules that must be followed in developing the plan.

Defined benefit plans falling under the jurisdiction of ERISA need to have provisions to ensure that the benefits will be available when payment is to commence. To discharge this obligation, companies either contract with an insurance company to provide insured benefits or set up a trust. The former is most common with smaller companies; the latter is used by the bigger plans.

Under a trusteed plan an actuary determines each year how much the company must contribute. This determination is made by making a number of assumptions regarding such items as mortality, salary increases, turnover, and investment gains in the portfolio as well as by adjusting for earlier errors in judgment. Once the money has been paid to the trustee, it can never be recaptured by the company.

Defined Contribution Plans. These plans indicate the amount that will be set aside each year for purposes of retirement. The value at time of retirement is usually dependent upon the market value of the investments at that later date. Such plans are usually described as either thrift (or savings) plans or profit-sharing programs. A critical difference is that with the former, the employee must set aside a

certain portion from his or her paycheck (e.g., 5 percent of salary) and the company will match this on a formula basis (e.g., 50 cents on the dollar). While employees usually have a choice of how their contributions will be invested (e.g., fixed income, common stocks excluding the company's, and/or the company's own stock), the company contribution is normally in the form of company stock.

Under a profit-sharing plan the company agrees to take a percentage of the profits (generally not to exceed 15 percent of covered payroll) and set it aside for the employee's termination. Some plans permit or require employee contributions. It should be noted that some plans pay off in shorter cycles, but these are not really directed toward providing retirement income. Profit-sharing and savings plans may be structured as salary reduction plans, thereby converting such employee contributions from after-tax to pretax income resulting in a lowering of current-year federal income taxes.

Another form of defined contribution plan is the employee stock ownership plan (ESOP), a leveraged form of financing. The company gives its stock to a trust in order to secure a loan, with the proceeds going to the company. The company makes regular payments to the trust (enabling it to pay off the loan); the trust in turn credits an employee account with the value of paid-off stock. A Tax Reduction Form of ESOP (TRAESOP) permits the company to set aside company stock worth prescribed amounts of payroll each year for employees.

Also available to employees is an Individual Retirement Account (IRA) permitting employees to set aside a tax-deductible amount within prescribed limits to provide a defined contribution retirement benefit. A Keogh Plan is a defined contribution plan that places self-employeds on a comparable basis with their company-employed counterparts under a defined contribution plan. The Simplified Employee Pension (SEP) is a hybrid IRA and Keogh permitting employer contributions to a plan established by the employee.

If these plans are not discriminatory in favor of higher-paid employees (other than in relation to direct compensation) and meet certain other requirements (e.g., ensuring payments will accrue only to employees and only at time of retirement), deductions can be taken by the company in the year in which it makes contributions either to the trust or to the insurance carrier, whereas the employees usually will have no tax liabilities until they actually receive payments.

Additional requirements dealing with disclosure, fiduciary responsibility, funding requirements, maximum benefits payable, reinsurance, and vesting (i.e., the nonforfeitable right of the employee to a benefit), and other items are covered in the 1974 Employee Retirement Income Security Act.

Another form of deferred income which is often

used to supplement retirement annuities is the qualified stock purchase plan, described in Section 423 of the Internal Revenue Code. This is somewhat similar in appearance to, but is not to be confused with, the incentive stock option, described in Section 422A of the same code. Under the qualified stock purchase plan, the employee contracts with the company to purchase, normally on an installment basis, a specified number of shares at a price as low as 85 percent of market at the time of each installment. Under an incentive stock option, the company agrees to allow the individual to buy up to a specified number of shares of stock not later than 10 years from the date of option at a price equal to the fair market value at the date of grant. While the company may pick and choose who will be eligible in an incentive stock option plan, essentially all employees must be afforded the opportunity to join if a qualified stock purchase plan is established.

Perquisites

Unlike employee benefits in general, which extend to all or most employees in the organization, perquisites are special "benefits" that apply only to a few executives at the pinnacle of the organization. They include such items as use of a company car and airplane, medical examinations, special life insurance plans, club memberships, financial counseling, and supplemental pension plans.

The reason for perquisites is to show that there is a difference between the very top executive level and everyone else in the organization. In some organizations these differences are openly flaunted; in most they are more discreetly observed.

Cost of Employee Benefit Programs

Recognizing the rising value of indirect compensation, the U.S. Chamber of Commerce in 1967 officially changed the name of its periodic analysis from the Fringe Benefits Report to the Employee Benefits Report.

To Company. In addition to calculating the annual total cost of each benefit, it is common to calculate three indicators of the cost per employee: (1) dollars per year per employee (total benefit dollars divided by average number of employees on the payroll during the year); (2) cents per payroll hour (total benefit dollars divided by total hours paid, thereby giving a cost for every hour paid, or by total hours worked, thereby giving a cost for every hour worked); and (3) percentage of pay (total benefit dollars divided by total payroll or total base payroll).

Following these approaches it is possible to cost not only the total benefit program but also each of the components. Results can be compared with the U.S. Chamber of Commerce's annual benefit survey.

To Employees. Employee costs fall into two categories: payroll deductions and noncovered costs. A payroll deduction is the amount the employee pays in order to participate in the program, an amount taken from each paycheck. When the employee pays a portion of the cost in this way, the plan is said to be contributory (i.e., the employee contributes toward part of the cost). When the company does not charge the employee for coverage, the plan is said to be noncontributory. In addition to the payroll deductions to support membership in various company benefit plans, the employee, of course, has various statutory deductions (e.g., Social Security and income tax withholding for federal, state, and possibly city taxes).

The second category, noncovered cost, is the amount in excess of plan benefits (e.g., the deductible and the coinsurance feature in a health care plan).

Because of the combined impact of all deductions, it is important that the benefits be considered worthwhile by the employee. It is this concern that has led to what some call flexible or customized compensation. This pick-and-choose benefit planning by the individual is present to some extent in almost every company. The various stages include the following: (1) the employee decides whether she or he wishes plan coverage; (2) the employee determines the extent of coverage by authorizing one of several possible payroll deductions; and (3) the employee chooses whether to waive normal protection with one benefit (thereby receiving lower minimum no-cost coverage), applying the value difference to obtain greater coverage in other benefits.

Such programs are optimally structured when an employee is able to purchase benefits with pretax dollars. Amounts not used for benefits may remain in a reimbursement account to cover expenses not paid under health care and other programs or to be returned to the employee as salary. The latter, of course, would be taxable income. While design problems and record requirements are significant, there has been an increased level of activity in this area and it will probably continue as companies strive to maximize the cost effectiveness of benefit expenditures.

Tax Effectiveness. Benefit expenditures fall into one of three categories: no expense (or tax credit), tax deductible, or nondeductible. A tax credit is a reduction in tax liability; a tax deduction is a reduction in income before taxes. Income received for employee benefits is nontaxable (or fully deductible if taxable), taxed as long-term capital gains, taxed as a lump-sum distribution, or taxed as ordinary income. Due to the progressive tax structure, the after-tax value is lower at the highest taxed income. By dividing the employee's after-tax value by the company's after-tax cost, one can calculate a tax-effectiveness rating. The higher the rating, the more efficient the dollar benefit provided by the company.

Summary

Employee benefits are a part of the whole—one segment of the compensation an individual receives in return for his or her work efforts. Their prominence is due to a combination of factors: (1) at several times in the last 50 years or so there have been periods when it was easier to grant benefit improvements than to provide direct compensation improvements (i.e., during World War II, the Korean conflict, and the periods of wage controls during the early 1970s); (2) a number of benefits can be provided at less cost on a group basis than on an individual basis; and (3) timing and extent of income tax liability, if any, provide additional appeal for such forms of compensation.

Because benefit plans are very visible, unlike salaries and incentive plans, they are easy reference points for a person considering alternative career opportunities. However, since the level of participation in employee benefit programs is usually not correlated with performance, they have very little motivational impact for most. Justification for adding new programs and improving features of existing plans essentially stems from competitive pressures (i.e., what other companies are doing). For some the competitive pressure is very direct—as in the bargaining sessions.

Because of the high cost of employee benefits and their complexity, many companies have developed sophisticated communication programs to explain them. These include bulletin-board coverage, group meetings, plan booklets, and personalized statements detailing the exact nature of benefit coverage for each individual. The inference is that benefit expenditures are better appreciated by employees when the company goes beyond governmental reporting and disclosure requirements.

See also Compensation, executive; Compensation, wage and salary policy and administration; Personnel administration; Wages and hours legislation.

REFERENCES

Ellig, Bruce R.: "Defined Benefit Retirement Annuities: Testing Competitiveness," *Compensation Review*, 1982.

Ellig, Bruce R.: *Executive Compensation: A Total Pay Perspective*, McGraw-Hill, New York, 1982.

McCaffery, Robert H.: *Managing the Employee Benefits Program*, American Management Associations, New York, 1983.

112   Bruce R. Ellig, *Pfizer Inc.*

Compensation, Executive

Executive compensation plans are special pay vehicles developed to motivate and reward an organization's key management employees. In today's typical corporation, executive compensation programs can include as many as 25 or more possible plans. Most compensation plans, however, tend to group into five broad categories: base salary, annual incentive or bonus, long-term incentives and executive stock plans, employee benefits, and perquisites. This article discusses executive compensation plans in four sections as follows.

1. Annual incentive or bonus plans are plans in which executives are eligible for awards, in addition to salary, based upon short-term performance (usually annual). The amount of award varies with the level of performance from year to year. The plan typically is designed to stimulate executives to improve short-term company profitability.

2. Long-term incentives and executive stock plans are plans in which executives are eligible for awards based upon level of performance over a multiyear period, typically 3 to 5 years or longer. The purpose of these plans is to motivate and reward executives for a corporation's long-term growth, profitability, and well-being. They align executives' interests with those of stockholders, balance the short-term profitability objectives of annual incentives or bonuses, and provide executives with opportunities to build net worth.

3. Deferred compensation is an arrangement under which executives earn (or in some cases voluntarily defer) income that is payable in the future. The purpose is to minimize current taxes and provide a source of retirement income or capital accumulation.

4. Executive benefits and perquisites are benefits and privileges designed specifically for executives. Sometimes they extend coverage provided under regular employee benefit plans, and other times they provide types of coverage not available to other employees. Perquisites often provide indirect, and sometimes tax-favored, compensation for executives. In many instances they connote status and are emoluments of rank.

Basic Concepts.   Underlying the typical executive compensation program are a number of concepts, some of which affect all forms of executive compensation; others relate to specific types of pay or common design approaches.

1. Compensation should be hierarchical; that is, at each successively higher position level, the total pay opportunity should increase. Execu-

tive compensation plans provide a means of achieving a more hierarchical pay structure since they restrict eligibility to executives at a certain salary or title level. Moreover, the use of several plans can create a "tiered" approach to compensation, thus motivating individuals to progress in the organization to where not only their salary increases, but also their eligibility for extra rewards.

2. Executive pay should vary with performance in a given year and over time and do so more sharply than is possible through salaries alone. This concept helps explain the popularity of the incentive bonus, executive stock plans, and other long-term performance plans which with varying degrees of precision match reward with performance.

3. At successively higher levels of responsibility, more of the executive's total reward should be at risk. This concept affects the design and award patterns of most plans, increasing the size of the target bonus or stock award at each higher level and thereby reinforcing the hierarchical concept of pay.

4. The professional manager should have a proprietary stake in the business, and his or her interests should be aligned directly with those of the stockholder. This concept provides one of the principal rationales for the adoption of an executive stock plan.

5. An executive's compensation should facilitate the building of personal net worth. This concept helps explain the prevalence of executive stock plans and deferred compensation plans that provide capital accumulation opportunities.

6. The compensation vehicles used by the company should be cost effective in a way that has the least impact on company earnings; that is, they should take advantage of those provisions of the law that enable corporations to provide tax-free or tax-favored compensation—thus delivering more net after-tax reward for every dollar of compensation expenditure. This concept has contributed to the popularity of certain forms of executive stock options and perquisites.

7. Compensation plans should be used to retain key executives. This concept has led to the development of plans that make the realization of actual gain or payout contingent on the recipient's continued employment. Some form of exercise or vesting provision is particularly common in most executive stock and deferred compensation plans.

8. Because of their position, executives have unique needs that the company should help them meet in order to spare them concern about personal affairs and free them for company matters. This concept underlies some of the additional indirect rewards that come as part of a total pay package; for example, special forms of insurance such as kidnap insurance and perquisites such as free assistance in personal tax preparation.

9. Executive compensation needs to be competitive both in the level of total reward and in the types of plans that are made available. In applying this concept, most companies attempt to relate their executive compensation program to that of companies within their industry.

10. In total, an executive compensation program should be designed to reinforce each company's business strategies in the light of its particular strengths, needs, and challenges. In most instances, this will require a strong commitment to performance, an approach that links compensation with performance standards and measures that facilitate the organization's business needs and strategic direction, and consistent administration of compensation plans to reinforce longer-term goals while striking a balance with short-term profit objectives.

In addition to these broad principles and concepts, one other factor has affected the evolution of executive compensation programs in the United States: the considerable and growing body of tax legislation and regulation. This consideration has affected the mix of pay, the popularity of specific pay vehicles, and often the design of plans and provisions. To a lesser extent, accounting rulings and precedents have had a similar result. Occasionally these tax and accounting considerations will be given more importance than basic principles, often to the detriment of good plan design.

The Incentive Bonus

The incentive bonus is a highly individualized form of executive compensation used in most companies today. This was not always the case. Originally, incentive bonus plans were, for the most part, limited to those industries in which the business cycle is relatively short-term and management decisions in a given year can affect profits substantially, such as the automobile and retail trade industries. Rarely were they used in heavily regulated industries or in industries where results can only be measured over several years.

In the past decade, however, large corporations in industries that do not meet all these criteria—e.g., commercial banks, property and casualty insurance companies, oil companies, airlines, and, more recently, health care organizations—have increas-

113

ingly adopted incentive bonus plans. In many instances the plans in these industries (or poorly designed or administered plans in any company) do not provide a true incentive, but rather a yearly "lump sum" salary payment.

Varied Features. Most incentive bonus plans are tailored to the organization structure and profit economics of the business. Five features, taken together, help characterize a given plan.

1. An incentive bonus is either formal (that is, the amount and basis of payout are defined and communicated to participants) or judgmental.

2. The aggregate monies available for payout (called the bonus pool) are based on corporate performance (usually profits before or after taxes), unit performance (operating income of a business group, division or subsidiary), or a combination of both. Alternatively, the aggregate payout may be determined simply by the sum of individual opportunities without the use of a funding formula.

3. The degree of leverage also distinguishes plans. Leverage in the aggregate pool is usually achieved by (a) setting a minimum performance hurdle or "set aside" that must be met before any bonuses can be paid and then accruing a percentage of profits above that level or (b) accruing the bonus pool with a variable percentage of profits that increases at successively higher levels of performance.

   Individual leverage is achieved by varying the size of a participant's bonus on the basis of her or his accomplishments during the plan year. Some plans are highly leveraged, with individual awards that can range from zero to two or three times a "normal" award. In plans without individual leverage, awards vary only slightly from year to year.

4. Some plans use fixed formulas, at times setting out a very specific and complex formula for the calculation of the fund. Others are target- or goal-based; that is, management and the board set a target related to their annual budget or profit plan, and the degree of attainment of this target governs the fund payout that year. Some companies combine the two approaches by using a fixed formula that determines the maximum payout (often called an umbrella fund or stockholder protection formula), and then setting specific targets to guide the actual payout each year.

5. An incentive plan can be designed to complement the base salary program so that the salary plus the normal bonus provide competitive cash compensation. This is sometimes referred to as a discounted plan because the salary structure is set on a discounted basis; that is, it is lower than it would be normally. Alternatively, a plan can be designed as an extra incentive to provide compensation opportunities substantially above competitive levels when results are superior.

Program Design. Because of these variable features, few incentive bonus plans, even within the same industry, are identical, and designing an effective plan is a complex task. It involves:

1. Evaluating the competitiveness of existing pay levels and ensuring that the base salary plan is sound (otherwise the incentive could compound inequities in base pay).

2. Determining eligibility criteria and selecting participants. The principal criteria should be (a) the impact of the position on business results and (b) the ability to measure the individual's contribution in a plan year.

3. Determining the magnitude of the award in a normal plan year for each level of participant. This award is often referred to as the target award or normal bonus. It is the dollar payment or percentage of salary that the company will award if it achieves its target profit objective and individual performance is standard. The sum total of these normal awards constitutes the target bonus pool.

4. Developing a formula for generating the bonus pool and varying its size at different levels of performance. This step should involve a detailed analysis of past performance, comparisons of the company's results with those of its competition, and a thorough review of different methods of measuring corporate or unit results. The decisions made in this step will affect the plan leverage discussed above.

5. Developing stockholder protection features. Many companies set other control features beyond the basic formula; for example, they limit the aggregate bonuses that can be paid to a percentage of common stock dividends.

6. Determining how individual performance will be judged and what the degree of leverage will be in individual awards.

7. Deciding on all award provisions, such as the form (usually cash) and timing of awards (most companies pay awards in full at the end of the plan year, but some pay the earned award over several years or defer a portion until retirement). Other decisions have to be made on how individual accrued awards will be handled in the event of promotion, death, or termination during the plan year.

8. Describing the bonus plan in detail in a formal plan text and administration guide; reviewing this guide with appropriate legal counsel.

9. Securing approval of the board compensation committee and the full board of directors.

(Unlike an executive stock plan, an incentive bonus usually does not require stockholder approval—although some companies take this step.)

10. Implementing the plan; i.e., setting a specified profit target and individual goals for the first plan year, communicating the details of the plan to participants, and establishing all necessary administrative procedures.

Operational Considerations. A well-designed and effectively administered incentive bonus plan can be a powerful motivation for the key executive group. It also adds a variable element to the company's compensation cost. An incentive bonus is, however, one of the most difficult forms of executive compensation to develop and manage. It is not uncommon, for example, for the actual award process to become somewhat arbitrary and therefore lose its motivating power, or for the plan to evolve over a few years into a type of group profit sharing, with limited year-to-year variation. Furthermore, studies have shown that incentive plans can increase total cash compensation 15 to 20 percent above the compensation levels prevailing in companies with just a salary plan, although year-to-year variations will exist.

An incentive bonus plan should not be adopted for vague philosophical reasons or for any me-too reasons. Unless executive decisions can substantially affect business results, unless management performance can be evaluated fairly on an annual basis, and unless senior management has the discipline to make the tough administrative decisions required, a company will not benefit from an incentive bonus.

Long-Term Incentives and Executive Stock Plans

Long-term incentive practices in the United States have undergone a long and complicated evolution since the Du Pont stock purchase plan was introduced in 1904. The Du Pont plan was one of the first attempts of modern business to make the managers see their actions through the owners' eyes. Since then, equity-oriented compensation plans—through the restricted stock options of the 1950s, the qualified stock options of the 1960s, up to the incentive stock options of 1981—have developed largely as reactions to rapidly shifting tax laws, often without significant attention to the design of incentives that can spur performance.

During the past decade, while stock options continue to be the most widely used form of long-term incentive, many companies have adopted alternative, or additional, vehicles which provide true incentives for sustained performance, with equity building opportunities, regardless of stock market perfor-

mance. The current trend is toward the design of programs utilizing multiple forms of long-term incentive techniques with an emphasis on tailored flexibility to satisfy varying strategies and to motivate varying levels and types of executives.

Basic Plans. The following basic plans are currently in use:

Incentive Stock Options. Executives are granted the right to buy stock during a period of not more than 10 years at the fair market value at the time of grant. If special holding and other requirements under Internal Revenue Code Section 422A are satisfied, the executive realizes no taxable income until shares are eventually sold, at which time any gain is taxed as a long-term capital gain.

Nonqualified Stock Options. Executives are granted the right to buy stock during a period, generally up to 10 years, usually at the fair market value at the time of the grant, although a lower price can be set. Because no special IRS requirements need be met, capital gains tax treatment is not available on gains at exercise; any gain at time of exercise is taxed as ordinary income.

Stock Appreciation Rights (Linked to Options). Executives may elect to receive payment of all or part of the appreciation on the underlying option in lieu of exercising the option. During the early 1980s, two-thirds or more of stock option plans included this additional feature. The use of SARs, however, has declined recently as the result of changes in tax legislation, adverse accounting consequences, and the increased use of alternative financing techniques; e.g., stock swaps and low-interest loans.

Phantom Stock. Executives are granted units which entitle them to payment—at some future time, usually upon retirement or the expiration of 5 to 15 years after the grant—of an amount based upon the appreciation, income (dividends paid), or basic starting value of the artificial shares, units, or rights. The units may be valued according to the market value of company stock, book or other nonmarket value, or some other formula value. Payment may be in cash and/or stock.

There are numerous variations of phantom or artificial stock and even more numerous combinations thereof—in fact, the flexibility available in tailoring phantom stock plans is one of the major attractions of this longer-term incentive. Phantom plans are particularly valuable for companies which have no public market for their stock.

Restricted Stock. Executives receive outright grants or are permitted to purchase company stock, but ownership is subject to risk of forfeiture and the right to sell is restricted for a specific period. In recent years, some restricted stock plans have incorporated a performance mechanism similar to that used in a performance unit plan in which shares are forfeited if objectives are not achieved, or restrictions lapse early if objectives are achieved.

Book-Value Shares. Executives buy shares, or are granted shares outright, at a price equal to book value rather than market price; subsequently the company either repurchases the stock at a price equal to book value at the time or makes cash or stock payments in the amount of the book-value appreciation.

Performance Shares. Executives are awarded shares of common stock or their cash equivalent, contingent upon the achievement of specified multi-year performance objectives. Objectives are often stated as a compound increase in earnings per share or a return on investor capital measure. A few companies use a relative performance measure over a performance period of from 3 to 5 years. These plans typically provide that a certain growth must be achieved in order to earn 100 percent of the executive's award, with somewhat lower growth to earn varying lesser percentages of the award, and finally with a minimum threshold below which no units will be earned.

Performance Units. Executives are awarded long-term dollar bonus opportunities with earn-out depending on achievement of specified objectives. The plan is structured in the same manner as a performance share plan; however, the value the executive receives relates to the value placed on the units at the time of grant and does not fluctuate with fluctuations in the market value of the corporate stock.

A plan of this kind, coupled with equity opportunities provided by incentive and nonqualified stock options, has become one of the most popular programs during the late 1970s and early 1980s.

Junior Stock. Executives are granted, sold, or given the option to buy shares of a special series of common stock which has limited voting rights, dividend rights, and liquidation rights. The junior shares are restricted against transfer and automatically convert to regular common shares contingent upon the achievement of specified long-term performance objectives. Since the applicable restrictions and conditions reduce the immediate fair market value of junior shares, the arrangement provides unique opportunities for highly leveraged long-term capital gains with little or no investment up front by executives. Originally adopted by a few high-technology companies, junior stock plans are starting to spread to other companies in an attempt to provide selected executives and key technical employees with the equivalent of founders' stock.

Program Design. The range of available plans and the many possible combinations complicate the task of selecting the right vehicle(s) and designing a program that meets the unique needs of a given company. For example, one company may need to emphasize the holding power of a program, while another needs to reinforce long-term growth objectives. More often than not, a company's program has several needs to meet. In developing an executive

long-term incentive, a company should take the following steps:

1. Analyze the need the program should satisfy and clearly define program objectives. This step usually requires reviewing the design of the existing long-term incentive program and the *total* executive compensation program; comparing the form, timing, and level of reward with competitive patterns; and determining the changes required. Compensation program design should focus on a number of strategic variables, including:

   - Positioning of total compensation, by company and business unit
   - Appropriate mix of short-term, mid-term, and long-term compensation
   - Mix of "at risk" and "fixed" element
   - Degree of relationship between reward and performance
   - Selection of performance standards and criteria
   - Degree of payout flexibility
   - Role of stocks or equity-related plans

2. Decide on the specific design requirements that will be used to screen available types of plans and review and test various plans against them. When these requirements are being formulated, a number of broad aspects of a corporation should be considered, including:

   - Ownership structure
   - Stage of growth
   - Stages of business and overall strategy
   - Industry
   - Overall management style, culture, and human resource environment

3. Establish eligibility ground rules and estimate the likely number of participants initially and over the term of the plan.

4. Concurrently, develop award guidelines and estimate the total award, share, or share-equivalent requirements.

5. To narrow the plans being considered further, make a detailed evaluation of them, comparing their inherent characteristics with the needs of the corporation, developing cost estimates, and projecting the potential gain for various levels of participants under a number of performance assumptions.

6. Select a specific plan and describe it in detail in a formal plan text and an administrative guide.

7. Submit the proposed plan to a thorough legal review.

8. Present the plan to a board compensation committee and the full board of directors.

9. Upon approval of the plan by the board, prepare proxy material describing the new plan and send it to shareholders to solicit their approval.

10. After final plan approval, make the initial awards and implement appropriate administrative procedures. Pay particular attention to effective communication, since these plans (and their personal, financial, and tax implications) are often difficult for most executives to understand.

Risk of Long-Term Plans. Any corporation considering the adoption of an executive long-term incentive plan should recognize that this type of reward and incentive carries risks as well as benefits. One risk is that the cost will be excessive and out of proportion to the benefits. This is particularly true with respect to stock plans. Since most executive stock plans increase the total amount of common stock outstanding, they have a dilution impact. Moreover, with the exception of stock options granted at market, all executive stock plans involve a cost to the corporation and thus can reduce reported earnings. Often this cost is not fixed; for example, where basis for gain is related to stock price in the future, the total cost can escalate sharply.

Another risk associated with stock plans is that they are not always effective long-term incentives. For example, factors outside the company's control or unrelated to its program (such as overall stock market trends) may wipe out the gain or payout to participants. This situation can lead to executive dissatisfaction and even contribute to turnover, particularly if other companies have better-designed plans or have moved faster to update their plans as circumstances change.

Finally, there is a particularly acute risk for both the company and the individual executives if they adopt a plan that requires participant investment (as all option plans do, for example). If the stock price drops precipitously after the executive exercises the option, the individual can suffer a substantial loss if unable to dispose of the stock. Corporate officers and other insiders are especially vulnerable to this risk under applicable SEC rules. If they have taken out loans to acquire the stock, the personal financial risk is obviously much greater.

Deferred Compensation

A premise underlying most deferred compensation plans is that an executive with high current income, taxed at the maximum rates, will benefit from the deferral of some of that income until retirement. Presumably his or her tax rate will then be lower, par-

ticularly if payout of the deferred funds is spread over a number of years. With the lowering of the maximum federal tax rates (currently at a maximum rate of 50 percent) this tax savings rationale has been weakened.

Additionally, with improvement made in employee retirement income plans in recent years and significant benefits offered by a myriad of long-term incentive programs, many top executives are likely to have postretirement incomes at the maximum tax rate level. Nevertheless, executive deferral arrangements are commonly used for a number of purposes.

Basic Plans. The basic types of deferred compensation plans in use today are:

Voluntary Deferral Plans. Under these plans, the company permits certain executives (usually at a stated position or earnings level) to defer a portion of the income they would normally be paid currently (in salary or incentive). Generally, this voluntary deferral is specified annually, before each tax year, in conjunction with IRS guidelines in order to avoid issues of constructive receipt. Most arrangements provide for the crediting of some investment return on deferred amounts. This opportunity for investment return, on a pretax basis from the individual executive's perspective, often is the reason behind the current attractiveness of deferred compensation.

Incentive Deferrals. These plans are integrated with an incentive bonus under which a portion of the bonus is mandatorily deferred. Often under an incentive deferral, the basis of appreciation is related to company performance, and return on stockholders' equity or growth in earnings per share, for example, is used to determine the annual change in the value of the deferred funds.

Nonqualified ERISA Excess Benefit Plans. Under these plans top executives are paid the difference between the benefits they would otherwise be entitled to receive under the company's tax qualified retirement program and the annual benefits they are permitted to receive under the plan pursuant to maximums established for qualified pension benefits under the 1974 Employee Retirement Income Security Act (ERISA). Annual maximums are currently set at $90,000, with cost-of-living adjustment (COLA) scheduled starting in 1986.

Other Supplemental Retirement Plans. Other nonqualified supplemental retirement arrangements are used to provide executives as a group or individually with retirement benefits in flat amounts, based on income investments, at guaranteed dollar or percentage of income replacement including all company-provided sources, or based upon defined contributions or defined benefit accruals geared to service. These arrangements are usually highly tailored to the needs of a particular company and its individual executives.

117

Program Design. The steps to be taken in designing and implementing a deferred compensation plan are similar to those outlined in the preceding sections. Three steps are particularly critical, however, in most deferral arrangements:

1. Determining the basis of appreciation of the deferred funds in voluntary or incentive deferral plans. Some companies use a variable external return measure (e.g., the prime rate or AAA bond rates); others set a fixed rate, which is reviewed periodically; still others use some measure of company performance. If this provision is not thought through carefully in the context of current interest rate trend and tax and investment trends, a deferral decision can be a poor *investment* decision for the individual and the company.

2. Carefully analyzing all tax consequences both to the company and to the executive.

3. Integrating the deferred plan with other compensation vehicles that pay off in the future, such as executive stock plans, pensions, and qualified profit-sharing plans.

Program Risks. Deferred compensation can meet legitimate executive compensation objectives if properly designed, but it does involve risks. If the corporation goes into bankruptcy, the accrued deferred funds can disappear (as happened at Penn Central). If the income tax structure changes after the deferral decision has been made, the inherent economics of the decision may be altered or an individual's projected income may vary sharply from what was assumed.

Even where the circumstances are right or the benefit seems worth some risk, participation in a deferred compensation plan is, in the final analysis, an investment decision and should be evaluated against other investment choices.

Executive Benefits and Perquisites

Long before the advent of the corporate form, human institutions were granting special privileges to key personnel to meet perceived needs and often to denote rank in the organization. With the coming of the income tax, these special privileges, or "perks," began to multiply rapidly. Under U.S. tax laws and regulations, a corporation can deduct legitimate business expenses. Even if the executive gains some personal benefit, she or he is often not taxed or not taxed fully on it. Thus an executive can receive tax-favored, indirect "compensation."

Among the more common executive perks used by corporations today are the following:

Company Loans. The corporation either lends an executive money directly or guarantees a bank loan, usually at a low interest rate and with liberal repayment terms. A relatively recent compensation form, this device is most commonly used to help an executive finance stock options and build personal net worth.

Company-Sponsored Tax Shelter. This is a fairly rare compensation device under which the company, often privately held, organizes a special limited partnership for its executives, usually to provide them with both a tax shelter and an opportunity to build personal net worth.

Executive Dining Room. Many organizations make an on-premise company eatery available to certain levels of executives as both a perquisite and a convenience. In commercial banks, for example, three or four classes of dining rooms can often be found, ranging from a cafeteria to private dining suites for senior officers.

Executive Housing. Company-provided housing is typically offered when executives are on temporary assignments away from their home base or when they can be expected to encounter unusual costs or difficulty in finding accommodations. Occasionally, executive housing, such as an in-town apartment or permanent hotel suite, is offered as an indirect form of compensation for high-level executives.

Executive Physical Program. Executives are provided free periodic physical examinations, exercise rooms, and other services. Frequently the policies and procedures governing the program become more liberal with rank.

Personal Financial Counseling. An independent professional firm advises an individual executive or a group of executives on financial matters under a plan organized and/or partially paid for by the company. The counselor analyzes financial affairs, suggests investment strategies, reviews estate plans, and gives advice on specific financial decisions.

Company Cars. Under this perquisite, an automobile (and on occasion a driver) is provided for the individual's use. Usually the company pays all insurance, maintenance, and operating expenses.

Tax Preparation Assistance. The corporation, through its staff or an outside professional firm, assists executives in preparing their personal tax returns.

Special Expense Accounts. This is a plan or individual arrangement under which executives are permitted more liberal reimbursement of business-related expenses (including entertainment) or are given a specific sum each year for expenses which they need not account for.

Education Reimbursement. Funds are set aside for self-development, the education of dependents, or educational leaves.

Personal Services. This category of perquisites covers the many, and occasionally special, personal services provided executives at company cost, including a company barber, free clothing, free tickets to cultural or sporting events, and free checking accounts.

Company Plane. An executive can use corporate aircraft for both business and personal reasons but must generally reimburse the corporation for at least part of the cost.

Spouse Travel. Spouses are permitted to accompany executives on business trips, to conventions, and so on, at company expense.

Excess Life Insurance. Many corporations have adopted additional group term or whole-life plans, restricted to a certain salary or position level, that provide insurance coverage substantially in excess of the basic amounts provided under general employee programs.

Split-Dollar Insurance. This is a life insurance arrangement involving permanent insurance written under an individual contract with an executive. In this plan, the company pays the portion of premium each year equal to the increase in the policy's cash value and the executive pays the balance, if any. In the event of the executive's death, his or her beneficiaries receive the insurance benefits in excess of the cash value.

Personal Liability Insurance. This form of insurance is usually provided to certain levels of executives to protect them against personal liability up to a stated maximum, generally $1 million or more. It is designed to cover executives against suits growing out of a car accident, for example, or some other liability they could incur as individuals. It is distinguished from director or officer liability coverage, which protects key executives from stockholder or consumer suits growing out of their role in the corporation.

Kidnap Insurance. As the term implies, this insurance provides a source of funds for the payment of a ransom in the event an executive is abducted. It is set up as an individual or group policy.

Executive Medical Reimbursement Insurance. This plan provides key executives with a coverage beyond the company's medical plan.

Evaluation of Need. A company should not adopt a perquisite unless it fills a clear and justifiable business need. Moreover, before implementing any such arrangement, a corporation should seek legal counsel. There is an extensive body of IRS rules and regulations governing most perquisites, and individual executives may find themselves liable for additional taxes. Even where business rationale and precedent in other companies support adoption of perquisites, a corporation should assess their impact on the business environment. Many corporations maintain that perquisites create too hierarchical a structure, reduce cost consciousness within the company, and engender adverse reactions from employees.

In evaluating the need for one or more forms of executive benefit or perquisite, a company should carefully review the income and age profiles of the executive group and the extent of benefit coverage under other company plans. Often it faces difficult trade-off decisions between improving the basic employee benefit coverage for all categories of employees and responding to the special requirements of key executives.

Another consideration is cost. Unlike incentives, executive benefits and perquisites are not performance-related and thus, in most instances, cannot justify a large portion of the corporation's executive compensation expenditure. Because of these circumstances, individual company philosophy has a greater bearing on the prevalence of these than it has on other compensation vehicles.

When dealing with executive insurance arrangements, companies should take particular care to:

1. *Select the right insurance carrier* and negotiate the best possible rate (wide variations in cost are not unusual).

2. *Coordinate the coverage* with other company plans and see that the individual recipient gets proper advice on integrating the company coverage with personal coverage.

3. *Examine the plan's annual cash-flow requirements* and the impact of any special insurance on the company's asset and liability structure. Since permanent insurance can require substantial cash outlays, the financial implications for the company need professional analysis, particularly in a smaller company.

In summary, insurance can play a special, but limited, role in the total executive compensation program. The most common mistake companies make is to adopt plans that they do not need or that respond poorly to their total requirements and priorities. Thus they increase costs unnecessarily or perpetuate more basic weaknesses in their overall compensation program.

See also Compensation, employee benefit plans; Compensation, sales; Compensation, wage and salary policy and administration; Motivation in organizations; Search and recruitment, executive; Tax management.

REFERENCES

Ellig, Bruce R.: *Executive Compensation,* McGraw-Hill, New York, 1982.

McLaughlin, David J.: *The Executive Money Map,* McGraw-Hill, New York, 1975.

Patton, Arch: *Men, Money and Motivation,* McGraw-Hill, New York, 1961.

Rock, Milton L.: *Handbook of Wage and Salary Administration,* McGraw-Hill, New York, 1983.

DAVID J. MCLAUGHLIN, *McLaughlin and Company, Inc.*

Compensation, Sales

A company may have sound product lines, appropriate marketing strategies, and a well-positioned sales organization, but without a motivated sales force, it will have difficulty reaching its sales goals. An integral part of a motivational system is a sales compensation package that complements and reinforces the overall marketing objectives. While the best sales compensation package will not overcome poor products or ineffective pricing, a well-designed package can have a direct impact on sales volume, profit margins, or market penetration.

The choices of sales compensation plans are wide, and the final design should always be tailored to support the overall marketing strategy of the company. The specific package should also be coordinated with the overall compensation policy of the company. As such, it should combine functional inputs from both marketing and personnel.

Historically, there are two basic methods of rewarding salespeople: straight salary and straight commission. Straight salary is simple to administer, but it provides limited incentives for greater sales productivity and generates a largely fixed cost of a sales force rather than a variable one. Straight commission, traditionally on volume, encourages the sales force to hustle but at the cost of decreasing the company's control over field salespeople, since it affects only one factor and gives rise to personal anxiety because there is no assurance of income. Beyond volume, neither system encourages the achievement of specific multimarketing and sales objectives. Consequently, enterprises typically develop combinations of base salary and incentives to get "the best of both worlds."

To develop an appropriate sales compensation plan, a number of distinct phases must be considered:

1. Review marketing objectives, analyzing them for clarity and consistency, getting agreement, and spelling out in detail the sales aims. Vague generalizations about increasing sales and reducing selling costs will not suffice; neither will exhorting salespeople "to concentrate on the most profitable products." Rather, you should have concise written statements of all the marketing goals and strategies which management agrees are desirable and attainable within a reasonable time. For example, one large agricultural equipment concern predicated its sales reward plan on the following corporate objectives:

    To increase the utilization of available production capacity through upgrading of sales volume and product mix.

    To upgrade the marketing and sales force effectiveness through improved goal setting, performance measurement, and communication processes.

    To upgrade the coordination and utilization of the various sales forces leading to improved market share.

    To lead to increased motivation of the sales force through emphasis on a reward system that balances the compensation rewards with career development rewards, within the marketing and work-force strategies of the company.

2. Study marketing-related areas, each of which can present important issues and complex variables which must be addressed. Of particular importance is an evaluation of the marketplace, the internal climate, the organization, and the organization's competition.

3. Establish the internal worth of a sales position to the company. To this end, job evaluation—such as the Hay Guide Chart-Profile Method, which rates jobs according to their know-how, problem-solving, and accountability content—is often utilized.

4. Reconcile the inputs from the earlier phases so that the sales compensation plan is one in which an appropriately competitive total earnings opportunity is established, base salary levels and ranges are set, methods of incentive payout are determined, and the timing of payouts is agreed upon.

5. Follow through with implementation, communication, and administration. The plan must be "built up" and communicated to the sales force. Its legal ramifications should be gauged; an employee may successfully sue for the recovery of earned incentives under certain conditions.

6. Once the plan has been put into effect, evaluate it routinely (typically annually) and update it to reflect changes in company strategies and competitive challenges.

The Sales Force Climate

The design of a sales compensation program will be mechanical and often ineffective if it is not based on a sound understanding of the sales force's environment. Furthermore, management must be aware of the perceptions of each level in the sales organization so that reward structures responsive to their specific needs can be planned. A not infrequent misconception of top executives who used to be salespeople is that every salesperson is motivated the way they used to be. What they forget is that they belong not to the average but to a minority who made it to the top.

Recent climate surveys have revealed contradictions to conventional wisdom regarding the character and compensation preferences of salespeople. It appears that most salespeople, when thinking about their own compensation, have a reasonably clear perception of what an equitable income is. They appear to know where they want to go; to some extent, how they get there is secondary.

Further survey data suggest that the traditional notion of the salesperson as a risk-oriented entrepreneur has to be substantially revised. In fact, the average field salesperson is much more security-oriented and noninnovative than is generally assumed. Sales forces are intensely interested in security and stability. There are salespeople, of course, who are highly achievement-oriented. For them, however, the earning of substantial incentive rewards appears to be sought as much for the personal fulfillment and recognition it brings as for the increased income per se.

It is possible that economic downturns are a factor influencing salespeople to favor security. A substantial economic upturn might create more enthusiasm for compensation structures with a high ratio of incentives to base salary. No one, therefore, least of all salespeople, suggests doing away with incentive compensation. But when one manages a force of more security-oriented salespeople, the design of the base salary and perquisite aspects of a compensation program becomes important. When plans with a significant base salary component are used, they should include an effective performance appraisal system to make base salary adjustments meaningful and motivational.

Where Incentives Work Best

An early decision in developing a compensation package is to establish the basic compensation approach. The five most common ones are:

Entrepreneurial Plan. In this approach, the company provides a product or know-how in return for part of the revenues. Typically, such plans cover general insurance agency, real estate, and manufacturing representatives. The company has only limited control in the marketing efforts of the participants.

Straight Commission (with or without a draw against commission). These are typically provided from "dollar one" on volume of sales with occasional adjustment for profit margins. Real estate and encyclopedia salespeople are often paid this way. The changing social and marketing environment makes it less common elsewhere.

Basic Salary plus a Managed Variable Incentive. Such plans are increasing in number. Incentive plans, whose purpose is to stimulate and motivate action, are causal in nature and contractual in a formula that equates individual incentive earnings to predetermined levels of performance. Incentive award levels are set before the effort is expended,

resulting in motivational pull toward desired earnings levels.

Base Salary plus Bonuses. This differs from managed variable incentives in that bonuses are usually paid annually (versus quarterly or monthly) and levels are usually determined after the fact. Consequently, payouts are far removed from the event and the judgments on which they are based are often perceived as subjective or unrelated to performance by the recipient. Thus they are often of questionable motivational value.

Variable Base Salary. This approach is an attempt to reward performance through periodic increases in the base salary. In the right sales environment it can be the preferred approach, and appropriately, it is widely used in complex sales situations. See Fig. C-3.

In selecting a specific approach, one must raise the eligibility issue. A good rule is to restrict incentive plan participation to those positions with line accountabilities designed to impact directly on the desired end results of sales volume, sales profitability, market penetration, or other clearly defined sales goals. To extend a plan beyond the sales force can rarely be justified; it generally weakens the program through confusion of, and difficulty in, setting objectives. Temptation to do so should be resisted.

Field sales-force incentives imply the need for variable compensation for all ranks of sales management. Aside from the logic of it, an incentive program for management is a practical necessity in order to avoid creating problems of career development and promotion, as well as to ensure equity of total compensation.

Relation to the Market Life Cycle

A principal concern in designing incentives is the nature of the market served combined with the fundamental sales challenge. A rapidly expanding market with limited competition is one thing; a mature market fully exploited by a number of competitors is another. Such factors have a bearing on total earnings opportunity, base salary levels, and the degree of plan elasticity. A general view of the applicability of the ratio of incentives to base salary may be seen in Fig. C-4, which represents a normal growth curve as it might apply to a product line, market segment, or company growth.

During a *start-up period* (phase A), competition is usually light, there is no track record, and forecasts are likely to be highly inaccurate. Ideally, this period calls for a relatively high base salary (to attract high-performance staff), with some discretionary-type, after-the-fact bonus. Phase B is the period of *high-growth* acceleration. This is the phase of the high-commission plan, with a market responsive to sales efforts. At this point, minimum performance levels

Influencing Factors

Use incentives as <u>less</u> of a percentage of total compensation		Use incentives as <u>more</u> of a percentage of total compensation
No	Clear goal setting and monitoring process	Yes
High	Number of different objectives	Low
Yes	Multiproducts	No
Very long	Time span between interest, booking, and shipment	Short
Large	Size of order or unit sale	Small
Mature	Market maturity	Developing
Low	Salesperson independence	High
No	Defined selling territories	Yes
High	Need for repeat business	Low
Significant	Continuous service to accounts	Limited
High	Special support by staff (engineering, finance, technical service)	Low
High	Technical know-how required	Low

FIG. C-3 The applicability of incentives.

may be established. In the U.S. economy, many companies and products are in phase C, that of *decelerating growth rates*, where exceptionally high earnings for star performers are no longer justified. Other companies find themselves, or their products, in phase D, that of *market maturity*, calling for stiff, sustained competition in maintaining market share. Typically, phases C and D either call for a "managed" incentive plan or emphasize base salary.

The general evidence suggests that sales incentives should be modified as market conditions evolve rather than remain fixed for long periods of time.

Plan Elasticity and Earnings Opportunity

In designing sales incentives, we find that income variability and earnings levels appropriate for the various performance levels are closely related. As a rule, the higher the earnings opportunity and the more variable an individual's income, the greater the motivation. Following this heuristic, high performers may attain comparably high earnings but must continuously perform at this level to maintain them. If the volume of business generated justifies such earnings, a workable plan can be put into effect. Conversely, the more secure a salesperson's income is, the lower the maximum earnings opportunity should be. Additionally, total incomes must be externally competitive as well as internally equitable. Special sales compensation surveys conducted within an industry or a geographic area will reveal appropriate earnings levels as well as industry peculiarities regarding the weight given the various components of cash compensation. An industry survey, in fact, is a good place to start when undertaking the design of an incentive plan, after which the company must get down to setting earnings levels.

Maximum earnings opportunity sets the top income level that the highest performers can

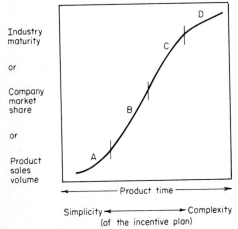

achieve. It should strike a balance between how much the additional business is worth to the company and the amount of incentive it is reasonable to pay as a cost of acquiring it. Usually, the more responsive the market is to direct sales effort, the higher the earnings opportunity may be without loss of sales productivity, i.e., the ratio of incentives paid (the cost of generating additional sales volume) to the volume of business produced.

Average earnings opportunity varies in most cases directly with the degree of maximum incentive opportunity and should be communicated to the participants. To establish proper maximum and projected average incentive levels the following must be considered: industry practice, flexibility of the market, nature of the sales event, considerations of internal and external equity, and productivity factors.

When incentive plans are installed within sales organizations with straight salary plans, base salaries are usually reduced. This can be done by an immediate downward adjustment or by gradually phasing in incentive opportunities while freezing base salary levels. National surveys which compare salaries for field salespeople with those of other employees in the organization (e.g., the Hay Compensation Comparison) often disclose a tendency to discount salary levels when sales incentive plans are in use. Many companies find it useful to retain a portion of a salary range to recognize the junior-senior nature of some sales organizations.

Performance Standards and Sales Goals

A significant overall objective for many incentive plans is management's desire to focus clearly the attention of the sales force on a few well-established goals critical to the enterprise's marketing plans and to reward their attainment amply.

Performance Standards. The most prevalent component of incentive payout is the achievement of *sales volume objectives* on either a quota or an absolute volume basis. In an intensely competitive environment, or in those industries subject to major cyclical changes, *overall market position/market penetration* is often a much better indicator of the success of the field sales force than is volume or growth. The problem with its use as the primary objective is the timeliness and accuracy of measurement.

Other incentive components include new business, customers, new product introduction, repeat business, profit and margins volume, and ROI. As competition increases and the available share of the remaining market decreases, considerations of profitability shift from volume alone to the selective marketing of more profitable product lines. Multiple-rate commission plans, featuring different rates for differ-ent products or territories, are often applicable to such situations.

As long as an essential objective can be defined and measured clearly, there appears to be no limit to the sophistication of incentive plans.

Sales Goals. Several methods are available to define sales goals.

Sales forecasts commit the sales force to obtaining precalculated volumes. Of course, sales forecasting is a critical management process essential to market planning and should be kept as objective as possible. A substantial advantage is gained if calculations of incentive remuneration are divorced from the process of sales forecasting. A salesperson becomes a natural pessimist when asked to forecast future volumes if he or she is aware that one use for the forecast will be to establish sales objectives which will determine future incentive earnings.

Sales quotas are more autocratic. Required total sales volume is set on the basis of (1) amount of available business and (2) desired profit margins implying a certain level of plant utilization.

Sales bogeys begin incentive payments "one step off par." Incentive earnings commonly commence between 70 to 90 percent below planned territorial objectives. The bogey system can be utilized to allow salespeople to increase income as they build their territories. This provides a long-term motivation and increases career opportunity for the salespeople.

Territorial standards are generally used in well-established markets. Territories are grouped into small, medium, and large categories whose volume levels are fixed for an extended period of time. Incentives may be paid to the degree that actual sales exceed certain norms or sales volume.

Whatever the goals a company selects, it is important to review and adjust them periodically to reflect changes in the market, objectives, or strategies.

1. In determining the proper components and rates for incentive payout, the overriding considerations are simplicity and the ability of the individual salesperson to compute quickly and accurately future incentive earnings on the basis of assumed performance levels.

2. An appropriate variable may be derived by relating desired incentive earnings levels to anticipated territorial volumes which have been adjusted to compensate for a sales goal or quota.

3. An important general rule is this: The lower the sales goal, the lower the variable rate required and the stabler the plan. As an illustration of this principle, assume the following two incentive plans, A and B (Fig. C-5).

    Plan A had a high minimum sales objective and consequently a high variable rate to ensure the required planned average payout (assumed to occur at the median volume level). An unstable situation occurred because incentive earnings

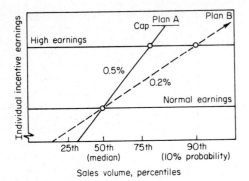

FIG. C-5 Determining incentive rates.

increased at too rapid a pace relative to increased sales volume. Too many people ordinarily got no commissions for a given period (approximately 35 percent of the sales force), and too many (those with sales above the 75th percentile, or about 25 percent) earned top dollar. For the latter, a ''cap,'' or maximum earnings level, was established. This was a poor incentive plan because it put 60 percent of the sales force at the extremes of income potential. Salespeople were provoked by what they considered an illogical earnings cap, and some encouraged customers to delay bookings until the outset of the following sales period. This created havoc in planning and even customer unrest.

The company reacted to the problem by returning to the general rule: sales goals were lowered—and so were commission rates—to stabilize the plan. The company adopted plan B, with a lower sales objective (now called a *bogey*) fixed at 70 percent of the normal sales goal, and a reduced commission rate. It found that the cap could be eliminated under the new system, since only about 10 percent would be expected to achieve high earnings and at a much slower rate of increase in earnings. Normal incentive awards in each case turned out to be about the same.

4. Commission rates do not necessarily have to be linear (e.g., proportional). A much sharper motivation program will result if the commission rate is allowed to increase in steps as higher volume levels are achieved. Such plans may prove useful, but they usually are less stable and tougher to control than single-rate plans.

Payout Periods

As a rule, the payout should be as close as possible to the event generating the reward. A highly variable compensation plan combined with a relatively short

incentive payout period provides the highest motivation levels. The limiting factor is practically determined by the size of the payout available and administrative procedure. Obviously, the more frequent the payout, the less the amount of the payout; thus a balance must be struck between payout level and frequency. Monthly incentive plans are common; even biweekly plans are not unusual in the case of straight commissions. Many firms quite sensibly choose to pay base salaries in weekly or biweekly increments, supplemented by quarterly payment incentive earnings. If variable earnings levels are determined to some extent by overall corporate or divisional performance, a common practice is to split incentive payouts, with the bulk of variable earnings paid quarterly and the portion that relates to overall performance paid annually.

The larger the portion of an individual's total earnings tied to incentives is, the shorter the payout period should be. Deferred payment of part of earned incentives is a common practice, however, wherever a contingency exists on the part of full customer commitment or where true sales performance cannot be fully determined until some later date.

Evaluation. Design of a sales compensation plan is not without pitfalls. The following, in particular, should be avoided: overly complex plans; plans that pay off only at quota or above; straight percentage commission plans; plans with high risk; plans which reward too few or too many results; plans which set unrealistic goals; plans which are wrong for the life cycle of the product; and plans which encourage counterproductive behavior. Other mistakes are (1) to have a plan at all where it is not possible to forecast, (2) not to change the plan when the business itself changes, and (3) not to have and properly use salary ranges.

See also Compensation, employee benefit plans; Compensation, executive; Compensation, wage and salary policy and adminstration; Job evaluation; Sales management; Wages and hours legislation.

REFERENCES

Bobrow, Edwin, E., and Larry Wizenberg (eds.): *Sales Manager's Handbook*, Dow Jones-Irwin, Homewood, Ill., 1983. Pt. 4, ''Training, Development, and Compensation of the Sales Force.''

Robertson, Dan H., and Danny N. Bellenger: *Sales Management*, Macmillan, New York, 1980.

Welch, Joe L., and Charles Lapp: *Sales Force Management*, South-Western Publishing, Cincinnati, 1983.

C. Ian Sym-Smith, *Hay Associates*

Avner M. Porat, *Hay Associates*

Robert J. Davenport, Jr. *Hay Associates*

Compensation, Wage and Salary Policy and Administration

The primary purpose of wage and salary administration is to assure both management and employees of equitable compensation for services rendered. This purpose, although simply stated, is difficult to translate into a practical program for implementation. Furthermore, wage and salary administration is not entirely an internal company matter. The design and function of the compensation plan are influenced greatly by outside forces, such as the government and labor unions.

The skillful management of wage and salary compensation is also essential to ensure attaining cost or profit objectives. These cost or profit objectives can be achieved by maintaining proper balance between the input costs and the resultant revenue from output. An immediate conflict of objectives arises, since the wage administrator's aim is to satisfy employer, owner or stockholder, employees, and such outside interests as suppliers and consumers.

Program Objectives. With these factors clearly in mind, one can subdivide the objectives of a sound wage and salary administration program into specific subgoals that represent milestones along the path to successful and equitable wage and salary compensation:

1. Equitable wage and salary payment in proportion to each person's relative worth to the organization
2. Consistency of wages between comparable occupations
3. Adjustment of wages in relation to changes in the labor market
4. Recognition of individual capability and proficiency
5. Comprehension of the plan by supervision and management
6. Procedure to solve compensation problems rationally

Organizational Status

The organizational form of wage and salary administration varies, depending on the industry and the emphasis placed on the function by executive management. It is normally an integral part of the human resources department and plays an important role in the total policy making of this department. The principal responsibilities of wage and salary administration are (1) establishing policies and procedures, (2) researching new and changing concepts in this field, and (3) auditing the operational levels of wage and salary administration to ensure adherence to policies and procedures.

Compensation Systems

There are numerous types of compensation systems. They cover the entire spectrum: straight hourly wages, salaried scales for clerical employees, productivity plans, daywork and measured daywork, and individual and organizationwide incentive plans. Each of these plans requires a different management style which must be recognized and incorporated into the overall corporate training and development of supervision and employees. For example:

1. A pure daywork plan has no relationship between compensation and output. It does not utilize work measurement or formal labor control. To maintain productivity, pure daywork requires an excellent relationship between employee and supervisor. This relationship has been enhanced in recent years by incorporation of the concepts of job enlargement, job enrichment, work design, and other motivational aspects.

2. A measured daywork plan also does not have a direct relationship between compensation and output. This plan does, however, utilize close supervision, work measurement, work standards, and formal labor controls.

3. An incentive plan, whether group or individual, compensates employees on the basis of output. This plan strongly utilizes work measurement and formal labor controls. It offers financial incentives for improvement of output or for reaching productivity goals. Profit-sharing plans are a form of incentive plan based on the measurement of the improvement of profits. Most incentive plans, whether group or individual, are based on output easily measured and distinguishable, such as total units shipped or number of production parts produced. The concept of incentive plans is based on the motivational effect of more pay for more work. However, many incentive plans lose effectiveness after a number of years owing to the pressures from employees, union, or supervision. The inclusion of an incentive plan in the overall compensation structure of the company must be considered over the long term, since the compensation relationship between employees is difficult to maintain in the face of annual increases and cost-of-living increases.

4. The salaried compensation plan is similar to the pure daywork plan, with little or no relationship between compensation and output. However,

motivational plans have had great success in these areas. And there still are a number of companies that pay extra compensation in the form of year-end bonuses based on attainment of company profit objectives. Only in companies using broad forms of incentive plans (such as profit sharing, the Scanlon Plan, etc.) would a salaried compensation system for technical, engineering, and professional employees be incentive-oriented. And typically, these plans are not based on measured individual output or contribution.

Employee Benefits. In recent years the importance of benefits other than wages and salary has come to the forefront. These are now considered an integral part of the overall compensation system and must be maintained in line with changing living conditions and competition.

Program Components

A sound wage and salary program can only materialize when the plan is well thought out, thoroughly understood by employees at all levels, properly executed by management, and flexible to the requirements of the personnel involved. The typical wage plan is complex when viewed in its entirety, but the key to comprehension for the manager is knowledge and understanding of the components it comprises. These components, along with the important core of the program—namely, the necessary planning, the fundamental policies, and the operational procedures—are illustrated in Fig. C-6.

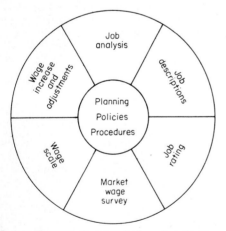

FIG. C-6 Elements of wage and salary administration.

Planning. The planning for implementation of a new or revised wage and salary plan must be executed carefully. The success or failure of the program depends heavily on this foundation. A number of questions require immediate answers:

Who will develop the program?

What jobs will be included?

Which specific plan should be selected?

Answers to these questions will take many forms, depending on the character of the company and the environment in which it operates. In most organizations—and following the thoughts developed previously—the wage and salary administration department will be responsible for developing the program. To achieve the objective of equitable compensation, it is imperative to include *all* hourly and salary paid jobs in the program. The form of the plan will vary considerably, depending on type of work performed, skills required, availability of labor, etc.

Policies and Procedures. The development of the plan requires competent wage and salary administration personnel. The approval and implementation of the plan requires equally competent and dedicated top management and supervision. The importance of comprehensive and effective decision making in wage and salary matters cannot be overemphasized.

Policies and procedures are normally reviewed and approved by a wage committee consisting of the wage administrator and other members of management. In cases where specific coverage is included in the labor contract, union officials may also serve in this capacity. The policies and procedures must be clear and understandable and permit quick reaction to questions and problems by supervision and workers. To assist in the communication of policy, all new employees are normally given an orientation that includes wage and salary matters. To augment this, training classes are conducted for supervision on the subject.

Job Analysis. Job analysis is the step that follows planning, and it initiates the mechanics of the wage plan. During this process, all the pertinent factors are collected and analyzed by the job analyst. To help the analyst to procure the necessary information, a questionnaire or work sheet is normally utilized. This work sheet is designed specifically to stimulate the analyst's approach by investigating the four basic aspects of the job—namely:

1.   What work is performed?

2.   How is this work performed?

3.   Why is it performed?

4.   What are the skills required to perform it?

Job Descriptions. The end result of the job analysis function is a clear and concise job description, which must accurately portray the basic and necessary skills and duties inherent in performing the job. This information is found in many forms in industry. But whatever the form, the following basic items must be covered:

Job Title.   The title should briefly describe the job and be definitive in nature. A typical example of a job title would be "Drill Press Operator—Multiple Spindle."

Summary of the Job. The summary should be in the form of a brief statement covering the purpose and function. A summary of the job titled above could be the following: "Set up and operate a multiple spindle drill press to machine gray iron casting parts, including drilling, reaming, boring, tapping, etc., to close tolerances."

Job Duties and Work Performed. This should include an accurate description of the specific tasks of work performed and the occurrence factor associated with them.

Equipment, Tools, and Material. A good description of equipment, tools, and material is essential to indicate the nature and complexity of the job.

Working Conditions. The physical surroundings and job-related hazards should be carefully described.

Job Requirements. The general requirements of education and experience necessary for job performance should be stated.

Job Evaluation. The process of job rating establishes the relative worth of the job. This is a beginning point for the eventual determination of rates of pay. The criteria for determining relative worth can be classified as either quantitative or nonquantitative.

Quantitative Methods. Typical of the quantitative types of job rating is the job evaluation technique. This technique subdivides each job into its essential job factors. These factors are then weighted in accordance with a rating scale. Other types of evaluation plans include the comparison of these factors of each job and the ranking of these factors between jobs.

Nonquantitative Methods. The main difference between this form of job rating and the quantitative method approach is that the latter determines the essential factors which constitute the job, while the former compares one job with another on the basis of a total approach of job content. Each separate job is ranked by the overall evaluation of all its elements and is ranked with the other jobs. The chief advantage of this method is its simplicity and ease of application.

The choice of either of these methods should reflect management's knowledge of the particular working environment of the company.

Market Wage Survey. Once the internal relative worth of the job has been established, it becomes necessary to compare this worth with the prevailing wage for comparable jobs in the industry or community. This is accomplished by a survey of the labor market to determine current compensation rates and practices.

Methods and Format. The formats used are as numerous as the industries they survey, but some basic information is inherent in each form. Because the survey cannot be exhaustive, it becomes extremely important to select *key* jobs for comparison. In addition to key jobs, a truly representative sample of companies must be selected and this sample should include companies having similar wage policies and objectives. The survey can be conducted by personal contact (including telephone) or by mail. Other important sources of wage and salary information are organizations that periodically conduct compensation surveys. Typical of these are personnel associations, chambers of commerce, trade and employee associations, and various governmental organizations such as the U.S. Department of Labor.

The primary use of the information obtained in the market survey is to establish a comparison between similar jobs in different companies. There are, however, many additional uses for this information. These include (1) establishment of minimum hiring rates, (2) current assessment of pay rate trends and their effect on product cost, and (3) the determination of nonwage benefits offered in industry.

Wage Scales. The final step in the determination of the relative worth of the particular job requires a review of some of the important parameters inherent in the company's business picture, such as the following:

1. The current anticipated profit potential
2. The availability of an adequate labor supply
3. The effects of collective bargaining
4. The benefits of paying a leading wage
5. The important effects of nonwage benefits

After careful review and study, the information compiled in all the preceding steps can be correlated to formulate an equitable wage scale designed to reach the overall objectives of the company or organization.

Graphic Method. A graphic method for developing the wage and salary curve starts with the selection of key comparison jobs that cover the entire wage structure from nonskilled laboring jobs to highly skilled trades that use apprentices and upward to technical, engineering, and professional positions. The midpoints of each key job become a graphic point of comparison to the ascending wage scale. In this manner the range of labor grades can be determined graphically; the smoothness of the wage curve can be ascertained by using mathematical correlation methods. A typical wage and salary curve is illustrated in Fig. C-7.

Wage Increases and Adjustments. The culmination of the preceding steps in the wage process is the equitable distribution of wages. The vehicle for achieving this result is a thorough understanding of the process by supervision and employees. This should be augmented by fair and equitable compensation on an individual basis where possible. **127**

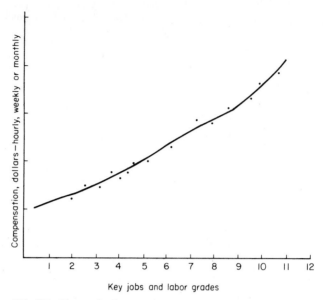

FIG. C-7 Wage and salary curve. Determination of line of best fit to wage data of key jobs.

Although many jobs are paid on a single-rate basis and leave no room for merit consideration, individual performance on these jobs should be given definite consideration toward future promotion.

There are a number of causes for wage adjustments, such as a change in internal relative worth of a job or a change in job worth in outside companies; however, the most common type of adjustment comes from changes in the general structure of the economy. As technological advances occur, the benefits of total productivity gains are usually shared with the wage earners in the form of periodic wage increases. In addition to or in conjunction with this, wage increases or decreases have been related to changes in the general cost of living. These usually stem from formulas based on the consumer price index published by the U.S. Department of Labor.

Automatic Wage Increases. In many of the jobs assigned to rate ranges, the beginning portion of the rate range is used for automatic wage increases. These occur on the basis of time spent on the job and often bear no relationship to skill or ability. This concept began with the lower-rated occupations but has spread even to those requiring apprenticeships and salaried positions.

Supplementary Compensation Methods. In addition to the real wage received by employees, supplemental pay policies have had an increasingly important effect. Payment for the employee benefits of paid vacation, holidays, life insurance, hospitalization, pension, etc., has a definite effect on product costs and the resultant profit. Therefore the wage administrator must remain cognizant of this effect

and take employee benefits into consideration when altering or instituting the wage plan. *See* Compensation, employee benefit plans.

Control and Appraisal

A compensation program must constantly be surveyed and appraised. The conditions that affect its important factors are dynamic and change almost continuously. New product or service models are introduced and processes change; these cause changes in work requirements, materials, specifications, and methods. In turn, these changes cause shifting values of job skills and job conditions, which influence job descriptions and standards.

Internal Implications. A constant appraisal is mandatory to maintain the goal of equitable wage and salary compensation. This appraisal can be an active program of internal company wage surveys. These surveys must be established in accordance with a firm schedule to review all job assignments at least once a year. The survey itself takes the form of a continuous job analysis, with the check sheet serving as the means of assessing the success of the program. As changes are discovered in job content, immediate reaction should be forthcoming. Rapid feedback goes a long way toward ensuring employee understanding and cooperation.

Legal Implications. In addition to constant internal knowledge of changing conditions, the wage administrator must maintain complete cognizance of government regulations and other legal aspects. As new legislation becomes law, the wage administrator must react immediately to implement the necessary changes. At the same time, the cost effects of these changes must be evaluated and reported to executive management.

Labor Contract Implications. Wage matters are being included in labor contract coverage at a rapid pace. With the increase in national labor contract negotiations and wage pattern setting, the results of the collective bargaining become an integral part of the labor contract. These often include the procedural aspects of wage matters, as the following example of typical wage contractual language illustrates.

Article XII—Section 1(b)
JOB CLASSIFICATION

If an appropriate classification does not exist in the appropriate Works Occupational Rating Book of the Works involved for new daywork or piecework, and in the case of changed daywork or piecework if the change has made the former classification inappropriate under the principles of the arbitration awards on classification under the prior Contract, the Company shall initially determine the classification, job description and wage group, including those cases under Article VII of this Contract in which an Arbitrator has decided that no appropriate classification exists. Such determination by the Company shall become final unless challenged by the Union within a thirty (30) day period after the Company informs the Local Union and the International Union of such determination. If challenged by the Union within such period, the issue shall become the subject of collective bargaining between the Company and the Local Union without undue delay. However, at the request of either the International Union or the Labor Relations Department of the Company, negotiations will be conducted on a central level. The Company's determination shall continue to be applied unless changed as the result of such collective bargaining.

As this coverage is extended, more collective bargaining sessions are likely to include details of the wage and salary administration plan. This will necessitate including the administrator in many of the face-to-face negotiation sessions.

Legal Regulation. A number of federal laws directly affect wage and salary administration. Of particular importance are the following:

Davis-Bacon Act (Prevailing Wage Law). This protects the wages paid employees in the construction or repair of federal buildings.

Walsh-Healey Act (Public Contracts Act). This sets minimum wages for all work performed on government contracts that exceed $10,000.

Fair-Labor Standards Act (Wage and Hour Law). This and its many amendments set minimum wages for most employment along with a provision that time and one-half the base rate be paid for all hours over 40 worked in one week.

Equal Pay Act of 1963. This amendment to the Fair-Labor Standards Act established that women must be paid the same wage rate as men for performing the same work.

Title VII of the Civil Rights Act of 1964, as amended in 1972. This legislation prohibits the unequal payment of wages because of race, color, religion, or national origin.

Age Discrimination in Employment Act of 1967. This law, as amended in 1978, protects employees between the ages of 40 and 70 from discrimination in wages and wage-related matters.

See also Affirmative action; Appraisal, performance; Compensation, employee benefit plans; Compensation, executive; Compensation, sales; Job analysis; Job evaluation; Labor legislation; Labor-management relations; Personnel administration; Wages and hours legislation; Work measurement.

REFERENCES

Mahoney, Thomas A.: *Compensation and Reward Perspectives*, Richard D. Irwin, Homewood, Ill., 1979.

Rock, Milton: *Handbook of Wage and Salary Administration*, 2d ed., McGraw-Hill, New York, 1984.

Wallace, Marc J., and Charles H. Fay: *Compensation Theory and Practice*, Wadsworth (Kent), Belmont, Calif., 1983.

GUY J. BACCI, II, *International Harvester Company*

Competition

Competition, in the sense of rivalry, is inherent in all social organizations and throughout the biological world. This basic rivalry can be enhanced, directed, utilized, and guided to assist in achieving the goals and objectives of organizations.

Regulated Rivalry. The focus here is upon competition among businesses and enterprises in countries, such as the United States and other Western nations, which have national economic policies of competition. In such countries, all business enterprises, unless specifically exempted, are to some degree under "the rule of competition" along with governmental rules and regulations. Competition in this sense expresses itself in market forms of organizations as opposed to bureaucratic, centrally directed operations. It springs almost spontaneously out of private property rights, the freedom and guarantee of contracts, and freedom of choice and of enterprise. The competitive market system through which free choices and enterprise are expressed and coordinated is inherently a highly flexible, adaptable, interacting system. It responds both to internal interactions and to its numerous environments, including governmental rules and regulations. The competitive market system, while regulating and enforcing its own discipline, is also controlled by rules enunciated by government and, to some extent, of course, by customs and conventions.

Competition is not a simple or single force, set of **129**

forces, or form of organization. The variety of expression is so great as to defy precise, universal definition and would require a long list of adjectival qualifications, depending upon the special interests, vantage points, or purposes of the users of the term. In this entry the interest is essentially in competition as rivalry under the rules of the game established by government.

Competition Rather than Cooperation. The Supreme Court of the United States in the Philadelphia Bank Case in 1963 reiterated clearly that "subject to narrow qualifications, it is surely the case that competition is our fundamental economic policy, offering as it does the only alternative to the cartellization or governmental regimentation of large portions of the economy." But how and why did this come about in the United States and other Western nations that have a national economic policy of competition?

The answer lies only in part in the rationalizations of the presumed benefits of competition: better allocation of resources, increased efficiency, higher quality of goods and services, lower prices, and so on. The answer in the United States may be found in the complex of institutions and ideologies which the early settlers brought from Western Europe, especially Great Britain. The United States became the magnificent success story of the transition from a society based on feudal status to one based on contract and free private enterprise and choice.

From Trading and Rural Society to Modern Industrial Society. The rule of competition in the United States can no longer be understood merely in terms of its common-law origin and tradition. Following the Civil War of the 1860s, the United States quickly began to move away from a relatively loose rural society into an integrated, complex industrial society. The Interstate Commerce Act of 1887 and the Sherman Antitrust Law of 1890 represented the first stages of the increasingly complex set of regulations imposed by the federal government in reaction to the new industrialization. The Sherman Act of 1890 was not a radical law, for it merely gave federal statutory form to the common law. It was symptomatic, however, of the intrusion of the federal government into the regulation of competition. This intrusion has continued step by step, statute by statute, tribunal by tribunal, and case by case ever since. As a consequence, the diverse expressions of market competition are now under the aegis of a labyrinth of federal and state regulations, intended both to (1) maintain and enhance competition and to (2) establish its plane and its essential quality and characteristics. Deregulation of banking, trucking, and the airlines illustrates this trend.

The two leading enforcement agencies are the Antitrust Division of the Department of Justice and the Federal Trade Commission. There are, in addition, numerous other agencies with overlapping responsibilities and numerous areas of special jurisprudence and of limited and partial exemption, plus the varied laws and regulations of the 50 states. The traditional negative requirements—the "thou shalt nots"—are increasingly being supplemented by positive, affirmative requirements. There is also a growing host of rules and regulations arising out of consumer, conservation, ecology, and broad welfare needs and issues. In retrospect, the relatively simple rules of the common-law tradition arising out of the adjudication of private grievances are overlaid by a complex variety of governmental regulations and requirements in the ceaseless efforts to adapt to the full needs of our democracy under the conditions of modern, complex, industrial society. A curious, almost paradoxical, development in recent years, however, has been the tremendous increase of private actions reminiscent of common-law procedures.

Application to Management

To live under the rule of competition involves two sets of interlinked rules:

1. Business policies and practices of a given firm in relation to those of its actual and potential competitors are expressions of the rule of competition between competitors. These policies must be effective in terms of the requirements of each product line, division, geographical area, situation, and so on. All business firms are in continuing processes of gathering the market and other intelligence data essential for appraising and adjusting their product lines, policies, and practices in relation to those of (a) direct and indirect competitors and (b) the needs and wants of buyers and users. The benefits to economic society accrue out of these continuing competitive compulsions.

2. All firms must also live under the rules enunciated by the various governmental agencies as interpreted by the courts. The fact findings and interpretations in this second area require a different form of expertise, including the advice of legal counsel supported by legal intelligence sources and services.

For large, diversified, national and multinational enterprises, the provision of adequate market and legal intelligence is an enormous task. Fortunately, the computer has come to the rescue, almost as if timed to coincide with the increasing complexities of the burden of fact finding and interpretation. It appears that we are moving into a regulative state of affairs in which the two great bodies of intelligence, market and legal, are becoming better integrated both in business enterprises and in law regulation. The portents are that Western nations are about to emerge out of the common-law tradition with its rules and regulations derived under simpler conditions into a coordinated pattern more appropriate to the complexities of modern industrial society.

Internal Organization and Decision Rules in Relation to Those of Law and Regulation. The United States economic policy of competition effectuated through the competitive market system cannot survive in recognizable form unless the rules of acceptable, effective private competition and those of governmental law and regulation complement each other, instead of thwarting each other. This does not mean that governmental regulations must play merely secondary or passive roles. It does mean that both sets of rules must be appropriate to (1) the basic tenets of a national economic policy of competition and (2) the circumstances and conditions of markets. This can happen only if there are basic understandings and appropriate working relations between the private and public sectors. There are some reasons for optimism on the possible outcome. Business management increasingly is expected to explain in federal courts the internal organization and policies and practices of their enterprises in terms of the rationale of effective competition. Increasingly, business executives are being deposed and appear as witnesses in trial cases. Discovery procedures digging deeply into internal organization and policies are an accepted part of corporate life. And there is an enormous stress on more adequate disclosure.

Out of the present sound and fury it is likely that established procedures better understood both on the private sides and by government will emerge, and these procedures will aid in bringing the regulation of competition more fully into the modern world. If this occurs, market intelligence and legal intelligence will, for the most part, run together. Business management will be reasonably expected to explain and interpret its organization, policies, and practices in the framework and setting of the market action.

The Market Structure Framework of Analysis. The framework appropriate to such interpretation has become well recognized in recent years under the guise of so-called market structure analysis. In this analysis, the elements of the setting of the market action are portrayed as the basis for interpreting the nature and results of market competition. These elements include (1) the number and size distribution of the market participants in both buying and selling, (2) the degree of product and enterprise differentiation, and (3) the conditions of entry into the market, including potential competition. In a complete approach, the vertical channel structures and relations and geographical submarkets and competition are also brought into the analysis. In this setting and perspective, allowance can be made for

unique historical episodes, for basic trends, and especially for internal organization and decision factors.

Competition Among the Few. One must not underemphasize, however, the problems and difficulties in the use of this type of analysis, especially in the great areas of "competition among the few," or *oligopoly*, and the case of broadly diversified enterprises. When there are only a few competitors, some uniformities in pricing (and in other vectors of competition) may appear out of the recognition of interdependence, without formal agreement. This is all the more reason for careful, detailed, conjoined analysis of structure and internal organization. There are many possible variations of oligopolistic market structures as well as those of product, price, service and territory policies and practices. The basic issues have to do with possible violations of the established so-called rules against cartel-type agreements. A careful analysis of the record over a number of years usually provides evidence as to whether there was active, effective competition or explicit or tacit agreements.

Diversification and Merger. Cases arising out of the diversification and conglomeration of assortments and of enterprises, especially in merger cases, also require a similar type of market structure analysis by product lines, divisions, or whatever internal organizational breakdowns are employed. Insofar as there are relatively discrete product lines or divisions, it is possible to relate the market categories reasonably to the internal organizational accounting. A difficult problem arises when, in managed and planned diversification, product line and other relationships with possible synergistic effects are emphasized. As yet, very little solid analysis and evidence have emerged in this area. It is likely, however, that market economies or advantages arising out of such planned relatedness would lead to the development of similar competitive enterprises, as has occurred historically in the case of department stores and supermarkets. In this event, the regulative issues would usually be those of competition among the few (oligopoly).

Furthermore, the increasing diversification of enterprises has raised regulatory issues that are unique to such enterprises. Allegedly, firms with wide assortments are able to employ practices such as cross-subsidization (out of so-called deep pockets of profits), coercive reciprocity, predatory pricing, tying arrangements, and so on, whereby specialized competitors are placed under unfair handicaps. Although such potentialities exist, they need not be exercised in fact. Regulations appropriate to unfair forms of competition are in the process of development or are already in effect. For example, coercive, organized reciprocity through trade relations departments has largely disappeared from the American scene. This whole set of problems beautifully illustrates the great need for updating the regulation of competition from its simple, common-law base.

Outlook

The vitality of competition and of the competitive market system derives from the ceaseless processes of dynamic innovation and flexible adjustments to the needs of buyers and to the policies and practices of competitors. This is in sharp contrast to the rigidities of governmental state-directed bureaucracies. Although one cannot be certain, the present portents are that emerging conjoined rules of private competition and of governmental rules and regulations will aid and complement each other instead of subverting or thwarting each other. In these conjoined sets of rules however, management must be prepared and able to explain and interpret its internal organization and decision processes in relation to the requirements of law and regulation. This can have a sobering, salutary effect on management.

In any event, looking ahead, there will be important learning processes on both sides that should, with goodwill, assist in maintaining and enhancing competition as our national economic policy, while updating the panoply of private and governmental rules from its common-law base to the requirements of complex industrial society. If this occurs, a national economic policy of competition, in terms of the dictum of the Supreme Court of the United States, will continue as the alternative to "the cartelization of governmental regimentation of large portions of the economy."

See also Acquisitions and mergers; Consumerism and consumer protection legislation; Economic concepts; Economic systems; Government regulations, federal regulation of competition; Product and service pricing; Profits and profit making; Regulated industries, management of; Social responsibility of business.

REFERENCES

Jacoby, Neil, E. T. Grether, Lee E. Preston, et al.: "Competition Policy: Looking Ahead Worldwide," California Management Review, vol. XVI, no. 4, Spring 1974, pp. 52–130.

Kintner, Earl, W.: An Antitrust Primer, 2d ed., Macmillan, New York, 1973.

Steckmest, Francis W., and the Business Roundtable: Corporate Performance: The Key to Public Trust, McGraw-Hill, New York, 1982.

E. T. GRETHER, University of California, Berkeley

Computer-Assisted Instruction

With the increased availability of affordable, reliable microcomputers, *computer-assisted instruction* (CAI)—teaching with the aid of a computer—is being increasingly applied in both education and industry to meet educational and training goals. In CAI, the trainee interacts directly with the computer by typing responses on a typewriterlike keyboard. Messages typed by the trainee are displayed on a TV-like monitor screen as they are transmitted to the computer. The computer then communicates with the trainee by displaying preprogrammed text on the monitor screen.

Adoption of *computer-managed instruction* (CMI)—application of the computer for management of tasks such as test scoring, monitoring of student progress, providing learning guidance, and routine record keeping—will further increase the usefulness of the computer in training programs. Computer-assisted instruction, when combined with computer-managed instruction, can improve training programs through its ability to provide (1) individualization of instruction through self-pacing, (2) diagnosis of a trainee's strengths and weaknesses in the development of desired skills and attitudes, and (3) prescription of appropriate instructional content.

Forms of CAI. The decision to implement computer-assisted instruction should be based on its potential for achieving specific training objectives. The traditional forms of CAI most easily adapted to training programs are drill and practice, tutorial, simulation, and games. Under the *drill-and-practice mode* the trainee is presented with exercises designed to provide practice in or to test knowledge gained from instruction received from a source other than the computer itself. Multiple-choice questions are a common format in this mode. Under the *tutorial mode*, instruction is presented directly by the computer. Highly individualized instruction is possible in this mode. *Simulations* are designed so that the trainee may study some real situation or environment, such as operation of an expensive or dangerous piece of equipment. *Games* are simulations which allow for competition between participants.

Going beyond these traditional categories of CAI, today's computer can be linked with other media, such as video, slide tape, or film, to present multimedia instructional programs controlled directly by the computer.

Computer System. The computer-assisted learning system may be composed of (1) computer hardware (the physical equipment), (2) software (the programs which tell the computer what to do), (3) courseware (the programs and subject content which deal with the subject being taught), (4) authors of system courseware, (5) trainers, and (6) trainees.

Criteria for selection of hardware include (1) amount of memory required for courseware to be employed and records to be kept, (2) expandability of memory capacity for future needs, (3) video display requirements, (4) the need for color and graphics, (5) requirements for interface between the computer and a printer, modem, disk drive, or audiovisual equipment, and (6) availability of courseware.

Courseware programs to meet specific training objectives may be available directly in ready-to-use prewritten packages from software suppliers, may be developed or tailored to your needs by outside consultants, or may be developed in-house. Directories of commercially available software, compatible with specific hardware, are available from hardware retailers. Cost-benefit analysis should be applied in decisions involving purchase and/or development of courseware. Development of "user friendly" authoring languages (special programming instructions designed to simplify writing courseware), such as PILOT or ENCORE, and authoring systems (special programs designed so that nonprogrammers can develop lessons in a fixed format), such as AUTHOR or PASS, have been designed to facilitate in-house production of courseware packages.

Types of programs to be developed, the need for computer response capability, the need for graphics, the need for computer-based management features, and characteristics of the users should be considered before choosing an authoring language or system. Specialized directories, such as *Data Sources* (annually from Ziff-Davis, New York), can be used to locate courseware consultants, specialized programming languages, and authoring systems.

See also Computer software packages; Development and training, employee; Simulations, business and management.

REFERENCES

Burke, Robert L.: *CAI Sourcebook,* Prentice-Hall, Englewood Cliffs, N.J., 1982.

Dean, C., and Q. Whitlock: *The Handbook of Computer-Based Training,* Nichols, New York, 1982.

Lewis, R., and E. Tagg: *Computers in Education,* Elsevier, New York, 1982.

INEZ RAMSEY, *James Madison University*

Computer Hardware, Mainframes

Computer, mainframe, central processing unit (CPU), and processor are all interchangeable terms used to describe a large calculating device that takes in data, processes them (using *application software*), and returns to users final product *(output)*. Thus a mainframe can be used to gather large amounts of accounting and budgetary information, tabulate totals, and generate monthly budget reports on what an organization spent. Typically, the term *mainframes* refers to the largest computers one might have, computers that cost over $400,000 apiece. They are usually installed in a *data center* along with a variety of peripheral equipment. Mainframes are most frequently taken care of by a data processing department which has *operators* (those who run a computer), *systems personnel* (those who ensure that the computer has the right kinds of programs running it), and *programmers* (those who write software applications for the computer to use, such as an accounting *package*).

Mainframes are typically located at regional, divisional, or corporate headquarters. They most frequently are used to support computerized applications that are available to large parts of an organization. They are also used for special tasks, such as supporting a variety of manufacturing applications in a plant. In either situation, one thinks of large computers as being at a *host* or *central site* within an organization. They range in purchase price from several hundred thousand dollars to $6 or $8 million.

The primary distinction between a mainframe and a *minicomputer* or *microcomputer* is its much larger size. By size is meant the ability to store more information within the system (mainframe and its associated peripherals) or the capability to process greater amounts of data. Some will even make the distinction that a mainframe is a computer that can process more than one application at the same time. That feature is increasingly becoming available, however, in minicomputers and microcomputers (*See* Computer hardware, micros/personal; Computer hardware, minis.)

Physical Description. A mainframe is part of a *computer system* all parts of which are necessary for any of the main components to work. A system consists of *input* devices, which are machines that take information from outside the system and give it to the computer; the central processing unit (computer), which uses the data to do what it was instructed to; *storage* devices, in which data are stored by the computer either before or after the CPU has performed its functions; and *output* units, which transmit information to people, usually in the form of printed reports, cards, or data on a *cathode-ray tube* (CRT) terminal. Finally, the computer has within it a set of programs, called the *system control program* (SCP), which coordinates all activities, software, and machines of the system, much like a traffic police officer at a busy intersection.

The mainframe itself, better known as the computer or "brains" of the system, is really divided into two parts. First, there is *memory*, where information is temporarily stored from input or storage devices and to which the computer can go immediately. The second part of a computer is the *processing unit*, which is the "logic"—that part of the machine that actually does the computations or "thinking," using data from memory. In memory, programs are also stored for use by the computer. Like data, these programs can also be moved in and out of memory either to the processor of the CPU or from storage devices in the same building.

Capability Measures. A mainframe is usually described by its size. Processing capability is measured by the speed in fractions of a second in which a computer can process information. Memory is measured in terms of the amount of storage space it has. Since most computer manufacturers sell various size computers, one can quickly spot larger from smaller devices by model numbers. For example, an IBM 4331 is smaller than an IBM 4341.

Within a particular size machine, one might have different numbering designations for the amount of memory it has. This is important because as one increases usage of a particular mainframe, the need to have more memory becomes critical. This increase can be obtained by adding on memory up to a certain amount, limited by the CPU's design. After that, acquisition of a bigger or another computer is necessary.

Compatibility Characteristics. A *family of computers* means that a variety of computers exist which are *compatible.* That is, programs written for one computer model will run on a different size machine within the same family. Also, peripheral equipment (input-output devices for example) can attach to other members of the same family. Finally, the same *operating system* (SCP) can be used on numerous machines. The ability to move information, SCPs, and peripherals (also called I/O devices) from one machine to another avoids any or most conversions which otherwise would be expensive and complicated. In the 1950s and early 1960s, before computer families existed, *migration* to new or bigger machines often cost as much as the computer if not more.

Peripheral Equipment. Storage devices attachable to a mainframe might consist of *tape drives* on which data are stored much as on a reel-to-reel tape unit connected to a stereo system. Tape, although slow, allows for inexpensive sequential processing of data. More frequently, data are stored on devices called *disk drives* which house information on racks of platters that look like lp record albums and which have needles that drop onto a platter exactly where the information wanted is stored. Thus, unlike tape, in which one has to read all information in front of the piece wanted, with disk (also called DASD), the computer goes directly to the item wanted, saving time. Information accessed via a terminal (such as a CRT) is always stored on disk. The more information made available to end users at terminals (kept *on-line*) the greater the number of disks needed.

Input devices for a mainframe are varied. The most common include *keypunching* units to put data on computer cards, terminals that fire data directly to disk, and even scanners such as supermarket terminals which also send information to disk. Card readers that take data off computer cards and transmit to

mainframes and tape drives are also used. Output devices could be tape and disk drives, CRTs, or printers.

In addition to these devices there are often attached to a mainframe configuration special units for communications. Thus, if there are terminals scattered across the country that use application software housed on a particular mainframe, these might be attached to the computer by way of a telephone line. That link comes into a *control unit* in the computer room which in turn is attached via cable to the mainframe. Other control units in the same room may manage banks of disk or tape drives, printers, and terminals.

Uses of Mainframes. Computer applications vary widely across all organizations, depending on the management philosophy governing data processing. Some organizations prefer to do all their processing at one location or in just a few locations. Each would thus have a computer to which all work is brought. This would be done in batches at prescheduled times by the data center. With the introduction of terminals in the late 1960s and their heavy use by the mid-1970s, the demand on the part of users to do processing instantaneously when they wanted led to *real-time* or *on-line* systems in which both *batch* and on-line work took place. Terminals would be attached via cables in a building or connected by telephone. By then computers could do *multiprocessing* (more than one job at a time).

As the cost of computing dropped during the 1970s, a new use of computers came into being, called *distributed processing.* This meant that computers of various sizes could be installed throughout an organization, linked to each other and to a host computer via telephone. With the introduction of microcomputers, easy to use by the late 1970s, it became possible to establish a *network* of CPUs beginning with a little one in an office on a desk talking to a mini in the building and, possibly, through a *teleprocessing* network of phone and satellite communications, to a large mainframe in another part of the country.

Large-Scale Applications. Mainframes are typically used for organizationwide applications and those that require vast amounts of power. Typical applications might include an accounting system, a companywide order entry system, and one that could handle all the various computing needs of a company within one computer. Frequently, complex applications may require their own CPU. A manufacturing plant's system is one of the most obvious. On-line engineering design work (CAD/CAM systems) usually has its own *dedicated* CPU. One application that for years always had its own is airline reservation systems.

When computers first were used in the late 1940s, the most common users were universities and government agencies. As costs dropped and ease of use rose during the 1950s, commercial customers acquired CPUs to automate tasks that previously required large amounts of labor, such as accounting. By the early 1970s, large calculations, modeling, and other tasks which either improved decision making or a person's productivity became common.

By the early 1980s it had also become routine to establish mainframe data centers, called *information centers*, in which an organization stored vast quantities of information *(data bases)* and software tools, such as report generators, which a large number of people could use on demand. As computing costs dropped, more computer power could be offered to larger numbers of people. This meant a variety of different size computers could be, and had to be, linked together from the very largest to the smallest (which might be a terminal with memory and a processor within it).

Broadening Usage. Mainframes are as common as telephones. Hardly any organization with sales of over $50 million or more than 100 employees is without one. Most with sales of under $300,000 also have smaller devices (minis or micros), and it is estimated that, by the end of the 1980s over one-third of all homes in the United States will have at least one micro. The implication is that computers are being used for a large variety of applications.

Usage began with scientific work, accounting, and payroll and moved on to manufacturing and sales, decision modeling, financial analysis, medicine, and reporting. Recently within the business community, usage has extended to computerized training, robotics (use of robots and computers in a plant), on-line designing and drafting, and, most explosive, the office.

The introduction of computers to help increase productivity in the office promises to be the most widely developed application in the 1980s. The fastest growing portion of the work force comprises office employees. Yet today the average blue-collar worker has about $35,000 in capital investments to support him or her while white-collar employees have less than $3500 in support. Office workers are paid more than factory personnel. When these facts are taken into account, it is easy to understand why there is a rapid push toward office automation. Often, the centerpiece of this technology is the mainframe and its software applications.

Selection of a Mainframe. The acquisition of a computer often is influenced by many of the same considerations as the purchase or lease of other capital machinery. Yet there are some special considerations management keeps in mind.

1. *Compatibility with already installed equipment.* Frequently the acquisition of a mainframe is as a replacement for an older or smaller unit. Essentially, management wants to pull out the old device and replace it with a newer, bigger one without disturbing much or any of the peripherals. Neither does management want to do any conversion of programs. Heart transplant changes of this kind are frequent and can usually be made over a weekend. Thus, for a variety of reasons, hardware and software compatibility is an important criterion against which to measure acquisitions.

2. *Vendor support.* No matter how efficient and sophisticated mainframes are, they still break down, and the uses to which they are put are complex. It is essential that the manufacturer of the computer provide maintenance of the hardware and frequently, of the software, to ensure that the device works and is being utilized correctly. A vendor's support and maintenance have to be measured in terms of cost, availability of resources in the community in which the CPU is installed, and services available at the remote sites that have terminals and other minis and micros attached which communicate with the host computer. Quality of such service must also be taken into consideration.

3. *Availability of prewritten software packages.* Increasingly within the data processing industry, large numbers of software packages covering a wide variety of applications are coming onto the market which are less expensive for an individual company to purchase than to write. However, they do not indiscriminately run on any computer—only on the most widely used ones for obvious marketing reasons. A computer may cost just so much, but a whole system with software packages costs a lot more of which the mainframe is often only a small part of the expense.

4. *Availability of people to operate the computer and write software for it.* This is critical if the machine is to be installed and utilized. Exotic CPUs for which personnel are hardly available are useless. This often is the case with devices manufactured 15 or more years ago. Such units need to be replaced quickly.

5. *Expense of a computer versus its benefits.* While cost justification could be an entry in itself, let us at least point out several factors. One must decide how long the mainframe is to be kept. In the 1960s and 1970s, for tax reasons, out of ignorance, or because of cost, computers were leased for 4 to 7 years with concrete contracts that could not be modified, or they were purchased and depreciated over 7 to 10 years. Managers thought that such tactics were appropriate, believing their organizations would keep the computers around that long, driving down costs.

By the mid-1970s, it became increasingly obvious that with the cost of computers dropping, along with maintenance charges, and at a time that dependence on data processing was rising sharply, (a) managers could not keep machines for so many years and (b) breaking contracts to get newer, bigger ones was too expensive. Thus they learned to depreciate such devices in shorter periods (5 or less years) and to consider leasing with purchase accrual clauses and upgrade capability. Managers by the early 1980s had also learned to buy more machine than their capacity studies suggested to ensure a buffer against miscalculation in either demand or accounting.

As a consequence of these considerations, management today typically will look at a variety of financial alternatives before selecting one in the acquisition of a computer. Managers plan to keep a computer for less than 5 years and will depreciate it accordingly. They recognize that the cost of a system (including all devices, software, people, and maintenance) far exceeds the expense of a computer and thus will take into account a variety of financial issues in making a decision. Today, for example, the cost of a mainframe is about a third of the expense of a system, and often only several percentage points or less of a data processing (DP) department's budget.

Management increasingly is finding that its major hardware expenses are elsewhere. Up to the mid-1970s, clearly the most expensive component of a system was the computer. Now it is common to spend as much or more on data storage devices, terminals, and large quantities of minis and micros. It is also becoming more common to have several mainframes in the same data center, linked to each other for the purposes of sharing information and work. In fact, mainframes are bought in bulk at quantity discounts much like terminals and micros.

6. *Long-range plans for computing in general.* Is an organization going to continue most of its processing at a centralized site or is it decentralizing? In a centralized environment, larger mainframes are needed for longer periods of time. Is the software being poured into these machines becoming more efficient and cost effective? What impact does the selection of a particular computer have on the cost of such software and its maintenance? How reliable (in terms of ability to stay running) are such computers and their software over older technologies? What additional applications or increased usage of existing applications can be expected on a mainframe? Such capacity studies are easy to do today and are an essential component of any acquisition decision.

Trends and Conclusions. Some trends to consider in mainframes and their systems are:

Costs. Since the early 1950s, when computers became commercially available in large numbers,

their costs have declined. Instructions that cost $1.50 to execute on a CPU in 1953 today are a fraction of a penny. In comparing one device against another over several decades, it is not uncommon to see compounding declines in cost of 20 to 40 percent.

Growth. The new waves of technology or families of computers are commonly referred to as *generations.* We are today in the fourth generation of technology and on the verge of the fifth. Each new one brought with it dramatic cost reductions and typical increases in capacity of memory or speed of processing of a third or better. Growth in the use of computers has paralleled such developments. Thus, it is still not uncommon for the DP industry to grow between 17 and 25 percent each year, regardless of whether the economy is in good shape or not.

Technology. The increased supply of computers and their declining costs have also been accompanied by significant improvements in their technology. In the early 1950s, computers broke down often (every day was not uncommon), while today they are designed to malfunction less than 1 or 2 percent of the time. If anything, it is software that breaks down more frequently. Reliability has been made possible by technological improvements, redundancy of parts (made possible because of cheapness of cost) that allow CPUs to switch instantaneously from a broken part to a backup before you know it, and finally to improved diagnostics which can either correct problems or quickly identify them for maintenance personnel.

To illustrate the impact of technological change just in the past few years, consider the following. The horsepower contained in computer systems which in 1975 sold for $1 million (peripherals and software included) and that might have been used by a company with sales of $100 million can now be purchased for under $10,000 in the form of microcomputers. The trends in declining costs, increased quality, and expanded capability show no signs of slowing down during the 1980s. The software going into these machines over time has required less technical personnel to support and fewer people to manage it. It increasingly is being made part of the hardware, especially SCPs (When buried in the machine, they are often called *firmware*). Management can expect to see more of this as the years pass, requiring less personnel to baby-sit mainframes.

The application programs which end users work with are also becoming easier to understand and more powerful. This allows one to dump into a mainframe larger varieties of inexpensive software tools for end users which they can select to use from their terminals. The computer is becoming a tool being used at will much like inexpensive hand calculators.

See also Automation; Computer hardware, micros/personal; Computer hardware, minis; Computer software, data-base management; Computer software, languages; Computer software packages; Control systems, management; Management information systems, transaction processing systems; Office automation; System concept, total.

REFERENCES

Cortada, James W.: *Managing DP Hardware: Capacity Planning, Cost Justification, Availability, and Energy Management*, Prentice-Hall, Englewood Cliffs, N.J., 1983.

Cortada, James W.: *Strategic Data Processing: Considerations for Management*, Prentice-Hall, Englewood Cliffs, N.J., 1984.

Dunlavery, Richard F.: ''Workload Management,'' *EDP Performance Review*, vol. 6, no. 5, 1978, pp. 1–6.

Schaeffer, Howard: *Data Center Operations*, Prentice-Hall, Englewood Cliffs, N.J., 1981.

Schiller, D. C.: ''System Capacity and Performance Evaluation,'' *IBM Systems Journal*, vol. 19, no. 1, 1980, pp. 46–67.

JAMES W. CORTADA, *IBM Corporation*

Computer Hardware, Micros/ Personal

In less than a decade, the ability to encapsulate large amounts of integrated circuitry into a single electronic microchip has produced what is probably the most significant industrial revolution of all time. This single chip, which now contains over one-half million individual electronic circuit elements, is more powerful than a complete roomful of the last generation of computer technology. Microminiaturization has enabled a growth of electronic computing power, which can be harnessed to support a wide range of new, exciting, and broad-reaching management and industrial applications. This entry examines (1) microtechnology, (2) its utilization in computing systems, and (3) the use of such computing systems in support of managerial applications.

Technology

Microcomputing itself is not all that exciting in terms of its technological breakthroughs. The basic beginning is to take an existing computer model and compress the circuitry into a high level of integration, such that it can be inscribed upon a single element of semiconductor material. The inscription on the semiconductor material represents the circuit elements necessary to perform the main computational process. This is often called the CPU, for central processing unit. Additional functions needed for computing—such as large amounts of memory, input-output interface units, peripherals, and power supplies—are usually separate from the main microcomputing chip.

By the time all these necessary elements are added to the central processor micro circuit, however, the microcomputer itself becomes a much larger package. Nevertheless, these circuits can be packaged on a single printed circuit card, housed within a small box, and made to rest either on top of a desk, beside a desk, or in a small enough case to be portable (more often called luggable).

Microcomputer Logic. Technology used in microcomputer circuits is fairly standard computing logic. There are an arithmetic unit, an input-output unit, various levels of stored direct access memory, a programming logic unit, and some dedicated instructions that represent the operational repertoire of the computer unit. In many cases the logic design for a microcomputer is a scaled-down version of that for an existing larger-scale computer. This makes good sense because it uses a proven design and concentrates on wrestling with the issues of packaging technology in order to provide a product that will work effectively in its operational space.

The Memory Factor. The excitement of having a small, fast, lower-cost implementation of a large computer is an intriguing and interesting technological fact. It turned out, however, that the first microcomputer products were not particularly useful in real-world applications. Originally, the memory associated with such a computer consumed considerably more space than the computer chip itself, and it was available only at a cost of several orders of magnitude greater than the microcomputer. In addition, the memory lacked adequate reliability and might fail at inopportune times, bringing the complete system to a catastrophic halt.

Fortunately, random access memory has come to benefit extensively from the same micro circuit encapsulation concepts that brought us the microcomputer chips. Today's memory chips reach a level of 256K (256,000 bits of stored information in one small integrated circuit element). They are quickly moving on toward an establishment of a next generation where each chip will contain 1 million bits of storable and accessible information. This compression brings the price of memory down dramatically (about a 40 percent per year decline) and makes it reasonably compact in the amount of space needed to support the microcomputer processor. As memory declines in price and size, however, the microprocessor still hungers for larger and larger amounts of memory in which to produce its intriguing and exciting applications performance. Today the memory norm is 256,000 bytes, or characters, with millions, even billions, of characters coming soon.

Peripherals

Early microcomputers were also handicapped by having few available peripherals. The original peripheral was a good, old, solid, slow, noisy, but cheap and reasonably reliable ASR33 Teletype. This machine had a long and useful service life and was the perfect device to fit to a microcomputer. It provided the keyboard input for generating characters which were immediately passed to the microcomputer; it could provide remote storage of data through punched paper tape which could be both punched and read through most of the teletypes; and, of course, the teletype would loudly clank its type wheel to produce a plodding 10-character-per-second output. Needless to say, this limited the overall flexibility of the microcomputer system. However, it did provide an access window and a simple mechanism that would allow users to begin to harness the power of the machine.

Floppy Disks. Fortunately, the same design intellect that was applied to the compression of circuitry to produce microchips also applied energy and attention to the various peripherals needed to support a truly viable microcomputer system's environment. The invention—by IBM—of a floppy disk allowed lower cost, smaller packaging, and reasonably speedy access to a rotating magnetic memory storage device. Although not nearly as fast and agile as its larger and hard disk cousins, the floppy disk was hundreds of times faster than any paper tape storage. It was also faster than the other early data storage facility, the magnetic tape, which was usually a modification of an audiocassette tape device functioning at very slow speeds. It should be pointed out, however, that that cassette tape was about five times faster than paper tape, so even it provided some performance advantage to the early micro systems' users.

The floppy disk allowed for random storage in information and the development of real files that could be stored on disks, libraried, copied, split apart, added to, appended, compressed, and, of course, used for generating extensive reports. Once the floppy disk was perfected in its original version (the full 8-inch), designers began to work to store more and more information of the disks. They expanded the densities; they increased the number of tracks that could be stored in the same amount of space. Next, the disk was reduced to 5 ¼ inches. It originally had about as much storage as the early 8-inch; then it proceeded to increase in capacity and storage density as well as use both sides. Today, almost all microcomputer systems support 5 ¼-inch disks, and only a few diehards in special situations use the larger 8-inch variety. There are continuing reductions in size even now, with 4-inch, 3-inch, 3 ¼-inch, and 3.9-inch varieties of various (usually nonstandard) disks which can hold extensive amounts of randomly accessible information. These further reduce the price of the disk units and offer a high level of service to the user in smaller and smaller amounts of space.

Hard Disks. While this activity continued, the original disk drives, those that used hard aluminum platters, were now making parallel improvements. Original drives were 14-inch platters usually stacked five to eleven high (called PACKS). These were first compressed to an 8-inch minidisk able to contain anywhere from 5 to 10 million characters of information. It provided a much larger capacity than a floppy disk, and it also turned much faster and had no contact between the head and the disk, thereby allowing up to 15 to 20 times faster access speed than can be found on a floppy disk. Such devices are of extremely high precision and were usually sealed units, from which the disks could not be removed (a significant drawback over the floppy disk, which, of course, could be removed and stored in library form).

The mini hard-disk vendors soon followed the pattern set by the floppy disk vendors. They extended the densities and added more tracks. Before long, the 8-inch hard disk was handling anywhere between 40 and 80 million characters of information. The designers also started to stack their disk platters three, four, and five high, thus increasing the amount of information stored up to 300 million characters on a single disk drive.

Then came the 5¼-inch *micro* hard disk. It originally contained 3 to 5 million characters of information but soon escalated to the point where a single 5¼-inch disk could handle up to 20 million characters of stored information. The popularity of these units, from a size performance and cost level, has made them a volume leader. As a consequence, prices on these disks have dropped to the point where they can be supported even in a home computer environment, where budgets are extremely limited.

Magnetic Tape Components. There are compact versions of large-scale half-inch magnetic tapes that have migrated across from the large-scale computer environment and are used to store extensive amounts of information in a sequential file form. The problem is that such devices cost on the order of $10,000 to $20,000—well beyond the budget of most microcomputer users. Although reel-to-reel units have been found in smaller, reduced capacity, and less costly versions, they still represent a significant investment that is not very often used in the microcomputer systems' environment.

Engineers from the 3M Company, however, have created the first cartridge data tape. This has now been expanded to include a full-scale and a mini-scale version. This tape is self-contained and sealed, and offers high speed, very good reliability, and reasonable cost. In addition, because it is not a replacement version of the audio tape, it does not run in just any home unit and is less susceptible to pilferage. The other main advantage of the cartridge tape is that it has good storage capacities, on the order of 15 to 65 million characters on a single tape, which is compatible with the amount of data storage needed for backup of a micro-level hard-disk system.

It is often frustrating to see microcomputer systems with either cassette tape or floppy disks (each containing approximately 100,000 to 300,000 characters of information) being used to back up the information on a sealed hard disk containing 20 million characters of information. It requires up to 20 floppy disks or cassettes to make the backups. This process becomes long and arduous and the amount of generated floppy disks or cassette tapes becomes very large and burdensome to manage, label, identify, and store. The option of having a single cartridge tape that can contain all the data from a single-disk file system is extremely attractive, and an operationally efficient way to organize one's backup.

Printer Technologies. The last peripheral, the lone holdout that probably caused the most difficulty and stymied the microcomputer development longer than others, was the availability of low-cost, high-reliability, reasonable-speed printers. Printers as a technology are extensively mechanical in form, having high costs and questionable reliability. There is an extensive array of large-scale computer printers, but at more than $60,000 for a typical unit, it places them well out of the range of microcomputer users.

Dot-Matrix Printers. Fortunately, some bright engineers discovered the technique of firing matrix pins through small holes, hitting a ribbon and making small pressure dots on paper. The early matrix printers, however, were noisy, relatively expensive, and unreliable and produced less than eye-pleasing results. The development needed in the microcomputer printer environment soon began. Early breakthroughs were spearheaded from Japan: Their first models were at $1000 to $2000, and this, in itself, was considered a breakthrough. Daisy wheel printers, the previous lowest-cost machine, which had been imported from the word processing marketplace, operated more slowly than matrix printers and normally cost two or three times as much as the matrix models. Arrival of the inexpensive matrix printer opened new markets at adequate speeds, reasonable quality, and low price.

As the matrix market developed, these printers were enhanced with the ability to fire the pins closer and closer together, giving an image of nearly letter-quality perfection. In addition, by firing the pins in varying patterns, one could generate normal characters, plus variable fonts, foreign-language character sets, and finally graphic symbols. Some matrix printers today allow the firing of as many as 200 pin impressions per inch, giving an almost complete shading of the paper.

As the quality and price of these printers were dropping, someone remembered that in the past typewriters came with ribbons in two colors, red and black. Although there was only one typeface, it was

noted that the ribbon was allowed to jump up and down between two positions to make different character colors. Engineers found they could build a movable ribbon mechanism covering four to seven different positions, and using small thin strips of different colored ink on a single ribbon, they could produce color output. Now there are matrix printers that perform high-speed draft printing, slower-speed multiple-pin-firing correspondence, or near-letter-quality printing, and extensive graphics; a few of them even have multicolored outputs.

The range of printers today is extensive. Few computer manufacturers actually are masters of their market when it comes to the printer environment. Printers represent a very demanding mechanical technology requiring precision and high accuracy, as well as extensive reliability engineering to perform adequately in their strenuous shock-oriented environment. Many of the successful printer vendors today are of international repute, and their products tend to be generalized so that they can run on a wide range of different machines. It is not unusual to see a U.S.-based computer, for example, coupled to a multinational printer from a different manufacturer operating in a working configuration.

The dot-matrix printers have become broad spectrum products that support micro/personal computers with a good match of capabilities, performance, flexibility, costs, and reliability. Much of this performance is due to the use of on-board microprocessors and buffer memories to handle the character generation, sizing, placement, operational movement, optimization, status management, and other activities within the printer. Other improvements in small printers include reduction in size for desktop use, portable use, and integration into transportable computer system packages.

Increasing Capabilities and Versatility. The focus of the next generation of small printers will be on reducing noise levels and improving their near-letter-quality output. Their option lists will also grow with multiple-character sets (U.S., foreign, etc.), different character fonts, graphic symbols, color ribbons, etc. The current technology trend in small printers is in the area of ink-jet systems. By squirting a tiny burst of ink under precise positional control, ink-jet printers can produce good images at reasonable speeds with minimal sound pollution. Cost and reliability problems appear to be solved, with new units appearing at a price at $1000 per unit and a 5000-hour mean-time-between-failure rating. Repair and maintenance are usually simple and user-performed by snapping in a cartridge ink supply with an integrated jet and pressure generator. In addition to their invaluable silence, the ink-jet systems can have multiple jets to produce quality color outputs.

The next printer technology on the horizon is the electronic laser. Among its advantages will be increased precision of image (for graphics, fonts, forms, etc.), good throughput speeds, reliability, communications, interfacing, image integration, copier replacement, and low noise. Used today in high-speed, large-computer systems (due to their high costs), the laser printers are the workhorses of EDP computer output systems. As their size and price are scaled down, they will become a key element in the output process of microcomputers.

Graphic Outputs. The generation of high-precision graphic outputs, such as product/engineering drawings, charts, schematics, and layouts, has usually been processed by electromechanical pen plotters operating under extremely high positional tolerances and movement controls. Such devices have been priced in the $40,000 and up class, putting them out of reach to microcomputer systems. However, by using microprocessor technology, coupled to large control memories and new, lower-cost servo motors, the plotter industry has undergone its own technological transformation. Recent products have moved down the price scale, stopping at $10,000, $5000, $3000, $2000, $1500, and now under $1000 for a two-pen, 8 ½ × 11, good-quality, modest-speed plotter. By changing pens, the user can obtain a broad spectrum of colors and the generation of hard-copy, overhead vu-graphs, velum reproduction masters, and other excellent-resolution image outputs. Areas such as computer-aided design (CAD), computer-aided engineering (CAE), business graphics, educational presentations, and professional reports will benefit greatly from the evolution of low-cost plotters.

Display and Keyboard Developments

Perhaps the subtlest evolution and impact of microcomputer technology on managerial users has been its almost total dedication to using interactive processing by means of a keyboard and video display screen (CRT, VDU, etc.). Although the keyboard is still a stumbling block to many users, due to lack of skills training and confusion with the illogical order of keys, the video display screen has been accepted almost without question.

Video Technology. The evolution of video technology has produced better-quality images, increased the display detailing to support graphics, and held to a controlled pricing with moderate declines. The most dramatic impacts are occurring in the color video screens, where detailed resolutions have greatly increased and costs have dropped from $10,000 to $400 per unit. In addition, a large amount of today's application software provides optional support for color monitors to enhance their user interfacing and message content.

Keyboard Technology. The keyboard product remains probably the major unchanged part of the microcomputer spectrum. It also presents the largest mental block to most managerial users. Based on an alphabetic arrangement that is standardized around the logic of slowing operators down (needed to make the original 1873 typewriter invention a viable product), it presents confusion, frustration, and a difficult learning and acceptance process. This old and poor key placement (commonly called QWERTY after the first six letters on the top letter row) is coupled to nonstandard additions of special functions, numeric pads, control and cursor keys, plus differing key shapes, angles, pressure levels, tactile feedback, colors, and placements. In short, a poor basic keyboard structure has been made nonstandard, confusing, complicated, unique, and a form of mental torture for users.

Some vendors have moved to ease the pain by using other keyboard orders. DVORAK, for example, is statistically organized for optimum finger motion, i.e., the alphabet order is more logical and easier to remember. Other vendors are offering substitutes for user-interface mechanisms, such as light pens, a rolling mouse, and touch-sensitive screens.

Direct-Voice Technology. The most significant future-user interfacing technology appears to be the direct-voice input concept enabling the user to speak to the computer. In this mode the computer processes the analog sound patterns, interprets the phonics, constructs word phrases, computes the meaning, and then executes the artificially derived action(s). The processing of spoken input is a complex mathematical analysis problem coupled to an intelligent search-and-select process to discern the proper command and intentions. Its practical delivery is still a few years away.

Applications

An enormous revolution in processes and technologies has come together to form the micro/personal computer systems of today. These systems open new vistas of individual and corporate uses of computing services. Coupled to the advances in available software tools and packages (word processing, spread sheets, graphics, data-base management, and thousands of specialized applications packages), this level of computers provides a powerful productivity tool. When these units are tied into networks of other computers (micros, minis, and large systems), applications and services from the local micro/personal computer can be expanded to unlimited horizons.

The next step is to increase the awareness, motivation, excitement, and energy levels of professional managers so that they will selectively convert their needs and applications into information-based activities that can use these available and affordable computing tools. This can only be done by a progression of (1) defining needs, (2) trying out possible uses, (3) conceiving relevant data and logic organizations, (4) practicing keyboard usage, (5) testing various software products, (6) building operational and protection procedures, and (7) developing a comfort and competency with the available tools. All this must be pursued on a personal, professional, and organizational basis. The results available from skilled and knowledgeable use of the tools described above make possible a broad range of personal and professional productivity improvements.

See also Computer hardware, mainframes; Computer hardware, minis; Computer security; Computer software, languages; Computer software packages.

REFERENCES

Glossbrenner, Bert I.: *The Complete Handbook of Personal Computer Communications,* St. Martin's Press, New York, 1983.

Popular Computing, McGraw-Hill, Peterborough, New Hampshire, monthly.

Webster, T.: *Microcomputer Buyer's Guide,* McGraw-Hill, New York, 1983.

RAYMOND P. WENIG, *International Management Services*

Computer Hardware, Minis

The first computer sold commercially was purchased in 1951. This was a very large computer; it weighed approximately 30 tons, occupied 1500 square feet of floor space, and required an air conditioning unit of approximately the same size to keep it from burning itself up with the heat generated during its operation. That machine cost the purchaser $1 million.

Minicomputers date to somewhere around the early to mid-1960s. They are primarily an outgrowth of the space effort. There was an obvious need for a smaller, more durable, yet highly powerful machine that could be used in aircraft and space capsules.

The first commercial uses of these physically smaller computers was in the area of process control. It was in the early to mid-1970s before organizations began to realize that there was a large potential use for minicomputers in administrative applications. Today, they represent a significant portion of the total computer market.

Over the 20-year history of minicomputers there has been a lack of agreement as to exactly what a minicomputer is. This uncertainty still exists today. Essentially, a minicomputer is whatever the manufacturer says it is. The following section lists some of the characteristics of machines currently listed as minicomputers. Selecting an appropriate device will not be an easy task. By the early 1980s more than 70 firms were manufacturing minicomputers.

Current State of the Art. Lack of standard definitions makes it difficult to compare hardware. Early minicomputers had 4K (K = 1024 storage positions, each capable of storing one character) of main memory, were often limited to punched-card input and punched paper tape for auxiliary memory, and cost from $100,000 up. Today, it is appropriate to talk about three categories of minicomputers: mini, midi, and maxi or super minicomputers. There is no specific guideline to use in assigning a computer to any of these categories. Assignment is based roughly on main memory size and processing speeds. Main memory ranges from 64K to 1Mbyte in size. Typically, minis offer almost full support of all available input and output devices (which is generally a major factor in differentiating them from microcomputers); they offer fairly large instruction sets; they are capable of operating in high-speed communication networks; and they cost from $50,000 to $500,000. Minicomputers normally have significant expansion capability, and software support is widely available.

Typical Applications. Because of their relatively low cost, wide software support, and ability to support numerous input-output devices, minicomputers are used in almost every way imaginable:

- Their processing power has allowed a number of firms to use minicomputers to support computer-aided design/computer-aided manufacturing (CAD/CAM).

- A number of educational institutions are using minicomputers to support computer-aided instruction programs, since the machines are capable of supporting a number of terminals simultaneously.

- Standard business applications, such as inventory management, accounts receivables, accounts payables, and general ledger, are often found on minicomputers. The processing power of the machines allows them to be used in areas such as production scheduling and marketing research.

- Firms setting up computer networks will often use their minicomputers to handle data communications or to act as a front-end processor for their mainframe. This takes some of the routine processing load off the mainframe to make it more productive.

Input-Output Options. Minicomputers are capable of supporting almost any of the multitude of input devices available. These include punched card, punched paper tape, magnetic tape, keyboard, optical mark readers, optical character readers, vocal input devices, digitizing tablets, and pressure-sensitive cathode-ray tube screens.

The only output device designed for computers that is not well supported by minicomputers is the laser-based printer. With this exception, minicomputers are quite capable of outputting to magnetic tape, magnetic disk, floppy disk, character printers, line printers, audio units, color graphic terminals, plotters, or data communication networks.

Software: Applications and Languages. Minicomputers were originally limited to assembly-level languages—very difficult to use, time-consuming, error-prone languages. A major reason for this was the mini's limited main memory size. The increasing memory size available today makes it possible to use virtually any language on a minicomputer. For administrative applications, the most popular minicomputer languages are COBOL, FORTRAN, RPG, and BASIC.

Application programs may be written in-house or purchased from an outside source. The wide popularity of minicomputers has resulted in a great variety of programs offered commercially. These range from standard payroll programs to complete sets of programs for a particular industry. Some of these package programs will be available free. Others may cost $100,000 or more. Commercially available programs are generally error-free and well documented; they can be up and running quickly and maintenance support is available for them. Serious consideration should be given to the purchase of commercially available programs before developing a program with your own staff.

Selection Criteria. A number of factors should be considered in selecting a minicomputer.

Cost of Acquisition. This is often a primary selection criterion. A rough guideline is that data processing expenses should be about 1 to 3 percent of gross revenues for the organization. Minicomputers can be acquired by renting, leasing, or outright purchase. The specific acquisition method should be chosen in connection with someone from your finance department.

Price per User. Although the price of a microcomputer might be cheaper, it often supports only a single user at a time. In contrast, a minicomputer can support a number of users at the same time. The price per user of the minicomputer might be significantly cheaper.

Software Availability. Although thousands of package programs are available, they are not equally available for all manufacturers' computers.

Memory Capacity. As demands on the system grow, it is often necessary to expand main memory. The ease of expansion of the system—main memory as well as peripheral devices—should be looked into.

Other Factors. The selection decision should also include (1) service availability, (2) vendor reputation, (3) delivery availability, (4) number of machines previously installed in your area so you can locate a backup computer in case yours goes down, and (5) processing speeds of the minicomputer.

See also Computer hardware, mainframes; Computer hardware, micros/personal; Computer software, data-base management; Computer software, languages; Computer software packages; Management information systems (MIS); Management information systems, transaction processing systems.

REFERENCES

Isshiki, Koichiro R.: *Small Business Computers: A Guide to Evaluation and Selection*, Prentice-Hall, Englewood Cliffs, N.J., 1982.

Joslin, Edward O.: *Computer Selection: Augmented Edition*, Technology Press, Fairfax Station, Va., 1977.

Silver, Gerald A.: *Small Computer Systems for Business*, McGraw-Hill, New York, 1978.

CHARLES P. BILBREY, *James Madison University*

Computer Security

Establishing a computer security program for a company requires making several important business decisions. Not only do computer "hardware" (computers themselves and peripheral equipment) and "software" (programs that make the computers work) represent a substantial investment of company resources, but the information stored in computer systems is often irreplaceable and essential to the continuity of an enterprise. At the same time, however, many computer security measures are expensive and of questionable value. Unwary business managers can easily find themselves spending money they cannot afford for products that don't work to protect against risks that do not exist.

There are four general threat classifications, often called *impact areas*. They are (1) destruction, (2) modification, (3) disclosure, and (4) denial.

Destruction refers to permanent deprivation of all or part of an asset; its manifestations include fire, water damage, and theft. The assets most frequently affected are hardware (especially microcomputers, terminals, and test equipment) and removable magnetic media (tapes, cassettes, disk packs, and floppy disks).

Improper modification refers to intentional or inadvertent changes to computer programs, data records, or hardware. Fraud and embezzlement frequently entail improper modification. Common "ripoffs" are payroll and benefit fraud; payment of fraudulent invoices; and theft or diversion of receipts, where the loss is covered up by application of more recent payments ("lapping").

Unauthorized disclosure from computer-stored files can result in compromise of trade secrets and proprietary computer programs, privacy-act violations, or legal liability when the information belongs to a third party.

Denial of data-processing service or access to

information can bring business to a standstill, with resultant loss of revenue, opportunity for profit, and market share. A common form of service denial occurs when a group of data-processing employees go into business for themselves, using their boss's hardware and software. Sometimes they undertake jobs for which their employer might have been in contention.

Threats also arise from natural causes like tornadoes, "global" accidents like a fire next door, "local" accidents like a burst water pipe, careless or malicious actions by employees, or malicious actions by outsiders. The most frequent causes of loss are those most easily controlled by management: local accidents and employee actions.

Security Measures

Computer security measures fall into five categories: (1) administrative, (2) physical, (3) environmental, (4) communications-related, and (5) systemic.

Administrative Security. There are four rules to follow to ensure administrative security:

1. Begin by making someone responsible for it. Computer security may be a part-time, full-time, or supervisory responsibility, depending on the magnitude of the computer resources of the company. The computer security officer will require access to top management and good working relations with corporate security. To do the job properly she or he may have to inconvenience some important middle managers.

2. Avoid putting inept, disloyal, or unreliable people into sensitive computer-related positions. This implies identifying those positions and carefully screening candidates for them.

3. Make people in sensitive positions aware of their responsibilities. This implies writing those responsibilities into job descriptions, executing appropriate preemployment agreements (e.g., nondisclosure, patent and copyright assignment, and bonding), conducting a continuing program of security training and awareness, dividing duties (e.g., operators don't program and programmers don't operate), enforcing vacations, and maintaining at least a one-over-five span of supervisory control.

4. Fix responsibility for all security-relevant actions. This can be implemented by audit trails, sign-in sign-out logs, and double sign-offs on program changes and other measures. Audit trails and logs must be reviewed regularly and follow-up action must be taken.

Physical Security. A computer room should be a restricted area into which only persons with legiti-

mate business, like operators and maintenance personnel, are admitted. These people should be required to show identification in all cases and to sign a visitors' log if not regularly employed there. Users should obtain service at counters. The computer room should be windowless to prevent unauthorized visual intrusion.

Doors should be kept locked; often electrically actuated digital combination locks or card-entry systems are used. There should be locks on consoles, keyboards, terminals, telephone closets, and equipment cabinets.

During "quiet hours," the area should be guarded or alarmed (passive or active infrared systems are preferable to microwave or ultrasonic systems). Informal portals such as ventilating ducts and under-floor and over-ceiling spaces should be stopped against entry. The area should be on an upper floor in the interior of the building. No exterior identifying signs should be posted.

A secure library separate from the computer room should be provided to store removable magnetic media such as tapes and disk packs. Backup copies of programs and data should be stored in a secure location off site. Provision should exist for secure destruction of sensitive waste, like printouts and carbons (using shredders or an incinerator), and secure storage of computer-produced negotiables, like checks and insurance policies.

Environmental Security. A computer should have a reliable supply of constant-voltage, well-filtered electrical power. This is best supplied by an "uninterruptable" power supply (UPS). A UPS converts incoming power to direct current, charges a bank of batteries, then converts the battery power back to alternating current. It not only decouples the computer from external power fluctuations but in case of power failure provides 45 minutes to switch to an emergency alternator or to power down in an orderly manner.

A computer also requires a supply of conditioned air to avoid problems from heat, excessive humidity, excessive dryness (static electricity), and dust. Usually this is provided by several air conditioners so that work can continue if one fails. Instruments should be installed to record voltage, electrical frequency, temperature, and relative humidity so that processing discrepancies arising from environmental causes can be properly attributed.

Fire can devastate a computer room. Smoke, heat, and flame detectors should be installed in ceilings, ventilating ducts, under-floor spaces and over-ceiling spaces. A Halon 1301 fire-suppression system should be installed under the raised floor (computer-room floors are elevated to make room for cables that interconnect equipment cabinets). There should be an adequate number of carbon-dioxide fire extinguishers. A floor-tile lifter should be available to reach under-floor spaces. A dry-pipe sprinkler system should be installed. Sites in high-rise towers should be avoided because of the difficulty of fighting fire there.

The reason for using dry-pipe sprinklers is to avoid water damage from premature discharge. For the same reason, water, sewage, and steam pipes should not traverse a computer room. Basement sites should be avoided because of the danger of flooding.

There should be an alternate data-processing site in case of fire, flood, or inability to maintain a proper machine environment. This could be realized by a contract with a service bureau, cooperative arrangement with a noncompetitive company, buying into a "shell" plan (empty computer center in which replacement equipment can be installed when needed), or a supplementary company-owned site.

Communications Security. Most computers are now accessed from remote locations. This makes them vulnerable to entry by persons who can falsely obtain access credentials or by wiretapping on data-communications lines. Access is usually controlled by requiring the user to give a password and by breaking off communications if he or she doesn't get it right in three tries. This system can be defeated by a combination of four hardware aids: a "blue box" or tone generator that illegally makes free long-distance telephone calls, a redialer that automatically reconnects if the computer hangs up, a microcomputer that can be programmed to try all likely passwords until it finds a valid one, and a "cheese box" to permit working from an unattended phone in case the repeated calls are traced.

Password identification can be supplemented by requiring insertion of a magnetic-stripe card or biometric identification (palm geometry, thumbprint, voice, or signature). However, cards can be forged or stolen and signals from biometric sensors can be simulated.

The only secure way to control remote entry is to have the user identify himself or herself, then have the computer hang up and call the user back on his or her regularly listed phone line. This scheme is known as *call back*.

The only effective defense against wiretapping is encryption. See *Data Encryption Standard, Federal Information Processing Standard 46*, National Bureau of Standards, Gaithersburg, MD, January 1977.

Even if no communications lines leave a computer center, an intruder can obtain information by "bugging" the computer room (either by turning a telephone into a listening device or by installing clandestine radio transmitters) or by recording and deciphering signals radiated by the computing equipment.

The defense against bugging is to keep all telephone instruments out of the computer room and to have the room "swept" regularly for hidden transmitters by specialists using panoramic receivers or special radars to detect semiconductor junctions. The

defenses against interception of undesired signal data emanations consist of denying an adversary a convenient "listening post" (have company occupancy on the computer-room floor and adjacent floors) and by thoroughly shielding the computer room.

Systems Security. There are many ways that skillful and unscrupulous persons with some level of legitimate access to a computer can (1) extract from it information they are not entitled to see or (2) make it do things it is not intended to do (like improperly issuing them checks).

A few of these techniques are well known:

- The "trap door" makes use of secret entry points to the operating system left by developers so they can get in to repair flaws.

- The "Trojan horse" hides instructions within a legitimate program belonging to a legitimate user that grant improper privileges to the penetrator.

- The "logic bomb" consists of hidden instructions that do something nasty, like wiping files, when triggered by an event like the disappearance of the perpetrator's name from the payroll.

- The "French roundoff" credits the fractions of cents of interest calculations to the perpetrator's account.

- The "misguided missile" turns the control of the system over to the penetrator. It grants her or him all the privileges of the operating system so that that person can get into any file she or he fancies and do anything she or he likes.

- The "limp" ties up all computer resources so that the system grinds to a halt ("crashes"). In the ensuing confusion the perpetrator may gain useful information.

- "Scavenging" occurs when one user is able to read information left in the computer's main memory by the preceding user.

In general, all operating systems have some peculiarities that can be exploited by well-informed penetrators. Most manufacturers correct them when they are discovered. However, some very old systems cannot be fixed. It is best to choose an operating system that is new enough to possess the benefits of modern software design techniques and still old enough to have been used by enough customers to have had its worst flaws corrected.

The most comprehensive specifications for selection of a secure computer system are contained in *Trusted Computer System Evaluation Criteria*, published by the Department of Defense Computer Security Center, Fort Meade, MD, January 27, 1983.

Risk-Analysis

To avoid either paying too much for computer security or overlooking serious threats, federal agencies are required to carry out a risk analysis. An annual expected dollar loss is obtained by multiplying the cost of loss of assets by the annual likelihoods of adverse events that could affect them. Computer security measures must be cost-justified by comparing their annual cost with the reduction they make in annual expected dollar loss. For a step-by-step approach to risk analysis see *Department of the Navy ADP (Automated Data Processing) Security Manual,* Navy Data Automation Command, Washington, DC (OPNAVINST 5239.1A).

See also Security management.

JOHN M. CARROLL, *University of Western Ontario*

Computer Software, Data-Base Management

Starting in the 1960s, a revolution has been occurring in the manner by which companies process and administer their computerized data. The concepts of data base, data-base management system, and data-base administrator are central to this revolution. A *data base* is a logically related collection of data concerning some aspect of an enterprise. A *data-base management system* (DBMS) is a software system for processing data bases which provides its users with simplified *logical views* of data bases. A DBMS is expected to support data sharing, data independence, and the convenient accessing of the data base. An important benefit of the use of DBMS has been the development of the *data-base administration approach to data processing.* With this approach, data control is centralized under a person or group of people called *data-base administrators* (DBAs), instead of being dispersed throughout the various applications groups which use the data.

Data Bases

Records and Relationships. Data bases represent records and the relationships between records.

A *record* is defined to be a logically related collection of data items, where a *data item* (also called a *field* or *attribute*) is the smallest named unit of data in the data base. For example, the CUSTOMER-PRODUCT-INVOICE data base described in Fig. C-8 contains three types of records, INVOICE, CUSTOMER, and PRODUCT, each consisting of appropriate numeric and alphanumeric data items. An INVOICE record contains three data items which describe a particular invoice: an identification number for the invoice (I#), the date the invoice was issued (DATE), and the amount of money the customer owes on the invoice (AMTDUE). Below each

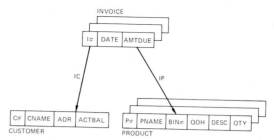

FIG. C-8 Hierarchical CUSTOMER-PRODUCT-INVOICE data base.

INVOICE record, to the left, is the related CUSTOMER record and, to the right, the *set* of related PRODUCT records for the products involved in the invoice. A CUSTOMER record contains four data items: the customer's identification number (C#), name (CNAME), address (ADR), and the total amount owed by the customer for all invoices (ACT-BAL). A PRODUCT record contains six data items: the product number (P#), name (PNAME), the number of the bin in which the product is stored (BIN#), the quantity on hand of the product (QOH), the product description (DESC), and the quantity of this product ordered on the invoice (QTY).

Hierarchical, Network, and Relational Data Bases. Data bases are classified into three categories according to the way they represent relationships between records: hierarchical, network, and relational.

A data base, such as the one in Fig. C-8, which represents relationships between records by placing these records on a hierarchy (or *tree*), is called a *hierarchical data base.* A connection between two records on the hierarchy is called a *link.* The data base in Fig. C-8 contains two links, labeled IC and IP.

Network data bases have a similar, but more general, structure than hierarchical data bases: Relationships between records in a network data base are represented by links, but the structure resulting from the linking of records need not be a tree. For example, the data base in Fig. C-9 is not tree structured because the same type of record (INVOICE) is directly below two different types of records (CUSTOMER and PRODUCT). Note that the subordination

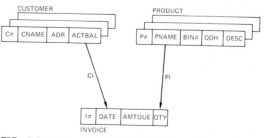

FIG. C-9 Network CUSTOMER-PRODUCT-INVOICE data base.

of INVOICE to PRODUCT forces the QTY data item into INVOICE.

A *relational data base* is a collection of *tables* (or *relations*), where a *table* is a collection of records of the same type. A relationship between records is represented by a table containing data items which identify the records being related. For example, in the Fig. C-10 relational data base, the table IC is used to relate invoices and customers, and the table IP is used to relate invoices and products.

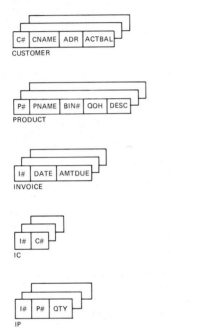

FIG. C-10 Relational CUSTOMER-PRODUCT-INVOICE data base.

DBMS Languages

There are three types of DBMS users: DBAs, data base programmers, and casual queriers. Each of these users must have languages with which to communicate with the DBMS. A DBMS usually provides several such languages.

Data Definition Language (DDL). The DBA, who sets up the structure of a data base, requires a data-definition language (DDL). A DDL is used by the DBA to define the logical views and the physical view of the data base. In a *logical view*, the view seen by data-base programmers and casual queriers, the data base is presented as being hierarchical, network, or relational as discussed in the previous section. Thus, for defining a logical view, the DDL must support ways of describing the data items within a record and the relationships between records. The *physical view* of the data base pertains to representational details by which the data base is stored on magnetic disk (the currently predominant hardware device on which data bases reside). For example, in the logical view given in Fig. C-8, the first five fields for a particular PRODUCT record are repeated every time that PRODUCT record is related to a different INVOICE record. Such redundancy may be convenient in a logical view, but actually storing the data that way could be extremely wasteful. Therefore, in the physical view, these five fields could be replaced by a pointer to (i.e., the address of) the disk location where this information can be nonredundantly stored.

Data Manipulation Language (DML). A data manipulation language (DML) is used to retrieve, insert, delete, and modify data in the data base. A DML may be either stand-alone (i.e., usable by itself) or hosted (i.e., callable from programs) within an applications programming language like COBOL or PL/I.

Ad hoc queriers, such as managers wishing to obtain some decision support information, may desire a simple retrieval-oriented interface to the DBMS. Such a user may be a nonprogrammer and may therefore wish to avoid using a full-scale programming language. A stand-alone DML would certainly be appropriate for this type of user.

On the other hand, data-base programmers write (possibly complicated) programs which generate reports or process-clerk-oriented on-line transactions (such as airline reservation transactions). These programs often require more computational and logical power than is available in the stand-alone DMLs of the DBMS, and thus must be written as applications programs with calls to a hosted DML.

Data Independence and Data Sharing. The fact that applications programs are written against a logical view instead of the physical view supports two very important objectives of DBMS: data independence and data sharing. Data independence and data sharing significantly reduce the cost of developing and maintaining applications.

Data independence is the immunity of the correctness of applications programs to changes in the data which these programs access. We have seen that some physical details (such as pointer information) are absent from the logical view. These details can thus be changed without affecting the correctness of programs.

The capability of a DBMS to provide different logical views of the same data base allows programs which require different views to be provided with them instead of with duplicate copies of that data base. Therefore, a DBMS encourages *data sharing;* i.e., the sharing of the same data by different applications programs, resulting in a reduction of redundancy.

Hierarchical, Network, and Relational DBMS

A DBMS is considered hierarchical, network, or relational according to whether it can provide a hierarchical, network, or relational logical view of the data base. The hierarchical and network DBMS predate relational DBMS, the first ones appearing in the 1960s. In 1971, the Data Base Task Group (DBTG) of the CODASYL Programming Language Committee published a report proposing a standard network DBMS.[1] Subsequently, the terms network DBMS, CODASYL DBMS, and DBTG DBMS have become somewhat synonymous. Strictly speaking, however, the terms CODASYL and DBTG should only be applied to a DBMS which conforms to the standards in the CODASYL report.

In 1970, E. F. Codd described the relational approach to data management.[2] The advantages of the relational approach over the network and hierarchical approaches include ease of use and increased data independence.

Although lacking some physical details, the logical views in network and hierarchical systems still are encumbered by (sometimes arbitrarily chosen) logical representational details, such as one record being linked under another. However, the relational view consists of only tables and records, ideally containing only those details inherent in the data. This causes relational systems to enjoy more *logical data independence*—i.e., more immunity to changes in logical views—and to have simpler, easier to use DMLs. However, there are some who feel that the sparseness in relational views will cause the relational approach to be less efficient than the hierarchical or network approaches.

Examples of hierarchical systems include IMS (IBM), RAMIS (Mathematica), and SYSTEM 2000 (INTEL). DMS 1100 (UNIVAC), TOTAL (CINCOM), and IDS (Honeywell) are network systems. IBM's SYSTEM R (an experimental system), SQL/DS (a commercial version of SYSTEM R), Relational Technology's INGRES, RSI's ORACLE, and Ashton-Tate's dBASE II are relational systems. Some systems, such as IDMS (Cullinet), are intended to support both network and relational views.

DBMS Features

In order for a DBMS to be a practical tool, it should support the following features:

Integrity Controls. *Integrity controls* check the correctness of the data in the data base. Typically, the DBA defines a set of constraints which the data in the data base must satisfy. If the data base satisfies these constraints, it is said to be in a *consistent state*. At appropriate points in time, the data base and inputs to the data base are tested to help ensure that the data base remains in a consistent state. For example, in the CUSTOMER-PRODUCT-INVOICE data base discussed earlier, it may be impossible for the QOH of a product to be negative. When the QOH for a product is entered into the data base, the DBMS could check to ensure that it is nonnegative.

Another reasonable integrity constraint for the CUSTOMER-PRODUCT-INVOICE data base is that the sum of the INVOICE AMTDUE fields for a customer must be equal to the ACTBAL field for that CUSTOMER. An integrity control called an *automatic consistency control* can enforce this constraint by causing a CUSTOMER ACTBAL field to be appropriately updated whenever an INVOICE AMTDUE field for that customer is updated.

It is clear that, although they may be desirable, integrity controls can slow down the execution of the DBMS.

Security Controls. *Security controls* check unauthorized access to a data base. Unauthorized accesses include computer crimes which can rob a company of millions of dollars. Data encryption and password exchanges are commonly used security controls.

Concurrent Transaction Processing. In many applications the DBMS must allow for concurrently executing transactions; that is, transactions which execute at the same time. In this case, not only is there data sharing by different programs, there is data sharing by different programs *at the same time*. Such data sharing requires regulation by the DBAs, so that concurrently executing transactions do not interfere with each other.

The execution of on-line transactions requires the availability of *data communications software* which controls the flow of information between terminals and the DBMS. Many DBMS contain data communications software, but some do not, necessitating its availability from other sources. A *distributed DBMS* supports transactions executing, and data stored, on different computers which may be geographically distant. A distributed DBMS requires particularly complex data communications software.

In the concurrent processing environment it is often very difficult to determine why a particular transaction is executing slowly. If the DBMS has *performance monitoring* capabilities which trace the movement of the transaction through the system, solving these problems can be greatly simplified.

Crash Recovery. *Crash recovery* is the ability of the DBMS to restore the data base to a consistent state after a system failure (or "crash"). There are two types of crash recovery: hard recovery and soft recovery.

Hard recovery is the ability to recover after a crash which has damaged the hardware device on which the data base is stored. Soft recovery is the ability to recover from a crash in which the hardware device is not damaged, and typically occurs when the DBMS or operating system suffers an abnormal termination.

A common technique for hard recovery is to periodically make a duplicate copy of the data base (called a *dump*) and have the DBMS maintain a log of all updates performed against the data base (called a *transaction log*). Then, after a hard crash, the transaction log can be applied against the dump to restore the data base to a current, consistent state. Soft recovery is provided by having the DBMS update the data base in such a way that, after a crash, any transactions running when the crash occurred can either be run to completion or be undone.

NOTES

[1]C. J. Date, *An Introduction to Database Systems*, 3d ed., Addison-Wesley, Reading, Mass., 1981, ref. 23.1

[2]Ibid, ref. 4.1.

REFERENCES

Date, C. J.: *An Introduction to Database Systems*, 3d ed., Addison-Wesley, Reading, Mass., 1981.

Kroenke, D. M.: *Database Processing: Fundamentals, Design, Implementation*, 2d ed., Science Research Associates, Chicago, 1983.

Lyon, J. K.: *The Database Administrator*, John Wiley, New York, 1976.

MARTIN K. SOLOMON, *Florida Atlantic University*

DBMS Advantages and Disadvantages

The major data processing alternative to DBMS is *file management systems*. File management systems cluster records into collections called *files* and supply software which only operates at the file level, not across files at the data-base level. The inadequacy of file management systems in providing logical views at the data-base level, and the resulting lack of data independence and data sharing, yield the principal advantages of DBMS over file management systems.

In addition, the availability of DBMS has encouraged the development of the data-base administration approach to data processing; i.e., the centralization of data control under the DBAs. This approach supports the management of data as a critical corporate resource. *Data dictionaries*, which keep track of the different views of the data base and the programs which access the data base through these views, are widely used by DBAs in such data management. Data dictionaries may be part of the DBMS or may be used in conjunction with a DBMS. Not only are data dictionaries useful in finding out the structure of the data, but many can be used as DDLs to define this structure.

On the other hand, a DBMS may suffer several disadvantages due to the complexity of its software and to data sharing. The former can cause increased run times and greater expense in purchasing and maintaining a DBMS. The latter can increase the vulnerability of the data base to recovery, integrity, and security problems.

By and large, the advantages of DBMS outweigh the problems, and their use is spreading at a rapidly increasing rate.

See also Computer security; Computer software, languages; Computer software packages; Control systems, management; Information sources; Management information systems (MIS); Management information systems, transaction processing systems; System concept, total.

Computer Software, Languages

More than 200 separate and distinct languages are available for use on computers. The count is even higher if the various "dialects" are included. As with spoken languages, each has its own history and special characteristics, each its strengths and weaknesses. Even the ones normally classified as outdated are self-perpetuating because of the enormous investment in existing programs.

A good way to make sense out of this confusing diversity and bring order to the seeming chaos is to categorize the various languages according to their characteristics and applications. Some broad categories into which the various languages can be divided include (1) low level versus high level, (2) general versus special purpose, (3) procedural versus nonprocedural, (5) structured versus unstructured, and (6) interactive versus noninteractive.

No computer language, of course, can be pigeonholed neatly into any one of these categories; most actually fall at some point along the ranges defined by these extremes. Nonetheless, this approach yields a valuable overview both of the individual languages and of their relationships to one another. And as the following review of the major computer languages that have evolved since the early 1950s illustrates, such categorizations also provide a framework within which intelligent choices can be made.

Low Level Versus High Level. Low-level languages give programmers direct control over the details of computer hardware, such as memory locations, microprocessor registers, and input-output ports. High-level languages provide some distance between the programmers and such details, using symbols which relate more to the function to be performed than to the specifics of how such functions are performed at the machine level. The lowest level is machine language; the highest level (at least in theory) is a "natural language" such as English.

The most basic and fundamental way of communicating with a computer is with a *machine language,* which consists of a computer's instructions, represented in binary form as on-off patterns of electronic switches. *Assembly language* is one step higher and uses alphabetic abbreviations for instructions and symbolic names for memory circuits and data. Programmers work more efficiently and accurately in assembly language than in machine language—an assembler program translating assembly code into machine language.

Machine or assembly language allows the most flexibility in tapping and in using a computer's resources. For example, a section of program code can be treated as data, or vice versa. And program code can be modified even while a program is running. Machine-level language programs can harness the specific strengths of a computer and its I/O facilities.

Counterbalancing these benefits are a number of drawbacks to low-level languages. First of all, they require a great amount of technical knowledge and attention to detail. This creates potential stumbling blocks for beginning programmers. Even professional programmers find assembly and machine-level programming slow and tedious work compared with programming in high-level languages.

By comparison, high-level languages are much more machine independent and require no knowledge of the particular machine code being used on the computer. Therefore, a high-level language is easier to use and easier to transport from computer to computer. With this convenience, however, comes an inevitable loss of efficiency and flexibility. Few programs written in high-level language offer the speed of those written in machine or assembly code. A few high-level languages such as C and FORTH offer some of the efficiency of machine language. These languages, however, are suited to only the most experienced programmers.

General Versus Special Purpose. Most high-level computer languages are created to serve specific purposes, such as teaching programming concepts, controlling industrial robots, or creating graphics. Many are extraordinarily flexible, however, and their ultimate use far exceeds the concrete plans of their designers. Indeed, most general-purpose languages started as special-purpose languages.

General-purpose languages include BASIC, FORTRAN, and COBOL, and more recently ALGOL, PASCAL, ADA, APL, and PL/I. The majority of programming applications have been written in BASIC, FORTRAN, or COBOL.

Special-purpose languages (also called problem- or application-oriented languages), on the other hand, are designed to enable programmers to solve narrowly defined problems and unusual applications. Special-purpose languages include C, FORTH, MODULA 2, and SMALLTALK (all for systems programming); PILOT, for computer-aided instruction; PROLOG, for logic programming; GPSS, DYNAMO, SIMSCRIPT, and SIMULA, for systems simulation; APT, for numerical control; LISP and SNOBOL, for list processing; and STRESS and ICES, for engineering design.

Special-purpose programs which have shown, or will show, promise for more widespread application include C, FORTH, MODULA 2, SMALLTALK, PROLOG, LISP, and PILOT.

Procedural Versus Nonprocedural. Procedural languages, which include most of today's general-purpose languages, require that the user specify a set of operations to be performed in a specific sequence. Unlike machine and assembly-level languages which require instructions in a form specific to particular computers, procedural languages are designed to be independent—relatively speaking—of particular machines. These languages relate to the procedures being coded, not to the specifics of the computer's architecture. A program written in a procedural language can be executed on any computer that has a translator for that programming language.

Where a procedural language specifies *how* something is to be done in terms that a computer can interpret, a nonprocedural language is more concerned with *what* is to be solved in terms and concepts relevant to the problem. The closer a programmer can come to stating a problem without specifying the steps that must be taken to solve it, the more nonprocedural the language. Examples of nonprocedural languages developed for microcomputers include program generators, such as SYSTEM 80, THE TOOL, SAVVY, THE PROGRAMMER, CORP, THE FORMULA, AUTOGRAMMER, and THE LAST ONE; for minicomputers CREATE, DATAFORM, ENGLISH, ADAM, and ESCORT; and for mainframes RPG, NOMAD, MAPPER, RAMIS, GENYASYS, MIMS, TAPS, SPIRES, and FOCUS.

Many professionals who program in procedural languages say that so-called nonprocedural languages are not programming languages at all and that their use does not qualify as true programming. However, according to many experts who have studied the problem—including James Martin[1]—the net effect of nonprocedural programming is exactly the same as that of any other programming. Just as high-level procedural languages were developed to relieve programmers of the burdens of dealing with machine or assembly-level coding, nonprocedural languages make it unnecessary for the user to get involved in specifying the programming steps that must be taken to solve a problem. Moreover, just as procedural languages generate object code written in the computer's machine language, nonprocedural language systems generate programs written in a particular symbolic code, whether assembly or procedural.

Interpreted Versus Compiled. A computer can only execute instructions written in its native machine code. Thus, a program written in a high-level language must be translated into machine code before it will run. Two types of high-level language translation schemes have been developed to do this: compilers and interpreters.

A compiler does the translation in two steps. First, it translates the whole program into machine language. Then the machine language code is executed by the computer. An interpreter performs the operations contained in the program as it reads them line by line, using a built-in dictionary that gives machine language equivalents of high-level commands.

While the interpreter must repeat the translation of a given statement every time it occurs—a rather inefficient process—the compiler can repeat the necessary statements without translating each time; this is a much faster process. The drawback of compilers is that it is much more difficult to modify or alter statements with a program. Usually the entire program must be translated over again if changes are required. An interpreted language, on the other hand, permits interaction with the program during execution and makes changes immediately.

Depending on the specific application, various programming languages tend to fall more into one category than the other. COBOL and FORTRAN, for example, are usually compiled, while APL is generally interpreted. Of the BASIC translators available, about half are compilers and half interpreters.

Structured Versus Unstructured. In the same way that it is relatively easy to pick up the grammar and syntax of a foreign language, it is not too difficult to master the basics of a particular programming language. What is not so easy is writing a program in a clear, logically organized manner.

According to Kenneth Orr,[2] a program is well structured if it satisfies three requirements:

1. Its routines and subroutines are written in a modular form in which each module is a program segment containing a complete logical thought.

2. Its modules are hierarchically organized in such a way that within each module are nested logical subunits that are themselves structured and contain further subunits.

3. It uses straightforward, readable code rather than slightly more efficient, but obscure, code.

A well-structured program has at least four advantages. First of all, it's easier to debug during development because the logical connections between various instructions, routines, and subroutines are clearly visible. Second, it is more likely to be correct the first time around because of the care that went into its design. Third, it takes less time to create because there are fewer bugs to find and fix. Finally, it is far easier to maintain, that is, to update and correct at a later date.

Most programming languages allow the design of well-structured programs, and many books have been written on how to do so. But what many programming languages—particularly the older ones—also allow is the design of poorly structured programs. Only the newer computer languages such as PASCAL and recent versions of older languages such as SBASIC actually prevent the user from implementing procedures that lead to illogical program structures. Similarly, many of the nonprocedural program generation languages also require information about an application to be entered in a logically consistent and structured manner.

Interactive Versus Noninteractive. As with structured programming, all the advantages lie on the side of interactive languages. In an interactive language the user can communicate directly with the computer, both when typing in the program and when running it. In addition, interactive languages offer the advantages of interactive editing and immediate error detection.

The process of developing a program alternates between running the program and changing or editing to correct the errors the preliminary run turns up. Where noninteractive languages separate the editor and the translator, the interactive language integrates the two, eliminating a number of time-consuming intermediate steps.

If a user types an incorrect line, a good interactive language will report it immediately. This allows correction of the error while the purpose of the line is still fresh in mind. Noninteractive languages support the detection and subsequent correction of errors only after the entire program has been typed in.

Despite these obvious advantages, only APL and BASIC, of the traditional general-purpose procedural languages, were designed from the start for interactive operation. And of the newer generation of languages, only LOGO, PILOT, and SMALLTALK can be characterized as truly interactive.

Chronological Survey of Languages

Most computer programming languages fall into more than one of the categories delineated above. This is particularly the case for the more recently developed languages. Moreover, the boundaries between the various categories are likely to get even fuzzier in the future. As the following chronological survey of a few of the more widely used programming languages indicates, the newer languages tend to be the furthest removed from machine level and closer to a "natural language" syntax and structure. They are also likely to be less procedure oriented, more natural and Englishlike in their syntax, and more structured than older languages.

FORTRAN (1956). Developed initially for solving problems in mathematics, engineering, and science, this language has found its way into business and educational applications because of its popularity as a teaching tool in colleges and universities. Its grammar, symbols, rules, and syntax are most similar to mathematical and English-language conventions. FORTRAN treats arithmetic operations with commands that evaluate expressions and substitute the results for current values of variables. Graphics processing programs, data-base management systems, and word processing programs have been written in this language.

COBOL (1960). Developed specifically for business and commercial applications, COBOL is characterized by programs stated in precise, easily learned natural words and phrases that can be read by nontechnical users. The language offers many important file organizing features and can deal with variable data lengths. I/O procedures and report generation are its strongest points.

ALGOL (1960). A particularly powerful language, ALGOL was originally developed as a general-purpose language for expressing formal problem-solving procedures known as algorithms. Similar to FORTRAN, it is more comprehensive and flexible and, thanks to its more formal structure, it poses fewer exceptions and is more readable.

LISP (1960). This language was designed specifically for the manipulation of nonnumeric data that often changes considerably in length and structure during the course of a computer run. Because it defines a list as simply a set of items given a specific order, LISP offers a convenient way of representing such data as English sentences, mathematical formulas, positions in a game, logic theorems, or computer programs. It is the language of choice of researchers in artificial intelligence.

BASIC (1964). Designed to be very simple to learn and inexpensive to implement and use, this language incorporates features of both ALGOL and FORTRAN. From the start it has been an interactive language. Its major advantage to beginning programmers is that it is available in both interpreted and compiled versions.

PL/I (1964). Designed as a multipurpose programming language for solving business and scientific problems, PL/I incorporates features of both FORTRAN and COBOL. Similar to FORTRAN, it has simple concise statements, but like COBOL, it has the ability to manipulate and input or output grouped records and files quite easily. It can handle strings of either alphanumeric characters or bits. It also allows programmers to describe data in terms of arrays and other sophisticated "pointer" structures.

APL (1967). Of all the general-purpose procedural languages, APL has the most comprehensive set of primitive operators to carry out such functions as random number generation, index generation, factorial computation, and matrix formation and inversion. Very popular among statisticians because of the speed with which algorithms can be developed and tested, APL is also used in a wide range of business applications, such as document production, graphic analysis, data retrieval, and financial analysis.

PROLOG (1970). Just now beginning to be recognized as a useful tool for artificial intelligence research and for writing "expert system" programs, this language is beginning to gain ground in an important application area previously dominated by LISP. Based on simple logic assertions, PROLOG has many of the aspects of a nonprocedural language in that the user tells PROLOG what is to be done, not how. The programmer has only to describe the problem in a series of simple facts stated in the form of syllogisms. This information is entered into a data base. And when PROLOG is asked questions about this information it will answer them on the basis of the information in the data base.

PASCAL (1971). Designed to encourage—some would say demand—structured programming, this language has a syntax very similar to ALGOL. A "small" language in that it does not allow a large number of different syntactic constructs, PASCAL is intended to be easy for programmers to learn and retain. Of all the high-level languages, PASCAL is among the most machine independent. PASCAL programs are first compiled into an intermediate code, called a P-code, which in turn is interpreted on various systems. The only code that needs to be written that is machine specific is a small interpreter.

SMALLTALK (1972). Conceived as a tool for allowing students to explore a subject or solve a problem, this language uses a wide range of graphic "objects." As recently as 1980, it was considered a special-purpose language. But now that a number of personal computer manufacturers and software firms have used it to design their newest "integrated software" products, it is well on its way into the mainstream of general-purpose applications languages.

PILOT (1973). Originally designed to introduce children to the fundamentals of computer operation, PILOT is now most often used in writing programs for computer-aided instruction in all subjects. It is especially useful in such instructional tasks as drills, tests, and dialogs and allows convenient comparisons between words or portions of words.

C (1974). A structured programming language that lends itself to systems programming, C produces code that approaches machine language in density and efficiency while offering some high-level features. A C compiler is simple, compact, and easily written—a professional programmer using current technology can prepare such a compiler for a new machine in no more than a few months. Because it is as independent as any procedure-oriented language can be from any machine's architecture, C is suitable for writing programs that can be expected to be transported from machine to machine.

ADA (1975). Developed under the auspices of the U.S. Department of Defense to reduce software development and maintenance costs, this language was designed to support structured programming. Including the most popular and desirable features of PASCAL, ALGOL, and Pl/I, an ADA compiler permits a range of software components to be easily attached to it, much as hardware modules are added to a computer bus. This allows ADA to be adapted to a wide variety of applications without losing compatibility with other existing software components.

FORTH (1975). Like C, FORTH is a high-level assembly language designed for systems programming. It is unusual in that it offers many interesting features not normally associated with interpreted languages, such as allowing the addition of new commands. It maintains a system library of command calls that is actually a list of addresses of routines that execute the commands.

Future Trends

It is clear that over the short term, traditional procedural languages will continue to dominate in most computer applications. But despite the enormous proliferation of personal, home, and small-business computers, the development of new programming languages will be much slower than in the past. This is because the rapid increase in the number of computers per capita has drastically altered the environment in which computer languages are developed. For one thing, the software companies find themselves unable to produce enough canned programs to satisfy the demands of all the new users of computers. They are looking for ways to increase the productivity of their professional programmers. For another, many computer users want to write their own programs but have neither the time nor the inclination to learn a procedural language. According to experts such as J. E. Sammet,[3] the above demands will favor the increased development of nonprocedural program generation languages.

One drawback—if it can be called that—of the present nonprocedural program generation languages is that they relieve the user of only the coding chores. It is still necessary to go through the process of developing the overall design of the program. Artificial intelligence research centers and software companies are, however, working on "expert systems" that not only relieve the user of the coding, but also aid the user in analyzing problems and structuring the programs. Typical of such efforts are MODEL and

NOPAL, under development at the University of Pennsylvania; PSI and CHI, at the Krestel Institute in Palo Alto, California; and GIST, at the University of Southern California.

See also Computer software packages; Data bases, commercial; Management information systems (MIS); Management information systems, transaction processing systems.

NOTES

[1]Martin, James: *Applications Development Without Programmers*, Prentice-Hall, Englewood Cliffs, N.J., 1982.

[2]Orr, Kenneth: *Structured Systems Development*, Yourdon Press, 1977.

[3]Sammet, J. E.: *Programming Languages: History and Fundamentals*, Prentice-Hall, Englewood Cliffs, N.J., 1969.

BERNARD CONRAD COLE

Computer Software Packages

The declining prices of computing equipment have brought custom-developed software to the point of becoming the biggest cost, largest total investment, most time-consuming, and most difficult aspect of information systems today. With lengthy procedures needed to establish software requirements and long periods of time to shake out bugs from custom-built software, it is no wonder that users have become stymied and frustrated at their inability to use their cost-saving computing investment. A reasonably viable alternative to custom software, however, is prebuilt (pretested) computer software "packages."

Only a few years ago, software packages were relatively few in number and woefully deficient in their capabilities and performance. That situation has changed considerably. There are now packages on the marketplace that are more flexible, powerful, and performance-proven than much of the custom-built software coming out of today's development projects. This sophistication in software products is due to (1) the growing maturity of the marketplace and (2) the fact that the demand for such software is becoming so great that it is now possible to put a much greater investment in packaged software than might be available for a custom product. In addition, some software packages are moving into their fourth, sixth, and even tenth generation, providing a maturity and flexibility that is unmatched in custom software designs.

Spectrum of Growth

The advent of computer application software packages has led to the development of whole new growth industries and to new opportunities for end users to acquire and use more of their computing resources as personal support systems and managerial aids. Certain marketplaces are totally dependent on the capabilities of packaged computer software. Consider, for example, the word processing marketplace. In this area a standard small computer product was taken and given a series of user-friendly, flexible, easy-to-use, relatively dynamic, computer software packages to process text and characters into user-defined formats. These software packages have created a whole new industry as well as an environment in which users seldom think about the fact that they are actually dependent on a computer software application package.

In areas such as microcomputers, where the machine cost has become so low that even a few days of programming cost can grossly exceed the cost of the hardware, it has become even more important that computer software packages be available to support the utilization of the equipment. Fortunately, the number of microcomputers and personal computers that will be built and sold is so large that it becomes an attractive volume market for software developers. They can create and produce software products for these systems, price them low to be compatible with the equipment, and depend on sheer volume of sales to ensure their success. Everyone looks to the classic cases of success—namely, VISICALC, which has currently sold more than 1 million copies; Lotus 1-2-3, more than 400,000 copies; and several others. Although it may be difficult to duplicate the VISICALC feat, there is still plenty of room in the micro/personal market for good software to secure a significant volumetric business return.

Range of Packages. Computer software packages originated with selected applications for large-scale computers. Applications that were consistent and similar from industry to industry, such as payroll, were obviously the earliest situations to use applications software. Soon to follow were such areas as general ledger, accounts receivable, order entry, inventory management, and other generalized business applications.

In actual fact, however, before these packages were popular many other specialty packages existed in the marketplace. Consider, for example, the packages that were used for project management (i.e., the programs that processed PERT, CPM, and other project task data). In addition, programs were developed in the early 1960s that supported activities such as mathematical and linear programming. There were also statistical analysis systems and many others that were used for specialized service processes. However, most users did not think of these as applications packages.

It wasn't until the late 1970s that people began to understand that the development of custom software would lead to a situation in which system aging would require extensive modification and eventual replacement with another custom system. Many users found this to be an ongoing treadmill that would get more and more expensive as each generation of software became more sophisticated and more complicated to replace than the previous generation.

Advantages of Packaged Software. The development of computer software packages means that users can not only select systems that match their needs, but they can also develop an ability to share with other users the ideas and costs for implementing new concepts and services in the existing software architecture. A true test of the maturity of the software package products if dound when the update versions exceed the flexibility and capability of most new custom products.

Another advantage in the use of packaged software systems is that they tend to be updated much faster than the internal system would be. Consider a software package that may have 200 or 300 users, each wanting to have certain improvements placed into that software package. The vendor will generate a considerable amount of business by providing an ongoing update and/or customization service to these users so that the package is continually moving through new generations.

The vendor can fund such generation movement through subscription updates or the release of new versions with a fee requirement for users to go through the upgrade process. The marketing of the software package now becomes an activity that attempts to respond to user needs so as to derive an adequate revenue flow from the sale of new, updated packages.

It is always easier to sell an existing client than to develop a new one. Thus in a few years popular software packages will have moved progressively through multiple updates. Some packages on the market today are in their tenth full generation. Very seldom will internal software age either so fast or so completely. After two or three major generations, the internal software is completely replaced and a brand new package is written for the user.

Several of the generations of software packages may also be completely new, with significant changes from the previous version. However, instead of considering the product obsolete and taking a totally new tack, most package vendors usually perform a "soft" upgrade of the product to maintain their user base and make it easy for existing clients to accept and implement the new version. Over a period of several years, the software package may go through more versions and will probably contain a greater latitude of variations than would be found inside similar custom-built systems that were designed and maintained on an internal basis.

Disadvantages of Packages Software. Of course, several compromises and weaknesses must be considered in using software packages. Probably the greatest one is that the user will be forced to utilize procedures, formats, mechanisms, and modus operandi that are dictated by the off-the-shelf package. Although most packages are kept as general as possible to permit the vendor broad market coverage, the package still must process data in certain fixed ways and produce logical outputs.

There are, of course, ways to enhance the flexibility through the use of variations of input formats and output report generators. Various query processors and the use of imbedded data bases can also help in providing some level of flexibility for the ultimate user. Nevertheless, in most cases, it is far simpler to use a fixed package, minimize the customization, and simply move aggressively toward the implementation and acceptance of the end result. This can be a problem for many sophisticated users who feel that their approach to business is unique and that they must have a software system that is completely compliant to their particular needs.

On the other hand, it is not uncommon in the development of an internal custom system to discover that the users do not fully understand their needs; thus, they inaccurately describe requirements and end up with a product that is not matched to their full expectations. Often, the appropriateness and fit of a software package to the internal user practices and needs can be critiqued at the beginning. If the package is complete and well tested, it may prove to supply an orderly solution for the user.

Although the package may not operate the way the user is accustomed to doing things, it may supply a proven and logical approach to the business process. In some cases the package "compromise," once it has been utilized for a period of time, becomes an accepted discipline, and the user does not really notice that it varies from the previous way of doing business. This is especially true for packages that have considerable field experience by various users.

Dependency. Another problem with computer software packages is the dependency on an external in the form of the sourcing of new changes, modifications, customization of the software packages, documentation, training, and other factors. In internally developed systems, this responsibility falls clearly on the internal data processing department.

It is true, of course, that questionable performance has often been experienced by users in some of these areas, due to the high turnover and busy condition of most internal EDP departments. Nevertheless, it is comforting to users to know that they have a local source and considerable political leverage that can be applied to obtain an adequate level of internal support. Once they purchase a package from an outside vendor, they lose most of their leverage.

Most observers agree that the institution of fee-based subscription services for support, modifications, maintenance, and bug chasing is a good business decision on the part of package vendors. However, there is a tendency to provide only a weak or blanket type of linkage for satisfying users' immediate needs relative to the software system. For example, should a user need a significant change in the package to meet a current requirement, it could be next to impossible to get the vendor to place adequate resources in soon enough to provide the necessary modifications. Vendors prefer the user to submit a request for modification, the request to be filtered through user groups and finally placed into one of the vendor's future update releases. This process can take several years.

Modification Problems. There are alternative courses to make up for this lack of affinity on the part of the vendor, but these, too, present problems. For example, the user can acquire the source rights to the system and then depend upon its internal data processing department to make the required changes. This becomes difficult because of the uniqueness of the actual code and the fact that it was generated by someone not in the internal organization. The software package documentation, organization, logic structure, etc., are likely to be considerably different from those followed inside the user's own organization. It takes considerable time for a systems professional to inspect someone else's programs and decide exactly what and how they were done.

In addition, there is a high occurrence of failures when modifications are made to a software package. The changes often end up causing significant destruction to other parts of the program. It is sufficient to say that it is not only difficult but also very risky to begin to modify, change, or extend someone else's programs.

Search and Selection

A major problem with computer software packages is to find one that is suited to the user's particular needs. Today's market has more than 70,000 computer software packages of all sizes, shapes, varieties and qualities. It is difficult to perform a search to find even a reasonable set against which to make a detailed analysis.

For example, if one wanted to acquire an inventory control system to be used for managing and controlling material in an industrial plant, one would find more than 350 packages from which to choose. The time to review 350 packages, to conduct a thorough evaluation of their quality, content, and usefulness, and to rank them would probably be greater than the time it would take to sit down and design and build a new system to suit the user's requirements. This means that in the search for computer software packages, one must be willing to take fast-paced shortcuts in order to arrive at a manageable group of three to seven packages that can be evaluated within a reasonable amount of time.

Search Procedure. It is a good idea to follow a systematic approach in the search for a software package:

1. Review two or three major computer software directories that are appropriate either to the application area, the size of the equipment, or the type of equipment that is in place or will be acquired to support the application. One that may be of value is *Data Sources,* published annually by Ziff-Davis.

2. Establish contact with industry groups, trade associations such as the Boston Computer Society, and/or other local users who are known to be using computer software packages in their business. Ask them for references and lead-ins on who they feel would be a reliable candidate or product for the particular application area.

3. Seek out one major general-package vendor and ask for a comparative list of how its software stacks up against the other main contenders in its particular area of specialization. This way, you will find out about its particular products and also learn the identity of its key competitors, who can be pursued further for evaluation and review.

4. Review the literature that is appropriate for the particular application and attempt to locate journal articles that review various software packages and provide additional details on their characteristics and options. Such reviews have been published for popular types of software such as those for accounting, inventory control, manufacturing, CAD/CAM, project management, word processing, and spreadsheet. Several magazines, such as *Computer Decisions* and *Popular Computing,* tend to specialize in regularly providing software package reviews and professional critiques.

5. Continue the search until you have built an adequate list of 3 to 20 packages.

Seeking a Proper Fit. The next problem becomes one of narrowing the initial package list down to a subset that is worthy of consideration. The best way to do this is to contact the vendors and, either through a telephone survey or through the process of sending out a short mail questionnaire, determine whether their software products have the key features you want. It is important to spend time in evaluating only those products than can reasonably be expected to cover the range of services you are looking for. It is wasteful to look at every single product with the hope that it might have some new feature that might be desirable. It is better to stick to the basics and acquire a package that has a sound and proven mechanism for meeting *most* user requirements, especially those that are listed as "musts"

and, hopefully, a goodly number of those that are in the "wants" category.

With the large number of software packages on the market today, it is possible to sort the packages quickly into those that are potential candidates and those that do not support an adequate range of services to suit the user's needs. A detailed evaluation should be made only on those packages that are considered adequate—a list of three to five. Short lists are better to work with than long lists because they allow you to concentrate on a few products and to conduct thorough evaluations.

Detailed Evaluation. In conducting detailed evaluations of software packages, it is important to:

1. Obtain complete documentation of the software system or package being evaluated.

2. If possible, obtain a demonstration disk and/or a demonstration arranged by the vendor or its agent at some convenient time and place.

3. If the software package is large enough (i.e., greater than $5000 in purchase value), conduct a site visit of at least one, and preferably more, existing users.

4. Have an informed professional examine the source code to review the detailed construction philosophy used inside the package. Although this step is not mandatory, it provides a quick review of the quality of the program and its likelihood for survival as a long-term system.

5. Give adequate consideration to the capability and reputation of the software package vendors. As they are a critical link to ongoing support enhancements and problem solving, it is important that they be viable, performance-proven, and user-friendly.

6. Carefully examine the published evaluation materials for comparative reviews and commentaries on the products being inspected. Vendors are usually aware of these and can supply copies or a list of any they consider fair or favorable to their product.

7. Construct a ranking matrix containing criteria for valuing "must" and "want" features, operation, and options of the selected packages. This should be applied subjectively and objectively to all package contenders. It helps to define and refine differences in products and focus on the user's critical success factors.

8. Identify and stipulate any mandatory modifications required of the two or three top packages. Test the leading vendors on their support of and response to the needed changes. Review their detailed plans for implementation and postimplementation support.

9. Prepare a selection-team decision proposal to management based on the "best" (or compro-

155

mise) product package to be acquired and implemented.

10. Negotiate a contract with the approved vendor.

11. Work hard on the implementation process to see that the package system is properly installed, understood, and accepted at the internal user levels.

Summary

The marketplace of computer software packages is likely to continue to grow into giant proportions: $12 billion by 1990 is in sight.

The advantages of software products in general far outweigh the disadvantages. As organizations build their expertise in selecting and using software packages, they will encourage the producers to generate better products and offer more flexibility to suit individual and unique needs. The introduction of integrated software products for accounting and personal services provides a clear basis for the next generation of software package designs. These products will offer a new range of user-driven services and will reduce the user learning times. In turn, this will build a far-reaching user-driven service expectation through the implementation of new process/action generators, reporters, and concepts like artificial intelligence.

Software application packages are an important key to more and more aspects of information services. They are critical to the supply of computer communications interconnections, office automation, information retrieval, public data bases, personal computers, robotics, computer-based education, and a host of other application and service areas. As these software products grow in power, flexibility, ease of use, and adaptability, more and more users will depend on them for support rather than using the lengthy and problem-fraught custom development approach.

The underlying key to successful use of application software packages is the ability to: (1) quick search the marketplace, (2) firmly define "musts" and be willing to compromise "wants," (3) spend major amounts of time implementing and adjusting to the package, (4) develop good working relationships with software product vendors, (5) cooperate with other systems users in building improvements for the package, and (6) migrate to other packages as new and better products evolve.

There is no perfect solution in the selection and use of software packages, so a spirit of compromise is a necessary ingredient. However, the growing wealth of good packages on the marketplace, the creativity reflected in the products, the quality of support and implementation service, and the speed with which package software can be delivered make this approach an alternative worthy of consideration in a growing number of systems applications.

See also Computer security; Computer software, languages; Control systems, management; Data bases, commercial; Management information systems (MIS); Management information systems, transaction processing systems; Office automation; Paperwork simplification; Systems and procedure; Word processing.

RAYMOND P. WENIG, International Management Services

Conference Leadership

The effectiveness of conference leadership depends as much upon preparation and procedure as upon personal communications skills.

Preparation. Seven factors should receive careful attention, whether the conference is formal or informal, intraorganization or public:

1. *Location.* Convenience to participants, atmosphere, adequacy of size, and other accommodations should be reviewed for appropriateness of the conference's purpose.

2. *Purpose.* Like all organizational activities, a conference's objectives should be clearly identified as a first step and provide the basis for all other factors.

3. *Frequency.* Executives and employees alike complain of being "meetinged to death." Obviously, there can be too much of even a good thing; but regularity of organizational conferences helps to establish their relevance to programs of which they are a part.

4. *Duration.* Single-purpose meetings can be of any duration, but experience suggests that 1 to 2 hours is optimum for most purposes.

5. *Participants.* A conference implies participation. Those invited should be in a position either to contribute information and join in problem solving or to benefit from exposure to the communications and interactions.

6. *Agenda.* Whether agendas are published or not, the conference should proceed on the basis of a carefully thought out sequence that anticipates the information participants will need and the subjects and issues to be covered.

Checklist. Any number of major and minor elements may contribute to a conference's success or failure. A key aid to planning its effectiveness is a detailed checklist such as the one shown in Table C-4.

Procedure. Conferences typically proceed according to one of five basic plans.

TABLE C-4   Checklist for Conference Leader Preparation and Planning

Have you	Yes	No
1. Fixed in your mind the objectives to be attained through the conference discussion?	_____	_____
2. Secured, prepared, or thoroughly familiarized yourself with the necessary conference aids:		
a. Charts ready?	_____	_____
b. Case studies prepared?	_____	_____
c. Check sheets to be distributed ready in sufficient quantities?	_____	_____
d. Demonstrations predetermined?	_____	_____
e. All special materials obtained?	_____	_____
f. Visual aids to be used previewed and a plan made for their use?	_____	_____
3. Prepared for your opening talk?	_____	_____
4. Carefully studied your conference agenda or outline?	_____	_____
a. Determined the important points to be emphasized?	_____	_____
b. Considered anticipated responses and group reactions?	_____	_____
c. Determined points at which quick summaries will be made?	_____	_____
d. Considered experiences and stories to be used for emphasis?	_____	_____
e. Determined ways and means of getting conferee participation, stimulating thinking, and creating interest?	_____	_____
f. Considered what the summary of the group's thinking might be?	_____	_____
5. Planned carefully to be sure adequate time has been allotted?	_____	_____
6. Notified everyone concerned of time and place of meeting?	_____	_____
7. Checked physical requirements for conducting meeting?	_____	_____
a. Blackboard or chart paper available?	_____	_____
b. Seating arrangement conforms to good conference procedure?	_____	_____
c. Facilities for showing films in readiness?	_____	_____
d. Ashtrays provided if smoking is permissible?	_____	_____
e. Chalk, crayon, scotch tape, thumbtacks, erasers, paper, pencils, etc., on hand?	_____	_____
f. Ventilation, heat, light, conferee comfort adequate?	_____	_____

Informational Conferences. These are selected to convey information and to ensure an understanding of its content and implications. Four steps contribute to this understanding:

1. Make the announcement. This can be a straightforward statement of the information to be conveyed, but it should always emphasize why the information is important and how it will affect the participants.

2. Ask for, and stimulate, questions. If the announcement stage has been handled empathetically, participants usually will not need to be prodded for questions. If questions are not forthcoming, they can be stimulated by the speaker's own questions directed toward individuals and phrased as follows: *How* will you go about making this change effective in your department? In *what* way will this affect your operating procedures? *Which* part of the new directive is least clear?

3. Summarize. Before closing the conference, the leader should restate the main points of the announcement and any clarifying information that developed during the question period.

4. Follow up. When the background data are voluminous or complex or when confirmation seems desirable, the information presented should be reproduced for distribution or publication.

Problem-Solving Conferences. These are selected to deal with operational or planning problems in situations where involvement in planning and decision making is genuinely desired. These conferences should follow a fairly inflexible sequence in order not to short-circuit the course to valid conclusions:

1. Decide on the real problem. General problems should be narrowed down to specific ones. A problem of high costs, for example, should pin down exactly which costs are high and what *high* actually means in those instances.

2. Present and discuss the facts. All relevant information should be gathered beforehand by the

leader or his or her staff. It should be stated precisely—together with its date and source. At this point, participants should be invited to challenge the information if they wish.

3. List advantages of solving the problem. This step is mainly motivational in that it provides participants with some idea of how much it may be worth to them to solve the problem.

4. List obstacles to solving the problem. These are the *causes*—apparent or hidden—that seem responsible for the problem's existence. Typically, there are many causes, although only one may be truly critical.

5. Suggest possible solutions. These are the ideas or programs that might remove or overcome the obstacles or causes. The solutions should match up with the obstacles developed, either singly or collectively.

6. Decide what to do. This is the decision, or choice, step. The action or program chosen as a solution should be as specific as possible. It should identify those responsible for carrying out the action and establish definite timetables for implementation.

7. Follow up. This stage should never be omitted. A written summary of the conference highlights should be prepared and distributed—with special attention to action plans, responsibilities, and timetables.

Open-Agenda Conferences. These are selected to provide a medium of information or problem exchange where group involvement is especially beneficial. Such a conference can deal with vague intuitions about morale, the market, changing environments, and the like. If such is the case, they provide an opportunity for participants to ask general questions for which there is no other forum, to make general observations, or to invite suggestions for uncertain projects or conditions. Formats for this kind of conference stress informality. The leader simply senses interests, and issues, and moves the discussion only so long as direction seems necessary or desired.

Brainstorming Conferences. These are selected to stimulate ideas for a particular problem, project, or product. Ideally, a brainstorming conference should adopt the following four guidelines:

1. Do not criticize ideas. Negative thinking is discouraged, and its expression is penalized. Any idea, thought, or suggestion is accepted without judgment.

2. Encourage serendipity. Sometimes, the wilder the idea, the more provocative it will be to other participants. The theme should be: "Can you top this?" Participants should use others' ideas as jumping-off places.

3. Strive for quantity. Experience shows that the more ideas there are generated, the better they are likely to be. Even seemingly remote ideas often contain the seed for more fruitful thoughts.

4. Combine and improve. Ideas are like building blocks. Participants should be encouraged to suggest how others' ideas can be improved—how two or more ideas can be combined into a single one that is better than either.

On-Record Conferences. These are the strictly formal ones required to conduct official business such as to establish goals and policies, appropriate funds, elect officers, or take any sort of certified action requiring recorded minutes. Seven factors are typically included:

1. Opening, such as a call to order.

2. Quorum, in which the minimum number of officially designated participants is verified.

3. Agenda, of old business and new business and an invitation to place issues in registry for "old" business at the next meeting.

4. Reading of the record, or minutes, of last meeting.

5. Controlled procedure (often using Robert's Rules of Order as a guide), in which (*a*) the leader or chairperson only may recognize speakers and invite or cut off discussion and (*b*) action is taken and/or decisions are made only after a supporting motion is made and seconded and relevant discussion is permitted, followed by a vote to accept or reject.

6. Closing, only upon a formally introduced and approved motion.

7. Records, or minutes, prepared and distributed, of main items of discussion and their disposition, especially issues voted upon.

Personal Skills. Conference leadership is not public speaking. Instead, it depends upon interpersonal skills in developing rapport with participants so that each individual makes his or her greatest contribution and derives the maximum benefit from participation. Neither should the conference leader become an entertainer. Often this role is most effective when it is least discernible to participants. Several techniques will contribute to this effectiveness:

1. Draw out reticent or inarticulate individuals. Do not press for participation immediately. Wait until the conference has warmed up; then ask open-ended questions of them directly. For example: "Sam, *where* have you observed that trouble has occurred in the past?" "Mary, *what* do you feel is the reason for poor sales this month?"

2. Try not to answer questions. If there is someone else of authority present, direct the question to her or him, or try turning the question back to the group.

3. Ask open-ended questions, those that cannot be answered by a simple yes or no. Ask questions that begin with *why, where, in what way, when,* or *how.*

4. Do not argue. Let others reply to challenges. Disagreements are best cleared up by participants, not the conference leader. Arguing destroys rapport and free discussion.

5. Do not try to cover too much ground. People will participate and make conferences productive if the conferences are pointed and results are obtained. Better to hold a second or third meeting than to try to accomplish too much in one.

6. Start and finish on time. Respect for participants' other time commitments puts them at ease and helps to ensure continuing attendance.

Audiovisual Aids and Support Material. The major purpose of audio and/or visual aids such as charts, three-dimensional models, sound tapes, slides, and motion pictures is to help the conference leader to:

1. Demonstrate and clarify complex or difficult concepts

2. Reduce presentation time

3. Dramatize and reinforce major elements

4. Provide additional interest or change of pace

Aids should be selected for their contribution to the above objectives. They are often expensive and time-consuming to design and prepare, although there is an abundance of materials and equipment that can simplify and reduce their cost of construction. Unless properly rehearsed, aids can be cumbersome to manipulate and distracting to the leader's main purpose. Simplicity and ease of use are usually good criteria to establish in their application.

See also Communications, organizational; Conferences and meetings, planning for; Development and training, employee; Quality circles.

REFERENCES

Carnes, William T.: *Effective Meetings for Busy People,* McGraw-Hill, New York, 1980.

Hon, D.: *Meetings That Matter,* John Wiley, New York, 1980.

Jeffries, James R., and Jefferson D. Bates: *The Executive's Guide to Meetings, Conferences, and Audiovisual Presentations,* McGraw-Hill, New York, 1983.

LESTER R. BITTEL, *James Madison University*

Conferences and Meetings, Planning for

Conferences and meetings should be planned only after a thoughtful response to the one-word question: *Why?* A rigorous answer inevitably leads to the rest of Kipling's "six honest serving men": who, what, when, where, and how. The answer to these, in turn, will cover all essential factors, such as the composition of the group, the nature of the facilities, and the style of leadership. But unless "why?" is answered honestly, the meeting may have been unnecessary and may have become not only a failure but a disaster.

There are many wrong reasons for holding a meeting: sometimes it is easier than writing a memo; it's a good excuse to break the monotony of routine; it's pleasant to "kick ideas around"; it often gives the pleasurable sensation that something significant has happened when, in fact, it has not.

Valid reasons for holding a meeting include:

1. Inform

2. Get information

3. Provide direction or give orders

4. Identify and/or solve problems

5. Create and/or develop ideas

6. Plan

7. Provide a training experience

It is always important that the specific reason (or reasons) for the meeting be conscious and be known to each member of the group beforehand.

Nonsubstantive Dimensions of Meetings. Objectives represent one axis of a matrix. Meetings designed to serve these objectives also have other dimensions, each of which can be identified on a continuum, and each of which represents special problems (Fig. C-11). These are:

1. Size, from small to large

2. Degree of structure, from low to high

3. Degree of participation desired, from active to passive

4. Behavior of chairperson, from permissive to autocratic

It is absolutely essential in planning a meeting to have the objective clearly in mind and to be prepared to deal with the special problems posed by the session's position on each of the four continua.

Advance Preparation. After determining objectives, the first step in preparing for any meeting is to inform those who are to attend and to let them know the purpose. The advance expectations of those who are to take part have a very direct bearing on the qual-

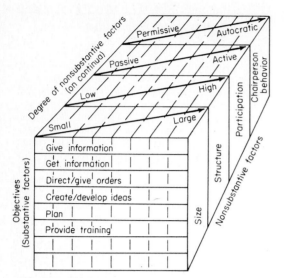

FIG. C-11 Meeting planning matrix.

ity of their participation and (to the extent that this is important) their ultimate satisfaction.

1. If the meeting is one of which action is expected, it may be very important to have some involvement of the group in doing the planning. For instance, either in person or by questionnaire, the participants might be asked for agenda items related to the objective from the standpoint of their special knowledge or interest. This gives them a stake in the outcome and ensures a degree of interest. An attempt to involve participants in advance, however, must be genuine and must be followed through. Otherwise, it will be seen as manipulative and the backlash will defeat the entire purpose.

2. The person in charge should set a realistic schedule to ensure that time is distributed properly within the allotted time frame. The schedule should admit a degree of flexibility; no one can really tell in advance just how much time will be required, especially if group participation is required.

3. It is absolutely essential, however, that the meeting start on time and adjourn no later than the announced time. It is a matter of simple courtesy to the attendees, makes it possible for them to plan their time efficiently, and establishes credibility for the chairperson. Attendees are much more apt to be prompt (and enthusiastic) at future meetings. One way to preserve flexibility is to allow somewhat more time for breaks than will be necessary; another is to allocate discussion time, which can be abbreviated.

4. An agenda should be worked out in advance and circulated so that attendees can prepare themselves effectively. The sequence of the agenda should be thought through rather than being allowed to occur by chance. More time should be allotted to the more complex items. Items which contribute to the understanding of other items should come first. Controversial items may be placed first so that the group will be fresh; on the other hand, they may be placed just before a break or adjournment so that discussion can be cut off gracefully.

5. Sometimes the time of a group can be conserved by sending out work to be done before the meeting to stimulate advance thought about the substance and thus bring about more informed participation. At the other end of the meeting, carry-over value may be extended and implementation improved by the provision of work to be done after the meeting is over.

6. It is important for members of a meeting group to know each other or be able to identify each other. Where members are not already acquainted and the group is small, place cards (with names in large block letters) are helpful. An opening routine in which each member also states her or his name and organizational identification is a convenient icebreaker and helps others to identify faces and voices with names. In large groups, badges with names and identification in nothing smaller than jumbo typewriter type are appropriate.

Special Problems of Small Groups. Small groups—usually 7 to 15 members, and not more than 20—have to be treated differently from larger assemblies. It is almost always desirable for members to sit facing each other, generally around a table. A round table is ideal, but it does not use space economically or lend itself to flexible arrangements; that is, it cannot be expanded, made smaller, or set up in a different shape. Therefore, a round table is used only in unusual situations.

U-, V-, and T-shaped tables are among the variations. At U- and V-shaped tables, do not seat members on the inside, because they will then have their backs to at least part of the group. In some training situations, the trainer may be tempted to walk into the "slot." This may provide an effective change of pace but must be done quickly (in and out) because obviously the trainer, too, will be facing only part of the group.

Most commonly, a rectangular conference table is used or is made up of combinations of square or rectangular tables. The first problem here is to avoid having legs so located that they constrict the spacing and movement of group members. Tables are available with legs near the center, rather than around the perimeter (pedestal tables).

Most people do not sit still in any meeting, nor do they sit neatly facing the center of the table. They tend to move and shift their bodies in keeping with the focus of discussion. Therefore, swivel chairs are preferred over straight chairs, and the kind used should be as well padded, seat and back, as possible. Because people shift positions (seat directions) even in straight chairs, adequate space provision must be made. Simply allowing the width of one chair for each person will result in intolerable cramping. Twice the width of a chair is a more reasonable allocation of space. By all means, make certain that there is room between occupied chairs and the walls so that members may enter and leave without inconveniencing the others.

There are certain housekeeping details which must not be overlooked; place cards if indicated (and crayons for filling them out), ashtrays and matches, fresh water and glasses or paper cups, provision for emptying ashtrays and refreshing water at major breaks, and note paper and pencils.

Small-Group Leadership. If an autocratic leadership style is adopted in the small group, it tends, by definition, to take care of itself. However, in most small-group meetings a degree of participation by the group members—ranging from *some* to *full*—may be desired, and this poses many problems for the group leader. Certain fundamental principles stand out. One is that the leader must put aside the traditional assumptions that the leader knows more than anybody else or that the leader must have all the answers. Instead, the leader performs certain functions—or makes sure that they are performed by members of the group—such as gatekeeping (making sure that each member has a fair chance to speak), pacing, stimulating, summarizing, and avoiding premature voting or polarization. The leader also protects the members, not only by assuring them "entry to the board" by gatekeeping, but by decreasing any threat which might result from participation and by avoiding or deflecting "put-downs." In this role, the leader is very much an "officer of the court"—in favor of justice, but not for or against either side.

Special Problems of Large Meetings. The large meeting—75 to 100 or even several hundred people—also has its own special problems.

1. *Simple logistics.* Has consideration been given to the traffic flow of people into and out of the main meeting room? Is the route clearly marked with direction signs? Are there bottlenecks in the form of narrow hallways or hallways blocked by desks, chairs, signs, or exhibits? Are there enough aisles in the room so that latecomers can get in without walking over an undue number of early arrivals? In large, auditorium-size meetings, it is useful to have one or more ushers for each aisle to indicate open seats to late arrivals. Many registrants will prefer to cluster, standing, in the rear rather than look for seats but will take seats willingly when they are pointed out.

2. *Registration procedure.* If registration is necessary, set up the registration procedure so that it is convenient but does not impede the traffic flow. Make sure that all related records and pieces of equipment, such as typewriters, are ready at hand and that there is enough staff to handle the peak loads. If large numbers are anticipated, break the registration area up alphabetically to avoid jams. Provide a staff phone where outside inquiries can be answered. Make adequate provision for hats and coats, either through formal checking facilities or hat and coatracks in individual rooms. The "nitty gritty" of seemingly endless, petty, and thankless details is unfortunately a major influence in the perception of the effectiveness of a meeting—frequently as important as the substance and presentation.

3. *Necessity for briefing attendees.* Attendees should know the time schedule (if it is not in a printed program, notebook, or handout) and the location of phones, rest rooms, and meal service, if any. Operating procedures should be set forth, such as how phone messages will be handled, how questions will be dealt with, and how supplies such as notepads and pencils may be obtained. A conference planner may think these matters are covered adequately if they are put in writing as part of a notebook or handouts. Unfortunately, this runs counter to human nature; in general people cannot be counted on to read material. If it is something they should know, it should be presented orally, even if it is summarized in print. It is also desirable for staff members responsible for the program and/or facilities to be identified by a distinctive badge so that attendees will know where to get information or make requests.

4. *Adhering to the announced time schedule.* Sessions that start late and run overtime convey an impression of sloppiness, poor planning, and lack of concern for the audience. There are many ways to control this. They start with *clear advance briefing* of the chairperson *and the speakers.* The chairperson should start on time, and if he or she realizes a speaker is running overtime, a note should be slipped to the podium to that effect. A speaker should know in advance what the assigned time is and how much of it is for speaking and how much for questions and answers, if that is the pattern.

A question-and-answer period provides a measure of flexibility, since it can be shortened, if necessary. Scheduled midmorning and midafternoon breaks provide similar flexibility. A 30-minute break can be shortened by 10 minutes; however, a clear announcement should be made to that effect, and the following session should start on time without waiting for stragglers. Similarly, the time allotted for lunch can be shortened, provided the lunch service can accommodate it. If an afternoon program has run long, it is possible to adhere to the schedule at the end of the last presentation by announcing, "This concludes the formal part of our day, but Ms. So-and-so has kindly consented to stay here for those of you who want to ask questions."

5. *Breaking the meeting up into smaller groups.* Smaller groups provide for more intimate, face-to-face communication. Although there are many names for this procedure, *subgrouping* and *buzz-grouping* are most common. Subgrouping, admittedly, has become almost a ritual, undertaken as a matter of routine without real thought. Executed in this way, it may cause more harm than good. *Do not* subgroup unless there is a good reason for it. *Do* make sure that group assignments are clearly stated and will have value to the members: superficial or make-work assignments will be seen as just that and will lower the standard of the entire meeting.

Visual Aids. Visual aids are a complicated enough problem to justify a full volume devoted only to them, and books on the subject are the place to look for technical information. However, some general caveats should be observed.

1. By far the greatest crime is to have aids which are too small. Texts on the subject of visuals contain tables specifying the minimum size of letters or numbers for visibility at varying distances. An illegible visual is not only useless but irritating to the audience. To achieve the proper size, cut the length of the copy or split the copy into more segments. In very rare cases—a mathematical table, for instance—breaking up the material might destroy the point of the table. The best thing to do in such an instance is to have the material reproduced and distributed as a hand-out. The projected or poster chart can still be exhibited; the speaker may draw attention to specific areas with a pointer while the audience then looks at the precise detail on the individual copies.

2. The second greatest crime is to use visual aids just to be using them—or to use aids which are not directly relevant to the subject.

3. Another crime is to fail to position a poster or the projection screen so that everyone in the audience can see it. It must be remembered also that the illumination intensity on certain types of projection screens falls off drastically when they are viewed from angles of less than 90 to 45 degrees.

Working with Hotels, Motels, and Conference Centers. The nature of hotels changed drastically after World War II. Hotels found that they could not survive on bedrooms, dining rooms, and social events. At the same time, companies growing rapidly in size and holding more meetings of various kinds found their own facilities inadequate. The companies turned to hotels to use their auditoriums and private dining rooms for meeting functions and began to discover that they were substantially below par in facilities, type of service, etc. Meanwhile, growing air travel with airports outside cities plus central-city congestion led to the growth of motels on the periphery of major cities. In such cases, a new position came into being, that of convention or meeting manager, someone devoting his or her staff and institution to new needs. The final step in this evolution has been the construction of buildings or building clusters intended solely as conference centers.

Today's institutional meeting manager has probably received professional training and can be a real help (but only a help) to the individual planning a meeting. This person is not infallible and any advice given should not simply be taken without question. The final responsibility is yours. Some tips:

1. Before making commitments, personally inspect any and all rooms to be used (not "one just like this").

2. If possible, obtain a copy of the floor plans (to scale).

3. Ask to meet personally the people who will be on duty during your meeting. (Meetings often start on Sunday afternoon or evening and the weekend hotel staff is most frequently not the same as the Monday–Friday staff.) Get their names and telephone extension numbers and the locations where they may be reached.

4. Find out when your rooms will be set up. Beware of the manager who tells you that the rooms will be set up at 7:30 A.M. for a 9:00 A.M. meeting. (If that *is* your answer, be there by 8:00 to be sure it's happening.) Try to have rooms set up the night before.

5. If you are promised chalkboards, ask to see them, just to be sure they are not chip board painted with chalkboard paint. In the same vein, check on all other promised equipment.

Meticulous Attention to Detail. It is probable that the single most significant factor in the success of meetings and conferences—large or small—is meticulous attention to detail. Take *nothing* for granted; make no assumptions! The hotel has assured you that coffee will be served at 10:45 A.M.? At 10:15 A.M., be on the phone, reminding the floor captain. So he thinks you're a slave driver? It's your meeting, isn't it? Count the number of chairs at the speakers' table; count the number of glasses, pitchers of water, and ashtrays. Are the table coverings clean and properly centered? Snap your fingers on the public address mike—is it working? *Always* check far enough in advance to allow time for remedial action if necessary.

Check beforehand to ensure that speakers' and chairpersons' arrangements are complete. Check the correspondence files. *All arrangements should have been confirmed in writing.* If arrangements were set more than 3 or 4 weeks before—even if in writing—a phone call to ask if everything is all right represents a tactful reminder and may spare many an ulcer. The name of the meeting game is check, check, and double-check. Checklists are among the references at the end of this entry. Don't spurn them. Even the most experienced veterans may tend to become complacent and take something for granted; they shouldn't.

Evaluation of Meetings. The needs for evaluation—and therefore the methods used—vary widely. For most in-company staff meetings, there is no need for evaluation. As the content becomes more complex, however, and the group more numerous or diverse, the need increases.

At the very least, the evaluation should provide information as to the extent to which the meeting's objectives were attained. The kinds of feedback received constitute part of a lifelong learning experience for meeting conveners, because even though responses may be the same over time, there is often some new element in each situation. Soliciting comments about a meeting, either orally or in writing, is evidence to the group of the convener's interest in the session and in them. Again, this interest must be genuine. If it is simply part of a routine, used manipulatively, it will do more harm than good. To state it bluntly, don't ask questions if you are not prepared to live with the answers.

1. *Substance.* Questions should deal with the subject matter, its coverage in breadth and depth, its relevance to the attendees' needs, its clarity, its internal consistency, and its logical development. It may be desirable to find out which elements were strongest, which were weak, and where there were gaps or overlaps.

2. *Methods.* Comments should be solicited on the methods of presentation, the effectiveness of presenters, and the usefulness of visual aids and supplemental materials.

3. *Logistics.* This concerns the schedule itself, the physical comfort of the meeting facilities, the meals, the clarity of instructions, and the adequacy of arrangements.

In addition to whatever detailed questions there are, it is useful to have an overall "umbrella" question dealing with the respondent's reaction to the meeting as a whole. This is desirable because the response may turn out to be much more than the sum of the responses to the specific questions.

Questionnaires are often criticized on the grounds that they are subjective. But subjective feeling is real to the respondent and will govern his or her subsequent behavior, no matter how many statistics may argue otherwise.

Effectiveness. All that has been said in this entry may be summarized as follows: *An effective meeting is one in which the subject matter is relevant to the participants' concerns and is logically developed, internally consistent, and competently presented within a logistical environment which is smooth and unobtrusive.*

A final word should be said regarding the role of participants' expectations in their evaluation of a meeting. An international meeting organization systematically analyzed the responses of a scientific sample of registrants in its meetings in an attempt to isolate those factors associated with highly regarded meetings and those associated with poorly regarded meetings. Although many factors were predictable, the single factor with the highest correlation to both good and bad meetings was the degree to which advance expectations were realized. This reinforces the need for clear objectives for a meeting—the answer to the question "why?" If the objectives are not clear in the mind of the convener, it is unlikely that they will be realized. And, unless clear objectives are clearly communicated and then lived up to, an attendee has every right to feel frustrated.

See also Communications, organizational; Conference leadership; Nominal group technique; Quality circles; Shareholder relations.

REFERENCES

Bradford, Leland: *Making Meetings Work: A Guide for Leaders of Group Meetings,* University Associates, La Jolla, Calif., 1976.

Carnes, William T.: *Effective Meetings for Busy People,* McGraw-Hill, New York, 1980.

Hart, Lois Borland: *Conference and Workshop Planner's Manual,* American Management Associations, New York, 1979.

Jones, Martin: *How to Organize Meetings: A Handbook for Better Workshop, Seminar, and Conference Management,* Beaufort Books, New York, 1981 (paperback).

EDWARD O. MALOTT, *American Management Associations*

Conformity in Management

A major problem with conformity is that the term often has a negative image. Some may believe that conformity is bad but that following the rules is all right; such simple positions often influence discussion of the topic and hinder an understanding of it. It should be made clear, first of all, that conformity is a neutral concept and must be considered as such without the value judgments that often color the use of the term.

Conformity is, to put it simply, the adherence of the individual to group norms through the influence of that group. The key word is *influence,* but people in a society seldom, if ever, act without being influenced by a group of others with whom they live and work. Analysis of any social activity—in business as elsewhere—must therefore focus upon the nature of the group, its norms, and the roles of individuals within it.

Response Differentiation. Students of behavior should also be cautioned to differentiate between types of human response.

1. Adherence can be in behavior only—without underlying attitudes and beliefs.
2. Actions may represent true feelings that fit and support the situation.

Obviously, the recognition and measurement of behavior are much easier than the determination of attitude and the beliefs supporting it. Behavior *without* congruent attitudes can be called *compliance.* The fuller state of behavior *with* attitudes is often referred to as *acceptance.* It is possible to analyze a situation further as to whether (1) compliance or acceptance is created by the situation or (2) it has been there below the surface all along waiting to emerge. Conclusions from scientific studies differ considerably as a result.

Group Differentiation. Groups were described long ago as "basic units of interacting personalities"[1] and later as units "with an interdependent sharing of an ideology."[2] Members of groups are aware of this belonging with others and of their sharing of attitudes and values with those in the group. A true group differs from casual aggregates or a crowd with no cohesive forces; a group is composed of individuals who interact in a meaningful and knowing way.

Groups exist because they provide a means of fulfilling needs—individual and group needs. If membership in a group provides something positive for the persons in it, there should be no surprise in the fact that the influence of a group is an important factor in society.

Groups are of many types. The first that usually come to mind are those groups officially organized under some authority; that is, *formal* groups. Beyond the official groupings, and often more important, are the *informal* groupings that can arise in an organization. Aggregates structured outside of regular channels can exert an influence even if they do not appear on the organization chart. Based upon intimacy or intensity of interaction, the distinction may also be made between primary and secondary groups. *Primary* groups are those with persons in close, face-to-face relationships, as in families or work teams. *Secondary* groups are broader, and there is less intense interaction in them. Universities or corporations in the aggregate are a bit more remote in their impact upon individuals and are typically secondary groups. *Membership* groups are the actual entities to which persons belong; *reference* groups are those toward which individuals may be drawn or which they may wish to join.

Group Norms. Norms are simply the rules or guidelines for behavior in connection with group activity. These may vary (1) from the very simple to the more complex and (2) from ones of little importance to those that are critical to the continued existence of the group. At whatever level, norms indicate to group members what should or should not be done. In addition, they provide a system of rewards and punishments which is assimilated by the individual who identifies with the group. In an industrial setting, the determination of a fixed number of units produced per day by a work group as a *fair day's work* (a norm) carries with it sanctions if that norm is either exceeded or not met. Higher up, in the executive suite, the norms may be more numerous and more complex, ranging from the appropriate color for a manager's socks to the elaborate patterns of deference to the president of the company at a meeting. These behavior guidelines may seem facetious to the outside observer when compared with the practical rules for organizational functioning, but they play a significant part in the process.

Group Influence. The influence of the group toward conformity to social norms has often been demonstrated. One of the earliest experiments to show this was conducted by Asch.[3] A task called for members of a group to make simple judgments involving matching of one of three lines with a standard. Ordinarily, people by themselves got perfect scores; when accomplices were put into a group of naive subjects and instructed to give occasional wrong responses, the pattern of responses changed dramatically. While there were variations by individual or number in the group, the number of choices that agreed with the incorrect ones given by the accomplices increased greatly. If not supported by another member, however, the incorrect responses were given less often, or ceased entirely. The strong lesson that emerges is that if the group induces conformity in such obvious choice situations, it can easily be deduced that the influence is even greater in work and social situations where the "correct" choices are not so easily identifiable.

Differences in Conformity. Are there any differences between individuals in the extent to which they conform? Some researchers have found that authoritarian personalities conform more than nonauthoritarians and strong needs for social approval, as well as authoritarian leanings, induce conformity more often.[4] Females, younger subjects, and those at lower intellectual or educational levels tended to conform more than others.[5] The structure of groups and the kind of situation are also important factors. Influence of the group is greater when it is cohesive. This may be based upon attractiveness of the group for its members. The more cohesive and homogeneous the group, the more consistent the criteria for behavior; that is, the clearer the norms. This reduces anxiety and provides greater security for individuals, since the ''right'' responses are more easily identifiable. The fewer the changes in membership, the stronger the cohesiveness; and the greater the membership communication, the closer the bond. All these factors reinforce each other and tend to continue the pressure toward conformity.

There is more of a tendency to conform to group norms when an individual is required to take a public stand than when asked to come to a conclusion in private. An early study[6] showed that listeners to a speech tended more to agree with a speaker when told that the results of a questionnaire on their views would be publicized. More recent research[7] found similar definite differences in the extent of conformity between private and public settings.

Participative Influences. Much interest in work situations over the years has focused upon participation by members in group activity. The classic Hawthorne studies[8] started out as research on the effect of physical factors upon work output. The surprised experimenters discovered that social factors were much more important in work performance. The workers, involved as they were in every phase of the development of the work process, adhered easily to group norms and worked effectively. Productivity and satisfaction both were at high levels. While the studies are characterized as research on participation and productivity, the interrelationship of these factors and norms is clear. Participation in structuring the rules and procedures makes for more cohesiveness of a group in adhering to those norms. A revival of these concepts is under way in various applications in industrial settings. Techniques such as ''quality circles'' or ''Q groups'' have built upon the basic lessons of the Hawthorne researches.

Recent interest in the workings of the Japanese corporation has led to widespread analyses, most of which have traced the effectiveness of the work units to social factors that emphasize conformity to group norms. One view of the Japanese experience[9] emphasizes the concept of *wa*, or group harmony, a situation that may be described as the unity or cohesiveness that comes from interdependence of individuals in the group. A complementary analysis[10] focuses upon the basic concept of collective values that influence adherence to social norms in the corporation

through the recognition that the end product is the result of collective rather than individual effort.

Productive and Nonproductive Conformity. At times, statements are made to the effect that conformity to group norms means a reduction of individual fulfillment with a concomitant decline in societal well-being. That can and does happen, but those simple statements miss the valuable, or even necessary, features of conformity. The pressures for conformity provide stability in the functioning of the group because the norms give the members an idea of the information they need to reach a goal. Adherence of the group members to the ''correct'' information builds that stability.

At the same time it must be pointed out that norms can be so complex or contradictory that they hinder the group, not help it. Norms can be counterproductive in an additional way if there is so much emphasis on adhering to the norms that the main purpose of the group—reaching the goal—is subordinated to the conformity to group norms. This phenomenon is often seen in business and other organizations. The insistence upon sticking to the rules may overshadow the real reason for those rules; it often interferes with getting the job done. Purists for rules miss this implication and often stand in the way of having informal methods do the work more effectively.

See also Affirmative action; Authority, responsibility, and accountability; Control systems, management; Discipline; Innovation and creativity; Interpersonal relationships; Leadership; Motivation in organizations; Organization structures and charting.

NOTES

[1] E. Burgess, ''The Family: A Unit of Interacting Personalities,'' *Family*, vol. 7, pp. 3–9.

[2] D. Krech et al., *Individual in Society*, McGraw-Hill, New York, 1962.

[3] S. Asch, *Social Psychology*, Prentice-Hall, Englewood Cliffs, N.J., 1952.

[4] B. Strickland and D. Crowne, ''Conformity under Conditions of Simulated Group Pressure as a Function of the Need for Social Approval,'' *The Journal of Social Psychology*, vol. 58, 1962, pp. 171–181.

[5] F. Di Vesta and L. Cox, ''Some Dispositional Correlates of Conformity Behavior,'' *The Journal of Social Psychology*, vol. 52, 1960, pp. 259–268.

[6] H. Kelley and E. Volkart, ''The Resistance to Change of Group-Anchored Attitudes,'' *American Sociological Review*, vol. 17, 1952, pp. 453–465.

[7] T. Nosanchuk and J. Lightstone, ''Canned Laughter and Public and Private Conformity,'' *Journal of Personality and Social Psychology*, vol. 29, 1974, no. 1, pp. 153–156.

[8] F. Roethlisberger and W. Dickson, *Management and the Worker*, Harvard University Press, Cambridge, Mass., 1939.

[9] R. T. Pascale and A. G. Athos, *The Art of Japanese Management; Applications for American Executives*, Simon and Schuster, New York, 1981, p. 125.

[10] W. G. Ouchi, *Theory Z; How American Business Can Meet the Japanese Challenge*, Addison-Wesley, Reading, Mass., 1981, pp. 47–51.

BLAIR J. KOLASA, *Duquesne University*

Consultants, Management

Experts of all kinds frequently refer to themselves as "consultants to management," but only those who advise on the management process itself can legitimately be called *management consultants*.

A definition that is gaining widespread acceptance has come, and only recently, not from the consultants themselves but from academia:

> Management consulting is an advisory service contracted for and provided to organizations by specially trained and qualified persons who assist, in an objective and independent manner, the client organization to identify management problems, analyze such problems, recommend solutions to these problems, and help, when requested, in the implementation of solutions.

That the authors of this definition find it necessary to follow with a more practical definition and note that they are only half joking illustrates the difficulty that even practitioners themselves have in explaining what they do:

> Management consulting is an uncertain and evolving process conducted by a foreign intruder who muddles through by performing various problem-solving activities, while trying to maintain high professional standards and still attempting to meet the needs of the client.[1]

What is explicitly stated as well as what is implied in these two definitions points to some key conclusions:

1. Management consulting is an advisory service, not a "take charge" or decision-making mode.
2. Not everyone is qualified to give this advice.
3. Objectivity and independence are essential to the consultant.
4. Not much is known about the actual process of management consulting.
5. Outsiders can be a big help in defining the problems they are called upon by insiders to solve.

A Large Competitive Market. Management consulting is at least a $3½ billion business in the United States. As a usually optional outside service that is easily postponable in tight times, management consulting finds itself prey to the economic cycle. Growth has averaged about 15 percent annually, and in recession times revenue reductions of 25 percent or more are not uncommon. It can be a volatile business indeed.

The consulting market is divided almost equally into thirds among large independent firms, the management consulting divisions of public accounting (CPA) firms, and small independents. University professors and captive (internal) consulting groups also share small portions of the pie. (See Fig. C-12.)

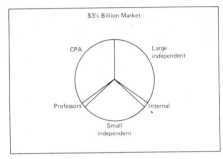

FIG. C-12 Consulting market.

At least 50,000 management consultants are operating in the United States, but many of these are unidentified because they operate part-time or in secret ("low profile," as they say). The largest 30 firms employ a good third of these, and this is where the career opportunities lie: some 17,000 to 20,000 jobs. Accounting firms—largely the Big Eight—employ another 8000 to 10,000 consultants. The 700-odd other firms and solo operations that can be identified account for perhaps another 6000 to 7000 professionals.[2]

The Major Consulting Associations. Not everyone self-proclaimed as a management consultant is a legitimate one, however, and relatively few have identified themselves with the professional associations in the field:

- *Institute of Management Consultants.* This is the certifying body for individuals, granting the *certified management consultant* designation. It has about 1500 members and was founded in 1968. It is organized regionally and undertakes some training functions (i.e., a seminar on fundamentals of management consulting).

- *ACME.* This is an association of management consulting firms, formerly the Association of Consulting Management Engineers. It was founded in 1929 and has about 60 members, mostly medium-sized firms. It helps its members with matters of firm management and undertakes an external educational role as well. Entry requirements are strict.

- *Association of Management Consultants (AMC).* This is the group for smaller firms. Founded in 1959, it has about 100 members, a significant portion of which are solo operators.

Other Specialized Groups. These serve specialized constituencies:

- *Association of Internal Management Consultants (AIMCO).* This group consists of some 200 individuals employed as consultants within nonconsulting firms, many of them blue-chip companies.
- *Academy of Management, Division of Managerial Consultation.* This organization consists of some 800 business-school professors who consult part-time and have developed their own code of ethics.
- *Society of Professional Management Consultants (SPMC).* This is a small group of largely solo consultants who have been meeting monthly in New York for a number of years and also once had an active California wing.
- *American Institute of Certified Public Accountants, Management Advisory Services Division (AICPA).* This is the center for information and education concerning formal management consulting activities engaged in by public accountants.

Selecting a Management Consultant. After doing the requisite homework to identify the problem and outline the possible parameters of assistance, it is a good idea to achieve some sort of internal consensus on the acceptability of bringing in outsiders at all. Nothing can decimate the effectiveness of external consulting aid more quickly than active or passive resistance from within. Once there is unified agreement to seek consultation, the following procedure will help to bring felicitous results:

1. Conduct your search for a consultant with all the seriousness attendant on selecting a brain surgeon: no room for mistakes!

2. Start with business associates, suppliers, customers, friends, and others familiar with your operations and industry. Ask for recommendations backed by specific references.

3. Widen your search by contacting your industry groups and the appropriate associations of management consultants. Do not overlook the yellow pages and any available directories of management consultants with meaningful cross-indexes.

4. Ask your lawyer, banker, accountant, and other professionals for recommendations.

5. Prune this initial combined list and then start contacting the consultants. Use a third party to make the contacts if this makes you feel more comfortable and if you want to avoid aggressive follow-up. Ask for the firm's brochure and other background material so you can begin to determine if its services and experience meet your needs. (Being too specific at the onset can tempt the consulting firm to distort and/or amplify its capabilities.)

6. Analyze these responses and write the most likely firms, asking them to respond to a more detailed description of your actual needs. Then invite those who pass this second screening to visit and possibly present a preliminary proposal.

7. Study the proposals carefully and be sure to check not only proffered but any other references you can identify. These are the sorts of questions you should be asking at this point: *(a)* Who will do the actual work? (Get resumes and, if possible, meet these people.) *(b)* How much internal administrative support will be required? (Your people and facilities cost less than buying on the outside, but you should know the extent of such assistance.) *(c)* What quality control procedures does the consulting firm have? (Experienced consultants build in supervisory and double-check points along the way to recognize and correct "souring" before it becomes irreversible.)

Fees and Billing Practices. Management consultants are essentially paid for their time, like other professionals. Some charge on an hourly or daily or weekly basis. Others quote a fixed or project fee, sometimes with a range or cap. Expenses—as detailed in the proposal—are extra.

There are as many fee arrangements as there are consultants, but beware of "guaranteed" savings or so-called contingent fees (i.e., fees dependent on certain results). Because consulting is by definition an advisory role, the outsiders must work through management, which itself is responsible for action and results. Tying consulting fees to specific savings, for example, can lead to all sorts of arguments about how the savings were figured.

Fees are a matter of mutual trust. No amount of documentation on an invoice can erase lingering doubts in the client's mind about the consultant's integrity.

Users of consulting services should not multiply the consultant's daily rate by 365 to estimate annual income. Even allowing for obvious weekends and holidays, most consultants do not manage to bill even 5 days a week. Like other businesses, consultants incur overhead for training, research, scheduling problems, selling, and administration.

See also Audit, management; Search and recruitment, executive.

NOTES

[1] Larry E. Greiner and Robert O. Metzger, *Consulting to Management*, Prentice-Hall, New York, 1983.

[2] *Directory of Management Consultants*, Consultants News, Fitzwilliam, N.H., 1983.

James H. Kennedy, *Consultants News*

Consumer Behavior, Managerial Relevance of

In developing different marketing strategies, management can adopt one of three different orientations: a selling orientation, a product orientation, and a consumer orientation. In adopting a *selling orientation*, management presumes that consumers will not buy the product unless there is a substantial promotional and selling effort. This approach is based on the "if you can make it, I can sell it" school of thought. Emphasis is on advertising, promotion, personal selling, and point-of-purchase displays. If carried to an extreme, this orientation evolves into a "hard sell" approach which can be offensive to many consumers.

The second orientation, the *product orientation*, is embodied in the "build a better mousetrap" school of thought. Characteristic of this approach are heavy research and development costs, an emphasis on higher technology, and frequent product failures. Consequently, the marketing mix variables receive minimal attention, and almost no consumer research is undertaken.

The third orientation is the *consumer orientation*, which arises from the "find out what they want and give it to them" school of thought. The key tasks in this orientation are (1) determining the needs and wants of the consumers within the target market and (2) motivating the company to satisfy market needs and wants more effectively and efficiently than the competitors. The primary emphasis is on market research, but product development, promotion, and other marketing mix variables are equally important. Thus a fully integrated marketing plan is utilized in the consumer-oriented philosophy of marketing management.

Benefits of a Consumer Orientation. Several specific and tangible benefits result from the adoption of a consumer orientation:

1. The company obtains a better picture of the structure of its market. Because consumer needs are more durable than products, they will reveal the true substitutability and complementarity of products. These relationships based on consumer needs often transcend the traditional industry viewpoint of competition.

2. There will be less waste and greater efficiency of the marketing effort, thereby decreasing marketing costs and increasing profitability. By providing the consumers with what they need or want, you cut out the need for persuasion. Further, receptivity of marketing communications will increase, reducing the amount of promotion necessary.

3. Product development stems from changes in the wants of consumers rather than from changes in

technology. Product research becomes more structured and meaningful, and product failure is less likely.

4. Products that are no longer desired in the marketplace are more easily discarded and replaced by new, more quickly successful products. The company becomes a leader instead of a follower.

5. Customer satisfaction is increased because customers have been provided with what they want. This increased satisfaction leads to favorable word-of-mouth communications, probably the most effective form of promotion for the generation of new demand. Increased satisfaction also leads to brand loyalty and a more positive public opinion.

6. There is less pressure on product development personnel for "spontaneous" new ideas because the consumer is the catalyst for most new products. Similarly, promotional personnel face less stress because they are no longer responsible for unloading products which fulfill no needs in the marketplace.

Criticisms of a Consumer Orientation. Recently a few marketing scholars have voiced what they believe to be some potential drawbacks of the consumer orientation. They argue that the consumer orientation has resulted in an excessive emphasis on minor product changes epitomized by the label of "new and improved." Also, as a result of looking to the consumer for new product ideas, companies have almost completely ceased all research efforts to develop revolutionary new technological advances. Thus, they conclude that the consumer orientation is one of the main explanations for the United States' loss of technological leadership to other countries, such as Japan.[1]

While these criticisms may appear to possess some merit, they are based largely on a faulty interpretation of the consumer orientation. The consumer orientation posits that a company not only must identify current consumer needs but must also anticipate future needs. Therefore, by following the consumer orientation a company should continue development of new technology which has the *potential* for solving present and *future* consumer needs.

Defining Consumer Behavior

Consumer behavior is not merely the use of goods and services marketed by profit-seeking companies and individuals; nor is it restricted to the actual act of consumption, such as the eating of french fries; nor is it restricted to the individual consumer. To understand the complete scope and complex nature of consumer behavior more fully, we need to examine its three aspects separately.

Objects of Consumption. The most typical objects of consumption are those products and services provided by companies or individuals who have a profit motive. Included among these are (1) nondurable goods such as groceries, personal care items, and household cleaning supplies; (2) semidurable goods such as clothing; (3) consumer durables such as furniture, appliances, and automobiles; and (4) private services such as doctors, lawyers, and beauticians. Additionally, the products and services of companies regulated by government, exemplified by the utility and transportation industries, should be included in this group.

However, people also consume public services provided by "nonprofit" organizations catering to such needs as health and recreation. Also included are those goods and services freely provided by the public sector such as highways, personal safety services, and educational facilities. The last, and subtlest, addition is the group of goods and services satisfying the political, moral, and religious values of society. Included in these are the marketing of churches, politicians, and astrology.

This expansion to less traditional goods and services is relevant for managers because they are all competing for pieces of the same well-defined pie; namely, the consumer's time, interest, and money.

Consuming Units. It is not enough to consider only individuals when discussing consumption behavior. Groups of individuals formed as social living units are important focal points for analysis. Usually most attention is directed at the traditional family as a consuming unit, but within the past decade the nontraditional household composed of single parents, unmarried couples living together, or communal groups has emerged as a major factor.[2]

Organizations must also be considered as consumers of products and services. The dominant types of organizations in our economy are industries, public institutions (hospitals, schools), private institutions (retail stores, clubs, restaurants), and government (local, state, and national). The single most important, and the largest, member of this group of consuming units is the national government. In addition, it is critical to remember that other living creatures are consuming units even though they are not the actual purchasers of the goods and services. Pets and livestock require such diverse items as food, shelter, medical services, and transportation.

Behavioral Roles. Having delineated the *who* (consumers) and the *what* (goods and services), it now remains to classify the *how* and *why* (activities and processes) to complete the complex picture of consumer behavior. Consumer behavior can be categorized broadly in two distinct ways: (1) by the nature of the activities and processes (behavioral roles) and (2) by the underlying motives and characteristics (behavioral types). Within the activities and processes, seven behavioral roles can be identified: problem recognition, establishment of goals, information gathering, decision making, purchasing, consuming, and postpurchase evaluation. These roles are important because they represent distinct parts of the total process, parts that permit specialization enabling them to be performed by different people in a household or organization in different places at different times.

Problem recognition involves the discernment of a need or problem that requires a solution. The triggering mechanisms for problem recognition may be internal physiological or psychological states of being, or they may be external stimuli provided by such sources as advertising messages, friends' comments, or salespeople's suggestions. A problem exists for a consumer when the desired state of affairs is different from the actual state of affairs. Because this is clearly a matter of personal interpretation, it is difficult to predict which conditions will lead to problem recognition for a specific consumer.

Once a problem is recognized, the role of *establishment of goals* becomes important. The delineation of goals for solving the problem typically revolves around consideration of desired benefits, permissible costs, acceptable risks, and an allowable time frame. For example, goals for resolving a transportation problem may include buying a car that gets at least 30 miles per gallon, costs less than $10,000, has a 5-year warranty, and can be bought straight off the dealer's lot.

The role of *information gathering* includes all activities regarding the collection, sorting, and evaluation of information concerning the benefits, risks, and consequences of the different alternatives. Information may be actively sought or passively received and can be obtained from many sources, including advertisements, point-of-purchase displays, and word-of-mouth communications. Of importance to management is the ability of the decision maker to be selective in information gathering. This selectivity can result in perceptual biases of the information received, causing a difference between objective information presented and the information perceived. For example, many consumers believe that there is a qualitative difference between national brands and store brands even though they are made by the same company.

Another behavioral role is *decision* or *choice making*. The process of choice making can be represented as a series of sequential steps. First, the decision maker must decide whether or not the product should be bought, depending on the existence of the need, desire, and ability to buy the product. Second, he or she must narrow the number of alternatives down to a manageable few. Next, a choice of brands must be made from among the selected set of alternatives. Finally, he or she must decide on the place and method of purchase.

While the decision maker, purchaser, and user

may all be the same person, frequently this is not the case. Almost always in organizational buying, the three roles are separated. For example, in the consumption of raw materials, the decision is made by the quality control department, the procurement by the purchasing department, and the consumption by the production department. This separation is also frequently evidenced in family buying behavior, most notably in the case of goods consumed by children, where the decision making and purchasing are usually done by the parents.

Purchasing refers to all the activities related to the procurement of the product or service. The most common activities include going to the store, physically searching for the product, picking the product up off the shelf, paying for the product, and transporting the product to the place of consumption. Consuming and purchasing do not have to occur at the same place or at the same time. Goods are frequently stockpiled for later consumption, and while usually purchased at the seller's place of business, they are most often consumed elsewhere. This discontinuity in time and place is important because the satisfaction obtained at the time of consuming may not equal the expectation at the time of purchase.

Consuming includes all the activities related to the actual utilization of the product or service. It can occur instantaneously or over a period of years. For example, an automobile burns gasoline, a child eats a candy bar, and a family wears out its living room rug.

After the product or service is purchased and at least partially consumed, there is usually a process of formal or informal *postpurchase evaluation* in which the performance of the product or service is compared against the consumer's goals and expectations. If the evaluation is positive, the consumer will be satisfied with her or his specific choice and will probably give strong consideration to purchasing that particular product or service when the problem arises again in the future. However, if the consumer's expectations are not realized, dissatisfaction will occur. Depending on the level of dissatisfaction, the consumer may pursue a range of options, including avoiding future purchases of that product, voicing displeasure and demanding compensatory action from the supplier of the product, and expressing disappointment to friends and relatives.

Types of Behavior. In addition to behaviors being separated into different activities, they can also be categorized by the underlying motives of the buying process. The six most common types of buying behavior are described below. Each type of behavior has different implications for marketing management.

1. *Impulse purchasing* is the simplest type of buying behavior. It is completely unplanned and involves no previous search, deliberation, or systematic choice. For example, a person randomly selects a candy bar while waiting at the checkout counter. While the marketer has less direct influence over this type of buying behavior, the most relevant aspects of the marketing mix are point-of-purchase displays and package designs.

2. *Habitual buying behavior* refers to those purchases that have become routinized and are performed almost mechanically. The behavior is fully learned, involves highly repetitive purchases, and occurs over short time cycles. While it is somewhat more involved than impulse purchasing, there is no information gathering or decision making done by the consumer. A common example is the consumer who always buys the same type, size, and brand of bread at the same grocery store. The most relevant marketing strategy is to ensure good distribution so that the product is always available.

3. *Problem-solving behavior* refers to the deliberative and calculated decision-making approach to purchasing, and includes the following steps: (*a*) the recognition of needs, (*b*) the establishment of goals to meet the needs, (*c*) the collection of information, (*d*) the determination of a set of alternatives, (*e*) the calculation of the potential of each of the alternatives to meet the goals, (*f*) a decision rule for choosing one of the alternatives, and (*g*) the purchase of the chosen alternative. The purchase of a home for most people involves problem-solving behavior. The total integrated marketing concept becomes most relevant in this type of buying behavior.

4. *Curiosity-motivated buying behavior* arises from a state of satiation or boredom with existing situations, which creates a need for change or increased complexity. This behavior is most susceptible to environmental stimuli (information). The product is tried because it is new or different. Many new products in a test market attain substantial first-time purchases but not enough repeat purchases to sustain the product because people buy the product owing to its novelty rather than its intrinsic superiority over existing products.

5. *Innovative buyer behavior* refers to the adoption of a new product or idea which may result in fundamental changes in the individual's lifestyle. The activities involved are similar to those of the problem-solving behavior but refer primarily to new areas of consumption. Because of the fundamental change required, adoption is more difficult than ordinary problem solving. The adoption process will be developed more fully later.

6. *Collective decision making* is performed jointly by several people. It requires special attention, for in addition to the previously discussed activ-

ities involved in the decision-making process, there are two new aspects. First, the roles are often more differentiated, indicating a separation of the marketing strategies. Second, interpersonal conflict results, making conflict resolution relevant for the marketing manager. Two specific types of collective purchasing, family buying and organizational buying, will be developed more fully later.

Explanations of Consumer Behavior

Within the last several decades, many theories have been developed in an attempt to explain and predict consumer behavior. Often derived from different discipline perspectives, all have had varying degrees of success and their own advantages and disadvantages. Although highly divergent in nature and scope, most theories can be classified into one of the following categories: learning and habit formation, demographic and socioeconomic theories, social class theories, cultural and reference group theories, motivation research, perceived risk, cognitive dissonance, and attitude theories.

Learning and Habit Formation. One of the most intriguing phenomena in consumer behavior is brand, store, or supplier loyalty. A variety of approaches has been introduced in an attempt to explain this phenomenon of repeat purchasing, and while differing substantially in their formulations, they are all derived from the psychological theories of learning and conditioning.

Learning, in psychology, refers to the change in an individual's response pattern which results from past experience. Thus, learning implies that the future purchases of an individual will be determined by his or her past purchases. Past experience can affect future responses in two ways. Based on the classical conditioning theory, the first approach postulates that the individual "learns" to make the same responses when confronted with the same stimuli by doing them over and over. For example, in the checkout line at the supermarket, when the clerk asks for money, the consumer gives the amount requested rather than making a counter offer and then bargaining for the price to be paid. The consumer does this because it is what she or he has always done.

Furthermore, the outcomes of past behavior also have an effect on future behavior. Based on the operant conditioning theory (reinforcement theory), a suggestion has been made that past behaviors that have resulted in favorable outcomes are more likely to recur than those resulting in less favorable or unfavorable outcomes. If a consumer buys a brand of detergent and finds that it gets clothes very clean, he or she is more likely to buy it again than if it did not get clothes clean.

Thus, the amount of learning will depend on both the habit strength—the number of previous stimulus-response associations—and on the incentive motivation—the expectation of reward based on past experience. In addition, both the internal state of the individual and the strength of the stimulus will affect the response tendency. It has been found, for example, that people tend to purchase more unplanned groceries when they are hungry (e.g., right before lunch) than when they are not hungry. Similarly, the aroma of fresh pastries that is coming from a bakery with open doors is more likely to bring about the purchase of some bakery products than a billboard advertisement several blocks away.

Socioeconomic and Demographic Factors. One of the more traditional approaches to explaining consumer behavior is the use of socioeconomic and demographic (SED) factors. SED variables are characteristics by which an individual may be described, and they include physical characteristics, social characteristics, and economic characteristics. Generally, they can be separated into two categories: those that are ascribed, i.e., outside the control of the consumer for the most part, and those that are attainable, i.e., within the control of the individual. The ascribed SED variables include sex, race, religion, ethnic origin, physical characteristics, and age. The attainable SED variables include income, education, occupation, marital status, home ownership, family occupation, and place of residence.

The theory holds that various aspects of consumer behavior such as brand choices and preferences, media habits, and shopping habits can be explained through differences in the SED characteristics of consumers. That is, people with the same SED characteristics are more likely to behave in the same manner.

Advantages of SED Models. SED models have several advantages:

1. They are easy data to collect and communicate. Respondents have a better understanding of what is being asked than they do with questions involving attitudes, beliefs, and values.

2. Because they are objective, SED variables generally elicit more reliable responses.

3. Because this type of data is collected by the Census Bureau, results can easily be generalized to entire populations.

4. By analyzing SED variables related to potential target markets, marketing managers gain a better understanding of the background and motivations of their customers.

5. Because we live in a highly dynamic and open culture, SED variables help marketers to anticipate and respond to major trends in product usage on the basis of demographic shifts. For

example, two critical movements in the United States in recent years have been the increased number and importance of older consumers and the emergence of Hispanic consumers as a powerful economic force.

6. SED variables help to guide the selection of promotional media that will "deliver" a particular audience in a cost-efficient manner.

Limitations of SED Models. SED variables present two major problems in explaining consumer behavior, however. First, they have proven to be poor correlates of brand choice in the past, and second, they are outside the control of marketing management. Therefore, SED variables should be used in the explanation of consumer behavior with the following considerations:

1. They are probably more relevant at the product level. While not differentiating well between brand users, they may help explain differences in product usage.

2. Owing to the increasing affluence of the lower classes, some SED variables are becoming obsolete. This is true for income, for example; however, race, sex, age, and religion are still very relevant SED variables.

3. Some marketing managers feel "handcuffed" when they discover that the SED profile for their target market is not dramatically different from the profiles of the nontarget groups. In such cases, assuming that the target group does have a legitimate unfulfilled need, the marketer should proceed by using a "shotgun" rather than a "rifle" approach. In other words, it may be more difficult and less efficient to reach the particular target market because general viewership media may be required.[4]

4. Finally, these variables will at best provide only a partial explanation; hence idealistic models developed using only SED variables will be unrealistic.

Social Class. Closely related to SED variables is the concept of social class. Most societies have some form of categorization system that groups members of that society into fairly distinct classes. Typically a person's social class placement is based on a composite of her or his income, occupation, education, and perhaps family background. Of particular relevance to marketers is the fact that consumers perceive strong connections between certain products or brands and certain social classes. For example, most respondents would probably agree that a Rolls Royce is an upper-class car, while a Chevrolet Chevette is a lower-class car. Research has also shown that even elementary-age children develop for many product classes a linkage between brands and social class.

The concept of *social mobility* relates to a person's movement from one social class to another. Typically most consumers aspire to move up on the social class ladder by means of occupational advancement, educational achievement, income expansion, or even marriage to a spouse from a higher social class. The potential for social mobility varies across cultures. The United States offers a high degree of social mobility, while other, more traditional cultures, such as Mexico and France, allow very little chance for social mobility. In an attempt to utilize consumers' desires for upward social movement, advertisers often suggest that the ownership of their product will enhance a consumer's social class position.

Culture and Reference Groups. The consumption behavior of an individual is determined in part by the social forces acting on her or him. The two major social forces in consumer behavior are culture and reference groups.

Culture. Culture refers to the learned response patterns and feelings of a homogeneous group of individuals which collectively reflect their values and meaningful symbols as they are transmitted from one generation to the next. Thus, culture is an attempt by each society to adapt to its particular environment.

The most common identification of culture is with national boundaries. However, culture can transcend national boundaries. More than one nation may belong to the same relevant culture, as for example the industrialized Western European nations, or more than one culture may be found within the same country—especially true in the United States and India where there are many large ethnic groups, each with its own culture and traditions.

There are numerous dimensions along which cultures vary which are significant to marketers.[5] Six relevant factors are orientation toward nature, activity orientation, time perspective, sex roles, role of children, and willingness to delay gratification.

1. Some cultures believe that human beings should control and utilize the natural environment, while other cultures believe that human beings should attempt to coexist with nature and avoid harming the environment. As pollution increases and the supply of natural resources decreases, this debate will continue to intensify.

2. The United States has a penchant for a high level of activity in work and recreation. Many other cultures pursue a more passive approach to life.

3. Another crucial distinction among cultures is their time perspective. Most modern, industrialized countries adopt a very strict approach to time utilization which is typified by precise beginning and ending times for events and rather severe sanctions for time misuse. Meanwhile, the more traditional, agrarian societies utilize a

more relaxed style in which time is more loosely construed. Many enlightening—and sometimes humorous—anecdotes can be cited about the frustrated U.S. businessperson who cannot understand why foreign businesspeople are so nonchalant about appointments and time pressures.[6]

4. The roles of men and women vary greatly across cultures. The emergence of equal rights for women has resulted in dramatic changes in product usage and purchasing behavior by American consumers. However, in most cultures the male is still the dominant decision maker, especially for major consumer durable purchases.

5. One source of variance that is often ignored is the role of children in a culture. In some cases children are highly treasured and glorified as symbolic objects of love and are sheltered from life's realities. But other cultures believe that children are primarily an economic asset which should be utilized for the benefit of the broader family unit. The level and pattern of child care and gifts for children will obviously vary greatly given different roles for children.

6. Finally, a culture's willingness to delay gratification has interesting implications. If a culture believes in the potential of the future, a high emphasis will be placed on education and savings. If, however, the future appears bleak or uncertain, people will "live for today" and reap as much immediate gratification as possible.

Reference Groups. A social force with a more direct impact on consumption behavior is the reference group. A *reference group* can be defined as any aggregation of people that influences an individual's attitudes or behaviors by serving as a point of reference. While reference groups may be classified in many ways, the most relevant types are membership groups, aspirational groups, disassociative groups, and primary groups.

Membership groups, those groups to which an individual belongs by a voluntary choice, are the most general form of reference group. *Aspirational groups* are groups to which an individual desires to belong, as, for example, the local country club. In such instances, the individual will emulate the members of this group, especially in the consumption of conspicuous products. The impact of aspirational groups is best demonstrated by the effectiveness of advertising endorsements. Just the opposite, *disassociative groups* represent those groups with which an individual does not want to be identified. Consequently, the individual will go out of his or her way to avoid using products and brands that would indicate membership in one of those groups. Finally, *primary groups* are those groups whose members all have face-to-face interaction. They represent the

most forceful social influence on patterns of consumption. Their influence is exerted through group roles and group norms. Each group member will have one or more roles which she or he is expected to perform. The parameters of a role are the acceptable limits of behavior for the person performing that role. The parameters may be quite wide; for instance, when a person is in charge of entertainment for a social club. Or they may be quite narrow, as for a soldier who has to get a haircut. If a person exceeds these parameters, the group usually imposes some form of sanctions upon the violator.

A person may also experience difficulty with group roles when he or she discovers that membership in multiple groups creates role conflict. This is especially relevant to working mothers who find that they cannot adequately meet the demands of their roles as wife, mother, and employee simultaneously. Norms exist in groups because they serve as guides to acceptable behavior for all persons within that group. For example, most religious groups have a norm regarding appropriate dress for religious services. An intriguing facet of norms is the attempt by marketers to influence group norms. In some instances, particularly in the personal care and fashion industries, such attempts are highly successful.

Motivation Research. While culture, reference group, and SED explanations of consumer behavior involve the identification of explicit consumer characteristics, motivation research refers to the understanding of human motives which are hidden, deep-rooted, and otherwise not obvious, but at the same time are determinants of product choices. Relying on the theory and methodology of clinical psychology, motivation research has evolved into three major types in studying consumption behavior:

1. *Psychoanalytic theory* seeks hidden motives. it postulates that the human personality structure is composed of the id, the ego, and the superego. The id represents the force acting in the body to satisfy the biological needs; the ego acts as the mediator between the demands of the id and the person's environment by determining behaviors that can satisfy the needs; and the superego provides the societal and personal norms that constrain behavior. Behavior is a result of the unconscious motivation resulting from the interaction of these three parts. Psychoanalytic theory has prompted the use of sexuality in the design of both products and promotion.

2. *Projective techniques* represent a method whereby the hidden and socially unacceptable or objectionable motivations of an individual can be determined. It assumes that in addition to sex, a human being can be motivated by such things as the need for power, achievement, money, and social acceptance. The technique consists of having an individual playact—for example, describ-

ing what he or she sees in a picture, or completing a short story. The individual's motives are then determined through the subjective analysis of his or her responses.

The purpose of these first two types of motivation research can be seen as only exploratory. They provide a means for pretesting and developing new ideas. They are too costly to perform in large numbers, are highly subjective, and are difficult to quantify.

3. *Personality characteristics* represent the major influence of motivation research on consumer behavior. Personality traits are those characteristics that cause two people to behave differently in the same situation. Thus, personality is an individual difference variable. For the theory to be useful, it is necessary to assume that many individuals will have the same personality characteristics, that these characteristics will be stable over time, and that they will consistently influence a wide variety of behaviors.

Personality traits can be measured through the use of specially designed instruments called personality tests. The traits are then used as independent variables in an attempt to find the relationship between them and product or brand choice.

Perceived Risk and Cognitive Dissonance. Two distinct cognitive theories that attempt to explain a consumer's choice behavior are (1) perceived risk theory and (2) cognitive dissonance theory.

Perceived Risk. This refers to the individual's evaluation of the negative consequences which are likely if she or he makes a wrong choice among available alternatives. Thus, perceived risk is a function of two components: (1) aversive consequences and (2) degree of uncertainty. The theory posits that the consumer will act in such a way as to reduce the risk involved in the choice situation.

Five general types of risk have been identified in the product choice situation: physical risk, social risk, economic risk, functional risk, and psychological risk. *Physical risk* is the risk that something may happen to harm the individual physically; for example, injury due to product failure. *Social risk* refers to the undesirable social effects resulting from a wrong choice; for example, ridicule for wearing outlandish clothes. *Economic risk* can result from either loss of money or loss of time. The risk that the product or service will not perform as expected is *functional risk (performance uncertainty)*. Finally, consumers may face *psychological risk (ego)* if they discover that they cannot master the use of the product or service, as in the purchase of a home computer or dance lessons.

Because people will act to decrease risk, the the-

ory has the following implications for consumer behavior:

1. The greater the perceived risk, the more likely the development of brand loyalty. People will stick with something they are sure of.

2. The greater the perceived risk, the more extensive the individual's search for information; hence, the greater the impact of advertising.

3. The greater the perceived risk, the greater the importance of word-of-mouth communications.

4. The greater the perceived risk, the more thorough the deliberation an individual will engage in; therefore, the less likelihood there is of impulse purchasing.

5. The greater the perceived risk, the more likely it is that the consumer will attempt to reduce the potential negative consequences of the purchase by seeking strong warranties or buying only a small trial amount of the product or service.

6. The greater the perceived risk, the more likely the consumer is to "go with the flow" and buy a very popular brand that has been on the market for a long time.

Cognitive Dissonance. This refers to the psychological discomfort experienced immediately following a choice decision between two or more attractive alternatives. While perceived risk is relevant to predecision behavior, cognitive dissonance is more applicable to post decision activities. In order for cognitive dissonance to occur, the following antecedent conditions are necessary:

1. There must be a number of desirable alternatives; that is, a choice must exist.

2. The unchosen alternatives must in fact have some desirable features that are not obtainable in the chosen alternative.

3. There must be some commitment to the choice, and the choice must be seen as irrevocable.

4. The individual must not feel forced into the particular decision, but rather must believe that the choice was of his or her own volition.

Under such circumstances, the individual will experience mental discomfort and will act in such a way as to reduce this tension after making the choice. The methods of dissonance reduction are very relevant for marketing management. First, the individual may psychologically decrease the attractiveness of the unchosen alternative and increase the attractiveness of the chosen one. Thus, cognitive dissonance should lead to the development of brand loyalty. The individual can also search for information to support or rationalize the choice. Thus, he or she will prefer consonant to discrepant information. This implies that marketing should not stop with the act of purchase but should continue to *reinforce* the decisions of those customers who have bought the product. Consumers will want to rationalize their choices. Advertising's greatest impact is often on loyal customers.

Attitudinal Theories. An attitude may be defined as some mental state of the individual which reflects favorableness or unfavorableness toward an object and includes her or his predisposition to behave in specific ways toward that object. Because attitudes represent predispositions, they can be used to predict future behavior. An individual's choice among products or brands will be determined by personal attitudes toward them, resulting in a choice of the most favorable. To understand choice behavior one must understand the underlying attitudes.

Attitudes are presumed to be determined by a number of factors. This determination of attitudes has been a major source of controversy in social psychology, resulting in four major schools of thought: the behavioral school, perceptual school, functional school, and cognitive consistency school.

1. The *behavioral school* hypothesizes that attitudes are a direct result of the experiences of past behaviors. Attitudes are the result of behaviors rather than the cause.
2. The *perceptual school* holds that attitudes are determined by the relative position of products to each other and to an ideal product within some defined product space. An individual's attitudes are estimated from this product space by comparing the distances between different products and the individual's ideal point. The individual is said to have the most favorable attitude toward that product which lies closest to his or her ideal point. Attitude change is brought about by changing the individual's perception of the products in the product space.
3. The *functional school* deals with the possibility that many people have the same attitude toward a particular product but for different reasons. The functional school posits that attitudes serve four functions for the individual. The *utilitarian function* of an attitude is to express a feeling about the usefulness of an object for satisfying an individual's functional and physical needs. The *knowledge function* of an attitude is to help individuals cope with a complex world. This function permits the stereotyping of objects into categories of like or dislike so that when confronted with them in future situations, the individual will not have to engage in extensive decision making. The *expressive function* of an attitude is to reflect the individual's self-concept. It is this function which often results in the purchase of products not so much for their functional utility as for the expression of social psychological needs by conspicuous consumption behavior. The final function of an attitude is to protect the individual from internal anxieties. In this sense, the attitude serves as an *ego-defensive mechanism,* often leading to the perceptual biasing of information.
4. The last school of thought, the *cognitive consistency school,* has had the greatest influence on consumer behavior theory and research. This theory posits that attitudes are based on three factors: a cognitive factor, an affective factor, and a conative factor. The *cognitive factor* represents an individual's information about an object, consisting of two basic types of beliefs: beliefs in the existence of an object (awareness) and beliefs about the object (evaluative beliefs). The *affective dimension* of attitude is the overall feeling of like or dislike. In consumer behavior, it is generally believed that this overall affect is a direct function of the person's evaluative beliefs. Specifically, affect for a product is hypothesized to be the sum of the evaluative beliefs (weighted according to their importance) over all the relevant product attributes.

   Research in this area has focused on the method of selecting salient product attributes, the method of measurement of both the evaluative beliefs and the importance of those beliefs, the inclusion or exclusion of the weights in the model, and the manner in which the beliefs are combined to form the overall affect toward the product. The apparent uncertainty is due in part to the inability of evaluative beliefs to predict affect, and hence product choice, exactly. It has thus been suggested that the conative factor mediates affect and behavior. This *conative factor* is the gross behavioral intention of the individual.

Sheth[7] has observed that there are situations in which people's attitudes and behavior are not consistent (see Fig. C-13). For example, many people have

		Attitude: Positive	Attitude: Negative
Relevant behavior	Engaged	Reinforcement strategies	Rationalization strategies
	Disengaged	Inducement strategies	Confrontation strategies

FIG. C-13 A typology of strategy mix choice.

a positive attitude toward carpooling, but they fail to take any steps toward the appropriate behavior. In such cases, the strategy of *inducement* is the most appropriate strategy to utilize. It refers to minimizing or removing organizational, socioeconomic, time, and place constraints which intervene between the positive attitude and the consequent behavior. For carpooling, this may involve establishing a mechanism for locating other potential car pool users or changing the time and place dimensions of the person's work schedule.

Conversely, a person may currently be engaged in a behavior even though he has a negative attitude toward it. To improve this situation, a *rationalization* strategy is effective. Rationalization strategy includes using persuasion and propaganda principles in which information is packaged in a biased way in favor of the desired behavior. Additionally, this strategy may include the use of economic incentives to encourage the continuation of the engaged behavior. An example is the use of propaganda regarding the benefits of physical exercise and gift coupons awarded for each visit for people who belong to a health club but do not enjoy the strain of exercising.

Of course, marketing managers desire the optimal situation, one in which the consumer purchases the company's product on a regular basis and also has a positive attitude toward the purchase behavior. To ensure this continued state of affairs, a manager should use *reinforcement* strategies which reward the consumer for her actions. This may involve such rewards as maintaining consistent, high-quality standards for the company's products, applauding the wise judgment of the loyal consumer in the company's advertisements, or even presenting personal awards of recognition to long-time buyers.

Finally, when both attitude and behavior are negative, the appropriate strategy is the *confrontation* strategy. This situation, which often occurs in social marketing contexts, requires the unlearning of old habits and the learning of new, desirable behaviors and attitudes. This radical transformation may involve the use of economic disincentives, behavior modification, and mandatory rules and regulations. For example, to minimize the level of drunk driving, the government may increase the tax on alcohol, place offenders in therapy sessions, and limit the hours of liquor store sales.

The Diffusion of Innovations

Diffusion theory is concerned with the adoption of new products. There are three compelling reasons why the study of diffusion of innovations is relevant to marketing management. First, by understanding the diffusion process, managers may be able to minimize the number of new products that do not achieve full dissemination in the marketplace. Second, the rate of diffusion is of interest because it has a major impact on a firm's ability to maintain steady sales and profits performances. Finally, the field of social marketing is concerned with the diffusion of socially desirable products, services, or ideas in a society, such as proper nutritional habits and effective birth control techniques.

The major components of theories of diffusion, from a marketing perspective, are (1) the innovation and its characteristics, (2) the process by which the new product is accepted, (3) the sources of communication relevant for the adoption process, and (4) the characteristics of different types of adopters.

Defining an Innovation. The most important of these elements is the innovation. Most marketers define an *innovation* as any new product, but this definition is misleading. A better definition of innovation is a product which is *perceived* as new by the potential adopters. Several characteristics of an innovation determine whether or not the product will be adopted and, if it is adopted, the rate of adoption—the speed at which it is diffused throughout the society.

1. *Relative advantage* of a new product is the extent to which it is perceived as being superior to existing alternatives. Relative advantage is a multidimensional concept based on many factors, including initial cost, maintenance costs, risk, time and effort savings, discomfort reductions, and speed of gratification.

2. *Compatibility* refers to the extent the new product blends in with current behavior patterns, values, beliefs, and attitudes. The less disruptive of current life an innovation is, the faster it will be adopted.

3. *Complexity* of a product refers to the amount of knowledge necessary for the use and understanding of a new product. If a new product is too complex, and therefore very difficult to understand, relatively few people will be able to adopt it initially, and the rate of diffusion will be very slow. Furthermore, more complex products are more difficult to communicate.

4. *Trialability* refers to the extent the consumer can experience the product firsthand before a decision to adopt must be made. Innovations that must be accepted without trial will diffuse more slowly than those that can be tried. Trial can occur through a division of the product into smaller units (such as in the adoption of new food products) or through use without commitment to adopt (such as the test driving of a new automobile).

5. Finally, *communicability* is also an important characteristic. The more easily the new product can be communicated to individuals, the faster it will be adopted. Communication can be of three forms: demonstration of the product itself, pictorial descriptions of the product, or verbal descriptions. Of these, demonstration will have the greatest effect.

Process of Adoption. There are several theories describing the process an individual goes through in accepting a new product. The best-known theory of the adoption process is that developed by Rogers and Shoemaker.[8] Their paradigm consists of four stages in the individual's acceptance process. The first stage, *knowledge,* consists of the individual's awareness of the product's existence and knowledge about its characteristics. The second stage, *persuasion,* refers to the process of forming an attitude or opinion toward the product. The attitude may be either positive or negative. In the third stage of the adoption process, the *decision,* the individual will decide either to adopt the product or to reject it. However, the decision need not be final. In some instances it is possible to discontinue use after adoption, and in some instances it is possible merely to postpone the decision. Because of the lack of finality, the adoption process does not stop with the decision. If the consumer does accept the product, he or she will desire support for the decision. Therefore, in the fourth stage, *confirmation,* the consumer seeks reinforcement for the decision to adopt, and this reinforcement can come from actual use of the product, from social sources, or from commercial sources.

Sources of Communication. Sources of communication affecting the adoption process can be either interpersonal or mass media. Because of the nature of the adoption process, interpersonal communication, especially from a social source, is often crucial in the acceptance of new products. However, it is impossible for everyone to obtain information from social sources prior to adoption; hence a two-step flow of communication has been proposed to explain the communication process. The fundamental principle of the two-step flow process is that some people will rely more on mass media and commercial sources for information regarding a new product while the rest will depend more on interpersonal and social sources.

The people who use mass media extensively are the ones the rest of society relies upon for information; they are called the *opinion leaders.* They constitute a fundamental part of the diffusion process.

A person becomes an opinion leader because she or he has a high level of involvement or interest in the specific product class. Although opinion leaders may possess any socioeconomic background, they all tend to be rather gregarious and to utilize specialized publications that relate to their particular product class of interest. Opinion leadership for any one individual is usually restricted to one or at most a few related product classes. Rarely is a person an opinion leader in many product areas (although we probably all are familiar with some people who believe they are universal opinion leaders!).

Adopter Characteristics. Because many new product adoption curves follow a cumulative normal distribution (the so-called S-shaped curve), the most common classification system of adopters is based on the time of adoption (relative to others) and consists of innovators, early adopters, early majority, late majority, laggards, and nonadopters.

Innovators are the first people to adopt a new product and represent the first 3 to 5 percent of the population. They are venturesome, like to take risks, and generally have control of their financial resources and are able to withstand a possible financial loss. They are also able to understand the use and nature of the new product easily.

Early adopters are more respectable in the community than innovators and are the next 13 to 15 percent of the population. They are more integrated into the social structure and often serve as models for the rest of society. They exhibit the greatest amount of opinion leadership.

Members of the *early majority* (the next 35 percent) are more deliberate. They want more information, especially from a social source; hence they have more frequent social interactions. However, their social interactions seldom occur outside their own area.

Those members of the *late majority* and *laggards* are more tradition-oriented and exhibit a high degree of product and/or brand loyalty. The demonstration of the perceived advantages of the new product is necessary for these individuals to adopt a new product.

It is important to remember that not all people will eventually adopt every new innovation. The reasons for *nonadoption* include lack of a perceived need and possibly lack of access to the innovation because of inadequate purchasing power or a poor product distribution system.

A consumer's placement in an innovator category is product specific. For example, Mr. Jones may be an early adopter for solar-powered calculators but a laggard for graphite tennis rackets.

At the collective societal level the concept of attitude toward innovations is also relevant to marketing managers. In most modern social systems, such as the majority of the United States, there is a high degree of acceptance and appreciation of new product innovations. Such innovations are perceived to be a sign of progress and success. However, more traditional social systems, such as those of the Amish in the United States and the devout Muslims in Mideast countries, view many innovations as a threat to their cultural heritage and traditions.

Innovation Resistance. Recently, Sheth[9] has proposed a theory of innovation resistance (Fig. C-14) in order to explain why consumers resist adoption of new technologies, new programs, or new ideologies. Sheth has postulated that resistance to innovations can arise either because there is a strong habit or tradition associated with the existing behavior that the innovation tries to displace or because the innovation is too risky.

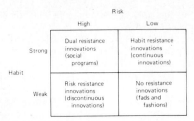

FIG. C-14 A typology of innovation resistance.

The maximal resistance is encountered when the perceived risk is high and there is also a strong prior habit. Many social programs regarding education, welfare, nutrition, and conservation fall into this category. Even when the perceived risk is low, there may still be a strong habit which may inhibit the acceptance of innovation. This is commonly confronted for products which are continuous innovations that represent only a slight change from the existing products the consumer is already using. The reverse circumstance, when the risk is high and the habit is weak, will often occur for discontinuous innovations which are major technological improvements over past products. Examples include nuclear energy, picture phones, and birth control pills. Finally, the least resistance arises when the risk is low and there is a weak habit, as for fads and fashions.

Family Buying Behavior

The most relevant aspect of the family buying process, as opposed to the individual process, is that the decision may be made either autonomously by a single individual or jointly by two or more members of the family. It is, therefore, necessary to separate those instances when a joint decision is more likely from those when an autonomous decision will be made.[10]

There are three *family determinants* of the decision-making process: (1) social class, (2) life cycle, and (3) role orientation. It is found that there is more joint decision making among members of the middle class than among families in either the upper or lower classes. Similarly, joint decision making tends to be more prevalent as the family moves up the family life cycle. Newly marrieds without children are less likely to make joint decisions than couples with young children are. Finally, the more separated the family role structure is, the more likely family members are to make autonomous decisions.

In addition to the family determinants of the decision-making process, there are three *product determinants:* (1) time pressure, (2) perceived risk, and (3) importance of purchase. As the amount of time available for a decision decreases, the likelihood of an autonomous decision increases. However, as the perceived risk inherent in a product increases, the likelihood becomes greater that the decision making will be joint.

A second and more important part of the theory revolves around the *concept of conflict.* Conflict will occur in the family decision process first, if there is a felt need for joint decision, and second, if there is a difference in goals or perceptions among family members. The type of conflict resolution depends on the reason for the conflict.

When conflict occurs because of a disagreement on the evaluation of different brands to satisfy the motives, its resolution will be by the *problem-solving process.* The consequences of problem-solving resolution is that family members will seek additional information from outside to support or refute the alternatives. They may even search for new alternatives.

However, the disagreement may be deeper than just the evaluation of the alternative brands. The members may disagree as to the criteria with which they should be evaluating the alternatives. Resolution in this instance occurs through a *process of persuasion.* For example, the teenage son may want a car of his own for reasons of prestige, but the other family members may persuade him that he will need his money for college, which is much more important to him. Thus, in effect, they demonstrate to him the inconsistency of his motives.

If two members have motives that are irreconcilable, resolution involves a *process of bargaining.* In this type of situation one member of the family may be given the permission to make an autonomous decision in return for some favor granted to the other members. Thus, the father gets to buy a new set of golf clubs for recreation if he takes the whole family on a vacation.

Finally, the disagreement may go beyond even differences in motives. Conflict may occur over the very style of life. When disagreement is this deep, resolution is only possible through the *process of politicking.* This style of resolution usually involves the formation of coalitions and subgroups within the family, but may also result in the dissolution of the family.

There are two plausible explanations for a particular family member's level of influence on family decision making. The resource contribution perspective states that the greater a person's contribution to the family in terms of income, status, expertise, or physical effort, the greater the amount of influence that person will have in the family. The alternative viewpoint, the sociocultural perspective, asserts that different cultures assign differential levels of influence to family members based on tradition. For example, in countries such as Greece, Japan, and Mexico, the husband is deemed to be the dominant decision maker. Conversely, in Sweden and Denmark husbands and wives exert relatively equal levels of influence in decision making.

The question of who possesses the strongest influence in family decision making is critical to effective marketing, especially in the field of personal selling. The salesperson must endeavor to identify the dominant influence in the family and then pattern her or his sales presentation accordingly.

Organizational Buyer Behavior

Although the volume of goods and services purchased by organizations exceeds the volume bought by consumers, until recently relatively little attention was directed to organizational buyer behavior. Now, fortunately, this deficiency is being rectified.

One of the paramount questions to be resolved is whether organizational buyer behavior is different from consumer buyer behavior. A popular notion holds that the organizational buyer is a more rational decision maker than the consumer. However, a significant amount of evidence indicates that the organizational buyer is far from rational.[11]

Probably the biggest difference between organizational and consumer buyer behavior is the predominance of conflict within the organizational buying process. Conflict is almost always a part of organizational buying because of the fundamental differences between the groups that normally engage in the decision-making process. The buying decisions are usually made by members of the purchasing department, the quality control department, the financial analysis department, and the manufacturing department. Conflict arises because of the fundamental differences in the purchasing criteria of these groups. The purchasing agent is most concerned about the price of the product, desiring to minimize cost. Quality control wants the best quality product on the market. And manufacturing wants the product to be the safest and the easiest to use. These criteria are often mutually exclusive, leading to conflict.

Other relevant distinctions between organizational behavior and consumer behavior include:

1. Organizational buying usually involves larger-volume purchases.

2. The organizational buyer may be very concerned about service after the purchase.

3. Women play a more dominant role in consumer buying than they do in organizational buying, although this situation is gradually changing.

4. The decision process in organizations is often more complicated and lengthier.

5. There is usually a closer interaction between buyers and sellers in organizational marketing,

particularly in terms of product design, price negotiation, and delivery schedules. However, there are numerous exceptions to this generalization.[12] While consumer goods are typically subject to mass marketing and industrial goods are usually subject to direct marketing, it is important to note that some industrial goods, such as oils, hand tools, and electric motors, do receive mass marketing treatment. Also, direct marketing is the norm for certain consumer goods, like homes.

Conclusion

Consumer behavior is highly complex and full of variety. The manager who believes that she or he fully understands consumer behavior for an organization's products and services is often in the same situation as the proverbial seven blind men and the elephant. It is best to hold a conservative view about the mystique of consumer behavior. Not only is consumer behavior complex, but it is also a dynamically changing phenomenon. What the manager knows about the firm's customers today may not necessarily hold true in the future.

See also Advertising concepts; Brands and brand names; Market analysis; Marketing concepts and systems; Marketing, direct; Marketing management; Marketing Research; Product and service pricing; Product planning and development.

NOTES

[1] R. Bennett and R. Cooper: "The Misuse of Marketing: An American Tragedy," *Business Horizons*, vol. 24, November–December 1981, pp. 51–61.

[2] Jagdish N. Sheth, "Marketing Megatrends," *Journal of Consumer Marketing*, vol. 1, 1983, pp. 5–13.

[3] Jagdish N. Sheth, "Demographics in Consumer Behavior," *Journal of Business Research*, vol. 5, March 1977, pp. 129–138.

[4] Frederick Winter, "Market Segmentation: A Review of Its Problems and Promise," in D. Gardner and F. Winter (eds.), *Proceedings of 11th Paul D. Converse Symposium*, American Marketing Association, Chicago, 1981, pp. 19–29.

[5] Harry Triandis and Richard Brislin (Ed), *Handbook of Cross Cultural Psychology: Social Psychology*, vol. 5, Allyn and Bacon, Boston, 1980.

[6] E. T. Hall, *The Silent Language*, Fawcett World Library, New York, 1959.

[7] Jagdish N. Sheth, "A Behavioral Model for Strategies of Planned Social Change," *Academic Psychology Bulletin*. vol. 5, March 1983, pp. 97–114.

[8] Everett Rogers and F. Floyd Shoemaker, *Communication of Innovations*, Free Press, New York, 1971.

[9] Jagdish N. Sheth, "Psychology of Innovation Resistance," in J. Sheth (Ed.), *Research in Marketing*, vol. 4, JAI Press, Greenwich, Conn., 1981, pp. 273–282.

[10]Jagdish N. Sheth (Ed.), *Models of Buyer Behavior,* Harper & Row, New York, 1974.

[11]Jagdish N. Sheth, "A Model of Industrial Buyer Behavior," *Journal of Marketing,* vol. 37, October 1973, pp. 50–56.

[12]Jagdish N. Sheth, "The Specificity of Industrial Marketing," *P.U. Management Review,* vol. 2, January–December 1979, pp. 53–56.

REFERENCES

Assael, Henry: *Consumer Behavior and Marketing Action,* Kent, Boston, 1981.

Bourne, Francis: *Group Influences in Marketing and Public Relations,* Foundation for Research on Human Behavior, Ann Arbor, Mich., 1956.

Cox, Donald F.: *Risk Taking and Information Handling in Consumer Behavior,* Division of Research, Harvard Business School, Cambridge, Mass., 1967.

Engel, James, and Roger Blackwell: *Consumer Behavior,* Dryden Press, Chicago, 1982.

Festinger, Leon: *A Theory of Cognitive Dissonance,* Stanford University Press, Palo Alto, Calif., 1957.

Fishbein, Martin (Ed.): *Attitude Theory and Measurement,* John Wiley, New York, 1967.

Hansen, Flemming: *Consumer Behavior: A Cognitive Approach,* Macmillan, New York, 1971.

Howard, John A., and Jagdish N. Sheth: *The Theory of Buyer Behavior,* John Wiley, New York, 1969.

Kassarjian, Harold, and Thomas Robertson (Eds.): *Perspectives in Consumer Behavior,* 3d ed., Scott, Foresman, Boston, 1981.

Kotler, Philip: *Marketing Management,* 4th ed., Prentice-Hall, Englewood Cliffs, N.J., 1980.

Woodside, Arch, Peter D. Bennet, and Jagdish N. Sheth (Eds.): *Consumer and Industrial Buying Behavior,* American Elsevier, New York, 1977.

Worcester, Robert M. (Ed.): *Consumer Market Research Handbook,* McGraw-Hill, London, 1972.

JAGDISH N. SHETH, *University of Southern California*

DENNIS E. GARRETT, *University of Illinois at Urbana-Champaign*

Consumerism and Consumer Protection Legislation

Consumerism provides business with a challenge to take the offensive and to reexamine its marketing philosophy, practices, and programs which affect short- and long-run customer satisfaction in a manner consistent with the public welfare. So enduring is today's consumer protection movement that it can be counted on to operate as a major force of influence in the years ahead.

Persistent Activity. Consumerism is a form of advocacy that seeks to protect and broaden the rights and powers of consumers. Since its inception in the early 1960s, the scope and impact of this modern-day consumer movement continues to evolve. It encompasses basic consumer rights which were first articulated in 1962 by President Kennedy as the right to safety, the right to be informed, the right to choose, and the right to be heard. In the intervening years, other presidents have restated them, while Congress has acted on them through consumer protection legislation (*see* Appendix at end of this entry).

Corporate managers and executives no longer ask whether consumerism is here to stay, but rather how to respond constructively to the problems and dissatisfactions of consumers. To an increasing number of executives, consumerism is viewed as an opportunity in the market arena, rather than as a threat. Correspondingly, new programs designed to meet the challenges of consumerism need to be analyzed, planned, and implemented.

Consumerism in the Eighties

Recent surveys of the public at large and of experts in the field reveal that consumerism is still strongly endorsed by the public. In general, research studies show that consumerism has become engrained in the American consciousness and will continue to be a vital force in society, regardless of the prevailing regulatory climate in Washington.

Surveys regarding attitudes on consumer issues and the state of the marketplace point to the following overall conclusions:[1]

- The public does not want a change in pro-consumer posture on the parts of government and the business community.

- Public support for consumerism is and will continue to be broad.

- Business retreat or de-emphasis on consumer issues would not only seriously misread consumer opinion and expectations, but would risk a backlash of prospectively major proportions.

- Enlightened business firms will recognize that consumerism is here to stay and address continuing and evolving consumer concerns in areas such as product safety and information.

An extensive look at consumerism in the eighties is provided by Louis Harris and Associates. Harris conducted a study of randomly selected adults across the United States to determine the many aspects of public opinion about new and changing consumer issues. Selected highlights (see Table C-5) of this research indicate that consumer concern is strong and growing; the consumer movement is rated positively; many government leaders and agencies are seen as not doing a good job in protecting the consumer; and support of government regulations in general has declined, but not in the area of consumer

TABLE C-5 Selected Consumer Trends and Issues in the Eighties

Consumer Concern Is Strong and Growing

- The public is even more concerned today about a number of consumer problems than it was in the mid-seventies.
- Consumers think they get a worse deal in the marketplace and receive less value for their money than they did a decade ago.
- Consumers also think that the safety of most products has improved, as has the labeling and information given for products.

The Consumer Movement is Rated Positively

- The accomplishments of the people in the consumer movement are rated high, although criticism of consumer leaders has grown.
- A plurality of people think that consumer protection has raised prices, but a majority also believe that the costs of consumer protection are worth it.
- Public participation in the organized consumer movement is modest, but the potential for involvement is high.

Government Is Seen as Not Doing a Good Job in Protecting the Consumer

- The administration and Congress are viewed as not doing a good job in protecting the interests of the consumer.
- The Consumer Product Safety Commission is the only arm of government that receives a clearly positive rating on protecting the consumer.
- Consumers Union tops the list of 11 agencies and organizations rated on the job they are doing to protect the consumer.

Support for Government Regulation in Consumer Protection Continues

- Consumers overwhelmingly endorse regulation for safety and protection; they are less keen on economic regulation in the marketplace.
- Virtually no support is found for rolling back or dismantling consumer protection regulation.
- A solid majority wants the government to do more to protect consumers against companies that fail to live up to their advertising claims.

Source: "Consumerism in the Eighties," A National Survey of Attitudes Toward the Consumer Movement, Conducted for Atlantic Richfield Company by Louis Harris and Associates, Inc., 1983.

protection. Another noteworthy finding is that consumerism cuts across traditional social and political battle lines and produces new or modified kinds of coalitions.

It seems safe to predict that consumerism will adapt and prevail as an essential force in society. It will continue to have significant implications for consumers and the business community, irrespective of the prevailing winds in Washington. Consumerism in the eighties can (and should) serve to bring consumers and companies closer together. Staying close to the customer is, after all, the core concept underlying the market orientation.

Widening Parameters. The challenge of consumerism today includes not only the demands of consumers for safer, higher quality and more effective goods and services, but also an insistence upon corporate responsibility in meeting a host of noneconomic and social concerns. Such matters as pollution of the environment, quality-of-life considerations, and even multinational business relations frequently appear under the banner of consumerism. In short, the parameters of consumerism continue to expand in response to ever-escalating consumer demands and expectations. The increased sophistication of consumers, the gap between product performance and marketing claims, the depersonalized nature of the marketplace (consumers repeatedly decry the lack of personal attention to their problems), and the failure of normal marketplace operations to satisfy consumers pose tremendous challenges to management operating in an environment that is characterized by *caveat venditor.*

Continuing Surveillance. If management is to address basic consumer issues rather than surface symptoms, it must have an information system that enables it to identify and predict underlying consumer issues and discontent. To understand the problems facing a company's customers and to stay current with consumer opinion trends, many companies have found it useful to conduct surveys, even if informally, on a periodic basis. From the responses of such surveys, important problem areas and worthwhile opportunities can be identified and compared with survey findings from trade associations, public opinion polls, and academic efforts. While the relative importance of consumer issues varies among and within manufacturing, retail, and service industries, corporate responses in terms of constructive consumer programs need to be developed by all firms. This requires top management commitment, not only in budget resource support but also in terms of philosophy and personal attitude.

Top Management Commitment. Management's basic attitudinal requirement is to accept consumerism and reject the notion that since "we have always been customer-oriented," there is really nothing new about consumerism. Additionally, adequate funding for specific, ongoing consumer programs should become part of the annual budget. These requirements pose a formidable task since direct corporate benefits may be difficult to measure, appear nonexistent, and are generally deferred. Consequently, there is a need to establish operational objectives and performance measures for improving or establishing on a first-time basis a consumer affairs program.

Establishing a Consumer Affairs Unit

A specialized consumer affairs unit now appears on the organization chart of a number of companies in

181

different industries. This unit is given various titles, including Office of Consumer Affairs (RCA, Motorola), Department of Consumer Affairs (Firestone, Grand Union), Consumer Services Office (Nabisco), Customer Relations Department (Westinghouse, Hertz, Scott Paper), Consumer Affairs Department (National Can Company), or simply Customer Services Department (Polaroid, Gillette). While these units are virtually new entities in many companies and are not always concerned with the same range of responsibilities, they are usually directly involved in one or more of the following activities: (1) responding to consumer complaints; (2) disseminating consumer education materials; (3) dealing with outside consumer interest groups; (4) coordinating programs and developing standards with respective trade associations; and (5) advising management on consumerism issues. The overall purpose of such consumer affairs units is to improve relations and communications with consumers and to make the company more responsive to the needs and problems of consumers, thereby helping to increase customer prepurchase, purchase, and postpurchase satisfaction.

Consumer Education. Company-sponsored consumer education programs and materials have now become an integral part of consumer protection. Numerous companies publish and distribute buying guides, pamphlets and booklets, posters, charts, and "fact sheets" for home use and/or educational programs administered by others. Additionally, films, newspaper features, television film clips, and public service radio announcements are prepared to keep consumers better informed and thereby more knowledgeable in shopping and consumption alike.

Concentrated efforts are increasingly made to deal with the problems facing specific groups of consumers, especially children, the economically disadvantaged, and the elderly. These groups should be the focus of special corporate consumer protection efforts. Reliance on existing or proposed consumer protection legislation and industry guidelines or codes is insufficient. Special educational and research efforts are called for, directed to such consumer problems of children as sweetened foods and nutrition, toy safety and promotion, and television programming. Similarly, tailored consumer protection efforts via educational programs need to be directed toward the poor and the elderly.

It should also be recognized that educational programs can easily be viewed as being too self-serving, and thus they become self-defeating. This occurs when undue emphasis is placed on promoting the firm's own products and brands.

Handling and Resolving Consumer Complaints. For the companies that have separate consumer affairs units, handling and resolving customer complaints or establishing policies and procedures to be followed by others is of primary concern. Regardless of which units have final responsibility for consumer complaints, however, all firms should establish a formal complaint control system. Unfortunately, some companies still harbor a negative attitude toward consumer complaints. They are often accorded a low-budget priority and viewed as outside the mainstream of the firm.

A 1980 nationwide survey of 2500 households conducted by the U.S. Office of Consumer Affairs revealed that 70 percent of consumer complaints regarding shoddy products and services are never remedied. The research study indicated that most private industries and government agencies are inept when it comes to handling consumer complaints and do an inadequate job of informing the public on how to file and follow through on their protests. (A different study showed that only about 4 percent of dissatisfied customers complain to a manufacturer.)

Inept handling of consumer complaints results in dissatisfied customers and loss of business. One study of 175,000 communications received from consumers by a leading soft-drink company pointed out that customers who complained and were not satisfied with the response typically told 9 or 10 friends or associates about their experience. Not only did complainers gripe, 30 percent said they stopped buying the particular company's products altogether and 45 percent said they would buy less in the future.

Benefits of Effective Consumer Complaint-Handling Programs. Responsive complaint-handling programs provide significant benefits for customers and business alike.

- *They serve as a real selling point.* Businesses are always looking for new ways to attract customers. Letting potential purchasers know you have a responsive customer complaint-handling program is clearly a strong selling point.

- *They keep customers satisfied and loyal.* A national consumer survey showed that customers who complained about their problems and received satisfactory results displayed the highest degree of continued brand loyalty. (One company indicates that a typical satisfied caller using its "800" number passes the word to five other people within 10 days. Conversely, a dissatisfied customer who does not complain usually stops buying the product and will bad-mouth it to others.)

- *They provide built-in warning signals.* Customer complaints provide early warning signals that products may have unforeseen safety defects or that a business may be in violation of consumer laws. Such an early warning system allows a firm to correct the problem promptly.

- *They provide valuable information.* Information obtained through a complaint-handling system can serve as a substitute for costly marketing surveys to help evaluate the quality of products, services, and personnel.

- *They help improve business-consumer-government relations.* Effective complaint-handling programs can improve a firm's relationships with government and private consumer protection groups.
- *They help lessen possible lawsuits.* A well-run complaint-handling procedure gives a firm an opportunity to correct customer problems before they lead to bruised relationships or, worse, to lawsuits.

Selecting a Complaint-Handling Program[2]

Each firm has different needs and resources and will therefore want to select a complaint-handling program which accounts for these factors. A firm should consider the benefits of both in-house complaint-handling programs and third-party dispute resolution programs. While most complaints can be handled effectively within the framework of the business (in-house), complaints that are not thus resolved can best be settled through the services of an independent person or persons; i.e., through a third party.

Organizing an In-House Program. Generally, there are two principal methods of organizing an in-house complaint-handling program: (1) the centralized approach, which places responsibility for all complaints in a specific department, and (2) the more informal, decentralized approach, which gives each employee or branch office broad responsibility for resolving complaints. To be sure, many businesses have found their needs are best met with a combination of the two approaches.

Regardless of the in-house approach adopted, it is important to keep the following checklist of design considerations in mind:

- *Consistency.* Establish uniform procedures for receiving, acknowledging, and resolving complaints. These policies should, if possible, be put on paper.

- *Accessibility.* Develop ways to publicize your program. Provide information in both English and other languages, as appropriate. Make the system simple, clear, and convenient.

- *Promptness.* Complaints should be acknowledged quickly, within 2 or 3 days if possible. The longer it takes to resolve a complaint, the more time is lost from business operations and the more likely frustrated customers will take their future business elsewhere.

- *Objectivity.* The customer should have an opportunity to present his or her case. Each customer should also have the chance to answer questions or respond to any conflicting information received by the complaint handler.

- *Monitoring.* Data obtained from an in-house complaint-handling program can be extremely helpful in a number of ways. Particular problem products, suppliers, stores, or employees can thus be systematically analyzed.

While it is prudent to attempt initially to resolve customer complaints through in-house complaint-handling procedures, there are good reasons to consider supplementing such programs with a third-party review procedure. Third-party approaches provide impartiality, greater customer confidence, more responsive employee complaint-handling performance, less litigation, and improved relations with consumer offices.

Third-Party Approaches. Third-party approaches use one or more of the following well-established dispute resolution techniques: conciliation, mediation, and/or arbitration. Figure C-15 shows the flow of complaints from the business's in-house program through a third-party dispute resolution process.

A *conciliator* is an independent person bringing the parties together and encouraging a mutually acceptable resolution of the dispute. The conciliator normally does not become actively involved in negotiations or make recommendations regarding a settlement.

A *mediator* is similar to a conciliator but may play a more structured and active role in the mediation process. The mediator conveys each party's views to the other in an attempt to arrive at a mutually acceptable resolution. A mediator may propose terms to settle a dispute but does not have the power to dictate a settlement.

An *arbitrator* is an independent person or panel reviewing the facts on both sides of the dispute and rendering a final decision by which both parties previously have agreed to abide. In so-called one-way binding arbitration, the business, but not the customer, is bound by the arbitrator's decisions.

Most businesses using third-party programs subscribe to an independent organization offering conciliation, mediation, and/or arbitration services. Among the benefits of this approach are the credibility such an organization lends to the dispute resolution process and the wide availability of such programs. The Better Business Bureau and the American Arbitration Association, as well as a growing number of state and local government consumer affairs offices and citizen-based groups, offer conciliation, mediation, and/or arbitration services at no or low cost to the business, while all are free to the customer.

Successful third-party programs have certain elements in common. Each of the following points should be considered "essentials" of such a program:

- Mediation or conciliation as an effective first step.
- Arbitration as a final decision-making step.
- Selection of a credible and competent third party. **183**

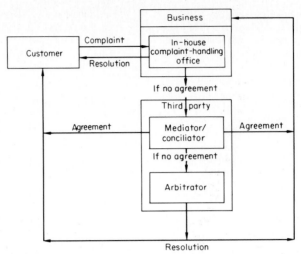

FIG. C-15 Flow of customer complaints from in-house to third-party resolution.

- Selection of fair arbitration procedures.
- Promotion of customer awareness and use of the program.
- Enforcement of agreements or decisions by the third party.
- Measures to ensure promptness.
- Follow-up and record keeping to maintain effectiveness.

Marketing Opportunities

Increasingly, executives view consumerism as representing new opportunities and profit potential, notably in the firm's marketing efforts. The basic consumer rights to have a choice, to be safe, to be informed, and to be heard suggest a framework for specific corporate actions to fulfill customer needs and create satisfied consumers.

New Product Opportunities. Today's consumer protection climate brings into focus new product opportunities aimed at protecting the consumer's short- and long-run health and safety. As more consumers express concern for their own and society's long-run welfare, totally new products or reformulations of existing products that fulfill both immediate satisfaction and long-run benefits will find a profitable niche in the marketplace.

New product opportunities may be identified by creating special task forces which continually monitor products on the basis of suggestions coming from the Consumer Products Safety Commission, congressional and regulatory agencies' hearings and investigations, consumer groups, and customers. Efforts might also be directed to the active solicitation of ideas from various experts, including nutritionists, home economists, safety engineers, and chemists. Bringing "outsiders," including customers, into the decision-making process is recommended.

Advertising Guidelines. Responsible, informative advertising benefits the consumer and contributes to a positive image among the buying public. All too frequently, however, advertising creates expectations about the performance of products that are not (or cannot be) fulfilled. To be sure, in a survey conducted by the Council of Better Business Bureaus, a majority of those polled responded that the business practices which annoyed them most were products not performing as represented and advertisements making exaggerated claims.

It is essential that a company determine its advertising credibility from a consumer's point of view and develop its advertising policy accordingly. In developing such policy, management should listen to consumer complaints and cooperate with outside industry and consumer groups.

The flow of persuasive information needs to emphasize not only what the consumer wants to know, but also what should be known to make intelligent choices in the marketplace. There are many examples of advertising which contain information directed at consumer education. Such advertising can be especially efficacious as a substitute for the present appeals to self-esteem and irrationality.

While advertising materials are in preparation, they are normally reviewed by the legal department for conformity to all relevant laws and regulations. In addition, a company's advertising policy should deal with accuracy, completeness, and usefulness of advertisements and other promotional materials. Those responsible for corporate consumer affairs should participate in periodic review of policy and in the ongoing assessment of specific advertising compaigns.

Product Information. There are a number of ways in which customers can be provided with useful product information. Among the methods currently employed are buying guides (nutritional information, performance criteria, open dating, unit pricing, etc.), installation and assembly guides, and product use and care instructions. The objective is to provide information that helps customers choose the "right" product in the first place so as to achieve better and prolonged product use. Accomplishing the task of providing the proper product information requires a coordinated effort between marketing, advertising, and consumer affairs.

To make it easier for the consumer to receive timely product information, a number of companies have established or are experimenting with toll-free telephone arrangements. Pioneered several years ago by Whirlpool, Polaroid, Clairol, and Procter and Gamble, use of "800" phone lines spread rapidly in the early 1980s. Among those that have recently introduced or are testing them are Drackett, Pillsbury, General Mills, Buick, Sony, Coleco, Atari, Kraft, General Foods, and Campbell Soup.

Consumer Warranties. A major problem facing consumers pertains to existing warranty practices. Congressional hearings and consumer complaints have repeatedly shown that sellers have been too preoccupied with the precision of the legal language used in warranties, rather than with the extent to which the document communicates to the buyer. The ongoing problems of customer understanding of difficult legalities and the existing loopholes continue to lead to customer dissatisfaction.

Whether or not the 1975 Consumer Product Warranties Act will accomplish its objective of resolving warranty problems remains to be seen. In the meantime, considerable progress can be made by adopting a concise, straightforward warranty, rather than continuing to add to the confusion with legal jargon and complicated loopholes. Whirlpool Corporation, for example, has simplified the language of its warranties so that they clearly explain what is to be done and who will do it. Similarly, General Electric moved in the direction of warranty simplification by removing the restrictions and legal language and replacing them with clear and concise statements. Corning Corporation even dropped the words *warranty* and *guarantee* and replaced them by the term *promise.*

It is useful for management to reflect upon the functional role of warranties in today's marketplace and to recognize that a warranty (or guarantee) is essentially an assurance made by the seller to the customer. It should not be perceived as a legal instrument that limits the seller's obligation to the consumer according to the terms of the warranty. In short, a warranty should give consumers some assurance, prior to sale, that the product will live up to the claims indicated in the advertising and sales promotion. If, for whatever reason, the product does not perform up to the customer's expectations, recourse should be readily available.

A Corporate Program

On the whole, consumerism is a positive development for consumers and business alike. As an enduring force in the marketplace, consumerism is responsible for far-reaching changes in business orientation and practice. Some generalizations on how to bring about constructive, positive corporate responses are:

1. It is necessary to adopt the proper managerial orientation and to listen conscientiously to consumer proposals. The role of consumerism should be viewed in terms of long-run corporate, consumer, and public welfare.

2. It is useful to establish a corporate mechanism, such as a consumer affairs unit, which represents the consumer interest in product planning, implementation of marketing programs, and review of customer policies. This unit should be an independent corporate entity reporting directly to top management.

3. Consumer complaints should be processed promptly and properly. Special effort should be undertaken to see that correspondence with customers is personalized and that complaints have indeed been satisfactorily resolved.

4. An effective response to consumerism calls for an integrated program of quality products, meaningful consumer information, and reliable postpurchase service. Product performance should match customer expectations; advertising and promotion should yield more factual and usable product information; warranty and service policies should be clear and comprehensive.

5. A control system should be established to help prevent corporate practices that inadvertently produce consumer complaints when product performance and buyer expectations are not harmonious.

6. A consumer information system should periodically inform top management of consumer problems which are the derivative of the firm's marketing practices and products.

7. Management should recognize that immediate, measurable results from its consumerism-oriented initiatives may not be forthcoming. Measuring dividends in terms of increased customer satisfaction and long-run welfare calls for extended information systems and new interpretations of existing data.

185

See also Advertising concepts; Consumer behavior, managerial relevance of; Environmental protection legislation; Ethics, managerial; Government regulations, business law; Government regulations, uniform commercial code; Insurance and risk management; Product liability; Product planning and development; Product and service pricing; Public and community relations; Social responsibility of business.

Appendix

Significant Consumer Protection Legislation

1872 *Mail Fraud Act:* made it a federal crime to defraud through the use of mail.

1906 *Food and Drugs Act:* regulated interstate commerce in misbranded and adulterated foods, drinks, and drugs.

1914 *Federal Trade Commission Act:* established the Federal Trade Commission and declared "unfair methods of competition" illegal.

1938 *Food, Drug, and Cosmetic Act:* strengthened the Food and Drugs Act (1906) by extending coverage to cosmetics and therapeutic devices; authorized standards of identity and quality for food products.

1938 *Wheeler-Lea Act:* amended the Federal Trade Commission Act by making it possible to prosecute for deceptive advertising or sales practices.

1939 *Wool Products Labeling Act:* provided for proper labeling of the kind and percentage of each type of wool used in products.

1951 *Fur Products Labeling Act:* provided that all furs show the true name of the animal from which they were produced.

1953 *Flammable Fabrics Act:* prohibited the shipment in interstate commerce of any wearing apparel or material which is highly flammable.

1958 *Automobile Information Disclosure Act:* required automobile manufacturers to post the suggested retail price on all new passenger vehicles.

1958 *Food Additives Amendment:* amended the Food, Drug, and Cosmetic Act (1938) by prohibiting use of new food additives until manufacturer establishes safety for human consumption and FDA issues regulations specifying conditions for use.

1959 *Textile Fiber Products Identification Act:* required identification of most textile products not covered by the Wool or Fur Products Labeling acts.

1960 *Hazardous Substances Labeling Act:* required prominent warning labeling on hazardous household chemicals.

1960 *Color Additives Amendment:* amended the Food, Drug, and Cosmetic Act (1938) by allowing the FDA to establish by regulations the conditions of safe use for color additives used in foods, drugs, and cosmetics.

1962 *Kefauver-Harris Drug Amendments:* required drug manufacturers to file all new drugs with the FDA, to label all drugs by generic name, and to require pretesting of drugs for safety and efficacy.

1965 *Fair Packaging and Labeling Act* ("Truth-in-Packag-ing"): regulated the packaging and labeling of consumer goods and provided that voluntary uniform packaging standards be established by industry.

1966 *National Traffic and Motor Vehicle Safety Act:* authorized the Department of Transportation to establish compulsory safety standards for new and used tires and automobiles.

1966 *Child Safety Act:* strengthened the Hazardous Substances Labeling Act (1960) by preventing the marketing of potentially harmful toys and permitting the FDA to remove inherently dangerous products from the market.

1966 *Cigarette Labeling Act:* required cigarette manufacturers to label cigarettes: "Caution: cigarette smoking may be hazardous to your health."

1967 *Wholesome Meat Act:* required states to upgrade their meat inspection systems to stringent federal standards and to clean up unsanitary meat plants.

1968 *Wholesome Poultry Products Act:* required states to develop inspection systems for poultry and poultry products which meet federal standards.

1968 *Consumer Credit Protection Act* ("Truth-in-Lending"): required full disclosure of annual interest rates and other finance charges on consumer loans and credit buying, including revolving charge accounts.

1968 *Hazardous Radiation Act:* required the secretary of HEW to establish performance standards for electronic products in order to limit or prevent the emission of radiation.

1969 *Child Protection and Toy Safety Act:* amended the Hazardous Substances Labeling Act (1960) to broaden its coverage to provide for the banning of toys and other articles used by children that pose electrical, mechanical, or thermal hazards.

1970 *Fair Credit Reporting Act:* stated conditions for the maintenance and dissemination of consumer credit records.

1970 *Poison Prevention Packaging Act:* authorized the establishment of standards for child-resistant packaging of hazardous substances.

1972 *Consumer Product Safety Act:* established the Consumer Product Safety Commission to protect consumers against unsafe products. Empowered the commission to set safety standards for a broad range of consumer products and to levy fines for failure of compliance.

1974 *Equal Credit Opportunity Act:* banned credit discrimination because of sex or marital status.

1975 *Equal Credit Opportunity Act:* outlawed credit discrimination on the basis of age, race, color, religion, or national origin.

1975 *Truth-in-Leasing Act:* provided disclosure in detail of all terms and costs of leases so that consumers can compare lease offers with other options such as installment buying.

1975 *Consumer Product Warranties Act:* set federal standards for consumer product warranties and established procedures for FTC rule making and legal action.

1975 *Fair Trade Laws:* repealed federal exemptions that protected state "fair trade" laws from challenge under antitrust laws.

1976 *Credit Card Surcharges Act:* amended the Fair Credit Billing Act to prevent merchants from imposing surcharges on purchases made with credit cards during a 3-year trial period.

1977 *Debt Collection Act:* protects consumers from late-night phone calls, harassment, and threats of violence by debt collectors.

1981 *Product Liability Risk Retention Act:* allows product manufacturers, sellers and distributors to purchase product liability insurance on a group basis.

NOTES

[1]See Stephen A. Greyser, Paul N. Bloom, and Steven L. Diamond, "Assessing Consumerism: The Public's and the Experts' Views," in Paul N. Bloom (Ed.), *Consumerism and Beyond: Research Perspectives on the Future Social Environment,* Marketing Science Institute, Cambridge, Mass., 1982, p. 4.

[2]This section is adapted from Lemuel Dowdy, Jill Goodrich-Mahoney, and Kerry Stoebner, *Handling Customer Complaints: In-House and Third-Party Strategies,* U.S. Government Printing Office, Washington, D.C., 1980.

REFERENCES

Bloom, Paul N. (Ed.): *Consumerism and Beyond: Research Perspectives on the Future Social Environment,* Marketing Science Institute, Cambridge, Mass., The Conference Board, 1982.

The Conference Board, *The Consumer Affairs Department: Organizations and Functions,* Report no. 609, New York, 1973.

Day, Ralph L., Thomas Schaetzle, Klaus Grabicke, and Fritz Staubach: "The Hidden Agenda of Consumer Complaining," *Journal of Retailing,* vol. 57, fall 1981, pp. 86–106.

Dowdy, Lemuel, Jill Goodrich-Mahoney, and Kerry Stoebner: *Handling Customer Complaints: In-House and Third-Party Strategies,* Superintendent of Documents, Washington, D.C., 1980.

Technical Assistance Research Programs: *Consumer Complaint Handling in America: Summary of Findings and Recommendations,* U.S. Office of Consumer Affairs, HEW, Washington, D.C., 1979.

RALPH M. GAEDEKE, *California State University, Sacramento*

Continuing Education Unit (CEU)

The *continuing education unit* (CEU) was conceived of in the late 1960s as "a uniform module for the purposes of recording and recognizing individual participation in noncredit learning experiences." The intent was for people to be able to document their learning activities beyond the last diploma or degree.

An ad hoc task force, purposefully national in scope, defined the CEU as "the equivalent of ten hours of participation in the recitation mode of instruction." The definition went on to include the further academic qualifiers of an appropriate sponsorship, capable administration, and qualified instruction.

The initial task force, itself an outgrowth of a National Planning Conference on the issue in July 1968, was reorganized into the Council on the Continuing Education Unit (CCEU) in 1977. The nonprofit CCEU now has a sustaining membership of over 400 individuals, affiliates, and major educational organizations. Interested parties are encouraged to become members in the appropriate category. The permanent offices of CCEU are at 13000 Old Columbia Pike, Silver Spring, MD 20904 (301: 338-7190).

Some of the specific objectives of the council are to:

1. Promote the development, interpretation, and dissemination of the best methods, standards, and ideals of the use of the CEU.

2. Assist in strengthening educational and professional standards in the fields of continuing education and training.

3. Serve as a forum for policy development and act as a clearinghouse for developments and methods relating to the CEU and its use in continuing education and training.

4. Engage in research that will provide more reliable and valid information about the CEU and continuing education and training at large.

Acceptance and Use. Estimates are that up to 1500 of the nation's colleges and universities routinely award CEUs. A similarly large number of associations, companies, hospitals, and organizations are also awarding CEUs for their in-service and related training programs. However, the great potential for the CEU still rests with the user sector of society. The principal qualifiers of an individual for the many forms of recognition that are related to career advancement include: (1) the level of formal education, (2) the experience background and a proven record of accomplishment therein, and (3) the demonstrated commitment to a lifetime of learning through participation in continuing education. A vast opportunity awaits the incorporation of CEUs of an appropriate content and achievement as one of the particularly current parameters in recognizing individuals for contemporary rewards. Such rewards may include initial hire, merit increases, promotion, qualification for membership or grade of membership, peer acceptance or acclaim, certification or licensure, and periodic recertification or relicensure.

Criteria and Guidelines. Criteria and guidelines for assigning CEUs to a noncredit learning experience have been published since 1974 by the founders and now the current membership of the council. The publication has been maintained up to date through several editions and is available for a nominal sum from the CCEU offices. Issues dealt with in the publication are needs analysis, the planning process, course content and objectives, instruction, completion requirements, record keeping, and the performance assessment of both the course and its learners upon completion.

Annual Conference. The parent council sponsors an annual conference on the CEU. The conference is intended for people in leadership positions as well as for planners and administrators of continuing education programs. Conference proceedings have generally been accessed by ERIC, where they are now available on microfiche.

Research. With the aid of limited outside support, CCEU has sponsored a 2-year research project that included a national survey of more than 5000 providers and others interested in quality continuing education. There has also been a collection and analysis made of existing pertinent standards. A national review panel has been enlisted for the development of a conceptual framework applicable to the newly evolving standards. A working task force has also been used to write standards and criteria for good practice in continuing education. With the publication of this research in late 1983, both the CEU and its guardian council have come of age.

See also Development and training, career path planning for managers; Development and training, management.

REFERENCES

Criteria and Guidelines, Council on the Continuing Education Unit, Silver Spring, MD., 1980.

Grogan, Paul J.: "Future of the CEU—Who, What, Where, When, and How," *Continuing Education Study Series,* Report no. 8, American Society for Engineering Education, Washington, D.C., 1974.

PAUL J. GROGAN, *University of Wisconsin–Extension at Madison*

Contracting Out

Periodically, since 1955, the issue of "contracting out" of internal government services to members of the small business community undergoes congressional scrutiny. It continues in a state of flux today with pressures to contract out government business counterbalanced by arguments that the proper way to fulfill commercial/industrial (c/i)[1] needs is with in-house federal employees.

Historical Background. In 1938, a special committee of the House of Representatives reported find-ing "232 business-type operations" of the federal government that were "carryovers from World War I."[2] It seems that major warfare generated pressure for the government to produce the additional goods and services it consumed. On the other hand, during World War II, the "tremendous expansion of requirements and the increased complexity of weapons caused the Government to rely much more heavily on private items."[3]

In 1955, a Bureau of Budget bulletin set national policy in the problem, stating, " . . . (since the) competitive enterprise system (is the) primary source of national economic strength (it) continues to be the general policy of Government to rely on commercial sources to supply products and services (for the) Government's needs. . . ." Subsequent bulletins in 1957 and 1960 carried the same policy statement. The Office of Management and Budget (renamed) said it again in its Circular A-76 in 1966 and revised it in 1967 and 1979. The current version of A-76 was introduced into the Senate on August 8, 1983, as "Freedom from Government Competition Act S. 1746" by New Hampshire Senator Warren S. Rudman. It was read twice and referred to the Committee on Governmental Affairs.

Prior to 1979, a government agency could contract out any private-sector purchase of goods or services simply because it was more cost effective to use the private sector. Since then, "The extensive changes made in the Circular and its procedures in 1979 and 1983 have served primarily to restrict the authority of agencies to convert Government commercial activities to private sector contract performance."[4] This is basically because of the time-consuming cost-effective studies which are now required.

Early on, the Defense Department, which still performs the bulk of the government's in-house c/i functions, made a commitment to Congress that it will not convert any in-house activity to an outside contract without a cost study which demonstrated cost savings. As Russell wrote,[5] taking into consideration the difficulty in making any kind of "revolutionary change in a large bureaucracy no matter how beneficial or desirable . . . and the fact that only minimal implementation was achieved in 28 years. . . . at best we can expect a slow, evolutionary change. . . ."

Senate Bill 1746. Perhaps the most significant change brought about by Senator Rudman's Senate Bill 1746 is the introduction of A-76 into Congress for the first time in its long history. Given congressional approval, it may put more teeth into the mandate that "the Federal Government procure from the private sector . . . the goods and services necessary for the operations and management of certain Government agencies. . . ." On the other hand, the exceptions given to agencies such as the Department of Defense and the Veterans' Administration's network of hospitals, plus the specific and detailed methodology prescribed for agency cost evaluation and comparison will almost certainly delay—and possibly negate—concurrence from agencies which plead for additional staffing as an alternative to contracting out.

For the Bill. In the opinion of David Muzio, a high official in the Office of Federal Procurement Policy, the requirement for agency cost-effective management study "is a policy designed to achieve economic and advanced productivity in the performance of commercial activities for the Government, whether they be performed by Government employees or by contractors. . . ."[6] The government agency establishes the scope of work and the performance standards. If it is efficient, the management study should be a simple one. If not, from 2 to 5 months will be required every 5 years to analyze the organization and its performance from every angle. The third advantage of A-76 to an agency, in this official's words, is "the Government determines whether competing contractors are technically qualified to perform to standard . . . only the lowest-priced contractor who is qualified to the Government's satisfaction will compete against the Government's most efficient organization."[7] In other words, government managers are given an opportunity to prove their efficiency and cost effectiveness.

Against the Bill. Not surprisingly, Kenneth T. Blaylock, president of the American Federation of Government Employees, does not agree with Muzio.

"Contracting out enables Federal Agency heads to conceal the real size of the Government from the taxpayers," is his expressed opinion. Others opposed to contracting out feel (1) it may bring a decline in the quality of services; (2) it is unfair to many federal workers; and (3) it undermines the controllability of federal programs and costs. In the 1970s a Rand Corporation study on security personnel found that "in-house personnel are more loyal and have a stronger sense of responsibility to the firm they are protecting." Others question whether contractors hire fewer people—younger, more blue-collar workers—at lower wages and benefits than government workers are accorded and whether in a fully employed economy they will be able to secure qualified employees at the same low wages that they are paying now.

Small-Business Task Group. Critical of what they called "the Government's growing intrusion into the marketplace," a group of small-business people met together under the auspices of the Small Business Administration in 1980 to discuss the problem of government competition as a threat to small business. The end result was a document issued through the Office of Interagency Policy by the Office of SBA's chief counsel for advocacy.[8] Some of the highlights of that report may be relevant. They wrote of government's frequent lack of appreciation for the differences between small and large businesses and

between tax-paying organizations and nonprofit, tax-exempt organizations. They cited examples from their personal experiences. The following is typical.

A high-tech, well-known testing service found its business dropping after a federal agency underwrote competitive testing services by funding nonprofit universities who could test for less money. A second federal agency granted equal de facto accreditation to all testing firms who requested it, despite the proven superiority of one. The final straw came when the state in which the testing service did most of its business established a monopoly by doing all testing itself, even offering its testing services at a reduced rate on an interstate basis!

Among the government facilities deemed most competitive to the small-business private sector are the following:

Military Post Exchange	Retail Stores
In-House Printing	Printing Firms
Advertising Circular Distributors	Retail Stores
General Services Administration	Printing Firms
U.S. Employment Service	Private Employment Agencies
Federal, State, and Local Parks	Private Campgrounds
Nonprofit Child Care Centers	Private Child Care Centers

On the Local Level. Within the last decade, state and local governments have greatly increased the number of services they contract out. During the 1981 U.S. Conferences of Mayors, 58 percent reported they had already reduced—or would soon be forced to reduce—many long-term community services because of their cities' weakened financial positions. Once they began contracting out, many found the idea favorably received by their citizens.

Today, the most often contracted out services by cities are solid waste collection and various other related services. In Tulsa, penalties are assessed to the contractor if solid waste collectors do not respond to a householder's complaint within 24 hours. Specialized skills and/or specialized equipment for short-term or seasonal use are probably the next most frequently contracted out. These, like those mentioned above, are "tangible services with clear-cut specifications . . . rather than intangibles."[9] Communities which have infrequent snowfall need no longer purchase expensive equipment which requires extensive storage space most of the year on the chance that it may be required for a few days.

Many innovations have developed among the cities which exchange information on their use of outside contractors for work formerly done by full-time city employees. In 1978, Gainesville, Florida, contracted out its vehicle repair work. Former city employees found jobs in the contracting private firms. The city saved about 20 percent in dollars, but more significant savings were achieved through lower vehicle downtime and fewer repeat repairs.

Widely used contracting services in large cities and small include the areas of public works, transportation, health and human services, parks, and recreation. Among the support functions most widely used, 45 cities contract out their legal services; 23 percent, labor relations; and 23 percent, some portion of data processing and tax billing. To retain a modicum of control, many cities assign a portion of a specific kind of work to a minimum in-house staff and contract out the rest as the work load increases.

No one pretends that the local contracting out picture is entirely rosy. Its favorable aspects include (1) forcing down of costs by multiple bids; (2) innovation and quality service if no monopoly is given; (3) avoidance of large initial costs to the city for equipment; (4) greater flexibility; and (5) better management.

Opponents of the idea say contracting out (1) may cost more; (2) may result in poor service; (3) may increase chances of corruption; (4) may result in an incomplete contract; (5) displaces public employees; (6) raises opposition from municipal unions; (7) entails problems in drawing contracts; (8) may be restricted by law; (9) may create problems in enforcing public policy; and (10) may fail to guarantee adequate competition for certain contracts.

Looking Ahead. it would be futile to hazard a guess about the outcome of the federal contracting out confrontation when—and if—it gets its day in Congress. Proponents of Senate Bill 1746 favor contracting out on the assumption that it could achieve budgetary savings approaching $545 million the first year. Opponents say the revised A-76 already exempts some 300,000 workers in the Department of Defense and the Veterans' Administration, because of military readiness in the first instance, and of the well-being of American veterans in the second. These two agencies alone could probably furnish as many small-business contracts as, or more than, all the other government agencies combined.

The U.S. Chamber of Commerce-sponsored Business Alliance on Government Competition, which favors the bill, considers in-house performance of commercial activities by government employees the biggest threat to small business. And small business, they say accurately, accounts for 65 percent of the nation's new jobs each year. Some small business owners say passage of the bill will not guarantee that small businesses will get their fair share of government contracts. They cite records which show[10] that government facilities which prefer to deal with a single large contractor can manage this by methods such as combining several contracts into one too large for a small business to handle.

Arguments on both sides are valid and made in good faith. There seems to be only one certainty at the present time: Contracting out on the local level will continue and probably increase.

See also Field services management; Government relations; Government services; Markets, government; Public administration; Small Business Administration.

NOTES

[1]Commercial/industrial (c/i) is an activity operated and/or managed by a federal agency involving a product or service that could be obtained from a private industry.

[2]From an unpublished study group staff paper, supporting *Utilization of Resources,* Commission on Government Procurement, Washington, D.C., 1972.

[3]*Ibid.*

[4]David Muzio, "Improved Management Through Competition," *Federal Manpower Quarterly,* Fall 1983.

[5]*Ibid.*

[6]*Ibid.*

[7]*Ibid.*

[8]"Government Competition: A Threat to Small Business," *Report of the SBA Advocacy Task Group on Government Competition with Small Business,* March 1980.

[9]"Alternate Service Delivery Approaches Involving Increased Use of the Private Sector," abstract of report prepared by the Greater Washington (DC) Research Center, Washington, D.C., 1982.

[10]"How Selected DOD Consolidation Effects Affected Small Business Opportunities"; *GAO Report to the Honorable Sam Nunn, United States Senate,* August 12, 1983.

HARRIET PREMACK SOLL, *Small Business Administration*

Contracts Management

All contracts, particularly those that are large and complex, must be managed. These are not limited to government's management of defense, space, or building contracts. Large-scale computer users; aircraft, ship, or bridge builders; architects; real estate operators; and hospital administrators routinely practice contracts management. The less successful firms give it only minimal support and attention. More successful firms formalize this activity. However, expert contracts management does not ensure a successful venture. It is not an elixir capable of magical alchemy. But its sound practice improves the possibility of success. Buyers' and sellers' interests are diverse with respect to private and public contracts. Each of these diversities calls for specialized attention. Due to the constraint of space, however, this article will concentrate on the phases, activities, and principles that thread through all the varied points of view of the contracting parties.

Contracts management is the control and influence of legally binding commitments—i.e., a contract by a second party to provide a product or perform a service—in furtherance of the first party's interest. Typically, the commitments are mutually binding, in that the first party pledges to do, or refrain from doing, some act in connection with requests for offers to perform; offers; negotiations and acceptances; monitoring of contractual performance; administration of claims, changes, and disputes; and control of assets.

Varied Perspectives. Control and influence of contracts are often the work of many people with varied titles. In all probability, they will represent many aspects of project management, including marketing, manufacturing, finance, law, engineering, procurement, and administration. Each person looks at contracts management from his or her vantage point. A financial executive sees contracts management as assets control—the commitment of assets to a project with a plan to maximize the financial return. A lawyer has preventive law in mind; if there must be litigation, the lawyer wants contracts management to provide reliable claims, counterclaims, and defenses. Engineers want to define, measure, and evaluate; they favor the procedural techniques used in contracts management. Marketing managers want sales and customer satisfaction: they will use contracts management to produce a winning proposal. A buyer will use contracts management to audit a seller's performance; in order to ensure a reliable future source, the buyer may use prudent contracts management to obtain costs and to grant the seller a reasonable profit. There's compatibility among these viewpoints. Each party wants to control and influence legally binding commitments, to his or her ends.

Universal Principles. Ten general principles help to describe and guide contracts management. They are common to all organizations and interests and give cohesion to the field of contracts management:

1. Contracts management embraces all commitments between the parties.
2. Contracts management is not automatically beneficial; its practitioners must regularly demonstrate its worth.
3. Contracts managers must be sensitive to extra-contractual matters.
4. Contracts managers must convert the contract into separately identifiable events.
5. Contracts managers must examine the contractual meaning of precontractual events and documents.
6. Contracts managers must evaluate all relevant surrounding circumstances to understand the other party's reasonable expectations.
7. Contracts managers must convert contractual commitments into financial values, subject to the policies of their organization.
8. Contracts managers must translate the language of the contract into the language of the organization.
9. Contracts managers must make a business, not a legal, decision as to how far to pursue their contractual rights.
10. Contracts management is often an unpopular element in a team effort.

Phases of Contracts Management

Legally binding commitments appear all along the contracts trail. They begin at the *precontractual phase* with invitations to make offers and the making of offers. They appear in the *contractual phase,* which includes acceptance, negotiation, and contract execution. And they play a large role in the third phase, *contracts monitoring,* which addresses the auditing of performance, disputes, claims, changes, subcontracts, and contract close out.

The Precontractual Phase. The federal government provides a good example here. It uses Standard Form 33, "Solicitation, Offer and Award," to start the contractual process. The procuring agency can select either a "sealed bid" or "negotiated" award approach. If a "sealed bid" is selected, any offer made is susceptible to acceptance without further contact between the parties. If "negotiated" is selected, the firm that tenders the offer has not made an irretrievable commitment. This choice of offer approach shows how commitments begin to take form before the contract is struck between the parties. It's an illustration of principle No. 5, that contracts managers must examine the contractual meaning of precontractual events and documents.

Proposal Procedures. In another part of the precontractual phase the process starts with the offer. It may be a bid, quotation, or proposal. In any case, it may be solicited or unsolicited. The offer will seldom represent the work of one person or organization. If it is a complex proposal, it will include the following steps:

Plan the proposal, with an outline and time schedule.

Develop technical, sales, and financial responses.

Establish the proposal's format and layout.

Write the material.

Direct the artwork.

Ensure quality and consistency.

Coordinate the data from various groups.

Obtain internal reviews and approvals.

A proposal must be believable and satisfy a need. **191**

If it meets those criteria, it will jump the first hurdle and be in the race for selection. In its development, several contracts management principles apply. For instance, how helpful can the contracts manager be? There are abundant opportunities for contributions, but there's nothing automatic about the contracts manager's value. He or she will have to demonstrate a knowledge of drafting, contracts, the seller's organization, and the seller's products. Here is principle No. 2: contracts management is not automatically beneficial; its practitioners must regularly demonstrate its worth.

Proposal Conditions. During the proposal process the contracts manager must evaluate foreseeable conditions. Will the buyer want a stronger warranty? If so, the additional warranty must be priced. In other words, the seller's contracts manager must be able to convert the buyer's wants into financial values. This is principle No. 7. But what if the seller's management won't, as a policy matter, accept a more stringent warranty? In that case, the contracts manager must establish a price for an alternative offer—again, principle No. 7 at work.

Another foreseeable condition is the anticipated contract. The contracts manager for the buyer and seller must examine those early letters, meetings, and sample products. They can have contractual meaning. These instances emphasize the importance of principle No. 5: contracts managers must examine the contractual meaning of precontractual events and documents.

The Contractual Phase. Legally binding commitments appear in this phase. For example: "I'll charge you $1000 to paint your barn red and you can pay when I'm finished." And the answer can be, "O.K., start when ready." There has been an offer and an acceptance—a traditional fixed-price contract. The painter, as his own contracts manager, will seek to "control and influence the legally binding commitments to further his interests." He will select workers, purchase paint, and use overtime and supplies as best suits him. But if he wants to be paid, he ought to know what this barn owner expects and be guided by that knowledge. That is principle No. 6: contracts managers must evaluate all relevant surrounding circumstances to understand the other party's reasonable expectations.

Negotiations. There may not always be a straight acceptance of an offer. Instead, there may be a negotiation. A successful negotiator is typically credible and knows his product, organization, and adversary. Additionally, he is a good listener, quick-witted, calm, patient, and persevering, a team leader, and organized.

A negotiator can learn tactics, but he or she must start and finish with the primary quality of credibility.

Graphic Support. Sometimes that quality can be exhibited by use of graphics. For example, assume the seller proposes a project on a cost-incentive basis. He or she estimates costs at $100,000 and would like a fee of $6000. A typical incentive would be for the seller to contribute 20¢ for every dollar overspent and receive 20¢ from the buyer for every dollar underspent. On the other side of the bargaining table, the seller might want full cost reimbursement, and a fee range of zero to $12,000. The shorthand description of this negotiation would be:

Target cost	$100,000
Target fee	6,000
Minimum fee	0
Maximum fee	12,000
Fee adjustment formula	80/20

This formula is displayed graphically in Fig. C-16. The fee is either increased or decreased by the seller's cost performance. Because the minimum fee is zero, however, the penalty will not exceed the fee and cut into cost reimbursement no matter how large the

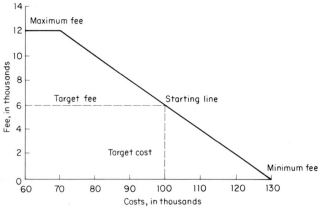

FIG. C-16 Graphic illustration of limited-cost incentive formula.

cost overrun may be. There are points at which the incentive formula becomes ineffective: the seller receives no added fee for spending less than $70,000, and won't be penalized for spending more than $130,000. As costs move up or down between these limits, the seller's fee will vary.

Impact on Others. Whatever his or her title may be, the leader of the negotiation team will be forming the basis for the contract. The leader will help determine which functions will be included and excluded and the size of the project. On the selling side, the "contracts manager" will normally be reducing the anticipated work of several team members as he or she agrees to cost reductions. That will not enhance his popularity. On the buying side, the contracts manager may have to agree to costs or fees higher than anticipated; surely, that will create a negative impact on his or her team members. Principle No. 10 will be at work: contracts management is an unpopular element in a team effort.

During negotiations, each side learns something about the other. For instance, the seller may learn of an opponent of the project within the buyer's organization; the buyer may learn of a patent infringement suit against the seller. This information must be stored, not forgotten. Each party should influence its actions so as not to be injured by these negative situations. That illustrates principle No. 3: contracts managers must be sensitive to extracontractual matters.

The Postcontractual Phase. This embraces several activities.

Contract Monitoring. To monitor contracts, a contracts manager must first execute two conversions:

1. The initial conversion (principle No. 4) is to express the contractual transaction in separate identifiable events. This gives a clearer view of the various commitments and permits them to be audited and controlled.

2. The second conversion (principle No. 8) calls for translating the contractual language into the language of one's organization. This is necessary so that assignments can be distributed to, and understood by, the subgroups performing or monitoring the work.

Thereafter, monitoring falls into a routine of periodic progress checks. These should focus on key areas such as completion of events by target dates, compliance to specified standards of quality and workmanship, and adherence to costs and budget limits. It is at this stage, of course, that such techniques as PERT, CPM, line of balance, milestone charting, and the like are applied.

Resolution of Disputes. Suppose a seller presents a contested claim of $50,000 for a change in specifications. The buyer agrees to pay only $25,000. Should the seller sue? Before deciding, the seller must quantify the cost of the suit in terms of legal expenses, loss of executive time, questionable publicity, and other factors. As expressed in principle No. 9, contracts managers must make a business, not a legal, decision as to how far to pursue their contractual rights.

See also Contracting out; Control systems, management; Field services management; Grants management; Line of balance; Network planning methods; Project management.

REFERENCES

Dib, A.: *Forms and Agreements for Architects, Engineers, and Contractors,* 2 vols., Clark Boardman, New York, 1981.

Hirsch, William J.: *The Contracts Management Deskbook,* American Management Associations, New York, 1983.

Spinner, M.: *Elements of Project Management,* Prentice-Hall, Englewood Cliffs, N.J., 1981.

Treuger, P. M.: *Accounting Guide for Defense Contractors,* 7th ed., Commerce Clearing House, Chicago, Ill., 1981.

WILLIAM J. HIRSCH, *Hirsch Associates*

Control Systems, Management

A management control system is concerned with the comparison of actual versus planned performance and the initiation of steps to correct any significant deviations from the plan. Such systems operate at all levels of an organization. At the lower operating levels the control system deals with detailed plans, while at the higher levels of the organization the system deals with broad, aggregate plans.

Management Control Concepts

Development of Plans and Standards. A measurement of performance is meaningful only when it can be compared with a standard. In some instances a standard may only be implicit and informal, but the emphasis in designing a management control system should be on explicit and formal standards. Ideally, every control variable should have a corresponding standard or plan against which it can be compared. For example, output of a manufacturing plant should be measured against scheduled production, actual sales should be compared with forecasted sales, and the actual cost of raw materials should be compared with standard costs.

Control standards are established through the organizationwide planning process. For example, production schedules are created through a complex process of forecasting the needs for products and determining planned outputs that meet these needs consistent with available capacities, existing inventories, relative costs of production, production lead times, and the like. Schedules are generated in increasingly fine detail through a hierarchical planning process in which each level adds details to higher-level plans. Many variables do not necessarily change during each planning period; for instance, standard material costs and policy-determined operating standards (such as the target inventory) remain in effect until conditions change or policies are revised.

Control as a Feedback Process. Planning is a forward-looking process, and therefore some uncertainty always exists as to the degree of attainment of a plan. Actual performance never matches plans exactly. Deviations arise because of unpredictable and uncontrollable factors in the environment of the organization, errors in execution, or imperfections in the plans themselves.

If a deviation becomes significant enough, corrective action should be taken. The corrective action may call for lower-level steps to bring performance back to the plan—such as working overtime to make up for a schedule slippage. A large deviation may require revision in the plan itself, rather than action aimed at achieving the plan. If, for example, an equipment failure in the factory causes a major delay in production, a revised shipping schedule may be the best way of coping with the deviation.

The greater the deviation from a current plan, the greater the potential penalty. The exposure to serious penalty can be reduced by maintaining tighter control. An important means of achieving such control is by reducing the *time interval* between the measurement of performance and the reporting of deviations. Figure C-17 illustrates how more frequent

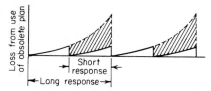

FIG. C-17 Effect of more frequent planning.

monitoring can reduce the penalties of deviations from plans. When a plan is created, it incorporates available information about internal and external conditions, such as current rates of sales, existing inventory levels, and raw material prices. As time goes on, deviations accumulate between the actual and planned conditions; the corresponding penalty similarly grows over this interval. If replanning takes place more frequently, the penalty is reduced. The shaded area in Fig. C-17 shows the total reduction in the penalty when the planning interval is cut in half.

Tighter control can also come from reducing the *size of the deviation* that is permitted before initiating more detailed scrutiny. In an "exception report-

ing system" (discussed more fully below), a deviation is not reported at all unless it exceeds some threshold (10 percent of the planned value of a variable, say). If the threshold is reduced (to 5 percent, for example), the situation is more likely to be reviewed and thus tighter control is exercised.

The *level of detail* of reporting also affects the degree of control. In a highly decentralized organization, top management might monitor only aggregate financial data pertaining to each autonomous unit; detailed variables dealing with such physical quantities as production output and inventory levels would not be reported. In a centralized organization, on the other hand, detailed physical and financial variables may be reported for purposes of coordinating action among lower-level units of the organization.

Trade-off Between Loose and Tight Control. Setting the proper degree of control involves a complex trade-off between the pros and cons of tight control. On the one hand, if control is too loose, a deviation between actual and planned performance may result in poor coordination among organizational subunits and the failure to respond in time to unforeseen problems or opportunities. Loose control may also reduce some of the incentives for managers to meet their plans.

On the other hand, tighter control generally calls for additional data collection, information processing, and management reporting. The cost and inconvenience of the "red tape" associated with tight control is likely to be resented by the persons being controlled. Tight control may restrict the ability of lower-level managers to exercise imagination and initiative in response to changed conditions. Close monitoring of detailed performance may also lead to behavior that is not in the best interest of the organization as a whole. For example, an organization that closely watches the travel expenses of its employees may prevent needed face-to-face coordination among geographically dispersed activities.

The improved coordination of a tight control system may sometimes prove to be more apparent than real. For example, the seemingly tight control provided by more detailed and frequent monitoring may in fact be spurious. A control system deluged with masses of data may not be able to screen out the trivia from the significant information. In the presence of random fluctuations in variables being monitored, frequent reporting may not provide a sufficient sample of events on which to draw valid inferences. For example, daily sales reporting for a national distribution system would rarely make any sense, since the sales figure for a particular day is subject to random variation in the market and vagaries in the shipping and billing cycles. The "noise" component of daily sales data tends to be smoothed out when the data are aggregated over periods of a week or longer.

A trade-off obviously exists between tight and loose control. The ideal is to strike the proper balance between the risks and penalties of insufficient control and the costs and disruption of overly tight control. The correct choice in any specific case depends on a variety of considerations, but in general the following factors should be taken into account:

Factors Favoring Tight Controls. These include:

1. Strong interrelations between organizational subunits (e.g., one unit supplying another with a basic raw material).

2. Significant potential penalties for deviations from plans.

3. The existence of an integrated computer-based planning system that reduces the incremental cost of close monitoring and frequent replanning.

Factors Favoring Loose Controls. These include:

1. Organizational subunits that are relatively independent of one another (e.g., selling in separate markets; using no common raw materials, technology, or manufacturing facilities).

2. Profit figures or a few other aggregate financial variables that provide adequate measures of performance and incentives for lower-level managers to behave in a way that contributes to the performance of the organization as a whole.

3. Unpredictable changes in the environment that have a significant effect on performance and call for rapid responses on the part of managers closely involved in the activities affected by the changes. (In an uncertain environment, lower-level managers may require tight controls to detect significant changes and trigger a response. Higher-level managers, however, need not be made aware of the changes if they are not involved in replanning.)

Design Issues

The design of a management control system basically comes down to the questions of what should be measured, what should be reported, and what the timing should be.

What to Measure. The management control system deals primarily in quantitative variables that can be measured and processed. Typical examples are sales in dollars or physical units, dollars of various categories of expense, number of employees hired, and the current volume of back orders. The objective in designing a control system is to choose the minimum set of variables that conveys the essence of what is going on of relevance to management.

The choice of variables depends in part on the level of management. At the lower operating levels of the organization, the variables are highly detailed, such as the sale of five units of item X to customer Y. The higher levels, on the other hand, deal in summary or aggregate variables, such as $5 million sales of product group ABC.

A variable may give either status or operating information (also called *level* or *rate* variables, respectively). A *status* variable defines a condition as of a given point in time, such as a cash balance of $17,000 at the end of the year. An *operating* variable defines a rate of activity during a given time period, such as sales of $73,000 during the month of April. A financial balance sheet typifies status or level variables, and an income statement illustrates operating or rate variables.

The proper choice of variable to describe a given condition requires a great deal of thought. Consider, for example, a variable (or set of variables) to describe *delivery performance* in a manufacturing plant that produces custom-ordered products. Performance might be described in terms of the percentage of jobs shipped on time. Such a variable ignores, however, the amount of lateness for a job shipped after its scheduled time. A variable such as *average days late per shipment,* or perhaps a composite variable weighted by a nonlinear function of lateness, gives a more complete, yet concise, measure of delivery performance. Similar variables must be chosen for all other aspects of performance that management deems relevant.

What to Report. Reporting occurs when a variable is displayed on a printed report or a transient display device (such as a cathode-ray tube). Not every measurement should necessarily be reported. Ideally, a variable should be reported only when it requires the attention of a decision maker. If a system monitors a large number of variables, it is desirable that the system filter out the insignificant data and only report information that will lead to improved decision making. In practice, however, it is impossible to identify all the relevant information and nothing but the relevant information. A compromise must be made between reporting too much (and hence not filtering out all insignificant data) and reporting too little (and hence overlooking significant information).

Timing Considerations. Measurement of a status variable occurs when the data base of which it is a function is updated. In a batch processing system, various transactions that affect the data base are accumulated over a time interval (such as a day or a week). At the end of the interval, the transactions are processed together and the results are reflected in the data base records. For example, inventory transactions (withdrawals, receipts, etc.) are processed against inventory records, with the resulting inventory balances reflecting the net addition to or reduction of inventory levels.

The age of status information depends on two **195**

components: (1) the batch processing interval and (2) the processing lag (the time period from the end of the batch interval until the updating is complete). If I is the processing interval and L is the processing lag, the minimum age is L, the maximum is $L + I$, and the average is $L + \frac{1}{2}I$. The average age of status information can thus be reduced by reducing the processing interval (i.e, by updating more frequently, perhaps even in "real time" as transactions enter the system) or by reducing the processing lag (e.g., by collecting the data more quickly and transmitting them more rapidly to the processing point).

Similar reasoning applies in determining the age of operating information, except that in this case the age is increased by half the length of the operating time period (since some of the events being reported occur toward the beginning of the operating period, others occur toward the end, and the average occurs halfway into the period). Thus, even with instantaneous processing, the average age of sales reported monthly will be a half-month.

If events of relevance to the system occur frequently and unpredictably, reducing the average age of information will give a more faithful representation of actual conditions. This, in turn, permits better coordination and faster response to unexpected conditions. In an airline reservation system, for example, events occur frequently, and so the value of up-to-the-minute information is very considerable. If, on the other hand, the situation changes relatively slowly or in predictable ways, more timely data may not be of much value. This is true, for example, of the typical inventory system for which daily updating is usually quite adequate.

Behavioral Issues

Measurement and reporting of performance always have behavioral effects. Their purpose is, of course, to motivate behavior consistent with the goals of the organization. Unless great care is taken, however, the control system may motivate dysfunctional behavior.

Compatibility of Individual Goals with Organizational Goals. When a variable is given serious attention, a manager will tend to behave in a way that makes the performance measure appear favorable. If improved performance in terms of the variable contributes to the achievement of the organization's goals, compatibility exists and the control system induces desirable behavior. If, on the other hand, "improvement" in terms of the measured variable actually reduces performance of the organization as a whole, the control system provides undesirable incentives. Although compatibility between control variables and the organization's goals is an obvious design objective, in practice it is impossible to achieve perfect compatibility.

It is not difficult to find examples of incompatibility. For example, a sales manager might be measured in terms of sales revenue, which induces behavior aimed at increasing sales rather than selling products having a favorable profit margin. Similarly, a production superintendent whose delivery performance is measured in terms of the percentage of jobs completed on schedule might be motivated to slight jobs already late and instead concentrate on jobs that can be completed on time. Flagrant incompatibilities such as these can usually be avoided, but subtler examples exist throughout almost any management control system.

Multiple Goals. A manager must deal simultaneously with multiple, and often conflicting, goals. Even in a private firm, in which a profit goal normally predominates, variables in addition to short-term accounting profit have to be considered. Undue attention to profit might motivate a manager to ignore the longer-term health of the firm; i.e., growth in sales, expenditures for research and maintenance, product quality, and personnel training and development. If trade-offs between accounting profit and the other variables were known, everything could be translated into a profit measure. Such relationships are not known in general, however, and so multiple goals must be established.

Surrogate Goals. A strong bias exists in favor of quantifiable goal variables. Thus, in order to measure progress in personnel development, the organization may use such surrogate goal variables as expenditures for training, number of training courses attended, or number of advanced degrees earned by employees. A surrogate goal tends to take on an importance of its own, independent of its relation to the underlying real (but unmeasurable) goal. For example, the personnel manager may become more concerned with the number of course offerings than with the quality of instruction or the relevance of material learned in furthering the long-term interests of the organization.

Limited Numbers of Goals. The goal variables that apply to a given manager should be limited to a relatively small number—perhaps a half-dozen or so. Beyond that number, goals cease to have much meaning as a guide to action; the manager would instead have to deal simultaneously with only a limited subset. It is therefore desirable to identify a few of the most critical goal dimensions for each manager. For a manufacturing vice president, for example, the critical dimensions might be cost, product quality, schedule performance, personnel development, and long-term improvements; for the dean of a community college, the critical dimensions might be the number and quality of entering students, the quality of teaching, salary costs of instruction, other costs of instruction, and contribution to the community.

Critical Goals. An effort should be made to choose a set of critical goals that are incommensurable and exhaustive. If an explicit trade-off can be established between two goals, a single composite goal should be used instead of the two separate goals, since this would reduce the number of goals with which a manager would have to deal. An exhaustive set of goals is needed to prevent undue attention to measured goals at the expense of unmeasured ones. For example, if an inventory manager were controlled only in terms of dollars of investment, the tendency would be to reduce stocks at the expense of poorer stock-out performance.

Each critical goal should, in general, be defined in terms of a composite variable. This is relatively straightforward in the case of profit or cost goals that can be broken down into components that have a monetary measure. Other goals, however, may require judgments concerning the weighting of goal components—such as a weighting of late jobs according to their lateness in measuring delivery performance. Since the trade-offs among components of a goal define desired performance of the organization, it is critical that they reflect the best combined thinking of the personnel most closely concerned with the goal in question. In the case of delivery performance, for example, the views of marketing and production control managers should certainly be considered.

Increasing the Usefulness of Control Information

Control information has value to the extent that it (1) provides some "surprise," (2) causes a decision maker to take action that otherwise would not have been taken, and (3) leads to improved performance. The ideal control system would thus report only unexpected situations that call for management action.

The information reported in a management control system always reflects a compromise between too much and too little information. If the system is too selective, it will fail to report valuable informa-tion; if it is not selective enough, it will report data with little surprise content and with little relevance to action. The proper balance depends on the relative penalties of overlooking relevant information versus reporting irrelevant data. The bias in most systems is toward reporting too much, on the (often mistaken) grounds that the recipient of a report can always filter out useless data. In fact, valuable information immersed in a sea of irrelevant data might just as well not exist if the recipient does not have an efficient means of selection. A well-designed reporting system can significantly increase the selectivity of displayed information.

Condensing Detailed Data. Transaction data are typically far too detailed to be useful for control purposes; they must first be condensed in various ways. The most common means is simple aggregation of detailed items within a broader category. Figure C-18 shows a typical summary report, in which detailed inventory items are aggregated within such product categories as "Major Appliances" (refrigerators, washers, etc.).

Summary Reports. A control system should allow the comparison of actual performance with a standard. A summary report should therefore give an aggregate standard corresponding to the aggregate actual value of a variable. If standards are available for the detailed items that make up an aggregation, the standard for the aggregation can be calculated by summing the detailed standards (the standard inventory level for all major appliances, say). In other cases, the standard may be a function of an aggregate variable (for example, a standard inventory of major appliances equal to 3 months' supply at the current aggregate rate of sales).

Supporting Detail. Summary reports always run the risk of hiding useful details. In order to reduce this risk, it is desirable for the system to provide easy access to the details that are included in a summary report. Figure C-19, for example, shows the breakdown of major appliances into dryers, freezers, refrigerators, and washers. The two reports are properly "nested," in the sense that each entry in the high-

---

INVENTORY REPORT

23 April 198X

Status	Number of products	Balance, $000	Standard, $000	Deviation from standard, $000	Percent of standard
In Control	9,242 (84%)	2,330 (71%)	2,405	− 75	97
Short (<50%)	1,025 (9%)	135 (4%)	415	− 280	33
Surplus (>200%)	779 (7%)	822 (25%)	271	+ 551	303
Total	11,046 (100%)	3,287 (100%)	3,091	+196	106

FIG. C-18 A typical summary report.

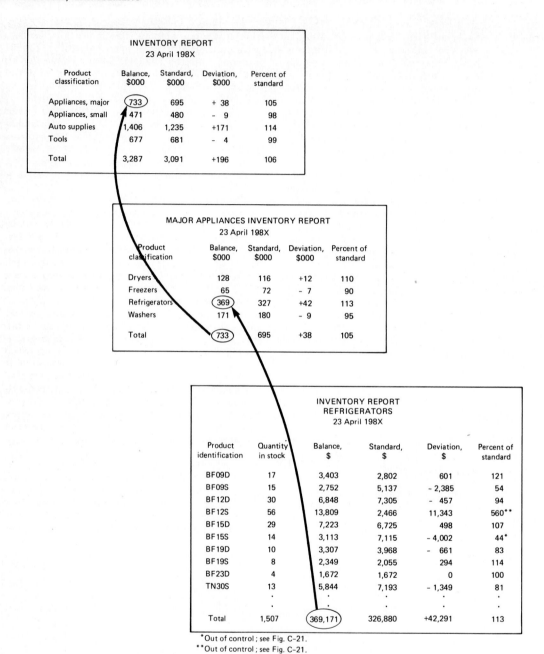

FIG. C-19 A hierarchical nesting.

*Out of control; see Fig. C-21.

**Out of control; see Fig. C-21.

level report has a corresponding sum in the lower-level report. This nesting of reports might continue several levels down to the most detailed level (individual products in an inventory system, for example). A hierarchy of nested reports thus provides condensed information, while still allowing a user to penetrate into the level of detail necessary to identify and deal with a problem.

An improper choice of aggregation categories may wash out significant information. In Fig. C-18, for example, the aggregate inventory is shown to be 106 percent of standard, with no product category seem-

INVENTORY REPORT
23 April 198X

Product classification	Balance, $000	Standard, $000	Deviation, $000	Percent of standard
Appliances, major	733	695	+ 38	105
Appliances, small	471	480	− 9	98
Auto supplies	1,406	1,235	+171	114
Tools	677	681	− 4	99
Total	3,287	3,091	+196	106

FIG. C-20   Aggregation within decision-oriented categories.

ingly in any significant trouble. In fact, however, the aggregation process may simply balance items with surplus inventory with items suffering from short supply. In order to avoid this problem, the aggregation categories could be defined in terms of the current inventory status of each individual item, as illustrated in Fig. C-20. Thus, the current balance of items in short supply (defined as less than half their standard) is aggregated separately; a similar process is used for surplus items and those items "in control" (that is, neither short nor surplus). Such a report provides a concise picture of inventory status and illustrates the importance of choosing relevant aggregation categories.

Exception Reports. If the deviation is small between the actual value of a control variable and its standard or desired value, a report of this fact is unlikely to lead to new action and therefore it has little value. It is only when the deviation becomes significant that action is likely and information about the deviation becomes valuable. An exception report only displays the variables having a large enough deviation for the information to have potential value. Figure C-21 shows an inventory report that only lists the items having either a shortage or surplus of inventory.

Standards for Comparison. One of the requirements for exception reporting is the availability of a standard with which a control variable can be compared. The standard should be the same as used in planning. Any planning variable can be subjected to exception reporting, whether it is an input variable or a planning outcome. For example, in a production scheduling system, standard raw material costs and standard processing times are basic input variables used in generating a schedule; an exception reporting system could therefore report when actual material costs or processing times deviate from the standard. The system could also report when actual production deviates significantly from the schedule. The control system thus monitors significant changes in the environment as well as failures in the execution of a plan.

Significance of Deviation. The second requirement for exception reporting is a means of determining when a deviation is significant enough to report. In principle, the threshold should be set at the point at which the penalty of not replanning when a deviation occurs is just matched by the cost of replanning. In practice, however, these costs can seldom be estimated with any accuracy. Normally a simple percentage threshold is set more or less arbitrarily.

INVENTORY REPORT
REFRIGERATORS
Items Out of Control
(Below 50% of standard or above 200%)

Product identification	Quantity in stock	Balance, $	Standard, $	Deviation, $	Percent of standard
BF 12S	56	13,809	2,466	11,343	560**
BF 15S	14	3,113	7,115	4,002	44*

FIG. C-21   An exception report.

In a sophisticated exception reporting scheme, standards can be determined dynamically by a model that takes changing conditions into account. For example, an inventory model might determine the optimal inventory balance based on current costs and current sales forecasts.

Adjustable Criteria. A system should allow the recipient of a report to define the (perhaps complex) criteria by which an exception is defined; furthermore, the recipient should be able to change the criteria as conditions or interests change. For example, when working capital becomes tight a manager may want to reduce the control limits that govern the reporting of items having surplus inventory. Rather than defining a surplus inventory item solely in terms of its percentage surplus (over 25 percent of standard, say), the manager may also want to know about all items having a surplus dollar amount that exceeds some threshold (e.g., $5000), whether or not it is over 25 percent surplus. By permitting a manager to adjust exception criteria, the system provides an effective filter between the detailed data base and the decision makers.

Ad Hoc Reports. Most control reports require someone to define in advance the information that will be reported (in terms of either content or exception criteria); the designers then implement a system that provides the specified information. Subsequent changes in report content are often expensive and time-consuming to make.

This inflexibility is guaranteed to cause problems. By the very nature of many unstructured management tasks, it is impossible to anticipate all desirable ways of reporting information. Even if designers could correctly determine future information needs, the variety of requirements would be large enough to preclude the routine preparation of anything other than the most commonly used reports. Information needs not satisfied by the standard periodic reports can usually not be satisfied at all within reasonable cost and response time limits.

Information System. The solution to this problem is to implement an information system capable of responding to unanticipated, or ad hoc, requests for information. The person entering a request expresses the desired information in terms of a retrieval language. For example, an ad hoc inventory report might be expressed as

LIST PRODUCT, BALANCE, STANDARD,
BALANCE − STANDARD
WHERE BALANCE/STANDARD > 1.25
OR BALANCE − STANDARD > 5000

Such a request is then translated into a program that a computer executes to generate the specified report. The system may allow "on-line" retrieval, in which case the report is prepared almost immediately, or (more often) it can be processed in batch

fashion and the results returned within, say, one working day.

An obvious requirement of such a system is a data base that contains the necessary raw data to process an inquiry—detailed inventory data, in the above example. In order to provide flexibility in preparing a wide variety of reports, the data should be maintained in disaggregated form; they can then be aggregated according to each specific ad hoc inquiry. Because of this flexibility, it is only necessary to anticipate the general nature of inquiries in order to provide the necessary raw data. This is much easier than trying to anticipate the exact nature of a report. Since the output from an ad hoc inquiry is in direct response to a specific request for information, the likelihood of its being useful is much greater than a standard periodic report (just as the response from a telephone directory assistance operator is much more likely to be used than a randomly selected name from a telephone book).

Use of Decision-Support Models. A decision-support model can be viewed as a particularly effective filter between the detailed data base and the decision maker. Output from the model might be either an optimal decision (such as the optimal production schedule) or, in the case of an interactive person-machine system, the predicted consequences of a proposed alternative plan (the cash flow consequences of a proposed budget, say). In either case, the output displayed to the decision maker is very much more condensed than the input data used by the model. By its very nature, model output is decision-oriented and therefore likely to lead to (desirable) action. As information systems evolve toward more direct decision support, decision makers will be less subject to the flood of irrelevant data that many current systems still inflict upon them.

Other Issues. The reporting system serves as the interface between the information system and decision makers. It is important, therefore, that reports take account of the principles of good human engineering. For example, careful attention should be given to the labeling of reports. When possible, a standard format should be used so that a recipient can grasp the content of a report more quickly. Graphic displays, rather than tabular formats, are becoming increasingly common. They are particularly valuable when displaying complex relationships among variables that need not be presented with great precision—a common requirement for information needed to support decision making.

See also Accounting, managerial control; Audit, management; Auditing, financial; Budgets and budget preparation; Exception, management by; Marginal income analysis; Standards and standardization programs.

REFERENCES

Anthony, Robert N., and John Dearden: *Management Control Systems,* 4th ed., Richard D. Irwin, Homewood, Ill., 1980.

Emery, James C.: *Organizational Planning and Control Systems: Theory and Technology*, Macmillan, New York, 1969.

Naylor, Thomas H.: *Corporate Planning Models*, Addison-Wesley, Reading, Mass., 1979.

Pritsher, Alan B., and C. Elliott Sigal: *Management Decision Making*, Prentice-Hall, Englewood Cliffs, N.J., 1983.

JAMES C. EMERY, *University of Pennsylvania*

Cost-Benefit Analysis

Cost-benefit analysis is a logical procedure for weighing the pros or benefits of an alternative program against the cons or costs of the alternative. Cost-benefit analysis (CBA) comes from economics and the optimal allocation of resources. It is related to capital budgeting in financial management. This entry discusses cost-benefit analysis within the context of program planning and the formulation of regulatory policies in government.

CBA was developed by European economists in the nineteenth century. In the United States it has been employed in connection with federal projects, especially water resource projects, since the turn of the century. It has gained particular attention since the mid-1960s, when attempts were made to rationalize federal spending through the planning, programming, and budgeting systems (PPBS) approach. Recently, both the Carter and Reagan administrations have asked for evidence that the benefits of a program outweigh the costs. Regulatory policy also has become dependent on CBA analysis ever since President Ford mandated that major regulatory policy proposals of executive agencies undergo CBA.

Cost-Benefit Analysis Procedure

The benefits and costs of a proposed program or project can be stated in both quantifiable and nonquantifiable terms. In CBA, emphasis is placed first on estimating and then on comparing the dollar value of all benefits and costs connected with program alternatives. Any significant benefits or costs that cannot be estimated in dollar terms are also identified and considered by the decision makers. A final decision is made on the basis of both the quantified and the nonquantified factors. The overall decision-making process in which CBA is used is described below.

Identification of Wants. Government programs are created to satisfy certain social wants. Carrying out programs generates satisfactions or benefits and costs.

Adherence to Objectives. Two basic objectives that guide governments toward optimal program choices are: (1) effectiveness; i.e., the expectation that wants will be satisfied, and (2) efficiency or economy; i.e., for a given amount of cost the most benefits will be provided or for a fixed level of benefits the program that costs the least will be used.

Choice of Alternatives. Marginal analysis in economics is directly related to CBA. In general, given limited resources on the one hand, and virtually unlimited public wants on the other, investments in various government programs should be made so that the greatest public welfare is produced. CBA guides decision makers toward an optimal mix of programs covering various public wants through indicating how well benefits compare with costs for each of the prospective programs. Also, CBA can be used to assist in the selection of an optimal program structure connected with a specific want.

Evaluation of Alternatives

Several approaches can be taken in evaluating alternative courses of action.

Monetary Valuation of Benefits and Costs. The guiding principle in valuing benefits and costs is what prices people would be willing to pay for government-provided goods or services. Valuations of benefits and costs can be made if competitive markets exist from which prices can be obtained. For example, the benefits of government-provided water recreational services for consumers could be estimated by using prices charged by businesses that provide similar services. In another example, the primary gain to society from an irrigation project comes from improved crop productions. The value of these gains would be estimated by multiplying the prices of the commodities by the additional output.

Sometimes existing market prices do not provide an accurate measure of the social value of benefits and costs. Problems are encountered when existing market prices involve the following: subsidization (e.g., passenger transportation), government policies (e.g., rent controls), a large recovery of taxes (prices too high), lack of effective competition (prices too high), industries with costs that decline over time (current prices higher than future prices), and presence of substantial external costs or benefits such as pollution (market prices do not reflect real costs or benefits). A difficult issue arises in the case of unemployed resources: what is the real cost of using resources that would otherwise be idle? In such a case analysts have to make price and demand adjustments to estimate the real social gains and costs of a program accurately.

Often there are no markets for the kinds of goods and services that will be provided by government programs. Some examples include highway safety (value of lives), saving time (value of time), improving the environment (value of clean air and water and less noise). For such cases the costs and benefits have to be estimated from imputed prices (e.g., ask people what they would be willing to pay to save travel time or to have a cleaner river). In regulatory cases involving safety, health, or pollution, where human lives are at issue, CBA can sometimes be employed to choose the alternative that for a given cost saves the most lives, obviating the necessity to value life. That variant of CBA is called cost-effectiveness analysis.

Present Value. Most program alternatives have expected lifetimes of at least several years, perhaps as long as 25 years or even more. The estimated streams of benefits and costs will differ from one alternative program to another. Lifetimes will sometimes differ among alternative programs. Moreover, money has a time value; i.e., the sooner benefits from a program are realized, the better; and the later cost outlays are experienced, the better. Variations in benefits and costs streams, program lifetimes, and values related to time call for the use of a common standard in evaluating alternatives.

Applying the concept of *present value* transforms the total lifetime benefits and costs into present dollars for each alternative. Thus all alternatives can be compared on the same basis. The present value, PV, of a stream of future values, FV, is determined by

$$PV = \sum_{t=0}^{N} FV_t \left[\frac{1}{(1 + i)^t} \right]$$

where t is a particular year from the present time ($t = 0$) through the end of the program lifetime, year N, and i is a discount (or interest) rate.

General Format. The estimated costs and benefits of a program are summarized year by year over its projected lifetime. All the estimates are made in current or constant dollars. The general assumption is that the benefits and costs of all alternatives are equally affected by inflation. Adjusting for inflation is done only when the values of one program alternative would be especially affected by inflation. One-time or nonrecurring costs are distinguished from recurring costs. Recurring costs and benefits and future nonrecurring costs are all expressed in both constant dollars and discounted dollars; i.e., present values.

Criteria for Evaluation. Several criteria exist to gauge how well program alternatives would be expected to perform in meeting the basic objectives of effectiveness and efficiency. Four criteria are:

1. Benefit-cost ratio (benefits/costs).
2. Net benefits (benefits − costs).
3. Internal rate of return (annual compound rate of return based on a comparison of net benefits stream with investment in a program).
4. Payback period (the time it would take for the cumulative undiscounted benefits to equal the cumulative undiscounted costs).

A program may be justified on economic grounds if (1) the CBA ratio in present-value form is equal to or greater than one, (2) the present value of the net benefits is equal to or greater than zero, (3) the internal rate of return is equal to or greater than a certain percentage (10 percent is the federal policy), and (4) the payback period is less than or equal to a specified number of years (usually between 2 and 5 years). The program that promises the most on the basis of the criteria would be the best economic choice. One program is sometimes superior on one criterion but not as good on a different criterion. For example, suppose program A is expected to generate $1.5 million in benefits at a cost of $1 million while program B is expected to produce $800,000 in benefits at a cost of $500,000. Program B would produce the better benefit-cost ratio (1.6 versus 1.5), but program A would yield the greater net benefits ($500,000 versus $300,000).

Sensitivity Analysis. Important variables are identified, assumptions are made, and variables are used in estimating the values of the benefits and costs. The basic analysis requires making assumptions about the future that the analysts believe are most likely to occur. Changes in key assumptions can lead to quite different indications about which programs are justified and which ones would be best to employ as reflected in CBA criteria. Therefore, the sensitivity of the criteria to the assumptions made in the analysts' model should be tested. Each key assumption should be changed to see what would happen to the criteria if the assumption were different. For example, both the estimated costs and the estimated benefits of cancer detection programs depend on the assumed percentages of the population expected to develop cancer.

Nonquantifiable or Intangible Factors. Significant benefits and costs that cannot be translated into dollars are identified and reviewed in CBA. It is the responsibility of the decision makers to weigh both dollars and nondollar-valued factors.

Application Issues

Several issues arise, and require consideration, during application of CBA.

Regulatory Field. In the regulatory field, CBA can be utilized to help determine the appropriate standard to set. It provides systematic answers to questions like what the extra costs and benefits are of setting the standard for ozone emissions at 0.01 parts per million instead of 0.02 parts per million. CBA has helped clarify the issues surrounding passive restraining devices in automobiles. CBA can often clarify the difficult trade-off between jobs and health. In some areas, like food additives linked to cancer, no CBA is permitted. Accordingly, Congress recently had to pass a law to allow saccharine to continue to be marketed. Economists have in general advocated more extensive use of CBA in the regulatory field.

Distribution of Benefits and Costs. A common implication of CBA is that if social gains outweigh social costs, a program is worthwhile. This conclusion is not necessarily valid. It may be vitally important for example, for the benefits or costs that particular segments of a society experience to be weighed more heavily than the same kinds of benefits or costs realized by other segments. The importance of distribution effects is easily seen in connection with assisting certain disadvantaged groups with job training programs, health care programs, and so on. Therefore, differential weights may be used to emphasize or de-emphasize the net benefits received by particular groups. The use of differential weights can substantially affect the computations of the CBA criteria mentioned earlier and thus show decision makers which programs would be expected to produce a desired distribution of benefits and costs.

The Discount Rate. Current federal policy requires the use of a 10 percent discount rate in computing present values and a 10 percent or higher internal rate of return. The 10 percent rate is a real rate since constant dollars are used in estimating future benefits and costs. Economists have noted that the long-term real rate of return in private industry is roughly 3 to 4 percent; consequently, some experts believe that the 10 percent rate is too high. Moreover, the highest costs of a program tend to come early, while the highest benefits tend to come later, where heavy discounting occurs, especially when using a higher discount rate.

Should Cost-Benefit Analysis Be Used? Requiring CBA to justify government programs or regulatory policies is very controversial. Opponents of CBA stress the difficulties as well as the impossibilities of measuring all benefits and costs accurately, particularly such intangibles as saving lives or preserving public lands for future generations. They feel that the quantitative information aspects will tend to outweigh the nonquantitative aspects. Proponents hold that decision makers are in a better position to make optimal decisions when they are given all the quantitative and/or economic facts in an organized and summary fashion. They believe that as a result both the quantitatively stated CBA and the nonquantified criteria will be weighed fairly and combined in evaluating government programming.

See also Accounting, cost analysis and control; Budgeting, capital; Cost improvement; Decision-making process; Environmental protection legislation; Program planning and implementation; Public administration; Social responsibility of business; Technology, management implications.

REFERENCES

Gramlich, Edward M.: *Benefit-Cost Analysis of Government Programs*, Prentice-Hall, Englewood Cliffs, N.J., 1981.

WILLIAM A. DEMPSEY *Temple University*
ERWIN A. BLACKSTONE, *Temple University*

Cost Improvement

Cost improvement is a positive approach to a continuous problem of all companies, that of reducing and keeping costs down through efficient and effective operations in all phases of management.

Fundamental Elements

A systematic approach to improving work methods and procedures can best be accomplished through the problem-solving techniques which are variations of the scientific method—analysis, hypothesis, testing, synthesis, and application. The early scientific management pioneers advocated "seeking the one best way." Later, the attack was on "waste," with the admonition to "work smarter, not harder." Early techniques were first applied by specialized "efficiency experts" or by industrial engineers and consultants. Today, the trend is to train the workers themselves to apply the more conceptual techniques of work improvement, work design, and the total systems approach. Workers, aided by specialists, put work simplification techniques into practice on the job, thereby enhancing the quality of working life through participation.

Work Design. From a cost improvement point of view, work design is a systematic analysis of the work performed in order to formulate the most effective way to approximate an ideal system of utilizing people, machines, and materials in the working environment. The four areas for improved utilization are (1) space and environment, (2) technology and energy, (3) product and raw material, and (4) time and people.

Space and Environment. This encompasses physical facilities, the plant itself, the layout, material handling, the workplace, and the flow of work. The social environment is equally important, including attitudes and interpersonal relationships of workers among their peers and with their supervisors.

Technology and Energy. This involves utilizing the most appropriate technology and equipment so that the human resource uses minimum effort to yield high energy.

Product and Raw Material. This area encourages the introduction of new ideas for the product, product mix, or raw materials that can change operations and work activities. The specific effects of changes in raw materials or maintenance and operating supplies can be evaluated through value analysis, value engineering, and standardization.

Time and People. Examination of these elements can reveal needs to (1) minimize time lost in waiting and traveling and (2) increase production through better methods, technology, or use of the human resource. Behavioral approaches also focus on motivation methods to build job satisfaction, high morale, and self-fulfillment.

Planning. Planning for work design encompasses all the following:

1. Design of the product, including size, shape, weight, material, and ultimate use.

2. Design of the process, since this determines the production system, the operations required and their sequences, dimensions and tolerances, machine tools, gauges, and equipment required.

3. Design of the work method, which establishes worker-job relationships by determining how the work is to be performed, the workplace, flow, and economic considerations.

4. Design of tools and equipment, which determines the fixtures, dies, gauges, tools, and machines needed to perform the operations.

5. Design of plant layout, which determines the total space required in terms of overall location of equipment, inventory service centers, work space, material-handling equipment, and worker/machine relationship.

6. Determination of the standard time for doing the work, which makes control of the job possible.

Organization. The planning process for work design may be organized by a team, or matrix organization, composed of design engineers, industrial engineers, and manufacturing and production specialists, to arrive at some optimal operation involving the above six factors. The broad functional areas of marketing, finance, and purchasing may be added to the matrix organization for coordination.

Installation. Following this phase, preproduction trials may be made before establishing the continuing production system involving people, machines, and tools for the most effective outcome. This applies to either product or service installations.

Control. The control function should indicate when methods deteriorate from planned methods so that corrective improvement action can be taken. Thus a constant analysis of current methods is required to follow up the improvement and installation.

Staff Role. The role of the industrial engineer or other staff specialist is to reduce costs by increasing productivity through continuing improvements. The role is that of the creator, motivator, innovator, trainer, facilitator, and catalyst.

Management of Cost Improvement. Planning, organizing, and controlling cost improvement programs should originate from top management, emphasizing an awareness of work improvement as a tool of management and promoting a companywide positive attitude and support. To this end, a training program taught by qualified industrial engineers should be available. Middle management should be offered an intensive course in techniques of methods study and its practical application for results. Supervisors should study work simplification and all its ramifications—work measurement, process planning, and managerial and motivational techniques.

Quality Circles. Groups of rank-and-file employees voluntarily meet together on a regular basis to identify, analyze, and solve quality and other problems in their area. Prevalent in Japan, these quality circles are growing in popularity in the United States. Motivational and behavioral research has found that employees involved in the improvement of their own jobs derive self-satisfaction and fulfillment with ready adoption and little or no resistance to changes. By means of quality circles, many companies teach problem-solving and work simplification methods to production and clerical workers, who participate in improvements to their own jobs. Quality circles promote creative thinking within the groups. Other techniques such as job enlargement and job enrichment have become increasingly useful devices for creating positive attitudes about work and jobs and thus for increasing productivity.

Techniques

Cost improvement typically follows a seven-part approach, as illustrated in Fig. C-22.

Analyze. After the problem is defined, a systematic analysis is made based upon the scientific method. This reveals the overall effectiveness of the total process and its flow. *Charting techniques* help to arrange detailed information and observations systematically so that the work study can easily be managed. Graphic analysis may take the form of a flow process, flow diagram, gang, or multicolumn chart. *Equipment analysis* using worker-machine charting and activity charts visualizes the relationship between workers and the equipment they are utilizing. In very precise and/or complex studies (from macromotion to micromotion) the workplace operation is analyzed through action-work breakdown, presented on micromotion, simultaneous (right-hand and left-hand), and operator charts. *Work distribution charts* help to show how well the work is allocated to individuals, particularly on clerical and service tasks.

Question Every Detail. Evaluation of the analysis requires asking the following questions: What is its purpose? Who is best qualified to do it? What is

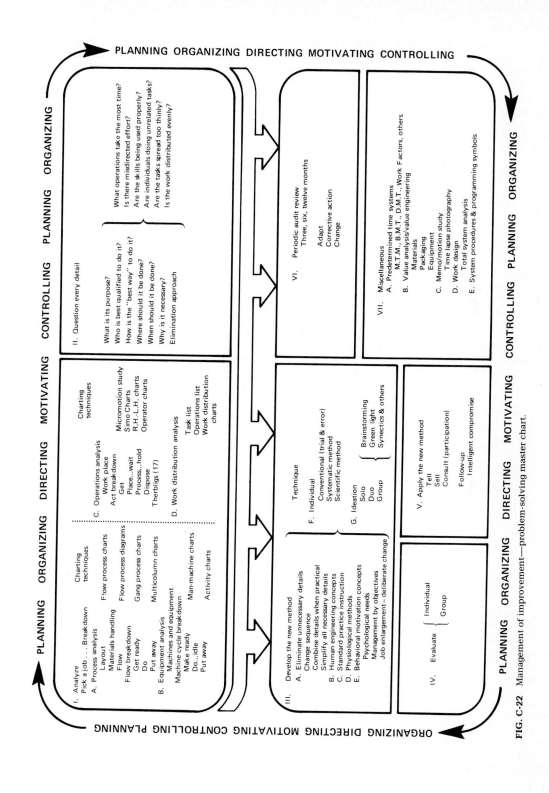

FIG. C-22 Management of improvement—problem-solving master chart.

the "best way" to do it? Where should it be done? When should it be done? And especially, why is it necessary? This last question often provides the starting point for elimination of tasks or parts.

For work distribution, further questions are appropriate: Which operations take the most time? Is this effort misdirected? Are skills being used properly? Are the individuals doing unrelated tasks? Are the tasks spread too thinly? Is the work distributed evenly?

Develop the New Method. When all information has been detailed systematically, essential procedures will stand out, clarifying the following options: (1) elimination of the whole task, (2) elimination of unnecessary work, (3) utilization of the most effective sequence of operations, (4) combining of steps, and (5) simplified work.

Sources. In developing the new method, human engineering concepts (motion economy principles) along with new discoveries in biomechanics involving physiological needs (ergonomics) can emerge as deliberate change is continuously sought out. Knowledge of models and statistical and mathematical techniques can be applied creatively to work flow, layout, material handling, and other functional activities for highest productivity. Once an improvement is identified, standard practice instructions, materials, tools and equipment, working conditions, and procedures should be formalized and followed.

Brainstorming. To bring forth ideas for improvements of all kinds, one may apply such creativity techniques as brainstorming, Mogenson's Green Light (Go Signal), synectics, and other applied imagination methods, either on an individual, a duo, or a group ideation basis.

Evaluate. Evaluation and testing of improvement ideas may be an individual or a group team effort. After approval or synthesizing of many components, a report is necessary, either to reject or to promote acceptance of the idea. Reports made on successful accomplishments, as well as on failures, indicate where more attention should be concentrated. Specifically, reports compare, review, evaluate, and provide feedback so that plans can be made to improve departmental operations.

Apply the New Method. Assuming approval of the work improvement plan, acceptance by members of the organization depends on the philosophy of management toward bringing about changes in behavior. Resistance to change can be expected and anticipated. Employees fear the unknown, especially the possibility of job elimination. This fear can foment insecurity and worries about whether change may entail new skills, new habits, different hours, or a different work environment. Antagonisms are often aroused when employees are shifted into a new area where their acceptance may be in doubt.

Managerial personnel may silently feel that the training and attention necessary to promote and plan the program is time-consuming, and may fail to acknowledge any gains in adopting a new idea or program. It is easier for many to "let things ride," to feel that "if things are going all right, why change?"

Union opposition must be anticipated, particularly where "changes" are part of the work rules contract provisions. Discussing program objectives and techniques and securing union cooperation in advance are very important.

Authoritarian directives should be avoided. Diplomatic "selling" of the change may be effective, but participation by inviting consultation and requesting input of ideas from users of the improvements will yield greater acceptance with the least resistance. Behavioral research favors participation in the decision process at all levels, and the development of work improvement is no exception. Workers vitally involved with decisions about their day-to-day work activities tend to accept changes more readily when job security is guaranteed and incentives provided for cooperation.

Follow-up. Once changes are installed, follow-up must be made to ensure success. The departments and people affected may have objections and challenge the adoption of changes. Intelligent compromise may be good strategy. Negotiations or even waiting for better timing may be justified. A follow-up at this point may reveal that a proposed change would have an adverse effect on other operations and departments. For this reason, the total system should be reexamined.

Periodic Audit Review. In a dynamic organization changes are constant. A periodic audit will reveal whether methods and products, materials, and equipment are obsolete or improperly utilized. Adaptations, corrective improvements, and changes can be instituted to keep the organization dynamic and viable and meet current demands of the market and competition.

Miscellaneous. Work measurement—with all its techniques of time study, standard data, predetermined time systems, work sampling, etc.—can be used for setting standards, scheduling work, estimating costs, and installing incentive systems. The use of these techniques points up areas for improvement, revealing inefficient methods and unnecessary work. The micromotion approach, using predetermined time systems, also reveals inefficiencies so that improvements can be adopted as a by-product.

Value analysis and value engineering, on a more technical level, can be of great help in reducing costs in materials, packaging, and equipment.

Memo-motion study will reveal inefficiencies of work effort over longer periods of time which are too time-consuming for individual monitoring. Also called time-lapse photography and generally known as production study, the slow film sequences of this technique record the ever-present occurrences of wasted effort and wrong methods.

Work design, as conceived by Gerald Nadler, is a total systems analysis intended to crystallize an ideal system which may then be suboptimized. This is the opposite of breaking down individual parts for examination. Instead, the individual parts are integrated into a total operating system for a synergistic effect.

The computer and computer graphics can be valuable tools in systems procedures and flow charting.

Cost Improvement Programs

By using all the management techniques described above, an optimum work design may be put in operation. There still exists, however, a need for improvement to offset rising wage and materials costs. Typically, a cost improvement program should be initiated simultaneously in order to maintain resilience and flexibility in constantly changing economic times.

At its core, a cost improvement program is one of increasing productivity, a need so great that the United States government established the National Center for Productivity and Quality of Working Life. However, this agency has been supplanted by White House conferences on productivity, which make recommendations embracing all forms of ideas to enhance the productivity of industry and government agencies.

Communications. A philosophy of work improvement must be communicated to all levels of management and labor to ensure success of the program. The expected benefits and goals should be specified so that understanding and appreciation will lead to shared enthusiasm and better employer-employee relationships. Emphasis should be placed on achieving goals of better and faster service through lower costs of materials and labor.

Suggestion Systems. For a cost reduction program to be fruitful, top management should initiate and completely support channels and procedures for an ongoing suggestion system. A responsible review committee with authority to reward and implement worthy suggestions can cut across departments and across levels of management, in order to elicit participation. *See* Suggestion systems.

Training of employees by industrial engineers in techniques of value analysis and creativity can be helpful to implant awareness of possible improvements and to establish a receptive climate for suggestions. Specialized forms (Fig. C-23), comparing present method and proposed method, with estimated cost savings, simplify the effort for workers proposing an improvement by spelling out the correct procedure for submitting ideas with supportive drawings or sketches.

Successful Programs. The National Center for Productivity and Quality of Working Life, during its brief existence, found that in companies successfully utilizing programs to improve productivity, a pattern emerged: (1) company support for the effort at top management levels; (2) recognition of the key role of the company's employees; (3) a full understanding at all levels of the purposes and objectives of the productivity improvement program; (4) establishment of goals and the development of valid measurements to reveal whether, and to what extent, the goals were being met; and (5) improvement in productivity sought to the extent possible without impairing job security.

Although company approaches differ, Beech Aircraft Corporation typifies what an all-out program of cost reduction can accomplish. The overall improvement program at Beechcraft is under the direction of the controller-cost management. The budget for each phase must be procured from savings realized. A work simplification administrator has plantwide responsibility to organize, train, direct, and follow up the program. Training in work simplification techniques makes all employees aware of the possibilities of job improvements. After employees learn the basic tools, they achieve results that amount to as much as a half-million dollars a year. Beechcraft also has a separate suggestion program, headed by its own administrator, with monthly and semiannual awards made by a committee reviewing and evaluating the suggestions. A strong program of management by objectives, with work measurement for control standards, is another factor in successful cost improvement programs. Quality circle groups can also suggest improvements and correct inefficient methods and processes.

See also Forms design and control; Human factors engineering; Marginal income analysis; Office automation; Paperwork simplification; Production/operations management; Profit improvement; Quality circles; Quality of work life; Records management; Suggestion systems; Therbligs; Work simplification and improvement.

REFERENCES

Barnes, Ralph M.: *Motion and Time Study, Design and Measurement of Work,* 7th ed., John Wiley, New York, 1980.

Lehrer, Robert N.: *Participative Productivity and Quality of Work Life,* Prentice-Hall, Englewood Cliffs, N.J., 1982.

Reports of the National Commission on Productivity and Quality of Work Life, Government Printing Office, Washington, D.C., 1975–1978.

Rosow, Jerome (Ed.): *Productivity, Prospect* for *Growth,* Van Nostrand Reinhold, New York, 1981.

Rukeyser, William (Ed.): *Working Smarter,* Viking Press, New York, 1982.

White House Conferences on Productivity: Reports, The White House, Washington, D.C., 1983.

HAROLD F. PUFF, *Miami University*

COST—REDUCTION REPORT

DESCRIPTION OF ITEM INVOLVED   FILE   11-B
DEPT.   Finished stock & shipping   DEPT. NO.   64   DATE
OPERATION   Marking with name and address of cosignee   PRODUCT   Cartons to be shipped
OBJECT OF ANALYSIS   To determine possible savings through stamping instead of stenciling

---

Comparison

Present method	Proposed method
Machine	Machine
Tools: Fountain stencil brush and precut stencil	Tools: Rubber stamp and stamp pad
Description: Stencils are prepared in advance and kept on file for all major cosignees, and name and address are stenciled on each carton	Description: Rubber stamps would be made up for all major cosignees, and name and address are stamped on each carton

Cost of operations involved:	$ per	Cost of operations involved:	$ per
Labor	carton	Labor	carton
0.16 minute per carton @ $3.00 per labor-hour	0.0080	0.05 minute per carton @ $3.00 per labor-hour	0.0025
Materials		Materials	
Miscellaneous		Miscellaneous	
Total of above items	0.0080	Total of above items	0.0025

Estimate of savings:
     Saving with proposed change ($0.0080 − $0.0025) equals $0.0055 per carton
     Probable yearly requirements 1,250,000 cartons   Estimated by   Sales dept.
     Estimated savings per year (based on 1,250,000 per year) $6875.00
     Probable savings per year $6500.00

Estimated cost of change:
   Design $ est. by   Less total cost of change . . . . $ 500.00
   Equipment $500   "   "   Net savings first year $6000.00
   Installation $ "   "   New method would pay for itself in months   1
     $ "   "
     $ "   "   Note: 100 rubber stamps required at $5.00 each
   Total cost
   of change $500.00   Suggested by   John Ryan

         Report prepared by   T. A. Wilson

cc to	Attached are	Date	Date
	1 Sheets drawings	First considered	Expen. appr.
	Sheets prints	Investgn. started	Installed
	2 Sheets details	Rept. submitted	Final rept.

FIG. C-23   Cost-reduction report. (Source: Ralph M. Barnes, *Motion and Time Study*, 6th ed., John Wiley, New York, 1968, p. 39.)

Credit Management

Credit is defined as the delivery of goods, money, or services today in exchange for a promise to pay at an agreed-upon future date. *Credit management* determines the degree of probability that payment will be received as promised and takes appropriate collection action when it is not.

Accounts Receivable Management. When credit is extended an account, or when a note receivable is accepted and it remains open until payment is received, an account receivable is created. Credit management is directed toward the management of this important asset.

Objectives. Credit management objectives should harmonize with those of the organization as a whole. They should include protection of the account receivable investment through (1) the avoidance of bad debt loss, (2) the acceleration of cash flow through intelligent collection efforts, and (3) the enhancement of profitable sales through the wise extension of credit.

Records. An accounts receivable aging record keeps track of individual customer (and total) amounts due by month in which the billing originated. At intervals, an aged total of each customer's account is run. This aging shows the total amount owing, broken down by (1) amount not yet due, and by (2) amounts 30, 60, and 90 days past due. By totaling the account agings of all customers, it is possible to arrive at an accounts receivable aging for a sales territory, a division, or the company as a whole.

Measurements. The condition of accounts receivable is measured by applying a percentage to each of the aging categories. An Accounts Receivable Aging report looks like this:

| Customer | Total | Current | Accounts past due, in days | | |
			30–60	60–90	Over 90
ABC Co.	$25,000	$15,000	$5000	$3000	$2000
DEF Co.	35,000	30,000	3000	2000	0
Total	$60,000	$45,000	$8,000	$5,000	$2,000
Percent	100%	75%	14%	8%	3%

Accounts receivable can also be measured as a comparison against sales. This method calculates the number of average days *credit* sales represented by accounts receivable. The result is the *collection period* and/or *days sales outstanding* (DSO), for which the formula is:

$$\text{Days sales outstanding} = \frac{\text{Accounts receivable}}{\text{Average days credit sales}}$$

$$\text{Average days credit sales} = \frac{\text{Credit sales for period}}{\text{No. of days in period}}$$

Factors affecting the collection period are (1) credit worthiness of sales prospect list, (2) terms of sales and early payment discount, and (3) collection follow-up.

Generally speaking, DSO should be no greater than one and one-third of the days stipulated in the terms of sale.

The Credit Decision. Credit management requires a decision: (1) credit approval on regular terms, (2) credit refusal with cash payment required, or (3) something between the two.

The credit decision is based upon an appraisal of the *three Cs of credit:* character, capacity, and capital. *Character,* most important of the three, is the debtor's determination to live up to commitments even when the going gets rough. *Capacity* is the ability to operate successfully so as to meet obligations. *Capital* relates to the finances available to the debtor.

Credit limits. Making the decision effective in a situation that includes repeated demands for credit requires establishing a credit line, or credit limit, in advance. Otherwise, each individual order must be approved or declined as it occurs. Once a credit limit is set up, orders go through automatically until the total of unpaid orders reaches the credit limit.

Credit Information. The credit decisions must be based upon an objective evaluation of facts. Therefore, the credit manager must know and examine key fact sources.

1. *Internal sources,* in the case of an existing customer, come first. What has the volume of sales been, have the sales been profitable, and has payment been prompt?

2. *If the customer is new,* the credit investigation will look to outside sources. Suppliers can be required to furnish their payment experience. The customer's bank—at the customer's request—can furnish general information concerning the soundness of the relationship.

Collections. Collection efforts are required when an account remains unpaid past the due date. Who makes the contact will depend on organizational policy. A contact between salesperson and purchasing agent may be desired, or a follow-up on the part of the credit department with the customer's accounts payable department may be more effective.

Collection by phone is usually effective. The collector should be well-prepared in advance, and the approach should be forcefully diplomatic. The objective is to reach agreement on the payment date; if payment is not received as promised, there should be immediate follow-up.

Collection by letter should include a follow-up sequence. Form letters can be effective; they are essential when amounts are small, as in retail accounts. In any case, the letter should state the amount owing and when it is due and make demand for payment.

Collection agencies are available to render assistance. Fees are on a sliding scale and contingent on collection.

Out-of-court arrangements can be worked out in the case of a debtor temporarily unable to pay. An installment note can be taken to allow a breathing spell. Or an extra amount on each new order can be required to apply on the old account.

Commercial attorneys, members of the Commercial Law League of America, specialize in collection matters as well as cases involving the Bankruptcy Reform Act of 1978. Chapter 7 of the act covers straight liquidation, while Chapter 11 involves financial reorganization and continued operation.

When an account is uncollectable, it must be written off as a bad debt. This can be done as a direct charge against operations or as a charge against a previously established bad-debt reserve.

See also Accounting, managerial control; Cash management; Consumerism and consumer protection legislation; Financial management, bank relations; Financial statement analysis; Sales management.

REFERENCES

Beckman, Theodore, and Ronald S. Foster: *Credits and Collections*, 8th ed., McGraw-Hill, New York, 1969.

Christie, George N., and Albert E. Bracuti: *Credit Management*, Credit Research Foundation, Lake Success, N.Y.

Prochnow, Herbert V. (Ed.): *Bank Credit: An In-Depth Study of Credit and Loan Practices*, Harper & Row, New York, 1981.

WILLIAM H. BRYAN, *Orleans, Massachusetts*

Data Bases, Commercial

Computerized data bases can provide quick access to information needed to make business and investment decisions. A *data base* is a comprehensive listing of information on a given subject stored in a computer. Users access the data base directly, using a personal computer, time-sharing terminal, or communicating word processor with a telephone hookup. Computerized data bases offer not only speed in acquiring information but also the ability to perform multiconcept searches. For example, marketing information on poultry product trade with the People's Republic of China for the last 5 years could be obtained by searching appropriate data bases.

There are two types of data bases: reference and source. A *reference data base* provides bibliographic citations to, or abstracts of, articles in periodicals, journals, newspapers, scientific and technical reports, and other sources. The complete text of an article may have to be obtained from a corporate, research, or public library. Some data base services, however, offer the full text of an article on request. A reference data base may also provide descriptions of projects, expertise of individuals, and other nonprint sources. A *source data base* may provide both text

and numeric information—including full text of an article, charts and graphs, and dictionary and handbook type of information.

Many companies produce specific information-content data bases for commercial distribution. Examples are: (1) IDS (HARFAX Database Publishing, Cambridge, Massachusetts), a data base which provides marketing and financial statistics on 65 key industries; and (2) DISCLOSURE ONLINE (Disclosure Incorporated, Bethesda, Maryland), a data base of corporate information which includes extracts of significant data filed by companies with the Securities and Exchange Commission.

The proliferation of data bases has resulted in the growth of data base vendors or companies which provide on-line access to hundreds of individual data bases. Examples include:

1. DIALOG (Dialog Information Services, Inc., Palo Alto, California), which operates the world's largest system with access to over 170 data bases, covering all major subject areas

2. BRS (Bibliographic Retrieval Services, Latham, New York), which provides access to major scientific, medical, social science, and business databases

3. DOW JONES NEWS/RETRIEVAL (Dow Jones and Company, Inc., Princeton, New Jersey), which provides business and financial information in four information groups of business and economic news, Dow Jones quotes, financial and investment services, and general news and information

4. ORBIT (SDC Information Services, Santa Monica, California), which provides reference and source information primarily in the fields of chemistry, pharmaceuticals, energy, engineering, and government

5. THE SOURCE (Source Telecomputing Corporation, McLean, Virginia), which provides communications and financial services, including commodity news services, market indicators, business news, and currency exchange rates; and information services, including access to current UPI news searches and abstracts from 27 business journals

These and other vendors offer a wide variety of services, including on-line ordering of documents located through searching; current awareness service, in which updated references on a subject are automatically received by a requestor; and consultancy services. Users of these data bases may require some specialized training (often provided by the vendors) in how to use the system. Contract options for obtaining services may include purchase, rental, or subscription plans.

For further information on data bases, data base producers, and data base vendors, consult: (1) *Information Sources* (The Information Industry Association, Washington, D.C.), the annual directory of the Industry Information Association; (2) *EUSIDIC Database Guide* (Learned Information, Inc., Medford,

New Jersey), a directory which lists over 1400 data bases available worldwide; and (3) *Directory of Online Databases* (Cuadra Associates, Santa Monica, California), a quarterly publication which describes the over 1400 data bases of all types and the 200 on-line services available throughout the world.

See also Computer software, data base management; Information sciences; Information sources; Management information systems (MIS).

REFERENCES

Guillet, D.: "On-Line Databanks," *Administrative Management*, July 1980, pp. 44–47.

Trenchard, B.: "New Data Bases for Management," *Administrative Management*, February 1979, pp. 59–61.

Inez L. Ramsey, *James Madison University*

Decision-Making Process

Decision making is a mental process by which a manager gathers and uses data. By questioning others, sifting the answers to find relevant information, and analyzing data, managers, individually and in teams, manage and control information and ultimately their business environment.

There are basically two types of decisions, and each requires a different process. *Strategic* decision making determines *what* the organization wants to be. It is a framework that guides those choices that determine the nature and direction of an organization. *Operational* decision making determines *how* the organization should get where it wants to go. It is a framework that guides how individual managers or

| What | | Strategy | |
How	Clear		Unclear
Effective	Clear strategy and effective operations have equalled success in the past and will in the future		Unclear strategy but effective operations have equalled success in the past, but success doubtful in the future
Ineffective	Clear strategy but ineffective operations have sometimes worked in the past in the short run, but increasing competition makes success doubtful in the future		Unclear strategy and ineffective operations have equalled failure in the past and will in the future

FIG. D-1 Strategy and operations: A what/how relationship.

teams organize information, investigate situations, arrive at choices, and implement decisions. Figure D-1 illustrates the relationship between strategy and operations. Each is critical to an organization's success, and each requires a separate process.

Strategic Decisions

Setting strategy is a task that belongs to top management. Only senior executives have the responsibility for determining where the organization is headed, though key line and staff executives must be sure that their respective functions have a clear strategy that is in line with the overall direction of the organization. If top management is not in control of the strategy formulation process, the nature and direction of the organization will be determined implicitly and haphazardly by others inside or outside the organization. Government regulations, banks, competition, labor unions, or middle management will in effect usurp the role of senior managers. The consequences can include poor product and market decisions which may eventually cause serious harm to the health of the whole organization.

The strategy formulation process begins with the concept of the *driving force,* the primary determiner of the organization's product or service scope and market scope. The driving force is the key controlling concept of the organization's strategy.

There are nine strategic areas that influence the nature and direction of any organization. They are sources for an organization's driving force. They can be grouped into three basic categories.

Category	Strategic Area
Products/markets:	Products offered
	Market needs
Capabilities:	Technology
	Production capability
	Method of sale
	Method of distribution
	Natural resources
Results:	Size/growth
	Return/profit

Once the organization's driving force is determined, a coherent strategic framework can be defined integrating products and markets, capabilities to support them, the organization's growth and return targets, and the allocation of its resources.

An example of how the driving force determines the future product and market scope involves a company that provides various products to the electrical

energy field. It developed a production capability driving force and redefined and broadened its product characteristics to reflect that force. These product characteristics included:

Industrial products

Electrical, mechanical, metallurgical properties

High-quality, high-reliability requirements

After-sale service requirements

Compatibility with high technology inputs

Low content of ferrous metals

In addition, several of the organization's market characteristics changed significantly. It shifted its focus to industries with a few large customers. It also sought specific customers who could not supply their own after-sale service and who required a system rather than a single product. Geographically, the company decided it would no longer cover the entire country, but would concentrate on major industrial areas.

After the driving force is determined and a strategic framework is put in place, strategy must be implemented. Implementation requires communication of the strategy. Mission statements for departments or business units must reflect the organization's strategy. Individual managers must be able to carry the organization's strategy in their heads and to make day-to-day decisions according to the strategy.

The implementation of strategy is an ongoing process. Besides the communication of strategy throughout the organization, implementation requires the recognition and resolution of critical issues. *Critical issues* are those major changes, modifications, and additions to the organization's structure and systems, to its capabilities and resources, and to its information needs and management that result from setting strategy. These issues must be resolved for the strategy to succeed.

Critical issues fall into four broad categories:

The Alignment of Business Units. The strategy of the organization may require a realignment of the existing business units or product/market groups. In some instances, these groups will be emphasized, in other instances, deemphasized, reorganized, or regrouped.

Communications. Getting the word out means more than talking or writing a memorandum. Sometimes part of the strategy should not be communicated to everyone. In other instances, communication, understanding, and commitment to the strategy is a critical issue because of such factors as different points of view, language, or geographic barriers.

Resource Capabilities. An organization's strategy will bring to the surface strengths and weaknesses of its human resources. In some instances, new skills or new people are required. In addition to human resources, an organization must keep pace with the technology of the industry. New equipment, procedures, or suppliers may be indicated.

The External Environment. Competition, the economy, the political climate, and the attitudes of managers and employees have a major effect on organizations. Each of these factors can influence the organization's capability to achieve its strategy.

Strategic decision making is a process. It begins with the role of top management—the people in an organization with the responsibility to establish the framework which guides the choices that determine the nature and direction of an organization. The first part of the strategy formulation process is to determine the organization's driving force, the primary determiner of the organization's product or service scope and market scope. From this driving force, top management sets the strategic framework, an integrated definition of products and markets, capabilities, growth and return targets, and allocation of resources. This strategic framework must be communicated and implemented. During the implementation, critical issues will surface and must be resolved.

Operational Decisions

Once the strategy is set, the organization must determine *how* to carry it out. Operational decision making is equally critical to an organization's success. Excellent organizations (listed in the upper left quadrant of Fig. D-1) are proficient in *both* strategic and operational decision making.

Operational decision making involves four rational processes. The first concerns organizing. Effective managers sort out situations by asking pertinent questions and setting priorities among situations. Second, in addition to their ability to organize, capable managers are good at investigating. They follow a logical sequence that allows them to determine what information is relevant and critical. A third rational process concerns making choices. Effective managers set criteria for choices, evaluate alternatives against these criteria, and consider the risks associated with their choices. The fourth such process is implementing decisions. Good managers anticipate what might go wrong and take specific actions to prevent adverse consequences or to minimize their effect.

These four patterns of thinking cover all the operational decision making that managers and employees perform day to day. Table D-1 shows these processes and their relationship to time.

Situation Appraisal

Situation appraisal is a rational process for setting priority among concerns. In addition to setting prior-

ity, situation appraisal helps a manager decide which type of rational process should be used to resolve each concern:

Problem: Something is not performing as expected.

Decision: A course of action must be selected from a range of alternatives.

Potential Problem: Something might go wrong that will affect a decision adversely.

Situation appraisal is a four-step process: (1) recognizing concerns, (2) separating concerns into manageable pieces, (3) setting priorities, (4) planning the resolution of concerns.

A *concern* is anything that prompts managers to act. How do managers or teams recognize concerns? Most concerns are fairly obvious. An employee reports that a piece of equipment has broken down. A memo from higher management identifies an action to be taken or defines a problem that must be solved. Organizational changes bring a need to select more people or equipment. A problem-solving team decides to improve productivity in the plant. A manager thinks through how he or she can exceed performance targets. But, other concerns are more difficult to recognize. The actions of competitors or technological changes, once recognized, may carry a responsibility for individual managers or whole departments within an organization to take action. Opportunities may be particularly difficult to recognize, but they also require action. Changes in consumer preference or the availability of unanticipated resources, for example, may allow managers to expand their effectiveness.

After recognizing a concern, managers must break it down into manageable pieces so that they can take action. Concerns do not always appear in managea-

TABLE D-1 The Rational Processes

Patterns of thinking	Time	Rational process
Organizing: Setting priorities among various concerns	Present	Situation appraisal
Investigating: Finding out why something went wrong	Past	Problem analysis
Making a choice: Setting criteria and evaluating alternatives	Present	Decision analysis
Implementing: Anticipating what might go wrong and protecting the decision	Future	Potential problem analysis

ble form. Sometimes they are stated very broadly: "a communications breakdown," "a morale problem," "a new distribution plan." Concerns are most often presented along with someone's opinion of how to resolve them: "We ought to raise salaries because we have high turnover," or "Where can we transfer Jill to? She's performing so poorly."

To proceed effectively, managers must be able to tackle manageable concerns. By asking questions, they can separate fact from fiction and arrive at specific concerns which they can act on. These questions are particularly helpful:

What evidence do you have that this is a concern?

What do we mean by . . .?

What is actually happening?

Do we think one action will resolve this concern?

Can we improve on the way we have handled this situation?

What could go wrong with this decision?

For example, by asking these questions a committee might learn that the "morale problem" really involves three separate concerns: deciding how to communicate company policies more effectively; finding out why turnover has increased; and negotiating fairly on the new labor contract.

The third step in situation appraisal is to set priorities. Priority is determined by investigating three aspects of each concern:

Seriousness: How much money or equipment and how many people are involved?

Urgency: Is there a deadline?

Growth: Will the situation get worse if we do not act?

Using these criteria, the high-priority concerns will stand out from the others. Those concerns that are highest in seriousness, urgency, and growth must be addressed first.

The final step in situation appraisal is to plan the resolution of concerns. By using the criteria in Table D-1, managers can determine which rational process will help them resolve the concern. If a choice must be made, use decision analysis. If a decision is to be implemented, use potential problem analysis. If this concern requires finding out why something went wrong, use problem analysis. Now the person or group is ready for resolution.

Decision Analysis

Choosing a course of action that provides maximum benefit within acceptable limits of risk is the purpose of *decision analysis.* It provides managers with an objective tool with which to analyze fact and opinion. Decision analysis is the model most widely applied to the vast number of decision-making situations encountered every day.

There are three major components to decision making:

1. *Establishing objectives.* Objectives are the goals which the selected course of action seeks to achieve. The degree to which these goals are missed, met, or surpassed will determine the success of the decision.

2. *Generating alternatives.* Alternatives represent the various routes available to reach the goal. Processes for generation and evaluation of alternatives identify the alternative that best meets the objectives.

3. *Examining adverse consequences.* Almost every possible course of action is inherent in each alternative. This part of decision making establishes peril, enabling the manager to determine whether the risk is prohibitive.

Decision Levels. A key determinant in the process is to establish the correct level of the decision. The level determines the range of alternatives that will be under consideration. For example, the simple decision to buy a new car implies that several prior decisions have already been made: The car will be *new,* and it will be *bought.* The probable starting point was a recognition of the need for transportation. Here is another example of how prior decisions affect current ones. A major insurance company entered the casualty field not long ago. Its entry was the result of a conscious decision to increase profits. Its decision chain might have looked like this:

1. Examine need to increase profits
   Raise premiums
   Cut staff
   Enter new line
   Cut dividends
2. Select a new line
   Marine
   Casualty
   Variable annuity
3. Decide how to enter casualty business
   Retain staff
   Buy out casualty company
   Hire new people

The next step in the decision sequence might be to select which company to buy. Note that as the decision maker moves down the chain, the range of available alternatives becomes less global. In this example, management has moved from broad profit-generating alternatives to specific plans to purchase a company. Examining the level of the decision will also keep managers out of a rut. By asking, "Why are we making *this* decision?" a manager can determine whether or not the level ought to be raised or lowered.

Establishing Objectives. Once the proper level has been set, objectives can be established. There are two sources of objectives: (1) the *resources* and the limits on resources to which managers have access, and (2) the *results* that the manager expects from the decision. By considering both resources and results, managers are in a position to try to maximize the latter with minimum investment of the former.

Musts and Wants. Objectives are not equal. Sound decision making requires a means to distinguish more important from less important objectives. Objectives are of two types: "musts" and "wants." Musts are absolute minimum standards, critical to the success of the decision. Any alternative that fails to meet a must standard cannot provide a satisfactory degree of success, no matter how well it may meet other objectives. Musts should always reflect such critical factors as budgetary limits, i.e., maximum expenditure of *x* dollars, and time constraints, i.e., availability within *y* days.

Wants are those objectives which are noncritical but desirable. Sometimes they may reflect a minimum standard established in the musts, e.g., minimizing expenditure, and sometimes they may represent entirely new goals, e.g., increasing the corporate image in the community.

Generating Alternatives. Alternatives should not be considered until after objectives have been established and classified. This is essential to a rational decision-making process. This approach avoids the pitfall of establishing objectives around a pet alternative. Common sources for the generation of alternatives include experience, superiors, subordinates, consultants, creativity, competition, research, peers, technical literature, and government regulations.

Once the alternatives are generated, the decision maker evaluates them by asking how well they satisfy the objectives. An alternative that does not meet the must objectives is immediately eliminated, since it cannot meet goals critical to the success of the decision. Those that meet must objectives are then compared against the wants to determine those that do the best job of meeting these desirable goals.

Examination of Adverse Consequences. Those alternatives that meet the must objectives and are most successful in meeting want objectives are then examined for adverse consequences. Each alternative will probably entail some risk. Using experience and judgment, managers estimate future difficulties, consider how probable and serious they are, and determine what might be done to eliminate or minimize those problems.

The final decision will result in that alternative that provides the most benefit (that best meets the want objectives) with the least damaging risks (adverse consequences that the manager is willing to accept). Consequently, the final decision involves more than just a paper exercise. Managers must exer-

cise judgment as to the degree of risk that the organization and individual managers are willing to undertake in return for various benefits. No amount of computer output and no simulation can replace the responsibility of management for decision making.

Other Applications. Another key aspect of decision analysis is the degree to which various parts of the process can be used.

Conflict Resolution. When conflict among individuals or departments occurs, the immediate question should be, "Is this conflict over alternatives or over objectives?" This will separate the conflict into one of two more manageable concerns which require different approaches.

1. If the conflict is over alternatives, it is helpful to refocus on the objectives. Since, presumably, there is agreement on objectives, this approach will defuse the hostility by concentrating on common ground. In so doing, it is possible to attempt to combine the best features of the alternatives that were in conflict or perhaps generate a new alternative on which all parties can agree. In any case, conflict over alternatives should be handled by reestablishing the agreement on the objectives and working toward compromise.

2. Conflict over objectives, however, requires a more basic approach. An assessment must be made as to the proper origin of the objectives. Is it up to the parties involved to establish them, or are they to accept objectives from a third party or a superior? If objectives originate elsewhere, they should be rechecked with the source. If objectives are to be established by the parties in conflict, then it is necessary to examine critically the level of the decision and what is to be accomplished. In many cases, an impartial third party might be needed.

Meetings Design. While most meetings have an agenda, few have results objectives to guide participants toward what results need to be achieved rather than merely to the activities to be performed. Results objectives for meetings allow participants to consider the proper resources to be invested to achieve the results desired, including knowing whom to involve in the meeting and what their role should be. Finally, results objectives also allow managers to track and monitor progress and to determine when the meeting is over. The absence of results objectives, which is typical of quality circle meetings, carries the risk of lengthy, irrelevant discussion.

Potential Problem Analysis

Potential problem analysis is used for implementing and protecting plans or decisions. In using this technique while examining the sequence of steps in any plan, managers can identify threats, perhaps as a result of the adverse consequence elements in decision analysis. *Potential-problem analysis,* then, is a process designed to enable managers to systematically plan actions to deal with the risks associated with decisions.

Once managers identify future, or potential, problems, they can use their experience and judgment to establish what the likely causes of those problems might be. This step is undertaken because the effects of a problem cannot be eliminated unless the cause is removed. Hence, likely causes are established so that preventive actions can be taken.

For example, if fire is a potential problem, two probable causes might be smoking in dangerous areas and electrical malfunction. Preventive actions might include posting NO SMOKING signs and setting electrical provisions which exceed normal safety standards. But if the fire were to occur anyway, either because preventive action failed or because of some unanticipated cause, the contingent actions which would minimize the effects might be a sprinkler system, emergency exits, and first-aid facilities. Note that the contingent actions address the effects of the fire itself, since the effects will be the same no matter which cause was responsible.

Two other concepts of special usefulness in potential problem analysis are triggers and mileposts.

Triggers. A trigger is the activating agent for contingent action. In the example of the fire, the fire alarm might be the trigger which prompts the emergency first-aid facilities to be set up by the designated personnel. In the case of the sprinklers, the trigger is automatic since heat activates the device. Triggers are employed to ensure that contingent action will occur at the appropriate time.

Mileposts. Mileposts are used to keep track of the plan and the status of the actions proposed. In the example of the fire, mileposts might include "Install sprinkler system by March 1" or "Check for presence of NO SMOKING signs on the first of each month." Perhaps more important, they are useful in determining when contingent actions are no longer needed. For example, if insurance is one of the contingent actions against fire damage in a building, the milepost might be the monthly insurance premium which keeps this action in effect. If the building is sold, the contingent action will no longer be needed. The next insurance premium—the milepost—reminds managers that this action should be discontinued. By making clear that contingent actions have outlived their usefulness, mileposts can be extremely valuable in conserving scarce resources.

Problem Analysis

Problem analysis is a search for cause. A problem exists when there is a deviation from an expected performance norm, or a "should"; when the cause for

that deviation is unknown; and when the situation requires the manager to act, as established in the situation appraisal process. This last point is critical, since a problem to one manager might not be a problem to another, as one is prompted to action by it and the other is not. The "should-actual" relationship is shown graphically in Fig. D-2.

FIG. D-2 Deviation from an expected performance norm.

The steps in the problem-solving process may be simply stated as:

1. Recognizing the problem (deviation)
2. Describing the problem (definition)
3. Determining causes of the problem (distinctions and changes)
4. Verifying the cause (testing) and eliminating the problem (correction)

The recognition step is accomplished when the manager perceives that actual circumstances deviate from expected performance norms, a problem for which the cause is not known and about which the manager is concerned. The description of the problem entails defining it in terms of its identity, location, timing, and magnitude in two dimensions: (1) where the problem is actually occurring, and (2) where it could have been expected to occur but in fact did not.

Changes and Causes. In comparing the problem's existence with what might have been its existence, managers can ascertain facts about the person, process, or machine that constitutes the problem. They can then search for changes that affected those facts, because if nothing had changed, the problem would never have come into being. Some change had to occur at or before the point at which the deviation was observed. Since thousands of changes occur in the typical workplace every day, the deviations allow us to focus only on relevant changes—the ones that relate solely to the definition of the problem and, therefore, can be responsible for the problem. Changes that affect both the "is" and "is not" dimensions cannot be responsible for the problem.

The search for a cause, then, is a search for the change or changes responsible for driving performance from expected (or "should") performance. Figure D-3 shows this relationship.

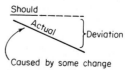

FIG. D-3 How changes cause deviations.

Testing and Verifying. As these causes are developed from the relevant changes that surface in the analysis, they are tested against the facts contained in the "is" and "is not" data. Causes which fail to explain why only the "is" was affected and not the "is not" are eliminated from consideration. The cause which best explains the description provided by the "is" and "is not" data is the most probable cause and is then verified by looking more closely at the problem and the change that caused it. Once the verification has proved that the most probable cause emerging from the process is actually the cause, appropriate steps are taken to remove the cause and eliminate the problem.

Problem Elimination. Eliminating a problem's effects can be accomplished only by finding and eliminating the cause of the problem. This is called *corrective action.* It may take some time to isolate the cause. In trying to live with or mitigate the effects while the cause is sought—or because corrective action is impossible or too expensive—managers can take *adaptive action.* For example, the National Aeronautics and Space Administration (NASA) has had a long-standing problem with thunderstorms during launches. Corrective action—changing the launch or stopping the storm—is impossible. The adaptive actions of lightning arresters, last-minute fueling, and minimum personnel exposure save the day. The critical point is that managers' best actions can be adaptive only until and unless the cause of the problem is determined.

Corrective action resembles preventive action in potential problem analysis; both address cause. Adaptive action resembles contingent action; both address effect. The difference is that corrective and adaptive actions address causes and effects that have already occurred; preventive and contingent actions address causes and effects that have yet to occur. This relationship is shown in Table D-2.

Problem analysis is not confined to hardware and machine problems. It applies to a diverse array of conditions, including the search for causes of inadequate human performance. In fact, in situations where there are fewer tangibles and few hard facts, the ability to focus on hard data is doubly important. Clear expectations are critical to the manager if standard operating procedures are to be realistic and achievable. Too few organizations address this need. Instead, they squander time and money trying to correct situations for which no standards exist.

TABLE D-2 Potential Problem Analysis

	Past	Future
Cause	Corrective	Preventive
Effect	Adaptive	Contingent

By using these three rational, systematic processes—decision analysis, potential problem analysis and problem analysis—managers can resolve any of the concerns they have identified in situation appraisal. Decision making in an organization is seldom an isolated process performed by a solitary individual behind a closed office door. Decision making is a dynamic process. Two or more people share information, raise questions, challenge one another and either commit themselves to a course of action or continue the decision-making process until they find an acceptable alternative.

Team Building

Most organizational decisions today are made by teams which typically consist of specialists from various functional areas of the organization—finance, sales, marketing, research and development, manufacturing. All these people were hired because they had different contributions to make. But how do you coordinate their efforts? The best method for coordinating the inputs of managers and employees with different functional skills is to provide simple, common, sensible guidelines and procedures. These guidelines should be used jointly to carry out responsibilities without inhibiting individual contributions.

Effective teams don't just happen. They must be *managed* into being. The first part of creating a smooth-running team is to install and teach a common approach and a common language for addressing management concerns. Beyond this, continual shared use of the concepts must be planned for and made to happen by the organization if these benefits are to be achieved and maintained. For example, the president of a large pharmaceutical company budgeted to have all managers and selected employees trained in systematic problem solving and decision making. He made sure their common approaches were used throughout the company by requiring all major recommendations to be presented in that systematic format. When he returned recommendations unapproved, his own comments were phrased in terms of the common, systematic approach—"Needs a financial objective," "What are the consequences?" "Is the cause known?"

Installing a Rational Problem-Solving and Decision-Making System

In order to make the decision-making process a vital element in how an organization operates day to day, there are seven conditions that should be met. These conditions were discovered through observation of

3000 companies that to a greater or lesser extent have achieved success with a systematic approach to problem solving and decision making.

1. The results to be obtained and the objectives to be achieved through use of a rational process have been clearly defined and are understood and accepted by top management and participants alike. All personnel are committed to their use at all levels and in all kinds of management situations within the organization.

2. The rational process ideas are presented in such a way that they are immediately recognized as practical and beneficial to those who will use them, relevant to their specific jobs, and, finally, easy to transfer to the real, everyday situations with which they must deal.

3. The application of rational process ideas to real concerns is not left to chance but is guided and guaranteed through techniques that incorporate real problems and choices as teaching vehicles. In this way the first uses of the ideas occur as part of the process of learning them, ensuring success in their use as practical tools.

4. Systems and procedures within the organization are modified and redesigned to fit with, and capitalize on, the rational process ideas, thus institutionalizing their use. The four patterns of thinking—situation appraisal, decision analysis, potential problem analysis, and problem analysis—become standard ways of operating.

5. Rewards and personal satisfaction are provided to those who use rational process ideas to deal with the organization's concerns and decisions, and to those who supervise and manage the use of those ideas. The rational process thus becomes first the preferred way, then, eventually, the automatic way of thinking and working.

6. There is continued follow-on activity to reinforce and sharpen capabilities already acquired, to extend application to new areas of organizational concern, and to reaffirm top management's commitment to the use of rational process.

7. There is continued monitoring and evaluation of the results of the use of rational process, assessing progress against initial objectives and providing feedback about these results to all concerned.

The installation of a common rational process for problem solving and decision making is not unlike the acquisition of a major piece of capital equipment. Once it is acquired, you can expect it to work and produce as predicted only if it is properly installed and integrated into the functioning of the rest of the organization. Successful installation comes about through careful planning and preparation.

Leadership and Performance

Developing a team or an organization that runs smoothly is a major challenge. Exposing managers and workers to a systematic process and encouraging them to use that process can be enhanced by developing the leadership skills of those managers and key employees who will guide teams and individuals in implementing the systematic approach.

The extent and nature of involvement by others in decision making should be determined by two key questions: "Does the leader now have adequate information to make a high-quality decision?" And "Is the commitment of others critical to effective implementation of the decision?" Answers to these questions will allow leaders to determine *who* else, if anyone, should be involved in the decision; *what* that involvement should be; and *how* that involvement should be structured.

In addition to the need for effective leadership, smooth-running organizations support individual and team performance by creating a work environment that encourages sound performance. Sometimes individuals who are thoroughly trained and highly motivated are unable to reach their performance targets because of factors in the work environment. To illustrate, managers and workers may have too much work to do; the consequences of performance may discourage them from performing as they should; feedback may not reach workers until long after a task is completed. For example, a team representing three departments recommends a new piece of equipment to improve quality control procedures but is reprimanded for not obtaining prior approval (negative consequences) and waits 2 months for higher management to approve or disapprove its recommendation (slow feedback). These factors discourage workers from recommending new quality improvement procedures in the future. The five factors in the performance system are shown graphically in Fig. D-4.

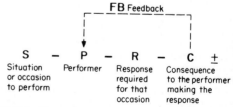

FIG. D-4 The performance system has five factors.

Training workers to use a systematic decision-making process does not guarantee that they will use it. By providing rewards, feedback, adequate resources, and skills, an organization can create a work environment that supports sound performance.

Summary

The goal of rational management is to make full use of the thinking ability of the people in the organization and to direct that ability toward resolving the organization's problems and concerns and achieving its strategy.

Once the strategy is in place, these goals are achieved by giving people the conceptual tools they need to do the job: a set of methods and techniques they can share as they gather and handle information to resolve problems, make choices, anticipate future concerns, and break complex situations into manageable components. In addition, the organization must provide its people with a supportive framework within which coordinated use of these ideas by the team can flourish.

Rational management cannot just happen. It must be managed into being as a planned intervention. It represents a major change in the way the organization operates, so it must be introduced by top management. If rational management is to succeed fully, a major commitment must be made and particular conditions must be met.

It is the role of top management to set an organization's strategic direction, to communicate that strategy, and to provide managers and workers with the operational decision-making skills to make that strategy a living document.

The four patterns of thinking most widely used in the day-to-day work of an organization—finding the cause of a problem, choosing the best course of action, foreseeing future problems, and rendering a complex situation manageable—can be sharpened and made more productive through installation of rational process. When this is carefully done through the commitment and guidance of top management, the productivity of the entire organization increases. Responsibility for quality moves in ever-widening circles from the organization's center. More people contribute in a significant way because they learn how to coordinate their thinking with the thinking of others for the good of all.

Rational management presides over no miracles. It releases intellectual resources that have been hidden, unused, or underused. It opens channels of communication among people by giving them common approaches and a common language for dealing with the ordinary and extraordinary situations they face in their jobs. Installation of rational process ideas makes it possible for the organization to be more nearly what every manager always believes it can be but too seldom is: an effective, efficient, and dynamic entity.*

See also Cost improvement; Cost-benefit analysis; Decision support systems; Management information systems (MIS); Risk analysis and management; Simulations, business and management; Work simplification and improvement.

REFERENCES

Gilbert, Thomas F.: *Human Competence*, McGraw-Hill, New York, 1978.

Kepner, Charles H., and Benjamin B. Tregoe: *The New Rational Manager*, Kepner-Tregoe, Princeton, N.J., 1981.

Tregoe, Benjamin B., and John W. Zimmerman: *Top Management Strategy: What It Is and How to Make It Work*, Simon and Schuster, New York, 1980.

Vroom, Victor, and Philip Yetton: *Leadership and Decision Making*, University of Pittsburgh, Pittsburgh, 1973.

BENJAMIN B. TREGOE, *Kepner-Tregoe, Inc., Strategic and Operational Decision Making*

Decision Support Systems

Although decision support systems (DSS) are still in an early stage of development and no clear consensus exists on what constitutes these systems, several features are emerging as common to most DSS. First, they are interactive. That is, an exchange of inputs and outputs between the user and the system takes place over a relatively short period of time—a few seconds, for example. This interactive nature requires that the user have access to a terminal or, perhaps, a microcomputer. Second, the user must have access to data. Data that are internal to the organization—sales volume, receipts, inventory levels, and so forth—may come from the transaction processing system (*see* Management information systems, transaction processing systems). Data that are external (interest rates, market forecasts, economic indicators, and the like) must, however, be furnished by the user. Next, the user must have access to decision models with which to manipulate these data. DSS models are usually mathematical in nature and more complex than the models used in management information systems (MIS). Finally, the decisions supported by the DSS tend to be semistructured or unstructured in contrast to the structured decisions made by MIS. In DSS, the word "support" should be stressed. The very nature of an unstructured decision requires a human decision maker. The DSS merely performs much of the analysis on which the decision is predicated, it does not actually make the decision.

DSS Levels

There are three distinct levels of DSS: (1) tools, (2) generators, and (3) specific DSS.

Tools are the fundamental capabilities of the computer hardware and software used in DSS. Examples of tools include programming languages, graphics packages, risk analysis, data base management systems, and statistical subroutines.

A DSS generator is a packaged collection of tools designed for a particular class of problems. Many of these collections are available as proprietary packages, with names like "Interactive Financial Planning System" or "Executive Information System."

A specific DSS is a combination of tools and generators designed to support a specific organizational decision. For example, portfolio management can be supported by the Interactive Financial Planning System generator and the specific tool of risk analysis. Specific DSS may also aid in decisions involving marketing mix, capacity planning, and venture analysis.

DSS Personnel

The three levels of DSS are also useful in explaining the role of personnel associated with DSS.

Users. The persons associated with specific DSS are users—probably management personnel. They have much greater involvement in their system than do users of other systems. DSS users are actually operators in the sense that they initiate the use of the DSS from a keyboard and obtain output directly from a screen or local printer. If the DSS users are upper-level managers, they may have staff assistants carry out some of the interactive work for them. Even so, the final decision based upon the DSS rests with the upper-level manager.

Builders. The builder is a member of the information systems staff who is knowledgeable in DSS generators and tools and, to a lesser extent, the decision environment of the user. The builder assembles the specific DSS from an existing inventory of hardware and software. The builder is somewhat analogous to the systems analyst, who designs other information systems.

Technical Support Personnel. In large organizations or in those with a very strong information systems function, there may also be technical support personnel who can modify or adapt existing tools and generator capabilities for a specific DSS. There might also be a "toolsmith" who develops the tools and generators needed, although most companies leave this expense to computer manufacturers and software development firms.

DSS Development

Successful DSS development has followed an iterative design process. The process is initiated by the user who approaches the builder with an information

need that cannot be satisfied by an existing system. Without the formality of feasibility studies, written plans, or contracts between the user and the developer, the builder makes available to the user some existing capabilities—perhaps a microcomputer and a DSS generator such as "The Executive Package" designed for the IBM PC. This "quick fix" can be made available on the day of the request. If it is unsuccessful, little has been lost. If, on the other hand, it shows promise, the user may return for additional DSS capabilities. In theory, a DSS developed in this manner is never finished but is continually modified and improved. Obviously, this process depends very heavily on the ability of users and builders to communicate precisely. The user must know something of DSS capabilities in order to state the requirements, and the builder must know something of the decision process in order to assemble a useful DSS. This concept of mutual understanding must be developed for a DSS process to function effectively.

DSS Applications

There are a number of immediate and practical applications for decision support systems.

Forecasting. One of the keys to successful decision making is the ability to resolve uncertainty—uncertainty about what the future will bring. One way in which managers attempt to do this is by forecasting future events. For example, Fig. D-5 shows a

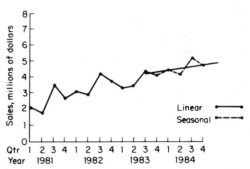

FIG. D-5 Forecasting with DSS.

trend analysis of sales. A simple analysis might establish a linear trend (shown by the solid line), or a more sophisticated analysis might incorporate seasonal patterns (shown by the broken line) evident in the historical data. Other forecasting capabilities found in DSS generators may include econometric methods or simple and multiple regression models.

Optimization. In some problems, it is possible to calculate the single best solution out of the hundreds or thousands that are possible. Optimizing models do this. Figure D-6 shows a classic optimiza-

Warehouse

Factory	Boston	Chicago	St. Louis	Memphis	Supply
Cleveland	3 / 3500	2 / 1500	7	6	5000
Bedford	7	5 / 2500	2 / 2000	3 / 1500	6000
York	2 / 2500	5	4	5	2500
Demand :	6000	4000	2000	1500	13,500

Total cost: 39,500

FIG. D-6 Optimization with DSS.

tion technique, called the transportation algorithm, which will minimize transportation costs when a number of destinations must be served by a number of sources, and supply, demand, and costs are known. The computer, of course, would solve this problem mathematically, without the graphical representation, and could accommodate many more factories and warehouses. The transportation algorithm is a special case of a broad class of optimizing techniques known as *linear programming.*

Data Base Management. One of the most powerful DSS capabilities is data base management. Figure D-7 shows an application in which all members of a purchasing department are displayed from a personnel data base. A typical DSS application of data base management might find a credit manager asking for all accounts past due over 60 days, or an inventory manager looking for all items under a certain minimum quantity. DSS are particularly useful when they are able to access the data bases used by other organizational information systems as well.

Goal Seeking. Sometimes decision makers are more interested in what inputs are required to yield a given answer than they are in what answers will result from a given set of inputs. In such cases, they use *goal-seeking* or *backward iteration* models. In the example in Fig. D-8, a financial planning model holds all other variables constant and solves for the market share necessary to yield a 20 percent return on investment. A production planning model might determine the cycle time required to balance an assembly line at a specified level of production.

Statistics. Statistical analyses are incorporated into almost every DSS generator. At a minimum, statistical analysis packages will organize data into arrays or frequency distributions, compute measures of central tendency and variability, and determine probabilities. The example in Fig. D-9 shows the probability that one person's income is greater than $22,500 when the income in the community is normally distributed with a mean of $18,750 and a standard deviation of $3,275. The answer of 12.6 percent

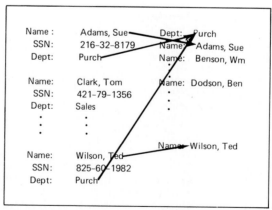

FIG. D-7 Data base management with DSS.

Goal: Return on investment = 20%

Variables: Price = 18.75
             Fixed cost = 2,250,000
             Variable cost = 5.6 × VOL + .03 × VOL²

             .
             .
             .

             Total market = 5,000,000/YR
             Market share = ?

FIG. D-8   Goal-seeking with DSS.

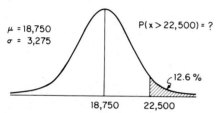

$\mu = 18,750$
$\sigma = 3,275$

$P(x > 22,500) = ?$

12.6 %

18,750   22,500

FIG. D-9   Statistical analysis with DSS.

would be useful to the marketing manager of a luxury product.

Financial Planning. Financial planning is a popular application area for DSS. Figure D-10 represents an analysis of a project that has $200,000 in start-up costs and sustaining costs of $50,000 a year. Revenue will be $100,000 per year starting in year 2 with an additional $75,000 in salvage value in year 7. This model has the advantage of showing both the undiscounted value ($175,000) and a discounted net present value ($19,000). It also assumes a discount rate of 15 percent. The DSS model easily allows

recalculation for, say, 12 percent and 18 percent for managerial comparisons.

DSS and MIS

DSS has a number of advantages over the typical management information system. DSS are special, rather than general-purpose, and are aimed at decision making rather than information gathering, analysis, and distribution. DSS may be temporary and quickly put together; they do not normally require the large computers and massive investment in hardware and software necessary for MIS. Finally, DSS function in unstructured situations where MIS require highly structured environments.

DSS are not intended to replace MIS; instead, they represent a useful complement to MIS for management decision making.

See also Computer hardware, micros/personal; Computer hardware, minis; Computer software, data base management; Computer software packages; Data bases, commercial; Decision-making process; Management information systems

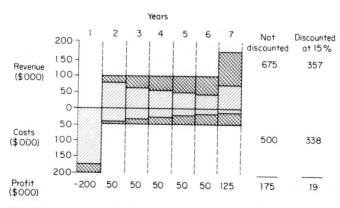

FIG. D-10   Financial analysis with DSS.

(MIS); Management information systems, transaction processing systems.

REFERENCES

Kroeber, Donald W., and Hugh J. Watson: *Computer Based Information Systems: A Management Approach.* Macmillan, New York, 1984.

Sprague, Ralph J., Jr., and Eric D. Carlson: *Building Effective Decision Support Systems,* Prentice-Hall, Englewood Cliffs, N.J., 1982.

Thieranf, Robert J.: *Decision Support Systems for Effective Planning and Control: A Case Study Approach,* Prentice-Hall, Englewood Cliffs, N.J., 1982.

DONALD W. KROEBER, *James Madison University*

Delegation

Delegation is essentially the task of farming out one's work to one's subordinates and of making sure that the subordinates successfully accomplish the projects or tasks thus assigned. Being proficient at the art and skill of delegation is probably the single most useful management tool for the person attempting to get work done through other people.

Many people make a complex issue of the subject of delegation by focusing their attention on the methods used in delegation rather than on the concept itself. In its simplest form, the art of delegation is the process of establishing and maintaining effective working arrangements between a manager and the people who report to him or her. Delegation takes place when the performance of specified work is entrusted to another and the expected results are mutually understood.

Decentralized Decision Making. The basic principle behind delegating work to one's subordinates is that of decentralizing decision-making responsibility throughout the organization. There are many reasons to decentralize such decision making:

1. It reduces costs throughout the organization.

2. It enables the executives to devote time to executive-level work (rather than the "doing" activities which would otherwise constitute the executive's workaday functions).

3. It often results in a better decision because in most cases, people who are on the spot have closer insights and more relevant information.

4. It tends to get the best out of people, since most people like to have some say in how they are going to do their job.

Roadblocks to Delegation. While many people understand very well the *need* for decentralization of decision making within an organization, many managers still find it difficult to delegate. At the root of this difficulty are certain mental blocks that managers frequently have toward making subordinates responsible for activities for which the manager bears the ultimate accountability. These include:

1. *The need to be needed.* A person who has an intense desire to make or keep subordinates dependent will find it difficult to give free rein to subordinates for job achievement.

2. *Fear of losing control.* When a manager delegates responsibility and authority to a subordinate, she or he runs the risk of the subordinate's not doing the job well or otherwise failing to perform as required. In such instances, the manager feels that delegation has removed control of performance for which he or she is accountable.

3. *The desire for reward.* Many managers enjoy the rewards that are usually associated with the achievement of functional, "doing" work. Delegating such work to one's subordinate necessarily means that the subordinate will get the reward—particularly the self-satisfaction from performing a task with "hands on" application.

4. *The feeling of a need to work.* Many managers have the notion that being weary at the end of the day from having worked hard is an indicator of meritorious job performance. They fail to recognize that the intellectual work of activating others effectively is far more productive of results than having done the work themselves.

5. *Fear of competition.* Still other managers are afraid that if they assign work for which they are responsible to their subordinates, their subordinates may, in fact, outperform them and, indeed, possibly end up becoming their supervisors.

Managerial Attitudes. Most managers who are ineffective delegators of work have yielded to one or more of the above mental blocks. Perhaps a still more fundamental reason for the inability of some managers to make effective work assignments is their latent feeling about people themselves. In short, many bosses fail at delegation because they do not have an effective attitude toward working with other people, especially their employees. The basic requirements for developing the appropriate attitude in the matter of delegation include:

1. *Receptiveness to other people's ideas.* A good delegator does not feel that his or her ideas are necessarily better than anyone else's or, more specifically, that other people's ideas are unworkable.

2. *A sufficiently placid disposition.* A good manager must be able to accept others' doing things in a way that she or he would not do them. This does not mean that the manager will accept absolute mistakes on a subordinate's part. It does mean

that the manager must be willing to see others attempt to do things their way. Further, the manager must be willing to forgo prejudging that way as unworkable when it in fact is still viable.

3. *A forbearance for mistakes.* An effective manager must forgo the luxury of irate criticism of subordinates. Wreaking havoc is futile when a subordinate has erred. Good delegation means encouraging people to do things their way. This implies, of course, encouraging them to do them in an operable manner. It does *not,* however, imply insisting that one's own way, no matter how effective, is the *only* way to accomplish a task.

4. *Powers of self-restraint.* The good delegator must resist the temptation of stepping in and taking over even though the subordinate's way of doing things seems inconsistent with what the manager thinks would be an optimal procedure.

Essential Requirements. Effective delegation of work is based upon six essentials. These are:

1. *Policies must be stated clearly and explicitly.* The subordinate must understand the operational guidelines within which he or she must operate. This requires that the manager clearly state what authority the subordinate has and the limits of the subordinate's responsibilities for task performance.

2. *Jobs and tasks must be carefully defined.* Nothing is more destructive of effective delegation than the manager's failure to define succinctly the performance expected of the individual on the delegated task. Failure to be explicit in this regard is confusing to the subordinate, who may then become frustrated. Such poor practice often results in the subordinate's inability or unwillingness to shoulder the delegated responsibility.

3. *Specific goals for completion of job performance must be established.* Job or task performance objectives should contain specific deadlines as to when, how well, how much, and under what governing restraints the task will be done.

4. *Ideas must be communicated to one's subordinates.* Effective delegation implies effective communication. This usually requires discussion and an exchange of ideas as to what the manager expects the subordinate to accomplish. This is particularly true, for example, when there are unique requirements for material handling or for relating the project to factors outside the manager's control. Without such guidance, both the superior and the subordinate may be frustrated. Often a subordinate will be disappointed at the superior's seeming unappreciativeness for the work which is done.

5. *Controls must be established to monitor progress toward the accomplishment of objectives.* It would be a mistake to delegate if there were no way to ensure that the work delegated is actually going to be (or has been) accomplished. If, for example, the sky diver has no way of determining whether the parachute rigger who has packed the diver's chute has done so correctly, then sky divers must either pack their own chutes or not make the jump. But when controls are established (riggers of parachutes are trained specifically in the art of packing the chute), and control efforts are exerted (riggers are required to jump some chutes they have packed), a degree of control is also exerted over the individual's motivation to accomplish the objectives. This is an extreme example, but in business, control would normally be executed by the manager's making use of various techniques including requiring progress reports on work performed; making comparisons of planned budgets against actual expenditures; analyzing indicators of performance against established norms (e.g., comparing scrap reports against standard scrap rates or comparing customer complaints or requests for adjustments on poor merchandise against the normal level of such complaints).

6. *Whole tasks must be delegated rather than pieces of tasks.* It is impractical for any individual to accept an incomplete assignment of work. This is particularly true when someone else is to be working on the assignment, especially if that individual is also unaware of the desired end result. No individual can be expected to function effectively on any job task if it must become an integral part of someone else's total job responsibility, or if the outcome desired is not known. Indeed, assigning pieces of one job to many people can, in fact, violate the basic rule of unity of command.

Figure D-11 is an example of the steps of delegation which might be taken by a company's personnel department manager in developing a personnel policy manual. Note that each level in the delegation chain breaks out in greater detail the "doing" tasks necessary for the satisfactory completion of the whole project. The unseen factor is the control (also time and length of statement requirements) and other constraints which the personnel department manager would level on each subordinate in ensuring that the work will be accomplished on time as required by the board of directors.

Pros and Cons of Delegation. The principal advantages of effective delegating include freeing up executive time to work on more important projects; leveraging one's talents throughout a whole organization; and making it possible to accomplish functional details which exceed the limits and capabilities of any one person in that organization. The

225

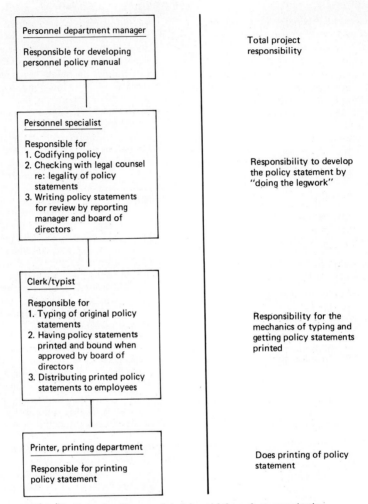

FIG. D-11 Example of how work is delegated through an organization.

disadvantages to delegation are essentially mental rather than instrumental. Some managers simply cannot stand what they perceive to be loss of control over their own work. Primarily, they cannot tolerate relying upon other people for results for which they retain ultimate responsibility. Because of this trait, many managers live in constant fear that a subordinate will botch an assignment, or that work will not be done on time, or that other embarrassing circumstances will occur.

Effective managers recognize that one cannot live in today's society without accepting the need to delegate tasks effectively to other people. In an ultimate sense, no one is self-sufficient. All people, in the final analysis, depend upon others to produce their food, provide their medication, supply their heat, light,

and water, and the like. Modern organizations are built on that premise. Effective delegation relies on the fact that everyone can do something useful. Failure to delegate is not only unintelligent behavior upon the part of a manager who wishes to be self-sustaining only in her or his own right; it is also an abuse of the law of comparative advantage. It is clear that no matter how limited a person is, he or she can do some one thing better than others. That person's time, therefore, should be devoted to doing that task. Thus, that person will be a productive citizen.

See also Authority, responsibility, and accountability; Exception, management by; Interpersonal relationships; Objectives, management by (MBO); Organizational analysis and planning; Work design, job enlargement, and job enrichment.

REFERENCES

Dalton, Gene W.: *The Distribution of Authority in Formal Organizations,* The M.I.T. Press, Cambridge, Mass., 1973.

McConkey, Dale D.: *No-Nonsense Delegation,* American Management Association, New York, 1974.

Steinmetz, Lawrence, L.: *The Art and Skill of Delegation,* Addison-Wesley, Reading, Mass., 1976.

LAWRENCE L. STEINMETZ, *High Yield Management, Inc.*

Developing Countries, Management in

Managers in developing countries (sometimes referred to as lesser-developed countries or LDCs) face challenges which surpass in complexity and severity most of those met by their counterparts in technologically more advanced societies. These challenges include:

Capital scarcity

Lack of a trained work force

Inadequate access to technology

Poorly articulated, often politicized, legal systems

Government intervention in the private sector

Limited consumer markets

Underdeveloped supporting services: banking, insurance, accounting, communications, transport, engineering, technical, secretarial

Legal and physical constraints on access to raw materials, components, and supplies, and to information of all kinds

None of these is entirely missing from the daily concerns of managers in more advantageous settings, but their omnipresence and intractability in many developing countries give to management in these societies a distinctive difficulty. This difficulty is only partially offset by the presence of some unique resources and opportunities.

Definition of Developing Countries. While there is no universally accepted classification of countries as "developing," an authoritative listing is that maintained by the World Bank. The Bank currently categorizes 94 countries having populations of at least 1 million as developing.[1] Thus defined, these countries, together with at least 30 other, smaller nations[2]—sometimes collectively referred to as the *Third World*—are to be contrasted with 21 countries with industrialized market economies (the *First World*),[3] with 8 eastern European countries with centrally planned or nonmarket economies,[4] and with 4 high-income oil-exporting countries.[5]

Managerial Environment of the Developing Countries

The variation among the developing countries in the conditions which affect management is enormous; only a little imagination is needed to visualize the differing managerial environments of, say, Upper Volta, Brazil, Saudi Arabia, Yugoslavia, and the Philippines—each of them is on the World Bank list. Nonetheless, some generalizations are valid. In many of these countries annual per capita incomes are low (in the range of $270), population growth is rapid (2 to 3 percent per annum), disparities among the highest and the lowest income groups are wide and still growing, average educational attainment is limited. Legacies (some helpful) from prior colonial status abound—in legal systems, language, cultural orientations, educational structure, and international market relationships. Growth since the 1950s in international telecommunications, in the availability of other mass media, and in air travel is breaking down intellectual isolation and stimulating aspirations previously dormant. Manifold interdependencies in economic and political relationships with other countries are emerging.

Amid this welter of ideas, interests, aspirations, demands, and frustrations, national governments in most developing countries must struggle to maintain political and social stability. The depth of poverty in many countries makes resort to extensive government intervention in the economy nearly inevitable. Strongly felt nationalism and the related demand for national economic and political autonomy lead to government intervention in any event, since it will be seen as required to constrain the power of foreign capital and technology. Authoritarian rule is widespread. Independence of the judiciary is the exception. These circumstances shape management practice.

Management Practice in Developing Countries. Most domestic firms in the private sector are small and usually family-owned, a condition that limits the scale of operations, career opportunities for professional managers, and the growth of a managerial class. Large-scale operations are generally in the control of government or multinational corporations.

Finance from domestic sources tends to be short-term and high-cost. Securities markets are thin and largely unregulated. Coupled with high rates of inflation, these conditions frequently demand that a large share of management attention be focused on rolling over short-term financing. Government plans and expenditures are often crucially important in market forecasts and marketing programs.

Technological research is rarely performed within the firm, and reliance on foreign technology available under license is the usual practice. Imported technology is often poorly adapted to developing country conditions, having been conceived in societies where labor cost outweighs other factors. In the limited instances in which government supports research, it tends to do so in laboratories oriented strongly to academic rather than practical interests. Domestic consulting firms are small and tend to stress accounting, industrial engineering, or market research.

With important exceptions, education for management as a profession is available only abroad, and the social status of managers—in comparison with that of doctors, lawyers, engineers—is low. As in other professions, the relative attractiveness of careers in management in the countries where advanced management training is available has induced management talent to emigrate.

Opportunities for Developing-Country Managers. This litany of difficulty is partially offset by unique positive factors and opportunities for the developing-country manager. Bilateral and multilateral foreign aid agencies and development banks provide capital resources and technical assistance of kinds not usually available in the industrialized countries. A generation of managers equipped with powerful tools such as systems analysis and operations research, backed up by growing computer power, is entering the scene. Management by task force is replacing, in some organizations and countries, the more traditional, hierarchical methods.

Managers in the private sector in the developing countries often have access to government-sponsored financial incentives for investment and growth in the form of tax holidays, capital grants for plant and equipment, subsidized personnel training programs, preferential financing terms, and other cost-reducing privileges, provided their enterprises are in activities to which government gives priority. In many countries, development banks and similar institutions offer subsidized technical assistance in connection with financing. There is a special opportunity for managers of business in some developing countries because natural resources in minerals, forests, and agricultural land have only recently been opened for development; they are usually reserved for exploitation by nationals. For the well-trained manager in a developing country, an advantage of great importance is the fact that the competition is thin; more than normal opportunity exists both for the manager and for the enterprise.

A recent trend in developing countries has been toward increased interest in applying management principles and techniques (developed originally in and for private sector enterprise) to the management of government organizations and government-owned enterprises. This is particularly significant because so much of total employment and overall economic activity in those countries is concentrated in government institutions. Moreover, there is growing recog-

nition that a large proportion of management principles and techniques originating in the industrialized, Western-oriented societies are transferable to, and are effective in, developing countries despite wide divergences in cultures and political structures. These trends substantially broaden career opportunities for developing-country managers, extending them well beyond the relatively narrow range available in the private sector in many of these economies.

See also Economic systems; International operations and management in multinational companies; International trade.

NOTES

[1]See World Bank, *World Development Report 1983*, "Definitions," p. IX; "Annex, World Development Indicators," Table 1; and "Technical Notes," p. 204. The 94 developing countries are subdivided into three classes.

Low-income economies [US$80 to US$400 annual gross national product (GNP) per capita, arranged in ascending order of per capita GNP for 1981]: Kampuchea, Bhutan, Laos, Chad, Bangladesh, Ethiopia, Nepal, Burma, Afghanistan, Mali, Malawi, Zaire, Uganda, Burundi, Upper Volta, Rwanda, India, Somalia, Tanzania, Viet Nam, China, Guinea, Haiti, Sri Lanka, Benin, Central African Republic, Sierra Leone, Madagascar, Niger, Pakistan, Mozambique, Sudan, Togo, Ghana.

Lower middle-income economies (US$420 to US$1620 annual GNP per capita, arranged in ascending order of per capita GNP for 1981): Kenya, Senegal, Mauritania, Yemen Arab Republic, Yemen PDR, Liberia, Indonesia, Lesotho, Bolivia, Honduras, Zambia, Egypt, El Salvador, Thailand, Philippines, Angola, Papua (New Guinea), Morocco, Nicaragua, Nigeria, Zimbabwe, Cameroon, Cuba, Congo Peoples Republic, Guatemala, Peru, Ecuador, Jamaica, Ivory Coast, Dominican Republic, Mongolia, Colombia, Tunisia, Costa Rica, Korean Democratic Republic, Turkey, Syrian Arab Republic, Jordan, Paraguay.

Upper middle-income economies (US$1700 to US$5670 annual GNP per capita, arranged in ascending order of per capita GNP for 1981): Republic of Korea, Islamic Republic of Iran, Iraq, Malaysia, Panama, Lebanon, Algeria, Brazil, Mexico, Portugal, Argentina, Chile, South Africa, Yugoslavia, Uruguay, Venezuela, Greece, Hong Kong, Israel, Singapore, Trinidad and Tobago. An anomaly is Taiwan, not listed by the Bank, but unquestionably having the characteristics of an upper middle-income economy with per capita GNP in the range of US$2500.

[2]These 30 smaller nations, with low annual GNP per capita for 1981, all have populations of less than 1 million but are members either of the World Bank or the United Nations. They are not included in the listing of developing countries in the Bank's 1983 report because of their small populations, but they unquestionably are developing countries for all practical purposes. Listed in ascending order of GNP per capita for 1981, from a low of US$180 to a high of US$5920, they are: Equatorial Guinea, Guinea-Bissau, Maldives, Comoros, Cape Verde, Vanuatu, The Gambia, São Tomé and Principe, Djibouti, Saint Vincent and the Grenadines, Western Samoa, Solomon Islands, Guyana, Dominica, Swaziland, Grenada, Saint Lucia, Botswana, Belize, Mauritius, Antigua and Barbuda, Seychelles, Fiji, Surinam, Barbados, Malta, Bahamas, Cyprus, Gabon, and

Oman. Two others with populations less than 1 million are excluded because of their relatively high GNP per capita: Bahrain and Qatar.

[3]There are 19 large countries with industrialized market economies. Listed by the World Bank in ascending order of GNP per capita for 1981 (the range is US$5,230 to US$17,430), they are: Ireland, Spain, Italy, New Zealand, United Kingdom, Japan, Austria, Finland, Australia, Canada, Netherlands, Belgium, France, United States, Denmark, Federal Republic of Germany, Norway, Sweden, and Switzerland. Two countries with less than 1 million population have similar characteristics: Iceland and Luxembourg.

[4]The eastern European nonmarket economies are: Albania, Hungary, Romania, Bulgaria, Poland, the USSR, Czechoslovakia, and the German Democratic Republic. Presumably, they constitute a "Second World," although this term does not seem to be widely used.

[5]The four high-income oil-exporting countries, which nevertheless exhibit many of the characteristics of developing countries and are often spoken of as part of the Third World, in ascending order of GNP per capita for 1981 (the range is US$8,450 to US$24,660) are: Libya, Saudi Arabia, Kuwait, and the United Arab Emirates.

REFERENCES

Bryant, Coralie, and Louise G. White: *Managing Development in the Third World*, Westview Press, Boulder, Colo., 1982.

Gordon, David: "Development Finance Companies, State and Privately Owned: A Review," World Bank Staff Working Paper no. 578, in *World Bank Staff Working Papers*, Management and Development Series no. 13, Washington, D.C., 1983.

Shirley, Mary M.: "Managing State-Owned Enterprises," World Bank Staff Working Paper no. 577, in *World Bank Staff Working Papers*, Management and Development Series no. 13, Washington, D.C., 1983.

Vernon, Raymond, and Louis T. Wells: *Managers in the International Economy*, 4th ed., Prentice-Hall, Englewood Cliffs, N.J., 1981.

World Bank, *World Development Report 1983: Part II, Management in Development*, Oxford University Press, New York, 1983.

WILLIAM A. W. KREBS, *Arthur D. Little, Inc.*

Development and Training: Career Path Planning for Managers

The word "career" suffers from surplus meanings. To some, it means advancement up the organizational pyramid. To others, a career entails a certain class of occupation: professions, such as medicine, law, engineering, and management. A third view is that a career is a person's experience in one particular organization or occupation, so that changing jobs means changing careers. In most management writings and in this entry, however, the term *career* is defined as follows:

The career is the individually perceived sequence of attitudes and behaviors associated with work-related experiences and activities over the span of the person's work life.[1]

It is important to note that in this context a career involves (1) work experiences, not other facets of a person's life; (2) a long period of time, the person's entire work life; (3) both attitudes (e.g., job involvement and satisfaction) and behaviors (such as performance and decision making); and (4) the person's own perceptions of career processes, rather than an external observer's description. Although there is a great deal of current interest in lifestyles, career path planning does not entail as broad a concern as life planning. The latter includes social activities as well as work. There are legitimate questions about the right of an organization to get involved in an employee's entire life, and, therefore, this entry is restricted to career planning applied to the field of work.

Impact on Operations. Careers are important because they affect employees' job behavior significantly. If employees see no career growth opportunities, however, positive attitudes and performance will eventually weaken among those persons most inclined to seek greater opportunities for responsibility and contribution to the organization's objectives.

Organizations pay a price for poor career growth opportunities in several important ways:

1. *High turnover among recently hired employees.* One company hired 120 new M.B.A.s each year in order to have 20 left at the end of the year.[2] The cost of such turnover is enormous, considering recruiting expenses, travel, testing, lost output before replacement, and reduced performance during orientation of new employees. One authority has estimated the cost of replacing a middle manager at around $25,000.[3] Therefore, a company that loses 40 good managers each year adds an extra $1 million to operating expenses just to stay even with last year's operation.

2. *Decreasing employee involvement.* In a declining economy and job market, some people may remain on the job in the face of poor growth opportunities, but they will adapt by "turning off" (becoming less involved in their work), with a corresponding drop in the quality of their work performance.

3. *Inefficient utilization of people's skills.* With poor development and matching of people with jobs, performance is subpar and frustration is high. In today's era of the "lean and mean" organization, no company can afford such inefficiency.

Responsibility. Management might ask, "Should career planning be something people do for themselves?" Perhaps, but in practice people tend to give little attention to planning their own careers, in spite of the importance of career fulfillment to them. In one study of executives and other professionals who had recently switched jobs, the researchers were surprised to find how few people had made the change on their own initiative. Most of the changes were externally initiated—e.g., better job offers elsewhere, termination, job transfers, family problems which required relocation. The study gathered very little evidence of career planning, even among these high-powered people who continually practiced corporate planning and planning for subordinates but not for themselves.[4]

Personal Values. Careers are also important because career fulfillment is more important now than formerly. Lifestyles are changing, and more employees are willing to turn down transfers or promotions in order to stay in desirable geographic areas.

Developing Career Competence in the Organization

For a management determined to provide assistance to employees in their career planning, a number of options are possible. A firm may establish its program independently. A small firm which cannot afford an internal program may wish to hire a consultant. Even large firms may benefit from a consultant's assistance, especially in designing their programs.

Career Planning Workshop. A 2- to 5-day career planning workshop is a basic approach. The focus here is on an organized internal program; the basic elements of any comprehensive program will be similar in purpose, while the activities pursued will usually vary substantially among programs. The framework employed is Crites's five components of career competence.[5]

Self-Appraisal. The first step, the most crucial by far and the one most frequently overlooked, is self-appraisal. There are few occupations which provide opportunities for people to assess themselves systematically, and most relationships at work are too impersonal to provide the candid, insightful feedback necessary to encourage self-appraisal. The career planning program, then, usually begins with some combination of occupational interest tests and small-group interaction to generate the data needed for self-assessment. It is in this phase that professional counseling assistance is most essential. Interpreting scores, designing group experiences to facilitate open feedback, and leading the group are all skills requiring professional expertise.

Occupational Review. As participants pursue their self-appraisal, they develop a need to obtain occupational information. There are a few publications (the *Dictionary of Occupational Titles* and the Department of Labor's *Occupational Outlook Hand-*

book) that may prove useful for persons seeking general vocational information. Within the organization, job descriptions or discussions with job incumbents may be the most practical sources. Statistical information on numbers of jobs in various parts of the organization can also be extremely useful. Deciding which of these sources will be most suitable will largely depend upon management's objectives in sponsoring the program. General information may encourage people to consider career changes to jobs not available within the organization.

Goal Selection. This is the central focus, once participants have achieved a tentative notion about the optimal job-person fit feasible. Argyris identified four key characteristics of goals which produce genuine personal development.[6] Goals are more effective to the extent that they are (1) challenging (but attainable), (2) related to more central psychological needs, (3) chosen by (rather than imposed on) the person involved, and (4) achieved by the person's own efforts. Setting such goals requires thorough self-awareness and knowledge of occupational opportunities. Goals should be chosen with the expectation that some will be achieved, some not, and some changed as needs and the situation change. Hence, the career planning program needs to be designed to encourage revising or setting new goals from time to time.

Several career planning exercises have been developed to facilitate the goal-setting process. Working with others is an important adjunct to the goal-setting activity. Making a public commitment to achieve the goal makes it more likely that the goal will be pursued. Furthermore, a support group can be developed to provide encouragement to persevere when the goal is truly challenging. Coworkers can provide much of this support, but increasing recognition is being paid to the role of the participant's family as the most crucial support group in most instances. Goal-setting modules in the career planning program should be structured so that participants' families can be active in the decision making.

Planning. Having selected their goals, the participants next enter the planning phase, the development of action steps to achieve the goal. Again, working in a group is helpful for the same reasons that the group improves the goal-setting process. Moreover, the group can be a useful source of ideas for alternative strategies which otherwise might be overlooked. Development of skills in planning, per se, is one of the most valuable things that participants may learn from the planning exercises usually assigned. *Force-field analysis*, a technique for identifying factors which discourage or encourage progress, is typical of the techniques employed at this point.[7]

Problem Solving. The resolution of problems encountered in achieving the career plan is the last step. Problem solving occurs largely after participants leave the career planning workshop. The problem solving, however, should be based upon the self-awareness, job information, and plans developed in the workshop. The workshop can further subsequent problem solving to the extent that participants are encouraged to develop contingency plans, support groups are established, and a system of progress charting is provided. Organizational superiors can also be of substantial assistance where participants are encouraged to seek their aid in pursuing the career plan.

Examples of Successful Applications

The *management assessment program* (MAP) at the 3M Company uses assessment centers not just for selecting employees but also for identifying (1) career goals, (2) developmental needs, and (3) placement opportunities. Normally, young nonmanagerial employees who have completed 3 years of employment meet in groups of 15 for 2 days. During this time, they complete various tests, exercises, and interviews, and are also evaluated by a staff of professional psychologists. After 2 days, each participant has a private feedback interview with a staff member, who reports the general results and suggests specific areas for development efforts by the employee. This information is also available to management for future career counseling and guidance. Here, the focus is on the individual, with the resulting information made available to the company.[8]

The Travelers Insurance Company also uses *career planning conferences* with an individual emphasis, but the information is not used for corporate personnel decisions. In fact, the information is not made available to anyone in the company. Employees who have completed 3 to 7 years of employment (and who are often found to be at an initial plateau) first complete a battery of interest, personality, skill, and ability tests. They then meet in a university setting with trained professionals from outside the company for 8 days. Much of the time is spent with participants and professionals in one-to-one counseling sessions. Class sessions discuss employees' perceptions of what goes on in the company, the realities and imperfections of everyday organizational life, ways to cope with the boss, strategies a person can build into his or her own behavior, etc. These discussions also cover such issues as family relationships and work versus family tensions.

Each participant develops a 6-month plan, with a follow-up contract made 6 months later. These experiences are shared anonymously with all participants and provide for more learning from peers. The results seem to include more personal self-direction and an increased sense of personal achievement, according to Dr Andrew Souerwine of the University of Hartford, director of the program.[9]

AT&T puts more stress on the work environment than the 3M and Travelers approaches. One program for high-potential employees involves first completing the company's regular *assessment center*. Based on the results of the assessment center, the employee, the boss, and a corporate staff person draw up a career plan which includes a target job, training needed, interim assignments, and a time frame. This plan is reviewed by all three parties every 3 months.

Ford Motor Company is developing career workshops with a strong focus on *organizational realities*. With a 1983 work force approximately half the size it was in 1979, there is a concern that the employees who remain might develop either unrealistically low or high expectations about career progress. A career workshop, directed by Dr. Phyllis Horner, focuses on the statistical likelihood of various types of moves, on ways to work within the system to create career movement, and on self-assessment activities. Supervisors are also trained—in a separate workshop—in coaching and counseling employees who have attended the career workshop.[10]

Other career programs also utilize assessment center data for input and are based on the following principles.[11]

1. Emphasize the development of high-potential people only. Do not try to change people who lack management potential.

2. Set specific developmental objectives. Identify specific job experiences and specific skills the person needs to acquire (e.g., the ability to supervise a central office PBX group).

3. Train the supervisor to provide day-to-day job experiences (e.g., job challenge, performance appraisal) which promote development.

4. Structure and monitor a *process* of career planning and development, but allow the supervisor and the employee to provide the *content*. Thus, a personnel staff member responsible for the program often plays a third-party, nondominant role in the process.

Considerations in Implementation

Organizations interested in sponsoring career planning need to be aware of several considerations:

1. Travelers Insurance, despite generally favorable results, found that some participating employees decided to leave the organization.

2. Out-of-pocket costs are determined largely by the number of employees participating, since the primary cost is usually the wages of the participants.

3. There is presently an almost total lack of empirical research on the effectiveness of career plan-

ning, save for a number of case studies reporting positive results in the sponsoring organizations.

4. Management must be willing to follow through and integrate the career planning program with other, related activities.[12] In order to assure that career planning does not become just another isolated program advocated by the personnel department, management should at the very least (a) provide training in coaching skills for managers and supervisors and systematically reward those who encourage employees to pursue their career goals; (b) revise work-force planning and performance appraisal systems to provide meaningful opportunities for employees to pursue and achieve their career goals; and (c) provide for periodic refresher activities at 2- or 3-year intervals to assure that employees reassess and revise their objectives. Ideally, the program should also be tailored to the unique concerns of employees at different stages of their careers. New management trainees and older managers approaching retirement will have different interests and priorities.

5. A job-posting system may be appropriate to ensure that employees know when opportunities to advance toward their career goals are available. The career planning process tends to raise employees' aspirations, and if opportunities to fulfill these aspirations are not available in the organization, they may look elsewhere.

6. Career planning works best when it is part of an integrated *strategic human resource planning process*. Companies such as IBM, General Electric, AT&T, and Monsanto, which are well-known for systematic human resource planning, have been successful in providing supportive career management opportunities to qualified people who have participated in individual career planning activities.[13]

7. Advancement systems should not be the only focus; lateral moves, organizational exit, and even downward moves may provide more career growth than staying in the current job.[14]

Career planning as a means of developing a more involved and committed work force appears to be a powerful tool. It should be undertaken only by a management willing to assume the added risks that arise when employees begin to seek greater opportunities to take initiative and responsibility and desire more chances for achievement and personal growth in their work.

See also Appraisal, performance; Assertiveness training; Assessment center method; Continuing education unit (CEU); Development and training, employee; Development and training, management; Health, mental; Outplacement; Stress management.

NOTES

[1]D.T. Hall, *Careers in Organizations*, Goodyear, Santa Monica, Calif., 1976, p. 4.

[2]Ibid., p. 75.

[3]D. T. Hall and F. S. Hall, "What's New in Career Management," *Organizational Dynamics*, vol. 5 (1), 1976, pp. 17–33.

[4]A. Roe and R. Baruch, "Occupational Changes in the Adult Years," *Personnel Administration*, vol. 4, 1957, pp. 212–217.

[5]J. O. Crites, *Theory and Research Handbook, Career Maturity Inventory*, McGraw-Hill, New York, 1973.

[6]C. Argyris, *Integrating the Individual and the Organization*, John Wiley, New York, 1964.

[7]A. Blumberg and R. T. Golembiewski, "Laboratory Goal Attainment and the Problem Analysis Questionnaire," *Journal of Applied Behavioral Science*, vol. 5, 1969, pp. 597–600.

[8]Hall, op. cit., pp. 165–166.

[9]Hall, op. cit., pp. 167–169.

[10]J. Turner, "Coping with Career Development in an Industry in Transition," paper presented at the meeting of the Academy of Management, Dallas, August 1983.

[11]Hall, op. cit., p. 167.

[12]T. G. Gutteridge and F. L. Otte (with the assistance of B. Williamson), *Organizational Career Development: State of the Practice*, American Society for Training and Development, Washington, D.C., 1983. Also see M. London and S. A. Stumpf, *Managing Careers*, Addison-Wesley, Reading, Mass., 1982.

[13]D. T. Hall, "Negotiation in Human Resource Management," in M. H. Bazerman and R. J. Lewicki (eds.), *Negotiating in Organizations*, Beverly Hills, Calif., Sage, in press.

[14]B. L. Kaye, *Up Is Not the Only Way: A Guide for Career Development Practitioners*, Prentice-Hall, Englewood Cliffs, N.J., 1982.

REFERENCES

Haldane, Bernard: *Career Satisfaction and Success: A Guide to Job Freedom*, American Management Association, New York, 1978.

Pearse, Robert F., and B. Purdy Pelzer: *Self-Directed Change for the Mid-Career Manager*, American Management Association, New York, 1975.

Donald D. Bowen, *University of Tulsa*

Douglas T. Hall, *Boston University*

Development and Training, Employee

The solution to the productivity problem facing the Western economy in the decade ahead lies in two areas—technological advances and a better work force. Improved productivity from the labor force itself will result from either better-trained workers or better-motivated workers. This entry addresses the question of how employees can be better trained so as to increase their potential for greater productivity.

Employee training programs are designed to provide the knowledge, attitude, or job skills that will help employees perform their present jobs. Training has immediate practical application on the job.

Employee development programs are designed to assist employees in preparing themselves for future responsibilities of a different nature, or a higher degree of proficiency in their present jobs. Whereas training has an early and often visible payoff, development is future-oriented. Consequently, development programs represent an investment, with the attendant risks of uncertain returns.

Basic guidelines governing the area of employee training and development have been distilled, in the following paragraphs, from experience and research. These are presented in prescriptive form as principles, followed by brief explanations and illustrations. Five topical areas encompass the field of training: (1) needs analysis, (2) learning principles, (3) training techniques, (4) evaluation of effectiveness and (5) transfer of training.

Needs Analysis

All training should be justified on the basis of a prior needs analysis. This is true of both new and existing programs. The reason is obvious: too often organizational training programs have been created and perpetuated for the wrong reasons. Examples of poor justification include these: because a supervisor asked for it; because there were resources available that we wanted to use; because our competitor initiated a program like this first; or (worst of all) because we *thought* there was a need for such a program.

A good needs analysis provides data relevant to five issues. It identifies the trainee group (or individual), the type of change desired, the topical area (content) of the training, the degree of improvement desired, and the overall priority placed upon this particular program.

Knowledge, Attitudes, and Skills. It is important to clarify here the difference between (and interrelatedness of) the three types of change. *Knowledge* includes the fundamental information needed to understand the job adequately. It describes what is to be done, under what conditions, with which resources, and with whom. It is the acquisition of technical facts prerequisite to effective job performance.

Attitudes are predispositions of employees to view their jobs and work environment either favorably or unfavorably. A positive frame of reference is an important prerequisite to using job knowledge effectively. Common examples include employee attitudes toward the value of safe work habits, toward a

superior or coworker, and toward the organization in general.

Skill is the capacity to perform a task at an acceptable level of speed and quality. Adequate job knowledge and proper job attitudes are normally viewed as prerequisites to skill development. All three must be considered in a satisfactory needs analysis program.

Techniques of Needs Analysis. Many techniques of needs analysis have been developed and used successfully. Those described below represent the most practical ones.[1]

Data Analysis. This is a technique that uses existing records and requires minimal expertise. The process involves examination of job descriptions for entry-level positions to determine the knowledge, skills, and attitudes required of new employees. This information is then compared with data describing the actual (or probable) qualifications of new employees. The difference between these two levels, if significant, represents a training need from which training programs can be designed.

Observation. This is an approach that requires a trained observer. This person, either a line supervisor or a staff specialist in training, physically observes the job behavior of the employee to determine whether upgrade training is necessary and, if so, what kind. A hybrid of observation and data analysis exists when records of an employee's behavior are examined (e.g., productivity, rejects, or absenteeism), and from this secondary information, a training need is inferred.

Surveys. These may take at least two forms.

1. *Written questionnaires* may be distributed asking employees to identify problems in their jobs, areas in which they wish they had more expertise, or their desires for future advancement. A key assumption is that the employees have an accurate perception of their needs and will report those perceptions honestly.

2. *Structured interviews* are surveys in which a staff specialist explores similar needs-oriented questions with each employee. The questionnaire has the merits of gathering objective data that are recorded for later analysis and are often collected anonymously. Its greatest constraint is the tight structure it often places on the respondent. The interview is more flexible in that it can adapt to emerging information. The results are difficult to record and often subjective in their interpretation, however.

An example of the written questionnaire often used in business and government organizations is the *skills inventory.* It may take the form of a checklist for employees to indicate the skills in which they have various degrees of proficiency. As an illustration, a clerk-typist may designate skill with an electric typewriter and 10-key adding machine, familiarity with a memory typewriter and electronic calculator, and no knowledge of how to operate a word processor. The data from this self-record of skills may then be used to assess training needs.

Learning Principles

Training programs should incorporate as many fundamental principles of learning as are relevant. Extensive research, both in experimental settings and in organizations, has validated the utility of several basic principles of learning. Each of these, when understood and carefully applied, will increase the effectiveness of a given training program. Learning will generally tend to be facilitated when:

1. *Multiple senses are stimulated.* The most probable ones are sight, sound, and touch, with smell and taste used far less often. It is for this reason that visual aids become a critical factor in training-program success, for they stimulate the sense of sight during what might otherwise be a boring presentation. Examples of *visual aids* include the chalkboard, overhead transparency projector, felt board, flip chart, videotape, and movie projector.

2. *Objectives of training are delineated in advance and are known by both trainer and trainee.* Objectives allow the participants to anticipate what comes next and to relate the content and methodology to an overriding purpose.

3. *Trainees' desire to learn.* Interest will occur more readily when the need for training has been made apparent to the employees. They can then better understand how the training program relates to more effective job performance and/or personal satisfaction.

4. *Content of the course is arranged in ascending order of difficulty and logical order.* This permits the trainee to absorb the easy material first and build upon it as the material becomes more complex. It also allows for the existence of natural *plateaus in learning* or times when no new skill development seems to take place.

5. *Trainees receive feedback on their progress.* They need to know how they are doing. That information should be specific, relevant, timely, and accurate. This feedback allows the trainees to organize their thoughts or generate a new burst of enthusiasm for the program.

6. *Trainees are reinforced for appropriate behavior in the training program.* A word of praise or encouragement from the trainer or peers can be highly effective at solidifying the learning that has taken place and stimulating future effort.

7. *Trainees are given adequate time to practice.* Repetition of a new skill facilitates its retention and improvement. The old axiom "practice makes [tends to make] perfect" captures the essence of this principle.

8. *Trainees are actively involved in the training process.* Techniques that require at least intellectual involvement (e.g., question-and-answer discussion periods) if not also physical participation (such as practicing transactions on a simulated bank-teller computer) are far more effective than those that allow passivity by the trainees.

9. *The skill to be learned is challenging, yet within the range of achievement.* The task must be difficult enough to stimulate interest and arouse a competitive spirit, but not so demanding that it is out of reach of the trainee.

10. *The training program is personalized to fit individual needs.* Trainees vary in terms of their background, experience, and capacity to learn. An ideal training program has entry capacity at different skill levels, as well as a flexible pace to accommodate varying speeds of learning.

11. *Unlearning can take place.* Unlearning is the process of reducing or eliminating preexisting knowledge or habits that would otherwise represent formidable barriers to new learning.[2] Strategies for facilitating unlearning include peer pressure, passage of time, public exposure of intentions to change, and direct barriers.

Training Techniques

Careful analysis of the pros and cons should precede the selection and use of any training technique. One of the most critical decisions to be made by the trainer concerns the selection of the appropriate training technique. Effective trainers utilize a more rigorous decision process in their selection decisions. One approach is to classify, in advance, the various training techniques according to the degree to which they match a set of relevant criteria.[3] These criteria might include, but not be limited to, the following:

1. Whether the technique is oriented toward knowledge, attitudes, or skills.

2. Whether the technique is generally applied on the job or off the job.

3. The degree to which the technique incorporates the major principles of learning.

4. The relative expense involved in development and administration of the program.

5. The flexibility inherent in the technique in terms of the size of training group that can be simultaneously accommodated.

6. The unique trainer skills required.

7. The extent to which specialized equipment or facilities are necessary (and available).

8. The degree to which the technique lends itself to evaluation by some of the more sophisticated criteria of effectiveness (as outlined later).

9. The time duration over which the training technique usually extends.

Several of the more common employee training techniques are briefly described below and evaluated by application of these nine criteria.

Off-the-Job Techniques. The trainee is typically not producing a product or service while engaged in these forms of training.

Orientation Training. Objectives of this technique vary from firm to firm but typically include an attempt to develop a positive attitude toward the firm (loyalty). The length of formal orientation programs ranges from less than 1 to several days' duration. Orientation usually precedes the beginning of any productive work experience. Its content includes such diverse topics as the history of the organization, company policies and procedures, employee benefits, career paths available, a tour of organizational facilities, a review of resources (counseling, cafeteria, recreational programs), and major organizational philosophies and programs.

Two major issues pervade the design of orientation programs. One is the question of how much material should be included and in what form (written, verbal, or visual). The answer to this question depends heavily on the trainer's assessment of how much content will likely be retained (if that is the objective) or how much "selling" must be done to develop a positive attitude. Experience suggests that short, rather than long, orientation programs are better received by most employees, who are probably anxious to begin work and demonstrate their usefulness to the organization.

The other major issue concerns the ease of evaluating the effectiveness of orientation programs. If the objective is to communicate content-oriented materials, then it is possible to test the new employees on their retention at the end of the training seminar (or later). Alternatively, if the objective is to reduce future employee turnover by developing more loyal employees, then not only will the evaluation be delayed substantially, but so many other factors will intervene as to make objective evaluation almost worthless.

A recent innovation now included in some orientation programs is the *realistic job preview*. When new (or prospective) employees are candidly told about both the positive *and* negative aspects of their work environment, they develop more realistic expectations. Consequently, turnover often declines.

Vestibule Training. Used almost exclusively for skill development, vestibule programs involve setting up realistic, productionlike equipment and

materials away from the actual workplace. It reproduces the workplace tasks in an environment conducive to close observation and individualized instruction. Many of the learning principles are incorporated (participation, practice, feedback), and the assessment of skills developed is readily observable or measurable. The time required is typically flexible, depending on the learner's pace of development and the job's complexity. The costs of development and operation may both be high, however, and prohibitive for the small firm. Vestibule training is most appropriate for those positions requiring use of mechanical equipment ranging from punch-press machines to key-punch machines.

Films. Films are often used to demonstrate appropriate supervisory behaviors, to communicate the essential elements of a procedure, or even to convince the viewers to change their perspective on a given issue. Purchased commercially, films typically cost $500 to $800, or rent for approximately 15 percent of that amount. They have frequently been misused organizationally, as fillers or as entertainment rather than for true learning purposes. A projector, screen, and suitable room are required, as is a trainer who has, at a minimum, previewed the film, prepared introductory comments, and developed a thoughtful plan for stimulating focused discussion subsequent to the showing.

Videotape. A technique closely aligned with films is the use of videotape equipment, available in either black-and-white or color playback, with sound. This equipment is typically used to provide feedback to trainees on their actual behavior; therefore, it is more clearly skill-oriented. Costs can range up to several thousand dollars of initial investment, but the operating costs are relatively low and the uses limited only by the trainer's imagination. Several learning concepts are directly incorporated, such as participation, feedback, and reinforcement. A dysfunction is that the technique is most effective when applied to each individual trainee (as in the development of personal selling skills) and less effective as simply a group demonstration device.

Lecture. The lecture is singularly useful for transmitting knowledge, and impractical for attitude change or skill development. It is widely used, economical to develop, flexible in application with regard to both time required and group size, and its effectiveness can be readily assessed by objective tests of knowledge. It incorporates very little of good learning theory, and perhaps is most blatant in its violation of the concept of trainee involvement. Although no special facilities other than an auditorium or classroom are required, the importance of platform presentation skills are often underestimated, thereby depreciating the value of the technique in practice.

Programmed Instruction. This technique (PI) has acquired increasing popularity. Oriented primarily toward knowledge acquisition, PI most clearly (of all techniques discussed) incorporates the major principles of learning. Its highlights are self-pacing, individualized entry at the appropriate background level, immediate feedback, correction and reinforcement, active involvement of the trainee, and arrangement of the material in ascending order of complexity. The essence of the PI technique is the systematic presentation of small units of material (one or more sentences) coupled with the requirement of an overt response (filling in the blank or choosing one of several alternative answers) from the trainee. After self-checking the response, the individual is directed on to the next material. Mastery at one level, then, is a prerequisite to further learning.

Programmed instruction requires minimal trainer supervision, but it is time-consuming to properly prepare materials. PI texts can be used with almost any size group. A PI program is inexpensive to administer although relatively costly to develop. Its effectiveness, particularly in reducing the total time required for learning, has been well documented.

Correspondence. This method involves the receipt of input (texts, manuals, instructional guides) by mail and requires the student to absorb the material and, usually, to submit a completed examination before receiving the subsequent phases of the material. The objectives are typically twofold: (1) acquisition of knowledge and (2) development of basic skills. Frequently, a certain amount of technical equipment (e.g., electronic test devices) will be included as part of the package so that the trainee can practice the skill while at home. Training costs are fixed (the cost of the course is known in advance), supervision required is minimal or absent, and any number of trainees can be simultaneously handled. Trainee participation, self-pacing, and feedback are typically incorporated. The most serious weakness is probably the difficulty (time lag) in obtaining answers to student questions. In other words, the student can become extremely frustrated at the lack of on-the-spot supportive feedback and redirection when needed. Effective correspondence courses are often expensive to develop (especially for small groups of employees or in specialized areas), and, therefore, many organizations rely on commercial programs or those offered by colleges and universities or by trade schools.

On-the-Job Techniques. These techniques are defined as those that allow the worker to produce a product or provide a service while the training takes place. This "learn as you earn" approach has great appeal to organizations and trainees alike, from the dual perspectives of cost effectiveness and motivation of the student (feeling of contribution). In general, total training time using on-the-job techniques is quite extended. Also, the usual orientation of the programs is toward skill development, in sharp contrast to several off-the-job approaches.

Apprenticeship. As typically practiced, apprenticeship programs combine the features of on-the-job and off-the-job techniques. New workers joining the organization (and entering the craft, trade, or occupation for the first time) are provided with a balance of the theoretical and practical through both instruction and experience. Persons in sales, clerical, managerial, or professional occupations would normally not participate in apprenticeship programs. Examples of these programs of 1 to 5 years' duration abound in careers such as mechanics, hairdressing, drafting, plumbing, and printing.

The administrative cost of apprenticeship programs is a function of several factors, but primarily the length of the program, the proportion of classroom hours to work hours, the number of individuals enrolled, and the expected level of productivity of the trainees while they are working. The training staff includes trained workers in the occupation who supervise the trainees while they work. This can be a strength or weakness of the program, depending upon the technical knowledge and ability of these trained workers to effectively develop subordinate workers. Little, if any, specialized training equipment is needed. The learning principles highlighted are participation, logical progression from step to step, feedback, the use of multiple senses, and adequate practice time.

Job Instruction. This method (JIT) of training trainers to train workers has been used for over 4 decades. Appropriate for both white- and blue-collar workers, the prerequisites to JIT are evaluation of the trainees prior to instruction, thorough job analysis to determine the important components, and a detailed schedule of instruction.

There are four major steps in JIT: (1) The trainer explains the task thoroughly. (2) The trainer demonstrates the performance of the skill. (3) The trainee is asked to explain the steps involved. (4) The trainee is asked to perform the operation. Steps 3 and 4 may be repeated as many times as necessary until the frequency of mistakes reaches a satisfactory level.

The costs of JIT can be substantial in terms of both the analysis required and the high ratio of trainers to trainees in the early phases. Time usage is quite efficient, however, since the trainer can gauge the progress of the trainee through direct observation. Skill development is the primary objective, although the existence of proper job attitudes (e.g., adherence to safety) can also be evaluated. In terms of learning principles, JIT utilizes feedback, correct sequencing of tasks, practice time, communication of learning objectives, and the opportunity for reinforcement of appropriate behavior.

Job Rotation. This technique involves the *systematic* movement of an individual from one job to another after sufficient time intervals to allow for basic competency (if not proficiency) in each succeeding job. The jobs may or may not be arranged in ascending order of difficulty or skill requirements. The purpose is to acquaint the employee with the nature of, and interrelationship between, each of several jobs. This can have a motivational effect in terms of developing the trainee's skill in several areas (job enlargement). It also has a beneficial effect on the organization in that it produces backup employees who can be called upon when other employees are ill, on vacation, are terminated, or when extra workload demands arise.

All three training objectives may be accomplished through job rotation. Multiple skills are developed, the trainees accumulate knowledge of several jobs, and the trainees' attitudes are expected to improve by virtue of better understanding a variety of jobs. The primary expense factor is the relative inefficiency (low productivity, disruption of work flow, possible safety threat) of the workers as they become acclimated to the new position. Little or no direct expenses are involved, nor is a formal trainer required. In terms of time, some job rotation programs are almost endless; however, the more structured ones typically last 1 to 2 years, with rotation taking place at intervals of 2 weeks to 6 months.

Unless carefully constructed, job rotation programs seldom fit neatly into a format of planned progression from simple to complex. Also, the limited amount of time spent in each position virtually precludes the opportunity to practice newly acquired skills adequately. Objectives of each phase must be carefully delineated to each trainee and reviewed at the conclusion. Although job rotation has the capacity to individualize itself to fit personal needs, it typically disregards trainee backgrounds and preferences and, instead, forces each person into each phase in lockstep fashion. On the positive side, the factors of feedback, active participation, and opportunity for reinforcement may be present.

Coaching. This method involves the formal pairing of a skilled person with an unskilled trainee, with the coach being made responsible for the trainee's skill development. This has the merit of being inexpensive from a direct cost standpoint, and it effectively utilizes the years of experience that older workers may have. It is highly personalized from the standpoint of teacher-student ratio (often 1:1) and requires no special equipment or facilities. It is similar to job rotation in its multiple objectives of skill, knowledge, and attitude development.

Coaching incorporates the use of multiple senses, makes it easier to gauge the trainee's desire to learn (because of the extensive degree of coach-trainee contact), and provides opportunity for feedback, reinforcement, involvement, and practice. Perhaps the single biggest drawback is the difficulty of discovering or developing persons with effective coaching skills who can not only demonstrate but also explain why they work as they do.

Evaluation of Training

All training programs should be evaluated. Few persons argue with the desirability of evaluation; they do, however, disagree regarding the method to use, or else contend that the cost of evaluation exceeds the benefits to be gained.

The reasons for evaluation are clear-cut. The trainer and the organization wish to know whether or not the objectives have been achieved (and if not, why not?); the trainer also seeks information on how the program (or the trainer's techniques) can be improved.

Training can be evaluated at any of three stages: input, throughput, or output. In terms of input, the costs (expense) of training can be assessed, either in comparison with other programs or against a budgeted figure. In terms of throughput, organizations often assess the numbers of trainees processed in a given time period. Far more effective, however, is the evaluation of output, which can be assessed by one of four criteria.[4]

1. *Reaction* measures the emotional response of the trainee to the program, through attitude surveys, typically immediately after the program.

2. *Learning* measures the acquisition of knowledge. This is measured by objective or subjective tests administered to the trainees.

3. *Behavior* measures the change in skills that occurs as a result of training. It is often assessed by direct observation of the trainee or by self-report.

4. *Result* measures the organizational effect of training. This is assessed through direct calculation of costs, sales, profits, etc.

With the exception of reaction (which by definition follows the training) the criteria can be assessed before, during, and after the training program, and again at a follow-up date. The ultimate purpose of evaluation is to demonstrate whether a change occurred in the positive direction—one that is significant, practical, and can reasonably be assumed to have occurred as a direct product of the training program.

Transfer of Training

Training can be judged effective only if it is transferred to the job. Sometimes trainees learn the required material and skills during a training program, but forget, fail to apply, regress, or relapse upon their return to the pressure-filled work environment.[5] A number of tactics can be used to increase the likelihood of transfer, however. Pretraining tasks can be assigned to heighten their interest; training contracts can be used to elicit commitment; support groups can be created; progress reports can be solicited from the trainees; or various methods of direct reinforcement can be implemented to establish habits.[6]

See also Appraisal, performance; Assessment center method; Attitude surveys; Computer-assisted instruction; Continuing education unit (CEU); Development and training, career path planning for managers; Development and training, management; Human resources planning; Personnel administration; Testing, psychological.

NOTES

[1] A contingency approach to evaluating the strengths and weaknesses of 12 needs analysis methods according to 5 criteria is presented in John W. Newstrom and John W. Lilyquist, "Selecting Needs Analysis Methods," *Training and Development Journal,* October 1979, pp. 52–56.

[2] John W. Newstrom, "The Management of Unlearning: Exploding the 'Clean Slate' Fallacy," *Training and Development Journal,* August 1983, pp. 36–39.

[3] See either John W. Newstrom, "Selecting Training Methods: A Contingency Approach," *Training and Development Journal,* October 1975, pp. 12–16; or Chip R. Bell, "Criteria for Selecting Instructional Strategies," *Training and Development Journal,* October 1977, pp. 3–7.

[4] Donald L. Kirkpatrick, ed., *Evaluating Training Programs,* American Society for Training and Development, Madison, Wis., 1975.

[5] Robert D. Marx, "Relapse Prevention in Management Education," in Kae H. Chung (ed.), *Academy of Management Proceedings '83,* Academy of Management, Dallas, Aug. 14–17, 1983, pp. 91–94.

[6] Melissa S. Leifer and John W. Newstrom, "Solving the Transfer of Training Problems," *Training and Development Journal,* August 1980, pp. 42–46.

REFERENCES

Craig, Robert L. (ed.): *Training and Development Handbook,* 2d ed., McGraw-Hill, New York, 1976.

Ribler, Ronald I.: *Training Development Guide,* Reston Publishing Company, Reston, Va., 1983.

JOHN W. NEWSTROM, *University of Minnesota, Duluth*

Development and Training, Management

Management development is the process of gradual, systematic improvement in the knowledge, skills, attitudes—and performance—of those individuals in an organization who carry management responsibilities. Management development is generally acknowledged as essential for improved results as well as the growth of an organization. In principle, it is noncontroversial. It does become controversial,

however, as soon as an organization faces up to six fundamental questions that are critical to the implementation of management development programs. These are:

1. Who should be developed?
2. For what purpose?
3. Whose responsibility is it?
4. What should be done?
5. How and where should it be done?
   a. On the job or off the job?
   b. In-house or by sending managers to outside programs?
6. How can management development efforts be evaluated?

Who Are Managers? According to Lawrence Appley, former president of the American Management Association, a manager is one who gets things done through others. For management development purposes, a *manager* may be defined as a person who supervises one or more other people. It would include a staff person who supervises a secretary, but not a district sales manager who manages a district with no one else there. By this definition, then, a first-line supervisor is just as much a manager as the president of the organization.

For What Purpose? Management development is done for two (often related) reasons. *First,* and most common and most important, managers are developed to perform their present jobs as effectively as possible. The present job may be changing for one reason or another (more complicated, computer-involved, etc.), but the basic job is essentially the same. The *second* purpose for management development is to prepare people for higher-level management jobs. These are the special cases. Even though many of the same principles and approaches apply, this entry is devoted to the first purpose—to help managers perform their current jobs most effectively.

Whose Responsibility? Some organizations suggest that all development is self-development and that the initiative is up to the individual. This view is rarely sufficient for the effective development of managers. It is far better for an organization to adopt a philosophy (and write a policy) that includes three areas of responsibility for management development:

1. Each manager is responsible for his or her own development. This means that some effort, time, energy, and possibly money should be spent by each manager for self-development.
2. Each manager is responsible for the training and development of subordinates. That is, middle-level managers have a responsibility for the development of lower-level managers (first-line supervisors), and top executives have a respon-

sibility for the development of middle-level managers. This responsibility can be discharged informally through coaching or formally through such programs as performance review and management by objectives.

3. The organization itself has a responsibility for the training and development of its managers. This means that the organization must provide time, money, and other resources to help the development take place. Examples of such help are tuition refund plans for attendance at evening classes, hiring outside consultants to conduct in-house training courses, sending people to outside seminars and workshops, and hiring a full- or part-time training and development staff to plan, coordinate, and teach in-house management development courses. Also, a library of management books should be maintained.

What Should Be Done? Management development programs and activities should be planned and developed to meet the needs of each organization. Many different approaches can be used to determine the needs. Each organization should use those approaches that are practical and effective.

1. *Recognize universal needs.* Most organizations can safely assume that their managers can stand improvement in such areas as planning, communications, motivation, and decision making.

2. *Ask the managers themselves.* Interviews and surveys can be used to find out the needs that managers feel they have. If this step is done well, valuable quantitative data about these felt needs can be obtained.

3. *Ask the bosses.* Interviews and surveys can also be made of the bosses of those managers to be trained. They may or may not agree with the managers themselves. There is no guarantee as to which of them will be right. If there is agreement, this is a good indication that the need does exist. If there is a difference of opinion, someone must make the decision. If the managers who are being trained do not feel the need, then special efforts should be made to sell them on the value of such training.

4. *Ask the subordinates.* Probably the best source of information about the training needs of managers is their subordinates. Managers, understandably, are not usually enthusiastic about, and are easily alienated by, this approach. Therefore, confidential attitude surveys made by outside organizations on an indirect basis may be effective. Results of attitude surveys, however, must be interpreted to indicate management training needs. Exit interviews of people who are leaving an organization may also be helpful.

5. *Analyze the manager's job.* Some organizations (Exxon, for example) carefully analyze the job functions and responsibilities of each manager to determine the knowledge, skills, and attitudes necessary to do the job. Training needs are then determined on the basis of specific performance requirements. Where indicated, performance deficiencies can be converted to training needs.

6. *Use an advisory committee.* One of the most effective ways of determining needs is to use an internal advisory committee representing different departments and levels in an organization. These people can provide input from a number of points of view. In using an advisory committee, the person who makes the final decision on needs (usually the training professional) should first provide the committee with ample quantitative data to consider in making their recommendations.

7. *Use performance appraisal information.* If an organization has an effective performance review procedure, information from appraisal forms can provide valuable indicators. The needs of each manager can be identified and tabulated to determine group training needs.

8. *Analyze problems and records.* An analysis of problems and records can provide some valuable clues regarding training needs. Examples include too much scrap, too much turnover, costs over budget, lack of productivity, and too many accidents.

Development Programs

The question of on-the-job versus off-the-job training has been debated widely in the training and development profession. In almost all cases, the same conclusion is reached: Both are necessary.

On-the-Job Development. One thing is sure: On-the-job training is taking place all the time. Lower-level managers are learning from middle-level managers, and middle-level managers are learning from higher-level managers. The question is, How *effective* is this training? The answer, of course, is that it varies from excellent to poor. Some managers do an excellent job of developing their subordinates. Others do a poor job—either by setting a poor example or by teaching and coaching the wrong things, or the right things improperly. Many of the reasons for poor on-the-job development can be attributed to the manager's immediate supervisor. For example, there are:

Bosses who do not want to develop subordinates. Often, they are afraid the subordinate will become too good and will outperform (and perhaps be promoted over) the present supervisor.

Bosses who do not feel that development is important. They believe only in self-development and thereby leave the subordinate alone.

Bosses who do not get around to doing it. They are too busy with seemingly more important functions, such as report writing, decision making, attending or conducting meetings, planning, putting out fires, and keeping on top of everything.

Bosses who do not know how to develop subordinates effectively. They are willing but not able.

Analysis of these conditions makes it obvious that effective on-the-job training requires:

1. Bosses who *want* to develop subordinates
2. Bosses who *will find the time* to do it
3. Bosses who *know how* to do it

Performance-Oriented Development. Two currently popular approaches include both a philosophy and a set of procedures for effective on-the-job development. They are closely related and sometimes used or interpreted almost interchangeably. They are called *management by objectives* and *performance standards, appraisal, and review.* In either case, a similar approach is followed:

STEP 1: Agreement is reached in advance between the manager and the superior of what the manager is expected to accomplish. It may also include what to do to accomplish these objectives, goals, or standards.

STEP 2: After a designated period of time, a comparison is made between the manager's performance and the objectives, goals, or standards that were set in advance.

STEP 3: An analysis is made of areas where standards and objectives were not met. Plans for improved performance are established and agreed on, and the superior coaches the subordinate to help implement these plans.

Off-the-Job Development. A great variety of options for training and development take the manager away from the job, the office, or the regular workplace. These include:

1. *Job rotation.* Some organizations (AT&T, for example) make extensive use of job rotation as a training and development approach. Managers are moved into responsible positions in other departments where they must learn by doing the new job. Their coaching comes from supervisors, subordinates, and peers.

2. *Reading materials.* Hundreds of management books and thousands of articles are available which provide information on philosophy,

approaches, and procedures that managers might follow to be effective.

3. *Programmed instruction.* Although programmed instruction is used most extensively by nonmanagerial people, there are programmed instruction courses for managers. These are available with or without program learning machines and allow an individual to study and learn at the individual's own pace. The main difference between programmed instruction and reading is that the former has a built-in requirement that the individual learn the material before continuing.

4. *Correspondence courses.* This, too, is an individualized approach. The manager selects a course and pursues it by mail—studying the material, completing papers and tests, and receiving grades from the instructor. This approach, like programmed instruction, is seldom used by managers. Many who begin a correspondence course do not finish it.

5. *Professional societies.* Some managers in professional and/or specialized areas like accounting, engineering, data processing, marketing, personnel, and purchasing learn by active participation in the related professional society. Not only do these managers learn from speakers at meetings, but they also learn by exchanging ideas and experiences with other managers in their profession. They may also learn management skills by "doing"—by becoming a local or national officer in the society. There is, of course, one professional society in particular that is devoted exclusively to human resource development. It is the American Society for Training and Development (Suite 305, 600 Maryland Avenue S.W., Washington, D.C., 20024).

6. *Evening classes.* Some managers take advantage of evening classes to improve their management knowledge and skills. They select courses that will help them improve their performance on their present jobs and/or enhance their chances for promotion to higher-level management. This is a demanding approach and requires dedication on the individual's part.

Far more popular than any of these approaches are in-house courses and outside seminars, both of which are discussed in detail below.

In-House Courses. For off-the-job training and development of managers there is the in-house training program. The term *in-house* indicates that the program is restricted to managers from the same organization. The instructors may be from inside or outside the organization, and the program may be held on or off the premises of the organization. Programs for lower-level managers generally use in-house facilities if adequate conference rooms are

available. Programs for middle- and top-level managers are more frequently held off the premises.

Generally, the organization employs full-time training and development professionals who become instructors for in-house programs for lower-level managers. Where the participants are middle- or top-level managers, the instructors are frequently hired from outside the organization.

Scheduling of these programs varies, depending on the availability of the participants as well as the preferences of those who plan the programs. There seems to be no pattern as to the timing or the length of the training and development course. In general, however, in-house courses are held on company time, although some organizations schedule the programs on Saturdays. In some cases, managers are paid for attending on their own time, in others, they are not.

Effectiveness of these programs depends on a number of factors—listed here in order of importance:

1. Subjects that meet the needs of participants
2. Leaders who are effective as instructors
3. Scheduling that fits the participants
4. Physical facilities that are adequate

In addition to these four basic requirements, the effectiveness of in-house courses is enhanced by top-management support, a favorable job climate, effective audiovisual aids, and related handouts and other prescribed reading materials.

Outside Seminars and Conferences. These outside programs vary from 1 day to as much as 13 weeks. The University of Wisconsin Management Institute, for example, specializes in programs of 1, 2, or 3 days. Northwestern University offers a 4-week course for managers, while Harvard University offers a 13-week management development course.

Outside seminars are costly, from an out-of-pocket view, at least. Are the benefits worth the costs? The obvious answer is sometimes yes and sometimes no. In order to be sure that benefits exceed costs, it is important to do the following:

1. Carefully select programs of verifiable quality. Examine the cost of the program, content of the bulletin (the promised benefits and subjects to be covered), and the brochure description relating to the effectiveness of the instructor. Investigate the reputation of the organization offering the program and, if possible, check with people who have previously attended.

2. Carefully select the participants. The most important qualities are (a) a desire to attend and (b) the subject content that will help improve the manager's performance.

3. Orient the participant beforehand to program details and the opportunities it affords. Also, explain what is expected when the participant returns—such as a written or oral report, discussion with the participant and supervisor, and on-the-job application of what was learned.

4. Discuss the program with the participant after the program is over. This can be done by the individual's supervisor and/or the training professional to determine the value of the course and to encourage on-the-job application.

5. Provide encouragement and help in getting the participant to apply the practical ideas that were learned.

6. Use the feedback from the participant to decide whether to send other participants to the same program or other programs offered by the same organization.

Evaluating Management Development

Evaluation of on-the-job development is difficult to accomplish, but every effort should be made to do so. For example, a main objective of most performance appraisal programs is to improve the performance of those being appraised. If the program is properly planned and implemented, evidence should be sought to document improved performance. Likewise, a management-by-objectives program should be studied rigorously to determine whether the time and money spent are paying off in improved performance and results.

Four possible ways to evaluate management development programs, especially in-house classroom training, are listed here.

Reaction. How do the participants feel about the program? Are they satisfied customers who feel that their time and effort were well spent? Those managers who have participated are in a good position to judge the extent to which they have been helped. Use the following guidelines to evaluate their reaction:

1. Determine what you want them to react to. (For example, subject, leader, facilities, schedule, meals.)

2. Use a written comment sheet including factors determined in item 1.

3. Get quantitative reactions that can be tabulated and quantified. Ask participants to check boxes such as ☐ Excellent, ☐ Very good, ☐ Good, ☐ Fair, ☐ Poor instead of asking open-ended questions such as, "How did you like the leader?"

4. Encourage written comments to explain and amplify the boxes that were checked. A simple

but effective question is, "What suggestions do you have for improvement?"

5. Seek honest reactions. This usually requires that the forms be anonymous because many participants are fearful of giving frank and critical reactions if they can be identified.

Learning. To what extent did the participants learn the facts, principles, and skills that were taught? Use the following guidelines to evaluate learning:

1. The learning of each participant should be measured.

2. The learning should be measured *objectively* (i.e., compare what participants knew after the course with what they knew before). Use such techniques as a pretest and posttest. Sometimes a standardized test, such as Kirkpatrick's *Supervisory Inventories,* on "Human Relations," "Communications," or "Safety" can be used. If standardized tests are not related to the subject content of the course, a pretest and posttest must be developed. If skills, such as oral communications or interviewing, are being taught, actual performance tests must be used on a before-and-after basis.

Behavior. To what extent did the job behavior of the participant change because of the course? This area is more difficult to evaluate because so many factors cause changes in behavior. Use the following guidelines to evaluate behavior:

1. The before-and-after behavior of the *participants* should be measured. This is preferred to an approach that only measures behavior *after* the program and determines how your present behavior differs from what you were doing before you attended the program.

2. The before-and-after behavior of a *control group* (those not attending the training program) should also be measured. These results should be compared with the participant (experimental) group in order to identify, and then eliminate, behavior changes that came from sources other than the training program.

Results. What final results were achieved because of the training course? This is the most significant and most difficult type of evaluation. It implies an evaluation on a cost-versus-benefit basis, where benefits include such desired results as reduced costs of operations, improved productivity, improved quality, reduction of accidents, reduction of absenteeism, reduction of turnover, improved sales, increase in profits, and improved return on investments.

Desired results such as these are affected by so many different factors that it is difficult, if not impossible, to relate the training course directly to the improved results. Efforts should constantly be made to do so, however, and the following guidelines may prove helpful:

1. Desired results should be established before the training program is presented.

2. Before-and-after measurements should be made and compared.

3. The before-and-after results of a control group should be made and compared with the experimental group.

Selecting and Training Future Managers

Selection of managers is, of course, the foundation upon which future development is based. It is evident, too, that many current managers, should not be managers at all. Many were selected because of one or more of the following qualifications: a good performer as a doer (production worker, salesworker, engineer, accountant, researcher, etc.); seniority within the organization; and cooperation with higher management—i.e., doing what the boss asks without asking why or suggesting a better way. Many organizations, accordingly, are faced with the impossible task of trying to develop unsuitable people into efficient managers.

The solution to this common problem lies in preventing the same thing from happening in the future. In other words, an organization should carefully select its future managers on the basis of more and better criteria than past performance, seniority, and cooperation. It should look for generally accepted indicators of management potential. These qualification criteria might include such identifiable qualities as a desire to be a manager, communications skills, intelligence, desire to work with people, emotional stability, and demonstrable leadership effectiveness. Each organization should first determine the qualities its managers need to be successful. Then it should develop a selection process for identifying the qualities and potential of candidates for managerial jobs.

More and more organizations are using the assessment center approach to determine qualifications for various levels of management. This approach utilizes interviews, stress situations, decision-making exercises, tests, and other techniques for measuring management potential. (*See* Assessment center method.)

Once a candidate has been screened and selected for promotion from doer to manager, at least some minimal management training should be provided before the candidate takes over the job. This can be accomplished by working along with a present man-

ager (as at General Motors Corporation), or those selected can be given classroom training while they are still hourly workers. A combination of both approaches is better than either one.

See also Appraisal, performance; Assessment center method; Development and training: career path planning for managers; Human resources planning; Leadership; Objectives, management by (MBO); Organization development (OD); Professionalism in management; Search and recruitment, executive; Testing, psychological.

REFERENCES

Kirkpatrick, Donald: *How to Improve Performance Through Appraisal and Coaching,* Amacom, New York, 1982.
Kirkpatrick, Donald: *A Practical Guide for Supervisory Training and Development,* 2d ed., Addison-Wesley, Reading, Mass., 1983.
Laird, Dugan: *Approaches to Training and Development,* Addison-Wesley, Reading, Mass., 1978.
Watson, Charles E.: *Management Development Through Training,* Addison-Wesley, Reading, Mass., 1979.

Donald L. Kirkpatrick, *University of Wisconsin—Extension, Milwaukee*

Discipline

Discipline (as a formal managerial control device) describes those measures or sanctions used to penalize, and thus control and influence, employee behavior. Typically, these measures include (1) suspension (such as time off without pay); (2) discharge; (3) assignment of unpleasant or undesirable tasks; (4) withholding of promotion or advancement; or (5) direct or indirect criticism (warnings and reprimands), either orally or in writing.

The basic purpose of discipline is to regulate employee behavior so as to direct it toward the best interests of the organization and its objectives. The mechanisms for discipline stem from the organization's policies and programs (as well as those imposed upon the organization by outside influences such as the government, customers, or suppliers) and usually take the form of regulations and rules.

Regulations prescribe the way in which activities, functions, duties, and tasks should be carried out in conformance with operating procedures. They are best when they are positive in language and intent. *Rules* tend to be more restrictive and are thus more likely to be negative in concept and expression. Rules cover a wide range of subjects, including attendance, theft, drinking and drugs, gambling, and safety.

Excessive discipline destroys motivation and invites resistance and defiance, either open or covert. Laxity in discipline tends to erode an organization's

unity and purpose. Over the short term, strict discipline may succeed with some leaders in some situations. Over the long haul, however, a more reasonable, participative approach is likely to be more effective.

Disciplinary Failures. Attempts by management to discipline employees are increasingly subject to review, either internally by labor unions or externally by various federal agencies, especially those concerned with equal employment opportunity and its ramifications. Failure to sustain disciplinary decisions are often attributable to the following:

1. *Absence of clear-cut breach of a rule.* Rules must be specific and their infractions demonstrable.

2. *Inadequate warning.* Rules and regulations should be published in writing and be made part of routine employee orientation and training.

3. *Lack of positive evidence.* Opinions and inferences may be correct, but they hold little weight in arbitration proceedings.

4. *Acting on prejudices.* Real or imagined discrimination or favoritism weakens a disciplinary ruling.

5. *Inadequate records.* The value of written records cannot be overemphasized. An accumulation of warnings and reprimands helps to support the "final straw" incident.

6. *Too severe punishment.* Especially for a first offense, a severe penalty may be viewed as unjust. Arbitrators tend to favor progressive discipline, which grows increasingly severe with subsequent infractions.

Positive Objectives. Most discipline is, in fact, negative, but to be judged effective, it should have a long-term positive effect upon employee behavior. A number of generally accepted guidelines support that objective:

1. The act, rather than the employee who performs it, should be the focus of the disciplinary decision.

2. The disciplinary action should provide a guideline to all employees for future behavior.

3. Application of rules and regulations should be consistent and uniform. Conversely, an element of flexibility should be incorporated in the discipline policy so as to allow for extenuating circumstances when they are validly present.

4. Disciplinary action should not be taken hastily in the heat of the moment, but it should be prompt. Delays dull the employee's acceptance of the connection between the infraction and the penalty.

5. The procedure should attempt to allow the individual to save face with his or her peers. Negative

discipline—especially personal criticism—is best handled in private.

6. Disciplinary interviews should be conducted in the sense of ultimate employee development, so far as is possible, with the overriding view that most employees desire to perform effectively and to conform to reasonable standards of organizational behavior.

See also Labor-management relations; Motivation in organizations; Personnel administration; Power and influence.

REFERENCES

Bittel, Lester, R.: *What Every Supervisor Should Know*, 5th ed., McGraw-Hill, New York, 1985, chap. 20, "How and When to Discipline."

Grote, R.: *Positive Discipline* (cassette program), McGraw-Hill, New York, 1979.

Ruud, Ronald C., and Joseph J. Woodford: *Supervisor's Guide to Documentation and File Building for Employee Discipline*, Advisory Publishing, Crestline, Calif., 1981.

LESTER R. BITTEL, *James Madison University*

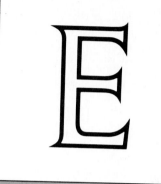

Economic Concepts

Economics may be defined as the social science which deals with scarcity and choice. While economics is not the only social science to deal with these two items, it is the only social science which presumes rational behavior on the part of individuals when they interact with one another to make choices through the social mechanism of the market.

Rational Behavior. By the term *rational behavior* an economist means an individual's actions designed to achieve self-interest. Rational behavior tends to be systematic, while irrational behavior tends to be unpredictable. Economists assume that individuals recognize the constraint of their scarce resources and that they will seek to select situations that best advance their own interest. Rational individuals will seek to accomplish their objectives at the least possible cost. When choosing among alternatives that yield equal benefit, a rational individual will select the cheapest option. Rationality assumes that individuals have some knowledge on which to base their evaluation of possible outcomes.

Self-Interest. Economists are sometimes criticized for assuming that individuals are self-interested, because many people equate this with saying that individuals are completely selfish. Such a criticism is unfair. Charity is certainly an important feature in many individuals' lives, but overall charity accounts for only a very small part of the aggregate expenditures of individuals. The assumption of self-interest does not rest upon empirical study by psychologists, but rather upon a process that might be called *intelligent introspection.* That is, economists justify their principle of self-interest by assuming that their own experiences are typical ones.

Human Wants and Resources. While the definition of economics focuses on the way in which scarce resources are allocated to satisfy human wants, a perfectly satisfactory definition must include the meanings of scarce resources and human wants. *Resources* are those items which can be used to produce economic goods. They include machines, natural resources, land, and any other productive factors. These resources are scarce because nature provides far less of them than human beings in the aggregate would like to have. *Human wants* are the goods and services, situations, and things that people desire. They vary from individual to individual as well as over time. While economists assume that the continuation of the desire for any particular good over a period of time is not infinite, they also assume

245

that human wants in the aggregate are indeed infinite.

Microeconomics versus Macroeconomics. A distinction is often drawn between microeconomics and macroeconomics. *Microeconomics*, often called *price theory*, used to be all there was to economics. The term *macroeconomics* refers to examining the aggregate level of activity of the economy. Macroeconomics developed in the 1930s with the ideas of John Maynard Keynes. The meanings of the prefixes *micro-* and *macro-* imply that microeconomics is a close-up look at the field, while macroeconomics is a broad overview of a much larger field. The distinction between microeconomics and macroeconomics can be described as the difference between (1) a detailed study of the behavior of individual decision-making units in the economy and (2) a study of the behavior of the broad aggregates in the economy: inflation, unemployment, and gross national product.

Tasks of an Economic System. It is not very likely that the human race would still be on planet Earth if each individual or each family unit had merely tried to remain self-sufficient over time. Instead, there is a great deal of variety and ingenuity in the techniques people have devised to perform the economic function of allocating scarce resources to competing uses. Each economic system has its own way to solve this particular problem. Three distinct categories of economic systems characterized by their institutional mechanisms can be identified: (1) decision by a central authority, (2) decision by tradition, and (3) decision by some automatic control mechanism. Economics of the twentieth century are most realistically described as combining all three of these forms of control.

Regardless of the method of control, however, each economy must solve the central economic problem and perform related functions dealing with production and distribution of the goods and services. The economic decisions facing all economies are what to produce, how to produce it, and for whom to produce it. Answering these questions requires some understanding of how goods are chosen and how resources are allocated and organized in a particular society. In societies controlled by a central authority, the economic decisions are dictated to the separate firms, families, and individuals by the central authority. In those societies dominated by tradition, previous experience offers the solution to current economic decisions. In many economies, including that of the United States, economic decisions are made through (1) the decentralized market system or (2) the centralized public sector. Goods and services desired by consumers are the ends toward which the private economy is directed. Resources are allocated in this private economy according to the dictates of *consumer sovereignty*, which means the consumer guides the determination of which goods are to be produced, how they are to be produced, and for whom they are to be produced. If all resources were available in abundance, that is, if they were not scarce, the tasks of economics in terms of choosing alternatives would disappear. The procedure by which decisions are made in a decentralized economy is, of course, of great significance. Economics is important as a social science because it is a process by which the ends are chosen and the scarcity of the resources is examined relative to those ends. While there are a number of qualifications, the United States economy is primarily market-oriented; that is, the composition of goods and services provided is largely the result of private decisions exercised in a network of private markets where free choice is permitted within limits.

Problem Solving with Economics. Economics as a social science deals with the problem of predicting the impact of changes in economic variables. When these predictions are considered to be value-free, the economic approach is strictly *positive*. *Normative* issues are those that include value judgments about "what ought to be." Such issues also require economic analysis. *Positive economic statements* may take the form "A will surely follow B" or "If the price of automobiles rises, all other things being equal, people will buy fewer automobiles." *Normative economic statements* emphasize a particular point of view and will normally advocate only one side of a proposition. These statements may be of the form "A should follow B" or "The federal government should support higher education." Observers of economic policy statements should be aware of the difference between positive and normative economics. Positive economic statements rely on facts to determine whether the statement is correct or incorrect. Normative economic statements are often philosophical and cannot be "proven" or "disproven" by reference to the facts.

Experimentation. The facts in economics are not oftentimes established through experimentation similar to the laboratory experiments in the natural sciences. The reason these experiments are not performed is that they would be unreasonably costly. In order to observe economic phenomena in a laboratory situation, the economic incentives facing individuals would have to be similar to real-world incentives. Such reproduction would, in all probability, be exceedingly costly. In lieu of laboratory experiments, then, economists most often determine facts by means of statistical inference through model building.

Models. An economist's model is an abstraction that is simple enough to understand and manipulate and yet close enough to reality to yield correct predictions. In most cases, it is just not possible to represent an entire economic system in all its complexity. Abstraction is the hallmark of model building. A theory and a model are in many ways synonymous. Each attempts to identify key variables and establish

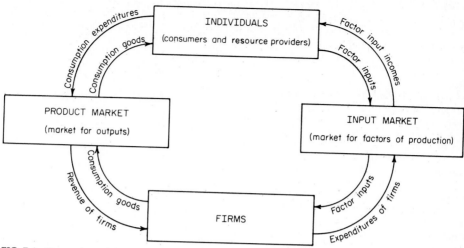

FIG. E-1 Economic model.

relationships among these variables. Each provides a framework which allows scientists to examine the complexities of a real-world situation with greater insight than if they were to try to work with all the variables and relationships at a single point in time. Models are tested by returning to the real world and examining whether the predictions of the model conform to observed events.

The models used by economists in problem solving may be models of individual markets where the prices of individual consumer goods are determined and the quantities provided of those individual consumer goods are examined. Models dealing with individual consumer goods or factor markets are termed *microeconomic* models. *Macroeconomic* models, on the other hand, concentrate on the employment level, the rate of inflation, and the total amount of goods and services produced in the economy as a whole. Macroeconomic models often lead to prescriptions for policy to be followed in order to achieve stable prices, low unemployment, and reasonable economic growth.

Figure E-1 is an economic model by which the relationship between macroeconomics and microeconomics may be described. The model shows how "consumption" goods flow from firms to individuals and "factor" inputs flow from individuals to firms. In the opposite direction, money flows from individuals to firms and back again to individuals. There are opposite circular flows of money and goods as indicated by the arrows. This model incorporates both macroeconomic and microeconomic descriptions.

Macroeconomic Interpretation. It is possible on the one hand to view the overall opposite flows of money and of goods and to describe the situation in which the flow of dollars increases relative to the

flow of goods as inflation. If the model were made more complicated, it would be possible to break down the individuals' incomes into the portions saved and portions spent and to insert into the stream of money the effects of actions by the central bank to increase or decrease the flow of money. It would also be possible to show the government as a purchaser of factor inputs or of consumer products and also as a tax claimant upon individuals' incomes. Finally, it would be possible to incorporate into the model the effects of international trade on the flow of goods and on the flow of money. Each of these matters is the domain of macroeconomics, which deals with the system as a whole.

Microeconomics, or price theory, on the other hand, concerns itself with the individual aspects of the system and generally assumes that the system as a whole is operating at the full-employment level. Microeconomics would seek to determine prices of the factor inputs and of the consumer products and to see how the prices and outputs are affected by the degree of competition. Instead of taking an overall view of the system, microeconomics considers its parts.

Microeconomics

The basic economic model, illustrated in Fig. E-1, shows that the economic problem of an individual is twofold. The individual faces the product market as a demander of consumer goods and she or he must decide how to spend that income over the consumer goods and services which are available in the market. At the same time, the consumer's income must be derived from the factor market where he or she is a **247** supplier of resources. Viewing the economic model in this way, the concentration is on the individual as consumer and as resource owner. Economists classify this view of the economic problem as microeconomics.

Utility. Each individual in this economic model attempts to maximize self-interest within the limits of the information available. Each consuming unit establishes hierarchies that indicate the order in which the needs and desires of the individual are to be met. A well-known hierarchy of human needs frequently cited in the literature of industrial psychology is given by Abraham H. Maslow. Economists, however, abstract from such observations and hypothesize the existence of something called *utility*, which represents the satisfaction derived by individuals from the various goods and services which they consume. The *law of diminishing marginal utility* has been derived from observations that after a certain amount of a good or service has been consumed, additional units of the good or service will yield diminishing increments of utility. A consumer existing in a world of diminishing marginal utility will maximize self-satisfaction by exchanging money for commodities that yield greater utility than holding on to the money would yield, such that additional utility per dollar spent is equal for each of the commodities purchased. Economists do not actually measure utility because the concept is wholly abstract. The only objective gauge of utility available to the economist is the *price measure,* that is, the amount of money, time, effort, or other commodities which an individual is willing to sacrifice to obtain an item. Models predicting the amounts of a commodity that would be purchased by consumers in a market over a period of time and at different prices are consumer demand models.

Demand. Consumer demand for a particular item is a schedule of the amounts that consumers would purchase at various prices. The relationship between the rate of purchase of a commodity and the price of a commodity is often diagrammed as a demand curve. Figure E-2 depicts the relationship of the quantity demanded as a function of price. Demand curves for an individual consumer simply describe that consumer's willingness to make certain rates of purchase at a particular time as some function of price. This inverse relationship between price and quantity demanded has been observed so often that the negative slope of the demand curve is referred to as the *law of demand.* A market demand curve is the sum of individual rates of purchase at various market prices. The negative slope of the market demand curve has also been verified empirically. The analysis of consumer demand is of critical importance to business managers in pursuing the firm's goals of maximizing profits, sales, the value of the firm, earnings per share, share of the market, or some combination of these goals.

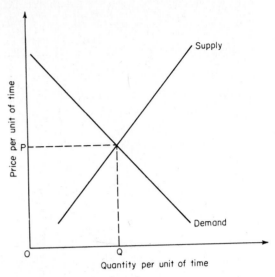

FIG. E-2 Demand and supply.

Three different approaches are used by researchers to estimate market demand empirically. First, direct interviews are sometimes undertaken in order to secure information about consumer preferences. Second, market experiments can be conducted to obtain information about a product's demand function. The most commonly used market experiment involves a series of price changes over time in one market to determine how these changes affect demand. Finally, the most often used technique to estimate market demand is regression analysis of existing data.

Supply. Just as individuals face a budget constraint—according to consumer demand theory—when they make decisions concerning which items and what quantities of those items to purchase, so do firms face technical constraints in producing the goods and services which individuals are willing and able to purchase. These technical constraints are exhibited in production functions which outline the physical relationships between a firm's input of factors and its output of goods and services over a given time. A firm's production function relates the magnitude of a flow of output to the magnitude of the corresponding flow of input which is required to generate it. A firm is assumed to employ this production function in such a way as always to obtain the greatest output from each alternative combination of inputs. Knowledge of the production function is of particular importance to a firm because it is the production function from which the supply curves of firms and product markets and the demand curves of firms and factor markets are derived.

The supply curve of a firm focuses on the price-quantity relationship—the rate at which a producer is willing to supply a product as a function of the expected market price of the product. A supply curve applies principally to competitive markets where price responds freely to market forces and where individual producers react to the price established by the market. In market situations which are not competitive but, rather, are dominated by a few large producers, the functional relationship economists call supply may cease to be meaningful. The supply function is then the quantity a producer would be willing to supply in a given period as a function of price. The positive slope of the supply curve in Fig. E-2 represents the empirical fact that sellers will offer more of their product as the price increases. A *market equilibrium* in Fig. E-2 is represented by the intersection of the demand and supply curves whose coordinates are *P*, the price, and *Q*, quantity demand of the item. The economists' justification that the intersection of supply and demand is an equilibrium position for the market is that neither suppliers nor consumers tend to move from such a position. The position is acceptable to both parties because it lies on their respective schedules.

Markets. Economists use the term *market* to define certain aspects of an individual firm's external environment within which the firm must operate in order to fulfill its objectives. A market is a process by which buyers and sellers interact for the purpose of (1) obtaining information about what they are willing to buy and sell and (2) determining the terms of trade. Most markets involve transactions on a continuing basis. Often there are technical problems in trying to determine where one market ends and another begins. The *perfectly efficient market* is one where adjustments in terms of price and quantity are instantaneous as the result of perfect knowledge of market conditions by buyers and sellers and of perfect factor mobility.

Pure Competition. A purely competitive market is one in which price and output determination are the result of the impersonal forces of supply and demand, not the result of individual actions of buyers and sellers. Economists refer to an individual firm in a purely competitive market as a *price taker*. Market demand and supply are defined as separate and distinct, interacting to determine the price-quantity combination which is the equilibrium of the market. The demand curve in Fig. E-2 may be viewed as the industry demand for a particular item, and the supply curve may be viewed as the industry's supply for a particular item. The price *P* and quantity *Q* would be the equilibrium price and quantity for this competitive market. An individual firm in this competitive market would be required to sell at price *P*. If the firm chose to raise its price, buyers would defect to the other firms in the market. If it chose to lower its price, it would sell its entire output at less than the price it would be able to get. For a market to be purely competitive, a number of conditions must prevail:

1. There must be many firms in the market, each acting independently and each unimportant enough relative to the size of the market so that a single firm's decision either to cease producing entirely or to produce to capacity will not cause a noticeable change on market supply or a change in market price.

2. Firms must be allowed to enter or exit the market at will.

3. The products offered for sale in this market are assumed to be homogeneous; that is, the output of any one firm is the same as the output of any other firm in the market.

4. There are also assumed to be many individual buyers in the market—so many, in fact, that individual buyers and sellers are assumed to act independently. That is, there is no collusion between buyers and sellers.

Real-World Competition. The purely competitive market is an abstraction from the real world. It is a particular way of looking at the operation of market forces and is often used as the standard by which to judge real-world markets. Most economists agree that under rather restrictive assumptions, the resource allocation within the purely competitive market is ideal from society's point of view. In a competitive market, sellers are induced to produce efficiently, and rewards are offered to those sellers who produce what consumers desire. The abstract idea of a purely competitive market is important to economists precisely because it explains why competitive forces are consistent with economic efficiency.

In a purely competitive market, price alone determines the basis for competition. In the real world, however, the basis for competition may be product quality, convenience of location, quickness of service, or any of a number of nonprice variables. Nonprice competition in the real world may be just as intense as the price competition in the perfectly competitive model.

Monopoly. One real-world variation from the competitive market is monopoly. This is the situation in which only one firm produces and sells a particular product. The study of monopoly focuses on situations where the barriers to entry into the industry are high and the existing firms have some protection from the competition of new firms entering the industry. In a monopoly market, the consumer must either buy from the monopolist or do without the product. Economists view this reduction in the choices available to the consumer as less efficient than the purely competitive situation.

Oligopoly. Oligopoly is the term used to describe a market in which there are only a few sellers. There are a number of real-world industries which could qualify as oligopolistic. While economics has a general theory of perfectly competitive markets and a general theory of monopoly, there is no general theory of oligopoly because of the possibility of close interaction between firms.

Macroeconomics

Macroeconomics deals with aggregate measurements which are the result of individual decisions made in the economy. The most often used measure of the nation's pulse is the *gross national product (GNP)*. GNP is the measure of the market value of all the goods and services produced in the United States over a specific period of time, usually a year. The importance of GNP is that it acts as an indicator of short-term changes in productive activity. Without some measure of business fluctuations, government policy could not be formulated and long-run prescriptions could not be made. The focus in macroeconomics is clearly on income and expenditure flows rather than on individual markets.

Keynesian Influence. John Maynard Keynes probably had more influence on macroeconomic analysis than any other economist. His book *The General Theory of Employment, Interest and Money* was published in 1935 after 5 years of severe economic depression in the United States. While many points Keynes made in the book had been mentioned previously, and while the book was confusing and contradictory in some sections, it transformed modern economic theory. The two important contributions of the book were that (1) it explained the existence in equilibrium of involuntary unemployment in a competitive economy like the United States economy, and (2) it suggested policy tools for eliminating that involuntary unemployment. Keynes suggested that industrialized economies like that of the United States could suffer from high unemployment and large underproduction and be unable to rid themselves of the unemployment unless they were bailed out by government action in the form of public works. The mainstream economists of Keynes's day felt that the economy would pull itself out of a depression with little or no government interference. Their prescription, then, was to do nothing, i.e., laissez faire.

Keynesian versus Monetarist. There are two approaches to studying the aggregate level of income and output in the economy. These two approaches are referred to as the Keynesian model and the monetarist model.

Keynesian Approach. The Keynesian model of income determination concentrates on the behavior of households and their consumption-saving choices and on the behavior of firms in their investment decisions. The quantity of money in the economy is not ignored by the Keynesians, but its effect on income and output is indirectly felt as a result of its altering the behavior of economic agents. The determination of consumption expenditures, that is, expenditures by households for goods and services, is central to the Keynesian model. Personal consumption expenditures by households are the largest component of the United States gross national product. In the Keynesian model, great importance is placed on the proposition that the consumption function is stable. Aggregate consumption, according to Keynes, is a stable function of aggregate disposable income. That is, as the rule and on the average, as individuals find their income increasing, they will also increase their consumption but not by as much as their income increases. This stability of the consumption function indicates the important influence of income as a determinant of both consumption and its counterpart, saving.

Monetarist Approach. The monetarist approach to studying the level of income and output in the economy is often called the *quantity theory of money*, and the approach concentrates on measuring the quantity of money and the velocity of money, that is, the speed with which money is spent or changes hands. The link in the monetarist model between the quantity of money and the level of income is the velocity of money, which is defined as the level of income divided by the quantity of money in the economy. The monetarist model rests on the assumption that velocity is either constant or very stable and predictable. If this is true, then the quantity of money will be a very important policy variable determining the level of income and output in the economy.

Keynesians believe that the major cause of unemployment and inflation in the economy is the instability of the investment function—that is, the private business sector. Monetarists believe that the major source of the business cycle is inappropriate monetary policy. The Keynesian view of an economy assumes that the macro system is inherently unstable. Keynes's prescriptions and those of his followers were that government could play the role of stabilizer in the economy by adopting (1) proper tax and expenditure policies, called *fiscal policy*, and (2) appropriate monetary growth, called *monetary policy*. The monetarists, on the other hand, view the macro system as inherently stable and attribute most of the disturbances in the form of inflation or unemployment to government intervention in the market economy. Their often-expressed proposal for stabilization involves a stable and predictable rate of growth in the money supply.

Impact on Managerial Decisions. Macroeconomic models today are well suited to serve management decision makers in large American corporations. Managers often deal with decisions which involve assumptions about the future aggregate level of economic activity, tendencies toward consumer saving, the intentions of corporations to increase their level of investment, and the liquidity preferences of firms and individuals. These same variables and others are included in most analytical models in the United States economy. Thus, macroeconomic models are a highly relevant tool for organizing and using economic information and forecasts in decision making. Perhaps the most important aspect of economic models is that they help to explain economic phenomena. In most business problems, management has some degree of control over a number of variables which are present in the relationship being examined. When forecasting the sales of a product, for instance, a firm must take into account the price of the product; it is the firm itself, however, which will set that price. Only when management clearly understands the interrelationships involved in an economic situation can it hope to forecast accurately and make optimal decisions by selecting correct values for the variables over which it has control.

Special Influences

Public finance and money and banking are two special areas in economics which do not clearly fall into either the microeconomic or the macroeconomic category.

Public Finance. Public finance is the economists' study of government considered as a unit. The objective of the field of public finance is to explain how the collective decision-making process operates. Public finance economists develop theories which link individual choices to collective action and analyze the implications of that theory. Just as microeconomists have traditionally studied the pricing mechanism and how it works, so do public finance economists explain how public choices are made. An individual makes private choices while going about ordinary personal business. He or she makes public choices when selecting among alternatives for others as well as for himself or herself. Traditional economic theory in the sense of microeconomics and macroeconomics is narrowly defined to interpret only the private choices of individuals in a market process. Public finance concentrates on the outcome of collective decisions even as they influence outcomes in the market.

Public finance economists view the government as a means of aggregating individual preferences. In addition to studying the social goals for aggregated preferences of individuals, public finance also studies the decision process used to arrive at such goals. Fiscal policy, that is, the expenditure and taxation policies of the government, is also the domain of public finance.

Money and Banking. Money and banking is the study of the role of money in the economy with the emphasis on monetary process. It is not the study of bank management or financial institution management. The study of money and banking involves the study of monetary process including (1) the institu-

tions which make up the monetary sector, (2) monetary theory, and (3) monetary policy prescriptions.

See also Competition; Economic measurements; Economic systems; Financial management; Forecasting business conditions; Marginal income analysis; Productivity; Profits and profit making; Regulated industries, management of; Risk analysis and management; Value-added tax.

REFERENCES

Friedman, Milton, and Rose Friedman: *Free To Choose,* Avon Books, New York, 1981.

Gordon, Robert J.: *Macroeconomics,* Little, Brown, Boston, 1978.

Keating, Barry, and Maryann O. Keating: *Not-For-Profit,* Thomas Horton, Glen Ridge, N.J., 1978.

Mansfield, Edwin: *Principles of Microeconomics,* Norton, New York, 1980.

Samuelson, Paul A.: *Economics,* 11th ed., McGraw-Hill, New York, 1980.

BARRY P. KEATING, *University of Notre Dame*

Economic Measurements

Various indicators are available which are routinely used to measure and to predict economic conditions. These indicators are described and examined in this entry.

Measures of Economic Activity

While there are many alternative measures of overall economic activity, three general categories of measures are most frequently used: measures of output and income, measures of production, and measures of employment and unemployment. Measures of economic performance are those variables which economic agents attempt to forecast. Generally, they themselves are of limited usefulness in predicting economic performance.

Measures of Output and Income. Measures of output and income are considered jointly in macroeconomics. In theory, the sum of all expenditures should equal the sum of all incomes, since one individual's expenditure is another's income. The most comprehensive of these aggregate measures is *gross national product* (GNP). GNP is the dollar value of final goods and services produced during some specified period, generally a year or a quarter of a year. From an expenditure approach, only sales to final users, either for consumption, investment, exports, or government expenditures, are included in GNP, while intermediate sales are excluded to avoid double counting. From an income perspective, GNP comprises all sources of income, including wages and salaries, dividends, interest, rent, and income from unincorporated businesses. GNP is the broadest measure of aggregate economic well-being of a nation.

Personal income is a second common measure of aggregate economic well-being. As defined by the U.S. Department of Commerce, personal income refers to the amount of income received by individuals during a specified time.[1] It includes money income from wages and salaries, rental income, dividends, interest, income from unincorporated businesses, and the difference between transfer payments (social security benefits, unemployment compensation, etc.) and income earned but not received (such as personal contributions for social security). Personal income differs from GNP primarily by excluding depreciation allowances (capital consumption allowances) and indirect business tax and nontax liability.[2] (A nontax liability is a payment such as a fine or a royalty.) Personal income represents approximately 84 percent of GNP.[3]

The statistical series on personal income is reported prior to allowance for personal tax and nontax payments and is of interest to the business community primarily as a reliable indicator of general business trends. Personal income figures are the only United States income and product series currently estimated on a monthly basis. These data are published in a monthly news release by the U.S. Department of Commerce, Bureau of Economic Analysis, and subsequently in the *Survey of Current Business*.[4]

The term *disposable personal income* connotes the income remaining in the hands of individuals after payment of all taxes levied directly on the individual.[5] Such taxes include federal, state, and local income taxes, property taxes, sales taxes, etc. Hence, disposable personal income is essentially the same as *take-home pay* and is the amount of income that individuals are free to spend or save as they see fit. Disposable personal income is the pool of private consumer purchasing power for which all members of the business community (including banks and financial institutions) compete. Total U.S. disposable personal income in the United States amounts to 85 percent of the nation's total personal income and to approximately 70 percent of its total GNP.

Components of Output. The largest component of GNP consists of *personal consumption expenditures,* which refers to that portion of disposable income that is spent for goods and services. Disposable personal income minus interest paid by individuals, personal transfer payments to foreigners, and personal savings equals personal consumption expenditures. The changes in these expenditures tend to coincide with turning points in GNP. Therefore, personal consumption expenditures are not useful in forecasting GNP. Consumption ranks among the most important economic statistical variables that must be forecast. The value of the nation's total personal consumption expenditures is estimated

quarterly by the U.S. Department of Commerce on a seasonally adjusted, annual basis and is published in the *Survey of Current Business.*[6]

This nation's personal consumption expenditures are approximately 64 percent of GNP and approximately 94 percent of disposable income. By contrast, U.S personal savings for the 5 years from 1978 through 1982 averaged 6.1 percent of disposable income, increasing toward the end of the period to 6.5 percent.

Consumption expenditures primarily depend on the level of disposable income. Consumers' spending decisions relate in large part to the income currently at their disposal as well as to their tastes and preferences,[9] which are substantially shaped by their previous levels of disposable income. In addition, increases in disposable income have tended to lead to predictable shifts in patterns of personal consumption. Since World War II, the pattern of consumption has changed first toward the purchase of more durable goods and later toward the consumption of more services, including education, medical services, and entertainment. For example, the distribution of personal consumption expenditures in 1946 was 11 percent on durable goods, 58 percent on nondurable goods, and 31 percent on services. During the 1960s, durable expenditures rose to 15 percent, while by 1982 expenditures on services had risen to 49 percent of consumer spending.

The decision to consume, to save, or to borrow also depends on the interest rates at which consumers can borrow or lend. Increasing interest rates will both make borrowing more expensive and increase the return to savings, thus decreasing consumption. Consumption decisions are also influenced by consumers' assessments of trends in general business conditions and their expectations concerning their personal future economic and financial conditions. Consumers' changing moods are measured on a quarterly basis by indexes of consumer confidence.[7] When consumers become pessimistic, they defer purchases of durable goods, reduce outstanding installment credit, and increase savings. Consumer confidence indexes are classified as leading economic indicators and, hence, are useful in business forecasting. However, their record of accuracy at forecasting major swings in general business activity is less than perfect because consumer confidence measures are substantially more variable than general business conditions.

The other major components of GNP are government expenditures (including federal, state, and local expenditures) and investment. Government expenditures in 1982 were 21 percent of GNP. (They are discussed in more detail below.) *Investment* is defined as expenditures for new plants and equipment *(capital spending)* plus changes in business inventory *(inventory investment)*. Both types of investment are regarded as lagging indicators. Inventories continue to increase even after a downturn has begun, and they remain low in the initial stages of an economic recovery. Capital spending tends to rise after the need for new capacity has ceased and to remain low for a while even after an upturn in general business conditions has begun. Data relative to capital spending are regularly collected and reported by the U.S. Department of Commerce[8] and by McGraw-Hill Publications, Department of Economics.[9] Investment spending accounts for 14 percent of GNP, while changes in business inventories typically alter gross investment by no more than 5 percent (or by less than 1 percent of GNP).

Measures of Production. The most popular measure of industrial output is the Federal Reserve Board's (FRB) "Index of Industrial Production," which sets production in 1967 = 100. Published monthly in both the *Federal Reserve Bulletin* and in the *Survey of Current Business,* it is an average of industrial production in different sectors of the economy.

The volume of output measured by the FRB index turns down at the same time general business conditions weaken, while the upturns tend to occur before improvements in overall business conditions are apparent. The usefulness of the index in forecasting general upturns is limited by the fact that it represents the average of diverse trends. In addition, preliminary data are at times subject to rather substantial revision. Nevertheless, by means of the FRB index, management can compare its own performance with that of the industry in which it is a member, and it can obtain valuable information about trends in supplier and customer industries that is not readily available elsewhere.

Measures of Employment and Unemployment. In the United States, the *civilian labor force* is defined as the nation's noninstitutional population 16 years of age and over (excluding members of the armed forces) that is either employed or actively seeking employment. The 1983 percentage of the noninstitutional population satisfying these qualifications was approximately 64 percent; this percentage is termed the *labor force participation rate.* There is substantial variation among these rates by age, sex, and race. For example, the participation rate for males was approximately 77 percent in 1983, for females 53 percent. Variations in participation rates may be due to differences in training, productivity, and wage offers, availability of jobs, discrimination, etc.

The *unemployment rate* is defined as the percentage of the labor force members without employment who are actively looking for work and who have not been recently laid off with the expectation of being quickly rehired. Unemployment rates also differ substantially by age, sex, and race group for reasons similar to those causing variations in participation rates. In 1982, the unemployment rate varied from 7.3 percent for nonteenage white females to 44 percent for teenage blacks. The aggregate unemployment rate is one of the most frequently used measures of overall economic welfare, but given the dispersion of unemployment, it should be considered an imperfect measure of economic welfare. Statistical data concerning the labor force, labor force participation rates, employment, and unemployment, as well as data on wages and hours, are published in the *Monthly Labor Review* and *Employment and Earnings.*[10]

Unemployment is generally viewed as the result of excess supply of labor at the prevailing wage. Thus, high unemployment rates are expected to lead to moderation in wage demands, which will eventually lead to decreases in the unemployment rates. However, while unemployment does play a considerable role in the determination of wages (and the rate of growth of wages), other factors are also significant. In particular, unions, market structure, regulations, foreign competition, and the potential for automation are also important determinants of wages.

Measures of Economic Policy

There are two general types of policy instruments used to stabilize the economy, fiscal policy and monetary policy. *Fiscal policy* is simply defined as changes in government spending and revenues (generally taxes) to influence aggregate economic variables such as GNP, unemployment, and inflation. By contrast, *monetary policy* consists of actions taken to change the money supply, thus indirectly influencing short-term and long-term interest rates. As a rule, Western nations attempt to maintain balanced economic growth with minimum inflation through a combination of fiscal and monetary policies.

Fiscal Policy. Changes in either government spending or taxes are termed *fiscal policy.* Government expenditures are one component of GNP. Any change in government spending will immediately change GNP, although valid questions have been raised concerning how long and how large a change in GNP will result. Changing taxes will also influence aggregate economic variables, albeit indirectly. For example, lowering taxes will increase disposable income, thus increasing personal consumption and possibly investment.

The term *fiscal policy* is generally reserved for spending and taxing decisions of the federal government. However, changes in state and local government expenditures and taxes have the same impacts. States and localities do not generally conduct any systematic stabilization policies. Rather, their spending and taxing decisions are motivated by other variables.

A number of factors may limit the effectiveness of fiscal policy. For example, the method of financing government expenditures may constrain the effectiveness of fiscal policy. An increase in government spending, financed by an increase in borrowing, may raise interest rates and result in an offsetting decrease (either partially or totally) in investment. In addition, if a particular spending or taxing decision is expected, businesses and households may alter their behavior in such a way that the desired policy is frustrated. It is also important to distinguish between automatic and discretionary policy changes. Changes in government spending and taxes need not always be the result of conscious government actions, i.e., *discretionary policies*. In a recession, GNP will automatically decrease and tax revenues will likewise automatically fall. Government spending on programs such as unemployment compensation will also automatically increase. By contrast, in inflationary periods, individuals will have higher money income and will be pushed into higher tax brackets, thus automatically increasing tax revenues. These are two examples of the automatic stabilizing properties of fiscal policy.

Statistics on government expenditures and taxes by type of expenditure and by level of government are available in the *Survey of Current Business*. Taxes minus government spending yields the government surplus (or deficit, if negative). The deficit, sometimes viewed as the net effect of fiscal policy, is also published in the *Survey of Current Business*. However, the deficit includes the effects of both discretionary and automatic fiscal policies. For 1982, federal expenditures were $762.6 billion while receipts were $614.7 billion, thus yielding a deficit of $147.9 billion. During the same time, state and local governments spent $405.4 billion and incurred a surplus of $31.9 billion.[11]

Monetary Policy. Monetary policy is concerned with altering the macroeconomy by changing the money supply (or the money stock). A gradual increase in the money supply is necessary to accommodate growth in the volume of a nation's production of goods and services. The Federal Reserve currently has four major alternative measures of the money supply. The narrowest definition of the money stock, *M1*, includes only checkable deposits in banks and currency in circulation. It is the most frequently used measure of the money supply, in large part because it is the most consistent with the prevailing definition of money as anything generally accepted in payment for goods and services. *M2*, the second measure of the money stock, is M1 plus savings deposits and small time deposits. *M3*, a third aggregate, includes M2 plus large denomination time deposits (also called certificates of deposit). The final aggregate, *L*, includes M3 plus other relatively liquid assets such as U.S. savings bonds. Data on all these measures of the money stock are published in the *Federal Reserve Bulletin* and in the *Survey of Current Business*. In 1982, M1 was $478.5 billion, M2

$1991.1 billion, and M3 $2403.7 billion. The reader should be aware that, in keeping with the 1981 financial deregulation, the Federal Reserve has twice recently changed the money stock definitions and may change them yet again. The precise current definition of all measures of the stock of money may be found in the *Federal Reserve Bulletin*.

The Federal Reserve can influence the money stock primarily by changing the banking system's *excess reserves* or *free reserves*. Excess reserves are bank's holdings of vault cash or deposits with the Federal Reserve in excess of their legal requirements. Excess reserves in large part determine the availability of credit and the willingness of bankers to make additional loans. Higher levels of excess reserves, other things equal, imply that bankers will be more willing to lend and to put those funds into assets which will earn them a higher rate of return.

Excess reserves plus currency in circulation is defined as the *monetary base*. The monetary base is a key in determining the money supply and the Federal Reserve focuses on the monetary base in its attempts to control the money supply. Changes in the monetary base are generally a good predictor of coming changes in the money stock. Data on both excess reserves and the monetary base are available in the *Survey of Current Business* and in the *Federal Reserve Bulletin*. The Federal Reserve releases data weekly on the monetary base. However, there is so much variability in the weekly figures that interpretation and forecasting based on those numbers are difficult at best.

The Federal Reserve has three principal instruments of monetary policy, all of which attempt to influence excess reserves and the monetary base and thus, indirectly, the stock of money. The most important of these instruments are open-market operations. *Open-market operations* are defined as the Federal Reserve's buying and selling U.S. government securities in an open market. Buying government securities gives banks and the public smaller holdings of government debt but greater holdings of Federal Reserve notes, i.e., currency. This action increases the monetary base and allows banks to make additional loans, thus raising the money supply. The discount rate and reserve requirements are the other two principal instruments of monetary policy. The *discount rate* is simply that interest rate at which banks can borrow from the Federal Reserve. *Reserve requirements* are the minimum reserves required by Federal Reserve regulation. Both instruments also work by changing the availability of credit. Detailed data on open market operations, the discount rate, and reserve requirements are published monthly in the *Federal Reserve Bulletin*.

When the Federal Reserve changes the monetary base and thus the stock of money, it is attempting to indirectly influence the availability and price of credit. The central bank of any nation (in the United

States, the Federal Reserve Banking System) has some power to regulate changes in the money supply. However, its control is far from complete. Individuals' holdings of alternative assets and the banks' willingness to make loans also play a critical role. When a bank extends credit (makes a loan), it also creates a checkable deposit and thereby increases the money stock, since all the definitions of the money stock include checkable deposits as a component of money. Thus the Federal Reserve's control over the money stock stems from its ability to make more (or less) funds available for banks to lend, but the Federal Reserve is but one actor in determining the money supply.

Measures of Prices and Inflation

Several factors influence these sensitive indicators of a nation's economy.

Prices. In modern, developed economies, the price of a good or service is stated as an amount of money a seller is willing to accept in exchange for the good or service. When the quantity supplied of a good is scarce relative to the quantity demanded, the price of the good will be high relative to similar goods and often (for example, in the case of a rare art object) also relative to the intrinsic value of the materials out of which the object is made. Under normal conditions, a high price will ration a scarce supply. Any high profit stemming from a high price is expected to attract new producers into the field, to bring the shortage to an end, and probably to lower the price. In general, an increase in supply relative to demand is accompanied by reductions in price.

In competitive markets, the price of a good (or service) is determined by the interaction of the sellers' desired prices and consumers' responses to those prices. In competitive markets, the price of a given good (or service) consists of the sum of all costs of production (labor, raw materials, tax and nontax payments, overhead costs, etc.) and an allowance for normal profit. Comprehensive statistical data on corporate profits are published quarterly by the Federal Trade Commission.[12]

Price Indexes. A price index is a ratio that expresses the relationship between the price of a given good at a specific time and the price of the same good during a period selected as a base year or reference point. A price index is derived by dividing the current price by the base year price and adding 100 to the quotient. An index number larger than 100 indicates an increase in the price under study (e.g., an index of 110 indicates a 10 percent increase over the base year), and an index number less than 100 indicates a decrease from the base year level (e.g., 95 indicates a 5 percent decline).

A price index generally measures changes in the price of a weighted average of products or a so-called market basket of goods and services. Price changes are only loosely related to changes in general business conditions; for example, in the late 1970s and early 1980s prices continued to rise while the volume of output declined. However, movements in price indexes are predictable in the sense that a change in the price of one or more raw materials is, as a rule, reflected with a time lag in the U.S. Bureau of Labor Statistics *Producer Price Index* and, after a further time lag, in the *Consumer Price Index.*

The *Producer Price Index* and its components are of interest to the business community for the role they may play in product-price, contract-escalation clauses. Similarly, the *Consumer Price Index* (often erroneously called the cost-of-living index) often plays a role in wage contract negotiations.

Real versus Nominal Values. This entry began by focusing on measures of output and income including GNP, personal income, disposable income, consumption, and investment. In fact, there are two measures for each of these series, one in real terms and one in nominal terms. For example, *nominal GNP* (or *current dollar GNP*) is simply the value of GNP denominated in current dollar values. *Real GNP* (or *constant dollar GNP*) is nominal GNP divided by, or deflated by, a price index to yield GNP figures holding prices constant. Thus, comparing 1972 and 1982 real GNP gives a perspective on the difference in real output produced in the 2 years. By contrast, nominal GNP from 1972 to 1982 may change as a result of real output changes or price changes. Real personal income, real disposable income, real consumption, and real investment are all calculated in the same manner. Both the nominal and the real series, as well as the price deflator series used to calculate the real values, are published in the *Survey of Current Business* and in *Business Conditions Digest.* The real series should be used to compare economic welfare in different years, holding prices constant.

When the general price level rises faster than nominal disposable income, real disposable income (effective purchasing power and therefore an indicator of final demand) declines. The series representing total U.S. real disposable income and real disposable income per capita is of vital interest to management since increases or decreases in real purchasing power influence both the amount of money spent rather than saved and the composition of goods and services that are purchased by consumers.

Inflation. Most economists do not describe a price increase that can be traced to a specific, temporary cause (such as a crop failure) as inflation. The term *inflation* usually refers to a persistent rise in the general price level of a nation. Inflation is described as being "cost push" when it can be traced to increases in the costs of key inputs and as "demand pull" when it can be traced to existing monetary purchasing power that exceeds the total value of goods available for sale at a given point in time. However, in practice it may be very difficult to distinguish cost push inflation from demand pull.

Inflationary expectations have been an additional source of inflation. Consumers', workers', and firms' expectations of inflation will cause them to take actions which may lead to inflation. For example, if consumers expect significant inflation, they may increase current purchases to try and "beat" the coming inflation. However, the resulting rise in demand may also cause the inflation which they expect.

Inflation is considered undesirable because it arbitrarily redistributes income and wealth, in particular, eroding the purchasing power of people living on fixed incomes such as pensions. Inflation is also undesirable to the extent that it raises domestic prices and renders the involved nation's products less competitive in world trade. The following figures represent changes that have occurred in the general price levels (as measured by the consumer price indexes) of the nations shown between 1971 and 1981.[13]

Germany	10.4%
Japan	8.9
Mexico	17.9
United Kingdom	14.0
United States	8.4

Indicators of Aggregate Profitability

A number of indicators must be considered in order to obtain a comprehensive picture of profitability. *Profit* is defined as an amount of money that remains (a residual) after all costs of production have been recovered. Profits tend to decline at peaks of economic activity when output is pushed above optimum rates and to improve when rates of production are increased from low levels. Profits are regarded as a leading indicator relative to trends in general business.

Manufacturers' Sales, Inventories, and Unfilled Orders. Data covering the dollar value of manufacturers' sales, inventories, and unfilled orders are collected and published monthly by the U.S. Department of Commerce, first in a special report and subsequently in the *Survey of Current Business.* Data are shown with and without seasonal adjustment for the two-digit standard industrial classifications (SIC) by stage of fabrication, and for several special market groupings. The main value to management of this body of data lies in a continuing study of the relationship among trends in sales, inventories, and unfilled orders, since these data can signal, at a fairly early date, the accumulation of burdensome inventories (overproduction relative to

effective demand) or emerging shortages as evidenced by growing order backlogs.

Capacity Utilization Rates. A *capacity utilization rate* represents the percentage of a company's or an industry's plant and equipment that is actually being used to produce goods and services during a specific period of time (e.g., as of a given date). Statistical data for capacity utilization are published monthly in the *Survey of Current Business* and *Monthly Calculation of Industrial Operating Rates* and quarterly in the *Federal Reserve Bulletin.*[14] Capacity utilization rates are a leading indicator at cyclical peaks, while upturns tend to coincide with upturns in general business.

Productivity. The term *productivity* identifies the volume of goods or services produced per unit of labor input, capital input, or both. The most popular measure of productivity is the ratio of any given volume of output to total worker-hours of labor input published by the U.S. Bureau of Labor Statistics. The *United States Department of Labor News*[15] contains information on both aggregate labor productivity and labor productivity by major industry group.

Efficiency as measured by labor productivity tends to decrease as maximum levels of output are approached and to remain low during the initial stages of a general business slowdown because employers are reluctant to discharge workers in response to short-term declines in output. Efficiency tends to rise during the upswing after a general business slowdown because rehiring lags behind increases in output.

See also Economic concepts; Forecasting business conditions; Input-output analysis; Market analysis; Productivity; Profits and profit making.

NOTES

[1]*Dictionary of Economic and Statistical Terms,* U.S. Department of Commerce, Social and Economic Statistics Administration, Washington, D.C., 1972.

[2]*Economic Report of the President,* Washington, D.C., February 1983.

[3]All data come from the *Economic Report of the President* and, except where noted, refer to 1982.

[4]*Survey of Current Business,* U.S. Department of Commerce. Historical data for many series are available in *Business Conditions Digest,* U.S. Department of Commerce, Bureau of Economic Analysis, Washington, D.C.

[5]*Dictionary of Economic and Statistical Terms,* op. cit.

[6]The most up-to-date values for all series will generally appear in the *Survey of Current Business* and *Business Conditions Digest* except for detailed labor statistics, which are contained in *Employment and Earnings,* U.S. Department of Labor, Bureau of Labor Statistics. An alternative, easily accessible source for yearly historical series is the statistical supplement to the *Economic Report of the President.*

[7]*Business Conditions Digest,* op. cit.

[8]*Survey of Current Business*, op. cit.

[9]*Annual Survey of U.S. Business' Plans for New Plant and Equipment*, McGraw-Hill Publications, Department of Economics, New York.

[10]*Monthly Labor Review*, U.S. Department of Labor Statistics, Washington. Also see *Employment and Earnings by States and Areas*, op. cit.

[11]*Economic Report of the President*, 1983, Table B-75.

[12]*Quarterly Financial Report for Manufacturing, Mining, and Trade Corporations*, Federal Trade Commission, Washington, D.C.

[13]*International Economic Conditions*, Federal Reserve Bank of St. Louis.

[14]*Monthly Calculations of Industrial Operating Rate*, McGraw-Hill Publications, Department of Economics, New York.

[15]*United States Department of Labor News*, Office of Information, Washington, D.C.

RICHARD G. SHEEHAN, *Federal Reserve Bank of St. Louis*

Economic Systems

Economic systems are distinguished from one another by the way they answer the three basic questions that every economy must answer, namely:

1. *What to produce and in what quantities.* All economies have to decide the kinds of things they want to produce both in general (such as consumer goods, military goods, and capital goods) and specifically within each category (the kinds of consumer goods, whether football fields, beverages, wheat, automobiles, television sets, medical services, and the like; the kind of capital equipment required to produce consumer and defense output that society wants). All these decisions must, of course, be made within the constraints of the resources available for productive activity. In addition to decisions about what kinds of things to produce, every economy must decide the relative quantities of each, again within the limits of the resources available.

2. *How to produce each category of goods and services.* The questions here are what technology to adopt, whether to use much labor and little capital or much capital and little labor, and whether to use the latest techniques available or so-called secondhand techniques.

3. *Who should get what.* In its traditional form, this is the problem of income distribution. Goods and services go to those who have the income to purchase them in a money economy, and the distribution of income determines the claims against the output of the economy.

Custom, Command, and Demand Economies. Prior to the industrial revolution (during the last quarter of the eighteenth century and throughout much of the nineteenth century), these kinds of questions were answered at various times and in various places by a mixture of what may be referred to as *custom and command*. Thus the answers could be provided by following traditions and customs passed along from generation to generation. Feudal society in Western Europe (from the tenth to the thirteenth century) and many past (and some present) primitive economies operated largely on this basis. On the other hand, the questions of what, how, and to whom could also be answered by command or the dictates of (1) a single person in the form of a monarch, commissar, dictator, or religious leader, or (2) a group (usually relatively small) such as a military junta, ruling elite based on royalty, wealth or age, or a politburo.

It was only following the early phases of the agricultural and industrial revolutions in England that differentiation started to develop between types of economic systems, and terms with a more contemporary ring came into use, namely, capitalism, socialism, communism, and fascism. All involved variants of custom and command, although applied to *nation-states*. Capitalism was unique in that it added a third way to answer the basic economic questions, namely, by the demands of the citizens of the society in their roles as suppliers of services or products and consumers thereof.

All actual economies, of course, employ mixtures of custom, command, and demand. Distinctions between economies then rest upon the extent to which the basic economic questions rely mainly on one or another of these methods. Though all economies have substantial elements of custom or tradition embedded in economic (and especially noneconomic) processes, almost all economies strive for rapid economic growth and thus seek to overcome the inertia (or stability) of traditional productive processes; most seek to "modernize," to raise output per head and to change both the quantity and quality of human wants. We may therefore exclude custom in the economies of contemporary nation-states as a major and deliberate way to answer the questions what, how, and to whom, even though the desirability or even the possibility of continuous economic growth and change is being questioned.

The two dominant forms of economic organization thus involve demand and command.

Capitalism. In its pure or theoretical form, a demand-oriented (capitalistic) economy relies upon the institutions of private property, the profit motive, competitive markets, free consumer choice, and minimal role of government to answer the three basic questions.

1. *What?* In such a system, the prices of goods and services relative to their costs of production,

which in turn represent the prices and quantities of the resources required to produce them, determine the absolute and relative profitability of particular products. The profit motive ensures that only those goods yielding a positive profit will be produced, with the relative quantities depending upon relative profitability. If consumer tastes and preferences change, their demands will change, thereby altering the profitability of particular commodities. Producers will respond to such price changes under the profit motive. The price mechanism, determined as it is in the pure form by the impersonal forces of supply and demand, provides the signals to which producers respond. This is the meaning of a consumer sovereignty economy—the monetary votes (demands) of the consumers determine what will be produced and in what quantities.

2. *How?* How things will be produced depends largely upon the profit incentive as well. Each producer has an incentive to reduce production costs. A producer who succeeds in so doing will increase profits. Other producers will be induced to adopt the more efficient production technique (unless barred by such things as patent laws, entry restrictions, secrecy, and the like). Thus, over time, least-cost techniques tend to remain consistent with the factor endowments of the economy.

3. *To whom?* To whom such output goes depends upon incomes generated in the productive process. If factor prices (i.e., wage rates, interest rates, rents, and profit rates) are determined in competitive markets, claims against the output of society are equivalent to one's productive contribution to society.

In short, the things that people want (as determined by their willingness to pay a price equal to or above the costs occasioned) are produced in the appropriate amounts by the least costly methods.

Such, in crude summary form, is the message that Adam Smith presented in 1776, which provided the *economic* rationale for the private enterprise, or capitalistic, system. The message included much more, of course, such as scathing attacks on monopoly, private or public, a political justification of an atomistic organization of industry in terms of maximum dispersal of economic and thus political power, and so on. But in his strictly economic message, Smith demonstrated not only (1) that government controls, planning, and intervention were unnecessary and contributed to inefficiency but also (2) that a completely unregulated economy, *if competitively organized,* would maximize output consistent with consumer tastes, preferences, and incomes—the last being a measure of the consumer's productive contribution.

The Rise of Other Isms. Smith's rationale was heeded increasingly by the British government as it came to be influenced by the interests of the rising commercial and business class. Capitalism, accompanied by the industrial revolution in England—and later in North America—put great stress on individualism (itself a product of the American and French revolutions and developments in political philosophy), private property, the profit motive, and the minimum role of government. The results, in terms of total growth of output, were spectacular in the United Kingdom. Indeed, growth rates some 5 times higher than in previous centuries were recorded. Why the industrial revolution and the capitalist form of economic organization developed first in England is unknown. However, it soon spread to other countries in Western Europe as well as North America, Australia, and New Zealand with similar results in terms of overall growth of output.

Modern Problems. Even before 1850, certain problems of such an economic system as was developing were perceived. Three principal problems came to dominate the concern of social thinkers as well as major segments of society, especially labor. These were (1) periodic instability in the sense that the society was subject to waves of expansion and contraction, or, as we would now refer to it, the business cycle; (2) apparently growing inequality of income distribution which led to a few extremely wealthy persons and a very large mass of poor people, with, however, a growing middle class (rising inequality seemed, indeed, to be part of the economic system that was evolving during this period); (3) persistent poverty related to inequality in the sense that if an economy is expanding rapidly overall and at the same time exhibits a growing inequality, this must mean that most of the fruits of economic growth end up in the hands of a relatively few people, leaving large numbers at a fairly low level of living.

Protest and Dissent. The awareness of these problems, whether due to the capitalist system itself or to the very process of rapid industrialization, led to various forms of protest and dissent and, ultimately, to alternative systems. These took the highly ambiguous terms *socialism* and *communism* with several versions of each, such as guild socialism, scientific socialism, syndicalism, anarchism, and the like. The two major versions persist: socialism and communism. Socialism and communism, however, did not differ fundamentally from command systems as they had existed in previous centuries except to the extent that they were more rationally conceived and systematically applied to nation-state systems as a whole. In their more modern form, socialism and communism are essentially reactions against (1) the specific problems of capitalism noted above as well as (2) the growing concentration of industry and (3) the apparent decline of markets that were perfectly or workably competitive.

Communism. As used in reference to *economic* planning in some contemporary nation-states, communism refers mainly to the *goal* of a classless society with public ownership of the means of production where the distributive ethic of "from each according to his abilities and to each according to his needs" *can* be realized. Achievement of this goal requires not only a high level of production per head and nearly equal distribution of income but also a change in human attitudes away from self-interest toward the larger interests of society as a whole, toward "community." Ultimately, the state, viewed as an instrument of coercion especially under capitalism, will wither away: it will no longer be needed to maintain social order once human nature has been transformed within an economy of abundance.

Transformation of Human Nature. As a goal, proclaimed by various contemporary nations, this transformation presupposes a path along which the economy as well as the entire social order should be propelled. There is, however, little agreement concerning the nature of such a path. Clearly, it calls for more than simply economic planning, essential as that may be under a system of widespread public ownership. To transform human nature may require either coercion or a set of novel inducements. Capitalist theory, à la Adam Smith, viewed human nature as "essentially selfish" and sought to create or maintain a set of institutions—the competitive market system and private property—which channeled selfish motivations along lines that contributed to the public well-being. Not so is the path to communism: Prices and outputs are to be centrally or administratively determined; production for use rather than for exchange and private profit is to prevail; selfishness is to be eradicated; and a new spirit is to be generated through education or reeducation.

Ambiguities of Approach. The ambiguities concerning the appropriate route to communism have quite naturally given rise to sharp differences in the approach among those nations proclaiming the same or similar goals. This is true even for those nations professing to be Marxist or to follow Marxist-Leninist principles. Indeed, the word "communism" in this sense was introduced in England as early as 1841 and was then used to define the more militant and radical wing of the socialist movement rather than to specify any blueprint for economic planning. The *Communist Manifesto* of 1848 was so designated by Marx and Engels to distinguish it from the various socialist movements they believed to be "utopian" and inadequate to overthrow or replace the capitalistic institutions.

Similarities and Differences. Centralized economic planning that specifies what will be produced even in very broad terms is, of course, a form of command economy, the details of which vary sharply from nation to nation aspiring to communist objectives. But, as indicated earlier, both socialism and communism were reactions against the perceived problems of England and Western Europe during the industrial revolution. Furthermore, they involved beliefs that the system designated as capitalism could not resolve the problems of poverty, inequality, and instability without radically changing its basic institutions and in a sense transforming itself into a different "ism." Communists at the time believed strongly that capitalism sooner or later would destroy itself but sought to hasten the process by fomenting revolution and violence. Socialists tended to be somewhat less militant.

Socialism. Those believing in communism as a goal view public ownership and operation of the instruments of production as merely one step "beyond" capitalism. *Socialism* sometimes has this meaning, which implies that much work remains to be done to complete the voyage to communism. In the meantime, under this view of socialism, certain amounts of productive assets can be left in private hands, some reliance upon market forces may be necessary, and pecuniary incentives may still be required with their resultant income inequalities. This view also contends that until the productive power of the economy has expanded greatly, human greed has been eliminated, and self-discipline and restraint have been inculcated, it will not be possible to realize the goal of "to each according to his needs." Thus the Soviet Union and the People's Republic of China continue to rely upon coercion and monetary incentives, in varying degrees, in order to create the new "socialist man (and woman)," who is cooperative, not competitive; honest; hardworking; disciplined; and incorruptible. Until these traits are achieved, some coercion and regimentation will be required to eliminate the last vestiges of bourgeois or capitalistic attitudes.

The Western world is liable to view societies holding the views just described as communist even though Russia refers to itself as socialist and China calls itself a "people's democratic republic." Other nations—such as Cuba, Albania, the Indochina States, and those in eastern Europe—are also designated as communist, although internally the adjective "socialist" is used more often.

"Democratic" Socialist States. There are, however, many other nations and political parties designated as socialist that differ sharply from the above vision and even more sharply in terms of their actual economic, social, and political policies and procedures. Sweden and the United Kingdom under the British Labour party are examples. In virtually all countries of the Western world, there are socialist parties that periodically come to power via the electoral process instead of revolution. The distinction between communism and this view of socialism is less one of economic planning and administration than it is of the extent to which coercion is exercised to realize centrally established economic and non-

economic objectives. Indeed, Soviet communism may best be defined as totalitarianism dedicated to economic growth and is vastly different from Swedish socialism

There are many so-called democratic socialist states—democratic in the sense that alternative political parties exist, dissent is tolerated, elections are regularly held, and the results are accepted. In economic terms, such socialist nations emphasize the traditional problems of capitalism. They stress, however, the need for more detailed planning, more public ownership of industrial assets, or at least more public participation in price, output, and investment decisions of major industries, especially those producing capital goods and those providing "basic" services. The goals of democratic socialism are usually less radical than communists aspire to and more concerned with problems of inequality, instability, and poverty. The goals, in short, are more confined to economic matters under the belief that only a higher degree of deliberate intervention in the marketplace, more progressive taxation combined with more publicly provided services (health, education, power, transport, communication, etc.), and more control over investment will suffice to redress the defects of a full-blown market system. There are, of course, serious concerns with efficiency in publicly owned and operated industries and in investment decisions in the public sector (as is also true in the Soviet Union though much less so in the People's Republic of China). But it is believed that better decisions can be made using *social* cost-benefit analysis rather than relying on private profit as a guide. This belief is especially strong where markets are not "workably" competitive and where external effects are large, such as when pollution and other social costs are not considered by the private firm in making price and output decisions.

In addition, democratic socialism leaves a good deal more of society's productive activity in private hands, especially in the consumer goods sector, than communism and retains some (often substantial) reliance upon market forces where these seem to be functioning well or satisfactorily.

The Isms in Reality. As should be apparent, it is no easy task to define economic systems with much precision, even in the abstract. If one examines the isms as actually practiced, the difficulties of definition and distinctions between them mount rapidly. One should not study communism, capitalism, etc., in the abstract when attempting to unravel basic differences. Instead, one should examine Russian, Chinese, or Yugoslav communism, all of which differ substantially, as is true of United States, German, or Canadian capitalism; British, Swedish, or French socialism; Spanish, Argentinian, or German (under Hitler) fascism. Forms of economic organization vary with any nation's history, culture, and traditions.

Indeed, "the economy" is not something separate from the whole society: it is part of an entire social, legal, political, and religious system. Collectivism in the Soviet Union, the "rights" of private property in England, and individualism in the American colonies, for example, all antedated the beginnings of industrialization.

Coercion and Repression. The degree of coercion or repression in any economy also depends partly upon the means by which a new regime comes to power. If it is by revolution, coercion is liable to be greater and last longer than if it is by peaceable transition. Most of the present regimes in the communist bloc acquired power after internal struggle and thus continue with a higher degree of coercion and centralized administration than socialist regimes democratically elected. This fact has obviously different implications in terms of economic planning and ensuring that plans are fulfilled in a communist or socialist economy, even though both may loosely be called command economies. It is particularly the case that democratic socialist regimes pay more attention to consumer sovereignty and individual rights than do highly centralized communist regimes.

Economic Convergence. Not only are all the industrialized economies shaped by the whole set of past and present institutions, values, and customs, as well as the method of political power transference, but all industrialized economies are also mixed. This is in the sense that central governments now play a substantially greater role in capitalistic economies than envisioned by the original rationale, while central governments often take a somewhat lesser role in socialist or communist economies than originally thought desirable or necessary. Many of the changes that have taken place since the late nineteenth century, and especially since the 1930s, within capitalistic economies have constituted attempts to redress the problems associated with instability, inequality, and poverty. These changes have involved a considerable expansion in the role of government and, to a lesser extent, its size. Similarly, attempts to administer a socialist or communist state have run into increasing problems of bureaucracy, inefficiency, and excessive centralization, which may retard the overall rate of economic growth. Attempts to redress these problems have pushed such economies to a greater or lesser extent in the direction of decentralization, or market socialism, as it is sometimes called. These general tendencies have given rise to a belief in the confluent or convergent economies. The industrialized, capitalistic economies of the Western world and Japan and the industrialized communist countries of eastern Europe and the Soviet Union have in fact moved away from the extremes of individualism and collectivism, respectively, in the economic sphere. To the extent that these trends continue, the *economic* distinctions among the isms become even more blurred.

Political, social, and cultural distinctions, however, are far less convergent, but they relate more to specific nation-states than to any general form of economic organization. Indeed, economic systems have become less generalizable and exhibit rather unique characteristics better explained by national history, national values, and so on.

Variance in Nonindustrialized Nations. The relevance of the terms *capitalism, socialism, communism,* and *fascism* is even more questionable when applied to nonindustrialized states. India refers to itself as a socialist state, yet little of its industry is publicly owned. The People's Republic of China refers to itself as a communist state, yet little detailed planning takes place at the center. Several of the Central American republics describe themselves as "market-oriented" if not capitalistic, but given the political systems, the large role of the military, and the high concentration of property ownership in a few families, *fascist* would be a somewhat more descriptive term. Likewise, South Korea and the Philippines, while stressing private property and the market system, have political regimes that tend to be more dictatorial than democratic, and so on.

Categorization Difficulties. The present realities therefore suggest that economic systems cannot be so neatly categorized as implied by the terms *capitalism, socialism, communism,* and *fascism.* Indeed, these designations appear to be far more polemical and emotive than descriptive. This is true even in the purely conceptual and economic aspects. With reference to particular nation-states, the terms are not only nondescriptive but misleading. All countries "plan" in one way or another. All countries have "markets" that are more or less free and extensive. To what degree either mix exists in any economy is more the result of circumstances and the immediate past than any ideological principles associated with economics. Freedom, coercion, tradition, the level of economic development, the extent and kinds of natural resources, the quality of human resources, the extent of inequality, aspirations, and so on, are more determinative of the specific mix and forms of demand and command than ideologies of capitalism, communism, and socialism developed more than 100 years ago.

Political Differentiation. It is in the noneconomic realm that sharp differences exist to some extent in concepts but especially in real situations. For example, the states that are designated as capitalist or market-oriented tend to be the political democracies of the Western world. They have two or more political parties and conduct elections at more or less regular intervals. They frequently bring to power a socialist or a labor party. In some local or provincial elections, communist parties are elected.

A communist party achieving power by such processes is likely to behave in a much different fashion from one achieving power by war or revolution.

The states designed as communist, on the other hand, tend to be one-party states or even subject to one-person or small-group rule. There may be considerable dissent *within* the party or group on economic issues, but once decisions are made, dissent ceases. Virtually every existing communist state arose following a revolution or external takeover by an existing communist power. Some sought, or are seeking, a radical transformation of previous social relations. The collective farms, the communes, the people's courts, the one-party press, political indoctrination, and so on, are pushed at various times and with varying degrees of ruthlessness among communist states. The attempt is to create a "new" order to replace the old, which all too often was identified with repression, exploitation for private gain, enormous inequality, colonial status, and similar conditions. Some states go to great lengths to eradicate the institutions of the past, such as China in the "Great Leap Forward," Russia in neutralizing the kulaks, and the Khmers in forcibly depopulating Phnom Penh, abolishing money, and establishing a short-lived, harsh, repressive regime. Other communist states work more pragmatically at the process of social and economic transformation.

Misleading Economic Labels. Whether public or private ownership of industrial assets is emphasized, whether economic decision making is centralized or decentralized, and whether coercion or incentives are used to ensure production are more matters of pragmatic judgment for any nation at any point of time. Furthermore, these (and other) attributes are not uniquely related to one another. Indeed, it is possible to have widespread public ownership of assets and, at the same time, decentralized decision making and reliance upon incentives. Similarly, private ownership is consistent with centralized decision making and coercion.

Unfortunately, the terms *capitalism, socialism, communism,* and *fascism* have had much more than economic matters attributed to them. Since it is possible to have varying political, social, and religious institutions associated with any given set of economic institutions, the isms have become nondescriptive and not only fail to distinguish between economic and noneconomic matters but also neglect important differences in the economic sphere itself.

Late twentieth-century capitalism bears little resemblance to the system so effectively analyzed by Adam Smith 200 years ago. In fact, the major specific proposals for economic reform made by the *Communist Manifesto* in 1848 have been almost completely adopted by the present market-oriented economies of the Western world. Since socialism and communism were largely reactions to the real and apparent defects of the early phases of industrialization of the West, their contemporary relevance is severely attenuated, as is the Smithian rationale of the capitalistic system. Economic systems cannot therefore be meaningfully distinguished by use of such terms.

See also Economic concepts; Economic measurements; Exchange, foreign, management of; Forecasting business conditions; International operations and management in multinational companies; Productivity improvement; Profits and profit making; Technology, management implications.

REFERENCES

Campbell, Robert W.: *Soviet Economic Power: Its Organization Growth and Challenge*, 2d ed., Houghton Mifflin, Boston, 1966.
Grossman, Gregory: *Economic Systems*, Foundations of Modern Economic Series, Prentice-Hall, Englewood Cliffs, N.J., 1967.
Marx, Karl, and Friedrich Engels: *The Communist Manifesto*, various sources. No contemporary U.S. businesspeople should miss reading this classic if they want to understand something about communism as an ideology.

GEORGE W. WILSON, *Indiana University*

Employment Process

The employment process can be conceptualized as consisting of eight essential steps. If these are observed, job misfits can be avoided, and equally important, good potential employees will not be overlooked. It provides a procedure for matching applicants and jobs which is thorough, expeditious, and objective. It is a positive process, which aims to put persons in the jobs for which they are best qualified in terms of what they *can* do and what they *will* do. It requires, however, that the interviewer have a thorough knowledge of the job demands, the human environment on the job, and the quantity and quality of supervision needed and given. Thus, the interviewer first makes a diagnosis, then a prognosis of possible job success.

Establishing Specifications. Formal job descriptions and specifications give only a superficial picture of what a job actually entails. In addition, the following questions must be considered:

How often is this person supervised?

What type of supervision will be provided?

How does the supervisor wish to see the job done?

Is the supervision provided by someone with the same specialty?

Is there a rule book to go by?

What are the practical possibilities for promotion?

With what types of people must the new employee get along?

How much pressure does the job entail?

How much interference is there with normal family life?

To what extent is initiative desirable?

To what extent is creativity essential?

How much does the job involve exercise of authority over people?

To what degree is administrative know-how required?

What is the most difficult aspect of this particular job?

What are the political aspects of the job?

Recruiting. The one fundamental rule for successful recruiting is this: The more candidates there are for any available job, the greater the opportunity is to fill that job with the right person the first time. There is no one best recruiting technique for all firms for all situations. Many methods can be used, including newspaper classified and display ads, radio announcements, handbills, company bulletin boards, the state employment service, private employment agencies, college and university placement bureaus, industrial and professional organizations, billboards, job offers to present employees, the company publication, trade and technical magazine advertising, and motion picture and TV advertising. Each, or all, of the methods should be used experimentally until the most appropriate and best one is found.

Genuine affirmative action requires that the recruiting process—as well as the screening, testing, interviewing, and evaluation processes—be as unbiased as possible toward minorities, women, the handicapped, and older workers. In order for employers to assure equal opportunity of employment, recruiting searches should not be based upon preconceived notions. The remainder of the employment process should look beneath surface impressions and attempt to find rational ways to screen minority applicants into the firm, rather than to exclude them because of superficial differences between them and nonminority incumbents.

Screening. An applicant screening form should be compiled for each job opening. It is designed to get the factual information needed to make judgments about qualifications. The form should request the applicant's name, address, telephone number, past three jobs (over three jobs in the past 5 years often indicates instability), present employed status, availability to begin work, earning requirements, ability to travel, freedom to relocate, driver's license number, bonding history, etc. The specification sheet should be reviewed for elements which may prove to be "knockout" factors. To expedite the screening process, much can be done on the telephone to screen out unqualified candidates.

Testing. Tests are of value, particularly in helping to evaluate what a person *can do* based on intelligence, aptitudes, and proficiency. Tests are also valuable in evaluating *will-do* factors, which are based on personality, temperament, and motivation. Projective techniques are helpful if a qualified professional psychologist interprets the test results in the light of job conditions and demands. Tests and testing procedures must meet Equal Employment Opportunity Commission (EEOC) requirements.

Reference Checking. Consciously or unconsciously, people are not always truthful in telling about themselves. They tend to put the most favorable interpretation upon whatever has happened to them in the past. At least three telephone reference checks should be conducted to verify employment history only. Inquiries about performance tread on dangerous ground and, generally, should be avoided. In any event, it is best to check with the person's former supervisor or operating official rather than with persons in the personnel department. Also, utilize college transcripts, credit reports (with the person's permission as required by law), a bonding company, and the individual's W-2 form. Checking personal or character references is almost uniformly futile.

Interviewing. A *guided interview form* should be utilized to aid in eliciting all the information needed about a particular person. It differs from the screening form in that it is far more comprehensive, for it is designed to learn about the attitudes and feelings of the person and is used only with previously screened prospects. The interview lends itself to analysis of what the individual will do by reviewing what the candidate has done in the past.

Evaluating the Candidate. Interpreting the guided interview information enables the interviewer to forecast what an individual will do. Behavior patterns that are important (in variable degrees) in most jobs relate to job tenure, work habits, tenacity, competitive spirit, loyalty, planning, organizing activity, relations with others, and the ability to lead.

Selecting the Right Person. At this point the several qualified candidates may be rated on a four-level scale:

1. Almost perfectly qualified
2. Well qualified—no serious deficiencies
3. Marginally qualified—seriously deficient in at least one will-do requirement
4. Unqualified

The question of whether or not a particular applicant should be employed depends also upon certain factors outside his or her qualifications. For example, if there are a large number of level 1s, the firm can afford to be selective. Urgency in filling the position without delay may necessitate hiring someone rated 3. One should not, however, be tempted to raise the rating to a 2. Instead, the individual who was given the 3 rating should be hired with the total understanding that the chance for success and permanence is the same as the individual's qualifications: marginal.

Summary. Shortcuts are not advisable. The important thing is to go through all the eight steps. There is no substitute for systematic thoroughness.

See also Affirmative action; Equal employment opportunity, minorities and women; Interviewing, employee; Job analysis; Job evaluation; Personnel administration; Testing, psychological.

REFERENCES

Farmer, Anthony X.: "How to Hire the Right Person the First Time," *Training Management and Motivation*, Spring 1976.

Fear, Richard A., and James F. Ross: *Jobs, Dollars, and EEO: How to Hire More Productive Entry-Level Workers*, McGraw-Hill, New York, 1983.

Flippo, Edwin B.: *Principles of Personnel Management*, 5th rev. ed., McGraw-Hill, New York, 1980, part 3, "Procurement."

ANTHONY X. FARMER, *The Personnel Laboratory, Inc.*

Energy Management

Energy management is a systematic approach for controlling the energy utilization of a facility so as to reduce energy waste in a cost-effective manner without adversely affecting the facility's functional requirements.

The results of continued efforts at energy management can be significant. From 1972 to 1979, for example, the 10 industries that are the heaviest consumers of energy improved the efficiency of their energy use by 15.4 percent. The potential for savings continues to be great. In commercial buildings, for instance, which number more than 4 million in the United States, a 15 to 50 percent reduction in energy consumption is generally possible. The greatest potential for energy savings is in buildings built between 1945 and 1973, which account for approximately one-third of all commercial space in the United States. These buildings will spend $5 billion to $7 billion annually for energy throughout the 1980s.

Energy Audits. * The first phase in an energy management program involves an energy audit of the facility. An energy audit serves the purpose of identifying where a building or plant facility uses energy and where energy conservation opportunities exist.

There is a direct relationship between the cost of the audit (depending on the amount of data collected and analyzed) and the number of energy conservation opportunities to be found. Therefore the first decision to be made is on the cost of the audit, which determines the type of audit to be performed.

The second necessary decision relates to the type of facility. For example, a building audit may emphasize the building envelope, lighting, heating, and ventilation requirements. On the other hand, an audit of an industrial plant stresses the process requirements.

Most energy audits fall into one or more of three categories: walk-through, mini-audit, or maxi-audit.

Walk-Through Audit. This is the least costly audit and identifies preliminary energy savings. A visual inspection of the facility is made to determine maintenance and operation energy-saving opportunities, and to collect information to determine the need for a more detailed analysis.

Mini-Audit. This type requires tests and measurements to quantify energy uses and losses and determine the economics for changes.

Maxi-Audit. This procedure goes one step further than the mini-audit. It contains an evaluation of how much energy is used for each function, such as lighting or process. It also requires a model analysis, such as a computer simulation, to determine energy-use patterns and predictions on a year-round basis, taking into account such variables as weather data. The chief distinction between the mini-audit and the walk-through audit is that the mini-audit requires an accounting system for energy to be established as well as a computer simulation.

Energy Accounting. A significant part of the overall energy auditing program is the ability to measure starting conditions and to establish specific savings targets. Accordingly, it is vital to establish an energy accounting system at the beginning of the program. It is important to account for (1) total consumption, (2) cost, and (3) how much energy is used for each utility, such as steam, water, air, and natural gas. This procedure enables the development of an appropriate energy conservation strategy.

Energy efficiency ratios alone cannot, however, answer the kinds of questions asked by business managers and/or government authorities:

- If we are conserving energy, why is our total consumption increasing?

- If we are wasting energy, why is our total energy consumption decreasing?

- If we have made no change in energy efficiency, why is our energy consumption changing?

Thus there is a need to evaluate several impacting factors such as weather, volume mix, and pollution control, all of which affect energy consumption.

Weather Impact. The effect of weather changes (colder winter or hotter summer) on the energy consumption is defined as the change in degree-days multiplied by the heating or cooling efficiency during the periods used as the basis for the analysis. The financial impact of weather is the impact calculated (as above) multiplied by the cost per unit of energy last year-to-date. That is, the impact of weather changes on energy use, or cost, is the difference between this and the last period's weather times the heating or cooling energy efficiency in the last, or base, period. The result ignores improvements in efficiency (identified later as energy conservation effects) and inflation (identified later as price effects), and isolates the effect of weather.

Volume/Mix Impact. The impact of volume and/or product mix changes is the amount of energy that is used currently as compared with previously, solely as the result of producing more (or less) product or proportionately more (or less) energy-intense products.

Pollution Control Impact. The impact of the energy increase or decrease to control pollution in the current period versus any other time period is simply the difference in the energy used in the two periods. The financial impact is the impact (calculated above) multiplied by the cost per unit of energy in the last period. The result ignores conservation and price effects as before and isolates the effect of pollution control.

Other Impacts. The impact of other energy uses, such as experimental or start-up of product lines without history of base loads, is simply the difference in energy used between the two periods being compared. The economic impact is the impact (calculated above) multiplied by the cost per unit of energy in the prior period.

Conservation Opportunities. Energy conservation opportunities lie in three main categories:

Category 1: Quick Fix. This category includes operation and maintenance measures, lighting reduction, change in maintained temperature conditions, insulation, etc. Category 1 offers the highest payback and is the easiest area to implement.

Category 2: Established Building and Equipment Modification. This category includes reduction in ventilation requirements, time clocks, night setback, and upgraded automatic temperature controls. Cate-

---

* Adapted with permission from Thumann, Albert: *Handbook of Energy Audits*, 2d ed., Fairmont Press, Atlanta, Ga., 1983.

gory 2 opportunities can be accomplished at a modest cost.

Category 3: Major Investments and New Technologies. This category is probably the most important, but it requires major capital authorization funds. It is usually implemented only after categories 1 and 2 are completed. Examples in this category include building energy management systems, heat recovery systems, and conversion to variable air-volume systems.

Creative Financing Opportunities. Building owners and managers who reach category 3 may wish to use one of the several "creative financing mechanisms" now available. For example, a simple alternative to purchasing an energy management system is to lease it from the equipment manufacturer. A second option is to have the equipment installed by a limited partnership that owns the equipment. The building owner pays a monthly fee for use of the equipment based on an agreed-upon shared-savings formula. The decision as to whether to use a shared-savings program depends in part, of course, on the building owner's willingness to take risk. For example, installation of an energy management system (EMS) usually offers a high rate of return on the investment. If building owners are confident in the energy analysis for the EMS equipment, then it pays them to purchase the system instead of having to pay a third party a monthly shared-savings fee.

Energy Consultants. Building owners and managers often turn to an energy consultant in evaluating the energy cost reduction opportunities which exist. As when choosing consultants, generally it is important to evaluate whether the consultant (1) has specialized knowledge in your type of building; (2) has a proven track record; (3) offers an unbiased appraisal of the facility, or also represents an equipment manufacturer. One good way to identify qualified energy consultants and staff energy managers is to look for individuals certified by the Certification Program for Energy Managers, inaugurated in 1980 by the Association of Energy Engineers.

Setting Energy Goals. Energy management objectives must be translated into clear goals. Since funds are limited, the financial goals as well as the energy goals need to be defined. These goals should be communicated to the individuals who are familiar with the detailed operation. They are in position to make the greatest contributions. They need to be informed of the potential for saving yearly operating expenses and how it will affect the profitability of the company.

When setting priorities, it is necessary to make sure that competing energy conservation projects are evaluated on the same basis. This means all life-cycle cost analysis should be based on the same fuel costs and the same assumptions of escalation. In addition, financial factors, such as depreciation method and economic life, need to be evaluated the same way. Competing projects can be ranked in order of (1) best rate returns on investment, (2) best pay-out period, and (3) best ratio of BTU-per-year savings to capital cost.

Organizing for Energy Management. Energy management affects almost every major activity of a facility, such as electrical engineering; cost control; control systems engineering; utility engineering; piping design; mechanical engineering; chemical engineering; heating, ventilation, and air-conditioning engineering; building design; environmental engineering; operations; maintenance; and accounting and financial management.

Each facility should assign individuals to be responsible for one or more of the above functions. The problem facing management is how to organize the energy management activity so that all functions are moving in a common direction. The situation becomes more complex, however, when several plants or facilities are involved. Since unified direction and coordination for the program are needed, the position of energy manager emerges in many organizations. Many companies, however, rely upon forming a committee and assigning an internal coordinator. Regardless of approach, a successful program requires an unqualified commitment from top management.

Program Essentials. The following checklist provides an outline of essentials for developing an effective energy management program.

1. *Inform line supervisors of:*
   a. The economic reasons for the need to conserve energy.
   b. Their responsibility for implementing energy-saving actions in the areas of their accountability.
2. *Establish a committee having the responsibility for formulating and conducting an energy conservation program. This committee should consist of:*
   a. Representatives from each department in the plant.
   b. A coordinator appointed by, and reporting to, management.
   Note: In smaller organizations, the manager and his or her staff may conduct energy conservation activities as part of their management duties.
3. *Provide the committee members with guidelines as to what is expected of them, namely, to:*
   a. Plan and participate in energy-saving surveys.
   b. Develop uniform record keeping, reporting, and energy accounting.
   c. Seek and develop ideas for ways to save energy.

  d. Communicate these ideas and suggestions to all parties responsible for implementation.

  e. Establish challenging, but achievable, goals for energy saving.

  f. Develop ideas and plans for enlisting employee support and participation.

  g. Plan and conduct a continuing program of activities to stimulate organizational interest in energy conservation efforts.

4. *Set goals in energy saving, including:*

  a. A preliminary goal at the start of the program.

  b. A revised goal later on, based on savings potential estimated from results of surveys.

5. *If necessary, employ external assistance in surveying the plant and making recommendations.*

6. *Communicate periodically with employees regarding management's emphasis on energy conservation action and report on progress.*

Energy management relies on creatively applying existing technology in new ways. A questioning ("Why?") approach must be promoted. A team of engineers representing several disciplines should meet periodically to brainstorm the various energy management proposals. The challenges facing the energy management team are great, but the stakes are equally high.

See also Audit, management; Budgeting, capital; Cost-benefit analysis; Environment, physical; Productivity improvement; Real estate management, corporate.

REFERENCES

Meckler, M.: *Energy Conservation in Buildings and Industrial Plants*, McGraw-Hill, New York, 1980.

Thumann, Albert: *Handbook of Energy Audits*, 2d ed., Fairmont Press, Atlanta, 1983.

Turner, W. C.: *Energy Management Handbook*, John Wiley, New York, 1982.

  ALBERT THUMANN, *Association of Energy Engineers*

Engineering, Industrial

Industrial engineers, trained in the principles of administration, behavioral science, computer science, economics, ergonomics, manufacturing systems, operations research, quality control, statistics, systems analysis and design, work study, and many other specialized fields, apply their unique skills to improve productivity in every type of business, manufacturing, or service industry.

Industrial engineers perform a variety of tasks in industry, including (1) scheduling traffic and maintenance, (2) improving the flow of work in large offices, (3) developing more efficient methods for the distribution of goods and services, (4) locating and laying out new facilities, (5) selecting processes and methods, (6) developing work standards, (7) designing and installing management information and data processing systems, (8) developing materials requirement planning systems, (9) performing economic analyses, (10) designing job evaluation systems, (11) instituting adequate safety and health procedures, (12) systems integration, and the design of production systems in the manufacuring industry, where two-thirds of the industrial engineers work.

Depending on the area of specialization, an industrial engineer may work under many different titles, including methods engineer, systems engineer, and sometimes manufacturing or production engineer. Regardless of title, the industrial engineering profession is best distinguished by the confluence of historical and modern engineering principles creatively applied to productivity improvement. Although the principles of industrial engineering were practiced long before the industrial revolution when civilized people first began to organize and improve their labor efforts, the definition adopted by the 43,000-member Institute of Industrial Engineers reflects the work of many industrial engineers, scientists, and academicians, beginning with the work of Frederick W. Taylor in about 1890. This definition reads:

> Industrial Engineering *is concerned with the design, improvement, and installation of integrated systems of people, material, equipment, and energy. It draws upon the specialized knowledge and skills in the mathematical, physical, and social sciences together with the principles and methods of engineering analysis and design to specify, predict, and evaluate the results to be obtained from such systems.*

Taylor, the father of scientific management, began a systematic study of ways to improve labor productivity among steelworkers in the late 1890s. He eventually developed a series of principles of scientific management. During the early 1900s, many pioneers in the scientific approach to management added to the body of knowledge, forming the foundation of modern industrial engineering. Henry L. Gantt developed management procedures and principles and a humanistic approach to management. Frank and Lillian Gilbreth worked extensively with motion study and methods improvement. Harrington Emerson evolved a set of efficiency and organization principles and a bonus-payment incentive plan.

The modern industrial engineer now has the option to use computers, robots, and other technology to more effectively solve industrial engineering–related problems in the design, improvement, and installation of integrated systems.

See also Cost improvement; Job analysis; Paperwork simplification; Production/operations management; Productivity improvement; Systems and procedures; Therbligs; Value analysis; Work measurement; Work sampling; Work simplification and improvement.

REFERENCES

Emerson, Harrington: *The Twelve Principles of Efficiency*, The Engineering Magazine Company, New York, 1912.

Rathe, Alex W., ed.: *Gantt on Management*, American Management Association and American Society of Mechanical Engineers, New York, 1961.

Salvendy, Gavriel: *Handbook of Industrial Engineering*, John Wiley, New York, 1982.

Taylor, Frederick W.: *The Principles of Scientific Management*, Harper & Brothers, New York, 1911.

GREGORY BALESTRERO, *Institute of Industrial Engineers, Inc.*

Engineering Management

Engineering, which can be defined as the adaptation of natural forces and materials to their beneficial use by human beings, is practiced in a wide range of industrial, institutional, and governmental organizations. In the normal industrial firm, engineering may be found in the organization structure in facilities design, product design, service engineering, and maintenance or plant engineering. In institutions such as hospitals, universities, and public school systems, facility and maintenance engineering also plays a key role. Another important area is consulting and design engineering provided by professional firms. *Engineering News-Record* reported that its listing of the top 500 design firms in 1983 represented billings of approximately $8.5 billion and staffs of 124,000 people. These firms engage primarily in the construction design of new facilities and in planning and economic feasibility studies. In addition, there are numerous firms in the "design-construct" classification which provide turnkey services from initial design of a plant or facility through construction and start-up.

While the broad concepts of managing these activities are the same as those for management in general, some special conditions and tools of managing must be recognized and used by the successful engineering manager. Professional engineering resources are available as time, such as worker-hours or worker-days. They cannot be stored or inventoried. They must be used effectively or they are wasted. The engineering manager's principal goal is to optimize the utilization of the professional and technical resources in an organization when guiding that organization toward meeting its objectives.

Although the specific examples that follow are based upon the management of a professional consulting and design firm, the concepts and approaches apply to engineering activities in all types of organizations.

Overall Planning

The first step in planning is to establish the broad goals and objectives of the engineering organization. For a professional design firm, the general objective may be stated as follows: to provide multidisciplined consulting engineering and design services of the highest quality to a wide range of industrial, utility, health care, and institutional clients, on a profitable basis. This broad objective may then be made more detailed by establishing dollar-volume goals of billings and profit over a 5-year period. This first year's planning activity breaks down the totals by type of client (*see* Table E-1).

Organization Structures. To achieve this projected level of operation requires an organization and staffing plan. Figure E-3 shows the type of organization for a typical design firm that would be needed to attain these objectives. Position descriptions, as shown in Table E-2, supplement the organization chart. An engineering organization, however, needs to be flexible. Rigid adherence to the organization

TABLE E-1 Example of an Engineering Firm's Objectives

XYZ Design Inc.—1985 objectives				
Total billings $4,500,000				
Profits (net after taxes) $300,000				
Breakdown of billings and profit				
Type of client	Billings	%	Profit	%
Industrial clients	$1,575,000	35	$120,000	40
Utility clients	$1,125,000	25	$ 90,000	30
Institutional clients	$1,800,000	40	$ 90,000	30
Totals	$4,500,000	100	$300,000	100

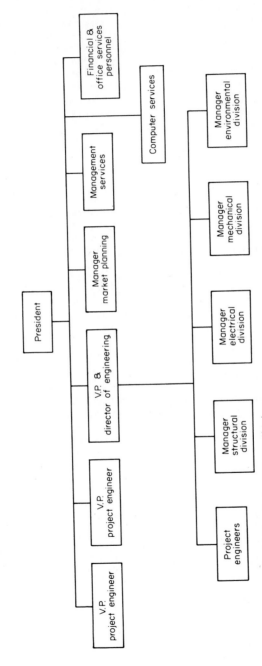

FIG. E-3 Typical consulting-design firm organization.

TABLE E-2 Example of a Position Guide

POSITION: Director of Engineering
REPORTS TO: President
PURPOSE OF POSITION: To provide overall technical and administrative control of corporate engineering activities.
DUTIES: 1. To provide overall technical direction and coordination of engineering design activities—mechanical, electrical, structural-civil,and environmental.
2. To maintain overall cost control of all engineering design activities through administration of project budgets, cost reports, and other similar tools.
3. To maintain top quality of engineering design work through procedures to eliminate errors and omissions in design, calculations, specifications, and drawings.
4. To improve efficiency of engineering operations through use of techniques in standard specifications and computer-aided design and drafting.
5. To maintain schedules and ensure completion of work on schedule.
6. To administer and implement engineering personnel policies and procedures such as job classifications, merit reviews, hiring procedures, worker utilization, and training.
7. To maintain liaison with project engineers on project schedules, costs, quality of work, and client problems.
8. To deal with clients as required.
9. To undertake business development and promotional activities as required.

chart can create problems rather than avoid them. Organizational changes may be necessary to meet special conditions.

For carrying out major projects, a project-type organization, as shown in Fig. E-4, may be used. The project engineer or project manager assembles a multidisciplined team to provide the talents and resources needed for the project. The project manager has responsibilities for successful technical completion as well as for cost control and adherence to schedule. The project-type organization is used within the more traditional organization structure.

Total worker needs to meet the billing and profit objectives are determined by using billings per employee. If experience indicates that $30,000 per year per employee represents normal billings and produces a net profit of 6.6 percent, an average staff of 150 would be required to produce the target of $4,500,000 shown in Table E-1. The specific mix of work force among the functional departments will depend upon the mix represented by the typical work level, tempered by any prospects for new projects which may represent a bias toward one particular discipline.

Detailed Planning. One of the first requirements is to see that job schedules and budgets are established for individual projects. For each project, an analysis must be made to determine the total number of worker-hours of engineering and technical (usually drafting) time required to complete the project. These requirements are broken down by the various disciplines, i.e., mechanical, electrical, structural, civil, and the like. As part of this procedure, a detailed list of drawings, with worker-hour estimates required, is prepared by each department manager. Also, she or he prepares estimates of the time required for preparation of the necessary specifications and cost estimates. The project manager or project engineer for the project then assembles these into a composite drawing list and composite worker-hour requirement. The drawing list is prepared in such a fashion that it then becomes the basis for the departmental schedules for a specific project. Figure E-5 shows a typical drawing schedule which is commonly used in construction design engineering activities.

The project manager, with the detailed information developed for scheduling, then prepares a budget for the specific project, indicating the hours and costs allocated to each department. Once this budget is established, it becomes a key tool in the process of controlling the costs and progress of the particular project.

Execution and Control

It is difficult to separate the execution and control stages of engineering management, as they work together in conjunction with planning in a feedback-type system. The following, however, will outline some of the more significant steps involved in the execution and control of engineering projects.

Work Flow. Individual work assignments are prepared from the detailed schedules. The engineering or project manager has the responsibility of coordinating the sequence of work and interrelationship of work carried out by the various disciplines. For example, on a project involving the construction design for an industrial steam plant, the first step is to develop the flow sheet for the plant and determine and specify the major items of equipment, such as the boilers, feedwater pumps, coal-handling equipment, stokers, and the like. A general arrangement drawing is then prepared, usually by the mechanical department, showing the relative positioning of the items of equipment and piping for the plant. As this general arrangement drawing is being completed, information is passed to the structural department so that it can begin to develop the design of the foundations, supporting structures, and the housing for the complete plant. As this work progresses, the electrical engineering department is working to develop the power distribution design based upon mechanical information giving the sizes and types of motors

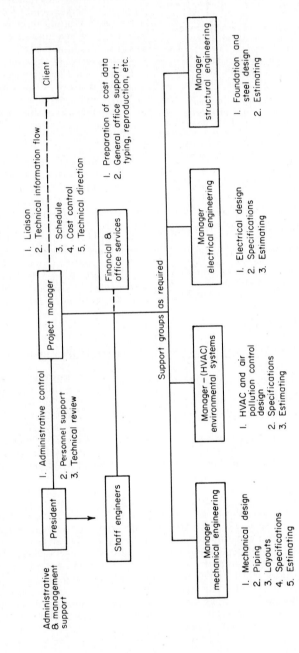

FIG. E-4 Example of a project organization.

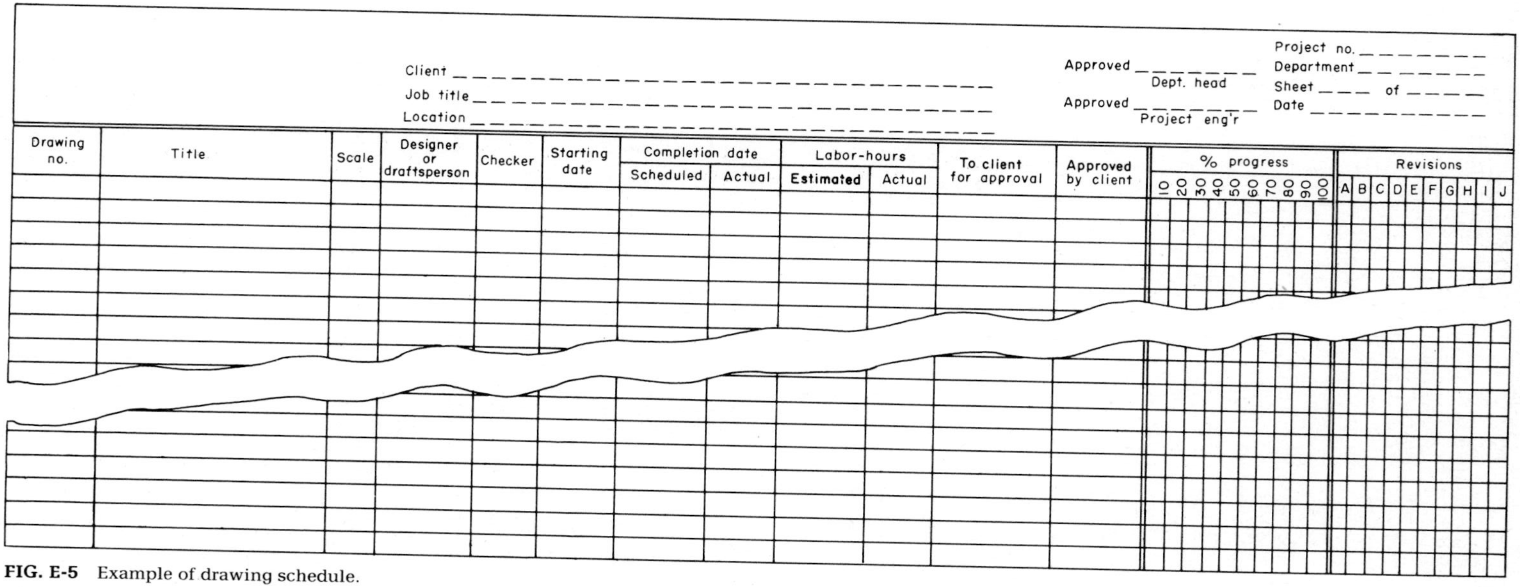

FIG. E-5 Example of drawing schedule.

TABLE E-3   Example of Project Budget Control Report Through 10/31/8X

PROJECT NO. 448-6   Title: Plant Addition
PHASE WORKING DRAWINGS   Fee: $102,530   PROJECT ENGINEER: John Doe

Department	Budget hours	Budget cost	Percent complete	Budget to date		Actual to date		Variance	
				Hours	Cost	Hours	Cost	Hours	Cost
Electrical	6100	32500	30	1830	9840	1216	6505	614	3335
Environmental	5700	34000	25	1425	8500	1599	9275	−174	−775
Mechanical	3300	18740	30	990	5622	755	4229	235	1393
Structural	440	2400	30	132	720	39	249	93	471
Computer	70	350	15	10	52	70	346	−60	−294
Staff	780	5200	30	234	1560	299	2046	−65	−486
Others	0	9040	25	0	2260	0	1596	0	664
Totals	16390	102230		4621	28554	3978	24246	643	4308

Remarks:

and controls required throughout the plant, as well as the details on the necessary instrumentation which may require electrical design and drafting work.

Progress Controls. In a typical operation, biweekly meetings with all key management personnel are held to discuss project progress and any particular problems that may arise in the course of design. These progress meetings provide an opportunity for the various department heads to ask questions regarding particular design problems or lack of information from other departments. Also on a biweekly basis, estimates of percentage of completion are prepared by each of the engineering department managers. These estimates are then incorporated in the biweekly budget control printout (Table E-3) so that the project manager and the director of engineering have an indication of how the job is progressing from the standpoint of both cost and hours expended. These estimates of percentage completion are made prior to the printout or distribution of information on *actual* hours spent or cost incurred, so that the percentage-of-completion figure is a genuine estimate of progress rather than an arithmetic calculation based upon ratio of hours expended to total hours available for the job. This report gives the engineering manager an effective, short-interval tool for taking action before costs get too far out of line by providing an indicator of project progress against the actual cost and hours expended to date.

Work Force Utilization

In order to utilize a professional work force effectively, overall detailed projections of work force requirements must be made at least monthly—with overall projections for a minimum forward period of 3 months and possibly 6 months. These projections then can be revised on a monthly basis to incorporate

new projects that have been received during the previous month and to allow for projects that have been completed and will no longer require the work force.

Projections. Figure E-6 shows a typical chart for such projection made on a monthly basis by individual projects with totals on a departmental basis being compared against available work force resources. The net result may indicate a balance, a surplus, or a deficit. A deficit, particularly on a continuing basis, indicates the need for additional workers. It alerts the engineering manager to secure the additional work force either by new hirings or scheduling of overtime. On the other hand, a surplus indicates the need for additional projects. If the prospects for additional projects are not forthcoming, some steps may have to be taken by the engineering manager to reduce staff to bring it in line with the job work force requirements.

Nonproductive Time. Another tool that is extremely useful to the engineering manager in controlling work force utilization is a daily report of standby, or nonproductive, time. This records the available professional, or technical, time that is not chargeable to specific jobs or projects because of either the lack of available work or inadequacies in departmental scheduling and work force assignment. The daily standby report time provides an immediate signal to the engineering manager to begin to determine why the available engineering time was not utilized. With a computerized system, this information can be available the day following that on which standby time occurred.

Work Sampling. In many instances, even though time is reported as chargeable to a job and is considered productive, the engineering manager may wish to determine exactly how the professionals and technicians are really spending their time. The technique of work sampling is a most effective tool for seeking areas for improvement in engineering and drafting operations (*see* Work sampling). Table E-4

_ _ _ _ _ Electrical _ _ _ _ Department
Year _198X_ as of January 7

Project no.	Client	Jan	Feb	Mar	April	May	June	July	Aug	Sept	Oct	Nov	Dec	Jan	Feb	Mar	April	May
1	"A"		(Hold)															
2	"B"	1	2	3	3 2 2													
3	"C"	19 19	19 19	19 19	19 19													
4	"D"	20 20	20 20	20 20	20 20													
5	"E"	2 2	2 2	2 2	2 2													
6	"F"	4 4	4 4	4 4	4 4													
7	"G"		(Hold)															
8	"H"	2	2															
9	"I"			1	1													
	Vacations			1	1 1													
	Workers required	48 49	49 49	48 48	46 45													
	Workers available	50 50	50 50	50 50	50 50	(Including 1 on loan from Structural Department)												
	Worker surplus	2 1	1 1	2 2	4 5													
	Worker shortage		None															

FIG. E-6 Example of work force projection schedule.

shows the results of work sampling of engineers and draftspersons in the design and application groups of a machine tool engineering department. The significant results of this work sampling study showed that 42.3 percent of the available time was spent in activities which were not directly productive. Investigation of nonproductive activities indicated that a certain portion were directly associated with the engineers' jobs. Some were caused by confusion with customer requirements, particularly the high percentage of discussion with others (32 percent). Information retrieval was another problem area since 7.5 percent of the overall time was spent in getting information from the vault or files.

Personnel Administration. One of the key factors in engineering personnel administration is the use of a sound job evaluation program. Position descriptions should be developed for the various functions in the organization, and appropriate wage or salary scales should be developed for each position. Job evaluation should be supplemented by a merit review program in which each individual in the organization is reviewed at periodic intervals.

Professional performance can be encouraged by

TABLE E-4 Work Sampling Study

Results of Work Sampling of Engineers and Draftspersons in Design and Applications Groups		
Productive elements		57.7%
Drafting	30.4%	
Study customer information, specifications	19.9%	
Write	6.8%	
Calculate	0.6%	
Nonproductive elements		42.3%
Discussion with others	32.0%	
Discussion with engineers	22.1%	
Discussion with shop	6.0%	
Discussion with supervisors	1.7%	
Discussion with sales	1.6%	
Discussion with methods	0.3%	
Discussion with planning	0.3%	
Get information from vault or files	7.5%	
Personal and miscellaneous		2.8%

273

one or all of the following: providing an education allowance for advanced study, paying for membership in professional societies, encouraging professional engineering registration, permitting and encouraging presentation and publication of technical papers, keeping professionals working on professional work, and maintaining good lines of communication.

Quality Control

A successful and well-managed engineering organization must provide a finished product—a construction design package, a product design, or a design for plant modifications—of the highest quality. Quality can be achieved in a number of ways. An unequivocal definition of the scope of the specific engineering project is important so that all involved have a clear concept of what is expected as the final result. Detailed departmental checklists of design items and factors that should be inspected and verified will limit design errors and omissions. Adequate checking of design calculations, design drawings, and specifications is as critical to the control of quality in an engineering operation as are inspection and checking of components and finished products to quality control in a manufacturing operation.

Methods and Procedures

Of considerable importance in an efficient and well-managed engineering operation are the methods and procedures employed in achieving the output of completed design as well as the equipment that is made available to the personnel. Sound engineering standards for making drawings—which include such items as dimensioning, lettering, preparing title blocks, issuing drawing numbers, processing vendor and purchased equipment drawings—are factors of importance. The specific standards and methods employed will vary from one type of engineering operation to another.

The use of *CADD (computer-aided design and drafting)* has dramatically increased in all types of engineering organizations. A CADD system uses a computer to perform engineering analysis and design as well as to do the work of a draftsperson (producing drawings). Productivity increases of 300 to 400 percent have been achieved with well-planned and highly utilized CADD systems. Improved quality of design and drawings also results. Drawings can be stored on tapes for future retrieval.

Specifications can also be prepared on the computer or on advanced word-processing equipment such as tape-controlled typewriters. Many parts of a typical construction design specification can be standardized and stored either in a computer or on the word-processing tapes. Duplication of those parts of the specification by the specification writer is avoided, and the time required for the actual typing or reproduction of the specification is reduced.

For those engineering organizations not using CADD systems, the use of modern drafting equipment including drafting machines (which automatically prepare electrical schematics and mechanical piping drawings), tilt-top tables, reference tables, and chair-type seats contribute to improved drafting output.

See also Human resources planning; Program planning and implementation; Project management; Work sampling.

REFERENCES

Cleland, D. I., and D. F. Kocaoghi: *Engineering Management*, McGraw-Hill, New York, 1981.

Coxe, Weld: *Managing Architectural and Engineering Practice*, John Wiley, New York, 1980.

Shannon, Robert G.: *Engineering Management*, John Wiley, New York, 1980.

William K. McAleer, *Peter F. Loftus Corporation*

Environment, Physical

Management concerns regarding the physical environment center mainly on material supplies, chemical pollutants, and energy conversion residuals. Material and fuel supplies are essential inputs for the industrial process. Pollutants and residuals load the physical environment with added wastes, which must be assimilated or transferred to an ultimate sink. As added waste loads, these residuals may alter the ecology or nutrient cycles upon which living species depend for survival.

Ecology is concerned with the interactions by which energy is transferred into materials or nutrients through successive living processes. As such, ecology covers a wide range of human and biological activity, as well as disciplines. Basically, ecological processes may be viewed as successive stages of development from energy or material sources to biological species, populations, and communities. Thus, a simplified view of ecological systems may be obtained by tracing the flow and balance of materials, or nutrients, as they are embodied successively in species or return as residuals to the earth, air, or water. For example:

The parent material of all living processes is the geochemical composition of the earth, from which all biological species draw their chemical and mineral requirements.

The primary energy source for converting geochemicals into cellular nutrient material is solar radiation. The biological conversion efficiency of solar radiation into usable energy is generally low, amounting to a few percentage points or less of the incoming radiation, with the balance of the sun's rays being reradiated back into the atmosphere.

The most basic of the energy converters are the autotrophs, such as green plants on land and photoplankton in the sea, which have the ability to fix carbon by photosynthesis into carbon molecules (living cells) with the use of solar energy and carbon dioxide in the atmosphere. The residuals of this process are respired back into the ecosystem as oxygen, water vapor, heat, and unassimilated gases.

The herbivores, such as rodents, deer, and cattle, consume the autotrophic species; then they combust the carbon nutrient and energy in them by digestion and oxidation. The residuals are carbon dioxide, vapor, heat, and solid waste.

The carnivores utilize the nutrients in herbivores by a similar consumption-combustion process and use a large part of the energy to maintain their own movement and respiration.

Entropy. In this process, energy moves through these ecological linkages and material forms from a higher to a lower energy state, from more concentrated to more diffused, in accordance with the second law of thermodynamics. This diffusion of energy state is called *entropy*. Living species temporarily reverse the entropic process by storing or concentrating nutrient energy reserves in their cells by high rates of consumption.

The consequence of energy diffusion in ecology has two important implications for management: (1) The cost of energy or materials increases the farther it moves through successive stages; thus the protein cost of beef is higher than that of soybeans, just as the energy cost of carbon steel is higher than the cost of iron. (2) The concentration of chemicals in cellular structure increases as energy is diffused (i.e., energy is being converted into materials), with the result that low levels of pollution in the environment may concentrate into high levels of chemical pollution in successive species higher in the food chain.

Or, more simply, the ecological system confronts management with (1) cost problems for energy conversion of all types, and (2) chemical contamination problems for residuals that concentrate to toxic levels in living species, thus causing health damage or death.

Management Implications. Management of an industrial economy compounds these physical phenomena multifold by pumping into the ecosystem (1) additional industrial heat with its added residuals; and (2) synthetic chemicals which are not biodegradable, with the result that they concentrate as pollutants in the food chain. For example, an oyster concentrates materials 70,000 times; thus one part per billion of DDT or PCBs (polychlorinated biphenyls) in sea water becomes 70 parts per million in the oyster. Eagles, as carnivorous birds of prey at the high end of the food chain, have been measured with 240 parts per million of PCBs in their muscle.

The management problems regarding the physical environment essentially come down to trying to reduce the residuals from manufactured combustion, either by (1) reducing the emissions or the intensity of energy use, or (2) reducing the concentration of hazardous chemicals, as pollutants, and (3) at the same time, maintaining adequate material supplies.

Environmental Resource Forecasts

An industrial economy operates by intensive use of energy for high rates of materials conversion. Hence, management is interested in future availability of materials and fuel supplies. A forecast of resource requirements depends upon (1) available energy sources and use rates, (2) availability or scarcity of raw materials, (3) the pollution damage effects constraining ecosystem productivity, and (4) the human population and consumption growth rate. Or, in economic terms, the withdrawal rate and supply of any given resource depend upon the following variables: energy costs, material costs, damage costs, and price (human demand).

The world population in 1980 reached 4.5 billion people. The population doubled in the prior 45 years and is expected to double again in the next 35 years. Of this growth, 90 percent was in the developing countries of the world and only 10 percent in the industrial nations. Of the 3 billion persons in the developing countries, 20 percent do not receive the daily requirement of calories or proteins, 60 percent are illiterate, and 85 percent have no access to basic health or family-planning service.

Food. On the supply side, the food available per person has increased only by 4 percent in 20 years. World grain output is about 1.2 billion tons. People in developing nations consume about 300 to 500 pounds of grain per year, mostly as grain. The United States consumption of grain is 1650 pounds per person per year: 200 as grain and 1450 as meat. To produce 1 pound of meat, animals eat from 2 to 10 pounds of grain. By the year 2000, world grain production will have to increase to 2 billion tons to keep up with population with no improvement in diets. In 1972, the world experienced a slight decline in food production, with massive crop failures in Russia and Eastern Europe. Since then, disappointing crops have been experienced in India, Ethiopia, the Sahel of West Africa, and to a lesser extent, in Western Europe. Some climatologists speculate that the weather is becoming more variable because of a cooling and drying trend in world climate. Other causes of food shortages are the high birthrates, high oil prices limiting power for food production, and leveling off of the production stimulus from the "green revolution" with its high-yielding wheat and rice.

The countries of the world have turned to the United States and Canada to fill their food deficits. The consequence has been rising domestic and world food prices.

Materials. The world's consumption rate of materials is growing faster than its population by a ratio of about 2½:1 as all nations seek to raise production and living standards. From 1980 to the year 2000, world population is expected to increase by 40 percent; materials consumption, as reflected in the gross domestic product, by 100 percent; and fuel requirements by 115 percent. The United States has large reserves or potential for the production of foods, fiber, coal, feldspar, gypsum, copper, magnesium, titanium, molybdenum, and iron. It currently has scarce reserves of, or imports, substantial aluminum, antimony, asbestos, bismuth, cobalt, fluorine, gold, lead, mercury, nickel, petroleum, phosphorus, platinum, potassium, sulfur, thorium, tungsten, uranium, vanadium, and zinc.

Energy. The United States used 76 quadrillion (10^{15}) Btu's (British thermal units) of energy in 1980, which is projected to become 130 quadrillion by 2000. The current supply of energy is 45 percent from petroleum, 26 percent natural gas, 21 percent coal, 4 percent hydropower, and 4 percent nuclear or other sources. The new energy supplies are expected to come from nuclear energy, low-sulfur Western coal, high-sulfur Eastern coal, oil shale, and geothermal energy, in that order of importance. With nuclear and coal being the major new sources of fuels, environmental pollution will be aggravated by more particulates, nitrogen oxides, sulfur dioxide, solid wastes, and radiation hazards. Petroleum will continue to provide approximately the same supply of energy, about 35 quadrillion Btu's, with 40 percent of the oil imported.

Land. The land supply in the United States comprises 2.3 billion acres, of which the federal government owns one-third, mainly in Western states and Alaska. Of the total United States acreage, 57 percent is classified as agricultural, but only 17 percent is cropland; the remainder is mostly grassland and grazed forest. Of the 43 percent nonagricultural land, more than half is in forest, and the balance in marsh, open swamp, desert, tundra, and the like. Urban land comprises 60 million acres, 3 percent of the total, and is the most valuable commercially. The land area for human settlement has been increasing at a rate 1.7 times faster than the population growth, with the result that population densities (at 3376 persons per square mile) have been declining by about 1.3 percent per year. Metropolitan areas have experienced a slower growth rate than nonmetropolitan counties since 1970, and the suburban growth has shifted to the nonfarm segment of rural areas. About 1¼ million acres of rural land, one-third of which is cropland, are withdrawn from agricultural use annually for more intensive settlement use.

Water. The water resources of the United States originate in the 4750 million acre-feet of rainfall which fall annually. Of this amount, 70 percent falls on nonirrigated lands: about 30 percent on cropland and the balance on forest and open land vegetation. The rest of the precipitation (30 percent, or 1370 million acre-feet) enters the streamflows. About 1000 million acre-feet are not withdrawn from streams and flow to the sea. Of the water withdrawn from streams, approximately 160 million acre-feet are used for irrigation, 160 million acre-feet for industry, and 30 million acre-feet for municipal water. While these withdrawals appear small relative to the total, very little of the water is consumed (100 million acre-feet) and the balance is discharged back into streamflows as effluent. There are 22 major river basins, which drain 70 percent of the nation's land area, into which these effluents are repeatedly discharged, with the result that stream qualities deteriorate under the waste loads of nitrates, phosphates, pesticides, and nutrients from agriculture; chemicals and trace metals from industry; and fecal coliform bacteria and carbonaceous wastes from municipalities. The carbonaceous wastes impose a biochemical oxygen demand upon the stream for their decomposition, a usage that tends to deplete the oxygen supply in the water for aquatic life.

Solid Waste. The solid waste, or gross discard, generated annually amounted to 150 million tons in 1978, or 3.8 pounds per person per day. The gross discard of solid waste by 1990 is expected to rise to 225 million tons annually, or 5 pounds per person per day. About 6 percent of the solid waste is currently recovered, mostly as paper, glass, metals, or rubber. The recycling by 1990 is projected at a 25 percent resource recovery. However, many of the voluntary and commercial recycling activities went out of operation in the mid-1970s with the fall in waste paper and scrap metal prices. The bulk of solid waste is disposed of by landfill, which is the lowest-cost disposal method. However, close-in landfill sites are becoming scarce, and transportation is a major disposal cost. The result may be rising landfill costs, which would make alternative forms of disposal, such as pyrolisis or recycling, more competitive.

Conservation Measures

Conservation measures, such as resource recovery from solid waste, have been encouraged by government as all forms of material have become scarce. However, the economic incentives have not always encouraged the degree of conservation expected by government goals. This has been true in energy conservation and land conservation, as well as in solid waste recycling. The government's role as conservationist has been more effective through regulation or public ownership, as in the case of public lands.

The conservation movement began in the late nineteenth century primarily to preserve timberland. The national forest reserves, national parks, grazing regulation on public lands, mining regulations, and wildlife preserves have tended to regulate multiple uses and sustainable yields on the public domain. The clear-cutting of private forest lands is still common among small operators, although large timber companies practice sustained yield timber harvesting for their own long-run interest. The timber case illustrates that conservation is effective either when government is the proprietor and regulator, or when economic incentives make conservation a self-interest in the private sector. These conditions do not regularly exist in the new areas in which conservation is currently attempted, such as solid waste, energy, land use, or materials conservation.

Energy. Rising fuel prices caused a conservation of energy following the oil crisis and price increases of 1973. Energy consumption per dollar of GNP decreased 9 percent between 1973 and 1980, reflecting greater energy efficiency in usage. Residential and personal transportation consumptions of energy have fallen from the 4 percent annual growth rate before 1973 to less than 1 percent since then. Industry has tended to reduce its intensity of energy use in response to higher prices by utilization of waste heat or materials substitutions when possible. Conservation of energy in construction or home maintenance by better insulation, tighter windows, new designs, or lower thermostat temperatures has gradually materialized. Thus, the internalized economic incentive to conserve energy has been realized to some degree. The preembargo cost of electricity was of the order of 10 mills per kilowatt-hour at the busbar for fossil fuel plants. This has risen to over 40 mills per kilowatt-hour at 1976 prices for oil-fired plants, in which the cost of oil itself at $30 per barrel accounts for 30 mills of operating cost. The new energy sources are likely to range in cost (at 1976 prices) from 30 mills per kilowatt-hour for geothermal and 40 mills per kilowatt-hour for coal and nuclear plants.

Water. Water conservation by recycling is occurring under the permit system and the Water Pollution Control Act Amendments of 1972 as industry effluents are controlled by regulation. Industry must obtain permits for water withdrawal and effluent discharge into streams, and the level of effluent discharges is controlled by water-quality standards. The effect is to impose on industry the investment cost required to abate effluents to the tolerable standard. This internalization of waste water disposal costs within industry has tended to produce gradual improvement in stream quality.

Land. Land conservation is being attempted through open-space, estuary, wildlife, and coastal zone regulations, much of which is experimental under state law rather than federal legislation. Such land conservation is selective in area and restrictive as to purpose. The broad use of land conservation measures is yet to be developed. Only a few states even have a land-use plan for inventorying land use and identifying uses of more than local concern. Meanwhile, research studies by the Environmental Protection Agency have shown that better land use (i.e., 0.3 acres per housing unit rather than 0.6 acres) could reduce private and public investment in housing by 44 percent, operating costs by 18 percent, energy usage by 40 percent, and pollution by 50 percent.

Pollution Control and Abatement

The incremental resource abatement costs amount to 1.1 to 1.5 percent of gross national product (GNP) in the 1974 to 1983 period. These costs include investment in pollution control equipment plus operating and maintenance costs. These costs average about $50 per capita, which, for a median income family, amounts to 2 to 2.5 percent of gross family income. Two-thirds of these costs are for air pollution control, 30 percent for water pollution abatement, 3 percent for solid waste, and minor amounts for radiation, surface mining, and noise abatement. Industry bears the highest incremental costs for water- and air-quality improvement. The federal government costs are mainly in water treatment through matching grants to state and local governments.

Distribution of Cost. The distribution of environmental abatement costs by industry shows the heaviest burden for utilities, petroleum refining, metals, paper, chemicals, stone, clay, and glass. For the most part, these abatement costs correspond with the energy intensity of the industry. Those industries with high pollution and energy intensity characteristics are encountering abatement costs ranging from 0.2 to 1 percent of the value of their shipments.

The citizenry, of course, ultimately pays all these costs as they are passed on by industry or government in higher prices or taxes. The automobile pollution abatement costs, for example, are $5 billion per year to consumers, made up of about $1 billion in car price or investment, $1½ billion in maintenance, and $2½ billion in the fuel penalty cost. The retail price increase for air pollution control on automobiles amounts to about $200 per car.

The net impact of these costs on the citizenry is somewhat regressive, bearing more heavily on the lower-income groups. The environmental costs are progressively distributed to the extent that the federal income tax is the transfer medium. But federal pollution control costs amount to only about 4 percent of the total. The balance of the cost is distributed mainly by price increases or sales and property taxes, which tend to be regressive.

Impact on Growth. The effect of environmental cost upon economic growth is a source of opposition to environmental regulation because growth is seen as necessary to improve productivity and living standards. Here the argument by industry is that the capital markets will be strained in the future to meet energy requirements, capacity expansion, and productivity needs. Thus, pollution control expenditures could potentially displace normal private investment for productive purposes.

The counterargument is that pollution control expenditures are small, averaging only about 4.6 percent of total private investment in the next decade. Moreover, a Brookings Institute study concludes that the capital demands of industry can be met in the next decade to satisfy normal growth.

Also, according to a macroeconomic analysis sponsored by the Council for Environmental Quality, pollution control expenditures at mid-decade with underemployment have stimulated the economy so that GNP is higher than it would otherwise have been. In the future as the rate of pollution control investment slows and slightly higher prices result, environmental costs will have a minor depressing effect on the economy. However, this effect will disappear as incomes adjust to prices, and GNP will end up at the same level it would have been without environmental improvement programs.

Impact on Inflation. The extra inflation rates attributable to pollution control costs are about 0.3 to 0.5 percent per year, which are small compared with the general inflation rates running from 6 to 12 percent during the decade. The effect of the extra inflation rate for pollution abatement upon the wholesale price index is projected at about one-tenth of the price increase.

Unemployment. Unemployment which is attributable to environmental costs has been caused by plant closings among older and smaller facilities, which were only marginally profitable in any case. An Environmental Protection Agency (EPA) study indicates that, from 1971 to 1975, 75 plants closed because of environmental costs, affecting 13,600 workers (0.0015 percent of the labor force). Offsetting these unemployment impacts, moreover, are new jobs created by producing equipment for pollution control investment. For example, about 85,000 additional jobs have been created by the construction of sewage treatment plants alone, plus additional jobs for other water- and air-quality improvement equipment. On balance, it would appear that the immediate impact of environmental regulation has been to create more jobs than those terminated. However, those employed in newly created pollution control jobs are not the same persons as those who became unemployed through plant closings, and therein lies the individual and political sensitivity of environmental unemployment.

In summary, then, the direct and indirect economic costs of environmental regulation amount to about 1 percent of GNP, plus very small effects on economic growth, inflation, and unemployment.

Health and Damage Effects of Pollution

The most serious, sensitive, and elusive effects of pollution damage are upon human health. A variety of studies have attempted to assess health damage to human beings. The valuations are based mainly upon medical costs and income losses due to excess morbidity and mortality. Such costs total at least $4.5 billion per year, comprising $1.8 billion for cancer, $2.1 billion for respiratory diseases from air pollution, and $0.6 billion for drinking-water diseases.

Materials. The identifiable damage to materials and property is about $6.5 billion per year, and the additional loss in property values due to air pollution is from $1.5 to $5 billion per year. Roughly, the total losses are about $10 billion annually. The material damage losses are the following: for rubber products, $0.2 billion; textile fibers and dyes, $0.2 billion; metals, $1.5 billion; paints, $0.7 billion; and other materials, $3.8 billion.

Much of this damage comes from sulfur oxides in the presence of particulates and moisture, forming sulfuric acid, which is corrosive to metals and many materials. The balance is attributable to ozone, which oxidizes materials and turns them into oxides such as ferric oxide or iron rust.

Biota. Ozone also oxidizes living tissue, such as human lung tissue, causing it to harden and age. The effects of oxidation are most easily seen on delicate plant leaves like lettuce or grape leaves, where oxidation of cell tissue results in a brownish scaling of the surface. The crop and ornamental damage in the nation from pollution is estimated to be over $130 million a year.

Of biota, generally, the economic costs are more difficult to estimate than the species count. The species count is indicative of the size and range of the gene pool from which future evolution may occur.

The Department of Interior estimates that 1 out of every 10 species native to the United States may be endangered or threatened. Hawaii, with a smaller species set, already finds 12 percent of its species extinct and another 38 percent endangered or threatened.

Among wildlife animals the situation is much the same. Among the animal species, 85 have become extinct. In the United States, 185 will probably be extinct, and another 718 may possibly become extinct, by the year 2000. Some species nearing extinction have been recovering as a result of hunting regulations or wildlife management, but the list of recovering species is small compared with the endangered.

Coping with Social, Political, and Regulatory Pressures

Environmental decisions represent a conflict, in many cases, between economic goals and health or ecological goals. The parties involved include business and labor on the economic side against factional interests in health, consumerism, environmentalism, conservation, recreation, and ecology and adversely affected property groups. These factional interests combine on some issues to press for tightening environmental standards or enforcement. Coalitions are most likely to be successful when demonstrable dangers exist to human health or wildlife or when there is local propertyowner opposition.

The focus for these pressures within the political structure usually occurs within the framework of (1) environmental impact cases, (2) regulatory hearings, or (3) jurisdictional disputes.

Environmental Impact Cases. Environmental impact cases may be heard in the courts when a plaintiff seeks to show that environmental damage is demonstrable in order to obtain an award of monetary damages or to obtain an injunction preventing the defendant from taking an environmental action until further facts or proofs are established. An award of monetary damages is usually difficult to obtain because the direct causation of adverse impacts is hard to prove in anything so interlinked as ecological networks. However, environmental groups have been relatively successful in delaying projects by obtaining injunctions. Often these delays so compound the costs and uncertainties that the project is abandoned.

An administrative method of examining environmental impact cases takes the form of prepared statements, clearances, and hearings under the National Environmental Policy Act of 1970 (NEPA) or its state counterparts. Section 102 of NEPA provides that federal agencies shall prepare environmental impact statements on all projects, particularly construction, which have ecological consequences. These statements are to describe the nature of the work to be done, its effects upon the ecology, its probable impacts on health or species, means of avoidance or abatement of impacts, and alternative courses of action. Environmental impact statements, once prepared, are circulated among concerned governmental agencies or constituencies for recommendations. The environmental impact statement and its comments form the basis of a hearing in which interested parties can further argue their cases prior to an administrative ruling.

Environmental impact statements have proved to be time-consuming, costly, and voluminous. Some federal agencies, such as the Army Corps of Engineers with its many construction projects throughout the country, estimate that 1 to 2 percent of their total expenditures go into the preparation of environmental impact statements. Business has also encountered the costs and delays of environmental impact statements as state laws have required state or local governments to review the environmental impacts of new projects, particularly construction. Electric utilities especially have found that environmental requirements, along with new fuel technologies, have stretched out the lead time on siting new power plants from 5 to 7 or 10 years.

Although the environmental impact statement is not a precise decision document and is prone to costliness and delays, it does serve the purpose of airing and resolving conflicts among the many interested parties over environmental issues.

Regulatory Hearings. The regulatory hearings of environmental protection agencies serve somewhat the same purpose of reconciling conflicts. Regulatory hearings occur when an agency proposes new environmental standards or enforcement procedures as, for example, with automotive engine emission controls, banning DDT, regulating offshore drilling, or monitoring the Alaskan oil pipeline. Here the agency proposes a compromise stand, business appears as proponents for a more favorable ruling, and environmentalists appear for more stringent rulings. These hearings or administrative deliberations may go on for several years before resolution.

Jurisdictional Disputes. The jurisdictional issues regarding environmental affairs occur most frequently among federal, state, and local governments. Most environmental decisions, particularly those involving construction, are highly localized, and ecological conditions are unique to each biome or biological community. Moreover, land-use decisions have historically been in the jurisdiction of local governments. The federal government, in attempting to enforce environmental programs or standards, has sought to delegate much of the implementation to state or local government, for reasons of both practical politics and administrative necessity. Indeed, the environmental program has brought a number of innovations and new dimensions to intergovernmental relations, but conflicts do occur since a state or local government is expected to implement federal regulations or legislation. Local governments frequently feel, however, that the regulatory measures are not applicable to the local case, that communication is poor in clarifying standards or procedure, that financial and administrative support is not adequate, that decisions are not forthcoming, or that local politics runs counter to federal practice. Thus, jurisdictional conflicts, apathy, or counterproductive practices develop.

On the whole, environmental problems present a

wide order of social, political, and regulatory pressures among diverse groups throughout the private and public sectors as people try to learn to live together under the limits which resources and ecology impose as population densities increase.

Technical Health and Operational Implications

The technical and operational problems imposed by environmental regulations include (1) establishing the biological and medical research base from which to adequately measure ecological damage for the purpose of setting environmental quality standards; (2) developing the technical instrumentation and monitoring networks which will measure ambient environmental quality against the standards; (3) developing new industrial technology to reduce emissions or effluence in products or equipment; and (4) devising the administrative incentives and penalties which will encourage individuals and business to modify their behavior toward the reduction of pollution. These several operational problems are perhaps best illustrated by examining the trends in environmental quality, which demonstrate some of the standards-setting, monitoring, research, and administrative problems which occur.

Air Pollution. Air quality has shown some improvement in recent years in particulates, sulfur dioxide, and carbon monoxide, but rather little improvement in nitrogen oxides or hydrocarbons. The problem is, of course, that the average nitrogen oxide emissions of automobiles have not decreased very much owing to technical obstacles, and the number of cars continues to increase.

The air pollution problem is very general throughout the United States, despite common impressions that the problem is limited to a few cities, such as Chicago for sulfur dioxide or Los Angeles for nitrogen oxides. At least 80 cities, large and small, throughout the United States exceed national standards for oxidants. Indeed, even rural areas are not immune. EPA monitors unexpectedly found rural oxidant levels exceeding 1-hour standards in western Maryland and eastern West Virginia while studying air pollution damage to Christmas trees. Additional studies showed air pollution to be significant throughout rural Maryland, Ohio, Pennsylvania, and West Virginia.

Water Pollution. Although water quality has improved over the past two decades for drinking purposes, one-third of all community water sources in 1980 did not comply with federal microbiological standards and 17 percent did not comply with turbidity standards.

The nature of the water pollution is indicated by the frequency of observed violations of EPA's proposed standards. The highest rates of violation were observed for fecal coliform bacteria (67 percent of observations), ammonia (11 percent), and sulfate (18 percent). For trace metals, the highest violation rates were for iron, lead, manganese, and zinc.

Hazardous Pollutants. Among the hazardous pollutants, environmental regulation has focused upon four—DDT, aldrin/dieldrin, PCBs, and mercury—as scientists have attempted to find the dose rates at which these pollutants become carcinogens or damaging to human health.

The dietary intake of DDT from meat, fish, poultry, and dairy products has been declining since restrictions on production and use were established. The older population, aged 50 years and over, still retain about 8 to 9 parts per billion of DDT in human fatty tissue from applications and usage of DDT 20 to 30 years ago. The young population, below 15 years of age, have only half the body weight of DDT of their elders.

Aldrin/dieldrin, which is used as a pesticide, is of concern because it is carcinogenic, i.e., cancer-inducing, in human beings. The dietary intake of aldrin/dieldrin is declining slightly as sales of the pesticide are restricted; but the levels of dieldrin in surface waters and as residues in fish continue to rise.

Polychlorinated biphenyls (PCBs) have been widely used since the 1930s as coolants, insulators, inks, adhesives, hydraulic fluids, and pesticide extenders. They have no counterpart in nature and, therefore, are not biodegradable, which makes them very persistent in nature. Their persistence causes them to cumulate in the food chain. PCBs, up to 20 parts per million, have been observed in seal blubber and 240 parts per million in muscle of the white-tailed eagle. PCBs are toxic to wildlife at varying dosages, as low as 0.1 parts per million to young shrimp. They have been correlated with mortality in game birds and reduced reproduction among fish-eating mammals. Recent studies indicate they may be carcinogens. PCBs in surface waters of the North Atlantic have been measured at around 30 parts per million in recent years; PCB residues in Lake Michigan fish range from 5 to 20 parts per million. About 4 percent of all human foods had traces of PCBs in 1974. The dietary intake of PCBs ranges from 1 to 3 parts per million. The health implications of these data are not yet known.

Mercury occurs in natural state in rocks and minerals whose decomposition produces background mercury measurements of 0.03 to 2 parts per billion. In addition, 60,000 to 70,000 flasks of mercury are produced annually for such uses as agricultural biocides, paint, electrical apparatus, and electrolytic processes. Mercury circulates readily through air, land, water, and living things. Mercury poisoning affects aquatic life, animals, and human beings by attacking the nervous system and is fatal in varying dosages. The mercury level in surface United States waters is about 1 part per billion, with similar levels as residues in freshwater fish. The human dietary intake of mercury in foods is now about 2.8 micrograms per day, down one-third from 1972 when mercury was banned from agricultural biocides.

Cancer. The presence of hazardous pollutants in the environment is a significant factor in rising cancer death rates. From 60 to 90 percent of all cancers are related to environmental factors, such as exposures to chemicals, cigarette smoking, natural and induced radiation, and asbestos fiber. The death rate from cancer has doubled since 1900, until now it is the no. 2 killer in the United States after heart disease.

Of some 2 million known chemicals, only about 6000 have been laboratory tested for carcinogenicity. Several thousand new chemicals are discovered annually, and several hundred go on the market each year without testing. The known chemical classes of carcinogens include aromatic amines, chlorinated hydrocarbons, tars, radioactive elements, metal dusts, and steroids. Federal agencies are sponsoring research models to speed up the work and reduce the cost of testing from 2 to 3 years at tens of thousands of dollars to 1 week at perhaps $1000 per compound.

Meantime, the rise in cancer death rates since 1950 has offset the reduction in mortality from other diseases, so that for 25 years there has been no improvement in life expectancy.

Management Responsibilities

The management responsibilities for environmental affairs are manifold in both private and public institutions because ecology is complex. Management has responsibility for organizing the decision information needed on all the problems discussed in previous sections, namely, (1) to forecast accurately its own resource requirements in the light of available energy sources, materials availability, pollution damage costs, and human consumption rates; (2) to minimize the cost of energy in materials by more efficient energy utilization or by substituting materials lower in the successive nutrient chains; (3) to reduce the concentration of chemicals in their ambient state; (4) to recycle water and materials; (5) to reduce land-use costs in terms of social investment, energy usage, or pollution; (6) to ascertain pollution abatement costs and make trade-offs against product development or health damage costs; (7) to help develop an objective basis for environmental decisions by better research inputs into environmental impact statements and hearings; (8) to undertake research which will establish the biological and medical base for environmental standard setting and monitoring; (9) to direct industrial research toward compliance with environmental standards as well as to maximize near-term demand; and (10) to devise incentives and administrative implementation

which will modify human behavior toward reducing ecological damage. These substantial responsibilities are a recognition that management and its institutions, as well as individuals, survive in the long run by living compatibly within an ecology which has limits and constraints to its waste assimilation capabilities. The ecological limits and constraints impose rising costs upon materials and fuels. Management, therefore, has both short- and long-term interests in ecology, namely, to minimize costs in the short term and to survive over the long run.

See also Energy, management; Environmental protection legislation; Facilities and site planning and layout; Technology, management implications.

REFERENCES

Edmunds, Stahrl W., and John Letey: *Environmental Administration*, McGraw-Hill, New York, 1973.

Environmental Quality, Annual Reports, Council on Environmental Quality, Washington, D.C., 1970–1981.

Massachusetts Institute of Technology: *Man's Impact on the Global Environment,* The M.I.T. Press, Cambridge, Mass., 1970.

Stahrl W. Edmunds, *University of California, Riverside*

Environmental Protection Legislation

Public concern over the deteriorating condition of the environment finds support among federal and state lawmakers who, since 1970, have enacted a wide range of environmental legislation. Legislation passed in the early 1970s focused on pollution abatement control and environmental protection. Recently, however, the character and content of environmental laws, either as amended or newly legislated, have changed. Closer attention is being given to protecting human health and safety by minimizing the environmental risks individuals (or society) may encounter in daily life. Restrictions on the disposal of toxic substances and regulation of new chemicals are examples of these risk-reduction efforts. While ecosystem management continues as the focal point of environmental legislation, there has been a noticeable shift to the control of specific materials and production processes. For business managers, incorporation of risk and liability considerations into managerial decisions is necessary in order to respond to current environmental legislation and public concern.

Environmental Legislation

Since 1970, the number of federal, state, and local laws enacted to protect and enhance the environment has steadily increased. The concerns and expectations of the citizenry with regard to environmental quality for all generations are set forth in the National Environmental Policy Act (NEPA). NEPA and state environmental protection legislation require both private and public managers to consider the consequences of their actions through the filing of environmental impact reports. A reevaluation of air-quality and water pollution laws and an appraisal of other pressing environmental problems were set in motion by the passage of NEPA. As a result, regulatory legislation directed at noise abatement, coastal zone management, occupational safety, hazardous waste management, and premarket testing of chemicals, for example, has been enacted by Congress. Beginning in the late 1970s and continuing to the present, environmental legislation has been periodically amended by Congress or adjusted by administrative edict in order to "fine-tune" regulatory requirements. This article briefly covers four major areas of environmental concern highlighting key aspects of federal legislation.

Air Quality. The Clean Air Act (1970, as amended) sets forth a federal and state regulatory approach designed to achieve primary and secondary National Ambient Air Quality Standards (NAAQS). Primary standards are based on scientific evidence and are targeted to protect human health. Secondary standards are also established to protect human safety but are predicated on inconclusive scientific evidence. The EPA has established NAAQS for six major pollutants: sulfur dioxide, carbon monoxide, nitrogen oxide, hydrocarbons, photochemical oxidants, and particulate matter. Responsibility for attaining and maintaining air-quality standards resides with state and local governments, the latter working together within defined air-quality management districts. States are required to develop implementation plans (SIPs) outlining how NAAQS will be achieved.

Existing sources are required to install "reasonable available control technology" with some flexibility provided through a loading-based formula allowing offsets, bubbles, and banking. (See page 284.) New pollution sources face stiffer controls, as they must meet technology-based equipment standards. Congress passed amendments during 1977 which imposed additional requirements on the states. In "nonattainment areas" where standards are not likely to be met, mandatory vehicle inspections (controls) and construction bans (penalties) were authorized. Nondegradation requirements to thwart deterioration of air quality in areas where ambient air-quality standards were already being met or exceeded were also included. Civil and criminal penalties could be assessed against individual dischargers for noncompliance or periodic knowing violations of SIPs.

Hazardous substance emission standards are cov-

ered not by SIPs, but on a pollutant-by-pollutant basis. Emission standards for vinyl chloride, mercury, asbestos, and beryllium, for example, have been promulgated by the Environmental Protection Agency (EPA), and other substances are being reviewed. Risk-generated standards for controlling toxic airborne pollutants were proposed, but they had not been adopted by 1984.

Water Pollution Control. Congress has enacted water-quality legislation intended to improve the quality of the nation's surface waters such that these waters would be fishable and swimmable by 1985. Legislation has been primarily oriented toward controlling point sources through permits and technologically imposed standards. Under the National Pollution Discharge Elimination System (NPDES), permits are issued to dischargers for the purpose of controlling and monitoring the amount and nature of substances being discharged into waterways. Each permit specifies the amount of acceptable discharge, and the act imposes mandatory self-reporting requirements if those levels are exceeded. Pollution limits for each industry are based on technologically obtainable levels. For existing point sources, *best practicable technology* (BPT) establishes the level of performance that was to have been achieved and maintained by 1977. For each firm selecting BPT, benefit-cost considerations were applicable. By 1983, however, each industry was to have adopted *best available technology* (BAT) irrespective of benefit-cost relationships. The focus of BAT requirements was changed by 1977 amendments to deal specifically with toxic substances. *Best conventional technology* (BCT) requirements were added to control traditional effluents such as fecal coliform bacteria, suspended solids, and those that increase biological oxygen demand. The EPA has broad regulatory discretion with respect to new source dischargers. In addition to imposing specific technologies, the EPA can require that alternative production processes or operating methods be installed.

As a result of a lawsuit brought by the Natural Resources Defense Council [*NRDC v. Train, 8 E.R.C. 2120*(D.D.C. 1976)], pollution standards were updated to include toxic pollutants. For toxic pollutants not already covered by an NPDES permit, discharge into waterways has been curtailed. Discharger responsibilities and liabilities in case a release of harmful amounts of a chemical occurs are delineated in amendments to the Clean Water Act.

Hazardous Waste Management. Control of hazardous substances has its antecedents in the Solid Waste Disposal Act (1965), which was superseded by the Resource Recovery Act (1973). When the RRA proved ineffective in handling hazardous wastes, Congress enacted the Resource Conservation and Recovery Act (RCRA) in 1976. RCRA contains previously legislated solid waste programs as well as a regulatory program for hazardous materials. RCRA's main objective is to monitor currently used chemicals from their conception through their disposal. The notification system which pertains to all generators, transporters, and owner-operators of treatment, storage, or disposal (TSD) facilities is the heart of RCRA's regulatory program. The law requires generators (those who produce hazardous wastes): (1) to keep records on the amount and use of a hazardous chemical; (2) to properly label all wastes; (3) to use appropriate containers for each waste produced; (4) to provide information on waste composition; (5) to employ a manifest system which can trace waste; and (6) to submit periodic reports on the final disposition, including amount of hazardous waste generated.

Transporters have a similar set of guidelines, with additional requirements of maintaining records of travel routes and delivery points and of disposing of waste at an approved facility. TSD facility operators are required to follow a more rigorous set of guidelines, which include personnel training, contingency planning, facility security systems, and liability insurance. Insurance is intended to cover any claims initiated while the TSD facility is in operation.

RCRA covers only hazardous substances currently being generated and disposed. A great deal of controversy exists, however, over abandoned hazardous waste sites. The Superfund or Comprehensive Environmental Response, Compensation and Liability Act (1980) has identified who is responsible for cleaning up these sites. Through contributions from industry, two funds are being established (1) to respond to spills of hazardous substances, and (2) to clean up closed or abandoned disposal sites. Persons responsible for the handling of hazardous wastes must demonstrate that they are financially capable of covering the costs of cleanup and the restoration of the environment. Actual fault does not have to be demonstrated to establish liability.

Regulated Chemicals. The EPA is mandated by the Toxic Substances Control Act (TOSCA) to evaluate and regulate chemicals prior to the time when they are commercially produced. The intent of TOSCA is to test new chemicals or old chemicals that are being considered for new uses for their environmental and human health effects. While TOSCA's legislative intent is very broad, there are two major regulatory mechanisms: (1) *premanufacture notification* (PMN) and (2) *substantial risk notification* (SRN). EPA has not officially announced final PMN guidelines, though exemptions for small businesses have been provided. PMN procedure currently in effect in 1984 requires manufacturers of chemicals not included on the EPA inventory to report the chemical substance (identification) and toxicological tests (risk assessment) within 90 days of production or change in use. Throughout the reporting period, EPA makes every effort to maintain the confidentiality of the chemical being reviewed. The manufactur-

er's report and results from any special tests required by EPA are used to evaluate whether the chemical is reasonably safe to produce and use.

Because the PMN requirements generate volumes of information which takes time to assimilate, manufacturers are required to report any adverse effects immediately. Substantial risk notifications do not require any risk assessment or scientific evidence to trigger an evaluation of a chemical. The EPA has assigned corporate officials the full responsibility for reporting adverse effects.

Authorization for regulation of all pesticide products resides in the Federal Insecticide, Fungicide, and Rodenticide Act (FIFRA). The goal of FIFRA is to prevent "unreasonable adverse effects" to the environment from pesticide use. The determination of unreasonableness is based on both the costs and the benefits of using a pesticide. Pesticide manufacturers submit the results of long- and short-term tests to the EPA. If the tests show that the chemical can be used without causing an unreasonable hazard, the chemical is registered and classified for general or restricted use. If the test results should trigger one of EPA's risk-based criteria for adverse effects, the pesticide will be carefully reviewed.

The manufacturer and users bear the burden of proof for demonstrating that the product's detrimental effects are not unreasonable. This is mandated as part of a comprehensive risk/benefit analysis conducted on the suspect chemical. If the pesticide's normal uses are determined to cause unreasonable adverse effects, those uses may be restricted, suspended, or canceled.

The 1978 amendments to FIFRA called for simplification of the cumbersome chemical-by-chemical registration process. The EPA has initiated a registration standards program which seeks to register generic groups of chemicals sharing the same active ingredient. A data call-in program has been established whereby registrants are notified of missing chronic toxicology studies well before the standard for that active ingredient is promulgated. This gives manufacturers 2 to 4 years' advance notice so that long-term tests can be completed or underway before the pesticide is reviewed for reregistration.

Environmental Management Strategies

Public concern over the deterioration of the environment, particularly the presence of hazardous substances, has not abated. Public and private managers continue to seek new ways to minimize risks to health, safety, and the environment. Dissatisfaction with traditional regulatory mechanisms and confusion arising from changing requirements have resulted in a gradual change in the focus of regulatory programs. Managers now have available to them a wider array of strategies to use to meet their environmental responsibilities. Adoption of market-type regulatory procedures has allowed pollution rights to be traded and has introduced greater flexibility into management's environmental programs. Liability insurance is one example of an alternative that may be a practical means of modifying environmentally damaging actions and covering claims brought against the firm. The environmental review still remains a solid strategy for evaluating the long-term consequences of management decisions and plant production processes. Even though managers are faced with an enormous body of environmental statutes, the climate supports the innovation of new strategies to protect the environment.

Technical Flexibility. In early 1979, the EPA announced new policies for the attainment of air emission standards by existing plants. Convinced that controlling plantwide emissions rather than single sources would be more effective, the EPA instituted a *bubble policy*. The bubble covers the entire plant, and a maximum emission limit is established. Plant managers are then free to adjust any aspect of the production process or adopt control devices best suited for particular aspects of plant operation. For example, a plant which relies heavily on high-sulfur coal can continue to discharge sulfur dioxide by reducing the level of other emissions. The bubble concept has now been extended to companies discharging to waterways.

This approach fits into an emerging regulatory scheme within EPA. In 1976, an *offset policy* was instituted whereby a firm could enter an area or expand by reducing pollution from existing sources. Firms have been allowed to trade or sell pollution rights, termed *offsets*, to other firms. *Banking*, or maintaining a reserve of pollution rights, is also becoming popular. The bubble policy extends the use of offsets by creating a more active market for pollution rights.

The flexibility provided by offsets and the bubble will greatly influence the strategy that managers can follow. Rather than be restricted to a limited set of options, managers can select from a wide array of possible production alternatives to meet plant discharge standards. With flexibility comes complexity, however, in that the number of interactions among all aspects of production rise. As a result, the possibility of not complying with existing statutes may also increase. Managers will be able to employ optimization modeling (linear programming) as one means of keeping apprised of the possible implications of their decisions. Bodily and Gabel (*see* References) provide an example of how linear programming can be utilized to optimize the allocation of resources among various environmental management options.

Liability Insurance. The use of insurance to protect the public welfare is not new, there being an indemnity plan included in the Price-Anderson Act

(1956) which applies to nuclear energy facilities. Until federal hazardous-waste legislation, environmental statutes had not specifically required insurance as a regulatory mechanism, unless implemented at the state level. One of the issues arising from the Love Canal incident and problems with other abandoned waste sites was the question of responsibility for paying damages resulting from the improper disposal of wastes. Owners and operators seldom carried liability insurance and could often avoid their responsibilities. Changes in federal common law make it easier to hold prior owners and waste generators responsible for damages. Therefore, insurance is now being considered in several situations as a regulatory mechanism for promoting environmental regulations.

As a management strategy, several features of insurance make this mechanism appealing. Court settlements for personal and property damages and legal fees can be very high. High liabilities may be enough incentive for managers to closely examine production processes and waste disposal procedures and to take steps to minimize the risks of negatively impacting the environment. Risk minimization or avoidance of an environmental accident may be economically rational. Second, mandatory insurance ensures that the perpetrator of the accident can meet the financial responsibilities resulting from the incident.

Because the role for insurance is relatively new, not enough information is available on how useful it will be as a regulatory tool or in what situations it will be most appropriate. Baram presents an argument that insurance as a regulatory mechanism seems applicable for hazardous-waste situations. Managers still need to evaluate its merits as a management tool for meeting their environmental responsibilities.

Environmental Review. A commonly used strategy to anticipate compliance and evaluate consequences of a management decision or a production process is the *environmental audit*. Usually performed by an external review team, an audit can be viewed as a "good faith" effort to comply with the law. This effort may reduce the possibility of costly litigation. Audits also reveal potential liabilities that management may have overlooked. At a time when public concern over hazardous substances runs high, the audit provides management with the information necessary to take corrective action.

Audits can be conducted on specific substances, a particular production process, disposal procedures, or the entire plant operation. Each of these approaches generates different information on company activities. For example, a product-based audit on a chemical would determine whether the chemical was being properly handled, stored, and disposed. An audit of a production process which is broader in scope examines leakages within the process and impacts on other production areas. Advocates of the environmental review argue that an integrated approach that evaluates products and processes within the entire corporate structure provides the most useful information.

To be used effectively, the audit needs to be incorporated into the overall organizational structure and policy context of the company. The unit within the company that is to be responsible for carrying out environmental mandates has to be identified. In some cases, a decentralized approach in which each division has its own environmental staff may be appropriate; in others, the staff can be centralized within the corporate structure. Corporate policy relating to environmental mandates, including information policy decisions, must be explicitly articulated to the audit team.

For an example of how an audit can facilitate managerial decisions, consider this case which dealt with implementing the Resource Conservation and Recovery Act. During the early implementation stage of this act, companies were required to register as a generator, transporter, or TSD operator. Many companies, believing they could not meet the generator 90-day maximum on-board storage requirement, opted for TSD status because a backlog of waste could be maintained. In fact, the EPA advised companies to obtain TSD facility permits. However, some companies were confused over the long-term implications of this strategy. In one California corporation with several major divisions, division managers disagreed over which permit to obtain. An independent consulting firm was retained to conduct an audit of hazardous waste operations. In the audit, the firm recommended that generator status would be the most appropriate means of compliance with RCRA. The audit also contained a program for meeting packaging, labeling, and marking requirements. Initial costs to the company were high, but in light of subsequent events with respect to the incrementally imposed TSD requirements by EPA, the long-term costs were minimized. Audits do work well and should be an integral part of corporate strategy.

See also Energy management; Environment, physical; Site selection; Social responsibility of business; Technology, management implications.

REFERENCES

Baram, Michael S.: *Alternatives to Regulation: Managing Risks to Health, Safety and the Environment,* Lexington Books, Lexington, Mass., 1982.

Bodily, Samuel, E., and H. Landis Gabel: "A New Job for Businessmen: Managing the Company's Environmental Resources," *Sloan Management Review,* Summer 1982, pp. 3–18.

Environmental Law Handbook, 7th ed., Government Institutes, Inc., Rockville, Md., 1983.

PHILIP D. GARDNER, *University of California, Riverside*

LINDA L. MAY, *University of California, Riverside*

Equal Employment Opportunity, Minorities and Women

The EEO climate of the sixties was one of equal opportunity. The seventies stressed affirmative action. In the eighties, affirmative action remains an issue, but with new and reactionary concerns about reverse discrimination. Demonstrable progress has occurred, but there are still many gaps and poor representations of minorities, especially in middle and higher levels of management.

The management of equal employment opportunity (EEO) is a specialized function by which a company, both voluntarily and to comply with federal law and regulations, systematically tries to provide fair and equal opportunity in the employment of ethnic minorities, women, the handicapped, veterans, and older people. The function also includes affirmative action to introduce more of these "protected groups" into all levels of the corporation where they are not proportionately represented.

Company EEO officers and staffs must work with line management for programs, monitoring, and documentation if success is to be achieved, although everything depends on top-management support and leadership. EEO managers should be familiar with EEO laws, particularly Title VII of the Civil Rights Act and the Executive orders which govern EEO policy. (*See* Affirmative action; Labor legislation; Women in business and management.) Although these laws are not likely to change in the near future, their interpretation frequently varies. For example, a new trend to watch is that with people living longer and with continuing company mergers, issues of age discrimination in the 1980s may dominate those of race and sex discrimination.

The Reagan administration has been accused of ignoring minorities and women. However, the Equal Employment Opportunity Commission, as the major enforcement agency, still seems to be aggressively concerned with eliminating discrimination. It is now, however, more realistically aware that federal laws alone cannot solve many of the problems of the depressed groups. A larger part of the solution in the eighties may have to come from action by such groups themselves. For example, the collapse of family structures, the alarming increase in the number of unwed mothers, whose children lack male role models, can lead to poor early education and inadequate job qualifications.

Regulations under the Executive orders may become somewhat simplified with potential changes by the Office of Federal Contract Compliance Programs (OFCCP) if, indeed, these new guidelines ever appear. Nevertheless, regulations will remain in effect. Therefore, it is prudent for the EEO staff to include lawyers, although a diversified staff of experts is most desirable.

The EEO management staff will also have to become familiar with the investigatory policies of the two major federal agencies: The Equal Employment Opportunity Commission (EEOC) and the Department of Labor's Office of Federal Contract Compliance Programs (OFCCP).

Continuing Challenges to Achieve Fair Employment

Many issues remain unresolved. Five, in particular, continue to be challenges to government and business alike.

Measurement. The law requires that all companies with 100 or more employees report yearly to the EEOC the number of minorities and women at the various levels of employment. However, raw statistics can be deceiving. One must also consider the employee's education, qualifications, location, desire for the job, culture, and supply in the labor market, which is the realistic labor pool. Another pitfall in measurement is the annual "snapshot" use of the EEO-1 profile. The relevant supply of minority applicants, the number of job openings, the growth or decline of the business, company recruiting efforts, and the possibility of backlash must also be considered to make annual "snapshots" meaningful.

A third pitfall is the problem of variations within the EEO-1 categories. Let us take the example of the EEO-1 category "Officers and Managers." A worldwide bank might require highly experienced officers and managers; a small local bank would not have the same requirement. The larger bank could find it much more difficult to fill this category than the smaller bank. Therefore, these two banks should not be compared on the basis of raw percentages alone.

Underutilization and Availability. Underutilization can be defined as "having fewer minorities or women in a particular job group than would reasonably be expected by their availability." Availability refers only to persons who are qualified and willing to work, have the skills for the job, and live near enough to come to work. In many cases, honest and fair measurement of underutilization and availability is not easily accomplished, but management must be prepared to defend any underutilization that may be charged to it.

Targets, Goals, Quotas, and Timetables. Targets and goals have always been important essentials in planning any kind of organizational management.

Targets, however, require no precise floor or ceiling if there is good faith toward achieving them. Quotas do have both floors and ceilings. The key to the difference between targets and goals is *rigidity of interpretation* in imposing certain requirements. In spite of the *Weber* decision (described in the next section), quotas will probably be resisted by American EEO specialists.

Selecting and Testing. Tests, selection procedures, and performance evaluations must continue to be free from any discriminatory bias. Company EEO staffs should regularly consult the federal "Uniform Guidelines on Employee Selection Procedures" (1978) or a revised edition of it.

Recruiting, Promoting, and Terminating. Compliance requires familiarity with both EEOC and OFCCP regulations. Management will need, therefore, to keep careful records of applicant flow, hirings, promotions, and terminations and must be prepared to defend their fairness.

Major Obstacles

Progress toward better equal employment opportunities must clear two imposing obstacles:

1. *Legalism.* Americans have a continued tendency to resolve problems by an excessive resort to tribunals, with high cost and delayed justice, rather than by mediation, conciliation, and compromise between the parties themselves.

   However, under the Reagan administration, both the EEOC and the OFCCP have tried to simplify their regulations and requirements of paperwork and to make their approach to management less adversarial. But legalism is still a problem. It usually arises when an employee or a group of employees brings suit. Sometimes these suits broaden individual claims into class-action suits that are based on sheer raw statistics, inadequately analyzed, with costly, sometimes frivolous, and always time-consuming litigation.

   Legalism invites game playing; it can draw corporate managers and attorneys away from positive efforts for working out creative affirmative action plans. Companies may perhaps lessen legalism by establishing clear-cut policies and practices to guard against discriminating in the first place. They then must develop supportive, creative, and voluntary affirmative action plans. Whether management likes it or not, however, EEO in the 1980s is thoroughly enveloped by laws, and management will have to deal with that fact.

2. *Affirmative Action (Preference) versus Reverse Discrimination.* This issue will probably be the major obstacle facing management throughout

this decade. The issue needs to to be thought through and worked out from the point of view of ethical equity, law, and practical industrial relations. A good starting point in this regard is the EEOC's "Affirmative Action Guidelines" of 1979 and any later, updated guidelines.

Ambiguity in the Law. The Civil Rights Act of 1964 neither expressly requires nor forbids preferential treatment. Revised Orders 4 and 14 of the OFCCP and practices from the EEOC do, however, call for preferential practices. Some companies (such as A.T.&T., Sears, and Kaiser) have deliberately worked preferential practices into their affirmative action plans.

As for the courts, the *Bakke* decision did not settle the matter. A more important decision is the *Weber* v. *Kaiser Aluminum* case. In the *Kaiser* case, the company and the union (the United Steelworkers), in a 1974 collective bargaining agreement, decided that entrance into Kaiser's skilled crafts training program would be based on seniority but drawn from two lists, one for whites and one for minorities. Thus, 50 percent of the program participants would belong to minorities until the percentage of minorities in the craft would approximate their percentage in the area surrounding each Kaiser plant. The plan—with a seemingly rigid quota—was challenged.

But in 1979 the Supreme Court decided that *voluntary* affirmative action plans, even those containing such numerical quotas, do not automatically violate the Civil Rights Act of 1964. The Court said:

> It is not necessary in this case to define the line of demarcation between permissible and impermissible action plans; it suffices to hold that the challenged Kaiser-USWA plan falls on the permissible side of the line. . . . At the same time, the plan does not unnecessarily trammel the interest of white employees, neither requiring the discharge of white workers and their replacement with new black hirees, nor creating an absolute bar to the advancement of white employees since half of those trained in the program will be white. Moreover, the plan is a temporary measure, not intended to maintain racial balance, but simply to eliminate a manifest racial imbalance.

The matter of race-conscious hiring, promotion, and layoff quotas will remain a 1980s issue. In *Williams* v. *The City of New Orleans*, there was a court-sanctioned consent decree to promote one black police officer for every white officer until blacks made up 50 percent of the supervisors in the department. This one-to-one provision was denied by the district court on the ground that such a practice was an inequitable infringement on the legitimate interests and expectations of innocent nonblack employees. It seemed to go far beyond the relief required for identifiable victims of discrimination.

In an action virtually duplicating the New Orleans case, an appeals court was asked to invalidate the Detroit police department's promoting blacks and whites on a one-for-one basis until blacks constituted 50 percent of lieutenants of the Detroit force. Unlike New Orleans, however, the Detroit plan was *voluntary* before being endorsed by the courts. These two cases may go to the Supreme Court.

Cases involving layoffs by race instead of by seniority are more serious. The *Boston Firefighters* case, for example, involved whites being laid off ahead of blacks in order to maintain the effects of previous affirmative action hiring, even though whites had greater seniority. The Supreme Court declared the *Boston* case moot, since the whites were rehired. But a similar case by the Memphis firefighters has come before the Supreme Court. If cases like these are declared moot, the seniority/race layoff issue will remain unresolved. In the author's opinion, violations of bona fide systems of seniority in order to retain racial balance will not survive.

Other cases are also pending and the courts will probably not finish clarifying this matter for years to come. However, "the law floats on a sea of ethics." Therefore, it may be productive to consider an ethical approach to reverse discrimination versus affirmative action.

An Ethical Approach. It is the author's position that preferential practices are ethically justified under certain carefully described limits and conditions. The minority person should be qualified for the job or promotion, according to a single standard of minimum qualifications applicable to everyone. Standards should not be lowered, but they should be clearly and honestly job-related.

Each case or group of cases should be considered in an ad hoc manner with appropriate preferential targets and goals, but not with rigid quotas. If minority and majority persons are clearly qualified but the majority person is more qualified in job-related abilities, then two variables must be carefully analyzed and considered simultaneously. They are (1) the strategic or *risk* importance of the job, and (2) the *differential* in qualifications.

1. When the job is of lesser strategic or risk importance, the author suggests selecting the minority person who is indeed qualified, but less qualified than the majority person. As the job becomes more critical, one should pick the *more* qualified person. For example, when choosing applicants for an airline pilot's job, one would prefer the more qualified person more readily than when choosing applicants for a flight attendant's job.

2. Consider the differential in qualifications. Suppose a very small but perceptible gap appears, with the majority person being slightly more qualified (and job risk or importance is not a critical factor). It is suggested here that the minority

person nevertheless be given preference. For example, a combination of test scores, plus subjective judgments, might put a majority person at 87 on the scale of 1 to 100 and a minority person at 85—a very slight difference.

Preferring the qualified, but less-qualified, minority person when both the job risk or importance and qualifications gap are significant would be reverse discrimination. Preferring the more qualified majority person when both the job importance and qualifications gap are minimal would be unaffirmative, or reverse affirmative action.

One might take a cost-benefit approach to the ethical problem of drawing the line between reverse discrimination and reverse affirmative action. If preference would lead to alarmingly high potential costs to the firm and society as a whole (the case of the airline pilot), this choice would surely outweigh the benefits society needs to provide for minorities and women.

Of course, managers need prudence, wisdom, and good faith to make fair judgments concerning both job importance and qualifications for hiring and promotion, since these two factors cannot be perfectly quantified or mechanically evaluated.

Preference is not necessarily reverse discrimination. Neither the qualified majority nor the qualified minority person has an absolute right to either distributive or exchange justice in being considered for a specific job or promotion. Fair consideration does not always require the employer to hire or promote the qualified person. *If the employer has a good and valid reason, called for by the common good, for employing or promoting the qualified, but less-qualified, person, this selection does not violate the rights to justice of the person passed over.*

When encrusted patterns of discrimination put most individuals of certain groups at a special disadvantage *solely because they are members of such groups,* it is just to give acceleration-preferential aid to those qualified individuals *precisely because of their group membership, not* with rigid quotas, but according to good faith targets and goals.

Not every group needs or should get preference. To ascribe "groupness" to every individual employee would lead to chaos in hiring and promoting. The five groups designated by the EEOC—namely, blacks, Hispanics, American Indians, Asians, and women—are groups in singular need of help in the United States. Not all, but most, individuals from these groups are disadvantaged regarding employment at this time.

It is not clear, in early 1984, whether or not the Reagan administration is against all forms of preference, advocating totally color-blind employment practices. The author's ethical stance may seem unpalatable to some. However, he agrees with the Supreme Court in the *Weber* case: that carefully

delineated preferential practices are just as "a temporary measure not intended to maintain racial balance, but simply to eliminate manifest racial imbalance." Company preferential practices, such as those at Sears, General Electric, and Kaiser, are very probably not going to be revoked in the near future.

The Future

The future of equal employment opportunity in the United States depends on many factors independent of management: the leadership of the President in influencing the civil rights climate; actions of the House, the Senate, and the courts; the problems of cities and their schools; the 55 percent of black one-parent families; white flight from the cities; but especially fuller employment.

Managers and federal laws have only moderate influence on some of these issues. Progress will be slow. Realistically, there are relatively few openings for minorities and women at higher-level jobs. Lack of professional and technical education and experience will keep many back. The American trend toward "high tech" industries, such as computers, will call for job qualifications not easily or quickly supplied. In all probability, special efforts on management's part will need to be continued to the year 2000. The future may give us, however, more sophisticated human resource management systems that will benefit *all* employees, whether majority, male, minority, or female, and thereby benefit the entire American economic system.

See also Affirmative action; Appraisal performance; Compensation, employee benefit plans; Compensation, wage and salary policy and administration; Development and training, employee; Employment process; Labor legislation; Older employees, management of; Personnel administration; Testing, psychological; Wages and hours legislation; Women in business and management.

REFERENCES

Anderson, Howard J., ed.: *Primer of Equal Employment Opportunity,* 2d ed., Bureau of National Affairs, Washington, D.C., 1982.

Purcell, Theodore V., S.J.: "Policies on Minority Employment: A Psychologist's View," *Professional Psychology,* vol. 11, no. 3 (June), 1980.

————, and G. F. Cavanagh, *Blacks in the Industrial World,* The Free Press, New York, 1973.

Rev. THEODORE V. PURCELL, S.J. (deceased), *Georgetown University*

Ethics, Managerial

Managerial ethics are concerned with what is deemed acceptable or unacceptable—and by whom—in the realm of business action (behavior) and decision making. Ethics are the collection of moral principles or views about acceptable or unacceptable actions in a given field of human activity. Thus medical ethics and legal ethics indicate what is acceptable or unacceptable behavior in the fields of medicine and law. The term *management ethics* refers to the collection of ideas or thoughts about acceptable or unacceptable behavior by managers. The focus of examination here is on managers in business organizations, keeping in mind that much applies also in government, education, and other types of organizations in our society.

Ethical Issues

Degrees of acceptability of management behavior suggest other terms also: that which is good or bad, fair or unfair, just or unjust. Taken together, these terms clearly identify managerial ethics as a concern with what behaviors and decisions of managers are considered *right* or *wrong.*

Judgments. Judgments about what is right or wrong, moreover, are the crux of the problem in talking about ethics. An individual may agree that the subject of managerial ethics is precisely as described, but *who decides* what is right or wrong, acceptable or unacceptable? Herein lies the problem. Value judgments of people—as individuals or, most usually, as groups—make the determination. They make this determination by comparing managerial actions against standards or norms. Standards or norms evolve from group consensus or agreement.

Consensus. The clearest case of group consensus might be said to be a country's laws. Though it is true that some people in any society do not agree with or like its laws, the legal process is the method by which a people formally establish norms or standards of acceptability. Thus, judgments about managerial ethics are made by value-based comparisons of behavior or actions with standards or norms (which in the final analysis are themselves based upon a set of values).

Unfortunately there is no clear consensus in our society as to what is acceptable or unacceptable regarding all the situations managers face. There are laws, of course, but laws cover only the grossest violations. In many decision arenas, no laws exist at all. For example, there are no clear-cut guidelines of acceptability in such gray areas as: What constitutes deceptive or misleading advertising? What responsibility does the manager have with respect to hidden product dangers? What about using company services for personal use? What about taking longer than necessary to do a job?

Guidelines. The real quandary in business, then, is that there are no clear-cut guidelines for behavior and decision making. Faced with this dilemma, the manager frequently responds to those guidelines which are clear. As an illustration, take the case of the spate of overseas bribery scandals by business firms in the late 1970s. Many businesspeople felt—perhaps rightly—that society had not made clear what is acceptable or unacceptable behavior in the international business arena. Thus, when in doubt, managers tend to respond to the norms of competition and profit, which, unlike ethics, are quite clear.

Level of Abstraction. While society may reach consensus on certain values at a high level of abstraction, this consensus tends to break down as the issues move from the general to the specific. At a high level of abstraction, for example, all agree that one should not take another person's life. As one moves to particular situations, however, there are circumstances under which we rationalize killing as justifiable, e.g., self-defense and war.

As another example, at a high level of abstraction most people tend to agree that one should not take another person's property. When examining specifics, once again there is trouble drawing the line. Is it all right to take home pencils? pens? paper? staples? adding machines? One recent cartoon illustrates a similar dilemma. In the first panel a father speaks to his son, who stands before him with a load of pencils in his hands. The father says, "You know how I feel about stealing, Wilberforce! Now tomorrow I want you to return every one of those pencils to school!" In the second panel the father says: "I'll bring you all the pencils you need from work."

So the problem develops. The manager has no clear-cut standard or norm as to what is acceptable and unacceptable. In the absence of such guidelines, the manager applies personal standards to the predicament, which sometimes mean no standards or standards motivated by self-gain, expediency, or perhaps fear of reprisal by superiors.

Current State of Managerial Ethics

The bulk of the evidence today suggests that the major ethical problem for managers is the constant pressure to compromise personal standards or acceptable ethics in order to accomplish organizational goals. Support for this view can be found both in anecdotal reports and in research studies.

Three brief examples illustrate the "pressure cooker" atmosphere many managers perceive exists today to please the boss. A plant manager of a glass-container plant in Gulfport, Mississippi, reports that he inflated the value of his plant's production by about 33 percent because he feared the company would close the aging facility and throw him and 300 other employees out of work. While working for a major automaker, managers performed unauthorized maintenance on engines undergoing federal certification tests so that they would pass government emission standards. The managers who engaged in this practice reported that senior management had put the squeeze on them to get the engines certified. At another large automaker's truck plant in Flint, Michigan, three plant managers installed a secret control box in a supervisor's office so they could secretly speed up the assembly line and meet the production standards that were being set for them by higher management. In all three of these cases, the managers reported that their unethical practices were in response to what they perceived as unreasonable demands being placed on them by supervisors.[1]

Research studies support the findings seen in these three cases. A survey conducted by Carroll disclosed that a majority of the managers surveyed felt that "managers today feel under pressure to compromise personal standards to achieve company goals." The survey showed also that these pressures were perceived most prevalently at the lower levels of management.[2] A study by Brenner and Molander supported this general finding by revealing that relations with supervisors made up the primary category of ethical conflict.[3] Finally, a study by Lincoln, Pressley, and Little found a high proportion of executives who believed they had to engage in questionable practices in order to advance in their organizations.[4]

These research studies, taken together with the reported examples of unethical behavior, suggest that (1) senior executives may not understand how far their subordinates will go to please them or to achieve organizational goals—perhaps out of a misguided sense of loyalty or fear of reprisal; (2) a serious problem exists with respect to the current state of managerial ethics; (3) the major responsibility for the ethical climate in the organization rests squarely in the hands of top management.

Improving Managerial Ethics

Though some adhere to the belief that good ethics cannot be taught or improved by management, there are a number of levels on which the problem can be effectively addressed: (1) the individual level, (2) the organizational level, (3) the association level, and (4) the societal level. These levels must be approached simultaneously, however, rather than in the sequential order presented here.

Individual Level. It is frequently asserted that good ethics ultimately depend on the individual. Ethical decision making may be improved by carefully engaging in self-analysis with respect to the following tests that business managers have suggested have been useful in recent years:

1. Test of common sense. Does the action I am getting ready to engage in make sense? That is, is it an action a reasonably responsible person would take?

2. Test of negative impact. Will the action harm others or have an irresponsible negative impact on them?

3. Test of self-concept. Does the action conform with my best concept of myself?

4. Watergate TV test. Could my action stand up under close public scrutiny? Would I be embarrassed if what I am getting ready to do became public?

5. Test of ventilation. Would my actions hold up under the scrutiny of ventilation with my colleagues? That is, if I got divergent views in a gray area, would my proposed behavior hold up as acceptable?

6. Test of the purified idea. Am I simply hiding behind my superior's judgments—assuming that the idea is "purified" or made acceptable by a superior's approval?[5]

Organizational Level. There are a number of actions which can be taken by management at the organizational level to improve ethical performance and climate:

1. *Exercise of leadership by top management.* L. W. Foy, former chairman of Bethlehem Steel, has suggested, "It is a primary responsibility of business management to instruct, motivate, and inspire their employees to conduct themselves with honesty, probity, and fairness. Starting at the top, management has to *set an example* for the others to follow." Foy elaborates, " . . . management has to *make company policy absolutely clear* to all employees. People have to be told and retold, in unmistakable terms, that the company is firmly committed to integrity in all its activities."[6] And Fred T. Allen, former chairman and president of Pitney-Bowes, Inc., has stated, "It is up to the leader to make sure that ethical behavior permeates the entire company. Employees must know exactly what is expected of them in the moral arena and how to respond to warped ethics."[7]

2. *Establishment of realistic sales and profit goals.* Allen remarked, "Under the stress of patently unrealistic goals, otherwise responsible subordinates will often take the attitude that anything goes." Goals should be set that are *realistic* and *achievable* within accepted business practices.

3. *Development of codes of ethics.* Codes which transcend the lip-service level of commitment can be established. These codes then must be communicated, adhered to, and made into "living documents."

4. *Encouragement of "whistle blowing."* An effective ethical climate is contingent upon employees having a *mechanism* for and top-management *support* of blowing the whistle on violators of the organization's codes of ethics.

5. *Creation of an ethical ombudsman or advocate.* Theodore Purcell held that ethical expertise be institutionalized at the executive level by creating a position of "ethics advocate."[8] The primary responsibility of this individual would be to identify the general questions of an ethical nature that should be constantly brought to the attention of top management along with the conventional marketing, financial, and legal questions.

6. *Dismissal of unethical managers.* Responding to the question "How should the corporation respond to the individual who is guilty of deliberately and flagrantly violating its ethical code?" Fred T. Allen asserted, "From the pinnacle of the corporate pyramid to its base, there can only be one action: dismissal. . . . When a company fails to take strong action against an employee—at whatever level—most people think the employee had the implicit—if not the explicit—consent of management."[9]

Association Level. Associations are groups of businesses that have a common interest based upon membership in the same trade, industry, or profession. Associations can take leadership in the ethical arena by the development of professional codes of ethics which are designed to bring about norms of behavior and ethical uniformity among a group of businesses; for example, the codes of ethics of the American Institute of Certified Public Accountants, the American Psychological Association, and the American Bar Association.

Efforts to provide leadership in other ways are also recommended. For example, the Chamber of Commerce of the United States Institute for Organization Management offers courses on "ethics for association executives."

Societal Level. Law is the primary instrument of ethical advocacy at the societal level, but management should not view law as the means of ensuring ethical behavior and practices. A section of the Code of Worldwide Business Conduct, issued by Caterpillar Tractor Co., is cogent here. It reads, "The law is a floor. Ethical business conduct should normally exist at a level well above the minimum required by law."[10]

See also Competition; Profits and profit making; Social responsibility of business.

NOTES

[1] George Getschow, "Some Middle Managers Cut Corners to Achieve High Corporate Goals," *The Wall Street Journal,* Nov. 8, 1979, pp. 1, 34.

[2] Archie B. Carroll, "Managerial Ethics: A Post-Watergate View," *Business Horizons,* vol. 18, April 1975, pp. 75–80.

[3] Steven N. Brenner and Earl A. Molander, "Is the Ethics of Business Changing?" *Harvard Business Review,* January–February 1977, pp. 57–71.

[4] Douglas J. Lincoln, Milton M. Pressley, and Taylor Little, "Ethical Beliefs and Personal Views of Top Level Executives," *Journal of Business Research,* 10, 1982, pp. 475–487.

[5] Ibid.

[6] L. W. Foy, "Business Ethics: A Reappraisal," Distinguished Leaders Lecture Series, Columbia University Graduate School of Business, New York, Jan. 30, 1975. (Italics added.)

[7] Fred T. Allen, "Corporate Morality: Is the Price Too High?" *The Wall Street Journal,* Oct. 17, 1975, p. 16. (Italics added.)

[8] Theodore V. Purcell, "A Practical Guide to Ethics in Business," *Business and Society Review,* no. 13, Spring 1975, pp. 43–50.

[9] Allen, loc. cit.

[10] Ibid.

REFERENCES

Beauchamp, Tom L., and Norman Bowie (eds.): *Ethical Theory and Business,* 2d ed., Prentice-Hall, Englewood Cliffs, N.J., 1983.

Benson, George C. S.: *Business Ethics in America,* Lexington Books, Lexington, Mass., 1982.

Bowie, Norman: *Business Ethics,* Prentice-Hall, Englewood Cliffs, N.J., 1982.

Jones, Donald: *Doing Ethics in America,* Oelgeschlager, Gun & Hain, Cambridge, Mass., 1982.

Velasquez, Manuel G.: *Business Ethics: Concepts and Cases,* Prentice-Hall, Englewood Cliffs, N.J., 1982.

ARCHIE B. CARROLL, *University of Georgia, Athens*

Exception, Management by

Management by exception is an information and control technique that provides management with signals that tell when a condition or operation is within its prescribed standards and when it is not. Certain refinements may enable the system to indicate the degree of variance and the particular level of management attention required, as shown in Fig. E-7. The principle, as conceived by Frederick W. Taylor, provides leverage for the use of management time and enables managers to accomplish far more than if they were to apply themselves indiscriminately to every problem that arose.

Management by exception implies the use of delegation, since subordinates typically handle conditions that are within the lower ranges of variance. Frank B. Gilbreth suggested that various control levels—or zones of variance—be established for each key condition and that responsibilities for appropriate action within each zone be prearranged.

Most budget and variance reports incorporate some form of management by exception in their information systems. These range widely in (1) degree of specificity (some reports simply indicate

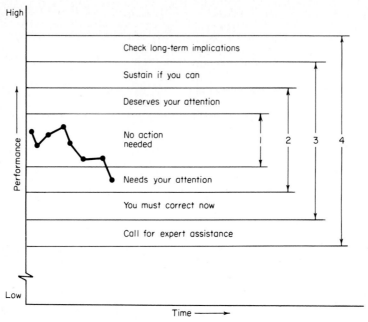

Establishment of zone limits is key to performance control.

Zone 1 — Expected and acceptable performance.

Zone 2 — Unusual performance. On the low side, needs surveillance. On the high side, needs verification.

Zone 3 — Unacceptable performance. On the low side, needs action to correct now. On the high side, look for evidence of changed conditions that indicate standards should be raised.

Zone 4 — Vitally disturbed performance. On the low side, ask for staff help to analyze and correct. On the high side, full-scale investigation indicated to assure that performance isn't being attained at expense of long-term goals.

FIG. E-7 Action-indicator chart.

under or over budget); (2) speed of reporting (instantaneous with on-line process controls and daily, weekly, or monthly with typical budgetary controls); and (3) format [ranging from handposted quality control charts to computer printouts to visual cathode-ray tube (CRT) indicators.]

See also Accounting, cost analysis and control; Control systems, management; Delegation; Gantt charts; Objectives and goals; Objectives, management by (MBO).

REFERENCES

Bittel, Lester R.: *Management By Exception*, McGraw-Hill, New York, 1964.

Gilbreth, Frank B.: "Graphical Control on the Exception Principle for Executives," Paper 1573a, American Society of Mechanical Engineers, New York, December 1916.

Swenson, Dan H.: *Business Reporting*, Science Research Associates, Chicago, 1983, p. 13.

Taylor, Frederick W.: "Shop Management," reprinted in *Scientific Management*, Harper & Row, New York, 1947, p. 126.

LESTER R. BITTEL, *James Madison University*

Exchange, Foreign, Management of

The necessity of dealing with matters concerning foreign exchange is one of the principal dimensions that distinguish international business transactions from their domestic counterparts. *Foreign exchange* deals with the relationships of the monies of one country to those of another; it is a generic term, used in conjunction with procedures and documents as well as prices and institutions. The actual purchase of the money of one nation with that of another is called *conversion.* The price at which the sale takes place is the *exchange rate.* If no real purchase or sale takes place, but merely the changing of accounting statements from an expression of values in one money to equivalent values in another, the process is called *translation. Money* refers to anything that is generally accepted to make payments for goods or services or to discharge obligations; it includes bills of exchange and bank drafts as well as bank notes (currency). Business assets and liabilities are expressed in the monetary units, or the *units of account,* of a particular country. If an eventual conversion must take place, the possibility of a change in the value of exchange rates gives rise to potential gain or loss of assets, or to a *foreign exchange risk.* The total amount of money subject to foreign exchange risk is called the *foreign exchange exposure.*

Exchange Rate Variation

Consideration of the shifting values of foreign exchange rates should begin with a recognition that any quoted rate, unless otherwise qualified, could represent an official rate or a free-market rate. The *official rate* is the value that the issuing government places on its own currency. The assignment of this value by a government can be quite arbitrary, but the use of that value can be enforced by the government's control of the banking system, with severe penalties for trading outside of prescribed channels.

The *free-market rate,* as the term implies, is the value determined by the forces of supply and demand. However, the greatest single force in the market affecting supply or demand is often a government action, even for currencies that are designated as freely convertible. A *convertible* currency is one that may be freely exchanged or converted into other foreign currencies.

Amount of Rate Variation. Some exchange rates do not vary at all over long periods, but other currencies may fluctuate widely over short periods of time. The United States dollar is legal tender in Panama, on par with that country's own balboa; therefore, one dollar has equaled one balboa since the inception of the balboa in 1904. On the other hand, the French franc fell about 5½ percent in value relative to the Japanese yen between the end of February and the middle of March 1976.

A change can also come quickly in both directions, as illustrated by the performance of the Italian lira and the French franc, where the franc appreciated about 12½ percent between the end of February and the end of April 1976, only to fall back more than 8 percent of its peak value the following month. Rapid price variations such as these are not unusual in free markets for commodities, including those for the commodity of foreign exchange. But the official rates of controlled currencies usually maintain their values, changing seldom but changing precipitously when the governments involved are finally forced to act. The United States dollar, for example, was devalued 7.89 percent in December 1971, and another 10 percent in February 1973, after having maintained its previous official value in terms of gold since 1934.

Fixed versus Floating Exchange Rates. Most Western nations do not now attempt to maintain a stable value of their currencies solely by edict and the exercise of police power, since this control results in the development of black markets or chokes off desirable commerce. Instead, they take part in elaborate economic measures that include direct operations by government in the exchange markets,[8] working arrangements between central banks, and participation in international agreements such as the International Monetary Fund (IMF) or the European Monetary Agreement. The fundamental objectives of these agreements are to promote commerce by providing exchange stability and orderly markets and a sufficient supply of foreign exchange (*international liquidity*). The choices of available means for establishing a new world monetary order fit on a continuum between administratively determined *fixed exchange rates* on the one hand and flexible or *floating exchange rates* established by the marketplace on the other.

Fixed exchange rates have the advantage of stability: businesses have assurances that foreign money will cost the same next month regardless of market conditions. But fixed rates, if different from what free markets would dictate, must be maintained by government action. This means restrictions,[1] with concomitant evasive behavior by citizens, or it could be accomplished by *pegging,* or direct government intervention in the market to maintain a particular rate of exchange (the *parity* rate). When governments or, more precisely, their agents, the central banks, peg the market by buying or selling the currency in question, they make the transaction with gold (especially in the past) or reserves. *Reserves* are drawable funds held by central banks or other financial institutions such as the IMF. Thus, in the fixed exchange rate system, rates remain fairly constant, but there is a fluctuation in the level of available reserves. In situations where the conditions underlying the market pressures are chronic, a central bank may exhaust its supply of available reserves. If this happens, a sharp adjustment of exchange rates becomes necessary. Floating rates, therefore, adjust daily and reflect the market at any moment; fixed rates are stable in the short run but risk precipitous changes in the long run.

Spot and Forward Exchange Rates. Foreign exchange resembles other commodities in an important respect besides price fluctuations. Exchange transactions may take place on the basis of a spot or forward contract defined as in commodities trading. A *spot* transaction is one in which immediate delivery of, and payment for, the currency takes place; because of procedural delays, "immediate" is generally taken to mean within 2 business days of the trade date. A *forward* transaction is a contract wherein the currency is to be delivered and payment made at a designated future date at a price set at the time when the contract is drawn. The period of the contract can be of any length, but 30, 60, or 90 days is the most common.

The spot and forward exchange rates are related to one another. At least two theories are currently available to explain the magnitude of the premium or discount at which the forward sells relative to the spot value: (1) *the interest rate parity theory,*[3] which holds that the difference in forward and spot prices is determined by the differences in short-term interest rates in the respective financial centers; and (2) the *interest parity plus speculation theory,*[3] which holds that in addition to the above, the forward rate reflects the expected future value of the spot rate, with speculators entering the market to shift the prices away from their "natural" interest parity values. The interest parity idea makes sense because when banks take one side of a forward contract, they typically, and must in some instances (such as is the case with British banks), offset the contract by a second transaction to cover any exposed position. For example, if an American bank sells a client a 90-day forward contract for British pounds, it has acquired an obligation to come up with a designated number of pounds in 90 days; to ensure that the pounds will be available 90 days hence without suffering an exchange loss, the bank can offset the forward contract by purchasing a British treasury bill (denominated in pounds). The bank earns interest at London rates on that British treasury bill; but it likewise has sacrificed the opportunity to put the same funds in a U.S. treasury bill at New York interest rates. Therefore, if New York interest rates are higher, the client must reimburse the bank for this loss—or pay a premium equal to the difference in the rates—when buying the forward contract. Conversely, if London interest rates are higher, the client's promise to deliver dollars in 90 days provides the bank with the opportunity to take advantage of the higher London rates without incurring exposure; hence, the forward contract would sell at a discount. Speculators, however, by the very nature of that operation, do take *open* (i.e., uncovered) positions; therefore, to the degree that the forward market is represented at any time by open positions, the interest parity plus speculation theory is reasonable. Also, since a forward contract depends upon the ability of the participants to deliver, credit standing of participants can be reflected in the price of a given transaction.

Why Spot Rates Fluctuate. Granting the above relationship between spot and forward rates, the question still remains as to the determinants of the spot rates of any two currencies. The most immediate impact on the supply and demand for currencies is produced by the *balance of trade* between the respective nations, or more precisely, the *balance of payments,* which includes, in addition to the difference between exports and imports, the net of all other money flows. This flow of payments is in turn affected by the differences in inflation rates (one of the best leading indicators), productivity, available reserves, interest rates, traders' attitudes, taxes, money supply, restrictions, and political considerations, all of which are to some extent interdependent.

Foreign Exchange Markets

The very word "marketplace" denotes a location where trading takes place. And indeed, the New York Stock Exchange, the Chicago Board of Trade, and Billingsgate in London all call up visions of specific buildings or areas with their own unique sights and sounds and character. Physically, the major portion of a foreign exchange market can best be described as a mass of telephone lines, cable, and radio systems located within and connecting the major financial centers of the world. The closest thing to a "place" in the foreign exchange market is the trading room of a major bank, wherein the bank's currency trading specialists are congregated for convenience and greater efficiency, along with their desks, telephones, and perhaps posting boards or electronic terminals. But the bank trading room usually represents only a part of any given transaction; the other parts involve the participants on the other ends of the telephone wires. These participants are, aside from the ultimate buyer and seller, another bank and often a broker specialist who connects the bank that has currency to buy with the one that has currency to sell. A central bank can also be a participant as a buyer or seller, and in countries with exchange controls, it may be a required link in clearing any transaction.

The One World of Foreign Exchange. Because of the capabilities of modern communications, the connection between financial centers in effect creates a single world marketplace for currencies. A businessperson in a small town in Alabama can place an order for Spanish pesetas with a local banker. The local banker probably does not have foreign exchange trading facilities, or even published market reports on currencies, but this doesn't matter. The order is relayed through a correspondent or perhaps is placed directly with a major New York or Chicago commercial bank that executes the order. The entire operation can be completed within minutes.

This capacity for communication also serves to keep the rates in one financial center in line with those at another. If the pesetas sold for a cheaper price in Frankfurt than in Chicago, a trader would make a quick profit by buying pesetas cheaply in Frankfurt and immediately selling them dearly in Chicago, thereby affecting the supply-demand relationships in both centers and bringing about equilibrium. This simultaneous purchase in one market and sale in another to take advantage of price discrepancies is called *arbitrage.*

Arbitrage also takes place to make the exchange rates mutually consistent among the various currencies. That is, if the British pound sells for $1.80 and the French franc sells for $0.20, a British pound should also buy 9 French francs, or the ratio of $1.80:$0.20. The relationship of the exchange rates of two currencies derived from their values in terms of a third currency is called *cross rate.* Because of arbitrage transactions, principally by commercial bank traders, cross rates do not usually maintain significant differences for more than a few minutes.

The worth of a particular currency can be determined daily by a local banker by checking his or her bank's own internal daily rate sheet, or by making a phone call to the trading room if it is a large bank, or through a correspondent if it is not. Exchange dealers in the trading rooms of some of the large commercial banks also give up-to-the-minute information directly to their more important clients. For most clients, the information on currency rates supplied by various publishers and advisory services should

suffice.[5,7] The most widely available daily reporting of exchange rates in the English language appears in *The Wall Street Journal* and the *London Financial Times.*

Translating Accounts and Measuring Exposure

There are a number of ways of translating accounts for consolidation purposes, or of calculating exposure to determine how much is at risk. The following four methods are illustrated in Table E-5, assuming a balance sheet of a British subsidiary of an American firm with all entries denominated in pounds sterling.

Current Rate Method. Sometimes referred to as the *closing rate method,* this procedure translates all items on the balance sheet at the current (i.e., closing) rate of exchange. Since the past is dead, this method has considerable appeal to the practitioner and is indeed favored by British firms and many European firms. With this philosophy, only net equity is exposed, since losses on assets are compensated for by corresponding gains on liabilities if the foreign currency depreciates, and vice versa.

The major problem with this approach is that it is not usually valid to assume all classes of assets and liabilities represent the same risks, either under inflation or exchange fluctuation. Fixed assets such

TABLE E-5 Comparison of Methods of Measuring Foreign Exchange Exposure

Example, Ltd. Balance sheet as of Dec. 31, 1977 (in pounds sterling)		Exposed item			
		Current rate method	Working capital method	Monetary-nonmonetary method	Temporal method
Assets:					
Cash	150	150	150	150	150
Accounts receivable	200	200	200	200	200
Inventory	400	400	400		
Prepaid expenses	50	50		50	
Plant & equipment	1000				
Less depreciation	−100 = 900	900			
Goodwill	80	80			
Total assets =	1780	1780			
Liabilities:					
Accounts payable	170	170	170	170	170
Short-term debt	120	120	120	120	120
Long-term debt	700	700		700	700
Total liabilities =	990	990			
Net worth:	790				
Total liabilities & NW =	1780				
Total exposure		790 Net assets	460 Net assets	(590) Net liability	(640) Net liability
Definition of exposure		Total assets less total liabilities	Current assets less current liabilities	Monetary assets less monetary liabilities	Temporal assets less temporal liabilities

Note: Preferred stock, if any, would have been a monetary liability.

as plant and equipment would tend to increase in money terms if the unit of account were depreciated, as would their replacement costs. Also, the use of this method disturbs accountants since it departs from the traditional cost basis of valuation.

Working Capital Method. For translation, consider current assets and liabilities at current rates, fixed assets and liabilities at historical rates. Since this method has an application of rates and accounting classification that appears to be consistent in time frame, it likewise has appeal to many firms, especially in the United States. *Current,* of course, means within a 1-year period. It is called the working capital method because the exposure is defined as current assets less current liabilities, or the firm's *working capital.*

The argument here is that it is the short-term items that are subject to rate fluctuation. But with this method, inventory becomes an exposed item, whereas long-term debt does not. Yet inventory is carried on the balance sheets only as a value near current costs when first-in, first-out (FIFO) inventory valuation is used; and the trend in inflation-prone environments is away from FIFO procedures. And long-term debt remains an obligation whose ultimate payment changes with rate fluctuations; hence a risk is involved.

Monetary-Nonmonetary Method. Exposure equals monetary assets less monetary liabilities. In translating accounts, monetary assets and liabilities are translated at current rates, nonmonetary assets and liabilities at historical rates. This method divides assets and liabilities according to their nature: physical or financial. It is based on the concept that physical items have an economic value that is independent of the unit of account; if inflation (or currency depreciation) occurs, physical items merely obtain a proportionately higher value in the depreciated currency. A classification of balance sheet items is as follows:

Monetary assets	Monetary liabilities
Cash	Accounts payable
Marketable securities	Short-term notes
Accounts receivable	Long-term debt
Prepaid expenses	Preferred stock

This method is based on good economic logic, and it is internally consistent if inventory is valued on last-in, first-out (LIFO) accounting procedures, hence carried on the balance sheet at historical cost. The method does increase exposure sharply for firms with high debt-to-equity ratios. Today, this is the method recommended by most authorities for exchange exposure measurement but not for accounting translation.[10]

Temporal Method. This method was introduced by the Financial Accounting Standards Board and made mandatory for consolidating financial statements for United States reporting that requires auditor approval. It is defined as follows: "The temporal method translates cash, receivables and payables, and assets and liabilities carried at present or future prices at current rate and assets and liabilities carried at past prices at applicable historical rates."[12] That is, if an item (such as inventory) is carried on the balance sheet at historical rates (which it is under LIFO), it should be translated at historical rates. Since most monetary items are carried on most firms' balance sheets at what amounts to current or future rates in a foreign exchange context and nonmonetary items are carried at historical rates, the results of the temporal method will usually coincide with those of the monetary-nonmonetary method. One exception, as seen in Table E-5, consists of prepaid expenses. The temporal method emphasizes consistency in accounting principles and usage; the monetary-nonmonetary method emphasizes economic decision making.

Comparison of the four methods with the example in Table E-5 illustrates the wide divergence in total exposure that can result. The first two show a risk of loss if the pound depreciates but a chance to gain if the pound increases in value relative to the dollar; the last two indicate the reverse! Here is an example where the international monetary manager would be expected to take entirely different protective actions depending on which exposure measurement system were in use. Which would be correct?

As mentioned earlier, the monetary-nonmonetary method is the method of measuring exchange exposure that is most *generally* appropriate for *economic* decisions. But it is worth remembering that this economic validity is based on a number of assumptions, so the following are among the questions that should be asked: Can you really raise prices in your markets if currency depreciates? Are your fixed assets a good inflation hedge, and does their value really go up as much as the value of the currency goes down? Are debts really debts when owed to the parent or a sister subsidiary? Do tax effects alter the picture? Do exchange restrictions limit repatriation of funds? What is the actual cost of replacing inventories and other assets today?

Dealing with Exchange Exposure

Once the method of measuring exposure most appropriate to the situation has been selected and the magnitude of the exposure calculated, the question remains: How best to deal with it? Several of the more popular devices are outlined below.

Hedging. A *hedge* is an offset. The term can be used generally to indicate any offsetting action, but in the context of foreign exchange, "hedging" generally refers to the use of a purchase or sale of a currency in the forward markets to offset an exposed position. For example, if an American exporting firm signed a contract for which it would be paid 1 year hence in Italian lire, it would have a risk of loss if the lira declines in value. So the firm can sell the lire forward at a price known today and thereby remove the exchange risk. Two parties, such as a parent and subsidiary, can lend each other currencies by a simultaneous spot purchase and forward sale or vice versa; this form of the hedge is called a *swap* transaction. For example, the American exporter can lend its Italian subsidiary lire by buying them spot and making the loan; this creates an open position that is immediately covered by the simultaneous forward sale.

Hedging is a direct financial device for reducing exchange risk. Its use has minimal interference with operational considerations. However, hedging can be expensive; the forward contract will probably cost at least as much as the interest rate differential between the two centers, as discussed previously. And hedging can increase the credit risk. Note what would happen in the example above if the exporter were not paid for its goods; it is out its payment and must also deliver lire according to the conditions of the forward contract!

Forward contracts are readily available for most major currencies. The International Monetary Market of the Chicago Mercantile Exchange trades contracts in British pounds, Canadian dollars, Japanese yen, Swiss francs, and West German marks. But forward markets in minor currencies, especially in less developed countries with chronic inflation and balance of payments problems, can be thin or nonexistent.

Monetary Balance. The previous discussion of methods for measuring exposure and the illustration in Table E-5 show the offsetting effects of assets and liabilities. Exposure can be managed by eliminating it, with actions that alter the magnitudes of the balance sheet items themselves. Such actions include:

Credit policy, to adjust accounts receivable

Payments policy, to adjust accounts payable

Factoring, to dispose of accounts receivable

Cash management, to reduce soft currency assets

Inventory management and pricing

Local borrowing of soft currency

Refinancing debt denominated in hard currency

A number of these actions can be considered good management practices to be followed regardless of the foreign exchange issue. Some companies routinely use credit policy, for example, as a source of funds by (1) slow remittance on accounts payable and (2) pressure for quick payment on receivables. This approach may also be useful in currency management; however, when the payables and receivables are denominated in currencies subject to appreciation, the reverse policy is followed. Speeding or slowing payments and receipts is called *leading* or *lagging* in money management vernacular.

Problems associated with altering monetary balance include financing costs, such as the interest required in obtaining soft currency loans (where interest is normally high), and disruption of a firm's financial structure, which can affect not only cost of capital but also return on investment. Inventory reduction to reduce exposure can cause stock-outs and loss of sales. Tight credit policy and price rises to compensate for currency depreciation can lose sales. Factoring can be expensive and is not available in many countries. In countries where currency fluctuations are expected, borrowing is likely to be difficult. And leads and lags in payments and receipts are harder to orchestrate when everyone is following these policies. In addition, many nations now regulate leads and lags.[11]

Netting. Multinational companies have an important advantage: with branches in many locations, exposed assets in one branch can be offset by exposed liabilities in another, thereby reducing the *net* exposure for the multinational entity. Also, payments may actually flow between branches, and the cost of these transfers may be reduced if only net amounts are involved. Exposure netting need not rely exclusively on matching identical currencies among branches; currencies that are tied together by the respective governments can be used as equivalents.

Netting can save substantial sums in exchange commissions and provide the advantages of centrally controlled money management, optimizing at the corporate level. But a large volume of transactions is usually required to justify the executive time required. Netting is also legally curtailed in many countries.[11]

Dollar Invoicing. A simple means for an exporter to avoid foreign exchange risk is to invoice in dollars or, more generally, in the currency of its home country. This is the most common procedure for American exporters for reasons of tradition and lack of knowledge, as well as currency risk aversion. This method presents obvious legal and operational problems for companies with subsidiaries abroad. Competitive marketing pressures and dollar weaknesses may make this procedure less attractive in the future, even to exporters.

Accepting Risk. The ultimate alternative for dealing with foreign exchange risk should always be considered by the international money manager, and that is simply to accept it.

A final caveat applicable to all the previous discussions of measuring and dealing with foreign exchange regards taxation. The necessity of integrating foreign exchange management with tax strategy is illustrated by the fact that tax rate *differences* can be as high as the American tax on corporations; this is considerably higher than the overwhelming majority of exchange rate fluctuations within a year. Therefore, although foreign exchange management is an important topic for the multinational manager, tax considerations can easily predominate.

See also Economic systems; Financial management; Financial management, bank relations; International operations and management in multinational companies; International trade.

NOTES AND REFERENCES

[1]*Annual Report on Exchange Restrictions*, International Monetary Fund. Summary of restrictive practices by country.

[2]Antl, Boris, and Richard Ensor, *Management of Foreign Exchange Risk*, Euromoney Publications, 2d ed., 1982.

[3]Einzig, Paul, *The History of Foreign Exchange*, Macmillan & Co., Ltd., London, 1968.

[4]*IMF Survey*, International Monetary Fund, Washington. Newsletter published twice monthly. Economic and monetary events, exchange rates.

[5]*International Currency Review*, Currency Journals, Ltd., 11 Regency Place, London. Published bimonthly. Also available from same source: *Economic Data Service*, with monthly updates of data pertinent to currency; *London Currency Reports*, with charts, data, and significant events affecting the major world currencies.

[6]*International Financial Statistics*, International Monetary Fund, Washington. Published monthly. Statistics on exchange transactions, international reserves, interest rates, world trade, balance of payments, and other data, by country.

[7]*International Reports on Finance and Currencies*, International Reports, Inc., 200 Park Ave. South, New York, 10003. Published weekly.

[8]*Monthly Review*, Federal Reserve Bank of New York. Contains articles in every third issue which discuss Federal Reserve foreign exchange operations, and developments in the markets for major world currencies.

[9]Pick, Franz, *Pick's Currency Yearbook*, Pick Publishing Corp., New York. Annual encyclopedia of the world's currencies. Includes historical data on exchange rates, black market rates, currency in circulation, currency restrictions, data on gold; also a monthly update, *Pick's World Currency Report*, on official and black market rates.

[10]Selling, Thomas I., and George H. Sorter, "FASB Statement No. 52 and Its Implications for Financial Statement Analysis," *Financial Analysts Journal*, May–June 1983, pp 64–69. Superseding FASB No. 8, FASB 52 specifies the temporal method for foreign subsidiaries whose "functional currency" is the dollar, and the current rate method for those whose "functional currency" is local.

[11]*Solving International Financial & Currency Problems*, Business International, One Dag Hammerskjold Plaza, New York, June 1976.

[12]*Statement No. 8—Accounting for the Translation of Foreign Currency Transactions and Foreign Currency Financial Statements*, Financial Accounting Standards Board, Oct. 1975.

EDWARD A. NELSON, *Northern Arizona University*

Facilities and Site Planning and Layout

Site planning and facilities layout encompass the conceptual planning of the new plant, office, institution, and/or warehouse. The principles discussed herein are fundamental to the effective transition from objectives and goals to the completion of plans and layouts for an operating unit. It is essential to planning and layout procedures that objectives and parameters be set forth and that certain standards of performance for the project itself (the planning and implementation process) be established. With the completion of this work, those charged with the architectural engineering design phase will have clear and accurate directions.

The vital relationship of buildings, site, and equipment represents the total environment in planning of facilities.

1. The site must accommodate immediate and long-term requirements for the proposed operating unit in terms of

    a. traffic, access, utilities, services

    b. adherence to governing covenant and regulations

    c. provisions for flexibility and growth in later site developments

2. The buildings must accommodate production operations effectively, represent the desired corporate image, and be adaptable to revisions in use and requirements for expansion.

3. Layouts of equipment must reflect the same factors plus the need for efficiency of operations, effective employee and administrative services, and provisions for security and quality control.

It is popular to observe that a facility should be designed from the inside out, that production equipment determines the building configuration; in practice, building design and plant layout are mutually dependent. The ideal layout in terms of production flow can be costly in terms of supervision, security, or lack of flexibility. Although the process will govern, facility planning prepares for the demands of future product and business needs within the confines of the site for future expansion.

Program Direction Phase

Facilities planning is the key to the success of the capital investment opportunities; any significant **299** allocation of funds and energy requires detailed goal setting and establishment of parameters for the program. Management (1) directs in general, but clear, terms the size of the facility in reference to production capacity or similar measure, relating this projection to return on investment (ROI) policy; and (2) establishes the order of magnitude of anticipated capital investments. The project manager proceeds to identify equipment, plant, services, staffing, and estimated costs. The ROI policy is the basic checkpoint and is monitored throughout the planning process.

It is essential that policy be established both for initial cost versus operating cost considerations and for utilitarian versus quality image determinations. This policy formulation addresses the question of low-cost start-up versus high energy consumption and inordinate maintenance costs. Complete estimates of project operating costs should be included in the ROI statement, as a poor judgment in equipment and materials selection can cut deeply into profit margins of even a new plant.

Objectives. The basic objectives of planning and layout are set forth prior to the planning process. These objectives relate to performance levels for the facility and the role of the facility within the corporate structure. Growth policy determines what provision is to be made for expansion and added capacity.

Data Base. It is essential that data be compiled, correlated, and subscribed to, in order that the planning process can be based upon factual information. The data will be in many forms and cover a wide range of material. The content depends upon the type of facility being planned, the complexity of the process, and whether the facility is a modification or an addition to existing facilities or a new one. Typical forms of data are suggested by the following:

1. Capacity or production rate(s) of the facility.

2. Number of product lines or areas of service of the facility. Planning must include a close evaluation of the performance goals and the equipment and services that will be required.

3. Identification of assemblies represented and manufactured and purchased parts. This information leads to assessments of production and storage requirements.

4. Estimates of the percentage of the product falling into active versus occasional classifications, that is, the approximately 20 percent of the products that usually provide 80 percent of sales versus the 80 percent that provide little profit.

5. Equipment requirements. Planners must determine what existing equipment can be reused and what must be purchased (with special reference to technologically advanced equipment).

6. Number of employees (by classifications) initially and as anticipated over the foreseeable life of the facility. These data should include evaluation of visitor access and all traffic and parking requirements.

7. Utilities and services. This item should include comprehensive listings of utility and service requirements with usage rates, quantities by period and characteristics, and the amount and physical description of wastes to be discharged.

8. Criteria for special building services such as air-conditioned areas, clean rooms, high-pressure steam service, compressed air service, and the treatment and/or disposal of hazardous materials.

9. Fire prevention requirements in detail, developed in consultation with the underwriting agency.

10. Reference data for governing restrictions, as required by building codes, zoning, the Environmental Protection Agency (EPA), and the Occupational Safety and Health Act (OSHA). A widening range of special requirements must be followed, and the only reasonable approach is to learn of the requirements at an early date, move to meet them, and arrange to discuss or appeal requirements which could abort the program.

These are only samples of the data that must be developed for analysis. Specialized handbooks will provide checklists, and company staff must furnish special data for specific operations of the company. The pertinence and accuracy of the information will determine in a large measure the efficiency of the total planning picture.

Technical Phase

The technical phase relates policy, objectives, and data needed to serve proposed production requirements by department and function. This work develops the optimum-sized facility with equipment, systems, and staffing for what can be considered a model of the proposed facility. Against this model, all considerations of alternatives and trade-offs will be measured.

Flow Diagrams. The first step in the plant layout process is the development of flow diagrams of principal operations. Flow diagrams show relationships of individual processing and production operations in sequence and with interacting functions. Although an established set of symbols is used to indicate operation, transportation, storage, delay, and inspection, the technique is less important than an understanding of the diagramming exercise. The diagrams' graphic representation of steps in a manufacturing and materials flow procedure, including interdependent functions, uncovers inefficiencies and, more important, opportunities for improvement.

Relationship Charts. The second major step is the preparation of a relationship chart showing relative importance of proximity between departments and functions. Essentially, a relationship chart will list each area on an X and Y axis similar to the mileage chart in a road atlas. In the intersecting square opposite two areas, the relative value of a close proximity between the areas is noted using a scale from 1 ("no importance") to 10 ("very critical"). The values are determined by priority factors, such as difficulty in product movement, quality control considerations in any moves, necessity of joint supervision or coordination between certain departments, and common use of critical services. A second set of indicators (usually letters) can be used to indicate types of moves. Color coding of similar values (using high-importance values) will further illustrate key relationships. Thus a pattern emerges indicating key areas for close (or remote) proximity, and trade-off judgments on location priorities can be made from these factual data.

The application of materials-handling systems in conjunction with the plant layout work, and with special reference to the relationship values among functions, is most important. (*See* Material handling.)

Block Layouts. The flow diagrams, relationship chart, and an understanding of material-handling system opportunities are preludes to the actual plant layout work. A series of general block layouts now can be accomplished. The blocks should be to a scale that indicates the floor area required for each function. By their shape, they also may indicate a production line or other special configuration.

There are many computer-assisted design (CAD) software programs for minicomputers that replace the manual/template systems of block layout planning. (*See* Production planning and control.)

The blocks—in template form or via CAD and to common scale (representing departments, operations, and functions)—can be assembled to represent the total plant. They are then arranged and adjusted to reflect the flow of material and information, relationships, and other factors governing efficient operation. The general layout of the plant will emerge from the practical procedure of study, critique, and refinement.

Overlays. Another tool in this phase is the use of overlays to represent services, distribution, and management patterns. With the general layout as a base plan, a series of transparent overlays should be developed using drafting techniques or CAD if a large-size plotter is available. They should indicate distribution systems for services and utilities, employee population of each department and func-

tion, and traffic patterns of employees and visitors. Overlays represent the principal traffic patterns of material, supplies, and parts from receiving, through the operations and into storage and shipping. They test the layouts and demonstrate where adjustments are required.

Working with the plant layout, it is possible to modify the operating sequences (and the flow diagrams) if new problems and opportunities are uncovered. Changes sometimes can be made in sequences to assist in layout solutions without adverse effect on production. An existing procedure should not dictate against improvements, and the plant layout effort is the correct time for such evaluation.

Office Planning. As work on the production areas takes shape, a parallel operation is the planning of office areas. The relationship of manufacturing, warehousing, and employee services to the office is integrated into the total facilities planning effort. (*See* Office space planning.)

Computer Programs for Plant Layout. In addition to the CAD software (mentioned for replacement of greatly improved graphics), several computer programs are available to accomplish the data processing of areas, growth, and relationships into a schematic plant layout. These programs include computerized relative allocation of facilities techniques (CRAFT) and computerized relationship layout planning (CORELAP). Generally, they tend to lack capability for judgments and trade-off considerations, and their graphic printouts require considerable massaging. For complex plants, however, a computer program can reduce a mass of data to comprehensible form and also can provide a useful check for many manual efforts.

Equipment Layouts. The final step in planning the facility involves developing detailed layouts by working from revised plant layouts and overlays. This planning has traditionally been done with ¼-inch scale templates, available commercially for most production machines, equipment, and furniture. The use of CAD and a library of equipment, conveyor, and storage system outlines provides the flexibility not achieved through previous systems. Analysis of equipment layouts includes (1) the ability to operate and serve the equipment efficiently, and (2) certainty that aisle widths are generous and that provisions are advantageous for maintenance and housekeeping work. A reproducible print of the equipment layout is used to indicate specific services required for each machine and the locations of connections. This information again checks the layout and is used by engineers for the design of distribution systems.

Use of three-dimensional models may be worth considering where there are questions of clearly demonstrating interaction of equipment, personnel, and services. Models are invaluable when dealing with management people who may have difficulty visual-

301

izing from plans and diagrams. They are also useful as employee indoctrination aids.

Site Planning

It now is possible to relate the plant requirements to the site. Here, even to a greater extent than in the plant itself, plans are critical to the long-term usefulness of the facility investment.

Nonproductive areas.   For effective use of land, an effort must be made to minimize nonproductive areas, as in setbacks and excessive landscaping. Locating a building in the center of a site may not leave surrounding areas of suitable size for expansion. Usually, it is better practice to locate the buildings forward and to one side, providing optimum alternatives to future planners.

Critical Factors.   Several factors should be considered in approaching the site-planning phase:

1. The total site and facility (whether a plant, a distribution center, or a headquarters) should convey to the public the functional and favorable image the company wishes to project.

2. Landscaping, roads, and parking areas must provide for ready identification of visitor destinations, clear views for security and safety, and screening for trucking and yard storage areas.

3. Access to the site should be planned for separation of dissimilar traffic as far as practical. Parking areas should be convenient to building entrances. It is realistic to provide a parking space for each employee unless there are public transportation and existing car pools. The EPA is working to mandate the reduction of available parking, and these regulations should be carefully researched.

A *preliminary site plan* showing principal uses on the site is developed for study. The buildings (with expansion shown as a dotted extension), shipping and receiving, roads, parking, railroad siding, utilities, fire prevention systems, etc., all can be sketched into the plan. The site plan is related to the building plans in order clearly to indicate relationships of employee parking and building access.

A *completed site plan* will provide sufficient direction for the designers (engineers, architects, and landscape architects) to execute the detailed plans.

Expansion and Flexibility

A 5-year forecast is about the limit for accuracy in specific planning of equipment layouts. In fact, a totally efficient layout for a high-production operation can be justified on a short-term basis, even allowing for extensive changeover costs on comple-

tion of the production run. Product changes, new marketing programs, and technology breakthroughs may put unforeseen pressure on the facility. Good facility planning provides diverse opportunities for the future planner, as specific future requirements can only be theorized. It is in the present planning effort that the future viability of the plant is established. Later changes in the functions will be reasonable or costly, depending on the alternatives provided in the original plan.

To provide for expansion and flexibility, the more permanent operations and services should be so located as to avoid blocking options for change. Power plants, substations, and equipment requiring special foundations or underfloor services should receive special attention also. Requirements for contiguous location of departments can be overcome through the use of conveyor systems and other accommodations. Often it is wise to locate departments with the common characteristics of immobility in a central core area—even when such a choice may not be indicated in the flow diagrams or relationship charts.

Growth and flexibility factors apply to site planning as well as to production areas. Parking areas provide logical expansion space if the road system has foreseen this eventuality. Underground water mains should be located away from areas that seem logical for building expansion. Railroad sidings and truck docks require special attention.

Managerial Control

Planning requires the continual analysis of all available cost data.

Cost Control.   Early development of policy for return on investment, combined with performance specifications for the facility, is a basic requirement. It will help management ascertain that the facility, as it emerges in greater detail, falls within the mandated economic guidelines. While cost estimates will be rough and generally will be provided only on a square-foot and unit-cost basis, these figures suffice for warning or confirmation purposes. Estimates always should be developed within a plus or minus 10 percent of actual cost.

Monitoring the Planning Process.   The planning functions are cyclical in nature, running from policy determination and data collection through a series of exercises in design and refinement, reevaluation of data, review of policy, and further refinements. It is essential that management monitor these cycles of effort and that participation of all staff functions and manufacturing and operating interests be assured so that planning of the facility is consistent with the interests of those charged with its operation. It is a severe error to expect a planning group, no matter how expert, to work in a vacuum while devel-

oping a solution for the long-term—or even short-term—interests of the company. The planning process is a total concern for the company.

See also Inventory stock-keeping systems; Material handling; Office space planning; Project management; Real estate management, corporate.

REFERENCES

Buffa, Elwood S.: *Modern Production/Operations Management,* 7th ed., John Wiley, New York, 1983.

Higgins, Lindley R., ed.: *Maintenance Engineering Handbook,* 3d ed., McGraw-Hill, New York, 1977.

Laufer, A. C.: *Production and Operations Management,* 3d ed., South-Western, Cincinnati, 1984.

Muther, Richard: *Practical Plant Layout,* McGraw-Hill, New York, 1956.

Society of Manufacturing Engineers: *CAD/CAM,* Publication Sales, One SME Drive, P.O. Box 930, Dearborn, Mich.

DAVID C. STEWART, *Carlisle Engineering Management, Inc.*

Field Services Management

Management of field services is an activity carried out at two overall administrative centers—the service deliverer and the service receiver—and entailing two distinct sets of objectives. Both deal with the handling, at some facility, of specialized personnel assigned by a fabricator, designer, or manufacturer to a client's site as a temporary supplement to the item or system being furnished. Both have the ultimate goal of transforming a manufactured product into an efficiently operating on-site entity. There are exceptions to this definition, involving the supply of general services, such as security or contract maintenance, and requiring management at both ends of the activity. But the management requirements, at each end, are reasonably similar for both the normal and exceptional circumstances.

Managing a Delivered Service. Two very important factors govern the management of field services by the service-supplying organization:

1. Members of field service teams must be regarded by management, and by themselves, as extensions of the supplying firm's sales force—the projectors of company image and the ultimate source of repeat business. Moreover, this is just as true for assigned security personnel or for contracted-equipment maintenance coverage people.

2. Because of this "sales" connotation, management by the service supplier requires a sort of "tip-of-the-iceberg" approach in which most management training and personality orienta-

tion occur *before* team members ever leave their home base. This means that they must know their own equipment thoroughly and must remember their "company representative" role at all times.

Supplementing and reinforcing these essential factors is the need for both parties to this service—deliverer and receiver—to have a fully understood, and written, agreement about scope of work; duration of stay; host-firm responsibilities for supplying tools, material, personal and business storage facilities, on-site meals; and for making quality inspections.

If the supplied activity is essentially a service (e.g., security guards), the agreement must include a very firm set of rules governing the division of authority and responsibility between the two agencies involved. And, since nearly all industrial activities carry some degree of physical risk, responsibility for accident-related injury must be covered by this joint agreement.

At the heart of top management's ability to administer its field service activities lie the reports made by field people and transmitted back to the home office. For any multimembered crew, one person must be designated as leader and should have the responsibility for making these reports. Reports must include time (chargeable or not) spent at the client's service; business and personal expenses, including any requisite purchases; and a day-by-day log of events and activities. In some instances, it may prove expedient to provide the client with a copy of such a report. However, unless the client approves, in writing, each transmitted report thus presented, ambiguities can easily provide a source of future litigation.

The real key to successful field service management by the supplier rests, however, with the preassignment training of personnel—the "tip-of-the-iceberg." It should go almost without saying that each field service team member have a firm and thorough understanding of the equipment or activity furnished. Any deviation from this recommendation, while it may not turn into an actual disaster, can do untold damage to the supplier's image and future relations with the client. This is true even when the service is considered "free." In addition, service people are salespeople. As one working spokesperson for the National Association of Service Managers (NASM) notes, "Service is also support of the product after it is sold to keep it sold and to ensure new sales when the customer needs more product."

Managing a Received Service. By definition, *received field service* is a purchased (or negotiated) commodity consisting of managed labor, inherent technical skills, materials, parts and subassemblies, and tools—all brought into a facility on some form of contract basis to perform some aspect of service, such as putting a machine or system on-stream effi-

ciently or providing some type of general upkeep or protection.

The cardinal rule for the client should be to make sure that complete satisfaction is obtained. In simple terms, the client must be sure to get his or her money's worth. In transforming a purchased machine or system into an efficiently operating element of the facility, field service may be regarded as the single tool for achieving this end. To ensure true full value for the service receiver, that person must learn from the service team quickly and thoroughly so that the latter's expertise may be absorbed for future utilization.

In managing a purchased service, the key is constant and competent monitoring to make sure a real service is being performed. This type of service usually involves a sizable number of nonemployees working on the premises for relatively long periods. The hired contractor (field service deliverer) should furnish supervisory people as well as workers. But this should not exempt in-house management from exercising evaluation and control. Also, in-house union representatives should be fully apprised of the presence of the field service team and their cooperation should be enlisted whenever possible. Use of in-house facilities (employee cafeteria or eating areas, washrooms and lavatories, lockers, proper entrances and exits) must be spelled out in detail before any service contract goes into effect. At the same time, special safety practices must be fully understood and followed by field service personnel and supervisors.

See also Contracts management; Contracting out; Engineering management.

REFERENCES

Berry, Dick: *Service Management for Results,* National Association of Service Managers, Chicago, 1983.

Feldman, Edwin B.: *Housekeeping Handbook for Institutions, Business & Industry,* Frederick Fell Publishers, New York, 1978.

Level, William B., and Joseph D. Patton, Jr.: *Service Management: Principles and Practices,* National Association of Service Managers, Chicago, 1980.

LINDLEY R. HIGGINS, *Piedmont Publications Company*

Financial Management

Modern financial management is concerned primarily with the commitment of funds to various uses in the business and with the best possible combination of types of financing. It serves to maximize the profitability of the firm within the limits of prudent risk exposure. To the extent that management of financial affairs contributes to this goal, the total value of the firm is increased. In earlier years, in contrast, the financial manager typically had as basic functions the custody of funds and the obtaining of money for the firm's operations and expansion. The increasing complexity of operations has dictated a vast increase in responsibility for financial management; mounting pressure on the nation's capital markets indicates that this responsibility will continue to grow. The establishment of profit goals, the direction of cost control programs, and the measurement of results have fallen primarily in the finance function. In short, financial management is now directly related to active profit seeking through participation in the planning, organization, administration, and control of company affairs.

Scope and Organization

An indication of the breadth of the finance function is reflected in Table F-1. This table, based on a survey of America's 1000 largest industrial companies, reflects the activities of chief financial officers. It is interesting to note the growth in importance of the planning function from 1975 to 1981.

The organizational structure of the finance function may take many forms. Not only do the size and nature of the business enterprise influence the organizational arrangement, but there is also a wide

TABLE F-1 Functions of Chief Financial Officers

	1981	1975
Financial planning	48.9%	46.7%
Administration of financial department	25.8	16.1
Analysis of mergers and acquisitions	5.5	3.1
Acquisition of funds	3.9	8.3
Accounting	2.2	2.7
Cost control management	1.7	2.1
Money management	1.7	5.1
Investor relations	0.5	6.2
Resisting takeover	0.5	NA
Tax administration	0.5	NA
Other	8.8	9.7
	100.0%	100.0%

Source: Profile of a Chief Financial Officer, Heidrick and Struggles, Inc., New York, 1981, p. 11.

diversity among firms within similar industries and among businesses of the same size. Each business attempts to establish a structure that will best serve its purposes. Typically, however, the chief financial officer reports directly to a company's chief executive officer and, in some cases, to the board of directors or committee of the board. The chief financial officer may carry the title of financial vice president, treasurer, or controller. A common arrangement is for both the treasurer and the controller to report to a financial vice president. For companies with several operating divisions, the purchasing, production, and marketing functions may be carried out with a high degree of independence of central headquarters. The financial executives of these divisions, however, rely heavily upon corporate headquarters for direction of their activities, and although they may report directly to division heads, there remains in most instances a divided responsibility between the division and corporate headquarters.

System Development

The advent of electronic data processing has introduced a wide range of planning and control devices little known in earlier times. Through the use of the computer, it is now possible for managements to base their decisions upon information that may be only a few hours old. Not only is planning enhanced, but deviations from plans may be quickly noted and corrective action taken. *Budgeting* has become far more meaningful as a plan for action and as a control device in noting departures from financial plans. The *budgetary process* may be described as the itemizing of planned expenditures along with the expected sources of funds from which expenditures are to be met. The *cash budget* is a special budgeting process designed to show how much cash the firm will have on hand by days, weeks, or months and the timing of financing necessary to supplement cash flows. The cash budgeting process has gained increasing importance as interest rates have increased and as the availability of loan funds has become more restricted. For many firms, the availability of cash may govern the overall operations of the firm, dictating the amount and timing of purchasing and work-processing activities and, in some cases, the nature of the production itself. The *internal auditing* function of businesses is that of preventing and disclosing error and fraud. This approach has been made particularly effective through the use of modern financial systems. Further, the effectiveness of the internal auditing function facilitates the work of independent auditors and reduces the cost of independent audits. Finally, periodic reports to top management are now available on a more timely and useful basis.

Specific Aspects of Financial Management

Beyond the aspects of planning, organizing, administering, and controlling for finance, it is helpful to explore specific activities of finance as they relate to business operations. It is important to keep in mind that there is a constant search in these activities for an optimum balance between profit maximizing and prudent risk assumption. The language of finance is most conveniently reflected in the financial statements of the firm. Although the modern balance sheet has a host of special accounts, the basic items as shown below will serve our purpose in describing specific financial activities.

Current assets	Current liabilities
Cash	Accounts payable
Receivables	Short-term borrowing
Inventory	Long-term debt
Fixed assets	Ownership capital
	Preferred stock
	Common stock
	Retained earnings

Cash Management. Cash management is a most important function and one that is capable of significant contribution to the dynamic management of business affairs. As for any asset, the more efficient the use made of cash, the smaller the necessary investment therein. Cash management functions may be classified as custodial responsibility, flow of funds control, arrangements for banking services, and investment of surplus cash.

Custodial Functions. Perhaps the oldest responsibility of cash management is that of protection of company funds. This task remains an important function and involves the careful selection of banking facilities, vault depositories, and internal auditing controls. Like the loss of any asset, a major cash loss may endanger the existence of the firm.

Controlling Cash Flows. To the extent that collection of cash from customers can be speeded, the cash balances of the firm are increased. The wire transfer of funds from divisional banks to headquarters banks and among the banks of the nation enables firms to minimize their bank balances. Just as an acceleration of the collection of money reduces the amount of required cash, so, too, a carefully devised plan of disbursements may make a similar contribution. The most obvious of these plans is to make payments at the latest possible moment compatible with obtaining discounts on purchases and otherwise maintaining a reputation for payment of obligations on schedule. Although the clearance of checks among banks has been speeded, it is still true that until a check is presented for payment at the bank on which it is written, the firm's deposit bal-

ance in that bank is not reduced. It is the balance shown on the bank's books that determines the services to which the business is entitled. Under special circumstances, so-called *zero accounts* or *automatic balance accounts* may be useful. Under these systems, dual accounts are maintained at the bank, with one of the accounts being drawn upon to maintain specified balances in the account on which checks are drawn. By such a system, a single general bank account may serve to prevent several special clearing accounts from falling below specified levels. Some firms make extensive use of *drafts* in paying bills. Under this arrangement, the business is not required to have funds on hand to meet the drafts until they are presented for payment. The daily cash report is the principal tool by which cash balances are managed most effectively.

Bank Services. Banks, of course, provide a host of services for their customers, not the least of which is the handling of the firm's payment and disbursement transactions through check clearance. Such services are typically paid for by the firm through credits received for balances maintained at the bank. Thus, if the firm has two or more banks of deposit on which checks may be drawn, it is important to allocate balances among the banks in such a way that credits offset the cost of each bank's services to the firm. Some banks are in a position to provide a greater variety of services than other banks, and a careful choice among banks may expand the range of services to which the firm is entitled by virtue of the balances it maintains. Finally, most banks require balances to support lines of credit. It is important to choose banks with lending capacities adequate for the needs of one's firm, and this, in turn, requires a careful distribution of deposits among the banks so that the balances are maintained at agreed-upon levels.

Investment of Surplus Cash. At certain times, cash balances may be far above needed levels. If these balances are not too large, they may be offset by below-normal balance levels at other times. Most banks are willing to measure bank balances on an average rather than a minimum balance basis. It is often to the advantage of a firm to invest excess cash balances until they are needed. To this end, the manager of the cash account must be familiar with the types of investments available and the methods by which these investments can be made. Ordinarily, temporary excesses of cash are invested in high-quality short-term obligations such as treasury bills, commercial paper notes, bankers' acceptances, bank certificates of deposit, and other highly liquid short-term obligations.

Receivables Management. Accounts and notes receivable are the second most liquid form of assets of the firm. These receivables come into being as a result of credit sales and constitute one of the largest assets of most firms. Studies have revealed that of all determinable causes of bankruptcy, one of the most important is the inability to collect receivables. Skillful administration of the receivables account is, therefore, of prime importance to the business. As in the case of cash management, however, the goal is not simply to minimize losses on receivables but to contribute to the overall profitability of the firm. The very reason for credit sales is to expand sales volume, and if too tight a rein is maintained by the credit manager in the approval of customer credit purchases, many sales may be lost that would otherwise contribute to the profits of the firm. It is the responsibility of credit management to effect a strategic balance between preservation of the investment in receivables and the maximizing of profitable sales.

Inventory Management. Although the finance function typically has complete control of cash and receivables management, it plays only a supportive role in inventory management. Inventory accumulation is primarily a purchasing and production function, but the finance function must make payment for the inventories. To this end, close cooperation between the purchasing and finance functions is called for. At times when there is extreme pressure on cash resources, the financial executive may substantially influence the timing and extent of purchases. Ordinarily, however, such cooperation is manifested by a constant exchange of information concerning cash position and inventory accumulation plans.

Fixed-Asset Management. As for inventory management, the financial executive plays a supportive role in the determination of expenditures for fixed assets. This general process is called *capital budgeting.* The importance of skillful fixed-asset expenditures is due to the fact that such expenditures are typically large and the economic lives of the assets quite long. Mistakes, therefore, must be lived with for many years.

The special contribution of the finance function to capital budgeting is in the determination of prospective rates of return on alternative investment projects and the establishment of minimum return levels. Further, since most firms will have more investment alternatives than their resources will accommodate, it is important to choose among the alternative proposals in such a way as to maximize the overall profitability. A key factor in the investment selection process is a consideration of the *timing* of the revenue flows from each investment proposal. While the relative speed with which an investment may pay back the capital committed to it is important, profits can be maximized only if the prospective returns over the economic life of the investment can be appropriately analyzed. Basic to the finance function in this respect is the determination of the firm's cost of capital. The *cost of capital*

may be described as the composite cost of the forms of financing on which the firm relies for expansion.

Many firms continue to use a simple *payback* measure of investment attractiveness—that is, a determination of the relative speed with which the capital committed to the project will be recaptured over the years. More sophisticated techniques such as the *net present-value* method or the *internal rate-of-return* method usually provide a better basis for evaluation of long-term investments. Although these techniques add a measure of complexity to the analysis, the importance of proper decisions warrants all possible constructive effort. The *net present-value* method of investment analysis involves the discounting of cash flows. This is accomplished first by a determination of the firm's cost of capital and the use of this cost for purposes of determining the present value of all expected net cash flows from an investment. If the present value of a series of net cash flows over the years discounted at the firm's cost of capital exceeds the cost of the investment, then it is assumed that the project will provide a positive return. If the present value of the stream of net cash flows is equal to or less than the necessary investment to implement the project, the project must be rejected or justified on some basis other than prospective profitability. The *internal rate-of-return* method involves the determination of that interest rate that equates the amount of the project investment with the current value of the anticipated net cash receipts. This rate, then, may be compared with the firm's cost of capital to determine whether the project has the potential for a return greater than that currently being experienced by the firm. While the net present-value method and the internal rate-of-return method have much in common, the circumstances involved in a particular decision may cause one technique to be more satisfactory than the other.

It is also important to recognize that the risk characteristics of alternative investment proposals will differ widely. Thus a group of projects with similar return expectations may have different degrees of attractiveness based upon the riskiness of the project. The introduction of risk adjustment in the capital budgeting process is complex, but procedures are available to accommodate such adjustments.

Current Liabilities. Obligations of the business that must be satisfied within a period of 1 year are classified as current liabilities.

Accounts payable are the first form of current liability and derive primarily from the purchase of goods by a business on credit terms. The term *trade credit* is customarily used to describe this form of financing and is by far the most substantial form of short-term liability for most businesses. Careful administration of accounts payable requires that discounts offered by the supplier be taken but that payments be scheduled in such a manner that as little advance payment as possible is made. Payments made beyond due dates, of course, may quickly be reflected in a reduced credit rating by suppliers and credit rating agencies.

The second principal form of current liability is *short-term borrowing.* For most businesses, this takes the form of borrowing from commercial banks on a line of credit. *Lines of credit* are established in advance on the basis of the prospective borrowing requirements of the business during seasonal peak demands of the year. Short-term funds are also obtained from commercial finance companies, ordinarily on the basis of a pledge of the firm's receivables as collateral. Large business firms may issue *commercial paper* notes directly or through dealers for purposes of short-term financing. Dealers, or commercial paper houses, purchase the promissory notes of the business and resell them to other banks or businesses, charging a fee based upon the amount of the notes. Short-term financing in the commercial paper market is not a substitute for bank credit, but rather, a supplement to it. Ordinarily, purchasers of commercial notes insist that the issuers maintain an unused bank line of credit to back such commercial paper notes.

Long-Term Debt Management. Some businesses borrow on a long-term basis because it is the only form of financing available to them to support investments in long-term assets. Beyond the matter of availability, however, long-term borrowing is used for other reasons. Long-term debt contracts usually include "call" provisions to make retirement of the debt possible if the need for the funds should cease to exist or if advantageous refunding opportunities should occur. It is also true that long-term lenders to the business do not have voting rights. Long-term borrowing may be carried out at times when the stock market is depressed and management wishes to avoid the sharing of ownership interests with new stockholders at depressed stock prices.

Most important, however, in the matter of strategic management of long-term borrowing is cost, especially as it affects *income taxes.* The interest paid on debt capital is a financial expense for tax purposes, in contrast with earnings on the equity capital of the firm. For most businesses, therefore, the after-tax cost of interest payments on long-term borrowing is approximately half the nominal rate. This assumes, of course, that the firm has taxable profits against which interest expense may be charged.

Beyond the tax advantage is the *financial leverage* that may be exerted on the earnings of the stockholders if the cost of long-term borrowing is less than the return on the total assets of the firm. This relationship is sometimes referred to as *trading on the equity.*

Hazards. While long-term debt financing may offer a substantial cost advantage to the firm, it should be recognized as a two-edged weapon. Just as the return on capital invested by the common stockholders may be benefited through the use of leverage financing, so too, their return may be severely depressed if the overall earnings on the company's assets fall below the cost of the long-term debt financing. There is a limit beyond which debt financing should not be carried. By way of generalization, it may be said that leverage financing—that is, financing with long-term debt capital or other fixed-cost types of capital—should be utilized to the fullest possible extent compatible with the safety of the firm. The level of long-term debt financing, of course, will differ with the type of business. Some firms with stable revenues find it possible to borrow as much as 60 or 65 percent of their asset requirements without undue risk to the stockholders. Other businesses find that long-term borrowing should be limited to a very modest level.

Form. The forms of long-term debt financing will also differ among businesses. Smaller firms will ordinarily arrange long-term borrowing on the basis of a *mortgage* placed with a single lender. Larger firms may issue *mortgage bonds* based on the collateral value of a mortgage, such bonds being sold to many investors. *Debenture bonds* differ from mortgage bonds in that they are secured by the general credit of the firm rather than by the backing of a mortgage on specific assets.

Term Loans and Leases. Commercial banks may provide long-term debt financing to a business in the form of term loans. *Bank term loans* usually have maturities from 1 to 10 years and may provide for installment payments throughout the life of the loans. Unlike mortgage and bond financing, term loans usually have floating rates, that is, rates that vary in relation to the prime bank rate. Bank term loans are especially useful to the firm as an intermediate form of financing. The *lease of fixed assets* is not a form of long-term debt financing, yet it bears a resemblance. The use of lease financing has grown to large proportions in recent years as a result of pressure on the capital markets. Many firms have found it possible to obtain long-term assets for expansion or replacement purposes only through the lease device. Substantial tax advantages may at times arise from a properly drawn lease arrangement.

Ownership Capital Management. The second form of long-term financing is that arising from the owners' investment in the business. For the sole proprietorship and partnership, it may involve little more than the contribution of owners' capital to the firm along with appropriate bookkeeping entries. For the corporation, on the other hand, ownership interest is represented by the issuance of stock. *Preferred stock* generally carries a limited dividend specified as either a percentage of par or a fixed number of dollars a year. It ordinarily has priority over common stock shares upon the liquidation of the business. *Common stock,* on the other hand, represents the basic ownership in the business and has a residual claim on profits after creditors' obligations have been met and the dividends on preferred stock shares have been paid. If the firm experiences losses, the common stockholders bear the initial brunt of such losses. Common stockholders of the corporation ordinarily exercise control over the policies of the firm through the election of a board of directors. *Retained earnings* in the business result from the declaration of dividends in an amount less than that of earnings. Such earnings retained in the firm are invested for the benefit of the firm's operations and are classified as a part of the common stockholders' ownership interest. Dividend payout policies differ widely among types of businesses.

Special Financial Responsibilities

The nature of the finance function is such that many new responsibilities have been added to financial managers' traditional activities. The financial manager, by training and by activity, has been in the best position to assume the responsibility for the growing importance of financial relations, mergers and acquisitions, multinational matters, and pension and profit-sharing management.

Financial Relations. The financial manager must spend a significant amount of time developing and maintaining good relations with all facets of the capital markets. To this end, frequent reports are made to commercial banks, dealers in commercial paper, and investment bankers. Not the least of the responsibilities of the financial manager is that of communicating with and maintaining constant contact with rating agencies. Among these rating agencies are Dun & Bradstreet, Inc., primarily for short-term credit ratings, Moody's Investor Service, Inc., and Standard & Poor's Corporation for long-term ratings.

Mergers and Acquisitions. Mergers and acquisitions may be carried out for a variety of reasons. Among them may be diversification of product lines, acquisition of management talent, or improvement of operating incomes as a result of economies of scale of operation. As a result of growth through merger and acquisition, financing may be made easier as access is gained to the public securities market. Financial management plays a key role in negotiations for merger or acquisition and also must make recommendations as to how such mergers and acquisitions are to be financed.

Multinational Financial Management. Many corporations have engaged in worldwide business operations for generations. In recent years, however, there has been a vast increase in multinational operations by firms that have heretofore limited their operations entirely to domestic affairs. It has become necessary for the financial manager not only to study specific foreign business activities and their prospective profitability, but also to analyze the governmental processes of the nations in which business operations are to be carried out. In addition to the general attitude of governments toward foreign business interests, much attention must be given to the matter of duties and taxes imposed by foreign countries. The repatriation of profits and restrictions on reinvestment vary greatly from one country to another, and changes in attitudes with changing administrations must also receive careful attention. The decision as to how foreign operations are to be financed is a key problem for the financial manager. Finally, almost daily attention must be given to exchange rates between nations for purposes of protecting bank balances and other short-term investments. The expectation of a devaluation typically demands quick action to prevent the loss of value of bank deposits.

Pension and Profit-Sharing Fund Management. The rate of growth of pension funds and profit-sharing funds has dwarfed that of all other investment forms. Many companies manage such funds internally and maintain large staffs for purposes of analysis and fund allocation among bonds, stock, real estate, and other investments. More common, however, is the use of banks, insurance companies, or individual investment managers to handle these funds. The placement of funds with professional money managers, however, does not relieve the corporation or the financial manager of responsibility. It remains an important function to work with the money managers in evaluating their performance, as well as in determining the degree to which the objectives of the funds are being carried out.

The Employee Retirement Income Security Act (ERISA), signed into law by the President on Labor Day, 1974, has added significantly to the financial manager's responsibility. Among other things, this act provides that pension claims are not limited to pension assets and that, under certain circumstances, up to 30 percent of a company's net assets may be legally claimed for pension liabilities.

Financial Analysis

All financial analysis begins with the study of the basic financial statements of the firm. These statements—the balance sheet and the income statement—however, are only a starting point in the analytical process. It is important, for example, to know how the balance sheet and the income sheet were prepared and the assumptions made therein. In analyzing the statements of other businesses for purposes of granting trade credit or for other reasons, it

is necessary to engage in much research in order to have a clear understanding of the statements.

Trend Analysis. The most common form of financial analysis is that of studying the trend of individual accounts over a period of years. By so doing, one can identify changing conditions. Following the trend of a single item may provide information relating to that particular item, but it fails to reveal interactions that may be taking place with respect to other items in the financial statements; hence, what may appear to be a deteriorating condition in one respect may be completely offset by a close analysis of other items. To this end, the financial manager often resorts to ratio analysis in addition to trend analysis.

Ratio Analysis. Although it is possible to express hundreds of relationships among accounts in the balance sheet and the income statement, the challenge has been to identify especially significant ratios. To do this, financial managers may compare certain well-defined ratios for their own business with those of similar businesses for purposes of determining possible problem areas. It is important to look at a group of ratios to form a composite profile of the position of the firm. Ratio analysis, or course, does nothing to correct a weakness in business operations, but diagnosis is a critical step in any corrective process. The financial manager has many sources of financial ratios which can be used for comparative purposes. Perhaps the best known of these sources is Dun & Bradstreet. This firm has for many years compiled a group of 14 ratios for 125 lines of business activities including retailing, wholesaling, manufacturing, and service enterprises. Ratios are reported for the median and quartile ranges. Another useful source is provided by Robert Morris Associates in their annual statement studies. The Federal Trade Commission has for many years published quarterly financial reports which present composite figures for a large sample of manufacturing corporations in ratio form and by asset size. Many commercial banks also provide such information. Trade associations have found that the preparation of financial ratios for their members is a valuable service. It is important to remember that ratio analysis is only one tool in the process of analysis. As an illustration of the types of ratios available to the financial manager, a small section of the Dun & Bradstreet *Ratios for Selected Industries* report is shown in Table F-2.

Analysis of Return on Investment. Of special interest in studying the return on investment is the relationship between the margin of profit on sales and the turnover of the firm's net operating assets. If the margin of profit on sales is multiplied by the number of times the net operating assets turn over during a specified period, the result is the earning power of the firm for the period under study. More precisely stated, the margin times the turnover

TABLE F-2 Types of Ratios Available to the Financial Manager

Retailing

Line of business (and number of concerns reporting)	Quick ratio	Current ratio	Current liabilities to net worth	Current liabilities to inventory	Total liabilities to net worth	Fixed assets to net worth	Collection period	Net sales to inventory	Total assets to net sales	Net sales to net working capital	Accounts payable to net sales	Return on net sales	Return on total assets	Return on net worth
	Times	Times	Percent	Percent	Percent	Percent	Days	Times	Percent	Times	Percent	Percent	Percent	Percent
5251 Hardware stores (109)	2.8 / **1.4** / 0.6	8.4 / **5.1** / 2.7	9.7 / **20.5** / 45.2	19.6 / **30.6** / 54.2	14.3 / **38.0** / 82.6	6.5 / **16.6** / 34.4	— / — / —	5.7 / **4.0** / 2.6	39.6 / **54.0** / 67.9	5.0 / **3.2** / 2.3	2.7 / **4.8** / 6.7	7.6 / **4.2** / 2.0	11.6 / **7.5** / 4.8	17.2 / **12.0** / 7.2
5311 Department stores (102)	2.2 / **1.0** / 0.5	5.1 / **3.1** / 2.1	20.0 / **45.0** / 79.5	34.4 / **60.3** / 87.7	33.3 / **61.5** / 137.0	8.3 / **20.6** / 48.3	— / — / —	6.9 / **4.7** / 3.8	35.7 / **44.4** / 59.6	7.9 / **4.6** / 3.0	1.8 / **4.3** / 6.4	5.7 / **2.6** / 1.0	11.8 / **5.9** / 2.9	21.4 / **11.2** / 5.0
5411 Grocery stores (105)	1.3 / **0.7** / 0.4	3.9 / **2.3** / 1.5	21.0 / **36.1** / 84.6	44.7 / **73.9** / 116.9	27.9 / **61.4** / 124.0	33.5 / **55.2** / 99.9	— / — / —	25.8 / **17.7** / 12.4	12.6 / **16.8** / 25.3	31.0 / **18.0** / 10.2	1.3 / **2.1** / 3.5	3.6 / **1.8** / 1.0	15.1 / **8.8** / 6.1	20.6 / **17.6** / 10.7

Wholesaling

Line of business (and number of concerns reporting)	Quick ratio	Current ratio	Current liabilities to net worth	Current liabilities to inventory	Total liabilities to net worth	Fixed assets to net worth	Collection period	Net sales to inventory	Total assets to net sales	Net sales to net working capital	Accounts payable to net sales	Return on net sales	Return on total assets	Return on net worth
5083 Farm & garden machinery & equipment (107)	0.6 / **0.3** / 0.1	2.0 / **1.5** / 1.3	80.4 / **164.1** / 274.7	66.3 / **81.3** / 97.9	98.4 / **192.9** / 336.2	12.6 / **21.9** / 38.1	8.7 / **15.3** / 31.3	4.1 / **2.7** / 1.9	43.2 / **58.3** / 79.3	8.4 / **5.7** / 4.1	1.3 / **3.8** / 13.5	5.8 / **2.6** / 1.2	9.3 / **4.8** / 2.1	23.6 / **12.5** / 5.5
5084 Industrial machinery & equipment (105)	1.9 / **1.2** / 0.8	3.5 / **2.1** / 1.6	30.7 / **72.8** / 134.8	67.7 / **100.5** / 158.2	40.1 / **115.5** / 189.8	8.4 / **21.2** / 41.9	32.1 / **42.7** / 56.2	11.9 / **7.3** / 5.0	29.8 / **40.3** / 64.5	10.2 / **6.5** / 4.2	4.1 / **6.1** / 9.8	7.3 / **3.8** / 2.1	12.8 / **8.2** / 3.9	24.7 / **15.5** / 11.2
5094 Jewelry, watches, diamonds, & other precious stones (123)	2.0 / **1.0** / 0.6	4.3 / **2.2** / 1.5	21.4 / **69.5** / 172.3	51.5 / **100.9** / 146.0	29.7 / **93.1** / 203.5	1.9 / **8.9** / 21.3	13.5 / **36.5** / 61.7	13.6 / **6.1** / 3.1	28.6 / **44.3** / 73.0	10.3 / **5.0** / 2.6	2.1 / **6.6** / 12.0	7.7 / **2.5** / 1.0	14.8 / **5.3** / 1.9	38.6 / **13.4** / 5.8

Manufacturing

2511-2519													
Household													
2.0	3.9	27.6	55.6	31.3	19.7	18.2	13.2	29.0	10.9	2.5	6.1	13.5	25.9
1.1	**2.5**	**46.9**	**83.6**	**71.3**	**35.9**	**34.1**	**9.4**	**42.2**	**6.9**	**3.7**	**3.0**	**7.0**	**13.3**
furniture (116) 0.7	1.8	97.2	130.2	148.4	70.3	47.4	5.2	51.8	4.2	6.5	0.9	2.6	4.2
2651-2655													
Paperboard containers 2.1	3.3	28.1	81.1	39.6	32.6	30.2	21.9	31.5	14.0	3.1	5.0	9.7	18.7
& boxes (115) **1.3**	**2.1**	**56.3**	**146.8**	**99.6**	**58.3**	**41.5**	**13.1**	**43.8**	**8.8**	**4.8**	**3.4**	**7.0**	**12.5**
0.9	1.5	110.0	248.0	197.4	107.7	46.3	7.6	55.8	4.8	7.6	0.9	2.6	4.6
2731-2732													
Books (101) 1.9	4.2	20.4	57.1	30.0	5.6	32.1	14.1	45.0	6.8	2.6	12.6	14.8	20.7
1.2	**2.7**	**42.2**	**98.0**	**69.4**	**20.1**	**48.5**	**7.3**	**62.7**	**3.7**	**6.0**	**6.7**	**9.3**	**13.5**
0.7	1.8	90.0	167.8	150.5	45.4	81.3	3.6	97.7	2.4	10.6	2.8	5.4	7.6

Services

7011													
Hotels, motels & 2.9	4.8	5.0	—	25.6	68.2	—	—	102.1	19.4	2.1	26.5	8.4	23.2
tourist courts (108) **1.1**	**2.0**	**14.7**	—	**95.5**	**136.1**	—	—	**146.8**	**8.3**	**3.4**	**9.0**	**3.2**	**11.0**
0.2	0.9	47.9	—	326.7	305.5	—	—	318.3	4.0	6.2	2.6	1.5	3.5
7216													
Dry cleaning plants, 4.3	6.9	4.1	—	9.8	40.9	—	—	29.7	15.8	1.0	13.4	15.7	22.3
except rug cleaning **1.9**	**3.5**	**12.5**	—	**22.5**	**74.7**	—	—	**46.9**	**9.6**	**1.8**	**6.8**	**10.1**	**13.9**
(118) 1.0	1.6	28.2	—	47.4	94.9	—	—	91.9	4.3	3.0	3.4	6.0	8.2
7261													
Funeral service & 4.0	6.2	7.4	—	16.6	21.6	41.9	—	63.8	6.5	1.9	15.0	16.2	22.4
crematories (109) **2.3**	**3.3**	**18.4**	—	**38.6**	**49.6**	**56.5**	—	**88.6**	**4.2**	**3.6**	**7.9**	**7.9**	**12.9**
1.5	2.0	30.2	—	74.1	90.5	76.2	—	152.3	2.4	6.9	4.1	3.3	7.2

Source: Dun & Bradstreet, Inc., *Selected Key Business Ratios*, 1981. By permission of Dun & Bradstreet Credit Services, a company of The Dun & Bradstreet Corporation.

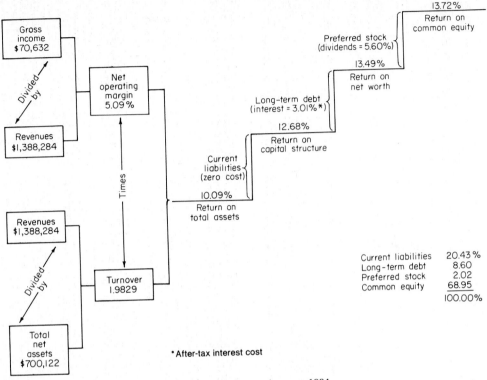

FIG. F-1 Analysis of return on investment for ABC Corporation, year 1984.

equals the return on investment. Of special interest in this relationship, however, is the derivation of these individual components, as shown in Fig. F-1. The return on investment may have the benefit of leverage, as discussed earlier, giving rise to an increasing percentage return to the common stockholders of the business. The leverage contributed by each class of preference capital (current liabilities, long-term debt, and preferred stock) is shown in this chart as a hypothetical example.

Sources and Uses of Funds Statement. Study of the balance sheet and the income statements of a firm will usually fail to provide a clear picture of all the sources of funds acquired by the business during a particular period of time and of the disposition of these funds. The source and use of funds statement serves to provide this particular information. It is particularly valuable to the financial manager attempting to determine the credit characteristics of a customer to which trade credit is to be extended, or to a lending officer in a commercial bank attempting to determine the probability of repayment of a prospective loan to a customer of the bank. Ordinarily, an applicant for credit will be required to provide not only a current source and use of funds statement but also a projection or pro forma statement.

Break-Even Analysis. This interesting type of analysis relates fixed costs and variable costs to total revenues for purposes of determining the level of revenues that must be achieved if the firm is to operate successfully. Break-even analysis not only provides a knowledge of the revenue level required to break even but also may reveal the point at which operations of the business should cease. Firms may at times operate at a substantial loss, however, in anticipation of prospective improvements in business conditions and in order to avoid the loss of skilled employees and other operating essentials dependent upon continuous business activity. Basically, the theoretical shutdown point for a business is that point at which revenues fail to cover the variable costs of operation. The assumption is that fixed costs are sunk and will exist irrespective of the level of sales. Break-even analysis, then, may serve to identify levels of revenues that will minimize losses as well as those levels that will maximize profits.

See also Accounting, financial; Auditing, financial; Budgeting, capital; Budgets and budget preparation; Credit management; Exchange, foreign, management of; Financial management, bank relations; Financial management, capital structure and dividend policy; Financial management, financing; Financial statement analysis; International trade;

Marginal income analysis; Profit improvement; Risk analysis and management; Shareholder relations.

REFERENCES

Johnson, Robert W., and Ronald W. Melicher: *Financial Management.* 5th ed., Allyn and Bacon, Boston, 1982, part 3.

Smith, Keith V.: *Guide to Working Capital Management,* McGraw-Hill, New York, 1979.

Welshans, Merle T., and Ronald W. Melicher: *Finance: Introduction to Markets, Institutions, and Management,* 6th ed., South-Western Publishing Company. Cincinnati, 1984.

MERLE T. WELSHANS, *Washington University*

Financial Management, Bank Relations

The quality of a financial relationship can often determine a company's capital structure, interest cost, and competitive position. Even the best-managed corporation may overlook simple ways to get more from its banking ties. Every business, large or small, should continually seek to establish a more profitable bank relationship while maintaining flexibility and alternative sources.

The Bank's Viewpoint

In the banker's eye, credit worthiness is a composite snapshot, a mixture of both quantitative and subjective facts. Nearly all lenders intuitively follow the same thought process to arrive at a final picture. By understanding the key elements of this process, a company can assess its own standing.

Relationship Profitability. A bank makes money from a business account in three ways: (1) fees, (2) interest on loans, and (3) reinvestment of deposits. Money market conditions will often determine which of the three is most profitable. For example, in periods of high interest rates (tight money), deposits will be worth more than in periods of lower rates. To improve its own profit and liquidity, the bank will often ask its borrowers to keep deposits equal to a prenegotiated percentage of the loan rather than charge the borrower a higher rate. Historically, the percentage has been around 20 percent; however, risk, length of maturity, and money market conditions can alter the balance arrangement.

Operating services are often paid for by balances. The bank should provide a monthly statement of services used, the service cost, and the balances required to pay for them. When comparing banks, a company should check both the price of the service and the rate that is used to convert its balances into a fee. Both the price and the rate vary from bank to bank. The industry trend is to fully price all services, including credit. The implications of this are far-reaching. In the past, bankers sometimes shrouded their prices in mystery by suggesting that some unquantifiable amount of surplus balance was necessary to keep the relationship profitable. But with full pricing, a bank's profit is built into the price, so the corporate customer knows exactly how much it has paid and that the bank has been fairly compensated. No business should settle for some vague understanding of the price. It should know in advance how much it will be charged for credit or services: if more convenient, the customer should ask if it can pay in fees. A good lender does not necessarily provide the most efficient operating services, so the client should place its business accordingly.

Full-product pricing applies to credit as well as services. Sophisticated banks will guarantee the availability of money (subject to continuing credit worthiness) even in capital-short markets. The usual cost is a commitment fee of ½ percent on the amount of funds to be reserved. In spite of recent attempts to price every product, banks still have some services which defy the cost accountant's calculator; credit information and financial consulting are examples. A business may wish to keep some surplus deposits at the bank to ensure that these and other intangibles are fairly covered.

Management Capability. Executive skill is an elusive and broad category which cannot be totally dissected. In general, however, the two most important qualities of good management are depth and dependability. One special problem is worth noting, however. Many banks have experienced loan losses because of a particular kind of manager—the self-important entrepreneur. Steady turnover in the lower management ranks of a business usually confirms this problem.

Financial Position. Traditional measures of financial risk, such as excessive leverage and earnings volatility, have not changed over the years. However, several analytical trends have recently emerged which underscore the need to support credit worthiness in depth:

1. Off-balance sheet financing per se will not increase borrowing capacity. If it does, the company lives with the risk of an inopportune reassessment when its capital structure is finally understood.

2. Subordinated debt is not equity. Too often, senior and junior positions in liquidation confuse the right of any creditor to accelerate because of a missed payment.

3. Deferred taxes are not equity. They are a legitimate obligation which, in an earnings slump, may compete for corporate cash with any other liability.

4. The current ratio is only a weak proxy for more reliable measures of liquidity. Management should regularly assess the permanency of both current assets and bank lines. Growing companies often find that inventory and receivables are really fixed investments, which should be financed on a permanent basis. Too often lines of credit are thought of as term loans—rolled over on an annual basis ad infinitum. In fact, the bank has no legal obligation to lend money under a line of credit, and most lines can be extinguished at the bank's option. If a company cannot "clean up" its line at least annually, it may be in trouble. More bankers are looking beyond the current ratio to test liquidity, and an annual current-debt retirement is one such test.

Controls and Information. The best management in the world would be helpless without reliable information about its business—not minutiae, but expressive data. A massive and complex system is not necessary. The lender wants to see the reports firsthand to be assured that they fit into the corporation's overall objectives and represent a simple, manageable picture. An accounting firm can provide valuable assistance in this process. In fact, most banks will expect a complete audit by a recognized public accountant when borrowings exceed $1 million.

Planning Process and Capability. Planning flows from the information base. If borrowing is on a term basis, projections covering the loan period should be provided. A detailed cash budget is the foundation of this process. Forecasting is inherently subjective, but well-managed companies seem to have consistent luck in their ability to predict their financial future. The most common indicator of poor planning is an *urgent* need for funds.

Corporate Structure. Complex legal structures frequently cloud and impede borrowing relationships. Holding companies that own operating companies that own holding companies, for example, can accidentally create several classes of creditors, which forces the bank to rely on more comprehensive loan agreements. For the best borrowing posture, the corporate structure should be kept clean and simple.

Openness and Honesty. Honesty is the cornerstone of the credit system. It is uncompromising. The lender should be told the good with the bad and at regular intervals. Openness is a form of honesty. Company management must be prepared to discuss every facet of the business and to provide supporting information. This openness does not mean that the client should not question the reasonableness of any information request that seems unnecessary. Lenders are usually sympathetic to adversity when they have been apprised of all events as they occurred. The lender may, in fact, be able to offer constructive suggestions as well as money.

Loan Applications

When preparing an application for a term loan, a company should incorporate its response to the bank's viewpoint into an information package. This package should include the following: (1) amount; (2) purpose; (3) repayment plans and source; (4) organizational and legal structure; (5) business description in a 10-K format; (6) historical financial statements with sales and profits by business line; (7) financial forecast; (8) background of key management; and (9) accountant's management letter.

The entire credit process requires something more than a series of cold, analytical steps. The essence of credit is a relationship—a working understanding between the bank and the borrower. In a sense, it is the summary of all the factors just mentioned but placed in the context of a company's personality. Unless the lender knows and understands that personal side of a business, it is difficult to seal the relationship. Making sure that the banker knows and interacts with several levels of management within the client company is a very sound practice.

How Many Banks?

Competition is healthy. Even though most companies work hard to maintain multiple vendors, the philosophy is not always extended to their bank, one of their most important suppliers. When does a company reach the critical mass required to justify a multibank relationship? Two guidelines might be useful:

1. Does the bank sell part of your loan to another bank?

2. Does your company borrow more than $1 million?

On the surface, the cost of establishing two profitable relationships may appear to outweigh the advantages. However, that cost will easily be eliminated as each institution scrambles to justify its position.

When a company diversifies its banking ties, it should consider several points.

Geographic Location. Sometimes banks in the same city find it difficult to compete constructively. Likewise, regional economic factors can shut off funds in one area and not in another.

Bank Size. Size can affect both the quality of attention and availability of funds; however, at a minimum, each bank should be capable of handling a significant portion of the customer's financial needs.

Operating Capability. This factor varies from institution to institution. Basic services like money transfer or cash management can be prohibitively expensive if the bank makes repeated mistakes or overcharges. It is sometimes a good idea to split a company's operating services until one organization proves to be superior.

Reputation. Successful banks rarely achieve their position by default. A better-managed bank will readily reflect its skill through the income statement. It makes sense to seek out the leaders in the field.

The Customer's Viewpoint

It is vital for the chief financial officer (CFO), at least, to know the basic workings of the company's bank. At the minimum, the CFO should know:

1. Who makes the credit decisions and how fast?

2. Are there quality and depth among the bank's key personnel?

3. How does the bank prioritize the importance of the company's account?

4. What kind of business is appreciated?

Whether the answers to these questions are favorable or not, the company's reactions should be communicated to bank officials. The CFO should visit with the account manager at least 4 to 6 times each year. The CFO, accompanied on occasion by other top-management personnel should meet with senior bank managers biannually—if they are in any way involved in the decision process.

The ideal relationship is one of balance: honest and open, but competitive. The borrower should negotiate pricing or credit with candor and know what issues are important and where a compromise may be struck. Overkill is counterproductive. In the end, the most profitable relationship will be well balanced between the bank's interests and those of the lender.

See also Accounting, financial; Audit, management; Auditing, financial; Credit management; Financial management, financing.

JAMES H. GRAVES, *First National Bank in Dallas*

Financial Management, Capital Structure and Dividend Policy

Planning the capital structure of a company poses two basic questions: What portion debt (borrowings)? What portion equity (stockholder purchases)? In the past the decision-making process which structured a company's financing was relatively simple. Equity was good; debt was bad. Current circumstances have changed those assumptions and have also made the science and art of planning a capital structure one of the fundamental decisions in business management.

Capital Needs. As a company grows and as the nature of its business changes, so will its capital needs. Technological advances and increased labor costs can change a labor-intensive industry with little need for debt into a capital-intensive industry greatly dependent on debt financing. Optimum debt-to-equity ratios will vary with each corporation's unique capabilities to service a debt while still paying a reasonable dividend. What is right for one business will not necessarily solve another's problems. The level and type of debt at one point in time may not be proper in the future.

Debt Ratios. The debt ratio of a company is an important indicator of its financial soundness. If it is too high, investors and lenders both become concerned with the borrower's ability to service the debt in periods of low business activity. If it is too low, the capital structure is heavily weighted with higher after-tax cost of equity. In either case, additional capital for growth may be costly and difficult to find.

Debt Structure. Another major consideration must be the structure of the debt. Just a few of the possibilities include bank loans, private placement of debt with financial institutions such as insurance companies and pension funds, public issues of debentures (both convertible and straight debt), and lease financing. Bank loans are further divided into revolving credit agreements, new types of term loans, and international currency loans.

When the debt strategy is effective, the income-producing base of the company is expanded, and the earnings generated by this added debt capital will prove to be substantially higher than the interest payments on the debt.

Planning for Capital Requirements. Every organization should formulate plans to manage growth and at the same time cope with the shocks of variations in business cycles. Some key factors in establishing a financing plan are:

1. *Suitability of capital.* The types of funds obtained must be in harmony with the operating assets employed.

2. *Risk.* Fluctuations in business cycles affect the ability to service debt already incurred or the ability to incur new debt.

3. *Income.* A major objective is to provide a reasonable current yield as well as potential appreciation to the shareholders.

4. *Maneuverability.* An ability to be selective as to sources of future capital requirements (debt or equity) will depend on maintaining debt levels below acceptable peaks.

5. *Timing.* Stock, bond, and money markets change constantly, making "when to act" an important criterion.

Capital Structure

Leverage. Equity shareholders benefit from the ability of a company to borrow funds and invest them at a rate of return higher than the cost of borrowing. Doing so results in increased earnings per share of stock outstanding and is commonly known as *leverage.*

Leverage should be carefully planned since the impact on earnings per share when business declines can be substantial.

Debt Levels. Financial decision making determines what debt level is optimum for a particular industry or corporation. There are no clear-cut rules or formulas to make this determination. In a chemical company, for example, parameters might be established between 25 and 35 percent of debt to total capitalization. The company may feel this level gives the shareholder the advantages of leverage without an undue risk in the event of a business downturn. As debt levels approach the targeted peak, sources of equity financing are explored. Means of accomplishing such financing are (1) acquisitions of other business in exchange for equity securities and (2) public marketing of equity securities.

Generally, while a business is expanding and until a determination is reached as to the amount of capital that will be permanently invested in such expansions, medium-term financing can be used to advantage. The funds permanently invested in fixed assets (i.e., plant equipment, buildings) should be covered by long-term financing, both equity and debt in the agreed-upon proportion.

Working Capital. The funds invested in working capital should be divided into two categories: (1) a minimum base load and (2) the additional amounts required to support levels of high business activity. Admittedly, this division is somewhat arbitrary but nevertheless necessary. The minimum base load should be financed on a long-term basis. However, the working capital required during high levels of business activity should be financed with debt which can be liquidated in the event of a business decline.

Seasonal Aspects. Another factor to be taken into account in financing working capital is one of a seasonal nature. Where peak working capital requirements occur during certain periods of a year, short-term debt, such as commercial paper or short-term bank loans, should be used. This allows for complete liquidation of this liability during the off-peak season.

Capital Stock. The prudent use of a company's equity securities can reap considerable advantages for both the company and its shareholders. The company can generate funds to finance future growth, and from this growth the individual investor can receive income and appreciation gains.

An obvious way to obtain a more favorable debt-equity ratio is to issue more stock. This move is usually a practice in times when market enthusiasm is high and the company's earnings performance is good. Adverse consequences are that (1) new stock issues can potentially dilute earnings per share and (2) they must be serviced with dividends. Long-range planning should take into account these possible drains on earnings from new stock issues.

Tax Considerations. Income taxes are an important consideration in sourcing financing (i.e., debt or equity). Interest payments on debt securities are tax-deductible, while dividends are not. As a consequence, debt financing, used judiciously, remains the least costly, after provision for taxes.

Analyzing the Capital Structure. The return-on-investment (ROI) approach to earnings analysis is the most widely used method of analyzing performance. The earnings before interest charges and income tax expenses are related to the total investment (i.e., total assets minus current liabilities). This calculation measures the return in relation to all the assets employed regardless of the source of financing—debt or equity. This is a sounder approach than measuring performance on earnings per share of stock outstanding or as a return only on the equity employed.

Another significant measurement is the cash payout (the sum of after-tax earnings plus depreciation) related to the total investment. This measurement is extremely important during times of high inflation. The more rapidly an investment can be recouped, the less deterioration there is in the money received as a result of inflation.

Dividend Policy

Two characteristics dominate the image of a stock and its owner's reasons for investing—income and appreciation in market value.

In establishment of a dividend policy, an eye to the future is of paramount importance. Investors usually will seek both current yield and long-term appreciation, but in varying degrees. In an inflationary economy, current yield becomes more important. On the other hand, an enterprise exists on profits; it grows only when those profits are reinvested wisely. A high dividend payout ratio can rapidly deplete the base that provides such profits.

A continuing dividend payout without frequent retractions is fundamental. Current payout should take into account current yield of other investment opportunities available to the investor, needs for growth of the company, and ability to sustain such a payout except in times of protracted adversity. As the earnings record of the corporation improves, increases in dividends should follow. Such a pattern reflects concern by management for a reasonable payment for the use of the stockholders' money as well as confidence in the corporation's future earnings potential. Proper consideration of these two factors should result in dividend increases being made on the basis of sound financial decisions and not wishful thinking.

Dividend Payout Ratio. Because of the dynamic changes—both advances and declines—experienced in business conditions, percentage payout targets should be avoided. Much of the profit reported by corporations in the late 1970s and early 1980s has been inflationary in nature and not a sound basis on which to structure a percentage payout target. Depreciation charges reflected in such reported profits do not adequately cover the future costs of replacing fixed assets. Thus, targeted payout ratios based upon inflated profits would lead to eventual liquidation of the corporation's assets. While the extent of inflation has declined substantially in the recent past, inflation still remains with us. It is important that management communicate to shareholders that the retained earnings not be paid out as dividends in order to assure the future growth of the company and also to maintain its position in the marketplace.

The basic rule is to determine the character of your business and its future capital requirements. Measure these against the competitive money markets and attempt to arrive at a solution to satisfy both dividend and growth capital demands. One possible solution is to fix dividends at a competitive yield based on the current market price of the company's stock, rather than as a fixed percentage of earnings. This approach also provides for regularity of dividend payments—a vital concern to investors seeking income.

Extras. Extra dividends (those paid above the regularly stated dividend) are another tool for the financial manager. They allow for a temporary boost in dividends—reflecting unusually high temporary earnings or those of a cyclical nature. It is important to reserve extra dividends only as an occasional issue. When declared too often, they lose their impact, and the marketplace will regard failure to declare them as tantamount to a dividend cut.

Stock Dividends and Splits. The general distinction between a stock dividend and a stock split is that the former generally refers to smaller distributions made as a supplement to, or substitute for, a cash dividend. The stock dividend requires that an amount equal to the fair market value of the stock distributed be transferred from the retained earnings account to the common capital stock and capital surplus accounts. A stock split reduces the par value per share with no change in the capital stock or capital surplus accounts.

Some reasons for stock dividends are to conserve cash, permit shareholders to defer income taxes, and increase future dividends to shareholders. Normally in a stock dividend, the cash dividend per share remains unchanged and is paid in the future on the additional shares issued as a stock dividend.

Reasons for stock splits include reducing a high-priced stock to a more popular selling range (around $20 to $40 per share), making round-lot purchases (increments of 100 shares) easier for individual investors, increasing or broadening the shareholder base (thus creating more marketability for the stock and normally increasing trading activity), and facilitating sale of new offerings because of broadened ownership.

Dividend Administration. The authority to declare dividends is usually vested in the board of directors. Practically, however, the administration of dividend policy depends on company management input and advice.

Several factors should be considered in establishing dividend policies.:

1. Both the historical record of earnings and the future prospects should be examined in setting a dividend policy.

2. Maintenance of a stable rate of dividends per share is generally advisable. Where earnings fluctuate substantially, a minimum regular dividend can be established with extra dividend payouts added when appropriate.

3. Cash flow, current cash positions, and anticipated need for asset replacement funds should be taken into consideration in determining whether a dividend should be paid in cash or stock or possibly a combination of both.

4. Also of importance are restrictions in current loan agreements, income tax considerations, and excess accumulation of earnings penalties and factors relating to the stock market.

Stock Repurchases

A company buys its own stock usually to employ a cash surplus at a favorable rate of return. However, this purchase has a negative implication: it can indicate that a company has run out of growth opportunities and new ideas for employing its funds. There may be times, however, when such an action is justified, such as buying one's shares for (1) future stock option or profit-sharing plan requirements and (2) an acquisition program which may require stock.

See also Acquisitions and mergers; Budgeting, capital; Financial management; Financial management, financing; Financial statement analysis; Markets, securities; Risk analysis and management; Shareholder relations.

REFERENCES

Archer, S. H., G. M. Choate, and G. Racette: *Financial Management*, 2d ed., John Wiley, New York, 1982, part 2, "Cost of Capital and Capital Structure."

Bierman, Harold, Jr.: *Financial Management and Inflation*, Collier Macmillan International, New York, 1981.

Conference Board, The: *Corporate Capital Structures and Financing Patterns: 1977–1980*, Report No. 734, New York, 1977.

Walsh, Francis, J., Jr.: *Planning Corporate Capital Structure*, The Conference Board, New York, 1972.

A. WILLIAM CAPONE, *Koppers Company, Inc.*

Financial Management, Financing

As used here, *financing* refers to actions undertaken to supply an enterprise with the money and/or credit it wants or needs in order to carry out its affairs. Financing, therefore, is a necessity. Effective financing requires skills, and intuitive apperception so that a company is financed at the least possible total cost over the longest significant period. According to period of time or source, financing may be classified five ways: (1) short-term, (2) intermediate-term, (3) long-term, (4) government, and (5) off-book. Each is examined separately below.

The financial officer must know more about the financing goals of the company than anyone else. Strategic counsel or technical advice may be obtained from many sources, but financing decisions should be those of the chief financial executive. This responsibility stems from his or her conception of the financing profile of the company.

Financing Profile

The basic purpose of financing is to contribute to the maximum extent toward corporate objectives, specifically to increase profit after tax by minimizing the direct and indirect costs of money and credit.

Rank Order of Company Objectives. There are circumstances, however, in which the immediate or intermediate corporate objective bears little direct resemblance to long-term profit. Examples include the following:

1. The need to stay in business at almost any cost.
2. A desire to pay for a very large call upon debt so as to be able in the future to take some important corporate step, such as investing in a new product or service or acquiring a new division.
3. An undertaking to improve balance sheet ratios to meet existing loan covenants or to give the company a healthier look.
4. A plan to weaken the balance sheet with a heavy burden of expensive debt in order to make the company less vulnerable to an expected takeover bid.

Since these purposes can be antithetical to one another, and since more than one can exist at the same time, the fundamental and paramount requirements of the financing officer are complete understanding of company objectives and the ability to rank-order them where necessary.

Impact on Company Capital. All financing becomes a part of the capital structure of a company. For this reason, it is important that financing alternatives be evaluated against their effect on company capital as reflected in the balance sheet.

Capital consists of equity and debt, with some capital instruments embracing attributes of both. Examples of the latter include convertible debentures issued with warrants for the purchase of common stock and cumulative preferred stock. *Equity* capital consists of common stock, which may exist in more than one class, perhaps with differing voting rights, and/or preferred stock in various forms, including participating and convertible. *Debt* may appear on the balance sheet as long term or short term; it may be mentioned only in a footnote, or—depending upon its form and significance—it may be unmentioned. Since potential lenders and investors are likely to examine the balance sheet and the footnotes to the financial statements closely, the underlying capital therein reflected should be assembled to appeal to those whose support is important.

Trial-and-Error Testing. Unfortunately, the building of a corporate structure cannot be preprogrammed with precision, because the financial environments in which a company operates are in a continuous state of flux. Equity markets ebb and flow. Long-term and short-term interest rates go up and down, not always in concert. The rate of inflation and the absolute availability of funds vary. Sources of capital change their business cycle expectations, and various means of financing (or investing) swing fad-like into and out of favor. For these reasons, financing plans must be tested like tax plans on a trial-and-error basis. The financing officer must define the alternatives, establish the limits within which they appear realistic, and then apply each one in turn to the company's operations as they may develop in the future. The better the company's forward plan, the more likely its financing proposals will prove appropriate, but trial-and-error testing against ranges of possible operating performance may prove better than no attempt to foresee the future.

Checklist for Borrowing. The desirability of pretesting a financing alternative suggests the importance not only of profit and cash forecasts, but also of the use of checklists. Many bank and institutional lenders use and frequently update a *loan agreement checklist*, and a similar reminder will prove helpful to most financing officers. Since such a list should be tailored specifically to the industry, geographic location, company, and financial structure involved, it is not practical to try to develop here a checklist which would meet the needs of every reader, or even readers in general. The illustrative listing in Table F-3 may

TABLE F-3 Illustrative Borrowing Checklist

1. General
   a. Purpose of loan
   b. Amount desired
      Minimum
      Maximum
   c. Preferred term
      Minimum
      Optimum
      Maximum
   d. Type of loan preferred
2. Useful background data
   a. Summary of existing indebtedness
   b. Covenants presently in force
      Affirmative
      Negative
   c. Current working capital
   d. Major ratios at present
      Current
      Debt/equity
      Coverage of fixed charges
3. Alternatives available
   a. Loan elements
      Placement costs
      Commitment fee
      Compensating balance
      Prepayment
      Sinking fund
      Collateral
      No financial call
      Affirmative covenants
      Negative covenants
      Apparent effective cost
   b. Forecast of major ratios at year-end
      19XX
      Current
      Debt/equity
      Coverage of fixed charges
      19XX
      Current
      Debt/equity
      Coverage of fixed charges
      19XX
      Current
      Debt/equity
      Coverage of fixed charges

  Attachment: 5-year summary forecast, prior to loan, with space in which to insert effect of alternative loan possibilities.

prove useful, however. The list refers only to borrowing, but a similar list can be drawn up when equity capital is being considered. The entries in Table F-3 have been listed compactly in order to save space; in practice, the table requires several pages to make room for all the information.

Short-Term Financing

Short-term financing traditionally is used for seasonal purposes, for example, to build up inventory. If a business is healthy enough to be able to repay its short-term borrowing each year, as after the sale of the inventory, it will be able to obtain all the short-term money it needs. But when short-term funds are used to meet long-term needs, difficulties arise.

Trade Credit. One normal source of short-term financing for all businesses is trade credit. Unfortunately for the cash-short company, it works both ways: a company can increase its working capital by not paying its suppliers, but it may also have to let its customers use some of the money they owe it.

Leads and Lags. The term *leads and lags* is used to describe the use of trade credit, but at times it implies some manipulation. A company which extends only 30-day credit but pays on 60-day terms may be ahead, depending on the value it adds to the products it buys, but this is not practical in many instances. Indeed, if a company knows in advance that it is facing a tight cash situation, it probably is well-advised to discuss payment expectations with each supplier in order to reach an understanding on the use of trade credit before serious questions can arise.

The one area in which leads and lags may have substantial merit is that involving multicurrency cash flows. Here there is special reason for prepayment or withholding payments if one can anticipate changes in currency parities.

Cash Discounts. A subordinate question related to trade credit involves cash discounts: Should or should not one take the "1 percent, 10-days" or "2 percent, 20 days" offered by some suppliers for prompt payment? The answer devolves from discounted cash flow analysis of the cost or saving involved. Usually, the discounts offered are greater than the company's cost of capital, a situation suggesting that they should be taken and, conversely, should not be offered.

Secured Borrowing. Secured borrowing is likely to provide more money to most companies than trade credit. A secured loan involves borrowing against accounts receivable, inventory, machinery, equipment, vehicles, construction, buildings, or a contract of some type. Such loans are available from banks, commercial finance companies, and (in the medium-term range) a few other financial intermediaries.

Commercial Finance Company. Since every company has a banker and every banker can explain the secured and unsecured financing offered by the bank, it seems desirable to shape this discussion primarily in terms of the less familiar services of a commercial finance company. As a general statement, a finance company often is willing to consider secured lending to a potential borrower that cannot arrange bank borrowing. The reason for the borrower's difficulty may be that it is in an undercapitalized seasonal business, has an insufficiently clear track record with the banking community, wants to make an acquisition of which the borrower's banker does not approve, or simply needs to be tided over a bad period. The finance company charges something on the order of 6 percent over the prime rate (more or less, depending upon circumstances), but this charge need not necessarily be considered exorbitantly high, particularly if alternative borrowing from a bank would cost the same borrower 2 or 3 percent over prime, plus compensating balances (and if the bank would not lend the money anyway).

Factoring. Finance companies are particularly known for factoring. This involves the buying of accounts receivable, with the assumption of the credit risk by the purchaser, or *factor*. There normally are three aspects to the arrangement:

1. The factoring company advances the face amount of selected invoices prior to their maturity.

2. It may take over the ancillary bookkeeping and collection services required.

3. It also may provide credit insurance where it establishes credit limits for selected customers.

Accounts Receivable Financing. This solution involves lending against accounts receivable that are secured by a floating loan registered under the Uniform Commercial Code. In this case, the lender does not collect the accounts directly nor assume credit risk, and the account debtors are not aware that the accounts have been assigned. Accounts receivable financing is limited to a percentage of the total receivable, perhaps 80 percent, with the cushion established to provide allowance for disputed items, past-due accounts, and errors.

Inventory Financing. In the normal course of events, not many loans are made against inventory alone. For companies with sharp seasonal businesses, however, a straight inventory loan may be particularly appropriate.

Unsecured Borrowing. All the foregoing forms of lending also may be offered by commercial banks which provide, in addition, unsecured short-term loans, lines of credit, and revolving loans. These may be called "unsecured loans," but they are unsecured only in the sense that they are not tied to a specific asset or group of assets. In fact, of course, "unsecured credit" is *secured* by the general financial and operating strength of the borrower as evaluated by the lender. Since this general strength consists in large measure of specific assets such as receivables, inventory, and equipment, no company should be able to borrow twice against the same security; that is, a company may be able to get unsecured credit from its bank, or it may be able to borrow against its assets, but it should not be able to do both, excepting in part. The trade-off from the point of view of the financing officer will devolve from an evaluation of the alternative costs involved as well as from the value put upon the flexibility and comfort of unsecured borrowing.

Paper and Notes. Short-term money is also available through two-name and three-name paper of various types.

Acceptance Financing. The most common such paper, which can be used for illustrative purposes, is the bankers' acceptance. To borrow money through this mechanism, the borrower arranges a line of credit with a banker and then issues a series of notes payable in 30, 60, 90, 120, or 180 days. These notes are payable to bearer at a competitive interest rate published in financial papers each day. The borrower delivers each note to the bank, normally paying the bank an additional ⅛ percent per month for its assistance. The bank endorses, or "accepts," the note and may retain it in its own portfolio or sell it to the investing public. In the latter case, the purchaser of the note looks in the first instance to the credit worthiness of the accepting bank rather than to that of the issuing company. The borrower, in effect, is paying the bank for the privilege of borrowing against the bank's credit.

The bank may charge a commission or a facility fee in addition to the interest surcharge, but to date banks have not attempted to obtain compensating balances for acceptance financing. While acceptance financing, therefore, often is less expensive to a borrower than bank borrowing, the financing officer should recognize that the bank, in offering an acceptance facility, may be undercutting its own more profitable straight-loan business. Acceptance financing, therefore, should be considered only as one part of a financing package, since a business that insists on the cheapest possible borrowing when it can get away with it may find, when conditions are more competitive, that it has no borrowing opportunity at all.

Commercial Paper. Large, well-run companies also may be able to raise short-term funds by issuing commercial paper. This consists of unsecured promissory notes broadly similar to those which form the basis of acceptance financing, except that they are not countersigned or "accepted" by anyone. Commercial paper is sold by a corporation to or through a dealer, or directly to an institutional investor, at a discount (similar to a treasury bill), for a maximum term of 9 months. A company considering the issuance of commercial paper (which also means entering the market in competition with its banker) should obtain counsel from one of the half-dozen or so major brokerage firms which act as dealers in the commercial paper market. Typical commercial paper and other short-term interest rates are shown in Table F-4.

Captive Financing. Large companies which sell products against installment, lease, or rental payments may wish to consider establishing their own "captive" finance companies. While such a company initially will be lending rather than borrowing, a captive finance company with a good record of 5 years or

TABLE F-4 Average Short-Term Interest Rates

	1980	1981	1982
Prime rate of major New York City banks	15.31	18.81	14.79
One-month bankers' acceptances	12.91	15.72	11.85
Three-month commercial paper	12.66	15.32	11.89
Eurodollars: London interbank 6-month asking rate	14.03	16.80	12.36

more will be able to obtain highly leveraged borrowing against its own name, rather than that of the parent company. The argument probably never will be settled as to whether the use of a captive finance company increases or fails to increase the total debt capacity of the parent (removal of much of or all the receivables from the parent reduces its borrowing capacity as the capacity of the captive increases), but there are, nevertheless, instances in which a captive can prove profitable. There also may be nonfinancial benefits in a subsidiary finance company. For example, a parent company with imprecise credit, collection, and bookkeeping records may be able to start afresh and reduce the size of its problems by channeling new time-payment business through a captive. Similarly, a captive finance company may be structured to offer marketing and new business advantages.

Intermediate-Term Financing

Most intermediate-term financing in the United States is handled by the commercial banking system through lines of credit extending for periods longer than 1 year and term loans up to 5 or 7 years. An amalgam of these two financing vehicles also is common. An example would be a line of credit for 2 or 3 years which then becomes a 3- or 4-year term loan, either automatically or at the option of the borrower. Intermediate banking facilities of this nature cost more than shorter-term facilities and usually are priced higher for the later than for the earlier years.

Custom-Tailored. Intermediate loans depend in large measure upon predictions of the business climate, company operations, and cash flow. The extent to which lenders have confidence in the managerial control and forecasting abilities of borrowers is therefore crucial. Since each loan essentially is tailor-made for a specific situation, there is no reason for the borrower or the lender to start with any preconception about term, price level, interest escalation, prepayment penalty, or any other aspect of the proposed arrangement. If the two parties are intelligent and have confidence in one another, the borrower should be able to obtain the amounts needed at costs and under conditions that can be sustained, and the lender should be able to earn a reward suffi-

cient to pay for tying up funds for an intermediate period of time.

International Sources. Institutions other than banks may make intermediate-term loans in special circumstances, but traditionally in the United States, nonbank lenders have been in either the short-term market (a year or less) or the long-term market (15 years or more). The situation has not been quite the same internationally. Intermediate funding possibilities abroad include the placement of 5- or 10-year bonds through major Swiss or other banks, the occasional availability of 5- to 10-year money directly from noncommercial banking institutions, and possible Eurocurrency loans. Eurodollar commitments of 3- or 5-year loans are not uncommon, and there have been many 7-year loans. Unfortunately for the inflation-conscious borrower, it has become next to impossible to borrow intermediate-term Eurodollars on anything but a floating-rate basis.

Since the specific requirements and ramifications of foreign borrowing are quite complex, as well as changeable, the potential lender should approach foreign money through an intermediary in the banking, merchant banking, or underwriting community.

Leasing. One of the more popular methods of obtaining intermediate or long-term financing involves the use of leases. The principles involved are sufficiently complex to suggest some definitions:

A *lease* is an instrument which permits a lessee to use something (equipment or a building, for example) in return for payments which are made regularly, over time, to the owner.

A *finance lease* permits the lessee to use an asset for most of—but not all—its life. The user must maintain the asset, pay taxes and insurance, and also make lease payments to the owner. The lease payments over the life of the lease repay the owner for the cost of the asset and the interest costs to own it, as well as providing a profit.

A *net lease* is any lease which stipulates payments to be made to the owner net of any deductions. For example, taxes, insurance, and maintenance are paid by the user. Most finance leases are of this type.

An *operating lease* is an arrangement, usually short term, through which the lessee uses an asset for only a small portion of its life. Examples include 1-year leases of data processing equipment or copying machines.

A *true lease* is one which, by meeting selected Internal Revenue Service criteria, permits the user to obtain a tax deduction for lease payments while at the same time permitting the owner to claim the tax benefits of ownership, such as investment tax credit and depreciation.

A *leveraged lease* is the most complex of the leasing arrangements. It involves three parties: the owner who provides less than half the cost of the asset; an institutional investor, who provides most of the cost on a nonrecourse basis to the owner; and the user. The interest of the institutional investors is secured both by a first lien on the asset and by the assignment of the lease.

Leasing arrangements can prove beneficial to all parties. In many instances, for example, it is possible to structure the arrangement in such a way that tax benefits go to the party that can use them most advantageously. In return for these benefits, that party may be willing to share some of their effect with the other party, to whom they otherwise might have been of no direct benefit.

It should not be inferred from the foregoing that leasing is a magical financing vehicle or that it is always desirable. In fact, a cash purchase is always cheaper than leasing on a pretax basis, if for no other reason than that it avoids the need for profit by the lessor. On the other hand, leasing may offer useful options, including the possibilities of saving capital, of borrowing advantageously through another's credit, and of introducing tax flexibility.

Long-Term Financing

The longest-term financing is with equity capital, which occurs when investors turn over cash in return for a part ownership in the company. Evidence of the latter takes the form of a certificate of stock. There are various types of stock, but the fundamental difference is between common and preferred. *Preferred stock* has a first, but limited, call upon earnings in the form of dividends and perhaps upon payout in the case of liquidation. *Common stock* represents residual ownership after the company has met its obligations to creditors of all types and to holders of preferred stock.

Companies may raise money by placing equity with friends or institutions, but by far the most usual practice in the United States is to engage a brokerage firm to advise on the timing and amounts of equity which can be raised in specific markets, to help the company comply with government and exchange regulations, and, one hopes, to guarantee to "take" or "place" the stock in question. (Equity is discussed more fully in Financial management, capital structure and dividend policy.)

Debentures. By far the largest volume of long-term funds is made available to companies in the form of term loans, either unsecured or secured. Unsecured borrowing, such as that represented by debentures placed privately or sold to the public, essentially is secured by the general credit and financial strength of the issuing company. For this reason, debentures normally contain covenants to protect the holders against loss or diminution of their security. In addition, there normally is a trustee to check upon the financial well-being of the corporation on behalf of the holders and to be prepared, if necessary, to cry "default" on their behalf. Long-term debt

secured by assets, such as buildings and equipment, is similar to intermediate-term debt of the same nature, and the applicable convenants normally refer to the care and use of the underlying surety rather than to general corporate strength.

Conditions of Agreement. The documentation which sets forth the terms and conditions of any long-term borrowing must be examined with considerable care, since the obligation is long term in nature and the borrower wants a document which (1) will allow flexibility and (2) is unlikely to become burdensome in the not-quite-foreseeable and varying circumstances of the years ahead. If there is any general forewarning which is likely to prove helpful to all borrowers, it probably is this: *Nothing is absolutely necessary, nothing is free, there is a trade-off for everything, and the smallest things may cost the most.* This somewhat laconic stricture refers to the many considerations included in a long-term loan document, among them the positive and negative covenants, the sinking fund, the commitment fee, the prepayment penalty, the interest cost, and the call provision.

Even the novice at borrowing knows that one prefers a lower to a higher rate of interest, but the careful borrower will remain alert to every aspect of the agreement and to the fact that anything one wants will cost one something. A 5-year no-financial-call provision (the borrower cannot for 5 years pay off the loan by borrowing at a lower rate of interest) may mean a higher prepayment penalty or a less attractive restriction on the payment of cash dividends; keeping the stated interest rate below a predetermined level may be possible, but if this means selling the bond at a discount, forgoing a call provision, or agreeing to a sinking fund schedule which does not synchronize well with the company's long-term cash forecast, then the cost of the appealing rate of interest may be too high. In short, almost any specific provision is possible, even if it is said to be "not customary," but everything has its price. It is the total long-term cost of the borrowing, including indirect and contingent or potential costs, which should be the primary concern of the borrower.

Bond Ratings. Since in practice most executives will turn to a specialized financial intermediary for full and up-to-date information on how to borrow long-term money through bonds and how to add an *equity kicker* (a conversion feature or warrants) when appropriate, more will not be written on the subject here. Because of their importance, however, some comment on bond ratings is advisable.

Many investors—the buyers of the bonds the company wants to sell—rely heavily on bond ratings to help them evaluate security, quality, and risk. Bond ratings not only have a significant effect on the cost of borrowing, they also serve to some extent as indications of a company's general investment quality, including the value of its common stock.

There are three major rating agencies: Moody's Investor Service, Inc., Standard & Poor's Corporation, and Fitch Investors' Service, Inc. All have been publishing ratings for at least 50 years, and all now charge for their ratings. The rating agencies have slightly different ways of distinguishing among rated issues to identify those which are of the highest grade, those which lack the qualities of a desirable investment, and those which fall in between.

Rating agencies have maintained consistently that ratings cannot be deduced by formula, that the application of personal judgment to each company (for example, in the evaluation of management) is crucial; nevertheless, a few key ratios have been proved over time to give a good hint as to the rating likely to be achieved. The most important data are: (1) interest coverage, (2) debt/equity ratio, (3) absolute size of the company, (4) earnings volatility, and (5) relationship between funded debt and earnings. A company considering the issuance of rated indebtedness should be able to approximate the rating it is likely to receive by reviewing the aforementioned data on a reasonable basis, comparing the ratios derived objectively with those of other companies of similar size in its industry which have rated debt, and listening carefully to its external financial advisers.

The interest differential between debt rated at different levels varies from time to time—sometimes markedly—and over the last 50 years in the area above B each rating improvement has saved the borrower from one-fourth to a full percent. See Table F-5.

TABLE F-5 1982 Yield Spreads on New Corporate Bonds. Difference between Ratings of A and AAA, In Basis Points.*

	Average	Maximum	Minimum
Long-term utilities	88	125	63
Industrials	105	138	63

Additional Interest Paid over the Life of a 25-Year $50 Million Bond with No Sinking Fund

Incremental interest, in basis points*	Aggregate cash cost, dollars
10	1,250,000
25	3,125,000
50	6,250,000
75	9,375,000
100	12,500,000

*A *basis point* is 1/100th of 1%, or 0.01%; 50 basis points are 1/2%.

Government Financing

No financial officer looking for short-, intermediate-, or long-term money in the United States at the present time should fail to search out programs of the federal government which may prove helpful. There are so many of these—probably hundreds—that it would be an encyclopedic effort merely to catalog them. Some programs provide guarantees, some include interest subsidy, some involve nonrecourse loans, and there are no doubt many other special attributes in one program or another.

Federal Sources. Specific examples include the following:

1. The Bureau of Indian Affairs makes nonrecourse, low-interest loans for individuals and organizations qualifying as natives or native groups.

2. The Economic Development Administration of the Department of Commerce makes business development and trade adjustment assistance loans to companies located in "redevelopment areas" or harmed by foreign competition.

3. The Farmers' Home Administration of the Department of Agriculture makes business and industrial loans available for nonagricultural projects in rural areas.

4. From time to time, the Federal Aviation Administration has offered government guarantees to support long-term loans to small air carriers for the purchase of aircraft.

5. The Small Business Administration makes available sums of money and loan guarantees (generally under $1 million).

6. The Agency for International Development of the Department of State offers guarantees for investment abroad.

Most financial intermediaries are familiar with a few of these programs, and a persistent borrower probably can uncover leads to many of them.

In addition to direct government involvement, there are government programs which facilitate borrowing in other ways, such as by providing government-subsidized or supervised insurance programs. Flood insurance is a domestic example, as are the export credit insurance programs of various countries (ECGD in Great Britain, Hermes in Germany, COFACE in France, MITI in Japan, and the Export-Import Bank in the United States.)

State and Local Sources. The most important programs below the federal level are those handled under state regulations by counties, other subdivisions, or especially established authorities to facilitate the issuance of industrial revenue bonds to finance industrial development, including antipollution expenditures. While the formalities differ by geographic location and to some extent with the purpose of the funding, the arrangements in general permit a company to raise money on a tax-free basis, thereby saving from 2 to 6 percent as compared with its normal cost of raising such funds. The procedures are somewhat burdensome in some cases, and the costs in an issue below $1 million to $2 million might eat up the savings, but industrial revenue bonds always merit consideration. Assistance is available from underwriters, several of whom specialize in this type of financing.

Surveillance. There is no easy, guaranteed way of knowing without omission where one can borrow money most readily. This means that every financial officer must find some way to keep reasonably current on the subject, preferably personally, but at least through a staff. The only way this can be done is by reading a flow of reports on financing from a number of sources and maintaining personal contacts with financial intermediaries of various types and in several locations.

Off-Book Financing

This term refers to financing which does not appear on a balance sheet. For example, a relatively strong corporation may guarantee the indebtedness of a subsidiary or of a weaker company with which it has a business relationshp. The debt appears on the balance sheet of the company for which the guarantee is issued, but the guarantee is not recorded on the balance sheet of the issuing corporation; it may or may not be mentioned in a footnote, depending upon the materiality of all guarantees or related contingent liabilities in the aggregate.

Such a guarantee may be desirable for the guaranteeing corporation, particularly if its alternatives are to lend the funds itself directly, to take a risky equity position in the smaller firm, or to forgo a profitable business relationship. Guarantees may be in various forms, ranging from legally binding documents which explicitly state "We hereby irrevocably guarantee . . ." to implications of guarantee (sometimes called "monkey letters") in which the guaranteeing corporation advises the lender by letter that it is "aware" of a loan or proposed loan. The overriding need is to remember that each guarantee is a call upon financing, however indirect or improbable any actual cash outflow may seem, and that it therefore represents a diminution in the overall debt capacity of the guaranteeing corporation.

Information Sources

The financial officer has many sources to tap in the continual search for the most current information about financing opportunities. They include the following:

1. The most important source of information on *short-term borrowing,* and possibly on loans of up to 10 years, is the company's banker. It is from this person, or from a more sophisticated banker to whom the company's own banker will introduce the financing officer, that the officer can learn (with one exception) what short-term financing alternatives are available. The exception is that a company for which commercial paper is a viable alternative will have to turn for practical advice on the subject to one of the half-dozen or so brokerage firms which are prepared to act as intermediaries in selling such paper to the investing public.

2. Useful, up-to-date information on *long-term borrowing* may be obtained from the corporate finance department of any major, money-center bank, or from a similar department in the office of a major or regional broker. Sound companies with substantial needs may find it practical to talk directly with institutional investors, such as insurance companies.

3. Advice on the *placement of equity* is available from members of the underwriting fraternity.

4. In the area of *background reading,* excellent periodical and occasional papers are disseminated by leading banks and underwriters, usually gratis, and each financing officer should endeavor to receive a selection of these regularly. Examples include the following:

   a. *Bond and Money Market Comments,* A. G. Becker & Co., New York, N.Y., 10005.

   b. *Comments on Credit,* Solomon Brothers, New York, N.Y., 10005.

   c. *Financial Digest,* Manufacturers Hanover Trust, New York, N.Y., 10022.

   d. *Market Memo,* Investment Banking Division, First Company Bank, Atlanta, Ga., 30304.

   e. *Short-Term Money Memo,* Commercial Credit Company, 300 St. Paul Place, Baltimore, Md., 21202.

   f. *Weekly Economic Package,* Economic Research Department, Chemical Bank, New York, N.Y., 10005.

See also Accouting, financial; Budgeting, capital; Credit management; Financial management; Financial management, capital structure and dividend policy; Tax management.

REFERENCES

Childs, John F.: *The Encyclopedia of Long-Term Financing and Capital Management,* Prentice-Hall, Englewood Cliffs, N.J., 1976.

Hutchinson, G. Scott: *The Streategy of Corporate Financing,* Presidents Publishing House, New York, 1971.

Lebowitz, Martin L.: *The Analysis of Intermediate Term Bond Financing,* Salomon Brothers, New York, 1976.

Willard Allan, *Lanfri Company*

Financial Statement Analysis

Financial statement analysis, like other tools of financial analysis, is based on a logical relationship between underlying business operations and the accounting or financial representation of those activities. Analysis of the cash-flow cycle, for example, demonstrates how various business activities, such as the purchase of raw materials, production and manufacturing activity, the sale of goods on credit, and the collection of accounts receivable, all are reflected in corresponding changes in the financial statements. In a like manner, the operations of a business firm generally follow the same logic in that the underlying production, sales, personnel, and the other operations of the firm are reflected in their financial consequences. Five types of ratios tend to measure these consequences: activity, cost structure, leverage, liquidity, and profitability.

Logic of Financial Analysis. The logical relation between the financial ratios is shown in Fig. F-2. The top goal or objective which represents the key-

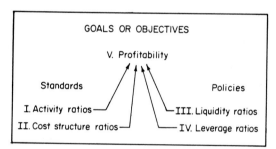

FIG. F-2 Relationships between financial ratios.

stone in the arch of planning and control is overall profitability (in its broadest sense). This is a result of two broad sets of forces.

1. *Standards.* The first set represents standards of performance (or operating) ratios. The activity ratios measure how effectively the firm is managing its investments in assets. The cost-structure ratios measure how effectively the firm is managing the control of its costs.

2. *Policies.* Leverage ratios measure the extent to which the firm finances its investments and operations by the use of debt. Liquidity ratios measure the balance in the firm's cash flows.

Profitability ratios measure the overall effectiveness of both the operations and policies of the firm. The liquidity and leverage ratios reflect management policies. Up to a point, decreasing liquidity and increasing leverage will increase the profitability of

the firm. But, if carried too far, leverage and illiquidity can lead to losses and insolvency of the firm. Therefore, each individual ratio is first explained in this entry, and then a broad view of the use of ratios in the effective management and valuation of the firm is discussed.

Computation Procedures

For each financial ratio, (1) the method of measurement or calculation, (2) the nature of the information conveyed by the financial ratio, and (3) the consequences of ratios that depart from industry averages are discussed.

To provide a concrete illustration of the calculations, the Jones Company is assumed to have been in operation for several years and to have reached a level of sales of $4 million per year. The financial statements of a firm are strongly influenced by its industry classification and by its size. In this initial presentation, the influences of size on the financial characteristics of a firm are emphasized. The ratios calculated for the Jones Company are based on the data in Table F-6 which presents the balance sheet data as of December 31, 1984, and the income statement for the year ending December 31, 1984.

The balance sheet composition and the income statement relationships presented in Table F-6 reflect the characteristic or "normal" pattern for a firm whose sales are in the $1 to $5 million range. (The sources utilized were the Federal Trade Commission—Securities and Exchange Commission, *Quarterly Financial Report for Manufacturing Companies,* U.S. Government Printing Office; and Robert Morris Associates, *Annual Statement Studies,* Philadelphia:)

Activity Ratios. These measure how effectively the firm is managing the investment in its assets. The underlying logic is that to manufacture goods, a firm necessarily uses plant and machinery, represented by fixed assets. The firm must also have some inventories in advance of making sales. Usually there is some lag between making sales and the actual receipt of cash, resulting in accounts receivable for some period of time. Thus the investments of business firms and assets are all required by the sales activity of the firm, so all activity ratios measure a relationship to sales. The amount of sales represents the basic forecasting, or causal variable, in financial ratio analysis, budgeting, and financial forecasting.

Inventory Turnover. The inventory turnover is measured by dividing inventories into sales:

$$\text{Inventory turnover} = \frac{\text{sales}}{\text{inventory}}$$

$$= \frac{\$4,000,000}{\$500,000} = 8 \text{ times}$$

325

TABLE F-6 Jones Company Financial Data

Balance Sheet, Dec. 31, 1984

Assets	Amount	Percent	Claims on Assets	Amount	Percent
Cash	$200,000	10	Accounts payable	$300,000	15
Receivables, net	500,000	25	Notes payable 8%	200,000	10
Inventories	500,000	25	Accruals	80,000	4
			Provisions for federal income taxes	20,000	1
TOTAL CURRENT ASSETS	$1,200,000	60	TOTAL CURRENT LIABILITIES	$600,000	30
Gross plant and equipment	1,500,000		Long-term debt at 8%	$300,000	
Less reserve for depreciation	700,000		Total debt	900,000	15
Net plant and equipment	800,000	40	Common stock	300,000	
			Retained earnings	800,000	
			Net worth	$1,100,000	55
TOTAL ASSETS	$2,000,000	100	TOTAL CLAIMS ON ASSETS	$2,200,000	100

Income Statement, for Year Ending Dec. 31, 1984

	Amount		Percent
Net sales		$4,000,000	100
Cost of sales excluding depreciation		2,800,000	70
Gross profit		$1,200,000	30
Less operating expenses:			
Selling and delivery expense	$400,000		10
Officers' salaries	120,000		3
Other general and administrative expenses	200,000		5
Lease rentals	40,000		1
Total operating expenses excluding depreciation		$760,000	
Net operating profit excluding depreciation		440,000	
Depreciation (8% of gross plant and equipment)		120,000	3
Net operating income		$320,000	10
Add: Other income			
Royalties		40,000	1
Earnings before interest and taxes		$360,000	9
Less:			
Interest on notes payable	$16,000		
Interest on long-term debt	24,000	40,000	1
Earnings before income tax		320,000	8
Tax at 40%		128,000	
Net income available to stockholders		$192,000	4.8

Two technicalities are involved in making this calculation. One is that while sales are made over some period of time such as a year, the inventory figure is a balance sheet item determined at the balance sheet date. Theoretically, if the turnover is calculated on an annual basis, the inventory figure for each day of the year will be averaged and this average figure will be divided into sales for the year. This method is unnecessarily cumbersome, so a number of alternatives are available. If inventories do not fluctuate greatly during the year, using the end-of-year inventory figure is accurate. If there is an upward trend in both sales and inventory each year, this trend will be reflected in both sales and inventories and can be approximated by averaging the beginning-of-year inventory with the end-of-year figure. If there is a strong seasonal pattern within the year in the firm's inventories, it will be desirable to calculate an inventory turnover at the time of the peak level of inventory and another at the time of the lowest level of inventory, then to calculate an average between the two for analysis.

A second technicality is that inventories are measured at cost. Logically, inventories at cost should be related to the cost of goods sold rather than to sales, but the published financial statements of many firms do not divulge the cost of goods sold. Therefore, the compilations of financial ratio statistics (such as those by Dun & Bradstreet) measure the inventory turnover on the basis of sales. Since one of the methods of evaluating the performance of an individual firm is to compare it with data for its industry, a firm's ratio should be calculated in such a way as to make possible the desired comparison.

If inventory turnover is low, there may be at least two possible causes, both undesirable. One is that inventories are excessive, indicating that the firm is inefficient in inventory control. This deficiency will have a depressing effect on profitability. If inventory turnover is low, the risk is higher that some obsolete or otherwise unsaleable inventories continue to be carried. If some inventories are obsolete, the current asset figure, which includes inventories and which is an overall indicator of liquidity, will be overstated.

On the other hand, if the sales inventory ratio is unusually high in relationship to the average for the industry, the firm may be losing sales because of lack of adequate inventory stocks on hand. Undesirable consequences would include reduced sales and underutilization of fixed assets.

Average Collection Period. The accounts receivable turnover is expressed as an average collection period because this number can be compared with the customary terms of sales in the industry. The degree of divergence is a measure of a firm's credit and collection performance. For example, if the general terms of credit in the industry are sales on net 30 days credit and a firm has an average collection period of 60 days, then the accounts of the firm were, on the average, 1 month overdue.

To measure the average collection period, one first determines credit sales per day by dividing total credit sales by 360. Then the resulting figure is divided into accounts receivable. The result is the average collection period.

$$\text{Sales per day} = \frac{\$4,000,000}{360} = \$11,111$$

$$\text{Average collection period} = \frac{\text{receivables}}{\text{sales per day}}$$

$$= \frac{\$500,000}{\$11,111} = 45 \text{ days}$$

An alternative convenient method of calculation is to find the accounts receivable turnover and divide this into 360 to determine the average collection period.

$$\text{Receivables turnover} = \frac{\text{sales}}{\text{accounts receivable}}$$

$$= \frac{\$4,000,000}{\$500,000} = 8 \text{ times}$$

$$\text{Average collection period} = \frac{360}{\text{receivables turnover}}$$

$$= \frac{360}{8} = 45 \text{ days}$$

The main basis for comparison, of course, is the general credit terms of the industry. An average collection period in substantial excess of the industry average term or duration of credit suggests the possibility that unsound credit policies exist or that the firm is experiencing serious collection problems with at least some of its accounts. An average collection period in excess of the industry average will be associated with a low receivables turnover. This may be an indicator of two potentially unfavorable developments. One is that bad debt write-offs may occur; the other is that if some of the receivables are in fact uncollectible, the balance sheet value of the accounts receivable is overstated. Therefore, the firm may not be as liquid as the total current assets figure would ostensibly indicate.

Fixed Asset Turnover. The fixed-asset turnover is measured by dividing the total net value of plant and equipment into sales.

$$\text{Fixed asset turnover} = \frac{\text{sales}}{\text{net fixed assets}}$$

$$= \frac{\$4,000,000}{\$800,000} = 5.0 \text{ times}$$

Decisions on investment of individual assets are made by the use of capital budgeting techniques. As

327

a rough overall measure of the soundness of capital budgeting decisions, the fixed-asset turnover ratio compared with the industry average is a useful guide. One other important consideration needs to be taken into account. To the extent that a firm leases its plant or equipment, a substantial portion of its fixed assets will not show up on the balance sheet. Therefore, without a consideration of lease rentals in conjunction with other financial ratios, the fixed-asset turnover of the firm cannot properly be evaluated. One method of taking account of the role of leases is to capitalize lease rentals and add the resulting figure to the firm's fixed assets and to its debt.

Total Asset Turnover. The total asset turnover ratio obviously reflects the resultant of all the preceding ratios.

$$\text{Total assets turnover} = \frac{\text{. sales}}{\text{total assets}}$$

$$= \frac{\$4,000,000}{\$2,000,000} = 2 \text{ times}$$

The total asset turnover will be greatly influenced by both the size of the firm and the nature of the industry. The largest firms tend to be found predominately in capital-intensive industries—industries that require heavy investments in plant and machinery to make their products. Examples of such industries are petroleum, chemicals, automobiles, and steel.

Small firms predominate in the least capital-intensive industries, so the ratios for such firms are likely to reflect their smaller use of fixed assets and their greater use of leased assets. Small firms would be expected to have a total asset turnover of 2 times or more. Large firms are more likely to have total asset turnovers of between 1 and 1½ times.

Cost-Structure Ratios. These ratios are the most critical of all financial ratios. Costs represent a continuous flow which, if out of control, can quickly lead to an erosion of profitability and result in bankruptcy for the firm. However, costs are also amenable to corrective actions by the firm's managers. While relatively little information is provided on the structure of the income statement, analysis of the structure of costs is highly important in internal operations. (Information on cost structures for a relatively large number of industries is provided in the *Annual Statement Studies* of Robert Morris Associates.) The four cost ratios presented are discussed as a group because their logic is intertwined:

Gross profit margin = sales less cost of sales (excluding depreciation and rentals) to sales

$$= \frac{\$4,000,000 - 2,800,000}{\$4,000,000} = 30 \text{ \%}$$

Selling expense ratio = selling expenses to sales

$$= \frac{\$400,000}{\$4,000,000} = 10\%$$

General & administration ratio

= general and administration expenses to sales

$$= \frac{\$320,000}{\$4,000,000} = 8\%$$

Depreciation plus lease rentals ratio

= depreciation plus lease rentals to sales

$$= \frac{\$120,000 + 40,000}{\$4,000,000} = 4\%$$

The first of the four cost-structure ratios is the gross profit margin. Since this figure is obtained by deducting the cost of sales from the total sales figure of the firm, it indicates the margin available for covering all the other functions that have to be performed to achieve the final sale of the goods. For most lines of business, the gross profit margin must be in the area of 30 percent, as is indicated for the Jones Company, because the other functions whose costs are not included in the cost of sales remain to be performed. Obviously, the required gross profit margin figures will vary widely among industries. For firms too small to have their own selling operations and that must pay 15 to 25 percent for the use of sales representatives or sales agents, the gross profits are to remain. For those particular industries in which research and development as well as considerable selling effort have to be performed, the gross profit margin may need to be as high as 50 percent.

The selling and delivery expense ratio is likely to be about 10 percent for most lines of business. If the firm has its own sales organization and the volume is high, and if technical engineering expenses involved in sales are relatively modest, the selling expense ratio may be somewhat less than 10 percent.

The general and administrative expense ratio measures the cost of the overall corporate level functions to be performed in the firm. It includes such items as officers' salaries, travel, and telephone. The control of general and administrative expenses is important because it involves a degree of self-regulation by the officers of the firm. Hence, it is a critical ratio to outsiders seeking to appraise the firm's performance.

All depreciation expenses have been separated from the previous income statement items. Depreciation plus lease rentals represents major elements of expense involved in the utilization of the firm's fixed assets. If most fixed assets have long lives, the ratio of depreciation to gross plant and equipment and to sales will be somewhat lower. The rentals have been added to the depreciation figure to account both for methods of obtaining the use and for utilization of assets.

In the Jones Company, for example, the figures for selling expenses, general administrative expense, and depreciation plus lease rentals total 22 percent.

Thus, of the 30 percent gross profit margin, 8 percent remains as the before-tax profit margin.

Leverage Ratios. Leverage and liquidity policies are influenced by the extent to which the firm has utilized its assets and to which it has managed the control of its costs. To some degree, the liquidity and leverage ratios are interrelated. For example, if a firm uses a considerable amount of current debt, it will decrease the current ratio, but it will also increase the total debt unless long-term debt is offset to an equal degree. This also illustrates the fact that liquidity ratios are not the same as leverage ratios. If a firm substitutes long-term debt for short-term debt, its current ratio will be increased; but if it has an excessive amount of long-term debt, it may face insolvency problems because of large fixed-interest requirements.

Short-term creditors of the firm are most concerned with liquidity ratios because they provide the key to the firm's ability to meet its maturing short-term obligations. Longer-term creditors of the firm are more concerned about its total debt and the performance of the activity and cost-structure ratios which will greatly influence the firm's long-term profitability—the ultimate source of paying its long-term obligations.

Fundamentally, leverage ratios measure the relative degree to which the owners versus the creditors have financed the firm's investments. The use of debt enables owners to utilize leverage in the sense that the firm is able to obtain the use of assets in excess of the amount that could be purchased by the owners' funds. This leverage of controlling a larger quantity of assets also results in amplifying the returns to the owners. For example, if assets earn 10 percent and debt costs 6 percent, the 4 percent differential benefits the owners of the firm. However, if the cost of debt remains 6 percent and the earnings on total assets fall to 4 percent, the returns to the owners of the firm will be less than 4 percent. Thus, when assets earn more than the cost of debt, leverage is favorable to the owners, and conversely.

Creditors also have a direct interest in leverage ratios because the percentage of total assets financed by the owners represents the margin of safety by which the value of total assets can decline on liquidation and still meet the obligations to creditors. The Jones Company balance sheet shows that the owners' funds have financed 55 percent of total assets. Therefore, on liquidation, total assets could decline in value by 55 percent and still meet all obligations to creditors. Creditors are also interested in the ability of the firm to meet its fixed obligations, which explains the use of two leverage ratios: (1) a leverage ratio based on balance sheet relations alone and (2) the fixed-charge coverage ratio.

Leverage Ratio. The debt ratio, or the degree of leverage employed by the firm, is the ratio of total debt to total assets. It measures the percentage of the firm's total investment that has been provided by creditors.

$$\text{Leverage ratio} = \frac{\text{total debt}}{\text{total assets}} = \frac{\$900,000}{\$2,000,000} = 45\%$$

A broad rule of thumb is that the owners should have at least as much funds in the business as the creditors. The Jones Company is approaching this limit. Creditors obviously prefer lower debt ratios since they provide a greater cushion against losses in the event of liquidation. Owners may seek high leverage in order to control more assets and to magnify earnings. Extremely high debt ratios may result in irresponsible "shoestring" operations by the owners. Thus, while owners may seek to have very high debt ratios, the financial market may be unwilling to provide debt beyond a safe limit.

Fixed-Charge Coverage. The fixed-charge coverage ratio is calculated by dividing the income available for meeting fixed charges by the total fixed charges. The total fixed charges include interest payments, lease payments, and before-tax sinking-fund payments. It is assumed that the sinking-fund requirement on the Jones Company long-term debt is $15,000 per year.

A *sinking fund* is a requirement of a bond issue; it consists of an annual amount set aside in connection with the repayment of the bond. Sinking-fund payments represent repayment of a debt and therefore are not deductible for income tax purposes. Thus, the firm must earn enough profit before taxes to be able to pay its taxes and then meet the sinking-fund requirements with the remainder. With a tax rate of 40 percent, $25,000 must be earned to meet the sinking-fund requirement of $15,000:

Before-tax income required for sinking-fund

$$\begin{aligned}\text{payment} &= \frac{\text{sinking-fund payment}}{1.0 - \text{tax rate}} \\ &= \frac{\$15,000}{1.0 - 0.4} = \frac{\$15,000}{0.6} = \$25,000\end{aligned}$$

The numerator in the fixed-charge coverage ratio represents earnings before interest and taxes plus fixed charges such as lease rentals. The before-tax sinking-fund requirement which appears in the denominator is not added back to earnings before interest and taxes in the numerator.

Fixed-charge coverage

$$\begin{aligned} &= \frac{\text{income available for meeting fixed charges}}{\text{fixed charges}} \\ &= \frac{\text{EBIT} + \text{rentals}}{\text{interest} + \text{rental} + (\text{before-tax sinking-fund payment})} \\ &= \frac{\$360,000 + \$40,000}{\$40,000 + \$40,000 + \$25,000} \\ &= \frac{\$400,000}{\$105,000} = 3.8 \text{ times} \end{aligned}$$

329

A broad rule of thumb of fixed-charge coverage for a manufacturing company is that it should range from 4 to 7 times. This ratio allows for some decline in gross income before financial embarrassment is encountered from inability to meet fixed charges.

Liquidity Ratios. These ratios measure the firm's ability to meet its maturing obligations. A large number of liquidity ratios could be employed, but most aspects of liquidity are conveyed by two ratios, the current and the quick ratios.

Current Ratio. This ratio is current assets divided by current liabilities:

$$\text{Current ratio} = \frac{\text{current assets}}{\text{current liabilities}}$$

$$= \frac{\$1,200,000}{\$600,000} = 2.0 \text{ times}$$

A widely employed "bankers'" rule of thumb is that the current ratio should be at least 2. This provides for a shrinkage in the value of the current assets by 50 percent before the firm is unable to meet its maturing short-term obligations. Such a rule of thumb, however, should not be used inflexibly—it is more of a checkpoint. Wide departures from the appropriate norm of a financial ratio are a signal for further investigation by the analyst.

Quick Ratio. In calculation of the quick ratio, inventories are deducted from current assets and the remainder is divided by current liabilities. The logic of this calculation is that inventories are likely to be the least liquid of a firm's current assets in that the loss ratio is likely to be higher on inventories if forced liquidation is required.

$$\text{Quick ratio} = \frac{\text{current assets} - \text{inventories}}{\text{current liabilities}}$$

$$= \frac{\$700,000}{\$600,000} = 1.2 \text{ times}$$

A widely used rule of thumb for the quick ratio is 1. It implies that inventories are normally about half of current assets, and a comparison between the norm of 1 and the actual quick ratio provides a guide for further judgment.

Profitability Ratios. These ratios reflect the results of the preceding four sets of ratios. They measure the joint effects of the extent to which the firm has met its standards with regard to activity and cost-structure performance, balanced against the policies the firm selects with regard to liquidity and leverage ratios. These four sets of ratios are interrelated since, if the firm fails to meet its objectives with regard to asset turnover and cost control, the levels it had set as policies for liquidity and leverage may be inappropriate at the altered levels of activity and costs. At least three profitability measures should be utilized because of variability in accounting measures of revenues and costs as well as in the measurement of balance sheet values: profit margin on sales, return on investment, and return on net worth.

Profit Margin on Sales. The profit margin on sales is net income after taxes available to the owners of the firm divided by total sales. It is shown in Table F-6 as the last item in the income statement presented in both absolute and percentage terms. The profit margin on sales measures the percentage by which the selling price of the firm's products can decline before the firm suffers losses:

$$\text{Profit margin on sales} = \frac{\text{net income}}{\text{sales}}$$

$$= \frac{\$192,000}{\$4,000,000} = 4.8\%$$

Return on Investment. The return on investment is measured by adding back interest to net income after taxes and dividing by total assets. It is a measure of the after-tax profitability with which the firm's total resources have been employed.

$$\text{Return on investment} = \frac{\text{net income} + \text{interest}}{\text{total assets}}$$

$$= \frac{\$192,000 + \$40,000}{\$2,000,000} = 11.6\%$$

Return on Net Worth. The return on net worth measures the overall results of operations from the owners' standpoint:

$$\text{Return on net worth} = \frac{\text{net income}}{\text{net worth}}$$

$$= \frac{\$192,000}{\$1,100,000} = 17.4\%$$

The return on net worth reflects both the profitability with which total investment or total assets have been employed and the effectiveness with which the firm has utilized leverage. Since leasing assets involves the simultaneous use of assets and the payment for them through lease payments, the net result of the use of leverage through leasing activity is also reflected in return on net worth. In analyzing two firms, one of which leases a substantial proportion of its fixed assets while the other does not, comparisons of profitability will require either the use of the measurement of return on net worth or the capitalization of lease rentals to include them both in total assets and in debt.

Evaluation of Financial Ratios

Two broad measures for the evaluation of the ratios for individual companies are used. One is to compare them with industry composites; a second is to analyze historical trends.

Industry Composites. A comparison of individual ratios with industry composites, as illustrated in the previous section, is useful as a starting point. It is not determinate, however. The product characteristics of the individual firm may differ somewhat from those of the industry as a whole. In addition, the firm may follow specific policies which make its situation somewhat different from that of the industry. An important value of comparing the individual firm with the industry, however, is that if differences are observed, they form a basis for raising the significant analytical questions. Why are the ratios different? What distinct and different policies are being followed? What is the basis for these different policies? Under what economic conditions would these policies be particularly advantageous? Under what economic and financial circumstances would different policies of the firm be undesirable or unfavorable? These are the kinds of questions that can be raised by a comparison of the individual firm's ratios with those of industry composites.

Analysis of Historical Trends. The use of the industry composites for historical analysis may be illustrated with reference to the Jones Company. For each of the five categories of ratios described, the pattern of composite ratios for the industry is set out graphically in Fig. F-3. These are the solid lines drawn in Fig. F-3, which charts 11 of the 15 ratios. To illustrate the idea in connection with planning, the years 1980 to 1983 are shown. The ratios are given slight time trends to avoid the implication that the industry ratios would not change. Starting with the ratios for the Jones Company in 1980, aspects of the use of industry composites can be seen by considering the effects of management performance on the ratios.

Suppose, for example, that the average collection period for the Jones Company went up sharply owing to the lengthening of credit terms or to slow collections in 1981, as illustrated in Fig. F-3, panel a.

The inventory turnover shown in panel b would not be affected, but the total asset turnover would decline. With the excessive investment in receivables, the gross profit margin would probably decline, as shown in panel c of Fig. F-3. Excessive receivables are likely to result in a higher bad-debt ratio and possibly increased office personnel expenses in the effort to return collections to normal. Thus, the general and administrative expense ratio, panel d, might also rise.

If the excessive receivables were financed by current debt, the current ratio, panel e, would also decline, even if receivables and current debt increased by the same amount. To illustrate this point, assume that the current ratio was 2:1 to start. If the same amount were added (for example, 1) to both the numerator and the denominator, the ratio would decline to 1.5:1. The quick ratio, panel f, would also decline for similar reasons. The total

debt-total assets ratio, panel g, would increase because current debt would have increased without a corresponding increase in equity. Furthermore, if the gross profit margin, panel c, has decreased and the amount of debt (and therefore the amount of interest) has increased, it is likely that the times-interest-earned ratio (h) will also decline. With the lower profit margins, the return on total assets (i) will also decline, and in addition the ratio of net profits to sales (k) will decline. Whether the return on net worth (i) declines depends upon the influence of the two opposing pressures. If profit margins decrease, the decline will tend to reduce the return on net worth (j). On the other hand, if the firm is earning more on total assets than after-tax cost of debt, the increased leverage the firm is utilizing may increase the return on net worth. This analysis assumes a slight decline in the net-worth-to-net-profit ratio.

In Fig. F-3 it is assumed that collections return to normal by 1982. If so, all the firm's ratios return to coincide with industry ratios. Thus, the charts illustrate graphically how unsound management policies in a single area can be reflected throughout many other financial ratios. In Fig. F-3, a substantial increase in the collection period, for example, is reflected in 9 of the 10 other ratios illustrated.

In a similar fashion, the impact of excessive inventories can be demonstrated. If this condition occurred in 1983, the impact of a decline in inventory turnover would be even more pervasive than that of excessive receivables. Indeed, attempts to sell obsolete inventory might lead to dissatisfied customers and make collection of receivables even more difficult. As a consequence, the average collection period might rise. Warehousing costs of holding the larger inventories and other additional expenses would cause the gross profit margin to decline. Also, the general administrative expense ratio, Fig. F-3, panel d, would rise as the average collection period, panel a, rose for the reasons indicated previously. In addition, insurance costs of holding larger inventories and expenses for additional warehouse and supervisory personnel would cause the general and administrative expense ratio, panel d, to increase. The excessive inventories are likely to be financed in part with increased accounts payable. To the extent that the current debt increases, the current ratio, panel e, would decline. The quick ratio, panel f, would decline even further than the current ratio because inventories are subtracted from current assets to obtain the numerator for calculating the quick ratio. Furthermore, since one or more forms of current debt have increased, the debt ratio, panel g, would rise. Hence, the fixed-charge coverage ratio, panel h, would decline. As in the analysis of the impact of excessive receivables, the consequences of inadequate control of inventories would result in a decline in all the profitability ratios, panels i to k.

Comparisons with industry composites need not

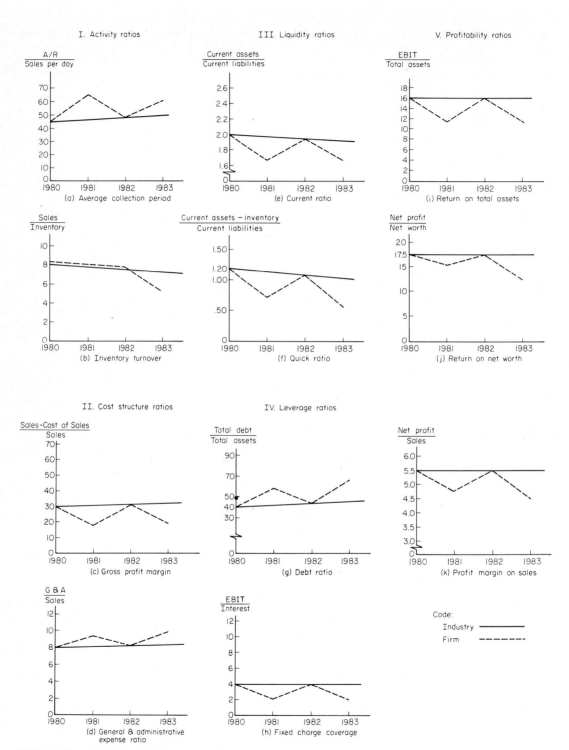

FIG. F-3 Financial trends and industry comparisons.

be determinative. Since there may be valid reasons for the financial ratios of a firm to depart from those of its industry, such divergences will not necessarily indicate a pathological condition in the firm. However, in such an instance, greater emphasis would be placed on the time trend of the individual firm's ratios. If over time the ratios are deteriorating independent of their relationship to the industry composites, the need for analysis and inquiry is increased.

Financial Market Tests

Profitability may be an incomplete measure of performance. The financial markets may capitalize the earnings stream of companies differently when their capital structures differ. Different leverage and liquidity policies may result in different capitalization ratios.

Related to the measures of profitability discussed in the preceding sections are four financial market tests which are often employed. They are (1) growth in earnings per share, (2) growth in market price per share, (3) the price-earnings ratio, and (4) the ratio of market to book value.

Any growth figure, of course, is greatly influenced by the choice of base period. From the early 1950s to 1965, earnings per share (EPS) for any stock index grew at about the same rate as the economy as a whole, 6 to 8 percent per annum. The growth in the market price per share, however, was at a somewhat higher rate, in the range of 8 to 12 percent per annum. This higher growth rate in market price per share for any group of companies reflects a rise in the price-earnings ratio on common stocks since the early 1950s. For a long period, the normal price-earnings ratio was about 10 times; this was its level in the 1950s. However, by the middle 1950s, the standard price-earnings ratio moved up to about 14 times. From the late 1950s to 1965, price-earnings ratios fluctuated in the range of 18 to 20.

Finally, there is the consideration of the ratio between the market price of stocks and their book values. Since book values reflect historical costs and earnings retention, they reflect in part the timing of asset purchases and earnings-retention policies. Although the ratios of market to book values fluctuate among firms, a well-managed firm should expect a market value from 1½ to 2 times its book value per share.

For a growth firm, the performance measures would be higher. The growth in earnings per share could be expected to be over 10 percent per annum. The growth in market price per share might be 15 percent or more per annum. The price-earnings ratio would be 25 to 30 times or better. Finally, the ratio of market to book value for growth companies

reaches as high as 3 times or more. These ratios for growth companies represent the upper ranges of financial market tests by which management may gauge the performance of its own company.

Market Position Tests

Much can be learned from an analysis of the firm's position in its own industry—market position tests. The relevant measures are (1) trends in share of market, (2) trends in quality of product, (3) productivity trends, (4) cost reduction trends, and (5) trends in relative selling price.

One of the performance measures frequently employed is the firm's share of its industry. The firm's industry reveals what the market potential for the firm may be. How well the firm exploits that opportunity is measured by its share of its total industry. Trends in that share represent a significant measure of performance in comparison with its competitors.

The other market position tests help determine the firm's share of its industry. One of the important factors is the firm's reputation for leadership in quality and performance of its products. For the producer of durable goods, reliability of performance and the availability of service are particularly significant.

Productivity measures the efficiency with which the firm utilizes labor and capital inputs. Productivity measures are output per unit of labor input, per unit of capital input, and per unit of total inputs. Over a long period of years, productivity in the American economy as a whole increased over 3½ percent per annum, although it leveled out in the late 1970s and early 1980s. Although variation among individual industries occurs, a firm should aim at an increase in productivity of at least 3½ to 4 percent per annum to compare favorably with the economy as a whole.

Related to productivity performance is cost reduction. Unit costs reflect the prices paid for labor and capital as well as their productivity. Characteristically, as an industry or a product line matures, many cost reductions are achieved. Hence, if a firm is to maintain its position in an industry or a product line, cost reduction is necessary.

As an industry matures, the rise of new and increased competition can be expected to put increased pressure on prices. Thus, cost reduction is related to selling price. The performance of a product line or company is likely to be greatly influenced by the ability to reduce prices over time.

These five factors are a part of and reflect a firm's market position over time. They are significant indicators, or barometers, of what is likely to show up in the more quantitatively oriented ratios discussed in the preceding sections.

Measure of Strategic Performance

Related to the measures of the firm's market position are measures of the strategic performance of the firm. The strategic performance measures discriminate among the causes of differential performance by the firm. Strategic planning emphasizes comparisons with individual close competitors rather than with industry standards. An industry is an average of a set of firms; some of these will be good, some poor. The aspiring firm seeks to compare itself with its close competitors.

The other important orientations of ratios for strategic production-market planning are distinctive in two respects. First, the ratios are oriented to the future. Second, emphasis is on economic characteristics of the product-market environment rather than the internal performance measures of the firm. Conventional financial ratio analysis focuses on the firm's internal operations. Financial ratios for evaluation of the strategic position of the firm emphasize characteristics of its external environment, are oriented to the future, and stress proper modeling of the characteristics of the firm to survival and growth in its economic environment.

Economic Environment. The tests of the firm's strategic position emphasize the economic environment. The economic variables considered should include the following:

1. Industry demand
   a. Growth
   b. Stability
   c. Stage in life cycle
2. Competitive trends
   a. Entry
   b. Size structure
   c. Growth-to-capacity relationships
3. Impact of dynamic change
   a. Political
   b. Technological
   c. Economic
   d. Social

The third set of factors overlaps the first two. The distinction is that in going through the appraisal for the first two, analysts make the best probabilistic judgments about the future as they see it. In analyzing the third set of factors, they take into account the fact that the environment, as viewed under the first set (with particular reference to the stage of the life cycle of the environment), and the capabilities which the firm possesses are other statements of the firm's strategic gap. One remedy for such a gap is found in diversification studies.

Sources and Uses of Funds Statements

The funds statement performs an important analytical function in conjunction with standard ratio analysis. On a historical basis, the sources and uses of funds statement indicates where the cash came from and how it was used. With it, the firm is able to answer the question often posed by possible lenders, "How has the firm used the funds it obtained in the past?"

Sources and uses analysis is also employed on a pro forma, or budget, basis for planning. It can explain the way funds will be employed in the future. Subsequently, the budgeted sources and uses statement can be used to determine whether funds were employed according to plan.

In constructing this statement, the category of *uses* of funds includes increases in asset items or of decreases in liability items. The category of *sources* of funds includes decreases in asset items or increases in liability items. Depreciation is a noncash outlay. Since it is deducted from revenues to calculate net income, it is added back as a source of funds in addition to net income. The financial statements in the annual reports of major corporations ordinarily will provide a sources and uses of funds statement for analysis along the lines indicated.

Limitations of Financial Statement Analysis

For a number of reasons, managers and analysts cannot place absolute reliance upon the results of financial ratio analysis. In general, "window-dressing" practices which will improve profitability in the short run may be utilized. Such practices include the postponement of the maintenance of fixed assets, which will decrease costs and increase profitability in the short run, but which will impact the firm severely when machine breakdowns occur and production processes are interrupted. A policy of delaying the purchase of modern equipment will decrease capital outlays and reduce depreciation expenditures in the short run. However, failure to keep pace with competitors that are installing modern, efficient, and low-cost machinery will result in a cost disadvantage at some point in time.

In addition, changing price levels and changes in the current values of assets can produce distortions in accounting measures of performance and financial position. It is desirable, therefore, to have on hand the kinds of additional information that are available regarding current replacement values. Additional information would be provided by the Financial Accounting Standard Board's program for general purchasing power reporting.

Nevertheless, even with the additional supplementary information, financial ratio analysis is not the complete answer to evaluating the performance of a firm. When financial ratio analysis indicates that the patterns of a firm depart from industry norms, this disparity is not an absolutely certain indication that something is wrong with the firm. Departures from industry norms provide a basis for raising questions and further investigation and analysis. Additional information and discussions may establish sound explanations for the differences between the pattern for the individual firm and industry composite ratios. Or the differences may reveal forms of mismanagement calling for correction.

Conversely, conformance to industry composite ratios does not establish with certainty that the firm is performing normally and is managed well. In the short run, many tricks can be used to make the firm "look well" in relation to industry standards. The analyst must develop firsthand knowledge of the operations of the firm and of its management to provide a check on the financial ratios. In addition, the analyst must develop a sense, a touch, a smell, and a feel of what is going on in the firm. Sometimes it is this "sixth sense" that uncovers weaknesses in the firm. The analyst should not be anesthetized by financial ratios that appear to conform with normality. Thus, financial ratios are a useful part of an investigative and analytic process, but they are not the complete answer to questions about the performance of any firm.

See also Accounting, financial; Audit, management; Auditing, financial; Financial management; Financial management, capital structure and dividend policy; Markets, securities; Markets, stock indicator series.

REFERENCES

Helfert, Erich A.: *Techniques of Financial Analysis*, 5th ed., Richard D. Irwin, Homewood, Ill., 1982.

Johnson, Robert W., and Ronald W. Melicher: *Financial Management*, 5th ed., Allyn and Bacon, Newton, Mass., 1982.

Weston, J. Fred, and Eugene F. Brigham: *Managerial Finance*, 7th ed., Holt, Rinehart and Winston, New York, 1981.

J. Fred Weston, *University of California, Los Angeles*

Forecasting Business Conditions

Forecasting is an essential managerial function that should be a continuing activity in any organization that produces goods or services. The executive responsible for corporate forecasting should consider the purposes, premises, priorities, and performance measures of the forecasting activities in the company and should conduct a periodic audit or review of those activities. Successful forecasting involves more than simply choosing and applying the best forecasting method. This entry presents pertinent management considerations and describes several of the most useful forecasting techniques.

Management of Forecasting

Forecasting should be considered an organizational function deserving careful managerial attention. This section briefly discusses five key aspects that require adequate, balanced attention to ensure satisfactory performance of a corporate forecasting system.

Purposes of the Forecast. The needs of management to be filled by forecasting should be clearly understood by all involved in the forecasting activities. Obvious as this may appear, in many cases the purpose of a forecast is not understood, and consequently the real needs of management are not filled completely or appropriately. The forecasting function may be an integral part of the *planning* process of an organization; on the other hand, forecasting methods may be used in management *control* systems to establish performance standards or to determine as early as possible when a process or pattern has shifted in some undesirable direction.

Planning. In a competitive environment, correct anticipation of future circumstances can give a corporation significant advantage. Resource allocation decisions in marketing, capital budgeting, cash management, work force planning, raw materials procurement, and production scheduling are often based in part on "anticipated circumstances." By analyzing historical trends and patterns in demand for products and services and by investigation of relevant economic data, a forecaster may project patterns and relationships into the future as a basis for product mix, promotion and advertising, plant expansion (or contraction), and other policies. The level of detail and precision of a forecast should be responsive to its intended purpose; the manager should avoid the pitfall of using a forecast created for one purpose for a significantly different purpose.

Control. Budgetary control and product quality control may be assisted by analytic methods which are able to predict and recognize changes in basic patterns at an early stage.

Premises of the Forecast. It is usually vitally important for the manager to recognize and understand the underlying assumptions or premises of a forecast, both at the time it is made and afterward. In addition to explicitly stated premises, there may be implicit, unstated assumptions; if managers are not aware of some of the implicit premises underlying forecasts upon which they are basing their decisions, they may not be adequately sensitive to shifts in factors that will affect the actual results. Premises are themselves "quasi-forecasts" often based on some earlier statistical work or investigation.

Internal premises concerning conditions within the corporation (e.g., "wages will increase annually by 7 percent" or "production yields on a particular product will improve by x percent during each of the next 2 years") may receive more attention from many managers than do the external premises. *External* premises usually include assumptions about economic, governmental, general environmental, market, and supply conditions that will affect the corporation.

A forecast should always be accompanied by an explicit list of internal and external premises. Successful use of a forecast will usually be enhanced by a systematic, timely, and satisfactorily dependable way of monitoring the status of internal and external premises.

Priorities for Forecasting. In many companies a large number of variables and factors are amenable to forecasting, but to try to forecast all of them is often not economically reasonable. In a large corporation, it is a significant management task to decide upon the priorities for the forecasting function on the bases of the *value* of anlaysis on the one hand and the *cost* of the analysis on the other.

The value of a forecast is a function of the *usefulness* of the forecast (in terms of its accuracy, appropriateness, and timeliness) and its *importance* to the firm. The cost of a forecast is composed of the costs of developing the associated forecasting process for a variable or factor, data acquisition and storage, and operating and maintaining the forecasting process.

Performance Measures. No matter how fancy and sophisticated a forecasting process, it is essentially worthless if the decision maker lacks confidence in it. Therefore, in developing performance measures for forecasting, one should first attempt to identify those aspects of the forecast that may affect the decision maker's confidence in the forecast.

There should be a "performance assessment component" in every corporate forecasting system. The usual basic measure in this regard is simply the difference between forecast results and actual results; this is designated the *forecast error.* Several other measures are often used to adjust the forecasting system to produce more accurate or more precise forecasts; some of them are the mean absolute deviation, the mean percentage error, the mean absolute percentage error, and the mean squared error.

One of the pitfalls of forecasting is to evaluate a forecasting method's performance relative only to the data used in constructing the forecast. To gain a fair assessment, one should evaluate a forecasting method with respect to data *not* used in developing the forecast.

Periodic Review. Considerable benefit can be derived from a periodic audit or review of an ongoing forecasting system to ensure that:

1. The value-cost considerations are still valid.

2. The priorities are still reasonable and consistent.

3. The premises of the forecasts continue to be correct.

4. Persons involved in forecasting are competent to perform their jobs.

5. The organizational structures and processes for forecasting are still appropriate and effective.

6. The data collection activities are supplying valid, reliable data for forecasting in a timely manner.

7. The correct forecasting methods are being employed.

8. The forecasts are being communicated effectively to management.

9. The predictive performances of the forecasts are being adequately assessed, and the necessary actions are being taken to adjust the forecasting process when forecast performance is unsatisfactory.

10. The needs of management are being filled by the forecasting function.

11. Corrective actions are taken as warranted by analysis of items 1 to 10.

Unfortunately, too many companies casually pass over this concept of a periodic review of their forecasting activities. This attitude may be a result of the feeling that such a review is a luxury or that the current forecasting practice is adequate without a full-blown review. Nevertheless, it is strongly recommended that every corporation systematically subject its forecasting to a periodic review (annually or every other year).

Forecasting Methods

A wide range of forecasting methods has been developed to help the manager anticipate future circumstances so that production, marketing, financial, and personnel decisions can be made as intelligently as possible. With the capability supplied by modern electronic computers and with the theoretically sound body of knowledge that now exists, forecasting methods are widely used and have practical value.

Subjective Assessments Using Experts. One of the practical challenges of forecasting involves the incorporation of expert judgment into the forecast. Judgment is certainly required in the use of many of the so-called objective forecasting methods to be described in later sections; however, the specific focus of this section is on ways to develop forecasts based entirely on expert judgment. There are numerous ways of doing this, and the present brief summary does not purport to mention them all. A good survey of judgmental forecasting methods is presented by Gross and Peterson.[1]

Some of the many reasons for using subjective assessment methods in addition to, or instead of, objective methods of forecasting are these:

1. Past behavior patterns for the variable being forecast have changed: new influences have emerged or old influences have changed.

2. Sufficient data are not available, or the data are incomplete or unreliable.

3. Data are available, but none of the quantitative methods works well in the specific forecasting situation.

4. The planning horizon is too far in the future to rely on time series or causal methods.

5. New technology is expected to exist in the future period being examined.

Probability Assessment Methods. Some companies have used probability assessment methods to forecast sales volume, market share, size of an aggregate market, and other variables. In one approach, an expert within the company is questioned about the most likely sales volume, level of sales for which there is less than a 1 percent chance of going above, the level for which there is less than a 1 percent chance of going below, the level of sales there is a 25 percent chance of exceeding, and the level there is a 25 percent chance of going below. These estimates can be translated into a cumulative probability curve by plotting on graph paper the 1, 25, 50, 75, and 99 percent estimates obtained above and connecting these points with a smooth curve. The curve can then be used as an aid in forecasting. There are several variations on this probability assessment approach.

Figure F-4 illustrates the cumulative probability curve assessed by a product manager for annual sales of a new product during its first year on the market. The product manager thought it was equally likely that annual sales would be greater or less than $5 million and also felt that there was a 25 percent chance that sales would be less than $3.5 million

and a similar likelihood that they would exceed $6 million. In no case did the manager feel that the first year's sales of the product would fall below $2.5 million or exceed $7.5 million.

In using subjective estimation procedures, the executive should try to "calibrate" the bias of the estimator by comparing the subjective forecasts with actual outcomes. If the estimator's bias can be determined, either allowances can be made for the bias or the estimator can be trained to reduce the bias of future estimates.

PERT Method of Estimating. The program evaluation and review technique (PERT) requires estimates of optimistic (O), pessimistic (P), and most likely (ML) future circumstances. These three estimates are weighted to form an expected value as follows:

$$\text{Expected value} = \frac{O + P + 4ML}{6}$$

The relative weights of 1 for O and P and 4 for ML are typically used; other weighting schemes are rarely used in this context. The corresponding standard deviation is computed as follows:

$$\text{Standard deviation} = \frac{O - P}{6}$$

This PERT-derived technique has been used in some companies to convert an expert's estimates of most likely and extreme values into measures of central tendency and dispersion. One rationale for using this approach is that many people find it easier to provide optimistic, pessimistic, and most likely values than to estimate a specific value. A second rationale is that the computed standard deviation enables the forecaster to estimate a confidence interval around the expected value.

The PERT approach is obviously only an approximation; however, it is quick and easy to use. It can often be valuable as a fast way to take expert opinion into account as a check on estimates produced by other methods.

The Delphi Method. An Air Force-sponsored Rand Corporation study, called Project Delphi, concerning the use of expert opinion was started in the early 1950s. Naturally, the earliest applications of the Delphi method dealt with defense questions, and later applications were aimed at research and development (R&D) questions where expert opinions were processed to gain better perspectives of long-range future circumstances. In recent years, there have been numerous business applications of the Delphi method in marketing and R&D long-term forecasting.

The Delphi method of forecasting operates as in the following example:

1. A panel of experts, whose members are kept physically remote from one another, is asked to respond in writing to a questionnaire dealing

FIG. F-4 Cumulative probability curve for first year's sales of a new product.

337

with a specific question, such as one asking for an estimate of sales of a product in some future year.

2. Each panel member is informed of the median (middle value) response (and perhaps is given other information about the responses), and if the panel member's forecast is significantly different from the median, she or he is asked to state her or his reasons for the significant difference in opinions. The panel members are asked to submit answers to the questionnaire again.

3. Step 2 is repeated until the median and the twenty-fifth (or twentieth) and seventy-fifth (or eightieth) percentile values stabilize so that further rounds do not greatly change the results of the preceding ones.

The Delphi method excludes many aspects of group behavior, such as social pressure, domination by a few members, undue optimism or conservatism, or argumentation. The result is usually a spread of opinions that can be used in decision making. Descriptions of applications of the Delphi method are provided by Linstone and Turoff.[2]

Causal Models. When the forecast variable can be explained as a function of explanatory or causal variables, a causal model may provide better forecasts than those generated by other forecasting techniques. The basic method used in causal models is usually *regression analysis*, which statistically describes the response of the forecast variable to changes in one or more explanatory variables. Beyond single-equation regression models, multiple-equation simulation models are used to forecast national, industry, company, or product variables. This latter approach is known as *econometric modeling*.

Regression Analysis. A regression model mathematically describes an "average" relationship between a variable (usually called the *dependent* variable) and one or more explanatory variables (usually called the *independent* variables). While the actual relationship among the variables will deviate from the average relationship, the regression model serves to explain some portion of the variance of the forecast (dependent) variable.

The *method of least squares* is used in regression analysis to fit the regression model to the historical data. It is worthwhile understanding that this method produces the best possible fit in terms of minimizing the sum of the squares of the errors (actual minus fitted values). Symbolically, for each historical observation of the variable being forecast there is a "fitted" value (produced by the regression model) such that

$$\text{Error (e)} = \text{actual (A) minus fitted (F)}$$

of, for the ith observation,

$$e_i = A_t - F_i$$

Where there were n historical observations, the corresponding errors may be symbolized as $e_1, e_2, \ldots, e_n$. The method of least squares minimizes the sum of the squares of these errors; that is, $e_1^2 + d_2^2 + \cdots + e_n^2$ is minimized (thus, the term *least squares*). A primary measure of performance in most forecasting systems is the *mean squared error*, which is simply the *mean* of the squared errors; i.e.,

$$\text{Mean squared error} = \frac{e_1^2 + e_2^2 + \cdots + e_n^2}{n}$$

Typically, the best forecasting method for a given situation is one that minimizes the mean squared error.

The *coefficient of determination* (usually symbolized as R^2) indicates the proportion of the variance (a common measure of dispersion) of the forecast variable that is explained by the regression model. When given a choice of two or more regression models, the forecaster generally will select the model which maximizes this coefficient of determination, for using it is tantamount to minimizing the mean squared error.

The independent or explanatory variables in a regression model may include leading indicators, time, marketing variables (such as price or advertising expenditures), demographic factors, or other indicators or variables that exhibit explanatory relationships with the forecast variable. One way to identify a possible relationship between variables is to plot a *scatter diagram* of one variable versus the other variable. Another way is to calculate the *correlation coefficient* which measures the degree of linear association between the variables. Most good computer programs for regression analysis will plot the scatter diagrams and calculate the correlation coefficients for a specified set of variables.

Consider, for example, the regression model for annual sales of a glass company in terms of two explanatory variables, building contracts awarded and number of automobiles produced, as follows:

$$\text{Sales} = 38.02$$

$$+ 10.59 \text{ (building contracts awarded)}$$

$$+ 33.25 \text{ (automobile production)}$$

where annual sales are in millions of dollars, building contracts are in billions of dollars, and automobile production is in millions of automobiles. The coefficient of determination (R^2) for this model was calculated to be .9479, meaning that the model explained nearly 95 percent of the variance in annual glass sales. (Again, any good computer program for regression analysis will calculate key coefficients, such as R^2; the manager should ask for this information in order to better judge the usefulness of the model.)

A measure of the statistical contribution of a variable to a regression model's explanatory power is called the *beta index* or the *beta coefficient*. This coefficient indicates the *relative* importance of each of the explanatory variables in the regression model. When there are several explanatory variables, the beta coefficients can be used to decide which variables to retain in the model and which to exclude. For example, in the annual glass sales model, the beta coefficients were computed to be .8215 for building contracts awarded and .2496 for automobile production; thus, building contracts appear to be more than 3 times as important as automobile production in explaining annual glass sales for the company being studied. It follows that one would prefer to retain building contracts awarded as an explanatory variable over automobile production if one of the variables were to be dropped from the model. (The forecaster is often motivated to delete variables from a regression model to simplify the model or because reliable data are not available for the deleted variables.)

In interpreting the regression model for annual glass sales, one would say that *on average* for each billion dollars of building contracts awarded, annual glass sales would be expected to increase by $10.59 million. Similarly, for each million automobiles produced, annual glass sales would be expected to increase $33.25 million. The coefficients 10.59 and 33.25 in the model are called *regression coefficients*.

In using regression models, there is one particular trap into which some executives unknowingly fall; it is caused by a phenomenon called *multicollinearity*. This phenomenon occurs when one explanatory (independent) variable is correlated with one or more of the other explanatory variables in a regression model For example, if building contracts and automobile production were associated statistically, they would be said to be *collinear*. The simplest way to recognize collinearity is to have the computer calculate correlation coefficients for pairs of explanatory variables. An undesirable effect of multicollinearity is that it reduces the reliability of the regression coefficients and the beta coefficients defined earlier. On the other hand, multicollinearity generally enhances the predictive capability of a regression model. The main point here is to avoid interpreting literally the regression and beta coefficients as we did above if multicollinearity exists to any considerable extent. This problem can sometimes be eliminated by dropping some of the collinear variables from the regression model.

Econometric Models. Some forecasting models contain more than one equation. When the dependent variable in one equation is used as an independent variable in one or more of the other equations, the model is said to be a *simultaneous system* of equations and is often called an *econometric model*. Not only does each equation describe the relationship of a dependent variable with several independent variables, but the set of equations describes the *interactions* of these interrelationships.

The use of econometric models requires a good deal of knowledge about the process being modeled. Because of the complex technical aspects of this approach, econometric modeling is practiced only in the largest corporations and banks, in governments, and in federally supported university research centers. Forecasts of gross national product (GNP) and its components are produced by several organizations, among them Wharton Econometric Forecasting Associates (University of Pennsylvania); the Brookings Institute; Chase Econometrics, Inc.; Data Resources, Inc.; the Economic Research Department of Chemical Bank; Kent Econometric Associates, Inc.; General Electric Company; Goldman, Sachs and Company; Irving Trust Company; and Townsend-Greenspan & Company, Inc.

An increasing amount of work is being done in applying econometric approaches to company and product forecasting. Claycamp and Liddy[3] developed a model for predicting new-product performance using three simultaneous regression equations. Some companies, including General Foods, Inc., have experimented with the Claycamp-Liddy approach; specifically, decisions related to introducing the freeze-dried coffee Maxim were modeled using this approach.

Time Series Methods. When past behavior of a variable (for example, sales of a particular product) can be used to infer something about the future behavior of that variable, a time series method may produce satisfactory forecasts for that variable. *Time series methods* do not explicitly account for causal relationships that may exist between the variable of interest and other factors; rather, historical patterns (sometimes obscure to the human eye) are projected into the future. These methods are generally applicable to relatively short-term forecasting situations in which the planning horizon is less than 6 months, whereas causal methods often are used to forecast as far as 2 years into the future.

Characteristics of Time Series Data. Many series of consecutive data over time contain trend, seasonal, cyclical, and random components. A *horizontal* pattern exists when there is no trend in the data; there is no tendency for the series either to increase or decrease in any systematic way. Patterns that over several years exhibit a definite trend sometimes might be assumed to have a horizontal pattern over a short time (e.g., during a 2- or 3-month period).

A recurring *seasonal* pattern exists when a series fluctuates according to some seasonal influence. The "seasons" may be the days of the week, the days of the month, the months of the year, or the quarters of the year. Sales of fertilizer, paint, air conditioners, new cars, heating oil, and soft drinks and visits in hospital emergency rooms typically exhibit seasonal patterns.

A *cyclical* pattern is very similar to a seasonal pattern in some ways; however, the length of a single cycle is generally longer than 1 year, and cycles will often vary in length. Various economic indexes have cyclical patterns; forecasting the business cycle has challenged businesspersons and economists for several decades.[4]

A *trend* pattern exists when there is a pervasive increase or decrease in the value of a variable over a specified time. The sales of a company, the gross national product, and many other business and economic indicators follow a trend pattern. The underlying trend is often not linear; the life cycle of a product is an example of an underlying trend pattern that is not a straight line.

In many cases, time series data will contain a combination of trend, seasonality, and cyclicality; it may be desirable to "decompose" the raw series into its underlying "components."

Classical Decomposition Method. Two phases are involved in the decomposition method: (1) seasonal, trend, and business-cycle components are separated from the random aspects of a historical time series, and (2) a time series model is chosen on the basis of the information gained in the first phase to forecast future behavior of the variable. (It should be emphasized at this point that while many time series methods are cumbersome to use manually, inexpensive computer programs are available from most computer vendors to accomplish all the necessary computation.) At least 3 years' monthly data or 4 years' quarterly data are needed if a decomposition method is being used.

Each of the components of a time series is symbolized with the first letter of that component; that is, trend T, seasonality S, cyclicality C, and randomness R, where Y denotes the time series data. Symbolically, each point of the time series data is represented as the product of its components:

$$Y = T \times S \times C \times R$$

Subscripts are used to designate the time series value for a particular period. For example, Y_8 refers to the observed value in period 8, and Y_{15} refers to the observed value in period 15. Thus, the time series value in some period t can be represented as

$$Y_t = T_t \times S_t \times C_t \times R_t$$

The classical decomposition method proceeds as follows:

1. Determine the *seasonal indices* (S) by dividing each raw data value by the corresponding moving average composed of 1 year's observations, half of which occurred prior to and half after the period whose seasonal index is being calculated. (If annual data are used, there is no seasonality; the raw data would then be of the form $Y = T \times C \times R$, and one could begin the procedure at step 2.) Divide the raw data by the corresponding sea-

sonal indices to produce seasonally adjusted or deseasonalized data. In symbols,

$$\frac{Y_t}{S_t} = \frac{T_t \times C_t \times S_t \times R_t}{S_t} = T_t \times C_t \times R_t$$

For example, consider the monthly sales of the Roanoke Corporation (name disguised at the request of the subject company) for 1972 through 1976 as shown in Table F-7. Figure F-5 presents

TABLE F-7 Monthly Sales of Roanoke Corporation, 1972–1976*

Month	1972	1973	1974	1975	1976
January	48.78	45.82	47.96	50.10	60.19
February	35.94	43.58	43.98	49.18	54.49
March	37.03	44.91	45.21	48.96	58.49
April	42.01	55.32	52.06	53.55	68.12
May	48.60	59.56	57.05	62.08	80.73
June	50.83	60.90	58.84	64.90	80.77
July	50.23	55.69	54.31	58.01	75.46
August	49.88	57.12	57.27	63.69	80.89
September	54.04	57.99	59.92	65.90	83.51
October	48.38	50.95	53.60	60.59	74.01
November	41.77	44.02	48.61	52.69	67.37
December	44.70	44.76	47.30	51.71	68.49

*Sales in thousands of dollars.

a graph of these actual sales and corresponding 12-month moving averages; Table F-8 shows the monthly sales, corresponding 12-month moving averages, and the ratios of actual sales to moving averages. Figure F-6 illustrates the ratios of actual sales to moving averages, thereby giving a clearer picture of the seasonal behavior of sales with the effects of trend and cyclicality removed. The ratios for a particular month (say, January) are then averaged; these average ratios are recorded in column 1 of Table F-9. Finally, the average ratios are adjusted to sum to 1200; these adjusted average ratios (shown in column 2 of Table F-9) are called the *seasonal indices*. The January index of 92.7 means that, on average, January sales are about 92.7 percent of the sales level the Roanoke Corporation expects to achieve in a "normal" month (i.e., a month in which no seasonal effect is experienced). On the other hand, the June index indicates that, on average, June sales have been about 115.17 percent of the "normal" sales level.

2. Determine the trend pattern T in the deseasonalized data by fitting a curve or a straight line through those data. One popular mathematical technique for doing this, the *method of least squares*, was discussed earlier in the section on causal methods.

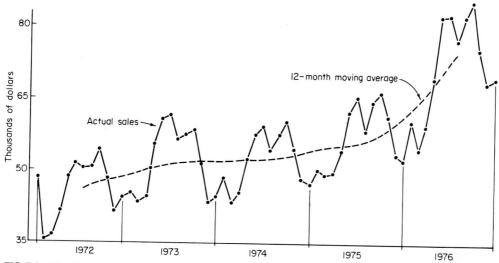

FIG. F-5 Monthly sales of the Roanoke Corporation, 1972–1976 (thousands of dollars).

TABLE F-8 Monthly Sales of Roanoke Corporation
Divided by Corresponding Moving Average, 1972–1976

Year	Month	Monthly sales, thousands of dollars (1)	12-Month moving average (2)	Ratio: (1) ÷ (2) × 100 (3)	Year	Month	Monthly sales, thousands of dollars (1)	12-Month moving average (2)	Ratio: (1) ÷ (2) × 100 (3)
1972	January	48.78				July	54.31	52.175	104.084
	February	35.94				August	57.27	52.354	109.392
	March	37.03				September	59.92	52.787	113.521
	April	42.01				October	53.60	53.099	100.936
	May	48.60				November	48.61	53.223	91.329
	June	50.83				December	47.30	53.642	88.185
	July	50.23	46.015	109.155					
	August	49.88	45.768	108.975	1975	January	50.10	54.147	92.521
	September	54.04	46.404	116.456		February	49.18	44.455	90.305
	October	48.38	47.060	102.797		March	48.96	54.990	89.026
	November	41.77	48.169	86.709		April	53.55	55.488	96.507
	December	44.70	49.082	91.065		May	62.08	56.071	110.711
						June	64.90	56.412	115.040
1973	January	45.82	49.921	91.775		July	58.01	56.779	102.165
	February	43.58	50.376	86.502		August	63.69	57.619	110.542
	March	44.91	50.979	88.089		September	65.90	58.025	113.564
	April	55.32	51.309	107.809		October	60.59	58.820	103.017
	May	59.56	51.523	115.592		November	52.69	60.034	87.770
	June	60.90	51.711	117.769		December	51.71	61.588	83.960
	July	55.69	51.716	107.676					
	August	57.12	51.895	110.060	1976	January	60.19	62.911	95.668
	September	57.99	51.928	111.681		February	54.04	64.365	83.960
	October	50.95	51.954	98.070		March	58.49	65.799	88.897
	November	44.02	51.682	85.175		April	68.12	67.266	101.272
	December	44.76	51.474	86.952		May	80.73	69.607	118.054
						June	80.77	69.607	116.031
1974	January	47.96	51.302	93.485		July	75.46	71.006	106.274
	February	43.98	51.187	85.912		August	80.89		
	March	45.21	51.200	88.308		September	83.51		
	April	52.06	51.361	101.362		October	74.01		
	May	57.05	51.581	110.605		November	67.37		
	June	58.84	51.963	113.228		December	68.49		

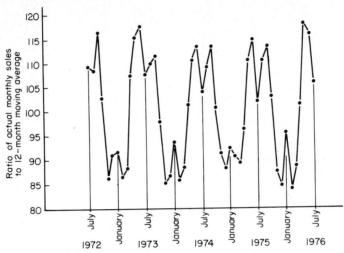

FIG. F-6 Ratio of actual monthly sales to 12-month moving averages, the Roanoke Corporation, 1972–1976.

TABLE F-9 Seasonal Indices for Roanoke Corporation

Month	Average ratio (1)	Seasonal index (2)
January	93.003	92.712
February	86.207	85.937
March	88.603	88.325
April	101.317	101.000
May	113.151	112.797
June	115.536	115.174
July	106.011	105.679
August	109.726	109.382
September	113.543	113.187
October	101.866	101.547
November	87.240	86.966
December	87.569	87.294
Total	1203.771	1200.000

3. Determine the cyclical component in the historical time series data by dividing each deseasonalized data point by the corresponding trend component (determined in step 2) and then fit a polynomial curve through this series of ratios to smooth out the effects of randomness. Thus,

$$\frac{T_t \times C_t \times R_t}{T_t} = C_t \times R_t$$

where for any point in time t, the corresponding *cyclical index* C_t can be determined from the fitted polynomial. A plot of the resultant series of cyclical indices should describe the cycle underlying the particular variable being analyzed.

The three steps just outlined constitute phase 1 of the classical decomposition method. This method provides *approximations* for seasonal and cyclical indices and for an underlying trend in the historical data. No claims are made regarding the precision and accuracy of this approach. It stands to reason that the forecaster's confidence in the results of the decomposition analysis will increase as more historical data are employed in the analysis.

A computer program, known as Census II, and instructions for decomposition analysis are available from the U.S. Bureau of the Census; this is probably the most generally used computer program for the decomposition type of time series analysis.

In order to forecast (phase 2 of the decomposition method), each of the components of the data must be reconstructed as follows:

4. Using a trend model, project deseasonalized T_t into the future. Often this trend model is the one developed in step 2 above; it is possible, however, that the trend will change and another trend model may be more appropriate. At this stage, the forecast should be adjusted for accounting-period changes, holidays, and abnormal events to the extent possible.

5. Multiply the trend component for a future time period t by the seasonal index corresponding to that period, that is, $T_t \times S_t$.

6. Decide on an estimate of cyclicality for the future period and multiply the value from step 5 by this cyclical index, thus, $T_t \times S_t \times C_t$. This produces a *point estimate* or *point forecast* for the future time period t. Random effects may be incorporated by describing an *interval* around the point forecast.

The last step of the decomposition method, namely, estimating the future impact of the cyclical influences, is usually the most challenging one in this forecasting method. Failing to anticipate a turn in the cycle correctly can result in the forecast overestimating ("overshooting") or underestimating the forecast variable. In this regard, the use of *leading economic indicators* to anticipate changes in the cycle is practiced by virtually every major U.S. corporation.

Economic Indicators. For a specific time series, it is usually possible to identify *leading, coincident,* and *lag indicators.* These indicators are statistics that tend to change value ahead of, at approximately the same time as, or after a change in the series being forecast. Of course, primary attention is generally focused on identifying and monitoring *leading* indicators pertinent to the forecast variable.

Many carefully prepared economic indicators are available from governmental, trade association, and university sources. Among the most used sources are the Bureau of the Census (especially the *Business Conditions Digest*), the Department of Commerce (especially the *Survey of Current Business*), the Bureau of Labor Statistics (especially the *Monthly Labor Review*), F. W. Dodge (especially dealing with construction contracts awarded), *Business Week* (weekly data on production, trade, prices, and finance), the Council of Economic Advisers (monthly *Economic Indicators* publications), and the 12 Federal Reserve banks. There are many, many more, and each business should identify those sources pertinent to its particular activities.

Business-Cycle Indicators. The indicator approach to business-cycle analysis was developed at the National Bureau of Economic Research (NBER) by analyzing the U.S. economy from the early 1800s to the present time. Researchers at NBER defined a business cycle as consisting of "expansions occurring at about the same time in many economic activities, followed by similarly general recessions, contractions, and revivals which merge into the expansion phase of the next cycle." Business cycles relate to aggregate economic activity as distinguished from the cycle of an individual series discussed earlier. A relationship may exist between an aggregate business cycle and the cycle of the time series data of a particular variable; it is in such matters that an executive should be advised by highly trained, experienced economists and other business forecast experts.[5]

Smoothing Methods. Many companies of every kind and size use smoothing techniques for short-term forecasting, especially for purposes of production and inventory control. Three categories of smoothing methods are moving-average, exponential smoothing, and adaptive filtering methods. These methods essentially remove the effects of randomness by averaging several consecutive data points together.

In the *moving-average* methods, a specified (constant) number of consecutive data points are averaged; as each new observation in the series becomes available, the oldest observation is dropped and a new average is computed. The latest moving average is used as the forecast for the next period. Table F-8 and Fig. F-5 illustrate moving averages. The 12-month moving average listed for July 1972, for example, was the average of sales for January 1972 through December 1972; as described in this section, this average would be used as the simple moving-average forecast for January 1973. Table F-10 shows 12-month moving-average forecasts for the Roanoke Corporation.

TABLE F-10 Twelve-Month Moving-Average Forecasts for Monthly Sales of Roanoke Corporation

Year	Month	Monthly sales, thousands of dollars (1)	12-Month moving average (2)
1972	January	48.78	
	February	35.94	
	March	37.03	
	April	42.01	
	May	48.60	
	June	50.83	
	July	50.23	
	August	49.88	
	September	54.04	
	October	48.38	
	November	41.77	
	December	44.70	
1973	January	45.82	46.015
	February	43.58	45.768
	March	44.91	46.404
	April	55.32	47.060
	May	59.56	48.169
	June	60.90	49.082
	July	55.69	49.921
	August	57.12	50.376
	September	57.99	50.979
	October	50.95	51.309
	November	44.02	51.523
	December	44.76	51.711
1974	January	47.96	51.716
	February	43.98	51.895
	March	45.21	51.928
	April	52.06	51.954
	May	57.05	51.682
	June	58.84	51.474
	July	54.31	51.302
	August	57.27	51.187
	September	59.92	51.200
	October	53.60	51.361
	November	53.60	51.361
	December	47.30	51.963

TABLE F-10   Twelve-Month Moving-Average Forecasts for Monthly Sales of Roanoke Corporation. (*Continued*)

Year	Month	Monthly sales, thousands of dollars (1)	12-Month moving average (2)
1975	January	50.10	52.175
	February	49.18	52.354
	March	48.96	52.787
	April	53.55	53.099
	May	62.08	53.223
	June	64.90	53.642
	July	58.01	54.147
	August	63.69	54.455
	September	65.90	54.990
	October	60.59	55.488
	November	52.69	56.071
	December	51.71	56.412
1976	January	60.19	56.779
	February	54.04	57.619
	March	58.49	58.025
	April	68.12	58.820
	May	80.73	60.034
	June	80.77	61.588
	July	75.46	62.911
	August	80.89	64.365
	September	83.51	65.799
	October	74.01	67.266
	November	67.37	68.384
	December	68.49	69.607
1977	January		71.006

A common trait of the numerous versions of the moving-average method is that they respond more rapidly to changes in the value of the variable as the number of periods used in the moving average decreases; conversely, as the number of periods increases, the moving-average estimates become more stable. A comparison of the relative merits of the responsiveness and the stability of the moving-average (and other smoothing) methods should be made in terms of the accuracy of the forecast. Stability is obviously an important attribute in situations in which sudden changes in production, labor force, or inventory levels are not desirable or tolerable.

Whereas simple moving averages place the same amount of weight on each of the components of the average, one may desire to put more weight on more recent data; *exponential smoothing* is an easy-to-use, economical approach to forecasting where exponentially decreasing weights are given to older observed values.

Exponential smoothing methods are probably the most commonly used time series methods. They are widely accepted because they place more weight on recent occurrences and because they require only the most recent value of the variable being forecast (whereas the moving-average methods require storage of data from several periods).

In its simplest form, the exponential smoothing formula is as follows:

Forecast for next period

$= \alpha$ (actual value for the most recent period)

$+ (1 - \alpha)$ (forecast value for most recent period)

where α (the Greek letter *alpha*) is the *smoothing constant* (weight), a number between 0 and 1. The larger α becomes, the more responsive the forecast will be to changes in the value of the variable being forecast. The value for α in exponential smoothing (and the value for n, the number of periods included in a moving average) should be chosen so that the mean squared error is minimized. (Experience has shown that smoothing constant values between .1 and .5 work best in most applications of exponential smoothing.) Higher-order exponential smoothing methods have been developed to handle underlying trends and seasonality.

One of the most recently developed methods for business forecasting is called *adaptive filtering*. The basic concept of adaptive filtering is to extend the smoothing techniques described earlier in order to determine the optimum set of weights to apply to past observations. While at least 5 years' data should be available to use this method effectively, it is an easy method to use in practice (with a computer) and will probably become one of the most-used time series methods.

Autoregressive-Moving-Average Methods. The so-called Box-Jenkins autoregressive-moving-average (ARMA) methods of time series forecasting are probably the most powerful of all the time series methods. At least 5 years' data should be used as the historical basis for the Box-Jenkins approach if it is to work effectively. The basic concept of the Box-Jenkins technique is that various classes of forecasting models are tested to determine which one minimizes the sum of the squared forecast errors; the challenge to the forecaster is to interpret skillfully the data patterns that are produced by alternative models so that incremental improvements can be made in the forecast.[6]

The ARMA approach essentially expresses the current value (Y_t) of the forecast variable as a function of previous values ($T_{t-1}, Y_{t-2}, \ldots, Y_{t-k}$) of that same variable. Systematic analysis of the characteristics of the time series data is accomplished by computing, graphing, and interpreting the *autocorrelation coefficients* of the data. Autocorrelation coefficients indicate the simple correlation between a particular variable value Y_t and some previous (lagged) value Y_{t-j} of that same (auto) variable; the meaning of autocorrelations is exactly the same as that of simple correlation coefficients computed in regression analysis. For example, the autocorrelation of Y_t and Y_{t-1} indicates how variables Y_t and Y_{t-1} are related to each other. If monthly data are seasonal, data for periods that are 12 months apart would be related to each other so that autocorrelations between Y_t and Y_{t-12} would show positive correlation. On the other hand, if the autocorrelation of 12 time lags is close to zero, it would indicate the absence of a relationship between the same months of successive years and, therefore, the lack of a seasonal pattern.

Stationarity. This term refers to the absence of a trend in the data; i.e., stationary data fluctuate around a constant mean, independent of time. The characteristic of stationarity in a data series can be easily identified by examining a graph of the autocorrelation coefficients. The autocorrelations of stationary data essentially drop to zero after the second or third time lag, while for a nonstationary series, they are significantly different from zero for several time periods. A graphical representation of the autocorrelation coefficients of nonstationary data shows a trend, indicating that successive values are highly correlated with each other. The *method of differencing* is used to remove trend from data in the ARMA scheme, thus transforming nonstationary data to stationary data.

A *series of first differences* is created by subtracting the most recent previous value from the current value of the forecast variable; symbolically,

$$Y'_t = Y_{t+1} - Y_t$$

and Y'_t represents the series of first differences. If this new series still exhibits nonstationarity (trend), the method of differencing must be applied again to produce a *series of second differences,* symbolized as

$$Y''_t = Y'_{t+1} - Y'_t$$

For most practical purposes, a maximum of two differences will transform the data into a stationary series.

If a stationary series has significant autocorrelations of lag greater than 3, there is a seasonal pattern whose length corresponds to the time lag with the largest autocorrelation. When seasonality is combined with other patterns such as trend, the stronger the trend, the less obvious the seasonality will be. This problem can be avoided by determining seasonality only when the data are stationary. As a rule, the presence of a trend in the data indicates that the data should be transformed to a stationary series using the method of differencing before determining seasonality.

A comparison of the ARMA and decomposition methods shows that many of the same things are accomplished by these two approaches. The decomposition method removes trend by dividing trended data by a moving average to obtain a series without trend. The ARMA method accomplishes this in a more computationally efficient manner by using the method of differencing. The ARMA approach incorporates a seasonal component into the model if there is a seasonal pattern in the data. The decomposition method develops a set of seasonal indexes which are used to adjust forecasts for the seasonality attributed to each forecast period. The ARMA method uses autocorrelation analysis to reveal the underlying characteristics of the data; existing computer programs make such an analysis computationally relatively easy. On the other hand, decomposition methods, while much less sophisticated (and therefore considerably less precise) than ARMA methods, are generally easier to apply. During the next decade, ARMA methods will very probably become increasingly popular for business forecasting, even though they are the most expensive time series methods currently available, and the technical competence required to use them successfully is considerably more than is required for other time series methods.

Multivariate ARMA Models. A highly promising development in business forecasting recently has been in the area of multivariate ARMA models (sometimes called *transfer functions*) as contrasted with the time series methods previously described, which pertain only to univariate *(single)* time series. Multivariate ARMA (MARMA) methods combine the time series approach with the causal (regression) approach to forecasting. The main aim of the MARMA approach is to identify some leading indicators of the series to be forecast that can be used to improve the predictions over those attainable with a univariate model; this model will prove to be especially valuable when sudden cyclical changes occur.

Intervention analysis, an extension of the MARMA approach, is aimed at identifying the type of response a forecast variable will exhibit, given some step or impulse change in an explanatory variable. A purpose of intervention analysis is to answer such questions as how sales will be affected if a promotional campaign is initiated on January 1 or how sales will be influenced if a price is increased by 25 percent. Whereas these questions could be considered using multiple regression analysis, regression analysis does not depict what happens during the transition period before a new equilibrium is reached. Rather, regression assumes that a new steady state (of sales, for example) is immediately achieved. In practice, the businessperson is often more interested in the transition period than in periods in which new equilibrium has been reached. Thus, intervention analysis, while still in the developmental stage, should prove to be an important forecasting method in future years.

Other Methods. While most forecasting methods used in business planning have been described in previous sections, several other forecasting approaches deserve brief mention in the concluding section of this entry.

Indirect Methods. Most of the attention in the discussion of time series, causal, and subjective assessment methods was spent on directly forecasting such variables as sales. Another approach is to base a forecast on estimates of national, regional, or industrial economic activity where the company's share of the larger activity is estimated. It should be noted that time series, causal, and judgmental methods are often used in conjunction with the indirect approach.

When a purchaser is a manufacturer or some other intermediate consumer unit, forecasts for demand for goods or services purchased by that unit may be based on demand for the unit's output. For example, the demand for glass may be derived from the demand for new automobiles and building contracts awarded.

Sometimes it is helpful to be able to gauge the "complementary consumption" of goods or services where the utilization of one product is related to that of another. Typical examples are such complementary products as beer and pretzels, tires and automobiles, grass seed and lawn fertilizer, and baseball bats and baseballs.

Some goods and services exhibit cycles of obsolescence or replacement such that forecasts can be based on knowledge of these replacement patterns. Publishers of textbooks, manufacturers of automobiles, and aircraft producers are examples of corporations that have attempted to use the concept of a replacement cycle to forecast future sales volumes. Time series and causal models have been used to analyze the replacement cycle phenomenon.

Closely related to derived demand and replacement cycle analysis, input-output analysis traces the flows of goods and services from one country to another, from one industry to another, from one sector of an economy to another, or, conceivably, between parts of a corporation. By understanding the magnitudes and paths of such flows, a forecaster can sometimes draw conclusions upon which to base forecasts. However, because of lack of data, technical limitations, and the expense involved, it is doubtful that input-output analysis will be useful to many corporate executives for forecasting purposes in the foreseeable future.

Survey Methods. Consumer surveys and test markets are widely used for forecasting in cases where historical data are not adequate. (*See* Marketing research.)

Normative Models. Policies are normative in nature, aimed at achieving specific objectives; that is, they indicate what should be done to accomplish the goals of an organization. Thus, *normative models* are prescriptive in nature. Most of the methods and models discussed in this entry are *not* prescriptive; rather, their usefulness is generally confined to assisting the forecaster to anticipate what *may* happen given certain assumptions and premises, *not* what *should* happen. In that sense, the methods discussed thus far could be called descriptive and diag-

nostic models. These models rely on previous experience, historical data, or both.

Mathematical programming techniques and decision-tree approaches could be considered to be normative methods, and certain uses of computer simulation and the Delphi approach could be considered to be normative. These are also sometimes referred to as *rational* methods. Normative or rational methods are used to best advantage when the uncontrollable variables have been forecasted and constraints (such as budget limitations) are known. If the uncontrollable variables and constraints can be assumed to be known with certainty, it may be possible to use a mathematical programming approach (such as linear programming) to make future resource allocation decisions and thus to project optimal policies.

If the future values of uncontrollable variables and constraints are not known with certainty, one may be able to use a decision-tree approach (or other decision analysis) or a Monte Carlo simulation model to determine the best policies in the face of the uncertainties surrounding the decision maker.*

See also Decision-making process; Economic measurements; Input-output analysis; Market analysis; Operations research and mathematical modeling; Production planning and control; Statistical analysis for management.

NOTES

[1]Charles W. Gross and Robin T. Peterson, *Business Forecasting*, Houghton Mifflin, Boston, 1978, chap. 2.

[2]Harold A. Linstone and Murray Turoff, *The Delphi Method: Techniques and Applications*, Addison-Wesley, Reading, Mass., 1973.

[3]Henry J. Claycamp and Lucien E. Liddy, "Prediction of New Product Performance: An Analytical Approach," *Journal of Marketing Research*, vol. 6, November 1969, pp. 414–420.

[4]Carl A. Dauten and Lloyd M. Valentine, *Business Cycles and Forecasting*, 4th ed., South-Western Publishing Company, Cincinnati, 1974.

[5]Elizabeth W. Angle, *Keys for Business Forecasting*, Federal Reserve Bank of Richmond, Richmond, Va., June 1975.

[6]Vincent A. Mabert, *An Introduction to Short Term Forecasting Using the Box-Jenkins Methodology*, Monograph, American Institute of Industrial Engineers, Atlanta, 1975.

REFERENCES

Chambers, John C., Satinder K. Mullick, and Donald D. Smith: *An Executive's Guide to Forecasting*, John Wiley & Sons, New York, 1974.

Mason, Robert D.: *Statistical Techniques in Business and Economics*, 5th ed., Richard D. Irwin, Homewood, Ill., 1982.

*The author acknowledges the guidance provided by Prof. Steven Wheelwright, Harvard Business School; Mr. Louis P. Pante, American Can Company; and Profs. John Forbes, Robert Landel, and Willis Ryckman, The Darden School, University of Virginia.

Makridakis, Spyros, Steven C. Wheelwright, and Victor E. McGee: *Forecasting: Methods and Applications,* John Wiley & Sons, New York, 1983.

Pindyck, Robert S., and Daniel L. Rubinfeld: *Econometric Models and Economic Forecasts,* McGraw-Hill, New York, 1976.

Curtis J. Tompkins, *West Virginia University*

Forms Design and Control

Business forms cover the entire spectrum of paperwork used to collect, process, record, and communicate organizational information in a standard or uniform way. Regardless of organization size, the cost of preparing, processing, and using business forms constitutes a sizable, ongoing investment in employee time. How productively that time is spent is largely determined by how well or poorly the forms are designed. Studies in government and private industry have shown that the costs of forms themselves are only 5 percent of the true overall cost of the typical clerical operation. The remaining 95 percent is the employee time required to process and use them.

Poorly designed forms are more expensive to process and invariably cost more than they should. If forms are not constantly reevaluated, they soon become obsolete; if their introduction is not closely supervised, forms tend to increase rapidly in number. In either case, the result is greater clerical cost. Clearly, all these factors point to the need for effective forms design and control.

Principles of Forms Design

The ideal form serves its function with a minimum of effort, expense, and waste. To achieve this goal, an analysis conducted by a forms designer (internally employed or a qualified vendor) must precede the design of a new form or the redesign of an existing one.

With the exact purpose of the form clearly in mind, and with nothing assumed, the designer should question and examine every aspect of it. Those who wish to initiate a new form as well as those who will process it are interviewed. The flow of each part of the form is traced from the time it is prepared until it is either sent out, filed, or discarded.

1. *Is the form truly necessary?* There is always the possibility that the information the new form would provide is available on an existing form.

2. *Does the form have more or fewer parts than are actually needed?* All too often, forms are routinely reordered with the same number of parts, although one or more no longer serve any pur-

pose. Eliminating only one part from an order for 10,000 multiple-part carbon-interleaved forms saves the cost of shipping, storing, processing, and filing 10,000 pieces of paper, in addition to the cost of the paper and carbon itself. Too few parts, on the other hand, result in costly trips to the copier.

3. *Is all the information on the form necessary?* Any data not required for a specific purpose should be eliminated. If not, the time and effort spent in gathering and recording that information are wasted.

4. *Can the form be combined with another form?* Dramatic savings of employee time and forms cost can be realized if two or more forms with similar information can be combined.

5. *Have all possible manual operations been eliminated by "building" them into the form?* Information or numbering that is repetitively written or stamped onto a form can be preprinted. Hand stapling can be eliminated by pregluing parts that eventually must be joined. File holes can be punched during form manufacture.

6. *What would be the most advantageous construction?* The volume of usage and the application, among other factors, will point to the best of a number of possible constructions. For instance, unit sets (multiple-part forms which come with carbon between parts) free the clerical worker of the tedious, time-consuming task of manually inserting carbons into each form before typing it. For larger volumes, the continuous construction does away with the need to insert, adjust, and eject each individual form. Only the first need be inserted and lined up in the machine. The rest follow one another in perfect alignment.

Upon completion of the analysis, the forms designer creates a form that reflects the answers to these and numerous other questions.

Case Histories

The benefits and savings to be realized from these principles and procedures can best be illustrated by a series of actual case histories.

Case History No. 1: Each of the approximately 150,000 shipments made annually by a large coffee company required a three-part bill-of-lading form which was prepared by hand in the shipping department. Shipments were subsequently billed on six-part continuous invoice forms prepared on computer terminals in the billing department. *Improvement:* Both the bill-of-lading and invoice forms are combined into a nine-part invoice/bill-of-lading form and continue to be prepared on the billing department terminals. A special type of very thin, carbonless paper is used to ensure legibility of all parts.

This change eliminates the time and expense of writing 150,000 bill-of-lading forms per year. Also gone are problems caused by illegible handwriting.

CASE HISTORY NO. 2: A large percentage of applications for new policies received by an insurance company required additional information from the agents who sent them in. The request for additional information came in a letter dictated by a sales executive and typed by a secretary. *Improvement:* A three-part unit-set "request for additional information" form was designed. It lists those items of information which an analysis of past letters revealed to be most frequently requested. To the left of each item is a check box; to the right, enough space for an answer. By using this form, the executive need only check one or more boxes for the information required of the agent. One copy is kept for follow-up, and the remaining two copies, with carbon intact, are sent to the agent. No additional typing of an envelope is required; the form is designed to be used with a no. 10 window envelope, which reveals the agent's name and address after the form has been folded and inserted. Upon receipt of the form, the agent simply fills in the items of information requested, removes the carbon, keeps one copy for the files, and returns the completed original to the insurance company. This form not only reduces executive and secretarial time; it speeds up replies.

CASE HISTORY NO. 3: A small but rapidly growing jewelry manufacturer had found that its forms failed to keep pace with the company's volume of orders. Each sales order required the preparation of a two-part production order, packing list, shipping label, and multiple-part invoice, each of which was individually prepared at different points and times in the operation. *Improvement:* All forms were combined into an eight-part typewritten unit set. At the start, the form is completely filled out except for the quantity shipped, extensions, and final totals. The production order copies, packing list, and shipping label are removed from the set as needed during the operation while the invoice section, with carbons intact, remains on file until final shipment of the order is made. At this point, with final quantities and shipping charges known, the invoice section is reinserted into the typewriter and completed.

CASE HISTORY NO. 4: A bottled-water distributor had a collection system consisting of three different 8½- by 11-inch continuous-form dunning statements. There were 30-, 60-, and 90-day past-due notifications. Large volumes of statements in each category were processed by computer each month, requiring a separate run for each of the three forms. After printout, the forms were separated from one another, folded, inserted into mailing envelopes along with a return remittance envelope, sealed, stamped, and mailed. *Improvement:* Through major revisions in layout and a more economical use of space, the length of the form was reduced from 11 to 5½ inches. The three different forms were redesigned into a single form so that all three categories are prepared in one pass through the computer, with the computer printout making the differentiation between the 30-, 60-, and 90-day statements. In addition, a continuous-mailer construction was introduced; the statements are manufactured so that each has already been sealed into its stamped mailing envelope, along with a return-remittance envelope, prior to being run through the computer. Now, after computer processing, these continuous envelopes need only be separated from one another and mailed. Form size is cut by 50 percent; monthly computer runs for the system are reduced from three to one; postcomputer processing is cut from 2 days to less than ⅛ day (thereby also improving cash flow), and the company has to order and store only one form instead of three.

Management and Forms Design

The price that must be paid for using inefficient forms is too high to be ignored. Effectively designed forms should be considered a necessity, not an option. Still, the mistaken notion persists that anyone can design a form, with paper and pencil the only prerequisites. Truly effective design, however, calls for professional knowledge and experience in the areas of systems analysis, layout, paper, carbon, printing, and forms manufacture, as well as the ability to deal with the capabilities and limitations of an everexpanding array of equipment for processing forms. The explosive growth in the use of computers, and the preoccupation with new, more glamorous office technologies, have tended to overshadow the need for properly designed forms, when everincreasing clerical employee costs make them more important than ever.

Forms Control

An organization with an awareness of the true cost of its forms (initial *plus* processing costs) and a desire to keep these expenses to a minimum can realize appreciable savings by initiating a forms control program. The size and scope of such a program will vary among companies, depending upon organization size, number of forms involved, and the degree of management's commitment to such an effort. A forms control program, on any scale, must have the total support of the highest levels of management if it is to succeed.

For smaller-sized companies, a forms control program carried out by a qualified design- and systems-oriented forms vendor will serve the purpose. Larger organizations, however, require an internal forms control unit, which can range in size from a single person to a full staff of analyst-designers headed by a forms manager.

Objectives. Ideally, the forms control group should have the necessary authority and staff to deal with and administer every aspect of the organization's paperwork and carry out these major objectives:

1. Collection and review of every form being used within the organization.

2. Elimination of all unnecessary forms, combination of forms wherever possible, redesign of existing forms as required for maximum efficiency and cost savings, and responsibility for analysis and design of all new forms.

3. Attainment of economies in purchasing by means of standardizing sizes wherever possible and combining purchases.

4. Assurance that forms are available as needed while inventories are kept at a minimal level.

Implementation. In order to implement and maintain a forms control program, the following steps are required:

1. Prepare and distribute a collection letter throughout the organization as a means of collecting samples of every form in use, along with a fully detailed account of how the form is presently being used and its volume of usage.

2. Set up and maintain a *numerical file* by initially devising an appropriate numbering system and then using it as the basis for assigning a number to each new form.

3. Set up and maintain a *functional file* as a means of sorting forms by function, such as "authorize," "acknowledge," "bill," "report." This file will uncover existing duplication of forms and also act as a tool to prevent future duplication. It is also a valuable reference file in which all forms which deal with a particular function or area can readily be found.

4. Establish the forms control unit as the sole authority in handling requests to initiate new forms and reorder existing ones, as well as in determining whether a form is to be supplied by an outside vendor or produced by an in-house printing facility.

5. Set up procedures and controls for procurement, inventory, storage, and distribution.

Initiating a forms control unit requires an investment of time, effort, and personnel, but there is a potential saving of from 30 to 50 percent of the total spent on forms and their usage. Initial savings are the most dramatic; subsequent savings tend to level off, however. For this reason, care should be taken

that forms control remains a permanent concern of the organization to ensure that economies gained and controls established are not lost.

See also Computer software, data base management; Paperwork simplification; Records management; Systems and procedures.

REFERENCES

Kramer, Seymour D.: "10 Ways to Improve Your Sales Control Forms," *Sales Management*, Special Report on Sales Control Forms, August 1975, p. 2.

Myers, Gibbs: "Forms as a Symptom of Business Health," *Journal of Systems Management*, February 1976, p. 16.

Pemberton, Roy F.: "Organizing the Forms Management Program," *Information-Records Management Magazine*, August 1975, p. 8.

SEYMOUR D. KRAMER, *Revere Business Graphics, Inc.*

Franchising

Franchised sales of goods and services in more than 463,000 outlets in the United States exceed $240 billion annually, and they are constantly increasing.

Under the franchising system, franchisors offer management expertise and marketing resources to small business enterprises with limited capital to help them achieve success. Many or all of the following services are offered to franchisees: advice on location choice; established name or reputation; standardized accounting and operating procedures, store equipment, and inventory; and continuing assistance in advertising, tax information, and store design. Franchisors are able to keep pace with shifting consumer markets by utilizing market techniques to survey potential customer demand. A typical arrangement calls for the franchisee to pay the franchisor a small percentage of gross sales or to agree to purchase equipment and inventory from the franchisor.

Useful definitions include:

Franchising. An arrangement under which the franchisor gives the franchise holder the exclusive right to sell specified products or offer specified services in a defined geographic territory in accordance with other terms of the contract.

Franchise. The right to operate a local "branch" of the parent company.

Franchisor. The manufacturer or the national or regional distributor that grants a franchise.

Franchisee. The local operator of the franchise.

Franchise Agreement. The legal contract which defines the relationship between the franchisor and franchisee, including the rights, privileges, and obligations of each.

349

The franchisee is a local, independent individual who establishes a reputation and relationship with the franchisor which are much closer than those of the usual independent intermediary. The franchisee is willing to subordinate personal identity because of superior advantages deemed attainable from the franchisor's reputation, training, and resources.

Thus, *franchising* is an arrangement where the franchisor, having developed a successful product or service plus a successful pattern or formula for the conduct of a particular type of business, extends to its franchisees the right or privilege of participating in that business as long as they follow the established pattern or formula of operation.

Advantages and Disadvantages to the Franchisor. In general, the franchisor achieves these benefits:

- Corporate growth with limited investment
- Increased market penetration
- Expanded volume and improved profits
- Dedicated entrepreneurial branch managers
- Improved utilization of company resources
- Divestment of locations, routes, markets
- Reduced costs of raw materials through quantity purchases

Franchising additionally has:

- Created markets for new products
- Developed markets for some products in a shorter span of time than otherwise would have been possible
- Altered the established channels of distribution for some products
- Enabled manufacturers to deliver new ideas and products with guaranteed high, uniform quality at the most distant location
- Enabled manufacturers to expand on less capital than would have been possible if outlets were company-owned.

On the other hand, franchising has these possible disadvantages to the franchisor:

- High cost of supervision. Franchisees often need more assistance and guidance than originally planned.
- Some loss of control. As an independent business, the franchisee often must be convinced or persuaded to do things in the prescribed manner. Some of the sensitive areas are likely to be (1) any procedure regarded as "standard"; (2) participation in sales promotion or advertising campaigns; (3) feedback of information, including weekly or monthly reports; and (4) franchisee's desire to handle other product lines, buy from nonapproved

sources, or go into other businesses and only "supervise" the franchise.

- Freedom of action. A major change in company policy, such as the addition of a product line, may have to be negotiated individually with each franchisee.
- Loss of initial drive. The franchisee may be satisfied with the initial profit being derived from the business and be unwilling to consider expansion or the future development of the market.
- Too rapid expansion. A franchisor can overextend itself financially.

Planning and Operating a Franchise Program

A careful plan must be established in advance. The major steps of such a plan should include:

1. An assessment of the feasibility of the product or service to be franchised and determination of the potential success of the franchise
2. A franchisee recruitment program
3. A determination of franchise locations
4. A complete set of financial projections
5. Advertising and promotion plans
6. A training curriculum

Franchise Feasibility Determination. An effective franchise program must be feasible to both the franchisor and the franchisee. Relevant questions should penetrate four especially important areas:

Production. Does the product or service have an element of distinctiveness, and does it have enduring customer appeal? Does it have a repeat factor, and have inventory requirements been minimized? Does the franchisor have the production ability to supply the franchisees, and can the franchisor arrange the supply of materials needed?

Finance. Is the pilot operation fully documented? Have realistic financial projections been made? Has viable franchisee financing been worked out? Does the franchisor have a record of financial stability, and is it able and willing to commit the necessary funds?

Marketing. Is the market position secure, and can it be projected to a national market? Is the industry in a growth position, and can the franchisee maintain a competitive position? Does the franchisor have adequate market research? Most important, is the current reputation of the product or service good?

Personnel. Can a franchisee with little experience be trained in the operation of the franchise? Does the franchisor have adequate staff to aid the franchisees?

Franchisee Recruitment. Successful franchise recruitment begins with a franchisee recruitment brochure, a presentation book, a franchisee agreement, a disclosure statement, and a recruitment control system.

The first step in recruiting is to generate leads by advertising. Such leads should be mailed a brochure and a franchisee qualification form. The qualification form should ask for financial information about the potential franchisee, identify requirements like being an owner-manager, etc. The use of a well-thought-out qualification form can separate those seriously interested from the casual shoppers.

After the receipt and evaluation of the qualification form, potential franchisees can be contacted, made a formal presentation, invited to visit an existing location, and given the franchise agreement and other legal forms. Final signing of the franchise agreement and discussion of the disclosure statement should involve appropriate legal counsel by both parties.

Franchise Location. As part of the original plan, the franchisor must decide where franchises are desired. For some services, one location in a large city is adequate. For other products or services, two locations in a small town may be reasonable. This decision is generally not difficult, and the use of government statistical data is of great help. The franchisor may also decide to grant a franchise for a region, or for each individual store or office.

As part of the franchise agreement, specification requirements of the exact site may need to be worked out. This item could include requirements of vehicular traffic, parking, land availability, zoning, competition, etc. In many areas, superior-quality franchise locations may not be available, and less than ideal locations may be necessary.

Financial Projections. Both the franchisor and the franchisee must have good financial projections in advance to determine if both are likely to be satisfied. For each franchise, a pro forma income statement and balance sheet should be determined, as well as a return-on-investment calculation.

Franchisors make their profit from a combination of items, such as a franchise fee, royalties on sales, and sale of equipment and supplies. It is to the franchisor's advantage to make sure the franchise is financially sound enough to improve the franchisor's profit.

Advertising and Promotion. A thorough advertising and promotion plan should be in place, both for the opening of a new franchise and for the franchisor in the long run. Advertising and promotion plans may be sponsored by the franchisor, by the franchisee, or jointly. National advertising, particularly television, is one major feature the franchisee may expect from the franchisor. The franchisor must make sure that franchisee participation in advertising and promotion programs is required in the contract and clearly identified.

Special attention should be paid to the new franchise's grand opening, where free publicity and good will can be generated.

Training. Franchisees must have a high degree of confidence in their ability to run the franchise and generate a profit. Training helps by generating this self-confidence. The franchisor must develop the training program and insist that it be followed rigorously.

Ideally, the franchisee will be brought to the home site for training, with a great deal of hands-on activity. In-store training can then apply the home-office training, though the franchisor's trainers should aid with the in-store training.

Specifically, franchisee training should include:

Business facts. Profit, the franchise agreement, the franchisor, legal considerations, etc.

Marketing. Customer relations, merchandising, advertising, grand opening, etc.

Production. Ordering equipment and supplies, sanitation, product processing, inventory control, etc.

Finance. Bookkeeping functions, cash registers (when appropriate), cash disbursements, bank deposits, payroll, insurance, lease. etc.

Personnel. Personnel recruitment, selection, training, motivation, legal considerations, etc.

Conclusion

Franchising is a proven way for many companies to increase sales and profits more rapidly than they could with internal growth. While many activities are now franchised, the potential for new franchisors remains high. Many franchisors are not successful, however, because they do not investigate and plan their franchises thoroughly. To be successful, both the franchisor and the franchisee must be satisfied that the relationship will work to both their advantages.

See also Advertising concepts; Facilities and site planning and layout; Financial management; Financial statement analysis; Market analysis; Marketing management.

REFERENCES

Boone, Louis E., and James C. Johnson: *Marketing Channels,* 2d ed., PPC Books, Tulsa, Okla., 1977.

Directory of Franchising Organizations and a Guide to Franchising, Pilot Industries, New York, 1977 and updates.

Seltz, David: *The Complete Handbook of Franchising,* Addison-Wesley, Reading, Mass., 1982.

    David Seltz, *Seltz Franchising Developments, Inc.*

Gantt Charts

The *Gantt chart* is a graphic method for planning and controlling production quantities and times. Originated prior to World War I by the industrial engineer Henry Laurence Gantt, the chart is widely used today in a variety of forms in every kind of organization.

The unique value of the Gantt chart is demonstrated in Fig. G-1, which deals with five production orders, stamped serially from 101 to 105. These orders indicate the machines the work must be processed on, the sequence that must be followed, and the estimated number of hours each machine will require to complete its work.

If the schedule planner were to load the machines with the assumption that each order must be finished before another one is begun (straight-line or point-to-point scheduling), the planner would come up with a schedule something like chart A in Fig. G-1. The flow of work would be orderly, but the equipment would be underutilized. Worse still, a great many orders would be delayed. To correct these deficiencies, Gantt *overlapped* orders, disregarding the sequence in which they were accepted while still rigidly adhering to the *operation* sequence that each

order specifies. Chart B in Fig. G-1 shows how the scheduler can juggle orders, starting no. 105 on machine B and no. 102 on machine C while at the same time beginning no. 101 on machine A. If the jobs are rearranged and overlapped, all five orders can be finished by Friday afternoon. Furthermore, the scheduler has greatly increased the overall machine utilization. Machine A is now scheduled to be in operation 18 of the first 24 hours of the work week (through Wednesday). It works 4 hours on no. 101, 4 hours on no. 104, is idle for 2 hours, then works 4 hours on no. 102, 6 hours on no. 105, and is idle again until the close of the shift on Wednesday. Machine B utilizes 22 hours during the same period: 4 hours on no. 105, 8 hours on no. 101, idle for 2 hours, 6 hours on no. 102, and 4 hours on no. 103. Machine C utilizes all 24 hours: 10 hours on no. 102, 2 hours on no. 105, 2 hours on no. 101, and 10 hours on no. 104. This schedule predicts utilization rates of 75 percent, 95 percent, and 100 percent. While the scheduler might not be able to juggle the work so efficiently all week long, this sequence is an indication of what judicious overlapping of jobs can accomplish.

Reserved-Time and Progress Control Chart. Gantt took his chart one step further in order to make it the basis for following progress of work through a

Chart A

	Monday	Tuesday	Wednesday	Thursday	Friday	Monday	Tuesday
Machine A	101			102		103	
Machine B	101			102	103		
Machine C		101 102				103	

Log of orders for Charts A and B

Order no.	101 (mask)			102 (knob)			103 (optic)			104 (pan)			105 (quoit)		
Operation sequence	1	2	3	1	2	3	1	2	3	1	2	3	1	2	3
Machine no.	A	B	C	C	A	B	B	A	C	A	C	B	B	C	A
Machine time (hr)	4	8	2	10	4	8	6	4	8	4	10	12	4	2	6

Chart B

	Monday	Tuesday	Wednesday	Thursday	Friday	Monday	Tuesday
Machine A	101 104	102 105		103			
Machine B	105 101		102 103	104			
Machine C	102	105 101 104			103		

FIG. G-1 Development of a Gantt chart from a series of production orders. Chart A shows jobs lined up in sequence as they were received. Chart B shows jobs rearranged (overlapped) for maximum machine loading, with prescribed sequences of operations for each job maintained. Each day represents 8 hours.

shop and providing each worker with a detailed schedule. The Gantt reserved-time and progress control chart in Fig. G-2 is identical in arrangement to the one in chart B of Fig. G-1. It applies the same data in the same way but is different in the way in which the individual rectangles are prepared. For each job scheduled on each machine, the scheduler lightly draws an open-topped rectangle. Inside the rectangle the name (and sometimes the part number) of the job to be run is marked. Where there are open, or unassigned, work blocks, the scheduler inserts an X in pencil that can be quickly found if a new job comes up which might fill the space. During the course of the week as each job progresses, the scheduler draws a heavy line across the bottom of the rectangle. This progress line is proportional to the *amount produced*, not to the time blocked out for its production. For example, on machine B, job no. 102 has been running since Tuesday afternoon; it is now Wednesday noon and the job should have been completed, but the heavy line at the bottom of the rectangle shows that the job is only two-thirds done (it has made only 450 of the 675 pieces scheduled). Examination of this chart, as of Wednesday noon, shows:

Jobs nos. 101 and 105 have been completed.

Job no. 102 is still running on machine B and is behind schedule.

Job no. 104 is running on machine C and is ahead of schedule.

Job. no. 103 has not been begun, but it is on schedule.

Finding that some jobs run behind and others run ahead of schedule is not unusual. This is one reason machines cannot be scheduled for 100 percent utilization. The scheduler, in this example, will have to keep modifying the reserved-time chart to take into account the realities of day-to-day operations. The scheduler also continually adds new orders as well as cancels others.

Order-of-Work Sheet. Figure G-3 shows how the scheduler can transfer the planned schedule on the reserved-time chart to an order-of-work sheet. This sheet becomes the detailed schedule for each machine and for each operator. It tells *what* will be run, *how much*, and *in what sequence*. Santo, for example, knows that she will operate machine B, that she will work on job nos. 105, 101, 102, 103, and 104 in that sequence. She also knows what *parts* she will work on and *how many* of each she must make to complete her portion of the order.

The Gantt Chart is, of course, the precursor of PERT, CPM, and other network planning methods.

See also Control systems, management; Network planning methods; Production/operations management; Production planning and control; Scheduling, short-interval.

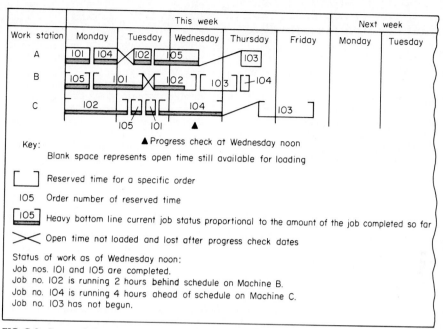

FIG. G-2 Reserved-time production planning and progress control chart.

REFERENCES

Clark, Mrs. Wallace: "The Gantt Chart," in H. B. Maynard (ed.), *Industrial Engineering Handbook*, 2d ed., McGraw-Hill, New York, 1963, chap. 7–3.

Henderson, Richard I., and Waino W. Suojanen: "Five Valuable Planning Tools for the Operating Manager," in *The Operating Manager*, Prentice-Hall, Englewood Cliffs, N.J., 1974, chap. 14.

Neuschel, Richard F.: "Planning and Controlling the Individual Systems Project," in *Management Systems for Profit and Growth*, McGraw-Hill, New York, 1976, chap. 8.

LESTER R. BITTEL, *James Madison University*

Dept. no.: ___135___   Date originated: Monday, Sept. 6
Period: Week of Sept. 6

Machine, operation, or bench		Order no.	Part		Operator's name	No. of pieces to make
Name	No.		Part name	Part no.		
Machine	A	101	Mask	276	Randolph	280
		104	Pan	654	″	410
		102	Knob	410	″	675
		105	Quoit	832	″	318
		103	Optic	721	″	1500
Machine	B	105	Quoit	832	Santo	318
		101	Mask	276	″	280
		102	Knob	410	″	675
		103	Optic	721	″	1500
		104	Pan	654	″	410
Machine	C	102	Knob	410	Trosk	675
		105	Quoit	832	″	318
		101	Mask	276	″	280
		104	Pan	654	″	410
		103	Optic	721	″	1500

FIG. G-3 Order-of-work sheet.

Government Regulations, Business Law

Business law includes a multitude of laws affecting the rights and obligations of those persons and organizations that engage in business. This entry is by no means encompassing, especially in view of the dynamic state of laws and legislation in the United States. It does include, however, basic but not exhaustive insights into selected elements of law that are most vital to business transactions.

Common Law and Equity

Common Law. At the heart of the American legal system is the body of law which originated with William the Conqueror in 1066: the common law. This system, or body, of law is composed of the decisions of judges in resolving real disputes. The distinguishing characteristic of the common law is the *doctrine of precedent,* which holds that prior decisions involving the same or similar facts should be followed in resolving present disputes. The United States adopted the common law as it had developed in England up to the time of the Revolution; since that time, the United States has carried on the tradition of common law in its own courts. The common law is also described as the *law of cases* and is to be distinguished from the acts of the various legislatures. This is not to say, however, that the two are unrelated, as any court decision which defines or interprets a statute is a part of the body of common law.

In a broader sense, common law distinguishes the jurisprudence in the United States and Great Britain from that of other nations and cultures.

Equity. *Equity,* or chancery, is—in the strictest sense—a system of law administered by courts separate and distinct from the common-law courts. The equity courts evolved to hear cases the common-law courts were unable to resolve, and they render justice unimpaired by the strict limitations imposed by the common-law courts. The distinguishing characteristics of the law of equity are the flexibility and broad range of remedies available, which include, for example, injunctions and decrees of specific performance. In the broader sense, equity has come to denote the ethical, as opposed to the strictly legal, resolution of disputes.

Torts

A *tort* is a private injury or wrong arising from a breach of duty owed by one member of society to a fellow member. It is a wrong to person or property not arising out of a contractual relationship. A wrongful act may be a tort and a crime at the same time, if the act transgresses the law. Torts may be classified as intentional and unintentional, and the latter group may be further divided into negligence and strict liability.

Intentional Torts. Intentional torts include assault, battery, defamation, false imprisonment, fraud, invasion of privacy, and infliction of emotional distress.

Against Persons. *Assault* is the intentional act of putting another in reasonable apprehension of the possibility of immediate bodily contact. *Battery* is the intentional act of touching another without justification or consent.

Defamation is the publication of false statements which impute some disreputable or immoral conduct to another. *Libel* is written defamation, whereas *slander* is spoken. Truth is a complete defense to an action of defamation.

False imprisonment is the wrongful denial of the physical liberty of another; the denial may be brought about by either acts or words.

Invasion of privacy is the unwarranted infringement upon a person's private life and includes the unpermitted use of a person's endorsement in an advertisement. Because one's peace of mind is being protected, the truth is not a defense in an action for invasion of privacy.

Emotional distress is actionable when a person has acted with the intention of causing the emotional disturbance of another. There need be no bodily contact in order to recover, but the plaintiff usually must demonstrate that the defendant's conduct has caused some illness.

Against Property. Torts for interfering with the property rights of another include: (1) trespass to land, (2) trespass to personal property, (3) conversion, and (4) fraud. *Trespass* is any unpermitted interference with another's possession of his or her land. The plaintiff need not demonstrate monetary loss; the interference alone is sufficient. The simple act of throwing a rock onto the property of another is a trespass. In an action for trespass to personal property, the plaintiff normally must prove that some damage has been done to the property. The distinguishing characteristic of *conversion* is the unlawful dominion of the personal property of another so as to deny the owner possession of the property. A person is guilty of conversion if he or she wrongfully, though mistakenly, takes goods belonging to another. *Fraud* is the knowing misrepresentation of a fact for the purpose of deceiving another person. Silence does not usually constitute fraud, but the law does impose a duty to speak when one occupies a position of trust. A statement of opinion or a prediction as to the future is not usually construed as the representation of a fact.

Unintentional Torts. These types of torts generally fall into two classifications.

1. *The law of negligence* imposes on every person the duty to act in such a way as not to harm others. The plaintiff in a negligence action must prove that the defendant has been negligent and that the negligent conduct was the cause of the plaintiff's injuries. Unlike the intentional torts, in an action for negligence there must be actual injury to the plaintiff. The duty the law imposes is to conduct oneself as a reasonable person would in the same or similar circumstance. Ignorance and honest mistakes are no excuse.

   The *doctrine of respondent superior* dictates that an employer is responsible for the torts of his or her employees that are committed in the course of performing their normal duties.

   Defenses to an action for negligence are contributory negligence and assumption of risk. In *contributory negligence*, the plaintiff, through her or his own negligent conduct, contributed to the cause of the accident. In *assumption of risk*, the plaintiff voluntarily enters into a situation where she or he knows there is a risk of injury. For example, a person attending a hockey game may have assumed the risk of being hit by a flying puck.

2. *Strict liability* means that the defendant, even though not negligent, can still be held liable for any damage resulting from his or her conduct. The law imposes strict liability upon a person when engaging in activities which are inherently dangerous yet provide a beneficial service. The spraying of crops from airplanes and the use of dynamite are traditional examples of strict liability. Recent years have witnessed the expansion of the doctrine of strict liability to sales of defective consumer products that may expose the consumer to unreasonable risks.

Contracts

A contract is a binding agreement between two or more people to do or not to do some particular thing; it is enforceable in a court of law. There are four requisites to every contract: (1) mutual assent, (2) capacity of parties, (3) consideration, and (4) legality of subject matter.

Mutual Assent. Mutual assent is arrived upon through an offer made by the offerer to the offeree who accepts the offer. The offer must be definite and certain, must be more than an invitation to negotiate, must be serious, and must be communicated to the offeree. The offerer may revoke the offer any time before it is accepted. An offer is terminated at the end of the time expressly stated or, if not stated, at the end of a reasonable period of time. The offerer determines the manner of acceptance, and acceptance of an offer must be in accordance with the terms of the offer. An offeree who does not accept the offer as communicated has rejected it; an offeree who attempts to accept but materially changes the terms has made a counteroffer.

Fraud, duress, and undue influence render a contract unenforceable by the guilty party. A salesperson's talk or "puffing" does not constitute fraud. Compelling a person to make a contract against his or her will is *duress*, whereas the improper use of power over the mind of another is *undue influence*. A contract is also unenforceable if there has been a mutual mistake as to the existence, but not value, of the subject matter.

Capacity. A contract with a party lacking capacity to contract is voidable at the option of the party having the incapacity. Infants, mental incompetents, and drunkards, when so intoxicated as to be unable to understand the nature of the transaction, lack legal capacity to contract. However, one lacking capacity is liable for the reasonable value (not the contract price) of "necessaries" furnished him or her. *Necessaries* are defined in terms of the party's normal needs for items such as food, clothing, and shelter. Upon reaching majority, an infant may ratify contracts by either a new promise or an act in which he or she recognizes contractual liability.

Consideration. *Consideration* is the price bargained and paid for a promise; it is the element of exchange in a contract; it induces another to enter into the contract. It may be an act, a forbearance to act, or promise given in exchange for a promise. Past consideration or a moral obligation will not support a promise. In the absence of fraud, the courts will not look into the value of the consideration.

Legality. An agreement is illegal whenever the agreement itself or the performance called for is illegal. Common examples include contracts made in violation of gambling, usury, and licensing statutes, as well as restraint of trade. Not all contracts in restraint of trade are illegal; restraint of trade is permissible when it gives necessary and reasonable protection to the benefiting party.

Other Factors. The essentials of an enforceable contract having been set out, there are two additional considerations of which businesspersons should be aware: the statute of frauds and the parol evidence rule.

Statute of Frauds. As a general rule, an oral contract is in every way as enforceable as a written one. However, the *statute of frauds* requires certain classes of contracts to be in writing and signed by the party to be charged. The statute of frauds does not pertain to fraud as such, but rather was designed to prevent fraud in certain types of contracts. Some of the more important contracts within the statute are these: contract for the sale of land or any interest therein; a promise to answer for the debt of another; agreements not to be performed within 1 year; contracts to sell goods having a value of $50 to $2500, depending on state law.

Parol Evidence Rule. The term *parol evidence* refers to any oral or written evidence which is extrinsic to the written contract. The parol evidence rule prohibits either party in a lawsuit from introducing any evidence which would change or contradict the written contract. The rule is designed to give effect only to those terms which the parties considered important enough to include in the writing.

The rule does not apply to:

1. Contracts partially in writing and partially oral
2. Sales receipts which do not purport to be contracts
3. Gross typographical errors
4. Evidence which tends to prove incapacity or fraud, duress, or undue influence

The parol evidence rule will never prevent the introduction of evidence which would explain or resolve an ambiguity in the contract.

Sales

Article 2 of the Uniform Commercial Code governs the sale of *personal* property; the sale of *real* property is covered in the section on property.

Contract of Sale. A *sale,* as the term is used in the Uniform Commercial Code, is the transfer of ownership of goods from the seller to the buyer for a price. The code defines "goods" as all things which are movable at the time of the identification to the contract, excluding money, investment securities, and *choses in action.* Rules governing the formation and requirements of contracts (discussed earlier) generally apply to contracts of sale. The courts will attempt to give effect to the intention of the parties as gleaned from the contract and the circumstances surrounding its formation. The code requires no particular form for a sales contract, nor does it require the contract to be in writing unless the statute of frauds so specifies. A contract for the sale of goods may be made in any manner sufficient to show agreement, including conduct by both parties which recognizes the existence of the contract.

The code differs from the general law of contracts in several areas:

1. An *acceptance,* which states terms additional to or different from those stated in the offer, will still form a contract.

2. An *agreement modifying a contract* of sale needs no consideration.

3. The code also establishes *separate rules which apply to transactions involving one or more merchants as a party.* There are 15 sections of the code regulating these transactions which demand a higher standard of conduct because of a merchant's presumed knowledge of the practices of commerce. If a court, for example, finds a contract of sale or any of its clauses to have been unconscionable at the time it was made, the court may refuse to enforce the contract, or it may enforce the remainder of the contract without the unconscionable clause.

4. *Risk of loss, insurable interest, and other rights and liabilities* under the code are no longer solely determined on the basis of who holds the title of the goods. Title may still be determinative, but only if the code expressly so states.

5. If not set out in the terms of the contract, *title passes when the seller has completed his or her performance.* If the contract calls for "delivery" by the seller, title passes upon delivery and tender to the buyer at the place designated in the contract. Where the contract calls for "shipment" by the seller, title passes to the buyer upon delivery to the carrier. If a buyer should reject goods, title revests in the seller.

Warranties. A warranty is a statement or representation made by the seller at the time of sale for the quality or suitability of the goods. A seller who limits statements to "sales talk," such as "This is an excellent buy," has not made a warranty, nor is the seller responsible for a mere opinion as to the quality of the goods. The seller must still be cautious, however, about any statements made to induce a sale.

The seller is considered to have such a strong advantage over the buyer that the law imposes implied warranties. Responsibility for these warranties exists even when the seller does not make any representation as to the quality of the goods. Under the code, there are two implied warranties: (1) the implied warranty of merchantability, and (2) the implied warranty of fitness for a particular purpose.

The *implied warranty of merchantability* applies only to merchants dealing in goods of the kind sold. Six criteria for merchantability are set out in the code; they basically require that the goods must be of "fair, average quality."

The *implied warranty of fitness* for a particular purpose is based on (1) the seller's having reason to know any particular purpose for which the goods are needed and (2) the buyer's reliance on the seller's skill or judgment to select suitable goods. This warranty will be implied to any seller, whether or not he or she is a merchant. Unless the seller expressly excludes or modifies an implied warranty, it becomes a part of the sales contract by operation of law. Both implied warranties may be excluded through express language of disclaimer.

Agency and Partnership

Agency Relationship. When one person, the *agent,* is authorized to perform some transaction for the benefit of another, the *principal,* an agency relationship arises. No particular formalities are required to create an agency; it may or may not involve a contract. Either party may be a corporation.

The law of agency governs the relationship of master and servant and that of principal and agent. Agents may be distinguished from servants in that they represent the principal in business transactions, whereas servants, or employees, perform physical activities under the control of the master or employer. The distinction is important in that it will determine the principal's liability for the torts of the agent. An *independent contractor* is neither an agent nor an employee; she or he does specified work for the employer but determines her or his own methods. The employer is not liable for the torts of an independent contractor.

The principal is liable for the authorized acts of the agent. The agent has the *express authority* to do as the principal has directed and also has the *implied authority* to undertake acts reasonably necessary in performing the express purpose of the agency. Furthermore, an agent's authority includes that which has apparently been delegated to him or her. If a principal intentionally or negligently allows the agent to lead third persons to believe justifiably that the agent has authority to act in the name of the principal, the principal is responsible for these acts of the agent.

Ratification is the subsequent approval of the unauthorized act of one person claiming to represent another. It is the granting of authority after the act and relates back to the time at which the act was performed.

An agent has a *fiduciary duty,* one of utmost loyalty and good faith, to the principal. In addition to fiduciary duties, an agent must obey all instructions, act with skill and care, and maintain proper accountings of all business done in the principal's behalf.

The principal owes a duty to pay the agent any compensation due and must reimburse the agent for all expenditures made in the performance of the principal's business.

An agency may be terminated:

1. At the will of either party, though this may be a breach of contract
2. At the accomplishment of the purpose of the agency
3. By the terms of the agreement
4. By the death or insanity of either the principal or the agent
5. By impossibility of performance

Upon termination of an agency, the principal should personally notify all persons who have dealt with the agent.

General Partnership. A *partnership* is the association of two or more persons to conduct a business for profit. No formalities are required to form a partnership. In determining whether a partnership exists, the courts will look for evidence of sharing of profits and having a voice in the management of the business. A corporation may become a member in a partnership.

In the absence of agreements to the contrary,

1. Each partner has an equal voice in the management of the business.
2. Each partner shares equally in the profits and losses of the business.
3. A simple majority can make everyday business decisions (unanimity is required for fundamental changes).
4. A partner is not entitled to wages for services rendered to the partnership.
5. Every partner is an agent of the partnership for the purpose of its business.

The law imposes a *fiduciary relationship* between the members of a partnership; this is a duty of utmost loyalty and good faith in all dealings with the partnership. A partner, for instance, may not take a partnership opportunity for himself or herself. The law also imposes equal liability on all partners for contracts of the partnership. They all are liable jointly and severally for the torts of the partnership.

A partnership is not a legal entity; rather, it is merely an aggregation of its members. Partnerships, unlike corporations, have limited existence. Death or bankruptcy of a member will cause a partnership to dissolve automatically. In most states, the admission of a new partner and the withdrawal or retirement of a partner dissolves the partnership. A partner always has the power to dissolve a partnership, although doing so may amount to a breach of contract. A partner may ask a court to dissolve a partnership on the grounds that (1) there are irreconcilable differences; (2) it is impossible to carry on the business at a profit; (3) a partner suffers from some incapacity.

After dissolution, a partnership continues to exist for the sole purpose of its winding up and termination. It will normally be wound up by the partners themselves. If a partnership has been dissolved by court decree, a receiver will be appointed to wind up the business. As a general rule, each partner must give actual notice of the dissolution to all persons who have done business with the partnership.

Limited Partnership. A limited partnership is a hybrid between the general partnership and the corporation. State statutes provide for the limited liability of one or more partners so long as the limited partner's name does not appear in the firm name and the limited partner does not participate in the management or control of the business. The limited partner does have the right to examine the books and may demand an accounting of partnership affairs.

Real Property

Real property is land and that which is erected or growing upon it.

Interests in Real Property. The law recognizes different degrees of ownership interest in real property:

1. *Fee simple.* This form entitles the owner to the entire property for an indefinite period. The owner may sell the property or devise it to another in his or her will. However, the owner of a fee simple is limited in the use of the land by the state's power of eminent domain and by zoning and building ordinances.

2. *Life estates.* The owner of a fee simple may create a life estate in the property whereby the owner gives another the right to occupy, use, and enjoy the land so long as he or she lives. The life tenant is obligated to maintain the property in the condition received and may use the land's natural resources only as necessary to keep up the property. The life tenant must pay all taxes and continue any mortgage payments due on the property. Unless the terms of the life estate specify otherwise, the interest may be sold or mortgaged, but the purchaser or mortgagee will receive only that which the tenant has himself or herself—an interest which terminates when the tenant dies. A *life estate pour autre vie* is a life estate measured by the life of someone other than the tenant. A *reversion* occurs when, at the end of the life estate, the property returns to the original owner or his or her heirs. If the property is to go to someone other than the owner or heirs at the end of the life estate, it is called a *remainder.*

3. *Leasehold.* A leasehold is the right to occupy and possess property for a fixed term of years. Leases may be oral or written, but where the period of the lease is to be in excess of 1 year, the statute of frauds in most jurisdictions requires the lease to be written. An *estate for years* runs for a certain number of weeks, months, or years from a specific date; it has a definite beginning and end. The lease terminates automatically; no notice is required. A *periodic tenancy* is a lease which continues automatically for periods of weeks, months, or years until terminated by proper notice by either party. The notice required to terminate the periodic tenancy varies from state to state—it is usually 30 days. A *tenancy at will* covers no specific time period and can be terminated by either party giving proper notice.

4. *Easements.* An *easement* is the right to use the land of another for a particular purpose. Two examples are a right of way over land and the right to extend power lines over land. An easement may be acquired by an express writing or by implication, necessity, or prescription. A *license* is oral permission to use the land of another and may be revoked at any time.

Coownership of Real Property. Coownership falls into two classes.

1. *Tenancy in common.* A tenancy in common is created whenever two or more persons take an ownership interest in the same piece of property. Tenants in common need not own equal percentages of the property. When a tenant in common dies, the interest in the property passes to his or her heirs. In most states, property taken by two or more persons is presumed to be a tenancy in common.

2. *Joint tenancy.* A joint tenancy is property taken by the same instrument and at the same time by two or more persons who share equal rights to its use and enjoyment. The distinguishing characteristic of a joint tenancy is that the interest of one tenant, upon death, goes to the survivor or survivors. A *severence* occurs when one of the joint tenants conveys her or his interest to some third person. The third person becomes a tenant in common with the remaining joint tenants. *Tenants by the entirety* are joint tenants who are husband and wife; however, neither the husband nor the wife has the power to sever by his or her individual actions. *Community property* is a statutory type of ownership for husband and wife recognized in several states.

Commercial Paper

Article 3 of the Uniform Commercial Code covers instruments known as *commercial paper.* The code recognizes two major classes of commercial paper: drafts and notes.

Drafts. A draft is an order to pay which involves three parties: one party, the drawer, orders a second part, the drawee, to pay a third party, the payee. The ordinary bank check is the most popular type of draft. A check is a draft drawn on a bank payable upon demand. Other types of drafts are bank drafts, trade acceptances, and cashier's checks.

Notes. A note is a promise to pay which involves two parties: one party, the maker, promises to pay to the order of a second party, the payee or bearer, a stated sum of money on demand or at some future date. Types of notes are simple promissory notes, collateral notes, installment notes, and mortgage notes. Article 3 of the code treats certificates of deposit as though they were notes.

Negotiability. If an instrument satisfies certain strict requirements, it will become *negotiable* and obtain certain characteristics which distinguish it from simple contracts. Article 3 specifies the following requirements of negotiability:

1. The instrument must be in writing.
2. The instrument must be signed.
3. The instrument must contain a promise to pay, if a note, or an order to pay, if a check or a draft.
4. The promise or order must be unconditional.
5. The payment required must be of a definite amount.
6. The payment required must be in money only.
7. The instrument must contain no other promise or order.
8. The instrument must be payable on demand or at a definite time.
9. The instrument must be payable to order of bearer.

The holder of a negotiable instrument acquires distinct advantages over a person who is the mere assignee of a contract. If the holder is one of the original parties, the holder has certain procedural advantages, such as not having to prove consideration.

Negotiation is a special type of transfer whereby the transferee becomes a *holder*. The two requisites for a valid negotiation are delivery and endorsement. *Delivery* is the voluntary transfer of possession; *endorsement* is a writing on the back of an instrument.

A *holder* is a person in possession of an instrument payable to the person, to the person's order, or to the bearer. He or she need not have given value in obtaining the instrument and may or may not be a holder in due course. A holder may transfer or negotiate an instrument in his or her possession.

A *holder in due course* is a holder who also meets certain additional requirements, which are the following:

1. The holder must have given value.
2. The holder must have taken in good faith.
3. The holder must have taken without notice of claim or defense.
4. The holder must have taken without notice that the instrument is overdue.
5. The holder must have taken without notice that the instrument has been dishonored.

A holder in due course takes the instrument free from personal defenses that one party to the instrument may have against another party. However, the holder takes the instrument subject to any real defenses. *Real defenses* are those which go to the very existence of the contract or which render it null or void. The defenses which may be raised against a holder in due course are:

1. Infancy
2. Other incapacity, duress, or illegality
3. Misrepresentation of the nature or terms of the instrument
4. Discharge in insolvency proceedings
5. Any other discharge of which the holder has notice when taking the instrument

The holder who does not meet the qualifications of a holder in due course takes the instrument subject to any defense which could be asserted under the general law of contracts. Many states are limiting the ability of becoming a holder in due course of a consumer's notes or drafts.

Makers of notes and acceptors of drafts are primarily liable for making payment. All other parties, such as endorsers, are secondarily liable.

Bankruptcy

The Bankruptcy Code of 1978 became effective on October 1, 1979. In 1984, there are eight chapters; the chapter under which a case is filed depends upon the qualifications of the debtor and the relief sought.

Chapter 7, or "Liquidation" or "Straight Bankruptcy," may be initiated by either a voluntary petition filed by the debtor or an involuntary petition filed by a creditor or creditors of the debtor. When the petition in a voluntary proceeding is filed, it constitutes an *order of relief*. A debtor need not be insolvent to file a voluntary petition; that person may merely seek relief from debts he or she is unable to pay.

An involuntary petition is filed by creditors seeking the distribution of the debtor's assets. However, an involuntary petition under Chapter 7 may not be filed against farmers or nonprofit organizations. If there are fewer than 12 creditors, an involuntary petition may be filed by one creditor. If there are 12 or more creditors, an involuntary petition must be filed by at least three creditors. The creditor or creditors must have valid claims totaling at least $5000. To be forced into involuntary bankruptcy, the debtor must have given the creditor(s) *grounds for relief*. Typically, these grounds consist of not paying debts as they become due.

The filing of a voluntary or involuntary petition operates as an *automatic stay* of various actions that creditors may be taking against the debtor's property.

When the petition is filed, the *debtor's estate* must be determined. In general, it includes all the debtor's legal or equitable interests in property. A trustee will be appointed to take possession of the estate. A *trustee* has a wide variety of powers, including the operation of the debtor's business as well as the power to assume or reject any contract or lease of the debtor. He or she may also set aside any fraudulent transfer of the debtor's assets made within one year of filing. The trustee reviews the claims being made against the estate and objects to the court if any are improper. The trustee sells nonexempt property in a fashion which is in the best interest of the creditors.

A debtor is not required to relinquish all his or her property. He or she may retain property exempt under either state or federal law. Federal law allows an individual to exempt $7500 of the equity in a residence, up to $1200 interest in a motor vehicle, household goods and furnishings, and other items including clothing, some jewelry, and up to $7500 in any tools or books of the debtor's trade.

Having collected all the nonexempt and unsecured property, the trustee will reduce it to cash and distribute it according to a system of priorities.

Higher-ranking claims are paid in full before any payment of a lower-ranking claim. The priorities are (1) administrative expenses and fees, (2) up to $2000 per individual of unsecured wages of employees earned within 90 days before the filing of the petition, (3) contributions due to employee benefit plans, (4) claims up to $900 each for deposits made on undelivered goods or for services not performed; (5) taxes; and (6) all other unsecured creditors.

A bankrupt person who has honestly complied with the provision of the code is entitled to the discharge of his or her debts. A *discharge* relieves the bankrupt of most debts and permits a fresh start.

Debts that will not be discharged are those that arise from (1) taxes, (2) fraudulent behavior, (3) educational loans, and (4) alimony and child support.

A debtor may not file again under Chapter 7 within 6 years of discharge. A corporation may not have its debts discharged under Chapter 7.

As an alternative to Chapter 7 liquidation, a wage earner may enter into a voluntary plan to pay her or his debts under *Chapter 13*. Repayment must normally be within 3 years. Unsecured creditors need not consent to the plan, but they must receive at least what they would get under Chapter 7. Secured creditors must consent to the plan if it modifies their security interest. If the plan is confirmed and the debtor makes all payments promised under the plan, he or she will be discharged of the debts.

Chapter 11 allows businesses to reorganize their debts and remain in business. The petition may be voluntary or involuntary. A committee of creditors is appointed by the courts to represent the various types of creditors. The creditors' committee consults with the debtor, investigates his or her conduct, and participates in the formulation of the payment plan.

The plan must designate classes of claims and specify which classes of creditors are going to be "impaired" and which are not. The courts will confirm the plan if it is fair and equitable, even though all classes of creditors have not accepted it. This is the so-called *cram down* provision of the code.

See also Boards of directors, legal liability guidelines; Credit management; Environmental protection legislation; Equal employment opportunity, minorities and women; Government regulations, federal regulation of competition; Government regulation, Uniform Commercial Code; Labor legislation; Legal affairs, management of corporate; Ownership, legal forms of; Patents and valuable intangible rights; Tax management; Wages and hours legislation.

REFERENCES

Kimbrough, R.: *Summary of American Law,* Lawyers Cooperative Publishing, St. Paul. Minn., 1981.

Moore, Russel F.: *Law for Executives,* American Management Association, New York, 1982.

Shartel, B.: *Introduction to Our Legal System and How It Operates,* Legal Publications, University of Michigan Law School, Ann Arbor, 1980.

ARTHUR J. HAMILTON, *James Madison University*

Government Regulations: Federal Regulation of Competition

The United States federal government, state governments, and local governments have the power to regulate business activity. This power is exercised through the lawmaking power of the legislative branch, and it is enforced by various administrative agencies. The Congress has enacted legislation to protect competition, prevent monopolies, and outlaw price discrimination; this area of law is known as *antitrust law.* The federal acts which are the basis of antitrust law are the Sherman Act, the Clayton Act, the Robinson-Patman Act, and the Federal Trade Commission Act.

Restraint of trade refers to business practices which tend to lessen free competition. Certain business combinations, such as monopolies and cartels, tend to restrain trade. Price fixing among competitors also tends to do so. Antitrust law has made many such activities illegal, but not all restraints of trade are illegal.

The Sherman Act. In 1890, Congress, under its power to regulate interstate commerce, passed the Sherman Antitrust Act. The act had two main provisions: (1) contracts, combinations, and conspiracies in restraint of trade were made illegal, as were (2) monopolies and attempts to monopolize. Restraints within the purview of the act include contract combinations or conspiracies to fix prices, limit production, and divide markets or clients. Still other activities may be illegal if, in light of the particular transaction and surrounding economic circumstances, the activity is found to unreasonably restrain competition. A common example of a permissible contract in restraint of trade is the covenant not to compete found in many contracts for the sale of a business.

The Sherman Act provides for three types of sanctions: (1) fines not to exceed $50,000, imprisonment not to exceed 1 year, or both; (2) injunctions to prevent violations; and (3) civil remedies of treble damages plus costs and attorney's fees to persons injured by violations of the act.

The Clayton Act. Soon after passage of the Sherman Act, the need for a more specific law was realized. Congress enacted the Clayton Act in 1914 to dispel confusion in the minds of businesspeople subject to the antitrust laws. The Clayton Act was broader in scope than the Sherman Act and attempted to prevent the harm to competition before it was done. The Clayton Act contained three major provisions:

1. Section 2 of the act made price discrimination between different buyers of commodities illegal "where the effect of such discrimination may be substantially to lessen competition or tend to create a monopoly in any line of commerce." Price discrimination is not illegal, however, if it is due to (a) legitimate differences in grade, quality, or quantity; (b) differences in cost of transportation; or (c) a good faith attempt to meet the price of the competitor. This section was amended and strengthened by the Robinson-Patman Act (discussed below).

2. Section 3 applies to exclusive-dealing contracts and to tying contracts. It prohibits a seller or lessor of a highly desirable product from forcing a buyer to purchase or lease a less desirable product in order to obtain the highly desired item. Section 3 applies only to sales of commodities and not to sales of services.

3. Section 7 as amended prohibits the acquisition by a corporation of the stock of another corporation engaged in interstate or foreign commerce when the effect substantially lessens competition or tends to create a monopoly. As long as there exists a reasonable probability that the merger will have anticompetitive effects, it will be prohibited under Section 7. However, purchases merely for investment are not prohibited. Additionally, a person may not be a director of two competing corporations if either corporation has assets in excess of $1 million.

The Robinson-Patman Act. In 1936, Congress closed several loopholes in Section 2 of the Clayton Act through passage of the Robinson-Patman Act. It was designed to ensure equality of treatment to all buyers by a particular seller. It prohibits price discrimination in commodities of like grade and quality shipped in interstate commerce. To be in violation, the price discrimination must substantially lessen competition or tend to create a monopoly. Section 2 of the Clayton Act allowed sellers to discriminate if they could justify their action on the ground that their selling or transportation costs were greater for some buyers or that they were selling at a lower price to meet the price of competitors. These shortcomings of the earlier legislation were eliminated in part by the Robinson-Patman Act.

The act applies only to commodities; it does not cover services or radio and newspaper advertising, for example. The act is also limited to commodities of like grade and quality. It also prohibits discounts, rebates, and allowances that are tantamount to discrimination.

The price of a commodity within the meaning of the act is the delivered price. Before a sale can be ruled as discriminatory, it must be shown to have been relatively close in time to a nondiscriminatory sale. The relevant time period will depend on the nature of the commodity, that is, on whether it is perishable or seasonal in nature.

The act prohibits not only discrimination among customers, but also discriminatory pricing to eliminate a competitor.

The act does permit (1) price differentials which reflect differences in the cost of manufacturing, selling, and delivery that are caused by differences in methods or quantities involved; (2) price differentials made in good faith to meet the price of a competitor so long as the competitor is not guilty of price discrimination; and (3) price differentials because of the deterioration of goods or when the seller is closing out a particular line of goods.

Finally, a buyer who knowingly accepts a discriminatory price is in violation of the act.

The Federal Trade Commission Act. In 1914, the Federal Trade Commission was created through the Federal Trade Commission Act. The commission is charged with preventing "unfair methods of competition in commerce and unfair or deceptive acts or practices in commerce."

The commission has the responsibility of investigating both violations of antitrust laws and unfair or deceptive trade practices. The commission has the power to issue cease-and-desist orders and levy fines. However, private suits for treble damages are not allowed. A cease-and-desist order by the commission has the force of an injunction and becomes final unless appealed to the U.S. Court of Appeals.

See also Acquisitions and mergers; Advertising concepts; Brands and brand names; Economic concepts; Government regulations, business law; Government regulations, Uniform Commercial Code; International operations and management in multinational companies; Legal affairs, management of corporate; Patents and valuable intangible rights; Product and service pricing; Profits and profit making; Regulated industries, management of; Social responsibility of business.

REFERENCES

Bankruptcy Reform Act of 1978: Lewis Kruger, Patrick A. Murphy, and Arnold M. Quittner, cochairmen, Practicing Law Institute, New York, 1981.

MacLachlan, James Angell: *Handbook of the Law of Bankruptcy,* West Publishing, St. Paul, Minn., 1979.

Murphy, Patrick A.: *Creditors' Rights in Bankruptcy,* Shepard's/McGraw-Hill, Colorado Springs, Colo. 1980.

ARTHUR J. HAMILTON, *James Madison University*

Government Regulations, Uniform Commercial Code

The *Uniform Commercial Code* (UCC) is a unified, comprehensive set of laws describing legal guidelines and limits for all business transactions from the time raw materials are purchased until finished merchandise is sold to a consumer.

Generally considered one of the major legal developments of this century in the United States, and clearly the most important legislative measure in United States commerce, the code is an attempt to systematize and bring uniformity to the voluminous, enormously complicated, confusing, and often contradictory and inequitable body of 800-year-old common law and statute law of the various states. The code expressly replaces the following uniform acts: Uniform Negotiable Instrument Law, Uniform Sales Act, Uniform Trust Receipts Act, Uniform Warehouse Receipts Act, Uniform Stock Transfer Act, Uniform Conditional Sales Act, and Uniform Bills of Lading Act. Additionally, it repeals any acts regulating bank collections, bulk sales, chattel mortgages, conditional sales, factors' liens, farm storage of grain and similar acts, and assignment of accounts receivable.

Objectives. Specifically, the purposes of the code are to (1) simplify, clarify, and modernize the law governing commercial transactions; (2) permit expansion of commercial practices through custom, usage, and agreement of the parties; and (3) make uniform the laws among the states and legal jurisdictions. In addition, the code asserts two important new legal concepts: (1) the duty of *good faith* imposed on every contract of duty subject to the code, and (2) the concept that the ordinary rules of contract law frequently need modification when applied to sales transactions involving one or more merchants who are presumably possessed of special "knowledge and skill" in the area of the transaction.

Scope. The code covers the following areas of commercial laws: sales, commercial paper and banking, letters of credit, bulk sales, documents of title, investment securities, and secured transactions. In addition, it deals with related transactions, such as movement of merchandise from one point to another, storage of goods, financing of commercial transactions, payments for merchandise, and the deposit and collection of checks, notes, and drafts.

Principal Coverage

The UCC contains 10 articles. Article 1, General Provisions, deals with general principles and definitions. Article 2, Sales, is the longest and possibly most radical article. It deals with the formation and modification of contracts and with assignments, delegations, and obligations of parties in general, including payment, price, delivery, quantity, time of performance, warranties, title, risk of loss, and general remedies.

Consumer Protection. Consumers rely upon Article 2 for protection. As a result, persons injured by a defective product have three possible warranties under the Uniform Commercial Code through which they may recover damages. *Express warranties* by the seller are created by an affirmation of fact or promise made by the seller to the buyer and by any description of the goods or any sample or model which relates to the goods and becomes part of the basis of the bargain. The seller warrants that the goods conform to the affirmation or promise. UCC 2-313.

Goods delivered under an agreement made by a merchant in a given line of trade must be of a quality comparable to that generally acceptable in that line of trade under the description or other designation of the goods used in the agreement. Under 2-314, this stipulation is considered an *implied warranty of merchantability* or *usage of the trade.*

UCC 2-315 indicates that there is an *implied warranty that the goods shall be fit for a particular purpose* when the seller, at the time of contracting, has reason to know any particular purpose for which the goods are required and the buyer is relying on the seller's skill or judgment to select or furnish suitable goods.

Commercial Paper. Another important section of the UCC is Article 3. This article focuses upon commercial paper. The code mentions four types of negotiable instruments: (1) drafts, (2) checks, (3) notes, and (4) certificates of deposit. Checks and drafts serve as a temporary safe and as an efficient substitute for money. In the United States today, the great majority of business transactions are settled by check. Drafts and checks involve three parties.

Drafts are used mainly for financing the purchase of goods and for transferring credits from one community to another. A *check* operates as a conditional payment of the obligation for which it is given and becomes final only when it clears the bank on which it is drawn. The right to sue is revived on the original obligation if the check is dishonored (i.e., not paid by the drawee bank) or if the drawer orders the bank to stop payment. *Notes* and *certificates of deposit* involve only two parties. The *promissory note,* one person's written promise to pay a sum of money to another person at some future date, is used primarily as a means of credit extension. A *certificate of deposit* is defined as "an acknowledgment by a bank of receipt of money with an engagement to repay it." By balancing the interests of the debtor and the creditor, Article 3 seeks to reduce the risks assumed by transferors of commercial paper and to enhance its marketability. When the risk of loss to the purchaser of commercial paper is reduced, it becomes more marketable. Consequently, negotiable instruments carry a greater value than nonnegotiable instruments. The risk of loss is reduced by cutting off most defenses and by obligating the transferor of the instrument if the debtor does not pay the obligation when it becomes due.

Negotiable Instruments. Because a substantial difference in legal efforts may exist between negotiable and nonnegotiable instruments, Articles 3-105 through 3-111 require eight things for negotiability. They must (1) be in writing, (2) be signed by the maker or drawer, (3) contain a promise or order to pay, (4) establish the unconditional character of that promise or order, (5) specify payment in money; (6) specify payment of a sum certain, (7) specify payment on demand or at a definite time, and (8) specify payment to order or to bearer.

Holder In Due Course. If these requirements have been met, the person to whom the instrument has been transferred may hold a special position in law—that of holder in due course—if the person meets other requirements. Such an individual takes free of most defenses, such as fraud or lack of consideration and has more rights than the original transferor of the instrument to the holder.

According to Article 3-302 (1), to be a *holder in due course,* a holder (or possessor) must take the instrument (1) for value, (2) in good faith, and (3) without notice that it is overdue, that it has been dishonored, or that there is any defense against or claim to it on the part of any person.

For the protection of consumers, a major change in the holder-in-due-course rule has been made by the Federal Trade Commission. Until this change, the credit purchaser of goods who executed an installment instrument, yet who had a legitimate defense, was still required to pay the holder in due course (frequently a collection agency) in full and then to seek a separate action against the consumer. By the new regulation, holder-in-due-course status is denied to anyone who purchases certain types of commercial paper. The regulation therefore allows the maker or the drawer of the note or check with a valid defense to withhold payment.

Bank Collections. The tremendous number of checks handled by banks and the countrywide nature of the bank collection process require uniformity.

Article 4 attempts to address this need. Banks frequently deal with negotiable instruments. Therefore the rules governing negotiable instruments (Article 3), their transfer, and the contracts are subject to the provision of Article 4. However, Article 8 (Bonds and Investments) governs provisions in Article 4 in the event of conflict.

The provisions of Article 4 apply to items handled by banks for purposes of presentment, payment, and collection. Unless a contrary intent clearly appears, the status of a collecting bank is that of an agent or subagent for the owner of the item. This status continues until the settlement given by it for the item is, or becomes, final.

Letters of Credit. *Credit* or *letter of credit* means an engagement by a bank or other party made at a customer's request that the issuer will honor drafts or other demands for payment upon compliance with the conditions specified in the credit. The engagement must be a documentary draft or a documentary demand for payment. *Document* means any paper, including documents of title, security, invoice, certificate, nature of default, and the like. Article 5 deals with some, but not all, of the roles and concepts of letters of credit.

Bulk Transfers. Like Article 5, Article 6 has a limited application. It deals with bulk transfers. A *bulk transfer* is any transfer in bulk (but not in the ordinary course of the transferor's business) of a major part of the materials, supplies, merchandise, or other inventory. Article 6 attempts to prevent fraudulent conveyance and to reduce the bulk-sale risk by giving notice to the seller's creditors that a bulk transfer is about to be made. Creditors of the transferor holding claims based on transactions or events occurring before the bulk transfer may then act to protect their own interests.

Warehouse Receipts. Warehouse receipts, bills of lading, and other documents of title are the subject matter of Article 7 of the UCC. Although not applicable to interstate or foreign commerce, Article 7 does provide guidelines for documents used to distribute goods which are lost, missing, or subject to the claims of others.

Document of title includes bill of lading, dock warrant, dock receipt, warehouse receipt or order for the delivery of goods, and any other document which in the regular course of business or financing is treated as adequate evidence that the person possessing it is entitled to receive, hold, and dispose of the document and the goods it covers.

The *warehouse person,* engaged in the business of storing goods for hire, may issue negotiable and nonnegotiable warehouse receipts. A carrier that issues a bill of lading, whether negotiable or nonnegotiable, and a warehouseperson who issues a warehouse receipt must each exercise the degree of care in relation to the goods which a reasonably careful person would exercise under like circumstances.

To be a document of title, a document must purport to be issued by, or addressed to, a bank and propose to cover goods in the bank's possession which are either identified or tangible portions of an identified mass.

Investment Securities. The law of investment securities is embodied in Article 8 of the UCC. In 1977, this article was amended to more adequately address the needs of brokers and dealers under the federal securities law.

A *security*, whether certified or uncertified, is defined as an instrument issued in bearer or registered form, of the type commonly dealt in on a securities exchange; it is either one of a class or a series evidencing a share or other interest in property. Guidelines for the issuance, negotiation, purchase, and transfer of securities have been set forth by the drafters of Article 8. New sections on the exchangeability of securities and on statements of uncertificated securities are also included in this article.

Secured Transactions. Article 9 rewrites the law of secured transactions. It was amended in 1972 in response to the widespread demand for revision because of the growth in credit transactions involving personal property. The aim of this article is to provide a simple and unified structure within which the immense variety of present-day secured transactions can go forward with less cost and with greater certainty.

A *security interest* is defined as "an interest in personal property of fixtures which secures payment or performance of an obligation." The principle test as to whether Article 9 applies is whether the transaction is intended as security.

Impact

The Uniform Commercial Code is a culmination of rules and statutes concerning commercial paper, sales, and secured transactions in personal property. A detailed discussion of actual applications is impractical because of the variety of factual settings. The code is, however, a living document, not a final statement. Therein lies its vulnerability. Managers are advised to keep themselves well informed and to refer to the code and its changes for guidance as they proceed in the daily transactions of business.

See also Consumerism and consumer protection legislation; Government regulations, business law; Product liability.

REFERENCES

"The Code and Comments," *Selected Commercial States*, West Publishing, St. Paul, annually.

Stone, Bradford: *Uniform Commercial Code: Nutshell Series*, West Publishing, St. Paul. 1975.

White, James, J., and Robert Summers: *Uniform Commercial Code: Horn Book Series*, West Publishing, St. Paul, 1972.

Daphyne Saunders Thomas, *James Madison University*

Government Relations

Government relations cover a broad spectrum of intercourse between private business and nonprofit institutions on the one hand and federal, state, and local governments on the other. Relationships will be affected by the particular branch of government involved—legislative, executive, or judicial. There are also many reasons why corporations, universities, and other organizations wish to relate productively to a government. Their purposes are these: to obtain protection; to obtain financial assistance; to obtain information; to sell products or services; to get laws passed, altered, or defeated; to buy something; to obtain a contract or a grant; to seek judicial remedy; to establish or modify public policy; to obtain health services; and to obtain licenses or permits.

Relating to the Federal Government

Relationships to the federal government can be organized in accordance with its three branches: legislative, executive, and judicial.

Legislative Branch. Concepts and techniques for relating to legislatures apply equally to federal, state, and local legislatures. The main idea is to establish effective relationships with legislators (senators, members of the House, assembly members, delegates, aldermen, or whatever). These legislators are the citizens' legally elected representatives in the government. As such, they are required by law to look after the well-being, safety, and welfare of all citizens, corporations, and institutions. In doing so, they have a basic need to communicate with their constituents. To be effective, these communications can and should flow in both directions.

Lobbying. Lobbying is the direct communication by individuals, corporations, universities, associations, and the like, with legislators. Lobbying implies that the lobbying group takes the initiative and originates the communication with the express purpose of getting specific legislation (laws) passed, modified, or defeated to suit the needs or requirements of that group. Effective lobbying will influence a legislator to vote a certain way on a specific bill (proposed law).

Lobbying can take various forms—from simply writing letters or telephoning a legislator's office to the retention of a professional lobbyist. Typically—but not necessarily—professional lobbyists are attorneys with expertise in certain facets of the law. Former members of a legislature often make good lobbyists because they are personally acquainted with current members of the legislature and are in a good position to communicate with them and influence them on a given issue.

While the press is replete with reports of lobbyists who use illegal, unethical, and sometimes immoral techniques to influence legislators, these cases are the exception. Most successful lobbyists rely on facts, persuasion, and reason to accomplish their goals.

One of the most widely used lobbying techniques is for a firm to join a trade association. These associations are usually located in the Washington, D.C., area or in a state capital, and they represent the interests of a particular group of individuals or companies. Examples include the National Association of Manufacturers, the American Petroleum Institute, and the American Association of University Professors. The District of Columbia telephone directory lists more than eight pages of associations, most of which perform lobbying functions.

Lobbying is also useful in establishing or modifying public policy on certain issues, such as environment, energy, health, education, transportation, and defense. Public policy can also be shaped or modified by dialog with executive branch agencies and departments as well as with legislators.

Suggestions for Lobbying. There are many actions in lobbying that an organization or an individual can take, such as (1) defining the issues or policies you wish to resolve or champion; (2) joining the appropriate trade associations; (3) contacting your congressperson and senators to let them know of your existence and of your position on certain issues and/or policies; (4) making contributions to the political campaigns of the legislators whose help you seek; (5) discussing issues and policies with your trade associations and legislators at conventions and public or private meetings; and (6) asking for specific lobbying help from these trade associations and legislators when you perceive a need.

Executive Branch. There is often more interest in relating to an executive agency because this branch of government administers the laws passed by legislatures. The executive branch is also much larger and performs many more functions. It is worthwhile to explore some of its functions to see how a corporation, for example, can relate to the appropriate departments, agencies, and commissions of this branch to accomplish its objectives.

Protection. Much government protection is provided automatically through the U.S. Department of Defense, the Department of Justice, and the Federal Bureau of Investigation, and other law enforcement

agencies on the state and local levels. If additional or immediate protection is needed, a call to the local police department will initiate a request for the appropriate degree of protection.

Financial Assistance and Health Services. Corporations, institutions, and other organizations can seek financial assistance from the executive branch through loans, grants, and contracts. Loans can be obtained by contacting any one of several agencies. For example, small businesses can seek and obtain loans from the U.S. Small Business Administration. Organizations can seek loans for international trade from the U.S. Export-Import Bank. Farmers can request loans from the U.S. Department of Agriculture. Many other federal and state loan and grant programs are available to qualified individuals and organizations for a variety of needs. Following is a partial list of contacts:

Information Office
U.S. Small Business Administration, Washington, D.C.
(202) 653-6460 or 6156

Information Office
U.S. Export-Import Bank, Washington, D.C.
(202) 566-8864 or 8860

Information Office
U.S. Department of Agriculture, Washington, D.C.
(202) 447-7454 or 472-1388

Information Office
U.S. Department of Health and Human Services, Washington, D.C.
(202) 472-7453

Selling to the Government

Perhaps one of the greatest opportunities for businesses and institutions is to sell their goods and services to the government through contracts, grants, and purchase orders. (The federal government alone spends well over $100 billion annually to purchase goods and services.) Every government office, each department, agency, and commission has a procurement office that provides information on such things as:

1. Bidders' mailing lists (BML)
2. Opportunities to bid on contracts through:
   a. Invitations for bid (IFB)
   b. Requests for proposals (RFP)
3. How to submit unsolicited proposals for grants and contracts
4. Government requirements for goods, materials, commodities, and services

Outright grants of monies may be obtained for education, research, training, and the purchase of equipment. Government contracts are available to build hardware, perform research and development, perform studies and analyses, and provide personal services. Purchase orders are issued by the government for equipment, components, and materials of every imaginable type. The government advertises almost all its requirements and needs through the *Commerce Business Daily* (CBD), available by subscription through the U.S. Department of Commerce, (312) 353-2950. One must make personal contact, however, and sell his or her product, organization, or institution to be successful in the government market.

Techniques for selling to the government include normal industrial marketing methods, of course, but certain aspects of government procurement need special attention. It is not easy, for example, for an organization that has never sold its goods or services to the government to break into the market. While there are regulations which govern procurement policies and practices and which are designed to offer "equal opportunity to all bidders," the real world of government procurement is difficult to penetrate. Government officials, for example, often have preferred or well-known and proven sources of supply for the goods or services required. Often, these sources are in a position to—and will—define the requirements or specifications for the government officials in advance of the procurement.

Training in selling to the government is available through courses and seminars, and consultants can be retained to assist in (1) understanding the government marketplace, (2) planning to enter it, (3) developing marketing techniques and strategies for successfully penetrating it, (4) preparing competitive bids and proposals, and (5) following up after submission of bids and proposals. Such courses and seminars can teach a firm how to sell hardware (both off-the-shelf and developmental hardware), research and development services, analytical and study services, architectural and engineering services, social and economic services, and computer services to agencies such as the U.S. Department of Defense (DOD), National Aeronautics and Space Administration (NASA), U.S. Department of Energy (DOE), U.S. Environmental Protection Agency (EPA), U.S. Department of Transportation (DOT), U.S. Department of Health and Human Services (HHS), General Services Administration (GSA), and many others with budgets for contracts and grants for goods and services. It is important that you learn not only how the government buys, but also how it plans, programs, and budgets to make purchases of goods and services. That way, you can better organize to sell to the government, and can perform the market research necessary to be ready to sell. Market research requires information, and, fortunately, the government has much of it—readily available and at nominal cost (sometimes free).

Obtaining Information from the Government

The federal government is one of the largest storehouses of knowledge and information in the world, and much of it is free or available at nominal cost. Contacting the appropriate department or agency can yield information useful in many areas, such as research, market planning and analysis, market intelligence, production planning, and personnel planning.

Principal sources of federal government information include the Library of Congress, the National Technical Information Service (Department of Commerce), the Defense Technical Information Center (DOD), NASA's Scientific and Technical Information System, the *U.S. Government Purchasing and Sales Directory* (available from the U.S. Government Printing Office), Bidders' Lists, *Commerce Business Daily*, agency small business offices, Tri-Service Industry Information Centers (DOD), Department of Energy Technical Information Center, government owner patents (U.S. Patent Office), agency freedom-of-information offices, and the public information offices and libraries of each agency and department.

Important ways to gather this information include (1) getting on mailing lists, (2) subscribing to appropriate government publications (lists are available from the U.S. Government Printing Office), (3) employing consultants who know how to obtain required information quickly and efficiently, and, most important, (4) making direct contact with appropriate sources of information.

Licenses and Permits

Ways of applying for and receiving licenses and permits are defined by certain government procedures. Following these procedures, however, is a complex, time-consuming process. If one waits for the bureaucracy to take its course, considerable time may pass—months or even years. Techniques for expediting the process exist. Unfortunately, they are not defined by the bureaucracy; they require knowledge of procedures, people involved, and appropriate pressure points and the ability to influence and persuade these people. For example, obtaining a license to export a product or service (research and development services and other technical services often require licenses) usually includes the following steps:

1. Determine whether or not the product or service is militarily oriented. If it is military in nature,

its export is governed by the "International Traffic in Arms Regulations" (ITAR: 22CFR121-128), and an export license must be obtained from the State Department, Office of Munitions Control. If it is nonmilitary, its export may be governed by the Export Administration Act (Public Law 96-72), and an export license may be required from the Department of Commerce or International Trade Administration, depending on the commodity and the country to which it is to be exported.

2. Obtain the necessary forms to apply for the license.

3. Complete the forms.

4. Review the completed forms, checking for accuracy and completeness with an official of the State Department or Commerce Department (this will ensure that they are not returned for corrections or omissions, which can delay a license by weeks).

5. Determine the list of government officials (sometimes eight or more) who must review the license application.

6. Contact each of these officials and offer to answer any questions to keep the application moving toward final approval.

7. If necessary, hand-carry the application and supporting paperwork between offices (government internal mail can take weeks).

8. Be aware that the squeaky—yet tactful—wheel often gets the lubricant.

See also Associations, trade and professional; Government services; Patents and valuable intangible rights; Political action committees (PACs); Regulated industries, management of.

REFERENCES

Bradshaw, Thornton, and David Vogel, eds.: *Corporations and Their Critics,* McGraw-Hill, New York, 1981.

Daly, John Jay: "How to Tell Your Story to a Legislative Body," in Tracy D. Connors (ed.), *The Nonprofit Handbook,* McGraw-Hill, New York, 1980, chap. 8.

Key to Public Trust, The Business Roundtable, McGraw-Hill, New York, 1982.

PETER J. CANNON, *Cannon Associates*

Government Services

Government regulation of business has historically been indirect in the United States. Adam Smith asserted that government fostering of unhindered action of individuals, controlled only by competition, was the best means of increasing the wealth of a nation. Thus the role of government in the economic sphere has been historically limited in the United States to (1) maintaining a safe environment for business; (2) providing for judicial relief for common law and statutory wrongs inflicted upon business; and (3) providing certain public works and institutions. Government regulation of business is provided for by Article I, Section 8, of the Constitution, vesting in Congress the power "to regulate Commerce with foreign nations, among the several States, and with the Indian Tribes."

The nature of the role of government initially in the United States was that of protector of business. Therefore, early tariffs were designed to protect infant industry. Government provision of public works was limited. Fire departments were financed by private fees; toll roads were common. As society became more complex, government was looked to for more public works, and it undertook to provide services in areas where the risk or capital need was beyond the reasonable capability of the private sector.

Rather than assume the role of provider of public services and public works, the government developed the policy of providing direct and indirect subsidy to the private sector. The limited role of government as a protector and promoter of business is consistent with a long-held implicit consensus that private decision making is the best way to accomplish economic gain for society generally. With passage of the Employment Act of 1946, the increased roles and responsibility of government in shaping the direction of economic activity, however, became a recognized and accepted policy.

Thus the impact of government relations upon management decisions and policies is felt as a result of government's acting for the following aims:

1. To protect business.

2. To regulate to (*a*) maintain competition, (*b*) maintain health and safety, and (*c*) implement public policy.

3. Promote and subsidize by furnishing (*a*) information, (*b*) services, (*c*) financing, (*d*) insurance against various risks, (*e*) a source of supply, and (*f*) a source of sales. As a result, government relations have an impact daily on a firm's decision making.

Relations with Government

The Executive Branch. There are few restrictions on, or guides to, relations with the executive branch. The Federal Election Campaign Act Amendments of 1976 (2 USC 431) provide restrictions upon contributions to candidates, political parties, and political committees. In 2 USC 441a *et seq.,* restrictions applicable to specific groups, such as national banks and government contractors, are set forth.

Regulations by some executive agencies against conflicts of interest provide limitations upon employment by industry of former employees of these agencies when the position would involve work on projects directly related to the employee's previous duties.

Influencing general and specific policies of government is vital to major industries, companies, and associations. Many companies and industries maintain offices in Washington. While some of the activity of these offices may involve lobbying, an important aspect is their furnishing regular access to the executive branch. They do so by frequent communication with staff personnel in the agencies that may affect the specific company. Most government offices desire whatever information their industry constituency can provide to resolve mutual problems. The astute Washington representative makes regular visits to the appropriate agency even when there are no immediate problems facing the company. (See Associations, trade and professional.) The Department of Commerce is the advocate of industry and commerce within the Cabinet. The role of the Office of Management and Budget (OMB) is substantial in developing the executive department's approaches to economic and fiscal policy and in formulating the positions of the executive branch and the White House on legislation. Thus, the many Washington representatives seek to persuade staff of the OMB of the legitimacy of the company or industry position. Most representatives seek a continuing dialog.

The Legislative Branch. This arm of government requires that any person who seeks to influence legislation file reports disclosing financial expenditures. The influence upon specific legislation is a small part of lobbyists' activities. Stating company position, problems, and needs, and information exchange are the major functions of the lobbyist.

The Regulatory Agencies. The Administrative Procedure Act serves to insulate the commissioners and administrative law judges from *ex parte* attempts to influence the outcome of specific hearings. These hearings are quasijudicial in nature, and all presentations must be a matter of record. It is important and proper, however, for industry to provide information to aid the independent regulatory commission to reach policy directions or positions.

Federal Regulatory Commissions

The 1983–1984 *United States Government Manual* lists a great many agencies in addition to many boards, committees, commissions, and quasiofficial agencies, all of which operate to some extent independently of the executive branch. Many are rarely heard from, but a few have substantial impact upon practically all business in the nation. The principal agencies impacting upon business decision making are shown in Table G-1, as are some of the regulatory functions of these agencies. A substantial amount of industry and business regulation is performed by the executive departments. Their activities range from antitrust enforcement by the Department of Justice to regulation of packers and stockyards by the Department of Agriculture and from regulation by the Food and Drug Administration within the Department of Health and Human Services to requirements for statistical reporting by the Department of Commerce.

Government as a Source of Assistance

Government, today, is a major source of assistance to business. The business that does not utilize this assistance to the greatest extent practicable is being competitively disadvantaged. The Department of Commerce is the source of most assistance to business in the form of services and information. A number of agencies have grant programs which aid business. Most programs are administered by grants to state or local governments or to nonprofit organizations. Industry cooperation with grant recipients, such as universities, is encouraged by some agencies, among them the National Science Foundation.

Loans. Some representative sources of loans and their purposes are these:

1. The Agency for International Development grants loans to certain foreign countries for development projects. These projects often utilize American industry.

2. The Agricultural Stabilization and Conservation Service (within the Agriculture Department) grants crop loans through county offices.

3. The Overseas Private Investment Corporation provides for some direct loans for United States investors in overseas projects. Such loans range from $50,000 to $2 million and run from 5 to 20 years.

4. The Small Business Administration provides various types of loans to qualified small business concerns and to disaster victims (see the following subsection).

Most loan programs provide for guarantee of loans made by or through commercial lending institutions. Loan applications, under either a direct loan or a guaranteed loan program, are processed through the district or regional office of the involved agency.

Insurance. Various agencies insure against certain risks too substantial for industry itself to bear. In most instances the agency guarantees through usual commercial channels. For example,

1. The Small Business Administration reinsures or guarantees surety companies against the major

TABLE G-1 Regulatory Agencies and Commissions

Name of commission	Year of formation	Number of members	Purpose
TRANSPORTATION			
Interstate Commerce Commission	1887	11	To regulate interstate surface transportation, to approve routes, grant certification, and ensure that rates and services are fair and reasonable.
Civil Aeronautics Board	1938	5	To promote and regulate civil air transportation, and to approve rates, routes, and agreements involving air carriers.
Federal Maritime Commission	1961	5	To regulate waterborne foreign and domestic offshore shipping of the United States and to ensure financial responsibility for indemnification of passengers and for cleanup of oil spills
UTILITIES			
Federal Communications Commission	1934	7	To regulate interstate and foreign communications by radio, television, wire, and cable. The commission grants operating authority and approves interstate communication rates.
Federal Power Commission	1920	5	To regulate interstate aspects of electric power and natural gas to ensure reasonable rates and adequate supply
CONSUMER PROTECTION AND COMPETITION REGULATION			
Federal Trade Commission	1914	5	To promote fair competition in interstate commerce, to prevent false advertising and deceptive practices, and to ensure true credit cost disclosure.
Consumer Product Safety Commission	1972	5	To protect the public against unreasonable risks of injury from consumer products, to establish product safety standards, and to ban hazardous products.
EMPLOYMENT			
Equal Employment Opportunity Commission	1964	5	To investigate charges of employment discrimination and to bring actions before the appropriate federal district court.
National Labor Relations Board	1935	5	To investigate and settle labor disputes and to prevent unfair labor practices.
Occupational Safety and Health Review Administration	1970	3	To adjudicate cases from the Department of Labor respecting safety and health inspections.
ENVIRONMENT AND TECHNOLOGY			
Environmental Protection Agency	1970	Administrator	To abate and control pollution through standard setting and monitoring.
Energy Research and Development Administration	1974	Administrator	To consolidate federal activities relating to research and development on the various sources of energy, to achieve self-sufficiency in energy.
Federal Energy Administration	1974	Administrator	To ensure a sufficient supply of energy to the United States, to evaluate allocation, to plan storage and rationing.
National Aeronautics and Space Administration	1958	Administrator	To conduct research on space flight and exploration.
FINANCE AND INTERNATIONAL COMMERCE			
Commodity Futures Trading Commission	1974	5	To strengthen the regulation of trading in futures and all commodities traded on commodity exchanges, to protect market users from fraud and other abuses.
Export-Import Bank	1934	President of the bank	To grant loans and issue guarantees and insurance so that exportation may be undertaken without undue risk.
Federal Deposit Insurance Corporation	1933	Chairman	To promote confidence in banks and to provide insurance coverage for bank deposits.
Securities and Exchange Commission	1934	5	To protect investors and the financial community against wrongful practices in the securities markets. The SEC relies on disclosure requirements to, as well as regulation of, securities dealers.
U.S. International Trade Commission (formerly U.S. Tariff Commission)	1916	6	To provide studies and recommendations concerning international trade and tariffs to the President, Congress, and other government agencies; to conduct investigations especially with respect to import relief for domestic industry and antidumping.

portion of losses on construction bonds issued for minority-owned businesses.

2. The Export-Import Bank guarantees repayment to commercial banks which finance medium-term transactions for exports.

3. The Overseas Private Investment Corporation insures U.S. lenders against both commercial and political risks by guaranteeing payment of principal and interest.

In addition to the indirect insurance, direct insurance is provided by the above agencies as well as others, such as the Federal Crop Insurance Corporation (within the Department of Agriculture), which insures crops against unavoidable losses. For domestic programs, applications are made through the agency's local offices. For international programs, application is made through the Washington office of the agency.

The consensus of most observers is that borrowers should first pursue all regular commercial sources of financing before seeking federal loans. This view prevails for several reasons:

1. In most instances the lending or guaranteeing agency requires that the applicant demonstrate nonavailability of customary commercial sources of financing.

2. Substantial time is involved in the processing of applications by a government agency.

3. The government agency frequently requires personal guarantees from the borrower even though the loan is for business purposes.

Management and Research Assistance. The major source of government assistance to the business entity is found in the Department of Commerce. The department states that its purpose is to encourage, serve, and promote the nation's economic development and encourage the competitive, free enterprise system. The department is a source of substantial aid and information. It is the first place to which business decision makers might look for market data. The Domestic and International Business Administration (DIABA) maintains field offices in over three dozen cities in the United States. It provides data on export opportunities, production, pricing, materials availability, and a myriad of other things. In addition, the department conducts other programs of aid to business. The National Bureau of Standards, the Economic Development Administration, the National Technical Information Service, the Patent and Trademark Office, the Bureau of the Census, the Office of Minority Business Enterprise, and the Economic Development Administration, all have programs of assistance to business by way of either information, research data, or financial aid.

The Small Business Administration provides financial assistance to small businesses through guaranteed direct or lender-participation loans. It also provides financial assistance to and regulation of small business investment companies (SBICs) and grants licenses (minority enterprise SBICs). In addition, it gives management assistance through conferences, workshops, publications, and courses. It maintains 10 regional and more than 80 local offices. (*See* Small Business Administration.)

Government as a Customer

The government is the largest single customer of business in the United States. The two agencies through which most procurement takes place are the General Services Administration (GSA) and the Department of Defense. Procurement for the nonmilitary agencies is subject to provisions of the Federal Procurement Regulation. Military procurement is covered by the Armed Service Procurement Regulation. Within the General Services Administration, the Federal Supply Service is the buying agent for standard or off-the-shelf items used by all government agencies.

The GSA also maintains business service centers in 10 major cities. These centers provide guidance to business interested in selling to or buying from the government. Another source of information is the *Commerce Business Daily* published by the Department of Commerce. In addition to requesting to be placed on the GSA bidders' list, one may ask to be placed on the bidders' list of other agencies which procure for government simply by writing to the Director of Procurement for the agency.

The General Accounting Office (GAO) is the congressional watchdog over the integrity of federal expenditures and procurement practices. For an unsuccessful bidder on a government contract, a protest to the GAO is one form of recourse.

Meaningful Relations

Any business of any size finds itself faced with the need to file significant numbers of reports with various federal agencies. These range from annual reports to the Securities and Exchange Commission and Internal Revenue Service to personnel practice reports. There is always the question of how much information one should voluntarily provide to a regulatory body which might eventually invoke sanctions upon one's business activities. Answers to this question are varied.

The channels of communication to government agencies are opened more widely than is generally recognized, both formally and informally. With respect to formal channels, for example, on antitrust or trade practices, both the Federal Trade Commission and the Department of Justice will render advisory opinions to guide business in advance of deciding upon a course of action. The IRS provides opinions concerning tax treatment of various transactions. These are obtained by request for a tax ruling. Informal channels are provided by trade associations and through one's representative in Congress. Many businesses fail to utilize fully the resources to be found in the offices of their congressional representatives or senators. The administrative or legislative aide in a Capitol Hill office is quite often a great source of information for the business decision maker.

There has been considerable discussion of the encroachment of government agencies upon business freedom in decision making. Frequently, there are moves to reduce the role of government, to deregulate or partially deregulate the regulated industries, and to revise antitrust laws either by repeal or by exemptions. Regardless of the ebb and flow of criticism of the governmental role in the management of economic enterprise, it is a fact of life that government will continue to have a meaningful role as a regulator, as a partner, or as an adversary.

See also Government relations; Markets, government; Public administration; Small Business Administration; Tax management.

REFERENCES

Katz, Robert N.: "Business Impact upon Regulatory Agencies," *California Management Review*, Summer 1974, pp. 102–108.

United States Government: *The Budget of the U.S. Government*, U.S. Government Printing Office, Washington, D.C., annually.

————. *The United States Government Manual*, U.S. Government Printing Office, Washington, D.C., annually.

Wiedenbaum, Murray: *Business, Government and the Public*, Prentice-Hall, Englewood Cliffs, N.J., 1977.

ROBERT N. KATZ, *Attorney-at-Law*

Grants Management

Research and development expenditures in the United States reached an estimated level of $87 billion in 1983, as reported by the National Science Board (NSB). The report stated that about half the research conducted in this nation is funded by the federal government. The study found that industry performed most research and development (R&D) accounting for an estimated 74 percent of all R&D expenditures in 1983. The emphasis in industrial research and development is on development. Nearly 50 percent of all basic research expenditures in the United States is conducted by colleges and universities, the report points out.

There is a growing trend of cooperative projects between industry and universities to solve the problems which require basic research discoveries, applied research, and the development of new products.

Federal agencies, such as the Department of Defense research offices, the Department of Health and Human Services, the National Institutes of Health, the National Aeronautics and Space Administration, and the National Science Foundation are major sources of support for grants. The national laboratories, such as Argonne, Oak Ridge, and Brookhaven, will provide greater support for sponsored programs than in the past.

Private foundations play a key role in supporting areas that do not receive attention from federal programs.

The principal organizations involved in funding and conducting research and development are the federal government, government laboratories, state governments, foundations, colleges and universities, nonprofit institutes, and profit corporations.

Grant proposal preparation is an act of persuasive communication to convey the ideas and plans of a researcher to a prospective sponsor. The grant proposal is simply the method employed to get the researcher and the sponsors of the research together.

Researchers often confuse the difficulty of preparing the proposals with the importance of the proposal itself. It is true that the funding decision—the facilitation and the very life of the research—may be based solely on this document, because it is the main means of communication. On the other hand, writing proposals does not require unusual skills, but some people are deterred because of the false belief that it does.

In preparing proposals, whether for research, development, or training programs, the most advisable narrative approach is direct, explicit, and comprehensive. The only way to master this communication style is through practice, and the basic rule is to present the case for support in a manner that would win your support if you were considering the proposal for funding.

Development of Grant Proposals

The submission of a proposal, if it is to be acceptable to a sponsor, will be the culmination of a well-planned process. The original idea of the proposer initiates the process. The formulation of a comprehensive strategy develops as the prospective proposer draws upon experience, reviews the professional literature, confers with colleagues, and investigates potential sponsors.

Investigating a potential sponsor thoroughly is wise strategy: a disinterested sponsor will not accept any proposal, well written or not. When preparing objectives and procedures of the proposal, the writer should be cognizant of the interests of a potential sponsor. The proposer should not, however, feel that the original thought or plan for research has been compromised. Funding agencies usually concentrate their resources in only a few areas, a fact that also warrants consideration in locating potential sponsors.

When the idea is fully crystallized, the composition of the written proposal is begun. The proposer usually works alone on the first draft.

The proposal should demonstrate a chain of reasoning and logic. Clarity of expression is essential. To communicate with both specialists and nonspecialists, the use of jargon or highly technical terms should be avoided when possible. If special terminology is necessary to present a complete, accurate picture of the activity to be funded, an explanation of each term should be included.

The written proposal, when submitted, must convince the reviewers that:

1. The project is appropriate for support by the sponsor considering the proposal. The relevance of the project to the sponsor's interest should be made explicit in the narrative.

2. The proposed activity is worthy of investigation. Its importance must be compellingly presented.

3. The proposed activity is likely to succeed. The proposal reflects the writer's plan for sound, cost-efficient procedures.

4. The author is well qualified to conduct the proposed activity. Bear in mind that the proposal permits the reviewers to judge the writer's ability to perform the specified activities and attain the proposal's objectives.

Contents of a Grant Proposal

An effective proposal, in addition to being clear and persuasive, must achieve the fine balance of detail and brevity. The basic questions of who, why, what, how, how long it will take, and how much it will cost must be answered in a businesslike fashion. Since most funding organizations seek about the same kinds of information in judging projects, a typical proposal will include the following:

Abstract. The abstract paraphrases the objectives and procedure. Although it appears first in the proposal, it is the last section to be written since it summarizes the contents. Because of time limitations, many reviewers read only the abstract.

Introduction. The introduction briefly states the qualifications and the pertinent experience of the staff which will undertake this project. It also describes the available facilities which might be used in the research. On some projects, it may be appropriate to include the consulting services of an established researcher to enhance the chances of obtaining a grant.

Problem Statement. This statement provides the justification for the project and its significance for the field. Funding agencies and organizations are usually interested in having a wide impact and are, therefore, more receptive to studies that have implications beyond the local scene.

Objectives. The objectives are what the researcher plans to accomplish. The expected outcomes of the project should be specifically stated and feasible. Objectives should relate clearly to the problem statement and should be listed in order of importance.

Procedures. This section outlines how the project will be organized and how the proposed objectives will be accomplished. A one-paragraph overview of the procedure section is helpful to the reviewer. The procedure description should include specific information on population and sample, design, and data and instrumentation. This section is especially important since it typically provides the primary basis for evaluating the proposal.

Analysis. The analysis will indicate the methods which will be used to determine how completely the objectives will be satisfied. A description of the method for obtaining evidence for evaluating each objective is essential.

Timetable. This schedule lists in chronological order the length of time to be employed for each major aspect of the study. The timetable contributes not only to the clarity of the proposal but also to the credibility of an author who has the knowledge to guard against possible pitfalls.

Budget. The budget simply states how much the project will cost. It is a detailed breakdown of the operational expenses. The more clearly the project is described and the more precisely the time schedule is prepared, the easier the development of an accurate budget.

Evaluation of Grant Proposals

The competition for grants makes it important that the proposal submitted be superior in content, style, format, and appearance. The analysis is based solely on what is on paper. Time must be allowed for the document to be critically reviewed by knowledgeable persons before the sponsor's deadline.

Proposal reviewers look for clarity and specific details. Before being submitted, the proposal should be compared with the following checklist of details in content and form:

1. Does the title of the proposal state clearly the purpose of the project in 10 to 20 words?

2. Is the proposal written appropriately for the reviewing audience: peer review, in-house review, or a combination of the two?

3. Does the organization and structure of the proposal follow the specifications of the sponsor?

4. Is the organization of the proposal unified and coherent?

5. Are the objectives realistic within the project's time limitations and the budget requested?

6. Does the proposal deal with as many specifics as possible without the use of broad generalities?

7. Does the abstract summarize the main body of the proposal, including the major objective and an overview of the plan of action?

8. Are there any spelling or grammatical errors within the proposal?

The extra time spent in making the proposal clear, concise, and specific and in checking for errors of any type will significantly increase the chances of the proposal's being accepted.

Grant proposal writers can always learn from experience. In all cases, whether the proposal is accepted or denied, a critique of it should be requested from the potential sponsor. Projects are often approved on their second, or even third, submission. The reviewing panel's evaluation of strengths and weaknesses of the proposal are helpful in developing success as a proposal writer.

Project Management

When a grant proposal is approved, the project director incurs the responsibility for satisfactory performance of the work for which funds are provided. The award document should be studied thoroughly, since the director is ultimately responsible for the total compliance of the project. During the operational phase of the grant, the project director will authorize all expenditures, including salary allocations for personnel on the project.

Initiating the Project. The project director is reminded that sponsors have different restrictions. It is therefore recommended that the director become familiar with the specific agency guidelines and the terms and conditions of the contract. A critique of the proposal from the agency should be requested immediately for any suggested improvements or changes in the project.

Financial Administration. All operating expenditures charged to the project account must be for items required solely to accomplish the purpose of the award and should be based on the budget as accepted by the sponsor. Personnel salaried by grant funds should be informed in writing, prior to commencement of employment, that the employment will cease with the expiration of the grant funds. Sometimes it is necessary to revise the way project funds are to be spent, to increase the time duration of the project in order to complete the work or to change personnel. Different sponsors have differing policies or rules about what changes can be made in the budget without sponsor approval.

Establishing a Budget. The budget *must* be established prior to any expenditure of grant or contract funds. It is the responsibility of the project director to initiate the appropriate documents of all funds for personnel and nonpersonnel expenditures.

Accounting and Control. It is essential that the project director review a monthly financial statement which reflects all transactions charged to the project account during the period and which provides a cumulative summary of expenses incurred from the time of the award. As a general rule, a sponsoring agency requires a regular report of expenditures.

Conducting the Project. The project director must be familiar with the general administrative requirements imposed by the funding agency when awarding the grant. The terms of the grant may govern all expenditures charged to the project, including costs of travel, supplies, equipment, consultant fees, and computer time. Research with human subjects and animals must comply with specific federal regulations.

Submitting Periodic Reports. The preparation and submission of progress and technical reports to meet the sponsor's time requirement are major responsibilities of the project director. If financial progress reports are not prepared by the director, they should be routed through him or her for review and approval prior to submission to the sponsoring agency. Prompt compliance with the requirements of the grant for subject matter and financial reporting affects not only the individual's chances of further support but also those of any colleagues who may be applying to the same agency for support. A number of agencies place primary emphasis on having publications appear in refereed journals, and they want very brief technical reports with reprints of publications forwarded to the agency project manager.

Closing the Project. This is an important step in conducting any sponsored activity. At the completion of a project, the project director should make sure that all final technical, financial, patent, and copyright reports required by the sponsor are completed as soon as practicable. Care must be taken to be sure that no obligations are made against a grant beyond the closing date.

See also Contracts management; Program planning and implementation; Project management; Public administration; Research and development management.

REFERENCES

Hall, Mary: *Developing Skills in Proposal Writing,* 2d ed., Continuing Education Publications, Portland, Ore., 1977.

Smith, C. W., and E. W. Skjei: *Getting Grants,* Harper & Row, New York, 1980.

White, V. P.: *Grants: How to Find Out about Them and What to Do Next,* Plenum Press, New York, 1975.

WILLIAM O. HALL JR., *James Madison University*

Health, Mental

This entry describes the symptoms of emotional stress and distress, their impact upon the work organization, and the strategies employed to prevent, abort, or ameliorate them. It views occupational stress in the context of people's continuous efforts to maintain their psychological equilibrium by balancing the forces which impinge upon them from within and without. When the "executive" function of the personality fails in the balancing-stabilizing process, the ensuing disease and distress are labeled *mental illness.* Executives at all levels of the organization must understand the process of change and the psychology of motivation if they are to perform the crucial managerial tasks of leading, motivating, and integrating human resources toward achieving mutual purpose. This understanding will help channel policies, goals, and decisions toward managing the stress of individual and organizational change.

The Meaning of Work

Work is a vehicle through which one maintains contact and interaction with the human physical environment. It facilitates a productive expression of innermost drives and deep aspirations. To the matrix of work a person brings a lifetime of experience with its attendant attitudes, expectations, and modes of behaving. In short, people enter the workaday world carrying their psychological baggage with them. The shift of focus from the economic to the psychological model of motivation implies that work serves different purposes for different people, as each "marches to a different drummer," and is a major device for maintaining psychological balance.

On Balancing

"What makes people tick?" They do not—tick, that is—they feel! All strive to maximize pleasure and minimize pain. To reach these goals, one must manage the feelings—love, hate, fear, dependency, and self-esteem—arising from the interfaces between one's desires and aspirations; reality's imperatives; societal and family rules, values, and expectations; and one's standards and principles. Normal behavior is a compromise between these competing forces within and without and requires constant balancing; this is the executive function of the personality.

The executive of the personality utilizes the functions of perception, thinking, memory, calculation, concentration, judgment, and planning to organize the intellectual and emotional spheres of life. We are most familiar with this function through its interface with reality where rational problem solving supposedly predominates. When rational thinking delays gratification of present desires in the interest of more effective long-term adaptation to reality, the personality is functioning on the *reality principle*. This is a difficult mode to maintain because there exist the buried remnants of unsolved and unresolved development tasks of childhood which incessantly press for time in conscious awareness, threatening to upset the delicate balance. The executive function must expend considerable energy in maintaining a constant vigil and in keeping out of awareness the painful skeletons in one's psychological closet. To complicate matters further, external events can, and often do, activate or escalate these buried emotional conflicts which are latent in all of us. Giving these conflicts such force are the powerful feelings, forged in childhood, which accompany them. These feelings can color our perceptions and result in thinking and behavior more appropriate to yesteryear. What distinguishes the emotionally disordered person from the average one is not so much the presence of imbalance per se, as is the tipping of the psychological scales toward repetitive constellations of maladaptive modes for managing stress or exaggerations of normally occurring responses. To a greater or lesser degree, everyone at one time or another is "off balance."

Signals. The executive function manages stress via its own early warning system linked to a variety of mental mechanisms designed either to channel, divert, contain, or reverse the two major drives of affectionate attachment on the one hand and assertive mastery and self-preservation on the other. The signaling system scans the internal and external environments for signs of danger and sounds an "audible" alarm—*fear,* when the threat is external and known—and a silent alarm when forbidden impulses from the drives or painful memories of early conflict threaten to surface. Fear provokes a constellation of physiological responses which prepares one for fight or flight. The silent alarm initiates one or several unconscious mechanisms, each having different consequences and import for the balancing process. For most of us most of the time, no blips appear on our psychological radar; when they do, defenses are initiated. If defenses prove inadequate at a given time, resulting in the imminent eruption of buried conflict and feelings, a general alarm is signaled—*anxiety.*

Defenses. A cardinal principle of the Oriental martial arts and of the science of conservation is to channel a potentially destructive force into constructive outlets. This is also the most constructive and efficient means of managing primitive impulses: channeling them into problem solving—*sublimation.* When this does not occur, the executive function contains impulses and memories through the process of "forgetting"—*repression.* In moderation, repression maintains a defense against internal threat with no difficulty; when abused, spontaneity of feelings is lost, and psychosomatic symptoms may appear in susceptible persons. Diverting feelings and impulses to alternative targets results in scapegoating or "kicking the cat," while reversing the impulse onto oneself can produce self-condemnation, self-punishment, accidents, or even suicide at the extreme. These latter modes of maintaining psychological balance along with the excessive application of repression are inefficient uses of energy and suggest the magnitude of the forces that the executive function is dealing with.

Defenses also ward off a special form of anxiety—*guilt.* This painful feeling arises from a part of the personality closely allied to the executive function, the censor-taskmaster.

The Censor-Taskmaster. This psychological "structure" is the repository of the moral and spiritual values of one's culture, the rules and regulations from family, and the "mind's-eye" attitudes toward oneself which are in part acquired from the reflected appraisal of others. Earlier, the mention of aspirations referred not only to one's explicit and acknowledged goals but also to that inner hidden taskmaster that drums out a measured beat, chastising us with pangs of guilt for errors of omission and commission alike. Each of us takes the measure of the distance between the way we perceive ourselves—our self-image—and the way we feel we ideally ought to be—our future best. The greater that distance, the lower is the self-esteem; the lower the self-esteem, the greater the incidence of illness. One strives toward one's future best along a road marked by the restraints and constraints of internalized ethics and values of parents and significant others that are grafted onto one's own personality. In order to understand the psychology of motivation, one must appreciate that the most vital motivating force for any human being is that person's insistent and persistent striving to attain the ideal self—one's future best. Often one perceives only dimly, if at all, the tune to which one marches.

Change and Loss. In addition to losing control of buried conflicts and feelings, and censure for running afoul of the "dos" and "don'ts," a major pervasive threat from within is the process of aging. It limits the rate at which new information can be acquired and dampens energy levels. One tends to become more inflexible in coping behavior and also less innovative. The greater the inflexibility, the greater the potential for becoming and remaining obsolete with its resulting lowered self-esteem. Lowered self-esteem makes one overly sensitive to rejection and defeat with an attendant unwillingness to take risks. Learning requires that we risk failure; failure to learn produces obsolescence—the cycle is complete.

We all have emotional conflicts which can be activated by an environmental event. The common denominator in most occupational stress is *change.* In this regard, Levinson's three axioms are pertinent: All change involves loss—"promotion, transfer, demotion, reorganization, merger, retirement, and most other managerial actions produce change"; losses in general, and particularly those which are long-standing and accompanied by feelings of hopelessness, often trigger significant illness which may be life-threatening; and last, people will try to compensate for their losses and can be aided in this process by management to the benefit of the organization.

Loss. People insistently and persistently minimize their attachments to faces, places, things and ways of thinking and doing. The losses of affection, supportive milieu, information networks, and of being "on top" of one's world are often the consequences of moving, career changes, and the severing of close work relationships. Loss requires a process of grieving before old attachments can be relinquished and new ones made. Appreciation of this process is essential to the management of loss and the stress of change.

Off Balance

Normal psychological growth is a continuous process of conflict resolution. One's personality is distinguished by the repertoire of methods employed. These methods apply to threats in the real world and to the ways we deal with buried, unresolved early conflicts and those aspects of current reality which threaten to uncover them. When the response to stress is so severe or frequent as to be disruptive, it is called a *symptom;* it can be present as feelings, behavior, or bodily dysfunction. In all instances, the capacity to love and/or work is impaired.

The executive must be concerned with the task at hand and most hold a worker accountable for resolving behavior that interferes with work; referral to a professional may be indicated.

Fear-Anxiety Response. Being white as a ghost, sweating bullets, having butterflies in the stomach, the runs, nervousness and heart palpitations—all describe the body's expression of fear or anxiety. When severe, concentration and overall intellectual efficiency are impaired; if mild, performance may be improved. When this response occurs in the absence of a palpable source of danger, we can infer the presence of unconscious conflict. In the milder cases

executives can help by calling the sufferer's attention to the events which preceded the onset of the distress and by facilitating discussion; it is always of some comfort to learn that one's emotional reactions are not unique.

When the severity of fear-anxiety reaches a level that is grossly disorganizing—*panic*—professional help should be sought through the organization's medical department or private sources. Under these circumstances the superior should take the initiative.

Sometimes, fear-anxiety is so predominant over time and situation that it is part of the character; persons with this syndrome are called "high-strung." More complex are symptoms of irrational fear and avoidance of experiences and things which have a neutral tone for most people—animals, heights, open spaces, elevators, etc. Professional help is indicated when the phobia limits the accomplishment of the task or becomes unacceptable to the sufferer.

Organizational Impact. The exercise of power inherent in executive functioning militates against being affectionately regarded. Those who are overly anxious about a loss in popularity avoid the use of power in order to please, thereby subverting their authority and position and creating further anxiety.

The anxiety of not being "on top" or in control of one's job results from responsibility-without-authority and not knowing what one is supposed to do, how it is to be done, or how one is performing—*role ambiguity.* This anxiety may lead to anger, withdrawal, or both.

Executive Action. Efforts should promote collaborative planning to reduce fear of the unknown; make problem solving and the task the competitive focus instead of internecine rivalry; initiate and maintain contact with subordinates to support them and to define job boundaries, and provide time daily to become aware of feelings and to talk them out.

Depressive Response. Sadness, dejection, pessimism, and loss of energy, interest, appetite, and sleep are all part of this most common of psychological symptoms. Actual or threatened loss underlies depression; loss is the "flip side" of attachment. When depression is of such severity and duration as to preclude involvement in work or other everyday activities of living, professional assistance is mandatory. This help is imperative if the person voices suicidal intent or, more seriously, has a plan and the means at hand to execute it. If the sufferer cries, allow this release by waiting patiently; this response communicates acceptance and understanding.

More commonly, we note individuals who consistently become angry with themselves over minor errors. One can infer that they hold themselves to very strict inner standards and suffer guilt and self-recrimination when they do not meet them. Minor events with major symbolic meaning can precipitate symptoms. One can help by lending a sympathetic ear, telling of one's own "goofs," or making contact with an outstretched arm; such efforts will often relieve some of the immediate burdens imposed by conscience. To be avoided is the tendency to prescribe "vacations" for depressed people; guilt is increased because they do not feel deserving. Exaggerated praise also increases guilt for the same reason; praise in moderation gives the approval sought and a sense of earned recognition.

The strict standards, high expectations, and strivings for perfection also make for very good employees and executives; one's strengths can often be one's point of vulnerability.

Organizational Impact. Many of even the most successful executives have feelings of inadequacy. This ubiquitous feeling can handicap a career if it leads to a paralyzing doubt of one's ability to assume greater responsibility. Also, a sense that one is in an occupational cul-de-sac is common in early middle age and may lead to compulsive competitive activities to assuage self-doubt. Such digressions prevent a necessary midlife reappraisal of goals.

When self-doubt turns to guilt and the need to expiate it, one may seek punishment via accidents, performance failure, aggression-provoking behavior, or behavior that invites imprisonment. When organizations act in ways that violate the consciences of workers, expiation may take the form of "leaks" to consumer or government agencies.

Executive Action. This solution requires an awareness of the prevalence of self-doubt and, if indicated, discussion of an alternative career path with a person versed in that alternative. If, after consulting with vocational guidance experts, talking with a trusted friend or spouse, and developing a course of action, one is still plagued by doubt, professional help should be sought.

Hostility Responses. A fearful, cornered animal will fight. A wild-animal trainer maintains a critical distance between self and animal in order to effect fearful retreat or compliance, knowing that "trespass" will invite attack. When one feels that one's turf or boundaries have been invaded or threatened, fear is evoked and anger follows. Note that although two feelings are present, overt behavior may express either or both of them.

The tendency to ascribe to others what one does not want to acknowledge in oneself is universal. In the extreme, some deal with their underlying feelings of helplessness and low self-esteem by attributing to others persecutory intent and responsibility for failure while maintaining for themselves a grossly distorted image of their own self-importance and omnipotence. Psychiatric intervention is mandatory in these cases and should be sought also when there is constant hostility in the absence of provocation.

Organizational Impact. People are most threatened by the possibility of losing control of their feelings, autonomy, power, and self-esteem. Such loss may result from change; rivalry with superiors, peers, or subordinates; increased responsibility; role ambiguity; and conflicting superiors. Anger often ensues in the forms of hostile withdrawal, irritability, or tension, becoming a "workaholic" to expend feelings, channeling the anger into productive competition, or boss-induced destructive intraorganizational rivalry expressed as defensiveness, refusal to communicate, guarding of territory, and fighting. At times, anger is staged to manipulate others or is displaced onto innocent, helpless substitute targets via scapegoating.

Executive Action. Be aware of your flash points and responses. Delay expression of your anger to avoid "shooting from the hip"; ask yourself, "What am I afraid of? What or who hurt my feelings?"

If you or your subordinates become the objects of displaced feelings, do not fire back, placate, or withdraw. If the other person seems embarrassed by the outburst, cushion the person's guilt by acknowledging that there *might* be a reason for it and that everyone feels angry at times. Remind the person that the joint concern is the task. When anger is explosive, insist that such loss of control must not be repeated but that discussion of grievances is welcome. Immediately abort destructive expressions of anger in the work group and search for causes, not culprits, by promoting an airing of problems.

Placing yourself in your "attacker's" shoes will provide a mirror of recognition and enable you to maintain perspective. One's anger can be defused in hobbies, sports, travel; it can be productively vented toward subordinates and associates in response to limit testings, and it can be used to accent one's position to help move the problem-solving process forward.

Withdrawal Response. Not uncommonly, people withdraw after a major life crisis; we all need privacy at times to recoup. But when one severs all contact with colleagues, friends, and usual activities—gradually or abruptly—there is cause for alarm, all the more so if there is no discernible precipitant.

Organizational Impact. Illness, accidents, absenteeism, apathy, high turnover, and frequent changes of employment may be disguised withdrawal. Fear of failure and of success can lead to avoidance of competition—slumps. The latter has its roots in threatening childhood competition with siblings and father, when unacceptable hostile impulses stimulated fear of retaliation. Those who have difficulty with rivalry feelings may be unable to work for others and elect to become entrepreneurs.

Executive Action. Be alert to the symptoms. Maintain contact by communicating your caring and a desire to keep in touch. Pressuring the person to be more sociable or active is counterproductive. Though childlike behavior may surface, avoid treating the person as a child, since this approach further reduces self-esteem. If withdrawal is a personality style, do not put the person into a position requiring continual or close relationships with others.

Drug Abuse. Overall decrements in performance, Friday and Monday absences, or erratic performance and emotional lability may signal drug abuse. Performance should be discussed with the worker; if alcohol or other abuse surfaces in these talks, treatment should be mandated as a condition of continued employment or sick leave provided during treatment. As with cancer, failure to act promptly will lead to progressive and possibly irretrievable physical, psychological, and social impairment. Close liaison between the medical department and a community drug treatment program is crucial.

Summary

Psychological forces are just beginning to be appreciated by management, as is the potency of unconscious motivation. It is not what you do *to* people but what you do *with* them that matters. We have learned, painfully, that one meddles with the balance of nature at one's peril and that we must court, not conquer, our physical environment. Managerial policies, goals, and decisions *must* be consonant with the ecology of the emotional environment.

See also Assertiveness training; Conformity in management; Human factors engineering; Interpersonal relationships; Motivation in organizations; Stress management; Transactional analysis.

REFERENCES

Claiborne, C., and L. Shapiro: *You Are Not Alone,* Little, Brown, Boston, 1976.

Hill, Norman C.: *Counselling at the Workplace,* McGraw-Hill, New York, 1981.

Levinson, Harry: *Psychological Man,* The Levinson Institute, Cambridge, Mass., 1976.

Layes, Peter, ed.: *Handbook of Health Education,* Aspen Systems Corporation, Germantown, Md. 1979.

STUART ROSENTHAL, *Harvard Medical School.*

Health Institutions, Management of

During recent decades, health has become one of the largest and most complex industries in the United States. According to figures compiled by the U.S. Department of Health and Human Services, health care expenditures as a percentage of gross national product have increased from 6 percent in 1965 to 10.5 percent in 1982. A great variety of health care units, institutions, and subsystems make up the health care industry. Some examples are hospitals; nursing homes; clinics; health maintenance organizations; medical centers; convalescent hospitals; mental and psychiatric institutions; federal, state, and local government units and review boards; third-party payers (the Blue Cross Associations, for example); professional standards review organizations; consultants; business and industry components; and educational institutions. All these units have a role to play in the total health care system and all of them require managerial knowledge and expertise.

Each of the health care system units has its own specific characteristics. For instance, hospitals tend to concentrate on the short-term care of patients, whereas nursing homes are concerned with long-term care. Different skills are needed, too, particularly among medical personnel. Most units in the health care system, however, tend to be both independent and nonprofit. Costs are important, but patient care is far more crucial. Each unit derives the bulk of its income from payments by those served, either directly or from a third-party payer such as an insurance company or the government in Medicare or Medicaid situations. On the other hand, each is dedicated to providing for all people presenting themselves insofar as rooms and time are available. Given the complex nature of these health care units, managers must develop and implement a framework within which medical personnel can provide patient-care services.

Managerial Responsibilities

In any health care unit, the role of the manager is to plan, organize, and control resources in order to achieve (1) the objectives of the individual unit and, in turn (2) the objectives of the total health system. Specifically, the manager's responsibility is to utilize leadership ability in such a manner that the inputs of human and material resources are combined to produce the desired outputs or goals.

Managerial positions in the health care system units have three basic components: the managerial component itself, a general health aspect, and an institutional or environmental component.

The Managerial Component. This component involves the basic managerial functions of planning, organizing, and controlling. The manager is concerned with organizational development and, more specifically, with the way people and the organization interact. Related managerial activities include determination of goals and objectives, financial management, personnel management, coordinating department operations, program review and evaluation, and planning—including both facility and program, public and community activities, health industry activities, and educational development. These activities all have similar basic performance aspects, although the implementation will vary in terms of the specific health care unit.[1]

The General Health Component. This component is concerned with knowledge about the health industry and the specific means of promoting and maintaining good health. In part, this component relates to a social responsibility concept as well as to information about the nature of health itself. The administrator, unless he or she is a physician, is generally not expected to be a certified expert in the field of health since the role is one of management. On the other hand, the administrator needs to be knowledgeable about such matters as the nature of the health industry itself and changes occurring within it, epidemiology, commonly used medical terms, approaches to improving health, health delivery systems, and relationships within the "health delivery" team. Specific knowledge of the health industry as it relates to the unit in which the manager is located is a necessity.

Each individual unit in the health care system has its own characteristics and state of development. The manager must relate to these characteristics and work toward the achievement of the goals of the unit managed.

The Environmental Component. Several changes are occurring in the manager's role. As is true with almost all management positions, the role is becoming more complex. This complexity is the result of many factors, including increased use of medical technology in the diagnosis and treatment of illness, larger units, extension of health care to growing numbers of citizens, rises in third-party payers, changes in government controls, and greater knowledge by and expectations from people themselves. These and other related forces have caused managers of health institutions to become increasingly concerned with external forces. No longer can they be involved exclusively in the day-to-day procedural internal operations but must also work with external planners, evaluators, and controllers. In this sense, they perform a boundary-spanning link between the health care unit and the external units of the health care system, including the government with whom the managers are in contact.

Governmental regulations, technological advances, consumerism, unions, third-party payers, and changes in the economy have caused health care managers to examine the external forces as they impact upon patient care and cost effectiveness. During the last 10 to 15 years, attempts have been made to control health care costs. For example, controls such as rate review/reimbursement control procedures, certificate-of-need reviews, and the voluntary effort have been instigated. A prospective reimbursement system was developed which became effective

in late 1983 for in-patient hospital-cost reimbursement under Medicare. This system is in contrast to the retroactive cost-based reimbursement approach under earlier programs. Changes such as this will create greater challenges for health care institution managers in the achievement of the organizational goals of high-quality health care that is cost-effective. The next decade will present many challenges to the health care manager as the industry develops an increasingly competitive climate.

Multi-Institutional System. Another factor in the growing complexity of the manager's role is the development of integrated or multi-institutional health care systems.[2] These systems are organized either on a horizontal or vertical basis.

1. *Vertical integration* involves different kinds of health care delivery units such as clinics, hospitals, ambulatory care institutions, long-term care, and/or mental health facilities (product lines). Combinations of various product delivery lines are involved in this vertical integration as well as the combination of administrative and medical technology in an integrated arrangement of multi-institutional systems.[3]

2. *Horizontal integration* involves the combination of similar health care units, such as a number of hospitals or long-term care facilities, in order to share administrative and medical technology. The relationship may be somewhat informal, although in many situations the individual units are combined or merged so that either a large organization results or new and complex organizational structures become necessary. Another form of relationship similar to vertical integration is the sharing among hospitals of services such as data processing and laundry facilities. This is a *cooperative* arrangement, and no merger or combination takes place.

Dowling, in a study of multihospital systems, projects a 4.5 percent growth rate for system hospitals and a 2.9 percent increase in beds when the American Hospital Association data are used as a base.[4] However, a data base from *Modern Healthcare* suggests a 7.8 percent increase in system hospitals and a 4 percent expansion in system beds. The two fundamental organizational motives of survival and growth appear to be underlying causes for increases in the number of multihospital systems. However, there are other pressures, such as competition, reduced governmental financing, and changes in medical practices. Most of the integration movements are horizontal in structure, although Starkweather has speculated that more vertical integration may come with the larger size of hospital systems.[5]

Situational Management. Given the complex character of the health care system and the need for managerial skills and knowledge appropriate to the unit in question, it is necessary to utilize a concept of management which will meet these goals. Called the *contingency* or *situational model of management,*[6] it begins with the assumption that organizations are complex arrangements and that, therefore, no single approach to management is necessarily universally best. Instead, the manager must deal with relationships and subsystems in such a way that the goals of the particular unit are attained. This concept implies that there are situational principles which are useful and applicable once the manager has determined the environmental characteristics within which she or he is operating.

The situational concept is very useful in the health industry during this period of rapid change because it enables the manager to develop skills in management and health generally, as well as to develop expertise in applying these skills to the specific health unit he or she manages. It implies that the manager must be able to influence policy decisions rather than merely to administer or implement the policies determined by others. In addition, a team approach, as opposed to a hierarchical, authoritarian method, is more appropriate. Most health care units combine the skills and abilities of a wide range of professionals. As health technology advances, the impact of this diversification on organizational units will be ever greater. An effective manager, consequently, must be a person who can mold together working teams of professionals so that the technology may be adequately delivered to those in need.

See also Nonprofit organizations, management of; Public administration.

NOTES

[1]Alton C. Johnson, Christopher R. Forrest, and John Mosher, *An Investigation into the Nature, Causes, and Implications of the Future Role of the Health Care Administrator: Final Report,* U.S. Department of Health, Education, and Welfare, Public Health Service, Bureau of Health Manpower, Washington, D.C., March 31, 1977.

[2]For more complete discussions about multihospital systems, see Montague Brown and Howard L. Lewis, *Hospital Management Systems—Multi-Unit Organizations and Delivery of Health Care,* Aspen Systems Corporation, Germantown, Md., 1976.

[3]Rockwell Schulz and Alton C. Johnson, *Management of Hospitals,* McGraw-Hill, 2d ed., New York, 1983.

[4]William L. Dowling, "Multihospital Systems Face Growth, Constraints, Unexplored Options," *Hospital Progress,* vol. 64, no. 4, April 1983.

[5]David Starkweather, "Health Facility Mergers: Some Conceptualizations," *Medical Care,* vol. 9, no. 3, November–December 1971, pp. 468–478.

[6]Rockwell Schulz and Alton C. Johnson, *Management of Hospitals,* 2d ed., McGraw-Hill, New York, 1983, pp. 182–187.

ALTON C. JOHNSON, *University of Wisconsin, Madison*

Hospitality Management

Manipulating the management wheel over the vast hospitality industry is *hospitality management.* The hospitality industry, a service industry, is the second largest retail industry in the United States. It routinely generates about $200 billion in sales or over 6 percent of the gross national product. Major components of the industry are food service, lodging, and tourism. Food service includes restaurants, industrial feeding, institutional feeding, catering, and fast-food outlets. The lodging segment consists mainly of hotels and motels. Tourism includes airlines, theme parks, cruise ships, campgrounds, resorts, casinos, travel agencies, bus lines, and auto rental. Clubs of all types and convention centers are also considered part of the hospitality industry.

Historical Link. The commercial approach to hospitality management began with the ancient Greeks and Romans in the years before Christ. Its principal purpose was to satisfy the needs of the traveler. The first travelers came on foot or on horseback. Today, the traveler may arrive by supersonic jet, and tomorrow, he or she may stop at a space station after a rocket trip from earth. Regardless of the means of transport, the traveler will still need food and shelter and will probably want entertainment. Throughout history, these needs of the traveler have been satisfied by what has grown into a giant industry. Hospitality management has been the key to this success and growth. *Webster's Third New International Dictionary* defines hospitality as the cordial and generous reception and entertainment of guests or strangers socially or commercially. It describes management as the executive function of planning, organizing, coordinating, directing, controlling, and supervising any industrial or business project or activity with responsibility for results. A merge of the two functions not only guided the proprietors of the posting houses of ancient Rome but also guides the chief executives of the integrated hospitality corporations of today.

International Involvement. International tourism is looked at in the United States and abroad as an immediate and positive way to influence the balance of trade. Most of the major hospitality chains in this country also have operations in Europe, Africa, South America, Asia, and Canada. European chains also operate in Canada, Asia, and the United States. China, which welcomed 400,000 tourists in 1983, is also increasing airline service and hotel accommodations to handle 2 million visitors. Within the United States, the major hospitality associations, the states, the federal government, large and small chains, and even individual properties are all intensifying their international marketing. This effort is expected to increase the popularity of the United

States as a travel destination. In an effort to facilitate tourism, many nations are also changing their entry and exit regulations for foreign travelers.

Service: A Major Obligation

During the early 1940s, the Cornell University Hotel School distributed a questionnaire on hotels. Guests were asked to indicate the item that concerned them the most about a hotel. The lack of good service was the universal complaint. Unfortunately, the hospitality industry either did not hear too well or was too busy accommodating very high hotel occupancies— 93 percent at the height of World War II. Since then, occupancies have dropped steadily. The occupancy rate, for example, for 1982 was 64.8 percent. As the various hotel and restaurant chains poll their guests, they are once again finding that service is the number 1 concern. The difference is that now hospitality management must adhere to the wishes of their guests or their guests will go elsewhere. When guests patronize any segment of the hospitality industry, whether it be a theme park, a hotel, a restaurant, or a cruise ship, they want good service. Good service is interpreted to mean prompt, courteous service; clean, safe facilities; reliable equipment; and appetizing food. Management must also ensure that, in addition to being courteous, employees be clean, neatly dressed, and well-groomed. The industry has learned that revenue lost from an unsold hotel room, an unoccupied restaurant seat, or an idle rental car is gone forever, and that poor service was probably the cause. Most companies are now concentrating on raising their services to a high level and plan to maintain them there.

United States Expertise. Early expertise in commercial hospitality, which originated with the Greeks and Romans and then spread throughout Europe, emphasized occupational skills rather than management. It was not until the hospitality industry began to grow in the United States that hospitality management was raised to a professional level. This stature was derived from innovations, conveniences, and efficiencies developed by noted hospitality managers in the United States. Industry giants such as Lucius Boomer of the Waldorf-Astoria, E. M. Statler, Howard Johnson, Conrad Hilton, J. W. Marriott, Kemmons Wilson, Vernon Stouffer, and Ray Kroc all shared in molding the profession to the level that its management expertise could be exported. World travelers, by their patronage, have indicated that hotels having American managers are preferred. Hospitality marketing was developed by United States managers as were today's efficient reservation systems.

Management Contracts. Many segments of the industry now use management contracts. A *management contract* (really a subcontracting arrangement) enables a hospitality company to operate a property without owning or renting it. This trend began in the hotel segment during the latter stages of World War II; today, the management contract is probably the most common method of hotel management. The popularity of such contracts has most likely been due to two major reasons: (1) The high cost of construction seriously limits the rapid expansion that many hotel companies have planned; and (2) companies with large sums of capital to invest in hospitality facilities, such as insurance companies, do not have the expertise to manage a large facility, nor do they have the worldwide marketing and reservation systems necessary to survive.

Major hospitality management companies (like Hilton, Sheraton, Marriott, and Hyatt) are able to walk into a hotel with their key personnel and begin to manage it under the contract. There will even be cash banks in the registers and inventories in the storerooms. On new construction, the management company will often plan the layout and design of the building, select the decor and furnishings, plan the menus, hire and train the employees, establish the operating procedures, and both plan and execute the preopening marketing campaign. The property owners gain from this arrangement, as they have an experienced company to manage the facility. It is not unusual to have conventions and guests booked long before the hotel opens.

Hotel management contracts are complex and detailed and extend for periods of up to 30 years. Contracts for industrial feeding, school feeding, hospital feeding, and restaurants are usually for a much shorter period. Typically, they may be contracted on a year-by-year basis with a limited renewal option. Many smaller hotels and motels contract out their food service operation, but maintain the lodging operation.

Youthful Managers. The hospitality industry is unique in that it gives more responsibility to young managers than any other large industry. It is not unusual for a young man or woman only 22 or 23 years old and only a few years out of college to be assigned responsibility for a $3 to $5 million facility. These managers may have 100 or more employees reporting to them and be totally immersed in the management of the facility. As a consequence, there is a relatively high burnout rate for young hospitality managers. Colleges and universities that educate managers for the hospitality industry—which requires about 20,000 new managers yearly—cannot meet the demand for these young professionals.

Trends and Outlooks. Hospitality managers continue to be conscious of the need to minimize their operating costs in order to operate profitably. In the face of ever-increasing costs of labor, utilities, equipment, food, and beverages, the manager of today is utilizing every means possible to forecast properly, conserve energy, purchase efficiently, and schedule only the required amount of labor. Skillful hiring, thorough training, and effective communications are more important than ever before. Budgeting now covers every operating area: labor, materials, time, etc. Computers are essential for inventory, accounting, status of rooms in hotels and tables in restaurants, and the provision of information to management on an increasing and timely basis.

The hospitality industry is dynamic and will remain in a state of flux for the balance of this century and probably longer. Hospitality managers and management will also remain in a state of change. The need for improvements in services and efficiency may force the leveling off of expansion. Marketing will both sharpen and increase. Integration of services within the industry will continue. However, the takeover of hotel companies by airlines has reversed, with the hotel chains becoming the aggressors. Government on all levels will attempt to tighten its regulation of the hospitality industry, which, in turn, will strive to contain most legislative efforts more than it has in the past. Occupancy rates should begin to rise in the mid-eighties. Meanwhile, the industry will segment itself very clearly into a budget segment; a large, profitable middle-class operation; and a smaller, highly profitable luxury segment.

See also Marketing of services, professional; Retailing management.

REFERENCES

Boomer, Lucius: *Hotel Management Principles and Practice,* 3d ed., Harper Brothers, New York, 1945.

Brymer, Robert A.: *Introduction to Hotel and Restaurant Management,* 3d ed., Kendall/Hunt, Dubuque, Iowa, 1981.

Lundberg, Donald E.: *The Hotel and Restaurant Business,* 3d ed., CBI Publishing, Boston, 1979.

JOHN J. BILON, *James Madison University*

Human Factors Engineering

Human factors engineering consists of a body of theories, experimental and empirical data, and methodology devoted to bridging the gap between human capabilities and limitations on the one hand and design of equipment, systems, and products on the other. Human factors engineering operates within the context of the development of systems or of products. It is an integral part of systems science and engineering; it interfaces with a number of other fields associated with the processes of analysis and design. As such, it cannot and must not be viewed out of context.

Human factors engineering is not a perfectly delineated field, and considerable controversy exists as to its exact content and boundaries. Controversy stems from the recent emergence of the field, from its origins both in the United States and in Europe, from the nature of the practitioners, and from the nature of problems dealt with. Difficulties with definition and terminology in no way diminish the fundamental importance of human factors engineering in designing equipment, products, and systems that are operable, maintainable, safe, comfortable, and consonant with human needs. Experience has shown that in the absence of effective human factors engineering, economic costs and costs in accidents and loss of life can be high.

Human factors engineering is an American term. Its history, methodology, and the problems chosen for study have been strongly influenced by experimental psychology; hence, there has been a strong emphasis on sensory, perceptual, and perceptual-motor processes. Human factors engineering received a strong boost from American military and space programs and has developed in the context of large and complex systems. Thus, implicit in the meaning of the term are considerations not only of worker/machine interrelationships but also of environmental considerations, staffing, and training. Related terms are *engineering psychology,* denoting a branch of psychology covering essentially the same breadth as does human factors engineering, and *human engineering,* which often refers to design only without also including staffing and training.

Ergonomics is a European term now widely used throughout the world. As its Greek roots indicate, it places a strong emphasis on the study and measurement of work, strength, and fatigue. Many of the problems originally studied by ergonomists were more physiological and medical than psychological. Ergonomics tended to be practiced in an industrial rather than in a military or space systems context. Today, these distinctions between human factors engineering and ergonomics are blurring because of the oscillations of the American aerospace industry; the concern over civil systems problems, relevance, and the quality of life; and the holding of international meetings and the exchange of scholars in recent years.

Systems psychology studies human behavior *and* experience in complex systems. It includes the domain of engineering psychology but, in addition, is more concerned with societal systems and the study of motivational, affective, cognitive, and group behavior than is engineering psychology. *Sociotechnical systems* are analogous to worker/machine systems but operate at a higher hierarchical level. Studies deal with the interactions among groups, organizations, and societies; technologies as a whole (rather than separate pieces of equipment); and the natural and social environments.

385

Human Factors Engineering in Systems Development

Human factors engineering in the practical setting of systems development consists of a dynamic, iterative sequence of analysis, data gathering, design, test, and evaluation. At each stage the human factors engineer interfaces as appropriate with other specialists, such as the program planner; systems manager; systems analyst; electrical and electronics, reliability, mechanical, or aeronautical engineer; and computer expert. The term *personnel subsystem* has been utilized to describe this situation wherein the operator-maintainer or crew subsystem (the personnel subsystem) is developed in parallel with, and in interaction with, the development of the structural, power, communications, support, and other subsystems. *Personnel subsystem* connotes a number of interacting elements including analysis and data base, human engineering, life support, staffing, training, and test and evaluation. Unfortunately, the term is passing into disuse.

Systems development can be divided into a number of stages. Although authorities differ in their subdivisions, the following are representative:

1. *Conceptual stage.* A need for the system is perceived, stemming, for example, from a new perception of enemy threat, societal deterioration, or technological change or from pressures by powerful interests in government, the military, or industry. Economic costing is made and schedules are laid out. Determination is made of the gross nature of system structure, that is, how people as well as other systems constituents will be incorporated into the system. Analyses, computer simulation, trade-off studies, and reference to human factors experimental findings and data banks help ensure that human performance will be the best possible, considering constraints of money and schedule and the needs and limitations of the other subsystems. Nevertheless, many systems do not get beyond this first stage.

2. *Initial design stage.* The ideas, analysis results, and other documentation produced in the conceptual stage now begin to be translated into design sheets, drawings, and specifications and into actual hardware components and subsystems. Human and human/machine performance requirements and constraints and functions are specified in greater detail. *Task descriptions* are begun. Testing is made of proposed alternative designs, using mock-ups and simulations if available.

3. *Major design stage.* An addition or change in the major contractor(s) may be made. Components and modules are fabricated or acquired from vendors or subcontractors and assembled into subsystems. Test and evaluation continue. Human

factors engineers engage in one of their principal activities, task analysis. *Task analysis* involves determining the behavioral consequences of the tasks required to operate, maintain, control, and manage the system. It is a bridge between the world of psychology, physiology, medicine, and anthropometry on the one hand and that of operating systems on the other. Although the literature details a number of steps in performing task analyses, the following outline captures the essence of this indispensable process: *(a)* Treat the person and machine as a closed-loop system, relating each machine display output as a stimulus to a human sense organ (such as the eye or the ear) and each human hand or foot response as an input to a machine control (such as a lever or pedal); *(b)* starting with the task descriptions which are typically outcomes of preliminary equipment design, back up and ask, "Given this task, what decisions must the person make before performing the task effectively, and what information must the person have before making the correct decision?"; *(c)* determine task criticalities, priorities, interdependencies, loadings, and constraints; *(d)* determine environmental requirements and features leading to performance degradation; *(e)* determine presence of feedback of satisfactory task performance; and *(f)* determine special skills needed.

Task analysis data can be expressed on sequential sheets, as flow diagrams, and in quantitative reliability form. Task analysis is a prerequisite to effective human engineering design of equipment, determining both the kinds and number of people required to staff the system and determining training requirements.

As the relative length of this section suggests, a preponderance of the human factors engineering effort typically occurs at the major design stage. The collective output of this stage is a prototype. Development may terminate at this point, or in some cases the prototype may be put directly into operation.

4. *Production stage.* Should the prototype pass critical tests, evaluations, and reviews, and should funding be available, the system can enter production. The human factors engineer is concerned with late design changes, quality control, and selection and training of personnel, including the development of the associated manuals.

5. *Operations stage.* Following final system test and evaluation incorporating user personnel, the system becomes operational. The human factors engineer continues to play an important role in the monitoring of operations, collection and analysis of error and accident data, and preparation for model changes and new generations of the system.

Management of the Human Factors Engineering Program

Successful management of a human factors engineering program requires a systems understanding of hierarchy, interfaces, and interrelationships, and an awareness of educational and personality differences among engineering and human factors specialists. This knowledge is in addition to the expected cognizance of procedures, methodology, and data, and is independent of whether the formal organization is line, staff, or matrix. Several features that can make or break a human factors program are reviewed here.

Personnel Subsystem. Whether the formal, somewhat obsolescent term *personnel subsystem,* a substitute, or no term is employed, the requirements of the user must be borne in mind from the earliest time of system conceptualization. User requirements must be progressively met in parallel with and interacting with the design of hardware and software. In actual practice just the opposite has often been the case—the human factors effort has come in too late when design is essentially frozen and at too low a system hierarchical level to have any significant effect. The single most important contribution of the human factors engineer will be answers to the question, "What will people *actually do* in the system?" "Knobs and dials" human engineering—concern only with simple displays, controls, and front-panel design—does not constitute effective human factors work.

Management's Understanding. The human factors engineering program will be severely crippled by the absence of understanding and full backing by top management. Management is increasingly aware that human factors engineering transcends "knobs and dials" work and that poorly human-factored systems, programs, and products can be associated with immense human, operational, economic—and, increasingly, legal—costs. This new understanding has been advanced by publicity given to dramatic accidents associated with human error and by lawsuits in which corporate negligence or lack of product safety was interpreted in terms of the absence of consideration of human factors.

Costs and Benefits. The costs of a human factors *program* always entail the salaries and support of the human factors professionals. The costs of having a human-factored system or product may entail substituting more expensive for less expensive (e.g., government-furnished or off-the-shelf) equipment. Costs *may* entail abandoning a tight schedule.

Benefits can be determined from both negative and positive events. The literature now documents numerous examples of costly system or operational failures associated with human factors deficiencies. For example, the crash of a DC-9 jetliner on September 11, 1974, at Charlotte, North Carolina, was the result of the pilot's misreading his altimeter by 1000 feet. The crash cost 72 lives. And the crash of a Turkish Airlines DC-10 on March 3, 1974, near Paris, which took 346 lives, was due to another display deficiency—the special instructions for proper closing of a design-deficient cargo door could not be read by an illiterate crewman.

Human factor deficiencies have contributed to the failure of large-scale, electrical-power generation systems. The most dramatic was the near meltdown, on March 28, 1979, of a nuclear reactor at Three Mile Island near Harrisburg, Pennsylvania. A potentially insignificant occurrence evolved into a serious accident. Deficiencies derived from the sheer size and complexities of control room panels. Alarm and other displays lacked integration, indication or priority, and even basic visibility. Operating procedures were also overly complex and contradictory. Operator selection and training, especially on how to handle system failures and contingencies, were sorely deficient. Management practices in the manufacturing firms, the operating utility, and the federal regulatory agency, together with a safety philosophy that neglected the operator role and stressed system infallibility, predisposed the plant to failure by "operator error." Consequences included severe reactor damage, continued plant shutdown, charges of criminal misconduct by the utility, and major public disillusionment with the nuclear power industry.

Alternatively, the presence of good human factors work has greatly improved many operations. Applications include aircraft, spacecraft, ships, command and control systems, the home, and products such as tools, stoves, the push-button telephone, biomedical instrumentation, and television sets. Benefits can often be defined in terms of applications beyond those originally intended, that is, in terms of *technological transfer.* For example, a number of tools designed for the National Aeronautics and Space Administration (NASA) for the weightless conditions of space are now useful in underwater operations and in confined or limited spaces. And techniques for detecting crew motions and limb positions in spacecraft can be applied to motions, space, and forces required in work, emergency, and recreational behavior on earth.

Worker/Machine Interrelationships

The determination of worker/machine interrelationships is the heart of human factors engineering. At the highest level, the integration of the following major activities is involved.

Theory and Research. Human factors engineers use and contribute to theories as varied as general systems theory, queuing theory, cybernetic theory, physiological theories of sensory function, information theory, decision theory, control theory, and reliability theory. For example, signal detection theory and the relative operating characteristic help determine the probability that a blip on a radar screen will be detected and whether vigilance will decrease over time spent looking at the screen. Control theory helps explain the flight behavior of pilots. And human reliability theory helps predict the probabilities of task success or failure.

Research continues actively in the traditional areas of display, control, and work station design. Representative new vistas include several areas of research on the worker/computer interface: the ways in which workers and computers interact to solve problems, the automatic recognition of handwriting, and the automatic recognition of speech. The last area involves not only syntactic and semantic interpretation of speech sounds but electromyographic analysis of the muscles used in vocalization and subvocalization (thinking the words) and electroencephalographic analysis of the associated brain waves.

Analysis and Simulation. The indispensable role of task analysis should be mentioned here. Human factors engineers engage in a number of other systems analyses and trade-off studies. These may involve, for example, alternative presentations of information visually or aurally, comparisons of manual and automatic control of vehicles, and trade-offs between design for operability and design for maintainability. Mathematical models have been derived for dynamic man-in-the-loop situations and for motions of the human body. Computer simulation models have been developed for people flying airplanes and for the behavior of multiperson crews. Simulators are invaluable in substituting less expensive simulator training time for more expensive training time spent actually flying. Without simulation for zero gravity and lunar landing, the Apollo moon landings might never have been possible.

Data Gathering and Use. Representative areas include errors, accidents, incidents, failures, and safety. Static and dynamic anthropometric data, used, for instance, in the design of work spaces, cockpits, escape hatches, ejection seats, and space suits, have long been available for healthy young men. The changing social picture now requires that more data be collected on women, children, the aged, the handicapped, and different races. There is a need for more base-line data from physiological measures. Human factors *data banks* contribute to a faster evolution of the field and lessen the redundancy of effort.

Findings and Principles. Human factors principles, derived from some four decades of work in both experimental and practical—but largely military—settings, are well documented in the design criterion literature. Good guides are the Department of Defense's Military Standard 1472 "Human Engineering Design Criteria for Military Systems, Equipment and Facilities"; Air Force Systems Command Design Handbook 1–3, "Human Factors Engineer-

ing"; and the guide edited by Van Cott and Kinkade (see this entry's references). These and similar works describe design principles applicable to traditional military situations. Most of them illustrate good (and sometimes for comparison, poor) designs and present underlying theoretical arguments and quantitative data corroborating the recommended designs. These guides find their best use as applied to visual and auditory displays, noise and speech, controls, work spaces, anthropometry, and maintainability. Systems concepts and methods, computer systems, and nonmilitary situations require additional sources.

Evaluation of Practices. Human engineering designs are successively *tested* throughout the systems development process. *Evaluation* is a broader-scale effort, involving criteria taken from the real world, not from the experimental laboratory. Representative criteria include performance measures of time and accuracy, economic costs, cost/effectiveness and benefit/cost ratios, and satisfaction.

Biomechanics

Biomechanics deals with the mechanical properties of the movement of organisms and with the effects of mechanical forces on them. Differentiation between this term and *biodynamics* does not appear necessary. A related field is *engineering anthropometry*, which treats of the static and dynamic dimensions of people. Data on people, nude and clothed, are available for the various positions of standing, sitting, crouching, and reaching. These data are applied to the design of such things as doorways, emergency exits, hallways, farm machinery, cockpits, rooms in homes, and furniture. Data are also applied to the design of special clothing such as arctic wear, pressure suits, and space suits. In all three cases, anthropometric data must apply not only directly to suit design but also secondarily to the design of controls and work space.

Biomechanical studies are made under conditions of normal gravitation, acceleration, deceleration, impact, vibration, and weightlessness. These forces, or lack thereof, affect both the whole body and specific organs and tissues.

Mathematical models and associated sensing equipment can be used to study limb and body motion and position, forces exerted on the body and required of the body, and work space required of the body during the performance of various tasks in normal work, recreational, and especially stressful settings. Instrumented vehicles, such as automobiles, used in conjunction with anthropometric dummies, are employed to study crashworthiness and the design of restraint systems and other protective devices. Rocket sleds have been used in studying the effects of acceleration, deceleration, and impact on body structure and function and on performance.

High gravitational forces and weightlessness can have major effects on the skeletal, muscular, cardiovascular, sensory, and nervous systems. For example, normal limb movements may be distorted or become impossible. Higher gravitational forces may lower the visual capability of pilots or cause them to lose consciousness or develop vertigo. The effects of environmental degradation must be compensated for in the design of the total worker/machine system. These areas are typically studied by physiologists and physicians trained in the specialty of *aerospace medicine*.

Environmental Considerations

A major principle of human factors engineering could be called *five-part interaction*, that is, the interactions among human, machine, medium, mission, and management factors. Here, *medium* substitutes for *environment*. The principle holds that the performance of a human/machine ensemble will be a function of its environment, the phase of the mission profile (e.g., takeoff, climb to altitude, cruise, descent, or landing of an aircraft), and the management of system resources.

The operating or working environment can be considered from two interrelated points of view: (1) normal environmental factors, the *extremes* of which greatly reduce or preclude normal body functioning and performance; and (2) atypical environmental factors, the *presence* of which greatly stresses both physiology and performance.

Limited-Range Environmental Factors. Human life itself can exist only within certain ranges of many environmental factors. Health and effective performance may require even narrower ranges. Examples are atmospheric composition and pressure, electromagnetic radiation, and acceleration and gravitation. Representative effects of the last have already been discussed in this category. Temperature is also in this category, but its effects are well known, and it will not be discussed here.

Atmospheric Composition and Pressure. The chemical composition and pressure of atmospheres are interrelated. Thus, at high pressures, both oxygen and nitrogen are toxic. Anoxia is fatal after about 4 minutes, and hypoxia can lead progressively to visual difficulties, poor judgment and memory, and death. Aerospace and undersea operations require special breathing mixtures, not only to provide oxygen but to eliminate or reduce the possibility of bends when nitrogen comes out of solution in the blood as a person goes from a higher to a lower atmospheric pressure. One hundred percent oxygen enhances combus-

tion. In January 1967, three astronauts were killed in a fire in an Apollo Command Module, leading to severe repercussions throughout the main contracting and monitoring agencies. This catastrophe provides a striking instance of the need for management to think in systems terms.

Explosive decompressions, depending on the altitude, may lead to loss of consciousness, rupturing of internal organs, or even boiling of the blood.

Electromagnetic Radiation. Extremes of electromagnetic radiation—x-rays, gamma rays, and microwaves (and perhaps radio waves)—can be dangerous to health and even fatal. Microwaves and infrared radiation produce the effects of heating. Ultraviolet radiation may lead to the production of cancers. Ionizing radiation progressively affects blood cell production, the skin and gastrointestinal tract, the central nervous system, and the testes. The composition of visible light must incorporate factors of brightness, contrast, target size, location, and distance. Red lighting, used to maintain dark adaptation in some aircraft cockpits and ship command centers, precludes the use of color codes both in documents and as surface paint. Visible light may be a stressor in the form of glare, illusions, flicker, or as a disruption of psychophysiological rhythms. All these forms of radiation have design implications in terms of level and placement of source(s), shielding, sensors, warning devices, and so on.

Stressors in the Environment. The main factors in this category are nuclear waste, toxic chemicals, and acoustic noise. Some substances are toxic when present in concentrations as low as a few parts per million or even a few parts per billion. Sources include nuclear reactors, pesticides, paints, engine emissions, mined materials, and fabrics. The effects of carbon monoxide are well known, as are black lung disease, silicosis, and asbestos poisoning. In some airplane crashes survivors have been killed by hydrogen cyanide released by burning upholstery.

Acoustic noise is defined as unwanted sound; hence, there is a strong subjective component in what any one person considers to be noise. Nevertheless, noise can produce distraction and annoyance, distort or mask speech, and at higher decibel levels and longer exposure times, cause temporary or permanent hearing loss.

The results of noise provide an excellent representative example to management of the effects of technology on occupational health and safety and on the external environment. Airport operations have been curtailed in many countries, and in some places (e.g., Los Angeles) billions of dollars in lawsuits have been generated because of airport noise. Other large lawsuits have been concerned with the release of pollutants into the environment. Thus, the environment may not only be a stressor on people but is itself stressed by human activities.

See also Health, mental; Job evaluation; Therbligs; Work design, job enlargement, and job enrichment.

REFERENCES

Behan, Robert A., and H. W. Wendhausen: *Some NASA Contributions to Human Factors Engineering,* U.S. Government Printing Office, Washington, D.C., 1973.

De Greene, Kenyon B.: *Sociotechnical Systems: Factors in Analysis, Design, and Management,* Prentice-Hall, Englewood Cliffs, N.J., 1973.

————, (ed.): *Systems Psychology,* McGraw-Hill, New York, 1970.

McCormick, Ernest J., and Mark S. Sanders: *Human Factors in Engineering and Design,* 5th ed., McGraw-Hill, New York, 1982.

The President's Commission on the Accident at TMI: *Report of the President's Commission on the Accident at TMI,* U.S. Government Printing Office, Washington, D.C., 1980.

Van Cott, Harold P., and Robert G. Kinkade, eds.: *Human Engineering Guide to Equipment Design,* U.S. Government Printing Office, Washington, D.C., 1972.

KENYON B. DE GREENE, *University of Southern California*

Human Resources Planning

The general goal of effective human resources planning is to provide continuous and proper staffing and to ensure that appropriate skills are available within the work force, when needed, to meet the organization's changing requirements. It also ensures that the organization meets its human resources obligations to society at large.

In its simplest forms human resources planning—or manpower planning, as it used to be known—has been practiced for centuries. Whenever a boss needed more "hands" on the following day and made arrangements for them to be taken on, or a superintendent recognized the need for an additional crew or shift to start the next week, crude labor-force planning was taking place. Today's dynamic economic and social environment clearly evidences the need for more sophisticated planning for human resources. Within industry, human resources planning is, or should be, an integral part of the total resources planning for the enterprise, on a par with planning devoted to financial affairs, capital development, materials and equipment purchases, and market development. Additionally, human resources planning now is often projected by the public sector as a step toward ameliorating social ills.

Plan Characteristics. An effective human resources plan must include (1) a mechanism for periodic monitoring and revision to adjust for changes either in the organization's objectives or in internal or external labor market factors; (2) established responsibility for its accomplishment; (3) authority appropriate for the task; (4) a certain degree of flexibility for effective implementation, particularly for on-job assignments at the operating levels; and (5) correlation with other organizational plans, especially because of its possibly substantial financial impact.

Planning Process

By definition, *human resources planning* is a process of forecasting future staffing requirements, developing action plans to meet them, and monitoring performance against the plan. In its basic form human resources planning includes the following components: (1) a forecast of the capabilities required on a given date in the future, (2) an inventory of current human resources, (3) an analysis of internal and external influences or actions that will occur during the intervening period, (4) a summary of the kinds of actions required to achieve the desired capabilities, (5) a comprehensive plan to implement these actions, and (6) monitoring techniques to ensure proper progress.

Forecast of Future Requirements. This procedure establishes the organization's goals to be achieved by the human resources plan. Introduction of new machinery, new product lines, or new facilities may provide requirements for these targets. Or, it may come about through establishment of an affirmative action plan or from a chief executive's wish to install a plan for top-management succession. When these requirements are being set, consideration should be given to internal and external forces and to making the ultimate goals realistic and attainable. This is particularly true when the time frame covers 3 to 5 years or longer. General economic and local labor market forecasts, changing product demand, and technological developments and obsolescence all must be considered. Their implications should be analyzed thoroughly before the forecast is finalized. Recommendations for human resources goals should be made by the planning staff, after obtaining input on the desired organization posture from the chief executive or key operating officers. These goals should then be refined into final statements by continuing discussion within top management regarding the "desired" and the "practical" or "possible."

Inventory of Current Resources. This component establishes the basis for all future actions under the plan. Depending upon ultimate requirements, the inventory can cover merely the number of people in certain job titles on each shift in an organization, or it may include breakdowns by race, sex, ethnic groups, age, length of service, degree of skill, promotional potential, educational background (and future plans for it), and the like. Off-job items, such as future career interests, outside leadership activities (in union, fraternal, civic, political, or professional organizations), and particular outside skills, interests, and hobbies can also be included. The items listed in the inventory should be geared to the objectives of the planning exercise—the future requirements of the organization.

Much of the inventory data usually is already in the organization files, noted on employment applications, and payroll and other records. However, all the desired data are seldom recorded, and rarely are they easily retrievable. As a result, a comprehensive data collection effort is usually required, using a broad-gauge questionnaire that covers all desired data elements for each employee. Alternatively, a smaller questionnaire may be used to pick up only missing items, but then additional work by the planners will be required to retrieve the other data from existing records. It is important, however, to be sure that the total requirements are known before data collection is started. Not only is the collection effort costly but it can also generate employee unrest stemming from concern on how the information will be used. Therefore, the questionnaire should collect all the desired information at one time, thus avoiding a second survey.

In situations with either a high volume of data or anticipated high frequency of use, computer-based storage and retrieval of the data are generally appropriate, using systems available from many sources. For smaller organizations with more limited data or use, a punch card system may be adequate.

Analysis of Internal and External Factors. After future requirements and current resources are established but before future actions are determined, internal and external factors which may impact on the plan must be identified and analyzed. They should include:

1. Projected retirements, layoffs, terminations, transfers and promotions, and other changes in the current work force. Such losses may provide opportunity for reassignments and transfers that will assist in the plan's effective operation.

2. Projected departmental expansions and contractions. Short-term requirements, with resulting dips and peaks, could lead to layoffs or emergency transfers that would void longer-term opportunities required in the total plan.

3. Anticipated changes in the external labor force or market from which the organization draws. Examples include relocation of major employers either into or out of the labor market area; an increase or decrease in the number of available engineers, accountants, scientists, or other specialists; and changes in legal Equal Employment Opportunity (EEO) requirements or in employment patterns of neighboring concerns which draw from the same labor market.

Assessment of Potential Actions. The human resources plan will include a variety of personnel actions designed to fill the development or staffing gap between the required population and skills and the current inventory. These actions generally fall into two basic areas: (1) development of current employees and (2) employment and placement of persons not now employed by the organization. Prior to development of the final plan, the planner should become familiar with these actions, particularly with their benefits and implications.

Development or Training of Present Employees. This component includes a broad variety of actions, with varying costs. Among the most widely used techniques are:

1. On-the-job training in a new assignment lets the individual learn necessary skills while functioning in the job. Assistance from the former job holder, a "buddy" at the next machine or desk, or extra attention from the immediate supervisor is usually needed and plays a key part in the success or failure of such a program.

2. Off-the-job classroom ("vestibule") training is often used to expose employees to new methods or ideas or to teach them new skills. This technique enables an organization to hire candidates who do not possess the necessary job skills, train them to an acceptable level in a simulated workplace, and then turn them over to the operating supervisors in production units for final on-the-job training. It also can provide an opportunity for employees to practice within a classroom setting before trying out such new skills in the workplace.

3. Formal apprenticeship programs combine on-the-job or vestibule training with off-the-job instruction, generally in a nearby vocational or trade school. These programs are usually offered to recently hired employees and often require specific prior education or experience as prerequisites.

4. Rotation among a series of jobs, either as a part of a job enlargement or an enrichment program, or in a longer-range career development process.

5. Tuition aid programs under which employees are reimbursed for certain expenses while attending outside academic programs, usually on a university level on their own time.

6. Special programs, conducted by universities, professional societies, and other organizations, assist middle- and upper-management personnel, in particular, to become better qualified in their present assignments or for promotion.

7. Correspondence courses may be particularly useful when potential participants are geographically remote from a training facility, work on rotating shifts, or face other circumstances that impede participation in other formal training programs.

Preemployment Efforts. Several preemployment techniques can be included in a human resources plan as sources of new employees.

1. Referrals can come from current employees or from organizations and agencies which specialize in identification of candidates with particular skills or qualifications. This technique applies equally to executive search firms which place top executives and to community groups which provide candidates with particular ethnic or racial backgrounds or special skills.

2. Employment advertising in either general or specialized publications which are read by the target population.

3. Visitation programs to academic and vocational high schools, junior and 4-year colleges, graduate schools, military separation centers, etc.

4. Temporary or contract personnel may be employed to bridge short-term gaps in order to level out the workload and maintain a stable work force, or when it is undesirable or impossible to hire employees with the needed skills. As well as providing clerical and secretarial temporaries, organizations now specialize in supplying drafters, engineers, computer programmers, laborers, etc. (A variant of this technique is the common practice of contracting to outside organizations work that is expected to be short-term or nonrecurring or that requires skills not readily available within the organization.)

5. Federally funded programs, under the Job Training Partnership Act and other statutes, may enable an organization to maintain its established standards for technical quality of new hires while opening doors to members of minority and disadvantaged groups in accordance with affirmative action programs.

6. Purchase of another company, division, or new product line may be appropriate to acquire an outstanding executive or an available work force. Conversely, development or purchase of a new product line may more effectively utilize an existing work force, particularly if existing product lines are strongly seasonal. Thus, a manufacturer of snow blowers for home driveways may diversify into power lawn mowers to reduce seasonal layoffs and provide a more constant work force requirement; addition of a line of canvas and leisure shoes by a maker of winter overshoes and boots could offer similar benefits.

Development, Implementation, and Monitoring of Plan

A human resources plan can be simple or complex; it can cover the next 2 weeks or the next 5 years, depending on the criteria set down by top management. The overall, or comprehensive, human resources plan is usually developed by a specialized staff in either the employee relations (personnel) or planning departments.

To be "real"—more than a piece of paper—the plan requires approval by the chief operating officer and concurrence by both line management and the financial staff, since the line organization will have responsibility for putting it into practice and the program costs will impact on the organization's financial performance. Within the framework of the comprehensive plan, the line organization will be responsible for implementation of several short-term plans. Thus, the line will need authority to make short-term adjustments to the plan to meet operating requirements. For best results key line managers should have been involved in all phases of the development of the plan, from collection of raw data in the inventory to agreement on ultimate objectives. They may even be charged with developing the short-term document, with the requirement that it fit into the broad guidelines of the overall plan.

The plan should define specific subgoals, with responsibilities and steps to achieve each goal within the requisite time period. It should also include necessary reporting and monitoring components, with preset opportunity for review and revision over time. Individual (development) plans may be appropriate within the overall plan, particularly in the area of top-management succession planning. These should spell out in fine detail the actions required, both by individuals and the organization, for employees to move from their present levels of skill to the desired levels within set periods of time. The staff personnel function usually has a major responsibility for coordination of these plans, which often involve more than one organizational unit. However, involvement of the line organization is necessary to make them work effectively.

Analysis and Control Considerations. Analysis of three kinds of internal and external factors was mentioned previously: (1) projected internal losses and/or lost time, (2) internal organizational changes, and (3) external changes (particularly in the local labor force). For each item data can be generated with varying degrees of accuracy and/or sophistication, depending upon the requirements of the plan. In most instances, comparison is required with a standard or similar historical period. Obviously, appropriate choice of the standard period is of prime importance for accurate forecasting.

Absenteeism. Projections of lost time (absenteeism) are vital to ensure that operating supervisors have adequate workers each day to accomplish the assigned output of goods or services. A realistic human resources plan may include a staffing requirement of 105 to 120 percent of the daily work force to compensate for lost time (both scheduled and random) because of vacations, jury duty, illness, training time off the job, unexcused absences, and other reasons. The actual percentage will depend on the age and length of service of the work force, the vacation policies, etc., and should be based on historical analysis. However, if the rate of overstaffing is considered too high, one subgoal in the overall plan may be to reduce it.

Turnover. In estimating turnover, staff planners can calculate the loss rate from data for the previous 3 to 5 years. Separate categories should be set up for deaths, discharges, releases (layoffs), and resignations. Also, separate rates can be calculated for unskilled, semiskilled, skilled workers or craftsmen, office workers, and lower, middle, and upper management, depending on the focus of the plan. The rates should be adjusted for the influence of known, nonrecurring external or internal pressures. For example, an economic downturn will reduce the resignation rate because other employment will be difficult to obtain. At the same time, it may increase the release or discharge rate if marginal performers are being replaced during this period as the work force is upgraded. A major employer's move into, or out of, the labor market area can also impact on turnover, as can a change in management philosophy to improve employee productivity.

In estimating turnover, it may be important to single out turnover caused by transfer and/or promotion within particular segments of the organization. Skills of such individuals are lost to their former supervisors and generally must be replaced just as if they had left the organization completely, yet they are available to their new supervisors. Statistics on such turnover are often difficult to obtain but can be developed from payroll records and other documents. (A computerized system is of particular benefit here.)

As part of the turnover analysis, the human resources planner should also analyze the impact of organizational changes—growth or retrenchment—on established or discontinued departments, sections, or units, etc. Layoffs due to temporary curtailment should be kept separate from other termination statistics, since this item is affected by the organization's marketing effectiveness and general market conditions. Layoffs may also be considered with organizational changes—the addition or elimination of a shift, product or product line, etc. Future production and marketing plans and their staffing implications are essential information at this point.

External Factors. In estimating external factors for 5 or more years in the future, the human resources planner may be forced to resort to almost pure conjecture. For example, technological advances, either in the state of the art or by introduction of new machinery into the production process, may impact on total staffing requirements, on required skill levels of the work force, or on both. In the fast-changing political and economic world, major changes in the availability of federal funds or in Equal Employment Opportunity emphasis can cause unexpected tilts in the labor market.

State and local development officials can provide information on their plans to attract new industry to the area within the plan's cycle. In addition, the U.S. Bureau of Labor Statistics, local and national chambers of commerce, the Engineers Joint Council, and other professional societies can provide local, statewide, or national labor market statistics and projections for particular job titles or categories.

Control. Effective implementation of a human resources plan requires a variety of control techniques to ensure compliance by all parts of the organization.

Staffing control is simple to initiate and flexible enough to be adapted to most requirements. A system of personnel requisitions for management and/or nonmanagement positions is a basic approach. Each requisition should require prior approval of one or more persons at higher levels than the supervisor to whom the added employee will report. Thus, the requisition system provides control of both the number and the quality (skill or other attributes) of new hires or internal transfers toward goals in the human resources plan. In the extreme, all such additions may require approval of a high operating executive if the goal is to shrink staffing in a particular department or plant, or certain jobs may be reserved for candidates with special desired qualifications.

One serious drawback occurs with strictly enforced hiring controls: Line supervisors generally resist the elimination of poor or marginal performers without prior, ironclad assurances of approval for replacements.

Their argument that "half a person is better than none" has a certain validity and can seriously impair a program to upgrade the effectiveness of a particular unit. Similarly, an internal job-posting program which gives preference to current employees may tend to perpetuate a level of skill or qualification that is contrary to the plan objectives.

Outlook

Recognition of the need for formal human resources planning has been widespread. Within the planning hierarchy of most organizations, however, it still ranks at, or near, the bottom of the list. Few organizations have comprehensive human resources plans. Few companies fully recognize the savings that can be realized in this area, although all have fragmentary or rudimentary plans. Looking toward the next decade, the cumulative effects of actions initiated by various branches of the federal government will continue to increase the recognition and importance of this function. Title VII of the Civil Rights Act of 1964 requires that most organizations set up affirmative action programs dealing with the employment and training of various minority groups. Court decisions in the AT&T and other cases forewarned industry of the cost of noncompliance. In its basic context, an affirmative action plan is a human resources plan with circumscribed objectives.

Surpluses of teachers and liberal arts graduates and shortages of engineers, doctors, and machinists point to a need for more effective communications on a national level regarding future requirements. Such information can assist students in secondary schools to prepare early for future careers.

In the past, ambitious federal human resources plans such as the programs of the Great Society and the Comprehensive Employment and Training Act (CETA) were largely ineffectual because their goals tended to be imperfect. They provided for training but paid too little attention to job development and placement. We must hope that mistake is not repeated in the future.

See also Affirmative action; Development and training, employee; Development and training, management; Forecasting business conditions; Organizational analysis and planning; Personnel administration; Work design, job enlargement, and job enrichment.

REFERENCES

Burach, Elmer H.: *Planning for Human Resources*, Brace-Park Press, Chicago, 1983.

————, and Nicholas J. Mathys: *Human Resources Planning: A Pragmatic Approach*, Brace-Park Press, Chicago, 1980.

Walker, James W.: *Human Resources Planning*, McGraw-Hill, New York, 1980.

JOHN S. JENNESS, *Consolidated Edison Company of New York, Inc.*

Information Science

Many economists, sociologists, and futurists have proclaimed that the United States and other advanced nations are rapidly entering into an information age. One of the resultant disciplines and professions of this phenomenon is information science. The *information science* discipline involves the body of knowledge concerning information and information transfer patterns and processes, structure and formats, organization and control, retrieval and access, and management. The profession, as a demonstration of this knowledge, deals with all aspects of information processes, particularly those involving recorded information. Such recorded information includes textual, numeric, and graphic data found in printed publications, in audio and visual systems, and in electronic data bases and knowledge bases. Some people in this profession are engaged in research, evaluation, planning, and design of information transfer systems and in the application of new technology. Others educate and train information professionals and other workers. But by far the largest number in the profession are information practitioners who manage information units or process and handle information on behalf of others.

Many of the information professionals who perform these functions do not call themselves information scientists, but they have a deep interest in information science and how it will affect their work.

Origin and Development. Information science, as it is known today, has two primary roots. One root is in the field of documentation, the other in the search for information associated with scientific research.

Documentation. This approach deals with the assembling, coding, and disseminating of recorded knowledge as a comprehensive process involving semantics and psychological and mechanical aids in order to make information readily accessible and useful. This approach, formally recognized in the 1930s in the United States, focused on new technology—such as micrographics—applied to documentation. Then, during and following World War II, the enormous generation and influx of documented information (some from Germany and Japan) required new methods of information management organization and control. Documentalists took on this task during the 1950s, applying knowledge and skills from such areas as linguistics, machine translation, abstracting and indexing, and information storage and retrieval. By the 1960s, many of the activities of documentalists involved new technology, such as computing and telecommunications. Large automated bibliographic systems were developed by the National Library of Medicine, the Library of Congress, and the National Aeronautics and Space Administration, among others. Advances in the use of new technology and extensive information research activities in the field led documentalists to seek a more appropriate title: information science. The principal professional society of documentalists in the United States, the American Documentation Institute, changed its name to American Society for Information Science; the National Science Foundation started a Division of Information Science and Technology; the Federal Commission on Library and Information Science was formed; and many library schools added information science to their names.

Search and Analysis. A parallel path for the development of information science as a profession had its genesis in the United Kingdom where it was recognized that information transfer was an inseparable part of scientific research. Thus, scientists who engaged largely in searching, retrieving, and making preliminary analyses of information were called information scientists. The title "information scientist" was soon adopted for those performing similar information functions for the fields of medicine, law, engineering, and, more recently, public and other community services. This title was used to distinguish such individuals from laboratory scientists. Even though, today, many of these information professionals have the title of information scientist, other occupational titles such as information specialist, information counselor—or those bearing the name of the profession served (chemist, statistician, etc.)—are actually more common.

Scope. Today, perhaps, the information science profession is best described by the membership of the American Society for Information Science. It consists of information researchers and technologists, educators, and practitioners. Information research and technology form the basic focal point of interest to the profession: the conduct of information research and the development of information technology as well as its potential application by information practitioners.

Research. Research consists of studies of the foundations of information science, information transfer patterns and relationships, organization and control of information, modeling of information transfer processes, human factors involved in the design of worker/machine systems, information-user behavior and needs, economics and evaluation of information transfer systems, and so on.

Technology. Technology involves computer and telecommunication applications to information systems, services, and products including library operations, on-line bibliographic and numeric systems, electronic publishing, and knowledge-base systems.

It also includes new systems such as videotex and teletext used in homes and office automation found in businesses and government agencies. Information scientists play a major role in the research, development, and operation of these systems.

Education. A number of library schools now include information science in their names and information science is a major course in other schools as well. There are approximately 25 schools in colleges and universities in the United States that have information science as part of their names. Many information scientists are educated in these schools, although a large number also have come from other fields, such as medicine, science, operations research, and computer science. Typical courses deal with theories of information definitions, structure and format, organization, retrieval, and management. They also emphasize current and future technology applied to information transfer processes. Many schools offer courses in (or about) other disciplines of information, such as computer science, cognitive sciences, linguistics, artificial intelligence, cybernetics, and system theory. Since the information field is growing so rapidly and new technology is changing so frequently, continuing education plays a substantial role in the education and training of information science professionals. Also, many information science professionals are themselves engaged in education and training of information professionals and other workers. Some of these professionals are located in universities and colleges, but an even greater number are employed by companies and government agencies.

Application. Practitioners in the information profession who are information scientists or who have a deep interest in information science are engaged in processing and handling information on behalf of others. Some of them are involved in creating or generating information, such as indexers, abstractors, catalogers, translators, and technical writers. Some are engaged in publishing as editors and information technologists, working on primary and secondary publications. Many practicing information professionals are employed in information organizations such as libraries, information clearinghouses, information analysis centers, records management units, and archives. A large number are involved in searching the thousands of available bibliographic and numeric data bases. Finally, management of information organizations is a principal function performed by information scientists and other information professionals who have particular interest in information science. This is true since so many companies and government agencies are combining all their information activities (e.g., traditional library, records management, computer files, word processing files, and marketing research) under a single information manager or into single information units. Thus, information resources manage-

ment is becoming an important specialty taught to, and practiced by, information scientists.

See also Computer software, data base management; Information sources; Management information systems (MIS); Records management; Research and development management; Word processing.

REFERENCES

Davis, Charles H., and James E. Rush: *Guide to Information Science,* Greenwood Press, Westport, Conn., 1980.

Encyclopedia of Library and Information Science, Allen Kent et al. (ed.), Marcel Dekker, New York, 1969.

Debons, Anthony, Donald W. King, Una Mansfield, and Donald L. Shirley: *The Information Professional: Survey of An Emerging Field,* Marcel Dekker, New York, 1981.

Machlup, Fritz, and Una Mansfield: *The Study of Information: Interdisciplinary Messages,* John Wiley, New York, 1983.

DONALD W. KING, *King Research, Inc., American Society for Information Science*

Information Sources

Major sources of problem-solving and decision-making information include books and reference materials, periodicals and newspapers, publications of the United Nations and various governmental agencies, trade association data, and on-line computerized data banks. Public, university, and business librarians can be especially helpful in locating and utilizing these resources.

Books and Reference Materials. A well-stocked library offers thousands of individual titles. The card catalog serves as the index to the library's collection. Books can be located by looking up the author, title, or subject in the catalog. Books on a specific subject will be shelved together. A listing of current books on a specific subject can be located by looking up the subject in the general reference book, *Subject Guide to Books in Print.* If a desired title is not part of the library's collection, it can often be obtained through interlibrary loan.

Reference books cover a wide range of business interests. For example:

- Biographical and locator information can be found in sources such as *Standard and Poor's Register of Corporations, Directors, and Executives, United States and Canada* and *Who's Who in Finance and Industry. The National Directory of Addresses and Telephone Numbers* can be quickly consulted for addresses or telephone numbers of persons in the areas of business and finance, government and politics, unions, transportation and hotels, and business services.

- Technical and scientific research sources include the *Research Centers Directory,* which lists university and nonprofit research organizations working in areas such as agriculture, business, engineering and technology, and conservation; and the *Industrial Research Laboratories of the United States,* which provides a guide to industrial research and research laboratories.

- Manufacturers are listed in directories such as the *Thomas Register of American Manufacturers,* which provides information on the manufacturers of more than 70,000 product items.

- Consultants' names can be found in directories published by many professional associations. Examples are *Information Sources,* a directory which lists company name, address, telephone number, officers, and services of the information industry; and the *Green Book,* which lists marketing consultants and researchers.

- Financial data are available through various business and financial services, such as *Moody's Industrial Manual,* which includes financial statements, stock issues, and other historical and financial information, and Standard and Poor's *Standard Corporation Descriptions,* which supplies data on balance sheets, earnings, and market prices for thousands of American and Canadian corporations. Both directories provide home-office addresses and names of directors and principal officers for each firm listed.

- Directories to meet specific needs include two especially useful titles: *Guide to American Directories,* which covers all industrial, professional, and mercantile categories; and *The Directory of Directories,* which provides an annotated guide to business and industrial directories and professional and scientific rosters.

Other specialized reference works, including dictionaries, encyclopedias, and yearbooks, are available in the subject areas of particular interest to businesses. A good overall general reference work is the *Encyclopedia of Business Information Sources,* which provides a detailed listing on primary subjects of interest to managerial personnel of sourcebooks, periodicals, organizations, directories, handbooks, bibliographies, and other sources of information.

Periodicals and Newspapers. Periodicals and newspapers provide the most up-to-date sources of information. They range from academically oriented journals to specific industry publications.

Titles of periodicals published in a particular area of interest can be located through *Ulrich's International Periodicals Directory* and its companion volume *Irregular Serials and Annuals,* which provide bibliographic information on more than 100,000 regularly and irregularly issued serials from around the world.

Business Periodicals Index lists, by subject and by company name, articles which have appeared in a large number of business publications.

Newspapers provide information on current happenings in industry and government, stock and bond quotations, and other data. The *Ayer Directory of Publications* provides a comprehensive listing of newspapers, magazines, and trade publications printed in the United States. The annual *Editor & Publisher International Year Book* includes a listing of newspapers published in the United States, Canada, and foreign countries. The yearbook also features a listing of clipping bureaus, another source of business information. Indexes to articles in specific major newspapers, such as the *New York Times Index* and the *Wall Street Journal Index*, are available.

Electronic news services, including *The Washington Post Electronic Newsletter,* a computer-based service that issues daily summaries of the *Post's* government and political coverage, may also be useful. Services such as NEXIS provide access to the full text and abstracts of hundreds of major national and international newspapers, magazines, newsletters, and wire services. Electronic news services are indexed in the directory *Information Sources*. Extensive coverage of back issues of periodicals and newspapers may be available on microfilm in one's local library.

United Nations and Governmental Agency Publications. The United Nations and various national, state, and local governmental agencies provide important sources of scientific, technical, and socioeconomic information. The *United Nations Document Index* may be helpful in locating specific publications of that body. A yearly checklist, "United Nations Publications in Print," is available free from United Nations Publications, New York, N.Y., 10017.

Large libraries serve as depositories for United States government publications. The volume that lists publications of all federal agencies is the *Monthly Catalog of United States Government Publications.* An index by subject, title, and the government agency that published the document appears in the back of each issue. A microfiche index, *Publications Reference File,* indexes all government documents currently in print. An index of specific articles which have appeared in more than 170 government-issued periodicals is provided in the *Index to U.S. Government Periodicals.*

A list of publications available through a specific agency can be obtained by writing directly to that agency. Comprehensive information on the agencies of the legislative, judicial, and executive branches of the federal government is provided in *The United States Government Manual.* The *Manual* also includes information on quasi-official agencies, international organizations in which the United States participates, and boards, committees, and commissions. A monthly brochure, "Selected U.S. Government Publications," is available free from the Superintendent of Documents, U.S. Government Printing Office, Washington, DC 20402. Although availability of data services may vary over time, investigation of government-developed data services may yield fruitful results. Examples are the Environmental Protection Agency's Chemical Substances Information Network (CSIN), designed to provide chemical information, and the Commerce Department's Worldwide Information and Trade System, designed to supply American firms with specific information on foreign markets. The Library of Congress maintains an extensive collection of books and periodicals available for public use.

State agencies are sources of "blue books," state statistical abstracts, and industrial and manufacturing directories. Some states offer checklist coverage of their publications which may be available at one's local library or may be obtained by writing to the state library. A *Monthly Checklist of State Publications* is also available; it lists all state publications received by the Library of Congress.

Information concerning a specific locality may be obtained by contacting the local chamber of commerce.

Trade and Professional Associations. In many industries, corporations and individuals sponsor associations to represent the industry or the profession and to provide information to members. Lists of publications—available to both members and nonmembers—can be obtained by writing to the association. The *Encyclopedia of Associations* contains a list of such organizations. A directory of trade associations is available in the *National Trade and Professional Associations of the United States and Canada.* The *Ayer Directory of Publications* lists trade publications.

On-line Computerized Data Banks. Larger libraries may offer computerized information search services which provide bibliographic information retrieved from data bases. This service (COM-SEARCH) can retrieve information from indexes and abstracts from many sources in the areas of biology, chemistry, published dissertations, education, management, medicine, psychology, and the social sciences. Hundreds of commercial information retrieval systems are also available. An example is the DIALOG system which contains millions of document references in fields such as technology/engineering, business, economics, medicine, science, social sciences, fine arts, and the humanities. A listing of commercial data bases is found in *Information Sources.*

See also Computer software packages; Decision support systems; Economic measurements; Forecasting business conditions; Information science; Management information systems (MIS); Marketing research; Records management.

REFERENCES

Ayer Directory of Publications, Ayer Press, Philadelphia, 1880–.

Business Periodicals Index, The H. W. Wilson Company, New York, 1958–.

DIALOG, Dialog Information Services, Palo Alto, Calif.

The Directory of Directories, Gale Research Company, Detroit, 1980.

Editor & Publisher International Year Book, The Editor & Publisher Company, New York, 1921–.

Encyclopedia of Associations, Gale Research Company, Detroit, 1982.

Encyclopedia of Business Information Sources, Gale Research Company, Detroit, 1980.

Green Book, American Marketing Association, New York, 1973–.

Guide to American Directories, B. Klein Publications, Coral Springs, Fla.

Index to U.S. Government Periodicals, Infordata International, Inc., Chicago, 1972–.

Industrial Research Laboratories of the United States, Bowker Associates, Washington, D.C., 1920–.

Information Sources, The Information Industry Association, Washington, D.C., Annual.

Irregular Serials and Annuals, R. R. Bowker Company, New York, 1982.

Monthly Catalog of United States Government Publications, U.S. Government Printing Office, Washington, D.C., 1895–.

Monthly Checklist of State Publications, Library of Congress, Washington, D.C.

Moody's Industrial Manual, Moody's Investors Service, New York, 1950–.

The National Directory of Addresses and Telephone Numbers, Concord Reference Books, New York, 1982.

National Trade and Professional Associations of the United States and Canada, Columbia Books, Inc., Washington, D.C., 1983.

New York Times Index, New York Times, New York, 1913–.

NEXIS, Mead Data Central, Dayton, Ohio.

Research Centers Directory, Gale Research Company, Detroit, 1965–.

Standard & Poor's Register of Corporations, Directors, and Executives, United States and Canada, Standard & Poor's Corporation, New York, 1928–.

Standard Corporation Descriptions, Standard & Poor's Corporation, New York, 1983.

Subject Guide to Books in Print, R. R. Bowker Company, New York, annually.

Thomas Register of American Manufacturers, Thomas Publishing Company, New York, annually.

Ulrich's International Periodicals Directory, Annual Supplement, R. R. Bowker Company, New York, 1969–.

United Nations Document Index, Dag Hammarskjold Library, New York, 1950–.

United States Government Manual, Office of the Federal Register, National Archives and Records Service, Washington, D.C., 1982.

Wall Street Journal Index, Dow Jones and Company, Inc., Princeton, 1961–.

The Washington Post Electronic Newsletter, Washington Post Company, Washington, D.C.

Who's Who in Finance and Industry, Marquis Who's Who, Chicago, 1936–.

INEZ L. RAMSEY, *James Madison University*

Innovation and Creativity

A distinction can be made between innovation and invention that helps clarify the meaning of innovation.

An *invention* is literally a creation, a new device or method, or a new idea. Or, if one believes that there is no such thing as a truly new idea, an invention is a new application or a new way of using existing knowledge. The use of fluoride to prevent tooth decay was a new application—an invention.

Innovation, by contrast, is concerned with introduction. Innovation is the process of bringing a new idea or new application into general use. If the fluoride idea was an invention, then Crest toothpaste became an innovation.

Distinguishing Characteristics. Innovation differs from invention in three important ways:

1. Innovation and invention are the same in that both are creative activities, but innovation is the more general activity. Invention is a creative *event;* innovation is a creative *process.* Innovation begins with an invention and then introduces that invention into general use. The computer was an invention, but the application of that invention to handle the information needs of a business firm has been an innovation.

2. Innovation applies to many areas in the organization. It is commonly thought of in connection with new-product development, but it applies more broadly than this. It is common also, for example, in production, distribution, and financial management.

3. The importance of innovation, in contrast to invention, is often underestimated. In many organizational settings, the challenge lies not in generating new ideas, but in finding and fostering the ability to introduce those ideas into general use. There is a saying among salespeople that "nothing happens until somebody sells something" that has its parallel in the invention/innovation field. No invention is worth much until someone persuades other people to use it. Innovation is the process of persuading people to adopt an invention.

Innovation versus Sustaining Operations. Another insight into the problems involved in managing innovation is to contrast it with maintenance, or sustaining, operations. The dominant concern of most organizations is the sustaining of current oper-

399

ations rather than innovation. Sustaining operations are concerned with today—with generating profits or output to serve the needs of today. Innovation is concerned with tomorrow—with making sure that there is a continuing profit stream in the future. Innovation and sustaining operations are inextricably linked: the profits from sustaining today's operations ensure the survival of the organization and provide the resources that make innovation, tomorrow's activity, possible.

Innovation and sustaining operations, however, are different in important ways:

1. Innovation is a highly creative process, highly qualitative, highly unstructured; sustaining operations are disciplined and lend themselves to quantification.

2. Maintenance operations outcomes are more predictable than innovation. Innovation activities, because they do not lend themselves to precise forecasts, are far riskier.

3. Sustaining operations are immediate and create demands for immediate action. Innovation is postponable because it is concerned with tomorrow. Innovation and sustaining operations are often not compatible because of this difference; the immediacy of sustaining operations tends to crowd out or force postponement of innovation activities.

Inherent Problems. The problem in managing innovation stems from the fact that most organizations are designed for management of maintenance or sustaining operations. This objective is only natural, as business organizations are in business to do business and that usually means to take care of today's customer needs. The consideration of innovation is not meant to diminish the importance of maintenance management since it is absolutely essential to the survival of the firm that it efficiently manage its ongoing business. The problem arises when management attempts to impose that ongoing management approach on the *other* activity of the organization—innovation.

Maintenance management systems have characteristics that do not apply very well to problems of innovation.

1. Maintenance management systems are fairly rigid and have a rather well-defined structure. Jobs tend to be clearly and rather narrowly defined. Work is divided functionally so as to carry out the process of specialization to improve the efficiency of the firm.

2. Maintenance management systems establish an orderly process for handling work because the work is repetitive and predictable. To handle this kind of work, the organization tends to utilize people with orderly minds who can cope with repetitive activities. Survival demands that this work be efficiently performed, meaning that performance must be tightly controlled and work performance measured. It is possible to do so because the work flows are predictable.

These systems do not work well when applied to management of innovation. Both the process and the people involved are different. It requires, therefore, a different management system attuned to the needs of the job to be done. This focus means a different structure and a different approach.

Successful Management of Innovation. A management system designed to support the process of innovation must be attuned to the nature of innovation and the nature of innovators. Both the process and the people are creative. An effective system will include these 10 essential characteristics:

1. *Less structure.* The organization for innovation must have an open structure that encourages the creative process. Creativity is concerned with doing things differently and thinking about things differently. It must not be inhibited by the barriers of a maintenance management structure. This openness is consistent with the personality and style of the people—entrepreneurs—who must be supported by the innovative organization. Entrepreneurs, the people who carry out innovation in an organization, are creative, work across disciplines, and are accustomed to dealing with uncertainty. Their efforts will not flourish in an inhibiting organization structure.

2. *Separation from maintenance responsibilities.* The innovation system must be separated from the sustaining organization. It is concerned with different tasks—one is concerned with today; the other with tomorrow—and it requires different skills. If the maintenance organization is joined with the innovative organization, the immediacy of maintenance problems will drive out the concern for building for tomorrow.

3. *An interdisciplinary, not functional, structure.* The problems facing the innovator are highly complex and require the application of multiple disciplines. The innovative organization must be interdisciplinary in its makeup. This means more than just having multiple disciplines available when needed. The interdisciplinary approach requires the *simultaneous involvement* of all relevant disciplines so that each problem in the innovative process is considered and solved in the broadest light. As a practical guide, the innovative organization cannot be structured along functional lines; it must be a task-oriented structure containing each of the relevant disciplines.

4. *Top-management commitment.* The biggest barrier to success in innovation is the lack of continuing commitment from top management. Top management must believe in the importance of innovation in shaping the future of the organization yet, at the same time, accept the risk that innovation efforts may fail. Acceptance of risk and the building of commitment can best be accomplished by continuing participation of top management in the process of innovation. This participation must go beyond the initial stages to a long-term involvement. To accomplish this, the innovation managers must have a direct and unhindered reporting relationship to the principal decision makers in the firm.

5. *Continuity of senior professionals.* The innovative organization must be staffed with senior professionals; it should not be treated as a training ground. The job demands experience because of both the risks involved and the importance of success. Maintaining continuity of senior professionals in the innovative organization requires an incentive and advancement system that establishes long-term career potential for innovation positions.

6. *Acceptance of qualitative control.* The output of the innovation process rarely is predictable and does not lend itself to quantitative control. It is essential that the management system accept, particularly during the early stages of the innovation process, a control system that is qualitatively based. The control standards cannot be based on output, profit, or cost control. Instead, they should focus on the timeliness of decisions, the momentum of the process, and the quality of the development work.

7. *Decision pressure.* Despite the absence of quantitative control mechanisms, it is also essential that pressure for progress be maintained in the innovative organization. This is probably best accomplished by insisting that decisions be made and milestones reached according to compressed schedules. To meet this requirement, decision-making ability must be located within the innovative organization so that communication lines are short and there is little opportunity to defer decisions by pushing them upstairs. The organization's ability to make timely decisions is a strong incentive to the innovative group and an important measure of its productivity.

8. *Entrepreneurial incentive.* The successful system must attract entrepreneurs—professionals who are able to accept marketplace risk and who are committed to effective introduction. The management system must contain incentives that will draw these extremely rare, yet highly prized, innovators. While the innovative organization must recognize the high risk of failure, the innovative system must reward success and drive the entrepreneurs to the decisions that will bring inventions into general use.

9. *Entrepreneurial leadership.* The innovative organization needs strong leadership that will motivate, encourage, and push the professional innovators. It needs a zealot, an individual committed to pressing forward, an individual who understands how to use persuasion to get decisions made and to sustain organizational commitment to innovation.

10. *Consumer orientation.* The system must recognize that products do not make markets; markets make products. The organization and the individuals within it must have strong marketing skills, sensitivity to the consumer, and a willingness to accept the risks of the marketplace. The innovative process must begin with the consumer or the user and work back to the drawing board to generate an idea or an application that will solve a real, rather than a make-believe, problem.

See also Communications, organizational; Conformity in management; Decision-making process; Product planning and development; Project management; Research and development management.

REFERENCES

Cafarelli, Eugene J.: *Developing New Products and Repositioning Mature Brands,* John Wiley, New York, 1980.

Calantone, Roger, and Robert G. Cooper: "New Product Scenarios: Prospects for Success," *Journal of Marketing,* vol. 45, Spring 1981, pp. 48–60.

Stancill, James McNeill: "Realistic Criteria for Judging New Ventures," *Harvard Business Review,* vol. 59, no. 6, November–December 1981, pp. 60–72.

DAVID W. NYLEN, *Stetson University*

Input-Output Analysis

Input-output analysis is a technique developed by the Harvard economist Wassily Leontief for measuring the effect of interindustry transactions on (1) the economy and (2) individual industries.

Figure I-1a shows a simplified input-output table in which each industry is designated by a number. (Only 15 are shown for purposes of illustration, whereas an actual table may cover several hundred.) *D* stands for total demand and *T* for total output; *H* designates household services, which are industry

Part A

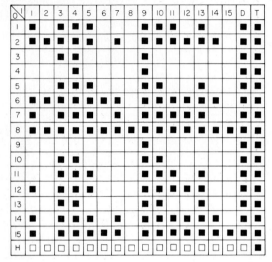

Part B

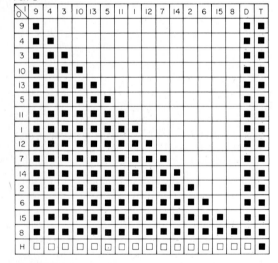

FIG. I-1 Examples of input-output tables. (Adapted from Wassily Leontief, "The Structure of Development," *Scientific American*, September 1963, pp. 148–166. With permission of the copyright holder.)

goes to the other industries appearing above it in the vertical column, as shown in Fig. I-1*b*, which is simply a rearrangement of Fig. I-1*a*. This rearrangement of the order in which the industries are listed will, in the case of an advanced industrialized country, produce the triangular pattern shown in Fig. I-1*b*, and from this it is possible to calculate how an increase in demand for the products of one industry will affect the demand for the products of its suppliers. Any increase in the demand for the output of one industry "cascades," as Leontief has said, down the triangle, affecting all the industries below it. Thus, if the demand for the products of industry 9 increases, industry 4, which is its supplier, will experience an increase in demand and will, in turn, purchase more from industry 3, and so on.

Of course, the increases in demand for the products of the supplier industries are not equal to the increases experienced by the customer industries above them, but coefficients have been developed to determine the effects on the supplier industries.

It has been found that all advanced economies, such as those of the United States and the industrialized countries of Western Europe, will exhibit a triangular pattern on an input-output table, whereas a table for a less developed country will show a more random design.

The U.S. Department of Commerce has developed input-output tables for the U.S. economy, and governments of other countries, including some of the less developed countries, have also charted the interindustry patterns of their economies. These tables, of course, give industry names and the actual figures for the transactions.

See also Economic concepts; Economic measurements; Forecasting business conditions.

REFERENCES

Leontief, Wassily: *Input-Output Economics*, Oxford University Press, New York, 1966.

Miernyk, William H.: *The Elements of Input-Output Analysis*, Random House, New York, 1965.

Survey of Current Business, "The Input-Output Structure of the U.S. Economy: 1967," February 1974, pp. 24–50.

JACKSON E. RAMSEY, *James Madison University*

requirements other than those for products from suppliers—requirements for labor, for example. Inputs *I* are read from the vertical columns; outputs *O* are read from the horizontal columns.

Each industry uses part of its output for itself and delivers another part to final demand (which includes demand for export), while the remainder

Insurance and Risk Management

No matter how well management sets its goals and executes its plans, the goals may be thwarted by unplanned events such as fires, hurricanes, liability suits, embezzlement, and other fortuitous losses. It was to fit the management of these risks of loss into the larger framework of general management that the techniques of risk management have evolved.

Risk Management Defined. After initial opposition from those who felt its use would conflict with other concepts of business risks, the term *risk management* has now achieved general acceptance as referring to pure, rather than business, risks. It can be defined as the art of selecting methods of loss control, risk finance (including insurance), and internal administration which develop the lowest long-term total cost of risk to the organization.

Loss control refers to preventive measures taken by the organization under the direct or indirect supervision of the risk manager to control all fortuitous losses. It encompasses fire protection, personnel safety, security, and control of claims adjustment.

Risk finance refers to techniques used to fund known or anticipated losses. The most common technique is insurance, but other methods include bank lines of credit, formal or informal pooling of risks among members of a single industry, and chronological stabilization plans. The last-named, sometimes called "spread-loss plans," are similar to insurance but call for the insured to repay, over a period of years, claims which have been paid. *Chronological stabilization* is thus a method of leveling high losses which occur in one year over subsequent years when losses may be lower, thereby enabling concerns to assume a higher degree of risk than would be the case under pure insurance.

Internal administration of risk is concerned with (1) record keeping of losses and values, (2) communications regarding claims and loss prevention procedures, (3) preparation and administration of corporate policy and manuals, (4) allocation of risk costs among operating units, and (5) administrative aspects of insurance purchasing.

Property. Risks of property loss are both direct and indirect.

Direct loss is (1) the amount the physical asset is diminished in value, as measured by the actual cash value (replacement cost less physical depreciation) or (2) the amount actually required to replace the destroyed property (replacement cost). To minimize cash-flow fluctuations, most organizations now insure on a replacement cost basis. Direct losses can occur to buildings, equipment, stock, vehicles, accounts receivable, valuable papers, boilers, cash, securities, cargo shipments, and any other tangible property.

Indirect losses include (1) loss of income, also known as business interruption, or the obsolescent term *use and occupancy*; (2) extra expenses (additional costs incurred to maintain activities as nearly normal as possible following destruction of property); and (3) loss of rent, loss of tuition fees, salesworkers' commissions, and power outage.

Disaster control is an element of risk management which establishes guides and procedures to follow when a fire, earthquake, airplane crash, or other disaster occurs. The risk manager should anticipate all possible cases and develop plans for immediate salvage and for communication with fire departments, police, the press, and important company officials. The plan should be checked periodically to see that emergency supplies are intact and all parties are familiar with procedures.

Personnel. The principal source of loss among personnel is on-the-job injuries, for which all states have statutory requirements for paying workers' compensation. Other sources of personnel loss are illnesses or off-the-job accidents, alcoholism, drug misuse, and strikes. Personnel safety is an important subject closely interwoven with government requirements (such as those stipulated by the Occupational Safety and Health Act), labor relations (labor contracts often have references to safety), and insurance. Technical assistance is frequently available from insurance carriers and their agents or brokers. It is the risk manager's job to act as adviser and coordinator to all persons involved with the safety program to see that undue emphasis is not given to one aspect at the expense of others.

The safety function seems to be predominantly with the labor relations department of a large organization, although many are now placing it under the direction of the risk manager.

Liability. The importance of public liability has grown enormously in recent years. The public has become increasingly aware that those whose negligence causes a loss can be held legally responsible. The courts have even gone beyond pure negligence and are holding many organizations legally responsible for damage where no negligence can be proved. This development is reflected in the growing number of lawsuits and in the increasing amount of awards. Multimillion-dollar judgments to single individuals are no longer rare.

The result has been to seriously undermine the stability of many important enterprises. The most prominent example is that of medical malpractice. Insurance companies underwriting this line have almost uniformly lost money and have withdrawn from the field. Those few remaining must charge premiums so high that they are prohibitive to many doctors and hospitals. As a result, many hospitals have formed their own insurance companies, and a significant number of doctors have placed their assets in outside trusts and are forgoing any insurance.

Product liability seems to be following close behind medical malpractice. Manufacturers are being held to an almost absolute standard of care: suits are being judged against a manufacturer even if all reasonable precautions were used. Retailers and lessors that have no part to play in the safety of the product are also being held responsible. (*See* Product liability.)

Municipal liability is also growing at such a rate as to cause some cities and counties to go without insurance and others to form pools in which to handle their losses.

The *conventional liabilities* have to do with bodily injury and property damage. The increasing emphasis on professionalism has also caused increased liability for professional acts. Persons who hold themselves as experts in any recognized professional line have been held responsible for failure to carry out their professional duties in an acceptable manner. Engineers, architects, accountants, attorneys, and many other professionals have considerable exposure to such loss for which professional liability insurance may be, but is not always, available.

An important aspect of professional liability is that which directors and officers of corporations owe to stockholders and the public. Insurance on a limited basis for this type of claim is available, and most large corporations purchase the insurance.

Insurance. Most of the risk manager's emphasis is placed on negotiating insurance within adequate limits, with coverage broad enough to include as many catastrophic losses as possible but not so complete as to insure minor losses which the organization could fund without insurance. Most organizations can readily absorb individual losses up to at least $\frac{1}{10}$ of 1 percent of their annual revenues, but where the loss potential exceeds the tolerable level, insurance is desirable.

The risk manager's first step is to select a skilled agent or broker. The manager then communicates to the agent or broker (jointly called *producers*) just what the needs are. In this process, the manager may be given considerable assistance by the producer or specialized consultant.

Property insurance is normally placed in several different contracts: (1) fire and extended coverage (wind, explosion, hail, aircraft, riot, vehicles, and smoke); (2) boiler and machinery; (3) crime (including employee fidelity, money, securities, and forgeries); and (4) difference in conditions (extends coverage to all risks rather than named perils and may or may not include earthquake and flood).

Liability insurance is usually separated into primary and excess.

Primary policies cover all claims up to the primary limit, varying from about $100,000 to $500,000. They can be written for general premises, manufacturers and contractors, automobile, aircraft, professional (errors and omissions) liability, directors and officers, and many others. The most effective primary policy is the comprehensive general liability policy which provides the broadest coverage of any of the primary policies.

The umbrella excess liability policy is then used to ride above all the primary policies, increasing their limits to the desired amount and providing even broader coverage than the primaries, subject to a major self-insured retention—at least $10,000. Most concerns are well advised to carry limits in excess of $50 million. Catastrophe protection is the most important function of insurance, and the higher limits are relatively inexpensive.

Insurance Carriers. There are four kinds of insurance carriers: stock, mutual, reciprocal, and Lloyd's. The organizational form is of little concern to the risk manager because there are strong and weak companies in all categories. *Stock companies* are owned by private investors and constitute the greatest percentage of insurers. *Mutual companies* are owned by the policyholders and usually pay dividends to them. *Reciprocal organizations* are similar to mutuals but act through an attorney in fact. *Lloyd's* is one organization consisting of many individuals, by far the most prominent of which is Lloyd's of London, who operate worldwide in almost all lines.

Insurance carriers can also be subdivided into those that write only through agents and brokers and those that write directly with the policy holders. Most stock companies are agency companies, but some write direct. Many mutual companies are direct writers, but many also write exclusively through producers. Lloyd's works only through brokers.

Selection of the insurer is an important function which the risk manager must assume. Considerable help can be obtained from producers, and the insured may want to retain the producer for advice even when dealing directly with the insurer, in which case the insured pays the producer a fee in lieu of the commission he or she would normally receive.

Self-Insurance. The rising costs of insurance have directed management's attention to the fact that insurance is not an economical way to handle small losses. Interest in self-insuring the lower levels has grown. The most prominent subjects for self-insurance are workers' compensation (relatively high-frequency, low-magnitude losses), automobile physical damage, money and securities, plate glass, medical payments, and low-valued properties. Although property and workers' compensation were the first areas to receive self-insurance emphasis, growing interest in public liability self-insurance has led to the formation of many service firms whose sole function is to provide claims adjusting and related services to self-insurers. The judicious selection of self-insurance service companies, loss prevention specialists, and properly worded excess insurance is an increasingly important aspect of the risk manager's responsibility.

Legal. The risk manager works within a structure of statewide insurance regulations. United States insurance companies must meet varying state requirements for forms of coverage and rates they may charge. In some cases, this regulation impedes their flexibility for the larger or more complex account, which then turns to the "surplus lines" or "nonadmitted" market. This market consists of United States or foreign insurers not licensed in the state involved.

Captive Insurance Companies. In large measure to by-pass this restrictive regulation, many large industrial firms have formed their own insurance companies—usually headquartered outside the United States, principally in Bermuda. These wholly owned insurance subsidiaries allow the risk manager direct access to the worldwide reinsurance market, which offers more flexible terms. They also may assume reinsurance from other insurers and develop a profit center.

The risk manager frequently works in tandem with the firm's legal advisers in analyzing major contracts and leases. The manager is concerned with provisions which require insurance as well as indemnity "hold-harmless" agreements, whereby one party assumes liability of the other. These contract conditions must be carefully coordinated with insurance coverage.

Summary. Every organization has a risk manager whose duties may range from the simple purchase of property and liability insurance to the most complex arrangements of internal funding, captive insurance companies, contract claims, and loss prevention services and worldwide accounting functions. In a small organization it may be the president who makes the decisions. In a larger organization it is usually the chief financial officer or a full-time risk manager reporting to the chief financial officer, though other orientations are used. The risk manager's work cuts across all lines of the organization. He or she must be aware of everything going on as well as plans for the future. The manager's background must be strong in insurance but should also include finance, accounting, engineering, and law. The goal of this responsibility is that of the organization itself: long-term conservation of assets and maximum profitability.

See also Financial management; Product liability; Real estate management, corporate; Risk analysis and management.

REFERENCES

Lenz, M., Jr.: *Risk Management Manual,* The Merritt Co., Santa Monica, Calif., 1977.

Practical Risk Management, P.O. Box 10093, Oakland, Calif. 94610, 1977.

Riegel, R., J. S. Miller, and C. A. Williams, Jr.: *Insurance Principles and Practices: Property and Liability,* 6th ed., Prentice-Hall, Englewood Cliffs, N.J., 1975.

Williams, C. A., Jr., and R. M. Heins: *Risk Management and Insurance,* 5th ed., McGraw-Hill, New York, 1984.

DAVID WARREN, *Risk Management Consultant, Orinda, California.*

International Operations and Management in Multinational Companies

A multinational company cannot operate effectively without a well-conceived philosophy to guide the people who manage its operations. Successful operations proceed from organizations that uniquely suit the individual company in its international marketplace. Four major functions—industrial relations, public relations, finance, and legal administration—deserve particular attention in international business. Finally, everything must be tied together by formulating written statements which set forth the various elements of the company's policy.

An International Business Philosophy Statement

As a starting point for entering the international arena, a company must first develop an underlying philosophy. This philosophy statement defines the fundamental convictions and commitments the company will adopt in meeting its unique responsibilities in the worldwide market. Equally important, the statement provides sound, constructive guidelines for corporate management of its international operations. An example of one such statement, which could apply to almost any multinational or international company, appears in Table I-1.

Forms of International Organization

Selection of the proper form of organization is critical to the success of multinational operations. Before describing three possible forms of organization—out of a myriad of possibilities—it is important to recognize the following:

1. The organization form must be structured so as to meet the needs of the individual company in terms of its own philosophies, strategies, objectives, priorities, markets, products, and technologies.

2. The organization form is and must be dynamic and evolutionary in nature; i.e., it must be flexible enough to be adjusted as the aims of the company and market conditions change. As a result, the risks inherent in rigid adherence to a formal organization chart can be minimized.

3. In a multinational, multimarket, multitechnology company, the organization form must provide for and accommodate efficient, timely dissemination and flow of information.

405

TABLE 1-1 Example of International Business Philosophy Statement

1. *International business responsibilities*
   a. We are dedicated to search worldwide for new products, services, markets, joint ventures, and acquisitions that add to our capabilities to move the corporation forward. We recognize that operations on a worldwide basis will have an ever-increasing role in our future growth. Consequently, we are charged with the responsibility of developing our business planning, manufacturing, and marketing in the perspective of the global marketplace.
   b. We shall be aware of, and responsible to, the impact our operations have on host countries, and we shall promote a successful long-term relationship with the host nations in which we operate. We shall strive to contribute to their economic development through the introduction of advanced technology, management planning and control systems, marketing know-how, and the training and promotion of qualified national personnel.
   c. Within the framework of our organization, the operating groups have individual product and profit responsibility on a worldwide basis, unless otherwise assigned to a multiproduct, multimarket geographical organization. Corporate-level coordination and policy guidance will be provided by the office of the president, which must be informed at all times of matters which might affect the corporation's overall business practices or reputation.
2. *Investments*
   a. Based on sound economic planning, the corporation intends to make investments on a long-term basis. Where economically viable, we shall invest in productive facilities to enhance our opportunity for continued growth and expansion. Investment decisions will take into account such factors as opportunities within the host country markets, exports from host country operations, sources of supply, possibilities for volume production, operating economics, and the availability of a trained or trainable work force.
   b. Should it become impractical to continue an operation for whatever reason, we shall make every effort to minimize any adverse impact on the host country.
   c. The support and cooperation of host governments are prerequisites of long-range growth and development. We look to host governments to promulgate policies and regulations on a fair and nondiscriminatory basis, to establish sufficient opportunity for reinvestment and expansion, and to provide for repatriation of earnings on an equitable basis.
   d. We recognize our responsibility to accept reasonable obligations that are placed upon business enterprises in the national interest. We shall respect the sovereign rights, customs, laws, and regulations of our host governments. Our local managements will be expected to make full use of the legal facilities of the corporation to assure compliance with the host country's statutory requirements.
3. *Markets, customers, and suppliers*
   a. As we participate in new or expanding international markets, we shall endeavor to develop and market products and services which are specifically tailored for host country markets and which are produced in the most economical manner possible. Underlying this important responsibility is our firm obligation to take every step to maintain our high standards of product quality and design as well as to service our customers in a manner superior to our competition.
   b. We shall utilize host country suppliers to the greatest degree possible where price, quality, delivery, and service meet our requirements for being a low-cost manufacturer.
   c. In our dealings with customers, the only factors to be considered are quality, price, delivery, and service. It is not our policy to utilize the corporation's position as a purchaser to promote sales. Conversely, a supplier's position as a customer is not a factor to be considered when making purchases.
4. *Research and technology*
   a. A key element in achieving our corporate goal is a steady outflow of innovative, high-technology products for our worldwide markets. In technology, as in manufacturing and marketing, we recognize the global challenge we face in maintaining a competitive position. To realize the maximum advantage from our technical competency and experience, we shall exchange technology from operation to operation, without regard to location, wherever possible. When technology is exchanged between two countries, each operation should benefit by improved profitability. By sharing technical skills and experiences, all operating units are made stronger and better able to achieve their goals.
5. *Facilities*
   a. Our operations will be located wherever it is economically sound to do so, recognizing that facilities are constructed and expanded to support local market needs, as well as to provide an enlarging basis for export to regional and area markets. Where feasible, multiproduct plants that can manufacture products for more than one market will be utilized.
6. *Human resources*
   a. We consider our human resources the essential element in the continuing success of the corporation. Wherever in the world our men and women are located, we are pledged to the following standards:
      (1) We shall strive always to attract, develop, and motivate people who demonstrate willingness, intelligence, and strong moral fiber in carrying out their responsibilities.
      (2) We shall hire, train, and promote qualified national personnel at all levels of the operation to the greatest extent possible. Race, color, creed, national origin, age, and sex will not be factors influencing our decisions on employment and advancement.
      (3) One of our highest priorities is the development of our employees, at all levels, to enhance their personal opportunities for career development.
      (4) Mutual respect and trust, prerequisites of effective teamwork, are basic to our ability to compete. This means taking the initiative in developing wholesome and productive working environments which recognize the importance of human dignity in a person's satisfaction with job and life.
      (5) We shall encourage two-way communications with all employees. Employees should be informed about matters that affect them or their jobs, management's position on relevant issues, and corporate actions which materially influence their long-range interests.
      (6) Our objective is to establish and administer wage and benefit programs which are equal to or above industry practices and national norms.

TABLE 1-1 Example of International Business Philosophy Statement (*Continued*)

7. *Finance*
   a. As a multinational corporation, we are necessarily involved in dealing in many of the world's currencies and in currency exchange. It is our policy to act to protect the corporation and its subsidiaries against exchange losses but not to seek speculative gains through currency transactions or similar activities unrelated to the nature of our business.
   b. Funds required for working capital and the growth of international operations should, where possible, be provided by borrowing in local currencies to protect against currency exchange losses and to avoid the complexity of currency conversions and exchange restrictions.
8. *Conflict of interest*
   Employees who are in a position to influence decisions must be aware of our policy concerning matters that may constitute a conflict of interest.
9. *Public responsibility*
   a. We believe our existence in the long term, and our role today in the many countries in which we operate, is dependent upon responsible citizenship in those societies. We have an obligation to use our resources in a manner which furthers an economically and socially healthy environment within our host countries.
   b. We shall conduct business in a manner which conveys the image of good neighbors and responsible, contributing citizens to our communities, governments, and the environment. Our objectives and accomplishments will be weighed by the measure of their contribution to the fulfillment of our social responsibility.
   c. In all cases, we shall abide by the spirit and letter of the local laws and customs of our host countries.
   d. Political contributions may be made only when permitted by the laws and regulations of the countries involved and by the laws of the United States. All significant contributions must be approved in advance by the appropriate United States headquarters authority.
   e. Public positions on issues relating to business operations will be communicated only through appropriate channels and in a manner consistent with corporate policy. We shall refrain from any involvement in partisan political activity or interference with national political decisions.

---

4. The form of organization must be determined and built from the bottom up rather than from the top down.

Certain organization forms are used more often than others. Three, in particular, warrant consideration.

International Company or International Profit Center. This approach is best suited to the single-product-line company or to the company utilizing common fundamental technology across a number of product lines. The markets served are most often similar, if not identical, in nature. Typical characteristics of this form of organization are:

1. Each international region has a senior operating executive in charge, reporting to the president who has responsibility for overall coordination.

2. The president has senior staff executives who provide specialized assistance to the regional executives as well as set and control policy in their respective functional areas. Senior staff executives report to the president.

3. Each region operates as a profit center within the company, and the company itself is an international profit center.

4. Finished products and components for the finished products often are transferred between regions on an intercompany basis.

5. The major part of the technology utilized is developed by the parent company. The same is true for systems and procedures; therefore, information flow and communication do not repre-sent severe problems, inasmuch as "common languages" are employed.

6. It is important to guard against duplicating functions in the international company where those functions are performed best in the parent company.

Divisional Worldwide Profit and Product Responsibility. This approach is best suited to the multiproduct, multimarket, multitechnology company where the application of the products is of paramount importance. Typical characteristics of this form of organization are:

1. The parent company is organized by product-oriented operating groups or divisions. The products in each division are related by technology and/or market.

2. Each operating division functions as a separate company, even though it is subject to overall corporate policy and broad directional control.

3. Each operating division has a worldwide responsibility for product and profit; therefore, it has its own international operations organization. It justifies and establishes its own international ventures and facilities.

4. A vast proportion of the technology is developed at the home base.

5. Information flow and communications are facilitated because common products are dealt with on a worldwide basis.

6. An inherent problem in this form of organization is the tendency toward building excess produc-

tive and/or marketing capacity in a particular country or region.

Geographic Area Administrative and Coordinating Organization. This approach is best suited to the multiproduct, multimarket, multitechnology company which recognizes the need to provide overall guidance and policy control within each major geographic area to the various groups and divisions operating within that area. Typical characteristics of this form of organization are:

1. A relatively small group of highly competent executives are headquartered in a major geographic international area. They have the area product and profit responsibilities for the products produced by several of the corporation's divisions.

2. The products for which area executives have responsibility are common (or compatible) in the areas of technology and/or manufacturing and/or marketing and/or application.

3. Multiproduct marketing organizations are utilized.

4. Multiproduct manufacturing plants are utilized in order to minimize excess productive capacity.

5. Technology develops and flows from the home base to the international geographic area, and vice versa.

6. Communications and flow of information will be two of the most difficult—and yet two of the most essential—aspects of the organization form.

International Industrial Relations

In most cases, the organization of the international industrial relations function should follow closely the general organization structure of the company at large.

Authority and Responsibility. The role of the industrial relations executive in a foreign country should be clearly defined, with specific areas of authority and responsibility carefully identified and agreed to by corporate operations and industrial relations officers. Time and thought given to function definition will be repaid many times over because the industrial relations executive and the executive's superiors know and understand the breadth and limitation of authority as well as the specific personnel policies and programs for which the activity is accountable. Line and staff relationships among international personnel managers and operating group and corporate industrial relations heads should receive the same careful attention.

Staffing Practices. The selection, promotion, and retention of personnel in the international operation are especially crucial. There is no single policy that fits every company's needs or every situation

within the full operation of a diverse multinational company. A uniform corporate staffing policy, however, applicable in most instances and under all but the most unusual conditions, is fundamental to sound international personnel management. As with organization style, the staffing of foreign operations is predicated largely on the company's general operational philosophy. Its choices range from developing a cadre of mobile international executives and functional specialists available for assignments throughout the world to employing exclusively local nationals at every level of the operation.

An emerging trend among many multinational companies is the utilization of local nationals in management and professional positions, thereby reducing or eliminating expatriate and third-country national personnel. While short-term indoctrination and training costs can be high, subsequent savings in expatriate and third-country national compensation and foreign service allowance costs can be substantial. Even more important in most cases, employment of host country nationals has cultural, social, and institutional benefits.

Training and Development. The reality of the company's beliefs about its community and social responsibilities is often evidenced by its education and training practices. A clear definition of the organization's social philosophy is an important prerequisite to the development of a comprehensive training program. Selection of particular training and development techniques hinges on the company's staffing policies, the availability of experienced and knowledgeable job candidates in the employment market area, the stage of maturity of the local organization, and the organizational style of the firm. Core programs for supervisory, management, and executive personnel can be conducted at home or abroad by the corporate management development staff. Additional seminars and instructional programs can be continued by component operating organizations. These courses can provide concentrated study of supervisory and management methods or address technical and professional matters in detail.

Compensation and Employee Benefits. Unquestionably, one of the most difficult and perplexing elements of international industrial relations management is the establishment and administration of compensation and benefit plans. The time, knowledge, and experience required in international compensation administration increase geometrically as the number of expatriates, nationals, and third-country nationals increases. This problem is compounded further by the rise in the number of countries in which the business operates. Subjects like tax equalization, foreign service allowances, moving and resettlement expenses, home leave practices, statutory benefit requirements, and host country customs and practices can be the bane of a salary and benefit plan designed for a domestic management structure. When operating abroad, a corporate policy of conforming to the host country's compensation customs and practices provides a logical basis for developing and administering specific salary and benefit plans. Except for the least developed parts of the world, a comprehensive analysis of national and local pay rates, coupled with the company's general philosophy on remuneration levels, can be a principal tool for determining the basic wage and salary structure of the organization. Refinements to meet the more unusual compensation circumstances of expatriate and third-country national personnel can follow, but *the core structure is the local or national pay scale and the compensation customs, practices, and regulations of the host country.*

Labor Relations. International labor-management relations remain one of the most unsettled areas of personnel management within the multinational business organization. The trend toward international unionism has accelerated with the internationalization of the business enterprise and with the formation of transnational management systems. At the same time, international management has become increasingly concerned with the rising power of organized labor abroad. By the same token, governmental regulations in such areas as wage-price controls, codetermination, and local ownership must be taken into account.

One of the essential questions facing multinational management, then, is the most effective way in which to administer the labor relations function. Should it be done at the local management level, by area or regional officials, or through representatives of the corporate industrial relations staff? Similarly, the multinational company must resolve the issue of the applicability of its basic labor relations policies, which frequently were developed to meet home country conditions, to a foreign environment.

In most industrial settings today, labor relations management can be delegated to the local organization, assuming that the necessary degree of competency has been developed. Generally, local management will be more familiar with shop conditions and competitive employment practices, as well as with the cultural, legal, and historic setting in which local labor relations are conducted.

With respect to the future, however, the placement of labor relations authority remains at question. The growing tendency to multinational unionism and international union cooperation may ultimately lead to the more frequent establishment of regional industrial relations offices that parallel the multinational union in authority and prestige.

International Public Relations

Today's international public relations management calls for a new perception of the world as countries develop their own resources and reach beyond their borders for materials, labor force, special skills, technology, and investment capital. As a consequence, there are at least two ways to view public relations management on an international scale. One is from the standpoint of a company or operation intent on achieving a business objective in a foreign country. The other is through the eyes of the multinational corporation, whose commerce crosses many national boundaries and whose relationships with the public have a profound impact on the management of the world enterprise as well as on international trade itself.

Evolution of Philosophy. In tracing the evolution of public relations philosophy, it is accurate to say that in the early days of the multinational company, overseas entities regarded themselves largely as islands, separate and distinct from both their parent companies and their counterpart subsidiaries in other countries. In those days, few companies recognized or acknowledged the public relations impact of their overseas activities. Those that did confined their concerns to the countries in which they were located. Usually, the host countries were content to have them operate in this manner.

The advent of the European Common Market and the actions of the Organization of Petroleum Exporting Countries, the Organization for Economic Cooperation and Development, the agencies of the United Nations, international environmental and labor groups, and various other government and private-interest organizations have changed this situation. The result is that if a change in corporate policy, an environmental problem, or a violation of ethical standards is important enough to be reported by the press of one country, it is likely to be transmitted widely to other countries.

Constituencies and Issues. The first step, then, is for a company to know its constituencies. They can be identified as segments of the general public with which most companies have continuing interaction. They are the source of both criticism and support and are the objects of any well-planned public relations program. Generally speaking, they include public media, government and agencies, employees, conservationists, the financial community, churches, labor organizations, suppliers, distributors, customers, competitors, pressure groups, stockholders, academia, minority groups, plant communities, and the voting public.

The issues that surround these constituencies are multitudinous and must be well defined and understood before public relations planning begins. Typical of the issues are prices and profits, consumerism demands, equal opportunities, nationalism, industrial democracy, industrial safety and health, truth in advertising, environment, energy and natural resources, exports and imports, taxes, incentives and restrictions, investments, employment, mergers and acquisitions, money and credit, business ethics, and the quality of management.

Policies and Procedures. Organizing a business for action on an international public relations front is essentially a three-phase procedure consisting of collection, evaluation, and dissemination or implementation: (1) In the collection phase, data, trends, and forecasts, such as customers' needs, market conditions, internal and external attitudes, and political, economic, and social projections form an information base; (2) the information is evaluated by a "think tank" composed of top management, public relations professionals, specialists, and consultants; (3) the output, in the form of policy and approved action programs, is communicated to constituent groups.

The foregoing suggest these specific actions:

Establish an information base. Specifically, determine how your company's policies and practices are perceived by the public which is in a position to influence your future course of business. At the same time, assess the social needs and expectations of both home and host countries.

Determine a common ground. Do so on the basis of your analysis of the information available. Make any nonpolicy changes that are indicated to accommodate local mores, customs, and traditions. Reevaluate other, broader policy questions with a view to making changes to improve the business environment.

Develop operational, economic, and ethical guidelines. These will assist your operating entities in their relationships with people inside and outside of the corporation. Make it clear that a good business reputation, like bottom-line results, is an operating responsibility and that managers will be measured, promoted, and rewarded according to their results.

Communicate values to your constituents. On an ongoing basis, show how your company's operations serve the needs of host countries. Do not neglect to report your efforts to shareholders, employees, citizens in the community, and other potential sources of support.

Demonstrate an interest in the locales from which you draw your employees, services, and materials. Do so by participating with others in efforts to improve these locales as places in which to live and work.

Assign specific responsibility for public relations management to your highest-rank operating manager in each country. Require that public relations problems, objectives, and strategies be included in the long-range planning cycle.

International Financial Management

Financial activities outside the home country include essentially the same elements as those in the domestic area. The structure and methods used to perform the financial functions are dependent on, and must be consistent with, the organizational relationships established for all the functions of the company.

Operation of a Typical System. In this section, an international financial management system which is functionally centralized in the world headquarters is described. The system is patterned, however, to serve and to utilize, where appropriate, the company's operating organization which is decentralized on a product-line basis but centralized geographically in major international areas. Product-line managers in the home country have worldwide responsibility for product-line profits.

Those groups with financial responsibilities that play major roles in this international management scheme are identified as field operating, field corporate, group operating, and home office corporate. Unit controllers or finance managers serving the operating divisions located outside the home country constitute *field operating* in this description. Their line-reporting relationship is to operating division management.

Field corporate staff is provided only in countries or areas where two or more divisions conduct substantial business. Field corporate staffs are competent in both accounting and treasury matters. They report directly to home office corporate.

Under this management scheme, foreign operating units report to home country operating divisions which, in turn, report to home country operating groups. *Group operating*, as used in this section, refers to financial staffs in both operating divisions and operating groups in the home country. Group operating is responsible on a line basis to group management and functionally to home office corporate.

At the home office, financial functions include accounting, treasury, taxation, financial public relations, insurance, and other financial specialties. All these functions are included in *home office corporate* in this description.

Forecasting and Accounting Practices. These functions are performed by field operating under the direction and surveillance of group operating. The latter consolidates all operations of the operating group for reporting to group management and to corporate headquarters. Field operating also advises field corporate on all financial aspects of its forecast and its operating requirements. Accounting must conform to host country standards as well as to the parent company's requirements.

Cash Management. Field corporate provides cash for all approved operating requirements in its geographic area, and it must invest or "dispose of" excess cash. It relies on forecasts from the operating units and manages cash within approved forecasts. It consults with home office corporate when significant deviations from forecasts appear, and it works under the general surveillance of the home office corporate, which has final responsibility for worldwide financial management.

In those areas where there is no corporate organization, field operating personnel are responsible for local cash management. In such instances, field operating reports to the home country group which looks to home office corporate to provide required financing for operating requirements.

Bank Relations. Responsibility for bank relations is shared by several of the financial groups. Field operating is responsible for relations with its own banks. Field corporate is responsible for relations with indigenous banks and local branches of the company's international banks used for corporate purposes. Home office corporate is responsible for establishing bank relations policy and for relations with the company's principal international banks.

Merchant bank contact and arrangements are the responsibility of home office corporate. Appropriate field corporate personnel, however, are made aware of any significant developments involving their local area merchant banks.

Contacts with important commercial and merchant banks are maintained in part by home office corporate visits with bank officials both in the corporate offices and in the bank offices in the home country and abroad. Home office corporate makes or approves major bank selections.

Currency Control. Control of currency exposure is a responsibility of home office corporate, although it is dependent on financial statements and supplemental currency reports from all field operations. The worldwide currency exposure position is visible only at home office corporate where final company consolidations are made. In making its currency judgments, however, home office corporate depends to an important extent on timely reporting and evaluation of the local economic and currency outlook by field operating and field corporate. Steps to remedy undesirable currency positions involve field operating through control of assets and liabilities, and may involve various field financial personnel if local loans are required. Hedging operations are directed and controlled by home office corporate.

Taxation Coordination. Home office corporate is responsible for coordination of taxation matters throughout the world. It relies on field operating and field corporate for preparation of local returns and routine relations with tax authorities. All significant tax returns are reviewed and all major tax negotiations are directed by home office corporate.

Credit Management. Credit matters are the direct responsibility of the various operating units. Home office corporate reviews credit performance, assists in negotiating special credit facilities, and provides other specialized credit services upon the request of operational units.

Insurance. Insurance matters worldwide are coordinated by home office corporate, and major insurance policies are arranged by it. Coverage requirements, employee benefit levels, pension funding, and similar matters are determined by home office corporate with the assistance of local management as required.

Stockholder Relations. These relations are the responsibility of home office corporate, although certain activities may take place in overseas areas with the assistance of local company personnel.

This financial management plan involves the financial staff at each level of the organization. The nature of needed services dictates this spread of responsibility. Furthermore, the multinational character of the financial community makes it necessary for the company to interface with the financial community on a worldwide basis. At the same time, the constraints of financial matters require worldwide compliance with company policy and effective surveillance by home office corporate.

International Legal Administration

For the typical multinational company having manufacturing, marketing, and service facilities in many countries, there are logistical problems in furnishing these operations with timely and effective legal services. Normally, these services are furnished either directly by in-house counsel, with assistance as required by outside foreign counsel, or through local foreign counsel. Aside from the careful selection and close monitoring of foreign counsel, it is essential that guidelines be established to distinguish (1) those matters which local operating personnel may handle directly with foreign counsel, without the necessity of reference to in-house counsel, from (2) those which must be referred first to in-house counsel. The fundamental premise underlying the determination of which matters must be referred first to in-house counsel is that such matters may involve legal or general corporate policy considerations, set a significant precedent, or involve unusual risk or significant loss exposure.

Local Administration. Examples of matters which might be handled directly by operating managers with foreign counsel are work permits, importation of products and supplies, immigration matters, limited currency control matters, collection matters where the amount involved is under $10,000, and holding of shareholder and directors' meetings.

Corporate Control. Examples of matters which might be referred first to in-house counsel are all patent, trademark, and trade name questions; all income tax matters and, where the amount involved is over $10,000, all other tax matters; formation or dissolu-

TABLE 1-2 Example of International Joint-Venture Guidelines

During recent years, we have entered into an increasing number of international joint-venture arrangements, and several new joint-venture opportunities are normally under study at any given time. Usually, joint ventures are entered into for one or more of the following reasons:

Local laws prohibit total ownership by foreign or foreign-owned companies.

The nature of the project, or the political or economic instability of the country in which the operation is located, makes it desirable to share risks with a local partner.

Growth potential is enhanced by the participation of local partners.

Partners can make a significant contribution by providing sources of raw materials, establishing marketing outlets, and, in some cases, technology.

It is important that all of us have a clear understanding of our corporate policy with respect to these arrangements. Therefore, the following general guidelines are set forth:

1. Sufficient equity is to be put into the joint venture to make it a viable economic entity. As a rule of thumb, equity capital should be equal to the investment in fixed assets, i.e., land, buildings, and equipment.
2. All joint-venture debt should be financed through local borrowing. Also, at times it may be desirable to finance a portion of our share of the equity capital through local borrowing. This is in keeping with our overall philosophy of providing funds required for growth of foreign operations in each major geographic area by borrowing in local currencies. By so doing, we are able to protect against currency exchange losses. In addition, debt can be serviced in the currency generated by the project without the complexity of currency conversions or exchange restrictions.
3. Any funds borrowed to finance fixed assets should be provided by long-term debt, preferably for a period of at least 10 years or a period corresponding to the useful life of the assets.
4. Working capital may be financed through short-term borrowing, such as bank overdraft facilities.
5. Joint-venture partners should have a controlling interest only where required by local law or when the partner is more critical to the success of the operation than is the parent company.

It is important to reemphasize that we want the joint venture to be a viable economic entity. Thus it should have sufficient equity to obtain working capital loans without partner guarantees. Also, in many countries, the ability to repatriate earnings in the form of dividends is directly related to the amount of equity investment.

We recognize that there may be extenuating circumstances which require deviation from one or more of the above guidelines. In order that we may properly coordinate operating unit objectives with overall corporate guidelines, all proposed capitalization and financing arrangements for joint ventures must be submitted to corporate headquarters for advance approval.

tion of companies; registration or termination of branches; changes in charters and bylaws; capital revisions; changes in directors, officers, and branch managers; granting of broad powers of attorney; initiation of new operations in a country; review and approval of shareholders' and directors' meeting agenda prior to the meetings for both wholly owned and jointly owned companies; collection matters over $10,000 or when the debtor is in a different country or where possible counterclaims are involved; trade regulation matters including antitrust and trading with restricted countries; licensing contracts; and product warranties which deviate from those previously approved.

Legal Reviews. A number of areas not listed above have legal aspects which must be examined by in-house counsel in support of other functional activities. The initial contact points, however, are with those departments having the prime responsibility. These matters could include such things as bank accounts; sales representatives and distributor agreements; insurance matters; purchase, sale, or lease of assets; and advertising and press releases.

International Acquisitions. Many multinational companies pursue growth through acquisitions and joint ventures. Prudence in such matters would apply as it does in domestic affairs, but with the expectation that acquisitions would be further complicated by local laws, contracts, customs, and obligations—especially as they apply to unwritten agreements between a local enterprise and its sup-

pliers and employees. Joint ventures represent especially delicate arrangements. Accordingly, a set of policy guidelines, as illustrated in Table I-2, is a useful instrument for approaching evaluation and negotiations. In fact, the development of policy guidelines in all particularly sensitive areas of operation is desirable, if not mandatory, for multinational companies and other firms engaged in international operations.

See also Developing countries, management in; Exchange, foreign, management of; International trade; Japanese industries, management in; Tax management.

REFERENCES

Cateora, Philip R.: *International Marketing,* 5th ed., Richard D. Irwin, Homewood, Ill., 1983.

Robock, Stefan H., and Kenneth Simmonds: *International Business and Multinational Enterprises,* 3d ed., Richard D. Irwin, Homewood, Ill., 1983.

Spronck, L. H.: *The Financial Executive's Handbook for Managing Multinational Corporations,* John Wiley, New York, 1980.

Rex A. Sebastian, *Dresser Industries, Inc.*

International Trade

International trade is a $2 trillion opportunity available to the relatively efficient producers of primary and manufactured goods. In an increasingly interdependent world economy, the opportunities for profitable exchanges of goods grow far more quickly than do governmental efforts to protect domestic firms and workers from the shocks of unrestricted import competition. There is growing recognition of the international benefits of an international specialization of labor. It is reflected in the continuing series of negotiations aimed at liberalizing the flow of trade. The successful outcomes of these negotiations have been a major factor in the unprecedented increase in the rate of world trade since 1950.

The Nature of Trade

International trade is the mutually profitable exchange of goods between citizens residing in different countries. Businesspeople are engaged in this practice for the same reason that they pursue domestic commerce: profits. Exports provide not only additional profits through increased sales, but the potential exists for introducing economies of scale to the production line. Importers, the international buyers, purchase foreign goods either for profitable resale or because foreign supplies provide cheaper or better raw materials and finished goods than those available domestically. In terms of export, companies are attracted to international trade when production and sales goals outgrow the potentials of the domestic market. Marketing strategies look upon foreign trade as an enormous extension of a finite home market. In many instances, foreign trade is the more appealing market in terms of size, growth, and profitability.

There are significant differences between international and domestic commerce, and the international trader must cope with new experiences and problems. Most important is the political reality that foreign trade is conducted among sovereign countries that jealously guard prerogatives to pursue national employment, price stability, economic growth, and industrial policies. Imports or exports may be arbitrarily controlled if they run askance of one or more of these policy priorities. Trade may be affected by foreign political policies or domestic health and safety standards. Sovereign countries also maintain proprietary laws and utilize different legal systems. National tastes vary widely in terms of needs and preferences. Language differences pose a number of problems in the marketing and distribution processes. Each country has its own currency. Accordingly, the price of all traded goods must be translated from the seller's currency into the comparable value of the buyer's currency. Floating exchange rates, the conversion and repatriation of foreign currencies, and the occasional use of exchange controls introduce additional complexities.

Except where state trading monopolies are involved, international trade is conducted by private business. Although transactions follow classic business patterns, international trade is specialized and specially structured. Transactions are routinely reported to the United States government for statistical purposes. In certain circumstances (e.g., strategic goods), exporter must first acquire export license approval. In every case, imports must be appraised by customs officials to determine what, if any, entry duty—tariff—is to be applied and whether quotas or other local statutes ban the product from entry altogether. Tariffs are usually imposed on an *ad valorem* basis, which means at a specified percentage of the import's value. In a few cases, tariffs are assessed on a per unit basis, for example, weight or volume. Only after the duty stipulated in the country's tariff schedule has been paid can the importer legally take possession of the merchandise. Tariffs sometimes exceed 100 percent of the assessed value, thus placing the imports at a price disadvantage. Obviously, the importer must pass part or all of the tariff cost to the consumer.

Historically, all nations have wanted to provide protection for domestically produced goods against those produced overseas. Thus, there is a correlation between tariff rates and a government's desire to encourage domestic production of a given product line. Conversely, raw materials and manufactured goods unavailable domestically will have little or no duty imposed on them. Finally, governments concern themselves with international freight rate schedules, lest a deviation from the norm discriminate favorably or unfavorably against the trade of a particular country.

Trade Concepts

Countries engage in international trade because it is a mutually beneficial process. At the macro level, national welfare improves. At the micro level, individual exporters earn profits, provide an additional source of employment, and supply convertible foreign exchange (read *dollars*) which is used to pay for imported goods and services. For some politicians, this sell side is the only desirable end of foreign trade: Exports provide domestic firms with jobs and capital, while imports provide *foreigners* with jobs and capital.

In terms of national welfare and economic common sense, imports are the ultimate rationale for trade. By definition, a good is unlikely to be imported unless it meets at least one of three criteria: (1) it is cheaper than domestically produced counterparts; (2) it is of better quality than its domestic competition; or (3) it is either unavailable or in short supply in the domestic market.

Obtaining goods from abroad at cheaper prices increases consumers' buying power, and, as a consequence, real incomes rise. This increase in turn

413

means a higher standard of living in the importing country. High tariffs and other barriers to imports increase costs to consumers, lower real incomes, and reduce their freedom at the marketplace. One of the major sources of price disciplines and incentives for innovation by domestic industry is import competition. By absorbing domestic demand, imports are intrinsically deflationary. Furthermore, since one country's imports are another country's exports, failure to import by country A reduces the supply of foreign exchange needed by other countries to buy A's exports.

Price Differentiation. The ultimate basis for international trade is price differentiation. Each country is endowed with a different relative mixture of the factors of production. Traditionally, differences in the relative abundancy or scarcity of land, labor, and capital determined the domestic price structure and production possibilities. For example, a country with abundant labor and land tends to be an efficient producer of agricultural goods, whereas an abundance of capital and a scarcity of labor encourages efficiency in sophisticated manufacturing that requires laborsaving machinery. Since international trade today is much more sophisticated than in simpler times when wine was swapped for cloth, many economists now accept a fourth and even a fifth factor of production: technology and managerial talent. The ability of a given country to be efficient in certain industrial products (e.g., Japan in electronics and the United States in computers) cannot be explained adequately only in terms of land, labor, and capital.

The theory of international trade is, therefore, dynamic. It must be continually modified to accommodate changes in business conditions. In the future, it will have to come to grips with the increasing role of foreign trade of multinational corporations. A growing volume of trade in manufactured goods is being achieved on the basis of an intracorporate transaction, not an arm's-length sale between nationals of two different countries.

Comparative Advantage. The essential elements of modern international trade theory are still intact. The theory holds that all countries have a *comparative advantage* in the production of certain goods, even if not an absolute advantage. World production, and therefore the world's welfare, will be increased if countries follow the dictum of an international division of labor: Concentrate on production of goods in which you are *relatively* efficient, and import the goods in which you are *relatively* inefficient.

Trade Restriction. Economic theory clearly indicates that a sound foreign trade policy is one which allows a maximum freedom of movement for goods in the world marketplace so that desired foreign-made products may be imported as simply and cheaply as possible, not unlike the transfer of goods

among the 50 states of the United States. In real life, this situation does not occur because politicians, not economists, promulgate trade policy. Visions of economic efficiency are subordinated to the domestic priorities of national security, full employment, etc.

The overriding international economic dilemma for national governments in today's sophisticated, interdependent world economy is how far to go in liberalizing the various barriers and distortions to world commerce that have been erected.

Trade Liberalization

The system of international trade which has evolved since the end of World War II has sought to reduce governmentally imposed trade barriers and distortions as fast as political sensitivities would allow. All industrialized countries have accepted in principle the advantages of freer trade. Subsequent to its creation in 1948, the General Agreement on Tariffs and Trade (GATT) has served as the negotiating and moral focal point for efforts at trade liberalization.

GATT. GATT is literally nothing more than a treaty having a small international secretariat, with headquarters in Geneva, Switzerland, to support it. Yet, as the world's premier treaty embodying reciprocal commercial rights and obligations, it is still the nucleus of international trade negotiations and consultations. The 80-plus signatory countries subscribe to three basic practices:

1. Nondiscrimination: Each country's negotiated concessions apply equally to all signatories; i.e., the products of all other countries receive the same treatment afforded to the most-favored nation.

2. Tariff protection: Tariffs, not quotas, are the sanctioned means of protecting domestic industries from foreign competition.

3. Consultations: Existing and potential trade disputes should be submitted for consultation. No new trade barriers should be implemented unannounced.

Impact on Tariffs. The international commitment to a rational utilization of the world's resources is mirrored in the results of seven rounds of tariff-cutting negotiations completed thus far within GATT. With the successful conclusion of the Tokyo Round in 1979, the average tariff rates of the major industrialized countries, Western Europe, the United States, and Japan, fell to the 4 to 7 percent range. For most products, tariffs are now more of a nuisance than an effective barrier to trade.

In regard to tariffs on industrial goods, the work of GATT is almost completed. However, much progress needs to be made on other existing distortions. Agricultural trade continues to be restricted in deference to the political sensitivity of domestic farm-support systems practiced throughout the world. A wide variety of nontariff distortions to trade are still in place. Also referred to as nontariff barriers or measures, they include such devices as arithmetic quotas, which arbitrarily limit imports to a certain level in complete disregard of price considerations. Governments employ a number of devices in their procurement procedures which discriminate in favor of domestic producers. In addition, safety, labeling, health, and antipollution requirements force foreign goods to conform to domestic specifications. Countries facing a balance-of-payments "emergency" may impose such financial requirements as advance deposits on imports or a special import surcharge tax.

On the export side, countries may adopt such diffuse measures as subsidies to increase exports or restrictive controls either to limit sales of goods in short supply or to attempt to raise the price paid by foreign buyers.

A major first step in reducing the impact of these nontariff distortions to trade flows was taken in the Tokyo Round of trade negotiations in 1979. Seven multilateral codes of conduct were negotiated regarding government procurement, customs valuation, technical barriers to trade (known as the standards code), export subsidies, antidumping, import licensing procedures, and liberalized trade arrangements in civil aircraft. Implementation and interpretation of these agreements will continue through most of the 1980s.

One of the Tokyo Round's major failures was the inability to conclude an international agreement on a standardized safeguards system under which uniform procedures would be established for use by countries that felt it necessary to take temporary import-restrictive measures so as to ease the adjustment impact of intense import competition.

Although GATT is the central international organization concerned with trade, several important regional organizations have come on the scene. In an effort to enjoy the fruits of freer trade and in recognition of the growing limits of the traditional nation-state as a viable market for large-scale industry, a number of countries have joined with their neighbors to form free trade areas and customs unions. The *free trade area* involves the negotiated elimination of all or most trade barriers among the member countries. The *customs union* carries the process one step further with the establishment of a common uniform tariff schedule for imports from all nonmember countries.

Common Market. The most significant of these regional trade groups is the customs union formed by the European Economic Community (EEC), often called the Common Market. The largest trading unit in the world, the EEC members consist of West Germany, France, Great Britain, Italy, the Netherlands, Belgium, Luxembourg, Denmark, Ireland, and Greece. Associate memberships of European and Mediterranean countries (e.g., Turkey), along with preferential market access agreements signed with developing countries (mainly former colonies of the full members), swell the number of countries affiliated with the EEC to well above 60. The member countries have nearly completed the process of developing a common international commercial policy (e.g., they negotiate as the Community in GATT, not as individual countries) and have committed themselves to the long-term process of full economic and monetary union. While the EEC is deeply committed to internal free trade, it is ambivalent in its policy toward outsiders. On the one hand, it consistently has lowered its common external tariff in GATT negotiations, but its common agricultural policy has had a significant impact on the farm trade of the Community, mainly in the form of excluding the competitive farm products of the United States and other efficient agricultural producers.

United States Policy. Closer economic relations with the EEC has been the overall priority item of United States trade policy since the early 1960s. The attempt to keep the EEC "outward looking" was the basis of the United States initiatives to spawn the Kennedy Round of GATT talks in 1964 and the subsequent Tokyo Round. As these initiatives imply, the United States has played the leadership role in promoting trade liberalization ever since the passage of the Trade Agreements Program in 1934, a historic milestone in international trade policy. The disastrous effect of the Hawley-Smoot Tariff of 1930, the highest in the country's history, led to the unprecedented extension of tariff-cutting authority by the legislative branch to the President. Previously, Congress had set all tariffs, generally on purely political grounds, by virtue of the Constitution's specific extension of authority to it to regulate foreign commerce and levy duties.

Trade Act of 1974. American international trade policy to this day rests on the delegation of trade-liberalizing authority to the President through periodic legislation. The current course of policy was charted in the Trade Act of 1974. In substance, the Trade Act does not affect the basic principles of policy: to reduce on a reciprocal basis American and foreign barriers to trade, to provide temporary protection to American firms and workers injured (or deemed about to be injured) by import competition, and to avoid discrimination among countries through application of the *most-favored-nation (MFN) principle*.

The statutory language by which American workers and firms are eligible for relief from foreign competition was eased considerably. The bill also authorized the United States to catch up with other industrialized countries by implementing tariff preferences, i.e., lower duties on imports of manufactured and processed goods produced by less developed countries.

TABLE I-3 World Trade: Exports (in billions of U.S. dollars)

	1955	1965	1975	1980	1982
United States	15.6	27.5	108.0	220.7	212.9
Canada	4.4	8.5	34.1	67.6	71.1
Japan	2.0	8.5	55.7	130.4	140.3
European Community	28.3	65.2	300.6	670.5	600.0
OPEC	n.a.	10.6	111.7	298.3	212.8
Other developing countries	n.a.	23.9	88.8	244.5	313.1
Communist countries	10.0	23.2	90.5	203.8	215.6
Global Total	93.7	187.5	874.9	2,030.5	2,062.1

Source: U.S. Bureau of the Census, *Highlights of U.S. Export and Import Trade*, FT990, monthly.

Magnitude of World Trade

The recurring efforts to liberalize trade have accelerated the underlying economic trend of increased international interdependence. In terms of sales, the real growth market has been in exports. In the 1960 to 1970 period, exports of the industrial countries grew at an average annual rate (9.5 percent) that was twice as fast as the value of real output, i.e., gross national product (GNP), which rose 4.8 percent.

As Table I-3 demonstrates, the total value of international trade increased more than twentyfold between 1955 and 1982.

Increases in the value of trade experienced by the United States have also been drastic. From their twentieth-century nadir in the early 1930s (when the average annual value was below $2 billion), American exports grew to $10 billion in 1950 and began doubling every 10 years thereafter: $20 billion in 1960 and $43 billion in 1970. By 1982, U.S. exports had increased fivefold to $212 billion. The value of American imports has grown even more rapidly, from a level of $15 billion to $270 billion in 1982. Nevertheless, the potential for further growth is still great. Despite these rapid increases in the value of trade, imports and exports account for only 8 and 7 percent, respectively, of total United States GNP, the lowest "penetration" of any industrialized noncommunist country. Potential on the export side is further demonstrated by the U.S. Department of Commerce estimate that only 8 percent of all American manufacturing corporations actually export and that 250 firms account for nearly 60 percent of total United States exports.

The major commodities exported by the United States in 1981 were agricultural products, valued at $43.3 billion (of which $19.5 billion was grain and cereal); chemicals, valued at $21.2 billion; machinery, with a total value of $63 billion (of which $11.5 was industrial, $11.5 electrical, and $9.5 power generating); and automobiles, mainly to Canada, with a value of $16.2 billion.

Major American imports in 1981 were petroleum, valued at $75.6 billion; agricultural products, costing $17 billion; chemicals, valued at $5.3 billion; iron and steel products, costing $11.2 billion; and motor vehicles, amounting to $22.1 billion.

Importing and Exporting

Few if any countries exert any official efforts on the import side other than to collect tariffs and administer various measures either to exclude imports altogether or place them at a competitive disadvantage in the domestic market. Imports, crudely speaking, are tolerated, not encouraged. Importers may be divisions of corporations or agents hired by exporting companies with active overseas sales programs. Occasionally, businesspeople actively seek out the products of overseas companies through foreign travel or via contacts with commercial officers assigned to the embassies and consulates of foreign countries. In any event, the job of the importer is to assure the safe entry of goods through customs at approved ports of entry and to arrange for distribution to wholesale or retail purchasers.

Protective Measures. Domestic industries and workers in the United States and other industrialized countries are protected from injury caused by increases in imports through a number of devices, all recognized as valid elements of international trade law. First, there is protection against illegal or unfair trade practices. Antidumping legislation prevents exporters from selling goods at sales less than fair value (e.g., to quickly dispose of domestic production overruns or to drive competitors in the importing countries out of business). A sale at less than fair value is generally measured as being equivalent to selling goods in foreign markets at prices below those prevailing in the home market or below production costs. Countervailing duty laws apply special rates on imports whose producers have been found to have received bounties or grants from their government that in effect subsidize the cost of the exports in question. Domestic business is supposed to compete only with foreign business, not foreign governments as well.

When American workers or firms feel threatened by completely fair foreign competition, they can petition for relief in the form of quotas or higher tariff rates under provisions of the "escape clause." Petitions for escape clause protection are made to the U.S. International Trade Commission (formerly the Tariff Commission), which conducts an investigation and renders a recommendation in conjunction with the law. Similarly, American workers or firms can petition for "adjustment assistance" in the form of government funds for retraining or plant modernization.

Exporting Procedures. The profit potential of exporting invariably justifies the initial expense and energy required to gain a foreign foothold. Any company interested in overseas sales can produce a preliminary assessment of its capabilities simply by considering industry trends, the position of the firm in the domestic industry, the effects that additional sales will have on production costs and schedules, the status of the company's resources, and a "guesstimate" of the export potential of the company's products. Inevitably, export aggressiveness is a function of the size of the domestic market.

Information and Assistance. Foreign marketing intelligence can be obtained from a number of sources. The official American source is the series of data on United States exports published in varying detail by the Department of Commerce. This department regularly issues detailed reports on the American market share of major manufactured goods for all major foreign markets and on the economic and financial outlooks for foreign countries. Extensive marketing surveys are issued periodically for those industries targeted by the Department of Commerce as being areas where this country is highly competitive internationally. The Department of Commerce also provides a number of export promotion services, ranging from trade fairs to individual business counseling to providing data on potential foreign distributors or agents for an American company's products. The above-mentioned publications and others, as well as information on all official export promotion efforts, are available at the Washington headquarters of the Department of Commerce or any of its district offices. The U.S. government provides tax deferrals for exporting companies, principally through the Foreign Sales Corporation.

Potential exporters can also obtain information and guidance from a number of private sources. These include local chambers of commerce, the international divisions of commercial banks, world trade clubs, trade associations, and export management companies.

Direct and Indirect Selling. Whether a company sells abroad on a direct or an indirect basis will depend on marketing strategy, experience, size, and commitment to exporting. *Direct export selling* techniques are the same, generically, as domestic efforts. Utilization can be made of sales representatives or agents, distributors, retailers, or state-controlled trading monopolies. *Indirect selling* efforts are especially attractive to the novice or small exporter. In this category are export agents and commission agents located in the foreign market or *export trading companies* located in the American market. Acting as the export departments of many companies simultaneously, these agents solicit and transact business on behalf of the manufacturer in return for sales commissions or retainers.

Financial Aspects

The financing of international trade is arranged through commercial banks. The two most common means of arranging payment between exporter and importer are drafts and letters of credit. The *draft* may be in the form of sight drafts for immediate payment or time drafts, requiring payment only after 30 or more days from the date in which the importer's bank receives all the requisite documentation. A *letter of credit,* when issued in irrevocable form by a bank in the buyer's country and confirmed by an American bank or when issued by an American bank on behalf of the importer, eliminates all credit risk for the seller. Unlike drafts, the letter of credit protects the exporter in this case against the contingency that the buyer will suddenly be unable to pay for the goods upon delivery.

Export-Import Bank. Commercial export financing is universally supplemented by official programs of export finance and insurance. The Export-Import Bank of the United States, with headquarters in Washington, operates two major programs:

1. *Direct loans.* Always in participation with commercial banks, these loans are for relatively large sales or for capital goods requiring longer-term financing; repayment terms vary from 5 years to longer periods.

2. *Guarantees and insurance.* On a medium-term basis, these guarantees protect the exporter (or the exporter's bank) against political and commercial risks. The privately operated Foreign Credit Insurance Association offers additional guarantees, particularly to exporters who for competitive reasons must sell on a deferred payment credit basis.

International Monetary System. The conduct of trade is heavily influenced by the workings of the international monetary system. It is here that countries reconcile receipts and payments made to one another in their respective currencies. A country's **417**

balance of payments is a complete accounting record of economic transactions between its citizens and residents of the rest of the world for a given period. If a country earns more abroad than it buys, it has a balance-of-payments surplus and, in effect, is a creditor country. A deficit results from net buying, produces a debtor status, and tends to diminish a currency's relative value (exchange rate). A balance-of-payments surplus will tend to produce an upward movement on a currency's exchange rate as buyers exceed sellers in the world's foreign exchange markets.

Fixed Rates. The means by which exchange rates are managed goes to the very heart of the international monetary system. Under the fixed-rate system which prevailed from the end of World War II until 1973, countries were obligated to keep their exchange rates fixed by having their central banks intervene in foreign exchange markets to assure an equilibrium supply-and-demand situation for their own currency. By this means, the competitive exchange rate depreciations of the 1930s were to be avoided. Reluctance of countries to change their rates despite structural disequilibria and the increased activities of international currency speculators doomed the fixed-rate system.

Float. Under the existing exchange rate regime, monetary authorities are free to allow their currency's exchange rate to "float" in response to changes in free-market pressures. In theory, a country could balance its external account merely by remaining aloof and allowing its exchange rate to move sufficiently higher or lower to find an equilibrium level. In practice, countries will not remain totally passive; they intervene in the foreign exchange markets whenever exchange rate movements are judged excessive. All this produces an element of uncertainty in international business. It is impossible to predict what the exchange rate is going to be between two currencies on that date in the future when the buyer is obliged to make actual payment to the exporter. Unless they are willing to gamble, international traders must *hedge* in the foreign exchange market. They do so by going to a commercial bank with a foreign exchange trading capability. An exporter will contract for the sale of a foreign currency (in which he or she expects eventual payment) on a specified future date for a specified rate. An importer will contract to purchase a foreign currency (the currency of the exporter's country) for delivery on a specified future date at a specified rate in terms of his or her own currency. By such an arrangement, no matter what exchange rate movements occur in the interim, international business executives will know beforehand the exact value of the foreign currency they are buying or selling in terms of their own currency. This is a potential business expense which must be taken into consideration in determining prices of internationally traded goods.

Impact of Trade Balance. When a country's exchange rate depreciates (loses value) or appreciates (increases in value), a direct impact is felt on its trade balance in the medium to long term. A currency depreciation (or devaluation) makes a country's imports more expensive and its exports cheaper. Appreciation (or revaluation) has the opposite effect. This was the rationale for the two devaluations of the dollar in 1971 and 1973. American industry was losing its competitiveness because the dollar's exchange rate had become overvalued vis-à-vis most West European currencies and the Japanese yen. Very simply, those countries by then had recovered fully from the devastation of World War II. The devaluations led to a lowering of the prices of American exports in these markets and an increase in the prices of our imports from those markets. The subsequent turnaround of the deteriorating American trade balance in 1975 was largely the result of the change in the dollar's exchange rate. By 1983, the United States trade account was suffering from the adverse competitive effects of an upsurge in the dollar's exchange rate brought on primarily by this nation's high interest and high economic growth rates.

Evaluation

Engaging in international trade can be a burden, a luxury, a necessity, or a major profit center for companies. It depends on individual circumstances. A company with a unique product or one in worldwide short supply can sit back and wait for foreign buyers to come to its doors. Others must make a decisive first step into this profitable growing market. Assuming governments do not regress into protectionism and, instead, choose to reduce further the barriers to trade, companies will find it increasingly difficult and costly to ignore the opportunities of foreign markets. The very successes of the private sector in conducting international trade occasionally lead to temporary obstacles inflicted by governmental authorities anxious to avoid sudden domestic disruptions. However, for corporations with aggressiveness and persistence, the challenge of exporting is seldom insurmountable.

When an industry is unable to sell profitably overseas, it is likely to be losing ground in its own home market. Such an industry is a prime candidate to begin feeling stiff import competition from abroad. International trade flows are becoming a key barometer of efficiency and growth.

See also Developing countries, management in; Economic systems; Exchange, foreign, management of; International operations and management in multinational companies; Japanese industries, management in; Small business administration.

REFERENCES

Daniels, John Earnest Ogram, and Lee Radebaugh: *International Business,* Addison-Wesley, Reading, Mass., 1976.

Exporters' Encyclopedia, Dun & Bradstreet Publications, New York, updated regularly.

U.S. Department of Commerce, *A Basic Guide to Exporting,* 1982.

————. *Export Bibliography,* 1983.

STEPHEN D. COHEN, *American University*

Interpersonal Relationships

Interpersonal relationships involve the content and quality of interaction among people and are defined by *both* their observable behavior in the interaction *and* the feelings that are associated with it. These exchanges are typically personal, person-to-person, and usually involve verbal communication channels. These relationships are characterized by a substantial influence of affect, as experienced by the individuals involved, in determining the nature of the relationships. The quality and content of these relationships are also influenced over time by the cumulative effect of a series of exchanges.

Substantial parts of managers' jobs involve them in person-to-person contact with people inside and outside their organizations. In one study, for example, managers reported spending over half their time in these kinds of exchanges.[1] The quality and effectiveness of the managers' interpersonal relationships will directly bear on the quality and effectiveness of their total performance, which, in turn, is highly influential in determining the effective performance of the organization unit.

Shortly after Frederick Taylor published *The Principles of Scientific Management*[2] and, in part, in response to Taylor's ideas, the human relations view of management began to take hold in American industry. An early study took place around 1930 in Western Electric's Hawthorne plant near Chicago. The Hawthorne Study investigated the effects of group and interpersonal relationships upon the productivity of workers.[3] It was found that informal relationships among workers can be a strong force in controlling the output of these workers, even, at times, inducing those on an incentive pay scale to produce less than they might in order to obey the group's "rules." More than anything else, the Hawthorne Study made clear the importance of social variables such as group interpersonal relationships in the practice of management. If such relationships can have a profound effect on worker productivity, the question was posed, is it possible that responsible people can come to understand and manage that effect to everyone's benefit? This question intrigued many managers in the 1930s, and it continues to intrigue them today.

Person Perception

What an individual senses and what that person perceives are not one and the same. Perceptions of people are impressions of others drawn in part from the input to the sense organs but reflected against past experiences and opinions. Every person is unique, yet the mind has its limits. One cannot think of all the unique characteristics of everyone encountered. In today's parlance, we tend to "put people in a bag." Social psychologists speak of creating invariances, by which they mean sets that simplify the world by giving order and stability to our perceptions. An example of an invariance is the notion that good people do good deeds. The dual processes of "bagging" people and creating invariances are facts of the subjectivity of human perception of others. One might observe the same behavior in two individuals and yet perceive that behavior very differently. Further, one person's perception of a second person may be very different from the perception a third party may have of that same individual. For example, assume a long-haired, bearded young man is attempting to jar open a partially closed window of a parked limousine, with its headlights on high beam, at a country club's rear entrance. An older woman observes the behavioral act. The woman perceives the behavior and concomitantly perceives the person. She might interpret the behavior as an act of vandalism and the person as a good-for-nothing individual. These perceptions are derived from experiences and opinions as well as from what has been observed. Suppose, too, that a young minister also observes the same behavioral act. Perhaps he may see it as a good deed: the efforts of a thoughtful young man to turn off the headlights before the car's battery runs down. The young man is thus perceived as a good samaritan. The same behavioral act can result in different perceptions of things and people. Such is the legacy of person perception.

When we perceive others, we attribute intent to them; that is, we perceive they are motivated to try to get somewhere or do something. *Our perceptions of others are dominated by our assumptions of their directedness, of their motives,* not by what we actually see them doing or hear them saying.[4] Our attribution of motives to others depends heavily upon our own cognitive models, invariances, and the way we go about "bagging" others. Much of what we see in others is really within ourselves. The world we perceive is the one we create. The people we perceive are, in part, characters of our own mind.

As well as attributing motives to others, people attribute abilities, emotions, and power to others. All these, too, grow in part from what is sensed and in part from individuals' cognitive models of the world.

Often, just one trait in a person can cause others to infer that person's entire personality. The development of this *implicit personality* in others can be accurate or very inaccurate.

What implications does this perception of others hold for management? First, and most important, managers must recognize the existence of these dynamics. They must realize that their perceptions of others are far from objective; rather, perceptions are highly subjective. In a manager's work, each day she or he must judge other men and women and make decisions on their ability and desire to see a job done right. Managers may have an intuitive feel for people, and the high quality of that intuition may explain many of their successes as managers. It is possible, however, to sharpen intuition about people if the source of that intuition is examined to determine whether it comes from a cognitive model or from their behavior.

Affiliation

A basic premise is that people are "needing" creatures and that their behavior reflects those needs. When we are denied something that we believe will satisfy a need we are experiencing, we become frustrated. (This unhappy sequence is discussed in more detail in the section "Conflict and Resolution" in this entry. For the dynamics of relationships between needs, behavior, and outcomes, *see* Motivation in Organizations.) A simplified explanation of motivation suggests that a person behaves in a manner which satisfies a need that has been aroused. People's behavior, therefore, is not random or capricious. Rather, it is goal-directed and purposeful.

This factor is of prime interest to managers because people's behavior can serve both their own individual goal and the objectives of the organization. The relative degree of overlap between individual and organizational goals is a variable over which managers exercise some control and influence.

One-to-One Relationships. One-to-one relationships are the fundamental basis of interpersonal relationships. Many of the dimensions of such relationships can be applied to more complex social situations involving three or more people. The essential point is that people engage in relationships with one another in attempts to satisfy their own particular needs. When satisfaction becomes reciprocal, the relationships can develop and flourish.

Trust and Intimacy. People vary in their capacity to trust others. Similarly, people vary in the degree to which they are trustworthy. Positive interpersonal relationships require, at minimum, a mutual trust. To engage in genuine relationships requires that each person allow a degree of vulnerability to the other. This often occurs through the increasingly complete expression of one's true self in the relation-ships. As relationships mature and trust in the other person is proved to be well placed, increasing amounts of vulnerability and trust will permeate the relationship. Interpersonal trust is a fragile thing which cannot take many jolts without suffering serious fractures. Just as increasing levels of trust can be built up, the cycle can be reversed, often permanently, by a violation of trust. There are some people who have been sufficiently disappointed by other people that they trust no one. They have become convinced or they have convinced themselves that people are essentially bad. This conviction can result in behavior that is so self-protective and abrasive that their prophecies about others are fulfilled in their interpersonal relationships.

A manager can build a reputation among the people in the organization for being trustworthy. This reputation will provide a substantial base upon which fulfilling and effective interpersonal relationships can be constructed. Managers cannot condone illegal or inappropriate behavior, nor can they ignore it in their attempt to be trustworthy. However, by being open about one's position and by respecting confidences when appropriate, a manager can develop and maintain a reputation as a trustworthy person. This reputation will prove invaluable in furthering the quality of his or her interpersonal relationships.

Empathy. Empathy is a capacity to see, understand, and experience the world as another person does. Empathy is definitely not the same as sympathy or even understanding. The latter implies an intellectual process. Empathy includes understanding *plus* the emotional aspect of another person's life experience. An important characteristic of empathy is that it is not primarily judgmental; it simply is the experiencing.

Empathy is a critical contributor to good interpersonal relationships because it fosters a situation in which one person can believe and genuinely feel that another human being knows what is going on inside oneself. Effective managers will have the capacity to empathize with others in the organization. At the same time, they will not find themselves hamstrung and unable to act or decide because of that empathic understanding.

Expression of Feelings. Interpersonal relationships that are on a good footing allow a wide range of feelings to be expressed. It is often toward the people with whom we are closest that we have the strongest emotional responses. Intense love, anger, joy, elation, and sorrow are seldom shared with strangers. Expression of extreme ranges of feelings is often considered unacceptable and unexpected behavior in organizations. The important point to recognize is that feelings are an unavoidable, real component of the human experience. To deny their existence or to require their complete suppression in the organizational setting is to ignore naively a powerful socioemotional force. Certainly, the unbridled expression of every fleeting emotion is not likely to improve organizational performance. At the same time, denial that emotions exist about organizational issues is equally absurd.

Attitudes and Values. *Attitudes* are generally described as a person's thoughts, feelings, or predisposition to act in regard to things. *Values* are generally assumed to be a little more basic than attitudes and usually include a judgmental quality about basic rights and wrongs. People's attitudes and values exhibit a general kind of internal consistency. Attitudes are usually easier to change than values, which are established early in life. Peer-group values will generally be included as a significant aspect of an individual's repertoire of values.

A dynamic relationship exists between behavior and attitudes. Generally, people try to keep them consistent with each other, so that if an attitude is changed, behavior will also alter to correspond. It also turns out that changing behavior can influence a change in attitude.

If people in an organization believe that the management is basically fair and trustworthy, they will usually behave in a way that is consistent with those attitudes. On the other hand, an employee who has a bad attitude may believe that management is unconcerned, incompetent, and antagonistic. That worker's behavior and job performance will probably reflect those attitudes, which can become a problem for the manager involved.

By and large, a manager's chances of quickly changing a person's attitude or values are relatively slight. This is particularly true when the attitude is central to a person's self-concept. Rather than undertake to change very central attitudes and beliefs, a productive direction for a manager to take is first to understand what the subordinate's attitude really is. With that understanding, the manager can proceed to create an environment in which the attitude and associated behavior either are appropriate to organizational goals or, alternatively, do not conflict with them. For example, assume a supervisor is convinced that a high level of participation in decision making is tantamount to abdication of managerial responsibility. It would be folly to force that person to engage in a participatory kind of managerial behavior. Instead, that supervisor could be placed in an organizational setting with a task and situation that call for strong, centralized decision making. In that way, the supervisor will not be required either to change the attitude, or to behave in a way inconsistent with the attitude.

Joint Goal Accomplishment

The relationship between managers and their immediate subordinates constitutes a major influence on the achievement of the group's goals. A central task of a manager is the coordination of the group's activities in the service of organizational goal achievement. It is essential, then, for managers to understand how groups function and to be able to use that understanding to promote achievement of organizational objectives. The problem for the manager is accentuated when a group's task calls for contributions by members whose skills, knowledge, and personal traits are very different. These differences will often lead to interpersonal difficulties. Management of such a group will require a firm understanding of the individual and group dynamics involved *and* an ability to apply those concepts effectively.

Types of Groups. In general, a group is a collection of individuals who share a sense of relationship. The nature of the relationship can range from high levels of interdependence, as occurs in a basketball team, to substantial independence, as occurs in a golf team. Types of groups can be identified which differ in the manner in which they come into being, in their purposes, and in the ways they conduct their affairs. These differences are important because they constitute leverage points that managers can consider as they perform their coordination tasks.

Formal and Informal Groups. Formal groups come into being as a consequence of overt organizational action. They typically have a prescribed organizational hierarchy which defines expected relationships among its members. Further, this kind of group will usually have its mission or area of activity spelled out.

Informal groups, on the other hand, develop in response to the needs of the people making up the group. As a consequence, they do not have an explicitly stated set of goals nor are there institutionally defined positions of authority. These aspects of an informal group develop as a consequence of group and individual activities. Informal groups serve a number of functions which formal groups do not address, such as (1) filling voids and details in decisions made by the formal organization; (2) establishing expectations for interpersonal relationships; and (3) fulfilling members' individual needs not met by the formal organizations, particularly needs for social contact. An informal group's goals and organizational goals may coincide, but they do not always do so.

Managers have authority over a wide spectrum of activities in formal groups. They have no direct control over emergent informal groups. In the latter case, prudent managers will recognize a group member's need for informal groups and will not try to outlaw or banish them. Rather, they will try to manage the situation so that the goals of the informal group complement organizational objectives.

Committees. Committees are common organizational groups. They often include representatives from several parts of the formal organization. They **421** have the advantages and disadvantages of a membership with diverse backgrounds, interests, needs, and loyalties.

Committees are criticized as being inefficient and inept; nevertheless, they survive and are continually called upon to serve organizational objectives. Problems with committees can be reduced when their leaders skillfully assist the group in assessing its progress toward its goals as well as in maintaining a clear understanding of those goals.

Project Teams. The *project team* is typically formed to complete a specific task; then it is disbanded. The members of a project team are usually assigned to the team because of special skills and knowledge they possess. The manager's task is to develop this group of individuals with their separate professional and personal ties into an effective working team.

Much of the success in managing a project team depends on effective communication channels and the unrestricted flow of information. People are not likely to feel they belong to a group when they do not know what is going on.

The team's approach to the project will have to be planned and then implemented. This critical planning phase often occurs so early in the group's development that its members have not had an opportunity to realize its potential as an effective working unit. Person perceptions have not been well established. Sources and bases of social need fulfillment have not been identified within the group. Both planning and implementation will require the coordinated application of individual team members' unique skills and knowledge. All other things being equal, the full and enthusiastic involvement of team members is highly desirable. Differences in approach, in personal style, and even in the definition of the problem at hand can be expected. Managers will use their best interpersonal skills as they nurture the development of a project team, work to resolve the inevitable conflicts, and see the project through to completion. This procedure can be helped by (1) facilitating open communications with adequate levels of trust and (2) ensuring sufficient time and attention to individual and group maintenance needs.

Dynamics of Groups

Besides classifying groups into types, it is useful to identify issues and processes that occur in most groups. These issues are of interest to managers, for they are the critical aspects which influence group performance.

Cohesiveness. Groups differ in the degree to which the members are attracted to one another and value their membership in the group. This quality is known as *group cohesiveness.* In general, cohesive-ness is higher (1) when group members are alike, sharing similar attitudes and values; (2) when they have ample opportunity to interact with one another; (3) when membership is relatively attractive; or (4) when the group is threatened from without. All other conditions being equal, a small group of four or five will interact more and be more cohesive than will a larger group.[5]

A highly cohesive group is a powerful social force in an organization. Its influence is substantial in guiding and prescribing members' behavior. Work groups which stick together are helpful to managers when the groups' purposes align with organizational objectives. When that alignment does not occur, managers will need to understand and, when possible, alter the factors supporting the group's antagonism to organizational goals. A work group which is not cohesive is a managerial problem in that group pressures for excellence in job performance are not present.

Norms. A *group norm* is a powerful social force influencing group members' behavior. Norms are rules and standards that describe how a "good" group member should behave. They are developed informally in a group through the interaction of its members. Members may deviate in some ways from group norms, but at some point more deviations will result in sanctions by the group. These sanctions have the objective of bringing a deviant member's behavior into line with the group's norms. Attempts to explain to the deviant member about "how things are done around here" are typical early warning devices used to bring a member's behavior into line. If the individual continues to violate norms, the group will isolate the person and, in the extreme, refuse to allow the deviant member to participate in the group's activities at all. Managers can expect that people will shape their behavior in a way that maintains their membership in desirable groups. If those behaviors happen to run counter to organizational goals, the extreme trade-off becomes group membership versus organizational goals. Managers will not help matters by forcing this dilemma or by denying its existence. Those who recognize group norms and their impact on behavior will be able to create situations which (1) minimize the either/or quality and (2) capitalize on these very powerful social forces in the service of organizational goals.

Decision Making in Groups. It is often said that increased participation of group members in decision making results in greater acceptance of those decisions and an increased likelihood that the decisions will be successfully implemented. In some instances, research has supported the assertion, and in other instances, it has not.[6] In situations where a manager and a work group are involved, the powerful impact of the organizational hierarchy with its potential rewards and punishments cannot be ignored. Because of this, it has been suggested that it is unethical and improper for managers to expect or assert that true participation in decision making has taken place at all.[7]

As a practical matter, the amount of participation in group decision making can range along a continuum.[8] At one extreme, the manager makes all the decisions. At the other extreme, the group has substantial responsibility for decisions. No matter how the decision-making chores are divided, managers continue to be accountable within the formal hierarchy for the performance of their parts of the organization. Managers therefore, have to be comfortable even when they do not have direct "hands-on" involvement in decisions.

The relative quality of group decisions is also of interest to managers. Whether or not a group makes a better decision than individuals do depends on (1) the nature of the problem, (2) the situation, (3) the availability of information, (4) the skills and knowledge of group members, and (5) their inclinations about involvement.

Task and Maintenance Activities. These two categories consume the major part of a group's time. *Task-related activities* have to do with the achievement of the group's goals and objectives. *Maintenance activities* are addressed to the socioemotional aspects that are necessary for the group to continue to function. At times, a third activity can gain a group's attention. It may do so when an individual captures the group's time and causes its members to deal with that person's own personal needs. The topics of these sorts of discussions have been termed *hidden agendas*, since the individual involved often puts the issue in a way that does not directly identify the personal (unsatisfied) need that lies behind the public agenda being discussed.

Managers will be concerned with all three types of group activities at one time or another. The task and maintenance activities are of central importance, since they will govern the quality of the group's goal attainment. Because groups serve a number of their members' social needs, and because socioemotional issues are generated as groups work, sufficient time and energy must be available to keep the group viable. While group maintenance activities, such as joking or humor, may seem inefficient and a waste of time, the severe denial or prohibition of these anxiety-reducing activities will reduce the effectiveness of the group over time. As with most managerial decisions, balance is the key. Both task *and* group maintenance activities are necessary for effective group performance.

Influence and Change

A large measure of a manager's job is concerned with influencing others. A manager may routinely ask an employee to change a work schedule in order to meet a new deadline. In the extreme, a manager may ask a person to move an entire family to another part of the country or across the sea. Each of these actions requires an ability and willingness to influence subordinates. A manager must also influence peers. Typically, managers find themselves in competition with other managers for the scarce resources of their company. In such cases, the manager must seek to modify the behavior of his or her associates. A manager often needs to influence superiors: the boss is about to make the wrong decision, or a situation should be reviewed one more time. In all of these tasks, the same dynamics are at play. Insights to these dynamics are provided by the process and philosophy of change and influence which draw heavily from the work of H. J. Leavitt[9] and are developed here from that source.

From a broad perspective, the process of influence involves the person or people being changed and the person or people doing the changing. Conclusions drawn from person-to-person relationships are generally transferable to larger collectivities of change agents and changes.

Person A, desiring person B to change, must have a specific motive or reason for wanting B to change. Person A must also diagnose what B's current behavior is, what that person's motives happen to be, and what A wishes B's future behavior to be. Further, person B will impute motives to person A, which may or may not be the real reasons A is trying to bring about a change in B. It is clear that both A and B may make errors in diagnosing each other's motives. Misdiagnosis on either side can cause difficulty and resistance in the change effort.

Once the changer A has diagnosed B's current behavior and motive constellation, a number of alternative philosophic approaches to influence and change B are open to A. Person A can (1) draw upon authority, (2) attempt to manipulate B, or (3) engage in collaboration.

Authority. The use of authority is the best-known approach to influence. In business relationships, it may be the most widely accepted philosophy. *Authority* means that A has the power to order B to change his or her behavior. When most employees join an organization, they agree psychologically (they make a psychological contract) to accept the authority of superiors. Thus, the use of authority is correct and proper. It is appropriate and is the most widely used means of influence and change between a superior and a subordinate. However, there are times when the influence and change can be less costly and the results more productive if superiors select collaboration rather than authority as the philosophy behind their efforts of change. When, for example, the influence is directed at an activity close to the ego of B, A might do well to tell B of A's motive to change B and not order B to change. This approach allows the decision to change to be made by B after getting a full picture of the pros and cons of the change from A's perspective. Collaboration does not always work, but when appropriate, it can be more effective than authority for the boss and the organization.

Manipulation. Unlike collaboration, *manipulation* is a philosophy of change in which A *does not* let B in on A's motives, including A's desire to change B. In an interpersonal relationship which is long term, manipulation is an irrational choice in that the costs of failure (even given a low probability of discovery and therefore failure) are so high as to make this an untenable alternative. In short-term interpersonal relationships, manipulation may be easier than collaboration, but it is still not recommended on the ground that one's reputation and ability to deal in future interpersonal relationships may suffer irreparably.

Collaboration. *Collaboration* is a philosophy of influence and change in which one seeks a candid and honest relationship with the person one wishes to influence. Suppose A makes known an intention to influence and change B's behavior *and* the reasons for that intention. The next step is up to B. B must choose to change. If B so decides, A reinforces the decision by sharing the burden of change with B, including overcoming resistances to change from others. Collaboration is a time-consuming procedure. It takes time to communicate to B the motive and viewpoint for the change. B will have questions. They must be answered with care and consideration. But the outcome of collaboration is very productive: the change, if B chooses to make it, will be firm. Collaboration has another benefit: it provides a test of A's ideas. In the use of authority, A's ideas are not exposed to evaluation and criticism. Collaboration forces A to make disclosure and opens the way to constructive evaluation.

Social Commitment. The dynamics of people working together in committees and groups open up one additional aspect of influence and change—that of *social commitment.* If A fully collaborates with a group of B's, tells them the expected cost and the benefits to be gained by the proposed change, A's motive for that change, and A's willingness to accept the group's decision—for or against the proposal—then A is engaging in an act of collaborative group participation. Because so many B's have an input on the final decision, the change finally adopted may not be exactly as A had proposed. If A can take a flexible stand on the change issue, collaborative group participation and change are the most desirable means of influence. Changes effected through collaborative means are supported by the social commitment of A and the group of B's. Their commitment to the change, to making it work, and to the relationship within which the change was designed gives the collaborative method its special value to managers. In the absence of managerial flexibility, however, this approach may be nonproductive and dysfunctional.

Conflict and Resolution

Conflict is a common occurrence in life. It occurs when a desired goal or objective is not reasonably available. It takes place (1) within a person (2) between people, (3) between organizational subunits, and (4) between organizations. The focus of this section is on the conflict issues of the first three levels.

Conflict at the Individual Level. An individual will experience frustration when a barrier hampers the attainment of a desired objective. For example, a desired promotion or transfer which is denied because of budget limitations will result in frustration for the person. A number of common ways in which people behave when frustrated have been identified.

Aggression. The frustrated person may attack the barrier itself. For example, a vending machine which accepts quarters with abandon while refusing to produce a candy bar may receive all sorts of punches, slaps, kicks, and verbal abuse. In organizations, people often feel unable to attack the barrier directly, so the aggression is displaced onto some other object or person. Raging at one's spouse, cat, or children might help relieve the immediate pressure caused by an uncooperative boss but does nothing toward reducing the real source of the internal conflict. In some extreme cases, people revert to infantile, maladaptive behavior—like plotting revenge or general negativism—when they have been severely frustrated.

Another alternative to being aggressive in response to frustration is to withdraw from the situation physically and/or psychologically. When this device is employed, people become withdrawn and apathetic. Clearly, this behavior is one that managers will not want to encourage in subordinates. When such behavior is observed in an organization, it may be a sign of a subordinate's frustration. Rather than try to cajole greater enthusiasm, the manager should seek to understand and change the organizational circumstances that lead to frustration and apathy.

Internal Dilemmas. Because people want different things and the wants themselves vary, people sometimes find themselves in conflict about their own goals. These internal conflicts can take one of three forms: approach-approach; approach-withdrawal; and withdrawal-withdrawal.

1. The person has two attractive goals which are mutually exclusive. When the attractiveness of the two choices is nearly equal, the tendency to be indecisive or to vacillate will be great. Choos-

ing between taking a new job in a small firm with growth potential and high risk or staying in the present position with its built-up retirement benefits and predictable promotion sequence is an example of the approach-approach dilemma.

2. A goal which has both positive and negative aspects can arouse conflict. A promotion which has all the rewards and gratifications normally associated with it but which requires a move to an undesirable geographical location is an example.

3. A person is involved in making a choice between two equally negative outcomes. An example is an organizational policy which calls for a pay reduction for failure to wear uncomfortable and unattractive protective goggles.

Reactions to internal conflict increase the levels of internal stress and tension. When managers see behavior that suggests such adaptive processes are occurring, they can take steps to alter relevant organizational factors. Energy not consumed in efforts to adapt to internal conflicts is potentially available for improving organizational performance.

Conflict at the Organizational Level. Conflicts between people in organizations and between organizational units cannot be avoided. Furthermore, organizational conflict is not necessarily bad nor counterproductive to organizational goal achievement. Groups tend to behave in different but consistent ways, depending on whether they consider themselves winners or losers of a conflict. A winning group is apt to become complacent, relaxing in its victory. It will often begin to attend to the maintenance of its members' socioemotional needs at the expense of group-task performance. The losing group will tend to rationalize the defeat or, failing that, to look inside the group for a cause of its loss. Fortunately, losing groups often are prepared to work harder to succeed and pay less attention to group members' individual needs.[10]

Stages of Conflict.[11] Organizational conflict stems from several unique sources and proceeds through several distinct stages. Identifying these stages and sources will assist the manager in designing an appropriate strategy for handling the situation.

1. Conflict has its genesis in an early latent state. The elements necessary for conflict are present in this stage, but they are not always visible. Where a latent conflict condition exists, one will probably find some combination of general uneasiness, perhaps apprehension, differences of opinion, different values, and limited resources.

2. The next stage occurs when the conflict is perceived and experienced by those involved. In this stage, people feel more tense, hostile, and aggres-

sive. They begin to see the dimensions of the conflict taking shape. Battle lines are sketched out and contingency plans are established. We/they distinctions become more important; good guys and bad guys are identified.

3. The final stage is one of manifest conflict where people are actually fighting. The fight will usually take place in the socially acceptable modes of verbal attack and defense and organizational intrigue. Occasionally, the fight gets to the physical aggression stage.

Sources of Conflict. Individuals and subunits in organizations may find themselves in disagreement about the facts of a situation, about the appropriate means and methods to be instituted, about the goals to be achieved, and about the relevant guiding values.

Competition for scarce resources is probably the most common source of organizational conflict. Conflict among claimants for resources can result in behavior and consequent resource distribution which is suboptimal for the organization. Winner-take-all battles can leave critical components of the organization with insufficient resources to operate properly. Management's concern is to achieve an orderly distribution of these limited resources and avoid the unnecessary costs of the competition.

A need for autonomy and independence will often spawn conflict within an organizational hierarchy. When a person joins an organization, some portion of autonomy and freedom of action is forfeited in deference to coordination and cooperation. Similarly, groups will have to subordinate some of their independence in deference to larger organizational objectives.

Managing Conflict. Resolution of conflict can take a number of different forms. Resolution will usually involve an investment of organizational time and energy. Avoiding unnecessary investments and disruptions is the critical managerial task.[12]

1. *Problem solving.* This technique for resolution relies on the open confrontation of differences among conflicting parties. It requires, at a minimum, open communications and the willingness of the parties to try to resolve the issues. When the conflict is based on differences in values, the problem-solving model is not apt to be successful. When differences occur over facts, methods, or goals, the confrontation, open communication, and problem solving have potential for finding resolution.

2. *Smoothing.* This technique does not truly remove or reduce the basic conflict. By emphasizing positive aspects in the situation and avoiding sensitive areas of difference, it is sometimes possible to smooth the situation sufficiently for

work to proceed. This technique is obviously a temporary solution.

3. *Referral to higher authority.* Resolutions of this sort will usually result in a winning and a losing side. If production and sales cannot agree about the appropriate percentage of rejects per order, the problem can be sent to the level of management that the two units have in common for resolution. When labor-management disputes are sent to arbitrators for solution, this general principle is being followed.

4. *Reduction in scarcity of resources.* Conflict based on competition for scarce resources can be resolved by increasing the pool of resources for all. Rather than fight over the relative size of portions, parties to the conflict can all enjoy increased portion size. This strategy will not be effective when there are status implications connected to relative amounts that a given unit gains. Furthermore, managers are often constrained by organizational budgets, so making changes in the total pool of resources frequently is a slow process.

5. *Avoidance.* This strategy is commonly found in interpersonal situations. One person, knowing another's sensitivities, can avoid a conflict by not bringing up topics in those areas. Nothing has changed, but a potential conflict has been avoided for a time during which progress may have occurred in other dimensions.

6. *Compromise.* The difficulty with compromise solutions is that all parties lose a little. The final solution may not be a particularly good one from any of the parties' points of view. Such solutions do permit conflicting parties to move beyond a stalemated situation. Compromises tend not to be permanent solutions to underlying problems.

7. *Changing the people in conflict.* This solution is not unanimously endorsed as practical by social scientists and organizational practitioners. People have a capacity for stubbornly clinging to their ways of being, believing, and behaving. To attempt to change people in the interest of conflict resolution is, at best, a long-term undertaking. By the time a conflict is manifest, people have usually taken positions publicly. To change one's position is to admit error and possibly lose face. Where conflict is based on an inaccurate view of the facts in the situation, changing people has some promise. New or more complete information may persuade people to alter their position. When conflicts are based in attitudes, beliefs, and values, hope for quick change in people is optimistic. Managers may occasionally be tempted to institute quick resolutions that do not address the basic sources of the conflict. In those cases, the manager is merely buying time; the

conflict will remain and will require attention again.

Organizational Effectiveness

Key to the management of excellence is the management of interpersonal relationships.[13] In a study of 62 American firms identified consensually by businesspeople, management consultants, and academics as being both innovative and excellently managed (that is, as top performers), a set of parameters of interpersonal relations, the key to their excellence, was isolated. This key was believed to be, most notably, the interpersonal relationships between organizational members and their clients (customers) and the interpersonal relationships between managers and supervisors and the "average" employee. Instrumental in this effort are (1) meeting the needs for self-esteem through appropriate but authentic use of praise and through reinforcement; (2) understanding the importance of individual cognitive models; (3) seeking to manage an organizational climate which facilitates the experience of "ownership" in the goals and future of the organization; and (4) trusting others' abilities sufficiently to allow autonomy of action.

Conclusion

Interpersonal relationships are a key element in management. Scientific study of these relationships in the managerial context is less than a half-century old, however. This field is still in a state of search. There appears to be a taxonomy which allows us to order the key dynamics of interpersonal relationships in a meaningful way, but that is only the beginning. The condensation in this entry necessarily leaves much unsaid. There is one general principle, however, to guide the study of interpersonal relationships: No person is a single entity; each person exists concomitantly in the other, and the study of management, as a substudy of humanity, is the study of that mutuality of existence.

See also Assertiveness training; Conformity in management; Control systems, management; Health, mental; Laboratory (sensitivity) training; Leadership; Motivation in organizations; Transactional analysis.

NOTES

[1]R. A. Webber, *Time and Management*, Van Nostrand Reinhold, New York, 1972.

[2]Claude S. George, *The History of Management Thought*, Prentice-Hall, Englewood Cliffs, N.J., 1968.

[3]Committee on Work in Industry, National Research Council, *Fatigue of Workers: Its Relation to Industrial Production*, Reinhold Publishing, New York, 1941, pp. 77–86.

[4]A. Hastoff, personal communication, 1968.

[5] David R. Hampton, Charles E. Summer, and Ross A. Webber, *Organizational Behavior and the Practice of Management*, rev. ed., Scott, Foresman, Glenview, Ill., 1973, pp. 220–223.

[6] H. R. Bobbitt et al., *Organizational Behavior: Understanding and Prediction*, Prentice-Hall, Englewood Cliffs, N.J., 1974, pp. 190–193.

[7] Harold J. Leavitt, "Applied Organizational Change in Industry: Structural Technological and Humanistic Approaches," in James G. March, ed., *Handbook of Organization*, Rand McNally, Chicago, 1965, pp. 1152–1153.

[8] Robert Tannenbaum and Warren Schmidt, "How to Choose a Leadership Pattern," *Harvard Business Review*, vol. 51, 1973, p. 164.

[9] Harold J. Leavitt, *Managerial Psychology*, 3d ed., The University of Chicago Press, Chicago, 1972.

[10] Edgar Schein, *Organizational Psychology*, 2d ed., Prentice-Hall, Englewood Cliffs, N.J., 1970, pp. 96–103.

[11] L. R. Pondy, "Organizational Conflict: Concepts and Models," *Administrative Science Quarterly*, vol. 12, no. 2, September 1967, pp. 296–320.

[12] Stephen P. Robbins, *Managing Organizational Conflict: A Nontraditional Approach*, Prentice-Hall, Englewood Cliffs, N.J., 1974, pp. 59–74.

[13] Thomas J. Peters and Robert H. Waterman, Jr., *In Search of Excellence*, Harper & Row, New York, 1982.

ROBERT H. DOKTOR, *University of Hawaii at Manoa*

MARVIN D. LOPER, *Hawaiian Telephone Co.*

Interviewing, Employee

The employment interview is a conversation—a conversation with the particular purpose of determining qualifications for employment, keeping in mind the needs of the applicant as well as those of the employer. Insofar as qualifications are concerned, it is important to ask three basic questions: (1) *Can* the applicant do the job or be trained to do it? (2) *Will* the person do the job and continue to do it? (3) *How* will the person fit in with the significant others on the job?

A second important objective of the employment interview is to promote good will regardless of whether or not an employment offer is made. Insufficient attention to this goal may discourage acceptance of a job offer, reduce the number of persons interested in seeking employment with a firm, make candidates for employment who are potential or current customers reluctant to purchase the product or services of that organization, and even precipitate legal action charging discrimination.

The costs of ineffective employment interviewing can be significantly high. Most studies indicate that it can easily cost several hundred dollars to place a nonexempt (or wage-roll) employee on the payroll and several thousand dollars for an exempt (professional) employee. These costs can be compounded when training and development are considered, particularly when the new employee is misplaced or turns out to be unmotivated, inept, or a troublemaker. Should an employer be found guilty or even be accused of discrimination against a prospective employee because of race, color, age, sex, place of national origin, handicap, veteran status, or religion, defense action and court-imposed costs can be many thousands, even millions, of dollars.

The Interviewing Process

Like any skill, interviewing requires that certain steps be taken or elements be included if the end results are to be achieved. These steps include preparing for the interview, establishing and maintaining rapport, gathering the necessary information, controlling the interview, and evaluating the data which have been collected in terms of the employer's and the applicant's needs.

Preparation. No interviewer plans to fail, but by failing to plan, the chances of failure are increased. Some of the most important steps to be taken before the start of the interview are these:

1. Develop your skills prior to any actual interviewing through supervised practice exercises, such as role playing, where valuable feedback is given by knowledgeable and experienced interviewers.

2. Determine the essential job requirements by carefully studying the job description and specifications, talking with persons doing the job, and observing the job being done.

3. Arrange the physical environment so that it is pleasant, comfortable, quiet, private, and free from interruptions and undue distractions.

4. Be alert to fair and equal employment considerations so that legal requirements as well as human and employment needs are met.

5. Plan your action in a way that allows for time efficiency but provides for a thorough exploration of the candidate's qualifications as they relate to the demands of the job.

Rapport. The interview should be relatively free from stress, at least from the kind of stress that is deliberately induced. The interviewee who is placed under pressure becomes more concerned with protecting his or her ego, avoiding criticism, or attacking than with communicating. Frequently, as a result of the applicant's being put on the spot through cross-examination techniques, the relationship deteriorates, the information becomes more guarded and slanted, the goodwill lessened, and the interviewee is more inclined to feel discriminated against.

A friendly smile, a firm handshake, a warm greeting, and some small talk about travel, the weather, and some common interests can get the interview started in a way that will enhance the relationship and the communications.

Continued attention to the candidate's comfort-level needs (temperature, lighting, seating, furniture arrangement, beverages, rest room), displaying an animated and responsive countenance, actively listening to what is being said, and making sincere compliments when appropriate can help the interviewee feel that she or he is being regarded as someone of importance and dignity.

Although the interview should be sustained as a pleasant conversation, it should be remembered that the goal of the interview is to obtain, retain, and analyze data so that a proper employment decision can be made; it is not just to fill time with easy talk that is light and enjoyable but not necessarily meaningful.

Gathering Information. Most effective in encouraging the applicant to talk freely and responsively is the use of the *funnel approach;* that is, the questioning moves from the general to the specific, from the public to the private knowledge area, and from the impersonal to the personal. By gently probing in this manner, there is less possibility that the candidate will feel that the interviewer is moving too quickly and probing too deeply into background areas that are sensitive and personal.

Open-ended questions that begin with what, how, and why are most useful in enlarging upon and enriching the fund of knowledge already available through the person's résumé or completed application. Some examples are, "What were some of your more challenging responsibilities in your last position?" "How did you handle them?" "Why did you take the approach that you did?"

Least useful are direct, closed-ended questions that provoke a one-word or yes or no response. Yet, the majority of questions asked by most untrained interviewers are of this type. While not ruling out closed-ended questions, the interviewer should use them very sparingly. Not only do they reveal less in-depth information than open-ended questions, they often put words in the mouth of the interviewee. For example, "Did you do well in your last job?" "Would you say that you have a good personality?" "Do you think you can do this job?" What person who is interested in being offered a job would say no to these questions?

Too many questions in rapid-fire succession may turn the conversation into a grilling, reduce the flow of spontaneous replies, and thus increase the number of distortions and untruths. To lessen the chances of doing this, the interviewer can make use of nonverbal actions, such as smiling, raising the eyebrows, pausing, employing pertinent comments such as verbal pats on the back, reflection of feelings, and brief restatements of what the interviewee has said. These techniques not only reduce the threatening aspect of continuing questions, they provide for a change of pace, force the interviewer to listen to what is being said, and convince the applicant that an attempt is being made to understand what he or she is saying.

Control. The interview should be a planned event, not a "happening." This not only keeps the interview on track, it reduces the possibility of forgetting or overlooking anything of importance. Additionally, the information obtained is sorted out in a systematic way so that the interviewer can absorb it more easily and make better sense out of it. Without a plan of action, there is more chance of a "happening" occurring where (1) the background data come forth at random without chronology and coherence, (2) control is weakened or lost, and (3) the interviewer becomes frustrated and confused.

After the initial greeting, welcome, small talk, and an opening question to learn what has transpired already and what the applicant's expectations are, broad-brush or lead statements can be used to describe to the candidate what is going to happen in the interview and the approach to be taken. These lead statements can be employed to introduce each major area, such as work, education, and even leisure if it appears relevant, as well as to summarize the highlights of the person's background and to close the interview.

Closing. During the closing, the interviewer should thank the interviewee and determine whether there is anything else the interviewee would like to tell about himself or herself. The interviewer then presents information about the job, the organization, and benefits and, finally, provides the applicant with an opportunity to ask questions.

The "sell" part of the closing should be based on the interviewer's evaluation of the candidate and directed to the personal and career needs of the applicant.

The applicant should leave feeling that he or she has been fully heard and fairly treated and that this has been a worthwhile investment of time and energy. Regardless of the decision, the interviewee should clearly know what the next step is and when it will be taken.

Interpretation. Interpretation is a mentally demanding task which is facilitated by learning the fundamentals for obtaining relevant and sufficient interview data. Once this is accomplished, the interviewer can concentrate on the process of evaluation.

As previously stated, the interviewer should ask three important questions when ascertaining a candidate's qualifications for employment. *Can* and *will* the candidate do the job, and *how* will she or he get along with superiors, coworkers, subordinates, and customers in terms of getting the job done?

Can do refers to the interviewee's abilities and work-related training, knowledge, skills, and experiences. *Will do* applies to motivation, initiative, drive, and aspiration. *How "fit"* is concerned with communications and interpersonal effectiveness.

Based upon these considerations, four steps are necessary to determine the candidate's suitability for employment:

1. A decision must be reached as to what the job requirements are; i.e., what the essential tasks are that must be done.

2. It is important to decide what *can do, will* do, and "fit" factors a new employee must have in order to do what is required on the job.

3. One must select the most effective approach, method, or questions for eliciting the required evaluative data from the applicant.

4. In as comprehensive fashion as possible, the information collected from the applicant must be matched against the job demands.

The evaluation should take into account the overall view of what the candidate has done, the strengths, weaknesses, likes, and dislikes evidenced as related to the opening available. It should in every way possible justify the employment recommendation and the possibilities of mutual success and satisfaction for the employer and candidate.

See also Employment processs; Equal employment opportunity, minorities and women; Outplacement; Personnel administration.

REFERENCES

Fear, R. A. and J. F. Ross: *Jobs, Dollars, and EEO,* McGraw-Hill, New York, 1983.

Morgan, H. H., M. H. Frisch II, and J. W. Cogger: *Seven Imperatives: Fair and Effective Interviewing,* Drake Beam Morin, Inc., New York, 1981.

JOHN W. COGGER, *Drake Beam Morin, Inc.*

Inventory Control

Despite the substantial shift in the United States from a manufacturing to a service economy, materials (for conversion or sale) continue to represent the major component of business costs. In manufacturing, this cost is in the neighborhood of 65 percent of the cost of goods sold; in retailing, about 82 percent; in wholesaling, about 93 percent; and in general service, 6 percent. The accumulation of these materials in the form of inventories is a significant variable for managers to monitor and control. In production processes especially, considerable cost is incurred when the right material is not in the right place at the right time and in the right quantity. A

number of control techniques are readily applicable to this end.

Inventory Theory and Modeling. Proper control of inventory requires a delicate balance and careful, detailed planning. To the controller who sees funds tied up in material in the warehouse, work-in-process inventory, and finished goods not shipped, the natural reaction is that inventories are too high. To the production superintendent faced with the prospect of interrupted deliveries or silent production lines due to inadequate raw, in-process, or finished materials, the response must be that inventories are too low. Therefore, a balance is needed between holding large quantities to satisfy the latter and frequent stock replenishment to satisfy the former. This might be represented, as in Fig. I-2, if the

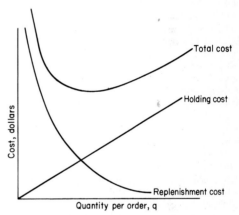

FIG. I-2 Cost-balance model.

replenishment quantity q is represented on one axis and the total inventory cost in dollars is represented on the other.

Many reasons exist for keeping inventory. They include: to improve customer service; to hedge against demand surges and variation of production level; to take advantage of favorable prices; to ensure against error and loss; and to avoid production stoppage.

Overproduction for any of these reasons can, on the other hand, increase costs through high investment and low capital turnover, material obsolescence, spoilage and deterioration, storage and handling excesses, and inefficient use of space due to overcrowding.

Inventory theory suggests that there are effective methods with which to do the careful planning necessary. The two most common approaches are the use of (1) economic order quantity techniques and (2) a more recent control measure called material requirements planning. The former is discussed in this entry, while the latter is described under Materials Management. More commonly, these are intermixed to achieve the objective: cost control through material control.

Factors in Inventory Control Modeling. To develop models which can be used in determining proper inventory levels and replenishment quantities, basic information describing the inventory using system must be identified. These factors are represented in Fig. I-3 as costs, demand, and replenishment. Since numerous variations can exist, however, those conditions must be identified which most closely define the inventory system to be modeled.

The following illustrates the selection process for the identification of the appropriate characteristic.

Costs. *Unit costs* may be constant within the planning period as reflected by accumulated manufacturing cost or purchase cost, or, alternatively, they may vary because of price discounting or economics of scale. *Storage cost* is an important factor and should reflect (1) the cost of capital invested in the stock item as well as (2) the physical costs to keep and protect the item. A third item of cost is *replenishment* (or ordering) *cost*. What is the cost of the clerical system to track the inventory use, initiate and process orders, and set up production processes, and what are the costs to initiate a replenishment order? These expenses occur only when a new order for replenishment is placed.

Finally, what is the penalty in terms of cost if the stock item is not available when it is needed? This *stock-out cost* can be very high, but it is also more difficult to determine. It is not unusual to use a stock-out level as a planning factor, but this implies a certain cost. For example, a policy that "we will not exceed a stock-out factor of 1 percent" suggests that *safety stock* should be such that only 1 in 100 replenishment cycles will result in a stock shortage. This implies that the cost of running out is 100 times greater than that of storing the amount necessary to prevent a shortage. Attention to this cost element, though difficult, is extremely important.

Demand. Demand may be known and fixed or be highly variable and require forecasting techniques. In materials requirements planning (MRP), forecasts are necessary for the final product, but component parts are determined from bills of material. Consequently, a mixed system may frequently be necessary. Other demand variables that impact on inventory control systems include: (1) whether the item is bulk or the items are individually controllable; (2) frequency of use; and (3) regularity of use.

Replenishment. To replenish inventory stock requires some knowledge of order lead time and the variability of that lead time in order to build in the proper safeguards or safety stocks. The nature of delivery is also a factor in planning and controlling inventory, e.g., partial shipments, frequency of shipments, and types of unit loads.

Use of Factors in Inventory Models. It is often necessary to rely on economic order quantity concepts in order to develop and retain that balance between stocking too much (high investment cost) and not having enough (production down owing to lack of material). The concept of economic order, or lot, quantities (EOQ) is based on knowledge of the previously discussed variables. An EOQ may be developed using (1) "quick and dirty" procedures and maintaining large safety stocks to accommodate error or (2) highly sophisticated techniques for close control. Needless to say, the former may be less costly to implement and can provide the necessary level of balance for some stock items, while very costly items would deserve the more costly control justified by the greater cost benefit. These concepts will be discussed further under "ABC Analysis" in this entry.

Two basic concepts of control models need to be recognized: transaction reporting and periodic review.

Transaction Reporting. Transaction reporting requires continuous, accurate updating of stock records to determine when a replenishment order should be initiated. Frequent stock activity, high volume requirements, and identifiable individual units may make this type of system more desirable. This system may entail *perpetual* (or continuous) record processing: e.g., reporting the use of each item and continuous monitoring of stock levels. When a predetermined reorder point is reached, an economic order quantity acquisition is initiated. This reorder point is set to ensure that sufficient stock is available to carry the production process until the replenishment supply is received.

Periodic Review. A second concept is that records will be reviewed periodically (weekly, monthly, quarterly, etc.) and if the level of inventory for that item has fallen below a certain target level, a new order will be placed. If it has not, the record will be returned to the file for review again at the end of the next period. Target levels, period lengths, and replenishment quantities are dependent on frequency of use, replenishment lead time, and criticality of item. This system is usually more difficult to establish but results in lower clerical cost to maintain stock control. Both transaction reporting and periodic review systems can be maintained manually or by computer, if the inventory system is of sufficient size to warrant computer control.

EXAMPLE: An example of a transaction system is the following: A manufacturer uses wooden pallets for unit load shipping of the product. These pallets are used regularly at a rate of 100 per month and purchased from a vendor at $3.50 per pallet. They are stored in an unheated but covered shed until needed, and it is estimated that it costs 20 percent of the unit value to pay for the investment and storage costs. A fixed cost of $50 in clerical time and processing is

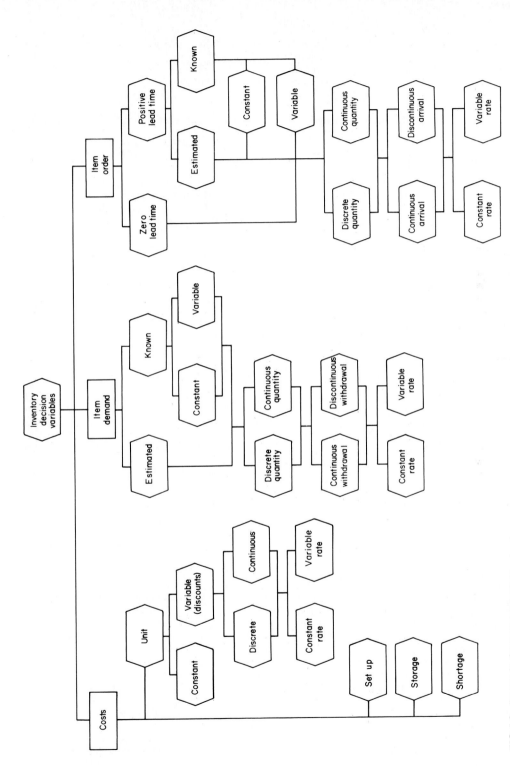

FIG. I-3 Factors in determining inventory level.

incurred every time a replenishment order is processed. If pallets are available when needed, rehandling of the unit load of final product is necessary at a cost of $10 per unit. Delivery normally takes from 6 to 10 days from the time of order, and 6, 7, 8, 9, or 10 days are equally likely.

To determine the EOQ, the following is considered:

Action	Result
Frequent orders	Frequent replenishment cost
	Low average inventory and low storage cost
	More frequent risk of running out
Infrequent orders	Infrequent replenishment cost
	High average inventory and high storage cost
	Less risk of running out

If C = replenishment cost

S = storage cost

I = number of inventory turnovers per year

T = total cost per year for storage and replenishment

R = rate of demand

Q = order quantity (EOQ)

then Q can be calculated to be the order quantity which results in the lowest cost T

$$Q = \sqrt{\frac{2CR}{S}}$$

$$= \sqrt{\frac{2(50)(100)}{(0.2)(3.50)}} = 120 \text{ pallets/order}$$

$$I = \frac{(R)(\text{number of months})}{Q}$$

$$= \frac{(100)(12)}{120} = 10 \text{ turnovers/year}$$

In this example, a transaction system is to be used, and a reorder point needs to be determined which will provide protection during the reorder period of 6 to 10 days. Since it is equally likely that delivery can be at any time between 6 and 10 days, inclusive, the reorder point will be selected at the point that gives a cost balance between overstocking during the lead time and understocking.

Each time period of days from 6 to 10 has 1 chance in 5 of occurring in the replenishment cycle. By weighting the chances of various delivery possibilities by the cost of overstocking versus understocking, a weighted average of delivery days can be computed which establishes a basis of the reorder points. In this example it may be computed as follows:

Number of items demanded per day = $100/20^* = 5$

*20 days assumes a 5-day workweek

Average cost of overstocking =

$$(5)(\$3.50)(1/5)(x - 5)$$

where x = delivery period between 6 to 10 days

Average cost of understocking =
$$(\$10 \times 1/5)[10 - (x - 5)]$$

Solving for x as the point where the weighted-average overstocking cost equals the weighted-average understocking cost:

$$(5)(\$3.50)(1/5)(x - 5) = (\$10)(1/5)(10 - x)$$

$$3.5x - 17.5 = 20 - 2x$$

$$5.5x = 37.5$$

$$x = 6.8$$

The weighted-average delivery period for the purpose of planning the reorder point is 6.8 days.

$$\text{Reorder point} = (100/20)(6.8) = 34.0$$

In summary, place an order for pallets when the pallet inventory drops to 34. Thus, you will provide an economical stock system for pallets as long as the costs and demand factors or the delivery time factors do not change.

ABC Analysis. It is not uncommon for an inventory system to have 30,000 line items in inventory control. These include supplies, packaging, maintenance parts, work in process, raw material, finished goods, and many other items. A *line item* includes an identifiable item and not the quantity of the item. For example, 500 rolls of 1-inch strapping tape for shipping purposes would be one line item for control purposes.

Clearly, a highly sophisticated inventory control system is not cost-effective for all items. Some items simply do not warrant the detailed record keeping, order quantity monitoring, stores keeping, or handling because the cost of the control system would far exceed the value of the item.

A rough classification to identify the line items which warrant a higher or lesser degree of control is commonly referred to as an *ABC analysis*. This analysis provides a method whereby the line items to be controlled can be classified according to *value* to provide indicators to the degree of control that can be justified. Characteristically, any inventory system will result in a relatively small percentage of the line items which constitute a large percentage of inventory value; e.g., 20 percent of the line items may constitute 95 percent of the inventory value. Therefore, these items may justify a greater degree of control.

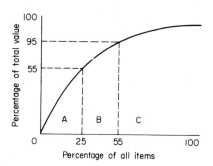

Fig. I-4 ABC curve.

Figure I-4 presents the percentage of total items and the percentage of total value in graphic form. In this example, approximately 25 percent of the line items constitute approximately 55 percent of the value, and 55 percent of the items make up approximately 95 percent of the value. Subjectively, these could be classified as A class, B class, and C class items. The A class items may require individual control and will warrant greater expenditure in a control system. The B class items might be controlled more on a group (or family) of items basis, and C class items could be controlled by a minimum expenditure system. Considerable care should be taken in the design of the total system to classify each line item and to establish proper control procedures to avoid paying $100 to control a $0.01 item or paying $0.01 to control a $100 item.

Productivity Measures for Inventory Control. A universal concept for productivity relates to labor productivity, i.e., units per labor hour. However, a concept of material productivity is equally important, as illustrated in the cost breakdown in the beginning of this entry. Some measures of material productivity include:

Turnover: The number of times per year inventory investment revolves.

Turnover =

$$\frac{\text{total annual material cost}}{\text{average inventory value on order and on hand}}$$

Economic order quantity: Equal to the size of the replenishment order to minimize total inventory control cost

Average inventory value: Equal to the average value of all inventory items in storage or on order

Material productivity:

Material productivity = $\dfrac{\text{total material cost}}{\text{total manufacturing cost}}$

Work-in-process productivity:

Work-in-process productivity =

$$\frac{\text{average total material value in process}}{\text{average total inventory value}}$$

Finished-goods productivity:

Finished-goods productivity =

$$\frac{\text{average total finished-goods inventory value}}{\text{average total inventory value}}$$

In establishing inventory value, two pricing policies are frequently used:

Last in, first out (LIFO): Establish value on the basis of the last quantity put in inventory.

First in, first out (FIFO): Establish value on the basis of the oldest item in the inventory.

The former tends to overvalue inventories in periods of inflating economies.

Interdepartmental Relationships. Inventory control is normally a function of production control. The interactions between these two organizational entities is crucial. Sales information is necessary to establish appropriate demand levels for planning purposes. Vendor pricing, lead items, and other replenishment information is equally vital to proper inventory planning and control. Production schedules become an integral part of the inventory controller's planning so that the *right materials* can be at the *right place* in the *right quantities.*

See also Accounting, financial; Control systems, management; Financial management; Financial statement analysis; Inventory stockkeeping systems; Material handling; Materials management; Purchasing management.

REFERENCES

Ammer, Dean: *Purchasing and Materials Management,* 4th ed., Richard D. Irwin, Homewood, Ill., 1980.

Jannis, C. P., C. H. Poedtke, and D. R. Ziegler: *Managing and Accounting for Inventories: Control, Income Recognition, and Tax Strategies,* 3d ed., John Wiley, New York, 1980.

Plossl, G. W., and O. W. Wight: *Production and Inventory Control,* Prentice-Hall, Englewood Cliffs, N.J., 1967.

Keith L. McRoberts, *Iowa State University*

Inventory Stockkeeping Systems

The cost of carrying inventory is a major one and is claimed to be anywhere from 15 to 60 percent of the value of the inventory. Of course, turnover makes these numbers more palatable. If the inventory can be turned 10 times each year, inventory carrying costs may be the equivalent of 1.5 to 6 percent of sales. It all depends on the point of view. Regardless of how much it costs to carry inventory, however, most of the control problems relate to turnover. The more turnover required, the more warehousing will likely present serious control problems.

The ideal condition would be to synchronize supply and demand so that supply coming in the receiving door would always be matched with demand going out the shipping door. Such ideal conditions are unlikely. Instead, thousands of warehouses and storerooms are busily stocking supplies in anticipation of shipping orders that do not always match the inventory waiting to be shipped.

Physical versus Accounting Control. The ability to satisfy demand efficiently is often directly related to the degree of control exercised by warehouse or storeroom personnel. Such control is defined as *physical control,* as opposed to *accounting control,* which is mainly concerned with financial responsibility and asset accounting. The firm's accounting department usually maintains a perpetual inventory control of some kind, and this inventory must be balanced periodically with the actual physical inventory. Balancing depends upon correctly accounting for receipts and withdrawals reported by the warehouse. This accounting normally takes place prior to issuing the shipping instructions, and entries are verified after the shipping documents or reports relating to shipping and receiving have been consummated. Periodically, physical inventories are taken to ensure that the actual inventory agrees with the perpetual book inventory. When discrepancies are found, adjustments must be made that will compensate for the overs and shorts detected, and the actual inventory is assumed to balance with the perpetual book inventory.

Overs and Shorts. In a very large warehouse where many stockkeeping units (SKUs) are stocked, all existing overs and shorts may not be detected, and new overages and shortages may be introduced unless careful attention is given to the establishment of a clean cut-off. Shortages and overages can also be introduced when verified counts are made of stacks in which all pallet loads are not uniformly loaded with the same number of warehousing units. In brief, a physical inventory cannot be assumed to be correct, because errors can be—and often are—found almost immediately following the completion of the inventory. Experience has also shown that errors can be made in adjustments; i.e., inventory is added that should be subtracted, and inventory is subtracted that should be added. It is a good practice to keep a file that includes *all* inventory adjustments, because this file can be used to account for mysterious disappearances as well as appearances.

Many over and short errors occur in order selection. Checking does not catch all selection errors. Errors also occur in receiving. More or less inventory than was actually received may have been reported.

Pilferage, or even large-scale theft, may account for some of the disappearances. Receiving may cooperate with inbound truck drivers and sign for more inventory that is in fact received. Truck drivers may detect overages not caught at checking time and deliver only what the shipping order calls for, keeping the remainder or overage to be disposed of later. Receiving clerks are more apt to catch and report shortages but to overlook overages, which then go unreported. Order selectors may also make errors involving substitution of one product for another; for example, 12/12-ounce pack is ordered, and 12/21-ounce pack is shipped. Checkers may not catch such errors because they are "natural" ones. In warehouses located adjacent to production, the production-run quantity may become the record when the actual quantity is either greater or less than the production-run quantity reported.

The more infrequently physical inventories are taken, the more likely it is that errors in overs and shorts will create problems that cannot be effectively dealt with by a remote central order processing system.

Central Order Processing (COP)

In an effort to resolve many of these problems, more and more firms have moved inventory control out of the warehouse and set up a *central order processing system* (COP) to gain greater control over the inventory. Typically, adjustments in the perpetual book inventory are not permitted unless a physical inventory is taken and verified. Consequently, many firms adopt the policy that changes in the records made necessary by overages and shortages cannot be made except at the time an inventory of the entire warehouse takes place.

Under this policy, more errors are likely to creep into the records because of the increase in the number of "cuts" and/or reduced quantities associated with (1) shipping orders and (2) the method of reporting by exception which is used by many large firms that employ central order processing systems to control a network of inventory locations.

Typical COP Process. In recent years, manual record-keeping systems which were used to maintain a perpetual inventory have been largely replaced by computers. COP is often designed to do away with this redundant record keeping on the grounds that costs are duplicated and no significant increase in accuracy or reliability is obtained. To understand the nature of the control problems encountered, it is necessary to describe briefly how COP works in many firms that use this method of accounting.

1. Perpetual inventories are maintained by COP for each warehouse or storeroom in the network.

2. When purchase orders are placed, COP updates an open purchase-order file.

3. When inventory is received at the warehouse or storeroom, a report stating what has been received is prepared (usually on punched tape or disk) and transmitted to COP together with a report of shipments made.

4. When this report is received, COP updates the files, clears the purchase order from the open purchase-order file, and updates the inventory to reflect receipts and issues reported.

5. All shipping orders are transmitted to COP for processing. COP compares demand with supply, allocates inventory, and chooses the warehouse to satisfy each order as inventory dictates. Orders are then transmitted to the respective warehouses or storerooms. Each shipping order is assigned a serial number for reporting purposes so that all orders shipped in full need only to be confirmed by serial number. When orders cannot be shipped in full, the exceptions are reported together with the serial number.

6. Once each working day or as frequently as service and volume requirements dictate, the warehouse calls COP and reports receipts and shipments. Upon completion of each cycle, the respective inventories are updated so that all receipts will be recorded to satisfy incoming shipping orders.

Advantages. When it is necessary to maintain a network of warehouses or storerooms, the main justification for COP is control. Customers frequently can be serviced from more than one location at little or no increase in cost, or as inventory conditions dictate. Centralized control allows for prompt invoicing and more effective cash flow. The cost of carrying inventory can be reduced with the flexibility allowed by the ability to allocate or dispense inventory on the basis of the total inventory. Where inventory is sensitive to packaging changes, promotions, deals, short shelf life, etc., it is highly desirable to clear inventories so that obsolete inventory does not build up and create additional problems.

Disadvantages. While COP easily accounts for and gains greater control over the total inventory in the network of warehouses, the individual warehouses and storerooms become almost totally dependent on COP for information relating to the inventory in their care.

Some large firms have found a way around this problem by partitioning COP so that individual warehouses can communicate directly with COP and retrieve information that may be needed between cycles. Still other firms have devised real-time systems in which the warehouse and storeroom can be continuously on line with the big computer. For many firms, however, this solution is either impractical or unaffordable. Here are some solutions that will prove helpful to large and small firms that cannot justify more elaborate or sophisticated systems of inventory control.

Fixed-Slot Order Selection. There is a practical rule called Pareto's law, or the 80-20 rule, that can help resolve many of the control problems encountered at the warehouse level when a perpetual inventory is maintained by COP. This rule can be used to demonstrate that about 80 percent of the items stocked in a warehouse are likely to account for about 20 percent of the volume of goods shipped. The remaining 20 percent of the items stocked account for as much as 80 percent of the volume, i.e., the bulk of the inventory handled through the warehouse. When one of these items is out of stock, everybody is likely to know it. Most of the problems relating to location are associated with the 80 percent of the items that account for 20 percent of the volume. The fixed-slot method can be used to resolve many, if not all, of the locator problems.

In this method a supply of each SKU (usually sufficient for one shift) is stored in a fixed location or slot. Each slot is numbered and chained to the product code number and/or description stored in the computer files. When shipping orders are processed by COP, items are arranged in slot sequence to facilitate sequential order selection and, thus, reduce travel and search time. This method allows each product to be stored in the selection line in the most efficient manner and facilitates order selection. For example,

1. Heavy items may be picked before lighter items.

2. Items can be arranged in the order of package height to facilitate loading pallets, containers, or carts.

3. Items can be arranged in order of dollar value to minimize the risk of loss, should one item be picked in place of another.

4. Items can be ranked by velocity, i.e., fast, medium, and slow movers.

5. Items can be categorized as being hazardous, perishable, fragile, etc., and grouped or sequenced to facilitate compliance with the requirements of the Department of Transportation (DOT), the Food and Drug Administration (FDA), or the Occupational Safety and Health Act (OSHA).

6. If cubic volume as well as weight is included in the master record, orders can be cubed for selection in terms of cart loads, pallet loads, etc. The computation of cubic volume on each shipping order can facilitate loading out and routing of shipments to minimize delivery cost and to comply with weight limits on carriers used.

All these benefits can be largely automatic once COP is programmed to accomplish these routine counting and computing tasks.

Reserve-Stock Locator System. When a fixed-slot system is used, it is seldom practical to keep all the stock of any given item in the pick-line or fixed-slot location. The reserve must therefore be stored elsewhere. The location of the reserve stock, however, must be readily available when needed.

A Rudimentary System. The most rudimentary system allows for chaining the reserve location to the fixed location as follows: (1) When stock is received, the fixed location is checked to determine whether the stock is needed; (2) if the stock is needed and no older stock is available, the pick-line location is filled; (3) if the stock is not to be placed in the fixed slot, the lift truck operator records where the reserve stock is to be located and leaves a record chained to the fixed slot; and (4) should a pallet load be needed, the forklift driver checks the fixed slot for the location to be used to retrieve a pallet load and then goes to this location after checking off the withdrawal on a tally card maintained at the fixed-slot location. Alternatively, the order selector can call for restocking and give the location to the lift truck driver, who will check off the location after completing the move.

Central Locator System. A more sophisticated system may be indicated when the rudimentary system does not work for some reason. For example, the effectiveness of the rudimentary system depends on cooperation of personnel and on accuracy. If the desired levels of cooperation and accuracy cannot be achieved, a central locator system can be used. In this method, reserve stock is recorded on commodity cards or records, one record for each pallet load of a commodity or product stored in reserve. No records need to be kept for stock stored in fixed slots, since these locations are maintained by COP.

In this system, it may be practical to prepare records in the form of punched cards. A master record is created for each item that will be received and stored in reserve on pallets. A supply of these records is maintained in a tub file in the receiving office. When stock is received and palletized, or prepared for storage, the load specifications (cartons per course times courses per load) are checked, and a record corresponding to the SKU number is pulled from the tub file to be used by the forklift operator to take the pallet to storage. When the pallet is placed in storage, the lift truck driver records the location and returns the record to receiving. When receiving has been completed, the records are placed in the commodity tub file. If a keypunch is available in the receiving office and one master record has been prepared for each item to be handled on pallets, a copy of the master record can be duplicated as needed. The unit records are then used to keep track of location and at the same time serve as the instrument for (1) instructing the lift truck operator to retrieve a load to be used for replenishment or (2) shipping when full pallet loads are required.

Minicomputer Applications

Another method for relieving COP problems would be to install a minicomputer at the warehouse. The minicomputer can be used as a stock locator system and warehouse controller. In this system, records relating to lot numbers, production codes, quality control information, quarantine, and other requirements can be integrated with the stock system, and a small printer can be used to prepare tickets referenced with warehouse locations. Cathode-ray-tube (CRT) terminals can be used to update records as inventory is received and to obtain location-referenced picking tickets for order entry when it is desired to ship orders. For example, if COP does not want to be bothered with the warehouse problems and is concerned only with network location problems, the minicomputer can be programmed to provide the auxiliary computer support the warehouse needs to cope with a growing variety of record-keeping requirements and physical inventory control problems. Some cost benefits may be realized by substituting the minicomputer for the terminal devices currently used by COP to transmit shipping orders to the warehouse and to retrieve information relating to receipts and data needed to maintain network control of the inventory.

Complexity of Record Keeping. The advent of many new regulations, such as those relating to the transportation and storage of hazardous materials, OSHA safety regulations, and FDA record-keeping requirements to facilitate product recall when products are found to endanger consumers, all combine to make record keeping a more detailed and costly function. The warehouse may be expected to keep more records relating to shipments. For example, pesticides must be accounted for by lot number as they are shipped from the warehouse. Food and other products that are consumed or used by people must be accounted for in terms of lot numbers and destinations. Normally, these data must be captured at the warehouse and recorded on the shipping documents. COP is so busy performing other tasks, it should be expected to be responsible only for data processing relating to overall accounting, perpetual inventory control in the network, and functions relating to the control of credit and accounts receivable. The warehouse, on the other hand, needs to be relieved of these functions so that it can effectively deal with the increasing demand for more records and record keeping that can be controlled only at the warehouse level.

Operational Control. Management at the local warehouse or storeroom level is just as concerned as COP with total inventory accountability. However, availability of the inventory to satisfy shipping orders is also of primary concern. Book inventory is not necessarily available inventory. Inventory can be damaged. Shelf life can have expired. Inventory may be in quarantine. Conditions not known to COP may make it impossible to ship orders which COP records indicate can be shipped. A more serious problem arises when COP transmits orders to the warehouse in anticipation of inventory being received. In this case, order selectors may search in vain for nonexistent stock.

Stock Locator Systems. When COP processes shipping orders, it generally arranges or sorts the items called for by the shipping order into product code-number sequence, which may not correspond to order selection or pick-line sequence. It is here that it would be useful to point out that the information contained on the shipping order has a great deal to do with labor productivity and the amount and quality of supervision required to manage the shipping function.

Order selector productivity is directly related to the design of the order selection system and the efficiency with which order selection or pick lines can be replenished. Computer-based COP systems can probably help the warehouse resolve some of the stock locator problems, provided its software can be modified to assign slot locations by warehouse when processing shipping orders.

Space Management. Invariably, every warehouse will find it no longer has sufficient space to keep pace with the increased demand. A minicomputer or warehouse controller can be used to make more efficient use of the available warehouse space. Experience has shown that selection of a slot with the right capacity can make more effective use of the available space. Furthermore, with a warehouse controller, it will be practical to maintain an inventory of empty slots and capacities to (1) facilitate choosing the most appropriate empty location or (2) determine which items are candidates for rewarehousing to make room for incoming lots. As data are processed to account for receipts and issues, an algorithm can be used to compute turnover. These and other data relating to warehousing specifications can then be used to optimize the use of storage space as well as to control the quality of the warehouse performance.

Performance Evaluation. One final contribution that can be expected of a minicomputer or warehouse controller is the ability to measure and quantify the performance of individuals, groups, or departments. For example, productivity can be measured more accurately and at less cost as an automatic by-product of processing transactions in real time, as opposed to the arduous and time-consuming manual methods that must be employed when no computing power is available at the warehouse level.

Partitioning the Large Computer. Many, if not all, of the benefits and control features described here can be obtained by partitioning the large computer. The same kind and quality of control can be achieved but probably at a much higher cost than necessary. The determination of the practicality and benefits of any of the systems or combinations of systems outlined above must be made on the basis of record maintenance cost, product turnover, and the impact of inventory discrepancies on profits.

See also Inventory control; Logistics, business; Management information systems, transactions processing systems; Marketing, channels of distribution; Material handling; Materials management; Production planning and control; Purchasing management.

REFERENCES

Brown, R. G.: *Materials Management Systems: A Modular Library,* John Wiley, New York 1977.

Buffa, Elwood F., and J. G. Miller: *Production-Inventory Systems: Planning and Control,* 3d ed., Richard D. Irwin, Homewood, Ill., 1979.

Hax, Arnoldo C., and Dan Candea: *Production and Inventory Management,* Prentice-Hall, Englewood Cliffs, N.J., 1984.

HOWARD WAY AND ASSOCIATES, INC. *Alexandria, Virginia*

Japanese Industries, Management in

Since 1968, Japan has been the third ranking economic power in the world. Its startling economic recovery from World War II and subsequent economic achievements have been widely attributed to the effectiveness of its management system. This effectiveness can be credited to at least three major elements: a unique industrial relations system, unique methods of financing industries and business groups, and the role the Japanese government plays in business through its unique industrial policy.

The Industrial Relations System

One of the key elements in the management of Japan's major industrial firms is the permanent employment system. The basic features of the system are that employees (primarily male) enter a large firm after junior high, high school, or college graduation; receive in-company training; and remain employed with that firm until the age of 55 to 57.

Payment according to length of service is the

basic practice which reinforces and maintains the permanence of employment among the workers within a firm. Usually only young, recent graduates can afford to enter the system at beginning wages (in 1982, the monthly starting salary of college graduates was about $500), and older workers cannot afford the loss of earnings a change of employer would entail. As a result, interfirm mobility is severely limited, and the vast majority of employees in large firms remain with the same employers throughout their careers.

The permanent employment system is the basic element providing the stability and continuity of human relationships essential to the behavioral effectiveness of the Japanese management style. Japanese permanent employees have reacted to their immobility by developing strong group loyalties, collectivism, a system of shared obligations, heavy dependence on powerful superiors, and an intense competitive drive. Among these employees—who are associated more by location and situation than by any other common factor—such cohesiveness, coordination, and effectiveness are established by several powerful behavioral control mechanisms—a rigid, hierarchical structure based on seniority; intense emotional involvement in the group ethos; total ful-

439

fillment of security needs; and economic interdependence.

Within this framework, certain limited areas of competition are permitted: among different firms within an industry, among separate work groups within a single firm, and among individuals for promotion within classes of employees who join a firm in the same year. This peculiar synthesis of cohesion and competition results in a remarkably effective work team.

The permanent employment system has other advantages as well. It makes extensive in-company training a profitable investment and provides large firms with the stability they need for long-range planning. Employees find it easy to accept the organizational changes required by technological innovation and growth because their firms are committed to retain and retrain them. Further, since the wage levels of employees are determined by age and length of service, labor costs are related to the average age of the work force; therefore firms with higher growth rates, having high proportions of young, starting workers, have lower wage bills. This cost advantage helps to keep firms vital by motivating them to grow and diversify.

The Extent of the Permanent Employment System. One of the most widespread misconceptions about this system is that it pervades the management of Japanese industrial concerns. Actually, the system is seldom operative in any but the larger Japanese firms and applies to less than 30 percent of the nonagricultural labor force. In order to keep wage costs down, the number of new permanent recruits is kept at a cyclically justifiable minimum, and additional needs for labor are met by extensive use of temporary, subcontract, daily, part-time (female), and retired workers, whose wages are from 10 to 50 percent less than those of permanent workers. This arrangement is known as the dual wage structure and labor market of Japan.

The Role of the Labor Movement. Just a little over 30 percent of Japanese workers are unionized. Japanese unions include manual as well as nonmanual workers and are organized on an enterprise basis, reflecting the structure of the enterprise entity and identifying with its interests. Most union members are permanent workers in large firms, while most untenured workers are outside the labor movement.

Union members are differentiated not by skills but by employing firm. Thus many of the standard issues in the collective bargaining of other industrialized countries—occupationwide bargaining, jurisdictional disputes, rigid work rules, technological change, and job assignments—are nonissues in Japan. Close identification between Japanese unions and their parent enterprises has led to an emphasis on emotional qualities in the relationship, such as mutual trust and good faith. The resulting collective bargaining agreements are rather general and abstract, and often obscure.

The majority of management-labor relations are collusive. It is not uncommon for union officials to be paid at least in part by management. Unions use company facilities for many of their activities, and many of their expenses are borne by management. The president of a Japanese enterprise union often serves as a kind of senior executive for labor relations in his parent firm. Strikes in Japan are generally of short duration, often lasting no more than an hour or two and seldom longer than one or two days. In the words of Robert J. Ballon, an expert on Japan, "Trade unions do not exist in Japan."

Methods of Financial Management

Bank Financing. One unusual financial feature of the Japanese management system is that 80 to 90 percent of the capital requirements of Japanese companies are financed by low-interest bank loans. The major obligation of the borrowing firms in the area of capital financing is the payment of debt-servicing charges. Except for this constraint, they are free to devote their energy toward market expansion and long-term growth without concern for stockholder pressure or predatory takeovers. Continued growth and diversification financed by further debt are easily encouraged.

Financing within Business Groups. Seven major groups of industrial firms dominate Japan's business world: Mitsubishi, Mitsui, Sumitomo, Fuyo, Daiichi Kangyo, Sanwa, and Tokai. Each of these groups embraces scores of companies and is continually expanding. Japan's Fair Trading Commission estimates that these seven groups control more than 40 percent of the nation's corporate capital and more than 30 percent of Japan's corporate assets.

Each business group is headed by a central management council composed of a core group of top executives who exchange managerial resources, maintaining carefully cultivated personal relationships with each other, staying out of one another's established markets, and buying and selling to one another. The individual firms are joined together under the financial leadership of a major bank. The major financial institution and trading firm in each group often take the lead in planning, implementing, and coordinating new ventures and are a constant source of leadership in the current business activities of member firms.

The risks of heavy debt financing are minimized in part by the business group system. The diversified nature of the industries represented in a group virtually guarantees that the fortunes of all the firms involved will not fluctuate alike, which reduces risk for the group as a whole and supports a higher debt capacity among members.

Another factor in the financial flexibility provided by Japanese business groups is the widespread cross-ownership of stocks among group members. Since less than 10 percent of new capital comes from the external issue of new stocks, Japanese corporations do not have to concern themselves with short-term shareholder interests as American firms do. This gives them a great deal of freedom to invest in long-term projects and outspend their competitors in promising new market situations.

Subcontracting. Another factor contributing to the financial stability of large Japanese corporations is the extensive use of subcontracting. This serves the twofold purpose of providing large firms with a valuable cushion against fluctuations in the business cycle and enabling them to make higher profits by manufacturing goods at lower costs.

These subcontracting arrangements often involve a pyramidal chain of relationships between a large master firm (usually part of one of the business groups) and a group of smaller firms, who may in turn subcontract with a group of even smaller firms. The Mitsubishi group, for example, consists of 27 core firms which control, through varying degrees of ownership, 2929 smaller firms, and the Daiichi-Kang-yo group consists of 57 core firms which exercise some degree of control over 3477 smaller firms.

The core firms and their lesser satellite firms mutually benefit from this arrangment. Smaller firms benefit by sharing the core firm's long-term goals and requisite technical know-how and can depend on the capital and market the core firms provide. Core firms derive a cost advantage from the arrangement since the untenured employees of the smaller firms in the hierarchy receive lower wages and fewer benefits than their own permanent employees. Smaller firms must resist their employees' demands for higher wages in order to produce at a price the large firms are willing to pay. In the event of a recession, the core companies simply reduce their orders from the smaller firms or reduce the limits on the prices they are willing to pay and allow the small firms to absorb the ill effects of the recession.

Government-Industry Relationships

The relationships between the various agencies of the Japanese government and Japanese business firms involve a degree of close interaction unrivaled among advanced nations. The Japanese government, in close consultation with the nation's major business leaders, determines Japan's economic goals and establishes the industrial policies with which to achieve them. This economic planning is purely advisory in nature, with no powers of legal enforcement attached. Nevertheless, the government manages to implement its policies very effectively in a number of ways.

Policy Formulation. The Economic Planning Agency is the clearing and coordinating organ which officially establishes Japan's long-range economic plan, the objective of which is to establish the most efficient and profitable direction the economy should take. Major concern is focused on identifying the coming generation of global growth industries and rendering special assistance to firms in those industries.

It is primarily two government agencies—the Ministry of International Trade and Industry and the Ministry of Finance—along with numerous consultative committees, whose members consist of both government and business leaders, who work out the actual policies to be followed. A group prominently involved in this process is Keidanren, which is a federation of business organizations representing industry as a whole. Numerous trade associations also participate.

As within business groups, many of the members of these organizations come from among the tenured elite, often having graduated from the same universities. They tend to maintain relationships at a personal level, constantly exchanging ideas and consulting one another so that each party knows the feelings of others on various issues and policy matters. There is a constant process of compromise and adjustment going on at this level, with government officials and top executives exchanging information and reactions on the economic plans of the major business corporations and proposed government policies that might affect the major corporations.

Methods of Obtaining Compliance. The Japanese government obtains compliance with its policies through consensus rather than enforcement, a process which is difficult for outsiders to understand. Through careful informal discussion, consensus is usually reached even before government policies become official and corporate plans are put into effect, so compliance is rarely an issue. Also, the Japanese are a very nationalistic people, and Japanese business leaders do readily concede to the national interest even when it seems to be in conflict with the interests of their own firms. Nevertheless, the Japanese government utilizes a number of very effective incentives to encourage Japanese firms to fall in line with government policy.

Monetary Policy. In industries where expansion is being encouraged, the apparent riskiness of heavy debt is largely offset by the fact that the Japanese government essentially guarantees the debts of Japan's major firms. While individual firms obtain their loans from commercial banks, these banks usually have nearly all their deposits on loan and are heavily dependent for funds on the Central Bank of the Japanese government (Bank of Japan) and extremely vulnerable to its policies.

When the Central Bank exercises influence by changing interest rates or required reserves for the commercial banks, the results are immediately felt by Japan's major firms. No large firm even requests a major loan without advance government approval. Because of its extensive control over the capital financing of Japanese industry, the Japanese government is able to play a major role in the direction and condition of its national industries, encouraging the expansion of firms in targeted growth industries and sponsoring the salvaging or mergers of troubled firms.

By guaranteeing the low-interest loans large firms need for expansion, the government makes it possible for large firms to forgo current profits in favor of the larger-scale profits to be earned from establishing a strong share in a new and growing market. The government also makes funds for basic research available to influence industries to expand into new product areas. Firms in those industries who compete in the marketplace often cooperate in doing basic research in areas they could not normally afford to investigate on their own.

Tax Incentives. The tax structure is utilized extensively by the Japanese government in influencing business outcomes. Devices such as rapid depreciation, special tax incentives for export, asset reevaluation, and multiple tax deductions for large firms are carefully formulated to encourage Japanese firms to work toward national economic goals. The government offers tax incentives for the rationalization of production facilities in inefficient firms and grants tax benefits to export firms and promising young growing firms to encourage them to become competitive in the international market. Debt-financed growth is encouraged by granting tax write-offs for loan interest payments.

Specialization and Economies of Scale. The Japanese consider product specialization an important element in their goal of rapidly, effectively, and efficiently opening up new growth markets. Large Japanese firms usually tend to concentrate their efforts on a single product line, which enables them to focus their attention on improving their production operations, upgrading the quality and design of their product, and identifying shifts in global market demand.

The financial institutions and trading firms associated with the firm's business group facilitate the single-minded pursuit of these goals by providing marketing and financial assistance. The concentrated effort made possible by product specialization has been an important factor in Japan's successful market penetration.

The high growth rate associated with firms which are expanding into new markets has the additional benefit of lowering product costs. Since growing firms take on many new workers at entry-level wages, their labor costs are lower than those of more mature and stable firms, which have a larger proportion of older workers. The large volume of production also results in increased productivity, which further lowers product cost.

The expansion of facilities that accompanies rapid growth also involves upgrading the means of production, which results in further efficiency. The benefits of high-volume production contribute importantly to Japan's market advances by enabling Japan to offer its goods at very competitive prices. Japan's single-minded pursuit of industrial growth has resulted in a phenomenal national growth rate, particularly in the government/business sector. In 1951, Japan's GNP was only one-twentieth of the U.S. level, but by 1982 it was half the U.S. level.

Protection from Foreign Competition. For years the Japanese depended on extensive trade barriers to protect their infant industries from foreign competition until they became internationally competitive. Due to foreign pressures and some structural industrial change, however, the Japanese government has had to reduce some of the tariff barriers and other protective measures for which it is so well known.

Nevertheless, for its key industries in targeted growth areas, the Japanese government still offers heavy protection from harmful foreign competition through explicit and implicit measures. Critical growth industries currently receiving strict government protection are computers, telecommunications, and biomedical products. Some domestically sensitive industries such as cigarettes, beef, and citrus fruits are also heavily protected by government measures. Large firms themselves establish a degree of protection through their control of the channels of distribution, whereby Japanese distributors are encouraged to overprice foreign goods. This strategy, coupled with the ingrained Japanese philosophy of buying only Japanese products, has limited foreign firms in most cases to a small and insecure segment of the market.

Domestic Competition. Even though the Japanese government protects its infant and sensitive industries from foreign competition, it does not ban competition altogether. When the Japanese government determines that competition will further Japan's interest by strengthening the firms involved, the process is encouraged. Domestic competition is often intense among different business groups and within industries, as when medium-small firms compete for the markets of large firms. By encouraging the survival of the fittest and sponsoring mergers among the weak, the government seeks to ensure the most efficient allocation of capital, technology, and human resources. But where the government establishes that competition is having a harmful effect on the Japanese economy, it calls instead for cooperation.

It is interesting to note that Japan earmarks most of its government assistance for its healthy, growing industries, while most U.S. government assistance falls into the hands of ailing industries. Nevertheless, Japan does not neglect its weaker firms and industries, but assists declining industries and sponsors mergers among weaker firms that lose out in the competition.

This peculiar coexistence of competition and cooperation results in part from the shared goals of government and industry in furthering Japan's economic and national interests. But the remarkable harmony with which the relationship is maintained can probably best be understood in terms of the unique Japanese social patterns which heavily sanction the resolution of nearly every human conflict through the process of consensus rather than through enforcement by a superior power.

Perspectives

Because of Japan's amazing economic achievements, both the popular press and academic journals have tended to invest Japanese management with an aura of mysticism. The impression has been given that Japanese management practices, such as quality control (QC) circles and the Kanban system or Ouchi's hybrid theory Z approach, can somehow offer magical remedies for the productivity problems of the United States. Many learned scholars as well as business executives have been influenced by this trend. But an accurate and balanced knowledge of Japanese management requires us to examine some factors which could dampen the current enthusiasm considerably.

First of all, the popular concern over U.S. productivity appears to be somewhat exaggerated. While it is true that the U.S. manufacturing sector has suffered some devastating losses in recent years, it is also a fact that the level of productivity per worker in the United States, although declining, is still more than 30 percent higher than the level of productivity per worker in Japan. It is also true that this margin still exists in spite of the cost to the United States of integrating large numbers of underqualified refugees into the work force—a humanitarian act motivated by national idealism rather than by a desire for profit.

Secondly, we need to consider that Japan's overall economic success cannot be attributed to any one single factor, such as the permanent employment system, but must be considered the result of a combination of all the elements of the Japanese management system and its environment which have been discussed here. These elements have all contributed in varying degrees to Japan's prosperity and must be seen as mutually interactive and reinforcing. Applying certain selected Japanese management practices to the management of firms in the United States should not be expected to alleviate U.S. industrial woes significantly.

An interesting question to ask is whether the Japanese themselves believe their management system could be applied profitably in the United States. A recent survey conducted by the Japan External Trade Organization (JETRO) suggests an answer. A study of 238 Japanese plants engaged in manufacturing operations in the United States in 1981 revealed that the overwhelming majority are not using such tried-and-true Japanese management techniques as consensus decision making, and only a few more than 20 have established QC circles. Clearly the Japanese do not consider their own system a magic formula which brings success in all situations.

Developing Problems in Japan. So far, the impression has been given that Japan's success in achieving rapid economic growth has been a totally positive phenomenon. A number of problems are currently developing, however, which cast a shadow over the rosy picture that has been so widely accepted.

Japan's rapid industrial growth has been realized at very high cost in terms of social welfare, public facilities, and air quality, to name a few. As the Japanese have become more and more aware of this, they have begun to demand improvements in their quality of life. New values, goals, and behaviors have begun to emerge, and some national attention has been diverted from the pursuit of growth to these overlooked areas.

In any case, the rapid growth rate Japan has so long enjoyed has recently begun to slow down. Since 1980, Japan's growth rate has declined to between 4 and 6 percent of the GNP. As a result, large Japanese firms, accustomed in the past to a high growth rate, are finding high levels of debt increasingly burdensome and have begun to seek other sources of equity and capital. This trend could weaken somewhat the government's influence on industry. If and when a venture capital market becomes firmly established in Japan, we can expect to see Japanese managers subjected to the same stockholder pressures and concern for current profits that beset their U.S. counterparts.

The reduced rate of economic growth has also resulted in rising labor costs. Large firms using the permanent employment system are hiring fewer young workers and so are having to pay out higher wages to a work force whose seniority level is growing. This trend could begin to threaten the competitiveness of Japan's prices in the global market. The lowered tariff barriers the Japanese government has been pressured into granting pose a further threat to Japan's global market position.

443

Problems of the Future. Japan has excelled primarily in the mass production of such items as small computers, home appliances, automobiles, semiconductors, and integrated circuitry. The Japanese cultural emphasis on groupism and the pursuit of group goals have made Japan particularly well suited to this type of industrial activity. Collectivism and behavioral control have been highly developed within Japan's rigidly hierarchical management system, and its highly disciplined work groups have been eminently successful in the exacting and detailed task of adapting foreign technologies to the demands of mass production, as well as innovating and improving upon their products.

There are other areas, however, in which the United States continues to outperform Japan on a substantial level, and some of these areas represent the coming generation of strategic industries. The rapid growth of knowledge-intensive industries, in which the United States is doing well, may pose a significant threat to the Japanese for several reasons. Their emphasis on collectivism is the antithesis of the atmosphere of individual creativity on which the high-tech industry thrives.

Rapid growth in the area of high technology also demands a deep and solid foundation in the basic sciences, which Japan lacks. Financing the growth of high-tech industries in Japan is a further problem: the trend toward high-tech, knowledge-intensive areas requires the frequent creation of new ventures by entrepreneurs, but the Japanese venture capital market is still in the embryonic stage, and bank financing has traditionally been available only to large, established firms with collateral.

Lastly, Japanese business leaders, who have been accustomed in the past to guiding their firms in the single-minded pursuit of growth, are faced today with the new challenge of responding to the many unpredictable factors emerging in the global market. Much imagination and creativity are required to make successful business decisions in this rapidly changing environment, and Japan's business leaders may have trouble adjusting to the situation. All these factors suggest that Japan's future prospects in this and other important growth areas are not as certain as its past success.

See also International operations and management in multinational companies; International trade.

REFERENCES

Johnson, Chalmers: *MITI and the Japanese Miracle,* Stanford University Press, Stanford, Calif., 1982.

Oh, Tai K.: "Japanese Management—A Critical Review," *Academy of Management Review,* January, vol. 1, no. 1., 1976, pp. 14–25.

Woronoff, Jon: *Japan—The Coming Economic Crisis,* Loftus Press, Tokyo, 1981.

TAI K. OH, *California State University, Fullerton*

Job Analysis

Job analysis involves (1) gathering information pertinent to the job and (2) defining the job by means of a *job description* which identifies the job, outlines work performed, and specifies requirements for those who seek to fill the job.

Job analysis is the fundamental first step in the job evaluation process. Thorough job analysis information is gathered about the "nature" and "level" of the work performed. The nature of the job refers to the principal tasks and duties as well as the discipline (e.g., production, engineering, or accounting) involved, and the level of the job refers to the necessary *skills* (education and experience), *effort* (both mental and physical), *responsibility*, and *work conditions* under which the job is performed. Job analysis is necessary to justify higher pay for higher-level jobs based on these job characteristics. Basic requirements for the job such as education, experience, inherent or acquired skills, working conditions which may be hazardous, and the supply-and-demand situation contribute to the differences in jobs which are systematically identified through job analysis.

In addition to wage-related use, job analysis can be used to improve work-force utilization by aiding in the assignment of time-consuming tasks to lower-paid jobs, by planning for worker-hours in order to ensure that all work assigned is essential, and by grouping tasks into efficient economic units. Job analysis is a managerial tool which can aid in the recruitment, selection, placement, and training of employees. It can help workers understand their jobs better, accept explanations for grievances, and agree to establish standards of job performance.[1] Thorough job analysis ensures accurate job descriptions, proper job classification within the organization, proper evaluation of jobs, and defensibility with respect to work-related laws and regulations.

The first step in job analysis is to obtain information about the job through interviews, observations, questionnaires, supervisory conferences, checklists, manuals, time-study reports, and descriptions of systems and organization charts. Job analysis may be performed by managers and employees trained by a professional job analyst, by outside consultants, or by committees of supervisors, workers, or both. The information gathered in job analysis is recorded in job descriptions.

Job Description. The job description contains the following information:

Identification. Job titles; persons employed on the job; location in the organization chart; location defined by plant, department, machine, etc.; and the number of personnel in the job category help identify the importance of the job to the organization.[2]

Work Performed. A concise description of what, how, and why a worker does a job defines the scope and purpose of the job. Detailed descriptions, including work assigned; specific tasks; area of responsibility; inherent authority; working relationships; specific methods, equipment, and techniques; scope and impact; working conditions; and specific examples are written on a chronological or functional basis.[3]

Job Specifications. Mental skills such as basic education, mental applications, job knowledge, and responsibility as well as physical requirements such as physical skills and working conditions constitute the basic factors of job specifications. Judgments regarding the presence of these attributes and their degree of importance are highly subjective because requirements are often inferred from duties.[4] Since existing laws and regulations require careful substantiation of these requirements as necessary for job performance, care must be taken when identifying jobs and hiring personnel on the basis of these requirements.

Procedure. The principal steps in job analysis are:

1. Use current titles to list all positions in the organization.

2. Gather sufficient information about each position to permit identification of discrete jobs.

3. Prepare job descriptions and verify their accuracy through review and "sign-off" by selected incumbents and their supervisors.

4. Retitle and classify all positions.

See also Affirmative action; Compensation, wage and salary policy and administration; Development and training, employee; Employment process; Job evaluation; Work design, job enlargement, and job enrichment.

NOTES

[1] Robert E. Sibson, *Wages and Salaries: A Handbook for Line Managers*, rev. ed., American Management Association, New York, 1967, p. 37.

[2] Charles W. Brennan, *Wage Administration*, rev. ed., Richard D. Irwin, Homewood, Ill., 1963, p. 101.

[3] David W. Belcher, *Compensation Administration*, Prentice-Hall, Englewood Cliffs, N.J., 1974, p. 125.

[4] Allan N. Nash and Stephen J. Carroll, Jr., *The Management of Compensation*, Brooks/Cole, Monterey, Calif., 1975, p. 115.

FREDERICK A. TEAGUE, *Frederick Teague & Company, Inc.*

Job Evaluation

Job evaluation is the process by which management determines the relative worth of jobs throughout the organization. Job evaluation emphasizes an organized and rational approach to determining job value. The underlying principle that an employee should be paid in relation to the job-related contribution assumes that pay should be assigned in accordance with the difficulty and importance of the job. Equal pay for equal work and more pay for more important work support this basic principle. Application of this principle helps to establish equitable internal pay relationships.[1] Companies that adopt job evaluation have decided that establishing a pay structure is important enough to justify the expense of undertaking a thorough and systematic study of job relationships. Participation in the program by representatives of all levels of the work force increases the possibility of good acceptance of salary differentials which, in turn, reduces a potentially serious source of employee dissatisfaction.[2]

Prevalence of Job Evaluation. Job evaluation was first used by the U.S. Civil Service Commission in 1871. It was not until World War II, however, that its use became widespread when the National War Labor Board permitted wage increases only to correct unfair pay relationships and some method of valuing jobs became necessary. Today, the use of one or more of several job evaluation techniques is practically universal throughout the public and private sectors of our economy.

Job-Related Contributions. Job evaluation examines the job-related contributions which employers and employees accept as the basis for employment exchange. There is general agreement that certain jobs have higher value and that individuals performing these jobs should receive more pay than those who perform lower-valued jobs. Some jobs require more education, special skills (inherent or acquired), or specific experience—and thus call for higher pay to compensate individuals for spending time, energy, and money to acquire these qualifications.[3] Other jobs involve adverse working conditions, which also support higher pay. Although economics (supply and demand) and social factors (collective bargaining) enter into the determination of job worth, the compensable factors usually measured in job evaluation emphasize the administrative concept (importance and difficulty) of job worth.[4] Job evaluation plans are based on implicit or explicit acceptance of compensable factors related to job contributions.

Job evaluation involves the measurement of job duties against some kind of yardstick in order to access relative job worth. The job, not the incumbent's performance, ability, background, potential, etc., is the quantity being measured.[5] Job evaluation attempts to compare the demands of normal performance of a worker in a particular job.

Job Evaluation Process. Complete job evaluation consists of the development, application, and ongoing administration of a five-step process: (1) job analysis (described in another entry); (2) determination of compensable factors; (3) selection of an appropriate job evaluation plan; (4) pricing of jobs internally and externally; and (5) implementation of the job evaluation plan and ongoing tuning and maintenance. This entry explains the second and third steps in the evaluation process and does not include pricing, implementation, and maintenance.

Determining the Compensable Factors

The compensable factors (or elements) to be used to compare jobs in the hierarchy should be the mutually accepted, job-related contributions rewarded by the organization.[6] Workers presumably accept the fact that certain jobs require differing amounts of contributions and that the wage-structure hierarchy is based on these factors. Generally, the basic factors of skill requirements, effort, responsibility, and working conditions can explain the variance in the worth of jobs in the pay structure. Employees' acceptance of pay structure decisions is improved if more factors that they feel better represent their jobs are included.

Factors should apply to all jobs in the organization or to large groups or classes of jobs. Factors chosen should embody the following characteristics:

1. Factors must not overlap in meaning.
2. Employer, employee, and union must understand and accept the importance of the factors.

TABLE J-1 Job Evaluation Methods

	Ranking	Classification	Point system	Factor comparison
Characteristics				
Nonquantitative	X	X		
Quantitative			X	X
Measure whole job	X	X		
Measure job factors			X	X
Rank	X			X
Measure against yardstick		X	X	
Advantages				
Inexpensive and installation time short	X	X		
Simple and easily understood	X	X		
Not necessary to determine absolute value of job	X	X		
Relative job differences determined without monetary considerations	X	X	X	
Consistent rating scales eliminate rater bias			X	
Employee acceptance aided by explanation of records of factors on point values			X	
Same job elements considered on all jobs			X	X
Factors limited to first or less avoids overlap				X
Employee acceptance aided by easily understood job comparison scales				X
Key job analysis ensures wage structure reflects the market				X
Monetary units in comparison system permit rapid determination of wage scales				X
Plan is tailormade for organization				X
Disadvantages				
Difficult to define overall job worth	X	X		
Difficult to justify results to employees because no record of judgments	X	X		
Raters may be inconsistent because factors not employed	X	X		
Difficult to write grade comparison		X		
Difficult to develop points and weights which are easy to understand			X	X
Expensive, installation time long, maintenance costly			X	X
Monetary units introduce bias in evaluation of key jobs				X
Few universal factors for all jobs is counter to concept of selecting factors which truly reflect job-related contributions				X

3. Factors selected must in some degree be found in all jobs and in varying amounts.[7]

4. Factors must be observable and measurable.

Factors frequently found in job evaluation systems for lower-ranking positions are education, supervision received, physical demand, working conditions, experience and training, complexity of duties, contact with others, and responsibility for equipment and tools.[8] For higher-level positions, additional factors include decision-making latitude, accountability for results, functional scope, and impact of discretionary actions.

Selection of Method

The third step in the job evaluation process is the selection of a system which will make it possible to list jobs according to the level of compensable factors present. There are four basic methods: ranking, classification, point system, and factor comparison. In ranking and factor comparison, jobs are compared with each other. In classification and the point system, jobs are measured against a scale. In the point system and factor-comparison method, elements or factors of the jobs are measured by quantitative point values. More complex plans are usually a hybrid of these plans. Ranking and classification plans are used less often than point system and factor comparison. A comparison of characteristics, advantages, and disadvantages of the four basic methods is found in Table J-1. Each method is explained below.

Ranking. This plan places jobs in order of organizational importance on the basis of the whole job from highest to lowest. Ranking has been made more sophisticated by employing computers to facilitate raters' comparisons. Since the system is so subjective, it is difficult to justify to employees and difficult to apply to large concerns.[9] It is not considered a very acceptable approach and is used by few companies.

Procedure. Steps in the ranking method include:

1. Obtain job information through job description and job specification employing compensable factors.

2. Select raters who know all jobs in the unit or specific departments.

3. Select compensable factors and outline a procedure for consistent application of factors.

4. Rank jobs by sorting or paired comparison. Sorting involves raters ranking jobs by ordering cards or lists on which job descriptions have been written. Paired comparison involves comparisons of each job with every other job (see Table J-2), either by comparing all possible combinations of two jobs or by checking the higher of two jobs indicated by the cells of a matrix. The rank is

TABLE J-2 Ranking Method

Step 4: Paired comparisons
Compare each job with every other job
Keypunch—*Stenographer*   *Stenographer*—Typist   *Typist*—Keypunch
Summary of comparisons

Job title	Times judged more difficult	Rank
Keypunch	0	3
Stenographer	2	1
Typist	1	2

determined by the number of times the job is favorably compared.[10]

5. Average observations of all raters to obtain a composite ranking.

Classification. In this method of job evaluation, classes or grades are defined verbally in terms of the types of jobs which fit into each class.[11] Jobs are classified by comparing each job with the descriptions.

The classification method has been used by the Civil Service Commission in the Classification Act of 1949, by the Westinghouse Electric Company, and by the Bell Telephone System.[12] The difficulty of explaining pay differentials based on the classification system has led to a decline in use.

Procedure. Steps in the classification method include:

1. Observe job analysis with job descriptions and job specifications.

2. Classify jobs into well-defined classes such as shop, sales, clerical, supervisory, and management.

3. Select compensable factors.

4. Write grade descriptions that differentiate each class in terms of levels of compensable factors.[13]

5. Classify jobs by comparing job information with grade descriptions. (See Table J-3)

Point System. The point system measures each job on a separate weighted scale for each factor. Point values assigned to each factor are summed for total job value. The popularity of the point system may be due partly to the fact that many ready-made plans of employer associations and consultants are available and can be adapted to a company's needs. The American Association of Industrial Management and the National Metal Trades Association have job rating plans for shop, service, office, technical, and managerial jobs. The plan of the National Electrical Manufacturers Association is widely used for factory jobs.[14]

447

TABLE J-3 Classification Method

Step 5: Example of grade description

Grade 2: Requires skill in handling relatively simple and precisely defined tasks. Requires general knowledge equivalent to a high school education plus skills in areas such as typing, blueprint reading, or operation of more complicated office or shop equipment. Position involves little or no administrative line responsibilities. Responsibilities require limited or no external contacts. Inadequate performance would have limited effect on cost of operations. Actions are reviewed regularly.

Procedure. Steps in the point-system method include the following:

1. Determine whether compensable factors should be applied to all jobs or job clusters and select the jobs to be evaluated.
2. Analyze the job description for each job.
3. Select the proper compensable factors which reflect job-related contributions and are accepted by managers and workers.[15]
4. Establish factor degrees with appropriate divisions so that each degree is equidistant from the two adjacent degrees. Two-dimensional degrees are sometimes employed to obtain maximum flexibility.[16] (See Table J-4.)
5. Determine the relative value of factors by establishing factor weights. This may be done by statistical means, such as linear regressions, or by using committee judgment. Key jobs should be evaluated to determine the number of degrees necessary.[17]
6. Assign point values to degrees by arithmetic or geometric progression. These values may be checked by noting the effect produced on key jobs.[18]

7. Write a job evaluation manual to aid raters in evaluating jobs.
8. Rate all jobs by means of the manual, job descriptions, and job specifications.

Factor Comparison. The factor-comparison method, an extension of the ranking method, employs distinctive factors, such as mental requirements, physical requirements, skill requirements, responsibility, and working conditions, which have numerical values assigned to them. In the factor-comparison method, jobs are compared with one another one factor at a time to determine which jobs contain more of certain compensable factors.[19] Evaluators rank all jobs on the job-comparison scale and sum points to determine the value of the job. Separate job-comparison scales should be developed for each job cluster.

Procedure. Steps in the factor-comparison method include:

1. Analyze the job and obtain job descriptions covering duties and job specifications based on factor definitions (30 to 40 percent of the jobs).
2. Select key jobs that are easily defined and compared and for which wage or salary data are clearly established.
3. Determine compensable factors and establish quantitative scales for factors, using either wage rates or point scores.
4. Rank key jobs by factors (see Table J-5).
5. Distribute wage rates by factors for all key jobs (see Table J-5).
6. Cross-check job-ranking judgment by comparing a company's difficulty rank with money rank to determine key jobs with consistent rankings (see Table J-5).
7. Construct the job-comparison scale by placing

TABLE J-4 Point-System Method

	Step 4: Two-dimensional degrees (skills and knowledge)				
Complexity of problem	General knowledge plus basic business skills	Knowledge plus competence in specialized fields	Scientific, professional, or management competence	Professional expertise	Extensive general management experience
Complex, loosely defined problem	23	24	27	29	31
Diverse and complex problem with solution by diverse principle	17	19	21	23	25
Difficult problem with solutions by diverse practices	12	14	16	14	20
Tasks with well-defined processes for solution	8	10	12	14	16
Simple, well-defined	5	7	9	11	13

TABLE J-5 Factor-Comparison Method

	Step 4: Jobs ranked by factors		
Job title	Knowledge and skills	Administration responsibility	External relations
Keypunch	3	2	3
Stenographer	1	1	1
Typist	2	3	2

	Step 5: Wage-rate distribution			
Job title	Knowledge and skills	Administration responsibility	External relations	Wage rate
Keypunch	2.25	.30	.20	2.75
Stenographer	3.10	.40	.65	4.15
Typist	2.70	.20	.40	3.30

	Step 6: Comparison of difficulty ranking (D) and money ranking (M)					
	Knowledge and skills		Administration responsibility		External relations	
Job title	D	M	D	M	D	M
Keypunch	3	2.25	2	.30	3	.20
Stenographer	1	3.10	1	.40	2	.65
Typist	2	2.70	3	.20	1	.40

key jobs opposite money positions or point values according to the factors (see Table J-6).

8. Evaluate the remaining jobs by placing them into the job-comparison scale one factor at a time.

9. Establish the wage structure by summing monetary or point values for all factors.

TABLE J-6 Factor-Comparison Method

Cents	Step 7: Job-comparison scale		
	Knowledge and skills	Administration responsibility	External relations
0.10			
0.20		Typist	Keypunch
0.30		Keypunch	
0.40		Stenographer	Typist
0.50			
0.60			Stenographer
0.70			
2.10			
2.20	Keypunch		
2.30			
2.40			
2.50			
2.60			
2.70	Typist		
2.80			
2.90			
3.00			
3.10	Stenographer		
3.20			

Other Techniques. Other methods for solving the wage-structure problem involve direct market pricing. The guidelines method bases relative job value on marketplace values. Often 50 percent of the jobs are selected as key jobs, and the appropriate market rates are determined. Market rates of key jobs are matched against midpoints and are placed into grades. The remaining jobs are placed by relating them to key jobs.[20]

See also Affirmative action; Compensation, wage and salary policy and administration; Job analysis; Personnel administration; Work design, job enlargement, and job enrichment.

NOTES

[1] David W. Belcher, *Compensation Administration*, adapted by permission of Prentice-Hall, Englewood Cliffs, N.J., © 1974, p. 87.

[2] Allan N. Nash and Stephen J. Carroll, Jr., *The Management of Compensation*, copyright © 1975 by Wadsworth Publishing Company. Adapted by permission of the publisher, Brooks/Cole Publishing Company, Monterey, Calif., p. 107.

[3] Charles W. Brennan, *Wage Administration*, rev. ed., Richard D. Irwin, Homewood, Ill., 1963, p. 64.

[4] Robert E. Sibson, *Wages and Salaries: A Handbook for Line Managers*, rev. ed., American Management Association, New York, 1967, p. 32.

[5] Ibid., p. 31.

[6] Belcher, op. cit., pp. 134 and 136.

[7] Ibid., p. 136.

[8] Nash, op. cit., p. 118.

[9] Ibid., p. 127.

[10]Belcher, op. cit., pp. 147 and 148.
[11]Ibid., p. 149.
[12]Brennan, op. cit., p. 118.
[13]Belcher, op. cit., p. 151.
[14]Ibid., p. 183.
[15]Ibid., pp. 175 and 176.
[16]Ibid., pp. 177 and 179.
[17]Ibid., pp. 179, 180, and 181.
[18]Ibid., p., 181.
[19]Ibid., p. 155.
[20]Ibid., p. 194.

REFERENCES

Bartley, Douglas L.: *Job Evaluation: Wages and Salary Administration*, Addison-Wesley, Reading, Mass., 1981.

Livy, Bryan: *Job Evaluation: A Critical Review*, Halstead Press, a division of John Wiley, New York, 1975.

Paterson, T. T., Jr.: *Job Evaluation*, vol. 1: *A New Method*, Cahners, Boston, Mass., 1972.

FREDERICK A. TEAGUE, Frederick Teague & Company, Inc.

Labor Legislation

Legislation affecting the employment relationship in the United States exists in several specific areas. Employment opportunity, wages, benefits, safety, health, and labor relations are regulated to some extent. A comprehensive interpretation of these regulations requires an understanding of statutes, court decisions, and regulatory agency policies.

Labor-Management Relations

The federal statute which provides the basic legal framework for labor-management relations in the United States is the Labor-Management Relations Act (LMRA). This legislation incorporates the National Labor Relations Act of 1935 (the Wagner Act) and the Labor-Management Relations Act of 1947 (the Taft-Hartley Act). The Labor-Management Reporting and Disclosure Act of 1959 (the Landrum-Griffin Act) makes further changes to the original legislation. The most recent amendment to the act (1974) brought all health care institutions, profit and non-profit, under LMRA coverage. The resulting statutory regulation of labor-management relations is complex. Court decisions and NLRB rulings interpret the language of the statutes. These laws establish the basic rights and obligations of employers, unions, and employees in the choice of a collective bargaining representative and the exercise of collective bargaining. The National Labor Relations Board (NLRB) is the administrative body which oversees the enforcement of the LMRA.

Section 7 establishes the right of an employee to engage in (or refrain from) union organization, collective bargaining, or concerted activities (e.g., strikes) free from undue influence or coercion by both union and management. Section 8, to further the objectives of Section 7, establishes a list of management and union actions which are illegal. These actions are called unfair labor practices.

Section 8(a) includes the following as unfair employer practices:

- Interference with, restraints, or coercion of employees in the exercise of their Section 7 rights.

- Domination or interference in the formation or administration of a labor union. Financial and other types of support are also prohibited.

- Encouragement or discouragement of union membership by discriminating in hiring, tenure or employment, or terms and conditions of employment. A proviso is included allowing for union shop agreements.

- Discharge of or discrimination against employees who testify before or file charges with the NLRB.
- Refusal to bargain collectively with the representatives of employees.

Section 8(b) provides a list of union unfair labor practices. These mirror Section 8(a). Section 8 also prohibits excessive dues or fees where a union shop exists, secondary boycotts, jurisdictional strikes, and organizational picketing under specific conditions (e.g., another certified union already has representation rights).

The NLRB and the courts have, through case decisions, given additional substance to Sections 7 and 8. The impact of the LMRA and NLRB is substantial for all covered employers.

LMRA Coverage. The NLRB has the constitutional authority to assert jurisdiction over any labor case affecting interstate commerce. The NLRB normally refuses to assert jurisdiction in cases which have only a minimal effect on interstate commerce. Dollar standards based on the volume of business have been established. The NLRB is unlikely to assert jurisdiction over firms which do not meet these dollar standards.

Union Organizing. The LMRA provides for freedom of employee choice in the selection of a collective bargaining representative. Secret ballot elections may be conducted by the NLRB with the simple majority choice of those voting being declared the winner. No election may be held if there has been a valid election within the previous 12 months or if there is a legally negotiated contract with an organization representing the employees in question (contract bar rule, 3-year limit),. Votor eligibility is determined by the NLRB. The employees to be covered by a proposed unit may be determined by the NLRB or by mutual agreement of the employer and the union(s) seeking to represent the employees. A union must demonstrate support for an election in the form of recognition cards signed by 30 percent of the employees in the proposed unit before the NLRB will hold such an election. An employer may voluntarily grant a union recognition based on recognition cards signed by a majority of employees in the proposed unit.

Election Campaigning. If a recognition election is to be held, both employer and union election campaign activities are likely to be scrutinized carefully by the opposition. Any interference with the free choice of employees, such as threats, promises, implied reward or punishment, or predictions of consequences which do not have a factual basis, are likely to lead to unfair labor practices charges of interference in the free-choice process. Severe interference with the process by an employer may result in the NLRB issuing an order to the employer to recognize and bargain with the affected union.

Decertification Petitions. Employees may also file decertification petitions indicating they no longer wish to be represented by a union. An employer with good faith doubts that the union represents a majority of the employees in the bargaining unit (for example, doubt based upon a decertification petition) may withdraw recognition.

Collective Bargaining. The LMRA requires both labor and management to bargain collectively in good faith. There are mandatory items (wages, hours, and working conditions), permissive items (items not related directly to wages, hours, or working conditions), and illegal items (for example, a clause calling for sexual discrimination) of negotiation specified. If either union or management raises a mandatory issue, the issue must be discussed. Bargaining to impasse and engaging in strikes or lockouts over mandatory items is permitted. Permissive items may be discussed if both parties are willing to negotiate over such items; bargaining to impasse over such items is not permitted.

Negotiation Procedure. Characterization of a typical negotiation procedure is not possible. The enormous array of items negotiated, the variety of tactics used, and the differing personalities and histories involved in a collective bargaining relationship cause each negotiation to be unique. For many years union leadership tended to emphasize the bread and butter issues in negotiation. Wages, hours, and working conditions are still likely to be the heart of any negotiation. Unions are increasingly addressing quality of work life issues and, in some industries, issues of foreign competition and managerial policies. No matter what the negotiation issue, the LMRA does not require either union or management to modify its collective bargaining position. Modification of positions normally occurs because of pressures brought to bear by the opposition in the collective bargaining process.

Strikes and Lockouts. Collective bargaining normally results in an agreement without resorting to economic force. While primary strikes (strikes directly aimed at the employer) are permitted, secondary strikes and boycotts are regulated. Jurisdiction disputes (strikes over the assignment of work to a particular group of workers) are prohibited. Organizational strikes are prohibited in some circumstances and regulated as to duration in other circumstances. While picketing is protected as free speech, picketing activity has been closely scrutinized by the NLRB and courts. And although the right of employers to engage in lockouts is protected by the LMRA, lockouts are infrequent.

Economic strikers (strikers seeking resolution of wage, hour, or working condition issues in the collective bargaining process) may be permanently replaced. Strikers must be placed on a recall list and offered employment as vacancies occur. If the former striker accepts employment, the individual is not considered a new employee and retains former seniority status. Unfair labor practices strikers (individuals striking due to employer unfair labor practices) may not be permanently replaced. Replacements are temporary only. An employer may continue to employ replacements at the conclusion of the strike, but replacements may not be retained in place of strikers. Unfair labor practices strikers or economic strikers who engage in serious misconduct during the strike may be discharged. Physically blocking the entrance to the workplace is normally not considered serious misconduct.

Contract Administration. The LMRA says little about contract administration. Section 301 provides for suits for the enforcement of contracts. Most collective bargaining agreements include arbitration clauses providing for third-party resolution of disagreements over contract administration. Supreme Court decisions have limited the scope of judicial review of arbitration awards and have given arbitrators broad powers in fashioning remedies for contractual violations. The details of grievance and arbitration clauses vary considerably from agreement to agreement. Federal and state court action may be taken to compel either party to submit issues to arbitration according to their contractual agreement.

Grievance issues may involve both an alleged contractual violation and an unfair labor practice issue. The NLRB has established a set of guidelines for deferral to arbitration. The unfair labor practice issue must be heard by the arbitrator and the decision must not be contrary to the LMRA.

Union Security. A union gaining recognition becomes the exclusive bargaining agent for the covered employees. The employer must bargain with the union. Individual employment contracts will not serve to undercut the bargaining status of a recognized union. Attempts to deal directly with the employee group and circumvent the union have been found to be unfair labor practices. All employees covered by the union's recognition are represented by the union regardless of their membership status in the union.

Membership as Condition of Employment. The LMRA permits agreements requiring union membership as a condition of employment. Under such an agreement, employees must join the union by the thirtieth day following the effective date of the contract or the beginning of their employment. In the construction industry the waiting period is 7 days. A union security contract clause such as this is commonly called the union shop. Maintenance-of-membership clauses (union members who do not resign within a specified time period must maintain their union membership as a condition of employment) and the agency shop clauses (nonmembers represented by the union must pay a fee to the union for their representational activities as a condition of continued employment) are two other forms of union security provisions. Section 14(b) of the LMRA gives

individual states the ability to pass laws prohibiting all or some forms of union security agreements. Most of the 20 states which have passed such "right-to-work" legislation are located in the South and Midwest.

Nonunion Employees. The LMRA gives protection to nonunion employees in organizational activities and in concerted activity which attempts to affect wages, hours, or working conditions. Supervisors are excluded from the coverage of the LMRA. Several authorities feel that the desire to remain a nonunion organization accounts for the excellent work environment in many nonunion organizations. Sound personnel practices can eliminate many causes of employee dissatisfaction, thereby reducing the appeal of unionization. While the percentage of the work force represented by unions has been declining, union impact in several industries remains substantial. The union movement has indicated intentions to increase organizational efforts in sectors of the economy which are growing. Labor has also announced plans to engage in a major organizational effort in the sunbelt states.

LMRA Reform. Amendment of the LMRA appears unlikely in the immediate future. The AFL-CIO, however, continues to lobby for changes in the act. Among the changes advocated by organized labor are a prohibition on federal contracts to violators of the act, expansion of the remedial powers of the NLRB, and legalization of common situs picketing (picketing at locations where employees of different employers work side by side at a common work site). There does not appear to be any movement by organized labor toward reducing traditional managerial duties, through either legislation similar to that existing in Western Europe or collective bargaining.

Employment Opportunity and Protection

The decades from 1960 to 1980 generated a great deal of significant legislation affecting employment opportunity, worker protection, and wages and benefit programs.

Equal Employment Opportunity. Numerous federal laws and orders deal with equal employment opportunity. The major pieces of legislation are:

- Civil Rights Act of 1964, Title VII
- Age Discrimination in Employment Act
- Equal Pay Amendment to the Fair Labor Standards Act
- Vocational Rehabilitation Act of 1973, 1974

These laws call for nondiscrimination in virtually all aspects of employment. The protected groupings are race, sex, religion, national origin, color, ages 40 to 70, and handicapped. The impact of one or more of these laws reaches virtually every employer. Equal

453

employment opportunity is required and affirmative action or reasonable accommodation may be required. Voluntary affirmative-action plans which give preferential treatment to a protected grouping have been upheld by the Supreme Court in *Weber v. Steelworkers.* Affirmative-action plans must meet specific guidelines enunciated by the Court. Executive Order 11246 requires covered federal contractors to develop affirmative-action plans. State or local nondiscrimination laws may also exist and may expand coverage to other groups (homosexuals, for example).

Worker Protection Laws. The Occupational Safety and Health Act of 1970 (OSHA) allows the administrative body to establish standards which can affect any aspect of the workplace. OSHA encourages states to develop and administer state occupational and safety laws. Employers are required to meet standards established by OSHA, to submit to OSHA inspections, to establish safety record-keeping procedures, and to report accident and illness statistics. An OSHA compliance officer may not inspect a workplace without a search warrant if the owner or manager requests a warrant.

Certain industries have been targeted by OSHA for more frequent inspection because of their high accident rates. These targeted industries are roof and sheet-metal work, longshoring, lumber and wood products, meat packing, foundries and castings, metal stamping, and miscellaneous transportation (mobile homes). Health hazard industries which have been targeted are those involving asbestos, cotton dust, carbon monoxide, lead, and silica.

The Unemployment Insurance Act and state workers' compensation acts are designed to protect workers from loss of income due to unemployment through no fault of their own or through work-sustained injury. Unemployment payments are funded by a payroll tax on the employer of at least 3.4 percent on the first $6000 earned by each employee. This can be a major labor cost. Workers' compensation laws are state laws. The specific content of each state law can vary considerably.

Compensation and Benefits. There are numerous pieces of legislation affecting the compensation and benefit levels of employees. The Fair Labor Standards Act (1938) is perhaps the most far-reaching. Minimum wage standards, overtime pay rates, child labor regulation, and reporting requirements are among the topics covered by FLSA. The Equal Pay Act (1963) prohibits discriminatory pay practices. Workers in identical jobs may be paid differing wages if wages are based on seniority or productivity. The Walsh-Healy and Davis-Bacon Acts require federal contractors to pay the prevailing wage level.

The most recent major legislation in the compensation and benefit area is the Employment Retirement Income Security Act (ERISA) (1974). This legislation ensures that employees covered by a private pension plan will receive promised benefits. ERISA does not require an employer to have a private pension plan. Employers with private pension plans must meet ERISA standards. Included in these standards are employee eligibility requirements, vesting requirements (three vesting alternatives exist), portability practices, funding provisions, and regulations concerning fiduciaries. Disclosure requirements are also established. While many employers discontinued private pension plans after ERISA passage, the act has focused attention on employee pension benefits and employer liability for those benefits.

Public Sector Labor Relations

Public employees are not covered by the LMRA. Controlling legislation for federal employees is the Civil Service Reform Act. State government employees and employees of subdivisions of state government are covered by state law. Many states have passed laws giving public employees the right to join unions and bargain with their employer. Eight states have given public employees a limited right to strike. Due to the sensitivity of the strike issue in the public sector, impasse provisions in public sector laws tend to be complex. Typical steps in impasse procedures are mediation, fact-finding, and in some states and for certain types of employees (usually uniformed services), binding interest arbitration over negotiation items at impasse.

Public sector labor relations have followed the private sector model in a somewhat modified form. There is a great deal of experimentation occurring. Some states have passed comprehensive laws with unique features. Some states continue to prohibit public sector bargaining and union activity. While bills to establish a federal statute regulating all public sector labor relations have been introduced, the probability of passage in the immediate future is low.

See also Affirmative action; Compensation, employee benefit plans; Compensation, wage and salary policy and administration; Employment process; Equal employment opportunity, minorities and women; Interviewing, employee; Labor-management relations; Labor (trade) unions; Personnel administration; Safety and health management, employees; Testing, psychological; Women in business and management.

REFERENCES

Feldacker, Bruce: *Labor Guide to Labor Law*, Reston Publishing, Reston, Va. 1980.

Schlei, B., and P. Grossman: *Employment Discrimination Law*, 2d ed., BNA (Bureau of National Affairs), Washington, D.C., 1983.

Taylor, B., and F. Whitney: *Labor Relations Law*, 3d ed., Prentice-Hall, Englewood Cliffs, N.J., 1979.

PETER A. VEGLAHN, *James Madison University*

Labor-Management Relations

The basic relationship between a company and a labor union consists of many complex variables built on past practice and future needs. It brings together individuals, groups, and institutions with different backgrounds, points of view, interests, and strengths. The balance of power is almost never equal; one party is usually dominant. These relative strengths will vary from time to time and situation to situation. Therefore, it is critically important that management establish, implement, and maintain a rational and objective strategy for dealing with the union; one that considers needs and interests of the company, union, and employees. Unions can only make demands or try to take control; it is the company that must agree to the demands or allow them to happen. Hence, a need exists for a regular, careful, and critical review of the overall labor relations climate in an organization. Because it has such a significant impact on the business, professional management input is required.

Labor relations decisions should be based on research and planning, just as is done with a new product concept before designing, manufacturing, and marketing it. Labor unions are staffed with members who have a high level of expertise and technical competence. Labor unions spend the necessary funds to research today's problems as well as to plan for the future. Management must do the same. These questions should be asked, "Are labor relations a mainstream operating activity in your company? Is the activity properly staffed? Is it held accountable for significant results? Does it support the business goals and objectives?"

Fundamental Factors Affecting Union-Management Relations

The relations between the parties must be carefully planned and thought through.

Basic Principles. A company's philosophy is the key factor that affects the relations between the company and union management. Several principles should guide the formulation of this philosophy.

Conflict of Objectives. The fundamental relationship between the union and the company is one of push and pull, most often in opposite directions, even though the company's continued success is essential for both parties. The union has as its primary objective the desire to obtain more in both economic (wages and benefits) and noneconomic (contract provisions and operating practices) areas. It expects to make these gains via the bargaining process, the grievance and arbitration procedure, and management default. The company, on the other hand, resists all efforts of the union to restrict management's freedom to make decisions necessary to run the business.

A Variety of Unions and Approaches. The numbers and types of unions that are present in industry are many. There are simple single-plant unions, multiple unions in one plant, craft and trade unions, companywide bargaining, industrywide bargaining, coalition and coordinated bargaining, and multiple variations of the above. Management must know its own business and its objectives and needs and then, after critical and careful examination, must determine what relationship is best for each situation.

Mutually Satisfactory Relationships. Once a majority of employees in an appropriate unit vote to be represented by a union, the company must determine the type of relationship it wants. Since the relationship is usually of long duration, serious consideration should be given to the various factors affecting it. Over the long term, these relationships require give and take by both parties.

Credibility. The axiom of credibility is to say what we mean and mean what we say; it requires telling both the good and the bad news. Management credibility does not interfere with hard bargaining and the primary responsibility for attaining it rests with the company. Experienced negotiators on both sides of the table can distinguish between bona fide bargaining on the one hand and vacillating uncertainty on the other.

Predictability. Surprises and sudden changes are natural enemies of good labor relations. Union leaders should be informed in advance of changes in important employee relations policies or practices and should be able to predict with reasonable certainty how the company will react to specific situations.

A Problem-Solving Approach. Successful labor relations are not so much a matter of *who* is right as *what* is right. Management must consider the specific problem and alternative solutions. Frequently, the solution initially proposed either by the company or by the union is not the best one. It is important to search out mutually acceptable solutions which, in many cases, are found somewhere between the positions of the two parties.

Open and Candid Communications. Discussion between company and union representatives occurs in various degrees of formality. Usually the more formal the discussion, the less effective the result. Effective communications usually can be improved by occasional informal business-related contacts between the parties. Such contact can lead to the development of mutual understanding and trust—essential factors in a continuing good relationship.

Understanding of Union's Political Considerations. One must accept the fact that unions are political organizations and that most union officials want to be reelected. In order to secure cooperation from them in the consideration of the company's problems, management must be willing to consider the union's problems. At the same time, the union must be required to accept management's responsibility to manage the business.

A Unified Management Front. Unions understandably strive to whipsaw and divide management. Operating management must be sufficiently informed of top management's position on any particular issue. Individually and collectively, all members of management must be able to defend that position in good conscience.

Carefully Thought-Out Negotiation Objectives. The primary objective in union contract negotiations is to reach a fair and equitable settlement without a strike, within company-established cost limits, and with contract terms that do not present unduly restrictive practices or obstacles to good management practices. One authority observes,

> Once written into a contract, the life of a provision is all but everlasting. In those rare instances where a company has been able to negotiate a provision out of an agreement, it has had to pay a high trading price.[1]

Fair and Consistent Practices. Whether questions of contract interpretation, discipline, job evaluation, or enforcement of productivity standards are involved, it is essential that they be dealt with fairly and consistently. Neither management nor the union can tolerate a failure to observe this principle.

Fundamentals of Management Behavior. In addition to its philosophical tenets, a prudent management will also follow certain guidelines in its dealings with union matters and labor union representatives.

Relationship Based on Mutual Respect. Each must treat the other party with dignity and respect. This should be the case at all levels in both the company and the union. One need not tolerate personal attacks or abuses.

Basis for Change. Constant change is a basic ingredient of business. When implementing changes that affect union relationships, management must try to have equity and moral forces working for it, not against it. Another authority comments,

> Management in the performance of its function is primarily an instigator of change. Change is its way of life. The union, on the other hand, serves more as a restraint on management and a protector of security for its members; therefore it is frequently cast in the role of forestaller of change.[2]

This can be, and often is, the cause of conflict.

Introduction of Change. Changes should be introduced at a pace that the company can manage and that the union can accept, however reluctantly. If the pace is such that the company exceeds the union's ability to react in the most rational way in which it is capable, the union will swamp the rela-

tionship with irrational behavior. Priorities for change should be based on operating needs and maximum long-range return.

Fairness and the Grievance Procedure. The primary purpose of a grievance procedure is to settle disputes fairly. The technicalities of the procedure should not be allowed to prevent justice. Walter Baer, in his book *Grievance Handling,* writes, "Grievance machinery is the formal process that enables the parties to attempt to resolve their differences in a peaceful, orderly, and expeditious manner."[3] The grievance procedure should be recognized and administered as a simple judicial process, not a political process.

> Grievance machinery is really a system of communications extending from the bottommost layers of the plant to the top and back down again. To the extent that a management avails itself of this listening device, it is in a better position to anticipate problems and read the mood of the labor force.[4]

Judge on Actions, Not Words. It is a sound practice to judge the union not on what it says but on what it does, carefully observed and averaged over a period of time. Unions were designed for the offensive, because of their origin as reformers and agents of change. When they become more conservative, they rest more on the status quo.

Labor Relations Charter and Strategy

In labor relations, just as in all other phases of business management, a company must know where it has been, where it is, and most important, where it is going. The company-union relationship is normally of long duration. It is established at both the bargaining table, where contracts are settled, and on the shop floor, where daily problems are resolved by understanding and/or conflict. As A. Blum says,

> Unions are real; they affect the system and process of management. They influence day-to-day policy and programs. Managers face an obvious need to understand unions, the reasons why members join them, and the rationale of union policy and practice. Unions are an important fact in the daily lives of managers, whether or not they like it.[5]

In simple terms, a company must develop an overall union relations charter and strategy. The strategy must be designed to supplement and fit the overall business plans and goals, both short and long term.

Once established, this basic approach must be documented, implemented, and revised as necessary. According to Dale Yoder, a labor relations policy must rest on certain major "planks." Among these are the right and obligation to bargain, employer rights and responsibilities, and union rights and responsibilities.[6]

These must be taken into consideration in developing the strategy.

Operating Goals and Strategy. All activities on the part of the labor relations staff must be directed to providing operating management with the latitude it needs to run a competitive business. If close coordination of objectives is not achieved, line and staff may well be working at odds with each other or, at best, putting emphasis on the wrong issues.

The long- and short-range labor relations strategy must consider certain business factors:

1. Nature of the business and where it is going.
2. Impact of short- and long-range business plans on the contract and practices. This includes employee levels, skill requirements or changes, technological changes, and product mixes.
3. Nature of the competition.
4. Customers' needs and requirements in terms of their impact on practices and the contract and on the company's ability to meet schedules and deliveries.
5. Seasonality of business and customer requirements.

Roles of Line and Staff. Primary responsibility for labor relations should rest with line-operating management. It sets the tone and, in fact, must run the facility. A high level of professional expertise must be provided by the employee relations staff, however, which is supportive of the line management's operating needs. Staff professionals must be knowledgeable in the contract and its administration, practices, negotiations, and legal considerations. They must be managers, tacticians, and strategists; not just administrators.

One of the union's favorite tactics is to whipsaw managers in one department against managers in another department; to ask the same question enough times and of enough different people to get the answer they want. Hence, the need exists for close coordination among management representatives.

Erosion of Practices. What is gained in negotiations often is lost through poor practices, sometimes called "sleeping on your rights." What established practices and the labor agreement say a company can do is important, but more important is how the company has applied the agreements. Most arbiters look at what the company is actually doing and how it applies the contract, not at contract language alone. Unions spend considerable time and effort making inroads into a number of seemingly insignificant areas; before management knows it, the union "owns" a whole practice. It is always costly to retrieve management rights which have slipped away.

Multiple-Union Situation. If a company has multiple unions and/or multiple locations, consideration must be given to coalition bargaining or multiplant bargaining. Expiration dates of contracts are extremely important in such instances. Accordingly, the company may want to have a *lead* or *pattern* contract expire first in order to establish benchmarks for later negotiations. Decisions in these matters have a high-level impact on the business and must be carefully evaluated.

Past Relationships. Since so much of the future is dictated by the past, it is important that management maintain and review the past history of the company's union relationship. Meanwhile, the union will also be predicting the future on the basis of the *company's* behavior. It wants to know where the company will stand firm and where it may give in to various levels of pressure. If management plans to change its basic relationship with the union, its position on important issues, its approach to the union and the relationship, the union should be informed in advance, with detailed and understandable reasons for the change.

The Union and Its Leadership. Just as the future is to some degree predicted by the past, so the relationship with the union is influenced by past behavior patterns of the two parties. An analysis of this type includes an understanding of the philosophies and operating practices of the local union— such things as timing and method for electing officers, contract ratification procedure, and involvement of the international union. Management should have knowledge of the behavior pattern of the local membership, stewards and officers, and international representatives. It should know the union's approach to handling situations, hot issues, normal reactions, reactions under pressure, internal political pressures, etc.

Union Decision Point. It is imperative that management also know the decision point at the various levels of the union organization. It must determine what individual or group makes decisions at the various levels of issues or problems. Otherwise, management may find itself addressing the right questions for resolution to the wrong level of decision making. The result can be disastrous.

Preparing the Written Policy. With the above considerations in mind, an overall labor relations policy or strategy should be formulated and put into writing. It should include the following elements:

1. *Significant past business or company relationship factors affecting the relationship:* New management, pending negotiations, past strikes at contract expiration, wildcat strikes, changes in business direction, etc.
2. *Fundamentals of relationship:* The overall fundamentals of the relationship with union or unions, such as type and nature of communica-

tions, operation of grievance procedure, and position on various management rights issues.

3. *Current business strategies:* Priorities, timetables, and responsibilities of current business objectives which impact on labor relations, organization and manning level changes, product and technology changes, etc.

4. *Policy-making group:* The specific individuals responsible for various levels and types of decisions; also a list of union counterparts.

5. *Role of supervisors:* Types and level of problems they should handle and level of union representatives with whom they should work.

6. *Union leadership:* Control and decision points; types of actions or reactions that can be expected; role of officers, stewards, and international representatives; membership needs and attitudes, etc.

7. *Grievance and arbitration procedures:* Analysis of past utilization and responses; judicial approach or trading device; company and union positions on classes of grievances such as back pay, discipline, etc.

8. *Negotiations planning:* The role of negotiations as it relates to ongoing labor relations. (See next entry.)

9. *Schedule of events:* Specific timetables, goals, and responsibilities necessary to implement strategies for the current year.

The policy should be used as a guideline for current actions and goals and long-range objectives. It should be a living document and control device. It should be revised and updated as necessary, but at least on an annual basis.

Collective-Bargaining Process

In terms of the business, stockholders, customers, employees, and public relations, no single employee relations event has as great an impact as contract negotiations. It is the culmination of all the activities, desires, needs, and frustrations of the past into a single finite point in time when the contract expires. Both parties position themselves and their constituents: for the union, its membership; and for the company, various levels of management. Both parties exchange thoughts and words, some logical and meaningful and other pure trivia and filler, which hopefully will result in a better contract for both. There is a certain ritual of collective bargaining, based on the particular situation.

The objective of collective bargaining, according to one authority, is

. . . to negotiate an agreement which will meet the needs of the company to remain competitive

and profitable, while at the same time being creatively responsive to individual interests, situations, and concerns of employees.[7]

It is a foregone conclusion that, in most instances, unions will achieve and/or claim improvements for their members in direct wage and benefit areas. However, in the critical areas of noneconomic operating practices, management must protect, and sometimes regain, their rights to make basic decisions necessary to running a competitive business. Getting back such management rights short of a confrontation is difficult, if not impossible. It is difficult to convince the union leadership,and often more difficult for them to sell the membership, to give back those rights.

There are a number of steps necessary to plan for and manage effective negotiations. Each is discussed briefly below.

Negotiations Schedule. Approximately 9 months to a year before negotiations begin, a detailed negotiations schedule should be prepared, setting forth each step to be taken, the individual responsible, and the completion dates.

Current Contract. Negotiation preparations should begin with a thorough review of present contract language, supplemental agreements, and a knowledge of any problems relating to its application. Issues presented in grievance or arbitration and their resolution should be analyzed as an aid in identifying potential union demands or possible company proposals. Finally, existing plant practices should be carefully considered.

Past Negotiations. Past negotiations should be reviewed to determine what demands were made by the company and union, and the results. This information may indicate types of settlements and union areas of concentration which will be helpful in developing company negotiations strategy. The role of outside parties such as mediators or arbiters should be carefully reviewed.

Status of Business. Needless to say, the current status of business and future company operating plans that may affect employees must be known. It is often essential in countering points raised by the union, as well as in constructing company proposals, to know what is necessary to reach business goals. Part of this review, of course, is obtaining information on current operating problems which are caused by present contract provisions or practices and which should be corrected in negotiations.

Survey of Practices and Economic Trends. Surveys should be made on the present level of economic items and changes that have occurred in them during the term of the contract. Care should be taken that a representative sample is obtained. Companies in the appropriate labor market, competitive companies, comparative industries, and national industry settlements and trends should be included.

Bargaining Unit Information. Understanding

and handling union demands, determining costs and effect on operations, and developing company policy and strategy can be done properly only with detailed knowledge of the work force and the union.

Review of Legal Requirements. It is essential that competent legal assistance be utilized throughout the early review of the current contract, proposed changes, the drafting of contract language, and as necessary to review legal questions on the bargaining process itself.

Review of Union Negotiation and Ratification Practices. Most unions follow an historical pattern in the negotiation and ratification practices. It is likely that a union will act about the same as it has in previous negotiations rather than follow a significantly different course of conduct. Knowledge of and strategy based on a union's pattern of conduct can often mean the difference between obtaining a settlement without a strike or being struck.

Union Negotiation Techniques. At the outset it is important to review past demands against actual settlements. This provides some insight into how much room the union typically leaves for itself to move. It is also important to review the degree of importance which the union has attached to dropped demands it may again bring up. However, if the union gave up on a demand only after hard bargaining, a repetition of the demand should be regarded as serious.

The pattern in which the union drops demands should be studied. A union may (1) rarely formally drop demands but simply stop talking about them; (2) make trades; (3) make few moves until the final hours of negotiations; (4) follow a fairly steady pace of movement from the start of negotiations; or (5) attempt to bluff through a "take it or leave it" position.

A related study should be made to determine if any traditional pattern exists by which the parties signal that they would be receptive to compromise proposals.

The negotiator should be aware, when the union stops talking about a demand, whether it is relatively certain that the issue has been dropped or whether there is a union practice of reviving a demand at the final hour.

Obtaining Union Committee Agreement. Obviously, the agreement of the union committee cannot be obtained unless the committee is convinced that the company has made its final offer. Traditionally, certain words, circumstances, and events indicate to the union when this point has been reached—and a variance by the company from an anticipated pattern of conduct may result in disastrous confusion. It is, therefore, highly important to know what previous negotiations have led the union to expect, who was involved, and where and when it was concluded. Further, mediation is traditionally a part of the final settlement process at some negotiations, and a final

offer would not be credible unless it evolved from the mediation process; at others this is not necessary.

Ratification. Ratification practices, like negotiation practices, tend to follow traditional patterns. Members, like leaders, learn to expect certain things to occur before the company's final offer is credible. The practice should be known if the final offer is to be timed correctly. It is also important to know whether the members are accustomed to waiting at the union hall while the negotiators work down to the last minute or whether they typically hold a ratification meeting the day after the contract expires. The time of day the meeting is traditionally held and the group of employees who attend the meeting should also be known.

Union Demands. It is important in planning company strategy and ascertaining the probable cost of reaching settlement to anticipate the demands the union may make in negotiations.

To anticipate union demands most accurately, the labor relations staff should (1) discuss the subject with supervisors who are in daily contact with bargaining unit employees; (2) attempt to get some advance hint from union officials; (3) review past grievances and past negotiation history; and (4) review settlements by other locals of the same union in the area or industry.

Once union demands have been received, each item should be analyzed and rated for (1) its impact on the business in terms of cost and operating restrictions and (2) the best appraisal of the priority which the union places on each demand.

Finally, a determination must be made of which union demands are strike issues. Once the company concludes and communicates that a demand is a strike issue, it must stand or fall with that position in order to protect its credibility in the future.

Company Negotiating Team. One of the primary requisites of successful bargaining is the makeup of the company negotiating team. The team should be of manageable size but large enough to contain a cross section of management representatives who are knowledgeable in all aspects of plant operations, union relations, and contract administration.

Committee Members. The line manager responsible for the employees concerned in the negotiation should be a member of the team or available to the company spokesperson at all times during negotiations. Other members of the team should be selected from the lower levels of management responsible for managing the various areas to be affected by the contract.

Company Spokesperson. One individual should be identified as the company spokesperson. Normally he or she is the cognizant employee relations manager although this is not a necessity. The individual must be articulate and have prestige with both the union and company representatives. The person

459

should be of a stature to make decisions which the union knows are final and binding, of a level to be able to discuss any item with top management, and in some cases have the company's positions changed when he or she feels it is necessary. Negotiations have both conflict and crisis; the spokesperson must be able to handle the buildup of pressure.

Training of Committee. After selection, the team members should be thoroughly briefed by their spokesperson in the role each is to play in negotiations as well as the overall strategy to be followed. It is essential that every member know the company's objectives and each step to be taken during negotiatons; however, it is not necessary for all members of the company committee to know the details of the company's economic authorization.

Conduct at Negotiating Table. At the negotiating table, no other member of the committee should speak unless pursuant to a plan worked out with the spokesperson in advance. During meetings outside of the negotiating room or in caucuses, other members of the negotiating team should understand that they are to participate fully in discussing, objecting to, or advancing proposals according to what they feel is proper. Once an item is discussed and agreed upon, however, all members of the team must act of one accord when discussing it across the table with the union committee.

Confidentiality of Negotiations. All items discussed in preparation for and during the actual course of contract negotiations must be held confidential by the members of the negotiating team unless specific authorization for certain types of communication is obtained from the company spokesperson.

Power of Commitment. Only the company spokesperson has the power to commit the company to an action. This must be clearly understood by the union negotiating committee as well as by the company committee members. The spokesperson in turn must receive approval from the designated higher-level manager.

Formulation of Company Objectives and Proposals. Development of company proposals to be given to the union should be the *last* step in the process of determining management goals and objectives in negotiations. Indeed, after the process is completed, it may be decided *not* to make any company proposals.

However, sometimes the best defense is a good offense. Sloane and Witney, for example, view collective-bargaining sessions:

> . . . as productive in terms of protecting the basic interests of management as they are in protecting the legitimate job rights of employees. These results, however, cannot be accomplished when management remains constantly on the defensive.[8]

The process begins with a review of the strengths and weaknesses of current plant practices and contract provisions. Simultaneously, top plant management should be requested to state what it desires the company to obtain in negotiations.

Setting Priorities of Company Proposals. After all this information is compiled, company objectives should be ranked in order of importance. Those items remaining should then be ranked (1) in order of importance to the company and (2) in order of the probability of obtaining union agreement. The list should then be pared to a manageable size. Items retained should be those that are the most important and have a reasonable probability of getting union agreement *provided* that a proposal not be made on any matter that, if unsuccessful, would put the company in a worse position than continuing the status quo—unless the company is willing to take a strike to get it. Some "droppable" proposals should be included purely for negotiating purposes.

Presenting Company Proposals. Company proposals are often stated in terms of the objective or as a discussion item, rather than in specific contract language, to provide more flexibility in negotiations. As indicated above, it is important not to ask for items or clarifications of things management believes it already has unless it is very important to do so. Any item considered to be a company strike issue should be clearly understood to be so before it is given such status in company negotiating strategy.

Factual Support Proposals. The negotiating team must be prepared to substantiate any proposal with facts. A weak presentation may mislead the union into thinking an important proposal is unimportant.

The Final Offer. This should consider the needs of the company, union leadership and membership, area wage rates, legal requirements, etc. The offer should go to the membership only if a majority of the union negotiators have approved it. Since offers made by the company bargainers cannot be withdrawn without running the risk of charges of "refusal to bargain," it is essential to obtain approval *prior* to making any offer and that all members of the company's bargaining committee be instructed not to make any proposal except as authorized and planned.

Negotiating Process. The negotiating process is a ritual that is peculiar to the given situation, the times, and the parties. It is a give-and-take process, but above all else, the parties must be realistic. The company must understand the union leadership and the membership and their desires and needs. The union must also understand the company and its needs. Someone observed

> The fact that collective bargaining is a two-way street is clearly evidenced in negotiation sessions. Some people hold the view that the collective bargaining process involves only the union's

demanding and the company's giving. On the contrary, . . . the company frequently will resist and refuse to concede to some issues. And when the company believes that the stakes are extremely important it will take a strike rather than concede to a particular union demand.[9]

The problem is that both parties view those needs and expectations from their own position or point of view. The process then becomes one of lowering or adjusting expectations so that they, in fact, meet the other party's ability to deliver. This modulating of positions takes a great amount of time, discussion, and often patient waiting. For some bargaining tips, see Table L-1.

TABLE L-1 Bargaining Tips

1. Never give a false signal.
2. Never indicate you will consider a demand on which you do not intend to move.
3. Spend plenty of time listening.
4. Be sincere about your motives—do not attempt to conceal the fact that you are in business to make money.
5. Do not indicate you cannot afford or cannot compete if a demand is given unless you are willing to show your books or are sure they will not be demanded.
6. Do not index economic items on a percentage base; negotiate on fixed cost so that you can negotiate on the item in the future, and both company and union gain credit for improvements.
7. Do not indicate you will not negotiate on a subject unless you are sure that you have no legal duty to negotiate on it.
8. Let the union drop its demands gracefully.
9. Do not lose self-control or attack any member of the union committee personally.
10. Do not take or give abuse; adjourn the meeting until tempers have cooled.
11. Work from the company's language.
12. Make sessions as long as is necessary to obtain satisfactory understanding.

Negotiations Communications Program

The communication of information regarding negotiations as well as communication in the event of a strike is a very sensitive subject. Therefore, early in negotiations planning, it should be decided what, how much, when, how, and by whom such information is to be communicated to managers and supervisors, employees, and the public.

Techniques to be reviewed are (1) letters to the home, (2) company newspaper, (3) bulletin-board notices, (4) supervisory meetings, (5) word of mouth, and (6) press releases.

Only *facts* and supporting arguments should be communicated; it is unwise to send up "trial balloons," engage in innuendo, or exaggerate. The key to any communications program is credibility. Further, consideration must be given to its effect on actual negotiations. Press releases should be issued through or coordinated with the cognizant public relations function.

Strike Preparation and Customer Contingency Planning

Major goals of strike preparation include maintaining the ability to meet customers' needs (to the greatest extent possible), preventing improper interference with company operations by striking employees, successfully concluding the strike, and resuming normal operations as quickly as possible. These goals require involvement in all management functions and close coordination with the labor contract negotiation process.

The company's preparations for a strike have the following main objectives, and a detailed written manual should be prepared as a guide should a strike occur. The objectives are:

1. To protect personnel and property and maintain essential maintenance, production, and service; thereby to minimize financial losses to the company and personal losses to employees.
2. To maintain the goodwill of customers, the public, and employees to the maximum extent practical.
3. To enable the company to deal fairly in terms of its personnel policies with both striking and nonstriking employees.
4. To enable the company to resume normal operations when the strike ends within the shortest possible time.
5. To demonstrate to the union that the company will take a strike if necessary in order to continue to manage the business effectively.

Critical Decisions. The following critical decisions should be made before the strike begins. All of them, and any other policy decisions, should be reviewed with the company spokesperson before they are implemented. These decisions include:

1. Whether to build up inventory and/or make advance shipments.
2. Whether to contract out or divert work to other plants.
3. Whether to attempt to get agreement from the union that certain essential employees (maintenance persons, for example) will be issued union passes permitting them to cross picket lines and work.
4. Whether to lay off certain nonstriking employees. (If a decision is made to allow nonstriking employees to continue to work, plans should be made to assign the work force to ensure its most

461

effective utilization. Consideration should be given to providing training sessions for otherwise idle factory supervision.)

5. Whether to continue to operate nonstruck portions of the business.

6. Whether to attempt to operate struck areas of the business with nonstriking employees and/or temporary hires.

7. Whether, and if so, when, to replace the strikers with new hires.

8. Whether to receive or ship material during a strike. If so, how.

If a strike should occur, the strike plan should be implemented and managed by the strike committee. Competent legal assistance should be available instantly for possible injunctive purposes.

Summary

The primary goal in union relations is to establish an overall plan, covering both daily contract administration and contract negotiations, which enables the company to remain profitable and competitive while providing employees with fair and equitable economic benefits and practices.

A delicate balance comes into play, since each party measures from its own point of view what is fair and equitable and what allows a company to remain profitable and competitive. A successful relationship takes years, not days, to develop; it takes facts, not half truths; it takes the ability to make a stand and not to vacillate; it takes an open mind, not arbitrary thinking; it takes a willingness to compromise, but not on an issue of principle. These actions and reactions must come from both parties, not just one.

Both the short- and long-run labor relations objective and strategies should be supportive of and should complement the operating goals of the company. In order to ensure this achievement, the labor relations function must be a part of the overall management planning and goal-setting process. It must be involved in and actively participate in the give and take of the decision-making process.

See also Human resources planning; Labor legislation; Labor (trade) unions; Negotiating; Personnel administration; Safety and health management, employee; Wages and hours legislation.

NOTES

[1]Dale Yoder, *Personnel Management and Industrial Relations*, Prentice-Hall, Englewood Cliffs, N.J., 1962, p. 482.

[2]H. D. Marshall and N. J. Marshall, *Collective Bargaining*, Random House, New York, 1971, p. 252.

[3]Walter Baer, *Grievance Handling*, American Management Association, New York, 1970, p. 2.

[4]A. A. Sloane and F. Witney, *Labor Relations*, Prentice-Hall, Englewood Cliffs, N.J., 1967, p. 169.

[5]A Blum, "Collective Bargaining: Ritual or Reality," *Harvard Business Review*, vol. 39, November–December 1961, pp. 63–69.

[6]Yoder, op. cit., p. 491.

[7]Marshall and Marshall, op. cit., p. 252.

[8]Sloane and Witney, op. cit., p. 169.

[9]Ibid.

REFERENCES

Kochan, Thomas A.: *Collective Bargaining and Industrial Relations*, Richard D. Irwin, Homewood, Ill., 1980.

Mills, D. Q.: *Labor-Management Relations*, 2d ed., McGraw-Hill, New York, 1982.

PAUL W. BOCKLEY, *Honeywell, Inc.*

Labor (Trade) Unions

The institution of unionism is rooted in the national concept of democracy. The principal distinctions that separate American and British democracies from autocracies may be subsumed into two basic concepts: (1) the participation of the governed in the formulation of the laws and regulations which accommodate individual freedom to group needs; and (2) the concept of *due process,* or a set of procedures instituted to resolve differences between the governed and the governors, with the added protection of a culminating decision vested in a judiciary that is completely independent of any pressure exercised by either group.

These concepts have been basic to political life in the United States since 1776, when the 13 colonies declared their independence from the British Crown. These concepts were institutionalized in the form of a national constitution in the last decade of the eighteenth century and in the various state constitutions at later dates. The Senate and the House of Representatives, the national legislative arms of the U.S. government, embody the participation of its citizenry in the legislative process.

Political Citizens and Economic Subjects. The judiciary resolves conflicts between citizens and their institutions and the executive branch of the political government in the event of conflict between individual citizens and the various areas of that government.

Paradoxically, the political citizen in the 1790s who was beginning to experience due process and participative decision making, albeit incomplete and rudimentary, in political life was subjected to complete autocracy in his occupational role as an employee. If his employer was benevolent, he enjoyed benevolent despotism. If his employer was harsh, he suffered from harsh despotism.

From the very beginning of the republic, some men revolted against this schizoid duality in their role as political citizen and economic subject if their labor was for hire. Their status as employee derived from the ancient law of master and servant. The contradiction between their political role and economic role led to the ultimate rejection of this status as servant. The vehicles which these workers created and which embodied the efforts at participation in deciding their fate became known as unions. They were industrial analogs of the legislature in the political domain.

Wages and Conditions. Because the economic demands which unions voiced were so much easier for the public to understand, their revolts were generally reported as a demand for a raise in wages. The demand for changes in rule making so that the workers could participate in the rules governing the workplace received attention largely from specialized scholars; nevertheless, this second demand was present from the start as one of the twin pillars of the labor movement.

The first record of an American strike goes back to 1786, when Philadelphia printers struck for a minimum income of $6 a week and indirectly for future participation in the determination of conditions of employment. They lost on both grounds.

Following this inconspicuous beginning, the labor movement waxed and waned throughout the years and assumed its modern form in 1881 with the formation of the Organized Trades and Labor Unions, renamed the American Federation of Labor (AFL) in 1886.

Emergence of Collective Bargaining. In 1890 the United Mine Workers of America pioneered the concept of the collective agreement, an instrument achieved through collective bargaining with the employer and which represented a focusing of hitherto diffuse union tactics into an effective means of addressing their problems. Surprising as it may seem, many of the notions of a collective agreement, however natural it seems to contemporary Americans, represented a new departure in labor-management relations.

The process of collective bargaining has been defined as follows by the leading scholar in the field, Professor Sumner Slichter, late of Harvard.[1] He divides collective bargaining into two separate basic functions:

1. It is a method whereby labor as union and capital as management define the price of labor.

2. It is a method of introducing civil rights for labor into industry; that is, of requiring that management be conducted by rule rather than by arbitrary decision. In a sense, it is a method of introducing a system of jurisprudence into industry in very much the same manner that the glorious revolution of 1688 substituted parliamentary

supremacy for the divine right of kings in political life. The labor movement extends this same constitutional concept to industrial life in very much the same manner that citizens instituted states in political life which define positive law, construct administrative procedures for carrying it out, and complement both statute law and administrative rule with a system of judicial review whose agent is *free* of any tie or obligation to either side.

The rise of the labor movement antedates the emergence of the institution of collective bargaining. The unions as a group within the labor movement *evolved collective bargaining after a long period of experimentation with other techniques.*

The unions first arose as a blind protest imbued with a purely adversary attitude. The progression from independent craft workers, owning and working with their own tools, to that of hired workers of faceless capital was stormy and had few precedents. It was only after a long period of experimentation with other devices and tactics that the institution of collective bargaining evolved. Earlier programs were predicated upon an antiprivate enterprise program.

The Cooperative Movement. The unions opposed the wage system as an institution and promoted producer cooperatives to escape the thralldom of the wage system. They rapidly became disenchanted with these cooperatives when they discovered that most of them failed because of lack of managerial competence. Those that succeeded presented an even more troublesome problem. Those who had pioneered the venture were loath to take on additional cooperators and give them the same ownership privileges enjoyed by the pioneers. Within a short time there was little to distinguish the enterprise that started as a producer's cooperative from any other private enterprise. For all purposes, the producer's cooperative had become a private partnership of the pioneers, who then employed latecomers to the institution on the same basis as any other private enterprise. This historic progression has been repeated in some of the manufacturing-oriented kibbutzim in Israel in the last decade.

Similarly, attempts to solve problems via the political route by alliance with farmers and small businesses led working people to discover that when the coalition succeeded, small business resented organization even more bitterly than big business did because the former operated at such a close margin to survival.

Management Under Law, or Work Rules. Finally, the adoption of collective bargaining was predicated on the frank acceptance of capitalism as an institution and the desire to improve the workers' status under that economic system. This meant an abandonment of any class-war doctrine and the adoption of a creed that acknowledged a simultaneous (1) **463** identity of conflict of interest with the employer and (2) identity of interest in the prosperity of the enterprise. In addition, it raised fundamental problems about the governance of the enterprise and the extent to which the employers participated in that governance. Management was acknowledged to be the industrial ruler, but this ruler was obliged to rule under law, or working rules, as they were called in industry. Conflicts over the interpretation of these laws, or rules, had to be resolved in accordance with the principle of due process.

This industrial law now pervades every facet of industrial management. Among the ideas are (1) entrance to the trade, (2) the method of production, and (3) the terms of the introduction of technological change. Each industry constitutes a local culture of its own and reflects the wide diversity of practices that fall under the rubric of industrial rights.

The American labor movement as we now know it can be dated from 1933 when President Roosevelt's election led to the revival of the labor organizations, many of which were left moribund by the great depression of the early 1930s.

The Norris-LaGuardia Act of 1932 had set the stage for this revival by sharply restricting the terms under which federal courts could issue labor injunctions—which had previously been capricious devices used by management to hobble labor.

Section 7(a) of the National Recovery Act of 1934, followed by the National Labor Relations Act of 1935, set the legislative climate in which unions could revive and flourish. The movement by and large confined itself to the private sector.

Arbitrable and Negotiable Issues. From the very beginning, management generally has stood for a containing strategy designed to restrict the subjects about which it is willing to talk in collective bargaining. It has sought to restrict the area of collective bargaining to wages and hours, arguing that all remaining areas constitute management prerogative. The labor movement, on the other hand, has argued that management is obliged to negotiate in any area that exercises an impact on worker welfare.

A Classic Confrontation. Some years ago these points of view received a formal expression in a controversy between Harold E. Phelps, at the time a Bethlehem Steel executive, and Arthur Goldberg, at the time the attorney for the United Steel Workers of America, later secretary of labor under President Kennedy, and still later Justice Goldberg of the U.S. Supreme Court. Phelps claimed that in the beginning all rights belonged to management, and management was therefore obligated to discuss only those areas which labor had managed to tear away and insert in the collective agreement.

Goldberg dissented, stating that in the beginning management was able to impose an absolute dictatorship on its workers, that collective bargaining broke this usurpation, and that equity had become the criterion for determining the area of collective bargaining upon which management was compelled to engage in joint decision making with the union.

Landmark Legislation. The conflict over the permissible areas of collective bargaining has resulted in a stormy history in the saga of U.S. industrial relations. Following World War I, President Wilson called an industrial relations conference in 1919 to head off a threatened outbreak of nationwide strikes. Management acknowledged the right of any individual worker to join a union but insisted that it remained management's right to deal with or refuse to deal with the union. After a series of bloody recognition strikes over the issue of whether management should or should not deal with the union, the U.S. government settled the controversy with the passage of the National Labor Relations Act of 1935. The act imposed upon management the obligation to bargain collectively with representatives of the workers who had been certified in an election procedure.

Arbitrable Issues. Now the controversy was transferred to the areas over which management was obligated to bargain. Almost every arbitration procedure over working conditions was bedeviled by management's claim that the dispute before the arbitrator was nonarbitrable because the areas were not specifically treated in the collective agreement.

A conference similar to the Wilson Industrial Relations conference of 1919 was called by President Truman in 1945 to avert anticipated post-World War II strikes. The conference foundered on the issue of management's insistence that labor must carefully restrict the collective bargaining subject area and recognize all other areas as management prerogatives. Labor demurred, insisting that such a move was impractical in a time when a rapidly changing economy disclosed that areas which had hitherto been management preserves had developed a powerful impact on working conditions.

In 1947 Arbitrator Harvey Shulman. late dean of Yale Law School, was called upon to resolve a strike called by the United Automobile Workers (UAW) against the Ford Motor Company over an alleged speedup of the assembly line. Shulman resolved this problem by drawing a distinction between *absolute management rights* and *conditional management rights*. He defined the setting of production standards as a conditional management right, and management's right was restricted to initially proposing a standard over which the union could present grievances. As an example of an absolute management right, he listed the location of a plant.

Narrowing Management Prerogatives. Yet, even this apparently compelling management right was subject to question. Even in 1947, the garment workers' union had a restriction of ancient vintage in their agreement with the garment employers. It imposed upon the management the obligation not to move its plant outside the 5-cent fare zone of New York City. This provision had been prompted by the predilection of garment employers to sign an agreement on Friday and then escape the union by moving their plant out of town over the weekend.

The auto workers, who thought nothing of plant location in 1947, were concerned with it by 1958. This came about because, as a result of the decline in auto sales, the primary layoffs were in the older areas like Detroit where older plants were located. What work was being performed was far from Detroit in plants of a much more modern vintage. Plant location, a matter of no interest to the United Auto Workers in 1947, had become a major concern in the late 1950s. Thus, the nature and definition of what constitutes a management prerogative is clearly changeable.

Implicit as Well as Explicit Matters. The matter of what areas are relevant to collective bargaining is generally linked to what is arbitrable under a collective agreement. The U.S. Supreme Court, in a trilogy of decisions,[2] struck down the strict construction that arbitrators are confined only to those issues specified in the contract. It defined the industrial relationship as a form of constitutional government in which the scope of arbitration is expanded to include contract implications as well as specific agreement subject areas.

The principles laid down in the trilogy by the U.S. Supreme Court in 1950 have been virtually eroded over the years, reaching their apogee in the case of *Charles Brown v. The American Postal Workers' Union.* By a 5-4 vote, the Supreme Court supported a verdict of a lower court awarding Brown damages of $30,000 against the union, of which he was a member, and a $23,000 award against the U.S. Postal Service.

Brown had been involved in a scuffle with a fellow employee. The union, feeling Brown had no case, refused to take his case to arbitration, but the lower court set itself up as the arbitrator (*Daily Labor Reporter #7*, 1/11/83), and the Supreme Court validated its verdict.

At the 1983 Arbitration Day Conference, management and union lawyers deplored the court's departure from the trilogy and noted that unions were in jeopardy unless they brought every triviality to arbitration, overloading the system so that it was becoming completely dysfunctional. It put a premium on union irresponsibility (*Daily Labor Reporter #100*, 5/23/83).

European Unionism. The system of industrial governance in U.S. collective bargaining is rooted in the shop or factory in which the worker participates in industrial government by means of the individual grievance. European unions, where organization does not reach into the shops, do not enjoy the same kind of rank-and-file participation in the everyday affairs of the union. For example, in Holland, as in Sweden,

Norway, the German Federal Republic, and the United Kingdom, the labor unions play a much more publicly significant role in political matters than they do in the United States. Yet, as Professor Barbash put it in 1972 after observing the Dutch system of industrial relations, "When it comes to the shop, management's sovereignty is absolute."[3] European unions have been attempting to overcome some of these problems by voicing a demand for codetermination or participative management. By and large, U.S. labor has eschewed that approach, settling instead for participation in shop governance via the grievance procedure. The threatened bankruptcy of the Chrysler Corporation led to the management's request that Douglas Frazier, president of the United Auto Workers, be elected to its board of directors, an unprecedented American change, closer to the pattern sought by Europeans.

The growth of huge transnational firms and the ease with which they transfer operations within countries and among countries have led U.S. unions to demand legislation to restrict management's freedom to move from place to place within the United States.

The Europeans have already instituted such restrictions within their own countries. The Europeans are demanding even more restrictions on the action of these transnational corporations by demanding that the office of Economic Common Development adopt the so-called Vredeling Amendment extending union participation in corporate decisions of the type between nations.

The automobile and steel industries, hitherto dominated by the Americans, are now in the process of being challenged by Japan and Europe. As the industries become subjected to more and more international competition, the unions are moving increasingly away from a position of open free markets to more protectionist positions.

Public Sector. Labor organizations in the United States developed later in the public sector. As early as 1912, the International Association of Machinists (among others) struck the Watertown Arsenal in the wake of efforts by the local management to introduce work measurements by time study into the plant. The result was that from that time to the 1940s all military appropriation bills carried a rider forbidding the expenditure of funds for any work-measurement purpose. However, the few unions that confined themselves to the government sector were relatively weak and ineffective, with the possible exception of the postal employees union. While all government unions eschewed the right to strike, the ubiquitous distribution of postal employees in every hamlet in the land gave them a lobbying influence in Congress that was more effective than any strike.

Restrictive Attitudes. The fundamental attitude toward labor unions in the public sector was laid down in 1919 by Calvin Coolidge, then the governor of Massachusetts, later president, who broke the Boston police strike, declaring that, "There is no right to strike against the public any time, anywhere, any place."[4]

In 1937, President Roosevelt, who was largely responsible for the revival of unionism in the private sector, expressed himself on collective bargaining for public employees as follows:

> The process of collective bargaining as usually understood cannot be transplanted into the public service. It has its distinct and insurmountable limitations when applied to public personnel management. The very nature and purpose of government makes it impossible for administrative officials to represent fully or to bind the employer in mutual discussions with government employee organizations. The employer is the whole people who speak by means of laws enacted by their representatives in Congress. Accordingly, administrative officials and employees alike are governed and guided, and in many cases restricted by laws which establish policies, procedures or rules in personnel matters. Particularly, I want to emphasize my conviction that militant tactics have no place in the functions of any organization of government employees.[5]

Yet, some 30 years later a Republican administration in Pennsylvania, led by Governor Schaeffer, put into effect Act 195, which granted to state employees the statutory right to collective bargaining, including the right to strike. The only exceptions to Act 195 were police, fire fighters, and prison guards. They were covered by Act III, however, which eschewed strikes but invoked joint fact-finding and binding arbitration over issues which the parties could not resolve in collective negotiations.

Facilitating Administrative Orders. President Kennedy issued Executive Order 10988, which set forth the procedures to facilitate union recognition and negotiation in the federal service. It directly stimulated employee organization and negotiations, not only in the federal service but also indirectly at the state and local levels. The order provided somewhat the same impetus for public-sector labor relations that the Wagner Act of 1935 did in the 1930s for labor relations in the private sector. Executive Order 10988 was superseded by President Nixon's Executive Order 14197, which revised some procedures and amplified others. This, in turn, was followed by Executive Order 11616.

At the present time, local governments are increasingly becoming accustomed to dealing with their employees on the basis of the customs and procedures of collective bargaining. Many individual states have passed legislation to do for their employees what President Kennedy did for federal employees during his term of office.

Public Process. Public workers (who, it was expected, could never make use of such an instrument) are today engaged in collective bargaining. For example, the federal government has adapted collective bargaining to the very special circumstances of the government employee. Quite obviously, wages for Civil Service are set by the Congress. The degree to which the government employee can participate in setting government wages is the same as every other citizen who acts through his or her congressional representative. At the work site, collective bargaining has been used to lend more reality to the appeals procedure, which Civil Service formerly furnished exclusively as a due process means of avoiding arbitrary, unreasonable behavior by the supervisory force. Although the Civil Service had long ago created an appeals procedure for individual federal workers, virtually all agree that the procedure was so weighted on the supervisor's side that it left much to be desired in terms of a due process criterion.

Unique Aspects. What is unique about collective bargaining in the public sector is that the Civil Service worker is represented by a person independent of the Civil Service against whom the employee's supervisor can exercise no power. In this respect, the federal Civil Service problem with collective bargaining is very similar to that of any manager who must cope with the problem of due process enjoyed by his or her employees. In the last decade or so, collective bargaining has become a regular tool, increasingly available to the public employee. Local government representatives, as a matter of course, today meet with the Policemen's Benevolent Association, the Fraternal Order of Police, and the International Association of Fire Fighters to determine the terms and conditions of employment for these public servants.

The railroad operating unions, the engineers, and the conductors started mutual societies for insurance purposes. The hazard of their occupations banned them from ordinary commercial insurance at the time of organization. In a short time, their preoccupation with safety led them to demand certain working rules from railroad management as a part of working conditions.

The letter carriers' union also started as a mutual welfare organization for insurance and recreation. The organization of letter carriers' musical bands were undertaken for this purpose.

Professional Organization. At times, professional organizations, organized for professional development, began by eschewing collective bargaining as a subprofessional activity, only to develop all the union functions under the pressure of the logic of events. The National Education Association (NEA), made up of teachers and administrators, was challenged by the American Federation of Teachers. The NEA found itself participating in election contests against the American Federation of Teachers for collective bargaining representation, an activity to which the association was allegedly opposed. NEA won the election, and before long, any differences between it and the American Federation of Teachers were reduced to a matter of rhetoric. In fact, both organizations have been discussing merger; the Los Angeles and New York State organizations have already merged. The administrators and principals, no longer comfortable in the teacher-dominated NEA, have organized their own association, which is assuming on their behalf very much the same functions that the NEA continues to perform on behalf of the teachers.

Engineering organizations, shaken by the vulnerability of their constituents in the labor market, have moved to imitate certain aspects of unionism at the same time that they eschew unions as being subprofessional. The engineers' need for due process asserts itself despite the reiteration of symbolic ideological pretension.

Gunnar Myrdal, the Swedish social scientist, has observed that we are moving closer and closer to a completely organizational society in which each group will bargain with the greater collective to define the condition and limitation governing their contribution of goods and services to the commonwealth.

See also Arbitration, labor; Labor legislation; Labor-management relations; Wages and hours legislation.

NOTES

[1]Sumner H. Slichter, *Union Policies and Industrial Management*, George Banta, Menasha, Wis., 1942.

[2]*USW v. American Manufacturing Company*, 363 U.S. 564 (1960); *USW v. Warrior and Gulf Navigation Company*, 363 U.S. 574 (1960); *USW v. Enterprise Wheel and Car Corporation*, 363 U.S. 593 (1950).

[3]Jack Barbash, *Trade Unions and National Economic Policy*, The Johns Hopkins Press, Baltimore, 1972.

[4]*The Public Papers and Addresses of Franklin D. Roosevelt*, 1937 vol., Samuel Rosenman (ed.), Macmillan, New York, 1941, p. 235.

[5]*Ibid.*

REFERENCES

Bok, Dereck C., and John T. Dunlop: *Labor and the American Community*, Simon & Schuster, New York, 1970.

Chamberlain, Neil, and James W. Kuhn: *Collective Bargaining*, 2d ed., McGraw-Hill, New York, 1965.

Kuhn, Alfred: *Labor, Institutions and Economics*, Harcourt Brace Jovanovich, New York, 1967.

(This entry is adapted from the author's chapter in *Military Unions and the United States Armed Forces*, University of Pennsylvania Press, Philadelphia, 1977.)

WILLIAM GOMBERG, *The Wharton School, University of Pennsylvania*

Laboratory (Sensitivity) Training

Laboratory training, also known as sensitivity training, is a form of leadership and personnel development which seeks to improve the ability of individuals to interact effectively with others by changing their attitudes through a strong emotional experience. This is accomplished by setting up training or T groups in a laboratory situation removed from the working environment and by encouraging confrontation between people and issues. This use of confrontation as a means of sensitizing participants to their own feelings and to those of others teaches them to accept these feelings consciously. By so doing, they are then able to understand and to promote the group process in order to achieve group goals.

Developed in the late 1940s and pioneered at the National Training Laboratories at Bethel, Maine, by Leland Bradford and his colleagues, laboratory training evolved from the experience of psychotherapists in treating individuals through group therapy. It is now a widespread practice throughout this country.

Laboratory training is characterized by (1) isolation from the work situation; (2) equal participation in leadership by all group members as peers; (3) no planned agenda or rules of procedure; (4) group sizes ranging from 10 to 16, with one or two trainers; (5) meetings lasting about 2 hours, twice daily, from 2 to 3 weeks. Experience has revealed a predictable pattern of the psychological states through which groups develop, although there is no guarantee that any group will progress through the entire pattern.

The disturbing vacuum created by the lack of agenda and lack of group roles apparently causes frustrations which force participants to reexamine the process of working with groups or influencing people. Attempts to express leadership or to determine the group's direction generally lead to confrontation, often to expressions of hostility and conflict, and frequently to deep anxiety. The trainer observes and endeavors to communicate to the members the nature of these feelings and interactions so that the group eventually begins to perceive, analyze, and handle them for itself. Although trainers differ, probing into subconscious motivation is usually discouraged.

Recent innovations bring laboratory training closer to work realities: the introduction of specific management problems into the agenda and the increasing practice of forming T groups from members of one organization, either of peers or of vertical groupings.

Opinions vary widely: laboratory training has clearly changed the focus in organizations from that of management versus employees to a realization that people, filling different roles, are engaged together in an enterprise which requires mutual understanding. "Gut level" training is more likely to cause real behavior change than is intellectual training, change which can often be carried over into the work situation; sensitivity training groups from one enterprise often do develop into cohesive and more efficient teams. The permanence of results has been questioned, however. Benefits are doubtful when the training attempts to prescribe behavior or attitudes and when it provokes deep anxieties and hostilities without resolving them.

The practice of sensitivity training has waned in recent years. Nevertheless, it was one of many related techniques that have led to the adoption of such bureaucratized, participative group activities as team building and quality circles.

See also Assessment center method; Interpersonal relationships; Motivation in organizations; Nominal group technique; Quality circles.

REFERENCES

Campbell, J. P., and M. Dunnette; "Effectiveness of T-Group Experiences in Managerial Training and Development," in W. E. Scott, Jr., and L. L. Cummings (eds.), *Readings in Organizational Behavior and Human Performance,* Richard D. Irwin, Homewood, Ill., 1973, pp. 568–594.

Klein, Stuart M., and R. Richard Ritti: *Understanding Organizational Behavior,* Wadsworth, Boston, 1980, chap. 19, "Changing Interaction Patterns for Organizational Improvement," pp. 464–500.

Tannenbaum, R. I., I. R. Weschler, and F. Massarik: "Sensitivity Training for the Management Team," *Leadership and Organization,* McGraw-Hill, New York, 1961, pp. 167–187.

LESTER R. BITTEL, *James Madison University*

Leadership

Leadership in business and industry is defined here as that part of management which deals with the direct supervision of subordinates. Given a reasonable equality in technical equipment and supplies, it is by far the single most important factor in determining the effectiveness of a group or organization.

This entry is concerned with leadership in formal organizations. It concentrates on the problems of professional managers and supervisors who obtained their position primarily by appointment rather than by election or by the force of their personality in informal organizations. Emphasis here will be on the leader's role in determining productivity and effectiveness rather than on the personal growth and development of his or her employees or their satisfaction with the job. This does not deny the rightful concern for these problems or the part the leader could or should play in furthering these goals. It simply is beyond the scope of this particular entry.

Search for Traits. Leadership holds an important place in philosophy and history for quite obvious reasons. The leadership of such men and women as Charles de Gaulle, Churchill, Golda Meir, Joan of Arc, Napoleon, Lincoln, Stalin, Mao Tse-tung, and Eisenhower made real differences. Similarly, the leadership of such men as the automobile manufacturer Henry Ford, the aircraft executive Boeing, and the film producer Samuel Goldwyn has had a critical impact on the success of their enterprises. It is not too surprising, therefore, that the ability to lead and direct has become identified in the popular mind with a personality type or certain traits. In fact, most psychological research on leadership from about 1900 to 1950 was devoted to identifying magic leadership traits or personality patterns that seem to have made a difference in organizational performance.

Absence of Evidence. In 1948 and again in 1974, Professor Ralph Stogdill published reviews of almost 300 empirical studies on leadership traits.[1] He was forced to conclude in both of these reviews that there was no evidence of a single trait or characteristic that identified a person as a leader. Furthermore, he could find no constellation of personality attributes or traits which identified a leader in all situations. To be sure, leaders tended to be somewhat brighter than their followers, somewhat taller, somewhat more outgoing and socially adept, but these differences were slight. Stogdill's conclusions were confirmed by a number of other researchers; e.g., Mann[2] and Bass.[3]

A moment of reflection will indicate why the trait approach does not seem to predict effective leadership. First of all, practically all people are leaders on some occasions and followers most of the time. The singularly successful chairperson of a Parent-Teacher Association committee will not necessarily succeed as the superintendent of a logging camp or a general manager of a savings and loan association. Further, among the traits often considered desirable, if not essential, for effective leadership, we usually include such things as being fair, honest, loyal, thoughtful, and judicious. While these traits undoubtedly are admirable and praiseworthy, they would as easily qualify one to become Mother or Father of the Year as to be appointed to manage an organization or a department. Sadly, we also know that some highly effective leaders have not necessarily been fair, honest, truthful, or loyal. In summary, leadership does not simply appear to be something with which an individual is born. First and foremost, it does seem to be a learned, interpersonal relationship.

Theories of Ideal Leader Types

If there are no personality traits which identify the successful leader, are there perhaps leader orientations or specific behaviors which make some individ-

uals successful in directing others? Theories which have postulated an ideal leader type are popular within the business community.

Theory X and Theory Y. Among the best-known theories of management is McGregor's concept of leaders who fall roughly into two camps on the question of how to deal with their subordinates. The older and more orthodox approach, known as *theory X*, refers to managers who believe their workers to be naturally lazy, resistant to change, requiring constant and closer supervision, and unmotivated to perform well. McGregor sees this as being the natural set of assumptions of managers and, in fact, the assumptions by which most managers attain their managerial position. Alternatively, McGregor proposes a new, more positive view of workers—*theory Y*. Under theory Y assumptions, the manager sees workers as basically mature, desirous of being productive, and wanting to contribute to the success of the organization (*see also* Theory X and Theory Y).

The obvious consequence of theory X assumptions is that managers believe that they must be authoritative and directive and that they must maintain a sufficient social distance from the employees to ensure their esteem. McGregor, in his well-known book, *The Human Side of Enterprise*,[4] held that this approach hampers organizational performance since (1) it relies on a small and select group of people for decision making and judgment and (2) it absorbs a great deal of organizational time and resources in ensuring compliance with prescribed standards.

The implications of *theory Y* assumptions, on the other hand, are that managers must be participative, democratic, and, above all, must concern themselves with creating the conditions which permit the worker to find fulfillment in the job. The manager is, in effect, admonished to create a democratic industrial environment. This approach, which has had a tremendous impact on academic thinking as well as on an important segment of business and industrial management, has been very influential in the philosophy of humanistic management. McGregor's theory, along with those of related thinkers,[5] has inspired a considerable amount of literature as well as some experimentation with industrial democracy which has become particularly prominent in the form of union participation in the managerial process in Europe. In some countries (for example, Germany and Sweden) union and worker participation in management is now mandated by law.

Unfortunately, McGregor himself had to abandon the style he espoused in his job as college president, and one of his strong supporters, Warren Bennis, also found that the theory Y assumptions do not apply in all situations. Moreover, recent studies show that most leaders tend to act on theory X assumptions at one time and theory Y assumptions at other times. In reviewing the literature on the subject, Stogdill concludes on the basis of several studies that the data

" . . . do not support the hypothesis that group productivity and cohesion are higher under permissive, *Theory Y* types of leader behavior than under more restrictive, *Theory X* patterns of behavior."[6]

Other Humanistic Approaches. Several major theorists emerged during the late 1950s and early 1960s who capitalized on the humanistic approach to leadership development. Among the most important was Rensis Likert,[7] who held that an employee-centered style of leadership (system 4) based on trust and participation will produce not only greater employee satisfaction but also increased organizational effectiveness.

Stimulating Employee Action. What, specifically, can the manager do to enhance employee contributions to organizational goal attainment? Generally one of two actions prevails.[8]

1. The manager can initiate structural changes in the physical working conditions, such as facilitating employee interactions with managers (e.g., common lounge and eating spaces), attending to job content, and reducing hierarchical organizational structure.

2. The manager can make changes in the organizational process, including the development of an organizational climate which recognizes and rewards employee contributions, the enhancement of interpersonal communication between superior and subordinate, acceptance of employee ideas, and the involvement of employees in decision making.

Leader as Facilitator. Likert[9] sees one important leader function as that of a "linking pin" between organizational levels. As such, the leader can act as a facilitator for the organization in planning, coordinating, identifying the needs of the organization at different levels, and translating these needs into task accomplishment by obtaining the employees' commitment to the organizational goals.

T-Group Training. One important outgrowth of the humanistic management approach has been the so-called *laboratory, sensitivity,* or *T-group* training. In large part as a response to a perceived need to humanize management, a number of well-known theorists and researchers in the leadership area, including, among others, Warren Bennis, Edgar Schein, and Chris Argyris, developed the T (training)-group [*see also* Laboratory (sensitivity) training]. Over the past 25 years, tens of thousands of managers have attended training programs which purported (1) to effect a change in values so that human factors and feelings came to be considered as legitimate and (2) to assist in developing skills among managers in order to increase interpersonal competence.[10]

In his summary of the literature in Stogdill's authoritative *Handbook of Leadership*, Bass, while acknowledging that T-group training does appear to

change attitudes toward subordinates, is quick to point out that there is shallow support for suggesting that individuals are more effective as leaders as a result of sensitivity training. In fact, he suggests that there is a good deal of evidence that sensitivity training may lead to *less* effective groups.[11]

In some countries, particularly Japan, the effect of such techniques appears to be far more convincing. However, the permanent employment system found in these countries also produces strong organizational loyalties necessary for productivity (*see also* Japanese Industries, Management in).[12]

The Managerial Grid®. A somewhat different approach was taken by Blake and Mouton,[13] who popularized a method of leadership training which became widely used. Although equally prescriptive in the area of humanistic development, Blake and Mouton capitalized on the findings of the Ohio State studies of leadership,[14] which demonstrated quite clearly that there are *two* fundamental dimensions of leader behavior in organizations. The first of these is *consideration of subordinates* and consists of employee-centered behaviors. The second is *initiation of structure*, sometimes referred to as task-oriented behaviors (see Fig. L-1a).

Unlike the proponents of the humanistic approach, Blake and Mouton stress that training in one dimension only—that is, in employee-centeredness—will not be sufficient to develop effective managers. Rather, the leader must also be trained in being concerned with getting the job done. This is not to say, of course, that Likert and others were unaware of or unconcerned about task-related aspects of the leadership job, but they considered this concern largely as given.

Blake and Mouton (see Fig. L-1b) provide popular terms for each of the extremes on the Grid. These are:

1. *Impoverished leadership* (1,1), which essentially represents no leadership at all.

2. *Country-club leadership* (1,9), which represents total concern for the needs of others and for creating a nonstressful work environment.

3. *Authority-obedience leadership* (9,1), which represents total concern for production with minimum concern for the people of the organization.

4. *Organization person leadership* (5,5), which reflects the maintenance of a satisfactory degree of concern, for people and for production.

5. *Team leadership* (9,9), which, of course, reflects the criterion for successful leadership—accomplishing the organizational task with committed people through a relationship of trust and respect.

To achieve the criterion—team leadership—managers, in a 5-day managerial Grid seminar, are first given a self-assessment scale to locate their current orientation on the Grid.[15] They are then provided with selected training techniques to give them the necessary skills to move toward the 9,9 style of leadership.

Although the managerial Grid has been used with mixed results in a variety of organizations, the primary support for the model comes from a year-long study of a large petroleum corporation in which 800 managers underwent 9,9 style of leadership training.[16] At the conclusion of the study, the company showed a considerable increase in profit and decrease in costs, which the authors interpreted as clear support for the Grid approach. Interpretation of the study by others, however, has pointed out critically that there was no control group upon which a comparison could be based. Consequently, other factors (e.g., a

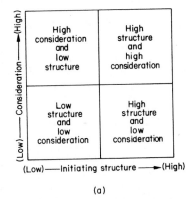

(a)

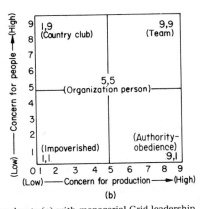

(b)

FIG. L-1 Comparison of the Ohio State quadrants (*a*) with managerial Grid leadership styles (*b*). (Paul Hersey and Kenneth H. Blanchard, *Management of Organizational Behavior: Utilizing Human Resources*, 4th ed., © 1982, pp. 89 and 90. Reprinted by permission of Prentice-Hall, Inc., Englewood Cliffs, N.J., and Gulf Publishing Co., Houston, Tex.)

generally more favorable economy) could have caused the increase in productivity.[17]

The simplicity of the Grid approach presents somewhat of a paradox. In the first place, it is very easily conceptualized by the practitioner, and it is, therefore, very appealing. This same simplicity, however, brings to mind the many exceptions that may be generated by situational differences. Is 9,9 always the best set of behaviors for the leader to follow? The entry of one situational variable, *stress*, into the model clearly demonstrates its weakness. In times of high task stress, behaviors that typically reflect concern for people may not be most appropriate. In such a situation, the group members may expect the leader to reduce the stress, which may require extreme 9,1 types of behavior.

Kerr, Schriesheim, Murphy, and Stogdill point out that researchers have uncovered a number of exceptions to the general rule that high consideration–high structuring leader behavior is to be preferred. They conclude that "the research suggests much more subtlety."[18]

In summary, therefore, prescriptive techniques that attempt to develop an ideal leader who will perform well in all situations leave much to be desired. General Patton was not notable for his consideration or his humanistic theory Y leadership approach, nor was Mahatma Ghandi known for his theory X approach. Different situations obviously call for different types of leadership.

Assessment Centers

A development in the leadership area which merits considerable interest is the assessment center method. The primary purpose of the assessment center is the selection and the promotion of managers or organizational leaders by means of interviews and such methods as role-playing and job-related simulations (*see also* Assessment center method). Although originally developed in World War II for selection of secret service agents, more recently such centers have been developed by several large corporations, notably AT&T; Sears, Roebuck and Co.; Standard Oil (Ohio); and IBM.[19] The procedures are basically atheoretical in nature and simply ask whether the center's assessment staffs are able to predict with reasonable accuracy the subsequent success of the assessee in the organization.

The most outstanding study along this line has been conducted by the staff of AT&T, which followed the careers of executives for over 15 years and is continuing the program. The results of the AT&T program have been impressive, and correlations on the order of .50 have been reported between predictions and results. While the specific procedures have been kept confidential, Bray and Grant[20] have reported that their success is well above chance levels when

evaluated on the basis of early promotion criteria and salary levels achieved after 5- and 10-year periods.

The assessment center method has its problems. It is, above all, fairly expensive, and the success of the assessment is undoubtedly due in large part to a highly trained and professional assessment staff. Where such a staff cannot be maintained, the results are likely to be poor.

The second problem is the unknown generality of the method. Does assessment work at AT&T because of the particular personnel requirements and expectations which this organization has of its managers, or would the same procedure also select as well the prospective managers of a candy factory or a hospital? At this time the extent to which the assessment center actually predicts leadership performance simply cannot be confirmed.

Situational Theories

A number of theories have been developed which tell us the conditions or organizational structures in which *any* leader is likely to be more effective than he or she would be under different conditions or situational structures. An example of these theories comes from communication net studies[21] which showed that a centralized communication net under controlled laboratory conditions is more effective for decision making than decentralized communication, regardless of the leader's style. Other theories prescribe a pyramidal organizational structure, proper span of control, line-staff relationships, or still other conditions. These are not leadership theories in the usual sense, however, and will not be discussed here.

Interactional and Contingency Theories

The term *contingency* has become something of a buzz word in the leadership and management literature. Essentially, *contingency* means that successful performance depends on the interaction of leader behavior *and* the given situation. That is, leader behavior that is successful in one situation may not be successful in another. Among the wide variety of theoretical positions that have been described as contingency theories are House's path-goal theory, Hersey and Blanchard's situational leadership theory, Vroom and Yetton's normative decision-making theory, and Fiedler's contingency model.

Path-Goal Theory. This theory[22] constitutes an extension of motivation theory and, in particular, the so-called "instrumentality theories." The theory is based on the premise that employees have certain goals which are meaningful and important to them and that these goals can be either intrinsically or extrinsically related to the work itself. That is, either the work itself may be motivating (e.g., the challeng-

ing nature of the managerial job) or the rewards associated with the work may be seen as desirable (e.g., the high pay and status of managerial jobs). The hypothesis is that employees make subjective estimates of the probability of attaining these valued goals. For example, employees may estimate how likely it is that they will find the work itself socially stimulating (a valued goal). If the likelihood is small, the employee may seek this goal elsewhere in ways which may be counterproductive to organizational aspirations. For example, the worker may spend time socializing with fellow workers rather than getting the job done.

According to the path-goal theory, the leader has the task of providing the subordinates either with the goals themselves (the rewards they seek) or with the means for attaining these goals by training, coaching, removing roadblocks, or guidance. In other words, the effect the leader has becomes *contingent* upon the psychological state of the particular subordinate and the situation in which leader and subordinate find themselves. House and Dressler cite an example of a subordinate who has a high need for affiliation and social approval, and they predict that this subordinate will find considerate behavior on the part of the leader to be a source of satisfaction.

Though several studies seem to provide support for this contingency approach, how to translate the theory into a usable prescription for the practitioner is still unclear at this point.

Situational Leadership Theory. Hersey and Blanchard[23] developed a model of leadership effectiveness that attempts to relate the maturity of the group to the prescribed leader behaviors. As in the path-goal theory, the important leader behaviors are defined as consideration and structuring.

Hersey and Blanchard hold that leaders must modify their behaviors as the maturity of their group changes. Maturity may be broken down further into (1) the members' ability to do the job (called *job maturity*) and (2) the members' motivation or willingness to do the job (called *psychological maturity*).[24] The members may be high in both, neither, or one but not the other (see maturity scale in Fig. L-2).

Situational leadership theory predicts a curvilinear (bell-shaped) relationship between group maturity and appropriateness of the leader's behavior. As can be seen in Fig. L-2, with an immature work group (perhaps a newly formed one with little or no training which shows an unwillingness to assume responsibility) the appropriate behavior of the leader is to be very directive and authoritarian, with very little concern for interpersonal maintenance. As the group begins to learn its job and mature along the listed dimensions, it is hypothesized that the leaders must maintain their concern with the task but must also begin to increase considerate behaviors. As maturity increases even further, the need for both structure (task behavior) and consideration (relationship

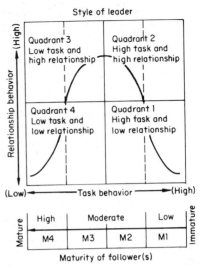

FIG. L-2 Maturity level and appropriate leader behavior. (Paul Hersey and Kenneth H. Blanchard, *Management of Organizational Behavior*, 4th ed., Prentice-Hall, Inc., Englewood Cliffs, N.J., 1982. Adapted by permission.)

behavior) decreases until, when the group is fully matured, the need for both, in theory, subsides completely.

In this last case, the leader's function is primarily that of a linking pin, a point of contact between echelons, planning future group activities and coordinating with various outside agencies or peers in order to facilitate the smooth functioning of the group. Such organizational phenomena as personnel turnover, a reorganization, or a change of mission may of course reduce the group's maturity—again requiring leader-specific action.

Hersey and Blanchard developed an instrument designed to give feedback on leadership style. By eliciting reactions to 12 written leadership situations, leader effectiveness and adaptability description (LEAD) purports to measure the individual's dominant leadership style based on the four quadrants of the Ohio State studies (see Fig. L-1a) as well as the associated "supporting style."[25]

Whether leaders are able to change their consideration or structuring behavior at will remains a question. Above all, however, virtually no known empirical research supports the theory, and the prescriptions are highly speculative.

A Normative Model of Decision Making. A quite different approach is taken by Vroom and Yetton[26] in their development of a normative theory of decision making. This is a highly detailed, real-world–oriented model which prescribes in detail the decisions a manager must make under various conditions in order to be effective. Implicit in the Vroom-Yetton argument are the assumptions that

better decision making on the part of the leader will result in greater productivity and that the leader is able to diagnose accurately the conditions in the situation which demand various types of reactions.

As is true for other interactional approaches, the Vroom-Yetton model predictions are *contingent* upon certain situational variables. It prescribes totally authoritarian procedures under some conditions (AI, AII), participative input of employees in others (CI, CII), and total collaboration with employees in still others (GII).

The model is represented by the rather complex lattice or decision tree shown in Fig. L-3. Eight considerations point the leader to the acceptable use of subordinates in the decision-making process. These are reflected in the form of questions shown in Fig. L-3 (A through G). In oversimplified form, if the problem at issue will have limited consequences on the people of the organization and the leader has all the information needed to solve the problem, he or she is advised to use an authoritative style of decision making. On the other hand, if the solution will have important consequences for subordinates, some degree of participation is required.

Another variable in the theory is time-efficient behavior. Essentially, the criterion for use of these decision-making behaviors (AI through GII) is the degree of pressure for a solution to the problem. Method AI, the authoritarian approach, is the most time efficient, while method GII, involving total group participation, is least time efficient. Conversely, GII is most developmental for employees, while AI is least developmental.

There are two fundamental problems with the Vroom-Yetton model:

1. While one would agree to the commonsense notion that decision making is an important leadership function, its relationship to overall organizational performance is not yet established. The evidence up to this point only shows that in retrospect successful managers describe themselves as having made decisions which are in conformance with the model.

2. The model assumes a great deal of flexibility on the part of leaders. Are they capable of changing their behavior as freely from an authoritative mode to a fully participative mode? Can all leaders effectively elicit the type of participative problem solving which the GII decision approach requires? Experience suggests that some people have a great deal of difficulty letting anybody else in on the decision-making act, while others find it very difficult to make their decisions without consultation and extensive discussion. The final verdict on this method must await convincing empirical studies that show improvement in organizational performance.

The Contingency Model

This theory holds that the effectiveness of a task group or of an organization depends upon two main factors: (1) the motivation of the leader (leadership style) and (2) the degree to which the situation gives the leader control and influence.

Leader Motivation. The leader's motivational structure (leadership style) is measured by the least-preferred coworker scale (LPC). This score is obtained by asking an individual to think of all people with whom he or she has ever worked and then to describe the *one* person who has been the *most* difficult to work with. The description of the least-pre-

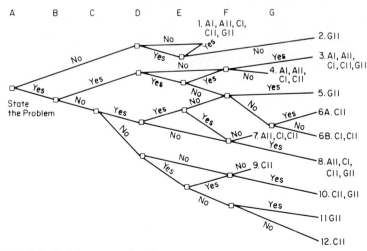

FIG. L-3 Decision-process flow chart.

ferred coworker is made on an 18-item, 8-point, bipolar adjective scale. The LPC score is the sum of the 18-item scores, for example,

Friendly $\underline{\ \ }:\underline{\ \ }:\underline{\ \ }:\underline{\ \ }:\underline{\ \ }:\underline{\ \ }:\underline{\ \ }:\underline{\ \ }:$ unfriendly
$\qquad\quad\ 8\ \ 7\ \ 6\ \ 5\ \ 4\ \ 3\ \ 2\ \ 1$

Pleasant $:\underline{\ \ }:\underline{\ \ }:\underline{\ \ }:\underline{\ \ }:\underline{\ \ }:\underline{\ \ }:\underline{\ \ }:$ unpleasant
$\qquad\quad\ \ 8\ \ 7\ \ 6\ \ 5\ \ 4\ \ 3\ \ 2\ \ 1$

High-LPC persons, that is, individuals who describe their least-preferred coworker in relatively positive terms, are primarily relationship-motivated. Low-LPC persons, who describe their least-preferred coworker in very negative rejecting terms, are basically task-motivated. The LPC score is not a description of leader behavior since the behavior of high- and low-LPC people varies as their control of the situation changes. Rather, it is a measure of goals and motivation (leadership style) or the leader's approach to the management situation.

Relationship-motivated people seem more open, more approachable, and more like McGregor's theory Y managers.[27] The task-motivated leaders tend to be more controlled and more controlling persons even though they may be as well liked and as pleasant as their relationship-motivated colleagues.

The median of 23 studies on LPC showed that the test-retest reliability coefficient was $+.64$.[28] That is, changes in LPC may occur, but in the absence of major upsets in the individual's life, changes tend to be gradual and relatively small.

Leadership Situation. The second variable, situational control or situational favorableness,[29] indicates the degree to which the situation gives leaders (1) control and influence and (2) the ability to predict the consequences of their behavior.[30]

Situational control is measured on the basis of three subscales. These are the degree to which

1. The leader feels supported by group members (leader-member relations).

2. The task is clear cut, programmed, and measurable (task structure).

3. The leader's position provides means by which compliance from subordinates can be obtained (position power).

Normative scores exist for each of the three dimensions, and their combination leads to an eightfold classification of situational control from very favorable (octant I) to relatively unfavorable (octant VIII) for the leader. A more recently used method for computing situational control is by the formula: Situational control = 4 (leader-member relations score) + 2 (task structure score) + position power score. The weighting of these three dimensions has been supported by several studies.[31]

The Leader-Situation Interaction. A schematic description of the contingency model is given in Fig. L-4. The leader's situational control is indicated on

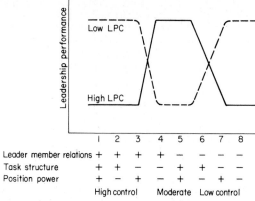

FIG. L-4 Schematic representation of the contingency model.

	1	2	3	4	5	6	7	8
Leader member relations	+	+	+	+	−	−	−	−
Task structure	+	+	−	−	+	+	−	−
Position power	+	−	+	−	+	−	+	−

the horizontal axis, extending from high control on the left to low control on the right side of the graph. The vertical axis indicates the leader's or the group's performance. The solid line is the performance curve of the relationship-motivated (high-LPC) leader, while the broken line indicates the performance of the task-motivated (low-LPC) leader.

Influence of Situations. These curves indicate that relationship-motivated as well as task-motivated leaders perform well under some conditions but not under others. Therefore, it is not accurate to speak of a good or a poor leader. Rather, a leader may perform well in one situation and poorly in another. Holding job skills constant, outstanding directors of research teams do not necessarily make good production supervisors, and good production managers may make poor advertising executives.

Influence of Job Assignment. The second major implication of Fig. L-4 is that the performance of leaders depends as much on the situation to which the organization assigns them as on the leadership style they bring to the job. As can be seen, certain leaders perform better with less rather than with more situational control. These are, for example, the people who constantly need the challenge of a new assignment in order to do well and who become stale and bored when they stay too long on the same job.

Validity of Contingency Model Predictions. A number of studies have tested the hypotheses derived from the contingency model and reviews of the literature indicate considerable support for the concepts proposed by this theory.[32]

Toward a Dynamic Theory of Leadership. Leadership must be seen as a dynamic process. Individuals change as they gain experience, training, and new perspectives about their job. Even more, however, organizations change. New personnel assignments, reorganization, and changes in the organizational mission demand a constant reassessment of a system in flux.

Impact of Experience on Performance. The schematic representation of the contingency model (Fig. L-4) illustrates the dynamic nature of the contingency model: As the leader's situational control changes, so will the match between leadership style and situational control and hence the performance of the leader. Therefore, various predictions can be made about the changes in leadership performance which are likely to occur as a result of events which take place in the organization or as a consequence of changes in the leader's own ability to control the situation.

The contingency model thus explains, in large part the lack of a consistent relationship between leadership experience and leadership performance.[33] It is not unusual, after all, for some young and aggressive managers and supervisors to get worse rather than better with each year of additional experience. The model suggests that some of these managers have been permitted to remain on their job too long and that they should have been rotated to a more challenging position which provides a better match between their leadership style and the situation.

Impact of Task Training on Performance. The model also predicts the effects of task training on leadership performance. This type of training should increase the structure of the task and hence the leader's situational control. A study by Chemers, Rice, Sundstrom, and Butler[34] supports this view. In this study, ROTC and psychology students participated in an experiment which involved deciphering a series of coded messages. Teams were divided into those led by high- and by low-LPC leaders, with half of each subgroup receiving simple but effective training on decoding.

The group-climate scores, indicating leader-member relations, were poor, largely because of the mixed ROTC and psychology student membership and the unexpected pressure which the officers in charge of the ROTC unit brought to bear on the leaders to perform well. The position power of the leader was low since this was a volunteer group, and the task structure for the untrained leaders was also low, but it was high for those who had been given task training.

The theory predicts that the task-motivated leaders should outperform the relationship-motivated leaders in the low situational-control condition (no task training), while the relationship-motivated leaders should outperform the task-motivated leaders in the trained condition. As Fig. L-5 shows, this was the case.

Leader Selection. The contingency model also has some important implications in leadership selection. Obviously, if the performance of leaders changes as they gain in experience or acquire appropriate training, different selection policies must be adopted. Specifically, the organization must ask, (1) Do we want leaders who will perform well right now, but who may become less effective over time? (2) Do

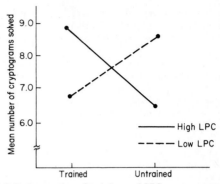

FIG. L-5 Interaction of training and LPC on group productivity. (From M. M. Chemers, R. W. Rice, E. Sundstrom, and W. M. Butler, "Leader Esteem for the Least Preferred Coworker Score, Training, and Effectiveness: An Experimental Examination," *Journal of Personality and Social Psychology*, vol. 31, no. 3, 1975, pp. 401–409. Reprinted by permission of the publisher.)

we want leaders who may not do so well in the beginning but who will later become top performers? The theory provides a framework for the development of more rational policies and procedures in the field of work force utilization and planning.

Shortcomings. As is true of the other models, the contingency model is not without valid criticism, but most of the criticism seems to stem from its derivation—its research base and Fiedler's interpretation (e.g., the model is a data-built model rather than a conceptualized model). Others feel that LPC is not a personality variable at all and that events such as training actually modify the leader and not the situation, as Fiedler proposes.[35]

The contingency model, however, is a compelling concept for the practitioner who is bent on improving organizational performance by selectively training subordinate leaders and by modifying certain elements of the situation rather than by attempting to change the leader's personality. To this end, the contingency model has been translated into a practical training program.

The Leader Match Concept

Fiedler, Chemers, and Mahar[36] developed a self-paced leadership training manual based on the notion that it is difficult, if not impossible, for leaders to change their leadership style every time their leadership situation changes. In contrast, it is much easier (1) to teach leaders to diagnose the situations in which they are likely to perform best and (2) to modify aspects of the situation so that it appropriately matches their leadership style.

The training, which takes about 6 to 8 hours of reading and responding time, first asks the individual to complete an LPC scale which he or she scores and interprets. The trainee is then taught how to fill out various measures which indicate leader-member relations, task structure, and position power, and how to compute situational control. The final sections provide detailed instructions on (1) *modifying the situation* so that it matches leadership style and (2) *applying the training* to subordinate leaders by changing their situational control to match leadership style.

Validation Studies. The leader match training program has been successfully validated in field as well as in experimental studies. The validation studies also provide evidence that the contingency model enables us to understand such previously puzzling findings as the fact that leadership experience typically does not correlate with leadership performance or that leadership training has not yielded the promised results. It also explains why rotation and transfer seem to improve the performance of some managers but decrease that of others. Above all, the contingency model training demonstrates that it is possible to improve leadership performance by teaching the leaders to diagnose and modify the leadership situation to match their leadership style. In effect, if an organization can teach leaders how to avoid or modify situations in which they are likely to fail, they are bound to be successful.

Unresolved Problems

None of the theories examined here covers the entire range of leadership problems. Some positions concentrate on the growth, well-being, and satisfaction of group members; others are more concerned with improving performance. Yet, such positions as, for example, path-goal theory, the decision-making theory, and the contingency model are not essentially incompatible in their implications. In addition, other important issues are just now beginning to claim the attention of researchers. These include the part played by moral values, inspiration, and commitment or intelligence and task abilities in determining organizational performance.

It is fairly clear at this time that the field of leadership is becoming considerably more cognitive. Studies of attribution[37] have shown that the evaluation of leadership performance depends in part on the eventual outcome. Thus, nurses who accidentally left a bed rail down were judged much more harshly if their patient fell out of bed and injured himself than if the patient did not fall out of the bed.

Fiedler, Potter, Zais, and Knowlton[38] conducted a series of studies of military personnel on the contribution of intellectual abilities and organizational experience to performance. These studies showed that stress with the immediate superior substantially decreased the correlation between leader intelligence

and performance but increased the contribution of experience. Low stress, on the other hand, led to high contribution of leader intelligence but a low contribution of leader experience to performance. In other words, when stress was high, leaders used their experience but not their intelligence; when stress was low, they used their intelligence but not their experience. Similar studies should clarify the role of intellectual abilities and job knowledge, which have been almost entirely neglected in leadership theory up to this point.

See also Assessment center method; Authority, responsibility, and accountability; Communications, organizational; Delegation; Interpersonal relationships; Japanese industries, management in; Laboratory (sensitivity) training; Management theory, science, and approaches; Managerial grid; Motivation in organizations; Theory X and theory Y.

NOTES

[1] R. Stogdill, "Personal Factors Associated with Leadership: A Survey of the Literature," *Journal of Psychology*, vol. 25, pp. 35–71, 1948; R. M. Stogdill, *The Handbook of Leadership*, The Free Press, New York, 1974.

[2] R. D. Mann, "A Review of the Relationships Between Personality and Performance in Small Groups," *Psychological Bulletin*, vol. 56, 1959, pp. 241–270.

[3] B. M. Bass, *Stogdill's Handbook of Leadership*, The Free Press, New York, 1981.

[4] D. McGregor, *The Human Side of Enterprise*, McGraw-Hill, New York, 1960.

[5] C. Argyris, *Six Presidents: Increasing Leadership Effectiveness*, John Wiley, New York, 1976; W. G. Bennis, "Goals and Meta-Goals of Laboratory Training," in W. G. Bennis, D. E. Berlew, E. H. Schein, and F. I Steele (eds.), *Interpersonal Dynamics*, 3d ed., The Dorsey Press, Homewood, Ill., 1973; T. J. Peters and R. H. Waterman, Jr., *In Search of Excellence*, Harper and Row, New York, 1982.

[6] R. M. Stogdill, *The Handbook of Leadership*, p. 375.

[7] R. Likert, *New Patterns of Management*, McGraw-Hill, New York, 1961.

[8] R. A. Sutermeister, *People and Productivity*, 3d ed., McGraw-Hill, New York, 1976, p. 107.

[9] Likert, op. cit.

[10] W. G. Bennis and E. H. Schein, "Principles and Strategies in the Use of Laboratory Training for Improving Social Systems," *Personal and Organizational Change Through Group Methods*, John Wiley, New York, 1965, p. 339.

[11] B. M. Bass, op. cit. p. 563.

[12] J. C. Abegglen, *Management and Worker: The Japanese Solution*, Sophia University, Tokyo, 1973.

[13] R. R. Blake and J. S. Mouton, *The Managerial Grid*, Gulf Publishing, Houston, 1964; R. R. Blake and J. S. Mouton, *Building a Dynamic Corporation Through Grid Organizational Development*, Addison-Wesley, Reading, Mass., 1969.

[14] R. M. Stogdill and A. E. Coons, *Leader Behavior: Its Description and Measurement*, Ohio State University, Bureau of Business Research, Columbus, Ohio, 1957.

[15] Blake and Mouton, *The Managerial Grid*, p. 1.

[16] R. R. Blake, J. S. Mouton, J. S. Barnes, and L. E. Greiner, "Breakthrough in Organizational Development," *Harvard*

Business Review, vol. 42, November–December 1964, p. 136.

[17]O. Behling and C. Schriesheim, *Organizational Behavior: Theory, Research and Application,* Allyn and Bacon, Boston, 1967, pp. 330–336.

[18]S. Kerr, C. A. Schriesheim, C. J. Murphy, and R. M. Stogdill, "Toward a Contingency Theory of Leadership Based Upon the Consideration and Initiating Structure Literature," *Organizational Behavior and Human Performance,* vol. 12, 1974, p. 63.

[19]W. C. Byham, "The Assessment Center as an Aid in Management Development," *Training and Development Journal,* December 1971.

[20]D. W. Bray and D. L. Grant, "The Assessment Center in the Measurement of Potential for Business Management," *Psychological Monographs,* vol. 80 (17), 1966.

[21]H. J. Leavitt, "Some Effects of Certain Communications Patterns on Group Performance," *Journal of Abnormal and Social Psychology,* vol. 46, 1951, pp. 38–50.

[22]R. J. House, "A Path Goal Theory of Leader Effectiveness," *Administrative Science Quarterly,* vol. 16, 1971, pp. 312–338; R. J. House and G. Dressler, "The Path-Goal Theory of Leadership: Some *post hoc* and *a priori* Tests," in J. G. Hunt and L. L. Larson (eds.), *Contingency Approaches to Leadership,* Southern Illinois University Press, Carbondale, 1974.

[23]P. Hersey and K. H. Blanchard, *Management of Organizational Behavior,* 4th ed., Prentice-Hall, Englewood Cliffs, N.J., 1982.

[24]Ibid.

[25]P. Hersey and K. H. Blanchard, "Leader Effectiveness and Adaptability Description," in J. W. Pfeiffer and J. E. Jones (eds.), *The 1976 Annual Handbook for Facilitators,* University Associates, LaJolla, Calif., 1976, pp. 87–99.

[26]V. Vroom and P. Yetton, *Leadership and Decision Making,* The University of Pittsburgh Press, Pittsburgh, 1973.

[27]L. K. Michaelsen, "Leader Orientation, Leader Behavior, Group Effectiveness and Situational Favorability: An Empirical Extension of the Contingency Model," *Organizational Behavior and Human Performance,* vol. 9, 1973, pp. 226–245.

[28]R. W. Rice, "Psychometric Properties of the Esteem for Least Preferred Co-worker (LPC Scale)," *Academy of Management Review,* vol. 3, 1978, pp. 100–118.

[29]F. E. Fiedler, *A Theory of Leadership Effectiveness,* McGraw-Hill, New York, 1967.

[30]D. M. Nebeker, "Situational Favorability and Environmental Uncertainty: An Integrative Study," *Administrative Science Quarterly,* vol. 20, 1975, pp. 281–294.

[31]Ibid.

[32]M. J. Strube and J. E. Garcia, *A Meta-Analytic Investigation of Fiedler's Contingency Model of Leadership Effectiveness,* University of Utah, Salt Lake City, 1981; M. M. Chemers and G. J. Skrzypek, "An Experimental Test of the Contingency Model of Leadership Effectiveness," *Journal of Personality and Social Psychology,* vol. 24, 1972, pp. 172–177; F. E. Fiedler, P. M. Bons, and L. L. Hastings, "The Utilization of Leadership Resources," in W. T. Singleton and P. Spurgeon (eds.), *Measurement of Human Resources,* Taylor and Francis, London, 1975, pp. 233–234.

[33]F. E. Fiedler, "Leadership Experience and Leader Performance—Another Hypothesis Shot to Hell," *Organizational Behavior and Human Performance,* vol. 5, 1970, pp. 1–14.

[34]M. M. Chemers, R. W. Rice, E. Sundstrom, and W. Butler,

"Leader Esteem for the Least Preferred Coworker Score, Training and Effectiveness: An Experimental Examination," *Journal of Personality and Social Psychology,* vol. 31, 1975, pp. 401–409.

[35]S. Kerr and A. Harlan, "Predicting the Effects of Leadership Training and Experience from the Contingency Model: Some Remaining Problems," *Journal of Applied Psychology,* vol. 57, 1973, pp. 114–117.

[36]F. E. Fiedler, M. M. Chemers, and L. Mahar, *Improving Leadership Effectiveness: The Leader Match Concept,* John Wiley, New York, 1976.

[37]S. G. Green and T. R. Mitchell, "Attributional Processes of Leaders in Leader-Member Interactions," *Organizational Behavior and Human Performance,* vol. 23, 1979, pp. 429–458.

[38]F. E. Fiedler, E. H. Potter, M. M. Zais, and W. A. Knowlton, "Organizational Stress and the Use and Misuse of Managerial Intelligence and Experience," *Journal of Applied Psychology,* vol. 64, 1979, pp. 635–647.

PAUL M. BONS, *Colonel, U.S. Army (retired)*

FRED E. FIEDLER, *University of Washington*

Learning (Experience) Curves

Improvement is a way of life. As any task or activity is repeated, the individual or organization should become more proficient at it. In particular, the cost of performing the activity should decrease as the activity is repeated.

The learning curve (often called an experience, improvement, or manufacturing process curve) is a concept that quantitatively models the amount of cost reduction with increases in volume so that future costs can be predicted in advance and used for management decision making.

Although Wright[1] developed the learning curve in terms of manufacturing direct labor costs, the learning curve was later shown to apply to total manufacturing costs[2] and then to all costs.[3] Attempts to measure total cost reductions, including overhead costs, are often obscured by the accounting system, although Bhada[4] and Morse[5] have suggested useful approaches.

Principles. The concept of the learning curve is straightforward: as the quantity of output is doubled, the cost per unit of output is decreased by a constant rate. That is, for an 80 percent learning curve, the cost of the ten-thousandth unit is 80 percent of the cost of the five-thousandth unit; the cost of the twenty-thousandth unit is 80 percent of the cost of the ten-thousandth unit, and so on.

An 80 percent learning curve for a hypothetical product is shown on an arithmetic scale in Fig. L-6 and on a double logarithmic scale in Fig. L-7. The log-log scale is a straight line, reflecting a constant decrease in cost, and is most useful for prediction.

A major question is the slope of the cost reduction line. Wright, in his original work, found an 80 per-

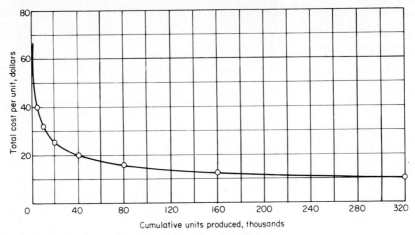

FIG. L-6 Eighty percent learning curve: arithmetic scale.

cent rate.[6] Hirschmann suggested that the labor-machine ratio determined the slope; that is, a 75 percent labor–25 percent machine mix gave an 80 percent curve, a 50-50 mix an 85 percent slope, and a 25-75 mix a 90 percent slope.[7] For total costs, it is suggested that the slope is a function of both the product and the industry, with values varying in the 70 to 95 percent range.[8]

Successful Applications. The learning curve was first developed for aircraft assembly. It is so widely used in airframe manufacture that it is required by the U.S. government in dealing with prime contractors and by these contractors in dealing with their suppliers.[9] Abernathy notes its applicability in automobile manufacture,[10] while Hirschmann

details its occurrence in petroleum refining, large plant maintenance, electrical power generation, basic steel output, and so on.[11] The Boston Consulting Group provides total cost data on 24 selected successful products, including transistors, diodes, integrated circuits, ethylene, polyvinylchlorides, and aluminum.[12] Additional applications have been widely noted in industrial and production engineering publications.

Successful application implies that the learning curve cost-reduction concept has been shown to apply to specific products. The firm's management may or may not recognize the fact and may or may not use it in formal future decision making such as price and profit planning.

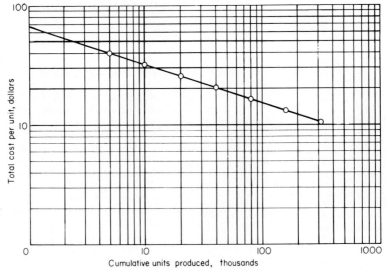

FIG. L-7 Eighty percent learning curve: log-log scale.

Application Opportunities and Techniques.
The widespread use of the learning curve suggests its applicability to almost any product. The Boston Consulting Group goes so far as to note that "the relationship has been analyzed for virtually every client over the past five years. The evidence is overwhelming. The relationship always exists."[13] Failure to identify the effect, they note, is usually a result of poor product market segment identification, rapid shifts in the importance of cost factors, use of an allocation cost accounting system, and failure of management to recognize that cost reductions can be predicted.

A straightforward framework can be used to estimate a learning curve:

1. A specific product or product market is identified.
2. The cost accounting system is modified to identify specific costs associated with the product.
3. The slope of the cost reduction curve is determined by analyzing the product's past history, the history of other similar products of the firm, and by other industry data available.
4. A curve is drawn by plotting unit cost versus total volume. From this curve, future unit costs at any volume level can be estimated and used in price and profit planning.

Evaluation. The learning curve is a valuable tool to predict future costs. As with any other tool, it should not be applied blindly. Although often used for small quantities of output (two or four aircraft), there are some suggestions that abnormal start-up costs may give a false cost picture. In addition, as a product is phased out, eliminating overhead costs and ending manufacturing costs may cause a curve variation. Also, changes in product characteristics, manufacturing technology, and so on, over a long-lived high-volume product could result in a change in slope of the cost curve.

Although learning assumes an inherent susceptibility of an activity to improve, no cost reduction will occur unless the cost reduction potential is exploited. Normal cost reduction techniques such as methods improvements, time studies, value engineering, and so on, are necessary to achieve these cost reductions. Most important, however, is a management environment aimed at stimulating employees to reduce costs by improving products and methods. In this context, the learning curve is a tool for estimating future costs for cost reduction goal setting as well as for price and profit planning.

See also Contracts management; Development and training, employee; Line of balance (LOB); Marginal income analysis; Product planning and development; Production planning and control; Productivity measurement; Purchasing management.

NOTES

[1]T. P. Wright, "Factors Affecting the Cost of Airplanes," *Journal of Aeronautical Science*, February 1936, pp. 122–128.

[2]Winfred B. Hirschmann, "Profit from the Learning Curve," *Harvard Business Review*, vol. 42, no. 1, January–February 1964, pp. 125–139.

[3]*Perspectives on Experience*, Boston Consulting Group, Boston, 1972.

[4]Yezdi K. Bhada, "Dynamic Cost Analysis," *Management Accounting*, vol. 52, no. 1, July 1970, pp. 11–14.

[5]Wayne J. Morse, "Reporting Production Costs that Follow the Learning Curve Phenomenon," *The Accounting Review*, vol. 47, no. 4, October 1972, pp. 761–773.

[6]Wright, loc. cit.

[7]Hirschmann, op. cit., pp. 126–128.

[8]*Perspectives on Experience*, loc. cit.

[9]Wright, loc. cit.; Hirschmann, loc. cit.; William J. Abernathy and Kenneth Wayne, "Limits of the Learning Curve," *Harvard Business Review*, vol. 52, no. 5, September–October 1974, pp. 109–119.

[10]Abernathy, loc. cit.

[11]Hirschmann, loc. cit.

[12]*Perspectives on Experience*, op. cit., pp. 69–101.

[13]Ibid, p. i.

REFERENCES

Good, T.: "Calculating and Using Learning Curves," *Accountant*, vol. 186, January 21, 1982, pp. 22–34.

Roberts, P.: "A Theory of the Learning Process," *Journal of the Operations Research Society*, vol. 34, January 1983, pp. 71–79.

JACKSON E. RAMSEY, *James Madison University*

Leasing, Equipment*

Equipment leasing became popular in the 1950s and has developed into a fast growth industry. This section discusses the advantages and disadvantages of equipment leasing, types of leases, and the basic tax aspects of leasing and provides a financial model for analyzing the lease-versus-purchase decision.

Rationale for Leasing

The decision to lease must be based on financial analysis, taking into consideration the specific needs of the firm, availability and cost of money, tax implications, and the like. Lessors have much to offer.

*Adapted, by permission of the publisher, from *Making the Lease/Buy Decision*, 2d ed., by Robert E. Pritchard and Thomas A. Hindelang, © 1984 by AMACOM Book Division, American Management Associations, New York. All rights reserved.

This fact is evidenced by the rapid growth of the equipment leasing industry. The American Association of Equipment Lessors' survey of memberships indicates that about 60 percent of its member leases are for assets costing $50,000 or more, while only 11 percent are for assets valued at less than $10,000. Generally, leasing is more economical for large-ticket items than for small because of the lessor administrative costs involved. Nonetheless, small businesses can and do lease everything from vehicles to personal computers to copy machines. Essentially anything that can be purchased can be leased.

Advantages. The advantages and disadvantages of leasing should be weighed carefully, as the relative value of each aspect of leasing will vary from company to company. The primary advantages are discussed below.

1. Leasing may be the only way to secure needed assets. Some companies do not have enough equity and/or the credit ratings necessary to borrow funds. Since leasing companies are marketing oriented (as distinguished from most banks), and since in a lease the ownership (equity interest) is retained by the lessor, many companies that are unable to borrow can lease. In such instances the financial evaluation is not utilized to choose between lease and purchase but rather is used to select the lessor offering the most advantageous lease terms.

2. Sometimes leasing may be less expensive than purchasing. There are three reasons. First, most lessors are large companies with excellent credit ratings and therefore may borrow at the most advantageous terms. The cost of borrowing to leasing companies is frequently 3 to 5 percent less than the cost to smaller businesses. Such differentials in borrowing rates can provide real savings to lessees. Second, nearly all equipment may be depreciated rapidly under the guidelines of the Accelerated Cost Recovery System. Further, investment tax credits may be taken. The relative value of the depreciation and credits varies from firm to firm, but the cost benefits of both are normally passed to the lessee. Thus, if a company is not able to take full advantage of the tax benefits of ownership, leasing may provide a way to enjoy those benefits. Third, the lessor may be able to secure the asset for a lower price. Examples of this situation are found among manufacturers which lease their products, such as vehicles, machinery, or equipment. Many manufacturers own captive leasing companies (called vendor lessors) which are organized to lease the manufacturers' products.

3. Maintenance may cost less when equipment is leased. Specialized equipment requiring particular expertise, tools, etc., to maintain may be serviced at a lower cost by a lessor. Not all companies perform maintenance but most vendor lessors do, while banks and independent lessors generally do not.

4. Leasing can smooth cash flow. Lease payments are normally constant throughout the life of the lease. This contrasts with the typical cash flow patterns associated with ownership (varying depreciation allocations from year to year and the probability of fluctuating interest rates). Further, leasing provides 100 percent financing, as opposed to borrowing, which requires an equity investment and an initial acquisition cash outflow to cover the down payment.

5. Leasing may avoid refinancing. Most equipment loans now incorporate balloon repayment features requiring loan renegotiation after 3 years. The frequent inclusion of balloon repayments may necessitate renegotiation two or three times over the life of the equipment and possibly at increasingly higher interest rates. Leases are usually written to cover the approximate useful life of the equipment. Further, many leases may be extended beyond their original period, normally at a lower rate.

6. Leasing may avoid the agony of borrowing. Lessors are sales oriented. They often require much less documentation than lenders, respond more rapidly, and are more open to negotiation.

7. Leasing can conserve existing credit lines.

8. Leasing reduces the risk of obsolescence. In a period of rapid technological change, ownership may result in unwanted assets as new models are introduced. A manufacturer-lessor may have sales channels available to dispose of such assets. However, the transfer of risk has a cost and the astute lessor will build a premium for potential obsolescence into the lease rate.

9. Leasing may provide periods for trial use, enabling the lessee to return the equipment if it does not meet expectations.

Disadvantages. There are two primary disadvantages to leasing.

1. Leasing almost always costs more than ownership. There are exceptions, as noted above. But lessors do have costs and do make profits and do bear the risks of ownership. These are built into the cost of leasing.

2. The lessor owns the asset at the end of the lease. Depending on the rate of inflation, possible technological obsolescence, etc., the asset may be nearly worthless or possibly have a high value at the lease end.

A thorough financial analysis must quantify the relative advantages versus the potential differences in costs at lease inception, during the life of the lease, and at its termination.

Types of Leases

The nomenclature used to identify leases is very confusing. This arises from the fact that lessors use certain names to identify leases for marketing purposes, the IRS identifies leases somewhat differently for tax purposes, and the Financial Accounting Standards Board further classifies leases for purposes of recording them on financial statements. A myriad of names such as operating, financing, capital, direct, middle-market, tax benefit transfer, and leveraged are commonly used.

For the purpose of most lessees, leases may be divided into two broad categories: operating and financial.

Operating Leases. These leases are frequently used to acquire computers, vehicles, copy machines, and other specialized equipment. Operating leases are characterized by

1. A relatively short lease term as compared with the life of the asset.
2. The availability of special services such as maintenance.
3. An option to cancel on the part of the lessee within reasonable restrictions.
4. Retention of all ownership risk by the lessor.

Financial Leases. Unlike operating leases, financial leases (as the name connotes) are leases designed to provide asset financing. The lessor extends credit to the lessee and concurrently transfers the responsibilities of ownership such as maintenance, insurance, taxes, and the life for a period roughly equal to the economic life of the asset. In most cases the lessor is a financial institution or an independent lessor and does not intend ever to take physical possession of the asset. At the end of the lease, the lessee normally re-leases or purchases the asset from the lessor.

Financial leases are normally full-payout leases. The lessor expects to recover the cost of the asset, the cost of financing, the cost of overhead, and an acceptable rate of return within the period of the lease, without relying on the salvage value of the asset. By contrast, operating leases are usually not full payout. The lessor does rely on the salvage value to cover purchase costs and achieve a profit.

Financial leases are closely analogous to mortgages wherein the payments consisting of interest and principal are constant over the life of the loan. Similarly, a financial lease payment may be thought of as consisting of two parts: a return to the lessor to recover the cost of the asset and a return the lessor requires to cover costs of money plus a profit.

Tax Aspects of Leasing

When a lease is a "true lease," as contrasted to a conditional sales contract, all the lease payments are deductible as expenses by the lessee. The lease payments are considered to be income to the lessor. The lessor may depreciate the asset, take advantage of any investment tax credits and pay tax on any recapture of depreciation and/or long-term capital gains, or enjoy a tax reduction based on any long-term capital losses at the termination of the lease.

Since passage of the Economic Recovery Tax Act of 1981 (ERTA), with its introduction of the Accelerated Cost Recovery System, it is possible to depreciate machinery and equipment fully in a period substantially less than its useful life. This rapid write-off, combined with more liberal treatment of investment tax credit, has reduced the cost of ownership. While the accelerated depreciation may only be taken by the lessor, the benefits should be enjoyed by the lessee in the form of lower lease payments. In addition, investment tax credits may either be retained by the lessor or passed through directly to the lessee. If the lessor retains the credit, the lease payments should be reduced accordingly.

ERTA also permitted the transfer of certain tax benefits through the mechanism of tax-benefit-transfer leases. Such leases were designed to assist companies facing severe financial difficulties by permitting them to sell the tax benefits of depreciation and investment tax credits. Passage of the Tax Equity and Fiscal Responsibility Act in 1982 essentially repealed tax-benefit-transfer leasing, which will be phased out completely over several years.

The Lease-Versus-Buy Decision

Within the context of the various advantages and disadvantages of leasing as described above, there are four basic issues which need to be addressed when making the lease-purchase decision:

1. Is the firm faced with a capital acquisition decision? Or has the decision been made to acquire the asset, and the firm is now faced with the problem of selecting the best financing package?
2. Have all of the cash flows related to each acquisition and financing decision been identified and estimated?
3. What is the appropriate discount rate to apply to each cash flow given the firm's cost of capital and the relative degree of risk surrounding the estimate of each cash flow?
4. What is the anticipated life of the asset within the context of its proposed use by the firm?

Figure L-8 provides a framework to assist in the **481**

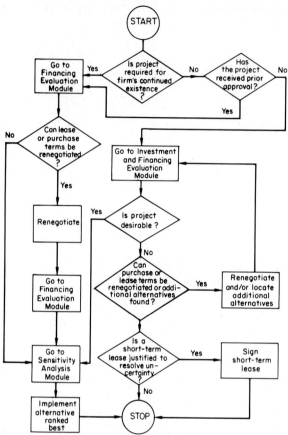

FIG. L-8 Overview of the lease-purchase decision analysis. (From Robert E. Pritchard and Thomas J. Hindelang, *Making the Lease/Buy Decision: A Guide to Leasing Under ERTA and TEFRA*, 2d ed., American Management Associations, New York, 1984.)

resolution of the four issues listed above and to deal with the possibility of utilizing a sensitivity analysis to provide for further exploration of the alternatives. Note in Fig. L-8 that two primary decision areas exist. The first, acquisition, is a capital budgeting problem. References in this area are provided at the end of the section. The second, financing, is where leasing fits into the decision model. Note further that the acquisition and financing decisions should not be made out of context since a proposed project could be rejected on the basis of normal corporate financing (equity and debt) but be acceptable when financed through a lease.

The decision process in Fig. L-8 is shown in terms of modules to assist in the logical analysis of the alternatives. The problem of asset financing (the financing module) would be called upon immediately if the firm has already decided to acquire the asset. If the decision to acquire has not been made, the acquisition and financing should be considered simultaneously (investment and financing module). The latter must examine both the expected benefits and the associated costs, while the former focuses on minimizing the costs.

Finally, as the alternatives are examined in each module, a need may arise to answer "what if" questions. "What if" questions include those relating to possible changes in sales, operating expenses, cost of capital, reinvestment rates, and the like. These questions are answered by means of a sensitivity analysis (sensitivity analysis module). Generally a sensitivity analysis is performed utilizing a computer model; otherwise the numerous calculations are very time-consuming.

Each of the modules is based on the concepts of discounted cash flow analysis. The several cash flows are discounted to their present value using discount rates appropriate to the riskiness of each. The result provides an accurate guide to both the acquisition and financing decisions.

See also Accounting, financial; Financial management, financing; Real estate management, corporate.

REFERENCES

Clark, John J., Thomas J. Hindelang, and Robert E. Pritchard: *Capital Budgeting; Planning and Control of Capital Expenditures*, 2d ed., Prentice-Hall, Englewood Cliffs, N.J., 1984.

Pritchard, Robert E., and Thomas J. Hindelang: *The Strategic Evaluation and Management of Capital Expenditures*, American Management Associations, New York, 1981.

Pritchard, Robert E., and Thomas J. Hindelang: *Making The Lease/Buy Decision: A Guide to Leasing Under ERTA and TEFRA*, 2nd ed., American Management Associations, New York, 1984.

ROBERT E. PRITCHARD, *Glassboro State College*

THOMAS J. HINDELANG, *Drexel University*

Legal Affairs, Management of Corporate

The number of attorneys employed directly by corporations more than doubled between 1970 and 1980. During this period, corporate management recognized that increasing the staff of in-house counsel can be economically advantageous. Recently, however, the phenomenal growth of the corporate legal department has come to a near standstill. A mentality of enhancing revenue by increasing the in-house corporate staff has given way to a more critical view of the efficiency and effectiveness of these departments. Concurrently, outside legal firms have started to respond to the competitive pressures generated by these new and increasingly efficient corporate legal departments. Outside firms have stimulated a drive toward lower costs, increased specialization, more efficient billing practices, and more effective marketing programs. Consequently, the management of corporate legal affairs is entering a new era in which competition will be keen and efficiency will be king.

Comparative Advantages of In-House Counsel. The objective of corporate management is to maximize the expected net revenue from various possible decision paths. Intimately associated with the selection calculus are three sets of legal concerns: (1) the requirements to comply with government statutes and regulations that may cover the various courses of action; (2) the risks that deleterious legal events may occur and the costs of preventing them; and (3) the costs of rectifying legal problems if they should happen to materialize. The in-house staff appears to have a comparative advantage in the first two areas, the so-called preventive law realm, since it can lessen the expenses of regulatory compliance, and it often can reduce the costs of dealing with the routine legal risks that affect the company.

Legal Compliance Procedures. One of the major responses by corporations to the high fees charged by outside law firms has been to increase efforts by their in-house staffs to create legal compliance procedures so that legal risks from business transactions transform into actual legal problems less frequently. Unlike outside lawyers, inside attorneys can concentrate very intensely on the full set of compliance regulations and record retention requirements that pertain to their particular corporation.

Coupled with this comparative information advantage, the in-house staff also has a more intimate understanding of the management structure and operating mechanisms of the corporation. Thus, the inside attorneys can apply their specialized knowledge to the proper executives and employees to achieve the most efficient results in terms of implementing legal compliance procedures and instituting effective record retention programs. Toward this goal of efficacious compliance, in-house counsel must (1) establish practical procedures to inform employees of the limits of permissible conduct and to monitor their compliance; (2) implement guidelines to ensure that documents needed in case of possible future litigation are not destroyed; and (3) closely follow any changes in government regulations affecting the corporation so that the above programs can be adapted swiftly to permit future compliance.

Routine Corporate Legal Affairs. In-house counsel also enjoys a competitive advantage in dealing with routine or repeated corporate legal issues. First, the inside attorney may handle similar problems which touch on the same legal grounds so often that he or she can generate almost instantaneous legal advice on these recurring issues. Second, in-house lawyers are part of the management team, and generally are well versed on the corporation's objectives, methods, personnel, and history. For general legal affairs, the attainment of this information by outside attorneys is time-consuming, expensive, and often incomplete and unsatisfactory. As part of the management team, the inside attorney knows whom to consult for information, and will have enough rapport with that person to obtain the necessary details more efficiently than outside counsel could. Third, inside attorneys are always present when a business decision has to be made. They are in attendance at corporate meetings and can deliver legal input while a business plan is under consideration. In this way, they can assist management in determining acceptable compliance cost and legal risk levels for various possible business activities. This process is more effective than one in which management first makes a business decision and then sets up a meeting with its outside counsel to approve the decision's legal viability.

Comparative Advantages of Outside Counsel. Although a sizable portion of corporate legal work can be performed most efficiently by in-house staffs, **483**

outside counsel still must play a large role in handling corporate legal affairs. Since its attorneys are usually paid on a salary basis, a corporation only will employ the requisite number of attorneys to handle its normal load of legal work. On those peak occasions when the legal work exceeds the parameters of the "base-load" staff, the excess requirements must be funneled to outside counsel.

The in-house staff is trained intensively to deal with the legal problems that most often accompany the corporation's activities. When a specialized legal concern attaches to the corporation, outside counsel, with expertise in the specialized field, should be approached to assist with the problem. Also, when the corporation is involved in a very significant legal matter, outside counsel can be valuable in verifying the quality and accuracy of the legal work performed by the in-house staff.

In addition, experience has shown that in-house counsel cannot, as yet, be used satisfactorily in certain legal areas. Most corporations have found that litigation can be handled most competently by outside counsel. Also, many corporate legal officers believe that tender offers and antitrust issues can be resolved more effectively through the use of outside counsel.

A final important instance in which outside counsel must be used is when there is a possible conflict of interest for the in-house attorney between his duty to the corporation and his allegiance to the corporation's management. In shareholder derivative suits, for instance, the in-house attorney theoretically should represent the corporation against possible misconduct by the management. However, the in-house counsel may have contributed to the management decision which eventually led to the derivative suit. In cases such as these, where the in-house staff may be biased or may have conflicting interests, the corporation should employ outside counsel for representation.

Management of the Corporate Legal Department. Currently, the major focus of corporations with respect to their corporate legal departments is on their efficiency in operations. The recession, in conjunction with deregulation, has had a profound effect. The corporate legal departments have not been immune to the overall corporate drives to cut costs across the board. In addition, corporations competing in an international context are feeling pressures to reduce domestic legal costs to the levels experienced in economies that do not have such complex legal environments.

Organization. The principal strength of the corporate law department is that it can effectively practice preventive law by being close to, if not a part of, significant business decisions. For this reason, if a corporation's decision-making units are decentralized, especially in a geographical sense, the legal department can engage in preventive law techniques

most satisfactorily by decentralizing in a similar fashion. In this way, the corporate attorneys will be present at the decision-making points.

However, decentralization of the legal department may create internal inefficiencies. Inefficiencies in space, support staff, and other resource usages are a substantial cost of multiple legal office operations. In addition, inefficiencies in legal practice itself may result from decentralization. Specialization by legal field generally leads to the most cost-effective legal solutions. In a centralized legal environment, such specialization can take place. However, in a decentralized framework, the attorneys must be legal generalists who are responsible for all the legal problems of their particular office.

Still, experience has shown that a decentralized staff is most effective in the decentralized corporation, while the centralized legal office, with full legal field specialization, is best in a centralized corporate environment. One should note, though, that the introduction of various computerized office and information linkages will improve the internal efficiencies of decentralized offices and will enable decentralized attorneys to specialize by legal field to a greater degree.

Management of Outside Attorneys. As indicated, the in-house corporate legal department frequently will have to call upon outside attorneys to meet peak demand loads, to provide special expertise, and to confirm critical legal decisions. When needed, outside attorneys must be selectively "leased" and properly managed.

The in-house counsel must be the planner and the leader of all legal operations. Outside attorneys are engaged to provide support to the inside staff; they are not an alternative to the corporate department. The duties of the outside firm must be specified clearly by the inside staff to encourage coordination between the two entities, and to prevent runaway expenses by the outside counsel. In-house counsel must make it clear that it has the final word on the legal objectives and the procedures to meet them. Periodic reviews of the outside firm's legal work product and itemized expenses should be the rule rather than the exception. In addition, all communications to the corporate business managers should be made by the in-house attorneys or strictly at the direction of the in-house counsel. This practice not only minimizes the number of repetitive communications with the business managers but also symbolically displays that in-house counsel does, indeed, run the show.

In-house counsel should start to depend less on the "retainer" system as a means of engaging outside counsel. Although there are some benefits to long-term relationships, especially in terms of the outside firm's understanding of the corporation's philosophy, rapid competitive developments in the private legal field have led to greater economies from forum shopping. Due to the tremendous growth in corporate legal departments, the advent of computerized legal clinics, the impact of microchip technology, the legalization and acceptance of law firm marketing, and the thrust of management consulting firms into the law firm domain, private law firms are entering an age of blossoming price and product competition. Law firms now are finding it necessary to establish their individual niches in the marketplace and to manage their costs strictly within that niche. This behavior is leading to various sets of competitive specialists in terms of both cost and legal expertise. Thus, for every legal problem that necessitates the use of an outside law firm, in-house counsel should take advantage of the opportunity to select a firm which most suitably meets its price, legal specialty, and support requirements.

Reduction of Internal Operating Expenses. The corporate legal department also should emphasize new methods to reduce internal operating expenses. Evolving computer technologies can have a tremendous impact on law department efficiency in terms of word processing, legal research, document searching, legal form manipulation, accounting, and communications, especially when the legal department can tap existing corporation computer facilities. The use of paralegals, rather than attorneys, to perform many routine legal tasks, such as due-diligence and blue-sky work, can lead to significant cost reductions. Also, various forms of alternative dispute settlement agreements can reduce the costs of litigation. For instance, arbitration agreements, direct negotiation without lawyers, and experimental minitrial procedures are starting to be used by corporations with some success.

See also Boards of directors, legal liability guidelines; Government regulations, business law; Patents and valuable intangible rights; Tax management.

REFERENCES

Banks, Robert S.: "Partnership Between Firms, Departments," *The National Law Journal*, vol. 5, no. 45, July 18, 1983, p. 24.

Perlman, Lawrence: "Corporate Legal Offices Must Stress Management," *Legal Times of Washington*, October 5, 1981, pp. 11–15.

"Preventive Lawyering Attracts Cost-Conscious Fans," *Legal Times of Washington*, Sept. 22, 1980, p. 28.

Reynolds, Ray: "Is In-House In?," *District Lawyer*, vol. 6, no. 5, May–June 1982, pp. 31–35.

Whitehead, G. Marc: "In-House, Outside Counsel," *The National Law Journal*, June 7, 1982, pp. 16–21.

LEE B. BURGUNDER, *California Polytechnic State University, San Luis Obispo*

Line of Balance (LOB)

A line of balance (LOB) is a charting device for planning and monitoring the progress of an order, project, or program to be completed by a target date. LOB contains elements of the program evaluation and review technique (PERT) in that the plan of operations is based upon establishment of critical dates at which materials must be on hand, contributing tasks accomplished, and subassemblies or subprojects completed. These tasks are represented by vertical bars of a length proportional to their production (or end point) requirements and are plotted sequentially on a Gantt-like vertical bar chart. The desired progress is the stairstep profile line derived by connecting the tops of the schedule bars: This profile line is the line of balance, shown in Fig. L-9. As the project is pursued, progress of each task is plotted on the LOB chart as a vertical bar (or sensor). At a particular

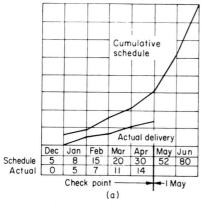

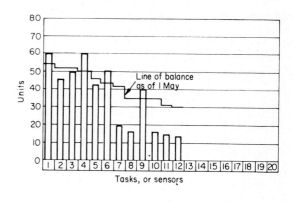

FIG. L-9 Line of balance charting: (*a*) objective chart; (*b*) line of balance chart. (Government Printing Office, Navy Special Projects Office.)

check date (May 1 in Fig. L-9) the gap between the top of a bar and the line of balance shows where a delay exception, or deficiency exists.

The LOB chart is usually studied in conjunction with an objective chart (Fig. L-9a), upon which is plotted the cumulative progress of the project (in terms of end units) toward its completion date. Figure L-9a shows that end units are far below schedule on May 1 (14 versus 30 units). Figure L-9b shows that tasks 2, 3, 5, 7, 8, 10, 11, and 12 are the critical reasons. A different line of balance is constructed for each check date and often for a number of closely related tasks (families).

See also Gantt charts; Network planning methods; Production planning and control.

REFERENCES

Dervitsiotis, Kostas N.: *Operations Management,* McGraw-Hill, New York, 1981.

Gaither, Norman: *Production and Operations Management,* 2d ed., Prentice-Hall, Englewood Cliffs, N.J., 1984.

JACKSON E. RAMSEY, *James Madison University*

Logistics, Business

Logistics is the management of the flow and interruptions in the flow of materials (raw materials, components, subassemblies, finished products, and supplies), services, and/or people associated with an enterprise. Conceptually, an *integrated business logistics system* consists of three operational areas: materials management (MM), conversion management (CM), and physical distribution management (PDM). MM is the logistical relationship between a firm and its suppliers. CM is the logistical relationship among the facilities of a firm (plant to warehouse or distribution center, plant to plant, etc.). PDM is the logistical relationship between the firm and its customers.

Basic Activities. These relationships consist of five basic activities which are common to the entire logistical process.

1. Traffic and transportation management is concerned with the physical movement of materials.

2. Inventory management entails responsibility for the quantity and variety of materials held to meet production and customer demand requirements.

3. Facility structure management involves strategic planning for the number, location, type, and size of distribution facilities (warehouse, distribution centers, and even plants).

4. Storage and materials handling management is concerned with the efficient use of inventory site space and the manual, mechanical, and/or automated means of physically handling materials.

5. Communications and information management entails the accumulation, analysis, storage, and dissemination of timely and accurate data relevant to logistical decision-making needs in an efficient and effective manner. Communications and information integrate the logistical operational areas and supporting activities into a system and enable system performance.

System Improvements. The output of logistical system performance is the provision of a clearly specified level or levels of customer service at the lowest possible total cost. The practical application of the total cost concept encourages system changes to improve performance in two ways. An improvement may increase the cost of performing one or more logistical activities, provided that the cost of performing one or more other logistical activities is reduced by an equal or greater amount such that total cost remains the same or is decreased. Alternatively, the total system cost may be permitted to increase, provided that there is an improved and more consistent level of customer service which can be used as a strategic competitive weapon to derive a greater overall profitability.

Organizational Position. The mission of the business logistics system is to provide customer service by supporting the production and marketing efforts of the firm. The logistical system is thus functionally subordinate to production and marketing, because the logistical system must respond effectively and efficiently to the operational and strategic requirements of these functions. The larger the firm and the greater the strategic importance of customer service to the nature of the business, however, the more important it becomes to position the logistics function organizationally on a par with the other major functional areas in terms of status and authority.

See also Inventory control; Inventory stock-keeping systems; Marketing, channels of distribution; Material handling; Materials management; Production planning and control.

REFERENCES

Lambert, Douglas M., and James R. Stock: *Strategic Physical Distribution Management,* Richard D. Irwin, Homewood, Ill. 1982.

Bowersox, Donald J.: *Logistical Management,* 2d ed., Macmillan, New York, 1978.

Coyle, John J., and Edward J. Bardi: *The Management of Business Logistics,* 2d ed., West Publishing Company, St. Paul, Minn., 1980.

KENNETH C. WILLIAMSON, *James Madison University*

Management, Definitions of

The most comprehensive definition views management as an integrating process by which authorized individuals create, maintain, and operate an organization in the selection and accomplishment of its aims. This basic concept has the advantage of denoting a process being carried out continuously over time. It includes the idea of a goal-oriented organization as the fundamental arena of managerial action as well as the concept of persons specifically charged with managerial responsibility.

Supporting Concepts. Other widely used definitions amplify the basic concept for use in practical settings:

1. *Management is getting things done through other people.* This definition stresses teamwork, delegation, and results.

2. *Management is partly an art and partly a science.* This definition recognizes the presence of intuitive, subjective skills in the management process and the growing importance of verified knowledge as a guide to managerial decision and action.

3. *Management is an academic and professional dis-*

cipline. This definition implies that a teachable body of knowledge is incorporated into the curricula of schools, colleges, and technical institutions. It includes the possibilities for the development of management as a profession.

4. *Management is a collective noun used to refer to the entire management group of an organization.* Used in this way, the term is convenient for designating a body of managers as a whole. For example, one may say, "the management of the Brown Corporation believes that . . ."

5. *Management is the performance of the critical functions essential to the success of an organization.* This definition essentially holds that management *is* what managers *do* in performing their roles as managers.

The first four variations of the management concept listed above are limited in scope, partial in content, and handicapped by oversimplification. The fifth definition is the most fundamental. It will now be explained in greater detail.

Management can usefully be viewed as a network of interrelated functional responsibilities. They are not a sequence of activities but rather a set of interacting activities that constitute a whole. One can single out a particular function only for analytical or descriptive purposes, but it should be recognized that activity in one function has an impact on one or more of the other functions.

The primary managerial functions are designated as planning, organizing, and controlling. Others include directing (leading), resourcing, activating, representing, coordinating, communicating, motivating, and, very important, decision making. Contributors to management knowledge do not agree on either the general or the relative importance of the various management functions. Some reject the functional approach on the grounds that the functions are only descriptive and are not precise enough for developing scientifically testable propositions. The concept of management, however, as a set of functional responsibilities performed by managers is an enduring one. Management scientists (operations researchers and decision theorists) stress decision making as the most important managerial function. Behavioral scientists focus on organization, organizational behavior, leadership, motivation, and communication. Other specialists in management utilize the traditional functions but draw upon management science and behavioral science contributors to extend and apply the functions.

The functions dramatize the differences between managerial and technical or other kinds of work. Planning, for example, is the manager's task because of the need to cope with change, but executing a plan to build a new plant also requires a grasp of technical elements such as layout, appearance, durability, and operating effectiveness. In almost every case, the manager's task is a mix of managerial (conceptual) behavior and the application of technical expertise. The higher the level of the manager, the greater is the proportion of managerial to technical content of the work.

Variations. For practical purposes, the terms *management* and *administration* are used synonymously. The term *administration* is widely employed in associations and in governmental, service, and nonprofit organizations, whereas *management* is more often used in business firms.

The term *industrial management* connotes an industrial setting, such as manufacturing, mining, or construction.

The term *entrepreneurial management* describes a type of risk-taking management geared to the development of new business enterprises or highly diversified conglomerates.

Management and Ownership. Business organizations are classified into three types according to their legal forms: (1) sole proprietorships, (2) partnerships, and (3) corporations. Management responsibilities and processes vary among the types.

In the sole proprietorship, the key manager is also likely to be the owner and to execute the two roles simultaneously. In partnerships, the active partners are the key managers as well as the owners. Both proprietorships and partnerships are generally but not necessarily small firms, with the owners actively involved in the direct management of the organization.

The management group in a corporation functions in a *fiduciary* capacity—entrusted by owners with virtually complete responsibility for running the organization. Many corporation managers are also owners by virtue of holding shares of their company's stock, but their role remains essentially that of a managerial employee of the company.

See also Audit, management; Boards of directors; Committees; Management theory, science, and approaches; Manager, definition of; Nonprofit organizations, management of; Officers, corporate; Ownership, legal forms of; Public administration.

REFERENCES

Koontz, Harold, Cyril O'Donnell, and Heinz Weihrich: *Management: A Systems and Contingency Analysis of the Managerial Functions*, 8th ed., McGraw-Hill, New York, 1984.

McFarland, Dalton E.: *Management: Principles and Practices*, 5th ed., Macmillan, New York, 1979.

Trewatha, Robert L., and M. Gene Newport: *Management*, 3d ed., Business Publications, Piano, Tex., 1982.

DALTON E. McFARLAND, *University of Alabama in Birmingham*

Management, Future of

The most exciting and challenging period of history is right now. Never before have societies, organizations, and people changed faster. No one can know for certain what the job of management will be like in the years ahead, but some futurists, management writers, and practicing managers are looking seriously at the future. Managers know that what they do or fail to do today can have an influence on the future.

Managers have inherited a great deal from the pioneers of management—Frederick W. Taylor, Henri Fayol, Chester Barnard, Douglas McGregor, Elton Mayo, and Frank and Lillian Gilbreth. But today's manager must face growing concern about social responsibilities, increasing government involvement, and increasing numbers of women and minority groups in the work force. The predictions about how society and managers will meet these new twentieth-century challenges are varied. Some scholars predict that civilization and its institutions are about to self-destruct. But others are confident that we have entered a new era in which people will not only be happier than ever before but will also create a more productive civilization.

The Manager's World in the Next Decade

The manager's job is *not* neat, routine, easygoing, clearly understood, and easy to evaluate. On the contrary—planning, organizing, and controlling functions are performed by managers in a rather hectic, fragmented, and complicated manner.

The Evidence.   The evidence as reported by practicing managers and research indicates that:

- Managers must often make decisions with incomplete information.
- Communication in organizations is often unclear and misleading.
- Considerations regarding individual differences get in the way of neat, orderly institutional programs.
- Managers need controls, but tight controls often destroy the motivation of employees.
- Innovative managerial ideas are rejected by top administrators because they are often threatening to philosophies or practices that have been in place for years.
- Groups have a significant influence on individual behavior, but many managers do not understand the characteristics and processes of groups.

In the future, the manager's job will probably be more closely scrutinized by researchers than it was during any other era. Through better and more thorough research, the manager's job will be made clearer to society. This should reduce the acceptance of the unfortunate myths that the work of managers is routine, neat, and orderly. The old cliché "Workers do, managers tell" will be revealed to be a silly misconception.[1] Managerial work described certainly requires a high level of energy, intelligence, and determination. It is managers who must convert technological, social, economic, and political changes into programs that improve the quality of citizens' lives. Managers must *do* and continue to *do* so that acceptable performance is achieved.

The Changing World

Significant changes have occurred in our society during the last two decades. Medical developments, technological advances, economic changes, social inventions, and political transformations have occurred rapidly (e.g., space shuttles, personal computers, laser surgery, gene splicing). Change has side effects that influence lifestyles and the quality of life. Some of the more pressing side effects of change that our nation now faces are the need for new energy sources, the depletion of crucial and natural resources, increased social activism and consumerism, rising educational levels, changing demographic patterns, increasing numbers of women and members of minority groups in managerial positions and professional occupations, increased governmental involvement in business transactions, and an expansion of international business and competition.

Changes in the form of trends, or what John Naisbitt refers to as "megatrends," will certainly have side effects which have implications for managerial activities. Managers in the future will have to adjust to these side effects. They will have to develop programs, policies, and actions to address special issues that can succeed in an environment that is changing rapidly and often unpredictably.

Special Issues and Management Action

Following are a few of the specific issues which will have to be addressed in the future by managers.

Women Workers and Managers.   The fall of 1978 was a landmark period in the history of women workers. It was then that their labor market participation rate surpassed 50 percent; i.e., more than half of all the women 16 years of age and over were in the work force.[2] Occupational choice has widened for women from a few jobs closely related to and often performed in the home to a wider range of employment possibilities. In 1880, 86.3 percent of all women workers were employed in 10 occupations; they were, for example, domestic workers, laundresses, dressmakers, teachers, and restaurant workers.[3] Today, while slightly more than half of all women are employed in just 20 traditional women's jobs, there are some women working in almost every occupation, from ironworker to professional baseball umpire to neurosurgeon in the famous Mayo Clinic.

Women, through their performance and managerial ability and with organizational encouragement, are gradually showing that the obstacles to their success can be overcome. There are also some companies that are helping women managers balance the job and home life. A balance is needed, because two-job couples are now a reality in many organizations. It is estimated that there are 25 million two-paycheck families in the work force. It is difficult for many of these couples to cope with career choices that involve relocation and excessive overtime. Women managers have had to turn down relocations and overtime opportunities because of family responsibilities or career complications created for their spouses. Unless organizations are considerate and tolerant of these kinds of refusals, careers of both men and women in management will be blunted.

Minorities in Work Organizations.   Although women still have problems in organizations, minorities have even more hurdles to overcome. Racial, ethnic, and sexual job discrimination has had a long history. Until the middle of the twentieth century, many organizations specified the desired sex and race

489

when advertising for employees. But recently businesses, as well as many citizens, have tried to minimize discrimination in employment.

Fortune listed 379,000 black managers in American businesses.[4] Yet many black managers still feel they are not doing meaningful jobs. Integrating more black managers into the organization mainstream is a continuous task that more companies will work on in response to government pressures as is voluntarily providing more challenging opportunities for blacks.

More and more black managers are entering key managerial positions. They are the success stories of the past decade's affirmative-action programs; they have moved from entry-level jobs into middle management. Now, along with their white peers, they stand on the brink of senior-level positions.[5] Yet progress has been slow and pressure on black managers is often intense. Blacks are now patiently waiting to see whether qualified black managers are allowed to enter senior management positions.

A Viable Work Ethic. There is general agreement that productivity in the United States has become stagnant. A number of reasons ranging from management inattention to government regulations have been cited as primary factors contributing to this problem. There are some who believe that another reason for the decline is the deterioration of the work ethic. If by work ethic—a very elusive term—we mean the desire to do a good job irrespective of financial reward, research shows that the work ethic in the United States is quite strong.

A 1980 Gallup study for the U.S. Chamber of Commerce showed that an overwhelming 88 percent of all working Americans feel that it is personally important to them to work hard and do their best on the job. The study concludes that there is widespread commitment among U.S. workers to improve productivity and suggests that there are "large reservoirs of potential upon which management can draw to improve performance and increase productivity."[6]

Although the work ethic remains strong, it appears that managers need to do something about the loss of pride in workmanship and about poor-quality outputs. America has become a land plagued by loose wires, missing screws, ill-fitting assembly, and things that don't work. Too many examples indicate quality problems.[7] For instance:

- Bolts supporting the Civic Center in Hartford, Connecticut, snapped and the entire steel and concrete roof plunged into the 10,000-seat auditorium.

- All 273 people on board a DC-10 died when an engine bolt snapped as the plane was taking off from Chicago's O'Hare Airport.

- At Three Mile Island, a relief valve got stuck in the open position and brought the nuclear core to the brink of a meltdown.

- In New York City, Houston, Los Angeles, Atlanta, and Santa Monica, 2500 brand-new Grumman buses costing $130,000 each developed cracks and sagging rear axles shortly after going into service.

The list goes on and on. It convincingly and sadly shows that major problems exist in the workplace. One researcher suggests that the problem lies in poor managerial implementation of reward systems that must be corrected in the future.[8] The Gallup study asked workers whom they thought would benefit from the improvements in their productivity; only 9 percent felt that they, the workers, would. Most assumed that the beneficiaries would be others—consumers, management, or stockholders. Management must educate workers about how they benefit from productivity improvements.

In principle, most Americans are willing to work harder, but they continue to work under reward systems that do not motivate them to do so. Why should workers make a greater effort if (1) they don't have to, and (2) they believe that others, not they, will benefit from such efforts? Managers need finally to realize that workers are responsive to other than economic rewards. The economic view is an obsolete and inaccurate image of the work force. Survey after survey shows this to be the case.

Unemployment: A Nagging Reality. During the past decade, more than 30 million jobs have been lost as a direct result of plant closings. Communities have been disrupted, workers' security undermined, and productivity reduced. Greater involvement and cooperation between labor, management, and the government are needed to deal not only with unemployment and retraining in a general sense but also with the shuttered factories, displaced workers, and ghost towns.[9]

The worker who accepts technology advances (i.e., robots and computers) and is willing to retrain for the future is far more likely to be employed than the worker who resists. There will be hardships along the way. More and more employees will have to change old habits, learn new skills, and move to new locations. Management must understand that some outstanding performers will openly resist technological change. A Booz Allen study of 300 executives at 15 companies concluded that 10 percent of the managers would refuse to accept electronic work stations. Booz Allen predicted that the 10 percent would lose their jobs without even understanding why they lost them.

Management needs to play a more active role in preparing employees for changes that could lead to more unemployment. Orderly planning, retraining, and communication of why changes are needed could provide employees with information, knowledge, and skills for the future. Also, management, together with the federal government and the labor movement, must look more into the future, forecasting the kinds of jobs that will be available and then establishing training programs for the work force needed to fill these jobs.

Conclusion

The manager of the future will be addressing the kinds of issues cited above and will be applying the functions of planning, organizing, and controlling in order to manage work and organizations, people, and production and operations more effectively. This is not an easy task. The following anonymous statement illustrates that the job of managing in an organization tomorrow will not be for the fainthearted. Instead, it is a job for the person who likes to face challenges and achieve the benefits that result from being successful.

> As nearly everyone knows, a manager has practically nothing to do except to decide what is to be done; to tell somebody to do it; to listen to reasons why it should not be done, why it should be done by someone else, or why it should be done in a different way; to follow up to see if the thing has been done; to discover that it has not; to inquire why; to listen to excuses from the person who should have done it; to follow up again to see if the thing has been done, only to discover that it has been done incorrectly; to point out how it should have been done; to conclude that as long as it has been done, it may as well be left where it is; to wonder if it is not time to get rid of a person who cannot do a thing right; to reflect that he or she probably has a family, and that certainly any successor would be just as bad, and maybe worse; to consider how much simpler and better the thing would have been done if one had done it oneself in the first place; to reflect sadly that one could have done it right in 20 minutes, and as things turned out, one had to spend two days to find out why it has taken three weeks for somebody else to do it wrong.

See also Ethics, managerial; Management, historical development of; Management theory, science, and approaches; Professionalism in management; Social responsibility of business; Technology, management implications.

NOTES

[1]Leonard R. Sayles, Leadership, McGraw-Hill, New York, 1979, p. 21.

[2]Seymour L. Wolfberg, "Planning for the U.S. Labor Force of the '80s," National Productivity Review, Spring 1982, pp. 228–239.

[3]"Job Options for Women in the 80s," U.S. Department of Labor, Women's Bureau, Pamphlet 18, 1980.

[4]Juan Cameron, "Blacks Still Waiting for Full Membership," Fortune, April 1975, p. 165.

[5]Robert S. Greenberger, "Many Black Managers Hope to Enter Ranks of Top Management," Wall Street Journal, June 15, 1981, pp. 1 and 15.

[6]Daniel Yankelovich, "The Work Ethic Is Underemployed," Psychology Today, May 1982, p. 5.

[7]Marvin Harris, "Why It's Not the Same Old America," Psychology Today, August 1981, p. 25.

[8]Yankelovich, op. cit., p. 8.

[9]Barry Bluestone and Bennett Harrison, The Deindustrialization of America, Basic Books, New York, 1982.

JOHN M. IVANCEVICH, University of Houston

Management, Historical Development of

Awareness of the importance of management skills dates back beyond the beginning of written history. Most historians, however, generally date the first recognized attempts at systematically studying the development of basic management principles to the last two decades of the nineteenth century. At that time, increased interest in management was paralleled by the growing economic and industrial development of the United States and Western Europe. The forces of expanding technology and commerce, paired with new advances in transportation and communication, dramatically increased the scope and complexity of business undertakings. For the first time in history, problems of managing large-scale organizations became widespread as industrial and commercial enterprises began to replace individual proprietors and partnerships as the usual forms of business. An unprecedented increase in the size of production facilities resulted in previously unexperienced problems of waste and inefficiency. These problems necessitated formulating and investigating new concepts for the scientific management of work.

The event most often referenced as the beginning of the search for a rational and systematic science of management came in 1886 with the presentation of a paper by Henry R. Towne, president of the Yale and Towne Manufacturing Company, on "The Engineer as Economist." His comments, delivered at a meeting of the American Society of Mechanical Engineers (ASME), stressed the importance of management as a field of independent study equal to that of engineering. Noting the almost complete absence of management literature, the virtual absence of a medium for the exchange of administrative ideas and experience, and the total lack of management associations, Towne urged that the ASME serve as a center for the development of an understanding of industrial management.Such a suggestion was considered nothing less than revolutionary.

Birth of Scientific Management. While

Towne's presentation is recognized as marking the beginning of the search for a science of management, the birth of the scientific management movement is generally credited to Frederick W. Taylor. His book, *The Principles of Scientific Management*, published in 1911, seriously questioned the traditional role of management. Synthesizing and refining the ideas and concepts developed in his earlier writings and experiments, Taylor envisioned a "mental revolution" in which the concerns of both management and the worker would be based on a philosophy of "mutuality of interests." He conceived of management's new duties as involving (1) development of a true science of managing complete with clearly stated laws, rules, and principles to replace old rule-of-thumb methods; (2) scientific selection, training, and development of workers (whereas in the past workers were randomly chosen and often untrained); (3) enthusiastic cooperation with workers to ensure that all work performed is done in accordance with scientific principles; and (4) equal division of tasks and responsibilities between the worker and management. Believing that the interests of employers and employees could be made to coincide, Taylor was resolutely committed to eliminating the inefficient and wasteful practices of the past and to transcending what at the time appeared to be irreconcilable conflicts of interests between labor and management.

Although the groundwork of Taylor's philosophy had been laid several years earlier, it was not until late 1910 that it began to receive widespread publicity. It was at this time that a number of Eastern railroads petitioned the Interstate Commerce Commission for an increase in their freight rates to offset recent wage hikes. Louis D. Brandeis (later associate justice of the U.S. Supreme Court), representing the opposing Eastern Shippers' Association, brought together a group of engineers in an attempt to have them agree upon a title to designate the principles and philosophy of Taylor's work. The term *scientific management* is said to have originated at this meeting.

As principal attorney for the freight shippers, it was Brandeis' strategy to prove by expert testimony that by adopting the methods of scientific management, the railroads could considerably reduce their costs while further increasing wages without increasing their rates. To this end, Brandeis presented a parade of expert witnesses, including Towne, Henry L. Gantt, Frank B. Gilbreth, and Harrington Emerson. The high point of the hearings was reached with Emerson's testimony that the railroads could save at least $1 million a day through application of scientific management. Such testimony had great appeal for the world press. The resulting widespread publicity served to provide the attention and support scientific management had previously lacked. Eventually even Lenin, writing in *Pravda*, told the Russians they should put scientific management into effect, too.

Early Contributors. Paralleling the work of Taylor, numerous other early pioneers contributed to the emergence and development of management thought. Henry L. Gantt's major contributions included the task and bonus pay plan, the Gantt Chart for production planning and control, and an early understanding of leadership theory. The most popular books of Gantt, a close associate of Taylor, were *Work, Wages, and Profits* (1910), *Industrial Leadership* (1916), and *Organizing for Work* (1919). His writings are characterized by a basic recognition of the human factor in industry and by his belief that workers should be provided with the means to find in their jobs a source of both income and pleasure. It was Gantt's belief that this ideal could only be achieved by providing a task for each worker, with a bonus to be awarded for its accomplishment.

Although influenced by Taylor, Harrington Emerson worked independently as an early efficiency expert. His major contributions to the field of management are embodied in two books, *Efficiency as a Basis for Operation and Wages* (1911) and *The Twelve Principles of Efficiency* (1913). The main thrust of his efforts was aimed at the elimination of waste and the creation of wealth. He presented his "principles of efficiency" as forming an interdependent and coordinated management system. Emerson made a contribution to the early development of management by identifying and describing its activities. In 1912, Emerson helped found The Efficiency Society of New York City, and in 1933 he helped form the Association of Consulting Management Engineers.

The work of Frank B. and Lillian M. Gilbreth is significant for several reasons. Through their efforts, they created an understanding of motion study and the significance of increasing output by reducing effort. Perhaps more significantly, however, their work emphasized the importance of the relationship between management and the social sciences. Frank Gilbreth was primarily interested in the new field of motion analysis, studying everything from bricklaying to surgical procedures to professional baseball and golf. His book *Motion Study* was published in 1911, followed by *Applied Motion Study* in 1917. He devised a system for classifying the motions of the hand into 17 basic divisions called *therbligs* ("Gilbreth" spelled backward with the *th* transposed). Lillian, his wife, a psychologist by training, pioneered in the new field of industrial psychology. Her book *The Psychology of Management*, published in 1916, is one of the most significant early contributions to the study of the human factor in industry.

The scientific management movement focused responsibility for work on management instead of on the individual worker or union. It emphasized task performance and the responsibility of management to plan, organize, and control employees' tasks.

Through the Mid-1920s. As outlined by Mee, the period from 1910 through the mid-1920s witnessed the full blossoming of the management movement. During this period, some of the more significant events to occur were:

1. Scientific management was recognized as a respectable university discipline. Courses in the "new" management movement were offered at institutions such as Columbia University, Cornell University, Pennsylvania State University, and the Massachusetts Institute of Technology.

2. The first formal assembly on management, a gathering of some 300 educators, industrialists, and consultants, was called in 1911 at the Amos Tuck School of Administration and Finance at Dartmouth College. The proceedings of this meeting served to outline possible future courses of action for management thinking within the United States, and are considered by many historians as somewhat of a "charter" for the fledgling management movement.

3. The first professional management association came into being in 1914 with the founding of the Society to Promote the Science of Management. It was reestablished as the Taylor Society in 1916 and in 1930 evolved into the present Society for Advancement of Management. The National Industrial Conference Board was started in 1916, followed by organizations such as the American Management Association in 1923.

4. The first management textbooks began appearing as early as 1910. Hugo Diemer's *Factory Organization and Administration* (1910) was followed by volumes such as John C. Duncan's *The Principles of Industrial Management* (1911) and Dexter S. Kimball's *Principles of Industrial Organization* (1913).

5. Writing in 1916, the Frenchman Henri Fayol was the first writer to classify the study of management into functional areas—such as planning, organizing, commanding, coordinating, and controlling. Unfortunately, Fayol's major contribution to management literature, *Administration industrielle et générale*, was not translated into English until 1930 and not widely distributed until a second English translation appeared in 1949.

6. In 1915, Horace B. Drury completed the first doctoral dissertation in management at Columbia University. It was entitled "Scientific Management: A History and Criticism."

7. The first textbooks dealing with the topic of industrial psychology began to appear. Prominent early volumes included Walter Dill Scott's *Increasing Human Efficiency in Business* (1911), Hugo Munsterberg's *Psychology and Industrial Efficiency* (1913), and Lillian M. Gilbreth's *Psychology of Management* (1916).

8. The first journals and magazines devoted largely to management and industrial psychology began to appear. Periodicals with titles such as *Management and Administration, Factory and Industrial Management*, and *Journal of Applied Psychology* steadily grew in number.

Hawthorne Study. One of the most outstanding milestones in the historical development of management was passed in connection with a study launched in 1924 at the Hawthorne plant of the Western Electric Company located near Cicero, Illinois. The study spanned an 8-year period in three phases.

Phase 1. Initiated in collaboration with the National Research Council of the National Academy of Sciences, the study's original intent was to investigate the relationship between illumination and worker productivity. It had been hypothesized that as illumination was increased, productivity would increase. The researchers systematically varied and recorded the level of illumination within the study's test room, fully anticipating individual efficiency to vary directly with light intensity. The study's results, however, demonstrated no such pattern. Rather, individual output increased continually throughout the entire experiment without regard to level of illumination. While it seemed clear at this point that no predictable relationship existed between productivity and light intensity, it was entirely unclear why productivity increased throughout the study's duration.

Phase 2. The inconclusiveness of the illumination experiments stimulated additional research at the Hawthorne plant. In 1927, Elton Mayo and Fritz J. Roethlisberger were asked to lead a group of researchers from Harvard Business School to explore further the unanticipated worker reactions earlier encountered. The thrust of their efforts was designed to determine the effects of working conditions, such as rest breaks and workday length, on employee productivity.

This phase of the study, known as the *relay-assembly test room study*, lasted 5 years. Like the illumination experiment, it also developed in quite an unexpected way. A test room was established, and six workers (five relay assemblers and a layout operator) were selected to participate in the experiment. In an effort to control test conditions more closely, careful measurements were made of variables such as the workers' blood pressure and vascular skin reaction as well as factors such as the humidity and temperature of the test room. Throughout the first 2 years of the experiment, the length and frequency of rest pauses and the length of the workday and workweek were continually changed. Seemingly without regard to experimental variation, however, just as in the illumination experiment, general productivity increased steadily.

These results strongly suggested to the researchers that something a great deal more potent than test conditions had served to influence the productivity of the relay assemblers. Only in retrospect, however, were they able to determine that not test conditions, but rather improved morale, a changed supervisory style, less worker control, and improved interpersonal relations accounted for the largest portion of the increase in output. In both the illumination and relay-assembly test room experiments the workers were isolated from the regular factory floor in special test areas. Throughout the relay-assembly test room experiment, the workers assumed an increasing share of their own supervision. This resulted in a supervisory style that was less restrictive and friendlier. The change in supervisory style was accompanied by less stringent control, with the relay assemblers actually participating in decisions affecting their jobs.

This change in orientation has since given rise to the concept of the *Hawthorne effect*, meaning essentially that the experimenters may have biased the study's outcome through their own personal presence and the simple novelty of their efforts. Additional factors believed by the researchers to contribute to the increased output of the relay assemblers were the formation of a cohesive group structure that stressed loyalty and cooperation and the general high morale that accompanied the entire experiment. The relay assemblers enjoyed and drew a great deal of intrinsic satisfaction from the special roles they occupied in the study.

Phase 3. The final phase of the Hawthorne study has become known as the *bank wiring observation* experiment. Begun in 1931 and lasting 6½ months, it essentially involved an analysis of spontaneous, informal social group behavior. An attempt was made to investigate the activities of a group of nine employees engaged in wiring switchboard equipment to determine the extent to which individual employee behavior was controlled by social groups that existed within each department. It was clear to the investigators from their early reports that several closely related phenomena were being encountered. In particular, it appeared that the group wage-incentive plan in effect for the department was being rendered ineffectual by collaborative group pressure to control output. The workers had established their own conception of a fair day's work and prevailed as a group upon one another not to exceed this predetermined level of output. In line with the behavior norms of the informal group, workers who exceeded the agreed-upon rate were known as "rate busters." Those workers whose production fell below the standard set by the group were known as "rate chiselers." The informal group enforced its norms of conduct through subtle forms of ridicule, sarcasm, and what came to be known as "binging." *Binging* was a practice in which a group member expressed displeasure with the actions of a coworker by hitting the coworker as hard as possible on the upper arm. In short, the researchers had previously been unaware of the implications of informal group behavior on management practices. The bank wiring observation experiment highlighted the significance of the informal group as a powerful organizational force.

The outcomes of the Hawthorne experiments carried with them numerous important implications for the management field. They stressed the importance of viewing the human element of an organization as part of a larger social system. They emphasized that the needs of employees are *both* physical and social in nature. They also underscored the existence of the informal social group as a natural outgrowth of the behavior patterns inherent in the formal structure of an organization.

In brief, the Hawthorne experiments, by emphasizing a new interpretation of work group behavior, ushered in the beginning of what was later to be known as the field of *human relations.*

Mid-1930s. By the mid-1930s, a change in the fundamental thinking of management, as expressed in the literature of the period, began to develop. Compared with the preceding three decades, a more mature philosophy of management had begun to emerge. Volumes such as Ordway Tead's *The Art of Leadership* (1935), Chester I. Barnard's *The Functions of the Executive* (1938), Charles P. McCormick's *Multiple Management* (1938), and Mary P. Follett's *Dynamic Administration* (1940) introduced concepts that replaced earlier, narrower themes and established the field of management within the total social framework of society in general.

1940s through Early 1950s. The period of World War II and its aftermath may perhaps be characterized best by a refinement of known principles and techniques and a focus on the activities of top management.

One of the first empirical studies in the area of top management was released in 1941 by Paul Holden, Lounsburg S. Fish, and Hubert L. Smith. Published under the title *Top-Management Organization and Control,* the study reported the general management practices of 31 industrial corporations. Based on their findings, the authors concluded that the primary responsibilities of top management involved: (1) long-range planning and the clear establishment of objectives; (2) the establishment of a sound organization structure; (3) the skillful training and development of all personnel; and (4) the establishment of effective control procedures. The significance of this conclusion lies in the fact that these are basi-

cally the same functions identified pragmatically by early writers such as Fayol. The Holden, Fish, and Smith study thus served to provide support for many earlier management theories that had been deduced through experience rather than through systematic research and experimentation.

Reflecting a broadening base of influence, significant contributions of this period included Burleigh B. Gardner's *Human Relations in Industry* (1945). Gardner, a veteran of 5 years of experience as a director of employee relations research at the Hawthorne plant of the Western Electric Company, drew upon his exposure to the ideas developed by Roethlisberger and Mayo to present a systematic discussion of the human element in industry. Published in 1947, Herbert A. Simon's *Administrative Behavior* represented a pioneering study of the basic concepts and framework of decision making as an organizaton process. Simon's work provided a foundation for the popularization of the quantitative techniques of the coming decade. Two additional books of this period that have enjoyed an enduring respect are Ralph C. Davis's *The Fundamentals of Top Management* (1951) and Peter F. Drucker's *The Practice of Management* (1954). The common objective of both Davis and Drucker was to present a general statement of business objectives and practices as they related to the basic business problems encountered by the practicing manager. It was in *The Practice of Management* that Drucker first introduced the popular concept of *management by objectives*.

Mid-1950s. The mid-1950s gave rise to a tremendous increase in the number of books and periodicals devoted to the field of management. The trend in the development of management thought was reflected by the spreading multidisciplinary roots of study that initially began to spread in the late 1930s and in the years following World War II. *On one front*, the seeds of the Hawthorne experiments continued to grow as anthropologists, psychologists, and sociologists expressed a continuing interest in applying the tools of the behavioral sciences to management. Significant works of this period include William F. Whyte's *Money and Motivation* (1956), Reinhard Bendix's *Work and Authority in Industry* (1956), William H. Whyte, Jr.'s *The Organization Man* (1956), Chris Argyris' *Personality and Organization* (1957), Harold J. Leavitt's *Managerial Psychology* (1958), and James G. March and Herbert A. Simon's *Organizations* (1958).

In a second direction, management theory continued to evolve from an emphasis on general theory to a greater stress on the development of management principles. The emergence of the first principles-of-management textbooks in the first half of the 1950s is a reflection of this trend. William H. Newman's *Administrative Action* was published in 1951, George R. Terry's *Principles of Management* in 1953, and Harold Koontz and Cyril O'Donnell's *Principles*

of Management: An Analysis of Managerial Functions in 1955.

A *third direction* of growth was in the areas of management science and operations research. Building on advanced solutions to World War II operational problems in logistics and tactics as well as on the theories of John von Neumann and Oskar Morgenstern (*Theory of Games and Economic Behavior*, 1944) and Norbert Wiener (*Cybernetics*, 1948), the areas of operations research and management science formally emerged in the early 1950s. Pioneer volumes in these areas include Phillip M. Morse and George E. Kimball's *Methods of Operations Research* (1951) and Joseph F. McCloskey and Florence N. Trefethen's *Operations Research for Management* (1954). *Operations Research*, the official journal for the Operations Research Society of America, was first published in 1953. *Management Science*, the journal of The Institute for Management Sciences, began publication in 1954.

The 1960s and 1970s. As the 1960s unfolded, various management thought streams that had developed in the preceding 60-odd years began to converge slowly. Quantitative techniques which developed within the areas of management science and operations research contributed conceptual methods that were employed by a steady stream of social scientists conducting research into areas such as motivation, leadership, and group behavior. The work of researchers such as Douglas M. McGregor in the development of theories X and Y (*The Human Side of Enterprise*, 1960), Tom Burns and George M. Stalker in the identification of mechanistic and organic systems of organization (*The Management of Innovation*, 1961), Frederick Herzberg in the introduction of the motivation-hygiene theory (*Work and the Nature of Man*, 1960), Rensis Likert in the popularization of employee-centeredness and production-centeredness (*New Patterns of Management*, 1961, and *The Human Organization*, 1967), Victor H. Vroom in the formulation of the expectancy theory of motivation (*Work and Motivation*, 1964), Joan Woodward in the cultivation of the so-called technological perspective (*Industrial Organization: Theory and Practice*, 1965), and Fred Fiedler in the development of the leadership contingency model (*A Theory of Leadership Effectiveness*, 1967) particularly stand out.

Building on this foundation, the 1970s were above all a period of introspection and refinement. Efforts of management theorists were largely directed at evaluating and verifying the work of preceding generations. Of particular note, an unprecedented number of researchers from other social sciences, especially sociology, psychology, anthropology, and economics, began to focus their efforts in the field of management. It is perhaps impossible to place the work of these more recent contributors into clear perspective without the benefit of a greater lapse in time. Their insights may come to be the basis for

another shift in the continual evolution of management history.

See also Management, future of; Management theory, science, and approaches.

REFERENCES

George, Claude S., Jr.: *The History of Management Thought*, 2d ed., Prentice-Hall, Englewood Cliffs, N.J., 1972.

Tillett, Anthony D., Thomas Kempner, and Gordon Wills, eds.: *Management Thinkers*, Penguin Books, Baltimore, 1970.

Wren, Daniel A.: *The Evolution of Management Thought*, 2d ed., New York, John Wiley, 1979.

ARTHUR G. BEDEIAN, *Auburn University*

Management Information Systems (MIS)

Management information systems attempt to provide managers at all levels with the information they need to guide their enterprises in the context of the 1980s. They typically require the use of sophisticated computer hardware and software—although theoretically a management information system (MIS) should be achievable without computer resources. Very few successful examples of an actual MIS exist; the potential of contemporary technology provides hope that more systems deserving of this designation will be developed. An actual MIS provides an organization with flexible, integrated tools for the planning and control functions of the endeavor, with the ability to respond to planned and unplanned information requirements at all managerial levels.

Genesis

The notion of management information systems originated during the early 1960s, largely through the efforts of Kennedy-era "whiz kids" in the Pentagon and other government agencies. The idea that the proper organization of data and the application of sophisticated computing equipment could yield reports and decision-making information of use to management for the purposes of planning and control was relatively new during that period; the name "computer" itself indicates the early restriction of data processing equipment to computational activities. The architects of John Kennedy's management policies—largely Harvard-trained businessmen—were among the first to realize the computer's potential as an information processing tool which could directly support management as well as the clerical

functions (i.e., payroll, accounts receivable/payable, and inventory) to which it was being applied.

Since the inception of the management information system (MIS) concept, Western culture has moved with increasing speed toward an *information-based* focus, following its evolution from an industrial to a postindustrial, service-based society.

Definition. Many writers have proposed definitions for MIS; most have had several features in common, such as the following:

1. A complex of human procedures and computer processes

2. Cutting across an organization's functional boundaries

3. To serve the information needs of management

These characteristics appear both necessary and sufficient to constitute a definition although there has been some controversy regarding the explicit mention of computers in item 1. Theoretically, it is possible to develop a management information system without the use of computer processing; practically in the 1980s this rarely if ever occurs. The ready availability of computer hardware and software makes automated support an implied if not explicit component of any contemporary MIS. A realistic definition, then, might read as follows: *A management information system is a combination of organizational resources which cuts across functional lines and serves the information needs of managers at different levels by providing information in a useful format on a timely basis to support planning and control requirements.* Such a definition makes the computer component of the MIS merely one of the organizational resources used. (Subsequent discussion will, however, assume a computerized context.)

Features. Perhaps the main features that distinguish an MIS from a more traditional clerical or record-keeping system are flexibility and integration. The *flexibility feature* requires that the successful MIS incorporate methods permitting *unanticipated* as well as known information needs to be met; this requirement imposes a heavy burden on the system designers. Fortunately, contemporary software packages display greater flexibility than their earlier counterparts. The *integration component* so essential to an MIS necessitates a consistent approach to the handling of data from different *vertical* levels in the subject organization as well as from varying *horizontal* slices. In other words, a comprehensive MIS should be equally capable of meeting the needs of a first-level marketing manager and those of the chief executive officer.

Features of a more technological nature include:

- User-oriented computer terminals (with graphics)
- Large-capacity direct-access storage devices

- Data communications capability (local and remote)
- Statistical analysis and simulation software
- Data-base management and report generation software

These system components, along with data representation standards, form the basis for a powerful MIS. Although such systems are rare in actual practice, the Pillsbury Corporation, United Airlines, and the U.S. Department of Agriculture are among the leaders in implementing such full-blown management information systems.

Evolution

Four technological factors distinguish the MIS of the 1980s from its precursors:

- Growth in number and power of microcomputers
- Increasing sophistication of data-base management systems
- Growing implementation of distributed processing systems
- Improvements in office automation

These factors are interdependent but can be discussed individually.

Microcomputers. When the MIS efforts of the early 1960s were undertaken, very few computer terminals existed. Most computer processing occurred in the "batch" mode, requiring the advance scheduling of computer time and the submission of data in punched card or magnetic tape format. In the latter part of the 1960s, *time-sharing* became popular as a means of accessing computer resources. A time-sharing system permitted multiple independent (and frequently remote) users to communicate with a large central computer facility through the use of typewriterlike terminals. These hard-copy terminals, although still in use, are less popular today than cathode-ray tube (CRT) terminals, frequently called video display terminals (VDTs). Most terminals used in early MIS applications were "dumb" in that they had no processing capability themselves; they were merely access points to a large computing system. For this reason (among others), managers were reluctant to learn the frequently complex sequences of commands necessary to invoke the processing capabilities of the central computer.

In the 1970s, microcomputers first began to appear in place of the typewriterlike terminals of the previous decade. Not only did they provide a "friendlier" interface to large computing systems, but they offered local processing capabilities which frequently required no host computer. Both their ease of use and the documentation describing their use were materially improved over earlier terminals, thereby encouraging the direct involvement of managers in the development and use of MIS applications.

Data-Base Management Systems. One of the constant requirements of a responsive MIS is a facility for sifting through large quantities of data and retrieving useful information through queries. The ability, without programming, to retrieve the part names of all items manufactured during the past quarter which had a quality control reject rate in excess of 10 percent is typical of data-base queries which can be framed quickly and easily. A data base is a repository of data which has been created from related computerized files and structured so that redundancy of information is minimized and retrieval by means of multiple identifying fields is possible. A *data-base management system* is a set of computer programs which enable the user to create, modify, and retrieve from the data base.

Distributed Processing. The linkage of terminals and data bases by means of data communications technology became a reality in the 1970s; subsequent improvements have permitted much processing and portions of the data base to be *distributed* or situated locally within the functional area they primarily serve. This arrangement enables the responsible area to maintain tighter control over the data most critical to its operations—although with a requirement to meet organizational standards for data-base structure so that other functional areas may access the data base as well. Distributed processing also implies a hierarchy of computing capability, with local processing of modest requirements and centralized processing of heavier demands. This hierarchy may include more than two levels, depending on the sophistication of the network structure implemented. Regardless of the design, distributed processing has made the MIS concept more viable than it was in earlier, monolithic computing environments.

Office Automation. Most managers were hesitant to exploit an information processing technology that was not integrated with the office environment. With the recent introduction of powerful word processing, electronic mail, and computerized calendars—and the ability of these applications to interface with data-base processing and other MIS components—the mystique of the MIS has been reduced and its utility to the manager enhanced. The office environment is a more comfortable arena for the manager; as MIS capabilities have entered the office, they have become more natural to the user/manager.

Application Problems

Four primary problems have denied MIS users the full potential theoretically possible through these

systems: (1) integration difficulties; (2) differing information requirements of managers at different organizational levels; (3) the communication gap between managers and systems specialists; and (4) lack of top management involvement.

Integration Difficulties. This primary benefit of MIS integration has also been one of its main obstacles to success. Most actual systems with the MIS designation have really been very loosely connected sets of subsystems, each serving a particular functional area of the organization. There is a real difficulty in attempting to reconcile the sometimes conflicting requirements of different users while still accommodating the needs of each. Contemporary data-base management systems have reduced the severity of this problem by prescribing data representation and definition standards across areas, but difficulties still exist in establishing linkages between such diverse applications (subsystems) as those serving the engineering, production, marketing, and accounting functions.

Differing Information Requirements. It is generally conceded that much of the difficulty surrounding successful MIS implementation results from the great variation in the "texture" of information required by the three classical levels of management: lower, or operational; middle, or tactical; and upper, or strategic.

Operational. Managers at this level require detailed, internally generated current information characterized by great precision; such information supports the short-term, localized decisions made by managers at this level.

Tactical. Middle managers demand a composite of internally and externally generated information, somewhat summarized, to support midrange decisions (those with a time horizon of 1 or 2 years in the future). Such information must be fairly up-to-date.

Strategic. Top managers utilize highly processed and summarized information, primarily from sources outside the organization. This information frequently represents a considerable period of past history; it is used to identify trends and shifts in the environment of the organization so that planning may take place for as much as 5 to 10 years in the future.

Communication Gap. It is well known that specialists in most disciplines develop jargon peculiar to their area of expertise; the more technical the discipline, the more arcane the jargon. The jargon of the computing environment is particularly frustrating to managers because they require close contact with the products of computing specialists—and on a continuing basis. This problem more than any other drove the manager to abdicate MIS responsibilities to technical specialists early in the evolution of MIS. Computer specialists have been shown to prefer communication with machines to conversing with other human beings; they also tend to avoid conflict and reflect other traits of temperament in direct opposi-

tion to the "meet and deal" characteristics of the typical manager.

Lack of Top Management Involvement. Partly because of the communication gap mentioned above, many managers have avoided involving themselves in MIS policy and development. It appears that most managers have traditionally spent less time dealing with MIS problems than with any element of their organization requiring such significant resources (typically between 1 and 2 percent of the entire budget). This has been particularly true of the top managerial levels, who have been inclined to leave direction of the MIS effort to the "experts," where, in fact, their own expertise in stating requirements has been essential, and their advocacy of the effort psychologically important at lower levels.

The Future

Technological advancements continue to fuel the application of MIS systems.

DSS and IRM. The term *MIS* is frequently used in conjunction with two related acronyms: DSS (decision support system) and IRM (information resource management). DSS is really a subset of MIS, that subset which attacks a specific, delineated problem requiring a decision. A DSS relies more heavily than a traditional MIS on the management science/operations research component. Experimentation is an essential attribute of the DSS concept; the form it takes is usually interactive computer simulation.

IRM, on the other hand, represents the broadest interpretation of the resources available to the MIS—from paper files to microform—and encompasses the policies in our information-based endeavors which have begun to view information as the fourth resource in an organization, on a par with labor, capital, and material. The management of information resources is a necessary prerequisite to the success of an MIS. Much research is under way focusing on these two variants of MIS, one a subset and the other a superset or umbrella concept.

Software Tools. MIS software has traditionally been tailor-made to the requirements of the organization. The explosion of proprietary software, much of it more flexible and usable than most customized software, frequently causes the make-or-buy dilemma to be resolved with a "buy" decision in the 1980s. Much of the current software is quite "user-friendly," offering a menu-driven format permitting users to descend to different levels of detail within the capabilities of a program and, most important, to extricate themselves when they cause an error or require assistance. A particularly useful feature is a "help" facility which guides the user through any operation of the program without requiring the abandonment of work already completed.

The *electronic spreadsheet* is probably the best example of a currently popular software tool which supports MIS (and DSS) activities. A spreadsheet program provides the user with a conceptual table whose rows and columns may be assigned meanings; as an example, a spreadsheet used for budgeting might have columns representing budget line items and rows representing years. Each cell in the table can be described in terms of other cells or provided an independent value. Any modifications to a cell will "ripple" to all dependent cells, permitting the user to experiment and ask "what if" questions with great ease. This type of software represents a powerful tool for the manager. Some versions permit interfacing with data-base and report generation packages, constituting a stand-alone MIS. Spreadsheet programs, available primarily on microcomputers, are a significant advance in the MIS arena.

Expert Systems. *Expert* or *knowledge-based systems* represent the current thrust in applied artificial intelligence (AI) research. Expert systems are focused computer-based applications that attempt to incorporate as much knowledge of a particular discipline in a data base as is held by expert practitioners and theorists in the field, and to implement heuristic (unstructured) approaches to solving problems within the subject area. To date, expert systems have been particularly successful in medical diagnosis and geological exploration. Much of the Japanese research into "fifth-generation" computer systems is predicated upon the concept of expert systems.

The future of MIS will doubtless be affected by the expert systems notion. If a manager's acquired wisdom could be incorporated into a computer application along with trial-and-error heuristic decision rules, much of what is now considered talent or intuition might be, in the future, transferred to an MIS. This possibility seems remote at present and, more important, possibly undesirable. Regardless of our value judgment, however, management information systems, while still falling short of our ideals, will continue to increase in capabilities.

See also Accounting, managerial control; Computer software, data-base management; Control systems, management; Information sources; Management information systems, transaction processing systems; Office automation; Production planning and control; Records management; System concept, total; Word processing.

REFERENCES

Riley, M. J.: *Management Information Systems*, Holden-Day, San Francisco, 1981.

Ross, Joel E.: *Modern Management and Information Systems*, Reston Publishing, Reston, Va., 1976.

Senn, James A.: *Information Systems in Management*, Wadsworth, Belmont, Calif., 1978.

FRED G. HAROLD, *Florida Atlantic University*

Management Information Systems, Transaction Processing Systems

Contemporary computer-based information systems (CBIS) are usually classified according to a specific organizational function. *Office automation systems* (OAS) support word processing, document handling, and other office tasks. *Management information systems* (MIS) typically maintain data and provide reports used to support operations and structured decision making. And *decision support systems* (DSS) provide assistance in making unique or unstructured decisions.

Underlying all these systems is a fourth, frequently unacknowledged system: the *transaction processing system* or TPS. Whereas MIS, DSS, and OAS have branched off to accommodate special needs, TPS—by and large—still perform the functions for which the earliest data processing (DP) systems were developed. These functions are carried out more quickly, more accurately, more thoroughly, and at much less cost in modern TPS, but conceptually they are not much different from DP functions. It is not surprising, therefore, that we can use the traditional DP model shown in Fig. M-1 to examine the functions of TPS: input, processing, and output.

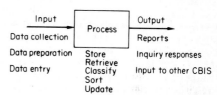

FIG. M-1 Functions of transaction processing systems.

TPS Input. To examine the input function of TPS, it is appropriate to look at the operational steps that must be performed to make transaction data available for processing. There are three such steps: *data collection, data preparation,* and *data entry.*

Data Collection. TPS input may be either direct or indirect. *Direct data input* implies that the transaction itself generates the data inputs for the TPS. For example, the act of an automobile passing through a tollgate is a service transaction—the use of the toll road—and also may activate a counter that provides input for financial and usage records maintained by the tollway authority. When TPS input is direct, the steps of data collection, data preparation, and data entry are combined with the transaction into a single function.

In *indirect data input,* the steps of data collection and preparation are distinctly different, although entry may still be combined with preparation. Data are generated at the point of the transaction, but they are maintained in an intermediate form, usually a document, and prepared later. Data pertaining to many business and government transactions are collected in this fashion. Industrial orders and sales, income tax returns, claims for unemployment benefits, and consumer credit card puchases are all recorded on documents at the time of the transaction and held for subsequent data preparation.

Data Preparation. Data preparation is the conversion of data into a form and/or format consistent with the data entry procedures. Just as direct data input eliminates the need for data preparation, some data preparation techniques also include data entry. For example, the data on credit card charge slips may be keyed into terminals or optically scanned at the credit card company. This procedure prepares the data and also enters them into the TPS for immediate or subsequent processing.

In other cases, data from transaction documents are re-recorded on a second document or other medium prior to entry. For example, if punched cards or optically scanned documents are the input medium for an inventory file, they must be prepared from the original bills of lading or "picking tickets."

Data Entry. Data entry is the step that makes transaction data available for processing. As explained above, it may occur automatically with data collection or data preparation, or it may be a separate, final step in the input function. The mechanics of data entry are dictated by the input medium and devices. For example, card input is entered through a card reader, magnetic ink characters are read through an MICR reader, data on other documents may be read optically or keyed in by a terminal operator, and so on.

Data entry also differs by the *timing* of the input. Some transaction data are saved and entered periodically while others are entered as they occur (or at least as they are prepared for entry). Both the medium and timing orientation of TPS are discussed in greater detail later in this article.

TPS Processing. Two characteristics that distinguish TPS from more sophisticated CBIS (such as MIS and DSS) are the relative simplicity of the transformation processes and the high volume of data. TPS tend to involve large numbers of simple, repetitive operations while DSS, for example, are more likely to use complex operations involving small volumes of data. There are exceptions in each case, of course. A transaction process could involve a small amount of data (reflecting a single transaction) and some DSS processes, such as simulation, often involve thousands of simple, repetitive operations. These exceptions aside, let us look at some typical TPS processes.

Storage. One of the most basic capabilities of TPS is that of storing data. In one sense, TPS act as superefficient, electronic filing cabinets that can accommodate the equivalent of hundreds of thousands or even millions of documents. Although TPS storage is accomplished with a fraction of the space

and cost normally associated with a manual storage medium, such as hard-copy files, it is not of itself a sufficient reason to develop and maintain TPS.

Retrieval. Any capability to store data must, of course, be complemented by the ability to retrieve them when needed. The comparative advantage of TPS over manual methods is even greater in the retrieval process than it is in storage, primarily because of the speed of computer-driven search methods. It simply is easier and faster to find specified data in a TPS than it is in a manual system. Retrieval is also the process that makes data in a TPS available to other CBIS.

Classification. To classify data means to group them according to some common characteristic. The characteristic may be an existing data element or it may be a new element derived from one or more existing elements. The "aging" of accounts by grouping them into categories of "under 30 days," "between 30 and 60 days," and "over 60 days" illustrates the derivation of a new element—"age"—from an existing one—"payment due date." Classification may be carried out in any data management environment, but it is particularly efficient when using a *data-base management system* (DBMS). (*See* Data bases, commercial.)

Sorting. A process somewhat related to that of classifying is sorting—the arranging of data into a specified sequence, such as numerical or alphabetical order. Sorting may be a separate process, as it is when addresses are sorted by ZIP code to facilitate bulk mailing, or it may be combined with classifying, as it is when the names of employees are sorted alphabetically within classifications of organizational departments. Sorting also is carried out with greater efficiency in a data-base environment.

Update. The term *update* is used generically to describe various processes that maintain the currency of data. TPS are used to *add* new data to existing records or files, *delete* obsolete or irrelevant data, and *change* incorrect or outdated values. The process of updating is described more completely later in this entry.

TPS Output. TPS processes result in a variety of output which, for practical purposes, can be grouped into three categories: reports, responses to inquiries, and input to other CBIS.

Report Generation. The preparation or generation of reports is a special form of retrieval that frequently follows the updating process. Reports produced by TPS are most likely to (1) be *scheduled* (produced on a regular, periodic basis) and (2) reflect *detail* information (the results of every transaction). In contrast, MIS are more likely to produce reports that are *on-call* (produced only when requested) and reflect *summaries* or *exceptions.* A weekly report showing the balance on hand for all items in inventory illustrates the concepts of both scheduling and detail reporting.

The term *report* usually evokes an image of a document—information printed on paper. Reports can be on other media as well. For example, the inventory report suggested above could be very bulky and inconvenient to use if printed on paper. Many organizations now output such reports on *microfilm* (rolls of film somewhat larger than 35mm camera film) or *microfiche* (sheets of film about 5 inches square). These media require special readers to illuminate and enlarge the printed matter, but they are convenient to use, more durable, and easier to store than reports printed on paper.

Inquiry Response. Although data maintained in TPS are usually made available to users in bulk, via reports, they often are required individually or in small volumes on short notice. The technique for outputting data on this basis is the inquiry response. Inquiries are handled best when operating in a data-base environment where the query language of the data-base management system provides ready user access to data. An airline reservation clerk confirming the availability of a seat on a specified flight, a sales representative checking the status of an unfilled order, and a university registrar looking up a student's grade point average all illustrate the use of inquiry response output in TPS.

Input to Other CBIS. Up to this point, we have considered transaction processing for the sake of transaction processing—a not altogether bad idea for organizations with very large volumes of data to process but one that does not fully consider the synergistic effect of several CBIS working in concert. One simple way in which TPS interact with other CBIS is in the role of an input system—a serial relationship, as shown in Fig. M-2, in which the output of one system (the TPS) becomes the input for another system (an MIS, in this example).

Other CBIS can use TPS output more readily when there is a common or *corporate* data base maintained by a data-base management system. Data in the data base are structured according to an overall *schema* and may be restructured for any given application by an appropriate *subschema*. But when data are maintained in application-oriented files, the applications of those other CBIS must be designed to use the existing TPS output file. This constraint severely limits the interface between TPS and other CBIS.

Manual TPS. Throughout this entry, there has been an assumption that the TPS is also a CBIS. This may not be true in every case. Much transaction processing is still done manually. For example, most

medical facilities—hospitals, clinics, doctors' offices, and the like—still maintain patients' records in file folders and update them with handwritten entries. We will not deal specifically with manual TPS here, but it is important to be aware that such systems do exist and that they pose a serious limitation on those other CBIS—MIS and DSS—that depend on TPS for input data.

Use with Application-Oriented Files

An *application-oriented file* is structured according to the processing requirements of a specific application and is normally used exclusively with its corresponding application program. In fact, it is common to store the application program at the beginning of the master file so both are readily accessible at processing time. This is the way data were managed in traditional DP systems and are still managed in many contemporary TPS.

Application-oriented files may be on punched cards, magnetic tape, magnetic disks, or some combination of these three media. Combinations can occur when different media are used in different stages of processing. For example, a billing application could use punched cards as transaction documents, transfer the data on cards to tape to use as a transaction file, and then use the tape to update a master file on disk. This is a rather extreme example, however, and in those that follow it will be assumed that the transaction and master files, at least, are on similar media.

Even if a single medium were always used throughout an application, differences among applications would necessitate a combination of media within a TPS. Most TPS have facilities for cards, tape, disks, and perhaps other media. The exact proportion of work carried out on the various media is determined by the mix of applications.

Card Systems. Card systems date back to the earliest days of data processing and represent something of an intermediate stage between manual and automated information systems. On one hand, cards can be read visually, sorted, filed, and handled like conventional transaction documents. On the other hand, they can also be read, sorted, merged, collated, and otherwise processed by machines. These characteristics give rise to a curious blend of manual and computer operations in transaction processing with cards.

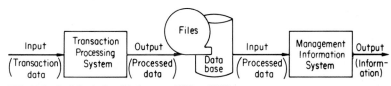

FIG. M-2 Serial relationship between TPS and MIS.

Updating a Card File. A pure card system does not use files in on-line storage. Instead, all data necessary for processing—the program, master file, and transaction file—are maintained off-line, in decks, until the time for updating. Since most card systems use a single card reader, some provision must be made for bringing the appropriate transaction record and master record into internal memory simultaneously. This is done off-line by first sorting both files into identical sequence and then merging the two decks into a single data deck. If every master record is to be updated, there will be alternate transactions or master records, but there may be consecutive transactions or master records if some master records need not be updated or if some new master records are to be opened.

Part of the output of a card system, in addition to any reports generated, will be a new master file on cards. In the next processing cycle, this file, along with the program deck and a new deck of transactions, will serve as input. The old transaction and master file may be saved as historical records or as back-up material to re-create a new master file should something happen to the current one.

Advantages and Disadvantages. Card systems are simple and somewhat reassuring to lay people because of the built-in backup capability. Furthermore, cards can double as turnaround documents; that is, they are output of one cycle that is "turned around" by a user or customer and become input for a subsequent cycle. These were distinct advantages in early data processing applications, particularly in finance and accounting, when computers were less reliable and auditors were inexperienced in computer operations. It is still common to use card systems in payroll and billing applications (look at your last paycheck or utility bill, for example), but cards are slowly and surely being replaced by other media.

One reason for the decline of card systems is, of course, the slow speed of card readers and card punches and the consequent underutilization of the computer's central processing unit (CPU). But cards are also bulky and difficult to use when damp (from humidity, for example) or dog-eared. Cards also require extensive off-line operations in the form of keypunching, verifying, sorting, merging, collating, duplicating, and the like—most of which can be done in the CPU or are unnecessary with other media. These off-line operations also involve special pieces of equipment that are increasingly idle as card usage declines, thereby creating further pressure to eliminate cards and their associated equipment.

Tape Systems. Tape represents a transition from cards to more sophisticated media, such as disks, in the same way that cards were a transition from manual to computer operations. To a certain extent, tape systems merely emulate the operation of card systems, but they use a technology (magnetic

impressions on an oxide of iron) like that of disks. Files in tape systems tend to be magnetic versions of card decks, but they can be read and written at speeds approaching those associated with disks. Like card systems, they preserve the old master file intact, and like disk systems, they use on-line storage and can accommodate very large files. For these and other reasons, tape systems have enjoyed a great deal of success and popularity in transaction processing and still carry a large share of the processing work load in TPS.

Updating a Tape File. In a typical tape operation the program and the master file are stored on one tape and the transaction file, organized into the same sequence as the master file, is on a second tape. After the program is read and rewritten onto a third tape (which will also hold the new master file), the first transaction is compared with the first record on the old master file. If the records match, transaction data and master file data are combined to create an updated record for the new master file.

If there is no corresponding transaction record for the master record, it is an indication that one or more master records are not to be updated and the master file is advanced (with the unchanged records being copied onto the new master file) until there is a match.

If there is no corresponding master record for a transaction record, it is an indication that a new master record must be created from the transaction data and written onto the new master file. The transaction file is then advanced for the next comparison.

All of these rules are dependent upon (1) accurate sequencing of records in both transaction and master files and (2) the absence of errors. In practice, additional steps, such as editing the transaction file and adding a data element to indicate the required updating process (to add, delete, or change a master record), are taken to ensure accuracy.

As records are updated, data to be included in any printed output are placed in a temporary storage area, either internal or external, until the updating process is completed and reports can be prepared according to program instructions. The new master file now becomes the basic source of data for the application. The old master file and transaction file are stored, off-line, for a few cycles as backup in the event of loss or damage to the new master file. The relationship among the several master files is often explained in family terms: the backup file is called the *grandparent* file, the one used in processing is called the *parent*, and the new one, naturally, is called the *child*.

Advantages and Disadvantages. Tape systems have several distinct advantages over card systems. Tapes can be read much faster than cards, they are less bulky for any given volume of data, and preliminary operations, such as sorting, can be performed by computer. But the biggest advantage of tapes is that they may be stored on-line, in quantity, subject only to limitations of the number of tape drives available and the capability of the CPU to support peripherals. Also, the creation of a completely new master file while preserving the transaction file and the old master file for backup purposes, a trait shared with card systems, is an advantage over the disk system described in the following section.

The biggest disadvantage of tape systems is that they are limited to sequential files. When many transactions are to be processed at once, as in the case of a monthly billing system or a payroll system, transactions can be sequenced as in the master file and processing with tape is quite efficient. However, if transactions must be processed serially, as they occur, tape systems are prohibitively slow.

A lesser disadvantage is that tape systems tie up a lot of equipment. In order to update a master file on tape with a tape transaction file, a minimum of three tape drives is required—one each for the transaction file, the old master file, and the new master file. If several tape applications are to be run concurrently, under time-sharing, the requirement for tape drives could easily exceed the number available.

Finally, pure tape systems cannot operate in a data-base environment. It is possible, of course, for a tape-disk system to use a data-base management system, but it is not possible to maintain a DBMS on a sequential access storage device.

Disk Systems. Disks are rapidly becoming the most popular medium for transaction processing. Disk drives, although somewhat more expensive than tape drives, are faster, have greater capacity, and offer more freedom in the choice of processing modes. Although disk drives are *direct access storage devices* (DASD) and are most commonly used with *random* files, it is also possible to create *sequential* files on disks.

Updating a Sequential Disk File. There are several reasons for using sequential files on disks. First, random files become inefficient when the disk is more than one-half full; with sequential files, the disk can be filled to capacity without loss of efficiency. Second, there is a limited capability to update a sequential master file on disk with a serial or other nonsequential transaction file. Finally, if all or most of the other applications in the TPS use random files, it may not be worth the bother to introduce tape just to support one or two sequential applications.

When both the master and transaction files are sequential, processing is conducted almost exactly as in a tape system with the obvious exception that disk drives are substituted for tape drives. The direct access capability of the disk drive is lost, of course, but the system can access the next record in physical order in much the same way that tape systems can read the next record on a tape. The comparison of records is conducted exactly as with tape. The new

master file is even created on a new disk—a departure from the more common random file procedures—although both old and new disks may be on the same drive.

Updating a Random Disk File. When the master file is organized randomly, the sequence of the transaction file is unimportant. When a transaction is read, the master record can be found by "key transformation" (a method of converting a numerical element in the record into a storage address) or by an index at the beginning of the file and brought into the CPU for updating. In contrast to processing with sequential files, the new master record is returned to the same location on the same disk from which the old master record came. The process of rewriting the new record over the old record effectively erases the old one although it does cut down on the total amount of storage space required for the application.

Advantages and Disadvantages. Disk systems are favored over tape or card systems because of their higher speeds, direct access capabilities, and large on-line storage capacities. They also permit greater flexibility in the choice of file organization and processing modes although it would be inefficient to use a disk system exclusively with sequential files and simply imitate a tape system.

The one major drawback of disk systems is the erasing of the old master file when updating a randomly organized file. Although it is now rare, disk drives are susceptible to "head crashes" in which a read or write head makes contact with the magnetized surface of the disk, scoring it and destroying any data recorded there. In such cases, it is difficult to reconstruct a new master file without an old one. Also, certain financial and other applications have auditing requirements that are difficult to carry out without historical files. In these instances, the master and transaction files must periodically be transferred onto a second disk, a tape, or even a printout and held in the data library to satisfy legal or operational requirements.

Use in a Data-Base Environment

The data processing ancestors of transaction processing systems were all application-oriented, and many TPS, even when they are part of a CBIS family that includes MIS and DSS, still use application-oriented files. Nevertheless, there is an ever-increasing trend to apply data-base concepts and data-base management systems concepts to transaction processing, especially where they are already incorporated into higher-level CBIS. Since data-base management systems are discussed elsewhere in this handbook, we will use a somewhat simplified model, shown in Fig. M-3, to point out the major differences between

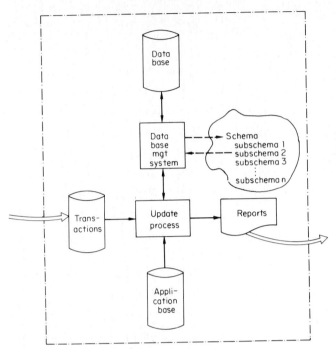

FIG. M-3 Updating in a data-base environment.

transaction processing with application-oriented files and with a data base.

The use of the symbol for a direct access storage device (DASD) to depict the data base in Fig. M-3 is not arbitrary. Data must be stored in DASD if they are to be structured and restructured constantly according to the various subschema required by the application programs. It should be borne in mind, however, that it is not the DASD per se that determines the extent of file independence; many application-oriented files are on disks or other DASD. Instead, it is the DASD working in conjunction with a DBMS that creates the data-base environment.

Updating a Data Base. Since the data base must be on a DASD, one expects the updating process to be somewhat similar to updating in a disk system with application-oriented files. It is, but there are several important differences. First, there is no permanent master file. An equivalent of a master file is defined by a subschema and is assembled as needed for the application. Second, application programs obviously cannot be stored at the beginning of the master file as they are in application-oriented TPS. Instead, application programs are drawn from an *application base* which is also maintained on a DASD.

The application base is the repository of application programs for all CBIS, although DSS often have a separate base of programs called a *model base*. This name derives from the fact that many programs used in DSS literally are mathematical or statistical models. The programs normally used for transaction processing, however, are little different from those used with application-oriented files. All that is unique about these programs in a data-base environment is the inclusion of program statements to identify the subschema by which data are structured for the application.

At this point, the system has all the characteristics of the disk system described earlier, to include the ability to update either a sequentially or a randomly organized master file. If the master file is sequential, the transaction file usually will be sorted in like sequence, but if the master file is random, the transaction file may be in any sequence—just as in any other disk system. Updating then proceeds as in the comparable application-oriented disk system.

When the updating process is complete, a third difference is evident. The "new" master file is disbanded and the individual data elements are returned—by the DBMS—to their original locations in the data base. For updated elements, the new values replace the former values and are the ones that will be used in any subsequent processing—even if it occurs only seconds later and involves a completely different application.

Advantages and Disadvantages. Data-base management systems (1) reduce redundancy in data collection, preparation, and storage; (2) simplify data maintenance; (3) reduce processing time; (4) improve consistency; and (5) facilitate the sharing of data. For transaction processing, which tends to serve as the primary source of CBIS data, the major advantage lies in the reduction of redundancy in data input. Data collection, preparation, and entry is perhaps the most time-consuming and error-prone phase of CBIS operations. Any reduction in data input is bound to improve DBIS accuracy and efficiency.

The disadvantages of a data-base environment for transaction processing are also similar to those for DBMS in general: DBMS are costly, security is more difficult, errors or breaches of security are more damaging, and greater control is required. No one of these disadvantages is more significant than the others in transaction processing; all must be considered in the decision to implement a DBMS.

Processing Modes

The *mode* of processing refers to the timing of the updating process with respect to the occurrence of transactions. Transaction data may be collected and processed periodically—say, at the end of each day—or as the transactions occur. In the first case, the mode is said to be *batch* while in the second it is called *transactional* or *on-line.** In the special case in which a transactional system processes some data and returns output in time to influence the remainder of the transaction, it is further identified as being *real-time.* A few examples will serve to illustrate the several processing modes.

Batch Processing. In most transaction processing applications, the updating interval is much greater than the interval between transactions. A payroll file, for example, may be updated weekly, although payroll transactions (the earning of pay) take place continuously. Credit card holders can charge purchases daily, but they are billed only monthly. In these and similar cases, transaction data are held until processing time and all records on the master file are updated in a batch, in a single run through the master file. Batch processing can be conducted with any medium (cards, tape, or disk) and with either application-oriented files or a data base.

Transactional Processing. When output is required for each transaction—say, to give a receipt to a customer—or when the data collection process is on-line, it is more efficient to process transactions as they occur. Many retail sales applications now operate in a transactional mode. Instead of punching sales data on cards or keying them onto tape or disk at the end of the day, transactions are recorded on point-of-sale terminals which double as cash regis-

ters. The operator may key in such data as the price, quantity, stock number, department, clerk identification, and sales tax, or some of these data may be read optically by a *wand.* Processes not apparent to the customer and the clerk also post the sale to department accounts, deduct the quantity sold from inventory, debit charge accounts, and maintain records for sales and marketing analysis. These latter functions also illustrate the manner in which transaction processing supports higher-level activities in MIS and DSS. Transactional processing requires a direct access medium such as a disk, but it may be conducted with either application-oriented files or a data base.

Real-Time Processing. Real-time processing, the ability to influence a transaction while it is taking place, is one of the most powerful capabilities of transaction processing. The first real-time systems were developed by the U.S. Air Force for air defense missile control, where only fractions of a second could be tolerated between the detection of an approaching aircraft and the decision to launch a missile against it. This application led many to equate "real time" with "instantaneous." This is not a bad definition for the air defense application, but in TPS much slower systems can be considered real-time.

Real-time processing is *interactive;* that is, there is an exchange of inputs and outputs at the source of the transaction. Real-time applications in business typically use a CRT or typewriter terminal to gain interactive access to a processor and master file.

Real-time systems are of necessity transactional or on-line. Indeed, such systems are often described as *on-line/real-time* although that terminology is somewhat redundant. Airline ticket reservation systems are excellent examples that demonstrate both real-time and transactional capabilities in a business application.

The ticket reservation system is real-time because the initial processing of a request for an airline ticket influences the outcome of the transaction—whether a ticket is sold or not. When a ticket request is keyed into a terminal at the reservation counter, the master file record for that flight is checked for the availability of a seat. If a seat is available, it is temporarily "booked" to prevent its commitment to another reservation office, and that information is displayed on a CRT screen. A second input at the reservation terminal confirms the sale and makes the booking permanent. The entire process may take a few minutes, but that is real-time in ticket reservation if not in air defense!

The ticket reservation system is also transactional since requests for tickets are processed individually, as they occur, instead of periodically in a batch. Different versions of this system can also print tickets, bill customers for tickets purchased on credit, and provide data for scheduling and route optimization.

---

*The term *transactional processing,* which means that transactions are processed as they occur, should not be confused with the similar term, *transaction processing,* which means literally the processing of transactions and may be either batch or transactional.

505

Again, in these latter uses, we see the value of transaction data in decision support and management information.

Computer booking on airlines often raises the question of overbooking. When more tickets are sold than there are seats on a flight, it is rarely due to a failure of the reservation system. More likely, it is a deliberate policy based on statistical evidence that a few ticket holders will not show up for the flight. This is an interesting example of another form of interface between the TPS and a higher-level system such as a DSS: the TPS furnishes data for analysis by the DSS and the DSS is the probable source of the criteria (such as overbooking) for processing transactions.

Summary

Transaction processing systems perform many of the functions originally associated with data processing, but in a CBIS environment they also are a basic source of data for the higher-level systems of MIS and DSS.

In the TPS function of *data input*, data are collected, prepared, and entered. When data input is direct, all three functions are carried out in a single step. In indirect data input, collection is a separate step but preparation and entry may still be combined.

Processing in TPS is typified by the storage, retrieval, classification, organization, and updating of transaction data. In general, these processes are less complex than those found in MIS or DSS.

The *output* of TPS is in the form of detail and scheduled reports, responses to inquiries, or input to other CBIS. The manner in which TPS output is made available to other CBIS depends on the approach to data management. A data-base approach provides much greater access than do application-oriented files.

Application-oriented TPS can use master files on cards, tape, or disk, but disk files are now the most popular. Application-oriented files are less costly and more secure, but are less accessible to other CBIS applications and may result in duplication of data.

TPS operating in a data-base environment must use master files on disk or other DSAD. Data bases and data-base management systems are costly, but they reduce much redundancy in the TPS data input and storage.

Transactions may be processed as they occur, in a transactional mode, or saved and processed periodically, in a batch mode. The transactional mode is further classified as real-time when the initial output of the process is received in time to influence the outcome of the transaction. The nature of the transaction process, to include the requirement for speed, will determine the best combination of file organization, medium, and processing mode to use in any particular application.

See also Computer security; Computer software, data-base management; Computer software, languages; Computer software packages; Data-bases, commercial; Decision support systems; Forms design and control; Information science; Information sources; Management information systems (MIS); Office automation; Paperwork simplification; Records management; Systems and procedures; Word processing.

REFERENCES

Awad, Elias M.: *Business Data Processing*, Prentice-Hall, Englewood Cliffs, N.J., 1980.

Kroeber, Donald W., and Hugh J. Watson: *Computer-Based Information Systems: A Management Approach*, Macmillan, New York, 1984.

Kroenke, David M.: *Business Computer Systems: An Introduction*, 2d ed., Mitchell, Santa Cruz, Calif., 1984.

Murach, Mike: *Business Data Processing with BASIC and FORTRAN*, 2d ed., Science Research Associates, Chicago, 1977.

Spencer, Donald D.: *Data Processing: An Introduction*, Charles E. Merrill, Columbus, Ohio, 1978.

Watson, Hugh J., and Archie B. Carroll: *Computers for Business*, 2d ed., Business Publications, Dallas, Tex., 1980.

DONALD W. KROEBER, *James Madison University*

Management Theory, Science, and Approaches

There may be no more important kind of human activity than managing. It is the basic task of all managers at all levels and in all kinds of enterprises to design and maintain an environment in which individuals, working together in groups, can accomplish preselected missions and objectives. In other words, managers are charged with the responsibility of doing those things which make it possible for individuals to contribute most effectively to attainment of group objectives.

In establishing this environment for group effort, the goal of all managers must logically and morally be productivity. In other words, whether managers are in a business or nonbusiness enterprise, whether they are presidents or supervisors, their principal task is to manage in such a way as (1) to accomplish objectives with a minimum input of money, materials, effort, time, or human dissatisfactions or (2) to accomplish as much of a mission or objective as possible with the available resources. Managers do so, of course, while being responsive to their entire external environment—economic, technological, political, social, and ethical. The purposes of an enterprise or department may vary, and these purposes may be more difficult to define in one situation than in another, but the basic managerial goal is the same.

In an activity as important and universal as managing, the nature of the basic knowledge—concepts, theory, and techniques—underlying its practice holds tremendous significance for managers, for those being managed, and, indeed, for the entire society.

Management as Art, Science, and Theory

In managing, as in any other field, unless practitioners are to learn only through trial and error, there is no other place they can turn to for meaningful guidance than the accumulated knowledge underlying their practice. Yet, in managing, much confusion remains about the nature of managerial knowledge. Questions are often raised about whether management is a science or an art, what theory exists, and in what way it can be useful to managers, how technology fits into theory and science, and why there are so many schools or approaches to management theory and knowledge. What can managers believe, and how can this belief be useful to them?

Both Art and Science. While these questions are often raised, a moment of reflection will indicate that they are really rather meaningless. Managing, like all other practices, is an art. It is know-how. It is doing things in the light of the realities of a situation. But the practice of managing must make use of underlying organized knowledge; and it is *this* knowledge, whether crude or advanced, whether exact or inexact, which, to the extent that it is well-organized, clear, and pertinent, constitutes a science. Thus, managing as practice is art; the organized knowledge underlying it may be referred to as science. Consequently, science and art are not mutually exclusive; they are complementary.

As science improves, so should art, as has happened in the physical and biological sciences. To be sure, the science underlying managing is fairly crude and inexact. This is true partly because the multitude of variables which managers deal with are extremely complex and partly because relatively little research and development have been done in the field of management. But such management knowledge as is available can certainly be used to improve managerial practice. Physicians without the advantage of science would be little more than witch doctors. Executives who attempt to manage without such management science as is available today must trust to luck, intuition, or what they did in the past.

Science and Theory. Science is organized knowledge. The essential feature of any science is that knowledge has been systematized through the application of the scientific method. Thus, the science of astronomy or chemistry, for example, involves clear concepts, theory, and other accumu-lated knowledge developed from hypotheses, experimentation, and analysis.

Scientific methods first require clarity of concepts. The meanings of words and terms must be clear, relevant to the phenomenon being analyzed, and meaningful to the scientist and practitioner alike. From this base, scientific method involves (1) determining facts through observation of events and verifying these facts through continued observation; (2) classifying and analyzing these facts; (3) identifying causal relationships which are believed to be true; and (4) testing these generalizations for accuracy and truth. When these generalizations appear to reflect or explain reality, and therefore to have value in predicting what will happen in similar circumstances, they are called *principles*. This does not always imply that these principles are unquestionably or invariably true; but it does imply that they are valid enough to be used for prediction and analysis.

Theory is a systematic grouping of interdependent concepts and principles which provides a framework or ties together a significant area of knowledge.

Role of Management Theory. In the field of management, the role of theory is to provide a means of classifying significant and pertinent management knowledge. In the area of designing an effective organization structure, for example, a number of related principles have a predictive value for managers. There are principles, for example, that provide guidelines for delegating authority: delegating by results expected; the coincidence of authority and responsibility and the unity of command. Likewise, to make comprehensible the task of managerial planning, theory will disclose that decision making must be related to objectives sought, must be made in the light of the expected environment in which the decision will operate, and must involve proper analysis of the most promising alternatives.

It should be noted that principles in management, like those in physics, are descriptive or predictive and are not prescriptive. For example, the principle of unity of command states only that the more exclusively an individual reports to a single superior, the more likely it is that he or she will feel a sense of loyalty and obligation and the less likely that there will be confusion in instructions. The principle merely predicts. It in no sense prescribes that an individual should *never* report to more than one person. It does suggest, however, that if this is done, a manager must expect some possible disadvantages which should be taken into account in balancing the advantages, in some instances, of having multiple command.

In applying theory to managing, managers, like engineers who apply physical principles to the design of a machine, must blend or compromise principles with realities. An engineer is often faced with the need to compromise considerations of weight, size, conductivity, and other factors in designing an instrument. Likewise, a manager may find that the advantages of giving a controller authority to prescribe accounting procedures throughout an organization outweigh the possible costs of disunity of command. By knowing the relevant theory, an informed manager will know that costs of disunity do exist and can undertake steps (such as making this functional authority crystal clear) to minimize the disadvantages.

Management Techniques. Techniques are essentially reliable ways of doing things, methods for attaining a given result. In all fields of practice, techniques are important. This is true in management, too, even though relatively few vitally important managerial techniques have been invented. Among the most notable are budgeting, network planning and control as in the program evaluation and review technique (PERT) or the critical-path method (CPM), rate-of-return-on-investment control, managing by objectives, and decision-tree analysis. As ways of doing things, techniques normally reflect theory and provide a means of helping managers to undertake activities most effectively.

By its very nature, managerial practice requires that managers take into account the realities of a situation when they apply theory or techniques. The task of science and theory is not to *prescribe* what should be done. Theories of management do not advocate the best way to do things in every situation any more than the science of astrophysics tells an engineer how to design the single best space vehicle for all kinds of applications. The manner in which theory and science are applied in practice naturally depends on the situation.

The Management Theory Jungle

Harold Koontz found over two decades ago that well-meaning researchers and writers, mostly from academic halls, were attempting to explain the nature and knowledge of managing from six different points of view, then referred to as "schools."[1] These were: (1) the management process school, (2) the empirical or "case" school, (3) the human behavior school, (4) the social system school, (5) the decision theory school, and (6) the mathematics school.

The varying schools, or approaches (as they are better called), have led to a jungle of confusing thought, theory, and advice to practicing managers. The major sources of entanglement in the jungle were often due to varying meanings given common words like "organization," to differences in defining management as a body of knowledge, to widespread casting aside of the findings of early practicing managers as being "armchair" rather than what they were—the distilled experience and thought of per-

ceptive men and women—to misunderstanding the nature and role of principles and theory, and to an inability or unwillingness on the part of many "experts" to understand each other.

Although managing has been an important human task since the dawn of group effort, with few exceptions the serious attempt to develop a body of organized knowledge—science—underpinning practice has been a product of the present century. Moreover, until the past quarter century almost all of the meaningful writing was the product of alert and perceptive practitioners—for example, French industrialist Henri Fayol, General Motors executive James Mooney, Johns-Manville vice president Alvin Brown, British chocolate executive Oliver Sheldon, New Jersey Bell Telephone president Chester Barnard, and British management consultant Lyndall Urwick.

But the early absence of the academics from the field of management has been more than atoned for by the deluge of writing on management from our colleges and universities in the past 35 years. For example, there are now more than 100 different textbooks purporting to tell the reader—student or manager—what management is all about. And in related fields like psychology, sociology, system sciences, and mathematical modeling, the number of textbooks that can be used to teach some aspect—usually narrow—of management is at least as large.

The jungle has perhaps been made more impenetrable by the infiltration in our colleges and universities of many highly, but narrowly, trained instructors who are intelligent but know too little about the actual task of managing and the realities practicing managers face. In looking around the faculties of our business, management, and public administration schools, both undergraduate and graduate, practicing executives are impressed with the number of bright but inexperienced faculty members who are teaching management or some aspect of it. It seems to some like having professors in medical schools teaching surgery without ever having operated on a patient. As a result, many practicing managers are losing confidence in our colleges and universities and the kind of management taught.

It is certainly true that those who teach and write about basic operational management theory can use the findings and assistance of colleagues who are especially trained in psychology, sociology, mathematics, and operations research. But what dismays many is that some professors believe they are teaching management when they are only teaching these specialties.

What caused this? Basically two things. In the first place, the famous Ford Foundation (Gordon and Howell) and Carnegie Foundation (Pearson) reports in 1959 on our business school programs in American colleges and universities, authored and researched by scholars who were not trained in management, indicted the quality of business education in the United States and urged schools, including those that were already doing everything the researchers recommended, to adopt a broader and more social science approach to their curricula and faculty. As a result, many deans and other administrators went with great speed and vigor to recruit specialists in such fields as economics, mathematics, psychology, sociology, social psychology, and quantitative methods.

A second reason for the large number of faculty members trained in special fields, rather than in basic management theory and policy, is the fact that the rapid expansion of business and management schools occurred since 1960, during a period when there was an acute shortage of faculty candidates trained in management and with some managerial experience. This shortage was consequently filled by an increasing number of Ph.D.s in the specialized fields noted above.

The Continuing Jungle

That the theory and science of management are far from being mature is apparent in the continuation of the management theory jungle. What has happened in the intervening years since 1961?[2] The jungle still exists, and in fact, there are nearly double the approaches to management that were identified only two decades ago. At the present time, a total of 11 approaches to the study of management science and theory may be identified. These are: (1) the empirical or case approach, (2) the interpersonal behavior approach, (3) the group behavior approach, (4) the cooperative social system approach, (5) the sociotechnical systems approach, (6) the decision theory approach, (7) the systems approach, (8) the mathematical or "management science" approach, (9) the contingency or situational approach, (10) the managerial roles approach, and (11) the operational theory approach.

Differences Between the Original and Present Jungle. What has caused this almost doubling of approaches to management theory and science? In the first place, one of the approaches found two decades ago has been split into two. The original "human behavior school" has been divided into the interpersonal behavior approach (psychology) and the group behavior approach (sociology and cultural anthropology). The original social systems approach is essentially the same, but because its proponents seem to rest more heavily on the theories of Chester Barnard,[3] it now seems more accurate to refer to it as the cooperative social systems approach.

Remaining essentially the same since Koontz's original article are (1) the empirical or case

approach, (2) the decision theory approach, and (3) the mathematical or "management science" approach. Likewise, what was originally termed the "management process school" is now referred to more accurately as the operational theory approach.

New approaches that have become popular in the past two decades include the sociotechnical systems approach. This was first given birth by the research and writings of Eric Trist and his associates in the Tavistock Institute in 1951 but did not get many followers to form a clear-cut approach until the late 1960s.[4] Also, even though the systems approach to any science or practice is not new (it was recognized in the original jungle as the "social systems" approach), its scholarly and widespread approach to management theory really occurred in the 1960s particularly with the work of Johnson, Kast, and Rosenzweig (1963).[5]

The managerial roles approach has gained its identification and adherents as the result of the research and writing of Henry Mintzberg, who prefers to call this approach the "work activity school."[6]

The contingency or situational approach to management theory and science is really on outgrowth of early classical, or operational, theory. Believing that most theory before the 1970s too often advocated the "one best way," and often overlooking the fact that intelligent practicing managers have always tailored their practice to the actual situation, a fairly significant number of management scholars have begun building management theory and research around what should be done in various situations, or contingencies.

Many writers who have apparently not read the so-called classicists in management carefully have come up with the inaccurate shibboleth that classical writers were prescribing the "one best way." It is true that Gilbreth in his study of bricklaying was searching for the one best way, but that was bricklaying and not managing. Fayol recognized this clearly when he said "principles are flexible and capable of adaptation to every need; it is a matter of knowing how to make use of them, which is a difficult art requiring intelligence, experience, decision, and proportion."[7]

Current Approaches. It is hoped the reader will realize that outlining the 11 approaches must necessarily be terse. Such conciseness may upset some adherents to the various approaches and some may even consider the treatment superficial, but space limitations make it necessary to be brief in identifying and commenting on most approaches.

The Empirical or Case Approach. The members of this school study management by analyzing experience, usually through cases. It is based on the premise that students and practitioners will understand the field of management and somehow come to know how to manage effectively by studying managerial successes and failures in various individual cases.

However, unless a study of experience is aimed at determining *fundamentally* why something happened or did not happen, it is likely to be a questionable and even dangerous approach to understanding management, because what happened or did not happen in the past is not likely to help in solving problems in a most certainly different future. If distillation of experience takes place with a view to finding basic generalizations, this approach can be a useful one to develop or support some principles and theories of management.

The Interpersonal Behavior Approach. This approach is apparently based on the thesis that managing involves getting things done through people, and that therefore the study of management should be centered on interpersonal relations. The writers and scholars in this school are heavily oriented to individual psychology and, indeed, most are trained as psychologists. Their focus is on the individual and his or her motivations as a sociopsychological being. In this schoool are those who appear to emphasize human relations as an art that managers, even when foolishly trying to be amateur psychiatrists, can understand and practice. There are those who see the manager as a leader and may even equate managership and leadership—thus, in effect, treating all "led" activities as "managed." Others have concentrated on motivation or leadership and have cast important light on these subjects, which has been useful to managers.

That the study of human interactions, whether in the context of managing or elsewhere, is useful and important cannot be denied. But it can hardly be said that the field of interpersonal behavior encompasses all there is to management. It is entirely possible for all the managers of a company to understand psychology and its nuances and yet not be effective in managing. One major division of a large American company put its managers from top to bottom through sensitivity training (called by its critics "psychological striptease") only to find that the managers had learned much about feelings but little about how to manage. Both research and practice are finding that we must go far beyond interpersonal relations to develop a useful science of management.

The Group Behavior Approach. This approach is closely related to the interpersonal behavior approach and may be confused with it. But it is concerned primarily with behavior of people in groups rather than with interpersonal behavior. It thus tends to rely on sociology, anthropology, and social psychology rather than on individual psychology. Its emphasis is on group behavior patterns. This approach varies all the way from the study of small groups, with their cultural and behavioral patterns, to the behavioral characteristics of large groups. It is often called a study of "organization behavior," and

the term "organization" may be taken to mean the system, or pattern, of any set of group relationships in a company, a government agency, a hospital, or any other kind of undertaking. Sometimes the term is used as Chester Barnard employed it, meaning "the cooperation of two or more persons," and "formal organization" as an organization with conscious, deliberate, joint purpose.[8] Chris Argyris has even used the term "organization" to include "*all* the behavior of *all* the participants" in a group undertaking.[9]

It is not difficult to see that a practicing manager would not be likely to recognize that "organizations" cover such a broad area of group behavior patterns. At the same time, many of the problems of managers do arise from group behavior patterns, attitudes, desires, and prejudices, some of which come from the groups within an enterprise, but many of which come from the cultural environment of people outside of a given company, department, or agency. What is perhaps most disturbing about this school of thought is the tendency of its members to draw an artificial and inaccurate line between "organization behavior" and "managing." Group behavior is an important aspect of management. But it is not all there is to management.

The Cooperative Social System Approach. A modification of the interpersonal and group behavior approaches has been the focus of some behavioral scientists on the study of human relationships as cooperative social systems. The idea of human relationships as social systems was early perceived by the Italian sociologist Vilfredo Pareto. His work apparently affected modern adherents to this school through his influence on Chester Barnard. In seeking to explain the work of executives, Barnard saw them operating in, and maintaining, cooperative social systems, which he referred to as "organizations."[10] He perceived social systems as the cooperative interaction of ideas, forces, desires, and thinking of two or more persons. An increasing number of writers have expanded this concept to apply to any system of cooperative and purposeful group interrelationships or behavior and have given it the rather general title of "organization theory."

The cooperative social systems approach does have pertinence to the study and analysis of management. All managers do operate in a cooperative social system. But we do not find what is generally referred to as managers in *all* kinds of cooperative social systems. We would hardly think of a cooperative group of shoppers in a department store or an unorganized mob as being managed. Nor would we think of a family group gathering to celebrate a birthday as being managed. Therefore, we can conclude that this approach is broader than management while still overlooking many concepts, principles, and techniques that are important to managers.

The Sociotechnical Systems Approach. One of

the newer schools of management identifies itself as the sociotechnical systems approach. This development is generally credited to E. L. Trist and his associates at the Tavistock Institute of England. In studies made of production problems in long-wall coal mining, this group found that it was not enough merely to analyze social problems. Instead, in dealing with problems of mining productivity, they found that the technical system (machines and methods) had a strong influence on the social system. In other words, they discovered that personal attitudes and group behavior are strongly influenced by the technical system in which people work. It is therefore the position of this school of thought that social and technical systems must be considered together and that a major task of a manager is to make sure that these two systems are made harmonious.

Most of the work of this school has consequently concentrated on production, office operations, and other areas in which the technical systems have a very close connection to people and their work. It therefore tends to be heavily oriented to industrial engineering. As an approach to management, this school has made some interesting contributions to managerial practice, even though it does not, as some of its proponents seem to believe, encompass all there is to management. Moreover, it is doubtful that any experienced manager would be surprised that the technology of the assembly line or the technology in railroad transportation or in oil companies affects individuals, groups, and their behavior patterns, the way operations are organized, and the techniques of managing required. Furthermore, as promising and helpful as this approach is in certain aspects of enterprise operations, it is safe to observe that there is much more to pertinent management knowledge than can be found in it.

The Decision Theory Approach. This approach to management theory and science has apparently been based on the belief that, because it is a major task of managers to make decisions, we should concentrate on decision making. It is not surprising that there are many scholars and theorists who believe that because managing is characterized by decision making, the central focus of management theory should be decision making and all of management thought can be built around it. This has a degree of reasonableness. However, it overlooks the fact that there is much more to managing than making decisions and that, for most managers, the actual making of a decision is a fairly easy thing—if goals are clear, if the environment in which the decision will operate can be anticipated fairly accurately, if adequate information is available, if the organization structure provides a clear understanding of responsibility for decisions, if competent people are available to make decisions, and if many of the other prerequisites of effective managing are present.

The Systems Approach. During recent years,

many scholars and writers in management have emphasized the systems approach to the study and analysis of management thought. They feel that this is the most effective means by which such thought can be organized, presented, and understood.

A system is essentially a set or assemblage of things interconnected, or interdependent, so as to form a complex unity. These things may be physical, as with the parts of an automobile engine; they may be biological, as with components of the human body; or they may be theoretical, as with a well-integrated assemblage of concepts, principles, theory, and techniques in an area such as managing. All systems, except perhaps the universe, interact with and are influenced by their environments, although we define boundaries for them so that we can see and analyze them more clearly.

The long use of systems theory and analyses in physical and biological sciences has given rise to a considerable body of systems knowledge. It comes as no surprise that systems theory has been found helpfully applicable to management theory and science. Some of us have long emphasized an arbitrary boundary of management knowledge—the theory underlying the managerial job in terms of what managers do. This boundary is set for the field of management theory and science in order to make the subject "manageable," but this does not imply a closed systems approach to the subject. On the contrary, there are *always* many interactions with the system environment. Thus, when managers plan, they have no choice but to take into account such external variables as markets, technology, social forces, laws, and regulations. When managers design an organizational structure to provide an environment for performance, they cannot help but be influenced by the behavior patterns people bring to their jobs from the environment that is external to an enterprise.

Systems also play an important part within the area of managing itself. There are planning systems, organizational systems, and control systems. And, within these, we can perceive many subsystems, such as systems of delegation, network planning, and budgeting.

Intelligent and experienced practicing managers and many management writers with practical experience, accustomed as they are to seeing their problems and operations as a network of interrelated elements with daily interaction between environments inside or outside their companies or other enterprises, are often surprised to find that many writers regard the systems approach as something new. To be sure, conscious study of and emphasis on systems have forced many managers and scholars to consider more perceptively the various interacting elements affecting management theory and practice. But it can hardly be regarded as a new approach to scientific thought.

The Mathematical or "Management Science" **511**

Approach. There are some theorists who see managing as primarily an exercise in mathematical processes, concepts, symbols, and models. Perhaps the most widely known of these are the operations researchers who have often given themselves the self-anointing title of "management scientists." The primary focus of this approach is the mathematical model since, through this device, problems—whether managerial or other—can be expressed in basic relationships and, where a given goal is sought, the model can be expressed in terms which optimize that goal. Because so much of the mathematical approach is applied to problems of optimization, it could be argued that it has a strong relationship to decision theory. But, of course, mathematical modeling sometimes goes beyond decision problems.

To be sure, the journal *Management Science*, published by the Institute of Management Sciences, carries on its cover the statement that the institute has as its purpose to "identify, extend, and unify scientific knowledge pertaining to management." But as judged by the articles published in this journal and the hundreds of papers presented by members of the institute at its many meetings all over the world, the school seems to be almost completely preoccupied with mathematical models and elegance in simulating situations and in developing solutions to certain kinds of problems. Consequently, as many critics both inside and outside the ranks of the "management scientists" have observed, the narrow mathematical focus can hardly be called a complete approach to a true management science.

No one interested in any scientific field can overlook the great usefulness of mathematical models and analyses. But it is difficult to see mathematics as a school of management any more than it is a separate school of chemistry, physics, or biology. Mathematics and mathematical models are, of course, tools of analysis, not a school of thought.

The Contingency or Situational Approach. One of the approaches to management thought and practice that has tended to take management academicians by storm is the contingency approach to management. Essentially, this approach emphasizes the fact that what managers do in practice depends on a given set of circumstances—the situation. Contingency management is akin to situational management and the two terms are often used synonymously. Some scholars distinguish between the two on the basis that while situational management merely implies that what managers do depends on a given situation, contingency management implies an active interrelationship between the variables in a situation and the managerial solution devised. Thus, under a contingency approach, managers might look at an assembly-line situation and conclude that a highly structured organization pattern would best fit and interact with it.

According to some scholars, contingency theory takes into account not only given situations but also the influence of given solutions on behavior patterns of an enterprise. For example, an organization structured along the lines of operating functions (such as finance, engineering, production, and marketing) might be most suitable for a given situation, but managers in such a structure should take into account the behavioral patterns that often arise because of group loyalties to the function rather than to a company.

By its very nature, managerial practice requires that managers take into account the realities of a given situation when they apply theory or techniques. It has never been and never will be the task of science and theory to prescribe what should be done in a given situation. Science and theory in management have not and do not advocate the "best way" to do things in every situation any more than the sciences of astrophysics or mechanics tell an engineer how to design a single best instrument for all kinds of applications. How theory and science are applied in practice naturally depends on the situation.

This is saying that there is science and there is art, that there is knowledge and there is practice. These are matters that any experienced manager has long known. One does not need much experience to understand that a corner grocery store could hardly be organized like General Motors or that the technical realities of petroleum exploration, production, and refining make impracticable autonomously organized product divisions for gasoline, jet fuel, or lubricating oils.

The Managerial Roles Approach. Perhaps the newest approach to management theory to catch the attention of academics and practitioners alike is the managerial roles approach, popularized by Henry Mintzberg.[11] Essentially this approach is to observe what managers actually do and from such observations come to conclusions as to what managerial activities (or roles) are. Although there have been researchers who have studied the actual work of managers, from chief executives to foremen, Mintzberg has given this approach sharp visibility.

By systematically studying the activities of five chief executives in a variety of organizations, Mintzberg came to the conclusion that executives do not act out the traditional classification of managerial functions—planning, organizing, coordinating, and controlling. Instead they engage in a variety of other activities.

From his research and the research of others who have studied what managers actually do, Mintzberg has come to the conclusion that managers act out a set of 10 roles. These are:

A. Interpersonal Roles
   1. Figurehead (performing ceremonial and

social duties as the organization's representative)
2. Leader
3. Liaison (particularly with outsiders)

B. Informational Roles
1. Monitor (receiving information about the operation of an enterprise)
2. Disseminator (passing information to subordinates)
3. Spokesperson (transmitting information outside the organization)

C. Decision Roles
1. Entrepreneur
2. Disturbance handler
3. Resource allocator
4. Negotiator (dealing with various persons and groups of persons)

Mintzberg refers to the usual way of classifying managerial functions as "folklore." As we will see in the following discussion on the operational theory approach, operational theorists have used such managerial functions as planning, organizing, staffing, leading, and controlling. For example, what is resource allocation but planning? Likewise, the entrepreneurial role is certainly an element of the whole area of planning. And the interpersonal roles are mainly aspects of leading. In addition, the informational roles can be fitted into a number of the functional areas.

Nevertheless, looking at what managers actually do can have considerable value. In analyzing activities, an effective manager might wish to compare these to the basic functions of managers and use the latter as a kind of pilot's checklist to ascertain what actions are being overlooked. But the roles Mintzberg identifies appear to be inadequate. Where in them does one find such unquestionably important managerial activities as structuring organization, selecting and appraising managers, and determining major strategies? Omissions such as these can make one wonder whether the executives in his sample were effective managers. It certainly opens a serious question as to whether the managerial roles approach is an adequate one on which to base a practical theory of management.

The Operational Approach. The operational approach to management theory and science, a term borrowed from the work of P. W. Bridgman,[12] attempts to draw together the pertinent knowledge of management by relating it to the functions of managers. Like other operational sciences, it endeavors to put together for the field of management the concepts, principles, theory, and techniques that underpin the actual practice of managing.

The operational approach to management recognizes that there is a central core of knowledge about managing that exists only in management: such matters as line and staff, departmentation, the limitations of the span of management, managerial appraisal, and various managerial control techniques involve concepts and theory found only where managing is involved. But, in addition, this approach is eclectic in that it draws on pertinent knowledge derived from other fields. These include the clinical study of managerial activities, problems, and solutions; applications of systems theory; decision theory; motivation and leadership findings and theory; individual and group behavior theory; and the application of mathematical modeling and techniques. All these subjects are applicable to some extent to other fields of science, such as certain of the physical and geological sciences. But our interest in them must necessarily be limited to managerial aspects and applications.

The nature of the operational approach can perhaps best be appreciated by reference to Fig. M-4. As this diagram shows, the operational management school of thought includes a central core of science and theory unique to management plus knowledge eclectically drawn from various other schools and approaches. As the circle is intended to show, the operational approach is not interested in all the important knowledge in these various fields, but only that which is deemed to be most useful and relevant to managing.

The question of what managers do day by day and how they do it is secondary to what makes an acceptable and useful classification of knowledge. Organizing knowledge pertinent to managing is an indispensable first step in developing a useful theory and science of management. It makes possible the separation of science and techniques used in managing and those used in such nonmanagerial activities as marketing, accounting, manufacturing, and engineering. It permits us to look at the basic aspects of management that have a high degree of universality among different enterprises and different cultures. By using the functions of managers as a first step, a logical and useful start can be made in setting up pigeonholes for classifying management knowledge.

The functions many theorists have found to be useful and meaningful as this first step in classifying knowledge are:

1. Planning: selecting objectives and means of accomplishing them.
2. Organizing: designing an intentional structure of roles for people to fill.
3. Staffing: selecting, appraising, and developing people to fill organizational roles effectively.
4. Leading: taking actions to motivate people and help them see that contributing to group objectives is in their own interest.
5. Controlling: measuring and correcting activities of people to ensure that plans are being realized.

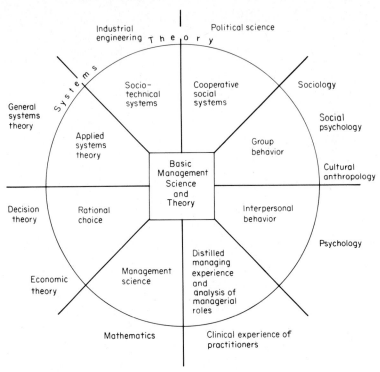

FIG. M-4 The scope of operational science and theory.

As a second step in organizing management knowledge, some of us have found it useful to propound basic questions in each functional area, such as:

1. What is the nature and purpose of each functional area?

2. What structural elements exist in each functional area?

3. What processes, techniques, and approaches are there in each functional area and what are the advantages and disadvantages of each?

4. What obstructions exist in effectively accomplishing each function?

5. How can these obstructions be removed?

Those who subscribe to the operational approach do so with the hope of developing and identifying a field of science and theory that has useful application to the practice of managing but is not so broad as to encompass everything that might have any relationships, no matter how remote, to the managerial job. Any field as complex as managing can never be isolated from its physical, technological, biological, or cultural environment. However, some partitioning of knowledge is necessary and some boundaries to this knowledge must be set if meaningful progress in summarizing and classifying pertinent knowledge is

ever to be made. Yet, as in the case of all systems analyses where system boundaries are set, it must be kept in mind that there is no such thing as a totally closed system and that many environmental variables will intrude on and influence any system proposed.

Toward a Convergence of Theories

As can be seen from the brief discussions above of the schools and approaches to management theory and science, there is evidence that the management theory jungle continues to flourish and perhaps gets denser, with nearly twice as many schools or approaches as were found over two decades ago. It is no wonder that a useful management theory and science has been so tardy in arriving.

The varying approaches, each with its own gurus, each with its own semantics, and each with a fierce pride to protect the concepts and techniques of the approach from attack or change, make the theory and science of management extremely difficult for the intelligent practitioner to understand and utilize. If the continuing jungle were only evidence of competing academic thought and research, it would not much matter. But when it retards the development of a useful theory and science and confuses practicing managers, the problem becomes serious. Effective managing at all levels and in all kinds of enterprises is too important to any society to allow it to fail through lack of available and understandable knowledge.

At the same time, there appears to be some reason to be optimistic in that signs exist indicating tendencies for the various schools of throught to coalesce. Although the convergence is by no means yet complete, there is reason to hope that as scholars and writers become more familiar with what managers do and the situations in which they act, more and more of these schools or approaches will adopt, and even expand, the basic thinking and concepts of the operational school of management.

While acknowledging that these are only indications and signs along the road to a more unified and practical operational theory of management, and that there is much more of this road to travel, let us examine briefly some of these tendencies toward convergence.

Greater Emphasis on Distillation of Basics Within the Empirical Approach. Within the many programs utilizing cases as a means of educating managers, there are indications that there now exists a much greater emphasis on distilling fundamentals than there was two decades ago. Likewise, in the field of business policy, by which term most of these case approaches have tended to be known, there has been increased emphasis in teaching and research toward going beyond recounting what happened in a given situation to analyzing the underlying causes and reasons for what happened. One major result of all this has been a new emphasis on strategy and strategic planning. This has been nowhere more noteworthy than at the Harvard Business School, which is regarded as the cradle of the case approach. This has led many empiricists to come up with distilled knowledge that fits neatly into the operational theorist's classification of planning.

Recognizing that Systems Theory Is Not a Separate Approach. When systems theory was introduced into the management field some two decades ago, it was hailed by many as being a new way of analyzing and classifying management knowledge. But in recent years, as people have come to understand systems theory *and* the job of managing better, it has become increasingly clear that in its essentials there is little new about systems theory and that practicing managers as well as operational theorists had been using its basics (although not always the jargon) for a number of years. Nonetheless, as those in the field of operational management theory have more consciously and clearly employed the concepts and theory of systems, their attempts at developing a scientific field have improved.

Recognizing that the Contingency Approach Is Not a New or Separate Approach. Although perceptive and intelligent managers and many manage-

ment theorists have not been surprised by the realization, it is now clear that the contingency view is merely a way of distinguishing between science and art—knowledge and practice. As I pointed out earlier, these are two different things, albeit mutually complementary. Those writers and scholars who have emphasized contingency approaches have, to be sure, done the field of management theory and practice a great service by stressing that what the intelligent manager actually does depends on the realities of a situation. But this has long been true of the application of *any* science.

That contingency theory is really application in the light of a situation has been increasingly recognized, as is evidenced by a recent statement by one of its founders. Jay Lorsch recently conceded that the use of the term *contingency* was "misleading."[13] He appeared to recognize that an operational management theorist would necessarily become a situationalist when it came to applying management concepts, principles, and techniques.

Finding that Organization Theory Is Too Broad an Approach. Largely because of the influence of Chester Barnard and his broad concept of "organization" as almost any kind of interpersonal relationships, it has become customary, particularly in some academic circles, to use the term *organization theory* to refer to almost any kind of interpersonal relationships. Many scholars attempted to make this field equal to management theory, but it is now fairly well agreed that managing is a narrower activity and that management theory pertains only to theory related to managing. Management theory is often thought of as being a subset of organization theory and it is now fairly well agreed that the general concept of organization theory is too broad.

This sign offers hope of clearing away some of the underbrush of the jungle.

The New Understanding of Motivation. The more recent research into motivation of people in organizational settings has tended to emphasize the importance of the organizational climate in curbing or arousing motives. The oversimplified explanations of motives by Maslow and Herzberg may identify human needs fairly well, but much more emphasis must be given to rewards and expectations of rewards. These, along with a climate that arouses and supports motivation, will depend to a very great extent on the nature of managing in an organization.

Litwin and Stringer[14] found that the strength of such basic motives as needs for achievement, power, and affiliation were definitely affected by the organizational climate. In a sample of 460 managers, they found a strong relationship between highly structured organizations and arousal of the need for power and a negative relationship with the needs of achievement and affiliation. Likewise, in a climate with high responsibility and clear standards, they observed a strong positive relationship, between this

515

climate and achievement motivation, a moderate correlation to power motivation, and an unrelated to negatively related relationship with affiliation motivation.

The interaction between motivation and organizational climate not only underscores the systems aspects of motivation but also emphasizes how motivation depends on what managers do in setting and maintaining an environment for performance. These researches move the problem of motivation from a purely behavioral matter to one closely related to and dependent on what managers do. The theory of motivation, then, fits nicely into the operational approach to management theory and science.

The Melding of Motivation and Leadership Theory. Another interesting sign that we may be moving toward a unified operational theory of management is the way that research and analysis have tended to meld motivation and leadership theory. Especially in recent years, leadership research and theory have tended to emphasize the rather elementary propositions that the job of leaders is to know and appeal to things that motivate people and to recognize the simple truth that people tend to follow those in whom they see a means of satisfying their own desires. Thus, explanations of leadership have been increasingly related to motivation.

This melding of motivation and leadership theories has also emphasized the importance of organization climate and styles of leaders. Most recent studies and theories tend to underscore the importance of effective managing in making managers effective leaders. Implied by most recent research and theory is the clear message that effective leaders design a system that takes into account the expectancies of subordinates, the variability of motives between individuals, and from time to time, situational factors, the need for clarity of role definition, interpersonal relations, and types of rewards.

As can readily be seen, knowledgeable and effective managers do these things when they design a climate for performance, when goals and means of achieving them are planned, when organizational roles are defined and well-structured, when roles are intelligently staffed, and when control techniques and information are designed to make self-control possible. In other words, leadership theory and research are, like motivation, fitting into the scheme of operational management theory, rather than going off as a separate branch of theory.

The New, Managerially Oriented Organization Development. Both *organization development* and the field ordinarily referred to as *organization behavior* have grown out of the interpersonal and group behavior approaches to management. For a while, it seemed that these fields were far away and separate from operational management theory. Now many of these scientists are seeing that basic management theory and techniques, such as managing by objec-

tives and clarifying organization structure, fit well into their programs of behavioral intervention.

A review of the latest organization behavior books indicates that some authors in this field are beginning to understand that behavioral elements in group operations must be integrated more closely with organizational structure design, staffing, planning, and control. This is a promising sign. It is a recognition that analysis of individual and group behavior, at least in managed situations, easily and logically falls into place in the scheme of operational management theory.

The Impact of Technology That technology has an important impact on organizational structure, behavior patterns, and other aspects of managing has been recognized by intelligent practitioners for many years. However, primarily among academic researchers, there has seemed to be in recent years a "discovery" that the impact of technology is important and real. To be sure, some of this research has been helpful to managers, especially that developed by the sociotechnical school of management. Also, while perceptive managers have known for many years that technology has important impacts, some of this research has tended to clarify and give special meaning to these impacts.

The impacts of technology are easily embraced by operational management theory and practice. And they should be. It is to be hoped that scholars and writers in the area of technological impacts will soon become familiar with operational management theory and incorporate their findings and ideas into that operational framework. At the very least, however, those who subscribe to the operational approach can incorporate the useful findings of those who emphasize the impacts of technology.

Defections Among "Management Scientists." It will be recalled that in the discussion of schools or approaches to management, one of them is identified as the mathematical or "management science" approach. The reader has also undoubtedly noted that "management science" was put in quotation marks; the reason for doing so is that this group does not really deal with a total science of management but rather largely with mathematical models, symbols, and elegance.

There are clear signs among the so-called management scientists that there are defectors who realize that their interests must go far beyond the use of mathematics, models, and the computer. These especially exist in the ranks of operations researchers in industry and government, where they are faced daily with practical management problems. A small but increasing number of academics are also coming to this realization. In fact, one of the leading and most respected academics, one widely regarded as a pioneer in operations research, C. West Churchman, has (in conversations with the author) been highly critical of the excessive absorption with models and mathematics and for this reason has even resigned from the Operations Research Society.

There is no doubt that operations research and similar mathematical and modeling techniques fit nicely in the planning and controlling areas of operational management theory and science. Most operational management theorists recognize this. All that is really needed is for the trickle of "management science" defectors to become a torrent, moving their expertise and research more closely to a practical and useful management science.

Clarifying Semantics. One of the greatest obstacles to disentangling the jungle has long been, and still is, the problem of semantics. Those writing and lecturing on management and related fields have tended to use common terms in different ways. This is exemplified by the variety of meanings given to such terms as "organization," "line and staff," "authority," "responsibility," and "policies," to mention a few. Although this semantics swamp still exists and we are a long way from general acceptance of meanings of key terms and concepts, there are some signs of hope on the horizon.

It has become common for the leading management texts to include a glossary of key terms and concepts and an increasing number of them are beginning to show some commonality of meaning. Of interest also is the fact that the Fellows of the International Academy of Management, composed of some 180 management scholars and leaders from 32 countries of the world, have responded to the demands of its members and have undertaken to develop a glossary of management concepts and terms, to be published in a number of languages and given wide circulation among many countries.

Although it is too early to be sure, it does appear that we may be moving in the direction necessary for the development of a science—the acceptance of clear definitions for key terms and concepts.

The Need for More Effort

Despite some signs of hope, the fact is that the management theory jungle is still with us. Although some slight progress appears to be occuring, in the interest of a far better society through improved managerial practice it is to be hoped that some means can be found to accelerate this progress.

Perhaps the most effective way would be for leading managers to take a more active role in narrowing the widening gap that seems to exist between professional practice and our college and university business, management, and public administration schools. They could be far more vocal and helpful in making certain that our colleges and universities do more than they have been in developing and teaching a theory and science of management useful to practicing managers. This is not to advocate making

these schools vocational schools, especially since basic operational management theory and research are among the most demanding areas of knowledge in our society. Moreover, these schools are *professional* schools and their task must be to serve the professions for which they exist.

Most of our professional schools have advisory councils or boards composed of influential and intelligent top managers and other leading citizens. Instead of these boards spending their time, as most do, in passively receiving reports from deans and faculty members of the "new" things being done, they should investigate managerially related teaching and research and insist on a move toward a more useful operational science of management.

See also Authority, responsibility, and accountability; Budgets and budget preparation; Communications, organizational; Control systems, management; Interpersonal relationships; Leadership; Management, definitions of; Management, historical development of; Manager, definition of; Motivation in organizations; Organizational analysis and planning; Planning, strategic managerial; Statistical analysis for management.

NOTES

[1]Harold Koontz, "The Management Theory Jungle," *Journal of the Academy of Management*, vol. 4, no. 3, December 1961, pp. 174–188; Harold Koontz, "Making Sense of Management Theory," *Harvard Business Review*, vol. 40, no. 4, July–August 1962, pp. 24ff.

[2]Harold Koontz, "The Management Theory Jungle Revisited," *Academy of Management Review*, vol. 5, no. 2., April 1980, pp. 175–187. Much of this entry has been drawn from this paper.

[3]C. I. Barnard, *The Functions of the Executive,* Harvard University Press, Cambridge, Mass., 1938, p. 65.

[4]See E. L. Trist and K. W. Bamforth, "Some Social and Psychological Consequences of the Long-Wall Method of Coal Getting," *Human Relations*, vol. 4, no. 1, January 1951, pp. 3–36.

[5]R. A. Johnson, F. E. Kast, and J. E. Rosenzweig, *The Theory and Management of Systems*, McGraw-Hill, New York, 1963.

[6]H. Mintzberg, *The Nature of Managerial Work*, Harper & Row, New York, 1973.

[7]H. Fayol, *General and Industrial Management*, Pitman, New York, 1949, p. 19.

[8]C. I. Barnard, loc. cit.

[9]Chris Argyris, *Personality and Organization*, Harper & Brothers, New York, 1957, p. 239.

[10]C. I. Barnard, op. cit., pp. 72–73.

[11]H. Mintzberg, "The Manager's Job: Folklore and Fact," *Harvard Business Review*, vol. 53, no. 4, July-August 1975, pp. 49–61.

[12]P. W. Bridgman, *The Logic of Modern Physics*, Macmillan, New York, 1938, pp. 2–32.

[13]J. W. Lorsch, "Organization Design: A Situational Perspective," *Organizational Dynamics*, vol. 6, no. 2, March 1977, pp. 12–14.

[14]G. H. Litwin and R. A. Stringer, Jr., *Motivation and Orga-*

nization Climate, Harvard Graduate School of Business Administration, Boston, Mass., 1968.

HAROLD KOONTZ (deceased), *University of California, Los Angeles*

Manager, Definition of

The term *manager* covers an enormous variety of persons because it is applied (1) in a variety of organizations, (2) at virtually every level within organizations, and (3) to persons who perform a wide range of duties and responsibilities.

A *manager* is best defined as a member of an organization whose tasks, duties, and responsibilities require the supervision of other people. Without subordinates, an organizational member works alone or, at best, cooperatively with others. The act of supervising others requires a reduction (but not elimination) of technical work and an increase in the relative importance of the managerial functions of planning, organizing, controlling, coordinating, and the like.

By delegating authority and responsibilities to subordinates, managers extend their personal influences and capabilities far beyond what they could accomplish alone. Only in this way can large-scale organizations be constructed and large-scale missions or tasks be pursued.

Types of Organizations. By custom and for analytical convenience, organizations are classified into types based essentially on their main purpose. Managers and management practices and problems vary among the several types.

Private-Sector Organizations. These are predominantly profit-seeking organizations, such as business firms. Profits are partly retained by the firm and partly distributed to the owners. Managers are employees of the organization under mutually agreed-upon conditions of employment.

Public-Sector Organizations. These are government organizations at local, state, and federal levels. Managers are often referred to as public servants. They are usually called administrators rather than managers. They are often subject to federal, state, county, or local civil service systems for purposes of personnel administration. They are subject to special constraints of the legislative mandates and missions which create the boards, jurisdictions, commissions, or government offices and bureaus they manage. *Military organizations* form a special category within the public sector.

Not-for-Profit Organizations. These include voluntary associations such as research foundations, mutual benefit societies, charitable organizations, fraternal groups, and a wide variety of community service organizations, such as the Red Cross, the March of Dimes, or the YMCA. Managers in these organizations are professional specialists dedicated to the kinds of activities for which their associations are created. They usually collaborate with selected lay persons who serve as advisers, resource people, and fund raisers, and help in policy guidance.

Institutional Organizations. Many organizations in the service or public sectors are termed institutions. This is a general term nearly synonymous with the term *organization.* An organization tends to be referred to as an institution when it is enduring and well-established, conforms to the typical features of its general class, has a history and tradition, and acquires a position of social importance in the culture of the society. Thus we speak of a particular hospital, school, or even business firm, as an institution. It is possible to describe a business such as the General Motors Corporation as an institution although this is a less-frequent use of the term. The managers in nonbusiness institutions are similar in their characteristics to those in not-for-profit or in public-sector organizations.

Voluntary Associations. An enormous group of organizations exist in which members are the clients rather than the employees of the organization. The Boy Scout organization is an example. Here the managers are few in number, and memberships are free or achieved informally at minimal cost. Voluntary associations are often, but not always, temporary or special-purpose groups. Managers are specialists or professionals with training and experience appropriate to the group's chosen areas of activity.

Mixed. Clearly the above categories are not mutually exclusive. All, however, have business problems in that they must obtain and husband scarce resources. All need managers of various types. Most voluntary associations are also not-for-profit organizations. An interesting type of mixed organization is *the quasi-public organization*—where the organization is a combination of government and private business ventures. An example is the U.S. Postal Service, which in 1970 was changed from a government bureau and set up separately from direct congressional control to operate more like an independent business, but subject to broad governmental directives and surveillance.

Hierarchical Level. Managers occupy specific positions at the different levels of an organization. Their responsibilities, authority, and status are roughly commensurate with their level in the organization.

At the lowest level are first-line managers, often called supervisors. At the middle levels are section managers or department heads, plant or division superintendents, general managers, and professionals, such as industrial psychologists or engineers. At the top levels, managers are often referred to as executives, and they are in charge of major groups or units within the organization. These managers hold such positions as vice president, division head, president, or executive vice president. The term *senior vice president* is often used to provide a special category between the vice president and president. Some executives are also corporate officers, elected as such by the board of directors.

Some managers appear high up on organization charts but fill relatively minor subordinate roles. An example is an assistant to the president. The power and influence of assistants-to vary greatly, depending upon their personalities, capabilities, and relationships with their superiors.

Managerial Responsibilities. Managers can be classified according to the nature of their skills, functional responsibilities, duties, and professional interests.

One category is that of the *line managers.* They are typically in operations, close to the central purposes of the organization. They have command authority within their domain. Examples are the managers in finance, marketing, and production.

A second major category consists of *staff specialists* who work in a service or advisory capacity or in a function that cuts across other functions. Examples are the personnel director and the manager of public relations. They function as researchers, advisers or idea people. They operate with a minimum of command authority. They work through planning, persuasion, and the application of specialized knowledge to the problems in their domain. Some staff groups may be delegated a control or other line-type function appropriate to their area of specialization, as in the case of a personnel officer who is expected to enforce safety rules.

Some managers belong to a *service* category, such as a data processing or computer services manager. Their chief source of authority is in their technical expertise.

Some managers are almost entirely *administrative,* such as those in central corporate headquarters, or, at a lower level, office managers.

See also Authority, responsibility, and accountability; Boards of directors; Committees; Leadership; Management, definitions of; Management theory, science, and approaches; Nonprofit organizations, management of; Officers, corporate; Public administration.

REFERENCES

Duncan, W. Jack: *Management,* Random House, New York, 1983.

Hampton, David R., Charles E. Summer, and Ross A. Webber: *Organizational Behavior and the Practice of Management,* 4th ed., Scott, Foresman, Glenview, Ill., 1982.

McFarland, Dalton E.: *Management: Foundations and Practices,* 5th ed., Macmillan, New York, 1979.

Dalton E. McFarland, *University of Alabama in Birmingham*

Managerial Grid

The *managerial grid®* is a two-dimensional model of the various styles of leadership. Based on the theory that managers can simultaneously and to varying degrees be both task- and people-oriented, the Grid permits analysis on a scale of 1 to 9 of the degree of a leader's concern for people and for productivity. (See Fig. M-5.) The optimum position is usually considered to be 9,9—a maximum interest for both people and production.

The well-known managerial Grid, registered, was developed by Robert R. Blake and Jane S. Mouton in 1962 in the course of research into leadership. They designed it as an alternative to the Ohio State University's quadrant model, which in its turn evolved from Rensis Likert's linear continuum model of leadership.

Blake and Mouton labeled the vertical axis of their managerial Grid *concern for people,* and the horizontal axis *concern for production,* and divided each into a scale of 9. Five basic leadership styles are highlighted in this conception. A 1,1 manager is abdicative, "impoverished," concerned neither for people nor for production, only for maintaining the status quo. The 1,9 manager, fairly or not, has often been called the country club type, who shows great concern for people by emphasizing a friendly atmosphere and harmonious relationships but shows little interest in production. In contrast, the 9,1 manager is a slave driver, the autocratic task manager. The middle-of-the-road 5,5 manager shows a balanced concern for people and their morale and for production, but the middle-of-the-road manager also needs to move in the direction of the 9,9 team manager who evokes high production from people committed to the goals of the organization and relating to one another in trust and mutual respect.

Blake and Mouton have used the managerial Grid both as a tool for the analysis of a leader's style and as an aid in setting goals and designing training for the development of effective managers. They have devised a six-stage training program to enable managers to move toward 7,7, 8,8, and 9,9 positions. The phases include laboratory-seminar training, team development, intergroup development, organizational goal setting, goal attainment, and stabilization, all factors to be measured in placing a manager on the Grid.

The research findings of Blake and Mouton, as epitomized in the managerial Grid, have changed the thinking of many theorists and led them to accept the concept that effective managers can be both hard and soft, both task- and people-oriented. Many companies have found the Grid to be a practical tool for helping managers to increase their effectiveness, particularly in redirecting their orientation toward peo-

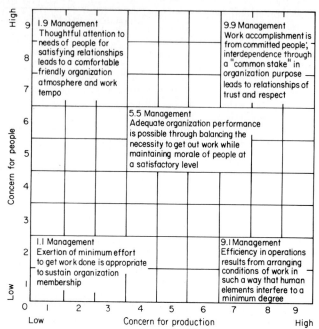

FIG. M-5 Managerial Grid. (From Robert R. Blake and Jane S. Mouton, "Managerial Facades," *Advanced Management Journal*, July 1966, p. 31. Reprinted with permission.)

ple, in the case of the 9,1 manager, or toward production, for the 1,9 manager. While the concept of the Grid itself is widely accepted, it has not been established that most effective managers are indeed at 9,9, although the research of Blake and Mouton reveals that 99.5 percent of managers in their seminars do believe that this is the soundest way to manage. (The second most popular style among these managers is 9,1, and the third is 5,5.) Follow-up research 2 to 3 years later in companies using the Grid finds managers retaining these opinions to the same degree. Blake and Mouton themselves, however, recommend the situational approach, using the style that works best in the particular situation.

See also Interpersonal relationships; Leadership; Motivation in organizations.

REFERENCES

Blake, Robert R., and Jane S. Mouton: *The Managerial Grid*, Gulf Publishing, Houston, Tex., 1964.

Harrison, Frank: "Reshaping the Managerial Grid," *University of Michigan Business Review*, vol. 29, no. 5, September 1977, p. 24.

Hersey, P., and K. H. Blanchard: "So You Want to Know Your Leadership Style?" *Training and Development Journal*, vol. 28, no. 2, 1974, pp. 22–37.

LESTER R. BITTEL, *James Madison University*

Manuals, Policy and Procedures

Policy and procedures manuals for an organization serve to record general and/or specific guidelines and operational elements and sequences for directive and/or reference purposes. Typically, these are active documents designed for ongoing managerial use and are subject to continual change and update.

Manuals are commonly prepared to include (and are often labeled as) the following:

Policy, covering general guidelines, for major aspects of the organization's activities.

Operations, covering procedures for the central conversion processes of the particular organizations, such as manufacturing or production, construction, loans, credit, sales, accounting, data processing, and customer relations.

Support, covering the service or ancillary functions, such as maintenance, purchasing, inventory control, quality control, production control, research and development, advertising, and traffic.

Administration, covering office or clerically related procedures usually associated with accounting, sales and purchase-order processing, and data processing.

Organization, setting forth the organizational structure with specific attention to position titles and descriptions along with specifications of responsibilities and authorities, especially as they pertain to financial and legal activities for disbursing funds, approving sales and purchase commitments, signing contracts, and hiring and firing employees.

Personnel, dealing with the entire range of people-oriented activities, especially wages and hours, safety and health, promotions and separations, and employee benefits.

Standards, including—generally or separately—standard specifications for cost, time, processes and products, design and engineering.

Content. The content of manuals varies widely according to their purpose, but all the following warrant consideration:

Statement of policy. For each item, a clear, concise delineation of the underlying policy provides the rationale for whatever specific implementation instructions follow.

Implementation instructions. These prescribe how the policy is to be carried out—the procedure or sequence—often in step-by-step order.

Variations. This acknowledges differences in application, as between home and branch offices, a main plant and a satellite, or a domestic and a foreign operation.

Explanations. These anticipate problems of interpretation about critical or complex aspects and handle them in question-and-answer style or with examples.

Forms. Wherever a standard form is employed, it is helpful to reproduce it and to illustrate its use.

Format. There are also common requirements of format that must be considered and resolved. These include:

Physical format. A looseleaf form is generally most suitable since it facilitates revision, but there is nothing wrong in issuing manuals periodically in bound form. Looseleaf format presupposes that holders of manuals routinely take care of the mechanics of updating, and this often does not occur.

Readability. Writing style, type selection, layout, and use of illustrations should aim toward the objective of clarity.

Ease of reference. Arrangement of material in the manual may be according to (1) function (assembly and finishing); (2) department (A shop and B shop); (3) problem (discipline and separation); or (4) any other way that conforms to the organization's typical way of thinking. Items and paragraphs may also be lettered and numbered, which helps in identifying material when revised. A comprehensive index and cross-index of terms and problems is especially useful.

Cost. The manual should not be designed to be a monument, and the cost of preparation and the format should be justified by the manual's intent and usage.

Preparation. In almost every instance, manual preparation is a costly, tedious, time-consuming, ongoing task. In its initial stages, a committee and subcommittee—at least for review purposes—are helpful. Usually, a single individual or department must be more or less permanently assigned to the task of assembling, integrating, rewriting, producing, distributing, monitoring, and updating.

Distribution. Two principal factors affect distribution: cost and control. The first is self-evident. The second depends upon both the degree to which information needs widespread dissemination and the degree to which the information is judged to be sensitive or privileged.

Revision. Policies need periodic review (annually is a good rule of thumb) in view of changing organizational objectives and strategies. Specific procedures need almost constant surveillance in view of the dynamic nature of most organizations and operations. On the one hand, revisions should be made as soon as a significant change in a critical element occurs. On the other hand, becoming aware of changes and making them accelerates the costs quickly. A determination of when or how often revisions should be made should relate to the true intent of the manual. If it is, in effect, a legal document, early change is probably warranted. If the manual deals with vital matters such as those affecting employee safety or product liability, early change is imperative. If, however, a particular matter is neither critical nor urgent and has been well-communicated by other channels, it can wait for a periodic review.

See also Communications, organizational; Organization structures and charting; Personnel administration.

REFERENCES

"How to Develop a Company Personnel Policy Manual," The Dartnell Corporation, Chicago, 1975.

"How to Prepare an Effective Company Operations Manual," The Dartnell Corporation, Chicago, 1974.

Lennox, Frederick E.: "Preparing the Maintenance Manual," in L. R. Higgins, *Maintenance Engineering Handbook,* 3d ed., McGraw-Hill, New York, 1977.

LESTER R. BITTEL, *James Madison University*

Marginal Income Analysis

Marginal income theory explains how to segregate costs according to the way in which they behave. The theory also explains the relationship between cost behavior and volume and the resulting effects on profits.

In practice, marginal income analysis provides the professional manager with important insights into the business that are not possible under more traditional accounting and cost analysis techniques: (1) a quick, graphic way to determine break-even points; (2) an accurate measure of a product's true profitability; and (3) a sound basis for making pricing and marketing decisions.

Marginal Income Theory

The concept of marginal income—or direct costing, upon which it is based—was not widely accepted until the early 1960s. In brief, marginal income theory holds that there is a natural and logical segregation of costs according to the pattern in which they behave. As illustrated in Fig. M-6, there are three categories of behavior:

Variable costs: those that vary directly with some measurable unit of production, such as the number of pieces produced or service transactions performed. The materials and labor used directly in manufacturing, shipping costs, and sales commissions are typically variable costs. (The examples cited here and below pertain to

a manufacturing business, but the theory holds true for service-related enterprises and financial institutions equally well.)

Fixed costs: those that are measured by or may change with time. Supervisory salaries, insurance premiums, and property taxes are examples of fixed costs. They represent the cost of being in business and will not vary directly with the volume of the business. *Period costs* is a more accurate but less generally used definition of fixed costs.

Semivariable costs: those that contain both fixed and variable elements. Utilities are typically semivariable costs. There is generally a base charge for electricity whether you use 500 or 500,000 kilowatts. The incremental cost beyond the base charge moves up or down with usage.

This segregation of costs according to the way they behave enables an enterprise to look at some interesting and highly important facets of its business:

Marginal income: the amount of sales dollar left after variable costs are covered. If a company is selling a product for $20 and the total variable cost (labor, materials, expenses) of producing that product is $12, its marginal income is $8. Marginal income is used to pay fixed costs and to contribute to profits when sufficient volume has been reached.

Marginal income ratio: marginal income expressed as a percentage of sales dollars. For the product described above, the marginal income ratio is 40 percent ($8 ÷ $20).

Break-even point: the level of sales volume where marginal income equals the total of fixed costs. Sales above this level contribute to profits. Sales below this level result in a loss.

In short, marginal income seeks to separate the direct out-of-pocket costs that go into the product from the fixed costs of being in business.

Marginal Income in Practice

As an example of the practical applications of marginal income, follow the hypothetical fortunes of The Orange Outdoor Grill Company, a manufacturer and distributor of fireplace grills. Examine how it uses marginal income in profit planning and in measuring the relative profitability of its product mix.

The Break-Even Chart. Unless a company systematically prepares a profit plan, it will simply be a matter of luck as to whether or not it obtains its profit objectives. The Orange Outdoor Grill Company, however, finds that the break-even chart based on mar-

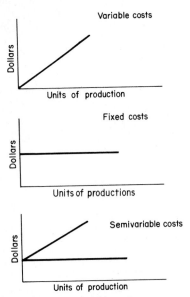

FIG. M-6   Fixed versus variable costs.

ginal income principles provides it with a clear, concise look at its profit picture. The information needed to construct the chart is shown on the abbreviated marginal income statement in Table M-1.

TABLE M-1 Example of an Abbreviated Marginal Income Statement

THE ORANGE OUTDOOR GRILL COMPANY
Marginal Income Statement, January 1978

Variable costs	$49,600
Fixed costs	43,100
Total costs	92,700
Net sales	139,000
Net profit before taxes	46,300
Marginal income	89,400
(Sales—variable costs)	
Marginal income ratio	64%
(Marginal income ÷ sales)	

A graph of the chart is given in Fig. M-7. The horizontal axis represents sales dollars. (This can also represent units of production if a single product is charted.) The vertical axis represents fixed costs, or the dollar volume of loss from the midpoint downward and the dollar volume of net profit from the midpoint upward. The profit path begins at the point on the vertical axis representing total fixed costs, in this case $43,100. If the plant had been shut down for a month, it would have incurred no variable costs and received no revenue, and, therefore, would have taken a loss equal to the fixed cost of $43,100.

The slope of the profit path is predicated on the marginal income ratio, or 64 percent. For every dollar of sales, 64 cents goes toward paying fixed costs and

contributing to profits. The break-even point is where the profit path intersects the midpoint of the vertical axis. It represents the volume of sales at which marginal income exactly equals fixed costs (64 percent × $67,300 = $43,100).

The break-even chart illustrates cost-volume-profit relationships graphically. With a profit objective in mind, a company can project alternative means to reach that objective. Here are some situations in which break-even charts are useful:

1. *When a pricing change is under consideration,* the break-even chart provides a means of determining the effects of the proposed change on profits and the break-even point. This is especially true where demand for the product has a high degree of elasticity; i.e., where the sales volume is sensitive to price changes. The break-even chart will not tell you how elastic your market is, but it will help picture the profit potential as well as the risks to which you may be exposed.

2. *During labor negotiations* the break-even chart helps to predict the effects on costs and profits of alternative bargaining proposals. An increase in fringe benefits will tend to increase fixed costs more heavily. A straight wage-rate increase will add to both fixed and variable costs proportionately.

3. *When a proposed capital expenditure (or alternative expenditures) is being evaluated,* the break-even chart will help evaluate the effects of the expenditure on the overall financial structure of the business.

Product Profitability. Marginal income theory

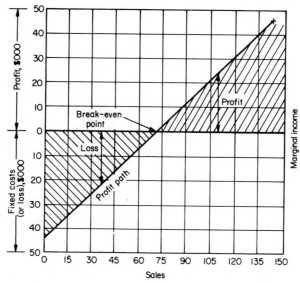

FIG. M-7 Example of a break-even chart.

TABLE M-2 Example of a Full Marginal Income Statement

THE ORANGE OUTDOOR GRILL COMPANY
Marginal Income Statement, Monthly

	Economy grill	Standard grill	Deluxe grill	Total
Variable costs				
Material	$6,000	$9,500	$10,700	$26,200
Labor	6,700	7,300	3,000	17,000
Expenses	2,200	3,200	1,000	6,400
Total	14,900	20,000	14,700	49,600
Fixed costs				43,100
Total costs	14,900	20,000	14,700	92,700
Net sales	45,000	58,000	36,000	139,000
Marginal income	30,100	38,000	21,300	89,400
Net profit before taxes				46,300
Fixed costs absorbed				
on labor dollars	16,800	18,500	7,800	43,100
Net profit before taxes	13,300	19,500	13,500	46,300

provides the most accurate measure of the true profitability of various products. Absorption-based accounting systems that attempt to allocate overhead costs among various products frequently give misleading signals about the true worth of a product and its contribution to profits.

Table M-2 shows the full marginal income statement for The Orange Outdoor Grill Company. The company sells three products—an economy grill, a standard grill, and the deluxe grill. At the bottom of Table M-2, the fixed costs of $43,100 are distributed among (or are "absorbed" by) the three products the company manufactures in proportion to the labor dollars expended on each product. This is the most common way of allocating overhead costs among absorption-based systems.

Table M-3 compares the relative profitability of the three products on a full absorbed basis. It would appear that the deluxe grill has the better earning power of the three, enjoying a 38 percent return on sales as compared with 34 and 30 percent, respectively, for the other two products.

TABLE M-3 Comparative Profitability of Products

	Economy grill	Standard grill	Deluxe grill
Sales	$45,000	$58,000	$36,000
Fixed and variable costs	31,700	38,500	22,500
Net profit before taxes	13,300	19,500	13,500
Net profit/sales	30%	34%	38%

If one looks at marginal income ratios, however, and cuts through the fog of allocating unrelated overheads to individual products, a much different and clearer picture is shown in Table M-4. Based on actual, out-of-pocket costs, the economy and the standard grills are clearly the most profitable prod-

TABLE M-4 Comparative Profitability with Marginal Income

	Economy grill	Standard grill	Deluxe grill
Sales	$45,000	$58,000	$36,000
Variable costs	14,900	20,000	14,700
Marginal income	30,100	38,000	21,300
Marginal income/sales	67%	66%	59%

ucts, and the deluxe grill the least. If, for example, the company plans to spend $50,000 on a promotional campaign, the economy grill represents the most attractive investment opportunity. An increase in economy grill sales of $75,000 will cover the cost of the promotion. On the other hand, an increase in deluxe grill sales of $85,000 would be needed to cover the same promotional expenditure.

Pricing Applications. Marginal income provides a valuable insight into product profitability when one is faced with pricing decisions. Under the marginal income concept, the standard direct cost of a product includes all out-of-pocket costs for producing that product. This is the rock-bottom figure for pricing purposes. If unused plant capacity exists, *any* price set above the standard direct cost will generate marginal income to cover fixed costs and contribute toward profits.

Assume that a national retailer approaches The Orange Outdoor Grill Company with an offer to buy 10,000 standard grills for delivery over the next 12 months under a private-label arrangement. Since it has the capacity to fill the order, the management at Orange thinks the offer represents an excellent opportunity—until it comes around to the question of price. The top price the retailer will pay is $30 a unit. Orange has produced an average of 1160 standard grills a month. If it looks only at the numbers generated by the traditional accounting systems (as shown in Table M-3), it would conclude that the cost of producing standard grills is slightly over $33 per unit ($38,500 ÷ 1160 = $33.19). As a result, it would appear that it would wind up losing over $30,000 on the order.

Marginal income (Table M-4), however, tells a completely different story. The variable out-of-pocket cost of producing a standard grill is actually $17.24 ($20,000 ÷ 1160), leaving a marginal income of $12.76 per unit on a selling price of $30. Instead of losing $32,000 on the deal, the company would gain an additional marginal income of $128,000 which would go toward covering fixed costs and contributing to profits.

Other Applications. The case studies described above illustrate the basic principles of the marginal income approach. There are many other situations that can be brought into clearer focus through the use of this technique:

1. *Distribution.* Analyzing marginal income, or cost-volume-profit relationships, at the production level tells one story for a manufacturing firm. When there are alternative distribution methods open to the firm, looking at marginal income ratios for merchandising costs also becomes important. A soft drink manufacturer, for example, has a wide variety of distribution outlets among which to choose: small grocery and confectionery stores, supermarkets, vending machines, taverns and bars, among others. While the profit contribution of the product on the shipping dock is the same, each outlet is likely to show a different profit picture in the final analysis.

2. *Product mix* has an important effect on profitability. This is especially true where there is a capacity constraint on production. Establishing the relationship between manufacturing run time and marginal income for each product provides the basis for planning the most advantageous product mix.

3. *Return on investment (ROI),* or return on assets employed (ROA), analysis lends itself well to the marginal income approach. After establishing the percentage of ROI desired, multiply that percentage by the average value of raw and finished inventories, by the average value of accounts receivable, and by the replacement value of your capital assets. To the sum of these three values, add the fixed and variable costs of manufacturing and distribution. The resulting figure is the sales goal you must reach to obtain the desired ROI. Adding in your ROI objectives as if they were a cost establishes a profit plan that both manufacturing and marketing can use to develop their strategies.

4. *The financial community* has found the marginal income approach to be a highly useful technique in improving its profitability. The "product" it deals with—money—differs in some respects from that of a typical manufacturing firm. But the techniques of segregating costs according to the way in which they behave is just as appropriate. Take the installment loan department of a bank, for example. A marginal income ratio can be developed for each transaction at the branch office level where the loan originates. A secondary marginal income ratio can be developed after the loan has been processed through the centralized installment loan department. This same approach applies to all the services a financial institution offers to its customers.

See also Accounting, cost analysis and control; Accounting, managerial control; Budgets and budget preparation; Financial management; Product planning and development; Product and service pricing; Profit improvement.

REFERENCES

Batty, J.: *Standard Costing,* McDonald and Evans, London, 1975.

Bittel, L. R., R. L. LaForge, and R. S. Burke: *Introduction to Business in Action,* 2d ed., McGraw-Hill, New York, 1984, pp. 210–212.

Lindemann, A. J., E. F. Lundgren, and H. K. von Kaas: *Encyclopaedic Dictionary of Management and Manufacturing Terms,* 2d ed., Kendall/Hunt, Dubuque, Iowa, 1974, pp. 5–19.

RANDOLPH B. MCMULLEN, *Cooper, Behrens & McMullen, Inc.*

Market Analysis

Market analysis encompasses activities directed toward the systematic study of the nature of (1) consumer needs and wants, (2) product characteristics (to what extent they do or do not meet the needs), (3) competitive market structure, and (4) consumer characteristics. The objectives of market analysis are to identify the consumer needs and wants, determine the degree to which the product characteristics meet these needs and wants, and examine how the products may be modified or redesigned or new products created to increase the degree to which consumer needs and wants are met—while at the same time trying to minimize the impact of competing products/brands. After finding the characteristics of the buyers of the product—i.e., the target market—it is possible to estimate the potential of the market by estimating the expected demand based on the size and the income and expenditure characteristics of the target market.

Market analysis helps to reduce the degree of uncertainty associated with the outcome of alternative marketing strategies. It is instrumental in enabling management to develop and select viable strategies for product screening, positioning, maintaining, and, if necessary, phasing out.

Market analysis is interrelated with a wide variety of associated activities, such as marketing research. This entry, however, is organized around the central aspects of the subject. These are: (1) market opportunity analysis, (2) market segmentation analysis, and (3) market potential analysis.

Market Opportunity Analysis

The marketing manager faces threats due to the actions of rival companies, sudden changes in the economic environment, shifts in consumer lifestyles, etc. Rather than reacting defensively, according to Kotler,[1] a more positive approach is to view these threats as veiled opportunities for revising ongoing marketing activities and examining alternatives. The process of the development and evaluation of alternatives is accomplished by means of market opportunity analysis. This process is characterized by (1) identification of alternatives; (2) determination of the value of each alternative relative to the objectives of the firm; (3) evaluation of each alternative with respect to the ability of the firm to adopt it and to take purposeful marketing action with a reasonable probability of success; and (4) formulation of feasible strategies for responding to the opportunity.

Market Needs Analysis. This concept is central to the identification and generation of opportunities. It is based on the premise that all products satisfy certain needs that consumers have and that the performance of products is directly proportional to the salience of these needs and the degree to which they are satisfied. Market needs analysis is hence primarily concerned with the assessment of issues such as:

What are the needs of the consumers?

How important are these needs?

How are these needs satisfied currently?

How do these needs vary by occasion?

What would be an ideal solution?

What would be an acceptable solution?

What needs are likely to develop in the future as a result of technological breakthroughs or changes in lifestyles?

Market needs analysis is usually performed at two levels. In conducting needs assessment at the *exploratory level,* all relevant inputs such as feedback from sales personnel, findings from ongoing marketing research, reports from the customer complaints and service departments, hunches, and expert opinions

(to name a few) should be used. Techniques such as focus-group interviews, group discussions, and brainstorming are quite adequate because the objective at the exploratory level is to identify, speculate, and formulate hypotheses to be researched further. Subsequently, more *advanced* techniques of marketing research can be used to test these hypotheses with consumers, using approved methodologies for research design, survey methods, and statistical inference.[2]

Product Position. In order to evaluate the attractiveness of any alternative, it becomes essential to examine market factors such as the ability of competitors to duplicate the product, the barriers to entry, and the trends that can be anticipated over the duration of the life of the product. A product's position, even the viability of its concept, depends on the needs of the consumer and the ability of the product (and its competitors) to satisfy those needs. Since both consumer needs and the nature of the competition are susceptible to changes over time, it is imperative to examine the profitability of products over their life span. This requires an examination of the historical performance of the product and a projection of what may happen in the future.

Product Life Cycle. This is a related concept that addresses these issues. Basically, it is an attempt to identify distinct stages in the history of the product. Most examinations of sales histories of products yield four stages in the product life cycle: introduction, growth, maturity, and decline. Each stage characteristically faces relatively distinct problems with respect to marketing strategies due to distinct patterns of profit potential and competitive market structure. Accordingly, it is feasible to make better marketing plans if one can identify the stage the product is in or will be in.

Figure M-8 illustrates the typical sales and profit trends associated with the product life cycle. The theory of diffusion and adoption of innovations[3] lends support to the shape of the sales curve. In the introduction stage there is resistance from the consumers, and the firm has to create awareness, stimulate inter-

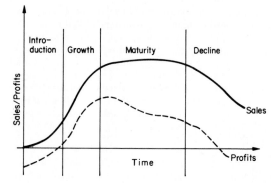

FIG. M-8 Sales and profit trends over the product life cycle.

est, etc. The product is adopted by a small proportion of potential customers (the innovators). Subsequently, as the product gains acceptability, there is a rapid increase in sales during the growth stage due to purchases by early adopters and early majority. The sales stabilize during the maturity stage when the major contribution to sales is due to replacement rather than initial purchase. Eventually, due to the emergence of new competing products, there is a decreasing interest in the product, leading to the decline stage.

Table M-5 contrasts some of the aspects of the four stages of the product life cycle that have implications for market opportunity analysis. Examination of Table M-5 reveals that products face varying levels of competition during their life cycle. The marketing manager will typically encounter different problem mixes over the four stages. Hence, at different stages of the product life cycle, different aspects of market analysis gain importance.

A key aspect in proceeding with analysis at this point is the concept of market segmentation, which allows management to devise strategies to meet the differential demands of various segments of the market and, in addition, to uncover the presence of unfulfilled consumer needs that furnish future opportunities.

Market Segmentation Analysis

The success of market segmentation approaches is centered on the validity of the following propositions: (1) consumers are different, and these differences are measurable; (2) differences among consumers are related to their differential behavior in the marketplace; and (3) segments of different consumers can be isolated in the market.[4]

Market segmentation in developed, competitive economies is an essentially viable strategy because it matches differential consumer needs with appropriate product characteristics or attributes. This by itself is not segmentation. Market segmentation also requires (1) the identification of homogeneous subsets of consumers that could be treated as target submarkets and (2) the accessibility of these subsets with distinct marketing mixes.

Advantages. Market segmentation is associated with numerous advantages. Some of these are: (1) understanding of the market, e.g., knowing who the customers are and why they purchase the product; (2) identification of new opportunities that may be exploited in the future; (3) enhancement of management's ability to identify and plan for changing market trends; (4) formulation of rational media plans; and (5) identification of strengths and weaknesses of competitors, and consequently the identification of segments that offer competitive advantages.

Problems. One of the main problems with seg-

mentation is that it leads to product disaggregation, which adversely affects economies of scale. Also, management has to formulate and monitor marketing mixes for different segments, which sometimes complicates decision making.

Segmentation Variables. A large number of variables, the choice of which is dictated by the product type and the objectives of the research, can be used to segment a market. These can be classified into six general categories: geographic, demographic, psychographic, product usage, perceptual, and brand loyalty variables.[5] The first three refer to consumer characteristics and the last three to consumer response. Table M-6 lists examples of these variables. Though not all variables are appropriate for every market, it is usually necessary to utilize a battery of measures of consumer characteristics (geographic, demographic, and psychographic variables) and response (product usage, perceptual, and brand loyalty variables).

Types of Segmentation. The type of market analysis employed depends on the type of information the researcher is seeking to aid in decision making. Correspondingly, the type of segmentation attempted depends on the objectives of the research.

Table M-6 lists some of the more common ways of segmenting a market, the variables used, the strategic implications, and the areas of market planning where they would be particularly useful. Depending on the complexity of the market situation, two or more of these ways of segmentation may have to be used. For example, the marketer may be interested in conducting market factor segmentation to develop promotional strategies and to allocate resources for the marketing-mix variables effectively. At the same time, the marketer may wish to conduct product-space segmentation to determine the need for product development and positioning.

As discussed earlier, the four stages in the product life cycle are characterized by different problem mixes that have varying information needs. Corresponding to these problem mixes, the various ways of segmenting a market will be differentially beneficial. For example, in the introduction stage we may be more interested in identifying adopters and non-adopters and in overcoming resistance to adoption. Therefore, the marketer could attempt to profile the adopters in terms of their demographic and psychographic characteristics, target communications toward this group, and subsequently achieve a higher rate of product adoption. Or, the opinion leaders could be identified, and the promotional campaign could be aimed at this group to obtain more effective dissemination of information. In the maturity stage, on the other hand, the marketer is interested in identifying the competitive advantages and disadvantages of the product and in spending the promotional dollars efficiently. Accordingly, product-space and market factor segmentation would be beneficial. If the

TABLE M-5 Some Aspects of the Product Life Cycle

			Stages		
Aspects		Introduction	Growth	Maturity	Decline
Profit levels expected		Losses can be expected due to heavy costs of research and development, etc.	Increasing profits due to higher sales and decreasing unit costs for promotion and production.	Profits peak early in this stage and then start to decline due to more firms joining the "bandwagon," which results in intense competition, price cutting, etc.	Rapid decline in profits due to decreased sales, cutthroat competition and decreasing economies of scale.
Competitive market structure		Little competition unless rival firms are introducing similar products. Promotional efforts by competitors are likely to promote product class rather than brands. Since consumer preferences are not stabilized, market share fluctuates.	Competition is still limited, especially for products requiring greater technological know-how. However, if the technological barriers are low, promotional efforts play an important role in determining the market share that will ultimately result.	Competition becomes much more intense, and market share stabilizes due to the development of preferences based on earlier purchases. Because of a larger number of products with similar characteristics, price plays an important part in determining market share.	Because firms have sunk costs and market sales are declining, competitors are willing to cut prices almost to the level of marginal costs. Generally, only strongly entrenched firms can hold on to their market share.
Typical problem mixes—information needs for pertinent decisions		1. Consumer resistance to adoption due to reluctance to change existing behavioral patterns, etc. 2. Uncertainty regarding the extent and nature of the market. 3. What product features are important to make it a success? How to emphasize them? 4. Distribution problems due to item 2.	1. Estimation of the impact of competitors' strategies. 2. Should profit levels or market share be maximized? 3. Who are the customers? How should they be cultivated? 4. Are any product improvements necessary? 5. Is the distribution system adequate?	1. How can we induce customers to use the product more frequently? 2. What are the characteristics of "heavy" users? 3. Can the product be modified or improved to stimulate sales? 4. Are there ways to increase the efficiency of the distribution system? Can profits of intermediaries be restricted without endangering market share? 5. Can we stress any attributes of our product to make inroads into competitors' market share?	1. How rapid is the decline expected to be? 2. Should the firm withdraw from the market? 3. Is it worth the expense to try to reawaken interest? 4. What are the advantages of new competing products? Can these be offset?

TABLE M-6 Types of Segmentation

Type of segmentation	Segmentation variables	Strategic implications	Relevant areas of marketing planning
Geographic: Segmentation is based on location of customers, sales territories, etc.	Geographic location regions, sales territories, rural/urban, etc.	Formulation of differentiated marketing strategies for dissimilar regions—could result in greater distribution efficiency and sales force effectiveness.	Physical distribution
Demographic: Distinct groups are identified on the basis of demographic characteristics.	Age, sex, race, education, family size, stage in life cycle, income, social class, etc.	Identification of target market in terms of salient demographic variables helps media selection; development of advertising copy to fit more desirable segments; choice of outlets to suit the desirable segments.	Media selection Advertising copy Retail store location
Psychographic: Distinct groups are identified on the basis of their personality, lifestyles.	Personality: leader/ follower, introvert/ extrovert, high/low achiever, conservative/ radical, swinger/plain Joe, spender/thrifty, etc.	Identification of desired segments in terms of personality characteristics of the members allows the design of advertising copy—especially for image development. Also useful to conceptualize product improvements, package designs to suit different psychographic segments.	Advertising copy Product development Package design
Benefit/occasion: Consumer groups are identified on the basis of the various benefits they are seeking from the product or the purposes (occasions) the products are used for (in). Subsequently, these groups are identified in terms of demographic characteristics, when possible.	Preference for various product attributes. For example, in the case of automobiles, preference for roominess, miles per gallon, power, etc.	By estimating the sizes of the various market segments, the manufacturer may redesign the product to suit a potentially more viable segment; the approach also helps identify the advantages/disadvantages relative to competing products. Knowledge of benefits desired by consumers allows the producer to design the product and the advertising message to emphasize the relevant benefits.	Product development Product positioning Advertising
Volume: Consumers are grouped in terms of their usage/consumption characteristics. Subsequently, an attempt is made to profile the segments on the basis of demographic data.	Usage rate: heavy users, medium users, light users, potential users, nonpotential users.	By identifying the heavy users and creating a profile for this segment in terms of demographic and/or personality variables, the marketer can develop viable advertising and media selection strategies. Also, if the size of the potential users (currently nonusers) segment is large, the manufacturer can conceivably tap this segment with a blend of promotion and product innovation.	Advertising copy Media selection Diffusion of innovation (penetration strategies)
Product space: Market is divided into segments according to similarities in attributes and product characteristics as perceived by the consumer. Consumers with similar perceptions/preferences are grouped and then identified on the basis of demographics, etc.	Similarities or preferences between products. Either overall comparisons or comparisons along several attributes (dimensions) may be used.	Provides competitive advantages/ disadvantages of product; identifies close competitors; may reveal areas in product space which have no competing products—i.e., lead to discovery of opportunities. Analysis of preferences will provide management guidelines for advertising.	Product development Idea generation (identification of opportunities) Product positioning

TABLE M-6   Types of Segmentation (*Continued*)

Type of segmentation	Segmentation variables	Strategic implications	Relevant areas of marketing planning
Market factor: Market is divided into groups susceptible to different mixes of marketing factors such as price deals, advertising, etc. Again, an attempt is made to profile the segments in terms of demographics.	Price, quality, service, packaging, advertising, etc. (Here either the consumers may be asked direct questions regarding their proneness to the marketing factors, or this susceptibility may be inferred through appropriate consumer choice models.)	Identification of segments based on their responsiveness to the different marketing factors enables the marketer to (1) develop strategies for each segment individually and (2) allocate resources according to the effectiveness of the marketing factors.	Promotional strategies Resource allocation for marketing-mix variables

product has too many disadvantages and few advantages relative to the competitor's product, and is in the decline stage (or close to it), it is probably time to withdraw from the market. Product-space segmentation will provide such indications.

Notice in Table M-6 that the more complex types of segmentation analyses (product space, market factor, benefit/occasion segmentation) use a two-stage procedure, where segmentation is initially done on consumer response or buyer behavior variables, and subsequently the segments are described (*profiled*) in terms of demographic and psychographic variables. The main reason for this is that it is usually prohibitively expensive, if not impossible, to estimate the size and hence the potential of the segments on purely consumer response variables. Also, in order to use segmentation for media selection and to design advertising strategies, one has to know to whom the message is to be directed. Since demographic variables are the only measures on which comprehensive statistics are readily available, most segmentation studies ultimately attempt to classify segments according to demographics.

Techniques Used in Segmentation Analysis. Since the use of market segmentation analysis entails the identification of groups (segments) of consumers who behave differently in the marketplace in terms of characteristic differences that are measurable, and the subsequent isolation of these segments in the market so that they can be reached by differentiated marketing strategies, the following techniques are typically used in segmentation:

1. Form groups or segments of consumers such that consumers exhibit similar buyer behavior within groups, while buyer behavior is distinctly different between groups.

2. Predict and classify into segments (above) on the basis of consumer characteristics that enable the marketer to identify and reach the different segments.

In step 1, the consumers are grouped together on the basis of their behavior, as measured by the consumer response variables (product usage, brand loyalty, preference, etc.).[6] Subsequently, in step 2, consumer characteristics (geographic, demographic, and psychographic variables) are used to identify the composition of these segments so that the marketer can devise differentiated marketing strategies to reach and influence these groups and to estimate their size and potential.[7]

Statistical Techniques. A host of mathematical techniques have been used at various stages of data analysis in segmentation studies. Factor analysis has been used to reduce the dimensionality; that is, to summarize the original variables by a smaller number of statistically independent variables while explaining a large proportion of the original data. Regression analysis has been used to predict group membership in instances where it is feasible to identify clusters based on an intervally scaled dependent variable. Nonmetric multidimensional scaling has been used to generate configurations of stimuli in product space, and these configurations have subsequently been used as input for cluster analysis to determine market segments.[8]

A combination of techniques may be used either sequentially (in tandem) or in parallel in segmentation studies. For example, cluster analysis may be used to classify consumers with similar preferences into segments. Subsequently, discriminant analysis may be used to find how these groups differ according to demographic and psychographic characteristics. The purpose of using a combination of multivariate techniques is not to go on a "fishing expedition." Rather, combinations of techniques, if used, furnish evidence that the results are not merely artifacts of the technique used or the algorithm employed.

The use of multivariate techniques in segmentation analysis requires that the researcher be conversant with marketing research literature and applications. Especially important are the statistical assumptions upon which the procedures are based, as it is only too easy to apply these techniques "correctly" while violating the data requirements.

Having identified the segments of the market, it is necessary to estimate the sizes of the segments and the income/expenditure characteristics of the consumers within them.

Market Potential Analysis

Market potential has been described as "the total amount of a product or product class that would be sold to a market in a specified time period under a given set of conditions."[9] The conditions referred to are both *controllable* aspects of the market, such as promotion, distribution, etc., and *uncontrollable* factors, such as environmental and competitive influences.

The major use of market potential in market analysis is to evaluate opportunities that a product has to offer. For example, it is important for management to identify those segments that offer the greatest opportunities. *Market potential* represents the opportunities that are available to the entire set of producers. In order to determine *sales potential* (that portion of the market potential that a firm can expect to obtain), it is necessary to estimate the market share that the company expects. *Market share* reflects the extent of competition that a firm faces and also measures the *market penetration,* a concept essential to strategic market planning. By assessing the sales potential of different market segments, the firm may obtain an estimate of the total sales potential of a product by aggregating across the segments.

Estimating Formula. In estimating the market potential of a product for a given segment, one examines the income/expenditure characteristics of the consumers in each segment. This estimation involves the following steps: (1) identification of market segments in terms of measurable consumer differences; (2) determination of the number of potential customers in segment i ($= N_i$); (3) determination of the average income per customer in the ith segment ($= I_i$); and (4) determination of the proportion of the income spent on the product class ($= E_i$).

The market potential of the product for segment i is

$$MP_i = N_i \times I_i \times E_i$$

If m_i is the market share of the firm in segment i, the sales potential of the firm in segment i is

$$SP_i = m_i \times MP_i$$

and the total sales potential of the firm is

$$SP = \sum_i SP_i$$

Sources of Data. In step 1 emphasis is placed on the need to identify the segments in terms of measurable consumer differences. That way, the size and income/expenditure characteristics of the segments can be used to determine the market potential. Unfortunately, the availability of data for steps 2 through 4 is limited in cases where the segments have been identified in terms of either demographic or geographic characteristics. For example, if one can identify the segments in terms of sex, income, educational level, etc., one can use census data (see Table M-7) to estimate the size of the segments and

TABLE M-7   Sources of Segmentation Data

For determining size of segments
U.S. Bureau of the Census, *County and City Data Book.* Rand McNally & Company, *Commercial Atlas and Marketing Guide.*

For income data
U.S. Bureau of the Census, *County and City Data Book.* "Survey of Buying Power," *Sales and Marketing Management,* annually. U.S. Department of Commerce, *Survey of Current Business.*

For expenditure data
U.S. Department of Commerce, *Survey of Current Business.* U.S. Bureau of Labor Statistics, *Survey of Consumer Expenditure.*

the income/expenditure characteristics. If the segments are described in terms of psychographic or consumer response characteristics, no such convenient data bases are available. However, it is feasible to create customer profiles by a two-stage procedure, where (1) segments are identified in terms of psychographic and/or consumer response variables, and (2) techniques such as discriminant analysis are used to characterize these segments in terms of geographic and demographic variables.

Conclusion

Application of the concepts discussed in this entry is not free from pitfalls. For example, segmentation analysis is not potentially productive if management has reasons to believe that the benefits of segmentation will be more than offset by the costs of reduced economies of scale. Also, market potential estimates are quite error-prone and sometimes must be tempered with managerial experience or expert opinions. The techniques and concepts suggested here merely *aid* decision making and are not substitutes for managerial experience. Indeed, the marketing manager must use all feasible and appropriate inputs, such as market potential, competitive product advantages and disadvantages, and the firm's ability to produce and distribute the product efficiently, to screen the alternative opportunities that are available.

See also Consumer behavior; Economic measurements; Marketing, concepts and systems; Marketing, industrial; Marketing research; Marketing of services; Marketing of services, professional; Markets, government; Positioning; Product planning and development.

NOTES

[1] Philip Kotler, *Marketing Management: Analysis, Planning, and Control,* 4th ed., Prentice-Hall, Englewood Cliffs, N.J., 1980.

[2] Robert Ferber (ed.), *Handbook of Marketing Research,* McGraw-Hill, New York, 1974; Glen Urban, and John Hauser, *Design and Marketing of New Products,* Prentice-Hall, Englewood Cliffs, N.J., 1980.

[3] Everett Rogers and Floyd Shoemaker, *The Communication of Innovation,* Free Press, New York, 1971.

[4] Wendell R. Smith, "Profit Differentiation and Market Segmentation as Alternative Marketing Strategies," *Journal of Marketing,* vol. 21, 1956.

[5] Yoram Wind, *Product Policy: Concepts, Methods and Strategy,* Addison-Wesley, Reading, Mass., 1982; Edgar Pessemier, *Product Management: Strategy and Organization,* 2d ed., John Wiley, New York, 1982.

[6] Glen Urban and John Hauser, *Design and Marketing of New Products,* Prentice-Hall, Englewood Cliffs, N.J., 1980.

[7] R. E. Frank, "The Design of Market Segmentation Studies," in R. Ferber (ed.), *Handbook of Marketing Research,* op. cit.

[8] D. A. Aaker, *Multivariate Analysis in Marketing: Theory and Application,* 2d ed., The Scientific Press, Palo Alto, Calif. 1981.

[9] William R. King, "Estimating Market Potential," in R. Ferber (ed.), *Handbook of Marketing Research,* op. cit.

RAJENDRA K. SRIVASTAVA, *University of Texas*

GERALD ZALTMAN, *University of Pittsburgh*

Marketing, Channels of Distribution

The distribution channel is composed of a linkage of institutions which collectively perform the essential functions in moving products from producers to consumers. In 97 percent of all product sales more than one firm participates. The concern that the company initiating the sale has for the product, while depending on other companies to cooperate, constitutes the heart of the channel problem. The task of channel management is to administer this collective effort in the interest of the product's favorable reception by the consumer. The initiating company cannot control the activities of other firms. However, by careful selection and by building and preserving effective relationships, it can influence the performance of these firms and achieve positive results.

Two Basic Flows in the Channel. There are two basic flows in the movement of the product through the channel: (1) the movement of the physical product from the point of production to consumption; (2) the informational flow both ways that precedes, accompanies, and follows the product. This flow can be of two classes: (*a*) deals with the purchase orders, bills of lading, invoices, payment for goods, and all other transactions essential to exchange; (*b*) relates to the promotional information about the product or institution.

The timing, economy, accuracy, and clarity with which these flows are administered measure the efficiency of the channel.

Savings Achieved by Intermediaries. Figure M-9 shows that firms using a retailing or wholesaling intermediary can serve five other companies with 20 transactions where it would require 50 transactions without the intermediary. A *transaction* includes an account receivable or payable, a purchase order, an

Without the intermediary

With the intermediary

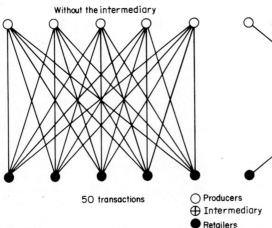

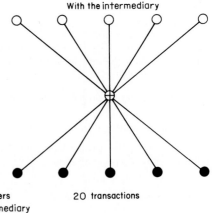

50 transactions   ○ Producers   20 transactions
⊕ Intermediary
● Retailers

532   **FIG. M-9** Savings resulting from the use of intermediaries.

invoice, a bill of lading, and the servicing by a salesperson. This reduction in the transaction flow brought about by the re-sorting and shipment by the intermediary would be multiplied 20 times if there were 100 retailers.

In the *physical movement* of the product, the manufacturer ships in carload lots to intermediaries. Otherwise the manufacturer would have to break the shipment into many parcels at high transportation rates in order to deal directly with each retailer. The intermediary, by re-sorting the shipments, can combine many products for one retailer into a large and more economical shipment. The institutions participating in the channel are retailers, wholesalers, and producers, or manufacturers.

Retail Institutions

Retailers are the terminal link in the distribution channel which ultimately sells to the consumer.

Price Competition. Competition has been the arbiter of the retailers' success. Because of the increasing complexity, the growing volume of sales, and improved management practices, recent changes in the retail structure have been dramatic. Powered by the competitive spirit, retailers have capitalized on the fact that net unit costs and prices can be reduced and profits increased by volume sales.

Nonprice Competition. Retailers also compete in the nonprice area. They offer options of differentiated products and differing qualities of products at stores where the quality of surroundings also varies. Different combinations of these factors have broadened the spectrum of competition so that the retail structure includes all sizes and classes of stores—from the austere price-competitive institution to the luxurious retailer.

Sales by Geographic Area. Retail sales shares by region correspond to population shifts during the last few decades to the west and south.

Sales by Legal Form. In spite of tax benefits of partnerships and proprietorships, retailers favor the power of largeness, access to money markets, and limited liability that come with the corporate form.

Retailer Classifications. The following classifications are most common:

Specialty Stores. Specialty stores that limit their offerings to one or a limited number of lines evolved with the general move to specialization. Since 1939 the categories which constitute specialty stores have increased in both number and size. The trends indicate continued growth in specializations within the respective categories by innovations in store decor, merchandise methods, and personalized customer services.

Department Stores. Department stores, classified with general merchandise stores, are stores offering a wide assortment of merchandise, with separate classifications divided into departments, each with a separate set of records. Department stores provide full services such as credit and delivery. Such stores have innovated constantly in design, services, and assortment of merchandise. Stores range widely in the clientele they seek. They have become big business: more than 90 percent of department store sales are made by firms with sales of $50 million of more. They have also become chains or multiunit systems, with 90 percent of all department store sales credited to firms owning 11 or more stores.

Direct-Marketing Operations. This field continues to expand and diversify from its initial base of mail-order. Sears and Ward began, and still dominate, the mail-order business, even though many other firms have entered the field. Only 1 percent of total retail sales is done by mail. Reasons for this segment not growing larger are (1) the availability of the automobile and hard surface roads to retail stores, (2) the inconvenience of filling out the order (although telephones and charge cards are vastly simplifying this process) and waiting for the merchandise, as compared with picking merchandise up immediately from an attractive display, and (3) the expense of preparing catalogs in an age of rapid change when unit sales and sales per catalog are small. Innovations such as in-store ordering desks and direct-wire service have firmed up the selling position of mail orders in the market, even though it is comparatively small.

Literally thousands of small, and hundreds of large, firms are engaged in catalog sales as well as in telemarketing and direct sales through newspaper, magazine, and television ads. Many such firms are, in effect, "paper" houses in that they do not stock or take ownership of the goods they sell; their orders are filled by the manufacturer or wholesaler by drop shipment.

Chain Stores. A chain or multiunit firm is defined as 11 or more retail stores under one owner. Advantages responsible for chain store success stem from (1) increased volume of sales, which enables several establishments with one set of overhead costs to sell for less and to attract and hold better management; (2) an ability to achieve a greater impact in advertising both by professional preparation of advertising and by one advertisement benefiting collective stores; and (3) mass buying and large-volume transportation rates. Some independent managers, in responding to competition, achieve the same low cost and high satisfaction goals.

Supermarkets. A supermarket is a complete departmentalized food store with a minimum sales volume of $1 million, with at least the grocery department being self-service. The supermarket concept is still evolving. Some large self-service units have remained food stores; others have popularized the one-stop shop concept and have organized massive distribution centers with virtually no limit to their offerings.

Discount Houses. The discount house offers both hard and soft lines in a store of over 10,000 square feet at a cost structure below that of the traditional store. Its beginning was the result of merchandise shortages and high prices following World War II. Fair trade laws also sustained such high prices. Many states have now abandoned such laws; others ignore them. The discount houses succeeded because, with no services or guarantees and in austere store surroundings, they were able to cut prices dramatically and still realize a profit.

Somewhat allied with the discount houses are *showroom stores* (especially popular for furniture marketing) and *catalog stores,* where merchandise is displayed and stocked on premises.

Wholesaling Institutions

A wholesale sale is a sale that is not a retail sale, or it may be a sale made for business purposes and not to the ultimate consumer. The wholesaler is the institutional intermediary whose re-sorting economizes transaction and transportation costs. In spite of these savings, in some kinds of businesses and some lines of merchandise—such as furniture or ready-to-wear apparel—due to volume sales and importance of prompt delivery, the wholesale intermediary is bypassed, and sales are made by the manufacturer directly to the retailer or consumer.

The institutions which perform the wholesale functions are classified by the U.S. census as merchant wholesalers, manufacturers' sales branches, agents and brokers, and petroleum bulk-tank stations.

Merchant Wholesalers. Merchant wholesalers take title to the products they sell and assume the risks of ownership. They have innovated constantly with up-to-date warehousing, electronic data processing, and additional services. They have broadened their lines and increased in size to correlate with the one-stop shop trends in retailing. They have evolved into large integrated systems in six general areas: (1) lumber and building materials; (2) paper goods; (3) automotive; (4) institutional sales to hospitals and restaurants and processors dealing with food, groceries, and paper supplies; (5) hard goods such as machinery, equipment, and industrial supplies; and (6) wholesale grocers who carry diversified lines and deal with the grocery and supermarket trade. Like innovators in retailing, merchant wholesalers have decreased their cost margins dramatically.

Manufacturers' Sales Branches. These firms are branches established by the manufacturer. They sell directly to dealers. Some perform the warehousing function. Sales branches are used by large firms where volume sales justify overhead, additional finance, and expanded management capacity. Firms such as Nabisco and General Electric are examples. They enjoy the following advantages: (1) product information and feedback is fast and dependable; (2) company gets suggestions for product and service improvements; (3) being close to the retailer enables the company to make accurate and short-term forecasts; and (4) as retailers get stronger, the company must stay close so as not to lose its influence. These reasons are considered by some firms as sufficient to offset the re-sorting and other advantages of the merchant wholesaler.

Merchandise Agents and Brokers. Merchandise agents and brokers buy and sell for the account of their principal. They do not take title or share the ownership risk. The brokers and manufacturers' agents represent the manufacturers to dealers by selling and arranging for shelf space and display. Their principal disadvantage is that they represent several manufacturers and must therefore dilute their efforts for one company. Their main advantage is that they work directly with dealers and retailers on a number of accounts and can therefore develop a closer relationship with them.

Conditions Influencing Channel Relationships

Usually one firm is dominant in taking the initiative to choose other firms for the channel and in planning the strategy. In the majority of cases, this dominant member is the manufacturer. There are instances, however, where initiative rests with the retailer (e.g., Sears) or the wholesaler (e.g., McKesson and Robbins).

Confusion Arising from Differing Expectations. As the result of competition, better communication, and improved management, the distribution channel is now perceived as a number of companies functioning as an interdependent unit. One company's performance influences all others. When serving a multitude of manufacturers, intermediaries have the problem of attempting to act consistent with the collective expectations of the manufacturers. The manufacturer also frequently fails to satisfy the expectations of the intermediary. The most common of these differences is the relationship between a manufacturer of a few products and the promotional effort of the wholesaler, who sells thousands of products. Other issues relate to maintenance of inventory, discount selling, bypassing intermediaries in selling large accounts, sales by factory-owned outlets, representational policies, national and private brands, promotional allowances, and service and warranty.

Channel Noise. These frustrations are so common, the trade has called them "channel noise." Channel noise may be minimized by (1) defining the company's target market, and selecting those intermediaries who will complement the need of the target market; (2) planning and executing a program that will keep the company's expectations of other channel members articulate and clear; (3) achieving market power with the consumer so the product will be in strong demand.

Intensive, Exclusive, and Selective Plans. In achieving market coverage, firms usually chooose one of three plans. An *intensive* plan is an arrangement which offers the product in as many retail outlets as possible. It is used when convenience and exposure to the public are important and high-volume sales are profitable (e.g., Coca-Cola). An *exclusive* plan is used when a company wishes to restrict the retail firms to a chosen few—and such firms will cooperate in a promotion plan. They are often required not to stock competitive products. Such a plan enables a company to protect its product's image and get more cooperation from its dealers. In the *selective* system, the manufacturer selects those dealers in a trading area who will represent the company products well, give them positive exposure, and respond positively to the company's goals for quality and market coverage.

Traditional Distribution Channels

Each firm selects and builds a channel for its line of products that is different from that for any other firm. The product line and its requirements, the competitive environment in which it sells, the characteristics of the other firms available with which to cooperate, and how the company wishes the product to be introduced to the target market are all relevant. The simplest plan is a direct contact with the customer.

Door to Door. The advantages of the door-to-door plan are that the company has complete control of its product. There is no danger of channel noise or information distortion by intermediaries. The main disadvantage is the difficulty of maintaining a satisfactory sales force. The per-unit costs of this method compared with using other intermediaries is usually greater, since the costs of travel and shipment must be borne by a single line of products. Approximately 1 percent of total retail sales in the United States are sold door to door.

Manufacturer to Wholesaler to Retailer. This channel is typical; it offers the manufacturers a large coverage of the market at both the wholesale and the retail level. It places at their disposal representatives who have solid relationships with both retail and wholesale trade. Companies that have new, dynamic, and vigorous programs use this channel most frequently because of their freedom to change products and outlets at will.

Manufacturer, Wholesaler, Broker, and Retailer. Small firms, or new firms, that do not have the market power to command the attention of wholesalers and retailers, and some large firms, often employ a broker or a *manufacturer's agent* to provide contacts with the retailer and to take orders from the retailer for the wholesaler.

Vertical Distribution Systems

The two channels which include the wholesaler are those channels which, unfortunately, that provide the base for role confusion and channel noise. In view of the facts that (1) the company gives up the ownership of its product to the wholesaler, and the wholesaler to the retailer and (2) these intermediaries deal in thousands of other products, there is always danger of confusion regarding the expectations of the initiating company. In solving this problem, progressive firms have built more reliable channels by adopting a vertical distribution system.

The vertical systems meet the problem of channel conflict by extending some control of the product through the channel. Formal arrangements with the wholesalers and retailers are often used. These vertical systems account for the sale of 64 percent of merchandise available for such sale. They are of three types: administrative, corporate, and contractual.

Administrative. Through administrative skills and unusual market power, some firms are able to win the cooperation of wholesalers and retailers by providing their products with administrative and selling support at each market level.

Procter & Gamble is an example. It holds the wholesalers and retailers into a unit by having its salespersons service and sell to the retailers but having all orders billed through the wholesaler. It sells directly to chain warehouses. It also sells directly to groups of large independent retailers if they will receive their goods in a single shipment. These shipments are billed through the wholesalers but are not warehoused. In addition to this program of *multiple channels* planned to satisfy the wants of the various channel members, the company advertises to the ultimate consumers and provides them with samples of new products and coupons redeemable at retail stores, thus creating a powerful consumer demand.

Corporate. In the corporate vertical system, the initiating company owns all, or a significant portion of, the firms that make up the channel. Sears owns an interest in many of its manufacturers. Sherwin-Williams Paint owns 2000 retail outlets. Hart Schaffner & Marx owns over 200 retail stores and maintains the loyalty of other retailers by a carefully managed exclusive policy. In these instances the companies' need to have control of their product justifies, in their view, a major commitment of capital, management talent, and risk.

Contractual. Cooperative voluntary groups and franchise systems provide a means of bringing greater harmony in channel communications.

Cooperative Voluntary Groups. In order to meet the competition and achieve the economies of the multiunit stores, some retail stores have formed groups which have adopted uniform improved management systems and have collectively warehoused, advertised, purchased, financed, and researched in the interest of increasing their market share. The wholesale intermediaries have taken the initiative in forming some of these groups (e.g., Independent Grocers Association); and in others, the retailers have set up a cooperative plan (e.g., Associated Grocers Association).

Franchise Organization. Under the franchise plan, successive stages of the production and distribution system are linked under one head, and franchises are granted by the franchisor to dealers who will conform to the franchisor's system. This concept is one of the fastest-growing areas of retailing.

There are three classes of franchise organizations: manufacturer-sponsored retailers (for example, the Chevrolet franchise from General Motors); manufacturer-sponsored wholesalers (for example, Coca-Cola Bottlers); and service firm-sponsored retailers (for example, McDonald's).

In each of these instances the franchisor establishes parameters which provide the control the system needs; yet there are many areas where the franchisee can use creative initiative and profit from extra effort.

Evaluation

In the interest of evaluating the effectiveness of the channel, management should frequently ask whether the channel (1) provides for the physical movement and storage of goods to achieve the greatest economy; (2) accommodates the distributional goals of the firm with a minimum of administrative transactional volume and confusion and maximum effectiveness; (3) guarantees an optimum amount and quality of promotional information to all prospective buyers and provides an adequate feedback; (4) has the flexibility to adapt creatively to company innovations; and (5) is sensitive to each company's role as it relates to the expectations of the other channel members.

See also Advertising concepts; Consumer behavior, managerial relevance of; International trade; Logistics, business; Marketing, industrial; Marketing of services; Product and service pricing; Retailing management.

REFERENCES

Evans, Joel, and Barry Berman: *Marketing,* Collier Macmillan, New York, 1982.

Ronan, Murray: *Telephone Marketing,* McGraw-Hill, New York, 1976.

Sroge, Maxwell: *Inside the Leading Mail Order Houses,* Maxwell Sroge Publishing, Colorado Springs, Colo., 1982.

Taylor, Weldon J. and Roy T. Shaw, Jr.,: *Marketing: An Integrated Approach,* 3d ed., South-Western Publishing, Cincinnati, Ohio, 1973, pp. 67–189.

WELDON J. TAYLOR, *Brigham Young University*

Marketing, Concepts and Systems

Market orientation—popularly referred to as the *marketing concept*—became a basic philosophy of American business during the 1950s and 1960s. Organizing a business to identify and serve the needs of the market was a necessary response to the rapid growth of the consumer economy which occurred during the 25 years following World War II.

Whether the marketing concept is adequate for the 1980s and beyond is a question that has been raised by marketing-thought leaders. Changes occurring during the 1970s/1980s—economic, environmental, social, and political—have posed new problems and challenges for the business community. Whether business response calls for a new concept or a revised marketing concept is not entirely clear. What is clear, however, is that business is operating under a different set of conditions from those that gave rise to the marketing concept.

Rise of the Marketing Concept

Marketing has been defined in a number of ways, but central to most definitions is that it includes the performance of business activities that direct the flow of goods and services from the producer to the consumer or user. This definition is sound as far as it goes, but it does not necessarily convey the now generally accepted idea that the process begins with identification of market needs, wants, and preferences, which in turn determine the goods and services the company should offer.

While it is axiomatic that for a company to succeed it must satisfactorily supply some market demand, the marketing concept has served to emphasize the idea that markets do not exist to serve the needs of business but that business exists to serve the needs of the market.

Although the idea of market orientation predates World War II, it was the General Electric Company that provided impetus to the idea when in 1951 it publicly embraced the marketing concept. General Electric proceeded to reorganize its businesses—both consumer and industrial—so as to identify and serve customer needs better. Other leading companies followed the General Electric model. Although the marketing concept was simple and easily understood, implementation took longer and was more difficult than most managements had envisioned.

A Response to Economic and Social Change. In retrospect the marketing concept can be seen as a response to an increasingly affluent society. Whereas the prewar economy concentrated primarily on providing basic essentials, the rapidly rising personal income of the postwar period provided dramatic changes in the nature of demand. Not only could consumers exercise more choice in supplying their basic wants, but their rising discretionary income enabled them to purchase many new products and services. Developments, such as more families in which both husbands and wives work and the shortening workweek, created demand for laborsaving devices, recreation, travel, education, and a variety of services. Services, for example, rose from 31 to 47 percent of the GNP between 1950 and 1980. Technological innovation was spurred by the new demands. New distribution systems evolved to serve the changing shopping patterns of a more mobile society.

The changes in lifestyles resulting from higher income, technology, and mobility were more dramatic than for any other comparable time period. Naturally the impact was felt by the business community. Although benefiting from the increased demand, most companies also had to modify their product lines and methods of marketing to take advantage of the new opportunities. And they found it necessary to have far better knowledge of consumers than previously.

Market Segmentation Concept. Nowhere was business practice more affected than by the growing consumer demand for variety. The relatively homogeneous markets of less-affluent times could be satisfied with limited product offerings. Increasing purchasing power, however, caused markets to become more heterogeneous and to demand greater choice. Recognition of this change led to wide acceptance of the concept of market segmentation.

This concept assumes that the market for any product or service can be divided into segments, each with its own discrete needs, wants, or preferences. Marketing strategy calls for a company to determine which segment(s) it can serve most efficiently and profitably and to orient its product development, pricing, distribution, and communications policies to the preferred segment or segments. The automobile industry's wide offerings of brands, models, prices, and combinations of colors and accessories illustrate responsiveness to market segments.

The market segmentation concept should not be confused with the product differentiation concept. *Product differentiation* refers to how different brands are perceived by the consumer. This may stem from real product differences or from purely perceived differences, which may be psychological in nature. Product differentiation is one means of appealing to a market segment.

The Changing Market Environment

While change in the 1950s and 1960s was stimulated by a rapidly growing economy, the 1970s and 1980s have seen very different developments—a slower growing economy, public concern over the physical environment, dwindling raw material resources, and changing social values.

Slower Economic Growth. A slower growing economy obviously affects overall market demand, but the nature of demand has been changing as well. For example, increasing average life expectancy (73 years in 1980) raised the demand for geriatric products and services, while a lower birth rate between 1955 and 1975 reduced demand for baby products and services. (The birth rate turned up again beginning in 1976. The total U.S. population is expected to increase by slightly less than 1 percent a year until the year 2000.) Longevity and birth rates affect many family purchases. The concept of the family life cycle helps to explain why.

From a marketing standpoint the *family life cycle* can be classified by at least five stages: (1) single stage; (2) newlywed stage with no children; (3) full-nest stage—married with dependent children; (4) empty-nest stage—married with no dependent children; and (5) solitary survivor stage. While each stage shows different characteristics of demand, stage 3—the full-nest stage—provides the largest expenditures for a wide variety of goods, particularly among those families with younger children.

If family formations are postponed or if couples have fewer children, demand is affected not only for baby products but also for products such as housing, appliances, home furnishings, and automobiles. Knowledge of the characteristics of consumption by life-cycle stages, combined with census bureau population projections by age bracket, is useful in forecasting demand for many consumer products. Industrial goods producers supplying consumer goods companies are also affected since their demand is *derived* from the basic consumer demand.

Environmental Concerns. There is growing awareness that the supply of most traditional raw materials and tillable land is insufficient to support the present world population and world economic growth over the long term. While new technology may resolve the problem before disaster overtakes us, the next few years seem certain to change many production and consumption patterns. Consumers and most industries will be affected either directly or indirectly. Rising petroleum prices during much of the 1970s provided an example of the worldwide economic disruptions that can stem from an impending raw material shortage. Not to be ignored, however, were the new markets created within the Middle East oil-producing countries as the result of their new purchasing power.

Environmental factors that affect the quality of

537

life such as pollution, overcrowding, noise, public safety, crime, addictive drugs, and delinquency have brought rising public concern. Public and governmental pressures to alleviate these problems increase business costs and contribute to inflation, which in turn influences unit demand. Many industries, such as packaging and automotive, are affected directly. Opportunities, however, have been created for companies in a position to fulfill new needs, such as pollution control, safety, and noise-abatement equipment.

New Social Values. The reasons for changing social values are involved and complicated, and their effects on marketing are apparent. Concern by some people over too much affluence, or overconsumption, has changed attitudes toward the purchase of many products. The choice of small cars and blue jeans by people who can afford more prestigious purchases has brought into question Veblen's *theory of conspicuous consumption*. It is possible, of course, that the examples of the theory have merely switched from expensive cars and fur coats to stereo equipment, foreign travel, and where one's children go to college. Increased criticism of advertising results, at least in part, from an attitude that questions whether the good life really requires so many products.

Consumers support more government control of business, with legislation affecting product safety, packaging, pricing, credit, warranties, service, and advertising claims. Increasing proportions of the GNP are being allocated to government, welfare, and education. Irrespective of their personal attitudes toward changing social values, marketing executives need to understand and respond wherever social values affect products, services, and marketing methods.

Modifying the Marketing Concept. In view of these new conditions, questions have been raised as to whether the marketing concept which seemed so appropriate in the past is right for the future. Some marketing authorities argue that what the customer wants may not always be good for society as a whole.

Examples of conflicts between individual consumer wants and the needs of the larger society are illustrated by the following types of questions: Should utilities promote the use of electricity in view of dwindling supplies of low-pollutant fuels? Should automobile companies promote the sale of larger cars in the face of scarce petroleum resources? Should container manufacturers promote disposable cans and bottles, or containers made of nonbiodegradable materials, in view of the problems of pollution and waste disposal? What benefit/safety criteria should determine whether a drug is to be sold? How should safety/cost issues be resolved? Should negative, as well as positive, product attributes be provided consumers by sellers?

Some argue that a societal-centered concept should replace the market-centered concept. Others point out that this would not work because in a free market economy the companies taking social leadership positions would be undercut by less socially concerned competitors. Others argue that the answer lies in more government control over business.

Public support appears to be declining for a market system so free that companies may supply any product or service that someone is willing to pay for. Despite the basic soundness of organizing a business around the customer, it would seem that management must modify the concept of customer sovereignty with considerations of social (public) sovereignty. Such a modified concept might be stated as *the purpose of a business is to create and serve customers in a socially responsible manner.*

Adapting to Future Market Change

The central idea that should be apparent from the previous discussion is that business management—and particularly marketing management—must be concerned with change constantly occurring in the external environment. While a company may influence the environment to a limited extent, a major objective should be to recognize and adjust to environmental change. Four concepts appear useful in dealing successfully with environmental change.

External Stimuli–Internal Response Concept. This concept proposes that several constantly changing external environments (stimuli) provide opportunities for the firm while at the same time exercising constraints over it. Each firm possesses a combination of resources (response mechanisms) which can be utilized to take advantage of the opportunities within the constraints imposed. This concept is sometimes discussed in terms of the noncontrollable elements (external environments) and the controllable elements (internal resources).

The external environments with which the firm must deal include the market, the economy, the industry, competition, and legal and ethical, political, technological, and societal factors. The firm's resources are its facilities, technology, financial position, market position and reputation, personnel, and management.

Management identifies the opportunities and constraints and establishes tentative market objectives. It then proceeds to evaluate the strengths and weaknesses of its internal resources in relation to its market objectives. Resources may be strong in terms of one objective and weak in terms of another. For example, the firm's resources may be considered strong for maintaining market share in its traditional market but weak in one or more areas if the objective is to enter a new market. The weaker resources should be strengthened before the company attempts to enter the new market.

Concept of the Marketing Mix. This concept is

similar to the one just described but directs attention to the marketing elements over which the firm has control. The concept of the marketing mix was developed by Neil Borden, although he gives credit for the idea to James Culliton.[1] Although Professor Borden listed some 12 elements of the mix, all but one (fact-finding and analysis) can be subsumed under the four major elements of product, price, distribution, and promotion.

The concept proposes that once market facts are known, marketing management can mix the four elements in proportions that will produce the most profitable marketing result. It assumes that the proportions of the mix will change as market conditions change or as the company's position in the market changes. Although the four internal marketing elements are controllable by the firm, it does not follow that marketing management may make decisions unconstrained by the external environment. Competitors' potential reactions, for example, limit the range of options open to a company.

The Systems Concept. The marketing process can be thought of as a system because the various functions and elements interrelate and interact. A change in one causes a response in others. The elements of the marketing mix interact not only with the external environments but also with internal functions such as production, research and development, and finance. Interest in marketing as a system has developed for two reasons. First, it is useful in describing the intricate workings of an involved process. Second, systems models can be used as marketing planning and decision tools.

Systems analysts think in terms of macro, micro, and total marketing systems. Macro systems describe the larger external environment, while micro systems describe the internal environment of the firm. A total system links the two. See Fig. M-10 for a graphic model of a total marketing system. Analysts also think in terms of marketing subsystems such as a distribution system.

Mathematical Models. While descriptions of marketing systems are useful in providing better understanding of the marketing process, operations

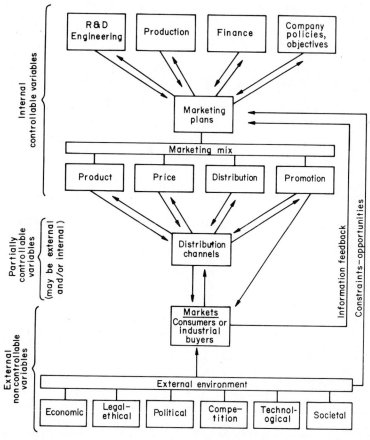

FIG. M-10 Simplified diagram of a total marketing system.

researchers and management scientists translate the descriptive models into mathematical models for use in planning and decision making. Computer-programmed models can be used to test various hypotheses by varying the inputs of the marketing mix and by using various assumptions about the likely reactions of the noncontrollable external factors. For example, the effect on sales of a change in price or a change in advertising expenditure can be projected in terms of several possible customer reactions and/or competitive reactions. A computer-programmed model can quickly project the likely outcome of any number of combinations of internal and external variables, from which management can choose the mix that appears best suited to its objectives.

Mathematical modeling has developed more slowly in marketing than in other business areas because of the large number of noncontrollable variables and the difficulty in predicting reactions from these variables to changes in the firm's marketing mix. A marketing subsystem, such as a distribution warehouse system, can be modeled more effectively, however, than a total marketing system because there are more factual data and the noncontrollable variables are more predictable.

Strategic Marketing Planning. Formalized marketing planning has developed concurrently with financial and other business planning necessary to support company sales forecasts, budgets, and profit forecasts. Formerly marketing planning dealt primarily with annual tactical plans, and more emphasis was given to the promotion mix—i.e., personal selling, advertising, sales promotion—than to the marketing mix. Some companies added longer-range marketing plans, although these usually ended up more as projections than as serious plans for achieving longer-range objectives.

The concept of strategic marketing planning, by way of contrast, places emphasis on the means of achieving predetermined longer-range goals. In strategic planning, management determines where it wants to be at some future time in terms of sales and profits. If projections for its current businesses do not match these longer-range objectives, alternative means of filling the void are developed. These may include improvements in present businesses, new products, entering new markets, or diversification into new businesses.

Strategic plans cover major means of achieving major objectives. Consequently, they require more in-depth and profit-oriented thinking than do shorter-range tactical plans. In strategic marketing planning, tactical plans become the means for implementing the broader strategies. Tactical plans are developed annually, or more often if needed. Strategies are reviewed annually for updating as changing market conditions may require. Strategic marketing planning must be coordinated closely with total business planning.

Product Life-Cycle Concept. This concept has been used in shorter-range marketing planning and may now be one of the reasons more companies are adopting strategic marketing planning.

The concept assumes that every industry goes through four stages—*introduction, growth, maturity,* and *decline.* Industry profit rates rise during the growth period but decline during the maturity period as price cuts and higher promotional costs become common. Profits drop more severely during the decline stage. Realizing that their principal product lines were in maturing industries has caused some managements to turn to strategic marketing planning in search of additional means to profitable growth.

Other Reasons for Strategic Planning. The factors discussed in the section "The Changing Market Environment" have also focused attention on the need for longer-range strategies, as have declining trends in profit margins and return on invested capital experienced by many companies.

Another factor affecting strategic thinking has been the finding of the profit impact of marketing strategies (PIMS) project that return on investment increases as market share increases and vice versa.[2] This finding has caused some companies to reevaluate their strategies in industries in which they have marginal market share positions.

Summary

The marketing concept remains a sound business philosophy, but business must increasingly consider the needs of society as well as the needs of the customer. Changes in the external marketing environment indicate an intensifying instability, and their impact on company operations requires continual surveillance. Every company faces marketing problems unique to itself. There are no prepackaged answers, and few marketing principles or techniques have universal application. Conceptual approaches provide a broader base and are proving helpful in analyzing problems, identifying opportunities, and developing profitable strategies.

See also Consumer behavior, managerial relevance of; Market analysis; Marketing, channels of distribution; Marketing, industrial; Marketing management; Marketing research; Positioning; Sales management.

NOTES

[1] Neil H. Borden, "The Concept of the Marketing Mix," *Journal of Advertising Research*, vol. 4, no. 2, June 1964.

[2] Sidney Schoeffler, Robert D. Buzzell, and Donald F. Heany, "Impact of Strategic Planning on Profit Performance,"

Harvard Business Review, vol. 52, no. 2, March–April 1974.

REFERENCES

Albert, Kenneth J. (ed.): *The Strategic Management Handbook*, McGraw-Hill, New York, 1983, particularly chaps. 9, 11, 12, 14, and 23.

Buell, Victor P.: *Marketing Management: A Strategic Planning Approach*, McGraw-Hill, New York, 1984.

Peters, Thomas J., and Robert H. Waterman, Jr.: *In Search of Excellence: Lessons from America's Best-Run Companies*, Harper & Row, New York, 1982.

Victor P. Buell, *University of Massachusetts; Editor, Handbook of Modern Marketing*

Marketing, Direct

Direct marketing is a business method used to sell merchandise or services directly to the consumer through advertising that requests an immediate response.

A Definitive Vocabulary. Direct mail, newspaper ads, magazine ads, and broadcast announcements generally include coupons or telephone numbers to facilitate immediate responses. These responses may be in the form of a sale accompanied by check or cash, a credit sale, a C.O.D. sale; an appointment for a sales visit at the prospect's or advertiser's premises; or an inquiry to be followed up by a salesperson, phone selling, or by one or more additional direct mail pieces.

When the response is furnished to a salesperson, it is called a *lead*. The lead may go to the advertiser's own sales organization or be furnished to an independent agent, retailer, or franchisee.

When the response is to be followed up by mail, it is called an *inquiry*, and the mailing piece or pieces sent in response are called *conversion mailings*, designed to convert the inquiry to a sale.

A defining characteristic of a direct marketing transaction is the ultimate identification of a purchaser, which enables the advertiser to assemble a mailing list—sometimes called a customer list, house list, or "data base"—of respondees and customers. These lists can be resolicited for additional merchandise and can be rented and exchanged with other advertisers. Such lists are key assets though they are seldom reflected in balance sheets.

Direct mail is a medium used heavily by direct marketers, but it can also be used for awareness-building and many other purposes.

Direct response applies to any type of advertising which asks for a response, whether or not that response is part of a direct marketing business. "Call for name of nearest dealer" is direct response but not direct marketing unless some effort is made to capture the caller's name and additional steps are taken to convert the inquiry into a sale.

Mail order refers to the business of selling through the mail (or through UPS or other direct-to-consumer shipping services). The defining characteristic here is the shipment of merchandise, not the way the order was solicited. A store which takes special orders at a counter and ships them to the customer is in the mail order business but is not in the direct marketing business.

Companies sell in several ways: *Mail order* is defined above. *Subscription*, a finite series paid for in advance, is used by magazine publishers. *Continuity*—meaning the customer gets and pays for each of a series of shipments which can end at any time—is used mainly with a series of books. *Negative option*, as in a record or book club, means the customer is offered shipments each month or so but can decline them. In *positive option*, the customer is offered periodic shipments, but nothing is shipped unless the customer sends in a notice. Both negative and positive options usually require *commitments* in return for a generous premium or pricing arrangement.

Applications. Direct marketing started out as a limited field used mostly by book publishers, correspondence schools, insurance companies, and encyclopedia companies, who solicited leads for conversion by their field forces.

Today direct marketing is used by almost every type of business. These include banks and other financial services, business-to-business marketers, appliance and other hard goods manufacturers, real estate developers, and telecommunications marketers. The list expands constantly.

Direct marketing has grown rapidly because of several sociological factors: the decline of retail sales ability; the shelf-space competition, which makes it difficult for a manufacturer's full line to be stocked and available to customers in most stores; and the trend to working women households, which mitigates against traditional shopping trips and makes the ease of ordering from magazines or catalogs more appealing.

Generally, direct marketing specialists can make significant contributions whenever a company is facing distribution problems. Direct marketing offers an alternative which can often make a dramatic difference in growth and/or survival for a corporation.

In business selling, for example, cold calls by salespeople cost more than $200 each on the average. If a salesperson gets one order out of 10 such calls, the *cost per sale* is $2000. A direct marketing lead generation program might produce leads—expressions of interest by prospective customers—at $20 each. If these are converted at a rate of 25 percent, the cost would be 10 sales calls at $200 each or

$2000, plus $200 cost of lead generation, for a total of $2200 times 25 percent, for a cost per sale of $550—as compared with the $2000 that each cold-call sale costs.

Measurability. One of the unique attributes of direct marketing, from a management point of view, is its definitive measurability. Because of the immediate, direct relationship between an advertising communication and the consumer's response, each advertisement or mailing piece can be measured for effectiveness. Coupons can carry key numbers; telephones can carry extension numbers; and computers can be programmed to measure the number of responses that come from each effort and the immediate and eventual sales which result. These results can be compared with the initial advertising investment, producing a *cost-per-response* figure which is the basis of all direct marketing measurement.

Pretested Profitability. All the rules of statistical validity, forecasting, projection, and return-on-investment analysis apply perfectly to direct marketing. As a result, it is much more of a science than most other advertising efforts and even distribution systems. Each investment can be evaluated in terms of profitability.

This has led to an entire system of media testing designed to minimize downside risk, creative and "offer" testing designed to indicate which variant is most productive, and new product introductions that can be tested before the major manufacturing investment has been committed.

As a result, the approach to advertising and investment decisions is very different. Where a packaged goods development may begin in a straight line, with development and rollout over a period of time leading to a go/no-go decision, direct marketing utilizes multiple product development. A direct marketing venture may develop, research, and test several alternative approaches to a marketing opportunity; determine which is the most effective by measuring consumer response; and then roll out those with the greatest promise. This approach requires alternative plans and the willingness to commit funds on a very flexible basis.

For example, a conventional advertiser might budget an entire year's advertising according to a plan that has been laid out in advance. A direct marketer would budget the dollars but not the specific media. The choice of specific media, creative approaches, and even the products selected to be featured would evolve as results come in. The advertiser has the ability to respond quickly to trends, seasons, and fads and to select investments where the consumer has indicated a willingness to buy. An inflexible approach mitigates this great advantage of direct marketing.

Even the accounting treatment requires a different approach. In direct marketing, advertising is an investment, which should be treated as such. Either the advertising expenditure is capitalized and expensed on the anticipated revenue curve, or it should be expensed with an offsetting future customer value to compensate it.

Multiple-Risk Decisions. Companies that have long been in the direct marketing field are geared for these considerations—as well as for the list maintenance, customer service, and product flexibility requirements—to maximize the direct marketing investment. That is why such entrepreneurial companies and companies in related fields such as publishing or entertainment—those geared to multiple-risk decision making—are often most successful in direct marketing. As more and more major corporations enter this field, they will have to consider the unique planning and administrative requirements of the direct marketing discipline just as much as the unique approaches to marketing strategy and advertising planning. Those who do so will find not only an important profit center but also critically needed insurance against impending difficulties in their existing distribution systems.

Interdynamic Marketing. One major change in the direct marketing field has been the integration of its principles with those of general advertising, a development brought about by general agencies starting up direct marketing agencies.

Some agencies have been successful in combining the research, data retrieval, and creative methods of general advertising with the traditional approaches of direct marketing. Resulting creative approaches have been successful at combining awareness-building objectives with those of achieving immediate measurable results and at utilizing emotional, nonverbal communication along with traditional "reason why" copy. Major breakthroughs have been attributed to this approach, so it is now no longer necessary to have one agency handle awareness objectives and another generate leads for salespeople; the direct marketing agency or a major agency which includes direct marketing in a closely integrated structure can do both.

See also Advertising concepts; Consumer behavior, managerial relevance of; Market analysis; Marketing management; Marketing research; Retailing management; Sales management.

REFERENCES

Nash, Edward L.: *Direct Marketing: Strategy/Planning/Execution,* McGraw-Hill, New York, 1982.

Posch, Robert J.: *The Direct Marketer's Legal Adviser,* McGraw-Hill, New York, 1983.

Stone, Bob: *Successful Direct Marketing Methods,* 2d ed., Crain Books, Chicago, Ill., 1979.

EDWARD L. NASH, *BBDO Direct*

Marketing, Industrial

Industrial marketing is concerned with the various aspects of selling products and services to industry. Industrial buyers include companies and institutions of all types, producers of agricultural products, and government agencies. The products and services they buy are used in or with products they make and sell or for their own consumption. Commercial businesses are also industrial buyers except in the case of consumer items purchased for wholesale or retail trade to nonprofessional users.

Definition. Industrial marketing encompasses those activities pertaining to the flow of goods and services from producers to industrial buyers.

Characteristics. Industrial products are characteristically different from consumer products, although a few items such as stationery and furniture appear in both categories. But, by definition, it is not products that define industrial marketing; it is the classification of the buyers. Industrial buyers have distinctive buying needs, roles, and behaviors that place them in a class by themselves, and therefore they require special marketing considerations. This section describes these marketing considerations and how sellers operate to provide them.

Industrial products can be classified as follows:

- Capital goods—property, plant, equipment, and furnishings
- Raw materials—basic and processed materials and chemicals used in manufacturing
- Fabricated products—components and assemblies used in manufacturing
- Manufacturing and processing services—subcontracted production services
- Operations supplies and support services—maintenance, manufacturing overhead, and utilities items
- Administrative and engineering supplies and professional and technical services

Selling these products and services to the industrial sector requires different approaches and activities from marketing to consumers.

Scope of Industrial Marketing

The primary activities of industrial marketing are: (1) sales and distribution; (2) market development; (3) product management; (4) advertising and sales promotion; (5) customer order service; (6) marketing information services; and (7) marketing administration. Some organizations merge several of these activities while others separate activities that have been combined. Occasionally, certain activities may be assigned to another organizational unit.

Purchasing Influences. No stereotypical industrial marketing organization exists. This is because of wide differences in the kinds of industrial products, in the size of selling companies and numbers of product lines sold, in market segments served, and in management philosophies. In the end, an organization's marketing approach and activities are determined by decisions on how to deal with the principal purchasing influences, including:

Purchasing personnel, who are concerned with all products, and are the dominant influence over nontechnical products.

Manufacturing engineering personnel, who are concerned with items used in production, production equipment and maintenance items, and manufacturing services.

Product engineering personnel, who are concerned with design and testing services and with the specifications of production materials and purchased items that affect product design. In some organizations the engineering department is also assigned the responsibilities for manufacturing engineering.

Quality assurance personnel, who have overlapping interests with manufacturing and engineering personnel, but from the viewpoint of supplier conformance to specifications.

Marketing personnel, who have a basic interest in items purchased for resale by the company.

Top management, which is often involved in the purchase of high cost items, particularly capital equipment.

Third-Party Influences. Third parties can also be important purchasing influences for certain products and marketing situations. Common third-party influences are the following:

Government agencies, which often supply prime contractors with names of qualified subcontractors. They also set a wide range of specifications and evaluate the acceptability of subcontractor bids.

Independent testing laboratories, which assess product qualities and characteristics.

Architects and engineers, who set product specifications and recommend on product acceptability.

Product design and packaging consultants, who are used in product engineering roles. In these cases, they exert significant purchasing influences on product materials and component parts.

Construction and trade contractors, who select

suppliers of common building and construction materials.

The industrial marketing job is complex, and this underlies the need to "sell in depth." Purchasing influences must be identified, and a coordinated marketing approach to reach them must be designed. The product concept, the marketing approach, and the promotional thrust constitute the essence of marketing strategy. Once this is determined, the company organizes to carry out these activities.

Selling and Distribution. This activity involves selecting the channels through which customers will be reached and supplied and carrying out the job. The principal approaches are (1) direct selling, (2) one-step distribution, and (3) two-step distribution. Selling through distributors is classified as indirect selling. Only a small portion of industrial sales—mainly common items and low-price supplies—are sold by mail and advertising promotion. In most industrial marketing situations selling relies heavily on personal attention and persuasion. While reorders may routinely be placed by mail, regular sales calls are necessary to sustain these accounts. Direct sales are invoiced by the company to nondistributor customers. A number of personnel can be involved; hence, the cliché, "Everyone sells." The following persons have sales responsibilities:

Field sales personnel. These are company sales personnel who are assigned to—and are usually based in—geographic territories.

National accounts sales executives. These are company sales personnel who are assigned accounts with multilocation operations, large purchasing potential, and some aspect of centralized purchasing or specifying influence. Usually these people are based at company headquarters.

Government market representatives. These are company sales personnel who are assigned the responsibility of serving government agencies and government prime contractors. Frequently, they are known as technical representatives to accommodate the notion that they provide the government with locally based technical support as opposed to selling influence. This has a bearing on what overhead costs are allowed in cost-plus contracts.

Service representatives. Industrial products often require technical servicing after the sale by service personnel. Frequently these company personnel also provide parallel support to the selling job.

Service parts sales personnel. Most sales of repair and service parts are placed by mail or telephone. The people who handle these orders also solicit such sales by telephone to prevent substitution of another manufacturer's parts.

Manufacturer representatives. These are independent sales professionals who work on behalf of manufacturers. As sales representatives, they do not physically handle the products they sell; nor do they take title to them or collect payments for them.

Wholesalers and Distributors. Wholesalers are intermediaries in product distribution. They purchase goods from manufacturers in their own accounts and resell them in their market areas. The roles of wholesalers in distribution are to:

- Provide local sales representation
- Provide local inventory
- Serve as a bulk-break center
- Take credit risks and perform billing and collection services for small-volume customers
- Act as a center for local service

The identities of sales by wholesalers are shielded from the manufacturers that distribute through them. This is a major difference in indirect selling. The wholesale channel can be one-step or two-step distribution. In *one-step distribution,* there is one wholesaler between the producer and the customer. *Two-step distribution* involves using large central wholesalers to sell to local wholesalers who, in turn, sell to industrial customers.

1. One-step wholesalers are known by a variety of titles: distributors, jobbers, supply houses, merchant wholesalers, and brokers. Occasionally, manufacturers also sell to dealers who operate like store-front businesses, mainly serving trade professionals.

2. In two-step wholesaling, the first-level members are known as regional warehouses, warehouse distributors, and master distributors; the second-step members are known as jobbers, subdistributors, and dealers.

3. Brokers are a separate class of buyers and resellers who function mainly in commodity items such as agricultural products and minerals.

Market Development. Market development usually is considered a part of product management, but there are noteworthy exceptions, mainly in large organizations. Persons having this responsibility are specialists in assigned market segments and they plan individual marketing programs for them. Building contractors, pipeline companies, construction companies, and municipalities are examples of different market segments for a construction machinery product line. Market development managers feed back special market requirements and intelligence to product managers, who must create overall product programs that meet the needs of all market segments.

Product Management. This is a cornerstone function in marketing. It has management oversight responsibilities for assigned product lines and is the source of their marketing strategy and plans. The following are product management's principal areas of responsibility:

Product marketability—product market specifications, price, and package design.

Product availability—finished inventory requirements and deployment, channels of distribution used, and distribution coverage.

The product marketing plan—marketing strategy, item mix, target markets, and promotional thrust.

Product performance accountability—share of market and product line profitability.

Product management is also the first level of technical expertise on the product line, backed up by product engineering. Typically, applications and proposal engineers report to product management. Frequently there is a question about the differences between product managers and brand managers. Because purchase decisions in industrial marketing are based most often upon critical evaluations of product specifications and attributes, the industrial product strategist is designated a product manager. By contrast, consumer purchase decisions are made more often on perceptions of brand position and on brand promotion than on product analysis. Hence, the consumer product strategist is called a brand manager. But the basic roles are the same—guiding product marketing.

Advertising, Sales Promotion, and Publicity. The task of advertising and sales promotion in industrial marketing requires analyzing the roles of various purchasing influences and then effectively communicating to them. The mix of tools and techniques available for this purpose includes:

- Catalogs, product bulletins, and price lists
- Technical data and instruction sheets
- Media advertising, publicity releases, and company reports
- Direct mail promotions, reprints of technical papers, and newsletters
- Shows and exhibitions
- Sales aids and traveling displays
- Remembrance advertising items

The role of advertising and sales promotion in industrial marketing is to achieve awareness, create interest, and provide helpful information. Personal contact is generally indispensable to industrial sales except when ordering standard, low-cost items. On the other hand, this personal attention will be low in productivity without appropriate use of advertising and sales promotion.

Customer Order Service. Entering and processing industrial product orders is usually more compli-cated than making entries of catalog numbers and customer data. Such orders need special attention and editing. For example, consider the following needs:

1. Requests for quotation, particularly for system-related items, usually require special proposals. These are prepared by customer order service or by product management when their complexities exceed the level handled by field sales personnel.

2. Industrial products often have technical specifications and options that must be precisely ascertained and specially priced before orders for them can be entered. Many times, field sales personnel are not prepared to handle this job.

3. Drawings and bills of material of industrial products and systems often require customer approval before production is authorized. Handling this administrative activity plus order expediting requests is done by customer order service personnel.

In some instances, when customer order service is clerical in scope, orders are preedited by product management for technical detail.

Marketing Information Services. This function includes doing market research, making sales analyses, maintaining marketing records and files, making forecasts, designing marketing models (computerized), and representing marketing on the company management information system committee. Many marketing organizations include only market research, forecasting, and modeling in the scope of information services. Integrated, computer-based systems are expanding the scope of this function, however.

Marketing Administration. Large industrial marketing organizations include a marketing administration function. When separately organized, it includes the following common responsibilities: (1) marketing budgets; (2) profit analyses; (3) marketing personnel administration; (4) incentives computation; (5) plans coordination; (6) systems and procedures administration; and (7) reports preparation.

The foregoing marketing activities are the most common in an industrial marketing organization. Two additional activities—product service and physical distribution—should also be mentioned because they appear in some organizations.

Product Service. Product service is concerned with the installation, troubleshooting, and repair of products after they are shipped. In some cases, product service is a separate product line and profit center. It then takes on an active selling role (as opposed to just being responsive) to augment the company's presence in the market and ensure a proper profit contribution for this activity. When product service is not included in marketing it is usually an arm of engineering or manufacturing.

Physical Distribution. Popular practice is to organize physical distribution as a part of operations rather than of marketing. Many companies, however, decentralize a number of marketing functions to the local warehouse level and, there, marketing personnel manage order entry and plan warehouse inventories. Operating personnel, on the other hand, perform all material handling, storing, and product movement tasks and are responsible for the physical plant and traffic function.

Summary

Marketing functions and organization structure vary according to circumstance. The different approaches are not important. What is important is that all essential functions in each situation are established and the overall job is carried out as a coordinated effort.

See also Advertising concepts; Contracting out; Field services management; Leasing, equipment; Market analysis; Marketing management; Marketing of services; Markets, government; Positioning; Product planning and development; Product and service pricing; Purchasing management.

REFERENCES

Haas, Robert: *Industrial Marketing Management,* Petrocelli, Charter, New York, 1976.

Stern, Louis W., and Adel I. El-Ansary: *Marketing Channels,* 2d ed., Prentice-Hall, Englewood Cliffs, N.J., 1982.

Westfall, Ralph, and A. John Ward: "Sales Control Research," in *Marketing Manager's Handbook,* 2d rev. ed., Dartnell, Chicago, Ill., 1983, pp. 443–449.

A. JOHN WARD, *The Austin Company*

Marketing Management

Marketing is the preparation and execution of objectives, strategies, and plans used in the development of products and services, and the efforts used in pushing or pulling these through channels of distribution into the hands of the customer or end user. The names of the key documents that carry these objectives, strategies, and plans are (1) the marketing plan and (2) action plans. *Pushing* occurs when a marketer applies promotional pressure against intermediaries (middlemen or the trade) in an attempt to propel the product or service through the channels of distribution. Examples are private labels and hospital supplies. *Pulling* occurs when the marketer spends promotional dollars to attract end users who, if the promotion is successful, pull the merchandise through the channels of distribution. Examples are fashion jeans and soap.

In marketing management, it is the process that

counts, not the structure of organization. The critical requirements are (1) that all functions of marketing be addressed in coordinated plans, (2) that these plans be prepared by those who will execute the plans, (3) that all decisions be based on sound marketing facts, and (4) that the basic plan be approved by top management. This is true whether the commodity for sale is soft drinks, computers, or financial services.

Responsibility of the Marketing Manager. It is a mistake for one individual to write a marketing plan. Even if the individual were capable of doing so, the motivation to execute this plan by other members of the marketing team would be low. Rather than write the plan, the principal marketing manager should be concerned primarily with the following tasks:

1. To provide an information system that ensures the availability of the necessary marketing facts to compile a fact book and the knowledge by all marketing personnel of the strategic plan or the long-term direction of the business.

2. To create a climate that ensures a coordinated effort in writing the marketing plan.

3. To obtain top management approval of the marketing plan.

4. To establish a process for the preparation and implementation of action plans.

5. To make certain that the plans are enthusiastically endorsed and executed by all members of the marketing team.

Each of these five tasks will be discussed on subsequent pages.

A Succinct Marketing Plan. A prevalent mistake is to produce huge marketing plans 200 to 500 pages long. These documents are impressive to the eye, but they are unwieldy. Their size discourages reading by top management and use by those in the field.

To be effective, a marketing plan should be short and precise. There are two ways to reach this objective. The *first* way is to put all the supporting marketing data in a separate document, usually referred to as the *fact book.* This document may number 250 pages, but it is the fact book, not the marketing plan. The fact book should always be readily available, however, so that if anyone questions a strategy in the marketing plan, the person being questioned can say, for example, "That is supported by the marketing data on page 210 in my fact book. Do you want me to show you?"

The *second* way to keep the plan short is not to insert extensive detail in the document. Whenever a section needs specifics, such as individual sales goals or the media plan, summarize the action in the marketing plan. Then, after the plan is approved by top management, put all the detail in a separate document, usually referred to as an *action plan* or *project plan*.

The Fact Book

The only part of the marketing planning process that takes considerable time is the preparation of the fact book. Given a well-prepared fact book, the development of the marketing plan is relatively easy. Typically, the fact book addresses three major components:

A. Industry
   1. Size
   2. Segments
   3. Growth rate
B. Competition
   1. Share of market
   2. Pricing
   3. Packaging
   4. Depth of line
   5. Distribution
   6. Promotions
C. Customer
   1. Heavy user
   2. Purchase process
   3. Benefits sought
   4. Benefits delivered

The terminology outlined under Industry (A) and Competition (B) is generally self-explanatory. The section on the Customer (C) requires further definition.

Heavy User. This describes the 20 percent of the current or potential customers who typically account for 80 percent of the total volume of sales. In practically every industry or product/service, approximately 20 percent of the purchasing universe will account for something like 80 percent of total sales. These are called the heavy users; market efforts should be directed at them rather than at the 80 percent of the universe that account for only 20 percent of the volume. Heavy users can be isolated within industries or industry segments according to size of company; demographics (age, income, sex, geographical locations); Standard Industrial Classification (SIC)—which are job descriptions set by the government; and psychographics—personality types such as morally concerned, socially concerned, aggressive, or passive.

Purchase Process. This is an analysis of all the individuals involved in the buying decision, ranked in order of priority or importance. For example: an engineer or child may *use* the product/service; it may be *purchased* by a purchasing agent or parent; and the model or brand selected may be *influenced* by the president, vice president, grandparents, physician, retailer, jobber, or current owners. All individuals should be listed, with the single most important indi-

vidual ranked first, the second most important individual next, and so on. For some products/services the *actual user* will receive the highest priority, such as children for cereals and secretaries for typewriters. Sometimes the *actual purchaser* (who could be the same as the actual user, such as for bread and spare parts for equipment) is ranked No. 1. Sometimes the *influencer* (such as doctors in the case of hospitals and consultants in the case of large computers) gets top ranking. The purpose of this ranking is to imply that no marketing funds should be allocated to the No. 2 priority until priority No. 1 is adequately covered, and no funds should be allocated to the No. 3 priority until both priorities No. 1 and No. 2 are adequately covered.

Benefits Sought. This is the process of determining what benefits the various individuals in the purchase process are seeking or what you think they will need. Of primary importance is the top-ranking benefit sought by the classification of individuals with the highest priority in the purchase process. If you can deliver on this promise, this benefit should become the basic thrust of all marketing communications (sales presentations, advertising, brochures, etc.) toward these people.

IBM, for example, concluded that the major benefit in owning a personal computer was that the buyer would not be embarrassed after the purchase because he or she could not make it perform. That is why IBM uses a look-alike for Charlie Chaplin as a spokesperson: "Even a clown can handle it." Contrast this powerful communications strategy with that of an electric typewriter manufacturer which mistakenly emphasizes cost when selling to small or medium-size companies. The secretary, who is No. 1 in the purchase process, doesn't rank cost as very important. After all, the secretary isn't going to pay for the typewriter; what he or she wants is ease of use and convenience.

The benefit that is the most important to the target audience or heavy user should become the basic thrust of all communications to this group of individuals. The marketer leads with the benefit, supported by the features—not the reverse. A common mistake, especially among industrial advertisers, is to emphasize features rather than benefits. Users don't buy a drill bit, for instance, because it is tungsten-tipped. They buy it because a tungsten-tipped drill bit enables them to drill more holes. The prudent marketer leads with "more holes," supported by the tungsten-tipped feature. "More holes" belongs in the heading of an ad and "tungsten-tipped" in the subhead or body copy.

Benefits Delivered. A marketer can't promote "more holes" if the product can't deliver on the promise. If a company has a competitive edge on delivering the most important benefit to the individuals who are ranked at the top of the purchase process, effective marketing is relatively easy. If a company is not that fortunate—and many are not—it has one of three choices. The *first* and most effective choice is to change or reformulate the product or service to correspond to the ideal marketing situation. If this can't be done, the *second* choice is to try to be *perceived* as delivering on the promise. A great many products/services are commodities. That is, they are inherently the same as competition. It is the marketing effort that enables the customer to perceive them as being different. Finally, then, if you can't deliver on the preferred benefit and you are not able to change perceptions, your *third* and least effective choice is to try to deliver on a benefit that is lower in rank. Unfortunately, the company that finds itself in this position normally has to offer the customer something additional, which is usually a lower price.

The Marketing Plan

Once the fact book has been assembled, attention can be directed to the development of the marketing plan. It should go without saying, however, that an effective marketing plan must be fully integrated with the company's strategic plan. This critical relationship bears examination since it provides the context for all marketing management.

Relationship to Strategic Plan. The strategic plan encompasses all components of the business—marketing, manufacturing, engineering, finance, operations, legal, and human resources. It establishes the long-term direction of the business and has a time span of from 3 to 15 years. Two factors that exert a major influence on the duration of the strategic plan are (1) how long it takes a business to change direction and (2) how far one can see into the future with some degree of accuracy. The strategic plan for Delta Airlines, for example, is for 20 years, and for IBM, for 5 years. If a strategic plan is, in fact, in place, a marketing plan is usually placed on a time frame of from 6 to 24 months. Twelve months is most common, although IBM uses 24 months. If there is no strategic plan, the marketing plan should try to fill the gap, at least in marketing, for a 3- to 5-year period.

Components of the Marketing Plan. The marketing plan has three major components: sales plan, communications plan, and research plan. The sales plan addresses pricing, packaging, channels of distribution, sales projections, and time management of the sales force. The communications plan is concerned with advertising, sales promotion, and public relations. The research plan is involved with marketing research, R&D, and communications research. Some companies may include pricing, distribution, and/or sales projections within a product plan, rather than the sales plan. Others may put public relations in a separate plan outside of the communications plan.

It is immaterial where the various functions of marketing are inserted in the marketing plan. What is critical is that each function be considered as a marketing tool and that each function that can have a positive effect on selling the product/service be coordinated with all other marketing functions and be included in this single document called the marketing plan. In this regard, some companies believe that they have a marketing plan when all they have is a sales plan. Sales is just one component of marketing. It is not the incorrect terminology that can cause a marketing problem; it is the misconception that sales is not a part of marketing. This can be disastrous if it results in a sales plan that is a separate document and not coordinated with—or shown to—other members of the marketing team.

Communications Plan. This section of the marketing plan consists of three separate areas of communications:

1. *Advertising plan.* This addresses the message and execution of the advertising campaign and could be subdivided into the creative strategy (what will be said in your advertising); the media strategy (how advertising monies will be spent, at what weight, during which period, and against which target audience); and the media plan (the specifics of where and when these monies will be spent—the actual names of the magazines, radio or television stations, newspapers, etc.). [The creative plan (like other components of the action plan) is *not* part of the communications plan because it specifies the actual ads or commercials to be run. It is usually difficult, if not impossible, to insert them inside the marketing plan. What should be remembered, though, is that the creative plan should never be started until the marketing plan has been completed and approved by top management. Hundreds of thousands of dollars can be spent by company advertising personnel and their advertising agencies on developing the creative plan, only to have the campaign killed at the last minute by the chief executive officer. If the CEO approves the creative strategy in advance, the chances of this happening are greatly diminished.] The responsibility for preparing the advertising plan belongs to either the advertising manager or the product/service brand or market manager.

2. *Sales promotion plan.* This encompasses the strategies and plans for the various aspects of sales promotion that will be used to help meet the marketing objectives. Choices are trade shows, direct mail, couponing, sampling, premiums, sweepstakes and contests, trade deals, price packs, brochures, sales aids, displays, and promotional activities directed at the company's own sales force. The responsibility for preparing the sales promotion plan belongs to either the

sales promotion manager or the product/service brand or market manager.

3. *Public relations plan.* This can consist of the strategies and plans relative to four basic areas of public relations: (*a*) *financial,* which concerns the company's posture with Wall Street, financial institutions, and business publications; (*b*) *external relationships* with the government, the business community, and the public; (*c*) *product or service publicity*—i.e., what can be done to get free publicity in magazines or on the air regarding specific products/services; and (*d*) *internal marketing,* which is concerned with what can be done to sell the company to the employees. The responsibility for preparing the public relations plan belongs to the director of public relations.

Research Plan. This section of the marketing plan can be sectionalized into three parts:

1. *R&D plan.* This is concerned with what activity should be completed on new product development to meet the targets stated in either the strategic plan or the marketing plan.

2. *Marketing research plan.* This states the type and scope of research studies that need to be completed to enhance the preparation of future marketing plans.

3. *Communications research plan.* This is a commitment to test the effectiveness of the various components of the communications plan. The results should answer such questions as, Is advertising actually increasing the desire to purchase the product? Is the value of the trade show, measured in quantifiable terms, exceeding the total cost of preparations and the exhibit? Is public relations enhancing the personality of the company? Responsibility for the preparation of the research plan belongs to the director of research.

Sales Plan. The components of the sales plan include such topics as sales goals, national accounts, segmentation, market development, customer service, distribution, pricing, packaging, sales training, sales meetings, sales aids, and telemarketing. Because so many marketing personnel receive their early training as sales representatives and are familiar with sales planning, the sales plan does not always require as much detail. The person normally responsible for the preparation of the sales plan is the sales manager.

Plan Preparation. The first step in preparing a marketing plan is to obtain agreement on what market segments will be developed, who is involved in the purchase or buying decision within each segment, and what benefits the product or service can deliver. The marketing facts that support these decisions are found in the fact book. Developing answers to these questions should be a joint effort of all mar-

keting personnel—sales managers, brand managers, marketing managers, advertising managers, sales promotion managers, communications managers, the director of public relations, and the director of research. If there is insufficient information to make these key decisions, a benchmark study should be conducted immediately to obtain the necessary facts.

Bottom-up Inputs. After agreement is reached on the profiles and ranking of the individuals involved in the purchase process by segment (sometimes there are different profiles within various segments), each specialist in the marketing team prepares a particularized plan on how to apply marketing pressure toward the top-ranking people in the purchase process. The sales manager and staff prepare the sales plan, the communications people the communications plan, and the research people the research plan, but there has to be constant dialogue between these teams to ensure an effective and coordinated plan. Otherwise, these teams may all go after different target groups with different messages.

Measurable Objectives. Typically, the first section of the marketing plan contains five to eight measurable objectives. These state in quantifiable terms what the marketing group expects to accomplish during the given period through the three functions of marketing: sales, communications, and research. Every objective should be measurable. Otherwise no one will ever know whether they have been reached, and, consequently, the objectives will be useless. An objective that states, "To increase sales or share of market," is too general to be measured. Measurable marketing objectives usually meet three requirements: (1) a *goal*—"To increase sales 10 percent . . ."; (2) an *expenditure*—"with a sales budget of $500,000 and a communications budget of $250,000 . . ."; (3) a *date*—"by June 30, 1985."

By using measurable objectives, a company learns from experience what it will normally take to reach its various goals. Admittedly, information obtained this way is through trial and error. But it provides realistic, rather than wishful, objectives. The process takes time, but after 3 or 4 years of constantly setting and revising objectives, the company should obtain a feel for what the ideal marketing mix is for a given objective for a particular product/service. This procedure has helped make Procter & Gamble the most astute and formidable marketing company in the world.

Action Plans

Action plans are documents separate from the marketing plan and the fact book. Action plans are prepared only after the marketing plan is completed and approved by top management. They delineate how each project will be completed, from beginning to end. Action plans contain the details that support the marketing plan and should include at least three key elements: (1) tasks or steps, (2) responsibilities, and (3) due dates. After each task or step, the person or department responsible for the particular activity is listed, along with the expected completion date. The composite of all the action plans for a marketing plan is the basis for the *milestone calendar*, which summarizes important completion dates. Operating budgets keep you on budget; milestone calendars keep you on time.

A set of action plans provides the company with two more benefits. First, it enables the marketing group to get the basic thrust of the plan approved before it spends time crossing all the t's and dotting the i's. Second, it further enhances bottom-up planning because the people who write the action plans are (or should be) the ones who are responsible for this particular specialty.

Summary

At the beginning of this chapter the five primary tasks of a marketing manager were listed. The first is to provide an information system that acquaints marketing personnel with the long-term direction of the business and enables them to construct a comprehensive fact book. The second is to provide a climate that allows for coordination between all members of marketing. The third is to obtain top management approval of the plan. If you are successful in accomplishing the first two tasks and keep your plan factual, specific, and terse, the third task should not be any problem. The fourth task, establishing a process for the preparation and execution of action plans, is also relatively easy since it enables the most knowledgeable and responsible people to write their own plans and programs. Finally, if you accomplish the first four tasks, you'll never have to worry about the fifth task—obtaining the enthusiastic endorsement and execution of marketing plans by all members of the marketing group.

See also Advertising concepts; Consumer behavior, managerial revelance of; Market analysis; Marketing, channels of distribution; Marketing, concepts and systems; Marketing research; Marketing of services; Product planning and development; Product and service pricing; Sales management.

REFERENCES

Chase, Cochrane, and Kenneth L. Barasch: *Marketing Problem Solving*, Chilton, Philadelphia, 1977.
Luther, William M.: *The Marketing Plan*, American Management Associations, New York, 1982.
McKay, Edward S.: *The Marketing Mystique*, American Management Associations, New York, 1979.

WILLIAM M. LUTHER, *Luther Company*

Marketing Research

Marketing research may be defined as the scientific acquiring of marketing-related information for the purpose of aiding managerial decision making. As such, it can be used by both business and nonprofit organizations. The scientific nature of marketing research sets it apart from other bases for decision making. In contrast to intuition, scientific decision making can be taught to others. It is cheaper than trial-and-error decision making because it can reduce the number of trials and cut the extent of error. Unlike copying the efforts of another organization, scientific decision making can help to show which similarities in efforts are likely to be beneficial and which are likely to be harmful. It is also superior to decision making by authority, experience, expert opinion, or majority vote, because it can reflect quickly the impact of environmental changes that affect organizational performance. Basically, the scientific method used in marketing research is a special approach to thinking. The reasoning is rational, logical, impartial, and based on verifiable evidence.

Marketing research typically deals with discontinuous projects rather than with ongoing information needs. However, the responsibility for gathering some regularly needed information may be given to marketing research when an organization has not yet established an information system for the periodic gathering of regularly needed information. The overall information system of an organization is discussed elsewhere in this handbook.

Application Opportunities

Marketing deals with the management of demand. Therefore, marketing research can deal with literally hundreds of different topics related to demand. Opportunities for marketing research occur within marketing, in its organizational environment, and in the outside environment.

1. Major categories of research within marketing are intended markets, product-service offerings, distribution, pricing, promotion, and marketing research itself.

2. Environmental categories within the organization worthy of marketing research are mission; goals; operating philosophy; organizational structure; communication networks; resource allocations; public image; and methods of planning, implementation, analysis, and control.

3. Opportunities concerning environmental influences outside the organization include competitors' actions, political and legal conditions, technological developments, economic conditions,

sociocultural influences, and natural conditions. For a discussion of several hundred specific topics covering the various categories of marketing research, see the outstanding marketing book by McCarthy and Perreault.[1]

Elements of a Research Project

Marketing research projects differ greatly in content and methods used. However, some parts should be included in the design of all such projects. A succinct definition is needed of the project objectives, relevant population, sampling unit, information sources, research design, sampling method, sample size, information collection media, structure, disguise, sequencing, layout, editing, tabulation mode, measurement level, analysis methods, interpretation of results, and reporting format.

Project Goals. A clear, concise statement of project goals is needed to guide the scope of research effort. Otherwise, essential information may be omitted, gathered in unusable form, or collected inefficiently.

Population Definition. The relevant population for a study depends on the objectives of the inquiry. It is the processes, events, things, or people to be measured in a study.

Sampling Unit. A sampling unit is the entity that will be used to represent a member of the population. Since different people in an organization have different knowledge and authority, specific members may be qualified to represent it on some issues and not on others.

Information Sources. Pieces of information differ greatly in their cost, appropriateness, accuracy, recency, and accessibility. No one source is best for all information needs.

Information inside an organization is usually easier and cheaper to gather than outside information. However, outside information is often needed for evaluation of activities by customers, competitors, and other aspects of the operating environment.

Information gathered previously for another purpose is usually cheaper to buy than new, custom-made information. Such data are widely available in libraries, in company records, and from syndicated data services. But new information may be bought because the past information is unknown to the organization, the coverage does not fit current needs, or the owner will not release the information for use by others.

Research Design. The specifications for obtaining information will affect how many different applications the information will have. Unfortunately, the simpler, less complex designs are also the ones that provide the least information.

An after-the-fact measurement can be used to describe an organization's condition at a point in time. However, a measurement of performance trends requires measurements from more time periods.

Even if results were measured in several time periods after a change in organizational strategy, there is still no indication that any changes in results were due to the change in effort. Part or all of the change in results may be due to other influences in the operating environment.

Trying out a new approach in one area and doing things the "normal" way in a similar area allows unknown and uncontrollable influences to continue. But the influence on both groups should be about the same, except for the deliberate difference in strategy. Therefore, the difference in results obtained could be attributed to the difference in strategy. Of course, the two areas or groups of people may have started out as different on some key characteristics. So, "before" measures are important to see whether the groups were similar prior to the intended influence being introduced.

As marketers know, when parts of the marketing strategy are put together their influence may be different from that of any of the parts alone. For example, an advertising campaign would involve choices of media, talking points, symbols used in the communication, and timing in delivery. A test of these variables in different combinations can be used to determine different response patterns.

The most useful research design involves several groups, "before" and "after" time periods, and combinations of strategy. However, such investigations are often impractical because of cost and time limitations.

Sampling Method. A sample uses a few population members to represent the many. In contrast, a census uses all population members to represent the population. Typically, surveys use a sample rather than a census because a sample usually is quicker and cheaper. Sometimes a sample is even more accurate than a census because time lags can be reduced and more of the project budget can be diverted from information collection to control of information collection efforts.

Random sampling gives each population member a known chance of being picked for a survey. It involves careful, deliberate selection of potential respondents. As a result, the accuracy of such samples can be estimated statistically.

Nonrandom sampling is usually quicker and cheaper than random sampling. If extreme results are expected, such a sample may be good enough to point the direction for management to make a "go" or "no-go" decision. But the representativeness of such studies cannot be estimated statistically.

A simple random sample gives each population member a known and equal chance of being selected for the survey. Such a sample might overrepresent and underrepresent some types of population members. But it does not require advance knowledge of the nature or size of subgroups in the population.

In contrast, a *stratified random sample* gives specified categories of population members a known, unequal share of the total sample. Stratification can help reduce the risk of inadequately representing important categories within the population. But stratification requires knowledge or assumptions on which population features are important, such as age, lifestyle, frequency of product use, or benefits sought. Normally a sample is too small to stratify on more than three or four variables, so choosing the bases for stratification can be a very difficult decision.

Proportional stratified samples are used to increase the accuracy of a sample for the purpose of describing the population. In contrast, *disproportional stratified samples* are used to obtain a larger representation of small or important categories in the population so that comparisons can be made.

Assume that chain stores account for only 10 percent of the businesses in a particular industry and independents account for 90 percent of the firms. A proportional, stratified sample based on number of businesses of each type would include one chain store for each nine independents in the total sample. A simple random sample might include more or fewer than one chain store per nine independents. In contrast, a disproportional stratified random sample could be used to include more chain stores intentionally so that comparisons could be made among them by region and floor space.

Sample Size. The size of a sample is dependent on goals of the study, size of the relevant population, proportion of the population included in the sample, extent of variability expected in the population, degree of exactness sought in the answer, level of confidence desired in the answer, time available for the study, and budget limitations. The technical and judgmental representation of the many influences requires careful communication between the researcher and research user. Nevertheless, here are three rules of thumb for setting sample size:

1. Use at least 400 for an overall representation of a large population.

2. Include a minimum of 30 in each category that is to be compared with another, to approximate representativeness in each category for the particular variable.

3. Use a sample size of at least 1000 when several variables are to be analyzed for both individual and combined influences.

Although setting an exact sample size can be mathematically tedious, it can be done quickly and cheaply by a skilled researcher. Careful calculation can be less costly than "weak" information value from too small a sample or wasted resources due to oversampling. Also, sample size formulas include estimates for variability in the population, confidence desired in the answer, and extent of exactness wanted in the answer. Therefore, trade-offs between accuracy, cost, and exactness can be simulated to see which combination is most agreeable to management.

Information Collection Media. Information can be gathered by phone, mail, face-to-face interviewing, or observation. No one medium is best for all types of situations. In fact, a combination of media can be very useful in gathering background information, prescreening respondents, obtaining the intended information, encouraging response, and verifying answers.

Some major characteristics of different information collection media are given in Table M-8. However, the actual results in a single study can vary greatly from what might be considered "normal."

Structure. A fixed list of possible answers can help people to recall important issues and to find words that express their ideas. Such questions with *closed-end answer choices* can be used to represent selected features of the relevant population.

TABLE M-8 Selected Features of Information Collection Media

Features	Media					
			Face-to-Face		Observation	
	Phone	Mail	Home	Mall	Personal	Machine
Cost per completed response	low	medium	high	high	high	high
Speed of data collection	high	medium	low	medium	low	low
Extent of wasted time between contacts	low	low	high	medium	high	high
Response rate	high	low	medium	high	high	high
Ability to adjust content during the contact	high	low	high	high	high	low
Quantity of information obtainable per contact	low	medium	high	high	high	high
Variety of information obtainable	medium	high	high	high	low	low

Open-ended questions can be used to explore for new ideas. But some types of people tend to volunteer more answers to an essay question than others. So the frequency of different answer choices obtained from essay responses should not be considered representative of the population.

Disguise. The purpose of a project can either be disguised or undisguised. An undisguised purpose can help interviewers save time by focusing the thoughts of respondents on the few issues of concern. But a disguised approach can be used to decide what the issues of concern should be by not prematurely narrowing the scope of consideration.

The sponsor of a project can also be disguised or undisguised. If a respected organization is indicated as the sponsor of a project, cooperation may be more likely. However, people usually do not want to offend the client, so many of them tend to slant responses in favor of the client. Generally, it is much less risky to disguise sponsorship than to identify the sponsor early in the survey contact.

Sequencing. The order in which issues are presented can affect the accuracy of answers and the willingness to respond. Simple, interesting questions are usually put at the start of an interview to allow respondents to warm up to the interview process. Questions that are hard, lengthy, or socially sensitive in content are typically placed near the end of the survey so that the likelihood of nonresponse will be reduced. Questions that distinguish between members and nonmembers of the relevant population are usually placed at the start of the question sequence so that time is not wasted on sampling units that are not within the scope of the study.

Layout. The accuracy of recorded data can be affected by the positioning, numbering, and highlighting of components on the recording form. Interviewer instructions and recording categories that should not be read to respondents can be put on a separate sheet, marked in color, or underlined. Aligning answer categories vertically near the right or left margin of the recording form can speed tabulation. The size of space allowed for an essay response on a mail questionnaire can encourage or discourage lengthy answers. Numbering questions can help interviewers to avoid losing track of which questions should be skipped if a respondent fits in some categories and not others. Ideally, recording forms should have printed words, vertical alignment of answers, numbered issues, clear distinction of instructions from questions, adequate spacing for easy reading, and designated positions where answers are to be recorded.

Editing. Checking answers prior to tabulation is often necessary. Essay answers may be given when a person does not know which structured answer category to mark or when categories have not been established. As a result, the answer has to be evalu-

ated to see if it fits in a designated category, if a new category should be set, or if the answer should be put in a miscellaneous category designated as "other."

Tabulation Mode. The choice between manual and machine tabulation is one of the easier project decisions to make. Manual tabulation is appropriate when a study involves few questions, few answers, a small sample size, few cross-tabulations of answers from different questions, some unclassified answers, no statistical analysis, and no intention to combine the information with information in other studies. If some of these criteria are not met, machine tabulation may be cheaper, faster, and more accurate than tabulation by hand.

Measurement Level. The level of measurement provided in survey answers is an important factor to consider in picking data analysis techniques. The more powerful analysis methods require high levels of measurement.

Nominal measurements are useful for identification purposes and counting the frequency in various categories. Breakdowns by occupation, industry, and race are some nominal measurements that may be useful in distinguishing which market segments are more responsive than others.

Ordinal measures suggest an order to answers. Such measures include heavy versus light use of a brand, rankings, and attitude ratings toward a product/service offering. Answers indicate the direction but not the amount of difference. As a result, statistical analysis that involves the averaging of scores is usually inappropriate.

Interval measurements provide more powerful information because they can be used for indicating the extent of difference. Temperature is one such measure. Since the zero point is arbitrary rather than natural, statistical routines that involve multiplication and division do not fit this type of information.

Ratio measurements have a natural zero point. So even more exacting statistical analysis methods can be used on such answers. Such information includes answers on age, income, and years of formal education when specific amounts are designated.

Analysis Methods. Tabulated information can be used by management to identify recent conditions, trends, interrelationships, and important differences. Sometimes results can be interpreted by visual inspection. But usually the information is so voluminous or the differences are so slight that the manager cannot distinguish easily between chance fluctuations and significant differences in the survey results.

The arithmetic mean, median, and mode are popular measures for representing average response. A frequency distribution represents the pattern of answers. The range indicates the greatest variation in scores, and the standard deviation provides a measure of the concentration in scores. The technical procedures for calculating such measurements for a single variable are described by Luck et al.[2]

When differences between two or more groups are to be determined on a single variable, other types of statistical analysis are needed. Several key questions need to be asked. Are the measurements only nominal or are they ordinal scaled? Do the groups to be compared have a different distribution pattern of answers? Are there substantial gaps between actual scores in either the population or the sample?

If any of these questions is answered with a "yes," *nonparametric statistical tests* should be considered. Otherwise, the more exacting parametric statistical tests should be given first consideration. Many nonparametric tests are described clearly in the classic book by Siegal,[3] and Luck et al.[2] aptly describe several parametric tests.

When more than two variables are to be considered in combination, multivariate statistics may be needed to identify the individual and combination influences. Such techniques are useful for investigating possible cause-and-effect relationships and the extent of similarity among different variables. Aaker[4] provides an outstanding book on multivariate tools and applications in marketing research.

Interpretation of Results. Some researchers believe that the results of a project should "speak for themselves" so that a client can make an impartial judgment of the content. Others prefer to add an interpretation of the findings to the report so that the client will be less likely to overlook or misinterpret key relationships. Conclusions reported by the analyst can provide managers with a major opportunity to double-check their own interpretation of the information.

Reporting Format. The final research report may be in oral or in written form. In either case it should include a very brief introductory overview of the purpose, methodology, findings, and conclusions of the study. If the client is reoriented to the project first, subsequent in-depth comments will be easier to put in perspective.

The design of a research report should be adjusted for the intended audience. If nontechnical managers are to use the information, statistical jargon should be avoided and technical calculations should be de-emphasized. When a report is also for use by technical personnel, statistical calculations, detailed definitions, and computer printouts can be included as appendixes.

The bibliography, figures, and appendixes in a written report are for supportive details, elaboration, and information of value to only a minor portion of the audience. A question-and-answer period in an oral presentation can serve a similar purpose as well as providing for clarification of issues raised in the body of the report.

Potential Misuse

Marketing research is a very important aid for decision makers. But it is underutilized by managers because of promotional abuses, fear, language barriers, impatience, and inaccurate results.

Promotional Abuses. When managers are reluctant to use marketing research, some researchers exaggerate the quality of information that can be provided. Short-term support for marketing research efforts may be increased. But long-term resistance will probably increase because of the suspicions created when unrealistic expectations are not fulfilled. Be wary of researchers who claim they can identify the "best" course of action for management. Marketing research cannot provide perfect information, because the cost, time, and environmental influences involved are too great.

Managers may also encourage distorted research reports by favoring positive reports and rejecting or attacking negative ones. Under such a reward system, the researcher quickly learns that managers want support for their personal preferences rather than objective information.

When biased reporting has become the norm in an organization, a reorientation to objective decision making and reporting can be very time-consuming. However, key managers can encourage the change by asking probing questions concerning how, what, when, where, why, how much, how many, and by whom. Challenging the objectivity of managers and researchers can be very embarrassing, but it provides a strong signal that wishful thinking and whimsical decision making are not acceptable substitutes for hard evidence.

Inaccurate Results. Regardless of how fast marketing research is done, the information is somewhat out of date by the time a client can react to it. Yet, some organizations will hold a manager responsible for a "wrong" decision even when it is in line with the best information that was available at the time. Such organizational behavior discourages objective decision making and can alienate high-quality managers. A more constructive approach is to make managers responsible for the quality of decision making, hold researchers accountable for the quality of information they provide, and recognize that the actual outcome is uncontrollable.

Research results may be presented in the form of exact numbers so that managers assume that one answer is very accurate even though the numbers are only approximations of what is being represented in the population. Researchers can encourage managers to recognize the inexactness of information by representing statistical findings with a range within which the actual amount is expected to be, instead of providing an exact answer that is quite likely to be wrong.

Fear. Some managers are afraid to use marketing research because it might conflict with what they want to do or what they have done in the past. As a result, the researcher may not be given access to potentially embarrassing information, misleading inputs may be provided, and attempts may be made to hide problems.

Marketing research can be given the power to operate in a business by providing it with a separate budget, giving top-management support, and allowing marketing research to suggest projects as well as respond to research requests. Reluctant managers can be encouraged to use marketing research by the company providing a training program in information use, requiring that managers at least consider research results in making decisions, or holding managers responsible for poor decisions that go against the information provided by marketing research and the rest of the management information system.

Language Barriers. Researchers are able to save time in talking to each other by using technical jargon. However, nontechnical managers are likely to be confused rather than enlightened by terms such as confidence level, stepwise multiple regression, degrees of freedom, and Likert scaling. As a result, much of the meaningfulness in a research report may be missed by the client. If a researcher forgets to "translate" the report for a nontechnical audience, a gentle reminder can be provided simply by asking, "What does that mean in a layperson's terms?"

Impatience. One of the major difficulties in developing a research project is in defining the problem. Managers generally are not detail-oriented, so they prefer to turn the project over to a researcher. But management needs to work with the researcher to clarify, revise, and screen the problem statement. Otherwise, the project developed by the researcher may not fit the information needs of the manager.

A major marketing research project is likely to take between 6 months and 2 years to complete. Therefore, information needs should be determined far in advance of when the information is to be used. Otherwise, the information may be unnecessarily expensive or unavailable when it is wanted.

See also Advertising concepts; Attitude surveys; Consumer behavior, managerial relevance of; Management information systems (MIS); Market analysis; Marketing, channels of distribution; Product and service pricing; Sales management; Statistical analysis for management.

NOTES

[1] E. Jerome McCarthy and William D. Perreault, Jr., *Basic Marketing: A Managerial Approach*, 8th ed., Richard D. Irwin, Homewood, Ill., 1984.

[2] David J. Luck, Hugh G. Wales, Donald A. Taylor, and Ronald S. Rubin, *Marketing Research*, 6th ed., Prentice-Hall, Englewood Cliffs, N.J., 1982.

[3] Sidney Siegal, *Nonparametric Statistics: For the Behavioral Sciences*, McGraw-Hill, New York, 1956.

[4] David A. Aaker, *Multivariate Analysis in Marketing*, 2d ed., Scientific Press, Palo Alto, Calif., 1981.

THOMAS M. BERTSCH, *James Madison University*

Marketing of Services

Services are defined by the American Marketing Association as "activities, benefits or satisfactions which are offered for sale, or are provided in connection with the sale of goods." Services, then, relate both to the sale of tangible goods and to intangible services themselves.

The marketing of services includes those activities which (1) accompany the sale of tangible goods and which are perceived to possess value for at least some of the customers (e.g., credit), and (2) are perceived to provide customer satisfaction without being tied to the sale of a tangible product (e.g., insurance).

Size and Scope of Services. The importance of marketing services is clearly reflected in employment and expenditure figures. Roughly half the consumer work force and half the consumer expenditures are committed to providing and consuming services—private and public. Opportunities for employment and expanded service offerings in such areas as finance, communications, health care, transportation, and recreation are strong.

Product-Related Services

For the most part, firms offer at least a limited number of services with the sale of a consumer good. Some of these—e.g., warranties—are required by law. Others are offered in an attempt to enhance sales and encourage selective demand for their product.

Consumer Products. Four types of marketing services are readily related to consumer product sales.

Credit. Consumers in the United States increasingly live in a cashless society in which the ability to pay for the purchase during, or even after, consumption of part or all of the product is extremely important. Credit permits the buyer to consume without initial payment of the product's total economic purchase value—whether the buyer lacks the money to pay for the item or prefers to hold the money personally and pay the seller a fee (interest) for delayed payment. Credit also enables the seller to commit a buyer now to future payments and thus to avoid the possibility of that customer's spending those dollars elsewhere at a later time. Hence, when judiciously used, credit is a mutually advantageous marketing service that retailers can offer customers.

Delivery. In some cases, delivery service is purely a convenience; for example, delivery of a sterling-silver bottle stopper from a local department store minutes away. In other cases, delivery service is a necessity; for example, delivery of a refrigerator. Sometimes delivery is included in the price; at other times it is not. Regardless of the cost to the buyer, delivery is a service for which a cost is incurred not only in time and related expenses for transportation but also in terms of proper installation and use as related to the explicit and implied warranty.

Warranty and Service. Even though a firm may not have extended an express warranty, such obligations are now imposed by law. A product must be of average quality and fit the ordinary purpose for which the product is typically used. The seller also has an implied warranty that the goods sold for a particular use will be fit for such purpose. Hence, in the United States a consumer is entitled to a product which meets reasonable expectations for performance as intended by purchase.

To ensure that products do work properly and are repaired if they do not, firms typically offer some form of warranty and repair services. As noted above, delivery service and installation often are included in the purchase price to minimize warranty repair work. The range of warranty-repair service alternatives varies from simple replacement to complex service repair systems. When it is cheaper to replace a product than to repair it, the former is often selected. This covers most products in which the labor costs are higher than the materials involved; e.g., low-priced cameras, children's toys, and small appliances. Depending upon the time since purchase and the retailer from whom the product was purchased, the exchange can be made at the place of purchase, the manufacturer's service outlet, or the factory.

For moderately priced or expensive items, repair is usually attempted. If the product is portable—e.g., a personal computer—repair is typically done at a service center which is owned by or under contract to the manufacturer. If the product cannot be transported easily—e.g., a refrigerator—service at the user's home is required. At the extreme are products which become part of a system, such as home air-conditioning units or central vacuum cleaner systems, which must be serviced completely at the place of use.

The alternatives available to manufacturers include central factory repair services, a company or contracted (independent) network of repair stations located in areas of population concentration, or retailer-dealer repair arrangements. Each implies varying financial commitments, control potentials, and consumer satisfaction possibilities.

User Instruction. In many cases, instructions for product use are rarely needed or read by the purchaser; for example, instructions for portable cassette players. However, as the complexity or hazard potential associated with use increases, as with hand tools and small appliances, the need for use instruction also increases, and elaborate instructions are included.

In some cases, doubt about how to use an item inhibits purchase. For this reason, Amana demonstrates its microwave ovens, and Cuisinart has distributor training sessions for its food mill operations.

Although the marketing services associated with consumer product offerings are frequently not sufficient in themselves to motivate continued selective demand, they are important in the overall product offering and marketing strategy.

Industrial Products. Marketing services associated with industrial product sales are generally more numerous and significant than those for consumer products. In addition to the four service categories previously mentioned, five other services are typically offered.

Financing. In the case of consumer goods, financing typically is short term. The retail establishment either approves credit for the particular item to be purchased or arranges for a limited amount of credit over an indefinite period of time. In the operation of most businesses the purchase of equipment and supplies is vital. The availability of attractive financing (or credit)—long-term as well as short—is extremely important and can become the differentiating factor in determining which supplier is selected.

Service Arrangements. In many instances, it is the availability of convenient and inexpensive service which becomes the major reason for industrial customers to choose one brand over another. In large installations the costs associated with product failure can be disastrous for a firm; thus, service becomes a crucial factor in the purchase decision of the businessperson.

The firm providing the service must determine the true value that effective service adds to a product and the effect of varying service levels on profit and sales. This includes analysis of the types of service, such as order filling, installation and training, and repair and maintenance.

Training. Consumer training is typically limited to an instruction booklet, sales personnel instructions when considering the purchase, in-store demonstrations, or succinct installation directions of service personnel. For simple consumer goods, these methods are usually adequate. In the case of industrial goods, frequently they are not.

Training in the use of a product is imperative for some products' sales. For example, in the case of office machines, such as reproducing equipment and microcomputers, the individual's knowledge about the machine directly influences the output obtained. Since many of the machines are operated by individ-

uals in positions where turnover is rather high, new operators must be trained to use the equipment properly if user satisfaction and continued use is to be expected. Thus, for many companies training is a necessary, ongoing process, and it represents a cost that must be considered by the seller as well as a desirable service by the purchaser.

Order Filling and Processing. Handling customer orders, processing the orders for subsequent production, shipping, and billing are services which can be offered as part of a sales program for industrial buyers. These services focus on the buyer and his or her needs. If they are properly administered, they lead to heightened customer satisfaction and long-term buyer-seller relationships. The strategy to supply such services represents a marketing orientation on the part of the seller, one in which the needs of the buyer are foremost in determining company policies. For example, where frequent deliveries are desirable for purchasers with limited inventory capabilities, product pricing which includes regular commercial carriers in place of company-owned truck deliveries every 10 days or so would be advantageous to the customer. So, too, would be supplier aid in proper inventory control and cost analyses.

Installation and Application Assistance. Unlike consumer goods, industrial equipment frequently involves installation procedures in the purchaser's plant. Installation may vary from delivery of an adding machine to a clerk's desk to installation of a complex and major piece of equipment. It could take only a few minutes, or months. Installation offers the seller an opportunity to build satisfying customer relationships—especially when the period of installation is extended, allowing auxiliary applications to enhance the purchaser's operations. Installation and application services can be offered through the manufacturer's personnel or authorized representatives (dealers or independents). Ideally, company-controlled and -trained staff members are the most desirable alternative. However, geographic dispersion of purchasers and uneven demand rarely make it economically feasible to operate an in-house service organization to cover all customers.

In summary, industrial sales require strong service support. Consequently, the marketing services offered with industrial sales are the key to product marketing strategy and corporate growth.

Organizational Services

In the prior section, the discussion of marketing services was in terms of activities related to the sale of tangible products. In this section, emphasis shifts to the marketing of services per se, that is, the marketing of what is frequently referred to as intangibles, such as insurance, banking, or travel.

Where the service itself is the product, the tasks traditionally associated with product marketing are still relevant. That is, the marketing management tasks (1) of determining the marketing mix and (2) of planning for effective strategy and organization for action are critical to the total marketing effort.

The Service Marketing Mix. The marketing mix—for services or for products—is composed of four key elements: product, promotion, price, and distribution. Marketing managers dealing with services must develop effective strategies in each of these areas.

Product. With a service, the product is an intangible good. Most services—for example, insurance, investment services, or protection services—cannot appeal to a buyer's sense of touch, smell, sight, taste, or hearing. Services can be considered perishable; that is, if they are not utilized, the potential can never be recovered. For example, an unused seat on a train or an individual's unrequested time to entertain an audience can never reoccur, for time is itself perishable. Moreover, services themselves are sometimes difficult to distinguish from the seller or the provider of those services.

Because of the characteristics, the job of attaining effective sales revolves around astute use of the marketing mix in total. That includes, of course, the differentiation of the service offering (product) as well as a thorough understanding of the environmental (customer, competitive, etc.) conditions.

Promotion. An organization's promotion efforts include personal selling, advertising, publicity, public relations, and other sales promotional activities. Promotional activities are capable of creating perceived differences among service offerings, for example, through imagery. Promotional activities are capable of directing the potential customer's attention toward the key attributes of the services as they relate to the potential buyer's needs; e.g., to sales or sales promotional literature. Promotional activities enable development of personalized relationships with the service organization, as with salespeople or public relations. Hence, promotional activities can be used by service organizations to (1) build a strong service image and (2) develop positively reinforcing personal relationships between the organization and its target market.

Price. Pricing objectives for a service organization are similar to those of product-oriented organizations; that is, to enable goal attainment. The goal, of course, will vary with the organization. For a privately owned, profit-oriented organization, it would imply traditionally defined economic profits. For a government welfare organization, it might imply operating within the budget and servicing x number of individuals. For a quasi-public–owned institution, it may mean perpetuation by covering costs and meeting the objectives established by the organization's leaders.

In the private sector, pricing depends primarily **557**

upon supply and demand. Prices are critically reflected in the cost of labor in the case of services. Negotiation, however, is a realistic activity in which buyers and sellers engage to determine price—especially in highly individualized and specialized service areas.

In the case of some services, such as home contractors, negotiation is expected. In the case of others, such as medical or legal, general guidelines of what might be charged are established by the group that speaks for the industry; for example, by the Bar Association, although its legality is being questioned. In still other sectors, like marketing research, proposals are prepared for prospective clients with details and cost of the services to be rendered.

Negotiation exists primarily because of the difficulty of differentiating one service offering tangibly from another and because of the individualization of the service offered to meet customer requirements.

On the other hand, very routine, organized service offerings that do not vary from one individual to another are often not subject to negotiation. For example, the services of a reducing gym, a dry cleaner, or a rug shampoo service typically have one-price (or multiple-service level) policies. In these cases, the price is determined by traditional cost plus return-on-investment, or target-return, pricing procedures.

Distribution. The distribution of a service is influenced by the characteristics of the service. Its perishability with reference to time and its intimate ties with the providers of the service place restrictions on the proliferation of outlets possible, unless marked standardization can be achieved.

In the case of fast-food outlets such as McDonald's, standardization of service levels and training is possible, which allows for mass distribution of the convenience service. In the case of reducing salons, the standardization is tempered by the emphasis on personal contact with the operation's manager. At the other end of the scale, an organization such as a consulting operation requires special knowledge and personal attributes as keys to success rather than mass distributive efforts.

Regardless of the type of service—from fast-food operation to welfare organization to insurance company—the placement of contact points, such as offices, salespeople, or places of operational contact, must meet the needs and desires of the population the organization hopes to serve. In this sense, it is no different from organizations offering products for sale.

Organizing the Service Function

Effective utilization of the total work force is especially critical in managing the service function, due to its high labor intensity and the difficulty in establishing performance standards.

Standards of Performance. The traditional attitude has been that standards of performance cannot be adequately set in the service industries. It may be difficult, but it is essential to have such standards. Alternative methods can be applied.

Past Performance Records. These are usually inadequate and inaccurate since they use averages. They do, however, provide guidelines, which can be modified by experienced judgment.

Time and Motion Study. The contributions of industrial engineering to manufacturing industries are gradually being felt in the service field. There is no reason such techniques as random sampling, time studies, workplace layout, and work flow cannot be applied equally to service operations.

Management by Objectives. In management by objectives (MBO), the basic concepts of self-evaluation and setting one's own standards could have important applications to the service industry, where individuals often have greater freedom of action than their industrial counterparts.

Control. Burgeoning costs in the service industry demand more effective marketing control systems. Beyond simple cost and financial controls, an exhaustive cost-effectiveness analysis of the function to be performed is demanded:

1. Can steps in, or parts of, the service be modified or eliminated?

2. Can the type of labor be changed from professional to technical to semiskilled?

3. Are the control systems too elaborate? Could they be replaced by simpler ones?

4. Are the costs allocated correctly?

5. Should some services be eliminated?

6. Is the supervisory structure too heavy or too expensive?

7. Can the product design be modified to allow more self-servicing by the customer; for example, by providing modular repair parts for a television set?

Organization Structure. Recent experiments have shown that there can be higher productivity with less, rather than greater, specialization of labor.

Organizing by Client or Geography. This allows a combination of tasks for one individual or for one group. Successful applications occur in telephone companies.

Autonomous Work Groups. This approach features setting overall objectives for a group of workers and letting them control work assignments, working conditions, and even the managerial function.

Flat Rather than Tall Structures. Increasing the span of control reduces the number of supervisors at

the risk of lessened control, but with the possibility of much higher motivation at lower levels.

See also Contracts management; Field services management; Leasing, equipment; Market analysis; Marketing of services, professional.

REFERENCES

Joseph, William: *Professional Service Management,* McGraw-Hill, New York, 1984.

Linden, Fabian: "The Consumer Market in the 1980s: Services," *Conference Board Record,* May 1972, p. 50.

Lovelock, Christopher: *Services Marketing,* Prentice-Hall, Englewood Cliffs, N.J., 1984.

Douglas C. Basil, *University of Southern California*

Burton H. Marcus, *University of Southern California*

Marketing of Services, Professional

Marketing concepts and practices have gradually been moving into service industries. Their role in this broad area is still limited, however, having achieved greatest utilization in banks and airlines and much less attention in insurance, brokerage, and public transportation. Marketing has received the least attention in the professional service activities of law, accounting, management consulting, medicine, architecture, and engineering. Even marketing research firms and advertising agencies tend to underapply marketing concepts to the marketing of their own services. On the other hand, evidence implies that marketing can be a most important function in helping professional service firms meet the unprecedented challenges they face.

Professional practitioners must now cope with three increasingly significant forces:

1. *Assaults on professional codes of ethics.* The Supreme Court has ruled that minimum fee schedules violate antitrust laws and stated, " . . . Federal law requiring price competition is applicable to legal services." Justice Douglas opined that, "For meaningful price competition the fees must be made known" rather than suppressed by rules against advertising.

2. *Changing expectations of clients.* Fewer clients today are in awe of the professional's credentials. Business executives are becoming more sophisticated in selecting, using, and—increasingly—replacing professional firms. They insist on client-centered performance in contrast to technical-centered service.

3. *Increased competition.* In today's uncertain economy, it is not unusual to encounter situations in which as many as six to eight professional firms submit proposals for new work. Some firms are willing to "buy in" to obtain off-season work; other firms are known to engage in questionable solicitation practices.

Professional service organizations are generally poorly equipped to cope with these forces due to three barriers to marketing:

1. *Disdain of commercialism.* Professionals do not like to think of themselves as businesspeople. Many show hostility to any suggestion that they are motivated by money rather than service to their clients. Discussion of fees is usually distasteful to them.

2. *Associations' codes of ethics.* Professional associations have erected stringent rules against commercial behavior. In three professions—accounting, actuarial, and law—an absolute prohibition has existed against anything resembling selling activity. Advertising, direct solicitation, and referral commissions have been banned. Other professional firms tend to adhere to certain standards of good practice which tend to limit the use of effective marketing and sales techniques.

3. *Equating marketing with selling.* Because of the bars or bans against *selling,* professional service firms show little interest in the subject of *marketing.* They make a major error in equating *marketing* with *selling.* Marketing is a much larger activity than selling. By remaining ignorant of the concepts and practices that make up modern marketing, these firms are often without the skill to adapt smoothly to a rapidly changing environment and to grow to their potential. Professionalism may be a blind spot that keeps them from doing what they must do to achieve their goals. Their position grows more precarious as more of their sister firms begin to learn and apply modern marketing techniques. It is bad enough not to understand marketing in a strong market and when no one else does; it can be fatal to ignore it in a down market and when competitors are beginning to use it.

As a preliminary step in explicating the role of marketing in professional services firms, the following definition is proposed: *Professional service marketing* consists of organized activities and programs by professional service firms that are designed to retain present clients and attract new clients by sensing, serving, and satisfying their needs through delivery of appropriate services on a paid basis in a manner consistent with creditable professional goals and norms.

Styles of Marketing for Professional Firms

Professional firms, like other business firms, have three major objectives: sufficient demand, sustained growth, and profitable volume. They must turn to some form of marketing to achieve these objectives. In fact, three different styles of marketing can be distinguished.

Minimal Marketing. A large number of professional firms practice minimal marketing. They avoid or minimize conscious development of a marketing program. The firms feel that they will attain their objectives by rendering the best-quality service to existing clients. They reason that a high quality of service will lead to satisfied clients. Satisfied clients will place their new business with the firm. Furthermore, satisfied clients will recommend the firm to others, thus leading to a substantial inflow of new clients.

This logic is appealing and allows the firm to feel it is adhering to the spirit of the ethical canons prohibiting direct selling activity. Unfortunately, however, minimal marketing is a decreasingly tenable philosophy for professional firms.

1. It places too much confidence in the assumption that quality speaks for itself. In marketing circles, this is known as the "better mousetrap fallacy."

2. It assumes that the firm will deliver distinctively better quality than competitors. But when several firms pursue the same philosophy, no firm may strike the client as particularly exceptional in this respect.

3. It assumes that competitors are not using sophisticated marketing techniques. An increasing number of firms, however, are turning to aggressive or professional marketing, and it is questionable that a firm with a minimal marketing effort can compete effectively.

4. It is a reactive rather than a proactive approach to marketing opportunities. The firm does little to shape its future clients or services. Minimal marketing means that the clients choose the firm, rather than the firm choosing its clients.

Hard-Sell Marketing. A few professional service firms practice hard-sell marketing. They engage in glad-handing, wining and dining, sharp pricing and discounting, slick brochures, partner bonuses for new clients, discreet bad-mouthing of competitors, and even some direct solicitation and possible referral commissions. There is a hustling for business that borders on, or is actually, a violation of the profession's code of ethics. Even if professional ethics are not violated, the majority of practitioners consider hard-sell marketing distasteful and predatory in nature.

Hard-sell marketing reflects a *sales orientation* rather than a *marketing orientation*. It may do more damage than good for the firm and the profession. It has some major faults: It does not use a disciplined approach to identify and cultivate the market; it confuses sales (which is an outside job) with marketing (which is an inside job); it neglects the marketing process, which is to choose targets, develop services, formulate plans, set up information systems, and establish controls.

Firms using this approach often get carried away with the problem of attracting new clients. This draws them into using more extreme techniques, which begin to violate the ethical code. Worse still, it may result in acquiring marginal-type clients.

Professional Marketing. This is a professional approach to the service/market opportunities of the firm that is consonant with the profession's canons of ethics. Its major attributes are listed here and developed later. It calls for the following:

1. Developing long-range marketing objectives and strategies.

2. Developing annual volume, growth, and profit objectives, and detailed plans and budgets broken down into individual responsibilities.

3. Holding regular training seminars to improve the professional person's effectiveness at marketing and personal selling.

4. Assigning formal responsibility to one or a few people to organize, manage, and motivate the marketing activity.

5. Allocating time and budget to support marketing activity.

6. Setting up a system of controls and rewards tied to individual and group performance in attaining marketing goals.

7. Making sure that the quality of professional work does not suffer as marketing activity is increased.

8. Using only those marketing tools and procedures that are consonant with the industry's code of professional ethics.

Professional Marketing Strategies

Six strategies are available to the professional firm that seeks disciplined growth.

Expanding Service to Existing Clients. Many professional firms see the key to growth in expanding their services to existing clients. A lawyer who prepares a client's taxes may uncover some poor asset management and propose estate planning. A public accountant may note an area of deficient performance and suggest that the client utilize the firm's management services division. Cross-selling of services is a major source of growth for the professional firm.

Identifying and Cultivating High-Potential Pro-

spective Clients. This strategy calls for identifying eligible and attractive potential clients and laying plans for their cultivation. Each professional firm can identify specific prospective clients whom it would like to serve. The criteria for good prospects include high growth and profit potential, actual or potential dissatisfaction with their current firm, a base for attracting further clients in that industry, and the availability of a good contact or referral source.

One firm divides the new client-development process into six stages: (1) generating and evaluating leads; (2) developing a plan for each good lead; (3) making contact with the prospect; (4) preparing and presenting the proposal; (5) closing the sale; and (6) follow-up work. Each stage is further modeled with specific procedures. For example, leads are evaluated with the following formula: Expected value of a prospect equals the probability of attracting the prospect with C dollars of effort, times the value of the prospect if he or she becomes a client, minus the cost C in dollars of trying to attract the pospect.

Widening and Deepening Personal Referral Sources. The professional firm also takes steps to cultivate key referral sources. Each professional firm has its own idea of which sources are most helpful. A lawyer in a medium-size law firm has ranked referral sources in the following way: Best sources for new business are bankers since bankers are often asked by their clients to recommend lawyers. Second-best sources are insurance agents; they recommend clients needing estate work and revised wills. Third-best sources are other lawyers with a high regard for this law firm's work in certain areas. Certified public accountants stand as a weak fourth in referral value to this law firm. This particular lawyer spends a lot of time with his referral sources, mostly in social settings. He practices reciprocity by recommending his clients to these firms when they need a bank, an insurance agent, a specialist lawyer, or an accountant. He carefully chooses his referral sources because he recognizes that his growth depends on their growth.

Favorable Awareness Programs. The professional firm also has to undertake steps to increase its overall market visibility and reputation. The first step is to assess its public image. Most professional firms have a distorted view of their image and are surprised to discover how they are actually perceived and talked about by competitors, referral sources, and clients.

Several methods are available to the professional firm seeking to increase its visibility and favorable image. The major method is *joining associations* by its members. Favored associations are business and trade groups, political parties, and charitable, religious, civic, and educational institutions.

A second method is that of *public speaking* and *writing.* Those partners who are effective at public speaking should seek out opportunities to speak to target industry groups, particulary those containing a high number of decision makers. Partners should be encouraged to write good articles for journals that reach a high number of potential clients.

A third method is *sponsoring seminars.* The professional accounting firm may build a seminar around a topical accounting subject, such as "Accounting for Inflation," a seminar directed at a target industry, such as "New Directions in Bank Accounting," or an annual seminar to summarize new developments, such as "What's New in Auditing Practices." Invitations are sent out to current clients, important referral sources, existing contacts, and attractive prospects.

A fourth method is through *sponsoring scholarships, awards, professional chairs, and professional training programs.* These goodwill gestures make a useful civic contribution and at the same time draw favorable attention to the firm.

A final way of achieving visibility is by *taking a controversial stand* on some public or professional issue. This brings immediate media attention and a flow of publicity to the firm. At the same time, this can be risky; a professional firm, in particular, must be on sure ground before staking out a role as iconoclast.

Service and Market Specialization. One of the major marketing errors of professional firms is to strike out in all directions for possible new clients. The partners join all kinds of associations, speak everywhere and anywhere, and accept all clients. This "total service" philosophy is counterproductive. It is an inferior strategy to that of service and market specialization. Specialization offers two distinct advantages to the professional firm: (1) it gives the firm a preferred position that places it automatically in contention for potential clients seeking that kind of expertise, and (2) it permits a greater profit on volume because the firm develops "cutting-edge" expertise and low-cost procedures for handling recurrent-type cases.

Replacing Clients. Replacing clients hardly sounds like a growth strategy, but under certain circumstances it is. Some of the clients of a professional firm are small, have little potential, require more attention during the "busy season," and may produce less than a normal rate of return. The firm needs an objective system to identify candidates for pruning. It also needs to know how to discontinue relationships with unattractive clients and discourage similar potential clients without damaging the reputation of the firm.

Implementing an Effective Marketing Program

Professional marketing strategies are ineffective unless the professional service firm undertakes spe-

cific steps to train and motivate some or all of its practitioners to devote some time to business development. There are three alternatives for such implementation.

Spontaneous Development. The first is to leave business development to those in the firm who are most interested in it and effective at it. Every firm has certain partners, managers, and staff who have a flair for spotting market opportunities and converting them into realized business. If the firm, however, is lacking in "natural marketers," it should make a point of looking for this trait when it hires new staff. The natural marketers should meet from time to time as a marketing committee to exchange information and develop plans. The trouble with this alternative, however, is that it really does not improve the business growth rate that currently exists. While it has the merit of not foisting a role on the staff that is unnatural or uninteresting to them, it has the fault of leaving business growth to spontaneous, rather than organized, forces in the firm.

A Specialized Marketing Office. The second alternative is to develop a special office for business development headed by a partner or specialist in marketing. This *director of business planning* would have the following responsibilities: (1) guide the development of a long-range and an annual plan for business development; (2) search in a systematic way for new business opportunities; and (3) provide incentives for, assist, and train members of the firm to perform better in business development activities. The creation of this center of responsibility for business development is a necessary step in the evolution of a more effective business development procedure, but it is not a complete solution.

A Pervasive Companywide Program. The third alternative is to develop a firmwide program for marketing training, providing incentives, planning, and control. The firm's leadership decides that every professional in the firm—with the possible exception of junior practitioners and specialists—should receive training and incentives in business development. A large public accounting firm recently decided that practitioners should spend approximately one-fourth of their time in practice development. Management, however, realized that this would be a pious utterance unless backed by incentives and budget. Practitioners could not be expected to work a longer day, nor could they be expected to cut down their current billable time. The solution was to create a budget account for business development which could support the practitioners' club memberships, luncheons, and charges to billable time. Furthermore, the desired behavior still would not come about unless practitioners found that their effectiveness at business development was a factor in determining their annual bonuses. In addition, the firm created an office that, among other things, orga-

nized seminars to help practitioners improve their planning and sales skills. The office designed planning forms that are filled out by the practitioners each year with their plans in the areas of cross-selling, prospecting, referral source work, favorable awareness activities, and so on. These plans are reviewed quarterly for accomplishment and for replanning where necessary.

Marketing Planning Model. A firm with many branch offices must introduce further mechanisms to build up business development effectiveness. Consider the following marketing planning model used by a public accounting firm:

The planning process starts with the home office gathering information on the economy, market, and other factors that will influence its objectives for the year. The home office also carries on informal discussions with the business development coordinator in each branch office about possible growth goals. Based on its information, the home office adopts a 5-year growth objective and specific growth and profit objectives for the coming year. These objectives are communicated to the branch offices.

Each branch office has a *business development committee* which looks at the firmwide growth objectives and develops specific objectives for the branch office on the basis of both the overall goals and local economic conditions. The *business development coordinator* in each office (who is a member of the business development committee) announces the branch's objectives to each department and practitioner. Each practitioner prepares an *individual business development plan* which states the individual's expected contribution in terms of fee objectives, expanded service to existing clients, potential new clients, planned work with referral sources, favorable awareness programs, and speaking, writing, and seminar work. The individual plans are reviewed by the business development committee, with suggested revisions through individual discussions. They are summarized for the branch office to make sure the time devoted to various marketing strategies is appropriate.

The branch office's business development plans are forwarded to the home office for review and approval. During the year, the home office receives branch office results and determines where consultation is desirable. The home office evaluates performance against objectives, using such measures as profitability, market share, the ratio of reported business development time to total hours, the hit ratio (ratio of successful proposals to total proposals), the percentage of lost clients, and the percentage of new clients.

See also Consultants, management; Ethics, managerial; Marketing of services; Professionalism in management; Public and community relations.

REFERENCES

Kotler, Philip, and P. N. Bloom: *Marketing of Professional Services*, Prentice-Hall, Englewood Cliffs, N.J., 1984.

Mahon, J. J.: *The Marketing of Professional Accounting Services*, John Wiley, New York, 1982.

Rathmell, John M.: *Marketing in the Services Sector*, Winthrop Publishers, Cambridge, Mass., 1974.

Wilson, Aubrey: *Marketing of Professional Services*, McGraw-Hill, New York, 1972.

PHILIP KOTLER, *Northwestern University*

Markets, Government

Although the government sector accounts for more than 20 percent of the gross national product in the United States, there is very little actual physical production in government-owned facilities. Under the principle that government should buy from private industry whenever possible in order to prevent duplication of functions or the necessity for the maintenance of staff to perform infrequent functions, almost everything used by the government is purchased from firms in the private sector. This makes the public market the largest market in the United States, with government purchasing hundreds of billions of dollars worth of output every year. A list of suppliers in the public market includes the giants in virtually every industry in the economy. In addition, many small firms enter into supply or construction contracts with federal, state, or local governments. Governments are usually buyers in the public market; however, governments, in particular the federal government, also enter the market as sellers of surplus personal and real property as well as strategic and critical materials which have been stockpiled.

Selling in the Government Market

Although the federal government is the largest single buyer in the public market, the purchases of other jurisdictions—taken together—are larger. Preliminary estimates for 1982 indicate that governments purchased $647 billion of goods and services ($345 billion exclusive of wages and salaries). Federal government purchases were $258 billion, of which about 69 percent was for national defense purposes; the remaining $389 billion was purchased by state and local governments. As an indication of the scope of the public market, as of 1982, in addition to the federal government, there were 50 state governments, 3041 countries, 15,032 school districts, 19,083 municipalities, 16,748 townships, and 28,733 special districts, all buying in the government market. The relative volume of purchases in these markets can be seen in Table M-9.

Governments make thousands of purchases on both current and capital accounts. In the case of the federal government, each item purchased has a single name, description, and identification known as *National Stock Number* or NSN. (See, for example, *Cataloging Handbook H2-1* of the Defense Logistics Agency.)

TABLE M-9 Direct General Expenditures of Governments 1976–1977*

	Amount, millions of dollars	Percentage of total
All governments	514,217	100
Federal	241,388	47
States	101,891	20
Counties	38,841	8
Municipalities	55,241	11
Townships	6,169	1
School districts	61,662	12
Special districts	9,016	2

*Compiled from the 1977 *Census of Governments*, vol. 7, table 1, p. 158. These data are not directly comparable to those in 1982 because they are for a different year and a different concept of expenditures.

General Procedures. Operations in the public market are very much like those in any other market, with a few notable exceptions. The activities of the government are not normally guided by the profit motive, nor does it usually purchase for resale. The budget constraint which is faced by the government, and in particular by the federal government, is also quite different from that of a private firm. Finally, government purchases are subject to legal restrictions, especially in the case of the federal government, where procurement procedures are based on public law from initiation of bids to final inspection and acceptance. An example of a legal constraint within which public market activity is conducted is the *principle of local preference.* Many larger cities and counties operate under this principle in awarding contracts to suppliers or contractors. Similarly, the federal government standard contract includes a Buy America clause.

Typically, contracts in public markets are awarded on the basis of competitive bids. The federal government, in principle, invites bids from all known responsible suppliers, who have an equal chance to compete for award of the contract. Procurement and construction intentions are publicized, and the federal government sends invitations for bids to all firms on its mailing lists. A bidder need not bid on the entire quantity.

In general, contracts are awarded to the lowest responsive bid by a responsible bidder, not necessarily the lowest bidder. A *responsive bid* is one which responds to the essential requirements of the invita-

tion for bids. Each government jurisdiction is free to define a *responsible bidder* in any way it chooses. Most definitions include reference to satisfactory past performance, dependability, quality of product, reliability of delivery dates, adequacy of plant, labor, and transportation facilities, and financial status. The federal definition of responsive and responsible bid can be found in Standard Form 33, "Solicitation, Offer and Award."

When an offer from a small firm is rejected for lack of responsibility, the contracting officer is required to notify the Small Business Administration (SBA), which may issue a *certificate of competency* if investigation reveals the firm to be able to do the job aside from capacity or credit consideration.

Current public law and executive orders now in effect provide several preferential federal procurement programs. For example:

1. For economically or socially disadvantaged businesses a special contract program is provided through the SBA.

2. Subcontracts to small and small disadvantaged businesses are required in all prime contracts larger than $500,000 ($1 million for construction).

3. Affirmative action is required in support of women-owned businesses.

4. Many programs have a small business *set-aside*.

5. Set-asides are provided for contract work to be performed in labor surplus areas; a firm's headquarters need not necessarily be located in the area.

There are some cases when bids are not taken and governments negotiate for the items required. Many state and local governments negotiate for very low-cost purchases, proprietary or patented items, and personal or professional services. The federal government also negotiates in these cases as well as under some special circumstances, such as (1) in time of national emergency, (2) when there is an unusual time constraint, and (3) for goods or services procured and used outside the country. In addition, negotiation is used if there is only one source of supply or if the bids are unreasonable or were determined not to be independent.

Procurement Regulations. The procurement regulations of the federal government are issued by the General Services Administration (GSA) or the deputy undersecretary of defense (acquisitions policy). The former agency issues the uniform procedures applicable to (1) procurement and construction by the executive agencies and (2) the "Federal Property Management Regulations," which describe the policies applicable to the management of federal government property and records. The "Defense Acquisitions Regulations" are issued by the deputy undersecretary. All these regulations are published

in the *Code of Federal Regulations.* There is no uniform code for state and local government procurement.

Specifications and Standards. Specifications—describing the product, service, or construction item—and standards have been set for hundreds of items purchased by the federal government. GSA publishes an *Index of Federal Specifications Standards and Commercial Item Descriptions*, which supplies an alphabetical listing. Specifications for state governments are found in *The Annual of State Specifications of Commodities*. Localities are influenced in their specifications and standards by the state and federal government requirements, but special requirements may exist in particular cases.

Contracts. Several types of contracts may be used in public markets. A contract may be for a nonrecurring purchase of a specific amount of a specified item. Or, the contract may be of a blanket nature concerning undetermined quantities of a product or service to be delivered as needed at a quoted price over a specific period of time or with no termination date stated. Most frequently, contracts are of a fixed-price type. These contracts may include a firm price statement or may allow for price adjustments according to an agreed-upon index or upon actual cost experience. In addition, incentive considerations may be included. Cost-type contracts are less often used.

Federal government contracts, in addition to the specific requirements pertaining to the contract, usually include a reference to general provisions. *Standard Form 32* contains the general provisions for supply and service contracts. The standard items cover such matters as inspection, payment procedures, assignment of claims and patents, and default and dispute settlement procedures. Also included are the relevant portions of the Buy America and Walsh-Healey Public Contract Acts.

Construction contracts are covered in *Standard Forms 19 and 23A*. The general provisions include specifications, inspection, and acceptance procedures for materials and workmanship, termination for default, damages for delays, and time extensions. Larger contracts contain labor standards provisions covering wages, hours, and employment conditions for labor. Copies of these standard contract forms can be obtained from any General Services Administration (GSA) Business Service Center.

Federal government contractors may not discriminate against any employee on the basis of race, color, religion, sex, national origin, or physical or mental handicap; discrimination is also prohibited against disabled or Vietnam veterans.

Becoming a Federal Government Supplier. By contacting the assistant regional administrator for external affairs in a regional GSA office, a potential supplier of regular items purchased by the federal government can receive what is needed—i.e., "Bidders Mailing List Application" (Standard Form 129),

the "List of Commodities" (Standard Form 1382), and the "Centralized Bidder's Mailing List Application Code Sheet" (Standard Form 3038). Once on the mailing list, the potential supplier will receive invitations to submit bids for those items purchased through GSA. Since 1949 the GSA has been responsible for purchasing those items used in common throughout the government, including many items used by the military. A potential supplier of an item which is not currently being purchased by the government, such as a new product, should send a detailed description of the item to the Regional GSA Business Service Center, and an "Application for Presenting New or Improved Articles" (GSA Form 1171) will be sent. There is no uniform way of making a product known to all agencies of the federal government, although many agencies make use of the bidders mailing list applications for soliciting bids. In addition to the 13 business service centers, there are more than 100 small-business information offices located in federal buildings throughout the country which can provide aid to potential suppliers.

Information about military procurement, including an alphabetical listing of the hundreds of products purchased in support of military operations and the addresses of procurement officers, is available in a Department of Defense publication, *Selling to the Military*, which is available from the U.S. Government Printing Office.

Bids for construction of buildings by the Public Building Service are solicited and opened by the GSA regional offices. Design contracts are solicited from architects or engineers who have filed with the GSA regional (and central) offices. Surveys, soil tests, etc., are usually subcontracted by the architect or engineer. Notice of opening of bids for construction contracts is publicized in the area where the construction is to take place and also in the *Commerce Business Daily*.

Notification of contract awards is normally sent by mail, along with directions to proceed. In the case of large contracts or those involving new departures or suppliers, notice of a contract award is delivered personally.

All items are inspected by the government before acceptance and final payment of the invoice.

Becoming a State–Local Government Supplier. States, counties, and cities may be able to supply lists of products which they normally purchase. If a list exists, it may be obtained from the purchasing officer. If no list is maintained, a potential supplier can obtain the information about a particular product from the same source. There is no uniformity among governmental jurisdictions as to who is responsible for procurement. It may be the city or county clerk, the controller, or the engineer. Some jurisdictions have a contract officer, a director of procurement, or a purchasing agent.

One difference between private markets and the public market is that all transactions in the latter must be matters of public record. Therefore, the potential supplier has information available in the state capitol, county court house, or city hall which will allow an estimate of the volume of purchases of any particular item by a government as well as the names of all contractors, particularly construction contractors, who are a source of potential subcontracts for materials, supplies, or services.

Buying in the Government Market

The main sales outlets of the federal government are GSA and the Department of Defense (DOD). There are some exceptions; for example, houses obtained by mortgage foreclosure under G.I. loans are sold by the Veteran's Administration, and properties obtained through other mortgage insurance programs are disposed of by the Department of Housing and Urban Development (HUD). The U.S. Postal Services and Maritime Administration also conduct their own sales. In general, announcements of sales and catalogs of items to be sold are available to anyone who has expressed an interest in bidding. GSA maintains a separate mailing list for each geographical region; to get on the mailing list, a firm must contact the business service center in the relevant region. DOD has a centralized mailing list; contact the Defense

TABLE M-10 Government Sales*

Category of good	How sold	To obtain information
Personal property	Sealed bid, public auction, or spot bid†	Consult U.S. government publication, *Surplus Personal Property Sales Programs*
Real property	Sealed bid, public auction, or brokers	Consult U.S. government publication, *How to Acquire Federal Real Property*
Strategic and critical materials	Sealed bid, negotiation, or fixed price	Contact Office of Stockpile Transactions, Federal Property Resources Service, GSA

*Compiled from information in *Doing Business with the Federal Government*.
†The bidder writes the bid and places it in a bid box.

Surplus Bidders Control Office. Information about government sales is summarized in Table M-10.

See also Government relations; Government services; International trade; Market analysis; Public administration; Small business administration.

SOURCES OF INFORMATION

An excellent source of general information is the U.S. government publication *Doing Business With the Federal Government,* 1981. Also see the pamphlet *Selling to the U.S. Government,* issued by the U.S. Small Business Administration, 1978.

Other important information is available in *Commerce Business Daily* (Monday through Friday), *Commerce America* (biweekly), and *U.S. Government Purchasing and Sales Directory.* Subscriptions to the former two and copies of the latter are available through the Superintendent of Documents, U.S. Government Printing Office.

Many departments and agencies of the U.S. government publish documents describing their individual procurement needs and procedures; for example, *This is Interior: Contracting Guide; NASA Procurement Regulations; Doing Business with the Department of Energy;* and *Selling to the Military.*

An extensive bibliography is available in *Council of Planning Librarians Exchange Bibliography Number 980,* "Contractual Services in Government: Selected Bibliography on Practices in Federal, State, and Local Agencies, Education and Foreign Countries," Monticello, N.Y., 1976.

EARL W. ADAMS, *Allegheny College*

Markets, Securities

The securities markets have much in common with markets of all kinds. A *market* is a means whereby buyers and sellers are brought together to aid in the transfer of goods and/or services. Several aspects of this general definition seem worthy of emphasis:

1. It is *not* necessary for a market to have a physical location. A market may simply be related by phones or some means of electronic communication. All that is necessary is for the buyers and sellers to be able to communicate regarding the relevant aspects of the purchase or sale.

2. The market does *not* necessarily own the goods or services involved. There is no requirement other than to provide for smooth and inexpensive transfer of goods and services. In the case of financial markets, those who establish and administer the market definitely do *not* own any of the assets; they simply provide a location for

potential buyers and sellers and help the market to function.

3. A market can deal in any variety of goods and services—from fish and vegetables to stocks and bonds. Any commodity with a diverse clientele, however, will develop a market to aid in its transfer.

4. Typically, both buyers and sellers benefit from the existence of a market.

Primary and Secondary Securities Markets

The markets for securities—stocks and bonds—are classified two ways according to whether they deal in (1) new or (2) outstanding securities.

Primary Markets. The primary market is one in which new issues are sold by companies to acquire new capital for the corporation through the sale of either corporate bonds, preferred stock, or common stock. These new issues are typically broken into two groups:

1. *Seasoned new issues.* These are issued by companies with existing public markets for their securities, such as General Motors selling a new issue of common stock in order to acquire additional external equity capital. In this case, there is an existing public market for General Motors stock, and the company is increasing the number of outstanding shares to acquire new equity capital.

2. *Initial public offerings.* This might take place when a small company sells common stock to the public for the first time. In this case, a public market does *not* exist for the stock; i.e., the company has been closely held.

Underwriters. New issues (seasoned or initial offerings) are typically underwritten by investment bankers, or underwriters, who acquire the total issue from the company and, in turn, sell the issue to individual investors. The underwriter provides advice to the corporation on the general characteristics of the issue, the pricing of the issue, and the timing of the offering. The underwriter also accepts the risk of selling the new issue, after acquiring it from the corporation.

The arrangements between the company and the underwriter typically take one of three forms:

1. The most common arrangement is when a corporation *negotiates* with a specified underwriter regarding the pricing and the arrangements for the new issue. This arrangement is typical for existing industrial corporations who have an underwriter, or investment banker, they work with on a continuous basis. When they decide to come out with a new issue of securities, they seek the advice of the investment banker, who

helps them set up the issue and, subsequently, forms an underwriting syndicate for the sale of the issues.

2. An alternative arrangement is when a corporation specifies the characteristics of an issue it is contemplating and then solicits *competitive bids* from alternative underwriting firms. This is typically done by utilities, where, in many cases, they are required to submit their issues for competitive bids. It is contended that the cost of the issue is reduced in this manner, although it is acknowledged that there is a reduction in the services provided by the underwriter. Although less advice is provided, the investment banking firm still underwrites the issue in that it buys it from the corporation and retails it through a syndicate.

3. A third arrangement is when an investment banker agrees to accept an issue and sell it on a *best-efforts basis.* This arrangement, which usually applies to a speculative new issue, arises when the investment banker is concerned with the possible success of the issue and will only become involved with the understanding that his or her best efforts will be used to sell the issue. The point is, the investment banker does *not* really underwrite the issue, since he or she does not buy the issue. In the best-efforts arrangement, the stock is owned by the company, and the investment banker acts more as a broker trying to sell what can be sold at the stipulated price.

Secondary Markets. These occur where there is trading in outstanding issues. In these markets, the issue has already been sold to the public and is traded between current and potential owners of the outstanding securities. Secondary markets are typically broken down into three major groups:

1. Major national exchanges, which include the New York Stock Exchange and the American Stock Exchange.

2. Regional exchanges, which include the smaller exchanges in cities like Chicago, Boston, Philadelphia, Washington, and San Francisco.

3. The over-the-counter market, which includes trading in securities that are not listed on an organized exchange.

Secondary Equity Markets

National exchanges and regional exchanges are similar in that they are referred to as listed securities exchanges; they differ because of size and geographic emphasis.

Listed securities exchanges are formal organizations that have a specified group of members who may use the facilities of the exchange and a specified list of securities (stocks or bonds) that have qualified for "listing" on the exchange. In addition to a limit on the membership and the securities eligible for trading, these exchanges also are similar in that prices are determined via an *auction* process, whereby interested buyers and sellers submit *bids* and *asks* for a given stock to a central location for that stock. The bids and asks are recorded by the specialists assigned to that stock, and the stock is sold to the highest bidder and bought from the individual with the lowest asking price (i.e., the lowest offering price).

National Stock Exchanges. The New York Stock Exchange and the American Stock Exchange are considered national in scope because of the large number of securities listed, the geographic dispersion of these issues, and the national nature of their buyers and sellers.

New York Stock Exchange (NYSE). This is the largest organized securities market in the United States and dates back to a constitution in 1817. As of the early 1980s, there were over 1700 companies with stock listed on the NYSE, and there were over 2400 issues with a total market value of approximately $900 billion. The average number of shares traded on the exchange has increased steadily over time, with an increase in the turnover of shares listed. Average daily volume was about 5 million shares in the early 1960s, increased to about 10 million shares in the second half of the 1960s, and averaged about 15 million during the period from 1970 to 1974. During the early part of the 1980s, trading increased to about 20 million shares a day.

The NYSE has consistently accounted for about 75 percent of all shares traded on listed exchanges, compared with about 10 to 20 percent for the American Stock Exchange (ASE), and about 10 percent for all the regional exchanges combined (the "other" category). Because the price of shares on the NYSE tends to be higher than prices on the ASE, the percent of value of the NYSE has averaged from 80 to 85 percent, with lower figures for the ASE, while the regional exchanges are comparable in shares and value.

American Stock Exchange (ASE). This exchange had its inception with the trading of unlisted shares at the corner of Wall and Hanover streets in New York City and was referred to as the Outdoor Curb Market. In 1911, formal trading rules were established, and in 1921, the members moved inside a building but continued to trade mainly in unlisted stocks. The dominance of unlisted stocks continued until 1946, when listed stocks finally outnumbered unlisted stocks. The current name was adopted in 1953.

While a small number of stocks are traded on both national exchanges, the overwhelming majority of stocks listed on the ASE are unique to that exchange.

567

Innovation. In addition to a different clientele of U.S. firms, the ASE has been innovative in listing foreign securities over the years. There were 68 foreign issues listed in 1972. Further, the ASE listed warrants for a number of years before the NYSE first listed them in 1970. The most recent innovation on the ASE has been the trading of call options on listed securities. This was introduced after option trading became widespread, following the establishment of the Chicago Board Options Exchange (CBOE). Because options were not traded on the NYSE, almost all the options traded on the ASE are for stocks listed on the NYSE.

Regional Exchanges. These have basically the same operating procedures as the NYSE and the ASE but differ in their listing requirements and the geographic distribution of the firms listed. Their listing requirements are less stringent than for either of the national exchanges because the main incentive for many of these exchanges is to provide trading facilities for geographically local firms that (1) are not large enough or (2) do not have a national stockholder list to qualify for listing on one of the national exchanges. These exchanges also list stocks from the national exchanges that are of substantial interest to the members of the exchange; i.e., AT&T and General Motors.

The major regional exchanges are as follows: (1) Midwest Stock Exchange (Chicago), (2) Pacific Stock Exchange (San Francisco–Los Angeles), (3) Philadelphia Exchange (Philadelphia–Pittsburgh), (4) Boston Stock Exchange (Boston), (5) Spokane Stock Exchange (Spokane, Washington), (6) Honolulu Stock Exchange (Honolulu, Hawaii), (7) Intermountain Stock Exchange (Salt Lake City), and (8) Cincinnati Stock Exchange (Cincinnati).

The fortunes of the regional exchanges have fluctuated substantially over time. They were popular during the late 1960s when there was strong interest in small, young firms. Their recent activity has been affected by institutional interest in stocks listed both on a national exchange and on a regional exchange.

Over-the-Counter Market (OTC). This market includes the trading in all stocks not listed on one of the listed exchanges. (It can also include trading in stocks that are listed on an exchange in an arrangement referred to as the third market, which is discussed in detail below.) The OTC market is *not* a formal market organization with specific membership requirements of a specific list of stocks that are deemed eligible for trading. In theory, it is possible to trade *any* security on the OTC market as long as someone is willing to take a position in the stock. To *take a position* means that an individual or firm advertises its willingness to buy or sell the stock; i.e., to make a market in the stock.

Size. Given the accessibility of the OTC market, it is not surprising that it is the largest segment of the secondary market in terms of the number of issues

traded and the most diverse in terms of quality. Estimates of the number of issues traded on the OTC market run as high as 20,000. Many of these issues are very inactive, but at least 5000 issues are traded actively.

Diversity. Since the OTC has no minimum requirements for listing, stocks traded on the OTC range from the smallest, most unprofitable company to the largest, most profitable firms. It is notable that all U.S. government bonds are traded on the OTC market; the vast majority of bank and insurance stocks are likewise not listed on any exchange but are traded only on the OTC. Finally, OTC handles some 150 dual-traded stocks of high quality, including AT&T and General Motors.

Operation. Participants in the OTC market act as dealers because they buy and sell for their own account. This is in contrast to the listed exchanges where specialists generally act as the agents for other investors—i.e., specialists keep the books and attempt to match the buy and sell orders left with them. As such, the OTC market is referred to as a *negotiated* market, where investors negotiate directly with dealers, in contrast to the exchanges that are auction markets with specialists acting as the intermediaries, or auctioneers.

The NASDAQ System. NASDAQ is an acronym that stands for National Association of Securities Dealers Automatic Quotations. Briefly, it is an electronic quotation system that serves the vast OTC market. It is entirely possible to have 10, 15, or more market makers for a given stock, and it is common to have three to five dealers. Given an interest in an OTC stock, a major problem has always been to determine what the general market is and also what the markets of the specific market makers are. Prior to the introduction of NASDAQ it was necessary to make phone calls to three or four dealers to determine the best market, and then after such a "survey," go back to the one with the best market. In cases where there were 10 or 15 dealers, a dealer was not certain which made the best market. With NASDAQ *all* the quotes by market makers are available immediately, and the broker can make one phone call to the dealer with the best market, verify that the quote has not changed, and make the sale or purchase. There are three levels specified by the developers of the NASDAQ system to serve firms with different interests.

Level 1 is for firms that want current information on the OTC stocks but do not often buy or sell OTC stocks for their customers and are not market makers. Level 1 provides a median quote for all stocks on the system.

Level 2 is for firms that are serious traders in OTC stocks for themselves or their customers. This system provides all the quotes by all the individual market makers.

Level 3 is for investment firms that make markets in OTC stocks. It has the capability of level 2 plus the ability to change the quote on the market-makers' stocks.

Third Market. This term is used to describe the trading of shares listed on an exchange on the over-the-counter market. When a stock is listed on an exchange, members of that exchange are generally required to bring all buy and sell orders to the exchange to be executed. At the same time, there is no reason why an investment firm that is *not* a member of an exchange cannot make a market in a listed stock in the same way as a market in an unlisted stock. The success or failure of such a venture will obviously depend upon whether the OTC market is as good as the exchange market and/or the relative cost of the transaction compared with the cost on the exchange. Volume on the third market varies. To understand this, two points must be known:

1. Almost all trading on the third market is by institutions. Most individuals do not even know that such a market exists, and if they know about it, they generally do not know how to use it.

2. Trading in the third market is concentrated in a limited number (less than 200) of stocks. The major stocks traded on the third market are the large active stocks of interest to financial institutions. Examples would be AT&T, General Motors, IBM, and General Electric.

The Fourth Market. This term is used to describe the direct trading of securities between two parties with no broker intermediary. In almost all cases, the two parties involved are institutions. The main reason any investor takes a transaction to a broker and through the broker to a listed exchange is that it is faster and easier; and the owner of the stock is willing to pay a fee for this speed and convenience. This fee is the brokerage commission.

The fourth market evolved for institutions because at some point, with very large orders, the fee became so large that it became worthwhile for institutions to attempt to deal directly with each other to save the fee. The arrangements for bringing two interested parties together take one of two forms: (1) an electronic system or (2) a third-party system, where the third party works for a flat fee for a group of institutions.

The *electronic system* allows its subscribers (large institutions) to advertise on the system using a code number indicating that they want to buy or sell a certain number of shares of stock at a specified price. Nobody knows which institution is trying to buy or sell. Any other subscribing member who has an interest in completing the proposed transaction can teletype to the original party (by code); only after both parties have agreed to final terms are the names revealed. The electronic system enables the parties to come together anonymously, and there is no specific cost for the transaction—the only cost is a flat annual fee to be a subscriber. The *third-party system* works in about the same way except that the annual fee is paid to an individual who makes the contacts for his or her institutional clientele.

Obviously, the major advantage of the fourth market for the participants is substantially lower commission costs on large transactions compared with costs on the exchange and even the third market. A major disadvantage is that it is necessary to expose your potential interest in selling or buying a stock with the possible effect this may have on the price.

Analysis of the Exchange Market

Because of the importance of the listed exchange market on national and international financial activities, this entry discusses in detail the several types of members on the exchange, the major types of orders used on the exchange, and the function of the specialist.

Breakdown of Exchange Membership. Listed securities exchanges typically have four major categories of membership:

1. *Specialists,* who constitute about 25 percent of the total membership and are responsible for maintaining a fair and orderly market in the securities listed on the exchange.

2. *Odd-lot dealers,* who stand ready to buy and sell less than a round lot of a stock (typically 100 shares). When individuals want to buy less than 100 shares, the order is turned over to odd-lot dealers who will buy or sell from their own inventory. Notably, odd-lot dealers are *not* brokers, but dealers, and are buying and selling from their own inventory. Recently this function has been taken over by the exchange or by the specialist in the stock. In addition, some large brokerage firms have begun handling the odd-lot business for their own customers.

3. *Floor brokers,* who can be either members or partners of a brokerage house. They can be brokers who sell for their own customers, they can transact for other members too busy to trade, or they can buy and sell for brokers who are not members of an exchange. When a brokerage house such as Merrill Lynch, Pierce, Fenner & Smith advertises that it is a member of the New York Stock Exchange, this is what one of its members does—executes orders given to Merrill Lynch registered representatives.

4. *Registered traders,* who are allowed to use their membership to buy and sell for their own account. They are allowed to save the commission in their own trading, and observers feel they have an advantage because they are on the floor.

The exchange and others feel they should be allowed these advantages because they provide added liquidity to the market—i.e., they will tend to trade against the crowd. At the same time, because of possible abuses, there are regulations regarding their conduct in terms of how they trade and how many registered traders can be in a trading crowd around a specialists' booth at a point in time.

Types of Orders. To understand the specialists' role, one must first have a full understanding of the different types of orders available to individual investors and to the specialist in the dealer function.

Market Order. This is the most heavily used order and is an order to buy or sell a stock at the best prevailing price currently available. An investor who wants to sell some stock and uses a market order indicates that he or she is willing to sell immediately at the highest bid available at the time the order reaches the specialist on the exchange. In contrast, a potential buyer who uses a market order indicates that he or she is willing to pay the lowest offering price available at the time the order reaches the floor of the exchange. Market orders are used when an individual wants to effect a transaction quickly and is willing to accept the prevailing market price.

Limit Order. This specifies a definite price that the buyer will pay for the stock or the price at which the individual will sell the stock. As an example, an investor submits a bid to purchase 100 shares of stock at $48 a share, when the current market is 52 bid–52½ ask, with the expectation that the stock will decline to $48 in the near future. Such an order must also indicate *how long* the limit order will be outstanding. The alternatives, in terms of time, are basically without bounds—they can be for a part of a day, for a full day, for several days, a week, a month, or open-ended, which means the order is good until canceled (GTC). These limit orders are typically given to the specialist to execute. Rather than have the broker wait for a given price on a stock, the broker will give it to the specialist, who will put it in his or her book and act as the broker's representative. When, and if, the market reaches the limit order price, the specialist will execute the order and inform the broker.

Short Sales. While most investors purchase stock with the expectation that they will derive their return from an increase in value, there are instances when an investor may believe that a stock is overpriced and would like to invest in order to take advantage of an expected decline in the price. The way to do this is to sell the stock short. A *short sale* is the sale of stock that is not owned with the intent of purchasing it later at a lower price. Specifically, the investor *borrows* the stock through a broker, from another investor, and sells it in the market. Subsequently, the investor will repurchase the stock

(hopefully, at a lower price than he or she sold it at) and replace the stock borrowed. The investor who lent the stock has the use of the money paid for the stock, because it is left as collateral on the stock loan. While there is no time limit on the short sale, the lender of the stock may want to sell his or her shares, in which case the broker will find another investor who will lend the stock.

Two technical points in connection with short sales are important:

1. A short sale can only be made on an uptick trade. The reason for this restriction is because the exchanges do not want to make it possible for traders to be able to *force* a profit on a short sale by pushing the price down through continual short sales. Therefore, the transaction price for a short sale must be higher than the last trade price (an *uptick*). If there is no change in price, the previous price must have been higher than its previous price (a zero uptick).

2. The short seller is responsible for the dividends to the investor who lent the stock. The purchaser of the short sale stock receives the dividend from the corporation, and so the short seller must pay a similar dividend to the lender.

Stop-Loss Order. This is a conditional market order, whereby the investor indicates that he or she wants to sell a stock *if* the stock drops to a given price. As an example, an individual buys a stock at 50 expecting it to go up. At the same time, if the stock does not go up, the individual wants to make sure that the losses are minimized or limited. Therefore, he or she would put in a stop-loss order at 45. If the stock dropped to 45, the stop-loss order would become a *market-sell order* and the stock would be sold at the prevailing market price. Notably, the order does not guarantee that the investor will get the $45. The investor can get a little bit more or a little bit less, because the order, as noted, is a conditional market order and becomes a market order only when a transaction takes place at 45. Because of the possibility of market disruption caused by a large number of stop-loss orders, the exchange, on occasion, has canceled all stop-loss orders on certain stocks.

Stop-Buy Order. A stop loss on the other side is called a *stop-buy order.* This is a conditional buy order by an individual who has engaged in a short sale. In this case, an investor has sold stock short and wants to minimize loss if a stock begins to increase in value rather than to decline as expected. This order makes it possible to place a conditional buy order at a price above the price at which the individual sold the stock short.

The Specialist. The stock exchange specialist is often referred to as the "center of the auction market" for stocks. The specialist is a member of the exchange who decides to fulfill the specialist function and applies for such a position by requesting the exchange to assign stocks to him or her. It is necessary for the specialist to possess substantial capital to carry out this function.

Specialist Functions. The specialist has two major functions. The first is that of a *broker* who handles the limit orders or special orders placed with member brokers. As noted previously, the individual broker who receives a limit order to purchase a stock $5 below the current market does not have the time or inclination to watch the stock constantly to see when and if the decline takes place. Therefore, the individual broker leaves the limit order (or a stop-loss or stop-buy order) with the specialist, who enters it in the book and executes it when appropriate. For this service the specialist receives a portion of the broker's commission on the trade.

The second major function is to act as a *dealer* in the assigned stocks in order to maintain a fair and orderly market. In this regard, the specialist is expected to buy and sell for his or her own account when there is insufficient public supply or demand to provide a continuous liquid market. As an example, if a stock is currently selling for about $40 per share, one could envision a situation in an auction market where the current bid and ask (without the specialist) might be 40 bid–41 ask. This means there is some public investor with a limit order on the books who is willing to buy stock at $40 per share, while another investor is willing to sell stock at $41 per share. If the specialist does not intercede and the market orders to buy and sell the stock come to the market in a random fashion, one would expect the price of the stock to fluctuate between 40 and 41 constantly—a movement of 2.5 percent between trades. Most investors would probably consider such a price pattern to be more volatile than desired; i.e., it would not be considered a very continuous market. The individual responsible for reducing the volatility and providing continuity in price changes is the specialist. The specialist is expected to provide an alternative bid and/or ask that will narrow the spread and thereby provide greater price continuity over time. In the above example this would entail *either* entering a bid of 40½ or 40¾ or an ask of 40½ or 40¼ to narrow the spread to one-half point or one-quarter point.

Specialist Income. Specialists derive their income from both their major functions. The actual breakdown between income from acting as a broker for limit orders and income from acting as a dealer to maintain an orderly market will depend upon the specific stock. In the case of a very actively traded stock (e.g., American Telephone and Telegraph), there is not much need for the specialist to act as a dealer because the substantial public interest forms a pretty tight market. In such an instance, the major concern (and the main source of income) of the specialist is maintaining the limit orders for the stock. In contrast, in the case of stocks with low trading vol-

ume and substantial price volatility, specialists would be called upon to interject themselves constantly into the market to close the spread. In these cases, their major income would depend upon their ability to trade profitably in the stock.

See also Auditing, financial; Financial management; Financial management, capital structure and dividend policy; Financial statement analysis; Markets, stock indicator series; Shareholder relations.

REFERENCES

Buckley, Julian G., and Leo M. Loll: *The Over-the-Counter Securities Market,* 3d ed., Prentice-Hall, Englewood Cliffs, N.J., 1981.

"NASDAQ and the OTC," National Association of Securities Dealers, New York, 1974.

Reilly, Frank K.: *Investments,* CBS College Publishing, New York, 1982.

Reilly, Frank K.: *Readings and Issues in Investments,* Dryden Press, Hinsdale, Ill., 1975.

FRANK K. REILLY, *University of Notre Dame*

Markets, Stock Indicator Series

A stock market indicator series (or index) is a composite measure of stock prices in an aggregate market. Although stock portfolios are made up of individual stocks, most stocks tend to move with the aggregate market. If the overall market rises or falls, it is likely that an individual's portfolio will also rise or fall in value. Furthermore, investors generally wish to know what the aggregate state—or trend—of the market may be. To monitor these aggregate movements, financial publications and other interested parties have developed market indicator series. The purpose of these composite indicators is to provide an overall indication of aggregate market changes or market movements.

Uses and Users. There are at least three important uses for stock market indicator series:

1. *Benchmarks.* Market indicator series serve those who examine total market returns over some time period and use the derived market returns as a benchmark to judge the performance of alternative individual portfolios.

2. *Relationships.* Security analysts and portfolio managers in particular examine the factors that influence aggregate stock price movements in order to determine the relationship between alternative economic variables and aggregate stock market movements.

3. *Predictions.* Technicians study past price changes to predict future price movements.

Differentiating Factors in Construction

Stock market indicator series are intended to indicate the overall movement for a group of stocks. Given this intent, it is necessary to consider what is important in computing any average intended to represent a total population.

Sample. The initial concern is the sample used to construct the market indicator series. Three factors must be considered: (1) the size of the sample, (2) the breadth of the sample, and (3) the source of the sample.

Weighting. The second concern is the weight given to each member in the sample. Three principal weighting schemes are used: (1) a price-weighted series, (2) a value-weighted series, and (3) an unweighted series, or what would be described as equally weighted series.

Computational Procedure. The final consideration is the computational procedure used. There are three basic alternatives: (1) a simple arithmetic average of the various members in the series; (2) a derivation of an index with all changes, whether in price or value, reported in terms of a basic index; or (3) the incorporation of a geometric average rather than an arithmetic average.

Alternative Indicator Series

A number of widely used series warrant closer examination.

Price-Weighted Series. These include the oldest and certainly most popular stock market indicator series—the *Dow-Jones industrial average (DJIA)*. The DJIA is a price-weighted average of 30 large industrial "blue chip" stocks listed on the New York Stock Exchange (NYSE). The value of this index is derived by adding the current prices of the 30 stocks and dividing that sum by a divisor that has been adjusted to take account of stock splits and changes in the sample average over time.

Because the series is price-weighted, a high-priced stock carries more weight in the series than a low-priced stock; i.e., a 10 percent change in a $100 stock ($10) will cause a larger change in the series than a 10 percent change in a $30 stock ($3).

In addition to a price series for industrial stocks, Dow-Jones also has a transportation average of 20 stocks and a utility average that includes 15 stocks.

Value-Weighted Series. A value-weighted index begins by deriving the initial total market value of all stocks used in the series (*market value* equals number of shares outstanding times current market price). This initial value is typically established as the base and assigned an index value of 100. A new market value is computed daily for all securities in the index. This new value is compared with the initial value to determine the percentage of change, and this percentage of change is applied to the beginning index value of 100.

There is an automatic adjustment for stock splits and other capital changes in a value index because the decrease in the stock price is offset by an increase in the number of shares outstanding. In a value-weighted index, the importance of individual stocks in the sample is determined by their relative market value; i.e., a given percentage of change in the value of a large company has a greater impact than a comparable percentage of change for a small company.

Standard & Poor's Indexes. The first company to employ a market-value index widely was Standard & Poor's Corporation. It developed an index using 1935 to 1937 as a base period and computed a market-value index for 425 industrial stocks. It also computed an index of 60 utilities and 15 transportation firms. Finally, it developed a 500-stock composite index. Subsequently, the base period was changed to 1941 to 1943 and the base value to 10. In July 1976, the Standard & Poor's series underwent a major change. Prior to this time, all the stocks in the Standard & Poor's series were companies listed on the NYSE, and there was no index of financial firms. In July 1976, Standard & Poor's revised the 500 index into four groups: 400 industrials, 40 public utilities, 20 transportation, and 40 financial. Several of the stocks added were from the OTC market. The net result of these changes is an index which is broader in terms of industry representation and of the total equity market.

In addition to its major market indicators, Standard & Poor's has constructed over 90 individual industry series that include from 3 to 11 companies within an industry group.

New York Stock Exchange. Several other market indicators now employ the value-weighted index concept. In 1966, the NYSE derived a market-value index with figures available back to 1940. In contrast to other indexes, the various NYSE series are *not* based upon a sample of stocks. Specifically, the NYSE series include *all* the stocks listed on the exchange. As such, the NYSE is not concerned with the number of stocks in the sample or its breadth because this series includes the total universe of stocks listed on the exchange. Nevertheless, because the index is value-weighted, the large companies still control the major movements in the index. As an illustration of this point, the 500 stocks in Standard & Poor's composite index represent *74 percent* of the market value of all stocks on the exchange although they are only about *28 percent* of the exchange in numbers.

American Stock Exchange. The exchange originally developed a price-change series in 1966 in which the price changes during a given day were added, and then this sum was divided by the number of issues on the exchange. This average price change was then added to or subtracted from the previous day's index to arrive at a new index value. Unfortunately, this procedure eventually caused a distortion in the series because the price changes were influenced by the values. The ASE subsequently created a value-weighted series similar to that used by the NYSE that includes all the stocks on the exchange. This new series was released in September 1973. The index was set at 100 as of August 31, 1973. Subsequently the exchange made figures available for the new series back to 1969.

NASDAQ Series. A relatively recent addition to the market indicator universe is the comprehensive price indicator series for the OTC market developed by the National Association of Securities Dealers (NASD). The NASDAQ-OTC price indicator series had an index value of 100 as of February 5, 1971. All active domestic OTC common stocks listed on NASDAQ are included in the indexes, as are new stocks added to the system. The numerous issues included in the NASDAQ-OTC price indexes have been divided into the following seven categories:

1. Composite
2. Industrials
3. Banks
4. Insurance
5. Other finance
6. Transportation
7. Utilities

The indexes are value-weighted series similar to the Standard & Poor's series and the NYSE series. Because the composite index is value-weighted, it is heavily influenced by the largest 100 stocks on the NASDAQ system.

Unweighted Price Indicator Series. In an unweighted index, all stocks carry equal weight irrespective of their price and/or the value of the stock. Specifically, a $20 stock is as important as a $40 stock, and the total market value of the company is not important. Such an index is most appropriate for an individual who would select stocks randomly for his or her portfolio. One way to visualize what transpires in an unweighted series is to assume that equal dollar amounts are invested in each stock in the portfolio (e.g., an equal $1000 investment in each stock). Therefore, the investor would own 50 shares of a $20 stock, 100 shares of a $10 stock, and 10 shares of a $100 stock.

Probably the best-known unweighted or equal-weighted stock market series are those constructed by Lawrence Fisher at the University of Chicago. Fisher and Lorie have carried out several studies examining the performance of stocks on the NYSE assuming that an investor bought equal amounts of each stock on the exchange. As suggested earlier, they concluded that the results in terms of appreciation or depreciation would be comparable to those derived by an investor who randomly selected a large sample of stocks from the NYSE.

Another unweighted price indicator series that has gained in prominence is the *Indicator Digest* index of all stocks on the NYSE. This series is more representative of all stocks on the exchange. In several instances, it reached a bottom earlier than other indicator series and continued to be depressed after some of the popular market indicator series resumed rising during a bull market. Such a difference indicates that the market rise only included the large popular stocks as contained in the DJIA or the Standard & Poor's market indicator series, which are heavily weighted and influenced by the large, well-known companies.

See also Economic measurements; Financial statement analysis; Forecasting business conditions; Markets, securities; Risk analysis and management.

REFERENCES

The Dow-Jones Investor's Handbook, Dow-Jones Books, Princeton, N.J., annually.

Fisher, Lawrence, and James H. Lorie: "Rates of Return on Investments in Common Stocks," *Journal of Business*, vol. 37, no. 1, January 1963.

Fisher, Lawrence, and James H. Lorie: "Rates of Return on Investments in Common Stock, The Year-by-Year Record, 1926–65," *Journal of Business*, vol. 41, no. 3, July 1965.

Khoury, Sarkis J.: *Investment Management*, Macmillan, New York, 1983.

Reilly, Frank K.: "Evidence Regarding a Segmented Stock Market," *Journal of Finance*, vol. 27, no. 3, June 1972.

Reilly, Frank K.: "Price Changes in NYSE, AMEX, and OTC Stocks Compared," *Financial Analysis Journal*, vol. 27, no. 2, March–April 1971.

FRANK K. REILLY, *University of Notre Dame*

Material Handling

The most commonly held view of what material handling involves is that material handling concerns the handling of materials between the receiving and shipping activities in an enterprise. This is a narrow-minded view, however. Actually, "material handling is handling material"[1] from anywhere, to anywhere, in any type of enterprise or situation. The handling of material may vary from a mere 5 to 10 percent of productive activity to nearly 100 percent in some types of industries. On the average, material handling in a typical manufacturing concern is judged to account for 40 to 60 percent of what goes on in the enterprise. It is a gold mine of potential savings most worthy of close examination and analysis. A 10 percent reduction of material handling is not at all difficult to achieve.

Scope. The scope of material handling in your

business properly encompasses all handling involved in any of these activities:

Packaging (consumer) at supplier's plant

Packing (protective) at supplier's plant

Loading at supplier's plant

Transportation to user plant

External plant handling activities

Unloading activities

Receiving

Storage

Issuing materials

In-process handling

In-process storage

Workplace handling

Intradepartmental handling

Interdepartmental handling

Intraplant handling

Handling related to auxiliary functions

Packaging

Warehousing of finished goods

Packing

Loading and shipping

Transportation to consumer

Interplant handling

Benefits. Improved material handling may yield any of the following:

Improved material flow

Fewer unnecessary moves

Less unnecessary handling

Reduced manual handling

Increased production capacity

More efficient material flow

Increased space utilization

Increased work force utilization

Increased equipment utilization

Reduced employee fatigue

Reduced safety hazards

Better customer survice

Controlled material flow

Improved housekeeping

Shorter production cycle

Reduced work in process

Higher inventory turnover

Reduced production cost

Increased profits

Principles of Material Handling

As in many other areas of work, there is much to be learned from those who have worked in the field of material handling in the past. This experience has been summarized in the principles of material handling, as follows:[2]

Related to Planning. Eight principles apply:

1. Planning principle: All handling activities should be planned.

2. Systems principle: Plan a *system* integrating as many handling activities as is practical and coordinating the full scope of operation.

3. Materials flow principle: Plan an operation sequence and equipment arrangement optimizing materials flow.

4. Simplification principle: Reduce or eliminate unnecessary movement and/or equipment.

5. Gravity principle: Utilize gravity to move material whenever practicable.

6. Space utilization: Make optimum utilization of the building cube.

7. Unit size principle: Increase quantity, size, and weight of load handled.

8. Safety principle: Provide for safe handling methods and equipment.

Related to Equipment. Nine principles apply:

1. Mechanization/automation principle: Use mechanized or automated handling equipment when practicable—including computer-controlled devices and programs.

2. Equipment-selection principle: In selecting handling equipment, consider all aspects of the *material* to be handled, the *move* to be made, and the *method(s)* to be utilized—all in terms of the lowest overall cost.

3. Standardization principle: Standardize methods as well as types and sizes of handling equipment.

4. Flexibility principle: Use methods and equipment that can perform a variety of tasks and applications.

5. Deadweight principle: Reduce the ratio of equipment deadweight to pay load.

6. Motion principle: Keep in motion equipment designed to transport materials.

7. Idle-time principle: Reduce idle, or unproductive, time of both handling equipment and work force.

8. Maintenance principle: Plan for preventive maintenance and scheduled repair of all handling equipment.

9. Obsolescence principle: Replace obsolete handling methods and equipment when newer meth-

ods or equipment will pay off in a reasonable time.

Related to Operations. Three principles apply:

1. Control principle: Use material handling equipment to improve production control, inventory control, and order handling.
2. Capacity principle: Use handling equipment to help achieve full production capacity.
3. Performance efficiency principle: Determine efficiency of handling performance in terms of expense per unit handled.

Survey Procedures

In surveying material handling activities to uncover improvement opportunities, the following procedures and techniques may be helpful:[3]

1. Record the flow of material(s) by means of the following:

   Assembly chart

   Operation process chart

   Multiproduct process chart

   Process chart

   Flow diagram

   Flow process chart

   From–to (trip frequency) chart

   Activity relationship chart

   Activity relationship diagram

   Procedure chart (information flow)

2. Identify violations of good practice (improvement opportunities) using

   Charts listed above

   Walk-through

   Check sheets (indicators, symptoms)

   Flow-planning principles

   Material handling principles

3. List worst violations (best opportunities).
4. Identify causes of violations.
5. Analyze causes and define problems.
6. Translate problems (causes) into projects.
7. Develop evaluation criteria.
8. Evaluate potential benefits.
9. Select most-likely project(s) to begin with.
10. Establish project sequence.
11. Review interrelated projects to ensure treatment from systems point of view.
12. Attack each problem.

13. Document and report all savings.
14. Periodically evaluate effectiveness of solution(s) for potential improvement.

Problem-Solving Procedure

In attacking a specific material handling problem, it is beneficial to follow a systematic approach:

1. Identify the problem(s).
2. Determine the scope of the problem(s).
3. Establish objective(s).
4. Define problem(s).
5. Determine data to be collected.
6. Establish work plan and schedule.
7. Collect data.
8. Develop, weigh, and analyze data.
9. Develop improvements (and/or design proposed system).
10. Select equipment (see section below).
11. Prepare justification.
12. Obtain approvals.
13. Revise as necessary.
14. Work out procedure for implementation.
15. Supervise the installation.
16. Follow up.

Equipment Concepts

Inevitably, many solutions to material handling problems require the use of equipment. There are over 570 kinds, types, and varieties of handling equipment. Fortunately, they fall roughly into three major categories:

Conveyors. These are gravity or powered devices commonly used for moving uniform loads continuously from point to point over fixed paths, where the primary function is conveying. Conveyors are generally useful when (1) loads are uniform, (2) materials move continuously, (3) route does not vary, (4) load is constant, (5) movement rate is relatively fixed, (6) conveyors can bypass cross-traffic, (7) path to be followed is fixed, and (8) movement is from one fixed point to another point.

Cranes and Hoists. These are overhead devices usually utilized to move varying loads intermittently between points within an area fixed by the supporting and guiding rails, where the primary function is transferring. Cranes and hoists are most commonly used when (1) movement is within a fixed area, (2) moves are intermittent, (3) loads vary in size or weight, (4) cross-traffic would interfere with conveyors, and (5) units handled are not uniform.

Industrial Trucks. These are hand or powered vehicles (nonhighway) used for intermittent movement of mixed or uniform loads over various paths having suitable running surfaces and clearances, where the primary function is maneuvering or transporting. Industrial trucks are generally used when (1) material is moved intermittently, (2) movement is over varying routes, (3) loads are uniform or mixed in size and weight, (4) cross-traffic would prohibit conveyors, (5) clearances and running surfaces are adequate and suitable, (6) most of the operation consists of handling (or maneuvering, stacking, etc.), and (7) material can be put into unit loads.

Selecting Equipment

In selecting handling equipment (step 10 of the problem-solving procedure above), the analyst should.[4]

1. Review material handling equipment and problem factors.
2. Identify move(s) to be made.
3. Collect data.
4. Relate all factors.
5. *a.* Determine degree of mechanization.
   b. Check computer capability or support potential.
6. Make tentative selection of equipment type.
7. Narrow the choice.
8. Evaluate alternatives.
9. Check each selection for compatibility with other equipment.
10. Select specific type of equipment.
11. Prepare performance specifications.
12. Consider lease or rent for trial period.
13. Develop tentative budget for implementation.
14. Prepare justification.
15. Obtain approvals.
16. Procure equipment.
17. Supervise installation.
18. Follow up.

Selection Criteria. It is important to review a number of criteria in selecting a specific piece of equipment. These criteria may be evaluated in the form of the following questions: Does the equipment

1. Fit into the handling system?
2. Combine handling with other functions, (production, storage, inspection, packing, etc.)?
3. Optimize the flow of materials?
4. Provide simplicity as well as practicability?
5. Utilize gravity wherever possible?
6. Require a minimum of space?
7. Handle as large a load as is practical?
8. Make the move safely, in terms of both work force and material?
9. *a.* Use mechanization judiciously?
   b. Integrate effectively with computer control system?
10. Offer flexibility and adaptability?
11. Have a low deadweight to payload ratio?
12. Utilize a minimum of operator time?
13. Require a minimum of loading, unloading, and rehandling?
14. Call for as little maintenance, repair, power, and fuel as possible?
15. Have a long and useful life?
16. Facilitate capacity utilization?
17. Perform the handling operation efficiently and economically?

Trends

In planning for better material handling, management should pay particular attention to these trends:

Increasingly wider scope of material handling activity.

Closer cooperation with and between manufacturers, carriers, vendors, customers.

Faster manufacturing cycles with resulting reduction of inventories.

Reduced handling by direct-labor employees.

Mechanization of indirect labor tasks.

Upgrading of job-skill requirements.

Vendor packaging to customer specifications.

More attention to unit load handling methods.

Increased attention to receiving and shipping.

Changes in layouts to improve material handling.

Increased emphasis on material handling at the workplace.

Higher integration of handling, processing, and information flow.

Greater use of continuous processing.

Greater use of handling equipment and higher degree of mechanization in warehousing.

Planned delivery to, and removal of materials from, the workplace.

Planning for flexibility, expansion, and growth.

Mechanized handling between departments.

Increase in number of production operations that are performed during handling operations.

Greater integration with computer-control systems.

See also Automation; Facilities and site planning and layout; Production/operations management; Production planning and control; Productivity improvement; Robotics; Site selection; Therbligs; Work design, job enlargement, and job enrichment; Work measurement; Work simplification and improvement.

NOTES

[1] James M. Apple, *Material Handling Systems Design*, Ronald Press, New York, 1972.

[2] Ibid. chap. 4.

[3] J. M. Apple, *Productivity Improvement for Profit*, American Institute of Industrial Engineers, Norcross, Ga., 1977.

[4] Apple, op. cit.

REFERENCES

Mallick, R. W., and W. R. Turkes: "Material Handling," in H. B. Maynard (ed.), *Industrial Engineering Handbook*, 2d ed., McGraw-Hill, New York, 1963.

Muther, Richard: "Plant Layout and Design," in H. B. Maynard (ed.), *Handbook of Modern Manufacturing*, McGraw-Hill, New York, 1970.

Shea, L. West: "Material Handling Devices," in H. B. Maynard (ed.), *Handbook of Modern Manufacturing*, McGraw-Hill, New York, 1970.

JAMES M. APPLE, (deceased) *Georgia Institute of Technology*

JAMES M. APPLE, JR., *SysteCon, Inc.*

Materials Management

The concept of materials management involves a total overview of industrial logistics. Materials management can be dealt with on a micro basis within a particular manufacturing function, department, or plant or on a macro basis relating to the entire flow of materials from the mine or farm through the industrial process and physical distribution system to the ultimate consumer and, in some cases, through recycling and back into the manufacturing system.

Materials managers who deal with the subject on a micro basis circumscribe their responsibilities with purchasing and shipping of finished goods. The macro system-oriented approach extends from commodity futures and mining and farming operations to physical distribution and retail marketing. This discussion looks at the business-oriented issues at both the micro and macro levels of the materials management configuration but restricts description of technique to the micro approach within the manufacturing organization.

General Business Concepts. The flow of material through a business sytem is the physical mani-

festation of cash flow, and its control is essential to the fluidity and responsiveness of the business as a whole. One of the unique characteristics of the management of material flow is the fact that most materials change in shape, cube or volume, condition, and value as they move through the system. Thus the materials management system must control not only units and value but also space and time as they relate to facility capabilities, supplier lead time, seasonality, and marketing policy.

Capital Allocation Options. An additional factor in the material management concept is related to the allocation of capital. Management has three fundamental options in dealing with the customer, and these options depend on a combination of market criteria and capital utilization. They are:

1. *Manufacture product into finished-goods inventory* on a planned production schedule which levels operating cycles and optimizes the relationships between capital equipment, facilities, and the work force. In this case the flexibility factor is in the finished-goods inventory, and in some cases in the raw material and work-in-process inventory. The marketplace always has instant finished-goods support. Examples of this alternative can be found in the food industry, automotive supplies, and industrial hardware, where customers expect on-the-shelf finished inventory, and suppliers can develop reasonably reliable sales forecasts.

2. *Invest in excess productive capability* and then stock raw materials to permit manufacture on a real-time demand basis. Examples of this type of operation can be found in electric power generation, soft drink bottling, and construction operations.

3. *Make the customer wait.* In this type of operation the manufacturer builds to order and does not buy supplies or raw materials until the customer has made a firm commitment. The manufacturer schedules work and tells the customer when deliveries will be made. Examples of this type of business are found in aircraft and heavy machinery manufacturing, custom tailoring, and art.

As might be expected, each option requires slightly different policies concerning materials management. Each needs a different level of information and operational prediction. In the serialized-type business, which is represented by food, automobile, and appliance manufacture, management usually can make reasonably dependable projections of sales by product item. These forecasts can be exploded upstream and used as a material demand forecast in the procurement operation. In the case of the high capital, facility-oriented business, the commitment is made on the basis of speculative investment in (1) production capability and (2) either captive raw material supplies or a high inventory of production materials. This situation frequently leads to the purchase of mines and farms by the manufacturer.

In the case of custom manufacturing, it is not uncommon for the manufacturer to push the inventory-holding function upstream to a supplier in order to (1) ensure quick response and (2) minimize dollar lockup in raw materials and supplies. In such instances a manufacturer might buy metals from a metal warehouse wholesaler, manufacturing hardware from a mill supply house, and other items from various wholesalers and jobbers. This would, of course, increase the price paid for these supplies, but at the same time it would reduce the manufacturer's cash lockup and ensure rapid response at the supply end of the manufacturer's materials management system. In addition, the use of credit purchasing could have the effect of the supplier financing the production.

Control Versus Ownership Costs. Another fundamental issue in the development of a materials management concept is the balance between the cost of the control system and the cost of owning inventory at fail-safe levels, which negates the need for precise control. Before the advent of the computer, the telephone, and the telegraph it was normal to buy inventories in quantities relative to transactions. This was necessary in order to preclude production delays and to accommodate the long lead times which were normal in the days of horses and sails. Some companies have not yet learned to trust modern communications and logistics capabilities, and they still protect themselves with high safety stocks as a hedge against unreliable supply situations.

Kanban Versus Materials Requirements Planning (MRP). The Japanese Kanban system of production with minimum or no work-in-process inventory is a notable application of control techniques and facility investment to ensure customer service without high inventory investment or storage costs. MRP provides for anticipatory work-in-process inventories to limit production interruptions.

Special Business Factors. Many other business issues affect the philosophy and policy of a company's materials management system. For example, a toy manufacturer who must do 70 percent of the annual business in a 6-week period cannot operate on the basis of economic lot quantities or marginal-inventory backup. The sales year of the toy manufacturer is short, and delivery must be guaranteed in time for Christmas sales. Conversely, a brewery can force the glass factory to deliver bottles and cartons on an hour-by-hour schedule and maintain as little as 4 hours of container inventory supply in the bottling plant, with the inventory guarantees in the hands of the glass company. Thus, the materials management philosophy and technique must be tai-lored to the manufacturing and marketing policy and business environment of the particular company.

Materials Management Structure

The starting point in the development of any materials management system must be in the development of a bill of materials for the particular product or products being manufactured. There are three basic classes of bills of material in current use, but only one of these has any significant value in the materials management structure. The three types are:

1. *A materials list or takeoff,* which is simply a list of the materials used to manufacture a product and is, more often than not, used primarily for purchasing and costing purposes.

2. *An engineering bill of materials,* which is generally structured according to engineering disciplines and is prepared by the designer. For example, an automotive engineering bill of materials could consist of no less than four or five separate engineering-discipline-type bills of materials. These might be mechanical or power train; structural, or frame and body; electrical and instruments; wiring and ignition; seating and upholstery; and appearance, or trim and paint.

3. *A manufacturing bill of materials,* in which the parts, materials, subassemblies, and components are arranged in level-by-level manufacturing or assembly sequence in the bill of materials. The stratified structure of the manufacturing bill of materials permits level-by-level manufacturing material control and production scheduling. *This bill of materials is the basis for any successful materials management system.*

Parts Standardization and Coding. One of the key materials management issues is the problem of parts and materials standardization. As a very fundamental example, the same ¼-20 one-inch socket head screw may be used at two or three levels in the manufacturing structure and in a whole variety of subassemblies at the same level. This screw might be used to fasten the spring shackles to the frame on all four wheels of a motor vehicle, to fasten the steering column to the body, and to fasten the body to the chassis. This example, although a very mundane one, points up the need for item identification. It prevents multiple inventories or multiple specifying of the same item, with the resulting increase in system complexity and product cost.

In order to achieve parts standardization it is essential to use some sort of worker-and-machine legible parts numbering system which will relate the part to its own identity, while at the same time providing a basis for level-by-level bill of materials structures and inventory control. Precise parts identification is essential for design retrieval, inventory control, scheduling, and procurement specifications. A good part-number coding system, then, is the second element in the development of a modern materials management system.

Inventory System and Data Bank. Production control is, by definition, level-by-level materials control or inventory management. Conversely, if level-by-level inventory control is in operation, by definition a degree of production control is in the system. Thus, the next building block in the materials control system is a sound level-by-level inventory control procedure with an adequate data bank. This data bank can be on ledger cards or in a computer, but it must contain certain fundamental elements in order to be effective. When used in combination with a well-structured manufacturing bill of materials and a communicative parts-numbering system, the inventory management structure becomes a keystone of the materials management system. The *data bank* should have no less than the following elements:

1. *On order balance*—in units, dollars, handling modules (pallets, tote boxes, cartons, etc.), cubic feet, and period or date of scheduled arrival into inventory.

2. *On-hand balance*—in units, dollars, handling modules (pallets, tote boxes, cartons, etc.), and cubic feet.

3. *Allocated or committed balance*—in units, dollars, handling modules (pallets, tote boxes, cartons, etc.), cubic feet, and scheduled commitment due date.

4. *Available balance*—in units, dollars, handling modules, and cubic feet currently available for commitment to scheduled use or sales.

5. *Miscellaneous information*—including dollar density (dollars per cubic foot), storage environment requirements (refrigeration, humidity control, security, red label, etc.), stackability, order picking location, and freight classification.

Each level of the inventory system from raw materials through finished goods (and in a captive distribution system, branch warehouses and retail stores) should have this same inventory system data bank. In each case all entries should be accompanied by the date of the entry, the identification or document number of the source of the entry, and any pertinent control date signals, such as projected out-of-stock date, engineering-change due date and configuration code, and order arrival or scheduled completion date. The master data bank (ledger card header or computer file) should also contain such information as a where-used list, vendor identity, vendor item number, specification codes, standard lot quantities, units per handling module (pallet, tote box, etc.), and standard costs.

If all these elements of information are properly built into the inventory control system, and if the system is based upon a *random access procedure* using either a random access computer or a ledger card technique, the inventory system can operate as the core or keystone of the overall materials management structure. It will provide the basis for production scheduling, procurement, and materials control. These techniques can be applied effectively and inexpensively in small operations by using a minicomputer or microcomputer.

Procurement Procedure. The fourth element of the materials management system is the procurement procedure. It should be recognized that purchasing performs three separate, but interlocking, roles in most organizations. Only one of these roles is legitimately a part of the materials management system, but all are a part of the materials management function. These roles are:

1. *Material and supply research* to identify suppliers and products and to qualify products for use in the manufacturing or marketing system.

2. *Negotiation of terms and prices* and liaison with vendors in relationship to business practices, delivery schedules, and contract arrangements.

3. *Material and product acquisition* to ensure that the right product, at the right time, in the right quantity, is in the right place. This is an administrative function which is a fundamental element of the materials management system and procedure. The procurement function must anticipate the material requirement quantities and dates based upon inventory position, must anticipate demand or requisitions, must arrange for purchase and delivery of the materials, and must monitor the vendor to ensure the proper quantity, quality, and scheduling of the inbound supplies.

Thus, the role of the procurement function in a materials management system is to interface requirements with the outside supplier and to ensure the vendor's proper response.

Internal and External Transportation. A fifth element of the materials management system is transportation. This function breaks into two primary elements: internal and external transport. The internal element is usually termed *materials handling,* and the external portion is generally known as *traffic.* The roles of these functions are basically the same, although they operate in different physical and business environments. Each has the responsibility to respond to schedule demand by having the right thing in the right place, at the right time, at the least cost, and in the right condition.

External movement is further broken down into inbound and outbound transportation. When private-vehicle fleets are involved, an additional breakdown is usually found in management, wherein the fleet operator is either separated and parallel to or under the direction of the traffic manager. The traffic manager usually performs the dual role of (1) transport purchasing and (2) movement scheduling, and handles both inbound and outbound cargoes. In modern materials management systems, it is not uncommon to operate with inventories in transit in rail cars or in trucks and to include the transport timing in the materials management scheduling structure. This is particularly critical in international operations. It is also a part of the technique used in such serialized operations as automotive manufacturing, bottling, and perishable food operations.

Shop-Loading Procedure. In the essential shop-loading portion of the system, material requirements, facility and labor capacity, inventory lot patterns, and time-related control elements are blended together to achieve an optimum balance between capital utilization, operating expense, supply availability, market demand, and the overall cash flow or financial structure of the business.

The variety of production rates between machines, operations, and components and the varying assembly schedules and cube-impact factors make the scheduling and loading of the manufacturing process particularly critical. *Imbalance* or erratic machine scheduling can have a major impact on inventories, cash lockups, and market response. *Underscheduling* can generate shortages and delays, while *overscheduling* can absorb available capital, reduce liquidity, and generate facility congestion.

Thus, the machine-loading procedures must recognize the economics of the production lot in terms of both (1) equipment and material utilization and (2) the relationship of a component to the schedule and the facility as a whole. Blind utilization of economic order quantities in facility scheduling or purchasing can result in disastrous distortions in the inventory/schedule pattern of the operation. Economic order quantities should be developed on a carefully researched local basis and should not be based blindly on the application of classical formulas or tables. The theory upon which these formulas are based depends upon academic assumptions which are nearly impossible to achieve in practice.

Materials Requirements Planning

In its fundamental form the concept of materials requirements planning relates a sales forecast to a production and a materials procurement schedule. In order to make this conversion, however, one must start with basically sound data. It is unfortunate that sales-forecasting techniques are generally less than precise; therefore the system begins with some built-in inadequacies which must be cushioned by inventories.

The basic function of an inventory is to adjust the material flow between nonlinearly related activities, such as manufacturing and retailing, procurement and manufacturing, or different production rates in process. Thus, if the sales forecast establishes a production schedule which is more optimistic than market performance, an inventory buildup occurs. Conversely, if the forecast is pessimistic and production schedules do not meet demands, inventory shortages will occur at many levels in the system.

It follows that the first and key step in any materials management or materials requirements planning system is the establishment of a reasonably dependable sales forecast on a product-by-product basis. If a fairly reliable sales forecast is obtained, the next step in the materials requirements planning system is the process of (1) exploding the forecast into a product-level production schedule and (2) further exploding this into materials requirements.

Multiple-Period Schedules. When the sales forecast is converted into a time-oriented product demand, it is then possible to establish completed product requirements on a period basis. The usual practice is to use either 12 or 13 months or periods, or in some cases to schedule on a weekly basis. Very few companies can achieve adequate precision for a daily schedule above the department level, and most product schedules are on a period or monthly basis. This approach allows for adjustments and slippages in the internal schedule to accommodate breakdowns, quality control problems, productivity variations, maintenance problems, and other unpredictable or difficult-to-anticipate occurrences.

Japanese Kanban techniques schedule materials on a constant flow, no-inventory basis and trust response reliability to close supervision and flexible production capacity.

The Kanban system treats inventory as a liability and ignores the "economic lot size" concept. The idea is to reduce setup cost to insignificance, use excess production equipment capacity, avoid queues, and require vendors and upstream operations to maintain zero defects and precise schedules. Lead times are minimized and the capacity/market inequities are accommodated by capacity variations instead of supply adjustments or finished goods and work-in-process inventories. The pure and very simple American example of this approach is a nuclear power plant which runs with minimum fuel inventory and no work-in-process or finished goods inventory, and varies turbine output with customer demand while maintaining maximum production capacity and flexibility.

Some authorities claim that Kanban can only succeed when highly repetitious products are being made. Conversely, the American-style materials requirement planning system (MRP) and manufacturing resource planning (MRPII) programs are expected to deal with all types of products, including engineered one-of items, build-to-order products, and manufacture-to-inventory goods. The MRP and MRPII concept use inventory, lead time, and lot size control (EOQ) to compensate for market and schedule variations within a fixed capacity environment. They also use make-or-buy procedures to vary capacity on the basis of a capital conservation philosophy.

Both systems do a good job when properly applied. Kanban requires more precise control and allows little market fluctuation. MRP requires more working capital and provides more market flexibility.

Consolidated Materials Requirements. When the product schedule is established for a given period, the manufacturing bill of materials for each product is exploded and extended to generate product and composite quantities of purchased materials and components and to identify parts manufacturing requirements. At this stage lead-time factors and lot quantities are entered into the system, and the demand (or requirement) dates for materials and purchased components is identified. By taking these data and applying them to the raw material and purchased component inventories, it is then possible to establish consolidated demands and procurement schedules for materials coming from outside vendors.

At this stage appropriate safety stocks are also introduced into the system to cope with vendor reliability factors and unforeseen delays and shortages. The result of this calculation is modified by purchasing to achieve the optimum balance between requirements, schedules, price, and transport expense. Variations in quantity and schedule are absorbed into the raw material and supply inventory patterns. In Kanban, no such inventory cushion is available and supplier discipline is required to ensure continuous and responsive operations.

Balancing Schedules and Capacities. At the next level the machine-loading procedures are used to balance facility capacity against production schedules. Appropriate make-or-buy decisions are also made at this time. In many instances production-lot quantities and manufacturing order consolidation of common parts result in the development of work-in-process inventories. Conversely, Kanban uses excess capacity instead of work-in-process inventories to ensure reliable schedules. These work-in-process inventories serve as the cushion between nonlinear manufacturing schedules. They also permit economies of scale to be applied to the fabrication and subassembly functions in serialized manufacturing, where common parts and components are used in a multiple of products. The economies of scale manifest themselves in more sophisticated tooling and more manufacturing-oriented part and component design.

The materials requirements planning concept provides control based upon (1) the multiple-period approach to scheduling and (2) the consolidation of materials and parts orders into a level-by-level inventory and production scheduling procedure.

Summary

Materials management, as a total concept, encompasses all elements of the business system. The ability to control or schedule raw materials can be enhanced by owning the mine or the farm; but in the case of agricultural products, nature schedules production, and the consumer must be accommodated by the choice of processing and preservation techniques. The primary consideration in materials management is the control of cash flow and capital lockup without impinging upon facility utilization and customer service. The materials manager must recognize that the primary function of a manufacturing business is to support marketing and that effective decisions must be market-oriented first and facility-oriented only in support of that objective.

See also Control systems, management; Inventory stockkeeping systems; Logistics, business; Material handling; Purchasing management.

REFERENCES

Orlicky, Joseph: *Material Requirements Planning*, McGraw-Hill, New York, 1975.

Plossl, G. W., and O. W. Wight: *Production and Inventory Control*, Prentice-Hall, Englewood Cliffs, N.J., 1967.

Pritzker, Robert A., and Robert A. Gring: *Modern Approaches to Production Planning and Control*, American Management Association, New York, 1960.

Tersine, Richard J.: *Materials Management and Inventory Systems*, American Elsevier, New York, 1976.

Yasuhiro, Munden: *Toyota Production System*, Industrial Engineering and Management Press, Norcross, Ga., 1983.

E. Ralph Sims, Jr., *The Sims Consulting Group, Inc.*

Matrix Management

Matrix management is an approach to organizing the authority and reporting structure of a firm so that short-run programs of the company can be carried out efficiently at the same time as the activities oriented toward the long run.

By the 1950s, the functional (chain of command) form of organizational structure had shown it could not cope with the increased technical demands brought about by complex processing plants and the sophisticated weapons systems being developed. The functional structure had difficulty in handling the increased coordination necessary among different functional groups. The project form of organizational

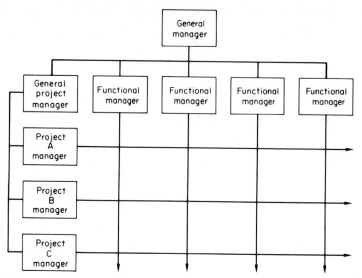

FIG. M-11   General matrix structure.

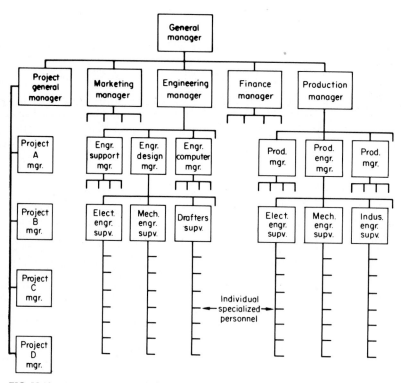

FIG. M-12   Matrix structure for a manufacturing company.

structure was first developed to overcome these coordination problems, but the pure project form had difficulty integrating with a firm's functional organizational structure. An increasingly viable solution to this problem is a hybrid of the old functional structure and the new project structure known as the matrix structure.

The general form of the matrix structure is shown in Fig. M-11. The typical vertical (downward) authority and reporting path of the functional manager is shown, crossed by the nontraditional horizontal (across) authority and reporting path of the project manager. The individual employee in the matrix thus reports to two superiors, a functional supervisor and a project manager.

The functional supervisor supervises a group of individuals in the same specialty, and is responsible for the technical skills of the individuals, the number of individuals, the equipment necessary, and so on. The project manager supervises the specialized individual on one specific project (package of work tasks), and supervises other specialized individuals who report functionally to other technical supervisors for work on the same project. Thus, the project

manager's authority cuts across department lines to coordinate all work on one project. The functional supervisor remains responsible for planning and developing the long-range skills of individuals and for supporting all projects in that functional area, while the project manager is responsible for getting the specific project completed.

Disadvantages of matrix management include: (1) the ambiguity of the balance of power between the project and functional sides of the organization; (2) the difficulty of integrating new employees into the system; (3) the uneasiness of many managers and supervisors with a dual reporting system; and (4) the additional cost of the project management personnel.

A Manufacturing Example

Matrix management has almost become the standard organizational form in large, technology-oriented companies, as well as in most military development and many production organizations. Figure M-12 shows a matrix structure for a typical manufacturing

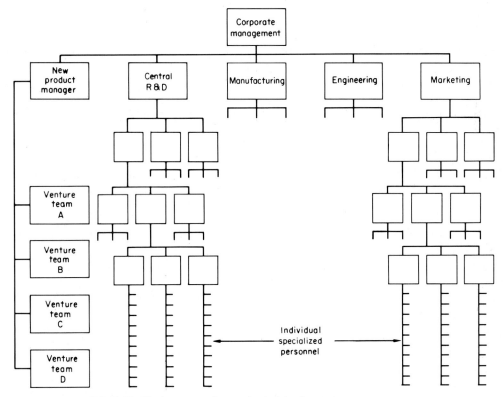

FIG. M-13 Matrix structure for new product development.

company. Running down through the organization chart are the main functional areas of engineering, production, and marketing. Along the left side are the project managers. In the engineering design group, design electrical engineers are assigned to work on project D, as are mechanical engineers and drafters. Likewise, in the production engineering group, electrical engineers, industrial engineers, mechanical engineers, and so on are also assigned to project D. These people are assigned to a project by their functional supervisor, who supervises the technical aspects of their work. The project D manager controls the work being carried out primarily by the use of budgets and time schedules, and supervises all types of technical work being carried out on project D.

Matrix management then combines the advantages of the technical specialization of the functional organization with the task orientation of the project organization.

A New Product Development Example

Many companies that regularly introduce new products use a matrix management structure, as shown in Fig. M-13. In this example, coordination is needed among the functional areas of research and development, manufacturing, engineering, and marketing. A new product or venture team functions in the project management position. This team coordinates the new product development throughout the entire development process to market introduction.

Conclusion

No form of organization structure can solve all problems. Matrix management in one of its forms exists in almost all large companies. It has been found to be the most practical way to achieve short-run product and project output consistent with the need for the organization to be prepared to respond to ongoing activities.

See also Authority, responsibility, and accountability; Contracts management; Engineering management; Network planning methods; Organization structures and charting; Program planning and implementation; Project management.

REFERENCES

Cleland, David I.: "The Cultural Ambience of the Matrix Organization," *Management Review.* vol. 69, November 1981, pp. 25–39; vol. 70, December 1981, pp. 48–56.

Knight, Kenneth: *Matrix Management*, Petrocelli Books, New York, 1977.

Kur, C. Edward: "Making Matrix Management Work," *Supervisory Management*, vol. 27, March 1982, pp. 37–43.

Jackson E. Ramsey, *James Madison University*

Motivation in Organizations

Motivation is a term that has been used frequently in many contexts. Thus, a precise unitary definition would not only be arbitrary but probably also dysfunctional. Generally speaking, however, persons who have thought and written about motivation have considered two distinct but interrelated sets of ideas.

1. One of these focuses on the environmental or personal characteristics that serve to energize, activate, or motivate the individual. These approaches have been referred to as *content* theories of motivation[1] since they aim at identifying classes of variables that serve to stimulate the individual.

2. A second approach has been concerned with explaining how the individual chooses to engage in a particular behavior. Campbell et al.[1] refer to these orientations as *process* approaches since they focus on the mechanisms linking content variables to specific actions that the individual may perform.

A bit of reflection will suggest that knowledge of both motivational contents and processes is important if we are to understand and ultimately influence motivation. In an organizational context, for example, we must have information on the needs people experience or the outcomes they seek (contents) in order to provide the types of rewards they will find attractive. At the same time, however, these rewards must be administered so that the people are encouraged to engage in the behaviors required by the organization. This requires knowledge of the motivational process.

This entry is concerned with motivation as it applies to organizational contexts. It is thus aimed at furthering understanding about motivational contents and processes as they apply to work-related behaviors such as job choice, job maintenance, and, particularly, job performance.

Motivational Contents

Content Theories. Motivational content can be viewed from two complementary perspectives.[2] One is to view contents in terms of the deficiencies, deprivations, imbalances, or needs that activate the individual to behave. This is the traditional way of considering contents; it views them as internal to the individual. In this entry it will be referred to as the *needs* approach. A second, more recent, approach focuses on rewards or outcomes that serve to satisfy needs. Thus this approach considers contents in terms of consequences of the individual's behavior and will be referred to as the *outcomes* approach.

Needs Approach. A number of theories have

emphasized taxonomies that purport to identify needs possessed by individuals. By far the best known of such theories to those interested in organizational behavior is Maslow's[3] *hierarchy of needs* theory. According to this theory, individuals may experience five classes of needs: (1) *physiological* (hunger and thirst); (2) *safety* (primarily bodily); (3) *social* (friendship and affiliation); (4) *esteem* (both self and the esteem of others); and (5) *self-actualization* (growth and realization of potential). These needs are hypothesized to be arranged in a hierarchy such that each lower-level need must be predominantly satisfied before the individual experiences higher-level needs. Moreover, Maslow hypothesized that as physiological-through-esteem needs are satisfied, they cease to motivate. Self-actualization needs, alternatively, are hypothesized to become more active as they are satisfied.

Outcomes Approach. Although explicitly aimed at identifying sources of satisfaction rather than motivation, Herzberg's *two-factor* taxonomy is the best-known attempt to identify motivating work outcomes.[4] According to this approach, there are two types of work outcomes: (1) *intrinsic* factors, which have to do with promotion, recognition of one's work, and the work itself; and (2) *extrinsic* factors, which have to do with the work environment, including formal rewards other than promotion, such as salary, relations with coworkers, supervision and organizational administration, and working conditions. In subsequent writings regarding this taxonomy, Herzberg[5] hypothesized that only the attainment of the intrinsic outcomes can initiate sustained motivation toward organizational goals.

Evaluation. The content theories identified above, particularly the two-factor taxonomy, have stimulated much research. While findings from this research are not, on balance, favorable to the hypotheses of either Maslow or Herzberg, they have shed light on a number of important content issues.[6]

In all probability there are greater differences between individuals in the needs they experience, and hence in the outcomes they are motivated to seek, than either theory acknowledges. Except at the physiological level, needs depend substantially on the reinforcement environment to which one has been exposed, particularly during the maturational years.[7] Since environmental experiences tend to be partially unique, so too do resulting individual need structures. Not surprisingly, therefore, studies investigating this issue have observed substantially greater individual differences in the relative salience of intrinsic versus extrinsic outcomes than hypothesized by Herzberg.[8]

As a corollary of the above, it should be noted that lower-level needs, or the value of extrinsic outcomes, are probably much more important than either Maslow's or Herzberg's analyses would suggest. *The importance of pay in the work environment has espe-cially been understated.* There is an impressive amount of evidence indicating that pay is a very important outcome for individuals in a wide variety of occupational groups.[9]

At present, less is known about how various needs or outcomes are connected to each other. There is little evidence, for example, supporting Maslow's hypothesis which states that satisfaction of needs decreases the importance of those needs. Indeed, some research findings tentatively indicate that needs strength and satisfaction are positively related. That is, the more satisfied one is with some need, the more important additional satisfaction of that need is.[10]

A provocative hypothesis has been formulated suggesting that the association of extrinsic outcomes with an activity may decrease the intrinsic outcomes associated with the activity. In a work setting, this might mean that the use of extrinsic outcomes such as pay to motivate higher performance levels would be partially or wholly self-defeating since the very act of linking pay to performance might reduce the intrinsic value of performing the work itself. Indeed, Deci conducted a series of experimental studies from which he concludes precisely this possibility.[11] While the work of Deci is interesting, it should be noted that his conclusions have been criticized severely[12] and that reviewers have indicated the need for more carefully designed research on this issue.[13]

Implications. The typical organizational environment has four characteristics that may serve as sources of motivational outcomes:

1. The *work itself* can provide intrinsic or task-mediated outcomes.

2. *Personnel policies and practices* pertaining to rewards and discipline constitute a source of outcomes.

3. Interpersonal relationships with one's *supervisor* and the extent to which the supervisor provides recognition and allows for participation are outcome sources.

4. One's *coworkers* are typically a source of socially oriented outcomes.

Content theories and their interpretations have too often emphasized one of these sources of outcomes to the exclusion of the others.

A more appropriate interpretation of employee outcome preferences would take into consideration the following observations: (1) As stated earlier, substantial differences exist between individuals in their preferences for outcomes. (2) Organizations probably have little influence on the types of outcomes employees find motivating.[14] (3) Employee preferences for outcomes, whatever the specific patterns, are likely to be fairly stable through time.[15]

Organizations interested in providing motivating outcomes for a majority of employees would do well to heed the implications of these observations. In some respects, these observations put organizations in a passive role. Rather than attempting to change outcome preferences through communication or development programs, for example, these observations suggest the importance of identifying preexisting preferences. Attempts to change outcome preferences of employees probably have to come over time through selection procedures aimed at changing the labor force of the organization.

Most important, these observations suggest that organizations maintain a balanced approach to the administration of work outcomes. For example, while job enrichment may be appropriate for certain tasks and employees, it cannot by itself solve an organization's motivational problems. Attention must also be paid to the other sources of outcomes.

Motivational Processes

Practical considerations of motivation inevitably lead managers to the question of how needs or outcomes can be harnessed or linked to behaviors the organization wishes to encourage. That is, how can needs or outcomes serve to motivate certain types of behavior? This is the basic question about the *process* of motivation.

Over the years, many process theories have been proposed in several different branches of psychology. Interestingly, however, it was not until fairly recently that industrial psychologists and others interested in human behavior in organizations began to consider and investigate seriously theories that are essentially aimed at understanding motivational processes. While a number of theories have been proposed, Vroom's[16] formulation of expectancy theory clearly has become dominant in recent years.

Expectancy Theory. Expectancy theory has been used to explain choices between different actions, such as decisions about what job to accept. It has also been used to explain levels of intensity regarding a single activity—such as whether or not an employee will attempt to be a high, average, or low performer.[17] The theory is thus obviously aimed at explaining behaviors of interest to organizations.

The theory is frequently referred to as a *cognitive* one in that it emphasizes the importance of the ability to think in determining voluntary activity. All told, one must consider three concepts that people presumably think about to understand the process of motivation according to this theory.[18]

Valence of Outcomes. One concept has to do with the attractiveness (or *valence*) of outcomes that may be associated with an activity. We have already discussed types of intrinsic and extrinsic outcomes that may occur in the work environment. Unlike the content theories discussed earlier, however, expectancy theory makes no a priori statements about what outcomes individuals will find valent or nonvalent.

Instrumentality Perceptions. A second concept has to do with individuals' beliefs about the connection or linkage between some activity and an outcome. These perceptions can be thought of as subjective probabilities and are referred to as *instrumentality* perceptions. In a work environment, for example, individuals would be expected to have instrumentality perceptions regarding the link between performance and potential outcomes such as salary increases. Note that there is a potentially unique instrumentality perception for each outcome.

Expectancy Perceptions. A third concept pertains to the individuals' beliefs about the connection (or linkage) between one's efforts to engage in an activity and the likelihood that the activity will be accomplished. These are called *expectancy* perceptions and may also be thought of as subjective probabilities. For example, an individual's expectancy perception regarding work performance might be thought of as his or her response to the question, "What is the likelihood of performing this task successfully if you exert a reasonable amount of effort?"

Expectancy theory states that motivation to engage in an activity will be high when an individual's expectancy perception regarding that activity is high and when instrumentality perceptions linking the activity to positively valent outcomes are high. Thus, we would expect an employee to be motivated to be a high work performer if that employee believed:

1. High performance was attainable through effort (high effort-performance expectancy).

2. High performance would lead to outcomes (high performance-outcome instrumentalities).

3. The outcomes were generally attractive (positively valent outcomes).

The major elements of the theory are diagrammed in Fig. M-14. Note that the motivational components

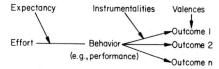

FIG. M-14 Motivational components in expectancy theory.

of the theory speak only to the effort an individual may be expected to expend toward the accomplishment of some activity. Actual accomplishment depends not only on motivation but also on ability.[19] Thus, the complete theory states that behavior (e.g., performance) = motivation $\times$ ability.

Evaluation. Since its formulation by Vroom in 1964, many studies have been conducted testing various aspects of the theory. For the most part, these studies have been conducted in actual public and private organizations. A wide variety of occupational groups have been investigated, including managers, professionals, and white- and blue-collar workers. Most of the research has been aimed at testing whether the theory can predict measures of employee performance and job choice.

By and large, findings from these studies have been favorable;[20] that is, it is frequently found that beliefs concerning valences of outcomes, and particularly concerning instrumentalities and expectancies, are associated with measures of effort and performance. Higher performers, or those exerting greater effort to perform, tend to have higher expectancies and higher instrumentalities that performance will lead to positively valent outcomes. While it is important to recognize that support for the theory has not been universal, nor always strong, it has been quite consistent.

Implications for Practice. Expectancy theory is very rich in implications for administrative action. Motivation can be enhanced to the extent that the organization is able appropriately to influence valence, expectancy, or instrumentality perceptions of employees. Since we have already indicated that organizations have little influence over the types of outcomes employees find important (valent), the discussion which follows will focus on the latter two perceptions.

It should be noted initially that employees' perceptions are ultimately influenced most importantly by the objective state of affairs. Thus, administrative policies will be unsuccessful if they communicate expectancy or instrumentality linkages that are not consistent with the actual implementation of those policies.

At the same time, however, individuals taken singly or as group members bring to the work environment a set of partially unique historical experiences. These experiences may tend to shade their feelings and beliefs regarding the important motivational components. Thus, majority relative to minority, rural relative to urban, female relative to male, advantaged relative to disadvantaged employees may hold somewhat different motivational perceptions regardless of organizational characteristics. Organizations must therefore show special sensitivity in establishing and implementing policy whenever persons of diverse backgrounds are employed.

Influencing Instrumentality Perceptions. There is little doubt that an organization can have the most immediate impact on motivation through its influence on instrumentality perceptions (beliefs regarding the links between behavior and outcomes). Instrumentality perceptions can be strengthened by making rewards contingent or dependent on desired behavior. Thus, if the organization wishes to encour-

age motivation to perform among its employees, it must reward the high performers with positively valent rewards. In addition, low performers must not be rewarded.[21] The key to establishing appropriate instrumentality perceptions is by *differentially* rewarding and not rewarding. Rewarding indiscriminately will not have positive motivational impacts.

Given the cognitive nature of expectancy theory, it follows that instrumentality linkages should be communicated. Employees need to be informed that behaving in desired ways will be rewarded. The more specific the organization is about the exact behavior desired and the exact rewards to be expected, the better. While contingent administration of rewards may influence behavior in any event, the impact can be more effective in a shorter time if it is explicitly communicated.[22]

There is substantial literature from reinforcement theory that has dealt with methods for linking rewards to desired behavior. This literature is frequently interpreted as suggesting that partial reinforcement schedules (i.e., where not every desirable behavior is rewarded) are most effective for motivation.[23] The evidence for this type of conclusion, however, has not been established on adults working in organizational settings. Field studies in the latter context suggest that continuous reinforcement (where every desirable behavior is rewarded) is at least as effective as partial reinforcement.[24] This latter observation is consistent with expectancy theory, which would hypothesize that instrumentality perceptions would be maximized when every desirable behavior was rewarded.

In summary, organizations can have positive impacts on their employees' instrumentalities by

1. Communicating in specific terms the linkage between the behaviors and the rewards.

2. Implementing the communicated linkages, including withholding rewards from persons who do not engage in the desired behavior.

3. Where possible, offering the rewards for every or nearly every desired behavior.[25]

While the organization probably has the greatest impact on instrumentality perceptions through the processes described above, keep in mind that individuals also differ in how they respond to these processes.

Influencing Expectancy Perceptions. Expectancy perceptions (beliefs regarding the links between effort and behavior) can also be influenced by the organization. Since they pertain to an individual's feelings about his or her capabilities to perform some activity, they will depend mostly on the individual's perception of his or her ability *relative* to the ability requirements of the activity. That is, expectancy perceptions depend jointly on the individual and the task to be done.

Such a formulation suggests that a number of organizational activities may have impacts on expectancy perceptions.

1. *Training and development programs* are an obvious method for attempting to change individuals. By sending employees through training programs, organizations typically attempt to increase their job skills. These changes, in turn, can frequently be expected to enhance expectancy perceptions.

2. *Selection* provides another method for changing, not individuals per se, but characteristics of the work force in the aggregate. By changing employment standards, organizations can influence the ability levels of those hired and consequently influence expectancy perceptions.

3. *Job simplification or enlargement* may also manipulate work content favorably. Simplification has been recommended as a mechanism for increasing productivity through an emphasis on employees' ability to perform. Recently, many people have advocated enlarging or enriching jobs (i.e., making them more demanding and difficult). Emphasis has been placed on employees' *motivation* to perform. Here it is sufficient to indicate that manipulation of the job is likely to influence the ability requirements of the job and hence employees' expectancy perceptions. Probable implications of job enrichment will be discussed in the last major section of this entry.

4. *The employee–job mix* may be changed by reallocation of persons within the organization. Transfers and promotions are frequently used as examples of this method for changing employees' relative ability to perform and hence their expectancy perceptions.

Viewing expectancy as proposed here suggests that it is a very dynamic construct. Employees change through time, jobs change, and hence expectancy perceptions change. It can frequently be assumed that expectancy perceptions will be fairly low for employees starting on a job. With experience and/or training, these perceptions are likely to increase. Changes in jobs, either through transfer or promotion or technological change, may dramatically alter expectancy perceptions of experienced employees, however. Thus, the organization must continually be alert to the implications of the congruence of worker abilities with job ability requirements for expectancy perceptions.

As with instrumentality perceptions, we can also expect individual differences in expectancy perceptions, primarily as a function of one's previous experience. Those who have a history of coping successfully with their environment in the past will probably have more positive expectancy perceptions than those who have been less successful.

Motivational Applications

The present section applies expectancy theory to two managerial strategies designed to enhance employee motivation: task redesign and compensation systems. Both have been characterized in the literature by successful *and* unsuccessful applications. By using expectancy theory, a manager can identify conditions in which each of these strategies might be expected to be effective in motivating high performance.

Task Redesign. The work itself, or the task, along with reward practices, supervisors, and coworkers, serves as a potentially important outcome source within the organizational environment. Recently, a large number of investigations have been conducted examining whether characteristics of the job itself influence employee attitudes and performance. Generally speaking, the results of those investigations have yielded ambiguous results. While there have been notable successes, there have also been notable failures.[26]

The task is a potential source of so-called "intrinsic outcomes," such as feelings of achievement, accomplishment, and competence. For these feelings to be generated, however, the person performing the task must probably believe the task to be psychologically important. To be so, it has been suggested, the job must be seen as meaningful, requiring worker responsibility and providing knowledge about work results. These requirements tend to describe enlarged and enriched jobs more than specialized jobs.

This then constitutes the major argument in favor of job enlargement or enrichment.[27] Enlarged or enriched jobs allow employees to experience intrinsic outcomes associated with doing them. In expectancy theory terms, job enlargement or enrichment increases instrumentality perceptions linking successful performance to intrinsic outcomes. To this extent, job enlargement has a positive motivational impact.

Expectancy theory also tells us, of course, that instrumentality perceptions are not of themselves sufficient. The associated outcomes must also be positively valent for motivation to exist. Thus, an organization should not always expect that the outcomes of job enlargement or enrichment will be motivating to all its employees.

Also, as has been suggested earlier, it is probable that changes in task scope will have an impact on expectancy perceptions. In the short run at least, broadening tasks through enlargement or enrichment programs is likely to result in reduced expectancy perceptions. This, in turn, can be expected to reduce motivation to perform unless the organization offsets these dysfunctional impacts through careful planning, including, in all likelihood, formalized training programs to facilitate the transition.

Compensation Systems. The impact of pay on motivation to perform has been controversial for reasons often not highly associated with the evidence. While there are examples showing pay systems failing, sometimes spectacularly so,[28] the evidence generally shows that adequately administered compensation systems which have been designed to motivate performance do so successfully.[29,30] A major reason for these successes is the high valence generally attached to pay.[31] High valence probably stems from the fact that pay is so generally transferable and frequently conveys other outcomes (e.g., recognition).

Since pay is generally valent to employees, the key to a motivating compensation system in terms of expectancy theory is to obtain high instrumentality perceptions that pay will be obtained if, and only if, the desired behavior is forthcoming. The closer the systems actually link pay to desired behaviors, the higher the instrumentality perceptions will be.[32] There is also evidence that employees with higher instrumentality perceptions regarding the link between pay and performance tend to be higher performers.[33]

If an organization desires to use compensation to motivate performance, a number of important conditions must be satisfied.[34]

1. The organization must be sure that employees are responsible for their own performance. It makes little sense to link any reward to performance if performance is essentially out of the employees' control.

2. The organization must be able to *define* and *measure* performance. Two types of procedures are in general use. One, frequently associated with individual and group-incentive systems, is based on quantitative indicators of physical productivity measured against engineering-based standards. The second procedure for measuring is through some sort of evaluation or performance appraisal system. Such systems are typical for nonmanagerial employees and involve the evaluation of one person by another.

3. The organization must actually link compensation outcomes to measured performance. This step is fairly direct in typical incentive systems using quantitative productivity measures. However, a frequent difficulty associated with such systems is unnecessary complexity. Employees may not know how their pay is specifically determined, and instrumentality perceptions linking pay and performance may be lower than they need be.

Another major difficulty has to do with changing production standards. Attempts to raise standards as production increases will be met by employee resistance and probable output restriction. Employee instrumentality perceptions for the intermediate and long run will be low if employees anticipate that standards will be raised as a consequence of increased productivity. This difficulty questions the advisability of incentive systems when production processes are subject to rapid technological change.

Performance appraisal procedures are generally connected to compensation through *merit-rating* systems. Policy regarding such systems frequently states that high performers can expect frequent and generous compensation increases, while low performers can expect infrequent and small, or nonexistent, increases. As Campbell et al.[35] have pointed out, however, organizations seldom follow through on these policies, so that too often little difference exists between the salary increases obtained by individuals receiving the most-favorable evaluations and those receiving the least-favorable evaluations. The consequences in terms of expectancy theory are predictable and necessarily dysfunctional. Pay–performance instrumentality will necessarily be weakened when salary increases are not differentially linked to evaluation results.

Undoubtedly, an important reason for the unwillingness to differentiate more rigorously on the basis of appraisal results is a concern about the validity of those results. Typical appraisal procedures are permeated with errors. These errors occur substantially because the evaluator has no clear-cut standards against which to compare the evaluatee's performance.

Management by Objectives (MBO). This is one procedure which attempts to generate clear-cut performance standards. It establishes, frequently with the evaluatees' participation, explicit individualized standards as a basis for subsequent evaluation.[36] Several elements of MBO have direct expectancy theory implications. One of the most consistent findings is that performance tends to increase as the goals established are made more specific.[37] In all probability, specific goals help the employee clarify expectancy perceptions linking effort to performance. Management by objectives can thus provide a double-barreled motivational impact if the goal setting is combined with a system of linking goal accomplishment to financial rewards so that performance–pay instrumentality perceptions are high.

Conclusion

Expectancy theory views motivation as a reasonably complex process involving multiple perceptions. As a consequence, analysis of administrative activities using this theory will yield multiple and sometimes conflicting impacts on organizational behavior. While initially this may seem frustrating to people who desire to understand and/or influence behavior in organizations, it is realistic in terms of the actual complexities. The alternative, attempting to understand organizational behavior in terms of unitary impacts, has always been doomed to failure.

See also Behavioral modeling; Discipline; Interpersonal relationships; Leadership; Theory X and theory Y; Work design, job enlargement, and job enrichment.

NOTES

[1]J. P. Campbell, M. D. Dunnette, E. E. Lawler, III, and K. E. Weick, Jr., *Managerial Behavior, Performance, and Effectiveness*, McGraw-Hill, New York, 1970, p. 341.

[2]L. L. Cummings and D. P. Schwab, *Performance in Organizations: Determinants and Appraisal*, Scott, Foresman, Glenview, Ill., 1973, pp. 22–23.

[3]A. H. Maslow, *Motivation and Personality*, 2d ed., Harper & Row, New York, 1970.

[4]F. Herzberg, B. Mausner, and B. B. Snyderman, *The Motivation to Work*, 2d ed., John Wiley, New York, 1959.

[5]For example, F. Herzberg, *Work and the Nature of Man*, World Book, Tarrytown-on-Hudson, N.Y., 1966.

[6]Interested readers will find summaries regarding the hierarchy of needs in J. P. Campbell and R. D. Pritchard, "Motivation Theory in Industrial and Organizational Psychology," in M. D. Dunnette (ed.), *Handbook of Industrial and Organizational Psychology*, Rand McNally, Skokie, Ill., 1976, pp. 97–100. Summaries regarding two-factor taxonomy will be found in E. A. Locke, "The Nature and Causes of Job Satisfaction," in M. D. Dunnette (ed.), op. cit., pp. 1309–1319, 1332–1333.

[7]R. V. Dawis, G. E. England, and D. J. Weiss, *A Theory of Work Adjustment: A Revision*, Minnesota Studies in Vocational Rehabilitation, Bulletin 47, Minneapolis, 1968.

[8]For example, M. D. Dunnette, J. P. Campbell, and M. D. Hakel, "Factors Contributing to Job Satisfaction and Job Dissatisfaction in Six Occupational Groups," *Organizational Behavior and Human Performance*, vol. 2, 1967, pp. 143–174.

[9]E. E. Lawler, III, *Pay and Organizational Effectiveness: A Psychological View*, McGraw-Hill, New York, 1971, pp. 37–59.

[10]For example, E. E. Lawler, III, and J. L. Suttle, "A Causal Correlational Test of the Need Hierarchy Concept," *Organizational Behavior and Human Performance*, vol. 7, 1972, pp. 265–287.

[11]E. L. Deci, *Intrinsic Motivation*, Plenum, New York, 1975.

[12]W. E. Scott, Jr., "The Effects of Extrinsic Rewards on 'Intrinsic Motivation:' A Critique," *Organizational Behavior and Human Performance*, vol. 15, 1976, pp. 117–129.

[13]Campbell and Pritchard, op. cit., p. 104.

[14]E. E. Lawler, III, *Motivation in Work Organizations*, Brooks/Cole, Monterey, Calif., 1973, p. 38.

[15]Dawis et al., op. cit.

[16]V. H. Vroom, *Work and Motivation*, John Wiley, New York, 1964.

[17]Campbell and Pritchard, op. cit., p. 74.

[18]Readers interested in the nuances of the theory are encour-

aged to read Vroom, op. cit., pp. 14–28, and Campbell and Pritchard, op. cit., pp. 74–84.

[19]Vroom, op. cit., pp. 196–204.

[20]For a review of studies on employee performance, see D. P. Schwab, J. D. Olian-Gottlieb, and H. G. Heneman III, "Between Subjects Expectancy Theory Research: A Statistical Review of Studies Predicting Effort and Performance," *Psychological Bulletin*, vol. 86, 1979, pp. 139–147. For a review of studies on job choice, see J. P. Wanous, T. L. Keon, and J. C. Latack, "Expectancy Theory and Occupational/Organizational Choices: A Review and Test," *Organizational Behavior and Human Performance*, vol. 32, 1983, pp. 66–86.

[21]This is not to suggest that low performers should be punished. Punishment does not generally influence behavior in a direction opposite to positive rewards and hence should not be thought of as falling on the opposite end of a continuum from positive rewards (e.g., Campbell and Pritchard, op. cit., p. 71).

[22]See, for example, A. Bandura, "Behavior Theory and the Models of Man," *American Psychologist*, vol. 29, 1974, pp. 859–869.

[23]See, for example, W. C. Hamner, "Reinforcement Theory and Contingency Management in Organizational Settings," in H. L. Tosi and W. C. Hamner (eds.), *Organizational Behavior and Management: A Contingency Approach*, St. Clair Press, Chicago, Ill., 1974, pp. 491–494.

[24]L. L. Cummings, "Reinforcement in Management: Principles and Cases," unpublished paper, Graduate School of Business, University of Wisconsin at Madison, 1976.

[25]This latter recommendation is the most tentative of the three because of the paucity of evidence from studies of human beings in work organizations.

[26]This literature has been reviewed by R. J. Aldag, S. H. Barr, and A. P. Brief, "Measurement of Perceived Task Characteristics," *Psychological Bulletin*, vol. 90, 1981, pp. 415–431.

[27]This analysis of task scope is based primarily on D. P. Schwab and L. L. Cummings, "A Theoretical Analysis of the Impact of Task Scope on Employee Performance," *Academy of Management Review*, vol. 1, no. 2, 1976, pp. 23–35.

[28]See W. F. Whyte, *Money and Motivation*, John Wiley, New York, 1955, pp. 20–27, 90–96.

[29]E. A. Locke, D. B. Feren, V. M. McCaleb, K. N. Shaw, and A. T. Denny, "The Relative Effectiveness of Four Methods of Motivating Employee Performance," in K. D. Duncan, M. M. Gruneberg, and D. Wallis (eds.), *Changes in Working Life*, John Wiley, New York, 1980, pp. 363–388.

[30]A. N. Nash and S. J. Carroll, Jr., *The Management of Compensation*, Brooks/Cole, Monterey, Calif., 1975, pp. 199–202.

[31]Lawler, 1971, op. cit., pp. 37–42.

[32]D. P. Schwab, "Impact of Alternative Compensation Systems on Pay Valence and Instrumentality Perceptions," *Journal of Applied Psychology*, vol. 58, 1973, pp. 308–312.

[33]See, for example, L. W. Porter and E. E. Lawler, III: *Managerial Attitudes and Performance*, Richard D. Irwin, Homewood, Ill., 1968; D. P. Schwab and L. D. Dyer, "The Motivational Impact of a Compensation System on Employee Performance," *Organizational Behavior and Human Performance*, vol. 9, 1973, pp. 215–225.

[34]Much of what follows is based on H. G. Heneman III and D. P. Schwab, "Work and Rewards Theory," in D. Yoder

and H. G. Heneman, Jr. (eds.), ASPA Handbook of Personnel and Industrial Relations, Bureau of National Affairs, Washington, D.C., 1979, vol. 6, pp. 1–22.

[35]Campbell et al. op. cit., 1970, pp. 51–54.

[36]S. J. Carroll, Jr., and H. L. Tosi, Jr., *Management by Objectives*, Macmillan, New York, 1976, pp. 1–16.

[37]R. M. Steers and L. W. Porter, "The Role of Task-Goal Attributes in Employee Performance," *Psychological Bulletin*, vol. 81, 1974, pp. 434–452.

DONALD P. SCHWAB, *University of Wisconsin, Madison*

Negotiating

Business requires two indispensable skills—managing people and making deals. Both involve *negotiation*, the process through which two or more parties arrive at a mutually acceptable resolution to a commonly recognized issue. Negotiating should be a means, not an end. Ideally, it is a mechanism to achieve goals and not a showcase for advancing ego. All participants to a negotiation should be satisfied on signing, committed during execution, and pleased on reflection. Solution sets that optimize nonconflicting objectives are always present in a negotiation and should be aggressively sought. Good negotiations enhance the reputation of all negotiators.

Negotiations Today

Negotiations in contemporary society affect all aspects of individual and collective life. Whether between members of a family, employees of a company, or nations of an alliance, negotiations are in constant session. No area of personal or organizational life is immune. Social and political environ-ments as well as economic ones are thick with overt postures and subtle cues of the negotiation process.

Getting the Edge. The popular press harangues us with predatory propaganda. If you're not a "gamesman," you're a pushover; if you don't "win through intimidation," you're a pansy; if you don't "look out for number one," you're a fool. Beating your customer, squashing your supplier, pinning your partner, squeezing your opponent are hailed as the apparent hallmarks of success, the pot of proverbial gold at the end of the crafty negotiator's rainbow.

Too many businesspeople pride themselves on besting their buddies; they must twist an advantage to feel successful; they must feel the turn of the screw to be content. You know the type. A fair price is never fair. Grinding never stops. Agreements are constantly changed; power plays never end. A done deal is altered on signing. Simple meaning is per-verted by complexity. Some of these characters like to intimidate; others prefer to hoodwink—the former want to see you squirm, the latter enjoy the painless slice. Priorities are always inverted, objectives pulled inside out, and goals flipped upside down.

An edge-getter is often vain, more turned on by the clever kill than by the extra meat. What counts is not the spending power of the bigger payoff but the puffing power of the smoother stroke. It's the edge itself that's sought, not the amount. Cutting a deal with a 1 percent nick is almost as gratifying as one with a 10 percent gouge. But whether the hit is 1 or 10 percent, the entire negotiations become more uncertain and closure less sure.

Riding the ego horse is fugitive and shortsighted. Today's quick buck may choke off a thousand tomorrow. Streams of dollars that could flow in the future are never seen. But what is not seen is not known; that is the irony. No negative reinforcement ever occurs; no long-term consequences of short-term actions are ever appreciated. The edge-getting negotiator struts blithely on his egotistical way, smug that he's played the perfect game won through intimidation, and looked after number one—whereas, in reality, he has flubbed the deal, lost the negotiation, and flattened number one. What happens here happens often. Commitment is attenuated and time is lost. Problems can erupt; days are wasted, deals lost, relationships ruptured, reputations ruined—all silly sacrifices on the altar of one-upmanship. Building the business takes a back seat when personal ego does the driving.

The "Good Deal." Being a sharp business person means being a sharp negotiator—someone who formulates, structures, and implements intercompany transactions and interpersonal arrangements with skill and finesse—someone who plans, organizes, and executes the interchange of products, services, and monetary considerations. Such an animal, it is assumed, lives in the marketplace jungle by wit and scheme—these being his claws and fangs—and only raw cunning can provide sufficient cover. Yet the best business people live by reputation, the evidence of their track records, the image of their integrity.

A "good deal," of course, does not necessarily require each party to play an equal role or even to make money. Natural power is distributed according to preexisting patterns. For example, a liquidator may buy end-of-season merchandise below cost; but, although the manufacturer loses money on this particular lot, unsalable inventory is being converted to ready cash, and if the manufacturer's overall costs have been covered, the transaction, in a real sense, produces pure profit.

Points of View

Negotiations have become a subject of both academic study and media interest. The behavioral sciences—from "game theory" to psychoanalysis—expand our understanding of why individuals think, feel, and act the way they do. "Decision theory," coming out of advanced business research, involves complex amalgams of logical analysis and computer simulations.

Appreciating the importance of "power" within organizations has greatly affected modern theory. Graham Allison, in *Essence of Decision* (about the Cuban missile crisis of 1962),[1] saw "bargaining games" and political jockeying among key advisers around President Kennedy and Premier Khrushchev as major determinants of the decision-making process. Power is the dominant motif in negotiations and the application to business is direct.

Recent years have seen several popular books on negotiation appear on board-room desks and bestseller charts. Their impact has been strong and warrants recognition. Examine the highlights of three; note that each promotes the benefits of a "win–win" attitude.

The Art of Negotiating. Gerard I. Nierenberg, an attorney, defines negotiations not as a game, but as a *cooperative enterprise,* and builds a "need theory" to optimize it. Successful negotiations recognize and fulfill *needs,* he writes, and all parties come out with some needs satisfied. Needs are understood within Abraham Maslow's well-known framework—physiological (homeostatic), safety and security, love and belonging, esteem, self-actualization, knowledge and understanding, aesthetic. Nierenberg articulates Maslow's general hierarchy of needs with the negotiator's specific orientation: A negotiator can choose to work for or against each level of her own needs, and for or against each level of her opponent's needs. Each approach may work under a given set of circumstances.[2]

You Can Negotiate Anything. Herb Cohen, a negotiation consultant, calls the world a "giant negotiating table." In every negotiation three crucial elements are involved: information (who knows more about the other?); time (which side is under greater deadline pressure?); and power (who has more authority and control?). *Power* is defined in terms of competition, legitimacy, risk-taking, commitment, expertise, knowledge of needs, investment, reward or punishment, identification, morality, precedence, persistence, persuasive capacity, and attitude. *Time* should be controlled, he writes; never reveal your deadlines, but be sure that the other side, no matter how serene outwardly, has deadlines of its own inwardly. Patience, in other words, pays. *Information* is the heart of the matter and all avenues of acquiring it should be explored (even "cues," whether unintentional, verbal, or behavioral).

Cohen defines the win–lose negotiation as "Soviet style," characterized by extreme initial positions, limited authority to make concessions, emotional tactics, adversary concessions viewed as weakness, stingy in concessions, and ignoring all deadlines. Negotiating for mutual satisfaction, on the other hand, stresses fulfilling needs of each party through harmonization and reconciliation. Win–win techniques involve building trust, gaining commitment, and managing opposition.[3]

Getting to Yes: Negotiating Agreement Without Giving In. Roger Fisher and William Ury, directors of the Negotiation Project at Harvard University, aver that the greatest detriment to successful negotiations is "positional bargaining," whereby each side locks itself into ever-hardening positions by constantly clarifying, supporting, and strengthening its original views. The authors advocate instead "principled negotiation" or "negotiation on the merits" and propose four basic elements: *people*—separate the people from the problem (deal with the former, not the latter); *interests*—focus on interests, not positions (seek compatible objectives hiding beneath conflicting ones); *options*—generate a variety of possibilities for mutual gain (brainstorm together to widen horizons before deciding what to do); *criteria*—insist that the result be based on some objective criteria (search for fair standards and procedures and use them collectively).[4]

Structure of Negotiation

Stages and mechanisms of negotiation are its structural foundations, the former more static, the latter more dynamic.

Stages. Any negotiation can be dissected into several independent stages, and although the boundaries between stages may be fuzzy, the critical issues indigenous to each are relatively constant.

Deciding. Too many people forget the preliminaries and lose the ball game before it begins. Determining *whether* and *what* to negotiate usually controls more of the outcome than all the strategies and tactics lumped together. What are your long-term goals and short-term objectives here? Verbalizing the "obvious" ahead of time often reveals things not so obvious.

Preparing. Doing your homework is essential. As much information as possible should be generated early on—and then boiled down before actual negotiations begin. (The problem in modern business is often too *many* data, not too few; the need is for data *reduction*, not data accumulation.) Specify superficial stances and discern underlying necessities, and think about dissociating the two. Get your hands on all numbers, public statements and reports, private opinions and interests. Treat your side and your opponent alike: do your self-analysis from your opponent's point of view.

Initiating. At the beginning of negotiations, postures and positions are established. Psychological structures are built in which the give-and-take will be conducted. Power plays of office design, seating arrangements, first proposals, and instant deadlines are well-known. They are often not effective and generate subliminal irritations more disruptive than useful. Professional negotiators establish people-rapport at the outset, articulating bottom-line needs of oppo-

nents with self-interests. Often such needs are not incompatible and win–win solution sets can be found. Establishing common ground is key.

Continuing. Persistence and patience are assets in any negotiations. Progress will never be linear, so don't expect it to be. Be satisfied to continue the process even if the direction appears temporarily to be wrong. Be aware of emotional ploys. Guilt trips, feints of precipitate disruption (or weakness), trumped-up issues—all are par for the long course. Overcoming frustration is an important orientation. Impasses can be surmounted by going back to first principles. Why are we here? What were our initial objectives? Sticking points are almost always the result of artificial ego hindrances (such as "face-saving" needs), not fundamental fact barriers. Novelty is an effective win–win tactic; try generating fresh sets of alternatives to overcome inertia, even in the middle of protracted negotiations.

Concluding. Have the sense to finalize when finished. Many deals have been ruptured after having been made because one side continued to press for advantages, which were invariably psychological, not substantive. What is your attitude on seeing your opponent achieve goals and fulfill needs? This is a marvelous test for the professional negotiator. If you feel genuine pleasure, you're well on your way.

Mechanisms. Attitudes and approaches to negotiating can be expressed by a series of spectra. Techniques vary, and properly so. In some situations, the "drip" is preferred, with one side letting out requirements little by little so as not to scare off the other side. In other situations, the "drop" is preferred, with the whole load being dumped at once.

Each of the following pairs of words reflects extremes of character. Most people, of course, function in between. The list is more descriptive than prescriptive. Though the first word may "sound" better, it is not always more effective or even more moral. Each situation determines its own truth. The word pairs are representational, not exhaustive: relaxed–nervous, calm–intense, patient–pressured, passive–active, recessive–dominant, objective–subjective, consistent–capricious, predictable–mercurial, rational–irrational, cooperative–competitive, guileless–manipulative, modest–conceited.

Strategies for Negotiation

The following general principles produce "positive negotiations," not self-importance. They help to produce a good deal and enhance the deal maker's perceived power among peers.

1. *Know what you want; don't worry what others get.* It's self-defeating to judge by comparison. Jealousy and envy are diversions and obstacles to successful business. With proper preparation

and self-confidence, a business person can segregate what he or she needs and wants from what others ask and get. For instance, if you sell your company at a price and at the terms you want, you should have no gripes if a friend sells her similar business for more.

2. *Understand the other side of the deal.* Project yourself into the place of those with whom you are negotiating. What are their real requirements, desires, and plans? What are they looking for here, what is their bottom line; and how important is it? Often, giving others what they want will not detract from what you want. If, say, the owner of a closely held firm wants to sell for retirement or estate-planning purposes, price can become secondary to terms and conditions. Such a person might well sell his business—his beloved baby—to a buyer offering a lower price if he believes that the new managers will take better care of his legacy (employees, products, reputation, customers, etc.).

3. *Seek win–win solutions.* Search for areas in which each side can achieve certain of its goals, desirably its primary goals, without adversely affecting the other. These optimal regions of "win–win" intersection can be surprisingly broad if one has the guts to seek them out and the insight to recognize them. When one structures negotiations with innovation and intelligence, "win–win" solutions emerge nicely. For example, the purchase price of an acquisition often can be allocated so that a greater percentage of the proceeds are taxed at lower rates for the seller without altering the cash requirements from the buyer. (In fact, the buyer can pay less and the seller receive more!)

4. *Be comprehensive in representation and conservative in projection.* Hype sometimes helps sell a first deal, but never a second. If all you have is one deal to make, have at it. But if you plan a career, not a caper, give heed. Hype always hinders subsequent negotiations. Exaggeration is a short-term, rapidly depleting asset and a long-term, quickly accruing liability. Don't be afraid to admit uncertainty about parts of your package—nothing can be that "perfect" and that "precise." Honesty enhances credibility and such admissions can be most disarming. Develop alternative scenarios: allow the other side choices; give room and keep options open. Use "sensitivity analysis" to show what might happen "if" various internal surprises or external shocks impact the proposed transaction (such as sales up or down 10 percent, 20 percent, 30 percent; gross-margin problems; escalating interest rates). Always make a conservative forecast of your most likely result; strive to exceed a somewhat pessimistic projection rather than to fall behind a somewhat optimistic one. Also, use sensitivity analysis to test the other side's options. Is the other side really at the wall or can it move a bit further?

5. *Address questions nobody has asked.* Few plays are more impressive than when one side brings up sensitive facets of its own proposition that the other side has not considered. In negotiating bank financing, for example, a company should enumerate all assumptions in its proposal, pointing precisely to areas of difficulty or ambiguity. The honesty shown—especially if the bank hadn't considered the point—will be potent. Problems should be exposed by design rather than hidden by default.

6. *Be frank but be fair.* Don't look to gain the upper hand—but don't appear to be a doormat either. Let others realize that you know the game, the rules, and the players. Being fair does not mean being weak. (Weakness, in fact, encourages disruption by tempting the other side to expand its position.) Some of the toughest business people are also some of the fairest. If you decide to buy from a certain supplier even though her price is not the lowest, be sure she knows that you know the score.

7. *Act as if the other side will become your public relations agents.* Act this way because it *will.* No matter how confidential the negotiations, no matter how secret the deal, other people will hear about it. Regardless of how you envision yourself, what circulates is how others see you. Above all, never boast about besting someone. A manager's reputation is his or her most valuable asset.

So it all comes down to this: what's your thing—getting the edge or building your business or career? You should always consider that when negotiating, you can "win" and still lose.

See also Arbitration, commercial; Arbitration, labor; Assertiveness training; Competition; Ethics, managerial; Interpersonal relationships; Labor-management relations; Motivation in organizations; Power and influence; Transactional analysis.

NOTES

[1]Graham T. Allison, *Essence of Decision*, Little, Brown, Boston, 1971.

[2]Gerard I. Nierenberg, *The Art of Negotiating*, Dutton, New York, 1968.

[3]Herb Cohen, *You Can Negotiate Anything*, Lyle Stuart, New York, 1980.

[4]Roger Fisher and William Ury, *Getting to Yes*, Houghton Mifflin, Boston, Mass., 1981.

ROBERT LAWRENCE KUHN, *University of Texas and New York University*

Network Planning Methods

Network planning methods are a family of techniques specifically developed to aid in the management of projects. For the purpose of definition, a *project* is a combination of interrelated activities that must be performed in a prescribed order to reach a specified goal. Some activities cannot start until others are completed. Activities require time and resources for completion. A due date may be prescribed for completion of the project.

Prior to recent developments, project planning and scheduling were accomplished using a method such as the Gantt bar chart, which specifies the start and finish times for each activity along a horizontal time scale. The Gantt chart is not suitable for use in planning large, complex projects, where there are numerous interdependencies between the activities and where time-cost trade-offs need to be investigated.

Network methods, on the other hand, are uniquely suitable for use in planning and scheduling projects. These methods construct arrow diagrams (or a network) representing the individual activities required to proceed from an initial event to an ultimate objective. The network shows all the interdependencies that exist among the individual activities. In modern management applications, a computer is utilized to assemble and sort the information on the precedence of activities, times, and costs, to provide scheduled completion times and earliest and latest start dates of each activity, with associated time-oriented costs.

Usefulness. Network planning methods evolved as a management tool with the development of the critical path method (CPM) and the program evaluation and review technique (PERT). Both methods are time-oriented network planning methods; in CPM, activity durations are assumed to be known, and in PERT, activity durations are given by probability distributions.

CPM is useful in obtaining trade-offs between cost and completion dates. In this case a relationship is established between additional resources (such as labor, equipment, and facilities) to reduce the durations of activities and the increased costs of these resources. PERT is useful in planning projects where uncertainty is the underlying factor, such as in the case of R&D projects.

Network planning methods are useful at all levels of management:

1. At the first level of supervision, network planning methods are useful for identifying the need for the project and the "how or where" to sequence the project better and thereby reduce times and/or costs.

2. At the middle management level, network planning methods serve as a planning tool in formulating and integrating the activities of a project. The middle manager is able to determine whether or not a project can be completed within specified time and cost schedules.

3. At the top management level, network planning methods are a control device providing for status reporting and progress evaluation. The updated network and periodic status reports provide a continual comparison of expected or required performance with actual or predicted performance. Project time-cost problems are highlighted and may be ranked in order of importance in achieving overall program objectives.

The networking approach provides management with information which answers many of the questions occurring during the life of a project, such as:

How long the project will take and what it will cost

When parts and materials are needed

Where a project should be expedited to save money

Where overtime should and should not be used

How much equipment (by type) is needed and when

How far a subcontractor or material delivery can slip

How to maintain a level work force

The effect on schedule of late design changes

When funds will be required to pay subcontractors

Properly used, the networking approach provides advantages and benefits to management which may be summed up as follows:

1. Provides an integrated "big picture" of project management.

2. Forces a more logical and analytical approach to planning projects.

3. Guards against not considering important activities.

4. Facilitates coordination between prime contractors and subcontractors.

5. Permits analyzing the effects of changes and slippages on schedules.

6. Simplifies replanning and rescheduling.

7. Provides a means for project cost control.

8. Provides a means for compressing schedules to meet deadlines and to reduce total cost.

9. Provides a means to estimate cash flow requirements.

Applications. A variety of project types may use either CPM or PERT. The following are examples of applications: (1) space vehicle construction and launching, (2) building or highway construction, (3) oil refinery turnaround and maintenance, (4) computer system installation and data center operations, (5) new product introduction, (6) monthly, quarterly, and annual closing of accounting records, (7) broadway show opening, (8) electric generator manufacture and assembly, (9) contract bid preparation and submission, (10) medical patient examination and treatment, and (11) ship repair.

Basic Definitions

In project management, network planning emphasizes the scheduled completion time and resource allocation. Project management is concerned with the basic managerial tasks of planning, scheduling, and controlling.

The planning phase is initiated by breaking down the project into the distinct activities. Resources requirements in the form of labor, materials, equipment, and facilities are estimated. The time estimates for these activities are then determined and a network (or arrow) diagram is constructed with each of its arcs (arrows) representing an activity. The entire network diagram gives a graphic representation of the interdependencies between the activities of the project. The construction of the network diagram at a planning phase has the advantage of analyzing the different activities in detail, perhaps suggesting improvements before the project is actually executed. Following the estimation of activity durations, costs are specified.

The ultimate objective of the scheduling phase is to determine the required start and finish times for each activity, as well as its relationship to other activities in the project, in order to achieve the project's anticipated completion date. In addition, the schedule must pinpoint the critical activities which require special attention if the project is to be completed on time. For the noncritical activities, the schedule must show the amount of slack (or float) times which can be used advantageously when such activities are delayed or when limited resources are to be used effectively.

The final phase in project management is project control. This includes the use of the network diagram and the time chart for making periodic progress reports. The difference between the scheduled and actual performance of each activity is reviewed. The network may thus be updated and analyzed and, if necessary, a new schedule may be determined for the remaining portion of the project.

Activities. An *activity* is any portion of a project which consumes time and resources and has a specific starting and ending point. It is the work necessary to progress from one point in time to another point in time. Activities consume time, money, human energy, facilities, equipment, and/or materials. Examples of activities may be tasks involved in office paperwork, processing plant machine operations, new highway construction, and corporate contractual negotiations. For each activity, the predecessor or successor activities must also be specified. Graphically, an activity may be represented by an arrow with the descriptions and time estimates written alongside the arrow. The representation of an activity is as follows:

$$\xrightarrow{\text{Drill 2-inch diameter holes}} \atop 12 \text{ minutes}$$

Events. An *event* denotes either the beginning or the completion of an activity or a group of activities, and it occurs at a discrete point in time. Events do not consume time or resources and are normally represented by a numbered circle. The beginning and end points of an activity are described by two events. Synonymous with the term *events* are the terms *nodes* and *connectors*.

An event is represented by a single number such as (1). An activity is represented by a pair of numbers such as (1,2). The direction of progress in each activity is specified by assigning a smaller number to the initiating event compared with the number of its ending event. The beginning and end points of an activity are described by two events.

Dummy Activities. In many projects, such as in chemical processing, an activity cannot be undertaken unless the product of the preceding activity is available. Therefore, *dummy* activities are needed to represent the logical dependencies of the network. In the network these are generally represented by broken (dashed) lines. In effect, the line indicates an activity where no real work is represented, but rather a dependency relationship in the form of a *zero time* activity.

The following are examples of situations where dummy activities are required:

In a steel mill ingots cannot be sent to the rod mill before being sent into a 12- or 8-inch rolling mill.

In building construction involving concrete plastering, the plastering cannot start before the poured concrete is set.

In automobile assembly-line production, the carburetor cannot be adjusted before the engine is installed.

In the example shown in Fig. N-1a, activities A and B have the same end events. The procedure is to introduce a dummy activity either between A and one of the end events or between B and one of the end events. The modified representations, after introducing dummy D, are shown in Fig. N-1b. As a result of

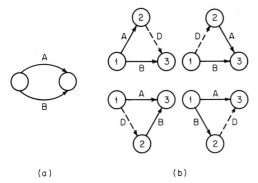

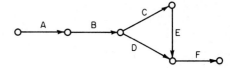

FIG. N-2 Elementary diagramming.

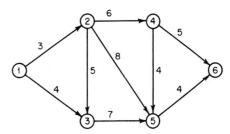

FIG. N-3 Diagram with six events and nine activities.

FIG. N-1 Dummy activities: (a) activities with the same end events; (b) modified representations.

using D, activities A and B can now be identified by unique end events. It must be noted that a dummy activity does not consume time or resources.

Network Construction

A graphic representation of the project plan, showing the interrelationships of various activities and associated times, is called a *network*. The time phase plan for accomplishing the activities in the network is called a *project schedule.*

To plan a project means to identify the component activities necessary for the performance and to determine and express the logical order in which they will be carried out. This requires a thorough knowledge of the particular project concerned, a systematic procedure which may be followed in expressing any project as a network. The activities should be listed in the approximate order of their performance and referred to by the labels A, B, C, etc. The logical sequence should be expressed in a table as follows:

Activity	Depends on (or is preceded by)
A	—
B	A
C	B
D	B
E	C
F	D,E

The network may be drawn in the manner shown in Fig. N-2.

Another example of a network is shown in Fig. N-3. There are six events: (1), (2), (3), (4), (5), and (6). The reader should identify the nine activities and the associated pairs of numbers: (1,2), (1,3), (2,3), (2,4), (2,5), (3,5), (4,5), (4,6), and (5,6). The time for each activity is indicated above the activity.

In the planning stage, while depicting the various interrelationships between the activities, the net-

work will also reveal the factors which affect the timing of the accomplishment of any given activity or group of activities and the consequent effects on the project schedule. Networks are used for planning, plan integration, completion time and analysis, and scheduling and resource analysis.

Time-Scaled Networks. A network may be represented in a time-scaled diagram, as shown in Fig. N-4. On a time scale the dashed arrows represent a slack. For example, both activities A and B must be completed prior to the initiation of C.

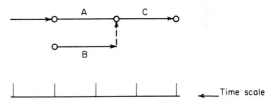

FIG. N-4 Time-scaled network.

Critical Path Method (CPM)

In planning the project, it has been indicated that it is necessary to identify the associated activities, events, and activity times. Key management questions are: (1) How long will the project take? (2) When may activities be scheduled? An important consideration in planning is the minimum time required to complete the project. It is necessary to find the longest path, or sequence of connected activities through the network, which is identified as the *critical path* in that it determines the duration of the project. The cumulative times of the activities along the critical path yield the length, or project duration.

As an example, consider the network in Fig. N-5, **599**

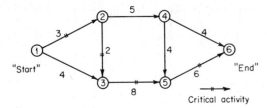

FIG. N-5 CPM diagram construction.

in which the work to be done is indicated by the direction of the arrows and the time to perform each activity is indicated above the arrow. The problem is to find the (critical) activities on the critical path.

The possible sequences from starting event (1) to terminal event (6) are given by:

Path Sequence	Path Length
(a)$1 - 2 - 4 - 6$	$3 + 5 + 4 = 12$
(b)$1 - 2 - 4 - 5 - 6$	$3 + 5 + 4 + 6 = 18$
(c)$1 - 2 - 3 - 5 - 6$	$3 + 2 + 8 + 6 = 19$ (maximum)
(d)$1 - 3 - 5 - 6$	$4 + 8 + 6 = 18$

The critical path is given by path (c), and the length of the critical path is 19. In the calculations below, the results are systematized as a sequence of similar steps.

Determination of the Critical Path. A critical path defines a sequence of critical activities which connect the start and end events. The critical path identifies all the critical activities of the project. The method of determining such a path is illustrated by the example in Fig. N-6, which starts at node 1 and terminates at node 6. The time required to perform each activity is indicated on the arrows.

The critical path calculations include two phases. The first phase is called the *forward pass* where calculations begin from the start node and move to the

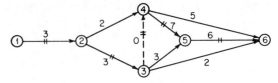

FIG. N-6 Critical path determination.

end node. At each node a number is computed representing the earliest occurrence time of the corresponding event *(ES)*. The second phase, called the *backward pass,* begins calculations from the end node and moves to the start node, representing the latest occurrence time of the corresponding event *(LC)*. After the forward and backward pass computations are completed, the float (free float and total float) can be computed for each activity, the critical path determined, and the individual activity schedules determined.

The critical path calculations, together with the floats for the noncritical activities, are summarized in Table N-1. The table gives a typical summary of the critical path calculations. It includes all the information necessary to construct the time chart. Notice that a critical activity—and only a critical activity—must have zero total float. The free float must also be zero when the total float is zero. The converse is not true, however, in the sense that a *noncritical* activity may have zero free float. Table N-1 shows that the total float is the same as the free float. This is accidental, since all the events of the project happen to be on the critical path. In general, this will not be true.

The positive values in the float columns of Table N-1 indicate the amount of time that the corresponding activity may be extended without affecting the duration of the project. For example, activity (4,6) may be extended from 5 to 13 without delaying the project, and the resources available for use in activity (4,6) may be partially utilized elsewhere.

TABLE N-1 Critical Path Calculations

		Earliest		Latest			
Activity (i,j) (1)	Duration D_{ij} (2)	Start ES_i (3)	Completion EC_{ij} (4)	Start LS_{ij} (5)	Completion LC_j (6)	Total float TF_{ij} (7)	Free float FF_{ij} (8)
(1,2)	3	0	3	0	3	0*	0
(2,3)	3	3	6	3	6	0*	0
(2,4)	2	3	5	4	6	1	1
(3,4)	0	6	6	6	6	0*	0
(3,5)	3	6	9	10	13	4	4
(3,6)	2	6	8	17	19	11	11
(4,5)	7	6	13	6	13	0*	0
(4,6)	5	6	11	14	19	8	8
(5,6)	6	13	19	13	19	0*	0

*Critical activity.

Program Evaluation and Review Technique (PERT)

Previously known as Polaris evaluation review technique, PERT was developed in 1958 to assist the U.S. Navy in development and production of the Polaris missile system. Since the existing facilities for integrated planning and control were not suitable for this assignment, Admiral W. F. Raborn sought the help of Lockheed Aircraft Corporation, the Navy Special Projects Office, and the consulting firm of Booz, Allen and Hamilton. This team evolved the PERT system from the consideration of techniques such as line of balance, Gantt charting, and "milestone reporting systems."

PERT involves considerations of duration times of activities which are subject to considerable variation. PERT provides the means to deal with these variations, making it possible to allow for choices in scheduling activities. PERT is used as a basis for determining the probability that the project, or key milestones in the project, will be completed on or before scheduled date(s).

The sources of uncertainty in activity completion times may stem from uncertainties in personnel (absenteeism, vacations, strikes), equipment (breakdown, acquisitions), facilities (delays in installation), materials (supplier delay), utilities (energy shortages, power breakdowns), and environmental conditions (temperature, snow, climatic conditions).

PERT uses probability theory in developing schedules to meet managerial objectives Although the activities are specified, there is uncertainty in activity times. In the PERT system, three time estimates are obtained for each activity:

a = the optimistic time, which will be required if execution goes extremely well.

b = the pessimistic time, which will be required if everything goes badly.

m = the most likely time, which will be required if execution is as expected.

The person most qualified to know, such as an engineer, a supervisor, or a worker, is requested to provide the estimates. The pessimistic estimate is based on the worst situation which may be encountered, where usual conditions are not likely to prevail. The optimistic estimate is based on the best possible situation, where everything goes right.

The range of times given by $(b - a)$ provides an indication of the degree of uncertainty associated with the time to perform an activity. The analyst is interested in deriving the probability distributions for the activity and project completion times. It is not possible to specify a definite time for the completion of a project; however, it is possible to state the probability of completing the project on or before a scheduled date. Utilizing the information on cost of not

meeting a scheduled due date and the cost of expediting the project, managers are able to develop sound plans at the start of a project and to control the project once it is under way.

The expressions for the mean $\overline{D}$ and variance V are

$$\overline{D} = \frac{a + 4m + b}{6} \quad \text{and} \quad V = \left(\frac{b - a}{6}\right)^2$$

The network calculations given in CPM can now be applied directly, with $\overline{D}$ replacing the single estimate D.

It is possible now to estimate the probability of occurrence of each event in the network. Let μ_i be the earliest occurrence time of event i. Since the times of the activities completed prior to i are random variables, μ_i is also a random variable. Let us assume that all the activities in the network are statistically independent; then we obtain the mean and variance of μ_i as follows. If there is only one path leading from the "start" event to event i, $E\{\mu_i\}$ is given by the sum of the expected durations $\overline{D}$ for the activities along this path, and var $\{\mu_i\}$ is the sum of the variances of the same activities. Complications arise, however, where more than one path leads to the same event. In this case, if the exact $E\{\mu_i\}$ and var$\{\mu_i\}$ are to be computed, we must first develop the statistical distribution for the longest of the different paths (that is, the distribution of the maximum of several random variables) and then find its expected value and its variance. This is rather difficult in general, and a simplifying assumption is introduced which estimates $\{\mu_i\}$ and var$\{\mu_i\}$ as equal to those of the path leading to event i and having the largest sum of expected activity durations. If two or more paths have the same $E\{\mu_i\}$, the one with the largest var$\{\theta_i\}$ is selected since it reflects greater uncertainty and hence more conservative results. To summarize, $E\{\mu_i\}$ and var$\{\mu_i\}$ are given for the selected path by

$$E\{\mu_i\} = \sum_k \overline{D}_k$$

$$\text{Var}\{\mu_i\} = \sum_k V_k$$

where k defines the activities along the longest path leading to i.

As μ_i is the sum of independent random variables, according to the central limit theorem, μ_i is approximately normally distributed with a mean $E\{\mu_i\}$ and variance var$\{\mu_i\}$. Since μ_i represents the earliest occurrence time, event i will meet a certain schedule time ST_i, specified by management with probability

$$P\{\mu_i \leq ST_i\} = P\left\{\frac{\mu_i - E\{\mu_i\}}{\sqrt{\text{var}\{\mu_i\}}} \leq \frac{ST_i - E\{\mu_i\}}{\sqrt{\text{var}\{\mu_i\}}}\right\}$$

$$= P\{z \leq K_i\}$$

601

where z is the standard normal distribution with mean zero and variance unity and

$$K_i = \frac{ST_i - E\{\mu_i\}}{\sqrt{\text{var}\{\mu_i\}}}$$

It is common practice to compute the probability that event i will occur no later than its LC_i. Such probabilities will thus represent the chance that the succeeding events will occur within the $(ES_i,\ LC_i)$ duration.

A PERT Example. Consider the project of the example given in Fig. N-6. To avoid repeating the critical path calculations, the values of a, b, and m shown are selected such that $\overline{D}_{ij}$ will have the same value as its correponding D_{ij} in the example in Fig. N-6. The mean $\overline{D}_{ij}$ and variance V_{ij} for the different activities are computed as shown in Table N-2.

The probabilities are given in Table N-3. The information in the St_i column is part of the input data.

PERT Simulations: Alternative Near-Critical Paths. The estimate of completion time of a project, using the times along the critical path, may not be a valid estimate of the project duration. A noncritical path may become critical if it has a higher variance than the "original" critical path. Accordingly, it would be desirable to investigate alternative near-critical paths. In these cases, estimates based on a single path may seriously underestimate the actual completion time up to 20 percent.

Computer simulation is an excellent method for finding the expected completion time as well as the frequency distribution of completion times. In this case, activity times are randomly selected for each activity from the corresponding frequency distribution. The project path length and duration and critical path are then calculated in the usual (CPM) way. The procedure is repeated several thousand times, using a computer program, and a record is kept of each run. An average project length and standard deviation are calculated on the basis of the simulation. The resulting simulation estimates are more reliable than the overly optimistic estimates produced by the standard (PERT) procedure, since the near-critical paths are considered in the simulation.

The simulation also provides a critical index for each activity. The critical index of an activity is the proportion of simulation runs in which the activity is critical. Although an activity may not be on the usual CPM critical path, it may have a critical index of, say, 0.5, indicating that 50 percent of the time it may be expected to be critical and therefore warrants managerial review. The simulation would also provide a probability estimation of slack values for each activity, again providing additional useful information for managerial review purposes.

Time-Cost Trade-offs

Although PERT is able to schedule projects which allow for variations in activity times as a result of unpredictable situations, it is desirable to consider alternative project schedules which result from the planned use of resources at different levels. Activity times may be reduced if additional resources such as labor, machines, and money are allocated.

There may be increased costs associated with the *crashed* activities, which may result in a project being completed earlier, particularly in the case of critical activities. However, if the activity is not critical and has slack (or total free float), the activity should be accomplished at the most efficient rate, say in the normal time. Accordingly, only the critical activities need to be expedited, and in these cases, only those where the returns justify the additional expenditures.

TABLE N-2 PERT Example, Estimated Times

Activity (i,j)	Estimated times (a,b,m)	Activity (i,j)	Estimated times (a,b,m)
(1,2)	(2,8,2)	(3,6)	(1,3,2)
(2,3)	(1,11,1.5)	(4,5)	(6,8,7)
(2,4)	(0.5,7.5,1)	(4,6)	(3,11,4)
(3,5)	(1,7,2.5)	(5,6)	(4,8,6)

Activity	$\overline{D}_{ij}$	V_{ij}	Activity	$\overline{D}_{ij}$	V_{ij}
(1,2)	3	1.00	(3,6)	2	0.11
(2,3)	3	2.78	(4,5)	7	0.11
(2,4)	2	1.36	(4,6)	5	1.78
(3,5)	3	1.00	(5,6)	6	0.44

TABLE N-3 Probabilities

Event	Path	$E\{\mu_i\}$	$\text{Var}\{\mu_i\}$	ST_i	K_i	$P\{z \le K_i\}$
1						
2	(1,2)	3	1.00	2	-1.000	0.159
3	(1,2,3,)	6	3.80	5	-0.512	0.304
4	(1,2,3,4)	6	3.80	6	0.000	0.500
5	(1,2,3,4,5)	13	3.91	17	2.020	0.978
6	(1,2,3,4,5,6)	19	4.35	20	0.480	0.584

The essential questions raised in time-cost trade-offs for project scheduling are the following:

1. What is the optimal project duration and schedule?
2. Which activities should be expedited?
3. Of these activities to be expedited, what are their optimal completion times?

Time-Cost Relationships. Project cost is composed of both direct and indirect costs. The direct costs are those associated with the individual activities, usually for elements such as labor, machine operation, and leased facilities. In addition, a project will have indirect costs such as managerial services, equipment rentals, and allocation of fixed expenses, which are affected adversely by the duration of the project. A project's contractor or customer may specify a due date, and delays beyond this date result in additional nonrecoverable costs to the project manager. For example, Lockheed's contract for the C-5A contained a $12,000-per-day late penalty clause, and General Dynamics received $800,000 for flying the F-111 10 days ahead of schedule.

Project schedules may influence two kinds of cost: direct costs associated with individual activities, which *increase* if the activities are expedited, and indirect costs associated with the project, which *decrease* if the project is shortened.

Project Control: Reviewing and Updating the Network Diagram. The network diagram should not be discarded when the time schedule is developed. In fact, an important use of the network diagram occurs during the execution phase of the project. It seldom happens that the planning phase will develop a time schedule that can be followed exactly during the execution phase. Quite often some of the activities are delayed or expedited. This naturally depends on actual work conditions. As soon as such disturbances occur in the original plan, it becomes necessary to develop a new time schedule for the remaining portion of the project.

It is important to follow the progress of the project using the network diagram rather than the time schedule alone. The time schedule is used mainly to check whether each activity is on time. The effect of a delay in a certain activity on the remaining portion of the project can best be traced on the network diagram.

Suppose that as the project progresses over time, it is discovered that delays in some activities necessitate developing a completely new schedule. How can this be effected using the present network diagram? The immediate requirement is to update the network diagram by assigning zero values to the durations of the completed activities. Partially completed activities are assigned times equivalent to their unfinished portions. Changes in the network diagram such as addition or deletion of any future activities must also be made. By repeating the usual computations on the network diagram with its new time elements, one can determine the new time schedule and possible changes in the duration of the project. Such information is used until it is necessary to update the time schedule further. In real situations, many revisions of the time schedule are usually required at the early stages of the execution phase. A stable period then follows in which little revision of the current schedule is required.

PERT/COST: A Network Costing Method

As described above, both PERT and CMP are time-oriented methods, which estimate the time required to complete a project. As scheduling techniques they provide a means of establishing time schedules for project activity. As control methods they allow managers to check scheduled time against actual times for activity durations or event occurrences. In CPM, a cost-time trade-off is considered, where costs are considered as a means of finding optimal activity times. No provision is made for compiling activity costs, either for predicting or control purposes. Thus the output of CPM models are optimal activity times (durations), generally associated with early or late start schedules.

PERT/COST is a general method for controlling the costs of projects. The basic concept of the PERT and CPM cost systems is simple but importantly different from activities; they should be divided into a sequence of two or more subactivities, each of which has a relatively constant expenditure rate. Then the cost per period of an activity may be approximated by dividing its total cost by its duration in periods. A project cost schedule is then prepared by adding all activity costs, period by period, according to the activity time schedule.

The PERT/COST method utilizes the CPM calculations for early and late start schedules. A month-by-month summary of cost requirements is calculated for both early and late start schedules. A schedule graph, in which the network is plotted on a time scale and in which the horizontal length and placement of activity arrows indicate activity duration and schedule, facilitates cost calculation.

When plotted as in Fig. N-7, the cumulative cost figures illustrate graphically the budget implications of the early and late start schedules. The area between the two curves represents a range of budgets which are feasible from a technological viewpoint. For budgetary or other reasons, it may be preferable to follow a relatively straight line of cumulative cost from start to finish. As long as this lies in the feasible region, it may be approximately achieved by juggling the scheduled starts of activities between their early and late start times.

The basic idea of the PERT/COST system is to measure and control costs in terms of the same enti-

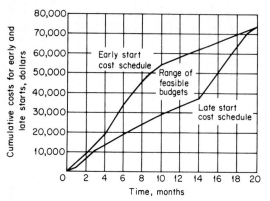

FIG. N-7 PERT/COST budget projections.

REFERENCES

Davidson, I. R.: "PERT—A Computer Simulation Approach," *Accountancy*, February 1982, pp. 93–104.

DOD and NASA Guide, PERT COST Systems Design, Secretary of Defense and National Aeronautics and Space Administration, Washington, D.C., June 1962.

Moder, J. J., and C. R. Phillips: *Project Management with CPM and PERT*, Reinhold, New York, 1970.

Phillips, Don T., and Alberto G. Diaz: *Fundamentals of Network Analysis*, Prentice-Hall, Englewood Cliffs, N.J., 1981.

Tanset, B. C., et al.: "Location on Networks: A Survey," *Management Science*, April 1983, vol. 29, pp. 482–541.

Wiest, J. D., and F. K. Levy: *A Management Guide to PERT/ CPM*, 2d ed., Prentice-Hall, Englewood Cliffs, N.J., 1977.

BURTON V. DEAN, *Case Western Reserve University*

ties of the project as are used for planning and scheduling purposes; that is, the activities. Actually, if a project has been broken down into activities small enough to be used for purposes of detailed planning and scheduling, many such activities will be too small to be used conveniently for cost control purposes. If so, several related activities may be grouped together into large *work packages*, which represent particular units of work for which responsibility can clearly be defined and which are still small enough to be manageable for planning and control purposes.

Applications. For planning and budgeting purposes, it is useful for a manager to know what the time pattern of expenditures will be for a project. If costs are estimated for each activity or work package, a projection of costs can easily be made, based upon an early start or a late start schedule or, for that matter, any other feasible schedule. To do this, the assumption is usually made that expenditures for an activity are incurred at a constant rate over the duration of the activity.

Project priority can also be viewed from a slightly different angle: How much is it going to cost if this project is not completed on time? How much can be saved or gained if it is completed ahead of time? The answers to these questions are crucial in the many areas of business where work projects are negotiated under bonus-penalty agreements.

Budget restrictions frequently limit the amount of expenditure or the amount of certain critical resources in any one period; if workers, materials, machinery, and resource constraints are such that even the late start cost schedule cannot be met, the finish date must be delayed. Once a schedule has been found which is feasible in terms of both technology and resource availabilities, however, a cost schedule may be calculated and plotted as above. A computer may be used to advantage for large projects.

See also Control systems, management; Engineering management; Gantt charts; Line of balance (LOB); Production planning and control; Project management.

Nominal Group Technique

Nominal Group Technique (NGT) is a formal, highly structured group decision-making process characterized by a face-to-face, yet largely noninteractive, group structure. The technique was developed to overcome the tendencies of some interactive groups to inhibit idea generation and limit decision quality. The technique will generally yield more ideas than brainstorming, while retaining many of the group participation benefits of the brainstorming technique.

Typical Procedure. NGT proceeds through either four or six steps, depending on the degree of precision that is desired in the final decision. Typically, the steps provide a highly structured format:

1. *Silent generation of ideas, in writing.* In this step, the group meets in a face-to-face setting. The problem or question to be addressed is presented to the group, and all individuals in the group silently and independently write down their ideas or thoughts on the problem or question.

2. *Recording of ideas.* A leader solicits one idea from one member at a time. All ideas are written down and displayed to the entire group. This step continues until all the ideas of all members are recorded and displayed. During the recording of ideas there is no discussion of the ideas; they are simply stated and recorded without comment.

3. *Group discussion for clarification.* The group then discusses each idea in turn, with the time for discussion divided equally among the ideas recorded. The focus of this discussion is on clarification of meaning, not on argumentation. In the discussion, a member may reveal the logic or analysis behind an item, while others may express their agreement or disagreement with the item. However, since all items must receive attention, such discussion is limited.

4. *Preliminary vote.* Each member selects individually the five, six, seven, eight, or nine most important items from the list. The number selected will depend on the length of the original list. Each member is asked to rank-order the items selected silently. The separate rank orderings are aggregated, and a mean rank is calculated for each item. This pooling technique yields an aggregate rank order of the items.

Many, if not most, NGT meetings would end with step 4. However, if additional precision and consensus are desired, two additional steps can be added.

5. *Discussion of preliminary vote.* In this step, items which the group felt received too few or too many votes can be discussed again. Widely split voting patterns may also be examined at this time.

6. *Final vote.* This step repeats and finalizes step 4.

Advantages. Many advantages may be derived from NGT:

- High-status or power people cannot dominate because item generation is individual and voting is anonymous. The result is equality of participation among group members.

- Silent generation of items results in a higher quantity of ideas, as opposed to the number generated in an openly interactive group.

- The meeting produces a tangible product; that is, a list of items rank ordered in terms of importance. Consequently, there is a high degree of closure and feeling of accomplishment on the part of the group members.

- NGT yields a consistency of output across groups because the structure of the technique eliminates variations in leader and group behavior.

Disadvantages. There are, however, several drawbacks to the NGT process:

- The technique requires advance preparation to identify the question to be addressed and to have materials available. NGT cannot be used on the spur of the moment at any group meeting.

- Usually only one topic can be addressed at a meeting.

- Some group members may be unwilling to conform to the tight structure of the meeting.

- The technique can be time-consuming; a typical meeting will last about 2 hours. In situations that call for a quick decision, NGT is not effective.

Applications. NGT is an appropriate technique to use in complex situations in which the ideas or judgments of a number of people need to be aggregated or pooled; for example, for establishing priorities, either in deciding in what order to undertake a set of actions or in deciding on areas of concentration. Fact-finding, or problem-finding, meetings are also prime candidates for NGT. In these instances, many people may have different views on the nature of the problem, and NGT becomes a useful tool to elicit those views.

See also Conference leadership; Conferences and meetings, planning for.

REFERENCES

Burton, G., D. Pathak, and D. Burton: "The Gordon Effect in Nominal Grouping," *University of Michigan Business Review*, vol. 30, Dec. 1978, pp. 7–10.

Delbecq, A. L., A. H. Van de Ven, and D. H. Gustafson: *Group Techniques for Program Planning*, Scott, Foresman, Glenview, Ill., 1975.

D. KENT ZIMMERMAN, *James Madison University.*

Nonprofit Organizations, Management of

The overall quality of life in the United States today depends on the collective human services provided by its more than 800,000 nonprofit organizations, of which more than 350,000 are also philanthropic. From hospitals to humane societies, symphony orchestras to environmental groups, nonprofit, voluntary action organizations provide the overall spice of American life. Never before have these organizations been so severely challenged to meet society's expectations and demands for human services, which now stretch from prenatal to postdeath. Only through better, more effective management can nonprofit organizations hope to meet these challenges successfully.

Better management of human service, nonprofit organizations (NPO) is the management issue of the so-called *third sector* (the other two sectors of the economy being business and government). Individual problems cited across the country are symptoms of the overall, sectorwide need for more effective management. For example, a human service organization may call in a consultant to ask about fund raising when the real problem may be a need for better financial management or long-range strategic planning.

A Growing Professionalism. Major strides in achieving more effective management for nonprofits will be made only through the efforts of more knowledgeable, professional managers—whether salaried staff or dedicated volunteers. Although there is a growing body of NPO management knowledge, there is currently a significant, overall lack of professional-caliber NPO management education and training. While there are seminars in abundance, few colleges offer NPO management courses, and fewer still do so as a coordinated group of courses leading to a specific NPO management degree program.

Until recently, few agreed or were aware of the fact that nonprofit organizations in general, regardless of the type of public service they provide, share certain basic management commonalties. At least seven management areas, however, are held in common by all nonprofit organizations, including:

- Leadership, management, and control
- Human resources management
- Revenue and support generation
- Financial management
- Public relations, marketing, and communication
- Organization and corporate principles
- Legal and regulatory matters affecting voluntary action organizations

Management thinking about the third sector appears to be moving away from a strict vertical—or category-specific—view of the nonprofit sector. Many authorities no longer feel comfortable in describing as separate disciplines such areas as ''arts management,'' ''hospital administration,'' or ''association management.'' Of course, major differences do exist in some areas between these categorizations in terms of the public services they provide. In management terms, however, they share much more than they differ; and the differences are primarily of degree rather than of basic principles.

What is emerging is an awareness of a ''horizontal view'' of management in the nonprofit sector. This consists of a concurrence that nonprofits share at least seven areas of management (itemized earlier), and that mastery of at least these areas is critical for the success of both the professional NPO manager and the organization he or she leads. The essential ingredient for success in managing apparently dissimilar organizations is a fundamental knowledge of operative management principles. Approaching NPO management improvement from a horizontal (management function) angle, as opposed to a vertical viewpoint, has a number of major ramifications, including:

1. Emergence of a new category of management professional—the ''nonprofit executive''—a professional, paid or volunteer, who has mastered the management basics of voluntary action organizations.

2. Ability to generate a curriculum designed to train the nonprofit executive—undergraduate and graduate; a curriculum which encompasses these management basics in one package of courses and studies. Heretofore, management training was approached from a vertical basis in terms of the category of public service provided by the

individual organization or in terms of function-specific areas such as fund-raising administration or volunteer administration.

An Emerging Educational Base. Efforts are under way at a growing number of colleges, some working with business organizations, to develop a basic curriculum of courses and skills in the seven areas of nonprofit organization management. The focus is on creating a core of courses which all managers of nonprofit organizations would be required to master in order to be considered minimally professionally qualified. This could then be linked to a sectorwide professional certification program to help ensure more effectively managed organizations as well as a better-defined career path or ladder for professional staff. The basic curriculum could be expanded and deepened in content and degree to provide postgraduate levels for both masters and doctoral programs.

There are certain basic commonalities of management which apply to any organized, goal-directed endeavor. These basic principles are typically taught to all students of management, regardless of the type of organization in which they will serve. Once these basic management courses have been completed, students will then move toward completion of a body of courses which will provide them with the management specifics applicable to the particular sector in which they wish to find employment.

Table N-4 illustrates the relation of a basic management curriculum and the various categories of specific management skills required in a typical nonprofit organization.

Translatability of Management Skills. Awareness of the commonality of management in nonprofit organizations has led also to an awareness of the translatability of management skills between one type of voluntary action organization and another. This is seen increasingly in the evolution of computerized jobs-bank services for a variety of nonprofit organizations across the country. These services are growing in utility and popularity since they imply that a successful manager of one type of voluntary organization could, with relative ease and effectiveness, move into a successful management role within an organization providing an entirely different type of public service. The success of the individual and of the organization, it is now widely recognized, is much more closely related to a knowledge and practice of successful management principles than to an in-depth knowledge of the particular human service provided by the organization.

High-Tech Opportunities. There has been a proliferation of ''high-tech'' grants to nonprofit organizations in recent years to help them computerize their operations. Funding for this purpose is much needed. The results of this incorporation of sophisticated technologies into the operation and manage-

TABLE N-4 College/University Degree Program, Nonprofit Organization management*

Core curriculum areas	Suggested course topics
ORGANIZATION AND CORPORATE PRINCIPLES	The History and Role of the Nonprofit, Independent Sector A Typology of Nonprofit Organizations Legally Constituting the Nonprofit Organization: Incorporation and Tax Exemption Structural Comparison: A Corporate and Organizational Analysis of Major Category-Specific Nonprofit Organizations (e.g., Health/Education/Culture)
LEADERSHIP, MANAGEMENT AND CONTROL	Leadership of the Nonprofit Organization: Board of Directors, Officers and Committees Planning, Analysis, Evaluation and Control in the Nonprofit Organization (includes (MBO for NPOs) Leadership and Management Roles/Styles in the Nonprofit Organization Comparison and Analysis of the Management Principles and Practices in the Nonprofit Sector, the Public Sector and For-Profit Organizations Management Problems and Challenges in the Nonprofit Organization
HUMAN RESOURCES	Personnel Management in the Nonprofit Organization Volunteer Administration: Recruitment, Orientation, Training and Evaluation The Human Resources Management Triad: Board of Directors/Volunteers/Staff Constituency Management: Planning, Development, and Utilization
REVENUE AND SUPPORT GENERATION	Revenue- and Support-Generating Methods for Nonprofit Organizations Fund Raising Laws and Regulations Fund Raising Management Grants and Contracts: Proposals Through Management Planned/Deferred Giving Programs Direct Mail/Marketing Corporate Funding and Support Programs: Planning, Research, and Implementation Foundation Funding Programs: Planning, Research, and Proposals Public Sector Funding: Planning, Research, and Proposals Specialized Revenue Sources: Merchandise Sales, Advertising, Special Events, and Membership Drives
PUBLIC RELATIONS, MARKETING COMMUNICATIONS	Marketing, Positioning, and NPO Fund Raising Planning the PR Program: Public Opinion and the Communications Process Public Information: Basics of Newswriting and Releasing News Utilizing the Electronic Media Special Events: Event Design/Implementation Communications and the Legislative Arena Positioning and Marketing Within the Nonprofit Organization Public Relations and Communications When the News Is Bad
FINANCIAL MANAGEMENT	The Financial Management Cycle: Long-Range Planning, Budgeting, and Accounting Budgeting for Nonprofit Organizations NPO Accounting Fundamentals: Bases, Standards, Elements, Financial Systems and Audits Record Keeping and Automated Data Processing in Nonprofit Organizations Investment Strategies for Nonprofit Organizations
LEGAL AND REGULATORY	Regulatory Aspects of Nonprofit Organization Management: U.S. Postal Service, Internal Revenue Service, and Other Governmental Agencies. The Law and the Nonprofit Organization: Office/Director Liability, Protection of Exempt Status, Litigation, Arbitration, and Dissolution

*The seven core curriculum areas which follow are based on management areas shared by all nonprofit organizations, regardless of the specific type of public or philanthropic service they provide.
It is suggested that degree students be required to successfully complete at least one course in each of these basic areas. To this total of 21 hours could be added at least three more courses in a specific area (e.g., Revenue and Support Generation) to provide further depth of study and a focus in management expertise.

ment of nonprofit organizations will have long-range effects on the organizations, their services, and their clients. Prudent NPOs with staff or volunteers having the requisite background are approaching businesses and asking for the use of their computers and associated equipment in addition to, or even in lieu of, actual funding for the organization.

Revenue and Support

In the aggregate, nonprofit organizations are a major economic force in the country. However, like the business sector of the economy, the third sector has had an increasingly difficult time generating the revenues to perform the public services for which it has collective and individual responsibility. Paradoxically, nonprofit organizations have a freedom which enables them to generate revenue from the widest possible variety of sources. In the past, this freedom was not thoroughly understood, appreciated, or developed.

Nonprofit organizations are now exploring and developing a wide variety of means to generate revenue and support. This effort ranges from actual ownership of for-profit organizations to better planning and development of their own assets. For example, it seems likely that real estate development will be a significant factor in long-range financial planning and revenue development for private colleges and other NPOs with land assets. (Nonprofit organizations own approximately one-ninth of all property in the United States!)

A Variety of Revenue Sources. Like their counterparts in business, nonprofit organizations run on money as much as on commitment and dedication. Their sources of revenue are generally different, however, from those of profit-making businesses, although this is not a legal restriction. In fact, nonprofits can generate revenue through all means allowable to profit businesses. This is in addition to those sources of revenue allowed and created by their designation as philanthropic organizations. Nonprofit organizations can own for-profit corporations, although the reverse is not the case. NPOs that generate revenue from sources not related to their charitable purpose can be taxed on this "unrelated business income," but they are not prevented legally from generating revenue from virtually any legal source.

While these activities are positive in themselves and undoubtedly will generate a great deal of much needed additional revenue for the NPOs, they are almost certain to produce a backlash of attention by government regulatory agencies such as the IRS. This agency can be expected to respond to a growing chorus of complaints of unfair competition from the for-profit sector. The IRS will surely police and enforce the letter of the tax law. In addition, this area of "unrelated" versus "related" (to the NPO's public purpose) business income can be expected to see increased legislative and regulatory activity at all levels of government.

The financial health of nonprofit organizations in future years depends to a great extent on the ability and skills of their managers—volunteer and paid professional—to apply specialized knowledge of a variety of revenue- and support-generating techniques in the context of a comprehensive, long-range master plan. Today, managers of nonprofit organizations are faced with (1) the challenge of having an enormous variety of revenue-generating options open to them, but with (2) the corresponding challenge of not knowing enough about the basic principles by which these sources of revenue and support operate to be able to build a diversified, coordinated, revenue-generation program. As a consequence, nonprofit organization managers have three basic tasks before them:

1. To select proper revenue sources from a great diversity of options.

2. To stay up to date in technical areas of financial management and development. Increasingly, these funding and support options—e.g., investment strategies and planned giving—are growing more technical and complex.

3. To protect the organization from the vulnerability inherent in having only a few (or worse still, only one) major sources of revenue or support. A diversified variety of these options needs to be developed in concert with each other. This requires a broad-based revenue-generation program whose components complement each other.

Erosion of Federal Funding. Nonprofit organizations and their leaders also face serious challenges in coming years from the ongoing pullback of the federal government from many grants program areas which nonprofits had come to view as traditional. Many NPOs, particularly those which had allowed federal funding to become the flywheel of their budgets, did not survive. Others, which had allowed their revenue-generating and traditional fund-raising "muscle" to grow flabby and weak, were severely tested. Hopefully, the lesson was learned: Truly effective nonprofit organizations create and maintain a balanced budget not dependent on too-few sources of revenue (and, therefore, vulnerable).

Optimum Funding Mix. The financial health of individual nonprofit organizations in the 1980s will depend not only on the manager's knowledge of revenue- and support-generating techniques, but also on his or her ability to target funding efforts to those sources exhibiting strong growth potential. A carefully considered funding mix strategy will increasingly become the hallmark of the successful NPO.

The funding mix is the proportion of income sources, including individuals, corporations, bequests, and foundations. These will grow at varying rates over the years.

Along the way, NPOs will face resistance from their internal constituencies as they move beyond the traditional bounds of revenue generation and support into new areas, such as real estate development. This resistance will arise both from the professional staff and from voluntary board members.

Public Relations, Communications, and Marketing

The ability to communicate successfully to a general public through the use of the mass news media—electronic and print—is a vital management skill of growing importance to NPOs. Sophistication in media relations and in public communications will increasingly determine which organizations flourish and which will wither and die from lack of support.

The mass media often see the third sector as a confusing mass of conflicting social goals and interests. The media rarely see the third sector as even having news value. Little concerted or coordinated effort has been made to date by leaders of nonprofit organizations to make the news media aware of NPO contributions and the economic importance of the third sector to the nation. As one news director summed it up succinctly, "There is no such thing as a nonprofit beat"—meaning that no one particular person is detailed by a newspaper, for instance, to provide coverage of the activities and events conducted by nonprofit, voluntary action organizations.

The evolution of the role of marketing in voluntary action, nonprofit organization management is certain to continue and to receive a great deal of attention. Marketing management will be recognized as a critical function that helps an organization change to meet the needs of those it has been established to serve. A population and an economy which is experiencing what Toffler called a "firestorm of change" expects and demands similarly fast changes in the voluntary action organizations which meet its human services needs. Only by an increased marketing effort can these changing needs be detected. Once these needs are determined or redefined, new client services can be designed and targeted to the specific segment of the public service market that the organization is best suited to serve. Then, these services can be publicized with similar accuracy through the appropriate communications medium.

Boards of Directors

One of the most important management challenges facing nonprofit organizations today is the composition and activities of their boards of directors. While obvious to the point of being trite, it is also widely ignored or overlooked.

The composition of skills, experience, and representation seen on the boards of directors of nonprofit organizations is a subject which requires a great deal of attention and research. The changing economy, changing social issues and needs, and a better understanding of the management role played by the board of directors have caused NPOs to question the composition and management of their boards of directors: Who is asked to serve on the board? What skills and/or representation should they bring to that role? What should they be asked to do as board members?

One thing that hasn't seemed to change a great deal, especially for institutional-sized nonprofit organizations, is the role of the individual board member in fund raising. That heavy responsibility is still there. The three G's—give, get, or get off—still apply in large part to most institutional boards of directors. What is changing rapidly is the technology and management science associated with today's fund raising—which should be more accurately labeled for what it is, *marketing*. Board members, especially, must become aware of this technology, particularly in the area of direct-mail marketing. In many cases, the technology has outstripped the knowledge of the typical board member. This means that, increasingly, the staff or the fund-raising consultant has to indoctrinate board members in the new processes, hardware, and software associated with today's highly sophisticated fund-raising campaigns.

Volunteers and Staff

Additional attention—in the form of research and published materials on the processes, the techniques, and the principles of managing in the context of a voluntary-action organization—must be directed toward the action and motivation which are not primarily generated by money per se.

The world of volunteerism has seen within itself major changes in thrust and motivation. For example, in a very few years there has been a shift away from volunteer corps composed almost exclusively of white, middle-class, noncareer women to volunteer corps that are much more representative of the population as a whole in sex, income, race, and ethnic background. There is also a healthy recognition that the services performed by volunteers, while not reimbursed by money, are nevertheless invaluable to the organization. There is general agreement, too, that those services and the people providing them should be given the same professional recognition as those who are paid for their services.

The volunteers, in turn, owe the organization the same degree of professionalism in the way they perform their volunteer jobs. This has resulted in a wide **609** variety of new, creative approaches to volunteer management, ranging from "employment contracts" and personnel files on volunteers to major organizations and the government giving career credit to volunteers and their services. And why not? Properly organized, voluntary service and volunteer management roles in a nonprofit organization are just as demanding and challenging and responsible as similar paid positions. They should be so recognized.*

See also Associations, trade and professional; Boards of directors; Boards of directors, legal liability guidelines; Cost-benefit analysis; Grants management; Health institutions, management of; Marketing of services; Professionalism in management; Public administration; Societies, professional.

*Portions of the above are adapted in part and with permission from article prepared by the author for: "Since the Filer Commission. . . ." Independent Sector, Washington, D.C.: 1983.

REFERENCES

Anthony, Robert N., and Regina Herzlinger: Management Control in Nonprofit Organizations, 2d ed., Richard D. Irwin, Homewood, Ill. 1980.

Connors, Tracy D.: Nonprofit Organization Handbook, McGraw-Hill, New York, 1980.

Connors, Tracy D., and C. Callaghan: Financial Management for Nonprofit Organizations, American Management Associations, New York, 1982.

Hardy, James M.: Corporate Planning for Nonprofit Organizations, Association Press, New York, 1980.

Unterman, Israel: Strategic Management for Not for Profit Organizations, Praeger, New York, 1984.

TRACY D. CONNORS

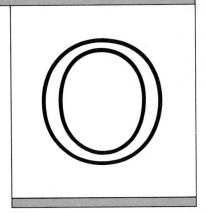

Objectives, Management by (MBO)

The system of *management by objectives* (MBO) is a process whereby the superior and subordinate managers jointly identify the organization's common goals, define each individual's major areas of responsibility in terms of results expected, and use these measures as guides for operating the unit and assessing the contribution of each of its members.

Typically, MBO starts at the top of the organization, where a sequence is established for setting and reviewing objectives. This sequence comprises a rudimentary calendar of events that take place cyclically in 2-year periods.

How to Set Strategic Objectives

The first step in goal setting is to determine the ordinary calendar of events which must be followed in the organization where MBO is to become the prevailing management system. This entails, as shown in Table O-1, some events that occur prior to the beginning of the target year and some events which will occur during that year.

Management by Anticipation. This term is used to describe goal-setting actions which are required of staff departments such as personnel, engineering, legal, traffic, finance, controller, and similar staff functions.

Collect Audit Information. This information, which includes program audits and overall reviews of the major strengths and weaknesses of each staff responsibility, should be reviewed to provide a basis for finding major opportunities and problems.

Prepare 5-Year Plan. The annual edition of the company's 5-year plan should be prepared for each of the major areas of responsibility. Thus the annual edition of the 5-year personnel plan, financial plan, technical plan, and the like should be prepared at a period about 3 months in advance of budget submission. For a company with a fiscal year starting in January, the close-off date for the annual 5-year plan would thus be about July 1 of the prior year. This permits an opportunity to revise budgetary plans, move resources to new uses, find new funding requirements, and make decisions about the abandonment of programs or plans.

Issue Annual Budgets. With audit information reviewed and the annual edition of the 5-year plan written and circulated, resources can be allocated. It permits more rational commitment of resources, including the use of zero-based budgeting for support services and cost-effectiveness methods for facility and program decisions.

611

TABLE O-1   Calendar Illustrating the Rudimentary MBO Strategic Planning Cycle
(For organizations on a calendar-year operating basis)

Date	Event	Comments/responsibilities
July 1	Prepare annual edition of the 5-year plan and review prior year's 5-year plan.	Responsibility of the top staff member and all major functional (staff) heads, assembled by planning department.
October 1	Submit budget to budget decision group (for the following year).	Upward from all units, starting with sales forecast, cost estimates, and profit forecast to budgeter.
	Review, revise, approve final budget figures.	Executive committee.
January 1	Start the new budget year; release resources.	Issue detailed, approved financial targets in final form.
January 15 to February 1	Complete individual operational objectives at all levels.	Sets standards for managerial performance for the year.
	Annual goals conference by managers of departments.	To share goals and devise teamwork.
	Annual message of the president.	To give a challenge.
April to July 1 October 1	Quarterly reviews of individual results against goals; make adjustments as required.	All managers at all levels.
April 15	Audits—including program.	Staff department.
Monthly	Hold meetings of the executive and finance committee to note exceptions and make corrective moves.	
Passim (or throughout)	Circulate and discuss position papers and note policy committee actions as major issues.	By staff experts or any responsible manager or professional or functional group.
July 1	Repeat the process.	

Strategic Objectives.   The three steps in management by anticipation are essential for the effective functioning of MBO. They ensure that sound strategic objectives are chosen. *Without strategic objectives stated in advance, measurable operational objectives may not be valid. The organization may simply be running a well-run bankruptcy.*

In formulating strategic objectives, the following points should be considered:

Strategic objectives should be stated in advance of budgetary decisions.

Strategic objectives should define strengths, weaknesses, problems, threats, risks, and opportunities.

Strategic objectives should note trends and missions and define strategic options, including the consequences of each option.

Good strategic objectives will answer the question, "Are we doing the right things?" in contrast to the operational objectives, which define "how to do things right."

Strategic anticipation of staff goals need not necessarily be measurable, but both words and numbers should be used with clarity to define long-run outcomes sought. Strategic goals are often established by groups such as the board of directors, the management committee, the personnel policy committee, and the like. An example of a strategic goal statement might be: Apex Corporation will become the leading seller of solid-state monitoring devices in the field by 1985.

As shown in Table O-2, specific questions are answered or anticipated in the strategic goals statement of every staff department and major business unit.

How to Set Operational Objectives

At the beginning of the operational year, each manager and subordinate manager conducts a formal dialogue on specific operational objectives for the coming year for the subordinate position. Prior to the discussion, each reviews the present situation, the

TABLE O-2   Format for Annual Strategic Objectives Statements

Statement should
1. Be prepared 3 months in advance of budgeting decisions.
2. Come up from below as proposed alternative strategies.
3. Be prepared annually at *half-year.*

OUTLINE FOR STATEMENT DEVELOPMENT	COMMENTS

1. Describe the present condition, statistically and verbally (and *add your professional opinion*) of:
    a. Internal strengths, weaknesses, and problems.
    b. External threats, risks, and opportunities.
2. Project today's trends: If we did not do anything differently in this area, where would we be in 1, 2, 5 years? (Do you like this possible outcome?)
3. What are we in business for? Who are our clients? What is our product? What should it be?

	What would the consequences be?		
4. What are some optional strategies?	Contribution	Costs	Feasibility
a. Do nothing differently.			
b. _____	____	____	____
c. _____	____	____	____
d. _____	____	____	____
e. _____	____	____	____
f. _____	____	____	____

(Press for multiple options)

5. Recommended action plan: To be turned into *strategic objectives.*

results of the previous year, and some of the more likely requirements for change. Each thus comes to the discussion prepared to make commitments and to assume and delegate responsibilities.

The superior is armed with information about budget limitations, strategic goals which have been agreed upon, and information about actual results obtained in the prior period.

The subordinate comes with some expectations and knowledge of his or her own performance strengths, weaknesses, and problems, as well as threats, risks, and opportunities.

Management by Commitment. Operational management by objectives adds a new dimension to the previous management by anticipation, which is the subordinate's face-to-face relationship with the superior and, through that superior, with the organization itself. This is management by commitment.

Commitment means making some promises of responsibility to somebody else whose opinion is important. This commitment is not general but specific, explicit, measurable, and worthwhile.

Responsibility means additionally the acceptance of full accountability for the outcomes produced during the commitment period, without reference to excuses or exculpatory explanations. Such a commitment does not guarantee that the responsible person will not fail for reasons beyond control. Regardless, this person assumes a "results" responsibility. This kind of responsibility implies adult behavior, professional effort, and mature self-control.

The superior is also committed. If the superior agrees in advance that the proposed operating goals are meritorious, those objectives must also be accepted as the criteria for judging performance at the end of the period. Thus, committed objectives could also include salary adjustments and merit-pay recommendations, bonus awards, appraisal, promotability notations, and similar rewards for achievement. In accepting objectives in the beginning, the superior thus cannot apply capricious or ex post judgments.

The key to management by commitment is that the hard bargaining about what constitutes excellence of performance is done up front, before the period begins, and not after a year or so of effort.

The process by which the operating goals (commitments) are established consists of (1) a dialogue and (2) a memorandum. The dialogue is one in which each brings something. It is neither solely top down nor solely bottom up, but a genuine discussion. It is most satisfactory when it is conducted on an adult-adult level rather than a parent-child model. The memorandum confirms the dialogue in specific terms and written form.

How to Write Objectives for Commitment

Operating objectives should constitute an ascending scale of excellence by which the manager can administer certain ongoing concerns in managing manag-

613

ers. For the subordinate it should be composed of a series of levels of excellence. This is best done when the superior has criteria for making year-end decisions for purposes of compensation, personnel records, defining promotability and assignments, coaching and training subordinates, and administering discipline and delegation.

For the subordinate, there are five questions to be answered or resolved:

What is expected of me? Let me know in advance.

What help and resources will be available to me in my work?

How much freedom may I expect, and what reporting times and form should I assume?

How can I tell how well I am doing in my work while I am doing it?

Upon what performance bases will rewards be issued?

Answers to these questions are best provided by placing them within a framework of three major goal categories. The commitment objectives should be written to cover all three.

Category 1. *Define* what the *regular responsibilities* of the position will be. These are the ongoing, recurring, repetitive, and measurable objectives of the job. These may range from dollar volume of sales at executive levels to units per shift at the supervisory level.

Category 2. *Identify the major problems* that should be attacked and solved in this position during the coming period. A problem can be a specific persistent deviation from a standard or simply something that somebody important wants to have fixed.

Category 3. *Specify the innovations* that will be attempted. These are not reactive but proactive goals. They are improvements, betterments, projects which will cause the organization under the subordinate's control to operate better, cheaper, faster, safer, at higher quality, or with greater dignity to people.

Some Typical Performance Measures

Starting with the regular objectives (category 1) of the general manager and his or her key subordinates, the goals chosen should lock the organization together through key indicators. Table O-3 shows a division general manager's sample objectives of an ongoing, recurring character together with related output indicators. Indicators of the regular category for this position include the following:

Dollar volume of revenue per month

Return on investment per quarter

Cash on hand at quarter end

Receivables, average age in days per quarter

Inventory, average dollar level over the quarter

Budget deviations as a percentage of capital budgets

Growth in dollar volume per quarter

Labor stoppages per year

There are no standard indicators, but those listed were found to be common among a sample of 50 general managers. Further study of Table O-3 highlights several features of regular operating objectives.

1. They are stated as *outputs for a time period.* Statements of *activities* to be performed are not objectives; they are means.

2. The specific number chosen to quantify an objective should be stated as a range. Start by establishing the middle figure first to define *normal realities.* Let the subordinate set the optimistic, or stretch, objectives. The superior chooses the pessimistic figure. This lower figure fixes the *exception point* at which the subordinate knows that the superior should be notified that things are not going according to plan. The middle point is usually based upon history, estimates, or industrial engineering studies or sales forecasts.

3. When deviations occur, the subordinate should (*a*) know it before anyone else, (*b*) know why the deviation has occurred, (*c*) take corrective action where it is possible, and (*d*) notify a superior and request help at an early instance.

4. On the other hand, when the subordinate is attaining the middle-level (normal realistic) goals, he or she should be left alone to operate without interference.

Problem-solving objectives (category 2) might look like those illustrated in Table O-4. It is usually wise to limit these commitments to one or two major problems that define the following:

Present level or condition

Desired level or condition

Date when problem is to be corrected (brought to the desired level)

Examples of innovative objectives (category 3) are also shown in Table O-4. These goals provide a statement of the present condition, the desired condition, and some time frame for the proactive, innovative goals to be attained, perhaps including some stages of study or development.

Organizational Objectives. The example given of the general manager's objectives must, of course, be supplemented (and complemented) by specific and explicit objectives for each of the key subordinates who report to the general manager. The man-

TABLE O-3 Example of Regular Objectives and Their Key Output Indicators

NAME _____ PERIOD _____

GENERAL MANAGER

REGULAR-BASIC INDICATOR OBJECTIVES

Responsibility		Level of result sought		
Output indicator	Time period	Pessimistic	Normal realistic	Optimistic
1. Dollar volume of revenue per month	Quarter			
2. Profit: ROI Dollar volume per month	Quarter Quarter			
3. Cash at month's end, dollars	Quarter			
4. Receivables: Dollars at month's end Days	Quarter Quarter			
5. Inventory: Dollars at month's end Turnover days	Quarter Quarter			
6. Capital budget, percentage of deviation	Quarter			
7. Labor problems—step 4 grievances	Quarter			
8. Share of market, percent	Quarter			
9. Other_____	_____			

RESULTS SCORE SHEET

Target no.	First quarter	Second quarter	Third quarter	Fourth quarter	Total
1					
2					
3					
4					
5					
6					
7					
8					

ufacturing manager, for example, might have a commitment to these regular objectives (category 1) as measured by key output indicators:

Average daily output per month

Units per shift per month

Indirect labor as a percentage of direct labor per month

Factory overhead as a percentage of total overhead per month

Average quality-reject rate per month

Warranty and policy costs per month

Number of step 4 grievances per quarter

Overtime hours per week per quarter

Hours of supervisory training per quarter

615

TABLE O-4 Requirements of Problem-Solving and Innovative Goals Statements

Category 2. Statement of problem-solving objective

1. Present condition or situation
2. Desired condition or objective if the problem is solved satisfactorily
3. Time commitment (always state as a range: pessimistic, realistic, optimistic)

Category 3. Statement of innovative project commitment

1. Present condition or situation
2. Innovation to be attempted
3. Results sought (condition which would exist if the innovation were to work well)
4. Time commitment (always state dates: pessimistic, realistic, optimistic)

The sales manager, on the other hand, does not have the same objectives as either the general manager or the manufacturing manager except for a few key result areas. The sales manager's objectives might include the following indicators:

Dollar volume per month and per quarter

Costs of producing the revenue per month and per quarter

New products introduced

Dollar level of bad debts per quarter

Days of sales training conducted per quarter

New customers added per quarter

Lost accounts per quarter

For each person reporting to the general manager, there are indicators which are unique to that position, but they follow a similar format: (1) indicators of output for the time period, stated in ranges, and including (2) problem-solving and (3) innovative goals.

Audit and Review of Objectives

Two forms of systematic evaluation are important in MBO: periodic audits and continuing and annual reviews.

Periodic Audit. The periodic audit is essentially a financial audit of a comprehensive nature, usually based upon a sampling of the numerically stated realities of the situation. It is closely related to the strategic objectives of the organization. It can be performed by professional internal auditors or by an outside audit group, such as a CPA firm. Program audits should be performed periodically not only for financial results and practices but for *program* operations as well.

Personnel audits and work force audits for such matters as affirmative action, replacements of key persons, compliance with company or organizational personnel policy, and similar matters, including labor relations, should be included in periodic audits. Safety audits performed internally against OSHA standards may prevent unfavorable audits by OSHA inspectors from enforcement agencies.

Other current practices of the best-run organizations include new forms of program audits such as the technical audit, community relations audit, public responsibility audit, purchasing practices audit, and legal compliance audit for antitrust or patent protection.

Continuing Reviews. Each manager, having made commitments, should be conducting ongoing reviews of his or her own performance. These reviews consist of observations and notations of actual results as compared with the statements of objectives to which one is committed. These reviews are made frequently and relate to the shorter time periods, for example, daily, weekly, monthly, and quarterly, in which supervisory management gets reports of outputs.

One of the major advantages of MBO is that it permits self-control by the manager against objectives agreed upon in advance. Self-control has powerful motivational effects; the tightest and most perfect form of control is self-control. Commitment is a means of motivation, and it is considerably enhanced when self-correction is built into the system.

As shown at the bottom of Table O-3, a manager should be able to post his or her own actual outcomes for the original objectives and should send a copy to the superior. The function of the superior is to respond with help and resources when requested or when notified that exceptions are present.

Annual Review. At the end of each year, the superior and subordinate pull out the objectives prepared in advance and formally review actual results. This is a preface to defining new objectives for the coming year. Such discussions should be treated as important events. They should be done free from distraction and should deal with objectives, results, problems, deviations, and improvements needed. They should avoid personality discussions or a manner which is exacting, hostile, judgmental, or punitive.

With actual results against objectives in hand, the superior can then make such personnel decisions as are required.

See also Appraisal performance; Budgets and budget preparation; Compensation, executive; Control systems, management; Exception, management by; Objectives and goals.

REFERENCES

MacDonald, Charles R.: *MBO Can Work!* McGraw-Hill, New York, 1982.
Mali, F.: *Managing by Objectives*, John Wiley, New York, 1972.

Odiorne, George S.: *Management by Objectives*, Pitman, New York, 1965.

———: "The Politics of Implementing MBO," *Business Horizons*, vol. 19, pp. 27–40, June 1974.

Reddin, W. J.: *Effective Management by Objectives*, McGraw-Hill, New York, 1971.

George S. Odiorne, *Eckerd College*

Objectives and Goals

In describing his corporation's promotion policy, the CEO of a large electronics firm recently cited three criteria: "Performance. Performance. Performance."[1] In obtaining performance, no factor is more important to managers than goals. Objectives and goals (the terms will be used interchangeably) are the starting points of the practice of managing. It is in their contribution to efficient and effective goal achievement that managers find the fundamental rationale for their jobs.

"Think goals" is a useful dictum for managers to practice, but the emphasis needs to be as much on *think* as on *goals*. How does one think about goals? The approach in this entry is to examine five aspects of goals: terms, contributions, criteria, classifications, and the goal-setting process.

Some Basic Terms

Goals are desired ends or results toward which behavior is directed. They are more than simply desired future states of affairs; goals are more than just "wouldn't it be nice" statements. The additional ingredient required of goals is evidence of behavior in support of the goals.

Suppose that an executive wants to become a vice president of industrial relations by the age of 40. That is a goal, in the practical sense of the term, only to the extent that it is backed up by behavior that is consistent with obtaining that position.

The statements of goals that individuals and people who represent an organization make are sometimes called *official goals*. These statements are public pronouncements about desired ends or results. They often appear in written form in a conspicuous place in offices and stores so that customers can see the goals. An important question to ask is, "Is behavior actually directed toward these goals?" If so, then the goals are not only official goals but also *operative goals*. They are goals supported by behavior. It is in the sense of operative goals that the term *goal* is used throughout this chapter.

For pragmatic purposes the terms *goals, objectives, aims,* and *purposes* are used interchangeably here. In practice, some firms find it useful to differentiate between these terms. They base the distinction on the level of generality and the period of time represented by the term. Thus, an aim or purpose may be a very broad, ultimate desired state of affairs that is only achieved, if at all, over a long period of time. Objectives may be more immediate desired results that can be subdivided into subobjectives. These subobjectives can become goals or *targets*. The problem with this use of terms is that it is not uniform from firm to firm, and there is no particular need for uniform usage; the basic idea of each term is the same.

How Goals Contribute to Managerial Effectiveness

All benefits of goals are only potential benefits; the mere presence of goals does not guarantee that they will play any role in improving managerial effectiveness. Most managers are familiar with situations in which official goals are loudly and enthusiastically proclaimed, only to be quickly ignored and forgotten. When considering the potential benefits of goals to managers, the practical question for managers to ask about these benefits is, "Are my goals actually achieving these benefits for my area of managerial accountability?"

All benefits of goals derive from their influence on behavior. Several of these potential influences on job behavior are discussed briefly below.

Direction and Motivation. Goals can focus attention; they can tell what individuals should be doing; they can serve as targets for behavior. To the extent that goals do these things, job behavior can become more purposeful and productive. The absence of well-defined organizational or departmental goals or objectives is commonly cited by executives as the *most common cause* of less-than-satisfactory executive productivity.[2] Such goals may not guarantee managerial effectiveness, but they are a necessary condition of it.

In addition to providing behavioral direction, goals can influence the level of motivation of managers and their employees. There is substantial motivational research supporting the finding that specific and challenging goals, coupled with feedback that induces the setting of higher goals, can lead to improved performance.

Standards. Goals can serve as the standards against which to evaluate managerial and employee job behavior. By providing behavioral direction, goals suggest what should be done; as standards, goals are useful in determining *how well* actual job behavior matches desired behavior. One reason executives may be reluctant to use goals is that goals *do* hold them to a standard of performance.

The prevalence of the use of goals as standards is suggested by the frequency with which executives mention goals and objectives as the most effective yardstick for measuring productivity and by the frequency with which achievement of goals is mentioned as the definition of success.

Foundation for Managerial Functions. What do managers do? A common, although incomplete, reply is to say that they plan, organize, staff, direct, and control. This set of managerial functions or activities provides a general way of identifying some of the behaviors managers are supposed to engage in if they want to achieve goals efficiently and effectively. The entire rationale for this classification is that these managerial functions are essential activities that need to be performed if goals are to be achieved efficiently and effectively. In this widely accepted view of managerial functions, goals are the foundation on which all functions are built.

Planning has no meaning apart from goals; indeed, some authors and managers consider goal setting as a part of planning. The essence of planning is to determine the what, how, when, where, and who of action necessary to achieve goals. Since *controlling* is inseparable from planning, it, too, depends on goals for its rationale. Controlling is the function of ensuring that actual behavior is contributing to goals.

The *organizing* function of managers has an influence on goals. On the one hand, the goals that guide behavior in organizations can have an influence on the way the organization is designed. On the other hand, the way the organization is designed can have an influence on what goals are selected to guide the behavior of the organization's members. In a similar way, the goals of an organization can influence the functions of *staffing* and *directing.* Who is hired and kept in an organization and how they are directed are partly determined by the organization's goals, but these goals are also influenced by the people in the organization who participate in formulating the goals.

Evaluating Change. In the absence of goals and the plans and controls that support the goals it is difficult to evaluate proposed changes that might affect managerial and organizational effectiveness. The presence of such goals provides a point of reference that can be used in evaluating the impact of the proposed changes on the organization's people, markets, resources, structure, operational processes, and overall effectiveness.

Evaluating changes against goals may help managers and organizations avoid changes that have as their only or major justification that they *are* changes. Change for the sake of change may on occasion be necessary or desirable, but it is, in general, a weak rationale for committing organizational resources.

Perspective. The four benefits of goals just discussed can be turned into obstacles to effective managing if goals are not kept in perspective. Goals that provide behavioral direction and focus attention can also become blinders. A kind of "goalopia" can set in that prevents managers from seeing the need for flexible, spontaneous behavior that may not be exactly consistent with goals but is essential to overall effectiveness. "Goalopia" can hinder a manager's capacity to evaluate the continuing relevance of particular goals.

Goals that serve as standards may become obstacles to improved performance if they are not changed in response to actual performance appraisal. Goals that provide the foundation for other managerial functions can lead to overly mechanistic and programmed approaches to planning, organization, staffing, directing, and controlling. Goals that are useful in evaluating change can also be used by managers as a basis for excessive resistance to change.

Finally, it is possible to place too much emphasis on goals. Unfortunately, there is no single key to effective managing. Neither goals nor any other idea or managerial tool is *the* key to the task of effectively managing systems having human, technical, and economic dimensions. Goals are a necessary but not exclusive condition for managerial effectiveness.

Criteria for Goals

If goals are going to be a useful tool for effective managing, they must meet certain criteria.

Acceptability. A certain minimum level of goal acceptance—enough to generate compliance behavior on the part of those responsible for achieving goals—is obviously essential. In short, no acceptance, no achievement. Beyond this minimum level, however, how much acceptance is necessary and/or desirable? How can this acceptance be acquired?

The "how much" question cannot be answered with specific terms. As a practical guide to goal acceptance, however, the idea of goal ownership is useful. *Goal ownership* reflects a good match between the goals of the organization and the personal goals and aspirations of those who are involved in reaching the goals.

How can goal acceptance be achieved? One approach to achieving goal acceptance is to make sure goals are communicated, known, and understood. Although these steps do not guarantee acceptance, they are a necessary precondition of it. Another approach to achieving goal acceptance is to involve those who are going to be responsible for achieving the goals in the process of goal setting. This involvement or participation can range from an advisory or consultative role to one in which participants actually make goal decisions. The participation can occur at the beginning or end of the goal-setting process or at any point in between.

Participation in goal setting is *a* way of obtaining goal acceptance because the participation process, by virtue of the inputs of the participants, may result in goals that are in fact, or are perceived to be, more in line with the personal goals of those persons involved. In addition, the participative process—a process that gives one a sense of being ego-involved—may serve to raise the aspiration levels of those involved. That is, a genuinely participative approach to goal setting can result in the setting of higher goals.

Precision. There is an *appropriate degree* of precision or specificity for every goal, and it is imperative that goals be stated with that degree of precision—and no more. It is just as much a mistake to impose more precision on a goal than it warrants as it is to undercut the usefulness of the goal by stating it with an insufficient degree of precision.

One of the most interesting and clearest findings from motivational research is that there is a definite positive relationship between job performance and the degree of precision in goals.

In a situation where managers and employees are given a very general goal (for example, to make a profit in this department) and told to "do your best," goal precision is very low. Job performance is likely to suffer because the goals do not provide behavioral focus or motivation or an adequate basis for planning and controlling.

However, when goals are appropriately precise in terms of *quantity*, *quality*, *time*, and *cost* (for example, to earn a 10 percent rate of return on the book value of total assets in this department in each of the next 2 years), it is more likely that goals will provide a source of motivation and focus and will be a foundation for effective planning and controlling.

In goal setting it is necessary to strike a balance between too little and too much precision. Excessive precision can stifle motivation, lead to poor job attitudes, and adversely affect job performance. A preoccupation with precision may lead to adopting trivial goals *because* they can be stated precisely at the expense of adopting more meaningful and challenging goals. In short, precision can be carried too far.

Attainability. This test of goals is concerned with the level of goal difficulty. Goals that are set too high may demotivate behavior, create frustration and anxiety, lower job performance, and lead to performance appraisal difficulties. Goals that are set too low do not contribute much to the satisfaction people experience when they achieve them. Further, achievement of easy goals may not lead to a favorable performance appraisal; an anybody-could-have-done-that attitude may characterize the appraisal session.

People are more likely to accomplish difficult goals if they can achieve, and be rewarded for achieving, subgoals that represent progress toward the larger difficult goal. In addition, difficult goals may require more effort on the part of managers to gain goal acceptance. As noted above, increased goal acceptance may result in an increased commitment to achieve goals. There is research support for the proposition that difficult, *but accepted,* goals lead to greater performance than easy goals do.

Congruency. Congruency means that all the internal goals within an area of accountability must be consistent with each other (internal congruence) and with the goals of other organizational units with which the area interacts (external congruence). For example, if departmental performance goals are inconsistent or nonsupportive of personal development goals, good performance is unlikely. Additionally, if goals of the production function, for example, are incompatible with goals of the marketing function, overall organizational effectiveness suffers.

A second meaning of goal congruence is that goals must be compatible with other characteristics of the organization. For example, a goal to increase the adaptability of an organization to changing environmental conditions may be inconsistent with the existing and rigid organizational structure. Goals that emphasize personal development and growth may be inconsistent with appraisal and reward systems that are based on subjective opinions and seniority. Human resource planning goals may be incompatible with current staffing practices.

Most complex organizations pursue so many different goals that it would be impossible for them all to be compatible with each other. It is not even possible to be aware of all goals being pursued. Thus, a certain amount of *goal conflict* is inevitable even in an organization whose members are committed to goal congruence.

Comparison with Alternatives. Goals selected for use in managing must be evaluated against alternative goals that were not selected. It is useful to state explicitly those goals that were rejected. This exercise helps managers become more aware of the *opportunity cost* associated with goals. Every goal involves some trade-off, and it is important for effective managers to be aware of what is being traded off. Quantity may be achieved at the expense of quality, quality may be possible only with higher costs, shorter customer delivery times may result in higher inventory carrying costs, and so on.

The trade-offs involved by selecting a particular goal are not always as obvious as in the cases above. All that may be necessary to highlight trade-offs, however, is the discipline of asking and answering this question, "What is the opportunity cost of this goal?"

Goal Classifications

Professionals frequently refer to a number of goals. Each of these types can be placed into one of five primary classifications. The goals within each class may be regarded as *types* of goals.

Time. The time period covered by goals is one basis for classification. Although this period can range from a few minutes to a lifetime, the most common managerial practice is to refer to short-run or *tactical goals,* mid-range or *intermediate goals,* and long-run or *strategic goals.* Typical, but arbitrary, time periods assigned to these goals are 1 year or less, 2 to 3 years, and over 3 years, respectively.

Primary Beneficiary. Organizations require goals for owners, employees, customers, suppliers, creditors, the local community, and society. Every organization has to achieve, in a satisfactory manner, a set of multiple goals. Each of these can be viewed as having a primary beneficiary, but none can be achieved unless all are satisfied to some extent. No one of these goals should be viewed as *the* goal of an entire organization, even though, at times, one goal may be given priority over others.

Priority. All goals are not equally important. In the most fundamental sense, every organization exists for some primary purpose. For business firms, this primary purpose is to provide customers with goods and services in sufficient quantity, acceptable quality and cost, and at a time when the goods and services are needed. This is the societal justification for the existence of the business firm, and it has the distinct characteristic that distinguishes business firms from other types of organizations.

In a similar way, schools exist to educate, hospitals exist to care for the sick, and so on. Every organization has a fundamental reason for existing that is, or should be, its highest priority goal.

This same line of reasoning applies to the smallest area of managerial accountability within an organization. Every such area has its primary objective(s). One of the manager's tasks is to identify the goal(s) from which all other goals derive their importance. Not only is it essential to assign priorities to these goals, but also the way in which priorities are assigned can differentiate effective from ineffective managers.

Social Unit. Goals range from individual or personal goals to organizational or systemwide goals, with a variety of social units between each of these two extremes. For convenience, we discuss goals of individuals, groups, and organizations. In a basic sense, every organization is a collection of individuals attempting to achieve their personal or *individual goals.* These individuals are members of the organization because they perceive membership in the organization as a vehicle for personal goal realization. In terms of human behavior, the most essential task confronting organizational leaders is that of harmonizing or integrating the personal goals of members with those goals of larger social units.

Group goals are goals that individual members of a group agree will serve as guides for the behavior of the group. Group goals are not identical to the individual goals of group members. Rather, they are goals agreed to by the individual members as behavioral guides for their role as members of the group.

Organizational goals are goals that serve to guide the decision behavior of key top managers on matters that impact the total organization or some major subsystem of the organization. The clearest example of such a goal in business firms is the profitability goal. This goal acts to constrain the decisions of top executives. Other major goals of business firms include growth, market share, and social responsibility.

Performance Area. Peter F. Drucker identifies the following eight key areas in which objectives are needed: (1) marketing, (2) innovation, (3) human organization, (4) financial resources, (5) physical resources, (6) productivity, (7) social responsibility, and (8) profit requirements. In listing these eight performance areas, Drucker presents the overall view that objectives need to be set in all areas on which the economic performance of the firm depends. The specific objectives set in any one of these performance areas will depend on the strategy of the individual business, but the areas are common for all businesses because, Drucker suggests, "All businesses depend on the same factors for their survival."[3]

The Goal-Setting Process

Goals do not just appear; they are the result of a continuous organizational goal-setting process. What does this process involve? In the first place, it has an overall purpose, which is to translate, through an ends-means chain, broad organizational goals into meaningful behavioral guides for people at each level of the organization. In the second place, the goal-setting process is a human behavior process and, as such, is never perfectly rational or mechanistic.

An Ends-Means Chain. Every organization has to have some process by which it arrives at a *hierarchy of goals* through an ends-means chain. The partial organization chart shown in Fig. O-1 illustrates the ends-means chain as it applies to the marketing function. The goal-setting process starts with the organization's top management. This group formulates goals applicable to the organization's top level. For example, a top-level marketing goal might be to reach sales of $2 billion. This marketing goal provides the basis for goal setting in marketing functions at the middle level of the organization. The sales function would then establish specific goals by product to support the top-level sales goal of $2 billion. Thus, the goals at the middle levels of an organization are the means used for achieving the goals, or ends, of the top levels. This ends-means chain continues throughout the organization.

A Human Behavior Process. Goal setting in organizations involves men and women in an interactive process in which they are looking out not only for the organization but for themselves as well. There is nothing wrong with this process; that is just the way it is. The key point is that goal setting cannot be

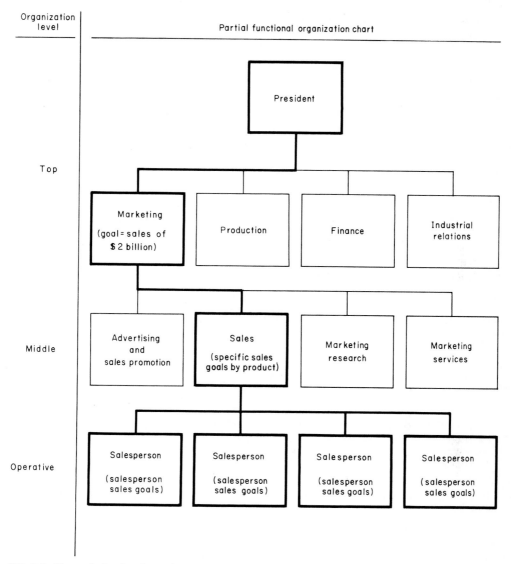

Organization level

Partial functional organization chart

Top

Middle

Operative

FIG. O-1 The marketing function ends-means chain.

viewed simply as a perfectly rational ends-means process that leads to a hierarchy of logically integrated goals. Rather, the hierarchy of goals results from an interactive human behavior process in which people have (1) a personal stake and (2) a limited perspective.

The personal stake concerns the perceived relationship between the goals that are being set for the organization and the personal goals of the people involved. It is inevitable and very rational for individual organization members to watch out for their personal and organizational "selfish" interests. In its extreme form, such behavior can ruin an organiza-

tion. More commonly, however, various nondestructive tactics are used by organization members to influence goals and the goal-setting process. Examples of these tactics include collective bargaining, informal negotiating, and temporary ad hoc groups or *coalitions* formed to push for particular goals.

These tactics may result in goals that are less than ideal or less than perfectly rational from a *total organization viewpoint*. The tactics may (will) generate conflict between individual members of the organization and between organizational units. The tactics and the conflict are an inevitable part of goal setting in organizations. They are part of the human behav-

621

ior process that results in goals that are the *best compromises* that can be reached in efforts to integrate the diverse interests of organization members.

Even if individual organization members had no personal stake in goals, goal setting would still be less than a perfectly rational process. That is because of the limited perspective of organization members. Once again, this is neither good nor bad; it is just a reality of organizational life. Individual members of the organization view what is going on in their organization from their particular frame of reference. Their perspective is determined largely by the scope of their responsibilities and by characteristics of their job specialization. This perspective, coupled with the limited ability of the human brain to process all the data that bombards it, means that every member brings a limited perspective to the goal-setting process. Some perspectives are more limited than others, of course, but all are limited.

The goal-setting picture presented so far has two themes. One theme is the need for organizations to develop a hierarchy of goals. The other theme is that the hierarchy of goals comes about as a result of an interactive human behavior process. One approach to the goal-setting process that takes these two themes into account and that is widely used is management by objectives (MBO).

See also Budgets and budget preparation; Control systems, management; Objectives, management by (MBO); Planning, strategic managerial.

NOTES

[1] Warren Kalbacher, "Computer-Age Trail Boss," *Success*, September 1983, p. 17.

[2] Herman S. Jacobs and Katherine Jillson, *Executive Productivity*, American Management Association, New York, 1974.

[3] Peter F. Drucker, *Management: Tasks, Responsibilities, Practices*, Harper & Row, New York, 1974.

REFERENCES

Albanese, R.: *Managing: Toward Accountability for Performance*, Richard D. Irwin, Homewood, Ill., 1981, chap. 2.

Latham, Gary P., and Edwin A. Lock: "Goal Setting—A Motivation Technique That Works," *Organizational Dynamics*, Autumn 1979, pp. 68–80.

Shetty, Y. K.: "New Look at Corporate Goals," *California Management Review*, Winter 1979, pp. 71–79.

ROBERT ALBANESE, *Texas A & M University*

Office Automation

Office automation is the application of computer hardware, software, and data communications technology to general office functions for the purpose of improving productivity in a cost-effective manner. The basic functions commonly found in an office environment include (1) data initiation and input, (2) data manipulation and calculation, (3) data storage and retrieval, (4) data reproduction, and (5) data transmission. These functions have, to some extent, been automated for years. It is the high degree of automation using today's technology, however, that has dramatically affected cost effectiveness and efficiency.

The technology that has initiated such advancements lies in the development of microelectronics, machine-ready software, and expanding data communication networks. From the 1950s until the late 1970s, computers made inroads into office applications, although these applications were generally limited to standard-cycle, large-volume processing. Computer application for office processing was simply too expensive, because the typical office had a relatively small volume and a somewhat unstandardized work cycle. Managers, for example, occasionally require information from the system that may not be needed regularly. Similarly, memoranda and other types of correspondence may be required under nonrepetitive, once-only conditions. In essence, the routine of the typical office was judged not to be as predictable as that in a high-volume business processing system.

As previously described, office automation deals with overall office functions. However, the term *word processing* is often confused with the concept of office automation when, in reality, it is only a part of office automation. Word processing is more commonly recognized because it represents the first direct application of computer technology to specific office processes. The first word processor was introduced in the 1960s by IBM. This device, called the Magnetic Tape Selectric Typewriter (or MT/ST), is capable of storing basic text which can be altered to create a more personalized correspondence. Like the more comprehensive word processors that followed, however, it is basically text- or correspondence-oriented. Its value to office automation is directly related to the percentage of quality correspondence developed in a particular office.

Automating Pivotal Functions. To appreciate fully the high degree of automation now possible it is appropriate to examine each of the five general office functions and the types of automated applications for each. A *function* is a group of activities or processes that change an input to an output. When a function is automated it does not necessarily mean that all the individual processes will carry over from the manual code. Certain functions, especially those requiring physical energy, do not lend themselves to automation.

Defining a function requires three things: recognition of (1) the output, (2) the inputs required for such outputs, and (3) the processes that will change the inputs to outputs. It is the manager's responsibility when developing an automated environment to identify each of the functions—and processes within each function—which make up his or her subsystem. The keys to identifying the most productive automated applications are to determine whether (1) the processes are routine and repetitive, (2) the quantity of data input is relatively high, and (3) the data-base manipulation is complex enough to make manual processing difficult.

Initiation and Input of Data. Initiation and input generally describe functions that are at the front end of office processing. Traditionally, data were initiated and put into the system by longhand draft or dictation, culminating in the use of a keyboard device such as a typewriter to capture the data. In the automated office, data are entered into a word processor or computer terminal. The major advantage of the latter is that the data can be checked, and only the errors need be retyped. This reduces the tremendous time and cost previously required to redo the entire source document. Another option for data input is *voice actuation.* This technology is not yet versatile and flexible enough to lend the degree of sophistication required, but it has important potential for input applications of the future.

Data Manipulation and Calculation. Data manipulation and calculation encompass a broad spectrum of processes, including revision, editing and correction, preparation of extracts, and data-base management. Word processors can do not only those types of data manipulation as they relate to text processing capabilities but also the direct accessing and manipulation of the organization's data base. Such capabilities involve calculation, searching, providing extracts, updating records, and generating reports. Incorporation of typical word processing and computer processing capabilities into a single system is fast becoming an everyday reality. Recent developments in software have expanded the capabilities of the basic word processing functions. *Records-processing software,* for example, can provide the capabilities of sorting, extracting, and merging of selected data elements into text output. The addition of "math packages" can turn the word processor into a sophisticated calculator. The "forms package" can assist in placing data elements in the proper location on a form. A "spelling package" with a vendor-created dictionary of 50,000 to 100,000 words assists in highlighting improper spelling.

Data Storage, Retrieval, and Reproduction. In the past, storage meant recording messages on paper and placing them in a file cabinet. The expense of the procedure could be minimized in some instances by substituting microfilm or microfiche. The main purpose of microfilm or microfiche was to reduce storage space and thus reduce cost. This is still true in many organizations, but to provide more flexibility and accessibility of data, automated storage is done by utilizing magnetic tape or disk media. In this way, the message can be electronically stored, manipulated, and, subsequently, retrieved. Moreover, the initial input and storage of data on the magnetic medium allow for future transfer of the data to other types of media at the press of a button.

Data reproduction formerly required photocopying or carbon copies of the original. In systems that used carbons or photocopying, copies of documents were mandatory to ensure that certain users in the system could examine and review them. Then as now, in many cases such reviews were unnecessary. With electronic storage, copies can be made on request or supplied for examination over a CRT. This approach reduces reproduction and storage costs and eliminates the proliferation of paperwork.

Transmission. The transmission of nonverbal messages using an electronic transmission medium is known as *data telecommunication.* Written words and pictures can be transmitted from one distant point to another just as voice is transmitted. TWX and Telex are telegraph systems that send and receive messages by wire. *Facsimile systems* can be used to transmit data or graphics. Electronic telecommunication of documents is usually performed among groups or organizational components in a formal manner. The newer, fast-growing area of *electronic mail* is a computer-based system. Electronic mail is generally informal, involving less structured communications. The drawback is that both the transmitter and the receiver must have access to the computer system. In the computer-based electronic mailbox, the messages are left until the user makes an inquiry.

Network Systems. The next generation of technology for developing automated offices appears to be network systems. In such networks, displays, terminals, and electronic files can be connected by a cable and directed by a controller. This provides the necessary integration of functions and the common use of organizational data. The use of communication systems extends the dissemination of data to various users and managers in the system. One such network system is *Local Area Networks* (LANS). Using specialized software, various terminals and computer systems can be linked by a technique called *protocol conversion.* Protocol conversion simply enables the translating of the communicating techniques of one system to be accepted by another. The network provides the means for controlling standards and expanding capabilities in small increments with fewer connection problems. LANS will use either a single communication channel or multiple channels. Necessary routing can occur with or without computer control. The present drawback of this technology is the lack of vendor agreements on standards.

Video Terminals and Ergonomics. All indications point to a very large percentage of office work being performed on video terminals (CRTs). One forecast is that by the 1990s some 75 percent of office jobs will be a human-machine interface. In the past the office, as opposed to the factory environment, was a relatively safe place to work. With terminals, computers, and other such electronic devices the frustrations and mental fears experienced by the factory worker are now being felt by the white-collar worker.

Developing a more acceptable office working environment by the integration of equipment design and the human physiology is the concern of the discipline called *ergonomics*. Ergonomics focuses on any interaction of human beings and electronic devices. Radiation from the CRTs was one of the primary concerns. Many studies done both here and abroad show, however, that the radiation levels are below established standards. Nevertheless, this has triggered an exploration of other health concerns. Such areas include the physiological stress in using video terminals and visual problems such as eyestrain, glare, screen flicker, and improper lighting. Compensations in design include the use of indirect lighting to reduce glare, colored screens to ease eye fatigue, and character arranging and formatting for better-readability. Similarly, hardware design focuses on reducing fatigue. Keyboards are sloped to accommodate the natural downward slope of the hands and fingers. Furniture is made adjustable to accommodate differing physical characteristics of the work staff.

Productivity and People. The optimum result of automation should be productivity improvement. Consideration of the organizational members should be an important factor in the planning stage, however, and not an unexpected afterthought. A cost-benefit analysis should be performed for each alternative. Viable alternatives should be the basis for recommendations presented for management's consideration. When members of the organization are involved in this planning it helps them to understand the proposed system's changes and goes one significant step toward having the staff accept them.

See also Computer software, data-base management; Forms design and control; Management information systems (MIS); Paperwork simplification; Records management; Systems and procedures; Telecommunications; Word processing.

REFERENCES

Kutie, Rita C., and Joan Rhodes: *Secretarial Procedures for the Electronic Office,* John Wiley, New York, 1983.

Lieberman, Mark A., Gad Selig, and John Walsh: *Office Automation,* John Wiley, New York, 1982.

Stallard, John J., E. Ray Smith, and Donald Reese: *The Electronic Office: A Guide for Managers,* Dow Jones-Irwin, Homewood, Ill., 1983.

Arthur Alkins, *U.S. Office of Personnel Management*

Office Space Planning

In planning a major office facility, a logical sequence should be followed: plan the project; gather and analyze requirements data; select the solution (build, lease, renovate); design; build; move.

Preliminary Planning. The project might require a few months for construction (for 20,000 square feet of leased space), 8 months (for a one-story simple structure on a suburban site), a year or year and a half (for 300,000 square feet of leased space), or 3 years (for a high-rise building on an urban site). Responsibility and authority should be defined and delegated from the start. An independent planning consultant and/or architect contribute greatly and should be selected as soon as possible. The consultant, architect, or some equally capable individual should have primary responsibility for setting up and monitoring the program and schedule.

Creating the Project Team. It is wise to select an in-house *project coordinator* who can take day-to-day responsibility for coordination among all parties: planners, brokers, landlords, architects, contractors, and your own departments. Appoint a *facility planning committee* to have ultimate responsibility. The facility planning committee should meet at least monthly to review progress and costs and whenever a major decision is needed: total requirements, budget, selection of space, approval of layout and design, and selection of major contractors.

Management's Preconceptions. Top management will probably have preconceptions about the project. Valid preconceptions will set the project limits and goals; invalid ones must be refuted tactfully by the project team. Preconceptions include total growth, a schedule, maximum rent, total costs, buildings preferred, what is right or wrong with the present space, open versus enclosed space, new versus existing furniture, a design look, and relationship of office sizes to titles.

Past Studies and Available Data. Recent past studies concerning personnel growth, organization, functions, and space should be sought and reviewed. Data listing personnel by department, title, and pay grade will be a good starting point for determining personnel requirements.

Budget Factors. Two types of costs affect the budget:

1. *One-time costs:* double rent, consultants' fees, construction, furniture, furnishings, art, telephone installation, electronic data processing (EDP), major utilities, audiovisual systems, move, move security, new office materiel, personnel relocation, personnel replacement and training.

2. *Recurring costs:* rent and rent escalation, elec-

tricity, telephone, cleaning and relamping, extra personnel, and extra services (not now required).

Organizing Data. Requirement data should be gathered and maintained in flexible increments. Restructure departments into *planning units.* Each unit should include those personnel and *special facilities* (conference rooms, food service, etc.) which must remain a physical unit to function effectively. A planning unit may be part of a department (e.g., an independent four-person group) or consist of an entire department. Assign an alpha code to each planning unit. (See Table O-5.) Select a series of *planning stages* to determine the years for which personnel and area projections are needed. Stage 1 is the present. Stage 2 might be the move date plus 1, 2, or 3 years (since the firm will not want to outgrow the space the day it moves in). Stage 3 would be the year more space is added, perhaps 5 to 7 years after the move. The team should also identify *hard areas* (areas that are expensive to build or to move, such as food service, EDP, board rooms, print shops) based on phase 3 needs, even though *soft areas* (typical private office and general office areas) are based on stage 2 needs and might be relocated when stage 3 occurs.

TABLE O-5 Typical Planning Units

A	Administration
AA	Executive group
AB	Public relations
AC	Government affairs
AD	Office services
B	Finance
BA	Controller's office
BB	Treasurer
BC	General accounting
BD	Payroll
C	Marketing
CA	Marketing administration
CB	Product 1
CC	Product 2

Review and Approval. Establish a procedure for review and approval of major decisions by the facility planning committee.

Gathering and Analyzing Base Data. The total space requirement (for a planning unit for a given planning stage) is composed of several types of data. Express data in terms of functional needs and not in terms of area; area is determined only after the base data are analyzed and approved and after space standards are selected. Once a department head has said, "I need a 400-square-foot office," it is difficult to assign space based on a uniform standard.

Personnel. Record personnel by work station categories related to a parity of function and/or status. The following categories and codings, listed in descending order of area normally required are recommended:

	Private stations
X	Chairman, president
A	Executive vice president, senior vice president
B	Vice president, general manager
C	Manager, top professional
D	Assistant manager, top clerical supervisor, professional needing privacy

	Nonprivate stations (O stands for open stations)
OSX	Executive Secretary
OA	Administrator, clerical supervisor, professional not needing privacy
OS	Secretary
OC	Clerk

	Special-facility stations
N	Special-facility personnel

Remember to include stations required by nonemployees: outside auditors, visitors, seasonal personnel, field persons.

Files, Storage, and Special Equipment. Files, bookcases, storage cabinets, and major machine requirements should be recorded if they are needed in an open area since they require additional space (but not if they are required in a private office). When these occur in a special facility, they should be recorded under the special facility (e.g., engineering file room: 40 legal drawers, 60 plan drawers, one 36 by 72 by 18 cabinet).

Special Facilities. Record the function, capacity needed, furniture and equipment to be accommodated, utilities and special construction, and special features for unique facilities. For example, conference-room requirements might be: to be used for client presentations; to seat 12 at single table; to have two working walls with pinup surface and chart rails; to have a motorized screen; to have a smoke exhaust and temperature control.

Utilities and Nonstandard Construction. These requirements will occur mostly in the special facilities list. Some occur in general office areas (e.g., separate circuits, ventilation for machines) and some in the X and A offices (e.g., ventilation, lighting, architectural features). These requirements affect the budget and must be considered when negotiating a lease.

Special Studies. Plans that affect long-range space needs should be reviewed in advance or simultaneously with your study of requirements. These include organization, automation, records management, methods, and work flow.

Adjacency Priorities. Determine adjacency priorities by asking planning unit managers to state these requirements or by analyzing the work flow. Work flow should consider only actual task interrelationships (e.g., accounts payable hand delivering batches to disbursement) or the need for face-to-face contact (e.g., research with applications engineering). Plot these on a *bubble diagram* (see Figure O-2), where a circle represents each planning unit, a rectangle each common-use special facility, and adjacency priorities are shown by connecting lines and numbers:

1. Essential: must be adjacent.
2. Desirable: should be on the same floor or an adjacent floor.
3. Convenient: helpful if adjacent, but separation would not hurt function.

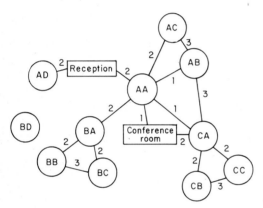

FIG. O-2 Bubble diagram. Adjacency priorities: 1—essential; 2—desirable; 3—convenient. See Table O-5 for identification of planning units.

Analysis and Approval of Base Data. Base data should be tabulated by planning unit and by planning stage. These tabulations should be reviewed by departments for their planning units, by divisions for their departments, and by top management for all divisions. Personnel totals should be confirmed. Parity in assigning space categories for similar functions and status should be positively checked; a single accidental deviation often results in charges of preferential treatment. Quantity of files and storage should be approved. Special facilities required should be compared with the size and capacity of present similar facilities.

Computing Space Requirements. Compute space requirements by applying space standards to base data, by extending and adding areas for each planning unit and planning stage, and by applying a circulation factor. Establish an area standard for each space category (if a building has been selected or designed) or a range of areas for each category (if several buildings are being considered) (see Table O-6).

Depending on the size of the company, the nature of its business, budget limitations, and the building's module, space standards can vary greatly. Establish area standards for files, storage units, and special equipment. Special facility areas should be based on a sketch for each. All standards should include access space (e.g., space to open a file drawer and stand in front of it) but not the pro rata share of common aisles.

Circulation Factors. Consider two kinds of circulation: *intraunit circulation,* or aisles connecting stations and special facilities within each planning unit; and *interunit circulation,* or aisles or corridors used by all planning units on one floor. The range of circulation factors to be applied to and added to basic space requirements could be the following:

	Intraunit Circulation
15 percent	Many large stations and special facilities; rectilinear layouts
25 percent	Many small stations, e.g., for clerks
35 percent	All small stations; irregular or "landscape" layouts
	Interunit Circulation
10 percent	A few large planning units on a floor
15 percent	Many small planning units; shallow space from window to core

As a practical matter, planners test layouts for three or four floors using typical requirements, compare the base requirements for all units accommodated with the usable area (see Usable and Rentable Area below) of each floor, and then select a combination of circulation factors to use for all planning units. If no test layouts are done, use 25 and 10 percent for typical rectilinear layouts; 35 and 12 percent for open-plan layouts that are not rectilinear.

Computing Usable Area. Table O-7 illustrates this computation for a typical planning unit.

Stating Adjacency Requirements. The adjacency data for each division (i.e., a group of departments) or for the entire company can be shown on one or two bubble diagrams.

Selecting Space

Three options should be considered: build, lease, or renovate.

Build a New Building. This option involves a commitment to a particular site and a permanent facility of limited size, as well as the risks of building (cost and schedule) and ownership (operating costs and responsibilities and change in resale value). It provides benefits such as tax shelter, depreciation, and, if you lease part of the building, cash flow. A building can be refinanced advantageously if its value goes up.

TABLE O-6 Computing Space Requirements

Space type	Typical user	Range of area, square feet From	Range of area, square feet To
		From	To
	Private space types		
X	Chairman, president	300	600
A	Executive vice president, senior vice president	275	400
B	Vice president, senior managers	200	300
C	Managers, top professionals	110	165
D	Assistant managers, other professionals	81	120
	General office space types		
OSX	Executive secretaries	100	200
OA	Administrators, clerical supervisors	65	100
OS	Secretaries, typists	55	75
OC	Clerks	45	65

TABLE O-7 Computation of Usable Area

Planning unit AA: Executive group

Title	Space type	Unit area	19XX Person	19XX Area	19YY Person	19YY Area
President	X	500	1	500	1	500
Executive vice president	A	300	1	300	2	600
Vice president	B	225	2	450	2	450
Administrative assistant	D	100	1	100	2	200
Executive secretary	OSX	100	2	200	3	300
Secretary	OS	75	2	150	2	150
Clerk	OC	55			1	55
Reception area			1	500	1	500
Board room			—	600	—	600
Subtotal			10	2800	14	3355
Intraunit circulation, 25 percent				700		839
Subtotal				3500		4194
Interunit circulation, 10 percent				350		419
Total				3850		4613

Lease Space. When leasing space and evaluating alternative lease choices, you should do a thorough analysis of each lease offer based on the company's requirements; this procedure can reduce costs significantly. Using the space, utility, and construction requirements, negotiate with a landlord to provide specific needs at little or no cost. Understand the difference between usable and rentable area and match the available area to the needs of the company.

Usable and Rentable Area. Landlords define *usable area* as the space within the glass line or exterior walls, less the enclosed areas within the core. Some of this, however, is not in fact usable; i.e., you cannot place furniture in the space required for convector enclosures, freight car and elevator lobbies, or corridors within the core line. For a tenant, the significant measure is the *assignable usable area* (AUA), which is the space within the line of the convector enclosure minus the entire core area. *Rentable area* is a term used by landlords to prorate all the areas within the core except stairs, elevators, and shafts to tenants. Thus, rentable area includes toilets, lobbies, utility rooms, and sometimes air-conditioning equipment rooms. Landlords define this according to rules recommended by the Building Owners and Managers Association International (BOMAI) or, in New York State, by the Real Estate Board of New York (REBONY), or by using arbitrary factors.

Floor Efficiency. Module and floor features also affect the desirability of one building over another. A building with a 5-foot window module results in C and B offices being 10 or 15 feet wide; if the window module were 4 feet 6 inches, similar offices would be 9 feet 0 inches or 13 feet 6 inches wide. If there are many C or B offices, the larger module results in more spacious offices but requires more space for each.

Work Letter. This is the portion of the lease that

specifies what construction the landlord will allow the tenant free or under a predetermined cost schedule. The standard work letter is usually a one- or two-page list giving the formulas for determining quantity allowances for necessary amenities: light fixtures, ceiling and floor tile, sheet-rock partitions, doors, electric and telephone wall outlets, and electric power. However, what is offered rarely covers everything needed and often covers some items or quantities that are not needed. The letter rarely provides a specification for quality. Negotiate for a work letter that gives you what is needed. Insist on product names, or "equal" if specifications for material are omitted. To start negotiations, present your own version of an optimum work letter.

Key Lease Clauses. The lease should provide for changes in work letter allowances with credits for unused allowances; the right to substitute similar items in place of the landlord's products; the cost basis for *additional work,* i.e., work beyond what the work letter offers (this should be at the *landlord's cost* plus a fixed profit-overhead factor); the right to use your own contractor for *tenant's installations* (e.g., cabinetwork, carpet, wall coverings). It should include a *rent commencement* clause, stating when rent begins (ideally, this should be when the landlord has completed all work that was undertaken for the tenant and when public areas and all building systems are complete). It should include terms for *rent escalation* (due to increases in operating cost and taxes), subleasing, options to cancel, options for more space, change to electric metering, hours and seasons for HVAC, and rights during construction and move-in (to power, trash removal, and use of elevators).

Renovate Space. A major renovation requires more planning than new construction. Work must usually be done in two or more stages, moving part of the office to temporary quarters while that part is renovated. Basic systems (HVAC, plumbing, power capacity, elevator service, etc.) must be evaluated and, if found inadequate for long-range needs, they should be replaced or corrected. If more than one-third of the original construction must be replaced, it usually pays to gut the space and build a totally new interior—since the unit costs of renovation (e.g., replacing one light fixture, building 1 foot of partition) are far more than the unit costs for new construction in space that has been cleared of existing walls and ceilings.

Final Design and Budget

These should be prepared simultaneously with the final layout. All three must be presented to top management at one time, since a change in layout or design affects the budget. The *final design* should include sketches and large-scale layouts of important areas, colored renderings, models or photos of models, perhaps full-size mock-ups of work stations, a color palette and sample boards of every fabric or material, photos of every piece of new furniture, and an exhibit of typical art proposed. The *final budget* should detail every cost, including allowances for delivery, storage, taxes, and contingencies. Following approval of these three final documents, documentation and procurement can proceed.

Documentation. A series of plans and related specifications must be submitted to the landlord or to your own contractors for costing. These could include plans for demolition, construction, electrical work and telephone, reflected ceilings, sections, elevations, and other details (of construction). In addition, a separate set of plans and details is needed for cabinetwork. Special plans will be needed for audiovisual facilities, security systems, speaker systems, communications networks, and any operations areas (EDP, dispatch centers, medical, kitchen, mail, print shops, etc.). New furniture should be documented by detailed specifications, suitable for getting competitive bids, by instruction to bidders, and (after selection of bidders) by purchase orders. Set up a cost control system at this time, covering budget amounts, amounts committed, construction revisions, field authorized work, and engineering changes. Document any controversies, changes, or delays that might become the basis for future claims.

Implementing the Design

There are four aspects to design implementation: technical, bids and estimates, procurement, and supervision.

Compliance. Plans and specifications must comply with fire and other local codes, and with the Office of Safety and Health Administration (OSHA), the national code on health and safety. A series of engineering reviews are needed: structural (for reinforced areas and stair openings), mechanical (for HVAC and plumbing), and electrical. Some design might be needed, and engineering plans must be prepared. A set of plans, based on the interior design and engineering plans, must be filed locally by a licensed architect or engineer and approved before construction can proceed.

Current Concepts

The following developments indicate the dynamic nature of space planning concepts.

Planning for Change. Most companies grow, reorganize, and change functions on a continuing basis. It is not unusual for 20 percent or more of all personnel to be assigned new space each year. Renovation costs are high, and even a minor renovation disrupts the work of most of the floor's personnel. A good plan is one that accommodates change with the least amount of renovation.

Hard Areas Versus Soft Areas. Identify the *hard areas;* i.e., those spaces that require unique or expensive construction: executive suites, food service, EDP, conference and training rooms, and medical facilities. Limit hard areas as much as possible; i.e., give vice presidents better furniture and furnishings rather than custom lighting or cabinetwork and use a standard-sized office for a secondary conference room. All other spaces are *soft areas;* i.e., they can be reassigned to any other location with little or no construction. Locate hard areas so that they do not inhibit expansion or contraction of space. Do not locate hard areas on floors that might be vacated in the future. Do not disperse them; try to group them all on just a few floors. If a floor must have a mix of hard and soft areas, group all hard areas adjacent to the core, or at one end of the floor.

Flexible Layout Patterns. If there are a large number of private spaces, changes in soft areas may be accommodated through a flexible layout pattern. This might require that all perimeter offices be two windows wide (a four-window office can be created by removing one wall and closing one door). Or set a rule that three-window offices will be permitted only in pairs (for easy conversion to 3 twos or to a four and a two). Require that all offices be the same depth. No planning system can be changed economically if the ceiling has to be modified or new outlets drilled in the floor whenever space is reassigned.

Open Plans. Frequently called *open landscape,* the term *open plan* covers several types of layout. The distinguishing feature of all the layouts is that there are few, or no, constructed or movable floor-to-ceiling partitions. These include the following:

Grid Plan. This is a rectilinear plan using less-than-full-height partitions. It creates an open look, since the entire ceiling can be seen from any point, but it results in acoustical problems.

Office Landscape. This layout is created by plotting traffic patterns among all work stations and all work groups, and then placing work stations at locations dictated by the traffic pattern. Screens are used to give visual privacy, but most work stations consist only of a surface and necessary storage units.

Verticality. With the development of the various open plan systems, manufacturers produced components to be used in combination with movable partitions. A significant change from traditional office furniture (i.e., desks, credenzas, two-drawer files, and bookcases used in a few combinations), this new furniture consists of one or two vertical panels from which the components are supported. The basic work surface (traditionally 30 by 60 inches) can be made smaller since it no longer serves a storage function; storage can be hung over the surface. Further, the employee faces the partition while working on a task,

achieving some visual privacy. The employee turns to work with visitors, usually across a small conference table.

Evaluation. The private office with its rarely closed door has become a status symbol and reward for professionals and managers. The productivity of such persons is not measured in terms of work units performed but in terms of general effectiveness. Professionals and managers often claim they are less effective in an open plan. As a result, the greater the number of older professionals and managers, the less successful open plan layouts have been. When a select few retain their private offices, it is particularly difficult to persuade other people that *open* is equal to *closed.* Where there are large clerical groups, open plan systems have been most successful. By the early 1980s, open plan layouts for managerial positions had gained broad acceptance. But by the mid-1980s the trend had reversed, as users concluded that only full-height partitions gave adequate acoustical and visual privacy to managers.

Middle Management Changes. The number of middle management positions is expected to decrease during the last half of the 1980s because of the competition and example of Japanese companies, which perform with greater efficiency by eliminating many middle management jobs, and because increased use of computers by senior management gives them direct access to the sources of data. New layout concepts should result.

Ergonomics. Furniture manufacturers and interior designers are focusing on the relationship of the office worker to the environment, particularly in chair design, orientation to the work material, and lighting. As the number of people using terminals increases, improvement in the work environment is needed to reduce fatigue, increase efficiency, and improve accuracy.

Electrical Distribution. Greater flexibility in relocating work stations at reduced cost will result from the use of fiber optics, flat wire, and multisignal loops for the distribution of electrical power and electronic/communications signals.

See also Computer security; Facilities and site planning and layout; Human factors engineering; Paperwork simplification; Real estate management, corporate; Systems and procedures; Word processing.

REFERENCES

Becker, Franklin: *The Successful Office,* Addison-Wesley, Reading, Mass., 1982.

Harris, Palmer, et al.: *Planning and Designing the Office Environment,* Van Nostrand Reinhold, New York, 1981.

Kleeman, Walter B., Jr.: *The Challenge of Interior Design,* CBI, New York, 1981.

HERBERT L. NEWMARK, *Planning Consultant,*
Corporate Headquarters Development,
Pompano Beach, Florida

Officers, Corporate

Corporate officers bear the company's heaviest responsibilities, for their decisions are legally binding on the corporation and they are the principal determinant of the company's destiny and performance. Since the officers are the top leadership group, their selection and performance are of critical importance.

State laws of incorporation without exception require boards of directors to elect the company officers. Corporate bylaws set forth the roles, duties, and titles of the corporate officers, together with procedures for their election or removal and other matters of governance. Bylaws, however, typically allow great flexibility in the board's determination of officer roles, duties, and titles. The specifications in bylaws are more general than typical job descriptions.

The titles and duties of officers are by no means standardized or uniform, but general patterns common to many enterprises have evolved. It is important to note that companies are empowered within the bylaws to change the roles and titles of officers to fit the changing status of people and the changing needs of the organization.

Definition and Types of Officers. The term *officer* is applied loosely, but it has come to be used to cover two main categories based on the focus of their responsibilities. The first is that of *officer of the board,* which includes officials who conduct the activities of the board itself or who come most closely under the direct authority of the board. The second category consists of *other officers* such as vice presidents, whose primary responsibilities are in the operating sectors of the company.

Officers of the Board. Officers of the board typically include the chairperson of the board, who serves primarily as the board's chief agent or representative, plus the heads of its various committees, and a secretary of the board.

Chairperson of the Board. Historically, the leadership of the board has been assigned to a chairperson of the board. The chairperson acts as the board's agent in the management of its own activities and also in the delegation of responsibilities to the top operations officers, principally the president or a person designated as the chief executive officer.

The chairperson of the board may be on a full-time or a part-time basis, depending on the scope of the role assigned to the chairperson compared with the roles of the other officers, especially that of the president. If the corporation decides to have only one top leadership position at the officer level, it is usually a full-time chairperson of the board. If it chooses a dual leadership pattern, the president is usually designated as the other top officer. In this case the chairperson of the board may be a part-time appointment, focusing on activities of the board itself and on the management of its retained powers and activities, while the president carries out operating responsibilities technically delegated by the board. In some companies, the selection of a chairperson in addition to a president is mandatory; in others, it is optional.

Chief Executive Officer. The use of this title is confusing because it is used in various ways. Its primary use is in the designation of an officer attached to operations, mainly the president, as in the combined title of president and chief executive officer. The term, however, is occasionally used for an individual performing a wider role than that of president. It is sometimes combined, for example, with the chairperson of the board.

The chief executive officer is the most important officer position, but the role varies widely from company to company. Some chief executive officers perform the dual roles of heading the board's activities with respect to powers it has reserved for itself and of carrying out the operational activities of the company. If the two top roles are separated, the chairperson of the board takes the former role and the chief executive officer usually has a wide latitude for actions within the delegated scope of responsibilities. The chief executive officer makes recommendations to the board on basic policies but can take specific actions on subsidiary matters. Since chief executive officers have wide latitude in formulating proposals going before the board, they occupy a very powerful position. The chief executive officer also predominates in the selection of all other officers, though in theory they are also elected by the board.

President. This role is usually combined with that of the chief executive officer, but it may be delegated to a separate officer. In either case, the president is a key link between the board itself and the other operating officers.

Other Board Officers. Under most bylaws the board is empowered to appoint other officers as are needed to manage the activities it retains and does not delegate. For example, the board may appoint a secretary of the board (not to be confused with the corporate secretary); it also elects the heads of its various committees.

Other Officers. In addition to the positions described above, the board usually elects the following officers: the corporate secretary, the treasurer, and the vice presidents of operating units.

The chief executive officer, except for the appointment of the officer who may be a possible successor, has a strong voice in choosing those who serve under him or her. This includes the other officers as well as nonofficer executives in top management. Boards, however, typically exercise careful control over the officer who is likely to succeed the chief executive officer—the president or an executive vice president.

Corporate Secretary. The traditional role of corporate secretary has been to keep minutes of board and stockholder meetings, to keep registers of stockholders and stock certificates, to send out meeting notices, and to keep the corporate seal. Sometimes the corporate secretary also serves as board secretary, preparing agendas, distributing working documents, planning meeting arrangements, and the like. In practice, the role of secretary has been expanded to include a variety of other duties, such as records management, office management, financial work, liaison with stock exchanges, and supervision of transfer agents and dividend disbursement agents. Some corporate secretaries direct legal work associated with contracts, leases, patents, and trademarks. Often the secretary is also the corporation's legal counsel. The secretary usually reports to the company's chief executive officer.

Treasurer. The treasurer receives and has custody of corporate funds and keeps accounts thereof, prepares financial reports, and directs accounting policies and practices. Other duties, such as credit management or real estate development, are sometimes assigned. One important responsibility is to make financial reports directly to the board and to the chief executive officer. The treasurer may report directly to the chief executive officer, but more often reports indirectly through a vice president for finance. The principal financial officer is often known as the chief financial officer (CFO).

Vice Presidents. The principal vice presidents in charge of the major functions or divisional units are usually elected officers. These include the vice presidents of finance, marketing, and production, group vice presidents, and senior vice presidents. Less frequently, vice presidents in staff functions such as personnel are elected as officers. In large, multidivisional firms, the chief executives of divisions or subsidiaries often hold the title of divisional president in addition to being elected vice presidents of the corporation.

Compensation of Officers. Full-time officers are compensated by a combination of salaries, bonuses, options, and other fringe benefits. (*See* Compensation, executive.) Part-time officers may be compensated by prorated salaries or by fees. Most boards have a compensation committee which guides all executive compensation policies for the company.

The board of directors usually approves the salaries of full-time officers, as well as bonus, profit sharing, or stock option plans. To avoid conflicts of interest, bonus and option decisions are generally made by a committee consisting of directors, none of whom will themselves benefit.

A problem exists in cases where officers are also directors and therefore in the position of fixing their own compensation. Sometimes independent judgments are then sought from outside directors or even

from majority stockholders. The salaries of officers who are not directors are largely influenced by their immediate supervisors, though board approval may be required by the bylaws.

See also Boards of directors; Boards of directors, legal liability guidelines; Committees; Compensation, executive; Organization structures and charting.

REFERENCES

Koontz, Harold: *The Board of Directors and Effective Management,* McGraw-Hill, New York, 1967.

Mace, Myles L.: *Directors: Myth and Reality,* Harvard Business School, Division of Research, Boston, 1971.

Vance, Stanley C.: *Corporate Leadership: Boards, Directors, and Strategy,* McGraw-Hill, New York, 1983.

DALTON E. MCFARLAND, *University of Alabama in Birmingham*

Older Employees, Management of

Older employees, whether management or nonmanagement, whether men or women, present both advantages and inevitable problems to the manager. While it is a mistake to characterize older employees as a completely special breed, there are clear differences between them and employees, for example, in their late teens or early twenties. Definitions of *older* can vary, and deviations from any broad pattern are frequent, depending on specific industry practice, union arrangements, and cultural influences.

Chronological Definition. By age 45, employees have become *older.* Typically, while in their twenties, they have completed their education or training and have made at least a tentative commitment to a career or trade or organization. In their thirties, they usually acquire both some solid experience in a field (depth) and some degree of variety in assignments (breadth). By their forties, they may take on major responsibilities associated with maturity and job seasoning. They usually already have family responsibilities, often heavy ones; signs of both physical aging and emotional wear are more evident. They are mature, settled, experienced, and usually well trained. Inevitably they are *older.*

Characteristics. In 1981 there were 25.8 million people between the ages of 45 and 64 employed in U.S. nonagricultural industries—14.8 million men and 11.0 million women—or 27 percent of the nonagricultural work force. Among men in the labor force, 91.0 percent between the ages of 45 and 54 were working, as were 64.4 percent between the ages of 55 and 64. Among women the percentages were 61.0 and 41.8 percent, respectively.[1] During those age periods, unemployment rates were at the lowest levels of the adult working years, at about 2.8 percent for men and 3.5 percent for women (1979 figures).[2]

Health. Older employees' health records are consistently better, and men's health records are better than women's. This shows up in the following measures per 100 employed persons: (1) days lost from work; (2) days of restricted activity associated with acute conditions; (3) incidence of acute conditions; (4) days of bed disability; and (5) days of restricted activity. Only in the average *duration of disability* and in days of restricted activities associated with injuries do older male employees show up worse than older female employees (8.4 days average versus 5.2 days average).[3] *Punctuality* records among older workers are also found to be better.

Job Stability. Older employees have considerable job stability but not significantly more than younger workers. A study of men 45 to 69 during the 3-year period 1966 to 1969 showed only 1 in 5 changing employers during that time, with 60 percent of the shifts occurring voluntarily.[4] Job changing was unrelated to race but closely tied to length of service, income, and occupation. Five years of service is a key stage in job stability, with men being eight times as likely to shift voluntarily and three times as likely to shift involuntarily before that period. Blue-collar workers shift more readily than white-collar workers, and higher wages are a significant motivation in changing jobs. Men who reported themselves as "content" with their jobs were less likely to shift.

Occupational Stability. Older workers also have occupational stability, with career shifts being less likely with advancing age.[5] One result is an overrepresentation of older workers in receding or nonexpanding occupations, including management and administration. Earnings peak in the 45- to 54-year-old category for managerial employees and in the 35- to 44-year-old category for craftsworkers. *Educational differences* are narrowing rapidly, being most pronounced among those over 55.

Legal Requirements. The Age Discrimination in Employment Act (ADEA) forbids discrimination against workers aged 40 to 70 who are working for commerce-related employers with 20 or more employees, for governmental units, in unions of 25-plus members or using hiring halls, or placed through employment agencies.[6] Discrimination based on age is forbidden in hiring, firing, promoting, classifying, paying, advertising, assigning, or eligibility for union membership. There are certain exceptions for apprenticeship programs, benefit plans, and clearly job-related age requirements. Sentiment is also growing for removal of mandated retirement at 70, either through an extension of this law beyond 70 or by court action. The law is hard to enforce, especially when employer action is linked to other factors, but government enforcement efforts are increasingly apparent. Equal opportunity laws can also apply in many of these situations.

Comparisons with Younger Employees. Older employees can learn as well as younger workers and can be retrained as easily.[7] Except in very special circumstances, physical impairment is insignificant and safety statistics are better. Older managers are as effective information processors as younger managers and diagnose data more accurately although more slowly.[8] However, they have also been shown to have poorer short-term mental retention.[9] They are also less effective than younger managers in operating in groups and in using groups to accomplish a task, perhaps because of the exposure of younger managers to more group-oriented education.

Job Satisfaction. Job satisfaction appears to affect job performance to a considerable degree in terms described by Herzberg as performance, turnover, interpersonal relationships on the job, and mental health.[10] Herzberg also found job satisfaction high when people started their first job; it then declined until about age 30, when it began to rise for the remainder of the work career. Otherwise, the relationship of age to job satisfaction is not nearly as clear as are, for example, the level of occupation, achievement, recognition, advancement, or the work itself.

Midlife Problems. It is evident that something special takes place in midlife. A Massachusetts study of industry's reluctance to hire middle-aged managerial candidates noted that middle-aged candidates had poor general health and appearance, relied excessively on outdated experience, were reluctant to undertake training, and performed poorly in training undertaken.[11]

The midlife crisis is a common observance. The period after 35 is the time of greatest expansion of the human personality, when mature adults are in widest contact with their surroundings. Yet psychological and physical aging is evident to the older person who subtly gives up on competition, emphasizes personal relationships, and substitutes new motivations for living. Older employees begin to adjust to the limitations of their organizational prospects. When satisfaction with life and job is lowered, job effectiveness is also lowered; and the two satisfactions are inevitably linked. At the same time, mobility or a fresh start are discouraged by corporate and social "freeze-in" devices, such as fringe benefits. There are few significant problems in managing older employees, however, who are at high or rising positions in the organization, have authority and position, receive satisfying monetary and symbolic rewards, and clearly are considered vital parts of the organization. This is as true of blue-collar workers as it is of white-collar employees.[12] The problem for management comes when employees of whatever level no longer look to the organization for satisfaction of important elements of their aspirations. They then react similarly to employees in their mid-twenties.

Managerial Responses. Correct and positive approaches to the management of older employees fit a number of categories:

1. *Health.* Despite favorable absence and health statistics among older employees, management must be alert to overall general health, which can point to incipient problems (weight, blood pressure, alcoholism, etc.), and to psychological well-being. Independent outside psychiatric consultants are recommended to handle midlife crises. The annual checkup is highly recommended.

2. *Obsolescence.* Executive development is widely used in industry and government, but it is often confined to rising or high-status managers. A full range of carefully considered programs make suitable provisions against obsolescence. If the employee *will not* adjust, there should be incentives to mobility, including early pensions, severance pay, placement services, etc.

3. *Promotions, transfers, salary treatment, etc.* It is fatal to give the best treatment to younger employees. It symbolizes to older employees that their worst fears are essentially correct. Of course, there are cases justifying bias, but the reasons must be evident to all, including the employees involved.

4. *Fringe benefits.* These are too often mere satisfiers rather than dynamic aspects of employee growth. For example, tuition reimbursement should be granted only when the result of the schooling fits into the plans of both the employee *and* management. Health plans should have prevention and examination features. Pension plans should encourage leaving as well as staying, especially at management levels. Vacations are vital to both physical and mental well-being: they are seldom managed other than routinely.

5. *Assignments.* Observers point out that older employees have a growing interest in other people. Japanese industry uses the "godfather" concept, linking older and younger employees rather than having them compete. The reward systems should encourage the development of the young to the benefit of the organization. It may be generally useful to downplay competition beyond a certain point in age or position.

6. *Leaves of absence.* In selected and carefully considered cases, a leave of absence can be the means of giving a new outlook to older employees. Academic sabbaticals are proven cases in point.

7. *Performance.* It is important that expectations of older employees be kept high, including level of output and quality of performance. There should be no rewards for age in terms of slackened performance, since experience and high-quality performance are precisely what older employees can give to the organization.

8. *Management attitude.* This will signal clearly whether the organization considers older employees valuable assets or burdens to be suffered. Younger employees will note this attitude in looking to their own commitment to the organization. Older employees will determine from it their own level of commitment.

See also Equal employment opportunity, minorities and women; Women in business and management; Younger employees, management of.

NOTES

[1] *Employment and Earnings*, U.S. Department of Labor, Bureau of Labor Statistics, Washington, D.C., March 1983, pp. 31, 49.

[2] *Handbook of Labor Statistics*, U.S. Department of Labor, Bureau of Labor Statistics, Washington, D.C., 1980, p. 77.

[3] *Vital and Health Statistics*. U.S. Department of Health and Human Resources, Public Health Service, Washington, D.C., Series 10, 970.141, 1981.

[4] *Monthly Labor Review*, U.S. Department of Labor, Manpower Administration, Washington, D.C., June 1973, pp. 60–61.

[5] Shirley H. Rhine, "The Senior Worker—Employed and Unemployed," *The Conference Board Record*, vol. 13, no. 5, May 1976, pp. 7ff.

[6] "Age Discrimination in Employment Act (ADEA) of 1967," Public Law 90-202, 181 Stat. 602, as amended in 1974 and 1978.

[7] Rhine, op. cit.

[8] Ronald N. Taylor, "Age and Experience as Determinants of Managerial Information Processing and Decision Making Performance," *Academy of Management Journal*, vol. 18, no. 1, March 1975, pp. 74ff.

[9] Wayne K. Kirchner, "Age Differences in Short-Term Retention," *Journal of Experimental Psychology*, vol. 55, no. 4, 1958, pp. 357–358.

[10] John W. Hunt and Peter N. Saul, "The Relationship of Age, Tenure, and Job Satisfaction in Males and Females," *Academy of Management Journal*, vol. 18, no. 4, December 1975, pp. 690ff.

[11] *The Aging Worker: Insights into the Massachusetts Problem*, John F. Kennedy Family Service Center, Inc., Older Worker Training and Employment Program, The Kennedy Center, Boston, 1969.

[12] Cyrus A. Altimus and Richard J. Tersine, "Chronological Age and Job Satisfaction: The Young Blue Collar Worker," *Academy of Management Journal*, vol. 16, no. 1, March 1973, pp. 53ff.

REFERENCES

Herzberg, Frederick, Bernard Mausner, and Barbara Block Snyderman: *The Motivation to Work*, John Wiley, New York, 1967.

Saleh, Shorekry D., and Jay L. Otis: "Age and Level of Job Satisfaction," *Personnel Psychology*, vol. 17, no. 4, Winter 1964.

Schultz, Duane: "Managing the Middle-Aged Manager," *Personnel*, vol. 51, no. 6, November-December 1974.

PHILIP T. CROTTY, *Northeastern University*

Operations Research and Mathematical Modeling

Since the early 1940s something called *operations research* in the United States and *operational research* in Great Britain (and *management science* in many university business administration or management schools) has emerged and developed to extraordinary dimensions. Operations research (commonly referred to as OR) has established itself as an activity that can and does bring new concepts, new ideas, new attitudes, and new approaches to the aid of management. Despite OR's rapid growth and increasing acceptance by all types of organizations, a great deal of confusion exists in many people's minds as to its nature and domain. In some aspects, it is similar to systems engineering and industrial engineering. It also depends heavily upon model building, applied mathematics, and applied economics. But these elements do not define OR. For example, *OR is not* (1) simply a collection of tools and/or mathematical techniques such as linear programming, theory of games, simulation, and queueing theory; (2) mathematical model building and manipulation, unless one wishes to conclude that all science is operations research; (3) utilization of interdisciplinary teams to study complex problems, although this approach is often followed; (4) a form of management. In fact, without the existence and participation of management, OR is a meaningless academic exercise.

Nature and Domain of OR. Operations research defies easy definition because it uses the methodology and tools of various fields of science and engineering to study operations that are not conventionally the province of the scientist. A partial but circular definition is that operations research is research on operations. But this does not specify the type of research, its purpose, or on what operations. Accordingly, *operations research* can be defined broadly as the study of complex systems of people, equipment, money, and operational procedures for the purpose of understanding how they function, in order to improve their efficiency and effectiveness. Such studies are conducted through the use of the scientific method, utilizing tools and knowledge from the physical, mathematical, and behavioral sciences. Its ultimate purpose is to provide the manager with a sound, scientific, and quantitative basis for decision making.

Purpose. Operations research is concerned with determining (1) how a system behaves under a wide range of conditions; (2) the relationships between the components which explain why the system behaves in this manner; and (3) how the manager can improve and control the behavior and performance of the system to achieve the desired goals and objectives. Thus, OR is concerned with the solution of executive-type problems. Its goal is to provide management with a scientific basis for solving problems involving the interaction of the different functional units of the organization in terms of the best interests of the total organization.

Technique. Operations research accomplishes these goals by providing management with pertinent information upon which to make decisions. This information is obtained by utilizing the diverse skills of a mixed (academic and experience) group of appropriate researchers. This mixed team utilizes the scientific method and any or all available tools and techniques which are appropriate, to gather and process this information so as to analyze the operations of complex systems. The critical point in all of this is the purpose, not the methods. If an operations research study has not resulted in better decisions by the manager, it has failed, no matter how elegant its approach or technique. The end goal and criterion by which it must always be judged is results.

Areas of Application

Operations research has been successfully applied in virtually every kind of business, industrial, and governmental organization.[1] When managers discuss decisions to be made, they often express a belief that their problems are different from those confronting other executives. They are correct in one sense. Problems can be viewed from two aspects—form and content. Two problems seldom have the same content, but they often have the same form. The following list illustrates some of the areas in which OR has been successfully applied.

Production. This includes: (1) production planning and scheduling, including decisions on product mixes, sequencing of jobs, overtime, scheduling, etc.; (2) allocation of production orders to different plants or departments on the basis of production or transportation costs; (3) scheduling of maintenance (both preventive and corrective) and replacement of equipment; (4) assembly line balancing and allocation of facilities and personnel; (5) raw material and in-process inventory management; and (6) analysis of waiting lines and bottlenecks.

Facilities Planning. This includes: (1) number and location of factories, warehouses, tool cribs, service yards, retail outlets, fire stations, ambulances, schools, etc: (2) internal allocation and layout of space; and (3) design of material handling systems.

Purchasing and Procurement. This includes: (1) development of rules for buying supplies with stable or significantly varying prices; (2) determination of quantities, timing, and source of purchase; (3) make-or-buy decisions of parts and components; (4) purchase-or-lease decisions on vehicles and equipment; and (5) spare-parts stocking requirements as well as problems associated with deterioration and shrinkage.

Investment and Finance. This includes: (1) cash-flow analysis, long-range capital requirements, alternative investments, and sources of capital; (2) development of automated data processing systems, accounting systems, and auditing procedures; (3) diversification and acquisition decisions; (4) stock and bond portfolio selection; (5) budgeting, planning, and control; and (6) financial forecasting.

Marketing. This includes: (1) advertising strategies, including selection of media, frequency of advertising, and allocation of budget to various media; (2) product selection and timing of new products; (3) forecasting demand; (4) pricing and bidding strategies; (5) number of salespeople, size of territories, and allocation of sales effort; (6) salespeople's compensation and incentive plans; (7) warranty and customer service strategies; (8) company-owned outlets versus franchising decisions; and (9) space allocation for display and stock accessibility.

Transportation and Physical Distribution. This includes: (1) multilevel inventory control systems; (2) worldwide logistics and supply systems; (3) development of transportation and support policies; and (4) determination of optimum routing of distribution and supply vehicles.

Research and Development. This includes: (1) evaluation of alternative designs; (2) determination of areas of research needed and technological forecasting; (3) selection of individual projects; (4) allocation of resources between R&D projects; and (5) coordination and management control procedures for complex R&D projects.

Personnel. This includes: (1) selection and recruiting policies of personnel, including determination of mixes of age and skills needed; (2) analysis of factors influencing labor turnover, absenteeism, and grievances; and (3) development of incentive, productivity improvement, and performance measurement schemes.

Governmental. This includes: (1) analyses of air, rail, highway, and waterway transportation systems, including routes; (2) development of waste pickup and disposal strategies, including vehicle routing; (3) determination of school districts and school bus routings; (4) traffic control studies; (5) urban planning, including land use, transportation, and community facilities; (6) economic planning; (7) cost-benefit analysis; and (8) evaluation of military weapons and strategies.

OR Methodology

Operations research emphasizes the application of the scientific method to the analysis and solution of decision problems. The *scientific method* is a rational, systematic method of approaching a problem and consists of the three phases of analysis, synthesis, and evaluation. Generally these consist of the following:

Analysis Phase. (1) Awareness and identification of needs; (2) definition in specific and detailed terms of the problem to be solved and the goals to be achieved; (3) gathering and structuring of information; (4) identification of the boundary conditions (i.e., what is and is not a part of the system); (5) identification of the relevant components of the system, including (a) input versus output variables, (b) controllable versus uncontrollable variables, and (c) decision makers and the decision-making process.

Synthesis Phase. (1) Determination of the criteria to be used for measuring effectiveness; (2) construction of an appropriate model; (3) data gathering; and (4) search for and derivation of feasible solutions from the model.

Evaluation Phase. (1) Evaluation of solutions derived from the model; (2) making a decision; (3) implementing the decision; and (4) closure to see if the problem is really solved.

The phases and steps listed above are by no means completely definitive or self-inclusive, nor do they always appear in the same order. All the steps represent continuing efforts throughout a study, with recurring interplay among the steps. There is an iterative nature to decision making, with a constant roving back and forth between generality and detail, as the practitioners continuously seek to improve their understanding and the description of the problem.

Analysis. In the execution of an OR project, the problem formulation, or analysis, is often the most important phase of a study. It is composed of the definition of the primary and subobjectives and the identification of the variables which significantly influence the performance of the system. Identification and consideration of uncontrollable variables such as the external business environment, competitors' actions, governmental regulations, and similar factors are also important. Another important aspect is that of determining the scope of the study in terms of long- or short-range planning.

Synthesis. In the second phase, a model is usually developed. A *model* is a representation of an object, system, or idea in some form other than that of the entity itself. Its purpose is usually to aid in explaining, understanding, or improving the system under study. In most OR studies, a mathematical model is used.

Mathematical models consist of equations or formulas derived to show the relationships between important factors in the operation under study. Such models can be analyzed and manipulated more easily than the real system. Proposed changes or hypotheses can be tested and evaluated using the model without disrupting the real-world system. For those who seek to understand, control, or manipulate the infinite complexities of the real world, mathematics is a very powerful tool. It is not, however, just one more tool among many. It is a conceptual tool more powerful than most others. Mathematics is the most precise, unambiguous language devised by the human race.

Underlying Principle. A number of specialized mathematical techniques are used in constructing OR models. Many of these will be discussed later. Even though OR models can take on many forms, their underlying principle is relatively simple. In symbolic expression, the basic form of most OR models is

$$P = f(C_i, U_j)$$

where the system's overall performance P is a function of a set of controllable aspects of the system C_i and a set of uncontrollable aspects U_j. This obvious oversimplification calls attention to the fact that the performance of the system is affected by variables outside the manager's control as well as those he or she can do something about. Once a model has been set up, one seeks those values of the controllable variables C_i that maximize (or minimize) the performance P.

Performance Measures. The most difficult part of an OR study may be the development of an adequate measure of the system's performance. Unfortunately, there are usually several possible measures, and the right choice depends upon which question is being asked. The measure of performance must reflect the relative importance of the many (and often conflicting) objectives involved in every management decision. These objectives are of two types—retentive and acquisitive. *Retentive objectives* are those which deal with keeping or preserving either resources (for example, time, energy, and skills) or states (for example, comfort, safety, and employment levels). *Acquisitive goals* concern acquiring resources (for example, profits, personnel, and customers) or attaining states (for example, share of market and deterrent position) that the organization or manager seeks.

Evaluation. The final phase involves an analysis of the sensitivity of proposed solutions to slight changes in assumptions, external and internal conditions, or levels of operations. It also consists of helping (1) to implement new policies and procedures and (2) to monitor the new system after implementation to ensure that the solution is correct and is solving the problem as anticipated.

Mathematical Models

In general, mathematical models useful in OR studies can be categorized as being either deterministic or probabilistic in nature. This distinction is based upon what is known about the values of the variables. In a *deterministic* model, the values of the variables are known or assumed to be known. Thus, decision theorists refer to the use of such models as decision making under conditions of certainty. The assumption of certainty implies that the consequence of selecting a particular alternative is a uniquely determined outcome. On the other hand, *probabilistic* models assume that the values of the variables are not all known with certainty but that probability distributions can be associated with each of them. These probability distributions may be derived from theoretical, empirical (actual data), or subjective (expert opinion) considerations. Decision theorists refer to the use of such models as decision making under conditions of risk.

The purpose of a good mathematical model is to help managers understand and evaluate alternative policies efficiently. The procedures used to derive a solution to the problem from the model depend upon the characteristics of the model. These procedures are either analytical or numerical. *Analytical procedures* are those in which the equation or set of equations is solved directly. For example, the researcher might differentiate the equation, set it equal to zero, and then solve for the variables of interest—or plug the values of the variables directly into the equation and evaluate the function.

Numerical procedures are iterative in nature (trial and error) and are usually referred to as algorithms. An *algorithm* is a systematic step-by-step procedure for finding a solution. Numerical techniques consist essentially of substituting different numbers for the symbols in the model and finding which set of substituted numbers yields the maximum effectiveness. Usually some set of rules (algorithm) is used to determine which set of numbers will be tried next. Such a procedure (which might be thought of as directed trial and error) is call *iteration.* Analytic procedures are essentially deductive in character, whereas numerical procedures are essentially inductive in character.

Classification of Mathematical Models. In order to discuss and understand the relationship between the various mathematical techniques and models, it is convenient to try to establish a framework or classification scheme. Any such attempt suffers, of course, from its inability to show models which fall into several categories.

I. *Deterministic models*
  A. Analytic (mathematical solution)
    1. Calculus
    2. Linear algebra
    3. Differential equations
  B. Numerical (iterative)
    1. Linear programming
      a. Simplex algorithm
      b. Transportation algorithm
      c. Assignment algorithm
      d. Goal programming
    2. Network optimization algorithms
      a. Maximum flow
      b. Shortest path
      c. Longest path
      d. PERT/CPM
    3. Integer programming
      a. Branch and bound algorithm
      b. Zero-one algorithm
    4. Nonlinear programming
      a. Search techniques
      b. Separable programming
      c. Quadratic programming
      d. Geometric programming
    5. Dynamic programming
    6. Heuristic algorithms
    7. Gaming theory

II. *Probabilistic models*
  A. Analytic (theoretical)
    1. Probability theory
    2. Queueing theory
    3. Markov processes
    4. Renewal processes
  B. Numerical (iterative and empirical)
    1. Simulation
    2. Expected value
    3. Decision trees
    4. Regression analysis

The characteristics of some of these models will be described below.

Deterministic Models. Many decision problems lend themselves to direct solution through the use of classical mathematical techniques. The system being studied can often be represented by an equation or set of equations which can be solved directly by calculus, linear algebra, or the methods of differential equations. For example, deterministic inventory control problems can be modeled as an equation which can be differentiated, set equal to zero, and solved for the decision variables of interest. Likewise, many control problems can be represented by a set of differential equations which can then be solved directly.

Mathematical programming is perhaps the most highly developed and widely used area of operations research methodology. It is a generic term mainly covering the topics of linear programming, network analysis, nonlinear programming, and dynamic programming. It is used to help solve those problems in which the decision maker must allocate scarce or limited resources among various activities in order to optimize some specified goal.

Linear programming deals with allocation problems where the goal can be expressed as a linear function (equation) of the alternatives subject to a group of constraints which can also be expressed as linear equations.[2] If there are multiple goals, the technique of *goal programming* can be utilized. Although there are several specialized linear programming methods (i.e., transportation and assignment methods) which can be used if the characteristics of the problem are correct, the most versatile (or general) is the simplex method devised by George C. Dantzig. The *simplex method* is a very powerful computational method which allows operations researchers to attack large-scale allocation problems. Commercial linear programming codes are available from most computer manufacturers and consulting firms. These computer programs will handle 16,000 or more constraints with no practical limit on the number of variables.

If there is the additional constraint, or requirement, that the resources can only be allocated as integers or whole numbers, the problem is classified as one of *integer (linear) programming*. If the resources are such that they are either used or not used (i.e., go–no go), it is a *zero-one linear programming* problem.

Many systems problems can be represented as a network. Transportation, communication, and distribution systems readily fall into this category. The analyst usually tries to find the shortest (or longest) path or the maximal flow through the network. The *program evaluation and review technique* (PERT) and the *critical path method* (CPM) are network techniques widely used in the planning, scheduling, and control of projects of various kinds. (*See* Network planning methods.)

Nonlinear programming methods are used when either the objective function (goal) and/or one or more of the constraints are expressed as nonlinear functions. Because many real-world problems contain nonlinearities, one might expect these techniques to be widely used. This is not the case, however, because of the computational difficulties inherent in solving nonlinear problems. A large family of *search* methods has been developed for seeking the solution to unconstrained nonlinear programming problems. Among the most widely used are the Fibonacci, golden section, Hooke-Jeeves, and gradient search techniques. These are sequential search methods which successively reduce the interval in which the maximum (minimum) value of a nonlinear function must lie. Although these search techniques usually work very well, their utility is limited by the fact that very few decision problems can be represented by a single equation with no constraints. **637**

Since most real-world problems contain constraints on the decision variables, a number of techniques have been developed for problems where the objective function and/or the constraints are nonlinear, such as *separable programming, quadratic programming,* and *geometric programming.* Of these, separable programming is probably the most useful at the present time. The separable programming technique approximates the nonlinear functions with piecewise linear functions and then uses a modified simplex linear programming algorithm to solve the resulting problem.

Dynamic programming is a mathematical technique (whose development is due largely to Richard Bellman) used for solving sequential decision problems. Primarily, these models deal with multiperiod decisions—those which occur only at certain points of time called "stages." The basic objective of most dynamic programming models is to provide the manager with a policy. That is, if the system is found to be in a certain condition at a given time, the derived policy tells which decision to make. Dynamic programming can also be used to solve problems which are single period in nature but which can be viewed as being solved through a sequence of decisions rather than a single decision; i.e., the decision-making process can be broken down into stages. This method is capable of handling either deterministic or stochastic (probabilistic) cases. In contrast to linear programming and other mathematical models, there is no standard form for dynamic programming models, nor is a generalized computer program available. Thus although theoretically it is one of the more powerful analytic tools of OR, in practice its use is limited by difficulties in problem formulation and the computational limitations whenever problems with a large number of constraints are to be solved.

Heuristic methods are those which utilize some commonsense rules of thumb to search for an acceptable solution. Heuristic methods do not guarantee an optimum solution (although they often achieve one); instead they strive for a good or above-average solution. Heuristic techniques are most often used when the problem is of such size and complexity that exact optimizing algorithms are not available or not practical. The heuristic approach seeks solutions based upon acceptability characteristics rather than optimizing rules.

Gaming theory (developed by J. von Neumann) has been considered by some to be the most significant mathematical development of the past century. It is concerned with competitive situations in which two or more participants are in conflict. Each of the participants of the conflict controls some of, but not all, the actions which can take place. This is a situation where a decision maker wishes to achieve some objective. The individual selects a strategy from among the alternatives available. This strategy, together with the chance events or states of nature which occur and the competitive or counter strategy employed by the opponent, determines the degree to which the individual obtains or fails to obtain the chosen objective.

The most practical and significant contribution of gaming theory has been to provide a conceptual and rational framework for decision analysis. The very process of analyzing a competitive situation in a gaming theory context will serve to provide a logical approach and aid in understanding—even though it provides solutions only for very simple problems.

Probabilistic Models. Some of the most commonly applied OR techniques come from probability theory and statistics. They include discrete and continuous probability, combinatorial analysis, and renewal theory. By introducing the notions of confidence limits and probability of occurrence, rather than by using simple averages, a much more realistic view of probable outcomes is presented. (*See* Risk analysis and management; Statistical analysis for management.)

Stochastic processes are those in which the probabilities of certain events change dynamically with time, distance, or other parameters. One of the important offsprings of the increasing ability to deal with stochastic processes is queueing theory. *Queueing theory* deals with the study of waiting lines of every conceivable kind and the need to reduce bottlenecks and congestion. Queueing theory deals with the capacity of an operating unit to perform some service. The units, or elements of interest, arrive at the service facility, wait in line if necessary, receive the desired service, and leave the system. These models are characteristic of toll booths, sales counters, tool cribs, docking facilities, etc. They are also usable where the service is brought to the unit, such as where machines break down and await the arrival of a repair crew. The objective of studies using queueing theory is to determine the optimal number of personnel or facilities needed to service customers who arrive randomly—and to balance the cost of service with the cost of waiting or congestion.

In general, queueing theory offers information on the probability that a certain number of units (people, machines, etc.) will have to wait in line, how long these units can expect to wait, and the percentage of idle time for the service facility. Such quantities can then be used to determine whether the size of the waiting space or speed of service should be increased.

Another useful form of stochastic models is the so-called *renewal process.* Studies related to the replacement of light bulbs according to their life expectancy or the overhaul of aircraft engines are examples. The studies of *renewal processes* involve the probability of failure or wearing out through time of some object. These renewal concepts are similar to those used by statisticians for life insurance actuarial studies. System reliabilty studies are also closely related and utilize many of the same concepts.

When the probable future state of a system is dependent only upon the present state, it is called a *Markov process*. In a Markov-dependent sequence of events, knowledge of the present makes the future independent of the past. If the system is known to have reached a certain state, it is immaterial what chain of events is passed through on the way to this stage as far as predicting the state it will enter into next. In other words, the system has no *memory* that would allow it to modify its behavior. A sequence of events, each of which is subject to the above-stated Markovian property, is referred to as a *Markov chain*. Markov chains have been used to study types of financial analysis. The model involves several over-simplifying assumptions, however, which limit its utility.

Of all the modeling methodologies available, the most powerful and widely used is simulation.[3] A *simulation* model is one which imitates the behavior and exhibits the characteristics of the process or system of interest. Simulation consists of developing a model of the system that shows the logical relationships between the different components of the system and how they affect each other. The model must be capable of showing the connection between the successive states of the system being studied. The model developed can either be a physical (iconic) or a mathematical (logical) one which is computerized. The model is then used to conduct experiments for the purpose either of understanding the behavior of the system or of evaluating various strategies for the operation of the system.

Physical simulation models may be (1) full-scale mock-ups, such as those used for airline pilot or automobile driver training, or (2) reduced-scale models, such as those used for aircraft wind-tunnel testing. The widespread practice in the chemical industry of building a small pilot plant of a new process before going into full-scale production is an excellent example of simulation using physical models.

Computerized simulation models use mathematical and logical relationships to portray and imitate the behavior of components of the system being studied. Corporate planning models are usually computerized simulation models of the marketing and/or production aspects of their operations. Computerized simulation models can either be deterministic in nature or contain probabilistic variables. Simulation is used when (1) mathematical techniques are inadequate or do not exist; (2) there is a need to understand how a complex system operates and a need to know the effect of different decisions; and (3) potential problems and methods of dealing with them must be anticipated.

The *expected-value technique* is more of a deci-sion-making criterion than a modeling method. The expected value of a particular decision or strategy is the sum of the values of each of the possible outcomes, each multiplied by its probability of occurrence. For example, if an individual were flipping a coin and received $1 for each head and forfeited $1 for each tail, the expected value would be equal to $.5(\$1) + .5(-\$1) = 0$. If the decision maker is considering several alternatives, each with different payoffs and probability distributions, the expected value for each alternative can be calculated so as to select the one with the highest expected payoff.

Decision trees are a special case of dynamic programming used for representing problem situations which require a sequence of decisions. In a decision tree, there is a sequence of decisions for which, after every decision is made, there is a result which is probabilistic in nature; once the result is known, there is a need for a further decision. In diagrammatic form, this is represented by Fig. O-3. In the tree there are two kinds of nodes: (1) decision points where the decision maker decides what to do next and (2) probabilistic nodes where someone or something else controls the outcome. A probability of occurrence is assigned to each branch at the probabilistic nodes. At the end of each of the branches of the decision tree, a value is placed which represents the utility of arriving at that point.

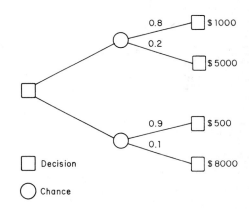

FIG. O-3 Decision tree.

The decision-tree approach then determines what decisions should be made by rolling back from the ends of the branches to the first decision point. An expected value for each decision alternative at a decision point is derived through the use of the expected-value technique.

Regression analysis is a widely used statistical technique to derive predictive equations from historical or empirical test data. It is essentially a line- or curve-fitting technique. If one suspects that the value of a variable is some function of one or more variables, regression analysis can be used to derive a predictive equation. Regression techniques are widely used by economists in econometric studies. (*See* Statistical analysis for management.)

See also Statistical analysis for management; System concept, total.

NOTES

[1] E. S. Buffa, *Modern Production Management*, 4th ed., John Wiley, New York, 1973; R. I. Levin and C. A. Kirkpatrick, *Quantitative Approaches to Management*, 3d ed., McGraw-Hill, New York, 1975; D. T. Phillips, A. Ravindran, and J. J. Solberg, *Operations Research, Principles, and Practice*, John Wiley, New York, 1976.

[2] R. E. Machol, *Elementary Systems Mathematics: Linear Programming for Business and the Social Sciences*, McGraw-Hill, New York, 1976; Phillips et al., op. cit.

[3] R. E. Shannon, *Systems Simulation: The Art and Science*, Prentice-Hall, Englewood Cliffs, N.J., 1975.

REFERENCES

Daellenbach, Hans G.: *Introduction To Operations Research Techniques*, 2d ed., Allyn & Bacon, Boston, Mass., 1983.

Stair, Ralph M.: *Production and Operations Management*, Allyn & Bacon, Boston, Mass., 1980.

ROBERT E. SHANNON, *Texas A & M University*

Organization Development (OD)

Organization development deals with organizational aspects of the behavioral sciences and may be known as, or associated with, human resource development, organization behavior, organization psychology, and organization renewal. OD also tends to overlap such fields as employee relations, sociology, anthropology, management, training, education, human relations, clinical psychology, and probably every other social and behavioral science.

Definitions of OD are many and varied. A particularly useful one is *any planned activity directed toward helping the members of an organization to interact more effectively in pursuit of the organization's goals.* In work organizations, improving or maximizing productivity and the quality of work life is usually part of the goals. Some practitioners insist that other provisions be stipulated, such as: *must be an organizationwide effort; must be directed toward more participative management; must provide for integrating the individual's goals with the organization's; must be considered an ongoing process—not an activity.* The real difference between OD activities and those technologically, economically, or administratively imposed to increase productivity is that

OD is intentionally based on a scientific awareness of human behavior and organization dynamics.

The Promise of OD. The great promise of OD lies in its ability to merge the interests of individuals and the organization and make both more productive. Much personal unhappiness can be traced to feelings of being inadequately integrated in organizations—particularly in work organizations. Similarly, much organizational inefficiency can be traced to member disinterest in, or even hostility to, the organization. In the past, organizations have been successful due largely to the intuitive talent of leaders or the fortuitous combinations of the many contributing factors. In the future, organizations will owe more of their success to those who aptly use OD concepts and techniques. While OD will not overcome such deficiencies as outdated technology, inadequate financing, or hostile and overwhelming external forces, it will enable organizations to cope more effectively with these negative influences. OD does this by releasing the power of people to work willingly together for the common good.

Background Theory and Assumptions. The definition of an organization, as used in this entry, is two or more persons interacting within some mutually recognized power relationship for some common purpose. This definition is intentionally broad in order to include all sizes and types of organizations, formal or informal, of either a temporary or more permanent nature. The power relationship may be hierarchical or that of equals.

Organizing is one of the oldest human activities. It is a phenomenon that will continue to be important to people. OD is based on the assumption that organizations influence human behavior and individuals influence an organization's behavior. OD also assumes that both individual behavior and organizational behavior can be modified, and with favorable results—if based on proper diagnosis and skillful interventions. The terms *climate* and *spirit (Orgeist)* are sometimes used in describing the mixture of individual and group feelings. Those who claim some professional expertise in positively influencing the behavior of an organization based on OD knowledge and skills are called *change agents,* practitioners, or consultants. Internal consultants are those who are also members of the organization, and external consultants are those who are independently contracted to serve the organization.

Organizations may be classified in many ways to fit the proclivities and motivations of the individual studying or working with them. One way to classify an organization is in terms of how it relates to its interest groups. The four interest groups are the owners, clients or customers, members, and the encompassing society. The same individuals may be part of two or more interest groups. Ideally, organizations should never be expected to serve one interest at the expense of the others. Most of today's leaders recognize the interdependence of the interests and consider each to various extents when making decisions. Quite often, the actual behavior of the members is at variance with the purpose of the organization. Cases like these are the proper targets for OD efforts.

Another way to classify organizations is on the basis of how the members are used to make and implement decisions. At one end of the continuum would be a plantation or slave camp where the members' decision-making skills are not used at all and behavior is motivated by deprivation, fear, or force. Next along the continuum would be highly structured organizations demanding member conformity to the wishes of those higher on the power ladder. Motivation in such organizations is effected through combinations of threats against nonconformity and rewards for cooperation. The source of the punishment and reward may be the leaders and peer group in either the formal or informal structure. Further along the continuum would be organizations of equals who make decisions based on the will of the majority. Here the majority is influenced by subgroups, factions, and powerful individuals. Motivation is usually based on anticipation of personal gain, be it selfish or altruistic in intent. At the farthest extreme of the continuum would be those organizations that strive for consensus of all members and interested parties in the decision-making process. The decision-making process is usually slower in such organizations, but implementation is faster because the members "own" the decision. While the value of any type of organization along the continuum may be relative, the consensus-seeking organization is superior in using members as a resource for solving problems. Most OD practitioners tend to view their mission as that of helping client organizations become more participative and consensus seeking.

OD Interventions and Techniques. The members of the organization are the primary target of the OD practitioner, even though they may ultimately be serving the interests of the owners or clients or society at large as well. While the practitioner knows the target group is influenced by technological and economic factors and that he or she is partly responsible for influences on these subsystems, the primary concern is with the social system—how people interrelate.

Client-Consultant Contract. The OD practitioner may intervene at any level or any process in the organization, but most prefer to start with the most powerful person. Without the initial and continuing support and supervision of the most powerful figures in the organization, an OD effort is likely to fail. The client-consultant contract may take many meetings to assume form, and it may end in failure. When the negotiations are successful, the consultant and one or more powerful figures and their agents agree on the goals of the effort, the roles to be played by the OD team, and the strategies to be used. They

also reach consensus on how the OD process can be evaluated with hard data at specific points in time.

The client and consultant should strive to build a relationship of trust in which each can level with the other in an open, risk-taking atmosphere without fear of being used, and in which both will grow in response to the challenges facing them. To accomplish this, the executive must avoid using the OD practitioner to take a problem off his or her hands. The executive must also avoid considering the OD practitioner as a temporary employee who must be closely supervised. Further, the OD practitioner must be supported during the early stages and beyond, when resistance to change, a natural by-product in the client system, is encountered. The OD practitioner, in turn, should be guided by professional standards, as illustrated by this excerpt from the code of ethics of one professional society.

> As an O.D. practitioner I strive to:
>
> Maintain a stance of concerned objectivity in all relations with my clients, keeping in mind the confidence and trust they place in me and the power my professional background gives me to influence their welfare.
>
> Serve the interests of both client organizations and those who are members of the organization, but not to serve one at the expense of the other.
>
> Help my clients understand and accept the ultimate responsibility for solving their own problems and realizing their own opportunities and never allow my clients to become dependent upon our continuing relationship.
>
> Help my clients reach meaningful and measureable objectives in the shortest possible time for the lowest possible cost.

Diagnostic Efforts. In the diagnostic stage of their work, OD practitioners use what seem to be well-known and commonplace tools: surveys, interviews, and direct observation methods. They also look at the traditional indicators of member dissatisfaction such as slumping production figures, delayed shipments, absenteeism, turnover, pilferage, poor housekeeping, grievances, and strikes.

In addition, they observe the *norms* operating within the organization—those unwritten rules of behavior that may be working contrary to official policy. They note the degree of openness among members communicating upward, downward, and with peers. They look for efficiency-sapping rivalries between groups within the organization or between members of the same group. They ascertain the extent to which individuals are matched by personality to those they report to and to those who report to them and the extent of the imposed or natural structure in their jobs and in the entire organizational climate.

The OD process may be a systematic, organizationwide planned effort tied to a productivity improvement program, or a relatively organic response to a specific need. In either case, OD practitioners tend to rely on a proven set of interventions. Some interventions have their origins in methods of clinical psychology, particularly those with a group orientation. Others have their origins in the fields of training and management. The former tend to be more people-centered and the latter more organization-centered.

Team building encompasses a broad range of activities directed toward helping the members of a specific group work together. Team building applies to the initial contract between the consultant and the client executive. It can also apply to the relationship between a leader and one or all of the followers, or to any group of any size that works together on a regular basis, such as executive committees or project-oriented groups of peers that are ad hoc in nature. The purpose of team building is to help the members become more compatible.

Problem-solving group training and development usually involves instruction in distinguishing between problem content, procedures, and processes. The *problem content* refers to the technical details of the group's concern; *procedures* refer to the steps involved in problem solving; and *processes* refer to the subconsciously motivated behaviors that tend to help or inhibit the ability of the group to work effectively on problems. Through the aid of a facilitator, the members are made aware of the processes influencing their behavior. The group strives to become self-facilitating.

Group networking is when all organization members are also members of one or more problem-solving groups and meet freely together, use members of other groups as consultants, and generally form a subculture of problem solvers.

Quality circles are an American invention made famous by the Japanese to involve first-line workers in the problem solving and decision making appropriate to their work.

Performance factor analysis is a method for focusing attention on the variables that influence organization behavior, particularly work performance. The factors are communication—understanding what is expected; training—knowing how to do what is expected; motivation—wanting to do what is expected; and structure—being supported and properly equipped by officials to do what is expected. The above may be expressed as: $C \times T \times M \times S = P$.

Reward system design, in an OD context, is a method of encouraging productive behavior through the right blend of intrinsic and financial rewards.

Management by objectives (MBO) is perhaps the most famous OD strategy which has been widely adopted. It has not been applied uniformly, and its results are very mixed. While the logic is perfect, the application is often mismanaged. MBO maximizes member participation in setting and integrating organization and individual goals. All participants theoretically know where they are going, why they are going there, their rate of progress, and how their efforts integrate with the efforts of other members. [*See* Objectives, management by (MBO).]

Norm modification is an OD strategy that starts with a view of the organization in terms of the norms that govern the behavior of the members. *Norms* are those unwritten behavioral rules that group members follow which may or may not be in tune with official organization policy. When negative norms, such as, "Everybody starts late around here," can be identified and replaced with positive ones, such as "We all put in a full day's work here," the members and the entire organization benefit.

Conflict resolution strategies are those directed toward helping individuals or groups in conflict within the organization to bring their feelings and expectations about each other to the surface and to deal with them in an open, problem-solving way.

Intergroup merging is a technique for encouraging the members of merged groups to integrate through recognizing the new power relationships, acceptance standards, norms, and functional expectations of all.

Feedback, in an OD context, is an interpersonal communications technique originally used in encounter groups. Its purpose is to sensitize members to their own feelings and to those of others. The technique involves reacting to others by discussing their behavior with them, and giving a personal assessment of the significance—and the results—of their behavior. Feedback is given in the spirit of welcoming feedback in return in order to promote mutual growth and understanding.

OD *team development* is the process of identifying those members of the organization who seem to have a natural proclivity for OD-type efforts. The process also includes recruiting and training those individuals to become either direct or indirect agents for positive changes in the organization's processes.

Multiple management is a relatively old organization design for fostering better communications and utilizing human resources. While the traditional pyramid structure is maintained to distribute responsibility and authority, peer-level councils are also used. The councils solve interdepartmental problems informally and provide a two-way channel of communication for policies, ideas, and general feedback among the power levels.

Training is not usually considered an OD strategy, mainly because it has been in use so much longer than OD. Indeed, the training field was one of the major fonts from which OD has sprung. Perhaps it would be truer to say that OD sprang from a recognized weakness in management and human relations training programs. All too often, changes made in an individual through traditional training methods are lost in a very short time once he or she returns to the original work environment.

Training, and periodic retraining, given within a systematic framework of an OD program, is essential to success. When all members in the organization receive the same general training, they have a common frame of reference from which they can constantly reinforce one another in their day-to-day interactions.

Training efforts such as those specifically designed to train supervisors or managers in handling their subordinates can readily be fitted into the broad definition of OD. So can those programs for members who must work effectively with many individuals in various departments or sections of the organization. Such programs have traditionally been called human relations programs but are currently being updated with behavioral science techniques.

Some other traditional organization activities that can justifiably be considered as OD strategies include:

Computer-assisted think tanks: the group problem-solving and decision-making processes and procedures structured and aided by interacting with special software and the organization's data base.

Brainstorming: a group idea-producing technique that also teaches individuals to work with each other in a noncritical, noncompetitive atmosphere.

Program evaluation review technique (PERT): a way of planning complex projects and also of showing the interdependence of all persons involved. It can be used to foster cooperation.

Planned meetings: used for the traditional reason of giving and getting information; may also be engineered through format and seating to foster feelings of mutual respect and equality among the participants. Schoolroomlike meetings, for example, promote teacher and pupil attitudes, whereas round table meetings tend to promote peer attitudes.

Communications systems analysis: a method for looking at the way messages are formally transmitted through regular channels and informally transmitted through linking pins in the organization. What messages are sent, how they are sent, who sends them, and who receives them all influence the organization in an integrative or disintegrative way.

Summary. OD is a relatively new, but very promising, science/art/profession that holds great promise for management. People still have the age-old need to be considered individuals. They must also be members of one or more organizations. Organizations are the vehicles through which people can improve their lot in the world. Executives have always recognized the importance of the organization phenomenon and have struggled, more than other people, with its problems. At present, only a small percentage of organization leaders are consciously employing the OD strategies described above. In the near future, however, these strategies and those still being developed will be common tools of the successful executive.

See also Authority, responsibility, and accountability; Interpersonal relationships; Matrix management; Objectives, management by (MBO); Organizational analysis and planning; Organization structures and charting; Transactional analysis.

REFERENCES

Lippitt, Gordon L.: *Organization Renewal*, 2d ed., Prentice-Hall, Englewood Cliffs, N.J., 1982.

Tagliere, D. A.: *The Participative Prince*, ODS Publications, 1980.

———: *People, Power and Organization*, American Management Association, New York, 1973.

DANIEL A. TAGLIERE, *Organization Development Services, Inc.*

Organization Structures and Charting

Structures are the functions, rules, relationships, and responsibilities which serve as a framework for organizational activities. Structures are important as they can, ideally, facilitate the attainment of organizational goals through the activities of organizational members. The focus here will be upon the formal structures and their features which are the result of deliberate strategies and designs. Unfortunately, in contemporary organizations, a considerable number of structures emerge in a haphazard manner. However, equally as bad are situations in which structural design approaches have been poorly taught and thus result in unexpected or undesirable consequences.

Structural Purposes. Structure is neutral; by itself, it is neither good nor bad. Yet, for many organization members, structure has come to mean rules or functions which restrict individual creativity. Many also think of structure as synonymous with bureaucracy, as a substitute for thinking, planning, or rational action. None of these negative meanings needs to be attached to structure. Structure is what the policymaker, managers, or organization designer make it or allow to happen.

Traditional View. The negative flavor often assigned to structure is not without foundation. Generations of organization members have been exposed to principles of organization structure which meant certain ratios of subordinates to supervisors, centralization of responsibilities, prescribed channels of communication, and fixed lines of authority relationships. Many organization members have witnessed the adherence to structural principles which were no longer delivering valued performances—if they ever did. In the traditional view, structure sought to lessen dependence on people and to substitute mechanisms for coordinating and controlling member activity to achieve high productivity and performance.

Contemporary View. Many social, economic, and environmental forces have combined to lessen reliance on pursuing purely structural approaches to performance. The position of most contemporary organization structure designers is that structure should facilitate both institutional and social processes. Thus the assessment of the functionality of organization structure will involve various economic performance measures (e.g., profits, costs, return on investment, productivity) and human performance measures (e.g., job-related satisfaction). The greater the complexity of organizational environments and activities, the greater the influence of human or social performance on economic performance.

Structural Features. Certain general considerations establish the overall structural features, or external shell, of an organization. A wide variety of authority structures emerge within the external shell, and subsequent sections of this entry will deal with some of their more important considerations. At this point, however, the basic concerns are: (1) What general factors shape the overall characteristics of the organization? (2) What dimensions underlie these general factors so that general guidelines can be developed?

General Descriptive Factors. Some general, and thus imprecise, descriptive factors impart a basic flavor to structure. Because of their nature, they offer only low predictive power. When considered in combination, however, these factors make possible a greater anticipation of structural specifics.

1. *Nature of the industry.* Basic steel, for example, has coking, hot melt, and basic rolling units—each suggests an organization segment. Intercity transportation systems (bus, air, rail) suggest some form of geographic decentralization in organization structure.

2. *Size, maturity, degree of physical decentralization.* Size (measured in dollars, assets, or people) provides a sense of the scope of operations, the complexity of organization structure, and the proportions of worker, administrative, and staff groups.

   Maturity may provide structural guidelines, indicating characteristic forms at different points in the growth cycle; for example, single products/single line (at an early point); increasing size of basic line and maturing of appropriate internal organizations; multiproduct structures; and finally, for some, conglomeration. The degree of physical decentralization—such as the number of field units, plants, or establishments—lends some degree of specification to structure.

3. *Legal considerations and restraints.* Federal and state laws, plus various regulating commissions, have established limits to size (e.g., in the area of economic competition) or branching (e.g., in banking).

Structural Determinants. Structure is dynamic and emerges in response to a wide variety of needs, environmental developments, and resource, market, and individual considerations. As changes occur over a period of time, structure provides a vehicle by which to capitalize on opportunity, to consolidate past growth, and to base future growth. At a general level, circumstances and factors shaping structure include:

1. Institutional goals and the particular work niche or product-service market segment to be serviced by the organization.

2. Functional work activities to secure the goals and product-service segment established for the organization.

3. Scope and sequence of functional steps in performing work and/or functional activities.

4. Economic size, physical dispersion of facilities or resources, and local, regional, national, or international character of operations.

5. Capability, depth, and limitations of the organization's management and professional members.

6. Prominence and relative importance of work and/or information technologies. Where production facilities or information processing is a major aspect of the organization, it shapes overall structural features.

Generally these points require little additional elaboration, since they fall within the general experience of a large number of managers and officials. Others which require more detailed explanation follow.

Organizational Maturity and Development. Many institutions fail to see the connection between structural evolution and business development and success. The point is simply that many organization structures grow and develop in systematic fashion. One theme, noted by Greiner, is that companies develop through alternate stages of prolonged growth (evolution) and considerable turmoil (revolution). According to Chandler, marketing opportunities and needs largely determine organization strategies, and these strategies determine structure. On the other hand, Greiner finds structure may determine strategy to the extent that existing functions, hierarchy, and deployment of facilities greatly influence strategy.

Viewing structure as a central feature of a developing organization leads to the identification of five dimensions which provide some degree of predictability regarding future directions: (1) organization size, (2) organization age, (3) evolutionary stages, (4) revolutionary stages, and (5) industry growth rate.

Greiner used these five dimensions to identify five typical stages of general organization development, as summarized in Table O-8. Organizations which are in fast-growth industries or are growing rapidly in size are likely to encounter all the indicated stages in a comparatively short period of time. Smaller companies or those that are part of slower-paced industries are not likely to progress through all the indicated stages. Organizations experience widely different needs for structure, depending on the immediate circumstances of size, stage of development, maturity, and general growth pace of their industry.

Philosophy of Management. The ambitions or interests of the owner or the organization's desire to meet individual motivational and growth needs better impact future characteristics of structure. A sense of personal competency, at times combined with a lack of high-talent people, can lead to a high level of centralized control. Under some conditions, the distinction between highly centralized control (e.g., in decision making and planning) and autocratic management may only be a fine line. When management's philosophy includes an emphasis on individual development and leadership growth, decentralized authority is likely to be favored. In some corporations these philosophical goals have allowed decentralization to remain despite economic benefits that would accrue from centralization.

Environmental and System Dimensions. Several newer research directions indicate promising results in accounting for *overall structural features* through environmental and systems analyses. Important concepts include an environmental uncertainty, task uncertainty, and a systems-notion interdependence.

Environmental Uncertainty. This refers to the variability and relative instability of the forces surrounding an organization; e.g., unpredictable competitive tactics, world tension, and sources of change that cannot fully be identified. The greater the uncer-

TABLE O-8 Stages of Structural Development*

Stage	Main focus	Structure	Communication, coordination, and control	Growing or central challenge	Founder, top management role
1	Birth, creativity, continuity	Informal	Informal and reactive to immediate needs	Resolving leadership and management growth needs	Make, or sell, or deliver product or service
2	Growth	Growing formalization—functionalization; centralized direction, budgets, standards	Growth of functional structures—accounting, inventory, formalization of communications	Centralized directions versus growing needs for flexibility in response to complexity	Professional management and direction
3	Decentralization and delegation	Decentralized by product, geographic area	Greater control and direction from officials of decentralized units—limits decentralization of information processing	Budget control by top management in face of autonomy of decentralized officials	Professional management—top management guidance, policy
4	Coordination and integration	Product groups, divisions	Expansion of centralized staff for analysis coordination, control, growing centralization of information processing	Credibility gap between headquarters and field, staff and field, or line personnel	Strengthen policy, planning and review
5	Collaboration and conflict resolution	Preserves previous authority structures but greater emphasis on processes such as matrix design	Group processes, conflict resolution, greater flexibility		Mediator, coordinator, moderator

*Adapted from the study of Larry E. Greiner, "Evolution and Revolution as Organizations Grow," *Harvard Business Review*, vol. 50, no. 4, July–August, 1972, pp. 37–46.

tainty, the greater the turbulence and unpredictability of events.

From the early work of Burns and Stalker we know that under turbulent conditions, organizations are forced to develop flexible and contingent approaches. Where environmental conditions are stabler and more predictable (low uncertainty), more traditional structures will usually suffice. Where environmental uncertainty can be ascribed to more specific factors, greater preciseness becomes possible in specifying its structural effects. For example, in a manufacturing firm, great uncertainty from technological innovations (of competition and new scientific breakthroughs) might lead to the creation of a department of technology.

Task Uncertainty.   According to Van de Ven, this concept refers to the variability and difficulty of the work performed. Variability occurs where a number of exceptional or unexpected situations emerge. The difficulty may involve (1) the clarity of steps that must be followed, (2) the predictability of knowing which is right or wrong, and (3) the time required to develop an approach. High task uncertainty forces the exercise of individual judgment or discretion (as opposed to predetermined rules) and pushes down (decentralizes) decision making in the organization. The practical result of high task uncertainty is to lower the amount of supervisory decision making and to increase nonsupervisory, or colleague, decision making.

Interdependence.   This characteristic relates to the extent that organizational units are dependent upon one another for performance resulting from the flow between units of work, materials, or information. A general relationship appears to exist between interdependence and the type and source of decision making. According to Galbraith, as interdependence grows, more complex communications structures are required and more mutual accommodation and adjustment must take place. Rules and regulations will be depended on to take care of some of the situations that come up. As contingencies grow, communication needs to go beyond programming (i.e., rules) to resolve the arising issues. Also, with increased interdependence, particularly with high task uncertainty, referring issues upward may not be beneficial as the only solution. The risk exists of overloading the hierarchy's limited capacity for processing information and of incurring delays in the work process. A basic bureaucratic mechanistic structure can be made adaptive in such situations by incorporating organic or matrix design alternatives. These involve the creation of lateral relations; group discussions and decision making are relied upon. By design, authority lines are cut across to bring the decision making to where the pertinent information exists. In matrix designs, organizational culture became a critical issue. This will be discussed in greater detail in a subsequent section.

A Stepwise Approach in Design

If anything has been learned from the efforts of organization theorists and designers, it is that there is no one best way of designing structures. Few modern organizations of any size are simple enough, or of such singular purposes, that only one design guide can be employed. Fortunately, however, few design problems involve a total organization. It is much more common to deal with matters confined to a particular department or division. Additionally, various portions of an organization must be handled in a way appropriate to (contingent upon) the needs of its situation. Thoughtful structural designs may use both contemporary and traditional approaches.

Another realization which has emerged is that a specific design or overall approach is best described as satisfactory and not optimum. The number of goals and/or criteria which must be satisfied simultaneously—combinations of economic and social considerations, complex environments, and varying degrees of uncertainty which are a result of change—rule out precise solutions. As a result, prudent organizations follow a contingency strategy, which incorporates flexibility or adaptability features in proportion to the unknowns or unexpected factors.

General Specifications.   Various general specifications are employed in most structures regardless of the particular needs involved. It seems unwise to label these specifications as principles, but these generalizations do provide some criteria to guide most design effort, as shown in Table O-9. The six points in Table O-9 are interrelated and cover points often ignored, although they may appear to be mostly a matter of common sense.

The Contingency Concept.   Contingency structuring focuses on management's main tasks and the relationships between them. Drucker has visualized these as (1) the work task, which is focused on today's activities and work performance; (2) the innovative task, which provides the ideas, products, and work accomplishments for tomorrow's organization; and (3) the task of ownership or top management, which provides the vision and guidelines for joining today's reality with tomorrow's possibilities.

A particular structural design serves organizational needs. Structural design follows strategy. Initially, it focuses on tasks and work activity, not the person who performs them. The final design, however, must meet the needs of both the organization *and* the individual, and some structural adjustments may have to be made.

The Contingency Approach.   There is no one best way to organize, yet alternative approaches are not equally effective. For any situation, contingency analysis presupposes that a relatively modest number of variables (of the many present) will be relevant to the problem at hand. The relevant variables are located in the environment (external and inter-

TABLE O-9 General Structural Specifications*

Clarity of purposes	Organizations have multiple rather than single goals, and these are acknowledged and understood by its members.
Adaptability	Change is pervasive and affects all organizations so that the question is one of degree of needed adaptation rather than of whether it is needed.
Flexibility	Structure displays the ability to shift or blend, avoiding rigidities which negate adaptability and build internal pressures.
Efficiency	Economy of effort for efficiency needs is met through joint economic and social objectives.
Stability	Structures (and the organization as a whole) incorporate mechanisms which seek to continually establish relationships, activities, and processes which are vulnerable to disruption because of change—stability represents a condition to be met by adaptability.
Organization renewal	Structural mechanisms, functions, and design incorporate needed change to permit survival and future growth.

*Adapted from Peter F. Drucker, "New Templates for Today's Organizations," *Harvard Business Review*, vol. 52, no. 1, January–February 1971, pp. 45–51.

nal), work systems, people, organization, and/or institutional philosophy "surrounding" the design matter. Organizations must be able to adapt to unplanned-for occurrences. A step-by-step contingency approach to organization design follows:

1. Review organizational goals: economic, social, long-range and short-range. Note also the niche the organization is to occupy in the future; the owner's philosophy; public regulatory restrictions; and historical criteria of performance.

2. Examine the firm's external environment: describe major forces, trends, and likely future occurrences; identify international, national, regional, and/or local forces for change which are likely to affect the organization, its customers, clients, mode of doing business, etc.; and determine which functional areas of the organization are likely to sustain change and their general approaches for coping.

3. Identify key end-accomplishments and means of achieving these.

4. Identify key (internal) subenvironments of the organization necessary for securing its niche. Determine the influence of key parameters such as size (number of people), geographic location, and physical dispersion on the scope and dispersion of the key subenvironments.

5. For each key subenvironment, determine (a) the pace of change, uncertainty, and complexity confronting it, (b) the quality and quantity of information and feedback vital to its functioning, and (c) the nature of communications. What has existed? Problems/dysfunctions? Future needs?

6. Formulate systems or work-flow models that relate the key subenvironments, indicating the step-by-step flow of major activities and key relationships. Also, determine organizational arrangements and functions (coordination, control, flexibility, etc.) needed to cope with change.

7. Determine the general organizational or structural requirements to achieve (a) *key functional activities* of planning, control, coordination, and direction; (b) *key offices*—research and development, finance, engineering, etc.; and (c) *key internal climate* features—reward, communications, and interaction. Utilize the models and prescriptions of the worker machine model, bureaucratic structure, and Rensis Likert's "system 4" organization.

8. Consider jointly (a) the organization's integration needs to coordinate activities and (b) the requirements for differentiation, which serve to strengthen areas of specialized expertise.

9. Examine job features, especially the motivational climate.

10. Modify structural design on the basis of a review of general design specifications and/or factors assigned high priority or urgency, yet not fully acknowledged previously.

Available Structural Designs. Although literally hundreds of variations of structural concepts and theories may apply to particular situations, these applications tend to draw from a comparatively small number of forms and concepts. Key models which have gained widespread usage follow.

Traditional designs include:

1. Centralized decision making and the functional format (e.g., marketing, finance, production, etc.).

2. Divisionalization and decentralization of operating authority and responsibility to heads of divisions (or departments), with the corporation or headquarters unit retaining general policy, capital allocation, coordination, and overall strategy responsibilities. Decentralization is commonly done along product/service or geographic lines.

Contemporary designs include:

1. Project or team approaches (involving multiple technical and social abilities) which are used in addition to, or beyond, traditional structural

designs for one-time projects or to deal with complex technical situations.

2. Colleague management, which visualizes situations of overall management among peers.

3. A matrix organization which combines both vertical authority relationships and horizontal or diagonal work relationships for dealing with complex work environments.

Underlying concepts include:

1. Specialization—gathering together or differentiating common skills or areas of knowledge to gain the benefits of concentrated effort.

2. Division of labor—the classical ideas of Adam Smith, in which work efforts are viewed in elementary form and so arranged or combined as to maximize overall economic performance.

3. Systems development, which emphasizes work/information flows and relationships. Where these flows or relationships are critical, traditional structural or hierarchical relationships are subordinated to these considerations.

4. Bureaucratic or structural nomenclature such as hierarchy, span of command, etc., which have tended to become more descriptive of a situation than definitive.

Contingency and classical models for structural design differ greatly in concepts, approaches, and specifics. Table O-10 summarizes the differences.

Traditionally Important Structures

Hierarchy, specialization, and control are among the key principles by which organizations have been structured in the past. Hierarchy is the vertical dimension of differentiated authority levels and responsibility. Horizontal differentiation distinguishes the departments, divisions, or functional units organized by product, activity, process, or location. Horizontal differentiation assumes that organizational effectiveness is best brought about through the grouping of like abilities, skills, or mission. Hierarchy is inherently pyramidal in overall shape, with a gradient from top to bottom of diminishing authority and responsibility.

Classic Design Principles. Five traditional principles of organizational structure still apply to many common design problems.

1. *Unity of command.* A participant should receive orders from only one individual.

2. *Commensurate authority and resonsibility.*

TABLE O-10 Contingency Versus Traditional Approaches in Designing Organization Structures

Contingency approach	Traditional approach
Direction of relations	
Develops relationships, communications, and interactions, whether horizontal, vertical, or diagonal	Places primary stress on hierarchical structure and vertically oriented authority
Number of supervisors	
Designs will sometimes involve multiple relationships with various supervisors assessing different aspects of individual performance	Emphasis on unity of command and only one boss for an individual
Locus of decision making	
Considers centralization or decentralization dependent on such things as individual abilities, available technology, and personal realizations	Focus on centralization of decision making
Span of control	
Depends on the situation, which encompasses people involved, communications needs, needed assistance time	Largely fixed, considering specific limits based on level of authority or point in hierarchical structure
Overall orientation	
Takes into account environmental, organizational, technological, and individual considerations; social, technical, and economic features	Basic focus on control and assumption of the inadequacies of people—when in doubt, rely on technology or structure but not on people

3. *Limited span of command* (control). The number of subordinates that can be controlled by a supervisor or official was thought to be largely fixed: at times, precise numbers or ranges of figures have been recorded as a function of the level of hierarchical authority.

4. *Centralization of major responsibilities.*

5. *Line-staff organizations.* Staff groups were to be organized around specialized areas of knowledge and ability to support the line operations of the work organization. Clear lines of responsibility were established among the two groups in order to avoid authority conflicts.

Structural Form: Tall, Flat. As indicated, top management's philosophy of the appropriate model for organization may lead to structural modifications, at times affecting overall organization features. One strategy, which assumes almost dramatic proportions, is the creation of a tall or flat structure.

In the *flat structure,* an attempt is made to reduce the number of authority levels, and considerable responsibility is laid at the door of middle management. In the *tall structure,* authority levels tend to be increased, spans of command reduced, decision making more centralized, and upper management's influence on control extended. (See Fig. O-4.)

Sears, Roebuck and Co. is probably the best-known example of a structural strategy as an outgrowth of philosophy of organization. It created an essentially flat structure to decentralize major operating responsibilities into the hands of its area and store managers, promote managerial development, and shorten the communications distance (authority levels) between customer, store management, and top management. Given the size of the Sears organization, the flat structure created extremely large

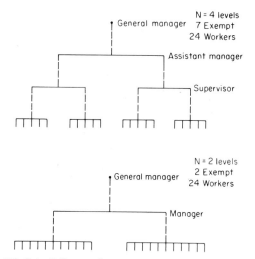

FIG. O-4 Tall versus flat structures.

spans of command at the middle management level of the structure. Middle-level managers were encouraged to develop self-reliance and to run their own shows.

This structural strategy was a contributing factor in the growth of Sears as it far outstripped its early rival, Montgomery Ward, in sales. Yet the decentralization of responsibilities and creation of a flat authority structure may well have outlived its utility at Sears; the recentralization of authority is currently being implemented. Additionally, upon a reconsideration of organizational mission, a conglomeration strategy is now also being pursued to increase profit potential.

Centralization Versus Decentralization. Generally, there are advantages and disadvantages to both centralization and decentralization strategies of major responsibilities. The most beneficial approach will be contingent on the specific situation. The identification of relevant variables and the priority assigned to each will determine which approach is best. Some important performance considerations are included in Table O-11. The approach which can potentially enhance each issue is identified. Again, the priority ascribed these considerations (others, not included) may be more relevant) will depend on the specific situation.

Product Versus Functional Organization. One of the oldest controversies in structural design concerns the choice between a product and a functional form of organization. Arguments can be advanced in favor of each.

Growth and Change. Viewing structure as a historical, evolutionary process suggests that both product and functional forms may be legitimate structural strategies. Similarly, it suggests that progress should be in evolutionary steps (from the functional form to the product form) as structural changes modify complexity. The recognition of these critical points for change is facilitated through size measures—the observance of general economic indicators (e.g., sales)—product-line diversification, geographic or organizational decentralization, and behavioral analyses of internal stress and conflict.

Traditional Arguments. Specialization of skills, equipment, products, or activities was frequently a basic guide for designing organization structures using traditional approaches.[1] For the most part, psychological and social consequences were ignored. The major trade-offs implicit in these arguments are the benefits of functional specialization versus the strengthening of coordination and control. The latter ensure greater integration of work-related or administrative functions.

If the contingency approach is used, the introduction of situational considerations of environment and work may assist in resolving this design problem. Functional organization is the logical choice where performance is relatively stable and administration

649

TABLE O-11 Centralization Versus Decentralization as an Organizational Strategy

Characteristic	Centralization	Decentralization
Flexibility in field decisions		✓
Field conditions diverse		✓
Technology is standardized	✓	
Monitoring and interpretation of broad trends in innovation and creativity	✓	
Developing middle-level managers		✓
Broad-based competition	✓	
Narrowly focused competition		✓
Legally (governmentally) mandated information gathering, processing, reporting	✓	
Economies of computer use	✓	
Overall control accessible	✓	
Overall coordination need	✓	
Uniformity in policies, plans, and programs	✓	

assumes (or can assume) a relatively routine basis. Integration can be achieved through preconceived plans and conflict can be handled routinely through hierarchical arrangement. Conversely, the more unstable the environment and the less predictable the task, the greater the need for flexibility and innovative planning and problem-solving approaches. The latter appears more feasible with the product type of structural model. Where both stable and unstable conditions exist simultaneously within different areas of a given organization, new structural roles may be indicated: committees, coordinators, or the use of a matrix-type organization.

Impact of Size. The sheer impact of size can outweigh technology, philosophy, and a great number of other forces already identified. For illustration consider a commercial bread unit—say, one producing 200,000 loaves of bread per day. A plant for producing 400,000 loaves would involve many more people, and the pieces of equipment would almost double; the organization structure would expand. However, in a different type of production unit—for example, in petroleum refining—increased size would only mean *larger* equipment rather than *more* equipment. Under these conditions, various personnel-supervisory relationships might remain the same despite the doubling of capacity.

Manner of Growth. The structural form to achieve large size varies greatly in each industry. For example, in some insurance companies and banks, growth in size is accomplished by adding more regional divisions or branches, while others in the same industry add to the work force and product line at a centralized headquarters unit. In basic steel operation, greater size may mean added capacity and/or integration (into the company) of related production operations. By definition, the conglomerate grows through acquisition of newer business enterprises, often unrelated to the initial core units.

Size Generalizations. Growth in size is typically accompanied by greater formalization of procedures and relationships and the need for better, more thor-

ough integration of activities for control and coordination. The question of whether greater size truly requires more centralization or decentralization of decision making, planning, etc., is far more complex to resolve. The answers are likely to be related to the following:

1. How organizations conceive of their competitive environment and work tasks (viz., uncertainty, turbulence, complexity).

2. The interdependencies between system elements, including organization, administrative, and work units.

Recent Structural Approaches

Historically, two major organizational models evolved to meet competitive and survival needs while delivering the amounts of internal coordination and control adequate for existing needs. In smaller organizations and simpler environments, the functional form of Henri Fayol proved adequate. As organizations grew in size and complexity, Alfred P. Sloan, Jr., of General Motors proposed and developed the divisionalized structure, which decentralized authority but retained overall corporate control centrally. Both models were copied and are used extensively even today.

Trends. The continuing pace of technical, economic, and social change, however, has brought about the need for newer structural arrangements, either in combination with traditional structure or as independent self-standing arrangements. In brief, the newer trends include:

1. Growth in service-type organizations (hospitals, schools, universities), where the work processes, assumptions, and relationships of manufacturing prototypes are inappropriate.

2. Conglomeration, where organizations compete in various markets simultaneously and also con-

tain multiple and distinct technologies, product lines, support facilities, and managements.

3. Multinational operation, where the distance considerations are compounded by multiproduct and/or multitechnology considerations.

4. Reduction in the relative proportion of blue-collar workers, with a corresponding growth in number and proportion of white-collar workers or professional staff.

5. Growth in environmental or organizational complexity, which has parlayed information needs to meet the requirements of multiproduct, physically decentralized, and/or multinational operations.

Contemporary Structural Models. Highly complex organizational environments and problems have spawned the development of various flexible, adoptive structural arrangements to cope with these situations. Two such structural models which have emerged are project organization (known for some years in technical or capital-intensive industries) and the newer matrix organization.

Project Organization. The essence of project organization emerges from the need for (1) considerable planning, (2) coordination or research to deal with a complex problem or task goal, and (3) completion in a specified length of time (say, several months to several years). It also assumes that routine organization procedures and formal structure are unable to deal with the situation in efficient or economic fashion. A temporary group is formed, combining and integrating diverse physical and social science talents with whatever equipment and procedures are needed to secure task goals. Group members return to their respective departments and positions at the completion of the project or their particular phase of the project. Project organization departs from traditional structure-authority arrangements in that it combines horizontal, vertical, and diagonal communications, work, and liaison interactions.

The utility and capability of the project group reside with the requisite self-containment and flexibility to meet project goals. The conceptualization and planning of newer-generation computers, construction projects, area redevelopment, energy from waste matter, new products, feasibility, etc., are examples of wide-ranging project situations which, for success, must combine diverse social and technical skills with various resources in flexible and creative fashion.

Project managers play a unique role, for they assume responsibility for successful project completion in conjunction with personnel who typically have no direct or formal authority relationship with them. A given project team may have engineers, architects, estimators, systems people, and a cost accountant—easily representing four or five different functional departments; even six or seven would not be unusual. The feasible number of team members requires contingency response; a team size can range from as few as three to upward of 40.

Thus, the project group superimposes a work and communication structure on a traditional hierarchical structure. The project manager evaluates individual performance on the task while each person's formal supervisor assesses other personal performance or activity features and assumes responsibility for preparation of an overall evaluation.

Understandably, ground conditions for great conflict exist here, and these become acute in the matrix design. Formal authority within the project team is largely on a colleague basis, which involves persuasion and demonstration of correctness. One's reputation is constantly put on the line in carrying out project functions such as goal accomplishments, efficiency, creativity, and timeliness. Project management and participation call for training in modes of communication and interaction which go far beyond the normal assertion of formal authority in traditional structures.

Matrix Organization. This structure is related to the project structure in the sense of flexibility, capabilities, work, and communication relationships but involves multiple and simultaneous undertakings in an organization. Additionally, a matrix organization may combine some project groupings having a temporary character with other arrangements having semipermanent working arrangements.

As an example, Fig. O-5 depicts a matrix organization involving three different groups (A, B, and C) which involve three organizational units and five different departments. Team members are drawn from all departments, and the composition of each team is unique. Consider, for example, team medicine. In this case each department represents a specialty, such as urology, ophthalmology, or geriatrics. The scientific developments in one specialty involve contributions of sister disciplines. The practice of a concept or technique may most easily be conveyed by seeking to integrate (for the patient in various treat-

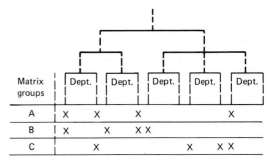

FIG. O-5 Matrix organization.

ment units) diverse bodies of knowledge. The elements of complexity, diverse knowledge, requirement to integrate, and continuing (semipermanent) need set out key elements of the matrix design. Needless to say, integration of knowledge domains involves far more than a mechanical mixing of (knowledge) fields. Table O-12 summarizes features

TABLE O-12 Features and Problems Associated with Matrix Organizations

Features	Problems, issues
Combine diverse skills.	Conflict in authority between formal roles and those assumed in matrix model.
Excellent basis for broadening participation and developing leadership.	Effective performance dependent on group processes involving leadership, working relationships, and communications.
Vehicle and framework for developing and presenting bodies of knowledge and information.	Leadership may not be accepted by group members.
Greater opportunity for individual job enrichment.	Traditional roles may be taken with growth in size, and so lead to problems of traditional structures.
Flexible format permitting change of membership and adaptability to a variety of situations.	Flexibility and, at times, transient composition difficult for some to accept.
Presents a good fit with the increasingly complex environment (internal and external) in modern organizations.	Matrix design may bleed off key performers from functional departments.
An effective basis to override traditional hierarchical relationships while permitting the preservation of this structure for other purposes.	Some view participation as added duties or responsibilities. To the extent design is successful, people may be reluctant to dissolve the matrix team.

and problems of the matrix organization, some of which also apply to project-type organizations.

Structure and Production Technology. It appears that a general relationship exists between structure characteristics (e.g., authority levels and ratio of first-line supervisors to subordinates) and technology. It exists because it reflects both economic and technical considerations. This relationship is more evident in a production organization (e.g., a manufacturing plant) and less so where the organization includes marketing and administration. The greater the organizational focus on production and directly related activities, the closer the expected relationships are.

The *level of technology* generally represents the degree of sophistication and controllability. A scale reflecting the level of technology would appear as shown in Table O-13.

In her first book, *Industrial Organization, Theory and Practice* (1965), Joan Woodward presented what is likely to be the largest and most representative study conducted of technology and structure. It involved 100 manufacturing companies. American studies appear generally to support the findings except where (1) larger units are included that involve nonproduction elements or (2) many different technologies are involved. The Woodward study provides two important measures of structural features which are related to the level of technology. Average (median) figures from this study (also reflecting firms with good profits performance) are as follows:

Level of technology	Low level	Intermediate level	High level
Authority levels	3	4	6
Subordinate-supervisory ratio (first level)	21–30	41–50	11–20

These figures serve as general guidelines for a wide variety of production units. The specific figures are not as important as the recognition that structure should be responsive to the level of technology.

TABLE O-13 The Technology Scale (Continuum)

Level of technology	Low level	Intermediate level				Advanced level
Description of technology	Unit production	Small-batch production	Large-batch production	Mass production (Detroit type)	Automatic, near-continuous processing	Continuous processing
Control features	Manual	Mechanical	Semiautomatic controls	Automatic	Feedback, manual adjustment	Feedback, automatic adjustment

Effects of Mixed Technologies. Few work systems consist of a single type of technology. Typically they contain a mixture of small-batch and mass production elements. Some plants may have large-batch and continuous-process elements. An automotive assembly plant, for example, contains many different work systems in addition to the final assembly line. The point is that structural features involving the first-line supervisory ratio (subordinates to supervisor) and authority levels will differ among departments. Structural planning for an entire plant will involve an analysis of the requirements of the different departments or suborganization. These will be gathered into an overall design.

Size and Technology. Advances in production technology result in curvilinear relationships with various aspects of plant structure.[2] Mass production work is more routine than most small-batch work; this leads to lower worker skill levels and changes in activity of plant staff. In updating mass production systems (i.e., units assuming greater process characteristics), further changes take place. Complex equipment must be maintained, monitoring functions are increased, and complex administrative structures emerge. Highly mechanized production technologies discourage decentralization by reducing the autonomy of plant managers in favor of higher authority levels and various staff support units. Centralization or decentralization, however, is still a matter of managerial philosophy and strategic choice.

The impacts of plant organization size and corporate affiliation are intertwined with these trends. For the most part, mass production plants tend to be larger than either batch or process-type plants (excepting petroleum), so that both size and level of technology may change simultaneously. Also, process-type plants tend to have (relatively) smaller direct labor components and fewer plant workers than mass production units.

Relationships between production technology and plant structure are further complicated by corporate form and disposition of corporate management and administrative staffs. In the United States, many manufacturing plants are a part of larger corporate systems. As such, substantial support staffs will often be found within corporate units, while plant staffs are only adequate enough to meet day-to-day operating needs.

Advances made in computer technology have provided new options in strategic choices of structural form. Aside from their use in upgrading production processes,[3] computers have had an impact on administrative structure by permitting choices between centralization and decentralization. When computers are provided at the plant level, their ability to support administrative control and coordinate activities permits the establishment of plant management autonomy. However, one consideration which has worked heavily against the decentralization choice has been the multiplication (and duplication) of computers across units of a given corporation.

Organization Manuals and Charts

Manuals and charts are central records in the documentation of organizational procedures and relationships.

Drawbacks. Through abuse, neglect, and misinterpretation, manuals and charts have probably caused as many problems as they have solved. Probably the greatest "sin" in procedural circles is that of allowing manuals and charts to get out of date. They are then relegated to dusty corners or desk drawers, infrequent reference, or complete disregard. Out-of-date material or charts force people to seek their own means of getting things done. A "sin" of almost equal magnitude—and a major area of abuse—is slavish adherence to manuals or charts when common sense and very little imagination suggest a modified approach to a situation. Overly detailed material often tries to answer everything and ends up answering little, if anything at all.

Manuals. Many companies have successfully devised manuals that bring together organizational policies, procedures, goal statements, and related documents. Manuals can provide an outstanding codification of what an organization stands for. They can provide needed guidelines for dealing with various situations without emotion or recourse to (high) authority figures. Additionally, memories are fragile, facilities are dispersed, and a myriad of situations arise in modern organizations which require reference to policy—all of which argue for useful manuals. In this sense, the manual is neutral and impersonal—if the contents are thoughtful and timely and permit imaginative actions for the unexpected or contingencies. Thoughtful, timely manual material is excellent for matters ranging from orientation of new employees to resolution of issues among managers.

Charts. We know a number of companies that change managerial offices so frequently that charts are maintained on magnetic boards. Additions, movements, or quits are readily disposed of by quick adjustments, snapping a picture, and producing a newly revised chart. Unfortunately, a preoccupation with mechanics may cause one to lose sight of the basic purposes of charting. Charts, like manuals, can (1) promote understanding of communication problems, (2) orient newer people to structural relationships and complexities, and (3) provide a graphic picture of the full sweep of organizational activities and services, and the units and personnel central to them.

Charts in their simplest form display only functional units and relationships. In their most complex state, job or office holder, major responsibilities, committees, and even communication relationships can be added. However, many modern organizations are so large and complex that only key positions or organizational segments are visible.

Decades of exposure to organizational principles and hierarchical authority have resulted in charts being interpreted in both an organizational and a social power sense. For example, if one job happens to be positioned slightly above another—say, a director of nursing higher than a medical director—adverse consequences are almost guaranteed. Thus, in chart construction, status, equity, power, and authority may be part of a *hidden agenda* in a particular organization—and in most organizations at least one of these notions might be involved. Thus charts must be developed with an eye to situations that exist in particular organizations. In some organizations, these matters have led to so much difficulty or a sense of inflexibility that charts are prohibited.

Toward the Future

Structural design in the not-too-distant future will involve more comprehensive, precise, and systematic approaches than those in evidence today.

Analytical Techniques. These new approaches will require more powerful analytical and behavioral theories and further advances in the application of contingency modeling. For example, the use of various multiple-regression models reflects the reality that numerous structure-related variables will have to be dealt with simultaneously in order to deal with the complex environments occasioned by various interacting variables. At the same time, these more-powerful analytical methods will have to capitalize on behavioral and structural theories which jointly encompass structural, technological, and behavioral considerations.

Participation Models. Another trend appears to be the use of structural models which further individual participation. As educational levels continue to rise, greater stress will be placed on colleague-type models and organic relationships which favor participation. Communications considerations will further affect structural designs by encouraging types which stimulate multidirectional flows and two-way interchange.

Design Constructs. Environmental and systems descriptions appear slated to receive much greater attention because of their potential power to systematize design and offer a broad latitude of application. Constructs such as environmental uncertainty, turbulence, and complexity are suggestive of one area for development. Systems-related notions with considerable promise include interdependence and various features of information processing. In conjunction with these constructs, organizations will direct more attention to developing their own data files of information on (1) factors shaping their structures, (2) the response of organization members to various designs, (3) economic performance under alternative structures, and (4) work force and career planning.

Organizational Culture. When considering past changes influencing organizations and new approaches to organizational structure, we find one concept which is becoming and will become increasingly important—organizational culture. It has attracted the attention of strategists and behavioralists alike. Simply, as a greater proportion of organization members become more directly involved in decision making, the attitudes, values, norms, and ideologies they share about their work participation become quite critical.

Structure and the graphic representations of relationships seen in charts and manuals provide the skeleton of an organization. It is the people enmeshed in the organizational culture who optimally provide the resources for its effective functioning.

When the value/ideology system of the organizational culture is congruent with organizational goals, it facilitates the prioritizing of tasks and the reinforcement of behaviors needed to reach these goals. When the value/ideology mix is incongruent with organizational goals, it can render the formal structure less than effective for goal attainment. Increasingly, organizations are attempting to develop strategies which encompass the needs of organization members to enhance the organizational culture. Correspondingly, members are now being perceived as human resources valuable for organizational growth, continuity, and renewal and adaptation. Career planning and participatory management strategies are examples of innovations which can allow individual and organizational needs to be integrated.

See also Authority, responsibility, and accountability; Committees; Delegation; Human resources planning; Matrix management; Objectives and goals; Organization development (OD); Organizational analysis and planning; Project management; Work design, job enlargement, and job enrichment.

NOTES

[1]Arthur H. Walker and Jay W. Lorsch, "Organizational Choice: Product vs. Function," *Harvard Business Review*, vol. 46, no. 6, November–December 1968, pp. 129–138.

[2]Peter M. Blau, Cecilia McHugh Falbe, William McKinley, and Phelps K. Tracy, "Technology and Organization in Manufacturing," *Administrative Science Quarterly*, vol. 21, no. 1, March 1976, pp. 20–40.

[3]E. Burack, *Organizational Analysis: Theory and Applications*, Dryden Press, Hinsdale, Ill., 1975.

ELMER H. BURACK, *University of Illinois at Chicago*

Organizational Analysis and Planning

An organization may be thought of as the coordinated actions of two or more people for the purpose of meeting an objective. The focus in this entry, however, is upon *complex organizations*, so named because they involve groups of people differentiated by their work, physical space, or levels of authority. The purpose of these complex organizations is to transform something—materials, information, people—in a manner which adds value to the thing transformed and allows the organization to survive and prosper.

Organizational Purpose

An organization does a variety of things:

1. *It establishes a repetition of desired actions.* By making rules, procedures, and reporting relationships formal, the organization simplifies the processing of information required and ensures that necessary actions occur automatically. Attention may then be shifted to issues which are new or nonrepetitive.

2. *It ensures that actions by organization members will be coordinated.* The desired actions will fit together in a systematic way, ensuring an efficient and effective pattern of collective effort.

3. *It makes behavior predictable.* Organization members may act with reasonable assurance that other members will act in the same manner. Thus members gain some degree of freedom, since their actions need not be based on the unpredictable actions of others.

4. *It stores information.* Organizations "learn" in the course of their existence, and the information gained is added to their fund of standing orders.

5. *It establishes an identity independent of the people within it.* The organization becomes more or less free of members deemed indispensable as long as replacement people are available. Thus, it ensures its existence in spite of members who leave.

6. *It allocates rewards to contributors and claimants.* The organization contains a complex system of bargains between itself and the people or groups who contribute to it or have claims upon it. It permits fair bargains to be struck for rewarding different kinds of work or levels of performance.

Organizational Types

Most discussions of organization design assume and encourage the development of professionally man-aged institutions with deliberate and conscious planning for survival and success. It may be noted, however, that there are at least three basic types of organization. Research by the author and others[1] has described and labeled these types as craft, promotion, and administrative.

Craft organizations are led by a chief executive who engages in technical rather than administrative duties and who seeks to make a comfortable living and to see the organization survive. Policies evolve by tradition, and the structure develops with little conscious planning. It is common for the organization to be layered by levels of power, with an elite group at the top, a group of long service and trusted employees in the middle, and a transient group of workers at the bottom. Members of craft organizations expect little change in their operations and, therefore, make minimal use of supervisory or indirect labor. They are not inclined to risk taking or innovation in their operations. Work technology is relatively uncomplex and tends to emphasize either an organization which sells something or an organization which makes something. Craft firms exist primarily at the mercy of a benevolent environment. They have great difficulty responding to important changes in technology, competition, or the market served.

In contrast, the *promotion* type of organization is strongly influenced by a chief executive who is charismatic to subordinates and a promoter of the firm's innovative advantage. Policies are fluid, changing from day to day at the discretion of the promoter, and the organization exists as an extension of the promoter's personality. He or she has contact and influence with most organization members. Middle management is bypassed by the promoter, and indirect labor provides technical or personal support for the chief executive. Basically, the organization exists to exploit a distinct market or product advantage, making planning or efficiency less important for organization survival and success. Such an advantage ends when competitors or imitators enter the field. Similarly, the enthusiastic support of the promoter by organization members early in the life of the promotion firm tends to diminish as the firm's competitive position changes. As implied, the promotion firm has a limited life. It must change or perish.

The third form of organization is *administrative*. This is the form described in this entry and, indeed, advocated here. It is managed professionally by a chief executive who directs a planned structure toward clearly defined goals. The organization becomes an institution with an absence of indispensable people. It is designed according to size and technological imperatives, to be described later, and it adjusts to changes in its market environment by means of planning.

Organizational Change. While craft firms may exist for many years in a stable market environment, a sudden shift in technology or competition may make survival dependent upon professional management. In addition, a change in company goals from comfort and survival to growth and profitability may stimulate development of the administrative form to be described.

A change in the promotion form is more pronounced and dramatic. As the promotion form loses its unique market advantage and must compete with other firms which may be considerably more efficient, the promoter-dominated form of organization will no longer suffice. The annals of business history are filled with examples of promoters who built and promoted their enterprises at the beginning, and then led them to the brink of disaster as conditions changed.

The material which follows suggests how the craft or promotion organization may be redesigned along administrative lines and how existing administrative organizations may be analyzed for further improvement.

Key Influences on Structure

In analyzing organization structure or in designing a structure, one might consider four basic influences which tend to shape it.

Competitive Basis for Survival. In general, there are two bases for organization survival: efficiency of operation or creativity and adaptability to client needs. Where the market for products is stable and predictable and where the company is providing products which are equal in quality to those of other suppliers, the organization will compete and survive on the basis of *efficiency*. Either its prices must be competitively favorable or else its prices must be equivalent to those of other suppliers, and the firm must be able to sell at those prices and make an adequate profit. Such organizations are designed to make or sell standard items.

In contrast, where the market for the products is unstable or hard to predict and where the company is providing products which are more or less unique, the organization will compete and survive on the basis of its *unique service*. In such cases, there is a great deal about the product that is "made to order," and it must do what it is supposed to do. Customers pay a premium to ensure that they get the service desired. For example, such organizations are designed to produce houses, special tooling, fashion items, or highly technical products.

This trade-off between efficiency and creativity in organization designs plays an important role within the organization as well. The efficiency and economy of some units within an organization will free the resources that can be devoted to creativity in other units. For example, making production or purchasing routine enables creative efforts to be expended in research and development or in the top executive team.

Technology. The technology of an organization is related to its design, and it appears that there are proper designs for different technologies. One classification of technology is provided by Woodward[2] who grouped the manufacturing organizations she studied into three classes: (1) custom and small-batch production, (2) large-batch and mass production, and (3) process production. She demonstrated that there were distinctly different patterns of organization for successful and unsuccessful organizations in each class.

A second classification of technology is provided by Thompson.[3] He identified three types of technology: long-linked, mediating, and intensive.

Long-linked technology, such as that found in mass production, typically has a functional organization design with units like production, sales, and purchasing subordinate to central planning and scheduling. Such firms will expand through vertical integration; e.g., through control of suppliers and sources of raw materials and through control of market channels. Such firms are expected to be highly organized and will try to protect their production operations from disruption. As Thompson pointed out, "The constant rate of production means that, once adjusted, the proportions of resources involved can be standardized to the point where each contributes to its capacity; none need be underemployed."[4]

Mediating is a second form of technology. Organizations that use it link clients or customers who are or wish to be interdependent. Banks, insurance companies, the post office, and retail chains are examples. Mediating technology requires that an organization operate in standardized ways, relying upon fixed rules and procedures. In addition, the operations tend to be spread in time and space. These organizations will try to increase the population served by expanding the geographic area which they serve or by adding additional product lines. The central offices of such organizations will engage in the development of the necessary plans and schedules.

Intensive is the third form of technology. Organizations using it combine a variety of skills and techniques to work upon a person or product in a special, unique, and customized way. Examples might include a hospital, a construction firm, or a research laboratory. It is important for intensive-technology organizations to include the right skills and to make them available at the right time. Such organizations make frequent use of teams, project groups, or task forces.

Size. There are a number of somewhat unrelated but parallel forces that encourage an organization to increase its size.[5] As might be expected, as organizations increase their size, they also tend to become more formal and more complex. For example, Child[6] reviewed the relationship between size and organizational characteristics in several different groups of manufacturing companies, finding that as size increased, there were also increases in the number of divisions, the division of labor, the formalization of rules and regulations, and the number of levels in the companies.

In academic circles, a virtual battle has been raging about whether size or technology is the main determinant of organization design. Some researchers[7] have argued that technology, not size, is the more salient influence on structure. Others[8] have argued that size, not technology, is more important.

It seems likely that both technology and size affect organization design, perhaps in different ways. It may also be noted here that increases in size may be an advantage in some organizations but not in others. In long-linked technology, for example, size may be expected to provide potential benefits for efficiency and profit. In contrast, an increase in the size of firms with intensive technology can create difficulties in processing information which might, in turn, interfere with the ability of the firm to provide customized and effective service to clients.

Markets or Environment Served. The internal character of an organization also depends greatly upon the kinds and degree of demands placed upon it by its environment. Where there are many changes in technology or many outsiders influencing or making claims upon the organization, the organization will be more differentiated. Where it can isolate or buffer itself from outside influences, the organization will be less differentiated. Considered in another way, one may see that where the organization provides a product which is more or less made to order, the attention of organization members will be more concerned with client needs and with the output to meet those needs than a company in which the organization mass produces a product. In the latter case, the organization will isolate its production processes so that it may produce a high volume of standard products without interruption or change.

Dimensions of Organization Design

The following design features provide the organizational pattern which affects the organization's success and survival.

Functional and Goal-Oriented Structures. There are two fundamental designs for organizing which apply to a total organization or to the units within the total organization. The first pools relatively large numbers of people doing similar work in the same department or organizational unit, and is called a functional structure. For example, the *functional organization* contains production, sales, engineering, and personnel departments.

Variations on the functional structure, particularly in large organizations, include the separation of the organization into product divisions or into geographically dispersed profit centers. In the former, each division contains the functions required to operate efficiently. In the latter, functionally organized stores or plants are contiguous to their markets. In manufacturing, such structures are appropriate in large-batch and mass production technologies. In nonmanufacturing, they are appropriate for long-linked or mediating technologies.

The second basic strategy for organizing is to be goal-oriented. *Goal-oriented organizations* direct member attention to specific outcomes or client services. They may be project teams containing people with different specialties combining their efforts to achieve a new and creative outcome. Job shop firms are also goal-oriented since they produce customized products to order. In addition, the specialized adaptation of organization services, as by regional contractors, is goal-oriented, since the design facilitates outcomes or services rather than functional processing.[9] in manufacturing, such structures are appropriate in unit and small-batch production. In nonmanufacturing, they are appropriate in intensive technologies.

The functional or goal-oriented alternatives may be observed in many other kinds of organizations as well. For example, a public utility commission is commonly organized into departments of legal services, engineering, rate setting, etc. (functional structure) or into a utilities department and a transportation department (goal-oriented structure).

Different parts of an organization will be organized using either of the two alternatives. For example, a research and development division may be organized into departments of data processing, chemistry, and engineering (function) or into project group A and project group B (goal-oriented). Secretarial services may be provided through a secretarial pool (functional) or by individual private secretaries (goal-oriented).

To reiterate, the essential logic of the two structures is that functional units contain people who emphasize their own specialty and its processes. In contrast, the goal-oriented unit often contains a mixture of skills, and its emphasis is upon the outcomes of work effort for creativity and adaptiveness.

Functional organizations typically have a very formal organization and relatively inflexible operations. Employees are likely to take a short-term view of their work since they focus on day-to-day job requirements. Conflict between departments is common. Departments are dependent upon each other, and scheduling and coordination between them is difficult.

The functional organization is most appropriate where organizational survival is based upon efficiency, where technology is routine and relatively

657

fixed, where size is great enough to permit standardized jobs and equipment, and where the market is stable and predictable.

The goal-oriented structure, on the other hand, has quite different characteristics. Unlike the functional organization, the goal-oriented structure is adaptive and creative, but not especially efficient. Equipment and personnel may be duplicated between units and are present because of potential need rather than full-time use.

Where the goal-oriented unit contains a mixture of different specialties, supervision is by a generalist or professional manager who can integrate the efforts of the various specialties. Thus, the goal-oriented structure may provide a training ground for top management of the organization. Teams are typically informal in their interactions and creative in their efforts. If successful, they take a long-run view since the measure of their effectiveness is evaluated on the basis of an outcome—construction of a building, completion of a piece of equipment, release of an advertising campaign, etc.

Goal-oriented units tend to meet schedules effectively because they are less dependent upon other units than functional organizations and because evaluation criteria include, importantly, the final result.

Matrix Organization Analysis. In addition to functional and goal-oriented structures, there is a third, hybrid form of organization structure which combines both organizing strategies. This strategy, the *matrix organization,* pools personnel and equipment within functional units, permitting subdivision in the specialties, advancement, effective use of resources, economies of scale, and the like. In addition, product responsibility is vested in product managers who coordinate and integrate the efforts in each department pertaining to a product. This goal-oriented strategy enhances adaptiveness and adherence to schedules and focuses on outcomes.

The matrix organization is well suited to situations in which time constraints are more important than maximum economy. It is also well suited to situations involving the use of temporary project groups which will terminate their existence once the projects are completed.

Matrix organizations generally exhibit conflict between the functional administrators and the heads of goal-oriented units. One way to manage such conflict is to maintain a balance of power between the two groups by budgeting money to the projects and by having most of the personnel in functional units assigned to and employed by the projects. Thus, the goal-oriented units have the power of money, which balances the functional units' power of expertise.

Matrix organizations also negate many of the old principles of management. Contrary to the principle that responsibility should equal authority, project or program managers have more responsibility than authority. In addition, contrary to the principle that each person should have only one boss, personnel assigned to goal-oriented units actually have two or more formal leaders—the heads of both the functional unit and the goal-oriented unit.

Centralization or Decentralization of Decision Making. A second design feature involves the extent to which key decisions are made at the top levels of the organization or are delegated to lower levels. For manufacturing organizations, such issues might include the following: capital acquisition, investment decisions, acquisition of subsidiaries, new product development, marketing strategy, pricing, research and development, hiring and firing of key personnel, and changes in corporate policy. Delegation probably ranges from exclusive control by the board of directors or top executive at one extreme to complete responsibility vested in a level below the chief executive without executive review at the other extreme.

A study of 79 manufacturing firms[10] considered the relationship between the technology of the firms, the degree of vertical integration involved, the size, the extent of decentralization, and the use of sophisticated controls. In addition, the study contrasted the patterns of organization in high-profit and low-profit firms.

The results showed that the more the technology of the firm was characterized by high volume and mass production and the larger the firm's size, the more it was vertically integrated. Further, the more vertically integrated it was, the greater the decentralization of decision making. Finally, the more decentralized it was, the more the firm used sophisticated controls for quality, costing, inventory, scheduling, finances, and evaluation of executive performance. Equally important, the more-profitable firms tended to follow this pattern more than less-profitable firms.

Line and Staff Organization. A third design feature has to do with the assignment and use of auxiliary services, generally called *staff.* In contrast to staff services, activities which are directly concerned with the creation or sale of a product are generally called *line.* The distinction between line and staff is clearest and most useful in manufacturing organizations.

Both size and technology are major determinants of staff use. Technology influences staff use through its influence on the application of sophisticated controls. Successful high-volume manufacturers use elaborate planning and control techniques,[11] and such planning and control are the primary responsibility of staff personnel. Size is also a factor, since the use of such specialized personnel is not feasible on a cost-effectiveness basis for small companies, and small size may not permit employment of staff personnel.

Staff units may be identified as one of two types: general and specialist.

1. *General staff.* These units are most readily identified in the corporate offices of large companies. Such corporate staff offices generally develop policies which affect all divisions of the organization and probably serve an adaptive function in an organization which is deeply embedded in a functional structure.

   Another form of general staff is the personal assistant, usually identified by an "assistant-to" title. Such positions do not have responsibility identified by function, as do other corporate staff offices. Instead, assistants perform a variety of duties within the responsibility and authority of the person they serve, expanding the administrative capacity of that person.

   General staff units, whether corporate staff or personal staff, report to the principal whom they serve. They provide a goal-oriented, adaptive function at the top of the organization, taking a long-run view, even if the rest of the organization is organized into functional units.

2. *Specialist staff.* These units are identified as engaging primarily in service, advice, or control activities. *Service staffs* are added when it becomes economical to employ a specialist rather than have the same functions performed by a line unit. A purchasing agent, a maintenance person, and a market research analyst are examples. *Advisory staffs* aid in problem solving by providing specialized information, such as legal advice or retirement counseling. Finally, *control staff* units provide special planning and control activities. Production control, cost control, and quality control are examples of the latter.

In addition, where a specialist staff unit engages in control over another unit, the head of the staff and the head of the unit controlled will report to a common superior. A quality control manager might not report to the head of a manufacturing department, for example, since a manufacturing department is evaluated by production volume and might bring pressure to bear against a quality control department to reduce its standards.

While the design questions regarding staff assignment or staff use are not difficult to answer, the question of how much staff to use is not easily answered. The latter depends upon issues of resource allocation. In other words, the creation of a staff unit depends upon whether staff functions are better performed by line managers themselves or by being assigned to a new or existing staff unit. In addition, some staff services may be purchased rather than provided internally.

Extent of Staff Use.   A few generalizations regarding the level of staff use are possible, however.

1. The distinction between line and staff and the emphasis on staff services will be greatest in high-volume mass production technologies. As indicated earlier, that type of technology requires decentralization of decision making and the use of sophisticated controls. Those controls are provided by specialist staffs engaged in planning and control.

2. As small organizations grow, the percentage of staff utilized will increase to some point and then remain at about the same percentage of total employment. The early growth of staff seems to occur as company size permits the economical use of fully employed staff units. Before such use is economical, the activities are performed by line managers or purchased externally. Finally, it is clear that the failure to use staff when needed can be a serious false economy.

Line and Staff Authority.   A manager's authority refers to the way in which the organization intends for him or her to influence others in the organization. Where a direct, formal reporting relationship is present, the superior is identified as having line authority over the subordinate. Thus, both the production manager and the personnel manager have *line* authority over their immediate subordinates. In contrast, where a manager is expected to provide service or advice or control outside the immediate reporting relationship, the authority is labeled *staff.*

Staff authority varies. At one extreme, a manager is empowered to give advice to others where it is requested. Next, where compulsory staff advice is a company policy, organization members are expected to ask for advice from designated sources before taking action, though they do not have to follow the advice. Such a policy ensures that appropriate sources of information are used. Next, some organizations require that concurrent agreements take place between two units before actions are taken. For example, this policy gives a finance department the opportunity to veto a capital expenditure by a production manager. Finally a manager may have functional authority over other units in the organization. Functional authority is a limited right to give orders and expect compliance outside the normal chain of command. For example, a safety engineer may be empowered to stop an unsafe operation or an inspector may have the right to reject products which do not meet quality standards.

Since staff executives generally have a great deal of power or informal influence in an organization even though they have relatively little formal authority, it is not uncommon for conflicts to occur between line and staff executives. This difficulty may be reduced by planning the degree of staff authority which executives may exercise over each other.

Organization Shape. The shape of an organization is influenced by the number of levels used and the span of control (number of people supervised) of each manager. Other things being equal, an organization with many levels will have smaller spans of control. Conversely, if the same number of people are organized into broad spans of control, the number of levels required will be reduced.

Number of Organization Levels. An analysis of organization design should consider the number of levels used. With too many levels of management, the organization experiences unnecessary administrative expense and channels of communication are lengthened. With too few levels, supervisory effectiveness is hampered and spans of control become too great.

Levels and Size. As one might expect, the number of levels in an organization is related to its size. In addition, in the smaller size range it takes a smaller increase in organization size to generate new levels than it does in size ranges of large organizations. Studies of business organizations consistently show high correlations between size and number of levels.

Levels and Technology. The number of levels is also influenced by technology, though not as clearly as by size. In her study of firms with more than 100 employees, Woodward[12] reported that firms with unit or small-batch production had a median of three levels of management, while large-batch and mass production firms had a median of four levels, and process firms had a median of six levels. Less successful firms deviated from those averages.

In contrast, another study[13] focused on the same three classes of technology and found just over five levels for unit production (average plant size, 421), mass production (average plant size, 631), and process production (average plant size, 326).

Levels and Employee Attitudes. While there is no clear and direct relationship between employee satisfaction and employee performance, there is a frequent relationship between satisfaction and the behavior of coming to and staying at work. That is, turnover and absenteeism rates are more favorable for satisfied employees than for dissatisfied employees. This being the case, it is useful to determine the effect of the number of levels upon measures of satisfaction.

Spans of Supervision. Another specific design issue involves the number of people supervised by any manager. As suggested earlier, the shape of the organization will be influenced by the spans used, affecting the cost of supervision and the quality of management exercised. Consider, for example, the difference between a span of control of 10 and a span of control of five. With one supervisor for 10 employees there is one level of supervision and the neces-

660

sary expense of one supervisor. But if the same 10 employees have two supervisors, each with a span of control of five, someone must be added to coordinate their work, and the result is two levels of supervision and the expense of three managers.

Executive Span of Supervision. The proper span of control for a chief executive depends upon his or her particular style of management and the organizing strategy of the company. Unlike the span of lower-level managers, it is not much influenced by the organization's size or technology. The organizing strategy plays a part because where units reporting to the executive are self-contained, many can be supervised without detracting from organizational effectiveness. Such is the case, for example, in a retail chain or a large divisionalized manufacturing firm.

To illustrate the way in which the relative spans within a single organization may be determined, the experience of the Lockheed Missiles and Space Company, a division of Lockheed Aircraft, is instructive.[14] Lockheed's organizational analysts selected seven factors which appeared to influence spans of supervision:

1. Similarity of function—the degree to which functions performed by the various components are alike or different (more similar = broader span).

2. Geographic contiguity—the physical location of the components and personnel reporting to a principal (more contiguous = broader span).

3. Complexity of functions—the nature of the duties being performed by the organization components or personnel. This takes into account the skills necessary to perform satisfactorily (simple duties = broader span).

4. Direction and control—the nature of the personnel reporting directly to a principal. This includes the degree of the principal's attention required for proper supervision of subordinates' actions (little supervision required = broader span).

5. Coordination—the extent to which the principal must exert time and effort in keeping actions properly correlated and in keeping his or her activities keyed in with other activities in the company (independent activity = broader span).

6. Planning—the importance, complexity, and time required to review and establish future programs and objectives (little planning = broader span).

7. Organizational assistance—the help received by the principal from direct-line assistants, staff activities, and assistants-to (more staff support = broader span).

In summary, while executive spans seem to have little systematic variation with organization size or

technology, the spans of supervision at lower levels do seem to vary with size, technology, and other characteristics of the job. If jobs are relatively routine and repetitive, broad spans may be used effectively.

Task Design and Worker Values. A fifth dimension in organizational analysis and design includes the job characteristics and the values of people holding the jobs. An important purpose of organizational analysis, therefore, is to establish congruence between the design of the organization, the design of jobs within the organization, and the values of jobholders. If these three parts can be matched properly, the result should be more effective performance by the organization and great satisfaction for its members.

Job Design. At the turn of the century, industry developed a major emphasis upon the use of mass production technology. It was felt, in many cases correctly, that if jobs could be routinized and made repetitive, the result would be high efficiency and low cost of operation. These benefits could occur because repetitive performance of simplified jobs would permit the use of relatively unskilled labor, ease of training and replacement, less physical effort, and predictable rates of production.

Such proved to be the case. However, the simplification of jobs was not without difficulty. For some workers, the routinized jobs were boring and monotonous, resulting in dissatisfaction and poor performance. High rates of absenteeism and turnover increased costs because of requirements for additional labor and the necessary expense of training and replacement.

In an effort to have the best of both worlds—efficient production and satisfied labor—a number of remedies have been tried. Human relations training, participative management, and job enlargement are examples of such remedies. In some cases, these actions did what they were supposed to do: satisfaction and worker performance increased. In other cases, they were obvious failures. The reason for success or failure is now becoming clear. If productivity and satisfaction are to be achieved, job design and worker values should match. This requires an objective assessment of job characteristics and the matching of different job designs with different kinds of employees.

Employee Values. A further contribution to successful job design efforts has been the assessment of employee values and the proper matching of employee values with different kinds of job design.

Research to date indicates that employees—particularly blue-collar workers—who have higher-order need-strength will probably respond favorably to challenging job designs. In contrast, employees low in higher-order need-strength will respond less favorably, or perhaps even negatively, to challenging jobs. If this is true, it suggests that employers should take pains to match different kinds of job designs with different kinds of employee values. Employees with higher-order need-strength should be rewarded with opportunities for interesting, varied, and challenging jobs. In contrast, employees low in such need-strength may be more productively and satisfactorily utilized in jobs where the performance requirements are clear and routine, and where employees can be rewarded with money and free time once standards are met.

Matching Organizational Design, Job Design, and Employee Values

It should be apparent at this point that an organization which seeks high levels of performance with satisfied employees should find a proper fit between the design of its structure, the design of its jobs, and the values of its jobholders. As indicated in Fig. O-6, the requirements for efficiency or adaptability, the nature of technology, the size of the organization, and the relative stability of the environment all influence the kind of organization design which will be appropriate.

This organization design will, in turn, influence the character of job design. For example, large functional organizations competing on the basis of efficiency will probably have fairly routinized jobs in many organizational units. It would appear that these jobs would be performed best by workers who do *not* seek challenge and autonomy in their work. Where the proper fit between job and values does not occur, it may be possible to redesign the jobs to provide needed challenge, to find new workers with requisite values, or, perhaps, to change worker values.

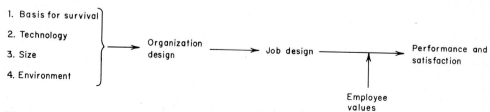

FIG. O-6 Balancing organization design, job design, and employee values.

See also Authority, responsibility, and accountability; Matrix management; Organization development (OD); Organization structures and charting; Project management; Work design, job enlargement, and job enrichment.

NOTES

[1] A. C. Filley and R. J. Aldag, "Characteristics and Measurement of an Organizational Typology," *Academy of Management Journal*, vol. 21, no. 4, December 1978, pp. 578–591; Alan C. Filley, Robert J. House, and Steven Kerr, *Managerial Process and Organizational Behavior*, 2d ed., Scott, Foresman, Glenview, Ill., 1976, chap. 22.

[2] J. Woodward, *Industrial Organization: Theory and Practice*, Oxford University Press, London, 1965.

[3] J. D. Thompson, *Organizations in Action*, McGraw-Hill, New York, 1967.

[4] Ibid., p. 16.

[5] Daniel Katz and Robert L. Kahn, *The Social Psychology of Organizations*, John Wiley, New York, 1966.

[6] John Child, "Predicting and Understanding Organization Structure," *Administrative Science Quarterly*, vol. 18, no. 2, June 1973, pp. 168–185.

[7] Howard E. Aldrich, "Technology and Organizational Structure: A Re-examination of the Findings of the Aston Group," *Administrative Science Quarterly*, vol. 17, no. 1., 1972, pp. 26–43; Woodward, *Industrial Organization: Theory and Practice*; William L. Zwerman, *New Perspectives on Organization Theory*, Greenwood, Westport, Conn., 1970.

[8] Peter M. Blau, Cecilia McHugh Falbe, William McKinley, and Phelps K. Tracy, "Technology and organization in Manufacturing," *Administrative Science Quarterly*, vol. 21, no. 1, March 1976, pp. 20–40; John Child and Roger Mansfield, "Technology, Size and Organization Structure," *Sociology*, vol. 6, 1972, pp. 369–393; D. S. Pugh, D. J. Hickson, C. R. Hinings, and C. Turner, "Dimensions of Organization Structure," *Administrative Science Quarterly*, vol. 13, no. 1., June 1968, pp. 65–105.

[9] Filley, House, and Kerr, *Managerial Process and Organizational Behavior*; Walter R. Mahler, *Structure, Power and Results: How to Organize Your Company for Optimum Performance*, Dow Jones-Irwin, Homewood, Ill., 1975.

[10] P. N. Khandwalla, "Mass Output Orientation of Operations Technology and Organizational Structure," *Administrative Science Quarterly*, vol. 19, no. 1, March 1974, pp. 74–97.

[11] Ibid.

[12] Woodward, *Industrial Organization: Theory and Practice*.

[13] Blau et al., "Technology and Organization in Manufacturing."

[14] J. Stieglitz, "Optimizing Span of Control," *Management Record*, vol. 24, no. 9, September 1962, pp. 25–29.

ALAN C. FILLEY, *University of Wisconsin*

Outplacement

Outplacement is a process designed to counsel people who have been displaced from their current jobs; to assist them through the trauma of termination and direct them in their job search. The corporation or organization may employ an outside consultant for this service or provide such counseling services itself to individuals or groups.

Rationale. An effective outplacement program frees management up to make decisions in a more timely manner about people who are not performing well in their careers. From an organization's point of view, early identification and severance of the poor performer can save the company unlimited dollars and a great deal of trauma. It eliminates the need to create shelved positions within the company that become stumbling blocks to the rest of the organization's personal growth. Outplacement also helps the manager to feel comfortable that the employee being terminated is not being hurt, thereby aiding the manager with his own feelings during the termination. A person who does not fit well in the job is also helped from a career development point of view by not being kept on in that job.

For the employer, there is always the risk that a termination will be handled poorly and invite litigation. A proper outplacement program anticipates and mitigates any particular legal problems that might arise. Most important, outplacement assistance helps the individual look to the future and to a new job rather than become preoccupied with the loss of the past job and the thought of legal redress.

Terminations often disturb the sense of security of other employees within the organization. If those left behind observe the fair treatment received by their terminated colleagues, they feel better disposed toward the company and tend to side with management in terms of the decision.

Another point for consideration is external public image. Public statements of an intimate or negative nature by a terminated executive can have a damaging effect on recruitment and on top management within the organization.

An effective outplacement program can also save money by reducing lengthy severance payments. Individuals tend to move to new jobs faster when they are properly counseled.

Typical Programs. Outplacement programs can be directed at individual executives or highly placed specialists or at groups of displaced employees.

For Individuals. An outplacement program can be designed for top-level executives up to and including chief executive officers, throughout business and government. Executive-level programs are usually conducted on an individual basis, with special attention given to the needs of the professional's progress through the program.

For Groups. Group programs and support systems can be designed for blue-collar, nonexempt, and exempt employees up through the middle-management levels. This process is referred to as *group outplacement* and has proved successful for companies faced with a "reduction in force" due to economic cutbacks. Group programs normally constitute a

three-day seminar for groups of 12 or more people. One-on-one counseling is also offered as an option to each member of the group so that anyone who is experiencing a high level of stress can be assisted.

Program Procedures. Outplacement programs must embrace two contingencies.

The Organization. This includes:

1. Pretermination consulting with personnel and line management about the entire severance process to ensure congruency with the company's policies and procedures.

2. Pretermination training with the person who will actually terminate the employee.

The Individual. This typically includes four steps:

1. Immediate consultation with the individual following the termination decision.

2. Career-path assistance with the aid of a trained counselor (often a licensed psychologist) to help each person assess his or her current career position. This includes: (*a*) evaluation of past work experience; (*b*) measurement of the individual's motivational characteristics, personality strengths, and aptitudes; and (*c*) provision of professional guidance in helping the terminated individual to understand which future positions are most appropriate.

3. Organizational support so that the individual has a feeling of continued work routine as a needed discipline to help with the trauma of displacement. This is supplied by making office space and support services available.

4. Job search activity through an integrated marketing plan that includes (*a*) résumé development and distribution, (*b*) training on how to make personal contacts, (*c*) sharpening of interview skills, and (*d*) ongoing personalized counseling.

Evaluation. Based on a national sample of approximately 200 people who received outplacement counseling services between 1980 and 1983, the average time to placement was 5.4 months. Some 72 percent of the candidates found new positions in 6 months or less, and 44 percent found positions in 3 months or less. Fully 64 percent experienced either no change or an increase in their base salary. The primary methods of obtaining a new position were use of personal contacts (63 percent), executive search organizations (14 percent), advertisements (13 percent), and direct letter contact (10 percent).

Advantages. New careers have often been successfully launched as a result of the motivation acquired by examination of self and of past work experience. The process allows individuals to reevaluate their skills and interests. It teaches them how best to apply themselves to finding the most suitable job. Employment parameters become defined and are backed up by self-awareness and the ability to handle interpersonal relationships during the job search. Ultimately, outplaced people become more effective on the job and, as statistics show, may earn higher salaries.

Disadvantages. An improperly planned and executed outplacement program can have a damaging effect on both the terminated individual and the employer. People are emotionally vulnerable to trauma and distress at the time of termination. If the program is not staffed with well-trained counselors, there is a likelihood that the terminated person will leave the program before its completion. The employer is then open to criticism and possible legal ramifications.

See also Development and training: career path planning for managers; Human resources planning; Personnel administration; Social responsibility of business.

REFERENCES

German, D., and J. German: *How to Find a Job When Jobs Are Hard to Find,* American Management Associations, New York, 1983.

Morin, W. J., and L. Yorkes: *Outplacement Techniques,* American Management Associations, New York, 1982.

Sweet, Donald H.: *Recruitment; A Guide for Managers,* Addison-Wesley, Reading, Mass., 1975.

WILLIAM J. MORIN, *Drake Beam Morin, Inc.*

Ownership, Legal Forms of

In a private enterprise system, economic decisions related to what shall be produced, how it shall be produced, and for whom, are usually made by organizations known as businesses. Generally speaking, businesses are economic organizations developed by individuals for the purpose of providing some good(s) or services(s) for a profit. In the American private enterprise system, profit-oriented firms can be classified as either unincorporated or incorporated businesses. The unique characteristics, as well as the advantages and disadvantages, inherent to each of these forms of business organization will be examined in this entry.

Unincorporated Businesses

Unincorporated businesses are the most popular form of business structure in the American enterprise system. However, the average size of unincorporated businesses is substantially smaller than the average size of incorporated businesses. Consequently, unincorporated businesses constitute a

smaller percentage of total business assets than incorporated businesses.

There are two primary types of unincorporated businesses in the United States: sole proprietorships and partnerships. Of these, the sole proprietorship is far and away the most popular. Indeed, there are approximately three times as many sole proprietorships in the United States as there are partnerships and corporations combined.

Sole Proprietorship. Sole proprietorships are, by definition, businesses run by one owner, or proprietor. Such businesses are usually small and usually operate in the services or retail goods business. One typical sole proprietorship is probably the "mom and pop" grocery store formerly found in abundance throughout America. The respective advantages and disadvantages of the sole proprietorship form of organization are discussed in more detail below.

Advantages of the Sole Proprietorship Organization. There are four primary advantages associated with the sole proprietorship form of organization. These are (a) ease of entry and exit, (b) full managerial powers, (c) rights to all profits, and (d) possible tax benefits. (See Table O-14.)

TABLE O-14 Characteristics of Sole Proprietorships

Advantages	Disadvantages
Ease of entry and exit	Limited life span
Full managerial powers	Limited size
Rights to all profits	
Tax benefits	Unlimited liability

Organizing and starting a sole proprietorship involves fewer obstacles than most other business forms. Other than the obvious start-up problems common to all businesses, the sole proprietor has few other obligations. In some communities and in some areas of business (for example, the retail liquor business) special licenses may be required by the local authorities, but such is not normally the case. In similar fashion, exit from business is a more simplified process for the sole proprietor than for other forms of organization. A sign in the window, a bolt on the door, and the business is closed.

A second advantage of the sole proprietorship is the right to full managerial say-so on the part of the proprietor. This advantage is usually a major factor cited by those who begin sole proprietorships. People, it seems, like to be their own boss. Nonetheless, this advantage contains a strong qualification, for it is one thing to desire full managerial authority and another to be a truly qualified manager. Indeed, statistics have shown that the major reason for the failure of small businesses has been managerial incompetence in one or more areas vital to success.

A third advantage to the sole proprietorship form of business enterprise is the right to all the profits of the business. Inherent with this advantage, however, is the undeniable fact that all losses also accrue to the sole proprietor. While all proprietors enter business with the expectation of making profits, the risk is always there that such profits may not materialize and that losses will result instead.

Should the proprietorship prove profitable, yet another benefit may result. This benefit relates to the tax treatment accorded sole proprietorship profits. The law does not distinguish between profits earned by the sole proprietor or the business. For tax purposes, all such incomes are treated as belonging to the individual proprietor and are thus taxed at the individual rate. For most proprietorships, this has the effect of taxing business profits at a lower rate than for incorporated businesses.

Disadvantages of the Sole Proprietorship Organization. Despite the many significant advantages inherent in sole proprietorships, certain disadvantages exist which tend to mute some of the overall attractiveness of this form of business organization. To begin with, sole proprietorships have the unfortunate characteristic of possessing a limited life span. Because the sole proprietorship has only one owner, the life span of the business cannot exceed that of the proprietor.

The limited life span of sole proprietorships tends to lead to yet another disadvantage; namely, the characteristic of limited size. Businesses become large only with the benefit of two factors: time and capital. Because a sole proprietorship's life span is limited, most such organizations lack sufficient time to grow large. Additionally, only one owner exists to provide the capital necessary to attain large size. When these two items are combined, the reason for the generally small size of most sole proprietorships becomes clear.

Finally, the sole proprietorship possesses the discomforting attribute of conveying unlimited liability to the proprietor. In essence, this means that under the sole proprietorship form of organization, the sole proprietor is personally responsible for all the debts and obligations accruing to the business. This liability extends to the full personal asset position of the sole proprietor and is indeed a major drawback to this form of business organization.

Partnership. The second major type of unincorporated business is the partnership. The partnership form of organization is characterized by the existence of two or more owners, or partners, at least one of whom must accept unlimited liability for the acts and obligations of the partnership. In addition to possessing characteristics unique only to this form of organization, partnerships possess advantages and disadvantages that can be clearly identified.

As noted, partnerships are distinguished by the existence of two or more owners, at least one of whom has unlimited liability for the debts of the business. Those partners who agree to accept unlim-

ited liability are known as *general partners.* They enjoy all the benefits of the partnership and are generally active in the management of the partnership. Unless specifically stated otherwise in the partnership agreement, all partners are assumed to be general partners.

On occasion, other types of partners (besides general partners) may partake in a partnership. *Limited partners* are individuals whose contribution to the management of the firm is restricted to a particular facet of the firm's operations. For example, a lawyer or an accountant may be a limited partner. Because the managerial role of limited partners is restricted, these partners are not subject to unlimited liability for the debts of the firm.

Similarly, *silent partners* and *secret partners* enjoy limited liability for the debts of a partnership. Silent partners are partners who do not play an active role in the management of the partnership but who allow the partnership to list their names as partners in the firm. Secret partners are partners who, although active in the management of the firm, are not recognized as partners by the general public. If for some reason the partnership status of the secret partner becomes known, that partner becomes a general partner and loses the limited liability status previously enjoyed. (See Table O-15)

TABLE O-15 Characteristics of Partnerships

Unique characteristics	Advantages	Disadvantages
Types of partners	Ease of entry Division of labor Tax benefits	Limited life Unlimited liability Personality conflicts

Advantages of the Partnership Form of Organization. Like the sole proprietorship, partnerships are relatively easy to form. Generally, a written agreement, known as the *articles of copartnership,* is drawn up by the various parties, outlining the duties, responsibilities, capital contributions, and profit sharing relationship of each of the partners. No other extensive legal formalities need to be undertaken (except in isolated industries) to begin the business.

A second advantage of the partnership form of organization is the possibility of achieving a division of labor in the management of the firm. With multiple partners in the firm, it is conceivable that one partner could assume responsibility for, say, marketing efforts, another could handle personnel, etc. Dividing responsibilities among the various partners can lead to improved business management.

Finally, partnerships possess the same tax advantages that accrue to sole proprietorships. That is, profits earned by the partnership are assumed to be earned by the various owners in proportion to the arrangement agreed on in the *articles of copartner-*

ship. Usually, this means the profits of the firm are taxed at a lower rate than that for an incorporated business.

Disadvantages of the Partnership Form of Organization. Generally speaking, partnerships suffer from many of the same disadvantages that are found in sole proprietorships. For example, partnerships tend to have a very limited life. If any of the general partners dies or becomes unable to function as a partner, the partnership comes to an end. Indeed, even the death of a special partner can, under some circumstances, terminate a partnership.

Another disadvantage is that all general partners are fully liable for all the debts of the business. As we have noted, this unlimited liability feature may even extend to secret partners, should word ever spread about their ownership position.

Finally, partnerships suffer from what can be called a "personality crisis." It is difficult to find a group of people who trust one another so much that they allow each other the freedom to commit acts which could result in a creditor suing them for the full extent of their wealth. It has often been said that a partnership is much like a marriage, in that the trust one partner must have in the others must be complete and total. Unfortunately, such trust is not easy to find.

Incorporated Businesses

The second major type of business organization in America is known as incorporated business. To create an incorporated business, it is necessary to obtain the permission of the appropriate legal authorities. Such permission, however, may obligate the incorporated business to follow certain rules and regulations, and possibly to adhere to the restrictions of regulatory agencies in the course of doing business.

Corporation. Perhaps the most important, and yet least understood, business structure in America is the corporation. By definition, a corporation is "an artificial being, invisible, intangible, and existing only in contemplation of law" (*Dartmouth College v. Woodward,* 17 U.S. 518). This definition, handed down by Chief Justice John Marshall in 1819, decrees that a corporation is, in fact, a legal person, possessing many of the rights and obligations of ordinary people. Thus, a corporation can sue or be sued, it pays taxes on its earnings, and in some ways, it even possesses abilities not radically different from married and divorced people. The characteristics—advantages and disadvantages—of the corporate business organization are noted in Table O-16.

When individuals desire to form a corporation, they must submit a charter to the state in which the corporation will be domiciled. This charter specifies the objective of the coporation, the nature of its business, the names of the organizers, the number of

TABLE O-16 Characteristics of Corporations

Unique characteristics	Advantages	Disadvantages
Corporate charter	Transfer of	
Stockholders	ownership	Organizational
Types of	Unlimited life	expense
corporations	Ease of expansion	Lack of privacy
	Division of labor	Double taxation
	Limited liability	

shares of ownership stock that will be issued, etc. Approval of the charter by the state government is necessary before the corporation can be created.

A second significant feature of the corporation is the existence of stockholders. By definition, the *stockholders* of a corporation are the owners of the firm. Such ownership is signified by possession of a certificate of ownership, known commonly as a *stock certificate*. Each shareholder's ownership consists of the percentage of the total shares of stock owned by that shareholder. Perhaps an example will clarify the situation.

Suppose a group of people desires to form a corporation. It submits a charter to the state, which gets approved. In that charter, assume the company asked for authorization to issue 1000 shares of stock at a price of $10 per share. Upon approval of the charter, the company offers the stock to the general public. Eventually, all 1000 shares are sold. The company has received a total of $10,000 (its initial capital) with which to begin business. Each of the people who bought the stock becomes known as a shareholder of the firm.

Because shareholders may live all over the world, it is impossible for them to engage in day-to-day management of the firm. As a consequence, the shareholders elect a team of professional managers to run the corporation for them. This team is known as the *board of directors*. The board has the responsibility of choosing a president and a vice president and watching over the interests of the shareholders who elected them.

A third unique characteristic of corporations is their diversity. For example, corporations may be public or private creations. *Private* corporations are typified by the large industrial corporations like General Motors. *Public* corporations, such as TVA or many large cities in the country, are less common. Recently, *quasi-public* corporations (Amtrak, for example) have also come into being. These are corporations created jointly by public and private interests.

Additionally, corporations can be classed as open or closed. An *open* corporation is one whose stock is widely owned and in which it is generally possible to buy shares from existing shareholders. *Closed* corporations are owned by only a few individuals who rarely sell their stock. Thus, the investing public has little opportunity to buy stock in these firms. An example of a closed corporation might be any of the professional sports teams operating in the country.

Corporations can also be classed as profit or nonprofit institutions. Most private, industrial corporations are *profit*-oriented concerns. By contrast, most hospitals, churches, and foundations and some schools are *nonprofit*-oriented institutions.

Finally, corporations can be classified as being either domestic, foreign, or alien corporations. A *domestic* corporation is one which is operating in the state in which it received its charter. A *foreign* corporation is defined as one operating in a state other than the one in which it was chartered. An *alien* corporation is one that received its charter in a foreign country. Volkswagen, Toyota, and Datsun are all examples of alien corporations in the United States.

Advantages of the Corporate Form of Organization. The corporate form of business organization enjoys many advantages over the unincorporated business. First, the corporation is the only business institution that allows for easy transfer of ownership from one person or institution to another. To transfer ownership, the two parties (the selling party and the purchasing party) need only make contact, agree on a price, make the sale, and notify the company of the sale. The company then removes the name of the selling party from its ownership records and replaces it with the name and address of the new shareholder. Moreover, for most of the large, public, industrial corporations, the securities markets provide an easy and efficient means for transfer of ownership.

Because of this ease of transferability of ownership, yet another advantage accrues to the corporation; that is, the potential for an unlimited life. The corporation, by virtue of its status as a "legal person," enjoys a life all its own. It is not dependent upon the life of its shareholders, since the demise of any shareholder merely transfers those ownership rights to his or her legal heirs.

A third advantage is the ease with which most corporations can expand and grow. A corporation can raise new capital by amending the charter and asking permission to issue more shares. If the state and the existing shareholders agree, the corporation may then offer more stock to the investing public and thus raise the desired new capital.

A fourth advantage of the corporation is the ability to enjoy a real division of labor. The owners of the corporation normally do not actively manage their business. Rather, this managerial task is assigned to a board of directors who are authorized to hire all those people they feel necessary to reach the goals of the firm. As a result, most corporations have well-defined organizational structures, with vast reservoirs of expertise available to run the business.

The corporation provides its shareholders with

one final advantage—namely, the right of limited liability. Because the corporation is a "legal person," it, and it alone, is responsible for its debts. The shareholders of the corporation can lose no more than their investment in the stock of the company.

Disadvantages of the Corporate Form of Organization. Although significant advantages exist with the corporate organizational structure, several major weaknesses are found with this form. First is the problem of organizational expense. Forming a corporation involves lengthy legal proceedings, the cost of which can often run into thousands of dollars.

Yet a second disadvantage is the loss of privacy of business operations. Because corporations are creations of the state, they must file regular reports and financial statements to the state of incorporation. These reports become part of the public record and are available for anyone, including competitors, to see.

Finally, corporations are subject to what is commonly known as "double taxation." When a corporation earns a profit, it pays taxes—at a rather high corporate tax rate—on those profits. From its after-tax profits, the corporation may then pay dividends to its shareholders. These dividends are considered to be income to the shareholder and, to the extent that they exceed presently allowed exclusions, are subject to personal income taxes. Thus, some of the profits earned by the corporation are taxed twice; once when earned by the corporation and again when earned by the shareholder.

Other Incorporated Businesses. Although sole proprietorships, partnerships, and corporations constitute the majority of business organizations, a few other types exist which deserve mention.

Cooperatives. Cooperatives are variations of corporations. Incorporated businesses, they differ from corporations in that (1) each shareholder is an active member of the co-op; (2) each shareholder has only one vote in co-op affairs, regardless of the size of his or her investment; and (3) in many cases they are not profit-oriented. Co-ops are not overly popular in America. The few that do exist are primarily in the agricultural fields.

Mutual Companies. Mutual companies are companies, organized under state law, which are usually found in the banking or insurance fields. These companies are owned by the policyholders or depositors of the firm. Profits earned from the business are returned to the members (policyholders or depositors) as a dividend. Participants in mutual companies may also be liable for debts incurred by the company, although the extent of that liability is usually limited.

Subchapter S Corporations. This option is open to small business owners. It enables them to retain limited liability protection while avoiding corporate income tax. A number of restrictions apply, however; among them are that there must be no more than 15 shareholders, 20 percent of the income must come from inside the United States, and no more than 20 percent of the income must come from investments.

See also Boards of directors; Economic systems; Franchising; International operations and management in multinational companies; Officers, corporate; Organization structures and charting.

REFERENCES

Millstein, Ira M., and Salem M. Katsh: *The Limits of Corporate Power*, Macmillan, New York, 1981.

Perlick, Walter W., and Raymond V. Lesikar: *Introduction to Business: A Societal Approach*, Business Publications, Dallas, Tex., 1979.

Smith, Randy Baca: *Setting Up Shop: The Do's and Don'ts of Starting a Small Business*, McGraw-Hill, New York, 1982.

WALTER W. PERLICK, *California Polytechnic State University*

Paperwork Simplification

Paperwork simplification is the organized application of common sense to eliminate waste and establish more effective and efficient ways of doing paperwork. It includes analytical techniques and a participative approach to applying them. One of the most widely used and productive of the techniques, procedure flow charting, is presented in this entry to illustrate the paperwork simplification approach. The rest of the techniques are simply enumerated with a few words of explanation.

Principles

The definition, as stated here, includes the basic concepts of organization, common sense, waste reduction, effectiveness, and efficiency. These concepts, in turn, establish the basic principles of paperwork simplification:

1. Organize the facts of the work for examination with analytical techniques, charts, and diagrams.
2. Utilize the common sense of people who are involved and affected by the procedures under examination (the users).
3. Carefully review the procedures step by step and eliminate waste of any kind, such as of time, energy, space, material, and equipment.
4. Reorganize the procedure, reflecting the best judgment of the involved users and participating specialists.

A Typical Improvement Project

Project Definition and Team Formation. Paperwork simplification projects begin for many reasons, such as to speed up processing, to ferret out and correct causes of processing errors, to adapt a procedure to meet new reporting requirements, to clean up a procedure for automation, or to clarify and document a procedure.

Projects are initiated by management. First the scope and objectives are agreed upon and users from the affected areas are formed into a project team. One team member is elected or assigned as team leader and another as recorder. These people are expected to participate 4 to 6 hours per week, assisted by an analyst (referred to as coordinator) who is trained in the techniques and works on the project full time. The team also receives assistance from specialists when their expertise is needed (i.e., in areas such as forms analysis, records management, computer systems, communications systems, word processing, and microform).

Training and Data Collection. A brief orientation is usually conducted by the coordinator, outlining project methods and the techniques to be used. This introduction is often reinforced with films depicting the paperwork simplification process and with short improvement exercises.

Data collection involves interviewing people at each step of the procedure. When procedure flow charting is employed, the data are collected on procedure data charts (Fig. P-1), one for each document involved in the procedure.

It is important to interview the people who do the work rather than people who may be unaware of details or may not be up to date about them. Managers' descriptions are often incomplete and occasion-ally erroneous. Using written procedures as a source—without checking them out—also risks being unrealistic. The objective is to record the facts accurately as they exist. It is necessary to "get it straight" from people who know.

Organizing the Facts. People involved in paperwork simplification are often surprised to discover that their existing procedures are far more complex than anticipated. Each step of the procedure had seemed so simple. Then, as the many facts pour in, they become overwhelming. This is the main reason why so many things go wrong with paperwork. There are so many details that pieces are often overlooked. When troubles surface, however, the solutions may be embarrassingly simple.

Since the problem is one of massive detail, the appropriate solution is to organize that detail, putting all the pieces in their places with a chart or diagram, usually prepared by the analyst. The alternative of ignoring the detail invites an unrealistic solution, mistakes of omission, and a lack of coordination. On the other hand, when people take the time to chart

SUMMARY	No.	Time
◉ Origin of record	0	
⊘ Add to operation	1	
◯ Handling operation	3	
○ Move	1	
☐ Inspection	1	
▽ Store, delay, dispose	2	
Total	8	

System number __12__
Chart no. __1__
Page __1__ of __1__
Date __XX XX XX__

System _Receiving_

Form name _Packing Slip_   No.   Copy name   No.

Prepared by _B.G._

Effect	Subject charted	Description	Notes – Questions	Distance	Quantity	Time
	◯○☐▽	1 Sitting on loading dock with materials				5. min
	◯○☐▽	2 Remove from carton and check quantities			200/da	8 hr
	◯○☐▽	3 Carried to receiving office		70 ft		
◉	◯○☐▽	4 Three-part receiving ticket and tape typed			200/da	6 hr
	⊘○☐▽	5 Receiving ticket no. entered on packing slip				
	☐○☐▽	6 Receiving ticket checked and parts separated				
	◯○☐▽	7 Part 3 of receiving ticket attached				
	◯○☐▽	8 File in desk				
	◯○☐▽	9 Hold 2 mo and dispose				2 mo
	◯○☐▽	10				
	◯○☐▽	11				
	◯○☐▽	12				

FIG. P-1 Procedure data chart.

their procedures in detail, alternatives become apparent as they see for the first time how the parts fit together. (*See* Fig. P-2.)

Analyzing the Facts. Before the team can effectively study the facts and produce recommendations, it must become familiar with the charts. The analyst first explains the charts step-by-step, and the team members may go over them several times. At the close of this familiarization session, the members may be given reduced copies of the charts to study and to mark up with ideas before the next meeting.

The actual improvement meetings begin with the team leader's reviewing the project objectives. Then the team begins a careful analysis of each step of the procedure. As each step comes under scrutiny, it is questioned as to what is done and why, where is it done and why there, when is it done and why at that time, who does it and why that person, and finally, how is it done and why in that way. When the answers to these questions do not satisfy the team's common sense, alternatives are suggested, and these are recorded by the team recorder as possible recommendations. It is important to record all recommendations whether they appear feasible or not. Selection among alternatives will follow.

Frequently, more information is needed, such as how often these things happen, whether there is a legal retention period, etc. To find answers to these questions, assignments are made by the team leader.

Preparing the Proposal. In a few weeks the team has enough recommendations to begin preparing a proposal. To accomplish this, the analyst prepares a new set of charts which incorporate the selected recommendations. Then, armed with two sets of charts, the analyst reviews the procedure (1) as it is and (2) as the team feels it should be. A reconciliation is then performed, listing step by step all the differences between the charts. These differences are analyzed in terms of costs and benefits, and together they make up the proposal.

Presentation of the Proposal and Approval. The proposal is presented by the project team to the managers and officials whose approval is needed. If the analysis has been carefully undertaken, the specific recommendations and their costs and benefits can be listed on three to five pages. This list is distributed to the authorities at the start of the presentation. Each of the recommendations is explained by a team member, usually from the area affected. Typically, about half the recommendations are approved immediately, while others require questions and discussion. Several issues must be worked out after the meeting.

Installation. When it is agreed which recommendations are approved, the charts of the proposal are adjusted to reflect those which were disapproved. Those which were approved are broken down into details for installation (e.g., forms, equipment, training, floor plans, policy statements, and procedure manuals). These details become the activities of the installation that will be organized in a network planning chart.

Techniques

Many techniques, charts, and devices are employed by the paperwork simplification analyst, including the following:

System study sheet. This is also known as a project definition sheet, a project request, etc. It is a form used to define the scope and objectives of a project.

Flow process chart. This chart shows the flow of a single item, which can be studied autonomously.

Flow diagram. This is a floor plan on which the route of a process or a procedure has been superimposed.

Operation chart. This chart shows the details of the methods of work done at a single workplace.

Right- and left-hand chart. This chart shows step-by-step the activities of the right and left hands.

Workplace layout. This is a workplace diagram, drawn to scale, showing location of materials, equipment, etc.

Procedure data chart. This chart is used to record the flow of a single document.

Procedure flow chart. This chart shows the flow of all the documents involved in a procedure.

Gantt chart. This is a chart plotting activities of work against a time scale.

Network chart. This is a PERT or CPM type of chart showing work activities arranged in the sequences in which they must occur (particularly useful where activities are highly interdependent).

Recurring data chart. This chart shows recurrence of entries on various forms and records.

Forms analysis checklist. This is a list of questions which suggest alternatives to existing forms.

Entries check-off list. This is a checklist employed when interviewing users about a form, entry by entry.

Typewriter analysis sheet. This sheet is used to develop efficient typewritten forms.

Print-cycle analysis sheet. This sheet is used to develop efficient forms for high-speed printers.

Responsibility chart. This detailed chart displays how individual responsibilities are aligned in a procedure.

671

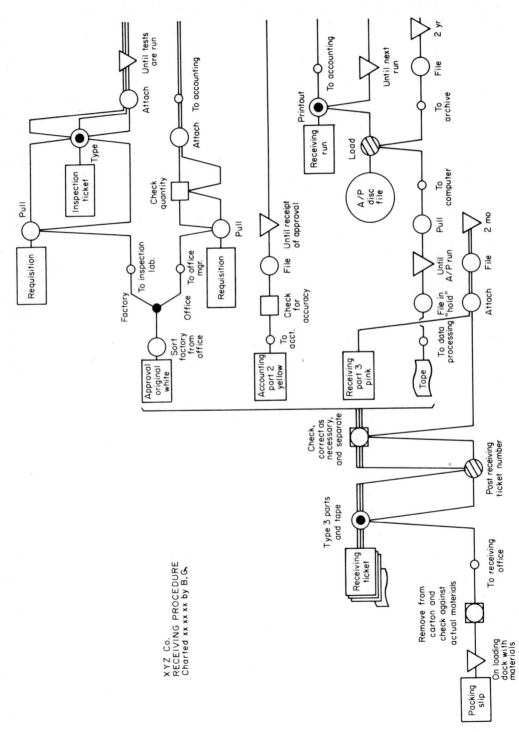

XYZ Co.
RECEIVING PROCEDURE
Charted xx xx xx by B.G.

FIG. P-2 Procedure flow chart.

672

Task data sheet. This is a form used to collect data on the time required to perform tasks.

Work distribution chart. This chart displays how much time is spent on each of the activities in a work unit.

Cost-benefit work sheets. These sheets enable project teams to calculate costs and benefits of their recommendations in terms of work force, materials, machines, processing time, error reduction, etc.

Benefits

Many organizations have used paperwork simplification charting and analysis techniques to achieve benefits typified by the following examples.

Personnel of the Federal Bureau of Drugs studied the procedures of reviewing, approving, and monitoring new drugs. In 5 months' time the bureau prepared a proposal that resulted in doubling productivity, reducing access time for documents from 2 days to 15 minutes, and eliminating two-thirds of the forms and records.

State Farm Insurance Companies use this approach with their agents and thereby have increased suggestions from this source over a hundredfold.

Abbott International trained project leaders from their Latin American affiliates and saved over $200,000 in a little over a year.

Hundreds of other organizations have recorded benefits such as doubling operating capacity with no increase in administrative staff; reducing the number of forms required by factors as large as 7:1; redesigning forms for faster typing or printing, easier mailing, filing, etc.; cutting process time to less than half; discovering and removing serious error sources; and reorganizing offices, files, workplaces, mail service, etc.

Limitations and Pitfalls

The basic limitation is the judgment and experience of the users. Analytical techniques, however, tend to extend their effectiveness. Nevertheless, there are always a number of potential pitfalls.

Management may believe that employees lack sufficient judgment and experience (an opinion which is often self-fulfilling as it allows employees little opportunity to demonstrate more than routine performance).

Management may be unwilling to support a participative effort, fearing this involvement will be construed as blanket approval of recommendations. Proper support means endorsing the study and listening to the recommendations. Beyond that, it is up to the teams to develop sound proposals and present them clearly.

The coordinator may take over the project, leading the users to lose interest or even become resistant.

The team may jump to conclusions without carefully reviewing the facts. As a result, problems which could have been resolved in weeks may hang on for years.

Interdepartmental rivalries and jealousies often interfere. Improvement requires responsible, adult behavior.

See also Cost improvement; Forms design and control; Management information systems (MIS); Management information systems, transaction processing systems; Office automation; Records management; Systems and procedures; Therbligs; Word processing; Work simplification and improvement.

REFERENCES

American Records Management Association: "Records Disposal Practices," *Records Management Quarterly*, vol. 16, October 1982, pp. 48–50.

Dower, J.: "Automated Office and Accurate Records," *Administrative Management*, vol. 42, March 1981, pp. 45–46.

Graham, Ben S.: "The Blue Book of Paperwork Simplification," The Ben Graham Corporation, Tipp City, Ohio, undated.

Miller, O. Owen: "Office Work Simplification," in Carl Heyel (ed.), *Handbook of Modern Office Management and Administrative Services*, R. E. Krieger, Huntington, N.Y., 1980.

BEN S. GRAHAM, JR., *The Ben Graham Corporation: Paperwork Simplification Division*

Patents and Valuable Intangible Rights

A *patent* is a limited monopoly right conferred by the government of a country in accordance with its own laws and regulations. Since a patent is issued by a government, it provides protection only within the territory of that government. A patent consists essentially of a specification and possibly drawing(s) to describe the invention and one or more claims. In the United States, claims specify the metes and bounds of the invention just as a property deed sets forth the property lines. This component is important so that third parties understand when and where they may be trespassing.

A patent is not a privilege to use an idea or invention, but rather, an exclusionary right, i.e., the right to exclude others from using the idea or invention described and claimed by that patent, at least within the territory of the government that issued the patent. The patent owner can exclude others from using the invention even if the owner is not using it. The owner may choose to manufacture directly or set up a joint venture, license third parties, or employ a combination of these possibilities. In the United States, a patent lasts for 17 years from the date it is issued.

Utility versus Design. The function and the design of an invention are subject to separate patents. Take a lamp, for example. Its electric circuitry, the switch, or other functional features relating to the lamp's use would be the subject matter of a utility patent. On the other hand, ornamental features of the lamp would pertain to a design patent. That is, a *utility* patent is concerned with functionality of either a process, a machine, a manufactured item, or a composition of matter; a *design* patent is concerned with ornamental features of an article of manufacture.

Valuable Intangible Rights. In addition to patents, there are other valuable, protectable types of ownership rights.

Trademarks. If a lamp happens to have a brand name identifying its manufacturer, that brand name is said to be its trademark. Because a trademark is synonymous with a brand name, it need not be registered to be protected. The only way to actually acquire trademark rights in the United States is by *use* of the trademark in connection with goods. That use can consist of either selling or advertising the goods under that trademark.

The trademark can be a word, name, symbol, device, or a combination of them. It is the means by which (1) manufacturers and merchants can identify their goods and distinguish them from others and (2) consumers can identify the source of the products they buy or of the services rendered them.

Copyrights. A copyright is the exclusive right to prevent the unauthorized use or copying of what the United States Constitution and the common law call *writings* of authors. Writings not only refer to literature but apply as well to photographs, musical compositions, labels, sound recordings, and works of art and their reproductions. A copyright does not relate to and does not protect ideas; it protects the *expression* of ideas. The ornamental features of a lamp may be protected by a design patent. However, a copyright can be obtained for the *artistic* features of the design on the lampshade and the artistry of the base of the lamp. Thus, there may be some instances where the right to a design patent and the right to a copyright overlap and both can be obtained. The patent is for the tangible embodiment of the "idea" involved; the copyright is for the artistic expression of that idea.

Know-How and Trade Secrets. Trade secrets constitute subject matter which is not generally known to the trade and which provides a competitive advantage. They may or may not be patentable. Trade secrets also can include business information, sources of supply, customer lists, and almost anything which is not known to competitors and which gives a competitive edge. Trade secrets are techni-

cally protected by common law. Know-how can be thought of as generic to trade secrets. It includes, as well, information which technically is not protectable as a trade secret because it is generally known to competitors, e.g., business acumen, but which may be valuable to a purchaser anyway. The purchaser might otherwise need months, if not longer, to acquire the same, albeit "public," information. A court will enjoin the disclosure of trade secrets but not after their publication. Contracts for the transfer of "public" information in the form of know-how, however, are enforceable in the absence of fraud.

When should one file for patent protection rather than rely on the common law of trade secrets? The classic case, of course, is Coca-Cola syrup, whose formula has successfully been maintained as a trade secret. For each such case, however, there are literally thousands of instances where information which was once a trade secret became public knowledge. Whether it is a disgruntled former employee, a slip of the tongue, or reverse engineering on the part of competitors, the fact remains that it is the exception, not the rule, that information can be maintained in secrecy. If the idea is patentable, then, as a general rule, patent protection is preferable. Exceptions can be made but only after the risks have been fully evaluated.

Application Requirements. In the United States, a patent application must be filed by the inventor within 1 year of the date that the inventor publicly uses or publishes the invention. Otherwise, the inventor forfeits the right to a valid patent. On the other hand, if the use or public disclosure was by some third party, the inventor would have a chance to prove that he or she was the first to conceive the invention and to reduce it to practice with appropriate diligence. Keep in mind, however, that a patent is invalid in the United States if the invention was published or publicly known or used by others more than a year prior to the date that the application was filed.

Interference Contests. The United States system is a "first to invent" patent system as opposed to "first to file" systems commonly found overseas. Accordingly, when there are two conflicting patent applications, an "interference" contest is held to determine who is the first inventor. The Patent and Trademark Office will inform an applicant when there is a conflict with one or more other applications claiming the same invention (or that there is a partial overlap of claimed subject matter) and will request information to help it decide who is the first inventor. The parties may take testimony and cross-examine each other's witnesses as well as submit affidavits and research records in an effort to establish prior right to the claimed invention. The need for detailed research records is apparent.

Obtaining Patents in Other Countries. Since patent rights are limited to those particular rights and privileges conferred by the country that granted the patent, separate applications have to be filed in each country in which patent protection is sought. There is an international convention, however, whereby the priority date of an application can be protected by filing in one member country, e.g., the United States, and then filing in other member countries within 1 year after the original filing. Safeguarding that filing date is important for asserting and enforcing foreign patent rights. The patent owner can look to the original filing date in the United States should a dispute arise as to whether the invention had been known or used in another nation before the owner applied there.

Where to Apply. Deciding where to apply for a patent is closely related to the inventor's objectives. It is wise to consider patent protection in every country in which one can reasonably anticipate doing business to a significant extent. Sometimes it is desirable to file in a particular country because of the legitimate concern that a third party will start manufacturing in that country and take advantage of trade parts which favor the free flow of goods across borders, exporting their goods into the patent owner's prime markets.

Patent Licensing or Assignment (Sale). Deciding whether to grant a license or self-exploit is largely a business decision. Licensing is not mandatory. While counsel can provide input as to the likelihood of enforcing the patent, the business philosophy and marketing strategy of the patent owner should take precedence. It is not always desirable to license, particularly where the patent owner would like to be alone in the market for a period of time and the patent position is apparently a good one. There are times, however, when the patent owner will take a hard look at the situation and decide that the costs of manufacturing and distribution, transportation, and, when selling overseas, customs and tariff duties, etc., are such that it is more economical to license rather than to attempt to do business directly.

Not every patent owner wants, or is financially able, to set up manufacturing facilities, particularly overseas. Often the initial capital investments are substantial, and the financial risk coupled with other business uncertainties or legal restrictions may prohibit self-exploitation of the patent. In some nations the law requires that citizens of that country own half or even a controlling interest in businesses exploiting patent and trademark rights. In some instances, nations block or restrict the transfer of their currency outside their country. Therefore, a decision to license or self-exploit requires a careful analysis of the objectives and capabilities of the patent owner in the light of the potential marketplace and the financial and legal risks in each case.

Tax Implications and Transfer of Ownership Rights. Licenses can take different forms, and each may have different tax consequences. For example, a nonexclusive license is essentially an agreement that the patent owner will not sue the licensee. Since the licensee acquires no "title" rights beyond freedom from a lawsuit, the licensor has transferred nothing in the eyes of the U.S. Internal Revenue Service (IRS) and must treat any royalty (or other consideration) as ordinary income.

In an exclusive license, the owner parts company with the right to grant further licenses and, therefore, the royalty (consideration) can qualify as capital gains. This is sometimes called *parting with equitable title* and *retaining bare legal title.* But note that the IRS imposes additional criteria to determine whether all substantial rights have been parted with. IRS reasoning is that if the patent owner can terminate the exclusive license at will (without default by the licensee) or retains other rights indicative of true ownership, the transfer of ownership rights is more apparent than substantive and, therefore, the transaction should not qualify for capital gains treatment.

A *patent assignment* is the "sale" of a patent. Since legal as well as equitable title is transferred from the patent owner, the transaction will ordinarily qualify for capital gains treatment. This will be true even if the owner (inventor) retains a right to part of the royalties derived from subsequent licensing by the assignee. Once more, the IRS looks beyond what the parties name the agreement to determine the true nature of the transaction from the terms of the agreement. Thus, the tax consequences can be determined only by examining the full agreement.

Royalty Charges. There is no legal restriction on the size of the consideration for a license, but discriminatory royalties have been challenged by the Federal Trade Commission as a form of unfair competition. In some industries there are accepted guidelines for the size of a royalty, but in any given case the consideration for a license will be determined primarily by the contribution of that technology to the licensee's business. For example, when a process saves a licensee a substantial sum in manufacturing costs, it would not be unusual to ask for anywhere from one-fourth to one-half the savings realized by the licensee. Generally, one intelligent approach to negotiating a fair royalty is to determine the probable benefit to the licensee and gear the royalty toward a portion of that benefit.

Major Licensing Terms. In addition to royalties, among the most important considerations are whether to (1) insist on minimums; (2) ask for grantback rights to any improvements made by the licensee; (3) provide for technical assistance and knowhow in addition to patent rights; (4) insist upon confidentiality (which should survive termination of the agreement) with regard to that know-how; (5) provide for appropriate warranties and indemnities; (6) define the responsibility for prosecuting third-party infringers; (7) define the licensee's right to subcontract or sublicense, or specify the absence of such right; (8) provide for payment of taxes (particularly in foreign licenses); (9) depending upon the circumstances, allow for transportation and shipping charges; and (10) provide for conditions under which the agreement can be terminated. Obviously, there are many other considerations which should be worked out to make for a clear understanding. A detailed agreement is sometimes not appreciated at the time a transaction is entered into, but in the event of a dispute, it will often help determine who was to do what as well as the rights of the parties. If the transaction cannot withstand the test of being specific (with all rights and obligations clear and in writing) at the time the agreement is first solidified, it is not likely to withstand the test of enforceability later on. While some understandings based on a handshake have lasted, most wind up in the courtroom.

Patent Validity and Infringement. A patent, once granted, is presumed valid until proved otherwise. This assumption gives the patent owner an advantage in a lawsuit since the burden of proof is on the one claiming its invalidity. A patent owner can seek a court-ordered injunction against third-party infringement on his or her patent and can seek damages (and sometimes costs) for losses sustained because of the infringement. Conversely, any member of the public who is threatened by the patent owner can challenge the patent and seek a judgment declaring it invalid. The challenger can also seek damages and sometimes costs.

Before bringing a lawsuit, the patent owner or challenger should have a validity study made of the patent. The U.S. Patent and Trademark Office, of course, performs a search of related subject matter to determine novelty and unobviousness before granting a patent. But the number of pending applications, coupled with limitations in staff and time, necessarily results in a limited search. A thorough validity study sometimes turns up relevant previous publications (*prior art*) that the patent examiner did not consider during evaluation of the application. The newly discovered prior art can be used to challenge the patent's validity in court and it is often a persuasive means of overcoming the presumption of validity. If so, the burden of proof shifts back to the patentee, who now must convince the court that the patent is still valid.

Antitrust Considerations. Treble damages can be obtained when it is shown that an antitrust violation occurred, such as fraud in obtaining the patent (e.g., the basis for more than 10 years of multimillion-dollar litigation in the tetracycline cases) or misuse of the patent (such as tying sale of the patented product to the purchase of unpatented goods). Thus, care should be taken when obtaining a patent to advise the Patent and Trademark Office of the best prior art known to the applicant. When licensing a patent or selling patented products, avoid the temptation to use the patent as leverage for some extra-

neous purpose. A patent grants its owner the right for a period of time to exclude others from using the claimed invention without his or her permission. The patent's use should be confined within the limits of that grant.

See also Brands and brand names; Government regulations, business law; Innovation and creativity; International trade; Legal affairs, management of corporate; Product planning and development; Research and development management; Technology transfer.

REFERENCES

Finnegan, M. B., and R. Goldsheider: *The Law & Business of Licensing,* 2 vols., Clark Boardman, New York, 1975.
Goldstein, P.: *Copyright, Patent, Trademark and Related State Doctrines,* Callaghan & Co., Chicago, 1973.
Kintner, E. W., and J. L. Lahr: *An Intellectual Property Law Primer,* Macmillan, Inc., New York, 1975.

STANLEY H. LIEBERSTEIN, *Ostrolenk, Faber, Gerb and Soffen*

Personnel Administration

Although all managers are intimately involved with, and held responsible for, "people" problems in their areas, it is generally agreed that for consistency, equity, and efficiency, a central unit provides supporting personnel services and guidelines for carrying out management's personnel function. The unit is termed the personnel department, employee relations department, or, more recently, the human resources department. Unionized companies usually call this unit the industrial relations department.

The need for a central unit becomes increasingly apparent as the employee count passes 20, at which time the personnel job is often assigned as an additional duty. The volume of related tasks, however, forces consideration of a full-time personnel staff as the employee count nears 200.

The many tasks which are comprised by the general term *personnel administration* may be divided into broad categories, such as the following cited by the American Society for Personnel Administration in its accreditation program: (1) employment, placement, and personnel planning; (2) training and development; (3) compensation and benefits; (4) health, safety, and security; (5) employee and labor relations; and (6) personnel research.

Personnel Policies

Personnel policies exist in every organization. The difference is the extent to which they are written, communicated, and consistently applied. Organizations interested in maintaining the trust and confidence of their employees strive to score high on these three counts.

The chief executive often insists that the personnel executive submit written personnel policies for adoption as corporate policies. The reasons for this requirement include the following: (1) to confirm that the policies to be implemented are acceptable to the corporation; (2) to assure the clarity, feasibility, and adequacy of the policies; and (3) to indicate to all concerned that the policies have been seriously considered and adopted as the policies of top management.

Personnel Manual. Personnel policies are best communicated to all levels of management by the issuance of a personnel policy manual. The manual provides a ready reference and facilitates consistent handling of similar situations throughout the organization. A common technique is to devote a separate section of the manual to each policy statement and a suitably detailed treatment of the personnel practices and procedures which are currently being utilized to implement that policy. Many firms consider it equally important to issue to all nonmanagement personnel an employee handbook which contains an appropriately written condensation of the same information. Both publications lend themselves to being published in loose-leaf binders in order to accommodate frequent changes in practice and procedure.

Impact of Regulatory Agencies

Compliance with the Fair Labor Standards Act (Wage-Hour Act) of 1938 was the primary legal concern of the personnel administrator for a number of years. Its provisions, applicable to employers engaged in interstate commerce, covered minimum wage standards, overtime pay, employment of minors, and definitions of exempt employees. The relatively simple administration of the act was assigned to the personnel staff for implementation; thus the provisions were of slight concern to top management. The section that prohibited unequal pay for equal work because of sex, however, did not take hold so that other legislation, the Equal Pay Act of 1963, was necessary to reiterate the provision.

That almost placid era came to an end in 1964 with the passage of the Civil Rights Act, or more specifically, Title VII of that act. The Civil Rights Act and its attendant executive orders, guidelines, and court decisions at the federal, state, and local levels (combined with several other major acts which have emanated from congressional concern with safety in the workplace, privacy, pension reform, and other social issues) have had an enormous effect on every organization's personnel operations. Virtually every personnel activity is now influenced by governmental regulation. If ever there was doubt that personnel administration was the concern not only of the personnel manager but of every manager in the organization, it has been dispelled since 1964. Legal penalties can be equally heavy for discriminatory acts by line supervisors and personnel executives.

Many organizations train all management personnel in the requirements and implications of personnel-related regulations. Among those regulations are the following:

Title VII, Civil Rights Act of 1964 (as amended), is applicable to private employers of 15 or more persons engaged in interstate commerce, educational institutions, state and local governments, employment agencies, and labor unions with 15 or more members. It prohibits discrimination based on race, color, religion, sex, or national origin in any term, condition, or privilege of employment (e.g., hiring, promotion, demotion, transfer, layoff or termination, rate of pay, benefits, and selection for training).

Executive Order 11246 (1965) as amended by Executive Order 11375 (1967) is applicable to federal contractors and subcontractors and requires affirmative action programs to implement Title VII. The programs of firms with contracts over $50,000 and having 50 or more employees must be written, and they are monitored by an assigned federal agency.

OFCC Revised Order No. 4 (1971) details the steps to be taken by firms required to implement affirmative action programs. Included in the steps are the identification of areas in which minorities and women are underutilized and the establishment of hiring and promotion goals.

Equal Employment Opportunity Act of 1972 (an amendment to Title VII of the Civil Rights Act of 1964) strengthens the power of the Equal Employment Opportunity Commission (EEOC) to enforce Title VII. EEOC receives, from individuals or organizations representing them, job discrimination complaints and attempts to conciliate them. When conciliation fails, EEOC may go directly to court to enforce the law. Sexual harassment, when related to hiring or promotion decisions, has been found to violate Title VII. A 1978 amendment, the Pregnancy Discrimination Act, prohibits dismissal of women because of pregnancy alone and protects their job security during maternity leaves.

Age Discrimination in Employment Act (1967) is applicable to employers of 25 or more persons. It prohibits discrimination in any aspect of employment against persons aged 40 to 65.

Title V of the Rehabilitation Act (1973) requires affirmative action of federal contractors and subcontractors with contracts of $2500 or more to hire and promote qualified individuals who have physical or mental handicaps which substantially limit one or more major life activities or have records of such impairments or are regarded as having such impairments.

Occupational Safety and Health Act (OSHA) (1970) authorizes the Secretary of Labor to establish mandatory safety and health standards in businesses engaged in interstate commerce.

Employee Retirement Income Security Act (ERISA) (1974), also called the Pension Reform Act, establishes and protects numerous employee benefit rights. Disclosure, eligibility, vesting, and fiduciary requirements for pension plans are covered.

In addition, there are state and local laws, often patterned after federal law. Hence, many small employers or those without federal contracts are facing the same requirements but from a different source.

Costs and Budgets

In addition to the normal overhead expenses, the personnel unit's budget often provides for the organization's total recruiting costs (e.g., advertising, agency fees, applicant expenses, moving expenses), training and development expenses, and employee service expenses (such as recreation, physical examinations, cafeteria, and service awards). Although salary administration and employee benefits may be engineered by the personnel staff, these costs are normally budgeted by all departments in order to facilitate functional cost analysis.

Performance Measures and Standards

It is highly desirable that performance standards exist for all segments of the personnel function against which current performance can be measured. They are, however, subject to questions of validity and relevance. This criterion stems from the fact that many personnel activity measures are influenced by uncontrollable factors, including the unpredictability of people and events. A recruiting time standard, for example, should consider job level, skills required, and availability of applicants among other factors.

Personnel measures must also take into account the influence of related personnel policies. A wage policy that results in paying less than going rates is apt to affect a recruiting time standard, for example.

The following are among the commonly utilized measures of the personnel functions:

1. Payroll as a percentage of total costs
2. Average wage rate, by several employee categories
3. Average annual percentage wage increase, by several employee categories
4. Employee benefit costs as a percentage of payroll
5. Selection ratio (number of hires per 100 applicants)
6. Recruiting lag (average number of days required to fill a job opening)
7. Personnel ratio (number of personnel workers per 100 employees)

The standards against which these and other measures are compared are based on in-house experience or on intercompany surveys.

Records and Reports

Personnel records are essential for many reasons and are often required by law. Yet, unless controlled, they can become redundant and unfairly damaging to the employee. Computerized record keeping is a means of greatly reducing the time and effort devoted to maintaining records and producing reports, but it is not until the work force approaches 100 that computerization is considered economically feasible. The microfilming of inactive records is another means of reducing the paper load.

Among the myriad of conceivable records, the following are essential:

An *employee personal file* is a folder containing papers related to an employee's affiliation with the organization. It may contain the employment application, physical examination results, attendance record, past performance appraisals, employee benefit records, payroll deduction authorizations, and correspondence. A common practice is to purge the file every 2 to 3 years to remove obsolete material, including adverse appraisal comments which are no longer applicable.

A *master employee record* is a quick reference device consolidating frequently needed employee information from other sources. It is often a computerized record or on cardstock. It shows personal data, employment and earnings history, test scores, special training, and skills data as well as attendance history and benefit entitlements.

Record of time worked, commonly called a time card, is legally required to be maintained for employees who are not exempt from provisions of the Wage and Hour Act of 1938. Although time clocks are still the most common means of recording time worked, they are giving way rapidly, especially in offices, to an honor system whereby the employee completes a time sheet by hand. Another method, approved by many local Department of Labor offices, is the exception method, requiring the employee to make time-card entries only when time other than published normal working hours is worked or when normal hours are not worked.

The U.S. Department of Labor requires employee information records to be retained for 3 years following separation. IRS requires earnings records to be kept 4 years after tax due date. ERISA, however, seems to supersede all other employee record retention regulations. Without specifying an obligatory retention period, ERISA requires maintenance of employee records sufficient to determine benefits which are due or may become due. Benefit vesting rights assured by ERISA for separated employees could require record retention for up to 50 years. EEOC regulations require records pertaining to hiring (applications, tests, etc.), promotion, termination, and other placement changes to be retained for 6 months from the date of record or action, whichever is later.

Reports can be divided into two groups: (1) those required for regulatory compliance and (2) those required by management. Federal and state laws, e.g., EEOC, OSHA, and ERISA, should be closely followed for changing report requirements. Management is interested in reports of such measures as those discussed in the preceding section. Many personnel executives originate an annual personnel report, which serves as an excellent future reference in their own area and presents a comprehensive report of the year's personnel activities to top management. In addition to abbreviated discussions of projects undertaken during the year, the report provides and analyzes annual statistics on such matters as employment, training, job evaluation, salary administration, benefits, attendance, turnover, and grievances.

Privacy. The issue of protection of an employee's privacy so far as work history goes has become an increasingly sensitive—and legal—one. The Privacy Act of 1974 gives everyone the right to examine records pertaining to himself or herself held by any federal agency or educational institution and to demand the correction of any erroneous information. Legislation has been proposed (and has, in fact, been passed in some states) to extend that right to include examination of records held within private industry. As a consequence, many private firms, either as a matter of stated policy (as at IBM and AT&T) or of prudent practice, make most of their employee files open to the individual concerned. Or, if they do not adopt such a policy or practice, they do maintain employee files carefully, replete with objective and defensible documentation.

Employment

In defining *employment* as the utilization of a person's services, it follows that the employment function goes beyond recruiting and placement. It includes the justification for employment, the most advantageous use of the person's services through promotion or transfer, and the termination of employment.

Employment Office. A designated employment office is highly desirable for several reasons, including avoidance of overlapping efforts, cost savings, and consistent application of employment policies and regulatory requirements. This function does not imply an infringement on the line manager's "right to hire": the final employment decision is usually made by the line manager. It does imply the value of a trained employment staff.

The employment office is often staffed by one or more interviewers and a receptionist whose duties may include providing applicants with employment forms, administering tests, and conducting pre-screening interviews. The prescreening interview is a brief exchange to determine whether or not the applicant possesses the most obvious qualifications for an available job. Totally unqualified applicants are usually released at this point, but a notation of the visit is made to assure complete applicant flow information.

Employee Requisitions. The employee requisition is a written request by a responsible manager for assistance in filing a specific job. A form is often used for the purpose of eliciting the job title, labor grade, rate of pay, desired starting date, and qualifications required. The employee requisition is looked upon as the employment office's authority to recruit and hire. It is the responsible manager's statement that an authorized job is vacant and that help is requested to fill it. Candidates for the job are then presented by the employment office to the manager. When the manager determines which candidate is to be offered the job, it is usually desirable for the employment office to make the offer in order to assure consistency, clarity, and adherence to corporate policy and practice in all terms of the employment agreement.

It is not unusual to have the employment office hire a person for a job without referring that person to the manager for consideration, especially for entry-level or junior jobs. This procedure is particularly true in large organizations or in firms committed to the hiring provisions of a labor contract. When feasible, however, the mutual benefits gained by the applicant-manager interview make it a desirable step in the employment process.

Recruiting. Recruiting is the process of soliciting the interest of potentially qualified people in an employment opportunity. It is not selective except to the extent that recruiting activity is limited and that published qualification requirements discourage inquiries. A number of sources of applicants are available to the employment office. Their use depends on the job level being recruited, recruiting policy, and costs.

In-House. The most obvious recruiting source is from within the organization. An internal search is usually the first recruiting step taken in a firm committed to a policy of promotion from within. A common tool for internal recruiting is job posting, which is the publication, often via bulletin boards, of openings within the company. A posting normally indicates the labor grade of the available job, qualifications required, and an invitation for employees on lower labor grades to apply. Critics of job posting cite the multiple training costs resulting from departmental turnover due to the program.

External Recruiting. Review of applications already on file is a logical first step in external recruiting. It is also recommended by EEOC as an affirmative action step.

Referral of applicants by employees is an excellent source. It can be a delicate one, however, in view of the EEOC opinion that it may be a discriminatory practice in a dominantly white organization. The offering of incentives for employment referrals in a largely white firm compounds the possibility of EEOC action.

Advertising a job opening in newspapers or trade journals is another common practice. The ad may be blind or open. A blind ad is one that does not identify the employer; a box number is provided for responses. Its advantages are that resentment by present employees is avoided and that responses to the ad need not be acknowledged. Open or signed ads are considered by some as a screening device; time is not wasted on those who prefer not to work in the employer's location, industry, or company. Radio, television, and billboard advertising are other, less-used media. In any case, the advertising message must be carefully worded to avoid any semblance of discrimination.

Campus recruiting at high schools and colleges is commonplace. Appointments are made through the guidance counselor or placement director on campus. The most promising students are invited to visit the firm, normally at company expense, for further interviews.

Employment agencies, which may be public or commercial, are of considerable assistance. Public agencies do not charge a fee for their service. In some states, employers are required to list all job openings with their local state employment service. Commercial agency fees, payable when an agency-referred applicant is hired, can run quite high and the trend is strong toward the employer's paying the fee rather than the applicant. It is not unusual for the fee to range from 7 percent of annual salary for junior jobs

up to 25 percent of annual salary for senior positions. Many employers build a close relationship with selected agencies to the extent that the agencies are, in effect, the recruiting arm of the organization for specified jobs. Listing an important position with an employment agency, like use of the blind ad, tends to assure the confidentiality of the search.

Executive search firms distinguish themselves from employment agencies in that they consider the employer, not the applicant, to be their client. All expenses and fees are borne by the employer rather than the applicant, who might otherwise be expected to pay the fee of an employment agency. This distinction becomes increasingly blurred, however, as employers pay more of the agency fees. Another difference remains in that executive search firms often provide consultant services in connection with the company's search for top-management candidates. The services may include a study of the company's history, organization, and objectives as well as extensive interviews to determine the personalities of company executives in an effort to introduce only the best-suited candidates for consideration. The process is attractive as a means of reaching into other firms for top people who are not actively seeking new employment and luring them away. If the employer were to do this directly at any level, it would be called pirating.

Finally, *temporary help agencies* should be noted as an excellent source of short-term help, especially when the need is urgent and time does not permit normal recruiting methods. These agencies maintain a call list of people with widely diverse skills and qualifications. Temporary workers obtained through this source are not employees of the company. They remain employees of the agency and are paid by the agency. In many cases, it is less expensive to pay the fees of an agency for temporary help than to put a temporary person on the payroll because of the savings in social security and other benefit payments.

Selection. Selection is the process of narrowing down the field of applicants to the one person to be offered the job. It has become, in many cases, a highly controversial activity as governmental agencies pursue claims of discrimination in hiring based on race, sex, age, and handicap. The common selection policy to hire the "best qualified" person is being challenged as a form of systemic discrimination against the Title VII–protected groups. Conversely, reverse discrimination cases are growing against firms that have struck the word "best" from their policy statements as an affirmative action measure. A clearly stated selection policy, announced by top management with every manager held accountable for its implementation, is an important step many organizations are taking to resolve the conflicting pressures present in the selection process today.

Opinions vary as to the proper sequence of selection steps in the employment office. Some insist that every applicant complete an application form prior to an interview. Others have the application completed only by those who interview favorably. Testing, physical examination, and reference checks are also inserted before, between, or after interviews. Regardless of the sequence utilized, good practice calls for (1) every applicant to be recorded for compliance and corporate statistical purposes; (2) each step to be clear of discriminatory implications toward Title VII–protected groups; (3) courteous, considerate behavior toward the applicant; (4) testing and interviewing facilities which are quiet and free from interruption; and (5) referring to line managers only those applicants considered to be reasonably qualified for the available job.

Application Form. An early step in the selection process is a study of the candidate's application form or résumé. EEOC–related laws require that questions which have a disproportionately negative effect on Title VII–protected groups not be asked on the application form or in interviews unless there is strong evidence of their job-relatedness or business necessity. Courts have upheld the banning of not only questions dealing with race, sex, national origin, age, and religion but also those dealing with non-job-related educational requirements, arrest and conviction records, credit rating, marital and family status, physical and experience requirements, and other potential areas of discrimination.

Résumés. A résumé is a nonstandardized, written presentation of one's qualifications for employment. Since it is originated by the applicant, its content is not restricted by law. Résumés are commonly requested of, or volunteered by, applicants for senior-level positions.

Interviewing. This is the most influential step in the selection process. To minimize bias, many firms use the patterned, guided, or *directed* interview in the employment office. This method fosters a uniform approach to eliciting pertinent responses by providing a guide list of questions to be asked. An application form may be the basis of the directed interview, or a separate interview form may be provided. In either case, employment office interviews are normally designed to elaborate upon the application form information and to correlate that information with the job requirements.

The unpatterned, unguided, or *nondirected* interview is essentially unplanned, and the interviewee's comments are unrestricted. Although its use is most appropriate in exit, grievance, or counseling interviews, a semblance of the unguided interview is frequently used by the line manager in an employment situation, especially for higher-level jobs. The line manager is interested in the applicant's work methods, attitudes, and ambitions, which can best be learned by asking brief questions that invite extended answers. It is a difficult technique to use effectively. The untrained interviewer can easily talk too much or ask leading, improper, or illegal questions.

Group interviews, in which several interviewers question the applicant in the same meeting, are common when filling a senior-level position. They offer the advantages of introducing the candidate to several prospective associates and allowing an exchange of opinion among the interviewers.

The *stress* interview should not be used by the untrained interviewer, nor is it applicable in the great majority of employment situations. Designed to test emotional control under trying circumstances, the stress interview calls for the interviewer to be openly hostile and irritating to the applicant. The technique may be applicable for police, sales, investigative, or clandestine work, but it is generally undesirable for common use.

Physical Examination. A physical examination today is more apt to be geared toward appropriate placement than toward a hire-or-reject decision. Many jobs can be performed by employees with physical limitations. This premise is given substance and the power of law by the Rehabilitation Act of 1973 (Title V), which affects federal contractors, and by several state laws.

References. The checking of an applicant's references, especially of former employers, is an important step. The value of a friend's, neighbor's, or minister's comment may be questionable. Face-to-face contact with the reference is most desirable. Telephone contact must often suffice. Written contact is least desirable because of the time element, most people's unwillingness to put unfavorable comments in writing, and the inability to pursue specific points of interest. In no case should the applicant's current employer be contacted without the applicant's consent. A most telling question to be asked at the end of a reference check is: "Is this person eligible for rehire at your firm, and if not, why?"

Credit Checks. These and other commercial investigative reports are utilized frequently when hiring a senior person. The Fair Credit Reporting Act, which became effective in 1971, provides that the applicant must be informed that such a procedure may be used, and if so, that the name and address of the reporting agency be provided to the applicant if as a result of the report the applicant is deprived of employment.

Tests. The use of tests in selection has always been controversial and has become more so since the advent of Title VII. *See* Testing, Psychological.

Placement. Placement begins with the acceptance of a job offer and does not end until termination of employment. It is the assignment of an individual to a job and, ideally, to the job best fitting his or her abilities and interests. It is the result of hiring, promotion, demotion, or transfer.

The job offer and its acceptance constitute a verbal contract. Because an understanding of its terms is so important, many firms put the offer in writing and ask for a written acceptance, especially for higher-level jobs. The job offer should include the job title, salary, starting date, name of immediate superior, exceptions to published employee benefits, special compensation terms, and any other unique terms of employment.

Affirmative action plans, whether legally required or voluntarily implemented, have a strong influence on placement. The legal and moral implications of equal employment opportunity impose an obligation on every manager to cooperate with efforts to place qualified minorities, women, individuals aged 40 to 65, and the handicapped at all levels in the organization. In meeting that obligation, many managers have been forced to realize that many traditional selection and placement criteria have been counterproductive. Excessive educational requirements, test cutoff scores, marital status, and sex and race preclusions are a few of the idols that have toppled.

Promotion, Transfer, Demotion. A *promotion* is an advancement to a position of increased status and responsibility. Increased earnings are usually associated with promotions, but this is not essential.

A *transfer* is the lateral movement of an employee to another job of essentially the same status but usually with different duties. The transfer may be initiated by the employer because of shifting production needs or requested by the employee because of changing career goals or personal reasons.

A *demotion* denotes movement to a position of lesser status and responsibility. Its use as a disciplinary penalty is generally considered inadvisable. A demotion may, however, be occasioned by circumstances wherein it is acceptable to the employee. A major reduction in work force with consequent bumping based on seniority is one such situation. Stepping down because of health reasons is another. A third is a situation where poor performance can be attributed to placement in a job that is beyond the employee's capacity. A reduction in earnings may or may not take place in a demotion, but if not, they are often frozen until other factors bring them in line.

Separations. *Separation* is a general term which encompasses all forms of termination of employment.

Resignation, or voluntary termination, is normally initiated by the employee. It is also offered at times as a face-saving device to spare a person from the stigma of a discharge. *Exit interviews* with resigning employees, conducted in the personnel department, are widely used as an indicator of employee morale and perceptions. Popular opinion is that comment from a resigning person is more apt to be frank and honest than that obtained under normal conditions. Others believe that either possible bitterness or a desire to leave with no ill feelings is apt to color exit interview comments. In any case, the exit interview is an appropriate means of delivering all final payments to the employee, explaining the disposition of benefits, and assuring the return of company property.

Layoff is a temporary or permanent involuntary termination due to a production cutback or stoppage. The order of layoff and recall back to work in a unionized organization is commonly based on seniority. Other labor contract provisions may provide supplemental unemployment benefits, accrued vacation pay, and other benefits to laid-off workers.

Discharge is a permanent involuntary termination usually due to a serious rule infraction or unsatisfactory performance. Because of its severity and finality, many firms follow a prescribed warning system prior to discharge in all but the most extreme cases. Solutions to performance problems are also sought prior to discharge.

Retirement may be a voluntary or involuntary termination of employment. Legislation is expected to change the mandatory retirement age (in many plans from age 65 to 70). Plans may, however, permit working beyond that age and/or voluntary retirement at an earlier age. An increasing number of firms offer preretirement counseling, seminars, and publications in an effort to assist in the transition to retired status.

Employee Rights. In almost every place of employment, evidence is growing that various United States laws are limiting traditional management prerogatives and increasingly giving legal status to the rights of employees. Accordingly, dismissals for frivolous reasons are not generally supported. Moreover, the laws seem to imply the assurance of due process in discipline and separation cases. Management must be prepared to justify and document actions that are based on perceived incompetence and wrong-doing as well as those based upon economic reasons, such as shifting operations from a high labor-cost area to another area.

Status Changes. The status changes resulting from promotions, transfers, demotions, and impending separations are reported promptly to the personnel department to assure proper salary payment and accurate employee records. In many cases, these status changes are made in consultation with the personnel staff to guarantee conformance with company policy and EEOC–related guidelines.

The following are other status changes that can result in confusion, extra cost, and embarrassment if not reported promptly: (1) transfer from or to permanent, temporary, full-time, or part-time employment; and (2) changes of name, marital status, address, telephone number, and other personal information required for benefit purposes.

Personnel Problem Indicators

The personnel department is expected to be alert to signs of employee discontent, problems generated by company practice, and other hindrances to productivity in order that appropriate action may be taken to overcome them. A number of indicators are used for this purpose. Among them are these:

Grievances. A *grievance* is an employee's expression to management of discontent or of a belief that an injustice is being suffered in a job-related matter. A formal system for handling grievances is followed in most companies. A periodic analysis of grievances to determine departmental frequency, the nature of the grievances, and the step at which each grievance was resolved is a prime problem indicator.

Disciplinary Actions. As used here, *discipline* is a negative term referring to the use of penalties to discourage unacceptable behavior. The exercise of discipline is a line manager's responsibility, but because it is a sensitive matter subject to corporate, legal, and union guidelines, personnel staff consultation is commonly sought. Penalties may include oral and written reprimands, loss of privileges, fines, suspension, demotion, and discharge. Discipline practices often outline offenses which warrant penalties, the sequence of penalties, and senior-management concurrence requirements.

Turnover. *Turnover*, or separation rate, is the number of separations during a period of time expressed as a percentage of the average employee count during that period. A degree of turnover must be expected and is healthy for the organization. It is also costly, and therefore employers are interested in keeping turnover in line with expectations as reflected by turnover surveys and in-house past experience. Turnover statistics are commonly analyzed by departments, employee levels, length of service, and cause of separation to determine problem areas. Exit interview data are used to supplement turnover analysis.

Absence. Job dissatisfaction sometimes results in excessive absence. Hence, departmental and company absence rates are analyzed periodically. Absence rates are computed and expressed in a variety of ways. A method preferred by some employers is to speak of average days absence per employee per period of time. It is found by dividing the total days of absence recorded by the group by the average size of the group during the period. Others choose to express the rate as a percentage: the number of days lost during the period is divided by the average number of employees times the number of workdays in the period, and the result is multiplied by 100.

Because lengthy illnesses may distort the absence rate, periods of absence rather than days of absence are also analyzed by some firms. The definition of excessive absence also varies widely among firms and industries—from as low as 9 days per year to as high as 3 days per month. To uncover problems, absence rates may also be analyzed by age, sex, years of service, reasons given, days of the week, and type of work assigned. Lateness, which is a partial day's absence, is often similarly analyzed.

Suggestion Boxes. Designed as a means of receiving productive or cost-saving ideas from employees, *suggestion systems* often reveal employee gripes, attitudes, or specific complaints. When they are examined for such content, problem areas can be uncovered.

Attitude Surveys. An *attitude survey* is an effort by management to determine employee perceptions of designated job-related factors. The survey may be accomplished by interview or questionnaire and may include a random sample of employee opinion or responses from the total work force. In all cases, anonymity of responses is assured. When interviews are used, outside consultants are generally utilized. Questionnaires are unsigned and sent to a central location. Survey content varies depending on the subjects management wants to explore. It might include questions related to job satisfaction, working conditions, supervision, training, opportunity for advancement, recognition, job security, pay, benefits, communications, company image, and personnel policies. It is generally agreed that survey findings should be reported back to the group surveyed and that the best method of doing so is through a series of meetings conducted by immediate supervisors. Feedback of unfavorable results is essential if employee trust is be maintained. Equally essential is a commitment by management to take action based on the results. A well-conducted survey can be an extremely valuable tool to uncover and respond to employee concerns.

See also Affirmative action; Appraisal, performance; Attitude surveys; Communications, organizational; Development and training, employee; Employment process; Equal employment opportunities, minorities and women; Interviewing, employee; Job analysis; Labor legislation; Older employees, management of; Safety and health management, employee; Search and recruitment, executive; Suggestion systems; Temporary help; Wages and hours legislation.

REFERENCES

Burack, E. H., and R. D. Smith: *Personnel Management: A Human Resource System Approach,* John Wiley, New York, 1982.

Katz, Alan S.: *The Professional Personnel Policies Development Guidebook,* Addison-Wesley, Reading, Mass., 1982.

Pigors, P., and C. A. Myers: *Personnel Administration,* 9th ed., McGraw-Hill, New York, 1981.

DAVID G. MULLER, *Ohio National Life Insurance Company*

Planning, Strategic Managerial*

Strategic planning is a process that includes a set of interactive and overlapping decisions leading to the development of an effective strategy for a firm. The process includes:

- The determination of the firm's mission

- The selection of goals or objectives the firm wishes to pursue

- The formulation of assumptions about changes occurring in the firm's external environment

- The identification of opportunities and threats emerging from the firm's external environment

- An assessment of the internal strengths and weaknesses of the firm

- The identification of feasible strategic alternatives available to the firm

- The choice of an alternative(s) the firm wishes to pursue

- The development of an implementation plan to facilitate achievement of the firm's objectives

- The design of a control or feedback system to monitor the firm's performance while the strategic plan is being implemented

Managers undertake strategic planning for a number of reasons. First, many managers believe that strategic planning will increase their firm's effectiveness, and there exists a substantial body of academic research to support this belief. Second, the strategic planning process itself promotes feelings of accomplishment and satisfaction. As managers and planners work together to formulate strategy and implementation plans, they develop confidence in their ability to understand and manage their situation. This tends to be very gratifying and satisfying. Third, strategic planning facilitates adaptation to change. Fourth, strategic planning is a process through which the efforts of divisions, functions, and individuals can be coordinated. Fifth, when major reorganizations or changes in top management occur, strategic planning can help to educate the new top-management team about the internal and external opportunities and constraints the team members face. Finally, when an organization is not performing well, strategic planning may be undertaken to identify the problems and solutions.

*The material presented in this article is synthesized from William F. Glueck and Neil H. Snyder, *Readings in Business Policy and Strategy from Business Week*, 2d ed., McGraw-Hill, New York, 1982.

Strategy Makers

Strategy makers are the people who formulate the firm's mission and the objectives the firm will seek to achieve. They also determine the way in which objectives will be pursued. Generally, the strategy-making group consists of the firm's top managers, selected members of the board of directors, and others who, because of particular skills or expertise, are asked to participate in the strategic planning process. Strategy makers do not have the freedom to choose a strategy arbitrarily without regard for internal and external constraints on the firm. The external environment offers both opportunities and threats. Strategy makers must avoid environmental threats while pursuing opportunities, but the firm's internal strengths and weaknesses will restrict the number of opportunities the firm can pursue. For example, if the strategy makers find an investment opportunity for which they need $10 million in capital and they can raise only $5 million, that investment opportunity is not a feasible alternative for the firm. Along a different vein, the values prevailing in the firm act as constraints on what the strategy makers can do.

Analyzing the Firm's Environment

Three sectors of the environment produce changes which strategy makers must monitor if their firms are to be successful in the long run: (1) the general environment, (2) the market, and (3) the supply sector.

The General Environment. The general environment includes the following forces affecting or potentially affecting the firm: the government, the economy, consumer pressures and attitudes, and population and wealth changes.

The Government. The government—federal, state, or local—can change its structure, pass laws, issue regulations, and become or cease to become a major customer or competitor of the firm. Government action or inaction is very important to business, and most knowledgeable people agree that the government sector will increase its influence on business over the next decade.

The Economy. The economy affects firms in many ways, including the following:

- Unemployment rates may affect the demand for the firm's products or services and the availability of labor.

- Inflation rates affect the pricing of the firm's products and services.

- The Federal Reserve's money supply policy can affect the availability of capital and the cost of capital.

The general status of the economy, which is a consequence of government policy, consumer decisions, and managerial decisions, affects different firms differently. Some products or services tend to hold up better in economic downturns than others.

Consumer Pressures and Attitudes. Consumer attitudes and values toward various products and services change over time. For example, some consumer attitudes toward cigarettes, liquor, drugs, gambling casinos, massage parlors, X-rated movies, bingo, and other products and services are frequently very strong. If the firm is involved in any of these businesses, it is likely to be affected by the changing values of its offerings to the public. These examples may be extreme, but consumer pressures and attitudes influence the demand for many other products as well. Consider the changes in consumer attitudes toward the following over the past few years:

- Oil companies before and after the energy crisis
- Oil company profits before and after deregulation
- Small cars before and after the energy crisis

Population and Wealth Changes. Changes in the characteristics of the population affect most firms. For example:

- Gerber Baby Food executives are quite concerned about the drop in the birthrate from 1957 to 1983.
- Coca-Cola Company executives are concerned about the population's getting older and drinking fewer soft drinks.
- Anheuser-Busch is concerned about the shift in adult drinking habits to wine from beer.
- Government executives are concerned about the population's getting older and not producing enough tax revenue to fund their programs.

The Market. The second factor most executives watch closely is the marketplace in which they compete to distribute their goods or provide their services. Some of the aspects of the market that the executives must analyze if they are to be effective strategists are these:

- Major new products and services introduced in the industry
- Major shifts in the pricing structure of the products or services
- Major shifts in the demand for the products and services
- Major shifts in consumer preferences affecting the firm's products and services
- Major competitors entering or leaving the industry

Most studies show that strategists examine the market environment very closely. In many industries, it is the primary factor. In others, governmental factors or shifts in the economy are most important.

The Supply Sector. The final environmental concern is the supply sector. This sector provides the raw materials, money, and equipment needed by the firm to offer its service or produce its product. Some components of the supply sector that strategists must monitor include:

- Changes in the availability of major raw materials, subassemblies, etc.
- Changes in the prices of raw materials, subassemblies, etc.
- Entry or exit of major suppliers, raw material producers, etc.
- Technological breakthroughs on the supply side

The gathering of supply sector information usually involves the executives' phoning or talking with knowledgeable people such as subordinates, bankers, industry analysts, and other executives in the industry. How intensely they seek information and on what factors depends on the executives and the industry. For example:

- If the company is clearly the most powerful firm (say, General Motors, Xerox, IBM) in the industry, it may be somewhat less concerned with competitors' moves than if it were the smallest, weakest firm.
- If the firm has millions of customers (General Foods, Goodyear) rather than a very few (McDonnell Douglas), it may pay less attention to each customer.
- If the firm is dependent on a few suppliers (such as firms using copper), it may pay close attention to the supply factor.

Executives tend to focus their environmental analysis on forces to which they are most vulnerable in the short run.

Analyzing the Firm's Strengths and Weaknesses

The organizational units most frequently examined for strengths and weaknesses are marketing, operations, finance/accounting, and personnel/management. Below is a list of factors managers can evaluate within each unit.

1. Marketing
   a. Competitive structure and market share
   b. Marketing research systems
   c. Product mix
   d. Product-services line
   e. Channels of distribution and geographic coverage, including international efforts
   f. Pricing strategy for products and services
   g. Sales force effectiveness
   h. Advertising effectiveness
   i. Marketing promotion and packaging

  j. Service after the purchase

  k. Marketing policies

2. Operations

  a. Raw materials cost

  b. Raw materials availability

  c. Inventory control systems

  d. Capacity utilization

  e. Integration of operations

  f. Management information systems

  g. Equipment utilization

  h. Location of facilities and offices

  i. Operations procedures

  j. Costs of operations compared with those of competitors

  k. Research and development

  l. Patents and similar legal protection for products, processes, and similar trade secrets

3. Finance/Accounting

  a. Cost of capital relative to industry

  b. Capital structure

  c. Relations with managers and stockholders

  d. Tax conditions

  e. Barriers to new entry because of high entry costs

  f. Financial planning, working capital, and capital budgeting procedures

  g. Accounting systems for cost, budget and profit planning, and auditing procedures

4. Personnel/Management

  a. Quality of employees and managers

  b. Labor costs

  c. Relations with trade unions

  d. Personnel relations policies

  e. Corporate image and prestige

  f. Organizational structure and climate

  g. Company size relative to industry

  h. Strategic planning system

  i. The firm's record for reaching objectives

  j. Relations with regulatory and governmental bodies

  k. Functional experience and track record of top management

Strategic Choice Decisions

The *strategic choice process* begins as strategy makers compare and contrast the data gathered during the internal and external analysis and identify feasible strategic alternatives for implementation. These alternatives should reflect a match between the firm's strengths and weaknesses and the opportunities and threats in its environment. Ultimately, one or more of these alternatives will be chosen and detailed implementation plans will be prepared.

If the environment offers major opportunities that match up with major internal strengths, the conditions are right for a *growth* strategy. If the environment offers threats that coincide with major internal weaknesses, the conditions are right for a retrenchment or *turnaround* strategy. If the environment and internal strengths signal growth in one part of the firm and weaknesses and threats produce strain in another part, the conditions are right for a *combination* strategy. If no major changes are indicated from the environmental and internal analyses, the firm will choose a *stability* strategy.

It is helpful to examine each of these strategies in greater depth.

Stability Strategy. A stability strategy is one a firm pursues:

- When it continues to serve the same or very similar customers

- When it continues to pursue the same or very similar objectives (adjusting the expected level of achievement about the same percentage each year)

- When its main strategic decisions focus on incremental improvement of functional performance

Strategy makers might choose a stability strategy for one or more reasons. For example:

- The strategy makers believe the firm is doing well, and they perceive no need to change.

- The strategy makers are risk averse, and a stability strategy is less risky than other strategies.

- The firm has grown rapidly in the past, and the strategy makers believe the time has come to consolidate and to focus on creating a more efficient and manageable operation.

- The firm is experiencing pressure from the government not to grow, at least in certain areas, because of potential antitrust violations.

Growth Strategy. A growth strategy is one a firm pursues when its strategy makers formulate objectives that are significantly more ambitious than the firm's past achievement level. The most frequent change in objectives in a growth strategy is to raise the market share or sales objectives.

A firm might pursue a growth strategy for these reasons:

- The strategy makers equate growth with success.

- The industry or industries in which the firm does

business is or are growing rapidly, and a choice not to grow is a choice to sacrifice market share.

- The strategy makers believe society benefits from growth.
- The strategy makers are achievement-oriented individuals.

There are many varieties of growth strategies. For example:

- Firms can grow by acquiring other firms (external growth).
- They can grow horizontally—that is, in the same type of business.
- They can grow vertically—that is, by moving forward and acquiring or developing firms in the market channel or by moving backward by acquiring or developing suppliers.
- Firms can grow internally by offering existing products to new markets or by creating new products for existing markets.

Retrenchment Strategy. A retrenchment strategy is pursued by a firm when its strategy makers decide to improve performance by:

- Focusing on functional improvement, especially reduction of costs (also called a turnaround strategy)
- Reducing the number of functions the firm performs by becoming a captive company
- Reducing the number of products it produces and/or markets it serves
- Liquidating part or all of the firm's assets (the ultimate retrenchment strategy)

Retrenchment strategies are used when strategy makers believe performance in a product line, division, or company in question is less than satisfactory and prospects for improvement are not good. By retrenching, the strategy makers free up some of their resources for more productive use elsewhere.

Combination Strategy. A firm pursues a combination strategy when its main strategic decisions focus on simultaneously using more than one of these strategies (stability, growth, and retrenchment) in one or more divisions of the company. Another form of the combination strategy uses several grand strategies over a period of time. For example, a firm's strategy makers may decide on a strategy which calls for rapid growth followed by stability.

Each of these strategies can be effective when the situation dictates its choice. The strategy makers select the strategy they believe represents the best match between their firm's strengths and weaknesses and opportunities and threats in the environment. Their choice is influenced by their past strategic choices, their willingness to take risks, and their power to make a choice.

Implementation and Evaluation

In the implementation phase, the strategy makers first make sure they have developed an appropriate organization structure. For example, in earlier stages of development, firms tend to organize functionally. That is, vice presidents reporting to the president have responsibility for particular business functions and have titles such as vice president—marketing. If the firm's strategy leads it to grow in product/service scope and/or geographically, it tends to shift to a decentralized divisional structure. In this stage, the staff members reporting to the president lead product/service, geographic, or similar units. The functional units then report to these executives.

The second implementation step is to place in key positions executives with the background and motivation to make the new strategy successful. Then functional policy decisions must be made to bring the strategic choice to fruition.

Policy Formulation. Policies are decision guides to action designed to make the strategy work. They connect strategic and implementation decisions by specifying how the strategic decisions will be implemented. In the policy formation process, it is crucial to explain the chosen strategy in terms of policies that are compatible and workable. It is not enough for managers merely to decide to change their firm's strategy. They must define precisely how they plan to get where they want to go, when they want to get there, and how efficiently they want to operate as they go. Managers do so by preparing policies to implement the strategy.

Policies must be developed for key functional decisions in the following areas:

- Operations/production
- Finance/accounting
- Personnel
- Marketing and logistics
- Research and development

Thus, if the strategic choice is to grow, policy decisions that are consistent with the growth strategy must be made. A sample list of policy questions in each of the functional areas follows:

Operations/Production

- Can we handle the added business with our present facilities and number of shifts?
- Must we add equipment, facilities, shifts? Where?
- Can we become more efficient by better scheduling?
- What is the firm's inventory safety level? How many suppliers does it need to obtain major supplies?

687

- What level of productivity and costs should the firm seek to realize?

- How much emphasis should there be on quality control?

- How far ahead should we schedule production? Should we guarantee delivery?

- Are we going to be operations or production leaders in the latest equipment and methods?

Finance/Accounting

- Where will we obtain additional funds for growth—internally or externally?

- If we wish to obtain additional funds externally, how should we obtain them? Where should we obtain them?

- What will growth do to our cash flow?

- What accounting systems and policies should we use (for example, LIFO or FIFO)?

- What capital structure policy (no debt or heavily leveraged) should we pursue? What policy should we pursue with regard to ownership?

- How much cash and other assets should we keep on hand?

Personnel

- Do we have an adequate work force?

- How much hiring and retraining are necessary?

- What types of individuals do we need to recruit college graduates? Minority groups? How should we recruit? By advertising? Personal contact?

- What should be the methods for selection? Informal interview? Very sophisticated testing?

- What should be the standards and methods for promotion? From within? By seniority?

- What incentive plans, benefits, labor relations policies, etc., should we have?

Marketing and Logistics

- Which specific products or services should be expanded? How?

- Which channels should be used to market these products or services? Should we use exclusive dealerships or multiple channels?

- How should we promote these products or services? Is it our policy to use large amounts of TV advertising? Heavy personal selling expenses? Price competition?

- Do we have an adequate sales force?

- What distribution policies do we want?

Research and Development

- What new projects are necessary to support our growth?

- Should we contract some of these functions out?

- How much should we spend on research and development?

There is also a time dimension in the policy formulation process. Some policy decisions can be made and implemented immediately (for example, changing from LIFO to FIFO, hiring unskilled workers). Others take long lead times to come to fruition (such as research and development, construction of new plants). In effect, managers create a cascade of policies. Long-range policy decisions guide and constrain them in the formulation of medium-range and short-range policies.

Evaluation of Strategic Planning. After the strategy is implemented, top managers must evaluate its effectiveness. Such evaluation is the phase of the strategic planning process during which top managers determine whether their strategic choice as implemented is meeting the objectives of the firm. Additionally, the evaluation can be qualitative or quantitative. For example, the quantitative criteria may include:

- Net profit
- Stock price
- Dividend rates
- Earnings per share
- Return on capital
- Return on equity
- Market share
- Growth in sales
- Days lost per employee as a result of strikes
- Production costs and efficiency
- Distribution costs and efficiency
- Employee turnover and absenteeism

If the top managers believe the strategy is working, they continue to implement it. If it is not, they shift to another strategy or adjust the current strategy to make it more effective.

Conclusion

Strategic planning is not a panacea, although it can be very helpful if it is implemented properly. Under certain conditions, however, strategic planning almost always fails to live up to the expectations of top managers. When this situation occurs, unnecessary frustration and anxiety set in. Why may strategic planning fail? Several reasons are suggested:

- Lack of top-management commitment
- Lack of critical skills in key areas
- Lack of coordination
- Inability to forecast accurately
- Overemphasis on short-run results
- Overemphasis on long-run results
- Failure to remain flexible to handle unanticipated contingencies
- Too complex and difficult to understand
- Failure to be specific about expected outcomes
- Failure to organize properly
- Poor communications
- Failure to evaluate and modify the strategy as needed

The material presented in this article is synthesized from *Readings in Business Policy and Strategy from Business Week*, 2d ed., by William F. Glueck and Neil H. Snyder, McGraw-Hill, New York, 1982.

See also Audit, management; Budgets and budget preparation; Control systems, management; Forecasting business conditions; Management information systems (MIS); Marketing, concepts and systems; Objectives and goals; Positioning; Product planning and development; Program planning and implementation.

NEIL H. SNYDER, *University of Virginia*

WILLIAM F. GLUECK (deceased), *University of Georgia*

Political Action Committees (PACs)

The democratic form of government of the United States of America derives much of its equitability and its vigor from large-scale participation of its citizens in the political process. Every law-abiding adult has a bona fide opportunity to become actively involved in the electoral process in a meaningful way. As a unique aspect of this process, political action committees (PACs) have been sanctioned by law—and regulated by the Federal Election Commission (FEC)—to provide interested individuals and/or organizations with a highly visible and focused influence on political issues and candidates for public office. PACs are loosely structured, voluntary membership organizations that solicit and accept financial donations from individuals who share similar

points of view about politics and government and/or—perhaps more pragmatically—similar economic and employment concerns. Thus, member-contributors to a particular PAC may be members of a trade union and have a "liberal" view toward politics and government. Member-contributors of another PAC may identify with corporate management and take a "conservative" view of politics and government. Regardless of political persuasion, however, the only source of PAC funding is from voluntary contributions from individuals. PACs use these funds to support financially candidates they prefer for public office or to oppose candidates whose political interests are judged to be contrary to those of the particular PAC.

PACs and the Law. Political action committees are authorized by the Federal Election Campaign Act of 1971 as amended in 1976. Essentially, the law was enacted to enable individuals to make effective political contributions: it specifically prohibits corporations, labor unions, and federal contractors to contribute to a PAC. Individuals may contribute up to $5000 per year, provided that the PAC supports more than a single political candidate. Individuals are allowed a tax credit for one-half of all their contributions to PACs up to a $50 credit—$100 for a joint return. No limit is set upon how much a PAC may receive. Each committee reports its receipts and disbursements to the Federal Election Commission on a quarterly basis.

Selection of Contribution Recipients. The main recipients of PAC money are candidates for public office or officeholders themselves. In order to make informed decisions about potential recipients, a PAC must gather relevant information about a candidate, his or her campaign, and anything else that is indicative of the outcome of a campaign. A PAC studies this information and tries to decide (1) whether a contribution is in its best interest, and (2) whether the contribution has the potential of making a difference in the outcome of the election. If the answers to these two questions are yes, the PAC will likely contribute to the candidate of its choice.

It is essential that the information a PAC gathers be correct. Otherwise, the committee can end up contributing money to candidates less likely to win, or to those whose interests are contrary to those of the PAC. Accordingly, PACs gather political intelligence from three basic sources:

1. The easiest, and sometimes most thorough, background information comes from the candidates themselves. In campaign circles, the information that a candidate sends to a PAC is contained in a "PAC kit." The kit contains an in-depth biography of the candidate, including positions on key issues and brief biographies of his or her family and campaign staff. Also included is the

amount of money raised from supporters within the district. A candidate who has been successful in raising money within the district indicates a broad base of support and is a potentially good PAC target. PACs examine a campaign budget to judge whether it is reasonable or not. They also look at where the campaign plans to spend the money that is raised, i.e., media, direct mail, phone banks, etc., to determine whether the money will be well spent or thrown away on unimportant and noncrucial projects. A map and demographic statistics of the district are also important to the PAC in understanding the district, as well as recent newspaper articles on the campaign. Newspaper articles often give the PAC a view of whether the people in the district perceive the race as winnable or not. Good PAC kits also include pertinent information on the opponents—brief biographical sketches in addition to positions on some major issues.

2. Also, a PAC gains information on campaigns through its own informal organizational network. The administrative hierarchy of a PAC is relatively simple, although there are minor variations. At the top of the hierarchy is a board of directors that typically includes members of the board of directors of the sponsoring association, corporation, or trade union. In addition, an administrative director sits on the board. This person oversees the PAC's day-to-day operations and makes recommendations to the board on specific contributions. There is also a political director, whose responsibilities include regular contact with other PACs and with ongoing campaigns.

3. Many major PACs also have a representative in Washington, D.C. Among PAC offices in Washington and throughout the nation, there is an informal, yet tightly knit, communication network into which most PACs are tuned. Various PACs represent different, often conflicting, interests, but they share their information on campaigns with one another. There are also a few very large PACs toward which other PACs look for leadership. If one (or more) of these larger PACs contributes to a candidate, the donation encourages the smaller PACs to contribute.

Types of PACs. Liberal and labor-oriented PACs were the first on the political scene. Their success and growth led the way for conservative associations and corporate PACs to evolve in the process of working for political candidates they favor.

The more liberal and labor-oriented PACs generally expound the views of blue-collar workers and labor unions, regarding social issues. In contrast, corporate and conservatively oriented PACs more typically promote free enterprise, business management, and a strong national defense. In addition, a number of PACs focus on a whole range of ideological issues from environmental concerns to abortion interests.

Pros and Cons. A recent count of political action committees put the number at 3700. In the 1982 congressional races, they contributed an estimated $85 million, up 85 percent from 1974. In 1982, 35 percent of the money raised by winning congressional candidates came from PACs. Many people look at these figures with alarm. They are concerned that political control, when associated with fundraising, will remove influence from the individual and place it in the hands of large organizations, both conservative and liberal. Another argument made against PACs is that they attempt to "buy" a candidate or an officeholder by demanding a specific vote or favor in return for a contribution.

On the other hand is the basic argument that PACs enable many individuals who otherwise could exert no influence to become directly involved in the political process.

Critics also complain that because of the large contributions they are allowed to make, PACs sometimes have undue influence over a candidate or an elected official. For congressional candidates, the figure is $5000 per PAC for each election cycle. In other words, a PAC may legally contribute $5000 for the primary, $5000 for the runoff if there is one, and $5000 for the general election. This regulation establishes a possible total of $15,000 per PAC. In fact, however, PACs rarely give so much money to one candidate. In 1982, for example, contributions to congressional candidates averaged $500 to $800 per PAC. PAC supporters argue that this contribution is not a lot of money when compared with the entire budget of congressional campaigns. These campaigns raise anywhere from $200,000 to $2 million. A $500 to $800 contribution may not even buy a full-page newspaper ad or a 30-second prime-time television commercial in a medium-size market of 200,000 citizens.

PAC supporters also contend that the contributions of many individuals are needed to support a PAC's activities. Accordingly, a PAC may contribute its legal maximum of several thousand dollars to a particular candidate, but this donation is simply the accumulation of many small, individual contributions to the PAC.

It appears that PACs are here to stay. Whether they will continue in their present structure depends in large part on the Federal Election Commission. Major reforms will probably be directed at the way a PAC can distribute its funds. Regulations are more likely to be tightened than loosened. The chance is that total contributions from PACs to the electoral process will continue to rise as new PACs are formed and as special-interest groups increase in number.

See also Economic systems; Government relations; Public and community relations; Social responsibility of business.

REFERENCES

Alexander, Herbert: *Financing Politics*, 2d ed., Congressional Quarterly, Inc., Washington, D.C., 1980.

Federal Election Commission: *Campaign Guide for Corporations and Labor Organizations*, Washington, D.C., January 1982.

————*FEC Reports on Financial Activity, 1981–82, Final Report: Party and Non-Party Political Committees*, Washington, D.C., November 1983.

Weinberger, Marvin: *Political Action Committees: PAC Directory*, Ballinger, Cambridge, Mass., 1982.

ROBERT DOUGLAS BAIN, *North American Marketing Corporation*

Positioning

Positioning is both a marketing term and a marketing concept. Definitions of the term vary, but a position typically implies the mental image which a product or service projects in a target market in relation to the images of other products or services competing in that market. In other words, it's what you do to the mind, not to the product. The authors, since 1969, have advocated a much broader application of the positioning concept. *Positioning,* in their view, is an indispensable element in marketing planning and strategy for the company or institution as well as for a particular product or service.

Essentials of Successful Positioning

There are any number of effective approaches used in positioning. The six principles stated below, however, appear to be the most compelling. They were advanced by the authors more than a decade and a half ago and have been confirmed by hundreds of successful corporate experiences.

1. *Today's marketplace is no longer responsive to strategies that worked in the past. There are too many products, too many companies, and too much marketing noise.* We have become an overcommunicated society. With only 5 percent of the world's population, the United States consumes 57 percent of the world's advertising output. The per capita consumption of advertising in the United States today is about $200 a year. If you spend $1 million a year on advertising, you are bombarding the average consumer with less than a half-cent of advertising, spread out over 365 days. This consumer is already exposed to $200 worth of advertising from other companies.

In an overcommunicated society, talk about the impact of advertising seriously overstates the potential effectiveness of a particular message. It is an egocentric view that bears no relationship to the realities of the marketplace.

In the modern communication jungle, the only hope is to be selective, to concentrate on narrow targets, to practice segmentation—in a word, to practice "positioning."

2. *As a defense against the volume of today's communications, the human mind screens and rejects much of the information offered it. In general, the mind accepts only that which matches its prior knowledge or experience.*

Millions of dollars have been wasted trying to change minds with advertising. Once a mind is made up, it is almost impossible to alter it. Certainly not with a weak force like advertising. "Don't confuse me with the facts, my mind's made up." That is a way of life for most people.

The average person can tolerate being told something about which he or she knew nothing, but the average person cannot tolerate being told he or she is wrong. The attempt at mind changing is the road to advertising disaster.

The computer industry is a good example of the folly of trying to change minds. Company after company tries to tell people its computers are better than IBM's. Yet, that doesn't "compute" in the prospect's mind. The computer position in the minds of most people is filled with the name of a company called IBM. For a competitive computer manufacturer to obtain a favorable position in the prospect's mind, it must somehow relate the company to IBM's position.

In other words, the strategy is not to try to change the prospect's mind at all. Accept what is up there and work around it. In positioning, the competitor's image is just as important as your own. Sometimes, it is more important.

3. *In the positioning era, the name of your company or product becomes more and more important.* No aspect of positioning has proved as controversial as the "importance of the name."

Eastern Airlines, for example, has a regional name that puts the company in a different category from other nationwide carriers (American, United, and Trans World Airlines). The name Eastern places the airline in the same category with airlines like Western, North Central, and Piedmont.

You see what you expect to see. Take any two abstract drawings. Write the name "Schwartz" on one and the name "Picasso" on the other. Then ask someone for an opinion on their respective values.

Pour a bottle of Gallo table wine into an empty 50-year-old bottle of French Burgundy. Then carefully decant a glass in front of a friend and ask for an opinion.

You taste what you expect to taste.

Were it not so, there would be no role for advertising at all. Were the average consumer rational instead of emotional, there would be no advertising. At least not as we know it today.

One prime objective of all advertising is to heighten expectations, to create the illusion that the product or service will perform the miracles we expect. And presto, it does.

Parallels in Industrial Advertising. It is a mistake to believe that the industrial customer buys on reason, logic, and facts, not emotion. Ask IBM's competitors—or Xerox's or General Electric's. Especially for high technology, such as high-priced products like computers and copiers, the average industrial buyer tends to be far more emotional than the average Charmin-squeezing housewife (who, more often than not, is downright practical).

Industrial customers are also cursed by a "play it safe" attitude. We cannot blame them. No housewife ever was fired for buying the wrong brand of coffee. But plenty of industrial buyers have been in deep trouble over a high-technology buy that went sour.

The trend in industrial products is toward more sophistication, more use of integrated circuits, fiber optics, lasers, etc. So you can expect the industrial buyer to buy more on feelings, hunches, and especially reputation and less on objective product comparisons.

This is why factual, expository advertising copy is growing less important in industrial advertising and positioning more important.

4. *Advertising programs have to go beyond just establishing a name. Many programs start and end there. To secure a worthwhile position for a corporate name, it needs a thought to go with it.* This combination leads directly to what is called the *line extension trap.* Line extension has swept through the marketing community for some very sound reasons. Logic is on the side of line extension. It utilizes arguments of economics, trade acceptance, customer acceptance, lower advertising costs, increased income, reduced costs, the corporate image. Truth, unfortunately, is not on this side.

The paradox of marketing is that conventional wisdom is almost always wrong. Xerox bought a computer company with a perfectly good name: Scientific Data Systems. And what was the first thing Xerox did? It changed the name to Xerox Data Systems. Then it ran an ad that said, " This Xerox machine can't make a copy." Obviously, any Xerox machine that couldn't make a copy was headed for trouble, believe us.

Singer did the same thing with the old, respected Frident name. One of its introductory ads declared: "Singer Business Machines introduces Touch & Know." Do you see the connection: Touch and know, touch and sew? Both Xerox and Singer committed the ultimate positioning mistake: to try to transfer a generic brand name to a different product sold to a different market. To top it off, Singer knocked off its own sewing machine slogan.

You can't hang a company on a name today. You need a position. So if your corporate name is inappropriate for the new product you intend to market, create a new one—and a new position to go with it.

5. *One thing that is worse than "just a name" program is one without a name. This error occurs when companies use initials instead of a name.*

The superiority of a name over a meaningless set of initials can generally be documented by market research. Happily, the initialitus that struck American business in the late 1960s and early 1970s has abated.

6. *It's almost impossible to dislodge a strongly dug-in leader that owns the high ground. It would be a lot better to open up a new front or position.* The big computer successes in the seventies were the companies that avoided going head-to-head with IBM—Digital Equipment Corporation and Data General, in particular, at the low end of the market.

Such positioning avoids competitors' high ground by outflanking them.

Creativity and Positioning

There is good reason to believe that positioning removed the often empty mystique from advertising creativity. In fact, we flatly stated in 1969: "Creativity is dead. The name of the advertising game in the seventies is positioning." In truth, the decade of the seventies might well be characterized as a "return to reality." White knights and black eye-patches gave way to such positioning concepts as Lite Beer's "Everything you've always wanted in a great beer. And less." Poetic? Yes. Artful? Yes. But also a straightforward, clearly defined explanation of the basic positioning premise.

Positioning and the Future

Just as positioning triggered a shift of emphasis and outlook in the 1970s, it will continue to provoke changes in the future, such as:

1. *The end of the traditional concept of marketing.* For at least 50 years now, astute advertising people have preached the marketing gospel: "The customer is king." Over and over again, there are wondrous arguments that to be "production"-oriented instead of "customer"-oriented is to flirt with disaster.

Plenty of companies that have dutifully followed this advice have seen millions of dollars disappear in valiant but catastrophic customer-oriented efforts. These firms include General Electric in computers, Singer in business machines, and Sara Lee in frozen dinners.

Typical explanations include "Product problems," "Not enough capital," or the ever popular "Not enough distribution."

Can it be that marketing, itself, is the problem?

Confusion has set in. In many categories, customers no longer perceive any large differences in products. Thus, brand choice will not be based on a rational search of all brands in the category but on a brand previously tried, or the leader, or the one positioned to the prospect's segment.

Once buying patterns are established, it is becoming more and more difficult to change them. The customer doesn't really want to accept any more information on a category that is already catalogued in his or her mind, no matter how dramatically or how creatively this information is presented. Today, every prudent company has become marketing-oriented. Knowing what the customer wants, however, is not too helpful if a dozen other companies are already serving those wants.

2. *To be successful, a company must shift its emphasis from the customer to the competitor.* A company must look for weak points in the positions of its competitors and then launch marketing attacks against those weak points. For example, while others were losing millions in the computer business, Digital Equipment Corporation was making millions by exploiting IBM's weakness in small computers.

There are those who would say that competitors are always considered in a well-thought-out marketing plan. Indeed they are, but usually toward the *back* of the plan under a heading entitled "Competitive Evaluation," whose inclusion seems almost an afterthought.

Up front with prominence is the major part of the plan: the details of marketplace, the various demographic segments, and a myriad of "customer" research statistics carefully gleaned from endless focus groups, test panels, concept and market tests.

3. *The marketing plan of the future will read more like a battle plan.* In this plan of the future, many more pages will be dedicated to the competition. The plan will carefully dissect each participant in the marketplace. It will develop a list of competitive strengths and weaknesses as well as a plan of action either to exploit or to defend against them.

4. *The name of the game in the 1980s will be "Marketing Warfare."* Successful marketing campaigns will have to be planned like military campaigns. Strategic planning and positioning will become more and more important. Companies will have to learn how to attack, defend, and flank their competition—and then to resort to guerrilla warfare.

They will need better intelligence on how to anticipate competitive moves. On the personal level, successful marketing people will have to exhibit many of the same virtues that make a great general— courage, boldness, loyalty, and perseverance. They will be the marketing people who know their competitors (and their positioning strategy and tactics) as well as they know their own customers.

See also Advertising concepts; Brands and brand names; Consumer behavior, managerial relevance of; Market analysis; Marketing management; Marketing research; Marketing, industrial; Product planning and development.

REFERENCES

Bradway, B. M., R. E. Pritchard, and M. A. Frenzel: *Strategic Marketing,* Addison-Wesley, Reading, Mass., 1982, chap. 4, "Positioning."

Ries, Al, and Jack Trout: *Positioning: The Battle for Your Mind,* McGraw-Hill, New York, 1981.

Trout, Jack, and Al Ries: "Positioning: Ten Years Later," *Industrial Marketing,* July 1979.

JACK TROUT and AL RIES, *Trout & Ries Advertising, Inc.*

Power and Influence

Power is generally viewed as the ability to compel obedience or cooperation. In its narrower sense, it is a delegated right or privilege, usually assigned legally and/or formally by an organization in the form of authority. In its broader sense, power is spoken of as the ability to prevail. Hence, organizational behaviorists prefer the term *influence* to *power.*

Power or influence may reside in an individual, or it may be a characteristic of a group as perceived by individuals within or outside the group. In the individual sense, power is associated with leadership and the requirement of management to plan and organize and especially to direct and control others. In the organizational sense, power represents the influence a group, such as a work group or an entire company, exerts upon its members to obtain participation and conformance while seeking its objectives.

Power may be described in several ways, according to its source, and be either real or as perceived by another individual:

Reward power is dependent upon the ability to provide incentives in the form of rewards such as pay increases, promotions, attractive assignments, and job security.

Coercive power reflects the ability to impose sanctions in the form of criticism, dismissal, unattractive assignments, and withheld rewards.

Referent power is a function of an individual's ability to project a personal form of appeal to followers and is based more upon faith and charisma than upon reward or coercion or identifiable logic.

Expert power stems from the possession of specialized knowledge or skills perceived by others to be valuable to them in their organizational activities and relationships.

Legitimate power is that conveyed by the organization to the various managers throughout its hierarchy in the form of designated titles and positions.

Perceptive Aspect. Power and influence form a two-way entity. There is, on the one hand, the power an individual holds as a result of personal qualities and/or those conferred legitimately upon him or her. On the other hand, there is the power that another individual *perceives* that the person holds for whatever reasons. In many organizational circumstances, there may be significant differences between the intrinsic power of an individual and the perception others have of this power. It is for this reason that organizations often strive so hard to establish the legitimacy of authority and to build up the reward and coercive prerogatives invested in its managers. It is also for this reason that legitimate, reward, coercive, and even expert power fall far short of being enough for managers lacking in referent power.

Power Needs. Individuals vary in their need for personal power. They also vary according to their response to the power of others. Some are influenced by one sort of power, such as charisma, and rebel against another, such as coercion. Others respond mainly to rewards and punishment. A bureaucrat may respect only legitimacy; a specialist, only expertise. Obviously, there may be followers and nonfollowers for each manager according to the needs of his or her organizational subordinates and associates.

Effect of Power. It is not certain how legitimate power will affect the individual who holds it and how he or she will use it. Some persons become more compassionate; others exploit their power. It appears that two factors may encourage the latter tendency. Many organizations seem to reward those who hold power, so the struggle to attain this valuable commodity can become rapacious. Furthermore, the larger the gap is between those who exert power and those who feel powerless, the easier—and thus greater—the exploitation is likely to be. Paradoxically, the feeling of powerlessness and overdependence often induces noncooperative behavior, perhaps because the less powerful individual no longer perceives benefits to be derived from his or her participation.

Typically, those who hold power in organizations resist the removal of that power. They do so by direct and indirect intimidation and by isolation of others who try to take it from them. Thus, the so-called power struggle is evident in many organizations where some degree of power equalization has not been developed.

The Use of Power

Exercise of Power. While the mere possession or nonpossession of power has an effect on an individual, the manner in which it is exercised and the kind of power employed can affect an organization's goals. Traditionally, organizations have depended on the right of the supervisor to require certain behavior (legitimate power) and his or her capability to impose sanctions (coercive power). While the use of legitimate power may elicit compliance from the subordinate, the compliance is apt to produce only "acceptable" levels of performance and is unlikely to result in increases in performance levels. The use of coercive power produces those feelings of powerlessness and overdependence in the subordinate that may lead to alienation and noncooperative behavior. The use of expert or referent power correlates most strongly with organizational effectiveness, employee satisfaction, and higher levels of performance.

Ideally, then, the supervisor's attempts to influence subordinates should be based upon expert or referent power. It should be emphasized, however, that in spite of a manager's belief that his or her influence attempts are based upon expert or referent power, the employee's perception of this basis may be more important. While the manager may, in fact, possess specialized knowledge and skills, the employee may comply mainly because he or she perceives the manager's ability to impose sanctions or grant rewards, or simply because the employee acknowledges the authority vested in the supervisor to require certain behavior. If an employee maintains either of these attitudes, the results of the compliance may be the same as if the manager had overtly used sanctions, rewards, etc., in the first place. Briefly, what is important in the influence attempt is the employee's perception of the basis of power and not the superior's. Since superiors do in fact possess legitimate, reward, and coercive power, it is very difficult for the employee in any given situation to perceive correctly the kind of power the supervisor intends to use.

Exchange Relationships. Students of organization behavior view social behavior as an exchange. They contend that an understanding of this concept will minimize power conflicts and maximize cooperation. Effective managers, they observe, recognize this implicit exchange in management-employee relations and seek to employ power from various sources accordingly. The employee or subordinate, in effect, trades certain prerogatives for certain privileges in relationship to personal and organizational values. Participative management approaches are based upon this view that power relationships are mutually determined. The offer of participation by a manager to subordinates is a sharing of power. It seeks a balance between (1) generally accepted managerial prerogatives and (2) freedom of the employee to develop his or her own expert power.

See also Authority, responsibility, and accountability; Delegation; Discipline; Interpersonal relationships; Leadership; Motivation in organizations.

REFERENCES

Grimes, A. J.: "Authority, Power, Influence, and Social Control: A Theoretical Synthesis," *Academy of Management Review*, vol. 3, 1978, pp. 724–735.

McFillen, J. M.: "Supervisory Power as an Influence in Supervisor-Subordinate Relations," *Academy of Management Journal*, vol. 21, 1978, pp. 419–433.

Pfeffer, Jeffrey: *Power in Organizations*, Pitman, Marshfield, Mass., 1981.

D. Kent Zimmerman, *James Madison University*

Privacy in the Workplace

Virtually every company maintains extensive personnel files on each of its employees. The information contained may include promotion records, performance evaluations, polygraph results, and medical records, to name but a few. Employers have many routes to gather information on their employees. Routinely, potential employees are required to complete extensive written questionnaires, to participate in face-to-face interviews, and to allow searches of records held by police and hospitals. Unfortunately, the large number of people who have access to these personnel records is astounding. The end result is that the employees are usually unaware of what specific information is contained in these data banks or who has examined the information.

As companies accumulate more and more data on employees and potential employees, a conflict arises between an employee's right to privacy and the employer's right to relevant information. This entry will provide background information on the legislation relevant to this conflict and examine some specialized topics pertaining to employee privacy.

Fair Credit Reporting Act. Companies today feel that it is necessary to gather as much background information as possible on potential and current employees. To accomplish this task, employers often utilize investigative consumer-report agencies. The activities of these organizations are regulated by the 1970 Fair Credit Reporting Act (FCRA). FCRA covers data based on the written records of an individual's financial history (bill payments, bankruptcies, and the like) and opinion data (statements made by past employers, friends, etc.). This legislation does not define what specific types of information are relevant to the employer.

Under FCRA, an individual who is being investigated is notified in writing that an investigative report may be requested. The job applicant, if rejected for a position, may secure the name of the investigating agency. The applicant can request accurate explanation of the substance of the information in the files and, under FCRA, ask for a reinvestigation where information is inaccurate.

Privacy Act of 1974. The Privacy Act of 1974, which applies to federal agencies, is aimed at promoting government respect for the privacy of individuals by regulating the collection, maintenance, use, and dissemination of personal information by federal agencies. Generally, an agency may not disclose to any other agency or individual any information pertaining to an individual contained in a Privacy Act record system without prior written consent of that individual. There are, however, 11 exceptions to this rule of nondisclosure.

The Privacy Act established a seven-member Privacy Protection Study Commission, budgeted at $1.75 million to make a 2-year study. Its purpose was to determine whether the act was effective in safeguarding personal privacy in federal agencies and whether Congress should consider similar legislation affecting state and local governments and the private sector.

The Privacy Protection Study Commission's lengthy report to Congress was announced on July 12, 1977, and included a variety of suggestions. The commission took the position that the private sector should exercise self-regulation concerning the protection of employee rights. It advocated voluntary controls because its members believed that overregulation and overlegislation existed. Some of the commission's specific recommendations included:

1. Prohibiting employers from requiring employees to submit to lie detector tests.

2. Denying to employers the arrest records of employees or job seekers, in most cases.

3. Establishing an independent government unit to monitor computer operations in the private sector.

4. Preventing government agencies from seeing records held by banks, hospitals, and utility companies without a person's consent or a subpoena.

5. Enacting legislation permitting an employee to sue for up to $10,000 if an organization gives out information without authorization and if the affected individual can prove a Privacy Act violation. At present, an employee can recover only provable losses incurred because of such a violation.

6. Requiring an explanation whenever an individual is denied credit, and allowing that person to see any information which a private firm has collected concerning himself or herself.

Arrest Records. Employers are very leery of any job applicant who has ever been arrested. For many employers, the fact that a person has come to the attention of the police is enough to justify not hiring that person. Application questionnaires frequently ask for a listing of all arrests, including those for juvenile offenses (which are supposed to be confidential, under most state laws) and those which were followed by a dismissal of charges or an acquittal. In addition, many applications ask for consent to a complete record search by the employer. Finally, some employers question applicants about arrests in a polygraph test.

Use of arrest record information creates a twofold problem. First, in some cases arrest records containing incomplete or inaccurate data are disseminated to an employer. Second, there is the general attribution of guilt to anyone who has an arrest record. In recent years, the courts have addressed some of these abuses and have offered various remedies to the victim.

A case in point was *Gregory v. Litton Systems, Inc.* (1970). A federal district court heard the complaint of a black sheet-metal worker who had been arrested 14 times but never convicted. Litton had rescinded a job offer to Gregory when it learned of his arrest record. The court found that Litton's apparently racially neutral inquiry into arrest records operated to bar employment to black job seekers in far greater proportion than to white job seekers. The court ruled Litton's rejection of Gregory a violation of the 1964 Civil Rights Act.

Polygraph. The so-called lie detector (or polygraph) is a machine that measures and records fluctuations in blood pressure, rate of respiration, and galvanic skin response. The theory behind the polygraph test is that the act of lying causes psychological conflict, conflict causes fear, and fear brings about certain measurable physiological changes, which are detected and recorded by the polygraph machine.

There are few legal protections for the job applicant or employee who is asked to take a polygraph test. Some labor unions have negotiated contracts banning its use. Just over a dozen states have enacted laws limiting or prohibiting the use of the polygraph for employment purposes. By 1984, Congressional efforts to enact legislation were so far to no avail.

Medical Records. The medical examination, along with the medical history taken from the applicant's physician and hospital records, places in the employer's hands information of an intimate nature. Traditionally, medical information has been considered as "privileged" between doctor and patient. However, the employer is legally free to use medical data to aid in decisions to hire, fire, promote, or reassign. In fact, except for government agencies subject to the federal Privacy Act or a similar state law, the employer may disseminate such information without any restriction at all.

Employers, furthermore, utilize psychological testing. Of particular interest to them is the personality or attitude test, used as a way of eliminating "misfits," "undesirables," and "dishonest employees." Despite the absence of evidence that these tests are predictive of either performance or honesty in an employment situation, their use is unrestricted except in federal employment.

Conclusion

This entry has tried to provide guideline information regarding the confrontation between the employer's right to information on employees and the employees' right to privacy. It appears that, in spite of various pieces of legislation and court rulings, the level of privacy enjoyed by employees is in the hands of their employers. Today, many companies are trying to work out practical regulations for maintaining the confidentiality of their employees' records. Also, some private sector efforts are being made to limit the information required of job applicants. Some companies no longer ask for arrest, conviction, physical, or mental records in an attempt to protect employee privacy. With the trend toward deregulation generally under the Reagan Administration, there appears to be little chance of a federal law governing employee privacy. For the time being, businesses will be left to regulate their employees' privacy as they see fit.

See also Assessment center method; Employment process; Equal employment opportunity, minorities and women; Interviewing, employee; Personnel administration.

REFERENCES

Hayden, Trudy: *The Privacy Report,* American Civil Liberties Union, New York, 1978.

Perham, John: "The New Push for Employee Privacy," *Dun's Review,* March 1979, pp. 112–114.

Raskin, David C.: "The Truth about Lie Detectors," *The Wharton Magazine,* vol. 4, no. 5, Fall 1980, pp. 29–33.

Roger A. Soenksen, *James Madison University*

Product Liability

The change in legal philosophy in the United States from *caveat emptor* (buyer beware) to *caveat venditor* (seller beware) has significant implications for the business executive. Nowhere has this change been more readily apparent than in the area of product liability. *Product liability* refers to the legal responsibility of a manufacturer or seller of a product to compensate a buyer who has been injured by the product. In recent years, the courts, regulators, and legislatures have extended liability to a wide range of product situations where it did not exist before.

In the 3-year interval between 1975 and 1978, product liability premiums paid by retailers and manufacturers increased from $1.13 billion to $2.75

billion. In 1976, over 1 million product liability claims seeking some $50 billion in total damages were filed against United States companies. In 1965, claims totaled only $500,000. More important from the firm's standpoint, the average award granted increased to $79,940 in 1973 from $11,644 in 1965.[1]

Compounding this problem is the fact that insurance companies, even with premium increases of 300 to 500 percent in 5 years, find it difficult to support the inflated awards and open-ended risk trend, and thus are becoming increasingly reluctant to provide product liability insurance. Although numerous reasons can be presented for the increase in the number of product liability cases, most experts recognize that it is primarily the result of the consumer's growing awareness of his or her right to sue and the increasing willingness to exercise that right. All evidence indicates that product liability as a critical concern for business is here to stay; therefore, it behooves the executive to acquire an appreciation of the contemporary legal concepts, the situations in which they are applicable, the defenses available, and specifically, what each firm can do organizationally to reduce its exposure to product liability and the associated claims and costs.

Widespread Vulnerability. Legislation, such as the Consumer Product Safety Act and the Magnuson-Moss Warranty–Federal Trade Commission Improvement Act, tends to give the impression that only firms manufacturing and distributing consumer products need to be concerned with product liability. This impression is erroneous, since an estimated 85 percent of all product liability suits have involved industrial rather than consumer products. In addition, the present application of legal doctrines by the courts has expanded product liability to the distributor as well as the manufacturer. In certain instances, legal suits may even include firms that are peripheral members of the channel of distribution, such as advertising agencies, endorsing firms, and testing firms.

Further compounding the product liability problem is the fact that exposure to liability is not a function of firm size. A small firm is at a decided disadvantage, and it is more likely to be forced out of business because it may be less able to satisfy a liability claim or unable to pay the high cost of liability insurance. Differences in risk, however, are related to types of products. Although some products, such as drugs, foods, chemicals, and selected types of machinery, inflict a greater risk for the firms that produce them, product liability presents a critical challenge for *all* firms.

Contemporary Legal Doctrines

In recent years, the liability of the manufacturer and seller for injury caused by defective products has increased substantially. When a suit is brought against a manufacturer or distributor, legal doctrines of negligence, breach of warranty, or strict liability in tort are usually at issue. Negligence and strict liability have their basis in tort law (law of personal injury or property damage), whereas breach of warranty is in contract law. Even though differences among these three doctrines exist, it is not uncommon to find all three at issue in a product liability suit.

Negligence Doctrine. The basis of liability for *negligence* is the failure of a manufacturer to design, manufacture, or market a product with reasonable care. Failure to exercise reasonable care allows buyers, users, and others within the foreseeable scope of product use to seek recovery for damages. Until the early 1900s, negligence was the only doctrine of liability available to an insured buyer. The courts protected manufacturers from these claims, however, by adopting a rule that required the injured person to be in privity of contract before he or she could bring suit. *Privity of contract* means that a direct contractual relationship must exist between the consumer (injured person) and the manufacturer. Since consumers do not usually purchase directly from a manufacturer, the cases were dismissed by the courts for lack of privity. The privity requirement of negligence cases was abolished by Judge Cardozo in the 1916 case *MacPherson v. Buick Motor Company.*[2]

Today, negligence still remains a major basis for product liability suits. Court decisions indicate that most negligence cases in product liability are based upon faulty production, poor product design, improper packaging, or inadequate warnings or instructions relating to dangers associated with the product.

Distributors may also be held liable for negligence by failing to inspect and give warnings for products, such as lawn mowers and chain saws, which may be inherently dangerous in their normal or foreseeable use. The duty to give a warning of a foreseeable danger of injury arises from the normal or probable use of the product and the likelihood that, unless warned, the user will not ordinarily be aware of such danger.

Breach of Warranty Doctrine. *Breach of warranty* refers to a failure by a manufacturer or seller to satisfy a contractual promise made in connection with the sale of a product.[3] Most managers consider only the express promises or warranties presented as a provision in a contract of sale, a statement in an advertisement or label, or, in certain circumstances, the oral representation made by a salesperson at the time of sale. The sale of products, however, may also be covered by implied promises or warranties which require that the seller's product is either merchantable or fit for a particular purpose as expressed by the buyer.

For a product to be *merchantable,* it must be fit for the "ordinary" purpose for which it is used. For **697** example, a package of hot dogs that contain glass fragments and cause injury to a consumer is not fit for human consumption (its "ordinary" purpose).

The *implied warranty of fitness* for a particular purpose differs from one of merchantability in that it is an indication by the seller that a product is suitable for a buyer's particular need, and the buyer relies on the seller's skill or judgment in making a purchase. For example, if a distributor sells a vehicle to a man knowing that he intends to use it as an off-the-road vehicle and the buyer is injured when the steering mechanism fails during off-the-road use, the seller is liable because the vehicle was not fit for the particular use.

Implied warranties do not apply to contracts for services. Any injuries incurred as a result of improper services must be based on negligence. However, it is not always easy to determine what is a product and what is a service.

Since breach of warranty as a basis for product liability is a contract action, it requires privity of contract and can work to the advantage of the manufacturer. Recently, though, the courts either have stretched the privity concept to a meaningless point or have chosen to abandon it altogether when dealing with implied warranties arising out of the sale of certain inherently dangerous products. For example, in the case *Henningson v. Bloomfield Motors, Inc.,*[4] an auto manufacturer was held liable for injuries caused by a defective steering wheel not only to the purchaser of the automobile but also to injured passengers and bystanders.

Strict Liability in Tort Doctrine. The doctrine of strict liability evolved from the doctrine of negligence in *Greenman v. Yuba Power Products, Inc.*[5] It imposes liability on a seller of defective products that cause injury to users or consumers even though due care has been exercised in their manufacture and sale. A manufacturer is also strictly liable for injuries caused by defective components purchased from others and merely assembled into the final products. In addition, courts have imposed liability on distributors and retailers—including those selling used products. At present, strict liability has normally been applied only to firms regularly engaged in the business of manufacturing, selling, or leasing products, but courts could expand application to include advertising agencies, product testing agencies, etc. Strict liability differs from negligence in that recovery does not require proof of negligence. Therefore, an individual injured by a defective product may recover damages if he or she is able to prove the following:

1. The product was defective.
2. Injury resulted from a defect in the product.
3. The defect existed at the time the product left the manufacturer's/supplier's control.

It is important to emphasize that although all reasonable care was exercised in the manufacturing and selling of a product, the courts may find it defective if it is not safe for expected use and an adequate warning is not provided. *Foreseeable product defects* are dangers that should have been anticipated by the seller, and either the product should have been redesigned or buyers should have been given adequate warnings. The critical factor to be determined in situations where foreseeability is an issue is the limit to what a manfuacturer/seller is expected to foresee.

At present, there is little guidance for most courts to make the final judgment. In the 1978 case of *Barker v. Lull Engineering Co., Inc.,*[6] however, the California Supreme Court developed a formula to determine whether a product is defective in design. First, a product can be deemed defective if it fails to perform as safely as an ordinary consumer can expect when used in a reasonably foreseeable manner. Alternatively, a product may be found to be defective in design when the plaintiff shows that the product's design was the proximate cause of his or her injury and the defendant fails to show that the benefits of the design outweigh the risk of the danger inherent in the design. In all probability, the use of strict liability by injured parties in product liability cases will continue to increase because it frees them from many of the requirements under the doctrines of negligence and breach of warranty.

Market Share Liability. A manufacturer identification problem can arise when an injured party is unable to identify which manufacturer made a defective product because it is essentially the same as that made by other manufacturers or when some time has passed between contact with the product and manifestation of the injury. The California Supreme Court attempted to solve this problem by delineating a new theory called market share liability where each manufacturer could be held liable for damages in proportion to its percentage market share.[7] Few courts have adopted the theory as doctrine because of many unanswered questions in the original decision.

Manufacturer/Distributor Defenses

As noted previously, a manufacturer of a defective product, or the distributor that sold it, may be held liable to the injured person on the basis of breach of warranty, negligence, or strict liability in tort. It is critical to establish which basis of liability is to be relied upon because such determination will govern the defenses available. The legislatures, in their interpretation of statutes, and the courts, in their interpretation of statutes and legal doctrines, have broadened the concept of what makes a product defective. In so doing, they not only have substantially increased the likelihood of product liability claims against manufacturers and distributors but also have limited many of the available defenses. The affirmative defenses that must be proven by manufacturers or distributors to avoid liability are identified below.

Defenses to Breach of Warranty. A number of defenses are available to the manufacturer of allegedly defective products in breach of warranty cases under the Uniform Commercial Code. However, the manufacturer must be aware that under breach of warranty, unlike negligence, the exercise of due care in the manufacture of a product is not a relevant issue. In effect, a manufacturer's liability is absolute if a defect in the product is proven in a breach of warranty case.

Disclaimer of Warranty. One of the principal defenses available to the manufacturer is that no warranties, either express or implied, were given. However, a *disclaimer of warranty* defense will be unacceptable if a prior agreement during negotiations indicated that express warranties existed. In addition, to effectively exclude liability for implied warranties, specific language must be used in the disclaimer. First, in order to exclude the warranty of merchantability, the disclaimer must mention the term *implied warranty of merchantability* and if in writing, it must be conspicuous. Second, to exclude the implied warranty of fitness, it is sufficient to use a general disclaimer indicating that no warranties are given.

Both types of implied warranty are excluded when expressions comparable to "as is" or "with all faults" are used in the disclaimer. Implied warranties are also excluded if the buyer has had the opportunity to identify discoverable defects by examining the product or a sample of it. Additionally, exclusion of implied warranties may exist if past and present contracts between parties exclude all implied warranties or it is industry custom to exclude all implied warranties.

Notice of Breach. A second defense available to the manufacturer is *notice of breach* to the seller. Under this defense, the buyer has a duty to notify the seller of a breach of warranty within a reasonable time after discovery of a defect.

Statute of Limitations. A third defense is the *statute of limitations.* Generally, this requires the injured product user to bring suit within 4 years after delivery of the product.

Defenses to Negligence. The most common defense used in negligence cases is contributory negligence. *Contributory negligence* refers to conduct by an injured product-user which is a contributing cause of the injuries because the user failed to exercise due care. For example, contributory negligence was successfully established in a case against a nightgown manufacturer. A woman suffered severe burns when a combustible nightgown caught fire while she was smoking in bed "in a semi-conscious state induced by . . . a highly potent sleeping pill." The court ruled in favor of the firm because the injured party's conduct contributed to the cause of the accident.[8] It is important to recognize that in most states, the proving of contributory negligence on the injured person's part prevents recovery of any damages for negligence of the manufacturer. This is true even though the manufacturer's negligence may be much greater than that of the injured product-user.

To avoid the seemingly harsh results of the strict application of contributory negligence on an injured product-user, some states have adopted the concept of *comparative negligence.* Under this concept, a jury will determine the percentage of each party's negligence and then allow recovery accordingly.

Another major defense available to the manufacturer in negligence cases is *assumption of risk.* Under this defense, an injured product-user may be denied recovery if he or she assumes the risk of any damage created by a manufacturer's negligence. However, in most cases, this defense requires the manufacturer to prove not only that the injured party knew of the defect creating the danger but also that he or she realized the full extent of the danger.

Defenses to Strict Liability in Tort. The only affirmative defense available to the manufacturer under strict liability in tort is also available in negligence cases: the assumption of risk. As stated previously, a manufacturer is not liable under this defense if an injured product-user had knowledge of the existence of a dangerous defect and voluntarily continued to use the product. The assumption of risk defense is strengthened when the manufacturer shows that adequate warnings were given for all foreseeable uses or misuses of the product.

In contrast to the breach of warranty statute of limitations, an action based on the doctrine of strict liability and negligence must begin within a given period from the time of injury. This period is usually shorter than that provided in product liability cases based upon warranty.

Prospects for Reform. As the courts continue to move from strict liability tort toward something that approaches absolute liability, business has begun to seek legislative relief at the state and federal levels. In 1979, a comprehensive package of product liability reforms was drafted by the Department of Commerce as the Model Uniform Product Liability Act.[9] By 1981, over half the states had passed some form of product liability tort legislation, but no state had adopted this act outright. At the end of 1981, two bills were being drafted in Congress that proposed a federal product liability law. Both bills were built on the provisions of the Model Uniform Product Liability Act. Some of the issues that these bills addressed were: (1) the establishment of the bases for manufacturer liability, (2) manufacturer defenses in liability actions, (3) a statute of limitations, and (4) punitive damages. In October 1982, neither bill passed as each encountered strong opposition from lawyer and consumer groups. Considering the composition of the opposition, it is not likely that a federal reform package will be enacted in the foreseeable future.

An Action Program

A prudent firm can take positive action at least to minimize and perhaps even to eliminate losses. It requires, however, a commitment by the firm to provide a comprehensive program—one that considers product safety from the perspective of the firm as a whole. The mere fact that most product liability suits are due to defective design, faulty production or assembly, improper packaging, or inadequate warnings or instructions relating to product use should be evidence enough to support this view (see Fig. P-3). Since suits normally cut across many functions in the firm, every department must play a key role in contributing to a corporate product safety program— including engineering (research and development), production, purchasing, quality control, advertising, sales and sales service. In addition, this program must be concerned with the entire life cycle of the product—including both the internal cycle (under the manufacturer's control) and the external cycle (after leaving the manufacturer's control).

The following is a framework and list of factors to be considered by a firm when establishing an action program to deal with the product liability challenge:

Establish Objectives. Specific objectives must be established in order to provide sufficient coverage and direction in approaching the product liability challenge. They should include the following:

1. Creation of a safe product
2. Assurance that the product will perform safely under ordinary circumstances
3. Assurance that the product will perform safely under extraordinary circumstances (foreseeable misuse)
4. Assurance of accurate and complete information to the buyer concerning:
   a. Product attributes
   b. Product usage
   c. Product warning
5. Assurance of coordination with channel members to provide:
   a. Accurate information
   b. Accurate training with regard to (1) transportation and handling, (2) demonstration, (3) installation, and (4) service
6. Acquisition of accurate product-market experience records
7. Assurance that when a product safety problem is identified, a contingency plan exists to take action with regard to (1) customers (users), (2)

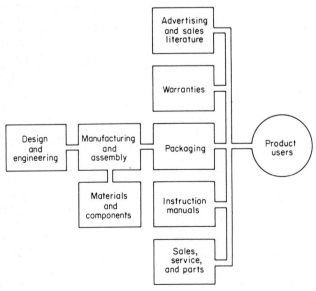

FIG. P-3 Where product liability suits arise. (Adapted from "How to Control Product Liability Losses," *Journal of American Insurance,* vol. 52, no. 2, p. 21, Summer 1976.)

product, (3) channel members, and (4) government agencies

8. Active support of constructive steps that can be taken to remove inequities relating to product liability (safety)

Assign Organizational Responsibility. The placement of organizational responsibility for product safety is critical to its success. It must be placed in the organization where those assigned responsibility can be held accountable. The foregoing comments suggest the following:

1. Responsibility for product liability must rest with top management, since it cuts across all functions and can arise at every stage of the product's development, manufacture, and service life.

2. Responsibility for product liability may be vested in one individual or a number of individuals brought together as a product safety committee (the size and structure of the committee must be adapted to the particular needs of the company).

3. The size and complexity of the organizational structure responsible for product liability is dependent upon the particular needs of the company. However, it must enable the firm to achieve its established product liability program objectives.

4. The product liability program actually assumes the appearance of a product liability audit. It is not a one-time affair, but rather, a continuous process used to isolate areas where additional work is needed. For example, it is necessary to evaluate not only new product designs but also older designs to ensure they incorporate current safety standards. Thus, the responsibility for accomplishment must be given organizational permanency.

Operationalize the Objectives. In order to achieve the established objectives, a plan of action must be developed that will identify these goals and describe how they are to be accomplished. The tasks include the following:

1. A written corporate policy on product safety should be communicated to all employees, stressing the company's commitment to design, develop, manufacture, and market safe products (product safety must be an integral part of all product decision areas).

2. Company standards should be developed for product design, development, and quality control. These standards should meet or exceed federal-, state-, local-, or industry-recommended or mandatory safety standards.

3. Quality standards should be stated in writing for all production-related tasks, including the purchase of raw materials and components, manufacture, assembly, packaging, and shipping.

4. Carefully supervised product-use tests should be performed, representing use of the product under both ordinary and extraordinary circumstances (foreseeable but unintended use).

5. Product information generated by the firm should be reviewed for clarity, accuracy, and completeness. This information includes technical manuals, instructions and directions, warranties, labels, advertisements, service manuals, and product claims (printed information must include complete disclosure of product information and must not overstate or misstate the product's capabilities).

6. Information intended to warn the user about hazards that cannot be eliminated by design should be conspicuously placed on the product, be presented in understandable language and symbols, and last the life of the product.

7. Close relationships with channel members should be promoted and maintained by providing:

    a. Relevant product literature to channel members (training sessions should be provided if necessary). Distributors, however, must *not* modify service or advertise a product without authorization.

    b. Skilled salespeople.

    c. Skilled field-service technicians.

8. The company should maintain a vital record file for each product, including sales records, sales literature, design specifications and drawings, purchase orders, technical manuals, instruction and training manuals, modification releases, performance tests, inspection controls, field-service reports, recall campaigns, and packaging and shipping instructions.

9. The company should monitor relevant environments, including:

    a. Product/customer environment by (1) reviewing submitted quality control reports; (2) receiving warranty-card purchase data and comments from customers; (3) reviewing customer complaints (a follow-up when an accident or near accident related to the product is reported); and (4) reviewing information gathered from salespeople, channel members, customers, and competitors.

    b. External environment by reviewing (1) professional and trade association reports; (2) industry journals; and (3) reports of government agencies (i.e., Consumer Product Safety Commission, Federal Trade Commission, etc.).

Prepare for Contingency Events. Implementation of programs in product liability does not eliminate entirely the risk of costly suits; it will, however, reduce the impact of suits. A successful program requires anticipating future events by:

1. Investing in adequate liability insurance written through a reliable company by a knowledgeable agent or broker.

2. Establishing a plan for quickly notifying distributors and customers when a defect is identified and specifying what procedure should be followed in order to have the product replaced or repaired. This information must also be relayed to meet the requirements of relevant government agencies.

3. Establishing a predetermined and tested product recall plan for a defective product, which includes the following:

   a. Task force responsible for product recall.

   b. Information systems for identifying sources and types of product-market information.

   c. Recall strategy for identifying, contacting distributors and customers, and picking up products.

   d. Financing strategy consistent with the company's resources and the potential costs of recall.

   3. Promotional program to minimize the effects of the product recall.

4. Establishing a plan for using corporate counsel not only in the development of product liability prevention programs but also as a defender of the company's existing lawsuits. (In the latter role, the corporate counsel is the liaison officer with the insurance carrier, assistant to trial counsel, and investigator and coordinator within the company.)

5. Supporting legislation that establishes time limits on product liability claims, dollar limits on certain types of damages, and limits on lawyers' contingent fees that are linked to the size of the settlement.

Conclusion

The trend of public policy as seen in new legislation and court decisions has established that the marketing of defective products results in a major risk of injury to customers. The trend has also established that the manufacturer and the distributor are better able than the consumer to assume or insure against the risk of loss arising from defective products. The critical issue management must recognize is that product liability is here to stay as a major and expensive risk of doing business. Given the diversity of business firms, the complexity of their product lines, and the varying level of resources available to them, only a general framework regarding product liability has been outlined here. To deal with this issue demands that each firm develop an intelligent, creative, and carefully planned program. Only through such an approach can management hope to establish an integrated and effective strategy to meet the challenge of product liability.

See also Consumerism and consumer protection legislation; Government regulations, uniform commercial code; Insurance and risk management; Product planning and development; Quality management.

NOTES

[1] "Calculating Your Liability Risk," *Modern Packaging,* vol. 48, October 1975, p. 10.

[2] First court decision which held that the privity requirement afforded no protection to a negligent manufacturer or seller if the product which caused injury was the type of product that is reasonably certain to be dangerous if negligently manufactured. *MacPherson v. Buick Motor Co.,* 217 N. Y. 382, 111 N. E. 1050 (1916).

[3] All warranties in the sale of goods arise from the Uniform Commercial Code—Article on Sales, enacted by essentially all states.

[4] *Henningson v. Bloomfield Motors, Inc.,* 32 N.J. 358, 161 A.2d 69 (1960).

[5] *Greenspan v. Yuba Power Products, Inc.,* 337 p. 2d 897 (1963).

[6] *Barker v. Lull Engineering Co., Inc.* 573 p. 2d 443 (1978).

[7] *Sindell v. Abbott Laboratories,* 607 p. 2d 924 (1980).

[8] *Dallison v. Sears, Roebuck and Co.,* 313 F. 2d 343 (Colorado Law) (1962).

[9] *44 Fed. Reg. 62,714 (1979).*

REFERENCES

Atkeson, Timothy, and George Neidich: "A Status Report on Proposals for a Federal Product Liability Act," *The Business Lawyer,* vol. 38, February 1983, pp. 623–639.

Gray, Irwin, with Albert L. Bases, Charles H. Martin, and Alexander Sternberg: *Product Liability: A Management Response,* American Management Association, New York, 1975.

Safety in the Marketplace, Washington, D.C.

Many associations have made available for a nominal charge product liability awareness pamphlets and program manuals, such as the following:

  Product Liability Manual, American Mutual Insurance Alliance, 20 North Wacker Drive, Chicago 60606. $2.

  Product Liability Pamphlet, Defense Research Institute, 1100 West Wells Street, Milwaukee, Wis. 53233. $.50.

Lonnie L. Ostrom, *Arizona State University*

Product Planning and Development

Product planning is a process, not a department. It is an integral part of the strategic management process of industry, education, and government. In some cases, it is heavily involved with the management of innovation (as with electronics)—while in others, it is concerned with reliably replicating successful business patterns (such as fast food). Regardless of the economic sector, it generates profits or benefits by identifying customer wants and needs and translating them into product and/or service specifications that provide the desired market share within each market segment (limited by the resources of the firm, the moves of competition, and other uncontrollable events). Figure P-4 sketches the process and organizes the discussion in this entry.

Broad-Gauge Monitoring

The process (of product planning) has to be aware of the world around it. Therefore, monitor systems are needed for technology, competition, customer values, the company's own capabilities, and uncontrollable external-force factors.

However, a problem arises: Most monitor assignments ask that you "watch everything—and still do your job." That is unrealistic, if not impossible. Monitor systems must be focused. They must say, "Engineering, look for this" or "If that doesn't happen by the third quarter, alert us." The job of developing a focus is what forecasting can do. Different forecasting methods, however, are needed for each type of monitor.

Technology forecasts can be based on expert judgments, extrapolations, Delphi surveys, decision models, or trend impact analysis. Competitive strategies can never be "known" (for legal and ethical reasons), but one can develop and vigorously test strategy hypotheses for each competitor, applying the scientific method to business. The customer value system can be estimated using conventional market research tools and then verified by successfully simulating historic purchase patterns using a decision model that relates customer values (weights) and competitive product/service ratings. Since this

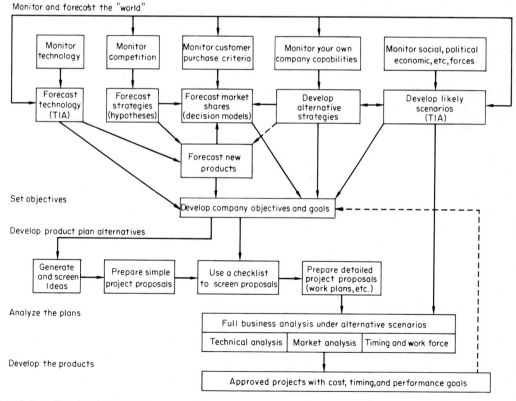

FIG. P-4 The planning process.

future cannot be accurately predicted, a monolithic view of the future is dangerous, and alternative scenarios must be developed. Finally, a company can develop meaningful strategies that anticipate expected events by using the forecasts to anticipate new products, new competitive pushes, new economic conditions, new customer values, and new market shares.

Skepticism is a typical reaction to such a comprehensive forecasting system. Nevertheless, each of the forecasts is implicitly assumed whenever a decision is made to develop a new product. By making the assumptions explicit—even without a single forecasting tool—it becomes possible to trace which assumptions were right (or wrong) and to rely more (or less) heavily on an expert for those assumptions (forecasts) in the future.

The process is always executed—but sometimes it is more intuitive than rational or procedural.

Set Objectives. When using monitors and forecasts, the setting of objectives and goals is easier. Goals should be clear and unambiguous, attainable but not too easy. Objectives like these help to build an atmosphere of success based on focused efforts and well-developed plans.

Develop Product Plan Alternatives. Without ideas, product alternatives cannot be generated. Developing alternatives requires a formal system to capture and screen ideas—otherwise, they escape. The system should also employ a screening checklist to keep engineers, designers, and others involved in the process focused on the needs of the organization.

Next, there should be a simple project proposal system. A one-page form provides enough "paperwork" to describe the idea, tell what it will accomplish, and estimate the research and development (R&D) effort needed. Marketing can estimate the sales impact(s). All these steps can be prepared quickly, with no fancy analysis. Precise numbers are not needed at this stage. Ranges of estimates are "good enough." The resulting project proposals can be screened using a checklist approach. Only then does a formal project proposal need to be prepared with enough detail for a full business analysis.

Developing a system that screens new ideas, and that screens project proposals before creating a formal project proposal (work plans, tasks, equipment needs, etc.), saves money and constantly teaches its values to the participants.

Prepare a Business Analysis. A business analysis can often be divided into four parts: (1) a technical analysis, (2) a market analysis, (3) a manufacturing analysis, and (4) a financial analysis. The first three are usually conducted in parallel, and are often "knockout" analyses.

Technical analysis asks: Can the technology be developed? Are new engineers needed? How many engineers are needed for how long? How can development be speeded? What is the probability of technical success? Who else is working on the technology(ies)?

Market analysis asks: What will the sales volume be in the first 5 years? What must the price be? Are the features right? What new sales tools are needed? What new sales personnel are needed?

Manufacturing analysis asks: What new equipment and facilities are needed? What new personnel are needed? What timing is involved? What new processes are needed? How will quality control, production control, purchasing, shipping/receiving, etc., be impacted?

Financial analysis is usually deterministic, using a "most likely" set of estimates. Using computerized "what-if" spread-sheet programs, several alternative scenarios can be analyzed deterministically. A more sophisticated approach generates a probabilistic forecast for each of the scenarios and results in a risk profile for each proposal for each scenario.[1] Figure P-5 shows three risk profiles under one scenario. Alternative 1 has high risk and high payback. Alternative 3 has low risk and low payback.

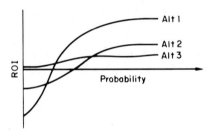

FIG. P-5 Risk profiles.

Using risk profiles expressed in return on investment (ROI) and/or monetary units, top management can focus on the reasons underlying the alternative curves and select one that best suits the needs of the business. Application of portfolio theory (spreading risk among alternative opportunities) can result in a set of new products that will best meet the objectives of the company.

A detailed financial analysis uses the refined estimates of effort that come from the technical analysis, market analysis, and manufacturing analysis, and generates estimates of effort for top management, finance, human relations, etc. It provides the basis for a complete analysis.

Project development should be initiated only after a successful business analysis. It requires a complete set of management controls on timing, staffing, progress, budgets, etc., and it is directly incorporated into the objectives and goals of the company.

The process of product planning having been described in sweeping terms, it is necessary to point out that no company has a product planner with such a scope of responsibility. Only the company president can have an overview of the entire process. Only by understanding the process, however, can a product planner be effective. Finally, the process of planning should develop alternatives, provide for contingencies, and allow for management flexibility.

Tools for Product Planning

Good product planning calls for the use of certain tools. This section examines some of the most effective ones and discusses the problems and advantages they present.

1. *Strategy Hypothesis Development and Competitive Monitors.* Porter, in his book *Competitive Strategy*, indicated that there are three fundamental strategies: market share dominance, lowest cost producer, and segment dominance.[2] Some other company product strategies to consider are technical leadership (Bausch & Lomb soft lens); best second-in or "don't rush to develop a new market" (IBM-PC); emphasis on cash flow or profits (perhaps to fund a major new development); acquisition; and divestiture.

There are dozens of ways to generate hypotheses: Conduct a computerized literature search; read; interview people in the industry, such as financial planners, editors, industry consultants, academics, suppliers, distributors, customers, and former employees of a company. Attend shows, meetings, and seminars. Find out who is leading in the technology, who is best at manufacturing, who has good sales and services, who is best at planning and strategy. Learn the names and backgrounds of the key decision makers, read their public statements, read the annual reports, analyze real productivity gains (versus pronouncements), determine their organizational strengths and weaknesses, look for labor problems, look for management's track record, etc.

The time to begin to generate alternative strategy hypotheses is while talking and analyzing. List them, combine them, test them. Meantime, muster facts to support or refute the hypotheses. Place emphasis on the search for fundamental characteristics that define the distinctive competence of the company and its products and/or services in the market. A recent price change, for example, is not significant unless it supports the strategic positioning of the company. Except when a new management team has taken over, strategies are often defined by long-term patterns. Look for them.

One last point: Strategies must be supportive of the reasons customers buy. These are documented later in the screening checklists in the subsection "Screening."

2. *Trend Impact Analysis (TIA).* This analysis is a way to change a basic forecast (trend extrapolation, regression model, etc.) by incorporating judgmental impacts for new events (surprises) that have some probability of occurrence. For example, the demand for diesel engines would change if another Middle East crisis created another fuel shortage. TIA relies upon expert estimates of the following: the probability of an event's occurring; the time until the first impact occurs (lags often occur); the time until the maximum impact; the level of the maximum impact; the time until the steady-state impact; and the level of the steady-state impact. A computer program can easily combine the probability of occurrence (by year) with the impacts for all possible events, and generate a new (probabilistic) forecast. The result is a forecast of a "most likely" future with confidence limits (10th, 50th, and 90th percentiles, for example).

TIA is also useful for developing sales forecasts, technical forecasts, and scenarios. One important feature is that the same event, with the same probabilities, can have a different impact on each of several different forecasts. It is this capability that makes internally consistent scenario development possible.

TIA models are fast and inexpensive to construct or use and are available via time-sharing or as a microcomputer program. They are excellent as a complement to spread-sheet, what-if models in that they provide a structured discipline for developing the alternatives.

3. *Decision Modeling.* Decision modeling is used to predict new-product market share based on a historic calibration of "why people buy" (based on the market's decision criteria). The criteria are listed and weighted. The historic products are listed and rated. Then (in one type of model, at least) the ratings are multiplied by the weights, and added together. The results of the addition of the multiplications are normalized so that the sum of all the historic products adds to 1. This number is called the relative perceived value (RPV) and is shown in Table P-1.

When RPV is plotted against historic market share, the S-shaped curve of Fig. P-6 occurs.

The reasons for the shape of the curve are rooted in human psychology, innovation diffusion, and marketing theory. The models can be additive, exponential, capacity-limited, or mathematically mixed. The model experts need to talk to the planners in enough detail to permit a model to be constructed. The calibration to history—the scientific testing of the hypothesis—gives the model credibility and allows it to be used for forecasting. The process of calibration is not simple. It requires that (1) the historically changing customer value weights be tracked and (2) different product attributes be identified in historic perspective. Forecasting with a decision model

TABLE P-1   One Calculation of Relative Perceived Value

Criteria	Weight	Product A	Product B	Product C	Sum
Price	10	6	8	10	n/a
Speed	8	9	10	4	n/a
Past experience	6	10	7	4	n/a
Multiplication sum		192	202	156	550
Relative perceived value		.35	.37	.28	1.00

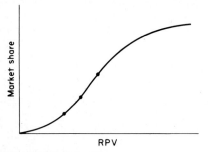

FIG. P-6   An RPV-market share curve.

requires forecasts (using TIA, expert judgments, etc.) of the future product characteristics *and* future customer value systems.

Unlike TIA, this powerful integrating tool is not inexpensive, but the results are impressive. It has resulted in a $300 million new-product venture, several acquisitions, and many changes in product directions. It is new—and it works.

Finally, it should be kept in mind that a market segment is, by definition, a homogeneous set of criteria weights. An added value of a decision model, then, is that it helps to sharpen the planner's understanding of market segments.

4. *Idea Generation.* Creativity and the innovation process have benefited from a great deal of attention ranging from brainstorming to forced relationships, from similes to word association, from Kepner-Tregoe problem solving to group dynamics, and from expert inventors to feature combinations/additions. This attention tends to ignore, however, a startling fact. The leaders in an industry rarely develop their own product replacements. For example, Detroit did not market fuel-efficient cars; the vacuum-tube makers did not invent the transistor; Bell Labs did not invent the integrated circuit; Texas Instruments did not invent the microprocessor; Intel did not invent the microcomputer (and neither did IBM or DEC); Kodak did not invent instant film; the steel industry did not invent plastics. The message is clear: Many obsoleted or weakened industries are routinely ''surprised'' by superior products from new competitors. The question for

innovators must be: What new idea can obsolete our business? Computer time-share services are already being made obsolete by microcomputer software. Fiber optics may replace both coaxial cable and satellites. High-powered satellite weapons may neutralize ballistic missiles. Voice-input computers and automatic spellers threaten secretaries. Sears is becoming the largest savings bank in the country. Thus, change is truly the only constant.

Turning from forecasts to idea management, the first task is to focus the idea-generating capabilities within the organization. This focus can be achieved by setting clear objectives and by stating evaluation-criteria weights. Regrettably, to prevent the stifling of ideas, most managements will not weight the criteria; some will not even identify them. Consequently, the planners must generate a list of criteria by examining past decisions. A list having been created, a vote can be taken (using a Delphi survey) to establish weights. The weights can be reviewed by top management after comparing them with the decision model weights found by calibrating market-share history. Alternatively, a set of criteria and weights can be taken from the literature, then modified as management accepts or rejects new-product ideas and preliminary proposals. In this manner, criteria weight can be inferred.

When the attention of the creative people has been focused, it is necessary to give them ways to submit their ideas. Log books are the historic approach, and they continue to be needed. However, an idea submission form compatible with both log book and patent disclosure requirements can be used to permit quick product planning feedback and idea evaluation. Finally, there is the requirement for the initial, simple, product development proposal forms discussed earlier.

5. *Scenario Development.* Scenario development should narrow its consideration to the two or three things that could most affect the business. For example, stockbrokers can worry about direct-stockholder or pension-fund computer access to the over-the-counter market (technologically possible); Digital Equipment Company can worry about 32-bit microcomputers from competitors like Radio Shack or IBM; Exxon can

worry about fuel surpluses and shortages; GM can worry about car designs that allow a foreign competitor to build a car with less than half the labor and one-third the capital required by GM.

Scenarios should first identify "big-swinger" items, but they cannot stop there. If a fuel shortage should occur, for example, fuel prices would increase; inflation would rise; social security would get into trouble again; taxes would rise; the gross national product (GNP) would slow, etc. To balance the trade deficit, agricultural exports would climb; plastics would convert to coal-based hydrocarbons; diesel engines would increase; airborne particulates would increase; unemployment would rise; Mexico would be coveted as a source of fuel and conflict could occur; etc. A comprehensive scenario reaches every part of the environment.

Using TIA, an organization can assure itself of internally consistent numbers, but the numbers are not the issue; attitudes are. The customer value system could shift dramatically, and the plan should be pliable enough to allow such change without obsolescence.

Since no one can really forecast the future, a company must be prepared for alternative futures. It is a good idea to build three scenarios and plan for them. They can be created internally or purchased. Each alternative strategy should be analyzed within each scenario. Surprisingly, some product strategies work well in all scenarios, while others work only in one or two. That realization provides true insight.

From an integrated planning standpoint, the same TIA events that cause scenario differences can also be used to impact the forecasts of customer value systems used in decision modeling. Thus, market shares, with and without new products, can be evaluated, as can competitive thrusts that are not countered by the new plans.

6. *Screening.* Screening criteria fall into three categories: (1) customer values; (2) company values; and (3) company capabilities.

Customer values include price (total and payment per month versus competition—"affordability"); performance/new features (speed, capacity, precision, etc.); ease of usage; familiar usage patterns; convenience, comfort, and economy of operation (including the cost of repairs and the time lost for repairs); reliability/durability (quality); appearance; safety (ease of error versus consequences); conspicuousness/inconspicuousness; delivery assurance; degree of market differentiation (suitability for good advertising copy); advertising awareness/credibility; social value (often low in importance to buyers); service availability/speed; brand/company credibility (past experience); and the credibility of the benefits.

Company values include legality (sometimes there are uncertainties); technical exclusivity (patents); potential competition (now and later); trade secrets; cost versus competition (now and later); investment required (compared with competition); integration (vertical or horizontal); ease of service; cost of warranty; market size; market growth rate, company sales potential (expected, minimum, and maximum by year); time to achieve 80 percent of plant capacity (assuming overtime or multiple shifts?); price trend (versus cost); expected market share by customer segment (now and later); market share of larger competitors (or the next two smaller competitors); product leadership (real or perceived); product importance to customers (critical products are worth more but delivery assurance and quality become more important as well); suitability/availability of sales/service organization; degree of current product substitution; expected life of the new product; expected life of the new investment; product line "fit" (all new?); customer "fit" (serving existing or new customer segments?); expected change in market share (with and without the new product); marketing effort versus competition; and R&D effort versus marketing effort. Finally, the financial values must be considered: profit, asset turnover, cash flow requirements, etc.

Company capabilities include availability of R&D personnel; suitability of existing plant, equipment, personnel, and processes; presence of a product champion with adequate resources for follow-on; market research, competitive analysis; prototype engineering; market testing; pilot production; production launch; market launch (advertising, promotion, collateral material, etc.); adequacy of financial resources; ability of sales to sell it.

These screening criteria are directly related to new-product success. R. G. Cooper analyzed 195 new industrial product successes and failures. He performed a regression analysis using 77 variables grouped into 18 categories.[3] He concluded that the single most important dimension leading to new-product success is product uniqueness and superiority. Market knowledge and market proficiency also play a critical role in new-product outcomes. The third most significant dimension that impacts on success and failure is the technical one, technical production synergy, and proficiency.

Note that the screening criteria are appropriate for decision modeling. For example, in studies performed for private clients during the last 6 years, The Futures Group (the author's firm) has found that it is possible to describe the value system of customer segments based on 6 to 12 factors that the market considers important. One study that forecasted the market share of competing office systems for the next 10 years, for example, identified the existence of 10 different market segments, each having a different value system that had an impact upon their evaluation of the alternative products. The attributes upon which each segment placed different weights were price, speed, durability, operating cost, ease of usage, product compatibility with existing system, product features, and product substitution impacts.

Summary Guidelines

In addition to the systematic approach to product development (outlined above), there are a number of other observations and admonitions that will improve the product planning process:

1. The greatest part of R&D expense is wasted because most new products fail, a fact that can be attributed to poor planning.

2. A different plan emphasis is needed for products in different stages of their life cycle; for example, quality during introduction, advertising during growth, cost reduction during maturity, new models and features during saturation, and service during decline.

3. Each market segment requires an integrated approach. A quality brand image, for example, does not belong in a discount store, should not be blister-packed, and should not be advertised in the classified ads; nor should it have the fewest features.

4. Market research should be treated with caution. It is limited by time, talent, money, objectivity, and the courage to produce results that may be unpopular. Be wary of your own sales "experts." Often they respond with one very costly word: "More" (more performance, lower price, more models, more . . .). Use their inputs, but check them to gain confidence.

5. A narrow view of competition is typical, yet every consumer knows that a new camera may be competing with a new stereo for his or her dollars; a new boat, with a camper; a new car, with a patio; crackers, with chips; furniture, with a vacation. The real competition is for the customer's expenditure, not for a percentage of the existing market; a good planner will try to expand the market (because profits rise faster then).

6. Pragmatism is a good watchword in product planning. Do not use sophisticated planning technology when simple methods are appropriate. Be aware of the techniques available, but choose a level of sophistication appropriate to your company and the problems at hand.

See also Brands and brand names; Consumer behavior, managerial relevance of; Forecasting business conditions; Innovation and creativity; Market analysis; Marketing research; Patents and valuable intangible rights; Product and service pricing; Research and development management.

NOTES

[1] David B. Hertz, "Risk Analysis in Capital Investment," *Harvard Business Review*, September–October 1979.

[2] Michael E. Porter, *Competitive Strategy*, The Free Press, division of Macmillan Publishing Company, Glencoe, Ill., 1980.

[3] R. G. Cooper, "The Dimensions of Industrial New Product Success and Failure," *Journal of Marketing*, Summer 1979.

REFERENCES

Carson, J. W., and T. Richardson: *Industrial New Product Development*, John Wiley, New York, 1978.

Douglas, G., P. Kemp, and J. Cook: *Systematic New Product Development*, John Wiley, New York, 1978.

Pessemier, E. A.: *Product Management: Strategy and Operations*, John Wiley, New York, 1982.

CHARLES J. MATHEY, *The Futures Group*

Product and Service Pricing

Price is the result of many influences. Effective pricing takes the combined skills of the economist, the accountant, the psychologist, the sociologist, the market researcher, and the lawyer. Many pricing concepts cross discipline lines, but for the sake of simplicity, they have been assigned in this entry to four groups: economic pricing concepts, accounting pricing concepts, marketing pricing concepts, and legal pricing concepts.

Economic Inputs to Pricing

There is no pricing idea more basic in economics than the concept of a *demand curve*. This is an expression of the relationship between various prices a firm might set and the quantity of goods or services it can sell at those prices. The expression can be a table, a graph, an algebraic equation, or a verbal description. Firms usually have some idea about their demand curve.

With few exceptions, however, these curves are not nearly so well defined as traditional economic analysis would require. Therefore, another economic concept is more useful in most pricing situations. To change price, a firm must consider its product's demand elasticity. *Demand elasticity* explains how a firm's quantity sold will change if it changes price. More precisely, the term can be defined as describing how revenue (item price times quantity sold) changes when price changes. Will revenue go up? That is, does quantity sold change only slightly if price goes up? Will revenue stay the same? Or, will it drop?

The reaction of buyers to price changes in part depends on several other concepts in the area of economics. The economist identifies at least four types of markets a pricer may face: perfect competition, monopolistic competition, oligopoly, and monopoly. These market structures exist because of reactions by competitors and because of characteristics of a firm's products.

Perfect Competition Conditions. In the perfectly competitive market, a firm is one of many relatively small sellers. Each firm's product is similar enough to those of other firms that forms of promotion, such as advertising, are of little importance. In this type of market, prices tend to be low enough so that extended price competition would gain little for any firm. In addition, the reaction of customers to a price rise by any one firm would be to buy elsewhere. The nature of the product is such that little brand loyalty exists.

The relatively small size of each firm in this type of market suggests another characteristic of the products that are sold: Usually, their manufacture requires little, if any, specialized skills or equipment. In other words, products or services requiring large inputs of equipment suitable for a specific production process or of highly trained people tend not to be sold in perfectly competitive markets. Generally, products or services sold in these markets permit two decisions:

1. If our firm is losing money, should we sell at the existing price or should we cease operations immediately?

2. Should our firm look for other ways to use the capital we have invested in this product?

The answer to the first question depends on whether or not the firm will do better by shutting down the product line immediately. To the extent a firm wishes to base an evaluation of "better" on income statement effects, the action chosen depends on whether the revenue it receives from operating exceeds the incremental cost (defined in the next section) of operating. Most firms have fixed commitments, such as rent, which they cannot avoid by shutting down. Therefore, a firm which shows a net loss from certain operations should consider the alternatives.

The second question involves a longer-range decision. Since the firm's equipment and/or skills are not unique to one product or service, the firm should frequently consider whether it is earning enough income to warrant staying with the existing product or service. Other potential uses of a firm's abilities should be considered.

Monopolistic Competition. The monopolistic competitor faces a slightly more responsive situation. Some brand loyalty can be created in markets of this type so that some price differences can exist among successful firms selling virtually the same physical product or service. Factors such as convenience of location, quality differences perceived by customers, and minor service differences can result in a monopolistic competitive market. In addition to the questions faced by the perfect competitor, the monopolistic competitor also must attempt to balance price adjustments unique to its firm with product differentiation.

Oligopoly Situations. The most complex pricing situation is faced by the oligopolist, which is one of few firms in a market where other competitors can and will retaliate to price adjustments. Having few firms in a market frequently means that the equipment is too costly and/or specialized for other firms to produce the product. Auto and steel manufacturers and petroleum refiners are classic examples. The costliness and the nature of the specialized equipment make it financially difficult, and also quite risky, to enter the market. If the venture fails, the entering firm cannot easily dispose of the equipment.

Because of the potential for retaliation, price adjustments are few and rigid. Oligopolists often resort to price leadership. By voluntary action, one firm's price adjustments are followed by all other firms in the industry. No formal agreement exists. In fact, there are cases in which a would-be price leader has had to recall an announced price change because others have failed to follow. Price leaders often announce their price changes in response to major events which tend to affect all firms in the industry, such as an oil embargo or signing a new labor contract. A popular pricing technique for the price leader is target rate-of-return pricing (defined later under "Full-Cost Pricing"). Price followers do not need a price computation method per se. Instead, they need a method to evaluate the proposed change by the price leader.

Monopoly Situations. The monopolist is almost like the price leader. Although the only firm in an industry, the monopolist still faces possible retaliation. One generally thinks of the monopolist as being created by the government and hence, as being severely regulated. It can also exist, however, because of geographic factors. In this case, the monopolist is the only firm close enough to supply the product or service. A computer repair specialist in an isolated community may be a monopolist.

Government-regulated monopolies face the retaliation of the regulating body if price adjustments are unreasonable. Geographic monopolies face the threat of competitors entering the market and destroying the monopoly position. Both these possibilities have to be considered when the monopolist sets a price.

The economist also provides definitions for intermarket reactions. In addition to the effect of the pricing decision on the firm's own markets, it must be aware that other markets may also be affected. The terms *complementary product* and *substitute product* describe two potential situations. Complementary products are those products whose unit sales respond in the same way to a price change in either one. Hamburger and hamburger buns may be an example of complementary products. If the price of hamburger rises, the quantity of hamburger sold tends to drop. Quite possibly, people will also buy fewer hamburger buns, too, because they plan to make fewer hamburgers. This situation creates several important problems. First, a firm may find price changes in other markets influencing its sales. Second, if the firm makes products that are complements (such as automobiles and auto parts), the impact of a change in one segment of the business on the other segment must be carefully considered. The effect of shutting down an unprofitable segment may be devastating. Suppose an auto manufacturer quits providing spare parts. One would expect a serious decline in the sales of that automobile.

Substitute products prompt the opposite behavior. A price rise in one product causes an increase in sales of a substitute product because buyers will switch to it. Once again, interfirm and intrafirm reactions to price changes must be evaluated.

Pricing Inputs from Accounting

Among the key inputs to pricing provided by the accountant is product–cost information. The role of product cost varies from market to market. For example, the perfect competitor may wish to know a cost representing a minimum below which production should be shut down. The price leader may use a cost as the base on which to set a price. For these different purposes, different costs are appropriate. In this section, several product costs that firms might use in various situations are described. Also, two price-setting methods which build directly on the accountant's cost figures are discussed.

Basic Accounting Methods. The first three cost terms—marginal cost, variable product cost, and incremental cost—have some definite similarities. *Marginal cost* is usually considered to be an economics concept, but it is a figure which a firm's accountant might approximate. It is the increase in total cost which will occur if the firm produces one additional unit. Two important points concerning marginal cost are: (1) Marginal cost is concerned with one-unit changes in output; and (2) marginal cost is dependent on the level of activity at which it is measured. A product's marginal cost may vary significantly over the levels of activity at which a firm usually operates. Since a firm usually does not attempt to decide whether to produce just one more unit or how to price just one of its units, the next two product costs are more useful in product pricing.

A *variable product cost* is a per-unit cost computed by adding together those unit-cost items, such as material, labor, and certain overhead items, which are incurred in increasing amounts as activity increases. For a merchandising firm, this cost would include such items as the cost of the product it sells plus the shipping cost incurred to obtain the product. There are two key differences between variable product cost and marginal cost. First, if, at a given level, a firm must incur a large cost to increase capacity, that unusual increase will be considered part of the marginal cost. It is not a part of the variable product cost. Only costs that respond to unit-by-unit changes in production over broad ranges are considered variable costing product costs. Second, variable product costs are usually averages; therefore, they are assumed to be the same for each unit over broad ranges of activities. This assumption is generally reasonable.

The *incremental cost* is the total amount of cost increase expected for a significant change in production. It, like the marginal cost, depends on the level from which a firm begins to measure the incremental cost. Unlike the marginal cost, it is the cost change resulting from a change of more than one unit.

Example of Differences. A brief example clarifies these differences. Suppose a firm faces the following situation:

Production, units	Total cost, dollars
400	4000
401	4010
402	5020
403	5030

The marginal cost of producing the 401st unit is $10 ($4010 − $4000), the change in total cost due to producing one more unit when the firm already produces 400 units. The marginal cost of the 402d unit is $1010 ($5020 − $4010). The variable product cost appears to be $10, which is the average increase observed except from unit 401 to 402. The incremental cost of producing two additional units when the firm already produces 401 is $1020 ($5030 − $4010).

For various forms of pricing, these costs represent minimums below which price should not be set. The result of pricing below these figures is receiving less from selling the product than the firm must spend to obtain the product to sell. Pricing below this level is the basis of the old joke of the retailer's saying, "I sell my widgets for $1 and I buy them from my wholesaler for $1.10, but I make up for that in volume." Each unit sold increases the firm's net loss. There is no way volume can improve this situation.

Below-Minimum Pricing. There are, however, several situations in which a firm may rationally price below this minimum. One such situation occurs when a firm has dropped a product and is trying to get rid of existing stock. Here, the firm has no intention of acquiring additional units, and the only question is how to dispose of the units at the best price. Even if the price is below the minimum, the firm is concerned with getting rid of the units, and any price received is usually better than not disposing of them.

A second below-minimum pricing situation can exist with complementary goods. If the firm prices below minimum on one good, it does so because its complementary good sells for well above its minimum. In this case, it has assumed that the low price of the below-minimum good increases the sales volume of the above-minimum good. One still needs to ask whether the sales of the above-minimum good are increased enough to justify selling its complement at all.

A third below-minimum situation exists when a firm temporarily prices low to gain sales from customers who are expected to develop brand loyalty. In this case, the firm must be sure that it will be able to successfully raise prices later to compensate for the temporary below-minimum price.

If a firm is pricing a group of units, such as a special order or a unique job to be bid upon, the incremental cost is the appropriate minimum to consider. For products that are part of its normal product line, the variable product cost, often increased by nonproduction variable costs such as commissions and shipping costs, is the appropriate minimum.

These costs do not, however, assure that the firm will earn a profit or that it should continue to stay in the product any longer than it takes to terminate existing production commitments such as rent or salaries. The full cost is a better figure for that purpose.

Full-Cost Pricing. The *full cost* is a unit cost which includes the variable product cost, variable nonproduction costs, and an allocation of fixed costs. It is an average operating cost. A price above this figure means the firm is earning a profit. Over the long run, this is the minimum a firm must receive if it is to consider remaining in the current product.

Markup Pricing. Two common pricing policies use the full cost as a basis for setting price. The most common policy is straight markup pricing. In *straight markup pricing*, the pricer adds an amount to the full cost which is believed to represent a sufficient amount of income per unit sold. This markup can be either a fixed dollar amount or a percentage of cost.

In some cases, the markup is added to a product cost, such as an absorption-costing product cost or a variable product cost, instead of to the full cost. These product costs include fewer cost items than does the full cost. The fewer the costs included in the product cost, the higher the necessary markup. For example, if a firm uses a product cost which does not

include the cost of shipping its product, the markup must represent not only an average profit per unit but also an average shipping cost per unit.

Target Rate-of-Return Pricing. The second method built on full cost is a refinement of straight markup pricing and tends to be used by larger firms. In target rate-of-return pricing, the markup is a per-unit average of a firm's desired return. The firm determines what rate of return it wishes to earn on its assets. This return is multiplied by the assets it uses in its operations. This amount is then divided by the projected annual sales or by an average of projected annual sales for several years to obtain the desired markup. When the markup is added to full cost, this sum yields the target rate-of-return price.

These two pricing methods yield a computed price for price leaders and firms whose sales volume is only slightly affected by price. Further, these figures may be used as long-range targets. If a firm cannot, on the average, sell at this price, it may wish to consider dropping the product line or making other major modifications in its operations. In making this decision, the firm should, of course, consider the effects of the decision on complementary products.

Incremental Pricing. Special-order or incremental pricing is done when the firm is approached to provide a batch of units outside its normal market. Two important points are the following: (1) multiple units are being sold, and (2) these units are not being sold through the normal distribution channel. Such a situation would exist if a large department store chain, such as Sears, Roebuck and Co., approached a major tire manufacturer to purchase a large quantity of tires similar to those made for the manufacturer's own brand but to be sold under the store's brand name.

The pricer must consider a number of consequences of providing goods for the special order. Can it be filled with existing capacity without giving up current sales? If not, what is the cost of giving up current sales or of obtaining additional production capacity both now and in the future? Will the special-order goods affect existing sales? They might, for example, be sold to customers who would otherwise buy the manufacturer's product. If sales will be reduced, what chance is there that another manufacturer will take on the order? This will have the same effect except that someone else will sell the special-order goods. Does the buyer of the special order intend to request other special orders in the future? Will these special orders grow in size until they require expanded capacity? What success will be had in raising the price on future special orders?

The answers to all these question affect how low a price on a special order the firm should be willing to set. Frequently, the buyer comes to the manufacturer with a suggested price. In this case, the manufacturer is in the position of either accepting or rejecting an offered price. Under almost all circum-

711

stances, a price below incremental cost should not be accepted. Perhaps the only situation in which a below-incremental cost price is acceptable is that in which the buyer will be making subsequent orders and the manufacturer is relatively sure of getting the future business and of being able to raise the price on future orders.

Special orders which require increased capacity or which in some way disturb existing sales have higher incremental costs than special orders that do not have these effects. The cost of increasing capacity or the contribution margin on existing sales given up for the special order is part of the incremental cost of the special order.

Bid pricers face many of the same problems as special-order pricers. The main difference seems to be that a bid pricer has to worry about bid prices developed by other firms. Therefore, the bid pricer must attempt to outguess other firms' bids and offer the lowest bid, but not bid so low as to be below the incremental cost of the bid. Probability assessments are particularly appropriate here.

A specialized form of bid pricing exists when one deals with the government. The problems of this area are highly specialized, and the reader is directed to *Negotiation and Management of Defense Contracts*, (especially chapter 3).[1]

Marketing Concepts Important to the Pricer

Among other factors one needs to keep in mind when pricing are the relationship of price and quality, the lure of prestige lines, brand loyalty, the public affinity for odd prices, and the danger of price wars.

Price-Quality Relationships. For some products, there seems to be some consumer belief that high price means high quality. This is certainly not the case for all products. If one is considering a small price reduction, however, one should be aware that instead of producing the desired result—increased sales volume—a lower price could result in reduced sales if the public perceives the price cut to be associated with a quality cut.

Prestige Factor. This price-quality relationship also has a parallel in high-priced prestige lines. It appears that some of the status associated with high-priced lines of any product is due to the high price. For this reason, a firm may choose to use higher markups on items that it views as top of the line in an attempt to add status appeal to the product rather than popular appeal. Having a status line sometimes can increase sales of the firm's cheaper lines also. This is undoubtedly why many firms label their cheaper lines with the tag "By the makers of ____." Some status rubs off from the prestige line to the less expensive, high-volume line.

Product Images. Brand loyalty has been indirectly described earlier. It is simply the public belief that one product is better or more desirable than similar or identical products available from competitors. Brand loyalty is frequently created by advertising. It can manifest itself in the public's paying higher prices for physically equivalent products. It appears that Bayer has successfully created brand loyalty for its aspirin. If all brands of aspirin are chemically the same and are all subject to the same purity requirements, brand loyalty must explain the higher price received by Bayer. Another interesting example of an attempt to establish brand loyalty involves the Dole banana. Bananas are not a product one would expect to be bought by brand. One does not buy fresh tomatoes or celery by brand, but Dole, through television and magazine advertising, attempted—with some success—to encourage the public to prefer Dole bananas.

"Right" Prices and "Odd" Prices. Associated with what people believe about a product is what they believe about price. Studies have demonstrated that some products have a price people associate with it as the "right" price. For other products, they have no idea what the price of the item should be or normally is.

Some prices are set to capitalize on the public's believed love of odd prices, set at $1.99, $3.09, and so on. It is generally thought that these prices are more effective than $2.00, $3.10, and so on. Whether the public feels that it is getting a bargain or that it is attracted to the unusualness of the price as it might be attracted to a hot orange-colored package is not certain. In fact, it may be that the odd price does nothing for the product sales but that pricers believe it does. Although frequently used, the real impact of odd pricing is unclear.

Price Wars. Price changes can result in unwanted competitor reaction and culminate in a price war. It is for this reason that competitor as well as customer reaction should be considered. A price war is a period of heavy and potentially destructive price cutting. In a price war, prices frequently drop to or below the minimum price. Continuation of prices at such a low level usually means that some firms can no longer stay in business. The personal computer wars of the early 1980s is a case in point; many smaller firms did not have the financial resources to sustain them and were forced out of business.

The initial reaction to a price war might be to shut down temporarily until the war is over and one's competitors have been severely weakened or forced out of business. But the difficulty in regaining lost customers usually keeps most participants in a price war until it ends or until they must cease business altogether. Since a price war is temporary in nature, prices will rise again. The firm that finds itself in a price war must hope that it can hold on until prices rise and that they rise enough to make up for the losses suffered during the price cutting.

Even after contending with the complexities discussed in this section, the pricer has still not solved all the problems. He or she must also consider the legal limitations imposed on pricers by various governmental bodies.

Legal Limitations on Pricing

Under the guise of promoting competition, the government has issued numerous restrictions which influence the way a pricer may set price. For this reason, a pricer may find a lawyer's input useful when product pricing.

Of the many terms which could be discussed in this section, three are most important: price fixing, price discrimination, and resale price maintenance. Firms have, on occasion, made explicit agreements concerning prices they will charge for their products. Such *price fixing* among supposedly competing firms is generally held to be illegal under the provisions of the Sherman Antitrust Act. The fines and damages authorized under the act can be extremely high and include a provision of triple damages to parties injured by price fixing. In the bid-rigging trials of highway construction firms in Georgia, for example, during 1982 and 1983, over 50 companies were fined and dozens of business executives were sent to jail.

Provisions of the Robinson-Patman Act restrict various forms of price discrimination. *Price discrimination* is the selling of the same product to different customers at different prices. The statute declares price discrimination on "commodities of like grade and quality" to be illegal "where the effect of such discrimination may be substantially to lessen competition or tend to create a monopoly in any line of commerce, or to injure, destroy, or prevent competition."

This part of the act seems designed to protect small retailers from large retailers that might be able to command significant price concessions from suppliers. Various states have also passed laws designed to protect the small store by requiring large stores to sell at no lower than cost. The overall intent of such legislation is to prevent large firms from forcing small firms out of business.

The Robinson-Patman Act also provides for resale price maintenance in states with fair trade laws. *Resale price maintenance* is the practice whereby manufacturers and sellers agree to the price the consumer must pay for a product and agree to enforce that price on all other sellers dealing in that product. These agreements, however, are only sporadically enforced, either by the parties involved or by the appropriate legal agencies.

Pricing in Review

There are no easy answers for the pricer, who must balance many inputs in order to be successful. The pricer must be aware of the market in which his or her product is sold and of the potential reaction of customers and competitors to price changes. He or she must be sure that the price is not "too low" as determined by various cost figures. Or, if the price is below the minimums suggested in this entry, then there should be a reason for the low price. Finally, the pricer must be careful not to violate the law.

See also Accounting, cost analysis and control; Brands and brand names; Economic concepts; Marginal income analysis; Marketing, channels of distribution; Product planning and development.

NOTE

[1]This book was written by Dean F. Price, published by John Wiley, New York, in 1970.

REFERENCES

Lere, John C.: *Pricing Techniques for the Financial Executive*, John Wiley, New York, 1974.

McCarthy, E. Jerome: *Basic Marketing: A Managerial Approach*, 7th ed., Richard D. Irwin, Homewood, Ill., 1981, chap. 19, "Pricing Objectives and Policies," chap. 20, "Price Setting in the Real World."

Monroe, K.: *Pricing: Making Profitable Decisions*, McGraw-Hill, New York, 1979.

JOHN C. LERE, *University of Minnesota*

Production/Operations Management

Production is any process or procedure used to create goods or services which have utility or value. A given process can be simultaneously physical, human, and economic, and it is designed to transform a given set of input elements into a specified set of output elements.

A *production system* is any cohesive collection of elements that are dynamically related for the purpose of production. Any such system has three distinguishable component parts: the inputs, the process, and the outputs.

By these definitions, production and production systems exist in hospitals, supermarkets, educational institutions, insurance companies, and airlines, as well as in manufacturing plants. *Inputs* may be materials, labor, and energy as existing in the manufacturing setting, but, under this broader definition, they may also be standard paperwork forms, clients, patients, or entire communities as found in service settings. The production *process* involves one or more separate operations, which may be mechanical, chemical, assembly, movement, personal contact, or the administration of help or treatment. The *outputs* may be completed parts, finished products, bulk chemicals, completed reports, serviced customers, or treated patients.

Production management deals with decision making as related to the design and control of production processes. In the managing process, the production manager is responsible for meeting (1) quantity requirements, (2) established delivery or completion dates, (3) quality levels placed on the outputs, and (4) the selection and application of the most economical methods for accomplishing these. This type of management holds true for profit and nonprofit organizations, private concerns, and forms of government, whether the output is tangible or intangible, a product or a service.

The knowledge of production management developed in the factory setting; hence, the traditional association of production management with manufacturing management. This same methodology, however, applies to production systems as found in hospitals, railroads, consulting firms, airlines, insurance companies, and so on, thus explaining the modern viewpoint which includes under production management *any* management concerned with *any* system whose function is to create tangible or intangible utility.

The term *production management* is being gradually replaced with the more general term *operations management*, or *production/operations management (POM)*, thereby transcending the manufacturing setting. Emphasis is on applicability to any type of production system.

Manufacturing (Production) Policies

A *policy* is a code, guide, or general rule which stipulates the preferred procedure to follow in handling a recurring situation or in exercising a delegated authority. It serves as a guide to decision making, as it defines a range wherein decisions may be made; as such, it enables top management to delegate authority while maintaining control through the policy statement. Theoretically, the underlying purpose of all policies is to ensure that decisions support organizational objectives and desired plans in a coordinated and consistent manner.

Characteristics of a Good Policy. A good policy has the following characteristics: (1) It reflects the objectives and plans of top management; (2) it represents a consistent pattern of thought; (3) it is stable but subject to change when change is needed; (4) it is sufficiently flexible to accommodate conditions which are unusual or unforeseen; (5) it is carefully thought out and clearly written; (6) it is well communicated and understood by those to be guided by it; and (7) it is controlled and consistently enforced. There are certain circumstances where it is advisable not to have a policy formalized in writing, such as when certain highly confidential matters are involved; however, control is very easily lost with informal policies, so written policies should be the general rule. A good policy program requires that policies be reviewed on a regular basis to determine whether or not they need updating, if they are complete and support current objectives, if they are understood, and if they are being complied with. Some large companies will assign this duty to a special group, department, or committee.

Hierarchy of Policies. Policies are needed at all levels of management; therefore there is a hierarchy of policies. The basic policies, which represent the prerogatives of top management, are at the top, with the lesser ones beneath but in harmony with and reflecting the former. The matter of *vertical integration* is a basic policy issue, and the decision here will establish the confines of the total activity in which the firm will be engaged. Will the firm push ownership back to raw materials by acquiring its own sources of materials? Will it reach out toward the market by acquiring its own retail outlets? *Horizontal integration* is another basic issue, which deals with the question of whether or not duplicate plants, each doing the same job, will be used to supply the firm's markets, or whether a single, general-purpose plant will be used. Other basic issues are the level of ownership of assets (owning versus renting or leasing), ground rules for guiding capital investments, and make-or-buy guidelines. Policies closer to operating management cover such matters as the following:

Inventory. Location of inventories; mix of items to be stocked; customer service–level targets; amount of allowed forward buying in anticipation of price increases or material shortages; limits on the use of inventories to level production; inventory turnover targets.

Equipment replacement. Interest rates to be used in various types of capital replacement requests; service-life estimates for classes of machinery, equipment, buildings, or other assets; sources of final approvals for various types and sizes of expenditures.

Quality control. Type of checking that will apply to specific outputs; the permissible level of risk for producing and shipping defective items and also for scrapping acceptable ones; application of quality control, whether during production or afterward in the form of 100 percent inspection.

Production control. Percentage goal of on-time delivery to customers and also from vendors; investment in inventory; degree of employment stability; process improvement program; cost-reduction programs.

Policy statements are also needed on purchasing, plant maintenance, plant security, safety habits, and housekeeping as well as on such common points as hours worked, attendance, overtime regulations, and so on.

Production Economics

The fundamental concept of production economics is that of utility of goods and services produced and either sold or dispensed. Utility in this sense is synonymous with the economic value assigned to these goods and services. While financial management is responsible for utility in terms of monetary value (i.e., cost and prices), production management sees utility as product availability in terms of quantity, timing, location, and the reliability of performance built into the product. The underlying premise is that the utility or value of the output is greater than the sum of the utilities or values of the inputs plus that of the investment in the production process when appropriately amortized.

Economics concentrates on the ways in which resources are, or can be, allocated to meet human needs, whereas economics of business concerns the allocations of organizational resources to meeting business needs. Production economics is a further refinement to production system needs where the allocation decisions arise from two broad areas of responsibility, namely, the designing of the production system and the operation and control of the system.

Functions of Production

Except for the most basic type of system, the modern production system is organized as a combination of line and staff functions.

Line operative functions are directly concerned with the primary objectives of the firm, and to define *line* one must know these objectives. In a manufacturing enterprise where the primary objectives are to make and sell products, the two basic lines are production and selling (and sometimes finance), whereas, in a retailing setting, the elements directly concerned with buying and selling constitute the line. The line production functions are directly responsible for the actual output of the firm through the operation of the production processes. The specific definition and character of a given line function are corollaries of the outputs to be made, the technology to be used, as well as the type and size of the organization of which it is a part.

Staff functions provide services to the line operative functions by advising, developing plans, counseling, coordinating, or performing specific tasks. A staff cannot order a line function to perform a specific task, nor is it ever directly responsible for the production performance, quality of output, timing of availability, or cost of production—these are line responsibilities.

The usual services-to-production functions which are provided by staffs are designing outputs, designing processes, providing materials and supplies, planning and controlling production, controlling quality (error), maintaining and repairing process components, and controlling cost. In the broad sense, the functions listed here, both line and staff, constitute production management.

Relationships

Since firms are traditionally organized in accordance with the principles of specialization and the division of labor, primary functional groups have evolved, such as marketing, finance, and manufacturing. Each function tends to be organized and managed as a separate activity, promoting functional traditions, methodologies, and points of view. The major concern of each function also tends to be the efficiency in performing its own tasks and responsibilities. In the past, top management assumed that if each function operated at top efficiency, the total organization would also operate at maximum effectiveness. Modern management recognizes that this assumption is not necessarily true and usually is not. Conflicts arise when functional efficiency takes precedence over overall enterprise effectiveness. Such efficiency-based conflicts must be resolved in accord with the firm's objectives. There must be an explicit structure of decision rules under which conflicting efficiency objectives will be traded off. There must be conditions under which exceptions to the rules will be allowed and an indication of the allowable extent of these exceptions. There must be a means for deciding whether or not the trade-offs are worthwhile from the organizational point of view. Finally, it must be assured that the component which is suboptimized, or whose local efficiency is curtailed, is not penalized for having yielded to the good of the total enterprise.

Relations with Marketing. Marketing interprets the demand for future periods, translates these into units of production output, and establishes desired delivery dates. Production management in turn provides production facilities (plant, personnel, and equipment) and acceptable quality, in addition to promoting growth in process improvement, technological advancement, and improvement in economic viability.

Conflicts arise between these two functions from their local efficiency viewpoints. Production management would like long design lead times, long production runs with few models, long and inflexible ordering lead times, strict production schedules, and infrequent model changes. On the other hand, marketing would prefer short design lead times, short production runs with many models, short order lead times, scheduling to meet emergency orders, and frequent model changes.

Relations with Finance. Financial management's concern is with the efficient use of the firm's capital resources. The design and operation of a production system entails various needs for capital for reducing operating costs, increasing yields, or otherwise improving processes. Conflict arises from questioning the value of these investments as well as the general availability of capital to production. Again, one turns to policy statements which establish procedures by which such conflict is to be resolved: the form of capital cost, the expected return, specific measures of merit, and so on.

See also Accounting, cost analysis and control; Automation; Budgeting, capital; Cost improvement; Learning (experience) curves; Material handling; Production planning and control; Scheduling, short-interval; Work simplification and improvement.

REFERENCES

Levin, R. I., et al.: *Production/Operations Management: Contemporary Policy for Managing Operating Systems,* McGraw-Hill, New York, 1972.

Mayer, R. R.: *Production and Operations Management,* 3d ed., McGraw-Hill, New York, 1975.

Moore, F. G.: *Production Management,* Richard D. Irwin, Homewood, Ill., 1973.

JAMES A. PARSONS, *American Cyanamid Company*

Production Planning and Control

Production planning is the process of translating a corporate business plan into an operating plan through such techniques as forecasting, master scheduling, and material/capacity requirements planning (MRP/CRP). The MRP triggers the release of purchase orders and shop orders. Shop orders are monitored by production activity control (PAC).

A Linkage of Techniques. Computerization and MRP have changed the basic approaches to production planning and control during the past decade. The logic of MRP has expanded from a narrow base of material requirements planning into total manufacturing resources planning (MRP-2). MRP-2 is seen, not as a tool of management, but as a new framework from which to manage. Emphasis is on uniting top-down planning with bottom-up planning and control. The computer has linked MRP with shop floor control, thus closing the loop. Shop floor control and Kanban (a Japanese technique discussed later under "Production Control") are assisting "just-in-time" minimization of inventory investment. Capacity requirements planning, combined with MRP, increases the productivity of capital. Theory Y/Theory Z human resource management (discussed under "Production Control" also) increases the productivity of labor.

Production planning begins with long-range decisions on products, markets, technology, plant location, and capacity. Capacity, production, and marketing are linked by the learning curve. Capacity and automation are linked in computer-assisted design/computer-assisted manufacturing (CAD/CAM), robotics, group technology, and computerized MRP information systems.

Learning Curves. The production decision overlaps the marketing strategy in deciding price and penetration and the choice of manufacturing methods. The learning curve, or manufacturing progress function, consists of the observation that progressively less labor is required per unit of production as experience accumulates. The learning curve reflects learning by workers, engineering changes, redesign of production methods, increased capital investment, and technology improvements.

If L is defined as the labor cost per unit produced, c the labor cost to produce the first prototype unit, x the number of units now being produced, and f the learning factor, the learning curve equation is

$$\text{Log } L = \log c + \frac{\log f}{\log 2} \log x$$

Calculation Technique. To illustrate the calculation, the first task is to estimate the value of f. Assuming that the firm has some preliminary production experience with this (or a similar) product, f may be determined by linear regression using the above logarithmic equation for L versus the logarithms of x, with $x = 1$ denoting the first unit of production for which records are at hand. The slope of the regression line is therefore a, which is $\log f/\log 2$, and the y-intercept of the regression is $\log c$, and the antilogs may then be found from log tables or a calculator having a log key.

For example, if c were found to be 90 minutes and f equal to 0.8, the time to produce the 100th unit could be calculated thus:

$$\text{Log } L = \log 90 + \frac{\log 0.8}{\log 2} \log 100$$

$$= 1.9542 - \frac{.09691}{.3010}(2.00)$$

$$= 1.31028$$

Then

$$L = \text{antilog } (1.31028)$$

$$= 20 \text{ minutes}$$

Similar calculations show that the 200th unit should require about 16 minutes, and the 500th unit roughly 12 minutes, of production time.

This calculation illustrates that a firm can strategically plan large production capacity and aggressively price low to capture a very large market share and rapidly "ride down the learning curve." If the value of f for a product is much less than unity, denoting that rapid learning is anticipated during manufacture, and if the potential market is large and responsive to price (elastic), then the long-range production strategy favors mass production of standardized product to capture market share. Conversely, if the learning rate factor f is close to unity, it may suggest pricing for high profit margin, low volume, and job-shop customized production.

Master Forecasting and Planning

The master production planning consists of the creation of the schedule of the items to be produced over the planning time horizon. Major tasks of master planning include (1) predicting sales demand using forecasting techniques; (2) deciding how much of the potential demand to produce; and (3) developing the master production schedule from which resource needs, with time, can be determined, coordinated, and implemented.

Forecasts. In production and inventory control, the objective often is to compute reasonably smoothed forecasts for many items on a routine basis. For doing so, exponential smoothing has proved very popular. *Exponential smoothing* computes a weighted moving average forecast with minimal data manipulation and minimal storage of information. The weights are easily modified. Forecasts can be automatically maintained by computer, with human intervention occurring only on an exceptions basis.

Exponential Smoothing. The exponentially smoothed average of past data at any point t in time is

$$F_t = \alpha D_t + (1 - \alpha)F_{t-1}$$

where D_t is the most recent data point and F_{t-1} is the smoothed average which was calculated in the period previous to t and was the basis by which D_t was forecasted before D_t became known.

The smoothing constant is α (alpha) which is a constant set at whatever value is found to give, on the average, the best forecasts. Alpha always lies between zero and 1, and often falls in the range of 0.1 to 0.3. The exponentially smoothed average can be made approximately equivalent to a moving average of any particular length by suitable choice of alpha.

Tracking Signals. If the system which is generating the time series data (such as sales demand) is not changing with time, we can predict the percentage of observations that should fall within plus-or-minus some number of MADs (sum of the mean absolute deviations) of the forecasts. Too many observations falling outside this range would signal that the model is not forecasting properly. Therefore a tracking signal is generally built into the calculations, which can be set at any degree of sensitivity to generate exception reports. The tracking signal equals the sum of forecast errors divided by the MAD.

Master Scheduling. The master schedule consists of a listing of the forecasted production requirements over time. The production forecast reflects the sales forecast, inventory adjustments, backlogs, and production leveling adjustments.

The master schedule is the plan from which all production activities are developed and coordinated, as distinguished from assembly schedules or work schedules. It must be updated as frequently as fluctuations occur in demand, priorities, raw material availability, and plant capacity in order to keep the master schedule credible and not be circumvented by informal scheduling. A master schedule should not, for example, show production backlog, since nothing can be produced yesterday. Instead, it is revised and reissued as often as necessary to remain the basic planning document for each period.

The master schedule shows the production plan to a time horizon that is at least as distant as the most lengthy production or procurement time for any end item or component. Time buckets may be of any suitable interval and typically consist of weekly periods for the present and near future, then monthly and quarterly periods for the more remote future.

A *bill of material* (BM) is a complete listing of the quantities of all the components of an end item. The end item may be a finished good or a component of a higher-level end item. In various industries, the bill of material may be called the furnish, formula, specification, or procedure. A firm with MRP stores the bills of material on computer disk files which are accessed by the bill of materials processor, a computer software package. The multiple levels of bills may then be quickly "chained" by computer to obtain a listing of all components and subcomponents of an end item.

The BMs are prepared from engineering drawings and parts lists, but often should be numbered differently from the engineering parts and assemblies. The reason is that every unique production end item should have its unique production bill of material number, but production end items may not correspond to physical end items. For example, a subassembly manufactured for in-process inventory might be a production end item, but would be only a collection of components from the engineering viewpoint.

Modular bills, also called *planning bills,* are based on defining the product at one or more levels below the end item, such as planning concerned with engines and transmissions insead of with finished automobiles. This approach may considerably reduce the number of bills of material to maintain for products that have many features and options, and the demand for lower-level modules is often easier to forecast. To simplify planning, groups of features and options may be gathered into *pseudobills*, also called *superbills*, under an artificial parent.

The *routing sheet* contains a heading of general information, followed by sequencing information which shows the work centers into which to route the job. Space is provided on the sheet for each work center to record the progress history of the job. Route sheets often are prepared and updated by punched cards and computerized systems.

If capacity and material are inadequate to supply demand, either additional resources must be procured or the master schedule must be reduced to less than demand. An iterative process may be performed to reconcile objectives to feasibility through simulation. One form of simulation consists of creating a tentative master schedule from which materials and capacity requirements are estimated, and then adjusting the plan until it becomes feasible. This method improves the leveling of the loading of the work centers and assigns more valid priorities to work in the queue.

Shop Layout and Automation

Production management varies with the product. At one end of a spectrum is the pure *job shop* which builds to order, with no two items identical. At the other end of the spectrum is *continuous production* by a process dedicated to a homogeneous product. *Repetitive manufacturing* lies toward the continuous production end of the scale. *Group technology* exploits similarities among different products to use *cells* of operations that are like repetitive operations within plants that are, overall, job shops.

CAD/CAM is useful with group technology.

1. CAD is *computer-assisted design* in which drafting is performed with graphics software on a monitor. The paper drawings may then be printed by computer. This procedure greatly improves the productivity in design because much time is often spent in redrawing or modifying existing designs.

2. CAM is *computer-assisted manufacturing.* The CAD also saves data about the manufacturing that can be transmitted to robots or NC (numerically controlled) machines, and compiles data on product structure for the MRP.

Inventory Optimization and Material Requirements Planning

The basic principle of inventory optimization and materials management is to minimize the competing costs of having either too little or too much in inventories of raw material, work in process, or finished goods. Inventories provide indispensable buffers to improve the leveling of production activity, but they constitute a major investment of the funds of most firms.

The traditional method of timing production runs and inventory replenishment has been by reorder point. Reorder point control should be replaced with MRP for production items, and by DRP (distribution requirement planning) for finished goods inventories. Under reorder point, total costs of inventory policy (TC) are generally taken to include the following as the most important cost elements:

TC = setup costs (or procurement costs)

+ holding costs + stockout costs

A first approximation to the cost categories of this equation is to specify the total cost to be

$$\text{TC} = \frac{cD}{Q} + \frac{ipQ(1 - d/r)}{2}$$

for an item that is never out of stock and has an annual forecasted demand for D units at a value of p per unit. The procurement or setup cost is c dollars per order, and the order or production run amount is Q units per batch. If the item is produced, it is at a daily rate of r and depleted at a daily rate of d. The value for the effective rate of interest, i, is often taken to be about 30 percent, to include the opportunity cost of capital, insurance, obsolescence, and other costs of holding.

Economical Production Quantity (EPQ). The above TC equation is minimized when

$$\text{EPQ} = \sqrt{\frac{2Dc}{ip(1 - d/r)}}$$

This equation is for the case of setting up a machine to run the item to a certain inventory level, then running that machine on another item until stocks are nearly depleted.

The *economical production quantity*, or EPQ, is the approximate optimal value of units per batch to manufacture, assuming simplistic uniform demand rates for finished goods with simplified work centers. Although reorder point continues to be commonly used, superior total planning and control are possible with computer-based MRP.

MRP and Dependent Demand Inventory. *Material requirements planning* (MRP) is an information and planning system to time the arrival of material and production so that stock-outs will never occur. MRP uses the data of the master schedule, the current inventory status report, and the bills of material of the items to be produced to determine the time phasing and priorities of production activity. Each end item (or group) that is to be produced is contained in the master schedule as to its time of need and its bill of material number. In the MRP procedure, each bill of material is broken down or "exploded" into a list of all the subassemblies and component parts (including the raw materials and purchases) which are required for the production of the end items. Manufacturing and procurement lead times are then estimated and controlled so that raw material and in-process inventories will be at the correct levels at the correct times.

MRP specifically minimizes two of the principal costs of the total inventory cost equation, namely, the holding costs and the stock-out or shortage costs. Holding costs are reduced both by reducing the average value of goods on hand at times they are not needed and by reducing the effective interest rate factor which contains allowance for obsolescence and losses. The third principal cost, which is ordering or procurement costs, is treated in MRP by various lot-sizing techniques.

MRP is more than an inventory control technique. It can be an element of a total data-based planning and production control system. Although the principles of MRP are not new, widespread interest in the system as a practical approach has developed only since about 1970, stimulated by the advent of more generally available computer software and the vigorous promotion of the concept by APICS (American Production and Inventory Control Society).

Just as the master schedule "drives" the MRP system, an MRP system can drive a capacity planning system. The MRP system displays the requirements for all raw materials and components in aggregate which are necessary for the production of the various end items. By inspection of this listing, management can ascertain whether the resources and the lead times are adequate to meet the master schedule or whether more capacity is required to meet objectives. The material capacity planning system is also implicitly a human resources planning system.

Cycle Counting. Successful MRP requires accurate information about inventory status. Cycle counting consists of counting inventory on a continuous frequency. ABC analysis may be used to count the high volume A items more frequently than the C items, or rules such as "Count whenever the item balance is reported zero" may be used to reduce some counting.

Capacity Planning

Capacity planning on the operational level consists of using the resources at hand to the best advantage. Planning provides for the timely accomplishment of work in the correct priorities, minimization of idleness of each aspect of the work centers, and utilization of the least-cost techniques for performing the tasks.

Capacity planning is performed by maintaining adequate data on the status of the production system and continually applying various heuristic rules of thumb, simulations, and mathematical and graphical techniques to attempt to determine the best procedures in the face of complex interaction.

Capacity Requirements Planning. Manufacturing production systems using material requirements planning use the information to perform capacity requirements planning. The procedure is to use the demand forecasts to develop a tentative master schedule, from which the material requirements planning is computed. This tentative MRP determines the tentative priorities of production and the capacities required to accomplish the production schedule. If these tentative capacity requirements are available and feasible, the (simulated) tentative master schedule becomes the actual master schedule for production. If these tentative capacity requirements are not available, the tentative master schedule must be revised until the plan is feasible.

Capacity requirements planning employs electronic data processing to maintain the files of information needed and to prepare the tabulated plans. This process allows revision of the production plan as frequently as desired (e.g., daily or weekly) to reflect current priorities and capacity changes.

This approach is a move toward central planning by removing production backlogs from the shop floor and replacing informal scheduling and control procedures by a formalized procedure. Difficulties include (1) the need for accurate data systems and (2) human factors, which tend to replace formal systems by informal ones.

Linear Programming. *Linear programming* (LP) is a general technique for optimally allocating resources. It is particularly useful for determining how to schedule various kinds of tasks through multiple work centers when each center has only a finite capacity. The "shadow prices" calculated by linear programming determine the additional profit contribution generated by scheduling more capacity, the potential profits due to changing the product mix, and the payoff of possible long-range capital expansion of facilities.

Simulation. The essence of *simulation* is to calculate the sequence of details of a possible situation before actually encountering it. By simulating, various scenarios can be investigated to see which courses of action would be best to implement. One form of simulation, in which the master schedule is simulated through the MRP system, has been outlined in the discussion of capacity requirements planning earlier in this section.

Other modes of simulation are also useful in capacity planning. Models can be constructed to represent complex interaction of production situations. *Monte Carlo simulation* refers to models where probabilities of interacting events are considered, and the model is recalculated many times on a computer to find the probabilities of the possible outcomes of a decision or situation. *Deterministic simulation* refers to calculating through a mathematical or computer model which does not include probabilities, but is usually too complex for routine analysis by intuition.

Simulation can be one of the most powerful tools for better understanding a system. Its importance has led to the creation of several computer languages designed especially for simulation, such as GPSS, GASP, SIMSCRIPT, GERT, Q-GERT, and DYNAMO. Of course, other more general languages such as FORTRAN can also be used, and very simple models can be simulated by hand calculation.

Queuing Models. The time that a job spends in a manufacturing process consists of waiting in a queue for the first operation, then setup, then machine operation time, then move time to the next queue of the second operation, and so forth through many operations.

One's tendency is to predict job completion times by summing the times for each work center operation. Usually, however, the time spent in the many queues is far greater than the actual operation times. This is one reason why most facilities have chronic backlogs and why expediting work can have dramatic results.

Queuing theory consists of the study of systems in which there are arrivals into the system bearing probability distributions, and service with (usually) different statistical features. Queuing theory provides for understanding of how waiting lines lengthen or shorten as functions of system statistics.

Until recently, queuing theory was too couched in mathematics for practical use in routine study of multiple-server, multiple-queue production processes. With the advent of high-speed computing, however, and with languages tailored for simulation modeling, queuing modeling is beginning to be a capacity planning tool for the practitioner.

PERT/CPM. Program evaluation and review technique (PERT) and critical path method (CPM) are network planning techniques for project management. They are most suited for complex extensive tasks, such as the production of a building or a ship. PERT and CPM differ from each other in their fine points, with PERT providing probability estimates of all the completion times for a job but with CPM restricting its focus to the control of the critical paths of the project.

The principal value of PERT/CPM is often the project definition and planning which occur during the development of the chart of sequential and parallel tasks that constitute the proposed project. This planning is usually much more critical than the updating control capability. Computer libraries are available for the periodic updating of the PERT/CPM network of a project for management control. *See* Network planning methods.

Job-Shop Loading Techniques. Various approaches have been pursued for better allocating capacity to work flow. These include operations research techniques, heuristic rules, and computer-based methods.

Allocation and scheduling problems can be studied by operations research techniques such as branch-and-bound methods, dynamic programming, and integer programming. These are more specialized approaches because of their technical complexities.

Production Control

Production control begins with techniques for organizing and conceptualizing information about the plan and the current status of events in pursuing it. The subsequent task of causing the system to react to this information rests upon the skill of the manager in interpreting the information that is presented and in reducing any variance between the plan and the actual status.

Charting Techniques. A simple but useful control technique is to use a calendar, time graph, or bar chart of some sort to visually present each task to be performed and the time schedule relationships. Examples include PERT and CPM, which can be displayed in different formats stressing "milestone" events and time-scaled activities. Other techniques include Gantt charts, line of balance charts, and combinations of them.

Gantt Charts. For assembly line operations, the simple Gantt chart is still often used to provide management with a quick impression of job status, priorities, and interdependencies.

Line of Balance. The line of balance (LOB) technique is a charting technique for monitoring assembly line progress. The four inputs which are required for an LOB chart are (1) the production plan, showing the key milestone events of the production process; (2) the cumulative schedule of time to reach each milestone; (3) the production progress, recorded on a vertical Gantt bar chart; and (4) the line of balance, which is a stairstep line obtained by calculating the cumulative number of units which must be completed to meet the schedule for each milestone.

Critical Ratios. Critical ratios are often maintained on work flowing through the shop to signal by exception reports which jobs should be expedited. Various formulas, invented for critical ratios, yield a number indicating the ratio of the time in which the job should be finished divided by the projected time in which the job will actually be finished. If the calculated critical ratio for a job is greater than 1.0, it indicates that the job is ahead of schedule; if it is equal to 1.0, the job is exactly on schedule; if it is less than 1.0, the job is behind schedule ("critical"). One way of ordering priorities might thus be to process in order of the smallest critical ratio.

Dispatch Lists. A dispatch list is a regular (usually daily) listing of the tasks to be done by each work center in order of priority. Firms with on-line computer inquiry terminals even allow the work centers to inquire at any moment regarding current job priorities. Jobs are taken from the top of the list, and as work is completed the work center creates a report to update the status.

Kanban. Kanban is a shop floor control technique developed by the Japanese for controlling materials movement in repetitive manufacturing. Stock movement occurs either in unit lots or in small containers bearing cards (called Kanban in Japanese). Kanban and MRP are complementary systems that strive ideally for small lot sizes and maximum productivity. MRP emphasizes planning and computerized information systems, and Kanban emphasizes control and manual information processing. Both are oriented toward JIT (just-in-time) production and minimal inventory of either raw materials or work in process. These systems have stimulated recent interest in broader concepts of JIT for reducing capital investment in inventory through improved information flow between vendors and customers as well as within the plant.

Theory Y and Theory Z. Advances in production planning and control, especially in MRP and Kanban, have increased managerial awareness that information systems rely on hardware, software, and "peopleware." Contrasted with Theory X carrot-and-stick motivation, Theory Y seeks worker enthusiasm for involvement in production, and Theory Z recognizes cultural foundations of productivity, particularly by comparing Japan and the United States. *Quality circles* and *quality of work life* groups are formalized ways to encourage workers to improve productivity.

Sources of Additional Information

Techniques which concentrate on the general optimization concepts and on the long-range or strategic aspects of production planning are described in textbooks on operations research, operations management, decision science, and managerial economics.

A principal source of literature on production planning and control is through the American Production and Inventory Control Society (APICS), which distributes educational material, bibliography on production management, the journal *Production Management*, and bound proceedings of the annual conferences of the society. The society maintains a national examination and certification program in production and inventory management. APICS sponsored the *Production and Inventory Control Handbook*.

See also Automation; Control systems, management; Gantt charts; Inventory control; Inventory stock-keeping systems; Learning (experience) curves; Line of balance; Logistics, business; Materials management; Network planning methods; Operations research and mathematical modeling; Production/operations management; Robotics; Scheduling, short-interval; System concept, total.

REFERENCES

Dilworth, James B.: *Production and Inventory Management*, Random House, New York, 1983.

Fogarty, Donald W., and Thomas R. Hoffman: *Production and Inventory Management*, South-Western, Cincinnati, 1983.

Greene, James H. (ed.): *Production and Inventory Control Handbook*, McGraw-Hill, New York, 1970.

Wight, Oliver W.: *MRP-II: Unlocking America's Productivity Potential*, CBI Publishing, Boston, 1981.

JAMES W. RICE, *University of Wisconsin, Oshkosh*

Productivity Improvement

Few issues that vie for the time and attention of managers in today's fast-paced and rapidly changing business world have generated the interest and concern that managers have expressed toward the issue of productivity falloff. Interest in and emphasis on improving operating results have soared. For some companies, the issue is survival. For others, the concern is maintaining profit margins when faced with declining sales and/or increasing costs. In all cases, it is basically an adjustment by management to the times—more competition, shrinking markets, rising costs, and increasing quality expectations among customers or clients. The purpose of this entry is to provide proven, practical guidelines for improving productivity in any situation without capital investment and not requiring the adoption of practices which are alien to our culture.

A Qualitative as well as a Quantitative Concept. Productivity is a measure of how well resources are combined and utilized to accomplish specific, desirable results. By the same token, it is a measure of what is received in return for what is given.

$$\text{Productivity} = \frac{\text{results achieved}}{\text{resources consumed}}$$
$$= \frac{\text{what is received}}{\text{what is given}}$$

The concept of productivity recognizes the quality as well as the quantity of results achieved. To produce more with a given amount of resources is not enough. The quality of whatever is produced must meet predetermined standards which reflect customer or client expectations. The productivity concept also recognizes the interplay between various factors in the workplace. While the results achieved may be related to many different resources in the form of various productivity ratios—output per labor hour, output per unit of material, or output per unit of capital—each of these ratios is influenced separately by a combination of many relevant factors. Those factors include the quality and availability of materials, the scale of operations and rate of capacity utilization, the availability and "through-put" capacity of capital equipment, the attitude and skill levels of the work force, and the motivation and effectiveness of management. The manner in which these factors interrelate has an important bearing on the resulting productivity as measured by any of many possible ratios.

Productivity Growth. Of all the issues confronting managers, none is more important, both in the near and the long term, than the issue of productivity growth. From a national perspective, productivity improvement is the only source of increased real national wealth. A better productive use of resources reduces waste and conserves scarce or expensive resources. Steady growth in productivity is the only way our nation can solve such pressing problems as inflation, unemployment, and a rising trade deficit.

In business, productivity improvements can lead to more responsive customer service, increased cash flow, larger return on assets, and greater profits. More profits provide investment capital for the expansion of capacity and the creation of new jobs. Improved productivity enables a business to be more competitive both domestically and abroad.

The Leverage in Controlled Costs. Business profit can be improved by either increasing sales, by reducing costs, or by a combination of both. It is not uncommon for management to focus on raising sales volume with a lesser emphasis placed on controlling, if not reducing, costs. This attitude is the result of conditioning brought about by the expanding markets and higher sales enjoyed by many businesses during the 1960s and extending, for some of those businesses, through the 1970s. The sale of additional units results in a diminished fixed cost per unit which automatically increases profit, provided there is no offsetting rise in variable cost per unit. It is generally easier for managers to ride the wave of increasing demand than it is for them to confront the issue of how better to control costs. Until we experience either a reduced demand for our products or services, or a demand that is growing at a lesser rate than that to which we are accustomed, productivity improvement and cost control tend to take a back seat to efforts to expand sales. Yet, in its broadest sense, productivity includes all resources and their costs and, as such, presents the best chance to improve profit in any for-profit business and to provide more service for every dollar spent in nonprofit organizations.

Cost control has a leverage on profit that few managers have stopped to consider. The positive impact of a single dollar of cost reduction has a far greater

TABLE P-2 Reducing Costs vs. Increasing Sales

Company's profit margin	Additional sales dollars required to equal profit-improving impact of $1 cost reduction
20	$ 5.00
15	6.67
10	10.00
9	11.11
8	12.50
7	14.29
6	16.67
5	20.00
4	25.00
3	33.33
2	50.00
1	100.00

effect than does an increase in sales of the same magnitude. (*See* Table P-2.)

Limiting Factors. Many factors act to limit productivity growth. While those factors may vary from one work situation to another, they can be combined into the following five broad categories which are common, in varying degrees of intensity, to most, if not all.

1. *Government regulation.* Increasing regulation, often of questionable value, has sapped resources which could better be applied to improving products, processes, and facilities.

2. *Organizational size and maturity.* As organizations increase in size, barriers to communication, singleness of purpose, and the achievement of results arise. As organizations mature, they develop a crusty rigidity, stubborn complacency, and reverence for the status quo, all of which diminish the organization's ability to respond to changing conditions.

3. *Physical resources and technological factors.* The facility, equipment, product design, materials, methods, and the level and effectiveness of research and development all affect productivity. The relationship between research and development which results in finding and implementing new and better ways of doing things and productivity growth is as crucial as it is apparent.

4. *Problems in implementing measurements.* Before many organizations have gotten around to designing and implementing meaningful measurements related to the outputs of their blue-collar workers, the work force has shifted to predominantly white-collar workers whose outputs are generally less tangible and more difficult to measure.

5. *Management practices.* How managers manage is the single most important of all the factors which affect productivity growth. A manager's day-to-

day interface with and direction of subordinates has the most influence on their willingness to contribute to the extent of their capabilities to the achievement of the organization's goals.

Improvement Guidelines

The limiting factors just mentioned are the most controllable ones from the managerial perspective—measurement and management practices.

Emphasis on Long-Term Results. Much has been said and written about management myopia or the emphasis on short-term results at the expense of the long-term outcome. What managers do in the near term *should* contribute to, rather than detract from, long-term results. In some organizations, however, this axiom is interpreted as license to avoid addressing today's problems today. The adage acts either to generate or to perpetuate a work climate void of the necessary sense of urgency. Emphasis should shift from long-term or future success to achieving enduring success, starting today.

Focus on Causes. Results are the consequences of the forces acting in and upon the workplace. Some of those forces—people, products, plant, and policies—are under the control of management. Acting separately or together, those forces create the conditions which determine the level of operating results. Before improved productivity can be realized, the conditions which restrict productivity must be identified and appropriately altered. While an element of risk is always associated with introducing change, the potential consequences from failing to implement necessary changes present a far greater threat to the organization's success. More damage has undoubtedly resulted from managerial acts of omission and failure to take the required action than from managerial acts of commission, or the managers having the courage to initiate and implement necessary changes.

An Awareness of Employee Needs. Ever since Abraham Maslow developed his hierarchy of human needs, there has been an increasing concern with fulfilling employee needs in the workplace. Practices such as lifetime employment and consensus decision making are being embraced by a growing number of managers. When attaching greater importance to meeting employee needs in the workplace, management must not lose sight of its responsibility to fulfill the organization's needs. A manager's job is to achieve results which are in the long-term best interest of the organization. Ideally, those results will be achieved in a manner consistent with the best interests of employees. Certain management practices are preferred because they simultaneously serve to fulfill the needs of the organization *and* its employees. Figure P-7 illustrates the hierarchies of both individual or employee needs and organizational needs. It also provides insight into the roles of communicating expectations, providing performance-related feedback based on objective measures, and basing rewards on performance. The following material provides more detailed explanations of how these practices can contribute to improving productivity in any work situation.

1. *The first, and often overlooked, step toward improving operating results is developing and then widely communicating a concise statement of the organization's mission, including how it intends to achieve its purpose.* A preliminary step in the strategic planning process is the generation of a statement that summarizes the organization's mission. Such a statement should pinpoint the function the organization performs as well as its purpose for being in business. It is important that the organization's mission be committed to writing, widely communicated in the written form, and verbally clarified in a manner which increases understanding by answering all related questions. Table P-3 provides exam-

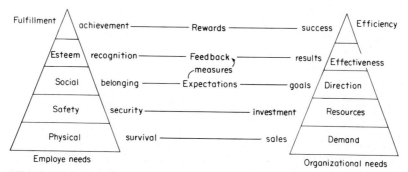

FIG. P-7 The role of communicating expectations, providing feedback based on objective measures, and basing rewards on performance in simultaneously fulfilling employee and organizational needs.

TABLE P-3. Sample Statements of Organizational Mission, Individual Responsibilities, and Goals

Type of organization	Factors in organization's business achievements
A manufacturer of fluid-handling equipment	*Mission:* to design, manufacture, and sell highly reliable fluid-handling equipment so as to realize a profit *Responsibilities of a buyer:* To purchase materials and services that will be delivered when needed and at the best possible cost, without compromising quality *Goals of the same buyer:* 1. to reduce the purchased materials and services cost as a percentage of net sales by 10% in the next year 2. to reduce the net sales to number of material shortages experienced by production ratio by 10% in the next year 3. to reduce the purchasing-responsible scrap and warranty expense as a percentage of net sales by 15% in the upcoming year
A wholesale distributor of electrical products and components	*Mission:* to distribute high-quality electrical products and components to the service sensitive maintenance and repair market in a manner that generates a profit and repeat business *Responsibilities of an order-processing manager:* to process all customer orders in a timely, accurate, and efficient fashion *Goals of that same manager:* 1. to fill customer orders in the next six months holding errors to a maximum of 2% of all lines filled as measured by internal point of shipment audits 2. during the next 6 months, to fill all orders which call for items in inventory within 2 working days; and to fill 95% of all such orders within 24 hours of receipt in the warehouse 3. during the next 6 months, to operate the order-processing department within the agreed-upon budget

ples of defined missions for two diverse organizations.

2. *Individual responsibilities must be expressed in terms of expected contribution to the achievement of the organization's mission.* The statement of the organization's mission provides general direction to its members. As an interim step in working toward specific direction in the form of goals, individual responsibilities need to be expressed in terms of expected contribution to the organization's mission. Statements outlining these individual responsibilities and expected contributions should be committed to writing. Preferably, they would be generated by employees at all levels of the organization and approved by each employee's immediate supervisor. Examples of such statements appear in Table P-3.

3. *Goals must be personal, realistic, specific, comprehensive, worthwhile, and written, if they are to serve as effective management tools.* The process of setting productivity goals provides direction to the efforts of all the organization's members. These goals inculcate a sense of order and purpose capable of generating and maintaining a high level of interest and motivation over long periods.

To be effective, goals must meet certain criteria. They must be (1) mutually agreed upon by manager and subordinate; (2) realistic in the sense that their achievement is difficult but attainable; (3) specific in that expectations are quantified and a deadline for their accomplishment is set; (4) comprehensive in that they are applied to all areas of activity within the organization; (5) worthwhile in the sense that they contribute to the achievement of the organization's mission by focusing on payoffs rather than activities; and (6) written so that they can be periodically referred to and not forgotten.

When setting goals, it is helpful to focus on three areas of common concern to most organizations: profit (or cost), quality (or accuracy), and service (or timeliness). At least one goal related to each of these three critical areas and incorporating the goal criteria should be set for each member of the organization. Table P-3 provides examples of individual goals which meet these requirements.

Measurement and Control

Designing and implementing meaningful measurements is commonly the most perplexing aspect of the productivity improvement effort. Measurements are required to track progress and identify problems. Managing without measures is like flying an airplane without instruments. In either case, you may not know where you are, where you are going, or if or when you are going to get there. As important as measurements are, few organizations have implemented them to the necessary extent. Those that have implemented some form of performance measurement often do not have meaningful measures and/or fail to apply them to all areas of the business. On one hand, some managers prefer to rely on subjective observation rather than on objective measurement as the basis for appraising performance. On the other hand, even managers that do embrace the measurement concept frequently experience undue difficulty in determining what those measures should be.

Criteria for Productivity Measurements. There are two key points to remember when designing performance measurements for any situation.

1. *Focus on end results rather than activities.* For example, measuring the dollar value of sales orders written is much more meaningful to a profit-oriented business than is the number of sales calls made. If the sales dollars booked are below expectations, you may want to look at the number of sales calls made; but dollars booked is the most meaningful measure because it best gauges the contribution to achieving the organization's mission—profit.

2. *Think in terms of the ratio of what "is" as compared with what "should be."* Even when outputs are tangible and easily quantified, the output/input ratio is meaningless until it is compared with the expected ratio or goal. For example:

$$\text{What ``is''} = \frac{\text{actual output}}{\text{actual input}} = \frac{22}{10} = 2.2 = ???$$

$$\frac{\text{What ``is''}}{\text{What ``should be''}} = \frac{\left(\dfrac{\text{actual output}}{\text{actual input}}\right)}{\left(\dfrac{\text{output goal}}{\text{input goal}}\right)} = \frac{\dfrac{22}{10}}{\dfrac{20}{10}} = \frac{2.2}{2.0} = 1.1$$

meaning goal was exceeded by 10%

When outputs are not easily quantified, performance can be measured by comparing what it actually cost to accomplish a certain task with what it should have.

$$\text{Performance} = \frac{\text{actual cost}}{\text{targeted cost}}$$

Note that performance ratios dealing with *costs*, unlike ratios not based on cost, indicate a better than targeted performance when the ratio is less than 1.00.

Visual as well as Verbal Reporting. Managers who depend solely on reports to communicate problems and motivate subordinates to improve their performance are frequently disappointed. In and of themselves, reports do not command attention. They also often fail to compare actual versus targeted performance or provide performance trends. While the

proper reporting format, coupled with managerial emphasis on performance, can go a long way toward overcoming these common shortcomings, the potential of reports to emphasize and draw attention to performance is limited. Graphs, on the other hand, have a much greater potential for being an effective management tool. The following points, when incorporated in a firm's graphs, will help it realize that potential.

1. Label the graph so that anyone who reads it can understand it.

2. Condense the graph horizontally and/or elongate it vertically to maximize fluctuations. Thus, changes are more apparent and attention is called to any lack of consistency or loss of control.

3. Make trends apparent by drawing either colored or dotted horizontal lines to indicate weekly averages. Draw other colored or solid horizontal lines to represent monthly averages.

4. Draw and label a horizontal line to indicate the goal, thus showing feedback related to actual and expected performances.

5. Have the graph updated each workday so as to include the previous day's operating results. The daily recording signals managerial interest and the importance of performance.

6. Display the graph in a prominent place and openly review and respond to it on a periodic basis. The more interest one displays, the greater will be the interest of one's subordinates.

Figure P-8 illustrates the difference between a graph which incorporates the above points and one which does not.

Managerial Surveillance. Managers must inspect what they expect. Reports, or even graphs, cannot be relied upon to provide all the required information. At best, they present only part of what any manager needs to know. The balance of the necessary information can be assimilated by periodically visiting each subordinate in his or her work area. Only then can the manager have a reasonably accurate understanding of what is really going on.

Participative Techniques. Before employees can be made to feel they are valuable members of the company team, managers at all levels must be made to feel they are an important part of the management team. Many companies have recently jumped into employee participation programs such as quality circles, and many of that number have failed. One revealing study found that after one year of operation, 28 of 41 quality circle programs in this country had failed to produce measurable results that exceeded their cost. This finding is not surprising. Supervisors whose personal inputs are not valued will naturally be hesitant to fulfill their required role

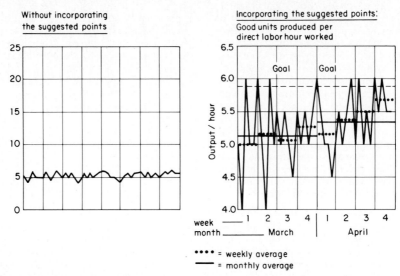

FIG. P-8 Making your graphs more meaningful. (Graph illustrating the same data both with and without incorporating the suggested points.)

to successfully solicit the inputs of their subordinates.

Problem-Solving Techniques. Triggering events, in the form of circumstances or situations, determine how persons will behave or perform in the workplace just as in any other setting. The consequences which follow that behavior either encourage repetition of that same behavior in response to similar, future circumstances, or motivate a different response to similar circumstances in the future. Analyzing performance problems to determine what precedes certain on-the-job behaviors, or *antecedents*, and what follows that behavior, or the resulting *consequences*, can often help managers resolve such problems. Figure P-9 illustrates some specific antecedents and consequences which affect behavior in the workplace.

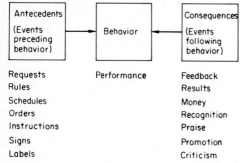

FIG. P-9 Common antecedents and consequences in the workplace.

Common sense indicates that the manner in which work is presented to a subordinate will have a bearing on that subordinate's performance. It also further suggests that good performance should be rewarded and that poor performance results in punishment or deprivation. The effect of certain management practices, however, may not be apparent without analyzing the antecedents and consequences. Management may, for example, be punishing the very behavior it is trying to encourage without realizing it. For example, consider the following chain of events:

Antecedent	Behavior	Consequence
An employee is asked to speed up an already fast work pace aimed at completing a special rush job.	The employee works diligently and quickly completes the assigned task.	The employee is asked to pitch in and help a lazier employee to complete his assigned task.

How do you think the employee who responded positively to the request to work faster will respond to similar requests in the future?

Management may also be unknowingly punishing more than the intended behavior to productivity's detriment, as is illustrated by the following example:

Antecedent	Behavior	Consequence
An employee experiences an equipment breakdown and, rather than wait, takes the initiative to find a repair person to fix the equipment.	In appreciation of the help provided, the employee buys coffee for the repair person before resuming work.	The employee's supervisor walks by and, unaware of what has happened, says, "Maybe if we had a little less coffee and more work around here, we would be on schedule."

What do you think are the chances that the employee will exhibit the same initiative should a similar breakdown occur in the future?

Summary

The current interest in and focus on improving productivity is destined, out of necessity, to be enduring. If managers are to protect their jobs, continue to raise the nation's standard of living, and overcome the nation's economic ills, they must improve productivity on a continuing basis.

Improving productivity is generally associated with tangible things—new and better equipment, for example. The most important factor, however, is that which controls all other factors: people. The roles of the managers are especially significant because their managerial skills determine the willingness of their subordinates to contribute, to the extent of their potential, to the achievement of the organization's goals.

See also Cost improvement; Paper work simplification; Profit improvement; Quality management; Systems and procedures; Work design, job enlargement, and job enrichment; Work measurement; Work simplification and improvement.

REFERENCES

Bain, David: *The Productivity Prescription*, McGraw-Hill Book Company, New York, 1982.

Higgins, Lindley R., and Ruth W. Stidger: *Cost Reduction from A to Z*, McGraw-Hill, New York, 1976.

Sutermeister, Robert A.: *People and Productivity*, 3d ed., McGraw-Hill, New York, 1976.

DAVID L. BAIN, *David Bain Associates*

Productivity Measurement

Productivity is generally defined as the relationship between output and any or all associated inputs measured in real (physical volume) terms. It may be measured for producing organizations (business firms, government agencies, or private nonprofit institutions) or their components for which separate records are maintained (divisions, departments, plants, cost centers). Likewise, it may be measured for industries, sectors, or entire economies. Early concepts and measures of productivity related mainly to the macroeconomic level. Since the late 1940s, there has been increasing emphasis on measuring productivity in plant units or companies. The underlying concepts and measurement techniques are the same, however, regardless of the level of aggregation, although the uses of the measures differ. At the macroeconomic level, the measures are used (1) to analyze the sources of productivity advances and their economic impacts as background for projections of outputs or input requirements and (2) for formulation of policies to promote relatively stable economic growth. In a particular company, productivity measures are used as a management tool (1) for promoting productivity and (2) for budgeting and longer-term projections. The following discussion focuses on productivity measures for the firm.

Concepts and Meaning. When output is related to all associated inputs (usually in ratio form converted to index numbers for successive time periods), the resulting *total productivity measures* reflect the net reduction of real costs per unit of output and thus the increase in productive efficiency. *Output* is generally a weighted aggregate of physical units of the various products of the firm. *Inputs* consist of the three major cost categories: labor, intermediate products (materials, supplies, energy, and purchased outside services), and capital—likewise expressed in real, constant dollars. *Partial productivity measures* are the ratios of output to individual classes of inputs. These reflect changes not only in productive efficiency but also in the mix of inputs, or factor substitutions. Thus, the most usual partial productivity ratio, output per worker-hour, reflects increases in capital and other inputs per worker-hour, as well as general efficiency changes.

A variant measure is *total factor productivity* (TFP), for which the constant-dollar intermediate product purchases are deducted from the real value of gross output to yield a measure of real value added. This real product measure is then related to the inputs of the basic factors of production, labor, and capital (including developed land). The advantage of TFP measures is that they are consistent among firms and coordinate with macroeconomic measures, since value added sums up to gross product of the business sector by industry. Nevertheless, total productivity measures seem preferable for company management purposes, since (1) all inputs must be considered in seeking least-cost combinations and (2) over time, managers try to reduce inputs of purchased goods and services, as well as of labor and capital factors, per unit of output.

Changes in total productivity in the short run reflect changes in rates of utilization of capacity over the business cycle. Over the longer run, productivity increase reflects technological and organizational advances resulting from cost-reducing innovations in the ways and means of production. These, in turn, derive from (1) research and development activities in the given firm and by suppliers of producers' goods; (2) the tangible investments in the capital goods in which technological improvements are embodied; and (3) intangible investments in education and training required to produce and apply advancing technology, and in the health, safety, and mobility of workers. In addition, economies of scale, changes in allocative efficiency, and changes in the average inherent quality of resources may affect productivity.

Measurement. Measurement of productivity involves converting estimates of the value and costs of production into constant prices. Since values represent price times quantities ($V = P \times Q$), measurement of the output numerator and the input denominator of productivity ratios involves separating the P's and Q's in a detailed operating statement, then recombining the Q's in successive periods by multiplying (weighting) them by the constant prices of a single *base* period. Alternatively, the values and costs of production may be divided (deflated) by index numbers of average prices received for the firm's output and prices paid for the inputs. By and large, the underlying data for productivity estimates can be obtained from the company's information systems. Various problems will be encountered, such as adjusting outputs for model or quality changes or determining the degree of detail to be used for the categories of outputs and of inputs.[1] Since each firm is unique, the estimator must still use his or her best judgment in applying general principles to special situations.

Applications. In the late 1940s, the U.S. Bureau of Labor Statistics conducted a series of studies comparing levels and rates of change in labor productivity among plants in a variety of industries. The estimates were used to analyze causes of differences, but they had the side effect of stimulating some firms to measure their own productivity. A number of private investigators also measured productivity of various firms in selected industries. Kendrick's manual,[2] in particular, further promoted company efforts to measure productivity, total as well as partial. Another flurry of activity was stimulated by phase 2 of the wage and price control program in 1971–1972, which initially required company productivity estimates as part of the cost justification in applications for price increases. Since 1970, productivity has been measured in U.S. federal government agencies, covering more than half of all their civilian workers. An increasing number of state and local governments are also applying productivity measurement at various organizational and/or functional levels.

Programs. A major benefit of organizational productivity measurement is the promotion of "productivity-mindedness." To have maximum impact, the periodic results must be circulated beyond management circles and be linked to companywide productivity improvement programs. In 1975, the U.S. National Center for Productivity and Quality of Working Life began publishing the series *Improving Productivity, A Description of Selected Company Programs.* These programs, initiated by top management to help meet special challenges or to reinforce continuing cost-reduction efforts, involved workers at all levels in programs featuring work measurement and simplification, special incentive schemes, job redesign, value engineering, waste reduction, salvage, improved quality, and (where unions were strong) joint labor-management productivity committees. These productivity improvement programs were generally linked to measurement systems which (1) provided psychological reinforcement and (2) enabled quantification of the program results.

Diagnosis. Productivity measures themselves, as a part of broader management information systems, serve as a tool for identifying adverse situations or trends requiring further investigation and possibly corrective action. This function of the measures is enhanced if they are prepared in considerable detail with respect to types of inputs and organizational units. Thus, when plants producing the same range of products are being compared with one another or with industry averages, lower productivity ratios or smaller rates of increase become red signal flags. The ratios may also be used to set goals for reducing input requirements per unit of output during a specified future period.

Projections. Productivity measures are particularly valuable as a background for projection. Past trends should not be mechanically extrapolated, however, but should be modified to take account of new investments and other planned cost-reduction measures, as well as of projected sales, output, and consequent changes in rates of utilization of capacity. When divided into projected output, the *total* and *partial productivity projections* provide projections of labor, materials, and capital input requirements. These are helpful in planning recruitment, purchasing, and investment policies. When multiplied by projected average hourly labor compensation and other input prices, the input projections yield cost estimates for the future period. They are thus a useful ingredient for budgeting as well as for longer-term projections.

See also Contracting out; Cost improvement; Economic measurements; Profit improvement; Quality circles; Value-added tax; Work measurement; Work simplification and improvement.

NOTES

[1]For detailed explanations of measurement techniques, see John W. Kendrick and Daniel Creamer, *Measuring Productivity: Handbook with Case Studies, Studies in Business Economics No. 89,* The Conference Board, New York, 1965.

[2]Ibid.

REFERENCES

Bailey, David, and Tony Hubert: *Productivity Measurement,* Westmead, Farnborough, England, 1980.

Chen, Gordon K. C., and Robert E. McGarrah: *Productivity Management,* The Dryden Press, Chicago, 1982.

National Research Council: *Measurement and Interpretation of Productivity,* National Academy of Sciences, Washington, D.C., 1979.

JOHN W. KENDRICK, *George Washington University*

Professionalism in Management

"Modern life ever to a greater extent is grouping itself into professions."[1] The words are those of the distinguished philosopher Alfred North Whitehead, written in 1933. Such activity did not begin in the twentieth century, however. Occupational licensure, a step in professionalizing work, has deep historical roots which can be traced back to the tenth century in Europe in the form of the worker associations called guilds.[2] Today, almost every field involving career preparation has its proponents claiming a measure of professionalism. Such claims run the gamut of careers from those of the established professions, theology, medicine, and law, to those fields with perhaps more tenuous claims to true professionalism.

This entry explores the topic of professionalism and examines the extent to which management may be deemed a profession. The concept of profession and professional standards will be considered, utilizing, to some extent, the model of established profession; professionalizing activity will be discussed including present-day certification efforts. Additionally, this entry will address the negative aspects of professionalizing, the practical obstacles to management's becoming a profession in the traditional sense, and the challenge and opportunity to management.

Profession versus Professionalizing. The question of professionalism is one replete with emotion-laden issues, stemming as often from semantical misinterpretation as from reasoned disagreement. No one would argue with the notion that a competent manager behaves professionally; yet, it is a large step from regarding certain behavior as professional to classifying the work as a profession. Traditionally, a *profession* may be defined as a "calling," often requiring extensive academic preparation, while the term *professionalizing* refers to the process of improving the various aspects of a field of endeavor to bring that field closer to the ideal model of a profession.

The lists of criteria for a profession are as numerous as writers on the subject; however, the following criteria are common to most listings: an organized body of knowledge, client recognition of the authority of the profession, a code of ethics, and a professional culture nurtured by professional associations.[3] The criteria may be considered as constituting an ideal model to which no field fully measures up. One can readily see that the field of management does meet all these standards to some degree, but the issue is precisely a question of degree. On the other hand, while management may not meet the standards as fully as the traditionally accepted profession, there is much evidence of professionalizing activity.

The Work of Professionalizing. Many are active in the work of *professionalizing* management. Some are engaged in better defining the work itself, the body of knowledge, and the role of the manager.[4] Others are engaging in activity to arrive at a consensus regarding standards of conduct.[5] Such activity is occurring in other countries as well as in the United States, as evidenced by the codes of the British Institute of Management, the Greek Management Association, and the RKW of the Federal Republic of Germany.[6] Another movement to professionalize is the attempt to certify managers. A model certification program, based upon present-day certification efforts might include such phases as an evaluation of the manager's experience and education credentials; participation in intensive workshops or seminars; an examination of management knowledge; the acceptance of a code of ethics; and provision for continuing education and development. Some of the most successful certification efforts have been made in the more technical functional areas of business management, such as accounting, insurance, and personnel.

While codes of ethics are considered essential for all professions, the proliferation of rules of behavior may appear to some to be sterile or ineffective. To those people, it may be suggested that there is an alternative or complement to this approach. It is the idea that the development of character is basic to the notion of ethics and ethical behavior. The origin of this idea lies in the classical philosophy of Aristotle. He suggested that moral virtue is the product of habit.[7] It is clear from this tenet that one can develop the virtues of integrity, justice, and loyalty, to name a few, all of which are central to professional behavior in the leader/manager. While this character development is ultimately personal, training and development programs can address the issue and assist in character formation. The leadership training at the United States Infantry School at Fort Benning,

Georgia, for example, encourages the development of these virtues (which the school calls leadership traits), as do the programs of many other institutions. All corporate development programs would do well to include this subject in their development curricula.

Obstacles and Problems. Although professionalism is considered a desirable end, there are problems associated with its attainment. The past provides dismaying evidence of how licensing and other restrictions of professions have, in some instances, denied entrance to those otherwise qualified, dampened competition, and placed profession as the end, rather than the means to an end, such as service to the client, patient, or organization.

In "The Informers' Tale," Benham and Benham present a satire on the extremes of professionalizing as the profession of "informing" the public on the best products and services. The professionalizing evolves to such a degree that the new professionals proclaim, "Who knows more than we about what we're doing?"[8] The classical admonition *"Quis custodiet ipsos custodes?"* (Who will guard the guardians?) comes to mind. Those involved in the work of professionalizing must avoid the state of mind mentioned earlier—that a profession is an end in itself rather than a means to an end.

Challenge and Opportunities. The work of the manager has become increasingly important in our complex world. While management may never become a profession in the traditional sense, the actions of countless individuals continue to professionalize the critical work of management. The process is ultimately personal, thus establishing as relevant the Aristotelean ideas of virtue development and character formation. Professional associations are a necessary complement, but it is on the individual level that managerial challenges will be met and that managerial opportunities will be successfully seized.

See also Audit, management; Ethics, managerial; Management, definitions of; Management, historical development of; Management theory, science, and approaches; Manager, definitions of; Social responsibility of business.

NOTES

[1]Alfred North Whitehead, *Adventures of Ideas*, The Macmillan Company, New York, 1933.

[2]Lee Benham, "The Demand for Occupational Licensure," in Simon Rottenberg (ed.), *Occupational Licensure and Regulations*, American Enterprise Institute for Public Policy Research, Washington, D.C., 1980, p. 13.

[3]Earnest Greenwood, "The Elements of Professionalization," in Howard M. Vollmer and Donald L. Mills (eds.), *Professionalization*, Prentice-Hall, Inc., Englewood Cliffs, N.J., 1966, p. 9.

[4]See Henry Mintzberg, "Managerial Work: Analysis from Observation," *Management Science*, vol. 18, no. 2, October 1971, p. B–97.

[5]Terry P. Brown, "Craft-Minded Chief at Bendix Tries to Set a Businessman's Code," *The Wall Street Journal*, vol. 186, no. 99, Nov. 18, 1975.

[6]Nancy G. McNulty, "And Now, Professional Codes for the Practices of Management," *The Conference Board Record*, Vol. 12, no. 4, April 1975.

[7]H. Rackham, *Aristotle: The Nicomachean Ethics*, Harvard University Press, Cambridge, 1962, p. 71.

[8]Lee Benham and Alexandra Benham, "The Informers' Tale," in Simon Rottenberg (ed.), *Occupational Licensure and Regulation*, American Enterprise Institute for Public Policy Research, Washington, D.C., 1980, pp. 317–325.

ANTHONY F. JURKUS, *Louisiana Tech University*

Profit Improvement

The key factor for a successful profit-improvement effort is the determination of the organization's chief executive. Voluntary programs initiated by the chief executive officer or down-the-line managers rarely achieve results interesting enough to write about. Although approaches to profit improvement vary from applying basic principles of good management to changing fundamental management tenets, individuals who have successfully implemented major profit-improvement programs seem to agree on three major steps:

1. Identifying specifically what has to be done and where, and securing a commitment from upper-level management

2. Building an environment for change

3. Implementing a number of profit-improvement projects and monitoring their progress

Identifying What Has To Be Done

Too many managers wait for problems to develop. Especially in new assignments, they tend to let valuable time slip by in get-acquainted meetings with colleagues and subordinates, visits to plant locations, and talks with customers. They read company literature and reports and gain familiarity with major activities, processes, and operations. But once the firefighting starts, they wish they had done more.

Starting from Scratch. The new executive should try to get a handle on an assignment in the first 30 to 90 days. Doing so will require four key steps:

1. Assess the company's present operations and outlook for future growth, and pinpoint overall industry and company problems.

2. Identify major profit-building opportunities for significantly improving near-term company per-

formance while maintaining or strengthening longer-term goals.

3. Evaluate the company's organization structure and its individual skills in terms of what is needed to realize the opportunities identified.

4. Reach agreement with the boss or the board of directors on specific improvement recommendations.

Step 1: Develop an economic and financial perspective. As a first step, the executive should develop such a perspective of his or her industry and company. This step will lay the groundwork for other steps that should be taken during this period.

For example, to establish an information base for this analysis, the executive of a large metal-fabricating company gathered financial and economic data by using *Thomas Register, Standard & Poor's Industry Surveys, Value Line* industry and company reports, *Wall Street Transcripts, Predicast* industry surveys, trade association material, and recent industry investment studies by securities brokerage firms and banks.

For industry data, he referred to *Census of Manufacturers, U.S. Industrial Outlook,* and *SEC-FTC Quarterly Reports of Manufacturing Corporations.*

For company data, he used *Moody's* and *Standard & Poor's Stock Reports,* his own company's and competitors' prospectuses, the Securities and Exchange Commission's detailed Form 10 KS and annual reports for the last 5 years, and available division, product-line, and plant financial statements.

With this information, the executive was able to develop an initial understanding of the industry, e.g., product-line characteristics, degree of vertical-horizontal integration, cyclical and seasonal influences, and four to six key factors for success broken down into their profit-making components. For example, if marketing effectiveness is a key success factor, the profit-building components might be a strong distributor organization, high market share, and a profitable product mix sold.

Many successful executives advocate conducting this profit-improvement analysis personally instead of relying on staff work. One marketing head used this approach and then invited the controller to participate in financial perspective meetings. These meetings included brainstorming sessions where "wild" ideas for improvement were encouraged, with evaluation postponed to keep the discussion on a positive note. Subsequently, the marketing chief classified the improvement ideas by functional responsibility and assigned the appropriate individuals to evaluate them.

Step 2: Identify profit-building opportunities. The next step is to evaluate the improvement ideas identified as part of the economic and financial analysis and to discard those that are obviously not feasible. The profit-improvement potential of each idea

is assessed, including the assignment of a dollar value to less tangible benefits. Implementation costs are estimated, and the next steps to be taken are outlined along with responsibility assignments and timing for complicated changes. Profit-improvement recommendations are then developed and classified as near or long term. Finally, priorities are established on the basis of profit-building impact.

Selection of High-Impact Projects. Faced with the need to improve near-term performance, the critical skill is to pinpoint and take action on those high-impact or dramatic and highly visible changes that can be accomplished quickly. In addition to their profit-building impact, these "quick and easy" changes both encourage subordinates to initiate a momentum for change and bolster senior management's confidence in the executive's ability to bring about change.

Another advantage of these actions is that they can often be taken in the absence of a well-formulated strategy, which is generally difficult (and usually not imperative) to define at the early stages of one's exposure. Thus, the executive can make some essential near-term improvements while wrestling with overall strategy.

Example of Short-Term Plans. One new marketer, for example, who was selling production items to off-road equipment manufacturers, had sound concerns about his company's capacity to compete in a particular product area in terms of costs and technology. While he gave this major strategic question due recognition, he resisted letting it obscure current improvement possibilities. These four immediate projects became the main elements of his plan for marketing improvements:

1. Raise prices 5 percent across the board on June 1 and again on December 1. It was thought that higher prices had a good chance of sticking without loss in volume because of the few sources of supply and the lengthy new-source approval processes followed by customers. The decision was made to have two rounds of smaller increases because one large increase might really invite new competition.

2. Institute minimum order quantities on June 1. Demand for replacement parts, in particular, had drifted so low that the plant was choking with uneconomical runs.

3. Shift promptly the burden of following major new business inquiries from the field sales force to the research and development laboratory. The technical skills of the sales force were not adequate to work with customer engineering. Training would take time. As volume was needed, the best stopgap measure was to make development personnel responsible for key inquiries.

4. Ask research to explore the feasibility of lowering raw material costs by December 1. This was

731

clearly a longer-range project that would have a major bearing on strategy; moreover, it could have a sizable influence on second-year results. The point now was to get it started.

This simple plan was straightforward and proved effective. It was not cloaked in an all-encompassing strategy. It dealt with immediate issues, yet it provided for input from research for strategy resolution.

Step 3: Evaluate the organization structure and personnel. The next step in the initial stage is to evaluate the company's organization structure and the skills and capabilities of its personnel in relation to the opportunities identified. This plan is essential to develop a complete business plan.

Organization. In serious turnaround situations where (as is frequently the case) structure is often conspicuously absent, it is imperative to establish one even if it is only temporary. If a formal organization is in place, it is still worthwhile to consider modification since the structure is probably designed to maintain the status quo rather than to bring about change.

One good way to start is by removing as many layers as possible between top management and first-line supervisors. In one situation, seven layers were cut to three with immediate benefits of improved communications and a better feeling for what was going on. It also improved the executive's own use of time because he now had more things to do than were feasible and had to decide which were vital and which could be put off. Span of control is also an area for organizational improvement. Where a great deal of change has to be managed, additional supervision is usually needed; where little change is required, span of control can typically be increased. In one company, for example, where product quality had eroded significantly, the newly appointed executive cut work sections of 20 to 30 people down to 12 to 14; sections where a great deal of change was required were reduced to 8 people. In another company, however, the manufacturing vice president found that his lower-level managers were supervising only 5 to 10 people. Investigation showed that this setup originated a few years back when the organization was expanding rapidly and new supervisors were scrambling simply to meet their basic responsibilities. But, as in any position, there is a learning curve over time, and the supervisors now knew their jobs. By increasing the span of control of some supervisors and assigning others to vital profit-improvement projects, work force utilization was greatly improved.

It should be cautioned, however, that wholesale organizational changes, particularly involving the field sales force, should be considered only as a last resort. It takes at least a year for most organizational changes to be effective—even when skilled managers are on board. One chemical company consolidated its autonomous selling units and soon found that volume in certain areas was dropping. The reason: There had been a sweeping change in customer contact continuity which eroded a substantial number of account positions where personal selling relationships were vital.

Personnel. Especially in the case of a new assignment, the executive should make an early evaluation of personnel. Many newly appointed—and incumbent—executives have difficulty coming to grips with an organizational evaluation of this nature. This indecision stems from the absence of three sets of guidelines:

1. Established standards for the specific management skills needed to accomplish demanding objectives

2. Objective appraisals of the individuals involved against these standards, asking the question, "Can the organization and its people do significantly more to improve results than is now being done?"

3. A consideration of all the alternatives to replacing personnel, such as training and job structuring

Once an evaluation is made, it is wise to determine through all available sources if any key lieutenants considered vital to a profit turnaround are thinking of leaving, since continuity is essential for success. Organizational change often gives rise to career evaluation on the part of the incumbent staff. It behooves the top executive to seek feedback and to take proper actions to hold good people.

Bringing in new people poses three problems. First, it takes time for a new manager to learn the operation, decide what has to be done, and begin doing it. Someone hired from a competitor may take 6 months to get up to speed; someone hired from a different industry may require twice that long. Second, the newly appointed executive will need all the inside knowledge available, and present members of his or her staff have valuable knowledge in their heads, not on paper. It was impossible, for example, for the president of a major publisher to replace his otherwise incompetent financial vice president at the outset of his appointment because he was completely dependent on the latter's knowledge. The larger the organization is, the more this becomes a factor. Third, the farther afield one looks for talent, the higher the risk is that the people brought in (1) will not meet expectations and (2) may damage the morale of the existing management team. In *The Will to Manage*, Marvin Bower, the former managing director of McKinsey & Company, Inc., supports this view:

Although I can't prove it, I believe that the insider who seems 65 percent qualified for the job is likely to outperform the typical outsider who seems 90

percent qualified. Such assessments are apt to be unbalanced, because the weaknesses of the insider are known, while those of the outsider are hard to learn accurately in advance. Since an insider's success will improve the morale and productivity of the executive group generally, it is usually worth taking a substantial risk on an insider, particularly if the only count against him is youth or lack of experience for the job.[1]

Step 4: Present the business plan to superiors. At this final step of the initial phase, the new executive must let his or her superior or the board know in what direction he or she is going—and why. There are two good reasons for this:

1. A logical formal action plan is a good indicator of likely results and, if it is approved, will help buy time for accomplishing objectives. The plan can similarly be used by the chief executive or the board, which may be under pressure from external sources, e.g., the financial press, stockholders, customers, to explain what is being done, what can be expected, and by when.

2. The superior officer may have some special insight as a result of more experience with the organization and its environment. For example, one newly appointed marketing chief failed to tell his superior of an important downward price that was planned. A competitor not only followed but went one step further—a reaction that the marketer's superior would have fully anticipated because of his familiarity with the competitor's market strategy.

Building an Environment for Change

When an organization is in profit trouble, its down-the-line managers are typically backed into a corner, defending themselves and the system. Their response to pressure for change is: "It worked in the past, it should work now; just give us a little more time and staff." In this situation, unless the incumbent can change the tone of the organization and get it off the defensive, there will be little chance for making improvements.

To build this climate for change, the executive in charge must assure the organization that it is with a winner and that the new directions are both sound and reasonable. The executive should plan steps to take charge, to gain the cooperation of other top executives, to motivate line managers, to win the confidence of rank-and-file employees, and to initiate profit-improvement actions.

Taking Charge. In every business, there are key decisions in which the executive must be directly involved. These decisions must be firmly established so that subordinate managers know on what and when to check before they move ahead. These "man-

agement guides" should cover such topics as work force levels; replacement of managerial or technical staff; compensation changes; organization changes in terms of either structure or promotion of key personnel; capital expenditure approval; changes in terms of sale; pricing; movement into new distribution channels; deferment of expenses; ethical conduct on the part of managers; and a host of other topics. Management guides will save a great deal of time and frustration and give down-the-line managers a clear idea of their freedom to act in the months ahead.

Motivating Executives. An operating chief must review the company's business situation in depth with his or her key executives, using facts and figures while carefully avoiding opinions and criticism. If the object is a turnaround, the manager must explain what has to be done to return to performance levels of prior years and must specify monthly profit goals for the next 6 months. There is a critical need to convince key people of the reasonableness of objectives and to indicate clearly what is expected of each staff member. Once this framework for action is established, its motivational impact can be maintained by:

1. Providing for daily, weekly, and monthly personal guidance to staff members as they give progress reports.

2. Helping them develop projects to increase profits. The job of any manager, including the chief executive officer, is largely one of teaching others how to attain objectives. In a turnaround situation, it may be assumed that staff members need extra coaching.

3. Motivating them through pride, compensation, stock options, growth, or survival in the job and with the company.

Motivating Middle Managers. One of the most powerful motivators is the opportunity to advance on merit. To this end, a mandatory annual performance review should be established for every managerial position in the company. Such a program ensures that responsibilities have been clearly assigned and authority has been properly delegated. In effect, it is a vehicle for planning each individual's job objectives so that they are in line with company objectives. That way, each manager knows what is specifically expected and can measure his or her own progress against these expectations.

The sooner the down-the-line managers are convinced that results will determine their future compensation increases and promotions, the sooner the cobwebs will disappear. Performance reviews open lines of communication that often do not (but should) exist, especially in an organization with significant turnaround opportunities. Every higher-level executive should read as many managers' performance reviews as possible and provide his or her own personal counsel on how to improve each review. Down-the-line managers should be expected to do the same with their staff members.

Another means of motivating managers is taking a one-on-one approach, instead of a committee approach, to problem solving. Executives should encourage subordinate managers to do the same in their problem-solving efforts. In committees, people may be reluctant to call a spade a spade, whereas on an individual basis, they will talk more freely and openly.

Stock options can also serve as powerful motivators, not only for top executives but also for supervisors. These managers will recognize the degree of importance placed on their thoughts and the results they produce.

Finally, there should be a careful review of the company's compensation plan, especially as it applies to the managerial group. More than one company has been hampered by an unfair plan. Raises may be in order for certain top performers. The existing incentive plan may need to be sweetened or even replaced.

Gaining Employee Confidence. Effective executives stress the importance of developing organizational "reach," that is, getting to know all, or as many as possible, of the people in the organization. Employees get a tremendous boost from talking directly to the company president and, better yet, from being addressed by name. Some newly appointed executives find that contact can be made with up to 1000 or more employees within the first 6 months on the job and is well worth the investment in time and effort.

Initiating Profit-Improvement Actions. A quick way to change the organizational environment is to initiate tangible profit-improvement actions such as the following:

Freezing Employment Levels. Establishing a holding action on costs is a straightforward task. In a labor-intensive operation, it means controlling head counts and wage increases. To control head count, the key executive should require that all requisitions for additional personnel bear his or her signature. This obligation will reduce the number of requests by 90 to 95 percent. In terms of controlling pay rates, an executive will have less leverage if the operation is unionized. It is possible, however, to put a lid on the costs of promotions by requiring that all salary increases due to promotion include the name of the person being replaced and his or her new assignment. This information prevents the promotion of people to new jobs created solely for the purpose of increasing their salaries.

Another sound approach is to have an analysis prepared of the work force levels as of the end of the month and on the same date for each year as far back as 4 years. This analysis should be developed on a department-by-department basis to see where head counts have risen in relation to the sales level, production level, or some other indicator of business activity appropriate to each department. This information should be presented to the managers with the request that they achieve former levels of employment in relation to the activity or (for those who have done a good job) with congratulations and encouragement to find new ways to increase the productivity of their organization.

Discontinuing Uneconomical Projects. This action requires sorting the work being performed in the company into two categories: (1) maintenance of the day-to-day business and (2) project work, such as that designed to develop new products, reduce costs, increase sales, strengthen employer-employee relations, and improve the company's computer system.

Obviously, business maintenance activities must go on, and steps should be taken to reduce the costs of performing these activities. One note of caution: The current selling-expense level will be a very sensitive area to tamper with. Sales activities are close to the customer, and many an emotional case has been presented for not cutting selling expenses for that reason. One approach is to establish a specific dollar amount that is to be spent and make sure that the marketing managers spend all of it in the most effective manner possible. Their job is to produce income, not to save on the budgeted amount for selling expense.

On the other hand, projects can be started or stopped without affecting the day-to-day business maintenance work, although they can affect the long-term levels of effectiveness and costs of performing the day-to-day activities. Each project should be evaluated on a cost-benefit basis. Too often, managers get carried away with projects that have little or no tangible benefits. Careful analysis will reveal many projects not worth doing, and they can generate substantial unanticipated extra costs once they are under way. Likewise, the potential benefits identified are often never realized for one reason or another.

Implementing Change

Once the right environment has been established, implementation of change should begin without delay. Many executives in turnaround situations rely upon change through sound project management, from the installation of a new piece of machinery to the development of a new data processing system. The value in the project-management approach is that it forces the participants to focus on the end results. Successful project management follows two principles: (1) Keep track of *what* you want to do, *whom* you want to do it, and the *date* you want it done; and (2) decide which of these three parameters you can afford to use as a safety valve.

Project Guidelines. In setting up projects, several guidelines should be kept in mind:

1. Make sure that if the project is successful, it will move the company toward a solution to the major problem outlined in the business plan.

2. Be careful not to saddle one individual with responsibility for more than one major project at a time. Within one key executive's area of responsibility, however, it is not uncommon for 20 to 30 major and minor projects to be going on simultaneously.

3. Offer assistance, and work with managers on projects. When managers and others see that mistakes can be made without prejudice, it reinforces their feeling that change is acceptable with minimum personal risk and maximum potential gain.

4. Keep in mind that 99 percent of the projects undertaken will never adhere to the original plan. In introducing change, there is usually very little historical (i.e., empirical) evidence on which to base a plan; therefore, executives should allow a little leeway and be prepared to give the project as much time and money as they think will be required. These are one-time expenditures that will soon be forgotten if the technical quality of the project is outstanding. For example, one executive implemented the first major real-time teleprocessing computer system for controlling work in process. Instead of winding up the project once it had met the original specifications, his staff spent several additional months redefining and reworking it. As a result, they were able to reduce related employment by 5 percent (approximately a 200 percent return on their investment) and gain much greater acceptance of the system by down-the-line managers.

5. Accept the fact that things will get worse before they get better. This is true whether computer software is modified, new equipment is introduced, or manual procedures are changed. The key executive should warn superiors, subordinates, and peers to expect additional problems and to avoid prejudice during a critical transitional period.

Tracking Progress and Taking Corrective Action

The basic reason for setting up a monitoring system is to enable an executive to take corrective action when required. Another reason is to establish a baseline—before-and-after measures for each activity—against which to report progress.

Indicators. Every time a major change is made, an indicator should be installed that will show whether the change (1) is being implemented and (2) is accomplishing its objective. Initial performance indicators need not be sophisticated or minutely accurate. The information does not have to be summarized, a process that causes delays and makes the information stale. Nor does it have to be machine-generated, for that often takes too long to get under way.

Overreaction. When a performance indicator identifies an impending problem, it is wise to avoid a drastic reaction that might destroy the fragile environment for change. If the indicators have been carefully set up, the problem area can be spotted before people outside the operation are aware of it. Early detection is a decided advantage and enables the executive to attack the problem in an orderly manner.

Pace of Change. In tracking progress, the pace of change is also important. If a change is not moving as fast as it should, perhaps managers are being asked to do too many things. If members of a management team are assigned more improvement projects than they can handle, they are likely to balk and retreat into their old roles and habits.

Reinforcement of Successes. Although many executives spend a great deal of their time modifying changes that are not effective, each change should be held up to appropriate members of the management team as an example of what can be done. In addition, some kind of visible reward should be provided for those responsible for implementation to reinforce the value of risking change.

Fine Tuning. Finally, executives should avoid fine-tuning improvements. When 80 percent of the targeted results are achieved, hand the project over to the appropriate down-the-line manager and concentrate on the remaining opportunity areas. Otherwise, it will be difficult, if not impossible, to achieve overall improvement objectives in the allocated time span.

Summary

Executives entering new positions charged with the responsibility for significantly improving earnings per share or for activities that are assigned to them often lack a sound concept of what they should be doing and how and when to do it during their initial 6 to 12 months on the job. Many tend to forgo formal planning and are satisfied in spending the initial "quiet period" on the job getting the feel of things, meeting other executives and subordinates, taking a look at some operations, and learning the business by osmosis before becoming forced into firefighting, attending meetings, and serving on project committees.

Without a sound and demanding concept of what

they should accomplish during their initial months, executives may lose the opportunity to gain a clear understanding of the economics of the company within its industry, identify the significant profit-improvement opportunities, develop hypotheses, and determine sound concepts of what is achievable by when. Without this background, the newly appointed executive is not in a position to evaluate his or her organization effectively against a demanding standard; i.e., whether the organization and its people can do significantly more to improve results than is being done—a key ingredient for accomplishing the turnaround objectives.

See also Accounting, cost analysis and control; Audit, management; Budgets and budget preparation; Cost improvement; Productivity improvement.

NOTES

[1]Marvin Bower, *The Will to Manage,* McGraw-Hill Book Company, New York, 1966, p. 170.

REFERENCES

De Bono, Edward: *Lateral Thinking for Management,* American Management Association, New York, 1971.

Eisenberg, Joseph: *Turnaround Management,* McGraw-Hill, New York, 1972.

Schaffer, Robert H.: "Demand Better Results—And Get Them," *Harvard Business Review,* vol. 52, no. 6, Boston, Mass., November–December 1974, p. 91.

Much of the information presented here is based on the successful profit-improvement experiences of E. Joseph Bensler, Citibank; Frederick J. Mancheski, Echlin Manufacturing Company; and John W. Priesing, Phelps Dodge Industries. Their help and advice are greatly appreciated.

JOSPEH EISENBERG, *Profit-Improvement, Inc.,*
Management Consultants

Profit Sharing

In the early history of the United States, the American economy was, by and large, an agricultural, small-craft economy. There was very little need for formal profit-sharing programs because cooperation and informal methods of sharing were inherent in the structure of family-owned farms, fishing, and small-craft partnerships. That is the way it was, but something happened on the road to the twentieth century. Corporations were created and as a general rule, the bigger they grew, the more impersonal they became. Corporations developed a wage relationship with their work force, but they usually forgot to forge an employee link to profits and ownership. Employ-

ees became wage earners—pure and simple—not concerned about the overall success of the business because they did not have a *direct* stake in profits or ownership.

One reason there is such great difficulty achieving cooperation between labor and management and mutuality of interest is our fragmented approach to motivation. Executives, salaried personnel, hourly employees, and stockholders are all focusing on diverse targets and are rewarded in different ways.

We have stratified our corporate pyramids and developed horizontal modes of motivating each stratum. We have driven artificial wedges between groups, and now we wonder why alienation, lack of cohesion, and loss of employee identification with the firm plague our corporations.

Individuals differ considerably. At different stages of their lives they respond to varying incentives—some of which are short-term, some long-term, some psychic, some financial, some stock, some cash. Different types of incentive hierarchies can be developed which complement or reinforce each other and together meet the diverse motivational needs of people. No one can motivate another person. Motivation is an engine that the worker turns on inside himself or herself.

The most management can do is to create a participative, sharing climate, a motivational environment in which this kind of "turn-on" will likely occur. This is where quality of work life (QWL) committees, quality circles, financial participation and employee share ownership fit in—as a way to create the climate in which excellence is recognized and rewarded financially and psychologically.

Types of Gainsharing Programs. There are a number of ways to achieve greater employee involvement and higher productivity. Compatible with direct worker participation in shop-floor discussions are gainsharing plans, such as Improshare®, Scanlon, Rucker, profit sharing (cash, deferred, or combination), employee stock ownership programs (ESOPs), and other hybrid plans like the Participative Management Plan at Motorola, Inc. For example,

Improshare® shares "physical productivity" gains.

Scanlon shares "labor cost" savings.

Rucker shares gains in "value added."

Profit sharing shares "bottom line" performance.

A review of characteristics reveals that there is not one "best" way to share. There are several options, depending on the circumstances in the particular case, and plans frequently work well together in tandem.

Procter & Gamble Co. has the oldest continuous profit-sharing program in the United States (1887). A number of other well-known profit sharing plans, still functioning today, were initiated between 1910 and 1917—e.g., Eastman Kodak Co. (1912); Andersen Corp. (1914); Yarway Corp. (1915); Harris Trust and Savings Bank (1916); Sears, Roebuck and Co. (1916); and Johnson Wax (1917). Scanlon and Rucker plans were developed in the 1930s and Improshare® came into being in the period from 1974 to 1976.

An Adaptable and Flexible Concept. Large companies as well as small companies share profits. Profit sharing today is practiced in a wide range of industries—i.e., manufacturing, retail trade, service companies, banks, and underground in the Mines of Mapco., Inc. Profits are shared in labor-intensive and capital-intensive enterprises, in mass production and job shop situations, in low- and high-technology firms.

Profit sharing can pay out rewards in cash—at frequent intervals with reserves set aside in case of deficit periods—with a short span between effort and reward (as under the Scanlon plan).

Profit sharing can also defer rewards—crediting the amounts to participants' accounts, investing these monies in stocks and bonds, and providing participants with an "investment wage" to complement their cash wage. Employees can be given an ownership stake in new technology—in the plant and equipment of their own companies and of the nation.

Profit sharing is the most common example of gain sharing, but only profit-sharing plans (deferred or cash) with fixed formulas should be considered gain sharing.

The Gain Sharing Philosophy. Gain sharing is a reflection of a management philosophy which recognizes the dignity and value of employees. The philosophy of participative gain sharing has support at both the macro and micro levels. Gain sharing makes compensation sensitive to the economic circumstances of the employer and adds flexibility to a significant component of total compensation. If the economy turns down, company profits will likely drop, less will go to employees in gainsharing, unit costs will automatically be cut, and the company's wage bill will shrink—without laying off people.

With gain sharing, there would be automatic concessions in a downturn, and automatic recoupment of concessions with recovery. The Japanese use this concept of wage flexibility through profit sharing to undercut competition in recessionary periods and to reward employees during upswings.

Profit sharing, at the micro level, meets the test of the market, focuses attention on all costs, and encourages the acceptance of change and technology. It also promotes teamwork among employees, management, and stockholders by providing a single target for all. There is no "double standard." Rewards are paid out only when the employer can afford them. A recent New York Stock Exchange study revealed that 86 percent of listed companies rated their profit sharing plans as successful in raising productivity.[1]

Union Attitudes. Union attitudes toward profit sharing historically have been hostile or indifferent while other goals have had higher priorities. Unions have, by and large, never espoused the concept of "contingent" compensation—i.e., contingent upon corporate profitability.

Nevertheless, in the Profit Sharing Research Foundation (PSRF) study *Profit Sharing in 38 Large Companies,* 24 out of the 38 companies were unionized to some extent, and unionized employees participated in the profit-sharing programs in 19 out of the 24 companies.[2]

While many companies with unions share profits, most very large unionized companies do not. Before 1981, negotiated profit-sharing plans were rare.

Recessionary Influence. During the time span from 1981 to 1983, many companies expressed a willingness to share profits they did not have in return for concessions from labor. Establishment of profit-sharing programs in weak companies rather than strong is a new phenomenon. In depressed industries like automobiles, farm implements, rubber, publishing, steel, trucking, mining and energy, profit-sharing plans were negotiated at General Motors, Ford Motor, International Harvester, Caterpillar Tractor, Uniroyal, General Tire (Waco, Texas), *New York Daily News,* McLouth Steel, Colorado Fuel and Iron, Wheeling–Pittsburgh Steel, and System 99.

Deferred Profit Sharing. In 1939, new interest in profit sharing was sparked by Senator Arthur H. Vandenberg's Senate Finance Subcommittee study of profit sharing. At that time there were only 37 qualified deferred profit-sharing programs and a few hundred cash programs in operation. After intense examination and hearings, the Senate subcommittee concluded that profit sharing can be "eminently successful, when properly established, in creating employee relations that make for peace, equity, efficiency and contentment"; it went so far as to declare profit sharing "essential to the ultimate maintenance of the capitalistic system."

Subsequent to the Senate report, encouragement was given to companies through favorable tax legislation to initiate deferred profit-sharing plans for employees. Considerable growth took place between 1939 and 1974, with plans doubling numerically every 5 years.

Impact of ERISA. The passage of the Employee Retirement Income Security Act (ERISA) on September 4, 1974, slowed this growth and precipitated many terminations. The intent of ERISA was to protect employee rights under qualified retirement income plans (i.e., corporate pensions, deferred profit sharing, stock bonus) and welfare plans. ERISA did not require any company to establish a plan, nor did it set any minimum benefit levels. ERISA did lay down many complicated provisions with respect to participation, vesting, funding, fiduciary standards, reporting/disclosure, and plan termination insurance. These provisions impacted all qualified plans, but the most adverse impact was on defined benefit pensions.

After ERISA much debate arose (and continues to the present time) as to whether ERISA and other subsequent legislation, like the Economic Recovery Tax Act of 1981 (ERTA) and the Tax Equity and Fiscal Responsibility Act of 1982 (TEFRA), would trigger a move toward defined-contribution plans [profit sharing, thrift, 401(k), stock bonus, ESOPs, and money purchase pensions] or toward defined-benefit pensions.

Some companies terminated their profit-sharing programs in favor of the apparent security of pensions, while others terminated their pension programs in favor of the flexible funding nature of profit sharing.

The argument is moot because both types of plans have their advantages and limitations, their strengths and their weaknesses. They also have their own distinct places in providing retirement income adequacy, and they work well together in the same company.

Defined-Benefit Pension Plans. Defined-benefit pensions satisfy specific needs, particularly for people with long past service who are close to retirement when the retirement income plan is initiated, people whose earnings rise rapidly in years immediately preceding their retirement, higher-paid executives, and employees who like the sense of security conveyed by the promise of fixed benefits related to final pay.

Immediately after the passage of ERISA, defined-benefit pension plan approvals fell significantly, but they rebounded well and have demonstrated considerable growth in recent years.

Numerically, more deferred profit-sharing programs were initiated in the six years (1977 to 1982) than any other type of retirement income plan, as shown in Table P-4.

- Defined-benefit pensions accounted for 27 percent of new plans (63 percent of participants).

- Money purchase pensions accounted for 29 percent of new plans (10 percent of participants).

- Profit sharing represented 44 percent of new plans (27 percent of participants).

Many large companies currently providing pensions do not want to increase their pension obligations with unpredictable cost implications for the future. Meeting pension commitments during a recession is a heavy burden for many companies. Firms in these categories are supplementing their pensions with profit sharing or thrift plans, frequently 401(k) plans.

Little benefit accrues to a young person's pension in the early working years. Accruals are skewed to older workers nearing retirement. Ten-year "cliff" vesting is common in pension plans and young people leaving the company before 10 years of service may get nothing from their pension plans.

Vesting Practices. Under profit sharing, individual accounts build up more rapidly for younger employees and this, combined with faster vesting, makes possible a more meaningful portable retirement benefit in our highly mobile society. Vesting in profit sharing is normally graduated, starting at 1 to 3 years of service and rising by 10 percent increments to 100 percent after 10 to 11 years of service.

Deferred profit-sharing plans emphasize profitability and affordability. Company contributions are directly linked to corporate performance. Profit sharing is an incentive approach to retirement income security.

The investment risk is carried by participants under a defined contribution plan and by the company under a defined benefit program. Profit-sharing participants, however, also share in investment gains. They participate more fully in the risk-reward system.

The PSRF study, *Profit Sharing in 38 Large Companies*, revealed the benefits that actually accrued to long-service, nonmanagement employees under profit sharing. Overall, only 6 companies (18 per-

TABLE P-4 Number of Newly Approved Profit-Sharing and Pension Plans and Participants 1977–1982*

Plan type	Plan approvals		Participants	
	Number	Percent of total	Number	Percent of total
Profit sharing	172,475	44%	3,948,274	27%
Money purchase	113,183	29	1,424,490	10
Defined benefit	103,263	27	9,031,692	63
Total	388,921	100%	14,404,456	100%

*Excluding stock bonus, ESOPs, TRAESOPs, bond purchase, and target benefit plans.

cent) out of the 33 that provided this data generated profit-sharing benefits that fell below the "pension standard." Of the 33 companies 27 (82 percent) have profit-sharing programs that have generated benefits from 102 percent to 1011 percent of the pension standard.[3]

Retirement Distribution Options. Fully funded, rapidly vested, individual account profit-sharing plans with no past service liabilities do not put a burden on social security, but rather greatly buttress the system.

Retirees under defined-benefit plans have only a promise of fixed dollars per month during retirement. These payments surely will be eroded by inflation. Only management goodwill and ad hoc adjustments will help the retirees to partially keep up with inflation.

Profit-sharing distributions may be taken in a lump sum in cash and/or company stock "in kind" or through installments with the balance contributing to investment returns through the years.

A participant who retired with $60,000 in a fixed-income fund and who elected to receive 15 annual installments would receive $4000 as her first installment ($\frac{1}{15}$ of $60,000). Under an assumption of an annual yield of 9 percent credited to her unpaid balance and the retiree receiving $\frac{1}{15}$, $\frac{1}{14}$, $\frac{1}{13}$, etc. of her revalued account each year, she would realize an increasing amount from interest and principal each year. The fifteenth and final installment would be approximately $13,364. The total settlement would have yielded the retiree more than $116,000.

Individuals would have additional options. The retirees could withdraw less of the interest and principal each year and stretch the installments out for a longer period, such as the joint life expectancies of the retirees and their spouses.

In other words, profit sharing permits the retiree's unpaid balance to continue to contribute to investment returns, and the power of compound interest continues to benefit the retiree directly. On the other hand, a distribution in a lump sum in cash in one taxable year at termination of employment or after age 59½ during employment may qualify for capital gains and/or 10-year averaging taxation.

Employee choice is a major aspect of profit sharing today. Employees, in many cases, can choose to participate or not to participate, to contribute or not to contribute (after-tax and/or before-tax dollars) and set the level, to receive the company contribution in cash or to defer it, to make withdrawals or loans, to exercise investment options (among funds made available to them), to transfer account balances among funds, and to select the mode of disbursement.

Legislative Impact. Recent legislation has impacted positively and negatively on qualified plans.

ERTA put the federal government squarely behind individual savings and investment by permitting qualified plan participants to make deductible contributions either to their employer's plan or to an individual retirement account (IRA) outside the employer's plan.

TEFRA imposed lower limits on contributions and benefits, reduced limits for multiple-plan participants, suspended cost-of-living adjustments, restricted loans from retirement plans, and introduced a new concept—i.e., top-heavy plans. Certain provisions of TEFRA are being debated in Congress currently and in all probability will continue to be debated.

Attributes of Deferred Profit Sharing. Profit sharing is no panacea, and it takes time to work its marvel of compound interest. It does, however, offer a number of advantages, especially for small businesses, with regard to flexible funding, vesting, reallocation of forfeitures, preretirement death benefits for spouses, and installment payouts during retirement (with the balance participating in investment earnings) as a way to help the retiree cope with inflation.

Deferred profit sharing (numbering 342,754 plans at end of 1982):

- contributes substantially to retirement income
- provides survivor and disability benefits
- aids capital formation
- encourages and adds to individual savings
- increases efficiency
- combats inflation
- reduces burden on Social Security system
- provides portability of retirement benefits to younger and short-term workers
- offers the most feasible method of providing retirement benefits to small and medium-sized companies, the area most in need of retirement programs

In conclusion, profit sharing is a versatile and adaptable program which can provide adequate retirement income and can simultaneously generate the enthusiasm, interest, involvement, effort—in short, productivity—to make the benefits affordable.

See also Compensation, employee benefit plans; Motivation in organizations; Ownership, legal forms of; Productivity measurement; Profits and profit making; Quality circles; Quality of work life.

NOTES

[1]New York Stock Exchange, Office of Economic Research, *People and Productivity: A Challenge to Corporate America*, New York Stock Exchange, New York, 1982, p. 36.

[2]*Profit Sharing in 38 Large Companies,* Profit Sharing Research Foundation, Evanston, Illinois, 1978.
[3]Ibid, pp. 44–49.

BERT L. METZGER, *Profit Sharing Research Foundation*

Profits and Profit Making

Profits may be loosely defined as the excess of sales revenue over the cost of providing a product or service to buyers. If the total cost of providing a product or service exceeds the amount for which it can be sold, the firm incurs a loss instead of a profit. Unfortunately, this simple, intuitive definition must not be used without thought of its implications.

Accounting Profit. The term *profit* is applied by accountants to the results of a firm's past performance. This accounting concept tells about the business history of the enterprise. From knowledge of past performance, managers and investors may draw conclusions about future performance, as well as gain clues about what changes in the firm's policies may be called for.

Accounting profit is not always a hard-and-fast, clearly defined concept because there are many options about how to calculate it. For example, a firm may set aside reserves or take special write-offs during a given year and thus reduce profits in that year but increase them in other years. Profit rates are also affected by methods of inventory valuation. During periods of inflation, prices of items used to produce products or services are rising; consequently, the inventory valuation method employed by the firm will affect accounting profits. If the firm assumes that the items sold first are those last added to the inventory (LIFO, or last in, first out), the inventory level will be frozen at historical costs and the items costing more will be sold first. In that way, current profits will be lower during periods of rising prices than if the firm assumed that the lower-cost items were sold first (FIFO, or first in, first out).

Taxes affect both apparent and actual profitability. For example, a firm financing with bonds is permitted by law in the United States to deduct the bond interest from its taxable income before computing corporate income taxes. A firm that finances through common stock, however, is not permitted to deduct dividends to stockholders before computing income tax. Since stockholders individually pay taxes on dividends, use of the stock alternative means that the stockholders and the firm combined pay higher income tax than if the bond alternative were used, other things being equal.

Profits and Decision Making. The term *profit* also applies to the criteria used by businesses and economists in making such *business* decisions as which price to set, where to locate a new branch, and whether to invest in a prospective opportunity. The simple, intuitive accounting concept of profit as the amount of revenue left after paying all expenditures does not suffice for business decisions. For example, assume that a publishing firm has been selling a book for several years, but sales have now tapered off to the point at which the publisher is almost ready to take the book out of print. Another firm comes along and offers to buy 2000 copies at $2 each for a total of $4000. The "out-of-pocket" printing, binding, and other production expenditures for the lot of 2000 books would be about $2200. The publisher refuses the deal, however, because the accountant rules that the sale would not be profitable, on the ground that when the original expenditures for editing and typesetting are allowed for, the cost of 2000 books comes to more than $2 apiece. Of course, the publisher would be better off accepting the deal, as is intuitively obvious to you. The editing and other overhead costs are all in the past. They cannot be affected by *this* sale, and hence they are no longer relevant. That is, the deal truly is profitable, even though the accountant says it is not.

Contribution to Profit Concept. To get around this difficulty, the concept of *contribution to profit* was invented. This term is really a redefinition of profit. Any decision that can be expected to lead to a higher end-of-year profit in the present year, taking into account only the relevant costs, is said to make a positive contribution to profit. Suppose, for example, a firm has unused capacity equal to 25 percent of its total capacity. Assume further that the variable costs (the additional costs from selling and producing an additional unit of output) are equal to $1 per unit, and overhead costs, if allocated, would raise the costs per unit to $3. This firm should not price the product of this *additional* production over $3 if market forces do not support a price of that magnitude. Instead, the firm should be content to sell the additional units at any price above $1 because the sale revenue would contribute to the profits of the whole organization; the particular price level should be set only after considering market pressure from competition. The essential point is that the profit-making process calls for price setting at something lower than full costs, but greater than the additional cost of the sale, if that lower price is required to make the sale. It must be understood, however, that this profit strategy cannot be employed for *all* products produced by a firm; overhead costs must finally be covered by the firm's operation. Obviously, if a firm sold all its output at a price only slightly over variable costs, the firm would suffer a loss on operations. Overhead must be covered in some market segments.

It should be noted that the contribution-to-profit concept itself presents problems. A major difficulty is the determination of which costs are relevant to a given activity of the firm. For example, is the sales manager's salary relevant to the proposed book deal mentioned earlier? One can get around the problem of figuring relevant or incremental costs by looking at the total revenues or total expenditures for a firm under the various alternatives, to see which alternative yields the greatest overall difference between revenues and expenditures.

Another major difficulty of the contribution-to-profit concept is that it refers only to the firm's revenues and expenditures in the present period. It is a fundamental fact of business life that all important decisions have ramifications far beyond the present year. There is no satisfactory simple way, therefore, to represent the future impacts in terms of this year's revenues and costs; normal accounting concepts are often misleading if one tries to do so. Hence, it is necessary to use a more general criterion.

The Appropriate Profit Criterion. The appropriate criterion for decision where impacts are spread over time (and this includes most business decisions) is the *discounted net present value* of the alternative, or simply the *present value*. This value may be defined in two ways:

1. Described in words, the present value of an alternative equals the sum of the net revenues of the entire firm in each future year under this alternative, after each year's net revenue is adjusted (discounted) to reflect the fact that a sum of money in the future is worth less than the same sum in hand at the present moment.

2. Stated algebraically, the present value of an alternative is determined as follows:

$$V_{T=0} = (S_{t=0} - E_{t=0}) + (S_{t=1} - E_{t=1}d)$$
$$+ (S_{t=2}d^2 - E_{t=2}d^2)$$
$$+ (S_{t=3}d^3 - E_{t=3}d^3)$$
$$+ \cdots + (S_{t=k}d^k - E_{t=k}d^k)$$
$$+ (W_{t=k}d^k - W_{t=0})$$

where $V_{T=0}$ = present value of alternative i at time T
S_t = expected gross sales revenue from alternative i in period t
E_t = total expenditure in period t
W_t = market value of firm's productive assets in period t

Comparison of Accounting and Decision-Making Concepts. The accountant's concept looks *backward* at history, to evaluate what happened. The purpose is to hold individuals and organizations "accountable" for auditing purposes and to judge whether they performed well or poorly. Although the information on past performance can be useful in the prediction of future performance, it is not in itself a good framework for making business decisions. In contrast, the business criterion is *forward-looking*. Its task is to evaluate what will happen in the future

and then to choose the best among the available alternatives.

In line with its own purposes, the accountant's concept of profit applies to a limited time period, such as a quarter of a year or a year. The concept of present value, however, refers to the entire future life of an alternative. Furthermore, accounting profit relates to what actually happened, whereas present value refers to what is *expected* to happen. The expected and actual outcomes do not always coincide. Also, the present value notion assumes that available sums of money are invested at the appropriate rate of return, whereas the accountant's one-period concept of profit does not need to make such an assumption.

Sources of Profits. How do opportunities for profits exist? Why does not competition squeeze firms to the point that no profits can be made? One part of the answer is that ordinary profits may be considered simply as a return to the invested capital, including returns to the ordinary risks involved. But sometimes a firm can make out-of-the-ordinary profits.

Unusually high profits may emerge from three possible sources: (1) a reward for risk taking, (2) a reward for successful innovation, and (3) a consequence of frictions and imperfections in the dynamic economy.

Variables that Affect Profits. Profits may be affected by a large number of variables. Essentially, these factors all reduce to those things which may affect a firm's costs, its ability to stimulate new business, and the amount of competition it faces from rivals. The following brief discussion presents only a few key forces which affect a firm's profits.

Market structure refers to the competitive environment in which a firm exists. Generally speaking, the larger the number of effective competitors, the smaller a firm's profits will be, and vice versa.

Extent of effective technology adaptation within both the firm and the industry itself is an important variable which affects profits of a firm. All firms in an industry may be able to earn very high profits if a high development of effective technology exists within the industry and all firms have adopted those improvements. At the same time, one firm in an industry may gain a substantial edge if it has adopted a more effective technology than its competitors. This distinction would provide the firm with a substantial cost advantage which would tend to increase its profits over those earned by rivals.

Tax laws and tax management practices, as mentioned earlier, also affect profit levels. For example, a firm using accelerated depreciation methods to reduce its tax liability during a year would tend to shift profits to a future time period, all other things equal. This effect is caused by the higher depreciation expense during the current period, causing profits to be lower; however, future depreciation deductions will be lower, causing higher profits for the business in the future time period.

In public utility industries, regulatory commissions attempt to control profits because the firms are usually free from competition. The effectiveness of this type of profit regulation has come under increased criticism during recent years.

Profits may also be affected by changes in a firm's efficiency, worker productivity, levels of advertising and sales promotion efforts, and management effectiveness, as well as a number of other factors.

Limiting Profits. Though businesses prefer larger over smaller profits, circumstances may sometimes make it seem wise to limit profits, in the short run at least. High profits attract competition; therefore, a firm may limit profits to discourage entry of additional rivals. Similarly, a firm may provide better working conditions than required in order to attract and hold superior employees; this step will also reduce profitability. A firm may also limit profits so as not to attract antitrust pressure. Anticipation of labor demands may be another reason for limiting profits; large profit levels sometimes signal labor to increase wage demands. Another reason for limiting profits is to maintain customer good will. If profits appear too large, there is the possibility that customers may view the firm unfavorably and seek other suppliers. A distinction must be made, of course, between long-run and short-run profitability. Many firms sometimes forgo short-run profits in order to attain larger, long-run profits.

See also, Accounting, financial; Competition; Economic concepts; Economic systems; Social responsibility of business.

REFERENCES

Haynes, W. W., and W. R. Henry: *Managerial Economics,* Business Publications, Inc., Dallas, Tex., 1974.

Newman, William H., and James P. Logan: *Strategy, Policy, and Central Management,* 8th ed., South-Western, Cincinnati, 1981.

Simon, Julian L.: *Applied Managerial Economics,* Prentice-Hall, Englewood Cliffs, N.J., 1975.

WALTER J. PRIMEAUX, Jr., *University of Illinois at Urbana*

JULIAN L. SIMON, *University of Illinois at Urbana*

Program Planning and Implementation

Planning is a process by which future actions are decided upon in terms of specific organizational or institutional goals. *Program planning* is a specialized planning process which is output-oriented and involves sets of resources encompassing a broader range of objectives than more traditional planning efforts. It combines long- and short-range planning while emphasizing the use of budgets in establishing priorities and in selecting alternatives. It is, in essence, a systematized way for organizations to deal with large-scale resource use and at the same time deal with dynamic, rapidly changing economic, political, social, and technological environments.

Program planning has been used for some time in the federal government of the United States, in particular, the Department of Defense. Other federal agencies have adopted program planning and implementation as a part of a formal planning-programming-budgeting system (PPBS). Although the concept was adopted from industry, indications are that program planning has been generally limited to the federal, and recently state, government organizations. This limitation may be short-sighted. Traditional planning tools are increasingly restrictive. Although PPBS systems are more complex than the systems needed in modern business organizations, program planning can provide a highly useful approach to restructuring a firm's total planning effort.

One must not confuse program planning with project planning, product planning, or brand management. *Project planning* is finite, dealing with a specific set of objectives. It ends when the project has been completed. *Product management* is tied to a specific product or product family and does not include the interrelationships between that particular product and other aspects of the firm's operation. *Brand management* is more narrow, dealing mainly with a very specific product or product line. Although these three terms are often used as synonyms for program planning, they are not the same.

The most important aspect of program management is that it is not tied to any specific period of time. Additionally, it (1) involves a significant amount of the firm's resources and (2) focuses on program interactions with a number of the organization's activities. A single functional area of the firm, for example, such as accounting or production, may be committed to a number of the firm's programs. Hence, the firm's goal setting, structure, resource allocation, and decision-making processes must take on a "systems view" in order to deal with the demands of program planning and implementation.

The Origins of Program Planning

Program planning has its roots in the PPBS system developed in the U.S. federal government during the mid-1960s. Even earlier evidence was presented during World War II when the National Defense Advisory Commission was formed in an attempt to expand American production efforts to support war efforts on both the Atlantic and Pacific fronts. Major goals were established for combat needs, essential civilian requirements, aid to friendly nations, and economic warfare. The analytical methods developed to deal with these resource allocation problems set the stage for later RAND Corporation efforts with the United States Air Force.

Program planning's goal was to understand and allocate more systematically the vast resources of the Defense Department. The result was to eliminate dual missions, minimize misallocation of resources, and most important, help each of the armed services to understand its contribution to the overall defense effort. Planning in this manner has withstood the test of time. It appears to have developed a better understanding of the military mission in terms of these broader goals rather than of the separate desires of each of the military services.

At the same time, PPBS reaped benefits which the planners had not proposed. People in government now look at results. More important, this goal orientation was extended from a fiscal year perspective to an evaluation of programs over an extended period, in some cases up to 10 or 20 years.

Along with the benefits came new problems. The most important of them was an inability to quantify or measure organizational outputs. For example, it is difficult for planners to fully document "success" with respect to strategic retaliatory forces. Many programs simply do not have dollar benefits that can be measured. Nonetheless, planners developed surrogate measures to evaluate goal achievement in each of the nine program areas. The success of the defense experience spilled over to all government agencies, and in 1965, all federal agencies were required to adopt a PPBS system.

Other federal agencies using program-planning techniques include the National Aeronautics and Space Administration, which adopted PPBS in early 1959. The program to land a man on the moon is the most notable example of this agency's attempt to use program planning. Similar success was enjoyed by the Department of Transportation when it developed five specific programs: general development of freight and passenger transportation in the United States, provision of better access to rural and remote towns and cities, relief of urban traffic congestion problems, creation of standby transportation capacity for war and other national emergencies, and promotion of national prestige and international trade. Program planning was readily accepted by these agencies because of the size of their efforts, diversity of resources, and multiplicity of goals.

Program Planning in Industry: A Historical Perspective

Program planning in industry can be traced back to the mid-1920s and the General Motors Corporation.

Its programs were developed not along product lines but, rather, in terms of price classes and categories of cars to be offered. Resources were allocated to each of the divisions so that certain models of Chevrolets could compete with Pontiac and Buick, for example. As a result, GM's objectives focused on a major segment of the market but without respect to a specific automobile product line. Further, because of the lead time in tooling for automobiles, program planning extended up to 5 years in the future. Interchangeability of parts and the need to allocate materials such as rubber, steel, and glass necessitated long lead times and allocation choices from among a number of alternatives.

Other companies that developed program planning were the Bell Laboratories, which initiated the concept of systems planning in the 1920s, and later, the Ford Motor Company under Robert McNamara, which introduced systems analysis into Ford planning in the 1950s.

The major thread running through each of these examples is that program planning and implementation were first used by very large organizations having a variety of resources and difficult allocation decisions. Given today's economy, the number of choices available to consumers, and the increased complexity of routine decision making, program planning has become a viable tool for a much broader range of industrial and nonindustrial organizations.

Implications for Today's Managers

Program planning provides new ways to look at a very old problem: how to evaluate the future. It structures the planning problem in such a way as to force the manager to consider all the environmental impacts on the organization's decisions. Finally, it provides alternative ways in which an executive can structure organizational decision making to deal more effectively with the complex future uncertainties.

1. Program planning forces a firm to reexamine its goals. In many organizations, goals have existed for a long time. Typically, they are expressed as some form of profit or growth. As a result, economic retrenchment or rapid advances in technology have caught many firms short. Today's plans become obsolete quickly. A manager must not be totally influenced by the past or even the present. Instead, he or she must take a look at the opportunities available in the scenario of the future. Is a national firm in the business of selling soap, or is it involved with the methods of cleaning clothes, dishes, walls, etc.? The crux of the program planning method is to force the organization to ask such questions as "Will there be a *need* for soap in the foreseeable future?"

"How might we clean clothes in the future?" "Will we be using dishes by the year 2000?" In essence, program planning asks, "What business are we *really* in?" Goal definition is often the most difficult task top management faces in constructing a program plan.

2. In evaluating alternative goals, a firm must study the rapidly changing economic, political, and social environments. The soap company would look at alternatives to today's chemicals, the economic viability of synthetic substitutes, and the social, political, and legal demands for nonpollutant ingredients. This way, attention is not focused on the competitiveness of a single product or product line, but on the firm's ability to deal with the program of supplying economically useful, competitive cleansing alternatives for the home and industry.

3. The organization must modify or adapt its structure to match the purpose of its program. Traditional hierarchies, functional organizations, project groups, and product or brand structures are increasingly found to be too myopic in dealing with environmental change. Because of the tremendous value of resources that enter today's technology (consumer and industrial), the cost of a mistake is similarly high. On one hand, the organization's response may be to take fewer risks. But in doing so, the company may lose its competitive edge. On the other hand, taking risks without systematically evaluating *all* the alternatives increases the chance of failure. Often, the organization form that emerges is one that focuses on the interrelationship between the functional support and the company's programs: a matrix form, where operational responsibility for a company goal rests with the program manager.

4. By carefully defining a firm's goals and arranging the resource allocation in a program structure, a manager can develop more precise ways of obtaining feedback and control. When resource use is assigned against a specific program, cause and effect relationships are more clearly understood. Adjustments to the program plan are more easily identified and better defined.

Risks, Problems, and Limitations

Many managers have great difficulty in reevaluating or redefining an organization's goals. Because business is so output-oriented, profit, whether short or long range, seems the most likely alternative. Reexamining a company's goals with respect to other alternatives, such as survival or social welfare, is time-consuming and difficult to articulate. Nonetheless, the process of asking the right question helps

the manager to understand the changing nature of organization goals. The clustering of common goals into program choices is often the result.

A second problem, and perhaps one of more import, is the use of annual or fiscal budgeting common to most organizations. Because programs extend over a number of years, budgets are really long-range projections. They not only include capital expenditures but involve all expenditures associated with program forecasts. It is difficult for many firms to define operating budgets for a period longer than a year, and resistance to program planning often focuses in this area.

A third problem involves resistance to structural changes. Although aerospace firms have used such concepts as project management and matrix management structures for a number of years, shared managerial responsibility and authority are relatively uncommon in the industrial and nonindustrial sectors. Tradition emphasizes the principles of "unity of command" and "one person–one boss." Because there is no one to blame when things go wrong, the concept of sharing resources and decision-making authority is difficult for many managers to accept. One popular alternative, committee management, rarely results in quick decisions. As a result, this alternative, too, is often discarded. Paradoxically, shared responsibility and resources are actually more definitive. Activities are directed toward specific program objectives; thus, control is greater and the effects of management actions are more clearly defined.

Finally, it is difficult to establish a thorough control system that accurately identifies critical deviations from the planned program. The tendency is to develop controls for all program activities. Experience has shown that feedback and control in the Department of Defense and other federal agencies often turn out to be cumbersome and unwieldy. A major management task is to design a useful control system and feedback process to support the program without their becoming the program itself.

Implementing the Program

In order to ensure a systematic program development, four specific steps are required: the establishment of goals, the definition of objectives, the allocation and structuring of resources, and the creation of a feedback and control mechanism. The relationship among these elements is portrayed in Fig. P-10.

STEP 1: *Goal setting.* The organization must decide upon its long-range goals and the timing of goal achievement. This decision requires asking and answering the question, "What business are we in now, and what business do we want to be in the future?" Top management must identify common sets of goals in such a way that clusters emerge and

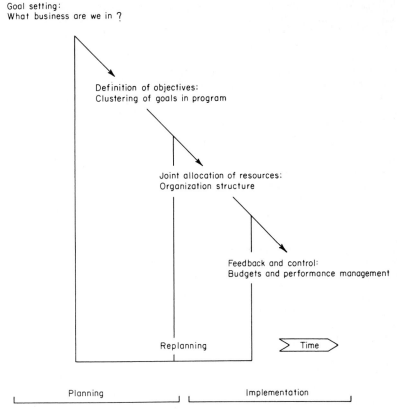

Goal setting:
What business are we in ?

Definition of objectives:
Clustering of goals in program

Joint allocation of resources:
Organization structure

Feedback and control:
Budgets and performance management

Replanning

Time

Planning

Implementation

FIG. P-10 A model of program planning and implementation.

programs are identified. An example of how this was done in one chemical firm is shown in Fig. P-11.

Goals that are similar with respect to home chemicals, pharmaceuticals, and industrial chemicals are identified and grouped according to the firm's program emphasis. When a long-range perspective is taken, this kind of goal identification can be done by almost any firm.

STEP 2: *Definition of objectives.* For each of the programs, alternative strategies must be identified. At this stage, planners seek answers to the question, "How will the firm meet its requirements in the next 5 years with respect to the home chemical industry or pharmaceuticals?" This approach avoids homing in on a short-term profit objective and encourages the firm to opt for a longer-term program development to

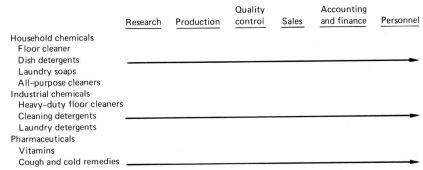

	Research	Production	Quality control	Sales	Accounting and finance	Personnel
Household chemicals						
Floor cleaner						
Dish detergents						
Laundry soaps						
All-purpose cleaners						
Industrial chemicals						
Heavy-duty floor cleaners						
Cleaning detergents						
Laundry detergents						
Pharmaceuticals						
Vitamins						
Cough and cold remedies						

FIG. P-11 Program structure in a hypothetical chemical corporation.

meet the projected needs. Thereby it concentrates on the future rather than on the present. The alternative strategies are, in essence, a set of program opportunities. They are evaluated with respect to the firm's long-range development criteria. New product lines, market expansion, and new product technologies are program opportunities that can be achieved in many different ways. The firm must evaluate present and projected resources, markets, and the competitive environment to select the strategy having the best complement of risk and return over the life of the program. A strategy can then be defined and short-run objectives established. These objectives become the goals for the immediate future and also fit into the long-range program. For example, the hypothetical firm portrayed in Fig. P-11 may decide that vitamins will play an increasingly important role in the pharmaceutical industry and choose to concentrate on the development of synthetic vitamins for home use. Meanwhile, as a part of its overall pharmaceutical program, it will monitor the environment for replacement of alternative opportunities.

STEP 3: *Joint allocation of resources.* To meet the defined objectives, both near and long term, resource allocation must be applied in such a way as to meet all defined programs. Manufacturing capacity is not the initial consideration, for example. Rather, the needs of each of the firm's programs must be established and the firm's manufacturing capacity must be allocated accordingly. Targets for each of the programs must be controlled by the program manager. Production, finance, marketing, engineering, and other functional managers must work to support the program managers in the accomplishment of their objectives. In the hypothetical firm, the decision to make a production run for household cleaning chemicals versus dish detergents would not be a production decision alone; it would be formulated in a joint meeting with the program manager. At that meeting, all aspects of this decision would be evaluated: production changeover problems, finance problems, raw materials availability, demand for the product, etc. Rather than suboptimize this production decision, the firm optimizes its activities with respect to the organization. Typically, this joint meeting will produce a decision that neither the program manager nor the chief of production would have made independently. Typically, neither had all the information necessary; joint planning forces organizational goal considerations in the chemical program.

STEP 4: *Feedback and control.* The final step in program implementation is the establishment of a feedback and control mechanism. A management information system may provide a great deal of computerized data, but unless it provides the right information quickly, it may be ineffective. Accordingly, an essential part of the program plan is to establish specific, quantifiable, and verifiable objectives. Milestones that identify when these objectives are to be accomplished are necessary, along with a specific measure that reflects the accomplishment of the goal. Thus, it is not the quantity of information available to the manager that is necessary, but the quality needed to make useful decisions.

The most important control mechanism is the budget. Inherent in the entire program planning procedure is a concern for financial administration. Cost estimating, revenue generation, and profit guides are integral to planning and control. Program budgets must be closely coordinated; they are at the heart of the entire process.

Replanning at frequent intervals is a necessary part of program implementation. The program plan is a long-term effort, and the environment changes rapidly. A good manager must not be afraid to start over again whenever environmental constraints make the current plan ineffective or obsolete.

Program Planning: A Tool for Any Organization

Program planning and implementation is not an ominous task, nor is it merely an academic exercise. It is a way of planning applied chiefly in public organizations that are characterized by an absence of accurate output measures or by requirements to budget from an output standpoint. Success in these organizations has led a number of business firms to adopt the tenets of program planning with substantial benefits.

Program planning and implementation involves time, managerial talents, and most important, organizational focus on the future. There are only four steps to the process, but these four steps imply a fresh understanding and a total restructuring of organizational planning. For those organizations that adopt program planning, the benefits far outweigh the costs.

See also Budgets and budget preparation; Control systems, management; Cost-benefit analysis; Matrix management; Planning, strategic managerial; Project management.

REFERENCES

Anthony, Robert N.: *Planning and Control Systems: A Framework for Analysis,* Harvard University Graduate School of Business Administration, Boston, 1965.

Cleland, David I., and William R. King: "Organizing for Long-Range Planning," *Business Horizons,* vol. 17, no 4, August 1974, pp. 25–32.

Gaither, Norman: *Production and Operations Management,* 2d ed., Dryden Press, Chicago, 1984.

King, William R., and David I. Cleland: "A New Method for Strategic Systems Planning," *Business Horizons,* vol. 18, no. 4, August 1975, pp. 55–64.

ROBERT L. TAYLOR, *United States Air Force Academy*

Project Management

Project Management is a set of techniques, procedures, and methods for systematically planning, organizing, monitoring, and controlling cost, time, and specifications of a project. The components of this approach also include processes for organizing project teams, managing conflict, and developing organizational structures, and computerized systems to assist in implementing the quantitative techniques.

Organizational Approaches. Implementing project management requires an evaluation and consideration of the organizational structure in which the system will be housed. Three organizational structures require elaboration: (1) the traditional organizational structure; (2) the project organizational structure; and (3) the matrix.

Traditional Structure. The usual approach to carrying out projects in this mode is to establish a task force consisting of individuals from the functional areas with the required knowledge and skills. The advantages of this type of structure in handling projects are efficiency, cost effectiveness, defined corporate policies and procedures, and well-defined lines of communication and authority.

The disadvantages include lack of project leadership, lack of project commitment, power residing with the strongest functional group, lack of project planning, poor project control, slow reaction time, and lack of teamwork.

Project Structure. This approach sets up the project team as a separate division, with a project manager and a team of project personnel assigned on a full-time basis to the project. The advantages of this approach include: (1) a project manager with sufficient authority and responsibility to manage all aspects of the project; (2) development of team spirit and project commitment; (3) greater flexibility and reaction time; (4) good training ground for promotion to upper-level management; (5) good control of cost, time, and performance; and (6) shorter communication channels.

Some of the disadvantages of the project structure are: (1) Resources are duplicated; (2) state-of-the-art technology suffers; (3) project wind-up and documentation may be slowed when people detect the final phases of the project and start looking for their next assignment.

Matrix. This structure attempts to combine the advantages and minimize the disadvantages of the other structures. The matrix, or "two-boss structure," has people reporting to the project manager for work on the project and to their functional manager for functional activities that are not project-related. A properly working matrix has the following advantages:

1. It is effective in carrying out the project mission and objective.
2. It is efficient in the use of resources.
3. It provides the channels of communication and coordination for state-of-the art technological innovation.
4. It does not pull an employee away from his or her functional area.
5. Project leadership is delegated to a project manager. The matrix, however, has some inherent problems. Davis and Lawrence[1] defined nine matrix pathologies: power struggles, anarchy, groupitis, collapse during an economic crunch, excessive overhead, strangulation of decisions, sinking, layering, and navel gazing.

The Planning Process. The most important phase of the project-management life cycle is the development of the project plan. The planning process can be broken down into these steps:

STEP 1: *Project definition.* This definition includes an outline of (*a*) the project title; (*b*) objectives; (*c*) specifications; (*d*) assumptions; (*e*) mission; (*f*) scope; (*g*) the estimate of project time and cost.

STEP 2: *Development of the work breakdown structure (WBS).* This structure is a procedure of systematically breaking down the work to a manageable level of detail. The WBS will then be used for estimating time and cost, delegating authority, assigning responsibility, developing budgets and schedules, and finally, monitoring and controlling the project.

STEP 3: *Determination of activity relationships.* With input from the work breakdown structure of a complete list of activities that have to be performed, it is necessary to determine the sequence in which they can be undertaken. This sequence is usually evaluated without the constraints of limited resources. The outcome will be a network indicating which activities can be worked on concurrently and which must be performed in sequence.

STEP 4: *Estimating.* This step consists of estimating the time, cost, and resources required to complete each task, function, or activity.

STEP 5: *Scheduling.* With input from the network and the estimate of the time and resource requirements, a feasible schedule can be developed. This development of the schedule is an iterative process requiring change as the constraints of resources are superimposed. The final schedule will indicate when each task will start and finish. It should also portray milestones or major points in time that require careful evaluation.

STEP 6: *Development of resource histograms.* Each resource (skill group, equipment, machinery, facilities, etc.) will require evaluation to determine whether it will be available when needed and whether it will be used efficiently. This procedure usually requires iterating steps 4, 5, and 6, before a feasible solution is developed.

STEP 7: *Development of the budget and cash flow.* As a result of the input from steps 4 and 5, a cash flow projection can be developed and the project budget determined.

STEP 8: *Commitment and approval.* The plan should be available in a format suitable to present to management for commitment and approval.

Quantitative Techniques. Two of the most important techniques to have been developed in the late 1950s are PERT and CPM. Both were developed independently in the 1957–1958 timeframe. They are both networking schemes used to graphically depict the relationship of project activities and to assist in the evaluation of project schedules. PERT is an acronym for program evaluation and review technique, and CPM stands for the critical path method. Both use one of the two types of networking schemes, either (1) the activity on the arrow (AOA) or (2) the activity on the node (AON) format. The difference between PERT and CPM is the estimation of activity times and the calculation of project time. CPM uses one time estimate for each activity; PERT requires three time estimates, which then can be converted to calculate a probabilistic distribution of project completion times.

Several other techniques have been devised and implemented with varying degrees of acceptance and success. They include (1) line of balance (LOB), used primarily for repetitive production jobs; (2) precedence diagramming; (3) graphical evaluation and review technique (GERT); (4) simulation; and (5) linear programming.

The Project Team. Basically, three component parts make up the groups of individuals necessary to support a project management system. They are (1) the project manager, (2) the project team, and (3) an administrative support group.

The *project manager* is the focal point of the project and the individual ultimately responsible for its successful completion. There are many characteristics that a good project manager should possess, but above all, proven managerial ability and human behavior skills are critical. Additionally, a project manager should be a planner, a communicator, a motivator, and a decision maker. Technically, the project manager should understand the project specifications and possess a comfort level with the budgeting, scheduling, and control processes.

The *project team* should consist of the individuals possessing the skills, talents, and knowledge necessary to complete the project. There are two other groups that should be considered for inclusion on the team. First, associate members who represent departments and divisions that will be affected by the project should be selected to be kept informed of the project's progress and repercussions. Second, the project manager should consider selecting various other individuals who can help promote and "sell" the project to the end users and other organizational units.

The *administrative support group* (project control group or project planning group) is charged with assisting the project with such functions as planning, data collection, status reporting, control of change, and issuing authorized work.

Project Control. The necessity of control systems is dictated by the simple fact that the project will be modified, changed, updated, and reevaluated because uncontrollable or unexpected things will naturally happen. Project control implies that a system is in place that will monitor progress and compare it with the plan. Any significant deviation will be evaluated and corrective action will be taken if necessary.

Cleland and King summarized

certain basic conditions that must be met in order to have a workable control system:

- *It must be understood by those who use it and obtain data from it.*

- *It must relate to the project organization, since organization and control are interdependent and neither can function properly without the other.*

- *It must anticipate and report deviations on a timely basis so that corrective action can be initiated before more serious deviations can occur.*

- *It must be sufficiently flexible to remain compatible with the changing organization environment.*

- *It must be economical, so as to be worth the additional maintenance expense.*

- *It should indicate the nature of corrective action required to bring the project back into consonance with the plan.*

- *It should reduce to a language (words, pictures, graphs, or other models) which permits a visual display that is easy to read and comprehensive in its communication.*[2]

Project Management Systems and Computers. In an era of rapid technological change, even small projects can be planned, monitored, and controlled by using computers. A significant number of software programs have been written for large main-frame computers, and the introduction of microcomputers has increased the need for self-contained, stand-alone project management systems. The major dilemma is that many of the systems are really pro-

TABLE P-5   Characteristics of Project Accounting and Project Management Systems

Characteristic	Project accounting system	Project management system
Purpose	To monitor and control costs	As an aid in planning, scheduling, and controlling resources, costs, time, and specifications
Detail of data	By phase	By activity or task
Frequency of information update	Weekly, biweekly, or monthly	Continually
Accessibility of information	Weekly, biweekly, and monthly	As required
Reporting formats	Specified by the system	Designed by the user
Special project management functions		Graphics, simulation, or "what if" analysis

ject accounting and not project management systems. The differences between the two are significant, as illustrated in Table P-5.

The differentiation between the *project accounting* and *project management* systems implies that a project management system is an integrated planning, accounting, scheduling, and resource allocation system. Computerized systems provide project managers with current, synchronous, and reliable information to allow them to make intelligent and timely decisions.

Project Management Applications.   Two decades ago, project management was limited to applications in the Department of Defense and the aerospace industry. Today, with the constraints of limited resources, the need for increased productivity, shorter product life cycles, the dramatic rise in technological innovation, the requirements for faster return on investment, and the legal, social, and environmental restraints, new management approaches are necessary. Project management has been adopted as the way to deal with these characteristics. The techniques, systems, and procedures have been useful in the public and private sectors, as well as in manufacturing and service industries, including construction, financial institutions, government agencies, hospitals, and consulting firms.

See also Engineering management; Grants management; Matrix management; Network planning methods; Program planning and implementation.

NOTES

[1] S. M. Davis and P. R. Lawrence, *Matrix*, Addison-Wesley, Reading, Mass., 1977, pp. 129–144.

[2] David I. Cleland and William R. King, *Systems Analysis and Project Management*, 3d ed., McGraw-Hill, New York, 1983, pp. 372–373.

REFERENCES

Kerzner, Harold: *Project Management for Executives,* Van Nostrand Reinhold, New York, 1982.

Stuckenbruck, Linn C. (ed.): *The Implementation of Project Management: The Professional's Handbook,* Addison-Wesley, Reading, Mass., 1981.

LARRY A. SMITH, *Florida International University*

Public Administration

The administration of government and of public affairs generally has existed since the beginning of organized society. As a self-conscious field of study and professional practice, however, the origins of public administration in the United States and Canada lie in the last decades of the nineteenth century. Important administrative reforms in cities and in the national government occurred in the 1880s. Reorganization of state governments also became a thrust of the movement by the "progressive era." The national government became a focus of change in World War I and much more so during and after the Great Depression. After World War II, activity extended to international and comparative administration, and by then its applications also encompassed many dimensions of public affairs which are tangential to government.

In intellectual terms, the origin of American public administration is most often identified with an 1887 essay by Woodrow Wilson, *The Study of Public Administration,* followed by Frank J. Goodnow's *Politics and Administration* (1900) and a few early treatises and texts, most notably W. F. Willoughby's *The Government of Modern States* (1919), Leonard D. White's *Introduction to the Study of Public Administration* (1st ed., 1926), and Luther Gulick's and Lyndall Urwick's *Papers on the Science of Administration* (1937). From these beginnings, one conclusion merits foremost attention: Public administration has been and remains heavily dependent upon its varied and complex environment; consequently, it is a broad field, drawing on many disciplines and based on a variety of models or paradigms, integrated **749** in the United States by some generally accepted public interest values of constitutional democracy.

Occupational Specialties

An influential delineation of program specialties and subject matter areas in public management was adopted in 1974 by the National Association of Schools of Public Affairs and Administration (NASPAA). Part II of that matrix lists program specializations at four levels of government: urban/local, state/regional, national, and international.

Competencies The elaborately detailed Part I of the NASPAA matrix lists the following five broad subject areas of professional competencies to be attained by public managers:

Political, social, and economic context

Analytical tools: quantitative and nonquantitative

Individual/group/organizational dynamics

Policy analysis

Administrative/management processes

For each of these five areas, the matrix identifies characteristics of the public manager in terms of four basic elements: (1) knowledge, (2) skills, (3) public interest values, and (4) behavior.

Occupations. Of the 13 million employees of state and local governments, the 2.75 million federal government employees, and 2.4 million military personnel in 1984, only a small proportion would normally identify themselves with the profession of public administration (PA). Indeed, only a fraction of 1 percent of the new entrants into public service are products of academic programs in public administration; many who initially enter government as professionals in various program specialties or who begin as nonprofessionals later engage in mid-career training and/or education for more responsible administrative responsibilities. The "PA professionals" are typically (1) general managers, such as city or county managers; (2) staff specialists in such fields as (a) budget, finance, or audits, (b) personnel and/or labor relations, (c) property and general services management, and (d) information systems; (3) policy/program analysts, often with program evaluation specialties; and (4) program managers, either out of other specialties, such as ballistics or health services, or with preparation as generalists in varied program areas.

Specialization. Although academic public administration has often stressed generalist functions, government in the United States has characteristically relied on specialists, even at the highest career levels. In the federal government, for example, 38 percent of the top career executives (the senior executive service) are in scientific and engineering specialties, and about three-fourths of the total are program managers, commonly drawn from the specialties managed (with obvious overlap of these groupings).

Executives. Typically, top executive positions in government in the United States represent a smaller percentage of total employees than the ratio in private enterprise. For example, only 0.5 percent of the federal government positions are at executive levels. Noncareer political appointees typically fill the highest-level positions in the federal government, state governments, and some politically managed local governments. In the federal government, for example, in 1984 there were about 600 positions at Executive Levels I through V (I = Secretary of Defense; II = Director, U.S. Office of Personnel Management; V = an assistant secretary of bureau director), nearly all of them filled by political appointees. There were about 8,200 executives in the senior executive service, and, of that total, at least 85 percent were supposed to be career personnel.

The Public Environment

The governmental/public affairs environment of public administration accounts for distinctions in its ideas and practices from "generic" administration. Changing social, economic, and technological contexts also condition the field, in many respects just as in business or other administration.

When government in the United States was relatively limited in powers and small in fact, "administration" per se was of little concern. But, by the 1970s, with over one-third of the United States gross national product consumed through governments, the field had become crucial. Political pressure for retrenchment in the late 1970s and early 1980s stopped public sector growth trends of the preceding 50 years, however, causing relocations at least for a time.

Constitutional Basis. The most basic values of American public administration are inherited from the ideas of constitutional democracy which define the political system. Those are the classic values of human dignity and rule of law, dynamic values which have been defined by changing aspiration and experience but which remain essential imperatives. American constitutional concepts designed to advance those values are likewise most fundamental: popular sovereignty and limited government, separation of powers, federalism, and judicial review.

Although these values and concepts are basic to American public administration, the field drew heavily on the ideas and practices of business at its beginnings, and it was deliberately moved in that direction by Leonard White and other leaders of the 1920s. With the emergence of a mixed private-public enterprise system in the United States by the post–World War II period, generic administration came to be common to much of business, government, and other organizations, with extensive exchange of ideas and practices.

Bureaucratic Context. The principal ideas of public administration from the 1880s through its first 60 years were centralization, economy and efficiency, and separation of politics from administration. Centralization became the bureaucratizing thrust of the field, most evident by the close of the "progressive era" in the city management movement and in state reorganization efforts. The field was then dominated by the ideas of scientific management, which likewise influenced business and engineering, and by aspirations to become a clear discipline. It thus sought to discover and to implement the "one best way" in government administration. The traditional bureaucratic model of public administration was born out of those efforts, with the following "principles" of organization more or less prescribed as guides by the 1930s:

1. External policy direction by a responsible legislative body and accountability through law

2. Hierarchical conformation and executive leadership

3. Coordinated staff services under a chief executive

4. Departmentalization according to functions

5. Merit selection and protection of personnel—and objective detachment

6. Organizational compliance based on internalization of society's basic values

Academic study of public administration at first relied heavily on case studies and comparison. The field also drew early on bureaucratic theory in sociology and law. The "human relations movement," which swept business after the Hawthorne Studies, also influenced public administration. Behavioral theory from the social sciences likewise affected the field enormously in the 1950s and 1960s.

Current Concepts. At the organizational level, modifications or alternatives to elements of the traditional bureaucratic model came into practice in the 1960s. By the 1980s, the following concepts were common:

1. Policymaking and implementation as interrelated activities within a context of different political and administrative roles

2. Dispersed authority and responsibility based on functions and expertise

3. Results-oriented management, balanced with concerns for efficiency and economical use of resources

4. Open management support systems with widely shared information and access to expertise and technical services

5. Emphasis on processes and functional relationships, with networks to resolve conflicts with minimal dissonance and to promote accomplishment of objectives

6. Futures orientation, with timely generation and adoption of changing policies, processes, and organizational structures[1]

Performance Effectiveness. One very important practical dimension of contemporary public administration began to emerge in the 1940s—a concern with effectiveness as an administrative responsibility, along with the traditional concerns of efficiency and economy. In effect, this view was a reflection of increasing limits on the practicality of separation of politics (and policymaking) from administration. In line with this changing orientation, budgeting and related management developments shifted from simple control and line-item budgeting to performance budgeting, beginning as an idea in the late 1930s and coming into general practice in the late 1950s. Program budgeting followed in the 1960s, often as a formal planning-programming-budgeting system (PPBS).

More varied, situational orientations followed in the early 1970s, with the adoption of an open approach to management by objectives (MBO) in the federal government. Program evaluation next became the dominant orientation, in part as a dimension of MBO, but also as a principal congressional concern. Zero-base budgeting and "sunset" provision for periodic review of needs for public programs thus became possible. Policy analysis supported these developments, drawing particularly on the discipline of economics and on information technologies and knowledge capabilities of cybernetics. By the 1970s, social indicators were being developed to add to economic indicators for macroperspectives on social problems and government policies.

Retrenchment pressures of the late 1970s and 1980s were complicated by the dominance of single-interest politics, which had grown since the 1960s. Hostility to expertise and professionalism in public administration increased, with a rise in pressures for politicization and deinstitutionalization. A movement called the "new public administration" started in the 1960s, focusing on administrators as change agents who should promote social equity through public policies and implementation. By the 1980s, that movement led to promotion of a "new civism," stressing linkages between civil servants and citizens for more responsible balances between popular involvement and professional expertise in government.

Trends

The future of public administration will be conditioned by its changing and varied contexts, as it has been from its beginning, with the following dimensions among the likely important influences on the last decades of the twentieth century in the United States:

1. Work force, productivity, and consumption trends, such as the shift between 1947 and 1984, from over 50 percent of United States workers producing tangibles to 70 percent producing intangibles, and the federal budget changes between 1960 and 1980 from over 50 percent to less than 25 percent for defense, space, and foreign affairs, and from less than 25 percent to more than 50 percent for human resources activities.

2. Scientific, technological, and cybernetic trends, such as the knowledge and information processing revolutions between the 1950s and 1980s.

3. Domestic social forces, such as the racial and sexual equality movements since World War II and the unionization movement, which has become much stronger in government than in the private sector, with over two-thirds of federal employees in exclusive units by the mid-1970s, and over half of all public employees unionized in 1984 compared with fewer than 20 percent in the private sector.

4. International forces, such as the past moves of the United States from isolationism to internationalism to world supremacy to a position in the 1980s of international economic interdependence without supremacy.

5. Probably most important, the nation's political and value frameworks. In the United States, as long as constitutional democracy survives, the most outstanding of these will remain the concept of popular sovereignty and limited government to facilitate people's seeking human dignity and rule of law or reasonableness in social relationships.

See also College and university administration; Government relations; Government services; Health institutions, management of; Nonprofit organizations, management of.

NOTES

[1] C. A. Newland, "Managing for Effectiveness, Efficiency, and Economy," *The Effective Local Government Manager,* International City Management Association, Washington, D.C., 1983, p. 77.

REFERENCES

Frederickson, H. George: *New Public Administration,* University of Alabama Press, University, 1980.

Mosher, Frederick C. (ed.): *American Public Administration: Past, Present, Future,* University of Alabama Press, University, 1975; *Basic Documents of American Public Administration, 1776–1950,* Holmes and Meier Publishers, New York, 1976; *Basic Literature of American Public Administration, 1787–1950,* Holmes and Meier Publishers, New York, 1981.

Waldo, Dwight: *The Administrative State,* The Ronald Press, New York, 2d ed., Holmes and Meier, New York, 1984. *The Enterprise of Public Administration,* Chandler and Sharp, Novato, Calif., 1981.

CHESTER A. NEWLAND, *University of Southern California*

Public and Community Relations

"Public Relations is the management function which evaluates public attitudes, identifies the policies and procedures of an individual or an organization with the public interest, and plans and executes a program of action to earn public understanding and acceptance." This is the official definition given in *Public Relations News,* the pioneer weekly newsletter in the field of public relations. There is another oversimplified definition that many practitioners use, which suggests that "public relations means doing good things and getting credit for it."

Organizations must communicate to survive. On the positive side, good communications can help sell products, improve worker productivity, maintain good relations with local, state, and federal governments, and enhance an organization's ability to attract the capital and employees needed to grow. On the other hand, poor communications can make the company more vulnerable to increasing external pressures from government, consumers, community groups, and the press.

Despite impressive progress and acceptance by a great many forward-thinking companies, public relations (PR) is frequently misused and underutilized. Sometimes there is resistance to giving public relations the full recognition and application that it deserves. This is not necessarily a conscious decision, but rather, the result of insufficient understanding and appreciation of underlying values. Over and over, PR capabilities are used randomly in only defensive, crisis-oriented situations.

Many managers have yet to perceive how public relations can be utilized to *avoid* crises. A case in point is the delayed and generally inadequate response of industry to environmental pollution criticisms. Proper PR perspective would have disclosed long in advance the public's impending ecological challenges. Furthermore, even after environmental activists created massive public concern, industry generally adopted a low-key, defensive posture. Even though many companies (voluntarily or otherwise) do an effective job in protecting the environment and have spent billions in the process, they fail, for the most part, to bring their accomplishments before the public.

The world often perceives a significant difference between two otherwise evenly matched competitors. One company seems to do everything right and get all the credit. The other produces raised eyebrows and quizzical looks when its name is mentioned. Such quick evaluation of organizations goes on all the time, and it can and does affect the bottom line. Public relations, therefore, is often a major factor in the development of what has come to be called the corporate image. For this reason, if no other, corporate management expects its key people to practice the art of public relations in the plant, in the community, among customers and suppliers, with government, and with special-interest groups of all kinds. This responsibility can be carried out with varying degrees of success, dependent on three chief elements: sensitivity, communication resources, and management leadership.

Sensitivity

Much has been written in the field of industrial relations on how management can keep its ear to the ground, how it can set up early warning systems to detect employee trouble before it happens, how it can use the ways and means of taking periodic morale readings, and so on. These activities constitute mechanisms for listening, a crucial component of the communication process. Listening helps isolate and define both the problems and the opportunities among the various publics important to the organization.

Listening Posts. In order to listen better, it makes sense to set up a structure for assessing the level of corporate acceptance among internal and external groups. This approach, in turn, helps define communication needs and opportunities.

In small companies, there is no need for an elaborate system. The top executive need only put the subject of public relations periodically on the agenda of operating committee meetings. In the smaller organizations, top management is also far less insulated by layers of management. Good and bad "vibrations" come through without much distortion—except when executives feel constrained about revealing imperfections in their areas of responsibility. To guard against this situation, top management must work hard to encourage straight talk rather than cover-up. Unfortunately, some managers deny the existence of communication problems until they are about ready to explode.

In the medium- and larger-sized organizations, it has become fairly common to conduct periodic attitude surveys, performed with the assistance of an outside firm. The attitudes surveyed are most often those of employees, but the same technique can be used effectively to determine the attitudes of community leaders, local press, and various levels of government. It is a truism that the very act of making an attitude survey is a mark per se of good public relations, since it suggests that the organization cares about its acceptance.

Communications Assessment. There should also be a continuing sensitivity to the need for better communications. When these needs come to the surface, either via some early warning technique or formal surveys, they should be analyzed and approached as major potential roadblocks to the forward movement of the organization. It is important to distinguish between words (what the company says) and deeds (what the company does) in the process of communicating. Deeds are often the best communicators in terms of getting the attention of the audience, but they alone do not necessarily tell the full story. Consider a negative example of the company that suddenly must close down one of its two plants in town, and then refuses to explain its action in anything more than a terse statement on the plant bulletin board. Typically, the community goes into a state of shock. Then come the rumors. Before the situation can be reversed, morale and productivity in the remaining plant have plummeted.

Corporate Visibility. Words and deeds must work together, one in support of the other. When there are deeds without words, there is incomplete communication, which can lead to a variety of misunderstandings. When there are words without deeds, the enterprise can eventually lose its credibility. It is also important to acknowledge that a firm is constantly communicating something, whether it is aware of it or not. Organizations have visibility from a number of sources:

1. *From the physical presence:* what people see of a company's buildings, parking lots, smokestacks, architectural and environmental impact

2. *From how an organization treats its people:* employees, customers, suppliers

3. *From what the media say about the organization:* in the local and regional press, newspapers and magazines, professional publications, radio and television, house organs, and club publications

4. *From how a company discloses itself:* through printed reports, bulletins, press releases, speeches, films, and participation in community activities

5. *From the reputation an organization has earned on the professional, political, industry and consumer levels:* how the people whose good will and approval are essential to an organization are talking about it

Internal Insights. Management must also give thought to its own attitudes and be sensitive to them at all times. It must ask such questions as: What kind of an organization do *we* operate? What do we think of external groups? Do we simply want to use them as part of our plan to achieve corporate objectives? Or, do we think they have something important to contribute? Do we say one thing, and do another? Do we feel a real sense of responsibility to employees and the community? Answers to these questions help form the basis for external judgment of a company and how people react to it and its management.

Press Relationships. Excellent sources of insights about a company's management are the press people locally and the business and trade press nationally. Public relations professionals often start with an audit of local press attitudes because it is the local reporter who can draw a graphic picture of community opinion, and sometimes even employee opinion, of the organization. It is true that editors and reporters sometimes see a company with bias. For example, a company may spend a lot of money to clean up emissions and yet be criticized by the press for not spending more. In being sensitive, however, the organization would be wise to listen to these critics and try to hear what they are really saying. Often what they truly mean are opinions like the following:

"You have *not* been a good neighbor, historically."

"Neither you nor your people take an active interest in community betterment."

"You don't ever give us the bad news, so we have to get it elsewhere."

"You try too hard to get your good stories printed, as if they were full-page advertisements."

"You haven't told the truth several times in the past."

"Your top people are inaccessible."

"You simply don't care."

The press is not the enemy. The real enemy is management's sense of frustration over its inability to convert the press to the company point of view. Yet, there are few situations where press relations do not improve significantly when a sincere effort is made by an organization to improve them.

Communication Resources

A perceptive management quickly recognizes the importance of good communications, organizes its people to meet the needs, and supports them with appropriate budgets. There is no good rule of thumb to suggest the kind of public relations staff or outside counsel that may be needed. Some very small organizations employ an internal staff and an outside agency as well. Some fairly large organizations may have neither. Both may say that they are "doing just fine."

The important point is that there should be at least one person in the company whose prime responsibility is (1) to assess communications on a continuing basis, (2) to make recommendations for improvement, (3) to develop the capability of executing such programs with or without help, and (4) to insist upon and justify the budget needed to support them. This individual needs the attention and full support of the chief executive. Without it, any program is doomed.

The Plan. Once such a person is on staff, management should demand an annual review of past activity, a critical evaluation of the company's relationship with its key publics, and a very specific public relations plan or program for the year ahead. From this kind of planning come the set of corporate public relations objectives, the strategy for achieving them, the tactics for carrying them out effectively, and the budgets and timetables that are required. The making of the plan forces management at least once a year to give due consideration to communication problems and opportunities.

Internal Expertise. The internal executive must try to understand the style or personality of the company and seek to project it in a variety of ways. There is more to public relations than publicity and more to publicity than press releases. This person often comes to the company from a newspaper, magazine, radio, or television background, but such past experience is by no means the sine qua non of a successful public relations executive. Journalism experience, however, is sound evidence of interest in, and awareness of, the art and science of communications.

Many companies, of course, function without internal staff by assigning certain communication responsibilities to key staff people. For example:

1. Responsibility for employee and community relations including the local press may be assigned to the chief of personnel.

2. The chief financial officer may deal with the financial community and with the financial press.

3. The sales manager (together with the advertising manager) may handle publicity about the company's products and/or services.

4. The president may typically speak for the company on larger questions, both within the industry and in the total business environment.

Unless the whole arrangement is coordinated by a single executive, however, this approach may result in community relations and publicity activities that are inconsistent or even counterproductive.

Outside Expertise. The use of outside counsel offers several advantages, whether or not there is an internal public relations staff. This counsel, under any circumstances, however, needs access to management.

Overview Function. Because the outside counsel is often thoroughly experienced in the full range of problems and opportunities facing corporate management, and can bring an objective outside viewpoint to sensitive issues, such counsel can be of especially great value as a key resource.

Program Responsibility. Outside counsel can relieve internal work loads by taking on full responsibility. If so, it makes an assessment of the company's needs, drafts the public relations objectives and program, implements it, and evaluates performance continually in the light of changing corporate requirements.

Audit Responsibility. Sometimes a company retains outside counsel solely for the purpose of (1) performing an objective audit of corporate communications and (2) preparing a specific long-range program for improving the entire spectrum of communications. Part of any agency assignment can be an evaluation of the existing communications structure, recommendations on the type of internal staffing required, and sometimes, even going out and finding the right people.

Specialized Skills. In many cases, it is too costly for a firm to employ on its own payroll such PR specialists as speech writers, financial relations experts, editorial relations people, researchers, arts counselors, and specialists in government relations, social affairs, and other vital areas. The full-service PR corporate firm typically has a battery of such specialists immediately available for client assignments.

Management Leadership

It is worth repeating that a PR program without the interest and participation of top management is doomed to failure. This is true because the chief executive officer personalizes the company and projects the attitudes, style, and personality of the organization. It is the chief executive officer who provides the impetus for serious public relations programs and then passes his or her standards, style, and enthusiasm down the line to other managers in the organization.

Top management typically recognizes its responsibility for the total communication function. Many company presidents spend the greatest part of their time communicating to their employees and managers, bankers and security analysts, mayors and city councils, engineers and suppliers, active and potential customers. These corporate executives do so because they recognize quickly enough that the public relations program supports short- and long-range corporate goals.

Reactive or Proactive? Some companies are content to handle public relations in a reactive manner so as to keep a low profile or "not to make

waves." These companies are often on the defensive in communications.

Other top managers refuse to sit still waiting for the occurrence of events to which they can respond. In contrast, they use creative means to generate news about their ideas, their company, and their products. These are the companies that want to "lead the pack" and to become industry leaders.

Both kinds of companies exist successfully. Regardless of approach, however, it is important to remember that public relations should not be turned on and off like a faucet. It is neither effective nor economical to bring in public relations people to solve a problem and then send them packing once the problem is solved. Use of PR for emergencies only paves the way for more crises. In the long run, it is less expensive and more efficient to accept the vital importance of the public relations function, to invite public relations thinking at key corporate meetings, and to support positive and continuing programs designed to help the company reach its objectives. In this way, an organization has a better chance to create a real deterrent to communication troubles and costly surprises for management.

Effective Guidelines. Managers who are sophisticated in public relations follow certain fundamental practices. Here are some of them:

1. Have a key person inside the company who is designated as its information contact person for both outsiders and insiders. That person becomes the conduit for receiving and disseminating information. Without some centralization of control, there can be chaos.

2. When outsiders, such as reporters or local groups, get in touch directly with executives other than the contact person, those executives should immediately report the nature of the discussion to the contact person. The information specialist should be kept apprised of all external contacts made with corporate executives. In that way, he or she can perform more effectively. A single responsible person can better evaluate the company's position in the community, can help capitalize on public relations opportunities, can coordinate company statements, and can clarify, when necessary, remarks that may have been confusing or in any way in need of improvement.

3. Maintain an early warning system to detect communication problems. This can take several forms:

    a. Regular meetings with the local, national, and trade presses are used by sophisticated executives just as much to get information as to give it.

    b. Monitoring of letters and evaluation of calls from customers and critics, while often disregarded, provide indicators of trouble trends.

c. Visits to Washington and to appropriate state capitals can provide signals of upcoming legislation that can affect the organization positively or negatively.

d. Regular sessions with investment bankers, commercial bankers, and security analysts are essential. Not only can the company story be presented to this vital public, but management can also listen to assessments of the organization, its performance, and its prospects. It is the job of the financial community to worry about its investments, and if it is worried about a business firm, that firm has ample cause to be worried about itself.

e. Sensitivity to rumors is essential. Sometimes, in listening, management will hear nothing more than vague rumors. Rumors left alone, however, can assume the substance of fact. Skilled information specialists need to deal immediately and forcefully with this kind of problem.

4. Make all executives aware of their public information responsibility. Are they allowed to speak directly to the press? Can they accept dates for speeches? Do they need to clear statements in advance of delivery? Are there company positions on certain crucial matters? The communications role of each executive should be clearly defined.

5. Do not try to use the press to solve company problems. Many executives feel that the only time to talk to journalists is when the company needs them to help sell its products or to explain its position or to correct misconceptions on the part of customers, employees, or the community. While these are certainly excellent reasons to be in touch with the press, it is also vital that there be continuing contact with reporters and editors to keep them informed of what the company is doing even if there is no important news to report. This contact provides an ongoing opportunity to create a better understanding of the company in an easy, relaxed atmosphere.

6. When trouble hits, try to get the whole story out fast. Everyone knows about the Watergate scandal. It was a disaster made worse by the attempt to cover it up. This maneuver triggered an almost endless succession of new discoveries, which made bigger and bigger headlines and destroyed the credibility of government people. Let good news linger as long as possible, but expel bad news—*all* of it—fast.

7. Do not forget the importance of communications to *all* employees. There is a grapevine through which they hear what is really going on inside

the company, so that it makes a lot of sense to carry out an employee communications program that carefully explains the rationale of corporate policies and programs. If employees are on the company's side, their support is a big help with everything from productivity to publicity. If employees are disaffected, the company can be in deep trouble, regardless of its external PR effort.

8. Continuing contact is also the secret of improving labor-management relations, customer relations, financial relations, etc. The corporate organization must be out there telling its story in good times and in bad. If the key publics understand what the company is doing and why, the company will more often than not find that it has some friends out there when it needs them most.

See also Associations, trade and professional; Attitude surveys; Communications, organizational; Conferences and meetings, planning for; Consumerism and consumer protection legislation; Government relations; Marketing of services, professional; Shareholder relations.

REFERENCES

Garbett, Thomas F.: *Corporate Advertising*, McGraw-Hill, New York, 1981.

Marston, J.: *Modern Public Relations*, McGraw-Hill, New York, 1979.

Moore, H. Frazier: *Public Relations*, 8th ed., Richard D. Irwin, Homewood, Ill., 1983.

Quinlan, Joseph C.: *Industrial Publicity*, Van Nostrand Reinhold, New York, 1983.

NORMAN WEISSMAN, *Ruder Finn & Rotman, Inc.*

Purchasing Management

Economics in the early 1980s adversely affected the United States, where production costs were out of line in competitive world markets. A reassessment as to American companies meeting the mounting international challenge for market share resulted in increased emphasis on the procurement role as part of an integrated global corporate strategic management. Previously, it was sufficient that a buyer be aware of the availability of United States supplies. But, as companies found their plants or competitors located in different countries, competition developed as to which plant or international supplier should produce the corporation's products. Because of the high impact of material costs and availability on major manufacturing decisions, headquarters management requires an intelligent purchasing overview with global supply and cost outlook.

Purchasing has been one of the last management functions to be handled by professionalized practitioners because it was one of the last responsibilities management delegated as companies grew in size. Previously, the function was retained at the very top because major buying decisions greatly affected profitability. Purchasing still has this tremendous leverage on profitability but, increasingly, top managers have had to let go of buying decisions. Yet, to one degree or another, management is always involved, especially on major procurements.

Resource Acquisition. One term frequently used for the procurement function is *resource acquisition*. Vendors or suppliers are "extensions" of a company's production line, manufacturing process, or service operation. A business can be thought of as acquiring its work force, its materials, its finances, and the like; and it is in this sense that the materials acquired have been termed *resources acquisitioned*.

The complete process, from the development of need to the end user, might more properly be termed *economic supply assurance* because purchasing has a long-range objective of both supply continuity and economic supply. Regardless of terminology and scope, with material costs at about 53 percent of many companies' sales dollar, recurring profit squeezes have focused greater emphasis on the savings potential in prudent purchasing and control of materials.

Organizational Position

There is no typical purchasing organization, but there are hybrids of all kinds. For purchasing personnel to perform successfully, the department must be well integrated within its parent organization. Much of purchasing's activities, however, occur in the marketplace in confrontation with conflicting interests. Thus, the place of purchasing within the organization has considerable impact on the function's effectiveness.

An example of an organization for a complex purchasing operation spending $200 million is depicted in Fig. P-12.

Initially, purchasing was the domain of the chief executive. As companies grew in size, however, the buying function was often assigned to the production department because it consumed most of the materials purchased. While some companies follow this practice today, there has been a clear trend since World War II to separate purchasing from production. By the late 1950s, independent purchasing departments had become commonplace. Today, most purchasing officials report to top management.

Corporate, or headquarters, purchasing is typically organized quite differently from plant or divi-

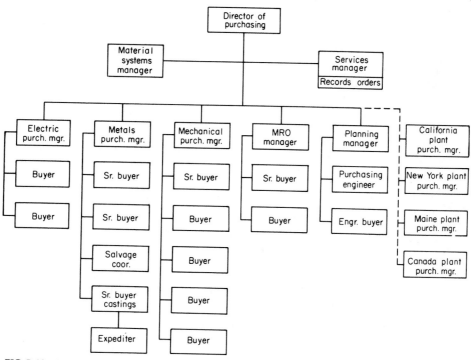

FIG. P-12 Organization chart of central purchasing operation located at headquarters with decentralized buying at branch plants.

sional purchasing. In simple, one-plant companies, purchasing can be a small department with one head reporting to either the president, the manufacturing vice president, or plant manager. Or, it can be considered part of a materials organization and can report to a materials manager. Some authorities who study the system of decision making pertaining to materials systems prefer to group all activities that play a role within one total system and under the control of one head. Other advocates extend the procurement scope to include physical distribution, traffic, warehousing, and stores; they use the term *materials* or *logistics management*. Considerable controversy exists as to whether such extension is desirable. Proponents claim conflicts are lessened and control is improved. Opponents argue that purchasing, representing the vendor interface, has more than enough in handling material acquisition alone. Usually, the determining factor is the magnitude of impact of purchased material on profitability, although inventory may sometimes be the more important area to be controlled.

Organization of the purchasing activity often depends on how management sees the purchasing function within its total operation. Purchasing does not exist in a vacuum; it operates within the framework determined by management. In practice, it reports to various management levels depending on whether the company is large or small, centralized or very diverse and decentralized. In short, purchasing mirrors management's philosophy and structure of its operations. At the same time, however, the purchasing function often affects other departments' performance. Accordingly, production frequently prefers to have purchasing under its control; others see it as part of the financial function. For this reason, it is not unusual to find purchasing reporting almost anywhere in an organization. As a general rule, where the purchasing dollar spent is a large percentage of expenditures, purchasing reports at a very high level.

Relationships with Other Functions. It is doubtful that any other function has greater interrelationships than purchasing, not only within its own company but with the outside supplier organizations. A variety of influences affect every buy. They range from one extreme where the buyer exerts total influence to one where the buyer has very little influence. This spectrum of buying influences properly reflects the composite needs of the operating concern. But this reality causes misunderstanding and ambiguity as to how purchasing operates and affects its relationships with other functions.

Settlement of Conflicts. Purchasing, on the fringe of the production sphere yet usually independent, might be described as being in conflict with two worlds: that of the company it represents and that of the supplying interests. It must frequently settle

material disputes, such as disagreements between requesting departments and vendors, as to whether quality is acceptable and whether the delivery requirement can be met and at what cost. Rejected purchases must be adjusted, costs controlled, and replacements made. While many operating functions have a large stake in what purchasing does, it often represents a very narrow interest to the vendor. Purchasing, then, must balance the interest of its own company with that of the vendor to protect long-range availability and to maintain its company's integrity. This is a role that may never completely satisfy everyone, neither management nor supplier. Yet, if purchasing is to adjust disputes, it has to find a common ground for settlement.

Impact on Performance. Purchasing cuts across every major function. As a result, purchasing capability greatly influences the performance of others. This impact makes its contributions and problems more apparent. Failures of purchasing to perform are immediately visible, and the information that top management receives too often appears to be negative. Purchasing's relationships are numerous and include those with the comptroller, finance, legal, plant management, production control, data processing, information systems, quality control, top management, traffic, logistics, audit, receiving department, engineering, stores, sales or marketing, international, government liaison, administration, and personnel. Each involvement is different. Engineering needs help with its new materials search and expects cost-reduction cooperation and guidance when seeking samples. The comptroller is interested in accurate estimates of cash discounts earned, what dollars of commitment need to be covered, and predictions as to future material cost trends, etc. Production control expects prompt processing of its needs: it wants vendor deliveries on time and assistance in keeping the inventories down. And so it goes. In turn, purchasing must secure maximum cooperation from all other departments in order to represent the company successfully. Purchasing is always responsible for supplier performance. How well it serves others will to a large degree determine how much authority it really can exert in buying control.

With Engineering. While the major interrelationship is with the production operation, the most vital relationship is usually with engineering. In the area of controlling material costs, the engineer plays a vital role by creating specifications and influencing source selection. There is no substitute for effective liaison between purchasing and engineering.

With Vendor Sales. A buyer must be firm when dealing with outside suppliers and vendor salespeople, but he or she must also be fair. A buyer must build a reputation for fair dealing and integrity and must give competition a chance. A buyer has to be open, making unbiased judgments and giving consideration to the seller's difficulties in trying to perform.

With Company Management and Marketing. Demands of company strategic planning require material inputs based on purchasing judgment. Statistics that facilitate a look ahead to future cost and supply availability are not readily available. Purchasing experts who study market trends and supply can best provide judgment on future price trends. Such judgments are essential if management is to properly assess both future product selling prices and profitability. Such knowledge of immediate and future cost levels helps determine strategy that marketing and management elect to follow.

Performance Measures

Purchasing performance can and should be measured. Experience indicates, however, that comparisons with other purchasing operations can be misleading. A better, more useful measure is to record the *trend* of performance with respect to past performance.[1] Trend measurements cover three basic areas: conceptual, behavioral, and resultant. Conceptual and behavioral measures are those associated with management-by-objective goals. Resultant measurements are the statistical ones: dollars saved, reductions of purchase orders issued, work load reductions, etc. No composite index seems to suffice or to replace interpretive judgment when using specific measurement information. Data for over at least a 5-year period should be used. Table P-6 illustrates some of the more useful data which can be incorporated as measurements of purchasing performance.

Standard cost performance as it pertains to material costs is also useful as a measurement of purchasing performance. Purchasing's control of its material

expenditures provides another meaningful measurement. A variance report in chart form is useful for indicating the trend of material costs. When this trend is compared to material indexes such as the wholesale price index (WPI), it gives some indication as to whether expenditures are higher or lower than the general material price changes.

Purchasing's contribution to return on invested capital for the company overall provides an interesting measurement. Calculations of the company's income statement with and without known purchasing savings show the effect of a purchase-saving dollar on the return on investment (ROI). It is magnified manyfold. A reduced cost of material purchased reflects in both the profit margin and the investment turnover, so there is a double-barreled effect on return on investment.

Purchasing Ethics

Because of the nature of the work, purchasing personnel are often confronted with questions of ethics. Buying decisions must stand scrutiny, especially when price discrimination may be an issue or where other legal technicalities prevail. And because the behavior of purchasing people is always subject to challenge, it should be above suspicion. High personal integrity and moral conviction are prerequisites in dealing with ethical buying questions. As in most ethical matters, there are no absolute guidelines. There *are* legitimate business expenditures for trade promotions, sales, and advertising, and many of these are aimed at the purchasing professional. Rightfully, a salesperson's purpose in contacting buyers is to influence the buyer's choice. One hopes that this influence is based mainly on the superior features, price or service, or other legitimate induce-

TABLE P-6 Data Chart on Indicators of Purchasing Efficiency

No.	Factor	Year				
		1	2	3	4	5
1	Purchases per year, $ mill.	12.4	16.6	20.4	16.8	18.0
2	Sales per year, $ mill.	24.3	33.0	41.5	33.6	35.7
3	$\frac{\text{Purchases}}{\text{Sales}}$ (%)	51.0	50.2	49.0	50.0	50.5
4	No. of purchase orders	24,909	25,350	25,655	26,230	26,000
5	$\frac{\text{Purchasing employees}}{\text{Total employees}}$	$\frac{1}{124}$	$\frac{1}{122}$	$\frac{1}{126}$	$\frac{1}{131}$	$\frac{1}{146}$
6	Cost of purchasing dept., $	120,000	140,000	153,500	150,000	152,000
7	Cost per purchase order, $	4.83	5.69	5.97	5.73	5.85
8	Saving per year, $	125,200	127,000	321,000	353,000	295,000
9	$\frac{\text{Saving}}{\text{Purchases}}$ (%)	1.01	0.77	1.58	2.10	1.64
10	Purchased material price index % increase (Base = 100)	50.1	51.2	55.3	58.1	61.0

ments. The gray area involving ethics occurs when side inducements are offered the buyer. Vendor influence, such as gifts or entertainment, is discouraged and frequently forbidden by company policy. When money is involved, it is generally illegal. Bribery or kickback is not condoned by any responsible company. Conflict of interest can be avoided by having key employees sign affidavits that they are not involved in investments with, or tied to, any supplier.

Unquestionably, the best answer for anyone involved in the buying profession is to stay away from situations judged by others to be an influence in reaching buying decisions. All business relationships should be conducted in such a way that no one has an opportunity to assume improper influence.

Purchasing Specifications

Without purchase specifications and a related identification code, the purchasing department would be doomed to verbal descriptions. Purchases would be either impossible to audit or a nightmare of detailed wordage. Specification sheets enable an item to be purchased repetitively and economically through a system of codes. Additionally, without concise, accurate, and complete specifications, the process of receiving and checking incoming shipments for quality would be ineffective.

Basically, a *specification* is simply a description of what is required. It may take the form of (1) a brand or trade name, (2) reference to explicit mechanical and/or chemical properties, (3) written description, (4) method by which the item is produced, or (5) end use intended and how the item is to perform. It may refer to certain industrial or society standard specifications already established, such as by American Society of Mechanical Engineers (ASME), American Society for Testing and Materials (ASTM), Society of Automotive Engineers (SAE), and the like. Another method of specification is by a sample that is to be reproduced.

Buying by brand or trade name places the trust entirely with the supplier's ability to produce quality. Preferably, two brands will be specified so there is some competition available.

Specifications are typically supported and detailed by code sheet and/or blueprint. These are the best specifications in that they illustrate the item precisely and in great detail. Detailed specifications are mandatory for such items as forgings, castings, dies, and special machine parts.

Specification by performance is very desirable because it holds the supplier liable for operation. It also leaves the vendor free to furnish whatever he or she deems satisfactory so long as it works. Giving some leeway to the vendor is often necessary if the buying company has little experience or knowledge as to how to specify what is required.

Specification by sample should be avoided if possible; it can be confusing as to what sample was submitted. There are times, however, when sample buying is the only method available.

A proper specification should be as simple and concise as possible to allow the supplier to provide what is required. It should have an identification so that it can be referred to. It should have reasonable tolerances that do not inhibit the supplier unnecessarily, causing increased cost. It must include quality requirements such as first-year survival rate and also any major points needing clarification. It should allow at least several companies to participate in the business. Above all, it should be capable of allowing inspection when the material is received.

Sources of Supply

Other than negotiating for the actual price, source selection is unquestionably purchasing's most vital function. It is the buyer's knowledge as to *who* can furnish the item to be procured that initiates the inquiry. A request for quotation may be initiated formally in writing or by phone or personal visit.

Vendor Selection. Factors to be considered in vendor selection and evaluation include the following:

Quality Factors. These include (1) consistent ability to meet specifications, (2) technical capability (including research), (3) performance, and (4) life expectancy.

Cost Factors. These include (1) total cost of using the product, (2) price, (3) price stability, (4) freight, (5) financial stability, and (6) ability to remain competitive and profitable.

Service Factors. These include (1) repair service availability, (2) delivery performance, (3) location as it affects transportation cost and transit time, (4) accuracy of information on progress of orders, (5) operation control (quality and inventory systems), (6) desire for business, (7) warranties and claims adjustments for faulty goods, (8) technical aid, and (9) compliance with needs.

Miscellaneous Factors. These include (1) production facilities and capacity, (2) ability to handle seasonal volume, (3) management, (4) reputation, and (5) performance history.

A vendor who serves well over an extended period makes potentially a better source of supply than one untried. On the other hand, there is a powerful need for alternative or multiple sources. When a company buys from one source only, competition is eliminated. Without warning, an act of God may render a particular vendor inoperative; a strike may idle the facilities; another supplier may develop a superior product. Without multiple sources, the buyer loses a powerful leverage on material costs—the ability to change sources quickly.

Standardization

An excellent way to control material costs is through *standardization:* simply the reduction of the number of different items purchased. If two will do the job of three, inventory control is simplified, obsolescence is reduced, and the entire administrative cost of purchasing, receiving, stores, etc., also decreases. Standardization is relatively simple. It is a matter of (1) listing all like items purchased and then (2) having engineering and technical people determine whether some of the lesser-used items can be cut out. For example, a firm uses five different bolts. One of them is bought in lots of 50 per year, whereas others are bought in 10,000 piece lots. The application for the 50 could use one of the other bolts but at a cost penalty. It would pay the company to eliminate the fifth bolt and inventory four items, thus reducing operating costs. Without standardization, over a period of time a company may end up with a multiplicity of items which are totally unnecessary.

Standardization also results from reducing the number of suppliers. This step may be especially effective where costly setups occur.

Purchasing Negotiations

If there is one key personal quality the professional buyer must possess, it is an ability to handle purchasing negotiations. The framework must first, however, exist for price analysis or other means for determining whether the price is fair, should be reduced, or perhaps even increased. The buyer then has at his or her option several techniques. They will be examined individually below.

Purpose. Negotiations vary depending on their purpose. They may be carried on to (1) establish a specific contract at a specific price, (2) revise prices either upward or downward, (3) change prices to meet adverse costs or operating changes, and (4) settle problems not covered nor anticipated in the purchase.

Price Analysis. This analysis comes through cost analysis or a breakdown of component costs. A simple analysis of price applies the formula that price is equal to material plus labor plus labor burden costs, plus selling and general administration costs, plus a profit. The process can be illustrated as follows:

Manufacturing cost

Price = material + labor + labor burden
+ selling and general administration cost + profit

Material	$1.00
Labor	.40
Labor burden	.80
Manufacturing cost	$2.20
Selling & GA @ 14%	.31
	$2.51
Profit at 10%	.25
Price	$2.76

Tooling and engineering costs may be itemized separately; so may many other items according to buyer or seller preferences.

Such analysis provides grist for negotiations.

Learning curve. This curve is a sophisticated mathematical form of price versus cost analysis. It is based on the fact that for a specific quantity, repetitive production can be produced with a percentage (for example, 80 percent) of previous labor cost, thus producing a *learning curve*, showing lower future costs with increased experience. *See* Learning (experience) curves.

Bids. Bids connote a formal buying approach. They may be closed or open. *Closed bids* indicate that the buyer reserves to himself or herself the opening and study of the bids in private so that competitive prices may not be revealed. In *open bids*, the buyer declares bids will be opened, with all bidders free to attend the bid opening so as to know all prices submitted.

Not to be confused with bids are *quotations*, which in effect represent the price a vendor *asks* for a product or service. A bid is what the supplier believes the price should be.

An approved bid list is sometimes kept for major construction or repair work. A firm is placed on the list by its previous or known performance or by meeting strict conditions. Bids are commonly used for governmental and publicly controlled buying. Quotations are more commonly used in industry.

Blanket Orders. Such orders are the means by which administrative and paperwork costs can be greatly reduced. By issuing a blanket order on an annual basis, a buyer can be freed of issuing routine releases and repetitive purchase orders. Blanket orders facilitate central buying and negotiations and enable multiplant decentralized operations to release their needs against the contract source and at the agreed price. The user may "release" a shipment from a supplier simply by specifying what quantity is wanted on what date. This method of buying frees the buyer of the releasing and expediting work load and allows the plant to control more directly its own input flow of materials.

So-called basket purchases occur when a grouping of items is negotiated and bought in toto. For example, all fasteners for a particular job might be bought at one lump sum. This method is similar to having the list of lumber required to build a home priced in one basket. Often, a better price can be achieved than by buying each item for the house individually.

Contracts. This term is general and may include not only purchase orders, which are themselves contracts, but also other formal legal contracts used to purchase. Contracts may be signed by the supplier or vendor and agreed to by the buyer. More often, the buyer simply uses his or her own purchase order form. When a contract is to exist for a period longer than a year or is more detailed in nature than can be covered through a normal purchase order, a formal legal contract is more desirable. For example, if there is a forklift truck lease of 5 years' duration, details may be far too involved to put on a standard purchase order form. In the case of special buying, such as in procuring private branded products, a legal contract may be preferable to the purchase order.

Make versus Buy. In past years, a factory often decided to *make* something if it could, and to *buy* if making the item was a problem. This solution has shifted to answering current questions such as: Should a factory (or which of several competing plants) be allowed to manufacture? Should certain items be combined to be made at specialized plants or, should they be made so as to control technology? Decisions made today must be reviewed periodically, as shifting economics can change the decision later. This is a very important management decision, especially for multiplant corporations which have several options as to where something may be made, or whether new sources may be acquired by acquisitions, and the like.

Systems Contracting. This technique is commonly used for maintenance, repair, and/or operating purchases. It greatly reduces the administrative costs of purchasing. It is accomplished by negotiating the purchase of all of a like commodity from available suppliers at a fixed markup. For example, all plumbing supplies are shopped with several plumbing supply houses. Frequently, the buyer will negotiate a supplier's profit. Upon agreement, a catalog of items to be purchased will be attached and made part of the systems contract. The buyer delegates to the using department authority to release directly from the supplier within the scope of the contract. A simplified format exists for releasing and invoicing, which cuts down the longer format of a formal purchase order. A systems contract pins down source and price: the requisitioner releases what he or she needs when it is needed.

Forward Buying. This buying method is used when a buy is made in advance, with full knowledge of what a future price will be since it has already been announced. It often requires reserving material well before needed. From this information, an economic analysis of holding costs, carrying costs, and

the like can be made to determine whether or not the buy should be made.

Speculative Purchasing. This approach is essentially an investment purchase of a speculative nature and has no place in ordinary industrial procurement. A speculative purchase is one made on the belief that prices might go higher, so it would be better to buy ahead. It should not be confused with a forward buy (defined above); otherwise a speculation exists, and that is not the intent of good material supply.

Hedging. A hedge position may assure that key costs are determined. For example, a food processor sells its output of canned pears in advance of the season. Prior to canning, if sugar costs rise sharply, no profit results. By buying sugar *futures* contracts on the Commodity Exchange, the processor covers its required sugar tonnage. The processor "fixes" this cost, since (in theory) the physical price of sugar and the futures price advance or decline an equal amount. While a decision to take physical delivery of sugar from the Commodity Exchange can be made, usually the processor will sell off its contracts prior to delivery time while continuing to buy from regular sources. If the physical price of sugar advances 5 cents per pound, the processor pays extra when it receives sugar from suppliers but makes 5 cents per pound when it sells an equal amount of its commodity futures. Conversely, if sugar prices decrease 5 cents, the processor spends 5 cents less but loses 5 cents on its futures. In either case, the two transactions cancel out, producing a non-change position for the processor's costs. This action thus hedges the costs.

In practice, no purchasing operation can hedge without management and financial involvement as to the business profit objective.

Capital Goods Procurement. This procedure applies to the acquisition of buildings, equipment, or large items which may be negotiated in a manner different from that used for other types of goods. For example, in this type of procurement, final price may be achieved through negotiations after preliminaries are out of the way. It contrasts with open bids, where the best price is presented the first time.

Discounting. This can apply to most of the purchases listed above. It is a term for the percentage deducted from the list price. It can be negotiated depending on volume and other economic factors. A company may price a motor at list price, for example, but very few people pay that price. An original equipment manufacturer will allow one discount to another equipment manufacturer and a different discount to the end user.

Reciprocity. Reciprocity exists when there is a relationship which ties what is bought to what is sold and is part of the negotiation or agreement to do business. It is now illegal. In past years, companies would frequently make buying and selling arrangements based on the volume given in exchange for purchases. Sales and purchases must be kept completely separate, with sales (and purchases) made on the basis of merit and value, but not tied together.

Purchasing Operations

Every purchasing operation is supported and facilitated by certain documents, records, ordering systems, and procedures.

Documents in common use include address books and/or vendor profiles listing addresses, phone numbers, key personnel, labor unions at suppliers' plants, plant locations, number of employees, and a variety of other statistical information which may be of some assistance in knowing a vendor company and in working with it.

The records most frequently kept include purchase price paid for items purchased, together with a listing of alternative vendors' prices. Such records are often kept by the buyer's secretary. On the other hand, some companies can justify data processing systems that make these data available for immediate recall at the buyer's request. The explosion in the use of personal computers and visual terminals for data processing and electronic mail has found acceptance in purchasing's operation. A transition to advanced information systems is underway in most progressive operations. There is really no such thing as a standard system, and many computer programs have been evolved to suit the needs of a particular corporation.

Expediting. In smaller organizations expediting may be done by the buyer who places the order. In larger companies, there is a tendency to set up special expeditors who spend all their time on this activity. When buyers place blanket orders and a plant releases against those blankets, the plant does the expediting. Regardless of who does the expediting, the buyer can never be totally divorced from responsibility for the procedure. Since delivery of the goods is a condition of the contract agreement, the buyer must always be held accountable ultimately for delivery performance.

Transportation. While transportation has always been part of the buying decision, two factors make it increasingly important: (1) the high cost of fuel and (2) deregulation of the industry, which has made the buying of transportation similar to that of a commodity. So transportation input has more cost impact than previously.

Purchasing Manuals. Most progressive purchasing operations are guided by their own purchasing manual. If there is a headquarters (or divisional) purchasing staff, the manual will be maintained and updated at central headquarters and distributed to decentralized plants. A manual generally consists of (1) general policies and procedures laid down by the purchasing head and (2) specific details of carrying out various purchasing routines.

Policies in the manual might cover such items as responsibilities and objectives of the purchasing function, relationships with other departments, gifts and ethical considerations, and the duties and organization structure with position guides. In particular, the policy as to authority to commit the company should be clearly detailed and approved by top management.

The manual's section on procedures explains such things as how buys are made, how long purchase orders are kept on file, what contracting forms to use, and special procedures, reports, and statistics deemed desirable.

Purchasing Inventory Control

Whether inventory controls are placed within purchasing or controlled elsewhere depends on organization policy and structure of the company or group served. Purchasing inventory controls, however, are essentially the same as inventory controls (see Inventory control). It is useful nonetheless to consider some necessary purchasing inputs to the inventory control process.

Forecasting. A vital input in determining inventory levels (whether from a standard cost base or actual cost base) can be provided by the purchasing department. Financial people know current prices paid, but they cannot project ahead except on a straight inflationary percentage basis provided by economic forecasts. The purchasing department can provide specific material cost forecasts either for each major item or for the overall material budget. These forecasts are based on the buyer's market knowledge and latest estimate of future cost trends. Many companies calculate their own material price index, which is weighted from the Industrial Wholesale Price Index.

Stockless Purchasing. This technique is similar to systems contracting and is used when purchasing people have persuaded suppliers to carry in stock sufficient quantities of items so that the purchaser may operate its production processes without considerable inventory of its own. These stocking programs are usually negotiable and produce savings by reducing the physical space needed for, and dollar value of, the inventory required to run the business.

Vendor Relations

Purchasing's relationship with vendors deserves particular attention. Newly initiated buyers often can be identified by an attitude of trying to "sock it to them." After operating through all levels of a business cycle, a purchasing professional learns that the best results come from relating well to the supplier. People make up organizations; if there is no one within the supplier's plant to speak well of the buyer, it may turn out that the vendor will not be able to meet the buyer's demanding delivery schedule. Sensitive areas that affect vendor relations include treatment of supplier's personnel during visits for sales or problem-solving purposes; unreasonable tolerances or specifications; late payment for goods; unreasonable delivery demands, especially after not allowing lead time; and method of handling complaints and rejections. In short, anything which allows friction to irritate or fester between supplier and consumer lessens a department's effectiveness. Diplomacy and tact are required.

Evaluation. Proper evaluation of vendor performance can assist suppliers to maintain required quality levels. The act of reviewing a supplier's performance tells the vendor that performance is important and watched, and it provides an incentive to do better. A high evaluation can be a source of pride and satisfaction, a low one a prod to improve (or lose out). Methods of evaluation include the use of control charts, standard deviation calculations, and audit inspections.

Mathematical formulas and rating systems have been utilized. Figure P-13 illustrates one such system. The consolidated index is flawed by judgment, which renders it questionable. But the indexes on (1)

quality, (2) cost, and (3) services and delivery are most constructively used.

Selecting Vendors. Source selection should result from controlled decision making; otherwise, it will happen haphazardly. To a large extent, the vendors selected determine the effectiveness of the purchasing job itself. As discussed earlier, the sourcing decisions stem from previous experience on delivery, quality, and price. Then, too, the vendor's current financial strength and potential profitability on the sale are important. Technical and service support lead the other variables in the selection process. Recognizing the multiple levels of input in vendor selection, some more formal organizations have developed vendor selection boards to ensure proper input of quality, engineering, production, and other activities as required. These vendor boards are chaired by purchasing, the inherent coordinator of such buying influence.

Supplier Partnering

Vendor relations, always of interest to purchasing people, is giving way to a broader concept that might be called *supplier partnering*. As suppliers and buyers work closely to achieve desired results, a more open, communicative relationship is needed. It may be necessary for several companies to pool their efforts because the cost of developing highly sophisticated items may be beyond the financial capability of an individual company to undertake total devel-

QUALITY RATING

Kind and class: iron CL 2. Period reported: 1st quarter

Vendors	3	16	21	27	35				
Factors	X	X	X	X	X	X	X	X	X
Received	126	243	132	98	57				
Rec. insp. rej.	10	28	31	36	2				
Line rej.	5	12	3	4	1				
Total rej.	15	40	34	40	3				
% accept	88.1	83.5	74.2	59.2	94.7				
Rating (% acc. x 40)	35.2	33.4	29.7	23.7	37.9				

COST RATING

Kind and class: iron CL 2. Period reported: 1st quarter

Vendors	3	16	21	27	35		
Factors	X	X	X	X	X	X	
Price 1 lb.	.19	.18	.16	.16	.20		
− Discount (10%)	.019	.018	.016	.016	.020		
	.171	.162	.144	.144	.180		
+ Trans.	.021	.046	.051	.039	.032		
+ Variance chgs.	.033	.056	.123	.142	.011		
net	.235	.264	.318	.325	.223		
Rating	33.2	29.6	24.5	24.0	35.0		

SERVICE RATING

Kind and class: iron CL 2. Period reported: 1st quarter

Vendors	3	16	21	27	35	
Factors	X	X	X	X	X	X
Promises kept	97	93	89	86	100.0	
Rating	24.3	23.3	22.3	21.5	25	

VENDOR RATINGS (consolidated)

Kind and class: iron CL 2. Period reported: 1st quarter

Vendors	3	16	21	27	35	
Factors	X	X	X	X	X	X
Quality	35.2	33.4	29.7	23.7	37.9	
Cost	33.2	29.6	24.5	24.0	35.0	
Service	24.3	23.3	22.3	21.5	25.0	
Consolidated rating	92.7	86.3	75.5	69.2	97.9	

FIG. P-13 Examples of numerical vendor ratings. These charts depict quality, cost, and service ratings, with an additional rating combining the three.

opment. Thus, many companies are entering into *strategic partnering.* Buyers and sellers team up in partnership to assure quality supply at reasonable cost.

Supplier Quality Programs. Purchasing should support every effort by suppliers to maintain effective quality assurance programs. Four basic responsibilities of the vendor's quality system are to (1) be of assistance to the engineering department so as to establish reasonable quality standards, (2) determine how well the standards are attained, (3) see that corrective action is taken when required, and (4) achieve improvements in quality when needed. Quality control efforts should be sufficient not only to specify the sampling plans and degree of protection against failures but also to determine where improvements need to be made. In similar fashion, they will identify good performance. Vendors should make use of such tools as statistical control charts, audit inspection, and reliability test laboratories, depending on the purchased item. Vendors should also identify the longevity of any item or its shelf life. In turn, purchasing must encourage its own quality people to assist vendors. They have a mutual concern, since the supplier's quality affects the buyer's end product quality.

Failure of the vendor to maintain an adequate quality program affects the buyer when failures disrupt the production schedule and tie up vital floor space where poor-quality units must be replaced or repaired. It is generally true also that the cost of repairs or replacements will not be totally recovered from the vendor. The vendor may replace a bolt but will not be responsible for the repeated tests, the teardown, and many of the auxiliary functions that have to be performed to overcome the vendor's defect.

The consumer's awareness of quality has sometimes made vendor failure devastatingly evident. Witness the myriad car recalls. When failure rates are perceived to be worse than in Japanese-produced goods, for example, sales of domestic goods suffer. But quality is more than an image. It must be supported at all times. It is affected by many vendors, so purchasing has to lead in maintaining high quality.

Vendor Visitations. Visits to a vendor's offices, plants, and warehouses provide an excellent means of buyer education, supplier awareness of the importance of the customer, an exchange of information, and an aid to improved relationships. Over a period of time, the purchasing department that makes it a practice to visit vendors—not solely to handle delivery problems when they occur but also to discuss how well the business is going—will outperform one that mails the order and uses the telephone exclusively. An observant visiting buyer can determine whether the vendors need new business and how well they are operating. The buyer can also make a point of noting the key people who control quality, pricing, and the like. Visits represent an extra cost to the buying company, but they repay in expertise, general business acumen, and better relations with suppliers' managements.

See also Contracts management; Inventory control; Inventory stock-keeping systems; Logistics, business; Materials management; Production planning and control; Quality management.

NOTES

[1]Victor H. Pooler, "Measuring the Purchasing Man," *TREND: Journal of Purchasing,* November 1973, p. 74.

REFERENCES

Aljian, G. W.: *Purchasing Handbook,* 4th ed., McGraw-Hill, New York, 1982.

Ammer, Dean S.: *Materials Management,* 4th ed., Richard D. Irwin, Homewood, Ill., 1980.

Dobler, Donald W., Lamar Lee, and David N. Beut: *Purchasing and Materials Management,* 4th ed., McGraw-Hill, New York, 1984.

Heinritz, E. F., and P. V. Farrell: *Purchasing: Principles and Applications,* 6th ed., Prentice-Hall, Englewood Cliffs, N.J. 1981.

Leenders, M. R. and W. B. England: *Purchasing and Materials Management,* 7th ed., Richard D. Irwin, Homewood, Ill., 1980.

VICTOR H. POOLER, *Carrier Corporation*

Quality Circles

The quality circles concept is based on the premise that people will take a greater interest in—and improve the productivity of—their work if they can become more involved in decision-making processes. In this way the workers improve both their self-image and their working environment. *Quality circles* are small groups of people who, under management sponsorship, volunteer to meet regularly to identify and solve work-related problems.

Circle Structure. Typical quality circles consist of small groups of employees from the same work area who meet regularly on company time but on a voluntary basis. Their purpose is to identify problems in their work area, analyze them, and develop a solution to them. The ultimate objectives of quality circles are to improve the quality of goods and services, encourage employee job involvement, and increase motivation, productivity, and morale.

Since quality circle *members* come from the same work area, the problems that they identify for study are common to all. An important requirement is that membership be voluntary. Each circle, ideally, consists of six to eight people, a size that allows all members to feel they have sufficient time to contribute to each meeting. However, quality circles have been known to vary in size from three to fifteen people. When a large number of employees within a work area wish to participate, it is best to divide them into several circles so as to keep the size of each circle within the specified limit.

Each circle has a *circle leader,* who is usually a team head or a supervisor of the circle members. Normally the first-level supervisor is selected as leader for the purpose of keeping the same authority structure within the organization and also to improve that person's skills as a leader. As the circle develops and progresses well, the supervisor may encourage another employee to be trained to assume responsibility for the circle's meetings. In such cases, the supervisor may allow the circle to elect a leader from within the circle.

A *facilitator,* who is the staff member reporting directly to management, is the link between the circles and the rest of the organization. She or he is responsible for the training of circle leaders in skills such as leadership, group dynamics, and group problem-solving methods. The facilitator also helps the leaders to train circle members in techniques that they need in order to analyze and solve problems that they have identified and selected to study.

Circle Impact. Quality circles encourage consciousness about quality; therefore, every organization can benefit from the implementation of this type of program. While emphasizing quality, an organization can show lower costs, improve productivity, and reduce defect levels, thus leading to increased customer or client satisfaction.

When employees become more involved with solving quality-related problems, they may effectively prevent or eliminate some of the factors that adversely affect other aspects of their job performance. This feeling of involvement increases employees' motivation and improves relations with all levels, resulting in more effective organizational communications. The individual who performs a job is likely to know more about improving it than anyone else. Involvement in decision making restores a worker's personal integrity and encourages his or her development in an atmosphere of mutual respect and trust. As a consequence, the entire organization can benefit from this approach.

Implementation of Quality Circles

The introduction of quality circles within an organization should follow an orderly sequence:

1. Selection of a well-organized steering committee, comprised of top-management officials and employee union representatives when a union is present: It is important that both groups be involved prior to implementation since the program's success depends on their cooperative support.

2. Selection, by the steering committee, of a facilitator who can interface between top-management personnel and the employees: The facilitator must have a strong commitment to the quality circle concept, be creative, and be fully aware of the political climate within the workplace.

3. Training of supervisors who have volunteered to become quality circle leaders: This training, conducted by the facilitator, includes methods of organizing, training, and maintaining the circles.

4. Presentation of the program, by these leaders, to their fellow workers: At that time, the leaders ask those interested to volunteer for circle membership. The workers are given a few days to decide, during which time the leader and the facilitator are available to answer questions.

5. Initial meetings: Once the circle is formed, members usually attend weekly meetings on company time although the frequency will vary. The meetings last about an hour, but management should allow sufficient time for the circle to conduct its business.

6. Member training: During the first few meetings, the circle leader trains the members in the techniques that he or she has learned. These skills include problem-solving methods such as data gathering, brainstorming, cause-and-effect analysis, check sheets, histogram construction, Pareto analysis, control charts, decision making, and techniques of presentation. Before each meeting, the leader discusses the proposed agenda and lesson plan with the facilitator. Typically, the facilitator attends each meeting so that he or she may provide feedback from the management at the next quality circle session.

7. Selection of a problem for study: Problems may be suggested by circle members, staff, management, other circles, or technical experts; however, it is important to note that actual problem selection is the decision of the circle members. The first project should be as simple as possible so that the group members may gain confidence. If a project becomes too involved, the facilitator may have to obtain the technical expertise of specialists to assist the circle in its problem solving. However, specialists should help the members but not solve the problem for them, or they will not gain the experience of problem solving themselves.

8. Development of a plan of action: Here is where circle members begin to use their acquired skills to solve the problem. It is important for them to keep a positive attitude in their problem solving, rather than to assume that management will not listen to their recommendations. Typically, large numbers of recommendations are approved by management. Quality circle members should approach their particular problem with the attitude that their recommendations have merit and will be accepted. It is also important that all members participate in the analysis since each person has different knowledge, experience, and opinions to contribute. As a matter of procedure, each member is encouraged to be open and receptive to other people's ideas.

9. Presentation of recommendations: When the study has been completed, employees make their recommendations, emphasizing results and addressing issues that are important to management. While facilitators are charged with keeping management advised of circle progress, members themselves should make presentations to management. They should do so at suitable intervals in order to advise management of project status as well as to improve communication. Such presentations give employees a chance not usually afforded them

to deal directly with management; at the same time, these contacts give management the opportunity to reaffirm their support for the quality circle program. Additionally, the presentations give the circle recognition for its contributions.

10. Follow-up: The facilitator continues to remain available to assist the leader during all phases of the project. Once the group's recommendations have been accepted by management, it is up to the facilitator to make sure that they are implemented quickly since it is important for the members to see the results of their labor. If their recommendations are not accepted, management must give its reasons to the circle members so that they do not feel that their suggestions are simply being ignored.

Case Example. When quality circles were first proposed at Norfolk Naval Shipyard (NNSY) in 1979, it was a relatively unknown concept for most people. A management review decided to conduct a pilot project consisting of nine separate groups. These groups would be evaluated for a one-year period. After the initial pilot project, quality circles were considered successful, and the program was allowed to expand as other groups became interested. By late 1980, there were four circle facilitators, each supervising approximately 10 quality circles, with several more groups hoping to participate. Since then, the NNSY program has served as a model for other public agencies.

In 1981, a decision was made to include quality circles under the auspices of NNSY's Productivity Programs Office, thereby making them a more permanent part of the shipyard operations. Today, there are currently over 70 such circles at NNSY. Their members often demonstrate their enthusiasm for the program by working on their projects on their own time, either at home or during their lunch breaks.

Quality circles were initiated at the Norfolk shipyard in an effort to address productivity problems. An underlying philosophy of the program, however, is that everyone should be given the opportunity to work in a stimulating environment. As a result, the quality circle became more than just a program; it gave people a chance to learn and to become part of the team effort. Once employees were involved, they were not only active in areas concerning productivity, but they also addressed issues such as morale, job satisfaction, quality, cost, and safety.

Program Evaluation

When implemented properly, a quality circle program can make individuals feel that they are important parts of the organizational team. Thus, they have a feeling of contribution and participation, many of them for the first time in their lives. Since the concept is based on mutual trust and respect, it can also strengthen the relations between management and organized labor.

In spite of the program's potential, however, if it is not managed well, it can be harmful to an organization. If, for instance, a particular circle does not have a strong leader, management itself tends to get too much involved in the circle's activities. In that case, its members are liable to feel that projects are not really their own any more but just another assignment from management. This reaction, in turn, can lead to lowered morale and a drop in productivity.

It is important, therefore, for the facilitator to make sure that each circle strictly follows procedures. Only this way leads to successful programs. When procedures are treated loosely, a circle will probably fail to solve problems and will eventually disperse.

If employees are represented by a labor union, it is important to involve union leaders in the planning stages of the circles. Almost any type of union opposition can be detrimental to the program. Union officials must be assured that the program is truly voluntary at all levels. Once they realize that effective quality circles can actually improve job security, unions and their members often become quite active in the program.

The manager's role in supporting quality circles is a vital one since the success of the program is dependent upon his or her genuine endorsement. Managers may initially feel that the program undermines their authority, or they may be concerned about the time that employees are away from their jobs. Once managers gain experience with the circles, however, they find that the circle concept actually makes their jobs easier. Workers become more aware of quality improvements and their enhanced morale leads to a subsequent increase in productivity.

Management's support, however, should not be turned into manipulation. While the quality circles need continual contact with management, managers must learn to recognize that their employees are truly capable of solving problems in their own work areas. Therefore, management's actions should always encourage self-reliance within the circle.

REFERENCES

Barra, Ralph J.: *Putting Quality Circles to Work*, McGraw-Hill, New York, 1983.

Ingle, Sud: *Quality Circle Master Guide*, Prentice Hall, Englewood Cliffs, N.J., 1982.

Thompson, Phillip C.: *Quality Circles: How to Make Them Work in America*, AMACOM, New York, 1982.

PHILIP S. BANNEVICH, *Norfolk Naval Shipyard*

Quality Management

Quality management is the functional management discipline responsible for defining and implementing professionally developed programs of (1) quality improvement, (2) elimination of nonconformances, and (3) defect prevention within an organization for the purpose of assuring that its products and services will conform to its requirements, that customers will be protected and satisfied, and that the cost of quality will be continually reduced.

A prudent company makes certain that its products and services are delivered to the customer by a management system that does not condone rework, repair, waste, or nonconformance of any sort. These are expensive problems and must be not only detected and resolved at the earliest moment but, if possible, prevented. To forestall these problems and accomplish these tasks, it is necessary to establish a quality management function to assure that the required professionally designed and implemented programs are conducted. These programs range from training new employees to inspecting current products and services, conducting quality improvement, performing design reviews, and assisting the finance department in calculating the cost of quality.

Organizationally, quality management must report to the senior executive of the company. This requirement is to make certain that the judgment of those involved cannot be adversely influenced by reporting arrangements. The basic rule is that no one should ever work for someone he or she is charged with evaluating. In its broadest sense, the quality function serves not only as the "conscience" of the company but also as a compelling force for continual improvement from within. Utilizing planned communication activities, the quality operation attacks conventional mind sets such as "error is inevitable" and "that's good enough."

Essential Definitions. A number of terms and concepts underlie the proper implementation of quality management. They are defined briefly below:

Absolutes of quality: Four concepts provide a realistic approach to managing quality. They are: (1) Quality is defined as conformance to requirements, not goodness. (2) The system for achieving quality is prevention, not appraisal. (3) The measurement of quality is the cost of quality, not an index. (4) The performance standard for quality is zero defects ("Do it right the first time").

ASQC: American Society for Quality Control.

Audit: A planned evaluation (or inspection) of any operation for the purpose of determining compliance with requirements. Audits are usually conducted by personnel trained for that purpose and are not routinely assigned to the unit being audited. Reports of audits are supplied to senior management as well as to the management being audited. *Product*

audits may include disassembly of the product for measurement of individual components and parts. *Process* audits include chemical analysis of fluids or ingredients used. *Procedural* audits include subjective evaluations; all subjective analysis should be reported as such.

Communications: The part of quality training which is involved with continually reminding all individuals of their personal responsibility to the quality process of the company and also of the absolutes of quality.

Complaint handling: Processing complaints communicated by customers and requiring that (1) they are satisfactorily resolved externally, (2) the cause of the complaint is eliminated by the organization responsible for the problem, (3) accurate records are kept, and (4) the results are followed up to verify effectiveness. It is necessary to be certain that all complaints are treated objectively.

Consumer affairs: Programmed activities (discussed in detail in this entry's last section) designed to assure that the customers of a company receive proper consideration when they need to complain or to seek information; also concerned with evaluating the effect of any company action on customers or other consumers; serves as ombudsman for consumers.

Corrective action: The systematic action taken to identify, evaluate, and resolve problems of nonconformance. Usually considered to involve five steps: (1) defining the nonconformance, (2) fixing the nonconformance, (3) identifying the root cause, (4) implementing corrective action, and (5) evaluating the results.

Cost of quality (COQ): A calculation showing the expense of nonconformance (of doing things wrong.) The COQ has two components: (1) the price of nonconformance, that is, the costs associated with nonconforming goods and services (e.g., scrap, rework, warranty); and (2) the price of conformance, or costs involved in ensuring that things are done right (e.g., training).

Design review: Evaluating a completed or planned design by presenting it to a team representing all functional operations that will have to deal with the product, such as manufacturing, quality, and applications. The review purpose is to verify the producibility of the product and to identify preventable errors that may be observed because of past experience.

Environmental quality: Concerned with (1) evaluating company performance against regulations concerning pollution created by company facilities, (2) preventing violations in new facilities, (3) increasing employee awareness, and (4) establishing communication between the company and the public.

Make-certain: An awareness program oriented toward white-collar functions in manufacturing plants and everyone in service industries. The program is conducted primarily by the supervisor and the employee. The key part of the program is helping the individuals to recognize that "most of the mistakes we commit are our own fault." This focus encourages all employees to make defect-prevention suggestions, since those who cause the problems are the most qualified to offer ideas to prevent them in the future.

Measurement: The planned recording of inspection, test, or other appraisal results in a systematic manner that enables management to determine status of conformance in any given area or operation.

Metrology: The general term encompassing the broad spectrum of the science of measurement.

Procedure proving: The verification of a new procedure, such as how to total the hotel cashier's receipts at the end of the shift, by having the procedure conducted exactly as it reads. The purpose is to help prevent future nonconformances.

Process proving: The act of taking a new process, such as a new marketing procedure and accomplishing the process exactly as described. The results are then subjected to environmental and other tests to determine that complying with the exact process will produce a conforming product.

Product acceptance: Sometimes called appraisal. Refers to all the planned inspections, tests, and other measurement actions conducted to verify that the product conforms to its requirements at various stages in its development. The actions are planned by quality engineering and conducted by professionally trained personnel. Part of product acceptance is the recording of results according to a prescribed procedure.

Product qualification: The planned conducting of tests and inspections (including environmental) to determine whether new or redesigned products will comply with all the requirements of performance and configuration attributed to them.

Product recall: The systematic process of identifying potentially harmful or nonconforming products already delivered to customers and retrieving all such material for replacement with a conforming product or repair to their satisfaction. Recalls are formally handled and recorded.

Product safety: The professional discipline dedicated to the continual evaluation of products for conditions that may cause harm to users even when they misuse the product. Product safety is primarily oriented toward prevention of unsafe characteristics but is heavily involved in internal communication and the formal handling of problems such as product recall.

Quality: Conformance to requirements.

Quality education: The planned process of informing all individuals in the organization about the quality absolutes and methods being utilized and their personal role in implementing them. Training activ-

ities include new employee orientation, executive training, quality engineering techniques and companywide quality improvement programs.

Quality engineering. The portion of quality management concerned with prevention planning and the correction of nonconformances within the production or service cycle. This function establishes all necessary measurement, analysis, and reporting actions and is continually concerned with getting things done right the first time.

Quality improvement process: The planned, long-range implementation by a company or organization of a formal program for (1) systematic reduction in the cost of quality, (2) improvement of the company's quality reputation, (3) increases in employees' awareness of the importance of quality in their jobs, and (4) elimination of nonconformance in product and services. The process (discussed in detail below) contains specific actions requiring participation by all levels of management and employees.

Reliability: The evaluation function concerned with calculating the performance life of a product at the earliest possible stage in its development. Practices are oriented toward prevention of system failures by assuring the competence of the components and subsystems.

Software qualification: A system of testing software to determine that it contains no errors and will cause the desired computer programs to operate.

Statistical quality control (SQC): The application of statistical concepts and specifically developed techniques to the control of processes and massproduced products. It is also utilized as the basis for sampling plans and problem evaluations.

Statistical quality control chart: Typical example of $\bar{X}$ (average of sample results) and R (range of sample results) charts to control the output of a machine or process. X marks the spot where the process or machine went "out of control." At this point, work is stopped until the assignable cause is discovered and corrected. In a different example, the range (R) might have been the indicator of an out-of-control condition, or it might have followed the mean and been out on the same sample. See Fig. Q-1.

Status reporting: The planned action of publishing evaluated measurement results in an agreed format so management can know the status of the pro-

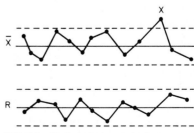

FIG. Q-1 Statistical control chart.

duct or service in terms of conformance to requirements with particular emphasis on problems and the actions being taken to resolve them. See Fig. Q-2.

Supplier quality: Most companies spend a third or more of their sales dollars on purchased material. Some actions involved are clearly spelling out the conformance requirements of a purchase, assisting the supplier in clarification or technology, conducting appraisal activities at the supplier's plant or in your own, and directing corrective action where applicable.

Zero defects (ZD): The phrase used in expressing the management standard: Do it right the first time. The ZD concept states that people expect errors to occur in their jobs because management expects them to happen; however, individuals have higher standards in their personal life. Management cannot use vague phrases when it establishes performance standards, or it will get vague results. The test is: "What standard would you set on how many babies nurses are allowed to drop?" ZD should be used in improvement programs to establish their goals clearly. It is not a "motivational" program. It is the attitude that nonconformance is not acceptable.

Implementing Quality Management

There are six specific actions necessary for installing a mature quality management process: (1) quality improvement, (2) supplier quality, (3) product acceptance, (4) service quality management, (5) quality engineering, and (6) consumer affairs.

Strategy. The primary problem most professionals face, however, is not so much determining the content of their programs as it is creating support of both management and employees for quality. To obtain that, it is necessary to involve all personnel in a deliberate quality improvement process so they can experience the value of such activities. Participation creates support for the establishment of the permanent programs of control and prevention.

Installation of defect detection and defect prevention programs in a company requires a genuine understanding of a complete strategy and the actions to implement it. Whether the "product" of a company is cast iron fittings or clean hotel rooms, the foremost quality management actions take place with people. Employees, customers, and suppliers are all involved as individuals and as corporate entities. Even in the most integrated manufacturing companies, half the people are involved in service and administrative functions. They never lay hands on the product itself during the manufacturing cycle. The only difference between programs in manufacturing and service is in what results are measured. Paperwork measurement requires special techniques, of course, but all things are measurable.

Three Basic Actions. To install a complete quality program in any organization, three basic actions are necessary.

Special programs

Item	Status or results
1. Quality department budget performance ($000)	1. YTD—$482.3 actual vs. $480.0 budget
2. Corrective action	2. New problems opened −29 Problems closed −32 Balance still open −28
3. Zero Defects program	3. QIT meeting this month reviewed and reached agreement on Marketing Department ZD goals.

Cost of quality summary

Months	J	F	M	A	M	J	J	A	S	O	N	D	Year end
													Monthly data — actual cost of quality, $(000)
Prevention	38.3	39.4	46.5										Previous years Actual
Appraisal	107.0	111.8	139.3										9.9
Failure	73.1	81.3	93.2										
Total cost of quality	218.4	232.5	279.0										Year-end target
Percentage of sales	9.1	9.3	9.0										8.9

Basic quality measurements (percent defective)

Area/Criteria	Previous year act.	J	F	M	A	M	J	J	A	S	O	N	D	Year-end goal
Recv. Insp.	8.7	9.5	8.5	7.0	6.0									5.0
Fabrication	0.75	0.50	0.70	0.60	0.45									0.3
PCB Insp.	12.5	12.0	14.0	13.5	11.5									6.0
Sub.assy.insp.	5.0	3.0	1.8	1.9	1.7									1.0
PCB test	11.0	10.0	10.0	8.5	9.5									6.0
Sub.assy.test	14.5	13.0	9.0	12.0	9.0									4.0
System test	9.6	7.0	6.0	8.0	4.0									2.0

Major items contributing to quality costs

Items	Responsibility and action plan
1. PCB rework approx. $4500.00/mo.	Industrial engineering continues a major task effort to incrementally improve the processes, parts control, instructions, and training aids.
2. Sub assy. test rejections $15,000.00/mo	Three (3) controlled lots of accepted PCBs are being carefully monitored to determine the cause of module rejections traced to PCBs.

Customer complaint summary

Items	Actions being taken
1. Customer rejections of lots of submitted reached zero (144 submissions) for the first time (average for 19XX was 0.3%).	1. Action not required.
2. Customer deficiency reports (from system audit results) continue below the goal of 2 per month or less.	2. Action taken on (1) QDR received.

FIG. Q-2 Quality status report.

1. Determination: All corporate management must recognize that quality is vital to the growth, prosperity, and even the survival of the company.
2. Education: Each and every employee of the company has to understand her or his role in the 14-step quality improvement process.
3. Implementation: The quality improvement process must be installed as a matter of a logical communication and action flow that requires no additional people or equipment.

Quality Improvement Process

There are 14 steps to follow in an effective process.

STEP 1: Management commitment

Action. Discuss the need for quality improvement with management people with an emphasis on the need for defect prevention. There are plenty of movies, visual-aids, and other material available to support this communication. (Do not confuse communication with *motivation.* Communication is long-lasting; motivation tends to be shallow and short-lived.) Prepare a quality policy that states that each individual is expected to "perform exactly according to the requirement or cause the requirement to be officially changed to what we and the customer really need." Agree that quality improvement is a practical way to profit improvement.

Accomplishment. Helping management to recognize personal requirement to participate raises the level of visibility for quality and assures everyone's cooperation so long as there is some progress.

STEP 2: Quality improvement team

Action. Bring together representatives of each department to form the quality improvement team. These should be people who can speak for their department in order to commit that operation to action. Preferably, the department heads should participate—at least on the first go-around. Orient the team members as to the content of the process, its purpose, and their role, which is to plan and administer the process in their departments and in the company.

Accomplishment. All the tools necessary to do the job are now together in one team. Appointing one of the members as the chairperson of the team works well for this phase.

STEP 3: Quality measurement

Action. It is necessary to find out the performance status of quality throughout the company. Quality measurements for each area of activity must be established where they do not exist and reviewed where they do. Nonconformance rates are recorded to show where improvement is possible and where corrective action is necessary, and to document actual improvement later on.

Nonmanufacturing measurements, which are sometimes difficult to establish (for example, in a hotel), can include the following:

Accounting
  Percentage of late reports
  Computer input incorrect
  Errors in specific reports as audited

Data processing:
  Keypunch cards thrown out for error
  Computer downtime due to error
  Rerun time

Engineering:
  Change orders due to error
  Drafting errors found by checkers
  Late releases

Finance:
  Billing errors (check accounts receivable overdues)
  Payroll errors
  Accounts payable deductions missed

Hotel front desk:
  Guests taken to unmade rooms
  Reservations not honored

Manufacturing engineering:
  Process change notices due to error
  Tool rework to correct design
  Methods improvement

Marketing:
  Contract errors
  Order description errors

Plant engineering:
  Time lost due to equipment failures
  Callbacks on repairs

Purchasing:
  Purchase order changes due to error
  Late receipt of material
  Rejections due to incomplete description

There are innumerable ways to measure any procedure. The people doing the work will respond with delight to the opportunity to identify some measurements for their work. A supervisor who says his or her area is completely immeasurable can be helped by asking how he or she knows who is doing the best work, whom to keep, and whom to replace.

Accomplishment. Formalizing the company measurement system strengthens the inspection and test functions and assures proper measurement. Getting the paperwork and service operations involved sets the stage for effective defect prevention where it counts. Placing the results of measurement in highly visible charts establishes the foundation of the entire quality improvement process.

STEP 4:   Cost of quality evaluation

Action. Initial estimates are likely to be shaky (although low), so it is necessary now to get more accurate figures. The comptroller's office must do this. It should be provided first with detailed information as to what constitutes the cost of quality. The cost of quality (COQ) is not an absolute performance measurement: it is an indication of where corrective action will be profitable for a company. The higher the cost, the more corrective action to be taken. The COQ is used to get management's attention, to direct corrective action, and to measure progress.

Accomplishment. Having the comptroller establish the cost of quality removes any suspected bias from the calculation. More important, a measurement of quality management performance has been established in the company's system.

STEP 5:   Quality awareness

Action. Management must share its concern about quality with the employees. It does so by training supervisors to orient employees and by providing visible evidence of the concern for quality improvement through communication material such as booklets, films, posters, and similar items. This should not be confused with motivation. There is no intent to manipulate people. It is a sharing process. This sharing is an important step; it may be the most important. Service and administrative people should be included on a first-class basis.

Accomplishment. The real benefit of communication is that it gets supervisors and employees in the habit of talking positively about quality. It aids the process of changing, or perhaps clarifying, existing attitudes toward quality. And it sets the basis for the corrective action and error-cause identification steps.

STEP 6:   Corrective action

Action. As people are encouraged to talk about their problems, opportunities for correction come to light. These problems include not only the defects found by inspection, audit, or self-evaluation, but also situations that require attention—as seen by the working people. The problems must be brought to the supervision meetings at each level, and the ones that cannot be resolved are formally passed upward to the next level of supervision for review at its regular meeting. If a specific functional area does not hold such meetings, the quality improvement team should take action to establish them in that department.

Accomplishment. Individuals soon see that the problems brought to light have the opportunity to be resolved on a regular basis. The habit of facing problems and correcting them is developing.

STEP 7:   Ad hoc committee for the zero defects event.

Action. Three or four members of the quality improvement team are selected to investigate the zero defects (ZD) concept and ways to implement it. The quality improvement team must understand that ZD is not a motivation program. Its purpose is to communicate to all employees the literal meaning of the words and the thought that everyone should do things right the first time. In particular, the ad hoc group should seek out ways to match the program to the company's personality.

Accomplishment. Improvement comes with each step of the overall process. By the time the ZD event is conducted, as much as a year may have gone by and the initial improvement will be flattening out. At that point, the new commitment to an explicit goal takes over and starts the improvement again. Setting up this committee to study and prepare the implementation actually installs the process with the thought leaders of the company.

STEP 8:   Quality education

Action. A formal orientation with all levels of management should be conducted prior to implementation of the next steps. All managers must understand each step well enough to explain it to their people; that is the test.

Accomplishment. Eventually all supervision will be tuned into the process and realize the value themselves. Then they will concentrate their action on the process.

STEP 9:   Zero defects event

Action. An event aimed at letting every manager and employee make visible their commitment to the performance standard of zero defects. The event should be fun, but it must also have a serious purpose. Do something different so that everyone will recognize it as a "new attitude day."

Accomplishment. Making an event of the zero defects commitment provides an emphasis and a memory that will be long-lasting.

STEP 10:   Goal setting

Action. During meetings with employees, each manager requests that they establish the goals they would like to strive for against their measurement. Usually, goals should be for 30-, 60-, and 90-day periods. All should be specific and relate to numbers.

Accomplishment. This phase helps people learn to think in terms of meeting goals and accomplishing specific tasks as a team.

STEP 11:   Error-cause removal (ECR)

Action. Using a simple one-page form, the manager asks individuals to describe any problem that keeps them from performing error-free work. This is not a suggestion system in that each person merely must list the problem; the appropriate functional group (i.e., industrial engineering) will develop the answer. It is important that ECRs are acknowledged quickly within 24 hours.

Typical inputs on the form might be:

1. "This tool is not long enough to work right with all the parts."

2. "The sales department makes too many errors on its order entry forms."

3. "We make a lot of changes in response to telephone calls, and many of them end up having to be done all over again."

4. "I do not have any place to put my pocketbook."

Accomplishment. People now know that their problems will be heard and answered. Once employees learn to trust this communication, the process can go on forever.

STEP 12: Recognition

Action. Award programs are established to recognize those who meet their goals or perform outstandingly. It is wise not to attach a value to the problem identifications. They should all be treated the same since they are not suggestions. The prizes or awards should not be expensive. The key element is the recognition of personal achievement.

Accomplishment. Genuine recognition of performance is something people really appreciate. They will continue to support the program whether or not they, as individuals, participate in the awards.

STEP 13: Quality councils

Action. The quality professionals and team chairpersons should be brought together regularly to communicate with one another and to determine actions necessary to upgrade and improve the solid quality process being installed.

Accomplishment. These councils are the best source of information on the status of the process and ideas for action. It also brings the professionals into a close affiliation.

STEP 14: Do it over again

Action. The typical process takes 1 year to 24 months to perform. By that time, turnover and changing situations will have wiped out much of the education effort. Therefore, it is necessary to set up a new team of representatives and begin again. The ZD event, for instance, should be marked as an anniversary. Nothing more than the notification and special lunch for all employees is necessary. But the process is never over.

Accomplishment. Repetition makes the process perpetual and thus "part of the woodwork." If quality is not that deeply ingrained in the organization, it will never develop.

Supplier Quality

The purpose of a supplier quality program is to eliminate the flow of unacceptable or unusable material and services from supplier to user. The service that supplier quality provides to the purchasing function may include any or all of the following: (1) surveys of supplier quality capabilities, (2) reviews of purchase order technical requirements, (3) itinerant or resident source inspection, (4) receiving inspection

and test, (5) supplier corrective action, and (6) quality rating systems. The key is to obtain the supplier's commitment to zero defect standards. *See* Purchasing management.

Product Acceptance

A company or organization producing a product or service must know that its output conforms to the requirements of the technical design, advertising literature, government regulations, and/or customer standards. *Product acceptance,* or the *appraisal* of a product, includes all the planned inspections, tests, and other measurement actions conducted to verify that the product conforms to its requirements during each phase of its development and production. Its primary purpose is to assure product readiness for proceeding into the next phase right up to its individual acceptability for delivery to a customer.

The extent of inspection in any given area is established by quality engineering. Inspection plans will normally by based on (1) those product characteristics that are critical to end-product performance, (2) those characteristics that are controlled by tooling, and (3) the extent of risk based on recent past performance.

Testing is an important part of the overall acceptance function for many companies. Its importance lies in its significant effect on the performance of a company's products. Its expense arises from the high level of skills and costly test equipment often involved. Testing starts with qualification testing of new designs and continues through the testing of purchased products, manufactured subassemblies, and final product testing. Like inspection, testing is always conducted by the quality department in accordance with specific plans and procedures.

For any acceptance measurement, there is always the possibility that nonconforming material will be discovered. When it is, acceptance cannot be achieved and the responsibility of the acceptance function becomes one of clearly defining and recording the exact conditions of nonconformance. This documentation is absolutely basic to effective corrective action.

Service Quality Management

Service quality management pertains to the service and administrative areas of manufacturing companies as well as to the entire service industry. Its specific objective is the prevention of nonconformances in service and administrative activities and the continual improvement of service operations. There is no basic difference between manufacturing and service management except that one has tangibles as its product and the other does not. Both require people to perform. All work is a process.

Service quality management is accomplished through the formal application of a quality improvement process. The improvement cycle will begin when each service activity center looks at itself as an individual entity with suppliers and customers. This examination will help to identify incoming, internal, and outgoing errors or deficiencies, which then become the basis for measuring the performance of this service activity. Measuring performance is the first step of improvement, and this measurement can be anything from the number of actual paperwork errors, such as wrong shipments, to a determination of the percentage of directly serviced customers who indicate satisfaction with the service.

Quality Engineering

The purpose of quality engineering might be briefly described as the application of the technology of quality systems to the specific technologies of a company's business. It is intended to supply the necessary engineering base to allow the fruits of quality improvement to achieve the maximum desirable effect on product or service quality. Organizationally, quality engineering embodies (1) activities of inspection and test planning, (2) data analysis and corrective action, and (3) the quality interface actions with marketing and engineering. In this capacity, quality engineers are responsible for continued state-of-the-art improvements in quality documentation systems, statistical techniques, testing systems, failure analysis techniques, reliability programs, vendor quality techniques, and many others.

Quality Planning. The first task of quality engineering is quality planning, which has the following purposes:

1. To provide the basic plan for the maintenance and improvement of product or service quality

2. To judiciously place available controls where they offer the most protection or prevention for the dollars spent

3. To exert maximum influence on the planning of others in an effort to make conformance to requirements and prevention of errors an inherent part of each company operation

4. To review and analyze results periodically and present them to management in such a way that improvements can be forthcoming

Visible evidence of the work of quality planning can be found in inspection and test plans, documentation systems, quality status reports, procedures for the control of quality, and the attitude of other planning groups with respect to the importance of quality.

Corrective Actions. For companies that deal in products, quality engineering's contribution to product quality improvement will be directly related to its ability to cause corrective actions. Without corrective changes, there can be no improvement. Opportunities for improvement begin with the first rejects or with nonconforming material found on the production floor. Quality engineers will (1) guide the acceptance function in requiring correction for obvious errors, (2) perform failed-product analyses to determine the causes of not-so-obvious errors, (3) direct supplementary investigative efforts for more complex product problems, and (4) ultimately require the commitment of responsible activities for specific corrective actions. Experience in this area of quality engineering is what qualifies them for doing customer problem analysis and making valuable contributions to the marketing and design engineering efforts.

Consumer Affairs

Companies will become more responsible to the needs and expectations of their customers through the implementation of a formal consumer affairs program. This extension of the quality management function is directed toward providing to ultimate consumers products and services which conform to agreed or implied requirements and reasonable expectations. The responsibility of this function is to promote and coordinate all efforts necessary to establish and improve communications, complaint handling, consumer and company education, and compliance with applicable consumer-oriented laws, regulations, and standards. The consumer affairs manager can then act as an internal consultant for consumer matters (the consumer's advocate). *See* Consumerism and consumer protection legislation; Product liability.

Guidelines. Typical guidelines for the consumer affairs program include the following:

1. Products manufactured, imported, exported, sold, or distributed must be in conformance with all requirements and in compliance with all applicable laws, regulations, and standards established for protection of users of such products.

2. Services provided must be (a) responsive to consumer needs and expectations, and (b) in compliance with applicable government regulations, codes, and standards.

3. Complaint handling must be swift and courteous and provide fair settlement of just claims.

4. Company activities which may have a significant impact on consumer satisfaction (such as marketing, advertising, product development, man-

ufacturing, and others) should be monitored by the consumer affairs activity.

5. The consumer affairs manager should prepare a manual containing written procedures to describe the activities required by all functions in the company necessary to carry out the consumer affairs program and to measure the status of the program at that particular point in time.

6. All the information processed by the consumer affairs activity should routinely be analyzed for identification of problems and system weaknesses. These results will become an important input to the corrective action system.

See also Consumerism and consumer protection legislation; Control systems, management; Product liability; Product planning and development; Production planning and control.

REFERENCES

Crosby, P. B.: *The Art of Getting Your Own Sweet Way*, 2d ed., McGraw-Hill Book Company, New York, 1981.

————: *Quality Is Free*, McGraw-Hill Book Company, New York, 1979.

————: *Quality Without Tears, the Art of Hassle-Free Management*, McGraw-Hill Book Company, New York, 1984.

PHILIP B. CROSBY, *Philip Crosby Associates, Inc.*

Quality of Work Life

Quality of work life (QWL) can mean different things to different people, but in recent years it has come to stand for a participative philosophy of work and organizations—a people and bottom-line philosophy. The QWL organizational philosophy centers on the dignity and respect accorded employees, the nature of their involvement in their work, and the goal of excellence for their organizations. QWL is employee involvement: a structured effort to enable employees at all levels in an organization to use their knowledge, skills, and abilities more effectively in their work and to participate more fully in decisions about it. For most organizations it is thus a new workplace culture.

In action, QWL is a planned, evolutionary, cooperative process—jointly undertaken by employees and management and, in unionized settings, with the union as an equal partner. It involves structural and systems changes, frequently featuring a network of "shop-floor" problem-solving groups supported by a top-level steering committee. Advanced sites may engage in a participative design—or redesign—process, structuring jobs and other organizational elements in accordance with sociotechnical systems principles. QWL efforts have twin goals: (1) enhancing the quality of life at work (in terms of dignity, learning, growth, participation, fulfillment, and engagement), and (2) improving organizational effectiveness in the areas of productivity, quality, cost effectiveness, creativity, and adaptability).* (See note on page 784.)

The Roots of QWL

The term "quality of work life" (or "quality of working life") was coined for its current usage in a series of conferences sponsored in the late 1960s and early 1970s by the U.S. Department of Labor and the Ford Foundation. These conferences were stimulated by the then widely publicized phenomenon of "worker alienation" as symbolized by work stoppages and disruption among the largely young work force at General Motors' new Assembly Division Plant in Lordstown, Ohio. The term "quality of work life" seemed to conferees to move beyond older concepts of job satisfaction to include such notions as participation in at least some decision making, enhanced autonomy in day-to-day work affairs, and the design of jobs and organizational systems and structures so as to foster learning, growth, and a more fulfilling form of engagement in work. Improved organizational effectiveness or "competitivity" was seen as a natural by-product of organizations that successfully pursued QWL as so defined.

The concept, however, remained ambiguous throughout much of the 1970s. To be sure, some companies (Mead Paper, Procter & Gamble, Cummins Engine, General Foods, etc.) used—and had previously been using—such ideas in new plant designs that resulted in startlingly effective and profitable operations. These companies featured unusually "flat" organizational structures along with semiautonomous or largely self-managing work groups whose members were deeply cross-trained and frequently paid on the basis of the number of skills at which they were proficient. While some of these plants achieved a certain celebrity, they were more generally viewed as freakish and inappropriate models for the transformation of most existing organizations.

More generally through the mid-1970s, QWL was rejected by management as "soft" and by organized labor as a potential "social science trick." Where it was embraced, it was often—with significant exceptions—cheapened into an effete form of fringe benefits (one Michigan company even touting its aerobic dance program for executives as its quality of work life program) or applied to the piecemeal and mechanical adoption of certain specialized techniques, such as flexitime.

The most important exception to this pattern was developed at General Motors. There, Irving Bluestone, vice president and director of the General Motors Department of the United Automobile Workers (UAW) Union—and one of the nation's most statesmanlike and innovative labor leaders—had suggested to General Motors in their 1970 negotiations, and again in 1973, that the union and the corporation enter into a joint effort to improve the quality of work life in automobile plants. This goal was desirable on its merits, he argued, and could, as well, avoid future disruption like that at Lordstown. In 1973, General Motors agreed; and Bluestone and his management counterpart, Dr. D. L. Landen, director of Organizational Research and Development for General Motors, subsequently fashioned one of the most effective QWL programs in the nation.

In the late 1970s, another innovative labor leader, Donald Ephlin, vice president of the UAW for Ford Motor Company, joined with an equally enterprising vice president for industrial relations at Ford, Peter J. Pestillo, to establish a Ford–UAW counterpart to the General Motors effort (calling it "Employee Involvement," or EI). Similar agreements were also concluded between the basic steel companies and the United Steel Workers union, and in telecommunications between the American Telephone and Telegraph Company and the Communications Workers of America. These developments added the theme of "labor-management cooperation" to QWL; more important, they moved QWL from its seemingly arcane applications in new plant designs—or in scattered partial use with managers or other specialized work populations—into the mainstream of basic industry and onto the shop floor.

In the late 1970s and early 1980s the worst recession since the great depression of the 1930s—combined with massive inroads into American markets by foreign competitors offering both low prices and high quality—caused widespread reexamination by both managers and labor leaders of fundamental assumptions underlying management theory and practice and labor-management relations. By then, the experience of the seventies had clarified the QWL concept sufficiently that hundreds of organizations in the public and private sectors—and thousands of workplaces—grasped for QWL or QWL-related activities. No accurate count exists, but separate surveys made available in 1983 by both the New York Stock Exchange and the Industrial Union Department of the American Federation of Labor—Congress of Industrial Organizations (AFL–CIO) reported widespread interest and involvement in participative organizational innovations.

Intellectual and Experiential Sources. In summary, QWL springs from several substantial intellectual and experiential sources:

1. *Theories and practices associated with small group behavior:* These may be said to have begun with the work of Lewin and his followers at the National Training Laboratories (NTL) in Bethel, Maine, and later at the Institute for Social Research (ISR) at the University of Michigan and other schools and associations of "organizational development" and "survey-feedback" professionals.

2. *Broader research on leadership, motivation, and effectiveness in organizations:* Here, the best-known work included that of Rensis Likert, Abraham Maslow, and R. R. Blake and J. S. Mouton, among numerous others. In general, they conclude that participatory management styles and structures provide higher orders of personal fulfillment and greater degrees of organizational effectiveness.

3. *Action research on semiautonomous work groups and sociotechnical systems:* During and after World War II, social psychologists at the Tavistock Institute near London examined small-group behavior in relation to technology. The work of Tavistock's Eric Trist and Fred Emery, joined later by Holland's Hans Von Beinum, Norway's Einar Thorsrud, and others developed the concept of *sociotechnical systems* (STS). This concept postulates that all organizations are composed of inherently interacting social and technical systems and that the highest levels of both human fulfillment and organizational effectiveness are attainable if the persons designing jobs and organizational structures seek to optimize jointly these interacting systems. This form of systems thinking reached its highest development in the "humanization and democratization of work" movements in Western Europe in the 1970s. Oslo's Work Research Institute under Thorsrud and Volvo's innovative assembly plant at Kalmar are notable. (*Note:* Such approaches concentrate on shop-floor redesign; they are not to be confused with "codetermination" legislation in Germany and elsewhere in Europe that placed various proportions of worker representatives on the boards of corporations. Such developments may have provided arguments for some people in the United States favoring broadened control over corporate decision making; but, in practice, they had little effect on daily work life or on organizational effectiveness.)

4. *Labor-management cooperation:* Labor-management relations in the United States have almost always been adversarial, often highly contentious, and sometimes violent to the point of bloodshed. But, they have seldom been ideological; hence, they have responded with quite opposite behaviors in crises or in the face of practical necessity. There is a thin, but almost century-old, history of labor-management cooperation—responses to war, natural disaster, worker welfare (safety and health, alcoholism treatment, pensions), training (including apprenticeships), etc. The vehicle for such cooperation has usually

been a joint labor-management committee. At the community level such committees have also existed—in small numbers—for decades. During the 1970s, they grew to over three dozen organized and active joint labor-management committees, located largely in the Northeast and Midwest and striving to better their communities in various ways. Of these, the area Labor-Management Committee (ALMC) in Jamestown, New York, is best known for its job training and employer-attraction successes.

5. *Innovative new plant designs:* New plants have often been designed along sociotechnical systems lines, as described earlier. The General Foods plant in Topeka, Kansas, designed with the aid of Harvard Business School professor Richard Walton, is perhaps the best known. Articles about it in various publications, including the *Harvard Business Review,* lent legitimacy and emphasis to QWL in the mid-1970s.

6. *Japanese experience with quality control circles:* Astute and adaptive Japanese managers quickly adapted the advice of American consultants regarding statistical process control techniques to small work groups in natural work units in order to boost quality and thus undergird their invasion of the markets of older industrial economies. The startling success of the Japanese over the last decade has done more than any single factor to excite fervent, albeit often shallow, interest in quality circles, from which thoughtful managers and unionists graduate to more comprehensive QWL processes. The recent successes of the Japanese circles have overshadowed the older European antecedents of QWL. Ironically, both draw heavily upon American ideas that failed, until recently, to elicit sympathy from American industrial and labor leaders.

7. *Joint labor-management participation and problem-solving experiences:* The recent successes of QWL in the automobile, steel, communications, and other industries as cited here have fueled much of the recent QWL impetus.

Work Life Characteristics Versus a Process of Change

As a term, quality of work life, or QWL, has an enduring ambiguity and a controversial implication that have both hindered and helped its advance. One axis of confusion runs between concepts of QWL as physical, social, psychological, or performance characteristics of work and work life on the one hand, and controversies over the scope, nature, and purposes of QWL change processes on the other.

Work Life Characteristics. For many American managers and union leaders, the quality of life at work seems to begin and end with pay, benefits, employment security, decent and relatively safe working conditions, and some rules of due process regarding job assignments, promotions, discipline, and the like.

Beyond such immediate and pragmatic concerns lie the rich literatures of industrial psychology and management theory and practice previously cited. Here, concepts of fulfillment, engagement, social interaction, participation, learning, and growth—as embodied in various approaches to job design—are important. So, too, are performance effectiveness and feedback regarding it.

QWL is not limited to such working conditions as the comfort and safety or hygiene factors of work. It embraces the broader social, psychological, and economic dimensions as well.

The work life characteristics of QWL may be summarized in the following list of work-related human needs:* (See page 784.)

1. *Fair pay.* People need compensation that is deemed equitable by the standards of their community.

2. *Good working conditions.* People need working conditions that are safe, healthful, and if possible, pleasant.

3. *Security.* People need a sense of confidence about their future job security, promotions, etc.

4. *Dignity and respect.* People need to be treated with dignity and respect at all times.

5. *Variety and challenge.* People need a degree of variety and challenge in their work.

6. *Wholeness.* People need a sense of wholeness, closure, or completion in their work.

7. *Learning and growth.* People need and respond to opportunities to learn and to grow in mental and physical competence.

8. *Participation.* People need and respond to opportunities to participate in problem solving and in decision making, at least about those aspects of work that directly affect them.

9. *Teamwork.* People need and respond to opportunities to work in teams or groups and not solely or mainly in isolation.

10. *Individuality.* People need to balance team and group values against their need for individuality—individual choice, idiosyncrasy, and recognition.

11. *Feedback on effectiveness.* People need to be effective at some things important to them, and they need to know promptly how well they are doing at those things.

12. *Social Utility.* People need to feel that their work has some larger social utility.

QWL theory and practice hold that "human fulfillment and well-being, responsible human behavior, and the effectiveness of organizations depend substantially upon the degree to which such needs are met in the culture, structures, and systems of day-to-day work life."* (See page 784.) (This is not to deny the importance of technology, materials, energy and its costs, capital and its costs, the role of government, and managerial acumen and entrepreneurship.)

The QWL Change Process. For those managers, workers, union leaders, scholars, and others with a narrow definition of QWL work life characteristics, the QWL "process" is simply putting into place, or negotiating for, improvements in pay, benefits, working conditions, etc. QWL "change" is thus adding improvements incrementally.

But, for those with a broader view of human needs at work, the QWL change process becomes much more. Some seek to humanize management through training in interpersonal communications, group dynamics, Theory Y (or, after the Ouchi bestseller, Theory Z), "Nine-Nine Managerial Grid" styles of management, etc. Others implement *quality* circle programs, which at their narrowest are voluntary groups of shop-floor employees, often trained in statistical process control techniques, who are allowed to seek improvements in product or service quality through solving quality-related work problems. Quality circle programs are now widespread throughout the United States, riding a wave of some managers' imitation of Japanese techniques (adapted by that nation from the advice of American consultant Dr. Richard Demming).

The successes of quality circles have been documented in the press, some scholarship, and the publications and conferences of the numerous local chapters of the International Association of Quality Circles. Press and other reports, however, also indicate high failure rates after sometimes short periods of accomplishment. The programs that fail seem to be those that narrowly limit the role of the circles, that are implemented in unionized settings without union involvement, that are seen by management as techniques to solve certain discrete production problems, and that lack broad commitment and support throughout the organization. The best quality circle programs approach, or evolve into, broader QWL processes; and the most experienced quality circle proponents advocate broader and more comprehensive organizational change.

The power of the quality of work life process lies in its comprehensiveness and in the fact that it is an amalgam of the intellectual and practical strains cited in a previous section, "The Roots of QWL." QWL is not a particular technique or "quick fix." It requires a conscious and deliberate shift in management style and philosophy, an acceptance of unions, where they exist, as legitimate stakeholders in the enterprise, and a commitment to viewing an organization as continually improving itself and continually adapting to a turbulent and changing social, technical, political, and economic environment. QWL is thus a process, not a program; it is a different way of organizational life—the purposeful and controlled evolution of organizational culture toward excellence and fulfillment. QWL in its broadest sense thus merges with the most advanced concepts of organizational development and systems theory. These are consistent with experience over the last decade, thus demonstrating that for QWL to be successful, it must be reflected not only in the philosophy and values of an organization but also in the concrete structures, systems, and job characteristics that determine the nature of day-to-day work life.

Implementing QWL

Key Elements of QWL* in Practice. (See page 784 for note.) As QWL has evolved over the last decade—especially in unionized settings—certain elements have emerged of central importance to the viability and effectiveness of these processes.

1. *Philosophy/purpose/goals:* A stated commitment by the organization to participative and humanistic management aimed at jointly pursuing and attaining economic, social, and individual goals. A clear understanding that while both human and economic improvements are expected, the latter are expected to derive from the former and that human betterment in both physical and sociopsychological terms is being pursued for its own value as well as for its economic by-products. An assumption that people want to be competent, responsible, and effective, and a commitment to structuring the organization to enable them to be that way.

   Such written philosophy statements exist at both the corporate and plant levels in organizations deeply into QWL processes. They vary from a few lines in length to a few pages. Some are carried by employees at all levels on plastic wallet cards. Such a written statement provides an important symbol of commonly held normative goals and purposes that guide the QWL process.

2. *Jointness/mutuality:* Acceptance of the legitimate role of the union, where there is one; acceptance by workers and their union of the importance of efficiency and profitability. Joint control of all aspects of QWL by management and the union; shared employee control where there is no union.

   For an effective QWL–employee involvement program, the program must be seen by workers and their union, if there is one, as a process in which they share so-called ownership. This jointness is reflected in all aspects of successful programs—particularly in governing bodies and QWL staff, with participants selected equally from both union and management ranks. It also has a strong role in planning and operational decisions regarding QWL. Funding, however, is normally provided fully by management although some exceptions exist where the union provides some degree of financial support.

3. *Demonstrated leadership support:* Clear, demonstrated, and continuous support by top-line management and top union leadership.

The strongest QWL processes have the strongest leadership support. A permissive or acquiescent role by such leadership sends ambivalent signals to mid-level and low-level organizational elements that bear the burden of making substantial changes if the QWL process is to succeed. Note, too, that leadership is normally lodged in line elements, not in staff officers such as those in personnel or industrial relations.

4. *Structural changes:* A joint steering committee, generally composed equally of union and management members and cochaired by the senior line manager in the facility and the union president. Worksite problem-solving groups such as GM's employee participation groups, Ford Motor's employee involvement groups, labor-management participation teams (as in the steel industry), and local workforce committees (as in the telephone industry). Supervisory and mid-management QWL structures, such as supervisor problem-solving groups, supervisor-steward coordinating committees, and operations support teams composed of supervisors, mid-managers, and relevant staff and support specialists responsible for effective operation of a natural work unit and adequate support of worksite problem-solving teams therein.

The steering committee normally sees its role as providing policy guidance to the QWL process, not in deciding on the merits of solutions or recommendations advanced by worksite problem-solving groups. Such worksite solutions or recommendations are normally decided upon and implemented by the groups themselves or by appropriate levels of management with the requisite approval authority for expenditure of funds, changes in methods, specifications, etc. Worksite groups are customarily voluntary, consist of 4 to 12 members drawn from natural work units, or in some cases cross-cutting sections or shifts where coordination is important. The supervisor is generally a member of the group but not normally its leader. The best practice is to have the group itself select the leader, with the supervisor providing assistance and support. The shop steward is authorized to sit in on group meetings, which are normally held once a week

for one hour on paid time. QWL structures for supervisors themselves, mid-managers, and specialists are often seen as essential in order to gain the understanding and support of such individuals and to help them meet their own QWL needs.

5. *QWL staffing:* Coordinators and facilitators from hourly and salaried ranks. Consultants for initial advice, training, and facilitation. Coordinators—one from management, one from the union—report to the steering committee and jointly manage the QWL process in accordance with its policy decisions. They also provide much of the internal QWL training and much of the facilitation for the first worksite problem-solving teams. Facilitators are assistants to the coordinators and concentrate on facilitating the interpersonal and intragroup interactions of the worksite groups. Except in the smallest organizations, these are full-time positions. Managers and union leaders from the strongest QWL organizations are virtually unanimous in recommending that outside consultants be retained to assist in the early phases of the process during which a catalyst may be needed to assist the parties to surmount issues of trust and communication, to establish a good working relationship, and to provide the expertise and knowledge lacking within the organization at the outset of a QWL process. Such leaders—and the best consultants—also stress that the organization should move rapidly to develop its own internal staff capacities so that the process is institutionalized more fully within the organization. Consultants can then recede to a less intensive advisory posture, assisting at difficult transition points and helping the steering committee to monitor progress.

6. *Training:* Extensive training for coordinators and facilitators. Orientation for all employees at all levels. Training in participative management styles and skills for managers and supervisors. Training in interpersonal communications, group processes, and problem solving for supervisors, group leaders, and group members. Coordinators and facilitators need from 1 to 3 weeks of training, for they must be the repository of the deepest knowledge and highest skills in the organization. Such training may begin with a 1-week residential course and be supplemented with 2 or more weeks of more advanced training in QWL principles and practices so that they have the skills necessary to function in the new, more participative approach envisioned by QWL. Group leaders and members need to understand problem-solving techniques to play their roles effectively.

7. *Participation, power sharing, and decentralization of authority:* Greater autonomy for employ-

ees. Power sharing by management and union over the governance of the QWL process. Power sharing by front-line employees and supervisors over problem solving and immediate production decisions. Decentralization of authority from top-management to mid-management to supervisors.

The essence of QWL is participation—some decisions are delegated downward, others are made with more intense consultation or on the recommendation of subordinates not involved in previous forms of decision making. While formal decision-making authority is retained by management, it may be wielded at lower levels, and it usually involves much more consultation and participation.

8. *Institutionalization and systems changes:* Examination over time of organizational systems (information systems, reward systems, performance evaluation, goal setting, training, etc.) for congruence with QWL and modification to align them. Additional structural changes to flatten hierarchies, redesign jobs, improve coordination and planning.

As a long-term process of organizational transformation, QWL requires organizational leadership to embark on a conscious process of redesigning all relevant aspects of their organizational structures, systems, and jobs to make them as consistent as feasible with the principles of QWL and of organizational effectiveness as defined earlier. This redesign may be in response to the needs of the slowly growing parallel structure of QWL groups, teams, task forces, and committees, or it may be undertaken proactively, before such new QWL structures are in place. In any event, both organizational theory and the practices of numerous large and medium-sized organizations demonstrate that QWL changes at any point in the organization require changes elsewhere, over time, if the process is to be sustainable and successful.

The Phases of a QWL Process. The QWL process normally proceeds through six phases* (See page 784), though some organizations may devote little attention to the last two phases, review and renewal and institutionalization.

1. *Phase 1: Exploration and commitment.* In this phase elements of management and/or the union are stimulated to explore the QWL process. The stimulus may be various forms of economic performance needs not being met by normal organizational processes, a perception of a need to improve excessively adversarial labor-management relations, or a concern for human needs at work as defined here. Increasingly, stimulus comes from publications in the business, labor, scholarly, or general press about QWL. Increasingly, too, stimulus comes from the higher headquarters of either a corporation or a union which has committed itself to explore or implement QWL. Sometimes local stimulus derives from a nationally negotiated agreement by corporate and national union leadership to initiate QWL.

This phase of exploration may involve individuals, task forces or committees, senior management groups, union executive boards, or both labor and management in some joint approach. Typically, QWL materials are reviewed, consultants are engaged to conduct exploratory workshops, visits to existing QWL facilities are made, and, after a few weeks, months, or a year or more, union and management leaders agree to attempt a QWL process.

This agreement is customarily sealed in some form of written agreement, often a letter appended to the contract.

2. *Phase 2: Laying the foundations.* In this phase, a joint steering committee is formed and engages in further self-education regarding QWL and the role of such a committee. Some ground rules are adopted, usually including provisions that the QWL process and mechanisms will be kept strictly separate from collective bargaining, the contract, and, particularly, grievances. An orientation program for the entire organization is designed and an active communications program of newsletters, bulletins, etc, is established to inform the organization fully and continually about developments in the QWL process. In all these activities, great care is taken to demonstrate the fully joint nature of the process where unions exist. QWL staff will be chosen and trained. Training for mid-managers and supervisors will be undertaken. This phase may last from several weeks to several months.

3. *Phase 3: Initial problem-solving groups.* In this phase, decisions are made about when and where to establish problem-solving groups. Normally, a few pilot sites are established first; they may vary in number from three to five or seven or more, depending on the size of the organization, its degree of preparation, and the training and facilitating resources available. Decisions are made by the steering committee with the aid of its staff and outside consultants about the size, composition, operation, training, and role of such groups. Usually, such decisions are general in nature, establishing guidelines and options for decision making within the groups themselves. The only two clear and common limits placed upon the worksite groups are that they not involve themselves with contractually negotiated matters and that they not deal with personality disputes. Guidelines also suggest, however, that the groups concentrate on dealing with problems they encounter in their daily work.

Problems to be considered by the groups will normally be suggested by group members themselves or by various levels of management, or be extracted from performance data made available to the groups. The decision as to what problems to work on generally resides within the group itself. Groups may initially spend time on working conditions, but experience shows that almost all, if well trained and oriented, move also to problems associated with the work itself.

Various support elements in the organization will need to be responsive to and supportive of the groups' efforts. Maintenance personnel, engineers, and others may attend group meetings upon request and provide information and assistance as needed by the groups.

Worksite groups are normally voluntary. Members and leaders are trained for at least 8 hours (preferably 24 or more, if possible) as described previously. Decisions within groups are made by consensus; decisions about implementing group solutions or recommendations are made as described earlier.

The pilot problem-solving groups may function for several weeks to several months under the close monitoring of the steering committee before it feels confident about moving to the next phase.

4. *Phase 4: Expansion of problem-solving groups.* In this phase, additional problem-solving groups are trained and brought on line in a phased manner dependent on the facilitating and training resources available and on the degree of readiness by the rest of the organization to support and respond to such expansion. This phase may take several months to a few years. Since the process is voluntary, it is uncommon for 100 percent of an organization to be directly involved in QWL structures. Indeed, it is far more common to encounter percentages ranging from 5 to 50 percent of the work force. Even 5 percent of a work force, when in a well-organized QWL program, can have a substantial effect on an organization. Moreover, the number or percentage of personnel directly involved is less important than the changes in management style, labor relations, and other supportive organizational practices that frequently do touch in significant ways all personnel in the organization.

5. *Phase 5: Review and renewal.* The steering committee and QWL staff will be closely monitoring the process during its early months. Effective QWL steering committees, however, periodically stand back and assess overall progress through an annual retreat or workshop and other means. Decisions may be necessary about additional training, changes needed at mid-levels, information flow, etc.

6. *Phase 6: Institutionalization.* This phase is continual and involves the ongoing strategic assessment of the organization and all its systems, structures, and job designs for congruence with QWL goals and principles and the redesign of such organizational elements to align them supportively. Some such changes may require negotiation in the collective bargaining arena.

QWL: A Preliminary Assessment

It has proven over the years uncommonly difficult to assess QWL. The organizational changes themselves are qualitative in nature and difficult to assess. The changes are also highly sensitive, involving union-management power relations and questions of authority up and down the organization line. The participants in many QWL processes decline to admit outside evaluators for just such reasons. Moreover, some fear that they will be held to quantitative measures of success that they feel to be inappropriate.

As a result, there are no comprehensive studies of how many organizations are engaged how deeply in what sorts of QWL, and these considerations are of central importance. Certain large corporations and their unions, such as General Motors, Ford Motor Company, and the UAW, do conduct internal surveys of employee attitudes associated with QWL and have on occasion invited outsiders to assess either particular plants or overall union/corporate QWL processes. General Motors expected to complete such a study in late 1984.

Many of the published academic evaluations—even those issued most recently—are of QWL "experiments" conducted as many as 10 years ago. At that time, the QWL concept was less fully developed and, most important, they were undertaken as isolated experiments lacking in full organizational support. Not surprisingly, many of them failed, and many of those that succeeded spectacularly in the short run failed in the mid to long run. Detailed studies are still lacking regarding the comprehensive corporate and union commitments to QWL that have occurred largely within the last 5 years.

Evaluators are left, then, with the testimony of participants and their own observations, when and where they can gain access to participating companies. The Ford Motor Company cites an almost 50 percent improvement in quality as measured by neutral industry observers. Its managers attribute much of this improvement to its joint employee involvement program with the United Automobile Workers. Executives of both Ford and General Motors claim unspecified millions of dollars in savings and improvements. Their internal, professionally performed surveys show impressive improvements in employee attitudes at all levels of their organizations, many of which are attributable to QWL. Visitors to individual plants may occasionally be provided with highly impressive data on productivity, quality, and other indices of performance. The testimony of hard-headed plant managers, supervisors, and union leaders is even more persuasive that QWL, done well, is both effective and satisfying. The literature on the less comprehensive quality circle approaches is filled with success stories.

There are, however, failures. The business press and certain scattered studies report relatively high failure rates of narrowly conceived quality circles. Practitioners in the management, labor, and consulting areas report failures in broader QWL efforts as well, though again the number and proportion are unclear. What seems obvious from the scattered and largely anecdotal testimony to date is that QWL is more likely to fail when any of the eight key elements listed above are lacking or insufficiently present.

Thus, if there is no firm commitment to a participative philosophy and a long-term process of change—if QWL is seen as a mere technique to attain specific improvements in performance—employees are likely to suspect the process as manipulative and managers are unlikely to provide it with the support needed for its sustenance. If top union and management leadership in unionized settings attain and sustain only a minimal degree of trust and communication, they will not be able to sustain the jointness necessary for QWL success. If top leaders are not actively supportive, the natural resistance of organizations to change will absorb the more limited pressures that lower-ranking leaders can bring to bear. If training is insufficient and QWL staff lacking in competence, the worksite groups are less likely to function well. If mid-management is not successfully engaged in the QWL process, it will successfully stifle what it sees as a threat. And, if the organization does not continue to assess its structures and systems and align them with QWL concepts, the process is not apt to attain its full potential and it may, over a longer time frame, run aground.

These requirements for success and these possibilities of failure constitute a massive challenge for American management and labor. Even among firms in the auto, steel, communications, and other fields that are adjudged to be leaders in the field, it is unclear whether all eight key elements are sufficiently in place. Changes in key leadership, shifts in government policy, a reduction in the economic pressures that have recently stimulated a willingness to

change, the inherent difficulty of such comprehensive cultural and structural change—any or all could flatten or reverse the curve of growth and success for QWL, and some observers discern that to be happening already.

A full abandonment of this concept, however, seems unlikely, for the emergence of world markets and the shifts in the values and expectations of a highly educated American work force are likely to continue to press QWL ideas upon labor and management leadership. In any event, those contemplating QWL need to be aware of the depth, complexity, and commitment that experience to date suggests are required for success. Clearly, it is possible, and desirable, to start down the QWL road slowly and to proceed at a comfortable pace. Those who travel that road will report substantial success in meeting both human and economic needs. The trip, however, is strenuous, the road is long, and the changes demanded of the traveler are substantial.

*The opening "Summary Definition of QWL," the list of "Work Related Human Needs," the list of "Key Elements of QWL", and the list of "Six Phases of QWL," are drawn from publications and training materials that are copyrighted by the Michigan Quality of Work Life Council, Inc., and its training arm, the Midwest QWL Institute. They are used here with the permission of the copyright holder.

See also Cost improvement; Innovation and creativity; Japanese industries, management in; Motivation in organizations; Nominal group technique; Organization development; Productivity improvement; Quality circles; Quality management; Suggestion systems; Work design, job enlargement and enrichment; Work simplification and improvement.

REFERENCES

Barbash, Jack, et al. (eds.): *The Work Ethic—A Critical Analysis*, Industrial Relations Research Association, Madison, Wis., 1983, (especially chaps. by Zuboff and Maccoby).

Davis, Louis E., Albert B. Cherns, and associates (eds.) *The Quality of Working Life*, 2 vols., The Free Press, New York, 1975.

Nadler, David A.: "Managing Organizational Change: An Integrative Perspective," *The Journal of Applied Behavioral Science*, vol. 17, no. 2, 1981, pp. 191–211.

BASIL J. WHITING, *Work Life Development Systems, Inc.*

Real Estate Management, Corporate

Almost all enterprises, whether they provide goods or services or are of an institutional nature, use real estate in some manner. Many organizations face decisions on real estate matters only infrequently; others must cope with realty matters regularly. In either instance, sound real estate decision making is often crucial to corporate profitability or institutional durability. Important aspects of real estate management requiring decisions include location strategy, leasing, development, appraisal, financing, law, taxation, maintenance, insurance, and disposition.

Location Strategy. For many organizations, location is the most critical aspect of real estate planning. Corporate income statements are sure to reflect the higher product cost due to poorly located manufacturing and distribution facilities and/or lower sales due to poor choices of store location. On the other hand, the location of some businesses is dictated by the location of something else. For example, a mining company must place operations where there are minerals; a hydroelectric company must be at a dam. For most businesses, however, the choice of a location is far more complex. Judgment and analysis are imperative.

Manufacturing. In selecting a site for manufacturing operations, important matters to be considered at state and local levels include the following:

1. Labor force availability and wage rates
2. Ad valorem and income tax rates
3. Municipal services: roads, police, and fire protection
4. Utilities: availability and cost of water, sewerage, gas, and electricity, both in the general area and at the specific site
5. Proximity and adequacy of transportation facilities: streets, highways, airports, railways, etc.
6. Transportation costs to and from customers and suppliers
7. Land and construction costs
8. Building codes, land use restrictions, and zoning
9. Ecological considerations
10. Political climate and policies

Retailing. For retail store location, considerations include area population, income levels, consumer buying habits, traffic and site accessibility, the location of competitors, and shifts that may take place in these matters.

Offices. Office space users should consider the proximity to necessary services such as parking and banking facilities and the location of legal and accounting counsel. Corporate managers must also decide whether a prestige address is important for some or all of the office operations.

Expansion. Regardless of the type of use, the availability of space for expansion must not be overlooked. Without adequate room for expansion at a given site, inefficiencies will be realized; obtaining larger facilities and moving to them may not be economically feasible.

Leasing. A lease is a device that transfers possession, but not ownership, for a period of time. Leases are usually categorized as net or gross. Under a *net* lease, the tenant must pay operating expenses; with a *gross* lease, operating expenses are the property owner's obligation. Since any provision may be written into a lease as long as it is legal, reading each lease is an essential step that prevents a misunderstanding of rights and obligations. For example, under some leases the property owner is obligated for insurance; yet the lease may be called net. Also, a gross lease may have *stop* clauses (also known as *escalation* clauses) that pass along operating expense increases to the tenant.

Provisions that allow the assignment of leases and the subletting of space should be in the original lease. Though these features do not relieve the tenant of his or her primary obligation, they will allow some flexibility in the use of space when it is no longer needed.

Since an established tenant often has more at stake in a particular location than the property owner has, provisions for the distribution of condemnation awards should be described in the lease. Renewal options and purchase options give the tenant the right to remain if he or she chooses; income tax implications of these clauses should not be overlooked.

Some leases require level rents throughout the lease term; others have step-up or step-down rental rates. Fledgling corporations often seek low rental rates in early years; thus a step-up lease can be satisfactory. Prestige space may be leased with step-down rates which acknowledge that the space will not be so valuable in coming years.

Percentage leases are typically used in conjunction with retail stores. The rental rate is a fixed percentage of retail sales, though a minimum base rental is also specified. Percentage overrides give a property owner incentive to properly maintain and promote a shopping center.

Development. An organization that elects to develop property typically seeks expert assistance. After choosing the best possible location with respect to the items noted previously, corporate managers must consult attorneys, architects, real estate brokers, accountants, and contractors. Selection of capable and reputable people for a development team is essential.

An agreement for the purchase of land should not be lightly entered into. Contingencies should be stated, such as "subject to rezoning for industrial use" or "contingent upon results from soil-boring tests that indicate that the land can support the intended improvements."

It is not uncommon for local attorneys and architects to be hired in addition to those on retainer to the corporation. Local professionals are more likely to be aware of peculiarities unique to their area and can often help to overcome public and political resistance.

Contractors may submit competitive bids based upon detailed project plans. A knowledgeable attorney should review all construction contracts. A performance bond provides important protection for the corporate developer. Contractor *draws* with holdback provisions assure that the contractor has a financial interest in seeing the project to fruition. A certificate of occupancy is needed to occupy a building; without one, property is useless. A corporate manager must therefore have assurances that one will be obtained for each building and must continually monitor the structure to assure maintenance of the certificate.

Appraisal. Before entering into an agreement for the purchase, sale, or lease of real property, it is a good policy to have the property appraised. An *appraisal* is a professionally derived estimate of value. The term *value* can take on many meanings. Most appraisals are estimates of fair market value, but, to many corporations, value in use or investment value, may be more significant.

Value in use is an estimation of property value to a user, given a specific type of use. A vacant structure intended for light manufacture might not be worth the same if it were intended for use as a warehouse. *Investment value* refers to the worth to a specific owner, considering the owner's individual investment needs. An appraiser must be advised of the type of value estimate sought.

There are three approaches to appraising:

1. Income, predicated upon the philosophy that present property value lies in the worth of anticipated future income.

2. Market (comparison), based on recent sales of comparable property.

3. Cost (summation), based on replacement cost (less depreciation) for improvements, plus the land value.

Appraisers often estimate value using all three approaches, then arrive at a final value estimate by weighting amounts from each approach. Greater weight is applied to the approach considered the most meaningful under the circumstances.

Financing. Long-term financing is available for most improved realty. Thinly capitalized corporations, especially those that require special-purpose buildings, may encounter difficulty in this respect. Real estate financing can be tailored to the company's needs and philosophy, of course. Some companies prefer to minimize fixed obligations, while others wish to minimize the amounts tied up in realty.

Mortgage bankers and brokers specialize in originating mortgage loans, including those on corporate realty. During the 1970s, investment bankers began to offer financing for pools of corporate real estate (real estate investment trusts, or REITS), which obviates the need for single-project financing. Sale-leasebacks, whereby property is sold to an investor and then leased back under a long-term lease, can be used to free working capital for other purposes. Industrial revenue bonds, popular in the 1960s, serve to pass on the benefit of tax-exempt interest rates to corporations that bring industry to a local area. Tax law changes have limited the use of this type of financing, however. Corporate managers should also be mindful of property refinancing or secondary financing, which can provide additional long-term funds at favorable rates.

Real Estate Law. Each state in the United States has real estate laws peculiar to it. That and the fact that such laws have evolved over many centuries make the practice of real estate law a challenge even to practicing attorneys. Corporate managers should be aware, however, of two provisions of real estate law that set the tone for transactions. The principle of *caveat emptor* (let the buyer beware) states that the buyer, being duty-bound to examine the property, assumes responsibility for defects except those that are hidden. The other provision is the Statute of Frauds, which renders verbal real estate contracts unenforceable. Corporate managers must therefore make a careful physical inspection of the property under consideration, and they are admonished not to accept the other party's word for anything—to be enforceable, agreements must be in writing. When in doubt, a buyer should consult an attorney; it is better to get legal advice before entering into a contract than to risk costly error.

Taxation. Income and ad valorem taxes will be imposed almost everywhere. Careful planning can help to minimize these expenses. Since corporations strive for income, income taxes (though costly) are preferable to genuine financial losses. Real estate ownership can help reduce a corporation's income tax burden.

Owners of depreciable property may claim a tax deduction for depreciation; the deduction requires no cash outlay and can reduce, postpone, or eliminate some taxes. Depreciation deductions, however, also apply to financial reporting, which is a matter that requires attention as well. Rent on a bona fide lease is tax deductible, but only the interest portion of mortgage loan payments is tax deductible. The trade-offs of buying as compared with leasing can be rapidly analyzed on an after tax present-value basis using a computer.

Ad valorem taxes are applied by municipalities against the value of property. The product of the millage rate and the fraction of value assessed establishes the effective rate of taxation. Local governments may woo a corporation into constructing a plant in their jurisdiction by offering reduced or deferred taxation. Corporation managers should remember, however, that the corporation does not vote for new schools, libraries, or other services; the public decides on such matters. It is best, therefore, to establish firmly the term and amount of tax reduction being offered before entering into an irrevocable location decision.

Maintenance. Proper maintenance is essential to retain property values. It is important to physically inspect facilities for necessary repairs and replacements. Periodic deposits into a replacement reserve account can smooth our income flows caused by events that occur irregularly. The curing of functional obsolescence is also necessary to keep up with competitors that have more modern facilities.

A periodic review of operating expenses is often rewarded. Expense-saving opportunities can be pinpointed by comparing current amounts of various expenses—oil, gas, electricity, water—with amounts paid the previous month and the same month of the previous year. Substantial changes in amounts offer clues to rate and/or consumption increases. A follow-up to detect reasons for the change can disclose worthwhile cost-saving opportunities.

Insurance. The soundness of a company rests heavily on the amount and type of real estate insurance coverage it has. Two important kinds of insurance for real estate are title insurance and hazard insurance.

Title Insurance. Whenever real estate is financed, the mortgagee will require title insurance to protect his or her interest. The property owner bears the cost of this insurance, which protects against valid claims of property ownership. The cost of title insurance is proportional to the value of the property; owners may also purchase title insurance to cover their equity.

Hazard Insurance. Insurance brokers offer hazard insurance. The simplest form is fire insurance; extended coverage covers other risks. But even policies that are called *all-risk* have exclusions written into them. Nearly all hazard insurance policies include 80 percent coinsurance clauses. These clauses require the insured to maintain insurance of at least 80 percent of the property value. To the extent that such a ratio is not maintained, the insured shares the risk of loss. Though some policies include automatic upward adjustments for inflation, coverage may be inadequate for the current property value; so the adequacy of hazard insurance should be reviewed periodically.

Disposition. The disposition of industrial, commercial, or office space requires the assistance of specially trained personnel who know that particular market. To locate a substitute tenant and/or owner for a special-purpose building is often difficult. Extra efforts are necessary to reach potential users; creativity as to possible alternative building uses may also be needed. It is not unlikely that losses will be sustained upon the disposition of special-purpose buildings, even though gains and losses are measured against the depreciated book value. Perhaps the best method of avoiding dispositions and potential losses is to analyze needs carefully and choose a suitable location and facility at the outset so that the likelihood of a disposition is reduced.

See also Budgeting, capital; Facilities and site planning and layout; Insurance and risk management; Leasing, equipment; Office space planning; Site selection; Tax management.

REFERENCES

Epley, D. R., and J. A. Millar: *Basic Real Estate Finance and Investment*, 2d ed., John Wiley, New York, 1980.

McMahan, John: *Property Development: Effective Decision Making in Uncertain Times*, McGraw-Hill, New York, 1976.

Wendt, N., E. N. Walker, and T. K. Rohdenburg: *Real Estate Investment Analysis and Taxation*, 2d ed., McGraw-Hill, New York, 1979.

ELBERT W. HUBBARD, *Georgia State University*

JACK P. FRIEDMAN, *The University of Texas at Arlington*

Records Management

The growing complexity of business operations, modern technology, and increasing government regulation have created massive paperwork problems. Typical indicators are the following:

- American business currently deals with 400 billion paper documents, and the number is growing by 70 billion each year.
- U.S. government agencies print over 25 billion sheets of paper a year to be used by businesses.
- Businesses with 50 employees or fewer complete approximately 75 types of forms annually.
- One major oil company annually files over 1000 reports excluding tax reports, to different federal agencies.
- A typical small business with a gross income under $100,000 is required to file over 50 tax forms each year.
- Official records stored around the country fill over 20 million cubic feet of storage space.

Impact of Technology. The modern filing system is indebted to Johann Gutenberg, whose invention of the printing press in the fifteenth century gave the world movable type. This new printing method meant that people could produce quickly and easily several copies of an original, without having to resort to laborious copying by hand. The first typewriter was manufactured in the United States in 1874. The invention of carbon paper helped to generate demands for more paper; and more paper meant that new filing methods would have to be found. At the turn of the century, Melvil Dewey created the system now used to classify knowledge. He divided learning into ten "100" categories, from 000 to 900. Each category divided into 10s, the 10s into 1s, and the 1s into an infinite number of figures stretching to the right of the decimal point. The invention of the punch card system in the 1920s provided machines that are able to file automatically when fed the right information. Today, magnetically recognizable marks on a check represent a language which machines understand. Today's electronic filing systems enable clerks to retrieve information in a few seconds. A laser-optical videodisk can store 10,000 pages of information with almost instantaneous access to any page. Electronic mail permits the simultaneous distribution (and creation of paper copies) of a message to thousands of individuals.

The extent to which modern technology has tamed the paperwork monster is a moot point. Through micrographics, we can reduce 3000 letters to a 100-foot roll of 16 mm microfilm. An entire document file can be stored on a 4- by 5-inch sheet of microfiche. Engineering drawings can be reduced to 35 mm and mounted on an aperture card, a card capable of machine sorting, selection, and printout. Word processing equipment is able to produce printed output at speeds from 100 to 450 words per minute. In computer-based systems, a high-speed laser printer often turns out more than 100,000 words per minute. The technology available is astounding, but it does not deal with the source of the problem.

Information Retrieval

It is the effectiveness of the information retrieval system that determines the difficulty of the records management problem. Planned well, with the users' needs in mind, an information retrieval system can be a highly effective corporate tool. It provides a company with a continuing capability to find, recognize, and utilize business intelligence—a major factor in how strongly a firm can compete for its share of the market. If poorly planned, the retrieval system may be a complex, glamorous toy, expensive yet of little help. The key to retrieval usefulness is not the machine used but the design of the system. For the average business firm, the problem is not one of machines at all, but how to identify and select information to be indexed and then how to file it so it can be found when needed.

Documents in Subject Files. There are two basic types of records: transaction and reference. *Transaction* documents, such as invoices, checks, requisitions, and purchase orders, lend themselves readily to simple patterns of numeric and alphabetic filing. *Reference* documents, however, are difficult to file and find again. It was for these documents—which account for about 10 to 15 percent of the paperwork load—that the retrieval system was developed.

There are two principal types of subject files: dictionary and functional. The *dictionary* pattern is a simple, straight alphabetic arrangement, self-indexing in nature and requiring a minimum of thought for filing and retrieving information. It is a perfectly valid system, but it becomes cumbersome when related documents get very widely separated, thus decreasing the speed and convenience of access. When the dictionary approach becomes unwieldy, most firms turn to a *functional* breakdown as a means of classifying, filing, and retrieving documents. Many functional approaches are possible; they vary with the size, complexity, and operations of a company. Functional systems are a hierarchical arrangement of related functional organization terms or subjects, i.e., Personnel, *a.* Benefits, *b.* Pension Plan, etc. Furthermore, most subject classifications are hierarchical; that is, each major subject is, in turn, divided into subordinate subjects. These, in turn, may be further subdivided. The Dewey decimal system used by many libraries is a hierarchical breakdown.

Drawbacks of Functional or Subject Files. The functional approach is excellent for retrieval in many cases; it is a logical breakdown, easy to understand. It does not require intensive training of personnel in indexing techniques if they already know the company's functions. It is a familiar type of breakdown to most people and helps those who classify information understand where each piece fits. Yet functional files also have severe retrieval disadvantages. Most important is their inherent inflexibility. By prescription, a functional classification is set up in advance; it is a closed system. New subdivisions may be added, but time has a devastating effect.

Imagine a scientific classification set up 500 years ago, and then picture the adjustment required to accommodate the new subjects of today—electronics, nuclear fission, ion propulsion, etc. Not only must a classification be adjusted, but the shift of thinking over a period of time reduces the chance of finding information of value. For example, consider a searcher trying to retrieve information in a subject that is now thought of in today's terminology. What is the likelihood that the subject will be defined in the same terms that an unknown indexer used years ago?

Concept Coordinating. One possible alternative to subject or functional classification is to allow the document to classify itself through key terms used in the title or text. Another is to apply a number of descriptors, using a combination of them to help define the document. Either way, whether external descriptors or internal terms are used, the system is known as *concept coordination* or *inverted indexing*.

Comparison with Subject Files. Simply expressed, in a subject classification, an item of information (a document) is indexed by a subject heading. This is an item entry because the basic record is the item itself. In a library catalog, the cards for a given book are filed under the author's name, the title, and subject headings. Inverted indexing merely makes the key term or descriptor the basic record; items or documents are listed on cards bearing applicable terms.

Applications. Inverted indexing, or *concept coordination*, is a fast, effective way to provide many retrieval handles for such items as reference documents, slides and photographs, specifications and samples, patents, legal precedents, directors' minutes and resolutions, laboratory notebooks, policies and procedures, personnel skills, inventories, and survey data. It also permits in-depth indexing of the contents or language of a document by means of relevant descriptors, which serve as convenient avenues of retrieval for other documents as well.

Under conventional indexing conditions, a separate index card is created and filed for each of the various concepts contained in a document. Yet, in a typical situation, you may want to provide many such retrieval handles. In a marketing research information center, for example, you may wish to retrieve a document by any of the following avenues: title, corporate author or issuing organization, individual author, geographic area, date of issue, industries or products, type of promotional programs, markets, brand names, type of selling outlet, or subject content. Using conventional techniques, it is not at all unusual to create as many as 10 or even 20 index cards for each input document. This means that if 10,000 reports and documents are fed into the collection, the index may contain 100,000 or more index cards. Thus it is difficult, from a retrieval point of view, to search the whole index.

Careful analysis of a file of conventional index cards will reveal that many basic subjects or concepts are repeated again and again. In other words, there are many more index cards than there are subjects. With an inverted indexing system, an index card is created for each subject or concept rather than for each document. As documents are processed into the system, they are identified on the relevant concept cards. This method greatly reduces the number of index cards; a system containing 10,000 documents may be thoroughly indexed with less than 1000 index cards.

Broad retrieval requests can be answered by producing all the documents listed on any one card. Specific requests are answered by matching two or more cards to determine documents that relate to both.

Variations. The *uniterm* approach is one type of concept coordination; the terms used in this approach are extracted directly from either the titles or texts of documents. Another approach is IBM's key-word-in-context (KWIC) index, developed by H. P. Luhn, which relies on identification of key words in the title as a means of indexing. The main advantage of KWIC is that cross references on all key words are machine-produced. The computer is programmed to ignore insignificant words in the title of the article and index the rest. The efficiency of the index depends on how relevant the words in the title are; if either the author or the publication uses a title to attract the reader rather than to describe the article accurately, the index will be less effective.

Mechanization. Concept coordination systems are easily automated. Devices and systems available for automating concept coordination include the following:

1. *Magnetic storage.* Indexing can be done by computer and stored on tapes or discs. This is a high-speed machine approach to retrieval and can be used in conjunction with other searching techniques.

2. *Photographic systems.* These use microfilm in roll form, microfiche, or aperture cards. Like magnetic storage media, photographic devices can be used in combination with other systems.

The number and variety of available devices call for a good fit between the user and the equipment. Specific user needs are of the utmost importance in selecting equipment.

Advantages. Some of the main advantages of the concept coordination approach, whether mechanized or manual, are the following:

Unlimited expansion capability. The inverted index is much more flexible than a hierarchical functional classification where the subjects must be defined in advance. It can be more eas-ily expanded to include new subjects, new products, and new ideas.

Fewer subject classification decisions. Term systems require less knowledge of the subject; documents almost index themselves. Hence, they do not require indexing personnel with as extensive an education as do hierarchical systems.

Adaptability to mechanization. Most of the information retrieval systems on the market and the drawing boards manipulate documents (or document images). They rely on concept coordination for programming input and providing document addresses for fast retrieval. Conversion to a manual system of inverted indexing provides a building block for future mechanization.

Limitations. In addition to the advantages of faster information input, faster search and response, and higher degree of use, concept coordination has these limitations:

False drops. When a search is requested based on any combination of several terms or descriptors, a number of documents having two or more of the descriptors will drop out. Some of these drops will be false; that is, they will not describe the concept the searcher is seeking.

For example, a search for material on copper-plated nickel is likely to retrieve false drops describing nickel-copper; hence, there is a word order difficulty. False drops also occur because of differing word meanings. The searcher looking for documents about outer space may receive those on advertising space if only the topic of space is specified. The viewpoint may cause false drops; does the searcher's interest in alcohol pertain to its use as a chemical, as a beverage, as an antiseptic, or as a fuel?

Specifics required. In requesting a search, the user must specify what terms apply. One must clarify the meaning of these terms; if information is requested about the substance *pitch*, the user's need must be identified in order to eliminate false drops about motion, acoustics, and angle.

Links and role indicators. To eliminate false drops due to syntactics or word order may require the use of links (for example, aluminum casting, casting aliminum; clock radios, radio clocks). Essentially, links define groups of words or ideas that are linked with one another in the original article. A dictionary or thesaurus may also provide role indicators, that is, a code showing the role or part each word plays in the concept of the original article.

Steps in Developing a Retrieval System

The basic objective is to file information for effective recall. A poor filing system is costly in terms of personnel, space, equipment, and information feedback. Most companies would be well advised not to jump into information retrieval immediately. First, they should develop a sound information program. They can start by taking these basic steps:

1. Clean up the company's overall filing system and develop a common filing language. To "clean up" includes destroying obsolete records and removing noncurrent records to storage.

2. Start with a manual process. Both the company and the people will gain experience; make requirements and adjustments along the way. This approach is a form of insurance that what works manually will automate easily. it avoids the limitations of a prematurely automated system.

3. Become aware of the company's unique information requirements. What do you need to know about your market, your competition, your products, and your industry? Which information is essential, which only "nice to have"? How do your users go about asking for information?

4. Learn about techniques and devices to see what might help you. Avoid a "canned" approach. Your people need information, not machines.

5. Inquire of other companies to learn what has worked for them. But do not build a system based on someone else's needs—this is an expensive shortcut.

6. Discuss your information needs with a management consulting firm that has sound experience in records, filing, and information retrieval. Advice from this source may be the least expensive path to effective information retrieval in your organization.

7. Bear in mind what the basic problem has been and continues to be; how to find relevant information in a reasonable time at a reasonable cost.

8. Whatever your filing or indexing system, train your employees; impress upon them the high cost of error. In a five-drawer file cabinet, 99 percent accuracy means 150 documents misfiled—possibly lost beyond retrieval.

9. Avoid complacency about what you have now, or what you install in the future. It pays to monitor an information program periodically and to inquire who uses it, why, and how much.

10. Recognize that in an information system, the user is the customer. Give your users information about how the system works and what is in it. Provide the language needed to articulate requests. Table R-1 is a useful list against which to audit present and future plans.

Integration with Management Information Networks. Records management increasingly assumes a vital management role in structuring and managing a companywide information network. This information network, under the most advanced concept, is a service designed to provide, at a single point of inquiry, access to all records, information, and data anywhere in the company, including selected outside sources such as subscription information services, outside data banks, and the like. The network links available information resources—customer and product information, technical information, market and financial information, etc.

Given this complexity of relationships, there is no clear-cut pattern of organizational position and reporting for the records management function—beyound the fact that it has acquired a much greater status than it had a decade ago. Whether or not a company recognizes information management by formal title, the records management function increasingly assumes integrated information management responsibilities.

Records Retention

There can be no quick and easy solution to the records retention problem. An effective schedule is as individual as a prescription for eyeglasses. However, some general rules or guideposts can be given.

Retention Schedule. Here are the basic factors to consider in the light of your own operations and experience:

Legal Requirement. Pay primary attention to what records must be kept for specified lengths of time in order to comply with federal, state, and local requirements. Also, there are instances where certain records should be kept even in the absence of a specific rule because of statutes of limitation. These laws prescribe the length of time after an action during which legal proceedings can be taken against a company or any of its personnel. Note that it is the information contained in a record that must be kept, not a record as such.

Administrative Requirements. In the main, your own operating needs should prevail. Your schedule must take into account your current practices. There are advantages to continuing procedures which are found to be satisfactory and with which your employees are familiar. Also, records of historical value, especially those indicating why certain decisions or policies were adopted in the past, may provide valuable future administrative guidance.

TABLE R-1   Audit Procedures List

PART 1.: GENERAL INFORMATION
Name of file.
Location.
Type of service rendered, e.g., engineering, executive, etc.
No. of people serviced.
No. of file drawers and cabinets.
History of files.
No. of items filed per day.
No. of references found per day or week.
No. of requests not found per day or week.
No. of folders prepared each day.
Analysis of references:
 Requesters.
 What requested
 Date
 Material provided.
No. of file personnel and salaries.
Cost of file space per year.
Retention period.
Check quality of classification system.
Check folder captions against approved subject headings.
Check folders for proper arrangement.
Check records within folders for classification markings, misfiles, and duplicates.
Is there a procedure for disposing of obsolete material? If so what?
Are duplicate copies filed? If not, how is it avoided?
Is each filed item recorded?

PART 2: FILES—CONDITIONS AND ACTIVITY
General appearance.
 Good housekeeping: no papers on top of files.
 Uniform equipment.
 Arrangement of file room.
 Legible labeling on drawers.
 Total number of cabinets or drawers.
File drawers.
 Check for overcrowding (about 3 inches free).
 Check for guides (10 to 15 per drawer).
 Check amount of material in folder (not more than 1 inch).
 Check labels for consistency in typing.
 Check for out cards.
 Check general condition of folders (old or new).
 Check for dust.
General Information
 How many items are filed per day?
 How many references per day?
 What type of system is used? (Dictionary Classified)
 If more than one system is used, how many?
 Ask to see their subject heading list and card file.
 What system is used to follow up charge-outs?
 Is there any difficulty in locating material, and if so, what type especially?
 How many file clerks and supervisors are there?
 Determine whether other copies are being filed elsewhere.
 What is the time period covered?
 Check follow-up system for charge-outs.
 Determine the distance of file from users.
 What is the method of delivery?
 Interview users for comments, suggestions, and degree of satisfaction.

PART 3: FILES SERIES AND ANALYSIS
Status analysis.
 Series name.
 Items composing series (forms nos., color, size, etc.)

Product (purpose).
Arrangement (primary, secondary, tertiary, etc.).
Volume.
Dates (range).
Cutoff period.
Retention (office and total).
Uses.
Equipment (type and amount).
Space.
Supplies (supplier's name and style).
Labeling Practices
Guiding practices
Paid worker-hours (includes all paid time including sick leave and vacations).
Operating costs
Duplicate items
Number of people
Housekeeping.
Accession analysis.
 List of contributors (dictators and secretaries).
 Frequency of incoming collections.
 Volume (postings and/or pieces of paper).
 Age (when received, range).
 Classifying (coding-marking) practices.
 Indexing practices.
 Cross referencing practices.
 Sorting practices.
 Filing practices.
 Worker-hours, accession activities.
 Number of people.
Reference analysis.
 Number of requests.
 Methods of request receipts (phone, visit, writing).
 Methods of request answers (phone, visit, copy, charge-out).
 Requests not answerable.
 Age of requested material.
 Request record.
 Requestors ranked by frequency.
 Charge-out practices.
 Follow-up practices.
 Request interrogation technique (phone particularly).
 Requester problems (user interviews).
 Worker-hours referencing activities.
 Number of people.
 Average charge-out time retained.
 Refile practices.

PART 4: RECORDS STORAGE FACILITIES
Physical conditions.
 Description of building or space in use.
 Shipping and receiving facilities.
 Fire protection.
 Office space.
 Floor load.
 Elevator facilities
 Sanitary and health facilities.
 Lighting conditions.
Equipment.
 Type of containers used for storing records, evaluated on the basis of the acitivty of records stored therein.
Storage system (description of records storage area):
 Height of files.
 Aisle space.

TABLE R-1 Audit Procedures List (*continued*)

Records accessibility.	Number of employees.
Area location system.	Salaries.
Arrangement and control of record containers.	Personnel costs per square foot.
Labels.	Cost for storing and maintaining each cubic foot of
Use of records.	records:
How are records referred to?	
What control is there for charged-out records?	$$\frac{Space + equipment + personnel + maintenance}{Cubic\ feet\ of\ records}$$
What types of service are provided by the records center?	
How is information transmitted?	$= cost\ per\ cubic\ foot$
What types of information are provided?	
Square footage of storage space.	Reference activity: number of references per cubic foot of
Cost per square foot.	records maintained.
Volume of records stored per square foot.	

Administrative Discretion. It is management's discretion that dictates which records will best satisfy all requirements. For example, the regulations of the Interstate Commerce Commission concerning certain carriers and freight forwarders contain retention clauses stipulating from 2 years to permanent retention for information about property. In addition, payrolls and material distribution sheets must be kept permanently, except when the data are transcribed to other permanent records. But whole series of records frequently contain this information—time cards, vouchers, job tickets, payroll work sheets—and it is within management's discretion to designate one or two of these for permanent retention. In this way, much space and equipment can be saved. Many statutes of limitation also leave room for discretion. In several states, the statute on open accounts is 6 years. Therefore, based on your own past experience, you may decide that it will be sufficient to keep vouchers for small sums (say under $50) for only 3 years.

Specific Record Groups. The following typical groups summarize some important factors to watch in setting a retention period for each type of record.

Accounting, general (journals, ledgers, trial balance). Journals and ledgers mean different things to different companies. The general ledger, as the basic summary accounting record, is usually retained permanently. The subsidiary journals and ledgers are required only through periods of actual use by the accounting department, auditors, or top management. Trial balances are working papers that need be retained only through final audit.

Accounts payable (general canceled checks, canceled payroll checks, vouchers). While general canceled checks may be retained for the number of years defined in each state's statute of limitations (average of 6 years), some companies keep payroll checks for only 2 years. Canceled payroll checks can create a volume problem. Activity is greatest in the first few weeks after issuance, and it usually falls to next to nothing after the first year. Vouchers are always a bulk problem. Rather than keep them all for 6 to 20 years, breaks can be made between plant vouchers (retained permanently), operating vouchers (retained until tax audits are complete, and petty cash vouchers (retained for an average of 1 to 2 years). The retention period holds for originals only. Further breaks may be made by dollar value. It pays to limit retaining copies of these vouchers for a minimum number of weeks or months.

Accounts receivable (billing copies of invoices, credit-memo invoices, accounts receivable ledger). Management's chief concern is with the unpaid invoices. Paid invoices, particularly large-volume, small-dollar-volume items, may often be disposed of within 6 months to 2 years. Most complaints on payment or amount of payment are received within this period. Equally important is minimum retention of any invoice files that duplicate the basic record (arranged by customer or by invoice number). Only those invoices connected with items of new design or the first item of a patentable product require long, indefinite retention. The accounts receivable ledger, as a basic summary of credit sales, needs to be kept only so long as it is a ready index to invoices or total daily sales. Where there is no other summary of sales, it may be useful to retain the ledger indefinitely for historical purposes.

Legal (contracts, copyrights, patents, trademarks, suits). Copyrights, patents, and trademarks are usually retained permanently. Contracts are more often kept for 6 years after expiration, but when renewed annually, are generally kept for shorter periods. Records on lawsuits are typically kept for 6 to 10 years after settlement. Bulky work papers and routine notes connected with contracts and suits should be cleaned out as soon as the matter is legally completed.

Payroll (earnings records, payrolls, pension records). The basic legal requirements are (1) Internal Revenue Service: 4 years for earnings records (Federal Insurance Contributions Act and Federal Unemployment Tax); (2) Department of Labor, Wage and Hour Division: 3 years for payrolls, 2 years for earnings records; and (3) the Department of Labor, Division of Public Contracts: 4 years of wage and hour records. Pension records are usually retained permanently and may often serve as the earnings record as well.

Personnel (applications for employment, attendance records, time clock cards, employee history records, personnel folders). Where a company maintains both employee history cards and personnel folders, the history cards may be destroyed within 1 year after termination of employment. An exception to the latter might be the top executive personnel data. Employment applications should be kept longer than 6 months only for jobs or persons where the company anticipates action in the near future. Attendance records, time clock cards, and related data should be handled as a package. Where this information is summarized on project or payroll records, the bulky initial records may be discarded within 1 to 6 months.

Production (job tickets, maintenance records, operating reports, production orders). Job tickets and production orders are really only of value in processing the order through the factory or when the customer raises questions on delivery or quality. These points come up in the initial months after shipping. Actual production orders are the only ones that warrant retention beyond 1 year. And of all the records for one order (e.g. job ticket, shipping ticket, bill of lading) only the original one need be retained. Most information is repeated from one form to the next. Maintenance records are usually retained for the life of the equipment on which the data are compiled. Monthly operating reports on production are valuable up to 2 years. Annual operating reports should be kept permanently for historical and management purposes.

Purchasing (bids, purchase orders, receiving reports, purchase requisitions). Purchase orders should be broken down into categories for retention purposes: major equipment, expendable supplies and materials, and so forth. Major purchase records, particularly where specifications are included, might be kept for 6 years. The retention period for routine items may be cut to 3 years and still stay within legal requirements on proof of local purchase and on records of use for tax purposes. Purchase requisitions need to be retained only until the items are received, since the data are covered on the purchase order. Receiving reports are usually supporting documents for the accounts payable vouchers and are retained accordingly. Bids are kept after a contract is let out only so long as management wants them for postau-

dit purposes, and so long as purchasing agents may need them as references for the next contract for the same service or items.

Real estate (deeds, leases). Deeds, right of way and easements are usually retained permanently; leases, for 6 years after expiration. If leases are renewed annually, they may be kept only for the current year plus 1 additional year.

Sales (correspondence, customer orders, sales staff reports). Sales correspondence on deliveries, acknowledgements, bids, and so on need be kept, at the most, 30 to 60 days for possible answer and follow-up policy. Policy letters should be segregated and retained permanently. Customer orders in sales departments are only copies of accounts receivable files and should be kept, if at all, for minimum periods. Sales staff reports on individual sales and expenses are important only for immediate review. They warrant keeping for only a few months.

Corporate (annual reports, bylaws, minutes of stockholders meetings, canceled stock certificates). The first three items are usually kept permanently. Canceled stock certificates are not governed by any federal legal requirement (except for regulated companies) and may be destroyed at the discretion of the company. However, most firms keep a formal certificate of destruction.

Tax (purchase-and-use tax returns, state and federal tax returns). Regulations on purchase-and-use taxes usually state that a city must announce its intentions to act on a company's returns within 3 years. There is no limitation, however, in cases of fraud. The same holds true for state and federal returns. The purchase-and-use tax statements are usually retained for 3 years. State and federal returns, being more involved, are retained at least 6 years, and often permanently. Work papers may be destroyed within the minimum periods.

Traffic (bills of lading, freight bills, packing lists). The only legal requirement on these items is on "order, shipping and billing records" (Department of Labor, Wage and Hour Division) for 2 years. However, there is rarely need for more than one official record to cover any one shipment (see the earlier paragraph on production).

Operating under a Retention Schedule. While the core of a sound record-keeping program is an accurate retention schedule, an efficient system also means the following:

1. Knowing what records and how many of them you have. A physical inventory should be taken of all your records, preferably under the direction of the person who is responsible for the entire operation. It is not necessary to examine every single piece of paper, only the different groups of records. Using a separate sheet of paper for every record type, record the following facts: (a) type

of record (checks, accounts payable, employment applications, and the like); (*b*) period covered, beginning and closing dates; (*c*) department that has jurisdiction over the record, such as sales, shipping, or accounting; (*d*) location of the record; (*e*) kind of equipment the record is in; (*f*) volume in cubic feet; letter-size drawers usually contain 1.6 cubic feet, legal-size 2 cubic feet; and (*g*) amount of space occupied by files and by shelving for records.

2. Learning how much use is made of each record type. Have a reference analysis made over 3 to 6 months to see how frequently a given type of record is actually used. This information will give you a factual basis for earmarking records for retention, destruction, or storage in a low-cost records center.

3. Setting up a low-cost records center. Once you know what records you have, how often they are used, and how long to keep them, you are prepared to realize substantial dollar savings in equipment, space, and personnel by scheduling inactive records for transfer to a new type of records center. Such a center can ensure both better reference service and economy if you locate it in low-cost space away from the office and institute a reference system. You can use the center for records that must be kept permanently and for those not yet old enough to be destroyed or sold as waste paper.

Essentials of a Records Center. An effective records center should include the following elements:

Cartons. Corrugated cardboard containers having $10 \times 12 \times 15$ inch dimensions are ideal. They may be used for either letter- or legal-size documents. Economical and sturdy, they may be obtained from a number of manufacturers.

Shelving. Space-saving shelves, preferably of metal, are used to store cartons of records. Ordinarily, 12 cartons can be stored satisfactorily, spaced 24 inches apart, on a 32×42-inch shelf.

Index. Records should be indexed as they are boxed for storage. Each cardboard box should have a number which designates the permanent location assigned to it in the records center and an inventory sheet showing the contents of the box.

System. A system for obtaining information on records from the center should be established. It should include procedures for finding material rapidly and for returning it to its proper place after use.

A well-planned records management program can provide an effective means for controlling the spiraling costs and volume of business information.

See also Computer software, data base management; Forms design and control; Inventory control; Inventory stock-keep-ing systems; Management information systems, transaction processing systems; Materials management; Office automation; Paperwork simplification; Production planning and control; Systems and procedures; Word processing.

REFERENCES

Diamond, Susan Z.: *Records Management: A Practical Guide,* American Management Association, AMACOM division, New York, 1983.

Johnson, Mina M., and Norma F. Kallaus: *Records Management,* 2d ed., South-Western, Cincinnati, 1974.

Maedke, Wilmer, Mary F. Robek, and Gerald F. Browne: *Information and Records Management,* Glencoe Press, Beverly Hills, Calif., 1982.

ROBERT A. SHIFF, *Naremco Services, Inc., Management Consultants*

Regulated Industries, Management of

All industries are regulated to some extent. Regulation of financial reports, occupational safety, environmental impact, and employment conditions is ubiquitous, but there are groups of companies that are also subject to regulatory control over the prices they charge for their products and the way they operate their businesses. These companies serve a public interest of a type that can best be satisfied if competition is limited.

The Regulated and Regulators. The scope of companies that are subject to price and operating regulations for the purpose of limiting competition is quite broad. The major groups are (1) energy distribution companies, such as electric and gas utilities and natural gas pipelines; (2) transportation companies, such as railroads and truckers, (3) communications companies, such as telephone, telegraph and cable TV systems. Until recently, airlines and banks also were subject to strict price regulation.

The agencies responsible for regulating prices and operating conditions for these companies are numerous. Each state has its own, as does the federal government. On the state level, energy distribution, transportation, and communications companies are usually regulated by a public utilities commission. The jurisdiction of these agencies over prices and conditions of service does not extend to activities over which the federal government claims jurisdiction, such as transactions in interstate commerce. Authority over such activities rests with federal agencies such as the Federal Power Commission, the Interstate Commerce Commission, the Federal Communications Commission and the Federal Reserve Board. The split between state and federal regulations sometimes produces conflicts.

Regulatory Intent. Regulated companies can be placed historically in two categories. The transportation companies and the financial companies were regulated to avoid the type of competition that would disrupt the vital services provided by these industries. In these industries, price competition was restricted and similar companies charged similar rates. The cost for assurance that service would be available even to individuals who are difficult or costly to serve was generally reflected in regulated prices that were higher than would result from unrestrained competition. Most companies of this type have been deregulated within the last few years.

Modern regulation of electric and gas utilities, telephone systems, and pipelines (the public utilities) is based on the prevention of competition that would result in unnecessary duplication by competitors of very expensive facilities. Regulated prices are based on the costs in each individual company and may vary widely from company to company. Price competition is avoided by granting each company an exclusive service territory. This type of regulation holds prices lower than would result from unrestrained competition.

Because of declining markets for their services, railroads are a special case, but they may be classified most readily with the other transportation industries. This classification is not so much because of the type of service they offer as because the goal of railroad regulation is to maintain railroad service; nevertheless, railroads have a number of the characteristics of the public utilities.

The rationale that regulation is a substitute for competition is only partially true in the real world of business. Competition is generally restricted or prohibited only between similar types of companies, such as telephone companies. It is not always restricted between different types of regulated companies within the same industry group, e.g., between an electric utility and a gas utility. In some cases the restriction is in one direction only, as when a natural gas utility that is prohibited from promoting sales of its product competes with an oil company that has no such restrictions.

Managements of regulated companies will, therefore, sometimes be operating in the same competitive climate facing any industrial firm and sometimes in a closely controlled noncompetitive atmosphere.

Regulatory Outlook. It is possible that some regulation of prices and operations will be extended to other industries in the future, but this is not necessarily so. New industries that develop within, or in competition with, one of the already regulated industries may find it difficult to escape such regulation. Other than this possibility, however, it does not seem likely that other industries face possible price and operations regulation unless they have some of the characteristics of public utilities. The antitrust laws should be adequate to take care of other circumstances.

Any industry, however, that believes it requires some protection from competition is a candidate for regulation, particularly if disruption of its service or product would have a widespread economic impact. In other countries, this set of circumstances has resulted in nationalization of industries such as coal mining or steel. In the United States regulation is more likely than nationalization.

Impact of Regulation on Management. To the extent that regulation replaces competition, it does so by protecting the customers from undue exercise of monopoly power.

Protection from monopoly power is accomplished by requiring the regulated company to provide a certain level of service and by regulating the prices that can be charged for such service to levels that reflect only a regulated company's or industry's cost to provide such service. These restrictions have significant impacts on management that are not felt by other industries.

Financial Aspects. The requirement to provide a certain level of service imposes financial as well as operating burdens on management. Public utilities have an obligation to provide service to anyone who applies for it. This responsibility imposes on utility management the burden of raising funds to provide facilities for that purpose regardless of economic, money market, or corporate financial condition at the time the funds are required. Some regulated companies, such as telephone systems, have considerable flexibility in meeting the levels of service required, since they can phase their purchase of new facilities and rearrange schedules. Others, such as natural gas pipelines, have little flexibility because every major investment in new facilities must be approved by the Federal Power Commission as being required to serve customers. However, all publicly owned regulated companies spend much of their management time raising money and maintaining good relations with the financial community. These activities are particularly important because most major regulated industries tend to be capital-intensive. For example, the average electric utility sells $1 of electricity each year for every $4 it has invested in fixed assets. In most industries, sales of $1 of product are backed by less than $1 of investment. A regulated company's earnings and financial stability therefore are more sensitive to capital structure policies and cash flow management than is true in most businesses. The adequacy of a company's earnings in a given year often depends on the success of management in setting and implementing policies in these two areas. It is not surprising that in many regulated companies, the chief financial officer has more authority and influence than anyone but the president.

Visibility. Price regulation also creates unique

problems for the public utility industries. Since such regulation is based on costs, anything necessary to determine those costs must be disclosed to the regulators. Once disclosed, the information usually becomes available to the public. Such information often covers management policies, operating practices, financial transactions, and plans for the future. It is the type of fishbowl atmosphere that requires significant management effort and expertise in external relations. It is important that senior management, particularly the chief executive, have a sensitivity to key public policy issues and be able to explain positions on them to the press and citizens groups that may be hostile.

Accounting Standards. Although financing and public affairs may be of more importance in regulated industry than in industry as a whole, the reverse is true in other areas, such as accounting for financial transactions. Each regulated industry has a uniform system of accounts that has been specified by its regulatory agencies and which it must follow in recording financial transactions. This requirement reduces the opportunities for "creative accounting" that are open to manufacturers. It also adds to the need for good, open, candid relationships with the financial community since uniform accounting invites superficial comparisons between regulated companies.

Pricing Structure. Price regulation is exercised through a process called *rate making.* Rates are complex price structures. A separate rate or series of rates is usually established for each type of service provided, e.g., for residential customers of a utility or for dry bulk shipments on a railroad. The rates are established to recover all costs associated with providing such service. The rates are generally structured, however, so that incremental or marginal costs, competitive influences, desired disincentives, and other factors are properly reflected in the final prices charged to individual customers; therefore, rates usually result in different unit prices for similar service to different customers. Designing such rates is a complex process that does not exist to anywhere near the same extent in other industries. Each major regulated company engages specialists in this field, but it is important for management to have a basic understanding of the economics and mechanics of rate making if rational pricing policies are to be established.

Regulatory Lag. New rates must be approved by the appropriate state and/or federal regulatory agencies after they have had a full opportunity to examine the basis for them in open hearings. The support for the new rates is based most commonly on past experience and known facts, although there has been some movement by regulatory agencies toward looking to the future. The hearings can be quite lengthy, a possiblity that leads to management problems not faced by other industries. By the time hearings are completed and a decision is rendered, the costs and economic conditions that were used to justify the rates are generally out of date. This regulatory lag not only ensures that a regulated company's rates will not be designed to match current economic conditions but also prohibits rapid adjustment of rates or prices to reflect rapidly changing costs. Past experiences have led to some attempts by regulators to speed up the process of rate adjustments especially for costs over which the regulated industry has no control, such as fuel costs in utilities. Nevertheless, regulatory lag places a heavy burden on company managements to forecast future conditions accurately and to stand ready to take appropriate action to cut costs and file for new rates early enough to compensate for these changes.

Information Exchange. Not all the impacts of price regulation are burdensome. Companies within a regulated industry are generally much freer to exchange information and to discuss policies and business practices among themselves. Trade associations for regulated industries have active committees, made up of industry executives, for exchange of information and discussion of matters that would be prohibited by antitrust laws in other industries. Even pricing information is exchanged, and the committees concerned with rate making are often among the most active. In fact, exchange of information among regulated companies is so widespread that it is possible that legal questions could be raised if one or more companies in a given industry were excluded from the exchange of information in that industry.

See also Consumerism and consumer protection legislation; Economic systems; Energy management; Environmental protection legislation; Social responsibility of business; Technology, management implications.

REFERENCES

Bonbright, James C.: *Principles of Public Utility Rates,* Columbia University Press, New York, London, 1961.

Kahn, A. E.: *The Economics of Regulation: Principles and Institutions,* vols. 1 and 2, John Wiley, New York, 1971, 1972.

Howard, R. Hayden, and Harry M. Trebling (eds.): *Rate of Return under Regulations: New Directions and Perspectives,* MSU Public Utility Studies, Institute of Public Utilities, East Lansing, Mich., 1969.

PETER J. McTAGUE, *Retired CEO, Green Mountain Power Corporation.*

Research and Development Management

Definitions of research and development (R&D) vary and are often controversial. The following will provide a basis for this examination of the subject.

Research: The two kinds of research consist of:

Basic: Searches for the understanding of a process or subject, with little expectation of a direct payoff.

EXAMPLE: Studies aimed at a better understanding of the mechanism by which detergents function.

Applied: Probes of the unknown for a specific goal or reason.

EXAMPLE: Studies to develop leather substitutes.

Development. Application of science and technology to take a successful applied research project to a commercial scale. Applied research often follows on the heels of basic research. Development is almost always preceded by applied research.

EXAMPLE: Transformation of applied research on leather substitutes to a commercially available product.

Discovery. An innovation—something new or a new application. Research and development are the search for discovery. Through discovery one can implement research or development.

Application. Engineering; the application of science, technology, art, and economics to the definition and solution of real problems.

Objectives and Policies

While most sophisticated organizations have objectives and policies, they often are not clearly stated nor do they relate to the concerns of research and development. In such far from uncommon instances, the practical answer for R&D is to generate its own objectives and policies. It can be done without rocking the corporate boat too much. In fact, such action is frequently taken by R&D without recognizing it as such. The act of questioning where the company is going can lead toward a set of priorities for research and development.

Interdependency of Company and R&D Goals. R&D may be its own best counsel in the establishment of specific goals. The R&D team, as a group, has more opportunity and time to contemplate the future than do operating divisions. Company objectives can be defined by active discussion in an atmosphere as open as possible with a minimum of "put-downs" for different ideas. In fact, R&D can lead a company to a set of goals—at the very least for the R&D group. Research staffers should meet, argue, and confer to establish an informal set of objectives. The group will then ask for comment and agreement on those goals. While probability of success is limited on the first attempt, perseverance can pay off later. Consider the alternative: Research sits on its thumbs while top management does the forward planning. Clearly, research input is needed. Research objectives and policies ought to be in agreement with the parent organization, but research cannot wait for a set of objectives to be formulated for it. It must be an active

part of, and often the initiator of, the planning dialogue.

R&D Organization

Organizational arrangement can enhance or retard R&D progress and productivity. While organization principles obviously apply to R&D, some are particularly pertinent:

1. Whatever the organizational arrangement is, its purpose is to bring workers together to get jobs done.

2. The overall purpose is to improve operations rather than to classify and categorize work.

3. The most effective organizational groups are frequently informal ones set up by research workers themselves, not by management.

4. Matrix-type systems can be effective, but they require extensive communication to operate well. (*See* Project management.)

5. Whatever the organization, communication should be free and open, and it should be encouraged to take place at the lowest possible level.

Informal Groups and Communication. Workers must feel free to consult with other researchers across organizational lines. Informal groups (not shown on any organizational charts) develop from these exchanges. Through such contacts can come good cross-fertilization of ideas, innovations, and problem solutions. This interchange is one of the underlying reasons for adopting matrix management.

Whenever organizations impede communications across lines, there is an inherent risk of lost opportunity. For example: Research is asked to solve a certain plant problem. Initial communication may take Path A, shown in Fig. R-1. Future communication can take several paths, from worst to best. One of the attributes of the "best" solution is that the plant problem will in fact be communicated to the researcher for his or her consideration. That does not necessarily follow for the other two arrangements. Additionally, the "best" solution enables the researcher to obtain a fuller picture of the plant problem. The solution to that problem may lie in a domain uncovered only by the dialogue between engineer X and researcher Y.

All communication channels, including the "best" arrangement, have their problems. Engineer X and researcher Y, supervisors A and B, the plant manager, and the research director may all be operating on three different channels, and confusion can result. For example, researcher Y finds out from her manager that there is a plant problem involving product quality. A specific kind of solution is proposed by management which Y is asked to pursue. Y

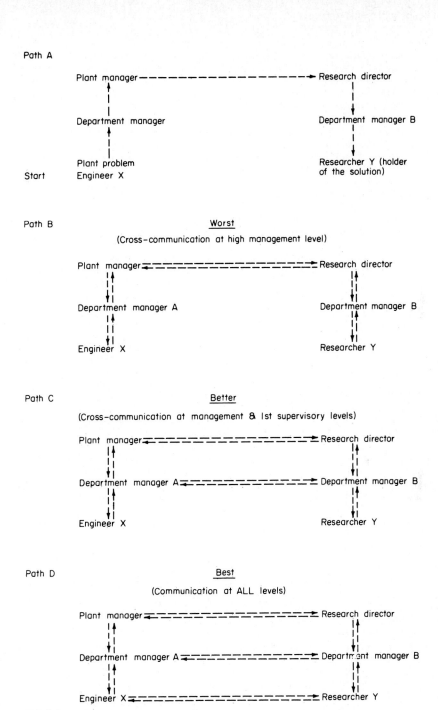

FIG. R-1   R&D communication paths.

talks to X. In the course of their dialogue, Y finds that the quality problem has its origin elsewhere in the plant and that the proposed solution is not only costly, but not as good as an alternative one. Here Y has to be sure to tell her boss what is going on and so does X. If they do so, all the participants can agree on the new solution. What often happens, though, is that plant manager A finds out from another source about the new solution. He calls research manager B and asks what is going on. B feels embarrassed at not knowing; he thinks he should tell researcher Y not to talk to engineer X so there will be less confusion. While such a move to control communication may be tempting, it should be resisted. Too much is lost by cutting the communication lines between X and Y. The problems which arise periodically from the "best" solution are generally not significant compared with the benefits derived from it.

Budgets

Budgets for R&D vary from industry to industry and from company to company within an industry group. Like those for other functions, the R&D budget reflects:

1. How much available money a company has
2. What a company feels it needs to accomplish its objectives
3. What its competition is spending

Typically, budget preparation starts some 3 to 6 months before the end of the fiscal or planning year. Actual methods differ from one firm to another, but most involve estimates of capital requirements and necessary expenses. These expected costs go hand in hand with the R&D program and are useful for historical perspective. They are also helpful in preparation of the next year's budget to the extent that there are no large changes in the scope of the R&D program. Since budgets are only projections, it is important not to get caught up in endless detail about the accuracy of forecasts. It is wise to keep a good perspective about the budget; once the budget is approved, the spending rules are generally less stringent than those used in its formulation.

Comparative Allocations. R&D expenditures by industry group are shown in Table R-2 as a percentage of sales, profit, and on a per employee basis. The range of expenditures within individual groups often is large, with the low spender at only 10 percent of the average and the high spender 2 to 3 times the average for the group. Among some groups, such as those involved with containers or cars and trucks, the spread is minimal and each member is close to the group average. These figures are useful to see how your company compares with the group average. The

National Science Foundation projects a 2 to 3 percent annual increase in spending for all R&D activities from 1983 to 1990. That is about half the annual rate of increase exhibited between 1975 and 1979.

Projects

Ideally, research money should be spent on projects that offer a good chance for a positive payoff. This is easier said than done. The research staff itself, however, may be the best source for sound project ideas. Unfortunately, some research people are uncomfortable with the notion that they are a valuable resource for future company activities. Nonetheless, the R&D staff itself is an excellent starting place. Good research ideas often come from unexpected sources, too. Consequently, management often has to force itself to be open to suggestions that come from seemingly unqualified sources. It is costly to think that those well versed in a specialty have a monopoly on all the good ideas in that specialty. Often the reverse is true; people outside the specialized area may have the most objectivity. They are not constrained by the knowledge of the specialty.

Marketing, for example, can be a fertile source for research projects. By its very nature, marketing contacts people with problems to be solved. These contacts should be regarded as research opportunities. Management, generally, is a good source for research ideas. While research, marketing, and management constitute the major sources of research ideas, they are by no means the only sources.

Project Selection. Successful research effort comes from the proper selection of projects—provided good projects are proposed. No culling process can produce good fruit from a poor vine. Projects are typically selected through a quasiformal procedure of project proposal, with backup data prepared on the proposed project for review by research management. Project selection is based on an assessment of payoff. Accordingly, there are critical questions to ask of a proposal:

1. What are the probabilities of success? Low? Medium? High?
2. What is the specific nature of the payoff if the project is a success?
3. What kinds of resources must be committed by the research group to support the proposal? What will they cost?
4. Will the company exploit the project if successful? How?
5. Will there be a market for the invention if successful?
6. Is the competition ahead or behind? Many companies may be working on obvious needs; e.g.,

TABLE R-2 R&D Expenditures by Industry Group

Type of industry	1982 expenditures		
	% Sales	% Profits	Dollars per employee
Aerospace	5.1	167	4091
Appliances	2.0	86	1469
Building materials	1.3	127	1217
Cars and trucks	4.0	−382	3845
Chemicals	2.9	82	3756
Computers	6.8	74	5112
Computer peripherals, services	7.2	130	4340
Conglomerates	2.8	67	1863
Containers	0.7	65	661
Drugs	6.0	60	4836
Electrical	2.8	45	1933
Electronics	3.8	86	2285
Farm and construction machinery	3.3	1628	3161
Food and beverage	0.7	18	834
Fuels	0.5	13	2628
Industrial machines	2.6	175	2025
Instruments	5.2	122	3142
Leisure time	4.8	70	3505
Metals and mining	1.2	−34	1516
Miscellaneous manufacturing	2.4	60	1687
Office equipment	5.1	130	3594
Oil service and supply	2.1	22	1885
Paper	1.0	42	1034
Personal and home care products	2.3	39	2568
Semiconductors	7.8	282	3535
Steel	0.7	−9	836
Telecommunications	1.3	13	850
Textiles, apparel	0.6	29	331
Tire and rubber	2.3	132	1695
All industry composite	2.4%	56%	$2562

Source: Business Week, "The U.S. Still Leads the World in R&D Spending," June 20, 1983, pp. 122–153.

"What this country needs is a good 5-cent cigar" or "Won't someone invent a really good gloss latex paint?" Thus an assessment of a sure market with a big payoff should be tempered by the thought that others are searching, too.

Backlogs and Timing. There has been deemphasis of longer-range, less specific research in American industry. This view poses real challenges. Pure research has lost its glamour; concrete results are being demanded. Technical service and short-term development have replaced longer-range work. While this may be good for next year's balance sheet, it can spell long-term trouble. There is probably no good formula for the correct mix of long- and short-term research. Nor is there a sure-fire method to achieve a given program. What seems clear is that research itself must support long-term research and argue in its own behalf. Even in companies where long-term goals are not popular, research must keep them in view while working on short-term projects.

One of the best ways to alleviate overemphasis on the short term is to conduct early exploratory work on a small scale. Cast project objectives in as general a way as possible. Keep a sufficently low profile and do the work necessary to get lead time on people who think only on the short term.

Structuring the R&D function so that research people have designated areas of long-range interest can help in this regard. Such a commitment has several advantages:

1. It indicates to the researcher that the company supports some longer-term objectives.

2. It lends perspective to the research and development program.

3. It is not a hard concept to sell to higher management. For example, to obtain commitment for research on new energy sources may not be difficult. After all, such sources are sorely needed. It is a broadly stated objective and easily accepted. On the other hand, a long-term, specifically delineated research project on fuel cells may elicit only corporate wrath because the same executives who encourage energy research may feel that fuel cells have little potential.

With the right research mix—both long and short term—there should be no problem with having a full docket of projects. If there is a problem of too few project proposals, several questions need to be asked:

1. Has management inhibited its people so often that they are reluctant to propose new work?

2. Has management force-fed its research group so much that they expect to be told what they will do next?

3. Is the work program so crash-and-crisis–oriented that no one has time or energy to contemplate the future?

4. Has the research group progressed with time? Have the innovators left and the dullards remained?

5. Are answers to all these questions yeses?

Program and Project Control. It is no easy task to keep an R&D program on a relevant path. Some never get on a good course; once there, they can easily fall off it. Review measures are necessary for all programs. These are often accomplished through periodic progress (monthly) reports. The frequency of those reports, however, makes them less effective as an overall control than semiannual reports of a more general nature. Periodic reviews of areas of research are excellent for both control and information. For the semiannual report and/or related critique sessions, some questions are appropriate:

1. Do the writers of project review reports really know why they are writing them? Do they know the intended audience? All too often, the researcher is not aware of either. Management, in turn, may respond negatively to a report if it is written primarily for research specialists.

2. Is the principal investigator invited to the review meetings about his or her project and perhaps to other closely associated ones? If not, a valuable resource is not being put to full use.

3. Is the management group getting out of its offices to talk to the R&D group face to face in an informal manner? Discussions held in the researcher's territory can be much more informative than those held in the manager's office.

Project Termination. Deciding when to stop a project is sometimes more difficult than determining when to start one. If there are regular program review sessions, the answer will be easier. Workers generally want to continue their projects; they cannot be relied on for an objective evaluation. Nonetheless, they should be asked their opinions; they should know more about their project than anyone else in the company. Negative answers to any of four key questions may help in making the termination decision.

1. Have the major objectives been accomplished? Is the project really finished but still hanging on because of inertia?

2. Have the major objectives been reduced as work has progressed? That is, "Six months ago we were aiming for Mars; now it is the moon. Perhaps we should throw in the towel."

3. Has the marketplace undergone changes that will cut the scope dramatically? A better "bias" tire has far less chance for success if the public wants radial tires.

4. Has the company itself undergone a change in philosophy, making an area of R&D not so vital? This is one time when quitting probably hurts the most. R&D may think it has a winner, but company attitudes have changed. It may be that the company position was never well defined to begin with; the definition came only when confronted with a real prospect for a new venture.

Evaluation of R&D Management Performance

Over the long haul, management of research and development must be judged by what the function accomplishes:

1. Is there a good flow of technology from the laboratory to operations?

2. Do operations personnel view R&D as an asset?

3. Does operations seek help from R&D or does it go outside the company for support?

Answers provide objective estimates of R&D performance and are good indicators of the quality of R&D management.

R&D management can also be evaluated by staff turnover and salary administration. Low turnover does not necessarily mean good management. The reverse may be true. A mediocre staff with mediocre management will have very low turnover. The clue is to look at who is leaving and why. Salary administration should provide similar indications. Some people should be expected to complain about their salaries. Are they the low achievers? Are they leaving? Or, are the high performers unhappy and moving on? What is important is *who* is unhappy and *why*.

Other indicators of management's influence on R&D performance involve a look outside the organization. Do R&D people participate regularly in conferences and professional activities? Is their organization highly regarded by other companies?

Finally, in evaluating research managers, these questions might be asked:

1. Are the people under each manager's supervision growing as professionals? Are their skills

increasing? Are their job assignments and projects changed from time to time?

2. Does the manager look ahead to new challenges, new ways to improve old things, and increases in productivity?

3. Does the manager represent his or her people well? Does the manager understand the projects they are working on? Will the manager stand up for these people when the going gets rough?

4. Does the manager anticipate or play catch-up? Are there future-oriented departmental goals? Is the manager interested in tomorrow or yesterday?

See also Engineering management; Innovation and creativity; Marketing research; Product planning and development; Project management; Technology transfer; Value analysis.

REFERENCES

Cook, C. F.: "Troubled Life of the Young Ph.D. in an Industrial Research Lab," *Research Management*, vol. 18, May 1975, pp. 28–31.

Gibson, John E.: *Managing Research and Development*, John Wiley, New York, 1981.

Parasurman, A., and L. M. Zeren: "R&D's Relationship with Profits and Sales," *Research Management*, vol. 26, January–February 1983, pp. 25–28.

Ramsey, Jackson, E.: *Research and Development Project Selection Criteria*, UMI Research Press, Ann Arbor, Mich., 1978.

Souder, W. E.: "Achieving Organizational Consensus with Respect to R&D Project Selection Criteria," *Management Science*, vol. 21, February 1975, pp. 669–681.

Carle C. Zimmerman, *Marathon Oil Company*

Retailing Management

Retailing management includes all business activities associated with providing the right merchandise at the right price at the right time and at the right place. A *retailer* is an independent merchant intermediary who stands between a producer and the consumer and, in effect, is the one who serves as the consumer's purchasing agent. The essence of a retailer's operation includes all the activities associated with the sale of goods and services for final consumption. Many functions, such as buying, selling, promoting, pricing, bulk breaking, warehousing, financing, and risk bearing are performed by the retailer, and the success of any retail store depends on the efficiency with which these and other retailing functions are strategically managed in response to changes in the marketplace.

A *retailing mix* is a combination of the store's goods and services, physical facilities, promotion, prices, merchandising, location, sales personnel, reputation, and image, which, when blended, create an atmosphere to satisfy customers and achieve store goals and objectives. Retail store managers must constantly adjust operating strategies in response to changing consumer expectations, lifestyles, tastes, and values.

Forms of Retailing. In adjusting to environmental influences, retailing takes a variety of forms. It has two major classifications: *in-store* or over-the-counter retailing and *nonstore* retailing.

Warehouse retailing usually involves a warehouse or a barnlike structure combining a showroom to display merchandise, contain extensive inventory, and offer consumers discount prices. Generally the facility is located on less expensive land, exists as one level, has free-standing buildings, and is designed to reduce handling and unloading costs. Merchandise samples are displayed in a "catalog" showroom, and a retailer's entire inventory is located in a storage room adjacent to the showroom. Typically, the warehouse retailer sells only a single line of merchandise, using price appeal to sell manufacturers' brands right from the carton.

Discount retailing emphasizes the sale of name-brand merchandise with price as the main appeal. Discount retailers, unlike warehouse retailers, carry a reasonably complete line of hard and soft goods with well-known, presold brand names, and this merchandise is consistently sold somewhat below the advertised or manufacturer's suggested retail price. The discount retailing concept is simplicity itself: a one-stop shopping center selling only fast-moving, branded merchandise at cut-rate prices. The discount retailer is often located in a free-standing store, and the rate of inventory turnover is much faster than for traditional retailers selling the same merchandise.

Department stores are large retail institutions handling many different product lines. Generally, department store management is divided into four functions: (1) operations, (2) sales promotion, (3) merchandising, and (4) control.

Chain stores are retail institutions which consist of two or more units, centrally owned and managed. Chain stores are usually large-scale retailers and often enjoy competitive advantages associated with their relative size. These advantages may include greater price discounts on buying merchandise for resale, financial strength, a greater number of resources, the ability to spread risks and, in some instances, the ability to sell goods at lower retail prices than some independents. One reason for the price advantage may be that chains sell many of their own brands rather than producer's brands.

Specialty stores specialize in a given line of merchandise. They provide consumers with a wide choice from a single merchandise line. The specialty store merchant is able to buy a larger assortment of goods for the same amount of money that must be invested by the retailer who carries several lines of merchandise. By specializing in one product line, the specialty retailer may have greater knowledge of consumer brand preferences, prices, styles, and fashion responsiveness than other types of retailers.

Nonstore retailing consists of mail-order, door-to-door, and automatic vending. *Mail-order* retailing (direct marketing) allows the consumer to purchase merchandise from a catalog. This type of retailing generally benefits from lower operating costs than in-store retailing. Delivery times, the effort of returning goods, and the inability to inspect the merchandise are major disadvantages for the consumer. Probably the oldest method of retailing is where the buyer and seller meet in a buyer's home. *Door-to-door* retailing is usually associated with producers, although some retailers also sell door to door.

Automatic vending retailing lends itself to an amazingly wide variety of products, usually low-unit value items such as cigarettes, candy, soft drinks, hosiery, cosmetics, and personal items. Automatic vending retailing is expensive for the retailer because of mechanical breakdowns, theft, and an initial equipment investment.

Franchise retailing has become an accepted and proven way of operating a retail business. A franchise is a contract which gives the retailer the right to do business under the name and image of a manufacturer or wholesaler. The party granting the license is called the franchisor; the party purchasing the license is called a franchisee. A franchise contract is an agreement between a franchisor (parent company) and a franchisee (individual) under which the franchisee is provided with the opportunity to conduct a business according to a definite *retail plan*, probably including the franchisor's name and method of operation, inventory requirements, record-keeping, etc. Franchise retailing has encouraged the growth of small independent retailers by providing them with managerial techniques, skills, training, and merchandising know-how. Through a franchise arrangement, the small independent retailer is provided with a proven retail business plan with the franchisor overseeing the operation of the retail store. For this guidance, aid, and instruction, the franchisee usually pays an initial fee and, in some instances, a percentage of the profits of the business. In essence, the franchisor and the franchisee become business partners although the franchisee often appears as an independent retailer.

Market Opportunity Analysis (MOA). This is a continuous process for most retailers. Existing markets must be constantly satisfied with new products and services. A retailer must increasingly identify market opportunities and evaluate the risks in the retail environment. Today's retailing environment is the most important single influence on a retailer's strategic business planning process.

There are several relationships between a retailer's environment and the strategic planning process, the retail business plan, and the policies and strategies. Today's retailers are concerned not only with economic, technological, political, and legal forces, but also with changing demographics, consumer attitudes, and social values.

A common cause of retail store failure is management's inability to determine market demand. An analysis of market opportunities and sales and profit potential within a trade area is one of the most difficult challenges facing retailers. MOA is a systematic and methodical search for a comprehensive, accurate, and useful description of a retailer's target market. *Retail market segmentation analysis* is one technique used to obtain useful information in predicting consumer demand within target markets. Retail market segmentation consists of dividing a heterogeneous market into homogeneous characteristics. Consumer products are classified into three groups based on buyer behavior:

1. *Convenience goods* are those products which are usually low in cost and are purchased with a minimum of effort.

2. *Shopping goods* are those products for which the consumer will shop and compare different product features, prices, warranties, colors, styles, and other characteristics.

3. *Specialty goods* are those products which a consumer will make a considerable effort to find. Usually there is a strong brand preference for specialty goods, and the consumer has full knowledge of the product.

Every retailer needs to know why consumers do or do not purchase certain goods and services. An understanding of consumer purchasing behavior is the retailer's foundation for developing a proper retailing mix. The disciplines of psychology, sociology, and social psychology will aid the retailer in better understanding consumers.

Retail Planning

Strategic retail business planning (SRBP) is a process whereby a retailer decides at present what to do in the future. It encompasses a determination of goals and objectives and includes the development of strategies and tactics for survival and growth of the enterprise. SRBP is matching and integrating what a retail firm can do with what it might do. Essentially, SRBP weighs the consequences of cause-and-effect relationships over time. From the whole planning process, a retailer can select the best alternatives for a certain set of market conditions.

In a strategic planning approach to retailing management, one visualizes a retailing institution as a total system of interacting and related business activities, each of which influences and affects the profitability of that enterprise. In other words, managerial decisions in any one area will directly or indirectly cause a chain reaction in all other activities within that firm.

The Retail Business Plan. A retail business plan is a written document that specifies systematic, orderly, and integrated procedures for achieving certain predetermined goals and objectives within a specified period of time. Briefly, the plan should state what is to be done, how it is to be done, by whom the work will be performed, and when it is to be completed. Strategic retail business planning leads to a number of benefits:

1. Goals and objectives for the business, stated in writing, serve as a means for measuring managerial abilities.

2. The plan results in improved coordination of retailing activities which, when combined, have a total greater effect on the business than does each of the activities taken independently. (The result is synergism.)

3. It leads to improved internal control through the development of more efficient and effective performance standards for the store's activities.

4. SRBP allows retail management to optimize labor, money, and physical facilities through the integrated, efficient use of each resource in developing strategies for achieving the store's goals and objectives.

5. It serves to mitigate inconsistencies and anomalies that may arise in the commitment of resources.

6. Through SRBP, management is able to evaluate the effects of alternative strategies and plans *before* a decision is implemented, isolate weaknesses in the organization, and correct misdirected or misplaced managerial efforts.

Common Elements. Every retail business plan is unique and distinctive since each reflects the firm's management philosophy as well as the special needs of a particular retail store; yet, each retail business plan contains the following common elements:

1. An assessment and measurement of the retailer's market potential, a survey of the customer profile of the market to be served, and a sales forecast by month for the forthcoming year. This statement becomes the retailer's fact base for the development of the strategic retail business plan. Market opportunities are identified, challenges are listed, problems are identified, and trade areas are analyzed.

2. A written, specific statement of goals and objectives for the retail store for the time frame covering the SRBP process. Assumptions are listed when appropriate.

3. An analysis and evaluation of the existing and/or potential site location of the store. Sites are never static; they either improve or deteriorate.

4. An assessment and appraisal of management's pricing policies, strategies, and tactics for the enterprise under current market conditions.

5. An examination and diagnosis of the store's promotional policies, strategies, and tactics, together with a current promotional campaign congruent with the existing retail environment.

6. A complete financial analysis and management audit of cash flows, revenues, product-line sales, profit by product line, and the preparation of an annual budget with weekly and monthly breakdowns.

7. The establishment of an expense control system, creating a chart of accounts and classification of all retail expenses, analyzing sales/expense ratios, operating profits, inventories, and expenses for soundness and accountability.

8. A survey and analysis of management's policies with respect to recruiting, screening, and hiring job applicants, and training, compensating, and evaluating employees. Any retail organization is only as good as its employees.

9. An assessment of the company's physical facilities, including exterior and interior layout and design, for efficiency and employee productivity commensurate with a psychologically stimulating work environment.

10. A review and analysis of the number of vendors and resources from which the company purchases products for resale. Also, an analysis and reevaluation of the store's policies with respect to negotiations with those same vendors and resources.

11. An evaluation of receiving operations with targeted goals of increased efficiency, reduction of waste and pilferage, and minimization in handling products upon arrival at the store. The establishment and maintenance of an inventory control system tailored to the store that will aid and facilitate managerial decision making by providing precise information on the movement of products, product lines, and the minimizing of stock losses.

12. The management of information in the office in order to organize input data into useful cate-

gories that can be utilized as management information.

Time Frame. *Strategic retail business planning* and the final product, the *retail business plan* itself, is an organized, systematic approach to marshaling the organization's resources and directing retailing activities toward the attainment of management's goals and objectives within a given time frame. The time frame may be on an annual or fiscal year basis. This is a matter of convenience and managerial choice, since most retail business firms are on a 12-month accounting cycle.

A Comprehensive but Uncomplicated Plan. Whatever a store's planning requirements, management can develop a sophisticated and comprehensive retail business plan, emphasizing each individual element in the plan to the degree that management desires. It is important to bear in mind that SRBP should be comprehensive, yet uncomplicated. The plan itself is a retail management tool to be used in making business decisions. The process of retail business planning facilitates organized thinking, takes the guesswork out of financial budgeting, zeros in on growth and profitability, and offers a means of measuring the firm's progress. It provides a base for corrective strategy and establishes a means for follow-up planning.

Future Challenges. Today's retailers are challenged on many fronts—intense competition, maturing markets, limited growth opportunities, energy shortages, escalating operating costs, consumer apathy, uncertain business conditions, declining employee productivity, rising cost of capital, and increasing social demands. Creative thinking, individual perception, corporate managerial vision, and management's ability to plan, organize, direct, and control the firm's activities and its possession of the ability to offer a differentiated merchandising mix are necessary in order to establish a comparative retailing advantage. What is needed is executive judgment which comes from experience, merchandising and managerial expertise, and provides a fine edge of distinction.

See also Consumer behavior, managerial relevance of; Franchising; Market analysis; Marketing, channels of distribution; Marketing, concepts and systems; Product and service pricing; Sales management.

REFERENCES

Arnold, Danny R., Louis M. Capella, and Garry D. Smith: *Strategic Retail Management*, Addison-Wesley, Reading, Mass., 1983.

Duncan, Delbert, Stanley C. Hollander, and Ronald Smith: *Modern Retailing Management: Basic Concepts and Practices*, 10th ed., Richard D. Irwin, Homewood, Ill., 1983.

Redinbaugh, Larry D.: *Retailing Management: A Planning Approach*, McGraw-Hill, New York, 1976.

806   LARRY D. REDINBAUGH, *Creighton University*

Risk Analysis and Management

Outcomes, or consequences, of human actions are rarely predictable even with perfect knowledge of them. Because management decisions do not have inevitable outcomes, these decisions are essentially wagers involving risk or uncertainty. At times, consequences of a particular course of action may be truly inevitable, but decision makers cannot include them in their plans because they do not have adequate knowledge of them. Decisions made under these circumstances are characterized as risky or uncertain.

Technically, risk and uncertainty do not mean the same thing. A situation is *risky* when a complete list of all possible outcomes and the associated chance of their occurrence are known in advance. When these conditions—knowledge of possible outcomes and the chance of their assurance—are not met, the situation is characterized as *uncertain*. The decision process under risk involves both the measurement of and attitude toward risk. The decision process under uncertainty involves listing the economic outcomes under differing conditions for every decision alternative and selecting the decision without weighting different outcomes by the chance of their occurrence. As will be demonstrated later, the original distinction revolving around measurement is no longer regarded critical; hence, the distinction between risk and uncertainty is practically ignored. The methods proposed for dealing with uncertainty are, however, of interest to managers, and they will be briefly described first.

Measurement of Risk

Risk is measured in terms of probabilities, reflecting relative changes in the occurrence of possible outcomes. For instance, if one rolls a die 1200 times, the number 6 is likely to appear 200 times. Thus the probability of number 6 appearing upon a roll of a die is $^{200}/_{1200}$ or $^{1}/_{6}$. The same holds true for numbers 5, 4, 3, 2, and 1. Because probabilities are ratios or relative numbers, it follows that when probabilities of all possible outcomes are summed, the sum equals 1. Although the notion of probabilities seems clear and straightforward, it involves one controversial issue. Instead of a detailed discussion of the issue, the description here will be limited to its practical significance.

Objective Versus Subjective Views. The issue is what happens when the die is rolled only once. In that case, either the number 6 appears or it does not. Is the notion of probability valid? Two different answers are provided. Those who believe in the *objective approach* regard probabilities as irrelevant in this instance. They argue that "valid" probabilities can be obtained only if the die is rolled many times. In business situations, such large numbers of trials are obtained when one deals with, say, insurance problems or machine replacement needs. The objectivists also maintain that probabilities are valid only when one additional condition is fulfilled: If the die is rolled the first time and the number 6 is obtained, that result should not create a bias for or against obtaining the number 6 in subsequent rolls. In other words, results obtained in earlier rolls or trials should not influence the outcomes in the subsequent rolls or trials. Those who believe in *subjective probabilities* regard this condition of a *large number* of *unrelated* trials as too restrictive. They believe that even when these conditions are not met, probabilities can be computed by considering the decision maker's experience, intuition, and judgment. Indeed, they consider the probabilities thus obtained are a valuable tool for systematic decision making. The following example illustrates the conflicting viewpoints.

A firm is considering introduction of a new product in the marketplace. This is the first new product that the firm has developed, and it does not think it can introduce another such product in the foreseeable future. The industry experience, however, is that 1 in every 10 new products succeeds. The objectivist is very likely to reject the idea of probability application in this situation because new products are not supposed to come on stream, and thus there is a violation of the condition regarding a large number of trials. On the other hand, the subjectivist may take the probability of success being $\frac{1}{10}$, or .10, on the basis of the industry experience as a starting point; then, depending upon the manager's confidence in the new product, the subjectivist will revise say, up to .20 or down to .05.

Suppose the subjectivist comes up with the figure of .20 as the probability of success of the new product. How is that figure obtained? The procedure is somewhat complex,[1] but essentially it boils down to the following proposition. Suppose the manager is offered a choice between two alternatives: (1) Sell the new product development to another firm in the industry for X, or (2) charge X to a gambler who gets the same payoff as the successful new product if that individual draws a white ball from a jar containing 2 white balls and 8 red balls of equal size, and nothing otherwise. If the manager is indifferent toward these two alternatives with equal payoffs for success or failure, then the probability of success or failure to these alternatives should be identical.

Expected Value. No matter how the probabilities are determined, it is clear that the larger the probability of an outcome, the more certain the occurrence of the outcome. The extreme values are 1 and 0. When an outcome is certain, the probability of its occurrence is 1. When the outcome is impossible, its probability is 0. This being so, it is reasonable to weigh each uncertain outcome with the associated probability—to discount, so to speak, the uncertainty contained in the outcome. When all possible outcomes are thus adjusted with their associated probabilities and summed, the resulting number is defined as the *expected value,* or mean. Because the expected value represents a discount for certainty, it is often a reasonable practice to compare two decision alternatives in terms of the expected value of the possible outcomes and regard as superior the alternative with a higher expected value.

Variance. Although the expected value can be an excellent index of risk, it may not always accurately reflect the riskiness of future outcomes. For example, alternative A in the situation shown in Table R-3 has the same expected value ($50) as alter-

TABLE R-3

(1) Alternative	(2) Probability of outcome	(3) Outcome, in dollars	(4) = (2) × (3) Probable weighted outcome, in dollars
A	.25	$ 49	$ 12.25
	.50	50	25.00
	.25	51	12.75
			50.00
B	.25	−50	−12.50
	.50	50	25.00
	.25	150	37.50
			50.00

native B. The decision maker may, however, regard alternative B as riskier than alternative A, because the spread from the expected outcome is much smaller for alternative A than for B. To put it differently, the losses and the gains would be much greater for alternative B than for A if the expected outcome did not occur.

This idea is systematically reflected in the measure of variance. The *variance* measures the difference between an outcome and the expected value. Since this difference may be positive or negative and since one's interest is in the spread, it is squared (a squared number is always positive). The squared difference is weighed with the probability of the outcomes so that a remotely possible outcome may not be weighed unduly just because of its large magnitude of difference from the expected value. The sum of the weighted squared difference is the variance. Often, the square root of the variance, called the *standard deviation,* is used as an alternative in place of the variance. It follows from this description that the larger the possibility that an outcome would differ from the expected value, the larger the variance, or the standard deviation. And the greater the risk, the larger the variance (the standard deviation). Often, a "relative" measure of risk is employed in the form of the ratio of the standard deviation to the expected value. This ratio is known as the *coefficient of variation*.

Distributions. Although the measure of variance adequately reflects risk under normal circumstances, it suffers from a conceptual problem as well as a practical difficulty. Conceptually, the measure is likely to be appropriate for symmetrical distributions (Fig. R-2a), but when the distribution is skewed (Fig. R-2b), other measures are called for. This discussion

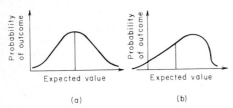

FIG. R-2 Two distributions. (a) symmetrical; (b) skewed.

will ignore these refinements. The practical problem is in terms of the requirement that the manager will be called upon not only to determine future outcomes possible for each decision alternative but also to assess associated probabilities. Even when the task is feasible, it is questionable whether the effort is worthwhile as to its time or cost. In this instance, a shortcut to measure both the expected value and the standard deviation may be taken: The manager is asked to predict (1) the most likely outcome (M); and (2) the highest possible outcome (H) and the lowest possible outcome (L). In that case:

$$\text{Expected value} = \frac{2M + (H + L)/2}{3}$$

$$\text{Standard deviation} = \frac{H - L}{6}$$

Sometimes the measurement is computed in this way:

$$\text{Expected value} = M$$

$$\text{Standard deviation} = \frac{H - L}{4}$$

These approximations are based on a *normal* distribution, one of the most widely used distributions. In a normal distribution, if the expected value is taken as a bench mark, say 0, 99 percent of the deviations from the expected value fall in the range 0 ± 3 (standard deviation), as shown in Fig. R-3.

FIG. R-3 Normal distribution.

In brief, dealing with risk requires measurement of either probabilities or probability-derived measures such as expected value and standard deviation (or variance).

Attitude Toward Risk

As shown above, sole reliance on the expected value may not lead to a choice of the most desirable alternative. The decision maker who strictly relies on the expected value is described as *risk-neutral*. One who prefers risk is called a *risk lover* or *speculator*. Most decision makers, however, do not fall into either of the two categories; instead they are risk averters. A *risk averter* may be defined as a person who prefers higher returns for a given amount of risk (or less risk for a given expected return). Since the attitude of risk aversion is most commonly encountered, this discussion will deal only with that category.

Risk Aversion. When the probability distribution is specified, the simplest possible way of arriving at a decision is to choose the alternative having the smallest chance of acceptable adverse results. For instance, avoiding stock-out in inventory management may be too expensive or even impossible. Hence, the manager has to indicate a willingness to take, say, 1 in 20 chances of being out of stock. In terms of the probability distribution, this means that the probability of stock below zero should be .05 or less. Suppose the current inventory policy leads to 1 in 10 chances of being out of stock, as shown by the cross-hatched axis in Fig. R-4a. If an alternative policy (with minimum cost increase) provides 1 in 20 chances, as shown in Fig. R-4b, the alternative policy

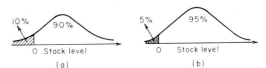

FIG. R-4 Alternative inventory policies.

should be selected by the manager. Decisions along this line can also be made for optimal debt in the capital structure of the company.[2]

Outcome Utilities. Although a variety of decisions can also be made along the above line, the decision process is awkward and at times does not lead to the most desirable decision. Suppose an investor is looking at two securities, each having a 5 percent chance of providing zero or even negative return. Should the investor remain indifferent toward the choice of the security? It is possible that the expected return is 10 percent on one security but 17 percent of the other. Thus, the choice may not be a matter of indifference or of purely noneconomic considerations.

One way out is to assign "utilities" to the value of outcomes, and weigh the utilities with probabilities associated with the outcome. The sum of all "weighted" utilities for a decision is the expected utility of that decision. The decision alternative with the highest utility is the most desirable alternative. How to measure utilities is the critical consideration in this decision process. One way is to define the worst possible and the most desirable outcomes. Suppose—$500,000 and $10 million are two such outcomes. Attach 0 utility units, or *utiles*, to −$500,000 and 1 utile to $10 million. The decision maker is told that a gamble has .10 probability of winning $10 million and .90 probability of losing $500,000; how much would the prospective purchaser be willing to pay for such a gamble? The decision maker's reply is, say, $400,000. In that case,

$$\text{Utilities of } \$400,000 = .9 \, [\text{utility } (-\$500,000)]$$
$$+ .1 \, [\text{utility } (\$10 \text{ million})]$$
$$= .9 \times 0 + .1 \times 1$$
$$\text{Utility } (\$400,000) = .10$$
$$= .10$$

Now the decision maker is asked how much it would be wise to pay for a gamble with payoffs of +$400,000 and −$500,000 with the respective probabilities of .3 and .7 (these probability figures are not pertinent except in the calculation of the utility of the price that the decision maker is willing to pay for the gamble). Suppose the decision maker expresses unwillingness to pay a single penny for the gamble. After some query, the investor admits that if *paid* $250,000 for playing the gamble, the purchase would be considered. In that case,

$$\text{Utility } (-\$250,000) = .7 \, [\text{utility } (-\$500,000)]$$
$$+ .3 \, [\text{utility } (\$400,000)]$$
$$= .7 \times 0 + 0.3 \times .1$$
$$= .03$$

Thus the decision maker attaches .03 utiles to the loss of $250,000 and .10 utiles to the profit of $400,000.

In this example, the range of the scale for utilities covers the values from 0 to 1. It does not matter if the scale, instead, is −10,000 to +500,000. What is critical is the ranking of the outcomes in terms of relative desirability. So long as that does not change, the final choice will remain the same irrespective of the scale. Of course, utile assignment does not necessarily remain identical for two individuals; it depends on each person's attitude toward risk.

One caution should be taken when utilities are determined in the way just described. The net utility of two outcomes combined is not the same as the sum of the utilities of each outcome considered separately. In other words,

$$\text{Utility } (A + B) \neq \text{utility } A + \text{utility } B$$

Thus, when several capital projects are being considered, their evaluation should not be made individually. Similarly, because capital projects are typically added to the existing pool of assets of the firm, they cannot be evaluated without considering the characteristics of the current mode of operations.

Certainty-Equivalent Values. One of the biggest limitations of the utility approach is the complexity of figuring out not only the probabilities but also the utility associated with each outcome. If, for measurement purposes, the probability distribution can be conveniently collapsed into two numbers, expected value and standard deviation, as shown earlier, the question is whether an effective way can be employed to reflect attitude toward risk in terms of these two numbers. When a decision maker is a risk averter, preferring higher returns for a given amount of risk, it is possible to determine the risk-return trade-off and thereby arrive at certainty-equivalent values adjusted for risk. If returns are designated by the expected value (EV), and risk by the variance (VAR), the certainty-equivalent value (CE) may be expressed as

$$CE = EV - a \cdot VAR$$

where *a* reflects the decision maker's attitude toward risk. The larger the value of *a*, the greater the decision maker's aversion toward risk. Determination of *a* can be shown graphically with the help of Fig. R-5.

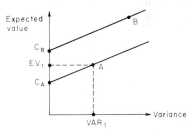

FIG. R-5 Risk-return trade-off and certainty-equivalent values in terms of expected value and variance.

Suppose the decision maker faces a risky outcome with EV_1 and VAR_1 as the expected value and the variance respectively. This is designated as point A in the figure. The decision maker is asked to give the maximum price (certain amount) that would be paid for this outcome. Equivalently, if he or she owned a business with risk-return characteristics of A, what would be the smallest offer that would be accepted for selling the business? This amount is designated by point C_A in Fig. R-5. Amount C_A is the certainty-equivalent amount (note that it is on the vertical axis with variance 0). The line $C_A{}^A$ represents an indifference curve on which the expected utility is constant (any point on line $C_A{}^A$ has the certainty-equivalent value C_A). If there is any other risky outcome, say B, its certainty-equivalent value C_B is easily found by drawing a line $C_B{}^B$ parallel to $C_A{}^A$ and passing through the point B. The value of a is provided by the slope of the line $C_A{}^A$ or $C_B{}^B$.

It is also possible to obtain the certainty-equivalent values in terms of the expected value and the standard deviation, as shown in Fig. R-6. The only

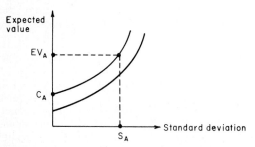

FIG. R-6 Risk-return trade-off and certainty-equivalent values, in terms of expected value and standard deviation.

difference is that the straight lines are now replaced by the curves.

In brief, the attitude toward risk can be incorporated in decision making in several ways. One way focuses on deviations from the expected value on the downside without explicitly considering the expected value. Another way considers utilities of possible outcomes and adjusts them for the probability of occurrence of outcomes. The third way described here is a special case of the second approach in that it takes into account two surrogates of the probability distribution, that is, the expected value and the variance (or the standard deviation). Two major areas of finance where these techniques have been extensively employed are securities selection and capital budgeting. In the next section, some applications in these two fields will be described.

Application: Securities Selection. When the choice is between a risk security and riskless investment, say, a treasury bond, the decision can be undertaken exactly along the line of reasoning suggested in the previous section. The certainty-equivalent rate of return on the risky security is thus compared with the return on the treasury bond, and whichever provides the higher return will be the choice of the investor.

When the number of risky securities is larger than one, the analyst cannot select these securities in terms of their *individual* risk (variance). The reason is that the risk of *all* securities combined is not necessarily the same as the sum of their individual risk measures. The variance of two securities, A and B

combined, for instance, is given by VAR(A + B) where

$$\text{VAR(A + B)} = \text{VAR(A)} + \text{VAR(B)} + 2\text{COV(A,B)}$$

and

$$\text{COV(A,B)} = \text{covariance of A with B}$$

In turn, the covariance is defined as follows:

$$\text{COV(A,B)} = \text{correlation coefficient (A,B)}$$
$$\times \, [\text{VAR(A)}]^{1/2} \times [\text{VAR(B)}]^{1/2}$$

Thus, if returns on two securities are highly positively correlated (the correlation coefficient approximately equal to $+1$), the covariance will be positive and large. On the other hand, if they are unrelated (with 0 correlation coefficient), the covariance will be 0. Finally, when the returns on the two securities are highly negatively correlated (the correlation coefficient in the neighborhood of -1), the covariance will be negative. Hence,

$$\text{VAR(A + B)} = \text{VAR(A)} + \text{VAR(B)}$$

only when returns on two securities are unrelated. When they are negatively correlated, the *overall* risk—VAR(A + B)—will be smaller than the sum of the individual security risks.

It follows, then, that individual securities should not be selected in terms of their *own* risk but in terms of their contribution to the risk of the bundle of the securities. A practical problem immediately arises. If there are *two* securities, then *two* expected values, *two* variances, and *one* covariance need to be estimated. If there are three securities, then three each of expected value, variance, and covariances are to be estimated. As the number of securities increases, the number of covariances to be estimated increases even faster; when there are 50 securities, the number of covariances to be estimated will be 1225!

An ingenious shortcut has been suggested by Sharpe, whereby he links the return on an individual security with a market index such as Standard & Poor's, and the linkage relationship in turn provides the covariance between two securities.[3] For different bundles of securities—portfolios—the overall expected return and the associated variance (or standard deviation) can be estimated. The portfolio that has the highest certainty-equivalent return (along Fig. R-5 or Fig. R-6) is the most desirable for the investor.

Application: Capital Budgeting. Capital expenditures involve cash flows over several time periods. Hence, their evaluation requires adjustment not only as to time but also for risk. A widely prescribed decision rule is in terms of the *net present value*, NPV, defined as

$$\text{NPV} = \text{cash flow (0)} + \frac{\text{cash flow (1)}}{(1 + d)^1}$$

$$+ \frac{\text{cash flow } (2)}{(1 + d)^2} + \frac{\text{cash flow } (N)}{(1 + d)^N}$$

$$= \sum_{t=0}^{N} \frac{\text{cash flow } (t)}{(1 + d)^t}$$

where cash flow (t) = positive or negative cash flow in period t associated with the project under consideration

d = discount rate

N = economic life of the project

Risk Adjustment. Risk involved in the project is adjusted in one of the three ways:

1. Shorten the economic life. If, for instance, a project has a 10-year life, cash flows for only, say, a 7-year time span are considered in decision making because, beyond the seventh year, the estimates are deemed too unreliable to be taken into account. The popular payback method is one extreme example where risk is reflected in the shortened life span of the project.

2. Modify the discount rate. Many companies, for example, employ a 12 percent discount rate for replacement expenditures, 16 percent for plant expansions, 18 percent for new products, and 24 percent for research and development.

A major problem with these two methods is that adjustments in the life span of the discount rate are arbitrary. Thus they are hardly related to the goals of the firm. Further, the payback method ignores not only cash flows beyond the payback period but also the *timing* of flows within the payback period. Similarly, risk adjustment in the discount rate requires it to reflect both the timing and risk considerations. As a result, a constant risk-adjusted discount rate implies that the inherent risk in the capital project increases at a constant rate over time. Introduction of a new product may have substantial risk for the first 2 years, but as the dust settles, the risk may not be as high as at the initial level. Thus, application of a high discount rate, such as 18 percent, may not accurately reflect the risk inherent in the new project.

3. Adjust the relevant cash flows of risk. This avoids the problems associated with the first two methods. Basically, the technique of the certainty-equivalent value is applied. There are, however, some interesting wrinkles in such an application. Although probabilities associated with the future periods may reflect substantial risk in isolation, they may have smaller risk once resolution of uncertainty *in the interim* is considered. For example, if one were to estimate cash flows in the fifth year of a new product, the range of outcome may vary, say, from −$2 million to $1 million. However, an ability of the firm to debug or modify the product within 3 years, to increase the advertising budget substantially if

the expected demand does not materialize in 4 years, or to modify the price as well as gain better knowledge of the market in the first 4 years may mean that *conditional* outcome in the fifth year would become more certain. A *decision-tree framework* is employed to consider risk modification over time to reflect not only better knowledge of the future but also the manager's ability to modify the eventual outcomes.[4]

The decision-tree method is, however, an extremely cumbersome way to reflect the basic risk characteristic of the capital expenditure decision: it has to consider not only the risk embodied in the variability of cash flows *within* each period, but also the covariability of flows *between* two periods. The simulation method is reasonable for tackling such a job.[5] However, the tremendous effort required in carrying out such work is economically justifiable only for big projects.

In a nutshell, none of the methods suggested for risk adjustment is perfect for *all* situations. For an important project, where the stakes are high, cash flow modification provides a great deal of flexibility. For routine projects, risk-adjusted discount rates are reasonably adequate. When managers do not trust their ability to assess risk or do not believe in the discount mechanism, they utilize a payback period— although its justification is hard to demonstrate in a typical situation.

Uncertainty and Decision Making

A manager who is ignorant of or unwilling to make subjective estimates of probabilities can still make decisions in a systematic way. The theory of games describes two such ways: the *minimax* (or *maximin*) principle and the *maximax* principle.

Suppose a certain decision maker is pondering over the alternatives of plant expansion or the status quo. For simplicity, this man thinks that the economy will either prosper if the government aggressively undertakes deficit financing or will have price stability but miniscule growth if the government tries to balance the budget. Further suppose that he chooses not to estimate the probability of the economy being in state 1 (prosperity and inflation) or state 2 (stability and slow growth), because the government action is likely to depend on his decision as well as decisions of other businesspeople like him. Finally, suppose that he determines the payoff of each decision corresponding to the two states, as shown in the following table.

Decision	State 1 (Prosperity)	State 2 (Stability)
Expansion	+$500	−$150
No expansion	+$200	−$ 70

Minimax. Under the minimax principle, the decision maker will choose the alternative that has the smallest worst loss. The worst outcome of the expansion decision is −$70. Since a loss of $70 is smaller and less painful that a loss of $150, the decision maker will choose not to expand. He has thus minimized the maximum loss.

Maximax. Under the maximax principle, he will choose the decision alternative that has the maximum most favorable outcome. In this instance, his strategy would be to opt for expansion (having the most favorable outcome of $500 versus that of $200 under the non-expansion alternative).

Mixed Strategies. A further refinement in the form of the *mixed strategies* principle is sometimes introduced. Suppose P_1 is the (as yet unknown) probability of prosperity, and P_2, the probability of stability. The outcomes have the *same value* when

$$500P_1 + (-150)P_2 = 200P_1 + (-70)P_2$$

$$300P_1 = 80P_2$$

$$P_1 = \frac{80P_2}{300}, \text{ or } .2667P_2$$

Since the sum of the probabilities is unity,

$$P_1 + P_2 = 1$$

Hence,

$$.2667P_2 + P_2 = 1$$

or

$$P_2 = 1/1.2667, \text{ or } .79$$

Hence, if the probability of stability were to be .79, the likely loss for the decision maker is the same as to what the government does. If the probability of stability is greater than .79, the likely loss is larger for the decision of expansion, and so it should be rejected. Notice that the minimax solution is obtained for the extreme case where the probability of stability is 1.0. On the other hand, if the probability of stability is less than .79, the expansion decision is preferred to the nonexpansion decision. Again, the extreme case of probability of stability being 0 is the same as the maximax principle. In this sense, the mixed strategy is only a generalization of the minimax and maximax principles.

The example can be easily extended to more than two states and/or decision alternatives. The procedure is cumbersome but does not involve any significant modification.

A question is reasonable at this juncture. Uncertainty was introduced because estimation of objective or subjective probabilities was ruled out, and yet the mixed strategy procedure showed that probabilities were called for either directly or indirectly. Then why not introduce probabilities from the start and follow the procedures suggested earlier? The answer lies in the calculation of probabilities. In the case of risk, it was implicitly assumed that the decision maker's action would not elicit any hostile response from the opponent so as to modify the probabilities of outcomes. In other words, the nature of the opponent was assumed passive. When the decision maker is faced with a hostile opponent who is, so to speak, out to wreck the decision maker's plan, the decision maker does not form the decision proceeding from probabilities but, instead, calculates the probabilities implicit in decision alternatives and reacts to them by making a choice.

See also Budgeting, capital; Decision-making process; Forecasting business conditions; Operations research and mathematical modeling; Statistical analysis for management; System concept, total.

NOTES

[1]Howard Raiffa, *Decision Analysis: Introductory Lectures on Choices under Uncertainty*, Addison-Wesley, Reading, Mass., 1968.

[2]Gordon Donaldson, "New Framework for Corporate Debt Policy," *Harvard Business Review*, vol. 40, March–April 1962, pp. 117–131.

[3]William F. Sharpe, "A Simplified Model for Portfolio Analysis," *Management Science*, January 1963, pp. 277–293.

[4]John F. Magee, "How to Use Decision Trees in Capital Investment," *Harvard Business Review*, vol. 42, September–October 1964, pp 79–86.

[5]David B. Hertz, "Risk Analysis in Capital Investment," *Harvard Business Review*, vol. 42, January–February 1964, pp. 95–106.

DILEEP R. MEHTA, *Georgia State University*

ROBOTICS

Current Technology

The development of industrial robots began in the late 1950s, based in part on George Devol's 1954 patent application for a "Programmed Article Transfer." The first robots to be used in manufacturing operations were installed in 1961. Thus, the technology has just entered its third decade.

Despite a great deal of interest, acceptance of industrial robots and their installation in manufacturing facilities proceeded at a slow pace during the 1960s and the early 1970s. Poor reliability, lack of experience, misapplication, and unrealistic expectations resulting, in part, from "overselling"—all were factors contributing to this slow growth. The total number of robots sold in North America in the first 10 years (1962 through 1971) was about 600 units, with a total value of around $16 million. The next 5 years (1972 through 1976) saw more than 1300 units sold for about $42.5 million. The market has shown steady growth since then, although nowhere near the potential for this technology.

The use of industrial robots is not limited to North America. Asia (particularly Japan), Western Europe, and Eastern Europe are all involved with robotics applications. Table R-4 shows the estimated

Table R-4. Estimated Programmable Robot Population by Region (Year end, 1982)

Region	Robot population	Percentage of total
Asia	31,935	61
Western Europe	9,480	13
North America	6,573	18
Eastern Europe	3,950	8
Total	51,938	100

Source: Based on data from *1982 RIA Worldwide Robotics Survey and Directory.*

industrial robot population, worldwide, at the end of 1982.

What Is a Robot?* The Robotic Industries Association (RIA) defines an *industrial robot* as "a reprogrammable, multi-functional manipulator designed to move material, parts, tools, or specialized devices through variable programmed motions for the performance of a variety of tasks." Industrial robots are available in a wide range of capabilities and configurations. Basically, however, they all consist of several major components: the *manipulator,* or *mechanical unit,* that actually performs the manipulative functions; the *controller,* or *brain,* that stores data and directs the movement of the manipulator, and the power supply, that provides energy to the manipulator.

The manipulator is a series of mechanical link-

---

* All definitions for this entry have been taken from the *RIA Robotics Glossary,* 1984 edition. Definitions for other italicized terms are given in Table R-5.

Table R-5. Slected Glossary Terms

Anthropomorphic robot: A robot with all rotary joints and motions similar to those of a human arm. (Also called jointed-arm robot.)

Cartesian coordinate robot: A robot whose manipulator arm's degrees of freedom are defined primarily by Cartesian coordinates.

Cartesian coordinate system: A coordinate system whose axes or dimensions are three intersecting perpendicular straight lines and whose origin is the intersection. (Also described as rectilinear.)

Control system: Sensors, manual input, and mode selection elements, interlocking and decision-making circuitry, and output elements to the operating mechanism.

Controller: An information-processing device whose inputs are both desired and measured position and velocity or other pertinent variables in a process, and whose outputs are drive signals to a controlling motor or actuator.

Cylindrical coordinate robot: A robot whose manipulator arm's degrees of freedom are defined primarily by cylindrical coordinates.

Cylindrical coordinate system: A coordinate system that defines the position of any point in terms of an angular dimension, a radial dimension, and a height from a reference plane. These three dimensions specify a point on a cylinder.

End-effector: An actuator, gripper, or mechanical device attached to the wrist of a manipulator by which objects can be grasped or otherwise acted upon.

Fixed stop robot: A robot with stop-point control but no trajectory control. That is, each of its axes has a fixed limit at each end of its stroke and cannot stop except at one or the other of these limits. Such a robot with n degrees of freedom can therefore stop at no more than $2n$ locations (where location includes position and orientation). Some controllers do offer the capability of program selection of one of several mechanical stops to be used. (Also called non-servo robot.)

Manipulator: A mechanism, usually consisting of a series of segments, jointed or sliding relative to one another, for the purpose of grasping and moving objects usually in several degrees of freedom.

Pitch: The angular rotation of a moving body about an axis perpendicular to its direction of motion and in the same plane as its top side.

Repeatability: Closeness of agreement of repeated position movements, under the same conditions, to the same location.

Roll: The angular displacement of a moving body around the principle axis of its motion.

Servo-controlled robot: A robot driven by servomechanisms, i.e., motors whose driving signal is a function of the difference between commanded position and/or rate and measured actual position and/or rate. Such a robot is capable of stopping at, or moving through, a practically unlimited number of points in executing a programmed trajectory.

Spherical coordinate robot: A robot whose manipulator arm's degrees of freedom are defined primarily by spherical coordinates.

Spherical coordinate system: A coordinate system, two of whose dimensions are angles, the third being a linear distance from the point of origin. These three coordinates specify a point on a sphere.

Working envelope: The set of points representing the maximum extent or reach of the robot hand or working tool in all directions. (Also called work envelope or robot operating envelope.)

Wrist: A set of rotary joints between the arm and end-effector which allow the end-effector to be oriented to the workpiece.

Yaw: The angular displacement of a moving body about an axis which is perpendicular to the line of motion and to the top side of the body.

Source: Adapted from *RIA Robotics Glossary,* 1984.

ages and joints capable of movement in various directions to perform the work of the robot. These mechanisms are driven by actuators which may be pneumatic or hydraulic cylinders, hydraulic rotary actuators, or electric motors. The actuators may be coupled directly to the mechanical links or joints, or may drive indirectly through gears, chains, or ball screws. In the case of pneumatic or hydraulic drives, the flow of air or oil to the actuators is controlled by valves mounted on the manipulator. Feedback devices are installed to sense the positions of the various links and joints and to transmit this information to the controller. These feedback devices may simply be switches actuated by the robot's arm or position-measuring devices such as encoders, potentiometers or resolvers, and/or tachometers to measure speed. Depending on the devices used, the feedback data are either digital or analog.

The *control system* has a threefold function: first, to initiate and terminate motions of the manipulator in a desired sequence and at desired points; second, to store position and sequence data in memory; and third, to interface with the "outside world." The heart of the controls system is the controller. Robot controllers run the gamut from simple step sequencers through pneumatic logic systems, diode matrix boards, electronic sequencers, and microprocessors to minicomputers. The controller may be either an integral part of the manipulator or housed in a separate cabinet. It initiates and terminates the motions of the manipulator through interfaces with the manipulator's control valves and feedback devices. It may also perform complex arithmetic functions to control path, speed, and position. Other interfaces with the outside world provide two-way communications between the controller and ancillary devices. These interfaces allow the manipulator to interact with whatever other equipment is associated with the robot's task.

The function of the power supply is to provide energy to the manipulator's actuators. In the case of electrically driven robots, the power supply functions basically to regulate the incoming electrical energy and to provide the direct-current (DC) voltages required by the electronic circuits internal to the robot controller and also by the drive motors. Power for pneumatically actuated robots is usually supplied by a remote compressor which may also service other equipment in the factory. Hydraulically actuated robots normally include a hydraulic power supply as either an integral part of the manipulator or as a separate unit. The hydraulic system generally follows straightforward industrial practice and consists of an electric motor-driven pump, filter, reservoir, and, usually, a heat exchanger.

Mechanical arrangements of robots are widely varied, but most fall into one of four configurations, which are generally described in terms of their coordinate systems (see Fig. R-7). The four common

robot configurations are: *Cartesian* or *rectilinear*, *cylindrical*, *spherical* or *polar*, and *anthropomorphic* or *jointed-arm*. These configurations describe the major axes or degrees of freedom of the robot. As many as three additional degrees of freedom may be provided at the extremity of the robot arm in a unit commonly called a *wrist*. Wrist axes may include *roll*, *pitch*, and *yaw*. A mounting surface is provided on the last axis of the wrist for installation of the tool or gripper with which the robot performs its intended task. These devices are usually unique to the robot application and are therefore provided by the user.

Robots may be generally classified as *servo-controlled* or *fixed-stop* (non-servo) robots. The significant features of a servo-controlled robot are:

- The manipulator's various members can be commanded to move and stop anywhere within their limits of travel, rather than only at their extremes.
- It is possible to control the velocity, acceleration, and deceleration of the various axes as they move between programmed points.
- Generally, the memory capacity is large enough to store many more positions than a non-servo robot.
- Both continuous path and point-to-point capabilities are possible.
- Drives are usually hydraulic or electric and use state-of-the-art servo-control technology.

The significant features of a fixed-stop or non-servo robot are:

- The manipulator's various members move until the limits of travel (end-stops) are reached. Thus, there are usually only two positions for each axis to assume.
- The sequencer provides the capability for many motions in a program, but only to the end-points of each axis.
- Deceleration at the approach to the stops may be provided by valving or shock absorbers.
- It is feasible to activate intermediate stops on some axes to provide more than two positions; however, there is a practical limit to the number of such stops that can be installed.
- Drives are usually pneumatic or hydraulic.

The range of capabilities of the available robots is wide. Payload capacities run from less than a kilogram to almost 1000 kilograms. Maximum end-of-arm speed can be as high as several meters per second, although an arm velocity of about 75 cm/sec is most common. *Working envelopes* range from about .03 cubic meter (30cm × 30cm × 30cm) to about 30 cubic meters (3 m × 3 m × 3 m). *Repeatability* ranges from ±1.5mm for larger units down to ±.1mm for smaller robots.

With as many as six axes, the robot can place a

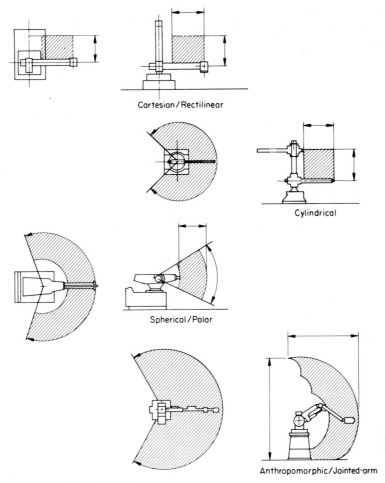

FIG. R-7 Robot configurations.

part or tool in virtually any position and orientation in its working envelope. Modern electronic controls provides for control of trajectory, velocity, acceleration, and deceleration. Large memories permit storage of more than one program and of thousands of spatial positions. Subroutines and branching are common and off-line programming with high-level language and interactive graphic simulation is becoming available. Adaptive control through external sensors (vision, tactile, force) is also emerging from the laboratory. Reliability is in the range of 97 percent.

On the other hand, the common industrial robot has some significant limitations. Robot arms have a power-to-weight ratio (lifting capacity to gross weight) of around 1 to 20; the average human arm can handle several times its own weight. Thus, on a task-for-task basis, robots tend to be larger than human workers. The industrial robot cannot travel from place to place or move freely about its workplace, although some limited mobility may be provided by placing the robot on a track-mounted, powered platform.

Basic robots lack external sensors; therefore the workplace must be structured and repeatable. Parts being handled by a robot must be presented one at a time at the same position and orientation or in a uniform array. Robot *end-effectors* lack the dexterity and adaptability of the human hand and often must be custom-designed for the specific task. Robots lack the capability for judgment and thus are unable to perform even simple visual inspection or sorting operations without peripheral devices. This combination of limitations often adds significantly to the cost of a robot installation. (See the later section, "Justification.")

Current Applications

Industrial robots are used to perform a wide variety of tasks, primarily in manufacturing operations. The most common industrial robot applications are shown in Table R-6.

Table R-6. Current Robot Applications

Application	Percentage of total installations
Welding	30
Material handling	19
Assembly	13
Machine load/unload	10
Painting and finishing	6
Casting	4
Other	18
	100%

Source: Based on data from 1982 *RIA Worldwide Robotics Survey and Directory.*

Parts Handling. Most of the simpler robot tasks involve the repeated manipulation, orientation, and positioning of objects. These are operations for which fixed-stop or non-servo robots are often as suited as the more complex servo-controlled units. In fact, for simple pick-and-place tasks involving small parts weighing 2 kilograms or less, fixed-stop robots have greater speed and precision than their servo-controlled counterparts. A number of common robotic parts-handling applications are described as follows:

Material handling is one of the most common applications of industrial robots, and operations range from very simple to very involved. Robots are used to advantage in handling heavy or fragile parts as well as parts that are very hot or very cold. Robots are used to palletize and depalletize parts, often utilizing contact sensors in the hand tooling. Material handling may involve loading and unloading moving conveyors. In some applications, one or more axes of the robot may be synchronized with the conveyor. Robots equipped with multiple tooling can handle more than one part at a time. A variety of tooling may be used, including vacuum cups, magnets, and mechanical grippers. Robots perform well in these applications. They offer advantages in handling heavy loads, reaching overhead, handling hot parts, and relieving people from tedious, repetitive, or difficult tasks.

Machine-tool loading and unloading is a growing robot application. The reliability and steady pace of the robot can significantly increase machine-tool utilization and productivity. In many cases, because of long machining cycle times, a single robot can load and unload several machines. The machines may be grouped about the robot or the robot may move from machine to machine on a traversing base. Dual-hand tooling may be used to load and unload a part at several different machines. Automatic gauging may be provided, with a robot loading and unloading the gage, which may be interfaced with the machine control for automatic tool adjustment. Spindle-orienting devices, chip blow-off systems, cycle timers, and power-actuated splash guards are machine modifications that may be required when a robot is installed. In addition, machines may have to be relocated and part feeder/orienters provided. Thus, these applications can be quite complex and so require careful planning.

Unloading die-casting machines and handling the castings and scrap are operations to which robots were first applied and, today, remain an important robot application area. The robot may merely remove a casting from the die-casting machine, placing it on a conveyor or into a container, or it may unload the casting, quench it, place it in a trimming press, and dispose of the sprue and runners after trimming. The robot may also load inserts into the dies, spray die lubricant on the dies, or ladle molten metal into the machine. A single robot may tend two die-casting machines, unloading each one alternately. Robots unloading die-casting machines can provide an excellent economic return by reducing or eliminating labor cost, decreasing scrap, and increasing the production rate of the machine.

Loading and unloading of stamping and forming presses, one of the earliest robot application areas, is being considered with renewed interest. Robots offer a means of complying with safety requirements and still have the flexibility to handle batch-run operations. They may not meet speed and accuracy requirements for some press operations; however, for press-to-press transfer and for handling large or heavy stampings, robots merit serious consideration. Vacuum systems are often used to handle parts and dual-hand tooling or dual-arm robots may be employed to increase efficiency. The major advantages of robots for press loading are related to releasing people from potentially hazardous, noisy, monotonous operations. As an alternative to other forms of press automation, robots may significantly reduce changeover time for batch-run parts.

In the investment casting or lost-wax casting process, industrial robots are used in the manufacture of shell molds. The shell molds are formed by dipping wax patterns into ceramic slurry and coating the wet slurry with sand. As many as six or more layers of slurry and sand may be applied to build up the shell to the desired thickness. Robots offer the advantages of carefully and consistently handling the shells through a series of complex motions, thereby promoting uniform shell thickness and a higher yield of good castings. Robots also significantly increase productivity through their ability to handle heavy loads. Some robots used in the production of investment casting shells are handling payloads in the range of 1000 kilograms.

Forging and heat treating are tasks where robots can relieve people from especially unpleasant working conditions. Heat, noise, dirt, smoke, heavy loads, fast pace, and monotonous routines may all be present in these operations. Robot applications in forging include die forging, upset forging and roll forging. The robots may load furnaces, forging presses, headers, and trim presses and lubricate dies. In heat-treating operations, they may load and unload furnaces and quench parts. Special attention is necessary to protect the robot from heat and shock loads: cooling of the robot's hand tooling may be required. Robots applied to these operations offer the user significant benefits not only in labor costs reduction, but also in leasing people from undesirable environments.

Plastic-molding operations involving robots include injection molding, structural foam molding, and compression molding. The robots load inserts and compression-molding charges, unload molding machines and presses, and perform secondary operations such as degating, trimming, machining, assembling, and packing. These secondary operations require die trimmers, gate cutters, and fixtures, rather than the simple hand tools generally used by human workers. Equipped with appropriate hand tooling, the robots can unload multiple-cavity molds in a single operation. They can reach into large machines that otherwise require a human operator to actually enter to unload. Robots can improve quality and reduce scrap in plastic-molding processes by operating at a consistent, optimum cycle rate.

Buffing, sanding, and polishing operations with robots involve parts ranging from brass plumbing fixtures such as faucets to stainless steel cookware and sinks. Programmable force application, continuous-path motion and complex manipulations may be required. In these applications, robots provide consistent quality and relieve workers from monotonous, fatiguing, and potentially disabling tasks.

Tool Handling. Tool-handling tasks generally require servo-controlled robots. Both point-to-point and continuous-path playback modes may be employed. A number of electrically driven robots have the capability of programmable force, as well as position, trajectory, and velocity. This capability allows the robot to exert a controlled force with a tool, thus opening up a number of new-applications opportunities. Some typical robotic tool-handling applications are described in the following paragraphs.

Resistance (spot) welding is one of the most extensive tool-handling applications of robots. It is one which often involves a number of robots, fixturing, and transfer devices integrated into a total system. It is a common joining method for light gage sheet metal, as in automobilies and home appliances. Robots are usually not quite so fast as human workers in handling spot-welding guns; however, the robots' consistent placement of welds may permit a reduction in the number of spot welds required, for the same net output.

Gas-metal arc welding (GMAW) is a robot-application area with great potential. Productivity of robot arc-welding operations may be 2 to 3 times as high as it is with people. Robot arc welding requires, however, more consistent, repeatable joint fit-up and positioning than does manual arc welding. The availability of practical, reliable joint-tracking devices, which are currently under development, will greatly increase the use of robots for these operations. This utilization will not only significantly improve arc-welding productivity, but will also relieve people from exposure to potentially hazardous fumes and from tasks that require high levels of concentration and skill.

Finishing operations with robots involve the spray application of paint, stain, plastic powder, plastic sealer, sound deadener, and a similar material. A recent robot operation is the flame spraying of metal film for the shielding of electromagnetic radiation (EMR) on plastic housings of electronic equipment. Application methods may utilize air-atomizing, electrostatic, or airless spray equipment. The robots involved in finishing operations are servo-controlled, continuous-path units, with six or seven degrees of freedom. They are hydraulically driven and intrinsically safe for use in a volatile atmosphere. Spray finishing with robots provides a number of advantages to the user. They include labor replacement, consistent quality, material savings, energy savings, reduced booth maintenance, and removal of workers from exposure to harmful or toxic substances.

Machining operations with robots are a relatively new application area. Production operations include deburring of machined parts and removal of flash from parting lines of forged and cast parts. Pneumatically or electrically driven tools are used, and the tools are usually compliantly mounted on the robot. In some cases, the robot may employ force-feedback as well. Other machining operations under investigation involve the drilling, profiling, and riveting of aircraft panels. At present, these operations require the use of drill fixtures and routing templates. The long-range objective, however, is to develop hardware and software capabilities that will do away with such machining aids. Robotic machining has the potential to eliminate what have primarily been hand operations and, eventually, costly tooling aids, too.

Combinations. There are also common robotic application areas that can involve both parts handling and tool handling. Several of these are described as follows:

In foundry operations, robots are used in a wide variety of applications in addition to die casting and investment casting. They unload core-making machines, handle cores through washing operations, and set cores in molds. They clamp and unclamp molds on pouring lines. They transfer hot castings from molding lines to shakeout machines. All these are typically parts-handling tasks. As tool handlers, robots dry and vent molds. They also remove gates, risers, sprues, and flash from castings, which may be done either by handling the part or a tool. In the foundry, an industrial robot can remove people from an environment characterized by heat, dust, smoke, noise, and, in some cases, potentially toxic materials.

Inspection is a relatively new application area, where the robot may have a passive (parts-handling) or an active (tool-handling) role. In the passive mode, the robot is used primarily as a handling device. It may load a gage or an inspection machine and then segregate or sort the parts, acting on the signals from the gaging system. In the active mode, the robot handles the measuring device itself, positioning the gage in programmed locations relative to the part being inspected. A data processing unit is often incorporated to record the gage readings for reference. Gaging devices may be either contact probes or noncontact devices, such as lasers. These robot systems can significantly increase productivity of inspection operations and assure high reliability of data as well.

Programmable assembly systems utilizing robots can effectively automate low- to medium-volume and batch-assembly operations. Assembly operations are a major use of labor in manufacturing and thus represent a robot-application area of significant economic potential. Both parts handling and tool handling are involved. A number of new, smaller, servo-controlled robots have recently been developed for use primarily in assembly operations. Tactile-, force-, and vision-sensing capabilities are being developed for this new generation of robots. In addition to robots and sensors, programmable parts-orienter/feeders, passive compliance devices, system control hardward and software, and interchangeable robot hand tooling are under development. Currently, few programmable assembly systems are in operation in production. However, research and systems development are underway at several major facilities. The potential economic benefits from labor replacement, improved quality, and increased productivity will encourage continued research and development in the assembly area.

Justification

In the justification of an industrial robot in a manufacturing environment, the major factor is economics. The robot is considered capital equipment; it is therefore expected to provide a return of capital and, the owner hopes, a profit within its useful lifetime. Factors other than economics are also sometimes cited for robot justification.

Noneconomic factors. The most common noneconomic factors are (1) increased productivity; (2) improved quality; (3) reduction of scrap; (4) performance of undesirable jobs; (5) advancement of technology; (6) competitive position; (7) management direction, and (8) safety. The following discussion of these factors discloses, however, that even the so-called noneconomic considerations are, in the final analysis, basically economic in nature.

Increased productivity through the use of a robot is, in many cases, more the result of the constant pace of the robot than of faster operation by a human. For many tasks, a human being is capable of working as rapidly as, or more rapidly than, a robot, particularly where complex motions or adaptive movements are required. The human's pace, however, tends to vary from cycle to cycle and, particularly on high-speed, repetitive tasks, fatigue will eventually reduce the person's work rate. The robot, on the other hand, will operate at a constant pace at all times. Thus, over the duration of a normal work shift, the robot's average cycle time may be less than a human's. The robot's higher productivity, measured in terms of increased parts per day, represents an economic gain.

Improved quality and reduction of scrap can result from the robot's consistent operation. In die casting and plastic molding, the constant cycle time of the robot allows die temperatures to stablize; operation without shutdown for breaks and shift changes avoids production of scrap upon restarting. In robot paint- and coating-spraying applications, a greater consistency in thickness of layers is achieved. Also, material losses due to overspray are reduced because of the increased accuracy and repeatability of the robot. Repair and rework are likewise reduced. The greater number of good parts produced per shift, avoidance of material waste and scrap, and reduction of repair needs are measurable economic gains.

Operation of a robot on an undesirable task also has economic advantages. Workers' complaints about poor working conditions such as noise, dust, fumes, heat, dirt, heavy loads, fast pace, or monotony, if unresolved, often lead to work stoppages or slowdowns, uncompleted operations, poor work quality, high labor turnover, absenteeism, grievences, or sabotage. All these problems will be reflected in higher than normal operating costs. Overtime may be required to make up production losses; rework and repair necessitate additional labor, and administrative costs are involved in processing grievances, hiring replacement personnel, and training new workers.

Advancement of technology may be cited as a reason for the introduction of a robot. Such a use, however, is commonly limited to only one or a limited number of robots in more-or-less developmental applications. The motivation here is to gain the knowledge required to implement similar robot applications in a true production setting where the usual economic criteria and measurements apply. In fact, the cost of developmental trials is often factored into the cost of the follow-on production applications.

Another consideration is *competitive position,* which has both direct and indirect economic implications. The direct economic saving is obvious: If a manufacturer can reduce the cost of producing goods by using robots, a profit or pricing advantage over competitors that do not use them will accrue. The indirect economic advantage lies in the inherent flexibility of robots. This flexibility gives a user the capability (1) to meet shifts in market demands by raising or dropping production rates on various products without increasing or decreasing the size of the work force, or (2) to introduce new products into existing manufacturing system quickly and easily, often with little change to production facilities.

A robot is sometimes justified on the basis of *management direction* without regard for economic considerations. In an effort to comply with the management directive, neither the robot nor the application may be carefully chosen. The application may turn out to be more complex than first anticipated, or the robot may not have the necessary capabilities to perform the chosen task. Aside from the obvious waste of capital, a bad experience may discourage management from further consideration of robots, even where other potentially successful (and therefore economically advantageous) applications may exist.

A robot is frequently used on an *operation that is* potentially *hazardous* to the human worker, particularly as a means of compliance with safety regulations. Such tasks include, for example, press loading or unloading; operation in toxic atmospheres, or extremes of ambient environment. Even under these strong pressures for applying robots, the astute prospective user will consider the economics of guarding or protecting the human worker as an alternative to using a robot and, other factors being equal, will usually choose the least costly approach.

Economic Factors. Generally, a potential robot application is evaluated on the economics involved, with the factors described previously as well as with projected labor cost reductions that are included in the financial analysis of the proposed installation.

Tyical cost elements of a robot installation are shown in Table R-7. These are the initial investments only. The on-going operating expenses for the robot are shown in Table R-8. For a relatively simple, stand-alone robot installation, the total initial investment will probably be about 2 to 2½ times the cost of the robot itself.

Savings will come from a number of sources, some of which are shown in Table R-7. Although the largest source of savings will generally come from a reduction in direct labor, the "noneconomic" factors previously discussed should be considered and quantified in the cost-savings analysis. If an increase in productivity can be projected for the robot, the number of parts per day can be estimated and, based upon their value, annual savings can be determined. Similarly, if quality improvement and/or scrap reduction

TABLE R-7. Typical Robot Project Cost and Saving Elements

Initial costs: capital and expense
Robot
Tooling: end-effectors, parts orienters, etc.
Engineering: application, design, etc.
Installation
Facilities rearrangements, additions, and revisions
Peripheral equipment: conveyors, containers, etc.
Equipment revisions: interfacing, controls, etc.
Training: maintenance and programming
Spare parts (initial complement) and special tools (maintenance)
Startup, debugging
Sources of savings
Direct labor: wages, fringe benefits, insurance, workers compensation, Federal Insurance Contributions Act requirements, shift premiums, relief allowances, etc. (i.e., *fully burdened labor rate*), including increases projected over the robot's life
Above-average administrative, hiring, and training for high-turnover positions
Indirect supplies and expenses: protective clothing, safety equipment, hearing and toxicology tests, etc.
Increased machinery and facility utilization
Scrap, rework, and repair
Increased productivity/throughout
Energy and other utilities
Investment tax credit
Depreciation
Supervisory costs
Inventory and work in process
Avoidance of obsolescence
Occupational Safety and Health Act compliance

Table R-8 Robot Operating Expenses

Cost per day, per robot	Large electric robot*	Large hydraulic robot†
Energy consumption	$ 2.00	$ 6.00
Hydraulic oil	-0-	2.00
Maintenance parts‡	6.62**	8.82
Maintenance labor§	15.11**	20.14
Total per day	$23.73**	$36.96
Hourly operating expense	$ 1.48**	$ 2.31

*Typical robot: ASEA IRb 60 S.
†Typical robot: Unimate 4000; Cincinnati Milacron HT3.
‡Maintenance parts allowance: $4.41 per robot, per shift.
§Labor standards: 0.645 hours per robot, one-shift, plant.
　　　　1.06 hours per robot, two-shift plant.
　　　　labor rate $19 per hour.
**Cost-estimation based on 75 percent labor and material of hydraulic robot.
Source: Based, in part, upon actual cost data accumulated by a major user of robots. The daily operating expenses were calculated for a two-shift operation, 260 days (4160 hours) per year.
Note: These costs do not include cost of capital (initial investment) for the robot installation, insurance, taxes, and similar expenses.

can be anticipated, the potential annual reduction in scrap or rework costs can be calculated. When a robot is applied on an undesirable operation prone to high labor turnover, a savings equivalent to the annual cost of hiring and training new personnel can be credited to the robot. Avoidance of overtime to make up for production losses is also attributable to the robot. Other areas of potential savings include normal costs of protective clothing, safety equipment, lighting and ventilation levels, parking, dining, washroom and locker room facilities, supervisory work loads, etc., that are inherent with human labor.

The Future

Robot installations and robot capabilities are both expected to show continued growth throughout the balance of the 1980s. Technological advances will make robots easier to implement, and will also open up opportunities for application to new tasks.

By 1990, between 70 and 90 percent of the industrial robots purchased (virtually all servo-controlled and some fixed-stop robots) will have computer controls, although most will still operate with a local controller rather than a central computer. About one-third of the robots in 1990 will be equipped with feedback sensors (mostly vision and tactile) and about 20 percent are expected to be capable of real-time adaptive decision making. Between 10 and 30 percent of the robots will be interfaced with CAD/CAM systems by 1990, and off-line programming will be almost as common as pendant-control teaching.

By 1985, bin picking, the acquisition and orientation of randomly arranged objects from a three-dimensional stack, will have reached a level of development suitable for use in factory environments.

Adaptive seam-tracking systems for arc-welding robots will reach acceptable performance levels by 1985. Interactive computer graphics systems will, by that year, allow a user to simulate robot applications in detail, checking for interferences, calculating trajectories, determining safe step velocities based upon robot arm kinematics, computing cycle times, and even generating the robot programs.

Industrial robots will become lighter and faster, while gaining greater accuracy and precision through the use of new materials, new drives, and new sensor-based feedback systems. Three-dimensional vision, scene analysis, and rudimentary mobility will provide greater flexibility for applications. By the end of the decade, robots will be performing service-oriented functions in areas of health care, law enforcement, and building maintenance, and they will likely be used in agriculture, forestry, mining, and construction as well.

See also Automation; Material handling; Office automation; Production/operations management; Technology, management implications; Therbligs.

REFERENCES

Engelberger, Joseph F.: *Robotics in Practice*, foreword by Isaac Asimov, American Management Association, AMACOM division, New York, 1980.

Hunt, H. Allan, and Timothy L. Hunt.: *Human Resource Implications of Robotics*, W. E. Upjohn Institute for Employment Research, Kalamazoo, Mich., 1983.

Susnjara, Ken: *A Manager's Guide to Industrial Robots*, Corinthian Press, Shaker Heights, Ohio, 1982.

Tanner, William R., ed.: *Industrial Robots*, vol. 1: *Fundamentals*, 2d. ed.; vol. 2: *Applications*, 2d ed., Society of Manufacturing Engineers, Dearborn, Mich., 1981.

Robotic Industries Association, *Dearborn, Michigan*

Safety and Health Management, Employee

Business employment has developed the need for specialists in the broad field of safety and health management. In general, they engage in protection of their employers' assets from loss which may result from accident, fire, or exposure of employees and members of the public to toxic substances, certain types of radiation, and noise. The common titles used in industry for these specialists are Safety Director, Occupational Safety and Health Manager, and Safety Engineer. In common practice, the term *safety engineer* has evolved into a generic term which is often used to designate safety specialists who may or may not be graduate engineers or registered professional engineers.

The yearly 100,000 accidental deaths and the $87 billion financial loss from accidents, including $32 billion from work-related injuries, have gained management's attention. These figures, coupled with occupational safety and health laws, consumer product safety laws, and environmental concerns, have had a positive impact upon the employment of safety and health specialists.

Organizational Responsibility. The duties, the titles, the reporting relationships and remuneration of safety and health specialists vary according to need. The need is a function of the size of the operation and the hazards involved. A woodworking shop with 25 employees could not normally justify a full-time safety professional, while the same type of operation with 2500 employees could. A foundry with 500 employees may be able to justify hiring a full-time safety professional, but an office operation with 1000 employees may be unable to do so.

Where an organization employs only one safety professional, the job is usually a staff position. In organizations where the services of many safety and health professionals are needed, it is common to find a line manager reporting to upper levels of management and heading up an occupational safety and health department. In large, multilocation organizations, this department may have safety and health professionals in the various locations reporting directly, but the more common arrangement is for those in the various locations to report administratively to the local line management and to have technical direction and support from the corporate headquarters' safety and health staff.

Occupational Safety Specialists. There are many technical specialty occupations in the broad field of occupational safety and health. Among them are:

Industrial Hygienist: One who is trained to recognize, evaluate, and prescribe controls for exposures to toxic substances, electromagnetic radiation, noise, and ergonomic stresses.

Health Physicist: One who specializes in protection of humans and their environment from unwarranted electromagnetic radiation.

System Safety Specialist or System Safety Engineer: One who applies appropriate practical and managerial skills to assure that a systematic, forward-looking hazard identification and control function are made an integral part of a project, program, or activity through all stages of its planning, design, production, testing, use, and disposal.

Fire Protection Engineer: One with expertise in the design and operation of facilities and management systems dedicated to the control of losses from fire and explosion.

Human Factors Engineer: A specialist in an area of knowledge and expertise, often termed *ergonomics,* who concentrates on designing products and work environments that will be most compatible with human usage and interface.

Product Safety Specialist: One with special expertise in the prevention and control of losses from personal injury or property damage caused by products. The specialty may involve design, quality control in manufacture, proper assembly, instructions and labeling for customers, product identification, recall, and legal considerations.

Fleet Safety Specialist: One who specializes in the prevention of losses arising out of the use of highway vehicles in business.

The safety and health management employee, or the safety director of the typical medium-sized organization that does not employ any of the above specialists, is expected to have enough expertise in the safety and health areas to be able to handle such problems as arise or to know where to get technical assistance.

Occupational Medical Specialists. Closely associated with the occupational safety and health manager's function are the occupational medical professionals. In larger organizations, the medical department or function is headed by an occupational physician. In some large firms, this physician heads the whole occupational safety and health function as well as the medical function. The head of the medical function usually reports directly to an upper level of management. The occupational nurses, located in the same facilities with the occupational physician, often report directly to the physician in a line-reporting relationship. In the multilocation organization, the occupational health nurses may report, administratively, to the local plant management but receive professional and technical direction from the company physician or a part-time local physician.

Professional Preparation. Prior to the 1970s, perhaps only about a dozen colleges and universities offered degree programs in occupational safety and health. The National Institute of Occupational Safety and Health (NIOSH) grants became available for developing the college and university programs about the same time the Occupational Safety and Health Administration (OSHA) was becoming active. NIOSH has established 15 Education Resource centers. Concurrently, the costs of accidents and occupation-connected illnesses were increasing rapidly. These factors stimulated a rapid increase in the number of degree programs so that in the early 1980s, some 150 United States colleges and universities were offering degree programs in occupational safety and health.

Accreditation. The American Society of Safety Engineers has developed an accreditation program, and the first accredited curriculum in occupational safety and health was offered in late 1983.

Professional Organizations. There are many professional organizations serving the safety and health professionals. It is not unusual for such professionals to be members of two or more. The principal societies include:

The *American Society of Safety Engineers,* founded in 1911 and now having 20,000 members, is the largest professional organization in the broad field of safety.

The American Industrial Hygiene Association has about 2400 members.

The *System Safety Society* is composed of about 1100 members.

The *Health Physics Society* and the *Human Factors Society* serve members of these specialty occupations.

Certification. The two primary certifying bodies in the United States are:

The *Board of Certified Safety Professionals of the Americas,* which certifies safety professionals with a broad knowledge of the many specialties in occupational safety and health.

The *American Board of Industrial Hygiene,* which certifies properly qualified industrial hygienists.

Elements of a Comprehensive Safety and Health Program. Like a business suit, each program must be tailored to fit the customer, but some elements are common to all programs in varying degrees. The following checklist will be beneficial to those developing a comprehensive occupational safety and health program and also for use in appraising existing programs. Negative responses to any of the questions may indicate a need for improvement in the program.

Executive/Upper-Management Role.

1. Does executive management recognize the need for its support of the safety program?
2. If not, has a cost-benefit analysis been made to evaluate the value of the safety program?
3. Did the cost-benefit analysis (if made) include the hidden costs of accidents that are generally considered to range from 3 to 6 times the direct cost?
4. When the need was evaluated, were intangible benefits, such as employee morale and community and customer goodwill, considered?
5. Does the company have a written statement of safety policy signed by a company executive and distributed to all employees?
6. Has executive management developed a workable safety organization, including:
   a. Definition of the responsibility and authority of principals (middle management, safety director, if applicable, medical staff, etc.)?
   b. Written reporting procedures?
   c. Safety performance standards?
   d. Safety performance as a part of the job descriptions and performance evaluation programs?
   e. A written plan for periodic review of safety program results?
7. Does executive management demonstrate support of the program by:
   a. Allocation of necessary funds to carry out the program?
   b. Recognition of better-than-average safety performance by providing for congratulatory letters, awards, and the like?
   c. Participation at safety functions, such as training meetings and accident investigations?

Middle Management / Supervisor / Shop-leader Roles.

1. Do mid-managers recognize the need to integrate safety in all their functions?
2. Does indoctrination of all workers who are assigned to new positions include company and departmental safety policy and practices?
3. Has a job safety analysis been completed for each job in the department?
4. Do the mid-managers monitor new employees

closely to ascertain that good work habits are established, including safe practices?
5. Do the managers have a written plan for routine workplace observations and inspections?
6. Is there a written plan for accident investigation by the manager?
7. Do the managers participate in professional development which updates their knowledge of occupational safety and health?
8. Do the managers provide periodic planned training to update the employees' knowledge of occupational safety and health?
9. Do the managers set a good example by personally adhering to safe practices?

The Employee's Role.

1. Do employees understand that doing the job safely is a part of doing it properly?
2. Are all employees thoroughly familiar with the job safety analyses of their own assigned areas?
3. Do employees freely report unsafe acts and conditions to management without fear of negative response?
4. Do all employees participate in periodic safety training programs?
5. Do all employees understand that rewards for good performance and disciplinary action for poor performance apply to safety as well as to other job factors?

The Safety Professional's Role. When an organization is large enough to justify a full-time safety professional, the following questions will apply:

1. Is the person assigned to the position technically qualified? That is, does the person have:
   a. Academic education with a baccalaureate degree, including mathematics, chemistry, and physics
   b. Certification as a safety professional or an industrial hygienist
   c. Experience, having worked 5 or more years in this field under qualified supervision
   d. Above-average oral and written communication skills
2. Does the position report (usually in a staff relationship) to someone high enough in the organization to command the respect of middle management?
3. Are adequate funds available for provision of training aids, safety equipment, and clerical assistance?
4. Does the safety professional engage in constant professional development to keep current on safety standards, government regulations, and the state of the art?

823

5. Does the safety professional hold frequent periodic meetings to pass along to management and employees pertinent occupational safety and health information?

6. Does the safety professional allow the line managers to totally manage safety along with the other job responsibilities in their respective areas?

Medical Facilities.

1. Have the medical facilities been established or reviewed by a qualified occupational medical doctor?

2. Where the size of the operation and nature of employment justify employment of occupational health nurses:

    a. Are the nurses qualified in occupational health, as well as being registered nurses (RNs)?

    b. Are the facilities adequately equipped?

    c. Are there written medical procedures defining which health conditions are to be treated directly and which are to be referred to outside medical facilities?

    d. Are there written procedures for response to medical emergencies and catastrophes?

3. Is there a close liaison between medical function and the safety professional or line management if there is no safety professional?

4. Are medical records kept in accordance with requirements of federal and state laws?

5. Are medical examinations used to place individuals properly throughout the organization?

6. Does the medical department know the physical requirements of all jobs in the operation?

Work Environment and Physical Hazards.

1. *Physical Plant*
   Have there been a thorough inspection and evaluation of the physical plant by a qualified safety professional, including:

    a. Layout and material flow?

    b. Stairs, walking surfaces, and exits?

    c. Material handling equipment and methods?

    d. Equipment maintenance?

    e. Fire and explosion hazard controls?

    f. Housekeeping practices and facilities

    g. Machine guarding?

    h. Electrical hazards?

    i. Boilers, pressure vessels, and elevators? Do they meet applicable standards, and are they inspected according to the applicable state and municipal codes?

2. *Occupational health hazards*

    a. Have all purchasing records been reviewed by a qualified safety professional or industrial hygienist to identify any materials that may be hazardous to health?

    b. Have material safety data sheets been obtained from suppliers for all hazardous or toxic materials being purchased?

    c. Have all work areas been surveyed by a qualified safety professional to identify areas of harmful exposure to toxic substances, radiation, noise, heat stress, or ergonomic stresses?

    d. Where exposures listed in item c have been identified, have they been evaluated by a qualified industrial hygienist or safety professional and controls instituted?

    e. Is there a written maintenance program for environmental control systems, such as dust collectors, paint spray booths, and the like?

    f. Where personal protective equipment is used, is there a program for training, fitting, and medical monitoring?

    g. Are all exposures of employees to toxic substances and radiation recorded and maintained when required by governmental agencies, such as the Occupational Safety and Health Administration?

3. *Special exposures*

    a. Are seasonal and infrequent functions, such as snow removal, major repairs, and new construction preplanned with review by a competent safety professional?

    b. Where employment involves use of highway vehicles, is there a vehicle fleet safety program designed by a competent fleet safety professional?

See also Compensation, employee benefit plans; Labor legislation; Personnel administration; Social responsibility of business.

REFERENCES

American Society of Safety Engineers: *Dictionary of Terms Used in the Safety Profession*, Park Ridge, Ill., 1981.

DeReamer, Russell: *Modern Safety and Health Technology*, John Wiley, New York, 1980.

McCormick, E. J.: *Human Factors in Engineering and Design*, McGraw-Hill, New York, 1976.

National Safety Council: *Fundamentals of Industrial Hygiene*, 2d ed., Chicago, 1979.

Peterson, Dan: *Techniques of Safety Management*, McGraw-Hill, New York, 1978.

JOHN E. RUSSELL, *Maryland Casualty Company*

Sales Management

Sales management is responsible for adding value to the organization by attaining financial objectives, contributory objectives, and market position. It achieves this added value by investing and managing the corporate resources of money, machines, materials, people, and time. The investment and management must take place within the definition of the organization's business, the policies governing the business, and the overall marketing strategy of the business through a coordinated and cooperative team effort with all other organization functions from production to engineering to research and development.

Planning Sales Growth

Sales planning is the continuous process (a series of risk-taking activities) of investing corporate resources in the ongoing business marketplace in order to satisfy client and customer needs and exploit opportunities so as to achieve the enterprise's long- and short-range objectives. The sales planning process consists of four action-oriented components: (1) structuring the planning base; (2) developing the sales organization's profiles; (3) writing the sales plan of action; (4) implementing and controlling. A sales organization, whether industrial, consumer, or service, cannot operate efficiently without a comprehensive, relevant sales plan.

Structuring the Planning Base. This component involves collecting and analyzing all the relevant data about the marketplace necessary for sales planning and decision making. The data are gathered by a six-step environmental examination. Sensitivity and response to the enterprise's environment appear in the written sales plan.

STEP 1: *Identify both the heavy-use customers of the enterprise's products and the light, or periodic, users.* The 80-20 rule, which states that generally 80 percent of a company's profitable sales can come from as few as 20 percent of the customers, remains valid. "Your heavy-user customers must determine two aspects of your sales growth planning: (1) your sales growth objectives, which will be largely dependent on the penetration you can make into heavy-user demand, and (2) your sales growth strategies, which must offer the highest value-to-price benefits to your heavy users."[1]

STEP 2: *Provide a marketing offering that heavy-user customers are willing to pay for.* The starting point is to recognize the needs of the key customers the company serves. Each customer segment (there are generally more than one) may have 15 to 25 needs that it wants satisfied. Sales management and

its sales force must resist the temptation of condensing the need list. Instead, the list should be extended and a value placed on each need as perceived by the customer. For example, does the need have high, medium, or low value in the eyes of the heavy user? Answers provide management with directional guidelines for planning, organizing, developing, and managing its sales force.

STEP 3: *Conduct a competitive audit.* This audit compares the company's marketing offering with those of the major and minor competitors. The objective is to determine the strengths, weaknesses, and uniquenesses of the company's offering versus those of the competitors as seen in the eyes of the marketplace.

STEP 4: *Search for changes in the marketplace.* Changes within an industry present the company with either an opportunity to pursue or a threat to defend against. Leaders in an industry *cause* change; followers *react* to change. Sales management and its sales force are the first to feel the impact of change. They play the important role of sounding a company's "change alarm."

STEP 5: *Identify environmental influences.* These are the changes that take place outside the industry over which sales management has no control. They are economic, political, technical, and social in character. Outside influences also come in two forms: opportunity and threat. Recognition of them will aid in the sales planning process and the development of a profitable sales plan of action.

STEP 6: *Determine industry dimensions.* These dimensions are found by diagnosing the following: total size of the industry of which the company is a member; company's share of the market in which it competes; company's share trend versus industry trend; competitor's share of market; competitor's share versus industry trends; industry trends for the various products being marketed; company's product performance versus those of the industry versus those of competition; and any other trend data that should be tracked on an ongoing basis. Until all the facts relative to the six planning steps are dug out, the sales plan of action cannot be written.

Developing the Sales Department's Three Profiles. These profiles encompass three critical factors: capability, opportunity, and performance.

The capability profile shows the sales department's strengths, limitations, and uniquenesses. Capabilities can be measured in terms of product performance, product availability, pricing, customer service, application technology, raw materials position, distribution system, financial status, personnel, etc.

The opportunity profile describes the opportunities that exist in the marketplace and those that the enterprise is capable of pursuing with a high achievement probability. Successful sales planning is always based on maximizing opportunities. Emphasis must focus on opportunity planning, which involves taking the initiative. *Caution:* Pursuit of an opportunity without the required resource and/or capabilities can result only in poor performance.

The performance profile states the sales department's record of opportunity achievement. Poor performance can be caused by one or more of the following: (1) inaccurate designation of opportunities, (2) deficiency in capabilities, and (3) ineffective management of capabilities.

Inability to assess realistically the sales department's three profiles versus those of the competition leads to the setting of unsound objectives, poorly designed sales strategies, and weak sales programming. Objective self-appraisal is a vital requirement of planning.

Writing the Sales Plan of Action. Diagnosis of the company's sales situation provides the platform on which to develop the sales plan of action.

Objectives. As the income-producing facts about the company's business are studied, sales objectives will come to light.

> There are three kinds of objectives that can add value to your sales growth. [See Fig. S-1.] The first is financial. *These objectives are the numbers that tell you how profitably you are managing your business. For this reason, financial objectives are primary objectives.* The second kind are sales objectives, *which underlie financial objectives. Sales objectives make financial objectives possible and for this reason can be regarded as contributory objectives.* Another contributory objective is the market position objective, *which underlies sales objectives.*[2]

Qualitative targets such as "Improve sales force communication," "Gather pertinent sales intelligence," "Change sales service policies," and "Introduce new credit policy" can also be established.

Primary Objectives
  1. Financial objectives
     1.1 Profit on sales
     1.2 Return on investment

Contributory Objectives
  2. Sales objectives
     2.1 Dollar sales volume
     2.2 Unit sales volume
     2.3 Share of market penetration
  3. Market position objectives
     3.1 Key customer's image of company

FIG. S-1 Hierarchy of objectives. (From Mack Hanan, Howard Berrian, James Cribbin, and Jack Donis, *Take-Charge Sales Management*, AMACOM—a Division of American Management Association, New York, 1976. Reprinted with permission.)

Criteria. When the final selection is made from a lengthy list of objectives, arriving at a manageable number is important. This can be done by considering the following criteria: (1) cost, (2) resource requirements, (3) long-term versus short-term payoff, (4) probability of achievement, (5) company's life-cycle position, (6) competitive obstacles, and (7) degree of "stretch."

Assumptions. A statement of assumptions follows the setting of objectives. Assumptions are agreed-upon forecasts about the future selling environment of the company. These assumptions become guidelines for anticipating developments that will have either positive or negative impact on the sales department's ability to achieve its objectives. Assumptions also reduce the risk of planning in a vacuum. They dictate that sales management focus on the future and also "look from the outside in" when planning.

Sales Strategies. Such strategies provide direction for sales management and the sales team. They are developed by focusing attention on the company's heavy-user customers and their needs while anticipating competitive marketing actions. Sales strategies, to produce results, must:

1. Be fixed firmly enough to operate over relatively long periods of time

2. Be identifiable and made clear in words and practice

3. Capitalize on the sales department's competence and resources, both present and projected

4. Exploit competitive weaknesses when and where possible

5. Speak to the significant needs of customers and have the customers recognize that their needs are being addressed

6. Project whatever "branded" image and posture the company wishes

7. Motivate a high degree of commitment from the personnel who have to implement them

8. Take advantage of marketplace opportunities

9. Be consistent with policies and systems of the company

Programs. The heart of the sales plan of action consists of the programs and actions that must be implemented to achieve the sales department's objectives. Each stated sales program encompasses four components: (1) What is it? (description of the program); (2) Who is to do it? (people involved and their tasks); (3) When is it to be done? (completion dates); (4) What is the estimated cost? (price tag for the program).

Dynamic and distracting business conditions, more than any other cause, require that the sales plan of action be committed to writing. Specifically, the program plan should include all the following:

1. Return-on-resource investment target

2. Individual and team responsibilities

3. Time scale for attainment of privacy and contributory objectives

4. Specified control measurement quantified in numbers and on a time scale

5. Costs established prior to investment on the basis of realistic estimates of the potential return

6. Accurate sales budgeting, the price tag placed on all the action plan programs

Implementing and Controlling. The sales plan of action should be monitored every 30-day period, every quarter, and, finally, at the year-end performance review. At each monitoring point, four controlling questions are asked: (1) What was the performance? (2) What are the reasons for plus or minus variances from the plan? (3) Was the budget adhered to? (4) What changes, if any, in the plan are called for?

Each monthly and quarterly evaluation session is also a key decision-making point. Planning decision possibilities at each review include: (1) no action required; (2) changes in environment requiring close 30-day surveillance; (3) adjusting objectives; (4) implementing contingency strategies; (5) adjusting objectives and implementing contingency strategies; (6) adjusting, adding, or eliminating tactical sales programs; and/or (7) revising the total plan.

Organizing the Sales Force

There are three prime ways of organizing a sales organization: line concept, line and staff concept, and functional concept. In order to increase the effectiveness of any of the three types of sales organization, many companies also extend the concept according to geographical coverage, product line, market served, or type of customer served.

Line Organization. In the line organization (Fig. S-2), authority flows directly from the chief sales executive to his or her subordinate and so on down the line.

Line-Staff Organization. The line-staff organization (Fig. S-3) evolves from the line organization in

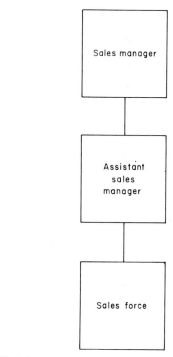

FIG. S-2   Line organization.

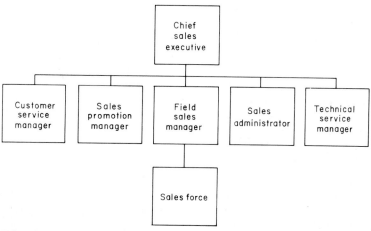

FIG. S-3   Line and staff organization.

order to extend its effectiveness. Staff assistants are added in key specialty areas. They act in an advisory or service capacity only and have no direct line authority over the sales force. Authority still flows from the chief sales executive through the field sales manager to the sales force.

Functional Organization. The functional organization (Fig. S-4) looks like the line-staff organization. The difference is that in a functional organization there may be a number of managers who give direct orders to the sales force. The functional organization is generally used in conjunction with a product structure or a geographic, market-served, or customer-type structure. It is an organizational structure that is used when line management may lack special expertise, when timesaving is vital, when heavy-user needs require special services and abilities, and/or when only a small part of the sales staff is involved with the line sales force.

Developing the Sales Force

Management know-how and leadership must be brought into play by the chief sales executive in the development of the men and women who actually make the sales. Specifically, sales management must assist each salesperson to:

1. Diagnose individual strengths
2. Diagnose individual weaknesses to reduce the development gap between performance and capability
3. Construct a development program that maximizes strengths and minimizes weaknesses
4. Commit himself or herself to a customized program work

Simultaneously, sales management must monitor and evaluate the program's effectiveness and demonstrate to each salesperson a high degree of concern for his or her personal growth.

Development Needs. Each member of the sales force has three sets of development needs: (1) technical skills (product application, technical advisor, product problem solver, trainer, service consultant, intelligence supplier); (2) interacting skills (understanding personalities, training people, reading interaction behavior, negotiating, building a climate of confidence, motivating individuals, handling groups); (3) management skills (time and territory management, budget and expense administration, customer sales planning, customer relations development, new business supervision, and self-management of talent, time, thinking, and energy).

Selling Needs. A sales force has to sell productively. The chief sales executive has the responsibility to develop this skill in the sales force. Selling effectively is a two-sided coin; one side is consultative salesmanship, the other is consultative selling.

Consultative Sales Method. This is the process of selling in a face-to-face sequential process that carries throughout the total sales transaction. It works in the following manner:

First, client needs are revealed.

Second, perceptual differences are reduced between customer and sales representative by the sales representative's putting himself or herself in the customer's place and assessing the sales situation from the customer's standpoint.

Third, customer needs are satisfied by demonstrating that the company's product/service system is superior to that of the competition and that the sales representative is a value adder.

Fourth, total customer satisfaction with the com-

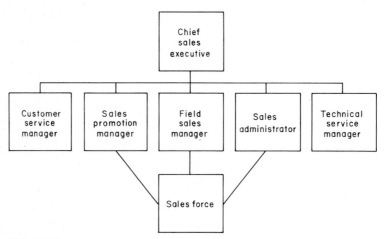

FIG. S-4 Functional organization.

pany's product/service system and with the sales representative's service is assured.

Consultative Selling. This is an operating behavior implemented by a sales representative in heavy-user customer situations. It is based on the concept that the ultimate customer benefit provided by a company and its sales team is profit improvement of the customer's business by reducing the customer's cost of doing business and/or increasing the customer's revenues. The sales representative accomplishes this by the application of six operating principles:

(1) Regards self as the manager of his or her own personal service business; (2) concerns self with the sum total of the customer's needs which his or her combined personal and corporate expertise can help make more efficient and/or more economical; (3) considers self as a marketeer knowing the markets of his or her key accounts, plus knowing the business of his or her customer's customer; (4) concentrates on profitable sales; (5) operates with a plan of action for all key accounts, and (6) provides the customer with innovative business development ideas based upon the customer's needs for new products, new service systems and new markets.[3]

Managing the Sales Force

The sales plan of action is translated into (1) external actions that are applied in key account situations and (2) internal actions, those management processes that the chief sales executive uses in managing the sales force. External and internal actions are (1) organizing territories, (2) assigning quotas, (3) establishing call patterns, (4) supervising, (5) evaluating performance, and (6) training.

Organizing Sales Territories. "Heavy-user customers are the focal point for territory organization making the best resolution of four factors: (1) types of accounts to be developed, (2) number of key accounts of each type, (3) profit value and gross sales volume of each key account, and (4) cumulative call time required to develop the full profit value of each key account."[4]

Quota Assignment. Every sales territory should carry an assigned quota indicating its contribution to profit and volume and its sales activity requirements. The three types of quotas for a territory are (1) profit quota by product line or by service; (2) dollar sales volume quota by product line or by service; and (3) activity quota in terms of demonstrations, tests, seminars, sampling, trade shows, etc.

Establishing Call Patterns. The number of calls per month is not the most important criterion in setting up territory call patterns. The best rule of thumb is to respect the 80-20 rule and call more frequently on heavy-user accounts that have high actual and potential profit value. Key accounts require intensive cultivation if full profit potential is to be realized. Sales representatives have to penetrate upward, downward, and horizontally in key accounts to achieve profit objectives. This approach requires a cumulative time-investment plan per key account. It must reflect the time required to reach and influence all decision makers and their influencers. To supplement the pattern of in-person calls, sales management and the sales representative can use telephone calls, direct mail support, letters, second-party assistance, service support calls, technical support calls, etc.

Supervising. Personal supervision, if properly applied, has high motivational value. The chief sales executive, field sales manager, and lower echelon sales management all play supervisory roles. Personal supervision aids monitoring of individual sales performance and is a major educational tool for improving individual sales performance. A personal supervision mix can include personal praise letters, on-the-job coaching, personal counseling sessions, telephone conferences, informal get-togethers, and performance review sessions.

Evaluating Performance. Evaluation of sales performance has one main objective—to help the sales representative improve. When setting performance objectives, from both a psychological and operational viewpoint each salesperson has to (1) participate in setting the objectives, (2) accept the objectives as being reasonable and attainable, (3) commit himself or herself to achieving these objectives and adhering to a plan of personal development.

Sales performance is measured from two aspects, effectiveness and efficiency. *Effective* performance accomplishes objectives within the allocated resources. *Efficient* performance achieves objectives profitably in terms of the time, materials, money, and efforts invested. Effectiveness can be evaluated by establishing (1) a sales revenue target per salesperson, (2) a sales revenue target per salesperson per day, and (3) an annual share-of-market objective. Efficiency can be evaluated by establishing (1) a monthly expense/volume ratio, (2) a monthly profit/volume ratio, and (3) a return on sales expenditure ratio (total margin of sales revenue over total sales budget).

Training. On-the-job training is a required complement to on-the-job experience. Training a sales representative in self-development requires a seven-component system: (1) one-on-one counseling, (2) job rotation, (3) special outside assignments, (4) teach-self programs, (5) training and teaching assignments, (6) club/association participation, and (7) job enrichment via increasing responsibilities and rewards.

See also Compensation, sales; Consumer behavior, managerial relevance of; Marketing, channels of distribution; Marketing management; Product planning and development; Retailing management.

NOTES

[1]Mack Hanan, Howard Berrian, James Cribben, and Jack Donis, *Take-Charge Sales Management,* American Management Association, New York, 1976, p. 107.

[2]Ibid, p. 107.

[3]Mack Hanan, James Cribben, and Herman Heiser, *Consultative Selling,* American Management Association, New York, 1973, pp. 8–10.

[4]Hanan, Berrian, Cribben, and Donis, op. cit., p. 83.

REFERENCES

Bobrow, E. C., and L. Wizenberg: *Sales Manager's Handbook,* Dow-Jones Irwin, Homewood, Ill., 1983.

Shapiro, Benjamin P.: *Managing the Sales Program,* McGraw-Hill, New York, 1977.

Welch, Joe E., and Charles Lapp: *Sales Force Management,* South-Western, Cincinnati, 1983.

HOWARD A. BERRIAN, *Berrian Associates, Inc.*

Scheduling, Short-Interval

Short-interval scheduling (SIS) is a system of scheduling work in small, timed batches. In each case the employee is told when the batch should be finished, and a record is kept of performance.

The first step in development of a system is the preparation of *activity reports*—a form of work measurement—showing how each employee spends the working day. (Figure S-5 is an activity report for a typist. The tally marks are entered by the employee.) When all employees have completed daily activity reports for a month, the amount of work each one may reasonably be expected to complete in a given time period and the total workload for each section can be determined. (The time allowed is "pure" working time: delays not attributable to the employee are excluded.)

Once reasonable time estimates have been determined, work is assigned in batches, each one accompanied by a *batch ticket* which indicates a scheduled time and upon which the employee records the start, stop, and elapsed times. In the case of clerical employees, a batch may amount to an hour's work; for others it may be larger. The supervisor checks on progress every 2 hours and enters the amount of work on the *schedule control form* which follows each employee's daily progress according to the planned output of work that is actually completed. A fourth form, the *schedule-miss chart,* shows at the end of the day which scheduled assignments were missed by each employee, the reason (e.g., shortage of supplies, poor instructions, a calculator that breaks down), and the corrective action taken.

Short-interval scheduling is most often applied to

Department: Sales order			Position: Typist		Lunch Hour	Individual: Amy Bittel	Date: Aug. 25	
Description of activity performed	How often performed	Unit of measure	8:00 A.M. to 10:00 A.M.	10:00 A.M. to 12:00 A.M.		1:00 P.M. to 3:00 P.M.	3:00 P.M. to 5:00 P.M.	Totals
			OUTPUT					
Type receipt forms	Daily	One page	///				/	3
Type inquiry letters	Daily	Form letter	/	//				3
Type envelopes	Daily	10 business envelopes	/				#####	6
Handle telephone calls	Daily	Call			////			4
Type order record cards	Weekly	10 cards		##### ///		##### ##### /		19
File order record cards	Weekly	100 cards					/	1
Cut form-letter stencils	Monthly	Stencil						0
Make copies on copying machine	Daily	1 piece 5-10 copies	/	//				3

FIG. S-5 Activity report for short-interval scheduling.

clerical work, but it has been used also for production and especially for maintenance.

See also Forms design and control; Paperwork simplification; Production planning and control; Records management; Systems and procedures.

REFERENCES

Batie, B. N.: "Short-Interval Scheduling," *Management World,* June 1973, pp. 22–23.

Bittel, Lester R.: *What Every Supervisor Should Know*, 5th ed., McGraw-Hill, New York, 1985.

Fein, Mitchell: "Short Interval Scheduling: A Labor Control Technique," *Industrial Engineering,* February 1972, pp.14–21.

Lester R. Bittel, *James Madison University*

Search and Recruitment, Executive

Executive search is a specialized management consulting service provided to corporate organizations, not-for-profit institutions, and governmental bodies, for a fee, to help them recruit management talent for specific executive positions. The consultant works on assignment to find executives for the client—not to find executive positions for individuals—and the fee is always paid by the client organization.

Like management consultants, accountants, and lawyers, executive search consultants charge for professional services rendered, plus expenses. A retainer allows search consultants to devote the time and resources necessary to complete a search objectively and to locate the best possible candidates.

Typically, the search process includes the following steps: (1) meeting formally with the client to determine the specifications of the executive position, (2) identifying prospective candidates, (3) interviewing and evaluating the most likely prospects, and (4) recommending the best two or three candidates. The client makes the final choice.

Emergence of Executive Search. Executive search as a profession is a post-World War II phenomenon. After 5 disruptive years of war, American industry faced the major task of identifying the executive talent required to rebuild the economy. As a natural extension of their organizational and auditing functions, management consultants and accounting firms were often asked to assist corporate clients to find the managers they needed. The skills required to evaluate executives are unique, and as requests became increasingly frequent, executive search emerged as a professional service in its own right. For many management consultants and accountants, however, search presented potential conflicts of interest. Some withdrew from the business they had created and others set up separate subsidiaries devoted to search. In this period, several major firms were organized specializing exclusively in executive recruiting.

Corporations quickly recognized the emergence of a new management tool and, as a result, executive search went through an initial surge of growth in the 1960s. In the 1970s, it entered a major expansion phase. The postindustrial society had emerged, creating a worldwide demand for competent executives in industrial operations, in financial and service institutions, and in the public sector. Corporations could no longer fill their management requirements by tapping the traditional "old-boy" network. They found that the most efficient way to recruit top managers was to engage the services of professional search consultants. Today, the four leading executive search firms each have annual revenues, from their domestic and international practice, of more than $20 million. Korn/Ferry International's yearly revenues approach $50 million. Other firms with revenues of more than $20 million each are Russell Reynolds, Spencer Stuart, and Heidrich & Struggles.

Corporate Use of Services. While approximately 75 percent of all executive vacancies are filled by promotion from within, even the best corporate planners cannot foresee all management needs. Economic and industry conditions change at a faster rate than corporations can develop internally the executive talent they require. Situations arise that call for a particular type of individual who is not available from within. The need to tap outside sources for top management is a positive indicator that an organization is evaluating itself realistically and determining ways to provide the human resources necessary to achieve its objectives.

Organizations seek the assistance of search consultants in order to save time, to preserve confidentiality, to obtain access to the greatest possible choice of candidates, and to have professional counsel in making the selection of the best candidate. Identifying candidates is a time-consuming process which, when done within an organization, can disrupt and distract the normal flow of work, often of the most important people in the firm. For search consultants, on the other hand, looking for executive talent is a full-time job, and they can provide the expertise to expedite the process. They can, for example, screen candidates, not only for specific skills and attributes, but also for the character and style that will make them compatible with the client, an appraisal frequently best made by an objective third party. Confidentiality is often a prime consideration, and search organizations can assure proper security. Finally, they not only offer an efficient, objective, and discreet method of locating the right person, but they can also tap a larger pool of talent than an individual organization as well as evaluate internal candidates.

The Search Process. Unlike employment agencies that find jobs for individuals, executive search firms work exclusively for organizations to find indi-

viduals for specific management positions. Typically, search firms follow a step process:

1. *Specification development.* The search firm first confers with the client to determine the specifications of the position, the required background of experience, and desired personality traits. Discussion of the client's industry, overall management needs, and company direction helps to clarify the assignment. Armed with all the relevant information, the search consultant prepares a detailed letter to the client which (*a*) includes a thorough job specification for the client's approval and (*b*) confirms the fee arrangement, typically 33⅓ percent of the first year's total cash compensation, plus out-of-pocket expenses at cost. A timetable and a search deadline may also be established at this time.

2. *Candidate search.* The next step is to locate potential candidates, who are identified in a variety of ways. Larger firms have research departments and computer data banks of executive profiles which can be scanned quickly to identify candidates with the desired background and experience. More important, however, are the many other sources developed over years of experience. These include industry and personal contacts, trade associations, etc.

3. *Candidate evaluation.* Working closely with the client and utilizing the search sources, the consultant develops a list of qualified prospects who meet the client's specifications and then selects the most promising to interview. Interviews reveal crucial information about each prospective candidate's managerial qualifications, track record, motivation, personal characteristics, and the likelihood of compatibility with the client.

4. *Candidate selection.* During the course of the search and evaluation, the consultant confers regularly with the client to report progress and to provide in-depth reports on the most promising candidates. Interviews are then arranged between the client and the top candidates. The client makes the final choice; the search consultant usually assists in negotiating the compensation and benefits package.

Current Trends. The search profession continues to evolve to meet the changing needs of society and business. In recent years, for example, the position of board director has been added to the standard group of top executive posts that recruiters are asked to fill. Independent and qualified directors are sought by companies, but increased responsibilities, liabilities, and much more demanding schedules have made it hard for corporations to attract and keep the top-quality directors they want. At the same time, many firms are seeking directors with highly specific experience and credentials. In addition, there is an increasing demand for individuals with a depth of expertise that qualifies them to fill very specialized senior management positions. Korn/Ferry International, for example, has established 10 specialty divisions, including board services, energy/petrochemicals, entertainment, financial services, government/not-for-profit institutions, health services, hospitality/leisure, real estate/construction, and retailing/fashion.

See also Compensation, executive; Consultants, management; Employment process; Manager, definition of; Personnel administration.

REFERENCES

Association of Executive Recruiting Consultants, Inc.: *Guidelines for Executive Recruiters*, New York, 1976.

Kennedy, James H.: *The Handbook of Executive Search*, Consultant News, Fitzwilliam, N.H., 1974.

Korn/Ferry International: *Korn/Ferry International's Executive Profile: A Survey of Corporate Leaders*, UCLA Graduate School of Management, 1979.

————, *National Index of Executive Vacancies*, published quarterly.

LESTER B. KORN, *Korn/Ferry International*

Security Management

Security management can be understood as the selection, employment, and supervision of human and material resources in the prevention or reduction of losses suffered from pure-risk loss events.

Pure-risk loss identifies those events which, should they occur, can result only in loss and never in gain. Examples of pure-risk losses are those resulting from crime, infidelity, disaster, catastrophe, civil disturbance, conflicts of interests and insurrection, war, or *force majeure.*

Human and material resources include (1) executive, supervisory, and administrative personnel actually employed by, or in direct support of, the security effort; and (2) items of equipment or supply employed for the same effort. Personnel directly employed in security include managers and functional supervisors, guards, investigators, receptionists, couriers, technicians, fire fighters, and fire prevention engineers, as well as clerical workers. Items of material and equipment include locks and keys, alarm and detection systems, photographic and television surveillance, perimeter and other barriers, protective and deterrent lighting, automated or semi-automated vehicle and personnel access controls, investigative equipment, vehicles, and communications gear.

In addition to the direct employment of staff and material resources, organizations with a comprehen-

sive understanding of establishing and maintaining a secure environment utilize all employees, particularly the line-management group. Line managers play a major role in the preliminary identification of loss exposures and in the successful implementation, within their respective units, of approved security countermeasures. First-line supervisors assure that workers under their control understand departmental and unit security objectives and contribute to their achievement. Individual workers, at all levels, learn and apply the security requirements as they relate to each worker's task. This unified approach is generally achieved through substantial "security awareness" training—on a sustained basis—throughout the organization.

Three-Phase Approach

Security management is a specialized area of enterprise management that supports the prime objectives of the organization by eliminating or reducing economic and social costs which might otherwise be expected from the occurrence of loss events. It is judged or evaluated, in large part, on investment (or cost-benefit) theory—how much has been saved or avoided in losses at what cost of resources. In implementing effective security programs, the security management activity is expended in three prime areas: (1) loss-risk assessment, (2) countermeasures planning and operation, and (3) program evaluation.

Vulnerability Analysis. The principal effort of the loss-risk assessment effort is in *vulnerability analysis.* This procedure consists of identifying those loss-risk events which could occur, assigning a frequency rate or occurrence probability to each such event and estimating the criticality or probable impact if the event does occur. Impact is measured in dollars of cost.

1. To identify loss-risk events, the combined skills of the security or assets-protection professional and the concerned line or staff manager are required. Working together, these managers (and others in their respective units) review the nature of the activity in the department or unit being analyzed, the type and amount of assets involved there, the exposure of those assets to loss-risk events springing from the environment, the nature of the asset, the style and level of operations, and all other relevant factors. For example, the risk event of theft is a concern in organizational units that process cash, precious metals, drugs and controlled substances, or other high unit cost or popular-appeal items. Flood damage and related business interruption would also be a concern for data processing operations installed in the ground or below grade areas of a structure located in a flood plain or other area with flood history. Fire and related damage would be a major concern in hydrocarbon refining and pipelining. Generally there is a wide mix of obvious, and not-so-obvious, loss-risk exposures in every enterprise. As a consequence, a high degree of competence is required to identify all those of significance.

2. Once the loss-risk events have been identified, they must be assigned some frequency rate (or probability of occurrence) so that the effect of multiple occurrences can be properly weighted. In considering frequency, various generic probability or frequency factors are used to direct the data collection. Thus, *physical factors* include the composition, size, shape, and physical environment; *procedural factors* include the way in which the exposed assets are handled or processed, the way in which accountability is maintained, and the general quality of record keeping; *sociopolitical factors* include the economic and demographic character of the general location, the type and quality of local government, especially police protection and law enforcement, type and quality of local fire protection, locally perceived identity of the enterprise (a popular local employer or a willful industrial polluter, for example); *historical factors* include the enterprise's own past history of pure-risk losses and known loss histories of like firms or the industrial or area loss records. The word "industrial" as used here does not imply limitation to industry as such. The same approach and management techniques are applicable, styled a bit differently, to government, not-for-profit, and general commercial entities.

3. As data are collected about exposed assets in the various categories, they are reduced to some convenient format to facilitate estimates of frequency. Matrix analysis, in which a particular asset is considered in terms of the various generic factors, is one method of presentation and is outlined below.

Criticality Assessment. *Criticality* is the net-cost impact of a loss event. Costs are both economic and social, although the latter are quite difficult to quantify. A good example of a social cost is the emotional and psychological effect of the assassination or kidnapping of a key employee. For measuring economic impact, the elements of permanent replacement, temporary substitute, consequent or related loss, and lost income opportunity should be included. Replacement or substitute costs are specific to the asset or assets lost. Temporary substitute costs usually add to permanent replacement. Consequent or related losses occur when the prime loss (say, of a production facility) results in later additional losses (e.g., idle time, contract penalties, debt service). Lost income opportunities are related to, but may often be separated from, consequent losses.

Matrix Analysis. A defined loss event should be given some combined rating for (1) its frequency rate (or probability level), and (2) its impact, so that a weighted value can be assigned. So rated, the loss events are those that will, or may, occur before consideration is given to security countermeasures. The universe of such weighted risks can then be presented as plot-points on a matrix which measures criticality (dollars of loss) on one axis against frequency (times of occurrence) per base period, usually a fiscal or calendar year, on the other. A smoothed curve will then show probable loss impact for the organization for that year.

Countermeasures Planning. In *countermeasures planning,* the asset protection or security professional identifies all those personnel, material, and procedural items which can be used or applied to eliminate or reduce the loss risks. These will include all or some of the following elements: *personnel,* consisting of guards, investigators, fire fighters, fire prevention engineers, technicians, receptionists, couriers, clericals; *material,* including closed circuit television, photography, fire detection and alarm systems, intrusion alarms, "panic" or emergency assistance alarms, radios, fences, gates, locks and keys, lighting systems, fire protection, and security vehicles, badges and passes, vaults, safes and storage containers, barriers and shielding; *procedures* such as access control for pedestrians and vehicles, document control and accountability, identification, property removal, loss reporting, key issues, and accountability. To the extent that they are useful or necessary, the basic objectives of the security program can be expressed in *security policies.* These are best issued by the chief executive or chief operating officer, although they will usually be drafted and prepared by the security staff or other staff persons. Areas in which enterprise policy should be stated to create a common baseline for implementing security procedures and programs include personnel screening, admittance to facilities, protection of proprietary information and intellectual property, use of identification devices, use and removal of company (or agency) property, loss reporting, and use or possession of contraband or illegal items or materials. Each enterprise must, of course, define its own list of required security policies.

Selection Criteria. In determining which countermeasures to use of all those available, attention should be paid to systems theory and to optimizing return on investment. Systems theory suggests that when relevant, different countermeasures are combined to deal with an array of security risks, they should be mutually supportive and complementary so that when employed together as a system, they offer greater protection than could be provided by their uncoordinated use. In other words, design of a security system should be integrated so that its elements enhance one another. For example, a television surveillance camera can provide not only detection of intrusion, but also the movement of materials or fire.

Optimizing Investment. In optimizing return on investment, the use of *fault tree analysis* is recommended. This analysis assesses the various individual risks and their combined effect in the total risk environment. Each set of conditions precedent to the ultimate risk event is stated so that essential combinations can be observed. When a loss event depends upon a number of precedent conditions that must exist simultaneously, the countermeasure selected must be specific to break the "and" connection. In the classical fire triangle, for example, there must *simultaneously* be (1) fuel, (2) ignition source, and (3) oxygen. Elimination of *any one of the three* will prevent or extinguish fire. Which one to eliminate, in a given case, would be dictated by required reliability and least cost. This technique, when applied to all security loss risks, will generally produce an integrated system of (1) the fewest necessary countermeasures, (2) at the required degree or reliability, and (3) at the least cost consistent with risk reduction objectives. As a general rule, the countermeasures arrays are considered in three primary domains: protection of persons, protection of physical assets, and protection of information or intellectual assets.

Countermeasures Evaluation. Once selected and implemented, security countermeasures must be evaluated as to their integrated effectiveness. Return on investment (ROI) analysis is helpful here to the extent it can be employed. It adds (1) the amount of losses avoided (or *probably* avoided under probabilistic formulas) to (2) the amount of post-loss recoveries actually obtained (as with recaptured inventories, or through payments or promises to pay by embezzlers or forgers, etc.); it then divides their total by (3) the cost of the program for the base period. The result is the return-on-expenditure ratio. Any ratio higher than 1 is considered desirable, the higher the better. Thus, a security program which avoided $250,000 in otherwise probable losses, recovered $75,000, and cost $200,000 to maintain for a year, will have a ratio of $\frac{(\$250,000 + \$75,000)}{\$200,000} = 1.625$. In economic terms, this program yields 62.5 per cent more than it costs. Other benefits, including the reduction of social costs, can also be given appropriate weight in the evaluation.

See also Computer security; Product liability; Risk analysis and management; Safety and health management, employee.

REFERENCES

Healy, R. J.: *Design for Security,* John Wiley, New York, 1983.

————, and T. J. Walsh: *Principles of Security Management,* Professional Publications, Long Beach, Calif., 1983.

Protection of Assets Manual, a continuing subscription service from The Merritt Co., Santa Monica, Calif.

TIMOTHY J. WALSH, *Harris & Walsh Management Consultants, Inc.*

Shareholder Relations

Shareholder relations is an essential management function for publicly held companies. The current economic environment, especially the trend of increasing tender offers, proxy contests, and leveraged buyouts among large corporations with many shareholders, has contributed to a reevaluation of many aspects of the function.

The philosophical underpinning of corporate shareholder relations programs has been that shareholders are an important source of capital and that management operates in the shareholders' interests and pursuant to the shareholders' wishes. However, the tenets of this philosophy have become increasingly subject to challenge.

Corporate shareholder relations efforts are generally directed at professional investors, such as security analysts, portfolio managers, and the financial officers of institutions and funds. Because this audience is relatively small, most corporations maintain direct contact, have a clear picture of its needs, and communicate effectively.

Information on institutional share ownership is relatively accessible and well organized (the Securities and Exchange Commission, or SEC, mandates 13G filings by most institutional investors on a quarterly basis). A number of commercial organizations, including Computer Directions Advisors, Inc., of Silver Spring, Maryland, collect this information and sell it in a variety of useful formats. (A company may, for example, analyze its own institutional holdings in the context of the institutional holdings of competitors in the same industry.)

This discussion will concentrate on communications to and from the segment of corporate ownership that is more difficult to identify and understand—individual shareholders.

A Variable Population. The individual shareholder is often ignored in these days of heavy institutional trading, and some executives question the need to pay any attention at all to this segment of their shareholder population. They point out that individual investors have been steadily leaving the market since 1970. The New York Stock Exchange reported that from early 1970 to mid-1975, the United States shareholder population dropped from 30.8 million investors to 25.3 million, an 18 percent decline. Stock held by individuals as of mid-1975 accounted for 52.7 percent of the total market value of all shares, down from 64.1 percent in 1970. But the number of individual shareholders rose nearly 20 percent between 1975 and 1980 to 30.2 million. In 1982, the New York Stock Exchange estimated the number of shareholders at 32.2 million (including those who hold shares through mutual funds). Experts believe the number of "active" individual investors (those who trade five or more times a year) is much smaller—probably about 1 million.

Benefiting from Successful Shareholder Relations. Individual investors can play an important role in a corporation's stability and well-being. The need to raise capital is a key concern for American businesses, and the individual shareholder's role in this area is significant.

The classic argument for the influence of shareholders is that the individual is one of the best prospective investors for a company's stock: the individual shareholder can provide liquidity in the marketplace, serve as a loyal ally in the case of unfriendly raids, provide important additional capital, and be a good customer, a loyal employee, and a supporter of corporate goals in the political and economic arenas.

However, as more individuals profit in takeover situations, evidence is growing that shareholder loyalty has its limits, particularly in the face of a generous cash offer.

It is also clear that the revolution in financial services is changing the shareholder-broker relationship; shareholders now have access to a wide and confusing array of financial products, which may or may not include equities. For this reason alone, many corporations have concluded that a relatively aggressive communications effort is necessary just to keep the attention of the investors they have.

Many companies have instituted active programs to communicate with this vital financial audience. Those that have not can find themselves in a proxy or tender fight and not understand why shareholders are not loyal to the company.

A basic concept in any well thought out shareholder relations program is first to find out who they are, why they are interested in the company and what makes them happy and/or unhappy, and then to make an effort to gain their trust and regard. As one would expect, different types of companies attract widely different shareholder populations.

Identifying the Stockholder Population. A report by the American Society of Corporate Secretaries indicates that fewer than 10 percent of the nation's corporations have undertaken stockholder identification studies.

Shareholder Profile. Alert companies attempt to build an in-depth profile of their individual shareholder community. They want to know, for example, whether their shareholders are primarily professionals or mostly unsophisticated individuals, as well as their geographic distribution, stability, and turnover. A company might consider the following data important in efforts to improve its shareholder communications program:

- What makes owners buy, sell, and hold stock in the corporation. For example, do they have specific investment goals or price objectives?
- How do they feel about the company's management—its dividend policies, products, and communications? Do they have misconceptions in these areas that can and should be corrected?
- To whom do the shareholders listen for advice on their investments?

Surveys. One simple approach to finding answers to these and other questions is to ask the stockholders through surveys.

In the survey approach, questionnaires tailored to a company's specific situation are mailed to a random sample of stockholders. When the questionnaires are returned, a smaller random sample is selected for telephone interviews in more depth. The sample size is important. It must be large enough to ensure representative and reliable results but not so large as to require an inordinate amount of time to complete the analysis. The survey questions should be objective. In sophisticated studies, the questions are designed to allow computer analysis of the responses. These refined approaches allow correlation between different data, providing answers to such questions as, "Do large shareholders feel differently from small shareholders about certain issues?"

Reply Cards. A simpler procedure is to include a stockholder reply card or questionnaire in regular shareholder mailings, particularly the annual report. While this approach is less expensive, it produces results that are less statistically valid.

In any case, merely asking shareholders their opinion often has a salutary effect on their view of the management and the company.

Reaching "Street Name" Holders. The shareholder population most difficult to reach is the group termed *"street name"* holders—that is, those stockholders whose stock is held in the name of a brokerage house. Twenty percent or more of all outstanding corporate stock is now held in street names, frustrating companies seeking more knowledge about their stockholders.

Because these individuals cannot be identified, companies have no way of communicating with them except through the holder of record. This often means a delay in communications, which can be a major problem in proxy or tender contests. One technique to reach these individuals is to include a return postcard in regular mailings (annual or quarterly reports) to street name holders. These cards ask the owners to identify themselves to the company in order to receive information directly and may also ask the number of shares held and date of purchase.

Under revised rule 14b-1(c) of the Securities Exchange Act of 1934, which will take effect in January 1986, brokers must provide a company, upon its request, with the names, addresses, and securities positions of customers who are "beneficial" owners of the company's stock and who have not objected to disclosure of such information. The company must, of course, use this information exclusively for purposes of corporate communications.

It remains to be seen how many beneficial shareholders will permit their names to be forwarded. Brokerage firms and transfer agents have historically opposed disclosure of this information for a variety of reasons—including their belief that these lists of customers have proprietary value. They are not likely to encourage strongly individual shareholders to disclose their names.

Transfer Sheet Analysis. Another way for companies to gain insight into which of its shareholders are buying and selling is to regularly study transfer sheets supplied to the company by transfer agents. The Depository Trust Company (CEDE & Co.) will, for a fee, supply a corporation, on a monthly basis, with a list of depositors who hold stock in the company.

It is difficult to identify trends within a single transfer system. However, several companies offer a clearinghouse function to evaluate transfers of many companies, pooling information gained in the examination of each. This computer-assisted process has ascertained the identity of an institutional investor accumulating shares.

Dividend Reinvestment. Automatic dividend reinvestment programs—offering shareholders the option of automatic investment of dividends in additional shares—have two advantages for corporations: (1) They help to regain part of the money paid out as dividends and (2) they promote shareholder goodwill. In some cases, shareholders pay a service charge for the transaction to the bank administering the plan. Where companies administer their own plans, stockholders usually purchase the additional shares at no cost—an attractive saving for investors. A few firms offer added enticements, such as permitting shareholders to reinvest cash dividends in new stock at a discount or allowing them to contribute cash toward the purchase of shares.

Participation in such plans ranges from 5 to 40 percent of a stockholder population and is usually favored by shareholders who own 100 to 300 shares, those to whom the investing convenience and commission savings are most attractive. These programs are being expanded by many companies to reach employees and customers.

Communicating Effectively with Shareholders. Modern business reporting is complex and demanding; a management has the responsibility to get across the most significant facts to its shareholders in order of importance. It is not enough merely to fulfill the regulatory requirements.

Corporate communications to shareholders must be open, giving the bad news as well as the good. Companies that communicate clearly, accurately, and thoroughly when things are bad find it easier to win support and influence with stockholders.

Annual Reports. The annual report is a corporation's most important communication tool. Many reports are aimed at security analysts and other professional investors, a group with whom corporate planners and writers usually are well acquainted. The result is that often the individual may not understand the report. Preparing an annual report that presents easily absorbed data in plainly written prose is not impossible. A number of approaches will increase an annual report's effectiveness and readability. Among them are:

- Using the report as an educational tool on such topics as financial statements, government regulations, or current national issues
- Combining the annual report with the form 10-K (the annual report a company files with the Securities and Exchange Commission) and supplementary statistical publications
- Printing interviews with members of such key audiences as security analysts, stockholders, and customers

Until very recently, the SEC took the position that annual reports should not be subject to regulation. However, in 1982, it adopted a system of "integrated disclosure," which imposed a number of specific disclosure requirements on the annual report. As a result, such reports today tend to look more alike than in prior years.

These disclosure requirements tend, again, to serve the needs of the more sophisticated investor. The SEC formally endorsed a "trickle-down" philosophy of annual report disclosure, under which the sophisticated investors "translate" the sophisticated information and pass it along in simpler form to other types of investors. Adoption of this philosophy has largely discouraged company efforts, common in the late 1970s, to write annual reports that would be easily understood by even those without in-depth understanding of economics or accounting. Nevertheless, the annual reports that win prizes each year and are widely admired seem to be those that provide at least some explanation and interpretation of financial information for nonprofessionals.

Most studies indicate that shareholders spend a very limited time reading an annual report. All agree, however, that at the top of the list of most frequently read report sections are the financial highlights and the company president's letter. The president's letter is a good opportunity to present the company's story. It should be brief and easy to read. More important, it should be candid and informative. It should, in general, be forward looking, not a mere report on the past year. For those shareholders who do not read the other sections, the president's letter should provide the significant data and leave the readers with a feeling that problems are being dealt with and that the company is well directed. It should set forth the company's objectives for the next year and how management views the company's future.

Interim Reports. Traditionally, quarterly reports to shareholders disclose only limited information. Although there are no rules stating that a company must issue a quarterly report to stockholders, the SEC has expanded the requirements for the quarterly 10-Q form (the report a company must file with the commission). As the 10-Q form has gained more attention from the SEC, the quarterly report to stockholders has grown in importance. Stockholders, too, are seeking detailed and informative interim data. New approaches include preparing quarterly features on new products and developments, utilizing the four quarterly reports together to yield an annual report, adding questions and answers from analyst meetings, and reprinting management speeches.

Management Letters. Just as companies write letters to potential customers, they might consider a similar effort to gain stockholder trust and regard. A company going through a difficult time, for example, may write brief letters to stockholders describing problems and outlining plans to solve them. Companies seeking approval from stockholders for a merger have sent out thank-you notes to shareholders who return proxies. Such unorthodox approaches receive surprisingly favorable comments from stockholders.

Welcoming letters to new shareholders offer another effective communication tool for management. These letters should be short, thank the individual for his or her support, and enclose the latest informational material about the company.

Personal Contact. In a stockholder relations program, there is no substitute for direct meetings with the stockholders. The company's regular annual meeting presents the most effective opportunity for such personal contact. Many corporate executives dread this meeting because it provides a forum for individuals who advocate a variety of corporate or social changes. Changes in Rule 14a-8 of the Securities Exchange Act of 1934, becoming effective in 1984, will reduce (but not eliminate) this kind of conduct and perhaps restore some balance to the annual meeting discussion.

Some companies hold their annual meetings in a different location each year in an effort to reach more shareholders. The cities are chosen according to their concentration of stockholders and location of company facilities. Another approach is to hold special regional stockholder meetings—inviting both street name and beneficial owners whenever possible. One interesting device used to promote a good turnout at these meetings is to engage retired employees to make invitation follow-up calls. Incidentally, the retiree group has another value; it can be mobilized for proxy solicitation.

AT&T has taken the personal touch even further. Representatives of the company have been calling on shareholders, at home and at work, since 1956—some 50,000 visits a year. The objective is to answer questions about the company and foster a feeling of belonging among its owners.

Telephone contact is also a good way for a company to maintain personal contact with its shareholders. A good time for calls is after the regular annual meeting or following the announcement of a major development, such as a dividend increase or a stock split. In addition to answering questions, company representatives can ask stockholders if they are satisfied with the company's performance and direction of its communication efforts.

Other Shareholder Communication Tools. Companies can use a few other communication techniques to reach shareholders. Some companies publish Political Action Committee (PAC) newsletters in an attempt to develop a politically active shareholder constituency. Occasionally, companies distribute product samples or product literature to shareholders. Advertising can reach shareholders but is more often used to reach the general investing public and is generally most effective when it simply builds name recognition for the company. In addition, companies increasingly are using public relations techniques to increase the visibility of company officials in the media (for example, when the chairperson gives a speech) and among shareholders through mailings of reprints of such talks.

Summary

Shareholder relations is, at best, an inexact science. The better programs are those in which the activities are planned, the messages to shareholders are refined to a few key points, and the overall effort is monitored to maintain effectiveness.

See also Boards of directors; Boards of directors, legal liability guidelines; Financial management, capital structure and dividend policy; Ownership, legal forms of; Political action committees (PACs); Public and community relations.

REFERENCES

Marcus, Bruce W.: *Competing for Capital in the '80s,* Quorum Books, New York, 1983.

New York Stock Exchange: *The New York Stock Exchange Fact Book,* New York, published annually.

Public Relations Society of America, Investor Relations Section: *Investor Relations Report,* published quarterly.

The SEC, the Stock Exchange and Your Financial Public Relations: Hill and Knowlton, New York, 1979.

RICHARD E. CHENEY, *Hill and Knowlton, U.S.A.*
ROBERT W. TAFT, *Hill and Knowlton, U.S.A.*

Simulations, Business and Management

The management (or business) game is essentially a pedagogical device that enables the individual to learn by participation and involvement. The simulation—or game—is a contest among participants, either as individuals or as teams, who must follow a set of rules and who aim to win the contest. The game is successful when the participants have obtained a better understanding of that portion of reality simulated within the game model.

Learning involves three successive steps:

1. Acquiring the *common language* and the facts expressed in the game

2. Learning the *process* simulated within the game model, including restrictions

3. Understanding the relative trade-offs—the costs, the advantages, and the disadvantages—required of the different *strategies* and *alternatives*

Games are usually conducted in three phases: (1) preplay description and briefing of the rules; (2) play itself—in sequential, discrete, and compressed periods of time; and (3) postgame critique of the decisions and consequences, possibly with participant suggestions to improve the realism of the game. Because of the competitive nature of the game, participants are usually motivated to learn by their desire to win.

Early Developments

Gaming has been used for some time to facilitate training in the military. From simple chesslike games employed in India many centuries ago to week-long simulated worldwide games employed today, military gaming has provided a rich antecedent to management and business gaming.

From the beginning, war games involved two or more teams of participants competing for the control of an area. By the mid-1800s, all the elements of modern war gaming had been developed: the inclusion of environmental factors, the passage of time, and the detailed simulation of activities.

The first business game, using a mathematical

model and a computer to facilitate calculation, was conceived in the mid-1950s by Frank M. Ricciardi, who was then manager of the finance division of the American Management Association (AMA). Following a visit to the Naval War College at Newport, Rhode Island, to see an existing war game facility, he secured a commitment within the AMA to develop a "business war game." The first model of the AMA game evolved early in 1956 and was tested for a year by staff members.

On May 2, 1957, under the aegis of the AMA, 20 company presidents took part in the first management game ever staged for corporate executives. Each team received some initial basic operating information, including the dollar resources available for expenditure. The five companies were assumed to manufacture a single identical product whose price was specified within the $5 to $10 price range in direct competition against one another. At the outset, each team had exactly one-fifth of the market, identical dollar value in assets, and the same range of available choices. Each team made decisions on a quarterly basis and decided how much to spend over the next period for production, marketing, research and development, and additional plant investment. The price for the product was also specified. After making its decisions, each team received a quarterly operating statement indicating the number of units sold and the costs incurred. They repeated the cycle, quarter by quarter, until the equivalent of three business years had elapsed. This initial game, like many games still in use today, concluded with a critique session wherein each group had the opportunity to compare its results with those of its competitors and to contrast strategies. In the initial AMA game, no winner was named, although the team which was most successful in increasing its assets was generally considered to have won.

Within a year, several games following the AMA simulation were introduced in various universities and other settings across the country. The University of California (Los Angeles) and the International Business Machines Corporation developed and made extensive use of two noteworthy games.

Features and Types of Games

A management game incorporates a mathematical model or replica of reality which establishes a set of relationships. The game does not *duplicate* reality but captures the *essence* of reality while remaining as simple as possible.

Features. Games usually reproduce reality through a compression of time or other resources. Like earlier games, some present-day games require decisions which then project over a quarter. Four

such decisions obviously represent a year in the existence of the firm. These decisions can be made in sequential ½-hour periods, and the total game, representing 4 or 5 years in the existence of the firm, can be completed within 1 day. The choice of the simulated time period depends on the function in question and can reflect a day, a week, a month, or even a year.

Games differ in their use of *interactive* or *noninteractive* relationships. Those that attempt to reproduce the competitive aspects of business and that include, in particular, a marketing component are likely to be interactive. Within this framework, the action taken by one team or firm may affect the results of an action taken by one or more opponents, as well as the action of the team in question. An interactive game is analogous to tennis where the tactics and success of an individual depend upon the strokes of the opponent. In golf, by contrast, all participants compete against a benign opponent, i.e., the golf course, and except for some psychological pressures introduced by a competitor through a particularly well-placed shot, no interaction of shots (or decisions) is possible. It should be obvious that it is not necessary to include interaction in order to introduce competition. The model itself can represent the golf course against which all participants compete, some with more success than others.

Games may or may not employ a computer. The advantages of using a computer are much the same as the advantages of using one for any day-to-day processing task: speed, accuracy, and comprehensive reports. The computer-based game is likely to be more complex because more complex relationships can be modeled and mathematically manipulated. However, the noncomputer game has the flexibility of being carried into the classroom or on the road without concern for computer accessibility and compatibility.

Types. Management games are conveniently classified by subject matter. While the earliest games were the so-called general management or total enterprise games, in recent years functional games and specialized or industry games have been developed either to meet a more specific pedagogical objective or to characterize the uniqueness of a business, industry, or other organizational entity. These three types will be discussed in turn.

General Management Games. The *general management game* is typically competitive, interactive, computer-scored, predominantly deterministic, and designed for team play. The players are usually divided into teams, each to represent the top management group of one of several competing companies. Each company starts in the same financial position with the same options available to it and is in direct competition with every other company in the manufacture of a single, identical product for sale in the same market. The players are provided financial data and an overview of the economic conditions which will influence the results of their decisions. They are usually asked to make quantitative decisions and, typically, must allocate dollars among the group of alternative expenditures—production, additional plant investment, research, advertising, and marketing effort—and they must designate the price for their product. The allocation of sales among the companies is in accordance with the model formulation and relates causally the implications of all decisions made by each team. The players are given the results in the form of financial statements representing the period in question.

Some of the general management games incorporate unique features. One provides for four marketing areas instead of one, permitting the use of different prices in sales expenditure strategies in each area. A second includes provisions for bank loans and corporate dividends, and a third requires labor negotiations. Still another general management game requires raw material purchases as a decision. Some games provide for a depreciation in production capacity and a corresponding investment just to maintain it. Further investment is needed to increase capacity. Finally, one game separates the process engineering expenditures from product development instead of grouping them under research and development. All general management games operate from the perspective of a top-management team within the organization.

Functional Games. Games have also been designed to develop skill in the performance of specific functions, e.g., inventory control, production scheduling, and quality control, while being aimed at the middle or lower level of management. These games tend to vary greatly in complexity and may be manual or computer-based, deterministic or random, interactive or noninteractive, and designed for team or individual participation. The university course in quality control might easily accommodate a simple exercise in which the participants are required to design a single sampling plan by attributes and then to test that plan against the simulated arrival of lots of materials of varying quality. Similarly, class participants might be required to schedule production in the face of a probabilistic sales requirement. Games as diverse as those requiring job-shop scheduling, machine loading, the scheduling of maintenance activities, and even the bidding of jobs in a construction industry lend themselves to the explicit reinforcement of the concepts to be developed within a more theoretical framework in the classroom. Through the game, the participants have the opportunity to test theory against a simulated requirement.

Industry or Specialized Games. The third class of games might be called "specialized." These games are either general management, developed to meet the requirements of an individual company or com-

panies in a specific industry, or functional, designed to display the uniqueness of a given situation. Numerous retail industry games have been developed, as have games involving service-station operations and automobile dealerships. A game requiring scheduling and work-loading within the maintenance department of an urban mass transit authority is more functional than management-oriented, but is unique to that industry. Finally, a number of games have been developed that capture banking, transportation, agribusiness, and even university functions.

The Uses of Games

The use and potential value of games may be illustrated in the context of a specific, specialized game. In the Academic Department Head game, participants are assumed to be directing a department of statistics within a large state university. Decisions are required on a semester-by-semester basis for 10 periods, simulating 5 years in the existence of this academic department. The game participant is provided with an initial roster of eight faculty members, including a personal sketch of each individual as well as an insight into his or her professional interests and abilities. Then, at any time during the game, these faculty members may choose to resign or, if nontenured, may be terminated. Additional faculty must then be secured, and it is not unusual for a department to change in composition over the 5 years of its existence. In the game, as in reality, the objectives of the department have to be achieved through the faculty. As a result, the critical decisions in this simulation exercise focus on the recruitment and retention of faculty and the assignment of faculty to teaching and research. The game participant is required to assign faculty to courses, which are diverse in number and level, and the subdiscipline within the field of statistics. The department head provides salary increases in varying amounts in accordance with his or her assessment of faculty productivity and is also able to recommend promotions and/or tenure, where warranted, or nonreappointment, if the individual is not tenured. If vacancies occur or the department increases in size, the department head (game participant) can recruit from an available pool of applicants. The measure of departmental progress is seen in the composite criteria, which include some proportion of teaching effectiveness, scholarship and research, and service to both the institution and the profession. The Academic Department Head game has been designed as both an orientation and a training device for the new or the aspiring department head. It can also be used to orient others, either within or outside the university, who might profit from a better understanding of some of the significant decisions required in the administration of an academic department. Obviously, the game excludes many decision situations that confront the department on a daily basis; for example, the situation in which a group of students complains about the length of the homework assignments required by a new assistant professor. Further, the department head is not required to respond to the excuses of the faculty member who cannot find a parking place and is habitually late for the first class. But the game does provide for a review of the more profound decisions required of a manager within this unique organizational setting. The game can be used as a vehicle for discussing the "real-world" situation.

The business game, in contrast to the more traditional teaching techniques, requires a pattern of decision, feedback, and new response. Not only do players have to live with the consequences of their decisions, but they also operate within a recurring pattern which represents a "dynamic" case study. Participants become highly motivated to do well in the game and will often hotly debate the merits of alternative strategies. In particular, games motivate the players to attempt to identify clearly what is to be maximized—what is important—and then attempt to devise mini-experiments to ascertain which few of the many controllable (and uncontrollable) factors seem to influence results. Gaming is potentially a powerful teaching tool. Whether all games do, in fact, teach is difficult to measure.

Games, by necessity, tend to ignore qualitative factors in order to permit the manipulation of a quantitative mathematical model which can easily be scored. With the exception of such games as the Academic Department Head game, the human element is entirely omitted. As a result, games tend to reproduce the idealized situation rather than the actuality of missed deadlines, equipment breakdowns, sales requirements lost owing to the inadvertent delivery of the product to the wrong market area, and so forth. Games are not usually offered within the framework of teaching the "correct decision." (In fact, a problem with some players is that they place an excessively high degree of faith in strategies developed from gaming situations.) Rather, they are offered as a framework within which discussion can proceed. Just as one seeks a solution to a case study, so, too, the winning strategy in a gaming situation is only a reference for discussion and the more general understanding of the "real-world" situation described within the game model.

See also Assessment center method; Decision support systems; Development and training, management; Management information systems (MIS); Operations research and mathematical modeling; Risk analysis and management; Statistical analysis for management; System concept, total.

REFERENCES

Carlson, John G. H., and Michael J. Misshauk: *Introduction to Gaming: Management Decision Simulations,* John Wiley, New York, 1972.

Shubik, Martin: *Games for Society, Business, and War: Towards a Theory of Gaming,* Elsevier, New York, 1975.

Torgersen, Paul E., and Robert E. Taylor: "The Department Head in Facsimile," *Engineering Education,* January 1974, pp. 245–249.

PAUL E. TORGERSEN and ROBERT D. FOLEY,
Virginia Polytechnic Institute and State University

Site Selection

Within the field of industrial site selection, two sets of criteria exist: (1) general or geographical factors and (2) specific or local factors. The former category concerns itself with comparisons of continents, countries, regions, states, counties, cities, and towns. The latter category comes into focus after a preferred general area has been identified and site selection is reduced to the comparison of the qualities of individual land parcels. The following discussion will deal with both general and specific site selection factors.

Acquisition Costs and Procedure. Total costs include those for land acquisition and preparation, construction, and interest on borrowed funds. If the new facility is to be leased instead of owned, lease terms are included under total costs.

Search. In assembling a land site, a good policy usually is to seek the assistance of a reputable industrial real estate broker who knows the land available and the prices being asked. This use of a broker does not preclude, of course, using railroad industrial development departments, banks, utility companies, chambers of commerce, and area, state, and local industrial development commissions. They all can be very helpful, especially in narrowing down the area of search.

Negotiations. Assembling an industrial site can be a sensitive matter. If more than one parcel is involved, each owner must be approached individually. At this time the industrial or land broker, serving as an agent, can explore whatever problems exist in each parcel of land while simultaneously maintaining the anonymity of the principal. If word leaks out during the investigative stage that a well-known company is interested in the site, the price almost automatically jumps upward as each succeeding land owner is approached. This problem may be successfully combated, however. If the agent lets it be known that the principal is indeed interested in the land but has established a rigid budget for acquisition, hard-bargaining land owners may be willing to accept the argument. The best policy, of course, is to keep the principal anonymous as long as possible so as to hold the acquisition price at its lowest possible level.

Site Configuration and Quality. The site should be large enough to permit an efficient operation at the outset, as well as to allow for future expansion. A land-to-building ratio, of from 3 to 5, i.e., 3 to 5 times as much land as building, is usually adequate for modern one-story facilities.

Requirement Specifications. More specifically, the size of the new structure will be determined by expansion requirements; code setbacks; employee and visitor parking, required truck-dock areas; railroad sidings, number and length of cars to be handled daily and radius of the track siding; and requirements for outside storage of raw materials, work in process, or finished products.

Topographical Considerations. The site's topography, soil, and subsoil conditions are important considerations. Land should never be purchased without prior inspection of a United States Geological Service survey and the results of soil testing. It can become very costly to rectify substandard conditions in a land site so that it will accept above-ground improvements. The costs associated with correcting a poor site can often amount to more than the initial cost of the land.

Deed Restrictions. The current or previous owner of the land site often has entered restrictions to the parcel in an attempt to guarantee the value of the property for future owners. Restrictions of this kind are a form of zoning that goes beyond ordinary local codes and ordinances. They usually concern aesthetic considerations, but sometimes are a whim of the owner. Some examples of private deed restrictions are: a requirement of approval of building plans by a developer or an architectural review board, prohibition of certain materials for use in exterior walls, denial of truck-dock construction facing a street or a demand that docks be enclosed, prohibition of outside storage, and a stipulation that extensive landscaping be undertaken.

Zoning. Building codes and other controls on land and building use are designed to protect industry from encroachment by commercial and residential development and to guarantee equitable and uniform enforcement. Some of the most common zoning ordinances deal with lot coverage or land-to-building ratio, setbacks from lot lines, uses permitted, parking requirements, and height restrictions. Almost all local building codes make reference to the requirements set forth by the Building Officials Conference of America or the National Association of Insurance Underwriters. With only minor variations, both codes cover the same items.

Utilities and Other Requirements. The following should be carefully investigated:

1. *Electric power.* Most suppliers construct lines free of charge up to the new industrial facility. Sometimes, however, there is an extra charge when service requirements go beyond a certain standard. The charge must be borne by the site owner or developer, landlord, or industrial user.

2. *Natural gas.* If gas for heating or power is required, an early inquiry to determine its availability is vital. Except for a few areas, a natural gas shortage exists which forces utilities either to put applications on a waiting list or to allot usage to those that are granted.

3. *Water supply.* Important items to check are main size, pressure per square inch, reliability of service, flow tests, mineral content, tap-on charges, and off-site extension costs. In most areas, enviromental protection agencies make judgments as to water utility plant capacities and quality.

4. *Sprinkler systems.* The degree of hazard involved in storing particular types of goods will determine whether ordinary or high-density sprinkler heads should be used. The height of the proposed structure will also have a bearing on whether sprinklering will be necessary within storage racking. The Factory Mutual Association (FMA) and similar insurance-rating agencies insist on certain requirements for a preferred rating. In areas where water pressure is low, FMA or another group will also require the installation of a pump or pumps to guarantee a proper water pressure.

5. *Sewer requirements.* These regulations include many of the same factors as with water supply. Main sizes, capacity of the local plant, the very important approval of the Environmental Protection Agency, and type of effluent permitted are the prime concerns.

6. *Storm drainage.* This need can be handled by storm sewers, an open ditch, swale, underground piping and drains, or natural runoff. The topography of the site will determine which method is best. Storm sewers are expensive, but they add to the value of the industrial property.

Transportation Facilities. It is the rule, rather than the exception, that proposed manufacturing and/or distribution facilities will require dependable and reliable railroad and trucking services tendered by local and interstate carriers.

Rail. It is usually wise to locate the new operation at a site where rail service can be accepted from a long-haul carrier or from a belt or switching line. *Other important points* are the number and frequency of daily car spots; direction of the turnout to avoid overshooting and backing up of cars for placement; ability of smaller belt or switching lines to handle the projected volume; eligibility of the site for reciprocal switching and favorable rate privileges; elevation of the site to the grade of the rail service roadbed—a 2 percent gradient or a 2-foot increase or decrease in elevation per 100 feet is allowable; ability of the proposed structure to accept a rail spur at the side or rear with no more than a turning radius curve of 12° or 475 lineal feet; and the policy of the rail carrier on acceptance of less-than-carload shipments.

Truck. Trucking requirements are equally influential in the planning of a new manufacturing and/or distribution operation. Management must determine whether the proposed location is within the commercial zone of a municipality or at least enjoys the rate basis of the nearby metropolitan area. If the proposed site is in a rural area, there probably will be additional freight charges on inbound and outbound shipments. The additional freight charges quite likely will be offset by other more favorable factors—a trade-off.

Load limits and height restrictions on arterial roads, highways, and bridges must be examined. In many cases, state, country, and local governing bodies will cooperate on these matters. Also of extreme importance are such factors as road widths, traffic congestion, rush-hour problems, and possible tie-ups at railroad crossings. If access roads must go through residential areas, problems can arise. A site should be chosen that will allow direct access to roads and highways on which truck traffic is accepted.

Labor Supply. Even with increasing automation, the availability and quality of the labor supply are important. Generally, 30 miles is the maximum distance workers can be expected to commute by automobile. Personnel managers of nearby industrial firms can shed light on such conditions as degree of difficulty in hiring labor, pirating of employees, wage levels, and aggressiveness of local unions. Routine investigation of help-wanted signs and advertisements and local employment agencies will also provide a valuable insight into prevailing labor conditions.

Taxes. Local real estate, personal property, and inventory taxes should be carefully considered. Present rates should be examined along with close scrutiny of the trend over a 5- to 10-year period. On real estate taxes, it is vital to investigate carefully previous years' changes in the assessed valuation percentage, rate per $100 of valuation, and, if applicable, the state's equalization factor for the area.

Community Services. If a site is selected in an established community, the nature and quality of public services are major considerations. Fire and police protection, road maintenance, and in a northern climate, snow removal should be evaluated. Of course, if a site is selected in an unincorporated area because of other favorable features, the company itself may be required to provide some form of these services at the new facility. An important point to remember is that the quantity and quality of these community services have a substantial effect on insurance rates and coverage.

Proximity to Sources of Supply and Markets. It should be self-evident that for any site to be consid-

ered for development, that site must optimize the relationship between these two factors.

Expressway or Highway Identity. To many enterprises there is a substantial public relations value in having a modern, attractive facility located adjacent to a major expressway or highway. This is especially true when a firm produces and distributes consumer goods. To other companies, such a location can be a hiring aid because employees like to be close to expressways for easy access in their daily traveling to and from work—and it extends the employment area.

Traffic Congestion. If a site or sites are near a metropolitan area, vehicular congestion (automobile, bus, truck, and railroad) must be investigated. It is important, not only in the inbound and outbound movement of goods, but also in the hiring and keeping of personnel.

Neighborhood. In a rural area, the surrounding neighborhood may not be a great factor. If the proposed site is located near a metropolitan area, however, a positive prognosis for the future is of value. Barring unusual overgrowth or unforeseen market conditions, the company should view the site as one that will take care of its needs for many years.

Cultural, Educational, and Recreational Facilities. These factors vary in importance according to the nature of employees' interests and expectations. If the site chosen is in a small community or rural area, the company may feel a responsibility for establishing some of these facilities for its employees—especially those it wishes to attract from metropolitan areas.

See also Energy management; Environment, physical; Environmental protection legislation; Facilities and site planning and layout; Real estate management, corporate; Security management.

REFERENCES

Browning, Jon E.: *How to Select a Business Site,* McGraw-Hill, New York, 1980.

Mills, John D.: *Site Selection,* Marketing Guidelines Company, Tulsa, Okla., 1980.

Schmenner, Roger W.: *Making Business Location Decisions,* Prentice-Hall, Englewood Cliffs, N.J., 1982.

William E. Linane, *Linane & Company, Inc.*

Small Business Administration

The United States Small Business Administration (SBA) fulfills many roles:

Financial institution. SBA makes equity capital—by guarantee or direct loan—available to members of the small business community to whom other credit sources are closed.

843

Vendor's advocate. SBA assures that small businesses will receive their fair share of contracts for the billions of dollars worth of goods and services federal agencies purchase from the private sector each year, and it helps them purchase an equitable proportion of the federal surplus merchandise sold to private companies annually.

Counselor and trainer. With a constantly growing network of proficient and dedicated volunteers who multiply its efforts many-fold, SBA sponsors and cosponsors hundreds of management and technical assistance workshops, seminars, and counseling sessions in the 50 states, Puerto Rico, and the Virgin Islands.

Avenue of public aid. The Equal Opportunity Act of 1964 mandates SBA to mobilize its resources to assure that socially and economically disadvantaged groups be given every opportunity to progress into the business mainstream. When a natural disaster strikes, personnel may be usurped from every program area so the agency can bring swift assistance to businesses and private individuals who have suffered major economic injury. These are continuing priorities. At the same time, special programs are devised on an "as needed" basis and administered for veterans, women, artists, truck drivers, handicapped individuals, etc. These become temporary priorities, or they may become permanent.

Surprisingly, perhaps, the SBA is relatively small as federal agencies go. Its total roster in 1983 was 4431 individuals of whom 1027 were in the Washington, D.C., central office at 1441 L Street, Northwest. The remainder were scattered in the field, which includes 10 regional offices, 70 district offices, 23 branch offices, and 19 posts-of-duty.

Small Business Loan Programs

From the SBA's inception, loan programs designed to assure a flow of funds to businesses whose "credit is not bankable under the prevailing standards of commercial banks" have been the heart of the agency's work. Today's loans are primarily guaranteed bank loans. SBA dollars for direct loans continue in short supply. In fiscal years 1972 and 1973, 32,375 loans were approved at a total dollar cost of over $1.9 billion, with Hurricane Agnes in 1973 accounting for nearly 52 percent of the total dollar value of all the loans during the preceding 20-year period. For three-quarters of the 1983 fiscal year, 21,718 loans were approved. Of these, 8,645 were disaster loans amounting to $144.9 million. Total loan dollars extended for the period totaled $1,872 billion.

Guaranteed Bank Loans. These are the agency's basic business loans. Eligible loans are approved quickly for eligible borrowers; any bank under state or federal regulation may now issue guaranteed loans following current SBA requirements and terms. They may be used for building construction, expansion, or conversion; purchase of inventory, equipment, and supplies; and/or working capital.

Non-Bank Lenders. This is a relatively new program which permits small business lending companies and their branch offices to make business loans guaranteed by SBA. These companies include credit unions, life insurance companies, savings and loan associations, development companies, and production credit associations.

Specialized Loans. This category includes loans for small general contractors, certified development companies, handicapped assistance, pollution control financing, solar energy and energy conservation programs, qualified employee trusts, disaster assistance, and others including special loans under the 7(a) section of the Small Business Act, such as the seasonal line of credit and the contract loan. The contract loan is a guarantee of credit extended by a bank so that a small business company may fulfill its construction or other assignable contract.

Loan Limits. SBA's participation in a regular business loan to any one applicant may not exceed $500,000. Its share in an immediate participation loan may not exceed $150,000. SBA's share of a guaranteed loan may not exceed 90 percent of the outstanding loan balance, or $500,000, whichever is less. The interest rate on an SBA loan may be fixed or variable. A maximum rate is set from time to time by SBA, depending on current New York prime rates and the loan's duration.

SBA may not extend or guarantee loans to small businesses that can obtain them at reasonable terms from private financial institutions. In addition, SBA loan funds may not be used:

1. To finance a newspaper, book, or magazine publishing company or similar enterprise involved in the creation, expression, or distribution of ideas, values, thoughts, or opinions

2. To finance charitable or nonprofit enterprises except those under the handicapped assistance program

3. To pay off creditors of applicants who are inadequately secured and in a position to sustain a loss; to be distributed or paid to owner, partner, or shareholder in the applicant's enterprise; to refund debt owed to the Small Business Investment Corporation; or to replenish working capital funds previously used for such purposes

4. For any reason, if any of the applicant's gross income stems from gambling activities except those small firms that obtain less than one-third

of their gross income from commissions through sale of official state lottery tickets under state license, or from gaming activities in states where they are legal

5. To finance the acquisition, construction, improvement, or operation of real property that is, or is to be, held for sale or investment

6. To encourage monopoly or inconsistency with accepted standards of the American system of free competitive enterprise

Equity Capital Financing. The Small Business Investment Corporation (SBIC) and the Minority Enterprise Small Business Investment Company (MESBIC)—the latter for socially or economically disadvantaged owners (see below)—are privately owned and operated companies. They are licensed and frequently funded by SBA to provide equity capital and long-term loans to small businesses. Both types of companies negotiate terms of financing with their individual borrowers. Some offer management assistance to their clients as well. As of April 1983, there were 359 SBICs with total private capitalization of $18.8 million and SBA capitalization of $758.2 million. On the same date, 130 MESBICs had private capital of $29.4 million and SBA funding of $159.5 million.

Doing Business with the Federal Government

A major charge of the SBA is to help small businesses obtain business from the government. This assistance is provided in a number of ways.

Federal and Civilian Procurement. SBA helps small businesses obtain a fair share of the billions of dollars worth of goods and services the government and large civilian corporations purchase from private companies each year. SBA procurement representatives at major military and civilian facilities (1) monitor future contracts whenever feasible; (2) refer small businesses to contracting officers; (3) work for the relaxation of unduly restrictive specifications; and (4) help small concerns overcome contracting problems. By law, all large prime contractors must commit a specific share of subcontracting to small businesses. In addition, government purchasing offices must set aside certain contracts or portions of them for bidding by small businesses only—sometimes for women or minority owners only.

Certificate of Competency. A small firm may be low bidder on a federal contract, yet face losing the award because of alleged financial or technical inability to perform satisfactorily. The firm's recourse is to apply to SBA for a certificate of competency (COC). The agency will then make an on-site study of the firm's facilities, performance record, and capacity to perform the contract in question. If it is determined that the firm can perform the contract as required, a COC will be issued by SBA requiring the contractor to award the contract to that business.

PASS. A master computerized list of small companies that can—or would like to—perform federal and civilian contracts and subcontracts is available on a system developed and maintained by SBA. Known as PASS, the Procurement Automated Source System lists the names of companies and their capabilities on terminals located both in SBA's 10 regional offices and in the offices of about 100 major federal procurement officials and private prime contractors. Small companies wishing to be on this list may fill out the appropriate forms in any SBA office.

Another SBA service is that of helping small business have the opportunity to purchase its fair share of the surplus real and personal property and natural resources that government agencies sell each year. The major thrust of this program assures that small firms can buy a fair proportion of timber sold from federal lands. It also ensures that small firms in energy-related industries receive an equitable share of federal energy-related mineral lease contracts.

Management Assistance

Management assistance (MA) offers diversified training and counseling for people considering going into business, new business owners, and experienced entrepreneurs who wish to update their skills or enlarge their operations. MA business counseling includes (1) initial counseling, usually in the SBA office with a member of the Service Corps of Retired Executives (SCORE), (2) a Small Business Institute (SBI) team counseling for a school term; and (3) the Small Business Development Center (SBDC) counseling and other assistance for as long as required.

MA Training. SBA's district and branch offices offer business courses, conferences, 1-day workshops, and special topic clinics on a wide variety of subjects. These are often cosponsored by chambers of commerce, banks and other lending agencies, and universities and colleges at little or no cost. Some SBI colleges and universities and most SBDC installations also offer training.

SCORE and ACE. Recently combined into one, these two organizations, the Service Corps of Retired Executives and the Active Corps of Executives (ACE), consist of 12,000 men and women executives—retired or active—who voluntarily share their management and technical expertise and experience with those who need it. They belong to more than 400 locally organized, self-administered chapters in the United States, Puerto Rico, and the Virgin Islands.

Their help in prebusiness counseling and workshops is significant. They also counsel and play an active role in most SBA training programs and in many SBDC and SBI programs.

The SBI Program. The SBI program currently uses the resources of 470 schools of business administration to provide sustained counseling to small businesses in the communities which house these schools. Guided by faculty advisors, 150,000 advanced and graduate students, working in teams, have assisted about 60,000 businesses for an entire school quarter, or semester, over the years. In some academic circles, SBA and the SBI program are credited with making the small business sequence a respectable part of the business administration curriculum where only a few classes existed "on sufferance" before. The program helps small businesses with counseling they might not otherwise be able to afford. Business students increase their learning from the "hands-on" experience provided by their program participation.

Small Business Development Centers (SBDCs). Designed to meet the specialized needs of small businesses in their individual states, SBDCs link the resources of federal, state and local governments, universities, and the private sector to assist small business owners and prospective owners resolve their management and technical problems. The thrust of the program has recently been broadened to focus on high technology, innovation, computer science, agribusiness, exporting, and economic development. Involvement in the design and management of the program by the local SBA district and regional offices ensures that each SBDC Program provides the services essential to the local small business community.

MA Publications. The Management Assistance program prepares and distributes publications in several categories. *Management Aids* (MA) is the title of a series of one-topic pamphlets that describe and recommend techniques for handling management problems and business operations. The *Small Business Bibliographies* (SBB) list reference sources for management subjects. The *Starting Out Series* (SOS) fact sheets describe the start-up requirements for specific businesses. The various aspects of starting, buying, selling, and running a business are treated in greater detail in the *Small Business Management Series* (SBMS) and the *Starting and Managing* (S&M) books. The *Business Basics* modules are self-study, how-to workbooks on 23 business topics such as inventory management, asset management, and marketing strategy. Nearly 7 million MA publications were distributed during 1983. Order blanks 115-A "List of Free Publications," and 115-B "List of For Sale Publications," are available at SBA offices.

MA Films. More than 50 different small business management training films are available to SBA field offices and, through them, to such SBA affiliates and volunteer organizations as SBI, SBDC, SCORE, and ACE, and to local cosponsoring educational institutions and nonprofit business organizations. Film subjects range from advertising, to crime prevention, to foreign trade. Central office personnel review new films constantly. Some are purchased. Others, to better meet specific needs, are made under agency direction, including "Very Enterprising Women" and "Credit and Collections," the English versions of which have been dubbed into Spanish.

Special Help for Special People

SBA's Office of Minority Small Business (MSB) and Capital Ownership Development (COD) make financial, management, and other assistance available to members of designated minorities and those persons who are socially and/or economically disadvantaged. Certain programs are limited to those who cannot obtain assistance in the economic mainstream and who meet the following eligibility criteria.

Eligibility. The lack of a precise legislation definition of "socially or economically disadvantaged" suggests that flexibility is warranted in the determination of who is eligible for these special programs; most decisions are made on a case-by-case basis. However, black, native, Hispanic, Asian-Pacific, and Asian-Indian Americans have been officially designated socially disadvantaged. Members of other groups must show proof of their ethnicity. All applicants must establish economic disadvantage, which is usually due to diminished capital and few credit opportunities.

Section 8(a) of the Small Business Act Contracting. This business development program was set up by law to help these small business owners obtain their fair share of government contracts. The SBA, acting as prime contractor for goods and services contracts set aside by other government agencies, awards them to qualified small businesses. To help these firms meet their contractual obligations, SBA makes financial assistance available to them in the form of loans, advance payments, and business development expenses. Management assistance is given to them through individual counseling, training seminars, and professional guidance. Rules established when the law was implemented in 1981 provide a fixed participation term of 5 years' maximum, with possibly one extension. The 5-year cut-off rule encourages businesses to become independent more rapidly, and permits more new companies to enter the program.

Section 7(j) Development Assistance. MSB makes grants, agreements, and contracts with professional management counseling firms, qualified individuals, educational institutions, and state and local governments to give managerial and technical aid to eligible small business firms. This professional assistance is provided primarily to businesses in the 8(a) program that need aid in specific areas of management that cannot always be handled by available SBA volunteer counseling personnel. In addition to 8(a) clients, other 7(j) assistance recipients may be socially or disadvantaged individuals or firms located in areas of high unemployment.

Section 301(d) MESmall Business Investment Companies. Privately owned and operated, these companies, familiarly called MESBICs, are licensed and partially funded by the SBA. They provide equity capital and long-term loans to other small firms. MESBIC loans are restricted to socially or economically disadvantaged small business owners. MESBIC companies may be established by industrial or financial concerns, community or business organizations, or private or public investors who combine money and management resources.

Advocacy

SBA was created in 1953 to be an advocate for the nation's small business community. Its charge was to help free enterprise survive in the face of capital markets that limited small entrepreneurs' access to funding and threatened their very survival. As the years went by, it became evident that small businesses needed strong representation. Many rules and regulations formulated by state and federal agencies for big business caused undue difficulties for the small business community, when applied to it without modification. As a consequence, the SBA's advocacy role has been strengthened in recent years.

Office of Advocacy. In 1976, Congress created the Office of Advocacy within the SBA. Headed by a chief counsel, the office was established to protect, strengthen, and represent small business within the federal government. It represents small business within the bureaucracy and monitors—protesting when necessary—the impact of government rules on small entities. Today, SBA has an advocate in each of its regional offices who serves as the chief counsel's direct link to the grass-roots communities.

Small Business Answer Desk. Recently, the office's information and referral service was enhanced by the addition of a nationwide Small Business Answer Desk. Using the toll-free number (1-800) 368-5855, it taps the expertise of SBA professionals and directs callers to appropriate government agencies and other resources for answers to questions outside SBA's scope. The Answer Desk is staffed Monday through Friday from 9 a.m. to 5 p.m. The Washington, D.C., number is (1-202) 653-7561.

Special Programs

At this writing, SBA has five "special" programs. A program may be in this category because it is impor-

tant and warrants priority treatment. It may be an exploratory pilot program that merits close attention. Or, it may be a permanent program which retains its "special" classification because of its importance to the small business community and, hence, to the agency.

Office of Veterans' Affairs. SBA has a permanent Office of Veterans' Affairs in its Washington central office. It is supplemented by a Veterans' Affairs officer (VAO) in each SBA field office, listed under "U.S. Government—SBA" in the white pages of local telephone directories. These officials expedite loans for business purposes to eligible veterans on a priority basis. They facilitate veteran participation in SBA prebusiness workshops, training programs, and special business-training projects. They help veteran owner-managers to obtain government contracts—with certificates of competency if need be—and to receive the benefits of all the programs SBA has to offer, with special consideration in each case. Recent financial assistance regulations also give qualified veterans higher priority in the processing and funding of loan applications, with particular attention to the handicapped and Vietnam-era veterans.

Office of Women's Business Ownership. The Office of Women's Business Ownership's primary purpose is to implement a national policy to support women entrepreneurs with the assistance of 81 coordinators and representatives working out of most of SBA's regional and district offices. Its major function is the development and coordination of a national program to increase the number and success of woman-owned businesses, making maximum use of existing government and private sector resources. Special programmatic needs of current and/or potential women business owners are explored and ways to meet them are developed.

Office of International Trade. Coordinated by its National Office of International Trade, SBA has programs to help members of the small business community enter international markets or expand their existing foreign operations. One-on-one counseling services, workshops, training programs, and publications for small exporters are available in many SBA field offices. Some offices will design an individual program of export assistance to meet the needs of a small manufacturer or distributor.

Financial assistance is restricted to firms based in the United States and in business for at least a full year. SBA funds cannot be used to establish new overseas ventures. The request for export financing must come from a small entrepreneur's bank or lending institution. Loans and/or loan guarantees may be used for equipment, facilities, working capital, and specified export market development activities, like the Export Revolving Line of Credit program.

National Advisory Councils. To increase the general awareness of the significance of small business and bring together the leadership elements that **847** represent it, SBA established the National Advisory Council and 10 Regional Advisory Councils. These councils act as two-way informational conduits, advising the administrator and staff of SBA about economic conditions in their areas and suggesting ways to improve current and proposed agency programs. Their members channel information to local business and commercial interests about specific SBA programs, and they act as small business advocates. They speak out on radio, TV, at civic and service clubs; they urge banks to make more capital available to small business; they call on state and local government units to give more equitable treatment to small businesses in such areas as taxation, regulations, and purchasing.

Office of Private Sector Involvement. This office was created late in 1982 to coordinate the resources of SBA and other agencies with private resources to stimulate private sector jobs and benefit small business. It has already established (1) local, state, and national public/private partnerships; (2) a national on-line data base on projects, techniques, people, and organizations; and (3) a strengthened SBA capacity—via education and training—to initiate and participate in public/private partnerships. Typical on-line demonstration projects include the study of successful existing projects and the exploration of the feasibility of statewide efforts to make advanced technology available to small businesses with such potential partners as corporations, university and research centers, local and state governments, and SBA.

See also Government relations; Government services; Markets, government; Ownership, legal forms of.

REFERENCES

Hayes, Rick Stephan, ed.: *Wiley Series on Small Business Management,* John Wiley, New York, 1980–1982.

Smith, Randy Baca: *Setting Up Shop: The Do's and Don'ts of Starting A Small Business,* McGraw-Hill, New York, 1982.

U.S. Department of Commerce: *The Vital Majority: Small Business in the American Economy,* AA/F & I, Washington, D.C., 1973.

Harriet Premack Soll, *United States Small Business Administration*

Social Responsibility of Business

The social responsibility of business is whatever society decides that it is. In recent years, society has been exceptionally ambivalent. Both its needs and its boundaries are uncertain.

The fundamental purpose of business in all societies is to produce and to distribute goods and services in such a manner that benefits exceed costs.

Communities at different times and in different places establish different constraints within which business is expected to fulfill this purpose. These constraints concern, for example, the nature and quality of goods and services, the characteristics and forms of production and distribution, the definition of a "cost," the allowable excess of benefits over costs (profits), and the allocation of that excess.

Situational Differences. These constraints reflect various situations: different characteristics of the real world within which business operates. In a situation of scarcity, for example, waste is a crime; in one of surplus, it is acceptable. Hevrat Ovdim, the business end of the Israeli Federation of Labor which accounts for about 20 percent of Israel's national product, is constrained and formed by a dedication to the growth, development, and independence of a Jewish state. Similarly, the structure and behavior of Japanese trading companies reflect the needs of that society. In the United States, business activity has reflected a particular situation at a particular time, and as that situation changes, so do the constraints on business. It is the change that raises the issues of social responsibility.

Society's Needs. The social responsibility of business is a function of the needs of the communities which the business serves and affects. These needs may be defined by individual consumers expressing their desires in an open marketplace, by investors seeking to maximize the return on their investments in capital markets, by the membership of the business—its managers and its managed—by government's allocating capital, natural, and sometimes government's allocating capital, natural, and sometimes human resources to those economic activities that it decides are most urgent, or, of course, by some mixture of these methods.

If a community's needs are clear and explicit, social responsibility is scarcely an issue; it is a well-understood given. When Thomas Aquinas told the medieval bankers that the maximum permissible interest which they could charge was 5 percent and no more, their social responsibility was clear. Similarly, in World War II, business in America was proudly dedicated to the fulfillment of a well-defined need; social responsibility was not an issue.

Changing Constraints. Today in the United States and elsewhere, social responsibility is a very real issue because the definition of the needs of the different communities which business serves and affects is as unclear as is the matter of who decides those needs and by what procedures. Consumer desires expressed in the marketplace are increasingly distinct from a variety of community needs for such things as clean air, pure water, and natural beauty. Old management/labor hierarchies, acceptable in an earlier time in which one worked to survive, are less well suited to a situation in which survival is in essence a right of membership in the community.

Layoffs in bad times to sustain dividend payments were once acceptable; today they are less so. The assembly line, once the glorious achievement of efficiency-minded production managers, is less acceptable as new human dimensions of cost are counted. The very idea of growth is in question. Some growth is desirable as, for example, in world food production. Other growth is obnoxious if it fractures ecological integrity and wastes increasingly valuable energy. And what is acceptable in one place may be unacceptable in another. The definitions of "development" in Brazil's Amazon jungle and in New Jersey are plainly different. There are a host of unmade trade-offs which obscure the constraints within which business activity can properly take place, particularly in the United States. The old rules which reflected the old situation are no longer acceptable. The new ones are neither clear nor explicit.

Multiple Relationships. The term *social responsibility* embraces a multitude of internal and external relationships of the corporation (and we are speaking here of the large, publicly held corporation, not the corner grocery store). Concern with social responsibility has risen as society's expectations of corporate activity have become increasingly ambivalent. Obeying the law has become at once vastly more complicated and at the same time insufficient. A multiplicity of interest groups bombard the corporation with complaints about which it is uncertain because society as a whole is uncertain. On many issues, the community has not spoken with a clear voice.

Corporate Response. In the midst of this uncertainty, corporations have taken a variety of actions. First, they have sought to improve their internal machinery for complying with new laws, especially those regarding racial and ethnic minorities, women, ecological effects of production, consumers, employee welfare, and their own general impact on the community. This machinery has included so-called social audits and other more-or-less formal procedures for monitoring corporate compliance with changing social demands. Second, business has attempted through advertising and public relations activity to explain and accentuate its consistency with various social objectives. And, finally, business has made an effort to increase its sensitivity to current and future pressures for changes in social expectations.[1]

Corporate efforts to cope with the question of social responsibility are greatly complicated by three factors:

1. The large corporation serves and affects a number of very diverse communities: shareholders, debt holders, employees, consumers, Detroit, New York, Brazil, France, and more.

2. There is considerable confusion about what the needs and rights of each of those communities are. What are the criteria for accountability, for legitimacy, for authority? The old notions of property rights, the bond of contract, competition to satisfy consumer desires, the limited state, and the glories of technological innovation and growth for their own sake are wearing thin. New ones are coming, but they are unclear.

3. In the meantime, who has the right and the competence to decide what these different communities need? Who has the right and the competence to determine, in short, the social responsibility of business? The answer to both questions does not seem to be business. It must be the community, acting through the political order in one way or another. It may be through government or through the pulling and hauling of interest groups. Business has some choice here, and it will probably prefer government because it is somewhat more orderly and predictable. It is not surprising that concerns are rising about alliance of big corporations and big government, corporate statism, as it were. But is there any real alternative? Do not the real issues revolve around what sort of an alliance? How open is it? Can everyone inspect and control it?

As we speculate about the future, it is useful to remember that we are discussing here age-old questions of *authority* and *control*.

Sources of Authority. The managers of business have no God-given rights. Their rights may derive from three sources. The *first* is property rights. This right continues satisfactorily to provide authority to managers of small, clearly owned enterprises. But with respect to great, publicly held corporations, the notion of property is a myth. Nobody "owns" them in any real sense. Consequently, their managers are extremely vulnerable. Their authority is weak because their legitimacy is questionable. At the same time, it is as unlikely as it is impractical to return to a simpler day when shareholders actually did own the companies in which they invested. Shareholder democracy attracts little enthusiasm from shareholders or anybody else. A *second* source of managerial authority is all the members of the enterprise—the managed. This source is somewhat more promising, and we see a wide variety of forms of worker participation in management, with or without unions, being tried throughout the Western world. *Finally*, there is the state. Whether we like it or not, it is difficult to deny that, increasingly, managerial rights are indeed deriving from government at various levels. The issues here are ones of degree, of centralization versus decentralization of forms of participation by business and other groups in governmental decision making. These three sources are the ones and the *only* ones from which managers may choose for the future.

Sources of Control. With respect to control, we **849**

are back to the matter of community need. Who decides and how? There are three ways.

Marketplace Reactions. The first is competition among a number of preferably small proprietors to satisfy individual consumer desires in an open marketplace. This is the way preferred in the United States; it lies at the heart of the antitrust laws. In practice, however, it presents difficulties. An increasing number of consumer desires may be irrelevant to, or inconsistent with, community need. Consumers also may not know what is good for them: in the days of Upton Sinclair's "jungle," business put rats in the hot dogs and consumers had no way of knowing that they were there. More recently, consumers in the mid-1960s had no special concern about increasing the safety of automobiles. They had been conditioned to desire other qualities: power, luxury, tail fins, and the like. Ralph Nader came along and said in effect, "It doesn't make any difference what consumers want. The community needs safety." Congress enacted stringent new safety regulations. Similarly, with respect to air and water pollution and other community contaminants, the old laws of competition are less reliable. In addition, efficiency may dictate bigness. The necessity of huge capital investments for research, development, and new plant and equipment; the economy of large production runs; the efficiency of managing worldwide production and distribution systems—all these tend to intensify the trend toward large, coordinated, and concentrated firms. Japan and Europe accepted this trend ideologically long ago; for the United States, it is still something of a shock and contributes to the debate about social responsibility.

Government Regulation. Where traditional marketplace competition does not work, a second alternative is regulation by government. But there are many difficulties here, too. From what level of government does the regulation emanate—the city, the state, the nation, or from many nations? Social and political pressures appear to be tending to push regulation up the governmental ladder. But government is unready. There is little multinational government of any sort, and national government in the United States has traditionally approached the problem of regulation in an ad hoc fashion, responding to separate crises as they occur. The result is that there is a good deal of regulation but little planning or coordination among the regulators, considerable intervention, and much visionless flailing. In such circumstances, large corporations have naturally devoted considerable time and effort to seeking to influence government. The Watergate investigations revealed that in many cases, this effort was illegal; society judged it irresponsible as well. Many corporate executives were removed from office.

Disappointment with regulation as a means of controlling business has caused increasing attention to be paid to the third means of control, which is through the corporate charter or some sort of partnership between government and business. The Tennessee Valley Authority and the Communications Satellite Corporation (COMSAT) are examples of corporations which are controlled through their charters. Large defense contractors and the major oil companies reflect partnership arrangements.

Charter Revision. In the early days of the republic, the normal source of corporate control was its charter. Corporations were created by state legislatures to do things that needed doing, mostly public works. As time went by, this process became both undemocratic and corrupt. Corporate charters tended to go to those who had the power and the influence to get them. Furthermore, growing America saw in the corporation an unquestionably efficient means of mobilizing capital growth and expansion, both of which were unquestionably good things. Every effort was, therefore, made to encourage the formation of corporations for virtually any purpose whatsoever. The corporate charter became a lifeless document generally kept in Delaware. Recently, however, attention is once again being focused on the charter as a means of stipulating the terms and conditions under which the nation will allow a corporation to exist. The assumption of proponents of federal chartering schemes is that the nation knows what those terms and conditions should be. In the mid-1980s, however, there still are some confusion and doubt; society seems to be having difficulty defining what it wants its corporations to do or to be—what, in fact, responsible behavior is.

One of the most vexing problems accompanying a closer connection between great corporations and national government has arisen from the extent to which those corporations had become global undertakings upon which the world depended for such vital resources as oil and food. As a consequence, it seems likely that pressures for multination or world governance of global corporate activity will increase. The definition of social responsibility must fit society, and society is evidently less national and more global as spaceship Earth continues its perilous course.

See also Consumerism and consumer protection legislation; Environmental protection legislation; Ethics, managerial; Government regulations, federal regulation of competition; Management, historical development of; Product liability.

NOTES

[1] Robert Ackerman and Raymond Bauer, *Corporate Social Responsiveness: The Modern Dilemma*, Reston Publishing, Reston, Va., 1976, pp. 3–42.

REFERENCES

Anshen, Melvin, ed.: *Managing the Socially Responsible Corporation*, The Free Press, Glencoe, Ill., 1974.

Farmer, Richard N., and W. Dickerson Hogue: *Corporate Social Responsibility*, Science Research Associates, Inc., Chicago, 1973.

Silk, Leonard, and David Vogel: *Ethics and Profits: The Crisis of Confidence in American Business*, Simon & Schuster, New York, 1976.

GEORGE C. LODGE, *Harvard University*

Societies, Professional

Professional organizations have played an integral part in the advancement of management thought and practice, particularly since the emergence of the professional managers and their ties to the professional associations.

Industrialization and Management. After the American colonies won their independence, the country began a gradual shift from a predominantly agricultural economy to include an emerging industrial economy. Industrialization was aided and encouraged by development of the means of production to support transportation, machinery manufacture, and the provision of industrial supplies. The increased industrial activity meant that greater numbers of people with engineering skill and administrative ability were required to staff and manage the new enterprises.

With the changes in manufacturing and administration, structural changes came about in the nature of organizations to accomplish the more complex task of managing the larger organizations. The corporate form of business organization was necessitated because of the large scale of business operations. And with the corporate form of management came the professional manager.

There also came problems of administration of operations, integration, and control of complex structures that management had not encountered previously. In their quest for solutions, the managers of these industrial complexes looked for help among their own colleagues. The professional engineer, with a grounding in the hard sciences and a training in the scientific method, frequently was identified as the most likely candidate for upper-management positions. As these professionals became involved in operational and general management, they realized that their technical backgrounds did not provide solutions to pressing organizational and human problems. When respected speakers with successful experiences in management began to write papers and to make presentations at the American Society of Mechanical Engineers, they found a receptive audience. Management papers during this era were few in number and were published almost exclusively in engineering journals.

Internationally, the professional organizations were serving a similar function. For example, Henry Fayol first offered his ideas about a system of management to his colleagues in France in 1916. Speaking before the Société de l'Industrie Minerale, he presented his now classic principles of management. This presentation was reworked as a book, published in 1925[1], on general and industrial management.

If the changing industrialization has spawned the demand for competent, nonowner general and operating managers, the associations clearly contributed to the increasing recognition of the professional managers and opened opportunities to share problems and ideas for solution among the members.

The Professional Manager. The professional manager may be characterized as a new type in charge of the management of the enterprise on behalf of the owners, the stockholders. The single business unit, because of its increased size, now needed a number of managers at the several levels of administration. Levels of managerial executive tasks evolved in the composite structure. With specialization of managerial tasks, there arose the need for collegial associations where problems could be examined and solutions proposed. The professional manager, although not clearly identified as such at the time, was expected to bring to the office most of the following qualifications:

Adequate formal preparation in the managerial field

A quieting spirit that will strongly motivate a search for and an application of new knowledge

Imbuement with a strong sense of ethics and social responsibility.[2]

During the latter part of the 1860–1900 period, the engineering schools were the early sources of formal preparations for management, if any was to be had. The formal education provided was predominantly technical with some industrial management concepts taught in the course of the discussions. It was through the association meetings of the established engineering profession, however, that the widest range of information needed by the emerging professional managers first became available.

Association Impact on Management Education. Before 1900, only three universities in the United States offered a curriculum in management education, and this was most limited in scope. Courses in economics, dealing with economic theory and principles of trade and commerce, were deemed beneficial. Practical solutions and needed guidance for day-by-day operating problems were not, however, transmitted at the college level.

Although it is difficult to pinpoint the role of professional associations in the early development of curricula in business management in colleges and universities, it may be inferred that there was an influence. Source information for teaching business administration courses was drawn from the business organizations. Published papers, association journals, presentations by speakers, and courses in management and administration taught by business persons served as sources of information for building business programs. The persistence of associations pressing for formal instructional programs leading to degrees in their special interest areas is felt even now in colleges and universities.

Role of the Professional Management Organization. The major contributions of the professional management organizations are to:

1. Provide a forum where current problems and new ideas may be proposed, evaluated, and reviewed by the professionals in management.

2. Provide channels for the distribution of information dealing with management problems and solutions. Papers presented at meetings are available for review by an audience that reaches beyond the organization membership. The journals of the professional management organizations alert the readers to impending problems, workable solutions, and new ideas. The Academy of Management, in particular, has performed this role exceedingly well for the academic area.

3. Maintain the collegial interaction that characterizes the professions. Associations give the specialists an opportunity to get together with their peers. Members may mingle with leaders in their profession who have similar interests.

4. Provide a special library service for the technical and professional areas of management. The American Management Association, for example, for years has maintained a professional library for the lending of books, magazine articles, and related publications pertinent to members' areas of interest.

5. Conduct seminars for management development. The Association for Systems Management, for example, is notable in this respect.

6. Provide the means for transmitting organizational needs for management skills to colleges and universities. The American Banking Association was an early leader in arousing interest in the promotion of higher education for business in the United States during the last decade of the nineteenth century.

7. Furnish an opportunity to conduct surveys and management science research, coordinated with the interests of the associations. Financing of research by professional organizations, or accessibility to selected business firms by the academic researcher, can be facilitated when endorsed by the local or national association officers.

8. Alert the profession to impending action by government or other power groups or influences which may have a significant impact on the management practices of members.

Status of Professional Associations. The contributions of the professional organizations can be clearly established historically. The role of the professional management associations indicates a strong potential for continued service to the members and to society. But recent experience of the professional organizations and attitudes expressed by members raise troubling issues.

Optimistic View. In 1974, *Nation's Business* surveyed the trade and professional associations and reported its findings. In general, it was found that, "Trade and professional associations' activities pay off for their members; but some of the extra benefits these groups provide may surprise you."[3] The article observed that the main purpose of any trade or professional association was to serve its members and that professional or commercial benefits occupy an important role in the continuation of membership.

Pessimistic View. A penetrating analysis of the current values of the strictly professional association was reported by Berkwitt.[4] He stated that after years of growth, professional societies are on the decline. He indicated that for many professionals, the typical benefits of membership are no longer significant or even relevant. Among the factors that may explain the decline in memberships in professional management associations are these implied from Berkwitt's study.

1. Needs of members are changing, but the associations are not. Membership benefits, such as attendance at meetings and seminars, and receipt of journals, and related publications are no longer regarded as compelling reasons to retain membership.

2. Changing expectations of members that the associations should play a more active role in the individual professional's concerns—locating jobs, protecting rights, or undertaking some such functions as the unions perform for their constituents.

3. Salespeople, consultants, and others who use the associations primarily as a place to do business have infiltrated them and monopolized their programs. Consequently, many of the "pros" have stopped attending because they refuse to be accosted by such practitioners. Additionally, members are bombarded with mail and solicitations from opportunists using the association roster to promote their own interests.

4. Memberships are often used primarily as a source of making commercial, rather than professional, contacts. Firms spend thousands of

dollars in membership fees for their members just so the "right" people are identified for the commercial follow-up.

5. Industry no longer is so certain the professional association has a valuable contribution to make to the development and professionalization of its management people. There is a noticeable cutting back in association memberships paid by employers since 1970. Companies reducing expenses where value cannot be pinpointed identify memberships in the associations as among the first to go.

6. Attendance is down in the local meetings owing to dull, lackluster, or irrelevant programs. The annual meeting is a showy, expensive affair that only a small percentage of the total membership does, or can, attend. The journals are boring, containing theoretical pieces written by professors who must publish or perish. Articles frequently fail to meet the needs of the readers.

7. Officers at the national level control the incoming national officers, and the "club" perpetuates itself for its own benefit rather than representing the membership's interests. At the local level, it is a struggle to find someone willing to run for office, with dwindling membership taking its toll of effective candidates.

Outlook. After proliferating since the 1900s to some 1000 organizations today, professional associations will decline in the specialties which are duplicated among the societies and associations. Nearly 200 management associations may be identified among the thousands of currently listed societies and trade associations.[5] Several of the current management associations evolved from mergers with smaller or single-purpose associations which were declining in their ability to attract and hold members. Others have survived by changing in those ways that were attractive to members and prospective members. Name changes, along with changes in organizational structure and types of services offered, seem to foretell the pattern for survival and growth. Mergers will continue as a means of survival for some associations. The shakeout caused by the recession and declining memberships at both national and local levels will strengthen the excellent associations and, one hopes, encourage them to emphasize professional aspects and reduce commercialization to a bare minimum. There is irrefutable evidence that the professional management organizations must contribute to the benefits professional managers expect from their associations if they are to occupy the role that the membership perceives they must fulfill.

See also Associations, trade and professional; Development and training, management; Ethics, managerial; Professionalism in management; Social responsibility of business.

NOTES

[1]Henry Fayol, *General and Industrial Management*, Pitman Publishing Company, London, 1949.

[2]Theodore Harriman, *Professional Management*, Houghton Mifflin, Boston, 1962, p. vii.

[3]"Professional Associations Busily Helping Business and Society," *Nation's Business*, vol. 62, December 1974, pp. 47–52.

[4]George J. Berkwitt, "Are Professional Societies Dead?" *Dun's Review*, vol. 99, March 1972, p. 46.

[5]*Encyclopedia of Associations*, vol. 1, National Organizations of the U.S., 18th ed., Gale Research Company, Detroit, 1984.

Loren E. Waltz, *Indiana University at South Bend*

Standard Industrial Classifications

Standard industrial classifications (SIC) constitute a numbering system developed by the U.S. Office of Management and Budget to facilitate collection and analysis of data on economic establishments and to ensure that statistics on activities in various economic areas are comparable. In this instance, an "establishment" is not necessarily, perhaps not even usually, a company. Rather, it is defined as "an economic unit, generally at a single physical location where business is conducted or industrial operations are performed." Thus, a single factory or a store would constitute an establishment.

Establishments are classified first into divisions, then into major groups, then into finer subdivisions. The SIC divisions and the numbers used for the major groups in each one are as follows:

Division A: Agriculture, forestry, and fishing, 01–09

Division B: Mining, 10–14

Division C: Construction, 15–17

Division D: Manufacturing, 20–39

Division E: Transportation, communications, electric, gas, and sanitary services, 40–49

Division F: Wholesale trade, 50–51

Division G: Retail trade, 52–59

Division H: Finance, insurance, real estate, 60–67

Division I: Services, 70–89

Division J: Public administration, 91–97

Division K: Nonclassifiable establishments, 99

The system of numbering the major groups and the subdivisions within the groups may be explained by some examples. An establishment manufacturing wood household furniture (except upholstered) **853** would be numbered 2511. The 2 indicates a manufacturing establishment; the 5 the major group, furniture and fixtures; the first 1, household furniture; and the second 1, wood except upholstered. The number 2512 indicates wood upholstered furniture. Office furniture numbers are 2521 for wood and 2522 for metal.

This system enables companies to identify the areas in which customers for their products exist, because the numbers are used in reports from the Census of Manufactures and the Census of Business, which show the number of establishments in each area, their size, and other facts about them. Thus, they can help a firm to determine the areas to which marketing efforts should be directed.

See also Economic measurements; Forecasting business conditions; Marketing, industrial; Marketing research; Standard metropolitan statistical areas.

REFERENCE

U.S. Office of Management and Budget, Statistical Policy Division: *Standard Industrial Classification Manual, 1972,* Washington, D.C., 1972.

LESTER R. BITTEL, *James Madison University*

Standard Metropolitan Statistical Areas

A *standard metropolitan statistical area* (SMSA) is an urban market of the United States as defined by the U.S. Office of Management and Budget. An SMSA is generally a city with a population of 50,000 or more and the county in which it is situated, although territory in contiguous counties may be included if it is socially and economically integrated with the city. Other tests are used in some cases. For example, a city of 25,000 and its environs may be an SMSA if the surrounding area meets certain criteria of population size and density.

Currently, there are 323 SMSAs in the United States including 5 in Puerto Rico. See Fig. S-6. The number changes constantly because of population growth and population shifts. Generally the number has been growing, but some areas have been dropped from the count because they have lost population.

A large amount of census data on these areas exists for use in pinpointing markets—data on the ages and incomes of the population, for example, and on the number of establishments in each of the industrial classifications of the Bureau of the Budget.

In addition, the Bureau of Economic Analysis (BEA) of the Department of Commerce has divided the whole country into what are called BEA economic areas, and a large quantity of government data on these exists as well.

See also Economic measurements; Forecasting business conditions; Market analysis; Marketing research; Standard industrial classifications.

REFERENCES

Federal Register: "Official Standards Followed in Establishing Metropolitan Statistical Areas," Jan. 3, 1980, part 6.

U.S. Bureau of the Census: "Metropolitan Area Concepts and Components," in *Statistical Abstract of the United States, 1982–1983,* Washington, D.C., December 1982, pp. 894–904.

U.S. Office of Management and Budget: *Standard Metropolitan Statistical Areas,* rev. ed., Washington, D.C., 1978.

LESTER R. BITTEL, *James Madison University*

Standards and Standardization Programs

Industry and business use standards to solve problems that occur again and again and to facilitate internal and external communications with everyone involved in an activity or operation. Application of standards increases profits, improves efficiency and safety of operations, and enhances the dependability and quality of products.

Companies adopt or adapt national, international, or industry standards to meet their needs and those of their customers. They also develop standards, as required, to solve unique problems. Formal standardization programs are generally established within companies to handle the development and adoption/adaptation processes; to promulgate and revise standards accepted for company use; to supervise application of standards on assignment; and to coordinate participation in external standards-developing activities at industry, national, and international levels.

Application and Benefits of Standards

Standards cover almost every field and discipline. They are invaluable to industry in design, production, quality control, procurement, materials handling, and construction and maintenance of plants and offices.

Dimensional and rating standards enable equipment produced by different manufacturers to be used together in individual and interconnected systems. Standards for parts and components reduce variety, thus resulting in longer production runs, reduced setup time, and rapid training of personnel. Other advantages are reduced inventory, decrease in purchasing transactions, and the freeing of engineering talent for innovative work. Application of standards for materials opens up new sources of supply and

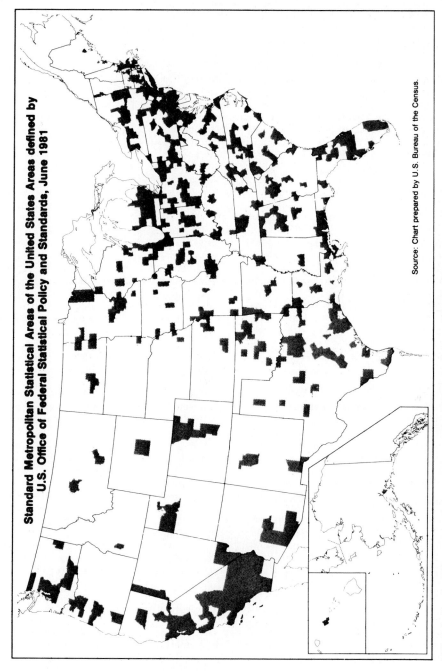

FIG. S-6 Standard Metropolitan Statistical Areas of the United States. (From *Statistical Abstract of the United States, 1982–1983*, U.S. Bureau of the Census, December 1982, Washington, D.C., p. 894.)

Standard Metropolitan Statistical Areas of the United States Areas defined by U.S. Office of Federal Statistical Policy and Standards, June 1981

Source: Chart prepared by U.S. Bureau of the Census.

reduces manufacturing costs. Uniform levels of product performance, reliability, and safety result from the use of standards for processing, inspection, and testing. By making mass production possible, standards reduce costs and selling price. Industrial workers are protected by the application of standards for construction and use of machinery, protective clothing, and ventilation, among many examples.

Manufacturing is, of course, not the only user of standards. Business uses them for information processing, purchasing, and establishing procedures; government, for procurement, to provide for safety and health of the public, to effect economies, and in providing for transportation and communication.

Company Standards Programs

Some type of formal standards program is required within a company to coordinate activities and supervise the application of standards. Uncoordinated development, selection, and use by various departments or divisions, acting independently, will result in waste and confusion and compound the problems that application of standards is intended to solve.

Organization. How a standards program is organized and administered depends on the needs of the company and its organizational structure. Whatever the organizational mode, adherence to certain principles is essential to the success of the standards activity:

1. The program should be made applicable to all company functions.
2. The program should be established by, report to, and have the active support of top management.
3. Standards approved for company use should be acceptable to all affected departments.

In small companies, administration of the standards program may be assigned to the head of a division or department—engineering or design, for example. Larger companies may establish a separate standards department, which should be coequal with other functional departments. Some companies assign administration of the program to a standards policy committee composed of department heads, chaired by a corporate-level executive, and supported by a standards department, which serves as secretariat.

Procedures. The first step in implementing a company standards program is to identify the problems that application of standards will solve. The next is to locate or develop standards that will meet these needs, achieve acceptance of the various departments that will be affected, and promulgate the standards for company use.

More than 8000 national consensus standards covering virtually every field and discipline are available in the United States. A search and evaluation should be made to determine if any fulfill the stated need, either as promulgated or with modifications. International standards or, on occasion, the national standards of other countries should be sought by a company that is multinational or engaged in export/import. If no applicable national (or international) standard can be located, a similar search and evaluation should be made of industry standards. If this search also proves fruitless, development work on a company standard should be considered. Another alternative, time permitting, is to petition the national/international coordinating organization to initiate a standards development project. If the proposed standard will affect more than one company, industry, or sector, this approach is essential.

Before a standards-writing project is initiated by a company, certain questions should be answered: Is the standard technically feasible? Is the development effort timely? What will be the overall costs of developing the standard, maintaining it, converting to it, and implementing it? What are the long term benefits of application? Will application be useful within the user's business environment?

The choice of who is to develop the standard—the standards department, standards policy committee, or designated subgroup—depends on the organization of the function within the company. Regardless of who develops the standard, extensive cooperation and consultation with affected departments are essential during the development process and reconciliation of differences. Also of vital importance is final acceptance of the standard for company use by all affected groups, whether the standard is developed internally or adopted or adapted from those available from outside sources.

When a standard has been accepted, it is issued to all affected departments. Distribution is usually carried out by the standards department, which serves as the clearing house for all company standards. Duplicate sets may be located in various departments or divisions. Ensuring that they are kept up to date is another responsibility of the standards department. Supervision of the application of standards within the company may be the responsibility of the standards department or may be handled through the company's normal management system.

Sources of Standards

Company Standards. Development of standards in the United States is a complex, interrelated process. They may be developed by a company to fulfill an individual need. If a particular standard is also found to serve the needs of many companies or industries or other affected sectors, it may be elevated to, or serve as the basis for, an industry or a national or international standard.

Thousands of standards also originate at the industry or national or international levels.

Industry Standards. Industry standards are developed and promulgated through trade, technical, professional, or scientific associations and societies that serve particular industries or disciplines and, in general, produce standards applicable to their particular fields.

In the United States, most of these organizations cooperate within the federated national standards system coordinated by the American National Standards Institute (ANSI). They submit to ANSI standards developed under their direction for recognition as national consensus standards.

National Standards. ANSI provides and administers the only recognized system in the United States for establishing standards—no matter what their origin—as American National (consensus) Standards. Its approval procedures ensure that all concerned interests have had an opportunity to participate in a standard's development or to comment on its provisions. They further ensure that the standard has achieved general recognition and acceptance for use. To date, ANSI has approved more than 8200 national standards encompassing virtually every field and discipline.

Other major ANSI functions are to coordinate the voluntary development of national standards and of U.S. participation in nongovernmental international standards efforts, and to serve as the source of information on availability of national and international standards.

International Standards. Two major nongovernmental organizations coordinate the development and approve a large proportion of the voluntary international standards used throughout the world. They are the International Organization for Standardization (ISO) and the International Electrotechnical Commission (IEC), located in Geneva, Switzerland. The IEC is responsible for standards in the electrical and electronics fields; ISO, for all other fields. Both maintain close liaison with each other and with other international organizations engaged in standardization. ISO and IEC have approved nearly 5700 standards that affect product acceptance throughout the world because they are adopted by many countries as the basis of product inspection, approval, and certification systems. These standards are available in this country through ANSI, the United States member of these organizations.

See also Inventory control; Production/operations management; Purchasing management; Quality management; Value analysis.

REFERENCES

American National Standards Institute: *ANSI Progress Report*, New York (annual).

————: *Catalog of American National Standards*, New York (annual).

Toth, Robert B., ed.: *Standards Activities of Organizations in the United States,* National Bureau of Standards, U.S. Government Printing Office, Washington, D.C., 1984.

Dorothy Hogan, *American National Standards Institute, Inc.*

Statistical Analysis for Management

Successful managing and planning in an increasingly complex environment requires more than intuitive, reactive approaches to decision making. Greater emphasis is now placed on analysis that applies mathematical and statistical techniques to the process. Experience and knowledge of operations still are essential, but they are being used with greater discipline.

Decision Theory. A wide range of quantitative techniques can be used to reduce an otherwise complex problem to manageable dimensions. The collection of these techniques has become loosely known as *decision theory*, although there certainly is no such thing as an integrated theory of how to make decisions. Nevertheless, the ultimate impact of these methods extends far beyond the decision tools themselves. In fact, there is a large body of opinion that maintains that the greatest impact of the quantitative approach will be, not in problem solving, but rather, in the area of problem formulation. It will radically alter the way managers think about their problems—how they analyze them, gain insights, relate them to other problems, communicate them to other people, and gather information necessary for solving them.

Decision Making Under Uncertainty

When all information relevant to a particular problem is gathered so that the outcome of each alternative action available to the decision maker can be predicted accurately, the analyst is said to be operating under conditions of *certainty*. The mathematical formulation used to help analyze such problems is called a *deterministic model*. For example, a purchasing agent might evaluate different suppliers on the basis of minimizing total acquisition costs or of shipping miles. In either case, the criterion for the best solution is expressed in known units. A wrong decision would be caused by either excessively difficult computations or errors in the formulation of the problem.

It is frequently necessary to make decisions when any one of several different outcomes possibly may occur following the selection of a particular course of action. These decisions are said to be made under conditions of *uncertainty* or risk. (Some statisticians draw a technical distinction between the terms *uncertainty* and *risk*. There is not a consensus on how or whether to differentiate, however, and the two terms will be used interchangeably in this discussion.) In some cases, all the possible outcomes of a particular course of action cannot be specified. In other cases, all outcomes can be specified, but nothing is known about the relative likelihood of the occurrence of each. Most quantitative techniques cannot be employed to analyze these situations. Formal analysis of a decision that can result in any one of several different consequences generally requires that each consequence and its associated probability of occurrence be specified. Probability assignments can be based on subjective judgment, historical data, or empirical forecasts. Analysis is conducted using what are commonly called *probabilistic models*.

The Decision Matrix

When decisions are made under uncertainty, any one of several outcomes can follow the decision to take a given action. The particular outcome that actually occurs will depend on what state of nature exists after the decision is made. For example, the return on an investment in a new product is dependent on the level of demand experienced after it is put on the market.

The outcomes of possible combinations of alternative decisions and ensuing states of nature can be shown concisely in a *decision matrix*. The alternatives available to the decision maker are referred to as *actions*, and the possible states of nature that can exist following the choice of a decision are *events*. The outcome associated with each action-event combination is referred to as a *payoff* (or *loss*).

A decision matrix portraying a situation with three alternative actions and four possible events is shown in Table S-1. Actions that can be taken by the decision maker are denoted by numbers; events that can occur following the selection of an action are denoted by letters. [It is generally, although not necessarily, assumed that the event that occurs is independent of the action that is taken. For example, the possibility (event) of having a fire is not affected by the decision (action) of whether to purchase fire insurance.]

TABLE S-1 Decision Matrix

	Actions, in dollars		
Events	1	2	3
A	4	−2	7
B	0	6	3
C	−5	9	2
D	4	−1	3

In a decision matrix, the payoff (outcome) of a particular action depends on the event that occurs. Because of this relationship, a decision matrix is sometimes termed a *conditional payoff table*. It specifies the payoff that will occur for each event *given*, or *conditional on*, the specification of a particular action. In Table S-1, for example, the payoff is a gain of $3 *if* action 3 is selected and event B occurs. This outcome is called a *conditional payoff*; i.e., it is conditional on selecting action 3 and having event B occur.

Models constructed to represent such problems are called *probabilistic models*. Since a multiplicity of outcomes can result from the choice of a particular action, the decision maker—in effect—is forced to gamble. Regardless of the quality of the analysis upon which the decision is based, the decision may turn out, after the fact, to have been wrong. No strategy will consistently lead to objectively correct decisions. Thus, a strategy for making decisions under uncertainty cannot be formulated until the manager first specifies what is meant by a "best" decision. While a "best" decision might mean different things to different people, the individual should devise a strategy that is consistent with the decision maker's personal judgment and preferences. Several different strategies are frequently used.

The Maximin, Minimax, and Maximax Principles

The best decision generally is not readily apparent. With the advantage of hindsight, it can be seen from Table S-1 that action 3 would have been the best decision if event A had occurred, action 2 would have been the best if either of events B or C had occurred, and action 3 would have been the best if event D occurred.

Unfortunately, at the time a decision must be made, it is not known which event will occur.

Maximin. One possible strategy is to select that action which would *maximize* the *minimum* gain, or payoff. This is the *maximin* principle, which is the basis for a conservative decision strategy. The decision maker behaves as though nature—or whoever or whatever else determines which event will occur—is acting as an adversary and will choose the most adverse event possible given the action that has been selected. The worst possible outcomes for actions 1, 2, and 3 are, respectively, −$5, −$2, and $2. According to the maximin criterion, therefore, action 3 would be selected; that is, the worst possible outcomes for actions 1 and 2 are less desirable than the worst possible outcome for action 3.

Minimax. An alternative decision strategy would be for the decision maker to select the action that would *minimize* the *maximum* loss (the *minimax* criterion) rather than maximize the minimum gain. *Loss* is defined as the difference between the minimum payoff for a given action and the highest minimum payoff for any of the actions available. The losses for the actions described in Table S-1 would be $7 for action 1, $4 for action 2, and $0 for action 3. Thus, action 3 would be best according to the minimax criterion.

Two general observations can be made from the example: (1) The maximin and minimax criteria will always give the same result; (2) the loss of the "best" action will be zero.

Maximax. A related decision strategy can be formulated from the opposite perspective of the maximin principle. That is, rather than minimize the minimum gain, the decision maker could select the action that would *maximize* the *maximum* gain (the *maximax* principle). This criterion would be used by a gambler or someone who expected nature to respond benevolently. Since the maximum payoffs for actions 1, 2, and 3 are, respectively, $4, $9, and $7, application of the maximax principle would lead to the selection of action 2.

Caution. Sometimes the blind application of decision rules such as the maximin or maximax criteria can lead to poor decisions. Suppose, for example, an investor is trying to decide whether to invest in a bond or a stock. The percentage returns on these two alternative investments, conditional on one of two possible states of the economy (E_1 or E_2) are given in Table S-2. The maximin principle would lead to investment in the bond, but this would not be a good decision unless the investor strongly feels that economic condition E_2 will occur. On the other hand, the use of the maximax principle would not be appropriate given the possible investment returns in Table S-3 unless a high probability of occurrence can be attached to economic condition E_1.

TABLE S-2 Investment Returns

	Bond, %	Stock, %
E_1	8	20
E_2	8	7

TABLE S-3 Investment Returns

	Bond, %	Stock, %
E_1	8	10
E_2	8	−5

Expected Value

It is generally appropriate to regard nature as being neutral, not malevolent or benevolent. An event will not be chosen in response to the selection of a given action. In fact, the probability of each event's occurring should not be affected by the choice of a partic-

ular action. It is therefore desirable to devise a decision strategy that, based on the neutrality of nature, will maximize benefits in the long run. Selecting the action with the largest *expected value* is a weighted average of the conditional values. The *weights* are the probabilities that each conditional value actually will be received (or that each associated event will occur). Thus, the expected value of a given action is the average outcome that would occur if the same action were repeated many times under identical circumstances. An example of the calculation of an expected value is given in Table S-4.

TABLE S-4 Calculation of Expected Value

Event	Probability	Conditional value, dollars	Expected value, dollars
X	.2	10	2
Y	.5	14	7
Z	.3	20	6
	1.0		Expected value = 15

Long-Run Averages. It should be obvious that no alternative action can provide greater total payoffs in the long run than the action with the highest expected value. (This is not to deny that alternative actions may, after the fact, have been superior for *some* decisions.) Note that the actual outcome will never equal the expected value. The expected value is simply the long-run average outcome that will result if the same situation is repeated numerous times. Thus, maximizing the expected value on each occasion will maximize the long-run average payoff. It is also true, however, that applying maximum expected value criteria to nonrepetitive decisions is the strategy that will maximize the expected total payoffs to the firm in the long run. Any other strategy might result in occasional spectacular gains but would be a suboptimal strategy over a prolonged period.

Assignment of Probabilities. The use of expected value to select from actions 1, 2, and 3 in Table S-1 requires that a probability of occurrence be assigned to each of the four possible events. Suppose the following probability distribution is assumed:

Event	A	B	C	D
Probability	.3	.2	.1	.4

Optimum Outcome. The objective is to determine which action leads to the optimum outcome (highest expected value). This is accomplished by calculating the expected payoff for each possible action. This is determined by summing the products of each conditional outcome and its associated probability of occurrence. The individual products and their sums are given in Table S-5. The table indicates that the decision maker's best alternative is action 3.

TABLE S-5 Calculation of Expected Values

Events	Probability	Actions, dollars		
		1	2	3
A	.3	1.20	−.60	2.10
B	.2	0	1.20	.60
C	.1	−.50	.90	.20
D	.4	1.60	−.40	1.20
	Expected value	2.30	1.10	4.10

This strategy has an expected value of $4.10, greater than the expected payoff of the other two available actions.

Loss Analysis. The same decision can be reached by means of a loss analysis (just as the minimax principle leads to the same decision as the maximin principle). The conditional loss table given in Table S-6 can be obtained directly from the decision matrix, or the conditional payoff table, given in Table S-7. The first step is to find the highest conditional payoff corresponding to each event. This payoff corresponds to the best action that could have been taken given that a particular event has occurred. The next step is to subtract all conditional payoffs in the event row from the optimal. Notice that all conditional losses will have values that are either zero (corresponding to the maximum payoffs for each event) or positive.

TABLE S-6 Conditional Loss Table

Events	Actions, dollars		
	1	2	3
A	3	9	0
B	6	0	3
C	14	0	7
D	0	5	1

TABLE S-7 Calculation of Expected Losses

Events	Probability	Actions, dollars		
		1	2	3
A	.3	.90	2.70	0
B	.2	1.20	0	.60
C	.1	1.40	0	.70
D	.4	0	2.00	.40
	Expected loss:	3.50	4.70	1.70

An expected loss table can be calculated for each possible action, using the same procedure employed to calculate expected payoffs. An expected loss table is presented in Table S-7. The appropriate decision criterion is now to select an action with the mini-

mum expected loss. This criterion leads to the selection of action 3.

Analysis of Payoff and Loss Tables. The expected opportunity loss of action A is $1.70. This is the smallest possible expected loss that can be achieved on the basis of available information, even though, over the long run, action A will turn out to have been the best choice only 30 percent of the time. That is, 70 percent of time events B, C, or D will occur, and on those occasions, either action 1 or 2 will give a smaller conditional loss (or larger conditional payoff) than action 3. Nevertheless, action 3 will give the smallest expected, or average, loss over time.

Cost of Uncertainty. Action 3's expected loss could be eliminated only if one knew in advance which event was going to occur—so that the appropriate action could be taken. Since this information is not available, the minimum expected loss can be thought of as the *cost of uncertainty.* In this example, the cost of uncertainty is $1.70 and, in the absence of additional information, it is an irreducible cost.

Perfect Information. Suppose, however, that it is possible to determine in advance which event will occur. Given the availability of this perfect information, it would be possible to select an action so that the conditional loss would always turn out to be zero. Action 1 would be taken 40 percent of the time (when it is known in advance that event D will occur); action 2 would be taken 30 percent of the time (when it is known that either event B or C will occur), and action 3 would be taken 30 percent of the time (when event A will occur). The expected, or average, payoff under conditions of certainty would be $5.80, as shown in Table S-8.

The computations in Table S-8 show that the average payoff over a long period would be $5.80 if perfect advance information were available as to which event would occur. In the absence of perfect information, the expected payoff would be $4.10. The difference between these amounts is the *expected value of perfect information* (EVPI). In this instance, a merchant could pay up to a maximum of $1.70 ($5.80 − $4.10) to obtain a perfect forecast of which event would occur. The $1.70 represents the increase in expected payoff that could be achieved if perfect advance information were available.

Notice that the EVPI and the cost of uncertainty are equal. They represent the same quantity interpreted in slightly different ways. It should also be noted that the sum of the expected payoff and expected loss is $5.80 for all alternative actions.

The EVPI can be used as a quick check of the advisibility of sampling to obtain additional information. If the cost of sampling would be in excess of the EVPI, it clearly would not be worthwhile. If sample information can be obtained very inexpensively, and if it will greatly improve the decision maker's ability to forecast the actual event that will occur, proceed-

TABLE S-8 Expected Payoff under Perfect Information

Event	Probability	Appropriate action	Conditional payoff, dollars	Expected payoff, dollars
A	.3	3	7	2.10
B	.2	2	6	1.20
C	.1	2	9	.90
D	.4	1	4	1.60
			Expected payoff:	5.80

ing will definitely be advantageous. But if the cost of taking a sample will be relatively expensive (although less than the EVPI) and/or the potential value of sample information is questionable, a more formal analysis should be conducted.

Cost of Irrationality. Suppose that, in the absence of perfect information, the decision maker selects action 2 instead of the optimal action 3. The expected loss due to this alternative is $4.70. The decision maker is using a suboptimal strategy and is therefore incurring a higher expected loss than would be necessary. The difference between this expected loss and the cost of uncertainty is called the *cost of irrationality*. In this example the cost of irrationality is $3.00 ($4.70 − $1.70). This is the *additional* loss, over and above the cost of uncertainty, incurred by the decision maker as a result of choosing a suboptimal, or irrational, action.

From the expected payoff table (Table S-5) the expected payoff of action 3 is $4.10. This is the highest expected payoff that can be achieved. A decision to select any other action will result in a lower expected payoff. For example, the expected payoff for action 2 is $1.10. The difference in the two payoff values is $3.00 ($4.10 − $1.10), or the cost of irrationality. This will always be true. The cost of irrationality is equal to both the increase in the expected loss and the decrease in the expected payoff that results from selecting a suboptimal action. Thus, the cost of irrationality of action 1 is $1.80 ($3.50 − $1.70 = $4.10 − $2.30).

Bayesian Analysis

The cost of uncertainty can generally be reduced if information can be obtained which allows the decision maker to better forecast the event that will occur. This explains why market surveys, investment analyses, sales forecasts, and other related activities are undertaken. Technically, from the view of decision theory, new information is collected to allow the reassessment of probability assignments in order to reduce the cost of uncertainty.

The initial probability assignments are called *prior* (before new information) *probabilities*. The probabilities determined on the basis of new information are called *posterior probabilities*. Thus a

mechanism is needed to revise the initial probabilities, given new information. The mechanism is called Bayes' rule. It can be written as:

$$P\frac{A_i}{B} = \frac{P(A_i)P(B/A_i)}{\sum_{i=1}^{n} P(A_i)P(B/A_i)}$$

where $A_i \ldots A_n$ is the set of possible events and B is the new or sample information.

Bayes' rule can best be illustrated by tabular analysis. Consider the situation where one feels that the probability a stock is a good buy is .4. That is, the prior (before new information) probabilities are P (good buy) = .4 and P (bad buy) = .6. Now an investment service that has a record of being right 80 percent of the time recommends purchase of the stock. What, then, would be the revised or posterior (after new information) probability that the stock is a good buy, i.e., P (good buy/investment service recommendation)?

The basic data can be structured as shown in Table S-9, since there are only two possible outcomes for the stock. Based on past records, the sample result "recommend" will occur 80 percent of the time when a stock is actually a good buy and 20 percent of the time when it is actually a bad buy. Such conditional probabilities of the sample result are called the *sampling probabilities.*

TABLE S-9 Information Necessary for Solution of Bayes' Rule

A_i Possible outcomes	$P(A_i)$ Prior probabilities	$P(B/A_i)$ Sampling probabilities
A_1 = good buy	.4	.8
A_2 = bad buy	.6	.2

The first step is to multiply each element in column 2 by its respective element in column 3, as shown in Table S-10. Each element in the new column (column 4) represents a joint probability, which is one of the terms in the numerator of the foregoing **861**

TABLE S-10 Tabular Analysis of Example

A_i	$P(A_i)$	$P(B/a_i)$	$P(A_i)p(B/A_i)$	$P(A_i/B)$
				$\frac{32}{44}$
A_1 = good buy	.4	.8	.32	$\frac{32}{44}$
A_2 = bad buy	.6	.2	.12	$\frac{12}{44}$
			.44	$\frac{12}{44}$

equation representing Bayes' rule. Thus, each element represents the probability of the row's outcome and B, and the sum of the column values equals the value of the denominator. Finally, division of the individual column entry by the column sum represents the conditional probability $P(A_i/B)$. Hence, using the Bayesian tabular analysis, one finds that the revised or posterior probabilities are $^{32}/_{44}$ that the stock is a good buy and, conversely, $^{12}/_{44}$ that it is a bad buy.

In analyzing the use of Bayes' rule to revise prior probability estimates in light of new information, the following relationship should be noted. The stronger the initial prior probabilities, the less effect the new information has on changing the probabilities. Conversely, the more conclusive the new information, the greater the impact on the revised probabilities. For example, if the prior probabilities are .99 and .01 for a good buy and a bad buy respectively, the revised probabilities will be $^{792}/_{794}$ and $^{2}/_{794}$ respectively. If the investment service is right 99 percent of the time, the revised probabilities will be $^{198}/_{201}$ and $^{3}/_{201}$ respectively.

Decision Trees

The alternative courses of action that will be available in the future are frequently determined by the decisions that are made today. Sometimes the interrelationships between current and future actions are known, and so strategies can be devised that will lead to an optimum sequence of decisions. Future decisions will be based on future events, certainly, but a well-devised strategy will indicate which action should be taken given the event (or sequence of events) that has occurred.

A situation may require a series of actions, and several different sequences (or strategies) can be followed. For example, the introduction of a new product or a new manufacturing process may require the construction of new plant facilities. The size of plant that will be needed will depend on the success of the new product or process. Three alternatives initially are open to the firm. A large plant can be constructed immediately, a small plant can be constructed, or the firm can decide to maintain the status quo and do nothing. The construction of a small plant would be a cautious decision. If future events are favorable, larger facilities could be provided by an expansion of the small plant.

A similar problem could be involved in marketing a new product. A strong national marketing effort could be undertaken immediately. Alternatively, the product could be test-marketed in one or more regions and, if successful, brought out nationally at a later date. Or, the firm could decide not to market the product at all. If cost figures and probability estimates of future demand are available, decision trees can be utilized in solving these problems.

Definition. A *decision tree* is a network representation of sequences of action/event combinations that are available to the decision maker. Each possible sequence of decisions and consequences is shown by a different path through the tree. Although some of the problems that are solved through the use of decision trees are very complex, the fundamental solution techniques are relatively straightforward. In fact, one of the major advantages of decision trees is that the problem is structured clearly. This clarity makes possible a systematic and logical attack on the problem of solving for the optimum strategy.

Just about any problem that can be solved using decision trees can also be solved with payoff tables. The two techniques have much in common. Payoff tables generally are used when only one decision must be made (or where a situation—and therefore decision—is to be repeated), whereas decision trees are used most often when a series of interrelated decisions must be made over time. Payoff tables quickly become unwieldy when used for the latter type of problem.

Application. Suppose a decision maker has identified two attractive projects (denoted by X and Y) but lacks the capital necessary to undertake both of them simultaneously. Because the two projects are independent, however, it is possible to undertake X first and then, if X is successful, undertake Y, or vice versa. Project X requires an outlay of $10,000, while Y requires an outlay of $12,000. Neither project will return anything if it is unsuccessful. Successful completion of X will return $8,000 (over cost); of Y, $11,000 (over cost). The probability of success for X is .7 and for Y is .6. *Strategies.* A full analysis of this problem would evaluate five alternative strategies: (1) Do nothing; (2) undertake X and then stop regardless of the outcome; (3) undertake Y and then stop regardless of the outcome; (4) undertake X and, if successful, undertake Y; (5) undertake Y and, if successful, undertake X.

In a decision tree, each decision, including components of an overall strategy, is analyzed individually. A decision tree depicting the above problem is presented in Fig. S-7. Notice that the tree consists of alternating *action/event areas*. The *action* area represents a time of decision for the decision maker. The *event* area that follows indicates the various consequences that can follow the action that is taken. These areas are also called *areas of choice and*

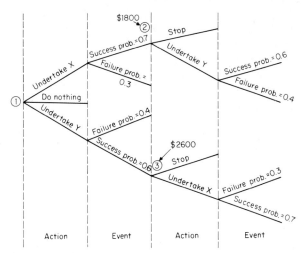

FIG. S-7 A decision tree.

chance. The probabilities of success or failure are shown in the tree following actions that can result in these two outcomes.

Rollback Method. A solution is obtained by working backward through the tree, i.e., from the most distant decisions sequentially back to the initial decision. This is sometimes called the *rollback* method. It is assumed that different decision points in the tree have been reached and, for each, the optimal decision is determined conditional on having reached the decision point being analyzed. Once a decision point has been analyzed, the next step in the procedure is to move backward along the path and analyze the preceding decision point. Each decision point is analyzed, taking into account both the immediate possible outcomes and the expected consequences of subsequent decisions.

The procedure for solving a decision tree can be illustrated with the problem concerning projects X and Y. The decision tree for the problem is given in Fig. S-7 where, for reference purposes, each decision point is identified by a circled number. Decision 3 will be evaluated first. This point is reached only after successful completion of project Y. The expected values of the two alternatives—stop or undertake X—are given in Table S-11. The expected value of stopping is $0 and the expected value of undertaking X is $2600. On the basis of the criterion of maximizing expected value, X should be accepted if Y is successful. Accordingly, a value of $2600 is assigned to the position corresponding to reaching decision point 3.

Decision point 2 will be evaluated next. (Since points 2 and 3 are not points along the same path, the order in which they are evaluated is arbitrary.) The alternative actions and their expected values are given in Table S-12. On the basis of the calculated

TABLE S-11 Evaluation of Decision Point 3

1. Undertake X

Event	Probability	Conditional payoff, dollars	Expected payoff, dollars
Success	.7	8000	5600
Failure	.3	−10,000	−3000
			2600

2. Stop
   Expected value = $0

TABLE S-12 Evaluation of Decision Point 2

1. Undertake Y

Event	Probability	Conditional payoff, dollars	Expected payoff, dollars
Success	.6	11,000	6600
Failure	.4	−12,000	−4800
2. Stop			1800
Expected value = $0			

expected values, the best decision would be to undertake Y. Thus the expected value of successfully completing X and being in a position to undertake Y is $1800. This potential expected gain is shown in Fig. S-7 by assigning a value of $1800 to the point corresponding to decision 2.

Two conditional decisions have been made: that X should be undertaken following successful completion of Y, and that Y should be undertaken if X is

863

TABLE S-13 Evaluation of Decision Point 1

1. Undertake X and then Y

Event	Probability	Conditional payoff, dollars	Expected payoff, dollars
		(8000 + 1800) =	
Success	.7	9,800	6860
Failure	.3	− 10,000	−3000
			3860

2. Undertake Y and then X

		(11,000 + 2600) =	
Success	.6	13,600	8160
Failure	.4	− 12,000	−4800
			3360

3. Do nothing
   Expected value = $0

successfully completed. The final step, shown as decision point 1, is to decide whether first to undertake X, first to undertake Y, or do nothing. The expected values of these three alternatives are given in Table S-13. The procedure is similar to that used above, but one additional factor must now be considered. Successful completion of X brings an immediate cash benefit of $8000 *plus* the opportunity to undertake investment Y. The expected value of accepting investment Y is $1800, so the total payoff of successfully investing in X is $8000 plus $1800, for a total of $9800. Likewise, if Y is accepted first and is successful, the total payoff is $13,600. This amount consists of $11,000, the immediate and direct benefit, plus $2600, the expected value of being able to continue and accept X.

On the basis of the computations in Table S-13, the best initial decision is to undertake X. The best overall strategy is to accept X and, if successful, then to undertake Y. The path through the tree that corresponds to this strategy has an expected value of $3860.

This example illustrates the usefulness of the rollback procedure. Although most problems are much more complicated than the one discussed here, the use of the decision tree approach enables a final solution to be obtained from the systematic solution of a series of small, individual subproblems. The computations become more time-consuming than difficult as the size and complexity of the decision tree grow.

Multiple Criteria

Up to this point, the exposition has always assumed that the objective was to maximize or minimize some single measurable outcome. Hence, the consequence at the end of each decision tree branch was a single

numerical value. Most frequently in routine business problems, one is minimizing costs or expected costs or maximizing the net present value of a profit stream or expected net present value of a profit stream. However, the concept of maximizing profit may be an oversimplification to top management. Business decisions are often made on the basis of consideration of various objectives. For example, an investor may wish to select the portfolio that maximizes expected return but minimizes risk. Here, there are two objectives or decision criteria; moreover, they tend to be conversely related. Another example is to minimize costs and maximize the quality of service. Still another is to decide where to build a new plant. The objectives may be to (1) minimize total construction costs, (2) minimize employee disruption due to the necessity of transfer to a new building, (3) maximize the availability of a qualified labor force, (4) minimize necessary transportation costs of goods received and shipped, and (5) maximize the environmental aspects for employee morale.

In sum, the *multiple-criteria problems*, often called *complex value problems*, are those where the consequences of a decision cannot be adequately described objectively by a single value such as dollars.

The multiple-criteria problem can be divided into two general parts. The first is the proper definition and measurement of the various criteria, and the second is the proper method of evaluating the importance and trade-offs of the various criteria to make the best decision.

Definition and Measurement. With respect to the first part—finding the correct definition and measurement of the criteria—the tasks are (1) to define objectives upon which an alternative action will be evaluated and (2) to measure the success of an alternative action with respect to each objective. Such measurements are called *attributes*. They might be *direct measures* (cost per unit produced), *proxy* measures (a direct measure of something correlated to the objective but not directly the objective), *subjective index of success* (the common social indexes for quality of life), or *direct preference measures* (the assignment of the expected utility of the outcome). These tasks are, of course, similar to that of a single-criterion problem, differing only in the number of objectives and attributes which must be defined. However, since one must ultimately evaluate jointly the various objectives through the attributes, a new dimension has been added to the task: that of structuring a set of attributes that (1) are *complete*, or cover all the important criteria; (2) *operational*, in a form that can be meaningfully used to assess trade-offs among objectives; (3) *decomposable*, such that the evaluation process can be simplified by breaking it down into parts; (4) *nonredundant*, so that double counting of impacts is avoided; and (5) *minimal*, so the dimensions of the task are as small as possible.

Evaluation. Three systematic approaches to finding an optimal action evaluated against multiple criteria are possible, as described below.

Cost Effectiveness. Here, no attempt is made to combine the criteria into a single composite measure to be maximized or minimized. One typically lists *aspiration levels* for each attribute and searches for a solution which meets the levels. If it cannot be found, the aspiration levels are decreased selectively until a solution is found. If a solution is found, investigation must proceed to determine whether any aspiration level can be increased such that a better solution can be found. This approach requires simulation and has two serious weaknesses: (1) It begs the question of what the aspiration levels should be and the appropriate trade-offs among the attributes; (2) it does not permit the introduction of uncertainty into the problem.

Cost-Benefit Analysis. In this approach, one combines the attributes into a single composite benefit measure by weighting the value of each attribute. The trick is to find suitable conversion factors which convert to commensurable units and reflect the appropriate trade-offs. In practice, the conversion is usually obtained by objective market mechanisms or by subjectively imputing dollar prices of monetary worth to each attribute. Cost-benefit is preferable to cost-effectiveness in that it makes arriving at an "optimal" solution easier—that is, the action that maximizes total benefits for a given cost constraint. Its weaknesses, however, are that pricing many attributes, such as goodwill or customer satisfaction, is often very difficult, and introducing uncertainty into the process is also difficult. Nevertheless, it is the most common approach used.

Joint Utility Theory. Here the decision maker must, in essence, assign a utility or develop a function for ordering the utilities for each possible set of attribute outcomes. Hence, the optimal action is the one that maximizes overall utility. This approach is theoretically appealing since it can systematically and effectively handle uncertainty. However, this approach is extremely complex and difficult (if not impossible in some cases) to use. Consequently, it is rarely used in practice.

See also Control systems, management; Operations research and mathematical modeling; Risk analysis and management; System concept, total.

REFERENCES

Anderson, David R., Dennis J. Sweeney, and Thomas A. Williams: *Statistics for Business and Economics*, 2d ed., West Publishing, St. Paul, Minn., 1984.

Johnson, Rodney D., and Bernard R. Siskin: *Quantitative Techniques for Business Decisions*, Prentice-Hall, Englewood Cliffs, N.J., 1976.

Levin, Richard I.: *Statistics for Management*, 3d ed., Prentice-Hall, Englewood Cliffs, N.J., 1984.

Mansfield, Edwin: *Statistics for Business and Economics*, 2d ed., Norton, New York, 1983.

RODNEY JOHNSON, *City of Philadelphia*
BERNARD R. SISKIN, *Temple University*

Stress Management

A manager's first responsibility is to become effective. The second responsibility is to maintain that effectiveness. In the maintenance of managerial effectiveness, stress is an increasingly significant threat. Stress is not new to managers, but there are at least three reasons for a new and enlightened concern.

First, there is the issue of change and adaptation. Organizations must respond continuously to a changing environment. They adjust, adapt, attempt to find new structures and new policies to meet changing constraints and opportunities. The need to adapt induces stress; and when organizations are under stress, managers are under stress.

The *second* reason for concern is that over the past 50 years, the nature of disease and disorder has changed. Chronic diseases are now the principal contributors to morbidity and mortality, and each day new evidence reveals the relationship of stress to chronic disease.

A *third* factor is that management jobs have become more complex—more difficult—because of global changes. Harlan Cleveland described three such changes:

1. The coming of the "horizontal society"
2. The blurring of what is public and what is private
3. The need for systems thinking, systems action[1]

These and other changes forebode more uncertainty and ambiguity in the future. They also require adjustment and adaptation, with resultant stress.

For managers and organizations, the issue of stress has many dimensions. The most obvious is simply health and longevity. The personal tragedy in premature death is obvious. The corporate loss is also significant. Many managers, having just risen to the point of assuming key positions, die of coronary heart disease. Thus, the bench strength dies on the brink of making its most significant contributions. Organizations must learn to nurture and be vigilant of such a valuable resource. They must respond to stress-related issues. Should managers have annual medical examinations? Do they know what they should about alcoholism, nutrition, exercise, and stress? Do they know how to survive in the twentieth century?

The Meaning of Stress. Most managers understand stress intuitively. It is usually an emotional discomfort accompanied by feelings of not being able to cope, that things are falling apart, that one is not in control. Or it may be just a general unease that all is not well, without an apparent cause. At the physical level, it includes loss of appetite, sleeplessness, sweating, ulcers, and other signs and symptoms.

In general, *stress is the result of the body's preparing itself for activity without the activity following.* As a consequence, the body's systems are thrown out of balance. Excess acid is secreted in the stomach. Adrenalin appears in the blood. Heart rates increase, and there are other inappropriate reactions. *Chronic* physiological preparation for action, without the action, leads to disease and disorder. Stress, then, is fundamentally a psychophysiological phenomenon. It has to do with our feelings and emotions and the way our bodies react to them.

Intense feelings and emotions are often the result of experiences we encounter within organizations. In addition, some types of experience are more stressful than others, and the same type of experience can be more stressful to one person than to another. Thus the *stress potential* of a situation can be defined as a function of two elements: (1) the situation and (2) the individual. Individuals, however, tend to differ in their abilities to cope with stress and job tension. Also, some techniques for coping tend to be more effective than others.

Coping with Job Tension. In studies we have done on job tensions, managers were asked to indicate the various methods by which they coped with potentially stressful job situations. Their answers were grouped into these 10 categories:

1. Build resistance by regular sleep, exercise, and good health habits.

2. Compartmentalize work and nonwork life.

3. Engage in physical exercise.

4. Talk through with peers on the job.

5. Withdraw physically from the situation.

6. Change to a different work activity.

7. Change strategy of attack on work.

8. Work harder.

9. Talk your feeling through with your spouse.

10. Change to a nonwork activity.

Most Effective Techniques. In follow-up studies, the effectiveness of each technique was determined by relating the usage of the technique to the incidence of stress symptoms. In terms of the average number of stress symptoms reported, the five best techniques for coping with job tensions were as follows:

1. Build resistance by regular sleep, exercise, and good health habits.

2. Compartmentalize work and nonwork life.

3. Engage in physical exercise.

4. Talk through your feelings with peers on the job.

5. Withdraw physically from the situation.

The most effective mechanism, building physical resistance, is highly significant in designing an action plan for coping with stress. It reflects an awareness of the demands of the job, a sensitivity to one's own limited physical resources, and a readiness to deal with tension as it arises. Individuals who have a preventive concern about their health will have energy available that they can use to help deal with problems rationally and effectively. Individuals who are healthy and alert have a much greater success potential as "managers of stress" than do the managers who neglect their health and, thus, their readiness to deal with stress.

Managing the Stress of Change. Change is a principal source of stress in the life of a manager, and coping effectively with it often requires a reassessment of attitudes and lifestyle. Research by the authors has shown that some individuals are more change-prone and that this same group is less efficient in dealing with the stress resulting from change. To become an effective manager of stress, the individual must maintain "change events" within tolerable limits. This is not to say that one should suppress change, as it constitutes the dynamics of life itself. Rather, one can consciously *plan* those events that are controllable so as to maintain a firm grasp on the events and activities of day-to-day living. At the same time, managers who are aware of the fact that the unexpected does occur prepare themselves by retaining a reserve of energy to cope with unanticipated events.

Active Participation versus Passive Reaction. One *can* make a conscious decision either to experience life as a series of inevitable, uncontrollable events or to actively control and anticipate occurrences in the present and in the future. The two extremes in attitude may be described as *active participation* and *passive reaction.*

The active participators simplify their lifestyles by consciously selecting and timing the occurrences of specific milestones in their lives. They are aware of, and consider, their personal energy level (psychological and physical capacity) and do not judge personal success by the number of activities and new events they can handle without first breaking down or burning out. They leave a reservoir of untapped time and energy for those unexpected events that otherwise might cause disruption and distress. They are "managers of change."

On the other hand, the passive reactors tend to leave their lives to fate. They seem to pride themselves on the number of activities and new undertakings they can cram into an already busy schedule. They do not anticipate the fact that, sooner or later, the one unexpected event will occur that is too large to fit into their chaotic and overburdened lifestyles. Change, therefore, not only occurs more frequently (from a self-inflicted source) but also tends to hit harder since it is often unanticipated.

From evidence collected in research by the authors, a continuum has been constructed, representing at its extremes the least and the most effective attitudes toward life and change, and the subsequent mechanisms used to cope and adapt. The ends of the continuum may be imagined as two hypothetical individuals composed of polar extremes in attitudes, actions, and coping dispositions. The summary of these constructs is presented in Table S-14.

If a manager is to cope successfully with a constantly changing environment and to adapt within the dynamics of an evolving lifestyle, he or she should attempt to move consciously toward the right-hand extreme of this continuum.

Development of Stress Management. A concerned manager can begin immediately a personal development program in the management of stress. Eight steps are particularly appropriate.

1. Consciously assess your own pace of life at present. Take inventory of all recent changes; include current or upcoming change events. Analyze job situations and identify those which you find particularly stressful. Ask yourself if you feel generally tense, overloaded, unsure about your job status, or confused by your state of affairs.

2. Try to become aware of your own psychophysiological threshold. Practice sensitivity in detecting stress symptoms (e.g., heart palpitations, headaches, rapid pulse, insomnia). Learn to identify a state of stress within yourself so you can begin to deal with it directly.

3. Simplify your life. Attempt to foresee the occurrence of specific stress-producing job events and try to schedule them so they do not occur simultaneously. In the same way, budget change events in such a way that they remain within your perception of controllable limits. Do not

TABLE S-14 Styles of Coping with Change

The passive reactor (least effective)	The active participator (most effective)
1. Reacts passively to life's events.	1. Participates actively in life.
2. Leaves life to "fate." Tends to "cram" rather than "plan" activities.	2. Maintains change events within tolerable limits by making a conscious selection of controllable activities.
3. Shows little foresight or anticipation of events.	3. Anticipates and prepares for likely events in the foreseeable future. Has good foresight.
4. Allows events to accumulate until unable to cope when the unexpected arises.	4. Builds and maintains a reservoir of untapped time and energy to deal with unexpected events.
5. Perceives the environment and most change events as generally threatening.	5. Views the environment objectively. Sorts events into categories of importance, urgency, and degree of actual threat.
6. When faced with potentially stressful change, tends to react compulsively, most often in a stereotyped manner.	6. When faced with potentially stressful change, takes time out to evaluate alternative strategies, perhaps even adopting a novel solution to a novel problem.
7. May unconsciously choose a coping mechanism that actually increases stress reaction through adverse consequences.	7. After careful evaluation, tries to adopt the mechanism of coping most apt to reduce potential stress and aid in successful adaptation.
8. Continues to tax his or her psychophysiological capacity to the limit. Stress symptoms accumulate.	8. Effectively eliminates or reduces stress. Continues to operate well within an adaptive range, and avoids overtaxing his or her psychophysiological capacity.

suppress all change and tensions; merely "manage" them. Leave job tensions at the office; compartmentalize work and home life. Become an active participator in controlling your life rather than a passive reactor to fate.

4. Leave room within your coping range for those unanticipated stress situations. Do not load your time or budget your energy completely to their quotas. Maintain a state of readiness by staying healthy and alert. Be prepared! Develop a preventive concern about your health.

5. When an unexpected stress situation or major change event arises, stop and think about it. Is it really as serious as it appears to be on the surface? Is it worth the expenditure of valuable energy resources in worrying and tension? Or, with the application of a little imagination and flexibility, can you adapt quite easily and readily?

6. Evaluate the various alternative mechanisms at hand for coping with tension. Are the old ways still working effectively? Or, is it time to take a break, get away from it all, and evaluate new courses of action objectively? Begin to design and apply a broad repertoire of alternative responses. Be flexible and imaginative; shy away from stereotyped reactions. Follow through by analyzing the implications and range of consequences in your responses.

7. Above all, be in conscious control of your life. Participate actively, imaginatively, and with flexibility. Remember that you, as a manager, are particularly exposed to tension and susceptible to stress.

8. Remember also that stress is not all bad. Some stress is both necessary and desirable. The basic issue is not its elimination but its containment and allocation—the management of stress.

See also Assertiveness training; Health, mental; Human factors engineering; Interpersonal relationships; Motivation in organizations; Transactional analysis.

NOTES

[1] Harlan Cleveland, *The Future Executive: A Guide for Tomorrow's Managers*, Harper & Row, New York, 1972.

REFERENCES

Janis, Irving: *Stress, Attitudes, and Decisions*, Praeger, New York, 1982.

Howard, John H.: "Management Productivity; Rusting Out or Burning Out?" *The Business Quarterly*, Summer 1975.

————, Peter A. Rechnitzer, and D. A. Cunningham: "Coping with Job Tension—Effective and Ineffective Methods," *Public Personnel Management*, September–October, 1975.

Marshall, Judi, and Cary L. Cooper: *Executives under Pressure: A Psychological Study*, Praeger, New York, 1979.

JOHN H. HOWARD, PETER A. RECHNITZER, AND DAVID A. CUNNINGHAM, *University of Western Ontario*

Suggestion Systems

A *suggestion system* is a formal program under which employees are encouraged to submit written suggestions to management and are rewarded for those which are adopted. Rewards are usually financial, either a set sum or a percentage of savings to the company affected by adoption of the suggestion.

An effective system requires that management (1) define precise objectives; (2) set a time frame for their attainment; (3) demonstrate prominent, widely communicated, and continual commitment; (4) provide prompt feedback to all suggesters (30 days for processing, 60 days at most for action); (5) publicize awards widely, in-house and locally; (6) thoroughly train middle management and supervisors (the critical elements in a suggestion system); (7) provide thorough and tailored communication to all employees about the system and its rules; (8) allocate sufficient budgeting for expert administration and complete record keeping (using data processing if more than 1500 files per year are generated); (9) specify in detail the evaluation process; (10) receive reports at least quarterly; (11) check on legal aspects of all steps before implementing a system; (12) lean over backwards to ensure that rewards are adequate (typical and recommended: a minimum of $50 or 15 to 25 percent of net savings earned the first year).

Effective systems can average impressive net returns on investment: 600 to 700 percent. They are a proved cost-reduction/profit-improvement tool, serve to locate both problem areas and talent, increase productivity and work quality, improve employee-management relationships, and develop employee motivation by providing direct communication upward and a medium for self-expression, achievement, and recognition—thus a feeling of involvement and responsibility to the company. Experts warn, however, that casual or half-hearted support of a suggestion system by management can actually harm the company by causing employee dissatisfaction and frustration. Furthermore, advocates of other types of work-related improvement programs, like work simplification and quality circles, deprecate suggestion systems because of their appeal to individual, rather than group, interests and their emphasis upon monetary rather than psychic rewards.

See also Attitude surveys; Communications, organizational; Quality circles; Work simplification and improvement.

REFERENCES

Gryna, Frank M., Jr.: *Quality Circles: A Team Approach to Problem Solving,* American Management Association, AMACOM, New York, 1981.

National Association of Suggestion Systems, Chicago. This nonprofit organization provides members with a wide variety of services for systems development, implementation, and administration.

Tatter, Milton A.: "Turning Ideas into Gold," Management Review, March 1975.

Lester R. Bittel, *James Madison University*

System Concept, Total

The total system concept represents a way of thinking rather than a precise methodology; accordingly, this entry emphasizes the system approach, which is closely linked with modern ideas on organization and information.

System Principles

Few words are so overworked and so often defined as *system,* which means: A set of interrelated components that function, together within constraints, toward a common purpose.

The term *total system* suggests components that interact dynamically to create a synergistic whole that is greater than the mere sum of its parts. The concept indicates that performance of a component cannot be evaluated by viewing it in isolation. It must be seen in context of contiguous functions and must be judged by its contribution to the achievement of the overall system objectives. A component may be either an individual element or an aggregation of them, known as *subsystem.* Subsystems may be arranged in a *hierarchy,* in which components are layered to form a complex network.

The Nature of Systems. Business and industry have become increasingly aware of the external influences on their organizations. Traditional organization theory assumed that it dealt with closed systems in the sense that destinies and performance were relatively deterministic and controlled from within. The modern concept is to view an organization as an *open system* which has significant interactions with the environment, depending on it for resources, and being constrained by its influences. The open system usually involves humans as developers, operators, and users who contribute to the uncertainty in func-

tion and results. While the open system has control guidance, it involves qualitative judgment and probabilistic performance.

Mission. The unifying force for the components of a system is a common purpose. The *mission* is expressed in terms of objectives and products, including both goods and services. The objectives are often general and subjective in nature, being concerned with such things as profit, growth, productivity, human need satisfaction, and public benefit. They are also concerned with the quantity and quality of the system output. A major point about the total system concept is that the hierarchy of subsystems exists solely to provide functions required to achieve the system purpose. Subsystem goals must be subordinate, and performance should be evaluated primarily on the subsystem contribution to the whole.

Environment. For a closed system, it is relatively easy to determine components necessary to achieve a given purpose. These components lie within a defined bounary and are under control of the system. All activities outside this boundary and control are classified as the environment, making the boundary more difficult to define as to purpose, components, and manageability. External constraints, such as social, government, market, technological, and legal changes become important parts of the definition of the system boundary.

Resources. The inputs to the open system are the various resources that must be transformed into the products or services to achieve the system purpose. Generally, the resources are described in terms of value and dimension of raw materials for the system process. More subjective inputs may include new opportunities and increased management skills.

Process. The functions needed to transform resources into desired output constitute the *system process.* Control over component operation is achieved by monitoring the state of activity; sensing output attributes; comparing actual results with those intended; and providing feedback to adjust inputs as necessary. Negative feedback makes corrections to return to an intended output characteristic, or essentially steady state. Positive feedback is utilized to change direction toward new goals.

Structure. Each system requires organization and procedures to define relationships among components and to provide channels for the flow of communications. Centralized authority is implied by the need to coordinate component performance. But broad understanding of objectives, coupled with effective communication, gives latitude for decentralizing both authority and responsibility. Adaptation to changes in purpose or environment is a management function crucial to the continued success of the system.

Modular Approach. The total systems approach is susceptible to a challenge of what is manageable in the "total" perspective. The degree to which one can integrate functions and still control operation is countered by the ability to describe functional modules without sacrificing objectives.

Application of System Principles

Two primary factors must be considered in applying systems principles.

Life Cycle. Advocates of the system approach imply that it applies equally to all activities. Experience tells us, however, that the approach has different ramifications for each phase of the life cycle of a system. This fact reinforces the time influence ascribed to the total system concept by indicating that relevance varies from inception to replacement.

During the operational stage, the system approach assumes the form of problem solving, decision making, and control functions of a system's life cycle (strategic, tactical, operational, and clerical).

Systems analysis is a methodical, reproducible way to identify significant problems from symptoms and to evaluate alternative solutions for situations in existing systems. In the process, resources are utilized in a way to optimize the time, cost, and quality issues. Output is sensed and compared with objec-

tives, and feedback is generated to control the process. Decisions are made toward improving productivity and maintaining the process through repair and minor alteration of components.

Activity Levels. Four different phases of system life are frequently encountered in project-oriented situations. Ongoing business, industry, and government institutions are more concerned with sustaining operations and adapting to changing conditions and opportunities. Evolution is usually accomplished while performing the organizational mission rather than through completely replacing obsolescent units, an approach common in physical systems. Table S-15 summarizes characteristics and implications of the systems approach for different levels of activity normally associated with a business organization. Some managers utilize quantitatively detailed estimates as a basis for decisions. Others are more comfortable when depending on intuition to generate new ideas, to assume risk, or to resolve subjective issues. The systems approach should be hardy enough to support these differing roles and attitudes.

Methodology

The systems approach must embrace the means to specify functions during design of the system and to

TABLE S-15 Activity Level Considerations

| Activity levels | System implication | | Performance measure examples |
	Organization	Information	
Strategic	Planning, future time periods Policy, mission-oriented Heuristic decision process Open system; probabilistic	Predictive models, representative samples Relevance Intuitive, qualitative, uncertainty Environmental influence	Satisfaction Share of market Change in risk
Tactical	Resource allocation, proximate time period Flexible, adaptive; choice among alternatives Revision of objectives Nonprogrammed decisions	Optimization models Sufficiency, conciseness, management decision Summary and analysis of functional performance	Delivery time Unit cost Utilization percent Scheduled task completion
Operational	Control of ongoing events and resource use Goal seeking, continuity of process or function Programmed decisions	Normative models Monitoring during operation cycle Reliability Feedback, output comparison	Downtime Time between failures Frequency of service requests Quality percent
Clerical	Productivity, cost displacement Conditioned reaction to input transactions Closed system, near deterministic	Descriptive models Data recording Accuracy	Error rate Capacity use Throughput volume Handling cost

assemble them into a unified whole at implementation. Because of the adaptive nature of organizations, heuristic decision processes are appropriate. The involvement of humans as decision makers stresses the need to apply modern ideas of organization and information systems. The *information system* is a set of rules and procedures designed to transform data into information which has utility in planning, organizing, and controlling activity. Such procedures do not require a computer, but its advent has made possible the handling of more variables and interactions. Thus, the systems approach has become more meaningful with the escalation of computer capability, especially data storage and management.

The problem of defining an open system is a major challenge in that clear and logical description of boundaries is difficult. Should customers be included in the marketing subsystem or vendors in the materials acquisition subsystem? If they are included, how does the system exercise control over their activities? If not, in what sense are we dealing with a "total" system? Assume that boundaries can be initially established to define the system of interest and to segregate it from other systems or suprasystems in a hierarchy. How can one accommodate the continual changes of state within the system and adapt to the influences that are associated with the environment? Expansion, variant inputs, and transient functions all cause overlaps and gaps among subsystems and also among those interacting systems that constitute the environment. Indeed, one never deals with a "total system"; consideration of the whole or its parts in isolation is always a matter of degree.

The systems approach must support compromise in perspective, but it should also promote an overview that keeps major corporate goals dominant. Even when components are isolated for manageable study, the assessment criteria should stress contribution to the whole rather than efficiency of the part.

See also Control systems, management; Decision support systems; Input-output analysis; Management information systems (MIS); Operations research and mathematical modeling; Simulations, business and management.

REFERENCES

Churchman, C. West: "Perspectives of the Systems Approach," *Interfaces*, vol. 4, no. 4, August 1974, pp. 6–11.

Johnson, Richard A., Fremont E. Kast, and James E. Rosenzweig: *The Theory of Management Systems*, 3d ed., McGraw-Hill, 1973.

Optner, Stanford I.: *Systems Analysis for Business Management*, 3d ed., Prentice-Hall, Englewood Cliffs, N.J., 1975.

WILLIAM A. SMITH, JR., *North Carolina State University*

Systems and Procedures

Systems and procedures analysis, which had its origin in the study and improvement of information, communications, and paperwork flow within an organization, has gradually extended its scope to include just about any kind of integrated analysis and improvement of the various functional aspects of an organization. Responsibility for it may be the domain of a separate systems (or systems and procedures) department; it may fall under the wing of an industrial engineering department; or it may be wholly the work of a management information systems activity. A fully operative systems function will include the talents of systems specialists such as operations research and statistical people, industrial and methods engineers, forms designers, records management analysts, and data processing and equipment experts. These talents may be those of full-time employees, or they may be obtained on a periodic consultative basis.

Activities. Systems analysis, design, and implementation draw from a wide range of activities and from many fields. Typically, these encompass a number of stages such as the following, but not necessarily in this order.

1. *Objectives verification.* Akin to strategic planning, a starting point for most systems studies is the identification of a company's long-term goals together with its implementation strategies. This study ranges downward from broad organizational goals to specific, functional, and departmental goals. In many instances, it focuses on the administrative aspects of information processing and management.

2. *Implementation analysis.* An effort is made to relate (a) the various processes and functions performed by the company to (b) its chosen goals. This procedure helps to uncover overlapping and superfluous activities as well as gaps in necessary coverage. The underlying questions are: Does every activity now performed contribute to identifiable objectives? In the most effective manner? While not omitting anything that is absolutely necessary? Industrial engineers are especially effective in this phase.

3. *Information analysis.* Assuming that the existing, or revised, operating system is effective, a determination must be made of the information needed at all decision points to keep it operative. Key questions are: What kind of information is needed? At what points? When? In what form?

4. *Communications analysis.* Each organization adapts itself to its own best communication channels, and information flow must respect

these channels, although it may bypass some channels and be redundant in others. Organization development specialists can make great contributions to phases 3 and 4.

5. *Systems design.* At some stage of analysis, it becomes imperative to put together—as well as possible, perfection being rarely possible—the implementation process activities (and structure), the communication channels, and the required information. The system must fit the restraints of all three elements. This is the stage in which operations research experts are best utilized.

6. *System transformation.* Only after the unifying system has been designed can data processing specialists convert the system to an information processing system. At this phase, those with know-how about hardware and software make their greatest contribution.

7. *Forms design.* This step calls for a determination of the best form or format upon (or with) which to collect information, transmit it through the system, and present it to the various decision makers. This is a specialty requiring knowledge ranging from that of human perceptions to the extensive mechanics of reproduction materials and devices.

8. *Records procedures.* The line between forms and records is indistinct, but the first tends to emphasize physical considerations while the second is more concerned with the sequences of information flow and with establishing policy about records dissemination, retention, and retrieval.

9. *Equipment specification.* Systems design recognizes the ubiquitous interface between person and machine and the need to delineate exactly what each will do. Ideally, the machine will be required to perform that portion of the work that it can do better, faster, or more economically than human beings. Therein lies the critical aspect of equipment specification and selection, a field of expertise dominated by equipment manufacturers and consultants.

10. *Electronic adaptation.* Electronic equipment—the computer and its ancillaries—is especially suitable for the data processing required by complex systems. Most systems ultimately must depend upon the computer's capabilities, and few systems should be accepted that do not acknowledge that eventuality.

11. *Work measurement.* Assuming that there is concern for the effectiveness of administrative systems (as distinguished from production systems, although a total systems approach would not view them separately), operating procedures and work requirements should be based

upon a systematic study of the human work involved. This study can be done by such techniques as time and motion study, predetermined time standards, activity charting, and work sampling.

12. *Work standardization.* The publication of procedures to be followed by those who operate the system requires that work be defined and routinized along with the specification of quantitative time and/or cost standards.

13. *Work simplification.* Somewhere along the line of system study and specification, thought should be given to improvement in—or simplification of—work methods, especially those related to paperwork and administrative services such as mail handling, word processing, key punching, and reproduction functions.

14. *Procedures preparation.* This is the phase that joins procedures to systems and in which all the previous decisions about design, forms, and equipment are formalized into a prescribed (and written) set of policies, standards, and procedures.

15. *Procedures publication.* Most organizations find it useful, if not absolutely necessary, to publish their policies and procedures in the form of manuals that are distributed to management and/or operations personnel in the various functional areas. These manuals are used for instruction, training, and reference and must be updated periodically as the system itself evolves or is redesigned. Communication specialists are especially useful in phases 14 and 15.

16. *Organization development.* In its ultimate form, systems and procedures analysis may begin with a study and redevelopment of the company's organization relationships and basic structure. This analysis involves the defining of new goals and the establishment of new strategies beginning at the top and cascading downward throughout the organization. If a company chooses this route, only after this phase is completed would the other 15 phases be considered. Organization development (OD) is typically conducted under the guidance of organizational and behavioral specialists.

Systems work, by its very designation, implies unification rather than fragmentation. It would be short-sighted, however, to suggest that the principles can be applied only to a company's total system. In many instances, because of internally or externally imposed restrictions, the systems approach can be applied effectively to the system that exists within a department or even a small work group. It is better first to design the overall system, of course, and then integrate the smaller system, but the work of any single function or department can be attacked independently.

See also Forms design and control; Gantt charts; Management information systems (MIS); Management information systems, transaction processing systems; Manuals, policy and procedures; Office space planning; Paperwork simplifications; Planning, strategic managerial; Records management; Scheduling, short-interval; System concept, total; Work design, job enlargement, and job enrichment; Work measurement; Work simplification and improvement.

REFERENCES

Grossman, Lee: *Fat Paper,* McGraw-Hill, New York, 1976.

Haslett, J. W.: *Business Systems Handbook,* McGraw-Hill, New York, 1979.

Heyel, Carl, ed.: *Handbook of Modern Office Management and Administrative Services,* R. E. Krieger, Huntington, N.Y., 1980.

Lester R. Bittel, *James Madison University*

Tax Management

Management responsibilities for federal income tax accounting are examined here from the standpoint of some of the critical topics and policy issues of concern to the generalist corporate manager. Emphasis is placed on what a manager should look for, be alert to, and identify in ongoing business transactions and planning as constituting either turning points for policy decisions or managerial danger signs. The tax law has been, and still is, undergoing constant changes; hence, there is a need for caution in using any publication addressing substantive topics. A number of changes in the law have occurred since 1978, with several of them having significance for the manager. Among the most important are the Economic Recovery Tax Act of 1981 (ERTA) and the Tax Equity and Fiscal Responsibility Act of 1982 (TEFRA). Subjects included in this entry, however, have a fairly high degree of fundamental stability, and the principles highlighted should have a continuing applicability. Constraints imposed by space cause the content here to be highly selective and, as to the substantive areas, only illustrative.

The Corporate Tax Department

An effective tax department must be directed toward the objective of meeting corporate tax obligations with a minimum of friction with the Internal Revenue Service (IRS) in the compliance areas that can be described as "no win."

The "no win" area means that failure to comply can result only in a disservice to the corporation; there can be no real benefits. Examples are failure to file required returns, failure to meet advance payment requirements, failure to make timely elections, and failure to properly execute tax and related forms so they will process through the IRS data processing system. Not only are interest and penalties significantly high for these kinds of failures, but the resulting deluge of computer-generated correspondence will be time-consuming and can result in compounding the error.

The managerial task of making certain the department is meeting the many recurring tax requirements imposed by government is, indeed, substantial. While this entry is concerned with federal income tax accounting, the multistate corporate operation must meet filing requirements in many states, as well as municipalities, townships, and counties. In terms of volume, these state requirements can exceed the federal by as much as 50 times in even the medium-sized, multistate operation. Thus, more department personnel must be assigned to state returns than to federal requirements.

One key to effective handling of these numerous recurring responsibilities is the use of a master tax calendar. The calendar carries due dates for every type of requirement that will have to be met during the year. In addition to the calendar, various cross-checks are maintained, including the alert provided by receipt of blank forms from the IRS or state tax agency, calendars offered by various commercial publications, and the use of a computer to provide work-load schedules.

The Tax Audit

Management does have a responsibility to set the climate in terms of relationships between the corporation and IRS, the administering agency. Management may unwisely abdicate this responsibility and leave it to the tax department, or worse, it may establish the climate by bad example, i.e., consistently skirting the edge of compliance or engaging in practices that smack of evasion. The best attitudinal stance is one of enlightened self-interest, vigorously asserting and protecting the corporate rights on the basis of "what's right" and, when necessary, disagreeing without being disagreeable.

Management can gain insight as to both the efficiency and the attitudinal stance of the corporate tax department as a result of an examination of corporate records by internal revenue agents. Normally, all the very large corporations are audited each year. The "team audit" concept is used; the team consists of various experts, such as engineers who are skilled in depreciable equipment, pension trust specialists, computer specialists who are able to cope with computerized records, and one or more revenue agents who are generalists in corporate examinations. If a corporate taxpayer is found to be in substantial compliance, the service may forgo an audit for one or more years.

Impact on Operations. An effective tax department will keep management apprised throughout the course of the audit as to the issues being raised. The audit may well proceed for several months, and, to the extent practicable, issues may be disposed of concurrently to avoid their being bunched at the conclusion. The issues are often those which involve shifts of income or deductions between or among years. The benefit of a deduction usually will not be lost but, rather, postponed. As to larger items of this kind that are conceded, management will be concerned with (1) what causal factors are responsible for the adjustment, and (2) what the impact of the deficiency will be on cash flow.

Other issues will have an adverse, irretrievable tax impact on the corporation or its officers or shareholders. If the amount is large, management usually regards these adjustments quite seriously and will carefully consider the likelihood of prevailing through further administrative and judicial action.

Audit Process. For various reasons, evaluation of the tax department and other related corporate functions, i.e., accounting, data processing, and internal audit, on the basis of results of an IRS audit can be difficult and frustrating. First, the issue list is often very long; it will change in the course of conferences at the agent level and, if protested, at higher administrative and/or judicial levels. Second, the procedure usually takes a great deal of time. Thus, even with current briefings, the manager will have difficulty tracking the process.

Additionally, the results of prior audits are only a partial guide to the current or future audits. This circumstance is the product of a number of factors: (1) While audits have become more thorough and more penetrating under the "large case" program, the effectiveness will vary among agents or "teams"; (2) the IRS is constantly gaining new insights into old problems, e.g., the computer-assisted audits have ensured that a mass of transactions recorded on magnetic tape is no longer free from scrutiny; and (3) new issues are constantly being identified which have industrywide significance.

Nonetheless, it is important that, to the extent feasible, the evaluation referred to earlier be undertaken. The effort may lead to routines within the accounting department where classification between repair and capital are the subject of inadequate instruction or where cost-accounting procedures have fragmentized transactions to the end that major capital items may be buried or in-house construction not properly classified as to repairs and new structures.

Management of the larger corporate entity must think in terms of internal and/or external audit entirely aside from IRS. This kind of tool can provide a realistic cross-check by professionals skilled in their function. Reports can be produced which provide management with an opportunity for corrective action. Whether such action will be taken depends on the quality of management itself.

Criminal Aspects. The corporate entity that has been indifferent to IRS oversight can be in for a major shock when an IRS audit uncovers proscribed campaign contributions, major executive use of corporate facilities for personal use, expenditures to influence potential buyer-representatives, or the use of false documentation.

TEFRA contains new, tough civil penalties for

substantial understatement of tax liability on returns and for aiding and abetting in the preparation or presentation of false documents. Criminal fines for evasion of tax, willfull failure to keep records, and filing and/or delivery of false documents to the government have been materially increased. The manager's only prudent course is to see that the organization turns "square corners" in meeting tax requirements, since the ability of the government to compel testimony and production of documents where a corporation is involved will, in general, either reveal the facts or result in a officer's or employee's being in contempt of court.

Tax executives of major companies are fully aware that IRS has a strong internal security program and that attempting to bribe an agent is not worth the risk. Agents are constantly indoctrinated as to methods of handling the bribe proffer. Some managers, however, may obtain an erroneous idea that the sophisticated way to handle a difficult issue is through bribing the agent. To those, we can say that even the amoral are deterred when the risk of detection is substantial. Regardless of whether it seems to have worked in the past, or the agent seems receptive, such a course should never be adopted. Entertainment of the agent(s), even in modest ways, is proscribed by the IRS.

Trust Fund Depositories

The delinquent trust fund problem is endemic to the corporation with a serious cash-flow problem. The sizable amounts of money involved in the withholding of federal income taxes and the ever-increasing rates and ceiling of salaries subject to the Federal Insurance Contribution Act (Social Security) involve a constant temptation for hard-pressed management to pay only the net salaries to employees and to defer the trust fund amounts for resolution at a future time. Under the prodding of various administrations, Congress has enacted an increasingly stringent series of remedies for failure of the taxpayer to make trust fund deposits.

In overall terms, management needs to be aware of the following provisions: (1) failure-to-file penalty, (2) failure-to-pay penalty, (3) interest rates on delinquent amounts, (4) mandatory deposit of trust funds, (5) the 100 percent penalty, and (6) criminal sanctions.

Pay-as-You-Go Requirements. The concept of "pay as you go," so well illustrated by individual withholding of federal income tax and Social Security tax (FICA) and their companion piece, the declaration of estimated tax (form 1040ES) for current payment of an individual's tax, has over the years not only been spread through nearly the entire system of federal tax liabilities, but it has often been accelerated so that now the funds are remitted to the U.S. Treasury at the earliest practicable date.

In general, corporations are required to deposit estimated tax payments with an authorized commercial bank depository or the Federal Reserve Bank during the taxable year if the corporation's estimated tax can be expected to be $40 or more. No estimated return as such is required, but the prepaid tax is claimed as a credit on the U.S. Corporation Income Tax Return, form 1120, filed for the taxable year.

With very limited exceptions, the corporation will, as an employer, also be liable for federal unemployment tax (FUTA). The return (form 940) is to be filed on or before January 31 following the calendar year, and during each year the corporation must make a computation to determine whether it is liable for quarterly deposits of the tax to an authorized commercial bank or the Federal Reserve Bank.

From a managerial standpoint, however, the most crucial depository requirements are those referred to above, involving income tax and social security tax withheld for employees, plus the employer's share of the latter tax. These are *crucial* because in any organization with a number of employees, large amounts will be involved, and the remedies available to the government for the corporation's failure to comply are, at least, extraordinary.

Deposits must also be made to an authorized commercial bank or the Federal Reserve Bank for these "collected" taxes. The return itself, form 941, Employer's Quarterly Federal Tax Return, is due quarterly. The timing of the deposit requirement, however, depends on the amount of taxes currently involved and ranges from quarter-monthly (approximately weekly) to monthly to quarterly.

Delinquency Penalties. Civil penalties for failure to deposit, failure to pay and failure to file the return when due, plus an interest rate which is now tied to the prime rate quoted by commercial banks, can have a significant combined dollar impact on the corporation. Under TEFRA, interest is currently compounded daily. From a tax policy perspective, the penalties and interest are designed to take any profit out of diverting resources to other applications in lieu of meeting the various depository and payment requirements.

Now, management must give consideration throughout the operating year to the requirements for cash flow to meet these depository responsibilities. In earlier years, the corporation could have the benefit of trust funds for the full calendar quarter and up to the actual filing of the employer's quarterly return. Similarly, corporate income tax liabilities and federal unemployment tax were payable annually, in contrast to the current "pay-as-you-go" system, which is also without benefit of interest to the corporation for money so deposited.

Management that is seriously hard pressed for

cash and that opts to pay only net salaries of employees while putting off the inevitable day of payment of the trust fund liabilities needs to be alert to the following extraordinary remedies available to the government.

Statutory authority and administrative procedure exist to require the corporation or other business entity which has employees, collects withholding of federal income taxes and social security taxes therefrom, and has a history of delinquency, to pay over such collections within 2 banking days to a designated depository in trust for the United States. Failure of a corporate officer or other responsible person to comply can subject such a person to a fine and imprisonment (on charges of misdemeanor).

The result of the imposition of the 100 percent penalty is usually the insolvency and bankruptcy of the corporation as either a "no-asset" case or liquidation without full discharge of outstanding trust fund liabilities. In these situations, the Internal Revenue Code authorizes the use of a penalty equal to the trust fund taxes unpaid—hence, the term *100 percent penalty.*

The penalty can be assessed only against responsible officials who "willfully" failed to collect and pay over to the United States such trust funds. It is usually not too difficult to show that one or more responsible officials had such knowledge. Those officials who claimed their conduct was not willful have found that this defense failed. The test adopted by the courts is whether the officer was responsible for determining which creditors should be paid. Note that a third party, often a creditor's representative, can also be liable if he or she exercised such control. Against an individual's personal estate, these assessments are often so large as to be devastating. The assessment also will be joint and several against all responsible officials who willfully failed in their duty.

Managerial Aspects of Tax Questions

It is customary for proposed corporate undertakings to be submitted to the firm's tax department for an opinion when the tax significance is not clear or the exact monetary impact is unknown. In order to formulate a sound opinion, the tax department may need to consult specialists for various facets of the problem.

At the same time, the tax department should, at its own initiative, be submitting staff papers, perhaps quarterly reports, and similar material to top management. In addition, however, the generalist executive can obtain an effective conceptual grasp of the tax significance involved in various projects, plans, and functions. This kind of viewpoint may actually contribute more to the quality of the managerial decision than the expert's opinion. Some examples follow of the methodology which can be used by the generalist in developing skill in this area.

Depreciation Policy. While there is a substantial volume of rules governing the treatment of depreciation of assets used in trade or business, in the context of financial planning the following information should meet the manager's needs. Over the last decade and a half, Congress (following initial action by the federal executive branch) moved to liberalize depreciation allowances for tax purposes, largely to make American manufacturing more competitive internationally. The liberalization occurred principally in the shortening, unifying, and stabilizing of estimated useful lives and enforcement by IRS through what became known as the Asset Depreciation Range System, plus the most generous allowances for depreciation during the initial years of acquisition of business property having a useful life of at least several years.

These evolved concepts were, however, dramatically changed by ERTA in an effort to further stimulate the economy. ERTA provides new opportunities for managerial decisions in that the 1981 act abandoned the old estimated useful-line method in favor of the new Accelerated Cost Recovery System (ACRS). Basically, this new system, to be utilized for property placed in service after 1980, relates classes of property to fixed recovery periods, not only eliminating traditional controversies with the IRS about estimated useful life but also, and more important, by providing short recovery periods to attract investors, coupled with larger deductions up front (declining balance). In brief, the deductions available through ACRS can reduce taxes sharply. For example, a fleet of business cars can be acquired and placed in service in December of a calendar-year taxpayer, and the cost can be fully recovered by the end of the following second year; salvage value is ignored. The cost (exclusive of land) of business real property can be recovered over 15 years, in contrast to prior periods ranging from 33½ to 50 years. The manager should proceed, however, on the premise that depreciated business property sold or disposed of at a gain will probably be taxable at ordinary, rather than capital gain, rates. Earlier, the reverse was true, but along with depreciation liberalization, depreciation recapture rules were enacted to tax at ordinary income tax rates the gain attributable to depreciation previously claimed. There is an important favorable exception to these rules in ERTA: If the taxpayer elects the straight-line (in contrast to the declining) balance method of recovery under ACRS for 15-year real property, no recapture is required; and on disposition at a gain, capital gain will be realized. The benefits of this provision were slightly eroded by TEFRA (a revenue-raising compliance act), but they still remain susbtantial.

Investment Tax Credit. The tax policy objective of investment tax credit has been to provide an economic incentive of some consequence to American business; managers, in turn, are concerned with ways to achieve the maximum benefit from the credit consistent with their business objectives.

Limitations and Restrictions. The investment credit is remarkable for the host of limitations and qualifications applicable in order to obtain this valuable direct subtraction from the corporate tax liability otherwise computed. These limitations affect the kind of property acquired, whether new or used, the class of property under ACRS, the type of business entity acquiring the property, the manner in which it was acquired, the maximum dollar credit in any one year, and a credit recapture for early property disposition. TEFRA also requires either a basis adjustment for a part of the credit (thus reducing depreciation), or a 2 percent decrease in the credit, for property placed in service after 1982.

The restrictions are ameliorated by provisions for the carry-back and carry-forward of unused (or unusable) investment credit and, in general, the pour-through of the credit to a lessee as it relates to new qualifying property.

Guidelines. Out of this complex web, there are certain facts the manager may usefully keep in mind. Depending on the applicable law in a given year, the credit ranges from 10 to 11.5 percent of the cost of tangible personal property subject to depreciation; of such credit, generally, the maximum deductible in any year is $25,000 plus 85 percent of the tax liability in excess of the $25,000. Unused credit can be carried back 3 years and forward 15 years. For property with an ACRS classification of 3 years, 60 percent of the cost is taken into account in computing the investment credit (ITC). Under ACRS, however, most tangible personal property will be recovered (i.e., depreciated) over a 5-year life; for this class of property, 100 percent of the cost will be taken into account in computing the credit.

On close questions relative to the acquisition of equipment, the management may be influenced as to whether the corporation already has unused investment credits available. Similarly, whether a property considered for acquisition is new or used may be important since only up to $125,000 of the cost of the latter may be used for investment credit purposes.

As indicated, in general, to qualify for the ITC the corporation must invest in tangible, personal (as contrasted with "real") property to be used in business, but an attractive exception, which may appeal to the innovative manager, is found in qualified rehabilitation expenditures to renovate a 30- or 40-year-old building or a certified historic building. For example, a qualified rehabilitation expenditure on a 40-year-old building can produce a 20 percent ITC credit, while the total cost (reduced by the credit) can be written off over 15 years. If the corporation cannot fully utilize the ACRS deductions and ITCs, it may

well consider forming a partnership (limited or regular) so these benefits can flow through to the partners; the completed structure can then be leased to the corporation.

True and Accurate Accountability. The objective manager's responsibility for a true and accurate accountability for federal taxes can be sorely tested in the closely held corporation. This is particularly true where such a manager reports to a strong, dominant majority shareholder-officer, either by virtue of outright holdings or family relationship among stockholders, and the majority shareholder is either hostile or indifferent to the strictures imposed by the federal tax laws.

It is not practical to cover in detail the numerous statutory, regulatory, and ruling provisions designed to control relevant transactions so as to preclude defeating the federal tax liabilities of corporations, shareholder-officers, and nonshareholder-officers. The manager can be alert, however, to certain categories of business practice that can result in an issue being raised by the IRS:

1. Classification of corporate disbursements as business expense which are in fact dividends in whole or in part, or additional compensation to a nonshareholder-officer.

2. Classification or handling of corporate receipts or disbursements so as to evade any corporate or individual tax liability.

3. Classification of transactions with the corporation so as to provide the appearance of a capital gain rather than a dividend.

4. Classification of corporate disbursements in violation of public policy as ordinary business expenses.

Examples of Requirements. In some instances, by proper planning and execution certain of these transactions can warrant the favorable tax treatment sought. But as the four categories imply, that is generally not the case.

1. *Personal Expenses.* There is a long history of abuses by some shareholder-officers and, in the larger corporations, nonshareholder-officers, of charging personal expenses to the corporation, usually under the heading of travel and entertainment. The current code does require adequate and complete documentation of these expenses; in the absence of records, the deduction will be denied. Personal and business expenses often will be commingled so as to provide a facade of "all business." Civil adjustments by IRS will be either in the form of a simple disallowance of the deduction claimed by the corporation or, in addition, for more blatant cases, the inclusion of the amount as a dividend in the income of the shareholder-officer.

879

Excessive compensation paid to a shareholder-officer is a potential issue where there is a question involving the reasonableness of the salary. This problem can occur where the shareholder-officer of a profitable corporation disburses funds from the corporation for personal use and classifies the total amount as salary, for which the corporation can obtain a deduction, in lieu of classifying a portion as dividends, wherein the corporation cannot obtain a deduction. In a civil tax case, the burden is on the corporation to show that the salary was reasonable. Where a shareholder has a personal interest in the underlying asset, other expenses of the corporation, such as rents and royalties, can raise a similar question as to reasonableness of the amount, i.e., whether there is really a dividend element involved in the claimed business expense.

Where the corporation is the obligor and a shareholder the obligee, the use of *interest-bearing debt* can be a device for obtaining an interest deduction for the corporation in lieu of a nondeductible dividend; the issue is generally described as "thin incorporation," where the debt greatly exceeds the stock, and IRS will contend that the corporation is undercapitalized.

2. *Common Evasion Schemes.* When the shareholder-officer siphons off corporate gross receipts, thus evading both corporate and individual tax liability, IRS is presented with criminal conduct, and the burden of proof shifts to the government. This kind of conduct is more commonly found in the small, closely held corporation in which internal control is either nonexistent or ineffectual. Two examples of this conduct are these:

The larger corporate entity may be misused by a corporate officer to *deflect miscellaneous receipts,* such as scrap sales, to his or her personal use or to require *kickbacks from suppliers* that are highly dependent on a single corporate vendee.

A potential civil issue is withdrawal of corporate funds by a shareholder as a *noninterest-bearing loan* from the corporation where the loan is not bona fide but simply an undeclared dividend.

3. *Capital Gains.* A shareholder's stock may be redeemed by the corporation, and the shareholder may obtain the benefit of capital gains treatment on the gain; conversely, the transaction may be a mere dividend. Assuming an ongoing corporation, one of the distinctions is whether the shareholder's relative standing as to control is the same after the transaction as before. If it is, a dividend is involved; if some change occurred, the rules must be consulted to determine whether it was a sufficient change to warrant capital gain treatment. If the transaction appears to the manager to be essentially equivalent to a dividend, an expert should be consulted as to the probable tax consequences if, in fact, capital gain treatment is being sought.

4. *Payments to Public Officials.* In recent years, extensive publicity of indictments and prosecutions of business executives has created a widespread awareness of the consequences of making proscribed payments to public officials or their agents. From a tax standpoint, deductions for the payoff, bribe, or campaign disbursements by a corporation are denied when they contravene some public policy, usually a state or federal law. When the proscribed payment is deducted and concealed or disguised, both civil and criminal sanctions can be applied to the corporation and the knowledgeable, responsible officers. Nontax statutes may also be applicable. A corporation can be convicted of a crime, although no confinement is possible.

Accumulated Earnings Tax. Since corporate dividends are nondeductible by the payer corporation and, in general, taxable to the shareholders, writers and speakers will often say corporate earnings are subject to "double taxation." As a consequence, corporate transactions may be shaped so as to avoid or evade such double taxation. Tax laws and enforcement efforts are designed to counter such tactics or require that the objective be achieved only in certain ways.

In this regard, one of the important statutory controls is the accumulated earnings tax. Directors need to know that they may be personally liable to the corporation for any imposition of such a tax, which is in addition to the regular corporate income taxes. This additional tax applicability turns on the answer to the question of whether earnings are available, and, if so, whether dividends have been declared, or, if not, whether the accumulated earnings have been appropriately applied to further the business purposes. The directors are responsible for the corporate dividend policy.

Leaving aside the many technical provisions, if the corporation has net income for the taxable year and earned surplus at the beginning of the year is more than $250,000 ($150,000 for certain personal services corporations), the manager should make note of whether the dividends declared or to be declared, plus earnings applied or to be applied to expansion, replacement, and similar business purposes, will be about equal to the net earnings available for the year. If the answer is no, management should consult its counsel.

Loans to shareholders, investments in securities, and the absence of any concrete plans for the application of earnings are additional flags that should spur the manager to check on the possibility of an accumulated earnings tax and ways to avoid it.

Carryback and Carryforward. Congress has recognized the need to ameliorate the result of treating, for tax purposes, each taxable year as an isolated unit. The situation is aggravated by the use of a graduated rate concept in taxing individuals and corporations. Income averaging was adopted to provide relief for the fluctuating income of individuals, and the net operating loss deduction was provided for trade or business. The latter has been made available to most business entities.

The financial manager is generally more concerned with the provisions relating to net operating loss. The basic concept, again subject to certain exceptions, involves a 3-year carryback and a 15-year carryforward for a net operating loss. The net operating loss is basically the excess of allowable deductions over gross income with some adjustments; in the carryback, carryover process, the income of the profit year also requires some adjustments. In general, the adjustments are designed to make certain that only a true operating loss is used to reduce taxable income.

Acquisitions. The acquisition of loss corporations, in a rather long-term climate of interest in growth-through-merger-and-reorganization, has been a matter of continual managerial interest. A successor corporation can obtain the benefit of unused net operating losses as a carry-over, but there is a requirement of continuity of ownership from the acquired loss corporation to the new entity. The Tax Reform Act of 1976 adopted new and generally tighter rules to determine whether all, part, or none of a net operating loss carry-over of an acquired corporation will be allowed. Since the passage of the Tax Reform Act of 1976, the effective date of these rules has been deferred three times and was to take effect on January 1, 1984, for reorganizations after that date, and on June 30, 1984, for post-1983 acquisitions. Where management anticipates obtaining the benefit of an acquired operating loss, it should consult its experts for an opinion of the impact of the limitations on its use.

Business Form. Perhaps the majority of managers will have little interest in business forms, e.g., proprietorship, partnership, corporation, owing to the popularity and general suitability of the corporate form of operation for the larger activity. The number of factors involved in exercising a choice as to business form is considerable; only the dominant aspects are discussed here.

From a tax standpoint, proprietorship and partnership net income are reflected directly in the individual or partner's personal federal income tax return. Under the federal income tax laws, the partnership is not a taxable entity, but the partnership is required to file an information return.

In contrast, the corporate form does permit alternative choices which involve both advantages and disadvantages. If the owners feel most of the net income will need to be distributed to them to meet their current personal needs, the corporate structure will yield a tax result to the owners substantially similar to a partnership, provided the corporate distribution to the owners is in the form of salaries. It should be recalled that salaries must be "reasonable." With the 50 percent income tax cap on an individual's earned and passive income now provided by ERTA, whether income is dividends or earned income has no tax significance to the officer-shareholder. (Previously, passive income was subjected to progressive rates of up to 70 percent.) The corporation, however, can obtain a deduction for only the salaries; dividends remain nondeductible. Thus, IRS still has an incentive to examine the "reasonableness" of salaries. Similarly, if the distribution will need to be some combination of dividend and salaries, the traditional form of corporate operation will be less favorable than a partnership because the divdends are nondeductible in computing corporate income. In the latter situation, the Subchapter S corporation is available for most small businesses with not more than 35 shareholders, and accords most of the benefits of both the corporate and partnership arrangement. By the Subchapter S Revision Act of 1982, the applicable rules were significantly revised to make this option more attractive to organizers.

If, however, the corporation involves a thriving activity with growth potential, the owners are willing to apply a good portion of retained earnings to attain such growth, and the owners are in higher tax brackets, the relatively lower corporate rates on the first $100,000 of taxable income, coupled with a number of fringe benefits the corporate form can offer to owners, can combine to make the corporate format a very viable choice for operations.

Lastly, it must be remembered that nontax considerations may well constitute the turning points in any decision as to which business form is most suitable.

Caution. Generalist managers can understand, consider, and decide the policy issues inherent in complicated tax questions as they can with any other managerial problem. But, as a practical matter, to do so they must insist that the tax department or tax counsel provide the relevant information in such a fashion that the policy questions are identifiable.

See also Accounting, financial; Auditing, financial; Budgeting, capital; Financial management; Financial management, capital structure and dividend policy; Financial management, financing; Financial statement analysis; Inventory control.

REFERENCES

Commerce Clearing House, Inc.: *Standard Federal Tax Reporter*, 70th ed.

————: *Standard Federal Tax Reports*, Revenue Act of 1978, no. 48, Nov. 2, 1978; Economic Recovery Tax Act of 1981, Aug. 9, 1981; Tax Equity and Fiscal Responsibility Act of 1982, Aug. 26, 1982; Subchapter S Revision Act of 1982, no. 45, Nov. 27, 1982.

Federal Tax Course, Prentice-Hall, Englewood Cliffs, N.J. 1976.

Income Tax Regulations, 26 Code of Federal Regulations, part 1.

Internal Revenue Code of 1954, Title 26, United States Code.

Tax Reform Act of 1976, Public Law 94-455, Oct. 4, 1976.

United States Internal Revenue Service: *Employer's Tax Guide*, Circular E, Publication 15, Washington, D.C.

DEAN J. BARRON, *Attorney at Law*

Technology, Management Implications

Technology and technological change have their most direct impact on human affairs through the development, conversion, management, and use of natural resources—food, water, materials, energy—for the benefit of human life. The enormous benefits of technology—and also, of course, the sometimes damaging side effects—so pervade modern society that it is almost impossible to imagine living otherwise, even so recently as a century or two ago. "No one in his senses," said the British historian J. H. Plumb, "would choose to have been born in a previous age unless he could be certain that he would have been born into a prosperous family, that he would have enjoyed extremely good health, and that he could have accepted stoically the death of the majority of his children."

Impact on Organizations. Great as is the impact of technology on individuals, it is even greater on men and women as social animals—on the organizations and institutional systems under which they live. In this arena, managers face a powerful challenge that to many people seems wholly new. In one sense, in the perspective of recent history, there is nothing new about today's problems *themselves*, but there is a great deal that is new about their size, their complexity, and their implications. These problems require mixed solutions that are not only technical, economic, and managerial, but political and social as well. The great failing of the solutions in the past—and a deficiency that is becoming dangerous in the present—is that they are victims of partial definition. There is too much emphasis first on one aspect of the problem and then on another so that momentum related to a balanced definition and solution cannot be sustained. It is the interconnections of technology and human systems that make for the complications. One always returns, however, to the central role played by technology in developing the resources on which every contemporary industrial society is based. But what of technology in the future? Will its importance diminish? How will it be managed? These are questions for which the answers are relevant to our own history, character, and mission. In reflecting on these questions in the context of our own society, my principal associates at Massachusetts Institute of Technology and I have said this:

Today, modern technology has for the first time brought us the power to achieve that just world, free of fear, disease, and hunger, of which men and women have long dreamed. We have turned to our use a remarkable range of materials and other resources from the environment in which we live; we have developed an effective economic system to spur technical and social development; we have a high standard of living; and we have made major commitments to social justice and welfare.

Yet the world is beset with threatened scarcity of resources; and as a result, with frustration and uncertainty. Many of our aspirations are yet unfulfilled; many of their implications are inadequately understood. Our efforts to solve old problems often create new ones, and some of these appear to be even more complex and intractable than those they displace. Problems increasingly cross national borders so that solutions are not under control of one nation, and actions taken far away for local reasons may have important effects close at home. In fact, the growing importance of the international dimension of the major issues of our society has served to complicate these effects even more.

Thus many people feel adrift, caught up in a system that seems to emphasize material goods beyond humanism. They fear that even today's standards of life cannot be brought equitably to everyone, or perhaps even sustained for the more affluent. Everything seems related to everything else in a web of such complexity as to defy our understanding and management. We are puzzled about next steps, and while we ponder them, we seem to find ourselves surrounded by constraints and complications that sap much of our momentum and confidence and freedom of action.

If today's problems are the consequences of our earlier successes and accomplishments, shall we solve them by renouncing those achievements and abandoning our technological society? Such a course is inconceivable; no clock can be turned back to an earlier era of history.

Clearly our purpose must be to direct our energy toward a more intelligent application of existing and new knowledge and toward a wiser and more responsible management of our technol-

ogy. It is our conviction that there still can be major advances in the human condition, and that the best ingredients for the future remain those which have brought us so far in the past—free human beings and innovative private industrial organizations functioning in a democratic society under a responsive government. We can do far more than we have done to improve people's lives. And we can strengthen the technological base that undergirds the whole by exploiting our technology more effectively and efficiently and by managing it more wisely.

In short, many of the problems facing the world are bound up with technology; and such issues cannot be understood adequately and dealt with effectively unless there is a deep and pervasive appreciation of this technology and of its impacts. For the future, then, the technology-relatedness of social and organizational problems can only increase.

The Largest Resource. Technology itself is, in a sense, the largest resource available to human beings. Most informed managers are convinced that the continued development of technology, of the great resources of research, of the ongoing advancement of science will continue to provide a major key to the world's future. People must have more science and engineering, not less, and have in addition the trained management to employ them to meet human needs if expectations for the enhancement of the quality of life, for the conservation and improvement of the environment, and for using efficiently and well our physical and human resources are to be met.

Growth or No-Growth. This optimistic view of the human capacity to cope with its problems contrasts with the gloomier prophecies of the limits of growth. Prophecy, of course, is extremely difficult—especially in regard to the future. Whatever the answer to our problems may be, it is assuredly *not at this time* a policy of no-growth. This is not to say that there is not somewhere a limit to our useful natural resources. But an absolute policy of no-growth now would be simplistic and probably unwise.

Putting the problem most starkly, the questions are: How much will nations of the world do without now for the rest of the world tomorrow? Or for the human race 200 years from now? Or 2000 years hence? That horizon is limitless. No-growth policies, as Roland McKean and others have stressed:

[W]ould undoubtedly reduce aggregate success in research and development and diminish the chances of solving particular technological problems. This sacrifice of knowledge might be terribly important . . . because technological developments, especially those pertaining to energy and biology, might reduce problems of pollution and exhaustible resources and contribute enormously to the well-being of posterity.[1]

Influence of Market Mechanisms. The arguments of the limits-of-growth school should not be taken lightly, of course. Management cannot deny their relevance; they have made a great contribution in focusing sharp attention on the basic problems of planning, of allocation, and of affording opportunity to the longer-range market mechanism to price scarce resources. In spite of projections of near-term limits, however, the market mechanism can continue to be a primary way in which further advance—and not only material advance—can be made. The record speaks eloquently to this point. Accordingly, present proponents of the limits of growth should pay attention to the mechanism of the market, and corporate capitalism must be equally concerned with the arguments of limits.

Role of Managerial Leadership. Businesses quite naturally tend to establish strong growth plans for their own futures. Thus, most organizations hope that they will grow at some significant rate over the years ahead. In these plans, unfortunately, many of them have not faced up to the fact that sheer economic growth, unrestrained by other influences, will probably become incompatible with the goal of achieving a proper balance between the effective use of the earth's resources and the needs of the earth's expanding population. This is a difficult and challenging domain. Society at large, as well as business, needs new explorations and new designs for the proper conservation and optimization of use *over the generations* of the whole of our resources for the future.

In these explorations, the leadership firms in business and industry have the responsibility to *lead* in thinking through the strategies society must adopt. Management must not shrink from this task. As Schumpeter often pointed out, the genius of capitalism is that it is flexible. It knows when to revise, and because it does not hesitate to change and adapt, it keeps the system vigorous. In that sense, it is a mechanism of humanism.

Managed Technology. If a continued and growing technology will be a requisite for handling future problems, it will have to be a new kind of managed technology. Tomorrow's technology must be defined differently from today's. Technology in the new era must take into larger account basic human, social, and environmental concerns, at a new level of awareness, and with a longer time frame in mind. The new definition will need to take into account also the international interconnections of technology and the aspirations of developing nations, as well as any given country's immediate and domestic present.

Requirements in Private and Public Sectors. Such a definition will place a much larger emphasis on the research base for technology, on understanding the scientific outcomes—biological, physical, and social—of the applications of technology, and in monitoring the ongoing effects of technology. Such a definition will place more emphasis, too, on the best ways to stimulate and encourage needed new technologies. In the longer run, such a definition will encourage a greater understanding on the part of developed countries for expanding wealth distribution beyond their borders and at the same time encourage the developing countries to understand the need for capital growth and wise expansion of technology within their own boundaries. The development of an enlightened, managed technology will necessarily require better performance from both the public and private sectors. Private companies—multinational companies—are likely to be the most effective mechanisms for the spread and development of useful technology in the sense used here. That kind of private development should be encouraged, and it must be monitored by a constructive governmental and, in some situations, intergovernmental, framework.

Large-scale technology requires the wise balancing of inputs from both private and public sources. Private effort, in the absence of effective competition, becomes too easily self-pressed for short-run gains. Government, on the other hand, left to its own bureaucratic tendencies uncontrolled by private standards of performance, slips too easily into the role of delayer, frustrator, inhibitor. What is needed to make managed technology useful, then, is a new spirit of positive leadership in both sectors.

Applications. The world's problems are manifold. They encompass the huge dilemmas of energy—its sources, storage, transmission—and, in general, of the allocation of other natural resources. They include the problems of the cities and their underachieving systems of housing, transportation, protection, education, and quality of life. And they cover the complex of problems related to medicine and health, to food and population. Yet we *can* bring these problems closer to solution, and technologies, old and new, can lead the way.

DEVELOPING COUNTRIES: Food supply is an example. Technologically, much can be done to improve the world food situation, but the attack on this problem should be enlarged. Particularly, there is a need to focus on increased food production in the developing countries through higher yields and new methods of efficient distribution. Even in the United States, which is the Saudi Arabia of food, important areas of research vital to strengthening food protein supply are either inadequately funded or entirely neglected. Priorities include application of new developments in biology and food technology to conventional agriculture, better identification of human protein needs, more comprehensive assessment of the protein value and safety of foods, and the long-range development of such novel protein resources as those from green leaves, yeast, bacteria, fungi, and chemical synthesis.

DEVELOPED COUNTRIES: For the developed countries, energy is almost as vital as food—and a problem of perhaps greater complexity. These countries have all obviously entered a difficult period of transition in their methods of energy supply and utilization. Lifestyles and productive technology have evolved on a basis of abundant and relatively cheap energy. Easily accessible domestic fuel resources have been exploited, and the national supply system has become vulnerable to outside control.

As with food, research must be accelerated over a broad spectrum of energy alternatives including more vigorous efforts at conservation. The research effort should include unconventional sources, such as solar energy, and continuing economic and technical feasibility studies of synthetic fuels. It should include also second- and third-generation potentialities, such as fusion, because if the basic research is not done now, energy-dependent nations will be caught just as short some years from now as they are today.

Interactive Relationships. With every opportunity for technological advance come problems of fallout and side effects that often loom large. For example, there are issues of privacy, of health effects, of environmental impact, and the like. They are an integral part of every technological assessment, of every advance. Typical questions demanding our attention are these:

Assuming that nuclear energy is a requirement, where do we site the plant and with what safeguards?

If some of the facts of citizens' lives are to be put into a computer, what facts should be chosen and who will have access to them?

As medical technology advances and becomes more specialized, when do we call a halt?

In genetic engineering, what is the next step and who will decide?

Such questions can become difficult and deep, and dealing with them—whether they be profound or mundane—is one of the requirements of managed technology. Governments, and in some cases international bodies, must have a primary responsibility for building the research base that permits better understanding of such dangers and what to do to ensure that they do not materialize.

Private companies must be concerned on their own in the development of technology, to understand and to prevent disastrous side effects. Companies should encourage their managers first to examine and think through the kind of regulation that serves the purpose and common good of all. Corporations entering upon this process could then propose to government, and expect of government, wise and effective regulation. The potential pollution of rivers, contamination of air, and production of unsafe devices are the proper concern of the manfacturers involved.

To make such a concern effective, important new ground must be broken. There is a growing need to define levels of safety or danger in many areas in the next decade. Though this is a rich world, it cannot afford zero risk; but, since we live in an impulsive world, we cannot afford all risk. The range of safety is a human decision based on good research data. No self-interest group or firm should make that decision on its own. Methods and mechanisms must be developed nationally where that approach is effective and proper—as they have been in the United Kingdom and in the Federal Republic of Germany—and internationally for the oil spill, the ozone layer, and the like, if progress in the management of technology is to be achieved.

Management's Responsibility. If progress is to be achieved, understanding and managing the complex interactions of technology and society are the very heart of the matter. There is a need, in this requirement for management, for human talent of breadth and quality. Assume that the world can develop a sense of the priorities reached on a basis of broad understanding. Assume, too, that with an appropriate research base, the world can develop the requisite technologies. There will still be the need for the quality of good management—for the people, for the trained leadership—to make the system function.

The constraints on an effective, functioning system by the twenty-first century will likely be more human than technical. There will, of course, be changes in the natural constraints upon the system. But the most difficult constraints will relate to the need for managers in all sectors of any society who can make the largest strategic judgments in positions that carry great visibility. Legal requirements, governmental pressures, and the decisive interests of many more people will combine to place extraordinary demands upon this management. Of all the factors that relate to the wise and humane future development of society, this requirement is the most complex. And at the heart of the complexity lies the question of incentives: making it worthwhile to get the extra level of performance. There must must be people with the highest sense of standards and values for the advance of our human society. There must be a clearer understanding in the leadership cadres of the world that wealth is the material basis of human advance and the crucial issue is not the wealth itself but the uses we are able to make of it.

Technological advance will not deal with all the world's problems. There remain the human problems of prejudice, greed, and sloth, the political problems engendered by nationalism, and spiritual decay that people inflict upon themselves. But technological advance can provide the optimum setting of the material and social world in which human growth can be protected and encouraged, and in which it can, in fact, take place.

See also Economic systems; Ethics, managerial; Social responsibility of business; Technology transfer.

NOTES

[1]*Daedalus,* Fall 1973, p. 222.

REFERENCES

Barbour, Ian G.: *Technology, Environment, and Human Values,* Praeger, New York, 1980.

Fried, J., and P. Molnar: *Technological and Social Change,* McGraw-Hill, New York, 1979.

Stephenson, R.M.: *Living with Tomorrow: A Factual Look at America's Resources,* John Wiley, New York, 1981.

HOWARD W. JOHNSON, *Massachusetts Institute of Technology*

Technology Transfer

Technology transfer is the process by which technology is conveyed from one geographical area or field of activity to another. When such transfer occurs across national boundaries, it is an international transfer of technology. Tehnology consists of society's pool of knowledge. It is made up of (1) knowledge concerning physical and social phenomena and (2) knowledge regarding the application of basic principles to practical work. Although the distinction between science and technology is imprecise, most authorities agree that *science* involves understanding, whereas *technology* involves use.

The rate of technological change in a particular field is affected by the amount of resources devoted to the advancement of knowledge in that field by individual companies, independent inventors, and government agencies. The money that government spends usually depends on how closely the field in question is related to the nation's defense, public health, and various other social needs, and on other, more purely political factors. The quantity of resources devoted to technology transfer by industry and independent inventors depends heavily on the expected profit from their use.

The dividing line between research and development is often ill-defined. *Research* is directed toward the pursuit of new knowledge, whereas *development* is oriented toward the capacity to produce a particular product or service. The outcome of research is generally more uncertain than the outcome of development. Nonetheless, development often entails considerable uncertainty as to cost, time, and the profitability of the result.

Innovation Process. Research and development (commonly known as R&D) is only a part of the process leading to a successful technological innovation. The first part of this process takes place in the interval between the establishment of technical feasibility and the beginning of commercial development of the new product or process. The second part occurs in the time interval between the beginning of commercial development and the first commercial application of the new process or product. It typically includes applied research, preparation of product specifications, prototype or pilot plant construction, manufacturing facilities, and manufacturing and marketing start-up.

Diffusion Process. Once a new process or product is introduced, the diffusion process—the process by which the use of an innovation spreads—begins. The diffusion of a new technique is often slow, and the rate of diffusion varies widely. Sometimes it takes decades for most firms in an industry to install a new technique; in other cases, most of them quickly imitate the innovator. The rate of diffusion of an innovation seems to depend on (1) the expected profitability of the innovation, (2) the size of the investment required to introduce the innovation, (3) the number of firms in the industry, (4) their average size, and (5) the amount that they spend on research and development.

Forms of Transfer. There are many types of technology transfers. *Vertical* transfer occurs when information is transferred between basic research and applied research, between applied research and development, and between development and production. *Horizontal* transfer occurs when technology used in one place, organization, or context is transferred and used in another place, organization, or context. *Material* transfer consists of the export of a new material or product by one country to another. *Design* transfer consists of the transfer of designs, blueprints, and the ability to manufacture the new material or product in the recipient country. *Capacity* transfer occurs when the capacity to adapt the new item to local conditions is transferred.

International Technology Transfers

International transfer includes all of the types just defined. The technologies transferred by firms based in the United States to their overseas subsidiaries can have benefits of various sorts to the host (and other foreign) countries. One type of benefit is a reduction of the costs to foreign users of the products or processes based on the transferred technology. Another type of benefit is a reduction of the costs of non-American firms that supply inputs used to produce the product or process based on the transferred technology.

Methods of Transfer

Because of the differences among nations in technological levels and capabilities, there is a continual process of international diffusion of technology. Knowledge can be transmitted by emigration of engineers and skilled workers, by exports of goods and services, by licensing, and by direct investment, among other means. Technology can be transferred across national borders in various ways. A considerable quantity of technology is transferred without any appreciable payment for it. Scientists and engineers exchange information at international meetings. Similarly, one country's scientists and engineers read the publications of other countries' scientists and engineers. Another important channel of international technology transfer is the export of goods. The existence or availability of a good in a foreign country may result in the transfer of technology since the good may provide information to the importers of the good. If the country that imports the good is able to take it apart to discover how it is constructed, there is the opportunity for further technology transfer.

Still another way of transfer occurs through the establishment and utilization of overseas subsidiaries. Firms typically become multinational because they want to exploit a technological lead. In some cases, the only way that a firm can introduce its innovation into a foreign market is through the establishment of overseas production facilities. A firm with a new product or process also may engage in licensing agreements with foreigners. Still another means of transfer is through the formation of a joint venture between the firm with the technology and a firm or agency in the host country.

Problems of Transfer. To the host government, direct investment creates problems because the wholly owned subsidiary of a foreign firm is partly outside its control. The investor can draw on funds and resources outside the host country and has a global strategy which may be at odds with the most appropriate operation of the subsidiary (from the host government's viewpoint). Joint ventures may overcome some of these disadvantages of direct investment, but they have a handicap in that the host country must invest more capital. Licensing arrangements eliminate many of the problems of control, but they have the disadvantage that the foreign firm with the technology has little incentive to help the licensee with the problems which may arise. When the technology is new, countries wanting it are under pressure to accept the firm's conditions, one of which often is its continuing ownership of the subsidiary. As the technology becomes more widely known, however, the host country can take advantage of competition among technologically capable firms to obtain joint ventures or, sometimes, licenses. Eventually, the technology may become available in plants that can be acquired by the host country from independent engineering firms.

Negotiable Aspects. The prevailing attitude toward multinational firms tends to be quite different in the host countries and in the parent country. To the host countries, the technological activities of multinational firms are often viewed with suspicion and fear. These countries sometimes fear that the multinational firm, in pursuit of its own profits, may engage in activities that are contrary to the host country's interests and policies. Before granting a license or charter to a firm, host countries may negotiate with the firm about taxes, amounts of capital to be raised locally, repatriation of profits, and other financial matters. In addition, they sometimes offer incentives for firms to establish R&D laboratories in the country, and apply pressure to get the firms to set up fully integrated plants to upgrade local skills. Also, a host country often forces firms to hire and train local workers and encourages them to purchase components from local suppliers.

Impact on Research and Development (R&D). The relative importance of foreign markets and utilization of the returns from a domestic firm's R&D program is directly related to the extent to which it depends on foreign sources for its current sales and to its ratio of R&D expenditures to sales. On the average, research projects seem to receive a somewhat larger share of their returns from abroad than development projects do. R&D projects aimed at new products apparently are the ones where foreign returns are expected to be most important. These firms are more hesitant to send overseas their process technology than their product technology, because they feel that the diffusion of process technology, once it goes abroad, is harder to control. If United States firms could not establish foreign subsidiaries (or transfer technology abroad in other ways), they would not carry out so much research and development. This would weaken their technological position. The percentage reduction would be relatively high among firms whose foreign sales are a relatively large proportion of total sales and where R&D expenditures (in absolute terms) are large. Furthermore, the reduction would be much greater for research and development of a product than for R&D of a process.

Costs of Transfer. Technology transfer costs are defined as the costs of transmitting and absorbing all the relevant unembodied knowledge. They include:

1. Cost of preengineering technological exchanges during which the basic characteristics of the technology are revealed to the transferee

2. Engineering costs associated with transferring the process design

3. Associated process-engineering costs in the case of process innovations, or, in the case of product

innovations, the cost of related product design and production engineering

4. R&D costs involved in adopting and modifying technology

5. Prestart-up training costs

6. Learning and "debugging" costs incurred during the start-up phase and before the plant achieves the design performance specifications

Many of the cost factors of international technology transfer are also characteristic of the technology transfer that occurs within national borders. A large proportion of the transfer costs will be incurred if the technology is transferred within the United States. However, because of such factors as language barriers, international differences in units of measurement and engineering standards, and cultural, attitudinal, and political differences, there generally are extra costs associated with transferring technology across national boundaries.

Rate of Transfer. Technology is being transferred across national boundaries more rapidly than in the past. In large part, this increase is due to the growing influence of multinational firms. Many of them are heavily involved in transferring technology. United States multinational firms, especially, are transferring their technology to their foreign subsidiaries much more quickly than in the past. For technologies transferring to subsidiaries in developing countries or for those transferring through channels other than subsidiaries, there is no evidence of a reduction in pace. For entire nations as well as for individual firms, R&D provides a window opening on various parts of the environment; this window enables the nation or firm to evaluate external developments and to react more quickly to them. In many important industries, the acceleration of international technology transfer is prompted by the fact that companies are carrying on an increasing share of their research and development overseas.

Transfer Changes. The principal channel through which new technologies are exploited abroad during the first 5 years after their commercialization is through foreign subsidiaries, not exports. In some industries, new products commonly are introduced by American firms more quickly in foreign markets than in the United States (owing, in part, to regulatory considerations). For new processes, on the other hand, the export stage continues to be important. Firms are more hesitant to send overseas their process technology than their product technology because they feel that the diffusion of process technology, once it goes abroad, is harder to control. In their view, it is much more difficult to determine whether foreign firms are illegally imitating a process than to detect a similar imitation of a product.

Many United States-based firms have come to take **887**

a worldwide view of their operations, as have foreign-based companies. Many of them have in place extensive overseas manufacturing facilities. Many also have substantial R&D activities located abroad. Given the existing worldwide network of facilities and people, firms are trying to optimize the implementation of their overall operations. This trend may mean that some of the technology developed in the United States may find its initial application in a foreign subsidiary. Conversely, an innovation developed in its subsidiary may find its initial application in that subsidiary.

Technology is becoming increasingly internationalized. The discovery phase, for example, frequently involves collaboration among laboratories and researchers located in several different countries, even when they are within the same firm. Testing also tends to become a multicountry project. Even in the later phases of development, work often is performed in more than one country.

Managerial Implications

There are several managerial implications for the multinational firm.

1. *Costs associated with separating production from development.* The especially high cost of transfer before first application favors the development location, at least for production of initial units. Transfer costs will be lowered once the first production run has been commenced. (Transfer costs decline with each application of a given innovation.)

2. *Technology transfer as a cost-reduction activity.* This purpose can be advanced as an explanation for the specialization often exhibited by engineering firms in the design and installation of particular turnkey plants, a characteristic especially noteworthy in the petrochemical industry.

3. *Criteria for the selection of a joint venture or licensing partner.* Although the evidence is limited, gigantic firms do not seem to have any appreciable advantage over firms of moderate size in absorbing technology at a relatively low transfer cost. Highly research-intensive firms do not appear to have more than a small cost advantage in absorbing technology over firms with much lower reasearch and development expenditures. However, manufacturing experience is important, especially for transferring machinery technology. In addition, there is evidence that transfers to governments in centrally planned economies involve substantial extra costs, sometimes because of high documentation requirements and differences in managerial procedures. The cost of designing, constructing, and starting up a manufacturing plant abroad, based on

American technology, depends on the time span between project commencement and project completion. There is a time-cost trade-off. The elasticity of cost with respect to time depends on (1) the duration of the preliminary planning stage of the project (relative to other stages), (2) the extent to which the relevant technology has been applied before, (3) the size of the primary transfer agent, (4) the size of the total project costs, and (5) whether or not the foreign market can be satisfactorily supplied by exports.

4. *Imitation versus innovation.* In some instances, technology is transferred from one organization to another with the help, or at least the consent, of the owner of the technology. In other instances, much or all of the technology is revealed by the innovation itself. In some fields, reverse engineering—which involves analyzing and tearing a product apart to see what it consists of and how it is made—is a well-developed art. Even when a new product is not subject to reverse engineering, it may be possible to "invent around" the patents on which it is based, if it is patented. Because much of the relevant technology frequently is transferred (more or less involuntarily) to potential imitators, the costs of imitating an innovation often are substantially lower than the cost of the innovation itself. Imitation costs are a very important, if neglected, topic. If imitation costs are substantially below the innovator's cost of developing the innovation, he or she may have little or no incentive to carry out the innovation. Imitation costs also affect concentration, since an industry's concentration level will tend to be relatively low if its members' products and processes can be imitated cheaply.

5. *Threats and opportunities.* The reduction of the United States technological lead presents opportunities as well as threats. The technological advances made by other countries can be of great value to the United States both directly and because they stimulate us to adapt and extend their, and our, technology. This fact has been true in the past, and it will be true in the future. For these opportunities to be exploited fully, however, it is important that United States firms be open, not hostile or indifferent, to foreign ideas. Prudent American companies find it worthwhile to monitor more closely technological developments abroad. According to some observers, they are not so adept at this as their foreign competitors.

See also Developing countries, management in; International operations and management in multinational companies; International trade; Research and development management; Technology, management implications.

REFERENCES

Botkin, James, Dan Dimanescu, and Ray Sata: *Global Stakes: The Future of High Technology in America*, Ballinger, Cambridge, Mass., 1982.

Fusfield, Herbert I., and Richard R. Nelson, eds.: *Technology Policy and Economic Growth Series*, Pergamon Press, New York, 1982.

Rosenbloom, Richard S., ed.: *Research on Technological Innovation, Management and Policy*, JAI Press, Greenwich, Conn., 1983.

Sahal, Devendra: *Patterns of Technological Innovation*, Addison-Wesley, Reading, Mass., 1981.

SAMUEL WAGNER, *Franklin and Marshall College*

Telecommunications

On January 1, 1984, the American Telephone and Telegraph Company (AT&T) was deregulated by order of a court decision. This action created a new competitive atmosphere in telecommunications marketing. There is no more federal control on telecommunications; state public utility commissions, however, still control rates for telecommunications services that originate and terminate in a particular state.

In the new environment, AT&T Technologies, Inc., provides research and development to other AT&T organizations, using Bell Laboratories and the plants and employees formerly utilized by Western Electric, which no longer exists. AT&T Technologies also provides financial and administrative support to other divisions and integrates strategic planning.

Divisions of AT&T Technologies, Inc.

AT&T Information Systems. This division (AT&T-IS) has laboratories for product development. It provides Enhanced Network Services such as Net-1000, a service that translates a transmitting computer's language into the language of the receiving computer. It sells, rents, or leases communications switching systems, such as the digital System 55 and System 85. AT&T-IS supervises the Phone Center Stores where products may be bought and serviced. Its National Business Systems offices sell telephone switching systems to those needing 40 or more instruments. Its General Business Systems staff sells to businesses using fewer than 40 instruments. Its Business Services people assist residential users who wish to rent or buy instruments to attach to the outside wiring brought to their homes by their independent Bell Operating Company (BOC).

AT&T Network Systems (AT&T-NS). This division carries long-distance calls to destinations outside the Local Access and Transport Area (LATA) of the BOC which provides telephone lines (trunks) from its central office to a termination at the wall of the customer's premises. AT&T-NS does not receive revenue from local or long-distance calls which originate and terminate within the "home" LATA of the BOC. That revenue is kept by the BOC. AT&T-NS has contracted with local BOCs to bill and collect for calls made on its facilities when the destination of the call is beyond the BOC's home LATA. The BOC's billing to the customer likewise includes cost of the trunk lines carrying calls from the local customer to the BOC's central office. Telephone switching systems or instruments formerly rented or leased from the BOCs were called "embedded base" and were transferred to AT&T-IS by the divestiture order. Thus, such charges are shown on another page of the customer's billing from the BOC; collected rent is remitted to AT&T-IS. If AT&T-IS so desires, it can offer the user an opportunity to pay off contractual obligations ahead of time to conserve accumulating interest, and perhaps to use the proceeds to acquire new equipment.

The Bell Operating Companies (BOCs)

The BOCs have joined together to form seven groups. The headquarters officers of each group make decisions on new products that can be introduced to customers by the BOCs, that have established separate marketing divisions that sell instruments, switching systems, and other equipment. These organizations likewise provide service for what they sell. Service on equipment sold prior to January 1st, 1984, is now provided by AT&T-IS technicians. In effect, BOC salespersons are competing directly with those of AT&T-IS and with the branch offices and dealerships of other telecommunications manufacturers, such as Northern Telecom, Rolm, General Telephone and Electronics, and many others.

Centrex Service. All the BOCs offer Centrex, as the equipment involved is housed in the central offices of the BOCs. Each Centrex "station" in the customer's premises requires a separate wire from the central office. Instruments can be purchased or leased from the serving BOC or other vendors. As Centrex is a profitable offering, BOCs are intensifying marketing and providing new features ("enhancements") to the service. Pricing usually is based on a guaranteed rate for a 4- to 6-year period, or less if the customer desires.

Access Charges. The Federal Communications Commission (FCC) has been considering an access charge which would be applicable to each telephone trunk or line connecting to another location. Suggested charges range from $2 to $25 monthly per line, depending on type of line. Centrex lines would carry a $6 surcharge. In 1984, BOCs were telling customers that the cost of Centrex would be adjusted downward to offset any access charges required by the FCC.

Bypassing the Telephone Utilities

Because private telephone circuits serving two different points are priced on a mileage basis, and because of the proposed additional access charge, large users of telephone service are building their own networks, using microwave and satellite circuits available from private carriers such as Satellite Business Systems, MCI, and GTE. Such bypasses could substantially reduce earnings of the BOCs and AT&T Network Systems. Technology improvements make such systems attractive and available.

Long-Distance Telephone Services

The cost of a long-distance call is determined first by the carrier chosen, then by the type of call, the time of day, the day of the week, and the airline mileage to the distant point.

Direct-Dialed Calls. Almost all calls are direct-dialed by the caller, both in the United States and to points abroad. Such calls cost the least of all calls.

Operator-Handled Calls. While all local and long-distance carriers provide for direct-dial calling, only AT&T–Network Systems offers operator-dialing to assist the caller. In most areas, you dial 1, then 0, then the number you wish to reach. On public push-button dial phones you then hear a chime. Now push the # button, which indicates that you want an operator; otherwise, you would have dialed your credit card number when you heard the chime if you had not inserted your coded card in the special slot of certain coin stations. There are two surcharges for interstate operator assistance. If you will talk to anyone at the distant number, the charge is $1.55 plus the direct-dial rate, with a 1-minute minimum. If you ask for a person by name or title (say, sales vice president) or a department (for example, the Repair Department), or give the operator an interior extension number (such as extension 291), a charge of $3 is added to the 1-minute direct-dial rate.

Bell System Credit Card Calling. The so-called Calling Card with its magnetic stripe can be used in special automated public phones, or you may dial 1, then 0 then your credit card number after you hear a chime. Calling Card surcharges in 1984 were $1.05 for interstate distances of 23 miles or more, 80 cents for 11 to 22 miles, 60 cents for 1 to 10 miles.

Time Periods for Calling at Decreased Cost. Direct-dial interstate and intrastate per-minute costs are reduced substantially in off-peak periods. A 40 percent discount applies to calls placed between 5 P.M. and 11 P.M., Monday through Friday, and on Sunday. A 60 percent discount applies daily from 11 P.M. to 8 A.M. and from 11 P.M. Friday to 5 P.M. Sunday. AT&T's competing long-distance carriers also offer discounts which may be more or less than those of AT&T. Be sure to obtain rate schedules from the carrier of your choice and compare these rates with those of other carriers. The effective time applicable to a discount is the time in the location where the call is originated.

Automatic Carrier Selection. In 1984, AT&T, through the BOCs, planned to offer customers their choice of a long-distance carrier, which would be accessed through single-digit dialing, namely, when the digit 1 is dialed first. Thus, instead of dialing a 7-digit number to reach the switching system of a carrier competing with AT&T, the customer would be automatically connected to that carrier after dialing 1. AT&T long-distance service continues to be offered if the customer does not choose another carrier.

Taking Advantage of Time Zone Differences. If a call originates in the Eastern time zone, the reduced rates applicable at 5 P.M. for all carriers permit connection to destinations in other time zones during normal working hours. Special working shifts, when workers come to the office later and do their calling after 5 P.M., may bring about substantial savings, as both direct-dial and services like WATS (Wide Area Telecommunications Service) will cost less.

Unit of Time Measurement. In general, a 1-minute call is charged even when the call is shorter. In 1984, however, a Bell competitor, Satellite Business Systems, charged calls at a 1-second interval.

Hotel-Motel Calling. As in Europe, United States hotels can add any surcharge they wish to a call made from a guest's room. Many hotels were routing those calls over their own WATS at low cost, but were charging guests at former Bell System operator-handled rates, which included a 3-minute minimum charge. Local-call charges varied from 50 cents upward. Timed local calls were charged higher rates in cities where message-unit charges apply. Guests can eliminate these surcharges by using lobby coin stations. Call costs can be reduced by calling before 8 A.M. and after 5 P.M. If a call straddles a rate period, AT&T computers raise or lower the rate on the portion of the call which continues into the next time-rate period.

Coin Station Calls. Automated equipment now accepts coded Calling Cards, so only the digits of the wanted number need be dialed. However, callers making coin or credit card calls in major metropolitan areas should first dial 0 and ask for the coin rate to the desired local area number before inserting the Calling Card. Use of the card will add a fixed surcharge, depending on distance. The AT&T maximum interstate surcharge is $1.05, with intrastate surcharges varying with each state.

"Wholesale" Telephone Long-Distance Services

In early 1984, there were three basic types of long-distance services. AT&T Network Systems manages the long-distance services used prior to the entry of other carriers into the long-distance market. AT&T connects direct-dialed and operator-assisted calls to any telephone in the world. Four Other Common Carriers (OCCs) have built their own networks and offer service both to network points priced on a network rate schedule, and universal service to "off-net" points, which they usually reach by foreign exchange or WATS circuits acquired from other carriers or AT&T. The four terrestrial OCC carriers are MCI, Sprint, ITT, and Western Union. Satellite Business Systems (SBS) offers originating service in certain cities, as do the other carriers, but SBS calls are sent to its satellite and are priced on usage levels rather than being distance-sensitive. All five carriers offer universal service, meaning that connections can be made to any telephone in the contiguous United States.

Other competitors of AT&T are called "resale" carriers. They may or may not employ direct circuits purchased outright, but all use WATS lines or similar circuits rented from other carriers; they secure their profits from higher loading of the circuits, thus gaining access to rate brackets with lower cost per minute than the customer can achieve, should similar circuits be employed. In 1984, AT&T was still servicing over 90 percent of offered long-distance traffic. Consequently, its rate setting is closely observed by its competitors. If it lowers long-distance rates, as was expected in early 1984, resale carriers with fewer customers and higher costs may leave the market. Users should never make cash advances to long-distance carriers, but should insist on paying bills after service is rendered. Mortality among resale carriers has been very high.

Wide-Area Telecommunications Service (WATS). WATS, the flagship of the long-distance service, produces AT&T Network Services' greatest profit; it is used by countless organizations on an inward (toll-free) basis and also for outward calls made to both interstate and intrastate destinations. WATS, properly designed, installed, controlled, and *utilized*, can dramatically reduce long-distance expense, perhaps 30 to 50 percent of former costs.

Each WATS line covers a defined band. Band 5 covers the continental United States, Puerto Rico, and the Virgin Islands; band 6 adds Hawaii and Alaska. Bands 1 through 4 are available for more limited coverage. Each numbered band covers its preceding bands. Band 4 includes bands 1, 2, and 3. Prices increase with distance covered.

Interstate WATS is furnished only by AT&T. Outward WATS covers states other than the originating state. A separate WATS circuit must be arranged through the local BOC for connection to intrastate phones. The serving BOC will also assist users in arranging interstate WATS circuits through the BOC's contacts with AT&T Network Services.

Inward WATS (800 service) has grown rapidly, as users recognize the marketing value of toll-free access to them by both customers and their own personnel. Prospective customers are much more likely to ask for information if the long-distance call is free. There are many optional extras available with the 800 service. One of them eliminates the need for a separate 800 number for customers calling within the state where the enterprise if located. The cost of this option in 1984 was $300 monthly. For 1984, WATS installation and ordering charges for a single interstate outward WATS line were $174.80 for outward service; for the required double-inward WATS interstate WATS lines, charges were $366.95. Monthly charges to keep each WATS in service were $31.65 for outward; $36.80 for inward WATS. Daytime (8 A.M. to 5 P.M.) rates for Band 5 (800) interstate inward lines ranged from $11.94 to $19.33 per hour depending on the geographic location of the business and total hours of usage. Usage is billed in one-tenth hour (6-minute) intervals. Rates for outward interstate WATS in Band 5 ranged from $10.78 to $21.50 in 1984, depending on location and distance. Both inward and outward WATS tariffs offer substantially reduced rates for usage between 5 P.M. and 11 P.M. on weekdays and from 11 P.M. on Friday to 5 P.M. Sunday.

Other WATS-like Services. Organizations with heavy long-distance phone requirements should also check with three other OCCs to determine whether they have switching systems in the user's city. MCI and GTE Sprint offer WATS-like services; SBS offers Message Service I. Properly used, these services may reduce costs beyond the reductions brought by a properly loaded group of WATS lines. In early 1984, the 800 service was available countrywide only through AT&T, but several of the OCCs were readying competitive inward calling services. AT&T also introduced 800 service from certain Canadian cities to United States destinations, likewise requiring two circuits for an initial installation. Express Call service is offered by AT&T at high-volume locations such as airports. Coin stations are used; cost is 50 cents per 30 seconds for calls to any United States destination, including Puerto Rico and the Virgin Islands. Dial-It 900 AT&T service permits calling simultaneously by a large number of callers, using a single telephone number. It is used by radio and TV advertisers. This service has a cost to the advertiser and a 50-cent charge to the calling person; the charge is placed on the monthly BOC billing for residential or business service. The service can be arranged to permit multiple minutes of calling for an added charge of 35 cents per additional minute.

Intrastate WATS. The BOC serving your area, or

AT&T–IS, can arrange WATS service, inward or outward, to and from points within your state. Costs vary widely, but billing is done similarly to WATS interstate billing. The $300 option for the universal WATS number, mentioned above, permits your intrastate callers to use your 800 number issued to your interstate callers, thus simplifying WATS advertising and eliminating a separate billing for the intrastate inward WATS service.

Foreign Exchange Service (FX). An FX line comes to your switching equipment from a telephone exchange different from that of your city. It may come from a close-by town or from across the country. You rent the line at the rate charged for a business trunk line in the distant community, plus a charge for each mile it travels to you, plus connection charges. You can furnish toll-free calling to customers in that city by giving them your local-line number, which routes the call directly to your switchboard. You can also dial the distant number and reach any telephone in the distant city at the cost of a local call. The line can be arranged only for inward calling if you wish to restrict your own people from using it to reach the distant city. Or, you can restrict the line to outward service only. Obviously, the number should not be released to your vendors. Conversely, such a line may help your purchasing department reach many vendors in the distant city, or you may call your customers. You may or may not wish to purchase a directory listing for your FX line, to be published in the directory of the distant city. An FX line is available on a 24-hour basis.

Tie-Line Service. A tie line is a circuit which connects two or more private telephone switching systems. A charge per mile is made, plus monthly connection charges at each end. A special code (say 21) can connect your desk telephone over your tie line to your office switching system in the distant city. You can then dial a 3- or 4-digit number to reach a specific person in that distant office. Tie lines can be one-way or two-way in operation. If the distant office is small, the tie line can be terminated on a button-equipped telephone instrument. You may choose to terminate the line at your switchboard or the distant one and have your operators connect calls to the wanted person or department. By proper arrangements, a tie line may also give you access to the dial tone of the distant switching system so that you can make calls to other numbers in that area. *Caution:* Be sure to block a tie line from long-distance access at the distant end. Your BOC can help you with all these arrangements.

Off-Premise Extensions (OPX). A travel agent may want to establish a direct connection to the travel office by installing a phone line from the travel agent's telephone switching system on the desk of the person arranging travel in a customer's office. The customer can now dial any agent's number in the travel bureau. Or, you may wish to equip your

own nearby branch office with a "station" on your headquarters system, so that office can use your WATS lines or other "wholesale" long-distance services. The circuit can be installed across your street or across the country. Ask your BOC for assistance.

Local Private Lines (LPL). Any desk telephone can be equipped with a special circuit to connect it with another telephone at any local or distant location. Pressing the LPL button and lifting the receiver will automatically ring the distant phone. Such equipment is widely used by investment dealers. Your BOC can furnish you with further information.

Choosing Your Private Circuit Carrier. While AT&T and BOC circuits may be the *best maintained* of your choices for the special circuits discussed here, the OCCs and many other specialized organizations offer to lease their facilities by providing full-time private lines for your use. The vendor maintains the line and arranges for "local loops" through your telephone company to connect its facilities to your office system. It is desirable to contrast AT&T costs and BOC costs with those quoted by OCCs such as MCI, GTE, ITT, and Western Union. You should ask for references in your city; these circuits may be "noisy" in operation. Satellite circuits are likewise available from SBS and a number of other specialized carriers.

Choosing between Carriers and Transmission Methods. To properly analyze sales presentations made to you, be sure you know your *cost per minute* of the long-distance services you are using *now*. Determine which OCC or Resale carrier has a direct connection, without switching the call, to cities that you call frequently. Points served by OCC networks differ widely, and if it is necessary to take your call "off-net" to reach your dialed destination, another rate schedule may apply which is higher than the cost of calling points on the vendor's private network. Also, ask for references of organizations already using the vendor's service. If you likewise calculate three monthly indicators, they will help you analyze and control your present and contemplated circuit usage and expense. The three factors are cost per minute, cost per call, and average length of call. The billings of your BOC, the OCCs, and Resale carriers all have the needed statistics to enable you to make this calculation.

Controlling Long-Distance Calling

Almost every large enterprise has now purchased or leased a new telephone switching system which offers an optional long-distance call accounting system. The part of the system which identifies and stores dialing impulses is called Station Message Detail Recording, or SMDR. To that "port" on the switch the user can connect additional equipment that will analyze the long-distance calls and print information in whatever form is needed by the management. Alternatively, the output of the SMDR port can be sent to organization that will process the data and mail reports to the user. As calls can always be traced back to the originating telephone station, employees learn that the company system should not be abused by their using it to make personal phone calls. Except in companies with unusually high personnel morale, such systems pay for themselves in reducing nonbusiness calls.

In addition to after-the-fact recording, modern switching systems likewise offer many different options in arranging software so that a particular phone is allowed only the dialing capability which that particular job requires. Thus, a user may be restricted to calls within the office, without access to outside trunks. Or the phone may be restricted from any kind of long-distance access. If long-distance calling is required, the computer can restrict the caller to a certain group of area codes, or to the use of only "wholesale" facilities like WATS, tie lines, or FX lines.

Once call restriction is in effect, the reports prepared by the accounting equipment should be carefully studied by executive personnel. Perhaps reports can be cut back to quarterly or semiannual printing if abuse is at a minimum.

The reports can be programmed to indicate the circuits used as well as call destinations. A WATS line, for example, should be used at least 20 hours monthly to ensure that its cost is lower than that of using the OCCs and Resale carriers as the first choice of routing. The feature of modern systems such as Automatic Route Selection will be helpful in controlling calling, as nothing is left to personal choice, and the least-cost channel is automatically chosen by the computer. Further, such automation eliminates the need to teach personnel the identification dialing codes that must be used in accessing the OCCs and Resale carriers when calls are dialed from a desk phone through the city's BOC central office. The user who permits such OCC dialing via the BOC central office should change identification codes regularly, so that discharged and unauthorized employees cannot dial personal calls via the OCC circuits.

The OCCs and the Resale carriers all offer to install direct lines from your switching system to their switches. Costs in 1984 were around $85 monthly for each line. These circuits eliminate dialing a 7-digit local number for the carrier and the 4- or 5-digit identification code. The tie line minimizes dialing, but only one call can be processed at one time. When carriers are dialed through the BOC's central office, a number of people can access the carrier simultaneously.

Remote Call Forwarding. This AT&T service requires the user to rent a telephone number in the city where the customer wishes to establish toll-free calling to the company office. The number may or may not be listed in that city's telephone directory. The caller is charged only for a local call; the BOC's computer forwards the call automatically to the destination switching system. The call is charged the direct-dial rate in effect at the time of origination. The circuit is billed at local trunk charges, plus a listing charge. Such a circuit costs less than WATS, but the service area is limited to subscribers in the selected city.

Third-Number Calls. The telephone number of a residence or an organization may be given to a telephone company operator with instructions to charge that number for a call being made to some other number. The operator is instructed to call the billing number to verify the correctness of the charge before the call can be placed. This requirement delays the call. Also, this procedure may be abused by outsiders or by employees making personal calls. If "third-number" calls appear on the monthly phone bill, and if the firm's employees have been told not to initiate such calls, you should refuse to pay until your BOC furnishes proof that your own people placed the calls.

Switching Systems for Smaller Companies

Switching systems are known as Key Systems. Each instrument has an arrangement of buttons. One button puts calls on hold; one or more give access to an intercom system which permits dialing a 1- or 2-digit number to reach another person within the office. Other buttons enable you to receive calls from the outside, or permit calls to be dialed to the outside. Modern key systems offer many different features, such as long-distance toll restriction, music on hold, hands-free conversation, and many other timesaving features. Systems such as ATT–IS's Merlin can be obtained for as few as 2 trunks and 5 instruments, and models range upward to more than 70 instruments. Larger systems are expensive; prospective users should check the cost of small switching systems for comparison. In operation, a designated person sees a button flash, depresses it, and answers the call. The call is placed on hold, and another button is pressed and an intercom number dialed. The called person is asked to "pick up the call on line 2." The call is now connected and the intercom is free for the next call. WATS trunks and other facilities may be terminated on key systems.

Switching Systems for Large Users

Most organizations are now using modern analog or digital switching systems, in contrast to so-called

893

step-by-step, crossbar, or electronic systems. A multitude of features are available. *Training* is essential for proper use of current technology. Persons new to the organization should be carefully briefed on feature operation.

Systems with digital architecture are preferable, as it is not necessary to send data through modems before the data are switched. Many manufacturers are producing equipment that will permit simultaneous transmission of voice and data over the same telephone wire. Local Area Networks help unify the use of technologically advanced systems within the organization. Features such as a "voice mailbox" pick up messages automatically when a user is away from the desk. Screens and keyboards may be included in the telephone desk instrument pad. The expensive instruments can be mixed with POTS (Plain Old Telephone Service), as the new technology can use a simple touch-dialing phone with no supplementary buttons. The user is taught to dial 2-digit codes to implement a desired feature built into the system. Substantial savings can be made by using such simple instrumentation and teaching the user how to utilize features built into the controlling computer.

Analog systems were still actively marketed in 1984, but knowledgeable, forward-looking users were choosing digital design. With the impact of increasing use of data communications, users carefully examine voice/data capabilities of the offered equipment. Many small manufacturers have entered the field; however, buyers should be sure that their chosen vendor is satisfactorily financed and thus able to survive the active competition by major companies.

All major manufacturers offer training to user personnel in maintenance procedures, as well as furnishing service from local parts and service offices. In-house maintenance skills are desirable. The vendor frequently can correct software problems by making a telephone call to the computer, and many vendors do this routinely each morning, to check operation of the equipment they have sold.

Vendor Selection. In 1984, leaders in the industry included AT&T Information Systems, which handled products manufactured by Western Electric, now a subsidiary of AT&T Technologies, Inc. Northern Telecom and Rolm Corporation have been other leaders; GTE Communications Corporation, Mitel (of Canada) Ericsson, the Harris Corporation, Inte-Com, United Technologies, and a number of Japanese manufacturers were prominent in the marketplace. The larger companies have opened their own direct marketing and servicing offices in major cities, and have also used dealerships, as have the smaller organizations. Prospective customers should be cautious: there have been many failures among "interconnect" distributors. References should be requested, and the

prospective user should visit organizations using the *exact* switching system recommended by the vendor.

Record Telecommunications

"Why should I pick up the phone at all?" is a question which everyone should ask when about to send one-way information by telephone. No answer or discussion is required. Modern methods of transmitting messages and data can accomplish delivery at the distant end in minutes, within the same day, or overnight.

Western Union Services. Telex I is a service timed in one-tenth-minute increments. Speed is 66 words per minute. Telex II is timed in 1-minute increments; speed is 100 words per minute. Modern terminals with message-composing screens create and dispatch messages at low cost to thousands of receiving terminals located throughout the world. In 1984, Telex I messages cost $0.3775 per minute; Telex II messages cost $0.43 per minute to domestic points. Per-word cost is minimal; there is no waste on social pleasantries so common to phone calls; speed is almost instantaneous.

The Western Union Telex services can likewise be used with Easy-Link, a feature which can connect a personal computer with the Telex network.

Western Union's Mailgram provides next-day postal delivery. Cost was $4.95 for 50 words in 1984.

Postal Services. Express Mail carries up to 2 pounds of contents to destination by 2 P.M. the next business day. The 1984 cost was $9.35 for envelopes delivered to a postal office. International Express Mail to certain foreign countries is likewise available.

Courier Services. Both Federal Express and Purolator offer overnight envelope (2-ounce limit) deliveries for much lower cost than standard overnight envelopes. In 1984, some couriers operated by both plane and truck, promising distant delivery by 10 A.M. Same-day service via customer delivery and pick-up from major airports was likewise offered by the postal service and by the couriers.

Facsimile Services (FAX). Sophisticated equipment transmits document copies over ordinary phone lines, using special modems. Less than 1-minute transmission time is promised by most major vendors. FAX is popular; management should be sure that material is single-spaced if possible, and supervisors of central FAX dispatching units should make sure that urgency of transmission justifies FAX costs as compared with the same-day or overnight delivery services.

International Communications. International video conferencing is offered by AT&T as well as domestic video conferencing service. Other vendors offer similar services. International direct dialing is reliable and available from any telephone. International Telex, inexpensive and effective for written messages, is used as a substitute for deteriorating international airmail. International facsimile transmission is available. The international carriers include RCA Globe-Com, ITT World-Com, Western Union International, Tropical Radio and Telegraph, and MCI International. Cablegrams are likewise offered by these carriers. The "letter telegram," which is billed at less expensive rates for next-day delivery, is available in certain countries.

See also Communications, organizational; Computer security; Information sciences; Management information systems (MIS); Management information systems, transaction processing systems; Office automation; Records management; Word processing.

REFERENCES

Periodicals:

Business Communications Review, 950 York Road, Hinsdale, Ill., 60521.

Communications News, 124 South First St., Geneva, Ill., 60134.

Office Administration and Automation, Geyer McAllister Publishing Co., 51 Madison Ave., New York, 10010.

Telecommunications, 610 Washington St., Dedham, Mass., 02026.

Telephone Engineer and Management, 124 South First St., Geneva, Ill., 60134.

Telephony, 53 Jackson Boulevard, Chicago, 60604.

FRANK K. GRIESINGER,
Frank K. Griesinger and Associates, Inc.
Superior Building, Suite 1412
815 Superior Avenue, Cleveland, Ohio 44114

Temporary Help

The term *temporary help* is used for employees supplied by an outside agency to (1) fill in for regular employees who are absent or on vacation, (2) assist during peak loads, or (3) handle work for which the regular employees do not have the skills.

Many contracting firms supply temporary clerical and office support staff employees on demand, and some of them have offices in more than one city. Other types of workers may be obtained as well, often from firms that specialize in providing one particular skill or group of skills.

Temporary workers are often used by maintenance departments, especially for cleaning work. In these cases, the company has a contract with the supplier which runs for a year or more. Generally, the agreement will specify the frequency with which var-

ious cleaning jobs will be performed and the standards of cleanliness.

Other types of contracts cover different kinds of work: construction and electrical work of various kinds, for example. It is also quite common for oil-refining plants to have contractors supply people to handle their "turn-arounds," periodic overhauls of major equipment. In a few cases, oil refineries have all their maintenance performed by an outside contractor.

Companies that use temporary help or contract labor generally pay a flat fee, sometimes an hourly or per diem rate to the contractor for each employee. The contractor then pays the employee and provides the fringe benefits.

In some instances, companies hire people for special types of work on a temporary basis and contract with the individual rather than with a firm for services at a per diem rate.

Employment of temporary help has the advantage of avoiding long-term commitments to employees. It limits the amount of employee benefits; flat wages or salaries are the compensation rule. It enables an organization to handle abbreviated work schedules (such as partial or short shifts) without paying overtime or other special premiums. The practice of employing temporary help rather than full-time employees, if abused, however, may cause resentment and lack of cooperation from a company's full-time employees.

See also Contracts management; Human resources planning; Wages and hours legislation; Work schedules, alternate.

REFERENCES

Feldman, Edwin B.: *Housekeeping Handbook for Institutions, Business & Industry*, rev. ed., Frederick Fell, New York, 1978, chap. 11, "Contract Cleaning."

Gannon, M. J.: "Profile of the Temporary Help Industry and Its Workers," *Monthly Labor Review*, May 1974, pp. 44–49.

LESTER R. BITTEL, *James Madison University*

Testing, Psychological

Although an estimate is difficult to make, there are at least 50,000 organizations in the United States that use psychological tests to help make decisions about people they consider hiring, placing, promoting. There may be abuses in these ranks, but generally, managers apply these tests in good faith to upgrade skills found in their work forces. Every organization wants to hire or promote the most qualified individuals, and a properly developed and executed testing program can contribute substantially to this goal.

Psychological tests are widely used but at the same time are quite misunderstood, not because testing is a mysterious or complicated subject, but because most people lack the basic knowledge to answer key questions: What makes a test good or bad? How can tests be used within the framework of the law? How can an organization benefit from using psychological tests? Which tests should be used for employment selection or evaluation?

Legal Issues

Sometime within the last decade, word spread throughout United States industry that it was illegal to use psychological tests. This allegation is not now true, nor has it ever been true. This idea is promoted somewhat by conservative lawyers and organizations that thought, erroneously, that they could avoid lawsuits by doing away with testing. The rumors were also fed by impractical federal agencies with unworkable testing guidelines which were so inconsistent in their enforcement practices that many multiunit organizations were under the impression that they had to abide by a different set of regulations in each region of the country. With all this confusion, it is no wonder that many organizations dropped psychological testing.

The fact is that any organization has the right to use psychological tests, and there has never been a law prohibiting this right. Section 703 (h) of Title VII of the 1964 Civil Rights Act, also known as the Tower Amendment, states quite clearly:

> Nor shall it be an unlawful employment practice for an employer to give and act upon the results of any professionally developed ability test provided that such test, its administration or action upon the results is not designed, intended or used to discriminate because of race, color, religion, sex or national origin.

The Uniform Guidelines on Employee Selection Procedures, published in the Federal Register by the Equal Employment Opportunity Co-ordinating Council, states the following:

> In addition, the guidelines are based upon the recognition that properly developed and validated tests can significantly aid in the development and maintenance of an efficient work force and in the effective utilization of human resource.

Two Basic Issues. Griggs et al. v. Duke Power Company is the most important court case to date regarding the use of psychological tests. Minority workers of the company involved were employed solely in the maintenance department; the other four departments employed only Caucasians. In order to advance to a higher level, an individual had to pass a test of general intelligence and a mechanical aptitude test, and have a high school diploma. These requirements made it difficult for black employees to advance, since few had high school diplomas. The company believed that it was not discriminating since it applied all three criteria equally, but the Supreme Court disagreed. The Court said that the issue was not that the promotion and hiring criteria were being applied unequally, but that these criteria were rejecting a disproportionate number of black applicants. According to the Court, the selection program may have been "fair in form" but it was "discriminatory in practice." The Court went on to say that the criteria were not job-related, since several white employees in advanced positions have never passed the tests nor achieved a high school diploma, but were able to function adequately on the job. Thus, two issues emerged from this case and became the overriding concern of government agencies and many organizations engaged in testing: Tests should (1) be job-related and (2) not have an adverse impact on members of minority groups. Government guidelines now call for a company to show evidence of job relatedness only when adverse impact exists. A test has adverse impact when it rejects a disproportionate number of minority group members. A company proves job-relatedness by validating its tests. Government testing guidelines spell out exactly what psychologists have maintained for years: Preselection tests or other data used to make employment decisions should be related to job duties.

It is important to realize that any selection criterion can have an adverse impact and can trigger the requirement of proof of job relatedness. The selection interview, education and training requirements, and physical requirements are but a few of the many preselection criteria that can adversely affect minority groups or women.

Characteristics of Psychological Tests

Psychological tests are measuring instruments that must possess certain characteristics in order to be useful. A good test must be both reliable and valid. If a test or another screening device does not possess these characteristics, it is useless. Publishers are required to present reliability and validity evidence in test examiners' manuals, and when such data are lacking, the tests should not be used.

Many companies have attempted to devise their own tests. This approach is not advisable unless expert advice is available. The vast proportion of in-house tests have not been researched well enough to justify their use. Test development is a long, involved, and expensive process which should be left to professionals.

Reliability. A prerequisite to validity, *reliability* refers to the consistency of a test in measuring a trait. An examinee's test score should not vary a great deal over a number of testings unless, of course, the trait being measured was strengthened by experience or special training. The examinee's actual raw score would not be exactly the same each time the test was taken, but would vary within an acceptable range. In practice, people usually take a test only once or twice; therefore, reliability is a theoretical concept that is verified with basic research and then becomes an assumption upon which the test is used.

A notorious example of an unreliable preemployment measure is the selection interview. It is difficult to maintain the same standards of judgment from interview to interview. An interviewer may evaluate or interpret the data differently with each interview, stressing the importance of one factor in one interview and deemphasizing or ignoring the importance of that same factor in the next interview. When this is the case, it makes the interview a useless measure of future job performance.

Validity. *Validity* simply means that a test measures what it is supposed to measure. When a test is published, the developer uses a variety of techniques to demonstrate that the test is a valid measure of the trait in question. Validity coefficients are generated in order to answer questions: Does the intelligence test measure intelligence? Does the mechanical aptitude test measure mechanical aptitude? This type of validity evidence is somewhat different from the type of evidence used to define a test as having job relatedness or validity as defined by federal guidelines. When a company tries to validate a mechanical aptitude test to be used in the selection of maintenance mechanics, its purpose is not to prove that the test measures mechanical aptitude. The publisher has already proved this fact. What it must prove is that mechanical aptitude is needed for anyone to succeed as a maintenance mechanic in this particular company.

Varieties of Psychological Tests

Psychological tests can be categorized as measures of *general ability* (intelligence), *aptitude* or *achievement*, *personality*, and *interest*. Each type of test may be used in an industrial setting depending upon existing needs. Personality and interest tests, however, are not used to make predictions regarding job performance, but they are used when personality or certain patterns of interest are known to be related to performance in a particular setting.

Tests can be administered either to groups of any size or to one person at a time. Group tests are common in industry, since they are usually less expensive and less time-consuming than individual tests.

General Ability Tests. These types of tests vary in their complexity and function. The best example of a sophisticated and comprehensive intelligence test is the Wechsler Adult Intelligence Scale R (WAIS-R). This test must be administered and interpreted by a trained psychologist, and it yields the traditional intelligence quotient (IQ) score. It is a very detailed test upon which many shorter tests are based. The WAIS-R is administered to executive and management personnel to assess particular styles and qualities of intellectual functioning. Normally it is not used as an absolute measure in deciding whether a person will be hired or promoted.

There are many shorter, less comprehensive tests of general ability. The Otis Self-Administering Test of Mental Ability, Wonderlic Personnel Test, SRA Verbal, and Thurstone Test of Mental Alertness are a few of the most popular. They estimate intellectual functioning and generally do not yield IQ scores.

Aptitude and Achievement Tests. These test types are often hard to differentiate. The way in which a test is used often indicates whether it is a measure of aptitude or achievement. Theoretically, an *aptitude test* measures ability to perform a particular kind of task and is used to predict future performance on the job or in training. The *achievement test* is a measure of present functioning and is used to determine to what extent a given trait has been learned or mastered through training or job experience.

Personality Tests. These tests should be administered by properly trained personnel; a master's degree in psychology is usually a minimum requirement, a doctorate is preferable. *Personality tests* measure abstract concepts such as aggressiveness, independence, support, conformity, passivity, and the like. More controversy is generated by personality tests than any other kind because personality testing is the most difficult area of psychological testing, especially in terms of development. Even the best personality tests are often criticized for lack of technical support, and for this reason it is extremely important to carefully scrutinize their use and to be sure that trained personnel administer and interpret them.

Interest Tests. These tests are seldom used to make predictions regarding job performance. They are, instead, inventories of a person's likes and dislikes and are generally used for career and vocational guidance. The best-known and most widely used interest tests are the Strong-Campbell Vocational Interest Blank and the Kuder Preference Record. These tests tell how a person's interests compare with the interests of others in various occupational groups. The assumption is that a person will be more satisfied working among people with similar likes and dislikes.

Conclusions

It is management's prerogative to use and act upon the results of professionally developed psychological tests. No law or government regulation can prohibit any organization from using psychological tests when those tests measure traits that are significantly related to job performance.

It is important to choose tests or any other selection device very carefully. The selection should be based upon a complete analysis of job requirements. The procedure must have proved reliability and validity. A testing program is not an absolute answer to all personnel problems. A properly developed and executed testing program, however, can contribute substantially to the development and utilization of human resources.

See also Affirmative action; Assessment center method; Development and training, employee; Employment process; Equal employment opportunity, minorities and women; Interviewing, employee; Personnel administration.

REFERENCES

Anastasi, A.: *Psychological Testing*, 4th ed., Macmillan, New York, 1976.

Cronbach, L.: *Essentials of Psychological Testing*, 3d ed., Harper & Row, New York, 1970.

Dunnette, M. D.,: *Handbook of Industrial and Organizational Psychology*, Rand-McNally, Chicago, 1975.

Fear, Richard A., and J. F. Ross: *Jobs, Dollars, and EEO—How to Hire More Productive Entry-Level Workers*, McGraw-Hill, 1983.

Ghiselli, E. E.: *The Validity of Occupational Aptitude Tests*, John Wiley, New York, 1966.

Kirkpatrick, J. J., R. B. Ewen, R. S. Barrett, and R. A. Katzell: *Testing and Fair Employment*, New York University Press, New York, 1968.

STEVEN J. STANARD, *Stanard & Associates, Inc.*

Theory X and Theory Y

Theory X and Theory Y are two theories of management which are based on antithetical assumptions about human nature and work. *Theory X*, the traditional, work-centered, authoritarian approach, assumes that employees dislike work and must be coerced by management. *Theory Y* believes that people can and will enjoy fully productive work if permitted to participate significantly in decision making. It is, as such, a people-centered, democratic, human relations approach.

Douglas McGregor first enunciated the two theories in 1960 in an attempt to explain the inadequacies of authoritarian types of management and to devise a better type on the basis of modern behavioral science and Maslow's definition of human needs and motivation.

The implicit assumptions of the managers of an organization will determine its modus operandi down to the smallest action. Theory X management assumes that (1) there is no intrinsic satisfaction for people in work; (2) humans will avoid work as much as possible; (3) therefore, management must direct, control, coerce, and threaten workers in order to achieve management goals; (4) the average human seeks to avoid responsibility, lacks ambition or imagination, craves direction and, above all, security. On the basis of these assumptions, theory X management must, to achieve its goals, apply external motivating force, or authority, which in turn determines that (1) the *locus of decision* will be solely in the nominal head of the organization; (2) the *structure* of the organization will be pyramidal, with authority flowing from the top down; (3) the *supervisor's* main functions are to transmit orders (not to make decisions) and to emphasize production; (4) the *role of the worker* is that of an isolated cog in the machine, communicating only with his or her supervisor.

Theory Y, at the opposite end of the continuum, assumes that (1) expenditure of effort in work and play is natural to humans; (2) external control and threat are not essential to bring about effort toward organizational goals to which humans are committed; (3) the satisfaction of individual ego and self-actualization needs can be direct products of efforts toward organizational goals; (4) the average human learns, under proper conditions, not only to accept but to seek responsibility; (5) the capacity for creativity is widely distributed in the population; (6) modern industry rarely utilizes the intellectual potentialities of the average human. Theory Y assumptions thus lead to a *participatory* organization in which authority is accepted by workers, not imposed on them. Accordingly, (1) the *locus of decision* may be widespread, at any level; (2) the group, including its supervisor, becomes the *primary organizational unit*; (3) the *supervisor* deals with groups; (4) the *worker* has become a group member who participates in setting organizational goals and therefore works willingly, intelligently. In sum, theory X management will rationalize problems by blaming the nature of its human resources, but a theory Y management assumes responsibility for the attitudes and productivity of its employees.

The concepts of theory X and theory Y have been of great service in defining the limits of the approaches to organization theory and in focusing attention on their opposing assumptions. Criticism centers on their extreme and rather sweeping generalizations. The theories pay insufficient attention to the specifics of interrelationships between particular jobs, to the great variety of conditions and of human individuals. Finally, neither theory X nor theory Y seems to be consistently supported by research findings.

As an outgrowth of theory Y, William G. Ouchi has dubbed the Japanese concept of "consensus management" as *theory Z*. Ouchi describes this theory Z as the belief that "involved workers are the key to productivity." McGregor would have said that this was theory Y carried to its ultimate.

See also Leadership; Motivation in organizations.

REFERENCES

McGregor, Douglas: *The Human Side of Enterprise*, McGraw-Hill, New York, 1960.

Ouchi, William G.: *Theory Z: How American Business Can Meet the Japanese Challange*, Addison-Wesley, Reading, Mass., 1981.

Wilcock, Keith D.: "Diagnosis and Treatment of Theory X Organizations," *World*, Peat, Marwick, Mitchell & Co., New York, Autumn 1972.

LESTER R. BITTEL, *James Madison University*

Therbligs

A therblig is the lowest indivisible work movement operation of the body; it is one of the 18 elementary subdivisions, physical, visual, and mental, which are supposedly common to all kinds of industrial manual work. The term *therblig* (Gilbreth spelled backward, almost) was coined by Frank Bunker Gilbreth, 1868–1924, in his pioneering work in motion study. The concept is in active use today in the highly developed science of time and motion study. While not a totally pure concept, it is very useful to the skilled industrial operations analyst.

In an effort to find the most economical (and least fatiguing) way of using the worker in combination with his or her tools or machine, the concept of the therblig is used as filmed motions performed by the worker in a manual operation are charted graphically and minutely analyzed. Examples of therbligs are "search"—during which the worker's hands or eyes are seeking the tool or object needed—and "find/select," the therblig which follows "search" and which may be either a mental or visual operation.

See also Human factors engineering; Work measurement; Work simplification and improvement.

REFERENCES

Barnes, Ralph M.: *Motion and Time Study*, 5th ed., John Wiley, New York 1963.

Gilbreth, Frank K.: *Motion Study*, D. Van Nostrand, New York, 1911.

LESTER R. BITTEL, *James Madison University*

Time Management

Time is the universal measure. It can be applied to each of an organization's inputs. The time value of facilities and equipment is rent. The time value of electrical energy is kilowatt-hours. The time value of money and materials is interest. The time value of labor is worker-hours. Similarly, output is valued in the number of units per minute, per hour, per week, per month, per year. Profits, too, are sized for a year's period of time. In almost all instances, time costs money.

Time is also an unforgiving measure of an organization's—and a manager's—effectiveness. It sets the restrictions on every operation and process. Time's two persistent questions are "How long will it take?" and "Was it finished on time?"

Time is a resource, too. As the late Ralph Cordiner, president of General Electric Company and architect of its massive reorganization in the 1950s, observed, "Time is an asset that all competitors share in common, but the management of time can be one of the decisive elements in success or failure." It follows that time can be wasted, or it can be conserved. An executive must manage time wisely whether it is the time allotted to processes or the limited personal time available for overseeing responsibilities. These two charges can be classified as time commitments and management of personal time.

Time Commitments. Specifically, three kinds of situations press a manager for a time commitment. These situations appear in almost all kinds of enterprises, regardless of the exact nature of the manager's responsibility.

Operating Schedules. Whether managers are held responsible for a product or service, they are routinely asked to meet certain operating schedules which usually call for a specific number of units of output per day, per week, or per month. These schedules act like a "go–no go" gauge of a manager's capability. Allowances will be made for interruptions and delays beyond the manager's control, but repeated failures will be held against the manager. The assumption is that a manager will alert the schedule makers to factors which contribute to delays so that the schedules incorporate enough time to allow for them. Put another way, if a manager regularly has problems meeting the schedules, initiative for corrective action must be provided by either (1) finding ways to meet schedules or (2) seeing that the schedules are adjusted beforehand.

Promised Delivery Dates. Routine schedules cover most time commitments; nevertheless, there are a number of nonroutine situations in which a manager is asked to see that the product or service is ready for delivery (or shipment) by a specific date. These promised delivery dates may be derived by the sales department, which has already made a commitment to a customer. They may be imposed upon the manager with apparent good reason by someone in higher authority. The manager may also simply volunteer. In any event, most of these promises are binding. Thus, a manager should try not to accept delivery dates that appear unreasonable without first making his or her own time estimates. If such promises imply that previously scheduled priorities must be rearranged, the proper time to speak of this need is when the commitment is accepted; if the problem is pointed out after the promise has been given, it is usually too late to complain about disruptions to routine schedules. The same advice goes for added costs—the costs of interrupting assembly runs, of overtime, or of expediting. These considerations should be brought up early in the negotiation rather than after the promise has been exacted.

Project Completion Deadlines. Many deadlines can best be described as *project completion dates.* These may be associated with such matters as (1) construction of a facility which must be ready for occupancy at a certain date: (2) installation of a new machine which must be in operation when the seasonal rush begins; (3) development of an information system which must be operative before the next accounting period begins; (4) preparation of a study or a report which is due when it is time to file appropriation requests; and (5) a test of a proposed process which must be completed before design plans are firmed up.

Project completion deadlines, like promised delivery dates, may be imposed upon a manager from above, or they may represent free choice. In either instance, the prudence and care the manager takes in establishing these deadlines go a long way toward ensuring that they can be met.

Factors Affecting Time Estimates. In cases where time measurements and calculations of the time needed to complete a task or an assignment are precise, many variable factors may reduce even the most careful approaches to rough estimates. In order to understand how this can be so, the variable time factors are examined one by one.

Inherent Time. Inherent in the conversion or production process are a number of nonproductive essentials. An order or instruction must be received and noted, for example. An individual or a machine (frequently both) must work on the material or paperwork form involved. The material or form must be moved from work station to work station. Finally, the finished product or form is ready for shipment or delivery. Industrial engineers call this total process the *order-delivery cycle* or the *manufacturing cycle.* This cycle has three inescapable elements:

Labor time or worker-hours needed to perform the recording, fabricating, transcribing, transmitting, assembling, finishing, inspecting, calculating, and packaging functions.

Machine time or machine hours to perform, or assist in performing, functions listed under labor time.

Handling time needed to move materials, supplies, parts, paperwork, and communications from one operation to another.

Setup Time. This is also known as "make-ready" time or, when it includes the beginning and the end of an operation, "setup and tear-down" or "get-ready and put-away" time. It is, of course, the time always needed to prepare an operation and to clean up after it is finished. The more often a schedule calls for a change in setup, the more time the department consumes in nonproductive work. Setup times may be necessary and unavoidable, but they consume time without actually producing a product or service. The best ways to attack this particular problem are to try to minimize the number of instances in which a line must be changed over and to direct work simplification efforts to that end.

Learning Time. Learning time can be viewed as a special version of setup time because it is typically associated with starting up—a new process, a new product, a new operation, a new organization, or a new employee. Output rates are always slower when starting up than after things are running smoothly. Employees have to learn the new operation or the new machine. Bugs show up that must be eliminated. Operations have to be coordinated. Unanticipated problems must be solved. Statistically, when anyone is learning, there is a uniform percentage drop (such as 10 percent) in the time needed to produce a single unit of output every time the total number of units of output is doubled. [See Learning (experience) curves.]

Lost Time. A manager's time plans must also accept the fact that the operations will lose time in two ways: (1) personal time lost from a scheduled 8-hour day for washup, rest periods, lunch periods, plus the time lost from the schedule for vacations, holiday, and sickness; (2) technical time delays caused by machine breakdowns, material shortages, and open spots on the schedule.

Costly Time. Certain practices often cause a manager to buy time in a costly fashion. These situations come about through:

1. Crash time or "red rush" when a product or service is forced into a schedule out of turn and hastened through the process with special attention and handling. Such instances usually arise from attempts to mollify favored customers, meet a competitor's delivery offer or make good on a delay caused by improper scheduling or oversight. In any event, rush jobs always cost more to complete because they do not move through normal channels.
2. Expediting time which employs the use of a manager or clerk to trace down so-called lost orders and/or walk them through the shop. Obviously this is a costly use of valuable time. It often occurs in conjunction with crash time and rush jobs.
3. Overtime which entails the use of costly worker-hours beyond 8 in a day or 40 in a week to complete schedules.

Managing Personal Time. Almost everything that can be said about conservation and utilization of operation and process times can also be said of a manager's own time. In many ways, this time is more valuable than all the other time put together. This is because a manager's interest, attention, and initiative are almost constantly needed to direct and maximize the total conversion process. Only a very determined person can maintain time headway each day in the face of distractions that come from every corner.

Personal Time Analysis. The best starting point in managing personal time is to find out where it goes. To do so, a work-sampling study should be made, similar to Fig. T-1. Observations should also be made at the same time each day in order to determine when these activities and functions take place. On the basis of the facts revealed in this study, a manager can prepare a fairly standardized personal time budget.

Personal Time Budget. This time budget may be basic, or it may be as complex as the individual feels is necessary. In a basic time budget (Fig. T-2, a manager's time is classified four ways.

1. *Routine paperwork.* This procedure includes checking time cards, filling out pay sheets, checking log books and tally sheets, and answering mail. While this activity should be held to a

Personal Time Analysis Sheet

Date:

Observed activity and function	Observation times 7:45	8:15	8:45	9:15	9:45	3:15	3:45	4:15	4:45	5:15	Totals	Percent of all observations
Activity												
A. Personal contacts												
B. Telephone												
C. Paperwork												
D. Meetings												
E. Personal (travel, lunch, etc.)												
F. Other												
Function												
1. Assigning work												
2. Reviewing subordinate performance												
3. Expediting orders and supplies												
4. Preparing and analyzing reports												
5. Preparing plans and schedules												
6. Organizational development												
7. Sales/customer development												
8. Product development												
9. Creative/self-improvement												
10. Other												

FIG. T-1 Personal time analysis sheet. For each observation time, place a mark in the activity and function group.

minimum, most budgets allocate between 10 and 20 percent of the manager's time to it.

2. *Overseeing duties.* These responsibilities make up the core of most management jobs and are often the most important part. They include, first and foremost, supervising employees and all that attends that task—assigning work, training, checking performance, counseling. Most managers should try to function in this capacity for at least 50 percent of their time.

3. *Special assignments.* For a manager who is well regarded, these extra activities will eat into the available time and also stretch the normal day from 8 to 9 or 10 hours. While a manager's record may benefit by his or her serving on safety and cost-reduction committes, or by being the person tagged for research on special projects, it does not pay to be too eager. Special assignments may erode the supervisory performance that is basic to a manager's survival. Generally, these special activities should be limited to about 10 to 20 percent of a manager's time.

4. *Planning and creative work.* These undertakings are the things managers do on their own initiative to smooth out the work flow, to improve layout and methods in operations, to train the staff for new assignments, and to make the most of the time available to all. Planning time also includes time for thought and reflection and for self-improvement. At a mimimum, a manager ought to allot 15 percent of the time to planning and creative work.

Conserving Personal Time   Personal time has a way of finding the leaks in the system. It drains away far more easily than it is utilized. There are, however, a number of ways in which an alert manager can plug these leaks.

1. *Control the telephone.* There is probably no demon more apt to chew up personal time than the telephone. Often, what begins as a brief exchange of business information degenerates into 15 minutes of irrelevant gossip. Time also is wasted when a manager accepts a nonurgent call during a meeting or is conducting business with a subordinate. Such calls can be handled by saying, ''Please call back later,'' or ''I'll return your call in 15 minutes.''

2. *Limit chitchat.* There is nothing like a 20-minute conversation about the weekend's ski trip to put a manager behind schedule the first thing Monday morning. It is difficult, of course, to sense when to lend an interested ear and when to cut a conversation short. It is probably best to develop a routine way of handling such situations by saying, ''I'd love to hear about it at lunch,'' or ''Let's

	Monday	Tuesday	Wednesday	Thursday	Friday
8	Routine	Routine	Routine	Routine	Routine
9	Inspection and supervision of operations	Individual work with staff / Regular	Inspection and supervision of operations	Individual work with staff / Regular	Special work
10		Inspection and supervision of operations / Regular		Control studies and reports	Inspection and supervision of operations / Regular
11	Regular	Regular	Division staff meeting / Regular	Regular	Staff meeting / Regular
12 / 1	L	U	N	C	H
	Interviews and contacts / Regular	Interviews and contacts / Regular	Interviews and contacts / Regular	Interviews and contacts / Regular	Creative work
2 / 3	Planning and organizing	Inspection and supervision of operations	Special work	Inspection and supervision of operations	
4	Regular	Regular		Regular	
5	Routine	Routine	Routine	Routine	Routine

FIG. T-2   Personal time budget.

get together during the coffee break, if we can, so that I can hear the whole story.''

3. *Decide quickly on small matters.* Most problems do not require a lot of time for a decision. On small matters especially, there is rarely justification for asking for time to think them over. A prompt yes or no saves time since it enables a manager to dispose of the matter without having to return to it later.

4. *Start early.* Many personal time problems can be avoided by beginning the workday a few minutes early. A great number of successful executives can testify to this fact. They say that they can accomplish more by getting to work ½ hour early in the morning than they can during any 2 or 3 hours during the day. Obviously, this is a good time for disposing of routine paperwork.

5. *Discourage interruptions.* If managers develop and follow time budgets, they can be justifiably firm about asking that their routines not be disturbed except in an emergency. They can do so because enough time has been allotted for the major duties. In this way, subordinates and others have a designated time during which they and their supervisors are free to discuss any problems which may arise during a day.

6. *Avoid overcommitting personal time.* A manager has an obligation to contribute to the organization's overall welfare but must avoid carrying these activities too far. Quite simply, a manager has to learn to say no when the time budget is overloaded.

7. *Utilize travel time.* A manager deserves rest and relaxation, of course. It makes good sense, however, to consider that the working day begins when a manager leaves home in the morning and ends upon reaching home at night. Many solutions can be effected more quickly by using extra times such as commuting hours, lunch periods, and waiting times in airports to think over problems encountered during the day.

See also Delegation; Learning (experience) curves; Work measurement; Work sampling; Work simplification and improvement.

REFERENCES

Douglass, Merrill E., and Donna N. Douglass: *Manage Your Time, Manage Your Work, Manage Yourself,* American Management Association, AMACOM, New York, 1980.

Ferner, J. D.: *Successful Time Management,* John Wiley, New York, 1980.

Mackenzie, R. Alec: *The Time Trap,* McGraw-Hill, New York, 1975. (Paperback.)

LESTER R. BITTEL, *James Madison University*

Transactional Analysis

Transactional analysis (TA) is the term used to describe both a theory and the application of that theory in the description and understanding of human behavior and interpersonal relations (''transactions''). It is used by management to heighten a trainee's ability to manage his or her own behavior and that of others and to build an atmosphere of mutual respect and trust.

Derived largely from Freud, developed and popularized by Dr. Eric L. Berne *(Games People Play)* and Dr. Thomas A. Harris *(I'm OK, You're OK)* in the 1950s, TA has been used by scores of corporations to train thousands of employees at all levels to use their rational abilities for problem solving and decision making more effectively. It is seen also as a management tool for improving in-house communications.

TA is a simplified approach to psychological therapy. The professional consultant teaches it as a basic language and trains small groups to use it to recognize and describe the ''child,'' ''parent,'' or ''adult'' ego state predominating in each participant in a simulated interaction. Trainees become aware of the consequences to other people of various behaviors and practice suggesting alternative behaviors in the optimal rational (''adult'') mode of transaction, thus leading to improved individual and group effectiveness and communication.

An important aspect of TA is the concept of ''stroking,'' the demonstration of compassionate behavior. TA advocates believe that such positive stroking, as compared with negative stroking or reprimand, helps to develop mutually supportive relationships.

Although its effectiveness is still difficult to measure, many corporations see positive benefits from TA training in improved customer relations, sharply decreased resignations (owing to improved managerial insights in handling subordinates—and bosses), increased enthusiasm for monotonous jobs, and in its uses as a nonthreatening ''gripe method.'' TA gives supervisors improved tools for selecting new hires, evaluating performance, and promoting. It sharply improves teams' abilities to perceive and manage their own processes. Conversely, as a technique that gives autonomy to people as a means toward productivity, it is not attractive to strongly autocratic managements. As a relatively shallow theory, it also needs a much stronger base in research than has yet been provided. When used in a firm, it sometimes causes new problems to surface, makes new demands on managers. Employees may suspect management of playing God or ''big brother''; nevertheless, the popularity of TA is symptomatic of the intense interest of people in their own behavior, and its future in business is probably assured.

See also Behavior modeling; Interpersonal relationships; Laboratory (sensitivity) training; Motivation in organizations; Nominal group technique; Theory X and theory Y.

REFERENCES

Berne, Eric L.: "Ego States in Psychotherapy," *American Journal of Psychotherapy*, 1957, pp. 11–293.

——————: *Games People Play*, Grove Press, New York, 1964.

Bradford, J. Allyn: *Transactional Analysis*, Addison-Wesley, Reading, Mass., 1977.

Harris, Thomas A.: *I'm OK — You're OK: A Practical Guide to Transactional Analysis*, Harper & Row, New York, 1967.

LESTER R. BITTEL, *James Madison University*

Valuation of a Firm

The valuation of a business takes place whenever a transfer of ownership is proposed, under negotiation, or actually agreed upon. This situation typically occurs when a company goes public, when it is up for sale or is sold, or when it is liquidated. Valuation is also important for estate and taxation purposes.

A number of methods are available to calculate the value of a business. In broad terms, these methods are discussed under three analytical approaches associated with either the balance sheet, the operating statements, or a comparison with similar businesses.

Normally, several of the various methods will be used to find a value for the company. The variation in values is looked at differently by the buyer and the seller. In any case, the calculated values are judged in the light of knowing if the business is (1) a "going concern," (2) being sold for its assets, or (3) filing for bankruptcy.

Balance Sheet Methods. Several methods of valuation are based on analysis of the balance sheet statement. In each method, the figures entered in the balance sheet are modified to obtain market values. Three principal methods of valuation from this source are as follows.

Book Value. The book value of a business is readily available and easily understood. It is found by subtracting all the liabilities from selected assets of the business. Liabilities include all the debts and nonequity accounts of the firm, such as current liabilities, long-term debt, and deferred taxes. Intangible assets, such as goodwill, new-product development, and patents, and assets not associated with the operation of the business are excluded from the asset total. From a practical viewpoint, book value rarely represents economic value and is not very useful in determining the real value of a business.

Market Value. A more logical method of valuation using the balance sheet is to modify each account to show its market value. That is, all liabilities are subtracted from selected assets. This procedure leads to substantial changes on the asset side of the balance sheet. Inventories, accounts receivables, plant, and equipment typically have market values that are different from their book values. These values may be higher or lower depending on obsolescence, deterioration, or other causes. Other real assets, such as land and mineral deposits, should also be recorded at their market values. The liability side of the balance sheet should be similarly modified. Much of the debt stated at book value has a very different value at the market. This is especially true

905

when there is a high fluctuation of interest rates. Accounts receivable are classified into several categories according to the degree of risk. Each class is then valued according to the likelihood of collecting on the account. Other real assets are valued by appraisers.

Liquidation Value. This valuation is a modified form of market valuation. It assumes that if the firm were forced into liquidation—either for business or personal reasons—many of the assets would be written down relative to what they are worth to an operating business. On the other hand, some firms are worth more when liquidated than they are as operating businesses. That is, the assets can be sold for more than the book value assigned to them in an operational situation.

Operating Statements Methods. Two methods prevail under this approach—the discounted cash flow and capitalization methods. Both employ a risk factor to discount or capitalize either earnings or dividends. Accordingly, these approaches are more theoretically sound, but much more difficult to use than the balance sheet methods.

Discounted Cash Flow. Forecasting is the basis for the discounted cash-flow method of valuation. The cash flows of the business are predicted for several years into the future, and the selling value of the business at the end of the period is also forecast. Each of these values is then discounted at the marginal cost of capital to the present time to get a value for the business. The cash flows for each year are calculated by adding depreciation charges to the pro forma net profit after tax and then subtracting loan amortization needs and additional working capital needs.

The present value factor used in discounting the cash flows and the termination value of the business is composed of (1) a risk-free factor and (2) a premium factor to take into consideration the risk associated with the business. For example, the United Stated Treasury bond rate can be used as the risk-free rate while an additional several percentage points can be used as the risk premium. As an alternative, the reciprocal of the price/earnings ratio can be used as the capitalization value. This ratio is found by calculating the price/earnings ratios of companies similar to the one being evaluated.

The discounted cash-flow method of valuation is inherently difficult to use except when cash flows are predictable and a disposal value of the business at the end of the period can be calculated. The predictions of cash flows are particularly hard to make if price changes and cost variations are common. The cost of capital also varies widely during times of inflation and can cause wide variations in valuation. However, this method does eliminate distortions that arise out of different methods of depreciation and amortization. It also should be noted that in some cases, dividends may be used in place of cash flows as the figures to be discounted to the present.

Earnings Capitalization. The value determined by this method is that amount that would give the stated earnings, using a specific rate of return. A reasonable approach is to (1) determine the pro forma net income after taxes over the next 5 years and average them; and (2) divide this average figure by the rate of return required for the riskiness associated with the business. The result is the capitalized value of the firm. In cases where the net income of the business is subject to large variations, however, a higher rate of return figure needs to be used for capitalization.

Comparison with Similar Businesses. This method is based on comparisons with similar, publicly traded companies. These companies should be of similar size, asset composition, debt/equity ratios, and products or services. The price of a common share of stock is then compared with both earnings and book value. Typically, the comparison can be computed in steps.

1. Initially, a price/earnings ratio is calculated for each of the publicly traded firms. It is necessary to assess the financial statements of the businesses for the past few years.

2. The average stock price for each year is then divided by the earnings per share. Thus a range of values of price/earnings ratios is obtained for the similar businesses.

3. An appropriate price/earnings ratio is selected using either the latest year or a weighted average. This price/earnings ratio is then multiplied by the net earnings of the business in order to get its value.

Similar calculations can be performed to obtain price/book value ratios. The results will also give another value for the firm.

If the risk characteristics of the firm being valued are different from those of the other companies, adjustments need to be made. In particular, the price/earnings ratio will be adjusted to take into consideration the different risks associated.

Application. In practice, all the valuation methods may be used in order to arrive at a range of values. Those that do not appear useful for the particular business being evaluated can be discarded. There will be differences of opinion at this point. The owner of the business will want a high valuation for selling purposes, yet a low value for taxation purposes. The buyer of the business is interested in paying a low price for the business. Since there will always be a range of values, subjective considerations will determine whether an acceptable price can be reached. In a great many cases, the assistance of experts in the fields of banking, appraisal, and taxation will be necessary to determine a firm and final figure for the value of the business.

See also Acquisitions and mergers; Budgeting, capital; Financial management, capital structure and dividend policy; Financial statement analysis; Risk analysis and management.

REFERENCES

Burke, Frank M., Jr.: *Valuation and Valuation Planning for Closely Held Businesses,* Prentice-Hall, Englewood Cliffs, N.J., 1981.

Pratt, Shannon P.: *Valuing a Business: The Analysis and Appraisal of Closely-held Companies,* Dow Jones-Irwin, Homewood, Ill., 1981.

Research Institute of America, Inc.: "What Is Your Corporation Worth?" *Research Institute Recommendations,* New York, Oct. 1, 1982.

Strischeck, Dev: "How to Determine the Value of a Firm," *Management Accounting,* January 1983.

PHILIP H. MAXWELL, *James Madison University*

Value-Added Tax

A value-added tax (VAT) is a multistage tax on the increase in the value of goods or services at each stage in the production and distribution process. The increase in value is measured by the difference between a firm's sales receipts and its purchases from other firms. The increase in value is also approximately equal to income received by owners of the factors of production at each stage of this process. Alternatively, a VAT can be applied to the sum of these payments at each stage of the process.

More specifically, three major types of VAT can be distinguished depending upon whether it is applied to (1) total production of final goods and service, (2) gross national product (GNP), or (3) only some portion of this aggregate. A GNP type of VAT can be applied to all final goods and services produced and sold, including both consumer and capital goods, at each stage of the production process. A second type of VAT allows firms to deduct their capital expenditures as well as their purchases from other firms in computing that VAT liability—a VAT on consumption goods. Application of a tax on net value added by each firm in the production process, applied to GNP less depreciation of existing capital assets, represents a third type of VAT.

European Consumption Type of VAT. During the late 1960s and continuing through the 1970s, the VAT became an important source of government tax receipts for countries that were members of the European Economic Community (EEC). Implementation of a VAT was considered as a condition for EEC membership. The VAT was intended to generate more uniform taxing systems, including border tax adjustments, to promote trade within the EEC. In addition, the VAT was used to replace ineffective sales taxes imposed on businesses in the member countries.

European countries that have instituted a VAT have chosen the consumption type of VAT system. Taxes are generally collected by all individual firms on their sales, while tax credits are received for taxes paid to their own suppliers. Invoices from suppliers must be used as documentation to qualify for tax credits. Because of concern for the regressivity of a VAT, special classes of goods and services are subject to differential tax rates or are exempt from the VAT. Preferential tax treatment has been generally applied to goods and services consumed in large quantities by lower-income classes. Goods and services consumed in large amounts by higher-income classes have received less favorable tax treatment.

Applicability in the United States. In this country, consideration for implementation of a federal VAT has experienced varying degrees of interest in Congress in recent years. The desirability for a VAT in the United States is conditioned by questions of economic efficiency, equity, and political expediency. Implementation of a consumption type of VAT involves consideration of the degree of uniformity of the tax rate for various classes of goods and services. A uniform tax rate would be expected to have a neutral effect on consumer choices between various classes of goods and services at market prices.

With a uniform tax rate on all goods and services, a VAT, while proportional to total consumption, would be regressive with respect to income. This regressivity results if the proportion of income allocated to consumption falls with rising income levels across income classes, a condition characteristic of this nation. Any reduction in regressivity through the use of exemptions or differential tax rates, following the European experience, would lessen the neutrality effects on consumption choice of a uniform rate. In addition, problems of administration might be expected to increase with the use of differential rates.

In considering the desirability of VAT for the United States, other questions concerning efficiency and equity must be addressed. Such questions include: Are existing tax systems going to be replaced by a VAT? Will existing government expenditure patterns be adjusted with a VAT? How can a VAT at the federal level be integrated with existing taxation systems at the state and local government levels?

Additional questions concerning the effects of a VAT of the macroeconomic performance of the nation's economy might also be addressed. Would a VAT be inflationary? Would it have detrimental effects on the longer-run income and employment performance of the economy? While evidence from the European experience does not suggest sustained price level, employment, and aggregate production effects associated with the introduction of a VAT, institutional differences probably preclude a direct application of this evidence to the United States.

Other questions of a more political nature concerning the desirability of a VAT might also be addressed. Both in recent years and in the foreseeable future, the federal government has experienced annual budget deficits in excess of $100 billion. Attempted reduction of such deficits through a VAT has been considered by some members of Congress as one potential solution. A consumption type of VAT, judging from the European experience, would represent a potential tax base in this country in excess of $1 trillion. The large size and cyclical stability of this potential tax base make it attractive to those members of Congress who are concerned with maintaining current levels of federal spending. These same characteristics can be viewed as undesirable by those members of Congress who favor a reduced role for the federal government in the American economy. While the VAT in the EEC replaced other taxing systems, it has been used in these same European countries to increase tax revenues during a period of rising government expenditures.

See also Economic concepts; Input-output analysis; Productivity measurement; Tax management.

REFERENCES

Aaron, Henry J., ed.: *The Value-Added Tax: Lessons from Europe,* The Brookings Institution, Washington, D.C., 1981.

Lindhold, Richard W.: *Value-Added Tax and Other Tax Reforms,* Nelson-Hall, Chicago, 1976.

McLure, Charles E., Jr., and Norman B. Ture: *Value-Added Tax: Two Views,* American Enterprise Institute for Public Policy Research, Washington, D.C., 1972.

DAVID SCHIRM, *John Carroll University*

Value Analysis

Value analysis is a proven management tool for profit assurance, but to be effective it must be part of the daily life of operating management. Value analysis has proven to be highly successful in many areas in addition to manufacturing companies. Substantial cost reductions have been achieved by hospital administrations, banking, and construction and by state and local governments.

Definition of Terms

Value programs have grown so rapidly in recent years that the terms *value analysis, value engineering, value control, value assurance, value management* and almost any program with the word "value" in

the title can be found in effect somewhere. The predominant term is the one coined in 1948 by Larry D. Miles at General Electric, Schenectady, where he pioneered the technique. *Value analysis* is an organized, creative approach to the problem of identifying and eliminating unnecessary cost, especially of a product or service. When applied to the design function, the activity is more commonly known as *value engineering.* In many cases, the terms value analysis and value engineering are used interchangeably, as will be done in this entry.

Elimination of unnecessary cost causes no adverse effect on quality, reliability, maintainability, or salability. The problem, however, is to identify what element of cost is unnecessary. The value analysis program is the technique for accomplishing this objective. All costs connected with the product design, material, manufacturing processes, and especially the specifications and requirements are subjected to the value analysis study. Specifically, the characteristics of value analysis are: (1) it is an organized, creative approach to cost reduction; (2) it places emphasis on function rather than method; (3) it identifies areas of excessive or unnecessary costs; (4) it improves the value of the product; (5) it provides the same or better performance at a lower cost; and (6) it reduces neither quality nor reliability. *Value* is the lowest cost needed to reliably accomplish the essential function.

Value Engineering Study. A value engineering study is an objective appraisal of all the elements of the design, construction, procurement, installation, and maintenance of equipment, including the specifications to achieve the necessary functions, maintainability, and reliability at the lowest cost. Value engineering entails a detailed review of product designs and specifications, placing a total dollar value on the costs of production and maintenance and relating these costs to the functional value of each part and assembly. Alternative designs, materials, processes, and methods of fabrication, together with standard products available from specialty suppliers are explored to find the lowest-cost way to achieve required functions.

Function. A function is that which makes a product work or sell. The function should be defined in two words, a verb and a noun; for example, "support cable." There are two reasons for restricting analysis to such a definition of function:

1. The use of two words avoids the possibility of combining functions and attempting to define more than one simple function at a time.

2. The use of two simple words will assure the achievement of the lowest level of abstraction possible with words; the identification of the function should be as precise as possible.

Primary or Basic Function. The *primary* or *basic* function is the most important essential function without the performance of which the product would be virtually worthless. If a function can be eliminated without preventing the achievement of the basic function, this function is secondary.

Five-Phase Approach

The first and perhaps the most important technique of value engineering is the organized approach—the value engineering job plan. If outstanding results are to be achieved in getting better value, and 30, 50, or even 75 percent of the original costs are to be removed, there must be a systematic plan of attack. The job plan consists of the following five phases:

The Information Phase. Each problem requires a phase in which all the facts are clearly determined. Get complete information concerning costs, inventory, usage, specifications, development history, material, manufacturing methods, and processes. Get drawings, manufacturing operation sheets, and actual samples. Define the primary function and secondary functions. Collect too much rather than too little information. Exhaust all possible sources of information. Separate facts from opinions. Do not "stack" the evidence.

The Speculation Phase. Here is where you put to use the creative approach. Try to answer the question, "What else will do the job?" Blast away old concepts. Make use of the brainstorming method. Exclude negative thoughts. Avoid analysis of ideas at this stage. Record all ideas; then forget them for the time being. To start the ideas flowing, try asking simple, suggestive questions such as:

In what form could this be?

How would I make it in my home workshop?

Should it slide instead of rotate?

What other layout might be better?

What if it were turned upside down? Inside out?

Record all ideas for achieving the function regardless of specifications, interchangeability, and so on. Many times, good ideas come from trying to develop others that obviously would not work.

Set a target to take out at least one-half the cost from functional areas and nine-tenths the cost from some of the components. By so doing, you will be forced into new areas—areas not previously explored.

The Analysis Phase. The primary objective here is to analyze and weigh the ideas generated with regard to cost, function, and feasibility. Establish a dollar value of each idea. Challenge each idea by applying the following tests for value:

Does its use contribute value?

Is its cost proportionate to its usefulness?

Can it or some of its features be eliminated?

Can its required function be achieved in a simpler manner?

Can a usable standard product be found?

Is it made on proper tooling, considering quantities used?

Will another supplier provide it for less?

Is anyone buying it for less?

Refine all ideas that show promise of providing improved value. Evaluate these ideas by comparison. Select for further consideration those ideas that have weathered the storm of evaluation.

Do not try to eliminate ideas. Instead, try to analyze them to see how they can be made to work. A positive approach must be used. Ideas emanating from a brainstorming session are not going to spring to life correct in all details. They are concepts only. Do not let an obvious fault hide the merits of a proposal and thus prevent its thorough analysis. With a small modification, it may become a promising idea.

The Decision Phase. Take the best ideas and plan a program to obtain the information needed to develop these ideas into sound, usable suggestions. What must be done is to recognize the problem and search for the person who can help. There are many specialists in a company, and the services of every specialist in industry are available on request. In drawing help from outside the company, from suppliers or specialists, do not just hand them a drawing and specifications and say, "What can you do with this?" Instead, inform them of the function you want, draw out their ideas on the problem, and give them some latitude to work in.

Certain ideas will develop and promise a future. Each idea should be reviewed with the thought, "Is this really the best idea?" "With this new information could a better job be done?" Now is the time to use your best judgment. Select those ideas showing the most promise, and plan your campaign for selling your proposals to top management.

The Execution Phase. In this phase, the idea must be sold. Be prepared to meet and triumph over considerable resistance. To do so, present a clear and concise picture of exactly what is proposed and what the proposal will mean to top management, its project, and the company. When making recommendations, always be prepared to give and take. Have an alternative plan ready in the event the primary proposal is rejected. Stress the technical capability of the proposal, and use cost reduction as an incentive.

Organization and Staffing

Location of the value engineering function within a company is dependent upon the type of industry. With complete backing of top management, location of the function is not so important as the personnel

909

selected to staff the organization. Most companies tend to place the value engineering operation within their engineering branch if the company is heavily design-oriented. Process-type industries more than likely will place the value operation within the procurement branch, where it is most often called *value analysis.* The reasoning behind this approach is based upon the higher percentage of dollar expenditure allocated to the procurement of materials in contrast to the cost of design, fabrication, and assembly operations. When value analysis is applied to manufacturing operations or to clerical systems and procedures, it is typically supervised by the industrial engineering organization.

See also Cost improvement; Productivity improvement; Profit improvement; Purchasing management; Quality circles; Work simplification and improvement.

REFERENCES

Miles, L. D.: *The Techniques of Value Analysis and Value Engineering,* 2d ed., McGraw-Hill, New York, 1972.

Mudge, A.: *Value Engineering,* McGraw-Hill, New York, 1972.

Ridge, Warren F.: *Value Analysis for Better Management,* American Management Association, AMACOM, New York, 1969.

FRANK J. JOHNSON, *Johnson Management Corporation*

Wages and Hours Legislation

Virtually every business in the United States is subject to legislative regulation of wages and working hours. As federal regulations do not preempt state action in the wage and hour area, most enterprises are within the ambit of overlapping statutes which generally mandate a minimum wage, equal pay for equal work, and payment of time and one-half after an employee has worked a certain number of hours. In the case of a conflict between federal and state requirements, the stricter wage and hour regulations always apply. The principal wage and hour law is the federal Fair Labor Standards Act [(FLSA) 29 U.S.C. 201 *et seq.*]. FLSA requires the payment of minimum wages and overtime pay for employees not specifically exempt who are (1) engaged in (interstate) commerce; (2) engaged in the production of goods for commerce; or (3) employed by an enterprise engaged in commerce or the production of goods for commerce.

Separate statutes provide somewhat more demanding wage standards for businesses that enter into government contracts. However, federal laws *do not* (1) limit the number of hours worked per week; (2) require payment for holidays, vacations, or sick leave, or (3) require different rates of pay for weekends or holidays.

Complaints that an employer has failed to pay minimum wage or overtime entitlements generally may be brought to a regulatory agency or to court either by employees or by governmental agencies (such as the Department of Labor's Wage and Hour Division) on the employees' behalf. Certain employees are exempt from wage and hour requirements. Objective, accurate job descriptions and evaluations help to (1) avoid liability for underpaying workers who are nonexempt, and (2) develop compensation programs which go beyond the requirements of law and aid the enterprise to gain the greatest return for its payroll dollar.

Employer liability for back wages and liquidated damages can be substantial. Basic steps for avoiding liability include (1) keeping accurate records in the format required, and (2) using honest and prudent judgment in determining employee exemptions.

Legislation and Regulation

Before the groundswell of social welfare and labor legislation during the Depression years, states and

911

the federal government made some attempts to mandate a minimum wage and maximum hours of work. It was not until the enactment of the Walsh-Healey Public Contracts Act in 1936, however, that base wage rates and overtime payment requirements for broad classes of workers became a part of American law. Legislative regulation of wages and hours has generally been prompted by the conclusion that a living wage is a means toward securing an acceptable standard of living. A wage floor is usually viewed as a desirable alternative to an extensive transfer payment system, where the government would pay some percentage of the difference between the cost of living and an employee's wages. The social welfare laws of the 1930s, which are the foundation for most subsequent wage and hour acts, also reflect concern that certain baseline conditions of employment must be mandated by statute.

The Fair Labor Standards Act, which is frequently amended and updated by Congress, is the most significant of all wage and hour laws. It establishes minimum wage, overtime, equal pay, child labor, and record-keeping standards for covered employment, unless a specific exemption applies.

FLSA Coverage. The coverage of FLSA is quite extensive, and its provisions affect the employees of almost every conceivable commercial entity. The act is an exercise of the congressional power to regulate interstate commerce, and employees are protected by the act, because of either their individual involvement in commerce or their employer's relationship with commerce. Any worker who is engaged in commerce or in the production of goods for commerce is within FLSA's *individual employee coverage. Enterprise coverage* adds those workers who are employed by an entity that performs related activities with other businesses which are under common control and which operate for the common business purpose of engaging in interstate commerce or the production of goods for commerce. *All* employees of an enterprise are covered, regardless of the relationship between their jobs and interstate commerce.[1] Coverage under the FLSA is broad. For example, the use of the interstate mails qualifies secretarial personnel as workers who are engaged in commerce. Coverage of all the workers of an enterprise may require that at least two workers be covered individually. Thus, enterprise coverage is somewhat keyed to the innumerable traditional coverage decisions.[2] The Courts and the Wage Hour Administrator have allowed some exceptions, but they are usually esoteric or obtuse and increasingly less common. Accordingly, no employer should assume an exception in the absence of prudent legal advice.

Minimum Wage. Under FLSA, covered employees must be paid at least the minimum hourly wage. In setting standards under wage and hour laws, legislators try to avoid the disappearance of marginal jobs which might occur if the minimum wage were set too high. The history of the statute shows differential minimum wages for employees in different industries. However, in 1985 the minimum wage is now the *same* for all covered employees—$3.35 per hour. Minimum wage figures will, however, be subject to constant revision. A telephone call to the Department of Labor's Wage and Hour Office can yield information on the current minimum, and regional administrators are usually familiar with proposed legislation which may affect payroll planning.

Overtime. The overtime provisions of FLSA stipulate that covered employees must be paid time and one-half for all hours worked in excess of 40 during a *workweek.* A workweek may begin at any hour of any day set by the employer and is a period of 168 hours running during seven consecutive 24-hour periods. The hours worked during two or more workweeks cannot be averaged to minimize overtime payments, except in certain exceptional occupations such as shipping and hospital employees. In computing overtime, the employer must pay 1½ times the employee's regular rate of pay. The regular rate is the employee's total weekly remuneration for work, minus statutory exclusions, divided by the total weekly hours worked for which such compensation was paid. "*Premiums* for regularly scheduled hours of work outside of the normal daytime shift are considered part of an employee's regular rate for the purpose of computing overtime."[3] For example, if a factory pays $3.00 per hour for the day shift and $3.10 per hour for the night shift, the night shift worker's overtime must be 1½ times $3.10, or $4.65 per hour.

Employers often incur substantial overtime liability merely by permitting work which they do not really want. For example, a nonexempt sales clerk who stays past official quitting time of his or her own accord to put away stock must be paid overtime if such extra efforts bring the hours of work over 40 per week. *The Portal-to-Portal Act* [29 U.S.C. 251 *et. seq.*] more precisely defines the time for which an employee must be paid. A shorthand rule is that any time spent by a worker for the benefit of the business must be paid for—as in the case of a factory hand who is preparing a machine for the day's work. Rather complicated rules control the inclusion or exclusion of bonuses from regular wage rates. On occasion, employers have intended a bonus as largess and yet have incurred disconcerting overtime liability because of the bonus payments. To avoid this result, the employer should maintain a maximum amount of discretion as to the payment and amount of any bonus.[4] Additionally, since exemption status is determined on a weekly basis, an employee can be exempt one week and nonexempt the next. This is particularly true in the case of exemptions from overtime. Under certain conditions, workers employed at piece rates, workers who do two or more jobs for which different hourly or piece-rate schedules have been established, and workers who have negotiated a special rate to be used expressly for overtime purposes may be paid on an alternative basis. The use of any of these alternative methods of overtime calculation requires the employee's consent.

Child Labor. FLSA prohibits "oppressive child labor"—that is, the employment of minors under the legal minimum ages. Sixteen is the basic minimum age for employment in any nonagricultural occupation not specifically designated *hazardous* by the Secretary of Labor. Sixteen-year-olds may work in hazardous agricultural occupations; a worker must be eighteen to work in other hazardous jobs. Persons 14 years of age may work in specified occupations outside of school hours. The act provides certain child labor exemptions for minors employed by their own parents, for juvenile actors, and for apprentices and students. Of course, unless an exemption applies, covered minor employees have to be paid the minimum wage and are entitled to overtime.

Equal Pay Act. Section 6(d) of FLSA, which was grafted on to the statute as the *Equal Pay Act of 1963*, is rapidly becoming one of the act's most important sections. The equal pay section stipulates that men and women performing jobs requiring equal skill, effort, and responsibility under similar working conditions be paid equal wages. Allegations of illegal wage discrimination based on sex have been on the rise during the past few years. Equal pay rules apply also to executive, administrative, and professional employees and to outside salespeople who are otherwise exempt from FLSA's minimum wage and overtime provisions. The Equal Pay Act expressly permits wage differentials which are based on (1) seniority, (2) merit, (3) measurement of earnings by quality or quantity of production, or (4) any factor other than sex. The crux of equal pay requirements is that male and female workers must be paid equally if the jobs they are doing are substantially equal. *Substantial equality* is a phrase that is usually quite broadly construed, casting suspicion on many pay differentials.[5]

Exemption Structure. The exemption structure of the FLSA is one of its most crucial and complex provisions. Any relatively complex question regarding an employee's exemption status is likely to require the advice of legal counsel. It is possible for an employee to be exempt from both the minimum wage and overtime dictates of the act or only from the act's overtime requirements. Of course, determination of the exempt or nonexempt status of employees has vital ramifications for compensation planning.

One of the most common and important exclusions from both minimum wage and overtime coverage is that for executive, administrative, and professional employees and outside salespeople. Academic administrative personnel and teachers are included in this category. Tests for exemption status have been devised to aid businesses in determining which of their employees qualify for these important exemptions. A bona fide *executive* must meet all the following criteria: The executive (1) has the primary duty for the management of an enterprise or a department thereof; (2) must customarily direct the work of two or more employees; (3) must have the authority to hire and fire, or to give important recommendations regarding hiring and firing; (4) must regularly exercise disoretionary powers; (5) must devote no more than 20 percent of his or her hours to nonmanagerial function;[6] and (6) must be paid at least $155 a week on a salary basis.[7] *Administrative employees* are exempt if they (1) perform responsible office or nonmanual work; (2) exercise independent discretion and judgment and have the authority to make important decisions; (3) regularly assist a proprietor or executive; (4) perform specialized or technical work or execute special assignments under only general supervision; (5) do not spend 20 percent of the workweek on nonexempt work; and (6) are paid at least $155 per week.[8]

The *professional employees* category includes the learned, artistic, and teaching professions. The law states that exempt professional work (1) require advanced knowledge in a recognized field of learning, usually obtained by a specialized course of study; or (2) be original and creative in character in a recognized artistic field; (3) be exercised with discretion and judgment; (4) be intellectual and varied, rather than routine and mechanical; (5) consist of nonprofessional duties for no more than 20 percent of the workweek; and (6) pay a salary of at least $170 a week. The salary requirement does not apply to doctors, lawyers, or teachers. An *outside salesperson* is exempt if he or she (1) is employed for the purpose of working, and customarily and regularly works, away from the employer's place of business; (2) is selling tangible or intangible items such as goods, insurance, stocks, bonds, or real estate; (3) is obtaining orders or contracts for services or the use of facilities, such as advertising, radio time, or typewriter repair; and (4) spends hours in nonoutside work that do not exceed 20 percent of the hours worked in the workweek by nonexempt employees of the employer.

Streamlined tests for exemption status are available in the cases of high-salaried executive, administrative, and professional employees, which may be found either in wage and hour handbooks or in federal publications.[9] For example, an executive paid $250 or more per week would, in general, be deemed to have met the requirements. Legislation to raise these wage levels has been proposed but postponed.

The remaining exemptions from minimum wage and overtime, or simply from overtime, are many. Perhaps the only fair advice that can be given about the FLSA's exemption structure is that Congress is *constantly* altering it, and that it is wise to consult sections 6, 7, and 13 of the act. Conflicts over the interpretation of the exemption structure generate hundreds of thousands of dollars worth of litigation every year. Caution and recourse to expert advice should be the executive's watchwords in making exemption decisions.

Trends. The trend in legislation for some years has been to extend coverage and to phase out exemptions. For example, the 1974 Amendments extended statutory coverage to employees of federal and state government(s) and their political subdivisions, to domestics, and to the employees of many retail and agricultural "conglomerates." But, state and local government employees (including those of state-run hospitals, institutions, and school systems), however, are *not* covered. The Supreme Court, (5–4) in *National League of Cities v. Usery*—426 U.S. 833 (Nos. 74-878, 879)—(1976), ruled that Congress unconstitutionally usurped state sovereignty by extending coverage to them. So, state and local governments are not bound by the federal wage and hour laws. Nevertheless, it is not yet clear that state and local governments can unilaterally set wage and hour standards for their employees.

To resolve troubling exemption questions, an employer should (1) consult the full text of applicable federal and state statutes; (2) obtain legal advice; and (3) solicit a written opinion from the Wage and Hour Administrator of the Department of labor.

Enforcement. The enforcement of wage and hour laws is usually the function of federal and state Departments of Labor. The enforcement of the Fair Labor Standards Act is the responsibility of the U.S. Department of Labor's Wage and Hour Division. The statute provides for three modes of assuring adherence: (1) the Secretary of Labor may seek an injunction to compel compliance with the statute and the payment of back wages to the aggrieved employee; (2) the Justice Department can bring criminal charges against *willful* violators; (3) employees themselves may sue for back wages due plus an equal amount in liquidated damages and reasonable attorney's fees. The statute of limitations for nonwillful violations is 2 years; it is 3 years for willful infractions. There is no statute of limitations applicable to injunctions. The Wage and Hour Administrator is empowered to issue interpretive bulletins construing the act, but has no power to simply issue compliance orders when violations seem evident.

For wage matters related to the various Equal Employment Opportunity laws, the Equal Employment Opportunity Commission may be the enforcing agency, either independently or in concert with the Department of Labor.

Other Federal Laws. Business relations with the federal government are controlled by a number of special wage and hour laws.

1. *The Walsh-Healey Public Contracts Act* [41 U.S.C. 35 *et. seq.*] sets basic standards for work done on United States government contracts greater than $10,000 in value. Minimum wages to be paid are set by the Secretary of Labor, based on standards in the industry. Overtime must be paid for all work over 8 hours a day or 40 hours a week, whichever number of overtime hours is greater. As under FLSA, in some situations subminimum wages may be paid to beginners, apprentices, student learners, and handicapped workers. Executive, administrative, and professional employees are exempt, and the Walsh-Healey Act does not cover contracts for utility services, common carriers under published tariffs, perishable agricultural products, or rentals.

2. *The Davis-Bacon Act* [40 U.S.C. 276(a) *et. seq.*] applies to federal construction contracts of about $2000 in value. The Secretary of Labor sets minimum wage rates and *required fringe benefits* based on similar work in the locality. It is not a valid defense for contractors to show that their employees accepted rates of pay below those set by the Secretary, and the government may withhold payments from any violating firm, for the benefit of the employees who have not been paid the required wages.

3. *The Miller Act* [40 U.S.C. 270 *et. seq.*] stipulates that any firm entering into a government contract for the construction, alteration, or repair of any public building or work in the United States valued at over $2000 must execute a payment bond with a surety to protect the wages of all persons supplying labor. A worker who is not paid within 90 days after the last labor performed may sue the contractor's surety in any federal district where the contract was to be performed and executed.

4. *The Work Hours Act of 1962* [5 U.S.C. 673(c); 28 U.S.C. 1499; 40 U.S.C. 327 *et. seq.*] provides an 8-hour workday and a 40-hour workweek, with overtime at 1½ times the basic rate, for all work involving the employment of laborers or mechanics, including security and guards: (1) on any federal public work; (2) for any contract to which the federal government is a party; or (3) for any contract financed in whole or in part by federal loans or grants and to which federal wage standard laws apply. The 1962 act is not applicable where the federal assistance is only in the nature of a loan guarantee or insurance.

5. *The Service Contract Act of 1965* [41 U.S.C. 351 *et. seq.*] stipulates that contracts for services entered into by any federal instrumentality must provide a minimum wage and certain fringe benefits. The wage/benefit package is established by the Secretary of Labor, based upon "standards prevailing in the community." Administrative, executive, and professional employees are exempt, and the Service Contract Act does not

apply to several types of transportation, communication, and public utility contracts. Contracts within the purview of the Davis-Bacon and Walsh-Healey legislation are also exempt. Examples of covered contracts are those for laundry and dry cleaning, mail transport, custodial and janitorial, packing and crating, food service, warehousing and storage, and support service arrangements for military personnel. The sanctions available to the government against violators parallel those of Walsh-Healey and Davis-Bacon.

6. *The Consumer Credit Protection Act of 1968* [15 U.S.C. 1671 *et. seq.*] gives wage earners protection from harassment or loss of work because of indebtedness. The act provides that *no* state or federal court may issue any order garnisheeing the aggregate disposable earnings of any individual for any workweek which is above the *lesser* of (1) 25 percent of disposable earnings for that workweek; or (2) the amount by which disposable earnings per week exceed 30 times the minimum wage under section 6(a) (1) of FLSA. The act does not apply to support orders, to court orders under chapter XIII of the Bankruptcy Act, or to any debt due for any state or federal tax. States may not garnishee above these rates, but if state law provides for a lower rate of garnisheement, that law must be applied. No employee may be discharged for being subjected to garnisheement for any one indebtedness.

7. *Age Discrimination in Employment Act of 1967, as amended in 1978.* This act establishes that employees between the ages of 40 and 70 cannot be denied pay increases, bonuses, or other benefits on the basis of age. The act is enforced by the EEOC.

8. *Title VII of the Civil Rights Act of 1964, as amended in 1972.* This law prohibits the payment of unequal wages to employees because of race, sex, color, or national origin. Exceptions can be justified only on the basis of proving a *bona fide occupational qualification* related to the designated characteristic. Enforcement is the responsibility of the EEOC.

9. *Employment Retirement Income Security Act (ERISA) of 1974.* This legislation establishes certain minimum management and reporting requirements for companies that choose to offer employees a pension plan as part of the total compensation package.

State Laws. State wage and hour laws often set minimum wages and require overtime payments. The requirements in the applicable jurisdiction should always be checked, because section 18 of the FLSA requires that if a state law establishes more generous wage and overtime levels, or a different set of coverage criteria, the state law must be followed.

Most states have statutes establishing additional pay practice requirements. Commonly, regular paydays are required, usually at least semimonthly. In many cases, employees must be paid in lawful money, and scrip is prohibited. Requirements that workers be promptly paid in the event that they are discharged, quit, or leave work owing to a labor dispute are also common. In many states, persons who have not been paid wages due them may assign their back-wage claims to a state agency, which will prosecute the claims for the aggrieved employees.[10]

Fringe Benefits. A general trend in both federal and state law is to require certain employee (or fringe) benefits. A case in point is the Davis-Bacon Act, which makes employers match fringe benefits to those of prevailing area standards. Noncash compensation often subject to such regulation includes medical care, pensions, myriad varieties of insurance, and vacation and holiday pay. In some cases, if benefits are not matched in kind, cash value must be added to the hourly rate for straight-time work, but not for overtime work.[11]

Record Keeping

Fortunately, the various wage and hour laws have similar record-keeping requirements. Usually, no particular form for the records is stipulated. The record-keeping requirements for FLSA are illustrative, and adherence to them will generally satisfy the provisions of other statutes. To satisfy FLSA, an employee's records must include:

1. The employee's full name and address.

2. The employee's birth date, especially if he or she is under 19 years of age.

3. The sex of the employee and the occupation in which employed.

4. The day of the week and time of that day when the employee's workweek begins.

5. The basis on which wages are paid (e.g., $3.75 per hour, $150 per week).

6. The regular hourly pay rate for any week in which overtime is worked. (If the employee is paid on a salary basis, the salary figure must be converted to an hourly rate for this purpose.)

7. The amount and nature of each payment excluded from the regular rate.

8. Total daily or weekly straight-time earnings.

9. Total overtime earnings for the workweek.

10. All additions to or deductions from the employee's wages for each pay period.

11. Total wages paid each pay period.

12. Dates of payment and the pay period covered by the payment.[12]

The record-keeping checklist for executive, administrative, and professional employees and outside salespeople is as follows:

1. The employee's full name and address.
2. The employee's sex and occupation.
3. His or her date of birth, if under 19.
4. The time of day and day of the week when the employee's workweek begins.
5. Data on fringe benefits, so that the employee's total remuneration for the position may be calculated.[13]

Records for all employees subject to the minimum wage provisions of the act must be kept, even if the employee is not subject to the law's overtime requirements. Records of hours worked must be kept, regardless of whether the worker is paid by the piece, hour, week, month, in tips, through commissions, or otherwise. Any complete and accurate timekeeping plan is permissible. Production workers may be paid on a salary basis, but for regulatory purposes, records indicating their compensation per hour must be kept.[14]

Under various EEOC laws and for companies engaged in affirmative actions plans, additional records must be maintained related to minority status—black, Hispanic, Native American, etc.

The minimum wage need not be paid completely in cash, but employers may not make a profit on non-cash payments. Tips will be credited up to 50 percent of the minimum wage rate. The cost of facilities primarily for the benefit of the employer, such as tools, may not be credited toward the minimum wage.

All information required by the Wage and Hour Department's regulations must be retained for 3 years. All data on which wage and hour computations are based must be kept for 2 years. Any enterprise having employees subject to the provisions of federal wage and hour laws must post a special informational poster, which is available free from the Department of Labor.

Relations with Regulatory Agencies

Successful relations with regulatory agencies require as a baseline an awareness of statutory wage, hour, and ancillary requirements *and* accurate, complete, and up-to-date records. The precise powers of different regulatory agencies at various governmental levels are somewhat dissimilar. However, the practices of the Department of Labor's Wage and Hour Division are again illustrative. Wage and hour compliance officers are empowered to investigate any business employing persons subject to the act. A complaint is *not* needed to trigger their inquiries. The Wage and Hour Office would like to direct the thrust of their enforcement effort so as to spend as much time as possible conducting field investigations and disseminating information. In practice, though, independent investigations usually take a back seat to the servicing of complaints.[15]

The Department of Labor also conducts a program of planned litigation to encourage compliance in the wage and hour area and to increase employer awareness of the law's various provisions. Allegations of sex discrimination in wage rates, in violation of the Equal Pay law, have been especially prevalent recently. It is imperative that employers formally determine that their pay structure is not sex-typed.

Questions regarding exceptions, records, and the like are the subject of comment by the Wage and Hour Administrator in special bulletins. Written inquiries to the Administrator's office could yield information helpful in coping with the law's subtle points. An employer has a defense to wage and hour charges where the employer pleads and proves that he or she acted in good faith, relying upon a written administrative regulation, interpretation, ruling, order, practice, or enforcement policy. In the case of the FLSA, the ruling relied upon must have been issued by the Wage and Hour Administrator. Under Davis-Bacon, an employer may rely upon a ruling by the Secretary of Labor. Reliance on rulings made by the Secretary of Labor or any other federal officer utilized by the Secretary in the administration of the act will suffice as a defense to charges brought under the Walsh-Healey Act.

Wage and Hour compliance officers are alert for an employer's allowing "work off the clock" and for inflated job titles which overstate a job's responsibilities in order to claim an exemption. The nonpayment of overtime to nonexempt salaried retail sales personnel is also a common violation.

The Impact of Wage and Hour Laws

The plethora of wage and hour laws tends to encourage traditional pay and hour practices—such as the 5-day workweek.[16] More important, the occasional complexity and the pervasiveness of these laws suggest that employers evaluate their entire compensation structure to make sure that it not only meets legal nuances but also advances company goals. Government regulations which require that certain employees be paid X dollars in Y fashion can never be more than a *component* of an enterprise's total compensation challenge. A good way for a company to help itself adhere to the law *and* to achieve its other employee reward goals is to obtain an objective evaluation of its compensation programs.[17] Reliance on a sophisticated job evaluation system helps in giving a wage and hour compliance officer a clear, reasonable explanation of why one position has been treated as exempt and another as nonexempt.[18] Job evaluations serve as a defense to allegations of wage and hour violations. In fact, in some equal pay cases, courts have intimated that job evaluations may provide the employer with a powerful tool for the defense of pay differentials.[19]

Once enterprise objectives have been defined and jobs formally evaluated, an executive can go about making wage and hour compliance a part of the organization's total compensation package. Refinements in pay and benefit structure may be considered at this point. Some companies, for example, may wish to develop incentive plans for nonexempt workers.[20] Some employers find it helpful to pay overtime to certain exempt employees.[21] Often, equity adjustments between some exempt and nonexempt workers must be made. In short, professional job evaluation is an excellent tool for linking wage and hour compliance efforts to the overall development of a company compensation program.

Compliance with wage and hour regulations generally requires few pay scales or record-keeping methods that any company which adheres to good business practices would ignore. Classification of jobs so as to conform to statutory strictures should be only a part of a precise, formal job evaluation program. Accurate job evaluations can provide a baseline for a compensation system which pays what employees *ought* to be paid, as well as what the law says they *must* be paid.

See also Affirmative action; Compensation, employee benefit plans; Compensation, executive; Compensation, sales; Compensation, wage and salary policy and administration; Equal employment opportunity, minorities and women; Human resources planning; Job analysis; Job evaluation; Labor legislation; Labor-management relations; Personnel administration; Women in business and management; Work measurement; Work schedules, alternate.

NOTES

[1] An employee engaged in commerce or in the production of goods for commerce during a workweek is entitled to protection under the act for that entire workweek regardless of the small amount of time that was devoted to interstate work. Mack A. Player, "Enterprise Coverage Under the Fair Labor Standards Act—An Assessment of the First Generation," 28 Vand L. Rev. 283 (1975), at 308. See also 29 C.F.R. 776.4.

[2] Ibid, pp. 286–287.

[3] Russell L. Greenman and Eric J. Schmertz, *Personnel Administration and the Law*, Bureau of National Affairs, Inc., Washington, 1972, pp. 24–25.

[4] *Guidebook to Federal Wage-Hour Laws*, Commerce Clearing House, Inc., Chicago, 1974, p. 25.

[5] *Brennan v. Houston Endowment* 7 EPD 9204. Female janitors who used vacuums were held to be engaged in work substantially equal to that of male janitors who used large power-driven machines such as floor buffers and carpet pile lifters.

[6] Less than 40 percent, if employed by a retail or service establishment.

[7] $130 per week in Puerto Rico, the Virgin Islands, and American Samoa, exclusive of board and lodging.

[8] Notes 6 and 7 apply.

[9] See *Guidebook to Federal Wage-Hours Laws*, Commerce Clearing House, Inc., Chicago, 1974; U.S. Department of Labor, *Executive, Administrative, Professional, and Outside Salesmen Exemptions Under the Fair Labor Standards Act*, WH Publication 1363.

[10] U.S. Department of Labor, *Growth of Labor Law in the United States*, 1967, pp. 101–114.

[11] Ibid., p. 119.

[12] 29 C.F.R. 516.

[13] 29 C.F.R. 516.3.

[14] Robert D. Hulme and Richard V. Bevan, "The Blue Collar Worker Goes on Salary," *Harvard Business Review*, vol. 53, March–April 1975.

[15] U.S. Department of Labor, *Minimum Wage and Maximum Hours Standards Under the Fair Labor Standards Act*, 1976.

[16] Janice Neipert Hedges, "How Many Days Make a Workweek?" *Monthly Labor Review*, vol. 98, p. 20, April 1975. The author discusses the contribution of FLSA to the prevailing 5-day, 40-hour workweek.

[17] See Milton L. Rock, ed., *Handbook of Wage and Salary Administration*, McGraw-Hill, New York, 1972, especially parts 1 and 2.

[18] See Jon Laking and Robin Roark, *Retailing Job Analysis and Job Evaluation*, National Retail Merchants Association, New York, 1975.

[19] See *Corning Glass Works v. Brennan*, 417 U.S. 188 (1974); Marsh W. Bates and Richard G. Vail, "Job Evaluation and Equal Employment Opportunity: A Tool for Compliance— A Weapon for Defense," *Employee Relations Law Journal*, Spring 1976, p. 535; Murphy, "Female Wage Discrimination: A Study of the Equal Pay Act 1963–1970," 39 U. Cin. L. Rev. 615, 634–637 (1970).

[20] Don R. Marshall, "Merit Pay without Headaches: How to Design a Plan for Nonexempts," *Compensation Review*, second quarter, 1975, p. 32; H. W. Lieber and Frederic L. Taylor, "Designing Incentives for Hourly Personnel," in Milton L. Rock, ed., *Handbook of Wage and Salary Administration*, McGraw-Hill, New York, 1972, pp. 7–14.

[21] Dennis S. Kennedy and H. Paul Abbott, "Establishing the Clerical Pay Structure" in Milton L. Rock, ed., *Handbook of Wage and Salary Administration*, pp. 4–44; David A. Weeks, *Overtime Pay for Exempt Employees*, National Industrial Conference Board, Inc., New York, 1967.

REFERENCES

Ledvinka, James: *Federal Regulation of Personnel and Human Resource Management*, Wadsworth Publishing Company, Inc. (Kent), Belmont, Calif., 1982.

Regulations, Part 541: Defining the Terms "Executive," "Administrative," "Professional," and "Outside Salesman," WH Publication 1281, rev. ed., U.S. Department of Labor, Employment Standards Administration, Wage and Hour Division, Washington, D.C., June 1983.

Rock, Milton L., ed.: *Handbook of Wage and Salary Administration*, 2d ed. McGraw-Hill, New York, 1983.

J. Robin Roark, *Hay Associates, Management Consultants*

Women in Business and Management

American women are found in almost all organizations and job categories. Their work history outside the home parallels United States industrial development. As industry replaced home manufacture, as compulsory education spread, and as the typewriter and telephone were developed, women have increasingly assumed larger work roles in the labor force. Progressive legislation has done much to improve the legal status of women in industry. Nevertheless, they still lag far behind men in terms of pay and status of the jobs they hold, although they represent an ever-increasing portion of the labor force.

Legal Status

The thrust of legislation in the last quarter-century has been to put pressure on both public and private enterprises to hire and promote women into jobs traditionally reserved for men only. United States federal laws enacted or modified during the 1960s and early 1970s to prohibit sex discrimination in employment include the Equal Pay Act, Title VII of the Civil Rights Act, Executive Order 11246, and Revised Order IV.

The Equal Pay Act (June 1963) amended the Fair Labor Standards Act (1938) to require the same pay for men and women doing similar work.

Title VII (of the Civil Rights Act of 1964) prohibits employers, unions, and employment agencies from sex discrimination in hiring; in wages, terms, conditions, or privileges of employment; in classifying, assigning, or promoting employees, and extending or assigning use of facilities; and in training, retraining, and apprenticeship.

Executive Order 11246, as amended by Executive Order 11375, prohibits discrimination in employment by contractors and subcontractors (including colleges and universities) that have $10,000 or more in federal contracts with the federal government. These government contractors and subcontractors must institute affirmative action programs. Specifically, they cannot:

Make any distinctions based on sex in employment opportunities, wages, hours, or other conditions of employment, including fringe benefits and pension plans.

Distinguish between married and single persons of one sex and not the other.

Advertise in sex-segregated help-wanted columns unless sex is a bona fide occupational qualification.

Deny employment to women with young children unless the same policy applies to men with young children.

Terminate an employee of one sex upon reaching a certain age, but not an employee of the other sex.

Penalize women because they require time away from work for childbearing (childbearing is justification for a leave of absence for a reasonable period of time whether or not an employer has a leave policy).

Maintain seniority lists based solely on sex.

Deny a female employee the right to a job for which she is qualified because of state "protective" legislation.

Revised Order IV (effective December 4, 1971) strengthened these guidelines. It requires that contractors (1) analyze their company work force to determine whether women are underemployed and (2) set numerical goals and timetables by job classification and organizational unit to correct any deficiencies. Goals, however, are to reflect the characteristics of the female work force in the relevant labor market and should not be used to force hiring of unqualified persons. Failure to meet certain goals is not noncompliance *if* good faith is demonstrated.

In summary, then, the U.S. Department of Labor can demand under present guidelines: (1) equality of opportunity in hiring and placement: (2) recruitment of women for all jobs or at all levels, skills, and pay rates; (3) equality of opportunity in transfers, promotions, upgrading, and protection from layoffs; (4) equality of opportunity for training; (5) equal application of seniority and retirement policies; and (6) special protection of women who need maternity leave. A problem is that, in many situations, it is not easy to make clear-cut cases to prove sex discrimination. In white-collar jobs, for example, equal work or precise reasons for promoting one person over another are difficult to define.

Employment of Women

Over the last 12 years, about 16 million women entered the work force, compared with 11 million men. Particularly in the last decade, the greatest growth in job holders has been among females. For instance, the number of men in the labor force increased by 7 percent, compared with a 33 percent increase for women. (See Table W-1.) By 1982, nearly half of all women aged 16 and over worked, holding 2 out of every 5 jobs in the United States. The trend indicates the employment of as many women as men in the work force by the year 2000.

Blue-Collar Positions. Since 1960, the number of women in skilled trades has increased dramatically. For example, in 1981 there were 802,000

TABLE W-1 Number of Civilian Labor Force Workers, by Sex, 1970 to 1982

Year	Male	Female
1970	51,228,000	31,583,000
1971	52,021,000	32,091,000
1972	53,265,000	33,277,000
1973	54,203,000	34,510,000
1974	55,186,000	35,825,000
1975	55,615,000	36,998,000
1976	56,631,000	38,856,000
1977	58,396,000	40,613,000
1978	59,620,000	42,631,000
1979	60,726,000	44,235,000
1980	61,453,000	45,487,000
1981	61,974,000	46,696,000
1982	62,287,000	47,904,000

Source: U.S. Bureau of Labor Statistics, *Employment and Earnings,* monthly; *Statistical Abstract of the United States, 1982–1983,* Washington, D.C., December 1982, p. 376.

women in skilled occupations, up from 222,000 in 1960 and 6 times the relative increase for men during the same period. Of all women workers, however, less than one-sixth (about 13.5 percent) are in blue-collar occupations, compared with about 44 percent of all males.

White-Collar Positions. Nearly two-thirds (about 65 percent) of all women workers are in white-collar jobs. In fact, most women employees are likely to be in retail sales and office work—e.g., as secretaries, typists, bookkeepers, receptionists, file clerks, telephone operators, bank tellers, and sales clerks.

Women account for more than three-fourths of all clerical workers. Not only is it the largest occupational group employing women, it has been one of the fastest growing occupational groups for women—increasing by about 134 percent between 1960 and 1981. By contrast, less than 6 percent of all male workers held clerical jobs in 1981.

Professional Work. More than 7.8 million women—or 1 out of 6 working women—are in

professional and technical occupations. Teaching and health fields account for about one-fifth of the professional and technical workers. And the number of women in the traditionally male-dominated areas is increasing. Conversely, the number of men is rising in the so-called women's professions—librarians, registered nurses, and school teachers.

Managerial and Administrative Opportunities. Women are also showing significant increases of employment in the male-dominated managerial occupations. For example, there were 1,323,000 female managers and administrators in 1970, or 4.5 percent of all working women; in 1981 the figures had risen to 3,168,000 and 7.4 percent. Males in similar jobs totaled 8,372,000 in 1981, accounting for 14.6 percent of all working men.

Income Comparisons

The 1980 reported median annual income for men was $18,612 compared with $11,197 for women. The overall pay gap between men and women has narrowed only slightly since 1974, when a woman earned 59 percent of a man's salary; in 1981, the percentage was 60. (See Table W-2 for a comparison of median incomes between men and women.)

Part of the difference in median income between men and women may be explained by the fact that women have not made substantial inroads into the most valued market occupations. They have been mostly in low-status, low-paying jobs with little advancement potential. Other reasons that have been traditionally given for the income disparity include lack of continuous full-time employment, job inexperience, limited vocational and training skills, lower educational levels, and inability to work full time. Institutional and attitudinal barriers—i.e., well-intentioned protective laws (overtime, weightlifting) as well as attitudes toward women's place and the value of women's work—have been extremely significant factors in the participation and

TABLE W-2 Comparison between Women's and Men's Earnings in 1980

Occupation	Women		Men		Ratio: Women to men	
	Number (1,000)	Median earnings	Number (1,000)	Median earnings	Number	Median earnings
Total	22,859	$11,197	41,881	$18,612	.55	.60
Professional, technical, and kindred workers	4,441	15,285	7,388	23,026	.60	.66
Managers and administrators	2,318	12,936	7,625	23,558	.30	.55
Sales workers	1,001	9,748	2,567	19,910	.39	.49
Clerical and kindred workers	8,991	10,997	2,586	18,247	3.48	.60
Craft and kindred workers	481	11,701	8,994	18,671	.05	.63
Operatives, including transport workers	2,387	9,440	6,432	15,702	.37	.60

Source: U.S. Bureau of the Census, *Current Population Reports,* series P-60, no. 132, *Statistical Abstract of the United States, 1982–1983,* Office of Management and Budget, Washington, D.C., December 1982.

marketable worth of women in the labor market. Pressures of changing social and economic conditions will cause these factors, however, to be examined and reexamined in the future.

Women in Management

While World War II and Title VII were decisive breakthroughs for working women in general, Revised Order Four may be the most significant turning point for women in management. For the first time in history, women must be recruited, hired, and promoted into management jobs. As a result, many changes in company policies and practices can be expected in the next decade.

Women make up almost half the labor force, but only a quarter of all managers and administrators are women. While this figure represents an impressive growth to 27 percent from 18.5 percent in 1974, the figures are somewhat misleading. One out of five of these women managers is either self-employed (she is an independent business person such as a realtor or a door-to-door salesperson) or an unpaid, titled employee in a family-owned business. Moreover, many of the women executives had titles more important than their functions.

Traditional Misconceptions. An overall labor force comparison shows nearly one out of seven men in managerial/administrative occupations, compared with one of twenty women. Social norms have kept women out of positions either competitive with, or superior to, those of men. Attitudes still range from one extreme, "Qualified women can perform adequately in any job," to the other extreme, "Women are excellent for handling details, but never for management." By 1990, however, the figure for women in management can be expected to double. Meanwhile, several erroneous beliefs must be overcome, particularly the following traditional assumptions.

Women Do Not Work Long Enough to Justify Management Training. A common argument against women in management has been that their turnover is too high. Comparisons with turnover of men in similar occupations, however, show almost no difference. Both unreliability and job-hopping appear to be related more to job satisfaction, salary, occupational level, and age than to one's gender. Polaroid Corporation, for example, reported not only that turnover rates were highest in its lower-level jobs but also that the rates were the same for both sexes.[1]

Upward mobility, equal pay, and various social factors—such as more female heads of households and acceptability of career-oriented mothers—have stimulated higher career aspirations and stability. With female life expectancy now over 75 years, the average family size barely two children, many women who interrupt their careers return to the work force by their forties with a quarter of a century left to contribute. The more attractive the job and the more valued the woman is, the more she wants to return.

Women Lack Skills, Training, and Education for Management. Because women are disproportionately concentrated at the lower occupational levels, the education of many women is not fully utilized. As pointed out in a Department of Labor report, 7 percent of employed women with 5 or more years of college education are services workers (including household), operatives, sales workers, or clerical workers. Nearly one-fifth of employed women with 4 years of college also work in these occupations, as do about two-thirds of those who had 1 to 3 years of college.[2]

Educated women have tended traditionally to cluster in the so-called helping professions—e.g., secretarial, nursing, teaching, social work, psychology, and occupational and physical speech therapy. Although commonly said that this work was the most appropriate for, or congenial to, women, the reality has been that only these professions have been open to women in any large numbers until recently.

Women Do Not Want Increased Responsibility. The general contention has been that, since marriage is their primary career, women work only to get away from home or for pin money rather than for intrinsic achievement or economic needs. The women's movement, legal changes, and recent legal actions (e.g., against AT&T, Bank of America, Bank of California, and the American Tobacco Company) strongly indicate that women are interested in assuming organizational responsibility. Few women were found in managerial positions prior to the 1970s because these roles were socially unacceptable for them. Before the legal pressures, few employers would put a woman in a managerial job. Few women trained for or applied for jobs in management more from their realism about the prospects for payoff of the training and application than from reluctance to assume management responsibility.[3]

Women Are Absent from Work More than Men. Many employers have felt that absenteeism is complicated by women's home responsibilities. Actually, men and women lose about the same number of days from work, including days lost because of pregnancy and childbirth. A Public Health Survey found that women tend to miss 5.9 days a year because of illness, whereas men tend to miss 5.2 days a year. Responsibility level appears to be the significant factor in absenteeism.

Moreover, younger women, while not choosing between marriage and career as perhaps many of their mothers did, are choosing between "being a super working Mom and not mothering at all." Many husbands of women with career aspirations find their wives rejecting pregnancy unless they get an assurance of partnership parenting—an agreement to help run the house and raise the children.[4]

Women Are Usually Unwilling to Transfer. Among most couples, geographic mobility has traditionally depended upon the male's career. Among many couples today, however, the male no longer arbitrarily determines where they will live. Some companies have begun to hire "executive couples" and to relocate them in concert. For other couples, a compromise is often made between two careers. Some husbands, for example, will accept a job transfer only if their wives' career will not be adversely affected. Some recent studies also show that many men with nonworking wives increasingly do not want to relocate because the wife has no job status of her own and suffers with each move.

Women Should Not and Usually Do Not Want to Travel. Willingness to travel depends on the individual, not on one's gender. The trip is business, regardless of whether both men and women are involved. Traveling together does not automatically mean intimacy.

Challenge to Organizations

Although there is no convincing evidence that one sex is brighter or more creative than the other or that there are innate differences in cognitive functioning, many people, nevertheless, still believe that women are different in ways that affect their managerial performance. A *Harvard Business Review* survey of 1500 subscribers revealed that social and psychological barriers still affect the employment, promotion, and effectiveness of women managers.[5] For example, women managers have been perceived to have different skills, habits, and motivations that make them undesirable leaders. The idea that neither men nor women like to work for women and that women have lower career aspirations than men, less commitment to work, more concern with friendships than with work itself, and make poor leaders because they are not assertive—or if they are, they are too dictatorial and bitchy—is prevalent in literature on women executives. These suppositions have been perceived this way because management has been viewed as a masculine occupation requiring traits more commonly thought to be masculine.

The organization's culture operates on perceptions that reflect conventional male and female behavior.[6] When a woman steps out of her traditional role, she upsets the balance of both roles for traditionally oriented people.

Probably the greatest initial problem for the woman manager is that few people can forget she is a woman—and different from a man. But if women are to be accepted as professional peers and managerial superiors, it is critically important that we come to truly believe that management skills are asexual and to recognize that few men or women learn to apply them effectively.

There are probably as many definitions of management as there are managers. But in its final analysis, the major responsibility of a manager is to direct, organize, and abet the activities of other people toward achievement of the objectives of the company that employs them. Thus, the function of a manager is to work with other people, developing their skills so that they grow more useful to themselves and to the company for which they work.

But women are generally not perceived as having management skills. The paradox is that the skills that women have socialized into them from early life are the very same skills required for success in the managerial sphere of activity. Females are socialized to be affiliative rather than independent; to give nurturance and support to others rather than to remain aloof; to find satisfaction in, and to stimulate, the achievements of others (e.g., children and husband). These same characteristics of affiliation, nurturance, and facilitation of the achievements of others are what most managers need in their moment-to-moment interaction with those whom they supervise.

The picture that emerges with respect to women as managers, then, is that they have the intelligence and motivation to assume and fulfill the managerial role; and equally important, by virtue of the socialization process which has feminized them, women have the interpersonal skills requisite to being effective managers. The same personality characteristics and skills that have made women excellent students, homemakers, and rearers of children are the skills managers desperately need. Indeed, many industrial corporations are trying to teach their male managers these same skills.

Of course, the setting for the application of these skills is different, and that makes a difference. Undoubtedly, the expectations placed on managers in the business world are different from the expectations on students, wives, or mothers. And because the setting and the expectations of the business world are different, the female managers cannot be expected to make an immediate and direct application of their problem-solving and nurturance skills. But those skills are there. The organization has moved into a postauthoritarian age where emphasis is upon growth, nurturance, creativity, communication, and the ability to mediate between forces that must work together but differ in purpose and approach. Women are particularly suited to meet these needs.

Management's challenge is to create an organizational climate in which male and female managers, along with their support teams, can effectively collaborate. To do this, top management must help people at all organizational levels to break through the sex-role stereotypes to develop professional relationships based on competency, personality, and a mutual commitment to the well-being of the organization.

What Organizations Can Do

The least-tried work relationships are women managing men and men working with women peers. Also, most male managers have supervised women who work in traditional women's jobs. Now, however, men face working for and with women; and some men must supervise and facilitate the development of women managers and help integrate them into male management groups.

How can an organization alter its culture? William H. Chafe[7] observed that people do not change from edict but from successful examples of people who do something that breaks the old cycle and starts a new one. To do this, top management must reflect, in its policies, procedures, and *practices,* a commitment to draw on the resources of *every* individual who wants and has the capacity and qualifications to make a management contribution. Direction from the top lowers role conflict and *by example* gradually increases "comfortableness" in the new working relationships with women as colleagues and superiors. Certainly, clear-cut patterns for guidance do not exist yet in most organizations. The following actions, however, can be a good beginning:

1. *Select the right person for the job.* Taking "cosmetic" action and moving women too fast are two dangers in hiring and promoting women as managers. Selection and promotion criteria should be the same for both men and women. This is easier said than done, however. Many men, for instance, feel they can spot technical and professional capabilities in another man but doubt their judgment about women.

2. *Sensitize male managers to the ambitions and potentials of women managers.* While male managers may be supportive of women managers who assume nontraditional roles, they may not see some of the more subtle forms of discrimination or know how to help women set goals, analyze their interests and abilities, or evaluate career alternatives. The manager of a woman manager, for example, needs to be aware of how male behavior can reinforce and perpetuate sex-role stereotyping; i.e., the informal behaviors that treat women as special or different (references to the woman's appearance during a business meeting, exaggerated chivalry—chair holding, cigarette lighting, introductions such as "our *woman* manager"). On the other hand, some well-educated and talented women who

have been taught to play dumb or to hide their light may have to be encouraged to raise their professional aspirations. Hence, the popularity of assertiveness training programs.

The goal is to realize that few differences exist between men and women managers. A number of recent comparative studies indicate that men and women managers have similar managerial styles, attitudes, and temperaments.[8] For instance, women can be as objective, decisive, and pragmatic in their decision making and can tolerate uncertainty and ambiguity as well as men.[9] The focus should be upon job demands and how a person's qualities will or will not enable him or her to meet them.

3. *Define her role.* If a woman's role is vaguely defined, she can never be sure of the extent and authority of her position, how she is evaluated, or exactly what she must achieve to be promoted or otherwise rewarded. Moreover, no one else can see the effects of her efforts, presence, and input. This affects not only others' evaluation of her performance but also their acceptance of her as well as her own self-concept and motivation.

4. *Announce new responsibilities.* When a man is given new responsibilities and authority, it is usually announced to subordinates and others in the organization. Women, again and again, report that when a woman is given a similar assignment, rarely is the change formally or informally announced. As a result, subordinates and peers often resist her intrusion. Publicizing her role legitimatizes her and shows top management's support. It clarifies her place in the hierarchy and helps ensure that her male peers treat her as an equal.

5. *Expect competency.* A woman manager's supervisor should expect the same performance from her as from her male counterparts. She should also receive the same help in areas where she needs help that would be given a male subordinate. Her superior should level with her, tell her the facts straight, what is good, what is bad—anything that affects her job performance. Competent, qualified, hard-working female managers *want* objective performance evaluation. Those who are not so qualified *need* it.

6. *Identify and sponsor women who have management potential.* Many companies use assessment centers to identify men as candidates for management positions. Some of the methods developed are proving to be accurate predictors among men over time. Little assessment center information, however, is available on women. Nevertheless, management might examine how men get ahead and compare this information with how women are advanced. For instance, women have not been a part of the informal sponsorship

system. A young man more often than not is a protegé of an older, established person. Executives have tended to identify a bright young man rather than a bright young woman as a protegé. This hesitancy toward women as protegés has been a major problem for them. Because a woman also tends to be seen as an assistant rather than as a colleague, her superior may fail to introduce her to his colleagues or sponsor her for jobs.

7. *Provide management training.* A woman cannot function as a good manager without appropriate training any more than a man can. She must develop her skills through higher levels of in-service training, related job rotation, and cross-functional assignments. She must be put into progressively more responsible positions where she can use her capabilities and be held accountable for the results.

Most women have advanced into management through specialized skills in a technical or staff area rather than through the general management training and development route through which most men have progressed. As a result, management skills most women managers reportedly need to improve tend to be in finance and budgeting, planning, and effective decision making.[10] Organizational skills that tend to need improvement are policy and budget-making guidelines.[11]

Lack of involvement in budget development and budget management may have special implications for the woman manager. Some men who fail to involve women in budget activities may have fallen prey to the sexual stereotype that women are inherently inept at dealing with numbers and money. If that is the case, it is bad enough on the face of it, but at least there is hope for changing the stereotype from which the behavior derives. Another reason women may not have been involved in budgeting and financial management is far more important. Money is power. Whoever controls the money through the budgeting process exerts considerable power in any organization. If some males resist women's assuming managerial positions, it would seem logical that the very last bastion of resistance would focus on the process of budgeting since that is a locus of power.

Summary

After more than 2 decades of federal legislation, relentless efforts from women, and shifts in public attitudes, women are beginning to move into corporate management. Within the next decade, it will not be an anomaly to see a woman walk down a corporate hallway with a briefcase.

People will adjust to women managers—if they are given the same training, responsibility, authority, staff, and other support that male managers receive.

To be an effective leader, every manager—man or woman—needs support from above and below in the organization. This support, more than sex or leadership style, determines one's effectiveness or ineffectiveness. It is needed to back up one's demands and decisions which, in turn, ensure the confidence and loyalty of subordinates—for if the boss has no influence, the department has no influence; so subordinates' attitude, more often than not, is one of "Why go all out?"

Women are capable of risk taking, decision making, and other managerial behavior usually attributed to men. These qualities describe *self-confident people* and are not confined to one sex or the other. By taking advantage of an exceptionally underutilized management resource, a firm can broaden its managerial base and, therefore, its competitive edge. Certainly, as highly motivated and qualified women directly compete with men on the way up, top management can come closer to eliminating mediocrity from its ranks. As this happens, top management will find its investment in talented women is worth that extra effort.

See also Affirmative action; Assertiveness training; Labor legislation; Equal employment opportunity, minorities and women.

NOTES

[1]Mike Tharp, "Improved Image; Women in Work Force Post Better Records for Stability in Jobs," *The Wall Street Journal,* Nov. 20, 1974, pp. 1 and 34.

[2]U.S. Department of Labor, *Underutilization of Women Workers,* Women's Bureau Workplace Standards Administration, 1971, p. 17.

[3]B. R. Bergmann and Irma Adelman, "Economic Role of Women," *The American Economic Review,* vol. 63, no. 4, September 1973, p. 510.

[4]Ellen Goodman, "Working Wives in 30s Shape New Generation," *The Plain Dealer,* Dec. 12, 1976, p. 15.

[5]*Harvard Business Review,* March–April 1974.

[6]Eleanor Brantley Schwartz and Walter B. Waetjen, "Improving the Self-Concept of Women Managers," *The Business Quarterly,* University of Western Ontario, Canada, Winter 1977.

[7]William H. Chafe, *The American Woman,* Oxford University Press, New York, 1972.

[8]W. E. Rosenbauch, R. C. Dailey, and C. P. Morgan, "Differences Among Women in Perceptions of Their Jobs," *Proceedings of the 36th Annual Meeting of the Academy of Management,* 1976, pp. 472–476.

[9]W. E. Rosenbauch, R. C. Dailey, and C. P. Morgan "Dispelling Some Myths and Stereotypes about Women in Business Management," *Colorado Business Review,* vol. 49, no. 9, September 1976, pp. 2–4.

[10]Martha G. Burrow, *Women: A Worldwide View of Their Management Development Needs,* American Management Association, New York, 1976, pp. 15–16.

[11]Ibid.

REFERENCES

Ginzberg, Eli, and Alice M. Yohalem, eds.: *Corporate Lib: Women's Challenge to Management,* Johns Hopkins University Press, Baltimore, Md., 1972.

Kanter, Rosabeth Moss: *Men and Women of the Corporation,* Basic Books, New York, 1977.

Stead, Bette Ann: *Women in Management,* 2d ed., Prentice-Hall, Englewood Cliffs, N.J., 1985.

ELEANOR BRANTLEY SCHWARTZ, *University of Missouri—Kansas City*

WALTER BERNHARD WAETJEN, *Cleveland State University*

Word Processing

Word processing is a term that describes the input, manipulation, storage, and output of text-oriented data resulting from the executed procedures of an office. The key part of this definition is the term "text-oriented." Word processing (WP), to many people, has become synonymous with the automated equipment specifically designed for the office. This is too restrictive a view. The more efficient systems are automated, but *all* word processing systems involve the controlled interaction of human and/or machine resources, data, and processes organized to meet standard office systems objectives.

Textual Data and Information. The substance of most of the data and information in an office can be classified as textual material. The text concept differs from other business data in that it communicates verbal information that can be structured, revised, and agreed to. This capability distinguishes it from business-processing data elements that form the basis for the recording, calculating, manipulating, and summarizing of output informaiton.

Basic Functions

The contemporary word processing applications include the basic functions found within all office systems: (1) origination of the textual data, (2) capture and storage of data, (3) handling and manipulation of the text, and (4) reproduction and display of the text as output.

Origination of Data. The origination of data is essentially the origination of a document. Assuming the originator believes a document is necessary, he or she formulates his or her ideas and chooses a means for communicating the textual message to a transcriber. The actual communication of the text must be directly given to the transcriber through dictation or by mechanically capturing the text first on dictation machines. The transcriber can also be the word processing operator.

Capture and Storage of Data. Once the originator has expressed the communication and captured it in some copyable form, the word processing operator goes to work. The equipment that is used may be as simple as an automatic typewriter or as sophisticated as an automated word processor. The main consideration is the capture and storage of the data in the word processing equipment so that manipulation and revision can be made with relative ease.

Initially, the word processor captures and records data by utilizing either a stand-alone or shared word processing system. The *stand-alone* system is a self-contained, input-output terminal, and does not need auxiliary devices or computer power to drive it. The basic electronic typewriter with limited storage and text-editing capabilities is one example of such a stand-alone system. The main purpose for this device is to help eliminate many first-time errors from being printed on the document. The more sophisticated work stations can provide a variety of capabilities through the use of peripherals and word processing software. Such capabilities include internal dictionaries, math packages, forms layout, and other software to be discussed later in this section.

Shared systems are designed as either (1) pure, shared-logic systems that include several terminal keyboards sharing one computer or (2) distributed-logic systems where computer capabilities are part of the terminal itself. The distributed system allows each work station to work independently of the central computer. Shared systems also share the resources of the system and, thus, can become extremely sophisticated and powerful.

Manipulation of Textual Data. Recording, calculating, extracting, and summarizing data are some of the basic functions performed routinely by a computer; functions performed by word processors are typically those required to manipulate and to format text-oriented data. Although process requirements differ between word and data, the basic capabilities of word processing and data processing are the same. The functions that can be performed by the former, however, depend on the design and capability of the particular word processing equipment available. Typical word processing capabilities include the following:

Systems/Operator Communications. The word processor can provide the operator with a list of functional selections commonly called a *menu.* This menu will progress from the general to the particular, with *functional prompts* that allow the user to choose the specific type of functions required. The *operator prompt* provides instructional messages that guide operators to choose the proper function or instruct them to perform a specific operation. Error messages will be displayed to indicate problems with a component, function, or command.

Typing New Text. The word processor keyboard is positioned exactly as a standard typewriter. The word processing output will be generated on a display screen, however, rather than on a paper medium. Errors can be immediately corrected before they are transferred to the final output medium. There are several features basic to the word processor that enable the operator faster input-correction and text manipulation. For example:

Word wrap allows the operator to enter the text into the system without regard to an end-of-line decision.

Centering is the ability to center headings or whole texts regardless of the right and left margin sets.

Superscript and *subscript* enable the operator to raise or lower, respectively, the upper or lower portions of the text as it relates to the regular text.

Pagination divides the document into pages and applies numbers to them.

Storing and Accessing Existing Documents. Documents are stored on a magnetic disk, and the document is given a name for future accessing of the disk. The names will appear on an index where future selection from the index can be made for document editing or printout.

Editing Process. Editing a document requires that the text be transferred electronically to the display screen. Editing capabilities include the following:

Type-over is the ability to replace a character or characters over existing text. Text will move left or right to adjust for character deletions.

Character insertion is the editing feature that allows new information to be entered where no characters had been previously. Again, the text will adjust left or right to compensate for the insertion.

Word-delete is also possible and, again, the text adjusts.

Paragraph rearrangement or *block movement* enables the operator to move whole portions of the text from one location of the document to another. In addition, *paragraph copying* is possible throughout various parts of the text.

String replacement is the ability to search for special parts of the text and to selectively or "globally" replace the character string with another set of characters.

Text justification means that the text fits evenly between the left and right margins.

Character pitch selection is the number of characters per inch of paper, whereas *proportional spacing* is the ability to allocate specific space for each individual character depending on its size.

Headers and *footnotes* can be provided separately or together on each page.

Forms Creation. Form entries can be measured to locate each field on the form and then stored in the machine. Data entry will automatically be placed into the proper location on the form as output. Thus, items can be placed into position on a preprinted form or the form and descriptive data can be placed on a clear sheet of paper.

Additional Manipulation. Certain functions that relate more with data processing than with word processing can also be accomplished with the newer word processing equipment. *Software integration,* for example, provides the capability to mix or integrate various functions associated with word processing and data processing functions in one application. *Merging* is still another capability, that of joining two separate components together. For example, a list of addresses can be merged with a standard form letter either selectively or automatically. *Textual sorting* can be accomplished numerically and/or alphabetically in either ascending or descending order and for more than one item, if required. An electronic *spelling dictionary*, dependent upon the software used, provides the operator with a searching routine that identifies and corrects misspellings within the text. *Mathematical functions* enable the performance of horizontal, vertical, or calculator math. These perform calculations across, or down, columns or tables, and any calculation can be inserted in the text.

Reproduction and/or Display of Output Texts. The possibilities for print or visual reproduction of the manipulated text material are almost limitless. Most dramatic, perhaps, is the "letter quality" correspondence that has replaced the traditional form letter. Whether the reproduction takes place on an electronic typewriter or printer or a laser printer, the choices of type fonts are enormous. Furthermore, the combined software and hardware enable the operator to generate and consolidate output from different data files. In turn, these can be transmitted to one or more users through a network of interconnected hardware. Moreover, "hard copy" documents can be printed on both sides and automatically collated, decollated, "burst," copied, reduced, or, if required, projected visually on a screen.

See also Computer software, data base management; Computer software packages; Data bases, commercial; Forms design and control; Management information systems (MIS); Management information systems, transaction processing systems; Office automation; Paperwork simplification; Records management.

REFERENCES

Bergerund, Marly, and Jean Gonzalez: *Word Processing,* 2d ed., John Wiley, New York, 1981.

Kutie, Rita C., and Joan L. Rhodes: *Secretarial Procedures for the Electronic Office,* John Wiley, New York, 1983.

Lieberman, Mark A., Gad Selig, and John Walsh: *Office Automation,* John Wiley, New York, 1982.

ARTHUR ALKINS, *U.S. Office of Personnel Management*

Work Design, Job Enlargement, and Job Enrichment

All the terms described in this entry refer to techniques for expanding the content of jobs by adding new functions and/or responsibilities. These techniques rest on the following common assumptions:

Many employees have more capability than their jobs require.

Many of them desire to use that capability.

Greater utilization of employee capabilities will benefit both the employees and the organization.

Job Design. Of the terms considered here, job design has enjoyed the longest period of use. It is best understood as a generic term under which all the others fit. Job design denotes exactly what it says: the design of jobs. The specific connotative meaning of the term has shifted with time and changes in management philosophy. F. W. Taylor advocated a scientific approach to the design of jobs which involved simplifying the work and specifying in great detail what was to be done and how it was to be done. Currently, the term *job design* is used to refer to any of a variety of approaches aimed at increasing the level of satisfaction with work by making jobs more challenging and interesting to do.

Most of the practitioners of job enlargement, job enrichment, and the establishment of autonomous work groups would be comfortable with having their efforts included under the heading of job design.

Job Enlargement. This term emphasizes the expansion of a job to include other related tasks of approximately the same level of difficulty. Its basic thrust is horizontal in that it involves combining into a single job the tasks that may have been performed by several different employees at the same level. It has the effects of reducing specialization and increasing the variety of tasks performed by the worker.

Job Enrichment. This approach is most often associated with the motivation theories of Frederick Herzberg and involves altering job content to give the worker more control and decision-making opportunity as well as improved feedback on performance. It may or may not include the addition of new tasks, as in the case of job enlargement.

The objectives of job enrichment are: (1) to build clearly defined and complete pieces of work (sometimes called *modules* of work); (2) to give the worker substantial opportunity to decide how that piece of work will be completed; (3) to give the worker appropriate information to help in making those decisions.

Autonomous Work Groups. These groups are an outgrowth of the sociotechnical systems approach to the design of work.[1] This approach has been advocated by those associated with the Tavistock Institute of Human Relations in London, England. The basic premise is that the social (human) system and the technical (machine and work technology) system are, in reality, *one* highly interlocked system, which is labeled a *sociotechnical system.*

The goal is to build relatively independent work groups (autonomous work groups) that can assert control over the technology involved in their work. The method of accomplishing this is to allow the work group to decide for itself how its objectives will be established and met and which group member will do what and when. Depending on how the group decides to structure its work, the result may include aspects of job enlargement, job enrichment, job rotation, or all three.

Application Opportunities. Job design techniques have their greatest impact under the following conditions:

When top management is knowledgeable about and willing to support experimentation with the design of the work.

When there is a feeling among many supervisors and managers in the area in question that things need to be improved or that some type of change is called for.

When many of the employees have more capability than their current jobs require.

When many of the employees indicate an interest in and desire for more challenging work.

When the basic needs of the employees for reasonable pay, benefits, working conditions, and fair treatment are being met.

Where the current structure of the jobs offers the opportunity to make significant improvements in their design.[2]

Application Procedures. The design, or redesign, of work can be and is accomplished in a variety of ways. Listed below, however, is a set of steps that are broadly representative of most approaches currently in use. Application procedures are most often carried out by task forces consisting of staff people trained in the processes of redesigning work (such as representatives of personnel or industrial engineering departments) and members of line management who are familiar with the jobs in question. In some cases, representatives of union groups and/or other employees who perform the jobs being studied are also involved in the planning.

Step 1: Feasibility Study: The feasibility study determines whether redesigning the work will be an effective activity in a particular organization or work unit. A complete study will usually require an examination of existing data on production, quality, absenteeism, turnover, etc.; an analysis of the work flow; interviews with employees to learn how they do their work and what they like and dislike about it; questionnaires to measure employees' satisfaction with the work;[3] interviews with supervisors and managers to determine their interest in and support for changes in work design; and the gathering of data concerning prospective changes in management, equipment, sales forecasts, etc., that might affect the advisability of becoming involved in an effort to redesign the work. A report is then written, based on this information, and a decision is made whether or not to proceed with the work design effort. Obviously, the following steps will be taken only if a positive decision is reached.

Step 2: Planning the Work Design Changes: The planning often begins with a workshop or seminar that may last anywhere from a few hours to a few days. The workshop typically features a discussion of job design principles and illustrations to stimulate the participants' thinking. In the case of job enrichment and job enlargement, a brainstorming approach is often used at this point. Its objective is to generate ideas for changes in the design of the work. In building autonomous work groups, an analytical procedure designed to identify sources of variance in the technological system is most often employed.

When a pool of ideas has been generated, the next step is to decide which changes merit implementation. This process is usually begun in the initial workshop, but most often it cannot be completed there because of the time involved as well as the necessity to gather additional information needed to assess feasibility of the proposals. As a result, the usual procedure is to set up a series of follow-up meetings to continue the planning. These meetings (from 1 to 3 hours each) are generally held on a weekly basis and may continue for a period of a few weeks to several months, depending upon the complexity of the work being designed.

Once a complete design has been agreed upon, a schedule of implementation must be laid out. If (as is usually the case) the changeover to the new work design is to be accomplished in phases rather than all at once, plans must specify which workers will be involved at which points, how and when any training will be accomplished, etc.

Quite often, in order to test the effectiveness of the new design, a pilot study is implemented. This involves trying out the new work methods with a small group of employees (1) to make certain the plan will work and (2) to anticipate potential difficulties.

Step 3: Implementation: During the implementation period, it is important for the task force to meet regularly. Its function now is to monitor the progress of the change and to make corrections as necessary. Depending on the number of unforeseen difficulties experienced, implementation may take from as little as a few weeks to as long as 3 years. An average implementation period ranges from 6 months to 1 year.

Step 4: Evaluation: Results of a work design change are usually of two kinds. First, there are often shifts in the job attitudes of employees. They can be measured by readministering the questionnaires used in the feasibility study, by reinterviewing some of the people, and by measuring shifts in such indicators as grievances, absences, and turnover. Second, there may be changes in the organization's effectiveness which can be measured by data on productivity, quality, customer complaints, waste, downtime, and unit costs. In all these measures, it is important that data be gathered *before* any changes are made and then again *after* the bulk of the change has been accomplished.

Examples of Work Design. In the United States, companies that have implemented work design changes include Texas Instruments, General Foods, Sherwin-Williams, General Electric, Cummins Engine, Prudential Insurance, American Telephone and Telegraph, PPG Industries, IBM, Cryovac Division of W. R. Grace, Procter & Gamble, and Monsanto, among many others. In other countries, organizations such as Olivetti, Volvo, Hallstavik Paper, Saab-Scania, Phillips, and Imperial Chemical Industries have been active in this area.

Some of these companies have been quite successful in their work design efforts, while others have experienced less satisfying programs. Walton[4] has described some of those which have failed to diffuse successfully, and Pasmore[5] has clearly summarized the conditions necessary for success.

Summary

Changes in the design of work have the potential to produce clear improvements in both workers' attitudes and organizational effectiveness. In addition, there are often benefits such as improved quality of supervision, greater cross-function cooperation, and improved customer relations. It is also important to note, however, that such benefits are frequently obtained only with significant difficulty.

The implementation of this type of change requires a great deal of time, patience, and follow-up support. This, of course, can be said of any attempt to change an organization, but it seems to be even more applicable to attempts to alter the design of work.

Specifically, this type of program fails in the absence of long-term support (for a period of *years*) on the part of top management. It also fails when it is not coordinated with a variety of other functions such as job evaluation and pay systems, career-planning systems, supervisory and managerial appraisal programs, and developments in data systems and machine technology.

Changes in work design or structure create ripples throughout an organization. For this reason, they should be undertaken with great caution and careful planning. Significantly, the failures in work design programs are generally not of the type that create great organizational difficulty; it is just that *nothing* happens. The potential benefits are great, but anything less than complete commitment appears unlikely to reap them.

See also Human factors engineering; Job analysis; Motivation in organizations; Organization development (OD); Productivity improvement; Quality circles; Work measurement; Work simplification and improvement.

NOTES

[1] L. Davis and J. Taylor, *Design of Jobs*, Penguin Books, Inc., Baltimore, 1972.

[2] D. A. Whitsett, "Where Are Your Enriched Jobs?" *Harvard Business Review*, January–February 1975.

[3] The most widely used questionnaire is the Job Diagnostic Survey (see J. R. Hackman and G. Oldham, *Technical Report No. 4*, Department of Administrative Sciences, Yale University, 1974).

[4] R. Walton, "The Diffusion of New Work Structures: Explaining Why Success Didn't Take," *Organizational Dynamics*, Winter 1975.

[5] W. Pasmore, "Overcoming The Roadblocks in Work-Restructuring Efforts," *Organizational Dynamics*, Spring 1982.

REFERENCES

Davis, L., and A. Cherns: *The Quality of Working Life*, 2 vols., The Free Press, New York, 1975.

Gilbert, Thomas F.: *Human Competence: Engineering Worthy Performance*, McGraw-Hill, New York, 1978.

DAVID A. WHITSETT, *University of Northern Iowa*

Work Measurement

Work measurement assesses the content of work, primarily physical work, although, in this context, work may include decisions or a series of thoughts usually regarded as mental activities. Work measurement also includes analysis and use of certain relevant data, i.e., machine and equipment operating rates and limitations.

Work content is usually stated in terms of time per physical unit, i.e., minutes per piece, pound, or foot, although it is sometimes expressed in unrelated form, i.e., per occurrence. *Work*, as examined in this entry, usually refers to those activities performed within a manufacturing or processing facility. It also includes, of course, those activities of clerical and other skilled and semiskilled office workers that are susceptible to analysis and measurement by direct visual observation and/or certain written records of a particular character and kind.

Concepts

Several concepts underlie work measurement and its applications.

Fair Day's Work.[1] This term, which is commonly used throughout industry, is a primary objective of work measurement and related techniques. In particular, it is related to compensation through the usual wording in a labor contract which includes the obligation to perform "a fair day's work for a fair day's pay."

A fair day's work is usually and best illustrated by motion picture films of common operations, such as walking, case handling, shoveling. These operations are physical in nature, and the apparent rate of work is easily judged, even by untrained observers. Films of many manufacturing, clerical, and other jobs and activities are available from a number of sources, such as the Society for the Advancement of Management. They are useful in providing supervisory, staff, and technical personnel with the approximate level of effort and skill associated with reasonable performance.

Various definitions of a fair day's work exist, but they are subjective in nature and employ terms such as *average* and *normal* without further definition.

Standard Time Date. The concept of standard time data, or standard data, is important to an understanding of work measurement. It is defined as a number of individually derived standards that are condensed into a tabular array to facilitate their storage, referral, and further use.

The array is generated by graphical or statistical analysis of elemental times and physical attributes of the operation/product, to ascertain valid existing relationships or functions. (See Fig. W-1.) These can be expressed in equation form, usually derived by fitting a scattergraph to a straight line, when done manually. The computer has made it possible to handle massive data inputs and, through regression techniques, to improve accuracy.

Standard time data also improve consistency in that human error inherent in the leveling—or judgment—process is, in some degree, reduced. Addi-

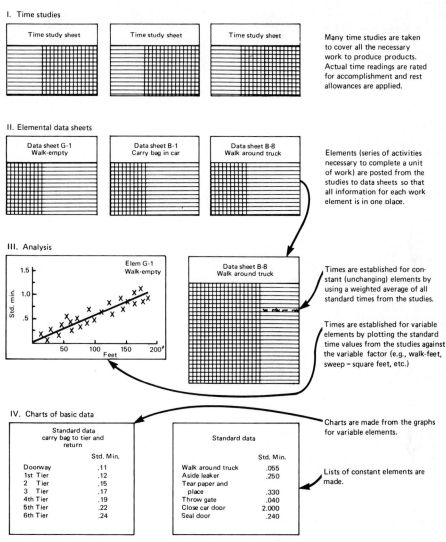

FIG. W-1 Standard data derivation.

tionally, these data reduce the time spent in observation of the task, once the relationship of time to physical attribute is established and verified. Interpolation can be employed to establish a time for an operation on a specific product without making an actual observation.

Techniques and Procedures

Selection of the work measurement technique to be used is an important decision, with serious cost implications, and involves significant considerations of a less tangible nature.[2]

Time Study. Basically, all time-study procedures are alike in that they constitute a time record of what, when, how, where, and by whom work was performed. Typically, the task is broken into smaller, logically sequenced subtasks, called *elements,* for which the time is recorded.

The technique of time study is usually accompanied by the estimates of the worker's effectiveness during observation. This step involves assigning a level-of-performance index, usually on a scale of 0 to approximately 150, with 100 being designated as normal or average. Among a dozen or so other terms, this mental comparison is often referred to as *leveling, accomplishment rating,* or *pace rating.*

929

In addition to the effort-leveling procedure, other allowances are usually added to time-study–derived data. They generally cover fatigue and personal needs, although the amount of delay judged to be inherent is sometimes factored similarly.

Enforced attention time involves an interrelationship between workers and machine(s), which then removes, in varying proportion, control of workers' performances from the individual or group. The amount of enforced attention time during which the operator must stay in the immediate area to tend to the equipment must be found and incorporated in the standard time.

Fatigue is the most variable and least understood of allowances. It is usually expressed as a factor to be multiplied by the leveled time for the element. It can range from a minimum of 1.05 to 1.10 to 2.00, or higher under extreme conditions. Less often, fatigue is accommodated in specified minutes per hour, ranging from a low of 5 to a high of 12 or more. Various tables exist which can be used. (*See* Table W-3.)

Personal allowances involve an estimate of the time needed to perform the human functions of elimination, quenching thirst, and related necessities. Washing, or clean-up, may or may not be included in this portion. If not, where it is significant and time-consuming, involving travel to facilities or very dirty working conditions, it is usually expressed as a flat allowance in minutes.

In continuous operations, lunch may be included in this allowed time. Recently, the Occupational Safety and Health Administration promulgated regulations that have brought about a spate of state laws affecting both rest and personal allowances. However, the main impact has been in the areas of extremes, e.g., the maximum weights that can be lifted under specified circumstances or the allowable exposure to certain environments for specified lengths of time.

Predetermined Time Systems. Since the beginning of detailed motion study, microelemental systems have proliferated. Essentially, these systems are constructed on the principles first articulated by Gilbreth. The principal objective is to reduce all human movement to its most fundamental discernible components. These factors can then be combined as necessary to synthesize a standard operational time. In addition, the task of estimating performance during time studies is eliminated.

Several of these systems have become well established and are extensively installed, often concentrating in particular industries. They are known by both public and proprietary terms. Each possesses certain features considered by the originators and/or proprietors to make them uniquely valuable. Basically, all deal in very small (micro) elements, with times expressed in decimal portions of minutes or hours, and are given a name.

The basic *microelemental time values* for elemen-

tal motions are often combined into clusters of modules to facilitate derivation and application of standards. This approach loses some degree of accuracy, but administration and application to written records of operations are simplified.[3]

It is common for practitioners very familiar with these techniques to check the derived time values by using a stopwatch or other means. This method is intended to insure that they have not misinterpreted the description of the operation under consideration or in some other way erred in the development of standard times.

Work Sampling. It has been found to be useful as well as reliable to observe human work activities in a noncontinuous mode, most often referred to as sampling.[4] This technique is capable of deriving standard times and/or allowances or delays for elements. (*See* Work sampling.)

Work sampling is often performed using random numbers as the basis for the time interval at which the work shall be observed; however, its validity when using fixed intervals has also been established.

Sampling is a convenient method by which the activities of many individuals can be observed readily and translated into meaningful information. It has advantages, mainly those of cost, over the detailed recording of work by orthodox time-study procedures. It is easily applied to (1) personnel visible within a particular area and (2) those who provide service to direct operations. It is also useful in examining the activities of personnel who are spread out over a much larger area, such as maintenance employees who may cover vast spaces of plants and grounds.[5]

Historical Data. Lacking any other reference materials or direct observational information, work content can be approximated, using past historical data related to rates of output, if these data are available in sufficient detail. This approach usually necessitates factoring by operations or groups, in order to correct historical rates or bring them into line.

Frequency Distribution Analysis. It is possible to plot standard times for elements as well as operations and from these to develop histograms and frequency distributions. The shape of the distributions, skewing, and other characteristics indicate the time for an operation which could be designated as standard. it is a useful technique for comparing (1) operator with operator or (2) similar methods for consistency, range, and other aspects of working times.

Multiple Regression. Some operations are of such nature that the length of time to perform them is reflected in more than one variable, sometimes several. The manual derivations of the influence of any one of several factors that influence the time necessary is laborious. The technique of multiple regression isolates and quantifies the independent variables.

Multiple regression often entails the development

TABLE W-3 Schedule of Fatigue and Personal Allowances for Factoring Elements

Selection Key for Handling Operations

From	Above head	Chest	Waist	Knee	Floor
Above head	4 / 1.18	5 / 1.15	4 / 1.12	3 / 1.12	3 / 1.14
Chest	5 / 1.23	5 / 1.12	3 / 1.13	3 / 1.12	3 / 1.14
Waist	5 / 1.18	5 / 1.17	1 / 1.10	2 / 1.15	2 / 1.15
Knee	4 / 1.19	4 / 1.18	3 / 1.22	3 / 1.14	3 / 1.19
Floor	4 / 1.22	3 / 1.22	3 / 1.25	3 / 1.33	2 / 1.20

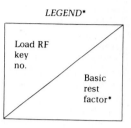

*LEGEND**

Load RF key no. / Basic rest factor*

Rest Factors for Transporting Operations

Element	Load RF key no.	Basic rest factor*	Load limit
Walking on level	1	1.10	75#
Ascending stairs	3	1.50	50#
Descending stairs	2	1.20	50#
Ascending rung ladder	3	1.60	25#
Descending rung ladder	2	1.40	25#
Walking up grade	3	$1.10 + [(.001) \times (\% \text{ up grade})^2]$	10% grade-75#
Walking down grade	2	$1.10 + [(.0005) \times (\% \text{ down grade})^2]$	10% grade-75#

Load Rest Factors

Load, pounds	Load rest factor key number				
	1	2	3	4	5
5	.01	.02	.02	.02	.03
10	.03	.04	.04	.05	.06
15	.05	.06	.07	.08	.09
20	.06	.08	.10	.11	.13
25	.09	.11	.13	.15	.17
30	.11	.14	.16	.19	.22
35	.13	.17	.20	.23	.27
40	.16	.20	.24	.28	.32
45	.19	.24	.28	.33	.38
50	.22	.28	.33	.39	.44
55	.25	.32	.38	.44	.51
60	.29	.36	.43	.50	.57
65	.32	.40	.48	.57	.65
70	.36	.46	.55	.64	.73
75	.40	.51	.61	.71	.81

Note: Rest factor = basic rest factor + load rest factor.
* *Use* basic rest factor for no load.
Source: Copyright 1946 by Albert Ramond and Associates, Inc., Chicago, Ill.

of exponential polynomial equations. Software programs have been developed and are available under proprietary ownership from several sources, facilitating the handling of cumbersome data inputs and derivation. (*See* Statistical analysis for management.)

Other Techniques. In special circumstances, linear programming, critical path methodology, and simulation are used in the general area of work measurement. Within a limited context, other terms and compilations are in use to indicate a rate of work which has been determined through a rational process such as *reasonable expectancy*, a task time used in conjunction with short-interval scheduling or incremental work assignment/loading; *ZIP standard data*, a block-type standard used when application expense is to be minimized and accuracy is of minimal importance; and *commercial industrial estimating manuals*, in which dollar estimates can be converted to useful standard time data.

Applications

Work measurement has a wide variety of practical uses, including the following:

Labor Utilization. The most frequent, and often the most productive, use of standard times derived from work measurement is the development of information for management control which reflects the rate of labor utilization.[6] This information can be collected over various periods of time and for various size groups of personnel ranging from total plants to individuals.

The classical definition of labor utilization is efficiency. *Efficiency* is the ratio of the earned hours generated by an employee, divided by the actual hours, i.e., clock hours, recorded during the time the corresponding work was performed. Thus, this definition corresponds directly to the engineering definition: output divided by input.

Earned hours is the term used to describe the product of the standard time(s) for operation(s) multiplied by the number of times the operation was performed. The term *earned hours* is generally used, although such times may be designated otherwise.

It is customary for most organizations to calculate the labor efficiency for any particular group on a continuing basis. It is not always possible for employees, however well motivated, to be at all times gainfully employed at desirable efficiencies. It is also impractical for work to be made available to all employees at all times. As a consequence, pure calculations of earned hours and actual hours cannot always be made.

Labor Analysis Sheets. In practice, workers report actual hours spent in other classifications, some of which are delay time, lost time, personal time, and union time. These classifications are recorded on labor analysis sheets, in various formats,

and distributed at periodic intervals (daily, weekly, monthly) as local procedures and needs may dictate. These displays of the performance of labor are provided to the various echelons of management for their information, analysis, and action. (See Fig. W-2.)

Standard Costs. Labor standards are widely used in the buildup of standard costs. They are usually posted on a card, or other format, by operations and also by product as the basis, together with material, upon which burden and other costs are allocated.

Production Control/Planning. In this area, labor standards are used in conjunction with production quantity requirements as they reflect sales demand. To order or release work to the manufacturing facility, incoming sales data are assembled and translated into internal operating orders. The production control/planning function combines the standards for labor performance and the customary or past performances of labor. This enables planners and schedulers to anticipate the completion of known product quantities and the sequence in which these will become available.

Methods/Equipment Analyses. Labor standard data are useful, and often essential, in the development of accurate cost comparisons directed toward the selection of equipment and methods.

Labor Disputes/Arbitrations/Grievances. It is very difficult to enforce labor performance clauses (as stated in labor contracts) unless the data gathered in the analysis of the situation are supported in adequate detail by labor standard times. Labor arbitrators have upheld the right of management to specify and to expect certain established levels of performance. Moreover, it has become possible to discipline, and ultimately to discharge, employees for failure to accomplish a certain defined level of performance, if their inefficacy can be demonstrated by an adequate and complete documentation of their work performance history.

Work Incentive Systems. Work measurement, accompanied by adequately developed supporting compensation systems, is the best foundation for incentive wage payment. In certain instances, standard times are supplemented by other factors, such as quality or yield parameters.

The labor content is used to establish a standard time which then becomes the norm—or that level of output which must be attained in order to earn above a certain level of pay in conformance with the governing clauses in the labor contract or incentive manual.

Budgeting. Standard labor hours serve as an accurate means of predicting certain variable costs, usually allocated to cost-center burden accounts. Expenditure levels are adjusted above or below the planned level of activity as measured by earned standard hours produced over a specified period of time.

	Period	Actual labor-hours				Earned std. hours	Performance					Savings	
	As designated	Daywork hours unmeasured	On standard hours	Lost time hours	Total labor-hours		% measured hrs. Excluding noncoverable	% measured hrs. Total labor-hours	% work perf.	% pay perf.	Cost per std. dollar	This week	To date
	Reference												
	Last quarter												
1	Feb.8	729.5	2155.2	57.1	2941.8	2218.9	85.0	73.3	103.0	119.0	1.18	3,987	3,987
2	15	793.7	2299.6	57.7	3151.0	2598.8	85.7	73.0	113.0	124.0	1.12	5,218	9,905
3	22	743.5	2462.8	57.5	3263.8	2857.4	88.6	75.5	116.0	125.5	1.10	5,948	15,153
4	Mar. 1	903.6	2345.4	54.6	3303.6	2602.3	85.9	71.0	111.0	123.0	1.13	5,124	20,277
	Month	3170.3	9263.0	226.9	12660.2	10277.4	86.1	73.0	111.0	123.0	1.13	—	20,277
5	Mar. 8	924.7	2173.4	54.3	3152.4	2427.1	82.7	68.9	111.7	123.5	1.13	4,784	4,784
6	15	780.5	2130.4	39.3	2950.2	2404.3	85.3	72.2	112.9	124.0	1.12	4,791	9,575
7	22	852.0	2459.5	55.3	3366.8	2798.3	86.2	73.1	113.8	124.5	1.11	5,582	15,157
8	29	745.2	2010.8	34.6	2790.6	2166.1	84.8	72.1	107.7	121.5	1.15	4,055	19,212
9	Apr. 5	796.3	2072.4	43.8	2912.5	2300.3	84.3	71.2	111.0	123.0	1.13	4,437	23,649
	Totals												
		1	2	3	4	5	6	7	8	9	10	11	12

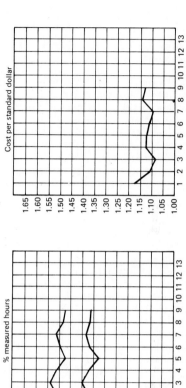

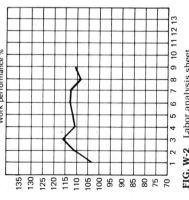

FIG. W-2 Labor analysis sheet.

These summaries are usually prepared on a monthly and accumulated (year-to-date) basis. Those accounts running over and below budgeted amounts are readily identified and analyzed.

Successful Applications—Work Measurement

The following three cases illustrate some of the fundamental uses of work measurement:

Manufacturer of Hydraulic Components.

Focus: Scheduling and productivity.

Period of observation: Over 20 years, with growth from 500 to over 3000 employees.

Purpose and techniques: Original program was a measured daywork system for all machining and assembly operations. A measured daywork system is simply the application of work measurement without wage incentives. Its primary purposes were (1) improvement of scheduling by means of standards and (2) improvement of productivity through a system of measurement and evaluation.

Administration: The system emphasized basic time-study standards and strong, comprehensive production controls. A methods evaluation and improvement activity used standards as a basis for identifying problem areas and corrective action. A follow-up system utilized decentralized dispatch booths strategically located throughout the plant for job-by-job and day-by-day review, evaluation, reporting, and control of work assignments.

Results: Before work measurement was undertaken, performance averaged 70 percent on measured work. Afterward, performance increased to 90 percent at current operating levels. Savings were over $2 million per year after deducting annual costs of system administration. Production output capacity for the existing plant facilities rose 28 percent.

Medium-Sized Steel Producer.

Focus: Cost control and profit improvement.

Period of observation: Covers a 12- to 13-year period.

Purpose and techniques: Original program was a work measurement system for all direct labor and indirect labor operations, including plant maintenance. Its primary purposes were to establish an accurate cost control and profit improvement system based on utilization of engineered standards for all operations.

Administration: This was designed to form the basis for a comprehensive standard cost system in which the labor and overhead costs were derived from engineered operating standards. They were developed using a variety of industrial engineering techniques. Profit improvement evaluation and review systems for decision making and corrective action were based on continual monitoring and an analysis of standard cost variances by all levels of management and supervision. An industrial engineering group, assigned by areas in the plant, maintained timely analysis and monitoring of day-by-day operations in support to line management.

Results: Before initiation of the program, overall effectiveness was 75 percent. One year after installation, and consistently thereafter, audits indicated performance averages of 92 percent. Yearly savings of over $2.5 million have been sustained. Production output increased 12 percent within existing plant facilities.

Specialty Rubber Goods Producer.

Focus: Direct labor.

Period of observation: Three years; approximately 300 employees.

Purpose and techniques: The primary objective of the program was to develop standard time data for all direct operations as the basis for a wage incentive system. These data were developed by time study and reduction to standard time data, motion-time measurement, and equipment capacity analysis.

The wage incentive system was implemented to motivate employees to increase their performance, thereby raising plant capacity. Also, very high turnover and absenteeism had become intolerable.

Administration: Efforts centered on the attainment of equitable pay performance relationships, despite considerable hostility from hourly employees. Supervisors were oriented to understand and support the standards published and released to the hourly employees. Monitoring by management identified potential troublesome areas. Communications were intensified.

Results: Before the program began, performance was controlled at a level of approximately 70 percent. Since then, performance has attained a plantwide average of 120 percent. Net financial impact has stabilized in the middle six figures per year. Absenteeism and turnover have been reduced by over 80 percent.

Outlook for Work Measurement

The main stream of effort in work measurement has shifted from the development of techniques for the derivation of work content to the following major areas of activity:

1. Simplified, cost-effective procedures concerning the application of standard times to production records

2. Improvement of management, supervisory, and staff roles in the administration of work measurement

3. Use of the computer and peripheral equipment in reporting time and production, processing data, and generating meaningful information for executive and operating action

4. Development, modification, and use of computer-oriented software systems incorporating standard time data

Administration. The day-to-day maintenance of reliable and accurate work measurement—related files, records, and reports—is that task which is most often defaulted. Employee pressures and understaffed functions often combine to erode well-conceived systems. This situation then induces a tendency to eliminate work rather than to demonstrate changes of less magnitude to unwilling employees. Thus, the phrase *engineered out* has come into common usage. This avenue, which emphasizes the development and installation of tooling, equipment, and capital goods, is less offensive than work measurement to unions and/or employees.

State of Development. While many examples of the successful development and use of work measurement exist, many executives ignore the subject completely and/or give it less than its rightful amount of attention.[7] Improvement, or the development, of techniques that overcome the persistent resistance to work measurement does not appear to be materializing. Admittedly, the behavioral sciences continue to contribute to an understanding of work and its management. It seems fair to conclude, however, that there is as yet no real agreement among leading observers and practitioners as to the degree of applicability feasible through various techniques.

Neither does there appear to be a resolution of the basic conflicts which revolve around (1) assessing the rate of work performance by direct time-study observation and (2) synthesizing the amount of work contained within a task through other avenues of approach, mainly those associated with predetermined motion-time systems.

Industry Variations. Without doubt, work measurement has had its greatest impact in the hourly work force within the factory. Acceptance of work measurement varies widely. In some industries, such as steel and garment making, work measurement and, further, incentive wage payment are traditional, common, and accepted in some degree by the work force affected. In other industries, neither is tolerable. Any measurement approach other than the crudest estimating procedure is sufficient to create a furor and often results in severe disruption.

The application of work measurement in those industries where it is little used still holds promise of great benefit. Process industries, for example, are increasingly using work measurement in any of several forms to increase the productivity of their facilities as engineering technology (with its large capital requirement) begins to approach the point of diminishing return.

Scope of Application. There is a pervasive feeling which makes many managers feel that work measurement is most useful, and indeed most accurate and trouble-free, when it is employed to assess the content of standardized work, specifically and especially with direct labor. There is also a conviction that indirect or unstandardized work cannot be measured adequately or properly controlled. This notion is probably derived from the early orientation of work measurement activists. They held that work must be very closely specified and analyzed in order to establish the one best way in which it must be performed. As a result, they left a vast area of unstandardized or peripheral work areas uncovered, normally designated as indirect or burden labor, or simply, services. Indirect or burden labor is meant to include those activities normally covered by the terms *maintenance, material handling, distribution* (shipping and receiving), *repair operations, janitorial work*, etc. Industry and management today suffer from this limiting, inaccurate view of the suitability of the application of work measurement. Much work is nonrepetitive and filled with variations from task to task and day to day. It is true that other activities, e.g., purchasing and engineering, have been measured with some degree of success, but these extensions of the concepts have been made on an extremely limited basis.[8]

See also Compensation, wage and salary policy and administration; Cost improvement; Engineering, industrial; Job analysis; Job evaluation; Therbligs; Work design, job enlargement and job enrichment; Work sampling; Work simplification and improvement.

NOTES

[1] B. W. Niebel, *Motion and Time Study*, Richard D. Irwin, Inc., Homewood, Ill. 1967, p. 192.

[2] John G. Hutchinson, *Managing a Fair Day's Work*, Bureau of Industrial Relations, The University of Michigan Press, Ann Arbor, 1963, pp. 58–59.

[3] K. B. Zandin, "Better Work Management with Most," *Management Review*, American Management Association, July 1975.

[4] G. Salvendy and G. P. McCabe, "Auditing Standards by Sample," *Industrial Engineering Magazine*, September 1976, p. 25.

[5] H. F. Allard, "Work Sampling, Valuable Maintenance Management Aid," *Plant Engineering*, Sept. 19, 1968.

[6] M. Fein, "Work Measurement and Wage Incentives," *Industrial Engineering Magazine*, September 1973, p. 49.

[7] Frank DeWitt, "Productivity and the Industrial Engineer," *Industrial Engineering Magazine*, January 1976, p. 21.

[8] C. N. Berton and J. E. Martin, "Work Measurement of Purchasing," *Industrial Engineering Magazine*, January 1976, p. 31.

REFERENCES

Buffa, Elwood S.: *Modern Production-Operations Management*, 7th ed., John Wiley, New York, 1983.

Gaither, Norman: *Production and Operations Management*, 2d ed., The Dryden Press, Chicago, 1984.

Stoner, James A. F.: *Management*, 2d ed., Prentice-Hall, Englewood Cliffs, N.J., 1982.

Roy Abel, *Albert Ramond and Associates, Inc.*

Work Sampling

Work sampling is a fact-finding technique which measures directly the overall activities of people or machines. It is of interest to the professional manager primarily because it can provide the answers to basic questions such as what percentage of their time maintenance craftworkers spend in actual craft work or what the utilization pattern for the fork trucks is in the warehouse. Work sampling is a form of work measurement but does not carry with it demand for the heavy involvement of trained personnel, nor is it related to problems of wage rate structures and incentives. It can be a means of supervisory development and is particularly applicable as a first analysis technique in attacking the cost of service and indirect labor activities.

Study Technique. A work-sampling study consists of a series of snap, or instantaneous, observations of each of the people or machines making up the group under study. The observer classifies whatever activity he or she sees into a predefined series of categories. These categories may be as simple as classifying a typist as either typing or other activity. Usually, for an initial study, there are fewer than 10 categories. As an example, in an analysis of typists, the categories might be:

1. Typing
2. Taking dictation
3. Transcribing from a dictating machine
4. Clerical activity at desk
5. Away from desk, but in office
6. Talking, telephoning
7. Personal
8. Not in office

Each of these categories will be defined in writing and discussed with the supervisors and typists before sampling. The procedure for taking the observations is straightforward. At randomly selected times during the workday, the observer looks at each of the typists in turn and decides for each individually which category of activity best describes what is being done (or not done) at that particular moment. The observer then writes the number of the category for each typist on a form similar to that shown in Fig. W-3. The names of the typists appear on the form for ease of recording but usually are not carried forward in any report. If there are five typists in the group, there will be five observations for each round of

Name of typist	9:07	9:53	11:21	1:17	2:46	3:38	3:49	4:22	4:31
Cain	7	8	1	1	3	5	6	3	1
Yeager	2	1	6	4	1	3	7	6	2
Cooke	7	4	5	1	8	1	1	3	8
Dooley	7	8	7	4	1	1	2	1	8
Macy	4	1	2	5	7	5	1	4	1

Random observation times

Date __7/16__   Supervisor __Hartke__
(Observer)

Categories:
1. Typing
2. Taking dictation
3. Transcribing
4. Clerical at desk
5. Away from desk
6. Talking
7. Personal
8. Not in office

FIG. W-3 Example of work-sampling observation sheet.

observations. Random times are used to determine the start of each round. Several rounds are made each day, perhaps eight or ten in an office and only three or four when studying widely dispersed groups such as maintenance craftworkers.

The results of a work-sampling study are given as a set of percentages or proportions for each category. These reflect the overall activity. Suppose in the example that for a group of 5 typists, the observer makes 9 rounds per day and that the study extends over a month of 22 working days. The total number of observations would then be 5 observations per round, times 9 rounds per day, times 22 days, or a total of 990 observations. Suppose the distribution of observations and the percentages of the total are as shown in Table W-4.

TABLE W-4

Category	Number of observations	Percent of observations
Typing	487	49.2
Taking dictation	23	2.3
Transcribing from machine	86	8.7
Clerical activity at desk	71	7.2
Away from desk, in office	36	3.6
Talking, telephoning	68	6.9
Personal	113	11.4
Not in office	106	10.7
	990	100.0

These results are in a form easily understood by all. The reliability (possible error) due to sample size can be calculated very simply. Although a work-sampling study does not provide much detail, it is a direct measurement that does give a form of bottom-line analysis that is of practical value to the executive. This is true because the end result of personnel practice, motivation, planning, scheduling, and control many times can be measured if management knows how people really spend their time.

Inputs versus Outputs. Work sampling, then, measures input in terms of hours spent at various activities. The other important element, output, must be measured also. Together, input and output measures enable management to determine unit costs and thus establish a *benchmark* for evaluating improvement. Organizations typically keep records of output in the form of an administrative measure. In the example, the number and classification of documents typed represent measures of output. Depending on the results of an initial analysis, the observer may make a more detailed analysis. In cases of studies made of indirect and service activities, work sampling and the concommitant analysis of units of output often provide the executive with the first truly structured approach to cost improvement.

Work Sampling Compared with Work Measurement. It is appropriate here to distinguish between work sampling as a form of work measurement and the more traditional work measurement techniques of stopwatch time study and of the use of predetermined human work times [such as Methods Time Measurement (MTM) or Work Factor]. These other techniques are all similar in the sense that each determines a standard time to perform a particular task. The term *standard* is the key, however, since the time to do a task depends directly on the method, tools, and equipment, the skill and motivation of the operator, and on environmental factors. All these must be standardized for conventional work measurement. When this is done, the result provides a time per unit of output, which is extremely useful for management purposes.

Technique for Improvement. Work sampling, in contrast, does not directly yield a time per unit. Nor does it provide the basis for methods improvement of a direct nature. It is not really an appropriate tool for the measurement of repetitive work. Instead, work sampling is most effective as a broad survey-type measurement technique. It can provide, for example, the first form of measurement in indirect cost areas. In such uses, it is common to find an unstructured pattern of activity. Methods may not be specified, and record keeping of units of output may be in terms of very gross units only; thus there may be very little real control of cost. Under these conditions, overstaffing is common, and great reliance is placed on the judgment of the individual who actually does the work. Managers are understandably uneasy in such situations. Without some sort of standards, managers cannot truly manage. Frederick W. Taylor observed that, "To manage we first must measure." This statement has withstood the test of time. Work sampling provides a means of taking the first important step in the management process where the absence of measurement is typical.

Technique for Development. One of the positive features of work sampling is that it can serve as an effective means of supervisory development. The supervisor is a logical candidate to act as the observer in those cases where a work-sampling study is made of indirect work. The supervisor knows the work and knows the people. Further, the supervisor is the one who is central to any steps taken toward work improvement. No matter who conducts the study, the supervisor must be convinced of its reliability. When supervisors take an active part in the study, it is much easier for them to accept the results and to explain the implications to their employees.

Many refinements have been made in the technique of work sampling, but it is only one of a series of measurement techniques, and the executive should devote more thought to being sure that it is used in an appropriate application than to the details of the study method.

See also Cost improvement; Statistical analysis for management; Work measurement; Work simplification and improvement.

REFERENCES

Buese, Frank A.: "Continuous Work Sampling," *IMS Clinic Proceedings*, Des Plaines, Ill., 1975, pp. 93–96.

Richardson, Wallace J.: *Cost Improvement, Work Sampling, and Short Interval Scheduling*, Reston Publishing Co., Inc., Reston, Va., pp. 87 and 153.

————, and Eleanor S. Pape: "Work Sampling," *Handbook of Industrial Engineering*, Wiley Interscience, John Wiley, New York, 1982, pp. 4.6.1–4.6.21.

WALLACE J. RICHARDSON, *Lehigh University*

Work Schedules, Alternative

In recent years, many people have questioned the logic of fixed work schedules for everyone. The increased use of alternative work schedules, such as flexitime, compressed workweek, part-time work, and job sharing are all evidence of this change in attitude.

Only since the middle of the nineteenth century have Americans known fixed schedules on such a wide scale. Before the modern era, most people were self-employed in various craft occupations or on family-run farms. Individual workers generally determined their own schedules. With the later trend toward working outside the home, workers relinquished this responsibility to their employers. A frequent result was fixed work schedules. The most obvious rationale for them was that fixed schedules allowed employers to coordinate the efforts of individual workers. Of course, this statement is valid even today in many situations—especially those requiring interdependence or involving assembly-line work.

An increased interest in scheduling innovations, however, reflects the concerns of managers, legislators, economists, and psychologists over issues of productivity and quality of work life. Many people feel that alternative work schedules address issues of both organization effectiveness and individual satisfaction. As such, these schedules have been incorporated into theories currently popular in the literature. For example, researchers have included alternative work schedules in their theory-building for quality of work life models (Ronen, 1981; Rosow, 1979), career development models (Van Maanen and Schein, 1977) and life-cycle stages within the context of the organization (Cohen and Gadon, 1978).

Three Alternative Approaches

Although factors like production processes, task interdependence, union contracts, and federal and state legislation may limit consideration of alternative work schedules in some cases, creative managers who are not bound by the constraints of traditional management philosophy have found sufficient space for manipulating the fixed work schedule. The most accepted and popularized alternatives include the compressed (or 4-day) week, part-time work and job sharing, and the many variations of flexible work hours. Each of these schedules represents variations in one or both of two dimensions of work scheduling. The first dimension is the *number* of hours worked during a given period of time—usually a day. The second is the *timing* of these hours of work; that is, when the required number of hours is scheduled within the work period.

The number of hours required is a decision rarely left to the individual employee; instead, either a provision of law or a particular organizational policy dictates it. Timing, on the other hand, is a sufficiently flexible dimension to allow the individual some freedom of choice.

The Compressed Workweek (CWW). This is an alternative work schedule designed to allow employees the standard number of weekly work hours in fewer than 5 days. The most common compressed schedule is a 10-hour day, 4-day week, often designated as the 4/40, although the number of hours worked per day and days per week varies considerably.

The basic concept behind the compressed week is a trade-off between the number of days worked per week and the number of hours worked per day. For the opportunity to work fewer days per week, the employee agrees to work more hours per day. However, beyond the designation of hours per week and days per week, there can be many variations in scheduling. For example, if a firm remains open to customers, 5 or 6 days a week, employees on a compressed week must work staggered schedules; different groups work different days to ensure full coverage.

The CWW has several clear implications. Some affect the employee. For instance, the CWW does not offer a choice of schedule, but it does offer potentially better utilization of leisure time for recreation, personal business, and family life. In addition, the extended workday and possible reduction in the work force present on a given day have the potential for changing job aspects such as the delegation of authority and task responsibility, cooperation, and increased job knowledge. Other implications concern the employer. Only a portion of the work force is available on certain days; this limitation may influence how a manager maintains coverage and supervision, delegates authority, and disseminates information.

The concept of the compressed workweek first gained acceptance in the United States during the late 1960's and early 1970's, and experienced a period of rapid growth early in that decade. This growth leveled off by the middle of seventies. Approximately 2 million American employees are now on some form of CWW. Despite the potential appeal of the CWW, however, certain environmental factors have limited its rate of adoption. For example, state and federal legislation designed to protect the worker's right to overtime payments has restricted the number of hours which an employee can work per day without overtime. (Recent legislation has relaxed these laws for Civil Service employees in order to allow experimentation with alternative work schedules.) Some unions have also been hostile toward the CWW, viewing it as a threat to overtime payments. Others, however, have been more receptive, regarding the system as a step toward further reduction in work hours and an eventual 4-day, 32-hour work week.

Part-Time Employment. This approach cannot be considered a recent innovation in work scheduling since it has been an accepted and popular alternative for many years. As of May 1977, part-time workers constituted 22 percent of the nonagricultural work force; that is, 13 million employees worked less than a full-time schedule. However, the influx of working mothers, older adults, students, and other groups with special needs into the labor force has required employers to evaluate the availability and the nature of part-time work.

Part-time employment is regular employment in which the employee works less than the full-time schedule. The schedule is not temporary, intermittent, or casual. Part-time employment is most common among sales, clerical, and labor jobs, and in the trade and service industries. It is less usual in such areas as management and the trades. A recent innovation in the part-time sector is job sharing, a situation in which two employees fulfill the duties of one job.

There are four distinct categories of part-time workers which represent different needs. First, one must distinguish between temporary and permanent part-time workers. Temporary part-timers include former full-time workers who have decreased their work hours for a period of time; for example, the working mother who has temporarily reduced her hours to simplify looking after a child. Alternatively, an individual may enter the work force on a temporary part-time basis; for example, students holding part-time jobs. Permanent part-time workers are those who have chosen part-time work as the optimal arrangement between work and nonwork obligations.

One must also distinguish between voluntary and involuntary part-time workers. Voluntary part-time workers are simply those who prefer to work part time. In contrast, involuntary part-timers are those who would prefer full-time work, but are unable to find full-time employment appropriate to their skills and education levels. Members of this group are typically young and often members of minority groups.

Of the total part-time work force, 64 percent are regular, voluntary part-time employees. Despite the competition for such jobs, however, managers often perceive part-time workers as extrinsically economically motivated, less than fully committed to their jobs, and lacking in career orientation. Reflections of this perception include the lack of benefits and paucity of professional or managerial jobs available to this sector of the labor force. Recent legislation in the federal government, however, requires the Office of Personnel Management to make part-time jobs available at all levels. These changes and the pressure from many professionals (especially women) for part-time opportunities should help to improve these attitudes.

Flexible Working Hours (Flexitime). This is an alternative work schedule which grants the employee certain freedom in choosing his or her times of arrival and departure. The organization usually defines the degree of variation possible. The simplest variation of the system allows the employee to determine starting and finishing times within a certain time range set by the employer, provided that the employee works the contracted daily attendance hours. (See Fig. W-4.) Conditions governing the degree of flexibility may include the total number of hours the company operates during the day, the hours an employee is required to be present, and the level of interdependence between jobs, between departments, and with suppliers and customers.

Note, however, that the employee's choices fall within certain restrictions. The employee may choose variations in the times he or she is present at work and in the distribution of working hours, but the employee may *not* vary the total number of work-

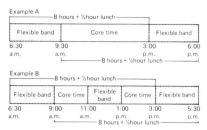

FIG. W-4 Two ways of designing flexitime schedules. (From Barbara L. Fiss, *Flexitime—A Guide,* U.S. Civil Service Commission, May 15, 1974.)

ing hours required by the employment contract. Furthermore, flexitime does not alter current management policies regarding vacations or sick-leave allowances.

Allowing the employee to create a better fit between individual needs and the work environment through scheduling affects many other aspects of the work experience. Flexitime can influence an employee's sense of autonomy by increasing his or her participation in decision making and responsibility for maintaining coverage for absent employees. It can also enhance group cohesiveness and orientation toward the organization's objectives, since employees must now interact in a cooperative mode to maintain work processes.

Because of the rapid rate of adoption of flexitime, it is difficult to estimate exactly how many employees and organizations currently use flexitime systems. A rough estimate by the U.S. Department of Labor, however, reported that as of 1981, nearly 10 million employees in the United States use some version of flexible scheduling. About 300,000 of them are public sector employees. An estimated 13 percent of all nongovernment organizations have some type of flexitime program for 50 or more employees, with a projected national usage rate of 17 percent in the near future.

Planning and Implementation. The outcomes associated with alternative work schedules are positive for both the individual and the organization. The few problem areas associated with this change can be avoided through rigorous planning and thoughtful implementation. Organizational change techniques should be utilized—especially for the training and preparation of first-line supervisors. Often, this particular group is less receptive toward the concept and needs special attention. It can be said, in general, that the more flexibility given to employees within the schedule, and the larger the variance between the organization's and the employee's schedules, the more changes the organization will be required to make.

In general, *all* levels of employees respond to a new concept better if they have had the opportunity to be included in the planning stages and to contribute their own ideas. This participation may also provide insights which might otherwise be overlooked at higher levels of management. In the same context, it is important to design *each* installation of an alternative schedule around the demands of the immediate work environment. Thus, different designs may be needed within an organization or even within a department.

See also Temporary help; Work design, job enlargement, and job enrichment.

REFERENCES

Cohen, A. R., and H. Gadon: *Alternative Work Schedules: Integrating Individual and Organizational Needs*, Addison-Wesley Company, Reading, Mass., 1978.

Ronen, Simcha: *Alternative Work Schedules: Selecting, Implementing and Evaluating*, Dow Jones-Irwin, Homewood, Ill., 1984.

————: *Flexible Working Hours*, McGraw-Hill, New York, 1981.

SIMCHA RONEN, *New York University*

Work Simplification and Improvement

Work simplification stems from the concept first expressed by this author in 1930, "that the person doing a job knows more about that job than anyone else, and is therefore the one person best fitted to improve that job." It is further extended by the observation of Dr. Lillian M. Gilbreth, "We spend far too much time studying operations that should not be done at all!" Originally called motion economy, the concept was later designated as work simplification by Erwin H. Schell, of M.I.T.

Philosophy

Work simplification (WS) consists of three parts: (1) the philosophy, (2) the pattern, and (3) a plan of action. Basic to the philosophy is a genuine belief in people. The furor today over job enrichment and quality circles simply reflects the WS belief in people.

Job Involvement. WS philosophy says that there are three ways of getting results through people. You can *tell* them, using force, fear, or authority. You can *sell* them, using persuasion or monetary rewards. Or you can *involve* them *in improvement*, thus providing them with the satisfactions they are looking for in their work. These satisfactions are found through a challenging job which allows a feeling of achievement, responsibility, growth, advancement, enjoyment of work itself, and earned recognition. The factors that most often dissatisfy workers are those that are peripheral to the job—work rules, lighting, coffee breaks, titles, seniority rights, wages, fringe benefits, and the like.

Confidence and Desire. Before one can put WS to work, one must sincerely believe that there is a vast, widespread, and largely untapped resource of ingenuity and creativity among almost all those in the work force. Most managers have little idea of how to go about unleashing this powerful resource. As has been demonstrated by the widespread failure of the conventional suggestion system with its boxes and prizes, more than hoopla is needed to bring forth substantial ideas that pay off on the bottom line.

Training. Unless *all* employees are given basic training in the principles and tools of WS, a company will wind up with results typical of a suggestion plan with only 25 percent acceptance of the ideas submitted. Under a good WS program, it is not unusual to *install*, not accept, 60, 70, and 80 percent.

Management Attitudes. Managers and supervisors must be given an opportunity to develop their capacity for handling the human relations problems involved. There is still a tendency to promote those employees who have demonstrated skill in the technology of their jobs. The result is that these people spend the majority of their time on the technological problems and only a small portion of time working on human problems.

Basic Problems. The two most vexing causes of many problems associated with WS are:

1. People resist change.
2. People resent criticism.

For years, the author has put these two statements on the board in front of many thousands of people all over the world and asked, "Do you believe them to be true?" The question never fails to get unanimous agreement. After discussion, however, some dissidents appear. Finally, they modify the two problems to read:

1. People resist *being* changed.
2. People resent *being* criticized.

When the work force becomes involved in improvement, the ideas become theirs and they will work very hard to see that they succeed. This is contrary to the traditional approach where new ideas and new methods are *imposed* upon people.

Commitment and Pledge. To ensure success with WS, it is essential to build *trust* in your organization. This requires a statement of policy on the part of the chief executive officer *and* the continuing demonstration of support. In most companies, it is customary to assure employees that no one will lose his or her employment as a result of a WS improvement.

Application Pattern

The pattern of WS develops the tools and techniques that make the difference between getting ideas that are flash improvements based on snap judgment and using an organized approach. The most commonly used pattern for improving methods follows five steps:

1. Select a job to improve.
2. Get all the facts
   Make a process chart.
3. Challenge every detail.
   What—*why?*
   Where—*why?*
   When—*why?*
   Who—*why?*
   How—*why?*
   List possibilities: Can we
     Eliminate?
     Combine?
     Change sequence? Place? Person?
   Improve necessary details.
4. Develop the preferred method.
5. Install it—check results.

Flow Process Analysis

The first and basic tool used within the framework of the WS pattern is the flow process chart.

Flow Process Chart. The beginning point is to examine critically the problem *as a whole.* Ask, *what* is the *purpose?* What function is to be carried out? What is to be accomplished? The entire process might be eliminated. It may be outmoded. If so, why look at details? Perhaps a technical development has made it obsolete. Is a new machine, process, or material now available that will make a better product or service at a lower cost? A plant making precision castings, for example, found that a centrifugal process would eliminate several machining operations. Another learned that welded steel stampings could replace cumbersome castings. A plastic plant adopted high-frequency heating, and a fixture plant, electrostatic paint spraying. An office noted that a revised computer program would eliminate many sortings, tabulating, and calculating operations. Perhaps the product itself can be eliminated as part of an assembly. The guide is to look at the overall objective first. Perhaps the chart of the details will not be necessary.

Select Symbols. Frank Gilbreth invented a sign language to visualize the steps on his flow process chart. Like the symbols a secretary uses in Pitman or Gregg, Gilbreth's shorthand symbols make it easy to pack a lot of information in a small place. The original Gilbreth set included about 40 symbols. As WS

programs developed, the list was simplified to five basic symbols as shown in Fig. W-5. They are used for steps performed on a material or by a person.

FIG. W-5 Flow chart symbols.

Chart the Information. To make a clear picture, the chart should show the *time, distance, person,* and *place* for each important step. The description should be as brief as a telegram. For a *person*-type chart, the action should be in the *active* form: drills, taps, grinds, types, posts, checks, etc. For a *material*-type chart, the action should be in the *passive* form: drilled, tapped, ground, typed, posted, checked, etc.

Pick an Important Problem. To get worthwhile results from a flow process chart, it is wise to pick an important problem, one with a payoff large enough to provide motivation and to demonstrate the efficacy of WS.

Decide on Person or Material. The chart can follow either one person or one material. In general, the person-type chart will be useful where the same person carries the action from place to place. This is the case of a maintenance person, a bank teller, or a messenger. The material-type chart is recommended where one material carries the action from place to place, as in most factory operations on a product or in clerical operations on some work paper in a procedure. For more than one person or one material, additional charts are made.

Pinpoint the Beginning and Ending. Pick a clear-cut starting point, where the action begins, and a clear-cut ending point. If an individual conducts the study, both points should be within his or her department. If the study is conducted by a team, the chart can include all the departments involved.

Making the Chart. Fill in the headings at the top of the chart (Fig. W-6). Walk from station to station where each step is performed. Do not depend on memory. Discuss each step with the person on the job as if you were a newspaper reporter. Avoid any criticism, but note any suggestions made by the operator or clerk. Make that person a partner in the search for the *one best way.* If the activity is important, try to estimate an average time for each work station. Count the steps to the next operation and convert them into feet traveled.

Flow Lines. To visualize the flow (or change of action) from step to step, and as an aid to analysis, a flow line is traced on the chart. The original Gilbreth charts were on a large roll of paper, the symbols made with a template. In 1940, the preprinted symbol chart was developed, thus simplifying the construction job. A line is drawn from the bottom of one symbol to the top of the next, as shown in Fig. W-6.

"Do" Operations. Operations are classified as *make ready* or *do* or *put away.* The "do" operations are those that alter the product or carry out the function of the process or procedure. The preparatory steps are called "make ready," and the clean-up or disposal steps are called "put away." On the chart, blacken in the symbols for the do operations. In this way they can be analyzed first. If a do operation is eliminated, this automatically eliminates both the make ready and the put away associated with it.

Summary. Now count the operations, inspections, etc., along with the time and distance where shown, and post the total in the "Summary" at the top of the chart. This will provide an overall picture of the process or procedure that the individual plans to improve.

Flow Diagram. In studies where the person or material moves from place to place, a picture of the movement may be shown on a *flow diagram.* This movement is drawn on a layout, or floor plan that shows the location of the workplaces. The movement from station to station is shown by dotted lines. The action, such as operations, inspections, etc., identified by a symbol with a number enclosed, to match the flow process chart. To avoid confusing details, only the *important* operations are diagrammed. Delays are usually omitted. The direction is shown by the head of the transportation arrow.

When a flow process is drawn for either a person or a material, it is usually evident that attention must

be paid to the work space layout. Unless the operation is such that it will be repeated many times over a long period or is one that involves large numbers of operators, it is not necessary to go to the detail of making an operator chart, or a right- and left-hand chart, as it is sometimes called.

Motion Economy. WS at this stage is vitally concerned with proper design of workplaces in factory, home, and office. The basic concepts of motion economy apply, as developed by William R. Mullee from the original Gilbreth principles:

1. Begin each element simultaneously with both hands.
2. End each element simultaneously with both hands.
3. Use simultaneous arm motions in opposite, symmetrical directions.
4. Use hand motions of lowest classification for satisfactory operation.
5. Keep motion paths within the normal work areas.
6. Avoid sharp changes of direction, with a smooth, curved motion path.
7. Slide or roll; do not lift and carry.
8. Locate tools and materials in proper sequence at fixed work stations.
9. Use method with fewest work elements, for shortest time with least fatigue.
10. Use rhythm and automaticity to increase output and reduce fatigue.
11. Relieve hands with foot pedals whenever practical.
12. Do not hold; use a vise or fixture, freeing hands to move pieces.
13. Provide foot-operated ejectors to remove finished product.
14. Use drop delivery to dispose of the finished product.
15. Shorten all transports and provide gravity-feed hoppers.
16. Preposition tools for quick grasp.
17. Preposition product for next operation.
18. Locate machine controls for convenience and ease of operation.
19. Design workplace height for sitting-standing operation, with posture seat and adjustable backrest and footrest.
20. Provide pleasant working conditions: illumination, air, noise, color, orderliness.

Each job should be checked against this list of principles to see what changes may be made to improve the method and reduce fatigue in the search for the one best way.

Summary

	Present No.	Present Time	Proposed No.	Proposed Time	Difference No.	Difference Time
◯ Operations	15					
⇨ Transportations	2					
▢ Inspections	2					
D Delays	5					
▽ Storages	1					
Distance traveled	600 ft.		ft.		ft.	

No. _1_
Page _1_ of _1_

Job _Fill out and approve form X_
▢ Person or ▢ Material _____
Chart begins _In A's desk drawer_
Chart ends _In A's out box_
Charted by _AHM_ Date _Oct 8_

Details of (Present / ~~Proposed~~) method — Possibilities (Eliminate, Combine, Sequence, Place, Person, Improve)

#	Details	Symbol	Notes
1	In A's desk drawer	◯⇨▢D▽	No definite location
2	Removed and placed on desk	◯⇨▢D▽	Cluttered desk
3	Filled out	●⇨▢D▽	Original & 5 copies
4	Placed in OUT box	◯⇨▢D▽	Long reach
5	Waits	◯⇨▢D▽	For messenger pickup
6	Picked up by messenger	◯⇨▢D▽	Difficult grasp
7	To B's office	◯⇨▢D▽	Delay in rest room
8	Placed in IN box	◯⇨▢D▽	
9	Waits	◯⇨▢D▽	
10	Picked up by B	◯⇨▢D▽	Difficult grasp
11	Examined	◯⇨▢D▽	
12	Signed	●⇨▢D▽	
13	Placed in OUT box	◯⇨▢D▽	Long reach
14	Waits	◯⇨▢D▽	For pickup
15	Picked up by messenger	◯⇨▢D▽	Difficult grasp
16	Back to A	◯⇨▢D▽	
17	Placed in IN box	◯⇨▢D▽	Location of box bad
18	Waits	◯⇨▢D▽	
19	Picked up by A	◯⇨▢D▽	
20	Read	◯⇨▢D▽	
21	Paper clips removed	◯⇨▢D▽	
22	Carbons and copies separated	◯⇨▢D▽	
23	Reassembled	◯⇨▢D▽	
24	Placed in OUT box	◯⇨▢D▽	Long reach
25	Waits	◯⇨▢D▽	For messenger pickup

FIG. W-6 Flow process chart.

943

Time Delays. Whenever machines or equipment are used, there are three ways to lose time: (1) operator waiting time, (2) machine waiting time, or (3) a combination of 1 and 2.

There is often a tendency to purchase a new piece of equipment without asking, "Can the job be done more effectively with the equipment already on hand?" It is a mistake to authorize purchase of elaborate or automatic equipment without thoroughly verifying its justification beforehand. Of particular concern are the time delays as they affect expensive equipment, where the loss of time on the part of the operator is less significant. As machines become more complex, the cost of idle time may spell the difference between profit and loss. Frequently, these idle times occur at intervals throughout their operating cycle, and are not readily apparent.

Preparation Time. There are three classes of work which occur most frequently with machines—make ready, do, and put away. (Those terms were mentioned earlier in discussing making a chart.)

1. *Make ready* is part of the operation in preparation for doing the work. It may include getting instruction, getting and checking materials, loading, setting up, and adjusting the machine. It includes all the work done before actually setting the machine in motion to do the specific task for which it was designed. Generally, the machine is idle while operators are making ready.

2. *Do* is the productive work done by the machine, such as winding, cutting, mixing, writing, computing, and printing. The operator is usually waiting while the machine is doing its work.

3. *Put away* covers the details necessary to remove the finished work and dispose of it, replace tools, and inspect. The machine is generally idle while operators are putting away.

Improvement Analysis. To analyze the chart for improvement, follow the same WS pattern as applied in the previous charts. Challenge every detail, asking the questions "What?" and "Why?," which lead to *elimination*; "Where?" and "Why?," which lead to a *combination* of details, *changes of sequence,* and possible *changes in work space*. The questions "Who?" and "Why?" lead to the possibility of having the machine perform details which the operator now does or having the operator perform details now performed by the machine. Where several operators are involved, they lead to the possibility of changing the person or the place with the work area. Finally, ask "How?" and "Why?" which lead to the possibilities of *improvement* (1) in tooling on the part of the machine and (2) in method on the part of the operator.

When all improvements have been listed and rearrangements of the make ready, do, and put away have been placed into their final sequence, the proposed or preferred method chart is completed as step 4 of the pattern.

Installation of Improvements. The final step in work simplification is actually to try out the job and put the improvements into effect. It is often assumed that workers will oppose such improvements because they will be regarded as "speed-up." If operators are taught how to use this tool and have been involved in the improvement, the feared opposition rarely materializes.

Summary

Work simplification is a human-oriented, systematic approach to the improvement of productivity, reduction of costs, and the enhancement of quality. Its concepts and methods precede and underlie many of the current concerns for the quality of work life. In many ways, the objectives, techniques, and results of WS are similar to job design, job enrichment, and/or quality circle programs.

See also Cost improvement; Paperwork simplification; Quality circles; Systems and procedures; Therbligs; Work design, job enlargement, and job enrichment; Work measurement; Work sampling.

REFERENCES

Barnes, Ralph: *Motion and Time Study: Design and Measurement of Work,* 7th ed., John Wiley, New York, 1980.

Bittel, Lester R.: *Improving Supervisory Performance,* McGraw-Hill, New York, 1976, chap. 13.

Maynard, H. B., ed.: *Industrial Engineering Handbook,* 2d ed., McGraw-Hill, New York, 1963, sec. 2. chaps. 1–10; sec. 5, chap. 3; sec. 10, chaps. 10 and 16.

ALLAN H. MOGENSEN, *Work Simplification Conferences*

Younger Employees, Management of

To develop and maintain high levels of motivation and productivity among younger employees require understanding and sometimes different techniques from those managers have typically used. Although the problems of integrating those under 25 years of age into the organization are not entirely unique to this group, it is increasingly apparent that young people cannot be supervised, motivated, or trained in traditional ways without creating substantial difficulties both for them and for the organization.

Insight into Younger Employees

There seem to be five general characteristics which young employees bring to their first full-time, formal job:

1. Greater mobility, which makes them potential candidates for turnover. They have fewer financial commitments. They are typically less affected by family considerations and less constrained by employee benefits based on length of service.

2. Changing attitudes and values, which cause them to expect more from an organization. They seem less tolerant of what they believe are imperfect managerial practices.

3. A relatively optimistic idea of what they can immediately contribute to an organization in terms of skills and abilities. They expect their talents to be utilized quickly. This expectation is especially true in recent college graduates.

4. An inclination to seek satisfaction of higher-order needs on the job, such as the psychological and self-fulfillment needs.

5. A desire to participate in decisions which affect their jobs and working conditions.

Job Expectations. Berlew and Hall have listed 13 expectations which new employees bring to the job. They are as follows: a sense of meaning or purpose in the job; personal development opportunities; extent of work that stimulates curiosity and induces excitement; challenge; power and responsibility; recognition and approval for good work; status and prestige; friendliness and congeniality of the work group; salary; a minimum of discipline and regimentation; a degree of security; advancement opportunities; and greater frequency of feedback and evaluation.[1]

High School Students. Scanlan surveyed high

school students between the ages of 17 and 19 who expressed interest in the following job aspects in descending order of importance: (1) interesting work, (2) wages, (3) pleasant working conditions, (4) advancement possibilities, (5) work associates, (6) job security, (7) recognition for a job well done, (8) tactful discipline, (9) good initial training, and (10) job importance.[2]

Blue-Collar Workers. Altimus and Tersine surveyed blue-collar workers and found the following differences between the younger workers (25 and under), middle-aged workers (26 to 35), and older workers (36 and over):

Younger workers were more dissatisfied with their work than older workers.

Younger workers exhibited a significantly greater dissatisfaction with the extent to which their esteem and self-actualization needs were met on the job than did the oldest age group.

Younger workers expressed greater dissatisfaction with pay, supervision, coworkers, and promotional opportunities than older workers.

Younger workers reported considerably less satisfaction than both middle-aged and older workers in the fulfillment of their security needs.

Younger workers indicated that their needs for esteem, autonomy, and self-actualization were higher than those of the older workers.

Younger workers tried to meet higher-level needs on the job (esteem, autonomy, and self-actualization), while older workers considered social needs more important.

Younger workers were more highly motivated by individually applied incentives, whereas older workers were more highly motivated by group incentives.[3]

College Students. Yankelovich surveyed college students and made the following observations:

The number of students who did not mind being bossed on the job has steadily dropped to 36 percent.

An ever-growing number of students find it harder to accept outward conformity for the sake of career advancement and to abide by rules with which they do not agree.

Students rank the opportunity to make a contribution, job challenge, the ability to find self-expression, and free time for outside interests as the most important influences on their career choices.

Some 69 percent of all students no longer believe hard work will pay off. A majority do not regard work as very important, ranking it well behind love, friendship, education, self-expression, family, and privacy.[4]

It seems obvious from the various research studies that younger workers have different perceptions, needs, expectations, and values than older workers and most managers. Even within the younger workers' group, there are substantial differences depending on age and education.

Practical Guidelines for Managing Younger Employees

To begin with, managers need to understand the differences among employees. These differences appear to be most acute in comparisons between younger and older employees. A really effective manager must also have insight into the differences among various groups of younger employees. Admittedly, gaining such insights is a complex job and requires substantial efforts from organizations and their managers. A failure to do this, however, results in a lowering of organizational effectiveness through reduced employee efficiency; lower productivity; higher absenteeism and turnover; reductions in creativity; increased superior-subordinate conflict, tension and miscommunication; and further erosion of the employee-employer relationship.

General Approaches. Scanlan suggests that managers consider the following general approaches:

1. Provide knowledge of what is expected. Jobs must be defined in terms of results expected. Knowing what to do is not enough; the individual must also know how performance will be measured.

2. Provide an opportunity to perform. Individuals should be given the freedom to exercise initiative and ingenuity in determining how to achieve objectives.

3. Provide feedback. Employees should be given continual appraisals of performance to maximize learning.

4. Provide assistance and support. Managers need to provide their subordinates with the necessary interdepartmental and intradepartmental coordination and guidance.

5. Provide rewards for results achieved. Both financial and nonfinancial rewards need to be distributed on the basis of performance. Accomplishment and improvement need to be recognized by the reward system in order to stimulate employee achievement.[5]

For Young Adults. Scanlan[6] further suggests the following as means to motivate young adults:

1. Provide interesting work. Job enrichment is a

promising means to challenge the young adult, as is the opportunity to participate as much as possible in decisions relating to how work should be performed.

Generally, the more ability the individual possesses, the greater his or her desire is to perform varied and challenging tasks. Thus managers must assess the individual's capabilities and needs, as people vary greatly as to what they consider to be challenging and interesting.

2. Provide a clearly understood wage system. Young adults, especially are concerned about equity in their wage plans. Satisfaction may result as much from a feeling of being treated fairly as from receiving an exceptionally high wage.

3. Provide good physical surroundings. Young people like to have a feeling of pride about the places where they work; a gloomy atmosphere is not conducive to such an attitude. Pleasant working conditions have been classified as a hygiene factor which has no motivational effect on employees, yet the absence can cause dissatisfaction.

4. Provide advancement opportunities. Most workers become unhappy with their jobs when advancement opportunites narrow or disappear. The young adult, particularly, finds it disconcerting to be in a dead-end job. Managers should make the ambitious young employees aware of advancement possibilities, yet care should be taken to avoid making promises that cannot be kept.

5. Provide opportunities for socialization. Most young adults prefer to work with other young adults, preferably ones with whom they have common interests and feel comfortable.

6. Provide job security. Although surveys do not show job security to be a primary concern of young adults, a sustained decline in business is likely to result in a motivation slump among all employees—youthful ones included. Rumors of layoffs and dismissals invariably cause restlessness. Only an exceptionally skillful supervisor will be able to keep the young employee contented when a loss of job appears imminent.

7. Provide recognition. Young people often feel the need for recognition with particular acuteness because they feel they are performing an "invisible" job. Recognition may come in varied forms—it may be positive, such as an increase in salary or oral or written appreciation from the individual's supervisor, or it may be negative in the form of correction. Improperly used as cheap praise, however, it accom-

plishes nothing. If appreciation is to be an effective tool in managing the young adult, the manager must believe in it and what it will accomplish.

8. Provide training. Young people appreciate the employer who spends time with them in training; the instruction they receive gives them self-confidence and the ability to perform their jobs more accurately.

9. Provide a sense of job importance. A person who feels that his or her job is significant is a much more effective employee than one who does not.

10. Be careful when criticizing and disciplining. Tactful discipline will produce good results, whereas inconsiderate discipline often results in defensive behavior in the rebuked employee and a loss of respect for the manager.

11. Communicate with employees. If one word were to be chosen as the key to effective management of young adults, that word would have to be *communication*. Young people need it even more than older employees do. They must have some feedback on their performance in their jobs. Morgan suggests several worthwhile elements in communicating with young adults: Communicate frequently, even if it is no more than to ask how things are going; when complex instructions are to be given, explain one portion at a time; recognize that minor problems may seem major to the young adult, and be willing to provide reassurance; make no promises that cannot be kept, and act on those made; when criticism is necessary, give it as impersonally as possible; be specific in instructions; and solicit questions and feedback, thus maintaining an open-door policy.[7]

For College Graduates. Schein suggests the following techniques for recent college graduates:

1. Provide opportunities for them to test their abilities with work that is clearly important.

2. Recognize the strength of the influence of the graduate's first supervisor. Select supervisors who are mature and secure in their knowledge as supervisors of new college graduates. Provide training for these supervisors so that they will be prepared to understand and work with these people.

3. Reform current approaches to the recruitment of college graduates to shift the emphasis from selling the student and, in the process, building up high and often unrealistic expectations to a more realistic dialogue. Also recruit on the basis of specific matches of talents to needs rather than just "good people."[8]

See also Affirmative action; Equal employment opportunity, minorities and women; Motivation in organizations; Women in business and management.

NOTES

[1] David E. Berlew and Douglas T. Hall, "The Socialization of Managers: Effects of Expectations on Performance," *Administrative Science Quarterly,* September 1966, pp. 207–223.

[2] Burt K. Scanlan, "Motivating Young Adults in Retailing," *Journal of Small Business Management,* vol. 4, no. 2, April 1976, pp. 46–54.

[3] Cyrus A. Altimus, Jr., and Richard J. Tersine, "Chronological Age and Job Satisfaction: The Young Blue Collar Worker," *Academy of Management Journal,* vol 16, no. 1, March 1973, pp. 55–66.

[4] Daniel Yankelovich, "The Student Revolution Permeates All Our Lives," *The Detroit News,* April 2, 1971, p. 1E.

[5] Burt K. Scanlan, *Principles of Management and Organization Behavior,* John Wiley, New York, 1973, pp. 428–429.

[6] ————, "Motivating Young Adults in Retailing," pp. 50–54.

[7] John S. Morgan, *Managing the Young Adults,* American Management Association, New York, 1967, p. 107; and "Communicating with Young Workers," *Supervisory Management,* May 1976, pp. 21–25.

[8] Edgar H. Schein, "The First Job Dilemma: An Appraisal of Why College Graduates Change Jobs and What Can Be Done about It," *Psychology Today,* March 1968, pp. 38–37.

BURT K. SCANLAN *University of Oklahoma*

ROGER M. ATHERTON, JR., *University of Oklahoma*

Z

Zero-Base Budgeting

Zero-base budgeting (ZBB) is an operating, planning, and budgeting process which requires each manager to justify his or her entire budget request in detail from scratch (hence, zero-base) and shifts the burden of proof to each manager to justify why any money should be spent at all, as well as how the job can be done better. This approach requires that (1) all activities be identified in "decision packages" (or programs) that relate inputs (costs) with outputs (benefits); (2) each one be evaluated by systematic analysis; and (3) all programs be ranked in order of performance.

ZBB is important because it reflects recent thinking in budgeting methodology. It is not just a method of budget cutting; it is a planning and budget control system as well. Not only is there an accounting of funds but also a description of how those funds will be used for the organization's goals and functions. Managers can be held accountable for both the planning and the use of funds.

The core concept of ZBB, building a budget up from ground zero, is not new in the budgeting literature. What is new is the methodology by which the ZBB system is implemented in an organization.

Basic Elements of the Process

ZBB is a bottoms-up planning and budgeting process that requires every manager or supervisor to reexamine each program or activity from the ground up each fiscal year before funds are allocated. The manager begins with the assumption that *all* resource needs must be justified. This justification is accomplished through a formal process of developing decision units, decision packages, and ranking.

The four basic elements in the ZBB system are:

Decision units. Each significant program, individual department, or level of an organization is identified.

Decision packages. Each decision unit manager draws up, in priority order, a number of packages, which together make up the total budget request for that unit.

Ranking process. All decision packages are ranked in order of decreasing benefits to the organization. The ranking process establishes priorities on the basis of functions described in each decision package.

Allocation of organizational resources. This procedure consists of the actual allocation of the organization's resources, using rank ordering at successively higher budget cutoff levels in the organizational structure and the preparation of detailed line-item budgets.

The corporate budget is derived from the establishment of a cutoff budget at the highest level of the organization, which in turn establishes the cutoff budgets at each lower level. The corresponding decision packages to be approved are above the cutoff budgets.

The use of decision units provides the organization with the identification of the specific organizational units or programs to be included in the ZBB process. Through decision packages, each manager identifies, reviews, evaluates, and justifies all programs, projects, and activities. The manager is required to consider the *alternative ways* of performing each identified activity and must also consider the different *levels* of effort and resource requirements that might be needed. Thus, in addition to reexamining the current level of service, the manager develops minimum (highest priority) and incremental decision packages that relate the costs and benefits of stepwise increased expenditure levels.

In ranking, each manager rates each decision package relative to all other packages and selects those packages to be included in the budget (resource) request. Decision packages are then consolidated and ranked by each succeeding level of hierarchical management. The final budget comprises a prioritized list of those packages proposed to be funded and selected from the total list of packages. During the fiscal year, each decision unit manager is responsible for achieving the specified performance objectives indicated in the decision package description and for doing so within the corresponding budget levels. ZBB provides an excellent cost control system.

Planning Assumptions and Requirements. As ZBB deals with a total budget request, not just an increase (or decrease) over the previous year, the existing activities are reviewed as closely as any proposed new activities. The emphasis is on the choice between alternative ways of providing a service as well as alternative funding levels for each proposed service. However, ZBB is not a strategic planning or corporate planning procedure.

The ZBB process requires the prior development of planning assumptions and objectives for the forthcoming fiscal period. Assumptions are provided to each of the operating or service departments for use in their individual budget preparation efforts. Each manager requires guidelines concerning inflation rates, fringe benefits, and salary increases. In addition, managers must have information concerning service-level requirements of related activities and departments.

Finally, planning information and guidelines are required concerning (1) the overall purpose of the organization, (2) specification of both short-term and long-range goals and plans, (3) definition of the organization's performance objectives, and (4) development of department, division, and subunit objectives.

Managing the ZBB Implementation Process

Initial implementation of ZBB is often accomplished by a task force of operating and financial managers who are responsible for the design and administration of the process in the organization. The inclusion of operating managers in the task force is essential, since they are the most knowledgeable about operating needs and problems, will be largely responsible for implementing the ZBB process, and will add credibility to the proposed zero-base implementation plan.

The task force manages the process by:

Designing the process to fit the specific needs and character of the organization

Preparing a simple, straightforward budget manual that illustrates the ZBB process and explains the decision unit, decision package, and ranking concepts

Presenting the process to management and teaching operating managers responsible for ZBB analysis of a decision unit how to apply the technique

Working with decision unit managers to improve and expedite the ZBB process

If required, designing, developing, and operating a computer system for ZBB

An important requirement in instituting a sound ZBB process is to manage carefully and efficiently the implementation of ZBB. The following are typical activities that must be performed in implementing ZBB:

1. Establish a ZBB task force responsible for the implementation of ZBB.

2. Develop a work plan and time schedule for implementation.

3. Review and document all current planning, budgeting, and control procedures.

4. Design a ZBB process that is adaptable to the organization's needs.

5. Prepare a manual that documents this process in simple, straightforward terms.

6. Conduct a training presentation to introduce decision unit managers to the process.

7. Assist decision unit managers in defining and formulating decision packages.

8. Work closely with decision unit managers to (a) specify current methods of operation, (b) spec-

ify performing measures, (c) develop alternative methods of operation, and (d) develop incremental cost-benefit analysis.

9. Assist decision unit managers to develop a procedure for ranking decision packages and to prescribe cutoff budget levels.

10. Assist in consolidating and summarizing the plan and detailed budgets.

See also Accounting, managerial control; Budgets and budget preparation; Program planning and implementation; Public administration.

REFERENCES

Austin, L. Allen: *Zero-Base Budgeting*, American Management Association, AMACOM, New York, 1979.

Dean, Burton V.: "Problems in Implementing Zero-Base Budgeting, *American Association for Budget and Program Analysis*, March 1977.

Hill, C. E., and T. Sharp: "Zero-Base Budgeting: A Practical Application," *Government Finance*, March 12, 1983, pp. 13+.

Pyhrr, Peter A.: *Zero-Base Budgeting; A Practical Management Tool for Evaluating Expenses*, John Wiley, New York, 1973.

Stonich, Paul J.: *Zero-Base Planning and Budgeting*, Dow-Jones Irwin, Homewood, Ill, 1977, p. 21.

Wildavsky, Aaron: *Budgeting — A Comparative Theory of Budgetary Processes*, Little, Brown and Company, Boston, 1975.

Burton V. Dean, *Case Western Reserve University*

INDEX